How to Write an Effective Essay about Literature: A Crash Course

Chapter Preview

After reading this chapter, you will be able to

- Approach the first draft of an essay purposefully
- Revise a draft effectively
- Participate in the peer review process
- Prepare a final draft of an essay

The Basic Strategy

Students have assured us that the following suggestions for writing analytical essays are helpful.

- **Choose a topic and a tentative thesis**, generating an *argument*. Aim to explore concepts that can be interpreted and developed rather than to summarize information.
- **Generate ideas through analysis**, engaging in a process of *inquiry, interpretation, and argument*. For instance, ask yourself inquiring questions such as "Why did the author—a woman—tell the story from the point of view of this male character rather than that female character?" and "Does this story give me some insight into family relationships?" Formulate interpretations based on your best questions and answers.
- **Select and evaluate evidence**, using specific details from the text to develop and support your ideas.
- **Make a tentative outline** of points that you plan to make.
- **Rough out a first draft**, working from your outline (don't worry about spelling, punctuation, etc.), but don't hesitate to depart from the outline when new ideas come to you in the process of writing.
- **Make large-scale revisions** in your draft by reorganizing, adding details to clarify and support assertions, or deleting or combining paragraphs.
- **Make small-scale revisions** by revising and editing sentences, and checking spelling and grammar.

- **Revise your opening and concluding paragraphs.** Be certain that they are *interesting*, not mere throat-clearing and not a mere summary.
- **Have someone read your revised draft** and comment on it.
- **Revise again**, taking into account the reader's suggestions. Read this latest version and **make further revisions as needed** so that your thesis—your argument—is evident.
- **Proofread** your final version.

All writers must work out their own procedures and rituals, but the following basic suggestions will help you write effective essays. They assume that you have made annotations in the margins of the literary text and have jotted notes in a journal, on index cards, or in a file of documents on your computer. If your paper involves using sources, consult also Chapter 10, "Research: Writing with Sources."

Reading Closely: Approaching a First Draft

1. **Carefully read and reread the work or works you will write about, annotating as you read.** Read with a pen in hand, and take notes in the margins of the text. Do not hesitate to reread the sections of the work that are most relevant to your subject, jotting down new notes and brainstorming new interpretations.
2. **Keep your purpose in mind.** Although your instructor may ask you, perhaps as a preliminary writing assignment, to jot down your early responses—your initial experience of the work—it is more likely that he or she will ask you to write an analysis in which you will connect details, draw inferences, and argue that such and such is the case. That is, almost surely you will be asked to do more than write a summary or to report your responses; you will be asked to engage with the conceptual ideas raised by the work. You probably will be expected to support a **thesis**, to make a *claim*, and offer an *argument*, for example: "The metaphors are chiefly drawn from nature and, broadly speaking, they move from sky and sea to the earth and to human beings, which is to say that they become closer at hand, more immediate, more personal."
3. **Choose a worthwhile and interesting subject, and work to generate a thesis argument about that subject.** As you determine what you will write about, choose something that interests you and is not so big that your handling of it must be superficial. As you work, shape your topic, narrowing it, for example, from "Characterization in Updike's 'A & P'" to "Updike's Use of Contrasting Characters in 'A & P.'"

Don't expect to have a sound thesis at the very beginning of your working on an essay. The thesis will probably come to you only after you have done some close reading and have stimulated ideas by asking yourself questions. Almost surely you will see that the initial thesis needs to be modified in the light of evidence that you encounter. It might be helpful to think of this writing as creating a *working thesis*, knowing that you will modify, expand, contract, and change the focus of your thesis as your ideas develop. In short, your thesis will evolve in the course of thinking about what you are reading.

An essay that analyzes a work will not only offer an argument but will also support the argument with **evidence**. Even an explication—a sort of line-by-line

paraphrase (see Chapter 6)—presents an argument, holding that the work conveys a certain meaning. Your analysis will break down the whole of the work into parts and investigate the relationships among those parts. Your argument will show off your critical thinking about the literary work, demonstrating how you engage in original interpretation by highlighting meaningful aspects of the text, drawing inferences, connecting details, and extrapolating larger concepts.

In thinking about your purpose, remember, too, that your **audience** will, in effect, determine the amount of detail that you must give. Although your instructor may, in reality, be your only reader, probably you should imagine that your audience consists of people like your classmates—intelligent but not especially familiar with the topic on which you have recently become a specialist. In putting yourself into the shoes of your imagined readers, think of reasonable objections the readers might raise, and respond appropriately to these objections.

4. **Keep looking at the literary work you are writing about, jotting down brainstorming notes on all relevant matters.**
   - You can generate ideas for writing about the issues raised by essays, stories, plays, and poems by asking yourself questions such as those given in the Checklists on pages 419–20, 455–57, 525–27, 554–55, and 783–85.
   - As you look and think, reflect on your observations, and record them.
   - As you look and think, move beyond plot summary and information-based reading. Move toward engagement with the concepts—the most compelling ideas, issues, and concerns—raised by the literary work.
   - When you have an idea, jot it down as a marginal annotation on the book or on a Post-it note attached to the margin of the book page. Don't assume that you will remember your ideas when you begin writing. Develop a strategy for collecting ideas that move beyond marginal annotations, allowing your notes to becoming more detailed and interpretive. Many people will keep a journal to jot down brainstorming ideas, develop a system of using 4-by-6-inch index cards, or take notes in electronic files on a laptop or iPad or similar tablet device.
   - As you develop your note-taking and brainstorming record, embed organizational techniques within it. For example, if you use index cards, put only one point on each card, and write a brief caption on the card (e.g., "Significance of title," or "Night = death????" Later you can arrange the cards so that relevant notes are grouped together. Similarly, if you take brainstorming notes in a journal, leave room to label each page or document; if you take notes on a computer, create a system of clearly labeled files and folders.
   - Become comfortable rereading your own notes and marking them up. Circle or highlight your best ideas. Jot down more notes next to your original notes, continuing to develop your thinking.
5. **When you are taking notes from secondary sources, do not simply highlight or photocopy.**
   - Take brief notes, *summarizing* important points and jotting down your own critiques of the material.
   - Read the material analytically, thoughtfully, and with an open mind and a questioning spirit.
   - When you read in this attentive and tentatively skeptical way, you will find that the material is valuable not only for what it tells you but also for the ideas that you yourself produce in responding to it.

6. **Sort out your notes, putting together what belongs together.** The process of rereading and rethinking your own ideas allows you to hone and strengthen your ideas as you organize them. As a first step, create groupings of like ideas. Three notes about the texture of the materials of a building, for instance, probably belong together. Note cards can easily be rearranged to bring connected ideas together. If you are working on a computer, cut and paste similar ideas into one document or one subsection of a document. If you are taking notes in a journal, skim through your earlier notes, and rewrite connected ideas on a fresh page. As you select your best ideas, set aside your weakest ideas. Don't hesitate to delete ideas, moving them into a different file, knowing that you can always return to them later. Reject notes that are irrelevant to your topic.

7. **Organize your notes into a reasonable sequence.** Your notes contain ideas (or at least facts that you can think about); now the notes have to be put into a coherent sequence. Think of the relationships among your ideas: Is one idea the overarching idea and must come first? Does one idea lead to the next, creating a sequence? Does one idea offer a minor observation and might best become a subpoint presented "under" a more important argument? Does one idea rely on information that is presented in another section and thus could come later in the argument? When you have made a tentative arrangement, review it; you may discover a better way to group your notes, and you may even want to add to them. If so, start reorganizing.

A tripartite organization for your analytical essay usually works. For this structure, tentatively plan to devote your opening paragraph(s) to a statement of the topic or problem and a proposal of your hypothesis or thesis. The essay can then be shaped into three parts:

- a *beginning*, in which you identify the work(s) that you will discuss, giving the necessary background and, in a sentence or two, setting forth your underlying argument, your thesis;
- a *middle*, in which you develop your thesis in a series of well-organized paragraphs, chiefly by explaining the ideas central to your argument, by offering evidence, and by taking account of possible objections to your argument; and
- a *conclusion*, in which you wrap things up, perhaps by giving a more general interpretation or by setting your findings in a larger context.

In general, organize the material from the simple to the complex in order to ensure intelligibility. For instance, if you are discussing the structure of a poem, it will probably be best to begin with the most obvious points and then to turn to the subtler but perhaps equally important ones. Similarly, if you are comparing two characters, it may be best to move from the most obvious contrasts to the least obvious. When you have arranged your notes into a meaningful sequence, you have begun a key step: dividing your material into paragraphs.

8. **Get it down on paper**. Most essayists find it useful to jot down some sort of **outline**, a map indicating the main idea of each paragraph and, under each main idea, supporting details that give it substance. An outline will help you to overcome the paralysis called "writer's block" that commonly afflicts professional as well as student writers. It does not necessarily have to be anything formal, with capital and lowercase letters and Roman and Arabic numerals, but merely key phrases jotted down in some sort of order. We provide numerous examples of jotted notes and outlines that lead to a rough draft and then a polished essay.

A page of paper with ideas listed in some sort of sequence, however rough, ought to encourage you. You will discover that you do have something to say. And so, despite the temptation to sharpen another pencil, surf the Internet, or have another cup of coffee, follow the advice of Isaac Asimov, author of 225 books: "Sit down and start writing."

If you do not feel that you can work from notes and a rough outline, try another method: Get something down on paper, writing (in a journal or on a computer) freely, sloppily, automatically, or whatever, but allowing your ideas about what the work means to you and how it conveys its meaning—rough as your ideas may be—to begin to take visible form. If you are like most people, you cannot do much precise thinking until you have committed to paper at least a rough sketch of your initial ideas. At this stage, you are trying to find out what your ideas are, and in the course of getting them down on paper, you will find yourself generating new ideas. We *think* with words. Capture your ideas in words, and then turn them into phrases and sentences. Later you can push and polish your ideas into shape, perhaps even deleting all of them and starting over, but it is a lot easier to improve your ideas once you see them in front of you than it is to do the job in your head. On paper, one word leads to another; in your head, one word often blocks another.

You may realize, as you near the end of a sentence, that you no longer believe it. Okay; be glad that your first idea led you to a better one, and pick up your better one and keep going with it. What you are doing, by trial and error, is moving not only toward clear expression but also toward sharper ideas and richer responses.

✔ CHECKLIST: *Generating Ideas for a Draft*

Have I asked myself the following questions?

☐ Have I double-checked my assignment, knowing what the purpose of my reading and writing is?

☐ Am I engaged in an active reading process? Have I read and reread the literary work that I am writing about?

☐ Have I annotated the literary work and written down brainstorming notes?

☐ Have I selected an interesting subject for my paper? Can I start to generate a working thesis for my paper, knowing that I will continue to revise it?

☐ Do my notes move beyond recording information and start to engage with conceptual ideas?

☐ Am I capturing my best ideas in my notes? Have I generated notes that explore the most compelling issues and concerns raised by the literary work?

☐ Are my note-taking techniques efficient? Do my notes allow me to sort and organize my ideas?

☐ Can my notes be organized into a sequence that has a beginning, a middle, and an end?

☐ Can I develop an outline from my notes, mapping the main idea of each paragraph and the supporting evidence that will be presented in each paragraph?

☐ Have I gotten ideas down on paper, no matter how rough they are? Can I move my ideas from words to phrases to sentences?

☐ Can I collect and reflect on my annotations, brainstorming notes, thesis, and outline, and start drafting my paper?

Writing and Revising: Achieving a Readable Draft

Good writing is *re*writing. The evidence? Heavily annotated drafts by Chekhov, Keats, Hemingway, Tolstoy, Woolf—almost any writer you can name. Of course, it is easy enough to spill out words, but, as the dramatist Richard Sheridan said 200 years ago, "Easy writing's curst hard reading." Good writers find writing is difficult because they care; they care about making sense, so they will take time to answer reasonable objections to their arguments and to find the exact words that will enable them to say precisely what they mean so that their readers will understand their key ideas in the right way. And they care about holding a reader's attention; they recognize that part of their job is to be interesting.

1. **Keep looking and thinking**, asking yourself questions and providing tentative answers, searching for additional material that strengthens or weakens your main point, and taking account of it in your outline or draft. As you return to the literary work and your outline, continue to add more ideas to it. Your draft will grow organically out of these notes.
2. **Continue to hone your thesis and develop your argument**. Generate a thesis that captures your main argument, making sure that your thesis engages with the most important conceptual ideas that you want to explore and makes a claim about those ideas. Your thesis paragraph should preview your development of your argument. Continue to revise your thesis as your paper evolves.

Now is probably the time to think about a title for your essay. It is usually a good idea to let your reader know what your topic is—which works of literature you will discuss—and what your approach will be. For instance, your topic might be Kate Chopin's "Désirée's Baby"—a story about the response to a white woman who gives birth to a mixed-race infant—and your approach might be that the story's theme of racial prejudice is still meaningful today. At this stage, your title is still tentative, but thinking about the title will help you to organize your thoughts and to determine which of your notes are relevant and which are not. Rather than the title "Chopin's Story about Race," a title "Chopin's 'Désirée's Baby' and Lessons about Racial Prejudice and Ignorance" starts to capture your unique ideas about the work. Remember, the title is the first part of the paper that your reader encounters. You will gain the reader's goodwill by providing a helpful, interesting title.

3. **With your outline or draft in front of you, write a more lucid version of your paper**, checking your notes for fuller details. If you wrote your draft on a computer, do not revise it on screen. Print a hard copy, and revise it with a pen or pencil. You need to read the essay more or less as your instructor will read it. True, the process of revising by hand takes more time than revising on a computer, but time is exactly what you need to devote to the process of revision. Time spent developing and clarifying your ideas is time well spent; it will save you time in the later stages of finalizing and editing the draft. When you wrote your first draft, you were eager to find out what you thought, what you knew, and what you did not know. Now, in the revising stage, you need to write slowly, thoughtfully. Later, you will type the handwritten revisions into the computer.

When you are revising an early draft, it is probably best to start by concentrating on *large-scale revisions*—reorganization and additions (for instance, you may now see that you need to define a term, or to give an example, or to quote further from the work that you are discussing). You will probably also make substantial deletions because you will now see that some sentences or paragraphs, although interesting, are redundant or irrelevant.

Although it is best to start with large-scale revisions (what teachers of composition somewhat grandly call "global revision"), the truth is that when most writers revise, whether they are experienced or inexperienced, they do not proceed methodically. Rather, they jump around, paying attention to whatever attracts their attention at the moment, like a dog hunting for fleas—and that is not a bad way to proceed. Still, you might at least plan to work in the following sequence:

- **Introductory and concluding sections:** Make sure that your title and opening paragraph(s) give your readers an idea of where you will be taking them. Is your thesis evident? Your concluding paragraph should tell them where they've been. Is your concluding paragraph conclusive without being merely repetitive?
- **Organization:** If some of your material now seems to be in the wrong place, move it by cutting and pasting. The Golden Rule is "Put together what belongs together." Make sure your ideas have a logical sequence or follow a natural flow in which one idea leads to the next.
- **Development:** Your ideas should not be repetitive and should not remain surface level. Rather, you should be presenting new but related ideas that add layers of depth and insight to your thesis.
- **Evidence:** Make sure that your assertions are supported by evidence and that the evidence is of varying sorts, ranging from details in the works to quotations from appropriate secondary sources.
- **Counterevidence:** Consider the objections that a reasonable reader might raise to some or all of your points, and explain why these objections are not substantial.
- **Coherence in sentences, in paragraphs, and between paragraphs:** Usually, this is a matter of adding transitional words and phrases (*furthermore, therefore, for instance, on the other hand*).
- **Tone:** Your sentences inevitably convey information not only about your topic but also about yourself. Do the sentences suggest stuffiness? Or are they too informal, too inappropriately casual?
- **Editorial matters:** Check the spelling of any words that you are in doubt about, check the punctuation, check sentence structure, and check the form of footnotes and bibliography (list of works cited).

If you find that some of your earlier notes are no longer relevant, eliminate them, but make sure that your argument flows from one point to the next. It is not enough to keep your thesis in mind; you must keep it in the reader's mind. As you write, your ideas will doubtless become clearer, and some may prove to be poor ideas. (We rarely know exactly what our ideas are until we write them down on paper or on the computer. As the little girl said, replying to the suggestion that she should think before she speaks, "How do I know what I think until I see what I say?") Not until you have written a draft do you really have a strong sense of what you feel and know and of how good your essay may be.

At this point, you can engage in a practice termed "reverse outlining." You read your draft and pull an outline out of it, in order to make sure that the draft is reasonably organized. A reverse outline works to capture what is actually written on the page. Jot down, in sequence, each major point and each subpoint as it is written in the draft. You may find that some points need amplification, that you have forgotten a key point, or that a point made on one page really ought to go on another page.

Later you will concern yourself with *small-scale revisions* (polishing sentences, clarifying transitions, varying sentence structure if necessary, checking spelling and documentation).

4. **After a suitable interval, preferably a few days, again revise the draft.** To write a good essay, you must be a good reader of the essay that you are writing. (We are not talking at this stage about proofreading or correcting spelling errors). Van Gogh said, "One becomes a painter by painting." Similarly, one becomes a writer by writing—and by rewriting and revising. In revising their work, writers ask themselves many questions:
   • Do I mean what I say?
   • Do I say what I mean? (Answering this question will generate other questions: Do I need to define my terms? Do I need to add examples to clarify? Do I need to reorganize the material so that a reader can grasp it?)

> *A Rule for Writers:* Put yourself in the reader's shoes to make sure not only that the paper has an organization but also that the organization will be clear to your reader. If you imagine a classmate as the reader of the draft, you may find that you need to add transition words (*for instance, on the other hand*), clarify definitions, and provide additional supporting evidence.

During this part of the process of writing, read the draft in a skeptical frame of mind. You engaged in critical thinking when you made use of the literary work and any secondary sources; now apply the same questioning spirit to your own writing. In taking account of your doubts, you will probably unify, organize, clarify, and polish the draft.

Reminder: If you have written your draft on a computer or a tablet, do *not* try to revise it on screen. Print the entire draft, and then read it—as your reader will be reading it—page by page, not screen by screen. Almost surely you will detect errors in a hard copy that you miss on screen. Only by reading the printed copy will you be able to see if, for instance, the ideas on page two are repeated on page four.

5. **With your draft in near-final form, turn to editing for correctness.** After producing a draft that seems good enough to show to someone, writers engage in yet another activity: They edit. **Editing** includes such work as checking the accuracy of quotations by comparing them with the original, checking a dictionary for the spelling of doubtful words, and checking a handbook for doubtful punctuation—for instance, whether a comma or a semicolon is needed in a particular sentence.

✔ CHECKLIST: *Writing and Revising a Draft*

Have I asked myself the following questions?

- ☐ Does the draft fulfill the specifications (e.g., length, scope) of the assignment?
- ☐ Does the draft have a thesis—a central focusing argument that gives my paper a purpose?
- ☐ Is the title interesting and informative? Does my title create a favorable first impression?
- ☐ Are the early paragraphs engaging, and do they give the reader a good idea of what will follow, naming the works of literature, the approach, and the argument?
- ☐ Are key concepts explained clearly and then developed with supporting observations, insights, and analysis?
- ☐ Is the organization clear, reasonable, and effective? Can I check the organization by making a quick reverse outline?
- ☐ Are arguable assertions supported with evidence? Is the evidence explained?
- ☐ Are my readers kept in mind, for instance, by defining terms that they may be unfamiliar with? Are possible objections faced and adequately answered?
- ☐ If quotations are included, are they introduced rather than just dumped into the essay? Are quotations as brief as possible? Might summaries (properly credited to the sources) be more effective than long quotations?
- ☐ Are *all* sources cited, including Internet material?
- ☐ Does the final paragraph nicely round off the paper, or does it merely restate—unnecessarily—the obvious?
- ☐ Does the paper include whatever visual materials the reader may need to see?

Revising: Working with Peer Review

Almost all professional writers get help—from friends, from colleagues, and especially from editors who are paid to go over their manuscripts and call attention to matters that need clarification. If possible, get a fellow student to read your manuscript and give you his or her responses. Do not confuse this sort of help—recommended by all instructors—with plagiarism, which is the unacknowledged use of someone else's words or ideas. Your reader is not rewriting the paper for you but merely suggesting that (for instance) your title is misleading, that here you need a clear example, that there you are excessively repetitive, and so forth. If you are unfamiliar with the process of peer review and uncertain about the nature of plagiarism, we urge you to read the discussions on pages 403-04.

If peer review is a part of the writing process in your course, the instructor may arrange for writing workshops to be held in or out of class. The instructor may also distribute a guide for peer review that offers suggestions and questions. The preceding checklist is an example of such a guide.

Preparing the Final Draft

1. **If you have received comments from a reader, consider them carefully.** Even when you disagree with them, they may alert you to places in your essay that need revision or clarification.

When a friend, a classmate, or another peer reviewer has given you help, acknowledge that person in a footnote or an endnote. (If you look at almost any book, you will notice that the author acknowledges the help of friends and colleagues. In your own writing, follow this practice.) Here are sample acknowledgments from papers by students:

> I wish to thank Anna Aaron for numerous valuable suggestions.

> I thank Paul Gottsegen for calling my attention to passages that needed clarification, and Jane Leslie for suggesting the comparison between Sammy in Updike's "A & P" and the unnamed narrator in Joyce's "Araby."

2. **If you have borrowed ideas, be sure to give credit**, usually in footnotes, to your sources. Remember that plagiarism is not limited to the unacknowledged borrowing of words; a borrowed idea, even when put into your own words, requires acknowledgment. (On giving credit to sources, see Appendix B.)

3. **Print a clean copy of your final draft**, following the principles concerning margins, pagination, footnotes, and so on, set forth in Appendix B.

4. **Proofread the hard copy, make corrections as necessary, and print it out again.**

All of this adds up to a recipe found in a famous Victorian cookbook: "First catch your hare, then cook it."

CHAPTER 2

How to Engage in Critical Thinking about Literature: A Crash Course

Chapter Preview

After reading this chapter, you will be able to:

- Define *critical thinking*
- Use close reading to investigate a literary work
- Engage in analysis, using inquiry, interpretation, and argumentation to come to a deeper understanding of a literary work
- Use comparison and synthesis to connect your ideas to other sources
- Reflect on your ideas and continually revise them to improve your writing
- Identify the differences between nonanalytical and analytical writing

The Basic Strategy

In order to develop your critical thinking skills, we suggest that you try the following strategies:

- **Annotate the literary work as you read**, engaging in *active reading*. Take notes in the margins of the text as you read; this will help you to remember key details but will also help to trigger insightful thinking as you read.
- **Make sure that you can summarize the literary work**, demonstrating that you understand its key ideas. If there is a passage that confuses you or a detail that you have forgotten, go back and reread the passage and clarify your thinking before you start to develop an interpretation of the text.
- **Ask questions about the literary work**, using an analytical approach to the text by asking conceptual "why" and "how" questions, rather than by asking informational "what" questions.
- **Argue with yourself** as you generate ideas. Continue to revise your understanding of the text by scrutinizing your assumptions, testing your evidence, thinking of counterarguments, and asking yourself follow-up questions.

- **Create an interpretation** that captures your sense of the meaning of the work. As you write your paper, develop a focused analysis of the work by selecting a key idea for exploration. Define, explain, and add depth to that idea.
- **Develop your interpretation by exploring both literary content and form.** Literary analysis examines both literary content (the thematic ideas presented by the work) and literary form (the structuring of those ideas through literary elements, such as voice, imagery, and symbolism, among many others). How does the form of the text shape its ideas?
- **Collect evidence that supports your interpretation. Look "inward" to literary form and content, and look "outward" to literary contexts and criticism.** As you develop your ideas, support them with details from the literary work and, if your assignment allows, information about the cultural context of the work or literary criticism written by scholars about the work.
- **Create an argument** that captures your most important analytical ideas about the text. Develop a thesis that takes a stand. Present your point of view on the key idea that you have selected for analysis.
- **Use comparison and contrast** to develop relationships among texts and to connect two or more texts by analyzing their similarities and differences. A comparison paper should lead to new insights about each text, clarifying the key ideas that you see in each.
- **When performing research, synthesize your sources.** Create relationships among your ideas and those of critics, working to interweave your sources in your paper.
- **Revise your ideas as you revise your writing.** An essential component of critical thinking is the ability to revisit and "re-see" your own ideas. Become your own best critic, and revise your ideas as you develop them.

What Is Critical Thinking?

When we engage in critical thinking, we are keenly aware of what we are doing. We are, for instance, studying an effect and searching for its causes. "This story bores me, but exactly why does it bore me?" "Is the plot too familiar?" "Are the characters unrealistic?" "Is the language trite?" "Is the language so technical that I can't follow it?" "Does the author use too many words to say too few?" Or: "I loved the book but hated the movie. Why?" Again, we start to consider the problem closely, probably (again) by examining the parts that make up the whole. And here we are at the heart of critical thinking. **Critical thinking** is a matter of separating the whole into parts in order to see relationships.

Having said that critical thinking does not necessarily involve faultfinding, we want to modify that statement. There is one writer whose work you should indeed judge severely. That writer is you. When you read a draft of your work, adopt a skeptical spirit. As you read, ask yourself if your assertions are supported with sufficient evidence, and ask if other interpretations of the evidence might reasonably be offered. When you engage in this process, you are engaged in critical thinking.

When we engage in critical thinking in an academic setting, we critique in order to come to a deeper understanding of complex ideas. Let's apply this to

literary study: When we engage in critical thinking about literature, we critique in order to come to a deeper understanding of a literary text's possible meanings, determine what meaning we find most interesting and important, explore how and why a text creates that meaning, and explore how and why that meaning might connect to a larger understanding of the world. Writing takes this critical thinking process one step further: It forces us to slow down and register how we understand and evaluate the text, how we develop an interpretation of the text, how we select evidence to support our ideas, how we construct an argument about the text, and how we compare texts and synthesize our ideas with those of others writers. Writing puts our critical thinking skills on display.

How Do We Engage in Critical Thinking?

We are constantly engaging with texts, ranging from stories to movies to blogs to YouTube clips, working to understand them and then express our opinions about them. When you go to a movie, you might come out from the screening telling a friend, "I really liked that character, except it was so unrealistic when he was able to overcome that warrior...." In moments like this, you are engaging in critical thinking without realizing it. You are showing that you understood what happened in the movie, and you are taking the next step of determining what the movie means by questioning its key elements and connecting it to your knowledge about how you think it should work. By explaining your opinions about the movie, you are showing that you've created your own interpretation of it. In other words, you've generated your own ideas—you've used someone else's work to trigger new ideas of your own.

In academic critical thinking, you take this general process of thinking and make it more directed and purposeful. You aim to understand and organize your thought processes and then apply those processes to challenging texts. You judge and critique those texts in order to hone your ability to develop ideas—and become an idea-creator and text-creator yourself. The process of critical thinking can be broken down into the following simplified stages of thinking:

- **Summary**, in which you restate the information conveyed by a literary text, demonstrating that you've carefully read the text and have fully understood its key ideas
- **Analysis**, in which you develop your opinion about the meaning of the text by questioning the text, interpreting the text, defining concepts central to the text, locating evidence that supports your ideas, and creating arguments that explain your unique understanding of the text
- **Synthesis**, in which you connect your reading of the text to other sources, developing relationships among your ideas and the ideas of others (such as critics)

Literature is widely understood to be one of the best ways to develop critical thinking because it is purposefully open-ended and encourages multiple interpretations. Literature does not tell you what it means in a straightforward way. It often raises more questions than it answers. It is often purposely complex or unclear. Why? Literature attempts to capture the complexity of the human experience, and human emotions, thoughts, dreams, and memories are far from straightforward. Crucially, literature does not tell you exactly what to think. Literature is

not a lecture, or a sermon, or a political speech, with a clear message or argument. Yet, that is exactly why we read literature—it gives us the freedom to think on our own.

Literature encourages you to come up with your own understanding of it—and this is where critical thinking comes in. When you are reading literature, you are able to develop your interpretation of the text and then create arguments that capture that interpretation.

Literature encourages the development of a particularly rich and multifaceted set of critical thinking skills. Let's explore these skills in more detail.

Close Reading

A strong literary analysis starts with a strong close reading. A **close reading** takes on a deceptively simple task: It attempts to accurately understand a literary work and then figure out what ideas the work explores. A close reading develops an understanding of the text and investigates how the text makes meaning.

In some ways, the close reading task is straightforward. For example, you know that the sentence, "Go to the store and buy a loaf of bread," means exactly that, and you do not have to attend to that sentence very closely to understand what it means. When you turn to literature, however, the close reading task gets more complex. For example, take the opening sentence of James Joyce's short story, "Araby": "North Richmond Street, being blind, was a quiet street except at the hour when the Christian Brothers' School set the boys free." We can provide a summary of the information in the sentence: A street named North Richmond Street is the site of a boy's school, and the street is typically quiet except when the boys are leaving school. However, a literary work encourages you to start a process of analysis. Instantly, questions pop up: What does "being blind" mean—how can a street be blind? What are the boys being set free from? Where are we—in what country and in what time period? Asking questions like this starts a process of thinking, interpreting, arguing—the process of critical thinking.

✦ Close reading asks you to become a detective, picking up clues that can help you figure out what you think the text's meaning is. **Annotating** the text, marking it up as you read, is the best way to collect those ideas. As you read, "notice what you notice," and note any interesting, strange, beautiful, or confusing moments.

In literature, the clues are the interesting words and the interesting ways those words are positioned in a text, such as repetition or sentence placement. Literary structure, literary genre, and literary elements call attention to certain ideas. In a poem, for example, the form that words take on a page (such as a sonnet form) is crucial to discovering the poem's meaning. A close reading examines not just *what* is being said but *how* the text is saying it.

If you reread that first sentence from "Araby," it starts to make sense. The street must be "blind" like a "blind alley" or a dead end; the boys are being set free from their school, which is holding them in like a prison; the school is in a town with clearly named streets and buildings. Slowing down and rereading the text for clues to its meaning is essential to the close reading process.

As you read "Araby," continue to notice key words and ask questions about them, connecting details to larger concepts. The second sentence reads, "An uninhabited house of two storeys stood at the blind end, detached from its neighbors in a square ground." "Araby" is not describing a street filled with happiness; the words "uninhabited" and "detached" are creating a feeling of loneliness or

uneasiness. The word "blind" seems important: It is repeated in the first two sentences. Is a pattern being set up? What does "blind" mean? In the story, maybe someone won't be seeing things clearly? Creating interpretations based on textual clues is the key outcome of close reading. With only two sentences to go on, we've already started to create an interpretation: We can hypothesize that "Araby" is going to explore loneliness or unhappiness, might feature a boy, and might be set in a city.

What literary forms are helping to create the text's meaning?

✔ **CHECKLIST**: *Close Reading*

How can I perform a close reading? As you think about your reading and writing process, ask yourself:

☐ Have I read with an open mind, asking questions as I read?
☐ Did I annotate the text, capturing my thinking in marginal notes?
☐ Have I slowed down my reading process, making sure that I am reading both to gather information and to generate new ideas?
☐ Did I read to understand the text? Make sure that you can accurately summarize the text. Reread passages that might be confusing or unclear on a first reading. Use annotations to keep track of important information about the literary work.
☐ Have I formulated ideas about the text's larger meaning? Collect clues to the text's meaning. Make sure to "notice what you notice," marking down any aspects of the text that you find interesting.
☐ Did I highlight specific evidence—words, phrases, images, structures—that seems to be signaling deeper meaning?
☐ Have I looked for patterns among details?
☐ Have I connected details to concepts? Make sure to jot down concept words in the margins of the text.
☐ Did I reread and rethink passages that seem particularly rich and passages that seem to be most connected to the concepts that I found interesting?

Analysis: Inquiry, Interpretation, Argument

Analysis is the process of thinking about (and rethinking and rethinking about!) a literary text in order to explore how it works, to examine the ideas that it raises, and to develop a unique interpretation of its meaning. Analysis asks you to investigate an issue raised by the literary work by breaking down the text into its component parts; you examine the text's parts in order to see how the text works as a whole to create its larger conceptual ideas. Analysis includes three critical thinking steps, which lead to and often overlap each other:

- **Inquiry:** the process of asking questions about a text in order to understand its meaning
- **Interpretation:** the development of a unique understanding of the text
- **Argument:** the presentation of a claim or a thesis about the text, which is then explained, developed, and supported with evidence

An analysis assignment might ask you to explore the ideal of beauty as presented in Michelle Serros's "Senior Picture Day," a short story that appears in Chapter 3. As soon as you start to explore "beauty" as presented in the story, it raises multiple questions and becomes a complex concept: In the story, how is beauty defined—is it defined only as appearance? Why does the narrator think her Mexican or Indian nose is not beautiful? How does American culture define beauty? How does her friend, Terri, reinforce that definition of beauty? Why would Native American beauty not be part of American beauty? How and why does her friend use her looks against her? Is beauty primarily about winning a boyfriend? This is just a start—the questions can keep coming!

As you think through your inquiry questions, you start to hypothesize answers to them. You might determine that you like the questions that connect ideas about friendship to ideas about beauty. Friends using beauty against each other is an unexpected concept. With some more thought, that idea could develop into an interpretation that explores how the story presents a character who uses beauty as a form of competition, showing that ideals of beauty can undermine friendship.

With a clear focusing idea and interpretation in place, you are ready to start writing your paper. When you are writing an analytical paper, you present your interpretation of the text in the form of an argument. You will need to create a central claim—an argument that captures your interpretation and conveys a position that can be debated. Your paper will work to develop and deepen that one idea. The central claim will become your thesis, serving as your paper's overarching and organizing principle. As you shape your thesis (such as with the argument that "Senior Picture Day" presents a character who uses beauty as a form of competition, showing that ideals of beauty can undermine friendship), you will need to examine any assumptions that you are making (such as the assumption that friendship should not be competitive) and define any terms that are essential to it (such as "beauty" and "American"). You will develop the thesis by explaining the different parts of the text that support your central idea, using details from the text as evidence and using sources that trigger further thinking. Analysis, then, is a process of using your observations about a text to develop a deeper understanding of the text and then presenting your new ideas and insights in a well-organized argument about the text's form and meaning.

As you read this description of analysis, you can see why it is at the core of critical thinking: It requires determining and exploring ideas, creating concepts, taking ideas apart and putting them back together again, making arguments, finding evidence, and developing ideas further. Let's look at each of these steps in turn.

Inquiry

Inquiry is the process of asking productive questions that lead to further thought and investigation, triggering new ideas and interpretations. The term "inquiry" captures the sense of a curious, inquiring mind asking open-ended questions that will lead to more questions and, ultimately, to the attempt to answer those questions. Inquiry is often positioned as the starting point of a discovery process that generates new ideas—inquiry encompasses a type of activity that we loosely call "brainstorming."

If you are trying to create new knowledge, you must be able to ask good questions about issues that you are observing, reading about, and researching. So, what is a "good" question? Inquiry-based questions cannot be answered with a quick "yes" or "no." They cannot be answered with a quick checking of factual information.

They cannot be answered with a plot summary or a restatement of the author's argument or findings. Instead, inquiry-based questions are often conceptual questions that seek to "open up" a topic to new thinking. Rather than asking for information, an inquiry-based question asks "why?" or "how?"

You can start to trigger interpretive thinking by asking general questions such as, "What is the main idea of this work?" or "What is the most important issue that this work explores?" and then moving toward more specific questions such as, "How does this story's character change to create a changing definition of this idea?" or "How does this poem's imagery show both positive and negative aspect of this idea?"

If we return to the story "Senior Picture Day," you might question how it presents "beauty," asking some of the questions that we've already noted. Those questions will become more specific as you reexamine the literary work and question it further. For example, as you reread your annotations on "Senior Picture Day," you might start to focus on the role the narrator's friend, Terri, plays in defining beauty. Why does Terri say to the narrator, "you look like you're more from Mexico than California"? How does the narrator counter that statement—does it show that she understands stereotypical ideals of beauty? When Terri is talking to Lightning Bolt, what are the ideals of female beauty that she references and why? Why does the narrator say about Terri, "She was saying things about a friend, things a real friend shouldn't be saying?" Why is Terri's reference to the narrator's nose the most painful comment? Why does the narrator leave Terri's house without telling her?

Inquiry-based questions wrestle with the ideas that are at the heart of the issue under consideration. Something meaningful is at stake in an inquiry-based question: An idea is being discovered and explained, an argument is being proven or disproven, a topic is being redefined, or a finding is being expanded.

✔ CHECKLIST: *Inquiry and Question-Asking*

How can I start my analysis by engaging in inquiry? As you think about your reading and writing process, ask yourself:

☐ Have I approached the text with a curious, inquiring mind? Remember that literary analysis is a process of discovery in which the reader uncovers meanings that he or she won't see at first.

☐ Have I asked as many questions as possible, big and small?

☐ Have I asked conceptual questions? Do not ask just fact-based "what" questions or "yes" and "no" questions. Instead, ask concept-oriented questions or "why" and "how" questions. Ask unexpected questions.

☐ Did I use brainstorming writing—jotting notes, making lists, writing response entries—to formulate answers to my questions?

☐ Have I argued with myself to continue the brainstorming process? Use questions to test your inferences, assumptions, and preexisting knowledge.

☐ Have I defined key terms?

☐ Did I use questions and answers to determine what a text might mean? At the same time, continue to be comfortable with ambiguity and indeterminacy, explore open-ended possibilities, entertain half-formed ideas, investigate opposing ideas, and notice what ideas seem too obvious and what ideas seem richly complex.

Interpretation

Analysis encourages you to maintain openness, asking questions while also predicting or hypothesizing the answers that you might discover as you continue your investigation. When you are working with literature, the most obvious outcome of the "questioning and answering" brainstorming process is that you interpret a piece of literature in an analysis paper. You use the annotating process of close reading and the note-taking process of inquiry to figure out what you think that literary text means, and you are then ready to turn to outlining and drafting a paper that solidifies your specific interpretation. Once focused and consolidated, your answers to your inquiry questions become your interpretation; your answers can serve as the arguments that structure your analysis paper.

Central to the interpretative process is evidence. Interpretation works with specific details in the text, asking, "What does this detail mean?" Literature trains you to look carefully at specific words and phrases, and at literary elements such as symbolism, setting, character, plot, and imagery. We discuss the literary elements central to each genre in detail in Chapters 11–15. All of these details become evidence for your interpretation, and you will evaluate and select the best evidence to support your ideas, quoting that evidence and citing it in your paper.

Literature also trains you to move back and forth between small details and big conceptual ideas, or to connect literary form (the literary elements) with literary content (the conceptual ideas, such as theme). Your interpretation will determine what ideas are represented by what details and what literary elements of the text are the most important. As you generate ideas, you will employ critical thinking skills, including drawing inferences, uncovering assumptions, connecting details, and entertaining and weighing competing interpretations.

If you look at the questions that we have been asking about "Senior Picture Day," you can see this movement from small details to larger concepts. An analysis will connect specific words, images, and elements from the story, such as Terri's comment about the narrator looking "Mexican" and not "blond," to larger ideas, such as the story's exploration of American ideals of female beauty and whether Native American women can fit those ideals. As you explore the story, you might analyze Terri's critique of her friend's body—how she mentions her being "skinny," then calls her "flat-chested," and then labels her nose "Indian." As you look at those phrases, you might form the opinion that Terri is purposely creating worse and worse insults about her friend. Your interpretation might show that, because the insults are presented in a series (skinny, flat-chested, nose), Terri knows that she is making insulting comments about her friend—they aren't unintentional. Your interpretation might determine that this is a strategic use of beauty by one friend to hurt another friend: Terri seems to move strategically toward the worst insult that she can make—and American ideals of beauty help her to do that.

Interpretation is the process of generating and testing your ideas. As you develop your interpretation, you should work to hone your ideas, making your interpretation more precise. We often think of "going deeper" into a text or "deepening" an interpretation, in that we do not want to remain at the surface level of the text and create an obvious or superficial interpretation of it; instead, we want to get to a deeper knowledge of what the text presents and understand its most important ideas. As you finalize your analysis, you will start to sort and organize your questions and answers, finding connections among your ideas. You will discover key ideas that repeat themselves, revealing that they are central to the literary work. You will also start to discard ideas that seem weak or off-topic. As your interpretation takes shape, it will become an argument, taking the form of a clear statement that will organize your paper.

✔ **CHECKLIST**: *Interpretation*

How can I continue my analysis, moving from inquiry to interpretation? As you think about your reading and writing process, ask yourself:

☐ Have I developed my understanding of the literary work, aiming for a focused explanation of the work's larger meaning? It can be helpful to ask, "What is one of the text's most important main ideas, and how does the text present and develop that idea?"

☐ Did I analyze both literary content and literary form as I created my interpretation? Literature not only presents complex ideas but also presents them in an artistic way, using specific literary forms. Make sure that your interpretation explores how the work makes meaning by attending to both form and content.

☐ Have I broken down the literary work? Separate the whole into parts in order to see relationships among the parts.

☐ Have I worked with concepts? Define, explain, and develop the work's key ideas.

☐ Have I worked with evidence? Explore the work's details, noting the ideas that they trigger. As you work with the evidence, you might:
  • draw inferences
  • uncover assumptions
  • connect details
  • organize evidence by categorizing it, locating similarities and differences
  • trace patterns and repetitions
  • entertain and weigh competing interpretations
  • note what seems to be missing, locating interesting gaps

☐ Did I create predictions or hypotheses concerning possible meanings?

☐ Did I create an interpretation? (Take a leap: What do you think the text means?)

Argument

An argument is a claim that offers a focused presentation of your interpretation of a literary work. A strong paper will take a specific position on, or make a specific proposition about, a carefully selected and narrowed topic, rather than present an obvious idea about a general topic. Your presentation of your claim and the evidence for your claim—and your attempt to win your reader over to your side through logical and well-organized writing—is argumentation.

When a main argument or claim is presented in an academic paper, we often label it a "thesis statement." A thesis statement allows you to show off your analysis by presenting it in a concise manner that highlights the strength of your ideas. This argument is then developed, typically through a series of supporting ideas or subpoints that present evidence and explain the reasoning behind the argument. A successful paper will answer the "so what" question and explain the significance of the argument.

Imagine yourself having to explain your ideas about a literary work to a friend, and then imagine your friend being somewhat resistant to your ideas so that you have to explain them in a more argumentative way, support them with clear evidence, and develop them with a series of related ideas. If you were exploring T. Coraghessan Boyle's "Greasy Lake," you might say something along the lines of, "The narrator seems really immature." If your friend questions you on this, you might decide to make your ideas more argumentative, explaining, "The narrator

represents immaturity because he doesn't think of the consequences of his actions—especially his violence toward the 'greasy character' and the 'fox.'" You might have to explain your ideas further, saying, "Although he can't handle responsibility, the narrator thinks that he is superior to everyone; he shows off how smart he is by making reference to art and literature. He thinks he is smart, but he is not smart about his actions and their consequences. Boyle wants to show that immaturity can't be rewarded, and that's why the narrator is punished with his car getting wrecked." With a bit of revision and development, this type of argument is already on its way to becoming a claim—a thesis—that can be further developed in an analytical paper.

Your thesis presents the main idea of your paper; it is the specific argument that you make about your selected topic. The best thesis arguments come from the ideas and evidence that you return to again and again in your brainstorming—the ideas that you are most interested in and passionate about. A thesis can result from your interest in a(n)

- *Pattern*: such as repeated images, ideas, or literary techniques
- *Problem*: such as a scene that raises but doesn't quite resolve a difficult issue
- *Insight*: such as a realization that an image might symbolize a specific idea
- *Question*: such as a questioning of a character's motivation
- *Formal element*: such as a careful charting of voice throughout a story
- *Conceptual idea*: such as a new insight into a universal concept, like love

Although we are concentrating on writing about literature, you can see how this type of writing develops larger critical thinking skills, such as learning to identify and analyze a problem, which are helpful in all fields and careers.

Once you have a thesis, you will want to develop it. The process of inquiry, of asking and answering questions about a text, can generate many insights. Those insights can be shaped—sorted, selected, and consolidated—into a pattern of ideas that can be developed into your argument. As you develop your interpretation of a text, your ideas can follow a logical order; for example, you might organize your ideas by subtopics, by facets of a topic, by "problems and solutions," from "most important to least important ideas," or from "big picture to smaller details."

✔ **CHECKLIST**: *Argument*

How can I use my analysis to generate an argument? As you think about your reading and writing process, ask yourself:

☐ Have I turned my interpretation into an argument by focusing on a specific aspect of the literary work and developing a position on that aspect?
☐ Did I create a strong thesis that presents a focused claim?
☐ Did I create a strong thesis that moves beyond an obvious statement or general idea?
☐ Have I developed my argument by selecting my best ideas and deepening them through further analysis?
☐ Have I organized my argument, most typically by breaking down my interpretation into a series of subideas or subconcepts, which I then have organized in a logical fashion? Remember to keep similar ideas together and work to

create a flow from one set of ideas to the next. You might create an organization in which you

- move from the most important idea to the least important idea
- move from the most obvious or understandable idea to the most complex idea
- trace a "cause/effect" or "causal" relationship, in which one idea leads to another because it causes it to occur
- explain the facets of one idea, showing how they connect (for example, "love" can encompass romantic love, platonic love, and familial love)
- perform an analysis of one literary element, such as a character analysis
- move from specific details to larger generalizations ("bottom up" or inductive reasoning)
- move from a general statement to smaller details ("top down" or deductive reasoning)
- follow a chronological order
- use a "pros/cons," "problem/solution," or "similarities/differences" structure

☐ Have I supported ideas with meaningful evidence that is analyzed and explained?

☐ Did I consider counterarguments?

Comparison and Synthesis

Comparison and synthesis connect together two or more sources, creating a relationship between them. In both comparison and synthesis, you are looking to find common concerns—areas of connection—that will allow different texts, authors, ideas, interpretations, or insights to be brought together.

Comparison is a well-known means of creating connections among sources, as most of us have written "comparison/contrast" papers at some point. Comparison focuses on finding similarities, while contrast focuses on finding differences among two or more sources. The development of relationships among texts encourages critical thinking; you cannot rely on a summary of the two texts but must evaluate each text in light of the other. Through comparison, you locate ideas and issues that might not be readily apparent in each text but that are revealed and then explored through the relationships you create.

Synthesis typically indicates a research paper in which multiple sources that comment on a topic are brought together in order to develop a new understanding of that topic. Rather than being compared and contrasted, the sources are often interwoven, taking the best ideas from each in order to help build an understanding of what has been discovered or debated about the topic at hand. When engaged in synthesis, you are connecting sources to your own thinking, showing how your ideas fit into larger critical debates. A synthesis will often serve as a strong foundation for further analysis, allowing you to show that your ideas are strong because they build on the ideas of critics. When working with critics' ideas, maintain a clear sense of your own ideas and arguments, explaining how you agree, disagree, or both agree and disagree ("Okay, but…") with the critics; further their ideas through your use of them; or apply their ideas to a new source. Use correct attribution and citation style, as detailed in Appendix B.

Synthesis requires several forms of critical thinking: You understand each source and can accurately convey its key ideas; you select only the most relevant

ideas from each source; you bring together sources in a way that clarifies how they agree, disagree, expand, develop, support, or contradict each other; you explain how each source connects to your thesis and arguments; and you create an organization for your synthesis that allows you to bring together sources without overwhelming your own ideas.

✔ **CHECKLIST** : *Comparison and Synthesis*

How can I engage in comparison and synthesis? As you think about your reading and writing process, ask yourself:

☐ Have I collected and selected sources that "speak to each other"—that address shared ideas and information, and thus can create meaningful connections?
☐ Did I create a relationship among my sources, explaining how they connect? Remember that comparison emphasizes similarities among sources, contrast emphasizes differences, and synthesis emphasizes an interweaving of sources.
☐ Have I maintained a strong sense of my own voice when performing research, clarifying how I agree with, disagree with, or further apply the critics' arguments?
☐ Did I create a strong thesis that emphasizes the relationship that I've created?
☐ Have I used the relationship that I've created to generate new insights into each text?
☐ Did I create a clear argumentative structure in which my paper works to integrate the sources to highlight ideas?
☐ Have I selected specific evidence from each source for quotation and analysis?
☐ Did I cite each source correctly?

Revision and Self-Awareness

An essential part of critical thinking is reflecting on your ideas and continually revising them in order to improve them. Each part of the critical thinking process should be repeated as needed: Reading should include rereading, inquiry should include asking follow-up questions, interpretation should include revisiting insights and reinterpreting evidence, argumentation should include a honing and reorganizing of key ideas, and synthesis should include reexamining the relationships created among sources.

The writing process ensures this rethinking by requiring revision. A paper is typically drafted and redrafted, moving from a rough initial draft through several intermediary drafts and then to a final draft that is polished before being submitted. Throughout this book, we provide multiple examples of papers being revised and improved as part of the writing process.

It might be helpful to think of paper "re-vision" as an opportunity to "re-envision" your ideas. Writing captures your thinking on the page. Writing also triggers new thinking: We have all had a lightbulb go off during the process of drafting—our mind is stimulated by the writing process to invent new ideas. When we are revising, we create new opportunities to improve our ideas. Make sure to see revision as an essential critical thinking skill and not a mere afterthought.

Revision forces you to step into the position of critic, asking you to analyze and criticize your own writing. The ability to create your own ideas and then to

step outside of yourself, reflect on, and critique those ideas requires advanced critical thinking skills that will serve you well in all of your academic courses and will later transfer into your career and beyond. Critical thinking encourages you to develop a sense of reflective self-awareness of yourself as a reader, writer, and thinker. As you engage in the writing process, use it to think carefully about your audience, the academic context of writing, your strengths and weaknesses as a writer, and how to push yourself to continually improve your thinking processes.

Standing Back: Kinds of Writing

Most writing about literature seeks to do one or both of two things:

- to inform ("This play was written only five years ago"; "The images of night suggest death.")
- to persuade ("This early story is one of her best"; "Despite the widespread view that the images of night suggest death, I will argue that here they do nothing more than indicate a time of day.")

Whether you are primarily concerned with informing or with persuading (and the two purposes can be nearly indistinguishable, because writers usually want to persuade readers that their information is significant), you ought to be prompted by a strong interest in a work or a body of work. This interest is usually a highly favorable response to the material (essentially, "That's terrific"), but an unfavorable response ("Awful!") or a sense of bafflement ("Why would anyone care for that?") may also motivate writing. In any case, because you have been stimulated by a work, you put words onto paper, perhaps first by jotting down observations in no particular sequence. Later, you will organize them for the benefit of an imagined reader, offering what D. H. Lawrence calls "a reasoned account of the feelings" produced by a work. Don't be embarrassed if a work produces strong feelings in you, pleasant or unpleasant.

Nonanalytical versus Analytical Writing

Writing about literature includes a range of types of writing. Some types of writing are nonanalytical-they try to avoid argument and attempt instead to inform, to describe, or to define. Some types of writing narrate personal responses. Although personal responses can hardly be argued about in rational terms, they can and must be set forth clearly and interestingly so that the reader understands—because the writer points to things in the literary work that evoke the responses—why the writer experiences these responses and why the writer evaluates the work as he or she does. Types of nonanalytical writing include the following:

- **Description and summary** ("The story is unusually brief, only a page long"; "The narrator explained his morning ritual of making coffee and then described riding the subway to work.")
- **Definition** ("The poem is a Shakespearian sonnet, since it is comprised of three quatrains and a couplet, following the rhyme scheme of abab, cdcd, efef, gg.")

- **Personal report or response** or what might be called "confession," a report of one's immediate response and perhaps of later responses ("The story reminds me of an experience that I had when I was about the age of the central character").
- **Review, evaluation, or judgment** ("The story is shocking" or "There is nothing here that holds my interest.") In Appendix A, we discuss critical strategies that underlie evaluation. Here, it is enough to say that the two most common sources for judging are: (1) a spontaneous personal response ("The death of a child is deeply disturbing") and (2) a principle that is alleged to be widely held ("A story ought to be unified").

Most academic writing about literature is chiefly explanatory and argumentative or, we can say, analytical: It is concerned with examining relationships (for instance, of the parts to the whole within a work, or of historical causes and effects) and creating arguments about how those relationships work and what they mean. Your instructors will probably ask you to write papers that are chiefly analytical, although some description, personal response, and review will almost surely be implicit (if not explicit) in your analyses. Analytical writing attempts to win over its audience through an interesting thesis, strong argumentation, compelling evidence, original insight, and clear organization.

- **Analysis** or explanation of the work, typically focusing on the conceptual ideas developed by the work and the internal relationships—the form and structure—of the work ("The second scene in this play has at least three functions"). As we have seen, an analytical paper results from close reading, inquiry, interpretation, and argumentation.
- **Comparison** ("While both poems present motherhood as challenging, the first emphasizes the negative feelings of overwork and the second emphasizes the positive emotions of support.")
- **Synthesis** ("These critics agree that the story presents a utopian vision of nineteenth-century farm life.") Synthesis can also include the application of critical concepts or theories to a literary work ("Freud's concept of the superego offers a way of understanding this character's motivations").

These analytical forms of writing aim to convince the reader of your interpretation of the work. Argumentation is central to these analytical forms of writing:

- **Argument** or writing that makes a strong claim and offers reasons advancing that specific understanding of the literary work. The reasons will be supported by evidence, notably references to passages from the literary works that you are discussing.

As you review the critical thinking process outlined in this chapter, the most obvious outcome of these steps is that you interpret a piece of literature—you figure out what you think that literary work means. In a literature-based class, the act of analysis is what it is all about! The ability to come to your own conclusions about a text's meaning is the foundation for all sorts of activities—class discussions, class debates, class papers—all of which typically present an argument that a text emphasizes as a key idea. More generally, note the skills that this process develops. A critical thinker learns not only to become a better reader and writer but also to notice details and patterns, to feel comfortable asking questions, to develop interpretations, to remain open to alternate interpretations, to test his or her own ideas, and to make arguments. Literature invites you to develop critical thinking skills at the most sophisticated level.

The Writer as Reader

Chapter Preview

After reading this chapter, you will be able to

- Explain the process of reading and responding to literature
- Use first responses, inquiry notes, and outlining to generate ideas for an essay
- Develop an analytical essay with an argumentative thesis
- Analyze an essay's argument, structure, and idea development
- Evaluate a student essay

Reading and Responding

Learning to write is in large measure learning to read. The text you should read most carefully is the one you yourself write—for example, an essay that makes an argument defending an interpretation. Your writing may start as jotting notes in the margin of a book that you are reading or in a journal, and it will go through several drafts before it becomes a finished essay. To produce something that another person will find worth reading, you must read each draft with care, trying to imagine the effect your words are likely to have on your reader. In writing about literature, you will apply some of the same critical thinking skills to your reading; that is, you will examine your responses to what you are reading, and you will try to account for them.

Let's begin by looking at a very short story by Kate Chopin.

KATE CHOPIN

Kate O'Flaherty (1851–1904), born into a prosperous family in St. Louis in 1870, married Oscar Chopin, a French-Creole businessman from Louisiana. They lived in New Orleans, where they had six children. Oscar died of malaria in 1882, and in 1884, Kate returned to St. Louis, where, living with her mother and children, she began to write fiction.

Ripe Figs

Maman-Nainaine said that when the figs were ripe Babette might go to visit her cousins down on the Bayou-Lafourche where the sugar cane grows. Not that the ripening of figs had the least thing to do with it, but that is the way Maman-Nainaine was.

It seemed to Babette a very long time to wait; for the leaves upon the trees were tender yet, and the figs were like little hard, green marbles.

But warm rains came along and plenty of strong sunshine, and though Maman-Nainaine was as patient as the statue of la Madone, and Babette as restless as a humming-bird, the first thing they both knew it was hot summertime. Every day Babette danced out to where the fig-trees were in a long line against the fence. She walked slowly beneath them, carefully peering between the gnarled, spreading branches. But each time she came disconsolate away again. What she saw there finally was something that made her sing and dance the whole long day.

When Maman-Nainaine sat down in her stately way to breakfast, the following morning, her muslin cap standing like an aureole about her white, placid face, Babette approached. She bore a dainty porcelain platter, which she set down before her godmother. It contained a dozen purple figs, fringed around with their rich, green leaves.

5   "Ah," said Maman-Nainaine arching her eyebrows, "how early the figs have ripened this year!"

"Oh," said Babette. "I think they have ripened very late."

"Babette," continued Maman-Nainaine, as she peeled the very plumpest figs with her pointed silver fruit-knife, "you will carry my love to them all down on Bayou-Lafourche. And tell your Tante Frosine I shall look for her at Toussaint— when the chrysanthemums are in bloom."

[1893]

Reading as Re-creation

If we had been Chopin's contemporaries, we might have read this sketch in *Vogue* in 1893 or in an early collection of her works, *A Night in Acadie* (1897). However, since we live more than a century later, we inevitably read "Ripe Figs" in a somewhat different way. This gets us to an important truth about writing and reading. A writer writes, sets forth his or her meaning, and attempts to guide the reader's responses, as we all do when we send a text or an e-mail home saying that we're thinking of dropping a course or asking for news or money. To this extent, the writer creates the written work and puts meaning in it.

But the reader, whether reading that written work as a requirement or for recreation, *re-creates* it in terms of his or her own experience and understanding. For instance, if your appeal for money is too indirect, the reader may miss it entirely or may sense it but feel that the need is not urgent. If, on the other hand, the appeal is direct or demanding, the reader may feel imposed upon, even assaulted. "Oh, but I didn't mean it that way," the writer later protests. Nevertheless, that's the way the reader took it. The text or e-mail is "out there," a physical reality standing between the writer and the reader, but its **meaning** is something that both the reader and the writer make.

Since all readers bring themselves to a written work, they each bring something individual. Although many of Chopin's original readers knew that she wrote chiefly about the people of Louisiana, especially Creoles (descendants of the early French and Spanish settlers), Cajuns (descendants of the French whom the British had expelled from Canada in the eighteenth century), African Americans, and mulattoes, those readers must have varied in their attitudes about such people. And many of today's readers do *not* (before they read a work by Chopin) know anything

about her subject. Some readers may know where Bayou-Lafourche is, and they may have notions about what it looks like, but most readers will not. Indeed, many readers will not know that a bayou is a sluggish, marshy inlet or outlet of a river or lake.

Moreover, even if a present-day reader in Chicago, Seattle, or Juneau knows what a bayou is, he or she may assume that "Ripe Figs" depicts a way of life that is still current, whereas a reader from Louisiana may see in the work a lost way of life, a depiction of the good old days (or perhaps the bad old days, depending on the reader's point of view). Much depends, we can say, on the reader's storehouse of experience.

Reading for Understanding: Collecting Evidence and Making Reasonable Inferences

As readers, we can and should make an effort to understand what an author is getting at. To begin, we should make an effort to understand unfamiliar words. Perhaps we need not look up every word that we don't know, at least on the first reading, but if certain unfamiliar words are repeated and thus seem especially important, we will want to look them up.

It happens that, in "Ripe Figs" a French word appears: "*Tante* Frosine," which means "*Aunt* Frosine." Fortunately, the meaning of the word is not crucial, and the context probably makes it clear that Frosine is an adult, which is all that we really need to know about her. However, a reader who does not know that chrysanthemums bloom in late summer or early autumn will miss part of Chopin's meaning. The point is this: The writer is pitching, and she expects the reader to catch on.

On the other hand, although writers tell us a good deal, they cannot tell us everything. We know that Maman-Nainaine is Babette's godmother, but we don't know exactly how old Maman-Nainaine and Babette are. Further, Chopin tells us nothing of Babette's parents. It *sounds* as though Babette and her godmother live alone, but readers' opinions may differ. One reader may argue that Babette's parents must be dead or ill; another may argue that the status of her parents is irrelevant and that what counts is that Babette is supervised by only one person, a mature woman.

In short, a text includes **indeterminacies** (passages that careful readers agree are open to various interpretations) and **gaps** (things left unsaid in the story, such as why a godmother rather than a mother takes care of Babette). As we work our way through a text, we keep reevaluating what we have read, pulling the details together to make sense of them, in a process called **consistency building**.

Whatever the gaps are, careful readers will collect evidence and draw many reasonable inferences about Maman-Nainaine. We can list them:

- She is older than Babette.
- She has a "stately way," and she is "as patient as the statue of la Madone."
- She has an odd way (is it exasperating, engaging, or a little of each?) of connecting actions with the seasons.
- Given this last point, she seems to act slowly, to be very patient.
- She is apparently used to being obeyed.

At this point, you may want to go back and reread "Ripe Figs" to see what else you can say about Maman-Nainaine.

What inferences can we list about Babette?

- She is young.
- She is active and impatient ("as restless as a humming-bird").
- She is obedient.

At this point, you may want to add to the list.

If you compare your additions with those of a classmate, you may find that the two of you disagree about what may reasonably be inferred from Chopin's words. Suppose, for instance, that your classmate says that, although Babette is outwardly obedient, inwardly she probably hates Maman-Nainaine. Would you agree that this is an acceptable inference? If you don't agree, how might you convince your classmate that such a response is not justified? What arguments (supported by what evidence) would you offer? We are speaking here of an activity of mind we call **critical thinking**, a topic outlined in Chapter 2 and that will be discussed throughout this book.

Reading with Pen in Hand: Close Reading and Annotation

It's probably best to read a work of literature straight through, enjoying it and letting yourself be carried along to the end. Then, when you have an overall view, you'll want to read it again, noticing (for example) how certain innocent-seeming details early in the work prove to be important later.

Perhaps the best way to read attentively is, after a first reading, to mark the text, underlining or highlighting passages that seem especially interesting, and to jot down notes or queries in the margins. (*Caution*: Annotate and highlight, but don't get so carried away that you highlight entire pages.)

The critical thinking skills developed by close reading are explored in Chapters 2, 4, and 6. Close reading encourages you to "notice what you notice," using annotation to remark on aspects of the text that seem to convey meaningful ideas, raise interesting questions, or offer rich opportunities for interpretation. Close reading also encourages you to notice how literary content (the ideas conveyed by the text) is created by literary form (the structuring of the text through literary elements, such as voice, imagery, setting, and word choice). By annotating the text, you'll start the process of asking questions, gathering evidence, and formulating opinions about the text.

Let's look at some sample annotations written by a student, Antonia Tenori, on "Ripe Figs."

Student Work: Annotation

KATE CHOPIN

Ripe Figs

Maman-Nainaine said that when the figs were ripe Babette might go to visit her cousins down on the Bayou- *?* Lafourche where the sugar cane grows. Not that the ripening of figs had the least thing to do with it, but that is the *strange* way Maman-Nainaine was.

It seemed to Babette a very long time to wait; for the leaves upon the trees were tender yet, and the figs were like little hard, green marbles.

But warm rains came along and plenty of strong sunshine, and though Maman-Nainaine was as patient as the statue of la Madone, and Babette as restless as a hummingbird, the first thing they both knew it was hot summertime. Every day Babette danced out to where the fig-trees were in a long line against the fence. She walked slowly beneath them, carefully peering between the gnarled, spreading branches. But each time she came disconsolate away again. What she saw there finally was something that made her sing and dance the whole long day.

contrast between M-N and B

When Maman-Nainaine sat down in her stately way to breakfast, the following morning, her muslin cap standing like an aureole about her white, placid face, Babette approached. She bore a dainty porcelain platter, which she set down before her godmother. It contained a dozen purple figs fringed around with their rich, green leaves.

another contrast ceremonious

Check this?

nice echo contrast like a song

"Ah," said Maman-Nainaine arching her eyebrows, "how early the figs have ripened this year!"

"Oh," said Babette. "I think they have ripened very late."

time passes fast for M-N slowly for B

is M-N herself like a plump fig?

"Babette," continued Maman-Nainaine, as she peeled the very plumpest figs with her pointed silver fruit-knife, "you will carry my love to them all down on Bayou-Lafourche. And tell your Tante Frosine I shall look for her at Toussaint—when the chrysanthemums are in bloom."

B entrusted with a message of love

opens with figs; ends with chrys. (autumn)

fulfillment? Equivalent to figs ripening?

Reading for Response: Recording First Reactions

Another useful way of getting at the meaning of a work of literature is to jot down your initial responses to it, recording your impressions as they come to you, in any order—almost as though you're talking to yourself. Since no one else is going to read your notes, you can be entirely at ease. You can write in sentences or not; it's up to you.

You can jot down your responses either before or after you annotate the text. Some readers find that annotating a text helps to produce ideas for further jottings; others prefer to jot down a few thoughts immediately after a first reading, and then, stimulated by these thoughts, they reread and annotate the text.

Write whatever comes into your mind, whatever the literary work triggers in your own imagination, and whatever you think are the important ideas or values, based on your own experience.

Here is Tenori's first response to "Ripe Figs":

Student Work: Response Writing

This is a very short story. I didn't know stories were this short, but I like it because you can get it all quickly and it's no trouble to reread it carefully. The shortness, though, leaves a lot of gaps for the reader to fill in. So much is not said. Your imagination is put to work.

But I can see Maman-N sitting at her table—pleasantly powerful—no one you would want to argue with. She's formal and distant—and definitely has quirks. She wants to postpone Babette's trip, but we don't know why. And you can sense B's frustration.

But maybe she's teaching her that something really good is worth waiting for and that anticipation is as much fun as the trip. Maybe I can develop this idea.

Another thing. I can tell they are not poor—from two things. The pointed silver fruit knife and the porcelain platter, and the fact that Maman sits down to breakfast in a "stately" way. They are the leisure class. But I don't know enough about life on the bayous to go into this. Their life is different from mine; no one I know has that kind of peaceful rural life.

Reading for Inquiry: Ask Questions and Brainstorm Ideas

After getting your initial responses down on paper, you are ready to start moving toward turning those reactions into an analytical paper by engaging in **inquiry**, or the process of active question asking. Inquiry-based questions aim to generate insights into a text and uncover new ideas. They are typically *open-ended conceptual questions* rather than *information-based questions*, asking "how" and "why" and trying to determine a text's meaning and how that meaning is created.

After reading the story, annotating it, and jotting down her first responses, Antonia reread her notes and highlighted any ideas that she thought were especially noteworthy. She then jotted down more analytical ideas on her laptop.

She generated a series of questions, placing each question on a new page so that she could further develop her thinking. Is "Ripe Figs" a story, or is it just a character sketch? (She put her responses on a page for that topic.) What contrasts are notable? (She recorded the material on another notebook page.) How should we define the relationship between Maman and Babette? (She recorded her ideas on another notebook page.) What words, phrases, or images are unusual? (She recorded this material on another notebook page.) A day later, when she returned to work on her paper, stimulated by another reading of "Ripe Figs" and a review of her notes, Antonia made additional notes that took this shape:

Student Work: Inquiry Notes

Is Ripe Figs a story, or is it just a character sketch?

Story = has a plot, events
—there is some conflict and resolution—there is the sense of moving forward
—there is a thematic emphasis on time

Character sketch = focuses on characters' key qualities
—this focuses mostly on describing the two characters and their interactions—
these interactions and their emphasis on time seem to make this more of a story

What contrasts are notable?

The contrast between age and youth: time
Between patience and impatience
Between Babette "restless as a humming-bird" and Maman with a "white, placid face"

Between seasons: spring and summer, unripe and ripe, warm and hot
　　Story emphasizes the cycle of seasons?
Between observing (the figs) and longing (for visit)

How should we define the relationship between Maman and Babette?

Godmother and goddaughter: wealthy, leisured
Mother figure and daughter figure
Old age and youth: the cycle of aging?
Solid and "stately" vs. energetic and "restless"
Sitting vs. dancing
Perceived passage of time as "early" vs. perceived changes as "late": time issue
　　—This raises another question: Why does Babette want to visit her cousins so
　　　much?
What is the relationship of Mamam and Babette to her cousins? Are they more fun,
　　youthful, energetic like Babette?

What words or phrases or images are unusual?

"ripening"
leaves: "tender"; figs: "hard"
"patient as a statue" vs. "restless as a humming-bird"
"Babette danced out," "sing and dance the whole long day"
"sat down in her stately way," "like an aureole about her white, placid face"
"bore a dainty porcelain platter"
"how early the figs have ripened this year" vs. "I think they have ripened
　　very late"
"peeled the plumpest fig with her pointed silver fruit-knife"
"when the chrysanthemums are in bloom"

Reading in Context: Identifying Your Audience and Purpose

Now, suppose that you are beginning the process of writing about "Ripe Figs" for someone else. The first question to ask yourself is, "For whom am I writing?" That is, who is your **audience**? (You are probably writing because an instructor has asked you to do so, but you must still imagine an audience. Your instructor may tell you, for instance, to write for your classmates or to write for the best teacher you had in high school.)

- If you are writing for people who are familiar with some of Chopin's work, you won't have to say much about the author.
- If you are writing for an audience that perhaps has never heard of Chopin, you may want to include a brief biographical note of the sort that we gave earlier.
- If you are writing for an audience that you believe has read several works by Chopin, you may want to make comparisons, explaining—arguing, really—how "Ripe Figs" resembles or differs from Chopin's other work.

In a sense, your audience is your collaborator and helps you to decide what you will say. You are also helped by your sense of **purpose**. If your aim is to introduce readers to Chopin, you will make points that reflect this purpose. If your aim is to tell people what you think "Ripe Figs" means to say about human relationships or about time, you will address that subject. If your aim is to have a little fun and to

entertain an audience that is already familiar with "Ripe Figs," you may decide to write a parody (a humorous imitation) of the story.

From Reading to Writing: Developing an Analytical Essay with an Argumentative Thesis

Let's assume that you want to describe "Ripe Figs" to someone who has not read it. You will briefly summarize the action, such as it is, and will mention where it takes place; tell who the characters are, including what their relationship is; and note what, if anything, happens to them. Beyond that, you'll try to explain as honestly as you can what makes "Ripe Figs" appealing or interesting—or trifling, or boring, or whatever. You will want to explain what the story means and how it has created that meaning. You will most likely focus on the conceptual ideas raised by the story that you find most important. That is, you will *argue* a thesis, even though you won't want to make so formal a statement as "In this essay, I will argue that . . ." or "This essay will attempt to prove that. . . ." Your essay will essentially be an argument because (perhaps after a brief summary of the work) you will point to the evidence that has caused you to respond as you did.

Student Analytical Essay: "Images of Ripening in Kate Chopin's 'Ripe Figs'"

Here is an essay that Antonia Tenori wrote for an assignment that asked for an analysis of "Ripe Figs" in a paper of "about 500 words (two double-spaced typed pages)."

Tenori 1

Antonia Tenori

Professor Lee

English 102

11 February 2016

Images of Ripening in Kate Chopin's "Ripe Figs"

Very little happens in Kate Chopin's one-page story, "Ripe Figs."

Maman-Nainaine tells her goddaughter Babette that she may "visit her cousins down on the Bayou-Lafourche" "when the figs were ripe"; the figs

---

ripen, and Babette is given permission to go (25). So little happens in "Ripe Figs" that the story at first appears merely to be a character sketch that illustrates, through Babette and her godmother, the contrast between youth and age. But by means of the natural imagery of the tale, Chopin suggests more than this: She asks her readers to see the relationship of human time to nature's seasons, and she suggests that, try as we may to push the process of maturity, growth or "ripening" happens in its own time.

The story clearly contrasts the impatience of youth with the patience and dignity that come with age. Babette, whose name suggests she is still a "little baby," is "restless as a humming-bird" (26). Each day when she eagerly goes to see if the figs have ripened, she doesn't simply walk but she dances. By contrast, Maman-Nainaine has a "stately way," she is "patient as the statue of la Madone," and there is an "aureole"—a radiance—"about her white, placid face" (26). The brief dialog near the end of the story also emphasizes the difference between the two characters. When the figs finally ripen, Maman-Nainaine is surprised (she arches her eyebrows), and she exclaims, "how early the figs have ripened this year!" Babette replies, "I think they have ripened very late" (26).

Chopin is not simply remarking here that time passes slowly for young people, and quickly for old people. She suggests that nature moves at its own pace, regardless of human wishes. Babette, young and "tender" as the fig leaves, can't wait to "ripen" (25). Her visit to Bayou-Lafourche is not a mere pleasure trip, but represents her coming into her own season of maturity. Babette's desire to rush this process is tempered by a condition that her godmother sets: Babette must wait until the figs ripen, since everything comes in its own season. Maman-Nainaine recognizes the patterns of the natural world, the rhythms of life. By asking Babette to await the ripening, the young girl is asked to pay attention to the patterns as well.

Tenori 3

Chopin further suggests that if we pay attention and wait with patience, the fruits of our own growth will be sweet, plump, and beautiful, like the "dozen purple figs, fringed around with their rich, green leaves," that Babette finally offers her godmother (26). Chopin uses natural imagery effectively, interweaving the young girl's growth with the rhythms of the seasons. In this way, the reader is connected with both processes in an intimate and inviting way.

[New page]

Tenori 4

Work Cited

Chopin, Kate. "Ripe Figs." *Literature for Composition*. Ed. Sylvan Barnet, William Burto, William E. Cain, and Cheryl L. Nixon. 11th ed. Boston: Pearson, 2017. 25-26. Print.

The Analytical Essay: Argument and Structure Analyzed

- The *title of the essay* is informative; it clearly indicates the focus of the analysis. Notice, too, that it is much more interesting than "An Analysis of a Story" or "An Analysis of Kate Chopin's 'Ripe Figs'" or "'Ripe Figs': A Study" or "An Analysis of Imagery." For your own essays, construct titles that inform and interest your reader.
- The *first sentence* names the author and title being written about. Strictly speaking, this information is redundant, since it appears in the essay's title, but it is customary to give the author's full name and the title of the work early in the essay, and it is essential to give such information when it is not in the title.
- The *second sentence* offers enough plot summary to enable the reader to follow the discussion. Notice, however, that the essay as a whole is much more than a summary of the plot. The **summary** is offered early in order to make the **analysis** intelligible. Chiefly, the opening paragraph presents one view (e.g., the view that Antonia Tenori believes is inadequate); then, after a transitional "but," it offers a second view and presents a thesis—the point that you will argue in the essay.

Perhaps the most common error that students make in writing about literature is to confuse a summary of the plot with analysis of the work. A little plot telling is acceptable, to remind your reader of what happens, but normally your essay will be devoted to setting forth a thesis about a work and supporting that thesis with evidence. Your readers do not want to know what happens in the work; they want to know what you make of the work— how you interpret it or why you like or dislike it.

- The *last sentence of the first paragraph* provides the **thesis statement**: Chopin "asks her readers to see the relationship of human time to nature's seasons, and she suggests that, try as we may to push the process of maturity, growth or 'ripening' happens in its own time." Note that this thesis is conceptual, exploring ideas of human time, the seasons, and maturity. Note also that the thesis is argumentative, maintaining that Chopin presents a specific understanding of time—that the process of maturity cannot be rushed.
- In the *second paragraph*, Tenori supports her thesis by providing brief quotations. These quotations are not padding; rather, they are **evidence** supporting her assertion that Chopin "contrasts the impatience of youth with the patience and dignity that come with age."
- In the *third paragraph*, Tenori develops her thesis ("Chopin is not simply. . . . She suggests. . . .").
- The *final paragraph* begins with a helpful transition ("Chopin *further* suggests"), offers additional evidence, and ends with a new idea (about the reader's response to the story) that takes the **analysis** a step further. The essay avoids the deadliest kind of conclusion, a mere summary of the essay ("Thus we have seen," or some such words). Tenori's effective *final sentence* nicely draws the reader into the essay. (Effective final sentences can be difficult to write; we give advice about writing them on pages 218 and 274.)

Tenori wrote this paper for an assignment that asked for five hundred words. If the first question to ask is "To whom am I writing?" the second question to ask is "What is the length of the assignment?" The answer to this second question will provide two sorts of guidance: It will give you some sense of how much time you should devote to preparing the paper—an instructor expects you to spend more time on a ten-page paper than on a one-page paper—and it will give you a sense of how much detail you can include. For a short paper—say, one or two pages— you will need to make your main point with directness; you will not have space for lots of details, just those that support the main point. This is what Tenori aims to achieve in her second and third paragraphs, where she highlights the term "ripens" and briefly, but effectively, develops its implications. For a longer paper of three to five pages or more, you can examine the characters, setting, and central themes in depth, and you can focus on more details in the text to strengthen your analysis.

The Writing Process: From First Responses to Final Essay

Antonia Tenori's essay is good because it is clear and interesting, and especially because it helps to develop a reader's understanding and enjoyment of Chopin's story. Now let's go backstage, so to speak, to see how this student turned her notes into an effective final draft.

Capturing Earliest Responses. After reading the story, Tenori annotated it, marking whatever she thought was especially noteworthy. She then captured her inquiry process by jotting down notes on her laptop, using note-taking software.

As seen, she asked interesting questions that pushed her thinking further: Is "Ripe Figs" a story, or is it just a character sketch? What contrasts are notable? How should we define the relationship between Maman and Babette? What words or phrases or images are unusual? Tenori started to answer those questions and then, a day later, returned to her reading and brainstorming and added additional notes.

Organizing Notes. When the time came to turn her notes into a draft essay, Tenori reviewed the notes and added further thoughts. Next, she organized the note pages, putting together into one section the pages about characterization and into another section the pages about the seasons. Reviewing the notes in each section, on the basis of her review (after making a backup copy), she deleted a few pages that no longer seemed useful and moved an occasional page into a different section (via the Contents view). She then started to think about how she might organize her essay.

As a first step in settling on an organization, she arranged the notebook sections into a sequence that seemed reasonable. It made sense, she thought, to begin with a brief biographical sketch of Chopin, but she soon decided not to include this material because the reader would probably already know it, it would take up too much of the paper's length, and, in any case, it was not relevant to the argument that she planned to set forth. She decided to go on to her major points about the story, then to refine some of these points, and finally to offer a conclusion. This organization, she felt, was reasonable and would enable the reader to follow her argument easily.

Preparing a Preliminary Outline. In order to get a clear idea of where she might be going, Tenori then typed an outline, following the sequence of her note packets—the organization of her chief points became an outline. In short, she prepared a map to confirm that each part of her paper would lead coherently to the next part.

Surveying her outline, Tenori became aware of points that she should have included but had overlooked. Her first outline and the revised version of it follow.

A tentative outline is a preliminary map that helps the writer to see not only pointless detours that need to be eliminated but also undeveloped areas that need to be worked up. As the two versions of Tenori's outline indicate, drafting her map enabled her to make important changes before she wrote a first draft.

Student Work: Outlining

First Outline	*Revised Outline*
Bio of Chopin	Little plot, emph. on contrasting characters
Plot summary	Characters related to seasons
Characterization	Contrasts
Babette	spring vs autumn
Maman-N	youth vs maturity
Contrasts	impatience vs patience (?)
Youth: activity, impatient	Significance, meaning
Age: stately, "statue"	Maman-N as teacher
Differences in perception of nature	some things can't be hurried
Point? Meaning?	implication that B is maturing, can
	carry message, will become aware of
	the changing seasons, and that there is a
	right time for each action

Writing a Draft. Working from her thoughtfully revised outline, Tenori wrote a first draft, which she then revised. The second draft, when further revised, became the final essay. Microsoft Word, for example, allows you to track the revisions made to a document and look at different versions of a document. However, many writers find comfort in having a printed copy of each draft to go over with a pen; the desired changes can then be made (and kept track of) on the computer.

Other Possibilities for Writing

You might write a paper of a very different sort, based on the same story by Chopin but emphasizing creative thinking in addition to analytical thinking. Consider the following possibilities:

1. Write a sequel, moving from fall to spring.
2. Write a letter from Babette, at Bayou-Lafourche, to Maman-Nainaine.
3. Imagine that Babette is now an old woman, writing her memoirs. What does she say about Maman-Nainaine?
4. Write a narrative based on your own experience of learning a lesson in patience.

From Reading to Writing: Moving from Brainstorming to Analytical Essay

BRUCE HOLLAND ROGERS

Bruce Holland Rogers, an American writer who has won numerous prizes for his short fiction, teaches in the MFA program of the Northwest Institute of Literary Arts. In 2001, a film, The Other Side, *was based on his short novel,* Lifeboat on a Burning Sea.

   The following story consists of three stories, each of which contains sixty-nine words. The form originated with a short-lived, Toronto-based magazine, NFC, *which set the limit of sixty-nine words, exclusive of the title. From this limit, there somehow evolved the story that consists of three thematically related stories, each of sixty-nine words, a form now known as the three-six-nine.*

Three Soldiers

1. The Hardest Question

My marines bring me questions. "When do we get to shower?" "Sergeant, how do you say 'Good afternoon' again?" "Sarge, where can I get more gun oil?"

   I have answers. "Tomorrow, maybe." "*Maysuh alheer.*" "Use mine."

   Answering their questions is my job. But when Anaya was shot and bleeding out, he grabbed my arm and said, "Sergeant? Sergeant?" I understood the question, but damn. I didn't have an answer.

damn, happens to everyone at the worst time

totally true [handwritten margin note]

2. Foreign War

No U.S. soldier who could see that kid would have shot him. But that's long-range ordnance for you. Calder stood next to me in the street, looking at the pieces. "We've come so far from home," he said, "that we'll never get back."

"You dumbass," I said. But a year later I stood on the tarmac hugging my child, thinking of that kid in pieces, and I wasn't home.

3. Decisions, Decisions

In morning twilight, far away, my men are making up their minds:

What's that guy carrying?
Friend or foe?

why isn't he there? what happened? [handwritten margin note]

I should be there, helping them decide. My wife and my parents do their best to make Christmas dinner conversation around my silence. An hour ago, I was yelling at Angie for turning on the damn news. My father, carving, won't meet my eyes. He says, "White meat, or dark?"

[2004]

The Writing Process: From Response Writing to Final Essay

Now, for the responses to "Three Soldiers" by a student who had been given only the biographical note that appears above the text and the suggestion that students begin by jotting down their first reactions to each story, such as:

- What puzzles you?
- What interests you?
- Are there significant connections among the three stories?

Here is the response of one student, Will Holly. Notice how he focuses on asking questions about the text and investigating the questions asked within the text. This is productive inquiry.

Student Work: Response Writing

This business of 69 words seems silly—crazy—to me. I wouldn't want to learn that Shakespeare wrote *Hamlet* because he was challenged to write a play of exactly such-and-such a number of words. Nutty—but I am glad that Rogers *did* write the stories, for whatever reason.

What sort of puzzles me is that I *like* them—even though I ought to be depressed by them—stuff about a soldier dying, a kid blown to pieces, soldiers who can't get over their terrible experiences. Why do we read this stuff, and—maybe a bigger puzzle—why do I like it?

In the first story, exactly what is "the hardest question"? I think the hardest question—not the first three questions but the question hidden in the word "Sergeant?"—the question asked but not asked in words, by the soldier who "was shot and bleeding out" (which I think means he is bleeding to death)—must be, "Why am I dying?" or something close to this. Maybe the question is "Why ME?" but in any case, it is a question about "bleeding out," and this question is a lot harder than "when do we shower" or "how do you say such-and-such in a foreign language?" or "where can I get oil?" Notice that

the sergeant does *not* have an answer for *this* question. Sure, we can give answers, but we realize that our answers cannot be adequate to the terrifying occasion.

In the second story, there is no question, but we are still concerned with death in war. A soldier is looking at the "pieces" of a kid who was killed by long-range gunfire. This soldier says, "We've come so far from home that we'll never get back." What does he mean? After all, most of the soldiers *will* actually get back to home. I think he means that we have had an experience—an experience we could not possibly have imagined when we were safe at home, maybe at college or maybe at some job, and now we can never be the same, we can never regain our naivete. We can *literally* go home, but we will be so changed by the experience that everything will look different. And in fact, in the last line of this very short story this soldier *does* get home, and he is hugging his own child, but his thoughts are in the warzone. So although he is physically home, he is not mentally home.

In the third story, the characters are also back home—the soldier is with his parents and his wife—but it is clear that his *mind* is still in the war zone. He is thinking—as any soldier in a combat area would think when he sees a stranger—"What's that guy carrying?" and "Friend or foe?" These questions are different, VERY different—from the trivial question that his father is asking, carving the chicken or turkey at the Christmas dinner, "White meat, or dark?" Again, he is home, but he is so changed from when he was last home that he is not home, he is in another world.

The order of the stories: The first story is set in—well, I don't know where, but I guess maybe Iraq. Certainly in a war zone. The second story, too, is set there, but they talk about home. The third story is set at home—but the soldier is still mentally at war. Further, there is a nice connection between the first and the last stories: The first story pretty much *begins with* a question, and the last story *ends with* a question, so, in a way, the wheel has come full circle. There is a sense of unity, of completion. It's sort of frightening, but, well, one would have to be crazy to think that the experience of war—which can include killing innocent children—is not horrible!

Student Analytical Essay: "Thinking about Three Soldiers Thinking"

The student ultimately wrote the following short essay.

Holly 1

Will Holly

Professor Cargill

English 101A

28 January 2016

Thinking about Three Soldiers Thinking

On the printed page Bruce Holland Rogers's "Three Soldiers" is three

very short stories, and each of the three can stand alone and can be read

---

with interest, but the three really go together and they form a whole that is greater than any of the parts.

All of the stories deal with soldiers who are engaged in killing people—maybe in Vietnam or Iraq, I think but I am not certain, and the exact locale does not really matter. The first story, "The Hardest Question," begins with some trivial questions that soldiers ask a sergeant ("When do we get to shower") but it ends, a few sentences later, with a soldier who is "bleeding out," and whose question—repeated—is only one word long, "Sergeant?" (37). The reader probably is supposed to understand that the soldier is bleeding to death, and the question in his mind is something like, "Sergeant, will I die?" or maybe it is, "Sergeant, why me?" The sergeant can easily answer the earlier questions, about showering, and so forth, but he gives no answer to what the title of the story calls "The Hardest Question."

When readers start to read a story called "The Hardest Question," they probably expect to hear the question stated fully, and they probably also expect some sort of answer to the question. Here, the question is never stated fully—we just get "Sergeant?"—and it certainly isn't answered (37). Does that mean we are disappointed with the story? No, the story, though painful, is complete. We know there is no satisfactory answer to the question of the soldier who is "bleeding out" (37).

The second story, "Foreign War," is also only a few sentences long. It begins by saying that a soldier is looking at "the pieces" of a "kid" who has been killed by "long-range ordnance" (38). A few sentences later the soldier is home, hugging his own kid, but his mind is back at the scene of the disaster, and he realizes that although he can return home physically, in another sense he can never be back home again, can never return to the place where he had been unaware of such horrors.

The third story, "Decisions, Decisions" continues this theme of being back home but not being *at home*. The soldier is with his family (wife and

parents), and is having Christmas dinner. But when we begin reading the story we do not know that this is the situation. The story begins, "In morning twilight, far away, my men are making up their minds" (38). And then we get two questions, "What's that guy carrying?" and "Friend or foe?" (38). Probably when readers first read these questions they think that even though the speaker says he is "far away" from his men he is still abroad with other soldiers—soldiers who quite naturally are suspicious of some "guy" carrying something—it could be a weapon—and who, seeing a stranger, wonder if it is "Friend or foe?" (38). We then learn where he is physically—although his *mind* is still on the battlefield, where his men are in danger, but he really is safe at home with his family. Here at home the decisions are not the life-and-death decisions of a soldier in combat ("What's that guy carrying?" "Friend or foe?") but are the utterly trivial decisions concerning whether one prefers the white meat or the dark meat of the Christmas bird (38). Bruce Holland Rogers is probably not saying that we should not express our preferences when it comes to food, but he is saying—or, rather, he is memorably *showing* us—that for someone who has gone through such experiences as seeing a man bleed to death, or seeing the blown-up pieces of a child—to be asked to make "decisions, decisions" about food preferences is almost intolerable (38).

   The three stories are separate and they can be read as separate things, but they are really three parts of one story. The title is "Three Soldiers," so we must assume that the characters in each of the three stories are different, but they really add up to one character, a soldier who has seen the unbearable, and who will carry the memories for the rest of his life, whether he is hugging his child or sitting at a family Christmas dinner. Put this way, the story sounds deeply depressing, and a reader might wonder why Rogers thinks we should read this, but in fact, the story is told so effectively, so vividly, so concisely, so memorably, that it comes across as something that one wants to tell one's friends they must read. It's not that it has an

---

Holly 4

encouraging moral (it doesn't) or a happy ending (it doesn't), but it is told

so skillfully—for instance, the first story begins with a question and the last

story ends with a question—and it is told with such apparent simplicity and

honesty that a reader feels he or she must share it with others.

[New page]

Holly 5

Work Cited

Rogers, Bruce Holland. "Three Soldiers." *Literature for Composition*. Ed. Sylvan

Barnet, William Burto, William E. Cain, and Cheryl L. Nixon. 11th ed. Boston:

Pearson, 2017. 37-38. Print

The Analytical Essay: The Development of Ideas Analyzed

Let's look at this short essay.

- The *title*, though not exceptionally good, is adequate. Will Holly tells us that, when he was working on his draft, he was very much taken with his perception that the stories are closely related—for instance, that questions begin the first story and a question ends the last story—and he thought he would title his essay "What Goes Around Comes Around." But, when he drafted the essay, he realized that this title sounded as though it referred to some aspect of a plot in which a character ends up where he or she started, or gets what he or she deserves, and Holly decided that it wasn't suitable. He then considered "Thinking About 'Three Soldiers'" but soon decided that this title was too vague. Holly says he was getting desperate until at the last minute he realized that he was *thinking* about soldiers who are *thinking*, and so he came up with his title, "Thinking About Three Soldiers Thinking." This title is accurate, and it involves a bit of wordplay, so in our view it is appropriate.
- The *opening paragraph* lets the reader know what author and what work(s) will be discussed—always a good idea!—and it makes the interesting **thesis argument** that the three works are independent yet also form a unified whole. The reader now expects that the rest of the essay will offer support for this *claim*.
- The *second and third paragraphs* discuss the first story. They briefly summarize the plot, but they do much more: They *explain* aspects of the story.

- The *fourth paragraph*, devoted to the second story, both summarizes and offers an **interpretation** of the significance of the plot. It tells the reader what the happenings *add up to*. The student is *thinking*, not just retelling what the story clearly says.
- The *fifth paragraph*, devoted to the third story, connects that story with the preceding story ("The third story . . . continues this theme of being back home") and then reports that here readers probably have to revise their sense of what is going on in the story. It's not that the author of the story is clumsy or careless; rather, Rogers wants to bring us back to the battlefield, so rather than offer an objective view of the setting, he puts us in the soldier's *mind*. Again, the essayist is thinking, analyzing, and offering **evidence** to support a thesis.
- The *final paragraph* begins by reasserting the thesis (the three stories are so connected by theme that they cohere as one story), and then it comments on *why* we are not depressed by reading a story (or three stories) on this theme. You may disagree with the author's conclusions, but we think you will agree that the essay goes beyond plot telling and offers interesting reasons to support its thesis.

From Reading to Writing: Moving from Preliminary Outline to Analytical Essay

RAY BRADBURY

Ray Bradbury (1920–2012) was born in Waukegan, Illinois, and was educated there and in Los Angeles. While a high school student, he published his first science fiction in the school's magazine, and by 1941, he was publishing professionally. The story printed here is from The Martian Chronicles *(1950), a collection of linked short stories. Among his other works are* Fahrenheit 451 *(1953),* Something Wicked This Way Comes *(1962), and* Death Is a Lonely Business *(1985).*

August 2026: There Will Come Soft Rains

In the living room the voice-clock sang, *Tick-Tock, seven o'clock, time to get up, time to get up, seven o'clock!* as if it were afraid that nobody would. The morning house lay empty. The clock ticked on, repeating and repeating its sounds into the emptiness. *Seven-nine, breakfast time, seven-nine!*

In the kitchen the breakfast stove gave a hissing sigh and ejected from its warm interior eight pieces of perfectly browned toast, eight eggs sunny-side up, sixteen slices of bacon, two coffees, and two cool glasses of milk.

"Today is August 4, 2026," said a second voice from the kitchen ceiling, "in the city of Allendale, California." It repeated the date three times for memory's sake. "Today is Mr. Featherstone's birthday. Today is the anniversary of Tilita's marriage. Insurance is payable, as are the water, gas, and light bills."

Somewhere in the walls, relays clicked, memory tapes glided under electric eyes.

Eight-one, tick-tock, eight-one o'clock, off to school, off to work, run, run, eight-one! But no doors slammed, no carpets took the soft tread of rubber heels. It was

raining outside. The weather box on the front door sang quietly: "Rain, rain, go away; rubbers, raincoats for today. . . ." And the rain tapped on the empty house, echoing.

Outside, the garage chimed and lifted its door to reveal the waiting car. After a long wait the door swung down again.

At eight-thirty the eggs were shriveled and toast was like stone. An aluminum wedge scraped them into the sink, where hot water whirled them down a metal throat which digested and flushed them away to the distant sea. The dirty dishes were dropped into a hot washer and emerged twinkling dry.

Nine-fifteen, sang the clock, *time to clean.*

Out of warrens in the wall, tiny robot mice darted. The rooms were acrawl with the small cleaning animals, all rubber and metal. They thudded against chairs, whirling their mustached runners, kneading the rug nap, sucking gently at hidden dust. Then, like mysterious invaders, they popped into their burrows. Their pink electric eyes faded. The house was clean.

10   *Ten o'clock.* The sun came out from behind the rain. The house stood alone in a city of rubble and ashes. This was the one house left standing. At night the ruined city gave off a radioactive glow which could be seen for miles.

Ten-fifteen. The garden sprinklers whirled up in golden founts, filling the soft morning air with scatterings of brightness. The water pelted windowpanes, running down the charred west side where the house had been burned evenly free of its white paint. The entire west face of the house was black, save for five places. Here the silhouette in paint of a man mowing a lawn. Here, as in a photograph, a woman bent to pick flowers. Still farther over, their images burned on wood in one titanic instant, a small boy, hands flung into the air; higher up, the image of a thrown ball, and opposite him a girl, hands raised to catch a ball which never came down.

The five spots of paint—the man, the woman, the children, the ball—remained. The rest was a thin charcoaled layer.

The gentle sprinkler rain filled the garden with falling light.

Until this day, how well the house had kept its peace. How carefully it had inquired, "Who goes there? What's the password?" and, getting no answer from lonely foxes and whining cats, it had shut up its windows and drawn shades in an old-maidenly preoccupation with self-protection which bordered on a mechanical paranoia.

15   It quivered at each sound, the house did. If a sparrow brushed a window, the shade snapped up. The bird, startled, flew off! No, not even a bird must touch the house!

The house was an altar with ten thousand attendants, big, small, servicing, attending, in choirs. But the gods had gone away, and the ritual of the religion continued senselessly, uselessly.

Twelve noon.

A dog whined, shivering, on the front porch.

The front door recognized the dog voice and opened. The dog, once huge and fleshy, but now gone to bone and covered with sores, moved in and through the house, tracking mud. Behind it whirred angry mice, angry at having to pick up mud, angry at inconvenience.

20   For not a leaf fragment blew under the door but what the wall panels flipped open and the copper scrap rats flashed swiftly out. The offending dust, hair, or paper, seized in miniature steel jaws, was raced back to the burrows. There, down tubes which fed into the cellar, it was dropped into the sighing vent of an incinerator which sat like evil Baal in a dark corner.

The dog ran upstairs, hysterically yelping to each door, at last realizing, as the house realized, that only silence was here.

It sniffed the air and scratched the kitchen door. Behind the door, the stove was making pancakes which filled the house with a rich baked odor and the scent of maple syrup.

The dog frothed at the mouth, lying at the door, sniffing, its eyes turned to fire. It ran wildly in circles, biting at its tail, spun in a frenzy, and died. It lay in the parlor for an hour.

Two o'clock, sang a voice.

25 Delicately sensing decay at last, the regiments of mice hummed out as softly as blown gray leaves in an electrical wind.

Two-fifteen.

The dog was gone.

In the cellar, the incinerator glowed suddenly and a whirl of sparks leaped up the chimney.

Two thirty-five.

30 Bridge tables sprouted from patio walls. Playing cards fluttered onto pads in a shower of pips. Martinis manifested on an oaken bench with egg-salad sandwiches. Music played.

But the tables were silent and the cards untouched.

At four o'clock the tables folded like great butterflies back through the paneled walls.

Four-thirty.

The nursery walls glowed.

35 Animals took shape: yellow giraffes, blue lions, pink antelopes, lilac panthers cavorting in crystal substance. The walls were glass. They looked out upon color and fantasy. Hidden films clocked through well-oiled sprockets, and the walls lived. The nursery floor was woven to resemble a crisp, cereal meadow. Over this ran aluminum roaches and iron crickets, and in the hot still air butterflies of delicate red tissue wavered among the sharp aroma of animal spoors! There was the sound like a great matted yellow hive of bees within a dark bellows, the lazy bumble of a purring lion. And there was the patter of okapi feet and the murmur of a fresh jungle rain, like other hoofs, falling upon the summer-starched grass. Now the walls dissolved into distances of parched weed, mile on mile, and warm endless sky. The animals drew away into thorn brakes and water holes.

It was the children's hour.

Five o'clock. The bath filled with clear hot water.

Six, seven, eight o'clock. The dinner dishes manipulated like magic tricks, and in the study a *click.* In the metal stand opposite the hearth where a fire now blazed up warmly, a cigar popped out, half an inch of soft gray ash on it, smoking, waiting.

Nine o'clock. The beds warmed their hidden circuits, for nights were cool here.

40 *Nine-five.* A voice spoke from the study ceiling:

"Mrs. McClellan, which poem would you like this evening?"

The house was silent.

The voice said at last, "Since you express no preference, I shall select a poem at random." Quiet music rose to back the voice. "Sara Teasdale. As I recall, your favorite. . . ."

There will come soft rains and the smell of the ground,

And swallows circling with their shimmering sound;

> And frogs in the pools singing at night,
> And wild plum trees in tremulous white;
>
> Robins will wear their feathery fire,
> Whistling their whims on a low fence-wire;
>
> And not one will know of the war, not one
> Will care at last when it is done.
>
> Not one would mind, neither bird nor tree,
> If mankind perished utterly;
>
> And Spring herself, when she woke at dawn
> Would scarcely know that we were gone."

45   The fire burned on the stone hearth and the cigar fell away into a mound of quiet ash on its tray. The empty chairs faced each other between the silent walls, and the music played.

At ten o'clock the house began to die.

The wind blew. A falling tree bough crashed through the kitchen window. Cleaning solvent, bottled, shattered over the stove. The room was ablaze in an instant!

"Fire!" screamed a voice. The house lights flashed, water pumps shot water from the ceilings. But the solvent spread on the linoleum, licking, eating, under the kitchen door, while the voices took it up in chorus: "Fire, fire, fire!"

The house tried to save itself. Doors sprang tightly shut, but the windows were broken by the heat and the wind blew and sucked upon the fire.

50   The house gave ground as the fire in ten billion angry sparks moved with flaming ease from room to room and then up the stairs. While scurrying water rats squeaked from the walls, pistoled their water, and ran for more. And the wall sprays let down showers of mechanical rain.

But too late. Somewhere, sighing, a pump shrugged to a stop. The quenching rain ceased. The reserve water supply which had filled baths and washed dishes for many quiet days was gone.

The fire crackled up the stairs. It fed upon Picassos and Matisses in the upper halls, like delicacies, baking off the oily flesh, tenderly crisping the canvases into black shavings.

Now the fire lay in beds, stood in windows, changed the colors of drapes!

And then, reinforcements.

55   From attic trapdoors, blind robot faces peered down with faucet mouths gushing green chemical.

The fire backed off, as even an elephant must at the sight of a dead snake. Now there were twenty snakes whipping over the floor, killing the fire with a clear cold venom of green froth.

But the fire was clever. It had sent flames outside the house, up through the attic to the pumps there. An explosion! The attic brain which directed the pumps was shattered into bronze shrapnel on the beams.

The fire rushed back into every closet and felt of the clothes hung there.

The house shuddered, oak bone on bone, its bared skeleton cringing from the heat, its wire, its nerves revealed as if a surgeon had torn the skin off to let the red veins and capillaries quiver in the scalded air. Help, help! Fire! Run, run! Heat snapped mirrors like the brittle winter ice. And the voices wailed, Fire, fire, run, run, like a tragic nursery rhyme, a dozen voices, high, low, like children dying in a

forest, alone, alone. And the voices fading as the wires popped their sheathings like hot chestnuts. One, two, three, four, five voices died.

60   In the nursery the jungle burned. Blue lions roared, purple giraffes bounded off. The panthers ran in circles changing color, and ten million animals, running before the fire, vanished off toward a distant steaming river. . . .

    Ten more voices died. In the last instant under the fire avalanche, other choruses, oblivious, could be heard announcing the time, playing music, cutting the lawn by remote-control mower, or setting an umbrella frantically out and in the slamming and opening front door, a thousand things happening, like a clock shop when each clock strikes the hour insanely before or after the other, a scene of maniac confusion, yet unity; singing, screaming, a few last cleaning mice darting bravely out to carry the horrid ashes away! And one voice, with sublime disregard for the situation, read poetry aloud in the fiery study, until all the film spools burned, until all the wires withered and the circuits cracked.

    The fire burst the house and let it slam flat down, puffing out skirts of spark and smoke.

    In the kitchen, an instant before the rain of fire and timber, the stove could be seen making breakfasts at a psychopathic rate, ten dozen eggs, six loaves of toast, twenty dozen bacon strips, which, eaten by fire, started the stove working again, hysterically hissing!

    The crash. The attic smashing into kitchen and parlor. The parlor into cellar, cellar into sub-cellar. Deep freeze, armchair, film tapes, circuits, beds, and all like skeletons thrown in a cluttered mound deep under.

65   Smoke and silence. A great quantity of smoke.

    Dawn showed faintly in the east. Among the ruins, one wall stood alone. Within the wall, a last voice said, over and over again and again, even as the sun rose to shine upon the heaped rubble and steam:

    "Today is August 5, 2026, today is August 5, 2026, today is. . . ."

[1950]

The Writing Process: From Outlining to Final Essay

Here is one student's response to Bradbury's story, preceded by the notes that the student used in preparing a draft. Notice that the final essay does not slavishly follow the notes. For instance, although the student jotted down four possible titles for her essay, none of them is the title that she settled on.

Student Work: Outlining

Possible title:

> *Bradbury's Meaning for Us*
> *Bradbury and Today*
> *Learning from Literature/Bradbury's Lesson*
> *Bradbury's Lesson for Us*

~~*Begin by quoting first sentence*~~
Begin with joke about airline??
~~*Define science fiction?*~~
Technology today—can do almost everything—but is this really LIVING?
Maybe such a life is a living death. Evidence??

End essay:
Does Bradbury show us our future?
A wake-up call. 2026 is not really very far away
~~*end with an example of unnecessary technology*~~

Student Analytical Essay: "The Lesson of 'August 2026'"

Working with this sort outline, the student produced the following essay. As the questions that follow the essay indicate, this essay makes an interesting argument, but it could have developed its ideas further. A more detailed outline might have led to a more fully developed paper. As you read the paper, consider how the writer might have expanded the paper by engaging more fully with the story and providing more evidence from the story.

Daniels 1

Esther Daniels

Professor Izzard

English 101a

14 January 2016

The Lesson of "August 2026"

Before discussing some of the implications of Ray Bradbury's short

story "August 2026: There Will Come Soft Rains," I want to tell a little joke.

The joke goes like this. Passengers are seated on the latest kind of airplane,

a plane that flies without a pilot because all of the controls are operated

mechanically, and the entire flight has been preprogrammed. After all the

passengers have boarded the plane, and the door has closed, and the

passengers, in accordance with the pre-recorded announcement, have

fastened their seat-belts, the plane begins to taxi for a take-off. As the

plane moves down the runway, the sound system says, in its flat mechanical

voice, "You are now beginning your flight on the most technologically

advanced airplane ever designed. There is no pilot or copilot, and there are

no flight attendants. Everything has been preprogrammed. The plane will

taxi for 60 seconds and then will take off. Nothing can go wrong . . . nothing

can go wrong . . . nothing can . . . nothing can . . . nothing can. . . ."

None of us has been on such a plane, but we probably all have had, in

a mild way, the sort of experience that the joke implies. We have bought

---

some wonderful gadget—let's say an alarm clock, and we have programmed it according to the complicated instructions, and it has failed to go off the next morning. Apparently we had set it for P.M. instead of A.M., but we still don't see what we did wrong. Or, try as we may we cannot change the margins on the computer. Or the airline has put our luggage on the wrong airplane. Or . . .

None of us wants to give up the wonderful devices we rely on—let's say the automobile, the computer, the iPod. We can even attend an English composition class, and, if we think it is boring, we can silently be exchanging messages with a friend a thousand miles away. Despite these pleasures and these great conveniences, there are times, I think, when most of us must wonder, "Are we really living, or are our machines doing the living for us?" In "August 2026: There Will Come Soft Rains," Ray Bradbury gives us a glimpse—with great exaggeration, of course—of what our lives may be like in the future when machines have become all-powerful.

In Bradbury's story, a preprogrammed house runs everything: sounds wake people up, mechanisms prepare food and clean the house, and other provide entertainment. If the people don't make a choice, a machine chooses something on their behalf. At the opening of the story, the house makes the people's breakfast, reminds the people of the weather and their work day, cleans itself with robot mice, and automatic sprinklers water the lawn.

Are the people who are served by these devices happy? We don't know, because there are no people in Bradbury's story. They have all been incinerated, and only their silhouettes survive on the wall of the house. We learn that some major disaster has happened in the future, as the ruined city near the house is giving off a radioactive glow. Although the preprogrammed house seems to fill the people's every need and want, we, as readers of the story, probably feel that these people could not really have been happy. Things are *too* programmed; the people who lived in this society must have become almost like machines themselves. With everything provided for them, how did

Daniels 3

these people think and feel for themselves? Probably none of us wants to say

that in our own lives we actually want difficulties, but, still, when we read

Bradbury's story we probably say that we would not want to live in a society

that was as highly programmed with labor-saving devices as Bradbury shows.

And yet, that is the way we seem to be going, with faster computers,

smarter houses. You can now, from your place of work, phone your home and

turn the oven on and set the temperature and the duration, so that when

you get home the beef has been roasted to medium-rare.

Bradbury first published the story in 1950, so the story was set

seventy-six years in the future. It was set, we can say, at a time when most of his

readers would probably not still be alive. But today, 2026 is not all that far from

us. Most of us who today are reading this story will still be alive in 2026, unless,

as the story warns us, we allow our technology—gadgets that can do just about

anything—to blow ourselves up. Bradbury's "August 2026: There Will Come Soft

Rains" is a wake-up call, a call that we ought to heed. We have somehow let our

technical knowledge outrun not only our wisdom but our sense of how to live

decent meaningful lives, lives of fun, truly human lives, not just lives in which

everything is easy, everything is done for us. We are allowing our gadgets to do

our living for us—and they may kill us. We are barely living, we are sleep-

walking. This cannot go on without some sort of catastrophic ending. To quote

the first line of Ray Bradbury's story, it is "time to get up, time to get up" (43).

[New page]

Daniels 4

Work Cited

Bradbury, Ray. "August 2026: There Will Come Soft Rains." *Literature for Composition*.

Ed. Sylvan Barnet, William Burto, William E. Cain, and Cheryl L. Nixon.

11th ed. Boston: Pearson, 2017. 43-47. Print.

Joining the Conversation: Critical Thinking and Writing

1. Has Esther Daniels done a good job in writing her title and opening paragraph? Please explain.
2. What is Daniels's thesis? Where does she state it?
3. Do you think Daniels has provided sufficient evidence for her thesis?
4. How could Daniels engage more fully with Bradbury's story to develop her ideas? What details from the story could she cite? Daniels does not explore several important events in the story, such as the poem that the house recites or the final fire that collapses the house. How could Daniels analyze and interpret these plot elements in her paper?
5. If Daniels added more analysis to each paragraph, what ideas could she emphasize and develop?
6. Daniels does not include direct quotations from the story, except in the last line of her paper. What passages from the story could she use to support and develop her ideas? Select one quotation from the story for each of her body paragraphs.
7. Evaluate the final paragraph. Is it effective? Why or why not?

Your Turn: Additional Stories for Analysis

MICHELE SERROS

Michele Serros (1966–2015), published her first book of poems and stories, Chicana Falsa and Other Stories of Death, Identity and Oxnard, *while she was still a student at Santa Monica City College. We reprint a story from her second book,* How to Be a Chicana Role Model *(2000), which achieved national attention.*

Senior Picture Day

Sometimes I put two different earrings in the same ear. And that's on a day I'm feeling preppy, not really new wave or anything. One time, during a track meet over at Camarillo High, I discovered way too late that I'd forgot to put on deodorant and that was the worst 'cause everyone knows how snooty those girls at Camarillo can be. Hmmm. Actually the worst thing I've ever forgotten to do was take my pill. That happened three mornings in a row and you can bet I was praying for weeks after that.

So many things to remember when you're seventeen years old and your days start at six A.M. and sometimes don't end until five in the afternoon. But today of all days there's one thing I have to remember to do and that's to squeeze my nose. I've been doing it since the seventh grade. Every morning with my thumb and forefinger I squeeze the sides of it, firmly pressing my nostrils as close as they possibly can get near the base. Sometimes while I'm waiting for the tortilla to heat up, or just when I'm brushing my teeth, I squeeze. Nobody ever notices. Nobody ever asks. With all the other shit seniors in high school go through, squeezing my nose is nothing. It's just like some regular early-morning routine, like yawning or wiping the egg from my eyes. Okay, so you might think it's just a total waste of time, but to tell you the truth, I do see the difference. Just last week I lined up all my class pictures and could definitely see the progress. My nose has actually become

smaller, narrower. It looks less Indian. ~~I look less Indian and you can bet that's the main goal here.~~ Today, when I take my graduation pictures, my nose will look just like Terri's and then I'll have the best picture in the year-book. I think about this as Mrs. Milne's Duster comes honking in the driveway to take me to school.

Terri was my best friend in seventh grade. She came from Washington to Rio Del Valle junior high halfway through October. She was the first girl I knew who had contact lenses and *four* pairs of Chemin de Fers. Can you believe that? She told everyone that her daddy was gonna build 'em a swimming pool for the summer. She told me that I could go over to swim anytime I wanted. But until then, she told me, I could go over and we could play on her dad's CB.[1]

omparing families

~~"You dad's really got a CB?"~~ I asked her.

5   "Oh, yeah," she answered, jiggling her locker door. "You can come over and we can make up handles for ourselves and meet lots of guys. Cute ones."

"Whaddaya mean, handles?" I asked.

"Like names, little nicknames. I never use my real name. I'm 'G.G.' when I get on. That stands for Golden Girl. Oh, and you gotta make sure you end every sentence with 'over.' You're like a total nerd if you don't finish with 'over.' I never talk to anyone who doesn't say 'over.' They're the worst."

Nobody's really into citizen band radios anymore. I now see 'em all lined up in pawnshops over on Oxnard Boulevard. But back in the seventh grade, everyone was getting them. They were way better than using a phone 'cause, first of all, there was no phone bill to bust you for talking to boys who lived past the Grade and second, you didn't have your stupid sister yelling at you for tying up the phone line. Most people had CBs in their cars, but Terri's dad had his in the den.

When I showed up at Terri's to check out the CB, her mama was in the front yard planting some purple flowers.

10   "Go on in already." She waved me in. "She's in her father's den."

I found Terri just like her mama said. She was already on the CB, looking flustered and sorta excited.

"Hey," I called out to her, and plopped my tote bag on her dad's desk.

She didn't answer but rather motioned to me with her hands to hurry up. Her mouth formed an exaggerated, "Oh, *my* God!" She held out a glass bowl of Pringles and pointed to a glass of Dr Pepper on the desk.

It turned out Terri had found a boy on the CB. An older *interested* one. He was fifteen, a skateboarder, and his handle was Lightning Bolt.

15   "Lightning Bolt," he bragged to Terri. "Like, you know, powerful and fast. That's the way I skate. So," he continued, "where you guys live? Over."

"We live near Malibu." Terri answered. "Between Malibu and Santa Barbara. Over."

"Oh, excuse me, fan-ceee. Over."

"That's right." Terri giggled. "Over."

We actually lived in Oxnard. Really, in El Rio, a flat patch of houses, churches, and schools surrounded by lots of strawberry fields and some new snooty stucco homes surrounded by chainlink. But man, did Terri have this way of making things sound better. I mean, it *was* the truth, geographically, and besides it sounded way more ~~glamorous~~.

---

[1] **CB** Citizens Band (a radio frequency used by the general public to talk to one another over a short distance).

REVEL™ for *Literature for Composition*

REVEL™ is Pearson's newest way of delivering our respected content. Fully digital and highly engaging, REVEL™ offers an immersive learning experience designed for the way today's students read, think, and learn. Enlivening course content with media interactives and assessments, REVEL™ empowers educators to increase engagement with the course and to connect better with students.

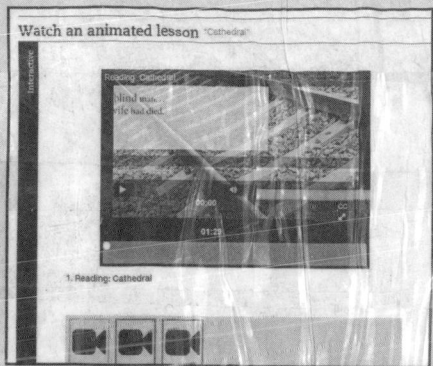

Video and Rich Multimedia Content

Videos, audio recordings, animations, and multimedia instruction provide context that enables students to engage with the text in a more meaningful way.

Interactive Readings and Exercises

Students explore readings through interactive texts. Robust annotation tools allow students to take notes, and post-reading assignments let instructors monitor their students' completion of readings before class begins.

Just-in-Time Context

Just-in-time context—encompassing biographical, historical, and social insights—is incorporated throughout, giving students a deeper understanding of what they read.

Integrated Writing Assignments

Minimal-stakes, low-stakes, and high-stakes writing tasks allow students multiple opportunities to interact with the ideas presented in the reading assignments, ensuring that they come to class better prepared.

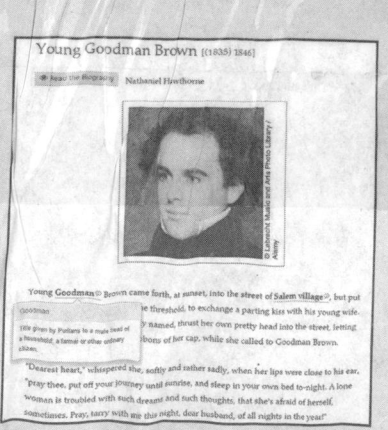

Walter B. Connolly, Stanley Corkin, Linda Cravens, Morgan Cutterini, Donald A. Daiker, Bruce Danner, Phebe Davidson, Thomas Deans, Beth DeMeo, John Desjarlais, Emily Dial-Driver, John Dobelbower, Ren Draya, James Dubinsky, Gail Duffy, Bill Elliott, Leonard W. Engel, William Epperson, Gareth Euridge, Martin J. Fertig, Shelley Fischer, Elinor C. Flewellen, Kay Fortson, Marie Foster, Donna Friedman, Larry Frost, Loris Galford, Charlene Gill, Esther Godfrey, Dwonna Goldstone, Jessica Beth Gordon, Kim Greenfield, Chris Grieco, Susan Grimland, Debbie Hanson, Dorothy Hardman, Sandra H. Harris, Syndey Harrison, Sally Harrold, Tom Hayes, Keith Haynes, Michael Hennessey, Mary Herbert, Ana B. Hernandez, Maureen Hoag, Allen Hoey, Diane Houston, Elizabeth Howells, Clayton Hudnall, Joyce A. Ingram, Craig Johnson, Michael Johnson, Angela Jones, Kristianne Kalata, Rodney Keller, Beth Kemper, Glenn Klopfenstein, Alison Kuehner, Donya Lancaster, Theresa René LeBlanc, Regina Lebowitz, Margaret Lindgren, John Loftis, Robert Lynch, Maria Makowiecka, Twister Marquiss, Phil Martin, Kate Massengale, Dennis McDonald, Sara McKnight Boone, Delma McLeod-Porter, Linda McPherson, Bill McWilliams, Martin Meszaros, Zack Miller, JoAnna S. Mink, Dorothy Minor, Owen Monroe, Wayne Moore, Charles Moran, Patricia G. Morgan, Nancy Morris, Jonathan Morrow, Christina Murphy, Richard Nielson, Sean Nighbert, David Norlin, Torria Norman, Marsha Nourse, Shanna O'Berry, John O'Connor, Chris Orchard, Phyllis Orlicek, Eric Otto, Suzanne Owens, Janet Palmer, James R. Payne, Stephanie Pelkowski, Elizabeth Gassel Perkins, Don K. Pierstorff, Gerald Pike, Kenneth Poff, Louis H. Pratt, John Prince, Sharon Prince, Michael Punches, David Raymond, Samantha Regan, Bruce A. Reid, Thomas Reynolds, Linda Robertson, Lois Sampson, Terry Santos, Daniel Schierenbeck, Jim Schwartz, Sigmar J. Schwarz, Robert Schwegler, Linda Scott, Herbert Shapiro, William Shelley, David Slater, Janice Slaughter, Martha Ann Smith, Tiga Spitsberg, Judith Stanford, Pam Stinson, Darlene Strawser, Geri Strecker, Jim Streeter, Timothy Stuart, Anthony Stubbs, David Sudol, Beverly Swan, Leesther Thomas, Raymond L. Thomas, Susan D. Tilka, Mary Trachsel, Dorothy Trusock, Billie Varnum, John H. Venne, Mickey Wadia, Nancy Walker, Betty Weldon, Patrick White, Jonathon Wild, Bertha Wise, Arthur Wohlgemuth, Cary Wolfe, Linda Woodson, Sallie Woolf, Kathy J. Wright, Rebecca Wright, Carlson Yost, Dennis Young, and Gary Zacharias.

No book of this kind gets done without a great deal of assistance from the publisher. We received insightful editorial guidance from Joe Terry and Anne Brunell Ehrenworth. Donna Campion (project manager at Pearson) kept things moving smoothly, and Donna Conte expertly copyedited the manuscript. Lois Lombardo (project manager at Cenveo) efficiently solved innumerable last-minute problems, and Gina Cheselka handled the difficult job of securing text permissions.

SYLVAN BARNET
WILLIAM BURTO
WILLIAM E. CAIN
CHERYL L. NIXON

Extensive material on research and the Internet: Because instructors are increasingly assigning research papers, the eleventh edition includes material on implementing a productive research plan that incorporates electronic resources, provides up-to-date instruction on evaluating, using, and citing electronic sources, and features a new student research paper that uses electronic resources.

Checklists: Twenty-two checklists focus on topics such as revising paragraphs, editing a draft, and using the Internet. Students can use these checklists to become peer readers of their writing.

Resources for Instructors

Instructor's Manual with detailed comments and suggestions for teaching each selection. This important resource also contains references to critical articles and books that we have found to be the most useful. ISBN 0134101642

REVEL™ is Pearson's newest way of delivering our respected content. Fully digital and highly engaging, REVEL™ offers an immersive learning experience designed for the way today's students read, think, and learn. Enlivening course content with media interactives and assessments, REVEL™ empowers educators to increase engagement with the course, and to better connect with students.

With an emphasis on critical thinking and argument, REVEL™ for *Literature for Composition* offers superior coverage of reading, writing, and arguing about literature enhanced by an array of multimedia interactives that prompt student engagement. Throughout REVEL's™ flexible online environment, the authors demonstrate that the skills emphasized in their discussions of communication are relevant not only to literature courses, but to all courses in which students analyze texts or write arguments.

Acknowledgments

We would like to thank the following reviewers, who provided their feedback during the revision of the eleventh edition: Karen Guerin, Bossier Parish Community College; Mary Hubbard, Northwest Arkansas Community College; Jennifer Laufenberg, Bossier Parish Community College; Megan Looney, Northwest Arkansas Community College; Joanna Mann, Northwest Arkansas Community College; Timothy McGinn, Northwest Arkansas Community College; Tabitha Miller, Pitt Community College; Stephanie Noll, Texas State University—San Marcos; John Padgett, Brevard College; and Jennifer Wiley, Pima Community College.

In preparing the first eleven editions of *Literature for Composition,* we were indebted to Cieltia Adams, Elizabeth Addison, Jonathan Alexander, James Allen, Alexander Ames, Kathleen Anderson-Wyman, Larry Armstrong, William D. Atwill, Patricia Baldwin, Mary J. Balkun, Daniel Barwick, David Beach, Daniel Bender, Billie Bennet, Mary Anne Bernal, Phyllis Betz, Kenneth R. Bishop, Margaret Blayney, Bertha Norman Booker, John P. Boots, Paul Keith Boran, Pam Bourgeois, Noelle Brada-Williams, Carol Ann Britt, Jennifer Bruer, Robin W. Bryant, Sharon Buzzard, Kathleen Shine Cain, Diana Cardenas, William Carpenter, Evelyn Cartright, Allan Chavkin, Mike Chu, Alan P. Church, Melinda Cianos, Dennis Ciesielski, Arlene Clift-Pellow,

More Student Samples of Works-in-Progress

* Throughout the text, every part of the writing process is demonstrated through student models. In addition, Part 3 contains four self-contained, genre-specific student writing portfolios that each showcase one student's writing process for a particular assignment.

Key Features

Here are the key features of the eleventh edition of *Literature for Composition*.

Extensive instruction in composition: Students are guided through the entire process of writing (especially writing arguments), beginning with generating ideas (for instance, by listing or by annotating a text), developing a thesis, supporting the thesis with evidence, and on through the final stages of documenting and editing. Twenty-four sample student essays are included; most are prefaced with the students' preliminary notes, some include first and revised drafts, and some are annotated or otherwise analyzed. Each literary genre chapter includes a new "Student Writing Portfolio" that collects sample materials generated by each step of the writing process, demonstrating how a paper evolves from initial note taking to a final draft.

Strategies for writing effective arguments: The eleventh edition focuses on argument and evaluation, not only in the case studies, but also in the discussion topics that follow *every* reading (headed "Joining the Conversation: Critical Thinking and Writing"). We emphasize the importance of questioning one's own assumptions—a key principle in critical thinking—and we also emphasize the importance of providing evidence in the course of setting forth coherent, readable arguments.

Wide range of literary selections: The book includes some three hundred selections, ranging from ancient classics such as Sophocles's *Antigone* to works written in the twenty-first century by authors such as Junot Diaz and Jhumpa Lahiri.

Abundant visual material, with suggestions about visual analysis: The book is rich in photographs. The images are chosen to enhance the student's understanding of particular works of literature. For example, we include photos of Buffalo Bill and a facsimile of a draft of E. E. Cummings's poem about Buffalo Bill. This edition also remains strong in its representation of graphic fiction.

Introductory genre anthology: After preliminary chapters on generating ideas and thinking critically, students encounter chapters devoted to essays, fiction, drama, and poetry.

Thematic anthology: The chapters in Part 4 are arranged under eight themes: The World around Us; Technology and Human Identity; Love and Hate, Men and Women; Innocence and Experience; All in a Day's Work; American Dreams and Nightmares; Law and Disorder; and Journeys.

Case studies: The three case studies presented in this book ("An Author in Depth") give a variety of perspectives for writing arguments and organizing research: Flannery O'Connor (page 500), William Shakespeare (page 640), and Robert Frost (page 817).

New Chapter on Research

- An extensive new Chapter 10 on research walks students step-by-step through the process, from creating a research plan and selecting a topic to locating and evaluating sources and avoiding plagiarism. Woven throughout the chapter is one student's writing process, culminating with a paper on Emily Dickinson's use of nature imagery.

New Chapter on Critical Thinking about Literature

- A streamlined Chapter 2 provides an overview of critical thinking early in the text, defining the term and discussing the importance of close reading, analysis, and synthesis.

New Chapter on Close Reading

- A revised Chapter 6 on close reading now includes discussions of both paraphrasing and summarizing, complete with new student samples.

New Chapter on the Pleasures of Reading, Writing, and Thinking about Literature

- A revised Chapter 5 designed to help students think productively about their writing, this material has been updated to reflect contemporary writing (such as blogging and texting) and now contains examples from each of the genres represented in the text, complete with a new personal response essay and new selections.

New Chapter on Comparison and Synthesis

- A new Chapter 9 on comparison walks students through drafting and revising to final production of this type of paper, with student samples throughout.

New Student Writing Portfolios

- Part 3 contains four unique, genre-specific student writing portfolios. These self-contained portfolios (located in Chapters 11, 12, 14, and 15) each present one student's writing process step-by-step, from assignment to finished product. Every portfolio is framed with a brief description of the paper "type," a short assignment that defines the writing, and helpful marginal annotations next to each step of the student's writing process, which highlight notable structures and provide guidance for readers to emulate in their own writing.

New Checklists

- Designed to help students produce successful writing, even more checklists are now included in the text at key points in the writing process, including ideas for generating a draft, revising a comparison essay, and evaluating sources for topic "fit."

Preface to Instructors

Literature for Composition is based on the assumption that students in composition or literature courses should encounter first-rate writing—not simply competent prose, but the powerful reports of experience that have been recorded by highly skilled writers of the past and present, reports of experiences that must be shared.

We assume that you share our belief that the study of such writing offers pleasure and insight into life and also leads to increased skill in communicating. Here, at the beginning, we want to point out that the skills we emphasize in our discussions of communication are relevant not only to literature courses but to all courses in which students analyze texts or write arguments.

What Is New in the Eleventh Edition?

Instructors who are familiar with earlier editions will notice that we retain our emphasis on critical thinking and argument. For the convenience of instructors who have used an earlier edition, we briefly summarize here the major changes:

New Essays, Short Stories, Poems

- Essays by Nicholas Carr ("Is Google Making Us Stupid?) and George Saunders ("Commencement Speech on Kindness").
- Short stories by Haruki Murakami ("On Seeing the 100% Perfect Girl…"), Junot Diaz ("How to Date a Brown Girl, Black Girl, White Girl, or Halfie"), Jhumpa Lahiri ("This Blessed House"), Dagoberto Gilb ("Love in L.A."), and Lan Samantha Chang ("Water Names"), among others.
- Poems by Billy Collins ("Twitter Poem"), Walt Whitman ("To a Locomotive in Winter"), Thylias Moss ("Tornados"), Sylvia Plath ("Blackberrying"), Seamus Heaney ("Blackberry-Picking"), Alberto Rios ("Nani"), and Helen Chasin ("The Word *Plum*"), among others.

New Thematic Chapter on Technology and Human Identity

- A new Chapter 17 in Part 4, comprised of selections from a mix of classic and contemporary authors, provides a lens through which students can see how technology both informs and impedes our lives. Several stories use science fiction elements to imagine utopian and dystopian futures. Authors in this chapter include Mark Twain, Stephen King, Maria Semple, Ray Bradbury, John Cheever, and Amy Sterling Casil.

Reimagined Thematic Chapters

- Thematic chapters have been collapsed and combined to promote ease of use and to avoid repetition. Each theme has been carefully cultivated to feature the most representative selections for that theme.

Graphic Fiction

Poetry

Drama

Contents by Genre

Essays

Short Stories

C H A P T E R **21** American Dreams and Nightmares 1125

CHAPTER **19** Innocence and Experience   986

CHAPTER **20** All in a Day's Work   1028

CHAPTER 17 Technology and Human Identity   862

CHAPTER 18 Love and Hate, Men and Women   948

PART IV

Enjoying Literary Themes: A Thematic Anthology

CHAPTER **12** Reading and Writing about Stories   440

PART III
Analyzing Literary Forms and Elements

CHAPTER 11 Reading and Writing about Essays   415

CHAPTER **10** Research: Writing with Sources   374

CHAPTER **8** Pushing Analysis Further: Reinterpreting
and Revising   **251**

PART II
Writing Arguments about Literature

CHAPTER **6** Close Reading: Paraphrase, Summary,
            and Explication   **165**

CHAPTER 5 The Pleasures of Reading, Writing, and
Thinking about Literature   **116**

Contents

Senior Editor: Brad Potthoff
Senior Development Editor: Anne Brunell Ehrenworth
Program Manager: Eric Jorgensen
Product Marketing Manager: Nicholas T. Bolt
Field Marketing Manager: Joyce Nilsen
Media Producer: Elizabeth Bravo
Content Producer: Julia Pomann
Media Editor: Christine Stavrou

Project Manager: Donna Campion
Text Design, Project Coordination, and Electronic Page Makeup: Cenveo® Publisher Services
Program Design Lead: Barbara Atkinson
Cover Designer: Cenveo® Publisher Services
Cover Illustration: marcusaires/Fotolia
Senior Manufacturing Buyer: Roy L. Pickering, Jr.
Printer/Binder: RR Donnelley/Crawfordsville
Cover Printer: Phoenix Color/Hagerstown

Acknowledgments of third-party content appear on pages 1417–1426, which constitute an extension of this copyright page.

Library of Congress Cataloging-in-Publication Data

Names: Barnet, Sylvan, editor. | Burto, William, editor. | Cain, William E., date-editor. | Pearson, Cheryl L. Nixon, editor.
Title: Literature for composition : an introduction to literature / [edited
  by] Sylvan Barnet, William Burto, William E. Cain, Cheryl L. Nixon Pearson.
Description: Eleventh edition. | Boston : Pearson, 2016. | Previous editions
  had other title information: essays, stories, poems, and plays. |
  Includes bibliographical references and index.
Identifiers: LCCN 2015048640| ISBN 9780134099149 (student edition) | ISBN
  0134099141 (student edition) | ISBN 9780134101774 (exam copy) | ISBN
  0134101774 (exam copy)
Subjects: LCSH: College readers. | English language—Rhetoric—Problems,
  exercises, etc. | Criticism—Authorship—Problems, exercises, etc. |
  Academic writing—Problems, exercises, etc.
Classification: LCC PE1417 .L633 2016 | DDC 808/.0427—dc23
LC record available at http://lccn.loc.gov/2015048640

2 16

Student Edition ISBN 10: 0-13-409914-1
Student Edition ISBN 13: 978-0-13-409914-9
A la Carte Edition ISBN 10: 0-13-431089-6
A la Carte Edition ISBN 13: 978-0-13-431089-3

www.pearsonhighered.com

ELEVENTH EDITION

Literature
for Composition

An Introduction to Literature

Sylvan Barnet
Tufts University

William Burto
University of Massachusetts at Lowell

William E. Cain
Wellesley College

Cheryl L. Nixon
University of Massachusetts at Boston

Boston Columbus Indianapolis New York San Francisco
Amsterdam Cape Town Dubai London Madrid Milan Munich Paris Montréal Toronto
Dehli Mexico City São Paulo Sydney Hong Kong Seoul Singapore Taipei Toyko

20   I took some Pringles from the bowl and thought we were gonna have this wonderful afternoon of talking and flirting with Lightning Bolt until Terri's dad happened to come home early and found us gabbing in his den.

"What the . . . !" he yelled as soon as he walked in and saw us hunched over his CB. "What do you think this is? Party Central? Get off that thing!" He grabbed the receiver from Terri's hand. "This isn't a toy! It's a tool. A tool for communication, you don't use it just to meet boys!"

"Damn, Dad," Terri complained as she slid off her father's desk. "Don't have a cow." She took my hand and led me to her room. "Come on, let's pick you out a handle."

When we were in her room, I told her I had decided on Cali Girl as my handle.

"You mean, like California?" she asked.

25   "Yeah, sorta."

"But you're Mexican."

"So?"

"So, you look like you're more from Mexico than California."

"What do you mean?"

30   "I mean, California is like, blond girls, you know."

"Yeah, but I *am* Californian. I mean, real Californian. Even my great-grandma was born here."

"It's just that you don't look like you're from California."

"And you're not exactly golden," I snapped.

We decided to talk to Lightning Bolt the next day, Friday, right after school. Terri's dad always came home real late on Fridays, sometimes even early the next Saturday morning. It would be perfect. When I got to her house the garage door was wide open and I went in through the side door. I almost bumped into Terri's mama. She was spraying the house with Pine Scent and offered me some Hi-C.

35   "Help yourself to a Pudding Pop, too," she said before heading into the living room through a mist of aerosol. "They're in the freezer."

Man, Terri's mama made their whole life like an afternoon commercial. Hi-C, Pringles in a bowl, the whole house smelling like a pine forest. Was Terri lucky or what? I grabbed a Pudding Pop out of the freezer and was about to join her when I picked up on her laugh. She was already talking to Lightning Bolt. Dang, she didn't waste time!

"Well, maybe we don't ever want to meet you," I heard Terri flirt with Lightning Bolt. "How do you know we don't already have boyfriends? Over."

"Well, you both sound like foxes. So, uh, what *do* you look like? Over."

"I'm about five-four and have green eyes and ginger-colored hair. Over."

40   Green? Ginger? I always took Terri for having brown eyes and brown hair.

"What about your friend? Over."

"What about her? Over."

Oh, this was about me! I *had* to hear this. Terri knew how to pump up things good.

"I mean, what does she look like?" Lightning Bolt asked. "She sounds cute. Over."

45   "Well . . ." I overheard Terri hesitate. "Well, she's real skinny and, uh . . ."

"I like skinny girls!"

"You didn't let me finish!" Terri interrupted. "And you didn't say 'over.' Over."

"Sorry," Lightning Bolt said. "Go ahead and finish. Over."

I tore the wrapper off the Pudding Pop and continued to listen.

50   "Well," Terri continued. "She's also sorta flat-chested, I guess. Over."
What? How could Terri say that?
"Flat-chested? Oh yeah? Over." Lightning Bolt answered.
"Yeah. Over."

Terri paused uncomfortably. It was as if she knew what she was saying was wrong and bad and she should've stopped but couldn't. She was saying things about a friend, things a real friend shouldn't be saying about another friend, but now there was a boy involved and he was interested in that other friend, in me, and her side was losing momentum. She would have to continue to stay ahead.

55   "Yeah, and she also has this, this nose, a nose like ___ like an *Indian.* Over."
"An, Indian?" Lightning Bolt asked. "What do ya mean an Indian? Over."
"You know, *Indian.* Like powwow Indian."
"Really?" Lightning Bolt laughed on the other end. "Like Woo-Woo-Woo Indian?" He clapped his palm over his mouth and wailed. A sound I knew all too well.
"Yeah, just like that!" Terri laughed. "In fact, I think she's gonna pick 'Li'l Squaw' as her handle!"

[handwritten: the root of the prob →]
[handwritten: ability to talk to mom/family]

60   I shut the refrigerator door quietly. I touched the ridge of my nose. I felt the bump my mother had promised me would be less noticeable once my face "filled out." The base of my nose was far from feminine and was broad, like, well, like Uncle Rudy's nose, Grandpa Rudy's nose, and yeah, a little bit of Uncle Vincente's nose, too. Men in my family who looked like Indians and here their Indian noses were lumped together on me, on my face. My nose made me look like I didn't belong, made me look less Californian than my blond counterparts. After hearing Terri and Lightning Bolt laugh, more than anything I hated the men in my family who had given me such a hideous nose.

[handwritten: mom trying to comfort her child]

I grabbed my tote bag and started to leave out through the garage door when Terri's mama called out from the living room. "You're leaving already?" she asked. "I know Terri would love to have you for dinner. Her daddy's working late again."
I didn't answer and I didn't turn around. I just walked out and went home.
And so that's how the squeezing began. I eventually stopped hanging out with Terri and never got a chance to use my handle on her dad's CB. I know it's been almost four years since she said all that stuff about me, about my nose, but man, it still stings.

65   During freshman year I heard that Terri's dad met some lady on the CB and left her mama for this other woman. Can you believe that? Who'd wanna leave a house that smelled like a pine forest and always had Pudding Pops in the freezer?

[handwritten: even perfect families have flaws]

As Mrs. Milne honks from the driveway impatiently, I grab my books and run down the driveway, squeezing my nose just a little bit more. I do it because today is Senior Picture Day and because I do notice the difference I might be too skinny. My chest might be too flat. But God forbid I look too Indian.

[handwritten: maybe ones becoming more accepting of herself]

[2000]

Joining the Conversation: Critical Thinking and Writing

1. How would you characterize the narrator of "Senior Picture Day"? Do you regard her with amusement, pity, contempt, sympathy—or all of the above, or none? Please explain.
2. Briefly recounted within this story about the narrator is another story about Terri's parents. Why do you suppose Serros included this story?

One of the most important Mayan portrait sculptures shows Pakal the Great, with an ample nose. Mayan portrait sculpture (mid-seventh century).

3. If someone asked you to write an essay about your body, would you find the assignment easy or difficult? Please explain.
4. a. Describe the impression that the portrait sculpture (shown above) of the most famous Mayan king, Pakal the Great, makes on you.
   b. When we say that someone is handsome or beautiful or striking looking, what do we mean? Is this just a strong feeling that we have, or is it a strong feeling that we could explain and support through an argument? Support your answer in an argument of 250–500 words (probably two or three paragraphs).
5. Which statement has the greater effect on you: "That person is very attractive" or "That person is highly intelligent"? Do you think that most people would agree with you? Could you present an argument that would convince others to agree with you? What would your argument consist of? What would your evidence be? Set forth your argument in 250–500 words.

HARUKI MURAKAMI

Born in Kyoto, Japan, in 1949, Haruki Murakami attended Waseda University in Tokyo, where he studied drama. In a well-known story told by Murakami, he was inspired to write his first novel when he attended a baseball game and saw an American player hit a double; he said he instantly knew he could write a novel and went home and started that night. A best-selling novelist, Murakami's work often uses surrealistic and experimental elements to capture the sense of alienation, uncertainty, and disconnection created by contemporary culture.

On Seeing the 100% Perfect Girl One Beautiful April Morning

One beautiful April morning, on a narrow side street in Tokyo's fashionable Harujuku neighborhood, I walked past the 100% perfect girl.

Tell you the truth, she's not that good-looking. She doesn't stand out in any way. Her clothes are nothing special. The back of her hair is still bent out of shape from sleep. She isn't young, either—must be near thirty, not even close to a "girl," properly speaking. But still, I know from fifty yards away: She's the 100% perfect girl for me. The moment I see her, there's a rumbling in my chest, and my mouth is as dry as a desert.

Maybe you have your own particular favorite type of girl—one with slim ankles, say, or big eyes, or graceful fingers, or you're drawn for no good reason to girls who take their time with every meal. I have my own preferences, of course. Sometimes in a restaurant I'll catch myself staring at the girl at the next table to mine because I like the shape of her nose.

But no one can insist that his 100% perfect girl corresponds to some preconceived type. Much as I like noses, I can't recall the shape of hers—or even if she had one. All I can remember for sure is that she was no great beauty. It's weird.

5   "Yesterday on the street I passed the 100% girl," I tell someone.

"Yeah?" he says. "Good-looking?"

"Not really."

"Your favorite type, then?"

"I don't know. I can't seem to remember anything about her—the shape of her eyes or the size of her breasts."

10   "Strange."

"Yeah. Strange."

"So anyhow," he says, already bored, "what did you do? Talk to her? Follow her?"

"Nah. Just passed her on the street."

She's walking east to west, and I west to east. It's a really nice April morning.

15   Wish I could talk to her. Half an hour would be plenty: just ask her about herself, tell her about myself, and—what I'd really like to do—explain to her the complexities of fate that have led to our passing each other on a side street in Harujuku on a beautiful April morning in 1981. This was something sure to be crammed full of warm secrets, like an antique clock built when peace filled the world.

After talking, we'd have lunch somewhere, maybe see a Woody Allen movie, stop by a hotel bar for cocktails. With any kind of luck, we might end up in bed.

Potentiality knocks on the door of my heart.

Now the distance between us has narrowed to fifteen yards.

How can I approach her? What should I say?

20   "Good morning, miss. Do you think you could spare half an hour for a little conversation?"

Ridiculous. I'd sound like an insurance salesman.

"Pardon me, but would you happen to know if there is an all-night cleaners in the neighborhood?"

No, this is just as ridiculous. I'm not carrying any laundry, for one thing. Who's going to buy a line like that?

Maybe the simple truth would do. "Good morning. You are the 100% perfect girl for me."

25   No, she wouldn't believe it. Or even if she did, she might not want to talk to me. Sorry, she could say, I might be the 100% perfect girl for you, but you're not the 100% boy for me. It could happen. And if I found myself in that situation,

I'd probably go to pieces. I'd never recover from the shock. I'm thirty-two, and that's what growing older is all about.

We pass in front of a flower shop. A small, warm air mass touches my skin. The asphalt is damp, and I catch the scent of roses. I can't bring myself to speak to her. She wears a white sweater, and in her right hand she holds a crisp white envelope lacking only a stamp. So: She's written somebody a letter, maybe spent the whole night writing, to judge from the sleepy look in her eyes. The envelope could contain every secret she's ever had.

I take a few more strides and turn: She's lost in the crowd.

Now, of course, I know exactly what I should have said to her. It would have been a long speech, though, far too long for me to have delivered it properly. The ideas I come up with are never very practical.

Oh, well. It would have started "Once upon a time" and ended "A sad story, don't you think?"

fairytale jargon

30 Once upon a time, there lived a boy and a girl. The boy was eighteen and the girl sixteen. He was not unusually handsome, and she was not especially beautiful. They were just an ordinary lonely boy and an ordinary lonely girl, like all the others. But they believed with their whole hearts that somewhere in the world there lived the 100% perfect boy and the 100% perfect girl for them. Yes, they believed in a miracle. And that miracle actually happened.

One day the two came upon each other on the corner of a street.

"This is amazing," he said. "I've been looking for you all my life. You may not believe this, but you're the 100% perfect girl for me."

"And you," she said to him, "are the 100% perfect boy for me, exactly as I'd pictured you in every detail. It's like a dream."

They sat on a park bench, held hands, and told each other their stories hour after hour. They were not lonely anymore. They had found and been found by their 100% perfect other. What a wonderful thing it is to find and be found by your 100% perfect other. It's a miracle, a cosmic miracle.

35 As they sat and talked, however, a tiny, tiny sliver of doubt took root in their hearts: Was it really all right for one's dreams to come true so easily?

And so, when there came a momentary lull in their conversation, the boy said to the girl, "Let's test ourselves—just once. If we really are each other's 100% perfect lovers, then sometime, somewhere, we will meet again without fail. And when that happens, and we know that we are the 100% perfect ones, we'll marry then and there. What do you think?"

"Yes," she said, "that is exactly what we should do."

And so they parted, she to the east, and he to the west.

The test they had agreed upon, however, was utterly unnecessary. They should never have undertaken it, because they really and truly were each other's 100% perfect lovers, and it was a miracle that they had ever met. But it was impossible for them to know this, young as they were. The cold, indifferent waves of fate proceeded to toss them unmercifully.

40 One winter, both the boy and the girl came down with the season's terrible influenza, and after drifting for weeks between life and death they lost all memory of their earlier years. When they awoke, their heads were as empty as the young D. H. Lawrence's piggy bank.

They were two bright, determined young people, however, and through their unremitting efforts they were able to acquire once again the knowledge and feeling that qualified them to return as full-fledged members of society. Heaven be praised, they became truly upstanding citizens who knew how to transfer from one subway line to another, who were fully capable of sending a special-delivery letter at the post office. Indeed, they even experienced love again, sometimes as much as 75% or even 85% love.

Time passed with shocking swiftness, and soon the boy was thirty-two, the girl thirty.

One beautiful April morning, in search of a cup of coffee to start the day, the boy was walking from west to east, while the girl, intending to send a special-delivery letter, was walking from east to west, but along the same narrow street in the Harajuku neighborhood of Tokyo. They passed each other in the very center of the street. The faintest gleam of their lost memories glimmered for the briefest moment in their hearts. Each felt a rumbling in their chest. And they knew:

She is the 100% perfect girl for me.

He is the 100% perfect boy for me.

But the glow of their memories was far too weak, and their thoughts no longer had the clarity of fourteen years earlier. Without a word, they passed each other, disappearing into the crowd. Forever.

A sad story, don't you think?

Yes, that's it, that is what I should have said to her.

[2010]

Joining the Conversation: Critical Thinking and Writing

1. In Murakami's short story, the narrator explains that he has passed his ideal match—the "100% perfect girl"—on the streets of Tokyo. How does he recognize her as the 100% perfect girl?
2. Why does the narrator not stop and talk to the 100% perfect girl?
3. The narrator imagines what he would have said to the girl and starts to tell a "once upon a time" story. Why would he tell a story to the girl? What would this story accomplish? Imagine being the girl listening to this story. Would this story intrigue and attract you, or would it confuse and repel you?
4. How does the "once upon a time" story connect to the first half of the short story? For example, are the characters in the "once upon a time" story the same people as in the original short story? How does the "once upon a time" story comment on the first half of the short story?
5. What do you make of the ending of the story and its statement, "A sad story, don't you think?"? Do you think this is a "sad story" and sad ending? Write a short response paper that analyzes and interprets the story's ending.

John Updike

John Updike (1932–2009) grew up in Shillington, Pennsylvania, where his father was a teacher and his mother was a writer. After receiving a BA degree in 1954 from Harvard, where he edited the Harvard Lampoon *(for which he both wrote and drew), he studied drawing at Oxford for a year until an offer from the* New Yorker *brought him back to the United States. He was hired as a reporter for the magazine but soon began contributing poetry, essays, and fiction. In 1957, he left the* New Yorker *in order to write independently full-time, though his stories and book reviews appeared regularly in it.*

In 1959, Updike published his first book of stories (The Same Door) *and also his first novel* (The Poorhouse Fair); *the next year, he published* Rabbit, Run, *a highly successful novel whose protagonist, "Rabbit" Angstrom, reappears in three later novels:* Rabbit Redux *(1971),* Rabbit Is Rich *(1981), and* Rabbit at Rest *(1990). The first and the last* Rabbit *books each won a Pulitzer Prize.*

A & P

In walks these three girls in nothing but bathing suits. I'm in the third checkout slot, with my back to the door, so I don't see them until they're over by the bread. The one that caught my eye first was the one in the plaid green two-piece. She was a chunky kid, with a good tan and a sweet broad soft-looking can with those two crescents of white just under it, where the sun never seems to hit, at the top of the backs of her legs. I stood there with my hand on a box of HiHo crackers trying to remember if I rang it up or not. I ring it up again and the customer starts giving me hell. She's one of these cash-register-watchers, a witch about fifty with rouge on her cheekbones and no eyebrows, and I know it made her day to trip me up. She'd been watching cash registers for fifty years and probably never seen a mistake before.

By the time I got her feathers smoothed and her goodies into a bag—she gives me a little snort in passing, if she'd been born at the right time they would have burned her over in Salem—by the time I get her on her way the girls had circled around the bread and were coming back, without a pushcart, back my way along the counters, in the aisle between the checkouts and the Special bins. They didn't even have shoes on. There was this chunky one, with the two-piece—it was bright green and the seams of the bra were still sharp and her belly was still pretty pale so I guessed she just got it (the suit)—there was this one, with one of those chubby berry-faces, the lips all bunched together under her nose, this one, and a tall one, with black hair that hadn't quite frizzed right, and one of these sunburns right across under the eyes, and a chin that was way too long—you know, the kind of girl other girls think is very "striking" and "attractive" but never quite makes it, as they very well know, which is why they like her so much—and then the third one, that wasn't quite so tall. She was the queen. She kind of led them, the other two peeking around and making their shoulders round. She didn't look around, not this queen, she just walked straight on slowly, on these long white prima-donna legs. She came down a little hard on her heels, as if she didn't walk in her bare feet that much, putting down her heels and then letting the weight move along to her toes as if she was testing the floor with every step, putting a little deliberate extra action into it. You never know for sure how girls' minds work (do they really think it's a mind in there or just a little buzz like a bee in a glass jar?) but you got the idea she had talked the other two into coming in here with her, and now she was showing them how to do it, walk slow and hold yourself straight.

She had on a kind of dirty pink—beige maybe, I don't know—bathing suit with a little nubble all over it and, what got me, the straps were down. They were off her shoulders looped loose around the cool tops of her arms, and I guess as a result the suit had slipped on her, so all around the top of the cloth there was this shining rim. If it hadn't been there you wouldn't have known there could have been anything whiter than those shoulders. With the straps pushed off, there was nothing between the top of the suit and the top of her head except just *her,* this clean bare plane of the top of her chest down from the shoulder bones like a dented sheet of metal tilted in the light. I mean, it was more than pretty.

She had sort of oaky hair that the sun and salt had bleached, done up in a bun that was unravelling, and a kind of prim face. Walking into the A & P with your straps down, I suppose it's the only kind of face you *can* have. She held her head so high her neck, coming up out of those white shoulders, looked kind of stretched, but I didn't mind. The longer her neck was, the more of her there was.

5   She must have felt in the corner of her eye me and over my shoulder Stokesie in the second slot watching, but she didn't tip. Not this queen. She kept her eyes moving across the racks, and stopped, and turned so slow it made my stomach rub the inside of my apron, and buzzed to the other two, who kind of huddled against her for relief, and then they all three of them went up the cat and dog food-breakfast cereal-macaroni-rice-raisins-seasonings-spreads-spaghetti-soft drinks-crackers-and-cookies aisle. From the third slot I look straight up this aisle to the meat counter, and I watched them all the way. The fat one with the tan sort of fumbled with the cookies, but on second thought she put the package back. The sheep pushing their carts down the aisle—the girls were walking against the usual traffic (not that we have one-way signs or anything)—were pretty hilarious. You could see them, when Queenie's white shoulders dawned on them, kind of jerk, or hop, or hiccup, but their eyes snapped back to their own baskets and on they pushed. I bet you could set off dynamite in the A & P and the people would by and large keep reaching and checking oatmeal off their lists and muttering "Let me see, there was a third thing, began with A, asparagus, no, ah, yes, applesauce!" or whatever it is they do mutter. But there was no doubt, this jiggled them. A few house slaves in pin curlers even look around after pushing their carts past to make sure what they had seen was correct.

You know, it's one thing to have a girl in a bathing suit down on the beach, where what with the glare nobody can look at each other much anyway, and another thing in the cool of the A & P, under the fluorescent lights, against all those stacked packages, with her feet paddling along naked over our checker-board green-and-cream, rubber-tile floor.

"Oh, Daddy," Stokesie said beside me. "I feel so faint."

"Darling," I said. "Hold me tight." Stokesie's married, with two babies chalked up on his fuselage already, but as far as I can tell that's the only difference. He's twenty-two, and I was nineteen this April.

"Is it done?" he asks, the responsible married man finding his voice. I forgot to say he thinks he's going to be a manager some sunny day, maybe in 1990 when it's called the Great Alexandrov and Petrooshki Tea Company or something.

10   What he meant was, our town is five miles from a beach, with a big summer colony out on the Point, but we're right in the middle of town, and the women generally put on a shirt or shorts or something before they get out of the car into the street. And anyway these are usually women with six children and varicose veins mapping their legs and nobody, including them, could care less. As I say, we're right in the middle of town, and if you stand at our front doors you can see two banks and the Congregational church and the newspaper store and three real estate offices and about twenty-seven old freeloaders tearing up Central Street because the sewer broke again. It's not as if we're on the Cape; we're north of Boston and there's people in this town haven't seen the ocean for twenty years.

The girls had reached the meat counter and were asking McMahon something. He pointed, they pointed, and they shuffled out of sight behind a pyramid of Diet

Delight peaches. All that was left for us to see was old McMahon patting his mouth and looking after them sizing up their joints. Poor kids, I began to feel sorry for them, they couldn't help it.

Now here comes the sad part of the story, at least my family says it's sad, but I don't think it's so sad myself. The store's pretty empty, it being Thursday afternoon, so there was nothing much to do except lean on the register and wait for the girls to show up again. The whole store was like a pinball machine and I didn't know which tunnel they'd come out of. After a while they come around out of the far aisle, around the light bulbs, records at discount of the Caribbean Six or Tony Martin Sings or some such gunk you wonder they waste the wax on, six-packs of candy bars, and plastic toys done up in cellophane that fall apart when a kid looks at them anyway. Around they come, Queenie still leading the way, and holding a little gray jar in her hand. Slots Three through Seven are unmanned and I could see her wondering between Stokes and me, but Stokesie with his usual luck draws an old party in baggy gray pants who stumbles up with four giant cans of pineapple juice (what do these bums *do* with all that pineapple juice? I've often asked myself) so the girls come to me. Queenie puts down the jar and I take it into my fingers icy cold. Kingfish Fancy Herring Snacks in Pure Sour Cream: 49¢. Now her hands are empty, not a ring or a bracelet, bare as God made them, and I wonder where the money's coming from. Still with the prim look she lifts a folded dollar bill out of the hollow at the center of her nubbled pink top. The jar went heavy in my hand. Really, I thought that was so cute.

Then everybody's luck begins to run out. Lengel comes in from haggling with a truck full of cabbages on the lot and is about to scuttle into the door marked MANAGER behind which he hides all day when the girls touch his eye. Lengel's pretty dreary, teaches Sunday school and the rest, but he doesn't miss that much. He comes over and says, "Girls, this isn't the beach."

Queenie blushes, though maybe it's just a brush of sunburn I was noticing for the first time, now that she was so close. "My mother asked me to pick up a jar of herring snacks." Her voice kind of startled me, the way voices do when you see the people first, coming out so flat and dumb yet kind of tony, too, the way it ticked over "pick up" and "snacks." All of a sudden I slid right down her voice into her living room. Her father and the other men were standing around in ice-cream coats and bow ties and the women were in sandals picking up herring snacks on toothpicks off a big glass plate and they were all holding drinks the color of water with olives and sprigs of mint in them. When my parents have somebody over they get lemonade and if it's a real racy affair Schlitz in tall glasses with "They'll Do It Every Time" cartoons stencilled on.

15   That's all right," Lengel said. "But this isn't the beach." His repeating this struck me as funny, as if it had just occurred to him, and he had been thinking all these years the A & P was a great big dune and he was the head lifeguard. He didn't like my smiling—as I say he doesn't miss much—but he concentrates on giving the girls that sad Sunday-school-superintendent stare.

Queenie's blush was no sunburn now, and the plump one in plaid, that I liked better from the back—a really sweet can—pipes up, "We weren't doing any shopping. We just came in for the one thing."

"That makes no difference," Lengel tells her, and I could see from the way his eyes went that he hadn't noticed she was wearing at two-piece before. "We want you decently dressed when you come in here."

"We *are* decent," Queenie says suddenly, her lower lip pushing, getting sore now that she remembers her place, a place from which the crowd that runs the

A & P must look pretty crummy. Fancy Herring Snacks flashed in her very blue eyes.

"Girls, I don't want to argue with you. After this come in here with your shoulders covered. It's our policy." He turns his back. That's policy for you. Policy is what the kingpins want. What the others want is juvenile delinquency.

20   All this while, the customers had been showing up with their carts but, you know, sheep, seeing a scene, they had all bunched up on Stokesie, who shook open a paper bag as gently as peeling a peach, not wanting to miss a word. I could feel in the silence everybody getting nervous, most of all Lengel, who asks me, "Sammy, have you rung up this purchase?"

I thought and said "No" but it wasn't about that I was thinking. I go through the punches, 4, 9, GROC, TOT—it's more complicated than you think and after you do it often enough, it begins to make a little song, that you hear words to, in my case "Hello (*bing*) there, you (*gung*) hap-py *peepul* (*splat*)!"—the *splat* being the drawer flying out. I uncrease the bill, tenderly as you may imagine, it just having come from between the two smoothest scoops of vanilla I had ever known were there, and pass a half and a penny into her narrow pink palm and nestle the herrings in a bag and twist its neck and hand it over, all the time thinking.

The girls, and who'd blame them, are in a hurry to get out, so I say "I quit" to Lengel quick enough for them to hear, hoping they'll stop and watch me, their unsuspected hero. They keep right on going, into the electric eye; the door flies open and they flicker across the lot to their car, Queenie and Plaid and Big Tall Goony-Goony (not that as raw material she was so bad), leaving me with Lengel and a kink in his eyebrow.

"Did you say something, Sammy?"

"I said I quit."

25   "I thought you did."

"You didn't have to embarrass them."

"It was they who were embarrassing us."

I started to say something that came out "Fiddle-de-doo." It's a saying of my grandmother's, and I know she would have been pleased.

"I don't think you know what you're saying," Lengel said.

30   "I know you don't," I said. "But I do." I pull the bow at the back of my apron and start shrugging it off my shoulders. A couple customers that had been heading for my slot begin to knock against each other, like scared pigs in a chute.

Lengel sighs and begins to look very patient and old and gray. He's been a friend of my parents for years. "Sammy, you don't want to do this to your Mom and Dad," he tells me. It's true, I don't. But it seems to me that once you begin a gesture it's fatal not to go through with it. I fold the apron, "Sammy" stitched in red on the pocket, and put it on the counter, and drop the bow tie on top of it. The bow tie is theirs, if you've ever wondered. "You'll feel this for the rest of your life," Lengel says, and I know that's true, too, but remembering how he made that pretty girl blush makes me so scrunchy inside I punch the No Sale tab and the machine whirs "pee-pul" and the drawer splats out. One advantage to this scene taking place in summer, I can follow this up with a clean exit, there's no fumbling around getting your coat and galoshes, I just saunter into the electric eye in my white shirt that my mother ironed the night before, and the door heaves itself open, and outside the sunshine is skating round on the asphalt.

I look around for my girls, but they're gone, of course. There wasn't anybody but some young married screaming with her children about some candy they didn't get by the door of a powder-blue Falcon station wagon. Looking back in the big windows, over the bags of peat moss and aluminum lawn furniture stacked on the pavement, I could see Lengel in my place in the slot, checking the sheep through. His face was dark gray and his back stiff, as if he'd just had an injection of iron, and my stomach kind of fell as I felt how hard the world was going to be to me hereafter.

[1962]

Joining the Conversation: Critical Thinking and Writing

1. In what sort of community is this A & P located? To what extent does this community resemble yours?
2. Do you think Sammy is a misogynist? Why, or why not? And, if you think he is, do you find the story offensive? Again, why or why not? Present your response in the form of a detailed argument.
3. In the last line of the story, Sammy says, "I felt how hard the world was going to be to me hereafter." Do you think the world is going to be hard to Sammy? Why, or why not? And, if it is going to be hard to Sammy, will this be because of a virtue or a weakness in Sammy?
4. Write Lengel's version of the story (500–1,000 words) as he might narrate it to his wife during dinner. Or write the story from Queenie's point of view.
5. In speaking of contemporary fiction, Updike said:

   I want stories to startle and engage me within the first few sentences, and in their middle to widen or deepen or sharpen my knowledge of human activity, and to end by giving me a sensation of completed statement.

   Let's assume that you share Updike's view of what a story should do. To what extent do you think "A & P" fulfills these demands? (You may want to put your response in the form of a letter to Updike.)

CHAPTER 4

The Reader as Writer

Chapter Preview

After reading this chapter, you will be able to

- Use a wide range of close reading and inquiry strategies to develop ideas for an essay
- Employ critical thinking to develop a thesis
- Engage effectively in the process of drafting and revising an argument
- Evaluate a student's analysis essay

Developing Ideas through Close Reading and Inquiry

Getting Ideas

How do writers "learn to have ideas"? Among the methods are these: reading with a pen or pencil in hand so that you can annotate the text; using brainstorming and freewriting notes to ask questions and develop answers; keeping a journal in which you jot down reflections about your reading; generating notes in the form of lists and outlines that organize your ideas; and arguing with yourself and talking with others (including your instructor) about the reading.

Let's take another look at the first of these methods, annotating.

Annotating a Text

When you're reading, if you own the book that you're reading, don't hesitate to mark it up, indicating (by highlighting or underlining or making marginal notes) what puzzles you, what pleases or interests you, and what displeases or bores you. If you plan to return the book, use sticky notes to add annotations to the text or take reading notes in a journal or on your laptop. Later, you'll want to think further about these responses, asking yourself, on rereading, whether you still feel that way, and if not, why not. These first responses, however, will get you started.

Annotations of the sort shown on pages 28–29, which chiefly call attention to contrasts, indicate that the student is thinking about writing an analysis of the story. That is, she is thinking of writing an essay in which she will examine the parts of a literary work either in an effort to see how they relate to each other or in an effort to see how one part relates to the whole.

Let's look at a story by Kate Chopin that is a little longer than "Ripe Figs," featured in Chapter 3, and then we'll discuss how, in addition to annotating it, you might get ideas for writing about it.

KATE CHOPIN

For a biographical note, see page 25.

The Story of an Hour

the wife of (handwritten)

could relate to a broken heart (handwritten)

Knowing that Mrs. Mallard was afflicted with a heart trouble, great care was taken to break to her as gently as possible the news of her husband's death.

It was her sister Josephine who told her, in broken sentences, veiled hints that revealed in half concealing. Her husband's friend Richards was there, too, near her. It was he who had been in the newspaper office when intelligence of the railroad disaster was received, with Brently Mallard's name leading the list of "killed." He had only taken the time to assure himself of its truth by a second telegram, and had hastened to forestall any less careful, less tender friend in bearing the sad message.

She did not hear the story as many women have heard the same, with a paralyzed inability to accept its significance. She wept at once, with sudden, wild abandonment, in her sister's arms. When the storm of grief had spent itself she went away to her room alone. She would have no one follow her. *grief does pass* (handwritten)

There stood, facing the open window, a comfortable, roomy armchair. Into this she sank, pressed down by a physical exhaustion that haunted her body and seemed to reach into her soul.

5 She could see in the open square before her house the tops of trees that were all aquiver with the new spring life. The delicious breath of rain was in the air. In the street below a peddler was crying his wares. The notes of a distant song which some one was singing reached her faintly, and countless sparrows were twittering in the eaves.

There were patches of blue sky showing here and there through the clouds that had met and piled above the other in the west facing her window. She sat with her head thrown back upon the cushion of the chair quite motionless, except when a sob came up into her throat and shook her, as a child who has cried itself to sleep continues to sob in its dreams. *dreams mirror feelings* (handwritten)

She was young, with a fair, calm face, whose lines bespoke repression and even a certain strength. But now there was a dull stare in her eyes, whose gaze was fixed away off yonder on one of those patches of blue sky. It was not a glance of reflection, but rather indicated a suspension of intelligent thought.

There was something coming to her and she was waiting for it, fearfully. What was it? She did not know; it was too subtle and elusive to name. But she felt it, creeping out of the sky, reaching toward her through the sounds, the scents, the color that filled the air.

Now her bosom rose and fell tumultuously. She was beginning to recognize this thing that was approaching to possess her, and she was striving to beat it back with her will—as powerless as her two white slender hands would have been.

10 When she abandoned herself a little whispered word escaped her slightly parted lips. She said it over and over under her breath: "Free, free, free!" The vacant stare and the look of terror that had followed it went from her eyes. They stayed keen and bright. Her pulses beat fast, and the coursing blood warmed and relaxed every inch of her body.

She did not stop to ask if it were not a monstrous joy that held her. A clear and exalted perception enabled her to dismiss the suggestion as trivial.

She knew that she would weep again when she saw the kind, tender hands folded in death; the face that had never looked save with love upon her, fixed and gray and dead. But she saw beyond that bitter moment a long procession of years to come that would belong to her absolutely. And she opened and spread her arms out to them in welcome.

There would be no one to live for her during those coming years; she would live for herself. There would be no powerful will bending her in that blind persistence with which men and women believe they have a right to impose a private will upon a fellow creature. A kind intention or a cruel intention made the act seem no less a crime as she looked upon it in that brief moment of illumination.

And yet she had loved him—sometimes. Often she had not. What did it matter! What could love, the unsolved mystery, count for in face of this possession of self-assertion which she suddenly recognized as the strongest impulse of her being.

15   "Free! Body and soul free!" she kept whispering.

Josephine was kneeling before the closed door with her lips to the keyhole, imploring for admission. "Louise, open the door! I beg; open the door—you will make yourself ill. What are you doing, Louise? For heaven's sake open the door."

"Go away. I am not making myself ill." No; she was drinking in a very elixir of life through that open window.

Her fancy was running riot along those days ahead of her. Spring days, and summer days, and all sorts of days that would be her own. She breathed a quick prayer that life might be long. It was only yesterday she had thought with a shudder that life might be long.

She arose at length and opened the door to her sister's importunities. There was a feverish triumph in her eyes, and she carried herself unwittingly like a goddess of Victory. She clasped her sister's waist, and together they descended the stairs. Richards stood waiting for them at the bottom.

20   Some one was opening the front door with a latchkey. It was Brently Mallard who entered, a little travel-stained, composedly carrying his gripsack and umbrella. He had been far from the scene of accident, and did not even know there had been one. He stood amazed at Josephine's piercing cry; at Richards' quick motion to screen him from the view of his wife.

But Richards was too late.

When the doctors came they said she had died of heart disease—of joy that kills.

[1894]

Brainstorming Ideas

Unlike annotating, which consists of making brief notes and small marks on the printed page, "brainstorming"—the free jotting down of ideas—asks that you write down whatever comes to mind, without inhibition. Don't worry about spelling, writing complete sentences, or unifying your thoughts; just let one thought lead to another. Later, you can review your jottings, deleting some, connecting those that are related, and expanding others, but for now you just want to get going. As we explored in Chapter 2, brainstorming starts the process of inquiry, working to move from your annotations about the text to open-ended writing that captures your questions and answers about the text. These writing strategies allow you to capture your thought process on paper, helping you to develop new insights that are worthy of further investigation.

Thus, you might jot down something about the title:

Title speaks of an hour, and story covers an hour, but maybe takes five minutes to read.

Then, perhaps prompted by "an hour," you might add something to this effect:

> *Doubt that a woman who got news of the death of her husband could move from grief to joy within an hour.*

Your next jotting might have little or nothing to do with this issue; it might simply say,

> *Enjoyed "Hour" more than "Ripe Figs" partly because "Hour" is so shocking.*

And then you might ask yourself,

> *By shocking, do I mean "improbable," or what? Come to think of it, maybe it's not so improbable. A lot depends on what the marriage was like.*

Focused Freewriting

Focused, or directed, freewriting is a form of brainstorming that some writers use to uncover ideas. Concentrating on one issue—for instance, a question that strikes them as worth puzzling over ("What kind of person is Mrs. Mallard?")—they write at length, nonstop, for perhaps five or ten minutes. They do not stop to evaluate the results or to worry about niceties of sentence structure or spelling. They just pour out their ideas in a steady stream of writing, drawing on whatever associations come to mind.

After the freewriting session, these writers reread what they have written, highlighting or underlining whatever seems to be of value. At this point, the writers are often able to make a rough outline and begin a draft.

Here is an example of one student's focused freewriting:

Student Work: Freewriting

What do I know about Mrs. Mallard? Let me put everything down here I know about her or can figure out from what Kate Chopin tells me. When she finds herself alone after the death of her husband, she says, "Free! Body and soul free!" and before that she said, "Free, free, free!" So she has suddenly perceived that she has not been free; she has been under the influence of a "powerful will." In this case it has been her husband, but she says no one, man or woman, should impose their will on anyone else. So it's not a feminist issue—it's a power issue. No one should push anyone else around is what I guess Chopin means, force someone to do what the other person wants. I used to have a friend that did that to me all the time; he had to run everything. They say that fathers—before the women's movement—used to run things, with the father in charge of all the decisions, so maybe this is an honest reaction to having been pushed around by a husband. I think Mrs. Mallard is a believable character, even if the plot is not all that believable—all those things happening in such quick succession.

Listing Ideas, Details, and Quotations

In your preliminary thinking, you may find it useful to make lists. In the previous chapter, we saw that listing the traits of the two characters was helpful in thinking about Chopin's "Ripe Figs":

Student Work: Listing

Maman-Nainaine
  older than Babette
  "stately way"
  "patient as the statue of la Madone"
  connects actions with seasons
  expects to be obeyed

Babette
  young
  active and impatient
  obedient

For "The Story of an Hour," you might list Mrs. Mallard's traits, or you might list the stages in her development. Such a list is not the same as a summary of the plot. The list helps you to see the sequence of psychological changes.

Mrs. Mallard
  weeps (when she gets the news)
  goes to room, alone
  "pressed down by a physical exhaustion"
  "dull stare"
  "something coming to her"
  strives to beat back "this thing"
  "Free, free, free!" The "vacant stare went . . . from her eyes"
  "A clear and exalted perception"
  rejects Josephine
  "she was drinking in a very elixir of life"
  gets up, opens door, "a feverish triumph in her eyes"
  sees B., and dies

Unlike brainstorming and annotating, which let you go in all directions, listing requires that you first make a decision about what you will be listing: traits of character, images, puns, or whatever. Once you make the decision, you can construct a list, and with that list in front of you, you will see patterns that you were not fully conscious of earlier.

Asking Questions

When you feel stuck, ask yourself questions. Questioning can help you to reenergize the process of inquiry. You'll recall that the assignment on "Ripe Figs" in effect, asked that students form questions about the work-for instance, questions about the relationship between the characters—and about their responses to it: "You'll try to explain as honestly as you can what makes 'Ripe Figs' appealing or interesting— or trifling, or boring."

If you are thinking about a work of fiction, ask yourself questions about the plot and the characters: Are they believable, are they interesting, and what does it all add up to? What does the story mean to you?

One student found it helpful to record the following inquiry notes:

Student Work: Inquiry Notes

Plot
  Ending false? Unconvincing? Or prepared for?
Character?
  Mrs. M. unfeeling? Immoral?
  Mrs. M. unbelievable character?
  What might her marriage have been like? Many gaps.
  Can we tell what her husband was like?
  And yet she loved him—sometimes" Fickle? Realistic?
  What is "this thing that was approaching to possess her"?
Symbolism
  Set on spring day = symbolic of new life?

You don't have to be as organized as this student. You may begin by recording notes and queries about what you like or dislike and about what puzzles or amuses you. What follows are the inquiry notes of a second student. They are in no particular order; the student is brainstorming, putting down whatever occurs to her, although it is obvious that one question sometimes leads to the next:

Title nothing special. What might be a better title?
Could a woman who loved her husband be so heartless?
Is she heartless? Did she love him?
What are (were) Louise's feelings about her husband?
Did she want too much? What did she want?
Could this story happen today? Feminist interpretation?
Sister (Josephine)—a busybody?
Tricky ending—but maybe it could be true.
"And yet she had loved him—sometimes. Often she had not."
Why does one love someone "sometimes"?
Irony: plot has reversal. Are characters ironic too?

These inquiry notes helped this reader think about the story, find a special point of interest, and develop a thoughtful argument about it.

Keeping a Journal

A critical thinking journal is not a diary. Rather, it is a place to store some of the thoughts that you may have inscribed in the margin of the text, such as your initial response to the title of a work or to the ending. It is also a place to capture further reflections, such as thoughts about what the work means to you and what was said in the classroom about writing in general or about specific works.

You may, for instance, want to reflect on why your opinion is so different from that of another student, or you may want to apply a concept such as *character* or *irony* or *plausibility* to a story that later you may write about in an essay. Comparisons are especially helpful: How does this story (or this character, or this rhyme scheme) differ from last week's reading?

A student who wrote about "The Story of an Hour" began with the following entry in his journal. When you are reading this entry, notice that one idea stimulates another. The student was, quite rightly, concerned with getting and exploring ideas, not with writing a unified paragraph.

Student Work: Journal Writing

Apparently a "well-made" story, but seems clever rather than moving or real. Doesn't seem plausible. Mrs. M's change comes out of the blue—maybe some women might respond like this, but probably not most.

Does literature deal with unusual people, or with usual (typical?) people? Shouldn't it deal with typical? Maybe not. (Anyway, how can I know?) Is "typical" same as "plausible"? Come to think of it, prob. not.

Anyway, whether Mrs. M is typical or not, is her change plausible, believable? Think more about this.

Why did she change? Her husband dominated her life and controlled her actions; he did "impose a private will upon a fellow creature." She calls this a crime, even if well-intentioned. Is it a crime?

Developing a Thesis
through Critical Thinking

Arguing with Yourself

In our discussion of annotating, brainstorming, freewriting, listing, asking questions, and keeping a journal, the emphasis has been on responding freely rather than on responding in any systematic or disciplined way.

The almost random play of mind in brainstorming and the other activities is a kind of thinking, but the term **critical thinking** (which we addressed in Chapter 2) is reserved for the process of moving these ideas toward analytical writing. When we think critically, we scrutinize our own ideas—for example, by searching out our underlying assumptions or evaluating what we have recorded as evidence. We have seen examples of this sort of analysis of one's own thinking in the journal entries in which a student wrote that literature should probably deal with "typical" people and then wondered if "typical" and "plausible" were the same, and then added "probably not."

Speaking broadly, critical thinking is rational, logical thinking. In thinking critically, writers

- scrutinize their **assumptions**;
- **define** their terms;
- test the **evidence** that they have collected and even look for **counterevidence**; and
- revise their **thesis** when necessary, in order to make the **argument** as complete and convincing as possible.

Let's start with **assumptions**. If I say that a story is weak because it is improbable, I ought to think about my assumption that improbability is a flaw I can begin by asking myself if all good stories—or all the stories that I value highly—are probable. I may recall that among my favorites is *Alice's Adventures in Wonderland* (or *Gulliver's Travels* or *Animal Farm*)—so I probably have to withdraw my assumption that improbability in itself makes a story less than good. I may go on to refine the idea and decide that improbability is not a fault in satiric stories but is a fault in other kinds of stories, which is not the same as saying bluntly that improbability is a fault.

The second aspect of critical thinking, **definition**, does not refer chiefly to defining technical terms, such as "meter," for readers who may be unfamiliar with the language of literary criticism; rather, here we are speaking about the need to define controversial terms. For instance, if you are arguing that a particular story is sentimental, you will have to define what you mean by "sentimental" because the word has several meanings.

The third aspect of critical thinking that we have isolated—testing the **evidence** and searching for **counterevidence** within the work—involves rereading the work to see whether we have overlooked material or taken a detail out of context. If, for instance, we say that in "The Story of an Hour" Josephine is a busybody, we should reexamine the work to make sure that she is, indeed, meddling needlessly and not offering welcome or necessary assistance. Perhaps the original observation will stand up, but perhaps on rereading the story we may feel, as we examine each of Josephine's actions, that she cannot reasonably be characterized as a busybody.

Different readers may come to different conclusions; the important thing is that all readers subject their initial responses to critical thinking, testing their responses against all of the evidence. Remember, your instructor expects you to hand in an essay that is essentially an **argument**, a paper that advances a thesis of your own, and therefore you will want to revise your thinking if you find counterevidence. Your **thesis** might be that

- the story is improbable, or
- the story is typical of Chopin, or
- the story is antiwoman, or
- the story is a remarkable anticipation of contemporary feminist thinking.

Whatever your thesis will be, it should be able to withstand scrutiny: That is what a good argument does. You may not convince every reader that you are unquestionably right, but you should make every reader feel that your argument is thoughtful. If you read your notes and then your drafts critically, you will probably write a paper that meets this standard.

Your first reading of the literary work probably *won't* be a critical reading. It is entirely appropriate to begin by reading simply for enjoyment. After all, we read literature (or listen to music, or go to an art museum, or watch dancers) to derive pleasure. However, in this course, you are trying to deepen your understanding of literature, so you are *studying* literature. On subsequent readings, therefore, you will read the work critically, carefully noting the writer's view of human nature and the writer's ways of achieving certain effects.

Arguing a Thesis

If you think critically about your early jottings and about the literary work itself, you will probably find that some of your jottings lead to dead ends but that others will lead to further ideas that hold up under scrutiny. What the thesis of your essay will be—the idea that you will assert and *argue* (support with evidence)—is still unclear, but you know that a good essay will need a thesis, or a claim that makes an argument. You ought to be able to state your point in a **thesis sentence**.

Consider the following candidates for a thesis sentence:

1. Mrs. Mallard dies soon after hearing that her husband has died.

True, but this is not a point that can be argued or even developed. About the most an essayist can do with this sentence is to amplify it by summarizing the plot of the story, a task not worth doing unless the plot is unusually obscure. An essay may include a sentence or two of summary to give readers their bearings, but a summary is not an essay.

2. The story is a libel on women.

Unlike the first statement, this one can be developed into an argument. Probably the writer will try to demonstrate that Mrs. Mallard's behavior is despicable. Whether this point can be argued convincingly is another matter; the thesis may be untenable, but it is a thesis. A second problem, however, is this: Even if the writer demonstrates that Mrs. Mallard's behavior is despicable, he or she will have to go on to demonstrate that the presentation of one despicable woman constitutes a libel on women in general. That's a pretty big order.

3. The story is clever but superficial because it is based on an unreal character.

Here, too, is a thesis—a point of view that can be argued. Whether this thesis is true is another matter. The writer's job will be to support it by presenting evidence. Probably the writer will have no difficulty in finding evidence that the story is "clever"; the difficulty will be in establishing a case that the characterization of Mrs. Mallard is "unreal." The writer will have to set forth some ideas about what makes a character real and then show that Mrs. Mallard is an unreal (unbelievable) figure.

4. The irony of the ending is believable partly because it is consistent with earlier ironies in the story.

The student who wrote the essay that appears on pages 73–75 began by drafting an essay based on the third of these thesis topics, but as she worked on a draft, she found that she could not support her assertion that the character was unconvincing. In fact, she came to believe that, although Mrs. Mallard's joy was the reverse of what a reader might expect, several early reversals in the story helped to make Mrs. Mallard's shift from grief to joy understandable.

✔ **CHECKLIST:** *The Thesis Sentence*

☐ Does the thesis sentence make a claim rather than merely offer a description?
☐ Is the claim arguable rather than self-evident, universally accepted, or of little interest?
☐ Does the thesis emphasize conceptual thinking? Does it focus on an important concept that can be developed? Does the thesis avoid an information-based statement, such as plot summary?
☐ Can evidence be produced to support the claim?
☐ Is the claim narrow enough to be supported convincingly in a paper written within the allotted time and at the assigned length?

From Reading to Writing to Revising: Drafting an Argument in an Analytical Essay

After making notes about your reading and then adding more notes stimulated by your rereading and further thinking, you should be able to formulate a tentative thesis. At this point, most writers review their preliminary notes and jot down brief statements of what they think their key points may be. These notes may include quotations of key phrases that the writer thinks will support the thesis.

Having reached this stage in considering irony in "The Story of an Hour," one student made the following notes:

> *title? Ironies in an Hour (?) An Hour of Irony (?) Kate Chopin's Irony (?)*
> *thesis: irony at end is prepared for by earlier ironies*
> *chief irony: Mrs. M. dies just as she is beginning to enjoy life*
> *smaller ironies:? 1. "sad message" brings her joy*
> *   2. Richards is "too late" at end*
> *   3. Richards is too early at start*

These notes are, in effect, a very brief **outline**. Some writers at this point like to develop a fuller outline, but most writers begin with only a brief outline, knowing that, in the process of developing a draft from their notes, additional ideas will arise. For these writers, the time to make a detailed outline is after they have written a first or second draft. The outline of the written draft will then help them to make sure that their draft has an adequate organization and that main points are developed.

Student Analytical Essay: "Ironies in an Hour" (Preliminary Draft)

Now for the student's draft—not the first version, but a revised draft with some irrelevancies of the first draft omitted and some evidence added.

The numbers in parentheses refer to the page numbers from which the quotations are drawn, though with so short a work as "The Story of an Hour," page numbers are limited. (Detailed information about how to document a paper appears in Appendix B.)

Bridas 1

Jennifer Bridas

Professor Lester

English 1102

22 February 2016

Ironies in an Hour

After we know how the story turns out, if we reread it we find irony at

the very start, as is true of many other stories. Mrs. Mallard's friends assume,

mistakenly, that Mrs. Mallard was deeply in love with her husband, Brently

Mallard. They take great care to tell her gently of his death. The friends mean

well, and in fact they do well. They bring her an hour of life, an hour of

freedom. They think their news is sad. Mrs. Mallard at first expresses

grief when she hears the news, but soon she finds joy in it. So Richards's

"sad message" (57), though sad in Richards's eyes, is in fact a happy

message.

Among the ironic details is the statement that when Mallard entered

the house, Richards tried to conceal him from Mrs. Mallard, but "Richards

was too late" (58). This is ironic because earlier Richards "hastened" (57) to

bring his sad message; if he had at the start been "too late" (58), Brently

Mallard would have arrived at home first, and Mrs. Mallard's life would not

have ended an hour later but would simply have gone on as it had before. Yet

another irony at the end of the story is the diagnosis of the doctors. The

doctors say she died of "heart disease—of joy that kills" (58). In one sense

the doctors are right: Mrs. Mallard has experienced a great joy. But of course

the doctors totally misunderstand the joy that kills her.

The central irony resides not in the well-intentioned but ironic

actions of Richards, or in the unconsciously ironic words of the doctors, but

in her own life. In a way she has been dead. She "sometimes" (58) loved her

husband, but in a way she has been dead. Now, his apparent death brings her

new life. This new life comes to her at the season of the year when "the tops

of trees . . . were all aquiver with the new spring life" (57). But, ironically,

her new life will last only an hour. She looks forward to "summer days" (58)

but she will not see even the end of this spring day. Her years of marriage

were ironic. They brought her a sort of living death instead of joy. Her new

life is ironic too. It grows out of her moment of grief for her supposedly dead

husband, and her vision of a new life is cut short.

[New page]

Bridas 3

Work Cited

Chopin, Kate. "The Story of an Hour." *Literature for Composition*. Ed. Sylvan Barnet, William Burto, William E. Cain, and Cheryl L. Nixon. 11th ed. Boston: Pearson, 2017. 65-66. Print.

Revising an Argument

Jennifer Bridas's draft, although thoughtful and clear, is not yet a finished essay. First, the draft needs a good introductory paragraph that will let the **audience**— the readers—know where the writer will be taking them. Doubtless you know from your own experience that readers can follow an argument more easily—and with more pleasure—if early in the discussion the writer tells them what the argument is. (The title, too, can strongly suggest the thesis.) Second, some of the paragraphs could be more effective.

In revising paragraphs—or an entire draft—writers unify, organize, clarify, and polish.

1. **Unity** is achieved partly by eliminating irrelevancies. Notice that, in the final version of the essay, which begins on page 78, the writer has deleted "as is true of many other stories."
2. **Organization** is largely a matter of arranging material in a sequence that will assist the reader to grasp the point.
3. **Clarity** is achieved largely by providing concrete details and quotations— evidence—to support generalizations and by providing helpful transitions ("for instance," "furthermore," "on the other hand," "however").
4. **Polishing** involves making small-scale revisions, such as deleting unnecessary repetitions. In the second paragraph of the draft, the phrase "the doctors" appears four times, but it appears only three times in the final version of the paragraph. Similarly, in polishing, a writer may combine choppy sentences into longer ones and break overly long sentences into shorter ones.

Later, after producing a draft that seems close to a finished essay, writers engage in yet another activity:

5. **Editing** includes checking the accuracy of quotations by comparing them with the original, consulting a dictionary for the spelling of doubtful words, and checking a handbook for appropriate punctuation.

Outlining an Argument

Whether or not you draw up an outline before writing a draft, you will be better able to improve your draft if you prepare an outline of what you have written. This revision strategy of pulling an outline out of an essay that has already been written in order to check its ideas, organization, and argument, is often termed "reverse outlining." For each paragraph in your draft, write down the main point of the topic sentence or topic idea. Under each of these sentences, indented, add key words for the idea(s) developed in the paragraph. Thus, in an outline for the first two paragraphs of the draft that we have just looked at, you might make the following jottings:

> *story ironic from start*
> > *friends think news is sad*
> > *Ms. M. finds joy*
> *some ironic details*
> > *Richards hastened, but "too late"*
> > *doctors right and also wrong*

An outline of what you have written will help you to see whether your draft is adequate in three important ways. The outline will show you

1. the sequence of major topics,
2. the degree of development of these topics, and
3. the argument, the thesis.

When you are studying your outline, you may realize that your first major point (probably after an introductory paragraph) would be more effective as your third point and that your second point needs to be further developed.

An outline of this sort is a short version of your draft, perhaps even containing phrases from the draft. Another sort of outline indicates not what each paragraph says but what each paragraph *does*. Such an outline of the three-paragraph draft of the essay on "The Story of an Hour" might look like this:

1. The actions of the friends are ironic.
2. Gives some specific (minor) details about ironies.
3. Explains "central irony."

We ought to see a red flag here. The aim of this sort of outline is to indicate what each paragraph does, but the jotting for the first paragraph only summarizes its content. Why? Because the paragraph doesn't do anything. It doesn't clearly introduce a thesis, or define a crucial term, or set the story in the context of Chopin's other work.

An outline indicating the function of each paragraph will force you to see whether your essay has an effective structure. We will see that this student later wrote a new opening paragraph for her essay on "The Story of an Hour."

Soliciting Peer Review, Thinking about Counterarguments

You may be asked to get a review from your peers. Such a procedure is helpful in several ways. First, it gives you a real audience-readers who can point to what pleases or puzzles them, who make suggestions, who may often disagree with you or with each other, and who frequently *misread*. Though writers don't always like what they hear about their work, reading and discussing their work with others almost always gives them a fresh perspective on their work, and a fresh perspective can stimulate thoughtful revision.

Your reviewers may suggest that you have overlooked evidence that works against your interpretation. Obviously, you will have to either revise your interpretation or show that, in fact, the supposed counterevidence really does not weaken your interpretation.

The writer whose work is being reviewed is not the sole beneficiary of a review. When students serve as readers for each other, they become better readers of their own work and consequently better revisers. As we said in Chapter 2, learning to write is, in large measure, learning to read.

If peer review is a part of the writing process in your course, the instructor may distribute a sheet of questions and suggestions. Here is an example of such a sheet.

QUESTIONS FOR PEER REVIEW   ENGLISH 125A

Read each draft once, quickly. Then read it again, with the following questions in mind.

1. What is the essay's topic? Is it one of the assigned topics or a variation from it? Does the draft show promise of fulfilling the assignment?
2. Looking at the essay as a whole, what thesis (main idea) is stated or implied? If the thesis is implied, state it in your own words.
3. Is the thesis plausible? How might the argument be strengthened?
4. Looking at each paragraph separately, answer the following questions:
   a. What is the basic point? (If it isn't clear to you, ask for clarification.)
   b. How does the paragraph relate to the essay's main idea or to the previous paragraph?
   c. Should some paragraphs be deleted? Should they be divided into two or more paragraphs? Should they be combined? Should they be put elsewhere? (If you outline the essay by jotting down the main point of each paragraph, it will help you to answer these questions.)
   d. Is each sentence clearly related to the sentence that precedes it and to the sentence that follows it?
   e. Is each paragraph adequately developed?
   f. Are there sufficient details—perhaps brief, supporting quotations from the text?
5. What are the paper's chief strengths?
6. Make at least two specific suggestions that you think will assist the author to improve the paper.

From Reading to Writing to Revising: Finalizing an Analytical Essay

Student Analytical Essay: "Ironies of Life in Kate Chopin's 'The Story of an Hour'" (Final Draft)

Here is the final version of Jennifer Bridas's essay. The essay submitted to the instructor was entirely retyped; but here, so that you can easily see how the draft was revised, we show the draft version with the final changes written in by hand.

Jennifer Bridas

Professor Lester

English 1102

4 February 2016

Ironies of Life in Kate Chopin's "The Story of an Hour"

~~Ironies in an Hour~~

 Despite its title, Kate Chopin's "The Story of an Hour" ironically takes only a few minutes to read. In addition, the story turns out to have an ironic ending, but on rereading it one sees that the irony is not concentrated only in the outcome of the plot—Mrs. Mallard dies just when she is beginning to live—but is also present in many details.

 After we know how the story turns out, if we reread it we find irony at the very start. /~~as is true of many other stories.~~ *Because* Mrs. Mallard's friends *and her sister* assume, mistakenly, that ~~Mrs. Mallard~~ *she* was deeply in love with her husband, Brently Mallard. / *They* ~~They~~ take great care to tell her gently of his death. ~~The friends~~ *They* mean well, and in fact they *do* well. / ~~They~~ bring*ing* her an hour of life, an hour of *joyous* freedom. / ~~They~~ *but it is ironic that* # *True,* think their news is sad. Mrs. Mallard at first expresses grief when she hears the news, but soon *(unknown to her friends)* she finds joy in it. So Richards's "sad message" (57), though sad in Richards's eyes, is in fact a happy message.

 Among the ironic details is the statement *small but significant* that when Mallard *near the end of the story* entered the house, Richards tried to conceal him from Mrs. Mallard, but "Richards was too late" (58). This is ironic because *almost at* ~~earlier~~ *the start of the story, in the second paragraph,* Richards "hastened" (57) to bring his sad message; if he had at the start been "too late" (58), Brently Mallard would have arrived at home first, and Mrs. Mallard's life would not have ended an hour later but would simply have gone on as it had before. Yet another irony at the end of the story is the diagnosis of the doctors. The doctors say she died of "heart disease—of joy that kills" (58). In one sense ~~the doctors~~ *they* are right: Mrs. Mallard *for the last hour*

Bridas 2

experienced a great joy. But of course the doctors totally

misunderstand the joy that kills her. *It is not joy at seeing her husband alive, but her realization that the great joy she experienced during the last hour is over.*

All of these ironic details add richness to the story, but
∧ ~~The~~ central irony resides not in the well-intentioned but

ironic actions of Richards, or in the unconsciously ironic words of
                              Mrs. Mallard's
the doctors, but in ~~her~~ own life. ~~In a way she has been dead.~~ She

"sometimes" (58) loved her husband, but in a way she has been
a body subjected to her husband's will   *Appropriately*
dead*./* Now, his apparent death brings her new life. ∧This new

life comes to her at the season of the year when "the tops of

trees . . . were all aquiver with the new spring life" (57). But,
She is "free, free, free"—but only until her husband walks through the
ironically, her new life will last only an hour. ∧She looks   *doorway.*

forward to "summer days" (58) but she will not see even the
                    If
end of this spring day. ∧~~H~~er years of marriage were ironic*/,*
bringing
~~They brought~~ her a sort of living death instead of joy*/,* ~~H~~er
          not only because
new life is ironic too*/,* ∧~~I~~t grows out of her moment of grief for
          but also because her vision of "a long progression of years"
her supposedly dead husband, ~~and her vision of a new life~~ is

cut short*/ within an hour on a spring day.*

[New page]

Bridas 3

Work Cited

Chopin, Kate. "The Story of an Hour." *Literature for Composition*. Ed. Sylvan Barnet,

William Burto, William E. Cain, and Cheryl L. Nixon. 11th ed. Boston: Pearson,

2017. 65-66. Print.

The Analytical Essay: The Final Draft Analyzed

As a review, let's look at several principles illustrated by Jennifer Bridas's essay.

- The **title of the essay** is not merely the title of the work discussed; it should give the reader a clue about the essayist's topic. Because the title will create that crucial first impression, make sure that it is interesting.
- The **opening or introductory paragraph** does not begin with the obvious, "In this story…" Rather, by naming the author and the title, it lets the reader know what story is being discussed. It also indicates the writer's *thesis* so that readers will know where they are going.
- The **organization** is effective. The smaller ironies are discussed in the second and third paragraphs, and the central irony is discussed in the last paragraph. The essay does not dwindle or become anticlimactic; the argument builds from the least important to the most important point. Again, if you outline your draft, you will see whether it has an effective organization.
- **Brief quotations** are used, both to provide evidence and to let the reader hear—if only fleetingly—Kate Chopin's writing voice.
- The essay is chiefly devoted to **analysis** (*how* the parts relate to each other), not to a summary (a restatement of what happened). The writer, properly assuming that the reader has read the work, does not tell the plot in detail. But, aware that the reader has not memorized the story, the writer gives helpful reminders.
- The **present tense** is used in narrating the action: "Mrs. Mallard dies"; "Mrs. Mallard's friends and relatives all assume."
- Although a **concluding paragraph** is often useful, when it does more than merely summarize, it is not essential in a short analysis. In this essay, the last sentence explains the chief irony and therefore makes an acceptable ending.
- Documentation follows the form set forth in Appendix B.
- If the author has proofread the final version of the paper carefully, it will contain no typographical errors.

From Reading to Writing to Revising: Drafting an Analytical Essay

KATE CHOPIN

Désirée's Baby

As the day was pleasant, Madame Valmondé drove over to L'Abri to see Désirée and the baby.

It made her laugh to think of Désirée with a baby. Why, it seemed but yesterday that Désirée was little more than a baby herself; when Monsieur in riding through the gateway of Valmondé had found her lying asleep in the shadow of the big stone pillar.

The little one awoke in his arms and began to cry for "Dada." That was as much as she could do or say. Some people thought she might have strayed there of her own accord, for she was of the toddling age. The prevailing belief was that

Armand represents society
shows how stupid the 1% rule is

she had been purposely left by a party of Texans, whose canvas-covered wagon, late in the day, had crossed the ferry that Coton Maïs kept, just below the plantation. In time Madame Valmondé abandoned every speculation but the one that Désirée had been sent to her by a beneficent Providence to be the child of her affection, seeing that she was without child of the flesh. For the girl grew to be beautiful and gentle, affectionate and sincere,—the idol of Valmondé.

It was no wonder, when she stood one day against the stone pillar in whose shadow she had lain asleep, eighteen years before, that Armand Aubigny riding by and seeing her there, had fallen in love with her. That was the way all the Aubignys fell in love, as if struck by a pistol shot. The wonder was that he had not loved her before; for he had known her since his father brought him home from Paris, a boy of eight, after his mother died there. The passion that awoke in him that day, when he saw her at the gate, swept along like an avalanche, or like a prairie fire, or like anything that drives headlong over all obstacles.

5 Monsieur Valmondé grew practical and wanted things well considered: that is, the girl's obscure origin. Armand looked into her eyes and did not care. He was reminded that she was nameless. What did it matter about a name when he could give her one of the oldest and proudest in Louisiana? He ordered the *corbeille*[1] from Paris, and contained himself with what patience he could until it arrived, then they were married.

Madame Valmondé had not seen Désirée and the baby for four weeks. When she reached L'Abri she shuddered at the first sight of it, as she always did. It was a sad looking place, which for many years had not known the gentle presence of a mistress, old Monsieur Aubigny having married and buried his wife in France, and she having loved her own land too well ever to leave it. The roof came down steep and black like a cowl, reaching out beyond the wide galleries that encircled the yellow stuccoed house. Big, solemn oaks grew close to it, and their thick-leaved, far-reaching branches shadowed it like a pall. Young Aubigny's rule was a strict one, too, and under it his negroes had forgotten how to be gay, as they had been during the old master's easy-going and indulgent lifetime.

The young mother was recovering slowly, and lay full length, in her soft white muslins and laces, upon a couch. The baby was beside her, upon her arm, where he had fallen asleep, at her breast. The yellow nurse woman sat beside a window fanning herself *they're wealthy and kind of racist*

Madame Valmondé bent her portly figure over Désirée and kissed her, holding her an instant tenderly in her arms. Then she turned to the child.

"This is not the baby!" she exclaimed, in startled tones. French was the language spoken at Valmondé in those days.

10 "I knew you would be astonished," laughed Désirée, "at the way he has grown. The little *cochon de lait!*[2] Look at his legs, mamma, and his hands and fingernails,— real fingernails. Zandrine had to cut them this morning. Isn't it true, Zandrine?"

The woman bowed her turbaned head majestically, "Mais si,[3] Madame."

"And the way he cries," went on Désirée, "is deafening. Armand heard him the other day as far away as La Blanche's cabin."

Madame Valmondé had never removed her eyes from the child. She lifted it and walked with it over to the window that was lightest. She scanned the baby

---

[1] *corbeille* wedding gifts from the groom to the bride.
[2] *cochon de lait* suckling pig (French).
[3] *Mais si* certainly (French).

narrowly, then looked as searchingly at Zandrine, whose face was turned to gaze across the fields.

"Yes, the child has grown, has changed," said Madame Valmondé, slowly, as she replaced it beside its mother. "What does Armand say?"

Désirée's face became suffused with a glow that was happiness itself.

"Oh, Armand is the proudest father in the parish, I believe, chiefly because it is a boy, to bear his name; though he says not—that he would have loved a girl as well. But I know it isn't true. I know he says that to please me. And mamma," she added, drawing Madame Valmondé's head down to her, and speaking in a whisper, "he hasn't punished one of them—not one of them—since baby is born. Even Négrillon, who pretended to have burnt his leg that he might rest from work—he only laughed, and said Négrillon was a great scamp. Oh, mamma, I'm so happy; it frightens me."

What Désirée said was true. Marriage, and later the birth of his son had softened Armand Aubigny's imperious and exacting nature greatly. This was what made the gentle Désirée so happy, for she loved him desperately. When he frowned she trembled, but loved him. When he smiled, she asked no greater blessing of God. But Armand's dark, handsome face had not often been disfigured by frowns since the day he fell in love with her.

When the baby was about three months old, Désirée awoke one day to the conviction that there was something in the air menacing her peace. It was at first too subtle to grasp. It had only been a disquieting suggestion; an air of mystery among the blacks; unexpected visits from far-off neighbors who could hardly account for their coming. Then a strange, an awful change in her husband's manner, which she dared not ask him to explain. When he spoke to her, it was with averted eyes, from which the old love-light seemed to have gone out. He absented himself from home; and when there, avoided her presence and that of her child, without excuse. And the very spirit of Satan seemed suddenly to take hold of him in his dealings with the slaves. Désirée was miserable enough to die.

She sat in her room, one hot afternoon, in her *peignoir*, listlessly drawing through her fingers the strands of her long, silky brown hair that hung about her shoulders. The baby, half naked, lay asleep upon her own great mahogany bed, that was like a sumptuous throne, with its satin-lined half-canopy. One of La Blanche's little quadroon boys—half naked too—stood fanning the child slowly with a fan of peacock feathers. Désirée's eyes had been fixed absently and sadly upon the baby, while she was striving to penetrate the threatening mist that she felt closing about her. She looked from her child to the boy who stood beside him, and back again; over and over. "Ah!" It was a cry that she could not help; which she was not conscious of having uttered. The blood turned like ice in her veins, and a clammy moisture gathered upon her face.

She tried to speak to the little quadroon boy; but no sound would come, at first. When he heard his name uttered, he looked up, and his mistress was pointing to the door. He laid aside the great, soft fan, and obediently stole away, over the polished floor, on his bare tiptoes.

She stayed motionless, with gaze riveted upon her child, and her face the picture of fright.

Presently her husband entered the room, and without noticing her, went to a table and began to search among some papers which covered it.

"Armand," she called to him, in a voice which must have stabbed him, if he was human. But he did not notice. "Armand," she said again. Then she rose and tottered towards him. "Armand," she panted once more, clutching his arm, "look at our child. What does it mean? tell me."

He coldly but gently loosened her fingers from about his arm and thrust the hand away from him. "Tell me what it means!" she cried despairingly.

25　　"It means," he answered lightly, "that the child is not white; it means that you are not white."

A quick conception of all that this accusation meant for her nerved her with unwonted courage to deny it. "It is a lie; it is not true, I am white! Look at my hair, it is brown; and my eyes are gray, Armand, you know they are gray. And my skin is fair," seizing his wrist. "Look at my hand; whiter than yours, Armand," she laughed hysterically.

"As white as La Blanche's," he returned cruelly; and went away leaving her alone with their child.

When she could hold a pen in her hand, she sent a despairing letter to Madame Valmondé.

"My mother, they tell me I am not white. Armand has told me I am not white. For God's sake tell them it is not true. You must know it is not true. I shall die. I must die. I cannot be so unhappy, and live."

30　　The answer that came was as brief:

"My own Désirée: Come home to Valmondé; back to your mother who loves you. Come with your child."

When the letter reached Désirée she went with it to her husband's study, and laid it open upon the desk before which he sat. She was like a stone image: silent, white, motionless after she placed it there.

In silence he ran his cold eyes over the written words. He said nothing. "Shall I go, Armand?" she asked in tones sharp with agonized suspense.

"Yes, go."

35　　"Do you want me to go?"

"Yes, I want you to go."

He thought Almighty God had dealt cruelly and unjustly with him; and felt, somehow, that he was paying Him back in kind when he stabbed thus into his wife's soul. Moreover he no longer loved her, because of the unconscious injury she had brought upon his home and his name.

She turned away like one stunned by a blow, and walked slowly towards the door, hoping he would call her back.

"Good-by, Armand," she moaned.

40　　He did not answer her. That was his last blow at fate.

Désirée went in search of her child. Zandrine was pacing the sombre gallery with it. She took the little one from the nurse's arms with no word of explanation, and descending the steps, walked away, under the live-oak branches.

It was an October afternoon; the sun was just sinking. Out in the still fields the negroes were picking cotton.

Désirée had not changed the thin white garment nor the slippers which she wore. Her hair was uncovered and the sun's rays brought a golden gleam from its brown meshes. She did not take the broad, beaten road which led to the far-off plantation of Valmondé. She walked across a deserted field, where the stubble bruised her tender feet, so delicately shod, and tore her thin gown to shreds. She disappeared among the reeds and willows that grew thick along the banks of the deep, sluggish bayou; and she did not come back again.

45　　Some weeks later there was a curious scene enacted at L'Abri. In the centre of the smoothly swept back yard was a great bonfire. Armand Aubigny sat in the wide hallway that commanded a view of the spectacle; and it was he who dealt out to a half dozen negroes the material which kept this fire ablaze.

A graceful cradle of willow, with all its dainty furbishings, was laid upon the pyre, which had already been fed with the richness of a priceless *layette*. Then there were silk gowns, and velvet and satin ones added to these; laces, too, and embroideries; bonnets and gloves; for the *corbeille* had been of rare quality.

The last thing to go was a tiny bundle of letters; innocent little scribblings that Désirée had sent to him during the days of their espousal. There was the remnant of one back in the drawer from which he took them. But it was not Désirée's; it was part of an old letter from his mother to his father. He read it. She was thanking God for the blessing of her husband's love:—

"But, above all," she wrote, "night and day, I thank the good God for having so arranged our lives that our dear Armand will never know that his mother, who adores him, belongs to the race that is cursed with the brand of slavery."

[1892]

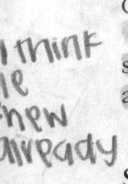

Student Analytical Essay: "Race and Identity in 'Désirée's Baby'"

Let's examine a student essay that analyzes "Désirée's Baby." The essay features a strong argument and an interesting uses of quotations. After the essay, we ask several questions that encourage you to evaluate the writing strategies used.

Hodges 1

Gus Hodges

Professor Durocher

English 125, section B

16 January 2016

Race and Identity in "Désirée's Baby"

"Désirée's Baby," says the literary scholar Emily Toth, is "a shocking story" that deals with the death of "a beautiful young woman"—the subject that, she notes, Edgar Allan Poe identified as "the perfect subject for poetry" (145). But in my view this story is shocking because it connects sexuality and race. It is not just that Désirée suffers a cruel fate, but that she does so because of her race, or, rather, the race that her husband Armand believes she belongs to. The tragic revelation is that Armand, not Désirée, is the person of mixed blood and thus is the cause or source of the mixed blood of their child.

In a key passage midway through the story, Chopin brings the Désirée/Armand relationship into focus:

When the baby was about three months old, Désirée awoke one day to the conviction that there was something in the air menacing her peace.

---

handwritten margin note: I think he knew already

It was at first too subtle to grasp. It had only been a disquieting suggestion; an air of mystery among the blacks; unexpected visits from far-off neighbors who could hardly account for their coming. Then a strange, an awful change in her husband's manner, which she dared not ask him to explain. When he spoke to her, it was with averted eyes, from which the old love-light seemed to have gone out. He absented himself from home; and when there, avoided her presence and that of her child, without excuse. And the very spirit of Satan seemed suddenly to take hold of him in his dealings with the slaves. Désirée was miserable enough to die. (82)

Chopin relates the action from Désirée's point of view—what she is seeing, thinking, feeling, fearing, as she and her husband grow estranged. But, at the same time, Chopin makes the reader aware of Armand. She prompts us to imagine, for ourselves, what might be leading him to shun his wife and child and, furthermore, what might account for his Satan-like treatment of his slaves.

This is a powerful insight on Chopin's part. As the story unfolds, it becomes clear that Armand has turned against Désirée because, to his horror and disgust, he has discovered that she possesses black—that is, "not white"—blood (83). To him, his family has been made impure, contaminated. He feels betrayed, and he takes out his wrath on his wife and child: he cannot bear to be in their presence. In addition, he unleashes his wrath on his slaves; they become the objects of his fury about his family, which is not what he thought it was.

Chopin is showing the tyranny of male authority and power, but, again, she is relating it to race. Armand becomes abusive—psychologically, emotionally, and physically violent—as a result of his reaction to the presence of blackness in his domestic life. This is intolerable to him, and he drives Désirée and the baby away, as if their disappearance could cancel out all memories of them.

The conclusion of the story is shocking: Armand learns that his child is "not white" (83) not because of Désirée but because of himself. It was his mother who was "cursed with the brand of slavery" (84) and she and her husband (Armand's father) sought to conceal this fact from him. Armand comes to despise his wife and child when he learns—or so it seems—that Désirée is black: this is the explanation that he gives to himself and to Désirée. He loathes himself for making such a marriage in the first place.

I am not sure I can prove this, but I have the feeling that Chopin wants us to perceive an ambiguity in the ending of her story. The meaning on the surface is that when Armand reads his mother's letter, he suddenly realizes what he had never known. But there may be a deeper meaning. Possibly it is the case that now Armand is finding confirmation from his mother of an identity—who he is—that he has known was, or could be, true. Driving away Désirée is, in truth, a desperate effort to cast out the self that is "not white" (84).

The more we delve into "Désirée's Baby," the more it becomes Armand's story: to me, he is its central character. In this respect, it is noteworthy that when the story was first published in a magazine, it was titled "The Father of Désirée's Baby" (Knights xxv). I think that this title is better than the one that Chopin settled on, because it puts the focus on Armand. It could be that in the end he learns the truth about who he is. It also could be that in the end he is forced to see something he might have suspected all along—something he could not believe ever could be possible.

We thus find ourselves asking a two-part question about Armand: What does he know, and what might he not want to know? Could he really have been so blind as never to have imagined the possibility that he at last discovers at the end—that the "not white" (83) blood is his own? Perhaps. To me, however, it seems just as likely that he suspected this possibility but could not face it. We do not want to accept the truth about who we might be, about who we are.

[New page]

Hodges 4

Works Cited

Chopin, Kate. "Désirée's Baby." *Literature for Composition*. Ed. Sylvan Barnet,

William Burto, William E. Cain, and Cheryl L. Nixon. 11th ed. Boston:

Pearson, 2017. 80-84. Print.

Toth, Emily. *Unveiling Kate Chopin*. Jackson: U of Mississippi, 1999. Print.

Joining the Conversation: Critical Thinking and Writing

1. Has Gus Hodges chosen a good title for his paper? Why or why not?
2. Do you think it is good strategy to begin a paper with a quotation from a secondary source? Why or why not?
3. The student begins his closing paragraph with a question. Is this strategy effective? Why or why not?
4. Do you agree with this student's decision to center his paper on a single lengthy quote? Please explain your answer.
5. Let's now consider the paper as a whole. What is the writer's thesis? Does the writer provide evidence? Does he prove his thesis?
6. If you were to give the writer of this paper one piece of advice for improving his paper, what would it be?
7. Hodges makes an intriguing claim about Armand. Do you agree with him or not? Can you locate evidence in the text to support the student's feeling about what Armand has known, or might have known, all along?
8. Is the final paragraph effective? Why or why not?

From Reading to Writing to Revising: Drafting a Comparison Essay

KATE CHOPIN

The Storm

I

The leaves were so still that even Bibi thought it was going to rain. Bobinôt, who was accustomed to converse on terms of perfect equality with his little son, called the child's attention to certain sombre clouds that were rolling with sinister intention from the west, accompanied by a sullen, threatening roar. They were at

Friedheimer's store and decided to remain there till the storm had passed. They sat within the door on two empty kegs. Bibi was four years old and looked very wise.

"Mama'll be 'fraid, yes," he suggested with blinking eyes.

"She'll shut the house. Maybe she got Sylvie helpin' her this evenin'," Bobinôt responded reassuringly.

"No; she ent got Sylvie. Sylvie was helpin' her yistiday," piped Bibi.

5   Bobinôt arose and going across to the counter purchased a can of shrimps, of which Calixta was very fond. Then he returned to his perch on the keg and sat stolidly holding the can of shrimps while the storm burst. It shook the wooden store and seemed to be ripping great furrows in the distant field. Bibi laid his little hand on his father's knee and was not afraid.

II

Calixta, at home, felt no uneasiness for their safety. She sat at a side window sewing furiously on a sewing machine. She was greatly occupied and did not notice the approaching storm. But she felt very warm and often stopped to mop her face on which the perspiration gathered in beads. She unfastened her white sacque at the throat. It began to grow dark, and suddenly realizing the situation she got up hurriedly and went about closing windows and doors.

Out on the small front gallery[1] she had hung Bobinôt's Sunday clothes to air and she hastened out to gather them before the rain fell. As she stepped outside, Alcée Laballière rode in at the gate. She had not seen him very often since her marriage, and never alone. She stood there with Bobinôt's coat in her hands, and the big rain drops began to fall. Alcée rode his horse under the shelter of a side projection where the chickens had huddled and there were plows and a harrow piled up in the corner.

diff. in classes

"May I come and wait on your gallery till the storm is over, Calixta?" he asked.

"Come 'long in, M'sieur Alcée."

10   His voice and her own startled her as if from a trance, and she seized Bobinôt's vest. Alcée, mounting to the porch, grabbed the trousers and snatched Bibi's braided jacket that was about to be carried away by a sudden gust of wind. He expressed an intention to remain outside, but it was soon apparent that he might as well have been out in the open: the water beat in upon the boards in driving sheets, and he went inside, closing the door after him. It was even necessary to put something beneath the door to keep the water out.

"My! what a rain! It's good two years since it rain' like that," exclaimed Calixta as she rolled up a piece of bagging and Alcée helped her to thrust it beneath the crack.

She was a little fuller of figure than five years before when she married; but she had lost nothing of her vivacity. Her blue eyes still retained their melting quality; and her yellow hair, dishevelled by the wind and rain, kinked more stubbornly than ever about her ears and temples.

The rain beat upon the low, shingled roof with a force and clatter that threatened to break an entrance and deluge them there. They were in the dining room—the sitting room—the general utility room. Adjoining was her bed room, with Bibi's couch along side her own. The door stood open, and the room with its white, monumental bed, its closed shutters, looked dim and mysterious.

[1]**gallery** porch, or passageway along a wall, open to the air but protected by a roof supported by columns.

Alcée flung himself into a rocker and Calixta nervously began to gather up from the floor the lengths of a cotton sheet which she had been sewing.

15 "If this keeps up, *Dieu sait*[2] if the levees goin' to stan' it!" she exclaimed.

"What have you got to do with the levees?"

"I got enough to do! An' there's Bobinôt with Bibi out in that storm—if he only didn' left Friedheimer's!"

"Let us hope, Calixta, that Bobinôt's got sense enough to come in out of a cyclone."

She went and stood at the window with a greatly disturbed look on her face. She wiped the frame that was clouded with moisture. It was stiflingly hot. Alcée got up and joined her at the window, looking over her shoulder. The rain was coming down in sheets obscuring the view of far-off cabins and enveloping the distant wood in a gray mist. The playing of the lightning was incessant. A bolt struck a tall chinaberry tree at the edge of the field. It filled all visible space with a blinding glare and the crash seemed to invade the very boards they stood upon.

20 Calixta put her hands to her eyes, and with a cry, staggered backward. Alcée's arm encircled her, and for an instant he drew her close and spasmodically to him.

"*Bonté!*"[3] she cried, releasing herself from his encircling arm and retreating from the window, "the house'll go next! If I only knew w'ere Bibi was!" She would not compose herself; she would not be seated. Alcée clasped her shoulders and looked into her face. The contact of her warm, palpitating body when he had unthinkingly drawn her into his arms, had aroused all the old-time infatuation and desire for her flesh.

"Calixta," he said, "don't be frightened. Nothing can happen. The house is too low to be struck, with so many tall trees standing about. There! aren't you going to be quiet? say, aren't you?" He pushed her hair back from her face that was warm and steaming. Her lips were as red and moist as pomegranate seed. Her white neck and a glimpse of her full, firm bosom disturbed him powerfully. As she glanced up at him the fear in her liquid blue eyes had given place to a drowsy gleam that unconsciously betrayed a sensuous desire. He looked down into her eyes and there was nothing for him to do but to gather her lips in a kiss. It reminded him of Assumption.[4]

"Do you remember—in Assumption, Calixta?" he asked in a low voice broken by passion. Oh! she remembered; for in Assumption he had kissed her and kissed her and kissed her, until his senses would well nigh fail, and to save her he would resort to a desperate flight. If she was not an immaculate dove in those days, she was still inviolate; a passionate creature whose very defenselessness had made her defense, against which his honor forbade him to prevail. Now—well, now—her lips seemed in a manner free to be tasted, as well as her round, white throat and her whiter breasts.

They did not heed the crashing torrents, and the roar of the elements made her laugh as she lay in his arms. She was a revelation in that dim, mysterious chamber; as white as the couch she lay upon. Her firm, elastic flesh that was knowing for the first time its birthright, was like a creamy lily that the sun invites to contribute its breath and perfume to the undying life of the world.

25 The generous abundance of her passion, without guile or trickery, was like a white flame which penetrated and found response in depths of his own sensuous nature that had never yet been reached.

---

[2]*Dieu sait* God only knows.
[3]*Bonté!* Heavens!
[4]**Assumption** a parish (i.e., a county) in southeast Louisiana.

When he touched her breasts they gave themselves up in quivering ecstasy, inviting his lips. Her mouth was a fountain of delight. And when he possessed her, they seemed to swoon together at the very borderland of life's mystery.

He stayed cushioned upon her, breathless, dazed, enervated, with his heart beating like a hammer upon her. With one hand she clasped his head, her lips lightly touching his forehead. The other hand stroked with a soothing rhythm his muscular shoulders.

The growl of the thunder was distant and passing away. The rain beat softly upon the shingles, inviting them to drowsiness and sleep. But they dared not yield.

The rain was over; and the sun was turning the glistening green world into a place of gems. Calixta, on the gallery, watched Alcée ride away. He turned and smiled at her with a beaming face; and she lifted her pretty chin in the air and laughed aloud.

III

30   Bobinôt and Bibi, trudging home, stopped without at the cistern to make themselves presentable.

"My! Bibi, w'at will yo' mama say! You ought to be ashame'. You oughtn' put on those good pants. Look at 'em! An' that mud on yo' collar! How you got that mud on yo' collar, Bibi? I never saw such a boy!" Bibi was the picture of pathetic resignation. Bobinôt was the embodiment of serious solicitude as he strove to remove from his own person and his son's the signs of their tramp over heavy roads and through wet fields. He scraped the mud off Bibi's bare legs and feet with a stick and carefully removed all traces from his heavy brogans. Then, prepared for the worst—the meeting with an over-scrupulous housewife, they entered cautiously at the back door.

Calixta was preparing supper. She had set the table and was dripping coffee at the hearth. She sprang up as they came in.

"Oh, Bobinôt! You back! My! but I was uneasy. W'ere you been during the rain? An' Bibi? he ain't wet? he ain't hurt?" She had clasped Bibi and was kissing him effusively. Bobinôt's explanations and apologies which he had been composing all along the way, died on his lips as Calixta felt him to see if he were dry, and seemed to express nothing but satisfaction at their safe return.

"I brought you some shrimps, Calixta," offered Bobinôt, hauling the can from his ample side pocket and laying it on the table.

35   "Shrimps! Oh, Bobinôt! you too good fo' anything!" and she gave him a smacking kiss on the cheek that resounded. "*J'vous responds*,[5] we'll have a feas' to night! umph-umph!"

Bobinôt and Bibi began to relax and enjoy themselves, and when the three seated themselves at table they laughed much and so loud that anyone might have heard them as far away as Laballière's.

IV

Alcée Laballière wrote to his wife, Clarisse, that night. It was a loving letter, full of tender solicitude. He told her not to hurry back, but if she and the babies liked it at Biloxi, to stay a month longer. He was getting on nicely; and though he missed them, he was willing to bear the separation a while longer—realizing that their health and pleasure were the first things to be considered.

---

[5]*J'vous responds* Take my word; let me tell you.

V

As for Clarisse, she was charmed upon receiving her husband's letter. She and the babies were doing well. The society was agreeable: ~~many of her old friends and acquaintances were at the bay. And the first free breath since her marriage seemed to restore the pleasant liberty of her maiden days.~~ Devoted as she was to her husband, ~~their intimate conjugal life was something which she was more than willing to forego for a while.~~

~~So the storm passed and everyone was happy.~~

[handwritten: no consequences]

[handwritten: if you think a story ends this way, its a fairytale]

[1898]

Student Work: Comparison Notes

A student in an "Introduction to Literature" class was asked to compare any two of three stories by Kate Chopin presented in this and the previous chapters ("Ripe Figs," page 25–26; "The Story of an Hour," page 65; and "The Storm," page 87). She settled on "The Story of an Hour" and "The Storm." We print the final version of her essay, preceded by a page of notes (a synthesis of earlier notes) that she prepared on her computer shortly before she wrote her first draft.

Resemblances or differences greater?
Resemblances
Theme: release from marital bonds; liberated women
Setting: nature plays a role in both
   springtime in "Hour," storm in "Storm"
Characterization: in both stories, no villains
   forces of nature compel
   Clarisse presumably happier without husband
   both seem to emphasize roles of women
Differences
Ending: "Hour" sad (LM unfulfilled); "Storm" happy
   all characters seem content
   But endings different in that "Hour" ends suddenly, surprise
   "Storm" not surprising at very end.
Overall view (theme?):
   "Hour" very restricted view; only one person is of much interest (LM); Josephine
   interesting only in terms of LM (contrast)
   In "Storm," Cal. and Alc. interesting; but also interesting are simple Bobinot and
   even the child, and also even Clarisse, who sort of has the last word
Possible titles:
   Two Women
   New Women
   Tragic Louise, Comic Calixta
   Louise, Calixta, and Clarisse
   Tone as key difference? Tragic vs. comic

Student Comparison Essay: "Two New Women"

Let's turn to the essay generated from these notes. This paper takes the ideas that conclude the brainstorming notes, specifically those that emphasize tone, comedy, and tragedy, and uses them to create a thesis and to organize the paper. As you read the essay, consider how it makes clear comparisons between the two stories and uses those comparisons to provide organization.

Linda Hernandez

Professor Welsh

English 150

18 February 2016

Two New Women

It is not surprising that two stories by an author somewhat resemble

each other. What is especially interesting about Kate Chopin's "The Story of

an Hour" and "The Storm" is that although they both deal with women who

achieve a sense of new life or growth outside the bonds of marriage, the

stories differ greatly in what we call tone. "The Story of an Hour" is

bittersweet, or perhaps even bitter and tragic, whereas "The Storm" is

romantic and in some ways comic.

The chief similarity is that Louise Mallard in "The Story of an Hour"

and Calixta in "The Storm" both experience valuable, affirming, liberating

sensations that a traditional moral view would condemn. Mrs. Mallard, after

some moments of deep grief, feels a great sense of liberation when she

learns of the death of her husband. She dies almost immediately after this

experience, but even though she is never physically unfaithful to her

husband, there is a sort of mental disloyalty, at least from a traditional point

of view. Calixta's disloyalty is physical, not merely mental. Unlike Louise

Mallard, Calixta does go to bed with a man who is not her husband. But

Calixta, as we will see, is treated just about as sympathetically as is

Mrs. Mallard.

Louise Mallard is sympathetic because she does grieve for her

husband, and because Chopin suggests that Mallard's sense of freedom is

natural, something associated with the spring, the "delicious breath of

rain," and "the tops of trees that were all aquiver with the new spring life"

(57). Furthermore, Chopin explicitly says that Mallard loved her husband.

But Chopin also tells us that one aspect of the marriage was a "powerful will bending her" (57). For all of these reasons, then—Mrs. Mallard's genuine grief, the association of her new feeling with the power of nature, and the assertion that Mrs. Mallard loved her husband but was at least in some degree subject to his will—the reader sympathizes with Mrs. Mallard.

In her presentation of Calixta, too, Chopin takes care to make the unfaithful woman a sympathetic figure. As in "The Story of an Hour," nature plays a role. Here, instead of nature or the outside world being a parallel to the woman's emotions, nature in the form of a storm exerts pressure on the woman. We are told that "the water beat in upon the boards in driving sheets" (82), and a bolt of lightning causes Calixta to stagger backward, into Alcée's arms. These forces of outside nature are parallel to a force of nature within Calixta. Chopin tells us that during the sexual union Calixta's "firm, elastic flesh . . . was knowing for the first time its birthright" (83). And in one additional way, too, Chopin guards against the reader's condemning Calixta. We learn, at the end of the story, that Alcée's wife, Clarisse, is quite pleased to be free from her husband for a while:

> And the first free breath since her marriage seemed to restore the
> pleasant liberty of her maiden days. Devoted as she was to her
> husband, their intimate conjugal life was something which she was
> more than willing to forego for a while. (84)

Since Clarisse is portrayed as somewhat pleased to be relieved of her husband for a while, we probably do not see Alcée as a villainous betrayer of his wife. The story seems to end pleasantly, like a comedy, with everybody happy.

In Louise Mallard and in Calixta we see two women who achieve new lives, although in the case of Louise Mallard the reader is surprised to learn in the last sentence that the achievement lasts only a few moments. By "new lives" I mean emancipation from their husbands, but what is especially

Hernandez 3

interesting is that in both cases Chopin guides the reader to feel that although in fact both women behave in ways that would be strongly condemned by the codes of Chopin's day, and even by many people today, neither woman (as Chopin presents her) is blameworthy. Mrs. Mallard is presented almost as a tragic victim, and Calixta is presented almost as a figure in a very pleasant comedy.

[New page]

Hernandez 4

Works Cited

Chopin, Kate. "The Storm." *Literature for Composition*. Ed. Sylvan Barnet,
    William Burto, William E. Cain, and Cheryl L. Nixon. 11th ed. Boston:
    Pearson, 2017. 87-91. Print.

—"The Story of an Hour." *Literature for Composition*. Ed. Sylvan Barnet, William
    Burto, William E. Cain, and Cheryl L. Nixon. 11th ed. Boston: Pearson, 2017.
    65-66. Print.

The Comparison Essay: Organization Analyzed

A few comments on this student's essay may help us to see how the student engaged in effective comparison.

- The title announces the topic.
- The first paragraph announces the thesis, the point that will be argued. The thesis provides a direct comparison of the two stories being analyzed, asserting how these two stories share similarities and exhibit a crucial difference.
- The paper's body follows a clear organization, devoting one paragraph to the similarities between the stories, followed by paragraphs on each of the stories that emphasize how they differ from each other.
- The second paragraph begins by getting directly to the point: "The chief similarity is. . . ." This paragraph continues to make direct comparisons between the two stories, often directly juxtaposing the stories' main characters in one sentence.

- The third and fourth paragraph each focus on one of the stories for analysis but develop the comparison by making references to the other story.
- The third paragraph advances the argument by giving evidence, introduced by a word that implies reasoning: *because*.
- The writer provides further evidence in the form of short relevant quotations from the story.
- The final paragraph summarizes but does not boringly repeat the paper's key comparison; that is, it does not merely say, "Thus, we see. . . ." Rather, it presents the argument in a new, fresh way.

Your Turn: Additional Stories for Analysis

DAGOBERTO GILB

Born in Los Angeles, California, in 1950, Dagoberto Gilb was raised by a Spanish-speaking mother from Mexico. While Gilb was working in the construction trades and as carpenter, he started writing stories that explored the Hispanic and working-class culture of the American Southwest. He has written several award-winning novels, short story collections, and nonfiction essays.

Love in L.A.

Jake slouched in a clot of near motionless traffic, in the peculiar gray of concrete, smog, and early morning beneath the overpass of the Hollywood Freeway on Alvarado Street. He didn't really mind because he knew how much worse it could be trying to make a left onto the onramp. He certainly didn't do that every day of his life, and he'd assure anyone who'd ask that he never would either. A steady occupation had its advantages and he couldn't deny thinking about that too. He needed an FM radio in something better than this '58 Buick he drove. It would have crushed velvet interior with electric controls for the L.A. summer, a nice warm heater and defroster for the winter drives at the beach, a cruise control for those longer trips, mellow speakers front and rear of course, windows that hum closed, snuffing out that nasty exterior noise of freeways. The fact was that he'd probably have to change his whole style. Exotic colognes, plush, dark nightclubs, maitais and daiquiris, necklaced ladies in satin gowns, misty and sexy like in a tequila ad. Jake could imagine lots of possibilities when he let himself, but none that ended up with him pressed onto a stalled freeway.

Jake was thinking about this freedom of his so much that when he glimpsed its green light he just went ahead and stared bye bye to the steadily employed. When he turned his head the same direction his windshield faced, it was maybe one second too late. He pounced the brake pedal and steered the front wheels away from the tiny brakelights but the smack was unavoidable. Just one second sooner and it would only have been close. One second more and he'd be crawling up the Toyota's trunk. As it was, it seemed like only a harmless smack, much less solid than the one against his back bumper.

Jake considered driving past the Toyota but was afraid the traffic ahead would make it too difficult. As he pulled up against the curb a few carlengths ahead, it occurred to him that the traffic might have helped him get away too. He slammed the car door twice to make sure it was closed fully and to give himself another second more, then toured front and rear of his Buick for damage on or near the bumpers. Not an impressionable scratch even in the chrome. He perked up. Though the car's beauty was secondary to its ability to start and move, the body and paint were clean except for a few minor dings. This stood out as one of his few clearcut accomplishments over the years.

Before he spoke to the driver of the Toyota, whose looks he could see might present him with an added complication, he signaled to the driver of the car that hit him, still in his car and stopped behind the Toyota, and waved his hands and shook his head to let the man know there was no problem as far as he was concerned. The driver waved back and started his engine.

5   "It didn't even scratch my paint," Jake told her in that way of his. "So how you doin? Any damage to the car? I'm kinda hoping so, just so it takes a little more time and we can talk some. Or else you can give me your phone number now and I won't have to lay my regular b.s. on you to get it later."

He took her smile as a good sign and relaxed. He inhaled her scent like it was clean air and straightened out his less than new but not unhip clothes.

"You've got Florida plates. You look like you must be Cuban."

"My parents are from Venezuela."

"My name's Jake." He held out his hand.

10   "Mariana."

They shook hands like she'd never done it before in her life.

"I really am sorry about hitting you like that." He sounded genuine. He fondled the wide dimple near the cracked taillight. "It's amazing how easy it is to put a dent in these new cars. They're so soft they might replace waterbeds soon." Jake was confused about how to proceed with this. So much seemed so unlikely, but there was always possibility. "So maybe we should go out to breakfast somewhere and talk it over."

"I don't eat breakfast."

"Some coffee then."

15   "Thanks, but I really can't."

"You're not married, are you? Not that that would matter that much to me. I'm an openminded kinda guy."

She was smiling. "I have to get to work."

"That sounds boring."

"I better get your driver"s license," she said.

20   Jake nodded, disappointed. "One little problem," he said. "I didn't bring it. I just forgot it this morning. I'm a musician," he exaggerated greatly, "and, well, I dunno, I left my wallet in the pants I was wearing last night. If you have some paper and a pen I"ll give you my address and all that."

He followed her to the glove compartment side of her car.

"What if we don't report it to the insurance companies? I'll just get it fixed for you."

"I don't think my dad would let me do that."

"Your dad? It's not your car?"

25   "He bought it for me. And I live at home."

"Right." She was slipping away from him. He went back around to the back of her new Toyota and looked over the damage again. There was the trunk lid, the bumper, a rear panel, a taillight.

"You do have insurance?" she asked, suspicious, as she came around the back of the car.

"Oh yeah," he lied.

"I guess you better write the name of that down too."

30   He made up a last name and address and wrote down the name of an insurance company an old girlfriend once belonged to. He considered giving a real phone number but went against that idea and made one up.

"I act too," he lied to enhance the effect more. "Been in a couple of movies." She smiled like a fan.

"So how about your phone number?" He was rebounding maturely.

She gave it to him.

35   "Mariana, you are beautiful," he said in his most sincere voice.

"Call me," she said timidly.

Jake beamed. "We'll see you, Mariana," he said holding out his hand. Her hand felt so warm and soft he felt like he'd been kissed.

Back in his car he took a moment or two to feel both proud and sad about his performance. Then he watched the rear view mirror as Mariana pulled up behind him. She was writing down the license plate numbers on his Buick, ones that he'd taken off a junk because the ones that belonged to his had expired so long ago. He turned the ignition key and revved the big engine and clicked into drive. His sense of freedom swelled as he drove into the now moving street traffic, though he couldn't stop the thought about that FM stereo radio and crushed velvet interior and the new car smell that would even make it better.

Joining the Conversation: Critical Thinking and Writing

1. Gilb sets his story on a traffic-filled highway in L.A. Why is this an interesting setting for Jake and his daydreams? How does this setting capture elements of contemporary life in L.A.?

2. How does Jake turn a negative event into an opportunity to pick up a woman? Trace the specific phrases that he uses to try to attract Mariana.

3. At the beginning of the story, Jake "was thinking about this freedom," and at the end of the story, Jake's "sense of freedom swelled." Why is freedom important to Jake? Does Jake achieve any form of freedom within this story? Write a short response paper that explores the concept of freedom and Jake's unique understanding of it.

4. Why does Mariana give Jake her phone number? How and why does Jake recreate himself for Mariana? What sort of identities does Jake construct? Why are Jake's fictional versions of himself successful?

5. Why is this short story titled, "Love in L.A."? How is this story a commentary on love?

Elizabeth Tallent

A professor at Stanford University in California, Elizabeth Tallent was born in Washington, DC, in 1954. Her stories explore the challenges of marriage and family, investigating the emotional complexities of human relationships. She has been published in magazines, including the New Yorker *and* Esquire, *and her work has been selected for the Best American Short Stories and Best American Essays collections.*

No One's a Mystery

For my eighteenth birthday Jack gave me a five-year diary with a latch and a little key, light as a dime. I was sitting beside him scratching at the lock, which didn't seem to want to work, when he thought he saw his wife's Cadillac in the distance, coming toward us. He pushed me down onto the dirty floor of the pickup and kept one hand on my head while I inhaled the musk of his cigarettes in the dashboard ashtray and sang along with Rosanne Cash on the tape deck. We'd been drinking tequila and the bottle was between his legs, resting up against his crotch, where the seam of his Levi's was bleached linen-white, though the Levi's were nearly new. I don't know why his Levi's always bleached like that, along the seams and at the knees. In a curve of cloth his zipper glinted, gold.

"It's her," he said. "She keeps the lights on in the daytime. I can't think of a single habit in a woman that irritates me more than that." When he saw that I was going to stay still he took his hand from my head and ran it through his own dark hair.

"Why does she?" I said.

"She thinks it's safer. Why does she need to be safer? She's driving exactly fifty-five miles an hour. She believes in those signs: 'Speed Monitored by Aircraft.' It doesn't matter that you can look up and see that the sky is empty."

5   'She'll see your lips move, Jack. She'll know you're talking to someone."

"She'll think I'm singing along with the radio."

He didn't lift his hand, just raised the fingers in salute while the pressure of his palm steadied the wheel, and I heard the Cadillac honk twice, musically; he was driving easily eighty miles an hour. I studied his boots. The elk heads stitched into the leather were bearded with frayed thread, the toes were scuffed, and there was a compact wedge of muddy manure between the heel and the sole—the same boots he'd been wearing for the two years I'd known him. On the tape deck Rosanne Cash sang, "Nobody's into me, no one's a mystery."

"Do you think she's getting famous because of who her daddy is or for her-self?" Jack said.

"There are about a hundred pop tops on the floor, did you know that? Some little kid could cut a bare foot on one of these, Jack."

10   "No little kids get into thiis truck except for you."

"How come you let it get so dirty?"

"'How come,'" he mocked. "You even sound like a kid. You can get back into the seat now, if you want. She's not going to look over her shoulder and see you."

"How do you know?"

"I just know," he said. "Like I know I'm going to get meat loaf for supper. It's in the air. Like I know what you'll be writing in that diary."

15   "What will I be writing?" I knelt on my side of the seat and craned around to look at the butterfly of dust printed on my jeans. Outside the window Wyoming was dazzling in the heat. The wheat was fawn and yellow and parted smoothly by the thin dirt road. I could smell the water in the irrigation ditches hidden in the wheat.

"Tonight you'll write, 'I love Jack. This is my birthday present from him. I can't imagine anybody loving anybody more than I love Jack.'"

"I can't."

"In a year you'll write, 'I wonder what I ever really saw in Jack. I wonder why I spent so many days just riding around in his pickup. It's true he taught me some-thing about sex. It's true there wasn't ever much else to do in Cheyenne.'"

"I won't write that."

20   "In two years you'll write, 'I wonder what that old guy's name was, the one with the curly hair and the filthy dirty pickup truck and time on his hands.'"

"I won't write that."

"No?"

"Tonight I'll write, 'I love Jack. This is my birthday present from him. I can't imagine anybody loving anybody more than I love Jack.'"

"No, you can't," he said. "You can't imagine it."

25 "In a year I'll write, 'Jack should be home any minute now. The table's set—my grandmother's linen and her old silver and the yellow candles left over from the wedding—but I don't know if I can wait until after the trout a la Navarra to make love to him.'"

"It must have been a fast divorce."

"In two years I'll write, 'Jack should be home by now. Little Jack is hungry for his supper. He said his first word today besides "Mama" and "Papa." He said "kaka."'"

Jack laughed. "He was probably trying to finger-paint with kaka on the bathroom wall when you heard him say it."

"In three years I'll write, 'My nipples are a little sore from nursing Eliza Rosamund.'"

30 "Rosamund. Every little girl should have a middle name she hates."

"'Her breath smells like vanilla and her eyes are just Jack's color of blue.'"

"That's nice," Jack said.

"So, which one do you like?"

"I like yours," he said. "But I believe mine."

35 "It doesn't matter. I believe mine."

"Not in your heart of hearts, you don't."

"You're wrong."

"I'm not wrong," he said. "And her breath would smell like your milk, and it's kind of a bittersweet smell, if you want to know the truth."

[1985]

Joining the Conversation: Critical Thinking and Writing

1. How would you describe the relationship at the heart of this story? Is this a love relationship? Is this a love story? The narrator states, "I can't imagine anybody loving anybody more than I love Jack." Notice that this line is repeated and appears twice in the story. Who makes this statement first? What does this statement reveal about the love it expresses?

2. The narrator and Jack try to predict what the narrator will write in her diary one, two, and three years in the future. What are the different stories they create about the future? The previous story in this chapter, "Love in L.A.," as well as the story in Chapter 3, "On Seeing the 100% Perfect Girl," also feature storytelling. In these stories, love seems to necessitate making up stories. Examine and compare the stories that are told in each story: What types of stories are told and why?

3. Why does the story open with the narrator being pushed to the floor of the pickup truck? What does this action represent?

4. The story contains vivid descriptions of several different settings: the setting of the dirty inside of the car, the Wyoming wheat fields outside the car window, and the imagined table set with wedding candles. Read each description closely, annotating the passage. What words seem most effective and meaningful?

5. What do you think the narrator will write in the diary in one, two, and three years' time? Engage in some creative thinking, and write those diary entries. Then, write Jack's response to each entry.

JUNOT DÍAZ

Considered one of America's most important contemporary authors, Junot Díaz is a Dominican American author whose writing often features characters who bridge American and Latin American culture. His novel, The Brief Wondrous Life of Oscar Wao *(2007), won the Pulitzer Prize for Fiction, and in 2012, he received a MacArthur "genius grant" fellowship. He majored in English and studied creative writing at Rutgers University and then earned an MFA in creative writing from Cornell University. He currently teaches creative writing at the Massachusetts Institute of Technology (MIT).*

How to Date a Brown Girl (Black Girl, White Girl, or Halfie)

Wait for your brother and your mother to leave the apartment. You've already told them that you're feeling too sick to go to Union City to visit that tía who likes to squeeze your nuts. (He's gotten big, she'll say.) And even though your moms knows you ain't sick you stuck to your story until finally she said, Go ahead and stay, malcriado.

Clear the government cheese from the refrigerator. If the girl's from the Terrace stack the boxes behind the milk. If she's from the Park or Society Hill hide the cheese in the cabinet above the oven, way up where she'll never see. Leave yourself a reminder to get it out before morning.or your moms will kick your ass. Take down any embarrassing photos of your family in the campo, especially the one with the half-naked kids dragging a goat on a rope leash. The kids are your cousins and by now they're old enough to understand why you're doing what you're doing. Hide the pictures of yourself with an Afro. Make sure the bathroom is presentable. Put the basket with all the crapped-on toilet paper under the sink. Spray the bucket with Lysol, then close the cabinet.

Shower, comb, dress. Sit on the couch and watch TV. If she's an outsider her father will be bringing her, maybe her mother. Neither of them want her seeing any boys from the Terrace—people get stabbed in the Terrace—but she's strongheaded and this time will get her way. If she's a whitegirl you know you'll at least get a hand job.

The directions were in your best handwriting, so her parents won't think you're an idiot. Get up from the couch and check the parking lot. Nothing. If the girl's local, don't sweat it. She'll flow over when she's good and ready. Sometimes she'll run into her other friends and a whole crowd will show up at your apartment and even though that means you ain't getting shit it will be fun anyway and you'll wish these people would come over more often. Sometimes the girl won't flow over at all and the next day in school she'll say sorry, smile and you'll be stupid enough to believe her and ask her out again.

5   Wait and after an hour go out to your corner. The neighborhood is full of traffic. Give one of your boys a shout and when he says, Are you still waiting on that bitch? say, Hell yeah.

Get back inside. Call her house and when her father picks up ask if she's there. He'll ask, Who is this? Hang up. He sounds like a principal or a police chief, the sort of dude with a big neck, who never has to watch his back. Sit and wait. By the time your stomach's ready to give out on you, a Honda or maybe a Jeep pulls in and out she comes.

Hey, you'll say.

Look, she'll say. My mom wants to meet you. She's got herself all worried about nothing.

Don't panic. Say, Hey, no problem. Run a hand through your hair like the whiteboys do even though the only thing that runs easily through your hair is Africa. She will look good. The white ones are the ones you want the most, aren't they, but usually the out-of-towners are black, blackgirls who grew up with ballet and Girl Scouts, who have three cars in their driveways. If she's a halfie don't be surprised that her mother is white. Say, Hi. Her moms will say hi and you'll see that you don't scare her, not really. She will say that she needs easier directions to get out and even though she has the best directions in her lap give her new ones. Make her happy.

10   You have choices. If the girl's from around the way, take her to El Cibao for dinner. Order everything in your busted-up Spanish. Let her correct you if she's Latina and amaze her if she's black. If she's not from around the way, Wendy's will do. As you walk to the restaurant talk about school. A local girl won't need stories about the neighborhood but the other ones might. Supply the story about the loco who'd been storing canisters of tear gas in his basement for years, how one day the canisters cracked and the whole neighborhood got a dose of the military-strength stuff. Don't tell her that your moms knew right away what it was, that she recognized its smell from the year the United States invaded your island.

Hope that you don't run into your nemesis, Howie, the Puerto Rican kid with the two killer mutts. He walks them all over the neighborhood and every now and then the mutts corner themselves a cat and tear it to shreds, Howie laughing as the cat flips up in the air, its neck twisted around like an owl, red meat showing through the soft fur. If his dogs haven't cornered a cat, he will walk behind you and ask, Hey, Yunior, is that your new fuckbuddy?

Let him talk. Howie weighs about two hundred pounds and could eat you if he wanted. At the field he will turn away. He has new sneakers, and doesn't want them muddy. If the girl's an outsider she will hiss now and say, What a fucking asshole. A homegirl would have been yelling back at him the whole time, unless she was shy. Either way don't feel bad that you didn't do anything. Never lose a fight on a first date or that will be the end of it.

Dinner will be tense. You are not good at talking to people you don't know. A halfie will tell you that her parents met in the Movement, will say, Back then people thought it a radical thing to do. It will sound like something her parents made her memorize. Your brother once heard that one and said, Man, that sounds like a whole lot of Uncle Tomming to me. Don't repeat this.

Put down your hamburger and say, It must have been hard.

15   She will appreciate your interest. She will tell you more. Black people, she will say, treat me real bad. That's why I don't like them. You'll wonder how she feels about Dominicans. Don't ask. Let her speak on it and when you're both finished eating walk back into the neighborhood. The skies will be magnificent. Pollutants have made Jersey sunsets one of the wonders of the world. Point it out. Touch her shoulder and say, That's nice, right?

Get serious. Watch TV but stay alert. Sip some of the Bermúdez your father left in the cabinet, which nobody touches. A local girl may have hips and a thick ass but she won't be quick about letting you touch. She has to live in the same neighborhood you do, has to deal with you being all up in her business. She might just chill with you and then go home. She might kiss you and then go, or she might, if she's reckless, give it up, but that's rare. Kissing will suffice. A whitegirl might just give it up right then. Don't stop her. She'll take her gum out of her mouth, stick it to the plastic sofa covers and then will move close to you. You have nice eyes, she might say.

Tell her that you love her hair, that you love her skin, her lips, because, in truth, you love them more than you love your own.

She'll say, I like Spanish guys, and even though you've never been to Spain, say, I like you. You'll sound smooth.

You'll be with her until about eight-thirty and then she will want to wash up. In the bathroom she will hum a song from the radio and her waist will keep the beat against the lip of the sink. Imagine her old lady coming to get her, what she would say if she knew her daughter had just lain under you and blown your name, pronounced with her eighth-grade Spanish, into your ear. While she's in the bathroom call one of your boys and say, Lo hice, loco. Or just sit back on the couch and smile.

20   But usually it won't work this way. Be prepared. She will not want to kiss you. Just cool it, she'll say. The halfie might lean back, breaking away from you. She will cross her arms, say, I hate my tits. Stroke her hair but she will pull away. I don't like anybody touching my hair, she will say. She will act like somebody you don't know. In school she is known for her attention-grabbing laugh, as high and far-ranging as a gull, but here she will worry you. You will not know what to say.

You're the only kind of guy who asks me out, she will say. Your neighbors will start their hyena calls, now that the alcohol is in them. You and the blackboys.

Say nothing. Let her button her shirt, let her comb her hair, the sound of it stretching like a sheet of fire between you. When her father pulls in and beeps, let her go without too much of a good-bye. She won't want it. During the next hour the phone will ring. You will be tempted to pick it up. Don't. Watch the shows you want to watch, without a family around to debate you. Don't go downstairs. Don't fall asleep. It won't help. Put the government cheese back in its place before your moms kills you.

Joining the Conversation: Critical Thinking and Writing

1. This story is written in the second person, with the narrator Yunior addressing you as "you." Do you find this effective? What does this voice do for the story? For example, does it make the story more direct or more energetic?

2. What are the interesting objects that fill Yunior's home? How do they function as symbols? What ideas do these objects express?

3. What are the interesting actions Yunior engages in as he prepares for dates? What ideas do the actions express? What activities do you like the most? What activities are the most humorous or the most unexpected?

4. Annotate the story carefully, noting the types of girls that Yunior imagines dating. What are the different types of girls? How and why does Yunior treat each type differently? Does this cataloging of different types of girls become offensive? Do you find the cataloging realistic? cruel? funny? Is Diaz critiquing or mocking this type of cataloging?

5. Although the story offers directions on dating and thus seems to grant the narrator authority on this subject, the story also reveals the narrator's self-doubt. Locate the moments in the story when the narrator reveals his anxieties and uncertainties about women and dating.

T. Coraghessan Boyle

The son of immigrants from Ireland, T. Coraghessan Boyle (the stress in his middle name is on the second syllable) was born in Peekskill, New York, in 1948. A graduate of the State University of New York, Potsdam, Boyle taught history and English in high school for several years. He then attended the Writers' Workshop at the University of Iowa and went on to receive a PhD in 1977. Boyle has won several awards for his fiction.

Greasy Lake

It's about a mile down on the dark side of Route 88.

—Bruce Springsteen

There was a time when courtesy and winning ways went out of style, when it was good to be bad, when you cultivated decadence like a taste. We were all dangerous characters then. We wore torn-up leather jackets, slouched around with toothpicks in our mouths, sniffed glue and ether and what somebody claimed was cocaine. When we wheeled our parents' whining station wagons out into the street we left a patch of rubber half a block long. We drank gin and grape juice, Tango, Thunderbird, and Bali Hai. We were nineteen. We were bad. We read André Gide[1] and struck elaborate poses to show that we didn't give a shit about anything. At night, we went up to Greasy Lake.

Through the center of town, up the strip, past the housing developments and shopping malls, street lights giving way to the thin streaming illumination of the headlights, trees crowding the asphalt in a black unbroken wall: that was the way out to Greasy Lake. The Indians had called it Wakan, a reference to the clarity of its waters. Now it was fetid and murky, the mud banks glittering with broken glass and strewn with beer cans and the charred remains of bonfires. There was a single ravaged island a hundred yards from shore, so stripped of vegetation it looked as if the air force had strafed it. We went up to the lake because everyone went there, because we wanted to snuff the rich scent of possibility on the breeze, watch a girl take off her clothes and plunge into the festering murk, drink beer, smoke pot, howl at the stars, savor the incongruous full-throated roar of rock and roll against the primeval susurrus of frogs and crickets. This was nature.

I was there one night, late, in the company of two dangerous characters. Digby wore a gold star in his right ear and allowed his father to pay his tuition at Cornell; Jeff was thinking of quitting school to become a painter/musician/head-shop proprietor. They were both expert in the social graces, quick with a sneer, able to manage a Ford with lousy shocks over rutted and gutted blacktop road at eighty-five while rolling a joint as compact as a Tootsie Roll Pop stick. They could lounge against a bank of booming speakers and trade "man"s with the best of them or roll out across the dance floor as if their joints worked on bearings. They were slick and quick and they wore their mirror shades at breakfast and dinner, in the shower, in closets and caves. In short, they were bad.

I drove. Digby pounded the dashboard and shouted along with Toots & the Maytals while Jeff hung his head out the window and streaked the side of my

---

[1]**André Gide** French novelist and critic (1869–1951), much concerned with unconventional behavior.

mother's Bel Air with vomit. It was early June, the air soft as a hand on your cheek, the third night of summer vacation. The first two nights we'd been out till dawn, looking for something we never found. On this, the third night, we'd cruised the strip sixty-seven times, been in and out of every bar and club we could think of in a twenty-mile radius, stopped twice for bucket chicken and forty-cent hamburgers, debated going to a party at the house of a girl Jeff's sister knew, and chucked two dozen raw eggs at mailboxes and hitchhikers. It was 2:00 A.M.; the bars were closing. There was nothing to do but take a bottle of lemon-flavored gin up to Greasy Lake.

5   The taillights of a single car winked at us as we swung into the dirt lot with its tufts of weed and washboard corrugations; '57 Chevy, mint, metallic blue. On the far side of the lot, like the exoskeleton of some gaunt chrome insect, a chopper leaned against its kickstand. And that was it for excitement: some junkie half-wit biker and a car freak pumping his girlfriend. Whatever it was we were looking for, we weren't about to find it at Greasy Lake. Not that night.

But then all of a sudden Digby was fighting for the wheel. "Hey, that's Tony Lovett's car! Hey!" he shouted, while I stabbed at the brake pedal and the Bel Air nosed up to the gleaming bumper of the parked Chevy. Digby leaned on the horn, laughing, and instructed me to put my brights on. I flicked on the brights. This was hilarious. A joke. Tony would experience premature withdrawal and expect to be confronted by grim-looking state troopers with flashlights. We hit the horn, strobed the lights, and then jumped out of the car to press our witty faces to Tony's windows; for all we knew we might even catch a glimpse of some little fox's tit, and then we could slap backs with red-faced Tony, roughhouse a little, and go on to new heights of adventure and daring.

The first mistake, the one that opened the whole floodgate, was losing my grip on the keys. In the excitement, leaping from the car with the gin in one hand and a roach clip in the other, I spilled them in the grass—in the dark, rank, mysterious nighttime grass of Greasy Lake. This was a tactical error, as damaging and irreversible in its way as Westmoreland's decision to dig in at Khe Sanh.[2] I felt it like a jab of intuition, and I stopped there by the open door, peering vaguely into the night that puddled up round my feet.

The second mistake—and this was inextricably bound up with the first was identifying the car as Tony Lovett's. Even before the very bad character in greasy jeans and engineer boots ripped out of the driver's door, I began to realize that this chrome blue was much lighter than the robin's-egg of Tony's car, and that Tony's car didn't have rear-mounted speakers. Judging from their expressions, Digby and Jeff were privately groping toward the same inevitable and unsettling conclusion as I was.

In any case, there was no reasoning with this bad greasy character—clearly he was a man of action. The first lusty Rockette[3] kick of his steel-toed boot caught me under the chin, chipped my favorite tooth, and left me sprawled in the dirt. Like a fool, I'd gone down on one knee to comb the stiff hacked grass for the keys, my

[2] **Westmoreland's decision . . . Khe Sanh** General William C. Westmoreland commanded U.S. troops in Vietnam (1964–68). When the North Vietnamese and Viet Cong in 1967 attacked Khe San (or Khesanh), Westmoreland chose to defend an area of little military significance.
[3] **Rockette** The Rockettes, a dance troupe at Radio City Music Hall in New York City, were famous for precision and for high kicking.

mind making connections in the most dragged out, testudineous[4] way, knowing that things had gone wrong, that I was in a lot of trouble, and that the lost ignition key was my grail[5] and my salvation. The three or four succeeding blows were mainly absorbed by my right buttock and the tough piece of bone at the base of my spine.

10   Meanwhile, Digby vaulted the kissing bumpers and delivered a savage kung-fu blow to the greasy character's collarbone. Digby had just finished a course in martial arts for phys-ed credit and had spent the better part of the past two nights telling us apocryphal tales of Bruce Lee types and of the raw power invested in lightning blows shot from coiled wrists, ankles, and elbows. The greasy character was unimpressed. He merely backed off a step, his face like a Toltec mask, and laid Digby out with a single whistling roundhouse blow . . . but by now Jeff had got into the act, and I was beginning to extricate myself from the dirt, a tinny compound of shock, rage, and impotence wadded in my throat.

Jeff was on the guy's back, biting at his ear. Digby was on the ground, cursing. I went for the tire iron I kept under the driver's seat. I kept it there because bad characters always keep tire irons under the driver's seat, for just such an occasion as this. Never mind that I hadn't been involved in a fight since sixth grade, when a kid with a sleepy eye and two streams of mucus depending from his nostrils hit me in the knee with a Louisville slugger,[6] never mind that I'd touched the tire iron exactly twice before, to change tires: it was there. And I went for it.

I was terrified. Blood was beating in my ears, my hands were shaking, my heart turning over like a dirtbike in the wrong gear. My antagonist was shirtless, and a single cord of muscle flashed across his chest as he bent forward to peel Jeff from his back like a wet overcoat. "Motherfucker," he spat, over and over, and I was aware in that instant that all four of us—Digby, Jeff, and myself included—were chanting "motherfucker, motherfucker," as if it were a battle cry. (What happened next? the detective asks the murderer from beneath the turned-down brim of his porkpie hat. I don't know, the murderer says, something came over me. Exactly.)

Digby poked the flat of his hand in the bad character's face and I came at him like a kamikaze, mindless, raging, stung with humiliation—the whole thing, from the initial boot in the chin to this murderous primal instant involving no more than sixty hyperventilating, gland-flooding seconds—I came at him and brought the tire iron down across his ear. The effect was instantaneous, astonishing. He was a stunt man and this was Hollywood, he was a big grimacing toothy balloon and I was a man with a straight pin. He collapsed. Wet his pants. Went loose in his boots.

A single second, big as a zeppelin, floated by. We were standing over him in a circle, gritting our teeth, jerking our necks, our limbs and hands and feet twitching with glandular discharges. No one said anything. We just stared down at the guy, the car freak, the lover, the bad greasy character laid low. Digby looked at me; so did Jeff. I was still holding the tire iron, a tuft of hair clinging to the crook like dandelion fluff, like down. Rattled, I dropped it in the dirt, already envisioning the headlines, the pitted faces of the police inquisitors, the gleam of handcuffs, clank of bars, the big black shadows rising from the back of the cell ... when suddenly a raw torn shriek cut through me like all the juice in all the electric chairs in the country.

---

[4]**testudineous** turtle-like (here, slow).
[5]**grail** the holy cup that, according to tradition, Jesus used at the Last Supper. Legend says that the person who finds this object will be saved.
[6]**Louisville slugger** a brand of baseball bat.

15   It was the fox. She was short, barefoot, dressed in panties and a man's shirt. "Animals!" she screamed, running at us with her fists clenched and wisps of blow-dried hair in her face. There was a silver chain round her ankle, and her toenails flashed in the glare of the headlights. I think it was the toenails that did it. Sure, the gin and the cannabis and even the Kentucky Fried may have had a hand in it, but it was the sight of those flaming toes that set us off—the toad emerging from the loaf in *Virgin Spring*,[7] lipstick smeared on a child: she was already tainted. We were on her like Bergman's deranged brothers—see no evil, hear none, speak none—panting, wheezing, tearing at her clothes, grabbing for flesh. We were bad characters, and we were scared and hot and three steps over the line—anything could have happened.

It didn't.

Before we could pin her to the hood of the car, our eyes masked with lust and greed and the purest primal badness, a pair of headlights swung into the lot. There we were, dirty, bloody, guilty, dissociated from humanity and civilization, the first of the Ur-crimes[8] behind us, the second in progress, shreds of nylon panty and spandex brassiere dangling from our fingers, our flies open, lips licked-there we were, caught in the spotlight. Nailed.

We bolted. First for the car, and then, realizing we had no way of starting it, for the woods. I thought nothing. I thought escape. The headlights came at me like accusing fingers. I was gone.

Ram-bam-bam, across the parking lot, past the chopper and into the feculent undergrowth at the lake's edge, insects flying up in my face, weeds whipping, frogs and snakes and red-eyed turtles splashing off into the night: I was already ankle-deep in muck and tepid water and still going strong. Behind me, the girl's screams rose in intensity, disconsolate, incriminating, the screams of the Sabine women,[9] the Christian martyrs, Anne Frank[10] dragged from the garret. I kept going, pursued by those cries, imagining cops and bloodhounds. The water was up to my knees when I realized what I was doing: I was going to swim for it. Swim the breadth of Greasy Lake and hide myself in the thick clot of woods on the far side. They'd never find me there!

20   I was breathing in sobs, in gasps. The water lapped at my waist as I looked out over the moon-burnished ripples, the mats of algae that clung to the surface like scabs. Digby and Jeff had vanished. I paused. Listened. The girl was quieter now, screams tapering to sobs, but there were male voices, angry, excited, and the high-pitched ticking of the second car's engine. I waded deeper, stealthy, hunted, the ooze sucking at my sneakers. As I was about to take the plunge—at the very instant I dropped my shoulder for the first slashing stroke—I blundered into something. Something unspeakable, obscene, something soft, wet, moss-grown. A patch of weed? A log? When I reached out to touch it, it gave like a rubber duck, it gave like flesh.

In one of those nasty little epiphanies for which we are prepared by films and TV and childhood visits to the funeral home to ponder the shrunken painted forms

[7]***Virgin Spring*** film (1960) by Ingmar Bergman.
[8]**Ur-crimes** primitive crimes.
[9]**Sabine women** women of an ancient tribe in Rome, raped by Romans and carried off to be their wives.
[10]**Anne Frank** German Jewish girl (1929–45) who hid from the Nazis in an attic in Amsterdam but was found and sent to a concentration camp, where she died. Her *Diary of a Young Girl* has become famous.

of dead grandparents, I understood what it was that bobbed there so inadmissibly in the dark. Understood, and stumbled back in horror and revulsion, my mind yanked in six different directions (I was nineteen, a mere child, an infant, and here in the space of five minutes I'd struck down one greasy character and blundered into the waterlogged carcass of a second), thinking, The keys, the keys, why did I have to go and lose the keys? I stumbled back, but the muck took hold of my feet—a sneaker snagged, balance lost—and suddenly I was pitching face forward into the buoyant black mass, throwing out my hands in desperation while simultaneously conjuring the image of reeking frogs and muskrats revolving in slicks of their own deliquescing juices. AAAAArrrgh! I shot from the water like a torpedo, the dead man rotating to expose a mossy beard and eyes cold as the moon. I must have shouted out, thrashing around in the weeds, because the voices behind me suddenly became animated.

"What was that?"

"It's them, it's them: they tried to, tried to . . . *rape* me!" Sobs.

A man's voice, flat Midwestern accent. "You sons a bitches, we'll kill you!"

25   Frogs, crickets.

Then another voice, harsh, *r*-less, Lower East Side: "Motherfucker!" I recognized the verbal virtuosity of the bad greasy character in the engineer boots. Tooth chipped, sneakers gone, coated in mud and slime and worse, crouching breathless in the weeds waiting to have my ass thoroughly and definitively kicked and fresh from the hideous stinking embrace of a three-days-dead-corpse, I suddenly felt a rush of joy and vindication: the son of a bitch was alive! Just as quickly, my bowels turned to ice. "Come on out of there, you pansy mothers!" the bad greasy character was screaming. He shouted curses till he was out of breath.

The crickets started up again, then the frogs. I held my breath. All at once there was a sound in the reeds, a swishing, a splash: thunk-a-thunk. They were throwing rocks. The frogs fell silent. I cradled my head. Swish; swish, thunk-a-thunk. A wedge of feldspar the size of a cue ball glanced off my knee. I bit my finger.

It was then that they turned to the car. I heard a door slam, a curse, and then the sound of the headlights shattering-almost a good-natured sound, celebratory, like corks popping from the necks of bottles. This was succeeded by the dull booming of the fenders, metal on metal, and then the icy crash of the windshield. I inched forward, elbows and knees, my belly pressed to the muck, thinking of guerrillas and commandos and *The Naked and the Dead*.[11] I parted the weeds and squinted the length of the parking lot.

The second car—it was a Trans-Am—was still running, its high beams washing the scene in a lurid stagy light. Tire iron flailing, the greasy bad character was laying into the side of my mother's Bel Air like an avenging demon, his shadow riding up the trunks of the trees. Whomp. Whomp. Whomp-whomp. The other two guys—blond types, in fraternity jackets—were helping out with tree branches and skull-sized boulders. One of them was gathering up bottles, rocks, muck, candy wrappers, used condoms, pop-tops, and other refuse and pitching it through the window on the driver's side. I could see the fox, a white bulb behind the windshield of the '57 Chevy. "Bobbie," she whined over the thumping, "come *on*." The greasy character paused a moment, took one good swipe at the left taillight, and then heaved the tire iron halfway across the lake. Then he fired up the '57 and was gone.

[11]***The Naked and the Dead*** World War II novel (1948) by Norman Mailer.

30   Blond head nodded at blond head. One said something to the other, too low for me to catch. They were no doubt thinking that in helping to annihilate my mother's car they'd committed a fairly rash act, and thinking too that there were three bad characters connected with that very car watching them from the woods. Perhaps other possibilities occurred to them as well—police, jail cells, justices of the peace, reparations, lawyers, irate parents, fraternal censure. Whatever they were thinking, they suddenly dropped branches, bottles, and rocks and sprang for their car in unison, as if they'd choreographed it. Five seconds. That's all it took. The engine shrieked, the tires squealed, a cloud of dust rose from the rutted lot and then settled back on darkness.

I don't know how long I lay there, the bad breath of decay all around me, my jacket heavy as a bear, the primordial ooze subtly reconstituting itself to accommodate my upper thighs and testicles. My jaws ached, my knee throbbed, my coccyx was on fire. I contemplated suicide, wondered if I'd need bridgework, scraped the recesses of my brain for some sort of excuse to give my parents—a tree had fallen on the car, I was blindsided by a bread truck, hit and run, vandals had got to it while we were playing chess at Digby's. Then I thought of the dead man. He was probably the only person on the planet worse off than I was. I thought about him, fog on the lake, insects chirring eerily, and felt the tug of fear, felt the darkness opening up inside me like a set of jaws. Who was he, I wondered, this victim of time and circumstance bobbing sorrowfully in the lake at my back. The owner of the chopper, no doubt, a bad older character come to this. Shot during a murky drug deal, drowned while drunkenly frolicking in the lake. Another headline. My car was wrecked; he was dead.

When the eastern half of the sky went from black to cobalt and the trees began to separate themselves from the shadows, I pushed myself up from the mud and stepped out into the open. By now the birds had begun to take over for the crickets, and dew lay slick on the leaves. There was a smell in the air, raw and sweet at the same time, the smell of the sun firing buds and opening blossoms. I contemplated the car. It lay there like a wreck along the highway, like a steel sculpture left over from a vanished civilization. Everything was still. This was nature.

I was circling the car, as dazed and bedraggled as the sole survivor of an air blitz, when Digby and Jeff emerged from the trees behind me. Digby's face was crosshatched with smears of dirt; Jeff's jacket was gone and his shirt was torn across the shoulder. They slouched across the lot, looking sheepish, and silently came up beside me to gape at the ravaged automobile. No one said a word. After a while Jeff swung open the driver's door and began to scoop the broken glass and garbage off the seat. I looked at Digby. He shrugged. "At least they didn't slash the tires," he said.

It was true: the tires were intact. There was no windshield, the headlights were staved in, and the body looked as if it had been sledgehammered for a quarter a shot at the county fair, but the tires were inflated to regulation pressure. The car was drivable. In silence, all three of us bent to scrape the mud and shattered glass from the interior. I said nothing about the biker. When we were finished, I reached in my pocket for the keys, experienced a nasty stab of recollection, cursed myself, and turned to search the grass. I spotted them almost immediately, no more than five feet from the open door, glinting like jewels in the first tapering shaft of sunlight. There was no reason to get philosophical about it: I eased into the seat and turned the engine over.

35   It was at that precise moment that the silver Mustang with the flame decals rumbled into the lot. All three of us froze; then Digby and Jeff slid into the car and

slammed the door. We watched as the Mustang rocked and bobbed across the ruts and finally jerked to a halt beside the forlorn chopper at the far end of the lot. "Let's go," Digby said. I hesitated, the Bel Air wheezing beneath me.

Two girls emerged from the Mustang. Tight jeans, stiletto heels, hair like frozen fur. They bent over the motorcycle, paced back and forth aimlessly, glanced once or twice at us, and then ambled over to where the reeds sprang up in a green fence round the perimeter of the lake. One of them cupped her hands to her mouth. "Al," she called, "Hey, Al!"

"Come on," Digby hissed. "Let's get out of here."

But it was too late. The second girl was picking her way across the lot, unsteady on her heels, looking up at us and then away. She was older—twenty-five or -six—and as she came closer we could see there was something wrong with her: she was stoned or drunk, lurching now and waving her arms for balance. I gripped the steering wheel as if it were the ejection lever of a flaming jet, and Digby spat out my name, twice, terse and impatient.

"Hi," the girl said.

40 We looked at her like zombies, like war veterans, like deaf-and-dumb pencil peddlers.

She smiled, her lips cracked and dry. "Listen," she said, bending from the waist to look in the window, "you guys seen Al?" Her pupils were pinpoints, her eyes glass. She jerked her neck. "That's his bike over there—Al's. You seen him?"

Al. I didn't know what to say. I wanted to get out of the car and retch, I wanted to go home to my parents' house and crawl into bed. Digby poked me in the ribs. "We haven't seen anybody," I said.

The girl seemed to consider this, reaching out a slim veiny arm to brace herself against the car. "No matter," she said, slurring the t's, "he'll turn up." And then, as if she'd just taken stock of the whole scene-the ravaged car and our battered faces, the desolation of the place—she said: "Hey, you guys look like some pretty bad characters—been fightin', huh?" We stared straight ahead, rigid as catatonics. She was fumbling in her pocket and muttering something. Finally she held out a handful of tablets in glassine wrappers: "Hey, you want to party, you want to do some of these with me and Sarah?"

I just looked at her. I thought I was going to cry. Digby broke the silence. "No, thanks," he said, leaning over me. "Some other time."

45 I put the car in gear and it inched forward with a groan, shaking off pellets of glass like an old dog shedding water after a bath, heaving over the ruts on its worn springs, creeping toward the highway. There was a sheen of sun on the lake. I looked back. The girl was still standing there, watching us, her shoulders slumped, hand outstretched.

[1985]

Joining the Conversation: Critical Thinking and Writing

1. Exactly what does "bad" mean in the first paragraph? Why would some young people think "it was good to be bad"? Notice that the first paragraph ends with a short sentence about Greasy Lake: "This was nature." Is the narrator saying that "bad" behavior is natural?

2. The third paragraph characterizes Digby as "dangerous" and "bad." How dangerous do you think Boyle wants us to think Digby is?

3. Suppose the story had a different title, and Greasy Lake was never mentioned in the story. Would anything be lost? In short, why does Boyle introduce the lake?
4. What do you make of the ending of the story? Why, in your view, do the boys reject the girl's offer?

MARY HOOD

Mary Hood is often categorized as a Southern writer and praised for capturing Southern voices, communities, and landscapes. In her essay, "On Being a Southern Writer," she explains that, when she writes fiction, she tries to "sound like the Southern talkers." Born in Georgia in 1946, Hood continues to call Georgia her home. She has published several short-story collections, novellas, and a novel. In 1984, she was awarded the Flannery O'Connor Award for Short Fiction for the short story collection, How Far She Went.

How Far She Went

They had quarreled all morning, squalled all summer about the incidentals: how tight the girl's cut-off jeans were, the "Every Inch a Woman" T-shirt, her choice of music and how loud she played it, her practiced inattention, her sullen look. Her granny wrung out the last boiled dishcloth, pinched it to the line, giving the basin a sling and a slap, the water flying out in a scalding arc onto the Queen Anne's lace by the path, never mind if it bloomed, that didn't make it worth anything except to chiggers, but the girl would cut it by the everlasting armload and cherish it in the old chum, going to that much trouble for a weed but not bending once-un begged-to pick the nearest bean; she was sulking now. Bored. Displaced.

"And what do you think happens to a chigger if nobody ever walks by his weed?" her granny asked, heading for the house with that sidelong uneager unanswered glance, hoping for what? The surprise gift of a smile? Nothing. The woman shook her head and said it. "Nothing." The door slammed behind her. Let it.

"I hate it here!" the girl yelled then. She picked up a stick and broke it and threw the pieces—one from each hand—at the laundry drying in the noon. Missed. Missed.

Then she turned on her bare, haughty heel and set off high—shouldered into the heat, quick but not far, not far enough—no road was *that* long—only as far as she dared. At the gate, a rusty chain swinging between two lichened posts, she stopped, then backed up the raw drive to make a run at the barrier, lofting, clearing it clean, her long hair wild in the sun. Triumphant, she looked back at the house where she caught at the dark window her granny's face in its perpetual eclipse of disappointment, old at fifty. She stepped back, but the girl saw her.

5   "You don't know me!" the girl shouted, chin high, and ran till her ribs ached.

* * *

As she rested in the rattling shade of the willows, the little dog found her. He could be counted on. He barked all the way, and squealed when she pulled the burr from his ear. They started back to the house for lunch. By then the mailman had long come and gone in the old ruts, leaving the one letter folded now to fit the woman's apron pocket.

If bad news darkened her granny's face, the girl ignored it. Didn't talk at all, another of her distancings, her defiances. So it was as they ate that the woman summarized, "Your daddy wants you to cash in the plane ticket and buy you something. School clothes. For here."

Pale, the girl stared, defenseless only an instant before blurting out, "You're lying."

The woman had to stretch across the table to leave her handprint on that blank cheek. She said, not caring if it stung or not, "He's been planning it since he sent you here."

10   "I could turn this whole house over, dump it! Leave you slobbering over that stinking jealous dog in the dust!" The girl trembled with the vision, with the strength it gave her. It made her laugh. "Scatter the Holy Bible like confetti and ravel the crochet into miles of stupid string! I could! I will! I won't stay here!" But she didn't move, not until her tears rose to meet her color, and then to escape the shame of minding so much she fled. Just headed away, blind. It didn't matter, this time, how far she went.

* * *

The woman set her thoughts against fretting over their bickering, just went on un-alarmed with chores, clearing off after the uneaten meal, bringing in the laundry, scattering corn for the chickens, ladling manure tea onto the porch flowers. She listened though. She always had been a listener. It gave her a cocked look. She forgot why she had gone into the girl's empty room, that ungirlish, tenuous lodging place with its bleak order, its ready suitcases never unpacked, the narrow bed, the contested radio on the windowsill. The woman drew the cracked shade down between the radio and the August sun. There wasn't anything else to do.

It was after six when she tied on her rough oxfords and walked down the drive and dropped the gate chain and headed back to the creosoted shed where she kept her tools. She took a hoe for snakes, a rake, shears to trim the grass where it grew, and seed in her pocket to scatter where it never had grown at all. She put the tools and her gloves and the bucket in the trunk of the old Chevy, its prime and rust like an Appaloosa's spots through the chalky white finish. She left the trunk open and the tool handles sticking out. She wasn't going far.

The heat of the day had broken, but the air was thick, sultry, weighted with honeysuckle in second bloom and the Nu-Grape scent of kudzu. The maple and poplar leaves turned over, quaking, silver. There wouldn't be any rain. She told the dog to stay, but he knew a trick. He stowed away when she turned her back, leaped right into the trunk with the tools, then gave himself away with exultant barks. Hearing him, her court jester, she stopped the car and welcomed him into the front seat beside her. Then they went on. Not a mile from her gate she turned onto the blue gravel of the cemetery lane, hauled the gearshift into reverse to whoa them, and got out to take the idle walk down to her buried hopes, bending all along to rout out a handful of weeds from between the markers of old acquaintance. She stood there and read, slow. The dog whined at her hem; she picked him up and rested her chin on his head, then he wriggled and whined to run free, contrary and restless as a child.

The crows called strong and bold MOM! MOM! A trick of the ear to hear it like that. She knew it was the crows, but still she looked around. No one called her that now. She was done with that. And what was it worth anyway? It all came to this: solitary weeding. The sinful fumble of flesh, the fear, the listening for a return that never came, the shamed waiting, the unanswered prayers, the perjury on the certificate—hadn't she lain there weary of the whole lie and it only beginning? and a voice telling her, "Here's your baby, here's your girl," and the swaddled package meaning no more to her than an extra anything, something store-bought, something she could take back for a refund.

15   "Tie her to the fence and give her a bale of hay," she had murmured, drugged, and they teased her, excused her for such a welcoming, blaming the anesthesia, but it went deeper than that; *she* knew, and the *baby* knew: there was no love in the begetting. That was the secret, unforgivable, that not another good thing could ever make up for, where all the bad had come from, like a visitation, a punishment. She knew that was why Sylvie had been wild, had gone to earth so early, and before dying had made this child in sudden wedlock, a child who would be just like her, would carry the hurting on into another generation. A matter of time. No use raising her hand. But she *had* raised her hand. Still wore on its palm the memory of the sting of the collision with the girl's cheek; had she broken her jaw? Her heart? Of course not. She said it aloud: "Takes more than that."

She went to work then, doing what she could with her old tools. She pecked the clay on Sylvie's grave, new-looking, unhealed after years. She tried again, scattering seeds from her pocket, every last possible one of them. Off in the west she could hear the pulpwood cutters sawing through another acre across the lake. Nearer, there was the racket of motorcycles laboring cross-country, insect-like, distracting.

She took her bucket to the well and hung it on the pump. She had half filled it when the bikers roared up, right down the blue gravel, straight at her. She let the bucket overflow, staring. On the back of one of the machines was the girl. Sylvie's girl! Her bare arms wrapped around the shirtless man riding between her thighs. They were first. The second biker rode alone. She studied their strangers' faces as they circled her. They were the enemy, all of them. Laughing. The girl was laughing too, laughing like her mama did. Out in the middle of nowhere the girl had found these two men, some moth-musk about her drawing them (too soon!) to what? She shouted it: "What in God's—" They roared off without answering her, and the bucket of water tipped over, spilling its stain blood-dark on the red dust.

The dog went wild barking, leaping after them, snapping at the tires, and there was no calling him down. The bikers made a wide circuit of the churchyard, then roared straight across the graves, leaping the ditch and landing upright on the road again, heading off toward the reservoir.

Furious, she ran to her car, past the barking dog, this time leaving him behind, driving after them, horn blowing nonstop, to get back what was not theirs. She drove after them knowing what they did not know, that all the roads beyond that point dead-ended. She surprised them, swinging the Impala across their path, cutting them off; let them hit it! They stopped. She got out, breathing hard, and said, when she could, "She's underage." Just that. And put out her claiming hand with an authority that made the girl's arms drop from the man's insolent waist and her legs tremble.

20   "I was just riding," the girl said, not looking up.

Behind them the sun was heading on toward down. The long shadows of the pines drifted back and forth in the same breeze that puffed the distant sails on the lake. Dead limbs creaked and clashed overhead like the antlers of locked and furious beasts.

"Sheeeut," the lone rider said. "I told you." He braced with his muddy boot and leaned out from his machine to spit. The man the girl had been riding with had the invading sort of eyes the woman had spent her lifetime bolting doors against. She met him now, face to face.

"Right there, missy," her granny said, pointing behind her to the car.

The girl slid off the motorcycle and stood halfway between her choices. She started slightly at the poosh! as he popped another top and chugged the beer in one uptilting of his head. His eyes never left the woman's. When he was through, he tossed the can high, flipping it end over end. Before it hit the ground he had his pistol out and, firing once, winged it into the lake.

25   "Freaking lucky shot," the other one grudged.

"I don't need luck," he said. He sighted down the barrel of the gun at the woman's head. "POW!" he yelled, and when she recoiled, he laughed. He swung around to the girl: he kept aiming the gun, here, there, high, low, all around. "Y'all settle it," he said, with a shrug.

The girl had to understand him then, had to know him, had to know better. But still she hesitated. He kept looking at her, then away.

"She's fifteen," her granny said. "You can go to jail."

"You can go to hell," he said.

30   "Probably will," her granny told him. "I'll save you a seat by the fire." She took the girl by the arm and drew her to the car; she backed up, swung around, and headed out the road toward the churchyard for her tools and dog. The whole way the girl said nothing, just hunched against the far door, staring hard-eyed out at the pines going past.

The woman finished watering the seed in, and collected her tools. As she worked, she muttered, "It's your own kin buried here, you might have the decency to glance this way one time. . . ." The girl was finger-tweezing her eyebrows in the side mirror. She didn't look around as the dog and the woman got in. Her granny shifted hard, sending the tools clattering in the trunk.

When they came to the main road, there were the men. Watching for them. Waiting for them. They kicked their machines into life and followed, close, bumping them, slapping the old fenders, yelling. The girl gave a wild glance around at the one by her door and said, "Gran'ma?" and as he drew his pistol, "Gran'ma!" just as the gun nosed into the open window. She frantically cranked the glass up between her and the weapon, and her granny, seeing, spat, "Fool!" She never had been one to pray for peace or rain. She stamped the accelerator right to the floor.

The motorcycles caught up. Now she braked, hard, and swerved off the road into an alley between the pines, not even wide enough for the school bus, just a fire scrape that came out a quarter mile from her own house, if she could get that far. She slewed on the pine straw, then righted, tearing along the dark tunnel through the woods. She had for the time being bested them; they were left behind. She was winning. Then she hit the wallow where the tadpoles were already five weeks old. The Chevy plowed in and stalled. When she got it cranked again, they were stuck. The tires spattered mud three feet up the near trunks as she tried to spin them out, to rock them out. Useless. "Get out and run!" she cried, but the trees were too close on the passenger side. The girl couldn't open her door. She wasted precious time having to crawl out under the steering wheel. The woman waited but the dog ran on.

They struggled through the dusky woods, their pace slowed by the thick straw and vines. Overhead, in the last light, the martins were reeling free and sure after their prey.

35   "Why? Why?" the girl gasped, as they lunged down the old deer trail. Behind them they could hear shots, and glass breaking as the men came to the bogged car. The woman kept on running, swatting their way clear through the shoulder-high weeds. They could see the Greer cottage, and made for it. But it was ivied-over, padlocked, the woodpile dry-rotting under its tarp, the electric meterbox empty on the pole. No help there.

The dog, excited, trotted on, yelping, his lips white-flecked. He scented the lake and headed that way, urging them on with thirsty yips. On the clay shore, treeless, deserted, at the utter limit of land, they stood defenseless, listening to the men coming on, between them and home. The woman pressed her hands to her mouth, stifling her cough. She was exhausted. She couldn't think.

"We can get under!" the girl cried suddenly, and pointed toward the Greers' dock, gap-planked, its walkway grounded on the mud. They splashed out to it, wading in, the woman grabbing up the telltale, tattletale dog in her arms. They waded out to the far end and ducked under. There was room between the foam floats for them to crouch neck-deep.

The dog wouldn't hush, even then; never had yet, and there wasn't time to teach him. When the woman realized that, she did what she had to do. She grabbed him whimpering; held him; held him under till the struggle ceased and the bubbles rose silver from his fur. They crouched there then, the two of them, submerged to the shoulders, feet unsteady on the slimed lake bed. They listened. The sky went from rose to ocher to violet in the cracks over their heads. The motorcycles had stopped now. In the silence there was the glissando of locusts, the dry crunch of boots on the flinty beach, their low man-talk drifting as they prowled back and forth. One of them struck a match.

"—they in these woods we could bum 'em out."

40   The wind carried their voices away into the pines. Some few words eddied back.

"—lippy old smartass do a little work on her knees besides praying—"

Laughter. It echoed off the deserted house. They were getting closer.

One of them strode directly out to the dock, walked on the planks over their heads. They could look up and see his boot soles. He was the one with the gun. He slapped a mosquito on his bare back and cursed. The carp, roused by the troubling of the waters, came nosing around the dock, guzzling and snorting. The girl and her granny held still, so still. The man fired his pistol into the shadows, and a wounded fish thrashed, dying. The man knelt and reached for it, chuffing out his beery breath. He belched. He pawed the lake for the dead fish, cursing as it floated out of reach. He shot it again, firing at it till it sank and the gun was empty. Cursed that too. He stood then and unzipped and relieved himself of some of the beer. They had to listen to that. To know that about him. To endure that, unprotesting.

Back and forth on shore the other one ranged, restless. He lit another cigarette. He coughed. He called. "Hey! They got away, man, that's all. Don't get your shorts in a wad. Let's go."

45   "Yeah." He finished. He zipped. He stumped back across the planks and leaped to shore, leaving the dock tilting amid widening ripples. Underneath, they waited.

The bike cranked. The other ratcheted, ratcheted, then coughed, caught, roared. They circled, cut deep ruts, slung gravel, and went. Their roaring died away and away. Crickets resumed and a near frog bic-bic-bicked.

Under the dock, they waited a little longer to be sure. Then they ducked below the water, scraped out from under the pontoon, and came up into free air, slogging toward shore. It had seemed warm enough in the water. Now they shivered. It was almost night. One streak of light still stood reflected on the darkening lake, drew itself thinner, narrowing into a final cancellation of day. A plane winked its way west.

The girl was trembling. She ran her hands down her arms and legs, shedding water like a garment. She sighed, almost a sob. The woman held the dog in her arms; she dropped to her knees upon the random stones and murmured, private, haggard, "Oh, honey," three times, maybe all three times for the dog, maybe once for each of them. The girl waited, watching. Her granny rocked the dog like a baby, like a dead child, rocked slower and slower and was still.

"I'm sorry," the girl said then, avoiding the dog's inert, empty eye.

50 "It was him or you," her granny said, finally, looking up. Looking her over. "Did they mess with you? With your britches? Did they?"

"No!" Then, quieter, "No, ma'am."

When the woman tried to stand up she staggered, lightheaded, clumsy with the freight of the dog. "No, ma'am," she echoed, fending off the girl's "Let me." And she said again, "It was him or you. I know that. I'm not going to rub your face in it." They saw each other as well as they could in that failing light, in any light.

The woman started toward home, saying, "Around here, we bear our own burdens." She led the way along the weedy shortcuts. The twilight bleached the dead limbs of the pines to bone. Insects sang in the thickets, silencing at their oncoming.

"We'll see about the car in the morning," the woman said. She bore her armful toward her own moth-ridden dusk-to-dawn security light with that country grace she had always had when the earth was reliably progressing underfoot. The girl walked close behind her, exactly where *she* walked, matching her pace, matching her stride, close enough to put her hand forth (if the need arose) and touch her granny's back where the faded voile was clinging damp, the merest gauze between their wounds.

Joining the Conversation: Critical Thinking and Writing

1. "How Far She Went" opens with the granddaughter yelling, "I hate it here!" Where is she, and why does she hate being there? Why is the granddaughter referred to as a "girl"?

2. What is the family history that defines the grandmother, her daughter Sylvie, and the granddaughter? What repeated pattern defines these three women? We learn of this family history when the grandmother is tending a grave. Why is this important?

3. Write a short essay that analyzes the character of the grandmother. What evidence can you find to support the argument that she is a strong and tough woman? What statements does the grandmother make that reveals her strength? What actions reveal the grandmother's strength?

4. Think about the title of the story. If we apply this title to the granddaughter, we could say that she clearly goes "too far" in encouraging the two motorcycle-riding men. When does the granddaughter realize that she has gone too far? How can we apply this title to the grandmother?

5. What does the grandmother do to her dog? Why? How does the grandmother explain her actions? Read and reread this section of the story, adding more detailed annotations to develop your interpretation.

6. The lake provides an important setting for the climactic action of the story. How does the lake provide an escape or "getaway" for the two women? How does the lake function on a symbolic level; for example, does the lake allow for a symbolic rebirth? Compare "How Far She Went" to "Greasy Lake." How and why do both stories feature lakes? In the two stories, how does the lake provide a backdrop for violence and sexuality? Do the lakes provide an escape from violence and sexuality, or do they heighten violent and sexual actions? Are the lakes a space of death or life, of love or hate?

CHAPTER 5

The Pleasures of Reading, Writing, and Thinking about Literature

Chapter Preview

After reading this chapter, you will be able to

- Connect the enjoyment of literature to the critical analysis of literature
- Consider how we interact with texts as readers and writers
- Use fiction to explore how literature creates connections
- Use graphic fiction to explore how literature makes and breaks rules
- Use poetry to explore how literature emphasizes language
- Use drama to explore how literature is a performance
- Use essays to explore how literature encourages discovery
- Write a personal response paper that captures your enjoyment of the literary work

The Pleasures of Literature

As you work to develop your writing skills by engaging in a careful analysis, we hope that you won't forget a starting point for this work: enjoyment! As you read a literary work for the first time, open yourself up to it as a pleasurable experience. Don't hesitate to ask yourself what characters you liked the most, what language you found most striking, what image seemed the most beautiful, or what plot twist was the most shocking. New insights often come from "gut reactions" to a literary work. As you start to think more critically about the work, your first responses will provide a foundation for more considered and careful analysis. You will start to ask *why* you reacted to a character, a word, an image, or a scene, and your enjoyment of the literary work will deepen as you think it through more fully. Ultimately, you'll enjoy the process of critical analysis itself, seeing it as an extension of your enjoyment of the literary work.

Let's read a microfiction that, although short, has many enjoyable elements.

ALLEN WOODMAN

Allen Woodman is a professor of creative writing at Northern Arizona University. He has published numerous short stories, including very short stories like this one, often called "flash fiction" or "microfiction." He has published six books, including a children's picture book and a collection of humorous short stories for adults, Saved by Mr. F. Scott Fitzgerald.

Wallet

Tired of losing his wallet to pickpockets, my father, at seventy, makes a phony one. He stuffs the phony wallet with expired food coupons and losing Florida Lottery tickets and a fortune cookie fortune that reads, "Life is the same old story told over and over."

In a full-length mirror, he tries the wallet in the back pocket of his pants. It hangs out fat with desire. "All oyster," he says to me, "no pearl."

We drive to the mall where he says he lost the last one. I am the wheelman, left behind in the car, while my father cases a department store.

He is an old man, trying to act feeble and childlike, and he overdoes it like stage makeup on a community-theater actor. He has even brought a walking stick for special effect. Packages of stretch socks clumsily slip from his fingers. He bends over farther than he has bent in years to retrieve them, allowing the false billfold to rise like a dark wish and be grappled by the passing shadow of a hand,

Then the unexpected happens. The thief is chased by an attentive salesclerk. Others join in. The thief subdued, the clerk holds up the reclaimed item. "Your wallet, sir. Your wallet." As she begins opening it, searching for identification, my father runs toward an exit. The worthless articles float to the floor.

Now my father is in the car, shouting for me to drive away. There will be time enough for silence and rest. We are both stupid with smiles and he is shouting, "Drive fast, drive fast."

[1996]

When we read this story, we found ourselves smiling with the characters, and we hope you did, too. Let's ask some general questions about the story, considering aspects of it that you might have found pleasurable.

- Did you find the story funny? At what points in the story did you laugh or smile?
- Did you like the setup of the plot—the idea that the father is creating a "sting" that will catch a thief?
- Are there elements of the story that struck you as true, capturing the way a real person might think or act?
- Did you like the father/son relationship? Does it seem to be a caring or a loving relationship?
- Are there details in the story that you found funny, such as the father pretending to drop packages of stretch socks?
- Did you find the ending of the story to be enjoyable? Would you label it a happy ending?

As we try to determine where our pleasure in the story comes from, we must dig deeper into the literary work. The more we look at the story, the more we see. Let's continue our questioning but make the questions more specific, trying to determine what details of the story we found most enjoyable and what ideas are triggered by those details.

- As we think about the planning of the "sting" operation, what elements of it are interesting: The idea of the father wanting the pickpocket to steal something? The father's creation of a false wallet that will be the pickpocket's "reward"? The father's desire to act like a victim?
- Let's take these questions about the sting operation one step further: Is the father's plan interesting because the father is taking justice into his own hands? Is the plan interesting because the father is creating his own form of punishment for the pickpocket? Rather than just catching the thief, does the father seem to want to play with the thief?
- What details of the fake wallet are funny—and interesting? Why are the food coupons "expired" and the lottery tickets "losing" tickets? Why does the wallet have to be "fat," and what does the phrase "fat with desire" mean? Why does the father say, "All oyster, no pearl"? What does that mean?
- Let's look at the wallet even more closely. Why does the fortune cookie fortune read, "Life is the same old story told over and over"? Because this fortune is placed within quotation marks at the beginning of the story, it seems important. Does the father seem to be accepting or rejecting this fortune?
- What do you make of the father's overacting when he sets himself up as a victim? How does the description of his overacting make the story even funnier?
- At the end of the story, "the unexpected happens." Although this story is very short, it plays with our expectations, setting up a plot twist that we— and the characters—don't expect. How does the salesclerk who catches the thief "ruin" the father's plan? Why would the father want the thief to take the wallet and *not* to be caught?
- The end of this story is even more unexpected: The father runs away! Why is this ending exciting? Like a snowball rolling down a hill, the plot seems to pick up speed. Why does the father *not* stay and explain himself and the wallet?
- Let's consider the plot as a whole. Why does the father set up an elaborate plan to have his son act like a "wheelman" and then, at the end of the story, run out to the car and yell "drive fast, drive fast"? Is the father acting like a thief who needs a getaway car? Why? Isn't the father supposed to be the innocent victim?

We hope that, as you reexamine the story and question it further, your enjoyment of it will increase. The story becomes more interesting as you look at its details: The father and son are acting like robbers, the father likes overacting and creating elaborate props, and the father seems to be in it for the chase and not for catching the thief. Ultimately, the story disproves the fortune cookie fortune: It is *not* "the same old story told over and over." Perhaps that's why we like it.

The Pleasures of Analyzing the Texts That Surround Us

We engage in the activity of responding to texts on a daily if not hourly basis. Reading for enjoyment is something we do so constantly that we almost don't even notice it. If you define a *text* as constructed material that conveys a message that can be read closely, almost anything that we watch or read can be seen as a text that is worthy of analysis: a film, a TV show, a video game, advertising campaigns, a Facebook page, a blog post, or a Twitter feed. These forms of text share many qualities of literature, borrowing literary elements to be successful forms of entertainment.

We assume that you enjoy these many forms of text. Film and TV shows are obviously contemporary forms of drama, using actors, plotted action, crafted dialogue, and staged sets to tell a story. A video game allows you to enter into a carefully constructed world that uses characters, setting, and symbols to make its fictional landscape feel real. An advertising campaign often connects its visual imagery to poetic language—compressed language that is carefully chosen and sequenced to create emotional reactions. Even the digital communication that surrounds consists of texts that have literary elements: A Facebook page often aims to create a perfected person, as if he or she were a character; a blog post is an essay that conveys ideas while emphasizing the writer's voice and personal style; and a Twitter post forces readers to use short bits of language in creative ways that become poetic. Some of these texts are more artistically constructed than others, to be sure, but they all can trigger our interest and critique.

Your reactions to these many texts are probably similar to your reactions to literature: At first, you might enjoy the text, but then you might slow down and think about its meaning and create a more *considered* response. You might love a character in a TV show, but when the character does something unexpected in an episode, you might find yourself disturbed by it, thinking, "Why did the show have him do that?" Or, you might initially laugh at a friend's text message but then find yourself returning to it again and again, asking, "What does she really mean?" Or, you might snap a photo of an advertisement and send it to your friends, finding yourself explaining why you found it beautiful or inspirational.

As you negotiate your text saturated world, your immediate reaction might be to like or dislike a text, but you might then ask questions about it, analyze it, and form opinions about it. This is the same type of inquiry and analysis process that underlies critical thinking and is also the process that we use to interpret literature and move toward writing about it.

The Pleasures of Authoring Texts

When you write an essay, you become an author yourself. Just as you respond to a text message by writing a quick text in return, you should respond to literary writing with writing—this is the best way to develop your critical thinking skills. Engage with thought-provoking writing by taking on the role of writer yourself. Unlike a short-story writer or poet, your essays will consist chiefly of

- **analysis** and
- **argument** (you want to persuade your reader that your analysis makes sense)

but your essay will surely also include

- **exposition** (you may have to define terms or summarize someone else's argument) and
- **narration** (you may have to summarize a plot)

and you will have to use an appropriate

- **style** (largely a matter of tone)

In short, when you are writing any essay, even when your emphasis is largely analytic and argumentative, you will probably use all the devices that all good writers use to hold the attention of readers and to convince readers that you have something to say that is worth hearing. Also, you *will* have something to offer when you think seriously about both the work you are discussing and the work you are producing that you will submit to your classmates and instructor. Read each draft in a mildly critical spirit; keep asking yourself if your imagined readers will find it convincing and engaging. Here are some of the questions that you should ask yourself:

- Have I located an interesting and engaging topic that I am excited to explore and that my reader will want to explore with me?
- Have I defined terms that may be crucial to my analysis (for instance, *immoral, realistic, pathetic, tragic, sentimental*)?
- Have I given just the right amount of evidence (*too little* evidence will leave readers unconvinced; *too much* evidence may bore them)?
- Do transitions take the reader easily from sentence to sentence and from paragraph to paragraph?
- Is my title engaging, does my opening paragraph arouse interest, and does my final paragraph provide an effective ending?
- Is my tone appropriate?

The point about tone is worth further comment. As a writer of arguments, you want your readers to trust you. How do writers gain the trust of readers? Usually, by being

- **knowledgeable** (the writer quotes accurately and does not make errors of fact),
- **fair** (the writer does not ignore contrary evidence), and
- **courteous** (the writer conveys an impression of goodwill and does not come across to the reader as a smart aleck).

Enjoy stepping into the role of author and taking on the challenge of writing a well-crafted essay.

The Pleasures of Interacting with Texts

We enjoy literature because we interact with it on many levels and in many ways: We can be entertained by it, question it, critique it, reread and reconsider it, memorize it, be inspired by it, and, of course, write about it. One of the pleasures of literature is that it forces us to think in unexpected ways—new thinking is often triggered by the interesting ways in which our minds interact with literature. Reading literature is an active endeavor, and the more that we see it as a dynamic pursuit that we can shape, the more we can enjoy it.

We interact with many types of texts in a typical day: informational alerts coming across social media, journalistic stories in the newspaper, opinionated blogs posted online, film clips on YouTube, and personal text messages received from friends. We know that different types of texts require different responses; we might quickly skim and reply to some texts, whereas we might carefully read and reread others. Literature, too, takes many forms that encourage many types of interaction. The major forms of literature include fiction, poetry, drama, and nonfiction. These types of literature can be subdivided further; for example, fiction includes short stories, novellas, novels, and graphic novels. These forms are often referred to as "genres" of literature, but genre is also used to indicate the content and style of the work, including the epic, comedy, tragedy, satire, or romance.

Let's examine the different genres of literature that we explore more fully in Part 3, Chapters 11–15: fiction, graphic fiction, poetry, drama, and the essay. Let us also look at some of the ways in which we can create active relationships with these forms of literature. Our goal is to create dynamic interactions with the sample literary works that we present here; to that end, we ask you questions in the "Joining the Conversation" section that immediately follows each work.

Interacting with Fiction: Literature as Connection

Literature often depicts human relationships, exploring characters defined by their emotional, psychological, familial, or social connections. When we read a narrative text—a poem, a play, or a piece of fiction that tells a story—we expect to encounter characters who are trying to connect with each other. The characters might achieve some sort of harmony or experience some sort of conflict and division, giving why they were or were not able to connect. What we might not think about are the ways in which the characters create connections with us.

A **character** provides one of the most powerful ways in which we connect to literature, giving the reader access to the emotions and thoughts that accompany a story, a poem, or a play. Characters make literature human, allowing us to put ourselves in the place of the fictional persons and imagine living in their world. While characters help us move "into" a story, characters also seem to step "outside" of the story, encouraging us to imagine them existing in our real world.

Characters are only one way in which we connect to literature. We might connect to the description of a specific place depicted in a story, be drawn to compelling images in a poem, or enjoy the patterns of sounds in a line spoken in a play. As readers, we create a multitude of connections with a literary work, and these connections are fertile ground for critical thinking and writing.

Let's turn to a short story by Jamaica Kincaid that features the relationship between a mother and daughter. In this story, you will hear two voices, one of which is that of a mother who is tutoring her adolescent daughter for her future role as a woman. In addition to this mother-daughter relationship, think about the connection that this story creates between its characters and you, the reader. The story captures a mother speaking to her daughter, but think about how that voice is also speaking to you.

JAMAICA KINCAID

Jamaica Kincaid was born in 1949 on the island of Antigua, in the West Indies, which at that time was a British colony. At the age of seventeen, she emigrated to the United States, where she still lives, although much of her writing continues to be set in Antigua. She has written several novels, including Annie John *and* Lucy, *and works of nonfiction, including essays on gardening.*

Kincaid informs us that benna, *mentioned early in the story, refers to "songs of the sort your parents didn't want you to sing, at first calypso and later rock and roll."*

Girl

Wash the white clothes on Monday and put them on the stone heap; wash the color clothes on Tuesday and put them on the clothesline to dry; don't walk bare-head in the hot sun; cook pumpkin fritters in very hot sweet oil; soak your little clothes right after you take them off; when buying cotton to make yourself a nice blouse, be sure that it doesn't have gum on it, because that way it won't hold up well after a wash; soak salt fish overnight before you cook it; is it true that you sing benna in Sunday school?; always eat your food in such a way that it won't turn someone else's stomach; on Sundays try to walk like a lady and not like the slut you are so bent on becoming; don't sing benna in Sunday school; you mustn't speak to wharf-rat boys, not even to give directions; don't eat fruits on the street— flies will follow you; *but I don't sing benna on Sundays at all and never in Sunday school;* this is how to sew on a button; this is how to make a buttonhole for the button you have just sewed on; this is how to hem a dress when you see the hem coming down and so to prevent yourself from looking like the slut I know you are so bent on becoming; this is how you iron your father's khaki shirt so that it doesn't have a crease; this is how you iron your father's khaki pants so that they don't have a crease; this is how you grow okra—far from the house, because okra tree harbors red ants; when you are growing dasheen, make sure it gets plenty of water or else it makes your throat itch when you are eating it; this is how you sweep a corner; this is how you sweep a whole house; this is how you sweep a yard; this is how you smile to someone you don't like too much; this is how you smile to someone you don't like at all; this is how you smile to someone you like completely; this is how you set a table for tea; this is how you set a table for dinner; this is how you set a table for dinner with an important guest; this is how you set a table for lunch; this is how you set a table for breakfast; this is how to behave in the presence of men who don't know you very well, and this way they won't rec-ognize immediately the slut I have warned you against becoming; be sure to wash every day, even if it is with your own spit; don't squat down to play marbles—you are not a boy, you know; don't pick people's flowers—you might catch something; don't throw stones at blackbirds, because it might not be a blackbird at all; this is how to make a bread pudding; this is how to make doukona; this is how to make pepper pot; this is how to make a good medicine for a cold; this is how to make a good medicine to throw away a child before it even becomes a child; this is how to catch a fish; this is how to throw back a fish you don't like, and that way something bad won't fall on you; this is how to bully a man; this is how a man bullies you; this is how to love a man, and if this doesn't work there are other ways, and if they don't work don't feel too bad about giving up; this is how to spit up in the air if you feel like it, and this is how to move quick so that it doesn't fall on you; this is how to make ends meet; always squeeze bread to make sure it's fresh; *but what if the baker won't let me feel the bread?*; you mean to say that after all you are really going to be the kind of woman who the baker won't let near the bread?

[1978]

Joining the Conversation: Critical Thinking and Writing

1. What is the relationship being dramatized by the story? How would you describe the connection between the mother and her daughter?

2. What are the essential lessons the mother wants to impart to her daughter? Some of the lessons relate to tasks and chores, such as washing clothes, sewing buttons, and ironing pants. However, other lessons relate to the maturation of a young girl, including how to connect to other people and relationships with men. What categories of knowledge is the mother sharing with her daughter, and why?

3. How does the mother's voice reach out and grab the listener? What are some of the ways in which the mother's voice is constructed to sound spoken? How does the voice become a dynamic, energetic force?

4. Try reading a section of "Girl" out loud in a rhythmical pattern, giving the two speakers distinctive voices. Then reread the story, trying to incorporate the rhythms mentally into your reading. How do the rhythms compare with speech rhythms that are familiar to you?

5. What do you make of the girl's second (and last) line of dialogue in "Girl," and what do you make of the mother's response to it?

6. Think of your own connection to the story. How does the story create a strong connection between you and its characters?

Personal Response Essay

One way to capture your enjoyment of a literary work is to write a *personal response* paper. A personal response paper emphasizes the reader's understanding of, and reaction to, the assigned literary text. In response-focused writing, the writer typically explains what he or she finds most thought provoking—most interesting, intriguing, confusing, enjoyable, or frustrating—about the text. A response paper often emphasizes emotional reactions and can overtly explain what the writer liked and didn't like about a text. It is thus often fun to write a response paper, as it allows more subjective self-expression than an analytical paper.

A response paper is more informal than an analytical paper, but it can serve as a good starting point for interpretation. As we've emphasized, personal response is often the first step toward critical thinking. If you were completing a response paper, your writing would explore the literary work by emphasizing the ideas, opinions, and emotions that it triggered. These insights could then be used to develop an interpretation and a more argumentative paper. By asking you to focus on a close reading of the text and the reactions that reading generates, a response draft helps you to avoid focusing on plot summary or ideas that are too general. Instead, the response draft allows you to chart and assess your specific reactions to specific literary elements or specific aspects of the text. Your responses demonstrate your comprehension of the text's information, your investigation into why certain parts of the text elicit certain reactions, and your ability to generate both emotional and intellectual insights about the text.

Student Personal Response Essay: "The Narrator in Jamaica Kincaid's 'Girl': Questioning the Power of Voice"

Let's look at a sample personal response essay to see how one student takes her immediate reactions to the story and turns them into writing. The essay captures the student's emotional response but also contains many excellent interpretations of the story. These ideas could become the basis of a more formal analytical paper.

Jackie Bracken

Professor Holmes

English 101

29 January 2016

The Narrator in Jamaica Kincaid's "Girl": Questioning the Power of Voice

Presented as a monologue, Jamaica Kincaid's "Girl" records a mother's

voice as she lectures her young daughter. The short story takes a unique

form: it is the mother's listing of all of the activities that the girl must be

able to do, from washing to eating to walking to cooking to attracting men.

The mother tells the girl exactly how to do each activity, giving her precise

directions. The short story is all one sentence, so that it takes the form of a

never-ending lecture that overwhelms the listening girl. This voice is a very

commanding one that overwhelmed me—it seemed to be commanding me as

I was reading the story. At first, I did not like this overwhelming nature of

the story. I think I was feeling like I was the daughter! But, on rereading the

story, I began to admire the mother and her knowledge. I think the story

captures the mother/daughter relationship very well, showing the power of

the mother over the daughter. As I reread the short story, I admired the

mother, but I also felt that the girl must be overwhelmed by the mother's

power. As a result, I think the story forces the reader to question the

mother/daughter relationship, asking if this is a healthy form of control.

The story shows the mother lecturing the girl, telling her all the tasks

she must do. On a first reading, I was overwhelmed by the number of tasks the

girl would be asked to do. The girl is being trained to be a woman and to take

on many domestic duties in the household. The tasks include specific

instruction on how to do numerous domestic chores such as cooking,

washing, and ironing shirts. For example, the girl is told, "This is how to sew a

button; this is how to make a button hole for the button you have just sewed

on; this is how to hem a dress when you see the hem coming down" (122).

The girl is under pressure to perform many different jobs. As a reader, I felt the pressure that the girl was under. The reader is made to feel the weight of those responsibilities.

The mother makes this control even more meaningful by connecting that control to the girl's sexuality. Interspersed within the mother's lecture are many comments about the girl becoming a "slut" and not being able to control her relationships with men. For example, the mother's lecture about the button holes continues to say, "this is how to hem a dress when you see the hem coming down and so to prevent yourself from looking like the slut I know you are so bent on becoming" (122). The use of the shocking word "slut" reveals that the girl's sexuality worries the mother. The girl's sexuality becomes a repeated issue. I am sure the daughter has no privacy. I think the mother wants to control her daughter's psychological, emotional and sexual maturation—and gives her instructions on all aspects of her life. We do not get to hear enough from the girl to know how she feels about it, but I think she might resent these instructions.

In addition to a long list of tasks, for each task, the mother makes sure to include all possibilities on *how* to perform that task. For example, the mother tells the girl how to cook fish—and then later includes instructions on how to catch the fish. As a result, the girl has a huge list of responsibilities. The pattern of the mother's lecture is to start with a small activity and to then keep broadening that task out to become bigger and bigger. The mother's lecture seems to start with just a few instructions about washing, but the instructions quickly grow to include almost any job the girl might have. For example, when the girl is told how to sweep, it starts with a focused act of sweeping, but then expands to include almost every type of sweeping: the mother says "this is how you sweep a corner; this is how you sweep a whole house; this is how you sweep a yard" (122). I expected her to

Bracken 3

next say, "this is how you sweep the world"! The mother's control is not only controlling the girls' physical tasks and sexual life, but also so large that it encompasses all aspects of her life—her entire world.

I was overwhelmed by the mother's non-stop voice. I think Kincaid is making the voice extreme to make the mother's control of her daughter clear. I can see that Kincaid wants the voice to come across as extreme even if it disturbs the reader. The mother's rapid-fire listing of the tasks makes it difficult for the girl to get a word in edge-wise. She answers back to the mother when she says, "but I don't sing benna on Sundays at all and never in Sunday school," but the mother seems to be ignoring and talking right over her (122). The girl's statement is ignored and lost in the stream of the mother's words. Toward the end of the story, the girl wonders what would happen if a baker won't let the he squeeze the bread. The mother finally answers back and gives a contradictory response: "you mean to say that after all you are really going to be the kind of woman who the baker won't let near the bread?" (122). She tells the girl that she must grow into a woman who will be allowed to squeeze the bread. Thus, the mother wants to control her daughter's sexuality, but also allow her to grow into an attractive woman

Once I understood that the mother's voice was supposed to be overwhelming, I wound up liking it and respecting that it was strong. But, the mother's voice is so strong, it left me wondering if the girl would ever be able to grow into that powerful, attractive woman. I can't imagine the girl ever getting free from that voice. I questioned if the mother would allow her daughter to take over her own life. I wondered if the non-stop directions meant that the girl would not be able to experiment with her own actions, test her own knowledge, and figure out her own direction in life. The mother's lecture proves that she loves her daughter by trying to teach her. However, the lecture is so all-controlling, it makes me wonder if the girl will be able to take control of her own life.

Bracken 4

Work Cited

Kincaid, Jamaica. "Girl." *Literature for Composition*. Ed. Sylvan Barnet, William

    Burto, William E. Cain, and Cheryl L. Nixon. 11th ed. Boston: Pearson, 2017.

    122. Print.

Interacting with Graphic Fiction: Literature as (Making and Breaking) Rules

Why do we play board games like chess and card games like solitaire? Perhaps we find it enjoyable to have both *structure* and *freedom*: We follow strict rules while also inventing new ways to use those rules. Or, perhaps, we find it satisfying to have predictability and unpredictability: We know the steps of a game, but we don't know when and how they'll be reached. Literature fulfills some of these same desires. It sets up rules and steps that the writer invents "within," allowing the writer to balance structure and freedom, predictability and unpredictability. As a reader, you are invited to enter into the game. You can be "in the know," predicting how the literary text's rules might work and being intrigued, even entertained, by the writer's inventiveness in following or breaking those rules.

Different literary forms or genres follow different rules. In fiction, we expect to connect with characters, follow a series of events or plot, imagine a setting, and interpret symbols. In fiction, it would be strange (but not totally impossible) for a character to suddenly start speaking in rhyme; in poetry, however, we might expect a persona to express him or herself in rhyme, and we wouldn't protest that a "real" person wouldn't speak that way. When we watch a play, we similarly don't protest when a character has to speak his or her internal thoughts aloud so that the audience can hear them. In drama, we expect ideas to be expressed through dialogue and movement on the stage, rather than in lengthy descriptions that we might find in novels.

In each of these genres, we know the "rules of the game" and expect a literary work to follow those rules, or conventions. At the same time, we enjoy when a literary work breaks those rules in a purposeful or artful way. For example, some plays will feature a moment when an actor turns to and directly addresses the audience, called "breaking the fourth wall." We might enjoy this moment when the actor disrupts the illusion that the play is real and reminds us that we are watching a piece of fiction.

Much contemporary literature likes to remind us that it is fictional—and remind us of the rules it is following or not following. We say that something is *meta* when it refers to or comments on itself. "Meta" is a term that signals that a work is self-referential; metafiction is thus "fiction about fiction." For example, a metafictional story might contain a character who shares the author's name and who interrupts the story to say, "Wait, let me rewrite this scene." Let's look at a short graphic text that calls attention to the storytelling it is engaged in.

LYNDA BARRY

Lynda Barry (born in 1956) is an award-winning cartoonist who started her career with a weekly comic strip, "Ernie Pook's Comeek." One of these comic strips is reprinted here. She has written illustrated and graphic novels, and most recently she has experimented with innovative how-to books that use collage, journal writing, poetic language, and comics to show people how to develop their creativity.

Before You Write

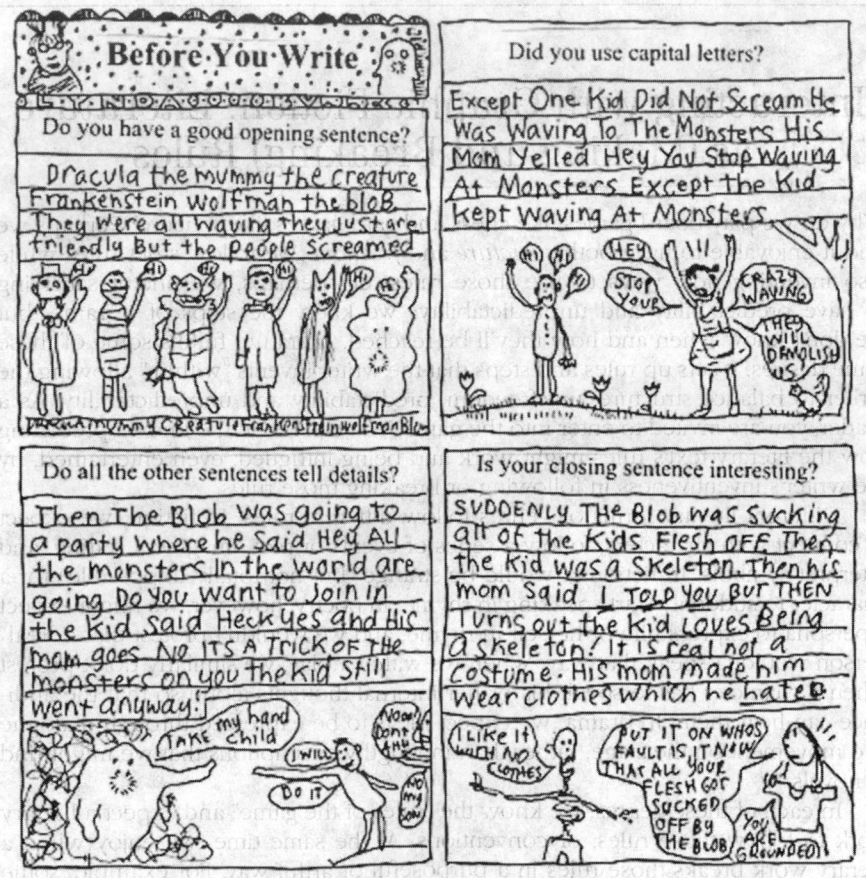

[c. 1990]

Joining the Conversation: Critical Thinking and Writing

1. This short graphic narrative is one of Barry's weekly comic strips published as "Ernie Pook's Comeek." It is a comic strip that is comic, or funny. What strikes you as funny about this graphic narrative? In literary terms, a "comic" story typically has a happy ending. Does this story have a happy ending?

2. What elements of the graphic narrative are unexpected and thus cause the pleasure of surprise? How does the story being told contain unexpected elements? How does the graphic imagery contain unexpected elements?
3. How is this graphic narrative an example of metafiction or metanarrative? How does the writing refer to itself as writing and call attention to the writing process? Consider the instructions at the top of each frame. How is the (supposed) young writer of this comic strip following and breaking these rules of writing?
4. Much of the humor of the comic strip comes from the disconnect between the writing instructions (presumably instructions typed on a worksheet by an adult teacher) and the story that comes under the instructions. How does the teacher who made the writing instructions think about the writing process? How does the kid writing the story think about the writing process?
5. Think of the relationship between the verbal text and the visual text. How do the illustrations add more meaning to the story? Look, for example, at what the mother is saying in the images.

Interacting with Poetry: Literature as Language

It seems obvious to state that literature is made out of language—but it seems important to emphasize that literature puts more pressure on the use of words than everyday communication. The artistic, creative, and imaginative use of language is an essential component of literary expression.

In literature, ideas are compressed into words that must be "unpacked," or analyzed, in a close and detailed manner that draws out all possible meanings. Literary language can be compared to a suitcase filled with layers of a traveler's belongings; words can be opened up and unpacked, with each layer examined for possible meanings. If we unpack a suitcase and remove hiking boots, we can guess that the traveler is going hiking. However, if, by digging deeper into the suitcase, we then unpack a Spanish phrase book, a guide to Aztec ruins, and a sketch book, we will have a much clearer, richer idea of the traveler's plans. Literary language encourages the reader to open up and tease out hidden meanings. If we explore a word long enough, we can locate its multiple meanings and come to richer conclusions about the larger meaning of the work. "Unpacking" opens up language and reveals ideas that we might have missed if we had only skimmed the surface.

Poetry makes literature's interest in creative language clear. While fiction and drama use words to build up their plots and characters, poetry strips thoughts, emotions, and actions down to their essential representation in words. A poem calls attention to language as its core element, emphasizing word selection, order, and sound. Specific words are carefully placed within the larger structures of the line, stanza, and whole of the poem. It is through these deceptively simple acts that literary meaning is created. When we are exploring the importance of literary language, it makes sense to examine poetry.

Let's turn to two poems that seem to be having great fun with language, specifically the new forms of language being created today through texting and tweeting. Texts and tweets feature short, compressed language that can take imaginative forms—an everyday parallel to poetry and thus great subjects for poetry itself.

JULIA BIRD

Born and educated in England, Julia Bird entered a poetry contest sponsored by a British publication, the Guardian. *The ground rules: Write a poem limited to the 160 characters of the mobile phone screen. Bird's poem won a Special Prize of £250 (about $400) for what the* Guardian *"called the most creative use of SMS 'shorthand' in a poem."*

14: a txt msg poM

his is r bunsn brnr b1%,
his hair lyk fe filings
W/ac/dc going thru.
I sit by him in kemistry,
It splits my @oms   5
wen he :-)s @ me.

Translation
14: a text message poem.
his eyes are bunsen burner blue,
his hair like iron filings   10
with ac/dc going through.
I sit by him in chemistry,
it splits my atoms
when he smiles at me.

[2001]

Joining the Conversation: Critical Thinking and Writing

1. How does this poem use language in unexpected ways? The use of "r" for "are" in line 1 is certainly not original, but do you find things in this piece that strike you as highly imaginative and especially entertaining?
2. How is the translation itself an interesting use of language? Which form of language do you prefer: the text message or the translation? Why?
3. Imagine that you are the person about whom Bird wrote her poem. Are you pleased, or not? Write a text poem in response.

With the rise of social media, contemporary poets have taken up the challenge of trying to make their creative writing fit within the constraints of internet-based communication. Just like the constraints provided by poetic forms such as the sonnet (which must be fourteen lines long that follow a set rhyme scheme) or the haiku (which is typically three lines following a pattern of 5-7-5 syllables), social media offers formal "rules" for writing that challenge the poet. For example, Twitter has a text limit of 140 characters. Let's look at how a famous contemporary poet, Billy Collins, accepts that challenge.

BILLY COLLINS

For a biographical note on Billy Collins, see page 245.

Twitter Poem

The poem creates a space.
It hides in a tent in a forest.
Making its own bed it falls asleep in the dark,
wakes up under a lamp or the sun.

[2011]

Joining the Conversation: Critical Thinking and Writing

1. If this poem was not labelled a "Twitter Poem," would you know that it follows the rules of a tweet?
2. Collins explains that a poem creates its own "space." Compare the space described in the poem to the space of the internet. Is this poem creating a space for poetry within the "forest" of social media? Can you continue to interpret the poem as a commentary on today's communication?
3. How does Collins characterize poetry? Is the poem strong and forceful? Or, is it meek and passive? Why would a poet imagine a poem hiding and sleeping? Does the poem have any positive qualities, such as self-reliance? How does the last line change the image of the poem? Does it offer a hopeful image of a poem coming to life? Why do you think the poem offers the images of both "a lamp" and "the sun"?

Interacting with Drama: Literature as Performance

Literature often encourages performance. All of us at times "perform" literary works when we tell stories in public. We read a fairy tale to children, or we tell a joke to a friend. When we were children, we recited nursery rhymes, perhaps even performing them by bouncing a ball or skipping rope to the accompaniment of the lines. Moreover, we sing lullabies, hymns, birthday greetings, and national anthems, and on New Year's Eve, we may sing Robert Burns's great poem, "Auld Lang Syne."

When Robert Frost said that a poem is "a performance in words," he was not speaking of poetry recitations, though Frost himself was an expert reciter and apparently a born showman. (If Frost had a weakness as a performer, it was that he insisted on being a soloist and never gave readings with other poets: "I only go / When I'm the show.") When Frost said that a poem was a performance in words, he was saying that the *writer* does things with words, more or less as a juggler performs with Indian clubs or balls, as a singer performs with vocal cords and air, and as a dancer or an athlete performs with the body. The writer's artistic materials are words, which the writer manipulates into something attractive and meaningful. All forms of literature can be seen as performances—artistic creations that come to life for an audience.

Drama is the literary genre that is most obviously connected to performance. A play is meant to be spoken aloud, presented in real time and space on a stage, and acted in front of a live audience. As with fiction and poetry, the dramatic work encourages us to create an active relationship with it. When we read a play, we can't help but envision actors following the stage directions, imagine lines being spoken aloud, and see sets and props used as part of the dramatic action. Our engagement with the play makes us, the readers, into its performers. Reading a short except from a famous play, *The Importance of Being Earnest*, demonstrates just how enjoyable "performing" a play—imagining it come to life as you read it—can be.

OSCAR WILDE

Famous for his razor-sharp wit, Oscar Wilde (1854–1900) was an Irish writer who composed plays, novels, poetry, and essays, He was one of the most popular play-wrights in London in the late nineteenth century. His brilliance did not spare him the prejudice of his times: He was involved in a libel trial that accused him of homo-sexuality; he was found guilty and imprisoned for two years, causing ill health that precipitated his death.

Excerpt from *The Importance of Being Earnest*

This excerpt from Wilde's play, The Importance of Being Earnest (1895), *features a young woman, Cecily, who has been creating a fictional romance for herself. In this scene, she meets the object of her predetermined affection, Algernon (whom she insists on calling Ernest), and explains how she has manufactured their love affair. The scene opens with the butler, Merriman, announcing that Algernon's one-horse carriage, called a dogcart, is ready.*

[*Enter* MERRIMAN.]

MERRIMAN: The dog-cart is at the door, sir.

[ALGERNON *looks appealingly at* CECILY.]

CECILY: It can wait, Merriman for . . . five minutes.

MERRIMAN: Yes, Miss. [*Exit* MERRIMAN.]

ALGERNON: I hope, Cecily, I shall not offend you if I state quite frankly and openly that you seem to me to be in every way the visible personification of absolute perfection.

CECILY: I think your frankness does you great credit, Ernest. If you will allow me, I will copy your remarks into my diary. [*Goes over to table and begins writing in diary.*]

ALGERNON: Do you really keep a diary? I'd give anything to look at it. May I?

CECILY: Oh no. [Puts her hand over it.] You see, it is simply a very young girl's record of her own thoughts and impressions, and consequently meant for publication. When it appears in volume form I hope you will order a copy. But pray, Ernest, don't stop. I delight in taking down from dictation. I have reached 'absolute perfection.' You can go on. I am quite ready for more.

ALGERNON: [Somewhat taken aback.] Ahem! Ahem!

CECILY: Oh, don't cough, Ernest. When one is dictating one should speak fluently and not cough. Besides, I don't know how to spell a cough. [Writes as ALGERNON speaks.]

ALGERNON: [Speaking very rapidly.] Cecily, ever since I first looked upon your wonderful and incomparable beauty, I have dared to love you wildly, passionately, devotedly, hopelessly.

CECILY: I don't think that you should tell me that you love me wildly, passionately, devotedly, hopelessly. Hopelessly doesn't seem to make much sense, does it?

ALGERNON: Cecily!

[Enter MERRIMAN.]

MERRIMAN: The dog-cart is waiting, sir.

ALGERNON: Tell it to come round next week, at the same hour.

MERRIMAN: [Looks at Cecily, who makes no sign.] Yes, sir.

[Merriman retires.]

CECILY: Uncle Jack would be very much annoyed if he knew you were staying on till next week, at the same hour.

ALGERNON: Oh, I don't care about Jack. I don't care for anybody in the whole world but you. I love you, Cecily. You will marry me, won't you?

CECILY: You silly boy! Of course. Why, we have been engaged for the last three months.

ALGERNON: For the last three months?

CECILY: Yes, it will be exactly three months on Thursday.

ALGERNON: But how did we become engaged?

CECILY: Well, ever since dear Uncle Jack first confessed to us that he had a younger brother who was very wicked and bad, you of course have formed the chief topic of conversation between myself and Miss Prism. And of course a man who is much talked about is always very attractive. One feels there must be something in him, after all. I daresay it was foolish of me, but I fell in love with you, Ernest.

ALGERNON: Darling! And when was the engagement actually settled?

CECILY: On the 14th of February last. Worn out by your entire ignorance of my existence, I determined to end the matter one way or the other, and after a long struggle with myself I accepted you under this dear old tree here. The next day I bought this little ring in your name, and this is the little bangle with the true lover's knot I promised you always to wear.

ALGERNON: Did I give you this? It's very pretty, isn't it?

CECILY: Yes, you've wonderfully good taste, Ernest. It's the excuse I've always given for your leading such a bad life. And this is the box in which I keep all your dear letters. [Kneels at table, opens box, and produces letters tied up with blue ribbon.]

ALGERNON: My letters! But, my own sweet Cecily, I have never written you any letters.

CECILY: You need hardly remind me of that, Ernest. I remember only too well that I was forced to write your letters for you. I wrote always three times a week, and sometimes oftener.

ALGERNON: Oh, do let me read them, Cecily?

CECILY: Oh, I couldn't possibly. They would make you far too conceited. [Replaces box.] The three you wrote me after I had broken off the engagement are so beautiful, and so badly spelled, that even now I can hardly read them without crying a little.

ALGERNON: But was our engagement ever broken off?

CECILY: Of course it was. On the 22nd of last March. You can see the entry if you like. [Shows diary.] 'To-day I broke off my engagement with Ernest. I feel it is better to do so. The weather still continues charming.'

ALGERNON: But why on earth did you break it off? What had I done? I had done
        nothing at all. Cecily, I am very much hurt indeed to hear you broke it off.
        Particularly when the weather was so charming.

CECILY: It would hardly have been a really serious engagement if it hadn't been
        broken off at least once. But I forgave you before the week was out.

ALGERNON: [Crossing to her, and kneeling.] What a perfect angel you are, Cecily.

CECILY: You dear romantic boy. [He kisses her, she puts her fingers through his
        hair.] I hope your hair curls naturally, does it?

ALGERNON: Yes, darling, with a little help from others.

CECILY: I am so glad.

ALGERNON: You'll never break off our engagement again, Cecily?

CECILY: I don't think I could break it off now that I have actually met you. [. . .]

[1895]

Joining the Conversation: Critical Thinking and Writing

1. According to Cecily, what are the elements of a romantic relationship? How has
    Cecily fulfilled all the criteria of a romantic relationship on her own?
2. Does Cecily reveal that a romantic relationship is a performance? Through this
    comedy, is Wilde encouraging us to conclude that all romance contains an
    element of performance?
3. Part of what make this scene funny is the completeness of Cecily's delusion: She
    maintains her deluded sense of romance even as she explains it to Algernon.
    How does Algernon react? Does he talk her out of her delusion? Wilde has obvi-
    ously created absurdly unrealistic characters. How does this rejection of realism
    make this a more enjoyable play?
4. How does the writing figure into this scene? How and why is Wilde mocking
    certain uses of writing? For example, what does Cecily plan to do with her
    diary? How does Cecily organize her letters?
5. Consider Frost's explanation that a poem is a "performance in words." How is
    Wilde using language as a performance? How does he juggle certain words for
    maximum effect? How do the words and ideas of loving "hopelessly," "charming"
    weather, and hair curling "with a little help from others" become comic?

Interacting with Essays:
Literature as Discovery

Literature is born out of our never-ending search for meaning—our search for the
"big ideas" that help us to think big thoughts. Importantly, this search is not one of
locating a single right answer put in place by an author. Rather, this search is an
act of interpretation, in which we help to create the meaning we seek. The big idea
of a literary work is not simply given to us; we must work to locate, define, and
question it. That activity is one of discovery: It allows us to determine what we
think the literary work is about. When we read a literary work, we hope to gain a
new idea or interesting insight: We want a reward for the intellectual effort of reading. That reward is not just for our new ideas, but also for our development of our
interpretive abilities.

The literary essay is a nonfiction essay that takes a personal, reflective, or narrative form. As we will explore in Chapter 11, essays can also take argumentative or expository forms, and the essays that you write analyzing literature fall into these categories. In all of these essay forms, the writer often wrestles with a "big idea" that is important enough to write about. In more literary forms of the essay, that exploration of ideas often features a process of personal discovery. The author is not arguing an idea that he or she has already decided but, rather, is often inviting us, the readers, to take a voyage and discover ideas along with the author.

Although the literary essay explores a factual issue, it often borrows the techniques and structures of fictional literature. For example, it might feel like a story; the essay might feature moments that are given a plot-like structure to emphasize their importance, interesting character-like persons that represent specific ideas, or concerns that become theme-like as they develop through realization and insight. The essay presents carefully *shaped* ideas, and that shaping aligns it with literature. Although it details factual ideas, the literary essay can embellish those ideas with imaginative elements because it is exploring ideas through the unique perspective of the author; that perspective can include creative interpretations, observations, reflections, dreams, hopes, fears, and delusions—all of the stuff that makes human thought an interesting and unique journey.

In the following essay, Anna Lisa Raya charts a process of discovery, specifically self-discovery, which focuses on language and race. Let's explore how her essay allows us, in turn, to discover new ideas about race and identity in America.

Anna Lisa Raya

Anna Lisa Raya, daughter of a second-generation Mexican American father and a Puerto Rican mother, grew up in Los Angeles, California, but went to Columbia University in New York. While an undergraduate at Columbia, she wrote and published this essay on identity.

It's Hard Enough Being Me

When I entered college, I *discovered* I was Latina. Until then, I had never questioned who I was or where I was from: My father is a second-generation Mexican-American, born and raised in Los Angeles, and my mother was born in Puerto Rico and raised in Compton, Calif. My home is El Sereno, a predominantly Mexican neighborhood in L.A. Every close friend I have back home is Mexican. So I was always just Mexican. Though sometimes I was just Puerto Rican–like when we would visit Mamo (my grandma) or hang out with my Aunt Titi.

Upon arriving in New York as a first-year student, 3000 miles from home, I not only experienced extreme culture shock, but for the first time I had to define myself according to the broad term "Latina." Although culture shock and identity crisis are common for the newly minted collegian who goes away to school, my experience as a newly minted Latina was, and still is, even more complicating. In El Sereno, I felt like I was part of a majority, whereas at the College I am a minority.

I've discovered that many Latinos like myself have undergone similar experiences. We face discrimination for being a minority in this country while also facing criticism for being "whitewashed" or "sellouts" in the countries of our heritage. But as an ethnic group in college, we are forced to define ourselves according to some vague, generalized Latino experience. This requires us to know our history, our language, our music, and our religion. I can't even be a content "Puerto Mexican" because I have to be a politically-and-socially-aware-Latina-with-a-chip-on-my-shoulder-because-of-how-repressed-I-am-in-this-country.

I am none of the above. I am the quintessential imperfect Latina. I can't dance salsa to save my life, I learned about Montezuma and the Aztecs in sixth grade, and I haven't prayed to the *Virgen de Guadalupe* in years.

5   Apparently I don't even look Latina. I can't count how many times people have just assumed that I'm white or asked me if I'm Asian. True, my friends back home call me *güera* ("whitey") because I have green eyes and pale skin, but that was as bad as it got. I never thought I would wish my skin were a darker shade or my hair a curlier texture, but since I've been in college, I have—many times.

Another thing: My Spanish is terrible. Every time I call home, I berate my mama for not teaching me Spanish when I was a child. In fact, not knowing how to speak the language of my home countries is the biggest problem that I have encountered, as have many Latinos. In Mexico there is a term, *pocha,* which is used by native Mexicans to ridicule Mexican-Americans. It expresses a deep-rooted antagonism and dislike for those of us who were raised on the other side of the border. Our failed attempts to speak pure, Mexican Spanish are largely responsible for the dislike. Other Latin American natives have this same attitude. No matter how well a Latino speaks Spanish, it can never be good enough.

Yet Latinos can't even speak Spanish in the U.S. without running the risk of being called "spic" or "wetback." That is precisely why my mother refused to teach me Spanish when I was a child. The fact that she spoke Spanish was constantly used against her: It prevented her from getting good jobs, and it would have placed me in bilingual education—a construct of the Los Angeles public school system that has proved to be more of a hindrance to intellectual development than a help.

To be fully Latina in college, however, I *must* know Spanish. I must satisfy the equation: Latina [equals] Spanish-speaking.

So I'm stuck in this black hole of an identity crisis, and college isn't making my life any easier, as I thought it would. In high school, I was being prepared for an adulthood in which I would be an individual, in which I wouldn't have to wear a Catholic school uniform anymore. But though I led an anonymous adolescence, I knew who I was. I knew I was different from white, black, or Asian people. I knew there was a language other than English that I could call my own if I only knew how to speak it better. I knew there were historical reasons why I was in this country, distinct reasons that make my existence here easier or more difficult than other people's existence. Ultimately, I was content.

10   Now I feel pushed into a corner, always defining, defending, and proving myself to classmates, professors, or employers. Trying to understand who and why I am, while understanding Plato or Homer, is a lot to ask of myself.

A month ago, I heard three Nuyorican (Puerto Ricans born and raised in New York) writers discuss how New York City has influenced their writing. One problem I have faced as a young writer is finding a voice that is true to my community. I was surprised and reassured to discover that as Latinos, these writers had faced similar pressures and conflicts as myself; some weren't even taught Spanish in childhood. I will never forget the advice that one of them gave me that evening: She said that I need to be true to myself. "Because people will always complain about what you are doing—you're a 'gringa' or a 'spic' no matter what," she explained. "So you might as well do things for yourself and not for them."

I don't know why it has taken 20 years to hear this advice, but I'm going to give it a try. *Soy yo* and no one else. *Punto*.[1]

[1994]

Joining the Conversation: Critical Thinking and Writing

1. Raya opens her essay by explaining how she discovers the different racial categories she might belong to. In her first paragraph, Raya says that, although her parents are American citizens, until she went to New York she "was always just Mexican" or "just Puerto Rican." Why do you suppose she thought this way? Then, when she goes to college in New York, she is a "Latina." What does this change in terminology represent?

2. In her second paragraph, Raya says that in New York she "had to" define herself as "Latina," and in her third paragraph, she says that many members of "minority" communities "are forced" to define themselves. In paragraph 10, she says, "Now I feel pushed into a corner, always defining, defending, and proving myself to classmates, professors, or employers. Trying to understand who and why I am, while understanding Plato or Homer, is a lot to ask. . . ." Is Raya saying that both the majority culture and the minority culture force her to define herself? Drawing on your own experience, give your views on whether it is a good thing or a bad thing (or some of each) to be forced to define oneself in terms of ethnicity.

3. Today, the words *Latino* and *Latina* are common, but until perhaps fifteen years ago, Spanish-speaking people from Mexico, Central America, and South America were called *Hispanics* or *Latin Americans*. Do you think these terms are useful, or do you think that the differences between, say, a poor black woman from Cuba and a rich white man from Argentina are so great that it makes very little sense to put them into the same category, whether the category is called *Latino, Hispanic,* or *Latin American?* Why, incidentally, do you think that *Latino/Latina* is now preferred to *Hispanic?*

4. In paragraph 7, Raya speaks of the Los Angeles bilingual educational program as "a construct of the Los Angeles public school system that has proved to be more of a hindrance to intellectual development than a help." If you have been in a bilingual educational program, evaluate the program. Did it chiefly help you or chiefly hinder you? Explain.

5. In her last two paragraphs, Raya explains that after an acquaintance told her to be true to herself, she concluded, "*Soy yo*" ("I'm me," or "I'm myself"). You may recall that in *Hamlet* Polonius says to his son Laertes, "This above all: to thine own self be true" (1.3.78). But what does it mean to be true to oneself? Presumably, one doesn't behave immorally, but beyond that, what does one do? For instance, if a friend suggested to Raya that she might enjoy (and intellectually profit from) taking a course in Latin American literature, in making a decision, what *self* would she be true to?

6. In your own life, you make many decisions each day. Are many of them based on being true to yourself? Again, putting aside questions concerning immorality, do you think you have a "self" that you are true to? If so, is this self, at least in part, based on ethnicity?

---

[1] *Soy yo . . . Punto* I'm me . . . Period. (Editors' note.)

Your Turn: Additional Poems, Stories, and Essays for Pleasurable Analysis

POEMS

JIMMY SANTIAGO BACA

Jimmy Santiago Baca, of Chicano and Apache descent, was born in 1952. When he was two years old, his parents divorced, and a grandparent brought him up until he was five years old, at which time he was placed in an orphanage in New Mexico. He ran away when he was eleven years old, lived on the streets, took drugs, and at the age of twenty was convicted of drug possession. In prison, he taught himself to read and write, and he began to compose poetry. A fellow inmate urged him to send some poems to Mother Jones *magazine, and the work was accepted. In 1979, Louisiana State University Press published a book of his poems,* Immigrants in Our Own Land. *Since then, he has published several other books.*

Green Chile

I prefer red chile over my eggs
and potatoes for breakfast.
Red chile *ristros°* decorate my door,
dry on my roof, and hang from eaves.
They lend open-air vegetable stands   5
historical grandeur, and gently swing
with an air of festive welcome.
I can hear them talking in the wind,
haggard, yellowing, crisp, rasping
tongues of old men, licking the breeze.   10

But grandmother loves green chile.
When I visit her,
she holds the green chile pepper
in her wrinkled hands.
Ah, voluptuous, masculine   15
an air of authority and youth simmers
from its swan-neck stem, tapering to a flowery
collar, fermenting resinous spice.
A well-dressed gentleman at the door
my grandmother takes sensuously in her hand,   20
rubbing its firm glossed sides,
caressing the oily rubbery serpent,
with mouth-watering fulfillment,
fondling its curves with gentle fingers.
Its bearing magnificent and taut   25
as flanks of a tiger in mid-leap,
she thrusts her blade into
and cuts it open, with lust

3 ***ristras*** strings.

on her hot mouth, sweating over the stove,
bandanna round her forehead,   30
mysterious passion on her face
as she serves me green chile con carne
between soft warm leaves of corn tortillas,
with beans and rice—her sacrifice
to her little prince.   35
I slurp from my plate
with last bit of tortilla, my mouth burns
and I hiss and drink a tall glass of cold water.

All over New Mexico, sunburned men and women
drive rickety trucks stuffed with gunny sacks   40
of green chile, from Belen, Veguita, Willard, Estancia,
San Antonio y Socorro, from fields
to roadside stands, you see them roasting green chile
in screen-sided homemade barrels, and for a dollar a bag,
we relive this old, beautiful ritual again and again.   45

[1989]

Joining the Conversation: Critical Thinking and Writing

1. *Sensory imagery* appeals to any of the five senses: touch, sight, smell, taste, and hearing. Reread "Green Chile," and annotate its sensory imagery, noting what senses are addressed. What words are used to trigger each sense? How and why does Baca appeal to the senses to capture the powerful appeal of the green chile?

2. In the second stanza, the poem uses sexual imagery to describe the grandmother's love of the chile. What does the grandmother do to the chile, which is compared to a "well-dressed gentleman"? Does Rios convey the sensuous nature of cooking and eating? What words do you find to be the most successful in conveying the sensual nature of food? Does Rios succeed in capturing the enjoyment of the chile?

3. The last stanza provides a sudden shift in setting, tone, and imagery. What ideas are addressed in this stanza? Why does Rios add this stanza? Do you like that it leaves the grandmother's kitchen behind? How does this stanza place eating green chile in a larger context? In your opinion, would the poem be more or less successful if it did not contain this last stanza?

4. Alberto Rio's Nani" and Jimmy Santiago Baca's "Green Chile" both describe eating food prepared by a grandmother. How would you compare the two poems? What is the relationship between the speaker and the grandmother that each poet is trying to capture? What is the relationship between food and family that each poet is trying to capture?

ALBERTO RIOS

The poems of Alberto Rios (1952–) capture his Mexican American heritage, often using magical realism to convey the experience of bridging two cultures. Rios teaches at Arizona State University and in 2013 was named the Inaugural Poet Laureate of Arizona. He has published several collections of poetry, three short-story collections, and a memoir. He has won numerous awards for his poetry, including six Pushcart Prizes and the Arizona Governor's Arts.

Nani*

Sitting at her table, she serves
the sopa de arroz° to me
instinctively, and I watch her,
the absolute *mamá,* and eat words
I might have had to say more   5
out of embarrassment. To speak,
now-foreign words I used to speak,
too, dribble down her mouth as she serves
me albondigas.° No more
than a third are easy to me.   10
By the stove she does something with words
and looks at me only with her
back. I am full. I tell her
I taste the mint, and watch her speak
smiles at the stove. All my words   15
make her smile. Nani never serves
herself, she only watches me
with her skin, her hair. I ask for more.

I watch the *mamá* warming more
tortillas for me. I watch her   20
fingers in the flame for me.
Near her mouth, I see a wrinkle speak
of a man whose body serves
the ants like she serves me, then more words
from more wrinkles about children, words   25
about this and that, flowing more
easily from these other mouths. Each serves
as a tremendous string around her,
holding her together. They speak
nani was this and that to me   30
and I wonder just how much of me
will die with her, what were the words
I could have been, was. Her insides speak
through a hundred wrinkles, now, more
than she can bear, steel around her,   35
shouting, then, What is this thing she serves?

She ask me if I want more.
I own no words to stop her.
Even before I speak, she serves.

[1982]

---

* **Nani** "grandmother."
2 **sopa de arroz** rice soup. 9 **albondigas** meatballs.

Joining the Conversation: Critical Thinking and Writing

1. The poem's speaker describes eating rice soup and meatballs served by his nani, or grandmother. This meal, however, seems to be more about language than food. He explains that he "eats words" (line 4). What does this mean? What does it mean that his nani's words are "now-foreign" (line 7)?
2. The poem's speaker offers the image that his nani's words are "a tremendous string around her, holding her together" (lines 28–29). How is his grandmother's identity connected to words? How does she use words? What does she do with words?
3. The poem's speaker connects the grandmother's words to his own identity, explaining that he wonders "what were the words I could have been, was" (lines 33–34). Does this realization give the poem an emotional resonance? For example, does this line convey a sense of sadness?
4. Examine the last stanza of the poem. Why does the speaker not stop his grandmother from serving more food? Write a response paper that explains the relationship between the speaker and his nani, using the poem's ending as a starting point.

WILLIAM CARLOS WILLIAMS

William Carlos Williams (1883–1963) was the son of an English traveling salesman and a Basque-Jewish woman. The couple met in Puerto Rico and settled in Rutherford, New Jersey, where Williams was born. He spent his life there, practicing as a pediatrician and writing poems in the moments between appointments.

This Is Just to Say

I have eaten
the plums
that were in
the icebox

and which   5
you were probably
saving
for breakfast

Forgive me
they were delicious   10
so sweet
and so cold

[1934]

Joining the Conversation: Critical Thinking and Writing

1. Williams's poem is famous for its simplicity. In your opinion, is this poem successful? How does this poem play with our expectations of poetry? Can a direct and straightforward statement be a poem? Or, do you expect a poem to be complex and difficult to understand? Try rewriting a stanza of the poem, using

your own words to convey the same images and ideas. Does your rewriting become longer and more complex than the original poem? Can stripping down a poem to its essential words be a difficult—and artistic—activity?

2. Why is the poem broken down into three stanzas? How does each stanza contain a different action or thought? Does each stanza add a new layer of meaning to the poem?

3. The last lines of the poem offer an excuse as to why the speaker has eaten the plums. Do these words help you to feel the attraction of the plums? Compare Williams's poem with Helen Chasin's "The Word *Plum*." How do both poets try to capture the appeal of the fruit? Which language appeals to you more: Williams's direct statement or Chasin's sensuous imagery? How would you explain each poet's strategy for, or approach to, describing a plum?

HELEN CHASIN

Born in 1938, Helen Chasin grew up in Brooklyn, New York, and attended Radcliffe College. In addition to teaching at Emerson College, she has served as a Bread Loaf Scholar in Poetry at Middlebury College and a Bunting Institute Fellow at Harvard University. Her poems are often praised for their use of warmth and playfulness to address serious aspects of social and personal change.

The Word Plum

The word *plum* is delicious

pout and push, luxury of
self-love, and savoring murmur
full in the mouth and falling
like fruit   5

taut skin
pierced, bitten, provoked into
juice, and tart flesh

question
and reply, lip and tongue   10
of pleasure.

[1968]

Joining the Conversation: Critical Thinking and Writing

1. Chasin's title and first line of the poem makes it clear that she is focusing on the word *plum* rather than on the plum itself. However, she also makes it clear that the word conveys the qualities of the fruit. What aspects of the fruit are captured in the word *plum*?

2. How is speaking the word *plum* like eating plum? How does Chasin make us think about the relationship between speaking and eating? For example, how does Chasin emphasize the mouth? What is "full in the mouth" (line 4)?

3. What are your favorite words in this poem? How does Chasin call attention to the power of words? As she investigates how the word *plum* conveys meaning, how does Chasin herself use evocative words? Look carefully at the words that

Chasin uses and how she organizes them. For example, note all of the verbs
that she uses to capture the action of speaking the word *plum*. Also, note the
sounds that are emphasized and repeated.

GARY SOTO

*Born in 1952, Gary Soto grew up in one of the barrios, or urban Mexican American
neighborhoods, of Fresno, California. His poetry often depicts the daily life of growing
up in this community. His parents and grandparents worked as farm laborers, and
Soto worked in the area's fields and factories. Inspired by the literature that he discovered in a library, including works by Hemingway and Steinbeck, Soto took creative writing classes at California State University, Fresno, and studied with the
famous poet Philip Levine. He earned a graduate degree in creative writing at the
University of California–Irvine. A prolific author, he has written eleven collections of
poetry for adults, three novels, a memoir, and numerous works for children and
young adults.*

Oranges

The first time I walked
With a girl, I was twelve,
Cold, and weighted down
With two oranges in my jacket.
December. Frost cracking   5
Beneath my steps, my breath
Before me, then gone,
As I walked toward
Her house, the one whose
Porch light burned yellow   10
Night and day, in any weather.
A dog barked at me, until
She came out pulling
At her gloves, face bright
With rouge. I smiled,   15
Touched her shoulder, and led
Her down the street, across
A used car lot and a line
Of newly planted trees,
Until we were breathing   20
Before a drugstore. We
Entered, the tiny bell
Bringing a saleslady
Down a narrow aisle of goods.
I turned to the candies   25
Tiered like bleachers,
And asked what she wanted—
Light in her eyes, a smile
Starting at the corners
Of her mouth. I fingered   30
A nickle in my pocket,
And when she lifted a chocolate

That cost a dime,
I didn't say anything.
I took the nickle from   35
My pocket, then an orange,
And set them quietly on
The counter. When I looked up,
The lady's eyes met mine,
And held them, knowing   40
Very well what it was all
About.

Outside,
A few cars hissing past,
Fog hanging like old   45
Coats between the trees.
I took my girl's hand
In mine for two blocks.
Then released it to let
Her unwrap the chocolate.   50
I peeled my orange
That was so bright against
The gray of December
That, from some distance,
Someone might have thought   55
I was making a fire in my hands.

                                                               [1983]

Joining the Conversation: Critical Thinking and Writing

1. What is the exchange that takes place with the shopkeeper? Is the exchange
   one of money or something more? Why is this exchange important?
2. How does Soto's word choice, or **diction**, capture the realities of the narrator's
   neighborhood? How would you characterize the style and level of the language:
   simple, ornate, complex, academic, or straightforward? Why is the style of Soto's
   language a good match for his subject matter?
3. Soto's last line describes the orange as "making a fire in my hands." Write a
   short interpretation of this image. How can an orange be a fire? Why does the
   narrator have a fire in his hands? Is this image positive or negative? Why does
   the poem end with this image?
4. Consider the young girl featured in the poem. How do we know that she enjoys
   this first neighborhood date? Why is her choice of the chocolate important?
   What does the chocolate represent?

SARAH N. CLEGHORN

*Sarah N. Cleghorn (1876–1959) was born in Manchester, Vermont. A Quaker, she
was active in pacifist, antivivisectionist, and women's suffrage movements. Among
her many books are* The True Ballad of Glorious Harriet Tubman *(1933) and an
autobiography,* Threescore *(1936).*

The Golf Links

The golf links lie so near the mill
    That almost every day
The laboring children can look out
    And see the men at play.

[1917]

Joining the Conversation: Critical Thinking and Writing

1. Check the meanings of *ironic, satiric,* and *sarcastic* in a dictionary, and decide which, if any, of these words applies well to Cleghorn's poem.
2. The poem was published in 1917, when child labor was common. (Children as young as ten years old worked as much as fifteen hours a day in mills. In 1916—a year before the poem was published—Congress had passed the Child Labor Act, but in 1918 the Supreme Court struck down the act, arguing that Congress did not have the right to control labor within a state.) Today, however, child labor in the United States is virtually nonexistent. Is there any point, then, in reading this poem? Set forth your response in a brief argument, perhaps of two paragraphs.

STEVIE SMITH

The British poet Florence Margaret "Stevie" Smith (1902–71) is known for using deceptively simple language to explore complex themes. Although her poems address topics such as death and religion, they are often light, witty, and playful, as seen in "Not Waving but Drowning." She wrote three novels and nine volumes of poetry, and she often published her poetry with accompanying doodles and drawings.

Not Waving but Drowning

Nobody heard him, the dead man,
But still he lay moaning:
I was much further out than you thought
And not waving but drowning.
Poor chap, he always loved larking   5
And now he's dead
It must have been too cold for him his heart gave way,
They said.

Oh, no no no, it was too cold always
(Still the dead one lay moaning)   10
I was much too far out all my life
And not waving but drowning.

[1957]

Joining the Conversation: Critical Thinking and Writing

1. What is the meaning of the title, "Not Waving but Drowning"? How does the title explain the poem's focus on "the dead man"? Did you find the poem's presentation of a dead man unexpected?

2. Who are the different speakers in the poem? Map the different speakers, stanza by stanza. How are these different speakers explaining the event of the drowning?
3. In line 9, the dead man explains, "I was much too far out all my life." What does this mean? How does this line connect a description of swimming to a more abstract description of how the man lived his life? Does this line help to explain his life and his death?

STORIES

AMBROSE BIERCE

Ambrose Bierce (1842–1914?) was born in Horse Creek, Ohio, but soon his family moved to Indiana, where at the age of nineteen he enlisted in the Union Army. In the next four years, he fought in several of the bloodiest battles of the Civil War, was wounded twice, and rose to the rank of lieutenant. After the war, he worked as a journalist in San Francisco, England, and again in San Francisco. In 1912, he went to Mexico to cover the Mexican Revolution, but he disappeared there, and it is assumed that he died in 1914.

Bierce's literary reputation rests chiefly on one story, reprinted here, but he wrote other stories of interest—some about the supernatural—as well as a witty, cynical book called The Devil's Dictionary. *Here is a sample definition: "Marriage. The state or condition of a community consisting of a master, a mistress, and two slaves, making in all, two."*

An Occurrence at Owl Creek Bridge

1

A man stood upon a railroad bridge in northern Alabama, looking down into the swift water twenty feet below. The man's hands were behind his back, the wrists bound with a cord. A rope closely encircled his neck. It was attached to a stout cross-timber above his head and the slack fell to the level of his knees. Some loose boards laid upon the sleepers[1] supporting the metals of the railway supplied a footing for him and his executioners—two private soldiers of the Federal army, directed by a sergeant who in civil life may have been a deputy sheriff. At a short remove upon the same temporary platform was an officer in the uniform of his rank, armed. He was a captain. A sentinel at each end of the bridge stood with his rifle in the position known as "support," that is to say, vertical in front of the left shoulder, the hammer resting on the forearm thrown straight across the chest—a formal and unnatural position, enforcing an erect carriage of the body. It did not appear to be the duty of these two men to know what was occurring at the center of the bridge; they merely blockaded the two ends of the foot planking that traversed it.

Beyond one of the sentinels nobody was in sight; the railroad ran straight away into a forest for a hundred yards, then, curving, was lost to view. Doubtless there was an outpost farther along. The other bank of the stream was open

---

[1] **sleepers** railroad crossties.

ground—a gentle acclivity topped with a stockade of vertical tree trunks, loop-holed for rifles, with a single embrasure through which protruded the muzzle of a brass cannon commanding the bridge. Midway of the slope between bridge and fort were the spectators—a single company of infantry in line, at "parade rest," the butts of the rifles on the ground, the barrels inclining slightly backward against the right shoulder, the hands crossed upon the stock. A lieutenant stood at the right of the line, the point of his sword upon the ground, his left hand resting upon his right. Excepting the group of four at the center of the bridge, not a man moved. The company faced the bridge, staring stonily, motionless. The sentinels, facing the banks of the stream, might have been statues to adorn the bridge. The captain stood with folded arms, silent, observing the work of his subordinates, but making no sign. Death is a dignitary who when he comes announced is to be received with formal manifestations of respect, even by those most familiar with him. In the code of military etiquette silence and fixity are forms of deference.

The man who was engaged in being hanged was apparently about thirty-five years of age. He was a civilian, if one might judge from his habit, which was that of a planter. His features were good—a straight nose, firm mouth, broad forehead, from which his long, dark hair was combed straight back, falling behind his ears to the collar of his well-fitting frock-coat. He wore a mustache and pointed beard, but no whiskers; his eyes were large and dark gray, and had a kindly expression which one would hardly have expected in one whose neck was in the hemp. Evidently this was no vulgar assassin. The liberal military code makes provision for hanging many kinds of persons, and gentlemen are not excluded.

The preparations being complete, the two private soldiers stepped aside and each drew away the plank upon which he had been standing. The sergeant turned to the captain, saluted and placed himself immediately behind that officer, who in turn moved apart one pace. These movements left the condemned man and the sergeant standing on the two ends of the same plank, which spanned three of the crossties of the bridge. The end upon which the civilian stood almost, but not quite, reached a fourth. This plank had been held in place by the weight of the captain; it was now held by that of the sergeant. At a signal from the former the latter would step aside, the plank would tilt and the condemned man go down between two ties. The arrangement commended itself to his judgment as simple and effective. His face had not been covered nor his eyes bandaged. He looked a moment at his "unsteadfast footing," then let his gaze wander to the swirling water of the stream racing madly beneath his feet. A piece of dancing driftwood caught his attention and his eyes followed it down the current. How slowly it appeared to move! What a sluggish stream!

5   He closed his eyes in order to fix his last thoughts upon his wife and children. The water, touched to gold by the early sun, the brooding mists under the banks at some distance down the stream, the fort, the soldiers, the piece of drift—all had distracted him. And now he became conscious of a new disturbance. Striking through the thought of his dear ones was a sound which he would neither ignore nor understand, a sharp, distinct, metallic percussion like the stroke of a black-smith's hammer upon the anvil; it had the same ringing quality. He wondered what it was, and whether immeasurably distant or near by—it seemed both. Its recurrence was regular, but as slow as the tolling of a death knell. He awaited each stroke with impatience and—he knew not why—apprehension. The intervals of silence grew progressively longer; the delays became maddening. With their greater infrequency the sounds increased in strength and sharpness. They hurt his ear like the thrust of a knife; he feared he would shriek. What he heard was the ticking of his watch.

He unclosed his eyes and saw again the water below him. "If I could free my hands," he thought, "I might throw off the noose and spring into the stream. By diving I could evade the bullets and, swimming vigorously, reach the bank, take to the woods and get away home. My home, thank God, is as yet outside their lines; my wife and little ones are still beyond the invader's farthest advance."

As these thoughts, which have here to be set down in words, were flashed into the doomed man's brain rather than evolved from it the captain nodded to the sergeant. The sergeant stepped aside.

2

Peyton Farquhar was a well-to-do planter, of an old and highly respected Alabama family. Being a slave owner and like other slave owners a politician he was naturally an original secessionist and ardently devoted to the Southern cause. Circumstances of an imperious nature, which it is unnecessary to relate here, had prevented him from taking service with the gallant army that had fought the disastrous campaigns ending with the fall of Corinth,[2] and he chafed under the inglorious restraint, longing for the release of his energies, the larger life of the soldier, the opportunity for distinction. That opportunity, he felt, would come, as it comes to all in war time. Meanwhile he did what he could. No service was too humble for him to perform in aid of the South, no adventure too perilous for him to undertake if consistent with the character of a civilian who was at heart a soldier, and who in good faith and without too much qualification assented to at least a part of the frankly villainous dictum that all is fair in love and war.

One evening while Farquhar and his wife were sitting on a rustic bench near the entrance to his grounds, a gray-clad soldier rode up to the gate and asked for a drink of water. Mrs. Farquhar was only too happy to serve him with her own white hands. While she was fetching the water her husband approached the dusty horseman and inquired eagerly for news from the front.

10   "The Yanks are repairing the railroads," said the man, "and are getting ready for another advance. They have reached the Owl Creek bridge, put it in order and built a stockade on the north bank. The commandant has issued an order, which is posted everywhere, declaring that any civilian caught interfering with the railroad, its bridges, tunnels or trains will be summarily hanged. I saw the order."

"How far is it to the Owl Creek bridge?" Farquhar asked.

"About thirty miles."

"Is there no force on this side the creek?"

"Only a picket post half a mile out, on the railroad, and a single sentinel at this end of the bridge."

15   "Suppose a man—a civilian and student of hanging—should elude the picket post and perhaps get the better of the sentinel," said Farquhar, smiling, "what could he accomplish?"

The soldier reflected. "I was there a month ago," he replied, "I observed that the flood of last winter had lodged a great quantity of driftwood against the wooden pier at this end of the bridge. It is now dry and would burn like tow."

The lady had now brought the water, which the soldier drank. He thanked her ceremoniously, bowed to her husband and rode away. An hour later, after nightfall, he repassed the plantation, going northward in the direction from which he had come. He was a Federal scout.

---

[2] **Corinth** Corinth, Mississippi, where Confederate forces were defeated, 3–4 October, 1862.

3

As Peyton Farquhar fell straight downward through the bridge he lost consciousness and was as one already dead. From this state he was awakened—ages later, it seemed to him—by the pain of a sharp pressure upon his throat, followed by a sense of suffocation. Keen, poignant agonies seemed to shoot from his neck downward through every fiber of his body and limbs. These pains appeared to flash along well-defined lines of ramification and to beat with an inconceivably rapid periodicity. They seemed like streams of pulsating fire heating him to an intolerable temperature. As to his head, he was conscious of nothing but a feeling of fulness—of congestion. These sensations were unaccompanied by thought. The intellectual part of his nature was already effaced; he had power only to feel, and feeling was torment. He was conscious of motion. Encompassed in a luminous cloud, of which he was now merely the fiery heart, without material substance, he swung through unthinkable arcs of oscillation, like a vast pendulum. Then all at once, with terrible suddenness, the light about him shot upward with the noise of a loud plash; a frightful roaring was in his ears, and all was cold and dark. The power of thought was restored; he knew that the rope had broken and he had fallen into the stream. There was no additional strangulation; the noose about his neck was already suffocating him and kept the water from his lungs. To die of hanging at the bottom of a river!—the idea seemed to him ludicrous. He opened his eyes in the darkness and saw above him a gleam of light, but how distant, how inaccessible! He was still sinking, for the light became fainter and fainter until it was a mere glimmer. Then it began to grow and brighten, and he knew that he was rising toward the surface—knew it with reluctance, for he was now very -comfortable. "To be hanged and drowned," he thought, "that is not so bad; but I do not wish to be shot. No; I will not be shot; that is not fair."

He was not conscious of an effort, but a sharp pain in his wrist apprised him that he was trying to free his hands. He gave the struggle his attention, as an idler might observe the feat of a juggler, without interest in the outcome. What splendid effort!—what magnificent, what superhuman strength! Ah, that was a fine endeavor! Bravo! The cord fell away; his arms parted and floated upward; the hands dimly seen on each side in the growing light. He watched them with new interest as first one and then the other pounced upon the noose at his neck. They tore it away and thrust it fiercely aside, its undulations resembling those of a water-snake. "Put it back, put it back!" He thought he shouted these words to his hands, for the undoing of the noose had been succeeded by the direst pang that he had yet experienced. His neck ached horribly; his brain was on fire; his heart, which had been fluttering faintly, gave a great leap, trying to force itself out at his mouth. His whole body was racked and wrenched with an insupportable anguish! But his disobedient hands gave no heed to the command. They beat the water vigorously with quick, downward strokes, forcing him to the surface. He felt his head emerge; his eyes were blinded by the sunlight; his chest expanded convulsively, and with a supreme and crowning agony his lungs engulfed a great draught of air, which instantly he expelled in a shriek!

20   He was now in full possession of his physical senses. They were, indeed, preternaturally keen and alert. Something in the awful disturbance of his organic system had so exalted and refined them that they made record of things never before perceived. He felt the ripples upon his face and heard their separate sounds as they struck. He looked at the forest on the bank of the stream, saw the

individual trees, the leaves and the veining of each leaf—saw the very insects upon them: the locusts, the brilliant-bodied flies, the gray spiders stretching their webs from twig to twig. He noted the prismatic colors in all the dewdrops upon a million blades of grass. The humming of the gnats that danced above the eddies of the stream, the beating of the dragon-flies' wings, the strokes of water-spider's legs, like oars which had lifted their boat—all these made audible music. A fish slid along beneath his eyes and he heard the rush of its body parting the water.

He had come to the surface facing down the stream; in a moment the visible world seemed to wheel slowly round, himself the pivotal point, and he saw the bridge, the fort, the soldiers upon the bridge, the captain, the sergeant, the two privates, his executioners. They were in silhouette against the blue sky. They shouted and gesticulated, pointing at him. The captain had drawn his pistol, but did not fire; the others were unarmed. Their movements were grotesque and horrible, their forms gigantic.

Suddenly he heard a sharp report and something struck the water smartly within a few inches of his head, spattering his face with spray. He heard a second report, and saw one of the sentinels with his rifle at his shoulder, a light cloud of blue smoke rising from the muzzle. The man in the water saw the eye of the man on the bridge gazing into his own through the sights of the rifle. He observed that it was a gray eye and remembered having read that gray eyes were keenest, and that all famous marksmen had them. Nevertheless, this one had missed.

A counter-swirl had caught Farquhar and turned him half round; he was again looking into the forest on the bank opposite the fort. The sound of a clear, high voice in a monotonous singsong now rang out behind him and came across the water with a distinctness that pierced and subdued all other sounds, even the beating of the ripples in his ears. Although no soldier, he had frequented camps enough to know the dread significance of that deliberate, drawling, aspirated chant; the lieutenant on shore was taking a part in the morning's work. How coldly and pitilessly—with what an even, calm intonation, presaging, and enforcing tranquility in the men—with what accurately measured intervals fell those cruel words:

"Attention, company! . . . Shoulder arms! . . . Ready! . . . Aim! . . . Fire!"

25   Farquhar dived—dived as deeply as he could. The water roared in his ears like the voice of Niagara, yet he heard the dulled thunder of the volley and, rising again toward the surface, met shining bits of metal, singularly flattened, oscillating slowly downward. Some of them touched him on the face and hands, then fell away, continuing their descent. One lodged between his collar and neck; it was uncomfortably warm and he snatched it out.

As he rose to the surface, gasping for breath, he saw that he had been a long time under water; he was perceptibly farther down stream—nearer to safety. The soldiers had almost finished reloading; the metal ramrods flashed all at once in the sunshine as they were drawn from the barrels, turned in the air, and thrust into their sockets. The two sentinels fired again, independently and ineffectually.

The hunted man saw all this over his shoulder; he was now swimming vigorously with the current. His brain was as energetic as his arms and legs; he thought with the rapidity of lightning.

"The officer," he reasoned, "will not make that martinet's error a second time. It is as easy to dodge a volley as a single shot. He has probably already given the command to fire at will. God help me, I cannot dodge them all!"

An appalling plash within two yards of him was followed by a loud, rushing sound, *diminuendo*,[3] which seemed to travel back through the air to the fort and died in an explosion which stirred the very river to its deeps! A rising sheet of water curved over him, fell down upon him, blinded him, strangled him! The cannon had taken a hand in the game. As he shook his head free from the commotion of the smitten water he heard the deflected shot humming through the air ahead, and in an instant it was cracking and smashing the branches in the forest beyond.

30   "They will not do that again," he thought; "the next time they will use a charge of grape.[4] I must keep my eye upon the gun; the smoke will apprise me—the report arrives too late; it lags behind the missile. That is a good gun."

Suddenly he felt himself whirled round and round—spinning like a top. The water, the banks, the forests, the now distant bridge, fort and men—all were commingled and blurred. Objects were represented by their colors only; circular horizontal streaks of color—that was all he saw. He had been caught in a vortex and was being whirled on with a velocity of advance and gyration that made him giddy and sick. In a few moments he was flung upon the gravel at the foot of the left bank of the stream—the southern bank—and behind a projecting point which concealed him from his enemies. The sudden arrest of his motion, the abrasion of one of his hands on the gravel, restored him, and he wept with delight. He dug his fingers into the sand, threw it over himself in handfuls and audibly blessed it. It looked like diamonds, rubies, emeralds; he could think of nothing beautiful which it did not resemble. The trees upon the bank were giant garden plants; he noted a definite order in their arrangement, inhaled the fragrance of their blooms. A strange, roseate light shone through the spaces among their trunks and the wind made in their branches the music of aeolian harps. He had no wish to perfect his escape—was content to remain in that enchanting spot until retaken.

A whiz and rattle of grapeshot among the branches high above his head roused him from his dream. The baffled cannoneer had fired him a random farewell. He sprang to his feet, rushed up the sloping bank, and plunged into the forest.

All that day he traveled, laying his course by the rounding sun. The forest seemed interminable; nowhere did he discover a break in it, not even a woodman's road. He had not known that he lived in so wild a region. There was something uncanny in the revelation.

By nightfall he was fatigued, footsore, famishing. The thought of his wife and children urged him on. At last he found a road which led him in what he knew to be the right direction. It was as wide and straight as a city street, yet it seemed untraveled. No fields bordered it, no dwelling anywhere. Not so much as the barking of a dog suggested human habitation. The black bodies of the trees formed a straight wall on both sides, terminating on the horizon in a point, like a diagram in a lesson in perspective. Overhead, as he looked up through this rift in the wood, shone great golden stars looking unfamiliar and grouped in strange constellations. He was sure they were arranged in some order which had a secret and malign significance. The wood on either side was full of singular noises, among which— once, twice, and again—he distinctly heard whispers in an unknown tongue.

35   His neck was in pain and lifting his hand to it he found it horribly swollen. He knew that it had a circle of black where the rope had bruised it. His eyes felt con-

---

[3] **diminuendo** decreasing in loudness.
[4] **grapeshot** a cluster of small iron balls fired from a cannon.

gested; he could no longer close them. His tongue was swollen with thirst; he relieved its fever by thrusting it forward from between his teeth into the cold air. How softly the turf had carpeted the untraveled avenue—he could no longer feel the roadway beneath his feet!

Doubtless, despite his suffering, he had fallen asleep while walking, for now he sees another scene—perhaps he has merely recovered from a delirium. He stands at the gate of his own home. All is as he left it, and all bright and beautiful in the morning sunshine. He must have traveled the entire night. As he pushes open the gate and passes up the wide white walk, he sees a flutter of female garments; his wife, looking fresh and cool and sweet, steps down from the veranda to meet him. At the bottom of the steps she stands waiting, with a smile of ineffable joy, an attitude of matchless grace and dignity. Ah, how beautiful she is! He springs forward with extended arms. As he is about to clasp her he feels a stunning blow upon the back of the neck; a blinding white light blazes all about him with a sound like the shock of a cannon—then all is darkness and silence!

Peyton Farquhar was dead; his body, with a broken neck, swung gently from side to side beneath the timbers of the Owl Creek bridge.

[1891]

Joining the Conversation: Critical Thinking and Writing

1. Characterize Peyton Farquhar. If you think Bierce makes him sympathetic, consider the *ways* in which Bierce does so.
2. Early in the story, the narrator says, "The liberal military code makes provision for hanging many kinds of people, and gentlemen are not excluded." How would you characterize the tone of this sentence? What, if anything, does the sentence contribute to the story?
3. Do you think that Bierce takes sides, suggesting that the North—or the South—is morally superior? What evidence can you offer to support your view?
4. Is the ending a complete surprise? Do some passages in the story suggest—at least on rereading—that perhaps Farquhar has not escaped? If so, point out a few.
5. What do you think of the title of the story? How does it compare with, for example, "Peyton Farquhar," or "Peyton Farquhar's Escape," or "The Hanging at Owl Creek Bridge"?

MARGARET ATWOOD

One of the most original and important voices in contemporary fiction, Margaret Atwood is a Canadian author who is best known for her novels, including The Handmaid's Tale *(1985),* The Robber Bride *(1993), and* Oryx and Crake *(2003). In 2000, her novel* The Blind Assassin *won the prestigious Booker Prize, England's annual prize for the best fiction in the English language. She also writes poetry, essays, and short fiction. Atwood explores difficult contemporary topics by weaving fantastical elements into stories that depict dystopian worlds, environmental crises, and suppressed peoples. Atwood was born in Ottawa, Canada, in 1939 and grew up in Ontario and Quebec. She received a BA from the University of Toronto and an MA from Radcliffe College.*

Happy Endings

John and Mary meet.
What happens next?
If you want a happy ending, try A.

A

John and Mary fall in love and get married. They both have worthwhile and remu-
nerative jobs which they find stimulating and challenging. They buy a charming
house. Real estate values go up. Eventually, when they can afford live-in help, they
have two children, to whom they are devoted. The children turn out well. John
and Mary have a stimulating and challenging sex life and worthwhile friends. They
go on fun vacations together. They retire. They both have hobbies which they find
stimulating and challenging. Eventually they die. This is the end of the story.

B

Mary falls in love with John but John doesn't fall in love with Mary. He merely uses
her body for selfish pleasure and ego gratification of a tepid kind. He comes to her
apartment twice a week and she cooks him dinner, you'll notice that he doesn't
even consider her worth the price of a dinner out, and after he's eaten the dinner
he fucks her and after that he falls asleep, while she does the dishes so he won't
think she's untidy, having all those dirty dishes lying around, and puts on fresh
lipstick so she'll look good when he wakes up, but when he wakes up he doesn't
even notice, he puts on his socks and his shorts and his pants and his shirt and his
tie and his shoes, the reverse order from the one in which he took them off. He
doesn't take off Mary's clothes, she takes them off herself, she acts as if she's dying
for it every time, not because she likes sex exactly, she doesn't, but she wants John
to think she does because if they do it often enough surely he'll get used to her,
he'll come to depend on her and they will get married, but John goes out the door
with hardly so much as a good-night and three days later he turns up at six o'clock
and they do the whole thing over again.

Mary gets run-down. Crying is bad for your face, everyone knows that and so
does Mary but she can't stop. People at work notice. Her friends tell her John is a
rat, a pig, a dog, he isn't good enough for her, but she can't believe it. Inside John,
she thinks, is another John, who is much nicer. This other John will emerge like a
butterfly from a cocoon, a Jack from a box, a pit from a prune, if the first John is
only squeezed enough.

One evening John complains about the food. He has never complained about
the food before. Mary is hurt.

5   Her friends tell her they've seen him in a restaurant with another woman,
whose name is Madge. It's not even Madge that finally gets to Mary: it's the restaurant. John has never taken Mary to a restaurant. Mary collects all the sleeping pills
and aspirins she can find, and takes them and a half a bottle of sherry. You can see
what kind of a woman she is by the fact that it's not even whiskey. She leaves a
note for John. She hopes he'll discover her and get her to the hospital in time and
repent and then they can get married, but this fails to happen and she dies.

John marries Madge and everything continues as in A.

C

John, who is an older man, falls in love with Mary, and Mary, who is only twenty-
two, feels sorry for him because he's worried about his hair falling out. She sleeps

with him even though she's not in love with him. She met him at work. She's in love with someone called James, who is twenty-two also and not yet ready to settle down.

John on the contrary settled down long ago: this is what is bothering him. John has a steady, respectable job and is getting ahead in his field, but Mary isn't impressed by him, she's impressed by James, who has a motorcycle and a fabulous record collection. But James is often away on his motorcycle, being free. Freedom isn't the same for girls, so in the meantime Mary spends Thursday evenings with John. Thursdays are the only days John can get away.

John is married to a woman called Madge and they have two children, a charming house which they bought just before the real estate values went up, and hobbies which they find stimulating and challenging, when they have the time. John tells Mary how important she is to him, but of course he can't leave his wife because a commitment is a commitment. He goes on about this more than is necessary and Mary finds it boring, but older men can keep it up longer so on the whole she has a fairly good time.

10   One day James breezes in on his motorcycle with some top-grade California hybrid and James and Mary get higher than you'd believe possible and they climb into bed. Everything becomes very underwater, but along comes John, who has a key to Mary's apartment. He finds them stoned and entwined. He's hardly in any position to be jealous, considering Madge, but nevertheless he's overcome with despair. Finally he's middle-aged, in two years he'll be bald as an egg and he can't stand it. He purchases a handgun, saying he needs it for target practice—this is the thin part of the plot, but it can be dealt with later—and shoots the two of them and himself.

Madge, after a suitable period of mourning, marries an understanding man called Fred and everything continues as in A, but under different names.

D

Fred and Madge have no problems. They get along exceptionally well and are good at working out any little difficulties that may arise. But their charming house is by the seashore and one day a giant tidal wave approaches. Real estate values go down. The rest of the story is about what caused the tidal wave and how they escape from it. They do, though thousands drown, but Fred and Madge are virtuous and lucky. Finally on high ground they clasp each other, wet and dripping and grateful, and continue as in A.

E

Yes, but Fred has a bad heart. The rest of the story is about how kind and understanding they both are until Fred dies. Then Madge devotes herself to charity work until the end of A. If you like, it can be "Madge," "cancer," "guilty and confused," and "bird watching."

F

If you think this is all too bourgeois, make John a revolutionary and Mary a counterespionage agent and see how far that gets you. Remember, this is Canada. You'll still end up with A, though in between you may get a lustful brawling saga of passionate involvement, a chronicle of our times, sort of.

* * *

15   You'll have to face it, the endings are the same however you slice it. Don't be deluded by any other endings, they're all fake, either deliberately fake, with

malicious intent to deceive, or just motivated by excessive optimism if not by downright sentimentality.

The only authentic ending is the one provided here:
John and Mary die. John and Mary die. John and Mary die.

* * *

So much for endings. Beginnings are always more fun. True connoisseurs, however, are known to favor the stretch in between, since it's the hardest to do anything with.

That's about all that can be said for plots, which anyway are just one thing after another, a what and a what and a what.

20   Now try How and Why.

[1983]

Joining the Conversation: Critical Thinking and Writing

1. "Happy Endings" is an example of metafiction: fiction that self-consciously comments on fiction, calling attention to its artificial and constructed status. How does "Happy Endings" call attention to storytelling conventions? For example, as the title emphasizes, readers want a story to have a happy ending. How does Atwood satirize that desire? What other expectations do we have for a plot? How does Atwood call attention to those expectations?
2. "Happy Endings" provides serious commentary on human relationships, but it is also very funny. Highlight the lines that you found humorous. Why are these lines funny? How do Atwood's language, character, and plot twists bring humor the story?
3. Variations "B" and "C" are quite dark. Is Atwood trying to convey a message about gender relationships and sexuality? Why does Atwood present plots that include unhappiness, mistreatment, getting "run-down," and being too "settled down"? Why do these stories end with violence? Continue this list of inquiry questions about these two sections, and use those questions to organize your note taking.
4. "Happy Endings" concludes what the statement, "That's about all that can be said for plots, which anyway are just one thing after another, a what and a what and a what. Now try How and Why." What does Atwood mean by "a what and a what and a what" and "How and Why"? How do these final lines address the purpose of storytelling?
5. Write a new variation, "G," for "Happy Endings." What would your variation emphasize? Can your variation satirize a certain genre or type of storytelling? Can your variation present a serious theme in a comic fashion?

ESSAY

GEORGE SAUNDERS

Born in 1958 in Amarillo, Texas, George Saunders worked as a geophysicist in the oil fields of Sumatra, Indonesia, and as a doorman, a roofer, and a "knuckle-puller" in a slaughterhouse before becoming a writer. He earned an MFA degree in creative writing from Syracuse University, New York, and started publishing his short stories while working as a writer for pharmaceutical and engineering companies. He now teaches in the Syracuse MFA program. His writing is widely praised for its use of unexpected perspectives to critique American culture's empha-sis on work, wealth, consumption, and the media. His short stories have earned him numerous accolades, including being named as one of the best writers under the age of forty by The New Yorker *magazine and one of the top one hundred most creative people in entertainment by* Entertainment Weekly *magazine. He was awarded a MacArthur "genius grant" Fellowship in 2006. He gave this convocation speech at Syracuse University in 2013.*

Commencement Speech on Kindness

Down through the ages, a traditional form has evolved for this type of speech, which is: Some old fart, his best years behind him, who, over the course of his life, has made a series of dreadful mistakes (*that would be me*), gives heartfelt advice to a group of shining, energetic young people, with all of their best years ahead of them (*that would be you*).

And I intend to respect that tradition.

Now, one useful thing you can do with an old person, in addition to borrow-ing money from them, or asking them to do one of their old-time "dances," so you can watch, while laughing, is ask: "Looking back, what do you regret?" And they'll tell you. Sometimes, as you know, they'll tell you even if you haven't asked. Some-times, even when you've specifically requested they *not* tell you, they'll tell you.

So: What do I regret? Being poor from time to time? Not really. Working terrible jobs, like "knuckle-puller in a slaughterhouse?" (And don't even ASK what that en-tails.) No. I don't regret that. Skinny-dipping in a river in Sumatra, a little buzzed, and looking up and seeing like 300 monkeys sitting on a pipeline, pooping down into the river, the river in which I was swimming, with my mouth open, naked? And getting deathly ill afterwards, and staying sick for the next seven months? Not so much. Do I regret the occasional humiliation? Like once, playing hockey in front of a big crowd, including this girl I really liked, I somehow managed, while falling and emitting this weird whooping noise, to score on my own goalie, while also sending my stick flying into the crowd, nearly hitting that girl? No. I don't even regret that.

5   But here's something I do regret:

In seventh grade, this new kid joined our class. In the interest of confidential-ity, her Convocation Speech name will be "ELLEN." ELLEN was small, shy. She wore these blue cat's-eye glasses that, at the time, only old ladies wore. When nervous, which was pretty much always, she had a habit of taking a strand of hair into her mouth and chewing on it.

So she came to our school and our neighborhood, and was mostly ignored, occasionally teased ("Your hair taste good?"—that sort of thing). I could see this hurt her. I still remember the way she'd look after such an insult: eyes cast down, a little gut-kicked, as if, having just been reminded of her place in things, she was trying, as much as possible, to disappear. After awhile she'd drift away, hair-strand still in her mouth. At home, I imagined, after school, her mother would say, you know: "How was your day, sweetie?" and she'd say, "Oh, fine." And her mother would say, "Making any friends?" and she'd go, "Sure, lots."

Sometimes I'd see her hanging around alone in her front yard, as if afraid to leave it.

And then—they moved. That was it. No tragedy, no big final hazing.

10 One day she was there, next day she wasn't.

End of story.

Now, why do I regret *that*? Why, forty-two years later, am I still thinking about it? Relative to most of the other kids, I was actually pretty *nice* to her. I never said an unkind word to her. In fact, I sometimes even (mildly) defended her.

But still. It bothers me.

So here's something I know to be true, although it's a little corny, and I don't quite know what to do with it:

15 What I regret most in my life are *failures* of kindness.

Those moments when another human being was there, in front of me, suffering, and I responded . . . sensibly. Reservedly. Mildly.

Or, to look at it from the other end of the telescope: Who, in *your* life, do you remember most fondly, with the most undeniable feelings of warmth?

Those who were kindest to you, I bet.

It's a little facile, maybe, and certainly hard to implement, but I'd say, as a goal in life, you could do worse than: *Try to be kinder*.

20 Now, the million-dollar question: What's our problem? Why aren't we kinder?

Here's what I think:

Each of us is born with a series of built-in confusions that are probably somehow Darwinian. These are: (1) We're central to the universe (that is, our personal story is the main and most interesting story, the only story, really); (2) we're separate from the universe (there's US and then, out there, all that other junk—dogs and swing-sets, and the State of Nebraska and low-hanging clouds and, you know, other people), and (3) we're permanent (death is real, o.k., sure—for you, but not for me).

Now, we don't *really* believe these things—intellectually we know better-but we believe them viscerally, and live by them, and they cause us to prioritize our own needs over the needs of others, even though what we really want, in our hearts, is to be less selfish, more aware of what's actually happening in the present moment, more open, and more loving.

So, the second million-dollar question: How might we DO this? How might we become more loving, more open, less selfish, more present, less delusional, etc., etc?

25 Well, yes, good question.

Unfortunately, I only have three minutes left.

So let me just say this. There *are* ways. You already know that because, in your life, there have been High Kindness periods and Low Kindness periods, and you know what inclined you toward the former and away from the latter. Education is good; immersing ourselves in a work of art: good; prayer is good; meditation's good; a frank talk with a dear friend; establishing ourselves in some kind of spiritual tradition—recognizing that there have been countless really smart people before us who have asked these same questions and left behind answers for us.

Because kindness, it turns out, is *hard*—it starts out all rainbows and puppy dogs, and expands to include . . . well, *everything*.

One thing in our favor: Some of this "becoming kinder" happens naturally, with age. It might be a simple matter of attrition: As we get older, we come to see how useless it is to be selfish—how illogical, really. We come to love other people and are thereby counter-instructed in our own centrality. We get our butts kicked by real life, and people come to our defense, and help us, and we learn that we're not separate, and don't want to be. We see people near and dear to us dropping away, and are gradually convinced that maybe we too will drop away (someday, a long time from now). Most people, as they age, become less selfish and more loving. I think this is true. The great Syracuse poet, Hayden Carruth, said, in a poem written near the end of his life, that he was "mostly Love, now."

30   And so, a prediction, and my heartfelt wish for you: As you get older, your self will diminish and you will grow in love. YOU will gradually be replaced by LOVE. If you have kids, that will be a huge moment in your process of self-diminishment. You really won't care what happens to YOU, as long as they benefit. That's one reason your parents are so proud and happy today. One of their fondest dreams has come true: You have accomplished something difficult and tangible that has enlarged you as a person and will make your life better, from here on in, forever.

Congratulations, by the way.

When young, we're anxious—understandably—to find out if we've got what it takes. Can we succeed? Can we build a viable life for ourselves? But you—in particular you, of this generation-may have noticed a certain cyclical quality to ambition. You do well in high-school, in hopes of getting into a good college, so you can do well in the good college, in the hopes of getting a good job, so you can do well in the good job so you can. . . .

And this is actually O.K. If we're going to become kinder, that process has to include taking ourselves seriously—as doers, as accomplishers, as dreamers. We *have* to do that, to be our best selves.

Still, accomplishment is unreliable. "Succeeding," whatever that might mean to you, is hard, and the need to do so constantly renews itself (success is like a mountain that keeps growing ahead of you as you hike it), and there's the very real danger that "succeeding" will take up your whole life, while the big questions go untended.

35   So, quick, end-of-speech advice: Since, according to me, your life is going to be a gradual process of becoming kinder and more loving: Hurry up. Speed it along. Start right now. There's a confusion in each of us, a sickness, really: *selfishness*. But there's also a cure. So be a good and proactive and even somewhat desperate patient on your own behalf-seek out the most efficacious anti-selfishness medicines, energetically, for the rest of your life.

Do all the other things, the ambitious things—travel, get rich, get famous, innovate, lead, fall in love, make and lose fortunes, swim naked in wild jungle rivers (after first having it tested for monkey poop)—but as you do, to the extent that you can, *err in the direction of kindness*. Do those things that incline you toward the big questions, and avoid the things that would reduce you and make you trivial. That luminous part of you that exists beyond personality—your soul, if you will—is as bright and shining as any that has ever been. Bright as Shakespeare's, bright as Gandhi's, bright as Mother Teresa's. Clear away everything that keeps you separate from this secret luminous place. Believe it exists, come to know it better, nurture it, share its fruits tirelessly.

And someday, in 80 years, when you're 100, and I'm 134, and we're both so kind and loving we're nearly unbearable, drop me a line, let me know how your life has been. I hope you will say: It has been so wonderful.

Congratulations, Class of 2013.

I wish you great happiness, all the luck in the world, and a beautiful summer.

Joining the Conversation: Critical Thinking and Writing

1. Saunders's speech examines the theme of regret. What are the events in his life that he should regret but doesn't? What is his biggest regret? Explain why his memories of Ellen have become a regret that he is still thinking about "forty-two years later."

2. Saunders's speech emphasizes kindness. Using Saunders's speech, define kindness. Continuing to work with this speech, provide examples of the type of kindness that Saunders wants us to practice. If you had to go out and engage in a specific act of kindness right now, what would it be?

3. As part of explaining why humans are not kinder, Saunders explains three "built in confusions" that shape us. Examine each of these confusions in turn. Do you agree that they define our approach to the world? Can you see these confusions operating in yourself or in those around you?

4. Reread the end of Saunders's speech, in which he offers his advice on how to replace the self with love and kindness. Now, put the speech aside and attempt to summarize its central ideas in your own words. What are the most important ideas that you would like to take away from this speech?

CHAPTER 6

Close Reading: Paraphrase, Summary, and Explication

What Is Literature?

Perhaps the first thing to say is that it is impossible to define *literature* in a way that will satisfy everyone. And perhaps the second thing to say is that, in the last twenty years or so, some serious thinkers have argued that it is impossible to set off certain verbal works from all others and, on some basis or other, to designate them as literature. For one thing, it is argued, a work is just marks on paper or sounds in the air. The audience (reader or listener) turns these marks or sounds into something with meaning, and different audiences will construct different meanings out of what they read or hear. There are *texts* (birthday cards, sermons, political speeches, magazines, novels that sell by the millions and novels that don't sell at all, poems, popular songs, editorials, and so forth), but there is nothing that should be given the special title of "literature."

Although there is something to be said for the idea that *literature* is just an honorific word and not a collection of work embodying eternal truths and eternal beauty, let's make the opposite assumption, at least for a start. Let's assume that certain verbal works are of a distinct sort—whether because the author shapes them or because a reader perceives them a certain way—and that we can call these works literature. But what are these works like?

Literature and Form

We all know why we value a newspaper or a textbook or an atlas, but why do we value a verbal work that doesn't give us the latest news or important information about business cycles or the names of the capitals of nations? About one thousand years ago, a Japanese woman, Shikibu Murasaki, or Lady Murasaki (978?–1026), offered an answer in *The Tale of Genji,* a book often called the world's first novel. During a discussion about reading fiction, one of the characters gives an opinion as to why a writer tells a story:

> Again and again writers find something in their experience, or see something in the life around them, that seems so important they cannot bear to let it pass into oblivion. There must never come a time, the writer feels, when people do not know about this.

Literature is about human experiences, but the experiences in literature are not simply the shapeless experiences—the chaotic passing scene—captured by a mindless, unselective video camera. Poets, dramatists, and storytellers find or impose a shape on scenes (for instance, the history of two lovers), giving readers things to value—written or spoken accounts that are memorable not only for their content but also for their *form*—the shape of the speeches, of the scenes, of the plots. (Later, we will see that form and content are inseparable, but for now, for our purposes, we can talk about them separately.)

Because this discussion of literature is brief, we will illustrate the point by looking at one of the briefest literary forms, the proverb. Consider this statement:

> A rolling stone gathers no moss.

Now let's compare it with a paraphrase (a restatement, a translation into other words):

> If a stone is always moving around, vegetation won't have a chance to grow on it.

What makes the original version more powerful, more memorable? Surely, much of the answer is that the original is more concrete and its form is more shapely. At the risk of being heavy-handed, we can analyze the shapeliness thus: *Stone* and *moss* (the two nouns in the sentence) each contain one syllable; *rolling* and *gathers* (the two words of motion) each contain two syllables, with the accent on the first syllable. Notice, too, the nice contrast between stone (hard) and moss (soft).

The reader probably *feels* this shapeliness unconsciously rather than perceives it consciously. That is, these connections become apparent when one starts to analyze a literary work, but the literary work can have its effect on a reader even before the reader analyzes the work. As T. S. Eliot said in his essay on Dante (1929), "Genuine poetry can communicate before it is understood." Indeed, our *first* reading of a work, when, so to speak, we are all eyes and ears (and the mind is highly receptive rather than sifting for evidence), is sometimes the most important reading. Experience proves that we can feel the effects of a work without yet understanding *how* the effects are achieved.

Most readers will probably agree that

- the words in the proverb are paired interestingly and meaningfully;
- the sentence is not simply information but is also (to quote one of Robert Frost's definitions of literature) "a performance in words";
- what the sentence *is*, we might say, is no less significant than what the sentence *says*;
- the sentence as a whole forms a memorable picture, a small but complete world, hard and soft, inorganic and organic, inert and moving;
- the idea set forth is simple—partly because it is highly focused and therefore leaves out a lot—but it is also complex;

- by virtue of the contrasts, and, again, even by the pairing of monosyllabic nouns and of disyllabic words of motion, it is unified into a pleasing whole.

For all of its specificity and its compactness—the proverb contains only six words—it expands our minds.

A Brief Exercise: Take a minute to think about some other proverb, for instance, "Look before you leap," "Finders keepers," "Haste makes waste," or "Absence makes the heart grow fonder." Paraphrase it, and then ask yourself why the original is more interesting and more memorable than your paraphrase.

Form and Meaning

Let's turn now to a work that is not much longer than a proverb—a very short poem by Robert Frost (1874–1963).

ROBERT FROST

For a biographical note, see page 246.

The Span of Life

The old dog barks backward without getting up.
I can remember when he was a pup.

[1936]

What makes this short statement a poem rather than a set of sentences? When we examine the lines for their literary elements, we notice several things:

- The poem is set off on the page by its title (somewhat as a picture is set off by a frame or a sculpture is set off by a pedestal) and the white space around it; it appears, so to speak, in a spotlight.
- The rhyme ("up/pup") is a device that distinguishes verse from ordinary prose.
- There is a contrast between the first words ("The old dog") and the last word ("pup").
- The two lines strike a balance: The first line describes the dog as it is now, old, and (after a reflective pause that the author forces on the reader by providing a period) the second line describes the speaker's memory of the young dog, leaving us with an implication about our own lives. Thus, the first line offers an observation, and the second line offers a meditation.
- The use of language is skillful, and not only in finding a rhyme. For instance, in "old dog," the speaker must pause a moment between the two words so that each *d* is sounded separately, and the *k* sounds in *bark* and *backward* make the first line (about an old dog) somewhat awkward and creaky, compared to the more speakable—let's say more jingling—second line (about a puppy). Moreover, in the first line, after the opening *The*, the next four syllables are all stressed fairly heavily ("old dog barks back"), and there are stresses on the second syllable of *without*, on the first syllable of *getting*, and on *up*, for a total of seven stresses in ten syllables—very effortful!—whereas, in the second line, there are at most four stresses: *I, mem* (in *remember*), *he*, and *pup* (*I* probably does not get much emphasis, so there are really only three significant stresses in the second line). Readers may differ about exactly

how much stress to put on a given syllable, but surely all readers will agree that the first line is heavier and requires more effort to say than the second, which is sprightlier. Most readers will agree that, in the first line, they may stress fairly heavily seven or eight syllables, whereas, in the second line, they may stress only three or four syllables:

The óld dóg bárks báckward withoút gétting úp.
Í can remémber when hé was a púp.

We can say, therefore, that the form (a relatively effortful, hard-to-speak line, followed by a bouncy line) shapes and is part of the content (a description of a dog that no longer has the energy or the strength to leap up, followed by a memory of the dog as a puppy).

Thinking further about Frost's poem, we notice something else about the form. The first line is about a dog, but the second line is about a dog *and* a human being ("*I* can remember"). The speaker must be getting on, too. And, although nothing is said about the dog as a *symbol* of human life, surely the reader, prompted by the title of the poem, makes a connection between the life span of a dog and that of a human being. Part of what makes the poem effective is that this point is *not* stated explicitly, not belabored. Readers have the pleasure of making the connection for themselves—under Frost's careful guidance.

Everyone knows that puppies are frisky and that old dogs are not—although perhaps not until we encountered this poem did we think twice about the fact that "the old dog barks backward without getting up." Or let's put it this way:

• Many people may have noticed this behavior, but
• perhaps only Frost thought (to use Lady Murasaki's words), "There must never come a time . . . when people do not know about this." And,
• fortunately for all of us, Frost had the ability to put his perception into memorable words.

Part of what makes this poem especially memorable is the *relationship* between the two lines. Neither line in itself is very special, but, because of the counterpoint, the whole is more than the sum of the parts. Skill in handling language, obviously, is indispensable if the writer is to produce literature. A person may know a great deal about dogs and may be a great lover of dogs, but knowledge and love are not enough equipment to write even a two-line poem about a dog (or the span of life, or both). Poems, like other kinds of literature, are produced by people who know how to delight us with verbal performances.

We can easily see that Robert Frost's "The Span of Life" is a work of literature—a work that uses language in a special way—if we contrast it with another short work in rhyme:

Thirty days hath September,
April, June, and November;
All the rest have thirty-one
Excepting February alone,
Which has twenty-eight in fine,
Till leap year gives it twenty-nine.

This information is important, but it is only information. The lines rhyme, giving the work some form, but there is nothing very interesting about it. (Perhaps you will want to take issue with this opinion.) The poem is true and therefore useful, but it is not of compelling interest, probably because it only *tells* us facts rather than *shows* or *presents* human experience. We all remember the lines, but they offer neither the pleasure of an insight nor the pleasure of an interesting tune. "Thirty days" has nothing of what the poet Thomas Gray said characterizes litera- ture: "Thoughts that breathe, and words that burn."

Close Reading: Reading in Slow Motion

Throughout this book, we focus on the skills required by a careful study of literary language. **Close reading** is perhaps the most familiar name for this technique of heightened responsiveness to the words on the page. But another, employed by the literary critics Reuben A. Brower and Richard Poirier, may be even better. They refer to "reading in slow motion." Brower, for example, speaks of "slowing down the process of reading to observe what is happening, in order to attend very closely to the words, their uses, and their meanings." This sort of reading, he explains, involves looking and listening with special alertness, slowly, without rushing or feeling impatient if a work puzzles us at first encounter.[1]

As Brower and Poirier point out, sometimes we are so intrigued or moved by a writer's technique and way with words that we are led to slow down our reading, lingering over verbal details and vivid images—"a watersmooth-silver/stallion" in Cummings's poem about Buffalo Bill (page 324), or "Babette danced out to where the fig-trees were," in Chopin's "Ripe Figs" (page 25). Or, we find that we want to return to a poem, or to a key section of a story or a scene in a play, to articulate— "slow motion" style—why it has affected us as powerfully as it has.

Close, or slow-motion, reading can help you to understand and enjoy a work that at first seems strange or obscure. When we examine a piece of literature with care and intensity, we are not taking it apart in a destructive way but, instead, are seeking to satisfy our curiosity about how the writer organized it. And, almost always, our increased *understanding* of the work results in increased *enjoyment*. Our understanding of a poem is almost always made better by close reading. That is, our ideas become deeper, more interesting, and more rewarding.

This point is clarified when we recall what it's like to watch a scene from a movie in slow motion, or a TV replay in slow motion of a touchdown run in a football game. In slow-motion film, we perceive details that we might otherwise have missed—the subtle changes in expression on an actress's face, for example, or the interplay of gestures among performers at a climactic moment in the action. Similarly, seeing a touchdown multiple times in slow motion, and perhaps from a half-dozen camera angles, reveals to us how the play developed, who made the crucial blocks, where the defense failed. The touchdown was exciting when it took place, and it remains exciting—and frequently it becomes more so—when we slow it down in order to study and talk about it.

This chapter and the next explore how we move from close reading to analy- sis. As we slow down our reading of a literary work, we are able to understand it more fully. We can demonstrate this understanding by being able to **paraphrase** or **summarize** its meaning. A paraphrase is a direct restatement of a specific idea in a literary text, whereas a summary is a more general overview of a literary text's

---

[1]The quotation is taken from Brower's introduction to *In Defense of Reading: A Reader's Approach to Literary Criticism*, ed. Reuben A. Brower and Richard Poirier (1962). See also Brower, *The Fields of Light: An Experiment in Critical Reading (1951);* and Poirier, *Poetry and Pragmatism* (1992).

main ideas. Both a paraphrase and a summary emphasize the correct understanding of the literary work developed though close reading.

Explication and analysis take that understanding of the text and use it as the foundation for arguments about the text's meaning. Explication and analysis emphasize the ideas, opinions, and interpretations generated by close reading. Both approaches are based on the principle that responding well to literature means

- acquiring the ability to read it closely;
- practicing this skill to become better and better at it;
- explaining and demonstrating in critical essays what we have learned.

However, the two terms, while related to one another, differ in their emphasis. An **explication** moves from beginning to end of an entire work (if it is fairly short) or of a section of a work; it is sustained, meticulous, thorough, and systematic. An **analysis** builds upon the habits of attention that we have gained from explicating texts and passages of texts, creating a focused argument about selected aspects of the text. Because an explication works through a text line by line, it is a good way to start working on the transformation of close reading into interpretation and argument.

Let's turn to explication first and learn what we can discover about literature through it. As you'll see, one of the things we quickly realize is that close reading of literary works makes us not only better readers but also better writers, attuned more sharply and sensitively to the organization of the language in our own prose.

Exploring a Poem and Its Meaning

Selecting a short poem for close reading will allow us to generate a paraphrase, summary, and explication of it. The following short poem is by Langston Hughes (1902–67), an African American writer who is well known for the central role that he played in the Harlem Renaissance.

LANGSTON HUGHES

For a biographical note, see page 429.

Harlem

What happens to a dream deferred?

> Does it dry up
> like a raisin in the sun?
> Or fester like a sore—
> And then run?
> Does it stink like rotten meat?
> Or crust and sugar over—
> like a syrupy sweet?

5

> Maybe it just sags
> like a heavy load.

10

> *Or does it explode?*

[1951]

Different readers will respond at least somewhat differently to any work. On the other hand, because writers want to communicate, they try to control their readers' responses, and they count on their readers to understand the denotations of words as they understand them. Hughes assumed that his readers knew that Harlem was the site of a large African American community in New York City. A reader who confuses the title of the poem with Haarlem in the Netherlands will wonder what this poem is saying about the tulip-growing center in northern Holland. Let's assume that the reader understands that Hughes is talking about Harlem, New York. Let's also assume that the reader understands that Hughes is exploring the dreams of African Americans who live in a society dominated by whites.

Explication is based on the assumption that the poem contains a meaning and that, by studying the work thoughtfully, we can unfold the meaning or meanings. Let's explore how the close reading of a poem can generate a paraphrase and a summary that convey the ideas of the poem accurately. Then, we can see how that close reading can lead to an effective explication.

Paraphrase

A **paraphrase** is a *direct restatement* of another text's ideas in your own words. Paraphrasing typically restates a focused portion of the text, rewriting it to clarify its meaning and express its ideas in your own style. A paraphrase does not analyze the text but, rather, conveys its key information.

You will want to use paraphrase to demonstrate your understanding of the text without copying the work's original wording and style. Paraphrase must not repeat the original text's words. If you do this, you must put the words inside quotation marks and cite the source. When you are writing a paraphrase, you must present the text's ideas in your own style and cite the source of the text, as it has provided the ideas that you are using. All paraphrases must be cited. A paraphrase is typically around the same length as the material that it is citing.

It might be helpful to think of a paraphrase as a type of translation in the same language—a translation of material that may in its original form be somewhat obscure to a reader. A native speaker of English will not need a paraphrase of "Thirty days hath September," although a nonnative speaker might be puzzled by two things: the meaning of *hath* and the inverted word order. For such a reader, "September has thirty days" would be a helpful paraphrase.

Although a paraphrase seeks to make clear the basic meaning of the original, if the original is even a little more complex than "Thirty days hath September," the paraphrase will, in the process of clarifying something, lose something because the substitution of one word for another will change the meaning. "Shut up" and "Be quiet" do not say exactly the same thing; the former (in addition to asking for quiet) says that the speaker is rude or perhaps that the speaker feels little respect for the auditor, but the paraphrase loses all of this.

Still, a paraphrase can be a first step in helping a reader to understand a line that includes an obsolete word or phrase, or a word or phrase that is current only in one region. In a poem by Emily Dickinson (1830–86), the following line appears:

The sun engrossed the East. . . .

"Engrossed" here has (perhaps among other meanings) a special commercial meaning, "to acquire most or all of a commodity; to monopolize the market," so a paraphrase of the line might say

The sun took over all of the East.

It is worth mentioning that you should always have at your elbow a good desk dictionary, such as the current *American Heritage Dictionary of the English Language*. Writers—especially poets—expect you to pay close attention to every word. When a word puzzles you, look it up.

Idioms, as well as words, can puzzle a reader. The Anglo-Irish poet William Butler Yeats (1865–1939) begins one poem with

> The friends that have it I do wrong. . . .

Because the idiom "to have it" (meaning "to believe that," "to think that") will be unfamiliar to many American readers today, a discussion of the poem might include a paraphrase—a *rewording* in more familiar language, such as

> The friends who think that I am doing the wrong thing. . . .

Perhaps the rest of the poem is immediately clear, but in any case, here is the entire poem, followed by a paraphrase:

> The friends that have it I do wrong
> When ever I remake a song,
> Should know what issue is at stake:
> It is myself that I remake.

Now for the paraphrase:

> The friends who think that I am doing the wrong thing when I revise one of my poems should be informed what the important issue is: I'm not just revising a poem—rather, I am revising myself (my thoughts, feelings).

Here, as with any paraphrase, the meaning is not translated exactly; there is some distortion. If "song" in the original is clarified by "poem" in the paraphrase, it is also altered; the paraphrase loses the sense of lyricism that is implicit in "song." Further, "Should know what issue is at stake" (in the original) is ambiguous. Does "should" mean "ought," as in "You should know better than to speak so rudely," or does it mean "deserve to be informed," as in "You ought to know that I am thinking about quitting"?

Granted that a paraphrase may miss a great deal, a paraphrase often helps you, or your reader, to understand at least the surface meaning, and the act of paraphrasing will usually help you to understand at least some of the implied meaning. Furthermore, a paraphrase makes you see that the original writer's words (if the work is a good one) are exactly right, better than any words we might substitute. It becomes clear that what is said in the original—not only the rough idea expressed, but also the precise tone with which it is expressed—is a sharply defined experience.

Student Work: Paraphrase

Bill Horner, a student taking a composition class, was asked to paraphrase the first line of Hughes's poem, "Harlem." He was asked to create a short paraphrase that he could then use in his paper assignment if needed.

He examined the first line of the poem:

> What happens to a dream deferred?

Although the line is short, the concept of a "dream deferred" is complex. Bill came up with the following paraphrase:

> What results occur when hopes are unfulfilled?

Bill then inserted this paraphrase into a sentence and added a citation:

> In the first line of his poem, Hughes asks us to consider what results occur when hopes are unfulfilled (1).

Bill has translated the phrase "dream deferred" into "unfulfilled hopes." As a paraphrase, this is excellent, but let's recollect that this translating of an author's words into equivalent words removes some of the power and meaning of the words. Hughes does not say "hopes"; he says "dream." And he does not say "unfulfilled"; he says "deferred." You might ask yourself exactly what differences there are between these words. Next, after you have read the poem several times, you might think about which expression is more meaningful, "unfulfilled hopes" or "dream deferred," and why.

Summary

A **summary** is a synopsis of the main points of a work. Compared to a paraphrase, a summary is a more *comprehensive overview* of the text's overarching ideas or arguments. A summary is usually much shorter than the original text. It must therefore select and condense the text's most important information into a coherent overview. You can position a summary as a short supporting section within an analytical essay. A summary typically provides an overview of a source's central ideas in order for you to then analyze, develop, or apply those ideas within your larger argument. As with a paraphrase, all summaries must be cited.

A summary of a work of literature usually gives the gist of the plot. It lets the reader know that X happened, then Y happened, and then Z happened, but it does *not* concern itself, for instance, with evaluating whether the happenings are plausible. Normally, in your analytic/argumentative essays, you will not summarize because you can assume that your readers are familiar with the works that you are discussing, but if, for instance, you are comparing an assigned text with another text that your readers probably don't know, you may want to offer a summary in order to help them follow the argument that you will be developing.

Consider this summary of Chopin's "The Story of an Hour" (page 65):

> A newspaper office reports that Brently Mallard has been killed in a railroad accident. When the news is gently broken to Mrs. Mallard by her sister Josephine, Mrs. Mallard weeps wildly and then shuts herself up in her room, where she sinks into an armchair. Staring dully through the window, she sees the signs of spring, and then an unnameable sensation possesses her. She tries to reject it but finally abandons herself to it. Renewed, she exults in her freedom, in the thought that at last the days will be her own. She finally comes out of the room, embraces her sister, and descends the stairs. A moment later her husband—who in fact had not been in the accident—enters. Mrs. Mallard dies—of the joy that kills, according to the doctors' diagnosis.

Here are a few principles that govern summaries:

1. A summary is **much briefer than the original.** It is not a paraphrase—a word-by-word translation of someone's words into your own. A paraphrase is usually at least as long as the original, but a summary is rarely longer than one-fourth of the original and is usually much shorter. A novel may be summarized in a few paragraphs, or even in one paragraph.

2. A summary **usually achieves its brevity by omitting almost all of the concrete details of the original** and by omitting minor characters and episodes. Notice that the summary of "The Story of an Hour" omits the friend of the family, omits specifying the signs of spring, and omits the business of the sister imploring Mrs. Mallard to open the door.
3. A summary is **as accurate as possible**, given the limits of space. It has no value if it misrepresents the point of the original.
4. A summary is **normally written in the present tense**. Thus, "A newspaper office reports . . . , Mrs. Mallard weeps. . . ."
5. If the summary is brief (say, fewer than 250 words), it **may be given as a single paragraph**. If you are summarizing a long work, you may feel that a longer summary is needed. In this case, your reader will be grateful to you if you divide the summary into paragraphs. As you draft your summary, you may find **natural divisions**. For instance, the scene of the story may change midway, giving you the opportunity to use two paragraphs. Or you may want to summarize a five-act play in five paragraphs.
6. The writer of a summary **need not make the points in the same order as that of the original**. If the writer of an essay has delayed revealing the main point until the end of the essay, the summary may rearrange the order, stating the main point first. Occasionally, if the original author has presented the elements of an argument in a disorderly or confusing sequence, a summary may be written to disengage the author's argument from its confusing structure.
7. Because a summary is clearly a report of someone else's views, it must be cited. **Use quotation marks and citations** for all direct quotations from the original. It is not necessary to specify "he says" or "she goes on to prove." From the opening sentence of a summary, it should be clear that what follows is what the original author says.

Summaries have their place in essays, but remember that a summary is not an analysis; it is only an overview of the information in the work, not an interpretation of that work.

Student Work: Summary

With these tips in mind, let's see how Bill tackles writing a summary of Hughes's poem. In contrast to a paraphrase, which focused on restating one line, a summary will attempt to encompass an overview of the entire work, especially when the work is short.

Bill reminds himself that he needs to convey the information in the poem and not express his opinions about the poem. He comes up with the following summary paragraph:

> Langston Hughes's poem explores the results that occur when hopes are left unfulfilled. The poem opens with a question that asks what happens to deferred dreams. The poem answers that question by offering a series of images, with each image filling a line or two of the poem. The dream is compared to a raisin drying in the sun, to a running sore, and to stinking, rotten meat. The dream is also compared to a sweet that gets a sugary crust on it and to a heavy load that sags. In the final line of the poem, Hughes asks if the deferred dream will explode.

This strikes us as a strong summary because it encapsulates the entire poem in a concise paragraph. It displays the following key characteristics of a summary:

- it demonstrate the writer's understanding of the original text;
- it demonstrates the writer's ability to convey the original text's information accurately; and
- it demonstrates the writer's ability to select and organize the most important information in the original text.

Because the poem is short, the summary is able to review all of the poem's main images. The summary moves through the images in order, repeating many of Hughes's words, without simply quoting each line verbatim. The summary emphasizes the opening and closing lines of the poem by putting information about those lines into their own sentences. By not offering an interpretation of the poem, the summary remains informative without becoming argumentative. The summary captures the central ideas and images of the poem, but, of course, much of the power of the poem has been removed.

Both summary and paraphrase are helpful in that, once performed, they ensure that you have read the literary work carefully and understand its central information. After having practiced writing a summary or a paraphrase, you are ready to write an explication, which allows you express your sense of the meaning of the work.

Explication

A line-by-line or episode-by-episode commentary on what is going on in a text is an **explication** (literally, an unfolding or spreading out). An explication does not deal with the writer's life and times, and it is not a paraphrase or a rewording, although it may include paraphrasing. Rather, it is a commentary that reveals your sense of the meaning of the work and its structure.

When we explicate a text, we attempt to create a detailed account of its meaning based on a careful *line-by-line close reading*. Because it focuses intently on the text at hand, explication often works with poetry, which rewards the line-level reading and rereading. We ask questions about the meanings of words, the implications of metaphors and images, and the speaker's tone of voice as we initially hear it and it develops and perhaps changes. How is the literary work put together? How did the writer organize it to prompt from me the response that I had (and am having) to it? How does it begin, what happens next, and what happens after that? And so on, through to the end.

It takes some skill to work your way along in an explication without saying, "In line one. . . . In the second line. . . . In the third line. . . ." This sounds mechanical and formulaic. Make good use of transitional words and phrases so that your commentary will feel to your reader more natural, with a better pace and rhythm. For example: "The speaker begins by suggesting. . . . The poem then shifts in direction. . . . In the next paragraph, however, the narrator implies. . . ."

An explication captures your understanding of the literary work, revealing your ideas about and interpretations of it. However, we would not label this type of writing as a fully "analytical" paper, as it is not selecting ideas for emphasis, not making a focused argument out of those ideas, and not organizing the paper around those ideas. Rather, an explication attempts to explain the original work as a whole and lets the work dictate the flow of ideas. Although an explication paper will have a thesis and advance an interpretation, and thus contain analysis, explication is best understood as a line-by-line commentary rather than an analytical paper.

Working toward an Explication

In preparing to write an explication, first type on a computer, or handwrite, the complete text of the work that you will explicate—usually a poem but sometimes a short passage of prose. *Don't* photocopy it; the act of typing or writing it will help you to get into the piece, word by word, comma by comma. Type or write it *double-spaced* so that you will have room for your annotations as you study the piece. It's advisable to make a few photocopies (or to print a few copies, if you are using a computer) before you start annotating so that, if one page gets too cluttered with annotations, you can continue working on a clean copy. Or, you may want to use one copy for a certain kind of annotation—let's say, those concerning imagery—and other copies for other kinds of annotation—let's say, those concerning meter or wordplay. If you are writing on a computer, you can highlight words, boldface them, put them in capital letters (for instance, to indicate accented syllables), and so forth.

Student Work: Annotations

Let's turn to the brainstorming writing that leads to an explication of the poem, a detailed examination of the whole. Here are Bill's preliminary jottings on the poem:

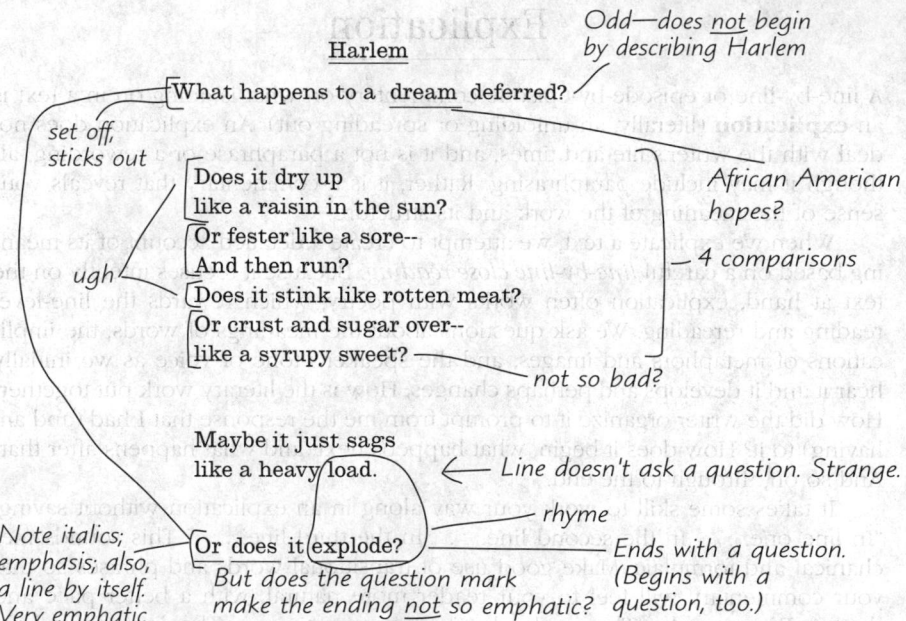

These annotations chiefly get at the structure of the poem, the relationship of its parts. Bill notices that the poem begins with a line set off by itself and ends with a line set off by itself, and he also notices that each of these lines is a question. Further, he indicates that each of these two lines is emphasized in other ways: The first begins farther to the left than any of the other lines—as though the other lines are subheadings or in some way subordinate to the first line—and the last is italicized.

Student Work: Journal Entries

Bill later wrote these entries in his journal:

> *Feb. 18. Since the title is "Harlem," it's obvious that the "dream" is by African American people. Also, obvious that Hughes thinks that if the "dream" doesn't become real there may be riots ("explode"). I like "raisin in the sun" (maybe because I like the play), and I like the business about "a syrupy sweet"—much more pleasant than the festering sore and the rotten meat. But if the dream becomes "sweet," what's wrong with that? Why should something "sweet" explode?*

> *Feb. 21. Prof. McCabe said to think of structure or form of a poem as a sort of architecture, a building with a foundation, floors, etc., topped by a roof—but since we read a poem from top to bottom, it's like a building upside down. Title is foundation (even though it's at top); last line is roof, capping the whole. As you read, you add layers. Foundation of "Harlem" is a question (first line). Then, set back a bit from foundation, or built on it by white space, a tall room (7 lines high, with 4 questions); then, on top of this room, another room (lines, statement, not a question). Funny, I thought that in poems all stanzas are the same number of lines. Then—more white space, so another unit—the roof. Man, this roof is going to fall in—"explodes." Not just the roof, maybe the whole house.*

> *Feb. 21, p.m. I get it; one line at start, one line at end; both are questions, but the last sort of says (because it is in italics) that it is the most likely answer to the question of the first line. The last line is also a question, but it's still an answer. The big stanza (7 lines) has 4 questions: 2 lines, 2 lines, 1 line, 2 lines. Maybe the switch to 1 line is to give some variety, so as not to be dull? It's exactly in the middle of the poem. I get the progress from raisin in the sun (dried, but not so terrible), to festering sore and to stinking meat, but I still don't see what's so bad about "a syrupy sweet." Is Hughes saying that after things are very bad they will get better? But why, then, the explosion at the end?*

> *Feb. 23. "Heavy load" and "sags" in next-to-last stanza seem to me to suggest slaves with bales of cotton, or maybe poor cotton pickers dragging big sacks of cotton. Or maybe people doing heavy labor in Harlem. Anyway, very tired. Different from running sore and stinking meat earlier; not disgusting, but pressing down, deadening. Maybe worse than a sore or rotten meat—a hard, hopeless life. And then the last line. Just one line, no fancy (and disgusting) simile. In fact, no simile at all. This is a metaphor, not a simile. Boom! Not just pressed down and tired, like maybe some racist whites think (hope?) blacks will be. Bang! Will there be survivors?*

Student Work: Listing

Drawing on these notes in his journal, Bill wrote down a list of several key ideas to guide him through a draft of his explication essay. The organization of the draft posed no problem; in an explication, the writer simply follows the organization of the original text. Bill thus focuses his notes on his understanding of the meaning of the poem rather than on the organization of his ideas. Although Bill's notes were written down on paper, you may find that composing such notes on your computer works just as well.

> *11 lines; short, but powerful; explosive*
> *Question (first line)*
> *answers (set off by space and also indented)*
> *"raisin in the sun": shrinking*
> *"sore"* ⎫
> *"rotten meat"* ⎬ *disgusting*
> *"syrupy sweet": relief from disgusting comparisons*
> *final question (last line): explosion?*
> *   explosive (powerful) because:*
> *   short, condensed, packed*
> *   in italics*
> *   stands by self—like first line*
> *   no fancy comparison; very direct*

Student Explication Essay: "Langston Hughes's 'Harlem'"

Here is Bill's final explication essay. See if you can trace his "unfolding" of the Hughes poem as he explains his understanding of it.

Horner 1

Bill Horner

Professor McCabe

English 122

6 January 2016

Langston Hughes's "Harlem"

"Harlem" is a poem that is only eleven lines long, but it is charged

with power. It explodes. Hughes sets the stage, so to speak, by telling us in

the title that he is talking about Harlem. In the first line of his poem,

Hughes asks, "What happens to a dream deferred?", encouraging us to

consider what results occur when hopes are unfulfilled. The rest of the poem

is set off by being indented, as though it is the answer to his question. This

answer is in three parts (three stanzas, of different lengths).

In a way, it is wrong to speak of the answer, since the rest of the poem

consists of questions, but I think Hughes means that each question (for instance, does a "deferred" hope "dry up / like a raisin in the sun?") really is an answer, something that really has happened and that will happen again. The first question, "Does it dry up / like a raisin in the sun?," is a famous line (2–3). To compare hope to a raisin dried in the sun is to suggest a terrible shrinking. The next two comparisons are to a "sore" (4) and to "rotten meat" (6). These comparisons are less clever, but they are very effective because they are disgusting. Then, maybe because of the disgusting comparisons, he gives a comparison that is not at all disgusting. In this comparison, he says that maybe the "dream deferred" will "crust over— / like a syrupy sweet" (7–8).

The seven lines with four comparisons are followed by a stanza of two lines with just one comparison:

Maybe it just sags like a heavy load (9–10).

So if we thought that this postponed dream might finally turn into something "sweet," we were kidding ourselves. Hughes comes down to earth, in a short stanza, with an image of a heavy load, which probably also calls to mind images of people bent under heavy loads, maybe of cotton, or maybe just any sort of heavy load carried by African Americans in Harlem and elsewhere.

The opening question ("What happens to a dream deferred?") was followed by four questions in seven lines, but now, with "Maybe it just sags / like a heavy load" (9–10), we get a statement, as though the poet at last has found an answer. But at the end we get one more question, set off by itself and in italics: "Or does it explode?" (11). This line itself is explosive for three reasons: It is short, it is italicized, and it is a stanza in itself. It's also interesting that this line, unlike the earlier lines, does not use a simile. It uses a metaphor. It's almost as though Hughes is saying, "O.K., we've had enough fancy ways of talking about this terrible situation; here it is, 'boom.'"

[New page]

Horner 3

Work Cited

Hughes, Langston. "Harlem." *Literature for Composition*. Ed. Sylvan Barnet, William

Burto, William E. Cain, and Cheryl L. Nixon. 11th ed. Boston: Pearson, 2017.

170. Print.

Joining the Conversation: Critical Thinking and Writing

1. Bill Horner's explication suggests that the comparison with "a syrupy sweet" deliberately misleads the reader into thinking that the ending will be happy, and it thus serves to make the real ending even more powerful. In class, another student suggested that Hughes may be referring to African Americans who adopt a smiling manner in order to cope with an oppressive society. Which explanation do you prefer, and why? What do you think of combining the two?

   Does some method or principle help us decide which interpretation is correct? Can we, in fact, talk about a "correct" interpretation, or only about a plausible or implausible interpretation and an interesting or uninteresting interpretation?

2. In *The Collected Poems of Langston Hughes* (1994), the editors title this poem "Harlem." But, in the *Selected Poems of Langston Hughes* (1959), published when the poet was still alive, the poem is titled "Dream Deferred." Which title do you think is more effective? Do you interpret the poem differently, depending on how it is titled? How might a reader—who knew nothing about Hughes—respond to the poem if he or she came upon it with the title "Dream Deferred"?

Explication as Argument

We have said that an explication unfolds or opens up or interprets a work by calling attention to such things as the speaker's tone of voice and the implications in images. It might seem, then, to be an objective report, the sort of explanatory writing that is called *expository* rather than *argumentative*.

But because literature makes considerable use of connotations and symbolic meanings—"A rolling stone gathers no moss" is not essentially a statement about stones and moss but about something else—readers may differ in what they understand words to mean. The writer of an explication not only examines the meanings of specific words and images but also, having come to a conclusion about what the details add up to, argues an interpretation and supports a thesis.

What distinguishes argument from exposition is this: In argument, some statements are offered as *reasons* for others. Because writers of arguments assume that their readers may not at the outset share their views, in their writing they offer evidence to support their assertions.

If you reread Bill Horner's explication of "Harlem," you will notice that in speaking of the line "Or does it explode?" Bill says, "This line is explosive for three reasons." He then specifies the three reasons. That is, he argues his case, presenting three pieces of supporting evidence: Hughes's line is short, it is italicized, and it is a stanza in itself.

True, much of Horner's explication is expository writing when he says that the poem consists of "three parts (three stanzas, of different lengths)." There can be little disagreement between writer and reader here, although perhaps a reader might respond, "No, the title is also part of the poem, so the poem consists of four parts." A reader who is looking for an argument—in the sense of a quarrel, not in the sense of a reasoned discussion—can find it with almost any piece of writing. But, again, our point is that because expository writing does not assume a difference of opinion, it chiefly sets forth information rather than seek to make a case. Argumentative writing, on the other hand, assumes that it must set forth information in a way that persuades the reader of its truth, which means that it must give evidence.

Pure exposition—let's say, information about how to register for classes or information about what is likely to be on the final examination—is not concerned with persuading readers to accept a thesis. But an explication, even though it might seem only to clarify the meanings of the words in a poem, argues a thesis about the work as a whole.

Notice Bill Horner's opening sentence:

"Harlem" is a poem that is only eleven lines long, but it is charged with power.

What is Horner's thesis? Certainly not that the poem is "only eleven lines long"—a writer hardly needs to argue for this assertion. Rather, Horner's thesis is that the poem "is charged with power." In the rest of the explication, he offers evidence that supports this assertion. To persuade us, he points out that certain lines are indented, that certain figures of speech have certain implications, and that the last stanza is italicized and consists of only one line.

You may disagree: You may not think the poem "is charged with power," and you may think that Horner has misread certain lines. We mentioned, in our first topic for "Critical Thinking and Writing," that when Horner offered this interpretation in class, another student saw a different meaning in "syrupy sweet" (line 8). But, if you disagree, whether with the reading as a whole or with the interpretation of a single image, it's not enough to assert that you disagree. You will have to offer an argument, which is to say, you will have to set forth reasons in your effort to persuade your readers.

Your goal in an explication is to present your insights about aspects of the poem's language. Even more, you want these insights to add up to a whole. When related to one another, they should enable your reader to understand the poem, overall, more clearly and to enjoy it more fully. Ask yourself, as you study the poem and develop your draft of the paper,

What is my **thesis** (my central point, my argument, my claim)?

This question will help you to make your essay coherent and unified. It is a reminder that an explication is more than a set of observations. The best explications make use of details to teach the reader something new about the poem as a whole.

✔ CHECKLIST: *Drafting an Explication*

Overall Considerations

☐ Does the explication work its way through the poem, line by line? Does the explication provide a commentary on the poem as a whole?

☐ Does the commentary support a unified interpretation of the poem? Is this interpretation positioned as the paper's thesis?

☐ Does the explication convey information about the poem accurately and then offer ideas and interpretations about that information?

☐ Does the poem imply a story of some sort, for instance, the speaker's account of a love affair or of a response to nature? If so, what is its beginning, middle, and end?

☐ If you detect a story in the speaker's mind, a change of mood—for instance, a shift from bitterness that a love affair has ended to hope for its renewal—is this change communicated in part by the connotations of certain words? By syntax? By metrical shifts?

☐ Do the details of the explication all cohere into a meaningful whole? If so, your explication will largely be an argument on behalf of this thesis.

Detailed Considerations

☐ If the poem has a title other than the first line, what are the implications of the title?

☐ Are there clusters or patterns of imagery, for instance, religious images, economic images, or images drawn from nature? If so, how do they contribute to the meaning of the poem?

☐ Is irony (understatement or overstatement) used? To what effect?

☐ How do the connotations of certain words (for instance, *dad* rather than *father*) help to establish the meaning?

☐ What are the implications of the syntax—for instance, of notably simple or notably complex sentences? What do such sentences tell us about the speaker?

☐ Do metrical variations occur? If so, what is their significance?

☐ Do rhyming words have some meaningful connection, as in the clichés *moon* and *June*, *dove*, and *love*?

☐ What are the implications of the poem's appearance on the page—for example, of an indented line or of the stanzaic pattern? (If the poem consists of two stanzas of four lines each, does the second stanza offer a reversal of the first?)

Student Argumentative Explication Essay: "Giving Stamps Personality in 'Stamp Collecting'"

Let's examine a student paper that provides another example of an explication essay, written in response to the following poem.

CATHY SONG

Born in 1955 and raised in Hawaii, Cathy Song is of Korean and Chinese descent. Her poetry often draws on this rich ancestry, exploring themes of family, gender, and identity. Her poems have been praised by reviewers for their compelling narratives and evocative imagery.

Stamp Collecting

The poorest countries
have the prettiest stamps
as if impracticality were a major export
shipped with the bananas, t-shirts and coconuts.
Take Tonga, where the tourists,   5
expecting a dramatic waterfall replete with birdcalls,
are taken to see the island's peculiar mystery:
hanging bats with collapsible wings
like black umbrellas swing upside down from fruit
trees.   10
The Tongan stamp is a fruit.
The banana stamp is scalloped like a butter-varnished seashell.
The pineapple resembles a volcano, a spout of green on top,
and the papaya, a tarnished goat skull.

They look impressive,   15
these stamps of countries without a thing to sell
except for what is scraped, uprooted and hulled
from their mule-scratched hills.
They believe in postcards,
in portraits of progress: the new dam;   20
a team of young native doctors
wearing stethoscopes like exotic ornaments;
the recently constructed "Facultad de Medicina,"
a building as lack-lustre as an American motel.

The stamps of others are predictable.   25
Lucky is the country that possesses indigenous beauty.
Say a tiger or queen.
The Japanese can display to the world
their blossoms: a spray of pink on green.
Like pollen, they drift, airborne.   30
But pity the country that is bleak and stark.
Beauty and whimsey are discouraged as indiscreet.
Unbreakable as their climate, a monument of ice.

[1988]

Let's examine how LaTina Johnson, a student in a composition course, uses an explication paper to make sense of "Stamp Collecting." Like the work by Bill Horner that we explored earlier in this chapter, LaTina's paper unfolds the meaning of a poem by tracing its ideas stanza by stanza and line by line. Unlike Bill's paper, this assignment tackles a longer and more complex poem, so every line of the poem cannot be addressed. This paper needs to be more selective and, as result, starts to shape its explication into a more analytical paper. In addition, this paper develops a strong thesis that emphasizes the poem's interest in a country's self-image and the poem's use of imagery. These focusing ideas are repeated throughout the paper and in the conclusion. This paper still uses the structure of the poem to structure its own ideas and organization, but it demonstrates just how argumentative an explication can become. As it becomes more argumentative and focused, an explication paper starts to evolve into an analytical paper. This paper serves as a good transition into our next chapter and its emphasis on analysis.

Paul 1

LaTina Johnson

Professor Wynne

English 122

1 February 2016

Giving Stamps Personality in "Stamp Collecting"

Cathy Song's poem "Stamp Collecting" uses the images on stamps to capture the cultures of different countries. She presents a series of three types of countries: poor countries, beautiful countries, and bleak countries. Each type of country is described through the stamp it might issue. As the poem shows, each country's hopes and failures are translated into the vivid imagery of a stamp. The stamp gives a personality to each country, describing the type of human emotions that country might have. Stanza by stanza, the poem moves through a series of stamps and describes the stamps' unique imagery, using that imagery to create a different cultural personality for each type of country.

Song shows how stamps use imagery that creates sensory impressions and creates cultural associations. In the first stanza, the poor countries are described as having the most exotic stamps. Song opens the poem by explaining, "The poorest countries/have the prettiest stamps/as if impracticality were a major export" (1–3). The stamps are impractical because they have excess beauty and detail, even though the poor countries have no resources. The stamps make the country seem human by expressing this human quality of "impracticality." In the first stanza, the stamps of Tonga are held up as an example. She shows how Tonga itself is exotic and strange by describing the strange bats that live there and are a "peculiar mystery" (7). Each stamp has a fruit that is presented in a uniquely memorable way: the "banana stamp is scalloped like a butter-varnished seashell," the "pineapple resembles a volcano," and the papaya looks like a "tarnished goat skull" (11–13). Song uses this list of similes to show how Tonga's exotic fruits are made even more exotic on their stamps. The stamps seem extreme and "over the top" in their imagery. The beauty, strangeness, and mystery of Tonga are captured in the imagery on their stamps.

These poor countries' stamps also show a second human quality: the belief in human progress. Song explains that these stamps will be placed on postcards: the countries "believe in postcards,/in portraits of progress" (19). The postcards show pictures of new dams, doctors, and hospitals. Although these countries' stamps and postcards express the hope for human progress, Song's poem makes it clear that the stamps do not match the reality of the country. The stamps are created by "countries without a thing to sell/except for what is scraped, uprooted, and hulled/from their mule-scratched hill" (15–17). Song's use of the strong verbs "scraped, uprooted, and hulled" shows how these countries are tough places to live, and the people are still dependent on land and human labor (16). Although the stamps put out a glamorous image, these countries have a culture of struggle. Song's poem shows that these countries' stamps are trying to make up for a lack of resources. The stamps and postcards seem to try to hide the poor country's reality, but wind up revealing that reality.

Song devotes these two stanzas to the poor countries' stamps, while the stamps of beautiful countries and bleak countries each receive only one short stanza each. Just like the stamps she describes, Song's first two stanzas are filled with visual beauty: they are long and detailed, and contain vivid, memorable images. These first two stanzas have a feeling of being "over the top," just like the stamps they describe.

The third stanza is shorter and describes the stamps of countries that are "predictable" (24). Song implies that these countries are more successful and wealthy. These countries can use images that show an "indigenous beauty./Say a tiger or a queen" (26). The image of a tiger conveys beauty and strength, while the image of a queen conveys beauty and stability. The poem states that countries that use these images are "lucky" (25). Such a country is lucky to have a culture that is more successful and predictable. Although that culture might not be as exotic or interesting as the culture of the poor counties, it can represent itself in beautiful stamps. Song uses a Japanese stamp to illustrate the idea of a predictable stamp created by an established culture. She describes the stamp's image of blossoms: "A spray of pink on green/Like pollen, they drift, airborne" (28–29). This image has a feeling of lightness and easiness. Unlike the exotic stamp from Tonga, this Japanese stamp does not have to try hard to impress or surprise its viewer. The Japanese culture seems secure and at ease.

The final short stanza describes the stamps of a country that is "bleak and stark" (30). Song prejudices us against this country by telling us to "pity" it (30). The stamps of this type of country are "serious" and filled with imagery of "factories, tramways and areoplanes" (34). The "beauty" and "whimsy" of the imagery of the other stamps is rejected (31). Instead, these stamps "issue serious statements" (33). The countries are described as "unbreakable as their climate, a monument of ice" (32). Compared to the exotic stamps of Tonga and the light stamps of Japan, these stamps are cold and unapproachable. Song captures the hard, cold nature of these countries in the image of a stamp that shows "athletes marbled into statues" (35). These stamps are empty of life. These stamps capture the personality of countries that "turn their noses upon the world." Instead of believing in progress or having a sense of beauty, these bleak countries try to present

Paul 3

their bleakness as a type of strength. The poem ends by describing how

these stamps and these countries offer "an unrelenting procession/of a

grim, historic profile" (37–38). These stamps reveal the cold unhappiness

that defines these countries.

Although a stamp might seem small and trivial, it can be a mirror of a

country. The stamp provides a way of personifying the country, showing how

a country can be exotic and hoping for progress, light and secure in its

identity, or cold and needing to convey its strength. Each stamp captures a

country's personality. "Stamp Collecting" uses vivid imagery to show how a

stamp gives a country a visual identity. The poem emphasizes that these

stamps reveal more than the country might want revealed—the stamps show

not only the strengths but also the weaknesses of a country. As Song's poem

convincingly shows, a stamp is a country's self-image.

[New page]

Paul 4

Work Cited

Song, Kathy. "Stamp Collecting." *Literature for Composition.* Ed. Sylvan Barnet,

William Burto, William E. Cain, and Cheryl L. Nixon. 11th ed. Boston:

Pearson, 2017. 183. Print.

Your Turn: Additional Poems for Explication

The basic assignment here is to explicate the poems, but your instructor may also ask you to respond to some or all of the questions that follow each poem.

WILLIAM SHAKESPEARE

William Shakespeare (1564–1616), born in Stratford-upon-Avon in England, is chiefly known as a dramatic poet, but he also wrote nondramatic poetry. In 1609, a volume of 154 of his sonnets was published, apparently without his permission. Probably he chose to keep his sonnets unpublished, not because he thought that they were of little value, but because it was more prestigious to be an amateur (unpublished) poet than a professional (published) poet. Although the sonnets were published in 1609, they were probably written in the mid-1590s, when there was a vogue for sonneteering. A contemporary writer in 1598 said that Shakespeare's "sugared Sonnets [circulate] among his private friends."

Sonnet 73

That time of year thou mayst in me behold
When yellow leaves, or none, or few, do hang
Upon those boughs which shake against the cold,
Bare ruined choirs° where late the sweet birds sang.
In me thou see'st the twilight of such day   5
As after sunset fadeth in the west,
Which by-and-by black night doth take away,
Death's second self that seals up all in rest.
In me thou see'st the glowing of such fire
That on the ashes of his youth doth lie,   10
As the deathbed whereon it must expire,
Consumed with that which it was nourished by.

　　This thou perceiv'st, which makes thy love more strong,
　　To love that well which thou must leave ere long.

[c. 1592, pub. 1609]

4 **choir** the part of the church where services are sung.

Joining the Conversation: Critical Thinking and Writing

1. In the first quatrain (the first four lines), to what "time of year" does Shakespeare compare himself? In the second quatrain (lines 5–8), to what does he compare himself? In the third? If the sequence of the three quatrains were reversed, what would be gained or lost?
2. In line 8, what is "Death's second self"? What implications do you perceive in "seals up all in rest," as opposed, for instance, to "brings most welcome rest"?
3. In line 13, exactly what is "This"?
4. In line 14, suppose in place of "To love that well which thou must leave ere long," Shakespeare had written "To love me well whom thou must leave ere long." What, if anything, would have been gained or lost?
5. What insights into your own feelings and experiences does this poem give you? Please explain, being as specific as you can.

JOHN DONNE

John Donne (1572–1631) was born into a Roman Catholic family in England, but, in the 1590s, he abandoned that faith. In 1615, he became an Anglican priest and soon was known as a great preacher. One hundred sixty of his sermons survive, including one with the famous line, "No man is an island, entire of itself; every man is a piece of the continent, a part of the main; if a clod be washed away by the sea,

Europe is the less . . . ; and therefore never send to know for whom the bell tolls; it tolls for thee." From 1621 until his death, he was dean of St. Paul's Cathedral in London. His love poems (often bawdy and cynical) are his early work, and his "Holy Sonnets" (among the greatest religious poems written in English) are his later work.

Holy Sonnet XIV

Batter my heart, three-personed God; for you
As yet but knock, breathe, shine, and seek to mend;
That I may rise and stand, o'erthrow me, and bend
Your force, to break, blow, burn, and make me new.
I, like an usurped town, to another due,   5
Labor to admit you, but oh, to no end.
Reason, your viceroy in me, me should defend,
But is captived, and proves weak or untrue.
Yet dearly I love you, and would be loved fain,
But am betrothed unto your enemy: 10
Divorce me, untie, or break that knot again,
Take me to you, imprison me, for I
Except you enthrall me, never shall be free,
Nor ever chaste, except you ravish me.

[1633]

Joining the Conversation: Critical Thinking and Writing

1. Explain the paradoxes (apparent contradictions) in lines 2, 3, 13, and 14. Explain the double meanings of "enthrall" (line 13) and "ravish" (line 14).
2. In lines 1–4, what is God implicitly compared to (considering especially lines 2 and 4)? How does this comparison lead into the comparison that dominates lines 5–8? What words in lines 9–12 are especially related to the earlier lines?
3. What is gained by piling up verbs in lines 2–4?
4. Are sexual references necessarily irreverent in a religious poem? Present a brief argument in which you say yes, and then another argument in which you say no. Make each argument as convincing as you can.

EMILY BRONTË

Emily Brontë (1818–48) spent most of her short life (she died of tuberculosis) in an English village on the Yorkshire moors. The sister of Charlotte Brontë (author of Jane Eyre*) and of Anne Brontë, Emily is best known for her novel* Wuthering Heights *(1847), but she was a considerable poet, and her first significant publication (1846) was in a volume of poems by the three sisters.*

Spellbound

The night is darkening round me,
The wild winds coldly blow;
But a tyrant spell has bound me
And I cannot, cannot go.
The giant trees are bending   5

Their bare boughs weighed with snow.
And the storm is fast descending,
And yet I cannot go.
Clouds beyond clouds above me,
Wastes beyond wastes below;   10
But nothing drear can move me;
I will not, cannot go.

[1837]

Joining the Conversation: Critical Thinking and Writing

1. What exactly is a spell, and what does it mean to be spellbound?
2. What difference, if any, would it make if the first line said "has darkened" instead of "is darkening"?
3. What difference would it make, if any, if lines 4 and 12 were switched?
4. What does "drear" (line 11) mean? Is this word too unusual? Should the poet have used a more familiar word?
5. Describe the speaker's state of mind. Have you ever experienced anything like this yourself? What was the situation, and how did you move beyond it?

LI-YOUNG LEE

Li-Young Lee was born in 1957 in Jakarta, Indonesia, of Chinese parents. In 1964, his family brought him to the United States. He was educated at the University of Pittsburgh, the University of Arizona, and the State University of New York, Brockport. He now lives in Chicago, where he works as an artist.

I Ask My Mother to Sing

She begins, and my grandmother joins her.
Mother and daughter sing like young girls.
If my father were alive, he would play
his accordion and sway like a boat.

I've never been in Peking, or the Summer Palace,   5
nor stood on the great Stone Boat to watch
the rain begin on Kuen Ming Lake, the picnickers
running away in the grass.

But I love to hear it sung;
how the waterlilies fill with rain until   10
they overturn, spilling water into water,
then rock back, and fill with more.

Both women have begun to cry.
But neither stops her song.

[1986]

Joining the Conversation: Critical Thinking and Writing

1. Why might the speaker ask the women to sing?
2. Why do the women cry? Why do they continue to sing?
3. Is this poem simple, or complex, or both? Please point to specific details to support your argument.

RANDALL JARRELL

Randall Jarrell (1914–65)—the accent in Jarrell *is on the second syllable—was educated at Vanderbilt University in Nashville, Tennessee, where he majored in psychology. After serving with the air force in World War II as a control tower operator, he taught in several colleges and universities, meanwhile establishing a reputation as a poet and a literary critic.*

The Death of the Ball Turret Gunner

From my mother's sleep I fell into the State,
And I hunched in its belly till my wet fur froze.
Six miles from earth, loosed from its dream of life,
I woke to black flak and the nightmare fighters.
When I died they washed me out of the turret with a hose.   5

[1955]

Jarrell has furnished an explanatory note: "A ball turret was a plexiglass sphere set into the belly of a B-17 or B-24, and inhabited by two .50 caliber machine-guns and one man, a short small man. When this gunner tracked with his machine-guns a fighter attacking his bomber from below, he revolved with the turret; hunched upside-down in his little sphere, he looked like the fetus in the womb. The fighters which attacked him were armed with cannon firing explosive shells. The hose was a steam hose."

Joining the Conversation: Critical Thinking and Writing

1. What is implied in the first line? In line 4: "I woke to . . . nightmare"? Taking account of the title, do you think that "wet fur" is literal or metaphoric, or both? Do you find the simplicity of the last line anticlimactic? How does it continue the metaphor of birth?
2. Why do you think Jarrell ended each line with punctuation?

CHAPTER 7

Analysis: Inquiry, Interpretation, and Argument

Chapter Preview

After reading this chapter, you will be able to

- Define *analysis* and describe the process for analyzing literary texts
- Use inquiry to ask productive questions about a literary text
- Develop an interpretation of a literary text
- Choose a topic and develop an analytical thesis
- Create a strong argument that expresses your interpretation of the text

---

Analysis

In the previous chapter, we explored explication, a form of writing that works its way line by line though a literary work to uncover its meaning. Explication is a method used chiefly in the study of fairly short poems or brief extracts from essays, stories, novels, and plays. In writing about works that are longer than a page or two, a more common approach than explicating is **analyzing** (literally, separating the work into parts in order to better understand the whole). Through literary **analysis**, we aim to come to a deeper understanding of the work, exploring the ideas and issues that it addresses. Through this exploration, we generate an interpretation that takes the form of an argument supported by evidence.

In an analytical essay, we cannot address all of the details in a complex literary text, so we select an element or facet of the text for in-depth exploration, explaining how understanding that part helps us to understand the larger meaning of the text. An analysis of, say, *The Color Purple* may consider the functions of the setting or the uses that certain minor characters serve; an analysis of *Hamlet* may consider the comic passages or the reasons for Hamlet's delay; an analysis of *Death of a Salesman* may consider the depiction of women or the causes of Willy Loman's failure. An analytical essay usually advances a central argument or thesis and offers supporting arguments—reasons, explanations, evidence—that develop the thesis.

Most of the writing that you will do in college—not only in your English courses but also in courses in history, sociology, economics, fine arts, and philosophy—will involve analysis, a method we commonly use in thinking about complex matters and in attempting to account for our responses to them. When we are watching Venus Williams play tennis, we may admire her serve, her backhand, or the execution of several brilliant plays, and then think more generally about the concentration and flexibility that allow her to capitalize on her opponent's momentary weakness. And, of course, when we want to improve our own game, we try to analyze our performance. When writing is our game, we analyze our responses to a work, trying to name them and account for them. We analyze our notes, looking for ideas that connect, searching for significant patterns, and later we analyze our drafts, looking for strengths and weaknesses. Similarly, in peer review, we analyze the draft of a fellow student, seeing how the parts (individual words, sentences, whole paragraphs, the tentative title, and so on) relate to one another and fit together as a whole.

Understanding Analysis as a Process of Inquiry, Interpretation, and Argument

It can be helpful to think of analysis as a natural process or method of thinking. Literature is inherently thought provoking: It encourages us to start analyzing it right away. Any time that we have asked, "Why did that character do that?" we have started the process of analysis. We want to harness this type of thinking and use it in our writing. Let's break down this process of analysis into concrete steps that you can take as you work with a literary work.

- Before you begin analysis, remind yourself that all work with literature begins with close reading. **Close reading** is a careful and attentive reading of literature. In close reading, you "notice what you notice" and start to select aspects of the text for further thought.
- **Analysis** starts with **inquiry**, or the process of asking interesting and revealing **questions** about the text. Analysis also encourages arguing with yourself—asking yourself questions about your inferences, assumptions, definitions, and evidence.
- **Analysis** then encourages **interpretation**, in which you determine what you think the text means as you form answers to your questions. Interpretation requires that you break down the whole into parts, explore the relationship between the parts, and put the parts back together again to determine key ideas. Interpretation often focuses on connecting the "big ideas" or **concepts** raised by the text to the specific details or **evidence** presented by the text.
- **Analysis** is typically best expressed in an **argument**, in which you present your opinions about the text as a well-organized, logical, and insightful sequence of ideas.

To develop an analysis of a work, we must engage in inquiry and interpretation; we must formulate questions and answer them. We can approach a literary work with a variety of questions that will help us start thinking analytically:

- What is the function of the setting in this story or play?
- Why has this character been introduced?
- What is the author trying to tell us?
- How has this idea been developed and made more complex?
- How exactly can we describe the work's tone?
- What is the difference in assumptions between this essay and another one?

After starting with helpful general questions such as these, your analysis will start to generate more specific questions, focusing on the ideas that you see as central to the text.

Analyzing a Story from the Hebrew Bible: The Judgment of Solomon

A brief analysis of a very short story about King Solomon, from the Hebrew Bible (often called the Old Testament), may be useful here. Because the story is short, the analysis can consider all or almost all of the story's parts, and therefore the analysis can seem relatively complete. ("*Seem* relatively complete" because the analysis will, in fact, be far from complete, since the number of reasonable things that can be said about a work is almost as great as the number of its readers. Also, a given reader might, at a later date, offer a different reading from what that reader offers today.)

The following story about King Solomon, customarily called the Judgment of Solomon, appears in the Hebrew Bible, in the latter part of the third chapter of the book called 1 Kings or First Kings, probably written in the mid-sixth century BCE. The translation is from the King James Version of the Bible (1611).

Two expressions in the story need clarification: (1) The woman who "overlaid" her child in her sleep rolled over on the child and suffocated it; and (2) it is said of a woman that her "bowels yearned upon her son," that is, her heart longed for her son. (In Hebrew psychology, the bowels were thought to be the seat of emotion.)

The Judgment of Solomon

Then came there two women, that were harlots, unto the king, and stood before him. And the one woman said, "O my lord, I and this woman dwell in one house, and I was delivered of a child with her in the house. And it came to pass the third day after that I was delivered, that this woman was delivered also: and we were together; there was no stranger in the house, save we two in the house. And this woman's child died in the night; because she overlaid it. And she arose at midnight, and took my son from beside me, while thine handmaid slept, and laid it in her bosom, and laid her dead child in my bosom. And when I rose in the morning to give my child suck, behold, it was dead: but when I considered it in the morning, behold, it was not my son, which I did bear."

And the other woman said, "Nay; but the living is my son, and the dead is thy son." And this said, "No; but the dead is thy son, and the living is my son." Thus they spake before the king.

Then said the king, "The one saith, 'This is my son that liveth, and thy son is dead': and the other saith, 'Nay; but thy son is the dead, and my son is the living.'" And the king said, "Bring me a sword." And they brought a sword before the king. And the king said, "Divide the living child in two, and give half to the one, and half to the other."

Then spake the woman whose the living child was unto the king, for her bowels yearned upon her son, and she said, "O my lord, give her the living child, and in no wise slay it." But the other said, "Let it be neither mine nor thine, but divide it."

5   Then the king answered and said, "Give her the living child, and in no wise slay it: she is the mother thereof."

And all Israel heard of the judgment which the king had judged; and they feared the king, for they saw that the wisdom of God was in him to do judgment.

Developing an Analysis of the Story

How can we analyze this story? Let's begin by analyzing the **form** or the shape of the story. One form or shape that we notice is this:

The story moves from a problem to a solution.

We can also say, still speaking of the overall form, that:

The story moves from quarreling and talk of death to unity and talk of life.

In short, the story has a happy ending, a form that (because it provides an optimistic view of life and also a sense of completeness) gives most people pleasure.

In thinking about a work of literature, it is always useful to take notice of the basic form of the whole, the overall structural pattern. Doubtless you are already familiar with many basic patterns, for example,

tragedy (joy yielding to sorrow) and
romantic comedy (angry conflict yielding to joyful union).

If you think even briefly about verbal works, you'll notice the structures or patterns that govern songs, episodes in soap operas, political speeches (beginning with the candidate's expression of pleasure at being in Duluth and ending with "God bless you all"), detective stories, westerns, and so on. And, just as viewers of western films experience one western in the context of others, so readers experience one story in the context of similar stories, and one poem in the context of other poems.

Looking at its form, we can start to explore the ideas that are expressed through that form. We can say that *The Judgment of Solomon* is a sort of detective story: There is a death, followed by a conflict in the testimony of the witnesses, and then a solution by a shrewd outsider. Consider Solomon's predicament. Ordinarily in literature, characters are sharply defined and individualized, yet the essence of a detective story is that the culprit should *not* be easily recognized as wicked, and here nothing seems to distinguish the two petitioners. Solomon is confronted by "two women, that were harlots." Until late in the story—that is, up to the time Solomon suggests dividing the child—they are described only as "the one woman," "the other woman," "the one," "the other."

Does the story suffer from weak characterization? If we think analytically about this issue, we realize that the point surely is *not* to make each woman distinct. Rather, the point is (until late in the story) to make the women as alike as possible so that we cannot tell which of the two is speaking the truth. Like Solomon, we have nothing to go on; neither witness is known to be more honest than the other, and there are no other witnesses to support or refute either woman.

Analysis is concerned with

- seeing the relationships between the parts of a work, but it is also concerned with
- taking notice of what is not in the work.

A witness would destroy the story, or turn it into an utterly different story. Another thing missing from this story is an explicit editorial comment or interpretation, except for the brief remark at the end that the people "feared the king." If we had read the story in the Geneva Bible (1557–60), which is the translation of the Bible that Shakespeare was familiar with, we would have found a marginal comment: "Her motherly affection herein appeareth that she had rather endure the rigour of the lawe, than see her child cruelly slaine." Would you agree that it is better, at least in this story, for the reader to draw conclusions than for the storyteller explicitly to point them out?

Solomon wisely contrives a situation in which these two claimants, who seem so similar, will reveal their true natures: The mother will reveal her love, and the liar will reveal her hard heart. The early symmetry (the competing identities of the two women) pleases the reader, and so does the device by which we can at last distinguish between the two women.

But even near the end there is a further symmetry. To save the child's life, the true mother gives up her claim, crying out, "Give her the living child, and in no wise slay it." The author (or, rather, the translator who produced this part of the King James Version) takes these very words, with no change whatsoever, and puts them into Solomon's mouth as the king's final judgment. Solomon too says, "Give her the living child, and in no wise slay it," but now the sentence takes on a new meaning. In the first sentence, "her" refers to the liar (the true mother says to give the child to "her"); in Solomon's sentence, "her" refers to the true mother: "Give her the living child. . . ." Surely we take pleasure in the fact that the very words by which the mother renounces her child are the words (1) that reveal to Solomon the truth and that (2) Solomon uses to restore the child to his mother.

In our analysis, we have talked chiefly about the relations of parts, and we have tried to explain why the two women in this story are *not* distinct until Solomon finds a way to reveal their distinctive natures: If the story is to demonstrate Solomon's wisdom, the women must seem identical until Solomon can show that they differ. We can start to imagine a paper that makes the argument that the two women must be seen as interchangeable in order for Solomon's discovery of the mother— and his use of a key question to differentiate of them—to have real power.

But our analysis could have gone into some other topic. Let's consider several possibilities. A student might begin by asking this question: Although it is important for the women to be highly similar, why are they harlots? (It is too simple to answer that the women in the story are harlots, because the author is faithfully reporting a historical episode in Solomon's career. The story is widely recognized as a folktale that is also found in other ancient cultures.) One possible reason for making the women harlots is that the story demands that there be no witnesses; by using harlots, the author disposed of husbands, parents, and siblings who might otherwise be expected to live with the women. A second possible reason is that the author wanted to show that Solomon's justice extended to all, not only to respectable folk. Third, perhaps the author wished to reject or to complicate the stereotype of the harlot as a thoroughly disreputable person. The author rejected or complicated the harlot by introducing another (and truer?) stereotype, the mother motivated by overwhelming maternal love.

Opening Up Additional Ways to Analyze the Story

One sign of a good analytical approach to a literary work is that it opens the work up for further thinking. Although in an analytical essay, you must ultimately select one idea for development, the brainstorming required by analysis will often lead to many good ideas that must be considered and put aside. As you formulate an analysis, you might imagine many alternative "ways in" to the work. Let's consider some of the other ways in which The Judgment of Solomon could be analyzed.

1. Another kind of analytical essay might go beyond the structure of the individual work, to the relation of the work to some larger whole. For instance, the writer might approach The Judgment of Solomon from the point of view

of gender criticism (discussed in Appendix A): In this story, it might be argued, wisdom is an attribute only of a male; women are either deceitful or emotional. From this point, the writer might set out to create a research essay on gender in a larger whole, using certain books of the Hebrew Bible.

2. We might also analyze the story in the context of other examples of what scholars call Wisdom Literature (the Book of Proverbs and Ecclesiastes, for instance). Notice that Solomon's judgment leads the people to *fear* him—because his wisdom is great, formidable, and God-inspired.

   It happens that we do not know who wrote The Judgment of Solomon, but the authors of most works of literature that came later are known, and therefore some critics seek to analyze a given work within the context of the author's life. Evidence drawn from the author's biography would be used to support an interpretation. For some other critics, the larger context would be the reading process, which includes the psychology of the reader. (Biographical criticism and reader-response criticism are discussed in Appendix A.)

3. Still another analysis—again, remember that a work can be analyzed from many points of view—might examine two or more translations of the story. You do not need to know Hebrew in order to compare an early seventeenth-century translation with a twentieth-century version, such as that of the New Jerusalem Bible or the Revised English Bible. You might argue that one version is, on literary grounds, more effective. Such an essay might include an attempt, by means of a comparison, to analyze the effect of the archaic language of the King James Version. Does the somewhat unfamiliar language turn a reader off, or does it add mystery, dignity, or authority to the tale—valuable qualities perhaps not found in the modern version? By the way, in the Revised English Bible, Solomon does *not* exactly repeat the mother's plea. The mother says, "Let her have the baby," and Solomon then says, "Give the living baby to the first woman." In the New Jerusalem Bible, after the mother says, "Let them give her the live child," Solomon says, "Give the live child to the first woman." If you prefer one version to the other two, why not try to analyze the reasons for your preference?

4. Finally, it should be mentioned that an analysis of the structure of a work, in which the relationships of the parts to the whole are considered, allows the work to be regarded as independent of the external world. If we argue, say, that literature should in all respects reflect life, and we want to analyze the work against reality as we see it, we may find ourselves severely judging The Judgment of Solomon. We might ask if it is likely that a great king would bother to hear the case of two prostitutes quarreling over a child or if it is likely that the false claimant would really call for the killing of the child. Similarly, to take an absurd example, an analysis of this story in terms of its ability to evoke laughter would be laughable. The point is this: An analysis will be interesting and useful to a reader only insofar as the aim of the analysis seems reasonable.

Analyzing a Story from the New Testament: The Parable of the Prodigal Son

Let's now look at another brief story from the Bible, this one from the Gospel according to Luke, in the New Testament. Luke, the author of the third of the four Gospels, was a second-generation Christian. He was probably a Roman, though some early

accounts refer to him as a Syrian; in any case, he wrote in Greek, probably composing the Gospel in about 80–85 CE. In Luke 15:11-32, the author reports a story that
Jesus told. This story, which occurs only in Luke's Gospel, is of a type called a
parable, an extremely brief narrative from which a moral may be drawn.

The Parable of the Prodigal Son

And he said, "A certain man had two sons: and the younger of them said to his father,
'Father, give me a portion of goods that falleth to me.' And he divided unto them his
living. And not many days after, the younger son gathered all together, and took his
journey into a far country, and there wasted his substance with riotous living.

"And when he had spent all, there arose a mighty famine in that land, and he
began to be in want. And he went and joined himself to a citizen of that country,
and he sent him into his fields to feed swine. And he would fain have filled his
belly with the husks that the swine did eat: and no man gave unto him. And when
he came to himself, he said, 'How many hired servants of my father's have bread
enough and to spare, and I perish with hunger? I will arise and go to my father,
and will say unto him, "Father, I have sinned against heaven, and before thee, and
am no more worthy to be called thy son: make me as one of thy hired servants."'

"And he arose, and came to his father. But when he was yet a great way off,
his father saw him, and had compassion, and ran, and fell on his neck, and kissed
him. And the son said unto him, 'Father, I have sinned against heaven, and in thy
sight, and am no more worthy to be called thy son.' But the father said to his servants, 'Bring forth the best robe, and put it on him, and put a ring on his hand, and
shoes on his feet. And bring hither the fatted calf, and kill it, and let us eat, and be
merry. For this my son was dead, and is alive again; he was lost, and is found.' And
they began to be merry.

"Now his elder son was in the field, and as he came and drew nigh to the
house, he heard music and dancing. And he called one of the servants, and asked
what these things meant. And he said unto him 'Thy brother is come, and thy father
hath killed the fatted calf, because he hath received him safe and sound.' And he
was angry, and would not go in: therefore came his father out, and entreated him.
And he answering said to his father 'Lo, these many years do I serve thee, neither
transgressed I at any time thy commandment, and yet thou never gavest me a kid,
that I might make merry with friends: but as soon as this thy son was come, which
hath devoured thy living with harlots, thou hast killed for him the fatted calf.' And
he said unto him, 'Son, thou art ever with me, and all that I have is thine. It was
meet that we should make merry, and be glad: for this thy brother was dead, and
is alive again: and was lost, and is found.'"

Asking Questions That Trigger an Analysis of the Story

Now that you've read The Parable of the Prodigal Son, how would you start to
analyze it? Looking at our analysis of The Judgment of Solomon, can you follow a
similar process to explore the form of this story and the ideas that it expresses?
What interesting situation does the story dramatize, and what ideas are revealed by
this situation? What parts of the story are most interesting to you? How do those
parts of the story come together to create the story's whole or its larger meaning?

In order to understand a literary work, we must question it. In sections following the literary works that appear in this anthology, we pose questions about them.
These questions may stimulate your thinking and thus help you write. Our concern

as teachers of writing is not so much with the answers to these questions as with your use of the questions to start a process of open-ended thinking. We believe, and we ask you to believe, that there are no "right" answers, only more or less persuasive ones, to most questions about literature—as about life. Our aim is to help you to pose questions that will stimulate your best thinking.

Inquiry—question asking—starts the process of analysis. Following are some questions that can help you to form your analysis of The Judgment of Solomon.

1. In talking about The Judgment of Solomon, we commented on certain repetitions (two women, for example) and contrasts (for example, troubled beginning, happy ending), which help to give shape to the story. What parallels or contrasts (or both) do you find in the parable of the prodigal son? What function does the older brother serve? If he were omitted, what, if anything, would be lost? (Characterize him, partly by comparing him with the younger brother and with the father.)

2. Is the father foolish and sentimental? Do you approve or disapprove of his behavior at the end? In a short argumentative essay (250–500 words), support your thesis.

3. Jesus told the story, so it must have had a meaning that was consistent with his other teachings. Christians customarily interpret the story as meaning that God (like the father in the parable) rejoices in the return of a sinner. What meaning, if any, can it have for readers who are not Christians? Explain your answer.

4. Does this parable present an argument? Can you offer a counterargument to the parable?

From Inquiry to Interpretation to Argument: Developing an Analytical Paper

If a story is short enough, you may be able to examine everything in it that you think is worth commenting on, but even if it is short, you may nevertheless decide to focus on one element, such as the setting, or the construction of the plot, or the connection between two characters, or the degree of plausibility. A close examination of one or more specific elements will allow you to explain the ideas that you feel are most central to the work. Let's read a story by Ernest Hemingway, one of America's most famous twentieth-century fiction writers, and see what elements of the story two different student writers choose to emphasize.

ERNEST HEMINGWAY

Ernest Hemingway (1899–1961) was born in Oak Park, Illinois. After graduating from high school in 1917, he worked on the Kansas City Star *but left to serve as a volunteer ambulance driver in Italy, where he was wounded in action. He returned home, married, and then served as European correspondent for the* Toronto Star, *but he soon focused on writing fiction. In 1922, he settled in Paris, where he moved in a circle of American expatriates that included Ezra Pound, Gertrude Stein, and F. Scott Fitzgerald. It was in Paris that he wrote stories and nov-*

els about what Gertrude Stein called a "lost generation" of rootless Americans in Europe. (For Hemingway's reminiscences of the Paris years, see his posthumously published A Moveable Feast.*) He served as a journalist during the Spanish Civil War and during World War II, but he was also something of a private soldier.*

After World War II, his reputation ebbed, though he was still active as a writer (for instance, he wrote The Old Man and the Sea *in 1952). In 1954, Hemingway was awarded the Nobel Prize in Literature; in 1961, depressed by a sense of failing power, he took his own life.*

Cat in the Rain

There were only two Americans stopping at the hotel. They did not know any of the people they passed on the stairs on their way to and from their room. Their room was on the second floor facing the sea. It also faced the public garden and the war monument. There were big palms and green benches in the public garden. In the good weather there was always an artist with his easel. Artists liked the way the palms grew and the bright colors of the hotels facing the gardens and the sea. Italians came from a long way off to look up at the war monument. It was made of bronze and glistened in the rain. It was raining. The rain dripped from the palm trees. Water stood in pools on the gravel paths. The sea broke in a long line in the rain and slipped back down the beach to come up and break again in a long line in the rain. The motor cars were gone from the square by the war monument. Across the square in the doorway of the café a waiter stood looking out at the empty square.

The American wife stood at the window looking out. Outside right under their window a cat was crouched under one of the dripping green tables. The cat was trying to make herself so compact that she would not be dripped on.

"I'm going down and get that kitty," the American wife said.

"I'll do it," her husband offered from the bed.

5   "No, I'll get it. The poor kitty is out trying to keep dry under a table."

The husband went on reading, lying propped up with the two pillows at the foot of the bed.

"Don't get wet," he said.

The wife went downstairs and the hotel owner stood up and bowed to her as she passed the office. His desk was at the far end of the office. He was an old man and very tall.

"Il piove,"[1] the wife said. She liked the hotel-keeper.

10   "Si, si, Signora, brutto tempo. It is very bad weather."

He stood behind his desk in the far end of the dim room. The wife liked him. She liked the deadly serious way he received any complaints. She liked his dignity. She liked the way he wanted to serve her. She liked the way he felt about being a hotel-keeper. She liked his old, heavy face and big hands.

Liking him she opened the door and looked out. It was raining harder. A man in a rubber cape was crossing the empty square to the café. The cat would be around to the right. Perhaps she could go along under the eaves. As she stood in the doorway an umbrella opened behind her. It was the maid who looked after their room.

"You must not get wet," she smiled, speaking Italian. Of course, the hotel-keeper had sent her.

---

[1]**Il piove** It's raining (Italian).

With the maid holding the umbrella over her, she walked along the gravel path until she was under their window. The table was there, washed bright green in the rain, but the cat was gone. She was suddenly disappointed. The maid looked up at her.

15   "Ha perduto qualque cosa, Signora?"[2]

"There was a cat," said the American girl.

"A cat?"

"Si, il gatto."

"A cat?" the maid laughed. "A cat in the rain?"

20   "Yes," she said, "under the table." Then. "Oh. I wanted it so much. I wanted a kitty."

When she talked English the maid's face tightened.

"Come, Signora," she said. "We must get back inside. You will be wet."

"I suppose so," said the American girl.

They went back along the gravel path and passed in the door. The maid stayed outside to close the umbrella. As the American girl passed the office, the padrone bowed from his desk. Something felt very small and tight inside the girl. The padrone made her feel very small and at the same time really important. She had a momentary feeling of being of supreme importance. She went on up the stairs. She opened the door of the room. George was on the bed, reading.

25   "Did you get the cat?" he asked, putting the book down.

"It was gone."

"Wonder where it went to," he said, resting his eyes from reading.

She sat down on the bed.

"I wanted it so much," she said. "I don't know why I wanted it so much. I wanted that poor kitty. It isn't any fun to be a poor kitty out in the rain."

30   George was reading again.

She went over and sat in front of the mirror of the dressing table looking at herself with the hand glass. She studied her profile, first one side and then the other. Then she studied the back of her head and her neck.

"Don't you think it would be a good idea if I let my hair grow out?" she asked, looking at her profile again.

George looked up and saw the back of her neck, clipped close like a boy's.

"I like it the way it is."

35   "I get so tired of it," she said. "I get so tired of looking like a boy."

George shifted his position in the bed. He hadn't looked away from her since she started to speak.

"You look pretty darn nice," he said.

She laid the mirror down on the dresser and went over to the window and looked out. It was getting dark.

"I want to pull my hair back tight and smooth and make a big knot at the back that I can feel," she said. "I want to have a kitty to sit on my lap and purr when I stroke her."

40   "Yeah?" George said from the bed.

"And I want to eat at a table with my own silver and I want candles. And I want it to be spring and I want to brush my hair out in front of a mirror and I want a kitty and I want some new clothes."

"Oh, shut up and get something to read," George said. He was reading again.

His wife was looking out of the window. It was quite dark now and still raining in the palm trees.

---

[2]**Ha . . . Signora** Have you lost something, Madam?

"Anyway, I want a cat," she said, "I want a cat. I want a cat now. If I can't have long hair or any fun, I can have a cat."

45   George was not listening. He was reading his book. His wife looked out of the window where the light had come on in the square.

Someone knocked at the door.

"Avanti,"[3] George said. He looked up from his book.

In the doorway stood the maid. She held a big tortoise-shell cat pressed tight against her and swung down against her body.

"Excuse me," she said, "the padrone asked me to bring this for the Signora."

[1925]

Close Reading

Careful close reading is the best way to start the analysis process. When you read a story—or, perhaps more accurately, when you reread a story before discussing it or writing about it—you'll find it helpful to jot an occasional note (for instance, a brief response or a question) in the margins and to underline or highlight passages that strike you as especially interesting. Here is part of the story, along with the annotations of a student in a college writing course, Tom Yanagi.

Student Work: Annotation

The cat was trying to make herself so compact that she would not be dripped on.

He doesn't make a move

"I'm going down and get that kitty," the American wife said.

Is he making a joke? Or maybe he just isn't even thinking about what he is saying?

"I'll do it," her husband offered from the bed.

"No, I'll get it. The poor kitty is out trying to keep dry under a table."

The husband went on reading, lying propped up with the two pillows at the foot of the bed.

still doesn't move

"Don't get wet," he said.

contrast with the husband

The wife went downstairs and the hotel owner stood up and bowed to her as she passed the office. His desk was at the far end of the office. He was an old man and very tall.

"Il piove," the wife said. She liked the hotel-keeper.

"Si, si, Signora, brutto tempo. It is very bad weather."

He stood behind his desk in the far end of the dim room. The wife liked him. She liked the deadly serious way he received any complaints. She liked his dignity. She liked the way he wanted to serve her. She liked the way he felt about being a hotel-keeper. She liked his old, heavy face and big hands.

She respects him and she is pleased by the attention he shows

to emphasize the bad weather??

Liking him she opened the door and looked out. It was raining harder. A man in a rubber cape was crossing the empty square to the café. The cat would be around to the right.

---

[3]**Avanti** Come in.

Inquiry Questions

Everything in a story is presumably important, but if you have read the story once, probably something has especially interested (or puzzled) you, such as the relationship between two people or the way the end of the story is connected to the beginning. On rereading, then, pen in hand, you'll find yourself noticing things that you missed or didn't find especially significant on your first reading and first annotation. Now that you know the end of the story, you will read the beginning in a different way.

If your instructor asks you to think about certain questions, you'll keep them in mind while you reread, and you'll find ideas coming to you. In "Cat in the Rain," suppose you are asked (or you ask yourself) if the story might just as well be about a dog in the rain. Would anything be lost?

Following are a few questions that you can ask of almost any story. (On pages 455–57, we give a fuller list.) After scanning the questions, you will want to reread the story, pen in hand, and then note your responses, either on a sheet of paper or on your computer. As you write, it will be helpful to go back and reread the story or at least parts of it.

1. *What happens?* In two or three sentences—say, in twenty-five to fifty words—summarize what happens in the story. What are the most important events?
2. *What sorts of people are the chief characters?* In "Cat in the Rain," the chief characters are George, George's wife, and the innkeeper (the padrone). Note the traits that each seems to possess, and next to each trait, briefly give some supporting evidence.
3. *What especially pleased or displeased you in the story?* Devote at least a sentence or two to the end of the story. Do you find the end satisfying? Why or why not?
4. *Have you any thoughts about the title?* If so, what are they? If the story did not have a title, what would you call it?

After you have made your own notes, compare them with responses to these same questions by the student, Tom Yanagi. No two readers will respond in exactly the same way, but all readers can examine their responses and try to account for them, at least in part. If your responses are substantially different, how do you account for the differences?

Student Work: Inquiry Notes

1. *What happens?*
   A Summary:
   A young wife, stopping with her husband at an Italian hotel, from her room sees a cat in the rain. She goes to get it, but it is gone, and so she returns empty-handed. A moment later the maid knocks at the door, holding a tortoise-shell cat.

2. *What sorts of people are the chief characters?*
   The characters and evidence:
   The woman.
   —kind-hearted (pities cat in rain)
   —appreciates innkeeper's courtesy ("liked the way he wanted to serve her") and admires him ("She liked his dignity")

—unhappy (wants a cat, wants to change her hair, wants to eat at a table with her own silver)

The husband, George.

—not willing to put himself out (says he'll go to garden to get cat but doesn't move)

—doesn't seem very interested in wife (hardly talks to her—he's reading; tells her to "shut up")

—but he does say he finds her attractive ("You look pretty darn nice")

The innkeeper.

—serious, dignified ("She liked the deadly serious way he received any complaints. She liked his dignity")

courteous, helpful (sends maid with umbrella; at end sends maid with cat)

3. *What especially pleased or displeased you in the story?*

   Dislikes and likes:

   —"Dislikes" is too strong, but I was disappointed that more didn't happen at the end. What is the husband's reaction to the cat? Or his final reaction to his wife? I mean, what did he think about his wife when the maid brings the cat? And, for that matter, what is the wife's reaction? Is she satisfied? Or does she realize that the cat can't really make her happy?

   —Now for the *likes*. (1) I guess I did like the way it turned out; it's sort of a happy ending, I think, since she wants the cat and gets it. (2) I also especially like the innkeeper. Maybe I like him partly because the wife likes him, and if she likes him he must be nice. And he *is* nice—very helpful.

4. *Have you any thoughts about the title?*

   The title:

   —I don't suppose that I would have called it "Cat in the Rain," but I don't know what I would have called it. Maybe "An American Couple in Italy." Or maybe "The Innkeeper." I really do think that the innkeeper is very important, even though he only has a few lines. He's very impressive—not only to the girl, but to me (and maybe to all readers), since at the end of the story we see how careful the innkeeper is.

   —But the more I think about Hemingway's title, the more I think that maybe it also refers to the girl. Like the "poor kitty" in the rain, the wife is in a pretty bad situation. "It isn't any fun to be a poor kitty out in the rain." Of course the woman is indoors, but her husband generates lots of unpleasant weather. She may as well be out in the rain. She says "I want to have a kitty to sit on my lap and purr when I stroke her." This shows that she wants to be affectionate and that she also wants to have someone respond to her affection. She *is* like a cat in the rain.

Tom's responses probably include statements that you want to take issue with. Or, perhaps you feel that the student did not even mention some things that you think are important. You may want to make notes on the student's inquiry notes and raise some questions about them in class.

Interpretation Brainstorming

Good inquiry questions trigger brainstorming and the development of ideas that move beyond the initial question. For example, Tom used his inquiry notes to develop the following detailed journal entry. His instructor asked the class to revisit their inquiry notes, to locate an interesting idea, and to continue to write about that idea in their journals. This more concentrated writing encourages interpretation or the explanation of your understanding of the meaning of the text. The interpretive stance, focused and developed further, can lead to a paper's topic. Let's take a look at Tom's developing analysis of the story in his journal writing.

Student Work: Journal Writing

As I look back on my inquiry notes and think about the story a second time, one of my "dislikes" becomes a "like." I like the way Hemingway shows the husband. I don't mean that I like the man himself, but I like the way Hemingway shows he is such a bastard—not getting off the bed to get the cat, telling his wife to shut up and read.

Another thing about him is that the one time he says something nice about her, it's about her hair, and she isn't keen on the way her hair is. She says it makes her look "like a boy," and she is "tired" of looking like a boy. There's something wrong with this marriage. George hardly pays attention to his wife, but he wants her to look like a boy. Maybe the idea is that this macho guy wants to keep her looking like an inferior (immature) version of himself. He doesn't seem to want to recognize her individuality or see her as a unique person with any power in the situation.

Perhaps this is represented by the way she is referred to as an "American wife." This term gets repeated. The word "wife" is repeated, but we never learn her name. That becomes her identity. George certainly doesn't seem interested in letting her fulfill herself as a woman.

I like the way Hemingway shows us the relation between the husband and wife (even though the relation is pretty bad), and I like the innkeeper. Even if the relation with the couple ends unhappily, the story has a sort of happy ending, so far as it goes, since the innkeeper does what he can to please his guest: he sends the maid, with the cat. There's really nothing more that he can do.

The more I think about it, the more I feel that the ending is as happy as it can be. George is awful. When his wife says "I want a cat and I want a cat now," Hemingway tells us "George was not listening." And then, a moment later, almost like a godmother the maid appears and grants the wife's wish.

The Argument-Centered Paper

In preparation for writing a draft for a paper, Tom reread the story and reexamined his annotations on the story, inquiry notes, and journal entry. As he looked over his own notes, he jotted down possible thesis ideas and subpoints that he could use to develop the body of his paper. His paper focuses on the idea of the main character being referred to as an "American wife" and how that term reflects her relationship with her husband. As you read this essay, see if you can see find traces of Tom's earlier inquiry and interpretation notes: What ideas did he start to develop in the brainstorming stages?

Student Argument Essay: "Hemingway's American Wife"

Tom Yanagi

Professor Costello

English 10B

21 December 2015

Hemingway's American Wife

My title alludes not to any of the four women to whom Hemingway was married, but to "the American wife" who is twice called by this term in his short story "Cat in the Rain." We first meet her in the first sentence of the story ("There were only two Americans stopping at the hotel"), and the next time she is mentioned (apart from a reference to the wife and her husband as "they") it is as "the American wife," at the beginning of the second paragraph of the story. The term is used again at the end of the third paragraph.

She is, then, at least in the early part of this story, just an American or an American wife—someone identified only by her nationality and her marital status, but not at all by her personality, her individuality, her inner self. She first becomes something of an individual when she separates herself from her husband by leaving the hotel room and going to look for a cat that she has seen in the garden, in the rain. This act of separation, however, has not the slightest effect on her husband, who "went on reading" (200).

When she returns, without the cat, he puts down his book and speaks to her, but it is obvious that he has no interest in her, beyond as a physical object ("You look pretty darn nice"). This comment is produced when she says she is thinking of letting her hair grow out because she is "so tired of looking like a boy" (201). Why, a reader wonders, does her husband, who has paid almost no attention to her up to now, assure her that she looks "pretty darn nice"? I think it is reasonable to conclude that he *wants* her to look like

Yanagi 2

someone who is not truly a woman, in particular someone who is immature. That she does not feel she has much identity is evident when she continues to talk about letting her hair grow, and she says "I want to pull my hair back tight and smooth and make a big knot at the back that I can feel" (201). Long hair is, or at least was, the traditional sign of a woman; she wants long hair, and at the same time she wants to keep it under her control by tying it in a "big knot," a knot that she can feel, a knot whose presence reminds her, because she can feel it, of her feminine nature.

She goes on to say that she wants to brush her hair "in front of a mirror." That is, she wants to *see* and to feel her femininity, since her husband apparently—so far as we can see in the story, at least—scarcely recognizes it or her. Perhaps her desire for the cat ("I want a cat") is a veiled way of saying that she wants to express her animal nature, and not be simply a neglected woman who is made by her husband to look like a boy. Hemingway tells us, however, that when she looked for the cat in the garden she could not find it, a sign, I think, of her failure to break from the man. At the end of the story the maid brings her the cat, but a woman cannot just be handed a new nature and accept it, just like that. She has to find it herself, and in herself, so I think the story ends with "the American wife" still nothing more than an American wife.

[New page]

Yanagi 3

Work Cited

Hemingway, Ernest. "Cat in the Rain." *Literature for Composition*. Ed. Sylvan Barnet, William Burto, William E. Cain, and Cheryl L. Nixon. 11th ed. Boston: Pearson, 2017. 200-02. Print.

Joining the Conversation: Critical Thinking and Writing

As you consider whether you liked the essay or not, a few comments and questions may be useful.

1. Do you find the essay interesting? Explain your response.
2. Do you find the essay well written? Explain your response.
3. Do you find the argument convincing? Can you suggest ways of strengthening it, or do you think the argument is mistaken? Carefully reread "Cat in the Rain," taking note of passages that give further support to this student's argument or that seem to challenge or qualify it.
4. We often say that a good critical essay sends us back to the literary work with a fresh point of view. Our rereading differs from our earlier reading. Does this essay change your reading of Hemingway's story?

From Inquiry to an Analytical Paper: A Second Example

Another student, Holly Klein, wrote about "Cat in the Rain," but she thought about it partly in terms of a familiar saying: "Love means never having to say you're sorry." Following are her inquiry notes, her journal writing, and the essay that she developed from these idea-generating steps. Holly did not use the general inquiry questions suggested above. Instead, while taking brainstorming notes on her computer, she generated her own questions and answered them. Her brainstorming is thus very personal, which guarantees a more original interpretation of the work. Notice how Holly includes lots of quotations in her questions and answers. She is already using evidence to support and develop her ideas, and that evidence will certainly appear in her essay.

Student Work: Inquiry Notes

1. *The cat:* Can we be certain that the cat at the end of the story is the cat that the woman saw in the rain? When we first hear about the cat in the rain we are not told anything about its color, and at the end of the story we are not told that the tortoise-shell cat is wet. I think there are two cats. I think this is important. She is willing to take any cat, as long as it is something she can love.

2. *The cat again!* What does the cat represent? The cat seems to represent the child that the wife wants to have. The way she talks about the cat makes it sound like a longed-for child: "Oh. I wanted it so much. I wanted a kitty." And: "Anyway, I want a cat," she said, "I want a cat. I want a cat now. If I can't have long hair or any fun, I can have a cat." She is wanting something to love. The way that she keeps repeating that she wants the cat reveals how unhappy she is.

3. *Relationship to padrone.* These lines struck me as really strange:

   "As the American girl passed the office, the padrone bowed from his desk. Something felt very small and tight inside the girl. The padrone made her feel very small and at the same time really important. She had a momentary feeling of being of supreme importance."

   What do these line mean? Is there anything sexual here? I guess I do think something sexual is happening here, but I'm not sure exactly why. The wife seems to feel this strange excitement when seeing the padrone. She feels both small and important. I think that Hemingway is trying to explain being attracted to someone else, even though you are married. So, Hemingway has to show the conflict that feeling creates in the wife. She feels both small and important. I think it is important that she feels both of these things and that she feels them inside, which makes it sound sexual.

4. *Happiness:* Is it true that love stories are about people who are happy in love, or are they mostly about people who are unhappy? I think Hemingway is showing us that love can lead to unhappiness. This is a very unhappy couple, but that is what makes them interesting. If Hemingway's lovers were happy and spent their time cooing at each other, the story probably would have been boring. Unhappiness seems to be the key idea that story is exploring—perhaps this is a good paper topic?

5. *Biographical information:* How can we connect biographical information to the story? How does knowing about Hemingway's own life help me to understand the story? As we learned in class, Hemingway wrote the story in Italy, when his wife Hadley was pregnant. In a letter to F. Scott Fitzgerald he said,

> Cat in the Rain wasn't about Hadley. . . . When I wrote that we were at Rapallo but Hadley was 4 months pregnant with Bumby. The Inn Keeper was the one at Cortina D'Ampezzo. . . . Hadley never made a speech in her life about wanting a baby because she had been told various things by her doctor and I'd—no use going into all that. (*Letters* 180)

> As we talked about in class, I think Hemingway knew his marriage was on the rocks and that he was going to get a divorce. This helps me to understand the story and makes the story more interesting. I think Hemingway wanted to show an unhappy couple, putting some of his own life into the story.

What types of questions and answers would you generate to help develop an interpretation of the story? No two readers will respond in exactly the same way, but all readers can examine their responses and try to account for them, at least in part. Can you imagine new questions or ideas that neither Tom Yanagi nor Holly Klein address?

Let's turn now to Holly's journal writing to see how she continues to develop her questions and answers, moving toward her own interpretation of the story.

Student Work: Journal Writing

Although this story features a married couple in a hotel at the sea, there is not much romantic passion in this story. Even though they seem to be on vacation, this couple seems unhappy. Are these people in love?

> *Is it true that love stories are about people who are happy in love, or are they mostly about people who are unhappy? Many lovers may suffer and some even die (Leonardo DiCaprio in Titanic), but aren't they happy anyway? They are happy in their unhappiness. (And Rose—Kate Winslet—survives, happy and unhappy in her love.)*

> *Is "Cat" really a love story anyway? Yes, in the sense it is about people who must at least at some time in the past have been lovers—happy lovers— but who now seem stuck with each other. The wife still seems to be in love, or maybe she is trying to bring a dead love back to life. But she is unhappy—and who wouldn't be, with a husband like hers? She says that she is going out in the rain to get the cat, and he doesn't even pay attention. He just goes on reading, obviously uninterested in what she is doing. Later, when she is talking about what she wants, he even tells her, "Oh, shut up and get something to read." This statement really struck me—it was here that I saw how much the husband*

ignored her. He wants the wife to be quiet and not bother him—not bother him
with her wants and desires. I think this is what is leading to her unhappiness.

The story seems to be focusing on the unhappiness that exists in any
relationship. The wife keeps mentioning unfulfilled desires: she wants a long hair,
a table with silver, and candles. These desires become focused on the cat. Her
desire for the cat becomes an expression of her unhappiness. She is able to show
her unhappiness—I think this is because women are more able to express their
unhappiness in words. Her husband keeps ignoring her, so she repeats her interest
in the cat again and again. She does not explicitly say that she is unhappy, but
she does express a desire for a life different from the one she is now living.

Student Analytical Essay: "Hemingway's Unhappy Lovers"

Here is the final version of Holly Klein's essay:

Klein 1

Holly Klein

Professor Chung

English 1102

17 December 2015

Hemingway's Unhappy Lovers

In class someone suggested that *Romeo and Juliet* is not so much

about how happy two people are but about how unhappy they are. This

statement, which at first I thought was ridiculous, now strikes me as true,

or for the most part true. The lovers in *Romeo and Juliet* and in *West Side*

Story, to name only some of the most famous lovers, would not give up being

in love, but during most of the time they are unhappy. I have heard a saying,

"Love means not ever having to say you are sorry," but some of these lovers,

and other lovers in daytime television programs, are always saying they are

sorry, and always feeling sorry for themselves. And we feel sorry for them.

Our interest in them is not in their happiness, but in their unhappiness.

Certainly in Ernest Hemingway's "Cat in the Rain" the woman is

unhappy—and who would not be unhappy, with a husband like hers?

She says she is going out into the rain to get the cat, and he says "Don't get

wet" (200), and he goes right on reading, obviously uninterested in what his wife is doing, or in her needs. The wife never explicitly says she is unhappy, but it is obvious that she is. Her husband pays very little attention to her, and then, when he does—he goes so far as to say "You look pretty darn nice"—it is only after she tells him she wants to change her appearance: "I get so tired of looking like a boy." When she adds that she wants to change her hair, his response is, "Yeah?" And a moment later he says, "Oh, shut up and get something to read" (201). At this point in the story, when the husband made this statement, I suddenly realized that these lovers are unhappy. If Hemingway's lovers were happy and spent their time cooing at each other, the story probably would have been boring.

What is interesting here is, paradoxically, the man's lack of interest in his wife—he is probably affectionate only when he wants sex—and the woman's basic unhappiness. Her unhappiness is revealed partly by her almost desperate attempt to give affection to the cat, and to receive some affection from it: "I want to have a kitty to sit on my lap and purr when I stroke her" (201). The wife keeps mentioning unfulfilled desires. For example, she explains that she wants long hair, and imagines eating at a table with silver and candles and imagines brushing her hair in front of a mirror. The husband does not want to be bothered with these desires, which leads him to tell her to "shut up." These unfulfilled wants become focused on the cat, and she repeatedly states that she wants the cat. The wife's desire for the cat, then, becomes an expression of her unhappiness.

Many people probably do not make a distinction between the attitudes of men and women toward love, and they therefore do not distinguish between the responses of men and of women to love stories. I think it is probably true that most love stories are chiefly about unhappiness, but it is probably also true that women in love are more likely than men to express in words their unhappiness. (I think there are psychological or sociological studies that support this view.) In any case, in

Klein 3

support of the idea that love stories are chiefly about unhappiness, I can say

that "Cat in the Rain" interested me not because the lovers keep expressing

their romantic passion but because the man does *not* express his love, and

the woman expresses her frustration. In this story about lovers, the man is

in bed—but he spends most of his time *reading* in bed, and (as I said) about

the best he can say to the woman is that she looks "pretty darn nice." The

wife holds our interest because she is unhappy, stuck with this guy, and she

is so grateful for a kind word from the hotel-keeper. She does not explicitly

say that she is desperately unhappy, but she does express very vigorously a

desire for a life different from the one she is now living, and we do feel that

(at least for her) love is not just a "mood," as it probably is for the man, but

is a matter of "life or death." She is, so to speak, dying to be loved.

[New page]

Klein 4

Work Cited

Hemingway, Ernest. "Cat in the Rain." *Literature for Composition.* Ed. Sylvan

   Barnet, William Burto, William E. Cain, and Cheryl L. Nixon. 11th ed.

   Boston: Pearson, 2017. 200-02. Print.

Joining the Conversation: Critical Thinking and Writing

We can ask about this essay the same questions that we asked about the previous
student essay:

1. Do you find the essay interesting? Explain your response.
2. Do you find the essay well written? Explain your response.
3. Do you find the argument convincing? Can you suggest ways of strengthening
   it, or do you think the argument is mistaken? Carefully reread "Cat in the Rain,"
   taking note of passages that give further support to this student's argument or
   that seem to challenge or qualify it.

4. We often say that a good critical essay sends us back to the literary work with a fresh point of view. Our rereading differs from our earlier reading. Does this essay change your reading of Hemingway's story?

We can also ask one additional question:

5. Sometimes writers make their essays far too impersonal, removing every trace of the writer as an individual human being, a distinct person. Do you think that this writer goes too far in the other direction, making the essay too personal? If you think that she does, what advice would you give her, to help her strike the right balance?

Breaking Down the Analytical Essay

Let's explore how inquiry and interpretation get written up as an argument. Each writing assignment will require its own kind of thinking, but let us provide a few principles that are relevant to analytical writing about literature:

1. Assume that your reader has already read the work that you are discussing but is not thoroughly familiar with it—and, of course, does not know what you think and how you feel about the work. Early in your essay, name the author, the work, and your thesis.
2. Do not tell the plot (or, at most, summarize it very briefly); instead, tell your reader what the work is about (not what happens, but what the happenings add up to).
3. Whether you are writing about character, plot, meter, or anything else, you will probably be telling your reader something about *how* the work functions, that is, how it develops. The stages by which a work advances may sometimes be marked fairly clearly. For instance, a poem of two stanzas may ask a question in the first stanza and give an answer in the second stanza, or it may express a hope in the first stanza and reveal a doubt in the second stanza. Novels are customarily divided into chapters, and even a short story may be printed with numbered parts. Virtually all works are built from parts, whether or not the parts are labeled.
4. In telling the reader how each part leads to the next or how each part arises from what has come before, you will probably comment on such things as (in a story) changes in a character's state of mind—marked perhaps by a change in the setting—or (in a poem) changes in the speaker's tone of voice—for instance, from eager to resigned or from cautious to enthusiastic. Probably you will not only be describing the development of character, tone, or plot, but also (and more important) you will be advancing your own thesis by offering evidence that supports the thesis.

Choosing a Topic and Developing a Thesis

As you move from your brainstorming and note-taking phases, you'll have to single out an appropriate topic for your paper. This topic will center your paper on a main idea, and your thesis will then present an argument about that idea. What is an appropriate topic? First, it must be a topic that you can work up some interest in, or your writing will be mechanical and dull. (We say "work up some interest" because interest is commonly the result of some effort.) Second, an appropriate topic is compassable—that is, it is something you can discuss with reasonable attention to detail in the few pages (and few days) you have to devote to it. If a work is fairly long, almost surely you will write an analysis of some part of it.

Unless you have lots of time for reflection and revision, you cannot write a meaningful essay of five hundred words or even a thousand words on "Shakespeare's *Hamlet* " or "The Fiction of Alice Walker." At that length, you cannot even write on "Character in *Hamlet*" or "Symbolism in Walker's *The Color Purple*." And probably you won't really want to write on such topics anyway; probably *one* character or *one* symbol has caught your interest. Think of something in your annotations or "response writing" (described in Chapter 3) that has caught your attention. Trust your feelings; you are likely onto something interesting.

In Chapter 3, we talked about the value of asking yourself questions as part of the critical thinking process. To find an appropriate topic, ask yourself such questions as:

1. *What purpose does this serve?* For instance, why is this scene in the novel or play? Why is there a comic grave digger in *Hamlet?* Why are these lines unrhymed? Why did the author call the work by this title? Why are these characters unable to come to an agreement?
2. *Why do I have this response?* Why do I feel that this work is more profound (or amusing, or puzzling) than another work? How did the author make this character funny or dignified or pathetic? How did the author communicate the idea that this character is a bore without boring me?
3. *Can I think both outward and inward—to both larger concepts and smaller details?* How does this scene allow me to both think about larger abstract ideas and look closely at the specific evidence that it provides? How does this work's imagery (or voice, or setting, or character) use specific words to introduce larger conceptual ideas?

The first of these questions, "What purpose does this serve?" requires that you identify yourself with the author, wondering, for example, whether the opening scene is the best possible for the story. The second question, "Why do I have this response?" requires that you trust your feelings. If you are amused, or puzzled, or annoyed, assume that these responses are appropriate and follow them up, at least until a rereading of the work provides other responses. If you make notes reporting your responses and later think about them, you will probably find that you can select a topic. The third question, "Can I think both outward and inward?" asks you to locate a topic that will allow you to explore larger conceptual ideas (such as love, envy, balance, or justice) while rooting them in the specific details of the text (such as, in "Cat in the Rain," that a spouse can express a need for love in how she responds to other people and animals).

A fourth valuable way to find a thesis is to test a published comment against your response to a work. Perhaps somewhere you have seen—say, in a textbook—a statement about the nature of fiction, poetry, or drama. Maybe you have heard that a tragic hero has a "flaw." Don't simply accept the remark. Test it against your reading of the work. Interpret the word *published* broadly. Students and instructors publish their opinions—offer them to a public—when they utter them in class. Think about something said in class; students who pay close attention to what their peers say learn a great deal.

Given an appropriate topic, you will find your essay easier to write and the finished version of it clearer and more persuasive if, at some point in your preparation, in note taking or in writing a first draft, you have converted your topic into a *thesis* (a proposition, a point, an argument) and have constructed a *thesis statement* (a sentence stating your overall point).

Let's dwell a moment on the distinction between a topic and a thesis. It may be useful to think of it this way: A topic is a subject (for example, "The role of Providence in *Hamlet*"); to arrive at a thesis, you have to make an arguable assertion (for example, "The role of Providence in *Hamlet* is not obvious, but it is crucial").

Some theses are more promising than others. Consider this thesis:

> The role of Providence in *Hamlet* is interesting.

This sentence asserts a thesis, but it is vague and provides little direction and little help in generating ideas and in shaping your essay. Let's try again. It's almost always necessary to try again and again, because the process of writing is, in large part, a process of trial and error, of generating better and better ideas by evaluating— selecting or rejecting—ideas and options.

> The role of Providence is evident in the Ghost.

This is much better, and it could stimulate ideas for an interesting essay. Let's assume the writer rereads the play, looking for further evidence, and comes to believe that the Ghost is only one of several manifestations of Providence. The writer may stay with the Ghost or may (especially if the paper is long enough to allow for such a thesis to be developed) alter the thesis thus:

> The role of Providence is not confined to the Ghost but is found also in the killing of Polonius, in the surprising appearance of the pirate ship, and in the presence of the poisoned chalice.

Strictly speaking, the thesis here is given in the first part of the sentence ("The role of Providence is not confined to the Ghost"); the rest of the sentence provides an indication of how the argument will be supported.

Every literary work suggests its own topics for analysis to an active reader, and all essayists must set forth their own theses, but if you begin by seeking to examine one of your responses, you will soon be able to stake out a topic and to formulate a thesis.

Developing an Argument

Introductory Paragraphs

As the poet Byron said, at the beginning of a long section of his poem, *Don Juan*, "Nothing so difficult as a beginning." Woody Allen thinks so, too. In an interview, he said that the toughest part of writing is "to go from nothing to the first draft."

We can give two pieces of advice:

1. *The opening paragraph is unimportant.* It's great if you can write a paragraph that will engage your readers and let them know where the essay will be taking them, but, if you can't come up with such a paragraph, just put down anything in order to prime the pump.

2. *The opening paragraph is extremely important.* It must engage your readers, and, probably by means of a thesis sentence, it should let the readers
   know where the essay will be taking them.

The contradiction here is only apparent, not real. The first point is relevant to the
opening paragraph of a *draft*; the second point is relevant to the opening paragraph of the final *version*. Almost all writers—professionals as well as amateurs—
find that the first paragraphs in their drafts are false starts. Don't worry about the
opening paragraphs of your draft; you'll revise your opening later. (Surprisingly,
your first paragraph may often be deleted altogether; your second paragraph, you
may find, is where your essay truly begins.)

When you are writing a first draft, you need something—almost anything—to
break the ice. In your finished paper, however, the opening cannot be mere throat
clearing. The opening must be interesting.

Among the commonest **uninteresting openings** are these:

1. A dictionary definition ("Webster says . . .").
2. A restatement of your title. The title is (let's assume) "Romeo's Maturation,"
   and the first sentence says, "This essay will study Romeo's maturation."
   True, there is an attempt at a thesis statement here, but there is no information beyond what has already been given in the title. There is no information about you, either—that is, no sense of your response to the topic, as
   there would be in, say, "*Romeo and Juliet* covers less than one week, but
   within this short period, Romeo is impressively transformed from a somewhat comic, infatuated boy to a thoughtful, tragic hero."
3. A platitude such as "Ever since the beginning of time, men and women
   have fallen in love." Such a sentence may be fine if it helps you to start
   creating a draft, but because it sounds canned and because it is insuffi-
   ciently interesting, it should not remain in your final version.

What is left? What *is* a good way for a final version to begin? Your introductory paragraph will be interesting if it gives information, and it will be pleasing if
the information provides a focus—that is, if it goes beyond the title to let the
reader know exactly what your topic is and where you are headed.

Let's assume that you agree: An opening paragraph should be *interesting* and
focused. Doubtless you will find your own ways of fulfilling these goals, but you
might consider using one of the following time-tested methods.

1. *Establish a connection between life and literature.* We have already suggested that a platitude ("Ever since the beginning of time, men and women
   have fallen in love") makes a poor beginning because it is dull, but you may
   find another way of relating the work to daily experience. For instance:

   Doubtless the popularity of *Romeo and Juliet* (the play has been with us for more
   than four hundred years) is partly due to the fact that it deals with a universal experience.
   Still, no other play about love is so much a part of our culture that the mere mention of
   the names of the lovers immediately calls up an image. But when we say that so-and-so is
   "a regular Romeo," exactly what do we mean? And exactly what sort of lover is Romeo?

2. *Give an overview that provides a focusing concept.* Here is an example:

   Langston Hughes's "Harlem" is about the destruction of the hopes of African
   Americans. More precisely, Hughes begins by asking "What happens to a dream deferred?" and then offers several possibilities, the last of which is that it may "explode."

3. *Include a quotation.* The previous example illustrates this approach. Here is another example:

> One line from Langston Hughes's poem "Harlem," "A raisin in the sun," has become famous, but its fame is, in a sense, accidental; Lorraine Hansberry happened to use it for the title of a play. Doubtless she used it because it is impressive, but, in fact, the entire poem is worthy of its most famous line.

4. *Use a definition.* We have suggested that a definition introduced by the phrase "Webster says . . ." is boring, but consider this approach:

> When we say that a character is the hero of a story, we usually mean that he is the central figure, and we probably imply that he is manly. But, in Kafka's "The Metamorphosis," the hero is most unmanly.

5. *Introduce a critical stance.* If your approach is feminist, or psychoanalytic, or Marxist, or whatever, you may want to say so at the start. Here's an example:

> Feminists have called our attention to the unfunny sexism of mother-in-law jokes, comments about women hooking men into marriage, and so forth. We can now see that the stories of James Thurber, long thought to be wholesome fun, are unpleasantly sexist.

We do not say that these are the only ways to begin, and we certainly do not suggest that you pack all five approaches into an opening paragraph. We are saying that, after you have done some brainstorming and have written some drafts, you may want to think about using one of these methods for your opening paragraph.

Middle Paragraphs

The middle, or body, of your essay will develop your thesis by offering supporting evidence. Ideas for the body should emerge from the sketchy outline that you made after you reviewed your brainstorming notes or journal.

1. *Be sure that each paragraph makes a specific point.* Each paragraph should contain a specific conceptual idea that works to develop your thesis. You can think of each paragraph as developing a subpoint that furthers the overarching idea in your thesis.
2. *Be sure that each paragraph contains meaningful evidence.* Each point should be sufficiently developed with evidence. A brief quotation is often the best evidence. Make sure to explain how your evidence develops your point. Do not simply "drop" the quotation into the paragraph without explaining how you are interpreting it or connecting it into the larger ideas of the paragraph. Make your understanding of the quotation a key part of the paragraph.
3. *Be sure that each paragraph is coherent.* Read each sentence, starting with the second sentence, to see how it relates to the preceding sentence. Does it clarify, extend, reinforce, or add an example? If you can't find the relationship, the sentence probably does not belong where it is. Rewrite it, move it, or delete it.
4. *Be sure that the connections between paragraphs are clear.* Transitional words and phrases, such as "Furthermore," "On the other hand," and "In the

next stanza," will often give readers all the help they need in seeing how your points are connected.

5. *Be sure that the paragraphs are in the best possible order.* A good way to test the organization of your paragraphs is to jot down the topic sentence or topic idea of each paragraph and then to see if your jottings form a reasonable sequence.

Concluding Paragraphs

Concluding paragraphs, like opening paragraphs, are especially important, if only because they are so conspicuous. Readers often skim first paragraphs and last paragraphs to see if an essay is worth reading. In conclusions, as in openings, say something interesting that captures your "key ideas." It is not interesting to say, "Thus, we see that Hamlet . . ." (and you go on to echo your title or your first sentence).

What should you do? When you are revising a draft, you might keep in mind the following widely practiced principles. They are not inflexible rules, but they often work.

1. *Hint that the end is near.* Expressions such as "Finally," "One other point must be discussed," and "In short" alert the reader that the end is near and help to keep the reader from feeling that the essay ends abruptly.

2. *Reassert the thesis, but put it in a new light that shows how your thesis has developed.* Replace "I have shown that Romeo and Hamlet are similar in some ways" with a more extended explanation, like the following:

> These similarities suggest that, in some respects, Romeo is an early study for Hamlet. Both are young men in love, both seek by the force of their passion to shape the world according to their own desires, and both die in the attempt. But, compared with Hamlet, who at the end of the play understands everything that has happened, Romeo dies in happy ignorance; Romeo is spared the pain of knowing that his own actions will destroy Juliet, whereas Hamlet dies with the painful knowledge that his kingdom has been conquered by Norwegian invaders.

3. *Offer an evaluation.* You may find it appropriate to conclude your analysis with an evaluation:

> Romeo is as convincing as he needs to be in a play about young lovers, but, from first to last, he is a relatively uncomplicated figure, the ardent lover. Hamlet is a lover, but he is also a good deal more, a figure whose complexity reveals a more sophisticated or a more mature author. Only five or six years separate Romeo and Juliet from Hamlet, but one feels that, in those few years, Shakespeare made a quantum leap in his grasp of human nature.

4. *Include a brief, significant quotation from the work.* Here's an example:

> Romeo has won the hearts of audiences for almost four centuries, but, for all his charm, he is in the last analysis concerned only with fulfilling his own passion. Hamlet, on the other hand, at last fulfills not only his own wish but also that of the Ghost, his father. "Remember me," the Ghost says, when he first appears to Hamlet and asks for revenge. Throughout the play, Hamlet does remember the Ghost, and, finally, at the cost of his own life, Hamlet succeeds in avenging his dead father.

Coherence in Paragraphs: Using Transitions

In addition to having a unified point and a reasonable organization, a good paragraph is *coherent*; that is, the *connections between ideas* in the paragraph are clear. Coherence can often be achieved by inserting the right transitional words or by taking care to repeat key words.

Richard Wagner, commenting on his work as a composer of operas, once said, "The art of composition is the art of transition," for his art moved from note to note, measure to measure, scene to scene. **Transitions** establish connections between ideas; they alert readers to the way in which you are conducting your argument. Here are some of the most common transitional words and phrases.

1. **Amplification or likeness:** *similarly, likewise, and, also, again, second, third, in addition, furthermore, moreover, finally*
2. **Emphasis:** *chiefly, equally, indeed, even more important*
3. **Contrast or concession:** *but, on the contrary, on the other hand, by contrast, of course, however, still, doubtless, no doubt, nevertheless, granted that, conversely, although, admittedly*
4. **Example:** *for example, for instance, as an example, specifically, consider as an illustration, that is, such as, like*
5. **Consequence or cause and effect:** *thus, so, then, it follows, as a result, therefore, hence*
6. **Restatement:** *in short, that is, in effect, in other words*
7. **Place:** *in the foreground, further back, in the distance*
8. **Time:** *afterward, next, then, as soon as, later, until, when, finally, last, at last*
9. **Conclusion:** *finally, therefore, thus, to sum up*

✔ **CHECKLIST:** *Revising Paragraphs*

☐ Does the paragraph say anything? Does it have substance, or is it mere padding?

☐ Does the paragraph have a topic sentence? If so, is it in the best place? If the paragraph doesn't have a topic sentence, might adding one improve the paragraph? Or, does it have a clear topic idea?

☐ If the paragraph is an opening paragraph, is it interesting enough to attract and hold a reader's attention? If it is a later paragraph, does it clearly evolve from the previous paragraph and lead into the next paragraph?

☐ Does the paragraph contain some principle of development—for instance, from the general to the particular?

☐ Does each sentence clearly follow from the preceding sentence? Have you provided transitional words or cues to guide your reader? Would it be useful to repeat certain key words for clarity?

☐ What is the purpose of the paragraph? Do you want to summarize, tell a story, give an illustration, concede a point, or something else? Is your purpose clear to you, and does the paragraph fulfill your purpose?

☐ Is the closing paragraph effective and not a restatement of the obvious?

From Inquiry to Interpretation to Argument: Organizing Ideas in an Analytical Paper

JAMES JOYCE

James Joyce (1882–1941) was born into a middle-class family in Dublin, Ireland. His father drank and became increasingly irresponsible and unemployable, and the family sank in the social order. Still, Joyce received a strong classical education at excellent Jesuit schools and at University College, Dublin, where he studied modern languages. In 1902, at the age of twenty, he left Ireland so that he might spend the rest of his life writing about life in Ireland. ("The shortest way to Tara," he said, "is via Holyhead," that is, the shortest way to the heart of Ireland is to take a ship away from Ireland.) In Trieste, Zurich, and Paris, he supported his family in a variety of ways, sometimes teaching English in a Berlitz language school. His fifteen stories, collected under the title of Dubliners, *were written between 1904 and 1907, but he could not get them published until 1914. (The story we present here, "Eveline," comes from* Dubliners.) *Next came a highly autobiographical novel,* A Portrait of the Artist as a Young Man (1916). Ulysses *(1922), a complex novel covering eighteen hours in Dublin, was for some years banned by the United States Post Office, although few, if any, readers today find it offensive. Joyce spent most of the rest of his life working on* Finnegans Wake (1939).*

Nine years before he succeeded in getting Dubliners *published, Joyce described the manuscript in these terms:*

> My intention was to write a chapter of the moral history of my country and I chose Dublin for the scene because that city seemed to me the centre of paralysis…. I have written it for the most part in a style of scrupulous meanness and with the conviction that he is a very bold man who dares to alter in the presentment, still more to deform, whatever he has seen and heard.

Araby

North Richmond Street, being blind, was a quiet street except at the hour when the Christian Brothers' School set the boys free. An uninhabited house of two stories stood at the blind end, detached from its neighbors in a square ground. The other houses of the street, conscious of decent lives within them, gazed at one another with brown imperturbable faces.

The former tenant of our house, a priest, had died in the back drawing-room. Air, musty from having long been enclosed, hung in all the rooms, and the waste room behind the kitchen was littered with old useless papers. Among these I found a few papercovered books, the pages of which were curled and damp: *The Abbot*, by Walter Scott, *The Devout Communicant* and *The Memoirs of Vidocq*.[2] I liked the last best because its leaves were yellow. The wild garden behind the house contained a central apple-tree and a few straggling bushes under one of which I found

[1]**blind** a dead-end street. (All notes are by the editors.)
[2]***The Abbot*** one of Scott's popular historical romances (1820); ***The Devout Communicant*** a Catholic religious manual published in the eighteenth century; ***The Memoirs of Vidocq*** the memoirs of the chief of the French detective force (1829).

the late tenant's rusty bicycle-pump. He had been a very charitable priest; in his will he had left all his money to institutions and the furniture of his house to his sister.

When the short days of winter came dusk fell before we had well eaten our dinners. When we met in the street the houses had grown sombre. The space of sky above us was the colour of everchanging violet and towards it the lamps of the street lifted their feeble lanterns. The cold air stung us and we played till our bodies glowed. Our shouts echoed in the silent street. The career of our play brought us through the dark muddy lanes behind the houses where we ran the gauntlet of the rough tribes from the cottages, to the back doors of the dark dripping gardens where odours arose from the ashpits, to the dark odorous stables where a coachman smoothed and combed the horse or shook music from the buckled harness. When we returned to the street light from the kitchen windows had filled the areas. If my uncle was seen turning the corner we hid in the shadow until we had seen him safely housed. Or if Mangan's sister came out on the doorstep to call her brother in to his tea we watched her from our shadow peer up and down the street. We waited to see whether she would remain or go in and, if she remained, we left our shadow and walked up to Mangan's steps resignedly. She was waiting for us, her figure defined by the light from the half-opened door. Her brother always teased her before he obeyed and I stood by the railings looking at her. Her dress swung as she moved her body and the soft rope of her hair tossed from side to side.

Every morning I lay on the floor in the front parlour watching her door. The blind was pulled down to within an inch of the sash so that I could not be seen. When she came out on the doorstep my heart leaped. I ran to the hall, seized my books and followed her. I kept her brown figure always in my eye and, when we came near the point at which our ways diverged, I quickened my pace and passed her. This happened morning after morning. I had never spoken to her, except for a few casual words, and yet her name was like a summons to all my foolish blood.

5   Her image accompanied me even in places the most hostile to romance. On Saturday evenings when my aunt went marketing I had to go to carry some of the parcels. We walked through the flaring streets, jostled by drunken men and bargaining women, amid the curses of labourers, the shrill litanies of shop-boys who stood on guard by the barrels of pigs' cheeks, the nasal chanting of street-singers, who sang a *come-all-you* about O'Donovan Rossa,[3] or a ballad about the troubles in our native land. These noises converged in a single sensation of life for me: I imagined that I bore my chalice safely through a throng of foes. Her name sprang to my lips at moments in strange prayers and praises which I myself did not understand. My eyes were often full of tears (I could not tell why) and at times a flood from my heart seemed to pour itself out into my bosom. I thought little of the future. I did not know whether I would ever speak to her or not or, if I spoke to her, how I could tell her of my confused adoration. But my body was like a harp and her words and gestures were like fingers running upon the wires.

One evening I went into the back drawing-room in which the priest had died. It was a dark rainy evening and there was no sound in the house. Through one of the broken panes I heard the rain impinge upon the earth, the fine incessant

---

[3] *come-all-you* a topical song that began "Come all you gallant Irishmen"; **O'Donovan Rossa** Jeremiah O'Donovan (1831–1915), a popular Irish leader who was jailed by the British for advocating violent rebellion.

needles of water playing in the sodden beds. Some distant lamp or lighted window gleamed below me. I was thankful that I could see so little. All my senses seemed to desire to veil themselves and, feeling that I was about to slip from them, I pressed the palms of my hands together until they trembled, murmuring: *O love! O love!* many times.

At last she spoke to me. When she addressed the first words to me I was so confused that I did not know what to answer. She asked me was I going to Araby. I forget whether I answered yes or no. It would be a splendid bazaar, she said; she would love to go.

—And why can't you? I asked.

While she spoke she turned a silver bracelet round and round her wrist. She could not go, she said, because there would be a retreat that week in her convent. Her brother and two other boys were fighting for their caps and I was alone at the railings. She held one of the spikes, bowing her head towards me. The light from the lamp opposite our door caught the white curve of her neck, lit up her hair that rested there and, falling, lit up the hand upon the railing. It fell over one side of her dress and caught the white border of a petticoat, just visible as she stood at ease.

—It's well for you, she said.

—If I go, I said, I will bring you something.

What innumerable follies laid waste my waking and sleeping thoughts after that evening! I wished to annihilate the tedious intervening days. I chafed against the work of school. At night in my bedroom and by day in the classroom her image came between me and the page I strove to read. The syllables of the word *Araby* were called to me through the silence in which my soul luxuriated and cast an Eastern enchantment over me. I asked for leave to go to the bazaar on Saturday night. My aunt was surprised and hoped it was not some Freemason[4] affair. I answered few questions in class, I watched my master's face pass from amiability to sternness; he hoped I was not beginning to idle. I could not call my wandering thoughts together. I had hardly any patience with the serious work of life which, now that it stood between me and my desire, seemed to me child's play, ugly monotonous child's play.

On Saturday morning I reminded my uncle that I wished to go to the bazaar in the evening. He was fussing at the hallstand, looking for the hat-brush, and answered me curtly:

—Yes, boy, I know.

As he was in the hall I could not go into the front parlour and lie at the window. I left the house in bad humour and walked slowly towards the school. The air was pitilessly raw and already my heart misgave me.

When I came home to dinner my uncle had not yet been home. Still it was early. I sat staring at the clock for some time and, when its ticking began to irritate me, I left the room. I mounted the staircase and gained the upper part of the house. The high cold empty gloomy rooms liberated me and I went from room to room singing. From the front window I saw my companions playing below in the street.

Their cries reached me weakened and indistinct and, leaning my forehead against the cool glass, I looked over at the dark house where she lived. I may have stood there for an hour, seeing nothing but the brown-clad figure cast by my imagination, touched discreetly by the lamplight at the curved neck, at the hand upon the railings and at the border below the dress.

[4]**Freemason** Irish Catholics viewed the Masons as their Protestant enemies.

impatience-childlike tendencies
debt/a iconolism-aware of adult issues
JOYCE • *Araby* 223

When I came downstairs again I found Mrs Mercer sitting at the fire. She was an old garrulous woman, a pawnbroker's widow, who collected used stamps for some pious purpose. I had to endure the gossip of the tea-table. The meal was prolonged beyond an hour and still my uncle did not come. Mrs Mercer stood up to go: she was sorry she couldn't wait any longer, but it was after eight o'clock and she did not like to be out late, as the night air was bad for her. When she had gone I began to walk up and down the room, clenching my fists. My aunt said:

20 —I'm afraid you may put off your bazaar for this night of Our Lord.

At nine o'clock I heard my uncle's latchkey in the halldoor. I heard him talking to himself and heard the hallstand rocking when it had received the weight of his overcoat. I could interpret these signs. When he was midway through his dinner I asked him to give me the money to go to the bazaar. He had forgotten.

—The people are in bed and after their first sleep now, he said.

I did not smile. My aunt said to him energetically:

—Can't you give him the money and let him go? You've kept him late enough as it is.

My uncle said he was very sorry he had forgotten. He said he believed in the old saying: *All work and no play makes Jack a dull boy.* He asked me where I was going and, when I had told him a second time he asked me did I know *The Arab's Farewell to His Steed.*[5] When I left the kitchen he was about to recite the opening lines of the piece to my aunt.

25 I held a florin tightly in my hand as I strode down Buckingham Street towards the station. The sight of the streets thronged with buyers and glaring with gas recalled to me the purpose of my journey. I took my seat in a third-class carriage of a deserted train. After an intolerable delay the train moved out of the station slowly. It crept onward among ruinous houses and over the twinkling river. At Westland Row Station a crowd of people pressed to the carriage doors; but the porters moved them back, saying that it was a special train for the bazaar. I remained alone in the bare carriage. In a few minutes the train drew up beside an improvised wooden platform. I passed out on to the road and saw by the lighted dial of a clock that it was ten minutes to ten. In front of me was a large building which displayed the magical name.

I could not find any sixpenny entrance and, fearing that the bazaar would be closed, I passed in quickly through a turnstile, handing a shilling to a weary-looking man. I found myself in a big hall girdled at half its height by a gallery. Nearly all the stalls were closed and the greater part of the hall was in darkness. I recognised a silence like that which pervades a church after a service. I walked into the center of the bazaar timidly. A few people were gathered about the stalls which were still open. Before a curtain, over which the words *Café Chantant* were written in coloured lamps, two men were counting money on a salver. I listened to the fall of the coins.

Remembering with difficulty why I had come I went over to one of the stalls and examined porcelain vases and flowered tea-sets. At the door of the stall a young lady was talking and laughing with two young gentlemen. I remarked their English accents and listened vaguely to their conversation.

—O, I never said such a thing!

—O, but you did!

30 —O, but I didn't!

church references=
admiration & awe

shop keeper flirts w/
shoppers — shows his
feelings for the sis are
not unique

[5]*The Arab's Farewell to His Steed* "The Arab to His Favorite Steed" was a popular sentimental poem by Caroline Norton (1808–77).

—Didn't she say that?

—Yes! I heard her.

—O, there's a . . . fib!

[handwritten: shopkeeper doesn't take him seriously]

Observing me the young lady came over and asked me did I wish to buy anything. The tone of her voice was not encouraging; she seemed to have spoken to me out of a sense of duty. I looked humbly at the great jars that stood like eastern guards at either side of the dark entrance to the stall and murmured:

—No, thank you.

The young lady changed the position of one of the vases and went back to the two young men. They began to talk of the same subject. Once or twice the young lady glanced at me over her shoulder.

I lingered before her stall, though I knew my stay was useless, to make my interest in her wares seem the more real. Then I turned away slowly and walked down the middle of the bazaar. I allowed the two pennies to fall against the sixpence in my pocket. I heard a voice call from one end of the gallery that the light was out. The upper part of the hall was now completely dark.

Gazing up into the darkness I saw myself as a creature driven and derided by vanity; and my eyes burned with anguish and anger.

[handwritten: not feelings of love but vanity & the desire for approval]

[1905]

Joining the Conversation: Critical Thinking and Writing

1. Joyce wrote a novel called *A Portrait of the Artist as a Young Man* (1916). Write an essay of about five hundred words on "Araby" as a portrait of the artist as a boy.

2. In an essay of about five hundred words, consider the role of images of darkness and blindness and what they reveal to you about "Araby" as a story about the fall from innocence into painful awareness.

3. How old, approximately, is the narrator of "Araby" at the time of the experience he describes? How old is he at the time he tells his story? On what evidence do you base your estimates?

4. The boy, apparently an only child, lives with an uncle and aunt rather than with parents. Why do you suppose Joyce put him in this family setting rather than some other?

5. The story is rich in images of religion. This in itself is not surprising, for the story is set in Roman Catholic Ireland, but the religious images are not simply references to religious persons or objects. In an essay of 500–750 words, discuss how these images reveal the narrator's state of mind.

Finding and Organizing an Interpretation

The short story "Araby" contains a complex exploration of a young man's love. Let's see how a student, Madelyn Mackenzie, captures her reactions to the story in inquiry notes, organizes them in an outline, and transforms them into an essay. Her essay provides a good example of a clearly organized approach to analysis. Madelyn selects a literary element—the setting—for close exploration. She develops a set of concepts relating to that literary element, focusing on the imagination and how it conflicts with reality. In order to develop her ideas, she creates three strong subpoints. Those subpoints become the organizational structure of her essay.

Student Work: Inquiry Notes

Questions: As I read this story, I had many questions:
–Why is the narrator so obsessed with his neighbor friend's sister? What triggers this obsession?
–Why does he focus on getting the girl a gift? Why does he want to show his love for her by giving her something?
–Why does he focus on the bazaar? Why does that become such a meaningful place?
–My main question has to do with the ending: Why does it have to end in such a negative way? He seems to realize that his ideals of love are shattered? Why?

In order to answer these questions, I could look at these literary elements:
–What is the main character's key qualities?
–What are the different settings that come into play?
–What imagery is used in the story?

As I think about my questions, I am coming up with three types of ideas. The first focuses on the narrator. He seems to be strangely obsessed with his friend's sister. But, the more I think about it, this seems to be a typical case of first love (like "puppy love" or a "crush")? His love is very unrealistic and very idealized. His love becomes an obsession (like when he looks at her by lying on the floor). What seems to be unique, and even positive, is his imagination. He has a powerful imagination that seems to be feeding into this love. For example, I love how he re-imagines the market. He can't help but imagine that his love will come true.

My second idea has to do with the setting. The setting of the story is actually negative. The street is described as dark and broken. His world seems to be one of routine. The home life is a bit depressing—he is told promises that aren't quite upheld. But, the bazaar seems to be a magical setting. It is very exciting and full of promise. This place becomes imagined as the solution to the narrator's drams of love: he will get the girl a wonderful gift at the bazaar.

As I noted in my questions, I am most concerned with the ending. This is my third idea. Why does it have to end in such a negative way? The narrator's dreams are shattered! The bazaar is not this magical place, but a place of frustration and fear. He realizes he isn't going to get the girl. I guess this is reality, but I was hoping for a happier ending. Perhaps this is the story's way of showing what the process of growing up is. Perhaps everyone's unrealistic first love has to end this way. We have to learn to deal with disappointment.

Student Work: Outlining

Initial Notes:

Setting as a key element in the story
—Setting of the town, the streets
—Setting of the house
—Setting of the bazaar
—Also settings are transformed by the imagination

So, these settings can be imagined as settings of love, possibility

—The story traces the narrator's belief that he can achieve love, but at the end there is the failure of that belief. The story turns negative at the end.

—The setting goes through a transformation, too? Does the way the setting is used change?

—At first, the setting is dark, but the imagination has hope—it is positive in the face of that dark setting.

—At the end, the setting is the magical and exotic bazaar. But, this space does not meet his expectations—not place of love/hope. So, this is the space where the narrator loses his hope for future love.

—The paper can track this shift.

<u>*Organizing ideas*</u>:

Contrast these settings: Daily, everyday world vs. World of imagination

Thesis topic: Reality vs. Imagination shown in setting
Subpoint development:
—Step 1. Imagination overcomes dark setting (imagination: hope for love)
—Step 2: Imagination becomes overactive, really wants love, starts to get frustrated
—Step 3: Imagination is overwhelmed by the setting of the bazaar. It is disproved or undermined by the setting, giving us the negative ending.

Student Analytical Essay: "Everyday and Imagined Settings in 'Araby'"

Let's take a look at the essay that Madelyn Mackenzie wrote using her inquiry notes and outlining.

Mackenzie 1

Madelyn Mackenzie

Professor Rodriguez

English 102-26

12 February 2016

Everyday and Imagined Settings in "Araby"

James Joyce's "Araby" features two settings: the daily world of the

narrator and the exotic world of the "Araby" bazaar. By contrasting these

two settings, the story is able to contrast the world of everyday work, which

is full of stress and broken dreams, and the world of the imagination, which

is full of hope and promised fulfillment. The world of the imagination is very

powerful, as it entices the narrator to the bazaar. The world of everyday

pressure proves more powerful, however, and it ultimately reveals that the
imagination creates false hopes. The setting emphasizes this conflict and its
resolution by showing how, first, the imagination overcomes the narrator's
dark setting by encouraging love; second, the imagination starts to become
too extreme and is replaced by frustration with the setting; and, third, the
imagination is undermined and disproved by the setting of the unwelcoming
bazaar. In each of these crucial developments, the setting shows the
narrator's conflicted emotions, which are the result of the conflict between
reality and the imagination.

    The story opens with the young narrator describing his dark,
depressing setting, and explaining how his love of his neighbor adds life to
that setting. The unnamed narrator's imagination is consumed by love for
the unnamed sister of his friend, Mangan. This love fires up his imagination.
As a first step in the story's exploration of imagination, the imagination is
powerful and transforms his setting from dreary to magical. Describing his
everyday setting, the narrator explains that he lives on a "blind" (i.e.
dead-end) street, in a "musty" and "littered" house where a priest died, and
with a yard filled with "a few straggling bushes" and a "rusty bicycle pump"
(221). His activities take place in this dark setting with associations of
death (the priest) and decay (the rusty pump). As he plays, it grows dark
and the "the houses had grown somber" (221).

    Against this depressing backdrop, the narrator's imagination conjures
up a magical world of love. The romance book he found in the dead priest's
room may have filled his thoughts with love and imagination. He describes
himself as watching Mangan's sister, going as far as lying on the floor and
watching her through a crack in the window sash (221). He then describes a
scene in which his romantic imagination transforms his everyday setting.
His love transforms the physical setting into a psychological setting. He

goes to the Saturday market, a setting that he describes as "most hostile to romance" (221). Although he travels through "flaring streets, jostled by drunken men and bargaining woman," and hears the sounds of "curses of labourers" and "the shrill litanies of shop-boys who stood on guard by the barrels of pigs' cheeks," his imagination transforms his setting (221). As if he was a knight in shining armor, he protects his sensation of love from these rude foes and "imagined that I bore my chalice safely through a throng of foes" (221). In this scene, the narrator shows his imagination's ability to transform his dark physical setting into a vivid psychological setting of love.

As the second phase in the development of the imagination, the imagination becomes so powerful that it starts to disturb the narrator's everyday life. When the girl finally speaks to the narrator, she makes an innocent remark that turns the narrator's imagination into a form of ecstasy and a form of torture. In his first conversation with the girl, she asks if he is going to the "Araby" bazaar; she imagines that it will be "splendid" and wishes she could go, which seems to increase the power of the narrator's imagination (222). He replies that he is going to the bazaar and promises to bring her something from it. After this exchange, he can think of nothing else. The story captures this mood of hope—the mood of a first crush. If he can bring home a worthy gift, he might win the girl's love. The bazaar becomes a setting so magical that it could give the girl to him.

Imagining the bazaar, the narrator explains that he becomes sick of his everyday setting: "I wished to annihilate the tedious intervening days. I chafed against the work of school" (222). His imagination becomes more and more powerful. He creates a romantic setting for "Araby," using the girl's enthusiasm as a starting point for a romantic image of the bazaar. He admits that his imagination has become extreme: "The syllables of the word Araby were called to me through the silence in which my soul luxuriated and cast an Eastern enchantment over me" (222). The setting reflects this psychological state: his fantasy has only briefly replaced the real setting of his real world. However, his description admits that this powerful imagination might not be positive; he hints that his psychological obsession had become out of control.

The conflict between his everyday world and his overactive imagination comes to a head when the narrator actually visits the "Araby" bazaar. The setting of the bazaar forces the narrator to confront both his dark and depressing everyday world and the tawdriness of triviality of what he had imagined as a romantic world. In this third development of the imagination, reality and fantasy are brought together, and reality must win out over imagination. Importantly, this conflict takes place in the bazaar setting. This setting has the potential to be magical: if an everyday market can be transformed by the narrator's imagination, why can't an exotic bazaar? However, this setting becomes the space that forces the narrator to realize that his dreams will not become a reality.

The bazaar setting shows the imagination becoming overwhelmed by the real world. The bazaar has imaginative possibilities; for example, the narrator must enter the "the large building which displayed the magical name." However, the narrator comes too late; it is already closing and whatever magic it might have had is disappearing. The bazaar is described as "Nearly all the stalls were closed and the greater part of the hall was in darkness. I recognized a silence like that which pervades a church after a service" (223). The magical bazaar, which promised exotic treasures and gifts of love, has become dark and silent. The setting of the bazaar has become like the narrator's everyday setting. The contrast between the imagination and reality becomes striking when the narrator looks at the bazaar stall. He can see nothing that he wants to buy. Instead, he must

Mackenzie 5

listen to the counting of coins and the arguing of the stall owners. There is

no magic and no romance in the bazaar space. At the end of the short story,

the narrator becomes surrounded by dark: "the upper part of the hall was

completely dark" (000). As darkness starts to settle into the bazaar, the

narrator looks into the darkness and sees himself. His dark setting has

captured his changed mood. He realizes he "is a creature driven and derided

by vanity," not driven by worthy romance and love.

The everyday setting overwhelms the romantic fantasies of the

narrator. The end of the story describes the narrator "gazing up into the

darkness" as though he sees the darkness of his setting for the first time.

The narrator cannot maintain his fantasy of love for the girl in such a dark

world. The setting shows the narrator's coming of age: he starts the story

able to transform his setting with his imagination, but ends the story with

his imagination crushed by reality. The story ends on a negative, but realistic

note. The narrator is forced to leave his childish imagination behind. The

setting of "Araby" becomes the crucial representation of this conflict

between reality and the imagination and shows the ultimate defeat of the

imagination.

[New page]

Mackenzie 6

Work Cited

Joyce, James. "Araby." *Literature for Composition*. Ed. Sylvan Barnet, William Burto,

William E. Cain, and Cheryl L. Nixon. 11th ed. Boston: Pearson, 2017. 220-24.

Print.

From Inquiry to Interpretation to Argument: Maintaining an Interpretation in an Analytical Paper

Aphra Behn

Aphra Behn (1640–89) is regarded as the first English woman to have made a living by writing. Not much is known of her life, but she seems to have married a London merchant of Dutch descent and, after his death, to have served as a spy in the Dutch Wars (1665–67). After her return to England, she took up playwriting, and she gained fame with The Rover *(1677). Behn also wrote novels, the most important of which is* Oroonoko, or The Royal Slave *(1688), which is among the first works in English to express empathy for enslaved Africans.*

Song: Love Armed

Love in fantastic triumph sate,
  Whilst bleeding hearts around him flowed,
For whom fresh pains he did create,
  And strange tyrannic power he showed:
5 From thy bright eyes he took his fire,
  Which round about in sport he hurled;
But 'twas from mine he took desire,
  Enough to undo the amorous world.
From me he took his sighs and tears:
10 From thee, his pride and cruelty;
From me, his languishments and fears;
  And every killing dart from thee.
Thus thou and I the god have armed
  And set him up a deity;
15   But my poor heart alone is harmed,
  Whilst thine the victor is, and free.

[16XX]

Maintaining Interpretive Interest Notes

The subject is Aphra Behn's "Song: Love Armed." In order to trace the development of an essay on this poem, we begin with a set of inquiry notes and two short entries in a journal kept by a first-year student, Geoffrey Sullivan. We then follow these entries with Geoffrey's completed essay.

Student Work: Inquiry Notes

Key questions:

1. *Who is speaking?*
   The speaker seems to be a man who talks of the suffering he is undergoing. I am thinking it is a man due to the convention of the man being active in love (but it could be a woman, reflecting Aphra Behn as the woman author.) Does he seem to

enjoy his plight? We often enjoy songs of unhappy love—maybe that is how the speaker is explaining his plight

2. *Who is he speaking to? How is she described/characterized?*
He seems to be speaking to the woman ("thee"). She is said to exhibit "pride and cruelty" (line 10).

3. *What is the action or event or issue being described?*
I am trying to figure out exactly what is going on, but it seems like Love has taken this pride and cruelty from the woman. Then, he seems to take "killing darts" from her. Are these being used against the speaker? Love is also taking "sighs and tears" and "languishments and fears" from the speaker. Love seems to be collecting all of these elements of broken love from the narrator.

4. *What images stand out?*
The description of the bleeding heart at the beginning works to grab the reader. The opening describes Love as a person, which is a powerful image (I like the idea of him having tyrannic power—of being a tyrant!).

5. *Further questions:*
Would men enjoy the poem more than women? Would a woman think this is unfair (that women are portrayed as mean)?

Student Work: Journal Writing

October 10. The title "Song: Love Armed" puzzled me at first; funny, I somehow was thinking of the expression "strong-armed" and at first I didn't understand that "Love" in this poem is a human—no, not a human, but the god Cupid, who has a human form—and that he is shown as armed, with darts and so forth. The poem focuses on key emotions: pride and cruelty, languishments and fears.

October 13. This god of "Love" is Cupid, and so he is something like what is on a valentine card—Cupid with his bow and arrow. But valentine cards just show cute little Cupids, and in this poem Cupid is a real menace. He causes lots of pain ("bleeding hearts," "tears," "killing dart," etc.). So what is Aphra Behn telling us about the god of Love, or love as an emotion? That love hurts? And she is singing about it! But we do sing songs about how hard life is. But do we sing them when we are really hurting, or only when we are pretty well off and just thinking about being hurt?

When you love someone and they don't return your love, it hurts, but even when love isn't returned it still gives some intense pleasure. Strange, but I think true. I wouldn't say that love always has this two-sided nature, but I do see the idea that love can have two sides, pleasure and pain. And love takes two people—the lover and beloved. Maybe there's also something to the idea that "opposites attract." Anyway, Aphra Behn seems to be talking about men vs. women, pain vs. pleasure, power vs. weakness, etc. Pairs, opposites. And in two stanzas (a pair of stanzas?).

Student Analytical Essay: "The Double Nature of Love'"

The following essay makes use of some, but not all, of Geoffrey preliminary notes, and it includes much that he did not think of until he reread his inquiry notes, reread the poem, and began drafting the essay.

Sullivan 1

Geoffrey Sullivan

Professor Morawski

English 2G

31 January 2016

The Double Nature of Love

Aphra Behn's "Song: Love Armed" is in two stanzas, and it is about two people, "me" and "thee," that is, you and I, the lover and the woman he loves.

I think the speaker is a man, since according to the usual code men are supposed to be the active lovers and women are the (relatively) passive people who are loved. In this poem, the beloved—the woman, I think—has "bright eyes" (line 5) that provide the god of Love with fire, and she also provides the god with "pride and cruelty" (10). This of course is the way the man sees it if a woman does not respond to him; if she does not love him in return, she is (he thinks) arrogant and cruel. What does the man give to Love? He provides "desire" (7), "sighs and tears" (9), "languishments and fears" (11). None of this sounds very manly, but the joke is that the god of Love—which means love—can turn a strong man into a crybaby when a woman does not respond to him.

Although both stanzas are *clever descriptions* of the god of Love, the poem is not just a description. Of course there is not a plot in the way that a short story has a plot, but there is a sort of a switch at the end, giving the story something of a plot. The poem is, say, ninety percent expression of feeling and description of love, but during the course of expressing feelings

Sullivan 2

and describing love something happens, so there is *a tiny story*. The first stanza sets the scene ("Love in fantastic triumph sate" [1]) and tells of some of the things that the speaker and the woman contributed to the god of Love. The woman's eyes provided Love with fire, and the man's feelings provided Love with "desire" (7). The second stanza goes on to mention other things that Love got from the speaker ("sighs and tears" [9]), and other things that Love got from the beloved ("pride and cruelty" [10]), and in line 13 the poet says, "Thus thou and I the god have armed," so the two humans share something. They have both given Love his weapons. But—and this is the story I spoke of—the poem ends by emphasizing their difference: Only the man is "harmed," and the woman is the "victor" because her heart is not captured, as the man's heart is. In the battle that Love presides over, the woman is the winner; the man's heart has fallen for the woman, but, according to the last line, the woman's heart remains "free."

We have all seen the god of Love on valentine cards, a cute little Cupid armed with a bow and arrow. But despite the bow and arrow that the Valentine Day Cupid carries, I think that until I read Aphra Behn's "Song: Love Armed" I had never really thought about Cupid as *powerful* and as capable of causing real pain. On valentine cards, he is just cute, but when I think about it, I realize the truth of Aphra Behn's concept of love. Love *is* (or can be) two-sided, whereas the valentine cards show only the sweet side.

I think it is interesting to notice that although the poem is about the destructive power of love, it is fun to read. I am not bothered by the fact that the lover is miserable. Why? I think I enjoy the poem, rather than am bothered by it, because *he is enjoying his misery*. After all, he is singing about it, sort of singing in the rain, telling anyone who will listen about how miserable he is, and he is having a very good time doing it.

[New page]

Sullivan 3

Work Cited

Behn, Aphra. "Love Armed." *Literature for Composition*. Ed. Sylvan Barnet, William Burto, William E. Cain, and Cheryl L. Nixon. 11th ed. Boston: Pearson, 2017. 231. Print.

Joining the Conversation: Critical Thinking and Writing

1. What do you think of the essay's title? Is it sufficiently interesting and focused?
2. What are the writer's chief points? Are they clear, and are they adequately developed?
3. Do you think Geoffrey Sullivan is too concerned with himself and that he loses sight of the poem? Or do you find it interesting that he connects the poem with life?
4. Focus on the writer's use of quotations. Does he effectively introduce and examine quoted lines and phrases?
5. What grade would you give Geoffrey's essay? What evidence can you offer to support your evaluation?

✔ **CHECKLIST:** *Editing a Draft*

- ☐ Is the title of my essay interesting?
- ☐ Do I identify the subject of my essay (author and title) early in the essay?
- ☐ What is my thesis? Do I state it soon enough (perhaps even in the title) and keep it in view?
- ☐ Is the organization reasonable? Does each point lead into the next without irrelevancies and without anticlimaxes?
- ☐ Is each paragraph unified by a topic sentence or a topic idea? Are there adequate transitions from one paragraph to the next?
- ☐ Are generalizations supported by appropriate evidence, especially by brief quotations from the text?
- ☐ Is the opening paragraph interesting and, by its end, focused on the topic? Is the final paragraph conclusive without being repetitive?
- ☐ Is the tone appropriate? No sarcasm, no apologies, no condescension?
- ☐ If there is a summary, is it as brief as possible, given its purpose?
- ☐ Are the quotations adequately introduced, and are they accurate? Do they provide evidence and let the reader hear the author's voice, or do they merely add words to the essay?
- ☐ Is the present tense used to describe what the author does and the action of the work ("*Shakespeare shows,*" "*Hamlet dies*")?

☐ Have I kept in mind the needs of my audience, for instance, by defining unfamiliar terms or by briefly summarizing works or opinions with which the reader may be unfamiliar?
☐ Is documentation provided where necessary?
☐ Are the spelling and punctuation correct? Are other mechanical matters (such as margins, spacing, and citations) in correct form? Have I proofread my essay carefully?
☐ Is the essay properly identified—author's name, instructor's name, course number, and date?

Your Turn: Additional Short Stories and Poems for Analysis

STORIES

EDGAR ALLAN POE

Edgar Allan Poe (1809–49) was the son of traveling actors. His father abandoned the family almost immediately, and his mother died when he was two years old. As a child, Poe was adopted—though never legally—by a prosperous merchant and his wife in Richmond, Virginia. The tensions were great, aggravated by Poe's drinking and heavy gambling, and, in 1827, Poe left Richmond for Boston. He wrote, served briefly in the army, attended West Point (but left within a year), and became an editor for the remaining eighteen years of his life. It was during these years, too, that he wrote the poems, essays, and fiction—especially detective stories and horror stories—that have made him famous.

The Cask of Amontillado

The thousand injuries of Fortunato I had borne as I best could, but when he ventured upon insult, I vowed revenge. You, who so well know the nature of my soul, will not suppose, however, that I gave utterance to a threat. At length I would be avenged; this was a point definitely settled—but the very definitiveness with which it was resolved precluded the idea of risk. I must not only punish, but punish with impunity. A wrong is unredressed when retribution overtakes its redresser. It is equally unredressed when the avenger fails to make himself felt as such to him who has done the wrong.

It must be understood that neither by word nor deed had I given Fortunato cause to doubt my good will. I continued, as was my wont, to smile in his face, and he did not perceive that my smile *now* was at the thought of his immolation.

He had a weak point—this Fortunato—although in other regards he was a man to be respected and even feared. He prided himself on his connoisseurship in wine. Few Italians have the true virtuoso spirit. For the most part their enthusiasm is adopted to suit the time and opportunity to practice imposture upon the British and Austrian *millionaires*. In painting and gemmary Fortunato, like his countrymen, was a quack, but in the matter of old wines he was sincere. In this respect I did not differ from him materially;—I was skillful in the Italian vintages myself, and bought largely whenever I could.

It was about dusk, one evening during the supreme madness of the carnival season, that I encountered my friend. He accosted me with excessive warmth, for he had been drinking much. The man wore motley. He had on a tight-fitting parti-striped dress, and his head was surmounted by the conical cap and bells. I was so pleased to see him, that I thought I should never have done wringing his hand.

5   I said to him—"My dear Fortunato, you are luckily met. How remarkably well you are looking to-day! But I have received a pipe[1] of what passes for Amontillado, and I have my doubts."

"How?" said he, "Amontillado? A pipe? Impossible! And in the middle of the carnival?"

"I have my doubts," I replied; "and I was silly enough to pay the full Amontillado price without consulting you in the matter. You were not to be found, and I was fearful of losing a bargain."

"Amontillado!"

"I have my doubts."

10   "Amontillado!"

"And I must satisfy them."

"Amontillado!"

"As you are engaged, I am on my way to Luchesi. If any one has a critical turn, it is he. He will tell me—"

"Luchesi cannot tell Amontillado from Sherry."

15   "And yet some fools will have it that his taste is a match for your own."

"Come, let us go."

"Whither?"

"To your vaults."

"My friend, no; I will not impose upon your good nature. I perceive you have an engagement. Luchesi—"

20   "I have no engagement; come."

"My friend, no. It is not the engagement, but the severe cold with which I perceive you are afflicted. The vaults are insufferably damp. They are encrusted with nitre."

"Let us go, nevertheless. The cold is merely nothing. Amontillado! You have been imposed upon; and as for Luchesi, he cannot distinguish Sherry from Amontillado."

Thus speaking, Fortunato possessed himself of my arm. Putting on a mask of black silk, and drawing a *roquelaure*[2] closely about my person, I suffered him to hurry me to my palazzo.

There were no attendants at home; they had absconded to make merry in honor of the time. I had told them that I should not return until the morning, and had given them explicit orders not to stir from the house. These orders were sufficient, I well knew, to insure their immediate disappearance, one and all, as soon as my back was turned.

25   I took from their sconces two flambeaux, and giving one to Fortunato, bowed him through several suites of rooms to the archway that led into the vaults. I passed down a long and winding staircase, requesting him to be cautious as he followed. We came at length to the foot of the descent, and stood together on the damp ground of the catacombs of the Montresors.

[1]**pipe** wine cask.

[2]**roquelaure** short cloak.

The gait of my friend was unsteady, and the bells upon his cap jingled as he strode.

"The pipe," said he.

"It is farther on," said I; "but observe the white web-work which gleams from these cavern walls."

He turned towards me, and looked into my eyes with two filmy orbs that distilled the rheum of intoxication.

30   "Nitre?" he asked, at length.

"Nitre," I replied. "How long have you had that cough?"

"Ugh! ugh! ugh!—ugh! ugh! ugh!—ugh! ugh! ugh!—ugh! ugh! ugh!—ugh! ugh! ugh!"

My poor friend found it impossible to reply for many minutes.

"It is nothing," he said, at last.

35   "Come," I said, with decision, "we will go back; your health is precious. You are rich, respected, admired, beloved; you are happy, as once I was. You are a man to be missed. For me it is no matter. We will go back; you will be ill, and I cannot be responsible. Besides, there is Luchesi—"

"Enough," he said; "the cough is a mere nothing: it will not kill me. I shall not die of a cough."

"True—true," I replied; "and, indeed, I had no intention of alarming you unnecessarily—but you should use all proper caution. A draught of this Medoc will defend us from the damps."

Here I knocked off the neck of a bottle which I drew from a long row of its fellows that lay upon the mould.

"Drink," I said, presenting him the wine.

40   He raised it to his lips with a leer: He paused and nodded to me familiarly, while his bells jingled.

"I drink," he said, "to the buried that repose around us."

"And I to your long life."

He again took my arm, and we proceeded.

"These vaults," he said, "are extensive."

45   "The Montresors," I replied, "were a great and numerous family."

"I forget your arms."

"A huge human foot d'or, in a field azure; the foot crushes a serpent rampant whose fangs are imbedded in the heel."

"And the motto?"

"*Nemo me impune lacessit.*"[3]

50   "Good!" he said.

The wine sparkled in his eyes and the bells jingled. My own fancy grew warm with the Medoc. We had passed through walls of piled bones, with casks and puncheons intermingling, into the inmost recesses of the catacombs. I paused again, and this time I made bold to seize Fortunato by an arm above the elbow.

"The nitre!" I said; "see, it increases. It hangs like moss upon the vaults. We are below the river's bed. The drops of moisture tickle among the bones. Come, we will go back ere it is too late. Your cough—"

"It is nothing," he said; "let us go on. But first, another draught of the Medoc."

I broke and reached him a flagon of De Grâve. He emptied it at a breath. His eyes flashed with a fierce light. He laughed and threw the bottle upwards with a gesticulation I did not understand.

[3]*Nemo me impune lacessit* No one dare attack me with impunity (the motto of Scotland).

55 I looked at him in surprise. He repeated the movement—a grotesque one.

"You do not comprehend?" he said.

"Not I," I replied.

"Then you are not of the brotherhood."

"How?"

60 "You are not of the masons."[4]

"Yes, yes," I said, "yes, yes."

"You? Impossible! A mason?"

"A mason," I replied.

"A sign," he said.

65 "It is this," I answered, producing a trowel from beneath the folds of my *roquelaure*.

"You jest," he exclaimed, recoiling a few paces. "But let us proceed to the Amontillado."

"Be it so," I said, replacing the tool beneath the cloak, and again offering him my arm. He leaned upon it heavily. We continued our route in search of the Amontillado. We passed through a range of low arches, descended, passed on, and descending again, arrived at a deep crypt, in which the foulness of the air caused our flambeaux rather to glow than flame.

At the most remote end of the crypt there appeared another less spacious. Its walls had been lined with human remains piled to the vault overhead, in the fashion of the great catacombs of Paris. Three sides of this interior crypt were still ornamented in this manner. From the fourth the bones had been thrown down, and lay promiscuously upon the earth, forming at one point a mound of some size. Within the wall thus exposed by the displacing of the bones, we perceived a still interior recess, in depth about four feet, in width three, in height six or seven. It seemed to have been constructed for no especial use within itself, but formed merely the interval between two of the colossal supports of the roof of the catacombs, and was backed by one of their circumscribing walls of solid granite.

It was in vain that Fortunato, uplifting his dull torch, endeavored to pry into the depths of the recess. Its termination the feeble light did not enable us to see.

70 "Proceed," I said; "herein is the Amontillado. As for Luchesi—"

"He is an ignoramus," interrupted my friend, as he stepped unsteadily forward, while I followed immediately at his heels. In an instant he had reached the extremity of the niche, and finding his progress arrested by the rock, stood stupidly bewildered. A moment more and I had fettered him to the granite. In its surface were two iron staples, distant from each other about two feet, horizontally. From one of these depended a short chain, from the other a padlock. Throwing the links about his waist, it was but the work of a few seconds to secure it. He was too much astounded to resist. Withdrawing the key I stepped back from the recess.

"Pass your hand," I said, "over the wall; you cannot help feeling the nitre. Indeed it is very damp. Once more let me implore you to return. No? Then I must positively leave you. But I must first render you all the little attentions in my power."

"The Amontillado!" ejaculated my friend, not yet recovered from his astonishment.

"True," I replied; "the Amontillado."

75 As I said these words I busied myself among the pile of bones of which I have before spoken. Throwing them aside, I soon uncovered a quantity of building-stone

[4]**of the masons** i.e., a member of the Freemasons, an international secret fraternity.

and mortar. With these materials and with the aid of my trowel, I began vigorously to wall up the entrance of the niche.

I had scarcely laid the first tier of masonry when I discovered that the intoxication of Fortunato had in a great measure worn off. The earliest indication I had of this was a low moaning cry from the depth of the recess. It was *not* the cry of a drunken man. There was then a long and obstinate silence. I laid the second tier, and the third, and the fourth; and then I heard the furious vibrations of the chain. The noise lasted for several minutes, during which, that I might hearken to it with the more satisfaction, I ceased my labors and sat down upon the bones. When at last the clanking subsided, I resumed the trowel, and finished without interruption the fifth, the sixth, and the seventh tier. The wall was now nearly upon a level with my breast. I again paused, and holding the flambeaux over the masonwork, threw a few feeble rays upon the figure within.

A succession of loud and shrill screams, bursting suddenly from the throat of the chained form, seemed to thrust me violently back. For a brief moment I hesitated—I trembled. Unsheathing my rapier, I began to grope with it about the recess; but the thought of an instant reassured me. I placed my hand upon the solid fabric of the catacombs, and felt satisfied. I reapproached the wall. I replied to the yells of him who clamored. I re-echoed—I aided—I surpassed them in volume and in strength. I did this, and the clamorer grew still.

It was now midnight, and my task was drawing to a close. I had completed the eighth, the ninth, and the tenth tier. I had finished a portion of the last and the eleventh; there remained but a single stone to be fitted and plastered in. I struggled with its weight; I placed it partially in its destined position. But now there came from out the niche a low laugh that erected the hairs upon my head. It was succeeded by a sad voice, which I had difficulty in recognizing as that of the noble Fortunato. The voice said—

"Ha! ha! ha!—he! he! he!—a very good joke indeed—an excellent jest. We will have many a rich laugh about it at the palazzo—he! he! he!—over our wine—he! he! he!"

80   "The Amontillado!" I said.

"He! he! he!—he! he! he!—yes, the Amontillado. But is it not getting late? Will not they be awaiting us at the palazzo, the Lady Fortunato and the rest? Let us be gone."

"Yes," I said, "let us be gone."

"For the love of God, Montresor!"

"Yes," I said, "for the love of God!"

85   But to these words I hearkened in vain for a reply. I grew impatient. I called aloud;

"Fortunato!"

No answer. I called again;

"Fortunato!"

No answer still. I thrust a torch through the remaining aperture and let it fall within. There came forth in return only a jingling of the bells. My heart grew sick—on account of the dampness of the catacombs. I hastened to make an end of my labor. I forced the last stone into its position; I plastered it up. Against the new masonry I reerected the old rampart of bones. For the half of a century no mortal has disturbed them. *In pace requiescat!*[5]

[1846]

---

[5]*In pace requiescat!* May he rest in peace!

Joining the Conversation: Critical Thinking and Writing

1. To whom does Montresor tell his story? The story he tells happened fifty years earlier. Do we have any clue as to why he tells it now?
2. At the end of the story, we learn that the murder occurred fifty years ago. Would the story be equally effective if Poe had had Montresor reveal this fact at the outset? Why, or why not?
3. Poe sets Montresor's story at dusk, "during the supreme madness of the carnival season." What is the "carnival season"? (If you are uncertain as to the meaning of "carnival," consult a dictionary.) What details of the story derive from the setting?
4. In the first line, Montresor declares, "The thousand injuries of Fortunato I had borne as I best could, but when he ventured upon insult, I vowed revenge." Do we ever learn what those injuries and that insult were? What do we learn about Montresor from this declaration?
5. How does Montresor characterize Fortunato? What details of his portrait unwittingly enlist our sympathy for Fortunato? Does Montresor betray any sympathy for his victim?
6. "The Cask of Amontillado" is sometimes referred to as a "horror tale." Do you think it has anything in common with horror movies? If so, what? (You might begin by making a list of the characteristics of horror movies.) Why do people take pleasure in horror movies? Does this story offer any of the same sorts of pleasure? In any case, why might a reader take pleasure in this story? Set forth your response in an argument of 250–500 words.
7. Construct a definition of madness (you may want to do a little research, but if you make use of your findings, be sure to give credit to your sources) and write an essay of 500–750 words, arguing whether or not Montresor is mad. (*Note:* You may want to distinguish between Montresor at the time of the killing and Montresor at the time of his narration.)

LESLIE MARMON SILKO

Leslie Marmon Silko was born in 1948 in Albuquerque, New Mexico, and grew up on the Laguna Pueblo Reservation some fifty miles to the west. Of her family she says,

> *We are mixed blood—Laguna, Mexican, white.... All those languages, all those ways of living are combined, and we live somewhere on the fringes of all three. But I don't apologize for this any more—not to whites, not to full bloods—our origin is unlike any other. My poetry, my storytelling rise out of this source.*

After graduating from the University of New Mexico in 1969, Silko entered law school but soon left to become a writer. She taught for two years at Navajo Community College at Many Farms, Arizona, and then went to Alaska for two years, where she studied Eskimo-Aleut culture and worked on a novel, Ceremony. *After returning to the Southwest, she taught at the University of Arizona and then at the University of New Mexico.*

In addition to writing stories, a novel, and poems, Silko wrote the screenplay for Marlon Brando's film Black Elk. *In 1981, she was awarded a MacArthur Foundation genius grant.*

The Man to Send Rain Clouds

One

They found him under a big cottonwood tree. His Levi jacket and pants were faded light-blue so that he had been easy to find. The big cottonwood tree stood apart from a small grove of winterbare cottonwoods which grew in the wide, sandy arroyo. He had been dead for a day or more, and the sheep had wandered and scattered up and down the arroyo. Leon and his brother-in-law, Ken, gathered the sheep and left them in the pen at the sheep camp before they returned to the cottonwood tree. Leon waited under the tree while Ken drove the truck through the deep sand to the edge of the arroyo. He squinted up at the sun and unzipped his jacket—it sure was hot for this time of year. But high and northwest the blue mountains were still deep in snow. Ken came sliding down the low, crumbling bank about fifty yards down, and he was bringing the red blanket.

Before they wrapped the old man, Leon took a piece of string out of his pocket and tied a small gray feather in the old man's long white hair. Ken gave him the paint. Across the brown wrinkled forehead he drew a streak of white and along the high cheekbones he drew a strip of blue paint. He paused and watched Ken throw pinches of corn meal and pollen into the wind that fluttered the small gray feather. Then Leon painted with yellow under the old man's broad nose, and finally, when he had painted green across the chin, he smiled.

"Send us rain clouds, Grandfather." They laid the bundle in the back of the pickup and covered it with a heavy tarp before they started back to the pueblo.

They turned off the highway onto the sandy pueblo road. Not long after they passed the store and post office they saw Father Paul's car coming toward them. When he recognized their faces he slowed his car and waved for them to stop. The young priest rolled down the car window.

5   "Did you find old Teofilo?" he asked loudly.

Leon stopped the truck. "Good morning, Father. We were just out to the sheep camp. Everything is O.K. now."

"Thank God for that. Teofilo is a very old man. You really shouldn't allow him to stay at the sheep camp alone."

"No, he won't do that any more now."

"Well, I'm glad you understand. I hope I'll be seeing you at Mass this week— we missed you last Sunday. See if you can get old Teofilo to come with you." The priest smiled and waved at them as they drove away.

Two

10   Louise and Teresa were waiting. The table was set for lunch, and the coffee was boiling on the black iron stove. Leon looked at Louise and then at Teresa.

"We found him under a cottonwood tree in the big arroyo near sheep camp. I guess he sat down to rest in the shade and never got up again." Leon walked toward the old man's head. The red plaid shawl had been shaken and spread carefully over the bed, and a new brown flannel shirt and pair of stiff new Levis were arranged neatly beside the pillow. Louise held the screen door open while Leon and Ken carried in the red blanket. He looked small and shriveled, and after they dressed him in the new shirt and pants he seemed more shrunken.

It was noontime now because the church bells rang the Angelus.[1] They ate the beans with hot bread, and nobody said anything until after Teresa poured the coffee.

Ken stood up and put on his jacket. "I'll see about the grave-diggers. Only the top layer of soil is frozen. I think it can be ready before dark."

Leon nodded his head and finished his coffee. After Ken had been gone for a while, the neighbors and clanspeople came quietly to embrace Teofilo's family and to leave food on the table because the grave-diggers would come to eat when they were finished.

Three

15 The sky in the west was full of pale-yellow light. Louise stood outside with her hands in the pockets of Leon's green army jacket that was too big for her. The funeral was over, and the old men had taken their candles and medicine bags and were gone. She waited until the body was laid into the pickup before she said anything to Leon. She touched his arm, and he noticed that her hands were still dusty from the corn meal that she had sprinkled around the old man. When she spoke, Leon could not hear her.

"What did you say? I didn't hear you."

"I said that I had been thinking about something."

"About what?"

"About the priest sprinkling holy water for Grandpa. So he won't be thirsty."

20 Leon stared at the new moccasins that Teofilo had made for the ceremonial dances in the summer. They were nearly hidden by the red blanket. It was getting colder, and the wind pushed gray dust down the narrow pueblo road. The sun was approaching the long mesa where it disappeared during the winter. Louise stood there shivering and watching his face. Then he zipped up his jacket and opened the truck door. "I'll see if he's there."

Ken stopped the pickup at the church, and Leon got out; and then Ken drove down the hill to the graveyard where people were waiting. Leon knocked at the old carved door with its symbols of the Lamb. While he waited he looked up at the twin bells from the king of Spain with the last sunlight pouring around them in their tower.

The priest opened the door and smiled when he saw who it was. "Come in! What brings you here this evening?"

The priest walked toward the kitchen, and Leon stood with his cap in his hand, playing with the earflaps and examining the living room—the brown sofa, the green armchair, and the brass lamp that hung down from the ceiling by links of chain. The priest dragged a chair out of the kitchen and offered it to Leon.

"No thank you, Father. I only came to ask you if you would bring your holy water to the graveyard."

25 The priest turned away from Leon and looked out the window at the patio full of shadows and the dining-room windows of the nuns' cloister across the patio. The curtains were heavy, and the light from within faintly penetrated; it was impossible to see the nuns inside eating supper. "Why didn't you tell me he was dead? I could have brought the Last Rites anyway."

Leon smiled. "It wasn't necessary, Father."

The priest stared down at his scuffed brown loafers and the worn hem of his cassock. "For a Christian burial it was necessary."

[1]**The Angelus** a devotional prayer commemorating the Annunciation (the angel Gabriel's announcement delivered to Mary of the Incarnation of God in the human form of Jesus).

His voice was distant, and Leon thought that his blue eyes looked tired.

"It's O.K., Father, we just want him to have plenty of water."

30   The priest sank down in the green chair and picked up a glossy missionary magazine. He turned the colored pages full of lepers and pagans without looking at them.

"You know I can't do that, Leon. There should have been the Last Rites and a funeral Mass at the very least."

Leon put on his green cap and pulled the flaps down over his ears. "It's getting late, Father. I've got to go."

When Leon opened the door Father Paul stood up and said, "Wait." He left the room and came back wearing a long brown overcoat. He followed Leon out the door and across the dim churchyard to the adobe steps in front of the church. They both stooped to fit through the low adobe entrance. And when they started down the hill to the graveyard only half of the sun was visible above the mesa.

The priest approached the grave slowly, wondering how they had managed to dig into the frozen ground, and then he remembered that this was New Mexico, and saw the pile of cold loose sand beside the hole. The people stood close to each other with little clouds of steam puffing from their faces. The priest looked at them and saw a pile of jackets, gloves, and scarves in the yellow, dry tumbleweeds that grew in the graveyard. He looked at the red blanket, not sure that Teofilo was so small, wondering if it wasn't some perverse Indian trick—something they did in March to ensure a good harvest—wondering if maybe old Teofilo was actually at sheep camp corraling the sheep for the night. But there he was, facing into a cold dry wind and squinting at the last sunlight, ready to bury a red wool blanket while the faces of the parishioners were in shadow with the last warmth of the sun on their backs.

35   His fingers were stiff, and it took them a long time to twist the lid off the holy water. Drops of water fell on the red blanket and soaked into dark icy spots. He sprinkled the grave and the water disappeared almost before it touched the dim, cold sand; it reminded him of something—he tried to remember what it was, because he thought if he could remember he might understand this. He sprinkled more water; he shook the container until it was empty, and the water fell through the light from sundown like August rain that fell while the sun was still shining, almost evaporating before it touched the wilted squash flowers.

The wind pulled at the priest's brown Franciscan robe and swirled away the corn meal and pollen that had been sprinkled on the blanket. They lowered the bundle into the ground, and they didn't bother to untie the stiff pieces of new rope that were tied around the ends of the blanket. The sun was gone, and over on the highway the eastbound lane was full of headlights. The priest walked away slowly. Leon watched him climb the hill, and when he had disappeared within the tall, thick walls, Leon turned to look up at the high blue mountains in the deep snow that reflected a faint red light from the west. He felt good because it was finished, and he was happy about the sprinkling of the holy water, now the old man could send them big thunderclouds for sure.

[1969]

Joining the Conversation: Critical Thinking and Writing

1. How would you describe the response of Leon, Ken, Louise, and Teresa to Teofilo's death? To what degree does it resemble or differ from responses to death that you are familiar with?
2. How do the funeral rites resemble or differ from those of your community?

3. How well does Leon understand the priest? How well does the priest understand Leon?
4. At the end of the story, we are told that Leon "felt good." Do you assume that the priest also felt good? What evidence supports your view?
5. From what point of view is the story told? Mark the passages where the narrator enters a character's mind, and then explain what, in your opinion, Silko gains (or loses) by doing so.

POEMS

BILLY COLLINS

Born in New York City in 1941, Collins is a professor of English at Lehman College of the City University of New York. He is the author of several books of poetry and the recipient of numerous awards, including one from the National Endowment for the Arts. Collins's Sailing Alone around the Room: New and Selected Poems *was published in 2001; in the same year, he was appointed poet laureate of the United States.*

Introduction to Poetry

I ask them to take a poem
and hold it up to the light
like a color slide
or press an ear against its hive.

I say drop a mouse into a poem   5
and watch him probe his way out,

or walk inside the poem's room
and feel the walls for a light switch.

I want them to waterski
across the surface of a poem   10
waving at the author's name on the shore.

But all they want to do
is tie the poem to a chair with rope
and torture a confession out of it.

They begin beating it with a hose   15
to find out what it really means.

[1988]

Joining the Conversation: Critical Thinking and Writing

1. Billy Collins has said of this poem, "It's about the teaching of poetry to students." What is Collins recommending? What is he objecting to?
2. One critic has said that "Introduction to Poetry" is a "good poem" but that lines 9–16 "should have come first"—that Collins should first have stated the bad way in which students often react and then come forward with the right way. Prepare an argument in which you agree with this critic's comment, and then prepare an argument in which you disagree. Which of the two arguments do you find more convincing?

3. Which image in the poem do you think is the most effective? Is there an image that you think is not effective, that is confusing or awkward, or that you cannot understand?
4. Are the final two stanzas disturbing? Too disturbing? In their tone, are these stanzas similar to, or different from, the preceding stanzas?
5. If someone asked, "What's the best way to teach poetry?" what would you say?
6. This is a relatively short poem, just sixteen lines long. Please try to memorize it. Is this hard or easy for you? Does memorizing poems help you to enjoy poetry more? A lot, or a little? Not at all?

ROBERT FROST

Robert Frost (1874–1963) was born in California. After his father's death in 1885, Frost's mother took the family to New England, where she taught in high schools in Massachusetts and New Hampshire. Frost studied for part of one term at Dartmouth College in New Hampshire, then did various jobs (including teaching), and from 1897 to 1899 was enrolled as a special student at Harvard. He later farmed in New Hampshire, published a few poems in local newspapers, left the farm and taught again, and in 1912 left for England, where he hoped to achieve more popular success as a writer. By 1915, he had won a considerable reputation, and he returned to the United States, settling on a farm in New Hampshire and cultivating the image of the country-wise farmer-poet. In fact, he was well read in the classics, in the Bible, and in English and American literature.

Among Frost's many comments about literature, here are three: "Writing is unboring to the extent that it is dramatic"; "Every poem is . . . a figure of the will braving alien entanglements"; and, finally, a poem "begins in delight and ends in wisdom. . . . It runs a course of lucky events, and ends in a clarification of life—not necessarily a great clarification, such as sects and cults are founded on, but in a momentary stay against confusion."

The Road Not Taken

Two roads diverged in a yellow wood,
And sorry I could not travel both
And be one traveler, long I stood
And looked down one as far as I could
To where it bent in the undergrowth;   5

Then took the other, as just as fair,
And having perhaps the better claim,
Because it was grassy and wanted wear;
Though as for that the passing there
 Had worn them really about the same,   10

And both that morning equally lay
In leaves no step had trodden black.
Oh, I kept the first for another day!
Yet knowing how way leads on to way,
I doubted if I should ever come back.   15

I shall be telling this with a sigh
Somewhere ages and ages hence:

Two roads diverged in a wood, and I
I took the one less traveled by,
And that has made all the difference.   20

[1916]

Joining the Conversation: Critical Thinking and Writing

1. If "The Road Not Taken" consisted of only the first and last stanzas, we would probably feel that Frost was talking about a clear-cut choice between two distinctive ways of life—for instance, the life of a poet or the life of a farmer. The poem does not consist only of the first and last stanzas, however. What do the two middle stanzas do? Do they complicate the poem in an interesting way? Or, do they make a muddle of it? Please explain.
2. The poem is often interpreted as Frost's statement that he chose the life of a poet. Yet, Frost on several occasions said that he was spoofing the indecisiveness of a friend and fellow-poet, Edward Thomas. Given the fact that the middle stanzas suggest that the two roads are pretty much the same, and given the fact that the speaker in the last stanza does seem to playfully mock himself ("I shall be telling this with a sigh / Somewhere ages and ages hence"), do you think that we should or should not take the poem as a serious statement about the decisions we must make? Please explain.

JOHN KEATS

John Keats (1795–1821), son of a London stable keeper, was taken out of school when he was fifteen years old and apprenticed to a surgeon and apothecary. In 1816, he was licensed to practice as an apothecary-surgeon, but he almost immediately abandoned medicine and decided to make a career as a poet. His progress was amazing: He published books of poems—to mixed reviews—in 1817, 1818, and 1820, before dying of tuberculosis at the age of twenty-five. Today he is esteemed as one of England's greatest poets.

Ode on a Grecian Urn

I

Thou still unravished bride of quietness,
    Thou foster-child of silence and slow time,
Sylvan historian, who canst thus express
    A flowery tale more sweetly than our rhyme:
What leaf-fringed legend haunts about thy shape   5
    Of deities or mortals, or of both,
        In Tempe or the dales of Arcady?
    What men or gods are these? What maidens loth?
What mad pursuit? What struggle to escape?
    What pipes and timbrels? What wild ecstasy?   10

II

Heard melodies are sweet, but those unheard
    Are sweeter; therefore, ye soft pipes, play on;

Not to the sensual° ear, but, more endeared,
    Pipe to the spirit ditties of no tone:
Fair youth, beneath the trees, thou canst not leave   15
    Thy song, nor ever can those trees be bare;
    Bold Lover, never, never canst thou kiss,
Though winning near the goal—yet, do not grieve;
    She cannot fade, though thou hast not thy bliss,
    For ever wilt thou love, and she be fair!   20

III

Ah, happy, happy boughs! that cannot shed
    Your leaves, nor ever bid the Spring adieu;
And, happy melodist, unwearied,
    For ever piping songs for ever new;
More happy love! more happy, happy love!   25
    For ever warm and still to be enjoyed,
    For ever panting, and for ever young;
All breathing human passion far above,
    That leaves a heart high-sorrowful and cloyed,
    A burning forehead, and a parching tongue.   30

IV

Who are these coming to the sacrifice?
    To what green altar, O mysterious priest,
Lead'st thou that heifer lowing at the skies,
    And all her silken flanks with garlands drest?
What little town by river or sea shore,   35
    Or mountain-built with peaceful citadel,
    Is emptied of this folk, this pious morn?
And, little town, thy streets for evermore
    Will silent be; and not a soul to tell
    Why thou art desolate can e'er return.   40

V

O Attic shape! Fair attitude! with brede°
    Of marble men and maidens overwrought,
With forest branches and the trodden weed;
    Thou, silent form, dost tease us out of thought
As doth eternity: Cold Pastoral!   45
When old age shall this generation waste,
    Thou shalt remain, in midst of other woe
    Than ours, a friend to man, to whom thou say'st,
"Beauty is truth, truth beauty,"—that is all
    Ye know on earth, and all ye need to know.   50

[1820]

13 sensual sensuous.
41 brede design.

Joining the Conversation: Critical Thinking and Writing

1. In the first stanza, Keats calls the urn an "unravished bride of quietness," a "foster-child of silence and slow time," and a "Sylvan historian." Paraphrase each of these terms.
2. How much sense does it make to say that "Heard melodies are sweet, but those unheard / Are sweeter" (lines 11–12)?
3. In the second stanza, Keats says that the youth will forever sing, the trees will forever have their foliage, and the woman will forever be beautiful. But what words in the stanza suggest that this scene is not entirely happy? Where else in the poem is it suggested that there are painful aspects to the images on the urn?
4. What arguments can you offer to support the view that "Beauty is truth, truth beauty"?
5. There is much uncertainty about whether everything in the last two lines should be enclosed within quotation marks, or only "Beauty is truth, truth beauty." If only these five words from line 49 should be enclosed within quotation marks, does the speaker address the rest of line 49 and the whole of line 50 to the urn or to the reader of the poem?

MARTÍN ESPADA

Martín Espada was born in Brooklyn in 1957. He received a bachelor's degree from the University of Wisconsin and a law degree from Northeastern University. A poet who publishes regularly, Espada teaches creative writing at the University of Massachusetts–Amherst.

Bully

Boston, Massachusetts, 1987

In the school auditorium,
the Theodore Roosevelt statue
is nostalgic
for the Spanish-American War,
each fist lonely for a saber,   5
or the reins of anguish-eyed horses,
or a podium to clatter with speeches
glorying in the malaria of conquest.
But now the Roosevelt school
is pronounced *Hernández*.   10
Puerto Rico has invaded Roosevelt
with its army of Spanish-singing children
in the hallways,
brown children devouring
the stockpiles of the cafeteria,   15
children painting *Taáno* ancestors
that leap naked across murals.
Roosevelt is surrounded
by all the faces
he ever shoved in eugenic spite   20

and cursed as mongrels, skin of one race,
hair and cheekbones of another.
Once Marines tramped
from the newsreel of his imagination;
    now children plot to spray graffiti   25
in parrot-brilliant colors across the Victorian mustache
and monocle.

[1990]

Joining the Conversation: Critical Thinking and Writing

1. What was Theodore Roosevelt famous for? If you are not sure, consult an encyclopedia. In the first stanza of "Bully," what words best express Espada's attitude toward Roosevelt?
2. In the second stanza, what does Espada mean when he says "Puerto Rico has invaded Roosevelt"? What does he mean by an "*army* of Spanish-singing children"? What are the *Taíno?*
3. What does "bully" mean as a noun? As an adjective?
4. Roosevelt was a great believer in America as a "melting pot." What is this theory? Do you think there is a great deal to it, something to it, or nothing to it? Why?
5. In one of Roosevelt's speeches, he states "Every immigrant who comes here should be required within five years to learn English or leave the country." What do you think of this idea? Why? Suppose that, for some reason (perhaps political, perhaps economic), you decided to spend the rest of your life in, say, Argentina, or Germany, or Israel, or Nigeria. Do you think the government might reasonably require you to learn the national language? Support your response with reasons.

CHAPTER 8

Pushing Analysis Further: Reinterpreting and Revising

Chapter Preview

After reading this chapter, you will be able to

- Define *interpretation* and describe the process for interpreting literary texts
- Evaluate your response to literature
- Use different strategies to develop your analytical writing, including rethinking first responses, exploring literary form, and emphasizing concepts and insights
- Use revision to strengthen your analytical thinking and writing

Interpretation and Meaning

We can define **interpretation** as

- a setting forth of your understanding of a literary work's meaning or
- a setting forth of your understanding of one or more of the meanings of a work of literature.

This question of *meaning* versus *meanings* deserves an explanation. Although some critics believe that a work of literature has a single meaning (the meaning it had for the author), most critics hold that a work has several meanings, for instance, the meaning it had for the author, the meaning(s) it had for its first readers (or viewers, if the work is a drama), the meaning(s) it had for later readers, and the meaning(s) it has for us today.

Take *Hamlet* (1600–01), for example. Perhaps this play about a man who has lost his father had a very special meaning for Shakespeare, who had recently lost his own father. Further, Shakespeare had earlier lost a son named Hamnet, a variant spelling of Hamlet. The play, then, may have had important psychological meanings for Shakespeare, but the audience could not have shared (or even known) those meanings.

What *did* the play mean to Shakespeare's audience? Perhaps the original audience of *Hamlet*—people living in a monarchy, presided over by Queen Elizabeth I—were especially concerned with the issue (specifically raised in *Hamlet*) of whether a monarch's subjects ever have the right to overthrow the monarch. But, obviously, for twenty-first-century Americans, the interest in the play lies elsewhere, and the play must mean something else. If we are familiar with Freud, we may see in the play a young man who subconsciously lusts after his mother and seeks to kill his father (in the form of Claudius, Hamlet's uncle). Or, we may see the play as being largely about an alienated young man in a bourgeois society. Or, we may see the work as a meditation on the character of a person who thinks too much and acts too little. The interpretations are countless.

This multitude of possible meanings is exactly what makes literature art. Literature encourages imagination and creativity on the part of the reader, not just the author. The analytical essay emphasizes the reader's meaning-making abilities. The reader creates his or her own understanding of the work and creates a convincing explanation of that understanding, to be shared with his or her own readers; in this way, the creative energy of the literary work informs the creative thinking shared through an analytical paper.

Is the Author's Intention a Guide to Meaning?

Shouldn't we be concerned, you might ask, with the *intention* of the author? The question is reasonable, but it presents difficulties, as the members of the U.S. Supreme Court find when they try to base their decisions on the original intent of the writers of the Constitution. First, for older works, we almost never know what the intention was. Authors did not leave comments about their intentions. We have *Hamlet*, but we do not have any statement of Shakespeare's intention concerning this or any other play. It might be argued that we can deduce Shakespeare's intention from the play itself, but to argue that we should study the play in the light of Shakespeare's intention and that we can know his intention by studying the play is to argue in a circle. We can say that Shakespeare must have intended to write a tragedy (if he intended to write a comedy, he failed), but we cannot go much further in talking about his intention.

Even if an author has gone on record expressing an intention, we may think twice before accepting the statement as definitive. The author may be speaking facetiously, deceptively, mistakenly, or unconvincingly. For instance, Thomas Mann said, probably sincerely and accurately, that he wrote one of his novels merely in order to entertain his family, but we may nevertheless take the book seriously and find it to be profound.

What Characterizes a Sound Interpretation?

Even the most vigorous advocates of the idea that meaning is indeterminate do not believe that all interpretations are equally significant. Rather, they believe that an interpretive essay is offered against a background of ideas, shared by essayist and reader, as to what constitutes a *persuasive argument*. Although a literary work encourages interpretation, there will be weak interpretations and strong interpretations. A strong interpretative essay (even if it is characterized as "interpretive free play" or "creative engagement") will have to be

- coherent,
- plausible, and
- rhetorically effective.

The *presentation*—the rhetoric—as well as the interpretation is significant. This means that the essayist cannot merely set down random expressions of feeling or unsupported opinion. The essayist must, on the contrary, convincingly *argue* a thesis—that is, point to evidence so that the reader will not only know what the essayist believes but also will understand why he or she believes it.

There are lots of ways of making sense (and even more ways of making nonsense), but one important way of helping readers to see things from your point of view is to do your best to face all the complexities of a work. Put it this way: Some interpretations strike a reader as better than others because they are *more inclusive*, that is, because they *account for more of the details of the work*. The less satisfactory interpretations leave a reader pointing to aspects of the work—to some parts of the whole—and saying, "Yes, but your explanation doesn't take account of. . . ."

This does not mean that a reader must feel that a persuasive interpretation says the last word about the work. We always realize that a work—if we value it highly—is richer than the discussion; again, however, for us to value an interpretation, we must find the interpretation plausible and inclusive.

Interpretation often depends on making connections not only among elements of the work (for instance, among the characters in a story or among the images in a poem), and among the work and other works by the author, but also on making connections between a particular work and a cultural context. The cultural context usually includes other writers and specific works of literature, since any given literary work participates in a tradition. That is, if a work looks toward life, it also looks toward other works. A sonnet is about human experience, but it is also part of a tradition of sonnet writing. The more works of literature you are familiar with, the better equipped you will be to interpret any particular work. Here is how Robert Frost put it, in the preface to *Aforesaid*, a book of verse published in 1954:

> A poem is best read in the light of all the other poems ever written. We read A the better to read B (we have to start somewhere; we may get very little out of A). We read B the better to read C, C the better to read D, D the better to go back and get something more out of A. Progress is not the aim, but circulation. The thing is to get among the poems where they hold each other apart in their places as the stars do.

Precisely because a literary work generates multiple meanings informed by details within the work and connections beyond the work, it provides an opportunity to develop your critical thinking abilities. Let's explore how to take an initial interpretation and continue to push it to become more meaningful, resulting in a stronger analytical paper.

Interpreting Pat Mora's "Immigrants"

Let's think about interpreting a short poem by a contemporary poet, Pat Mora.

PAT MORA

Of Mexican American descent, Pat Mora was born in 1942 in El Paso, Texas. She writes poetry, nonfiction, and children's books that explore the border between Mexico and America, emphasizing its cultural diversity and flexible bilingual language. A energetic advocate of the pleasure of reading books, which she calls "book-joy," Mora supports several literacy initiatives and founded what she calls "Children's Day, Book Day, El dia de los ninos, El dia de los libros," a literacy celebration often know as Día.

Immigrants

wrap their babies in the American flag,
feed them mashed hot dogs and apple pie,
name them Bill and Daisy,
buy them blonde dolls that blink
blue eyes or a football and tiny cleats   5
before the baby can even walk,
speak to them in thick English,
hallo, babee, hallo.
whisper in Spanish or Polish
when the babies sleep, whisper   10
in a dark parent bed, that dark
parent fear, "Will they like
our boy, our girl, our fine american
boy, our fine american girl?"

[1986]

Perhaps most readers will agree that the poem expresses or dramatizes a desire, attributed to "immigrants," that their child grow up in an Anglo mode. (Mora is not saying that *all* immigrants have this desire; she has simply invented one speaker who offers details about immigrants. Reader Jones may say that Mora says all immigrants have this desire, but that is Jones's interpretation.) For this reason, the parents call their children Bill and Daisy (rather than, say, José and Katarzyna) and give them blonde dolls and a football (rather than dark-haired dolls and a soccer ball). Up to this point, the parents seem a bit silly in their mimicking of Anglo ways. The second part of the poem, however, gives the reader a more interior view of the parents, and brings out the fear, hope, and worried concern that lie behind their behavior: Some unspecified "they" may not "like / our boy, our girl." Who are "they"? Most readers will probably agree that "they" refers to native-born citizens, especially the blonde, blue-eyed "all-American" Anglo types that until recently dominated the establishment in the United States.

By reviewing the ideas raised by the poem, we are well on our way to creating an interpretation of it. But it is crucial to reread the poem and continue to interpret it, developing a more sophisticated understanding of its ideas.

We can raise further questions about the interpretation of the poem.

- Exactly what does the poet mean when Mora says that immigrants "wrap their babies in the American flag"? Are we to take this literally? If not, how are we to take it?
- Why must the parent's whisper the last lines of the poem? Why can't they speak them loudly? Why are they whispered in a "dark parent bed?" What is the significance of that location?
- Why is the word "american" in the last two lines not capitalized? Is Mora imitating the nonnative speaker's uncertain grasp of English punctuation? (If so, why does Mora capitalize "American" in the first line and "Spanish" and "Polish" later in the poem?) Or, is she perhaps implying some mild reservation about becoming 100 percent American, some suggestion that, in changing from Spanish or Polish to "American," there is a loss?

A reader might seek out Mora and ask her why she didn't capitalize "american" in the last line, but Mora might not be willing to answer, or she might not give a straight answer, or she might say that she doesn't really know why—it just seemed right when she wrote the poem. Most authors do, in fact, take this last approach. When they are working as writers, they work by a kind of creative instinct, a kind of feel for the material. Later, they can look critically at their writing, but that's another sort of experience.

To return to our basic question: What characterizes a good interpretation? The short answer is *evidence* and especially evidence that seems to cover all relevant issues. In an essay, it is not enough merely to assert an interpretation. Your readers don't expect you to make an airtight case, but, because you are trying to help readers to understand a work—to see a work the way you do—you are obliged to

- offer reasonable supporting evidence,
- explain how the evidence develops your ideas, and
- take account of what might be set forth as counterevidence to your thesis.

Of course, your essay may originate with an intuition or an emotional response, a sense that the work is about such and such, but this intuition or emotion must then be examined, and it must stand a test of reasonableness. Your readers may not be convinced that your interpretation is right or true, but they must feel that the interpretation is plausible and in accord with the details of the work, rather than, say, highly eccentric and irreconcilable with some details.

✔ **CHECKLIST:** *Developing an Interpretation*

☐ Do I know the work well enough to offer a thoughtful interpretation? Have I looked up the meanings of words that were unfamiliar to me? Have I engaged in enough brainstorming to develop my own ideas about the text?

☐ Have I discussed the work with my classmates—or at least argued with myself—so that I can reasonably believe that my interpretation makes sense?

☐ Have I reread the literary text and rethought my original responses? Have I taken time to reinterpret the text, add new ideas to my interpretation, or develop my interpretation by introducing new concepts or evidence?

☐ What is my thesis, my main point? Can I state it in a sentence?

☐ Does my thesis express my understanding of the literary work? Have I expressed my insights about the work? Have I avoided general, obvious, or conventional interpretations of the work?

☐ Have I supported my thesis with evidence, using brief quotations from the text? Have I used the evidence to develop by interpretation?

☐ Have I taken account of evidence that may seem to contradict my thesis?

☐ Have I kept my audience in mind?

☐ Have I given credit to all sources for borrowed words and borrowed ideas? (On avoiding plagiarism, see pages 403–404. For citation style see Appendix B.)

Strategy #1: Pushing Analysis by Rethinking First Responses

Usually, you will begin with a strong *response* to your reading—interest, boredom, bafflement, annoyance, shock, pleasure, or whatever. Then, if you are going to think critically about the work, you will go on to *examine* your response in order to understand it, to deepen it, or to change it.

How can you change a response? **Critical thinking** involves seeing an issue from all sides, to as great a degree as possible. As you know, in everyday usage, *to criticize* usually means to find fault, but, in literary studies, the term does not have a negative connotation. Rather, it means "to examine carefully." (The word *criticism* comes from a Greek verb meaning "to distinguish," "to decide," "to judge.") Nevertheless, in one sense, the term *critical thinking* does approach the everyday meaning, since critical thinking requires you to take a skeptical view of your response. You will, so to speak, argue with yourself, seeing if your response can stand up to doubts.

Let's say that you have found a story to be implausible. Ask yourself the following questions:

- Exactly what is implausible in the story?
- Is implausibility always a fault?
- If so, exactly why?

Your answers may deepen your response. Usually, you will find supporting evidence for your response, but, in your effort to distinguish and to decide and to judge, try also (if only as an exercise) to find counterevidence. See what can be said against your position. (The best lawyers, it is said, prepare two cases—their own and the other side's.) As you consider the counterevidence, you will sometimes find that it requires you to adjust your thesis. You may even find yourself developing an entirely different response. That's fine, though, of course, the paper that you ultimately hand in should clearly argue a thesis.

In short, critical thinking means examining or exploring one's own responses, by questioning and testing them. Critical thinking is not so much a skill (though it does involve the ability to understand a text) as it is a *habit of mind* or, rather, several habits, including

- open-mindedness,
- intellectual curiosity, and
- willingness to work.

It may involve, too, a willingness to discuss the issues with others and to do research on writing a research paper, which will be discussed in Chapter 10.

Let's explore how you can revisit a first response and develop it into a successful interpretation that demonstrates your critical thinking skills. Students in a composition course noted their first impressions of a story and then, as part of a classroom exercise, revisited those first responses and developed them further. By examining their first and second responses, we can see what elements of thinking characterize interpretive writing. After writing the first response, the class was encouraged to reread the story and their notes and to work toward an interpretation that

- makes an argument,
- contains conceptual thinking, and
- selects supporting evidence.

Although the writing is rough, the elements of a successful analytical paper are in place.

Let's turn to the literary texts that triggered this interpretive process. Some years ago, Steve Moss, a writer, editor, and publisher, began having an annual contest in which contestants submitted stories of fifty-five words or fewer (plus a title that could be as long as seven words). Let's explore three entries that were accepted for publication.[1] Following each short story is a student's first response to it and then a more developed interpretation of it.

JEFFREY WHITMORE

Bedtime Story

"Careful, honey, it's loaded," he said, re-entering the bedroom.

Her back rested against the headboard. "This for your wife?"

"No. Too chancy. I'm hiring a professional."

"How about me?"

He smirked. "Cute. But who'd be dumb enough to hire a lady hit man?"

She wet her lips, sighting along the barrel.

"Your wife."

All readers will have their own responses to this story, and they will make their own evaluations as to whether it is effective. Here, we offer the first response of one of our students, followed by a more interpretive response. Although this is a rough brainstorming exercise, a comparison of the two responses reveals that the revised response is moving toward a more focused interpretation of the work. With a bit more work, it could be transformed into a compelling thesis argument.

Student Work: Response Writing Revisited

First Response: Clever; I expected a sort of child's nursery tale, and instead got a story that in part is about adults going to bed sexually—so I did get a "bedtime story" but not what I first expected. Sort of clever. The ending gets even more clever, because we didn't see it coming. The story creates a twist on the male/female relationship. The woman in the bed that he is having the affair with is the hired hitman—and he is the target! I didn't see that coming. Certainly it is clever.

Expanded Response: What do we make of the relationships set up between the man and the woman? There are only two characters—and a very very short story, so we don't expect elaborate characterization. But, even with this limited information, the man is neatly shown to be a self-satisfied jerk. He thinks he is smart—"Too chancy. I'm hiring a professional"—and he "smirked" when his girlfriend suggests she might act as a hit-man. He has a conventional superior-male idea that a woman can't do a difficult job—but at the end of the story he knows (if only for a few seconds!!) better. This is his key realization: that his lover has been hired to kill him AND that a woman can be a hired hit-man and do a good job of it. He didn't even suspect her! So, she's obviously been doing a great job of being a double-crosser. She probably even relied on his superiority complex, knowing she wouldn't even be suspected by him. Because of the way the woman has set up the last lines of the story, she is obviously smart. She's not just a "honey."

Here is the second story and a second student's response to it.

[1]**Steve Moss, ed.,** *The World's Shortest Stories* (Philadelphia: Running Press, 1998).

DOUGLAS L. HASKINS

Hide and Seek

At last he would really show them. He'd picked the very best place to hide. They'd all say he could play the game better than anyone. When they found him, they'd clap their hands.

The dopes. How dumb can they get? They should have looked here first! It's so obvious.

Here in the abandoned refrigerator.

After reading the preceding short story, the student made some free writing notes that she then reread and expanded. Notice how the student moves from a personal first response to an analytical assessment in the second response. Both responses focus on the main character, but the first response is emotional and focuses on conveying the facts of the story. The expanded response becomes analytical, containing an assessment of the qualities of the narrator and a clear focus on the concept of intelligence.

Student Work: Response Writing Revisited

First Response: This story is horrible! I guess it is "effective" because it really hits me, hurts me, but it is so cruel. As I understand it, the narrator hides in an abandoned refrigerator—and presumably he dies. This is horrific. It is showing the last thoughts of a child before he dies. I don't even want to think about this scene. Frankly, I don't think a story like this should be published. It is too frightening.

Expanded Response: When I get over the emotions of horror that this story triggered, I can start to focus on the narrator. The words "dope" and "dumb" leap out at me, making me realize that the story is exploring the idea of intelligence—who is the smart one here? This kid wants to show other kids that he is smart, that "he could play the game better than anyone." What we hear are the thoughts of the kid before he died—his attempt to be a winner at the game of hide-and-seek and have his friends "clap" for him. And I think we also hear, in a way, what is said after the other kids discover his dead body: We "should have looked here first! It's so obvious." The narrator thinks he is smart, but he makes (unfortunately) a dumb choice of a hiding place. The kids who, if they find him too late, would fulfill his expectations that they are dumb—they don't think to look in the refrigerator.

Finally, we have the third story from the same collection of stories of fifty-five words or fewer, this time with only the first response from a student. We offer a series of questions that encourage you to write an expanded response.

MARK PLANTS

Equal Rites

"Highly irregular," said the priest.

"The diocese allows them," replied one of the men.

Overcoming a visceral dislike of same sex unions, the priest agreed to hold the ceremony quietly. There was a harpist. Both men wore tuxedos.

But the priest, even while donning her vestments, still wondered if she was doing the right thing.

Student Work: Response Writing Revisited

> **First Response:** The twist in this story is that the priest is a woman. The story seems to be about same-sex unions, but then the story reveals that it is really interested in the gender of the priest. The shock is not that the church is allowing same-sex unions, but that the church allows woman priests. This story is obviously taking place in the not-too-distant future. I wonder if this is a comment on where the religion is headed? Maybe the church will allow women to be priests before allowing same-sex marriage?

Joining the Conversation: Critical Thinking and Writing

1. How would you expand this first response, making it more analytical?
2. What key concepts appear in the first response that could provide a foundation for further thinking? For example, are you interested in the idea of gender? Or, are you interested in the idea of religion? Are there additional concepts that you would want to address?
3. The first response does not contain any direct quotations from the story. What phrases or lines from the story do you feel are the most important and would thus include in your response?

Strategy #2: Pushing Analysis by Exploring Literary Form

One of the best ways to deepen literary analysis is to examine the literary work's structures—what we might call the artfulness of the work, such as the work's meter or use of figurative language—in addition to its themes. A literary work connects *form* (the shape and structure that it gives to language) to *content* (the ideas it wants to express). Literature asks us to pay attention to both form and content, and to think about how they work together to create meaning.

In an analytical paper, you will be expected not only to explore a literary work's key ideas but also to explain how those ideas are conveyed by form. If you are looking to improve, expand, or develop a paper, you should examine how you are building an analysis of form into your paper. In order to explore form, you must work closely with textual evidence. As a result, a careful attention to the formal qualities of literature will almost always improve your writing, as it will integrate meaningful evidence into your writing.

To explore how careful attention to a formal element can improve a paper, let's turn to poetry. Because it highlights form, poetry allows us to practice seeing the connections between form and content. A poem often uses rhyme, repetition, line breaks, and stanza breaks, taking a specific shape on the page. That shape, in turn, highlights or enacts specific ideas. For example, if you are analyzing a poem that expresses frustrated anger, you may notice that the poem features fragmented lines that "break off" in mid-idea; you will want to explain how the form of the fragmented lines expresses the idea of anger. As we say elsewhere in the text, an analytical essay answers the somewhat odd-sounding question, "How does a poem mean?" in addition to the expected question, "What does the poem mean?"

In an analytical paper on a poem, you'll want to use your knowledge about poetry by locating, naming, and analyzing the poetic devices that create the poem's meaning.

Let's consider an analytical paper assignment that focuses on the formal elements of a poem, asking you to explore the poem's imagery. You might mark up the poem, locating its key images and taking marginal notes that start to question and interpret those images. You might then expand your ideas, developing them into a set of inquiry questions that focus on the issue of form: What is the poem is about? What are the ideas being expressed by the imagery in the poem? What are its most thought-provoking images in the poem? What feelings do the images evoke? What specific words are used to convey its imagery? Does the imagery take on the significance of a symbol, as we discuss in Chapter 15? And, is that symbol conventional or unique?

When you are writing an analysis, review the literary structures you have been studying. Locate those structures in the literary work, and analyze how they convey ideas. If your instructor asks you to focus on a specific literary element—for instance, meter or figurative language—reread the text, focus on that element and how it contributes to the text's meaning. In your annotations and brainstorming notes, examine your selected literary element closely. Emphasize your overarching interpretation by transforming it into a thesis argument that you set forth at the beginning of your paper. If you are interpreting a specific literary element, make sure that element is central to your thesis argument. Then, create a hierarchy of ideas, in which your secondary interpretations become subpoints in your paper, continuing to analyze the selected formal element throughout the paper. Keeping focused on a specific literary element will benefit your paper; in addition to strengthening your use of evidence, it will help you to avoid inserting a summary and overly general ideas about the text.

✔ **CHECKLIST:** *Using Formal Evidence in an Analytical Essay*

☐ Did I review the literary forms and structures I have been studying? Do I understand the definitions of these forms? Do I understand the examples of that form provided by this literary work, and can I locate examples of those forms in other literary works?

☐ Did I read the literary work closely, annotating it for the selected literary forms?

☐ Did I consider what seems to be the literary work's most important formal element? Does the work call attention to, for example, its use of voice, imagery, plot, setting, characterization, or dramatic irony?

☐ Did I emphasize the ideas being expressed though these literary forms? Did I make sure to connect form to content?

☐ Did I create inquiry questions that focus on the issues of form and then use those questions to deepen my analysis of the text?

☐ Are issues of literary form central to my thesis argument?

☐ Did I use issues of form to push my analytical thinking? Did I address issues of form throughout my paper?

☐ Did I make my ideas specific by illustrating them with interesting quotations? Did I explain the formal elements used in those quotations?
☐ Did I use the analysis of form to come to a more sophisticated understanding of the poem's meaning?

Let's see how an exploration of literary form can be used to brainstorm ideas for a paper and develop a draft. We can turn to the annotations, inquiry notes, and final paper written by Ayn Brady, a first-year student in an introductory course on writing about literature. Her paper examines "Mother to Son," a poem written by one of the most important poets of the twentieth century, Langston Hughes. As Ayn's analysis of the poem's poetic devices shows, Hughes's poetry uses straightforward language to capture complex ideas.

LANGSTON HUGHES

For biographical information on Langston Hughes, see page 429.

Mother to Son

Well, son, I'll tell you:
Life for me ain't been no crystal stair.
It's had tacks in it,
And splinters,
And boards torn up,   5
And places with no carpet on the floor—
Bare.
But all the time
I'se been a-climbin' on,
And reachin' landin's,   10
And turnin' corners,
And sometimes goin' in the dark
Where there ain't been no light.
So boy, don't you turn back.
Don't you set down on the steps   15
'Cause you finds it's kinder hard.
Don't you fall now—
For I'se still goin', honey,
I'se still climbin',
And life for me ain't been no crystal stair.   20

[1922]

Student Work: Annotation Exploring Form

Ayn's class has been given an assignment asking them to explore how a poem's poetic form contributes to its meaning. Ayn's annotations on the poem show her first attempts to explore the poem's form. She takes notes on the poem's formal elements on the right-hand side of the poem and takes notes on the conceptual content on the left-hand side of the poem. This strategy allows her to make sure that she is giving enough consideration to the poem's form and allows her to see more clearly the patterns of poetic structure used by Hughes.

"Mother to Son"

Well, son, I'll tell you: ← *mother talking to son*
Life for me ain't been no crystal stair.

The Harsh Stairs

It's had tacks in it,
And splinters,   *strong images of*
                      hard stairs = hard climb = hard life
And boards torn up,
And places with no carpet on the floor–
Bare. ← *one word – harsh, lonely word*

The Climb

But all the time
I'se been a-climbin' on,   — *repetition of "and" and "in'" for "ing"*
And reachin' landin's,   *words become repeated like stairs*
And turnin' corners,   *are repeated – like repeated*
And sometimes goin' in the dark *sound of steps up stairs?*
Where there ain't been no light.

The Lesson!

So boy, don't you turn back.
Don't you set down on the steps — *don't give up – lesson for son*
'Cause you finds it's kinder hard.   *& African Americans*
Don't you fall now– — *repetition*

Strong voice of "I"

For I'se still goin', honey,
I'se still climbin',
And life for me ain't been no crystal stair. — *repeats line 2*

Student Work: Inquiry Notes Exploring Form

After completing her annotations, Ayn generates a series of inquiry questions that help her to analyze the poem's formal elements, including its imagery, voice, and diction. Notice how her inquiry questions help her to locate and organize evidence that she could use in her paper.

"Mother to Son"
What poetic structures or devices does this poem use to make meaning?
Right away, I notice the straightforward language, as if the speaker is speaking right at me (just like the voice is talking to the son) in everyday/colloquial language. The meaning of the poem is clear: it is conveying the difficulties of a tough life. This life is like climbing up a difficult staircase. But, how does this poem capture the difficulty of that climb? How does the poem make us feel that sense of difficulty? I guess that the question I want to answer by looking at the poem's form.

Imagery: How does the poem use imagery?
Central image = image of climbing stairs
Stairs are not glass stairs, but difficult, rough, not-easy stairs
**Does this become a metaphor? Life is like climbing stairs?

What are the specific words used by the poem to build up these images?
- –tacks
- –splinters
- –boards
- –no carpet, bare
- –landing
- –turnings
- –no light = dark

These images add up to the idea of a difficult climb—the stairs are rough and broken; they are all uphill. The words are easy to understand, but create a strong and clear image of a tough climb.

Voice: How does the poem use voice?
Poem has a strong speaking persona
Mother speaking directly to son—directly addresses him in the first line and again near end ("honey")
She directly addresses him and tells him what to do: "Don't you fall now"

Language: How does the poem use language?
The poem uses colloquial language—language that seems slangy and everyday
- –ain't
- –climbin'
- –reachin'
- –turnin'
- –goin'

Spoken language, as if talking directly to you.
Maybe the language itself is tired, not precise, due to difficult climb?

Pattern: How does the pattern of the words create meaning?
Repetition
- –And, and, and
- –I'se still, I'se still

Short lines
The poem starts to feel like the stairs, like the steps going up a staircase
Maybe the poem is meant to imitate the feel of step-by-step (line-by-line) action of going up the stairs

What seems to be the key content—the meaning—of the poem? Does the form capture that meaning?
The mother is giving a lesson to her son. The key lesson is "So, boy, don't you turn back," meaning that the boy cannot give up or turn back from difficulties. He must continue up the stairs, just as she has gone up the stairs. Do not turn back, rest, or give up! Keep going! The mother shows a successful climb—the poem acts out the climb–making it clear that the climb can be done.

Can the poem be connected to a larger context?
Harlem Renaissance
The poem could be read as a comment on the larger African-American struggle against prejudice—African-Americans have had a hard and difficult climb towards equality, but they cannot give up.

Student Analytical Essay: "Accepting the Challenge of a Difficult Climb in Langston Hughes's 'Mother to Son'"

Ayn takes the interesting insights that she has generated in her inquiry notes and turns them into the following paper:

Brady 1

Ayn Brady

Professor Singh

English 150-32

10 March 2016

Accepting the Challenge of a Difficult Climb

Langston Hughes's "Mother to Son" centers on the key metaphor that life can be compared to the act of climbing stairs. The poem develops this metaphor by using poetic devices, focusing on the poetic language of the poem's speaker. As the title reveals, the poem features the persona of a mother. The mother describes her life as climbing stairs and expresses the feeling of climbing stairs by using colloquial language and the repetition of words and sounds. The pattern of the language sounds like the pattern of climbing up stairs one after the other. The climbing of stairs is difficult and stressful, with no break. Thus, life for the speaker has been difficult and stressful with no break. "Mother to Son" conveys the feeling of this difficult life by creating a strong speaking persona, using repetition, using colloquial language, and developing a clear metaphor.

The poem creates the persona of a mother who is talking to her son. The poem's first line is "Well son, I'll tell you," creating a speaking situation in which the mother is talking directly to the son—and to the reader (1). The speaker's voice creates a strong connection between herself and her son. She even addresses the son as "honey" towards the end of the poem. As she shares the difficulties of her life with him, the mother's voice seems honest and open. As the poem progresses, it becomes clear that the mother is giving a lesson to her son. The speaker addresses the listener directly with the key lesson "So, boy, don't you turn back," meaning that the boy cannot give up or turn back from difficulties.

The poem is told from the perspective of this persona, using the language, experiences, and knowledge of the mother. The mother has had a difficult life, which is effectively presented through the metaphor of an upward climb. The poem sets itself up to feel like a set of stairs. The poem has very short lines, like the short steps a person takes on stairs. The language repeats itself, such as repeating the word "and" at the start of six of its lines (4-6, 10-12). The repetitive language captures the repetition of climbing upwards. In addition, the mother's colloquial language, such as the use of "I'se" for "I'm," reveals that the hard work of climbing happens in everyday life (9, 18-19). Life can feel like a constant struggle and the speaker's language captures this feeling.

Through its persona and poetic language, the poem develops the metaphor that life is a difficult staircase that requires a stressful climb. The poem opens and closes with a statement that makes the comparison between life and staircase clear: the mother says "Life for me ain't been no crystal stair" (2). The metaphor of "life as staircase" is set up through a negative statement; the mother sees the possibility that life could be a crystal stair, as for example in a TV spectacular musical, but knows that her life is *not* that. A crystal staircase would be glittering, precious, and handled delicately. However, this speaker's life is the opposite and she opens the poem with this idea of opposition and negativity.

The metaphor of life being a difficult set of stairs is developed through clear imagery. For lines 3-7, the poem creates a staircase of short lines and gives one image per line. Each image conveys the difficulty of the climb: the speaker's stairs has "had tacks in it;" followed by "Splinters," and

Brady 3

"boards torn up," and "places with no carpet on the floor" (3-7). Although these words describe the stairs, they are really describing the speaker's hard life. The mother has been challenged by a series of painful obstacles. Each of these lines starts with the word "and," making a repetitive pattern of sound—perhaps imitating the repetitive act of climbing a staircase. This repetition of "and," followed by strong descriptive words, makes the idea of stairs come alive. In a set of stairs, each stair is similar—and there is always another stair ahead.

The image of these difficult stairs culminates in a very effective line. Line 8 contains one word, left to stand all alone: "bare." The word "bare" is presented in a bare and lonely way that makes it meaning clear. The word can be seen as representing the mother, who must have had to stand "bare" and alone throughout her life.

After describing the stairs, the speaker explains her attitude: she continues to climb the stairs no matter what obstacles they throw in her way. Lines 9-12 shift from describing the stairs to her describing herself and her climbing activity. As the speaker describes her climbing activity, it feels real because the lines are presented in colloquial, everyday language. For example, the speaker explains "I'se been a-climbin' on," which captures the feeling of an everyday struggle that causes weariness but that has been accepted and is now part of life (9). The mother continues to describe her climbing through a list of active verbs that are presented in her unique voice: "And reachin' landin's/And turnin' corners./And sometimes goin' in the dark" (10-12). This use of "in'" for "ing" becomes a pattern. The stairs might continue one after another in repetitive pattern, but the mother will continue to climb them. The mother's description of her activity reveals that she will not give up, but sees the stairs as a challenge to be met and overcome.

In this speaking situation, the speaking mother wants to make sure that the listening son learns from her upwards climb. The mother addresses him directly, saying "So boy, don't you turn back/Don't you set down on the steps/'Cause you finds it's kinder hard./Don't you fall now—" (14-17). The mother wants her son to continue her climb. He must learn from her example and continue a forward, upward march. The mother does not want the son to take any backward steps, but urges him to continue without turning around or taking a rest. The strength of the mother's persona comes across in these lines. She ends her poem by saying "For I'se still goin' honey,/I'se still climbin'/And life for me ain't been no crystal stair" (18-20).

This final section of the poem describes the upward climb as if it were the mother's individual life, but the climb can also be read as describing the African-American experience. Knowing that Langston Hughes was African-American and wrote during the Harlem Renaissance can help to position the poem in the larger context of the African-American struggle to achieve recognition and equal rights. The mother's upward climb can be read as expressing the struggle to move forward in the face of prejudice. In this reading, the mother's climb becomes inspirational. Though faced with numerous obstacles, the mother has continued to tackle and overcome those obstacles. The boy must not let that legacy be forgotten. The boy must make sure that he picks up and continues from his mother's point in the upward climb—he cannot go backward. In this way, the boy can be seen as representing the next generation of African-Americans who are being urged to continue the struggle of the previous generation. Just like the boy, the newest generation must not lose the gains of their parents. When read this way, the metaphor of climbing stairs becomes a way of explaining the struggle for equality.

Brady 5

Hughes's "Mother to Son" is a powerful poem that makes the reader feel the difficulty of the speaker's life. The poem gains its power from the effective use of poetic devices, including voice, repetition, colloquialisms, and imagery. The challenge of constantly climbing stairs is an effective metaphor for the difficulty of moving forward in life. The poem is especially effective in expressing the difficulty of moving ahead in a life that is "bare" rather than bright with crystal. This is especially true if the speaker is an African-American woman. The speaker inspires her son and the reader to continue to fight for equality.

[New page]

Brady 6

Work Cited

Hughes, Langston. "Mother to Son." *Literature for Composition*. Ed. Sylvan Barnet, William Burto, William E. Cain, and Cheryl L. Nixon. 11th ed. Boston: Pearson, 2017. 261. Print.

Strategy #3: Pushing Analysis by Emphasizing Concepts and Insights

Because a literary text is open-ended—it does not come right out and say, "This is what I'm about"—literary analysis asks the student to create his or her own interpretation of the text; in essence, the student says, "This is what I think the text is about." A successful interpretation is grounded in a careful close reading but does not hesitate to reach for a unique understanding of the text. In an analytical paper, you are asked to develop your critical thinking skills—to use writing about a literary work in order to push your ideas to become richer, deeper, and more complex. In analysis, you build on close reading by using writing to define, explain, and develop your most meaningful interpretation of the text. You then present that interpretation as an argument, attempting to convince your reader of your interpretation's originality and importance.

How can you develop your analytical thinking and writing to make it more sophisticated? Perhaps your instructor or a peer has said to you, "Develop your ideas further." How can you do that?

Analysis emphasizes the reader's idea-based interpretation of the text and formulation of an argument about those ideas. In its broadest sense, an analytical paper allows you to investigate how a text makes meaning. As a result, you want to emphasize your insights about the text: What unique ideas is the text triggering in your mind? What strikes you as important and interesting about the text? One way to make sure that you are developing new ideas and not just regurgitating basic information (such as providing a plot summary) is to locate the *concepts* that you feel are more central to the text. Position yourself as a conceptual thinker, able to see the more abstract ideas that the literary text is exploring. For example, in her paper on Langston Hughes's "Mother to Son," Ayn Brady did not limit herself to arguing that the poem depicts a woman climbing stairs. Instead, she argued that the poem addresses the more abstract idea of rising to the challenge of a difficult life. Ayn pushed this idea further and connected it to the concept of equality, specifically the African American struggle for equality.

At the same time that you are exploring abstract concepts, you want to root those concepts in the specific details of the text. As we've discussed throughout this text, an analytical paper is a testing ground for your ability to explain how smaller details connect to larger ideas. An analytical paper often explores the relationships among specific "parts" of the literary text and the contributions of those parts to the text's "whole," or its conceptual meaning. These "parts" can be the literary elements (such as character or voice) that work together to create the text's larger, more overarching ideas.

Further, as we've just seen in Ayn's paper, an analytical paper that asks the student to explore a literary work often asks for an in-depth exploration of formal elements and structures. When you are working on the paper, you should locate and interpret meaningful details and patterns in the text, using those details and patterns to trigger original interpretations. These interpretations should express a larger understanding of the literary text, using the literary elements to illuminate larger conceptual concerns.

Let's read Robert Frost's "Stopping by Woods on a Snowy Evening" and then read two analytical essays written by first-year students. These two papers offer very different interpretations of the same poem, allowing you to see how one student's interpretation of a poem can lead to emphasizing concepts and evidence that differ greatly from another student's insights.

Robert Frost

For biographical information on Robert Frost, see page 246.

Stopping by Woods on a Snowy Evening

Whose woods these are I think I know.
His house is in the village though;
He will not see me stopping here
To watch his woods fill up with snow.

My little horse must think it queer   5
To stop without a farmhouse near
Between the woods and frozen lake
The darkest evening of the year.

He gives his harness bells a shake
To ask if there is some mistake.   10
The only other sound's the sweep
Of easy wind and downy flake.

The woods are lovely, dark and deep.
But I have promises to keep,
And miles to go before I sleep,   15
And miles to go before I sleep.

[1923]

Manuscript version of Frost's "Stopping by Woods on a Snowy Evening." The first part is lost.

Student Analytical Essay: "Stopping by Woods—and Going On"

Let's turn to our first analytical essay on Robert Frost's "Stopping by Woods on a Snowy Evening." This student, Darrel Jenkins, selects specific evidence to support his unique interpretation of the poem. See if you agree with his assessment of the poem's narrator.

Darrel Jenkins

Professor Conner

English 1102

21 December 2016

Stopping by Woods—and Going On

Robert Frost's "Stopping by Woods on a Snowy Evening" is about what

the title says it is. It is also about something more than the title says.

When I say it is about what the title says, I mean that the poem really

does give us the thoughts of a person who pauses (that is, a person who is

"stopping") by woods on a snowy evening. (This person probably is a man,

since Robert Frost wrote the poem and nothing in the poem clearly indicates

that the speaker is not a man. But, and this point will be important, the

speaker perhaps feels that he is not a very masculine man. For example, the

speaker uses the word "lovely," which sounds more like the word a woman

would use than a man.) In line 3 the speaker says he is "stopping here," and

it is clear that "here" is by woods, since "woods" is mentioned not only in

the title but also in the first line of the poem, and again in the second

stanza, and still again in the last stanza. It is equally clear that, as the title

says, there is snow, and that the time is evening. The speaker mentions

"snow" (4), and "downy flake" (12), and "downy flake", and he says this is

"The darkest evening of the year" (8).

But in what sense is the poem about *more* than the title? The title does

not tell us anything about the man who is "stopping by woods," but the poem—

the man's meditation—tells us a lot about him. In the first stanza he reveals

that he is uneasy at the thought that the owner of the woods may see him

stopping by the woods. Maybe he is uneasy because he is trespassing, but the

poem does not actually say that he has illegally entered someone else's

property. More likely, he feels uneasy, almost ashamed, of watching the "woods

fill up with snow" (4). That is, he would not want anyone to see that he actually is enjoying a beautiful aspect of nature and is not hurrying about whatever his real business is in thrifty Yankee style.

The second stanza gives more evidence that he feels guilty about enjoying beauty. He feels so guilty that he even thinks the horse thinks there is something odd about him. In fact, he says that the horse thinks he is "queer" (5), which means "odd," but also (as is shown by *The American Heritage Dictionary*) can mean "gay," "homosexual." A traditional man, he sort of suggests, would not spend time looking at snow in the woods when he has work to attend to.

So far, then, the speaker in two ways has indicated that he feels insecure, though perhaps he does not realize that he has given himself away. First, he expresses uneasiness that someone might see him watching the woods fill up with snow. Second, he expresses uneasiness when he suggests that even the horse thinks he is strange or different, or at least unbusinesslike. And so in the last stanza, even though he finds the woods beautiful, he decides not to stop and to see the woods fill up with snow. And his description of the woods as "lovely" (13).—a woman's word—sounds as though he may be something less than a he-man. He seems to feel ashamed of himself for enjoying the sight of the snowy woods and for seeing them as "lovely," and so he tells himself that he has spent enough time looking at the woods and that he must go on about his business. In fact, he tells himself twice that he has business to attend to. Why? Perhaps he is insisting too much. Just as we saw that he was excessively nervous in the first stanza, afraid that someone might see him trespassing and enjoying the beautiful spectacle, now at the end he is again afraid that someone might see him loitering, and so he very firmly, using repetition as a form of emphasis, tries to reassure himself that he is not too much attracted by beauty and is a man of business who keeps his promises.

Jenkins 3

Frost gives us, then, a man who indeed is seen "stopping by woods on

a snowy evening," but a man who, afraid of what society will think of him, is

also afraid to "stop" long enough to fully enjoy the sight that attracts him,

because he is driven by a sense that he may be seen to be trespassing and

also may be thought to be unmanly. So after only a brief stop in the woods he

forces himself to go on, a victim (though he probably doesn't know it) of the

work ethic and of an over-simple idea of manliness.

[New page]

Jenkins 4

Work Cited

Frost, Robert. "Stopping by Woods on a Snowy Evening." *Literature for Composition*.

Ed. Sylvan Barnet, William Burto, William E. Cain, and Cheryl L. Nixon.

11th ed. Boston: Pearson, 2017. 269-70. Print.

Analyzing the Analytical Essay's Development of a Conceptual Interpretation

Let's examine this essay.

The *title* is interesting. It tells the reader which literary work will be discussed ("Stopping by Woods"), and it arouses interest, in this case by a sort of wordplay ("Stopping . . . Going On"). A title of this sort is preferable to a title that merely announces the topic, such as "An Analysis of Frost's 'Stopping by Woods'" or "On a Poem by Robert Frost."

The *opening paragraph* helpfully names the exact topic (Robert Frost's poem) and says that the poem is about something more than its title. The writer's thesis presumably will be a fairly specific assertion concerning what the poem is about.

The *body of the essay*, beginning with the second paragraph, begins to develop the thesis. The **thesis** perhaps can be summarized: "The speaker, insecure of his masculinity, feels ashamed that he responds with pleasure to the sight of the snowy woods." The thesis introduces the key concept of masculinity. This is

Darrel's insight into the poem: that it addresses insecurities and, more specifically, insecurities about what constitutes manly thoughts and businesslike behavior. The writer's evidence in the second paragraph is that the word "lovely" is "more like the word a woman would use than a man." Readers of Darrel's essay may at this point be unconvinced by this evidence, but probably they will suspend judgment. In any case, he has offered what he considers to be evidence in support of his thesis.

The next paragraph dwells on what is said to be the speaker's uneasiness, and the following paragraph references the word "queer," which, Darrel correctly says, can mean "gay, homosexual." The question of course is whether *here,* in this poem, the word has this meaning. Do we agree with Darrel's assertion, in the last sentence of this paragraph, that Frost is suggesting that "A traditional man . . . wouldn't spend time looking at snow in the woods"?

Clearly, this is the way Darrel takes the poem, but is his response to these lines reasonable? After all, what Frost says is this: "My little horse must think it queer / To stop without a farmhouse near." Is it reasonable to see a reference to homosexuality (rather than merely to oddness) in *this* use of the word "queer"? Hasn't Darrel offered a response that, so to speak, is private? It is *his* response, but are we likely to share it and to agree that we see it in Frost's poem?

The next paragraph, amplifying the point that the speaker is insecure, offers as evidence the argument that "*lovely*" is more often a woman's word than a man's word. What do you think of Darrel's assertions that the speaker of the poem "was excessively nervous in the first stanza" and is now "afraid that someone might see him loitering"? In your opinion, does the text lend much support to Darrel's view?

The *concluding paragraph* effectively reasserts and clarifies Darrel's thesis, saying that the speaker hesitates to stop and enjoy the woods because "he is driven by a sense that he may be seen to be trespassing and also may be thought to be unmanly."

The big questions, then, are these:

- Is the thesis *argued* rather than merely asserted, and
- Is it argued *convincingly?*

Or, to put it another way,

- Is the evidence adequate?

Darrel certainly does argue (offer reasons) rather than merely assert, but does he offer enough evidence to make you think that his response is one that you can share? Do you think that he is correct to have positioned the concept of masculinity as central to the poem and to, more specifically, emphasized anxieties about masculinity? Has he helped you to enjoy the poem by seeing things that you may not have noticed, or has he said things that, however interesting, seem to you not to be in close contact with the poem as you see it?

Student Analytical Essay: "'Stopping by Woods on a Snowy Evening' as a Short Story"

Here is another interpretation of the same poem. In this paper, Sara Fong demonstrates how a poem can lead to differing interpretations by exploring two understandings of this one poem. Let's see what concepts this paper emphasizes.

Sara Fong
Professor Patel
English 102
3 December 2016

"Stopping by Woods on a Snowy Evening" as a Short Story

Robert Frost's "Stopping by Woods on a Snowy Evening" can be read as
a poem about a man who pauses to observe the beauty of nature, and it can
also be read as a poem about a man with a death wish, a man who seems to
long to give himself up completely to nature and thus escape his
responsibilities as a citizen. Much depends, apparently, on what a reader
wants to emphasize. For instance, a reader can emphasize especially
appealing lines about the beauty of nature: "The only other sound's the sweep /
Of easy wind and downy flake" (11–12), and "The woods are lovely, dark and
deep" (13). On the other hand, a reader can emphasize lines that show the
speaker is fully aware of the responsibilities that most of us agree we have.

For instance, at the very start of the poem he recognizes that the
woods are not his but are owned by someone else, and at the end of the
poem he recognizes that he has "promises to keep" (14) and that before he
sleeps (dies?) he must accomplish many things (go for "miles" [15]).

Does a reader have to choose between these two interpretations? I do
not think so; to the contrary, I think it makes sense to read the poem as a
kind of very short story, with a character whose developing thoughts make
up a plot with four stages. In the first stage, the central figure is an ordinary
person with rather ordinary thoughts. His very first thought is of the owner
of the woods. He knows who the owner is, and since the owner lives in the
village, the poet feels safe in trespassing, or at least in watching the woods "fill
up with snow" (4). Then, very subtly, the poet begins to tell us that although
this seems to be an ordinary person thinking ordinary thoughts, he is a
somewhat special person in a special situation. First of all, the horse thinks
something is strange. He shakes his bells, wondering why the driver doesn't

keep moving, as presumably ordinary drivers would. Second, we are told that this is "The darkest evening of the year" (8). Frost could simply have said that the evening is dark, but he goes out of his way to make the evening a special evening.

We are now through with the first ten lines, and only six lines remain, yet in these six lines the story goes through two additional phases. The first three of these lines ("The only other sound's the sweep / Of easy wind and downy flake" [12] and "The woods are lovely, dark and deep" [13]) are probably the most beautiful lines, in the sense that they are the ones that make us say, "I wish I were there," or "I'd love to experience this." We feel that the poet has moved from the ordinary thoughts of the first stanza, about such businesslike things as who owns the woods and where the owner's house is, to less materialistic thoughts, thoughts about the beauty of the nonhuman world of nature. And now, with the three final lines, we get the fourth stage of the story, the return to the ordinary world of people, the world of "promises" (14). But this world that we get at the end is not exactly the same as the world we got at the beginning. The world at the beginning of the poem is a world of property (who owns the woods, and where the house is), but the world at the end of the poem is a world of unspecified and rather mysterious responsibilities ("promises to keep" [14], "miles to go before I sleep" [16]). It is almost as though the poet's experience of the beauty of nature—a beauty that for a moment made him forget the world of property—has in fact served to sharpen his sense that human beings have responsibilities. He clearly sees that "The woods are lovely, dark and deep" (13). and then he says (I add the italics), "*But* I have promises to keep" (14). The "but" would be logical if after saying that the woods are lovely, dark and deep, he had said something like "But in the daylight they look different," or "But one can freeze to death in them." The logic of what Frost says, however, is not at all clear: "The woods are lovely, dark and deep, / But I have promises to keep" (13–14). What is the logical

Fong 3

connection? We have to supply one, something like "but, *because we are human beings we have responsibilities;* we can refresh ourselves by perceiving the beauties of nature, and we can even for a moment get so caught up that we seem to enter an enchanted forest ('the woods are lovely, dark and deep'), but we cannot forget our responsibilities."

My point is not that Frost ends with an important moral, and it is also not that we have to choose between saying it is a poem about nature or a poem about a man with a death wish. Rather, my point is that the poem takes us through several stages and that, although the poem begins and ends with the speaker in the woods, the speaker has undergone mental experiences—has, we might say, gone through a plot with a conflict (the appeal of the snowy woods versus the call to return to the human world). It is not a matter of good versus evil and of one side winning. Frost in no way suggests that it is wrong to feel the beauty of nature—even to the momentary exclusion of all other thoughts. But the poem is certainly not simply a praise of the beauty of nature. Frost shows us, in this mini-story or mini-drama, one character who sees the woods as property, then sees them as a place of almost overwhelming beauty, and then (maybe refreshed by this experience) rejoins the world of chores and responsibilities.

[New page]

Fong 4

Work Cited

Frost, Robert. "Stopping by Woods on a Snowy Evening." *Literature for Composition*. Ed. Sylvan Barnet, William Burto, William E. Cain, and Cheryl L. Nixon. 11th ed. Boston: Pearson, 2017. 269-70. Print.

Joining the Conversation: Critical Thinking and Writing

1. What is the thesis of the essay? The thesis seems to support two interpretations. Is this successful?
2. How is Sara's essay organized? How does the essay introduce and develop the concepts of nature and the concept of responsibility?
3. Does Sara offer convincing evidence to support her thesis?
4. How would you compare Sara's essay to Darrel's essay? Which interpretation do you find more convincing? Which interpretation do you find more original and thought provoking?
5. Compare the evidence given by both Sara and Darrel. For example, they both quote the narrator watching the woods "fill up with snow" and the description of the woods as "lovely, dark, and deep," but they create different arguments based on that evidence. How is this possible?

Strategy #4: Pushing Analysis through Revision

The writing process emphasizes revision as a way of improving your analytical ideas and your writing style. Writing encourages the discovery of new ideas; when we write, a "light bulb" will often go off in our head, and we suddenly gain a new insight. Revision should be seen as, first, a strategy used to continue this process of creating and shaping ideas, and second, a strategy used to improve the presentation of those ideas through correct writing. Make sure to use revision to improve your interpretation and develop your analysis.

Revising for Ideas versus Mechanics

Revision starts when you draft a paper, put it aside, and then return to it with a fresh perspective. Revision asks you to reread your own writing with a critical eye: What are the strengths and weaknesses of your paper? Using this self-critique, you then redraft the paper, reworking existing writing and adding new writing. As you revise your paper, it might be helpful for you to think of yourself as taking on two roles: *thinker* and *editor*.

Critique your draft as a thinker first. Make sure that your ideas are insightful, well developed, and supported by evidence. What are your best ideas? What are your weakest ideas? What ideas need more development? What ideas need more evidence? After you feel that your ideas are your best ideas, make sure that you show them off with a clear presentation. Are your concepts clearly defined, and do they follow a logical sequence?

After you have revised your paper for its ideas, then turn to writing mechanics. Take on the role of editor, and work on the correctness of your writing. Are your sentences grammatically correct? Are you choosing the best words to convey your ideas? Are you using an academic style?

Revising Using Instructor Feedback, Peer Feedback, and Self-Critique

Your instructor may ask you to turn in your paper's first draft and give you feedback on that draft. If your instructor gives you written comments, make sure that you understand the critique being offered and know how to use those comments in order to make changes to your paper. As you analyze your instructor's comments, consider how they can be applied to the paper as a whole: How can a comment written in the margins of one paragraph be used to strengthen ideas in other sections? If your instructor is not giving you feedback on this specific paper, you should look back at earlier papers, read the instructor's comments on those papers, and apply his or her comments to this new paper. See your instructor's comments as encouraging a dialogue about your writing; if you do not understand your instructor's comments, make an appointment to discuss them.

As part of the revision process, your class might include a *peer workshop* session that asks your classmates to provide feedback on your writing. Your classmates' reactions will indicate the parts of the paper that they found interesting and the parts that they found unclear, helping you to locate your paper's strengths and weakness. Again, consider the "thinker" and "editor" stages of revision: Try to distinguish between comments that will help you improve your ideas and comments that will help you correct your writing style.

Much of your revision will rely on your ability to engage in self-criticism. Work on developing ways to distance yourself from your own writing so that you can read it critically. Ensure critical reading by printing your paper out and reading the entire draft with a pencil in hand, annotating it as you would a literary work. This will ensure that you read your paper critically, and do not interrupt that self-criticism with typing, which will happen if you read your paper on the computer screen rather than from a printout.

Examining a Preliminary Draft with Revision in Mind

An early draft of a paper typically captures the writer's ideas in a rough form, which then will be revised and improved. Let's read the short story "Saboteur" by Ha Jin and then read a preliminary draft of an analysis of the story by a student in a composition course. The paper assignment asks for an analysis of approximately seven pages. How can a writer generate enough ideas to fill that many pages? The student, Owen Monroe, uses the revision process to deepen his thinking and to expand the ideas presented in his first draft. His final draft is also provided, allowing us to explore how he develops his ideas.

As we consider the revision process, let's review the essay's essential parts, which become the goals of revision.

An analytic essay's basic components include:

- a clear central argument or thesis,
- a sense of ideas becoming deeper or richer as the paper progresses,
- the use of evidence—specific details and quotations—from the literary work,
- a series of well-organized paragraphs that sequentially develop the thesis, and
- the presentation of original insights in the writer's voice and in a clear, correct writing style.

The revision process can include making large-scale changes, such as redefining the paper's central idea or rearranging the order of paragraphs, and small-scale changes, such as improving word choice. It is best to work on the level of ideas first and to save working on such issues as grammatical correctness for a final step. Let's look at Owen's first draft, noting ideas that he could develop further. We can then examine what ideas he chose to expand in his revised draft.

HA JIN

Ha Jin is the pseudonym taken by Xuefei Jin, who was born in China in 1945. Once his military service had ended, he studied the English language and then focused on English literature in his undergraduate and graduate work in Chinese universities. He came to the United States in the mid-1980s to attend graduate school at Brandeis University, and later he did advanced work in creative writing at Boston University. Ha Jin has published two books of poetry, three novels, and several collections of short stories, including Ocean of Words *(1996) and* Under the Red Flag *(1997). He is a professor in the English department at Boston University.*

Saboteur

Mr. Chiu and his bride were having lunch in the square before Muji Train Station. On the table between them were two bottles of soda spewing out brown foam and two paper boxes of rice and sauteed cucumber and pork. "Let's eat," he said to her, and broke the connected ends of the chopsticks. He picked up a slice of streaky pork and put it into his mouth. As he was chewing, a few crinkles appeared on his thin jaw.

To his right, at another table, two railroad policemen were drinking tea and laughing; it seemed that the stout, middle-aged man was telling a joke to his young comrade, who was tall and of athletic build. Now and again they would steal a glance at Mr. Chiu's table.

The air smelled of rotten melon. A few flies kept buzzing above the couple's lunch. Hundreds of people were rushing around to get on the platform or to catch buses to downtown. Food and fruit vendors were crying for customers in lazy voices. About a dozen young women, representing the local hotels, held up placards which displayed the daily prices and words as large as a palm, like FREE MEALS, AIR-CONDITIONING, and ON THE RIVER. In the center of the square stood a concrete statue of Chairman Mao, at whose feet were peasants were napping, their backs on the warm granite and their faces toward the sunny sky. A flock of pigeons perched on the Chairman's raised hand and forearm.

The rice and cucumber tasted good, and Mr. Chiu was eating unhurriedly. His sallow face showed exhaustion. He was glad that the honeymoon was finally over and that he and his bride were heading back for Harbin. During the two weeks' vacation, he had been worried about his liver, because three months ago he had suffered from acute hepatitis; he was afraid he might have a relapse. But he had had no severe symptoms, despite his liver being still big and tender. On the whole he was pleased with his health, which could endure even the strain of a honeymoon; indeed, he was on the course of recovery. He looked at his bride, who took off her wire glasses, kneading the root of her nose with her fingertips. Beads of sweat coated her pale cheeks.

5   "Are you all right, sweetheart?" he asked.

"I have a headache. I didn't sleep well last night."

"Take an aspirin, will you?"

"It's not that serious. Tomorrow is Sunday and I can sleep in. Don't worry."

As they were talking, the stout policeman at the next table stood up and threw a bowl of tea in their direction. Both Mr. Chiu's and his bride's sandals were wet instantly.

10   "Hooligan!" she said in a low voice.

Mr. Chiu got to his feet and said out loud, "Comrade Policeman, why did you do this?" He stretched out his right foot to show the wet sandal.

"Do what?" the stout man asked huskily, glaring at Mr. Chiu while the young fellow was whistling.

"See, you dumped tea on our feet."

"You're lying, You wet your shoes yourself."

15   "Comrade Policeman, your duty is to keep order, but you purposely tortured us common citizens. Why violate the law you are supposed to enforce?" As Mr. Chiu was speaking, dozens of people began gathering around.

With a wave of his hand, the man said to the young fellow, "Let's get hold of him!"

They grabbed Mr. Chiu and clamped handcuffs around his wrists. He cried, "You can't do this to me. This is utterly unreasonable."

"Shut up!" The man pulled out his pistol. "You can use your tongue at our headquarters."

The young fellow added, "You're a saboteur, you know that? You're disrupting public order."

20   The bride was too petrified to say anything coherent. She was a recent college graduate, had majored in fine arts, and had never seen the police make an arrest. All she could say was, "Oh, please, please!"

The policemen were pulling Mr. Chiu, but he refused to go with them, holding the corner of the table and shouting, "We have a train to catch. We already bought the tickets."

The stout man punched him in the chest, "Shut up. Let your ticket expire." With the pistol butt he chopped Mr. Chiu's hands, which at once released the table. Together the two men were dragging him away to the police station.

Realizing he had to go with them, Mr. Chiu turned his head and shouted to his bride, "Don't wait for me here. Take the train. If I'm not back by tomorrow morning, send someone over to get me out."

She nodded, covering her sobbing mouth with her palm.

* * * *

25   After removing his belt, they locked Mr. Chiu into a cell in the back of the Railroad Police Station. The single window in the room was blocked by six steel bars; it faced a spacious yard, in which stood a few pines. Beyond the trees, two swings hung from an iron frame, swaying gently in the breeze. Somewhere in the building a cleaver was chopping rhythmically. There must be a kitchen upstairs, Mr. Chiu thought.

He was too exhausted to worry about what they would do to him, so he lay down on the narrow bed and shut his eyes. He wasn't afraid. The Cultural Revolution was over already, and recently the Party had been propagating the idea that all citizens were equal before the law. The police ought to be a law-abiding model for common people. As long as he remained coolheaded and reasoned with them, they probably wouldn't harm him.

Late in the afternoon he was taken to the Interrogation Bureau on the second floor. On his way there, in the stairwell, he ran into the middle-aged policeman who had manhandled him. The man grinned, rolling his bulgy eyes and pointing his fingers at him as if firing a pistol. Egg of a tortoise! Mr. Chiu cursed mentally.

The moment he sat down in the office, he burped, his palm shielding his mouth. In front of him, across a long desk, sat the chief of the bureau and a donkey-faced man. On the glass desktop was a folder containing information on his case. He felt it bizarre that in just a matter of hours they had accumulated a small pile of writing about him. On second thought he began to wonder whether they had kept a file on him all the time. How could this have happened? He lived and worked in Harbin, more than three hundred miles away, and this was his first time in Muji City.

The chief of the bureau was a thin, bald man who looked serene and intelligent. His slim hands handled the written pages in the folder in the manner of a lecturing scholar. To Mr. Chiu's left sat a young scribe, with a clipboard on his knee and a black fountain pen in his hand.

30   "Your name?" the chief asked, apparently reading out the question from a form.

"Chiu Maguang."

"Age?"

"Thirty-four."

"Profession?"

35   "Lecturer."

"Work unit?"

"Harbin University."

"Political status?"

"Communist Party member."

40   The chief put down the paper and began to speak. "Your crime is sabotage, although it hasn't induced serious consequences yet. Because you are a Party member, you should be punished more. You have failed to be a model for the masses and you—"

"Excuse me, sir," Mr. Chiu cut him off.

"What?"

"I didn't do anything. Your men are the saboteurs of our social order. They threw hot tea on my feet and on my wife's feet. Logically speaking, you should criticize them, if not punish them."

"That statement is groundless. You have no witness. Why should I believe you?" the chief said matter-of-factly.

45   "This is my evidence." He raised his right hand. "Your man hit my fingers with a pistol."

"That doesn't prove how your feet got wet. Besides, you could have hurt your fingers yourself."

"But I am telling the truth!" Anger flared up in Mr. Chiu. "Your police station owes me an apology. My train ticket has expired, my new leather sandals are ruined, and I am late for a conference in the provincial capital. You must compensate me for the damage and losses. Don't mistake me for a common citizen who would tremble when you sneeze. I'm a scholar, a philosopher, and an expert in dialectical materialism. If necessary, we will argue about this in *The Northeastern Daily*, or we will go to the highest People's Court in Beijing. Tell me, what's your name?" He got carried away with his harangue, which was by no means trivial and had worked to his advantage on numerous occasions.

"Stop bluffing us," the donkey-faced man broke in. "We have seen a lot of your kind. We can easily prove you are guilty. Here are some of the statements given by eyewitnesses." He pushed a few sheets of paper toward Mr. Chiu.

Mr. Chiu was dazed to see the different handwritings, which all stated that he had shouted in the square to attract attention and refused to obey the police. One of the witnesses had identified herself as a purchasing agent from a shipyard in Shanghai. Something stirred in Mr. Chiu's stomach, a pain rising to his rib. He gave out a faint moan.

50   "Now you have to admit you are guilty," the chief said. "Although it's a serious crime, we won't punish you severely, provided you write out a self-criticism and promise that you won't disrupt the public order again. In other words, your release will depend on your attitude toward this crime."

     "You're daydreaming," Mr. Chiu cried. "I won't write a word, because I'm innocent. I demand that you provide me with a letter of apology so I can explain to my university why I'm late."

     Both the interrogators smiled contemptuously. "Well, we've never done that," said the chief, taking a puff at his cigarette.

     "Then make this a precedent."

     "That's unnecessary. We are pretty certain that you will comply with our wishes." The chief blew a column of smoke toward Mr. Chiu's face.

55   At the tilt of the chief's head, two guards stepped forward and grabbed the criminal by the arms. Mr. Chiu meanwhile went on saying, "I shall report you to the Provincial Administration. You'll have to pay for this! You are worse than the Japanese military police."

     They dragged him out of the room.

* * * *

After dinner, which consisted of a bowl of millet porridge, a corn bun, and a piece of pickled turnip, Mr. Chiu began to have a fever, shaking with a chill and sweating profusely. He knew that the fire of anger had gotten into his liver and that he was probably having a relapse. No medicine was available, because his briefcase had been left with his bride. At home it would have been time for him to sit in front of their color TV, drinking jasmine tea and watching the evening news. It was so lonesome in here. The orange bulb above the single bed was the only source of light, which enabled the guards to keep him under surveillance at night. A moment ago he had asked them for a newspaper or a magazine to read, but they turned him down.

     Through the small opening on the door noises came in. It seemed that the police on duty were playing cards or chess in a nearby office; shouts and laughter could be heard now and then. Meanwhile, an accordion kept coughing from a remote corner in the building. Looking at the ballpoint and the letter paper left for him by the guards when they took him back from the Interrogation Bureau, Mr. Chiu remembered the old saying, "When a scholar runs into soldiers, the more he argues, the muddier his point becomes." How ridiculous this whole thing was. He ruffled his thick hair with his fingers.

     He felt miserable, massaging his stomach continually. To tell the truth, he was more upset than frightened, because he would have to catch up with his work once he was back home—a paper that was due at the printers next week, and two dozen books he ought to read for the courses he was going to teach in the fall.

60   A human shadow flitted across the opening. Mr. Chiu rushed to the door and shouted through the hole, "Comrade Guard, Comrade Guard!"

     "What do you want?" a voice rasped.

     "I want you to inform your leaders that I'm very sick. I have heart disease and hepatitis. I may die here if you keep me like this without medication."

     "No leader is on duty on the weekend. You have to wait till Monday."

     "What? You mean I'll stay in here tomorrow?"

65   "Yes."

     "Your station will be held responsible if anything happens to me."

     "We know that. Take it easy, you won't die."

It seemed illogical that Mr. Chiu slept quite well that night, though the light above his head had been on all the time and the straw mattress was hard and infested with fleas. He was afraid of ticks, mosquitoes, cockroaches—any kind of insect but fleas and bedbugs. Once, in the countryside, where his school's faculty and staff had helped the peasants harvest crops for a week, his colleagues had joked about his flesh, which they said must have tasted nonhuman to fleas. Except for him, they were all afflicted with hundreds of bites.

More amazing now, he didn't miss his bride a lot. He even enjoyed sleeping alone, perhaps because the honeymoon had tired him out and he needed more rest.

70   The backyard was quiet on Sunday morning. Pale sunlight streamed through the pine branches. A few sparrows were jumping on the ground, catching caterpillars and ladybugs. Holding the steel bars, Mr. Chiu inhaled the morning air, which smelled meaty. There must have been an eatery or a cooked-meat stand nearby. He reminded himself that he should take this detention with case. A sentence that Chairman Mao had written to a hospitalized friend rose in his mind: "Since you are already in here, you may as well stay and make the best of it."

His desire for peace of mind originated in his fear that his hepatitis might get worse. He tried to remain unperturbed. However, he was sure that his liver was swelling up, since the fever still persisted. For a whole day he lay in bed, thinking about his paper on the nature of contradictions. Time and again he was overwhelmed by anger, cursing aloud, "A bunch of thugs!" He swore that once he was out, he would write an article about this experience. He had better find out some of the policemen's names.

It turned out to be a restful day for the most part; he was certain that his university would send somebody to his rescue. All he should do now was remain calm and wait patiently. Sooner or later the police would have to release him, although they had no idea that he might refuse to leave unless they wrote him an apology. Damn those hoodlums, they had ordered more than they could eat!

* * * *

When he woke up on Monday morning, it was already light. Somewhere a man was moaning; the sound came from the backyard. After a long yawn, and kicking off the tattered blanket, Mr. Chiu climbed out of bed and went to the window. In the middle of the yard, a young man was fastened to a pine, his wrists handcuffed around the trunk from behind He was wriggling and swearing loudly, but there was no sight of anyone else in the yard. He looked familiar to Mr. Chiu.

Mr. Chiu squinted his eyes to see who it was. To his astonishment, he recognized the man, who was Fenjin, a recent graduate from the Law Department at Harbin University. Two years ago Mr. Chiu had taught a course in Marxist materialism, in which Fenjin had enrolled. Now, how on earth had this young devil landed here?

75   Then it dawned on him that Fenjin must have been sent over by his bride. What a stupid woman! A hookworm, who only knew how to read foreign novels! He had expected that she would contact the school's Security Section, which would for sure send a cadre here. Fenjin held no official position; he merely worked in a private law firm that had just two lawyers; in fact, they had little business except for some detective work for men and women who suspected their spouses of having extramarital affairs. Mr. Chiu was overcome with a wave of nausea.

Should he call out to let his student know he was nearby? He decided not to, because he didn't know what had happened. Fenjin must have quarreled with the police to incur such a punishment. Yet this could never have occurred if Fenjin hadn't come to his rescue. So no matter what, Mr. Chiu had to do something. But what could he do?

It was going to be a scorcher. He could see purple steam shimmering and rising from the ground among the pines. Poor devil, he thought, as he raised a bowl of corn glue to his mouth, sipped, and took a bite of a piece of salted celery.

When a guard came to collect the bowl and the chopsticks, Mr. Chiu asked him what had happened to the man in the backyard. "He called our boss 'bandit,'" the guard said. "He claimed he was a lawyer or something. An arrogant son of a rabbit."

Now it was obvious to Mr. Chiu that he had to do something to help his rescuer. Before he could figure out a way, a scream broke out in the backyard. He rushed to the window and saw a tall policeman standing before Fenjin, an iron bucket on the ground. It was the same young fellow who had arrested Mr. Chiu in the square two days before. The man pinched Fenjin's nose, then raised his hand, which stayed in the air for a few seconds, then slapped the lawyer across the face. As Fenjin was groaning, the man lifted up the bucket and poured water on his head.

80   "This will keep you from getting sunstroke, boy. I'll give you some more every hour," the man said loudly.

Fenjin kept his eyes shut, yet his wry face showed that he was struggling to hold back from cursing the policeman, or, more likely, that he was sobbing in silence. He sneezed, then raised his face and shouted, "Let me go take a piss."

"Oh yeah?" the man bawled. "Pee in your pants."

Still Mr. Chiu didn't make any noise, gripping the steel bars with both hands, his fingers white. The policeman turned and glanced at the cell's window; his pistol, partly bolstered, glittered in the sun. With a snort he spat his cigarette butt to the ground and stamped it into the dust.

Then the door opened and the guards motioned Mr. Chiu to come out. Again they took him upstairs to the Interrogation Bureau.

85   The same men were in the office, though this time the scribe was sitting there empty-handed. At the sight of Mr. Chiu the chief said, "Ah, here you are. Please be seated."

After Mr. Chiu sat down, the chief waved a white silk fan and said to him, "You may have seen your lawyer. He's a young man without manners, so our director had him taught a crash course in the backyard."

"It's illegal to do that. Aren't you afraid to appear in a newspaper?"

"No, we are not, not even on TV. What else can you do? We are not afraid of any story you make up. We call it fiction. What we do care about is that you cooperate with us. That is to say, you must admit your crime."

"What if I refuse to cooperate?"

90   "Then your lawyer will continue his education in the sunshine."

A swoon swayed Mr. Chiu, and he held the arms of the chair to steady himself. A numb pain stung him in the upper stomach and nauseated him, and his head was throbbing. He was sure that the hepatitis was finally attacking him. Anger was flaming up in his chest; his throat was tight and clogged.

The chief resumed, "As a matter of fact, you don't even have to write out your self-criticism. We have your crime described clearly here. All we need is your signature."

Holding back his rage, Mr. Chiu said, "Let me look at that."

With a smirk the donkey-faced man handed him a sheet, which carried words:

95   I hereby admit that on July 13 I disrupted public order at Muji Train Station, and that I refused to listen to reason when the railroad police issued their warning. Thus I myself am responsible for my arrest. After two days' detention, I have realized the reactionary nature of my crime. From now on, I shall continue to educate myself with all my effort and shall never commit this kind of crime again.

A voice started screaming in Mr. Chiu's ears, "Lie, lie!" But he shook his head and forced the voice away. He asked the chief, "If I sign this, will you release both my lawyer and me?"

"Of course, we'll do that." The chief was drumming his fingers on the blue folder—their file on him,

Mr. Chiu signed his name and put his thumbprint under his signature.

"Now you are free to go," the chief said with a smile, and handed him a piece of paper to wipe his thumb with.

100   Mr. Chiu was so sick that he couldn't stand up from the chair at first try. Then he doubled his effort and rose to his feet. He staggered out of the building to meet his lawyer in the backyard, having forgotten to ask for his belt back. In his chest he felt as though there were a bomb. If he were able to, he would have razed the entire police station and eliminated all their families. Though he knew he could do nothing like that, he made up his mind to do something.

* * * *

"I'm sorry about this torture, Fenjin," Mr. Chiu said when they met.

"It doesn't matter. They are savages." The lawyer brushed a patch of dirt off his jacket with trembling fingers. Water was still dribbling from the bottoms of his trouser legs.

"Let's go now," the teacher said.

The moment they came out of the police station, Mr. Chiu caught sight of a tea stand. He grabbed Fenjin's arm and walked over to the old woman at the table. "Two bowls of black tea," he said and banded her a one-yuan note.

105   After the first bowl, they each had another one. Then they set out for the train station. But before they walked fifty yards, Mr. Chiu insisted on eating a bowl of tree-ear soup at a food stand. Fenjin agreed. He told his teacher, "You mustn't treat me like a guest."

"No, I want to eat something myself."

As if dying of hunger, Mr. Chiu dragged his lawyer from restaurant to restaurant near the police station, but at each place he ordered no more than two bowls of food. Fenjin wondered why his teacher wouldn't stay at one place and eat his fill.

Mr. Chiu bought noodles, wonton, eight-grain porridge, and chicken soup, respectively, at four restaurants. While eating, he kept saying through his teeth. "If only I could kill all the bastards!" At the last place he merely took a few sips of the soup without tasting the chicken cubes and mushrooms.

Fenjin was baffled by his teacher, who looked ferocious and muttered to himself mysteriously, and whose jaundiced face was covered with dark puckers. For the first time Fenjin thought of Mr. Chiu as an ugly man.

* * * *

110   Within a month over eight hundred people contracted acute hepatitis in Muji. Six died of the disease, including two children. Nobody knew how the epidemic had started.

Joining the Conversation: Critical Thinking and Writing

1. Reread the ending of this story, and then write a paraphrase of it. What happens in the last two lines of the story? Why did it happen?
2. What does the title of the story mean? What is a *saboteur*? Look up a dictionary definition of the word. After you analyze the ending of the story, how would you explain the title of the story?
3. What is the "crime" that Mr. Chiu commits at the beginning of the story? What makes the arrest unfair? How does the context of the arrest, such as the fact that Mr. Chiu is on his honeymoon, make the arrest seem particularly unjust? Is Ha Jin offering a critique of Chinese society? As depicted in this story, what elements of Chinese society seem most problematic?
4. How does Ha Jin convey Mr. Chiu's worsening health? Annotate the story, noting particularly vivid sentences that capture Mr. Chiu's physical state. Do these descriptions start to have an impact on you as a reader? Do the descriptions make you feel the illness?
5. Who is Fenjin? What role does he play in the story?
6. Why does Mr. Chiu sign the confession? What causes him to give in to the pressure of the police? Does he compromise his principles by signing the confession?

Student Analytical Essay: "Morals in Ha Jin's 'Saboteur'" (Preliminary Draft)

Ha Jin's short story "Saboteur" tells a story of revenge. The story questions if that revenge is morally correct. The story details the unfair arrest and imprisonment of Mr. Chui and, later, his lawyer-student, Fenjin. Mr. Chui confesses to the "crime" of disrupting public order, and is then released. After being released from the prison in Muji, Mr. Chui purposely eats at several food stands, infecting the dishes with the hepatitis disease he is carrying. At the end of the story, his revenge is complete: eight hundred people in Muji have contracted hepatitis and six people have died. The story asks its readers to judge Mr. Chui as an individual and to decide if his revenge is morally right or wrong.

"Saboteur" explores the individual, asking us to judge the individual's moral actions. The short story's third-person narrator focuses on Mr. Chui as the protagonist, keeping him at the center of the story and making him a sympathetic character. He represents the idea of the individual faced with a moral challenge. When he returns from his honeymoon, Mr. Chui is filled with "exhaustion," is feeling "worried," and has just gotten over a serious hepatitis attack. A restful lunch with his wife is interrupted when a policeman throws a bowl of tea at their feet; when Mr. Chui questions their actions, he is arrested for disturbing the peace.

"Saboteur" develops the idea of the individual by showing that Mr. Chui's individual rights are abused. Mr. Chui's is treated unfairly when he is locked in jail and forced to sign a confession to his "crime" of disrupting society, a crime he did not commit. The police chief demands that Mr. Chui confess, saying, "Now you have to admit you are guilty. Although it's a serious crime, we won't punish you severely, provided you write out a self-criticism and promise that you won't disrupt the public order again" (283). The story presents Mr. Chui as a person of integrity. At first, he maintains his innocence and demands an apology. Then, he becomes increasingly sick and feverish due to his hepatitis. However, even though he is in this physical pain, he still defends his innocence. The narrator presents a complex picture of the individual, showing how Mr. Chui's external actions must reveal his internal beliefs. Fenjin comes to help Mr. Chui and is physically abused after being handcuffed to a tree. Mr. Chui feels "Anger was flaming up in his chest; his throat was tight and clogged" (285). The police manipulate Mr. Chui, telling him that they will release Fenjin only if Mr. Chui signs a confession. Mr. Chui decides to sign the confession, even though it goes against everything he believes. The narrator describes Mr. Chui's internal struggle as he decides to go against his beliefs: "A voice started screaming in Mr. Chui's ears, "lie, lie!" Mr. Chui is willing to go against his beliefs for the higher purpose of saving his lawyer-student from physical abuse.

Although Mr. Chui has been mistreated and been forced to go against his principles, our sympathy for Mr. Chui is soon tested by his act of revenge. Immediately after signing the confession paper, Mr. Chui decides on revenge, thinking that he would tear down the police department and kills their families, but he immediately admits he can't do that. We know Mr. Chui has been wronged.

We are so sympathetic to Mr. Chui as an individual that we want him to have some sort of revenge against the police: he has used his hepatitis, which was triggered by the police, to seek revenge on the city.

Because the story focuses on Mr. Chui, it is easy to see the story as most concerned with the individual. The story shows an "individual vs. society" theme: Mr. Chui has been mistreated by society and, as an individual, he needs revenge or at least to find some justice. Because Mr. Chui is presented in a sympathetic light, we want him to achieve revenge. But, we need to think about the impact that revenge has on innocent lives. If we look at the individual lives of the people who die of hepatitis, it forces us to see Mr. Chui's revenge as immoral. Examining the story through the individual helps us to ask questions about the morality and immorality of revenge.

If we remain focused only on Mr. Chui as an individual, we lose sight of some of the story's moral questions. The story presents a society that has no sense of right and wrong. The story opens with the dramatic external conflict of the policeman throwing tea at Mr. Chui's feet and arresting him. Then, when Mr. Chui is in jail, he confronts a corrupt police force that manufactures false evidence and forces a false confession. The police represent a society that has no sense of justice. Mr. Chui lives in a society that doesn't believe in truth, order, innocence, and justice. Because his society does not believe in these values, does Mr. Chui have to live by those values? "Saboteur" shows us a society in which all sense of right and wrong has been lost. Mr. Chui's actions are part of a larger society that has no sense of morally correct behavior. Although we must question Mr. Chui's actions as an individual, the story also asks us to question the larger society that led to those actions.

Work Cited

Jin, Ha. "Saboteur." *Literature for Composition*. Ed. Sylvan Barnet, William Burto, William E. Cain, and Cheryl L. Nixon. 11th ed. Boston: Pearson, 2017. 280–86. Print.

Developing a Revision Strategy: Thesis, Ideas, Evidence, Organization, and Correctness

To guide your revision, think of the elements that make a successful paper, such as the creation of a thesis argument or the use of compelling evidence, and analyze your paper for those elements. One way of doing this is to use a checklist to guide your self-critique. We've created a checklist that outlines five basic revision steps. This list can be used to create a revision strategy, emphasizing the five elements of a paper that can be reviewed and strengthened: the thesis, idea development, evidence, organization, and correctness. We can apply this revision checklist to the rough draft of Owen's paper, exploring if and how he engages with these five revision steps as he moves toward a revised draft.

✔ REVISION CHECKLIST

Strengthen Your Thesis

☐ Add focus and depth to your central argument.

Develop Your Ideas

☐ Revisit your best responses to literary form and content, adding more thinking to those responses.

Integrate and Explain Your Evidence

☐ Select and analyze rich, interesting quotations to provide evidence for your ideas.

Improve the Organization

☐ Structure your ideas to follow a clear sequence.

Clarify Your Style and Edit for Correctness

☐ Use a consistent, professional style to explain your ideas, correcting sentence structure, word usage, and grammar.

Let's look at each of these revision goals in turn.

Strengthen Your Thesis. When you examine the draft of your paper, you should start with an essential question: "Does the draft present the main idea in the form of an argument or a thesis?" Reread the draft to see if its most important, overarching idea is captured in a thesis that (1) presents a focused argument or central claim, (2) is specific to the text under consideration, and (3) indicates some of the sophisticated thinking that will be developed in the paper. Although a thesis statement is typically one sentence in length, the paragraph that includes it should contain sentences that clarify and develop its ideas. The thesis argument will need to be concise, but the full explanation of that argument becomes the thesis paragraph.

When you examine Owen Monroe's revised paper draft, note that he expands his thesis paragraph to include new ideas that he generates about the morality of Mr. Chui's society. The paper's thesis shifts from focusing on individual morality to the more complex idea that individual morality is connected to social morality. The revision process has allowed Owen to "re-see" his thesis and realize that he can make it much more interesting by adding a new argument about social morality.

Develop Your Ideas. Although you have completed a draft, you should not assume that you are done with brainstorming but, instead, view your draft as a means to continue the idea development process. The writing process itself will generate new ideas. While writing, new insights will pop into your head while you are trying to wrestle your thoughts down on paper. Although you might wish that you could predetermine all of your ideas before you start a paper, that wish ignores the fact that revision is needed precisely because it will help you generate new ideas. Once your paper is in draft form, you can see the gaps, missing pieces, and unclear ideas that need fixing—and the hints of new ideas that need developing.

Note that Owen's revised draft has become much longer. He uses the revision process to expand his thinking, adding new arguments to his paper. In Owen's first draft, ideas concerning Mr. Chui's corrupt social context are mentioned in the last paragraph. Through the revision process, these ideas are expanded, generating several new paragraphs and a new thesis argument.

Integrate and Explain Your Evidence. The revision process also focuses on the textual evidence used to develop the paper's ideas. In almost every paper, the use of quotations from the text can be improved. Are the ideas in the paper supported with carefully selected and explained quotations? Does the paper show how your opinions, thoughts, and arguments evolve out of the literary text? Have you "digested" the quotations, integrating them into your own writing?

As he rereads his draft, Owen marks any ideas that seem unsupported, that could be made richer by citing from the text, or that seem to refer to the literary text without quoting from it. For example, Owen notes that the second half of his paper contains no direct quotations, signaling a weak use of evidence. He adds additional quotations and uses them to support the new ideas that he has been developing in the drafting process. Crucially, never engage in plagiarism, which is the undocumented use of another person's words or ideas. As shown in Appendix B the use of source materials must be documented through correct citation. Owen also checks his parenthetical citations and Works Cited list.

Improve the Organization. As you improve the ideas of your paper draft, the organization of the paper may need to change to capture those ideas. As part of the revision process, you may need to revisit the paper's original outline and determine if the paper's central arguments are changing, shifting, being emphasized, or being erased.

As Owen revises his paper draft, he realizes that one of his best ideas—that Mr. Chui lives in an unjust society, making it difficult to question his morality—is buried in his last paragraph. He decides to make that idea his thesis, a central part of his paper's overarching claim. Note how the topic and concluding sentences in his first draft's last paragraph have been moved forward to the thesis paragraph in his revised draft. These ideas are then fully developed in his new body paragraphs. Also note how Owen's first draft contains paragraphs of very uneven lengths: A very long body paragraph is followed by very short paragraphs, and one of his paragraphs is only one sentence long. In his revision, Owen creates a more balanced paragraph structure. He uses paragraph breaks to emphasize the introduction of new subpoints, and he connects together paragraphs that are working on the same idea. In his final draft, Owen presents ideas that are more complex than those in his first draft, and he also presents them in a more organized and balanced fashion.

Clarify Your Style and Edit for Correctness. A final revision strategy asks you to analyze a paper for its writing style. Does the draft explain ideas in a precise way? Does the draft clarify ideas by defining key terms? Does the draft avoid generalizations? Does the draft avoid overly general references to outside ideas and, instead, use specific references to specific aspects of the text? As part of clarifying the paper's style, you should revise a draft to avoid tentative-sounding "could be," "might be," or "perhaps" phrasing. You should strive to avoid the repetition of words or phrases. Finally, you should use academic language rather than casual expressions.

As part of his revision, Owen rereads his draft, looking for places where his ideas are hidden by very general sentences, tentative claims, or nonacademic phrasing. He continues to improve his ideas by polishing his language.

Student Analytical Essay: "Individual and Social Morals in Ha Jin's 'Saboteur'" (Final Draft)

As you read Owen's final draft, refer back to his first draft. He has expanded his paper's length, meeting the expectations of the assignment. Has this increased length allowed him to improve his ideas and argument?

Monroe 1

Owen Monroe
Professor Garcia
English 102
21 April 2016

Individual and Social Morals in Ha Jin's "Saboteur"

Ha Jin's short story "Saboteur" tells a story of revenge. The story ends with a successful act of revenge, but the story questions if that revenge is morally correct. The story details the unfair arrest and imprisonment of Mr. Chui and, later, his lawyer-student, Fenjin. Mr. Chui confesses to the "crime" of disrupting public order, and is then released. After being released from the prison in Muji, Mr. Chui purposely eats at several food stands, infecting the dishes with the hepatitis disease he is carrying. At the end of the story, his revenge is complete: we learn that eight hundred people in Muji contracted hepatitis, and "six died of the disease, including two children" (286). The story asks its readers to judge Mr. Chui as an individual and to decide if his revenge is morally right or wrong. However, if we remain focused only on Mr. Chui as an individual, we lose sight of some of the story's moral questions. "Saboteur" shows us a society in which all sense of right and wrong has been lost. Mr. Chui's actions are part of a larger society that has no sense of morally correct behavior. Although we must question Mr. Chui's actions as an individual, the story also asks us to question the larger society that led to those actions.

"Saboteur" explores the individual, asking us to judge the individual's moral actions. The short story's third-person narrator focuses on Mr. Chui as the protagonist, keeping him at the center of the story and making him a sympathetic character. He represents the idea of the individual faced with a moral challenge. The story uses direct presentation to describe his thoughts and feelings. We are explicitly told that, although he is returning from his honeymoon, Mr. Chui is filled with "exhaustion," is feeling "worried," and has just gotten over a serious hepatitis attack (280). A restful lunch with his wife is interrupted when a policeman throws a bowl of tea at their feet, wetting their sandals. The act is unfair to Mr. Chui. Although the story's two policemen are clearly provoking Mr. Chui, when he questions their actions, he is arrested for disturbing the peace. The policemen call him a "saboteur" and bring him to jail.

"Saboteur" develops the idea of the individual by showing that Mr. Chui's individual rights are abused. Mr. Chui's is treated unfairly when he is locked in jail and forced to sign a confession to his "crime" of disrupting society, a crime he did not commit. The police chief demands that Mr. Chui confess, saying, "Now you have to admit you are guilty. . . . Although it's a serious crime, we won't punish you severely, provided you write out a self-criticism and promise that you won't disrupt the public order again" (283). The story presents Mr. Chui as a person of integrity. At first, he maintains his innocence and demands an apology. Then, he becomes increasingly sick and feverish due to his hepatitis. However, even though he is in this physical pain, he still defends his innocence. He decides, "Sooner or later the police would have to release him, although they had no idea that he might refuse to leave unless they wrote him an apology. Damn those hoodlums, they had ordered more than they could eat!" (284).

The narrator presents a complex picture of the individual, showing how Mr. Chui's external actions must reveal his internal beliefs. Fenjin comes to help Mr. Chui and is physically abused after being handcuffed to a tree. Mr. Chui feels "Anger was flaming up in his chest; his throat was tight and clogged" (285). The police manipulate Mr. Chui, telling him that they will release Fenjin only if Mr. Chui signs a confession to the crime of disturbing the peace. Mr. Chui decides to sign the confession, even though it goes against everything he believes. The narrator describes Mr. Chui's internal struggle as he decides to go against his beliefs: "A voice started screaming in Mr. Chui's ears, "lie, lie!" But he shook his head and forced the voice away. He asked the chief, 'If I sign this, will you release both my lawyer and me?'" (286). Here, Mr. Chui is presented as a sympathetic character full of integrity. He is willing to go against his beliefs for the higher purpose of saving his lawyer-student from physical abuse.

Although Mr. Chui has been mistreated and been forced to go against his principles, our sympathy for Mr. Chui is soon tested by his act of revenge. Immediately after signing the confession paper, Mr. Chui decides on revenge, thinking, "If he were able to, he would have razed the entire police station and eliminated all their families. Though he knew he could do nothing like that, he made up his mind to do something" (286). We know Mr. Chui has been wronged. We are so sympathetic to Mr. Chui as an individual that we want him to have some sort of revenge against the police. However, we are not fully aware that Mr. Chui has decided on a form of revenge that will actually kill people. Because we want Mr. Chui to have revenge, we might at first support him: he has used his hepatitis, which was triggered by the police, to seek revenge on the city. However, if we look at

his revenge from the victim's perspective, we realize that his revenge is

morally wrong: his actions led to the deaths of six people. These innocent

people died as a result of one man being imprisoned for two days.

Because the story focuses on Mr. Chui, it is easy to see the story is

most concerned with the individual. The story shows an "individual vs.

society" theme: Mr. Chui has been mistreated by society and, as an

individual, he needs revenge or at least to find some justice. Because

Mr. Chui is presented in a sympathetic light, we want him to achieve

revenge. But, we need to think about the impact that revenge has on

innocent lives. If we look at the individual lives of the people who die of

hepatitis, it forces us to see Mr. Chui's revenge as immoral. Examining the

story through the individual helps us to ask questions about the morality

and immorality of revenge.

To take this thinking even further, we can look at the story as

questioning society in addition to the individual. The moral questions raised

by Mr.Chui's revenge become even more complex. Mr. Chui's social setting

makes us question his actions on a deeper level. Is there such a thing as

morally right and wrong behavior in a society where no one, not even the

police, upholds right and wrong? Is Mr. Chui's revenge wrong when he lives

in a society that does not seem to have any system of justice?

The story presents a society that has no sense of right and wrong. The

story opens with the dramatic external conflict of the policeman throwing

tea at Mr. Chui's feet and arresting him. The policeman also manipulates

ideas and words. When Mr. Chui asks why the policeman threw the tea, the

policeman exclaims, "You're lying. You wet your shoes yourself" (281). The

policeman replaces truth with lies. He represents a society that does not

believe in truth. When Mr. Chui is arrested, the second policeman charges,

"You're disrupting public order" (281). In reality, it is the police who are disrupting public order. The police do not uphold public order, but create disorder. The policemen have charged Mr. Chui with their own crime: they lie and create chaos. Although they call Mr. Chui a "saboteur," they are the saboteurs (281). When Mr. Chui says that his story could appear in a newspaper and get the police into trouble, the police say, "We are not afraid of any story you make up. We call it fiction" (285). This statement is ironic because the police are saying the exact opposite of what has really happened. It is the police who are making up stories and who are presenting fiction as truth.

When Mr. Chui is in jail, he confronts a corrupt police force that manufactures false evidence and forces a false confession. The police represent a society that has no sense of justice. In this society, just like truth can be turned into lies, innocence can be turned into guilt. When Mr. Chui maintains his innocence and argues, "I am telling the truth," the police argue back, "We can easily prove you are guilty. Here are some of the statements given by eyewitnesses" (282). When Mr. Chui realizes that "in just a matter of hours they had accumulated a small pile of writing about him," it becomes obvious that the police are making up materials for his case. The police go as far as writing Mr. Chui's confession and hand him a confession that states, "I hereby admit that I disrupted public order at Muji Train Station, and that I refuse to listen to reason when the railroad police issued their warning. Thus I myself am responsible for my arrest" (286). Each statement in this confession is false. Each of Mr. Chui's innocent acts has been turned against him and made into proof of his guilt.

Mr. Chui lives in a society that doesn't believe in truth, order, innocence, and justice. Because his society does not believe in these values, does Mr. Chui have to live by those values? This story could be arguing that Mr. Chui cannot be expected to uphold positive values if those values are not part of his society. If truth, order, innocence, and justice are not used when

Mr. Chui is in jail, can society expect Mr. Chui to use those values? If Mr. Chui's society creates lies, disorder, guilt, and unfairness, then that society should expect to have those values acted out. The story could be making the point that this society needs to be punished. If this society needs to be punished, then Mr. Chui's revenge can be seen as correct.

"Saboteur" can be examined on the level of the individual and on the level of society. Mr. Chui is presented as a very sympathetic character. We know he has been mistreated as an individual, and can understand his desire for revenge. Although we might want him to achieve revenge, we also can see that innocent people died as a result of his spreading hepatitis. When we think of those innocent individuals, we can see that Mr. Chui's revenge is wrong. However, when we focus on Mr. Chui's society, we might come to a different conclusion and argue that Mr. Chui's revenge makes sense in a society that encourages lying and disorder. Mr. Chui's society punishes positive values, and that society cannot expect to be treated with fairness and kindness. Although this is a negative conclusion, "Saboteur" might be asking the reader to think about when and why a society deserves to be punished, even if that punishment hurts the individual.

[New page]

Work Cited

Jin, Ha. "Saboteur." *Literature for Composition*. Ed. Sylvan Barnet, William Burto, William E. Cain, and Cheryl L. Nixon. 11th ed. Boston: Pearson, 2017. 280-86. Print.

Your Turn: Additional Poems and Story for Interpretation

POEMS

T. S. ELIOT

Thomas Stearns Eliot (1888–1965) was born into a New England family that had moved to St. Louis, Missouri. He attended a private school in Massachusetts, graduated from Harvard, and did further study in literature and philosophy in France, Germany, and England. In 1914, he began working for Lloyd's Bank in London, and three years later, he published his first book of poems (it included "The Love Song of J. Alfred Prufrock"). In 1925, he joined a publishing firm, and in 1927, he became a British citizen and a member of the Church of England. Much of his later poetry, unlike "The Love Song of J. Alfred Prufrock," is highly religious. In 1948, Eliot received the Nobel Prize in Literature.

The Love Song of J. Alfred Prufrock

S'io credesse che mia risposta fosse
A persona che mai tornasse al mondo,
Questa fiamma staria senza piu scosse.
Ma perciocche giammai di questo fondo
Non torno vivo alcun, s'i' odo il vero,
*Senza tema d'infama ti rispondo.**

Let us go then, you and I,
When the evening is spread out against the sky

Like a patient etherized upon a table;
Let us go, through certain half-deserted streets,
The muttering retreats   5
Of restless nights in one-night cheap hotels
And sawdust restaurants with oyster-shells:
Streets that follow like a tedious argument
Of insidious intent
To lead you to an overwhelming question . . .   10
Oh, do not ask, "What is it?"
Let us go and make our visit.

In the room the women come and go
Talking of Michelangelo.   15
The yellow fog that rubs its back upon the window-panes,

---

*In Dante's *Inferno* 27.61–66, a damned soul who had sought absolution before committing a crime addresses Dante, thinking that his words will never reach the Earth: "If I believed that my answer were to a person who could ever return to the world, this flame would no longer quiver. But because no one returned from this depth, if what I hear is true without fear of infamy, I answer you."

The yellow smoke that rubs its muzzle on the window-panes
Licked its tongue into the corners of the evening,
Lingered upon the pools that stand in drains,
Let fall upon its back the soot that falls from chimneys,
Slipped by the terrace, made a sudden leap,   20
And seeing that it was a soft October night,
Curled once about the house, and fell asleep.

And indeed there will be time
For the yellow smoke that slides along the street,
Rubbing its back upon the window-panes;   25
There will be time, there will be time
To prepare a face to meet the faces that you meet;
There will be time to murder and create,
And time for all the works and days° of hands
That lift and drop a question on your plate;   30
Time for you and time for me,
And time yet for a hundred indecisions,
And for a hundred visions and revisions,
Before the taking of a toast and tea.

In the room the women come and go   35
Talking of Michelangelo.

And indeed there will be time
To wonder, "Do I dare?" and, "Do I dare?"
Time to turn back and descend the stair,
With a bald spot in the middle of my hair—   40
[They will say: "How his hair is growing thin!"]
My morning coat, my collar mounting firmly to the chin,
My necktie rich and modest, but asserted by a simple pin—
[They will say: "But how his arms and legs are thin!"]
Do I dare   45
Disturb the universe?
In a minute there is time
For decisions and revisions which a minute will reverse.

For I have known them all already, known them all:—
Have known the evenings, mornings, afternoons,   50
I have measured out my life with coffee spoons;
I know the voices dying with a dying fall°
Beneath the music from a farther room.

So how should I presume?

And I have known the eyes already, known them all—   55
The eyes that fix you in a formulated phrase,
And when I am formulated, sprawling on a pin,
When I am pinned and wriggling on the wall,
Then how should I begin
To spit out all the butt-ends of my days and ways?   60

29 works and days "Works and Days" is the title of a poem on farm life by Hesiod (eighth century BCE).
52 dying fall This line echoes Shakespeare's *Twelfth Night* 1.1.4.

And how should I presume?

And I have known the arms already, known them all—
Arms that are braceleted and white and bare
[But in the lamplight, downed with light brown hair!]
Is it perfume from a dress   65
That makes me so digress?
Arms that lie along a table, or wrap about a shawl.

And should I then presume?
And how should I begin?

. . .

Shall I say, I have gone at dusk through narrow streets   70
And watched the smoke that rises from the pipes
Of lonely men in shirt-sleeves, leaning out of windows? . . .

I should have been a pair of ragged claws
Scuttling across the floors of silent seas.

. . .

And the afternoon, the evening, sleeps so peacefully!   75
Smoothed by long fingers,
Asleep . . . tired . . . or it malingers,
Stretched on the floor, here beside you and me.
Should I, after tea and cakes and ices,
Have the strength to force the moment to its crisis?   80
But though I have wept and fasted, wept and prayed,
Though I have seen my head [grown slightly bald]

brought in upon a platter,°

I am no prophet—and here's no great matter;
And I have seen the moment of my greatness flicker,   85
And I have seen the eternal Footman hold my coat, and snicker,
And in short, I was afraid.

And would it have been worth it, after all,
After the cups, the marmalade, the tea,
Among the porcelain, among some talk of you and me,   90
Would it have been worth while,
To have bitten off the matter with a smile,

To have squeezed the universe into a ball°
To roll it toward some overwhelming question,
To say: "I am Lazarus,° come from the dead,   95
Come back to tell you all, I shall tell you all"—
If one, settling a pillow by her head,

Should say: "That is not what I meant at all.
That is not it, at all."

81–83 But . . . platter These lines allude to John the Baptist (see Matthew 14:1–11).
92 To have . . . ball This line echoes lines 41–42 of Marvell's "To His Coy Mistress" (see
page 351). **94 Lazarus** See Luke 16 and John 11.

And would it have been worth it, after all,   100
Would it have been worth while,
After the sunsets and the dooryards and the sprinkled streets.
After the novels, after the teacups, after the skirts that trail along
     the floor—
And this, and so much more?—
It is impossible to say just what I mean!   105
But as if a magic lantern threw the nerves in patterns on a screen:
Would it have been worth while
If one, settling a pillow or throwing off a shawl,
And turning toward the window, should say:

"That is not it at all,   110
That is not what I meant at all."

No! I am not Prince Hamlet, nor was meant to be;
Am an attendant lord, one that will do
To swell a progress, start a scene or two,
Advise the prince; no doubt, an easy tool,   115
Deferential, glad to be of use,
Politic, cautious, and meticulous;
Full of high sentence,° but a bit obtuse;°
At times, indeed, almost ridiculous—
Almost, at times, the Fool.   120

I grow old . . . I grow old . . .
I shall wear the bottoms of my trousers rolled.

Shall I part my hair behind? Do I dare to eat a peach?
I shall wear white flannel trousers, and walk upon the beach.
I have heard the mermaids singing, each to each.   125

I do not think that they will sing to me.

I have seen them riding seaward on the waves
Combing the white hair of the waves blown back
When the wind blows the water white and black.

We have lingered in the chambers of the sea   130
By sea-girls wreathed with seaweed red and brown
Till human voices wake us, and we drown.

                                                           [1910–11]

117 full of high sentence See Chaucer's description of the Clerk of Oxford in the
Canterbury Tales. **112–117 Am . . . obtuse** These lines allude to Polonius and perhaps
other figures in *Hamlet.*

Joining the Conversation: Critical Thinking and Writing

1. How does the speaker's name help to characterize him? What suggestions—of
    class, race, or personality—do you find in it? Does the title of this poem strike
    you as ironic? If so, how or why?

2. What qualities of big-city life are suggested in the poem? How are these qualities linked to the speaker's mood? What other details of the setting—the weather, the time of day—express or reflect his mood? What images do you find especially striking?

3. The speaker's thoughts are represented in a stream-of-consciousness monologue, that is, in what appears to be an unedited flow of thought. Nevertheless, they reveal a story. What is the story?

4. In a paragraph, characterize Prufrock as he might be characterized by one of the women in the poem, and then, in a paragraph or two, offer your own characterization of him.

5. Consider the possibility that the "you" whom Prufrock is addressing is not a listener but one aspect of Prufrock and that the "I" is another aspect of Prufrock. Given this possibility, in a paragraph characterize the "you," and in another paragraph characterize the "I."

6. Prufrock has gone to a therapist, a psychiatrist, or a member of the clergy for help. Write a five-hundred-word transcript of their session.

THOMAS HARDY

Thomas Hardy (1840–1928) was born in Dorset, England, the son of a stonemason. Despite great obstacles, he studied the Classics and architecture, and in 1862 he moved to London to study and practice as an architect. Ill health forced him to return to Dorset, where he continued to work as an architect and to write. Best known for his novels, Hardy ceased writing fiction after the hostile reception of Jude the Obscure *in 1896 and turned to writing lyric poetry.*

The Man He Killed

"Had he and I but met
By some old ancient inn,
We should have sat us down to wet
Right many a nipperkin!°

"But ranged as infantry,   5
And staring face to face,
I shot at him as he at me,
And killed him in his place.

"I shot him dead because—
Because he was my foe,   10
Just so: my foe of course he was;
That's clear enough; although

"He thought he'd 'list, perhaps,
Off-hand—just as I—
Was out of work—had sold his traps°—   15
No other reason why.

4 nipperkin cup.
15 traps personal belongings.

"Yes; quaint and curious war is!
You shoot a fellow down
You'd treat if met where any bar is,
Or help to half-a-crown."   20

                                                                        [1902]

Joining the Conversation: Critical Thinking and Writing

1. What do we learn about the speaker's life before he enlisted in the infantry?
   How does his diction characterize him?
2. What is the effect of the series of monosyllables in lines 7 and 8?
3. Consider the punctuation of the third and fourth stanzas. Why are the heavy,
   frequent pauses appropriate? What question is the speaker trying to answer?
4. In the last stanza, what attitudes toward war does the speaker express? What,
   from the evidence of this poem, would you infer Hardy's attitude toward war to
   be? Cite evidence to support your argument.

ANNE BRADSTREET

Born in England in 1612 and educated by her father, Anne Bradstreet emigrated to
Massachusetts in 1630 and lived there until her death in 1672. She is considered the
first female poet of the New World. As a Puritan writer, Bradstreet often explored her
spiritual struggles and addressed themes of sin, death, and salvation. Her poetry
also expressed her devotion to her husband and deep love for her eight children.

Before the Birth of One of Her Children

All things within this fading world hath end,
Adversity doth still our joyes attend;
No ties so strong, no friends so dear and sweet,
But with death's parting blow is sure to meet.
The sentence past is most irrevocable,   5
A common thing, yet oh inevitable.
How soon, my Dear, death may my steps attend,
How soon't may be thy Lot to lose thy friend,
We are both ignorant, yet love bids me
These farewell lines to recommend to thee,   10
That when that knot's untied that made us one,
I may seem thine, who in effect am none.
And if I see not half my dayes that's due,
What nature would, God grant to yours and you;
The many faults that well you know I have   15
Let be interr'd in my oblivious grave;
If any worth or virtue were in me,
Let that live freshly in thy memory
And when thou feel'st no grief, as I no harms,
Yet love thy dead, who long lay in thine arms.   20
And when thy loss shall be repaid with gains
Look to my little babes, my dear remains.

And if thou love thyself, or loved'st me,
These o protect from step Dames injury.
And if chance to thine eyes shall bring this verse,   25
With some sad sighs honour my absent Herse;
And kiss this paper for thy loves dear sake,
Who with salt tears this last Farewel did take.

[1678]

Joining the Conversation: Critical Thinking and Writing

1. In this poem, Bradstreet addresses her fear of dying in childbirth. How does she come to terms with this fear? Reread the poem, and then make a list of the different ways in which she tries to prepare for death. For example, she starts by reminding herself that everyone must die. She then moves on to addressing her husband. What other rationalizations does she provide?
2. If she dies, what will Bradstreet leave behind? Find the lines that contain an explanation of her different legacies. Will these legacies help her to live beyond death?
3. Bradstreet writes many poems about her husband and children. Search the Internet for one of these poems. How would you describe Bradstreet's emotional connection to her family?
4. Look ahead to the next poem, Christina Rossetti's "After Death," which also discusses death. How would you compare these two different female narrators' stance toward death? Do these narrators ultimately accept or reject death?

CHRISTINA ROSSETTI

Christina Rossetti was a poet who experienced success during her lifetime, and she continues to be recognized as one of the most important poets of Victorian England. Born in 1830, she was raised in a well-educated family that valued the study of poetry, art, history, and languages. Rossetti and her three siblings pursued artistic and intellectual careers; her brother Dante Gabriel Rossetti is a famous Pre-Raphaelite painter. Christina suffered from ill health, and her poetry often features meditations on the body, death, and loss. Her poetry conveys these complex themes in a direct and powerful style. She is best known for her narrative poem, "Goblin Market," published in 1862.

After Death

The curtains were half drawn, the floor was swept
    And strewn with rushes, rosemary and may
Lay thick upon the bed on which I lay,
Where through the lattice ivy-shadows crept.
He leaned above me, thinking that I slept
    And could not hear him; but I heard him say,
    'Poor child, poor child': and as he turned away
Came a deep silence, and I knew he wept.

He did not touch the shroud, or raise the fold
    That hid my face, or take my hand in his,
      Or ruffle the smooth pillows for my head:
      He did not love me living; but once dead
    He pitied me; and very sweet it is
To know he still is warm though I am cold.

[1862]

Joining the Conversation: Critical Thinking and Writing

1. Who is the speaker of this poem? Where is she located? What is her physical status?
2. What is the relationship between the speaker of the poem and the man who visits her? Reread the poem to understand the emotions that underlie its direct style. What rather harsh insights does the speaker have into the man and his emotions? How have his emotions changed or evolved?
3. What are the actions of the male visitor? Why does he say "Poor child, poor child"? What are the actions of the speaker of the poem?
4. What do you make of the last line of the poem? The speaker states, "very sweet it is / To know he still is warm though I am cold." Why is this knowledge "very sweet"?

FRED CHAPPELL

A novelist and poet, Fred Chappell was born in North Carolina in 1936 and continues to live there. He taught at the University of North Carolina–Greensboro and served as the state's poet laureate from 1997 to 2002. Some of his most ambitious story and poem collections are autobiographical and take the form of linked multivolume works.

Narcissus and Echo

Shall the water not remember *Ember*
my hand's slow gesture, tracing above *of*
its mirror my half-imaginary *airy*
portrait? My only belonging *longing;*
is my beauty, which I take *ache*   5
away and then return, as love *of*
of teasing playfully the one being *unbeing.*
whose gratitude I treasure *Is your*
moves me. I live apart *heart*
from myself, yet cannot *not*   10
live apart. In the water's tone, *stone?*
that brilliant silence, a flower *Hour,*
whispers my name with such slight *light;*
moment, it seems filament of air, *fare*
the world become cloudswell. *well.*   15

[1983]

Joining the Conversation: Critical Thinking and Writing

1. A unique element of this poem is the ending of each line. Examine the italicized words closely. How do those words relate to the words that immediately precede them? What is the meaning of this relationship? After you read horizontally and understand how each italicized word connects to its line, read vertically and read the italicized words as connecting to each other in order to create a new set of lines.
2. Read the poem aloud. Then, try to write a few new lines for the poem, imitating the sound effect of the end of each line. Can you make your new lines work with both a horizontal and vertical reading?
3. The title of the poem refers to an episode in Ovid's *Metamorphosis* that retells the myth of Narcissus, the young man who is so beautiful that he falls in love with his own reflection when he gazes into a pool of water (he is memorialized with a narcissus flower, and we get the word *narcissist* from this myth). Do some Internet research on this story, learning Echo's role in it and how she earns her name. Now, return to the poem with this new understanding of its inspiration. How does the poem relate to the Narcissus and Echo story?
4. Analyze the word choice of the poem. For example, notice how the words "I" and my" are repeated. How does this word repetition emphasize the theme of the poem? What other word patterns do you notice?

STORY

JOYCE CAROL OATES

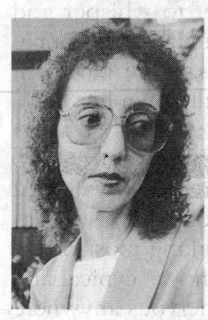

Joyce Carol Oates was born in 1938 in Millerport, New York. She won a scholarship to Syracuse University, from which she graduated (Phi Beta Kappa and valedictorian) in 1960. She then did graduate work in English, first at the University of Wisconsin and then at Rice University, but she withdrew from Rice University in order to be able to devote more time to writing. Her first collection of stories, By the North Gate, *was published in 1963; since then she has published many books— stories, poems, essays, and novels. She has received many awards, has been elected to the American Academy and Institute of Arts and Letters, and now teaches creative writing at Princeton University.*

Where Are You Going, Where Have You Been?

For Bob Dylan

Her name was Connie. She was fifteen and she had a quick nervous giggling habit of craning her neck to glance into mirrors or checking other people's faces to make sure her own was all right. Her mother, who noticed everything and knew everything and who hadn't much reason any longer to look at her own face, always scolded Connie about it. "Stop gawking at yourself, who are you? You think you're so pretty?" she would say. Connie would raise her eyebrows at these familiar complaints and look right through her mother, into a shadowy vision of herself as she was right at that moment: she knew she was pretty and that was everything. Her mother had been pretty once too, if you could believe those old snapshots in the album, but now her looks were gone and that was why she was always after Connie.

"Why don't you keep your room clean like your sister? How've you got your hair fixed—what the hell stinks? Hair spray? You don't see your sister using that junk."

Her sister June was twenty-four and still lived at home. She was a secretary in the high school Connie attended, and if that wasn't bad enough—with her in the same building—she was so plain and chunky and steady that Connie had to hear her praised all the time by her mother and her mother's sisters. June did this, June did that, she saved money and helped clean the house and cooked and Connie couldn't do a thing, her mind was all filled with trashy daydreams. Their father was away at work most of the time and when he came home he wanted supper and he read the newspaper at supper and after supper he went to bed. He didn't bother talking much to them, but around his bent head Connie's mother kept picking at her until Connie wished her mother was dead and she herself was dead and it was all over. "She makes me want to throw up sometimes," she complained to her friends. She had a high, breathless, amused voice which made everything she said sound a little forced, whether it was sincere or not.

There was one good thing: June went places with girlfriends of hers, girls who were just as plain and steady as she, and so when Connie wanted to do that her mother had no objections. The father of Connie's best girlfriend drove the girls the three miles to town and left them off at a shopping plaza, so that they could walk through the stores or go to a movie, and when he came to pick them up again at eleven he never bothered to ask what they had done.

5   They must have been familiar sights, walking around that shopping plaza in their shorts and flat ballerina slippers that always scuffed the sidewalk, with charm bracelets jingling on their thin wrists; they would lean together to whisper and laugh secretly if someone passed by who amused or interested them. Connie had long dark blond hair that drew anyone's eye to it, and she wore part of it pulled up on her head and puffed out and the rest of it she let fall down her back. She wore a pull-over jersey blouse that looked one way when she was at home and another way when she was away from home. Everything about her had two sides to it, one for home and one for anywhere that was not home: her walk that could be childlike and bobbing, or languid enough to make anyone think she was hearing music in her head, her mouth which was pale and smirking most of the time, but bright and pink on these evenings out, her laugh which was cynical and drawling at home—"Ha, ha, very funny"—but high-pitched and nervous anywhere else, like the jingling of the charms on her bracelet.

Sometimes they did go shopping or to a movie, but sometimes they went across the highway, ducking fast across the busy road, to a drive-in restaurant where older kids hung out. The restaurant was shaped like a big bottle, though squatter than a real bottle, and on its cap was a revolving figure of a grinning boy who held a hamburger aloft. One night in midsummer they ran across, breathless with daring, and right away someone leaned out a car window and invited them over, but it was just a boy from high school they didn't like. It made them feel good to be able to ignore him. They went up through the maze of parked and cruising cars to the bright-lit, fly-infested restaurant, their faces pleased and expectant as if they were entering a sacred building that loomed out of the night to give them what haven and what blessing they yearned for.

They sat at the counter and crossed their legs at the ankles, their thin shoulders rigid with excitement, and listened to the music that made everything so good: the music was always in the background like music at a church service, it was something to depend upon.

A boy named Eddie came in to talk with them. He sat backward on his stool, turning himself jerkily around in semicircles and then stopping and turning again, and after a while he asked Connie if she would like something to eat. She said she did and so she tapped her friend's arm on her way out—her friend pulled her face up into a brave droll look—and Connie said she would meet her at eleven, across the way. "I just hate to leave her like that," Connie said earnestly, but the boy said that she wouldn't be alone for long. So they went out to his car and on the way Connie couldn't help but let her eyes wander over the windshields and faces all around her, her face gleaming with a joy that had nothing to do with Eddie or even this place; it might have been the music. She drew her shoulders up and sucked in her breath with the pure pleasure of being alive, and just at that moment she happened to glance at a face just a few feet from hers. It was a boy with shaggy black hair, in a convertible jalopy painted gold. He stared at her and then his lips widened into a grin. Connie slit her eyes at him and turned away, but she couldn't help glancing back and there he was still watching her. He wagged a finger and laughed and said, "Gonna get you, baby," and Connie turned away again without Eddie noticing anything.

She spent three hours with him, at the restaurant where they ate hamburgers and drank Cokes in wax cups that were always sweating, and then down an alley a mile or so away, and when he left her off at five to eleven only the movie house was still open at the plaza. Her girlfriend was there, talking with a boy. When Connie came up the two girls smiled at each other and Connie said, "How was the movie?" and the girl said, "*You* should know." They rode off with the girl's father, sleepy and pleased, and Connie couldn't help but look at the darkened shopping plaza with its big empty parking lot and its signs that were faded and ghostly now, and over at the drive-in restaurant where cars were still circling tirelessly. She couldn't hear the music at this distance.

Next morning June asked her how the movie was and Connie said, "So-so."

She and that girl and occasionally another girl went out several times a week that way, and the rest of the time Connie spent around the house—it was summer vacation—getting in her mother's way and thinking, dreaming, about the boys she met. But all the boys fell back and dissolved into a single face that was not even a face, but an idea, a feeling, mixed up with the urgent insistent pounding of the music and the humid night air of July. Connie's mother kept dragging her back to the daylight by finding things for her to do or saying, suddenly, "What's this about the Pettinger girl?"

And Connie would say nervously, "Oh, her. That dope." She always drew thick clear lines between herself and such girls, and her mother was simple and kindly enough to believe her. Her mother was so simple, Connie thought, that it was maybe cruel to fool her so much. Her mother went scuffling around the house in old bedroom slippers and complained over the telephone to one sister about the other, then the other called up and the two of them complained about the third one. If June's name was mentioned her mother's tone was approving, and if Connie's name was mentioned it was disapproving. This did not really mean she disliked Connie and actually Connie thought that her mother preferred her to June because she was prettier, but the two of them kept up a pretense of exasperation, a sense that they were tugging and struggling over something of little value to either of them. Sometimes, over coffee, they were almost friends, but something would come up—some vexation that was like a fly buzzing suddenly around their heads—and their faces went hard with contempt.

One Sunday Connie got up at eleven—none of them bothered with church—and washed her hair so that it could dry all day long, in the sun. Her parents and sister were going to a barbecue at an aunt's house and Connie said no, she wasn't interested, rolling her eyes to let her mother know just what she thought of it. "Stay home alone then," her mother said sharply. Connie sat out back in a lawn chair and watched them drive away, her father quiet and bald, hunched around so that he could back the car out, her mother with a look that was still angry and not at all softened through the windshield, and in the back seat poor old June all dressed up as if she didn't know what a barbecue was, with all the running yelling kids and the flies. Connie sat with her eyes closed in the sun, dreaming and dazed with the warmth about her as if this were a kind of love, the caresses of love, and her mind slipped over onto thoughts of the boy she had been with the night before and how nice he had been, how sweet it always was, not the way someone like June would suppose but sweet, gentle, the way it was in movies and promised in songs; and when she opened her eyes she hardly knew where she was, the back yard ran off into weeds and a fence line of trees and behind it the sky was perfectly blue and still. The asbestos "ranch house" that was now three years old startled her—it looked small. She shook her head as if to get awake.

It was too hot. She went inside the house and turned on the radio to drown out the quiet. She sat on the edge of her bed, barefoot, and listened for an hour and a half to a program called XYZ Sunday Jamboree, record after record of hard, fast, shrieking songs she sang along with, interspersed by exclamations from "Bobby King": "An' look here you girls at Napoleon's—Son and Charley want you to pay real close attention to this song coming up!"

And Connie paid close attention herself, bathed in a glow of slow-pulsed joy that seemed to rise mysteriously out of the music itself and lay languidly about the airless little room, breathed in and breathed out with each gentle rise and fall of her chest.

15   After a while she heard a car coming up the drive. She sat up at once, startled, because it couldn't be her father so soon. The gravel kept crunching all the way in from the road—the driveway was long—and Connie ran to the window. It was a car she didn't know. It was an open jalopy, painted a bright gold that caught the sunlight opaquely. Her heart began to pound and her fingers snatched at her hair, checking it, and she whispered "Christ, Christ," wondering how bad she looked. The car came to a stop at the side door and the horn sounded four short taps as if this were a signal Connie knew.

She went into the kitchen and approached the door slowly, then hung out the screen door, her bare toes curling down off the step. There were two boys in the car and now she recognized the driver: he had shaggy, shabby black hair that looked crazy as a wig and he was grinning at her.

"I ain't late, am I?" he said.

"Who the hell do you think you are?" Connie said.

"Toldja I'd be out, didn't I?"

20   "I don't even know who you are."

She spoke sullenly, careful to show no interest or pleasure, and he spoke in a fast bright monotone. Connie looked past him to the other boy, taking her time. He had fair brown hair, with a lock that fell onto his forehead. His sideburns gave him a fierce, embarrassed look, but so far he hadn't even bothered to glance at her.

Both boys wore sunglasses. The driver's glasses were metallic and mirrored everything in miniature.

"You wanta come for a ride?" he said.

Connie smirked and let her hair fall loose over one shoulder.

"Don'tcha like my car? New paint job," he said. "Hey."

25 "What?"

"You're cute."

She pretended to fidget, chasing flies away from the door.

"Don'tcha believe me, or what?" he said.

"Look, I don't even know who you are," Connie said in disgust.

30 "Hey, Ellie's got a radio, see. Mine's broke down." He lifted his friend's arm and showed her the little transistor the boy was holding, and now Connie began to hear the music. It was the same program that was playing inside the house.

"Bobby King?" she said.

"I listen to him all the time. I think he's great."

"He's kind of great." Connie said reluctantly.

"Listen, that guy's *great*. He knows where the action is."

35 Connie blushed a little, because the glasses made it impossible for her to see just what this boy was looking at. She couldn't decide if she liked him or if he was just a jerk, and so she dawdled in the doorway and wouldn't come down or go back inside. She said, "What's all that stuff painted on your car?"

"Can'tcha read it?" He opened the door very carefully, as if he was afraid it might fall off. He slid out just as carefully, planting his feet firmly on the ground, the tiny metallic world in his glasses slowing down like gelatine hardening and in the midst of it Connie's bright green blouse. "This here is my name, to begin with," he said. ARNOLD FRIEND was written in tarlike black letters on the side, with a drawing of a round grinning face that reminded Connie of a pumpkin, except it wore sunglasses. "I wanta introduce myself, I'm Arnold Friend and that's my real name and I'm gonna be your friend, honey, and inside the car's Ellie Oscar, he's kinda shy." Ellie brought his transistor radio up to his shoulder and balanced it there. "Now these numbers are a secret code, honey," Arnold Friend explained. He read off the numbers 33, 19, 17 and raised his eyebrows at her to see what she thought of that, but she didn't think much of it. The left rear fender had been smashed and around it was written, on the gleaming gold background: DONE BY CRAZY WOMAN DRIVER. Connie had to laugh at that. Arnold Friend was pleased at her laughter and looked up at her. "Around the other side's a lot more—you wanta come and see them?"

"No."

"Why not?"

"Why should I?"

40 "Don'tcha wanta see what's on the car? Don'tcha wanta go for a ride?"

"I don't know."

"Why not?"

"I got things to do."

"Like what?"

45 "Things."

He laughed as if she had said something funny. He slapped his thighs. He was standing in a strange way, leaning back against the car as if he were balancing himself. He wasn't tall, only an inch or so taller than she would be if she came down to him. Connie liked the way he was dressed, which was the way all of them dressed: tight faded jeans stuffed into black, scuffed boots, a belt that pulled his waist in and showed how lean he was, and a white pullover shirt that was a little soiled and showed the hard small muscles of his arms and shoulders. He looked as if he probably did hard work, lifting and carrying things. Even his neck looked muscular. And his face was a familiar face, somehow: the jaw and chin and cheeks slightly darkened, because he hadn't shaved for a day or two, and the nose long and hawklike, sniffing as if she were a treat he was going to gobble up and it was all a joke.

"Connie, you ain't telling the truth. This is your day set aside for a ride with me and you know it," he said, still laughing. The way he straightened and recovered from his fit of laughing showed that it had been all fake.

"How do you know what my name is?" she said suspiciously.

"It's Connie."

50   "Maybe and maybe not."

"I know my Connie," he said, wagging his finger. Now she remembered him even better, back at the restaurant, and her cheeks warmed at the thought of how she sucked in her breath just at the moment she passed him—how she must have looked to him. And he had remembered her. "Ellie and I come out here especially for you," he said. "Ellie can sit in back. How about it?"

"Where?"

"Where what?"

"Where're we going?"

55   He looked at her. He took off the sunglasses and she saw how pale the skin around his eyes was, like holes that were not in shadow but instead in light. His eyes were like chips of broken glass that catch the light in an amiable way. He smiled. It was as if the idea of going for a ride somewhere, to some place, was a new idea to him.

"Just for a ride, Connie sweetheart."

"I never said my name was Connie," she said.

"But I know what it is. I know your name and all about you, lots of things," Arnold Friend said. He had not moved yet but stood still leaning back against the side of his jalopy. "I took a special interest in you, such a pretty girl, and found out all about you like I know your parents and sister are gone somewheres and I know where and how long they're going to be gone, and I know who you were with last night, and your best girlfriend's name is Betty. Right?"

He spoke in a simple lilting voice, exactly as if he were reciting the words to a song. His smile assured her that everything was fine. In the car Ellie turned up the volume on his radio and did not bother to look around at them.

60   "Ellie can sit in the back seat," Arnold Friend said. He indicated his friend with a casual jerk of his chin, as if Ellie did not count and she should not bother with him.

"How'd you find out all that stuff?" Connie said.

"Listen: Betty Schultz and Tony Fitch and Jimmy Pettinger and Nancy Pettinger," he said, in a chant. "Raymond Stanley and Bob Hutter—"

"Do you know all those kids?"

"I know everybody."

65   "Look, you're kidding. You're not from around here."

"Sure."

"But—how come we never saw you before?"

"Sure you saw me before," he said. He looked down at his boots, as if he were a little offended. "You just don't remember."

"I guess I'd remember you," Connie said.

70   "Yeah?" He looked up at this, beaming. He was pleased. He began to mark time with the music from Ellie's radio, tapping his fists lightly together. Connie looked away from his smile to the car, which was painted so bright it almost hurt her eyes to look at it. She looked at that name, ARNOLD FRIEND. And up at the front fender was an expression that was familiar—MAN THE FLYING SAUCERS. It was an expression kids had used the year before, but didn't use this year. She looked at it for a while as if the words meant something to her that she did not yet know.

"What're you thinking about? Huh?" Arnold Friend demanded. "Not worried about your hair blowing around in the car, are you?"

"No."

"Think I maybe can't drive good?"

"How do I know?"

75   "You're a hard girl to handle. How come?" he said. "Don't you know I'm your friend? Didn't you see me put my sign in the air when you walked by?"

"What sign?"

"My sign." And he drew an X in the air, leaning out toward her. They were maybe ten feet apart. After his hand fell back to his side the X was still in the air, almost visible. Connie let the screen door close and stood perfectly still inside it, listening to the music from her radio and the boy's blend together. She stared at Arnold Friend. He stood there so stiffly relaxed, pretending to be relaxed, with one hand idly on the door handle as if he were keeping himself up that way and had no intention of ever moving again. She recognized most things about him, the tight jeans that showed his thighs and buttocks and the greasy leather boots and the tight shirt, and even that slippery friendly smile of his, that sleepy dreamy smile that all the boys used to get across ideas they didn't want to put into words. She recognized all this and also the singsong way he talked, slightly mocking, kidding, but serious and a little melancholy, and she recognized the way he tapped one fist against the other in homage to the perpetual music behind him. But all these things did not come together.

She said suddenly, "Hey, how old are you?"

His smile faded. She could see then that he wasn't a kid, he was much older— thirty, maybe more. At this knowledge her heart began to pound faster.

80   "That's a crazy thing to ask. Can'tcha see I'm your own age?"

"Like hell you are."

"Or maybe a coupla years older, I'm eighteen." *Shes 15 still kid*

"Eighteen?" she said doubtfully.

He grinned to reassure her and lines appeared at the corners of his mouth. His teeth were big and white. He grinned so broadly his eyes became slits and she saw how thick the lashes were, thick and black as if painted with a black tarlike material. Then he seemed to become embarrassed, abruptly, and looked over his shoulder at Ellie. "*Him,* he's crazy," he said. "Ain't he a riot, he's a nut, a real character." Ellie was still listening to the music. His sunglasses told nothing about what he was thinking. He wore a bright orange shirt unbuttoned halfway to show his chest, which was a pale, bluish chest and not muscular like Arnold Friend's. His shirt collar was turned up all around and the very tips of the collar pointed out past his chin as if they were protecting him. He was pressing the transistor radio up against his ear and sat there in a kind of daze, right in the sun.

85   "He's kinda strange," Connie said.

"Hey, she says you're kinda strange! Kinda strange!" Arnold Friend cried. He pounded on the car to get Ellie's attention. Ellie turned for the first time and Connie saw with shock that he wasn't a kid either—he had a fair, hairless face, cheeks reddened slightly as if the veins grew too close to the surface of his skin, the face of a forty-year-old baby. Connie felt a wave of dizziness rise in her at this sight and she stared at him as if waiting for something to change the shock of the moment, make it all right again. Ellie's lips kept shaping words, mumbling along, with the words blasting in his ear.

"Maybe you two better go away," Connie said faintly.

"What? How come?" Arnold Friend cried. "We come out here to take you for a ride. It's Sunday." He had the voice of the man on the radio now. It was the same voice, Connie thought. "Don'tcha know it's Sunday all day and honey, no matter who you were with last night today you're with Arnold Friend and don't you forget it!—Maybe you better step out here," he said, and this last was in a different voice. It was a little flatter, as if the heat was finally getting to him.

"No. I got things to do."

90   "Hey."

"You two better leave."

"We ain't leaving until you come with us."

"Like hell I am—"

"Connie, don't fool around with me. I mean, I mean, don't fool *around*," he said, shaking his head. He laughed incredulously. He placed his sunglasses on top of his head, carefully, as if he were indeed wearing a wig, and brought the stems down behind his ears. Connie stared at him, another wave of dizziness and fear rising in her so that for a moment he wasn't even in focus but was just a blur, standing there against his gold car, and she had the idea that he had driven up the driveway all right but had come from nowhere before that and belonged nowhere and that everything about him and even about the music that was so familiar to her was only half real.

95   "If my father comes and sees you—"

"He ain't coming. He's at a barbecue."

"How do you know that?"

"Aunt Tillie's. Right now they're—uh—they're drinking. Sitting around," he said vaguely, squinting as if he were staring all the way to town and over to Aunt Tillie's back yard. Then the vision seemed to get clear and he nodded energetically. "Yeah. Sitting around. There's your sister in a blue dress, huh? And high heels, the poor sad bitch—nothing like you, sweetheart! And your mother's helping some fat woman with the corn, they're cleaning the corn—husking the corn—"

"What fat woman?" Connie cried.

100   "How do I know what fat woman. I don't know every goddam fat woman in the world!" Arnold Friend laughed.

"Oh, that's Mrs. Hornby. . . . Who invited her?" Connie said. She felt a little light-headed. Her breath was coming quickly.

"She's too fat. I don't like them fat. I like them the way you are, honey," he said, smiling sleepily at her. They stared at each other for a while, through the screen door. He said softly, "Now what you're going to do is this: you're going to come out that door. You're going to sit up front with me and Ellie's going to sit in the back, the hell with Ellie, right? This isn't Ellie's date. You're my date. I'm your lover, honey."

"What? You're crazy—"

"Yes, I'm your lover. You don't know what that is but you will," he said. "I know that too. I know all about you. But look: it's real nice and you couldn't ask for nobody better than me, or more polite. I always keep my word. I'll tell you how

it is, I'm always nice at first, the first time. I'll hold you so tight you won't think you
have to try to get away or pretend anything because you'll know you can't. And I'll
come inside you where it's all secret and you'll give in to me and you'll love
me—"

105   "Shut up! You're crazy!" Connie said. She backed away from the door. She put
her hands against her ears as if she'd heard something terrible, something not
meant for her. "People don't talk like that, you're crazy," she muttered. Her heart
was almost too big now for her chest and its pumping made sweat break out all
over her. She looked out to see Arnold Friend pause and then take a step toward
the porch lurching. He almost fell. But, like a clever drunken man, he managed to
catch his balance. He wobbled in his high boots and grabbed hold of one of the
porch posts.
    "Honey?" he said. "You still listening?"
    "Get the hell out of here!"
    "Be nice, honey. Listen."
    "I'm going to call the police—"

110 He wobbled again and out of the side of his mouth came a fast spat curse, an
aside not meant for her to hear. But even this "Christ!" sounded forced. Then he
began to smile again. She watched this smile come, awkward as if he were smiling
from inside a mask. His whole face was a mask, she thought wildly, tanned down
onto his throat but then running out as if he had plastered makeup on his face but
had forgotten about his throat.
    "Honey—? Listen, here's how it is. I always tell the truth and I promise you
this: I ain't coming in that house after you."
    "You better not! I'm going to call the police if you—if you don't—"
    "Honey," he said, talking right through her voice, "honey, I'm not coming in
there but you are coming out here. You know why?"
    She was panting. The kitchen looked like a place she had never seen before,
some room she had run inside but which wasn't good enough, wasn't going to
help her. The kitchen window had never had a curtain, after three years, and there
were dishes in the sink for her to do—probably—and if you ran your hand across
the table you'd probably feel something sticky there.

115   "You listening, honey? Hey?"
    "—going to call the police—"
    "Soon as you touch the phone I don't need to keep my promise and can come
inside. You won't want that."
    She rushed forward and tried to lock the door. Her fingers were shaking. "But
why lock it," Arnold Friend said gently, talking right into her face. "It's just a screen
door. It's just nothing." One of his boots was at a strange angle, as if his foot wasn't
in it. It pointed out to the left, bent at the ankle. "I mean, anybody can break
through a screen door and glass and wood and iron or anything else if he needs
to, anybody at all and specially Arnold Friend. If the place got lit up with a fire
honey you'd come runnin' out into my arms, right into my arms an' safe at home—
like you knew I was your lover and'd stopped fooling around. I don't mind a nice
shy girl but I don't like no fooling around." Part of those words were spoken with
a slight rhythmic lilt, and Connie somehow recognized them—the echo of a song
from last year, about a girl rushing into her boyfriend's arms and coming home
again—
    Connie stood barefoot on the linoleum floor, staring at him. "What do you
want?" she whispered.

120   "I want you," he said.

"What?"

"Seen you that night and thought, that's the one, yes sir. I never needed to look any more."

"But my father's coming back. He's coming to get me. I had to wash my hair first—" She spoke in a dry, rapid voice, hardly raising it for him to hear.

"No, your Daddy is not coming and yes, you had to wash your hair and you washed it for me. It's nice and shining and all for me, I thank you, sweetheart," he said, with a mock bow, but again he almost lost his balance. He had to bend and adjust his boots. Evidently his feet did not go all the way down; the boots must have been stuffed with something so that he would seem taller. Connie stared out at him and behind him Ellie in the car, who seemed to be looking off toward Connie's right into nothing. This Ellie said, pulling the words out of the air one after another as if he were just discovering them, "You want me to pull out the phone?"

125   "Shut your mouth and keep it shut," Arnold Friend said, his face red from bending over or maybe from embarrassment because Connie had seen his boots. "This ain't none of your business."

"What—what are you doing? What do you want?" Connie said. "If I call the police they'll get you, they'll arrest you—"

"Promise was not to come in unless you touch that phone, and I'll keep that promise," he said. He resumed his erect position and tried to force his shoulders back. He sounded like a hero in a movie, declaring something important. He spoke too loudly and it was as if he were speaking to someone behind Connie. "I ain't made plans for coming in that house where I don't belong but just for you to come out to me, the way you should. Don't you know who I am?"

"You're crazy," she whispered. She backed away from the door but did not want to go into another part of the house, as if this would give him permission to come through the door. "What do you . . . You're crazy, you . . ."

"Huh? What're you saying, honey?"

130   Her eyes darted everywhere in the kitchen. She could not remember what it was, this room.

"This is how it is, honey: you come out and we'll drive away, have a nice ride. But if you don't come out we're gonna wait till your people come home and then they're all going to get it."

"You want that telephone pulled out?" Ellie said. He held the radio away from his ear and grimaced, as if without the radio the air was too much for him.

"I toldja shut up, Ellie," Arnold Friend said, "you're deaf, get a hearing aid, right? Fix yourself up. This little girl's no trouble and's gonna be nice to me, so Ellie keep to yourself, this ain't your date—right? Don't hem in on me. Don't hog. Don't crush. Don't bird dog. Don't trail me," he said in a rapid meaningless voice, as if he were running through all the expressions he'd learned but was no longer sure which one of them was in style, then rushing on to new ones, making them up with his eyes closed, "Don't crawl under my fence, don't squeeze in my chipmunk hole, don't sniff my glue, suck my popsicle, keep your own greasy fingers on yourself!" He shaded his eyes and peered in at Connie, who was backed against the kitchen table. "Don't mind him honey he's just a creep. He's a dope. Right? I'm the boy for you and like I said you come out here nice like a lady and give me your hand, and nobody else gets hurt, I mean, your nice old bald-headed daddy and your mummy and your sister in her high heels. Because listen: why bring them in this?"

"Leave me alone," Connie whispered.

135   "Hey, you know that old woman down the road, the one with the chickens and stuff—you know her?"

"She's dead!"

"Dead? What? You know her?" Arnold Friend said.

"She's dead—"

"Don't you like her?"

140   "She's dead—she's—she isn't here any more—"

"But don't you like her, I mean, you got something against her? Some grudge or something?" Then his voice dipped as if he were conscious of a rudeness. He touched the sunglasses perched on top of his head as if to make sure they were still there. "Now you be a good girl."

"What are you going to do?"

"Just two things, or maybe three," Arnold Friend said. "But I promise it won't last long and you'll like me the way you get to like people you're close to. You will. It's all over for you here, so come on out. You don't want your people in any trouble, do you?"

She turned and bumped against a chair or something, hurting her leg, but she ran into the back room and picked up the telephone. Something roared in her ear, a tiny roaring, and she was so sick with fear that she could do nothing but listen to it—the telephone was clammy and very heavy and her fingers groped down to the dial but were too weak to touch it. She began to scream into the phone, into the roaring. She cried out, she cried for her mother, she felt her breath start jerking back and forth in her lungs as if it were something Arnold Friend were stabbing her with again and again with no tenderness. A noisy sorrowful wailing rose all about her and she was locked inside it the way she was locked inside the house.

145   After a while she could hear again. She was sitting on the floor with her wet back against the wall.

Arnold Friend was saying from the door, "That's a good girl. Put the phone back."

She kicked the phone away from her.

"No, honey. Pick it up. Put it back right."

She picked it up and put it back. The dial tone stopped.

150   "That's a good girl. Now come outside."

She was hollow with what had been fear, but what was now just an emptiness. All that screaming had blasted it out of her. She sat, one leg cramped under her, and deep inside her brain was something like a pinpoint of light that kept going and would not let her relax. She thought, I'm not going to see my mother again. She thought, I'm not going to sleep in my bed again. Her bright green blouse was all wet.

Arnold Friend said, in a gentle-loud voice that was like a stage voice, "The place where you came from ain't there any more, and where you had in mind to go is canceled out. This place you are now—inside your daddy's house—is nothing but a cardboard box I can knock down any time. You know that and always did know it. You hear me?"

She thought, I have got to think. I have to know what to do.

"We'll go out to a nice field, out in the country here where it smells so nice and it's sunny," Arnold Friend said. "I'll have my arms tight around you so you won't need to try to get away and I'll show you what love is like, what it does. The hell with this house! It looks solid all right," he said. He ran a fingernail down the screen and the noise did not make Connie shiver, as it would have the day before. "Now put your hand on your heart, honey. Feel that? That feels solid too but we know better, be nice to me, be sweet like you can because what else is there for a girl like you but to be sweet and pretty and give in?—and get away before her people come back?"

155   She felt her pounding heart. Her hand seemed to enclose it. She thought for the first time in her life that it was nothing that was hers, that belonged to her, but just a pounding, living thing inside this body that wasn't really hers either.

"You don't want them to get hurt," Arnold Friend went on. "Now get up, honey. Get up all by yourself."

She stood up.

"Now turn this way. That's right. Come over here to me—Ellie, put that away, didn't I tell you? You dope. You miserable creepy dope," Arnold Friend said. His words were not angry but only part of an incantation. The incantation was kindly. "Now come out through the kitchen to me honey, and let's see a smile, try it, you're a brave sweet little girl and now they're eating corn and hot dogs cooked to bursting over an outdoor fire, and they don't know one thing about you and never did and honey you're better than them because not a one of them would have done this for you."

Connie felt the linoleum under her feet; it was cool. She brushed her hair back out of her eyes. Arnold Friend let go of the post tentatively and opened his arms for her, his elbows pointing in toward each other and his wrists limp, to show that this was an embarrassed embrace and a little mocking, he didn't want to make her self-conscious.

160   She put out her hand against the screen. She watched herself push the door slowly open as if she were safe back somewhere in the other doorway, watching this body and this head of long hair moving out into the sunlight where Arnold Friend waited.

"My sweet little blue-eyed girl," he said, in a half-sung sigh that had nothing to do with her brown eyes but was taken up just the same by the vast sunlit reaches of the land behind him and on all sides of him, so much land that Connie had never seen before and did not recognize except to know that she was going to it.

[1966]

Joining the Conversation: Critical Thinking and Writing

1. Characterize Connie. Do you think the early characterization of Connie prepares us for her later behavior?

2. Construct an argument in response to the question, "Is Arnold Friend clairvoyant—definitely, definitely not, maybe?"

3. Evaluate the view that Arnold Friend is both Satan and the incarnation of Connie's erotic desires.

4. What do you make of the fact that Oates dedicated the story to Bob Dylan? Is she perhaps contrasting Dylan's music with the escapist (or in some other way unwholesome) music of other popular singers?

5. If you have read Flannery O'Connor's "A Good Man Is Hard to Find" (page 498), compare and contrast Arnold Friend and the Misfit.

CHAPTER 9

Comparison and Synthesis

Chapter Preview

After reading this chapter, you will be able to

- Define *comparison* and describe the process for comparing literary texts
- Evaluate a student interpretation
- Define *synthesis* and describe the process for analyzing and connecting literary texts
- Analyze and evaluate four student interpretations

Comparison and Critical Thinking

We synthesize texts when we create connections between them. Comparison is an effective tool for generating synthesis. An advanced critical thinking skill, **synthesis** builds on analysis by developing relationships among texts in order to illuminate a larger idea, issue, or theme. Synthesis is the process of bringing together separate literary texts and their analyses, locating points of meaningful connection between them, and creating interpretations and arguments that rely on and deepen those connections. Synthesis enacts the idea that new, often better, ideas come from seeing how two texts can work together rather than from seeing each text in isolation.

When we compare, we examine things for their resemblances to, and differences from, other things. Strictly speaking, if we emphasize the differences rather than the similarities, we are contrasting rather than comparing, but we need not preserve this distinction: We can call both processes **comparing.**

Although your instructor may ask you to write a comparison of two works of literature, the *subject* of the essay remains the two literary works; comparison is simply an effective analytical technique for showing the qualities in the works. We've examined a student paper that compares Chopin's exploration of women who are unfulfilled by marriage in "The Story of an Hour" (page 65) and "The Storm" (page 87). This paper created a meaningful comparison by locating a topic that connected the stories while revealing the subtle differences between them. A comparison of works that are utterly unlike each other can hardly tell the reader or the writer anything. One of the first steps in a successful comparison is selection: You will want to locate two or more literary texts that can work together to generate meaningful ideas.

A helpful way to think about synthesis is that you are aligning or juxtaposing two texts, positioning them against each other so that their overlapping ideas and interests can be revealed and analyzed. As its name implies, a comparison paper compares two texts, finding similarities between the two, while also finding revealing differences or contrasts between the two. Rather than simply locating points of comparison, followed by points of contrast, think of yourself as taking two multifaceted pieces of art and locating meaningful points of *connection*. As the texts are brought together, new insights are generated into each individual text and into the larger concepts that they explore together.

Organizing a Comparison Essay

Something should be said about organizing a comparison essay, say between the settings in two stories, between two characters in a novel (or even between a character at the end of a novel and the same character at the beginning of that novel), or between the symbolism in two poems. Probably, a student's first thought after making some jottings is to discuss one half of the comparison and then the second half. Instructors and textbooks (though not this one) usually condemn such an organization, arguing that such an essay breaks into two parts and that the second part involves a good deal of repetition of the categories set up in the first part. Often they recommend that students organize their thoughts along these lines:

1. First similarity
   a. First work (or character, or characteristic)
   b. Second work
2. Second similarity
   a. First work
   b. Second work
3. First difference
   a. First work
   b. Second work
4. Second difference
   a. First work
   b. Second work

You continue in this way, for as many additional differences as seem relevant. If you wish to compare *Adventures of Huckleberry Finn* with *The Catcher in the Rye*, you might organize the material thus:

1. First similarity: the narrator and his quest
   a. Huck
   b. Holden
2. Second similarity: the corrupt world surrounding the narrator
   a. Society in *Huck*
   b. Society in *Catcher*
3. First difference: degree to which the narrator fulfills his quest and escapes from society
   a. Huck's plan to "light out" to the frontier
   b. Holden's breakdown

Here is another way to organize a comparison and contrast:

1. First point: the narrator and his quest
   a. Similarities between Huck and Holden
   b. Differences between Huck and Holden
2. Second point: the corrupt world
   a. Similarities between the worlds in *Huck* and *Catcher*
   b. Differences between the worlds in *Huck* and *Catcher*
3. Third point: degree of success
   a. Similarities between Huck and Holden
   b. Differences between Huck and Holden

These outlines provide strong models of organization for a comparison essay, but a comparison need not employ either of them. There is even the danger that an essay employing either may not come into focus until the writer stands back from the seven-layer cake that he or she has created and announces in the concluding paragraph that the odd layers taste better. In your preparatory thinking, you may want to make comparisons in pairs:

- good-natured humor: the clown in *Othello*, the clownish grave-digger in *Hamlet*
- social satire: the clown in *Othello*, the grave-digger in *Hamlet*
- relevance of each character to theme X
- length of role and centrality of each character to each play

Before writing the final version, you must come to some conclusions about what your comparisons add up to.

The final version should not duplicate your thought processes; rather, it should be organized so as to make your point—the thesis—clearly and effectively. After reflection, you may believe that

- although there are superficial similarities between the clown in *Othello* and the clownish grave-digger in *Hamlet*,
- there are essential differences in the aims of their social satire, leading you to make an argument about how theme X is developed differently by each character.

In the finished essay, you will not want to obscure your main argument by jumping back and forth from play to play, working through all of the similarities and differences you've located. It may be better to discuss the clown in *Othello* and then to point out that, although the grave-digger in *Hamlet* resembles him in A, B, and C, the grave-digger also has other functions (D, E, and F) and is of greater consequence to *Hamlet* than the clown is to *Othello*. Some repetition in the second half of the essay ("The grave-digger's puns come even faster than the clown's . . .") will bind the two halves into a meaningful whole, making clear the degree of similarity or difference. The point of the essay will not be to list pairs of similarities or differences but to illuminate a work or works by making thoughtful comparisons in support of a larger argument.

In a long essay, the writer cannot postpone until, for example, page thirty a discussion of the second half of the comparison. In an essay of fewer than ten pages, the writer can set forth one half of the comparison and then, in light of it, the second half. The essay will break into two unrelated parts if the second half makes no use of the first half or if it fails to modify the first half. The second half of the paper must look back to the first half and call attention to differences that the new material reveals. As a student, you need to learn how to write an essay with interwoven comparisons, but you ought to know also that a comparison should be written in a simple and clear way.

Finally, a reminder: **The purpose of a comparison is to call attention to the unique features of something by holding it up against something similar but significantly different.** You can compare Macbeth with Banquo (two men who hear a prophecy but who respond differently), or Macbeth with Lady Macbeth (a husband and wife, both eager to be monarchs but differing in their sense of the consequences), or Hamlet with Holden Caulfield (two people who see themselves as surrounded by a corrupt world), but you can hardly compare Holden with Macbeth or with Lady Macbeth—there simply aren't enough points of resemblance to make it worth your effort to call attention to the subtle differences.

When the differences are great and apparent, a comparison is a waste of effort; you will be arguing about something that is not really arguable. ("Blueberries are different from elephants. Blueberries do not have trunks. And elephants do not grow on bushes.") Indeed, a comparison between essentially and evidently unlike things can only obscure your thesis, for by making the comparison, you imply that significant similarities do exist, and readers can only wonder why they do not see them. The essays that do break into two halves are essays that make uninstructive comparisons: For example, the first half tells the reader about five qualities in Alice Walker, and the second half tells the reader about five different qualities in Toni Morrison.

Comparison and Close Reading

Let's practice comparison by reminding ourselves that it is a natural analytical process that we engage in every day as we try to make sense of the texts that surround us. Our task is to use writing to make this process of comparison more rigorous and more generative of new insights. Let's examine a photograph, a visual "text" that we can examine closely and analyze for the ideas it conveys. We can apply a process of close reading, inquiry, interpretation, and argumentation to this photograph, just as we would to a written text. At first, the photograph seems to be a straightforward image of two people, but when we look at it more closely, we see that it contains several strange elements. The photograph becomes more interesting—and more enjoyable—the more we look at it. It invites close reading and inquiry.

An examination of this photograph demonstrates that comparison can take place within one text. Let's start the process of comparison by examining the two figures in the photograph and then move outward from the photograph, comparing it to a literary work. Later in the chapter, we will explore how to synthesize multiple literary works. In the next chapter, we will examine how research enacts a process of synthesizing primary sources (the literary work) and secondary sources (the critical article).

At a first glance, this photograph appears to be merely an old-fashioned image capturing a cowboy and an Indian standing side by side. But, almost instantly, the setup or premise of the photograph raises questions: Why would a cowboy and an Indian be standing side by side? If they fit into the stories we tell about the American West, aren't they supposed to be sworn enemies? As we look more carefully at the photograph, it becomes even more interesting. Are the cowboy and the Indian shaking hands? Are they clasping hands on top of a gun? Also, why are they dressed in such fancy clothes? Are they trying to impress each other—or impress us? As our curiosity about the photograph grows, these initial impressions and questions start to lead to an understanding of the text. For example, although the cowboy and the Indian seem to be just standing together, a close examination reveals that they are carefully posed, with the feathers on the headdress carefully spread out and their feet carefully arranged. Perhaps they are staging some sort of agreement or reconciliation?

William Notman, *Foes in '76, Friends in '85*. Photograph. The Sioux chief Sitting Bull appeared for one season in William F. Cody's show, *Buffalo Bill's Wild West*. Souvenir cards with this picture were sold.

Some basic information about the photograph can help us to come to understand it more fully. Rather than answer all of our questions, however, this information triggers more questions, encouraging us to become even more curious about the photograph's meaning.

The photograph that we are focusing on here, of Sitting Bull and Buffalo Bill, was taken by a Canadian photographer, William Notman (1826–91). Buffalo Bill—William F. Cody—got his name from his activities as a supplier of buffalo meat for workers on the Kansas Pacific Railway, but his fame came chiefly from his exploits as an army scout and a fighter against the Sioux Indians, and later from *Buffalo Bill's Wild West*. *Buffalo Bill's Wild West* was a show (though he never used this word because he insisted that the exhibition re-created recent Western history) consisting of mock battles with Indians, an attack on a stagecoach, and feats of horsemanship and sharpshooting. Sitting Bull, a Sioux chief, had defeated General George Custer at the Battle of Little Bighorn ten years before this picture was taken, but he had fled to Canada soon after the battle. In 1879, he was granted amnesty and returned to the United States, and, in 1885, he appeared in Buffalo Bill's Wild West. The photograph, titled *Foes in '76, Friends in '85*, was used to publicize the show.

With this information in mind, let's look at the photograph even more closely and inquire even more deeply about its meaning.

Comparison and Asking Questions

The writer Howard Nemerov once said, "If you really want to see something, look at something else." He was talking about the power of comparison to illuminate. We compare X and Y, not for the sake of making lists of similarities and differences, but for the sake of seeing X (or Y) more clearly. This book offers many writings for you to read with pleasure, and one source of pleasure is understanding. Your understanding of one work may be heightened by thinking about it in comparison with another work.

Suppose we want to think about the photograph of Sitting Bull and Buffalo Bill in order to deepen our understanding of it and to share our understanding with others. To say that the photograph's dimensions are such and such or even to say that it shows two people is merely to *describe* it, not to *think* about it. But, if we look more closely and compare the two figures in the photograph, our mind is energized. Comparing greatly stimulates the mind; by comparing X with Y, we notice things that we might otherwise pass over. Comparison leads to questions that deepen our understanding of the text:

- What resemblances and what differences do we see in the clothes of the two figures?
- What about their facial expressions?
- How do their poses compare?
- How are the two figures interacting?
- Is the setting significant?

As we try to answer these and other questions that come to mind, we may find ourselves jotting down phrases and sentences along the following lines:

> *Buffalo Bill is in fancy clothing (shiny boots, a mammoth buckle, a decorated jacket)*
>
> *BB is striking a pose—very theatrical, his right hand on his heart, his head tilted slightly back, his eyes looking off as though he is gazing into the future. He seems to be working hard to present a grand image of himself.*
>
> *Sitting Bull simply stands there, apparently looking downward. One feels that he is going along with what is expected of him—after all, he had joined the show—but he refuses to make a fool of himself.*
>
> *Sitting Bull lets BB have upper hand (literally—on gun)*
>
> *BB in effect surrounds SB (Bill's right shoulder is behind Sitting Bull and Bill's left leg is in front of him).*

Comparison and Analyzing Evidence

If we continue to look closely, we will probably notice that the landscape is fake—not the great outdoors but a set, with a painted backdrop and probably a fake grass mat. If we see these things, we may formulate the thesis that Buffalo Bill is all show biz and that Sitting Bull retains his dignity. If, in our essay, we support these assertions by pointing to evidence—specific details from the visual text that provide justification for our interpretation—we are demonstrating critical thinking. Let's look at some sample student interpretations of this photograph that rely on evidence-based comparison.

Student Work: Comparison Arguments

Here is the final paragraph from an informal essay that a student, Patricia Flynn, wrote on this photograph for her composition course.

> Buffalo Bill is obviously the dominant figure in this photograph, but he is not the outstanding one. His efforts to appear great only serve to make him appear small. His attempt to outshine Sitting Bull strikes us as faintly ridiculous. We do not need nor want to know any more about Buffalo Bill's personality; it is spread before us in the picture. Sitting Bull's inwardness and dignity make him more interesting than Buffalo Bill, and make us wish to prove our intuition and to ascertain that this proud Sioux was a great chief.

We think this analysis is excellent, but we also can see a student emphasizing different elements of the photograph and coming to different conclusions. If we reacted positively to the energetic pose of Buffalo Bill, we might come to the conclusion that he was a positive force for change in addition to being a showman. We can create an argument that advances this conclusion, as long as we have convincing evidence to support our ideas.

Here is the final paragraph from an informal essay written by Luis Torres, a student in the same composition course:

> The photograph conveys the positive energy that surrounds Buffalo Bill. By looking upward and out of the photo, Buffalo Bill seems to be welcoming the future and encouraging us to look forward to that future with him. Because he leans into and touches Sitting Bull, his future seems to be one of cooperation and working together. Sitting Bull is a solid presence, filled with dignity. But, it is Buffalo Bill's energy that might create a new future of connection between the white Americans and Native Americans.

Which interpretation of the photograph seems best to you? Can you create an interpretation that comes up with a new opinion or one that combines these two opinions? What details from the photograph do you feel are the most important to emphasize, and how do they shape your interpretation?

Comparison and Arguing with Yourself

Having compared the two figures in the photograph, we can extend the idea of textual comparison and interpretation further to connect the photograph to a poem. Let's look now at a short poem by E. E. Cummings, which was probably written in 1917, the year Buffalo Bill died, but was not published until 1920.

Cummings did not give it a title, but he included it in a group of poems called "Portraits." (In line 6, "pigeons" are clay targets used in skeet shooting or in exhibitions of marksmanship.)

E. E. CUMMINGS

For biographical information on e.e. cummings, see page 811.

Buffalo Bill 's

Buffalo Bill 's
defunct
   who used to
   ride a water smooth-silver
                     stallion
and break one two three four five pigeons just like that   5
                              Jesus
he was a handsome man
                   and what i want to know is
how do you like your blue eyed boy   10
Mister Death

Read the poem, preferably aloud, at least two or three times and with as open a mind as possible. *Don't* assume that, because the photograph shows us a man who seems to be all show biz, this poem necessarily conveys the same attitude. After we generate an understanding of the poem, we can start to make comparisons to the photograph, noting similarities and differences.

Critical thinking requires that we keep asking questions as we formulate an interpretation. One way to generate questions that develop your ideas is to imagine arguing with yourself. How would you question your own assumptions, your use of evidence, or your original opinions? You will want to ask your own questions about the E. E. Cummings poem and arrive at your own responses, but for a start you may find it useful to consider the following inquiry questions and jot down tentative answers. We say "tentative" answers because, when you think about them, you will almost surely begin to question them and thus improve your responses. Notice how each question leads to more questions that can be used to deepen your thinking.

1. What is the speaker's attitude toward Buffalo Bill? (How do you know? What *evidence* can you point to?)
2. In line 6, why do you suppose Cummings ran the words together? Does this new word create a new image or sound in your mind?
3. Why do you think Cummings spaced the poem as he did? One student suggested that the lines form an arrowhead pointing to the right. Do you find merit in this suggestion? If not, what better explanation(s) can you offer?
4. What do you make of the address to "Mister Death"? Why "Mister Death" rather than "Mr. Death" or "Death"? If Mister Death could speak, what answer do you think he might give to the speaker's question?
5. What do you make of the use of "defunct" (as opposed to "dead") in line 2? Imagine creating the argument that "defunct" is a word that adds depth to the poem, making us think about how a person might no longer be

functional or might have outlived his use. Now, imagine arguing with yourself and creating an opposing argument. Imagine arguing that "defunct" is a confusing word that starts the poem in an unclear fashion, making its description of Buffalo Bill difficult to understand. What word would you use in the second line to replace "defunct"?

6. What do you make of "Jesus" in line 7? What is the effect of placing the word on a line by itself? Is Cummings being blasphemous? Is he inviting us to compare Buffalo Bill with Jesus? Support your response with *evidence*.

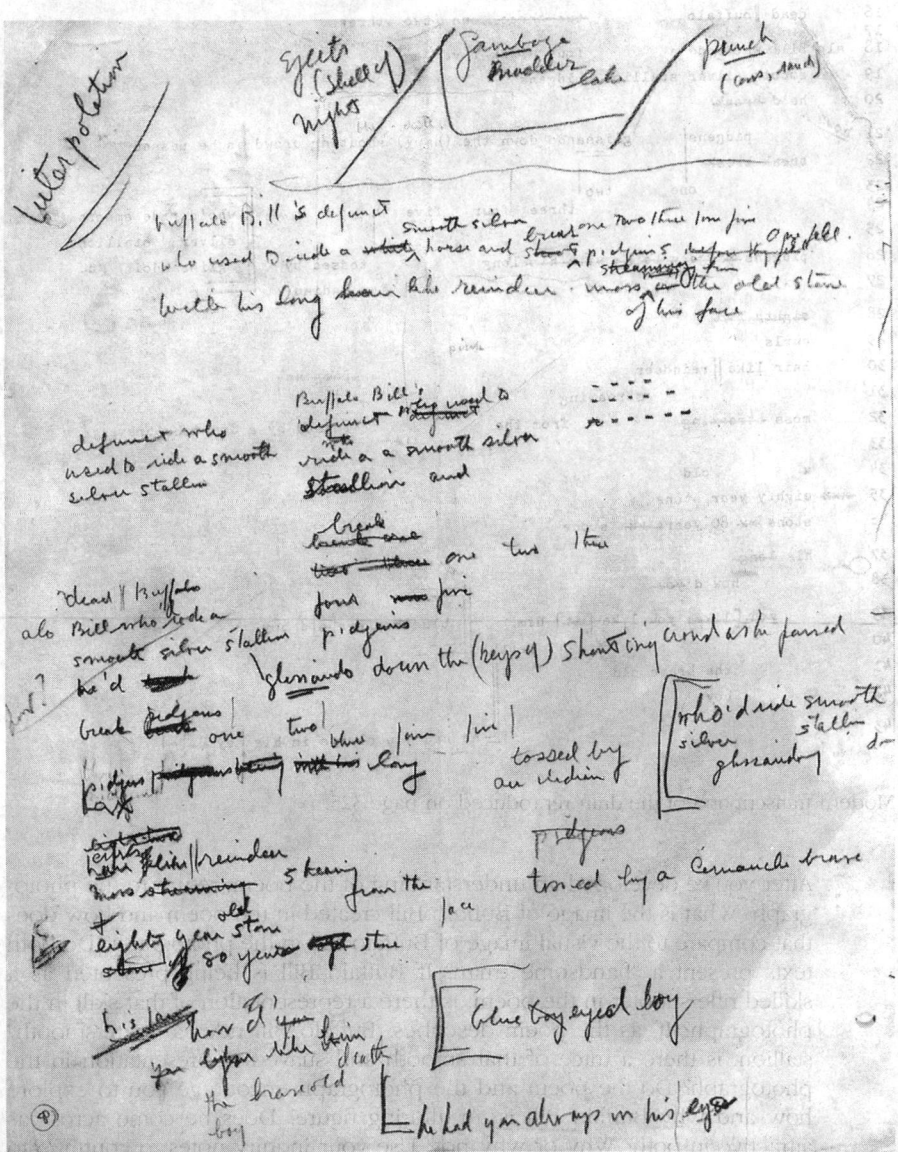

Manuscript of the draft of E. E. Cummings's poem (the final version appears on page 324).

```
1              buffalo Bill [is]'s defunct
2                          smooth silver  break one two three four five  one fell.
3       who used to ride a white horse and shoot pidgens before they fell.
4                                        streaming from
5                                           xxxx
6              with his long hair like reindeer moss in the old stone
7                                           of his face

8                              Buffalo Bill's          - - - -
9                                who used to
10      defunct who           defunct defunct           - - - - -
11      used to ride a smooth      who
12      silver stallion        ride a a smooth silver  r - - - - -
13                             [horse] stallion and

14                             break
15                             break one
16      dead ‖Buffalo          two three  one  two  three
17           'd
18  alo Bill who rode a        four xxxx five
19      smooth silver stallion pidgens
20      he'd break

21  how?       pidgens    glissando down the (happy) shouting crowd as he passed
22      break break

23                one    two
24                         three four    five      |
25                                                 |          who'd ride smooth
26      pidgens pidgens being with his long        |          silver ' stallion
27      ax                                 tossed by         glissandoing do
28      eighty two                         an indian
29      curls
30      hair like ‖ reindeer                        pidgens
31              streaming
32      moss streaming         from the             tossed by a Comanche brave
33                             face
34      x-        old
35  xxx eighty year stone
36      stone xx 80 years xxx stone
37      his long
38              how d'you
39      you [like] you like [it] him    | blue boy eye[e]d boy
40                          death        |_ _ _|
41          the brave old
42          boy
43                                    └ he had you always in his |ey[es]e|
```

Modern transcription of the draft reproduced on page 325.

7. After you've developed an understanding of the poem, return to the photograph. What is the image of Buffalo Bill created in the poem and how does that compare to the visual image of Buffalo Bill in the photograph? Do both texts present a "handsome" man? If Buffalo Bill is being presented as a skilled rifle shooter in the poem, is there a representation of that skill in the photograph? If, as the poem describes, Buffalo Bill rides a "watersmooth" stallion, is there a trace of that smooth and suave self-presentation in the photograph? Do the poem and the photograph encourage you to explore how and why Buffalo Bill is an alluring figure? Does he come across as attractive in both? Why or why not? Use your inquiry notes to continue to ask questions and develop answers that compare the poem and photograph.

8. Let's make another comparison. Compare the published poem with the manuscript draft. In the manuscript (see page 325); for a scholar's transcription of it, see page 326), you will notice that Cummings wrote, near the start, "with his long hair like reindeer moss streaming from the old stone of his face." These words do not appear in the final version. Do you think Cummings showed good judgment in deleting the line? Explain your answer.

9. Some readers say that Cummings is satirizing Buffalo Bill, and others say that he is satirizing death. Do you agree with either of these views? Why? (In a sentence or two, define *satire*—feel free to consult a dictionary—and perhaps give an example of it. By the way, it's possible to satirize the common human fear of death, but can death be satirized? How might that be done? And what would be the point?)

You may want to discuss some or all of these questions, as well as others that you generate for yourself, with classmates and with your instructor. It will be interesting to see whether differences of opinion can be resolved in discussion by pointing to evidence.

Finally, after you have thought about these questions, and any others that you may initiate, consider two opinions from published discussions of the poem:

1. Buffalo Bill, in the poem, functions as a destroyer, an agent of death.
2. The poem's image of Buffalo Bill on his "water smooth-silver stallion," riding to the center of the tent to accept the adulation of the crowd before his demonstration of crack marksmanship is acidly ironic.

Compare your own interpretations to these arguments. Do you agree with either statement, or with both? What evidence in the poem can you point to in order to support or rebut these assertions?

Buffalo Bill on a favorite horse.

✔ **CHECKLIST**: *Developing a Comparison*

☐ Have you selected appropriate works for comparison? Does it make sense to compare these texts?

☐ Will your comparison lead to meaningful analysis and synthesis? What question will the comparison help to answer? What do you hope your reader will learn?

☐ Have you located a key bridge concept that you can use to compare the literary works?

☐ Does a close reading of the two works reveal unexpected connections between them? Can you create connections between the works on the level of theme? Can you create connections between the works on the level of form and structure?

☐ What evidence can you select from each work to strengthen your comparison? Can you locate specific words that appear in each work? Can you locate specific phrases that resonate across both works?

☐ As you develop your comparison, have you moved back and forth between the two texts? Did you interweave the texts, rather than allow each text's analysis to stand alone?

☐ As you developed your comparison, did you argue with yourself, considering alternative interpretations? Did you consider counterarguments?

☐ Does your comparison achieve synthesis, creating a relationship between the two works that allows a larger idea to be explored—and explored in a more sophisticated way than if it were addressed through only one work?

Synthesis through Close Reading: Analyzing a Revised Short Story

Let's continue to work on using synthesis to create relationships between texts, moving on to a comparison of two literary works. As we explore the activity of synthesizing texts, we will examine several students' note-taking techniques and explore how they develop new ideas through synthesis. These students' notes take innovative forms, demonstrating that synthesis is a creative process that generates exciting ideas.

Here, we start developing the skill of synthesis by selecting two texts defined by a clear relationship: One story is a revision of an earlier version. Consider these two versions of a very short story by Raymond Carver. In 1977, Carver published the first version, "Mine." In 1981, he published a revised version with a new title, "Popular Mechanics," and in 1986, he published the same revised version under yet another title, "Little Things." After the two stories, we present an innovative note-taking technique that uses a table to capture the close reading and interpretation process.

Read "Mine," and then read "Little Things." Then go back and reread both stories, marking differences and jotting down your own responses. What changes were made? Why do you think the changes were made? Do different ideas emerge in each story due to revision? What words were added or subtracted in the revision, and what ideas are emphasized, added, modified, or taken away in the revision? You may want to jot down your responses to the titles: Do you think the new title is better, or not? Why?

RAYMOND CARVER

*Raymond Carver (1938–1988) was born in Clatskanie, Oregon. In 1963, he gradu-
ated from Humboldt State College in northern California and then did further
study at the University of Iowa.*

*As a young man, Carver wrote poetry while working at odd jobs; later he turned
to fiction, though he continued to write poetry. Most of Carver's fiction narrates
stories about bewildered and sometimes exhausted men and women.*

Mine

During the day the sun had come out and the snow melted into dirty water. Streaks
of water ran down from the little, shoulder-high window that faced the back yard.
Cars slushed by on the street outside. It was getting dark, outside and inside.

He was in the bedroom pushing clothes into a suitcase when she came to the
door.

I'm glad you're leaving. I'm glad you're leaving! she said. Do you hear?

He kept on putting his things into the suitcase and didn't look up.

5   Sonofabitch! I'm so glad you're leaving! She began to cry. You can't even look me
in the face, can you? Then she noticed the baby's picture on the bed and picked it up.

He looked at her and she wiped her eyes and stared at him before turning and
going back to the living room.

Bring that back.

Just get your things and get out, she said.

He did not answer. He fastened the suitcase, put on his coat, and looked at the
bedroom before turning off the light. Then he went out to the living room. She
stood in the doorway of the little kitchen, holding the baby.

10   I want the baby, he said.

Are you crazy?

No, but I want the baby. I'll get someone to come by for his things.

You can go to hell! You're not touching this baby.

The baby had begun to cry and she uncovered the blanket from around its
head.

15   Oh, oh, she said, looking at the baby.

He moved towards her.

For God's sake! she said. She took a step back into the kitchen.

I want the baby.

Get out of here!

20   She turned and tried to hold the baby over in a corner behind the stove as he
came up.

He reached across the stove and tightened his hands on the baby.

Let go of him, he said.

Get away, get away! she cried.

The baby was red-faced and screaming. In the scuffle they knocked down a
little flower pot that hung behind the stove.

25   He crowded her into the wall then, trying to break her grip, holding onto the
baby and pushing his weight against her arm.

Let go of him, he said.

Don't, she said, you're hurting him!

He didn't talk again. The kitchen window gave no light. In the near dark he
worked on her fisted fingers with one hand and with the other hand he gripped
the screaming baby up under an arm near the shoulder.

She felt her fingers being forced open and the baby going from her. No, she said, just as her hands came loose. She would have it, this baby whose chubby face gazed up at them from the picture on the table. She grabbed for the baby's other arm. She caught the baby around the wrist and leaned back.

30   He would not give. He felt the baby going out of his hands and he pulled back hard. He pulled back very hard. In this manner they decided the issue.

[1977]

how'd they decide? I'm confused

Little Things

Early that day the weather turned and the snow was melting into dirty water. Streaks of it ran down from the little shoulder-high window that faced the backyard. Cars slushed by on the street outside, where it was getting dark. But it was getting dark on the inside too.

He was in the bedroom pushing clothes into a suitcase when she came to the door.

I'm glad you're leaving! I'm glad you're leaving! she said. Do you hear?

He kept on putting his things into the suitcase.

5   Son of a bitch! I'm so glad you're leaving! She began to cry. You can't even look me in the face, can you?

Then she noticed the baby's picture on the bed and picked it up.

He looked at her and she wiped her eyes and stared at him before turning and going back to the living room.

Bring that back, he said.

Just get your things and get out, she said.

10   He did not answer. He fastened the suitcase, put on his coat, looked around the bedroom before turning off the light. Then he went out to the living room.

She stood in the doorway of the little kitchen, holding the baby.

I want the baby, he said.

Are you crazy?

No, but I want the baby. I'll get someone to come by for his things.

15   You're not touching this baby, she said.

The baby had begun to cry and she uncovered the blanket from around his head.

Oh, oh, she said, looking at the baby.

He moved toward her.

For God's sake! she said. She took a step back into the kitchen.

20   I want the baby.

Get out of here!

She turned and tried to hold the baby over in a corner behind the stove.

But he came up. He reached across the stove and tightened his hands on the baby.

Let go of him, he said.

25   Get away, get away! she cried.

The baby was red-faced and screaming. In the scuffle they knocked down a flowerpot that hung behind the stove.

He crowded her into the wall then, trying to break her grip. He held on to the baby and pushed with all his weight.

Let go of him, he said.

Don't, she said. You're hurting the baby, she said.

30   I'm not hurting the baby, he said.

Till items they're struggle over or not

The kitchen window gave no light. In the near-dark he worked on her fisted fingers with one hand and with the other hand he gripped the screaming baby up under an arm near the shoulder.

She felt her fingers being forced open. She felt the baby going from her.

No! she screamed just as her hands came loose.

She would have it, this baby. She grabbed for the baby's other arm. She caught the baby around the wrist and leaned back.

35   But he would not let go. He felt the baby slipping out of his hands and he pulled back very hard.

In this manner, the issue was decided.

Still don't understand

[1981]

Student Work: Innovative Listing

Let's examine how a student, Felix Tran, outlines the differences that he finds between the two stories. Felix uses a table format to list the changes that Carver made in the revision of the original story; he then adds a column to that table to capture his new ideas—his interpretation. In this way, his note taking encourages and captures both close reading and interpretation.

"Mine"	"Little Things"	My Interpretation
Line 1: melted	was melting	Revision: things are still under development, still in action
Line 3: Getting dark, outside and inside	But it was getting dark on the inside too	Revision: Emphasizes "inside"—makes you think more about that word
Line 4: and didn't look up	deleted	Revision: Makes sentence shorter? The reader has to figure out that he didn't look up.
Line 6: Then she noticed the baby's picture	New paragraph breaks	Revision: Makes writing more choppy? Captures stressful, broken relationship
Line 20: and he came up	Line 23: New paragraph break: but he came up	Revision: "But" emphasizes that he does things anyway. Makes writing choppy.
Line 28: He didn't talk again	Line 30: I'm not hurting the baby, he said.	Revision: Emphasizes idea of hurting baby. Do we believe the man? Is he protesting even though he knows he is hurting baby? Seems to make him even more argumentative and mean.
Line 28: This baby whose chubby face gazed up at them from the picture on the table.	Deleted	Revision: No image of happy child? Makes the revision even more depressing? I like the contrast set up between present and past in the first version.
Line 30: They decided the issue	The issue was decided	Revision: "They" connects the wife and husband. They = they are together. Revision deletes this idea, making them more separate. Revision makes it unclear who is to blame. (What happens—what is decided?)

After you annotate the two stories and think about your annotations, write a short essay arguing that, on balance, one version is superior to the other. You do not have to believe that every change was an improvement (or a worsening); in fact, you may want to argue that, in some ways, the earlier version is better and in some ways the later version is better. In any case, formulate a thesis sentence—a sentence that tells the reader the gist of your point—and then in 250–500 words support the thesis.

Synthesis through Building a Concept Bridge: Connecting Two Poems

By using synthesis, you often generate new ideas by comparing two literary works that are quite different. As you work to develop your skills of synthesis, remember that synthesis rests on the creation of relationships and that you need to select works that can generate meaningful connections. Then, as in any analytical writing, by means of synthesis, you will work to develop a thesis argument. In a comparison paper, the argument must find a meaningful point of connection between the two works and create an argument that highlights that connection. Comparison is a popular paper format because observation about what aspects two texts share and don't share, and why they are similar and different, can be used to create a strong argument.

As you prepare to write a comparison paper, reread your selected texts, and work to build bridges between them. Find literary concepts, structures, and devices that they have in common. At the same time, work to differentiate the two texts, showing how each contains unique elements. Make sure that your paper develops a larger understanding of each text through comparison: How does your thinking about a text become both clearer and more complex when you connect it to another text? How does your thinking about the concepts presented in each text become both clearer and more complex when you compare the texts?

Think of your writing as building a *concept bridge* between the two texts. For example, if two texts describe the same scenario of a pair of lovers on a beach, a juxtaposition may reveal how one creates a happy image by emphasizing the sunlight sparkling on the waves while the other creates an image of desperation by emphasizing the empty repetition of the waves. By bringing the two texts together, you can more clearly see how each is developing its ideas about love by using different images of the waves.

Let's turn to two poems that both feature the topic of tornadoes. This creates an obvious bridge between the two poems. Is there also a more conceptual bridge? After we read each poem, we can look at sample student notes, seeing the innovative responses inspired by these poems.

THYLIAS MOSS

A poet, playwright, filmmaker, and sound artist, Thylias Moss has won a MacArthur Fellowship and Guggenheim Fellowship, recognizing her experimental work in creating new forms of art that combine writing, visual work, audio work, and technology. She explains the goals and processes of this interdisciplinary work on her Limited Fork Theory website. Moss was born in Ohio in 1954, attended Oberlin College and the University of New Hampshire, and works as a professor at the University of Michigan.

Tornados

Truth is, I envy them
not because they dance; I out jitterbug them
as I'm shuttled through and through legs
strong as looms, weaving time. They
do black more justice than I, frenzy   5
of conductor of philharmonic and electricity, hair
on end, result of the charge when horns and strings release
the pent up Beethoven and Mozart. Ions played

instead of notes. The movement
is not wrath, not hormone swarm because   10
I saw my first forming above the church a surrogate
steeple. The morning of my first baptism and
salvation already tangible, funnel for the spirit
coming into me without losing a drop, my black
guardian angel come to rescue me before all the words   15

get out, *I looked over Jordan and what did I see coming for?*
to carry me home. Regardez it all comes back, even the first
grade French, when the tornado stirs up the past, bewitched spoon
lost in its own spin, like a roulette wheel that won't
be steered like the world. They drove me underground,   20
tornado watches and warnings, atomic bomb drills. Adult
storms so I had to leave the room. Truth is

the tornado is a perfect nappy curl, tightly wound,
spinning wildly when I try to tamper with its nature, shunning
the hot comb and pressing oil even though if absolutely straight   25
I'd have the longest hair in the world. Bouffant tornadic
crown taking the royal path on a trip to town, stroll down
Tornado Alley where it intersects Memory Lane. Smoky spirit-
clouds, shadows searching for what cast them.

[1991]

KWAME DAWES

Born in 1962 in Ghana, Kwame Dawes grew up in Jamaica and is currently the Chancellor's Professor of English at the University of Nebraska. He also serves as the Glenna Luschie Editor-in-Chief of Prairie Schooner, *an important literary magazine that features both a traditional book format and innovative online series. His publications include sixteen books of poetry, two novels, two collections of nonfiction writing, and several edited anthologies. His work is often inspired by the sights, sounds, and rhythms of Jamaica, and he has written an important study of the lyrics of the reggae musician Bob Marley.*

Tornado Child

For Rosalie Richardson

I am a tornado child.
    I come like a swirl of black and darken up your day;
    I whip it all into my womb, lift you and your things,

carry you to where you've never been, and maybe,
if I feel good, I might bring you back, all warm and scared,
heart humming wild like a bird after early sudden flight.   5

I am a tornado child.
  I tremble at the elements. When thunder rolls my womb
  trembles, remembering the tweak of contractions
  that tightened to a wail when my mother pushed me out   10
  into the black of a tornado night.

I am a tornado child,
  you can tell us from far, by the crazy of our hair;
  couldn't tame it if we tried. Even now I tie a bandanna
  to silence the din of anarchy in these coir-thick plaits.   15

I am a tornado child
  born in the whirl of clouds; the center crumbled,
  then I came. My lovers know the blast of my chaotic giving;
  they tremble at the whip of my supple thighs;
  you cross me at your peril, I swallow light   20
  when the warm of anger lashes me into a spin,
  the pine trees bend to me swept in my gyrations.

I am a tornado child.
  When the spirit takes my head, I hurtle into the vacuum
  of white sheets billowing and paint a swirl of color,   25
  streaked with my many songs.

                                                          [2001]

Student Work: Innovative Journal Writing

Let's examine how a student, Esther St. Pierre, uses a personalized form of journal writing to build a concept bridge between the two poems. Esther creates a form of note taking that feels right for the critical thinking task before her: She creates synthesis by locating bridge concepts, noting key quotes, and then writing out her ideas about each concept. Notice that the emphasis is on the *generation of ideas*.

RACE & GENDER = HAIR

"Tornados"	"Tornado Child"
"funneled through . . . legs"	"swirl of black and darken"
"do black justice"	"my womb"
"black guardian angel"	"contractions"
"nappy curl"	"mother pushed me out"
"hot comb . . . pressing oil"	"black of a tornado night"
"longest hair in the world"	"crazy of our hair"
"Smoky spirit"	"coir—thick plaits"

These poems connect tornadoes to black women. Race is central to both poems—right in the first stanza of each poem, we get the word "black." Then, each poem connects the idea of a tornado to a black woman's hair. The whole last stanza of "Tornados" is about hair. The poem's speaker describes the tornado as a "perfect nappy curl" and describes trying to tame her hair with a comb and oil. Her hair is a "bouffant tornadic crown"—at first I didn't get this image, but now I can see that her hair is like a tornado over her head, creating a crown. In "Tornado Child" the third stanza is all about hair. It explains "the crazy of our hair, / couldn't tame it if we tried." In the next line I think the hair is being put in a bandana because it is "anarchy." Again, the hair is out of control, like a tornado. I'd like to try to connect these two poems through these images of hair: the African-American woman's hair is wild, out of control— almost like it has a mind of its own.

POWER—STRENGTH

"Tornados"	"Tornado Child"
"frenzy"	"swirl of black"
"electricity"	"whip it"
"release /the pent up"	"scared,/heart humming"
"lost in its own spin"	"tremble . . . thunder"
"won't/be steered"	"din of anarchy"
"atomic bomb"	"whirl of cloud"
"spinning wildly"	"blast of my chaotic giving"
	"anger lashes me into a spin"

I think another key concept raised by both poems is the idea of power. The tornado is an incredibly powerful force of nature, able to cause fear and destruction. Both of the poems emphasize the tornado's power and especially that the power is out of control or almost out of control: "won't be steered" "anarchy." This is not a normal power, but a chaotic power full of energy. The use of words in each poem is great: frenzy, whip, whirl, release, spinning, wild, whirl—all of these capture the feel of the tornado. In addition, both poems use words that warn that the tornado might be on the verge of exploding: "atomic bomb," "blast of my chaotic giving." Threatens even more damage?

BAPTISM/BIRTH

"Tornados"	"Tornado Child"
"church . . . surrogate steeple"	"thunder rolls my womb"
"first baptism"	"contractions"
"salvation"	"mother pushed me out . . . tornado night"
"funnel for the spirit"	"born in the whirl of clouds"
"guardian angle"	
"Jordan"	
"tornado watches and warnings"	

> Both poems focus on a key event that involves tornadoes. "Tornados" describes a tornado that visits the speaker's church on the day of her first baptism. The tornado becomes the church's steeple. The poem's speaker was saying words at the baptism—but then she has to run underground to take shelter from the tornado. In "Tornado Child," the speaker describes being born, and it seems like the mother gave birth during a storm (or maybe the birth felt like a storm). The narrator keeps repeating "I am a tornado child" and says she is born in the "tornado night." In "Tornados," the poem connects the tornado to feelings of religion (like the idea of "funnel for the spirit"), but in "Tornado Child," the idea of birth is connected to sexuality (like the idea that "lovers know the blast of my chaotic giving"). Maybe the idea of baptism as rebirth can be connected to the idea of birth? In both poems, tornadoes seem to symbolize the female narrator, being connected to her sense of religion or sexuality (something deeper than her appearance/hair).

Now that you've read a student's attempt to create a concept bridge that connects the two poems, write a short essay that puts one or more of these connections into essay form. Can you create a thesis argument out of one of these concepts? Can you develop one of these concepts further? Can you find more evidence to support one of these concepts? Can you combine the concepts? You can, of course, develop your own concept bridge, locating evidence that supports an analytical response to the two poems. Write an essay of 250–500 words, remembering that the goal is synthesis—a connecting of the two texts to explore an important idea presented by both.

Synthesis Using Theme

As we've been exploring, with synthesis, you are developing relationships between texts, using those relationships to generate new insights into concepts that bridge the texts. Comparison offers a strategy for performing synthesis: It asks you to develop your ideas by locating similarities and differences among literary texts or parts of texts. Synthesis tests your critical thinking skills: How can you position texts alongside each other, using that relationship to reveal new ideas in each text?

When we turn to fiction, one of the first ways in which we might think about creating synthesis, then, is though theme. **Theme** is a *central concept, idea, or issue* explored by a story—a larger meaning or insight that the story reveals. A story will have one or more unifying or overarching concepts that it explores; theme is the presentation and development of those ideas. When we synthesize stories, we will often turn to their themes as a source of comparison.

Let's make the task of synthesis even more interesting by bringing together three pieces of microfiction. Let's see what themes emerge from these stories. As you read these very short stories by Sandra Cisneros, Maryanne O'Hara, and Jayne Anne Phillips, consider what themes might provide productive connections among all three.

SANDRA CISNEROS

Best known for The House on Mango Street *(1984), a coming-of-age novel told through short chapters filled with poem-like lines, Sandra Cisneros has written poetry, novels, short stories, a children's book, and a picture book for adults. Born in Chicago in 1954, Cisneros received a BA in English from Loyola University of Chicago (1976) and an MFA in Creative Writing from the University of Iowa (1978). Raised in a family that repeatedly migrated between Mexico and the United States, she is an advocate for Latina writing and has created foundations that support socially conscious writers and writers connected to Texas. The importance of her writing has been recognized by a MacArthur Fellowship, National Endowment for the Arts awards, and the American Book Award from the Before Columbus Foundation.*

Barbie-Q

Yours is the one with mean eyes and a ponytail. Striped swimsuit, stilettos, sunglasses, and gold hoop earrings. Mine is the one with bubble hair. Red swimsuit, stilettos, pearl earrings, and a wire stand. But that's all we can afford, besides one extra outfit apiece. Yours, "Red Flair," sophisticated A-line coatdress with a Jackie Kennedy pillbox hat, white gloves, handbag, and heels included. Mine, "solo in the Spotlight," evening elegance in black glitter strapless gown with a puffy skirt at the bottom like a mermaid tail, formal-length gloves, pink chiffon scarf, and mike included. From so much dressing and undressing, the black glitter wears off where her titties stick out. This and a dress invented from an old sock when we cut holes here and here and here, the cuff rolled over for the glamorous, fancy-free, off-the-shoulder look.

Every time the same story. Your Barbie is roommates with my Barbie, and my Barbie's boyfriend comes over and your Barbie steals him, okay? Kiss kiss kiss. Then the two Barbies fight. You dumbbell! He's mine. Oh no he's not, you stinky! Only Ken's invisible, right? Because we don't have money for a stupid-looking boy doll when we'd both rather ask for a new Barbie outfit next Christmas. We have to make do with your mean-eyed Barbie and my bubble head Barbie and our one outfit apiece not including the sock dress.

Until next Sunday when we are walking through the flea market on Maxwell Street and there! Lying on the street next to some tool bits, and platform shoes with the heels all squashed, and a fluorescent green wicker wastebasket, and aluminum foil, and hubcaps, and a pink shag rug, and windshield wiper blades, and dusty mason jars, and a coffee can full of rusty nails. There! Where? Two Mattel boxes. One with the "Career Gal" ensemble, snappy black-and-white business suit, three-quarter-length sleeve jacket with kick-pleated skirt, red sleeveless shell, gloves, pumps, and matching hat included. The other, "Sweet Dreams," dreamy pink-and-white plaid nightgown and matching robe, lace-trimmed slippers, hair-brush and hand mirror included. How much? Please, please, please, please, please, please, please, until they say okay.

On the outside you and me skipping and humming but inside we are doing loopity-loops and pirouetting. Until at the next vendor's stand, next to boxed pies, and bright orange toilet brushes, and rubber gloves, and wrench sets, and bouquets of feather flowers, and glass towel racks, and steel wool, and Alvin and the Chipmunks records, there! And there! And there! And there! and there! and there! and there! Bendable Legs Barbie with her new page-boy hairdo, Midge, Barbie's best friend. Ken, Barbie's boyfriend. Skipper, Barbie's little sister. Tutti and Todd, Barbie and Skipper's tiny twin sister and brother. Skipper's friends, Scooter and Ricky. Alan, Ken's buddy. And Francie, Barbie's MOD'ern cousin.

5 Everybody today selling toys, all of them damaged with water and smelling of smoke. Because a big toy warehouse on Halsted Street burned down yesterday—see

there?—the smoke still rising and drifting across the Dan Ryan expressway. And now there is a big fire sale at Maxwell Street, today only. So what if we didn't get our new Bendable Legs Barbie and Midge and Ken and Skipper and Tutti and Todd and Scooter and Ricky and Alan and Francie in nice clean boxes and had to buy them on Maxwell Street, all water-soaked and sooty. So what if our Barbies smell like smoke when you hold them up to your nose even after you wash and wash and wash them. And if the prettiest doll, Barbie's MOD'ern cousin Francie with real eyelashes, eyelash brush included, has a left foot that's melted a little—so? If you dress her in her new "Prom Pinks" outfit, satin splendor with matching coat, gold belt, clutch, and hair bow included, so long as you don't lift her dress, right?— who's to know.

[1991]

MARYANNE O'HARA

A novelist and short-story writer who lives in Massachusetts, Maryanne O'Hara earned an MFA from Emerson College and served as associate fiction editor for Boston's literary magazine, Ploughshares. *She often takes her inspiration from local landscapes, and her novel* Cascade *(2012) fictionalizes the real events of the flooding of central Massachusetts towns to create the Quabbin Reservoir.*

Diverging Paths and All That

In Dollar Saver, the aisles are empty, customers crowding Electronics watching Nixon resign on twenty TV sets. Dad dropped us off with three bucks to buy burgers but we've already spent it on fireballs and fudge.

While Nixon keeps the manager occupied, Billy demonstrates the "heads-up technique," the nonchalant gaze, his left hand filching Hershey bars and Bic pens while his right hand jingles pocket change. Billy grins, "I really save my dollars here."

Solo time. I head for Cosmetics, the wall of Peeper Sticks—blue and green and lavender eye crayons that've always cost dollars I don't have. My hand closes around Seafoam Green, hesitates, but what the hell, even the President's a crook, so I slip it up my sleeve. I try to sneak away natural as Billy, but my legs move too quick and stiff.

Billy meets me in Electronics, where Nixon's keeping his head up, not admitting a damn thing. Saying he'd be able to clear his name if he fought long enough, but he'll sacrifice his honor for the country. When he says he'll resign as of noon the next day, I check out all these adults who yelled, "Impeach the crook." Nobody cheers. The faces are solemn as gravestones. Billy's motioning, Come on on let's go, but I suddenly feel like I ate too much candy. I shake my sleeve, dropping the Peeper Stick onto a shelf, and follow Billy out the automatic doors. Dad's picking us up in two minutes, but Billy's headed someplace else.

[1996]

JAYNE ANNE PHILLIPS

Born in 1952 in West Virginia, Jayne Anne Phillips earned a BA from West Virginia University and an MFA from the University of Iowa. She is currently a professor of English and the founding director of the Rutgers University–Newark MFA in Creative Writing Program. Her work wrestles with the American experiences of coming of age, maintaining family relationships, and struggling with the legacy of war, and includes the short story collection Fast Lanes *(1984) and the novels* Machine Dreams *(1984) and* Lark and Termite *(2008).*

Sweethearts

We went to the movies every Friday and Sunday. On Friday nights the Colonial filled with an oily fragrance of teenagers while we hid in the back row of the balcony. An aura of light from the projection booth curved across our shoulders, round under cotton sweaters. Sacred grunts rose in back corners. The screen was far away and spilling color—big men sweating on horses and women with powdered breasts floating under satin. Near the end the film smelled hot and twisted as boys shuddered and girls sank down in their seats. We ran to the lobby before the lights came up to stand by the big ash can and watch them walk slowly downstairs. Mouths swollen and ripe, they drifted down like a sign of steam. The boys held their arms tense and shuffled from one foot to the other while the girls sniffed and combed their hair in the big mirror. Outside the neon lights on Main Street flashed stripes across the asphalt in the rain. They tossed their heads and shivered like ponies.

On Sunday afternoons the theater was deserted, a church that smelled of something frying. Mrs. Causton stood at the door to tear tickets with her fat buttered fingers. During the movie she stood watching the traffic light change in the empty street, pushing her glasses up over her nose and squeezing a damp kleenex. Mr. Penny was her skinny yellow father. He stood by the office door with his big push broom, smoking cigarettes and coughing.

Walking down the slanted floor to our seats we heard the swish of her thighs behind the candy counter and our shoes sliding on the worn carpet. The heavy velvet curtain moved its folds. We waited, and a cavernous dark pressed close around us, its breath pulling at our faces.

After the last blast of sound, it was Sunday afternoon, and Mr. Penny stood jingling his keys by the office door while we asked to use the phone. Before he turned the key he bent over and pulled us close with his bony arms. Stained finders kneading our chests, he wrapped us in old tobacco and called us his girls. I felt his wrinkled heart wheeze like a dog on a leash. Sweethearts, he whispered.

[1976]

Student Work: Innovative Mapping

As you read these three stories, you probably formulated ideas about how they might be connected. With three stories to compare, rather than just two, the relationships among ideas become more complex. How can you keep your ideas straight as you interweave and develop them?

Sample writing by a student offers an example of **mapping** ideas in a graphic, free-flowing fashion. Mapping allows connections between ideas to emerge through brainstorming and then allows those connections to be developed further. Mapping frees brainstorming from the linear thinking that an outline, list, or table supports. As you look at the mapping below, see if you think it generates interesting ideas that could lead to your writing a paper.

Young girls → Coming of Age
—play with Barbies
—wants candy and eye-liner
—Sunday movie

**Coming of Age Theme #1 =
Theme of Facing Moral Dilemmas**
—how to get doll clothes
can't afford
—stealing
—escaping Mr. Penny

Larger Moral Issues
—poverty
—stealing
—sexuality
**issues push them
closer to coming of age
and to adult world

**Coming of Age Theme #2 =
Theme of Expressing Desires/Wants**
—Barbies—Barbie clothes
—Cosmetics
—Movie
—**becoming more adult?

Desires not yet adult
—sexuality: dolls kissing
—cosmetics—make-up like adult
—movie: teenagers on dates

On verge of being adult
—knows adult world
—not part of adult world

Desires very female:
—sexuality, growing up
— ✗ the "consumer good" and
activities of growing up

**Theme of Adult World?
Larger Context**
—fire at toy factory
—Nixon, resignation
—gender-stereotyped movies
— ✗ Consumer goods part of this world

Mapping creates a *web of ideas* across all three texts. This student's mapping seems to be leading toward a thesis that emphasizes the theme of young girls coming of age, focusing on young girls facing a moral dilemma or an issue that pushes them closer to the adult world. This theme becomes more specific if, following the mapping, it emphasizes how girlish desires become more adult desires or how girlish desires are expressed through consumer goods. Using this mapping as a starting point for further synthesis, see if you can continue to make notes in a mapping format. Then, write an informal essay of 250–500 words that explains the ideas discovered by the sample mapping provided here and your own mapping.

Synthesis Using Form

Having emphasized theme, let's now turn to form—the arrangement, shape, and structure of the text—as a source of comparison and synthesis-based thinking. Form emphasizes *how* ideas are expressed by literature, not just *what* the ideas are. All good literary analysis and literary synthesis will include a discussion of form.

Let's read two poems that take specific formal shapes and thus encourage the reader to analyze form in addition to theme. Shakespeare's "Sonnet 18: Shall I Compare Thee to a Summer's Day?" takes the form of a sonnet, a fourteen-line poem that consists of three quatrains (a set of four rhymed lines) and a final couplet (a set of two rhymed lines), and uses iambic pentameter (a ten-syllable line, in which an unstressed syllable is followed by a stressed syllable). This sonnet rhyme scheme is noted as *abab, cdcd, efef, gg*. The sonnet structure organizes the flow of ideas though the poem and is thus important to recognize and analyze. Howard Moss's "Shall I Compare Thee to a Summer's Day?" provides a modern translation of the poem into contemporary English. Although it reworks Shakespeare's lines, the poem does not follow the sonnet form. It contains only thirteen lines and modifies the rhyme scheme. We can ask why Moss's poem references Shakepeare's sonnet form but ultimately does not use it. For example, Moss's poem quite literally "falls short" of Shakespeare's sonnet, containing one less line.

After reading these two poems, we can examine a sample student essay that uses form to connect the poems.

WILLIAM SHAKESPEARE

William Shakespeare (1564–1616), born in Stratford-upon-Avon in England, is chiefly known as a dramatic poet, but he also wrote nondramatic poetry. In 1609, a volume of 154 of his sonnets was published, apparently without his permission. Probably he chose to keep his sonnets unpublished, not because he thought that they were of little value, but because it was more prestigious to be an amateur (unpublished) poet than a professional (published) poet. Although the sonnets were published in 1609, they were probably written in the mid-1590s, when there was a vogue for sonneteering. A contemporary writer in 1598 said that Shakespeare's "sugared Sonnets [circulate] among his private friends."

Sonnet 18: Shall I Compare Thee to a Summer's Day?

Shall I compare thee to a summer's day?
Thou art more lovely and more temperate:
Rough winds do shake the darling buds of May,
And summer's lease hath all too short a date;
Sometime too hot the eye of heaven shines,   5
And often is his gold complexion dimm'd;
And every fair from fair sometime declines,
By chance or nature's changing course untrimm'd;
But thy eternal summer shall not fade,
Nor lose possession of that fair thou ow'st;   10
Nor shall death brag thou wander'st in his shade,
When in eternal lines to time thou grow'st:
So long as men can breathe or eyes can see,
So long lives this, and this gives life to thee.

[1609]

HOWARD MOSS

Howard Moss is best known for serving as the poetry editor at the New Yorker *magazine for over thirty-five years, an influential position that allowed him to publish many of the most important poets of the twentieth century. His editorial work nurtured the careers of writers that included Theodore Roethke, Anne Sexton, and Sylvia Plath. His own poetry earned him acclaim, with his* Selected Poems *being awarded a 1972 National Book Award. Known for their wit and intelligence, his poems show an evolution toward darker themes and a more fluid style over the course of his career.*

Shall I Compare Thee to a Summer's Day?

Who says you're like one of the dog days?
You're nicer. And better.
Even in May, the weather can be gray,
And a summer sub-let doesn't last forever.
Sometimes the sun's too hot;   5
Sometimes it is not.
Who can stay young forever?
People break their necks or just drop dead!
But you? Never!
If there's just one condensed reader left   10
Who can figure out the abridged alphabet,
After you're dead and gone,
In this poem you'll live on.

[1976]

Student Comparison Essay: "Condensing Shakespeare: A Comic Re-writing of a Shakespeare Sonnet"

Kathryn Werner, a student taking a composition course, wrote the following synthesis paper. Her paper compares the two poems by exploring issues of form and theme. In fact, concerns about form, such as the activity of abridging a literary text, becomes the main theme of the paper. Let's explore this paper and how it addresses issues of form, including language, structure, rhyme, and writing style.

Werner 1

Kathryn Werner

Professor Jones

English 102

23 October 2016

Condensing Shakespeare: A Comic Re-writing of a Shakespeare Sonnet

Howard Moss's "Shall I Compare Thee to a Summer's Day" is a comic re-writing of Shakespeare's "Shall I Compare Thee to a Summer's Day." A comparison of Shakespeare's sonnet to Moss's updating of it reveals just how much Moss has removed from Shakespeare's poem while still retaining much of its meaning. The humor of Moss's poem comes from this activity of making the original much shorter and more concise. In addition, Moss has also substituted comic words for Shakespeare's lofty language, translating Shakespeare's language into common, direct, and even crude phrases. Moss's poem also copies Shakespeare's themes and simplifies them while adding to them. Shakespeare's poem is about love and Moss gives us a comic version of that theme of love. However, Moss's poem is also a comic analysis of writing, specifically the act of shortening—or "abridging" or "condensing" (to use his words)—a text (10–11). Moss's poem is less about love and more about the activity of editing. Moss forces us to think about the act of abridging literature, and to question what can and cannot be changed in a poem before it loses its connection to the original.

Moss's first ten lines follow Shakespeare's sonnet, offering a line-by-line rewriting of the poem in short, modern English. If we focus on that rewriting, the theme of love remains crucial. However, lines 10–11 are key and reveal that Moss is exploring a second theme in his poem. Lines 10–11 read: "If there's just one condensed reader left / Who can figure out the abridged alphabet," and the poem continues to explain that if there is just this one reader left, the beloved will live on in the poem. These lines completely rewrite Shakespeare's poem. They are some of the longest lines in

the poem and contain the poem's most complex language, forcing the reader

to slow down and contemplate their meaning. These lines focus on the idea

of "condensing" and "abridging." They highlight what this poem is doing:

condensing and abridging Shakespeare. These lines ask us to focus on those

activities and think about how they work.

     In addition, these lines emphasize the reader and hint at the idea

that readers want condensed, shortened writing. Readers don't have the

energy or knowledge needed to figure out the complex language of

Shakespeare's sonnet. Today's readers, even more than when Moss was

writing his poem in 1976, want condensed language. In today's world of

texting and tweeting, who will find the time to read a complex poem like

Shakespeare's? Moss seems to be playing around with this idea, asking us to

think about the reader who will be able to figure out this poem. Will readers

prefer the condensed version? Will there always be readers who will know

that Moss's poem is not the original and re-writes a Shakespeare poem? Or, is

that knowledge in danger of being lost?

     With these ideas of annotation, condensing, and the reader's activity

in mind, we must go back to read the rest of the poem. The poem achieves

comedy by translating Shakespeare's evocative language into everyday

slang. Shakespeare's imagery is also reduced to a series of common images of

everyday life. Moss's poem seems to be making the point that simplifying

poetry makes it more common and everyday.

     Line-for-line, Moss follows and abridges Shakespeare's writing.

Shakespeare's poem opens with the line "Shall I compare thee to a summer's

day?" (1), which Moss re-writes as "Who says you're like one of the dog days?"

(1). Moss's first line makes it clear that he is writing an over-the-top comic

version of the original. The phrasing of "dog days" leaps off the page and emphasizes the idea of comparing a lover to the hottest days of summer. But, because the phrase also contains the word "dog," it hints at comparing the lover to a dog. Instead of creating the simile "my lover is like the summer," Moss creates the simile "my lover is like the summer" AND "my lover is like a dog"—an insulting idea! The first quatrain in Shakespeare's poem expands on this famous comparison between the beloved and a summer's day, proclaiming that the beloved is "more lovely and more temperate" (2). Moss translates this into the common phrasing "You're nicer. And better" (2). The downgrading of poetic language is exactly what makes Moss's poem humorous.

Shakespeare's second quatrain describes the failings of the natural world, failings which his lover does not have. When describing the sun, he writes that the "eye of heaven" can be "too hot" or can have its "gold complexion dimmed" (5–6). Moss condenses this into a straightforward line "Sometimes the sun's too hot;/Sometimes it is not" (5–6). The imagery of the "eye of heaven" and a "gold complexion" has been completely erased in favor of a straightforward statement. This condensed statement is true—of course, sometimes the sun is too hot and sometimes not—but it lacks beauty. When Shakespeare continues to explain that everyone's life must decline, Moss takes the idea of death and makes it comic, "People break their necks or just drop dead!" (8). Moss's poem removes beauty from a poem about a beautiful lover. Moss calls attention to the importance of poetic language by writing a poem that deletes it.

The third quatrain in each poem proclaims that the beloved will remain beautiful. Shakespeare writes, "thy eternal summer shall not fade" (9), while Moss exclaims, "But you? "Never!" (9). In Moss's abridgement, the line has become so short as to become almost meaningless. Not only is this line lacking poetic imagery, it also lacks a clear verb! The punctuation gives the line life, rather than the language. Each poem then explains that the beloved person will escape death by being written into the poem itself. The poem will preserve the beauty of the beloved, making it clear and accessible to future readers. While Shakespeare explains that his beloved "growest" in his "eternal lines" (12), Moss exclaims that he needs a "condensed reader" who can read the "abridged alphabet" of his poem (11). Moss has transformed "growing" into "condensing."

The form of Moss's sonnet calls attention to the act of condensing a text. While a typical Shakespearean sonnet has three quatrains totaling 12 lines, Moss's poem cuts the length of the sonnet short and gives the three quatrains only 11 lines. Immediately after he has stated that he needs a reader who can "figure out the abridged alphabet" (11). Moss makes an extreme abridgement to Shakespeare's sonnet: he cuts out an entire line. Moss calls attention to his "abridging" theme by acting out that theme in his sonnet's form.

Moss has not only abridged the sonnet, but has completely re-structured its form. Although he follows the "abab" rhyme scheme of the poem in the first couplet, throughout the rest of the sonnet he departs from that expected rhyme scheme. Perhaps he is making the point that if you abridge a sonnet enough, it stops being a sonnet. At what point does a poem stop being a poem?

The final couplet in Shakespeare's sonnet emphasizes that the beloved will live "So long as men can breathe or eyes can see," because his poem will "give life to thee" (13–14). Moss simplifies this idea into the lines "After you're dead and gone, In this poem you'll live on" (13). This captures the literal meaning of the poem, but it seems to miss what poetry is really about: capturing an image, creating a rich comparison, or evoking an emotion that will inspire future readers.

Moss calls attention to the act of abridging by condensing the sonnet's language, themes, and form. He questions that abridging by showing how much it can change a poem and how much it can even undermine the idea of poetry itself. In order for Moss's poem to be understood, he needs a reader who understands the original Shakespeare poem. The fun of Moss's poem is understanding the original and seeing how he has manipulated it. As a result, Moss really does need "one condensed reader" (10) who knows Shakespeare and knows how condensing works—he needs one reader who can "figure out" abridging in order for his poem to be understood. In this way, Moss's poem is about the reader and how the reader allows a poem to "live on." Moss's ideal reader would not be interested in just the beauty of a lover, but would be interested in thinking about what makes a sonnet a sonnet and what makes a sonnet, like Shakespeare's, live on throughout time. In this way, Moss offers a meaningful exploration of Shakespeare's ideas about the reader, and Moss makes them come alive in an unexpectedly fun and comic way.

[New page]

Works Cited

Moss, Howard. "Shall I Compare Thee to a Summer's Day?" *Literature for Composition*. Ed. Sylvan Barnet, William Burto, William E. Cain, and Cheryl L. Nixon. 11th ed. Boston: Pearson, 2017. 342. Print.

Shakespeare, William. "Shall I Compare Thee to a Summer's Day?" *Literature for Composition*. Ed. Sylvan Barnet, William Burto, William E. Cain, and Cheryl L. Nixon. 11th ed. Boston: Pearson, 2017. 342. Print.

✔ **CHECKLIST:** *Revising a Comparison*

☐ Is the comparison meaningful? Does this synthesis of two or more texts lead to the development of interesting conceptual ideas?
☐ Is the point of the comparison—the reason for making it—clear? Is the point stated in a thesis sentence?
☐ Does the comparison cover all significant similarities and differences?
☐ Is the comparison readable; that is, is it clear and yet not tediously mechanical?
☐ Is the organization used—perhaps treating one text first and then the other, or perhaps shifting back and forth between texts—the best way to make the comparison?
☐ Does the comparison feature specific evidence? Do you break down the evidence into short quotations? Do you explain your analysis of the evidence and use it to synthesize the texts?
☐ If the comparison offers a value judgment, is that judgment fair? Does the comparison offer enough evidence to bring a reader into at least partial agreement?
☐ Has the comparison been edited for correctness, using correct sentence structure, word choice, and grammar?

Your Turn: Additional Poems and Stories for Comparison and Synthesis

CARPE DIEM ("SEIZE THE DAY") POEMS

ROBERT HERRICK

Robert Herrick (1591–1674) was born in London, the son of a goldsmith. After taking a master's degree at Cambridge, he was ordained in the Church of England, and later he was sent to the country parish of Dean Prior in Devonshire, where he wrote most of his poetry. A loyal supporter of the king, he was expelled in 1647 from his parish by the Puritans, though in 1662 he was restored to Dean Prior.

To the Virgins, to Make Much of Time

Gather ye rosebuds while ye may,
   Old Time is still a-flying;
And this same flower that smiles today,
   Tomorrow will be dying.

The glorious lamp of heaven, the sun,   5
   The higher he's a-getting,
The sooner will his race be run,
   And nearer he's to setting.

That age is best which is the first,
   When youth and blood are warmer;   10

But being spent, the worse, and worst
   Times still succeed the former.

Then be not coy, but use your time;
   And while ye may, go marry;
For having lost but once your prime,   15
   You may for ever tarry.

[1648]

Joining the Conversation: Critical Thinking and Writing

1. Why did the poet write "rosebuds" rather than roses in the first line?
2. What sort of person seems to be speaking? Young or old? How do you know?
3. Doubtless this advice has something to commend it, but it is not the whole truth. Does the value of this poem depend on the soundness of its advice? Explain your answer.
4. Does the poem offer an argument? If so, how is the argument supported? Is it convincing? Explain your answer.

CHRISTOPHER MARLOWE

Christopher Marlowe (1564–93), English poet and playwright, was born in the same year as Shakespeare. An early death, in a tavern brawl, cut short what might have been a brilliant career.

Marlowe's "The Passionate Shepherd to His Love" is a pastoral poem; it depicts shepherds and shepherdesses in an idyllic, timeless setting. This poem engendered many imitations and replies, three of which we reprint after Marlowe's poem.

The Passionate Shepherd to His Love

Come live with me and be my love,
And we will all the pleasures prove,
That valleys, groves, hills, and fields,
Woods or steepy mountain yields.

There we will sit upon the rocks,   5
And see the shepherds feed their flocks,
By shallow rivers to whose falls
Melodious birds sing madrigals.

And I will make thee beds of roses
With a thousand fragrant posies,   10
A cap of flowers, and a kirtle
Embroidered all with leaves of myrtle;

A gown made of the finest wool
Which from our pretty lambs we pull;
Fair lined slippers for the cold,   15
With buckles of the purest gold;

A belt of straw and ivy buds,
With coral clasps and amber studs:
And if these pleasures may thee move,
Come live with me and be my love.   20

The shepherds' swains shall dance and sing
For thy delight each May morning:
If these delights thy mind may move,
Then live with me, and be my love.

[1599–1600]

Joining the Conversation: Critical Thinking and Writing

Read the poem two or three times, preferably aloud. Marlowe's poem is not to
be taken seriously as a picture of the pastoral (shepherd) life, but if you have
enjoyed the poem, exactly what have you enjoyed?

SIR WALTER RALEIGH

*Walter Raleigh (1552–1618) is known chiefly as a soldier and a colonizer—he was
the founder of the settlement in Virginia, and he introduced tobacco into Europe—
but, in his own day, he was known also as a poet.*

The Nymph's Reply to the Shepherd

If all the world and love were young,
And truth in every shepherd's tongue,
These pretty pleasures might me move,
To live with thee, and be thy love.

Time drives the flocks from field to fold,   5
When rivers rage, and rocks grow cold,
And Philomel° becometh dumb,
The rest complains of cares to come.

The flowers do fade, and wanton fields,
To wayward winter reckoning yields,   10
A honey tongue, a heart of gall,
Is fancy's spring, but sorrow's fall.

Thy gowns, thy shoes, thy beds of roses,
Thy cap, thy kirtle, and thy posies,
Soon break, soon wither, soon forgotten: 15
In folly ripe, in reason rotten.

Thy belt of straw and ivy buds,
Thy coral clasps and amber studs,
All these in me no means can move,
To come to thee, and be thy love.   20

But could youth last, and love still breed,
Had joys no date, nor age no need,
Then these delights my mind might move,
To live with thee and be thy love.

[c. 1600]

7 Philomel In Greek mythology, Philomela was a beautiful woman who was raped and later
transformed into a chattering sparrow, but, in most Roman versions, she is transformed into
the nightingale, noted for its beautiful song.

Joining the Conversation: Critical Thinking and Writing

1. What is the season in Marlowe's poem? What season(s) does Raleigh envision?
2. Some readers find puns in line 12, in "fancy's spring, but sorrow's fall." How do you paraphrase and interpret the line?
3. How would you describe the tone of the final stanza?
4. Now that you have read Raleigh's poem, reread Marlowe's poem. Do you now, in the context of Raleigh's poem, enjoy Marlowe's poem more than before, or less? Why? (You might think of it this way: Does Raleigh's refutation cause you to lose interest in Marlowe's poem?)

ANDREW MARVELL

Born in 1621 near Hull in England, Andrew Marvell attended Trinity College, Cambridge, and graduated in 1638. During the English Civil War (1642–1651), he was tutor to the daughter of Sir Thomas Fairfax in Yorkshire at Nun Appleton House, where most of his best-known poems were written. In 1657, he was appointed assistant to John Milton, the Latin Secretary for the Commonwealth. After the Restoration of the monarchy in 1659 until his death, Marvell represented Hull as a member of Parliament. Most of his poems were not published until after his death in 1678.

To His Coy Mistress

Had we but world enough, and time,
This coyness, lady, were no crime.
We would sit down, and think which way
To walk, and pass our long love's day.
Thou by the Indian Ganges' side   5
Should'st rubies find: I by the tide
Of Humber° would complain.° I would
Love you ten years before the Flood,
And you should, if you please, refuse
Till the conversion of the Jews.°   10
My vegetable° love should grow
Vaster than empires, and more slow.
An hundred years should go to praise
Thine eyes, and on thy forehead gaze:
Two hundred to adore each breast: 15
But thirty thousand to the rest.
An age at least to every part,
And the last age should show your heart.
For, lady, you deserve this state,
Nor would I love at lower rate,   20
     But at my back I always hear
Time's winged chariot hurrying near;
And yonder all before us lie

---

7 Humber river in England;   **complain** write love poems.   **10 conversion of the Jews** It was believed by Christians that the conversion of the Jews would occur just before the Last Judgment.   **11 vegetable** slowly growing.

Deserts of vast eternity.
Thy beauty shall no more be found,   25
Nor in thy marble vault shall sound
My echoing song; then worms shall try
That long preserved virginity,
And your quaint honor turn to dust,
And into ashes all my lust.   30
The grave's a fine and private place,
But none, I think, do there embrace.
    Now therefore, while the youthful hue
Sits on thy skin like morning dew,
And while thy willing soul transpires   35
At every pore with instant fires,
Now let us sport us while we may;
And now, like am'rous birds of prey,
Rather at once our time devour,
Than languish in his slow-chapt° power,   40
Let us roll all our strength, and all
Our sweetness, up into one ball;
And tear our pleasures with rough strife
Thorough° the iron gates of life.
Thus, though we cannot make our sun   45
Stand still, yet we will make him run.

[1641]

40 slow-chapt slowly devouring. **44 Thorough** through.

Joining the Conversation: Critical Thinking and Writing

1. What does "coy" mean in the title, and "coyness" in line 2?
2. Do you think that the speaker's claims in lines 1–20 are so inflated that we detect behind them a playfully ironic tone? Explain. Why does the speaker say in line 8 that he would love "ten years before the Flood," rather than merely "since the Flood"?
3. What do you make of lines 21–24? Why is time behind the speaker, and eternity in front of him? Is this "eternity" the same as the period discussed in lines 1–20? Discuss the change in the speaker's tone after line 20.

JOHN DONNE

John Donne (1572–1631) was born into a Roman Catholic family in England, but in the 1590s he abandoned that faith. In 1615 he became an Anglican priest and soon was known as a great preacher. One hundred sixty of his sermons survive, including one with the famous line "No man is an island, entire of itself; every man is a piece of the continent, a part of the main; if a clod be washed away by the sea, Europe is the less . . . and therefore never send to know for whom the bell tolls; it tolls for thee." From 1621 until his death Donne was dean of St. Paul's Cathedral in

*London. His love poems (often bawdy and cynical) are said to be his early work,
and his "Holy Sonnets" (among the greatest religious poems written in English) his
later work.*

The Bait

Come live with me, and be my love,
And we will some new pleasures prove
Of golden sands, and crystal brooks,
With silken lines, and silver hooks.

There will the river whispering run   5
Warmed by thy eyes, more than the Sun.
And there th'enamored fish will stay,
Begging themselves they may betray.

When thou wilt swim in that live bath,
Each fish, which every channel hath,   10
Will amorously to thee swim,
Gladder to catch thee, than thou him.

If thou, to be so seen, beest loath,
By Sun, or Moon, thou darknest both,
And if my self have leave to see,   15
I need not their light, having thee.

Let others freeze with angling reeds,
And cut their legs, with shells and weeds,
Or treacherously poor fish beset,
With strangling snare, or windowy net: 20

Let coarse bold hands, from slimy nest
The bedded fish in banks out-wrest,
Or curious traitors, sleavesilk flies
Bewitch poor fishes' wandring eyes.

For thee, thou needst no such deceit,   25
For thou thy self art thine own bait;
That fish, that is not catched thereby,
Alas, is wiser far than I.

[1633]

Joining the Conversation: Critical Thinking and Writing

1. In Donne's first stanza, which words especially indicate that we are (as in Marlowe's poem) in an idealized world?
2. Which words later in Donne's poem indicate what (for Donne) the real world of fishing is?
3. Paraphrase the last stanza, making it as clear as possible.

POEMS ABOUT BLACKBERRIES

GALWAY KINNELL

Pulitzer Prize–winning poet Galway Kinnell (1927–2014) is known for his explora-
tions of how personal philosophy and spirituality is rooted in the physical and social
world. His poetry often examines nature, and many of his most famous poems, such
as "The Bear," feature animals. His political poetry reflects his involvement in the
civil rights movement and his protests against the Vietnam War. Born in Provi-
dence, Rhode Island, Kinnell served in U.S. Navy, earned a BA from Princeton
University, and lived much of his adult life in Vermont.

Blackberry Eating

I love to go out in late September
among the fat, overripe, icy, black blackberries
to eat blackberries for breakfast,
the stalks very prickly, a penalty
they earn for knowing the black art   5
of blackberry-making; and as I stand among them
lifting the stalks to my mouth, the ripest berries
fall almost unbidden to my tongue,
as words sometimes do, certain peculiar words
like *strengths* and *squinched,*   10
many-lettered, on-syllabled lumps,
which I squeeze, squinch open, and splurge well
in the silent, startled, icy, black language
of blackberry-eating in late September.

[1980]

Joining the Conversation: Critical Thinking and Writing

---

1. Central to this poem is the comparison between blackberry eating and the
   inspiration of finding specific words when writing. How does the poem
   make this comparison? What specifically is being compared to blackberries?
   How is the physical body involved in both blackberry eating and locating
   words?
2. Examine the language used by the poem. Annotate the poem, noting how certain words are repeated. For example, how are the words "ripe," "icy," "squinch,"
   and "black" repeated? How does the poem capture the taste of blackberries?
   How does it capture the action in writing?
3. The poem contains the interesting phrases "black art" and "blank language."
   What do these phrases mean within the context of the poem?
4. Before moving on to other poems about blackberries, write a short response to
   this poem. What is the emotional content of the poem? What are the thematic
   issues central to the poem? After your understanding of Kinnell's poem is in
   place, turn to other poems in this section and work toward making meaningful
   comparisons among them, using the questions that follow each poem.

Sylvia Plath

Sylvia Plath (1932–63) was born in Boston, the daughter of German immigrants. While still an undergraduate at Smith College, she published in Seventeen *and* Mademoiselle *magazines, but her years at college, like her later years, were marked by manic-depressive periods. She details these difficulties in her semi-autobiographical novel,* The Bell Jar *(1963). After graduating from college, she went to England to study at Cambridge University, where she met the English poet Ted Hughes, whom she married in 1956. The marriage was unsuccessful, and they separated after having two children. She committed suicide at the age of thirty while living in London.*

Blackberrying

Nobody in the lane, and nothing, nothing but blackberries,
Blackberries on either side, though on the right mainly,
A blackberry alley, going down in hooks, and a sea
Somewhere at the end of it, heaving. Blackberries
Big as the ball of my thumb, and dumb as eyes   5
Ebon in the hedges, fat
With blue-red juices. These they squander on my fingers.
I had not asked for such a blood sisterhood; they must love me.
They accommodate themselves to my milkbottle, flattening their
    sides.

Overhead go the choughs in black, cacophonous flocks—   10
Bits of burnt paper wheeling in a blown sky.
Theirs is the only voice, protesting, protesting.
I do not think the sea will appear at all.
The high, green meadows are glowing, as if lit from within.
I come to one bush of berries so ripe it is a bush of flies,   15
Hanging their bluegreen bellies and their wing panes in a
    Chinese screen.
The honey-feast of the berries has stunned them; they believe in
    heaven.
One more hook, and the berries and bushes end.

The only thing to come now is the sea.
From between two hills a sudden wind funnels at me,   20
Slapping its phantom laundry in my face.°
These hills are too green and sweet to have tasted salt.
I follow the sheep path between them. A last hook brings me
To the hills' northern face, and the face is orange rock
That looks out on nothing, nothing but a great space   25
Of white and pewter lights, and a din like silversmiths
Beating and beating at an intractable metal.

                                 [1960]

21 Note: The third line of the third stanza has been corrected to read "Slapping its phantom laundry in my face" instead of "Grapping its phantom laundry in my face." [2/23/11].

Joining the Conversation: Critical Thinking and Writing

1. Plath's poem describes a walk along a lane filled with blackberries. Take notes on that walk, asking inquiry questions of each stanza. For example, how does the first stanza describe her interaction with the blackberries? What does she do with them? In the second stanza, what is up in the sky? What new sense does she introduce? In the third stanza, what is Plath's destination? What does she ultimately see, and how does she describe it? For each stanza, add to these inquiry questions and form answers for your questions.
2. What lines leap out at you that contain interesting words, phrases, images, or emotions? For example, consider the image of the wind "slapping its phantom laundry in my face." What lines catch your eye and ear? Why?
3. How would you characterize the speaker's motivations? Is the poem about the enjoyment of nature, or is it about the desire to reach a destination? What ideas or emotions motivate the speaker?
4. Compare this poem to Galway Kinnell's "Blackberry Eating." How does each poet describe picking blackberries? In each poem, do the blackberries seem excessive, such as being "overripe" in Kinnell's poem and a "honey-feast" in Plath's poem? How do blackberries connect the poems' speakers to nature? How do the blackberries connect to a larger quest or purpose on the part of the speaker?

Seamus Heaney

Seamus Heaney (1939–2013) was born in Belfast, Northern Ireland. He grew up on a farm and then went to Queens University in Belfast. Heaney lectured widely in Ireland, England, and the United States. He taught at Harvard (1985–2006) and was Regius Professor of Poetry at Oxford, a post that was held by Matthew Arnold and W. H. Auden. In addition to writing poetry, he wrote essays about poetry. In 1995, he was awarded the Nobel Prize in Literature. "Digging," the first poem in his first book, reveals his concern with getting to the bottom of things.

Blackberry-Picking

Late August, given heavy rain and sun
For a full week, the blackberries would ripen.
At first, just one, a glossy purple clot
Among others, red, green, hard as a knot.
You ate that first one and its flesh was sweet   5
Like thickened wine: summer's blood was in it
Leaving stains upon the tongue and lust for
Picking. Then red ones inked up and that hunger
Sent us out with milk cans, pea tins, jam-pots
Where briars scratched and wet grass bleached our boots.   10
Round hayfields, cornfields and potato-drills
We trekked and picked until the cans were full,
Until the tinkling bottom had been covered
With green ones, and on top big dark blobs burned
Like a plate of eyes. Our hands were peppered   15
With thorn pricks, our palms sticky as Bluebeard's.

We hoarded the fresh berries in the byre.
But when the bath was filled we found a fur,

A rat-grey fungus, glutting on our cache.
The juice was stinking too. Once off the bush 20
The fruit fermented, the sweet flesh would turn sour.
I always felt like crying. It wasn't fair
That all the lovely canfuls smelt of rot.
Each year I hoped they'd keep, knew they would not.

[1966]

Joining the Conversation: Critical Thinking and Writing

1. In the first stanza, how does Heaney capture the physical pleasures of black-berry picking? How does Heaney's language compare to Kinnell's and his description of "fat, overripe, icy" berries that fall onto his tongue? How does Heaney's language compare to Plath's description of berries that are "fat/with blue-red juices" and are part of a "blood sisterhood"? What sensory images does each poet use? What colors does each poet use? Are there any words or images that create a concept bridge between two or more of these poems?

2. In the first stanza, how does Heaney explain the "lust for picking"? Annotate the poem, making sure to highlight the phrases that convey that lust. What triggers that lust? How is that lust expressed in the collecting of berries, such as the types of cans used or the places visited to collect the berries?

3. What happens in the second stanza? Where are the berries hidden? What happens to them? What is the "fur" that the speaker finds?

4. With the outcome described in the second stanza, is Heaney encouraging us to think about human motivations, hopes, dreams, or failures? Is Heaney trying to impart a larger lesson?

5. How does this poem's ending compare to the ending of Kinnell's, Plath's, and (as the next poem in the series) Komunyakka's poems? Write a short analytical essay that compares the ending of two (or more) of these poems, creating an argument about how each ending explores a conceptual issue represented by the blackberries rather than the blackberries themselves.

YUSEF KOMUNYAKAA

Yusef Komunyakaa was born in 1947 in Bogalusa, Louisiana. After graduating from high school, he entered the army and served in Vietnam, where he was awarded the Bronze Star. On his return to the United States, he earned a BA at the University of Colorado and then an MA at Colorado State University and an MFA in creative writing at the University of California, Irvine. The author of several books of poetry, Komunyakaa teaches at New York University.

Blackberries

They left my hands like a printer's
Or thief's before a police blotter
& pulled me into early morning's
Terrestrial sweetness, so thick
The damp ground was consecrated 5
Where they fell among a garland of thorns.

Although I could smell old lime-covered
History, at ten I'd still hold out my hands
& berries fell into them. Eating from one
& filling a half gallon with the other,   10
I ate the mythology & dreamt
Of pies & cobbler, almost

Needful as forgiveness. My bird dog Spot
Eyed blue jays & thrashers. The mud frogs
In rich blackness, hid from daylight.   15
An hour later, beside City Limits Road
I balanced a gleaming can in each hand,
Limboed between worlds, repeating one dollar.

The big blue car made me sweat.
Wintertime crawled out of the windows.   20
When I leaned closer I saw the boy
& girl my age, in the wide back seat
Smirking, & it was then I remembered my fingers
Burning with thorns among berries too ripe to touch.

[1992]

Joining the Conversation: Critical Thinking and Writing

1. Like the poems by Kinnell, Plath, and Heaney, Komunyakaa's poem conveys the excitement of finding and eating berries. Annotate Komunyakaa's poem, circling and underlining key words and exploring how he uses language to describe the berries. How are his images similar to, or different from, the images used by the three other poets? What images can you use to create a concept bridge that connects these poems?
2. How does Komunyakaa describe the sweetness of the berries and the painful sting of their thorns? Why is something that is both sweet and painful a perfect object for exploring the speaker's maturation or coming of age? Do Kinnell, Plath, and Heaney also describe the undesirable thorns of the desirable berries? Compare and contrast each poem's exploration of the blackberries' thorns.
3. What does the speaker hope to do with his can of berries? Why is the speaker "repeating one dollar"? Why is the speaker "limboed between worlds"?
4. Read and reread the last stanza, and then write an explication of these final lines. Work your way through each line of the poem, explaining its meaning and noting how the poem's formal elements create that meaning. What event takes place? What ideas and emotions does this event trigger in the speaker? Why is this moment meaningful to the speaker?

POEMS ABOUT AMERICA

WALT WHITMAN

Walt Whitman (1819–92) was born on Long Island, New York, the son of a farmer. The young Whitman taught school and worked as a carpenter, a printer, a newspaper editor, and, during the Civil War, as a volunteer nurse on the Union side. After the war, he supported himself by doing secretarial jobs. In Whitman's own day, his poetry was highly controversial because of its unusual form (formlessness, many people said) and its often erotic implications.

I Hear America Singing

I hear America singing, the varied carols I hear,
Those of mechanics, each one singing his as it should be blithe
    and strong,
The carpenter singing his as he measures his plank or beam,
The mason singing his as he makes ready for work, or leaves off
    work,
The boatman singing what belongs to him in his boat, the   5
    deckhand singing on the steamboat deck,
The shoemaker singing as he sits on his bench, the hatter
    singing as he stands,
The wood-cutter's song, the ploughboy's on his way in the
    morning, or at noon intermission or at sundown,
The delicious singing of the mother, or of the young wife at
    work, or of the girl sewing or washing,
Each singing what belongs to him or her and to none else,
The day what belongs to the day—at night the party of young   10
    fellows, robust, friendly,
Singing with open mouths their strong melodious songs.

[1860; rev. 1867]

Joining the Conversation: Critical Thinking and Writing

1. What is Whitman doing in this poem?
2. How are the workers to whom Whitman refers similar to one another? How are they different?
3. Does Whitman's poem speak to us today? Explain why it does or does not.
4. Please write your own version of Whitman's poem, with your own choice of representative workers.

LANGSTON HUGHES

Langston Hughes (1902–67) was born in Joplin, Missouri. He lived part of his youth in Mexico, spent a year at Columbia University, served as a merchant seaman, and worked in a Paris nightclub, where he showed some of his poems to Alain Locke, a strong advocate of African American literature. After returning to the United States, Hughes went on to publish poetry, fiction, plays, essays, and biographies.

I, Too [Sing America]

I, too, sing America.

I am the darker brother.
They send me to eat in the kitchen

When company comes,
But I laugh,   5
And eat well,
And grow strong.

Tomorrow,
I'll be at the table
When company comes.   10
Nobody'll dare
Say to me,
"Eat in the kitchen,"
Then.

Besides,   15
They'll see how beautiful I am
And be ashamed—

I, too, am America.

[1926]

Joining the Conversation: Critical Thinking and Writing

1. How is this poem an answer to, or continuation of, Walt Whitman's "I Hear America Singing." At first these poems appear to be very different. How can you synthesize them? How does the Hughes poem bring race into the Whitman poem? Can the poems be compared in terms of both form and content? How do the poems connect? How do they *not* connect?
2. The activity of eating in the kitchen or at a table provides the poem with its central images. What does it mean to "eat in the kitchen"? What does it mean to eat "at the table"?
3. After reading Whitman's "I Hear America Singing," return to Hughes's "I, Too, [Sing America]." Can you ask new inquiry questions of Hughes's poem after reading Whitman's poem? For example, why does Hughes's speaker state that he sings America but then does not describe himself singing? In contrast, Whitman's poem describes many acts of singing. Continue to ask questions that compare the two poems. What other new insights can a comparison of the two poems generate?
4. Compare the first and last lines of the poem. What crucial change has been made? How does this change shift the meaning of the line and of the entire poem?

STORIES ABOUT READING AND WRITING

JULIO CORTÁZAR

In 1951, novelist and short-story writer Julio Cortázar left his native Argentina because of his disillusionment with its political leadership and class structure. Although Cortázar traveled widely, he settled in Paris and died there in 1984. His fiction is known for its experimental style, abstract and surreal ideas, and playful questioning of human existence. His 1963 novel, Rayuela (Hopscotch), *allows the reader to rearrange its parts, demonstrating Cortázar's interest in rethinking the meaning, structure, and purpose of storytelling. "The Continuity of Parks" plays with the trajectory of time and space, creating a sense of vertigo in the reader.*

The Continuity of Parks

He had begun to read the novel a few days before. He had put it aside because of some urgent business, opened it again on his way back to the estate by train; he allowed himself a slowly growing interest in the plot, in the drawing of characters. That afternoon, after writing a letter to his agent and discussing with the manager of his estate a matter of joint ownership, he returned to the book in the tranquility of his study which looked out upon the park with its oaks. Sprawled in his favorite armchair, with his back to the door, which would otherwise have bothered him as an irritating possibility for intrusions, he let his left hand caress once and again the green velvet upholstery and set to reading the final chapters. Without effort his memory retained the names and images of the protagonists; the illusion took hold of him almost at once. He tasted the almost perverse pleasure of disengaging himself line by line from all that surrounded him, and feeling at the same time that his head was relaxing comfortably against the green velvet of the armchair with its high back, that the cigarettes were still within reach of his hand, that beyond the great windows the afternoon air danced under the oak trees in the park. Word by word, immersed in the sordid dilemma of the hero and heroine, letting himself go toward where the images came together and took on color and movement, he was witness to the final encounter in the mountain cabin. The woman arrived first, apprehensive; now the lover came in, his face cut by the backlash of a branch. Admirably she stanched the blood with her kisses, but he rebuffed her caresses, he had not come to repeat the ceremonies of a secret passion, protected by a world of dry leaves and furtive paths through the forest. The dagger warmed itself against his chest, and underneath pounded liberty, ready to spring. A lustful, yearning dialogue raced down the pages like a rivulet of snakes, and one felt it had all been decided from eternity. Even those caresses which writhed about the lover's body, as though wishing to keep him there, to dissuade him from it, sketched abominably the figure of that other body it was necessary to destroy. Nothing had been forgotten: alibis, unforeseen hazards, possible mistakes. From this hour on, each instant had its use minutely assigned. The cold-blooded, double re-examination of the details was barely interrupted for a hand to caress a cheek. It was beginning to get dark.

Without looking at each other now, rigidly fixed upon the task which awaited them, they separated at the cabin door. She was to follow the trail that led north. On the path leading in the opposite direction, he turned for a moment to watch her running with her hair let loose. He ran in turn, crouching among the trees and hedges until he could distinguish in the yellowish fog of dusk the avenue of trees leading up to the house. The dogs were not supposed to bark, and they did not bark. The estate manager would not be there at this hour, and he was not. He went up the three porch steps and entered. Through the blood galloping in his ears came the woman's words: first a blue parlor, then a gallery, then a carpeted stairway. At the top, two doors. No one in the first bedroom, no one in the second. The door of the salon, and then the knife in his hand, the light from the great windows, the high back of an armchair covered in green velvet, the head of the man in the chair reading a novel.

[1967]

Joining the Conversation: Critical Thinking and Writing

1. Why does Cortázar not name his characters? What is the effect of not using names?
2. What is the man's situation? Reread the story closely, working to determine when you realize the man is reading. At what point does the story shift from the man's perspective to his reading? Are they ever separated?
3. What is the situation of the lovers? Are they in the man's novel, or are they real? Is the knife at the end part of the story, or is it real? Write an essay that makes an argument and defends your interpretation. Use quotations from the text to support your ideas.
4. How does this story fit the definition of "metafiction"? Write an essay that defines this term and then applies it to "The Continuity of Parks" and "Things You Should Know," the next story under consideration. In your opinion, which story provides the better example of metafiction?

A. M. HOMES

An award-winning fiction writer, essayist, and television writer and producer, A. M. (Amy Michael) Homes is known for creating extreme characters and imagining extreme acts, such as murder and arson. She explores the pressures of the American dream—having the perfect family and possessions—in darkly comic novels such as May We Be Forgiven *(2013) and* Music for Torching *(2000). Born in 1962, Homes was adopted at birth by a Maryland family and later reunited with her birth mother, an experience she details in her memoir* The Mistress's Daughter *(2007).*

Things You Should Know

There are things I do not know. I was absent the day they passed out the information sheets. I was home in bed with a fever and an earache. I lay with the heating pad pressed to my head, burning my ear. I lay with the heating pad until my mother came in and said, "Don't keep it on high or you'll burn yourself." This was something I knew but chose to forget.

The information sheets had the words "Things You Should Know" typed across the top of the page. They were mimeographed pages, purple ink on white paper. The sheets were written by my fourth-grade teacher. They were written when she was young and thought about things. She thought of a language for these things and wrote them down in red Magic Marker.

By the time she was my teacher, she'd been teaching for a very long time but had never gotten past fourth grade. She had'nt done anything since her Things You Should Know sheets, which didn't really count, since she'd written them while she was still a student.

After my ear got better, the infection cured, the red burn mark faded into a sort of a Florida tan, I went back to school. Right away I knew I'd missed something important. "Ask the other students to fill you in on what happened while you were ill," the principal said when I handed her the note from my mother. But none of the others would talk to me. Immediately I knew this was because they'd gotten the information sheets and we no longer spoke the same language.

5   I tried asking the teacher, "Is there anything I missed while I was out?" She handed me a stack of maps to color in and some math problems. "You should put a little Vaseline on your ear," she said. "It'll keep it from peeling."

"Is there anything else?" I asked. She shook her head.

I couldn't just come out and say it. I could'nt say, You know, those information sheets, the ones you passed out the other day while I was home burning my ear. Do you have an extra copy? I could'nt ask because I'd already asked everyone. I asked so many people—my parents, their friends, random strangers—that in the end they sent me to a psychiatrist.

"What exactly do you think is written on this 'Things to Know' paper?" he asked me.

"'Things You Should Know,'" I said. 'It's not things to know not things you will learn, but things you already should know but maybe are a little dumb, so you don't."

10   "Yes," he said, nodding. "And what are those things?"

"You're asking me?" I shouted. "I don't know. You're the one who should know. You tell me. I never saw the list."

Time passed. I grew up. I grew older. I grew deaf in one ear. In the newspaper I read that the teacher had died. She was eighty-four. In time I began to notice there was less to know. All the same, I kept looking for the list. Once, in an old bookstore, I thought I found page four. It was old, faded, folded into quarters and stuffed into an early volume of Henry Miller's essays. The top part of the page had been torn off. It began with number six: "Do what you will because you will anyway" Number twenty-eight was: "If you begin and it is not the beginning, begin again." And so on. At the bottom of the page it said, "Chin San Fortune Company lines 1 through 32."

Years later, when I was even older, when those younger than me seemed to know less than I ever had, I wrote a story. And in a room full of people, full of people who knew the list and some who I was sure did not, I stood to read. "As a child, I burned my ear into a Florida tan."

"Stop," a man yelled, waving his hands at me.

15   "Why?"

"Don't you know?" he said. I shook my head. He was a man who knew the list, who probably had his own personal copy. He had based his life on it, on trying to explain it to others.

He spoke, he drew diagrams, splintering poles of chalk as he put pictures on a blackboard. He tried to tell of the things he knew. He tried to talk but did not have the language of the teacher.

I breathed deeply and thought of Chin San number twenty-eight. "If you begin and it is not the beginning, begin again."

"I will begin again," I announced. Because I had stated this and had not asked for a second chance, because I was standing and he was seated, because it was still early in the evening, the man who had stopped me nodded, all right.

20   "Things You Should Know," I said.

"Good title, good title," the man said. "Go on, go on."

"There is a list," I said, nearing the end. "It is a list you make yourself. And at the top of the page you write, 'Things You Should Know.'"

[1998]

Joining the Conversation: Critical Thinking and Writing

1. How is this a story about reading? Compare the character of the reader in "The Continuity of Parks" to the character of the reader in "Things You Should Know." Are there any similarities?
2. Explain the premise of this story. The story's speaker believes that a paper labeled "Things You Should Know" has been circulated by her fourth-grade teacher. Explain this paper. Why is it so important to the reader? What sort of fantasy does this story feed into? For example, do we all wish that we were given a set of life instructions? What is the author's stance in the story toward this type of wish?
3. What details in this story strike you as interesting or funny? Select a detail, and write inquiry questions about it. How can you open up a seemingly small detail to larger meanings? For example, what do you make of the speaker's burnt ear? What does the "Chin San Fortune Company" paper represent?
4. What does this story suggest about the human search for meaning? Reread the last subsection of the story, and examine the last sentences closely. What are the wise sayings that the speaker is able to use?
5. How does both "The Continuity of Parks" and "Things You Should Know" explore confusion between fantasy and reality? How does each short story comment on the power of fiction over our real lives?

STORIES ABOUT GRANDMOTHERS

LAN SAMANTHA CHANG

Born in 1965 in Wisconsin to parents who emigrated from China, Lan Samantha Chang's fiction memorializes her Chinese ancestry. She earned a BA from Yale University, an MA from Harvard University, and an MFA from the University of Iowa. She currently works as the director of the prestigious Iowa Writers' Workshop. Her publications include two novels, Inheritance *(2004) and* All Is Forgotten, Nothing Is Lost *(2010), and the collection* Hunger: A Novella and Stories *(1998). In addition to being awarded a Guggenheim Fellowship, Chang has been honored as a recipient of the PEN Beyond Margins Award (now known as the Open Book Award).*

Water Names

Summertime at dusk we'd gather on the back porch, tired and sticky from another day of fierce encoded quarrels, nursing our mosquito bites and frail dignities, sisters in name only. At first we'd pinch and slap each other, fighting for the best—least ragged—folding chair. Then we'd argue over who would sit next to our grandmother. We were so close together on the tiny porch that we often pulled our own hair by mistake. Forbidden to bite, we planted silent toothmarks on each other's wrists. We ignored the bulk of house behind us, the yard, the fields, the darkening sky. We even forgot about our grandmother. Then suddenly we'd hear her old, dry voice, very close, almost on the backs of our necks.

"*Xiushilala*! Shame on you. Fighting like a bunch of chickens."

And Ingrid, the oldest, would freeze with her thumb and forefinger right on the back of Lily's arm. I would slide my hand away from the end of Ingrid's braid. Ashamed, we would shuffle our feet while Waipuo calmly found her chair.

On some nights she sat with us in silence, the tip of her cigarette glowing red like a distant stoplight. But on some nights she told us stories, "just to keep your Chinese," she said, and the red dot flickered and danced, making ghostly shapes as she moved her hands like a magician in the dark.

5   "In these prairie crickets I often hear the sound of rippling waters, of the Yangtze River," she said. "Granddaughters, you are descended on both sides from people of the water country, near the mouth of the great Chang Jiang, as it is called, where the river is so grand and broad that even on clear days you can scarcely see the other side.

"The Chang Jiang runs four thousand miles, originating in the Himalaya mountains where it crashes, flecked with gold dust, down steep cliffs so perilous and remote that few humans have ever seen them. In central China, the river squeezes through deep gorges, then widens in its last thousand miles to the sea. Our ancestors have lived near the mouth of the river, the ever-changing delta, near a city called Nanjing, for more than a thousand years."

"A thousand years," murmured Lily, who was only ten. When she was younger she had sometimes burst into nervous crying at the thought of so many years. Her small insistent fingers grabbed my fingers in the dark.

"Through your mother and I you are descended from a line of great men and women. We have survived countless floods and seasons of ill-fortune because we have the spirit of the river in us. Unlike mountains, we cannot be powdered down or broken apart. Instead, we run together, like raindrops. Our strength and spirit wear down mountains into sand. But even our people must respect the water."

She paused, and a bit of ash glowed briefly as it drifted to the floor.

10   "When I was young, my own grandmother once told me the story of Wen Zhiqing's daughter. Twelve hundred years ago the civilized parts of China still lay to the north, and the Yangtze valley lay unspoiled. In those days lived an ancestor named Wen Zhiqing, a resourceful man, and proud. He had been fishing for many years with trained cormorants, which you girls of course have never seen. Cormorants are sleek, black birds with long, bending necks which the fisherman fitted with metal rings so the fish they caught could not be swallowed. The birds would perch on the side of the old wooden boat and dive into the river." We had only known blue swimming pools, but we tried to imagine the sudden shock of cold and the plunge, deep into water.

"Now, Wen Zhiqing had a favorite daughter who was very beautiful and loved the river. She would beg to go out on the boat with him. This daughter was a restless one, never contented with their catch and often she insisted they stay out until it was almost dark. Even then, she was not satisfied. She had been spoiled by her father, kept protected from the river, so she could not see its danger. To this young woman, the river was familiar as the sky. It was a bright, broad road stretching out to curious lands. She did not fully understand the river's depth.

"One clear spring evening, as she watched the last bird dive off into the blackening waters, she said, 'If only this catch would bring back something more than another fish!'

"She leaned over the side of the boat and looked at the water. The stars and moon reflected back at her. And it is said that the spirits living underneath the water looked up at her as well. And the spirit of a young man who had drowned in the river many years before saw her lovely face."

We had heard about the ghosts of the drowned, who wait forever in the water for a living person to pull down instead. A faint breeze moved through the mosquito screens and we shivered.

15   "The cormorant was gone for a very long time," Waipuo said, "so long that the fisherman grew puzzled. Then, suddenly, the bird emerged from the waters, almost invisible in the night. Wen Zhiqing grasped his catch, a very large fish, and guided the boat back to shore. And when Wen reached home, he gutted the fish, and discovered, in its stomach, a valuable pearl ring."

"From the man?" said Lily.

"Sshh, she'll tell you."

Waipuo ignored us. "His daughter was delighted that her wish had been fulfilled. What most excited her was the idea of an entire world like this, a world where such a beautiful ring would be only a bauble! For part of her had always longed to see faraway things and places. The river had put a spell on her heart. In the evenings she began to sit on the bank, looking at her own reflection in the water. Sometimes she said she saw a handsome young man looking back at her. And her yearning for him filled her heart with sorrow and fear, for she knew that she would soon leave her beloved family.

"'It's just the moon,' said Wen Zhiqing, but his daughter shook her head. 'There's a kingdom under the water,' she said. 'The prince is asking me to marry him. He sent the ring as an offering to you.' 'Nonsense,' said her father, and he forbade her to sit by the water again.

20   "For a year things went as usual, but the next spring there came a terrible flood that swept away almost everything. In the middle of a torrential rain, the family noticed that the daughter was missing. She had taken advantage of the confusion to hurry to the river and visit her beloved. The family searched for days but they never found her."

Her smoky, rattling voice came to a stop.

"What happened to her?" Lily said.

"It's okay, stupid," I told her. "She was so beautiful that she went to join the kingdom of her beloved. Right?"

"Who knows?" Waipuo said. "They say she was seduced by a water ghost. Or perhaps she lost her mind to desiring."

25   "What do you mean?" asked Ingrid.

"I'm going inside," Waipuo said, and got out of her chair with a creak. A moment later the light went on in her bedroom window. We knew she stood before the mirror, combing out her long, wavy silver-gray hair, and we imagined that in her youth she too had been beautiful.

We sat together without talking, breathing our dreams in the lingering smoke. We had gotten used to Waipuo's abruptness, her habit of creating a question and leaving without answering it, as if she were disappointed in the question itself. We tried to imagine Wen Zhiqing's daughter. What did she look like? How old was she? Why hadn't anyone remembered her name?

While we weren't watching, the stars had emerged. Their brilliant pinpoints mapped the heavens. They glittered over us, over Waipuo in her room, the house, and the small city we lived in, the great waves of grass that ran for miles around us, the ground beneath as dry and hard as bone.

[1998]

Joining the Conversation: Critical Thinking and Writing

1. Compare this story to the "Jilting of Granny Weatherall" by Katherine Anne Porter that follows. Although these two stories are very different, each contains an elderly woman as its main character. Write an essay that compares these two characters, the stories they tell, and the effect that their stories have on the reader. What is the story that each grandmother tells, either aloud or in her head? How does each story explore big questions such as love and death? What is left unresolved in each story? How—and why—do you, the reader, have to guess at the meaning of each story?

2. What is the setting of "Water Names"? What is the setting of the grandmother's story? Are there any connections between the two settings?

3. How do the girls act toward their grandmother, Waipuo? Use annotations to trace the girls' actions and emotions. How do they act before the story is told? How do they act when the grandmother is telling the story? What do they do after the story is told?

4. Engage in a close reading of the description of the ring found in the fish and the beautiful daughter's interpretation of the ring. Why does the ring trigger a fantasy? What imaginative thinking does it encourage? What does it mean that "What excited her most was the idea of an entire world like this, a world where such a beautiful ring would be only a bauble"?

5. Write a response essay that explores what happened to the young girl. Did she drown? Did she run away? Could the story have a supernatural ending—could she have joined her beloved? Waipuo says that the young girl "was seduced by a water ghost" or "perhaps she lost her mind desiring." How do you interpret this ending?

6. Why does Waipuo not answer the question, "what do you mean?" at the end of the story? Imagine two different ways that Waipuo could answer this question. Write down these answers as if they were spoken by Waipuo.

KATHERINE ANNE PORTER

Katherine Anne Porter (1890–1980) had the curious habit of inventing details in her life, but it is true that she was born in a log cabin in Indian Creek, Texas, that she was originally named Callie Russell Porter, that her mother died when Callie was two years old, and that Callie was brought up by her maternal grandmother in Kyle, Texas. She was sent to convent schools, where, in her words, she received a "strangely useless and ornamental education." When she was sixteen years old, she left school, married (and soon divorced), and worked as a reporter, first in Texas and later in Denver and Chicago. She moved around a good deal, both within the United States and abroad; she lived for a while in Mexico, Belgium, Switzerland, France, and Germany.

Even as a child, she was interested in writing, but she did not publish her first story until she was thirty-three years old. She wrote essays and one novel (Ship of Fools), *but she is best known for her stories. Porter's* Collected Stories *won the Pulitzer Prize and the National Book Award in 1965.*

The Jilting of Granny Weatherall

She flicked her wrist neatly out of Doctor Harry's pudgy careful fingers and pulled the sheet up to her chin. The brat ought to be in knee breeches. Doctoring around the country with spectacles on his nose! "Get along now, take your schoolbooks and go. There's nothing wrong with me."

Doctor Harry spread a warm paw like a cushion on her forehead where the forked green vein danced and made her eyelids twitch. "Now, now, be a good girl, and we'll have you up in no time."

"That's no way to speak to a woman nearly eighty years old just because she's down. I'd have you respect your elders, young man."

"Well, Missy, excuse me." Doctor Harry patted her cheek. "But I've got to warn you, haven't I? You're a marvel, but you must be careful or you're going to be good and sorry."

5   "Don't tell me what I'm going to be. I'm on my feet now, morally speaking. It's Cornelia. I had to go to bed to get rid of her."

Her bones felt loose, and floated around in her skin, and Doctor Harry floated like a balloon around the foot of the bed. He floated and pulled down his waistcoat and swung his glasses on a cord. "Well, stay where you are, it certainly can't hurt you."

"Get along and doctor your sick," said Granny Weatherall. "Leave a well woman alone. I'll call for you when I want you. . . . Where were you forty years ago when I pulled through milk-leg and double pneumonia? You weren't even born. Don't let Cornelia lead you on," she shouted, because Doctor Harry appeared to float up to the ceiling and out. "I pay my own bills, and I don't throw my money away on nonsense!"

She meant to wave good-by, but it was too much trouble. Her eyes closed of themselves, it was like a dark curtain drawn around the bed. The pillow rose and floated under her, pleasant as a hammock in a light wind. She listened to the leaves rustling outside the window. No, somebody was swishing newspapers: no, Cornelia and Doctor Harry were whispering together. She leaped broad awake, thinking they whispered in her ear.

"She was *never* like this, never like this!" "Well, what can we expect?" "Yes, eighty years old. . . ."

10   Well, and what if she was? She still had ears. It was like Cornelia to whisper around doors. She always kept things secret in such a public way. She was always being tactful and kind. Cornelia was dutiful; that was the trouble with her. Dutiful and good: "So good and dutiful," said Granny, "that I'd like to spank her." She saw herself spanking Cornelia and making a fine job of it.

"What'd you say, Mother?"

Granny felt her face tying up in hard knots.

"Can't a body think, I'd like to know?"

"I thought you might want something."

15   "I do. I want a lot of things. First off, go away and don't whisper."

She lay and drowsed, hoping in her sleep that the children would keep out and let her rest a minute. It had been a long day. Not that she was tired. It was always pleasant to snatch a minute now and then. There was always so much to be done, let me see: tomorrow.

Tomorrow was far away and there was nothing to trouble about. Things were finished somehow when the time came; thank God there was always a little margin over for peace: then a person could spread out the plan of life and tuck in the edges orderly. It was good to have everything clean and folded away, with the hair brushes and tonic bottles sitting straight on the white embroidered linen: the day started without fuss and the pantry shelves laid out with rows of jelly glasses and brown jugs and white stone-china jars with blue whirligigs and words painted on them: coffee, tea, sugar, ginger, cinnamon, allspice: and the bronze clock with the lion on top nicely dusted off. The dust that lion could collect in twenty-four hours! The box in the attic with all those letters tied up, well, she'd have to go through that tomorrow. All those letters—George's letters and John's letters and her letters to them both— lying around for the children to find afterwards made her uneasy. Yes, that would be tomorrow's business. No use to let them know how silly she had been once.

While she was rummaging around she found death in her mind and it felt clammy and unfamiliar. She had spent so much time preparing for death there was no need for bringing it up again. Let it take care of itself now. When she was sixty she had felt very old, finished, and went around making farewell trips to see her children and grandchildren, with a secret in her mind: This is the very last of your mother, children! Then she made her will and came down with a long fever. That was all just a notion like a lot of other things, but it was lucky too, for she had once for all got over the idea of dying for a long time. Now she couldn't be worried. She hoped she had better sense now. Her father had lived to be one hundred and two years old and had drunk a noggin of strong hot toddy on his last birthday. He told the reporters it was his daily habit, and he owed his long life to that. He had made quite a scandal and was very pleased about it. She believed she'd just plague Cornelia a little.

"Cornelia! Cornelia!" No footsteps, but a sudden hand on her cheek. "Bless you, where have you been?"

20   "Here, Mother."

"Well, Cornelia, I want a noggin of hot toddy."

"Are you cold, darling?"

"I'm chilly, Cornelia. Lying in bed stops the circulation. I must have told you that a thousand times."

Well, she could just hear Cornelia telling her husband that Mother was getting a little childish and they'd have to humor her. The thing that most annoyed her was that Cornelia thought she was deaf, dumb, and blind. Little hasty glances and tiny gestures tossed around her and over her head saying, "Don't cross her, let her have her way, she's eighty years old," and she sitting there as if she lived in a thin glass cage. Sometimes Granny almost made up her mind to pack up and move back to her own house where nobody could remind her every minute that she was old. Wait, wait, Cornelia, till your own children whisper behind your back!

25   In her day she had kept a better house and had got more work done. She wasn't too old yet for Lydia to be driving eighty miles for advice when one of the children jumped the track, and Jimmy still dropped in and talked things over: "Now, Mammy, you've a good business head, I want to know what you think of this? . . . " Old. Cornelia couldn't change the furniture around without asking. Little things, little things! They had been so sweet when they were little. Granny wished the old days were back again with the children young and everything to be done over. It had been a hard pull, but not too much for her. When she thought of all the food she had cooked, and all the clothes she had cut and sewed, and all the gardens she had made—well, the children showed it. There they were, made out of her, and they couldn't get away from that. Sometimes she wanted to see John again and point to them and say, Well, I didn't do so badly, did I? But that would have to wait. That was for tomorrow. She used to think of him as a man, but now all the children were older than their father, and he would be a child beside her if she saw him now. It seemed strange and there was something wrong in the idea.

Why, he couldn't possibly recognize her. She had fenced in a hundred acres once, digging the post holes herself and clamping the wires with just a negro boy to help. That changed a woman. John would be looking for a young woman with the peaked Spanish comb in her hair and the painted fan. Digging post holes changed a woman. Riding country roads in the winter when women had their babies was another thing: sitting up nights with sick horses and sick negroes and sick children and hardly ever losing one. John, I hardly ever lost one of them! John would see that in a minute, that would be something he could understand, she wouldn't have to explain anything!

It made her feel like rolling up her sleeves and putting the whole place to rights again. No matter if Cornelia was determined to be everywhere at once, there were a great many things left undone on this place. She would start tomorrow and do them. It was good to be strong enough for everything, even if all you made melted and changed and slipped under your hands, so that by the time you finished you almost forgot what you were working for. What was it I set out to do? she asked herself intently, but she could not remember. A fog rose over the valley, she saw it marching across the creek swallowing the trees and moving up the hill like an army of ghosts. Soon it would be at the near edge of the orchard, and then it was time to go in and light the lamps. Come in, children, don't stay out in the night air.

Lighting the lamps had been beautiful. The children huddled up to her and breathed like little calves waiting at the bars in the twilight. Their eyes followed the match and watched the flame rise and settle in a blue curve, then they moved away from her. The lamp was lit, they didn't have to be scared and hang on to mother any more. Never, never, never more. God, for all my life I thank Thee. Without Thee, my God, I could never have done it. Hail, Mary, full of grace.

I want you to pick all the fruit this year and see that nothing is wasted. There's always someone who can use it. Don't let good things rot for want of using. You waste life when you waste good food. Don't let things get lost. It's bitter to lose things. Now, don't let me get to thinking, not when I am tired and taking a little nap before supper. . . .

The pillow rose about her shoulders and pressed against her heart and the memory was being squeezed out of it: oh, push down that pillow, somebody: it would smother her if she tried to hold it. Such a fresh breeze blowing and such a green day with no threats in it. But he had not come, just the same. What does a woman do when she has put on the white veil and set out the white cake for a man and he doesn't come? She tried to remember. No, I swear he never harmed me but in that. He never harmed me but in that . . . and what if he did? There was the day, the day, but a whirl of dark smoke rose and covered it, crept up and over into the bright field where everything was planted so carefully in orderly rows. That was hell, she knew hell when she saw it. For sixty years she had prayed against remembering him and against losing her soul in the deep pit of hell, and now the two things were mingled in one and the thought of him was a smoky cloud from hell that moved and crept in her head when she had just got rid of Doctor Harry and was trying to rest a minute. Wounded vanity, Ellen, said a sharp voice in the top of her mind. Don't let your wounded vanity get the upper hand of you. Plenty of girls get jilted. You were jilted, weren't you? Then stand up to it. Her eyelids wavered and let in streamers of blue-gray light like tissue paper over her eyes. She must get up and pull the shades down or she'd never sleep. She was in bed again and the shades were not down. How could that happen? Better turn over, hide from the light, sleeping in the light gave you nightmares. "Mother, how do you feel now?" and a stinging wetness on her forehead. But I don't like having my face washed in cold water!

30   Hapsy? George? Lydia? Jimmy? No, Cornelia, and her features were swollen and full of little puddles. "They're coming, darling, they'll all be here soon." Go wash your face, child, you look funny.

Instead of obeying, Cornelia knelt down and put her head on the pillow. She seemed to be talking but there was no sound. "Well, are you tongue-tied? Whose birthday is it? Are you going to give a party?"

Cornelia's mouth moved urgently in strange shapes. "Don't do that, you bother me, daughter."

"Oh, no, Mother. Oh, no. . . ."

Nonsense. It was strange about children. They disputed your every word. "No what, Cornelia?"

35   "Here's Doctor Harry."

"I won't see that boy again. He just left five minutes ago."

"That was this morning, Mother. It's night now. Here's the nurse."

"This is Doctor Harry, Mrs. Weatherall. I never saw you look so young and happy!"

"Ah, I'll never be young again—but I'd be happy if they'd let me lie in peace and get rested."

40   She thought she spoke up loudly, but no one answered. A warm weight on her forehead, a warm bracelet on her wrist, and a breeze went on whispering, trying to tell her something. A shuffle of leaves in the everlasting hand of God. He blew on them and they danced and rattled. "Mother, don't mind, we're going to give you a little hypodermic." "Look here, daughter, how do ants get in this bed? I saw sugar ants yesterday." Did you send for Hapsy too?

It was Hapsy she really wanted. She had to go a long way back through a great many rooms to find Hapsy standing with a baby on her arm. She seemed to herself to be Hapsy also, and the baby on Hapsy's arm was Hapsy and himself and herself, all at once, and there was no surprise in the meeting. Then Hapsy melted from within and turned flimsy as gray gauze and the baby was a gauzy shadow, and Hapsy came up close and said, "I thought you'd never come," and looked at her very searchingly and said, "You haven't changed a bit!" They leaned forward to kiss, when Cornelia began whispering from a long way off, "Oh, is there anything you want to tell me? Is there anything I can do for you?"

Yes, she had changed her mind after sixty years and she would like to see George. I want you to find George. Find him and be sure to tell him I forgot him. I want him to know I had my husband just the same and my children and my house like any other woman. A good house too and a good husband that I loved and fine children out of him. Better than I hoped for even. Tell him I was given back everything he took away and more. Oh, no, oh, God, no, there was something else besides the house and the man and the children. Oh, surely they were not all? What was it? Something not given back. . . . Her breath crowded down under her ribs and grew into a monstrous frightening shape with cutting edges; it bored up into her head, and the agony was unbelievable: Yes, John, get the doctor now, no more talk, my time has come.

When this one was born it should be the last. The last. It should have been born first, for it was the one she had truly wanted. Everything came in good time. Nothing left out, left over. She was strong, in three days she would be as well as ever. Better. A woman needed milk in her to have her full health.

"Mother, do you hear me?"

45   "I've been telling you—"

"Mother, Father Connolly's here."

"I went to Holy Communion only last week. Tell him I'm not so sinful as all that."

"Father just wants to speak to you."

He could speak as much as he pleased. It was like him to drop in and inquire about her soul as if it were a teething baby, and then stay on for a cup of tea and a round of cards and gossip. He always had a funny story of some sort, usually about an Irishman who made his little mistakes and confessed them, and the point lay in some absurd thing he would blurt out in the confessional showing his struggles between native piety and original sin. Granny felt easy about her soul. Cornelia, where are your manners? Give Father Connolly a chair. She had her secret comfortable understanding with a few favorite saints who cleared a straight road to God for her. All as surely signed and sealed as the papers for the new Forty Acres. Forever . . . heirs and assigns forever. Since the day the wedding cake was not cut, but thrown out and wasted. The whole bottom dropped out of the world, and there she was blind and sweating with nothing under her feet and the walls falling away. His hand had caught her under the breast, she had not fallen, there was the freshly polished floor with the green rug on it, just as before. He had cursed like a sailor's parrot and said, "I'll kill him for you." Don't lay a hand on him, for my sake leave something to God. "Now, Ellen, you must believe what I tell you. . . ."

50   So there was nothing, nothing to worry about any more, except sometimes in the night one of the children screamed in a nightmare, and they both hustled out shaking and hunting for the matches and calling, "There, wait a minute, here we are!" John, get the doctor now, Hapsy's time has come. But there was Hapsy standing by the bed in a white cap. "Cornelia, tell Hapsy to take off her cap. I can't see her plain."

Her eyes opened very wide and the room stood out like a picture she had seen somewhere. Dark colors with the shadows rising toward the ceiling in long angles. The tall black dresser gleamed with nothing on it but John's picture, enlarged from a little one, with John's eyes very black when they should have been blue. You never saw him, so how do you know how he looked? But the man insisted the copy was perfect, it was very rich and handsome. For a picture, yes, but it's not my husband. The table by the bed had a linen cover and a candle and a crucifix. The light was blue from Cornelia's silk lampshades. No sort of light at all, just frippery. You had to live forty years with kerosene lamps to appreciate honest electricity. She felt very strong and she saw Doctor Harry with a rosy nimbus around him.

"You look like a saint, Doctor Harry, and I vow that's as near as you'll ever come to it."

"She's saying something."

"I heard you, Cornelia. What's all this carrying on?"

55   "Father Connolly's saying—"

Cornelia's voice staggered and bumped like a cart in a bad road. It rounded corners and turned back again and arrived nowhere. Granny stepped up in the cart very lightly and reached for the reins, but a man sat beside her and she knew him by his hands, driving the cart. She did not look in his face, for she knew without seeing, but looked instead down the road where the trees leaned over and bowed to each other and a thousand birds were singing a Mass. She felt like singing too, but she put her hand in the bosom of her dress and pulled out a rosary, and Father Connolly murmured Latin in a very solemn voice and tickled her feet. My God, will you stop that nonsense? I'm a married woman. What if he did run away and leave me to face the priest by myself? I found another a whole world better. I wouldn't have exchanged my husband for anybody except St. Michael himself, and you may tell him that for me with a thank you in the bargain.

Light flashed on her closed eyelids, and a deep roaring shook her. Cornelia, is that lightning? I hear thunder. There's going to be a storm. Close all the windows. Call the children in. . . . "Mother, here we are, all of us." "Is that you, Hapsy?" "Oh, no, I'm Lydia. We drove as fast as we could." Their faces drifted above her, drifted away. The rosary fell out of her hands and Lydia put it back. Jimmy tried to help, their hands fumbled together, and Granny closed two fingers around Jimmy's thumb. Beads wouldn't do, it must be something alive. She was so amazed her thoughts ran round and round. So, my dear Lord, this is my death and I wasn't even thinking about it. My children have come to see me die. But I can't, it's not time. Oh, I always hated surprises. I wanted to give Cornelia the amethyst set— Cornelia, you're to have the amethyst set, but Hapsy's to wear it when she wants, and, Doctor Harry, do shut up. Nobody sent for you. Oh, my dear Lord, do wait a minute. I meant to do something about the Forty Acres, Jimmy doesn't need it and Lydia will later on, with that worthless husband of hers. I meant to finish the altar cloth and send six bottles of wine to Sister Borgia for her dyspepsia. I want to send six bottles of wine to Sister Borgia, Father Connolly, now don't let me forget.

Cornelia's voice made short turns and tilted over and crashed. "Oh, Mother, oh, Mother, oh, Mother. . . ."

"I'm not going, Cornelia. I'm taken by surprise. I can't go."

You'll see Hapsy again. What about her? "I thought you'd never come." Granny made a long journey outward, looking for Hapsy. What if I don't find her? What then? Her heart sank down and down, there was no bottom to death, she couldn't come to the end of it. The blue light from Cornelia's lampshade drew into a tiny point in the center of her brain, it flickered and winked like an eye, quietly it fluttered and dwindled. Granny lay curled down within herself, amazed and watchful, starting at the point of light that was herself; her body was now only a deeper mass of shadow in an endless darkness and this darkness would curl around the light and swallow it up. God, give a sign!

For the second time there was no sign. Again no bridegroom and the priest in the house. She could not remember any other sorrow because this grief wiped them all away. Oh, no, there's nothing more cruel than this—I'll never forgive it. She stretched herself with a deep breath and blew out the light.

[1929]

Joining the Conversation: Critical Thinking and Writing

1. In a paragraph, characterize Granny Weatherall. In another paragraph evaluate her claim that the anguish of the jilting has been compensated for by her subsequent life. Be sure to offer evidence to support your assertions.
2. The final paragraph alludes to Christ's parable of the bridegroom (Matthew 25:1–13). With this allusion in mind, write a paragraph explaining the title of the story.
3. Compare this story to Lan Samantha Chang's "Water Names." Both stories feature grandmothers. How would you characterize each grandmother? What does each grandmother convey as a meaningful lesson? When is the grandmother silent? What remains unclear or unresolved in each story?

CHAPTER 10

Research: Writing with Sources

Chapter Preview

After reading this chapter, you will be able to

- Create a research plan and select a topic
- Locate both print and online sources, and evaluate those sources
- Draft your paper and take precautions to avoid plagiarism
- Evaluate a student research paper

Creating a Successful Research Plan

Reading and writing about literature should generate questions. Often, those questions will require research because you cannot answer them using your preexisting knowledge; you need to generate new knowledge in order to answer them. Consider these questions: "Why do Hawthorne's stories often feature Puritans?" "How have readers interpreted the snake in Hurston's 'Sweat'?" "Why was the sonnet a popular form during the British Renaissance?" All of these questions can be answered by turning to scholars who have developed research-based information and ideas. Doing research encourages us to move beyond our own understandings and opinions, helping us to expand our knowledge about literature. Through research, we can join in academic conversations by implementing a plan that will locate reputable sources, assess those sources, learn from and select the best ideas in those sources, and integrate those sources into our own writing.

Academic research cannot begin without a plan. If you start your research with no plan, you'll fall back on "googling around" the Internet, which guarantees unfocused searching, general results, and unoriginal thinking. An undefined Internet search can waste hours of your valuable time. In contrast, a focused search of academic sources can return excellent results in a short amount of time. In order to perform productive research, start with an academic research plan.

Enter Research with a Plan of Action

Create a research plan that immediately defines your work as academic research. Start your research process by defining your assignment requirements, timeline, academic goals, and academic resources.

- *Create assignment-based research goals.* Use your research paper assignment to help set the parameters of your research. Does the assignment tell you the number of sources needed, the types of resources to consult, the research questions to consider, or the research approach to use?

- *Create a calendar of research tasks.* Know your assignment deadlines, and create a research calendar that works "backwards" from your due dates. Build time into your calendar for multiple database searches, source evaluation and selection, and source note taking—all to be done *before* starting to draft your paper.
- *Create a record-keeping system for your searches and sources.* Your research will generate multiple forms of material: lists of keywords used, lists of search results, scanned copies of articles, hard copies of articles, and stacks of books. You'll need a system to keep track of your searches and their results. Create a hard copy or electronic file to organize your findings.
- *Know your library's online resources, and select the best one for your topic.* Become familiar with your library's web page. Explore its links to online databases and reference resources. Understand how different links connect you to different types of information. Survey each resource, and select the best one for your research topic.
- *Select academic databases, and do multiple searches.* Academic research often relies on electronic databases; these databases provide access to full-text sources, such as journal articles. Know which electronic databases provide access to literary sources, such as EBSCOhost's *Academic Search Premier*, *JSTOR*, and *Project MUSE*. Search more than one database, keeping track of your work. Within each database, perform multiple searches with multiple keywords, keeping track of your work.
- *Know your library's on-site resources, and select the best one for your topic.* Become familiar with your library. Use the online catalog to locate useful books held by the library, and then go to the library to find and borrow those books.
- *Use the Internet sparingly and selectively.* Because your paper will have to use and cite academic sources, most sources that you find on the Internet will not have the type of information that you need. Carefully evaluate any site *before* spending time reading its opinions.

What Resources Does Your Institution Offer?

Your school's library—both its physical and virtual forms—is an amazing resource. It is set up to facilitate the academic research that you have to do for your classes. Create a research plan that will take advantage of its on-site and online resources.

Although colleges and universities offer a wide range of electronic materials and databases, make sure to do what may seem old-fashioned but remains the best way to access academic material: Get off-line and visit the library! Although you may be accustomed to working online late at night, try to break that pattern and spend an afternoon at the library. An hour or two that you spend in the library can result in a backpack full of high-quality books.

One of the best resources that you have is the librarian, who can help you locate sources that are perfectly matched to your topic. Also learn how to use the interlibrary loan system, which will often deliver scanned articles directly to your e-mail account, in addition to delivering books to you at the library. Sign up for a library tutorial at your school, and take a look at the library's home page and online catalog options.

What Type of Research Do You Want to Do?

Research employs well-known ways of approaching the available sources, which will help you to create clear research questions. When you create your research questions, consider the different types of research available to you.

Cultural Research. This type of research focuses on the cultural and historical context of a literary work. In cultural research, you locate historical material and examine how it helps you to understand the literary work.

- *Example:* Connecting Langston Hughes's poetry to information about the Harlem Renaissance.

Biographical Research. Biographical research focuses on the literary author's life. In this type of research, you connect the literary text to events in the author's life or ideas that the author has offered about his or her work.

- *Example:* Using an interview with Lorraine Hansberry to interpret her drama *A Raisin in the Sun*.

Critical Research. Critical research emphasizes the critical debate surrounding a literary text. Academic critics offer differing interpretations of literature. In critical research, you locate articles published in academic journals, assess the arguments expressed in the articles, and connect those arguments to your own interpretation of the literary work.

- *Example:* Comparing different interpretations of what the quilt represents in Alice Walker's short story "Everyday Use."

Theoretical Application. Theoretical research takes a widely recognized theory (which might not have been created for literature) and applies it to a literary work. This type of research explores how the concepts developed by the theory help to explain a literary work.

- *Example:* Applying Freud's theory on dreams to Katherine Anne Porter's short story "The Jilting of Granny Weatherall."

Appendix A offers an in-depth overview of critical strategies that can be employed when you are engaged in academic research.

Selecting a Research Topic and Generating Research Questions

Use Close Reading as Your Starting Point

A good literary research paper starts with a thoughtful close reading. Close reading encourages you to develop your own sense of the literary work, allowing you to determine the work's meaning, to notice how the work is structured, and to decide what aspects of the work you find most intriguing and worth further exploration. Research connects this process of personal exploration to external sources. Start your research with a close reading that generates your own understanding of the literature. Then, use research to connect your close reading to other critics' readings.

Select Your Topic

Your paper's topic should arise from the ideas and questions that you formulate as you read and reread the literary text. You want your topic to be "yours," so start with your original analysis and develop it before turning to other people's ideas. However, as you select the topic for your research paper, remember that your goal is to develop ideas about the topic by turning to other writers' arguments rather than by just relying on your own individual ideas. Thus, a successful research topic is one that remains flexible and can be developed by adding ideas, theories, and explanations that other writers provide. A research topic is also one that can be assessed from many points of view, allowing you to agree or argue with critics who have written about the topic.

Skim Resources through Preliminary Research

Perform preliminary research to "test" your topic and see if it can be developed through research. As you perform this research, you will translate your topic into keywords that you can enter into academic databases and Internet search engines. A research paper thus requires you to define your paper's topic by means of keywords. The keyword search is a good exercise, as it forces you to create a very concise, focused version of your topic. Perform preliminary searches on more than one academic database; these quick searches will allow you to test your topic ideas. See how many and what type of results are returned by your search. Skim the articles returned by your searches. The success of these searches can help you to formulate your topic—you don't want to create a topic that can't be researched.

Narrow Your Topic, and Form a Working Thesis

Based on your preliminary research, you will revise your topic, narrowing and focusing your research to inform your thesis. A research paper's thesis remains the expression of the paper's central argument. To develop your thesis, you will also engage in synthesis; you must synthesize your arguments with those of critics, allowing their ideas to help develop your ideas. As a result, a research paper must feature ideas that can be developed by engaging with other writers' ideas. A strong thesis will highlight the concepts that it will connect to research resources. Your thesis will evolve as you form those connections by locating, reading, and analyzing new sources. It is often helpful to think of your thesis as a "working thesis": an argument that is "in progress" and that will be revised based on the new information and ideas that you discover through research. Because your working thesis will change and evolve, you will need to take good notes in order to trace your ideas and show how they were influenced by, and connected to, critic's ideas. Your thesis will take final form as you start to draft your research paper.

   After you determine your research topic and create a working thesis, you are ready to start locating and evaluating sources. Your working thesis will change, depending on the materials you find. But, how do you even start to locate good sources and then engage with them in a way that connects them to your own ideas?

   In the sample research notes below, Mike Ramos, a student taking a first-year composition course, is working on an assignment that requires a six- to eight-page paper that analyzes two Emily Dickinson poems. The assignment asks the writer to select a theme that the two poems share. Then, the student must compare and contrast the two poems, using criticism to help interpret the selected theme and to create a strong thesis argument. The assignment requires that the student locate at least four scholarly sources and use MLA citation style. Mike feels that he writes best on his computer, so he creates a research folder on his desktop and opens new files for each step in his research process. As he starts the research process, Mike creates a document that states his research goals and creates a research calendar. He then starts the process of determining his research paper's working thesis by engaging in the type of prewriting note taking shown in Chapters 3 and 4. Let's turn to the materials in Mike's digital research folder, noting that he approaches his research and writing by reminding himself of the assignment's goals and clarifying his research resources and calendar.

Student Work: Digital Research Folder Assignment and Research Plan Notes

---

Assignment Goals:

2 Emily Dickinson poems
    –connect poems through theme → determine thesis
    –analyze literary elements
4 academic sources on Dickinson
    –academic articles
    –academic books
    –cite them

Research Sources:

Library databases—check out for journal articles, figure out keywords
    EBSCOhost's Academic Search Premiere
    JSTOR
    Project MUSE
    MLA database

Library catalog—check for book
    Catalog search on Emily Dickinson

Research Calendar:

Assignment Start Date: April 2

Week #1   Pick poems and topic
                Locate articles
                Skim articles
                Firm up topic and create working thesis

Week #2   Read articles closely
                Select articles—take notes and highlight key quotes
                Finalize thesis and create outline

Week #3   Draft essay

Week #4   Revise essay
                Proofread essay

Paper due date: April 27

After Mike has generated a research plan, he creates a new document to sort through his ideas and select his Dickinson poems. He starts this brainstorming by returning to his primary sources and rereading his favorite Dickinson poems. This rereading leads to rough note taking, which allows Mike to formulate a paper topic and working thesis, which he knows will be revised as he engages in more research. Let's take a look a Mike's preliminary research notes.

Student Work: Digital Research Folder "Working Thesis" Notes

Dickinson Poems I could work with:

A Bird came down the walk
A narrow fellow in the grass (snake)
There's a certain Slant of light
A Drop fell on the Apple Tree
The name—of it—is "Autumn"-
The wind begun to rock the grass

Possible Topic: Nature

> **Animals** ————————▶ Likes animals? Too basic?
> **Nature** ————————▶ Storms
> **Weather** ————————▶ Light Energy
> **Land (houses)** ————————▶ Natural vs. man-made?
> **Seasons** ————————▶ Spring, autumn, winter
> Change/cycle of seasons

Topic: Weather? Emotions with Weather?

> **Weather that changes**   The wind begun to rock the grass
> There's a certain Slant of light
> The name—of it—is "Autumn"-
>
> **Natural world that changes**

Topic could become Argument/Thesis:

> Emily uses weather, seasons, natural world to capture emotions
> ~~Esp. emotions that are female?~~
> ~~Esp. emotions that have conflict?~~
> Esp. emotions that change
> The emotions are negative? Maybe weather/nature is a way to get out those upsetting emotions or unsure emotions?
>
> Nature is ~~plants, animals,~~ weather
> What about seasons? Seasons that change? Cycle?
> Unpredictable? Change is difficult? (note word "despair" in "Slant of light")
>
> Puts emotions into imagery? Tone/mood?
> Bold emotions? Violent? (note blood image in "Autumn" poem)

(continued)

> Doesn't put emotions into people but into nature? Into images of nature?
> No other people in the poem
>
> No connection to people? But connection to nature, seasons
>
> **Working Thesis:**
>
> Dickinson uses imagery of changing nature—especially changing seasons and
> changing weather—to capture changing emotions. In two poems (There's a certain
> Slant of Light and The name—of it—is "Autumn"-) the emotions are violent in a way
> that is upsetting (despair) or bold. She can capture those emotions (mood) in nature/
> seasons/weather.

Generate Key Concepts as Keywords

After you have generated a working thesis that captures your understanding of a literary work, you are ready to consider critics' arguments and use them to help develop your interpretations. As part of your brainstorming process, generate a list of concepts that are central to your working thesis. Ultimately, this list of concepts will serve as keywords in your database, catalog, and Internet searches. As a first step in formulating his paper's argument, Mike selects the poems he would like to work with: Dickinson's "There's a certain Slant of Light" (page 857) and "The name—of it—is 'Autumn' (page 857). He is now ready to start formulating a thesis that connects these two works. If we reexamine Mike's working thesis notes, we can see that his ideas are starting to become conceptual and specific (such as "seasons that change in Dickinson's poetry" or "bold/violent emotions in Dickinson's poetry") rather than general or purely informational (such as "Emily Dickinson"). These concepts can serve as keywords in his library research. Mike opens a new document in his research folder and starts to list possible keywords. By using detailed keywords, Mike can make sure that his research remains focused and that he develops his working thesis. Mike's concept words should bring his research back to critics' arguments that can be clearly connected to his own ideas. He also lists synonyms for each concept word so that he is able to enter multiple terms as keywords in a database search. He aims for concept words that capture his ideas without being either overly general or too specific.

Create Inquiry Questions

Mike's assignment asks him to provide an argument that can be developed by exploring critics' interpretations of Dickinson; he knows that he is searching for critical interpretation rather than biographical or historical information. Mike starts to frame his topic through inquiry questions that emphasize interpretation. For example, rather than simply thinking, "I need to locate sources on Emily Dickinson," Mike starts his search by asking the analytical questions that he is interested in exploring for his thesis: "How have critics of Dickinson interpreted her nature imagery?" and "Do critics see Dickinson as inspired by nature or fearful of nature?" After he compiles a list of meaningful questions, he is confident that he can find critics' interpretations of that topic.

Student Work: Digital Research Folder "Research Keywords" and "Inquiry Questions" Notes

Working Thesis:

Dickinson uses imagery of changing nature—especially changing weather—to capture changing emotions. In two poems ("There's a certain Slant of Light" and "The name—of it—is 'Autumn'-"), the emotions are violent in a way that is upsetting (despair) or vivid. She can capture those emotions (mood) in nature/seasons/weather.

Key Concepts—Keywords:

Weather
Nature—environment—landscape—natural world—outdoors
Seasons—times of year—winter, autumn
Emotions
(key: changing emotions—despair)
Imagery
Mood/tone
Emily Dickinson
Titles of poems

Inquiry Questions for Research:

How have critics interpreted Dickinson's nature imagery?
Do any critics discuss Dickinson's use of weather?
Do any critics discuss Dickinson's use of the seasons?
Do critics see Dickinson as changing her emotions? Or having extreme emotions?
Do critics see Dickinson as inspired by nature or fearful of nature?"
~~Where did Dickinson live? (Biographical—no)~~
~~What was her daily routine?~~
Did Dickinson ever interact with nature (might be OK)?
How do critics think Dickinson uses imagery?
Do critics debate the meaning of the two poems?
Do critics think Dickinson puts emotions into nature rather than shows people and their emotions?

Locating Materials through Productive Searches

If you've created a research plan, created a working thesis, and generated a list of research questions, you'll enter into the research process with a purpose! You can quickly start the process of selecting resources that will fit your topic and help to develop your ideas. Academic research relies on the resources provided by your library: electronic databases and on-site, hard-copy resources. Start your research by consulting these materials first. Then, move to the Internet, and evaluate the sources that can be located there.

Generate Meaningful Keywords

Electronic databases and catalogs rely on keyword search engines. In order to access the materials within the database, you must enter the meaningful keywords that will allow you to locate specific sources that contain those keywords. The quality of your search results is thus dependent on the quality of your keywords. How can you create meaningful keywords?

✔ **CHECKLIST:** *Creating Meaningful Keywords for a Successful Search*

☐ Isolate your central ideas, and translate them into single words.
☐ Use concept-based words.
☐ Create a list of synonyms.
☐ Note information correctly, such as the author's name and the literary text's title.
☐ Use *and*, *not*, and *or* to narrow your search results.
  • These terms, known as Boolean operators, allow you to better direct your electronic searches.
  • Using *and* in a search for "Emily Dickinson and nature" will only return results that contain both keywords.
  • Using *not* in a search for "Emily Dickinson not plants" will return results that discuss Emily Dickinson but do not mention plants.
  • Finally, using *or* in a search for "Emily Dickinson or nature" will bring back results that include either term but not necessarily both.
☐ Use quotation marks to join key phrases.
  • By placing quotation marks around key phrases (for example, "Emily Dickinson"), you direct the search to only bring back results that include the entire phrase.

Using Academic Databases to Locate Materials

Your library subscribes to academic databases, such as the MLA database, *JSTOR*, and *Project MUSE*, which cite and reproduce sources that have appeared in peer-reviewed venues. A scholarly publication is referred to as a peer-reviewed source because it is written by a scholar and carefully reviewed by other scholars before it is published. Academic research requires work with these materials—sources that have been carefully written and reviewed by experts. Academic databases will better connect you to a wide variety of these peer-reviewed venues than an Internet search can.

Search the MLA Database

As noted, literary studies' most important database is the MLA or *MLA International Bibliography of Books and Articles in the Modern Languages and Literatures*, and most literary research starts with this database. The MLA, or Modern Language Association, is the professional organization that brings together professors of literature and language. It sets professional standards for elements of literary analysis, such as the citation style used in literary papers. In addition, it provides the most comprehensive and up-to-date bibliography in literary studies. The MLA database contains the most complete listing of journals and books published on literary topics, but it does not provide full-text scans of academic publications. However, most libraries now integrate their databases; as a result, an MLA citation can contain a library-provided link to a full-text scan of an article that is held in another database.

Search Full-Text Academic Databases

Databases that contain full-text journal articles include EBSCOhost's *Academic Search Premier*, *JSTOR*, and *Project MUSE*. These databases provide full-text scans of journal articles that have appeared in print. These scans typically take the form of PDFs that can be downloaded directly to your computer desktop. These academic databases use keyword searches and return lists of "results." Thus, they look and feel like the type of searching that you would do on the Internet. The benefit of doing your searching *within* an academic database (rather than on the Internet) is that you are assured of the integrity of the sources. None of the sources you locate in an academic database will have been created by an amateur writer (who might be writing out of passion rather than knowledge!); rather, academic databases collect published works by professional and academic writers.

Perform Advanced Keyword Searches

As you enter each database, you should start with an *advanced* keyword search, which will allow you to create a more focused search. The advanced keyword search page will allow you to select features such as the type of resource (article, review, or interview), the language of the article, and the year of publication. As a result, your search will be instantly more productive. For example, if your instructor asks you to find up-to-date articles, you can select to locate articles written in the last ten years and to deselect formats such as interviews.

Student Work: The Academic Database Search

Mike starts his research by looking for academic journal articles that he can locate electronically. He opens his library's website and reminds himself of the many electronic databases it owns. For his literary paper, he clicks on the "Browse by Subject" button and the subheading "Humanities." This leads him to databases that contain literary criticism, including the MLA database. When he clicks on a specific database's link, it opens to a home page that takes the form of a keyword search page. As he starts to enter keywords into the database's search engine, Mike's research begins in earnest.

Due to information that he has learned in library sessions held in his class, Mike knows to consult the MLA database for the most comprehensive search of literary sources. Because Mike's library connects the MLA citation database to other full-text databases, it proves to be a great starting place for literary research.

He starts his research with the keywords "Emily Dickinson and nature." Let's look at the different searches he performs and how he analyzes his results.

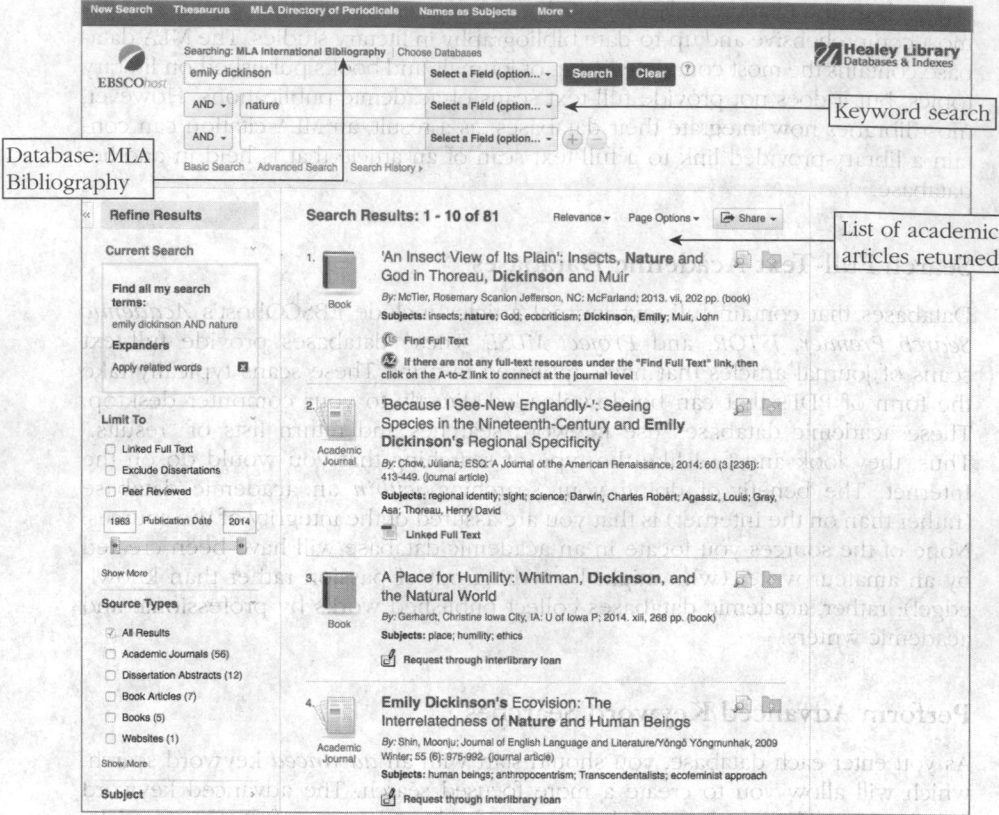

Evaluate the Results List, and Revise Your Search

A keyword search will return a list of results, typically citations of article titles. Mike analyzes his results according to several criteria: Did his search return articles that are "on topic"? Did his search return sources from appropriate journals? Did his search return a good number of results (not too many, not too few)? Mike continues to revise his keywords and invent new searches. He also tries searches that use two keywords: He uses *and* to create a more focused search that locates sources with both keywords; he uses *or* to create a broader search that will locate sources with either keyword.

Evaluate the Individual Titles

If a keyword search is successful, it will return a list of promising titles. Mike evaluates the list that his search returns, locating the sources that seem to be a good match for his paper's topic. He discards titles that are off-topic, are too confusing or filled with jargon, or are not of the right "type" (for example, a review of a poetry reading rather than an analysis of the poem itself). After he selects titles for closer analysis, Mike downloads each article into an electronic folder that he has created on his computer desktop to keep track of his research materials. He skims each article to determine if it connects to his working thesis before he reads it closely. Some journal articles open with an abstract that summarizes the article. Other journal articles will contain a clear title and headings that reveal its central argument. For most articles, he'll need to skim the first page or two to determine the article's thesis. As Mike skims, he evaluates how helpful the source will be for his topic and sorts his sources into folders that indicate this analysis (such as "most helpful," "OK," and "not helpful"). This type of sorting will help Mike limit the amount of reading that he needs to do as he moves toward writing his research paper.

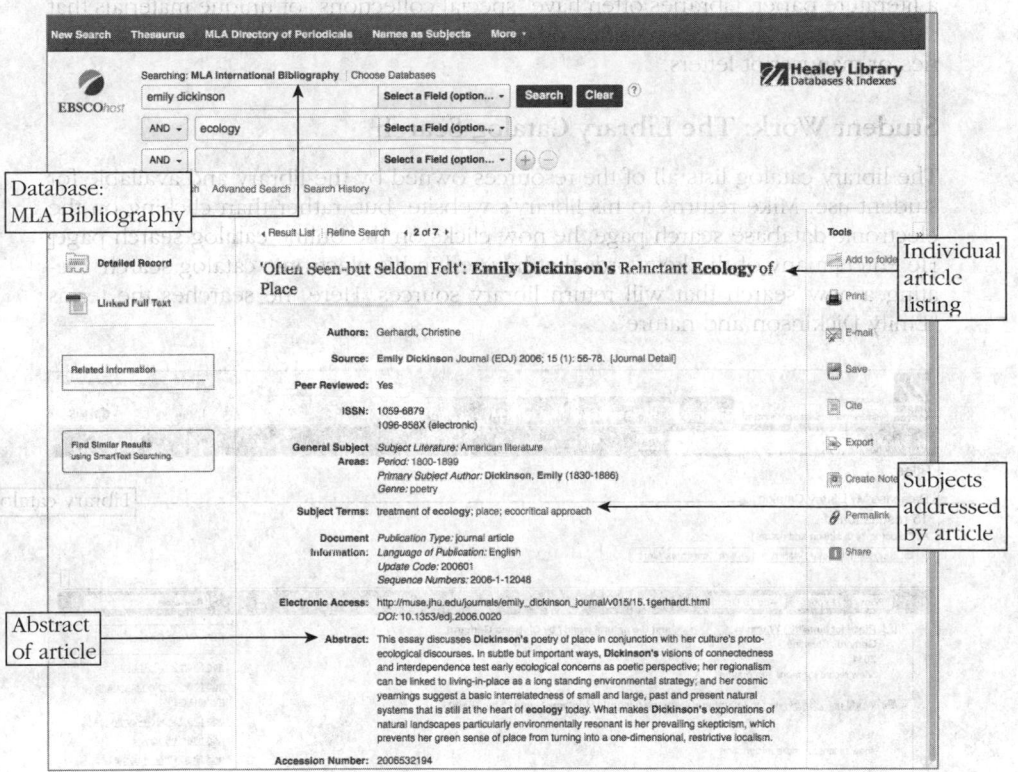

Using the Library Catalog to Locate Materials

Your school's library maintains an accessible and easy-to-use electronic catalog of the sources that it owns and that you can use or borrow. The library's website will prominently display its catalog, often by having a search screen right on its home page. Like the Internet or the library's academic databases, the library catalog is accessed through a keyword search. Enter the keywords that you have developed for your database search into the library's electronic catalog, and see what results are returned. Your library catalog will also allow you to search by author, title, and subject, among other categories; enter your keywords in more that one category to create the most comprehensive search.

Locate Books and Additional Resources

Mike's library catalog will connect him to materials that are not available online. The most important of these sources will be academic books. The catalog uses a call letter/number system to direct Mike to the book's location in the library; university libraries typically use Library of Congress (LoC) cataloging (for example, literary sources in English are categorized under the LoC call numbers PN, PR and PS). When Mike locates a source on a library shelf, he skims that shelf for additional books. Books on similar subjects are shelved together, so a book on Emily Dickinson will be shelved next to others on that same topic. In addition to books, an academic library will hold materials such as film and music that might be useful for a literature paper. Libraries often have "special collections" of unique materials that can help shape an entire research project; these collections can include oral histories or manuscript letters.

Student Work: The Library Catalog Search

The library catalog lists all of the resources owned by the library and available for student use. Mike returns to his library's website, but, rather than clicking on the electronic database search page, he now clicks on the online catalog search page. He enters many of the keywords that he used in his electronic catalog search, creating a new search that will return library sources. Here, he searches the terms "Emily Dickinson and nature":

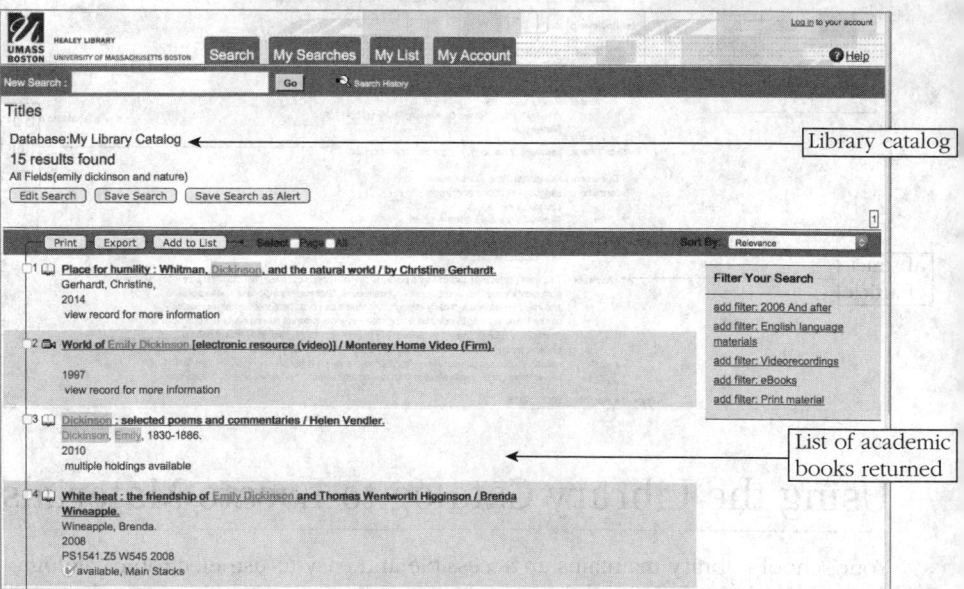

Use a Catalog Entry to Locate More Sources

As Mike searches the library catalog, he uses the same process of source evaluation and search revision that he used when he was searching for online resources. He works to focus his research process and improve his research results. As he engages in this process, he comes to see that the library's cataloging of its materials is, in itself, an excellent resource. A library catalog offers a comprehensive description of each item that it lists. Mike notices that the item description contains a list of subject words used to catalog the source. When Mike locates a good source, he clicks on its subject words to quickly find related materials.

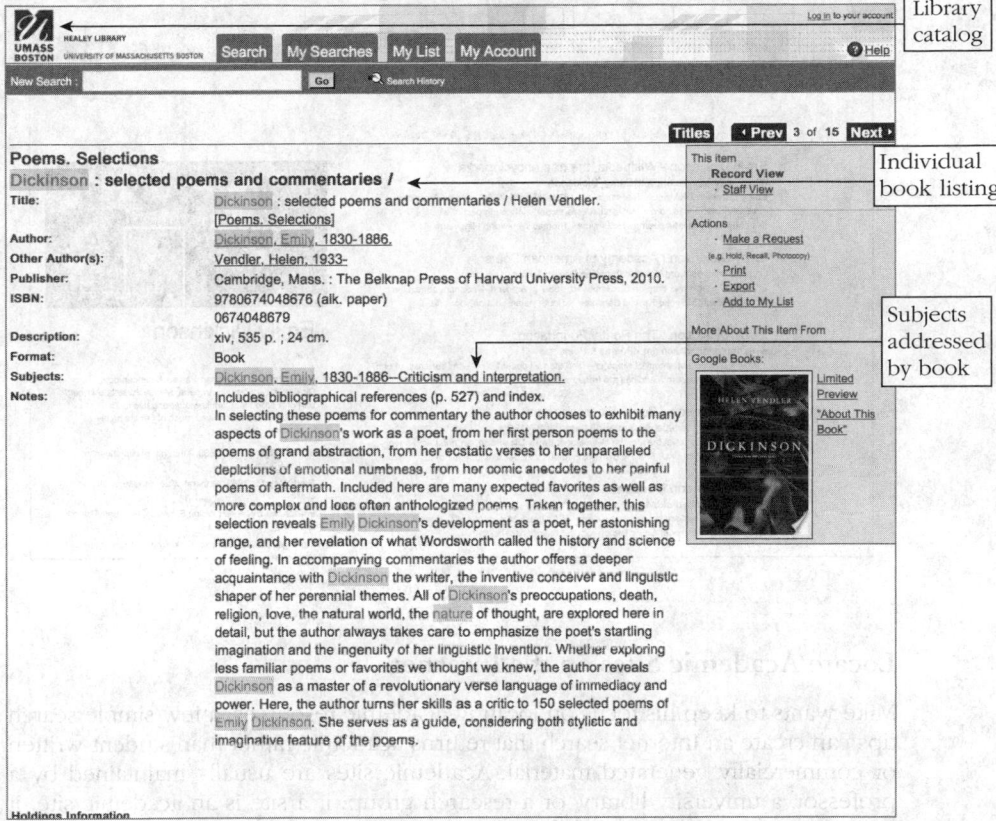

Using the Internet to Perform Meaningful Research

You are probably very familiar and comfortable with searching the Internet for information. That comfort can lead you to perform searches that return excellent resources. However, that comfort can also lead you to treat online academic research as if it were the same as googling your favorite celebrity topics for entertainment or researching local restaurants for tonight's dinner. When you search the Internet for information for a research paper, continue to think of that searching as academic work that must return academic resources.

Student Work: The Internet Search

The Internet can be a valuable source of information, but its use in academic work requires an extra level of caution and diligence by the researcher. The Internet is open for anyone to contribute. Unlike print sources, which are vetted by experts,

Internet sources may not be held to any quality standards. After typing "Emily Dickinson" into his search engine, Mike carefully evaluates each result for its academic reliability and it relevancy to his topic.

Locate Academic Sites on the Internet

Mike wants to keep his focus on locating academic resources: a few simple search tips can create an Internet search that returns academic rather than student-written or commercially generated material. Academic sites are usually maintained by a professor, a university library, or a research group; if a site is an academic site, it will always indicate its academic status. To find these academic sites, do the following:

- Search for sites that are connected to a college or university. Limit your search to the ".edu" domain using the advanced search options, or type "site. edu" into your search engine's basic search field. Check each site to ensure that it is written by a scholar, not a student.
- Search for sites that have an "About Us" page that lists the people who have created the site. An academic site will list the scholars involved and will often explain their editorial policy—how they select materials for inclusion on the site.
- Search for academic sites by starting your search in Google Scholar. Google Scholar is a drop-down menu on Google's home page. It limits its search to books, and does not include websites created by academic researchers.

Locate Information-Rich Sites on the Internet

In addition to academic websites, many types of nonprofit organizations dedicated to intellectual inquiry maintain excellent websites. For example, a museum dedicated to a literary author will often contain excellent resources, including a biography, information on cultural and historical context, and links to additional resources. Similarly, the official website maintained by a living author will often contain clear biographical information and an up-to-date list of literary works.

Avoid Commercial Sites on the Internet

When Mike types "Emily Dickinson" into an Internet search engine, it returns lots of sites produced by commercial entities. These sites aim to make money from students; they often contain annoying pop-up advertisements and bold advertisements at the top, bottom, and sides of the page. Even more obviously, sites aim to make money by encouraging the user to pay for their content. For example, many sites will show a small section of an essay and ask the user to pay to see the rest of it. Sites ask the user to pay for student-written papers with the understanding that the user will submit that paper as if it were his or her own. This is plagiarism. Very wisely, Mike simply stays away from these sites.

Locate Well-known Literary Sites on the Internet

The Internet has several well-known, long-standing, noncommercial websites that specialize in literary information. These sites contain a wealth of information and often act as clearinghouses that contain links to reputable websites. Well-known literary sites include:

> The Voice of the Shuttle: http://vos.ucsb.edu
> The Poetry Foundation: http://www.poetryfoundation.org
> Literary Resources on the Net: http://andromeda.rutgers.edu/~jlynch/Lit

Locate Primary Sources on the Internet

Although Mike doesn't plan to do extensive research on Dickinson's life, his Internet keywords lead him to Harvard University's website. Obviously, this is a reputable academic institution, and Mike is intrigued. Mike follows the links and finds his way to the Emily Dickinson Collection and, with a few more clicks, a rare document scanned by Harvard. He locates a full-image scan of a notebook owned by Emily Dickinson, filled with the plants and flowers that she collected and labeled. This resource shows that Dickinson had a deep interest in nature and offers insight into her connection to, and close observation of, the natural world. Although Mike won't make this resource central to his paper, he thinks he might be able to use it as part of his discussion of Dickinson's interest in nature.

The Internet contains academic websites that are dedicated to scanning original primary source documents related to literature. Many libraries are making parts of their collections accessible online through digital humanities initiatives. For example, you can now find scanned images of Shakespeare's First Folio and Walt Whitman's manuscripts online. These are rare materials that, only a few years ago, you could have seen only if you were a rare books scholar working in a rare books library. Search for these primary literary sources by adding the words *manuscript, archive, full text, digital,* or *scan* to your keyword search.

Evaluating Sources for Academic Quality

For sources found through Internet searches, as with print sources, you must evaluate what you have located and gauge how much or how little it will contribute to your literary analysis and argument. If you are using an Internet site as a source in an academic paper, you will want to make sure that the site maintains academic standards for presenting accurate, unbiased information. The information should be conveyed with the depth of understanding and analysis found in academic sources. In addition, the site should cite the sources of its information.

✔ CHECKLIST: *Evaluating Web Sites for Quality*

Focus the topic of your research as precisely as you can before you embark on an Internet search. Ask the following questions:

☐ Does this site or page look like it can help me in my assignment?
☐ Whose site or page is this? Is this a commercial, an academic, or a nonprofit site?
☐ Who is the intended audience?
☐ What is the point of view? Are there signs of a specific slant or bias?
☐ Is the site accurate? How good is the detail, depth, and quality of the material presented?

- ☐ Is the site well constructed and well organized?
- ☐ Is the text well written?
- ☐ Can the information be corroborated or supported by print sources? Does the site contain citations of its sources?
- ☐ When was the site or page made available? Has it been recently revised or updated?
- ☐ Can the person or institution, company, or agency responsible for this site or page receive e-mail comments, questions, and criticisms?

Student Work: Evaluating Sources for Academic Quality

Working with his school's electronic databases, Mike creates a list of keywords and enters them into three different databases: EBSCOhost's *Academic Search Premiere*, the *MLA International Bibliography*, and *JSTOR*. In each database, he clicks to the "Advanced Search" page, selecting qualities such as peer-reviewed sources. For each set of search results, Mike quickly skims the titles, evaluating them for their academic quality. He looks for articles that appear in noncommercial academic journals, are peer reviewed, and have been published recently. In his first search of Academic Search Complete, Mike uses the keywords "Emily Dickinson" and "Seasons." The third title returned sounds interesting, until he clicks on the title, views it, and sees that it is not an academic article. It is a short two-page article appearing in a popular writing magazine. He discards this source.

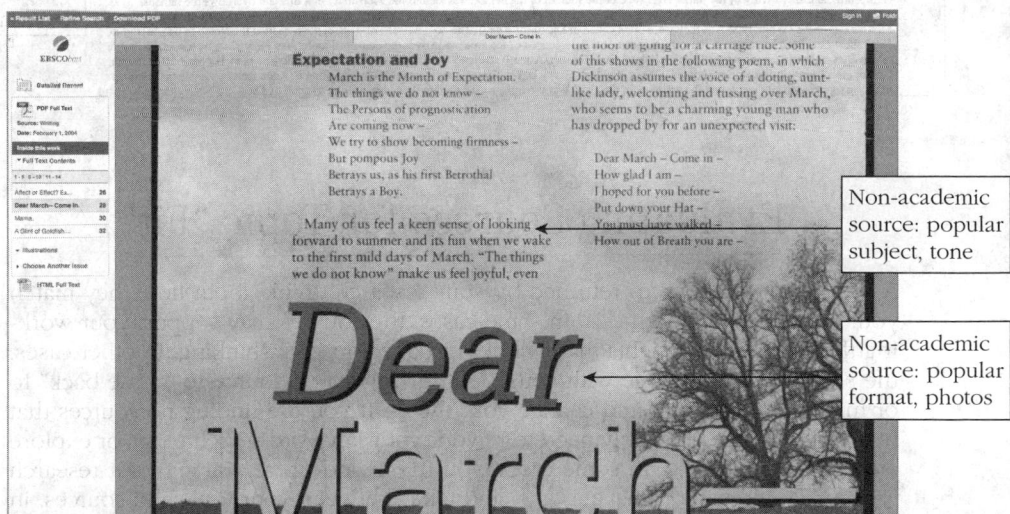

Non-academic source: popular subject, tone

Non-academic source: popular format, photos

In a later search on *Project MUSE*, Mike uses the keywords "Emily Dickinson" and "Autumn." He finds articles that address the specific poem "The Name—of it—is 'Autumn'-" that his paper will analyze. One article catches his eye because its title references the Civil War. When he clicks on the scanned article, he is happy to see that it is clearly an academic source; he downloads the article and saves it into a file that he's labeled "Research-Articles-Dickinson."

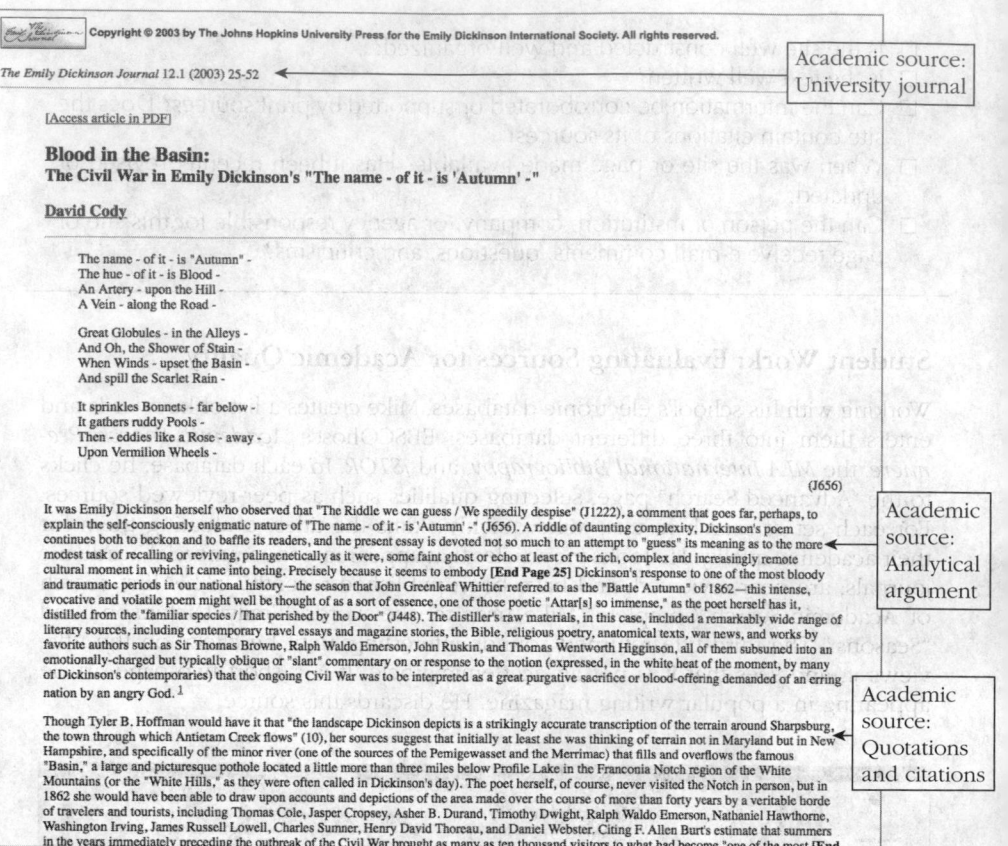

The Emily Dickinson Journal 12.1 (2003) 25-52 ◄───────────────

Academic source:
University journal

[Access article in PDF]

Blood in the Basin:
The Civil War in Emily Dickinson's "The name - of it - is 'Autumn' -"

David Cody

> The name - of it - is "Autumn" -
> The hue - of it - is Blood -
> An Artery - upon the Hill -
> A Vein - along the Road -
>
> Great Globules - in the Alleys -
> And Oh, the Shower of Stain -
> When Winds - upset the Basin -
> And spill the Scarlet Rain -
>
> It sprinkles Bonnets - far below -
> It gathers ruddy Pools -
> Then - eddies like a Rose - away -
> Upon Vermilion Wheels -

(J656)

It was Emily Dickinson herself who observed that "The Riddle we can guess / We speedily despise" (J1222), a comment that goes far, perhaps, to explain the self-consciously enigmatic nature of "The name - of it - is 'Autumn' -" (J656). A riddle of daunting complexity, Dickinson's poem continues both to beckon and to baffle its readers, and the present essay is devoted not so much to an attempt to "guess" its meaning as to the more modest task of recalling or reviving, palingenetically as it were, some faint ghost or echo at least of the rich, complex and increasingly remote cultural moment in which it came into being. Precisely because it seems to embody **[End Page 25]** Dickinson's response to one of the most bloody and traumatic periods in our national history—the season that John Greenleaf Whittier referred to as the "Battle Autumn" of 1862—this intense, evocative and volatile poem might well be thought of as a sort of essence, one of those poetic "Attar[s] so immense," as the poet herself has it, distilled from the "familiar species / That perished by the Door" (J448). The distiller's raw materials, in this case, included a remarkably wide range of literary sources, including contemporary travel essays and magazine stories, the Bible, religious poetry, anatomical texts, war news, and works by favorite authors such as Sir Thomas Browne, Ralph Waldo Emerson, John Ruskin, and Thomas Wentworth Higginson, all of them subsumed into an emotionally-charged but typically oblique or "slant" commentary on or response to the notion (expressed, in the white heat of the moment, by many of Dickinson's contemporaries) that the ongoing Civil War was to be interpreted as a great purgative sacrifice or blood-offering demanded of an erring nation by an angry God. [1]

◄── Academic source: Analytical argument

Though Tyler B. Hoffman would have it that "the landscape Dickinson depicts is a strikingly accurate transcription of the terrain around Sharpsburg, the town through which Antietam Creek flows" (10), her sources suggest that initially at least she was thinking of terrain not in Maryland but in New Hampshire, and specifically of the minor river (one of the sources of the Pemigewasset and the Merrimac) that fills and overflows the famous "Basin," a large and picturesque pothole located a little more than three miles below Profile Lake in the Franconia Notch region of the White Mountains (or the "White Hills," as they were often called in Dickinson's day). The poet herself, of course, never visited the Notch in person, but in 1862 she would have been able to draw upon accounts and depictions of the area made over the course of more than forty years by a veritable horde of travelers and tourists, including Thomas Cole, Jasper Cropsey, Asher B. Durand, Timothy Dwight, Ralph Waldo Emerson, Nathaniel Hawthorne, Washington Irving, James Russell Lowell, Charles Sumner, Henry David Thoreau, and Daniel Webster. Citing F. Allen Burt's estimate that summers in the years immediately preceding the outbreak of the Civil War brought as many as ten thousand visitors to what had become "one of the most **[End**

Academic source: Quotations and citations

Evaluating Sources for Topic "Fit"

As you skim the sources returned by your research, think about how they match your paper's topic and thesis. In some cases, the sources may support your working thesis, offering insights that will help to develop your thinking. In other cases, the sources may disagree with your ideas, giving you a source to "argue back" to or making you rethink and change your thesis. If you are finding no sources that fit your topic, you probably need to rework your keyword search terms or explore an alternate database. In some cases, you may wind up rethinking your research topic. You will want to have a "give and take" between your topic and sources, in which your topic evolves in response to the sources that you find and your sources are selected based on that evolving topic.

Analyze each source for its relevance to your topic—its "fit" with the ideas that you are developing for your paper. Start by skimming the source listing and then the source itself; as a next step, read the source carefully as you work it into your research paper. As you examine the materials that you have located, evaluate these aspects of the source.

✔ **CHECKLIST:** *Evaluating Sources for Topic "Fit"*

☐ **What is the title?** Does the article, essay, book, or chapter title address your topic? Does the title contain words or phrases that match your topic?

☐ **What is the journal's name?** If the source is an article, does the journal's name address your topic? Does the journal present itself as reporting research in an area relating to your topic?

☐ **What subject terms are listed?** All academic databases and catalogs use subject terms that are listed in the source's citation; explore these subject terms. Do the subject terms match your topic? Do the subject terms give you new ways of naming your topic?

☐ **Does the source use your selected literary text and/or author?** Does the source analyze the literary text and/or author that you are analyzing?

☐ **Does the source have a promising abstract?** Some academic sources provide an abstract—a one-paragraph overview of the source's central argument. Does the abstract reveal that the source connects to your topic?

☐ **What is the opening argument?** Skim the source's first few paragraphs. Does the source's opening thesis connect to your topic?

☐ **What is the closing argument?** Skim the source's last few paragraphs. Do the source's concluding arguments connect to your topic?

Student Work: Evaluating Sources for Topic "Fit"

After skimming his sources to make sure that they are reputable academic articles, Mike skims his sources a second time to see if they will help him to develop his paper's topic and working thesis. Rather than focusing on the first sources returned by a search, good researchers sift through a lot of material to locate the *best* material for the research paper. Mike becomes skilled at assessing his search results, using his research topic to decide which sources to read closely and which to discard.

Good keywords will help to locate sources that match your paper's topic. However, even the best keywords will return sources that are off-topic. Mike evaluates the results generated by each search. Before he reads the full-text scan of a journal article, Mike examines each article's title, subject terms, and abstract to help determine if that source will support his topic. If a source is not a good match for his paper's ideas, Mike discards it or keeps it in the database's search folder for future reference. If a source connects to his paper's ideas, he downloads it into his research folder and prints it out.

In one of his initial searches of the MLA database, Mike uses the keywords "Emily Dickinson" and "Nature" because these keywords seem to capture his paper's topic perfectly. These terms return a good number of hits. However, as Mike starts to look at the titles, some do not seem to connect to his paper's topic. For example, the first title returned seems to focus on Insects, not nature more generally. As he reads the first page of the article it becomes clear that this Book explores insects rather than the seasons or weather as aspects of nature.

Mike needs to dig deeper into his search results list. He continues to examine each source, getting to the article. This article seems to be off-topic because it compares Emily Dickinson's writing to that of another author, Alberto Manguel,

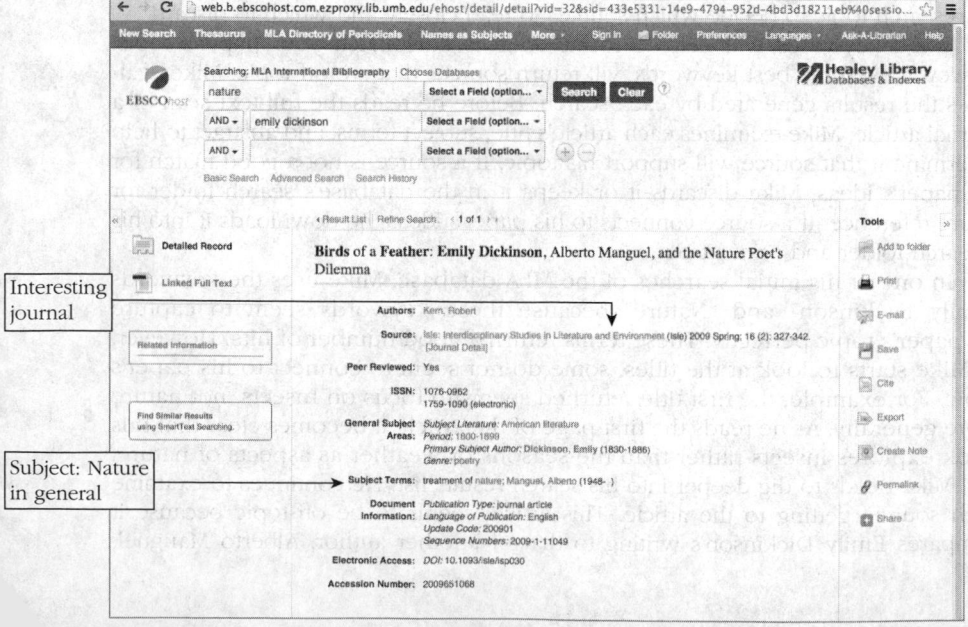

who Mike has never heard of. However, remembering that he can use aspects or parts of an essay, Mike takes a second look at the listing. He notes that the essay's subject term is "nature" and that the essay is published in a journal devoted to "Literature and the Environment." Mike decides that this article is worth a second look and saves it into his "Research-Articles-Dickinson" folder.

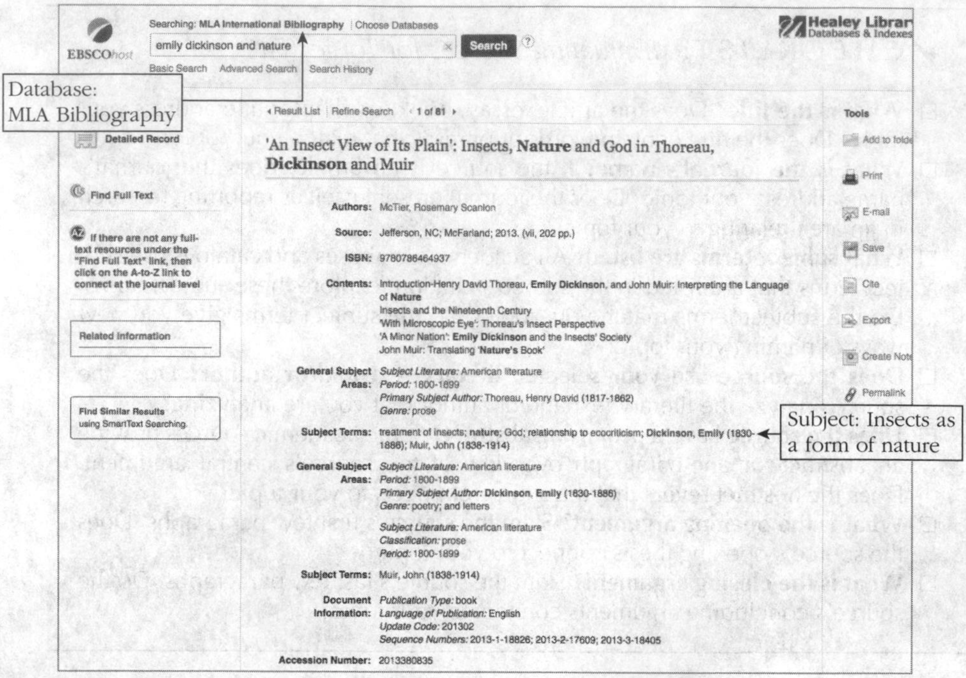

Taking Notes on Secondary Sources

Once you have consulted databases, books, and bibliographies, and have a fair number of references, read to find evidence and interpretations of the evidence in support of your thesis. Most researchers find it convenient, when examining bibliographies and the library catalog, to write down each reference on a 3-by-5-inch index card—one title per card. You may wish to record these references on your computer instead. Either way, in your entries, record the following information:

- the author's full name (last name first);
- the exact title of the book or journal (and, if a journal, the date of publication);
- the title of the chapter (if applicable) or journal article, and the page numbers; and
- (if using a book) the library catalog number on the card (this will save time if you need to get the item for a second look).

Start reading or scanning the materials that you have collected. Some of these items will prove to be irrelevant or silly; others will be valuable and may even provide further references. Be sure to photocopy any material—especially material that can't be taken out of the library—that you may want to refer to later.

A Guide to Note Taking *take a look @ this again*

Some students use note cards, but most now write their notes on a computer and then organize and rearrange this material by copying and pasting, moving the notes into a coherent order. (Be sure to keep all of your notes, even the irrelevant ones. When you write your paper, you may realize that a note you thought wasn't important might actually turn out to be quite valuable.)

Whichever method you prefer, keep in mind the following:

- **For everything you consult or read in detail, always specify the source** so that you know exactly from where you have taken a key point or a quotation.
- **Write summaries, not paraphrases** (See Chapter 6 for more on these terms).
- **Quote sparingly.** This is *your* paper—it will present your thesis, not the thesis, arguments, and analyses of someone else. Quote directly only those passages that are particularly effective, crucial, or memorable. In your finished paper, these quotations will provide authority and emphasis.
- **Quote accurately.** After copying a quotation, check what you have copied against the original, correct any misquotation, and then put a checkmark after your quotation to indicate that it is accurate. Verify the page number also, and then put a checkmark after the page number.

    Use an ellipsis (three spaced periods) to indicate the omission of any words within a sentence. If the omitted words are at the end of the quoted sentence, put a period where you end the sentence and then add three spaced periods to indicate the omission:

    If the . . . words were at the end of the quoted sentence, put a period where you end . . . .

    Use square brackets to indicate your additions to a quotation. Here is an example:

    "Here is an [uninteresting] example."

- **Never copy a passage by changing an occasional word**, under the impression that you are putting it into your own words. Notes of this sort may find their way into your paper, your reader will sense a style that is not your own, and suspicions of plagiarism may follow. (For a detailed discussion of plagiarism, see pages 403–04.)
- **Comment on your notes** as you work and also later as you reflect on what you have jotted down from the sources. Make a special mark—we recommend using double parentheses ((. . .)) or a different color to write, for example, "Jones seriously misreads the passage" or "Smith makes a good point but fails to see its implications." As you work, consider it your obligation to *think* about the material, evaluating it and using it as a stimulus for further thought.
- **In the upper corner of each note card, write a brief key**—for example, "Swordplay in *Hamlet*," so that later you can tell at a glance what is on the note card. If you are using a computer file, be sure to also label these files clearly and consistently.

Student Work: Annotation of Research Sources

Annotation is not just for the literary source! You can annotate the research source, using the same process of highlighting important passages and jotting down ideas in the margins. Rather than read his research resources on-screen, Mike prints them out and marks them up as he reads them. Although this may initially seem like a lot of work, it saves large amounts of time and effort when Mike starts to write, as he will only have to read his annotation and will not have to reread and rethink each source. As Mike annotates his source, he concentrates on locating the most crucial information: the thesis, subarguments, interesting ideas, interpretations of the literary source, and use of critics.

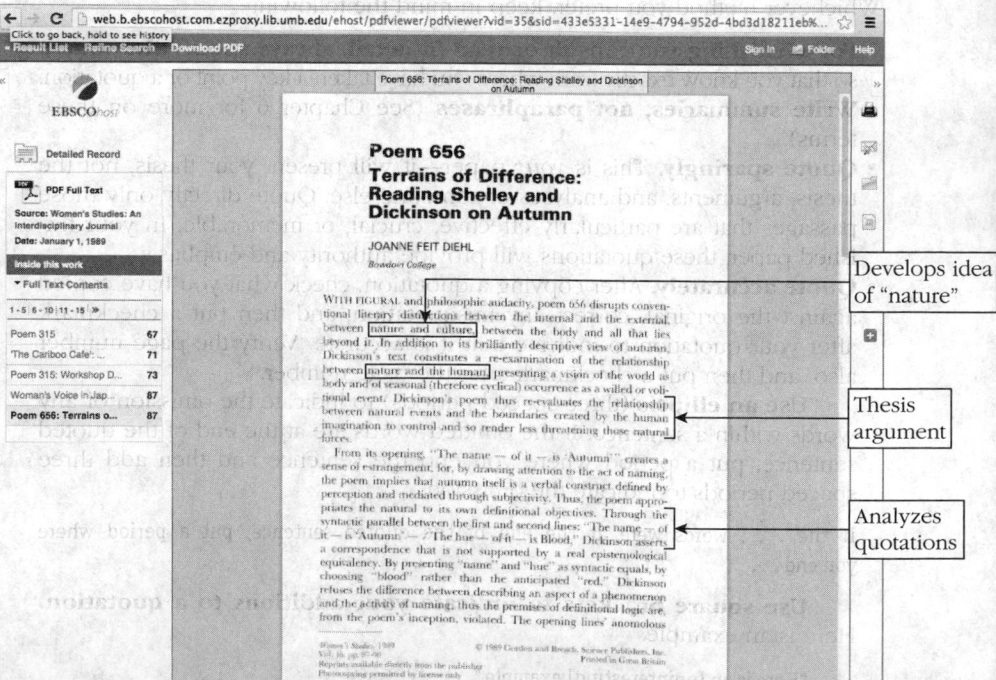

The critical thinking skills that you have developed by writing explications, analytical papers, and interpretation papers can be used to write a research paper, and the process of generating ideas through journal writing should be applied to the research paper. Now that Mike has read and annotated his articles that he thinks are critical to his research, he starts the process of deciding which ideas he wants to use from each source and of determining how those ideas will shape his working thesis. Let's examine how Mike transfers key ideas from his annotations into his research notes, capturing this critical thinking process. Notice how his research notes combine listing information and asking inquiry questions. He notes the ideas that he finds most interesting in the article, and then he records his reactions to those ideas, capturing his thinking about how he might use those ideas in his paper.

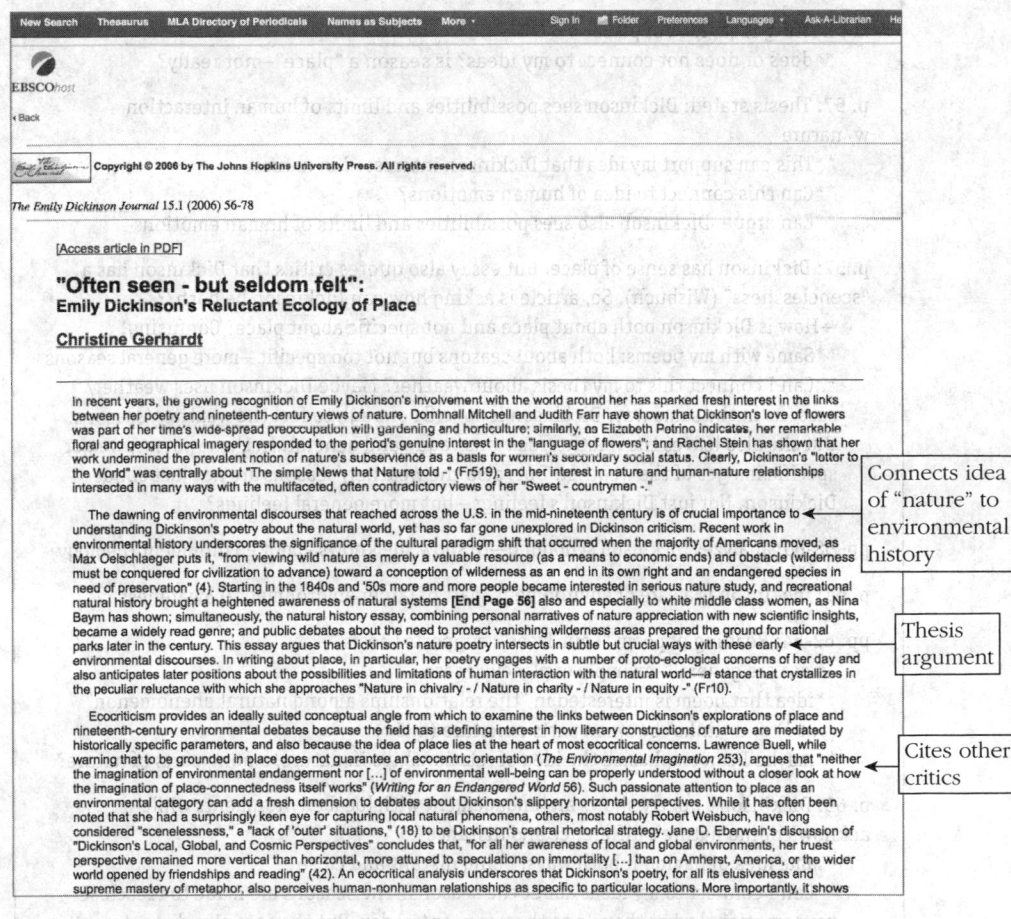

New Search   Thesaurus   MLA Directory of Periodicals   Names as Subjects   More ·   Sign In   📁 Folder   Preferences   Languages ·   Ask-A-Librarian   He

EBSCO*host*

‹ Back

The Emily Dickinson Journal 15.1 (2006) 56-78

[Access article in PDF]

"Often seen - but seldom felt":
Emily Dickinson's Reluctant Ecology of Place

Christine Gerhardt

In recent years, the growing recognition of Emily Dickinson's involvement with the world around her has sparked fresh interest in the links between her poetry and nineteenth-century views of nature. Domhnall Mitchell and Judith Farr have shown that Dickinson's love of flowers was part of her time's wide-spread preoccupation with gardening and horticulture; similarly, as Elizabeth Petrino indicates, her remarkable floral and geographical imagery responded to the period's genuine interest in the "language of flowers"; and Rachel Stein has shown that her work undermined the prevalent notion of nature's subservience as a basis for women's secondary social status. Clearly, Dickinson's "lottor to the World" was centrally about "The simple News that Nature told -" (Fr519), and her interest in nature and human-nature relationships intersected in many ways with the multifaceted, often contradictory views of her "Sweet - countrymen -."

The dawning of environmental discourses that reached across the U.S. in the mid-nineteenth century is of crucial importance to understanding Dickinson's poetry about the natural world, yet has so far gone unexplored in Dickinson criticism. Recent work in environmental history underscores the significance of the cultural paradigm shift that occurred when the majority of Americans moved, as Max Oelschlaeger puts it, "from viewing wild nature as merely a valuable resource (as a means to economic ends) and obstacle (wilderness must be conquered for civilization to advance) toward a conception of wilderness as an end in its own right and an endangered species in need of preservation" (4). Starting in the 1840s and '50s more and more people became interested in serious nature study, and recreational natural history brought a heightened awareness of natural systems **[End Page 56]** also and especially to white middle class women, as Nina Baym has shown; simultaneously, the natural history essay, combining personal narratives of nature appreciation with new scientific insights, became a widely read genre; and public debates about the need to protect vanishing wilderness areas prepared the ground for national parks later in the century. This essay argues that Dickinson's nature poetry intersects in subtle but crucial ways with these early environmental discourses. In writing about place, in particular, her poetry engages with a number of proto-ecological concerns of her day and also anticipates later positions about the possibilities and limitations of human interaction with the natural world—a stance that crystallizes in the peculiar reluctance with which she approaches "Nature in chivalry - / Nature in charity - / Nature in equity -" (Fr10).

Ecocriticism provides an ideally suited conceptual angle from which to examine the links between Dickinson's explorations of place and nineteenth-century environmental debates because the field has a defining interest in how literary constructions of nature are mediated by historically specific parameters, and also because the idea of place lies at the heart of most ecocritical concerns. Lawrence Buell, while warning that to be grounded in place does not guarantee an ecocentric orientation (*The Environmental Imagination* 253), argues that "neither the imagination of environmental endangerment nor [...] of environmental well-being can be properly understood without a closer look at how the imagination of place-connectedness itself works" (*Writing for an Endangered World* 56). Such passionate attention to place as an environmental category can add a fresh dimension to debates about Dickinson's slippery horizontal perspectives. While it has often been noted that she had a surprisingly keen eye for capturing local natural phenomena, others, most notably Robert Weisbuch, have long considered "scenelessness," a "lack of 'outer' situations," (18) to be Dickinson's central rhetorical strategy. Jane D. Eberwein's discussion of "Dickinson's Local, Global, and Cosmic Perspectives" concludes that, "for all her awareness of local and global environments, her truest perspective remained more vertical than horizontal, more attuned to speculations on immortality [...] than on Amherst, America, or the wider world opened by friendships and reading" (42). An ecocritical analysis underscores that Dickinson's poetry, for all its elusiveness and supreme mastery of metaphor, also perceives human-nonhuman relationships as specific to particular locations. More importantly, it shows

Connects idea of "nature" to environmental history

Thesis argument

Cites other critics

Student Work: Digital Research Folder Critical Thinking Notes

Christine Gerhardt article: "Often seen—but seldom felt: Emily Dickinson's Reluctant Ecology of Place" (The Emily Dickinson Journal)

This article connects Dickinson to environmental writing happening in 19th c (ecology).

This article argues that Dickinson has sense of place (New England) but also is reluctant to name places or make environment too specific—this shows that she is reluctant to show humans having power over environment.
   —"Reluctant" is keyword in conclusion

Interesting idea: she wants to be connected to nature, but not too connected—not too controlling
   —kinda wants to have both (connection, no connection)

Interesting idea: idea of place
   **does or does not connect to my ideas? is season a "place"—not really?

p. 57: Thesis stated: Dickinson sees possibilities and limits of human interaction w/nature
   **This can support my idea that Dickinson interested in nature
   **Can this connect to idea of human emotions?
   **Can argue: Dickinson also sees possibilities and limits of human emotions

p. 57: Dickinson has sense of place. But essay also quotes critics that Dickinson has a "scenelessness" (Wisbuch). So, article is asking how can Dickinson be both???
   —How is Dickinson both about place and not specific about place? Confusing!
   **Same with my poems: both about seasons but not too specific—more general seasons
   **Can I connect this to my thesis about weather? Maybe Dickinson uses weather/ seasons in the same way: Dickinson is specific enough to feel the weather/seasons. But she also leaves the weather/seasons vague and general. In these poems, we get specific images of the weather. But, also the weather/seasons are not just about Dickinson. Not just Dickinson's feelings—but more general feelings?

pp. 58-60: analyzes Dickinson schooling—to show she knows about environment (geology)

p. 61: Dickinson is aware of environment, part of larger environmental awareness

pp. 62-64: Reading of poem "Four Trees": supports thesis
   —trees are general—example of placelessness
   **idea that poem is interested in "the relationships among natural phenomenon" (p. 63) and "links" between parts of nature (p. 64)
   **maybe I can emphasize the idea of relationships in nature, among parts of nature?

p. 65: Dickinson's poetry shows an "engagement with local environments while acknowledging nature's difference and distance"
   —same idea of having it both ways: being distant and close
   **Can I connect to my ideas about the seasons? The seasons are made to feel close— very emotional what they do to the narrator/reader. But they are also distant.
   **the seasons/weather is not super-specific—it's abstract??

p. 65: Interesting quote: "Awareness of her limited insights acknowledges a respectful distance between human and nature, which grants nature a dignified autonomy. Through this tentative take on familiar places, the natural environment assumes a presence that goes beyond its role as a 'commodity' for the expanding nation to, for that matter, the observing mind" (65).

> **Dickinson keeps "respectful distance"—this idea could be applied to the weather/ seasons in the poem?
> **But what about when her emotions seem to get violent?

As you analyze academic sources, they should resonate with and start to shape your ideas. This is one of the primary reasons that the research paper is assigned: It teaches you to expand and strengthen your own thinking by creating meaning-ful relationships among ideas. As Mike reads his sources, he considers not only the ideas they contain but also how he wants to position those ideas in his paper. As Mike takes notes on his sources, he is determining how he can *use* those sources in his paper. He wants not only to understand the article but also to decide if he agrees or disagrees with the source. His note taking lays the founda-tion for his integrating the academic sources into his writing. Note taking allows Mike to engage in critical thinking about how he can use the sources to develop his ideas.

Drafting the Research Paper

look at this again

The difficult job of writing about your findings remains, but if you have taken good notes and have put useful headings on each note, you are well on your way to drafting your paper.

- **Read through your notes, and organize them into packets of related material.** Remove all notes that you now see are irrelevant to your paper. (Put them in a "Rejects" file in case you want them later.) Go through the notes again and again, sorting and resorting, putting together what belongs together.
- You may find that you have to do a little **additional research** because you aren't quite clear about something, but, after you have done this additional research, you should be able to arrange your notes into a reasonable and consistent sequence. You now have a kind of first draft, or at least a tentative organization, for your paper.
- **Beware of the compulsion to include every note in your essay**; that is, beware of telling the reader, "A says. . . . ; B says. . . . ; C says. . . ."
- **You must have a point—a thesis.** Make sure that you state your thesis argument early and that you keep it evident to your readers. Use your sourc-es to develop that argument, explaining how the critics help you to further your own ideas.
- **Make sure that the organization is evident to the reader.** By this point, with your notes arranged into what seems to be the correct sequence, ev-erything should add up. In the process of drafting, you will make important changes in your focus, but a draft is not complete until you think it says not only what you want to say but also in what seems to you to be a reasonable order. Your final paper should be a finished piece of work, without the in-consistencies, detours, or dead ends of an early draft. Your readers should feel that they are moving toward a conclusion (by means of your thoughtful

evaluation of the evidence) rather than merely reading an anthology of commentary.

• **Preface all or almost all quotations with a lead-in**, such as "X concisely states the common view" or "Z, without offering any proof, asserts that. . . ." Let the reader know where you are going and **how the quotation fits into your argument.**

Quotations and summaries should always be accompanied by your own analyses. By the end of the paper, your readers not only will have read a neatly typed paper (see pages 405–12.) and gained an idea of what previous writers have said but also will have been persuaded that, under your guidance, they have seen the evidence, heard the arguments summarized, and reached a sound conclusion.

A bibliography or list of works consulted (see pages 412–13.) is usually added at the end of a research paper so that readers may look further into the primary and secondary material if they wish. However, if you have done your job well, readers will be content to leave the subject where you have left it, grateful that you have set matters straight.

Focus on Primary Sources

Remember that your paper should highlight the *primary* literary sources, the materials that are your real subject, rather than secondary sources, the critical and historical discussion of primary materials. **The paper should be, above all, *your* paper**, in which you present a thesis that you have developed about the literary work or works that you have chosen to examine. By using secondary sources, you enrich your analysis, as you place yourself in the midst of the scholarly community interested in this author or authors, and you make your contribution to the ongoing conversation.

To help you succeed in balancing primary and secondary sources, when you review your draft, mark in red the quotations from, and references to, primary sources, and then in blue do the same marking for secondary sources. If, when you scan the pages of your paper-in-progress, you see a lot more blue marks than red marks, you should change the emphasis and the proportion to what they should be. Guard against the tendency to rely heavily on the secondary sources that you have compiled. **The point of view that counts is your own.**

Integrate Secondary Sources

A research paper asks you to use sources to develop your ideas: You connect your ideas to the source's ideas in order to "push" your own thinking forward. Let's explore how you integrate a source into your writing by using multiple critical thinking strategies.

Create a Relationship between Your Writing and the Source

As you reread your research notes, see yourself as creating a relationship between your ideas and another person's ideas. In order to create analytical relationships, consider your stance toward each of your sources. For example, in your opening analysis of a source, ask yourself if you are creating a relationship of agreement or disagreement. Do you agree or disagree with the source? Then ask yourself *why* you agree or disagree. How does that agreement or disagreement help you to think more deeply about your ideas and your working thesis? As you work with each source, think about how you can do the following:

- **Agree with the source:** Can you use the source to support your ideas?
- **Disagree with the source:** Can you argue "back" to the source?
- **Apply the source:** Can you "pick up" an idea from the source and apply it to a new text?
- **Show how the source provides a close reading of a literary work:** Can you examine how a critic reads the literary work, noting what elements the critic finds most interesting?
- **Position the source as an authority:** Can you explain how the critic offers crucial ideas and information?

Surround the Source with Your Writing

As Mike works with his selected articles, he wants to emphasize the bridges that he is building between his ideas and the sources' ideas. After locating specific passages that he wants to quote, he starts to draft paragraphs that integrate those quotations into his writing. He does not just drop a quote into a paragraph, but surrounds the quotation with his analysis and his writing. He has the goal of creating "quote sandwiches," which follows the pattern of "quotation set-up → quotation → quotation analysis." He makes sure to lead into and lead out of a quotation, explaining how the source connects to his ideas.

Agree with a Source in Order to Develop Your Ideas

Through his note taking, Mike discovers a critic whose argument he agrees with. He locates a quotation that states an idea that he agrees with and clearly connects to his thesis. He sets up the quotation by selecting parts of it to quote directly and then connects his agreement to the quotation. By leading into and out of the quotation, Mike is able to explain what ideas within the quotation he finds most useful and most worthy of emphasis.

Student Work: Source Integration
Agree with Source

Critics emphasize that Dickinson uses images of nature to express herself. In her analysis of "There's a certain Slant of Light," Paula Bennett explains, "The world becomes a partner in the poet's depression" (118). She continues to argue that the poem "is explicitly a projection of the poet's inner life, a massive transference to the landscape of her inner state of being" (Bennett 118). I agree with Bennett's idea that Dickinson projects her emotions onto the landscape.

Apply a Source in Order to Develop Your Ideas

Looking at the paragraph that he's just written, Mike realizes that he should not merely agree with the quotation but, instead, should use the quotation to develop or "further" his ideas. Rather than simply state his agreement with the critic, he can continue to analyze her ideas. He decides to explain how her ideas can be applied to the two poems that he has selected; her general ideas about nature can be applied to his more specific ideas about weather and the seasons. He "picks up" the critic's ideas and applies them to the new context of the two poems. This allows him both to further the critic's ideas and to develop his own ideas. He rewrites the last sentence of the paragraph and then continues it:

Student Work: Source Integration
Analyze and Apply Source

. . . Bennet makes the convincing argument that Dickinson projects her inner emotions onto the external landscape. Dickinson uses nature to show human emotions, and this can be seen in how she describes weather and the seasons. In "There's a certain Slant of Light," Dickinson reveals that winter afternoons "oppress" her "like the weight/Of cathedral tunes" (3-4). This passage clearly shows her use of the seasons to express the depression Bennett explains in her article. In "The name—of it—is 'Autumn',", the emotion is less depression and more of being upset or even thrilled by the violence of the seasons. Dickinson describes how the autumn wind has "upset the Basin" (7). The word "upset" can be used to describe her emotions, too.

Disagree with a Source in Order to Develop Your Ideas

Reviewing his sources and his note taking, Mike decides that he disagrees with one of the articles. He creates a paragraph that explains how his reading of the poems differs from the critic's interpretation, connecting his arguments to the critic's arguments. He aims to clarify how his ideas differ from the critic's and then to provide evidence of why his ideas are correct.

Student Work: Source Integration
Disagree with Source

Some critics emphasize that nature allows Dickinson to create a sense of distance in her poetry. For example, in her work on Dickinson's understanding of the environment, Christine Gerdhart emphasizes that Dickinson's writing creates "respectful distance between human and nature, which grants nature a dignified autonomy" (65). However, nature is not distant in "The name –of it—is 'Autumn'-" and "There's a certain Slant of Light." In these poems, the connection between humans and nature overwhelms any distance. Both poems use personification to make nature seem human. For example, in "There's a certain Slant of Light," nature seems cold and reserved, but it is given human qualities: the landscape "listens" and its shadows "hold their breath" (13-14). Nature is not distanced or "autonomous" from people, but acts like people. Nature remains close and connected to people.

Synthesize Critics' Ideas to Show Scholarly Debate

As Mike continues to work with the ideas in this paragraph, he sees an opportunity to compare these two critics' arguments. While Bennett emphasizes the landscape's connection to Dickinson's inner life, Gerhardt emphasizes Dickinson's distance from nature. Mike decides that he can try to show how the critics disagree and then integrate his own thinking into this argument. He creates a new transition paragraph that he can put between the paragraph analyzing Bennett and the paragraph analyzing Gerhardt.

Student Work: Source Integration
Synthesize Sources

Bennett emphasizes that nature becomes human-like, supporting the argument that Dickinson uses the seasons to represent human emotions. According to Bennett, Dickinson uses the landscape to reflect her mind. Therefore, Dickinson is close to nature and, in "The name—of it—is 'Autumn'- and "There's a certain Slant of Light," she connects her emotions to the seasons. However, other critics emphasize the distance between Dickinson and the landscape. Critic Christine Gerhardt argues that Dickinson's poetry shows an "engagement with local environments while acknowledging nature's difference and distance" (65). While Bennett might emphasize this idea of "engagement," Gerhardt emphasizes "difference and distance" (65).

In this paragraph, Mike achieves a complex form of synthesis, reviewing how two critics disagree and explaining his position with regard to that disagreement. As a next step in his writing process, he will revise these three paragraphs as he integrates them into his paper. As part of his revision, he will delete some repetition and make the flow of his ideas clear.

Avoiding Plagiarism

Honest scholarship requires that you acknowledge material that is not your own, not only when you quote directly from a work, but also when you use someone else's original idea (an idea that is not common knowledge). Not to acknowledge such borrowing is plagiarism. If in doubt, give credit.

You ought, however, to develop a sense of what is considered **common knowledge**. Definitions appearing in a dictionary and the date of first publication, for example, of *The Scarlet Letter* (1850) are considered to be common knowledge, so no credit is needed.

Suppose that, in the course of your research for a paper on Langston Hughes, you happen to come across Arnold Rampersad's statement, in an essay in *Voices and Visions* (edited by Helen Vendler), that

> books alone could not save Hughes from loneliness, let alone give him the strength to be a writer. At least one other factor was essential in priming him for creative obsession. In the place in his heart, or psychology, vacated by his parents entered the black masses. (355)

This is an interesting idea, and, in the last sentence, the shift from *heart* to *psychology* is perhaps especially interesting. You certainly *cannot* say, with the implication that the idea and the words are your own, something like

> Hughes let enter into his heart, or his psychology—a place vacated by his parents—the black masses.

Here, you are simply lifting Rampersad's ideas and making only minor changes in the wording. But making even more changes in the wording would still be unacceptable, unless Rampersad is given credit. Here is a restatement that is an example of plagiarism, even though the words differ from Rampersad's:

> Hughes took into himself ordinary black people, thus filling the gap created by his mother and father.

In this version, the writer presents Rampersad's idea as if it were the writer's own and presents it less effectively than Rampersad does.

What can the writer do? Give Rampersad credit, perhaps along these lines:

> As Arnold Rampersad has said, "in the place in his heart, or his psychology" where his parents had once been, Hughes now substituted ordinary black people (355).

You can use another writer's ideas, and even some of the writer's very words, but you *must* give credit, and you *must* use quotation marks when you quote. You can

- give credit and quote directly;
- give credit and summarize the writer's point; or
- give credit and summarize the point but include—within quotation marks—some phrase that you think is especially interesting.

Synthesizing Sources and Ideas: The Research Paper

Student Research Essay: "Dickinson's Representation of Changing Seasons and Changing Emotions"

Mike now has a multilayered research folder on his computer desktop, filled with his research plan notes, working thesis notes, research keyword lists, inquiry questions, and critical thinking notes. He has downloaded and saved the most interesting and relevant critical articles to a folder that he has labeled "Research-Articles-Dickinson," and he has sorted through those articles further to find the best ones for his paper. Mike also has printed out hard copies of these articles, knowing that he has had to carefully read and annotate the essays to fully digest their ideas. Those annotations have led to Mike's drafting of evidence-filled paragraphs that develop his own analysis of Dickinson's poems.

Mike's careful reading and note taking has paid off, allowing him to draft his paper quickly and efficiently. With so many materials at his fingertips, Mike has been able to jump right into the writing process with no fear of writer's block. He has produced a paper that engages in synthesis on many levels: synthesizing two Dickinson poems, synthesizing the poetry with critical articles, synthesizing the arguments in the articles, and, most importantly, synthesizing his ideas about the Dickinson poems with those of the critics.

Mike Ramos

Professor Ashland

English 102

3 May 2016

"Dickinson's Representation of Changing Seasons and Changing Emotions"

Emily Dickinson's poetry contains complex imagery that conveys

complex ideas. Dickinson's poetry describes nature, using images of the

external environment to explore internal emotions. This paper examines

Dickinson's use of nature imagery—especially images of the changing

seasons—to capture changing emotions. In her poems "The name—of it—is

'Autumn'-" and "There's a certain Slant of light," Dickinson imagines intense

emotions. She is able to explore bold, even violent and depressing emotions

by putting them into nature, rather than presenting those emotions as

human emotions. Critics such as Anna Priddy explain, "Dickinson is often

characterized as a nature poet. Certainly the love of the natural world

figures prominently in her work" (51). Wendy Martin also states that

Dickinson has a "simple love of nature" (87). This love of nature can be seen

in Dickinson's poetry featuring the seasons. However, these poems often

have a complex representation of her love of nature, showing nature as full

of power and conflict. In "The name—of it—is 'Autumn'-" and "There's a

certain Slant of light," the changing seasons express emotions that are not

always positive, but the seasons allow those emotions to be shown as natural

and common.

Dickinson's relationship with nature is often presented as a positive

source of inspiration for her poems. In *The Cambridge Introduction to Emily

Dickinson*, Wendy Martin explains, "The heavenliness of nature was a

constant subject for Dickinson's poems. Because she reverenced nature so

intensely, Dickinson constantly felt the need to describe and praise nature's

beauties" (93). She emphasizes Dickinson's "interest in nature's bounty," and

makes it clear that nature affects Dickinson's emotions (Martin 87).

Dickinson "embraced the slower rhythms of nature and rural life that allowed her to enjoy the world's sensory and synaesthetic richness" (Martin 87). Nature imagery allows Dickinson to explore her emotions. And, sensory imagery gives nature vividness, so that the reader feels Dickinson's ideas about nature.

However, as Martin explains, these senses are not always positive: "Although the harmony that Dickinson feels with nature allows her transcendent moments of communion, her love was not blind to its darker rhythms" (95). Neeru Tanson and Anjana Trevedi also emphasize this possibility of a dark side to nature. They argue, "In the poems of Emily Dickinson, nature appears through two basic moods—as a child's garden of flowers, plants, and birds, and as a symbol of mysterious process of death" (147). While nature can be happy and positive, "Dickinson finds that nature is not so gay, innocent and frolicsome as she appears on the surface" (Tanson and Trevedi 147). Under that surface, nature can be "terribly destructive" (Tanson and Trevedi 147). This idea of a more destructive nature can be seen in "The name—of it—is 'Autumn'-" and "There's a certain Slant of light."

Both "The name—of it—is 'Autumn'-" and "There's a certain Slant of light" show nature as full of emotions that can become violent or upsetting. "The name—of it—is 'Autumn'-" describes autumn as an energetic force that disrupts nature in a violent way. Autumn is given the imagery of "Blood" that seems to spill over the landscape (2). "There's a certain Slant of light" focuses on winter, and describes more quiet, less action-packed emotions. However, nature is still powerful and can lead to depression and "Despair" (10). These poems can be read, at first, as describing the seasons of fall and winter and the changing weather they bring. But, on a second reading, the poems can be seen as describing changing human emotions. Both poems provide clear images of how emotions work when they overwhelm people.

"The name—of it—is 'Autumn'-" presents vivid imagery of blood-red autumn leaves covering the ground. The first stanza describes autumn as if it were part of a larger body. That body can be seen as nature, the earth, or the environment. The season brings "Blood" that fills an "Artery" that is "upon the Hill" and a "Vein" that runs "along the Road" (3-5). This powerful image describes leaves filling the pathways up and down a hill, looking like arteries of pumping blood. Autumn is full of powerful change, giving those leaves movement. When those leaves are tossed by the wind and rain, Dickinson captures their movement in her second stanza:

> Great Globules—in the Alleys—
>
> And Oh, the Shower of Stain—
>
> When Wins—upset the Basin—
>
> And spill the Scarlet Rain— (5-8)

Dickinson uses violent imagery, in which autumn seems to be throwing globules of blood and knocking over basins of blood. Her repeated use of dashes captures this sense of movement and energy. The seasons force nature to change, constantly recreating it. The last stanza of the poem describes autumn as becoming calmer: it "sprinkles Bonnets," "gathers Pools," and "eddies like a Rose" (9-11). Autumn then leaves the landscape, moving away "upon Vermilion Wheels" (12). In its path, it has shaken the earth and left a path of blood-like leaves.

In "There's a certain Slant of light," Dickinson describes the season of winter and uses a more subdued set of images. She describes the light created by a winter afternoon as triggering a feeling that "oppresses, like the Heft/Of Cathedral Tunes—" (3-4). Winter causes a feeling of "Heavenly Hurt," but the feeler can "find no scar" (5-6). Thus, the winter afternoon causes strong emotions that are "internal" and difficult to trace (7). Dickinson continues to describe the "Despair" and "internal affliction" sent by the winter light—"sent us of the air" (10-12). The changing seasons obviously cause deep emotions and, as the seasons turn to winter, those emotions become depressing. Dickinson presented striking images to capture feeling of despair caused by winter. The despair is so striking that nature feels it. Nature stops, and "the Landscape listens—/Shadows—hold their breath—" (13-14). Dickinson makes the power of this depression clear by explaining that it connects the human to death. She ends the poem by saying that the landscape and its shadows are depressed by winter light that has "the look of Death" (16).

In her article in *The Emily Dickinson Handbook*, Judith Farr explains that Dickinson "prefers to describe nature in movement or change," and often shows nature sunsets or sunrises "in progress" and animals in "natural motion" (68). The use of imagery of the seasons allows Dickinson to create that feeling of movement or change. In both poems, the changing seasons are powerful because they create change. "The name—of it—is 'Autumn'-" shows the violent power of the rapidly changing seasons. The narrator persona seems to be in awe of nature and its ability to change the earth. The autumn winds are fast-moving and full of unexpected actions. In contrast, in "There's a certain Slant of light," Dickinson describes the season of winter and emphasizes that it causes slow changes that become increasingly depressing. The landscape is described as listening and full of "Shadows" that "hold their breath." This change is still powerful, but it is powerful because it is a slow, pressure-filled force. In "The name—of it—is 'Autumn'-," the imagery is violent, but the persona seems to be thrilled by that violence. In "There's a certain Slant of light," the imagery is more about pressure, and the persona seems to be feeling depressed by the seasons.

In both poems, these changing seasons are connected to human emotions by describing nature as if it were a human body. In "The name—of it—is 'Autumn'-," Autumn changes the earth into a huge human body. The red leaves become the blood pulsing through the body. In "There's a certain

Slant of light," nature is described as if it is a person who can listen and hold
her breath. The natural world is full of shadows that seem to be waiting for
death. The changing seasons can thus be connected to the idea of a person
and to the person's changing emotions.

Nature gives Dickinson a safe way to explore these complicated
human emotions. Her interest in a feeling of violence or the desire to see
blood spilling can be safely put into an image of nature. Her interest in
exploring depression and waiting for death can be safely put into the winter
landscape. Dickinson allows us to see these complicated emotions, but she
reassures us that they are part of nature. Feeling complex, changing
emotions is part of the natural world.

Dickinson's own life shows how she connected her complex emotions
to nature. "Emily Dickinson: The Writing Years (1855–1865)" reveals that
one of Dickinson's favorite hobbies was gardening. This Emily Dickinson
Museum biography explains that, during the years that she was writing the
most poetry, her father "added a conservatory to the Homestead, where
Emily could raise climate-sensitive plants. Now she could engage in her
beloved hobby of gardening year-round." At this same time, as the biography
shows, Dickinson is writing poems about "pain, grief, joy, love, nature, and
art." In addition, just like Dickinson made booklets of her poems, she made a
booklet that collected plants. This *Herbarium* is available on the Harvard
University website, and shows Dickinson's close work with nature. Dickinson
worked with nature through her gardening, and it was obviously an
important part of her life. As a result, she probably felt that nature
connected to her emotional life and even let her feel deep emotions.

Critics explain that Dickinson uses images of nature to express her
deepest emotions. In her analysis of "There's a certain Slant of light," Paula
Bennett explains, "The world becomes a partner in the poet's depression"
(118). She continues to argue that the poem "is explicitly a projection of the

poet's inner life, a massive transference to the landscape of her inner state of being (Bennett, 118). Bennet makes the convincing argument that Dickinson projects her inner emotions onto the external landscape. Dickinson uses nature to show human emotions, and this can be seen in how she describes weather and the seasons. In "There's a certain Slant of light," Dickinson reveals that winter afternoons "oppress" her "like the weight/Of cathedral tunes" (3-4). This passage clearly shows her use of the seasons to express the depression Bennett explains in her article. In "The name—of it—is 'Autumn'-," the emotion is less depression and more of being upset or even thrilled by the violence of the seasons. Dickinson describes how the autumn wind has "upset the Basin" (7). The word "upset" can be used to describe her emotions, too.

Bennett emphasizes that nature becomes human-like, supporting the argument that Dickinson uses the seasons to represent human emotions. According to Bennett, Dickinson uses the landscape to reflect her mind. Therefore, Dickinson is close to nature and, in "The name—of it—is 'Autumn'-" and "There's a certain Slant of light," she connects her emotions to the seasons. However, other critics emphasize the distance between Dickinson and the landscape. Critic Christine Gerhardt argues that Dickinson's poetry shows an "engagement with local environments while acknowledging nature's difference and distance" (65). While Bennett might emphasize this idea of "engagement," Gerhardt emphasizes "difference and distance" (65).

Gerdhart argues that Dickinson's writing creates "respectful distance between human and nature, which grants nature a dignified autonomy" (65). However, nature is not distant in "The name—of it—is 'Autumn'-" and "There's a certain Slant of light." In these poems, the connection between humans and nature overwhelms any distance. Both poems use personification to make nature seem human. For example, in "There's a certain Slant of light," nature seems cold and reserved, but it is given human qualities: the landscape "listens" and its shadows "hold their breath" (13-14). Nature is not distanced or "autonomous" from people, but acts like people. Nature remains close and connected to people. "The name—of it—is 'Autumn'-" goes even further in wanting to remove the "respectful distance between human and nature" that Gerdhart emphasizes (65). This poem seems to want to make the human and nature as close as possible. Nature is given all of the life of a human being, and becomes a human body.

In her article, "Poem 656: Terrains of Difference: Reading Shelley and Dickinson on Autumn," Joanne Feit Diehl explains that "Dickinson's text constitutes a re-examination of the relationship between nature and the human" (87). Emphasizing the reader, Diehl then explains how the poem impacts the reader, arguing, "Because the reader cannot distinguish between what lies within or beyond the self, the poem erodes both rhetorical and physical boundaries" (88). Diehl continues to argue that Dickinson re-maps the boundary between the self and environment, including the boundary between the internal imagination and external nature (89). The boundary between the human and nature is eroded—and Dickinson uses the imagery of changing seasons to do that.

Criticism shows how these poems' powerful images can be connected to even larger ideas about difficult human emotions. For example, in "Blood in the Basin: The Civil War in Emily Dickinson's 'The name—of it—is 'Autumn',"" David Cody explains that the imagery in the poem can be seen as representing the bloody battles of the Civil War or the Bible's idea of death and salvation (38-39). In her chapter on "There's a certain Slant of light," Priddy explains that the poem explores "the difference between the interior and exterior world" and allows Dickinson to explore ideas about pain, death, and mourning (79-80).

Ramos 8

Dickinson uses nature to represent human emotions. As seen in both 'The name—of it—is 'Autumn'-" and "There's a certain Slant of light," she uses images of the changing seasons to explore how human emotions change. 'The name—of it—is 'Autumn'-" depicts emotions as rapidly changing in a violent and thrilling way, while "There's a certain Slant of light" depicts emotions as slowly becoming more depressing. Critics show how Dickinson's nature imagery can use different strategies, including creating distance between humans and nature. In these poems, however, Dickinson erases the boundary between humans and nature. Dickinson relies on the seasons and their changing imagery to capture the force of changing emotions.

[New page]

Ramos 9

Works Cited

Bennett, Paula. *Emily Dickinson: Woman Poet*. Iowa City: U of Iowa P, 1990. Print.

Cody, Davis. "Blood in the Basin: The Civil War in Emily Dickinson's 'The name—of it—is 'Autumn'-." *Emily Dickinson Journal* 12.1 (2003): 25–52. *Project MUSE*. Web. 4 Apr. 2016.

Dickinson, Emily. *Herbarium, circa 1839-1846* (manuscript collection of pressed plants). Houghton Library. Harvard University, n.d. Web. 9 Apr. 2016.

—. "The name—of it—is 'Autumn'-." *Literature for Composition*. Ed. Sylvan Barnet, William Burto, William E. Cain and Cheryl L. Nixon. 11th ed. Boston: Pearson, 2017. 857. Print.

—. "There's a certain Slant of Light." *Literature for Composition*. Ed. Sylvan Barnet, William Burto, William E. Cain and Cheryl L. Nixon. 11th ed. Boston: Pearson, 2017. 857. Print.

Ramos 10

Diehl, Joanne Feit. "Poem 656: Terrains of Difference: Reading Shelley and

Dickinson on Autumn." *Women's Studies* 16.1 (1989): 87–90. *Academic*

Search Premier. Web. 5 Apr. 2016.

"Emily Dickinson: The Writing Years (1855–1865)." *Emily Dickinson Museum: The*

Homestead and the Evergreens. Trustees of Amherst College, 2011. Web.

1 Apr. 2016.

Farr, Judith. "Dickinson and the Visual Arts." *The Emily Dickinson Handbook.* Ed.

Gudrun Grabher, Roland Hagenbuchle, and Cristanne Miller. Amherst, MA:

The U of Massachusetts P, 2005. 61–92. Print.

Gerhardt, Christine. "'Often seen—but seldom felt': Emily Dickinson's Reluctant

Ecology of Place." *Emily Dickinson Journal* 15.1 (2006): 56–78. *Project*

MUSE. Web. 19 Apr. 2016.

Martin, Wendy. *The Cambridge Introduction to Emily Dickinson.* Cambridge:

Cambridge UP, 2007. Print.

Priddy, Anna. *Bloom's How to Write about Emily Dickinson.* New York: Infobase

Publications, 2008. Print.

Tandon, Neeru, and Anjana Trevedi. *Thematic Patterns of Emily Dickinson's Poetry.*

New Delhi: Atlantic Publishers, 2008. Print.

Joining the Conversation: Critical Thinking and Writing

1. What is the thesis of the essay? Where does it appear? Is it clearly stated? Is the thesis developed in the sentences that immediately follow it?
2. In paragraphs 2 and 3, Mike uses critics to help define and explain Dickinson's use of nature. How does he synthesize these critics? List each critic and the key idea that each critic presents that Mike uses in his paper. How does this use of criticism help to present Mike's ideas in his paper as valid?
3. In paragraph 7, Mikes uses the critic Farr to introduce the concept of change. How does he apply Farr's ideas to the two poems? In paragraph 14, Mike uses the critic Dehl to continue to develop his paper's analysis of Dickinson's presentation of nature. How does he use Dehl's ideas to continue to complicate the concept of nature?
4. How does Mike synthesize the critics Bennett and Gerdhart in paragraphs 11–13? Does he position these two critics as agreeing or disagreeing?

5. Examine Mike's close reading of the two Dickinson poems. Does he provide an interpretation of the poems that becomes his thesis concept and subconcepts? Does Mike's analysis of these poems shine through the critics' ideas?
6. How does Mike integrate his research findings on Dickinson's gardening and her "Herbarium" into the paper? Is this part of the paper successful?
7. Examine the formatting of the paper, the paper's parenthetical citations, and the works-cited page. Using Appendix B as a guide, apply its tips and rules to Mike's paper. Does Mike follow these guidelines correctly?

CHAPTER 11

Reading and Writing about Essays

Chapter Preview

After reading this chapter, you will be able to

- Identify types of essays and their elements
- Identify an essay's topic and thesis
- Analyze essays
- Write a successful paper about an essay, using a writing process that moves from first annotations to final draft

The word **essay** entered the English language in 1597, when Francis Bacon called a small book of ten short prose pieces *Essays*. Bacon borrowed the word from Michel de Montaigne, a French writer who in 1580 had published some short prose pieces under the title *Essais*—that is, "testings," or "attempts," from the French verb *essayer,* "to try." Montaigne's title indicated that his graceful and personal jottings—the fruit of pleasant study and meditation—were not fully thought-out treatises but, rather, sketches that could be amplified and amended.

If you keep a journal or write a blog, you are working in Montaigne's tradition. You jot down your thoughts, perhaps your responses to a work of literature, a current event, or a social trend, partly to find out exactly what you think and how you feel. Montaigne said, in the preface to his book, "I am myself the subject of my book," and in all probability you are the real subject of your journal or blog. Your entries—your responses to other writers, events, opinions, and ideas, and your reflections on those responses—require you to examine yourself.

Types of Essays

If you have already taken a course in composition (or even if you haven't), you are probably familiar with the chief kinds of essays. Essays are usually classified—roughly, of course—along the following lines: meditation (or speculation or reflection), argument (or persuasion), exposition (or information), narration, and description.

Of these kinds of essays, the **meditative essay** (or **speculative essay** or **reflective essay**) is the closest to what Montaigne wrote. In a meditative essay, the writer is chiefly concerned with exploring an idea or a feeling. The organization usually seems casual—not a careful and evident structure, but a free flow of thought—what the Japanese (who wrote with brush and ink) called "following the brush." The essayist is thinking, but he or she is not especially concerned with arguing a case, or even with being logical. We think along with the essayist, chiefly because we find the writer's tentative thoughts engaging. The writer may, in the long run, be pressing a point or advancing an argument, but the emphasis is on the free play of mind, not on an orderly and logical analysis.

In the **argumentative essay** (or **persuasive essay**), the organization probably is apparent, and it is reasonable: The essay may announce a problem, define terms, or present and refute solutions that the writer considers to be inadequate, and then, by way of a knockdown ending, offer what the writer believes to be the correct solution. Most academic writing takes the form of an argumentative essay and follows a logical structure that presents a thesis or a central claim, subpoints that explain ideas developing that claim, and evidence that works to prove or support that claim.

The **expository essay** (or **informative essay**), in which the writer is concerned with giving information (for instance, on how to annotate a text, how to read a poem, or how to use a computer), ordinarily has an equally clear organization. A clear organization is necessary in such an essay because the reader is reading, not in order to come into contact with an interesting mind that may keep doubling back on its thinking (as in a meditative essay), and not in order to come to a decision about some controversial issue (as in an argumentative essay), but in order to gain information.

The **narrative essay** and the **descriptive essay** are usually meditative essays. A narrative essay may recount some happening—often a bit of autobiography—partly to allow the writer and the reader to meditate on it. Similarly, a description, let's say of a spider spinning a web or of children playing in the street, usually turns out to be offered, not so much as information—thus, it is unlike the account of how to annotate a text—but as something for the writer and reader to enjoy in itself, and perhaps to think further about.

Most essays are not pure specimens of a single type. An informative essay, let's say on how to make the most out of a trip to New York City, may begin with a paragraph that seeks to persuade you to start your trip with a visit to the Metropolitan Museum of Art rather than the Statue of Liberty. Or, it may begin with a brief narrative, an anecdote of a visitor who loved the Metropolitan Museum of Art, again in order to persuade you to visit this site. Similarly, an argument—and probably most of the essays that you write in English courses will be arguments concerning the meaning or structure of a literary work—may include some exposition, such as a brief summary, to remind the reader of aspects of the work that you will be arguing about.

Elements of Essays

The Essayist's Persona

Many of the essays that give readers the most pleasure are, like entries in a journal, reflective. An essay of this kind sets forth the writer's attitudes or states of mind—the writer's **persona**—and the reader's interest in the essay is almost entirely in the way the writer sees things. It's not so much *what* the writer sees and says as *how* the writer says what he or she sees. Even in essays that are narrative—essays that recount events, such as a bit of biography—our interest is more in the essayists' *responses* to

Elements of Essays   417

the events than in the events themselves. When we read an essay, we might respond, "So that's how it feels to be you" and "Tell me more about the way you see things." The bit of history is less important than the memorable presence of the writer.

Voice

When you read an essay in this chapter or in a later chapter, try to imagine the person who wrote it, the kind of person who seems to be speaking it. Then, slowly reread the essay, noticing *how* the writer conveyed this personality or persona, or **voice** (even while he or she was writing about a topic). The writer's persona may be revealed in part by common or uncommon words, by short or long sentences, by literal or figurative language, or by familiar or erudite examples.

Let's take a simple, familiar example of words that establish a persona. Lincoln begins the *Gettysburg Address* with "Four score and seven years ago. . . ." He might have said "Eighty-seven years ago," but the language would have lacked the biblical echo, and the persona would then have been that of an ordinary person rather than that of a man who has about him something of the tone of an Old Testament prophet. This religious tone of "four score and seven years ago" was entirely fitting because

- President Lincoln was speaking at the dedication of a cemetery for "these hallowed dead," and
- he was urging the members of his audience to give all of their energies to ensure that the dead men had not died in vain.

By such devices as the choice of words, the length of sentences, and the sorts of evidence offered, an author can sound to the reader solemn, agitated, witty, genial, or severe. If you are familiar with the famous *I Have a Dream* speech by Martin Luther King Jr., you may recall that he begins the piece (originally it was a speech, delivered at the Lincoln Memorial on the one hundredth anniversary of Lincoln's Emancipation Proclamation) with these words: "Five score years ago. . . ." King is deliberately echoing Lincoln's words, partly in tribute to Lincoln, but also to help establish himself as the spiritual descendant of Lincoln and, further back, of the founders of the Judeo-Christian tradition.

Tone

Only by reading closely can we hear in the mind's ear the writer's **tone**—friendly, bitter, indignant, or ironic (characterized by wry understatement or overstatement). Perhaps you have heard the line from Owen Wister's novel *The Virginian* (1902): "When you call me that, smile!" Words spoken with a smile mean something different from the same words forced through clenched teeth. But, while speakers can communicate—or guide the responses of their audience—by body language, gestures, facial expressions, and changes in tone of voice, writers have only words on paper.

As a writer, you are learning control of tone when you learn to take pains in your choice of words, in the way you arrange sentences, and even in the punctuation marks that you may find yourself changing in your final draft. These skills will pay off doubly if you apply them to your reading by putting yourself in the place of the writer whose work you are reading.

As a reader, you must make an effort to "hear" the writer's tone as part of the meaning that the words communicate. Skimming is not adequate for that task.

Thinking carefully about the works in this book means, first of all, reading them carefully, listening for the sound of the speaking voice so that you can respond to the persona that the author presents.

Consider the following paragraph from the middle of "Black Men and Public Space," a short essay by Brent Staples. Staples is speaking of growing up in a tough neighborhood. Of course, the paragraph is only a short example; the tone depends, finally, on the entire essay, which will follow.

> As a boy, I saw countless tough guys locked away; I have since buried several, too. They were babies, really—a teenage cousin, a brother of twenty-two, a childhood friend in his mid-twenties—all gone down in episodes of bravado played out in the streets. I came to doubt the virtues of intimidation early on. I chose, perhaps unconsciously, to remain a shadow—timid, but a survivor.

Judging only from these few lines, what do we know about Staples? Perhaps you will agree that we can probably say something along these lines:

- He is relatively quiet and gentle. We sense this, not simply because he tells us that he was "timid," but because (at least, in this passage) he does not raise his voice either in denunciation of white society for creating a system that produces black violence or in denunciation of those blacks during his youth who engaged in violence.
- He is perceptive; he sees that the "tough guys," despite the fact that some were in their twenties, were babies; their bravado was infantile and destructive.
- He speaks with authority; he is giving a firsthand report.
- He doesn't claim to be especially shrewd; he modestly says that he may have "unconsciously" adopted the behavior that enabled him to survive.
- In saying that he is a "survivor," he displays a bit of wry humor. The usual image of a survivor is a guy in a Banana Republic outfit gripping a knife, someone who has survived a dog-eat-dog world by being tougher than the others. But Staples says almost comically that he is a "survivor" who is "timid."

If your responses to the paragraph are somewhat different, list them and try to explain them in a few sentences.

Topic and Thesis

Although we have emphasized the importance of the essayist's personality, essayists also make a point. They have selected a topic, the subject or issue that they want to address. They have a thesis or an argument, and an argument implies taking a specific viewpoint about that topic. In reading an essay, then, try to identify the topic. The topic of "Do-It-Yourself Brain Surgery" cannot really be about brain surgery; it must be about do-it-yourself books, and the attitude will probably be one of amused contempt for such books. Even an essay that is largely narrative, like Brent Staples's recounting a personal experience or a bit of history, will probably have an attitude toward the event that is being narrated. It is that attitude—the interpretation of the event rather than the event itself—that may be the real topic of the essay.

It's time to look at Staples's essay. At the end of this chapter, you will find a writer's portfolio that presents a student's note taking on the essay and her summary paper on the essay.

BRENT STAPLES

Brent Staples, born in 1951 in Chester, Pennsylvania, received a BA degree from Widener University in Chester, Pennsylvania, and a PhD from the University of Chicago. After working as a journalist in Chicago, he joined the New York Times *in 1985, and he is now on the newspaper's editorial board, where he writes on politics and culture. His essay was first published in* Ms. *magazine in 1986 and was reprinted in a slightly revised form—the form we give here—in* Harper's *in 1987.*

Black Men and Public Space

My first victim was a woman—white, well dressed, probably in her late twenties. I came upon her late one evening on a deserted street in Hyde Park, a relatively affluent neighborhood in an otherwise mean, impoverished section of Chicago. As I swung onto the avenue behind her, there seemed to be a discreet, uninflammatory distance between us. Not so. She cast back a worried glance. To her, the youngish black man—a broad six feet two inches with a beard and billowing hair, both hands shoved into the pockets of a bulky military jacket—seemed menacingly close. After a few more quick glimpses, she picked up her pace and was soon running in earnest. Within seconds, she disappeared into a cross street.

That was more than a decade ago. I was twenty-two years old, a graduate student newly arrived at the University of Chicago. It was in the echo of that terrified woman's footfalls that I first began to know the unwieldy inheritance I'd come into—the ability to alter public space in ugly ways. It was clear that she thought herself the quarry of a mugger, a rapist, or worse. Suffering a bout of insomnia, however, I was stalking sleep, not defenseless wayfarers. As a softy who is scarcely able to take a knife to a raw chicken—let alone hold one to a person's throat—I was surprised, embarrassed, and dismayed all at once. Her flight made me feel like an accomplice in tyranny. It also made it clear that I was indistinguishable from the muggers who occasionally seeped into the area from the surrounding ghetto. That first encounter, and those that followed, signified that a vast, unnerving gulf lay between nighttime pedestrians—particularly women—and me. And I soon gathered that being perceived as dangerous is a hazard in itself. I only needed to turn a corner into a dicey situation, or crowd some frightened, armed person in a foyer somewhere, or make an errant move after being pulled over by a policeman. Where fear and weapons meet—and they often do in urban America—there is always the possibility of death.

In that first year, my first away from my hometown, I was to become thoroughly familiar with the language of fear. At dark, shadowy intersections, I could cross in front of a car stopped at a traffic light and elicit the *thunk,* thunk, thunk, thunk of the driver—black, white, male, or female—hammering down the door locks. On less traveled streets after dark, I grew accustomed to but never comfortable with people crossing to the other side of the street rather than pass me. Then there were the standard unpleasantries with policemen, doormen, bouncers, cabdrivers, and others whose business it is to screen out troublesome individuals *before* there is any nastiness.

I moved to New York nearly two years ago and I have remained an avid night walker. In central Manhattan, the near-constant crowd cover minimizes tense one-on-one street encounters. Elsewhere—in SoHo, for example, where sidewalks are narrow and tightly spaced buildings shut out the sky—things can get very taut indeed.

5　　After dark, on the warrenlike streets of Brooklyn where I live, I often see women who fear the worst from me. They seem to have set their faces on neutral, and with their purse straps strung across their chests bandolier-style, they forge ahead as though bracing themselves against being tackled. I understand, of course, that the danger they perceive is not a hallucination. Women are particularly vulnerable to street violence, and young black males are drastically overrepresented among the perpetrators of that violence. Yet these truths are no solace against the kind of alienation that comes of being ever the suspect, a fearsome entity with whom pedestrians avoid making eye contact.

It is not altogether clear to me how I reached the ripe old age of twenty-two without being conscious of the lethality nighttime pedestrians attributed to me. Perhaps it was because in Chester, Pennsylvania, the small, angry industrial town where I came of age in the 1960s, I was scarcely noticeable against a backdrop of gang warfare, street knifings, and murders. I grew up one of the good boys, had perhaps a half-dozen fistfights. In retrospect, my shyness of combat has clear sources.

As a boy, I saw countless tough guys locked away; I have since buried several, too. They were babies, really—a teenage cousin, a brother of twenty-two, a childhood friend in his mid-twenties—all gone down in episodes of bravado played out in the streets. I came to doubt the virtues of intimidation early on. I chose, perhaps unconsciously, to remain a shadow—timid, but a survivor.

The fearsomeness mistakenly attributed to me in public places often has a perilous flavor. The most frightening of these confusions occurred in the late 1970s and early 1980s, when I worked as a journalist in Chicago. One day, rushing into the office of a magazine I was writing for with a deadline story in hand, I was mistaken for a burglar. The office manager called security and, with an ad hoc posse, pursued me through the labyrinthine halls, nearly to my editor's door. I had no way of proving who I was. I could only move briskly toward the company of someone who knew me.

Another time I was on assignment for a local paper and killing time before an interview. I entered a jewelry store on the city's affluent Near North Side. The proprietor excused herself and returned with an enormous red Doberman pinscher straining at the end of a leash. She stood, the dog extended toward me, silent to my questions, her eyes bulging nearly out of her head. I took a cursory look around, nodded, and bade her good night.

10   Relatively speaking, however, I never fared as badly as another black male journalist. He went to nearby Waukegan, Illinois, a couple of summers ago to work on a story about a murderer who was born there. Mistaking the reporter for the killer, police officers hauled him from his car at gunpoint and but for his press credentials would probably have tried to book him. Such episodes are not uncommon. Black men trade tales like this all the time.

Over the years, I learned to smother the rage I felt at so often being taken for a criminal. Not to do so would surely have led to madness. I now take precautions to make myself less threatening. I move about with care, particularly late in the evening. I give a wide berth to nervous people on subway platforms during the wee hours, particularly when I have exchanged business clothes for jeans. If I happen to be entering a building behind some people who appear skittish, I may walk by, letting them clear the lobby before I return, so as not to seem to be following them. I have been calm and extremely congenial on those rare occasions when I've been pulled over by the police.

And on late-evening constitutionals I employ what has proved to be an excellent tension-reducing measure: I whistle melodies from Beethoven and Vivaldi and the more popular classical composers. Even steely New Yorkers hunching toward nighttime destinations seem to relax, and occasionally they even join in the tune. Virtually everybody seems to sense that a mugger wouldn't be warbling bright, sunny selections from Vivaldi's *Four Seasons*. It is my equivalent of the cowbell that hikers wear when they know they are in bear country.

[1987]

Joining the Conversation: Critical Thinking and Writing

1. In a paragraph or two, set forth what you take to be Staples's purpose in "Black Men and Public Space." Do you think he was writing chiefly to clarify ideas for himself—for instance, to explore how he came to discover the "alienation that comes of being ever the suspect"? Or was he writing to assist blacks? Or to assist whites? Or something else? (You may conclude that none of these suggestions are relevant.)

2. The success of a narrative as a piece of writing often depends on the reader's willingness to identify with the narrator. From an examination of "Black Men and Public Space," what explanations can you give for your willingness (or unwillingness) to identify yourself with Staples? (Probably you will want to say something about his persona as you sense it from the essay.) In a five-hundred-word essay explaining your position, very briefly summarize Staples's essay and state his thesis.

3. Have *you* ever unintentionally altered public space? You may recall an experience in which, as a child, your mere presence caused adults to alter their behavior—for instance, to stop quarreling.

    After a session of brainstorming in which you produce some possible topics, you'll want to try to settle on one. After you have chosen a topic and produced a first draft, if you are not satisfied with your first paragraph—if you feel that it is not likely to grab and hold the reader's attention—you may want to imitate the strategy that Staples adopted for his first paragraph.

4. If you have ever been in the position of one of Staples's "victims," that is, if you have ever shown fear or suspicion of someone who, it turned out, meant you no harm (or if you can imagine being in that position), write an essay from the "victim's" point of view. Explain what happened, what you did and thought. Did you think at the time about the feelings of the person you avoided or fled from? Has reading Staples's essay prompted further reflections on your experience? (Suggested length: 750 words.)

✔ CHECKLIST: *Getting Ideas for Writing about Essays*

Persona and Tone

- ☐ What sort of persona does the writer create? Authoritative? Tentative? Wise-guy? Something else?
- ☐ How does the writer create this persona? (Does the writer use colloquial language, formal language, or technical language? Short sentences or long ones? Personal anecdotes? Quotations from authorities?)
- ☐ What is the tone of the essay? Is it, for example, solemn, or playful? Is the tone consistent? If not, how do the shifts affect your understanding of the writer's point or your identification of the writer's persona? Who is the audience?

Kind of Essay

- ☐ What kind of essay is it? Is it chiefly a presentation of facts (an exposition, a report, a history)? A meditation? Or is it chiefly an argument? If it is an argument, what persuasive devices does the writer use? Logic? Appeals to the

(continued)

emotion? (Probably the essay draws on several kinds of writing, but which kind is it primarily? How are the other kinds related to the main kind?) What is the overall purpose of the essay?

☐ What does the essay seem to add up to? If the essay is chiefly meditative or speculative, how much emphasis is placed on the persona? That is, if the essay is a sort of thinking-out-loud, is your interest chiefly in the announced or ostensible topic or in the writer's mood and personality? If the essay is chiefly a presentation of facts, does it also have a larger implication? If it narrates a happening (history), does the reader draw an inference—find a meaning—in the happening? If the essay is chiefly an argument, what is the thesis? How is the thesis supported? (Is it supported, for example, by induction, deduction, analogy, or emotional appeal?) Do you accept the assumptions (explicit and implicit)?

Structure

☐ Is the title appropriate? Propose a better title, if possible.
☐ Did the opening paragraph interest you? Why, or why not? Did the essay continue more or less as expected, or did it turn out to be different from what you anticipated?
☐ Prepare an outline of the essay. What effect does the writer seem to be aiming at by using this structure?

Value

☐ What is especially good (or bad) about the essay? Is it logically persuasive? Or entertaining? Or does it introduce an engaging persona? Or (if it is a narrative) does it tell a story effectively, using (where appropriate) description, dialogue, and commentary, and somehow make you feel that this story is worth reporting?
☐ Does the writer seem to hold values that you share? Or cannot share? Explain.
☐ Do you think that most readers will share your response, or do you think that, for some reason—for example, your age or cultural background—your responses are unusual? Explain.

Student Writing Portfolio

SUMMARY PAPER

Writing a Summary Paper

A summary is a condensation or abridgment; it briefly gives the reader the gist of a longer work. It boils down the longer work, resembling the longer work, for example, as a bouillon cube resembles a bowl of soup. A summary of Staples's "Black Men and Public Space" will reduce the essay, perhaps to a paragraph or two or even to a sentence. It will not call attention to Staples's various strategies, and it will not evaluate his views or his skill as a writer; it will merely present the gist of what he says. We discuss summary in detail in Chapter 6.

If, then, you are asked to write an analysis of something that you have read, you should not hand in a summary. On the other hand, a very brief summary may appropriately appear within an analytical essay. Usually, the reader will need some information, and the writer of the essay will briefly summarize that information. For example, a student, Anna Torres, who wrote about Staples's essay, is *summarizing* when she writes

> Staples says that he is aware that his presence frightens many whites, especially women.

Anna is summarizing because she is reporting, without comment, what Staples said. On the other hand, she is *analyzing* when she writes

> By saying at the outset, "My first victim was a woman—white, well dressed, probably in her late twenties," Staples immediately catches the reader's attention and sets up expectations that will be undermined in the next paragraph.

In this sentence, Anna is not reporting *what* Staples said but is explaining *how* he achieved an effect.

Anna might take her analysis even further by trying to engage in an argument with Staples or apply Staples's ideas to anther situation. For example, she might question how white people have been culturally trained to fear black men or extend Staples's ideas to current examples of black men being unfairly feared. However, these forms of critical thinking—argumentation and application—move beyond the goals and limits of summary.

A summary is information-based: It focuses on conveying the information in a text accurately and concisely. A successful summary demonstrates the reader's understanding of a text and Anna's ability to pass that understanding on to her own readers. Since a summary must condense the source's information, you must think carefully about what ideas you are selecting to explain in your summary. Always summarize the text's most important ideas, and leave out the less important details that are being used to illustrate those ideas. In addition to selecting information carefully, make sure that you are conveying information accurately. As accuracy is one of the central goals of summary, make sure to reread your source and your summary side by side, double-checking the correctness of your information.

In Chapter 6, we discussed principles that govern summaries (see the list on pages 419–20). Here is a summary of our comments on "summary":

> A summary is a condensation or abridgment. Its chief characteristics are that (1) it is rarely more than one-fourth as long as the original; (2) its brevity is usually achieved by leaving out most of the concrete details of the original; (3) it is accurate; (4) it may rearrange the organization of the original, especially if a rearrangement will make things clearer; (5) it is normally in the present tense.

Let's look at the assignment given to Anna, and then explore how she approached that assignment to create a successful summary.

Assignment

One-paragraph Summary:

- This paper asks you to write a concise one-paragraph summary of Brent Staples's essay, "Black Men and Public Space."

- Read "Black Men and Public Space" carefully, noting the most important information that it contains. Reread the essay, determining what information will be essential to convey in your summary. Select the information that you wish to convey carefully.

- Write a one-paragraph summary. Condense the key information in "Black Men and Public Space" into one paragraph. Note that you are capturing the main ideas of a thirteen-paragraph essay in a one-paragraph statement.

- Check your summary for accuracy.

Annotation: Reading for Information

As we explored in Chapters 3 and 4, annotating a text is the best way to increase your comprehension and appreciation of it. Annotation is the practice of reading with a pen in hand, marking up the text as you read it. Active annotation uses a wide variety of marks on the text—underlines, circles, arrows—and a wide variety of marginal notes on the side of the text—repetition of key words, questions, and notes about meaning. Annotation can be focused on the task of summary, noting the key information contained in the text and marking it up in a way that makes that information easy to retrieve.

Annotation marks help to ensure your understanding of the text. If you are reading a difficult, complex, and dense text, you might engage in reading and rereading, repeatedly marking up the text simply to make sure that you understand it. In addition, annotation typically leads to analysis; as a reader, you often can't help but start to question a text's ideas or isolate concepts for development as you read. As you write a summary paper, simply make sure to concentrate on the annotation marks that capture your understanding of the text rather than your analysis of it.

As Anna annotates Brent Staples's "Black Men and Public Space," she uses her marks to gather important information. She underlines sentences that she feels are critical to understanding the text. She also repeats key bits of information in her marginal notes. Some of this information will make its way into her summary, but not all. She must be selective, so she has added stars next to the most important information.

Student Work: Annotation
"Information Gathering" Marginal Notes

My first victim was a woman—white, well dressed, proba- | *victim: white*
bly in her late twenties. I came upon her late one evening on a | *female*
deserted street in Hyde Park, a relatively affluent neighborhood
in an otherwise mean, impoverished section of Chicago. As I
swung onto the avenue behind her, there seemed to be a discreet, uninflammatory distance between us. Not so. She cast
back a worried glance. To her, the youngish black man—a | *writer: black*
broad six feet two inches with a beard and billowing hair, both | *male*
hands shoved into the pockets of a bulky military jacket—
seemed menacingly close. After a few more quick glimpses, she
picked up her pace and was soon running in earnest. Within | *she runs*
seconds, she disappeared into a cross street.

That was more than a decade ago. I was twenty-two years | *he = age 22*
old, a graduate student newly arrived at the University of Chi- | *grad student*
cago. It was in the echo of that terrified woman's footfalls that I
first began to know the unwieldy inheritance I'd come into— | *change public*
the ability to alter public space in ugly ways. It was clear that | *space; fear*
she thought herself the quarry of a mugger, a rapist, or worse. | *(mugger, rapist)*
Suffering a bout of insomnia, however, I was stalking sleep, not
defenseless wayfarers. As a softy who is scarcely able to take a | *"softy"*
knife to a raw chicken—let alone hold one to a person's
throat—I was surprised, embarrassed, and dismayed all at once.
Her flight made me feel like an accomplice in tyranny. It also | *he = tyranny??*
made it clear that I was indistinguishable from the muggers | *unclear*
who occasionally seeped into the area from the surrounding | **he = mugger—*
ghetto. | *why? race*

Note Taking: Using Inquiry Notes to Summarize Information

Inquiry: Paragraph-by-Paragraph Notes

If the essay doesn't include its own summary, we suggest that, after rereading each
paragraph, you write a sentence summarizing the gist of the paragraph. (A very
long or poorly unified paragraph may require two sentences, but make every effort
to boil the paragraph down to a dozen or so words.) A paragraph that consists
merely of a transitional sentence or two ("We will now turn to another example")
you will lump with the next paragraph. Similarly, a series of very short paragraphs—for instance, three examples, each briefly stated, and all illustrating the
same point—you will probably cover with a single sentence. But if a paragraph
runs to half a page or more of print, it's probably worth having its own sentence
of summary. In fact, your author may summarize the paragraph in its opening sentence or in its final sentence.

Anna decides to use this paragraph-by-paragraph approach to starting her summary writing assignment. Here is Anna's paragraph-by-paragraph summary of Staples's "Black Men and Public Space." The numbers refer to Staples's paragraphs.

Student Work: Listing
Paragraph-by-Paragraph Summary Notes

Para #	Summary
1	"First victim" was a white woman in Chicago, who hurried away.
2	Age 22, he realized—to his surprise and embarrassment—that he (a "youngish black man") could be perceived by strangers as a mugger because he is large and black, and young. And, since his presence created fear, he was in a dangerous situation.
3-5	At intersections he heard drivers of cars lock their doors, and elsewhere he sensed hostility of bouncers and others. In NY, lots of tension on narrow sidewalks. Women are esp. afraid of him; he knows why, but that's "no solace."
6	He's not sure why it took him 22 years to see that others fear him, but prob. because in his hometown of Chester, Pa., there was lots of adolescent violence, though he stayed clear of it.
7	As a boy, he saw young toughs killed, and he kept clear, "timid, but a survivor."
8-10	Though he is gentle, he looks fearsome. Once, working as a journalist, he was mistaken for a burglar. Another time, in a jewelry store, the clerk brought out a guard dog. Another black journalist was covering a crime, but the police thought the journalist was the killer. Many blacks have had such experiences or have been treated worse.
11	He has learned to smother his rage—and he keeps away from nervous people.
12	Walking late at night, he whistles familiar classical music, trying to cool things down and reassure others that he is not a mugger.

When you have written your sentence summarizing the last paragraph, you may have done enough if the summary is intended simply for your own private use—for example, to help you review material for an examination. However, if you are going to use it as the basis of a summary within an essay that you are writing, you probably won't want to include a summary that is longer than three or four sentences, so now your job will be to reduce and combine the sentences that you have jotted down. Indeed, you may even want to reduce the summary to a single sentence.

Crafting a Thesis and Creating a Concise Summary

Drafting: Crafting a Strong Thesis

Summarizing each stage of an essay forces a reader to be attentive and can assist the reader in formulating a **thesis statement**, a sentence that (in the reader's opinion) sets forth the writer's central point. If an essay is essentially an argument— for example, an argument for or against capital punishment—it will probably include one or more sentences that directly assert the thesis. "Black Men and Public Space" is chiefly a narrative essay and is much less evidently an argument, but it does have a point, and some of its sentences come pretty close to summarizing that point. Here are three of those sentences:

> And I soon gathered that being perceived as dangerous is a hazard in itself. (2)

> The fearsomeness mistakenly attributed to me in public places often has a perilous flavor. (8)

> I now take precautions to make myself less threatening. (11)

We asked our students to formulate their own thesis sentence for Staples's essay. One student came up with the following sentence after first drafting a couple of tentative versions and then rereading the essay in order to modify them:

> In "Black Men and Public Space," Staples recognizes that because many whites fear a young black man and therefore may do violence to him, he may do well to try to cool the situation by making himself unthreatening.

Notice, again, that a thesis sentence states the *point* of the work. Don't confuse a thesis sentence with a summary of a narrative, such as "Staples at the age of twenty-two came to realize that his presence was threatening to whites, and he has since taken measures to make himself less threatening." This sentence, though true, doesn't clearly get at the point of the essay, the larger generalization that can be drawn from Staples's example.

Look again at the student's formulation of a thesis sentence (*not* the narrative summary sentence that we have just given). If you don't think that it fairly represents Staples's point, you may want to come up with a sentence that seems more precise to you.

Whether you use the thesis sentence that we have quoted or one that you formulate for yourself, you can still disagree strongly with what you take to be Staples's point. Your version of Staples's thesis should accurately reflect your understanding of Staples's point, but you need not agree with that point. For example, you may think that Staples is hypersensitive and thus question some of his conclusions.

A thesis sentence—whether the words are your own or the author's—is thus a capsule summary of the argument (not of the narrative) of the work. If you are writing an essay about an essay, you'll probably want to offer a sentence that reminds your reader of the point of the work that you are discussing or gives the reader the basis of an unfamiliar work. Here is another example of a summarizing thesis statement:

> In "Black Men and Public Space," Brent Staples uses his own experiences to show that black males, however harmless, are in a perilous situation because whites, especially white women, perceive them as threatening.

Let's look at how Anna drafts and redrafts a thesis statement for her summary paper. She wants to create a clear statement that summarizes the most important, overarching point of the essay, and she works through several revisions to hone that statement.

Student Work: Drafting
Crafting a Strong Thesis through Revision

Rough Draft:

Brent Staples is aware that many people see him as dangerous and see him as a threat. This causes him to be in danger himself, as he might get attacked, arrested, or worse. As a result, he recommends that black men try to be nonthreatening and cool everything down, such as in the example of whistling classical music.

key concept: seen as dangerous

too much explanation

unnecessary detail

First Revision:

Brent Staples is aware that many people see him as dangerous, which causes him to realize that he could be in danger himself, and which further causes him to recommend that black men try to adopt nonthreatening behavior and cool everything down.

unneeded detail deleted

tries to get all ideas in one sentence = confusing

Second Revision:

Brent Staples, in "Black Man and Public Space," tells how his awareness that many white people regarded him as dangerous caused him to realize that he was in danger. His recommendation is to reduce anxiety by adopting nonthreatening behavior and cooling everything down.

clarifies idea of danger uses 2 sentences to keep ideas clear

2nd sentence has repetitive ideas

Final Draft:

Brent Staples, in "Black Men and Public Space," tells how his awareness that many white people regarded him as dangerous caused him to realize that he was in danger. His implicitly recommended solution is to try to reduce this anxiety by adopting nonthreatening behavior.

keeps clear first sentence

adds the idea of "implicit" clarifies second sentence by deleting repetition

Drafting: Creating a Concise Summary

Sometimes a fuller summary statement may be useful. For instance, if you are writing about a complex essay that makes six points, you may help your reader if you briefly restate all six points. All six points can never be clearly explained in a sentence or two. The length of your summary will depend on your purpose and the needs of your audience.

The following principles may help you to write your summary:

1. After having written sentences that summarize each paragraph or group of paragraphs, formulate the essay's thesis sentence. Formulating the thesis sentence in writing will help you to stay with what you take to be the writer's main point.

2. Write a first draft by turning your summaries of the paragraphs into fewer and better sentences.

3. Write a lead-in sentence that opens your summary essay. The lead in sentence can incorporate the thesis sentence. Alternatively, it can be a more general statement that names the topic of the text being summarized, preparing the reader for the thesis statement.

4. After writing a lead-in sentence and your thesis statement, organize and revise your summary paragraphs. Read and re-read the draft of your summary as a whole. Revise the draft, eliminating needless repetition, providing transitions, and adding whatever you think may be needed to clarify the work for someone who is unfamiliar with it. Your summary will typically follow the order of ideas in the text being summarized. However, you may rearrange the points if you think the rearrangement will clarify matters.

5. Check the accuracy of your writing. Compare your summary to the original text, making sure that you have both overarching ideas and supporting details correct.

6. Edit your draft for errors in grammar, punctuation, and spelling. Read it aloud to test it once more for readability. Sometimes only by reading aloud do writers detect needless repetition or confusing phrases.

Student Summary Paragraph: Summary Paragraph on Staples (Preliminary Draft)

Anna follows these steps to create a draft of her one-paragraph summary. She rewrites her paragraph-by-paragraph summary notes and adds her thesis statement to the opening of that writing. Because she has broken down the writing process into steps that include lots of note taking and prewriting, she can quickly and efficiently create a rough draft of her summary paragraph.

Anna Torres
English 101
Professor Wynne
25 January 2016

Summary Paragraph on Staples—First Draft

Brent Staples, in "Black Men and Public Space," tells how his awareness that many white people regarded him as dangerous caused him to realize that he was in danger. His implicitly recommended solution is to try to reduce this anxiety by adopting nonthreatening behavior. Staples first frightened a white woman in Chicago. When she hurried away from him, he realized—to his surprise and embarrassment—that because he was large and black and young he seemed to her to be a mugger. And since his presence created fear, he was in a dangerous situation. Other experiences, such as hearing drivers lock their cars when they were waiting at an intersection, have made him aware of the hostility of others. Women are especially afraid of him, and although he knows why, this knowledge does not comfort him. Oddly, it took him twenty-two years to see that others fear him. Perhaps it took this long because he grew up in a violent neighborhood, though he kept clear, making sure to survive. Because he is black and large, whites regard him as fearsome and treat him accordingly (once a clerk in a jewelry store brought out a guard dog), but other blacks have been treated worse. He has learned to smother his rage, and in order to cool things down he tries to reassure nervous people by keeping away from them and (when he is walking late at night) by whistling classical music.

Revision: Using a Revision Strategy

Chapter 8 emphasizes the importance of revision as part of the writing process. Even for a short writing assignment, such as this assignment that asks for only one paragraph, you should allow some time for revision. Rereading and revising your work is an essential step in creating a successful piece of writing.

Chapter 8 provides this revision checklist, which can be applied to Anna's summary paragraph.

✔ REVISION CHECKLIST

Strengthen Your Thesis

☐ Add focus and depth to your central argument.

Develop Your Ideas

☐ Revisit your best responses to literary form and content, adding more thinking to those responses.

Integrate and Explain Your Evidence

☐ Select and analyze rich, interesting quotations to provide evidence for your ideas.

Improve the Organization

☐ Structure your ideas to follow a clear sequence.

Clarify Your Style and Edit for Correctness

☐ Use a consistent, professional style to explain your ideas, correcting sentence structure, word usage, and grammar.

Revision: Revising to Integrate Evidence

Anna has already engaged in revision as part of her drafting process. As seen, she reworked her thesis statement several times. Her paragraph-by-paragraph notes have allowed her to capture the essential ideas of Staples's essay and then to redraft those ideas as she wrote her summary. Anna has not, however, thought about how best to integrate evidence into her writing. Although her writing includes lots of details, it does not include any quotations. A summary should not include lengthy quotations, but it can include short key word or phrase quotations. Short quotations can capture the key ideas of the essay in a concise and effective way. Short quotations can also add liveliness to your writing style.

Student Summary Paragraph: "Exploring Racial Fear: A Summary of Brent Staples' 'Black Men and Public Spaces'" (Final Draft)

After reading her summary and looking back at her notes, Anna adds a few carefully chosen quotations to her draft. Her additions are in bold below. With these final touches in place, Anna's summary paragraph is complete.

Anna Torres
English 101
Professor Wynne
25 January 2016

Exploring Racial Fear: A Summary of Brent Staples' 'Black Men and Public Space'

Brent Staples, in "Black Men and Public Space," tells how his awareness that many white people regarded him as dangerous caused him to realize that he was in danger. His implicitly recommended solution is to try to reduce this anxiety by adopting nonthreatening behavior. Staples's **"first victim"** was a white woman in Chicago. When she hurried away from him, he realized—to his surprise and embarrassment—that because he was **"a youngish black man"** he seemed to her to be a mugger. And since his presence created fear, he was in a dangerous situation. Other experiences, such as hearing drivers lock their cars when they were waiting at an intersection, have made him aware of the hostility of others. Women are especially afraid of him, and although he knows why, this knowledge is **"no solace."** Oddly, it took him twenty-two years to see that others fear him. Perhaps it took this long because he grew up in a violent neighborhood, though he kept clear, **"timid, but a survivor."** Because he is black and large, whites regard him as fearsome and treat him accordingly (once a clerk in a jewelry store brought out a guard dog), but other blacks have been treated worse. He has learned to smother his rage, and uses **"tension-reducing measures,"** such as when he tries to reassure nervous people by keeping away from them and by whistling classical music.

Your Turn: Additional Essays for Analysis

LANGSTON HUGHES

Langston Hughes (1902–67) was born in Joplin, Missouri. He lived part of his youth in Mexico, spent a year at Columbia University, served as a merchant seaman, and worked in a Paris nightclub, where he showed some of his poems to Alain Locke, a strong advocate of African American literature. After returning to the United States, Hughes went on to publish poetry, fiction, plays, essays, and biographies.

Salvation

I was saved from sin when I was going on thirteen. But not really saved. It happened like this. There was a big revival at my Auntie Reed's church. Every night for weeks there had been much preaching, singing, praying, and shouting, and some very hardened sinners had been brought to Christ, and the membership of the church had grown by leaps and bounds. Then just before the revival ended, they held a special meeting for children, "to bring the young lambs to the fold." My aunt spoke of it for days ahead. That night I was escorted to the front row and placed on the mourners' bench with all the other young sinners, who had not yet been brought to Jesus.

My aunt told me that when you were saved you saw a light, and something happened to you inside! And Jesus came into your life! And God was with you from then on! She said you could see and hear and feel Jesus in your soul. I believed her. I had heard a great many old people say the same thing and it seemed to me they ought to know. So I sat there calmly in the hot, crowded church, waiting for Jesus to come to me.

The preacher preached a wonderful rhythmical sermon, all moans and shouts and lonely cries and dire pictures of hell, and then he sang a song about the ninety and nine safe in the fold, but one little lamb was left out in the cold. Then he said: "Won't you come? Won't you come to Jesus? Young lambs, won't you come?" And he held out his arms to all us young sinners there on the mourners' bench. And the little girls cried. And some of them jumped up and went to Jesus right away. But most of us just sat there.

A great many old people came and knelt around us and prayed, old women with jet-black faces and braided hair, old men with work-gnarled hands. And the church sang a song about the lower lights are burning, some poor sinners to be saved. And the whole building rocked with prayer and song.

5   Still I kept waiting to *see* Jesus.

Finally all the young people had gone to the altar and were saved, but one boy and me. He was a rounder's son named Westley. Westley and I were surrounded by sisters and deacons praying. It was very hot in the church, and getting late now. Finally Westley said to me in a whisper: "God damn! I'm tired o' sitting here. Let's get up and be saved." So he got up and was saved.

Then I was left all alone on the mourners' bench. My aunt came and knelt at my knees and cried, while prayers and songs swirled all around me in the little church. The whole congregation prayed for me alone, in a mighty wail of moans and voices. And I kept waiting serenely for Jesus, waiting, waiting—but he didn't come. I wanted to see him, but nothing happened to me. Nothing! I wanted something to happen to me, but nothing happened.

I heard the songs and the minister saying: "Why don't you come? My dear child, why don't you come to Jesus? Jesus is waiting for you. He wants you. Why don't you come? Sister Reed, what is this child's name?"

"Langston," my aunt sobbed.

10   "Langston, why don't you come? Why don't you come and be saved? Oh, Lamb of God! Why don't you come?"

Now it was really getting late. I began to be ashamed of myself, holding everything up so long. I began to wonder what God thought about Westley, who certainly hadn't seen Jesus either, but who was now sitting proudly on the platform, swinging his knickerbockered legs and grinning down at me, surrounded by deacons and old women on their knees praying. God had not struck Westley dead for taking his name in vain or for lying in the temple. So I decided that maybe to save further trouble, I'd better lie, too, and say that Jesus had come, and get up and be saved.

So I got up.

Suddenly the whole room broke into a sea of shouting, as they saw me rise. Waves of rejoicing swept the place. Women leaped in the air. My aunt threw her arms around me. The minister took me by the hand and led me to the platform.

When things quieted down, in a hushed silence, punctuated by a few ecstatic "Amens," all the new young lambs were blessed in the name of God. Then joyous singing filled the room.

15   That night, for the last time in my life but one—for I was a big boy twelve years old—I cried. I cried, in bed alone, and couldn't stop. I buried my head under the quilts, but my aunt heard me. She woke up and told my uncle I was crying because the Holy Ghost had come into my life, and because I had seen Jesus. But I was really crying because I couldn't bear to tell her that I had lied, that I had deceived everybody in the church, and I hadn't seen Jesus, and that now I didn't believe there was a Jesus any more, since he didn't come to help me.

[1940]

Joining the Conversation: Critical Thinking and Writing

1. Do you find "Salvation" amusing, or serious, or both? Explain your answer.
2. How would you characterize the style or voice of the first three sentences: childlike, sophisticated, or what? How would you characterize the final sentence? How can you explain the change in style or tone?
3. Why does Hughes bother to tell us, in paragraph 11, that Westley was "swinging his knickerbockered legs and grinning"? Do you think that Westley, too, may have cried that night? Give your reasons.
4. Is the episode told from the point of view of someone "going on thirteen" or from the point of view of a mature man? Cite evidence to support your position.
5. One of the golden rules of narrative writing is "Show, don't tell." In about five hundred words, report an experience that you had—for instance, a death in the family, a severe (perhaps unjust) punishment, or the first day in a new school—that produced strong feelings. Like Hughes, you may want to draw on an experience in which you were subjected to group pressure. Do not explicitly state your feelings; rather, let the reader understand them chiefly through concretely detailed actions. But, like Hughes, you might state your thesis or basic position in your first paragraph and then indicate when and where the experience took place.

LAURA VANDERKAM

Laura Vanderkam wrote this essay a few months after graduating from Princeton University. At the time that it was published in July 2001, she was working as a Collegiate Network intern with the editorial board of USA Today. *She is a member of* USA Today's *board of contributors, and her work has appeared in* Scientific American, Wired, *and other publications.*

Hookups Starve the Soul

The scene: my college dorm's basement bathroom on a Sunday morning early in my freshman year. As hungover girls crowded around the sinks, I caught a friend's eye in the mirror. What happened when she left last night's party with a boy neither of us had ever seen before?

"Oh," she said with a knowing look, "we hooked up."

No, not planes refueling in midair. Hookups are when a guy and girl get together for a physical encounter and don't expect anything else. They've all but replaced dating at most colleges, according to a study being released today by the Institute on American Values, a non-partisan family issues think tank. Only half of the women interviewed had been on six or more dates during college; a third had been on no more than two.

As a new college graduate, I can attest to this. I've had as many dates in my first 2 months in the real world as I had during my whole college career.

5   Lest you think college students are all libertines, hooking up doesn't mean having sex, although it can. The term includes all of the bases, and the ambiguity is intentional. Modest types can imply that less happened than did, and braggarts can hint at hitting a home run. Hookups are defined by alcohol, physical attraction and a lack of expectations in the morning.

While the study found that only 40% of the women interviewed admitted to hooking up, the practice pervades college culture. Dates and, for the most part, love affairs, are passé. Why bother asking someone to dinner when you can meet at a party, down a few drinks and go home together?

I hear the traditionalists clucking. Sex without commitment. Sounds like a male plot, right? But women are going along.

Some blame the sexual revolution. Some blame co-ed dorms and alcohol abuse. I blame something else. Hookups are part of a larger cultural picture. Today's college kids are the first generation to have had their entire childhoods scheduled. To them, dating is simply not a productive use of time.

Author David Brooks used the phrase "Organization Kid" in April's *Atlantic Monthly* to describe what he discovered at my alma mater, Princeton. After a lifetime of shuffling from soccer practice to scout meetings and piano lessons, today's college kids no longer want to spend hours debating the nature of good and evil, he noted. Once obsessed with getting into increasingly selective colleges—and now obsessed with getting great grades and even greater jobs—they no longer have hours to spend wooing a lover.

10   "I was amazed to learn how little dating goes on," Brooks wrote in the magazine. "Students go out in groups, and there is certainly a fair bit of partying on campus, but as one told me, 'People don't have time or energy to put into real relationships.'"

But 20-year-olds still have hormones, so they hook up instead. They stumble home together late Saturday night, roll around in bed, then pass out. The next morning, it's as if nothing happened.

Hookups do satisfy biology, but the emotional detachment doesn't satisfy the soul. And that's the real problem—not the promiscuity, but the lack of meaning.

People who don't bother with love affairs cut themselves off from life's headier emotions. What about Scarlett O'Hara's passion, or Juliet's? What about the mad jealousy of Dostoevsky's Dmitry Karamazov or even the illicit pleasures of Lady Chatterley and her lover? No great art will be inspired by the muse of Milwaukee's Best or a tryst that both parties are trying to forget.

In the same way, the Organization Kid's lack of soul-searching doesn't bode well for future poets and philosophers. Dostoevsky's Ivan wouldn't have had time to dream up the Grand Inquisitor if he spent his youth being carted from one sport to another and his early 20s obsessed with the perfect lab report.

15   Parents want the best for their kids—but some also want the perfect kid. Somewhere along the way to achieving these perfect children through structured activities, overachieving parents stunt the growth of their children's souls. Too much supervision creates kids who'd rather hook up than fall in love, who'd rather get the right answers on tests than ask the larger questions.

It's too late to bring back the dormitory mothers, curfews and traditional morals that forced courtships in the past. But the Organization Kid culture can be changed. If parents stop rigidly scheduling their children's lives, and if they no longer teach that life is only a series of concrete goals to be met and then exceeded, then there will be more real lovers and truth-seekers in the future—and fewer hookups.

[2001]

Joining the Conversation: Critical Thinking and Writing

1. Vanderkam's opening words—"The scene"—are unusual because they sound like the opening of a play. What other rhetorical devices does Vanderkam use in order to make her essay interesting?
2. In a sentence or two, state Vanderkam's thesis. (Please do not confuse a statement of the thesis—the point, the argument—with a summary of the essay.) Do you agree with her thesis? In whole, in part, or not at all? Whether you agree or disagree with Vanderkam's thesis, write your own five-hundred-word essay on hookups—or on a related topic, such as college dating.

STEVEN DOLOFF

Steven Doloff, a professor of English and humanities at Pratt Institute, has published essays on contemporary culture, education, and travel in numerous publications, including the New York Times, *the* Boston Globe, *and the* Philadelphia Inquirer.

The Opposite Sex

For just one day, imagine yourself a boy (wow!). A girl (ugh).

Having seen Dustin Hoffman's female impersonation in the movie "Tootsie," I decided to give myself some reading over the Christmas recess by assigning in-class essays to my English composition students on how each would spend a day as a member of his or her respective opposite sex. From four classes I received approximately 100 essays. The sample, perhaps like the movie, proved both entertaining and annoying in its predictability.

The female students, as a group, took to the subject immediately and with obvious gusto, while the male students tended to wait a while (in several cases half the period), in something of a daze, before starting. The activities hypothetically engaged in by the women, whose ages averaged about 20, generally reflected two areas: envy of men's physical and social privileges, and curiosity regarding men's true feelings concerning women.

In their essays, women jauntily went places *alone,* and sometimes stayed out *all night.* They threw their clothes on the floor and left dishes in the sink. They hung out on the street and sweated happily in a variety of sports from football to weightlifting.

More than a third of them went out to cruise for dates. Appointing themselves in brand names of men's clothing and dousing themselves in men's cologne I have never heard of (I was instructed to read *Gentleman's Quarterly* magazine), they deliberately and aggressively accosted women, *many* women, on the street, in discos, in supermarkets. Others sought out the proverbial locker room for the kinds of bull sessions they hoped would reveal the real nitty-gritty masculine mind at work (on the subject of women).

5   At least two female students in each class spent chunks of their essays under the sheets with imaginary girlfriends, wives or strangers, finding out with a kind of scientific zeal what sex is like as a man.

Some, but not all of the women ended their essays with a formal, almost obligatory sounding statement of preference to be a female, and of gratitude in returning to their correct gender after a day as Mr. Hyde.

The male students, after their initial paralysis wore off, did not write as much as the females. They seemed envious of very little that was female, and curious about nothing. Three or four spent their day as women frantically seeking medical help to turn back into men more quickly. Those who accepted the assignment more seriously, if unenthusiastically, either stayed home and apathetically checked off a list of domestic chores or, more evasively, went off to work in an office and engaged in totally asexual business office routines.

A small percentage of the men ventured into the more feminine pursuits of putting on makeup and going to the beauty parlor. They agreed looking good was important.

If they stayed home as housewives, when their hypothetical husbands returned from work they ate dinner, watched some television and then went right to sleep. If they were businesswomen, they came directly home after work, ate some dinner, watched TV and went right to sleep. A handful actually went out on dates, had dinner in the most expensive restaurants they could cajole their escorts into taking them to, and then, after being taken home, very politely slammed the doors in their escorts' faces and went right to sleep. Not one male student let anybody lay a finger on him/her.

10   Finally, the sense of heartfelt relief at the end of the male students' essays, underscored by the much-repeated fervent anticipation of masculinity returning with the dawn, seemed equivalent to that of jumping up after having been forced to sit on a lit stove.

Granted, my flimsy statistical sample is nothing to go to the Ford Foundation with for research money. But on the other hand, do I really need to prove that young people even now are still burdened with sexist stereotypes and sexist self-images not nearly as vestigial as we would like to think? (One male student rhetorically crumpled up his paper after 10 minutes and growled, "You can't make me write this!") What does that imply about the rest of us? What would *you* do as a member of the opposite sex for a day? This last question is your essay assignment.

[1983]

Joining the Conversation: Critical Thinking and Writing

1. In paragraphs 2–4, Doloff summarizes the essays that the women wrote, and, in paragraphs 7–10, the essays that the men wrote. Do you think that you would have written something fairly close to the essays that he attributes to the persons of your sex? Explain your answer.

2. Do you think Doloff's assignment is a good one? Please argue why or why not.
3. Write an essay that fulfills Doloff's assignment and that honestly represents your thoughts, but that does *not* largely fit the pattern that Doloff finds.

GRETEL EHRLICH

Gretel Ehrlich, born in 1946, was educated at Bennington College, the UCLA Film School, and the New School for Social Research. She has written fiction and poetry, especially about open spaces (she has lived in Wyoming, Colorado, and Greenland), and has received numerous awards. The following selection comes from The Solace of Open Spaces *(1985).*

About Men

When I'm in New York but feeling lonely for Wyoming I look for the Marlboro ads in the subway. What I'm aching to see is horseflesh, the glint of a spur, a line of distant mountains, brimming creeks, and a reminder of the ranchers and cowboys I've ridden with for the last eight years. But the men I see in those posters with their stern, humorless looks remind me of no one I know here. In our hellbent earnestness to romanticize the cowboy we've ironically disesteemed his true character. If he's "strong and silent" it's because there's probably no one to talk to. If he "rides away into the sunset" it's because he's been on horseback since four in the morning moving cattle and he's trying, fifteen hours later, to get home to his family. If he's "a rugged individualist" he's also part of a team: ranch work is team-work and even the glorified open-range cowboys of the 1880s rode up and down the Chisholm Trail in the company of twenty or thirty other riders. Instead of the macho, trigger-happy man our culture has perversely wanted him to be, the cow-boy is more apt to be convivial, quirky, and softhearted. To be "tough" on a ranch has nothing to do with conquests and displays of power. More often than not, circumstances—like the colt he's riding or an unexpected blizzard—are overpow-ering him. It's not toughness but "toughing it out" that counts. In other words, this macho, cultural artifact the cowboy has become is simply a man who possesses resilience, patience, and an instinct for survival. "Cowboys are just like a pile of rocks—everything happens to them. They get climbed on, kicked, rained and snowed on, scuffed up by wind. Their job is 'just to take it,'" one old-timer told me.

A cowboy is someone who loves his work. Since the hours are long—ten to fifteen hours a day—and the pay is $30 he has to. What's required of him is an odd mixture of physical vigor and maternalism. His part of the beef-raising industry is to birth and nurture calves and take care of their mothers. For the most part his work is done on horseback and in a lifetime he sees and comes to know more animals than people. The iconic myth surrounding him is built on American notions of heroism: the index of a man's value as measured in physical courage. Such ideas have perverted manliness into a self-absorbed race for cheap thrills. In a rancher's world, courage has less to do with facing danger than with acting spontaneously—usually on behalf of an animal or another rider. If a cow is stuck in a boghole he throws a loop around her neck, takes his dally (a half hitch around the saddle horn), and pulls her out with horsepower. If a calf is born sick, he may take her home, warm her in front of the kitchen fire, and massage her legs until dawn. One friend, whose favorite horse was trying to swim a lake with hobbles on, dove under water and cut her legs loose with a knife, then swam her to shore, his arm around her neck lifeguard-style, and saved her from drowning. Because these incidents are usually linked to someone or something outside himself, the westerner's courage is selfless, a form of compassion.

The physical punishment that goes with cowboying is greatly underplayed. Once fear is dispensed with, the threshold of pain rises to meet the demands of the job. When Jane Fonda asked Robert Redford (in the film *Electric Horseman*) if he was sick as he struggled to his feet one morning, he replied, "No, just bent." For once the movies had it right. The cowboys I was sitting with laughed in agreement. Cowboys are rarely complainers; they show their stoicism laughing at themselves.

If a rancher or cowboy has been thought of as a "man's man"—laconic, harddrinking, inscrutable—there's almost no place in which the balancing act between male and female, manliness and femininity, can be more natural. If he's gruff, handsome, and physically fit on the outside, he's androgynous at the core. Ranchers are midwives, hunters, nurturers, providers, and conservationists all at once. What we've interpreted as toughness—weathered skin, calloused hands, a squint in the eye and a growl in the voice—only masks the tenderness inside. "Now don't go telling me these lambs are cute," one rancher warned me the first day I walked into the football-field-sized lambing sheds. The next thing I knew he was holding a black lamb. "Ain't this little rat good-lookin'?"

5   So many of the men who came to the West were Southerners—men looking for work and a new life after the Civil War—that chivalrousness and strict codes of honor were soon thought of as western traits. There were very few women in Wyoming during territorial days, so when they did arrive (some as mail-order brides from places like Philadelphia) there was a standoffishness between the sexes and a formality that persists now. Ranchers still tip their hats and say, "Howdy, ma'am" instead of shaking hands with me.

Even young cowboys are often evasive with women. It's not that they're Jekyll and Hyde creatures—gentle with animals and rough on women—but rather, that they don't know how to bring their tenderness into the house and lack the vocabulary to express the complexity of what they feel. Dancing wildly all night becomes a metaphor for the explosive emotions pent up inside, and when these are, on occasion, released, they're so battery-charged and potent that one caress of the face or one "I love you" will peal for a long while.

The geographical vastness and the social isolation here make emotional evolution seem impossible. Those contradictions of the heart between respectability, logic, and convention on the one hand, and impulse, passion, and intuition on the other, played out wordlessly against the paradisiacal beauty of the West, give cowboys a wide-eyed but drawn look. Their lips pucker up, not with kisses but with immutability. They may want to break out, staying up all night with a lover just to talk, but they don't know how and can't imagine what the consequences will be. Those rare occasions when they do bare themselves result in confusion. "I feel as if I'd sprained my heart," one friend told me a month after such a meeting.

My friend Ted Hoagland[1] wrote, "No one is as fragile as a woman but no one is as fragile as a man." For all the women here who use "fragileness" to avoid work or as a sexual ploy, there are men who try to hide theirs, all the while clinging to an adolescent dependency on women to cook their meals, wash their clothes, and keep the ranch house warm in winter. But there is true vulnerability in evidence here. Because these men work with animals, not machines or numbers, because

---

[1] **Ted Hoagland** Edward Hoagland (1932–   ), American essayist and novelist.

they live outside in landscapes of torrential beauty, because they are confined to a place and a routine embellished with awesome variables, because calves die in the arms that pulled others into life, because they go to the mountains as if on a pilgrimage to find out what makes a herd of elk tick, their strength is also a softness, their toughness, a rare delicacy.

[1985]

Joining the Conversation: Critical Thinking and Writing

1. Early on, Ehrlich says: "In our hellbent earnestness to romanticize the cowboy we've ironically disesteemed his true character." What is she saying in this sentence? Do you find the sentence clear or confusing? Please explain your answer.
2. Later, Ehrlich says that cowboys are not like "Jekyll and Hyde." Identify and explain this reference. Where did you go to find this information?
3. In a paragraph of three or four sentences, summarize the main point that Ehrlich is making. Do you find it hard or easy to write this summary? What does your response suggest to you about Ehrlich's essay as a piece of writing?
4. Would you describe this essay as an argument? Or is it something different? After you read the essay, did your understanding of the topic change? In what way?

CHAPTER 12

Reading and Writing about Stories

Chapter Preview

After reading this chapter, you will be able to

- Define *fiction*
- Identify and analyze the elements of fiction
- Analyze stories
- Write a successful paper about a story, using a writing process that moves from first annotation to final draft

---

Stories True and False

The word *story* comes from *history;* the stories that historians, biographers, and journalists narrate are supposed to be true accounts of what happened. The stories of novelists and short-story writers, however, are admittedly untrue; they are "fiction," things made up, imagined, manufactured. As readers, we come to a supposedly true story with expectations that are different from those we bring to fiction.

Consider the difference between reading a narrative in a newspaper and reading one in a book of short stories. If, while reading a newspaper, we come across a story of, say, a subway accident, we read it for the information about an actual, relatively unusual event. Was anyone hurt? What sort of people are they? Do they live in our neighborhood? Whose fault was the accident? When we read a book of fiction, however, we do not expect to encounter literal truths; we read novels and short stories, not for facts, but for pleasure and for some insight or for a sense of what an aspect of life means to the writer. Consider the following short story by Grace Paley.

GRACE PALEY

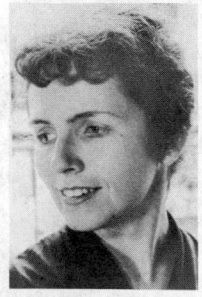

Born in New York City, Grace Paley (1922–2007) attended Hunter College and New York University but left without getting a degree. While raising two children, she wrote poetry and then, in the 1950s, turned to writing fiction. Her publications include Collected Stories *(1994).*

Paley's chief subject was the life of little people struggling in the big city. Of life she said, "How daily life is lived is a mystery to me. You write about what's mysterious to you. What is it like? Why do people do this?" Of the short story she said, "It can be just telling a little tale, or writing a complicated philosophical story. It can be a song, almost."

Samuel

[handwritten: social roles?]

Some boys are very tough. They're afraid of nothing. They are the ones who climb a wall and take a bow at the top. Not only are they brave on the roof, but they make a lot of noise in the darkest part of the cellar where even the super hates to go. They also jiggle and hop on the platform between the locked doors of the subway cars.

Four boys are jiggling on the swaying platform. Their names are Alfred, Calvin, Samuel, and Tom. The men and the women in the cars on either side watch them. They don't like them to jiggle or jump but don't want to interfere. Of course some of the men in the cars were once brave boys like these. One of them had ridden *[handwritten: how]* the tail of a speeding truck from New York to Rockaway Beach without getting off, *[handwritten: society]* without his sore fingers losing hold. Nothing happened to him then or later. He had *[handwritten: views]* made a compact with other boys who preferred to watch: Starting at Eighth Avenue and Fifteenth Street, he would get to some specified place, maybe Twenty-third and *[handwritten: roles]* the river, by hopping the tops of the moving trucks. This was hard to do when one truck turned a corner in the wrong direction and the nearest truck was a couple of feet too high. He made three or four starts before succeeding. He had gotten his idea from a film at school called *The Romance of Logging*. He had finished high school, married a good friend, was in a responsible job and going to night school.

These two men and others looked at the four boys jumping and jiggling on the platform and thought, It must be fun to ride that way, especially now the weather is nice and we're out of the tunnel and way high over the Bronx. Then they thought, These kids do seem to be acting sort of stupid. They *are* little. Then they thought of some of the brave things they had done when they were boys and jiggling didn't seem so risky.

The ladies in the car became very angry when they looked at the four boys. Most of them brought their brows together and hoped the boys could see their extreme disapproval. One of the ladies wanted to get up and say, Be careful you dumb kids, get off that platform or I'll call a cop. But three of the boys were Negroes and the fourth was something else she couldn't tell for sure. She was afraid they'd be fresh and laugh at her and embarrass her. She wasn't afraid they'd hit her, but she was afraid of embarrassment. Another lady thought, Their mothers never know where they are. It wasn't true in this particular case. Their mothers all knew that they had gone to see the missile exhibit on Fourteenth Street.

5   Out on the platform, whenever the train accelerated, the boys would raise their hands and point them up to the sky to act like rockets going off, then they rat-tat-tatted the shatterproof glass pane like machine guns, although no machine guns had been exhibited.

For some reason known only to the motorman, the train began a sudden slowdown. The lady who was afraid of embarrassment saw the boys jerk forward *[handwritten: she]* and backward and grab the swinging guard chains. She had her own boy at home. *[handwritten: wants]* She stood up with determination and went to the door. She slid it open and said, *[handwritten: them to]* "You boys will be hurt. You'll be killed. I'm going to call the conductor if you don't just go into the next car and sit down and be quiet." *[handwritten: safe]*

Two of the boys said, "Yes'm," and acted as though they were about to go. Two of them blinked their eyes a couple of times and pressed their lips together. The train resumed its speed. The door slid shut, parting the lady and the boys. She leaned against the side door because she had to get off at the next stop.

The boys opened their eyes wide at each other and laughed. The lady blushed. *[handwritten: why]* The boys looked at her and laughed harder. They began to pound each other's *[handwritten: do they laugh]* back. Samuel laughed the hardest and pounded Alfred's back until Alfred coughed and the tears came. Alfred held tight to the chain hook. Samuel pounded him even harder when he saw the tears. He said, "Why you bawling? You a baby, huh?" and laughed. One of the men whose boyhood had been more watchful than brave became angry. He stood up straight and looked at the boys for a couple of seconds. Then he walked in a citizenly way to the end of the car, where he pulled the emergency cord. Almost at once, with a terrible hiss, the pressure of air abandoned the brakes and the wheels were caught and held.

People standing in the most secure places fell forward, then backward. Samuel had let go of his hold on the chain so he could pound Tom as well as Alfred. All the passengers in the cars whipped back and forth, but he pitched only forward and fell head first to be crushed and killed between the cars.

10   The train had stopped hard, halfway into the station, and the conductor called at once for the trainmen who knew about this kind of death and how to take the body from the wheels and brakes. There was silence except for passengers from other cars who asked, What happened! What happened! The ladies waited around wondering if he might be an only child. The men recalled other afternoons with very bad endings. The little boys stayed close to each other, leaning and touching shoulders and arms and legs.

When the policeman knocked at the door and told her about it, Samuel's mother began to scream. She screamed all day and moaned all night, though the doctors tried to quiet her with pills.

Oh, oh, she hopelessly cried. She did not know how she could ever find another boy like that one. However, she was a young woman and she became pregnant. Then for a few months she was hopeful. The child born to her was a boy. They brought him to be seen and nursed. She smiled. But immediately she saw that this baby wasn't Samuel. She and her husband together have had other children, but never again will a boy exactly like Samuel be known.

[1968]

Joining the Conversation: Critical Thinking and Writing

1. Paley wrote the story "Samuel," but an unspecified person *tells* it. Describe the voice of this narrator in the first paragraph. Is the voice neutral and objective, or do you hear in it an attitude, a point of view? If you do hear an attitude, what words or phrases in the story indicate it?

2. What do you know about the setting—the locale—of "Samuel"? What can you infer about the neighborhood?

3. In the fourth paragraph, we are told that "three of the boys were Negroes and the fourth was something else." Is race important in this story? Is Samuel "Negro" or "something else"? Does it matter? Respond to these questions in a short argumentative essay.

4. Exactly *why* did a man walk "in a citizenly way to the end of the car, where he pulled the emergency cord"? Do you think the author blames him? What evidence can you offer to support your view? Do *you* blame him? Or do you blame the boys? Or anyone? Explain your answer.

5. The story is called "Samuel," and it is, surely, about him. But what happens after Samuel dies? (You might want to list the events.) What else is the story about?

(You might want to comment on why you believe the items in your list are important.)
6. Can you generalize about what the men think of the jigglers and about what the women think? Is Paley saying something about the sexes? About the attitudes of onlookers in a big city?

Elements of Fiction

You might think about the ways in which "Samuel" differs from a newspaper story of an accident in a subway. (You might even want to write a newspaper version of the accident.) In some ways, Paley's story resembles an account that might appear in a newspaper. Journalists write to give information about

- who,
- what,
- when,
- where, and
- why,

and Paley does provide this material. Thus, the **characters** (Samuel and others) are the journalist's Who; the **plot** (the boys were jiggling on the platform, and when a man pulled the emergency cord, one of them was killed) is the What; the **setting** (the subway, presumably in modern times) is the When and the Where; and the **motivation** (the irritation of the man who pulls the emergency cord) is the Why.

To write about fiction, you need to think about these elements of fiction, asking yourself questions about each, both separately and how they work together. Much of the rest of this chapter will be devoted to examining such words as *character* and *plot*, but before you read those pages, consider the questions we've posed about "Samuel" and respond to them. Your responses will teach you a good deal about what fiction is and the ways in which it works.

Character

In some stories, such as adventure stories, the emphasis is on physical action—wanderings and strange encounters. In Paley's story, "Samuel," however, although there is a violent death in the subway, the emphasis is on other things: for instance, the contrast between some of the adults, the contrast between uptight adults and energetic children, and the impact of the death on Samuel's mother.

The novelist E. M. Forster, in a short critical study, *Aspects of the Novel* (1927), introduced a distinction between **flat characters** and **round characters**. A *flat character* is relatively simple and usually has only one trait: loving wife (or jealous wife), tyrannical husband (or meek husband), braggart, pedant, hypocrite, or whatever. Thus, in "Samuel," we are told about a man "whose boyhood had been more watchful than brave." This man walks "in a citizenly way" to the end of the subway car, where he pulls the emergency cord. He is, so to speak, the conventional solid citizen. He is flat, or uncomplicated, and that is probably part of what the author is getting at. A *round character,* on the other hand, embodies several or even many traits that cohere to form a complex personality. In a story as short as "Samuel," we can hardly expect to find fully rounded characters, but we can say that, at least by comparison with the "citizenly" man, the man who had once been a wild kid, had gone to night school, and now holds a "responsible job" is relatively round. Paley's story asserts rather than shows the development of the character, but much fiction does show such a development.

Whereas a flat character is usually *static* (at the end of the story, the character is pretty much what he or she was at the start), a round character is likely to be *dynamic,* changing considerably as the story progresses.

A frequent assignment in writing courses is to set forth a character sketch describing some person in a story or a novel. In preparing such a sketch, take these points into consideration:

- what the character says (but consider that what he or she says need not be taken at face value; the character may be hypocritical, or self-deceived, or biased—you will have to detect this from the context),
- what the character does,
- what other characters say about the character, and
- what others *do*. (A character who serves as a contrast to another character is called a **foil**.)

A character sketch can be complex and demanding, but usually you will want to do more than write a character sketch. You will probably discuss the character's function, or trace the development of his or her personality, or contrast the character with another character. (One of the most difficult topics, the narrator's personality, is discussed later in this chapter under the heading "Narrative Point of View.") When you are writing on one of these topics, you will probably want to keep in mind the four suggestions for getting at a character, but you will also want to go further, relating your findings to matters that we will discuss later.

Most discussions of fiction are concerned with happenings and with *why* they happen. Why does Samuel die? Because (to put it too simply) his youthful high spirits clash with the values of a "citizenly" adult. Paley never explicitly says anything like this, but a reader of the story tries to make sense of the details by filling in the gaps.

Things happen, in most good fiction, partly because the people have certain personalities or character traits (moral, intellectual, and emotional qualities) and, given their natures, because they respond plausibly to other personalities. What their names are and what they look like may help you to understand them, but probably the best guide to characters is what they do and what they say. As we get to know more about their drives and goals—and especially about the choices they make—we enjoy seeing the writer complete the portraits, finally presenting us with a coherent and credible picture of people in action.

In this view, plot and character are inseparable. Plot is not simply a series of happenings, but happenings that come out of character, that reveal character, and that influence character. The novelist Henry James put it thus in his essay "The Art of Fiction" (1884): "What is character but the determination of incident? What is incident but the illustration of character?" James goes on to say: "It is an incident for a woman to stand up with her hand resting on a table and look out at you in a certain way."

Plot

Plot is the artful arrangement of a story's events for meaningful effect. A plot is not simply a well-organized explanation of an idea or a detailed description of an object; in a plot, something happens and seems to happen for a reason. When we hear or tell a story, we know it is a story because its narration follows a structure that makes use of patterns. And, typically, when we think of a story's structure, we think of the events that are being patterned, sequenced, or ordered. Events are purposefully arranged, and that organization gives the events meaning and encourages the reader's interpretation.

In order to try to explain how a plot makes meaning, critics have distinguished between story and plot. **Story** can be defined as the narration of all the details of what happened, in chronological order, leaving nothing out. **Plot**, in contrast, is the purposeful ordering of the story's events, in which many techniques can be used to tell that same story but shape it into an artful structure that emphasizes elements, highlights ideas, and encourages reactions. In essence, story is the raw material that plot organizes and makes into art. When you analyze plot, you will most likely focus on events, exploring how and why they happen by exploring sequencing and ordering. You might trace how events create a pattern, questioning how that arrangement creates expectations that are then fulfilled or broken. Plot often relies on **causality**, or the ordering of events into cause-and-effect relationships. In a famous formulation, E. M. Forster explains that the sentence "The king died and then the queen" is a story, whereas "The king died and then the queen died of grief" is a plot. The crucial difference between the two sentences is causation: In the second sentence, it is clear that the queen's death was caused by grief. In this "plotted" sentence, the queen died *because* the king died, not simply after the king died; we understand that the king's death led to her death because we are given a clear cause. All plots have a sense of causality, in which events do not simply follow each other but, rather, connect and lead to each other.

Foreshadowing

Although some stories depend heavily on a plot with a surprise ending, other stories prepare the reader to some degree for the outcome. The **foreshadowing** that would eliminate surprise, or greatly reduce it, and destroy a story that has nothing else to offer is a powerful tool in the hands of a writer of serious fiction. In "Samuel," the reader perhaps senses even in the first paragraph that these "tough" boys who "jiggle and hop on the platform" may be vulnerable and may come to an unfortunate end. When a woman says, "You'll be killed," the reader doesn't yet know if she is right, but a seed has been planted.

Even in such a story as William Faulkner's "A Rose for Emily" (page 415), in which we are surprised to learn near the end of the story that Miss Emily has maintained a strange relationship with her lover, from the outset we expect something strange; that is, we are not surprised by the surprise, only by its precise nature. The first sentence of the story tells us that, after Miss Emily's funeral (the narrator begins at the end), the townspeople cross her threshold "out of curiosity to see the inside of her house, which no one save an old manservant . . . had seen in at least ten years." As the story progresses, we see Miss Emily prohibiting people from entering her house, we hear that, after a certain point, no one ever sees Homer Barron again, that "the front door remained closed," and (a few paragraphs before the end of the story) that the townspeople "knew that there was one room in that region above the stairs which no one had seen in forty years." The paragraph preceding the revelation that "the man himself lay in the bed" is devoted to a description of Homer's dust-covered clothing and toilet articles. In short, however much we are unprepared for the precise revelation, we are prepared for something strange happening in the house; and, given Miss Emily's purchase of poison and Homer's disappearance, we have some idea of what will be revealed.

The full meaning of a passage will not become apparent until you have read the entire story. In a sense, a story has at least three lives:

- when we read the story sentence by sentence, trying to turn the sequence of sentences into a consistent whole;
- when we have finished reading the story and we think back on it as a whole, even if we think no more than "That was a waste of time"; and
- when we reread a story, knowing even as we read the first line how it will turn out at the end.

Setting and Atmosphere

Foreshadowing normally makes use of **setting.** The setting or environment is not mere geography, not mere locale: It provides an **atmosphere**, an air that the characters breathe, a world in which they move. Narrowly speaking, the setting is the physical surroundings—the furniture, the architecture, the landscape, and the climate—and these elements are often highly appropriate to the characters who are associated with them. Thus, in Emily Brontë's *Wuthering Heights* (1847), the passionate Earnshaw family is associated with Wuthering Heights, the storm-exposed moorland, whereas the mild Linton family is associated with Thrushcross Grange in the sheltered valley below.

Broadly speaking, setting includes not only the physical surroundings but also a point (or several points) in time. The background against which we see the characters and the events may be specified as morning or evening, spring or fall. In a good story, this temporal setting will probably be highly relevant; it will probably be part of the story's meaning, perhaps providing an ironic contrast to, or exerting an influence on, the characters.

Symbolism

When we read, we may feel that certain characters and certain things in the story stand for more than themselves or hint at larger meanings; that is, we feel that they are symbolic. But we must be careful. How does a reader know that this or that figure or place serves as a symbol and introduces **symbolism** into the story? In Ernest Hemingway's "Cat in the Rain" (page 200), is the cat symbolic? Is the innkeeper? Is the rain? Reasonable people may differ in their answers. Further, in Kate Chopin's "The Story of an Hour" (page 65), is the railroad accident a symbol? Is Josephine a symbol? Is the season (springtime) a symbol? Again, reasonable people may differ in their responses.

Let's assume, however, that if writers use symbols, they want readers to perceive—at least faintly—that certain characters, places, seasons, or happenings have rich implications and stand for something more than what they are on the surface. How do writers help us to perceive these things? They do so by emphasizing them—for instance, by describing them at some length, by introducing them at times when they might not seem strictly necessary, or by calling attention to them repeatedly.

Consider Chopin's treatment of the season in which "The Story of an Hour" takes place. The story has to take place at *some* time, but Chopin does not simply say, "On a spring day," or an autumn day, and let things go at that. Rather, she tells us about the sky, the trees, the rain, the twittering sparrows—and all of this in an extremely short story in which we might think there is no time for talk about the setting. After all, none of this material is strictly necessary to a story about a woman who hears that her husband was killed in an accident, who grieves, then recovers, and then dies when he suddenly reappears.

Why, then, does Chopin give such emphasis to the season? Because, we think, she is using the season symbolically. In this story, the spring is not just a bit of detail added for realism. It is rich with suggestions of renewal, of the new life that Louise achieves for a moment. But, here, we urge caution: We think that the spring in this story is symbolic, but this is not to say that whenever spring appears in a story, it stands for renewal, any more than whenever winter appears in a story it always symbolizes death. Nor does it mean that since spring recurs, Louise will be reborn. In short, in *this* story, Chopin uses the season to convey specific implications.

Is the railroad accident in "The Story of an Hour" also a symbol? Our answer is no, although we don't expect all readers to agree with us. We think that the railroad accident in "The Story of an Hour" is just a railroad accident. It's our sense that Chopin is *not* using this event to say something about modern travel or about industrialism. The steam-propelled railroad train could be used, symbolically, to say something about industrialism displacing an agrarian economy, but does Chopin give the train any such suggestion? We don't think so. Had she wished to do so, she would probably have talked about the enormous power of the train, the shriek of its whistle, the smoke pouring out of the smokestack, the intense fire burning in the engine, its indifference as it charged through the countryside, and so forth. Had she done so, the story would have been a different story. Or she might have made the train a symbol of fate overriding human desires. But, again, in our opinion, Chopin does not endow the train with such suggestions. She gives virtually no emphasis to the train, and so we believe it has virtually no significance for the reader.

What of Chopin's "Ripe Figs" (page 25)? Maman-Nainaine tells Babette that when the figs are ripe, Babette can visit her cousins. Maman-Nainaine may merely be setting an arbitrary date, but, as we read the story, we probably feel—because of the emphasis on the *ripening* of the figs, which occurs in the spring or early summer—that the ripening of the figs in some way suggests the maturing of Babette. If we do get such ideas, we will, in effect, be saying that the story is not simply an anecdote about an old woman whose behavior is odd. True, the narrator of the story, after telling us of Maman-Nainaine's promise, adds, "Not that the ripening of figs had the least thing to do with it, but that is the way Maman-Nainaine was." The narrator sees nothing special—merely Maman-Nainaine's eccentricity—in the connection between the ripening of the figs and Babette's visit to her cousins. Readers, however, may see more than the narrator sees or says. They may see in Babette a young girl maturing; they may see in Maman-Nainaine an older woman who, by almost collaborating with nature, helps Babette to mature.

Here, as we talk about symbolism, we are getting into the theme of the story. An apparently inconsequential and even puzzling action, such as is set forth in "Ripe Figs," may cast a long shadow. As Robert Frost once said,

> There is no story written that has any value at all, however straightforward it looks and free from doubleness, double entendre, that you'd value at all if it didn't have intimations of something more than itself.

The stranger and more mysterious the story is, the more likely we are to suspect some intended significance, but even realistic stories such as Chopin's "The Storm" and "The Story of an Hour" may be rich in suggestions. This is not to say, however, that the suggestions (rather than the details of the surface) are what count. A reader does not discard the richly detailed, highly specific narrative (Mrs. Mallard learns that her husband is dead and reacts in such and such a way) in favor of some supposedly universal message or theme that it implies. We do not throw away the specific narrative—the memorable characters or the interesting things that happen in the story—and move on to some "higher truth." Robert Frost went on to say, "The anecdote, the parable, the surface meaning has got to be good and got to be sufficient in itself."

Narrative Point of View

A writer must choose a **point of view** (or sometimes, several points of view) from which he or she will narrate the story. The choice will contribute to the total effect of the story.

Narrative points of view can be divided into two sorts: **participant** (or **first-person narrative**) and **nonparticipant** (or **third-person narrative**). That is, the narrator may or may not be a character who participates in the story. Each of these two types of narratives can be subdivided:

I. Participant (first-person narrative)
    A. Narrator as a major character
    B. Narrator as a minor character
II. Nonparticipant (third-person narrative)
    A. Omniscient
    B. Selective omniscient
    C. Objective

Participant Points of View Toni Bambara's "The Lesson" (page 654) begins:

> Back in the days when everyone was old and stupid or young and foolish and me and Sugar were the only ones just right, this lady moved on our block with nappy hair and proper speech and no makeup.

In this story, the narrator is a major character. Bambara is the author, but the narrator—the person who tells us the story—is a young girl who speaks of "me and Sugar," and the story is chiefly about the narrator. We can say, then, that Bambara uses a first-person (or participant) point of view. She has invented a young girl who tells us about the impact that a woman in the neighborhood had on her: "[Sugar] can run if she want to and even run faster. But ain't nobody gonna beat me at nuthin." The narrator is a major character. She, and not Bambara, tells the story.

Sometimes a first-person narrator tells a story that focuses on someone other than the narrator; he or she is a minor character, a peripheral witness, for example, to a story about Sally Jones, and we get the story of Sally filtered through, say, the eyes of her friend or brother or cat.

The first-person narrator, whether a major or a minor character, is a particular character who sees things in a particular way. The reader should not assume that the speaker is necessarily a reliable source. Some, in fact, are notably **unreliable narrators**—for instance, young children, mentally impaired adults, and psychopaths. A story told by an unreliable narrator, such as a man consumed with vengeful thoughts, depends largely on the reader's perception of the gap between what the narrator says and what the facts presumably are.

Nonparticipant Points of View In a nonparticipant (third-person) point of view, the teller of the tale does not introduce himself or herself as a character. If the point of view is **omniscient**, the narrator relates what he or she wants to relate about the thoughts as well as the deeds of all the characters. The omniscient narrator can enter the mind of any character; the first-person narrator can only say, "I was angry" or "Jack seemed angry," but the omniscient narrator can say, "Jack was inwardly angry but gave no sign; Jill continued chatting, but she sensed his anger." Thus, in Paley's "Samuel," the narrator tells us that Samuel's mother was "hopeful," but when the new baby was born, "immediately she saw that this baby wasn't Samuel."

Furthermore, a distinction can be made between **neutral omniscience** (the narrator recounts deeds and thoughts but does not judge) and **editorial omniscience** (the narrator not only recounts but also judges). An editorially omniscient narrator knows what goes on in the minds of all the characters and might comment approvingly or disapprovingly: "He closed the book, having finished the story, but, poor fellow, he had missed the meaning."

Because a short story can scarcely hope to develop a picture of several minds effectively, the writer may prefer to limit omniscience to the minds of a few characters or even to that of only one of the characters; that is, the writer may use **selective omniscience** as the point of view. Selective omniscience provides a focus, especially if it is limited to a single character. When thus limited, the writer sees one character from both outside and inside, but sees the other characters only from the outside and from the impact they have on the mind of this selected character. When selective omniscience attempts to record mental activity ranging from consciousness to the unconscious, from clear perceptions to confused longings, it is sometimes labeled the **stream-of-consciousness point of view**.

Finally, sometimes a third-person narrator does not enter even a single mind but records only what crosses an apparently dispassionate eye and ear. This is an **objective point of view** (sometimes called the **camera point of view** or **fly-on-the-wall point of view**). The absence of editorializing and of dissection of the mind often produces the effect of a play; we see and hear the characters in action. For example, "A Rose for Emily" (page 451) opens with dialogue between Miss Emily and town officials trying to collect taxes from her. The dialogue makes this section of the story look like a play:

> We are the city authorities, Miss Emily. Didn't you get a notice from the sheriff, signed by him?"
>
> "I received a paper, yes," Miss Emily said. "Perhaps he considers himself the sheriff. . . . I have no taxes in Jefferson."
>
> "But there is nothing on the books to show that, you see. We must go by the—"
>
> "See Colonel Sartoris. I have no taxes in Jefferson."
>
> "But, Miss Emily—"
>
> "See Colonel Sartoris."

Style and Point of View

A story told by a first-person narrator will have a distinctive style—let's say, the voice of an adolescent boy, or an elderly widow, or a madman. The voice of a third-person narrator—especially the voice of a supposedly objective narrator—will be much less distinctive, but if, especially on rereading, you listen carefully, you will probably hear a distinctive tone. (Look, for instance, at the first paragraph of Grace Paley's "Samuel.") Put it this way: Even a supposedly objective point of view is not purely objective, since it represents the writer's choice of a style, a way of reporting material with an apparently dispassionate voice.

After reading a story, you may want to think about what the story might be like if told from a different point of view. You may find it instructive, for instance, to rewrite "Samuel" from the "citizenly" man's point of view, or "Ripe Figs" from Babette's point of view.

Theme

We distinguish between story (or plot) and theme in fiction. *Story* is concerned with "How does it turn out? What happens?" But **theme** is concerned with "What is it about?" "What does it add up to?" "What motif holds the happenings together?" "What does it make of life, and what wisdom does it offer?" In a good work of fiction, the details add up—in Flannery O'Connor's words, they are "controlled by some overall purpose."

Suppose we think for a moment about the theme of Paley's "Samuel." Do we sense an "overall purpose" that holds the story together? Different readers will inevitably come up with different readings, that is, with different views of what the story is about. Here is one student's version:

Whites cannot understand the feelings of blacks.

This statement gets at an important element in the story—the conflict between the sober-minded adults and the jiggling boys—but it assumes that all of the adults are white, an inference that cannot be supported by pointing to evidence in the story. Further, we cannot be certain that Samuel is black. And, finally, even if Samuel and his mother are black, surely white readers *do understand his youthful enthusiasm and his mother's inconsolable grief*.

Here is a second version:

One should not interfere with the actions of others.

Does the story really offer such specific advice? This version of the theme seems to us to reduce the story to a too-simple code of action, a heartless rule of behavior, a rule that seems at odds with the writer's awareness of the mother's enduring grief.

Here is a third version:

Middle-class adults, acting from what seem to them to be the best of motives, may cause irreparable harm and grief.

This last statement seems to us to be one that can be fully supported by checking it against the story, but other equally valid statements can probably be made. How would you put it?

Let's look at Faulkner's story. At the end of this chapter, you will find a writer's portfolio that presents a student's note taking on the essay and writing of an analytical paper on the story.

WILLIAM FAULKNER

William Faulkner (1897–1962) was brought up in Oxford, Mississippi. His great-grandfather had been a Civil War hero, and his father was treasurer of the University of Mississippi in Oxford. The family was no longer rich, but it was still respected. In 1918, he enrolled in the Royal Canadian Air Force, though he never saw overseas service. After the war, he returned to Mississippi and went to the university for two years. He then moved to New Orleans, where he became friendly with Sherwood Anderson, who was already an established writer. In New Orleans, Faulkner worked for the Times-Picayune; *still later, even after he had established himself as a major novelist with* The Sound and the Fury *(1929), he had to work in Hollywood in order to make ends meet. In 1950, he was awarded the Nobel Prize in Literature.*

A Rose for Emily

I

When Miss Emily Grierson died, our whole town went to her funeral: the men through a sort of respectful affection for a fallen monument, the women mostly out of curiosity to see the inside of her house, which no one save an old Negro manservant—a combined gardener and cook—had seen in at least ten years.

It was a big, squarish, frame house that had once been white, decorated with cupolas and spires and scrolled balconies in the heavily lightsome style of the seventies, set on what had once been our most select street. But garages and cotton gins had encroached and obliterated even the august names of that neighborhood; only Miss Emily's house was left, lifting its stubborn and coquettish decay above the cotton wagons and the gasoline pumps—an eyesore among eyesores. And now Miss Emily had gone to join the representatives of those august names where they lay in the cedar-bemused cemetery among the ranked and anonymous graves of Union and Confederate soldiers who fell at the battle of Jefferson.

Alive, Miss Emily had been a tradition, a duty, and a care; a sort of hereditary obligation upon the town, dating from that day in 1894 when Colonel Sartoris, the mayor—he who fathered the edict that no Negro woman should appear on the streets without an apron—remitted her taxes, the dispensation dating from the death of her father on into perpetuity. Not that Miss Emily would have accepted charity. Colonel Sartoris invented an involved tale to the effect that Miss Emily's father had loaned money to the town, which the town, as a matter of business, preferred this way of repaying. Only a man of Colonel Sartoris' generation and thought could have invented it, and only a woman could have believed it.

When the next generation, with its more modern ideas, became mayors and aldermen, this arrangement created some little dissatisfaction. On the first of the year they mailed her a tax notice. February came, and there was no reply. They wrote her a formal letter, asking her to call at the sheriff's office at her convenience. A week later the mayor wrote her himself, offering to call or to send his car for her, and received in reply a note on paper of an archaic shape, in a thin, flowing calligraphy in faded ink, to the effect that she no longer went out at all. The tax notice was also enclosed, without comment.

5   They called a special meeting of the Board of Aldermen. A deputation waited upon her, knocked at the door through which no visitor had passed since she

ceased giving china-painting lessons eight or ten years earlier. They were admitted by the old Negro into a dim hall from which a stairway mounted into still more shadow. It smelled of dust and disuse—a close, dank smell. The Negro led them into the parlor. It was furnished in heavy, leather-covered furniture. When the Negro opened the blinds of one window, they could see that the leather was cracked; and when they sat down, a faint dust rose sluggishly about their thighs, spinning with slow motes in the single sun-ray. On a tarnished gilt easel before the fireplace stood a crayon portrait of Miss Emily's father.

They rose when she entered—a small, fat woman in black, with a thin gold chain descending to her waist and vanishing into her belt, leaning on an ebony cane with a tarnished gold head. Her skeleton was small and spare; perhaps that was why what would have been merely plumpness in another was obesity in her. She looked bloated, like a body long submerged in motionless water, and of that pallid hue. Her eyes, lost in the fatty ridges of her face, looked like two small pieces of coal pressed into a lump of dough as they moved from one face to another while the visitors stated their errand.

She did not ask them to sit. She just stood in the door and listened quietly until the spokesman came to a stumbling halt. Then they could hear the invisible watch ticking at the end of the gold chain.

Her voice was dry and cold. "I have no taxes in Jefferson. Colonel Sartoris explained it to me. Perhaps one of you can gain access to the city records and satisfy yourselves."

"But we have. We are the city authorities, Miss Emily. Didn't you get a notice from the sheriff, signed by him?"

10   "I received a paper, yes," Miss Emily said. "Perhaps he considers himself the sheriff. . . . I have no taxes in Jefferson."

"But there is nothing on the books to show that, you see. We must go by the—"

"See Colonel Sartoris. I have no taxes in Jefferson."

"But, Miss Emily—"

"See Colonel Sartoris." (Colonel Sartoris had been dead almost ten years.) "I have no taxes in Jefferson. Tobe!" The Negro appeared. "Show these gentlemen out."

II

15   So she vanquished them, horse and foot, just as she had vanquished their fathers thirty years before about the smell. That was two years after her father's death and a short time after her sweetheart—the one we believed would marry her—had deserted her. After her father's death she went out very little; after her sweetheart went away, people hardly saw her at all. A few of the ladies had the temerity to call, but were not received, and the only sign of life about the place was the Negro man—a young man then—going in and out with a market basket.

"Just as if a man—any man—could keep a kitchen properly," the ladies said; so they were not surprised when the smell developed. It was another link between the gross, teeming world and the high and mighty Griersons.

A neighbor, a woman, complained to the mayor, Judge Stevens, eighty years old.

"But what will you have me do about it, madam?" he said.

"Why, send her word to stop it," the woman said. "Isn't there a law?"

20   "I'm sure that won't be necessary," Judge Stevens said. "It's probably just a snake or a rat that nigger of hers killed in the yard. I'll speak to him about it."

The next day he received two more complaints, one from a man who came in diffident deprecation. "We really must do something about it, Judge. I'd be the last one in the world to bother Miss Emily, but we've got to do something." That night the Board of Aldermen met—three graybeards and one younger man, a member of the rising generation.

"It's simple enough," he said. "Send her word to have her place cleaned up. Give her a certain time to do it in, and if she don't . . ."

"Dammit, sir," Judge Stevens said, "will you accuse a lady to her face of smelling bad?"

So the next night, after midnight, four men crossed Miss Emily's lawn and slunk about the house like burglars, sniffing along the base of the brickwork and at the cellar openings while one of them performed a regular sowing motion with his hand out of a sack slung from his shoulder. They broke open the cellar door and sprinkled lime there, and in all the outbuildings. As they recrossed the lawn, a window that had been dark was lighted and Miss Emily sat in it, the light behind her, and her upright torso motionless as that of an idol. They crept quietly across the lawn and into the shadow of the locusts that lined the street. After a week or two the smell went away.

25   That was when people had begun to feel really sorry for her. People in our town, remembering how old lady Wyatt, her great-aunt, had gone completely crazy at last, believed that the Griersons held themselves a little too high for what they really were. None of the young men were quite good enough for Miss Emily and such. We had long thought of them as a tableau, Miss Emily a slender figure in white in the background, her father a spraddled silhouette in the foreground, his back to her and clutching a horsewhip, the two of them framed by the back-flung front door. So when she got to be thirty and was still single, we were not pleased exactly, but vindicated; even with insanity in the family she wouldn't have turned down all of her chances if they had really materialized.

When her father died, it got about that the house was all that was left to her; and in a way, people were glad. At last they could pity Miss Emily. Being left alone, and a pauper, she had become humanized. Now she too would know the old thrill and the old despair of a penny more or less.

The day after his death all the ladies prepared to call at the house and offer condolence and aid, as is our custom. Miss Emily met them at the door, dressed as usual and with no trace of grief on her face. She told them that her father was not dead. She did that for three days, with the ministers calling on her, and the doctors, trying to persuade her to let them dispose of the body. Just as they were about to resort to law and force, she broke down, and they buried her father quickly.

We did not say she was crazy then. We believed she had to do that. We remembered all the young men her father had driven away, and we knew that with nothing left, she would have to cling to that which had robbed her, as people will.

III

She was sick for a long time. When we saw her again, her hair was cut short, making her look like a girl, with a vague resemblance to those angels in colored church windows—sort of tragic and serene.

30   The town had just let the contracts for paving the sidewalks, and in the summer after her father's death they began the work. The construction company came with niggers and mules and machinery, and a foreman named Homer Barron, a Yankee—a big, dark, ready man, with a big voice and eyes lighter than his face. The little boys would follow in groups to hear him cuss the niggers, and the

454 *Chapter 12* *Reading and Writing about Stories*

niggers singing in time to the rise and fall of picks. Pretty soon he knew everybody in town. Whenever you heard a lot of laughing anywhere about the square, Homer Barron would be in the center of the group. Presently we began to see him and Miss Emily on Sunday afternoons driving in the yellow-wheeled buggy and the matched team of bays from the livery stable.

At first we were glad that Miss Emily would have an interest, because the ladies all said, "Of course a Grierson would not think seriously of a Northerner, a day laborer." But there were still others, older people, who said that even grief could not cause a real lady to forget *noblesse oblige*—without calling it *noblesse oblige*. They just said, "Poor Emily. Her kinfolks should come to her." She had some kin in Alabama; but years ago her father had fallen out with them over the estate of old lady Wyatt, the crazy woman, and there was no communication between the two families. They had not even been represented at the funeral.

And as soon as the old people said, "Poor Emily," the whispering began. "Do you suppose it's really so?" they said to one another. "Of course it is. What else could . . ." This behind their hands; rustling of craned silk and satin behind jalousies closed upon the sun of Sunday afternoon as the thin, swift clop-clop-clop of the matched team passed: "Poor Emily."

She carried her head high enough—even when we believed that she was fallen. It was as if she demanded more than ever the recognition of her dignity as the last Grierson; as if it had wanted that touch of earthiness to reaffirm her imperviousness. Like when she bought the rat poison, the arsenic. That was over a year after they had begun to say "Poor Emily," and while the two female cousins were visiting her.

"I want some poison," she said to the druggist. She was over thirty then, still a slight woman, though thinner than usual, with cold, haughty black eyes in a face the flesh of which was strained across the temples and about the eye-sockets as you imagine a lighthouse-keeper's face ought to look. "I want some poison," she said.

35   "Yes, Miss Emily. What kind? For rats and such? I'd recom—"

"I want the best you have. I don't care what kind."

The druggist named several. "They'll kill anything up to an elephant. But what you want is—"

"Arsenic," Miss Emily said. "Is that a good one?"

"Is . . . arsenic? Yes, ma'am. But what you want—"

40   "I want arsenic."

The druggist looked down at her. She looked back at him, erect, her face like a strained flag. "Why, of course," the druggist said. "If that's what you want. But the law requires you to tell what you are going to use it for."

Miss Emily just stared at him, her head tilted back in order to look him eye to eye, until he looked away and went and got the arsenic and wrapped it up. The Negro delivery boy brought her the package; the druggist didn't come back. When she opened the package at home there was written on the box, under the skull and bones: "For rats."

IV

So the next day we all said, "She will kill herself"; and we said it would be the best thing. When she had first begun to be seen with Homer Barron, we had said, "She will marry him." Then we said, "She will persuade him yet," because Homer himself had remarked—he liked men, and it was known that he drank with the younger men in the Elks' Club—that he was not a marrying man. Later we said, "Poor Emily" behind the jalousies as they passed on Sunday afternoon in the glittering buggy, Miss Emily with her head high and Homer Barron with his hat cocked and a cigar in his teeth, reins and whip in a yellow glove.

Then some of the ladies began to say that it was a disgrace to the town and a bad example to the young people. The men did not want to interfere, but at last the ladies forced the Baptist minister—Miss Emily's people were Episcopal—to call upon her. He would never divulge what happened during that interview, but he refused to go back again. The next Sunday they again drove about the streets, and the following day the minister's wife wrote to Miss Emily's relations in Alabama.

So she had blood-kin under her roof again and we sat back to watch developments. At first nothing happened. Then we were sure that they were to be married. We learned that Miss Emily had been to the jeweler's and ordered a man's toilet set in silver, with the letters H. B. on each piece. Two days later we learned that she had bought a complete outfit of men's clothing, including a nightshirt, and we said, "They are married." We were really glad. We were glad because the two female cousins were even more Grierson than Miss Emily had ever been.

So we were not surprised when Homer Barron—the streets had been finished some time since—was gone. We were a little disappointed that there was not a public blowing-off, but we believed that he had gone on to prepare for Miss Emily's coming, or to give her a chance to get rid of the cousins. (By that time it was a cabal, and we were all Miss Emily's allies to help circumvent the cousins.) Sure enough, after another week they departed. And, as we had expected all along, within three days Homer Barron was back in town. A neighbor saw the Negro man admit him at the kitchen door at dusk one evening.

And that was the last we saw of Homer Barron. And of Miss Emily for some time. The Negro man went in and out with the market basket, but the front door remained closed. Now and then we would see her at a window for a moment, as the men did that night when they sprinkled the lime, but for almost six months she did not appear on the streets. Then we knew that this was to be expected too; as if that quality of her father which had thwarted her woman's life so many times had been too virulent and too furious to die.

When we next saw Miss Emily, she had grown fat and her hair was turning gray. During the next few years it grew grayer and grayer until it attained an even pepper-and-salt iron gray, when it ceased turning. Up to the day of her death at seventy-four it was still that vigorous iron-gray, like the hair of an active man.

From that time on her front door remained closed, save for a period of six or seven years, when she was about forty, during which she gave lessons in china-painting. She fitted up a studio in one of the downstairs rooms, where the daughters and grand-daughters of Colonel Sartoris' contemporaries were sent to her with the same regularity and in the same spirit that they were sent to church on Sundays with a twenty-five cent piece for the collection plate. Meanwhile her taxes had been remitted.

Then the newer generation became the backbone and the spirit of the town, and the painting pupils grew up and fell away and did not send their children to her with boxes of color and tedious brushes and pictures cut from the ladies' magazines. The front door closed upon the last one and remained closed for good. When the town got free postal delivery, Miss Emily alone refused to let them fasten the metal numbers above her door and attach a mailbox to it. She would not listen to them.

Daily, monthly, yearly we watched the Negro grow grayer and more stooped, going in and out with the market basket. Each December we sent her a tax notice, which would be returned by the post office a week later, unclaimed. Now and then we would see her in one of the downstairs windows—she had evidently shut up the top floor of the house—like the carven torso of an idol in a niche, looking or not looking at us, we could never tell which. Thus she passed from generation to generation—dear, inescapable, impervious, tranquil, and perverse.

And so she died. Fell ill in the house filled with dust and shadows, with only a doddering Negro man to wait on her. We did not even know she was sick; we had long since given up trying to get any information from the Negro. He talked to no one, probably not even to her, for his voice had grown harsh and rusty, as if from disuse.

She died in one of the downstairs rooms, in a heavy walnut bed with a curtain, her gray head propped on a pillow yellow and moldy with age and lack of sunlight.

V

The Negro met the first of the ladies at the front door and let them in, with their hushed, sibilant voices and their quick, curious glances, and then he disappeared. He walked right through the house and out the back and was not seen again.

55   The two female cousins came at once. They held the funeral on the second day, with the town coming to look at Miss Emily beneath a mass of bought flowers, with the crayon face of her father musing profoundly above the bier and the ladies sibilant and macabre; and the very old men—some in their brushed Confederate uniforms—on the porch and the lawn, talking of Miss Emily as if she had been a contemporary of theirs, believing that they had danced with her and courted her perhaps, confusing time with its mathematical progression, as the old do, to whom all the past is not a diminishing road but, instead, a huge meadow which no winter ever quite touches, divided from the now by the narrow bottle-neck of the most recent decade of years.

Already we knew that there was one room in that region above stairs which no one had seen in forty years, and which would have to be forced. They waited until Miss Emily was decently in the ground before they opened it.

The violence of breaking down the door seemed to fill this room with pervading dust. A thin, acrid pall as of the tomb seemed to lie everywhere upon this room decked and furnished as for a bridal: upon the valance curtains of faded rose color, upon the rose-shaded lights, upon the dressing table, upon the delicate array of crystal and the man's toilet things backed with tarnished silver, silver so tarnished that the monogram was obscured. Among them lay a collar and tie, as if they had just been removed, which, lifted, left upon the surface a pale crescent in the dust. Upon a chair hung the suit, carefully folded; beneath it the two mute shoes and the discarded socks.

The man himself lay in the bed.

For a long while we just stood there, looking down at the profound and fleshless grin. The body had apparently once lain in the attitude of an embrace, but now the long sleep that outlasts love, that conquers even the grimace of love, had cuckolded him. What was left of him, rotted beneath what was left of the nightshirt, had become inextricable from the bed in which he lay; and upon him and upon the pillow beside him lay that even coating of the patient and biding dust.

60   Then we noticed that in the second pillow was the indentation of a head. One of us lifted something from it, and leaning forward, that faint and invisible dust dry and acrid in the nostrils, we saw a long strand of iron-gray hair.

[1930]

Joining the Conversation: Critical Thinking and Writing

1. Why does the narrator begin with what is almost the end of the story—the death of Miss Emily—rather than save this information for later? What devices does Faulkner use to hold the reader's interest throughout?
2. In a paragraph, offer a conjecture about Miss Emily's attitudes toward Homer Barron after he was last seen alive.
3. In a paragraph or two, characterize Miss Emily, calling attention not only to her eccentricities or even craziness but also to what you believe to be her moral values. Do the illustrations affect your response to her and to the story?
4. In paragraph 44, we are told that the Baptist minister "would never divulge what happened" during the interview with Miss Emily. Why do you suppose Faulkner does not narrate or describe the interview? Let's assume that, in his first draft of the story, he *did* give a paragraph of narration or a short dramatic scene. Write such an episode.
5. Suppose that Homer Barron's remains had been discovered before Miss Emily died and that she was arrested and charged with murder. You are the prosecutor, and you are running for a statewide political office. In five hundred words, set forth your argument that, despite the fact that she is a public monument, she should be convicted. Or, suppose that you are the defense attorney, also running for office. In five hundred words, set forth your defense.
6. Assume that Miss Emily kept a journal—perhaps even from her days as a young girl. Write entries for the journal, giving her thoughts about some of the episodes reported in Faulkner's story.
7. Does "A Rose for Emily" make you want to read more stories by Faulkner? Be as specific as you can in explaining your response.

Following are questions that may help to stimulate ideas about stories. Not every question will be relevant to every story; however, if, after reading a story and thinking about it, you then run your eye over these questions, you will find questions that help you to think further about the story and to get ideas.

As we have said before, it's best to do your thinking with a pen or pencil in hand. If some of the following questions seem to you to be especially relevant to the story you will be writing about, jot down your initial responses, interrupting your writing only to glance again at the story when you feel the need to check the evidence.

✔ **CHECKLIST:** *Getting Ideas for Writing about Stories*

Character

☐ Which character chiefly engages your interest? Why?
☐ What purposes do minor characters serve? Do you find some who by their similarities and differences help to define each other or help to define the major character? How else is a particular character defined—by his or her words, actions (including thoughts and emotions), dress, setting, narrative point of view? Do certain characters act differently in the same, or in a similar, situation?

(continued)

☐ How does the author reveal character? By explicit authorial (editorial) comment—for instance, by revelation through dialogue? Through depicted action? Through the actions of other characters? How are the author's methods especially suited to the whole of the story?

☐ Is the behavior plausible—that is, are the characters well motivated?

☐ If a character changes, why and how does he or she change? (You may want to jot down each event that influences a change.) Or did you change your attitude toward a character, not because the character changed, but because you came to know the character better?

☐ Are the characters round or flat? Are they complex or highly typical (for instance, one-dimensional representatives of a social class or age)? Are you chiefly interested in a character's psychology, or does the character strike you as standing for something, such as honesty or the arrogance of power?

☐ How has the author caused you to sympathize with certain characters? How does your response—your sympathy or lack of sympathy—contribute to your judgment of the conflict?

Plot

☐ Does the plot grow out of the characters, or does it depend on chance or coincidence? Did something at first strike you as irrelevant that later you perceived as relevant? Do some parts continue to strike you as irrelevant?

☐ How are the story's events sequenced and patterned? Do cause-and-effect relationships order the story's events, creating its plot?

☐ Does surprise play an important role, or does foreshadowing? If surprise is very important, can the story be read a second time with any interest? If so, what gives it this further interest?

☐ What conflicts does the story include? Conflicts of one character against another? Of one character against the setting, or against society? Conflicts within a single character?

☐ Are certain episodes narrated out of chronological order? If so, were you puzzled? Annoyed? On reflection, does the arrangement of episodes seem effective? Why, or why not? Are certain situations repeated? If so, what do you make out of the repetitions?

Setting

☐ Do you have a strong sense of the time and place of the story? Is the story very much about, say, New England Puritanism, or race relations in the South in the late nineteenth century, or midwestern urban versus small-town life? If time and place are important, how and at what points in the story has the author conveyed this sense? If you do not strongly feel the setting, do you think the author should have made it more evident?

☐ What is the relationship of the setting to the plot and the characters? (For instance, do houses or rooms, or their furnishings, say something about their residents?) Would anything be lost if the descriptions of the setting were deleted from the story or if the setting were changed?

Symbolism

☐ Do certain characters seem to stand for something in addition to themselves? Does the setting—whether a house, a farm, a landscape, a town, or a period—have an extra dimension?

☐ If you do believe that the story has symbolic elements, do you think they are adequately integrated within the story, or do they strike you as being too obviously "stuck in"?

Point of View

☐ Who tells the story? How much does the narrator know? Does the narrator strike you as reliable? What effect is gained by using this narrator?

☐ How does the point of view help shape the theme? After all, the basic story of "Little Red Riding Hood"—what happens—remains unchanged whether told from the wolf's point of view or the girl's, but if we hear the story from the wolf's point of view, we may feel that the story is about terrifying yet pathetic compulsive behavior; if we hear the story from the girl's point of view, we may feel that the story is about terrified innocence.

☐ It is sometimes said that the best writers are subversive, forcing readers to see something they do not want to see—something that is true but that violates their comfortable conventional ideas. Does this story oppose comfortable conventional views?

☐ Does the narrator's language help you to construct a picture of the narrator's character, class, attitude, strengths, and limitations? (Jot down some evidence, such as colloquial or formal expressions, ironic comments, and figures of speech.) How far can you trust the narrator? Why?

Style

☐ How has the point of view shaped or determined the style?

☐ How would you characterize the style? Simple? Understated? Figurative? Or what, and why?

☐ Do you think that the style is consistent? If it isn't—for instance, if there are shifts from simple sentences to highly complex ones—what do you make of the shifts?

Theme

☐ Is the title informative? What does it mean or suggest? Did its meaning seem to change after you read the story? Does the title help you to formulate a theme? If you had written the story, what title would you have given it?

☐ Do certain passages—dialogue or description—seem to you to point especially toward the theme? Do you find certain repetitions of words or pairs of incidents that are highly suggestive and helpful in directing your thoughts toward stating a theme? Flannery O'Connor, in *Mystery and Manners* (1969), says, "In good fiction, certain of the details will tend to accumulate meaning from the action of the story itself, and when that happens, they become symbolic in the way they work." Does this story work that way?

☐ Is the meaning of the story embodied in the whole story, or does it seem stuck, for example, in certain passages of editorializing?

☐ Suppose someone asked you to state the point—the theme—of the story. Could you? And if you could, would you say that the theme of the story reinforces values you hold, or does it challenge them to some degree? Or is the concept of a theme irrelevant to the story?

Student Writing Portfolio

ANALYTICAL PAPER

Writing an Analytical Paper

Writing about fiction allows you to develop a deeper understanding of why you enjoy storytelling while also encouraging you to develop your analytical skills. If you engage in literary analysis, you cannot help but become a more sophisticated critical thinker. Writing about a story asks you to be an interpretive thinker who can investigate a text, evaluate its ideas, and explain your perspective. Writing about a story also asks you to be a flexible thinker who can work with the text on the level of details and the level of big ideas, and move back and forth between those two levels. This type of writing encourages you to be a conceptual thinker, able to engage with a story's major issues, themes, and concerns. Finally, writing about a story asks you to be an argumentative thinker who is able to make claims about a text and support those claims with evidence.

John Martinez has been given an assignment to write a five-page analytical paper focusing on William Faulkner's "A Rose for Emily." The assignment asks John to write a paper that analyzes the murder revealed at the end of the story. In order to complete this paper, John must move from his initial reading of the story, captured in his annotations, to his inquiry strategies, such as note taking, to his paper drafting and revision, and then to the completion of his final draft. John's reading and writing materials are reprinted here, allowing us to see how his thinking evolves as he completes this assignment. Let's start by looking at the assignment.

Assignment

Five-page Analytical Paper:

- This paper asks you to investigate the ending of "A Rose for Emily" and how it encourages you to revisit and rethink the story. After you realize a poisoning has taken place, how does that make you rethink the characters and events of the story? For example, knowing what you do about the poisoning, how would you analyze Miss Emily and her actions, Homer and his courtship, the townspeople and their beliefs, or the Grierson family and their attitudes?

- Select one focused aspect of the story for continued investigation and analysis. Create an argument that explains your new thinking about the story.

- Make sure to analyze both form and content.

- Write a five-page analytical paper that uses a formal structure of a thesis, subpoints, and evidence.

- Include an outline with your draft.

Annotation: Reading for Form and Content

As we have stressed throughout this book, the easiest and most effective way to start your analysis of a text is to annotate the text. Annotation is the process of writing your responses directly on the text as you read it. Literary annotation should focus on both the content and the form of the text. Content is the information conveyed by the story, whereas form is the *way* that information is conveyed. Annotating for content focuses on the ideas of the story, whereas annotating for form focuses on the literary elements being used to tell the story.

   Knowing that he has to write a paper on "A Rose of Emily" that analyzes both form and content, John wants to use a more organized form of annotation. This annotating strategy highlights the contribution of both form and content to the story's meaning. As seen in John's notes below, in this type of annotation, the emphasis on form and content has clearly structured, with notes concerning form written on the left and notes concerning content written on the right. As in any form of annotation, John marks up areas in the text that contain important, complex, or interesting ideas; areas that encourage thinking and rethinking; areas that trigger questions; and areas that encourage strong opinions and interpretations. He writes most of these notes on the right-hand side of the text. But, after making these more conceptual notes, he double-checks the text's form and jots down a few notes about form on the left-hand side of the text.

Student Work: Annotation
"Form and Content" Marginal Notes

Form		**Content**
narrator—we: 1st person plural	Already we knew that there was one room in that region above stairs which no one had seen in forty years, and which would have to be forced. They waited until Emily was decently in the ground before they opened it.	closed, secret room = secrets
long, detailed description	The violence of breaking down the door seemed to fill this room with pervading dust. A thin acrid pall as of the tomb seemed to lie everywhere upon this room decked and furnished as if for a bridal: upon the valance curtains of faded rose color, upon the rose-shaded lights, upon the dressing table, upon the delicate array	room = tomb
dust imagery = symbol	of crystal and the man's toilet things backed with tarnished silver, silver so tarnished that the monogram was obscured. Among them lay collar and tie, as if they had just been removed, which, lifted, left upon the surface a pale crescent in the dust. Upon a chair hung the suit, carefully folded; beneath it the two mute shoes and the discarded socks.	details of items on table = aged, time
short, clear sentence	The man himself lay in the bed.	DEAD MAN?!

love in middle
of para = slow
realization

dust imagery
repeated

For a long while we just stood there, looking down at the profound and fleshless grin.
The body had apparently once lain in the
attitude of an embrace, but now the long sleep
that outlasts love, that conquers even the grimace of love, had cuckolded him. What was left
of him, rotten beneath what was left of the
nightshirt, had become inextricable from the
bed in which he lay; and upon him and upon
the pillow beside him lay that even coating of
the patient and biding dust.

theme of love

rotted body

shock saved
for end: closure
and surprise

Then we noticed that in the second pillow
was the indentation of a head. One of us lifted
something from it, and leaning forward, that
faint and invisible dust dry and acrid in the nostrils, we saw a long strand of iron-gray hair.

indent! Was
Emily sleeping
w/body?!!

Every successful reading starts with a close observation of the text and a way
to keep track of those observations and use them to brainstorm new ideas about
the text. Annotation allows you to record your ideas during and after your reading,
generating materials that will help you build toward a written analysis of a text.

As John annotates the text, he engages in several activities. He records specific
information from the text, making sure that his interpretive foundation is correct.
This type of prewriting ensures that he is working from the "inside out," that is,
working from inside the text out toward larger ideas, rather than bringing pre-
formed ideas into the text. John also actively searches for "jumping-off points" in
order to move away from plot summary, using prewriting to emphasize moments
in the text that call out for interpretation. This allows John to find areas that are rich
for conceptual investigation. He also traces interesting patterns, noting patterns in
literary elements and tracing how those patterns' meaning evolves. John's annotations add up to a method of tracking concepts, interpretations, and questions so
that he does not "lose" a good idea that could lead to further thinking and writing.
His annotations have already started the type of brainstorming and question-asking
inquiry work that additional note taking will develop.

Note Taking: Using Inquiry
Notes to Generate Ideas

Inquiry: Double- (or Triple-) Entry Notes

A productive way of taking notes is to follow the page-by-page development of a
story and create a "double-entry" or "triple-entry" notebook that allows you to keep
track of the page-by-page information that you find and the thoughts that you have
as you read. Knowing that he will need to organize his evidence and ideas for his
paper, John Martinez uses that form of note taking here. He uses the first column
to keep track of the page number and a key detail or quote. He uses the second
column to note his ideas and interpretations. He uses the third column as a space
for brainstorming, revisiting his original notes and adding more interpretative ideas,
questions, and observations.

Student Work: Inquiry Notes
Double- (or Triple-) Entry Notes

Page #, Quotation or Information	Interpretations/ Questions	Interpretation Revisited
p. 449: Emily dies, is described as "monument," "tradition"	Why is she described in these terms? Does she represent a dying tradition, a dying way of life?	
p. 449: House is described as "eyesore"	House is decayed, just like Emily has decayed	House's decay represents many types of decay: Is this decay of love, of life?
p. 449: History of Emily's taxes: "next generation" with "modern ideas" wants her taxes	This new generation, with its "modern ideas" seems to be being critiqued. This generation lacks old-fashioned sense of honor	But, is old generation to blame for Emily's isolation—and the murder?

Inquiry: Listing Notes

As seen in Chapter 4, listing is a common form of prewriting. John likes to record important details about the story in a well-organized list as he reads the story. By creating a blank list with well-defined categories and then filling in that list as he reads, John organizes his notes and ideas through the reading process. John uses listing to record details that he'll want to refer to later but might forget, such as complete character names, places, or dates. He uses literary elements to create his categories, allowing him to start to see how those elements come together to form the literary work. He then engages in brainstorming, using his list to trigger open-ended thinking about the meaning of the information that he's noted.

Student Work: Listing
Key Information Overview

Characters

Miss Emily Grierson (dies age 74)
Her father (dead)
Colonel Sartoris (mayor who forgives taxes)
Judge Stevens (mayor at time of smell)
Tobe (Emily's African-American servant)
Homer Barron (construction company foreman, courts Emily)
Two female cousins (come to stay during affair b/w Emily and Homer)
Unnamed narrator and unnamed people in town: gossiping, judging

Place/Setting

The Grierson house: decayed and dusty
Southern town

Time

1894 (date taxes forgiven, near father's death)
two years after father's death: the smell
thirty years after the smell: gets rid of men coming for taxes

Plot Events

Part I. Miss Emily dead in first sentence
Taxes remitted, but the Board of Alderman wants to reclaim taxes: turned away
Part II. The smell
Miss Emily doesn't go out after father's death
The smell starts; neighbors complain
Men secretly break open cellar door and put lime around Miss Emily's house
Window lighted: Miss Emily sees them
When father died, Miss Emily acted as if father wasn't dead

. . .

Questions

Why do the townspeople allow Miss Emily to intimidate them repeatedly?
Does the town respect Miss Emily's family and her past—or does it just fear her?

Inquiry: Journal Writing

Journal writing encourages an unstructured, brainstorming type of writing, but, because it is the first stage in writing a draft, it can be intimidating. If you are having trouble getting started with journal writing, turn to the literary text and let it inspire your writing. Consider starting with a specific quotation that has caught your attention because it is expressing a complex idea, a problem that needs to be thought through, or a dramatically important conflict, epiphany, or resolution. John decides to "dig deep" into a specific passage as a way of starting his brainstorming process. He records his intellectual reactions to the passage, explaining the key concepts that the passage seems to be exploring. John's brainstorming journal writing becomes "messy" as he works and reworks his ideas, but that type of reworking signals a deepening of ideas that will become part of the foundation of his paper's draft.

Student Work: Journal Writing
Key Quotation Brainstorming

Interesting quotations:

—*The Judge exclaims, "Will you accuse a lady to her face of smelling bad?" (451).*
  Why won't they confront her?
—*The men "slunk about the house like burglars" (451). Why do they slink to her*
  house? Why do they become like burglars?
—*Miss Emily is watching them from the window.*

—Gossip about courtship: "it was a disgrace to the town and a bad example to the young people" (453). Was Emily aware of the gossip?

The townspeople seem to know that Emily is up to no good—that she has something going on in the house. They knew the smell was connected to something bad, but are afraid to actually ask Miss Emily about it. The townspeople do not want to confront Miss Emily with the embarrassing fact of the smell. Rather than confront her, the Board of Alderman of four men go to her house and spread lime around the base of her house, hoping to stop the smell. The men do not have enough courage to face Miss Emily. They even seem to act like criminals rather than confront Miss Emily—rather than discover that she is a criminal, they act like criminals and slink around. What I found interesting about this scene is that Miss Emily was aware of it.

The townspeople think her courtship is a "disgrace." It seems like they are too quick to judge. There is a weird dynamic of them judging Miss Emily, but then not being able to actually confront her. But, they do have a Baptist minister go and talk to her—but he "refused to go back again" (453). It seems like they want to intervene in Miss Emily's life, but stop before they can actually figure out exactly what's going on.

Does the town push for them to get married, and then actually cause them to split up—and thus cause Miss Emily to poison Homer? Do they push her towards being a murderer? Do they ruin her happiness and her courtship—and thus push her towards her hideous crime?

End of story

Seems like whole town comes into house—why?
House is decaying, like a crypt
Shock of the dead body
Dead body set up to be married—connects to earlier gossip about courtship
Town likes to gossip about Emily

Drafting: Creating an Argument and Explaining Your Interpretation

John transforms his prewriting into a rough draft. As with every rough draft, his writing contains both strengths and weaknesses. A notable strength of John's paper is that it opens with a clear thesis argument; he argues that the townspeople bear some responsibility for Homer's murder. A sign of a good argument is that another person can disagree and argue back to it; you can answer John's paper by saying, "No! Miss Emily is clearly solely responsible for the murder." A paper that takes a stand and argues for its interpretation will be a lively paper.

In addition to having a central argument, John's paper has created a series of subpoints that support that argument—the paper is doing the hard work of proving its argument. In places, the subpoints are not completely clear; however, for a first draft, this paper is doing a good job of breaking its ideas down and creating an organized body. As you read John's paper, you'll notice that it uses a traditional, but often overly formulaic, structure: the five-paragraph essay. The paper has used the five-paragraph format to create three subpoints that are treated equally; each subpoint is set up to prove the thesis that the townspeople helped to "set the stage" for the murder. However, the draft notes that the final subpoint is not quite the same as the first two and this difference disrupts the flow of the paper's ideas. The paper's first two subpoints discuss the townspeople's actions that occur before the murder, and thus might lead to the murder. The third sub-point discusses the smell that happens *after* the murder, not an action that sets up the murder. This third subpoint does not seem to support the thesis argument that the townspeople bear some responsibility for the murder; this subpoint's connection to the rest of the paper becomes unclear. As a result, in his final draft, John may be able to create a better structure for his paper.

Student Analytical Essay: "Homer's Murder in 'A Rose for Emily'" (Preliminary Draft)

Let's examine John's preliminary draft, noting how it fulfills many of our expectations for a strong analytical paper. John creates a clear and compelling argument, and presents it in his thesis statement. His paper continues to develop and push his ideas, aiming for increasingly sophisticated interpretations of the story. He supports these interpretations with numerous short quotations from the story. And, as noted, he organizes his main ideas into clear subpoints; however, this organization might best be rethought as he develops his ideas. What are the elements of good writing that you expect to see in John's paper?

Martinez 1

John Martinez

English 200: Intro to Lit

Professor Murphy

February 20, 2016

Homer's Murder in 'A Rose for Emily'

At the end of William Faulker's "A Rose for Emily," it becomes clear

that a murder has taken place. Miss Emily Grierson, the central character,

has murdered her suitor, Homer Barron. It becomes clear that she murdered

him using poison, placed his body in a bedroom, and then visited, embraced,

and even slept with the body. The ending is a shock and leaves you focused

on Miss Emily, thinking about her as the main character and how she is now

seen as a criminal. Suddenly, she is no longer a sad character, avoided by the town, but she can now be seen as a criminal. This focus on Miss Emily makes

her be seen as a criminal and makes her seem to be the only person to blame

for Homer's death. However, the townspeople share responsibility for

Homer's death. The narrator, who explains the townspeople's reactions to

Emily, makes it sound like she is crazy. But, he also reveals that the

townspeople have done things that make them responsible for Homer's

death. First, the townspeople judged Miss Emily's relationship with Homer,

saying it was disgraceful. They intervened by talking about the affair and

calling her relatives in to stay with her. Second, the townspeople let her buy

the poison. This poison was obviously used to kill Homer. Third, they did not

investigate the smell. In fact, they went to Emily's house and covered up the

smell. As a result of trying to stop her affair and then not investigating the

poison or the smell, the townspeople helped to set the stage for Homer's

murder.

    Let's look at the first reason that the townspeople are semi-

responsible for Homer's death. The townspeople couldn't help but gossip

about Emily dating Homer, especially as Emily is upper-class and Homer is

working class and from the North: "Of course a Grierson would not think

seriously of a Northerner, a day laborer" (452). Miss Emily seemed to really

be enjoying her time with Homer, as they drove around town in a "glittering

buggy" (453). The townspeople start to "say that it was a disgrace to the

town and a bad example to the young people" (453). They had the Baptist

minister go and talk to her. I think something horrible must have happened

because he "refused to go back again" (453). Then, they decide to take

action, and write her relatives to have them come to visit. Two female

cousins come and stay with Miss Emily. The relatives seem to move things

forward towards a marriage, because Miss Emily buys a "man's toilet set in

silver" and a "complete outfit of men's clothing, including a nightshirt"

*writer creates
thesis
statement—
makes an
argument*

*writer uses clear
organization to
break down
ideas into
subpoints*

*writer creates
clear subpoints
by giving each a
strong focusing
idea*

*successful
integration of
quotations into
paper*

Martinez 3

(453). But, then the relationship seems to be over because the marriage never happens.

The second reason the townspeople are responsible for Homer's death is that they don't question why Miss Emily might be buying poison. When Miss Emily goes to the drugstore, she buys some poison. However, she does not explain the reason for buying poison. In this scene, a crucial piece of missing information is not followed up on: the druggist asks Miss Emily what she wants the poison for, and she refuses to answer, even though she is required by law to explain the use of the poison. The druggist gives in to her stare, gives her the poison, and writes "For rats" on the poison (452). If the druggist had refused to allow her to buy the poison, the entire murder plot might have been avoided. I think the druggist should have at least questioned Miss Emily—if the druggist had questioned the use of the poison more thoroughly, Miss Emily would have known her murder plot would be uncovered. If the druggist was stronger, he would not have allowed Miss Emily to purchase what becomes a murder weapon—he could have intimidated Miss Emily into giving up her murder plans.

writer develops interpretation by explaining own unique insights

The final reason that the townspeople are responsible for Homer's death is that they do not investigate the smell at Miss Emily's house. (This not checking on the smell does not make them responsible for Homer's death—he is already dead. The smell comes after the death. So, what does this reveal?) The townspeople do not want to confront Miss Emily with the embarrassing fact of the smell. The Judge exclaims, "Will you accuse a lady to her face of smelling bad?" (451). Rather than confront her, the Board of Alderman of four men go to her house and spread lime around the base of her house, hoping to stop the smell. The men "slunk about the house like burglars" (451). The men decide that they themselves should act like criminals rather than confront Miss Emily—rather than discover that she is a criminal, they act like criminals. What I found interesting about this scene

writer uses drafting to note issues in thinking—writer can "solve" these issues in later drafts

Martinez 4

is that Miss Emily was aware of it. When the men left the house, she was sitting in a lighted window, watching them.

The townspeople had a couple of different opportunities to turn Miss Emily away from her criminal act of murder. In the first place, they could have supported Miss Emily's courtship with Homer. Even if the courtship broke expectations or was inappropriate, it was far less criminal than murder! The townspeople should have let Miss Emily enjoy the relationship. A real opportunity to stop the murder occurred when Miss Emily purchased the poison. If the druggist had stood up to her and questioned her motives more closely, she might have given up on the idea of poison—and the entire idea of murder. After the murder occurred, the townspeople could have come to a greater understanding of what had happened in the Grierson house. They could have questioned Emily and forced themselves into the home to investigate. Instead, they participated in the "cover up" of the murder, covering up the smell and letting the whole town pretend nothing had ever happened. Although Miss Emily is clearly Homer's murderer, she might not have taken on that role if the townspeople had been more supportive of her and more questioning of her. The townspeople, although not directly acting like murderers, bear some indirect responsibility for Homer's murder. The townspeople set the stage for Homer's murder. Miss Emily is not the lonely, all-alone murderer that we thing she is; I think she has a "partner in crime" in the townspeople.

writer's interpretations are strong, direct—creates a lively paper

writer restates his thesis in the conclusion

[New page]

Martinez 5

Work Cited

Faulkner, William. "A Rose for Emily," *Literature for Composition*. Ed. Sylvan

Barnet, William Burto, William E. Cain, and Cheryl L. Nixon. 11th ed.

Boston: Pearson, 2017. 451–56. Print.

Revision: Using a Revision Strategy

Revision is essential to the drafting of a paper. Allow enough time and devote enough energy to revising your paper because revision allows you to "re-see" your writing as a critic and to improve your writing for its ultimate audience. A rough draft allows you to capture ideas in an essay form, but that draft must be improved through the revision of the ideas, evidence, and organization. Before we explore John's revision process, let's review the revision checklist in Chapter 8.

✔ REVISION CHECKLIST

Strengthen Your Thesis

☐ Add focus and depth to your central argument.

Develop Your Ideas

☐ Revisit your best responses to literary form and content, adding more thinking to those responses.

Integrate and Explain Your Evidence

☐ Select and analyze interesting quotations to provide evidence for your ideas.

Improve the Organization

☐ Structure your ideas to follow a clear sequence.

Clarify Your Style and Edit for Correctness

☐ Use a consistent, professional style to explain your ideas, correcting sentence structure, word usage, and grammar.

Revision: Revising to Strengthen the Thesis

The most crucial element of an analytical paper is its thesis argument. A paper's most important idea should be captured in a thesis statement that presents a focused argument about the text under consideration and previews the sophisticated thinking that the paper will develop. Although it is typically a short sentence or two, the thesis argument serves as an "umbrella" for the entire paper; all of the paper's ideas and development can fit "under" that "umbrella." A thesis must thus be interesting and complex enough to sustain the development of ideas that will take place throughout the entire paper.

Let's look at the first paragraph in John's draft of his paper. As indicated in the paper's title, John makes the argument that, as the paper states, "the townspeople share responsibility for Homer's death." This is a good working thesis because it is not restating an obvious idea; for example, a statement such as "Emily is a jilted lover" is not a good thesis because it is obvious and information-based, and it does not set up an interpretation-based argument. John's draft is off to a good start because it has a straightforward, but not obvious, argument. However, the thesis paragraph weakens after the thesis statement, since it does not clearly address a question that follows from the thesis: *How* are the townspeople responsible for the death? What do the townspeople do to share in Homer's death? The thesis paragraph contains the vague statement that the townspeople have "done things" that make them responsible. This is an idea that needs some work! Let's see how this idea can be developed through the revision process.

Student Work: Revision
Revising to Strengthen the Thesis

Rough Draft:

This focus on Miss Emily makes her be seen as a criminal and makes her seem to be the main person to blame for Homer's death. <u>However, the townspeople share responsibility for Homer's death</u>. The narrator, who explains the townspeople's reactions to Emily, makes it sound like she is crazy. But, he also reveals that the townspeople have <u>done things</u> that make them responsible for Homer's death.

concise thesis, explain further

clarify?

↓

First Revision:

The narrator's focus on Miss Emily makes her into a <u>criminal who is responsible for Homer's death</u>. <u>However, the townspeople share responsibility for Homer's death</u>. Although the narrator emphasizes Miss Emily's <u>elite attitude and her insane actions</u>, he also reveals that the townspeople have <u>encouraged Miss Emily's attitude and actions</u>.

better phrasing keep concise thesis, explain further better phrasing clarify?

↓

Second Revision:

The narrator's focus on Miss Emily positions her as a <u>criminal who is solely responsible for Homer's death</u>. Although she kills Homer out of <u>loneliness and isolation, Emily is not completely isolated in this murder</u>. <u>The townspeople share responsibility for Homer's death</u>. The narrator emphasizes Miss Emily's withdrawal from society and unstable actions, but he also reveals that <u>the townspeople encouraged that withdrawal and pushed her towards instability, which resulted in murder</u>.

better phrasing, explanation

concise thesis kept

thesis explained

Revision: Revising to Develop Ideas

A paper's draft will often contain ideas that need more work. Revision is crucial because it allows you to put your work aside, gain some distance from it, and return to it with fresh eyes. When you reread one of your paper's drafts, you can often locate ideas that are unclear, incorrect, or poorly explained; you might not have sensed that your ideas were weak when you were in the middle of inventing them, but, on a rereading, you can see their weaknesses and start to correct them.

Let's look at the long parenthetical comment in the body's third subpoint. John's own drafting indicates that the subpoint isn't quite right: The covering up of the smell doesn't show that the townspeople set the stage for Homer's death, since it happens *after* his death. The claim that the covering up of the smell *contributes* to Homer's death needs to be reworked. Rather than ignore the inconsistency between this claim and the previous two subpoints, John decides to explore his "chain of ideas" more thoroughly. As a result of thinking about the covering up of the smell, he revisits all three subpoints and engages in a deeper analysis of the townspeople. After further brainstorming, John realizes that the townspeople either directly intervene in Emily's life or refuse to confront Emily, and he decides that this dynamic of "intervening/giving in" is an interesting way of organizing the paper. He starts to outline his paper to emphasize this new idea.

Student Work: Revision
Revising to Develop Ideas

Rough Draft Outline:
Thesis paragraph: Emily committed murder; the town has some responsibility

Body:
Subpoint #1: Rumors and intervening in courtship with Homer
Subpoint #2: Allowing her to buy poison
Subpoint #3: Covering up the smell

Conclusion: Miss Emily committed murder, but the town set the stage for the murder

↓

Revised Outline:
Thesis paragraph: Emily committed murder; the town has some responsibility

Body:
A. *First Type of Action: The townspeople gossip and intervene in her courtship*   *adds two new categories re: townspeople's reactions to Emily*
  Subpoint #1: Rumors and intervening in courtship with Homer

B. *Second Type of Action: The townspeople let her make her own rules, give in too easily to her, and don't confront her*
  Subpoint #2: Allowing her to buy poison
  Subpoint #3: Covering up the smell

Conclusion: Miss Emily committed murder, but the town set the stage for the murder by intervening in her courtship and then giving in to her when she created her own rules

---

Revision: Revising to Improve Organization

As you develop new ideas, your paper's organization might need to change to capture those new ideas. Although you might be hesitant to make significant changes that reorganize your entire paper, remember that revision is about improving the ideas in your paper, not just tinkering with editing of words. In order to move a paper forward, you might need to make significant changes, but those changes will result in a better paper (and a better grade!).

As John works on the revision process, the outline for his draft paper has already changed to accommodate a new two-point emphasis on the townspeople's interactions with Miss Emily. In order to explain the "intervening/giving in" dynamic, the paper needs to emphasize those two ideas, causing it to break out of the five-paragraph essay (and its "three body paragraphs") formula. The draft is shaping up to have two main sections, with several subpoints under each section. As John revises his paper, he adds new subpoints that take additional evidence— key scenes from the story—into account. Crucially, the structure of John's paper reflects the new structure of his ideas.

Student Work: Revision
Revising to Improve Organization

Rough Draft Outline:

Thesis paragraph: Emily committed murder, but the town has some responsibility

Body:
Subpoint #1: Rumors and intervening in the courtship with Homer
Subpoint #2: Allowing her to buy poison
Subpoint #3: Covering up the smell

Conclusion: Emily committed murder, but the town set the stage for murder

$\downarrow$

Revised Outline:

Thesis paragraph: Emily committed murder, but the town has some responsibility

Body:
A. First *Type of Action: The townspeople gossip and scold/ judge her*
   Subpoint #1: Rumors about Homer

B. *Second Type of Action: The townspeople let her make her own rules, give in to her*
   Subpoint #2: Taxes ◄── **Locating this subpoint here follows the**
   Subpoint #3: Poison   **order of the story but makes it seem like**
   Subpoint #4: Smell   **she avoided taxes <u>before</u> murder.**

The writer uses revision to create an organization that captures his best ideas. Here, two new subsections are used.

Conclusion: Miss Emily committed murder, but the town set the stage for the murder by intervening in her courtship and then giving in to her when she created her own rules

$\downarrow$

Final Revised Outline:
Thesis paragraph

Body:
A. *First Type of Action: The townspeople gossip and scold/ judge her*
   Subpoint #1: Rumors about Homer

B. *Second Type of Action: The townspeople let her make her own rules, give in to her*
   Subpoint #2: Poison
   Subpoint #3: Smell
   Subpoint #4: Taxes

The writer uses revisions to position his new ideas correctly—he follows his ideas and not just the order of the story.

Relocating this subpoint here follows the chronological order of events, not the order in which story is told. Makes it clear that Miss Emily avoids taxes later in life, after the murder. The town allows her to create her own reality.

Conclusion: Miss Emily committed murder, but the town set the stage for the murder by intervening in her courtship and then giving in to her when she created her own rules

Student Analytical Essay: "The Townspeople's Responsibility for Homer's Murder in 'A Rose for Emily'" (Final Draft)

Now that we've explored three strategies for revising this paper, let's see how John has revised his entire draft. Compare this final draft to the first draft on page 466. Notice how John has strengthened several aspects of his writing. He has

- clarified and deepened the thesis argument;
- developed the series of connected claims;
- created an organizational structure that captures idea development;
- used evidence to support ideas; and
- improved phrasing, style, and grammar.

John has engaged in a true revision of his paper—he has not used the revision process to merely correct typos on his first draft. As a paper is revised, its ideas should evolve and feed back into the brainstorming process; new subpoints should appear, and new evidence should be added. A comparison to the earlier draft reveals how John has used the revision process to strengthen both his writing and his thinking.

Student Work: Outlining
Outlining to Reorganize Ideas

Thesis paragraph:

Emily committed murder
The town has some responsibility because they encouraged her instability

writer uses outline to state thesis strongly, succinctly

Body:

A. *First Type of Action: The townspeople gossip and scold/judge her*

    Subpoint #1: Rumors/scolding about Homer

      —The town tries to tell her that her running around with Homer is a disgrace

      —Baptist minister goes to see her

      —Minister's wife makes relatives come to see her

writer organizes paper's body by creating clear sub-points

B. *Second Type of Action: The townspeople let her make her own rules, give in too easily to her, and don't confront her*

    Subpoint #2: Poison

      —The druggist let her buy poison

      —The druggist gave in quickly after questioning her

writer develops paper by adding layers of ideas to thesis

    Subpoint #3: The Smell

      —The Board of Alderman wouldn't confront her

      —They secretly spread lime over her house to cover up the smell

writer locates interesting evidence to support his ideas

    Subpoint #4: Taxes

      —The town let her avoid paying taxes, creating a story that she doesn't owe them

      —This was a remaking of the rules, proving that rules don't apply to her

      —This also allowed Miss Emily to continue to create own reality

outline allows the writer to balance subsections— each contains ideas and evidence

Conclusion: The townspeople's way of interacting with Miss Emily is conflicted: they intervene and give in to her. This encourages Miss Emily's instability and her crime.

John Martinez

English 200: Introduction to Literature

Professor Murphy

March 4, 2016

The Townspeople's Responsibility for Homer's Murder in

"A Rose for Emily"

    At the end of William Faulker's "A Rose for Emily," it becomes clear that a murder has taken place. Miss Emily Grierson, the central character, has poisoned her suitor, Homer Barron, placed his body in a bedroom, and visited, embraced, and even slept with the body. The shocking ending creates a new perception of the story's main character. Suddenly, Miss Emily

strong opening— immediately starts a discussion about a specific aspect of the story is no longer a sad, lonely character, avoided by the town, but is a murderer. The narrator's focus on Miss Emily positions her as a criminal who is solely responsible for Homer's death. Although she kills Homer out of loneliness and isolation, Emily is not completely isolated in this murder. The

thesis is stated in a clear, succinct sentence

townspeople share responsibility for Homer's death. The narrator emphasizes Miss Emily's withdrawal from society and unstable actions, but he also reveals that the townspeople encouraged that withdrawal and pushed her towards instability, which resulted in the murder.

writer explains his paper organization, previews his ideas

The townspeople interact with Miss Emily in two seemingly opposite ways. First, they are overly judgmental about her relationship with Homer and involve themselves in that relationship. They try to make her conform to their expectations about proper courtship. Second, and in contrast to this intervening, the townspeople avoid confrontation with her and let her create her own rules and create her own reality. This giving in to Miss Emily can be seen in a series of key acts. Crucially, the druggist let her buy the poison that was used to kill Homer. In addition, the Board of Alderman did not confront her about the smell, but went to Emily's house and covered up the smell. Finally, many years later, the town does not force Emily to pay her taxes. As a result of trying to stop her affair and then giving in to her, the townspeople helped to create Miss Emily's instability.

writer stays "on track" by following his outline and restating the main focus of paper section A

The townspeople's involvement in Emily's courtship is the most direct way that they contribute to Homer's murder. The townspeople couldn't help but gossip about Emily dating Homer, especially as Emily is upper-class and Homer is working class and from the North. The townspeople gossip, "Of course a Grierson would not think seriously of a Northerner, a day laborer" (452). Miss Emily seemed to be in love with Homer, driving around town in a "glittering buggy" (453). The townspeople, however, label her "Poor Emily" because Homer is "not a marrying man" and Emily does not seem to have convinced him to marry her (452).

Martinez 3

In these gossiping scenes, the townspeople function as a "group character" in which individuals are connected into one larger group. The narrator typically refers to the townspeople as "we" (451–53). Although this character can be divided into individuals, the townspeople are most often portrayed as acting together, as when they gossip about Miss Emily. Sometimes, the group is defined more specifically, such as when "the ladies began to say that it was a disgrace to the town and a bad example to the young people. The men did not want to interfere" (453). Individuals within the group are briefly mentioned. For example, a "Baptist minister" goes and talks to her, and his wife writes her relatives to have them come to visit. Although these seem to be individual actions, the whole town is presented as participating in them; for example, the narrator explains, "So, she had blood-kin under her roof again and we sat back to watch developments" after the relatives arrived (453). Throughout the story, this "we" seems to be a large force that tries to shape Miss Emily. This "we" brings in the relatives who, in turn, make Miss Emily define her relationship with Homer and push her towards murder.

Although the townspeople seem to be involved in Miss Emily's life, a second dynamic takes place when they have to confront her directly: they seem afraid of her and give into her. This is seen in several scenes, including when Miss Emily buys poison. In this scene, a crucial piece of missing information is not followed up on. The druggist asks Miss Emily what she wants the poison for, and she refuses to answer; even though she is required by law to explain the use of the poison, she does not give that information. When the druggist explains the law, "Miss Emily just stared at him, her head tilted back in order to look him eye for eye, until he looked away and went and got the arsenic and wrapped it up" (452). The druggist is intimidated by her stare and, the reader learns, writes "For rats" on the poison and covers for Miss Emily (452). If the druggist had refused to allow her to buy the

a strong literature paper analyzes literary form

writer uses close reading to analyze specific words

writer restates the central argument of paper section B

writer follows his outline and develops subpoint #2

Martinez 4

*writer develops
his ideas by
making strong
arguments*
poison, the entire murder plot might have been avoided. He could have
questioned the use of the poison more thoroughly, and Miss Emily would
have known her murder plot would be uncovered. If the druggist was a
stronger character, he would not have allowed Miss Emily to purchase what
becomes a murder weapon.

The townspeople's willingness to not question Miss Emily is also
shown after Homer's death. The townspeople do not investigate the smell at
*writer follows his
planned
organization
and develops
subpoint #3*
Miss Emily's house, which the reader later learns is caused by Homer's
decaying body. The townspeople do not want to confront Miss Emily with the
embarrassing fact of the smell, and the Judge exclaims, "Will you accuse a
lady to her face of smelling bad?" (451). Rather than question her, the Board
of Alderman of four men go to her house and spread lime around the base of
her house, hoping to stop the smell. The men "slunk about the house like
burglars" (451). The men decide that they should act like "burglars" rather
than confront Miss Emily; rather than discover that she is a criminal, the
men act like criminals. Interestingly, Miss Emily was aware of the men
*writer analyzes
interesting
moments in the
story*
coming to her house, and watched them from a lighted window. However,
the men remained unable to ask her about the smell, but allowed her to live
above the law.

A final example of how the townspeople create a larger patterns of not
confronting Miss Emily appears in the opening of "A Rose for Emily." The
story opens with a scene that seems boring in comparison to the murder: the
*writer follows his
planned
organization
and develops
subpoint #4*
narrator explains why Miss Emily is allowed to avoid paying taxes. This scene
also explains that the townspeople see Miss Emily as "a tradition, a duty, and
a care; a sort of hereditary obligation upon the town" (449). This scene
shows that the town is connected to Miss Emily and that she is not as
*writer offers
evidence and an
interpretation of
that evidence*
isolated as she seems. In addition, it shows how the town tries to "care" for
her, but actually allows her to break town rules and live in her own reality.

The scene describes Miss Emily returning her tax notice, "without comment," followed by the Board of Alderman's visit to her house (449). Miss Emily's house is described as being "dim" and in "shadow," smelling of "dust and disuse—a close dank smell," and being filled with "cracked" leather furniture (450). This smell foreshadows the earlier smell that results from the murder of Homer—the smell that an earlier group of Aldermen try to cover up. When the Alderman visitors sit down, "a faint dust rose sluggishly about their thighs, spinning with slow motes" (450). The dusty scene foreshadows the discovery of Homer's body in the dusty, decayed room at the end of the story. The men explain that she owes taxes, but she responds by repeating three times, "I have no taxes in Jefferson" and telling them three times to go see a dead "Colonel Sartoris" (450). The men give in to her demands and do not force her to pay taxes. As the narrator explains, "she vanquished them, horse and foot" (450). By letting her not pay her taxes, these men allow Miss Emily to create her own reality—a reality in which she follows her own rules and ignores if people are alive or dead.

writer breaks down the quotes and integrates them into his writing

writer pushes his thinking to create inventive interpretations

The townspeople are a "group character" that has some responsibility for Homer's murder because of the way they interact with Miss Emily. As a first dynamic of interaction, they intervene in Miss Emily's courtship, gossiping and asking her relatives to come stay with her. Even if the courtship broke expectations or was inappropriate, it was far less criminal that murder. The townspeople should have let Miss Emily enjoy her relationship with Homer. As a second dynamic, the town did not stand up to Miss Emily when it should have. The town had an opportunity to turn Miss Emily away from her criminal act of murder. If the druggist had stood up to her and questioned her motives more closely, she might have given up on the idea of the poisoning. After the murder occurred, the townspeople could have come to a greater understanding of what had happened in the Grierson

writer creates unique phrasing to capture his ideas

writer reviews his arguments as needed

writer continues to phrase his ideas in an argumentative fashion

house. They could have questioned Emily and forced themselves into the home to investigate. Instead, they participated in the cover up of the murder, covering up the smell and letting the town pretend nothing had happened. Finally, the Board of Alderman's later reaction to her taxes shows that the town was willing to let Miss Emily create her own world and create her own rules. This tax issue reveals how the town was afraid to confront her directly.

Although Miss Emily is clearly Homer's murderer, she might not have taken on that role if the townspeople had been both more supportive of her and more questioning of her. The townspeople, although not directly acting like murderers, bear some responsibility for Homer's murder. Miss Emily is

paper ends with a strong argument.

not the lonely, all-alone murderer that she seems to be; she has a partner in crime in the townspeople.

[New page]

Work Cited

Faulkner, William. "A Rose for Emily," *Literature for Composition*. Ed. Sylvan
Barnet, William Burto, William E. Cain, and Cheryl L. Nixon. 11th ed.
Boston: Pearson, 2017. 451–56. Print.

Your Turn: Additional Stories for Analysis

KATHERINE MANSFIELD

Katherine Mansfield (1888–1923) was born in New Zealand. She published a book of stories in 1911, and in 1912 met and began living with the writer John Middleton Murry. In 1918, after divorcing, she married Murry. She died of tuberculosis in 1923 a few months after her thirty-fourth birthday.

Miss Brill

Although it was so brilliantly fine—the blue sky powdered with gold and great spots of light like white wine splashed over the Jardins Publiques[1]—Miss Brill was glad that she had decided on her fur. The air was motionless, but when you opened your mouth there was just a faint chill, like a chill from a glass of iced water before you sip, and now and again a leaf came drifting—from nowhere, from the sky. Miss Brill put up her hand and touched her fur. Dear little thing! It was nice to feel it again. She had taken it out of its box that afternoon, shaken out the moth-powder, given it a good brush, and rubbed the life back into the dim little eyes. "What has been happening to me?" said the sad little eyes. Oh, how sweet it was to see them snap at her again from the red eiderdown! . . . But the nose, which was of some black composition, wasn't at all firm. It must have had a knock, somehow. Never mind—a little dab of black sealing- wax when the time came—when it was absolutely necessary. . . . Little rogue! Yes, she really felt like that about it. Little rogue biting its tail just by her left ear. She could have taken it off and laid it on her lap and stroked it. She felt a tingling in her hands and arms, but that came from walking, she supposed. And when she breathed, something light and sad—no, not sad, exactly—something gentle seemed to move in her bosom.

There were a number of people out this afternoon, far more than last Sunday. And the band sounded louder and gayer. That was because the Season had begun. For although the band played all year round on Sundays, out of season it was never the same. It was like some one playing with only the family to listen; it didn't care how it played if there weren't any strangers present. Wasn't the conductor wearing a new coat, too? She was sure it was new. He scraped with his foot and flapped his arms like a rooster about to crow, and the bandsmen sitting in the green rotunda blew out their cheeks and glared at the music. Now there came a little "flutey" bit—very pretty!—a little chain of bright drops. She was sure it would be repeated. It was; she lifted her head and smiled.

Only two people shared her "special" seat: a fine old man in a velvet coat, his hands clasped over a huge carved walking-stick, and a big old woman, sitting upright, with a roll of knitting on her embroidered apron. They did not speak. This was disappointing, for Miss Brill always looked forward to the conversation. She had become really quite expert, she thought, at listening as though she didn't listen, at sitting in other people's lives just for a minute while they talked round her.

She glanced, sideways, at the old couple. Perhaps they would go soon. Last Sunday, too, hadn't been as interesting as usual. An Englishman and his wife, he wearing a dreadful Panama hat and she button boots. And she'd gone on the whole time about how she ought to wear spectacles; she knew she needed them; but that it was no good getting any; they'd be sure to break and they'd never keep on. And he'd been so patient. He'd suggested everything—gold rims, the kind that curved round your ears, little pads inside the bridge. No, nothing would please her. "They'll always be sliding down my nose!" Miss Brill had wanted to shake her.

5   The old people sat on the bench, still as statues. Never mind, there was always the crowd to watch. To and fro, in front of the flower-beds and the band rotunda, the couples and groups paraded, stopped to talk, to greet, to buy a handful of flowers from the old beggar who had his tray fixed to the railings. Little children ran among them, swooping and laughing; little boys with big white silk bows under their chins, little girls, little French dolls, dressed up in velvet and lace. And

[1]**Jardins Publiques** Public Gardens (French).

some-times a tiny staggerer came suddenly rocking into the open from under the trees, stopped, stared, as suddenly sat down "flop," until its small high-stepping mother, like a young hen, rushed scolding to its rescue. Other people sat on the benches and green chairs, but they were nearly always the same, Sunday after Sunday, and—Miss Brill had often noticed—there was something funny about nearly all of them. They were odd, silent, nearly all old, and from the way they stared they looked as though they'd just come from dark little rooms or even—even cupboards!

Behind the rotunda the slender trees with yellow leaves down drooping, and through them just a line of sea, and beyond the blue sky with gold-veined clouds.

Tum-tum-tum tiddle-um! tiddle-um! tum tiddley-um tum ta! blew the band.

Two young girls in red came by and two young soldiers in blue met them, and they laughed and paired and went off arm-in-arm. Two peasant women with funny straw hats passed, gravely, leading beautiful smoke-colored donkeys. A cold, pale nun hurried by. A beautiful woman came along and dropped her bunch of violets, and a little boy ran after to hand them to her, and she took them and threw them away as if they'd been poisoned. Dear me! Miss Brill didn't know whether to admire that or not! And now an ermine toque[2] and a gentleman in grey met just in front of her. He was tall, stiff, dignified, and she was wearing the ermine toque she'd bought when her hair was yellow. Now everything, her hair, her face, even her eyes, was the same color as the shabby ermine, and her hand, in its cleaned glove, lifted to dab her lips, was a tiny yellowish paw. Oh, she was so pleased to see him—delighted! She rather thought they were going to meet that afternoon. She described where she'd been—everywhere, here, there, along by the sea. The day was so charming—didn't he agree? And wouldn't he, perhaps? . . . But he shook his head, lighted a cigarette, slowly breathed a great deep puff into her face, and, even while she was still talking and laughing, flicked the match away and walked on. The ermine toque was alone; she smiled more brightly than ever. But even the band seemed to know what she was feeling and played more softly, played tenderly, and the drum beat, "The Brute! The Brute!" over and over. What would she do? What was going to happen now? But as Miss Brill wondered, the ermine toque turned, raised her hand as though she'd seen some one else, much nicer, just over there, and pattered away. And the band changed again and played more quickly, more gaily than ever, and the old couple on Miss Brill's seat got up and marched away, and such a funny old man with long whiskers hobbled along in time to the music and was nearly knocked over by four girls walking abreast.

Oh, how fascinating it was! How she enjoyed it! How she loved sitting here, watching it all! It was like a play. It was exactly like a play. Who could believe the sky at the back wasn't painted? But it wasn't till a little brown dog trotted on solemn and then slowly trotted off, like a little "theatre" dog, a little dog that had been drugged, that Miss Brill discovered what it was that made it so exciting. They were all on the stage. They weren't only the audience, not only looking on; they were acting. Even she had a part and came every Sunday. No doubt somebody would have noticed if she hadn't been there; she was part of the performance after all. How strange she'd never thought of it like that before! And yet it explained why she made such a point of starting from home at just the same time each week—so as not to be late for the performance—and it also explained why she had quite a queer, shy feeling at telling her English pupils how she spent her Sunday afternoons. No wonder! Miss Brill nearly laughed out loud. She was on the stage. She thought of the old invalid gentleman to whom she read the newspaper four afternoons a week while he slept in the garden. She had got quite used to the frail head

[2]**toque** a brimless, close-fitting woman's hat.

on the cotton pillow, the hollowed eyes, the open mouth and the high pinched nose. If he'd been dead she mightn't have noticed for weeks; she wouldn't have minded. But suddenly he knew he was having the paper read to him by an actress! "An actress!" The old head lifted; two points of light quivered in the old eyes. "An actress—are ye?" And Miss Brill smoothed the newspaper as though it were the manuscript of her part and said gently: "Yes, I have been an actress for a long time."

10   The band had been having a rest. Now they started again. And what they played was warm, sunny, yet there was just a faint chill—a something, what was it?—not sadness—no, not sadness—a something that made you want to sing. The tune lifted, lifted, the light shone; and it seemed to Miss Brill that in another moment all of them, all the whole company, would begin singing. The young ones, the laughing ones who were moving together, they would begin, and the men's voices, very resolute and brave, would join them. And then she too, she too, and the others on the benches—they would come in with a kind of accompaniment—something low, that scarcely rose or fell, something so beautiful—moving. . . . And Miss Brill's eyes filled with tears and she looked smiling at all the other members of the company. Yes, we understand, we understand, she thought—though what they understood she didn't know.

Just at that moment a boy and a girl came and sat down where the old couple had been. They were beautifully dressed; they were in love. The hero and heroine, of course, just arrived from his father's yacht. And still soundlessly singing, still with that trembling smile, Miss Brill prepared to listen.

"No, not now," said the girl. "Not here, I can't."

"But why? Because of that stupid old thing at the end there?" asked the boy.

"Why does she come here at all—who wants her? Why doesn't she keep her silly old mug at home?"

"It's her fu-fur which is so funny," giggled the girl. "It's exactly like a fried whiting."[3]

15   "Ah, be off with you!" said the boy in an angry whisper. Then: "Tell me, my petite chère[4]—"

"No, not here," said the girl. "Not *yet*."

On her way home she usually bought a slice of honey-cake at the baker's. It was her Sunday treat. Sometimes there was an almond in her slice, sometimes not. It made a great difference. If there was an almond it was like carrying home a tiny present—a surprise—something that might very well not have been there. She hurried on the almond Sundays and struck the match for the kettle in quite a dashing way.

But today she passed the baker's by, climbed the stairs, went into the little dark room—her room like a cupboard—and sat down on the red eiderdown. She sat there for a long time. The box that the fur came out of was on the bed. She un- clasped the necklet quickly; quickly, without looking, laid it inside. But when she put the lid on she thought she heard something crying.

[1920]

Joining the Conversation: Critical Thinking and Writing

1. Why do you think Mansfield did not give Miss Brill a first name?
2. What would be lost (or gained?) if the first paragraph were omitted?
3. Suppose someone said that the story is about a woman who is justly punished for her pride. What might be your response?

---

[3]**whiting** a kind of fish.   [4]***petite chère*** darling.

TIM O'BRIEN

Tim O'Brien, born in 1947 in Austin, Minnesota, was drafted into the army in 1968 and served as an infantryman in Vietnam. Drawing on this experience, he wrote a memoir, If I Die in a Combat Zone *(1973), in which he explained that he did not support the Vietnam War, considered dodging the draft, but, lacking the courage to do so, he served, largely out of fear and embarrassment. A later book, a novel called* Going After Cacciato, *won the National Book Award in 1979. "The Things They Carried," first published in 1986, was republished in 1990 as one of a series of interlocking stories in a book titled* The Things They Carried.

The Things They Carried

First Lieutenant Jimmy Cross carried letters from a girl named Martha, a junior at Mount Sebastian College in New Jersey. They were not love letters, but Lieutenant Cross was hoping, so he kept them folded in plastic at the bottom of his rucksack. In the late afternoon, after a day's march, he would dig his foxhole, wash his hands under a canteen, unwrap the letters, hold them with the tips of his fingers, and spend the last hour of light pretending. He would imagine romantic camping trips into the White Mountains in New Hampshire. He would sometimes taste the envelope flaps, knowing her tongue had been there. More than anything, he wanted Martha to love him as he loved her, but the letters were mostly chatty, elusive on the matter of love. She was a virgin, he was almost sure. She was an English major at Mount Sebastian, and she wrote beautifully about her professors and roommates and midterm exams, about her respect for Chaucer and her great affection for Virginia Woolf. She often quoted lines of poetry; she never mentioned the war, except to say, Jimmy, take care of yourself. The letters weighed ten ounces. They were signed "Love, Martha," but Lieutenant Cross understood that Love was only a way of signing and did not mean what he sometimes pretended it meant. At dusk, he would carefully return the letters to his rucksack. Slowly, a bit distracted, he would get up and move among his men, checking the perimeter, then at full dark he would return to his hole and watch the night and wonder if Martha was a virgin.

The things they carried were largely determined by necessity. Among the necessities or near-necessities were P-38 can openers, pocket knives, heat tabs, wrist watches, dog tags, mosquito repellent, chewing gum, candy, cigarettes, salt tablets, packets of Kool-Aid, lighters, matches, sewing kits, Military Payment Certificates, C rations, and two or three canteens of water. Together, these items weighed between fifteen and twenty pounds, depending upon a man's habits or rate of metabolism. Henry Dobbins, who was a big man, carried extra rations; he was especially fond of canned peaches in heavy syrup over pound cake. Dave Jensen, who practiced field hygiene, carried a toothbrush, dental floss, and several hotel-size bars of soap he'd stolen on R&R[1] in Sydney, Australia. Ted Lavender, who was scared, carried tranquilizers until he was shot in the head outside the village of Than Khe in mid-April. By necessity, and because it was SOP,[2] they all carried steel helmets that weighed five pounds including the liner and camouflage cover. They carried the standard fatigue jackets and trousers. Very few carried underwear. On their feet they carried jungle boots—2.1 pounds—and Dave Jensen carried

[1] **R&R** rest and rehabilitation leave.
[2] **SOP** standard operating procedure.

three pairs of socks and a can of Dr. Scholl's foot powder as a precaution against trench foot. Until he was shot, Ted Lavender carried six or seven ounces of premium dope, which for him was a necessity. Mitchell Sanders, the RTO,[3] carried condoms. Norman Bowker carried a diary. Rat Kiley carried comic books. Kiowa, a devout Baptist, carried an illustrated New Testament that had been presented to him by his father, who taught Sunday school in Oklahoma City, Oklahoma. As a hedge against bad times, however, Kiowa also carried his grandmother's distrust of the white man, his grandfather's old hunting hatchet. Necessity dictated. Because the land was mined and booby-trapped, it was SOP for each man to carry a steel-centered, nylon-covered flak jacket, which weighed 6.7 pounds, but which on hot days seemed much heavier. Because you could die so quickly, each man carried at least one large compress bandage, usually in the helmet band for easy access. Because the nights were cold, and because the monsoons were wet, each carried a green plastic poncho that could be used as a raincoat or groundsheet or make-shift tent. With its quilted liner, the poncho weighed almost two pounds, but it was worth every ounce. In April, for instance, when Ted Lavender was shot, they used his poncho to wrap him up, then to carry him across the paddy, then to lift him into the chopper that took him away.

They were called legs or grunts.

To carry something was to "hump" it, as when Lieutenant Jimmy Cross humped his love for Martha up the hills and through the swamps. In its intransitive form, "to hump" meant "to walk," or "to march," but it implied burdens far beyond the intransitive.

5   Almost everyone humped photographs. In his wallet, Lieutenant Cross carried two photographs of Martha. The first was a Kodachrome snapshot signed "Love," though he knew better. She stood against a brick wall. Her eyes were gray and neutral, her lips slightly open as she stared straight-on at the camera. At night, sometimes, Lieutenant Cross wondered who had taken the picture, because he knew she had boyfriends, because he loved her so much, and because he could see the shadow of the picture taker spreading out against the brick wall. The second photograph had been clipped from the 1968 Mount Sebastian yearbook. It was an action shot—women's volleyball—and Martha was bent horizontal to the floor, reaching, the palms of her hands in sharp focus, the tongue taut, the expression frank and competitive. There was no visible sweat. She wore white gym shorts. Her legs, he thought, were almost certainly the legs of a virgin, dry and without hair, the left knee cocked and carrying her entire weight, which was just over one hundred pounds. Lieutenant Cross remembered touching that left knee. A dark theater, he remembered, and the movie was *Bonnie and Clyde,* and Martha wore a tweed skirt, and during the final scene, when he touched her knee, she turned and looked at him in a sad, sober way that made him pull his hand back, but he would always remember the feel of the tweed skirt and the knee beneath it and the sound of the gunfire that killed Bonnie and Clyde, how embarrassing it was, how slow and oppressive. He remembered kissing her goodnight at the dorm door. Right then, he thought, he should've done something brave. He should've carried her up the stairs to her room and tied her to the bed and touched that left knee all night long. He should've risked it. Whenever he looked at the photographs, he thought of new things he should've done.

What they carried was partly a function of rank, partly of field specialty.

---

[3]**RTO** radio and telephone operator.

As a first lieutenant and platoon leader, Jimmy Cross carried a compass, maps, code books, binoculars, and a .45-caliber pistol that weighed 2.9 pounds fully loaded. He carried a strobe light and the responsibility for the lives of his men.

As an RTO, Mitchell Sanders carried the PRC-25 radio, a killer, twenty-six pounds with its battery.

As a medic, Rat Kiley carried a canvas satchel filled with morphine and plasma and malaria tablets and surgical tape and comic books and all the things a medic must carry, including M&Ms[4] for especially bad wounds, for a total weight of nearly twenty pounds.

10   As a big man, therefore a machine gunner, Henry Dobbins carried the M-60, which weighed twenty-three pounds unloaded, but which was almost always loaded. In addition, Dobbins carried between ten and fifteen pounds of ammunition draped in belts across his chest and shoulders.

As PFCs or Spec 4s, most of them were common grunts and carried the standard M-16 gas operated assault rifle. The weapon weighed 7.5 pounds unloaded, 8.2 pounds with its full twenty-round magazine. Depending on numerous factors, such as topography and psychology, the riflemen carried anywhere from twelve to twenty magazines, usually in cloth bandoliers, adding on another 8.4 pounds at minimum, fourteen pounds at maximum. When it was available, they also carried M-16 maintenance gear—rods and steel brushes and swabs and tubes of LSA oil—all of which weighed about a pound. Among the grunts, some carried the M-79 grenade launcher, 5.9 pounds unloaded, a reasonably light weapon except for the ammunition, which was heavy. A single round weighed ten ounces. The typical load was twenty-five rounds. But Ted Lavender, who was scared, carried thirty-four rounds when he was shot and killed outside Than Khe, and he went down under an exceptional burden, more than twenty pounds of ammunition, plus the flak jacket and helmet and rations and water and toilet paper and tranquilizers and all the rest, plus the unweighed fear. He was dead weight. There was no twitching or flopping. Kiowa, who saw it happen, said it was like watching a rock fall, or a big sandbag or something—just boom, then down—not like the movies where the dead guy rolls around and does fancy spins and goes ass over teakettle—not like that, Kiowa said, the poor bastard just flat-fuck fell. Boom. Down. Nothing else. It was a bright morning in mid-April. Lieutenant Cross felt the pain. He blamed himself. They stripped off Lavender's canteens and ammo, all the heavy things, and Rat Kiley said the obvious, the guy's dead, and Mitchell Sanders used his radio to report one U.S. KIA[5] and to request a chopper. Then they wrapped Lavender in his poncho. They carried him out to a dry paddy, established security, and sat smoking the dead man's dope until the chopper came. Lieutenant Cross kept to himself. He pictured Martha's smooth young face, thinking he loved her more than anything, more than his men, and now Ted Lavender was dead because he loved her so much and could not stop thinking about her. When the dust-off arrived, they carried Lavender aboard. Afterward they burned Than Khe. They marched until dusk, then dug their holes, and that night Kiowa kept explaining how you had to be there, how fast it was, how the poor guy just dropped like so much concrete. Boom-down, he said. Like cement.

In addition to the three standard weapons—the M-60, M-16, and M-79—they carried whatever presented itself, or whatever seemed appropriate as a means of killing or staying alive. They carried catch-as-catch-can. At various times, in various situations, they carried M-14s and CAR-15s and Swedish Ks and grease guns and

---

[4]**M&M** joking term for medical supplies.
[5]**KIA** killed in action.

captured AK-47s and Chi-Coms and RPGs and Simonov carbines and black-market Uzis and .38-caliber Smith & Wesson handguns and 66 mm LAWs and shotguns and silencers and blackjacks and bayonets and C-4 plastic explosives. Lee Strunk carried a slingshot; a weapon of last resort, he called it. Mitchell Sanders carried brass knuckles. Kiowa carried his grandfather's feathered hatchet. Every third or fourth man carried a Claymore antipersonnel mine—3.5 pounds with its firing device. They all carried fragmentation grenades—fourteen ounces each. They all carried at least one M-18 colored smoke grenade—twenty-four ounces. Some carried CS or tear-gas grenades. Some carried white-phosphorus grenades. They carried all they could bear, and then some, including a silent awe for the terrible power of the things they carried.

In the first week of April, before Lavender died, Lieutenant Jimmy Cross received a good-luck charm from Martha. It was a simple pebble, an ounce at most. Smooth to the touch, it was a milky-white color with flecks of orange and violet, oval-shaped, like a miniature egg. In the accompanying letter, Martha wrote that she had found the pebble on the Jersey shoreline, precisely where the land touched the water at high tide, where things came together but also separated. It was this separate-but-together quality, she wrote, that had inspired her to pick up the pebble and to carry it in her breast pocket for several days, where it seemed weightless, and then to send it through the mail, by air, as a token of her truest feelings for him. Lieutenant Cross found this romantic. But he wondered what her truest feelings were, exactly, and what she meant by separate-but-together. He wondered how the tides and waves had come into play on that afternoon along the Jersey shoreline when Martha saw the pebble and bent down to rescue it from geology. He imagined bare feet. Martha was a poet, with the poet's sensibilities, and her feet would be brown and bare, the toenails unpainted, the eyes chilly and somber like the ocean in March, and though it was painful, he wondered who had been with her that afternoon. He imagined a pair of shadows moving along the strip of sand where things came together but also separated. It was phantom jealousy, he knew, but he couldn't help himself. He loved her so much. On the march, through the hot days of early April, he carried the pebble in his mouth, turning it with his tongue, tasting sea salts and moisture. His mind wandered. He had difficulty keeping his attention on the war. On occasion he would yell at his men to spread out the column, to keep their eyes open, but then he would slip away into daydreams, just pretending, walking barefoot along the Jersey shore, with Martha, carrying nothing. He would feel himself rising. Sun and waves and gentle winds, all love and lightness.

What they carried varied by mission.

15   When a mission took them to the mountains, they carried mosquito netting, machetes, canvas tarps, and extra bugjuice.

If a mission seemed especially hazardous, or if it involved a place they knew to be bad, they carried everything they could. In certain heavily mined AOs,[6] where the land was dense with Toe Poppers and Bouncing Betties, they took turns humping a twenty-eight-pound mine detector. With its headphones and big sensing plate, the equipment was a stress on the lower back and shoulders, awkward to handle, often useless because of the shrapnel in the earth, but they carried it anyway, partly for safety, partly for the illusion of safety.

On ambush, or other night missions, they carried peculiar little odds and ends. Kiowa always took along his New Testament and a pair of moccasins for silence.

[6] **AOs** areas of operation.

Dave Jensen carried night-sight vitamins high in carotin. Lee Strunk carried his slingshot; ammo, he claimed, would never be a problem. Rat Kiley carried brandy and M&Ms. Until he was shot, Ted Lavender carried the starlight scope, which weighed 6.3 pounds with its aluminum carrying case. Henry Dobbins carried his girlfriend's panty hose wrapped around his neck as a comforter. They all carried ghosts. When dark came, they would move out single file across the meadows and paddies to their ambush coordinates, where they would quietly set up the Claymores and lie down and spend the night waiting.

Other missions were more complicated and required special equipment. In mid-April, it was their mission to search out and destroy the elaborate tunnel complexes in the Than Khe area south of Chu Lai. To blow the tunnels, they carried one-pound blocks of pentrite high explosives, four blocks to a man, sixty-eight pounds in all. They carried wiring, detonators, and battery-powered clackers. Dave Jensen carried earplugs. Most often, before blowing the tunnels, they were ordered by higher command to search them, which was considered bad news, but by and large they just shrugged and carried out orders. Because he was a big man, Henry Dobbins was excused from tunnel duty. The others would draw numbers. Before Lavender died there were seventeen men in the platoon, and whoever drew the number seventeen would strip off his gear and crawl in headfirst with a flashlight and Lieutenant Cross's .45-caliber pistol. The rest of them would fan out as security. They would sit down or kneel, not facing the hole, listening to the ground beneath them, imagining cobwebs and ghosts, whatever was down there—the tunnel walls squeezing in—how the flashlight seemed impossibly heavy in the hand and how it was tunnel vision in the very strictest sense, compression in all ways, even time, and how you had to wiggle in—ass and elbows—a swallowed-up feeling—and how you found yourself worrying about odd things—will your flashlight go dead? Do rats carry rabies? If you screamed, how far would the sound carry? Would your buddies hear it? Would they have the courage to drag you out? In some respects, though not many, the waiting was worse than the tunnel itself. Imagination was a killer.

On April 16, when Lee Strunk drew the number seventeen, he laughed and muttered something and went down quickly. The morning was hot and very still. Not good, Kiowa said. He looked at the tunnel opening, then out across a dry paddy toward the village of Than Khe. Nothing moved. No clouds or birds or people. As they waited, the men smoked and drank Kool-Aid, not talking much, feeling sympathy for Lee Strunk but also feeling the luck of the draw. You win some, you lose some, said Mitchell Sanders, and sometimes you settle for a rain check. It was a tired line and no one laughed.

20   Henry Dobbins ate a tropical chocolate bar. Ted Lavender popped a tranquilizer and went off to pee.

After five minutes, Lieutenant Jimmy Cross moved to the tunnel, leaned down, and examined the darkness. Trouble, he thought—a cave-in maybe. And then suddenly, without willing it, he was thinking about Martha. The stresses and fractures, the quick collapse, the two of them buried alive under all that weight. Dense, crushing love. Kneeling, watching the hole, he tried to concentrate on Lee Strunk and the war, all the dangers, but his love was too much for him, he felt paralyzed, he wanted to sleep inside her lungs and breathe her blood and be smothered. He wanted her to be a virgin and not a virgin, all at once. He wanted to know her. Intimate secrets—why poetry? Why so sad? Why that grayness in her eyes? Why so alone? Not lonely, just alone—riding her bike across campus or sitting off by herself in the cafeteria. Even dancing, she danced alone—and it was the aloneness that filled him with love. He remembered telling her that one evening. How she nodded and looked away.

And how, later, when he kissed her, she received the kiss without returning it, her eyes wide open, not afraid, not a virgin's eyes, just flat and uninvolved.

Lieutenant Cross gazed at the tunnel. But he was not there. He was buried with Martha under the white sand at the Jersey shore. They were pressed together, and the pebble in his mouth was her tongue. He was smiling. Vaguely, he was aware of how quiet the day was, the sullen paddies, yet he could not bring himself to worry about matters of security. He was beyond that. He was just a kid at war, in love. He was twenty-two years old. He couldn't help it.

A few minutes later Lee Strunk crawled out of the tunnel. He came up grinning, filthy but alive. Lieutenant Cross nodded and closed his eyes while the others clapped Strunk on the back and made jokes about rising from the dead.

Worms, Rat Kiley said. Right out of the grave. Fuckin' zombie.

25   The men laughed. They all felt great relief.

Spook City, said Mitchell Sanders.

Lee Strunk made a funny ghost sound, a kind of moaning, yet very happy, and right then, when Strunk made that high happy moaning sound, when he went *Ah-hooooo,* right then Ted Lavender was shot in the head on his way back from peeing. He lay with his mouth open. The teeth were broken. There was a swollen black bruise under his left eye. The cheekbone was gone. Oh shit, Rat Kiley said, the guy's dead. The guy's dead, he kept saying, which seemed profound—the guy's dead. I mean really.

The things they carried were determined to some extent by superstition. Lieutenant Cross carried his good-luck pebble. Dave Jensen carried a rabbit's foot. Norman Bowker, otherwise a very gentle person, carried a thumb that had been presented to him as a gift by Mitchell Sanders. The thumb was dark brown, rubbery to the touch, and weighed four ounces at most. It had been cut from a VC corpse, a boy of fifteen or sixteen. They'd found him at the bottom of an irrigation ditch, badly burned, flies in his mouth and eyes. They boy wore black shorts and sandals. At the time of his death he had been carrying a pouch of rice, a rifle, and three magazines of ammunition.

You want my opinion, Mitchell Sanders said, there's a definite moral here.

30   He put his hand on the dead boy's wrist. He was quiet for a time, as if counting a pulse, then he patted the stomach, almost affectionately, and used Kiowa's hunting hatchet to remove the thumb.

Henry Dobbins asked what the moral was.

Moral?

You know. *Moral.*

Sanders wrapped the thumb in toilet paper and handed it across to Norman Bowker. There was no blood. Smiling, he kicked the boy's head, watched the flies scatter, and said, It's like with that old TV show—Paladin. Have gun, will travel.

35   Henry Dobbins thought about it.

Yeah, well, he finally said. I don't see no moral.

There it *is,* man.

Fuck off.

They carried USO stationery and pencils and pens. They carried Sterno, safety pins, trip flares, signal flares, spools of wire, razor blades, chewing tobacco, liberated joss sticks and statuettes of the smiling Buddha, candles, grease pencils, *The Stars and Stripes,* fingernail clippers, Psy Ops leaflets, bush hats, bolos, and much more. Twice a week, when the resupply choppers came in, they carried hot chow in green Mermite cans and large canvas bags filled with iced beer and soda pop. They carried plastic water containers, each with a two gallon capacity. Mitchell

Sanders carried a set of starched tiger fatigues for special occasions. Henry Dobbins carried Black Flag insecticide. Dave Jensen carried empty sandbags that could be filled at night for added protection. Lee Strunk carried tanning lotion. Some things they carried in common. Taking turns, they carried the big PRC-77 scrambler radio, which weighed thirty pounds with its battery. They shared the weight of memory. They took up what others could no longer bear. Often, they carried each other, the wounded or weak. They carried infections. They carried chess sets, basketballs, Vietnamese-English dictionaries, insignia of rank, Bronze Stars and Purple Hearts, plastic cards imprinted with the Code of Conduct. They carried diseases, among them malaria and dysentery. They carried lice and ringworm and leeches and paddy algae and various rots and molds. They carried the land itself—Vietnam, the place, the soil—a powdery orange-red dust that covered their boots and fatigues and faces. They carried the sky. The whole atmosphere, they carried it, the humidity, the monsoons, the stink of fungus and decay, all of it, they carried gravity. They moved like mules. By daylight they took sniper fire, at night they were mortared, but it was not battle, it was just the endless march, village to village, without purpose, nothing won or lost. They marched for the sake of the march. They plodded along slowly, dumbly, leaning forward against the heat, unthinking, all blood and bone, simple grunts, soldiering with their legs, toiling up the hills and down into the paddies and across the rivers and up again and down, just humping, one step and then the next and then another, but no volition, no will, because it was automatic, it was anatomy, and the war was entirely a matter of posture and carriage, the hump was everything, a kind of inertia, a kind of emptiness, a dullness of desire and intellect and conscience and hope and human sensibility. Their principles were in their feet. Their calculations were biological. They had no sense of strategy or mission. They searched the villages without knowing what to look for, nor caring, kicking over jars of rice, frisking children and old men, blowing tunnels, sometimes setting fires and sometimes not, then forming up and moving on to the next village, then other villages, where it would always be the same. They carried their own lives. The pressures were enormous. In the heat of early afternoon, they would remove their helmets and flak jackets, walking bare, which was dangerous but which helped ease the strain. They would often discard things along the route of march. Purely for comfort, they would throw away rations, blow their Claymores and grenades, no matter, because by nightfall the resupply choppers would arrive with more of the same, then a day or two later still more, fresh watermelons and crates of ammunition and sunglasses and woolen sweaters—the resources were stunning—sparklers for the Fourth of July, colored eggs for Easter. It was the great American war chest—the fruits of sciences, the smokestacks, the canneries, the arsenals at Hartford, the Minnesota forests, the machine shops, the vast fields of corn and wheat—they carried like freight trains; they carried it on their backs and shoulders—and for all the ambiguities of Vietnam, all the mysteries and unknowns, there was at least the single abiding certainty that they would never be at a loss for things to carry.

40   After the chopper took Lavender away, Lieutenant Jimmy Cross led his men into the village of Than Khe. They burned everything. They shot chickens and dogs, they trashed the village well, they called in artillery and watched the wreckage, then they marched for several hours through the hot afternoon, and then at dusk, while Kiowa explained how Lavender died, Lieutenant Cross found himself trembling.

He tried not to cry. With his entrenching tool, which weighed five pounds, he began digging a hole in the earth.

He felt shame. He hated himself. He had loved Martha more than his men, and as a consequence Lavender was now dead, and this was something he would have to carry like a stone in his stomach for the rest of the war.

All he could do was dig. He used his entrenching tool like an ax, slashing, feeling both love and hate, and then later, when it was full dark, he sat at the bottom of his foxhole and wept. It went on for a long while. In part, he was grieving for Ted Lavender, but mostly it was for Martha, and for himself, because she belonged to another world, which was not quite real, and because she was a junior at Mount Sebastian College in New Jersey, a poet and a virgin and uninvolved, and because he realized she did not love him and never would.

Like cement, Kiowa whispered in the dark. I swear to God—boom-down. Not a word.

45 I've heard this, said Norman Bowker.

A pisser, you know? Still zipping himself up. Zapped while zipping.

All right, fine. That's enough.

Yeah, but you had to see it, the guy just—

I *heard*, man. Cement. So why not shut the fuck *up*?

50 Kiowa shook his head sadly and glanced over at the hole where Lieutenant Jimmy Cross sat watching the night. The air was thick and wet. A warm, dense fog had settled over the paddies and there was the stillness that precedes rain.

After a time Kiowa sighed.

One thing for sure, he said. The lieutenant's in some deep hurt. I mean that crying jag—the way he was carrying on—it wasn't fake or anything, it was real heavy-duty hurt. The man cares.

Sure, Norman Bowker said.

Say what you want, the man does care.

55 We all got problems.

Not Lavender.

No, I guess not, Bowker said. Do me a favor, though.

Shut up?

That's a smart Indian. Shut up.

60 Shrugging, Kiowa pulled off his boots. He wanted to say more, just to lighten up his sleep, but instead he opened his New Testament and arranged it beneath his head as a pillow. The fog made things seem hollow and unattached. He tried not to think about Ted Lavender, but then he was thinking how fast it was, no drama, down and dead, and how it was hard to feel anything except surprise. It seemed unchristian. He wished he could find some great sadness, or even anger, but the emotion wasn't there and he couldn't make it happen. Mostly he felt pleased to be alive. He liked the smell of the New Testament under his cheek, the leather and ink and paper and glue, whatever the chemicals were. He liked hearing the sounds of night. Even his fatigue, it felt fine, the stiff muscles and the prickly awareness of his own body, a floating feeling. He enjoyed not being dead. Lying there, Kiowa admired Lieutenant Jimmy Cross's capacity for grief. He wanted to share the man's pain, he wanted to care as Jimmy Cross cared. And yet when he closed his eyes, all he could think was Boom-down, and all he could feel was the pleasure of having his boots off and the fog curling in around him and damp soil and the Bible smells and the plush comfort of night.

After a moment Norman Bowker sat up in the dark.

What the hell, he said. You want to talk, *talk*. Tell it to me.

Forget it.

No, man, go on. One thing I hate, it's a silent Indian.

65   For the most part they carried themselves with poise, a kind of dignity. Now and then, however, there were times of panic, when they squealed or wanted to squeal but couldn't, when they twitched and made moaning sounds and covered their heads and said Dear Jesus and flopped around on the earth and fired their weapons blindly and cringed and sobbed and begged for the noise to stop and went wild and made stupid promises to themselves and to God and to their mothers and fathers, hoping not to die. In different ways, it happened to all of them. Afterward, when the firing ended, they would blink and peek up. They would touch their bodies, feeling shame, then quickly hiding it. They would force themselves to stand. As if in slow motion, frame by frame, the world would take on the old logic—absolute silence, then the wind, then sunlight, then voices. It was the burden of being alive. Awkwardly, the men would reassemble themselves, first in private, then in groups, becoming soldiers again. They would repair the leaks in their eyes. They would check for casualties, call in dust-offs, light cigarettes, try to smile, clear their throats and spit and begin cleaning their weapons. After a time someone would shake his head and say, No lie, I almost shit my pants, and someone else would laugh, which meant it was bad, yes, but the guy had obviously not shit his pants, it wasn't that bad, and in any case nobody would ever do such a thing and then go ahead and talk about it. They would squint into the dense, oppressive sunlight. For a few moments, perhaps, they would fall silent, lighting a joint and tracking its passage from man to man, inhaling, holding in the humiliation. Scary stuff, one of them might say. But then someone else would grin or flick his eyebrows and say, Roger-dodger, almost cut me a new asshole, *almost*.

There were numerous such poses. Some carried themselves with a sort of wistful resignation, others with pride or still soldierly discipline or good humor or macho zeal. They were afraid of dying but they were even more afraid to show it.

They found jokes to tell.

They used a hard vocabulary to contain the terrible softness. *Greased,* they'd say. *Offed, lit up, zapped while zipping*. It wasn't cruelty, just stage presence. They were actors and the war came at them in 3-D. When someone died, it wasn't quite dying, because in a curious way it seemed scripted, and because they had their lines mostly memorized, irony mixed with tragedy, and because they called it by other names, as if to encyst and destroy the reality of death itself. They kicked corpses. They cut off thumbs. They talked grunt lingo. They told stories about Ted Lavender's supply of tranquilizers, how the poor guy didn't feel a thing, how incredibly tranquil he was.

There's a moral here, said Mitchell Sanders.

70   They were waiting for Lavender's chopper, smoking the dead man's dope.

The moral's pretty obvious, Sanders said, and winked. Stay away from drugs. No joke, they'll ruin your day every time.

Cute, said Henry Dobbins.

Mind-blower, get it? Talk about wiggy—nothing left, just blood and brains.

They made themselves laugh.

75   There it is, they'd say, over and over, as if the repetition itself were an act of poise, a balance between crazy and almost crazy, knowing without going. There it is, which meant be cool, let it ride, because oh yeah, man, you can't change what can't be changed, there it is, there it absolutely and positively and fucking well *is*.

They were tough.

They carried all the emotional baggage of men who might die. Grief, terror, love, longing—these were intangibles, but the intangibles had their own mass and specific gravity, they had tangible weight. They carried shameful memories. They carried the common secret of cowardice barely restrained, the instinct to run or freeze or hide, and in many respects this was the heaviest burden of all, for it could never be put down, it required perfect balance and perfect posture. They carried their reputations. They carried the soldier's greatest fear, which was the fear of blushing. Men killed, and died, because they were embarrassed not to. It was what had brought them to the war in the first place, nothing positive, no dreams of glory or honor, just to avoid the blush of dishonor. They died so as not to die of embarrassment. They crawled into tunnels and walked point and advanced under fire. Each morning, despite the unknowns, they made their legs move. They endured. They kept humping. They did not submit to the obvious alternative, which was simply to close the eyes and fall. So easy, really. Go limp and tumble to the ground and let the muscles unwind and not speak and not budge until your buddies picked you up and lifted you into the chopper that would roar and dip its nose and carry you off to the world. A mere matter of falling, yet no one ever fell. It was not courage, exactly; the object was not valor. Rather, they were too frightened to be cowards.

By and large they carried these things inside, maintaining the masks of composure. They sneered at sick call. They spoke bitterly about guys who had found release by shooting off their own toes or fingers. Pussies, they'd say. Candyasses. It was fierce, mocking talk, with only a trace of envy or awe, but even so, the image played itself out behind their eyes.

They imagined the muzzle against flesh. They imagined the quick, sweet pain, then the evacuation to Japan, then a hospital with warm beds and cute geisha nurses.

80   They dreamed of freedom birds.

At night, on guard, staring into the dark, they were carried away by jumbo jets. They felt the rush of takeoff. *Gone!* they yelled. And then velocity, wings and engines, a smiling stewardess—but it was more than a plane, it was a real bird, a big sleek silver bird with feathers and talons and high screeching. They were flying. The weights fell off, there was nothing to bear. They laughed and held on tight, feeling the cold slap of wind and altitude, soaring, thinking *It's over, I'm gone!*—they were naked, they were light and free—it was all lightness, bright and fast and buoyant, light as light, a helium buzz in the brain, a giddy bubbling in the lungs as they were taken up over the clouds and the war, beyond duty, beyond gravity and mortification and global entanglements—*Sin loi!*[7] They yelled, *I'm sorry, motherfuckers, but I'm out of it, I'm goofed, I'm on a space cruise, I'm gone!*—and it was a restful, disencumbered sensation, just riding the light waves, sailing that big silver freedom bird over the mountains and oceans, over America, over the farms and great sleeping cities and cemeteries and highways and the Golden Arches of McDonald's. It was flight, a kind of fleeing, a kind of falling, falling higher and higher, spinning off the edge of the earth and beyond the sun and through the vast, silent vacuum where there were no burdens and where everything weighed exactly nothing. *Gone!* they screamed, *I'm sorry but I'm gone!* And so at night, not quite dreaming, they gave themselves over to lightness, they were carried, they were purely borne.

On the morning after Ted Lavender died, First Lieutenant Jimmy Cross crouched at the bottom of his foxhole and burned Martha's letters. Then he burned the two photographs. There was a steady rain falling, which made it difficult, but he used

---

[7]*Sin loi* sorry.

heat tabs and Sterno to build a small fire, screening it with his body, holding the photographs over the tight blue flame with the tips of his fingers.

He realized it was only a gesture. Stupid, he thought. Sentimental, too, but mostly just stupid.

Lavender was dead. You couldn't burn the blame.

85   Besides, the letters were in his head. And even now, without photographs, Lieutenant Cross could see Martha playing volleyball in her white gym shorts and yellow T-shirt. He could see her moving in the rain.

When the fire died out, Lieutenant Cross pulled his poncho over his shoulders and ate breakfast from a can.

There was no great mystery, he decided.

In those burned letters Martha had never mentioned the war, except to say, Jimmy, take care of yourself. She wasn't involved. She signed the letters "Love," but it wasn't love, and all the fine lines and technicalities did not matter.

The morning came up wet and blurry. Everything seemed part of everything else, the fog and Martha and the deepening rain.

90   It was a war, after all.

Half smiling, Lieutenant Jimmy Cross took out his maps. He shook his head hard, as if to clear it, then bent forward and began planning the day's march. In ten minutes, or maybe twenty, he would rouse the men and they would pack up and head west, where the maps showed the country to be green and inviting. They would do what they had always done. The rain might add some weight, but otherwise it would be one more day layered upon all the other days.

He was realistic about it. There was the new hardness in his stomach.

No more fantasies, he told himself.

Henceforth, when he thought about Martha, it would be only to think that she belonged elsewhere. He would shut down the daydreams. This was not Mount Sebastian, it was another world, where there were no pretty poems or midterm exams, a place where men died because of carelessness and gross stupidity. Kiowa was right. Boom-down, and you were dead, never partly dead.

95   Briefly, in the rain, Lieutenant Cross saw Martha's gray eyes gazing back at him.

He understood.

It was very sad, he thought. The things men carried inside. The things men did or felt they had to do.

He almost nodded at her, but didn't.

Instead he went back to his maps. He was now determined to perform his duties firmly and without negligence. It wouldn't help Lavender, he knew that, but from this point on he would comport himself as a soldier. He would dispose of his good-luck pebble. Swallow it, maybe, or use Lee Strunk's slingshot, or just drop it along the trail. On the march he would impose strict field discipline. He would be careful to send out flank security, to prevent straggling or bunching up, to keep his troops moving at the proper pace and at the proper interval. He would insist on clean weapons. He would confiscate the remainder of Lavender's dope. Later in the day, perhaps, he would call the men together and speak to them plainly. He would accept the blame for what had happened to Ted Lavender. He would be a man about it. He would look them in the eyes, keeping his chin level, and he would issue the new SOPs in a calm, impersonal tone of voice, an officer's voice, leaving no room for argument or discussion. Commencing immediately, he'd tell them, they would no longer abandon equipment along the route of march. They would police up their acts. They would get their shit together, and keep it together, and maintain it neatly and in good working order.

He would not tolerate laxity. He would show strength, distancing himself.

Among the men there would be grumbling, of course, and maybe worse, because their days would seem longer and their loads heavier, but Lieutenant Cross reminded himself that his obligation was not to be loved but to lead. He would dispense with love; it was not now a factor. And if anyone quarreled or complained, he would simply tighten his lips and arrange his shoulders in the correct command posture. He might give a curt little nod. Or he might not. He might just shrug and say Carry on, then they would saddle up and form into a column and move out toward the villages west of Than Khe.

[1986]

Joining the Conversation: Critical Thinking and Writing

1. What is the point of the insistent repetition of the words "the things they carried"? What sorts of things does Lieutenant Cross carry?
2. We are told that "Kiowa admired Lieutenant Jimmy Cross's capacity for grief" (paragraph 60). But we are also told that, although Kiowa "wanted to share the man's pain," he could think only of "Boom-down" and of "the pleasure of having his boots off and the fog curling in around him and damp soil and the Bible smells and the plush comfort of night." What might account for the different responses of the two men?
3. Near the end of the story (paragraph 82), Lieutenant Cross "burned the two photographs." Why does he do this?

GABRIEL GARCÍA MÁRQUEZ

Gabriel García Márquez (1928–2014) was born in Aracataca, a small village in Colombia. After being educated in Bogotá, where he studied journalism and law, he worked as a journalist in Latin America, Europe, and the United States. He began writing fiction when he was in Paris, and when he was twenty-seven years old, he published his first novel, La hojarasca *(Leaf Storm, 1955). During most of the 1960s, he lived in Mexico, where he wrote film scripts and the novel that made him famous:* Cien años de soledad *(1967, translated in 1970 as* A Hundred Years of Solitude*). In 1982, García Márquez was awarded the Nobel Prize in Literature.*

A Very Old Man with Enormous Wings: A Tale for Children

Translated by Gregory Rabassa

On the third day of rain they had killed so many crabs inside the house that Pelayo had to cross his drenched courtyard and throw them into the sea, because the newborn child had a temperature all night and they thought it was due to the stench. The world had been sad since Tuesday. Sea and sky were a single ash-gray thing and the sands of the beach, which on March nights glimmered like powdered light, had become a stew of mud and rotten shellfish. The light was so weak at noon that when Pelayo was coming back to the house after throwing away the crabs, it was hard for him to see what it was that was moving and groaning in the rear of the courtyard. He had to go very close to see that it was an old man, a very old man, lying face down in the mud, who, in spite of his tremendous efforts, couldn't get up, impeded by his enormous wings.

Frightened by that nightmare, Pelayo ran to get Elisenda, his wife, who was putting compresses on the sick child, and he took her to the rear of the courtyard. They both looked at the fallen body with mute stupor. He was dressed like a rag-picker. There were only a few faded hairs left on his bald skull and very few teeth in his mouth, and his pitiful condition of a drenched great-grandfather had taken away any sense of grandeur he might have had. His huge buzzard wings, dirty and half-plucked, were forever entangled in the mud. They looked at him so long and so closely that Pelayo and Elisenda very soon overcame their surprise and in the end found him familiar. Then they dared speak to him, and he answered in an incomprehensible dialect with a strong sailor's voice. That was how they skipped over the inconvenience of the wings and quite intelligently concluded that he was a lonely castaway from some foreign ship wrecked by the storm. And yet, they called in a neighbor woman who knew everything about life and death to see him, and all she needed was one look to show them their mistake.

"He's an angel," she told them. "He must have been coming for the child, but the poor fellow is so old that the rain knocked him down."

On the following day everyone knew that a flesh-and-blood angel was held captive in Pelayo's house. Against the judgment of the wise neighbor woman, for whom angels in those times were the fugitive survivors of a celestial conspiracy, they did not have the heart to club him to death. Pelayo watched over him all afternoon from the kitchen, armed with his bailiff's club, and before going to bed he dragged him out of the mud and locked him up with the hens in the wire chicken coop. In the middle of the night, when the rain stopped, Pelayo and Elisenda were still killing crabs. A short time afterward the child woke up without a fever and with a desire to eat. Then they felt magnanimous and decided to put the angel on a raft with fresh water and provisions for three days and leave him to his fate on the high seas. But when they went out into the courtyard with the first light of dawn, they found the whole neighborhood in front of the chicken coop having fun with the angel, without the slightest reverence, tossing him things to eat through the openings in the wire as if he weren't a supernatural creature but a circus animal.

5   Father Gonzaga arrived before seven o'clock, alarmed at the strange news. By that time onlookers less frivolous than those at dawn had already arrived and they were making all kinds of conjectures concerning the captive's future. The simplest among them thought that he should be named mayor of the world. Others of sterner mind felt that he should be promoted to the rank of five-star general in order to win all wars. Some visionaries hoped that he could be put to stud in order to implant on earth a race of winged wise men who could take charge of the universe. But Father Gonzaga, before becoming a priest, had been a robust woodcutter. Standing by the wire, he reviewed his catechism in an instant and asked them to open the door so that he could take a close look at that pitiful man who looked more like a huge decrepit hen among the fascinated chickens. He was lying in a corner drying his open wings in the sunlight among the fruit peels and breakfast leftovers that the early risers had thrown him. Alien to the impertinences of the world, he only lifted his antiquarian eyes and murmured something in his dialect when Father Gonzaga went into the chicken coop and said good morning to him in Latin. The parish priest had his first suspicion of an imposter when he saw that

he did not understand the language of God or know how to greet His ministers. Then he noticed that seen close up he was much too human: he had an unbearable smell of the outdoors, the back side of his wings was strewn with parasites and his main feathers had been mistreated by terrestrial winds, and nothing about him measured up to the proud dignity of angels. Then he came out of the chicken coop and in a brief sermon warned the curious against the risks of being ingenuous. He reminded them that the devil had the bad habit of making use of carnival tricks in order to confuse the unwary. He argued that if wings were not the essential element in determining the difference between a hawk and an airplane, they were even less so in the recognition of angels. Nevertheless, he promised to write a letter to his bishop so that the latter would write to his primate so that the latter would write to the Supreme Pontiff in order to get the final verdict from the highest courts.

His prudence fell on sterile hearts. The news of the captive angel spread with such rapidity that after a few hours the courtyard had the bustle of a marketplace and they had to call in troops with fixed bayonets to disperse the mob that was about to knock the house down. Elisenda, her spine all twisted from sweeping up so much marketplace trash, then got the idea of fencing in the yard and charging five cents admission to see the angel.

The curious came from far away. A traveling carnival arrived with a flying acrobat who buzzed over the crowd several times, but no one paid any attention to him because his wings were not those of an angel but, rather, those of a sidereal bat. The most unfortunate invalids on earth came in search of health: a poor woman who since childhood had been counting her heartbeats and had run out of numbers; a Portuguese man who couldn't sleep because the noise of the stars disturbed him; a sleepwalker who got up at night to undo the things he had done while awake; and many others with less serious ailments. In the midst of that shipwreck disorder that made the earth tremble, Pelayo and Elisenda were happy with fatigue, for in less than a week they had crammed their rooms with money and the line of pilgrims waiting their turn to enter still reached beyond the horizon.

The angel was the only one who took no part in his own act. He spent his time trying to get comfortable in his borrowed nest, befuddled by the hellish heat of the oil lamps and sacramental candles that had been placed along the wire. At first they tried to make him eat some mothballs, which, according to the wisdom of the wise neighbor woman, were the food prescribed for angels. But he turned them down, just as he turned down the papal lunches that the penitents brought him, and they never found out whether it was because he was an angel or because he was an old man that in the end he ate nothing but eggplant mush. His only supernatural virtue seemed to be patience. Especially during the first days, when the hens pecked at him, searching for the stellar parasites that proliferated in his wings, and the cripples pulled out feathers to touch their defective parts with, and even the most merciful threw stones at him, trying to get him to rise so they could see him standing. The only time they succeeded in arousing him was when they burned his side with an iron for branding steers, for he had been motionless for so many hours that they thought he was dead. He awoke with a start, ranting in his hermetic language and with tears in his eyes, and he flapped his wings a couple of times, which brought on a whirlwind of chicken dung and lunar dust and a gale of panic that did not seem to be of this world. Although many thought that his reaction had been one not of rage but of pain, from then on they were careful not to annoy him, because the majority understood that his passivity was not that of a hero taking his ease but that of a cataclysm in repose.

Father Gonzaga held back the crowd's frivolity with formulas of maidservant inspiration while awaiting the arrival of a final judgment on the nature of the captive. But the mail from Rome showed no sense of urgency. They spent their time finding out if the prisoner had a navel, if his dialect had any connection with Aramaic, how many times he could fit on the head of a pin, or whether he wasn't just a Norwegian with wings. Those meager letters might have come and gone until the end of time if a providential event had not put an end to the priest's tribulations.

10   It so happened that during those days, among so many other carnival attractions, there arrived in town the traveling show of the woman who had been changed into a spider for having disobeyed her parents. The admission to see her was not only less than the admission to see the angel, but people were permitted to ask her all manner of questions about her absurd state and to examine her up and down so that no one would ever doubt the truth of her horror. She was a frightful tarantula the size of a ram and with the head of a sad maiden. What was most heart-rending, however, was not her outlandish shape but the sincere affliction with which she recounted the details of her misfortune. While still practically a child she had sneaked out of her parents' house to go to a dance, and while she was coming back through the woods after having danced all night without permission, a fearful thunderclap rent the sky in two and through the crack came the lightning bolt of brimstone that changed her into a spider. Her only nourishment came from the meatballs that charitable souls chose to toss into her mouth. A spectacle like that, full of so much human truth and with such a fearful lesson, was bound to defeat without even trying that of a haughty angel who scarcely deigned to look at mortals. Besides, the few miracles attributed to the angel showed a certain mental disorder, like the blind man who didn't recover his sight but grew three new teeth, or the paralytic who didn't get to walk but almost won the lottery, and the leper whose sores sprouted sunflowers. Those consolation miracles, which were more like mocking fun, had already ruined the angel's reputation when the woman who had been changed into a spider finally crushed him completely. That was how Father Gonzaga was cured forever of his insomnia and Pelayo's courtyard went back to being as empty as during the time it had rained for three days and crabs walked through the bedrooms. The owners of the house had no reason to lament. With the money they saved they built a two-story mansion with balconies and gardens and high netting so that crabs wouldn't get in during the winter, and with iron bars on the windows so that angels couldn't get in. Pelayo also set up a rabbit warren close to town and gave up his job as bailiff for good, and Elisenda bought some satin pumps with high heels and many dresses of iridescent silk, the kind worn on Sunday by the most desirable women in those times. The chicken coop was the only thing that didn't receive any attention. If they washed it down with creolin and burned tears of myrrh inside it every so often, it was not in homage to the angel but to drive away the dungheap stench that still hung everywhere like a ghost and was turning the new house into an old one. At first, when the child learned to walk, they were careful that he not get too close to the chicken coop. But then they began to lose their fears and got used to the smell, and before the child got his second teeth he'd gone inside the chicken coop to play, where the wires were falling apart. The angel was no less standoffish with him than with other mortals, but he tolerated the most ingenious infamies with the patience of a dog who had no illusions. They both came down with chicken pox at the same time. The doctor who took care of the child couldn't resist the temptation to listen to the angel's heart, and he found so much whistling in the heart and so many sounds in his kidneys that it seemed impossible for him to be alive. What surprised him most,

however, was the logic of his wings. They seemed so natural on that completely human organism that he couldn't understand why other men didn't have them too.

When the child began school it had been some time since the sun and rain had caused the collapse of the chicken coop. The angel went dragging himself about here and there like a stray dying man. They would drive him out of the bedroom with a broom and a moment later find him in the kitchen. He seemed to be in so many places at the same time that they grew to think that he'd been duplicated, that he was reproducing himself all through the house, and the exasperated and unhinged Elisenda shouted that it was awful living in that hell full of angels. He could scarcely eat and his antiquarian eyes had also become so foggy that he went about bumping into posts. All he had left were the bare cannulae[1] of his last feathers. Pelayo threw a blanket over him and extended him the charity of letting him sleep in the shed, and only then did they notice that he had a temperature at night, and was delirious with the tongue twisters of an old Norwegian. That was one of the few times they became alarmed, for they thought he was going to die and not even the wise neighbor woman had been able to tell them what to do with dead angels.

And yet he not only survived his worst winter, but seemed improved with the first sunny days. He remained motionless for several days in the farthest corner of the courtyard, where no one would see him, and at the beginning of December some large, stiff feathers began to grow on his wings, the feathers of a scarecrow, which looked more like another misfortune of decrepitude. But he must have known the reason for those changes, for he was quite careful that no one should notice them, that no one should hear the sea chanteys that he sometimes sang under the stars. One morning Elisenda was cutting some bunches of onions for lunch when a wind that seemed to come from the high seas blew into the kitchen. Then she went to the window and caught the angel in his first attempts at flight. They were so clumsy that his fingernails opened a furrow in the vegetable patch and he was on the point of knocking the shed down with the ungainly flapping that slipped on the light and couldn't get a grip on the air. But he did manage to gain altitude. Elisenda let out a sigh of relief, for herself and for him, when she saw him pass over the last houses, holding himself up in some way with the risky flapping of a senile vulture. She kept watching him even when she was through cutting the onions and she kept on watching until it was no longer possible for her to see him, because then he was no longer an annoyance in her life but an imaginary dot on the horizon of the sea.

[1968]

Joining the Conversation: Critical Thinking and Writing

1. The subtitle is "A Tale for Children." Do you think that the story is more suited to children than to adults? What in the story do you think children would especially like, or dislike?
2. Is the story chiefly about the inability of adults to perceive and respect the miraculous world?
3. Characterize the narrator of the story.
4. Characterize Pelayo, Elisenda, their son, and the man with wings.

---

[1]**cannulae** from a Latin word meaning small reed or pipe; a narrow tube for draining off fluid, introducing medication, etc.

An Author in Depth: Flannery O'Connor

FLANNERY O'CONNOR

look @ more closely

Flannery O'Connor (1925–64)—her first name was Mary but she did not use it—was born in Savannah, Georgia, but spent most of her life in Milledgeville, Georgia, where her family moved when she was twelve years old. She was educated in parochial schools and at the local college, and then went to the School for Writers at the University of Iowa, where she earned an MFA in 1946. For a few months, she lived at a writers' colony in Saratoga Springs, New York, and then for a few weeks, she lived in New York City, but most of her life was spent in Milledgeville, where she tended her peacocks and wrote stories, novels, essays (posthumously published as Mystery and Manners *[1970]), and letters (posthumously published under the title* The Habit of Being *[1979]).*

In 1951, when she was twenty-five years old, Flannery O'Connor discovered that she had lupus erythematosus, an incurable autoimmune disease that had crippled and then killed her father ten years before. She died at the age of thirty-nine. O'Connor faced her illness with stoic courage, Christian fortitude, and tough humor. Here is a glimpse, from one of her letters, of how she dealt with those who pitied her:

> *An old lady got on the elevator behind me and as soon as I turned around she fixed me with a moist gleaming eye and said in a loud voice, "Bless you, darling!" I felt exactly like the Misfit [in "A Good Man Is Hard to Find"] and I gave her a weakly lethal look, whereupon greatly encouraged she grabbed my arm and whispered (very loud) in my ear, "Remember what they said to John at the gate, darling!" It was not my floor but I got off and I suppose the old lady was astounded at how quick I could get away on crutches. I have a one-legged friend and I asked her what they said to John at the gate. She said she reckoned they said, "The lame shall enter first." This may be because the lame will be able to knock everybody else aside with their crutches.*

A devout Catholic, O'Connor forthrightly summarized the relationship between her belief and her writing:

> *I see from the standpoint of Christian orthodoxy. This means that for me the meaning of life is centered in our Redemption by Christ and what I see in the world I see in its relation to that.*

A Good Man Is Hard to Find

why does she live w/ son?

why not go to Florida?

The grandmother didn't want to go to Florida. She wanted to visit some of her connections in east Tennessee and she was seizing every chance to change Bailey's mind. Bailey was the son she lived with, her only boy. He was sitting on the edge of his chair at the table, bent over the orange sports section of the *Journal*. "Now look here, Bailey," she said, "see here, read this," and she stood with one hand on her thin hip and the other rattling the newspaper at his bald head. "Here this fellow that calls himself The Misfit is aloose from the Federal Pen and headed toward Florida and you read here what it says he did to these people. Just you read it. I wouldn't take my children in any direction with a criminal like that aloose in it. I couldn't answer to my conscience if I did."

Bailey didn't look up from his reading so she wheeled around then and faced the children's mother, a young woman in slacks, whose face was as broad and innocent as a cabbage and was tied around with a green headkerchief that had two points on the top like rabbit's ears. She was sitting on the sofa, feeding the baby his apricots out of a jar. "The children have been to Florida before," the old lady said. "You all ought to take them somewhere else for a change so they would see different parts of the world and be broad. They never have been to east Tennessee."

The children's mother didn't seem to hear her, but the eight-year-old boy, John Wesley, a stocky child with glasses, said. "If you don't want to go to Florida, why dontcha stay at home?" He and the little girl, June Star, were reading the funny papers on the floor.

"She wouldn't stay at home to be queen for a day," June Star said without raising her yellow head.

5   "Yes, and what would you do if this fellow, The Misfit, caught you?" the grandmother said.

"I'd smack his face," John Wesley said.

"She wouldn't stay at home for a million bucks," June Star said. "Afraid she'd miss something. She has to go everywhere we go."

"All right, Miss," the grandmother said. "Just remember that the next time you want me to curl your hair."

June Star said her hair was naturally curly.

10   The next morning the grandmother was the first one in the car, ready to go. She had her big black valise that looked like the head of a hippopotamus in one corner, and underneath it she was hiding a basket with Pitty Sing, the cat, in it. She didn't intend for the cat to be left alone in the house for three days because he would miss her too much and she was afraid he might brush against one of the gas burners and accidentally asphyxiate himself. Her son, Bailey, didn't like to arrive at a motel with a cat.

She sat in the middle of the back seat with John Wesley and June Star on either side of her. Bailey and the children's mother and the baby sat in front and they left Atlanta at eight forty-five with the mileage on the car at 55890. The grandmother wrote this down because she thought it would be interesting to say how many miles they had been when they got back. It took them twenty minutes to reach the outskirts of the city.

The old lady settled herself comfortably, removing her white cotton gloves and putting them up with her purse on the shelf in front of the back window. The children's mother still had on slacks and still had her head tied up in a green kerchief, but the grandmother had on a navy blue straw sailor hat with a bunch of white violets on the brim and a navy blue dress with a small white dot in the print. Her collars and cuffs were white organdy trimmed with lace and at her neckline she had pinned a purple spray of cloth violets containing a sachet. In case of an accident, anyone seeing her dead on the highway would know at once that she was a lady.

She said she thought it was going to be a good day for driving, neither too hot nor too cold, and she cautioned Bailey that the speed limit was fifty-five miles an hour and that the patrolmen hid themselves behind bill-boards and small clumps of trees and sped out after you before you had a chance to slow down. She pointed out interesting details of the scenery: Stone Mountain; the blue granite that in some places came up to both sides of the highway; the brilliant red clay banks slightly

2.

the grandmother

~~Or~~ who was the first one ready to load up the next morning at six
o'clock. She had Baby Brother's bucking bronco ~~that~~ and ~~baxxxkima~~ what she
called her "*FXxe*" and Pitty Sing, the cat, ~~she was~~ packed in the car before
Boatwrite had a chance to ~~gaixxxxxiagxxiaxixx~~ ~~come out of the door with the~~
get the
~~rest of the luggage~~ out of the hall. They got off at seven-thirty, Boatwrite
and ~~Baby~~ the children's mother in the front and Granny, John Wesley, Baby Brother,
Little Sister Mayy Ann, Pitty Sing, and the bucking bronco in the back.

"Why the hell did you bring that goddam rocking horse?" Boatwrite asked
they were out of the city + on the smooth highway
because as soon as ~~the car began to move~~, Baby Brother began to squall to get
on the bucking bronco. "He can't get on that thing in this car and that's final,"
his father who was a stern man said.

"Can we open the lunch now?" Little Sister ~~Mayy Ann~~ asked. "It'll shut
Baby Brother up. Mamma, can we open up the lunch?"

"No," their grandmother said. *It's only eight-thirty.*

Their mother was ~~xxxxx~~ reading SCREEN MOTHERS AND THEIR CHILDREN. "Yeah,
sure," she said without looking up. She was all dressed up today. She had on
a purple silk dress and a hat and ~~gixxxxxxx~~ a choker of pink beads and a new
large
pocket book, and high heel pumps.

"Let's go through Georgia quick so we won't have to look at it much," John
Wesley said. ~~It wasn't enough of it wouldn't~~

"You should see Tennessee," his grandmother said. "Now there is a *beautiful* state."

"Like hell," John Wesley said. "That's just a hillbilly dumping ground."

"Hah," his mother said, and nudged Boatwrite. "Didjer hear that?" *she was*
from Tennessee
They ate their lunch and got along fine ~~after that~~ for a while until Pitty
Sing who had been asleep jumped into the front of the car and caused Boatwrite
to swerve to the right into a ditch. Pitty Sing was a large grey-striped cat
with a yellow hind leg and a ~~x large~~ *big* soiled white face. Granny thought that she
the truth was
was the only person in the world that he really loved but he had never ~~really~~
of
~~looked xxxxxxxxxxxxxxx~~ ~~any~~ farther than her middle and he didn't even
like other cats. He jumped snarling into ~~the front seat and Boatwrite's~~ shoulders

Typescript page from "A Good Man Is Hard to Find," with O'Connor's handwritten
changes.

streaked with purple; and the various crops that made rows of green lace-work on
the ground. The trees were full of silver-white sunlight and the meanest of them
sparkled. The children were reading comic magazines and their mother had gone
back to sleep.

"Let's go through Georgia fast so we won't have to look at it much," John Wesley said.

15   "If I were a little boy," said the grandmother, "I wouldn't talk about my native
state that way. Tennessee has the mountains and Georgia has the hills."

"Tennessee is just a hillbilly dumping ground," John Wesley said, "and Georgia
is a lousy state too."

"You said it," June Star said.

"In my time," said the grandmother, folding her thin veined fingers, "children were more respectful of their native states and their parents and everything else. People did right then. Oh look at the cute little pickaninny!" she said and pointed to a Negro child standing in the door of a shack. "Wouldn't that make a picture, now?" she asked and they all turned and looked at the little Negro out of the back window. He waved.

"He didn't have any britches on," June Star said.

20 "He probably didn't have any," the grandmother explained. "Little niggers in the country don't have things like we do. If I could paint, I'd paint that picture," she said.

The children exchanged comic books.

The grandmother offered to hold the baby and the children's mother passed him over the front seat to her. She set him on her knee and bounced him and told him about the things they were passing. She rolled her eyes and screwed up her mouth and stuck her leathery thin face into his smooth bland one. Occasionally he gave her a faraway smile. They passed a large cotton field with five or six graves fenced in the middle of it, like a small island. "Look at the graveyard!" the grandmother said, pointing it out. "That was the old family burying ground. That belonged to the plantation." "Where's the plantation?" John Wesley asked.

"Gone With the Wind,"[1] said the grandmother. "Ha. Ha."

25 When the children finished all the comic books they had brought, they opened the lunch and ate it. The grandmother ate a peanut butter sandwich and an olive and would not let the children throw the box and the paper napkins out the window. When there was nothing else to do they played a game by choosing a cloud and making the other two guess what shape it suggested. John Wesley took one the shape of a cow and June Star guessed a cow and John Wesley said, no, an automobile, and June Star said he didn't play fair, and they began to slap each other over the grandmother.

The grandmother said she would tell them a story if they would keep quiet. When she told a story, she rolled her eyes and waved her head and was very dramatic. She said once when she was a maiden lady she had been courted by a Mr. Edgar Atkins Teagarden from Jasper, Georgia. She said he was a very good-looking man and a gentleman and that he brought her a watermelon every Saturday afternoon with his initials cut in it, E.A.T. Well, one Saturday, she said, Mr. Teagarden brought the watermelon and there was nobody at home and he left it on the front porch and returned in his buggy to Jasper, but she never got the watermelon, she said, because a nigger boy ate it when he saw the initials, E.A.T.! This story tickled John Wesley's funny bone and he giggled and giggled but June Star didn't think it was any good. She said she wouldn't marry a man that just brought her a watermelon on Saturday. The grandmother said she would have done well to marry Mr. Teagarden because he was a gentleman and had bought Coca-Cola stock when it first came out and that he had died only a few years ago, a very wealthy man.

They stopped at The Tower for barbecued sandwiches. The Tower was a part-stucco and part-wood filling station and dance hall set in a clearing outside of Timothy. A fat man named Red Sammy Butts ran it and there were signs stuck here and there on the building and for miles up and down the highway saying, TRY RED

---

[1]*Gone With the Wind* a 1939 film about the plantation South and the Civil War that was adapted from Margaret Mitchell's 1936 novel of the same name.

SAMMY'S FAMOUS BARBECUE. NONE LIKE FAMOUS RED SAMMY'S! RED SAM! THE FAT BOY WITH THE
HAPPY LAUGH. A VETERAN! RED SAMMY'S YOUR MAN!

Red Sammy was lying on the bare ground outside The Tower with his head
under a truck while a gray monkey about a foot high, chained to a small chinaberry tree, chattered nearby. The monkey sprang back into the tree and got on the
highest limb as soon as he saw the children jump out of the car and run toward him.

Inside, The Tower was a long dark room with a counter at one end and tables
at the other and dancing space in the middle. They all sat down at a broad table
next to the nickelodeon and Red Sam's wife, a tall burnt-brown woman with hair
and eyes lighter than her skin, came and took their order. The children's mother
put a dime in the machine and played "The Tennessee Waltz," and the grandmother
said that tune always made her want to dance. She asked Bailey if he would like
to dance but he only glared at her. He didn't have a naturally sunny disposition like
she did and trips made him nervous. The grandmother's brown eyes were very
bright. She swayed her head from side to side and pretended she was dancing in
her chair. June Star said play something she could tap to so the children's mother
put in another dime and played a fast number and June Star stepped out onto the
dance floor and did her tap routine.

30   "Ain't she cute?" Red Sam's wife said, leaning over the counter. "Would you like
to come be my little girl?"

"No, I certainly wouldn't," June Star said. "I wouldn't live in a broken-down
place like this for a million bucks!" and she ran back to the table.

"Ain't she cute?" the woman repeated, stretching her mouth politely.

"Aren't you ashamed?" hissed the grandmother.

Red Sam came in and told his wife to quit lounging on the counter and hurry
with these people's order. His khaki trousers reached just to his hip bones and his
stomach hung over them like a sack of meal swaying under his shirt. He came over
and sat down at a table nearby and let out a combination sigh and yodel. "You can't
win," he said. "You can't win," and he wiped his sweating red face off with a gray
handkerchief. "These days you don't know who to trust," he said. "Ain't that the truth?"

35   "People are certainly not nice like they used to be," said the grandmother.

"Two fellers come in here last week," Red Sammy said, "driving a Chrysler. It
was an old beat-up car but it was a good one and these boys looked all right to
me. Said they worked at the mill and you know I let them fellers charge the gas
they bought? Now why did I do that?"

"Because you're a good man!" the grandmother said at once.

"Yes'm, I suppose so," Red Sam said as if he were struck with this answer.

His wife brought the orders, carrying the five plates all at once without a tray,
two in each hand and one balanced on her arm. "It isn't a soul in this green world
of God's that you can trust," she said. "And I don't count nobody out of that, not
nobody," she repeated, looking at Red Sammy.

40   "Did you read about that criminal, The Misfit, that's escaped?" asked the grandmother.

"I wouldn't be a bit surprised if he didn't attack this place right here," said the
woman. "If he hears about it being here, I wouldn't be none surprised to see him.
If he hears it's two cent in the cash register, I wouldn't be a tall surprised if he . . . ."

"That'll do," Red Sam said. "Go bring these people their Co'Colas," and the
woman went off to get the rest of the order.

"A good man is hard to find," Red Sammy said. "Everything is getting terrible.
I remember the day you could go off and leave your screen door unlatched. Not
no more."

He and the grandmother discussed better times. The old lady said that in her opinion Europe was entirely to blame for the way things were now. She said the way Europe acted you would think we were made of money and Red Sam said it was no use talking about it, she was exactly right. The children ran outside into the white sunlight and looked at the monkey in the lacy chinaberry tree. He was busy catching fleas on himself and biting each one carefully between his teeth as if it were a delicacy.

45   They drove off again into the hot afternoon. The grandmother took cat naps and woke up every five minutes with her own snoring. Outside of Toombsboro she woke up and recalled an old plantation that she had visited in this neighborhood once when she was a young lady. She said the house had six white columns across the front and that there was an avenue of oaks leading up to it and two little wooden trellis arbors on either side in front where you sat down with your suitor after a stroll in the garden. She recalled exactly which road to turn off to get to it. She knew that Bailey would not be willing to lose any time looking at an old house, but the more she talked about it, the more she wanted to see it once again and find out if the little twin arbors were still standing. "There was a secret panel in this house," she said craftily, not telling the truth but wishing that she were, "and the story went that all the family silver was hidden in it when Sherman came through but it was never found . . . "

"Hey!" John Wesley said. "Let's go see it! We'll find it! We'll poke all the woodwork and find it! Who lives there? Where do you turn off at? Hey, Pop, can't we turn off there?"

"We never have seen a house with a secret panel!" June Star shrieked. "Let's go to the house with the secret panel! Hey, Pop, can't we go see the house with the secret panel!"

"It's not far from here, I know," the grandmother said. "It wouldn't take over twenty minutes."

Bailey was looking straight ahead. His jaw was as rigid as a horseshoe. "No," he said.

50   The children began to yell and scream that they wanted to see the house with the secret panel. John Wesley kicked the back of the front seat and June Star hung over her mother's shoulder and whined desperately into her ear that they never had any fun even on their vacation, that they could never do what THEY wanted to do. The baby began to scream and John Wesley kicked the back of the seat so hard that his father could feel the blows in his kidney.

"All right!" he shouted and drew the car to a stop at the side of the road. "Will you all shut up? Will you all just shut up for one second? If you don't shut up, we won't go anywhere."

"It would be very educational for them," the grandmother murmured.

"All right," Bailey said, "but get this. This is the only time we're going to stop for anything like this. This is the one and only time."

"The dirt road that you have to turn down is about a mile back," the grandmother directed. "I marked it when we passed."

55   "A dirt road," Bailey groaned.

After they had turned around and were headed toward the dirt road, the grandmother recalled other points about the house, the beautiful glass over the front doorway and the candle lamp in the hall. John Wesley said that the secret panel was probably in the fireplace.

"You can't go inside this house," Bailey said. "You don't know who lives there."

"While you all talk to the people in front, I'll run around behind and get in a window," John Wesley suggested.

"We'll all stay in the car," his mother said.

60   They turned onto the dirt road and the car raced roughly along in a swirl of pink dust. The grandmother recalled the times when there were no paved roads and thirty miles was a day's journey. The dirt road was hilly and there were sudden washes in it and sharp curves on dangerous embankments. All at once they would be on a hill, looking down over the blue tops of trees for miles around, then the next minute, they would be in a red depression with the dust-coated trees looking down on them.

"This place had better turn up in a minute," Bailey said, "or I'm going to turn around."

The road looked as if no one had traveled on it in months.

"It's not much farther," the grandmother said and just as she said it, a horrible thought came to her. The thought was so embarrassing that she turned red in the face and her eyes dilated and her feet jumped up, upsetting her valise in the corner. The instant the valise moved, the newspaper top she had over the basket under it rose with a snarl and Pitty Sing, the cat, sprang onto Bailey's shoulder.

The children were thrown to the floor and their mother, clutching the baby, was thrown out the door onto the ground; the old lady was thrown into the front seat. The car turned over once and landed right-side-up in a gulch on the side of the road. Bailey remained in the driver's seat with the cat—gray-striped with a broad white face and an orange nose—clinging to his neck like a caterpillar.

65   As soon as the children saw they could move their arms and legs, they scrambled out of the car, shouting, "We've had an ACCIDENT!" The grandmother was curled up under the dashboard, hoping she was injured so that Bailey's wrath would not come down on her all at once. The horrible thought she had had before the accident was that the house she had remembered so vividly was not in Georgia but in Tennessee.

Bailey removed the cat from his neck with both hands and flung it out the window against the side of a pine tree. Then he got out of the car and started looking for the children's mother. She was sitting against the side of the red gutted ditch, holding the screaming baby, but she only had a cut down her face and a broken shoulder. "We've had an ACCIDENT!" the children screamed in a frenzy of delight.

"But nobody's killed," June Star said with disappointment as the grandmother limped out of the car, her hat still pinned to her head but the broken front brim standing up at a jaunty angle and the violet spray hanging off the side. They all sat down in the ditch, except the children, to recover from the shock. They were all shaking.

"Maybe a car will come along," said the children's mother hoarsely.

"I believe I have injured an organ," said the grandmother, pressing her side, but no one answered her. Bailey's teeth were clattering. He had on a yellow sport shirt with bright blue parrots designed in it and his face was as yellow as the shirt. The grandmother decided that she would not mention that the house was in Tennessee.

70   The road was about ten feet above and they could see only the tops of the trees on the other side of it. Behind the ditch they were sitting in there were more woods, tall and dark and deep. In a few minutes they saw a car some distance away on top of a hill, coming slowly as if the occupants were watching them. The grandmother stood up and waved both arms dramatically to attract their attention. The car continued to come on slowly, disappeared around a bend and appeared again, moving even slower on top of the hill they had gone over. It was a big black battered hearselike automobile. There were three men in it.

It came to a stop just over them and for some minutes, the driver looked down with a steady expressionless gaze to where they were sitting, and didn't speak. Then he turned his head and muttered something to the other two and they got out. One was a fat boy in black trousers and a red sweat shirt with a silver stallion embossed on the front of it. He moved around on the right side of them and stood staring, his mouth partly open in a kind of loose grin. The other had on khaki pants and a blue striped coat and a gray hat pulled down very low, hiding most of his face. He came around slowly on the left side. Neither spoke.

The driver got out of the car and stood by the side of it, looking down at them. He was an older man than the other two. His hair was just beginning to gray and he wore silver-rimmed spectacles that gave him a scholarly look. He had a long creased face and didn't have on any shirt or undershirt. He had on blue jeans that were too tight for him and was holding a black hat and a gun. The two boys also had guns.

"We've had an ACCIDENT!" the children screamed.

The grandmother had the peculiar feeling that the bespectacled man was someone she knew. His face was as familiar to her as if she had known him all her life but she could not recall who he was. He moved away from the car and began to come down the embankment, placing his feet carefully so that he wouldn't slip. He had on tan and white shoes and no socks, and his ankles were red and thin. "Good afternoon," he said. "I see you all had you a little spill."

75   "We turned over twice!" said the grandmother.

"Oncet," he corrected. "We seen it happen. Try their car and see will it run, Hiram," he said quietly to the boy with the gray hat.

"What you got that gun for?" John Wesley asked. "Whatcha gonna do with that gun?"

"Lady," the man said to the children's mother, "would you mind calling them children to sit down by you? Children make me nervous. I want all you to sit down right together there where you're at."

"What are you telling us what to do for?" June Star asked.

80   Behind them the line of woods gaped like a dark open mouth. "Come here," said their mother.

"Look here now," Bailey began suddenly, "we're in a predicament! We're in . . ."

The grandmother shrieked. She scrambled to her feet and stood staring. "You're The Misfit!" she said. "I recognized you at once!"

"Yes'm," the man said, smiling slightly as if he were pleased in spite of himself to be known, "but it would have been better for all of you, lady, if you hadn't of reckernized me."

Bailey turned his head sharply and said something to his mother that shocked even the children. The old lady began to cry and The Misfit reddened.

85   "Lady," he said, "don't you get upset. Sometimes a man says things he don't mean. I don't reckon he meant to talk to you thataway."

"You wouldn't shoot a lady, would you?" the grandmother said and removed a clean handkerchief from her cuff and began to slap at her eyes with it.

The Misfit pointed the toe of his shoe into the ground and made a little hole and then covered it up again. "I would hate to have to," he said.

"Listen," the grandmother almost screamed, "I know you're a good man. You don't look a bit like you have common blood. I know you must come from nice people!"

"Yes ma'm," he said, "finest people in the world." When he smiled he showed a row of strong white teeth. "God never made a finer woman than my mother and my daddy's heart was pure gold," he said. The boy with the red sweat shirt had come around behind them and was standing with his gun at his hip. The Misfit squatted down on the ground. "Watch them children, Bobby Lee," he said. "You know they make me nervous." He looked at the six of them huddled together in front of him and he seemed to be embarrassed as if he couldn't think of anything to say. "Ain't a cloud in the sky," he remarked, looking up at it. "Don't see no sun but don't see no cloud neither."

90   "Yes, it's a beautiful day," said the grandmother. "Listen," she said, "you shouldn't call yourself The Misfit because I know you're a good man at heart. I can just look at you and tell."

"Hush!" Bailey yelled, "Hush! Everybody shut up and let me handle this!" He was squatting in the position of a runner about to sprint forward but he didn't move.

"I pre-chate that, lady," The Misfit said and drew a little circle in the ground with the butt of his gun.

"It'll take a half a hour to fix this here car," Hiram called, looking over the raised hood of it.

"Well, first you and Bobby Lee get him and that little boy to step over yonder with you," The Misfit said, pointing to Bailey and John Wesley. "The boys want to ask you something," he said to Bailey. "Would you mind stepping back in them woods there with them?"

95   "Listen," Bailey began, "we're in a terrible predicament! Nobody realizes what this is," and his voice cracked. His eyes were as blue and intense as the parrots in his shirt and he remained perfectly still.

The grandmother reached up to adjust her hat brim as if she were going to the woods with him but it came off in her hand. She stood staring at it and after a second she let it fall on the ground. Hiram pulled Bailey up by the arm as if he were assisting an old man. John Wesley caught hold of his father's hand and Bobby Lee followed. They went off toward the woods and just as they reached the dark edge, Bailey turned and supporting himself against a gray naked pine trunk, he shouted, "I'll be back in a minute, Mamma, wait on me!"

"Come back this instant!" his mother shrilled but they all disappeared into the woods.

"Bailey Boy!" the grandmother called in a tragic voice but she found she was looking at The Misfit squatting on the ground in front of her. "I just know you're a good man," she said desperately. "You're not a bit common!"

"Nome, I ain't a good man," The Misfit said after a second as if he had considered her statement carefully, "but I ain't the worst in the world neither. My daddy said I was a different breed of dog from my brothers and sisters. 'You know,' Daddy said, 'It's some that can live their whole life without asking about it and it's others has to know why it is, and this boy is one of the latters. He's going to be into everything!'" He put on his black hat and looked up suddenly and then away deep into the woods as if he were embarrassed again. "I'm sorry I don't have on a shirt before you ladies," he said, hunching his shoulders slightly. "We buried our clothes that we had on when we escaped and we're just making do until we can get better. We borrowed these from some folks we met," he explained.

100   "That's perfectly all right," the grandmother said. "Maybe Bailey has an extra shirt in his suitcase."

"I'll look and see terrectly," The Misfit said.

"Where are they taking him?" the children's mother screamed.

"Daddy was a card himself," The Misfit said. "You couldn't put anything over on him. He never got in trouble with the Authorities though. Just had the knack of handling them."

"You could be honest too if you'd only try," said the grandmother. "Think how wonderful it would be to settle down and live a comfortable life and not have to think about somebody chasing you all the time."

105 The Misfit kept scratching in the ground with the butt of his gun as if he were thinking about it. "Yes'm, somebody is always after you," he murmured.

The grandmother noticed how thin his shoulder blades were just behind his hat because she was standing up looking down on him. "Do you ever pray?" she asked.

He shook his head. All she saw was the black hat wiggle between his shoulder blades. "Nome," he said.

There was a pistol shot from the woods, followed closely by another. Then silence. The old lady's head jerked around. She could hear the wind move through the tree tops like a long satisfied insuck of breath. "Bailey Boy!" she called.

[handwritten margin note: well, Bailey and John a dead]

"I was a gospel singer for a while," The Misfit said. "I been most everything. Been in the arm service, both land and sea, at home and abroad, been twict married, been an undertaker, been with the railroads, plowed Mother Earth, been in a tornado, seen a man burnt alive oncet," and he looked up at the children's mother and the little girl who were sitting close together, their faces white and their eyes glassy; "I even seen a woman flogged," he said.

110 "Pray, pray," the grandmother began, "pray, pray. . . ."

"I never was a bad boy that I remember of," The Misfit said in an almost dreamy voice, "but somewheres along the line I done something wrong and got sent to the penitentiary. I was buried alive," and he looked up and held her attention to him by a steady stare.

"That's when you should have started to pray," she said. "What did you do to get sent up to the penitentiary that first time?"

"Turn to the right, it was a wall," The Misfit said, looking up again at the cloudless sky. "Turn to the left, it was a wall. Look up it was a ceiling, look down it was a floor. I forget what I done, lady. I set there and set there, trying to remember what it was I done and I ain't recalled it to this day. Oncet in a while, I would think it was coming to me, but it never come."

"Maybe they put you in by mistake," the old lady said vaguely.

115 "Nome," he said. "It wasn't no mistake. They had the papers on me."

"You must have stolen something," she said.

The Misfit sneered slightly. "Nobody had nothing I wanted," he said. "It was a head-doctor at the penitentiary said what I had done was kill my daddy but I known that for a lie. My daddy died in nineteen ought nineteen of the epidemic flu and I never had a thing to do with it. He was buried in the Mount Hopewell Baptist churchyard and you can go there and see for yourself."

"If you would pray," the old lady said, "Jesus would help you."

"That's right," The Misfit said.

120 "Well then, why don't you pray?" she asked trembling with delight suddenly.

"I don't want no hep," he said. "I'm doing all right by myself."

Bobby Lee and Hiram came ambling back from the woods. Bobby Lee was dragging a yellow shirt with bright blue parrots on it.

"Throw me that shirt, Bobby Lee," The Misfit said. The shirt came flying at him and landed on his shoulder and he put it on. The grandmother couldn't name what the shirt reminded her of. "No, lady," The Misfit said while he was buttoning it up, "I found out the crime don't matter. You can do one thing or you can do another, kill a man or take a tire off his car, because sooner or later you're going to forget what it was you done and just be punished for it."

[handwritten margin note: Alzheimers?]

The children's mother had begun to make heaving noises as if she couldn't get her breath. "Lady," he asked, "would you and that little girl like to step off yonder with Bobby Lee and Hiram and join your husband?"

"Yes, thank you," the mother said faintly. Her left arm dangled helplessly and she was holding the baby, who had gone to sleep, in the other. "Hep that lady up, Hiram," The Misfit said as she struggled to climb out of the ditch, "and Bobby Lee, you hold onto that little girl's hand."

"I don't want to hold hands with him," June Star said. "He reminds me of a pig."

The fat boy blushed and laughed and caught her by the arm and pulled her off into the woods after Hiram and her mother.

Alone with The Misfit, the grandmother found that she had lost her voice. There was not a cloud in the sky nor any sun. There was nothing around her but woods. She wanted to tell him that he must pray. She opened and closed her mouth several times before anything came out. Finally she found herself saying, "Jesus, Jesus," meaning, Jesus will help you, but the way she was saying it, it sounded as if she might be cursing.

"Yes'm," The Misfit said as if he agreed. "Jesus thown everything off balance. It was the same case with Him as with me except He hadn't committed any crime and they could prove I had committed one because they had the papers on me. Of course," he said, "they never shown me my papers. That's why I sign myself now. I said long ago, you get you a signature and sign everything you do and keep a copy of it. Then you'll know what you done and you can hold up the crime to the punishment and see do they match and in the end you'll have something to prove you ain't been treated right. I call myself The Misfit," he said, "because I can't make what all I done wrong fit what all I gone through in punishment."

There was a piercing scream from the woods, followed closely by a pistol report. "Does it seem right to you, lady, that one is punished a heap and another ain't punished at all?"

"Jesus!" the old lady cried. "You've got good blood! I know you wouldn't shoot a lady! I know you come from nice people! Pray! Jesus, you ought not to shoot a lady. I'll give you all the money I've got!"

"Lady," The Misfit said, looking beyond her far into the woods, "there never was a body that give the undertaker a tip."

There were two more pistol reports and the grandmother raised her head like a parched old turkey hen crying for water and called, "Bailey Boy, Bailey Boy!" as if her heart would break.

"Jesus was the only One that ever raised the dead," The Misfit continued, "and He shouldn't have done it. He thown everything off balance. If He did what He said, then it's nothing for you to do but thow away everything and follow Him, and if He didn't, then it's nothing for you to do but enjoy the few minutes you got left the best way you can—by killing somebody or burning down his house or doing some other meanness to him. No pleasure but meanness," he said and his voice had become almost a snarl.

"Maybe He didn't raise the dead," the old lady mumbled, not knowing what she was saying and feeling so dizzy that she sank down in the ditch with her legs twisted under her.

"I wasn't there so I can't say He didn't," The Misfit said. "I wisht I had of been there," he said, hitting the ground with his fist. "It ain't right I wasn't there because if I had of been there I would of known. Listen lady," he said in a high voice, "if I had of been there I would of known and I wouldn't be like I am now." His voice seemed about to crack and the grandmother's head cleared for an instant. She saw

the man's face twisted close to her own as if he were going to cry and she murmured, "Why you're one of my babies. You're one of my own children!" She
reached out and touched him on the shoulder. The Misfit sprang back as if a snake
had bitten him and shot her three times through the chest. Then he put his gun
down on the ground and took off his glasses and began to clean them.

Hiram and Bobby Lee returned from the woods and stood over the ditch,
looking down at the grandmother who half sat and half lay in a puddle of blood
with her legs crossed under her like a child's and her face smiling up at the cloudless sky.

Without his glasses, The Misfit's eyes were red-rimmed and pale and defense-
less-looking. "Take her off and thow her where you thown the others," he said,
picking up the cat that was rubbing itself against his leg.

"She was a talker, wasn't she?" Bobby Lee said, sliding down the ditch with a
yodel.

"She would of been a good woman," The Misfit said, "if it had been somebody
there to shoot her every minute of her life."

"Some fun!" Bobby Lee said.

"Shut up, Bobby Lee," The Misfit said. "It's no real pleasure in life."

[1953]

Joining the Conversation: Critical Thinking and Writing

1. Explain the significance of the title "A Good Man Is Hard to Find."
2. Interpret and evaluate The Misfit's comment on the grandmother: "She would of been a good woman if it had been somebody there to shoot her every minute of her life."
3. O'Connor reported that once, when she read aloud "A Good Man Is Hard to Find," one of her listeners said that "it was a shame someone with so much talent should look upon life as a horror story." Two questions: What evidence of O'Connor's talent do you see in the story, and does the story suggest that O'Connor looked on life as a horror story?
4. What are the values of the members of the family?
5. Flannery O'Connor, a Roman Catholic, wrote, "I see from the standpoint of Christian orthodoxy. This means that for me the meaning of life is centered in our Redemption by Christ and what I see in the world I see in relation to that." In the light of this statement and drawing on "A Good Man Is Hard to Find," explain what O'Connor saw in the world.

Remarks from Essays and Letters

From "The Fiction Writer and His Country"

In the greatest fiction, the writer's moral sense coincides with his dramatic sense, and I see no way for it to do this unless his moral judgment is part of the very act of seeing, and he is free to use it. I have heard it said that belief in Christian dogma is a hin-drance to the writer, but I myself have found nothing further from the truth. Actually, it frees the storyteller to observe. It is not a set of rules which fixes what he sees in the world. It affects his writing primarily by guaranteeing his respect for mystery. . . .

When I look at stories I have written I find that they are, for the most part, about people who are poor, who are afflicted in both mind and body, who have little—or at best a distorted—sense of spiritual purpose, and whose actions do not apparently give the reader a great assurance of the joy of life.

Yet how is this? For I am no disbeliever in spiritual purpose and no vague believer. I see from the standpoint of Christian orthodoxy. This means that for me the meaning of life is centered in our Redemption by Christ and what I see in the world I see in its relation to that. . . .

The novelist with Christian concerns will find in modern life distortions which are repugnant to him, and his problem will be to make these appear as distortions to an audience which is used to seeing them as natural; and he may well be forced to take ever more violent means to get his vision across to this hostile audience. When you can assume that your audience holds the same beliefs you do, you can relax a little and use more normal means of talking to it; when you have to assume that it does not, then you have to make your vision apparent by shock—to the hard of hearing you shout, and for the almost-blind you draw large and startling figures.

From "Some Aspects of the Grotesque in Southern Fiction"

If the writer believes that our life is and will remain essentially mysterious, if he looks upon us as beings existing in a created order to whose laws we freely respond, then what he sees on the surface will be of interest to him only as he can go through it into an experience of mystery itself. His kind of fiction will always be pushing its own limits outward toward the limits of mystery, because for this kind of writer, the meaning of a story does not begin except at a depth where adequate motivation and adequate psychology and the various determinations have been exhausted. Such a writer will be interested in what we don't understand rather than in what we do. He will be interested in possibility rather than in probability. He will be interested in characters who are forced out to meet evil and grace and who act on a trust beyond themselves—whether they know very clearly what it is they act upon or not. To the modern mind, this kind of character, and his creator, are typical Don Quixotes, tilting at[1] what is not there.

From "The Nature and Aim of Fiction"

The novel works by a slower accumulation of detail than the short story does. The short story requires more drastic procedures than the novel because more has to be accomplished in less space. The details have to carry more immediate weight. In good fiction, certain of the details will tend to accumulate meaning from the story itself, and when this happens, they become symbolic in their action.

Now the word *symbol* scares a good many people off, just as the word *art* does. They seem to feel that a symbol is some mysterious thing put in arbitrarily by the writer to frighten the common reader—sort of a literary Masonic grip that is only for the initiated. They seem to think that it is a way of saying something that you aren't actually saying, and so if they can be got to read a reputedly symbolic work at all, they approach it as if it were a problem in algebra. Find *x*. And when they do find or think they find this abstraction, *x*, then they go off with an elaborate

---

[1]**tilting** at "tilting at windmills" is a popular expression that derives from Cervantes's novel *Don Quixote*, published in 1604–05.

sense of satisfaction and the notion that they have "understood" the story. Many students confuse the *process* of understanding a thing with understanding it.

I think that for the fiction writer himself, symbols are something he uses simply as a matter of course. You might say that these are details that, while having their essential place in the literal level of the story, operate in depth as well as on the surface, increasing the story in every direction. . . .

People have a habit of saying, "What is the theme of your story?" and they expect you to give them a statement: "The theme of my story is the economic pressure of the machine on the middle class"—or some such absurdity. And when they've got a statement like that, they go off happy and feel it is no longer necessary to read the story.

Some people have the notion that you read the story and then climb out of it into the meaning, but for the fiction writer himself the whole story is the meaning, because it is an experience, not an abstraction.

From "Writing Short Stories"

Being short does not mean being slight. A short story should be long in depth and should give us an experience of meaning. . . .

Meaning is what keeps the short story from being short. I prefer to talk about the meaning in a story rather than the theme of a story. People talk about the theme of a story as if the theme were like the string that a sack of chicken feed is tied with. They think that if you can pick out the theme, the way you pick the right thread in the chicken-feed sack, you can rip the story open and feed the chickens. But this is not the way meaning works in fiction.

When you can state the theme of a story, when you can separate it from the story itself, then you can be sure the story is not a very good one. The meaning of a story has to be embodied in it, has to be made concrete in it. A story is a way to say something that can't be said any other way, and it takes every word in the story to say what the meaning is. You tell a story because a statement would be inadequate. When anybody asks what a story is about, the only proper thing is to tell him to read the story. The meaning of fiction is not abstract meaning but experienced meaning, and the purpose of making statements about the meaning of a story is only to help you to experience that meaning more fully.

On Interpreting "A Good Man Is Hard to Find"

A professor of English had sent O'Connor the following letter: *"I am writing as spokesman for three members of our department and some ninety university students in three classes who for a week now have been discussing your story 'A Good Man Is Hard to Find.' We have debated at length several possible interpretations, none of which fully satisfies us. In general we believe that the appearance of the Misfit is not 'real' in the same sense that the incidents of the first half of the story are real. Bailey, we believe, imagines the appearance of the Misfit, whose activities have been called to his attention on the night before the trip and again during the stopover at the roadside restaurant. Bailey, we further believe, identifies himself with the Misfit and so plays two roles in the imaginary last half of the story. But we cannot, after great effort, determine the point at which reality fades into illusion or reverie. Does the accident literally occur, or is it a part of Bailey's dream? Please believe me when I say we are not seeking an easy way out of our difficulty. We admire your story and have examined it with great care, but we are convinced that we are missing something important which you intended for us to grasp. We will all be very grateful if you comment on the interpretation which I have outlined above and if you will give us further comments about your intention in writing 'A Good Man Is Hard to Find.'"* She replied:

28 March 61

To a Professor of English

The interpretation of your ninety students and three teachers is fantastic and about as far from my intentions as it could get to be. If it were a legitimate interpretation, the story would be little more than a trick and its interest would be simply for abnormal psychology. I am not interested in abnormal psychology.

There is a change of tension from the first part of the story to the second where the Misfit enters, but this is no lessening of reality. This story is, of course, not meant to be realistic in the sense that it portrays the everyday doings of people in Georgia. It is stylized and its conventions are comic even though its meaning is serious.

Bailey's only importance is as the Grandmother's boy and the driver of the car. It is the Grandmother who first recognizes the Misfit and who is most concerned with him throughout. The story is a duel of sorts between the Grandmother and her superficial beliefs and the Misfit's more profoundly felt involvement with Christ's action which set the world off balance for him.

The meaning of a story should go on expanding for the reader the more he thinks about it, but meaning cannot be captured in an interpretation. If teachers are in the habit of approaching a story as if it were a research problem for which any answer is believable so long as it is not obvious, then I think students will never learn to enjoy fiction. Too much interpretation is certainly worse than too little and where feeling for a story is absent, theory will not supply it.

My tone is not meant to be obnoxious. I am in a state of shock.

"A Reasonable Use of the Unreasonable"

Last fall I received a letter from a student who said she would be "graciously appreciative" if I would tell her "just what enlightenment" I expected her to get from each of my stories. I suspect she had a paper to write. I wrote her back to forget about the enlightenment and just try to enjoy them. I knew that was the most unsatisfactory answer I could have given because, of course, she didn't want to enjoy them, she just wanted to figure them out.

In most English classes the short story has become a kind of literary specimen to be dissected. Every time a story of mine appears in a Freshman anthology, I have a vision of it, with its little organs laid open, like a frog in a bottle.

I realize that a certain amount of this what-is-the-significance has to go on, but I think something has gone wrong in the process when, for so many students, the story becomes simply a problem to be solved, something which you evaporate to get Instant Enlightenment.

A story really isn't any good unless it successfully resists paraphrase, unless it hangs on and expands in the mind. Properly, you analyze to enjoy, but it's equally true that to analyze with any discrimination, you have to have enjoyed already, and I think that the best reason to hear a story read is that it should stimulate that primary enjoyment.

I don't have any pretensions to being an Aeschylus or Sophocles and providing you in this story with a cathartic experience out of your mythic background, though this story I'm going to read certainly calls up a good deal of the South's mythic background, and it should elicit from you a degree of pity and terror, even though its way of being serious is a comic one. I do think, though, that like the Greeks you should know what is going to happen in this story so that any element of suspense in it will be transferred from its surface to its interior.

I would be most happy if you have already read it, happier still if you knew it well, but since experience has taught me to keep my expectations along these lines modest, I'll tell you that this is the story of a family of six which, on its way driving to Florida, gets wiped out by an escaped convict who calls himself the Misfit. The family is made up of the Grandmother and her son, Bailey, and his children, John Wesley and June Star and the baby, and there is also the cat and the children's mother. The cat is named Pitty Sing, and the Grandmother is taking him with them, hidden in a basket.

Now I think it behooves me to try to establish with you the basis on which reason operates in this story. Much of my fiction takes its character from a reasonable use of the unreasonable, though the reasonableness of my use of it may not always be apparent. The assumptions that underlie this use of it, however, are those of the central Christian mysteries. These are assumptions to which a large part of the modern audience takes exception. About this I can only say that there are perhaps other ways than my own in which this story could be read, but none other by which it could have been written. Belief, in my own case anyway, is the engine that makes perception operate.

The heroine of this story, the Grandmother, is in the most significant position life offers the Christian. She is facing death. And to all appearances she, like the rest of us, is not too well prepared for it. She would like to see the event postponed. Indefinitely.

I've talked to a number of teachers who use this story in class and who tell their students that the Grandmother is evil, that in fact, she's a witch, even down to the cat. One of these teachers told me that his students, and particularly his Southern students, resisted this interpretation with a certain bemused vigor, and he didn't understand why. I had to tell him that they resisted it because they all had grandmothers or great-aunts just like her at home, and they knew, from personal experience, that the old lady lacked comprehension, but that she had a good heart. The Southerner is usually tolerant of those weaknesses that proceed from innocence, and he knows that a taste for self-preservation can be readily combined with the missionary spirit.

This same teacher was telling his students that morally the Misfit was several cuts above the Grandmother. He had a really sentimental attachment to the Misfit. But then a prophet gone wrong is almost always more interesting than your grandmother, and you have to let people take their pleasures where they find them.

It is true that the old lady is a hypocritical old soul; her wits are no match for the Misfit's, nor is her capacity for grace equal to his; yet I think the unprejudiced reader will feel that the Grandmother has a special kind of triumph in this story which instinctively we do not allow to someone altogether bad.

I often ask myself what makes a story work, and what makes it hold up as a story, and I have decided that it is probably some action, some gesture of a character that is unlike any other in the story, one which indicates where the real heart of the story lies. This would have to be an action or a gesture which was both totally right and totally unexpected; it would have to be one that was both in character and beyond character; it would have to suggest both the world and eternity. The action or gesture I'm talking about would have to be on the anagogical level, that is, the level which has to do with the Divine life and our participation in it. It would be a gesture that transcended any neat allegory that might have been intended or any pat moral categories a reader could make. It would be a gesture which somehow made contact with mystery.

There is a point in this story where such a gesture occurs. The Grandmother is at last alone, facing the Misfit. Her head clears for an instant and she realizes, even in her limited way, that she is responsible for the man before her and joined to him by ties of kinship which have their roots deep in the mystery she has been merely prattling about so far. And at this point, she does the right thing, she makes the right gesture.

I find that students are often puzzled by what she says and does here, but I think myself that if I took out this gesture and what she says with it, I would have no story. What was left would not be worth your attention. Our age not only does not have a very sharp eye for the almost imperceptible intrusions of grace, it no longer has much feeling for the nature of the violences which precede and follow them. The devil's greatest wile, Baudelaire has said, is to convince us that he does not exist.

I suppose the reasons for the use of so much violence in modern fiction will differ with each writer who uses it, but in my own stories I have found that violence is strangely capable of returning my characters to reality and preparing them to accept their moment of grace. Their heads are so hard that almost nothing else will do the work. This idea, that reality is something to which we must be returned at considerable cost, is one which is seldom understood by the casual reader, but it is one which is implicit in the Christian view of the world.

I don't want to equate the Misfit with the devil. I prefer to think that, however unlikely this may seem, the old lady's gesture, like the mustard-seed, will grow to be a great crow-filled tree in the Misfit's heart, and will be enough of a pain to him there to turn him into the prophet he was meant to become. But that's another story.

This story has been called grotesque, but I prefer to call it literal. A good story is literal in the same sense that a child's drawing is literal. When a child draws, he doesn't intend to distort but to set down exactly what he sees, and as his gaze is direct, he sees the lines that create motion. Now the lines of motion that interest the writer are usually invisible. They are lines of spiritual motion. And in this story you should be on the lookout for such things as the action of grace in the Grandmother's soul, and not for the dead bodies.

We hear many complaints about the prevalence of violence in modern fiction, and it is always assumed that this violence is a bad thing and meant to be an end in itself. With the serious writer, violence is never an end in itself. It is the extreme situation that best reveals what we are essentially, and I believe these are times when writers are more interested in what we are essentially than in the tenor of our daily lives. Violence is a force which can be used for good or evil, and among other things taken by it is the kingdom of heaven. But regardless of what can be taken by it, the man in the violent situation reveals those qualities least dispensable in his personality, those qualities which are all he will have to take into eternity with him; and since the characters in this story are all on the verge of eternity, it is appropriate to think of what they take with them. In any case, I hope that if you consider these points in connection with the story, you will come to see it as something more than an account of a family murdered on the way to Florida.

Reading and Writing about Graphic Fiction

Letters and Pictures, Words and Images

Literature is, literally speaking, made out of letters (*literature*, *literally*, *literate*, *literacy*, and *letters* all come from the Latin word *littera*, meaning "letter"). A person who can read letters is literate. Yet, today, we hear a good deal about "visual literacy," which means the ability to understand visual things. In this usage, *literacy* is metaphoric. You cannot literally (again that word!) read a picture; you can look at it and either understand it or not understand it. In order to help prepare you to read a story that is partly told by means of pictures, we will be talking about achieving visual literacy—that is, achieving the ability to understand pictures and to "read" pictures, specifically pictures that are used to tell stories.

The good news is that, if you have spent any time at all looking at comic strips or comic books, you already know a great deal about how to "read" pictures that tell stories.

- You know, for instance, that you should read the pictures and the words from left to right (if you were brought up in China or Japan, you would begin at the right and read the first column downward, then the next column, again reading downward, unless the book were a Western-style book).
- You also know that, in the usual comic strip, a box represents a particular scene; the next box may show the same characters but at a later moment in time.
- You know that human actions can be conveyed by showing figures in certain postures (walking, eating, and so forth) and making certain gestures (pointing or making a fist).
- You know that emotions can be conveyed by facial expressions (think Smiley Face, where two dots and a curve say it all).
- You know that the setting can easily be established (a tree indicates the outdoors, the Capitol indicates Washington, DC).

- You know that, when a heavy object is shown on the ground with the word *bang* in large thick letters next to it, a character has just dropped the object.
- You know that words enclosed in a circle over a character's head indicate words that the character is speaking.
- You know that a character is cursing or using dirty language when words are represented, not by letters, but by symbols such as @ and # and !
- You know that, when the line that encloses words is scalloped or looks something like a cloud, the words represent *thoughts* rather than utterances.

In short, you know the conventions that enable you to understand what the cartoonist/storyteller is doing, and you can follow the story, the narrative conveyed by words and pictures, all of which says that you are already visually literate. Yet, because you may not have developed the habit of reading images closely and taking in all the subtleties that they may offer, we will talk a bit about reading images.

Let's look at a single image that tells a story. Look, for instance, at this painting by Grant Wood, *Death on the Ridge Road*. The title—words!—tells you what the picture is about, but even if you found the picture in the attic, with no title affixed, you could infer what is about to happen, what story the picture tells.

A big black car, apparently a limousine, is going to collide with a truck.

Death on the Ridge Road (1935), Grant Wood (American; 1892–1942). Oil on masonite, frame: 39 × 46 1/16 in. (99 × 117 cm) Williams College Museum of Art, Williamstown, MA, Gift of Cole Porter, (47.1.3). Art © Figge Art Museum, successors to the Estate of Nan Wood Graham/Licensed by VAGA, New York, NY.

We think all viewers will agree with this statement, and perhaps we can go a *little* further. (First, let us note that the cars are black, the truck is red, the grass is green, and the sky is darkening.)

- Given the facts that the cars are black—in the context, an ominous color—that the sky shows a storm brewing, that the intersecting diagonals of the limousine and the truck imply conflict, and that the telephone pole appears at an angle, the picture makes the viewer uneasy.
- Apparently, the limousine was behind the car that is now at the bottom of the picture; in order to pass the car, the limousine must have crossed into the left lane, and it is now cutting to the right in order to return to its proper lane.
- The telephone poles, in this context of vehicles about to collide, we perceive as crosses, and thus they turn the pretty landscape with its winding road into a cemetery.
- The picture may cause us to moralize: "Death comes unexpectedly"; "Even in lovely rural surroundings, death can be present."

But, even when a viewer has such thoughts—and we think these thoughts are supported by the picture—the picture itself tells only a simple story:

- A car, having passed another car on the left, is cutting back into the right lane and will in a moment collide with a truck coming over a hill.

The picture does *not* tell us anything about the minds of the people involved in the accident to come. Conceivably, a viewer may conjecture that the driver of the limousine was impatient, driving behind someone in a dinky car going at twenty miles an hour, and—such is the personality of the rich men who drive big cars, or of their chauffeurs—that this driver confidently and recklessly crossed the dividing line marked on the road, entered the left lane, zoomed ahead of the slowpoke, and now (here, we return to the facts shown in the picture) is cutting back into the right lane but is too near the truck to avoid a crash. Clearly, this interpretation of the character of the driver cannot be supported by the picture. For all we know, the smaller car may have stalled in the middle of the road, and the driver of the limousine—maybe a very cautious woman—was forced to go around the stalled car.

As our thoughts about this single image show, we crave a complex story that we can interpret. In the next sections, we'll turn to two strategies that are used in graphic fiction to tell more complex stories: the use of words in combination with images and the use of sequential images.

Joining the Conversation: Two Topics for Creative Writing

1. Write two versions (each about five hundred to one thousand words) of a story based on Grant Wood's painting. In one version, tell the story from the point of view of the driver of the car that is being passed. This driver cannot know the exact thoughts of the other driver, but he or she can say such things as, "This guy was behind me, honking like crazy, so I deliberately slowed down, just to teach him a lesson." In the second version, use a *different* point of view—perhaps the point of view of the driver of the car that will be struck, or perhaps the point of view of a spectator, or, if you wish, an omniscient point of view.

2. Grant Wood's most famous painting is *American Gothic,* a picture that shows a man, holding a pitchfork, and a woman standing in front of their home, a house with a window shaped like a gothic (pointed) arch. (You can find the picture on the Internet.) Do you see a story, a narrative, or a sequence of events in this picture? If so, what is the story? If you do not see a story, invent a very short one that might plausibly use this painting as an illustration of some episode.

Now let's look at a picture that is accompanied by words.

Reading an Image:
A Short Story Told in One Panel

TONY CARRILLO

Tony Carrillo was born and raised in Tempe, Arizona. He conceived F Minus when he was a sophomore at Arizona State University. The comic strip is currently syndicated in more than one hundred newspapers.

F Minus

Tony Carrillo: "F Minus" © 2007 Tony Carrillo. Universal Uclick.

For now, let's pretend that the picture doesn't exist and that we have been given only some text:

> One day, in a quiet office building somewhere, a small calculator suddenly became self-aware.
> In eight seconds, it plotted the extinction of all mankind.
> Then the battery died.
> Two weeks later, it was thrown away.

We don't want to make extravagant claims, but we think this is pretty good as a mini-sci-fi story. We hear much about the possibility that someday there may be machines that "think," and we hear even more about technology possibly getting out of control and destroying its creators. In the words of Elias Canetti, winner of a Nobel Prize in Literature, "The planet's survival has become so uncertain that any effort, any thought that presupposes an assured future amounts to a mad gamble."

So, the graphic story begins with something fantastic yet something that we hear about and that we can imagine may become real:

> One day, in a quiet office building somewhere, a small calculator suddenly became self-aware.
> In eight seconds, it plotted the extinction of all mankind.

There is an engaging combination of vagueness ("One day," "somewhere") and of the highly specific ("In eight seconds"); that is, things in a leisurely once-upon-a-time land suddenly come down to a matter of seconds. The vague fairy-tale world of "one day" has been transformed into real time, and the "small calculator" is now a big threat. Like all good fiction, each sentence of this tiny story stimulates the reader to wonder, "What happens next?"

What does happen after the calculator "plotted the extinction of all mankind"? "Then the battery died." Well, that makes sense. We haven't anticipated this happening, but, again, the happening is a plausible one, and we are relieved, satisfied. In a sense, the story is over—the battery is dead, so what more can be said?—but we see additional words:

> Two weeks later, it was thrown away.

We think this ending is masterful. It is as if we heard a joke, laughed, and thought we had heard the end of the matter, and then the narrator went on to top the joke, giving us an unexpected joke that builds on the first joke—a line that, after we have heard it, seems inevitable. The calculator, once an enormous menace, fails to be of even the slightest significance because—as is entirely natural, if we can speak of naturalness in connection with a mechanical device—the battery dies. The story seems to be over, and there is nothing more to say. But there *is* more to say. The battery-dead calculator for two weeks is not even noticed, and, then, when presumably it somehow comes to some unspecified person's attention, it is unceremoniously discarded, "thrown away." The way of all flesh.

What is convincing is not simply that A is followed by B and that B is followed by C, but that there is a *logic* to the sequence, even (may we say?) a *truth* to the sequence. Notice, too, that the artist–writer does not moralize; rather, it is the reader–viewer who draws conclusions.

The theme is a great one, the humbling of the ambitious. Shakespeare often treated it—for instance, in *Richard II,* in which the king meditates on his "state" (that is, high status, exalted rank) and sees death as an "antic" (buffoon, jester) mocking even a king:

> Within the hollow crown
> That rounds the mortal temples of a king
> Keeps Death his court and there the antic sits,
> Scoffing his state and grinning at his pomp,
> Allowing him a breath, a little scene,
> To monarchize, be feared and kill with looks,
> Infusing him with self and vain conceit,
> As if this flesh which walls about our life,
> Were brass impregnable, and humored thus
> Comes at the last and with a little pin
> Bores through his castle wall, and farewell king!

We are not claiming that the story about the calculator is in the same league with Shakespeare's play, but we do find it memorable. We think the *text* of this graphic story makes a pretty good short, short story, even without the picture. Now let's examine the accompanying picture.

We think the accompanying picture is clever and cute. The cartoonist might simply have drawn a calculator, but he brilliantly put two eyes into the liquid crystal display and thus animated the whole thing. The calculator *does* seem to be aware, doesn't it? So, in our view, the story becomes enriched by the image. We can call this sort of thing "graphic fiction," but, to go back to our earlier point, the truth is that the picture doesn't tell the story. It merely enriches a story that is told in words.

That last sentence is, we admit, unfair. The image doesn't "merely" enrich the words. The picture is literally central to the story. If the story consisted only of text, or if all of the text were written above or below the story, the story would not be as effective. The image is integral.

And that's our point: The best graphic fiction does not merely illustrate the verbal story; rather, the images are inseparable from the words. The story is text-and-image, not just text-adorned-with-image.

Elements of Graphic Fiction

Graphic fiction often expands the structure of the single panel into a series of panels, taking the form of a sequential series of images and text. Graphic fiction often features narrative development and depth, translating the elements that we know from fiction—plot, character, setting, tone, style—into a visual form. The term **graphic fiction** is broadly applied and can encompass anything from a single panel, to a series of panels, to a novel-length story. Graphic literature can also encompass nonfiction, such as an autobiography or a historical account.

Visual Elements

Graphic fiction shares many literary elements with fiction, such as plot, character, and setting. However, because graphic fiction is told through a visual rather than a verbal form, it introduces a new set of formal or structural elements that can be analyzed. A graphic novel is typically constructed out of the following:

- *Panels:* the square or rectangles that contain a single image; the graphic novel page is made up of a series of panels that we read in sequential order.
- *Gutters:* the blank space between the panels, revealing the unillustrated white space on the page.
- *Captions:* the descriptive text that contains information about a scene or a character, often placed in a square at the top or bottom of the panel.
- *Dialogue balloons:* the balloon-like space that contains the spoken communication between characters.
- *Thought balloons:* the balloon-like space that contains a character's unspoken thoughts.
- *Sound effects:* the reproduction of sound through words, such as "pow!" or "crrrackkkk."

As you read graphic fiction, notice how these different visual elements work to convey key aspects of the story being told.

Narrative and Graphic Jumps

In *Understanding Comics*, Scott McCloud emphasizes that, due to its unique formal elements, graphic fiction requires imaginative engagement on the part of the reader. As graphic fiction shows a scene developing visually, it typically divides that scene up into a series of panels, separated by blank space, or **gutter**. This division into panels creates visual gaps on the page. As he or she reads graphic fiction's sequential images, the reader must, as McCloud says, "jump the gutter" and move from one panel to the next. The reader must fill in the information that takes place between the panels—information that, in a story, would often be provided by a narrator or central character. For example, if one panel shows a person standing at the bottom of a mountain and the next panel shows that person standing at the top of the mountain, we make an interpretive leap and assume that the character climbed the mountain, imagining the time and effort that climb took. As we "jump the gutter," moving from one image to the next, we would not, presumably, imagine that the character flew up to the top of the mountain. When we read graphic fiction, we often fill in lots of narrative information, understanding the story without realizing how extensively we have been guided by the skillful artist to make assumptions and interpretations based on visual cues.

Graphic Style

In graphic fiction, the artist's style quite literally leaps off the page. You can tell at a glance how a page reflects an artist's unique drawing style and how he or she uses that style to create an atmosphere for the story that it is telling. In some graphic fiction, the author and artist are the same; in others, the story is written by the author and the imagery is provided by an artist and sometimes completed by a colorist. Graphic style relies on numerous elements, but it is often helpful to start by asking how "realistic" the style is. Graphic works can employ a style that is highly detailed and looks similar to a fine art painting or a style that is very stripped-down and overly simplified, such as in the drawing of a stick figure. Graphic fiction often employs **icons**, or simplified images that can be understood at a glance. For example, comic strips often use variations of a round "smiley face" to represent a human face and its emotions. To take another example, if you were asked to draw an image of a house, you might draw a triangle for a roof on top of a square, with a window and a door and maybe a chimney. Even if houses don't really look like this, we have come to accept this as an easily recognizable image—or icon—of a house. How much or how little do graphic artists rely on icons, and varying levels of visual symbolism and realism, to define their style?

The most successful examples of graphic fiction marry style and content; the graphic style becomes a perfect match for the story being told. For example, *Persepolis*, told and drawn by Marjane Satrapi, purposefully employs a rudimentary drawing style that evokes the young age of its narrator as she comes of age in Iran. Drawn in black and white with the use of a relatively thick line, *Persepolis* evokes the harsh "black-and-white" contrasts between a rebellious girl and her surrounding repressive world. In contrast, Allan Moore's popular *Watchman* series, illustrated by Dave Gibbons and colored by John Higgins, is lush, multicolored, and full of action. *Watchman* imitates the style of a superhero comic in order to critique the idea of superheroes, imagining a world in which such heroes are manipulated by a corrupt government. As you read a graphic fiction, notice the elements of line, shading, and color and how they are used to convey meaning.

Reading a Series of Images:
A Story Told in Sequential Panels

Let's look now at an example of more complex sequential work of graphic fiction, consisting of eight panels. The artist–writer is Art Spiegelman.

ART SPIEGELMAN

Born in Sweden in 1948, Art Spiegelman was raised in New York City. His two-part graphic story (part novel, part memoir), Maus (1986, 1991), based on his Polish-Jewish parents' experiences during the Holocaust, was awarded a Pulitzer Prize in 1992. A highly inventive artist–writer, Spiegelman not only cofounded several outlets for comic books but also created Garbage Candy (edible candy in the shape of garbage, packaged in miniature garbage cans). In 2005, Time *magazine included Spiegelman in its list of the one hundred most influential people.*

If you were explaining *Nature vs. Nurture* to critters from outer space, you might point out the following conventions, moving from panel to panel:

- Spiegelman sets the scene at the extreme upper left, in the first panel, with some text in a small box. This text box, providing the reader–viewer with background rather than dialogue, is appropriately distinct in shape from the speech balloons.
- The little girl in the first panel is obviously happy. Her happiness is conveyed not only by the text's expressions of motherly love but also by the expression on her face. The father is also smiling.
- In the second panel, the well-intentioned, politically correct father takes the doll from the girl. The girl is puzzled (the balloon says "uk?" and the smile is gone from her face).
- In the third panel, the father is full of enthusiasm—his mouth is open, he has a big smile—and the text conveys his enthusiasm. Additional text, "Skreeee," in different lettering (to indicate it is not human speech) comes out of the fire truck. The father has presumably pushed a button or flicked a switch so that the fire truck emits a sound. The girl's face and posture show puzzlement.
- The enthusiastic father (still with a big smile) seeks to show the girl how to play with the fire truck. His talk is (how shall we put it?) male talk, loud and aggressive ("Clang! Clang! Clang! Everybody get outa the way!").
- In the fifth panel, the father, still teaching his daughter but evidently having a great time, is verging on the maniacal with his toothy grin and his "Vroom! Vroom!" A reader–viewer probably thinks, "Hmmm, boys will be boys," and may also think, seeing this father's childish enthusiasm, "You can't take the boy out of the man."
- The next panel shows the smiling—and complacent—father handing the fire truck to the girl, whose face conveys uncertainty.
- The bottom row begins with more uncertainty, indicated by a big question mark over the girl's head. She says nothing—there is no speech balloon—but we know that she is puzzled.
- The final panel shows that the girl has covered half the fire truck with a blanket instead of thrusting it crazily around and making loud noises, and the father is reduced to silence. His posture—hands thrust into pockets, head slightly turned down—shows that he has given up his attempt (the "nurture" of the title) to stifle the expression of motherly feelings (the "nature" of the title), and a balloon indicates that he is heaving a sigh of resignation. The sigh is conveyed by enclosing the word "sigh" within elongated dots, indicating that he is sighing rather than *saying* "sigh."

If we were to think about the story in terms of the elements of fiction, what might we say? Well, so far as **character** (personality) goes, each of the two figures is relatively simple: The girl is just a girl—at her young age, we hardly expect her to be a richly complex figure—and the father is essentially a well-meaning dad who wants his daughter to grow up free from gender stereotypes. Surely, that is an admirable ambition. The **plot**—the sequence of events—shows the father's attempt to free her by offering her an alternative, a fire truck instead of a doll. He is apparently rather pleased with his efforts (the seventh panel shows him smiling when his little daughter touches the fire truck), but, with the final panel, reality breaks in. The girl does not career around the room shouting "Vroom!" as the father did; rather, her maternal instinct manifests itself even toward the fire truck. But this is not quite the end of the story: At the extreme right-hand side, we see the father heaving a sigh, shoulders slumped and hands in pockets: He has been forced to accept reality. This is not always a bad thing, really, when you think about it. If we are asked what the **theme** of the story is—that is, "What does the story *add up* to?" (which is very different from the plot, which is "What *happens* in the story?")—we can say that the theme concerns (as the title of the story indicates) the conflict between Nature and Nurture, or, to put it a bit differently, biology versus socialization. We most emphatically do not wish to say anything like "Spiegelman shows that human nature is unchangeable." For one thing, Spiegelman doesn't "show" us (in the sense of prove or demonstrate) anything. He just drew some pictures and wrote some words; he didn't offer anything that can be called evidence. Even if the pictures represented something that happened in his own family, his graphic report of his experience would not prove that other fathers had the same experience with their daughters. Spiegelman is entertaining us, not arguing, not preaching. Still, one feels that Spiegelman's story—the events that he illustrates and the actions of the two characters—is plausible. One thing follows from another:

- The father sees his daughter playing with dolls, and
- being a good father, he wishes to free his daughter from stereotypical limited behavior, so
- he gives his daughter a toy that is usually associated with boys, but
- nature will have its way, and the girl turns the fire truck into an object that allows her to express her maternal instinct.
- Heaving a sigh, the father appears to recognize that his efforts have failed.

You have now instructed your Martian visitors in the language of graphic fiction. Yes, you knew it all along, and maybe the Martian visitors did, too.

Graphic fiction asks you apply your understanding of storytelling to a form that combines words and images. The questions in the following checklist may help you to focus on the unique elements of graphic fiction, analyzing how it uses pictures to create a narrative.

✔ **CHECKLIST:** *Getting Ideas for Writing Arguments about Graphic Fiction*

Elements of Fiction

☐ Does the graphic fiction feature a central character or a set of characters? How does this character or set of characters provide a focal lens for the story?

☐ How do the characters contribute to the graphic fiction's narrative progression? How are the characters developed? Do the characters have clear motivations? How do the characters change? What are the relationships among the characters? Are the characters defined by conflict?

☐ How are the characters represented graphically? How is characterization achieved visually? How do you recognize the characters? What are the key graphic features used for each character?

☐ What is the plot of the graphic work? What story is being told? What are the story's beginning, middle, and end?

☐ How do events structure the story? What are the story's most important "turning point" events? Do cause-and-effect relationships among events order the story?

(continued)

☐ How are these key events represented graphically? How do visual elements convey the importance of specific events? Do certain events take place "off-panel," or outside the graphic panels, forcing the reader to imagine and interpret the event that took place?

☐ What symbols convey meaning within the story? Are symbolic objects presented graphically? Are certain images repeated, gaining symbolic significance? What meaning do you ascribe to these symbols?

☐ How has the author used additional elements of fiction to convey meaning, such as point of view, mood and atmosphere, and setting?

☐ What is the thematic meaning of the graphic work? What conceptual ideas are being conveyed by the story? What is the point or message of the story? How do the elements of fiction and the story's graphic style come together to convey that meaning?

Visual Elements

☐ How do the visual elements of the graphic work together to create the story's meaning? What are the most important graphic elements being used by the artist to convey the story?

☐ How are the story's panels composed? How is the layout of the page broken into a series of panels or boxed images? Are the panels always the same size and shape, or do they vary? Why? How do we read the panels sequentially; for example, do they always follow a left-to-right order?

☐ How are the gutters used to sequence the story? Do the gutters become a graphic element that helps to organize the page?

☐ How are words introduced into the images? Do the words themselves become graphic, presented in an interesting font or a variety of styles?

☐ Does the graphic work use captions? Do the captions function as a narrator? What types of information do the captions convey? Are the captions used in a consistent way?

☐ How is dialogue presented graphically? How is dialogue presented in words but also presented through visual elements, such as balloons or a change in font?

☐ How are the character's thoughts presented graphically? How do you know that the words being presented are thoughts? How are thoughts presented through visual elements, such as balloons or a change in font?

☐ How are sound effects captured in the graphic fiction? Are sounds presented through words or images, or a combination of the two?

☐ How would you characterize the relationship between words and images in the graphic work? What sort of balance is created between the two?

Narrative and Graphic Jumps

☐ How does the graphic fiction rely on the reader's ability to provide narrative information that is not presented by the words or images on the page? Does the work contain few or many narrative and visual gaps?

☐ What meaning is conveyed in the gutter? Examine how the break provided by the gutter conveys different types of information. For example, is the gutter used to convey the passage of time or a change in location?

☐ How does the work use your ability to "jump the gutter"? Is there a moment in the story when this ability to make an interpretive leap seems especially important?

☐ Are there moments in the story when the sequence of panels becomes confusing? Is the graphic fiction purposely using the gaps created by panels to convey meaning, such as a feeling of disruption or confusion?

Graphic Style

☐ How would you describe the style of the graphic work? What seems to be the artist's signature style?

☐ How does the artist represent reality? Is the work realistic? Or, is it stripped down? Are objects and characters presented in realistic forms, or are they presented in more symbolic forms or as "icons"?

☐ How elaborate or simplified is the graphic style? Is the imagery detailed or stripped down? How does the level of detail relate to the size of the panel?

☐ How does the artist use elements of line, shading, and color? Are thick or thin lines used; when and why? Are smooth or jagged lines use; when and why? Is the imagery presented in black and white, or is shading used? How does shading contribute to the graphic style? Is color used? What is the color range? How does the color convey meaning, such as atmosphere?

☐ How does the style match the story being told? Is the style a good match for the themes and concepts being conveyed by the narrative?

Your Turn: Additional Graphic Fiction for Analysis

WILL EISNER

Born in Brooklyn, New York, Will Eisner (1917–2005) drew cartoons for his high school newspaper and after graduation studied for a year at the Art Students League of New York. He was soon publishing cartoons and comic strips, and he became an important figure in establishing the graphic novel ("sequential art") as a form of fiction. He taught at the School of Visual Arts in New York, and he published two highly informative books derived from his lectures, Comics and Sequential Art *(1985) and* Graphic Storytelling and Visual Narrative *(1996). In* Comics and Sequential Art, *Eisner includes a chapter titled "Expressive Anatomy." Among the illustrations in this chapter is* Hamlet on a Rooftop, *first published in June 1981. Eisner prefaces the* Hamlet *drawings with the following remark and then offers a running commentary on the pictures.*

Hamlet on a Rooftop

The Body and the Face

The employment of body posture and facial expression (both having equal attention) is a major undertaking and an area of frequent failure. Properly and skillfully done, it can carry the narrative without resorting to unnecessary props or scenery. The use of expressive anatomy in the absence of words is less demanding because the latitude for the art is wider. Where the words have a depth of meaning and nuance, the task is more difficult.

This represents an example of a classic situation — that of author vs. artist. The artist must decide at the outset what his 'input' shall be; to slavishly make visual that which is in the author's mind or to embark on the raft of the author's words onto a visual sea of his own charting.

HAMLET ON A ROOFTOP

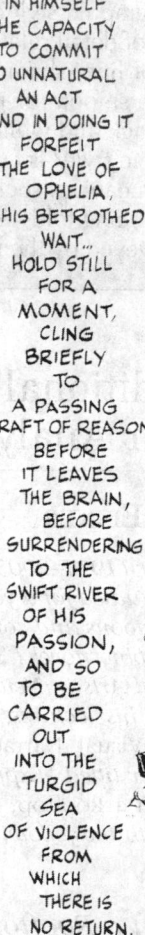

His father is dead, mysteriously! His mother, within but a month, marries his uncle! So soon?, so soon? Can there be anything other than **something rotten** here? Can it be anything but murder!? Well, then, if murder it be all he values, indeed, his manhood cries out for retribution ....Vengeance .. to honor the filial duty his father's voice demands in the hot cauldron of his mind! Aye, to punish them, to **murder his mother and uncle**... as they lay in violation of his code!!! ...or perhaps something more unspeakable within him.

Yet... can he find in himself the capacity to commit so unnatural an act and in doing it forfeit the love of Ophelia, his betrothed? Wait... hold still for a moment, cling briefly to a passing raft of reason before it leaves the brain, before surrendering to the swift river of his passion, and so to be carried out into the turgid sea of violence from which there is no return.

In this experiment, Shakespeare's words are intact. The soliloquy is broken up into balloons at the artist's discretion. The intent here is to permit a meaningful fusing of word, imagery and timing. The result should provide the reader with necessary pauses.

The artist here functions as actor and in the process gives his own meaning to the lines.

A gesture signifying contemplation.

Furniture employed in intimate involvement with the actor gives the 'background' story value because it is part of the action.

Submission . . . to a "heavy" thought.

Here, the postures are more than a classical portrayal of emotions. This man is not the Danish Prince Hamlet! His gestures and postures are derivative of his special background. The question of how he would deliver the standard gesture for self-doubt and internal agony is the artist's real challenge!

WHETHER 'TIS NOBLER IN THE MIND TO SUFFER THE SLINGS AND ARROWS OF OUTRAGEOUS FORTUNE...

OR...

TO TAKE ARMS AGAINST A SEA OF TROUBLES, AND BY OPPOSING **END** THEM!

Bravado . . . he envisions himself as challenging the forces of troubles.

Exhaustion — beaten by the enormity of his problems

Seeking comfort he lets his body slide down along the wall

Retreat . . . into his refuge . . . sleep

TO DIE... TO SLEEP...

NO MORE...

AND...BY A SLEEP TO SAY WE END THE HEARTACHE AND THE THOUSAND NATURAL SHOCKS THAT FLESH IS HEIR TO...

'TIS A CONSUMMATION DEVOUTLY TO BE WISHED!

TO DIE, TO SLEEP ...TO SLEEP PERCHANCE TO DREAM...

The language of posture is universal and inter-changeable — the application is not.

Wishing with all his might.

Withdraw-ing into sleep or oblivion, he assumes an almost fetal posture.

Anger . . . . now he builds his resolution

Arguing
. . . he
begins to
make a
case to but-
tress grow-
ing resolve.

Debating . . . the postures of a courtroom advocate

The use of a long-shot, here is meant to reinforce realism — and in that way try to deal with the problem of putting Shakespeare's language in the mouth of such a man.

Hesitation . . . a recurrence of doubt

RESOLVE!

AND ENTERPRISES OF GREAT PITCH AND MOMENT WITH THIS REGARD THEIR CURRENTS TURN AWRY AND **LOSE** **THE NAME OF ACTION**!!

...SOFT YOU NOW!

ATTACK . . .
he now moves
to act upon
his resolve.

This wedding of Shake-spearean language with a modern denizen of the ghetto may not be appropriate but the exercise serves to demonstrate the potential of the medium be-cause the emotional content is so universal.

Now let's examine a contemporary graphic treatment of an early twentieth-century short story, Franz Kafka's "A Hunger Artist." In one obvious way, the job of the illustrator of a classic text is easier than the job of the creator of an entirely original work, but in another way, it is also more difficult because the artist who illustrates a classic is in some sense putting himself or herself up against a classic writer: The reader–viewer will inevitably expect the artist to contribute something to the work, to do more than ride piggyback on the original author.

R. CRUMB AND DAVID ZANE MAIROWITZ

Robert Dennis Crumb, born in Philadelphia in 1943, worked for a while in Cleveland as a designer of greeting cards and then began drawing for underground newspapers. Some of his work is strongly sexual and highly satiric, but he has also drawn R. Crumb's Kafka *(1993), with a text by David Zane Mairowitz, illustrating several works of fiction by the writer Franz Kafka (1883–1924).*

David Zane Mairowitz, born in New York City in 1943, emigrated in 1968 to England, where he works as a freelance writer.

A Hunger Artist

In June 1924, his "phantoms" saw to it — with their usual irony — that while dying of *starvation*, he would be correcting the galley-proofs of an astonishing masterwork called...

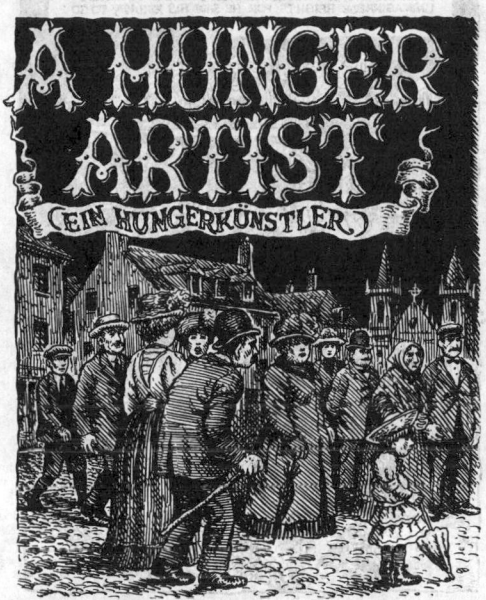

THE PERIOD OF FASTING WAS SET BY HIS IMPRESARIO AT FORTY DAYS MAXIMUM, BECAUSE AFTER THAT TIME THE PUBLIC BEGAN TO LOSE INTEREST. SO, ON THE FORTIETH DAY, WITH AN EXCITED CROWD FILLING THE ARENA AND A MILITARY BAND PLAYING, TWO YOUNG LADIES CAME TO LEAD THE HUNGER-ARTIST OUT OF HIS CAGE. WHEN THIS HAPPENED HE ALWAYS PUT UP SOME RESISTANCE...WHY STOP AFTER ONLY FORTY DAYS?!? WHY SHOULD THEY TAKE FROM HIM THE GLORY OF FASTING EVEN LONGER, OR SURPASSING EVEN HIMSELF TO REACH UNIMAGINABLE HEIGHTS, FOR HE SAW HIS ABILITY TO GO ON FASTING AS *UNLIMITED!*

THEN CAME THE FEAST, WITH THE IMPRESARIO TRYING TO SPOONFEED THE NEARLY COMATOSE HUNGER-ARTIST, ALL THE WHILE CHATTING CHEERFULLY IN ORDER TO DISTRACT ATTENTION FROM HIS CONDITION.

AFTER THAT THERE WAS EVEN A TOAST TO THE AUDIENCE, SUPPOSEDLY SUGGESTED BY THE HUNGER-ARTIST HIMSELF IN A WHISPER TO THE IMPRESARIO.

HE LIVED THIS WAY FOR MANY YEARS, HONORED BY ALL THE WORLD, YET TROUBLED IN HIS SOUL, DEEPLY FRUSTRATED THAT THEY WOULD NOT ALLOW HIS FASTING TO EXCEED FORTY DAYS. HE SPENT MOST OF HIS TIME IN A GLOOMY MOOD, AND WHEN SOME KIND-HEARTED PERSON WOULD TRY TO EXPLAIN THAT HIS DEPRESSION WAS THE RESULT OF THE FASTING, HE WOULD SOMETIMES FLY INTO A RAGE AND BEGIN RATTLING THE BARS OF HIS CAGE LIKE AN ANIMAL.

AS TIME WENT BY PEOPLE BECAME INTERESTED IN OTHER AMUSEMENTS, AND WERE REVOLTED BY PROFESSIONAL FASTING. THE HUNGER-ARTIST COULD NOT CHANGE JOBS, FANATICALLY DEVOTED TO FASTING AS HE WAS. SO, DISCHARGING THE IMPRESARIO, HE HIRED HIMSELF OUT TO A LARGE CIRCUS, WHERE HIS CAGE WAS PUT OUTSIDE, NEAR THOSE OF THE ANIMALS.

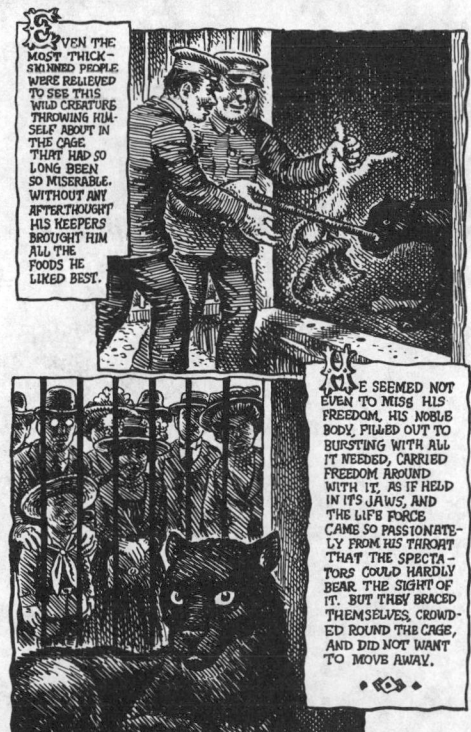

Joining the Conversation: Critical Thinking and Writing

1. Select one panel from the graphic version of *A Hunger Artist* for close examination. How do the visual elements and the narrative elements work together to convey the meaning of the story? Write an explication of your selected panel, describing specific visual and verbal elements in turn. Explain how these elements reinforce each other to convey the panel's key ideas.

2. Does R. Crumb and David Zane Mairowitz's graphic style seem to be a good match for the content of Kafka's story? Do the heavily lined and crosshatched images capture the emotional content of a story about fasting and starvation, exhibitionism and viewership? Why or why not?

3. Analyze *A Hunger Artist* as a sequential series of images that culminate in the final images of the dying artist and the panther. Consider how one panel leads to another, encouraging us to connect images across the panels. For example, notice the repeated imagery of cage bars. Also consider how the panels are separated by gutters, encouraging us to compare and contrast panels. Compare and contrast the last few images of the artist with the image of the panther, while also comparing and contrasting images of the viewers and images of the cage. How does the visual contrast between the dying man and the sleek panther convey Kafka's thematic ideas?

CHAPTER 14

Reading and Writing about Plays

Chapter Preview

After reading this chapter, you will be able to

- Identify and define the types of plays
- Identify and analyze the elements of drama
- Evaluate a dramatic production
- Compare filmed plays to stage productions
- Describe the conventions of Greek tragedy
- Write a successful paper about a play, using a writing process that moves from first annotation to final draft

Types of Plays

Most of the world's great plays that were written before the twentieth century may be regarded as one of two kinds: **tragedy** or **comedy**. Roughly speaking, tragedy dramatizes the conflict between the vitality of the individual life and the laws or limits of life. The tragic hero reaches a height, going beyond the experience of others but at the cost of his or her life. Comedy, on the other hand, dramatizes the vitality of the laws of social life. In comedy, the good life is seen to reside in the shedding of an individualism that isolates in favor of a union with a genial and enlightened society. These points must be amplified a bit before we go on to the further point that any important play does much more than can be put into such crude formulas.

Tragedy

Tragic heroes usually go beyond the standards to which reasonable people adhere; they do some type of fearful deed that ultimately destroys them. This deed is often said to be an act of **hubris**, a Greek word meaning something like "overweening pride." It may involve, for instance, violating a taboo, such as that against taking a life. But, if the hubristic act ultimately destroys the man or woman who performs it, it also shows that person (paradoxically) to be in some way more fully a living being—a person who has experienced life more fully, whether by heroic action or by a capacity for enduring suffering—than the other characters in the play. (If the tragic hero does not die, he or she is usually left in a death-like state, as is the blind Oedipus in *Oedipus the King*.) In tragedy, we see humans pushed to an extreme state; the hero enters a world unknown to most people and reveals magnificence. After the hero's departure from the stage, we are left in a world of smaller people.

What has just been said may (or may not) be true of most tragedies, but it is not true of all. If you were writing about a tragedy, you might consider whether the points just made are illustrated in the play about which you were writing. Is Willy Loman, in Arthur Miller's *Death of a Salesman* (page 1057), a tragic figure, or is he merely a pathetic figure? In our first paragraph, we said that a tragic figure "reaches a height, going beyond the experience of others but at the cost of his or her life," and, in our next paragraph, we said that "[a]fter the hero's departure from the stage, we are left in a world of smaller people." Do these words apply to *Death of a Salesman*? Or is Biff right when, in the second act (page 1117), he says to Willy, "Pop, I'm a dime a dozen, and so are you." If Biff is right, is the play not a tragedy? Or does our statement describing tragedy need to be emended? Is the tragic hero guilty of hubris? Does the hero seem a greater person than the others in the play? An essay examining these questions probably requires not only a character sketch but also comparison with other characters.

Tragedy commonly involves **irony** of two sorts: unconsciously ironic deeds and unconsciously ironic speeches. Ironic deeds have some type of consequence that are more or less the reverse of what the doer intends. In Shakespeare's *Macbeth*, Macbeth thinks that by killing Duncan he will gain happiness, but he finds that his deed brings him sleepless nights. In Shakespeare's *Julius Caesar*, Brutus thinks that by killing Caesar he will bring liberty to Rome, but his action brings tyranny. In an unconsciously ironic speech, the words mean one thing to the speaker but something more significant to the audience, as when King Duncan, baffled by Cawdor's treason, says

> There's no art
> To find the mind's construction in the face:
> He was a gentleman on whom I built
> An absolute trust.

At this moment, Macbeth, whom we have already heard meditating on the murder of Duncan, enters. Duncan's words are true, but he does not apply them to Macbeth as the audience does. A few moments later, Duncan praises Macbeth as "a peerless kinsman." Soon Macbeth will indeed become peerless, when he kills Duncan and ascends to the throne.[1] Sophocles's use of ironic deeds and speeches is so pervasive, especially in *Oedipus Rex*, that **Sophoclean irony** has become a critical term.

When a deed backfires or has a reverse effect, such as Macbeth's effort to gain happiness, we have what Aristotle (the first—and still the greatest—drama critic) called a **peripeteia**, or a **reversal**. A character who comes to perceive what has happened (Macbeth's "I have lived long enough: my way of life / Is fall'n into the sere, the yellow leaf") experiences (in Aristotle's language) an **anagnorisis**, or **recognition**. Strictly speaking, for Aristotle, the recognition was a matter of literal

---

[1] **Dramatic irony** (ironic deeds, or happenings, and unconsciously ironic speeches) must be distinguished from **verbal irony**, which is produced when the speaker is *conscious* that his or her words mean something different from what the speakers says. In *Macbeth*, Lennox says, "The gracious Duncan / Was pitied of Macbeth. Marry, he was dead! / And the right valiant Banquo walked too late. / . . . / Men must not walk too late." He *says* nothing about Macbeth's having killed Duncan and Banquo, but he *means* that Macbeth has killed them.

identification—for example, the recognition that Oedipus was the son of a man that he had killed. In *Macbeth,* the recognition in this sense is that Macduff, "from his mother's womb / Untimely ripped," is the man who fits the prophecy that Macbeth can be conquered only by someone not "of woman born." Does Willy Loman in *Death of a Salesman* ever experience a recognition? If not, does this lack of recognition indicate that the play is not a tragedy or, on the other hand, that the description of tragedy needs to be emended?

In his analysis of drama, Aristotle says that the tragic hero comes to grief through his **hamartia**, a term sometimes translated as **tragic flaw** but perhaps better translated as **tragic error**, since *flaw* implies a moral fault. Thus, it is a great error for Hamlet not to inspect the foils at the start of the deadly fencing match with Laertes; had he done so, he would have seen that one of the foils was blunt and one was pointed. If we hold to the translation *flaw,* we begin to hunt for a fault in the tragic hero's character, and we say, for instance, that Hamlet is gullible, or some such thing. In doing this, we may diminish or even overlook the hero's grandeur.

Comedy

Although in tragedy the hero usually seems to embody certain values that are superior to those of the hero's surrounding society, in comedy the fullest life is seen to reside *within* enlightened social norms. At the beginning of a comedy, we find banished dukes, unhappy lovers, crabby parents, jealous husbands, and harsh laws, but, at the end of the comedy, we usually have a unified and genial society, often symbolized by a marriage feast to which everyone, or almost everyone, is invited. Early in *A Midsummer Night's Dream,* for instance, we meet quarreling young lovers and a father who demands that his daughter either marry a man she does not love or enter a convent. Such is the Athenian law. At the end of the play, the lovers are properly matched, to everyone's satisfaction.

Speaking broadly, most comedies fall into one of two classes: **satiric comedy** or **romantic comedy**. In satiric comedy, the emphasis is on the obstructionists— the irate fathers, hardheaded businessmen, and other members of the establishment who at the beginning of the play seem to hold all the cards, preventing joy from reigning. They are held up to ridicule because they are repressive monomaniacs enslaved to themselves, acting mechanistically (always irate, always hardheaded) instead of responding genially to the ups and downs of life. The outwitting of these obstructionists, usually by the younger generation, often provides the resolution of the plot. Ben Jonson, Molière, and George Bernard Shaw are in this tradition; their satiric comedy, according to an ancient Roman formula, "chastens morals with ridicule"—that is, it reforms folly or vice by laughing at it. On the other hand, in romantic comedy (think of Shakespeare's *A Midsummer Night's Dream, As You Like It,* and *Twelfth Night*), the emphasis is on a pair or pairs of delightful people who engage our sympathies as they run their obstacle race to the altar. There are obstructionists here, too, but the emphasis is on festivity.

When writing about comedy, you may be concerned with the function of one scene or character. But whatever your topic, you may find it helpful to begin by trying to decide whether the play is primarily romantic or primarily satiric (or something else). One way of getting at this is to ask yourself to what degree you sympathize with the characters. Do you laugh *with* them, sympathetically, or do you laugh *at* them, regarding them as being at least somewhat contemptible?

Elements of Drama

Theme

If we have read or seen a drama thoughtfully, we ought to be able to formulate its **theme**, its underlying idea—and perhaps we can even go so far as to say its moral attitudes, its view of life, and its wisdom. Some critics have argued that the concept of theme is meaningless. They hold that *Macbeth,* for example, gives us only an extremely detailed history of one imaginary man. In this view, *Macbeth* says nothing to you or me; it tells only what happened to an imaginary man. Even *Julius Caesar* says nothing about the historical Julius Caesar or about the nature of Roman politics. Here we can agree; no one would offer Shakespeare's play as evidence of what the historical Caesar said or did. But surely the view that the concept of theme is meaningless and that a work tells us only about imaginary creatures is a desperate one. We *can* say that we see in *Julius Caesar* the fall of power, or (thinking of Brutus) the vulnerability of idealism, or some such thing.

To the reply that these are mere truisms, we can counter: Yes, but the truisms are presented in such a way that they take on life and become a part of us rather than remain things of which we say, "I've heard it said, and I guess it's so." The play offers instruction, in a pleasant and persuasive way. And surely we are in no danger of equating the play with the theme that we sense underlies it. We recognize that the play presents the theme with such detail that our statement is only a wedge to help us enter into the play.

Some critics (influenced by Aristotle's statement that a drama is an imitation of an action) use **action** as if it were equivalent to theme. In this sense, the action is the underlying happening—the inner happening—for example, "the enlightenment of a character," "the coming of unhappiness to a character," or "the finding of the self by self-surrender." It might be said that the theme of *Macbeth* is embodied in words that Macbeth himself utters: "Blood will have blood." This is not to say that these words and no other words embody the theme or the action; it is only to say that these words seem to the writer (and, if the essay is effective, to the reader) to bring us close to the center of the play.

Plot

Plot is variously defined, sometimes as the equivalent of *story* (in this sense, a synopsis of *Julius Caesar* has the same plot as *Julius Caesar*), but more often, and more usefully, as the dramatist's particular *arrangement of the story*. Thus, because Shakespeare's *Julius Caesar* begins with a scene dramatizing an encounter between plebeians and tribunes, its plot is different from that of a play on Julius Caesar in which such a scene (not necessary to the story) is omitted.

Handbooks on drama often suggest that a plot (an arrangement of happenings) should have a **rising action**, a **climax**, and a **falling action**. This sort of plot can be diagrammed as a pyramid: The tension rises through complications or **crises** to a climax, at which point the climax is the apex, and the tension allegedly slackens as we witness the **dénouement** (literally, *unknotting*). Shakespeare sometimes used a pyramidal structure, placing his climax neatly in the middle of what seems to us to be the third of five acts. In *Hamlet,* the protagonist proves to his own satisfaction Claudius's guilt in 3.2, with the play within the play, but almost immediately he begins to worsen his position by failing to kill Claudius when he is an easy target (3.3) and by contaminating himself with the murder of Polonius (3.4). In *Romeo and Juliet*, the first half shows Romeo winning Juliet; however, when in 3.1 Romeo kills Juliet's cousin Tybalt, Romeo sets in motion the second half of the play, the losing of Juliet and of his own life.

Of course, no law demands such a structure, and a hunt for the pyramid usually causes the hunter to overlook all the crises but the middle one. William Butler Yeats once suggestively diagrammed a good plot, not as a pyramid, but as a line moving diagonally upward, punctuated by several crises. Perhaps it is sufficient to say that a good plot has its moments of tension, but their location will vary with the play. They are the product of **conflict**, but it should be noted that not all conflict produces tension; there is conflict but little tension in a baseball game when the home team is ahead 10–0 and a pinch hitter comes to bat in the bottom of the ninth inning with two out and no one on base.

Regardless of how a plot is diagrammed, the **exposition** is that part that tells the audience what it has to know about the past, the **antecedent action**. Two gossiping servants who reveal that, after a year away in Paris, the young master is coming home tomorrow with a new wife are giving the audience the exposition. However, the exposition may also extend far into the play, coming to light in small, explosive revelations.

Exposition has been discussed as though it consists simply of informing the audience about events, but exposition can do much more. It can give us an understanding of the characters who themselves are talking about other characters, it can evoke a mood, and it can generate tension. When we summarize the opening act by treating it as "mere exposition," we are probably losing what is dramatic in it.

Exposition usually includes **foreshadowing**. Details given in the exposition, which we may at first take as mere background, often turn out to be highly relevant to later developments. For instance, in the very short first scene of *Macbeth*, the witches introduce the name of Macbeth, but, in such words as "Fair is foul" and "when the battle's lost and won," they also give glimpses of what will happen: Macbeth will become foul, and though he will seem to win (he becomes king), he will lose the most important battle. Similarly, during the exposition in the second scene, we learn that Macbeth has loyally defeated Cawdor, who betrayed King Duncan, and Macbeth has been given Cawdor's title. Later, we will find that, like Cawdor, Macbeth betrays Duncan. That is, in giving us the background about Cawdor, the exposition also tells us (though we don't know it when we first see or read the play) something about what will happen to Macbeth.

In writing about an aspect of plot, you may want to consider the following approaches:

- Is the plot improbable? If so, is the play therefore weak?
- Does a scene that might at first seem unimportant or even irrelevant serve an important function?
- If certain actions that could be shown onstage take place offstage, is there a reason? (A good way to approach this sort of question is to think of what your own reaction would be if the action were shown onstage.)

- If there are several conflicts—for example, between pairs of lovers or between parents and their children and also between the parents themselves—how are these conflicts related? Are they parallel? Or are they contrasting?
- Does the arrangement of scenes have a structure? For instance, do the scenes depict a rise and then a fall?
- Does the plot seem satisfactorily concluded? Are there loose threads? If so, is the apparent lack of a complete resolution a weakness in the play? Or does it serve a function?

Gestures

The language of a play, broadly conceived, includes the **gestures** that the characters make and the settings in which they make them. As Ezra Pound said, "The medium of drama is not words, but persons moving about on a stage using words." Because plays are meant to be seen, you'll want to make every effort to visualize the action when you read a play. Ibsen is getting at something important when he tells us in a stage direction that Nora "walks cautiously over to the door to the study and listens." Her silent actions tell us as much about her as many of her speeches do.

Gestures can be interpreted even more broadly: The mere fact that a character enters, leaves, or does not enter may be highly significant. John Russell Brown comments on the actions and the absence of certain words that in *Hamlet* convey the growing separation between King Claudius and his wife, Gertrude:

> Their first appearance together with a public celebration of marriage is a large and simple visual effect, and Gertrude's close concern for her son suggests a simple, and perhaps unremarkable modification. . . . But Claudius enters without Gertrude for his "Prayer Scene" (3.2) and, for the first time, Gertrude enters without him for the Closet Scene (3.4) and is left alone, again for the first time, when Polonius hides behind the arras. Thereafter earlier accord is revalued by an increasing separation, often poignantly silent and unexpected. When Claudius calls Gertrude to leave with him after Hamlet has dragged off Polonius' body, she makes no reply; twice more he urges her and she is still silent. But he does not remonstrate or question; rather he speaks of his own immediate concerns and, far from supporting her with assurances, becomes more aware of his own fears:
>
> > O, come away!
> > My soul is full of discord and dismay. (4.1.44–45)
>
> Emotion has been so heightened that it is remarkable that they leave together without further words. The audience has been aware of a new distance between Gertrude and Claudius, of her immobility and silence, and of his self-concern, haste, and insistence.[2]

Setting

Drama of the nineteenth and early twentieth centuries (especially the plays of Henrik Ibsen, Anton Chekhov, and George Bernard Shaw) is often thought to be

---

[2]John Russell Brown, *Shakespeare's Plays in Performance* (New York: St. Martin's, 1967), 139.

"realistic," but even a realistic playwright or stage designer selects from among many available materials. A **realistic setting** (indication of the **locale**), then, can say a great deal, and it can even serve as a symbol. Over and over again in Ibsen, we find the realistic setting of a nineteenth-century drawing room, with its heavy draperies and its bulky furniture, helping to convey Ibsen's vision of a bourgeois world that oppresses the individual who struggles to affirm other values.

Twentieth-century dramatists are often explicit about the symbolic qualities of the setting. Here is an example from Eugene O'Neill's *Desire Under the Elms;* only a part of the initial stage direction is given:

> The house is in good condition but in need of paint. Its walls are a sickly gray-ish, the green of the shutters faded. Two enormous elms are on each side of the house. They bend their trailing branches down over the roof. They appear to protect and at the same time subdue. There is a sinister maternity in their aspect, a crushing, jealous absorption. . . . They are like exhausted women resting their sagging breasts and hands and hair on its roof.

Not surprisingly, the action in the play includes deeds of "sinister maternity" (a mother kills her infant) and "jealous absorption."

In *The Glass Menagerie* Tennessee Williams tells us that

> the apartment faces an alley and is entered by a fire-escape, a structure whose name is a touch of accidental poetic truth, for all of these huge build-ings are always burning with the slow and implacable fires of human desperation.

Death of a Salesman opens with a long stage direction that includes this state-ment: "Before us is the Salesman's house. We are aware of towering, angular shapes behind it, surrounding it on all sides." Later, we will understand that this setting is a way of conveying Willy's sense that he is hemmed in, oppressed.

Characterization and Motivation

Characterization, or personality, is defined, as in fiction (see pages 351–52), by what the characters do (a stage direction tells us that "Nora dances more and more wildly"), by what they say (she asks her husband to play the piano), by what others say about them, and by the setting in which they move. The charac-ters are also defined in part by other characters whom they in some degree resemble or from whom they in some degree differ. Hamlet, Laertes, and Fortinbras have each lost a father, but Hamlet spares the praying King Claudius, whereas Laertes, seeking vengeance on Hamlet for murdering Laertes's father, says he would cut Hamlet's throat in church. Hamlet meditates about the nature of action, but Fortinbras leads the Norwegians in a military campaign and ultimately acquires Denmark.

Other plays also provide examples of **foils**, or characters who are structured to create a comparison that heightens our understanding of each character. Macbeth and Banquo both hear prophecies, but they act and react differently; Brutus is one kind of assassin, and Cassius another, and Casca still another. Any analysis of a character, then, will probably have to take into account, in some degree, the other characters who help to show what he or she is, and who thus help to set forth his or her **motivation** (grounds for action, inner drives, goals).

✔**CHECKLIST:** *Getting Ideas for Writing Arguments about Plays*

Plot and Conflict

☐ Does the exposition introduce elements that will be ironically fulfilled? During the exposition, do you perceive things differently from the way the characters perceive them?

☐ Are certain happenings or situations recurrent? If so, what significance do you attach to them?

☐ If there is more than one plot, do the plots seem to be related? Is one plot clearly the main plot and another a sort of subplot, a minor variation on the theme?

☐ Do any scenes strike you as irrelevant?

☐ Are certain scenes so strongly foreshadowed that you anticipated them? If so, did the happenings in those scenes merely fulfill your expectations, or did they also surprise you?

☐ What kinds of conflict are there? Is one character pitted against another, one group against another, or one part of a personality against another part in the same person?

☐ How is the conflict resolved? Is the conflict resolved by an unambiguous triumph of one side or by a triumph that is in some degree a loss for the triumphant side? Do you find the resolution satisfying, or unsettling, or what? Why?

Character

☐ A dramatic character is not likely to be thoroughly realistic, a copy of someone we might know. Still, we can ask if the character is consistent and coherent. We can also ask whether the character is complex or a rather simple representative of some human type.

☐ How is the character defined? Consider what the character says and does, what others say about him or her, and what others do to him or her. Also consider other characters who more or less resemble the character in question; the similarities—and the differences—may be significant.

☐ How trustworthy are the characters when they characterize themselves? When they characterize others?

☐ Do characters change as the play goes on, or do we simply know them better at the end?

☐ What do you make of the minor characters? Are they merely necessary to the plot, or are they foils to other characters? Or do they serve some other function?

☐ If a character is tragic, does the tragedy seem to proceed from a moral flaw, from an intellectual error, from the malice of others, from sheer chance, or from some combination of these factors?

☐ What are the character's goals? To what degree do you sympathize with them? If a character is comic, do you laugh *with* or *at* the character?

☐ Do you think the characters are adequately motivated?

☐ Is a given character so meditative that you feel he or she is engaged less in a dialogue with others than in a dialogue with the self? If so, do you feel that this character is to some extent a spokesperson for the author, commenting not only on the world within the play but also on the outside world?

Nonverbal Language

☐ If the playwright does not provide full stage directions, try to imagine for at least one scene what gestures and tones might accompany each speech. (The first scene is usually a good one to try your hand at.)

☐ What do you make of the setting? Does it help to reveal character? Do changes of scene strike you as symbolic? If so, symbolic of what?

Thinking about a Film Version of a Play

Although one might at first think that a film version of a play is pretty much the play caught on film, as soon as one realizes that movies use such techniques as close-ups and high and low angle shots (the action is seen from above or below), one realizes that the film version of a play can be very different from the stage version, even though in both forms a story is told by means of actors. In Laurence Olivier's *Hamlet* (1944), dream-like dissolves (the shot fades into the background while a new shot appears to emerge from beneath it) suggest the prince's irresoluteness. Or consider the use of black-and-white versus color film; Olivier made Shakespeare's *Henry V* (1944) in color but made *Hamlet* in black and white because, in Olivier's view, color conveyed a splendor appropriate to England's heroic history, whereas black and white seemed more suited to somber tragedy.

Filmmakers customarily "open out" plays, giving us skies, beaches, city streets, and so forth. In Olivier's *Hamlet*, we get shots of the sea and the sky. The camera descends from a great height just before Hamlet delivers his first soliloquy, and when the Ghost leaves at 1.5.96, the camera soars into the air, as though with the Ghost, and then, from above, the camera shows Hamlet fainting at the battlements. Even when the camera shows us scenes within the palace, it opens out the play by panning and traveling through long, empty corridors and over staircases, suggesting Hamlet's irresolute mind. (Kenneth Branagh's film version of *Hamlet* [1996] is very different; for a student's discussion of this film, see the essay by Will Saretta that appears on page 764.)

In the 1985 film (for television) version of *Death of a Salesman*, with Dustin Hoffman, perhaps the most impressive example of opening out the play comes at the very beginning, when the screen credits are given: We read the words while we see Willy, through the windshield of his car, driving home. Other examples of opening out the play show Willy walking the streets, muttering to strangers, and at least one scene shows the outside of Willy's house, with its paint peeling.

The 1987 film version of *The Glass Menagerie,* directed by Paul Newman, may suffer in part because the camera is not adventurous enough. Much of the play is shot in close-up, with the result that this film of Tennessee Williams's "memory play" has a realism and an in-your-face quality that is at odds with the dreaminess and fragility of the play. A stage production—usually set within a proscenium and making use of evidently theatrical lighting—has an illusionary or unrealistic quality that is appropriate to Williams's play, in which a narrator (Tom) conjures up scenes. Newman gives us almost all of Williams's dialogue, but he loses almost all of the magic of the play.

Getting Ready to Write about a Filmed Play

A mastery of the terminology does not make anyone a perceptive film critic, but it helps writers communicate their perceptions to readers. Probably an essay on a film will not be primarily about the use of establishing shots or wipes; rather, it will be about the reasons why a particular film pleases or displeases, succeeds or fails, seems significant or insignificant; and, in discussing these large matters, it is sometimes necessary (or at least economical) to use common technical terms. Large matters are often determined in part by such seemingly small matters as the distance of the camera from its subject or the way in which transitions are made, and one may as well use the conventional terms. However, a filmmaker's technique and technology alone cannot make a first-rate film. An idea, a personal vision, a theme must be embodied in all that is flashed on the screen.

Writing an essay about a new film—one not yet available for study on DVD—presents difficulties that are not encountered when we are writing about stories, plays, or poems. Because we experience film in a darkened room, we cannot easily take notes, and, because the film may be shown only once, we cannot always take another look at passages that puzzle us. When brief notes can be taken in the dark, however, it is best to amplify them as soon as light is available, while you still know what the scrawls mean. If you can see the film more than once, do so, and if the script has been published, study it. Draft your paper as soon as possible after your first viewing, and then see the film again. You can sometimes check hazy memories of certain scenes and techniques with fellow viewers. Even with multiple viewings and the aid of friends, it is almost impossible to get all the details right; it is best for the writer to be humble and for the reader to be tolerant.

Reminder: For a sample essay by a student, see the essay on Kenneth Branagh's *Hamlet,* which appears at the end of this chapter.

✔ CHECKLIST: *Writing about a Filmed Play*

Preliminaries

☐ Is the title of the film the same as the title of the play? If not, what is implied?

Dramatic Adaptations

☐ Does the film closely follow the original play and neglect the potentialities of the camera? Or does it so revel in cinematic devices that it distorts the original?

☐ Does the film do violence to the theme of the original? Is the film better than its source? Are additions or omissions due to the medium or to a crude or faulty interpretation of the original?

Plot and Character

☐ Can film deal as effectively with inner action—mental processes—as with external, physical action? In a given film, how is the inner action conveyed? Olivier used voice-over for parts of Hamlet's soliloquies—that is, we hear Hamlet's voice, but his lips do not move.

☐ Are shots and sequences adequately developed, or do they seem jerky? (A shot may be jerky by being extremely brief or at an odd angle; a sequence may be jerky by using discontinuous images or fast cuts. Sometimes, of course, jerkiness may be desirable.) If such cinematic techniques as wipes, dissolves, and slow motion are used, are they meaningful and effective?

☐ Are the characters believable?

☐ Are the actors appropriately cast?

Sound Track

☐ Does the sound track offer more than realistic dialogue? Is the music appropriate and functional? (Music may, among other things, imitate natural sounds, give a sense of locale or of ethnic group, suggest states of mind, provide ironic commentary, or—by repetition—help establish connections.) Are volume, tempo, and pitch—whether of music or of such sounds as the wind blowing or cars moving—used to stimulate emotions?

Student Writing Portfolio

COMPARISON PAPER

Writing a Comparison Paper

Comparison provides a popular means of generating an analytical paper. Bringing together two or more literary works encourages you to think about the relationships that can be created between authors, texts, and ideas. Comparing and contrasting texts allows you to see each text with new eyes. This form of critical thinking puts each text into a new context—the context of the other text—and reveals ideas that may be hidden when a text is considered in isolation. Writing a comparison paper allows you to explore how ideas are developed differently in two texts, how themes may work across texts to connect them, and how literary elements are used similarly or differently in two texts. Comparison/contrast allows you to stretch your thinking about a text by putting it into a relationship.

A comparison/contrast assignment asks for juxtaposition. The term "juxtapose" captures the idea of bringing two texts together, placing them side by side, and seeing how they resonate. Rather than thinking of comparing texts (finding similarities between them) and then contrasting texts (finding differences between them), think of putting the texts into a dynamic relationship. For example, you can think of the two texts as if they were talking to each other: What would they argue about; what would they agree on? Or, you can think of connecting the texts by asking where, why, and how the two texts connect. In juxtaposition, you create the relationship between the texts, explaining what connections are most important.

Before we explore one student's writing process for her comparison paper, let's look at the two selections that Yuki Chen was asked to compare: two versions of the same plot, as written and rewritten by Susan Glaspell in her play, *Trifles*, and in her short story, "A Jury of Her Peers."

SUSAN GLASPELL

Susan Glaspell (1876–1948) was born in Davenport, Iowa, and was educated at Drake University in Des Moines. In 1903, she married the novelist, poet, and playwright George Cram Cook and, with Cook and other writers, actors, and artists, in 1915 founded the Provincetown Players, a group that remained vital until 1929. Glaspell wrote Trifles *(1916) for the Provincetown Players, and she also wrote stories, novels, and a biography of her husband. In 1931, she won a Pulitzer Prize for* Alison's House, *a play about the family of a deceased poet who in some ways resembles Emily Dickinson.*

Trifles

SCENE: *The kitchen in the now abandoned farmhouse of* JOHN WRIGHT, *a gloomy kitchen, and left without having been put in order—unwashed pans under the sink, a loaf of bread outside the breadbox, a dish towel on the table—other signs of incompleted work. At the rear the outer door opens, and the* SHERIFF *comes in, followed by the* COUNTY ATTORNEY *and* HALE. *The* SHERIFF *and* HALE *are men in middle life, the* COUNTY ATTORNEY *is a young man; all are much bundled up and go at once to the stove. They are followed by the two women—the* SHERIFF'S WIFE *first; she is a slight wiry woman, a thin nervous face.* MRS. HALE *is larger and would ordinarily be called more comfortable looking, but she is disturbed now and looks fearfully about as she enters. The women have come in slowly and stand close together near the door.*

COUNTY ATTORNEY [*rubbing his hands*]: This feels good. Come up to the fire, ladies.

MRS. PETERS [*after taking a step forward*]: I'm not—cold.

SHERIFF [*unbuttoning his overcoat and stepping away from the stove as if to the beginning of official business*]: Now, Mr. Hale, before we move things about, you explain to Mr. Henderson just what you saw when you came here yesterday morning.

COUNTY ATTORNEY: By the way, has anything been moved? Are things just as you left them yesterday?

SHERIFF [*looking about*]: It's just the same. When it dropped below zero last night, I thought I'd better send Frank out this morning to make a fire for us— no use getting pneumonia with a big case on; but I told him not to touch anything except the stove—and you know Frank.

COUNTY ATTORNEY: Somebody should have been left here yesterday.

SHERIFF: Oh—yesterday. When I had to send Frank to Morris Center for that man who went crazy—I want you to know I had my hands full yesterday. I knew you could get back from Omaha by today, and as long as I went over everything here myself—

COUNTY ATTORNEY: Well, Mr. Hale, tell just what happened when you came here yesterday morning.

HALE: Harry and I had started to town with a load of potatoes. We came along the road from my place; and as I got here, I said, "I'm going to see if I can't get Harry and I had started to town John Wright to go in with me on a party telephone." I spoke to Wright about it once before, and he

The original Provincetown Players production (1916) of *Trifles*. The New York Public Library/Art Resource, NY.

put me off, saying folks talked too much anyway, and all he asked was peace and quiet—I guess you know about how much he talked himself; but I thought maybe if I went to the house and talked about it before his wife, though I said to Harry that I didn't know as what his wife wanted made much difference to John—

COUNTY ATTORNEY: Let's talk about that later, Mr. Hale. I do want to talk about that, but tell now just what happened when you got to the house.

HALE: I didn't hear or see anything; I knocked at the door, and still it was all quiet inside. I knew they must be up, it was past eight o'clock. So I knocked again, and I thought I heard somebody say, "Come in." I wasn't sure, I'm not sure yet, but I opened the door—this door [*indicating the door by which the two women are still standing*], and there in that rocker—[*pointing to it*] sat Mrs. Wright. [*They all look at the rocker.*]

COUNTY ATTORNEY: What—was she doing?

HALE: She was rockin' back and forth. She had her apron in her hand and was kind of—pleating it.

COUNTY ATTORNEY: And how did she—look?

HALE: Well, she looked queer.

COUNTY ATTORNEY: How do you mean—queer?

HALE: Well, as if she didn't know what she was going to do next. And kind of done up.

COUNTY ATTORNEY: How did she seem to feel about your coming?

HALE: Why, I don't think she minded—one way or other. She didn't pay much attention. I said, "How do, Mrs. Wright, it's cold, ain't it?" And she said, "Is it?"—and went on kind of pleating at her apron. Well, I was surprised; she didn't ask me to come up to the stove, or to set down, but just sat there, not even looking at me, so I said, "I want to see John." And then she—laughed. I guess you would call it a laugh. I thought of Harry and the team outside, so I said a little sharp: "Can't I see John?" "No," she says, kind o' dull like. "Ain't he home?" says I. "Yes," says she, "he's home." "Then why can't I see him?" I asked her, out of patience. "'Cause he's dead," says she. "*Dead?*" says I. She just nodded her head, not getting a bit excited, but rockin' back and forth. "Why—where is he?" says I, not knowing what to say. She just pointed upstairs—like that [*himself pointing to the room above*]. I got up, with the idea of going up there. I walked from there to here—then I says, "Why, what did he die of?" "He died of a rope around his neck," says she, and just went on pleatin' at her apron. Well, I went out and called Harry. I thought I might—need help. We went upstairs, and there he was lyin'—

COUNTY ATTORNEY: I think I'd rather have you go into that upstairs, where you can point it all out. Just go on now with the rest of the story.

HALE: Well, my first thought was to get that rope off. I looked . . . [*Stops, his face twitches.*] . . . but Harry, he went up to him, and he said, "No, he's dead all right, and we'd better not touch anything." So we went back downstairs. She was still sitting that same way. "Has anybody been notified?" I asked. "No," says she, unconcerned. "Who did this, Mrs. Wright?" said Harry. He said it businesslike—and she stopped pleatin' of her apron. "I don't know," she says. "You don't *know?*" says Harry. "No," says she. "Weren't you sleepin' in the bed with him?" says Harry. "Yes," says she, "but I was on the inside." "Somebody slipped a rope round his neck and strangled him, and you didn't wake up?" says Harry. "I didn't wake up," she said after him. We must 'a looked as if we didn't see how that could be, for after a minute she said, "I sleep sound." Harry was going to ask her more questions, but I said maybe we ought to let her tell her story first to the coroner, or the sheriff, so Harry went fast as he could to Rivers' place, where there's a telephone.

COUNTY ATTORNEY: And what did Mrs. Wright do when she knew that you had gone for the coroner?

HALE: She moved from that chair to this over here . . . [*Pointing to a small chair in the corner.*] . . . and just sat there with her hands held together and looking down. I got a feeling that I ought to make some conversation, so I said I had come in to see if John wanted to put in a telephone, and at that she started to laugh, and then she stopped and looked at me— scared. [*The* COUNTY ATTORNEY, *who has had his notebook out, makes a note.*] I dunno, maybe it wasn't scared. I wouldn't like to say it was. Soon Harry got back, and then Dr. Lloyd came, and you, Mr. Peters, and so I guess that's all I know that you don't.

COUNTY ATTORNEY [*looking around*]: I guess we'll go upstairs first—and then out to the barn and around there. [*To the* SHERIFF.] You're convinced that there was nothing important here—nothing that would point to any motive?

SHERIFF: Nothing here but kitchen things. [*The* COUNTY ATTORNEY, *after again looking around the kitchen, opens the door of a cupboard closet. He gets up on a chair and looks on a shelf. Pulls his hand away, sticky.*]

COUNTY ATTORNEY: Here's a nice mess. [*The women draw nearer.*]

MRS. PETERS [*to the other woman*]: Oh, her fruit; it did freeze. [*To the* LAWYER.] She worried about that when it turned so cold. She said the fire'd go out and her jars would break.

SHERIFF: Well, can you beat the women! Held for murder and worryin' about her preserves.

COUNTY ATTORNEY: I guess before we're through she may have something more serious than preserves to worry about.

HALE: Well, women are used to worrying over trifles.

[*The two women move a little closer together.*]

COUNTY ATTORNEY [*with the gallantry of a young politician*]: And yet, for all their worries, what would we do without the ladies? [*The women do not unbend. He goes to the sink, takes a dipperful of water from the pail and, pouring it into a basin, washes his hands. Starts to wipe them on the roller towel, turns it for a cleaner place.*] Dirty towels! [*Kicks his foot against the pans under the sink.*] Not much of a housekeeper, would you say, ladies?

MRS. HALE [*stiffly*]: There's a great deal of work to be done on a farm.

COUNTY ATTORNEY: To be sure. And yet . . . [*With a little bow to her.*] . . . I know there are some Dickson county farmhouses which do not have such roller towels. [*He gives it a pull to expose its full length again.*]

MRS. HALE: Those towels get dirty awful quick. Men's hands aren't always as clean as they might be.

COUNTY ATTORNEY: Ah, loyal to your sex, I see. But you and Mrs. Wright were neighbors. I suppose you were friends, too.

MRS. HALE [*shaking her head*]: I've not seen much of her of late years. I've not been in this house—it's more than a year.

COUNTY ATTORNEY: And why was that? You didn't like her?

MRS. HALE: I liked her all well enough. Farmers' wives have their hands full, Mr. Henderson. And then—

COUNTY ATTORNEY: Yes—?

MRS. HALE [*looking about*]: It never seemed a very cheerful place.

COUNTY ATTORNEY: No—it's not cheerful. I shouldn't say she had the homemaking instinct.

MRS. HALE: Well, I don't know as Wright had, either.

COUNTY ATTORNEY: You mean that they didn't get on very well?

MRS. HALE: No, I don't mean anything. But I don't think a place'd be any cheerfuler for John Wright's being in it.

COUNTY ATTORNEY: I'd like to talk more of that a little later. I want to get the lay of things upstairs now. [*He goes to the left, where three steps lead to a stair door.*]

SHERIFF: I suppose anything Mrs. Peters does'll be all right. She was to take in some clothes for her, you know, and a few little things. We left in such a hurry yesterday.

COUNTY ATTORNEY: Yes, but I would like to see what you take, Mrs. Peters, and keep an eye out for anything that might be of use to us.

MRS. PETERS: Yes, Mr. Henderson.

[*The women listen to the men's steps on the stairs, then look about the kitchen.*]

MRS. HALE: I'd hate to have men coming into my kitchen, snooping around and criticizing. [*She arranges the pans under sink which the* LAWYER *had shoved out of place.*]

MRS. PETERS: Of course it's no more than their duty.

MRS. HALE: Duty's all right, but I guess that deputy sheriff that came out to make the fire might have got a little of this on. [*Gives the roller towel a pull.*] Wish I'd thought of that sooner. Seems mean to talk about her for not having things slicked up when she had to come away in such a hurry.

MRS. PETERS [*who has gone to a small table in the left rear corner of the room, and lifted one end of a towel that covers a pan*]: She had bread set. [*Stands still.*]

MRS. HALE [*eyes fixed on a loaf of bread beside the breadbox, which is on a low shelf at the other side of the room; moves slowly toward it*]: She was going to put this in there. [*Picks up loaf, then abruptly drops it. In a manner of returning to familiar things.*] It's a shame about her fruit. I wonder if it's all gone. [*Gets up on the chair and looks.*] I think there's some here that's all right, Mrs. Peters. Yes—here; [*Holding it toward the window.*] this is cherries, too. [*Looking again.*] I declare I believe that's the only one. [*Gets down, bottle in her hand. Goes to the sink and wipes it off on the outside.*] She'll feel awful bad after all her hard work in the hot weather. I remember the afternoon I put up my cherries last summer. [*She puts the bottle on the big kitchen table, center of the room, front table. With a sigh, is about to sit down in the rocking chair. Before she is seated realizes what chair it is; with a slow look at it, steps back. The chair, which she has touched, rocks back and forth.*]

MRS. PETERS: Well, I must get those things from the front room closet. [*She goes to the door at the right, but after looking into the other room steps back.*] You coming with me, Mrs. Hale? You could help me carry them. [*They go into the other room; reappear,* MRS. PETERS *carrying a dress and skirt,* MRS. HALE *following with a pair of shoes.*]

MRS. PETERS: My, it's cold in there. [*She puts the cloth on the big table, and hurries to the stove.*]

MRS. HALE [*examining the skirt*]: Wright was close. I think maybe that's why she kept so much to herself. She didn't even belong to the Ladies' Aid. I suppose she felt she couldn't do her part, and then you don't enjoy things when you feel shabby. She used to wear pretty clothes and be lively, when she was Minnie Foster, one of the town girls singing in the choir. But that—oh, that was thirty years ago. This all you was to take in?

MRS. PETERS: She said she wanted an apron. Funny thing to want, for there isn't much to get you dirty in jail, goodness knows. But I suppose just to make her feel more natural. She said they was in the top drawer in this cupboard. Yes, here. And then her little shawl that always hung behind the door. [*Opens stair door and looks.*] Yes, here it is. [*Quickly shuts door leading upstairs.*]

MRS. HALE [*abruptly moving toward her*]: Mrs. Peters?

MRS. PETERS: Yes, Mrs. Hale?

MRS. HALE: Do you think she did it?

MRS. PETERS [*in a frightened voice*]: Oh, I don't know.

MRS. HALE: Well, I don't think she did. Asking for an apron and her little shawl. Worrying about her fruit.

MRS. PETERS [*starts to speak, glances up, where footsteps are heard in the room above. In a low voice.*]: Mr. Peters says it looks bad for her. Mr. Henderson is awful sarcastic in speech, and he'll make fun of her sayin' she didn't wake up.

MRS. HALE: Well, I guess John Wright didn't wake when they was slipping that rope under his neck.

MRS. PETERS: No, it's strange. It must have been done awful crafty and still. They say it was such a—funny way to kill a man, rigging it all up like that.

MRS. HALE: That's just what Mr. Hale said. There was a gun in the house. He says that's what he can't understand.

MRS. PETERS: Mr. Henderson said coming out that what was needed for the case was a motive; something to show anger, or—sudden feeling.

MRS. HALE [*who is standing by the table*]: Well, I don't see any signs of anger around here. [*She puts her hand on the dish towel which lies on the table, stands looking down at the table, one half of which is clean, the other half messy.*] It's wiped here. [*Makes a move as if to finish work, then turns and looks at loaf of bread outside the breadbox. Drops towel. In that voice of coming back to familiar things.*] Wonder how they are finding things upstairs? I hope she had it a little more red-up up there. You know, it seems kind of sneaking. Locking her up in town and then coming out here and trying to get her own house to turn against her!

MRS. PETERS: But, Mrs. Hale, the law is the law.

MRS. HALE: I s'pose 'is. [*Unbuttoning her coat.*] Better loosen up your things, Mrs. Peters. You won't feel them when you go out.

[MRS. PETERS *takes off her fur tippet, goes to hang it on hook at the back of room, stands looking at the under part of the small corner table.*]

MRS. PETERS: She was piecing a quilt. [*She brings the large sewing basket, and they look at the bright pieces.*]

MRS. HALE: It's log cabin pattern. Pretty, isn't it? I wonder if she was goin' to quilt or just knot it?

[*Footsteps have been heard coming down the stairs. The* SHERIFF *enters, followed by* HALE *and the* COUNTY ATTORNEY.]

SHERIFF: They wonder if she was going to quilt it or just knot it. [*The men laugh, the women look abashed.*]

COUNTY ATTORNEY [*rubbing his hands over the stove*]: Frank's fire didn't do much up there, did it? Well, let's go out to the barn and get that cleared up.

[*The men go outside.*]

MRS. HALE [*resentfully*]: I don't know as there's anything so strange, our takin' up our time with little things while we're waiting for them to get the evidence. [*She sits down at the big table, smoothing out a block with decision.*] I don't see as it's anything to laugh about.

MRS. PETERS [*apologetically*]: Of course they've got awful important things on their minds. [*Pulls up a chair and joins* MRS. HALE *at the table.*]

MRS. HALE [*examining another block*]: Mrs. Peters, look at this one. Here, this is the one she was working on, and look at the sewing! All the rest of it has been so nice and even. And look at this! It's all over the place! Why, it looks as if she didn't know what she was about! [*After she has said this, they look at each other, then start to glance back at the door. After an instant* MRS. HALE *has pulled at a knot and ripped the sewing.*]

MRS. PETERS: Oh, what are you doing, Mrs. Hale?

MRS. HALE [*mildly*]: Just pulling out a stitch or two that's not sewed very good. [*Threading a needle.*] Bad sewing always made me fidgety.

MRS. PETERS [*nervously*]: I don't think we ought to touch things.

MRS. HALE: I'll just finish up this end. [*Suddenly stopping and leaning forward.*] Mrs. Peters?

MRS. PETERS: Yes, Mrs. Hale?

MRS. HALE: What do you suppose she was so nervous about?

MRS. PETERS: Oh—I don't know. I don't know as she was nervous. I sometimes sew awful queer when I'm just tired. [MRS. HALE *starts to say something, looks at* MRS. PETERS, *then goes on sewing.*] Well, I must get these things wrapped up. They may be through sooner than we think. [*Putting apron and other things together.*] I wonder where I can find a piece of paper, and string.

MRS. HALE: In that cupboard, maybe.

MRS. PETERS [*looking in cupboard*]: Why, here's a birdcage. [*Holds it up.*] Did she have a bird, Mrs. Hale?

MRS. HALE: Why, I don't know whether she did or not—I've not been here for so long. There was a man around last year selling canaries cheap, but I don't know as she took one; maybe she did. She used to sing real pretty herself.

MRS. PETERS [*glancing around*]: Seems funny to think of a bird here. But she must have had one, or why should she have a cage? I wonder what happened to it?

MRS. HALE: I s'pose maybe the cat got it.

MRS. PETERS: No, she didn't have a cat. She's got that feeling some people have about cats—being afraid of them. My cat got in her room, and she was real upset and asked me to take it out.

MRS. HALE: My sister Bessie was like that. Queer, ain't it?

MRS. PETERS [*examining the cage*]: Why, look at this door. It's broke. One hinge is pulled apart.

MRS. HALE [*looking, too*]: Looks as if someone must have been rough with it.

MRS. PETERS: Why, yes. [*She brings the cage forward and puts it on the table.*]

MRS. HALE: I wish if they're going to find any evidence they'd be about it. I don't like this place.

MRS. PETERS: But I'm awful glad you came with me, Mrs. Hale. It would be lonesome for me sitting here alone.

MRS. HALE: It would, wouldn't it? [*Dropping her sewing.*] But I tell you what I do wish, Mrs. Peters. I wish I had come over sometimes when *she* was here. I—[*Looking around the room.*]—wish I had.

MRS. PETERS: But of course you were awful busy, Mrs. Hale—your house and your children.

MRS. HALE: I could've come. I stayed away because it weren't cheerful—and that's why I ought to have come. I—I've never liked this place. Maybe because it's down in a hollow, and you don't see the road. I dunno what it is, but it's a lonesome place and always was. I wish I had come over to see Minnie Foster sometimes. I can see now—[*Shakes her head.*]

MRS. PETERS: Well, you mustn't reproach yourself, Mrs. Hale. Somehow we just don't see how it is with other folks until—something comes up.

MRS. HALE: Not having children makes less work—but it makes a quiet house, and Wright out to work all day, and no company when he did come in. Did you know John Wright, Mrs. Peters?

MRS. PETERS: Not to know him; I've seen him in town. They say he was a good
man.

MRS. HALE: Yes—good; he didn't drink, and kept his word as well as most, I guess,
and paid his debts. But he was a hard man, Mrs. Peters. Just to pass the
time of day with him. [*Shivers.*] Like a raw wind that gets to the bone.
[*Pauses, her eye falling on the cage.*] I should think she would 'a wanted
a bird. But what do you suppose went with it?

MRS. PETERS: I don't know, unless it got sick and died. [*She reaches over and swings
the broken door, swings it again; both women watch it.*]

MRS. HALE: You weren't raised round here, were you? [MRS. PETERS *shakes her head.*]
You didn't know—her?

MRS. PETERS: Not till they brought her yesterday.

MRS. HALE: She—come to think of it, she was kind of like a bird herself—real
sweet and pretty, but kind of timid and—fluttery. How—she—did—
change. [*Silence; then as if struck by a happy thought and relieved to get
back to everyday things.*] Tell you what, Mrs. Peters; why don't you take
the quilt in with you? It might take up her mind.

MRS. PETERS: Why, I think that's a real nice idea, Mrs. Hale. There couldn't possibly
be any objection to it, could there? Now, just what would I take? I
wonder if her patches are in here—and her things. [*They look in the
sewing basket.*]

MRS. HALE: Here's some red. I expect this has got sewing things in it. [*Brings out a
fancy box.*] What a pretty box. Looks like something somebody would
give you. Maybe her scissors are in here. [*Opens box. Suddenly puts her
hand to her nose.*] Why—[MRS. PETERS *bends nearer, then turns her face
away.*] There's something wrapped up in this piece of silk.

MRS. PETERS: Why, this isn't her scissors.

MRS. HALE [*lifting the silk*]: Oh, Mrs. Peters—it's—[MRS. PETERS *bends closer.*]

MRS. PETERS: It's the bird.

MRS. HALE [*jumping up*]: But, Mrs. Peters—look at it. Its neck! Look at its neck! It's
all—other side *to*.

MRS. PETERS: Somebody—wrung—its neck.

[*Their eyes meet.* A look of growing comprehension of horror. Steps are heard
outside. MRS. HALE *slips box under quilt pieces, and sinks into her chair. Enter*
SHERIFF *and* COUNTY ATTORNEY. MRS. PETERS *rises.*]

COUNTY ATTORNEY [*as one turning from serious things to little pleasantries*]: Well,
ladies, have you decided whether she was going to quilt it or knot it?

MRS. PETERS: We think she was going to—knot it.

COUNTY ATTORNEY: Well, that's interesting, I'm sure. [*Seeing the birdcage.*] Has the
bird flown?

MRS. HALE [*putting more quilt pieces over the box*]: We think the—cat got it.

COUNTY ATTORNEY [*preoccupied*]: Is there a cat?

[MRS. HALE *glances in a quick covert way at* MRS. PETERS.]

MRS. PETERS: Well, not now. They're superstitious, you know. They leave.

COUNTY ATTORNEY [*to* SHERIFF, *continuing an interrupted conversation*]: No sign at
all of anyone having come from the outside. Their own rope. Now let's
go up again and go over it piece by piece. [*They start upstairs.*] It would
have to have been someone who knew just the—[MRS. PETERS *sits down.*

The two women sit there not looking at one another, but as if peering into something and at the same time holding back. When they talk now, it is the manner of feeling their way over strange ground, as if afraid of what they are saying, but as if they cannot help saying it.]

MRS. HALE: She liked the bird. She was going to bury it in that pretty box.

MRS. PETERS [*in a whisper*]: When I was a girl—my kitten—there was a boy took a hatchet, and before my eyes—and before I could get there—[*Covers her face an instant.*] If they hadn't held me back, I would have—[*Catches herself, looks upstairs where steps are heard, falters weakly.*]—hurt him.

MRS. HALE [*with a slow look around her*]: I wonder how it would seem never to have had any children around. [*Pause.*] No, Wright wouldn't like the bird—a thing that sang. She used to sing. He killed that, too.

MRS. PETERS [*moving uneasily*]: We don't know who killed the bird.

MRS. HALE: I knew John Wright.

MRS. PETERS: It was an awful thing was done in this house that night, Mrs. Hale. Killing a man while he slept, slipping a rope around his neck that choked the life out of him.

MRS. HALE: His neck. Choked the life out of him.

[*Her hand goes out and rests on the birdcage.*]

MRS. PETERS [*with a rising voice*]: We don't know who killed him. We don't *know.*

MRS. HALE [*her own feeling not interrupted*]: If there'd been years and years of nothing, then a bird to sing to you, it would be awful—still, after the bird was still.

MRS. PETERS [*something within her speaking*]: I know what stillness is. When we homesteaded in Dakota, and my first baby died—after he was two years old, and me with no other then—

MRS. HALE [*moving*]: How soon do you suppose they'll be through, looking for the evidence?

MRS. PETERS: I know what stillness is. [*Pulling herself back.*] The law has got to punish crime, Mrs. Hale.

MRS. HALE [*not as if answering that*]: I wish you'd seen Minnie Foster when she wore a white dress with blue ribbons and stood up there in the choir and sang. [*A look around the room.*] Oh, I *wish* I'd come over here once in a while! That was a crime! That was a crime! Who's going to punish that?

MRS. PETERS [*looking upstairs*]: We mustn't—take on.

MRS. HALE: I might have known she needed help! I know how things can be—for women. I tell you, it's queer, Mrs. Peters. We live close together and we live far apart. We all go through the same things—it's all just a different kind of the same thing. [*Brushes her eyes, noticing the bottle of fruit, reaches out for it.*] If I was you, I wouldn't tell her her fruit was gone. Tell her it *ain't.* Tell her it's all right. Take this in to prove it to her. She—she may never know whether it was broke or not.

MRS. PETERS [*takes the bottle, looks about for something to wrap it in; takes petticoat from the clothes brought from the other room, very nervously begins winding this around the bottle. In a false voice*]: My, it's a good thing the men couldn't hear us. Wouldn't they just laugh! Getting all stirred up over a little thing like a—dead canary. As if that could have anything to do with—with—wouldn't they *laugh!*

[*The men are heard coming downstairs.*]

MRS. HALE [*under her breath*]: Maybe they would—maybe they wouldn't.

COUNTY ATTORNEY : No, Peters, it's all perfectly clear except a reason for doing it. But you know juries when it comes to women. If there was some definite thing. Something to show—something to make a story about— a thing that would connect up with this strange way of doing it.

[*The women's eyes meet for an instant. Enter* HALE *from outer door.*]

HALE: Well, I've got the team around. Pretty cold out there.

COUNTY ATTORNEY: I'm going to stay here awhile by myself. [*To the* SHERIFF.] You can send Frank out for me, can't you? I want to go over everything. I'm not satisfied that we can't do better.

SHERIFF: Do you want to see what Mrs. Peters is going to take in?

[*The* LAWYER *goes to the table, picks up the apron, laughs.*]

COUNTY ATTORNEY: Oh I guess they're not very dangerous things the ladies have picked up. [*Moves a few things about, disturbing the quilt pieces which cover the box. Steps back.*] No, Mrs. Peters doesn't need supervising. For that matter, a sheriff's wife is married to the law. Ever think of it that way, Mrs. Peters?

MRS. PETERS: Not—just that way.

SHERIFF [*chuckling*]: Married to the law. [*Moves toward the other room.*] I just want you to come in here a minute, George. We ought to take a look at these windows.

COUNTY ATTORNEY [*scoffingly*]: Oh, windows!

SHERIFF: We'll be right out, Mr. Hale.

[HALE *goes outside. The* SHERIFF *follows the* COUNTY ATTORNEY *into the other room. Then* MRS. HALE *rises, hands tight together, looking intensely at* MRS. PETERS, *whose eyes take a slow turn, finally meeting* MRS. HALE'S. *A moment* MRS. HALE *holds her, then her own eyes point the way to where the box is concealed. Suddenly* MRS. PETERS *throws back quilt pieces and tries to put the box in the bag she is wearing. It is too big. She opens box, starts to take the bird out, cannot touch it, goes to pieces, stands there helpless. Sound of a knob turning in the other room.* MRS. HALE *snatches the box and puts it in the pocket of her big coat. Enter* COUNTY ATTORNEY *and* SHERIFF.]

COUNTY ATTORNEY [*facetiously*]: Well, Henry, at least we found out that she was not going to quilt it. She was going to—what is it you call it, ladies?

MRS. HALE [*her hand against her pocket*]: We call it—knot it, Mr. Henderson.

CURTAIN

[1916]

A Jury of Her Peers

When Martha Hale opened the storm-door and got a cut of the north wind, she ran back for her big woolen scarf. As she hurriedly wound that round her head her eye made a scandalized sweep of her kitchen. It was no ordinary thing that called her away—it was probably farther from ordinary than anything that had ever happened in Dickson County. But what her eye took in was that her kitchen was in no shape for leaving; her bread all ready for mixing, half the flour sifted and half unsifted.

She hated to see things half done; but she had been at that when the team from town stopped to get Mr. Hale, and then the sheriff came running in to say his wife wished Mrs. Hale would come too—adding, with a grin, that he guessed she was getting scarey and wanted another woman along. So she had dropped everything right where it was.

"Martha!" now came her husband's impatient voice. "Don't keep folks waiting out here in the cold."

She again opened the storm-door, and this time joined the three men and the one woman waiting for her in the big two-seated buggy.

5   After she had the robes tucked around her she took another look at the woman who sat beside her on the back seat. She had met Mrs. Peters the year before at the county fair, and the thing she remembered about her was that she didn't seem like a sheriffs wife. She was small and thin and didn't have a strong voice. Mrs. Gorman, sheriffs wife before Gorman went out and Peters came in, had a voice that somehow seemed to be backing up the law with every word. But if Mrs. Peters didn't look like a sheriffs wife, Peters made it up in looking like a sheriff. He was to a dot the kind of man who could get himself elected sheriff—a heavy man with a big voice, who was particularly genial with the law-abiding, as if to make it plain that he knew the difference between criminals and non-criminals. And right there it came into Mrs. Hale's mind, with a stab, that this man who was so pleasant and lively with all of them was going to the Wrights' now as a sheriff.

"The country's not very pleasant this time of year," Mrs. Peters at last ventured, as if she felt they ought to be talking as well as the men.

Mrs. Hale scarcely finished her reply, for they had gone up a little hill and could see the Wright place now, and seeing it did not make her feel like talking. It looked very lonesome this cold March morning. It had always been a lonesome-looking place. It was down in a hollow, and the poplar trees around it were lonesome-looking trees. The men were looking at it and talking about what had happened. The county attorney was bending to one side of the buggy, and kept looking steadily at the place as they drew up to it.

"I'm glad you came with me," Mrs. Peters said nervously, as the two women were about to follow the men in through the kitchen door.

Even after she had her foot on the door-step, her hand on the knob, Martha Hale had a moment of feeling she could not cross that threshold. And the reason it seemed she couldn't cross it now was simply because she hadn't crossed it before. Time and time again it had been in her mind, "I ought to go over and see Minnie Foster"—she still thought of her as Minnie Foster, though for twenty years she had been Mrs. Wright. And then there was always something to do and Minnie Foster would go from her mind. But *now* she could come.

10   The men went over to the stove. The women stood close together by the door. Young Henderson, the county attorney, turned around and said, "Come up to the fire, ladies."

Mrs. Peters look a step forward, then stopped. "I'm not—cold," she said.

And so the two women stood by the door, at first not even so much as looking around the kitchen.

The men talked for a minute about what a good thing it was the sheriff had sent his deputy out that morning to make a fire for them, and then Sheriff Peters stepped back from the stove, unbuttoned his outer coat, and leaned his hands on the kitchen table in a way that seemed to mark the beginning of official business. "Now, Mr. Hale," he said in a sort of semi-official voice, "before we move things about, you tell Mr. Henderson just what it was you saw when you came here yesterday morning."

The county attorney was looking around the kitchen.

15   "By the way," he said, "has anything been moved?" He turned to the sheriff. "Are things just as you left them yesterday?"

Peters looked from cupboard to sink; from that to a small worn rocker a little to one side of the kitchen table.

"It's just the same."

"Somebody should have been left here yesterday," said the county attorney.

"Oh—yesterday," returned the sheriff, with a little gesture as of yesterday having been more than he could bear to think of. "When I had to send Frank to Morris Center for that man who went crazy—let me tell you. I had my hands full *yesterday*. I knew you could get back from Omaha by to-day, George, and as long as I went over everything here myself—"

20   "Well, Mr. Hale," said the county attorney, in a way of letting what was past and gone go, "tell just what happened when you came here yesterday morning."

Mrs. Hale, still leaning against the door, had that sinking feeling of the mother whose child is about to speak a piece. Lewis often wandered along and got things mixed up in a story. She hoped he would tell this straight and plain, and not say unnecessary things that would just make things harder for Minnie Foster. He didn't begin at once, and she noticed that he looked queer—as if standing in that kitchen and having to tell what he had seen there yesterday morning made him almost sick.

"Yes, Mr. Hale?" the county attorney reminded.

"Harry and I had started to town with a load of potatoes," Mrs. Hale's husband began.

Harry was Mrs. Hale's oldest boy. He wasn't with them now, for the very good reason that those potatoes never got to town yesterday and he was taking them this morning, so he hadn't been home when the sheriff stopped to say he wanted Mr. Hale to come over to the Wright place and tell the county attorney his story there, where he could point it all out. With all Mrs. Hale's other emotions came the fear now that maybe Harry wasn't dressed warm enough—they hadn't any of them realized how that north wind did bite.

25   "We come along this road," Hale was going on, with a motion of his hand to the road over which they had just come, "and as we got in sight of the house I says to Harry, 'I'm goin' to see if I can't get John Wright to take a telephone.' You see," he explained to Henderson, "unless I can get somebody to go in with me they won't come out this branch road except for a price / can't pay. I'd spoke to Wright about it once before; but he put me off, saying folks talked too much anyway, and all he asked was peace and quiet—guess you know about how much he talked himself. But I thought maybe if I went to the house and talked about it before his wife, and said all the women-folks liked the telephones, and that in this lonesome stretch of road it would be a good thing—well, I said to Harry that that was what I was going to say—though I said at the same time that I didn't know as what his wife wanted made much difference to John—"

Now, there he was!—saying things he didn't need to say. Mrs. Hale tried to catch her husband's eye, but fortunately the county attorney interrupted with:

"Let's talk about that a little later, Mr. Hale. I do want to talk about that, but I'm anxious now to get along to just what happened when you got here."

When he began this time, it was very deliberately and carefully:

"I didn't see or hear anything. I knocked at the door. And still it was all quiet inside. I knew they must be up—it was past eight o'clock. So I knocked again, louder, and I thought I heard somebody say, 'Come in.' I wasn't sure—I'm not sure yet. But I opened the door—this door," jerking a hand toward the door by which the two women stood, "and there, in that rocker"—pointing to it—"sat Mrs. Wright."

30 Every one in the kitchen looked at the rocker. It came into Mrs. Hale's mind that that rocker didn't look in the least like Minnie Foster—the Minnie Foster of twenty years before. It was a dingy red, with wooden rungs up the back, and the middle run was gone, and the chair sagged to one side.

"How did she—look?" the county attorney was inquiring.

"Well," said Hale, "she looked—queer."

"How do you mean—queer?"

As he asked it he took out a note-book and pencil. Mrs. Hale did not like the sight of that pencil. She kept her eye fixed on her husband, as if to keep him from saying unnecessary things that would go into that notebook and make trouble.

35 Hale did speak guardedly, as if the pencil had affected him too.

"Well, as if she didn't know what she was going to do next. And kind of—done up."

"How did she seem to feel about your coming?"

"Why, I don't think she minded—one way or other. She didn't pay much attention. I said, 'Ho' do, Mrs. Wright? It's cold, ain't it?' And she said, 'Is it?'—and went on pleatin' at her apron.

"Well, I was surprised. She didn't ask me to come up to the stove, or to sit down, but just set there, not even lookin' at me. And so I said: 'I want to see John.'

40 "And then she—laughed. I guess you would call it a laugh.

"I thought of Harry and the team outside, so I said, a little sharp, 'Can I see John?' 'No,' says she—kind of dull like. 'Ain't he home?' says I. Then she looked at me. 'Yes,' says she, 'he's home.' 'Then why can't I see him?' I asked her, out of patience with her now. "Cause he's dead,' says she, just as quiet and dull—and fell to pleatin' her apron. 'Dead?' says I, like you do when you can't take in what you've heard.

"She just nodded her head, not getting a bit excited, but rockin' back and forth.

"'Why—where is he?' says I, not knowing *what* to say.

"She just pointed upstairs—like this"—pointing to the room above.

45 "I got up, with the idea of going up there myself. By this time I—didn't know what to do. I walked from there to here; then I says: 'Why, what did he die of?'

"'He died of a rope round his neck,' says she; and just went on pleatin' at her apron."

Hale stopped speaking, and stood staring at the rocker, as if he were still seeing the woman who had sat there the morning before. Nobody spoke; it was as if every one were seeing the woman who had sat there the morning before.

"And what did you do then?" the county attorney at last broke the silence.

"I went out and called Harry. I thought I might—need help. I got Harry in, and we went upstairs." His voice fell almost to a whisper. "There he was—lying over the—"

50 "I think I'd rather have you go into that upstairs," the county attorney interrupted, "where you can point it all out. Just go on now with the rest of the story."

"Well, my first thought was to get that rope off. It looked—"

He stopped, his face twitching.

"But Harry, he went up to him, and he said, 'No, he's dead all right, and we'd better not touch anything.' So we went downstairs.

"She was still sitting that same way. 'Has anybody been notified?' I asked. 'No,' says she, unconcerned.

55   "'Who did this, Mrs. Wright?' said Harry. He said it businesslike, and she stopped pleatin' at her apron. 'I don't know,' she says. 'You don't *know?*' says Harry. 'Weren't you sleepin' in the bed with him?' 'Yes,' says she, 'but I was on the inside.' 'Somebody slipped a rope round his neck and strangled him, and you didn't wake up?' says Harry. 'I didn't wake up,' she said after him.

"We may have looked as if we didn't see how that could be, for after a minute she said, 'I sleep sound.'

"Harry was going to ask her more questions, but I said maybe that weren't our business; maybe we ought to let her tell her story first to the coroner or the sheriff. So Harry went fast as he could over to High Road—the Rivers' place, where there's a telephone."

"And what did she do when she knew you had gone for the coroner?" The attorney got his pencil in his hand all ready for writing.

"She moved from that chair to this one over here"—Hale pointed to a small chair in the corner—"and just sat there with her hands held together and looking down. I got a feeling that I ought to make some conversation, so I said I had come in to see if John wanted to put in a telephone; and at that she started to laugh, and then she stopped and looked at me—scared."

60   At sound of a moving pencil the man who was telling the story looked up.

"I dunno—maybe it wasn't scared," he hastened; "I wouldn't like to say it was. Soon Harry got back, and then Dr. Lloyd came, and you, Mr. Peters, and so I guess that's all I know that you don't."

He said that last with relief, and moved a little, as if relaxing. Every one moved a little. The county attorney walked toward the stair door.

"I guess we'll go upstairs first—then out to the barn and around there."

He paused and looked around the kitchen.

65   "You're convinced there was nothing important here?" he asked the sheriff. "Nothing that would—point to any motive?"

The sheriff too looked all around, as if to re-convince himself.

"Nothing here but kitchen things," he said, with a little laugh for the insignificance of kitchen things.

The county attorney was looking at the cupboard—a peculiar, ungainly structure, half closet and half cupboard, the upper part of it being built in the wall, and the lower part just the old-fashioned kitchen cupboard. As if its queerness attracted him, he got a chair and opened the upper part and looked in. After a moment he drew his hand away sticky.

"Here's a nice mess," he said resentfully.

70   The two women had drawn nearer, and now the sheriff's wife spoke.

"Oh—her fruit," she said, looking to Mrs. Hale for sympathetic understanding. She turned back to the county attorney and explained: "She worried about that when it turned so cold last night. She said the fire would go out and her jars might burst."

Mrs. Peters' husband broke into a laugh.

"Well, can you beat the women! Held for murder, and worrying about her preserves!"

The young attorney set his lips.

75 　　"I guess before we're through with her she may have something more serious than preserves to worry about."

　　"Oh, well," said Mrs. Hale's husband, with good-natured superiority, "women are used to worrying over trifles."

　　The two women moved a little closer together. Neither of them spoke. The county attorney seemed suddenly to remember his manners—and think of his future.

　　"And yet," said he, with the gallantry of a young politician, "for all their worries, what would we do without the ladies?"

　　The women did not speak, did not unbend. He went to the sink and began washing his hands. He turned to wipe them on the roller towel—whirled it for a cleaner place.

80 　　"Dirty towels! Not much of a housekeeper, would you say, ladies?"

　　He kicked his foot against some dirty pans under the sink.

　　"There's a great deal of work to be done on a farm," said Mrs. Hale stiffly.

　　"To be sure. And yet"—with a little bow to her—"I know there are some Dickson County farm-houses that do not have such roller towels." He gave it a pull to expose its full length again.

　　"Those towels get dirty awful quick. Men's hands aren't always as clean as they might be."

85 　　"Ah, loyal to your sex, I see." he laughed. He stopped and gave her a keen look. "But you and Mrs. Wright were neighbors. I suppose you were friends, too."

　　Martha Hale shook her head.

　　"I've seen little enough of her of late years. I've not been in this house—it's more than a year."

　　"And why was that? You didn't like her?"

　　"I liked her well enough," she replied with spirit. "Farmers' wives have their hands full, Mr. Henderson. And then—" She looked around the kitchen.

90 　　"Yes?" he encouraged.

　　"It never seemed a very cheerful place," said she, more to herself than to him.

　　"No," he agreed; "I don't think any one would call it cheerful. I shouldn't say she had the home-making instinct."

　　"Well, I don't know as Wright had, either," she muttered.

　　"You mean they didn't get on very well?" he was quick to ask.

95 　　"No; I don't mean anything," she answered, with decision. As she turned a little away from him, she added: "But I don't think a place would be any the cheerfuler for John Wright's bein' in it."

　　"I'd like to talk to you about that a little later, Mrs. Hale," he said. "I'm anxious to get the lay of things upstairs now."

　　He moved toward the stair door, followed by the two men.

　　"I suppose anything Mrs. Peters does'll be all right?" the sheriff inquired. "She was to take in some clothes for her, you know—and a few little things. We left in such a hurry yesterday."

　　The county attorney looked at the two women whom they were leaving alone there among the kitchen things.

100 　　"Yes—Mrs. Peters," he said, his glance resting on the woman who was not Mrs. Peters, the big farmer woman who stood behind the sheriff's wife. "Of course Mrs. Peters is one of us," he said, in a manner of entrusting responsibility. "And keep your eye out, Mrs. Peters, for anything that might be of use. No telling; you women might come upon a clue to the motive—and that's the thing we need."

Mr. Hale rubbed his face after the fashion of a show man getting ready for a pleasantry.

"But would the women know a clue if they did come upon it?" he said; and, having delivered himself of this, he followed the others through the stair door.

The women stood motionless and silent, listening to the footsteps, first upon the stairs, then in the room above them.

Then, as if releasing herself from something strange, Mrs. Hale began to arrange the dirty pans under the sink, which the county attorney's disdainful push of the foot had deranged.

105   "I'd hate to have men comin' into my kitchen," she said testily—"snoopin' round and criticizin'."

"Of course it's no more than their duty," said the sheriff's wife, in her manner of timid acquiescence.

"Duty's all right," replied Mrs. Hale bluffly; "but I guess that deputy sheriff that come out to make the fire might have got a little of this on." She gave the roller towel a pull. "Wish I'd thought of that sooner! Seems mean to talk about her for not having things slicked up, when she had to come away in such a hurry."

She looked around the kitchen. Certainly it was not "slicked up." Her eye was held by a bucket of sugar on a low shelf. The cover was off the wooden bucket, and beside it was a paper bag—half full.

Mrs. Hale moved toward it.

110   "She was putting this in there," she said to herself—slowly.

She thought of the flour in her kitchen at home—half sifted, half not sifted. She had been interrupted, and had left things half done. What had interrupted Minnie Foster? Why had that work been left half done? She made a move as if to finish it,—unfinished things always bothered her,—and then she glanced around and saw that Mrs. Peters was watching her—and she didn't want Mrs. Peters to get that feeling she had got of work begun and then—for some reason—not finished.

"It's a shame about her fruit," she said, and walked toward the cupboard that the county attorney had opened, and got on the chair, murmuring: "I wonder if it's all gone."

It was a sorry enough looking sight, but "Here's one that's all right," she said at last. She held it toward the light. "This is cherries, too." She looked again. "I declare I believe that's the only one."

With a sigh, she got down from the chair, went to the sink, and wiped off the bottle.

115   "She'll feel awful bad, after all her hard work in the hot weather. I remember the afternoon I put up my cherries last summer."

She set the bottle on the table, and, with another sigh, started to sit down in the rocker. But she did not sit down. Something kept her from sitting down in that chair. She straightened—stepped back, and, half turned away, stood looking at it, seeing the woman who had sat there "pleatin' at her apron."

The thin voice of the sheriff's wife broke in upon her: "I must be getting those things from the front room closet." She opened the door into the other room, started in, stepped back. "You coming with me, Mrs. Hale?" she asked nervously. "You—you could help me get them."

They were soon back—the stark coldness of that shut-up room was not a thing to linger in.

120   "My!" said Mrs. Peters, dropping the things on the table and hurrying to the stove.

Mrs. Hale stood examining the clothes the woman who was being detained in town had said she wanted.

"Wright was close!" she exclaimed, holding up a shabby black skirt that bore the marks of much making over. "I think maybe that's why she kept so much to herself. I s'pose she felt she couldn't do her part; and then, you don't enjoy things when you feel shabby. She used to wear pretty clothes and be lively—when she was Minnie Foster, one of the town girls, singing in the choir. But that—oh, that was twenty years ago."

With a carefulness in which there was something tender, she folded the shabby clothes and piled them at one corner of the table. She looked up at Mrs. Peters, and there was something in the other woman's look that irritated her.

"She don't care," she said to herself. "Much difference it makes to her whether Minnie Foster had pretty clothes when she was a girl."

125   Then she looked again, and she wasn't so sure; in fact, she hadn't at any time been perfectly sure about Mrs. Peters. She had that shrinking manner, and yet her eyes looked as if they could see a long way into things.

"This all you was to take in?" asked Mrs. Hale.

"No," said the sheriffs wife; "she said she wanted an apron. Funny thing to want," she ventured in her nervous little way, "for there's not much to get you dirty in jail, goodness knows. But I suppose just to make her feel more natural. If you're used to wearing an apron—. She said they were in the bottom drawer of this cupboard. Yes—here they are. And then her little shawl that always hung on the stair door."

She took the small gray shawl from behind the door leading upstairs, and stood a minute looking at it.

Suddenly Mrs. Hale took a quick step toward the other woman.

130   "Mrs. Peters!"

"Yes, Mrs. Hale?"

"Do you think she—did it?"

A frightened look blurred the other thing in Mrs. Peters' eyes.

"Oh, I don't know," she said, in a voice that seemed to shrink away from the subject.

135   "Well, I don't think she did," affirmed Mrs. Hale stoutly. "Asking for an apron, and her little shawl. Worryin' about her fruit."

"Mr. Peters says—" Footsteps were heard in the room above; she stopped, looked up, then went on in a lowered voice: "Mr. Peters says—it looks bad for her. Mr. Henderson is awful sarcastic in a speech, and he's going to make fun of her saying she didn't—wake up."

For a moment Mrs. Hale had no answer. Then, "Well, I guess John Wright didn't wake up—when they was slippin' that rope under his neck," she muttered.

"No, it's *strange*," breathed Mrs. Peters. "They think it was such a—funny way to kill a man."

She began to laugh; at sound of the laugh, abruptly stopped.

140   "That's just what Mr. Hale said," said Mrs. Hale, in a resolutely natural voice. "There was a gun in the house. He says that's what he can't understand."

"Mr. Henderson said, coming out, that what was needed for the case was a motive. Something to show anger—or sudden feeling."

"Well, I don't see any signs of anger around here," said Mrs. Hale. "I don't—"

She stopped. It was as if her mind tripped on something. Her eye was caught by a dish-towel in the middle of the kitchen table. Slowly she moved toward the table. One half of it was wiped clean, the other half messy. Her eyes made a slow, almost unwilling turn to the bucket of sugar and the half empty bag beside it. Things begun—and not finished.

After a moment she stepped back, and said, in that manner of releasing herself:

145   "Wonder how they're finding things upstairs? I hope she had it a little more red up up there. You know,"—she paused, and feeling gathered,—"it seems kind of *sneaking:* locking her up in town and coming out here to get her own house to turn against her!"

"But, Mrs. Hale," said the sheriff's wife, "the law is the law."

"I s'pose 'tis," answered Mrs. Hale shortly.

She turned to the stove, saying something about that fire not being much to brag of. She worked with it a minute, and when she straightened up she said aggressively:

"The law is the law—and a bad stove is a bad stove. How'd you like to cook on this?"—pointing with the poker to the broken lining. She opened the oven door and started to express her opinion of the oven; but she was swept into her own thoughts, thinking of what it would mean, year after year, to have that stove to wrestle with. The thought of Minnie Foster trying to bake in that oven—and the thought of her never going over to see Minnie Foster—.

150   She was startled by hearing Mrs. Peters say: "A person gets discouraged—and loses heart."

The sheriff's wife had looked from the stove to the sink—to the pail of water which had been carried in from outside. The two women stood there silent, above them the footsteps of the men who were looking for evidence against the woman who had worked in that kitchen. That look of seeing into things, of seeing through a thing to something else, was in the eyes of the sheriff's wife now. When Mrs. Hale next spoke to her, it was gently:

"Better loosen up your things, Mrs. Peters. We'll not feel them when we go out."

Mrs. Peters went to the back of the room to hang up the fur tippet she was wearing. A moment later she exclaimed, "Why, she was piecing a quilt," and held up a large sewing basket piled high with quilt pieces.

Mrs. Hale spread some of the blocks out on the table.

155   "It's log cabin pattern." she said, putting several of them together. "Pretty, isn't it?"

They were so engaged with the quilt that they did not hear the footsteps on the stairs. Just as the stair door opened Mrs. Hale was saying:

"Do you suppose she was going to quilt it or just knot it?"

The sheriff threw up his hands.

"They wonder whether she was going to quilt it or just knot it!"

160   There was a laugh for the ways of women, a warming of hands over the stove, and then the county attorney said briskly:

"Well, let's go right out to the barn and get that cleared up."

"I don't see as there's anything so strange," Mrs. Hale said resentfully, after the outside door had closed on the three men—"our taking up our time with little things while we're waiting for them to get the evidence. I don't see as it's anything to laugh about."

"Of course they've got awful important things on their minds," said the sheriff's wife apologetically.

They returned to an inspection of the block for the quilt. Mrs. Hale was looking at the fine, even sewing, and preoccupied with thoughts of the woman who had done that sewing, when she heard the sheriff's wife say, in a queer tone:

165 "Why, look at this one."

She turned to take the block held out to her.

"The sewing," said Mrs. Peters, in a troubled way. "All the rest of them have been so nice and even—but—this one. Why, it looks as if she didn't know what she was about!"

Their eyes met—something flashed to life, passed between them; then, as if with an effort, they seemed to pull away from each other. A moment Mrs. Hale sat there, her hands folded over that sewing which was so unlike all the rest of the sewing. Then she had pulled a knot and drawn the threads.

"Oh, what are you doing, Mrs. Hale?" asked the sheriff's wife, startled.

170 "Just pulling out a stitch or two that's not sewed very good," said Mrs. Hale mildly.

"I don't think we ought to touch things," Mrs. Peters said, a little helplessly.

"I'll just finish up this end," answered Mrs. Hale, still in that mild, matter-of-fact fashion.

She threaded a needle and started to replace bad sewing with good. For a little while she sewed in silence. Then, in that thin, timid voice, she heard:

"Mrs. Hale!"

175 "Yes, Mrs. Peters?"

"What do you suppose she was so—nervous about?"

"Oh, / don't know," said Mrs. Hale, as if dismissing a thing not important enough to spend much time on, "I don't know as she was—nervous. I sew awful queer sometimes when I'm just tired."

She cut a thread, and out of the corner of her eye looked up at Mrs. Peters. The small, lean face of the sheriff's wife seemed to have tightened up. Her eyes had that look of peering into something. But next moment she moved, and said in her thin, indecisive way:

"Well, I must get those clothes wrapped. They may be through sooner than we think. I wonder where I could find a piece of paper—and string."

180 "In that cupboard, maybe," suggested Mrs. Hale, after a glance around.

One piece of the crazy sewing remained unripped. Mrs. Peters' back turned, Martha Hale now scrutinized that piece, compared it with the dainty, accurate sewing of the other blocks. The difference was startling. Holding this block made her feel queer, as if the distracted thoughts of the woman who had perhaps turned to it to try and quiet herself were communicating themselves to her.

Mrs. Peters' voice roused her.

"Here's a bird-cage," she said, "Did she have a bird, Mrs. Hale?"

"Why, I don't know whether she did or not." She turned to look at the cage Mrs. Peter was holding up. "I've not been here in so long." She sighed. "There was a man round last year selling canaries cheap—but I don't know as she look one. Maybe she did. She used to sing real pretty herself."

185 Mrs. Peters looked around the kitchen.

"Seems kind of funny to think of a bird here." She half laughed—an attempt to put up a barrier. "But she must have had one—or why would she have a cage? I wonder what happened to it."

"I suppose maybe the cat got it," suggested Mrs. Hale, resuming her sewing.

"No; she didn't have a cat. She's got that feeling some people have about cats—being afraid of them. When they brought her to our house yesterday, my cat got in the room, and she was real upset and asked me to take it out."

"My sister Bessie was like that," laughed Mrs. Hale.

190   The sheriff's wife did not reply. The silence made Mrs. Hale turn round. Mrs. Peters was examining the bird-cage.

"Look at this door," she said slowly. "It's broke. One hinge has been pulled apart."

Mrs. Hale came nearer.

"Looks as if some one must have been—rough with it."

Again their eyes met—startled, questioning, apprehensive. For a moment neither spoke nor stirred. Then Mrs. Hale, turning away, said brusquely:

195   "If they're going to find any evidence, I wish they'd be about it. I don't like this place."

"But I'm awful glad you came with me, Mrs. Hale." Mrs. Peters put the bird-cage on the table and sat down. "It would be lonesome for me—sitting here alone."

"Yes, it would, wouldn't it?" agreed Mrs. Hale, a certain determined naturalness in her voice. She had picked up the sewing, but now it dropped in her lap, and she murmured in a different voice: "But I tell you what I *do* wish, Mrs. Peters. I wish I had come over sometimes when she was here. I wish—I had."

"But of course you were awful busy, Mrs. Hale. Your house—and your children."

"I could've come," retorted Mrs. Hale shortly. "I stayed away because it weren't cheerful—and that's why I ought to have come. I"—she looked around—"I've never liked this place. Maybe because it's down in a hollow and you don't see the road. I don't know what it is, but it's a lonesome place, and always was. I wish I had come over to see Minnie Foster sometimes. I can see now—" She did not put it into words.

200   "Well, you mustn't reproach yourself," counseled Mrs. Peters. "Somehow, we just don't see how it is with other folks till—something comes up."

Not having children makes less work," mused Mrs. Hale, after a silence, "but it makes a quiet house—and Wright out to work all day—and no company when he did come in. Did you know John Wright, Mrs. Peters?"

"Not to know him. I've seen him in town. They say he was a good man."

"Yes—good," conceded John Wright's neighbor grimly. "He didn't drink, and kept his word as well as most, I guess, and paid his debts. But he was a hard man, Mrs. Peters. Just to pass the time of day with him—." She stopped, shivered a little. "Like a raw wind that gets to the bone." Her eye fell upon the cage on the table before her, and she added, almost bitterly: "I should think she would've wanted a bird!"

Suddenly she leaned forward, looking intently at the cage. "But what do you s'pose went wrong with it?"

205   "I don't know," returned Mrs. Peters; "unless it got sick and died."

But after she said it she reached over and swung the broken door. Both women watched it as if somehow held by it.

"You didn't know—her?" Mrs. Hale asked, a gentler note in her voice.

"Not till they brought her yesterday," said the sheriff's wife.

"She—come to think of it, she was kind of like a bird herself. Real sweet and pretty, but kind of timid and—fluttery. How—she—did—change."

210   That held her for a long time. Finally, as if struck with a happy thought and relieved to get back to everyday things, she exclaimed:

"Tell you what, Mrs. Peters, why don't you take the quilt in with you? It might take up her mind."

"Why, I think that's a real nice idea, Mrs. Hale," agreed the sheriff's wife, as if she too were glad to come into the atmosphere of a simple kindness. "There couldn't possibly be any objection to that, could there? Now, just what will I take? I wonder if her patches are in here—and her things."

They turned to the sewing basket.

"Here's some red," said Mrs. Hale, bringing out a roll of cloth. Underneath that was a box. "Here, maybe her scissors are in here—and her things." She held it up. "What a pretty box! I'll warrant that was something she had a long time ago—when she was a girl."

215   She held it in her hand a moment; then, with a little sigh, opened it.

Instantly her hand went to her nose.

"Why—!"

Mrs. Peters drew nearer—then turned away.

"There's something wrapped up in this piece of silk," faltered Mrs. Hale.

220   "This isn't her scissors," said Mrs. Peters, in a shrinking voice.

Her hand not steady, Mrs. Hale raised the piece of silk. "Oh, Mrs. Peters!" she cried. "It's —"

Mrs. Peters bent closer.

"It's the bird," she whispered.

"But, Mrs. Peters!" cried Mrs. Hale. "*Look* at it! Its *neck*—look at its neck! It's all—other side *to*"

225   She held the box away from her.

The sheriff's wife again bent closer.

"Somebody wrung its neck," said she, in a voice that was slow and deep.

And then again the eyes of the two women met—this time clung together in a look of dawning comprehension, of growing horror. Mrs. Peters looked from the dead bird to the broken door of the cage. Again their eyes met. And just then there was a sound at the outside door.

Mrs. Hale slipped the box under the quilt pieces in the basket, and sank into the chair before it. Mrs. Peters stood holding to the table. The county attorney and the sheriff came in from outside.

230   "Well, ladies," said the county attorney, as one turning from serious things to little pleasantries, "have you decided whether she was going to quilt it or knot it?"

"We think," began the sheriff's wife in a flurried voice, "that she was going to—knot it."

He was too preoccupied to notice the change that came in her voice on that last.

"Well, that's very interesting, I'm sure," he said tolerantly. He caught sight of the bird-cage. "Has the bird flown?"

"We think the cat got it," said Mrs. Hale in a voice curiously even.

235   He was walking up and down, as if thinking something out.

"Is there a cat?" he asked absently.

Mrs. Hale shot a look up at the sheriff's wife.

"Well, not *now*" said Mrs. Peters. "They're superstitious, you know; they leave."

She sank into her chair.

240   The county attorney did not heed her. "No sign at all of any one having come in from the outside," he said to Peters, in the manner of continuing an interrupted

conversation. "Their own rope. Now let's go upstairs again and go over it, piece by piece. It would have to have been some one who knew just the—"

The stair door closed behind them and their voices were lost.

The two women sat motionless, not looking at each other, but as if peering into something and at the same time holding back. When they spoke now it was as if they were afraid of what they were saying, but as if they could not help saying it.

"She liked the bird," said Martha Hale, low and slowly. "She was going to bury it in that pretty box."

"When I was a girl," said Mrs. Peters, under her breath, "my kitten—there was a boy took a hatchet, and before my eyes—before I could get there—" She covered her face an instant. "If they hadn't held me back I would have"—she caught herself, looked upstairs where footsteps were heard, and finished weakly—"hurt him."

245 Then they sat without speaking or moving.

"I wonder how it would seem," Mrs. Hale at last began, as if feeling her way over strange ground—"never to have had any children around?" Her eyes made a slow sweep of the kitchen, as if seeing what that kitchen had meant through all the years. "No, Wright wouldn't like the bird," she said after that—"a thing that sang. She used to sing. He killed that too." Her voice tightened.

Mrs. Peters moved uneasily.

"Of course we don't know who killed the bird."

"I knew John Wright," was Mrs. Hale's answer.

250 "It was an awful thing was done in this house that night, Mrs. Hale," said the sheriff's wife. "Killing a man while he slept—slipping a thing round his neck that choked the life out of him."

Mrs. Hale's hand went out to the bird-cage.

"His neck. Choked the life out of him."

"We don't *know* who killed him," whispered Mrs. Peters wildly. "We don't *know*."

Mrs. Hale had not moved. "If there had been years and years of—nothing, then a bird to sing to you, it would be awful—still—after the bird was still."

255 It was as if something within her not herself had spoken, and it found in Mrs. Peters something she did not know as herself.

"I know what stillness is," she said, in a queer, monotonous voice. "When we homesteaded in Dakota, and my first baby died—after he was two years old—and me with no other then—"

Mrs. Hale stirred.

"How soon do you suppose they'll be through looking for the evidence?"

"I know what stillness is," repeated Mrs. Peters, in just that same way. Then she too pulled back. "The law has got to punish crime, Mrs. Hale," she said in her tight little way.

260 "I wish you'd seen Minnie Foster," was the answer, "when she wore a white dress with blue ribbons, and stood up there in the choir and sang."

The picture of that girl, the fact that she had lived neighbor to that girl for twenty years, and had let her die for lack of life, was suddenly more than she could bear.

"Oh, I *wish* I'd come over here once in a while!" she cried. "That was a crime! That was a crime! Who's going to punish that?"

"We mustn't take on," said Mrs. Peters, with a frightened look toward the stairs.

"I might 'a' *known* she needed help! I tell you, it's *queer*, Mrs. Peters. We live close together, and we live far apart. We all go through the same things—it's all just a different kind of the same thing! If it weren't—why do you and I *understand?* Why do we *know*—what we know this minute?"

265   She dashed her hand across her eyes. Then, seeing the jar of fruit on the table, she reached for it and choked out:

"If I was you I wouldn't *tell* her her fruit was gone! Tell her it *ain't*. Tell her it's all right—all of it. Here—take this in to prove it to her! She—she may never know whether it was broke or not,"

She turned away.

Mrs. Peters reached out for the bottle of fruit as if she were glad to take it—as if touching a familiar thing, having something to do, could keep her from something else. She got up, looked about for something to wrap the fruit in, took a petticoat from the pile of clothes she had brought from the front room, and nervously started winding that round the bottle.

"My!" she began, in a high, false voice, "it's a good thing the men couldn't hear us! Getting all stirred up over a little thing like a—dead canary." She hurried over that. "As if that could have anything to do with—with—My, wouldn't they *laugh?*"

270   Footsteps were heard on the stairs.

"Maybe they would," muttered Mrs. Hale—"maybe they wouldn't."

"No, Peters," said the county attorney incisively; "it's all perfectly clear, except the reason for doing it. But you know juries when it comes to women. If there was some definite thing—something to show. Something to make a story about. A thing that would connect up with this clumsy way of doing it."

In a covert way Mrs. Hale looked at Mrs. Peters, Mrs. Peters was looking at her. Quickly they looked away from each other. The outer door opened and Mr. Hale came in.

"I've got the team round now," he said, "Pretty cold out there."

275   "I'm going to stay here awhile by myself," the county attorney suddenly announced. "You can send Frank out for me, can't you?" he asked the sheriff. "I want to go over everything. I'm not satisfied we can't do better."

Again, for one brief moment, the two women's eyes found one another.

The sheriff came up to the table.

"Did you want to see what Mrs. Peters was going to take in?"

The county attorney picked up the apron. He laughed.

280   "Oh, I guess they're not very dangerous things the ladies have picked out."

Mrs. Hale's hand was on the sewing basket in which the box was concealed. She felt that she ought to take her hand off the basket. She did not seem able to. He picked up one of the quilt blocks which she had piled on lo cover the box. Her eyes felt like fire. She had a feeling that if he took up the basket she would snatch it from him.

But he did not take it up. With another little laugh, he turned away, saying:

"No; Mrs. Peters doesn't need supervising. For that matter, a sheriff's wife is married to the law. Ever think of it that way, Mrs. Peters?"

Mrs. Peters was standing beside the table. Mrs. Hale shot a look up at her; but she could not see her face. Mrs. Peters had turned away. When she spoke, her voice was muffled.

285   "Not—just that way," she said.

"Married to the law!" chuckled Mrs. Peters' husband. He moved toward the door into the front room, and said to the county attorney:

"I just want you to come in here a minute, George. We ought to take a look at these windows."

"Oh—windows," said the county attorney scoffingly.

"We'll be right out, Mr. Hale," said the sheriff to the farmer, who was still wait-ing by the door.

290 Hale went to look after the horses. The sheriff followed the county attorney into the other room. Again—for one final moment—the two women were alone in that kitchen.

Martha Hale sprang up, her hands tight together, looking at that other woman, with whom it rested. At first she could not see her eyes, for the sheriff's wife had not turned back since she turned away at that suggestion of being married to the law. But now Mrs. Hale made her turn back. Her eyes made her turn back. Slowly, unwillingly, Mrs. Peters turned her head until her eyes met the eyes of the other woman. There was a moment when they held each other in a steady, burning look in which there was no evasion nor flinching. Then Martha Hale's eyes pointed the way to the basket in which was hidden the thing that would make certain the conviction of the other woman—that woman who was not there and yet who had been there with them all through that hour.

For a moment Mrs. Peters did not move. And then she did it. With a rush forward, she threw back the quilt pieces, got the box, tried to put it in her hand-bag. It was too big. Desperately she opened it, started to take the bird out. But there she broke—she could not touch the bird. She stood there helpless, foolish.

There was the sound of a knob turning in the inner door. Martha Hale snatched the box from the sheriff's wife, and got it in the pocket of her big coat just as the sheriff and the county attorney came back into the kitchen.

"Well, Henry," said the county attorney facetiously, "at least we found out that she was not going to quilt it. She was going to—what is it you call it, ladies?"

295 Mrs. Hale's hand was against the pocket of her coat.

"We call it—knot it, Mr. Henderson."

[1917]

Now, let's explore Yuki Chen's comparison paper, including the reading, brain-storming, and drafting steps that led up to the final paper. As previously men-tioned, Yuki's composition class explored two versions of the same plot as written and rewritten by Susan Glaspell in her play, *Trifles*, and her short story, "A Jury of Her Peers." The class has been assigned a six-page paper that asks for a compari-son/contrast of the play and the short story. The student, Yuki, must not only develop ideas on one text but also examine the two texts and decide how to weave them together. In order to do this, Yuki works her way through a series of reading and writing steps: After her first reading, she makes notes on the text itself and on her computer; then, she engages in freewriting that leads to her first draft; finally, she revises and reshapes her first draft into a final draft.

Assignment

Six-page Comparison/Contrast Paper (about 1,500 words):

- This assignment asks you to compare and contrast Susan Glaspell's play *Trifles* and her short story "A Jury of Her Peers." Create an argument that explores what changes Glaspell makes as she re-creates the play as a story. Explain how or why the plot, characters, and themes change as they are transformed from a play into a short story. Although the play and short story are very similar, there are changes. Locate changes that seem significant or meaningful to you. Then, explore why those changes might have been made.

- Write a six-page comparison/contrast paper that:
  1. creates an argument about differences and similarities between the play and short story;
  2. develops ideas about how and why the play and short story are different, showing an understanding of these different genres;
  3. compares specific moments from the play and short story; and
  4. quotes specific words and phrases.

Annotation: Marginal Notes

With the comparison/contrast assignment in mind, Yuki knows that she will have to find similarities and differences that connect the play and the short story. She decides to annotate both *Trifles* and "A Jury of Her Peers" by highlighting the differences between the two. A crucial moment occurs near the end of Susan Glaspell's play, *Trifles*. In this dramatic scene, the two central woman characters discover a rather grisly clue to a murder. Yuki's notes focus on this scene as a key point of comparison.

As we've discussed, annotating is the activity of marking up your text, noting your responses on the text as you read it. Annotation provides a way of capturing your ideas as you create them. Literary annotation explores both content, or the meaning of a text, and form, or the literary structures and devices used to convey that meaning. For example, Yuki notes that the play contains stage directions that reveal much of the important events, thoughts, and emotions in the play; as a result, she highlights all stage directions and underlines those she finds most interesting. In contrast, the short story contains descriptions; as a result, she highlights all of the descriptions in the story. After highlighting these differences, Yuki adds annotations that capture her thinking about what those differences might mean.

Student Work: Annotation
Marginal Notes on a Play

[They look in the sewing basket.]

Mrs. Hale: Here's some red. I expect this has got sewing things in it. [Brings out a fancy box.] What a pretty box. Look like something somebody would give you. Maybe her scissors are in here. [Opens box. Suddenly puts her hand to her nose.] Why—[Mrs. Peters bends nearer, then turns her face away.] There's something wrapped up in this piece of silk."

Mrs. Peters: Why, this isn't her scissors.

Mrs. Hale: [Lifting the silk.] Oh, Mrs. Peters—it's—[Mrs. Peters bends closer.]

Mrs. Peters: It's the bird.

stage direction = they are doing it together

action reveals bad smell, bad look

action = peeking need to bend closer = like a secret?

Mrs. Hale: [Jumping up.] But, Mrs. Peters—look at it! It's   *Jump = shock*
neck! Look at its neck! It's all—other side too.

Mrs. Peters: Somebody—wrung—its—neck.

[Their eyes meet. A look of growing comprehension, of   *eyes meet =*
horror. Steps are heard outside. Mrs. Hale slips box under quilt   *connection*
pieces, and sinks into her chair. Enter Sheriff and County   *KEY: hides box*
Attorney. Mrs. Peters rises.]

Now, let's turn to the same plot moment as it appears in Susan Glaspell's short story, "A Jury of Her Peers." The short story follows the play closely and is rewritten in prose form. Yuki uses annotation to highlight the differences that she finds.

Student Work: Annotation
Marginal Notes on a Story

They turned to the sewing basket.

"Here's some red," said Mrs. Hale, bringing out a roll of cloth. Underneath that was a box. "Here, maybe her scissors are in here— and her things." She held it up, "What a pretty box! I'll warrant that   *the pretty box* was something she had a long time ago—when she was a girl."

She held it in her hand a moment; then, with a little sigh,   *action described* opened it.

Instantly, her hand went to her nose.   *the smell!*

"Why—!"

Mrs. Peters drew nearer—then tuned away.

"There's something wrapped up in this piece of silk, faltered   *silk reaction* Mrs. Hale.

This isn't her scissors," said Mrs. Peters, in a shrinking   *voice described* voice.

Her hand not steady, Mrs. Hale raised the piece of silk. "Oh, Mrs. Peters!" she cried. "It's—"

Mrs. Peters bent closer.   *bends closer—*

"It's the bird," she whispered.   *this is in the*

But, Mrs. Peter!" cried Mrs. Hale. "Look at it! Its neck—look   *play* at its neck! It's all—other side too."   *jump in play?*

She held the box away from her.   *Held = not in*

The sheriff's wife again bent closer.   *play*

"Somebody wrung its neck," said she, in a voice that was   *voice described* slow and deep.   *strong*

And then again the eyes of the two women met—this time   *description* clung together in the dawning comprehension, of growing horror. Mrs. Peters looked from the dead bird to the broken door of the cage. Again their eyes met. And just then there was   *more looks* a sound at the outside door.

Mrs. Hale slipped the box under the quilt pieces in the   *KEY: hides box* basket, and sank into the chair before it. Mrs. Peters stood holding to the table. The county attorney and the sheriff came in from outside.

Comparison as a Form of Critical Thinking

When you compare and contrast the play and the short story, you might initially think that the two texts are very similar. At first, you might concentrate on the action that is at the center of each scene: the discovery of the dead bird. In both the play and the short story, this discovery is shocking. In both genres, there are the details of the bird: Its broken neck and it being covered in silk catch our attention. In both genres, a sense of surprise turning into horror is captured.

As you place the play and short story side by side, reading more closely and annotating as you read, you can highlight and analyze the differences and similarities between the two. In addition to reading to understand the plot, you can read to understand the two genres and their key features. A closer look at the play will reveal its use of a structural aspect of drama: stage directions. Because it relies on stage directions, the play might seem shorter and more action-packed: It puts the characters and their discovery into a series of actions. In contrast, the short story spends more time and space describing the women and their reactions. The story's prose form relies on description rather than on stage directions. With this observation in mind, you can start to generate ideas about how that difference might affect the meaning of the play and the short story.

By comparing the play and the short story, you can start to think about the larger differences between the two genres. In the play, the stage directions will be interpreted by the actors, who will bring the directions to life in a unique way. Every time the play is performed, the audience is watching a different enactment of those stage directions. In contrast, the short story offers more information, but that information will remain static and unchanging. How does the active nature of drama shape the story's plot? How does the more static, descriptive form of the short story change the plot?

Inquiry Notes: Comparison Grid

The inquiry process helps you to translate your reading into writing. It captures the questions that you see in the text and your attempt to develop answers. Yuki employs prewriting strategies that help her create a comprehensive comparison of *Trifles* and "A Jury of Her Peers." Although she understands the central events and characters of the play and short story, she needs to dig deeper to find out how best to connect the play and the short story. Planning for the comparison/contrast paper, Yuki wants to make sure her prewriting finds details that will reveal the similarities and differences between the two.

Yuki uses her note taking to trigger the comparison/contrast thinking process. She uses listing to start to bring the play and the short story together—to quite literally get them "on the same page." Working on her computer, she creates a grid-like comparison chart to capture the information that she sees as central to the short story and the play and to start the process of building a concept bridge between the short story and the play. The comparison grid allows her to organize those details to generate questions and ideas. Listing not only gets ideas down on paper but also leads to the creation of more ideas and shapes them for further analysis.

The comparison grid highlights which ideas are most interesting, clarifies those ideas by organizing them as a comparison/contrast, and allows those ideas to be digested and developed. In order to add organization and clarity to your thinking, consider creating a list or grid that collects and categorizes your ideas, as seen here.

Student Work: Inquiry Notes Comparison/Contrast Grid

Key Moment	Trifles vs.	"A Jury of Her Peers"
Opening	p. 558 Right into the action Men and women enter	p. 567 Starts with long description Describes Mrs. Hale leaving kitchen
	Men start questioning	Mrs. Hale doesn't want to leave things ½-finished
	Mr. Hale starts in on long story	Describes trip Describes characters Describes setting: lonesome Describes thoughts: should have visited Minnie Lots of info before Hale's story LOTS OF DESCRIPTION
Hale's story	p. 558 almost same	p. 569 almost same emphasizes "lonesome stretch of road"
Fruit that has burst jars	p. 560 Attorney criticizes mess women try to explain women draw together ACTION	p. 571 same women have "sympathetic understanding" women DESCRIBED DESCRIPTION AGAIN Attorney laughs
Unfinished Work	p. 561 Dirty towels, pans p. 561 Bread is set out Bread is out, not put back Why bread changed to sugar?	p. 572 same p. 573 Sugar part put away Job is not finished

---

Inquiry Notes: Journal Writing

As we explored in Chapter 4, journal writing is an exploratory stage of writing that enacts the crucial step of translating your ideas into sentences and paragraphs. As she starts her journaling, Yuki uses a technique presented in her class: She uses the category of "observations" and the category of "ideas," followed by the category of "analysis" to shape her thinking and move it toward an argument. The "observations" section captures the information that she feels is important to the play, while, in the "ideas" section, she starts to think about *why* that information might be important. The "analysis" section offers an interpretation that brings together the information and concepts. These categories start Yuki's ideas flowing and also help her to clarify her thinking. As Yuki puts these ideas into more complete sentences and paragraphs, she knows that she wants to emphasize the category of "analysis." Yuki avoids plot summary by avoiding repeating her observations; she uses those observations as evidence for her analytical ideas.

The process of journal writing is a process of discovery. Here, Yuki starts to discover her unique interpretation of *Trifles* and "A Jury of Her Peers." We start to see glimpses of original ideas, such as the difference between "seeing" and "describing" and, at the end, the idea that an audience is a "detective." These ideas will become central arguments in her paper's drafts.

Student Work: Journal Writing
"Close Reading → Inquiry → Analysis" Writing

Close reading (information)

1. There are NOT many changes from play to story.
2. Major changes are the opening of the story (a lot more detail on the characters and setting in the short story). A lot more detail on the travel to the house—page 567
3. Another major change is that the play has stage directions.

Inquiry Ideas (concepts)

1. The play must put the story's key ideas into actions—must show actions.
2. The short story describes the ideas. The story can also describe the internal thoughts of the characters. The play must make this into actions.
   Story = internal stuff Play = makes it into actions so you can see it
3. Audience can SEE the actions—can figure them out.

Analysis (developing information and concepts)

Trifles and "A Jury of Her Peers" are very similar, using the same characters and following the same plot. But, when you take a closer look, you start to notice small changes throughout the play and story that make the two versions start to feel different.

The beginning of the short story has the most changes compared to the play. The story adds a lots of details. Most importantly, it starts in a different place: Mrs. Hale's kitchen. It has her working in the kitchen—and then going to the murder scene. She needs to leave her work half-finished. She leaves her flour half sifted/unsifted. After she leaves the house, the story describes her trip. The story then describes the other characters on the trip. Then, as they approach the Wrights' home, it describes the home—and the fact that it is lonesome. It also describes Mrs. Hale's internal thoughts—that she wishes she had gone to see Mrs. Wright.

At first I liked all of these details because they gave insight into the characters. But, then I thought about the play and the fact that it puts you right into the action. Ultimately, I like the play's opening better. It is more action-oriented. The audience is in the action and needs to figure out what is going on. We are not told what is going on and what to think. As an audience, we would just see it. We would then have to figure out that we think is happening. So, we'd have to realize on our own that this is a lonely place. In a play, we'd have to SEE the differences between Mrs. Hale and Mrs. Peters and not be told about them.

A key difference between the play and the story is the idea that the play must SHOW IN ACTION all the ideas, making them come to life in actions and dialog. In contrast, the short story can DESCRIBE the ideas without having to make them come to life. Ideas can be described by the narrator. The characters' thoughts and emotions can be described— in a short story they don't have to be put into action. In the play, all the internal ideas of the characters must become outside. Become external.

In the play, the audience must SEE the actions. The play's audience must watch and figure out what is going on without being directly told. The audience is more active (???). The audience must observe and decide on their own. The audience is like a detective at the Wright murder scene—they are trying to figure out what has happened. The short story makes it easier on the reader.

Drafting and Revision: Using Comparison to Create Interpretation and Argument

Drafting provides a space of sustained analytical writing, in which you can generate ideas and push them to a higher level of insight, sophistication, or creativity. A final paper demonstrates your understanding of the literary text by showing that you have created an insightful, thought-provoking, and well-organized interpretation of it; however, you need to push your writing through several drafts before you can attain that ideal. Yuki's drafting of her paper moves her thinking toward this well-formed interpretation. Her paper contains a good thesis, emphasizing that the play is action-oriented while the short story is description-oriented. Using subpoints, she builds several layers of connections between the play and the short story. In addition, she uses several quotations from both the play and the short story.

As you read Yuki's draft, think about its strengths and weaknesses. Which ideas are Yuki's best ideas? Which ideas are less well formed? Which ideas should Yuki develop further? What evidence should Yuki add to this paper? Can the thesis or the conclusion be strengthened? How can Yuki continue to improve her thinking and her writing?

Student Analytical Essay: "*Trifles*, the Play, versus 'A Jury of Her Peers,' the Short Story" (Preliminary Draft)

This first draft of Yuki's is a rough attempt to reshape a series of ideas into an analytical argument. Yuki's draft still contains weaknesses that, through the revision process, will be deleted or rewritten. As we look at the first draft, we'll use marginal annotations to capture our observations, noting the strengths of the paper and making suggestions for how it could be strengthened even further.

Yuki Chen

English 102

Professor Dutta

April 2, 2016

Trifles, the Play, versus. "A Jury of Her Peers," the Short Story

In 1917, Susan Glaspell rewrote her 1916 play *Trifles* in the form of a short

writer names texts being compared

story titled "A Jury of Her Peers." Both the play and short story show a group

of people investigating the home of Mrs. Minnie Wright, a woman charged

with murdering her husband John Wright. By looking at the details of the

home, the women in the group are able to figure out that she must have

committed the murder. They also figure out the motive for the murder. The

story makes very few changes to the play's plot and characters. But, in the

play, the character's thoughts are shown through dramatic actions—the play

writer develops thesis that captures most important comparison between two texts

is about *showing*. First, the opening of the play jumps right into action,

while the opening of the story gives more description than the play. Then, in

the body of the play, big events such as the discovery of the bird, are put in

stage directions, meaning they'd be acted out (shown in action) by the

actors. In the short story, these events and the women's thinking about

them are described in ways that are more detailed. But they are less active.

When trying to portray how people think, the drama *Trifles* is more action-

oriented, while the story "A Jury of Her Peers" is more description-oriented.

The play is thus more interesting.

The play opens by putting the audience right into the middle of the

crime scene. The scene opens with a large group entering the Wright's

kitchen: Sheriff Henry Peters, County Attorney George Henderson, a

neighboring farmer Lewis Hale, Mrs. Peters, and Mrs. Hale. They immediately

start questioning the events that took place in the Wright's home. The

County Attorney and the Sheriff question Mr. Hale because he was the first

person to visit the Wright home after the murder; he described talking with

Chen 2

Mrs. Wright, realizing something wasn't right, and then discovering the

strangled Mr. Wright. Mr. Hale explains that when he first sees Mrs. Hale, she

doesn't respond, "I said, "How do, Mrs. Wright, it's cold, ain't it?" And she

said, "It is?" and went on pleating her apron. Well I was surprised; she

didn't ask me to come to the stove, or set down, but she just sat there, not

even looking at me" (559). Then, Mr. Hale asked for John: "I said, "I want to

see John." And then she—laughed. I guess you would call it a laugh" (559).

He then explains that he asked if he can see John and how Mrs Wright

responds: "I said a little sharp: "Can't I see John?" "No, She says, kind o' dull

like. "aint he home?" says I. "Yes," says she, he's home." "Then why can't I

see him?" I asked her, out of patience" (560). Then comes the shocking

reply: "'Cause he's dead, says she" (560). The scene then shows the men

criticizing the housekeeping of Mrs. Wright, criticizing her dirty towel and

dirty dishes. Right in this first set of actions, the women start to feel sorry

for Mrs. Wright. When they realize that the glass jars holding Mrs. Wright's

fruit preserves have broken, they realize all of her lost work.

"A Jury of Her Peers," or the short story version of the play, opens with

lots of description of the group of characters gathering together and

travelling to the Wright home before they arrive at the home and start to

discuss the house. The short story contains a lot more exposition, or

description of the characters and setting. The short story does not open with

the action-filled events of the play. The short story tells you about the

characters by having us see their actions and figure out who they are based

on their actions. For example, the short story describes how Mrs. Hale

perceives and thinks about Mrs. Peters: "She had met Mrs. Peters the year

before at the country fair, and the thing she remembered about her was

that she didn't seem like a sheriff's wife. She was small and thin and didn't

have a strong voice" (568). The short story also describes the setting as a

writer uses direct quotes as evidence, but uses quotes to provide plot summary; plot summary should be limited

discussion remains on level of plot summary—needs to be more analytical

writer integrates new analysis, highlighting formal aspects of story

Chen 3

lonesome place. The short story takes more time setting up the characters
and the location—and telling you what to think about them.

writer juxtaposes two texts; brings them into dialogue that can be developed further

    The opening of the short story is effective, but it delays the action-
filled events of the play. The short story tells you how to think about the
characters and setting. In contrast, the play must show you the characters
and the setting. You've gotta come to your own conclusion. In this way, the
play makes you into a detective-like person—the audience has to watch and
figure out things, just like the women do.

writer captures her unique reading in draft

    The stage directions read "The two women move a little closer
together" (561). Right from the beginning, the dynamic of the women being
together against the men is created. Importantly, the connection of the
women is shown by their movement rather than described. In both the play
and the short story, the women are described as moving close to each other.
But, in the play, the movement is part of the stage directions—the

paper emphasizes strong point of contrast between play and short story

movement would be seen. It would not be read. In the short story, the
movement must be described and left as a description. After the men leave
the women, in both the play and short story. Mrs. Hale explains, "I'd hate to
have men coming into my kitchen, snooping around and criticizing" (561).
The short story contains the same sentence but tries to convey the slang of a
spoken voice by having Mrs. Hale say, "I'd hate to have men comin' into my
kitchen . . . snoopin' round and criticizin'" (573). The short story surrounds
that statement with an explanation of some of Mrs. Hale's thoughts.

    As the plot in both forms develops, the women start to feel for
Mrs. Wright. They start to feel for her situation—and they even put
themselves into her situation. Ultimately, hiding the evidence that
Mrs. Wright murdered her husband is what they had then decided to do.
Her motive, the reason for murdering her husband by strangling him, would
have been understood by the women, and is realized by them, in a way that
the men would have not.

The men need the motive, and the women make an unspoken agreement to hide the motive from them. This understanding is shown through a series of unspoken agreements. These agreements take the form of actions. Because these agreements take the form of actions, the play is a more effective way to get the story across. The women show sympathetic actions, such as when they save an unbroken bottle of cherries to take to Mrs. Wright. Then, the women start to feel for Mrs. Wright by putting themselves into her place and understanding her emotional situation.

writer makes strong statement that judges effectiveness of play

For example, the women take out Mrs. Wright's bad quilt stitching and replace it with more organized quilt stitching. The women connect with Mrs. Wright and they also connect with each other. In the play, they look at each other as they discover the bad stitching. Mrs. Hale explains, "Why, it looks as if she didn't know what she was about!" and then the stage directions explain, "After she has said this they look at each other, then start to glance back at the door. After an instant Mrs. Hale has pulled at a knot and ripped the sewing" (576). The audience is expected to figure out that the women are connecting through the sewing. By glancing at the door, they are connecting. In the short story, the connection between the women is described and given more explanation: "Their eyes met—something flashed to life, passed between them; then, as if with an effort they seemed to pull away from each other. A moment Mrs. Hale sat there, her hands folded over that sewing which was unlike all the rest of the sewing" (576). The story has the women connecting.

writer supports ideas with specific quotations from text, followed by analysis of their meaning

At the end of the play, the women's understanding of Mrs. Wright slowly becomes actions that hide Mrs. Wright's guilt from the men. Ultimately, the women do not just feel for her and understand her, but decide to protect her. The play highlights these actions of sympathy, understanding, and protection. The climax of the play and short story is the women's discovery of Mrs. Wright's canary. The canary is dead. When inspected, the canary has a snapped neck. In addition, its cage door had

Chen 5

writer uses literary elements, such as symbolism, as foundation for draft's preliminary interpretation

been broken. The canary is an important symbol. Symbols are always important in literature. Symbols can represent important ideas. Because birds are sweet, innocent, and happy, it could represent the sweetness, innocence, and happiness of life. Life that is now gone.

The women's discovery of the motive for the murder is accomplished through a series of shared looks and actions. In the play, there is a discovery of the bird and the understanding that it is the motive for the murder—these are put in the stage directions. Right after Mrs. Peters says, "Somebody—wrung—its—neck," the stage directions state:

> Their eyes meet. A look of growing comprehension of horror. Steps are heard outside. Mrs. Hale slips box under quilt pieces, and sinks into her chair.
> Enter Sheriff and County Attorney. Mrs. Peter rises. (565)

The stage directions show the women connecting. The women do not just understand and feel for Mrs. Wright, but protect her.

writer continues to analyze in detail strong point of contrast between two texts

In the short story, the women's connection is described in similar way. But, in contrast to the play, this description will remain a description. It must explain what to think. The short story explains, "And then again the eyes of the two women met—this time clung together in a look of dawning comprehension, of growing horror. Mrs. Peters looked from the dead bird to the broken door of the cage. Again their eyes met. And just then there was a sound at the outside door" (578). The story puts together the pieces for the reader.

writer creates a strong argument in conclusion, leaving reader with strong sense of writer's interpretation of two texts

By comparing the play *Trifles* and the short story "A Jury of Her Peers," it becomes clear that the play is a better match for this plot and the plot's ideas. In the play, the audience members must see the clues being gathered. The play thus makes the audience into a detective who must figure out what is going on by watching it. In this way, the audience becomes like the two detective women, Mrs. Hale and Mrs. Peters. In contrast, the short story often tells the reader what the characters are thinking and tells the reader how to interpret the plot. The short story does not let the reader become like a detective.

[New page]

Chen 6

Works Cited

Glaspell, Susan. *Trifles. Literature for Composition*. Ed. Sylvan Barnet, William

    Burto, William E. Cain, and Cheryl L. Nixon. 11th ed. Boston: Pearson,

    2017. 558-67. Print.

Glaspell, Susan. "A Jury of Her Peers." *Literature for Composition*. Ed. Sylvan

    Barnet, William Burto, William E. Cain, and Cheryl L. Nixon. 11th ed.

    Boston: Pearson, 2017. 567-81. Print.

Revision: Using a Revision Strategy

As we saw in Chapter 8, the revision process gives the writer the time and space to rethink his or her reactions to the literary work, understanding of information in the text, insights into the ideas conveyed by the text, and questions about the text. Yuki uses revision to highlight which ideas are most interesting to her and then to further digest and develop those ideas. Before we explore Yuki's use of selected aspects of the revision process, let's revisit our revision checklist.

✔ REVISION CHECKLIST

Strengthen Your Thesis

☐ Add focus and depth to your central argument.

Develop Your Ideas

☐ Revisit your best responses to literary form and content, adding more thinking to those responses.

Integrate and Explain Your Evidence

☐ Select and analyze rich, interesting quotations to provide evidence for your ideas.

Improve the Organization

☐ Structure your ideas to follow a clear sequence.

Clarify Your Style and Edit for Correctness

☐ Use a consistent, professional style to explain your ideas, correcting sentence structure, word usage, and grammar.

Revision: Revising to Develop Ideas

Let's look at a paragraph that starts to develop a concept bridge between the short story and the play by describing the women coming together when the men criticize Mrs. Wright's housekeeping. As Yuki starts the revision process, she notices a critical flaw in her writing. She has spent much time and space giving a plot summary of Mr. Hale's explanation of the murder; her paper contains long quotes that distract the reader's attention from her thesis. This does not help to develop her thesis. She deletes this long section. She then replaces it with sentences that work to develop her best ideas: The women have an emotional connection and, in the play, that emotional connection must be shown through actions.

Student Work: Revision
Revising to Develop Ideas

Rough Draft

The County Attorney and the Sheriff question Mr. Hale because he was the first person to visit the Wright home after the murder; ~~he described talking with Mrs.. Wright, realizing something wasn't right, and then discovering the strangled Mr. Wright. Mr. Hale explains that when he first sees Mrs. Hale, she doesn't respond, "I said, "How do, Mrs. Wright, it's cold, ain't it?" And she said, "Is is?" and went on pleating her apron. Well I was surprised; she didn't ask me to come to the stove, or set down, but she just sat there, not even looking at me" (559). Then, Mr. Hale asked for John: "I said, "I want to see John." And then she laughed. I guess you would call it a laugh" (559). He then explains that he asked if he can see John and how Mrs Wright responds: I said a little sharp: "Can't I see John?" "No, She says, kind o' dull like. "Aint he home?" says I. "Yes," says she, he's home." "Then why can't I see him?" I asked her, out of patience" (560). Then comes the shocking reply: "'Cause he's dead, says she" (560).~~ The scene then shows the men criticizing the housekeeping of Mrs. Wright, criticizing her dirty towel and dirty dishes. Right in this first set of actions, the women start to feel sorry for Mrs. Wright. When they realize that the glass jars holding Mrs. Wright's fruit preserves have broken, they realize all of her lost work.

As part of revision process, writer locates and deletes unnecessary plot summary

↓

First Revision

The County Attorney and the Sheriff question Mr. Hale because he was the first person to visit the Wright home after the murder. The scene then shows the men criticizing the housekeeping of Mrs. Wright, criticizing her dirty towel and dirty dishes. <u>Right away, in this first set of actions, the women start to feel sorry for Mrs. Wright</u>. When they realize

writer locates areas of interpretation that could be expanded through more analysis

that the glass jars holding Mrs. Wright's fruit preserves have broken, they realize all of her lost work and they have even more sympathy for her. Because this is a play, the characters have to talk to each other to explain their thoughts. This is most important for Mrs. Hale and Mrs. Peters, who start to connect through their actions and dialogue.

writer adds new sentences that develop ideas

↓

Second Revision:

The County Attorney and the Sheriff question Mr. Hale because he was the first person to visit the Wright home after the murder. The scene then shows the men criticizing the housekeeping of Mrs. Wright, criticizing her dirty towel and dirty dishes. Right away, in this first set of actions, the women start to feel sorry for Mrs. Wright. When they realize that the glass jars holding Mrs. Wright's fruit preserves have broken, they realize all of her lost work and they have even more sympathy for her. Because this is a play, the characters have to talk to each other to explain their thoughts. This is most important for Mrs. Hale and Mrs. Peters, who start to connect through their actions and dialogue. Mrs. Peters says, "Oh her fruit; it did freeze" and explains, "She worried about that when it turned so cold. She said the fire'd go out and her jars would break" (560). The men dismiss the women's feelings. The Sheriff says, "Well, can you beat the women! Held for murder and worryin' about her preserves (561). Mr. Hall dismisses the women's sympathy as "worrying over trifles" (561).

writer supports new ideas with focused evidence

Revision: Revising to Clarify Style

As one of the last steps in revision, you should edit your paper for style and correctness. An academic paper should show off the writer's ability to express his or her ideas in a clear, convincing, and professional manner. When you are revising to improve your writing style, you can work on the paragraph level, aiming for focus and flow; the sentence level, crafting clear structure and using correct grammar; and the word level, strengthening your word choice. Let's distill these ideas down into a Writing Style Checklist featuring three distinct style tips:

✔ WRITING STYLE CHECKLIST

Style Tip #1: Keep focused on your best ideas

☐ Delete generalizations.
☐ Delete "filler" ideas and phrases.
☐ Delete repetition (don't be afraid to delete!).

Style Tip #2: Make your ideas active and energetic

☐ Move the subject noun/verb to the front of the sentence.
☐ Use present-tense verbs.
☐ Use active verbs and strong nouns.

Style Tip #3: Express your ideas in an academic, intellectual way

☐ Replace colloquialisms.
☐ Replace tentative phrases.
☐ Use precise references.
☐ Use correct grammar.

Let's look at how Yuki revises three specific sentences, applying these goals of bringing focus, energy, and intellectual sophistication to her writing. Although we focus on only three sentences here, her final draft reveals that she has used these three style tips to revise her entire draft.

Student Work: Revision
Revising to Clarify Style

Style Tip #1: Keep focused on your best ideas: Delete generalizations; delete "filler" ideas and phrases; delete repetition (don't be afraid to delete!).

The canary is an important symbol. ~~Symbols are always important in literature. Symbols can represent important ideas. Because birds are sweet, innocent, and happy, it could represent the sweetness, innocence, and happiness of life. Life that is now gone.~~

in revising for style, writer deletes overly general statements

↓

Thus, the canary becomes an important symbol. First, the bird symbolizes an act of violence, and reveals that violence can lead to death. Second, it symbolizes Mrs. Wright herself. Mrs Hale explains, "She—come to think of it, she was kind of like a bird herself—real sweet and pretty, but kind of timid and—fluttery" (565). Third, the bird symbolizes that Mrs. Wright cared for it and wanted some happiness in her life. The women realize that the canary must have been killed by Mr. Wright. Through this symbol, they understand Mr. Wright must have been cruel, even violent to Mrs. Wright.

The writer improves her paper by making her interpretation more specific to the text being analyzed.

Style Tip #2: Make your ideas active and energetic: Move the subject noun/verb to the front of the sentence; use present-tense verbs; use active verbs and strong nouns.

Ultimately, hiding the evidence that Mrs. Wright murdered her husband is what they had then decided to do. Her motive, the reason for murdering her husband by strangling him, would have been understood by the women, and as had been realized by them, in a way that the men would have not.

writer locates and revises past tense verbs

Ultimately, they decide to hide the evidence that Mrs. Wright murdered her husband. The women realize that they understand her motive for murdering her husband in a way that the men do not.

writer improves paper by using present tense and active verbs

Style Tip #3: Express your ideas in an academic, intellectual way: Delete colloquialisms; delete tentative phrases; use precise references; use correct grammar.

The short story tells you how to think about the characters and setting. In contrast, the play must show you the characters and the setting. Then, it's up to you to come up with your own conclusion. In this way, the play makes you into a detective.

writer locates and replaces informal language and colloquialisms, such as referring to "you"

The short story tells the reader how to think about the characters and setting. In contrast, the play opens with action and the audience must decipher what is happening. The play shows the characters and the setting on the stage, and must let the audience come to its own interpretation of them. In this way, the play makes the audience figure out clues, and the audience starts to think like a detective.

writer uses more precise and academic language, such as "the reader"

Student Analytical Essay: "The Dramatic Action of *Trifles*: Making the Audience into Detectives" (Final Draft)

Compare this final draft to the preliminary draft on page 588. Notice in this paper how Yuki continues to strengthen her ideas and improve several aspects of her writing. In this final draft, she has

- clarified and deepened the thesis argument,
- developed the series of connected claims,
- created an organizational structure to capture the development of ideas,
- used evidence to support her ideas, and
- improved her phrasing, style, and grammar.

Yuki Chen

English 102

Professor Dutta

April 21, 2016

The Dramatic Action of *Trifles*: Making the Audience into Detectives

In 1917, Susan Glaspell rewrote her 1916 play *Trifles* in form of a short

story titled "A Jury of her Peers." Both the play and short story show a group

of people investigating the home of Mrs. Minnie Wright, a woman charged

with murdering her husband John Wright. By looking at the details of the

home, the women in the group, Mrs. Hale and Mrs. Peters, are able to figure

out that she must have committed the murder. They also figure out the

motive for the murder. The main difference between the story and the play is

that the story has a narrator who reveals the unspoken thoughts of the main

characters and explains the plot's main ideas. In the play, this information is

given through dramatic action that is shown to the audience. As a result, the

drama *Trifles* is a more action-oriented, while the story "A Jury of Her Peers"

is more description-oriented. This difference between the play and the short

story can be seen in the opening of the plot, and the different strategies

each genre uses to set up the idea that the Wright home is cheerless. The

play's use of action can also be seen in events that show that the women are

connecting and bonding. In addition, the play's use of action is also central

to the events that show the women protecting Mrs. Wright: they re-sew her

stitches and they hide the dead bird. In the short story, these key moments

are described in more detail, but are less active. Because the plot relies in

the actions of the women, the action-filled play is the better genre for this

plot. The play fits the idea of the women needing to act on their ideas, and

not just describe them, and as a result the play is the best genre.

The contrast between the play and the short story shows that the play

Trifles encourages the audience to experience the actions of the women. The

writer creates a clear comparison/ contrast argument

writer develops a strong thesis statement that presents a clear argument

Chen 2

play has the women characters show their ideas to the audience rather than describe those ideas to the audience. The play puts the women's thoughts into action. This is especially important because the play is all about thinking—it is about two women who become detectives, think through the clues before them, and solve a crime by thinking about it. The play encourages the audience to think along with the women. By comparing scenes from the play and the short story, it becomes clear that the play puts ideas into action in the stage directions.

paper now develops, explains the writer's best insights

    The play opens by putting the audience right into the middle of the crime scene. A large group enters the Wright's kitchen: Sheriff Henry Peters, County Attorney George Henderson, a neighboring farmer Lewis Hale, Mrs. Peters, and Mrs. Hales. They immediately start questioning the events that took place in the Wright home. The County Attorney and the Sheriff question Mr. Hale because he was the first person to visit the Wright home after the murder. The scene then shows the men criticizing the housekeeping of Mrs. Wright, criticizing her dirty towel and dirty dishes. Right away, in this first set of actions, the women start to feel sorry for Mrs. Wright. When they realize that the glass jars holding Mrs. Wright's fruit preserves have broken, they realize all of her lost work and they have even more sympathy for her. Because this is a play, the characters have to talk to each other to explain their thoughts. This is most important for Mrs. Hale and Mrs. Peters, who start to connect through their actions and dialogue. Mrs. Peters says, "Oh, her fruit; it did freeze" and explains, "She worried about that when it turned so cold. She said the fire'd go out and her jars would break" (560). The men dismiss the women's feelings. The Sheriff says "Well, can you beat the women! Held for murder and worryin' about her preserves" (561). Mr. Hall dismisses the women's sympathy as "worrying over trifles" (561).

paper now keeps plot summary short and moves quickly to analysis

    The women's emotions are not trifles and lead them to solve the murder. In the play, their emotions are put into dialogue so that the

writer uses strong topic sentences to develop the paper's arguments

audience can experience them. Right after feeling sorry for Mrs. Wright and her lost preserves, the women explain that the household was not a cheerful place. Mrs. Hale says, "It never seemed a cheerful place" (561). She then criticizes John Wright, explaining that "I don't think a place'd be any cheerfuller for John Wright's being in it" (561). The play must put the women's ideas into active dialogue. In contrast, in the short story, the cheerlessness of the place is shown in description that is less active and more passive.

"A Jury of Her Peers," the short story version of the play, opens with a long description of the group of characters gathering together and travelling to the Wright home. Before they arrive at the home, the short story contains a lot more exposition, or description of the characters and setting. The short story does not open with the action-filled events of the *writer continues to make comparison/ contrasts as she analyzes each text* play. The short story tells the reader about the characters by describing them. For example, the short story describes how Mrs. Hale perceives and thinks about Mrs. Peters: "She had met Mrs. Peters the year before at the country fair, and the thing she remembered about her was that she didn't seem like a sheriff's wife she was small and thin and didn't have a strong voice" (568). The short story also describes the Wright home's setting; Mrs. Hale "could see the Wright place now, and seeing it did not make her feel like talking. It looked very lonesome this cold March morning. It had always been a lonesome-looking place. It was down in a hollow, and the popular trees around it were lonesome looking trees" (568). The short story takes more time setting up the characters and the location—and telling the reader, what to think about them. In contrast, the play does not describe the setting, but shows the setting.

The opening of the short story is effective, but it delays the action-filled events of the play. The short story tells the reader how to think about

Chen 4

the characters and setting. In contrast, the play opens with action and the audience must decipher what is happening. The play shows the characters and the setting on the stage, and must let the audience come to its own interpretation of them. In this way, the play makes the audience figure out clues, and the audience starts to think like a detective. The women must figure out the motive for the murder, and the audience must, too.

paper has been revised to strengthen the juxtapositions that bring the two texts together

The play shows complicated ideas through actions, such as the development of a strong connection between the women. Early in the play and short story, the women start to bond together against the men. After the women are criticized for worrying about trifles, the stage directions read "The two women move a little closer together" (561). Right from the beginning, the dynamic of the women being together against the men is created. Importantly, the connection of the women is shown by their movements. In both the play and the short story, the women are described as moving close to each other. But, in the play, the movement is part of the stage directions—the movement would be seen and not read. In the short story, the movement must be described and left as a description. After the men leave the women, Mrs. Hale explains, "I'd hate to have men coming into my kitchen, snooping around and criticizing" (561). The short story contains the same sentence but tries to convey the slang of a spoken voice by having Mrs. Hale say, "I'd hate to have men comin' into my kitchen . . . snoopin' round and criticizin'" (573). The short story surrounds that statement with an explanation of some of Mrs. Hale's thoughts. For example, before she criticizes the men, Mrs. Hale is described as experiencing a strange emotion: "Then, as if releasing something strange, Mrs. Hale began to rearrange the dirt pans under the sink" (573). The play cannot provide description of emotions, but must show them as actions.

final paper continues to interpret specific literary details

As the plot of the play and the short story develops, the women start to sympathize more and more with Mrs. Wright. They start to feel for her situation—and they even put themselves into her situation. Ultimately, they decide to hide the evidence that Mrs. Wright murdered her husband. They realize that they understand her motive for murdering her husband in a way that the men do not. The men need the motive, and the women make an unspoken agreement to hide the motive from them. This understanding is shown through a series of actions. Because these agreements take the form of actions, the play is a more effective way to get the story across.

paper analyzes genre as a way of making a strong argument

Mrs. Hale and Mrs. Peters start to feel for Mrs. Wright by putting themselves into her place and understanding her emotional situation. For example, the women take out Mrs. Wright's bad quilt stitching and replace it with more organized quilt stitching. The women connect with Mrs. Wright's

writer develops ideas by adding layers to them (here, the idea of "connection" is used)

emotions through this action. They also connect with each other. In the play, they look at each other as they discover the bad stitching. Mrs. Hale explains, "Why, it looks as if she didn't know what she was about!" and then the stage directions explain, "After she has said this they look at each other, then start to glance back at the door. After an instant Mrs. Hale has pulled at a knot and ripped the sewing" (563). The audience is expected to figure out that the women are bonding through the sewing. By glancing at the door, the women are becoming allies against the men. In the short story, the connection between the women is described and given more explanation: "Their eyes met—something flashed to life, passed between them; then, as if with an effort they seemed to pull away from each other. A moment Mrs. Hale sat there, her hands folded over that sewing which was unlike all

paper also includes revisions for style; direct, concise statement emphasizes the paper's main argument

the rest of the sewing" (576). The play shows the women in action. The short story must describe those actions and thoughts and give them an interpretation.

At the end of the play, the women's understanding of Mrs. Wright slowly becomes actions that hide Mrs. Wright's guilt from the men. Ultimately, the women do not just feel for her and understand her, but

Chen 6

decide to protect her. The play highlights these actions of sympathy, understanding, and protection. The climax of the play and short story is the women's discovery of Mrs. Wright's canary. The canary is dead, but it has been carefully wrapped up in a piece of silk and stored in a special box. When inspected, the canary has a snapped neck. Mrs. Hale explains, "Look at it! Its neck! Look at its neck" (565). In addition, the cage door had been broken. Thus, the canary becomes an important symbol. First, the bird symbolizes an act of violence, and reveals that violence can lead to death. Second, it symbolizes Mrs. Wright herself. Mrs. Hale explains, "She—come to think of it, she was kind of like a bird herself—real sweet and pretty, but kind of timid and—fluttery" (565). Third, the bird symbolizes that Mrs. Wright cared for it and wanted some happiness in her life. The women realize that the canary must have been killed by Mr. Wright. Through this symbol, they understand Mr. Wright must have been cruel, even violent to Mrs. Wright. The bird, one of the few things to bring cheer to Mrs. Wright's cheerless life, is now gone. Mrs. Wright has a reason to murder her husband—she needs to seek revenge on the murderer of her bird.

writer has used organizational structure within paragraphs to keep ideas clear

The women's discovery of the motive for this murder is accomplished through a series of shared looks and actions. In the play, the discovery of the bird and the understanding that it is the motive for the murder is put in the stage directions. Right after Mrs. Peters says, "Somebody—wrung—its—neck," the stage directions state:

> Their eyes meet. A look of growing comprehension of horror. Steps are heard outside. Mrs. Hale slips box under quilt pieces, and sinks into her chair. Enter Sheriff and County Attorney. Mrs. Peter rises. (565)

The stage directions show the women connecting with each other. The women do not just understand and feel for Mrs. Wright, but protect her. Because this information is put in the stage directions, it must be acted out

writer presents the most important evidence in her selected quotations

writer introduces and follows the quotations with interpretation

Chen 7

and shown. It is not described to the audience, but would be shown to the audience through the acting. The women decide that they must hide the evidence of Mrs. Wright's motive.

The play is very effective in getting across the idea that an unspoken agreement can be important. The audience must see actions that reveal this unspoken agreement—it will not be described and explained to them. So, in a way, the audience shares in that unspoken agreement. The audience saw the same things as the women, and had to come to the same understanding of the same evidence in the same way. The audience is included in the women's realization.

In the short story, the women's connection is described in a similar way. But, in contrast to the play, this description does not become active

and remains a description. It must explain what to think. The short story explains, "And then again the eyes of the two women met—this time clung together in a look of dawning comprehension, of growing horror. Mrs. Peters looked from the dead bird to the broken door of the cage. Again their eyes met. And just then there was a sound at the outside door" (578). The story puts together the pieces for the reader. The reader does not have to do much interpreting. The short story explains that the two women have bonded by using the phrase "clung together." The short story also explains exactly how the two women are connecting the clues of the murder—it explains that the women look at the dead bird and the broken birdcage. The short story makes the connections between the clues obvious. So, in the short story, the reader has to do less thinking and less connecting of the clues—and thus less

detecting. The reader of the story is less of a detective.

By comparing the play *Trifles* and the short story "A Jury of Her Peers," it becomes clear that the play genre is a better match for this plot's ideas. In the play, the audience members must see the clues being gathered, with no description to tell them what the characters on stage are thinking

Chen 8

and no description telling them how to interpret the plot. The play thus

makes the audience into a detective who must figure out what is going on by

watching it. In this way, the audience becomes like the two detective

women, Mrs. Hale and Mrs. Peters. In contrast, the short story often tells the

reader what the characters are thinking and tells the reader how to interpret

the plot. The short story lets the reader be more passive and less active. It

tells the reader what to think. As a result, the short story does not let the

reader become a detective. The play is a more successful version of the plot, *writer concludes*
with a strong
as it makes the audience become more active in interpreting the plot. In the *argument that*
juxtaposes the
play, the audience becomes a detective. *two texts*

[New page]

Chen 9

Works Cited

Glaspell, Susan. *Trifles*. *Literature for Composition*. Ed. Sylvan Barnet, William

Burto, William E. Cain, and Cheryl L. Nixon. 11th ed. Boston: Pearson,

2017. 558-67. Print.

Glaspell, Susan. "A Jury of Her Peers." *Literature for Composition*. Ed. Sylvan

Barnet, William Burto, William E. Cain, and Cheryl L. Nixon. 11th ed.

Boston: Pearson, 2017. 567-81. Print.

Your Turn: Additional Plays for Analysis

A Modern Comedy

DAVID IVES

David Ives, born in Chicago in 1950, was educated at Northwestern University and at the Yale Drama School. Sure Thing *was first publicly staged in 1988, and it was later staged with six other one-act plays, grouped under the title* All *in the Timing.*

Sure Thing

This play is for Jason Buzas

BETTY, *a woman in her late twenties, is reading at a café table. An empty chair is opposite her.* BILL, *same age, enters.*

BILL: Excuse me. Is this chair taken?

BETTY: Excuse me?

BILL: Is this taken?

BETTY: Yes it is.

BILL: Oh. Sorry.

BETTY: Sure thing.

[*A bell rings softly.*]

BILL: Excuse me. Is this chair taken?

BETTY: Excuse me?

BILL: Is this taken?

BETTY: No, but I'm expecting somebody in a minute.

BILL: Oh. Thanks anyway.

BETTY: Sure thing.

[*A bell rings softly.*]

BILL: Excuse me. Is this chair taken?

BETTY: No, but I'm expecting somebody very shortly.

BILL: Would you mind if I sit here till he or she or it comes?

BETTY [*glances at her watch*]: They do seem to be pretty late. . . .

BILL: You never know who you might be turning down.

BETTY: Sorry. Nice try, though.

BILL: Sure thing.

[*Bell.*]

Is this seat taken?

BETTY: No it's not.

BILL: Would you mind if I sit here?

BETTY: Yes I would.

BILL: Oh.

[*Bell.*]

Is this chair taken?

BETTY: No it's not.

BILL: Would you mind if I sit here?

BETTY: No. Go ahead.

BILL: Thanks. [*He sits. She continues reading.*] Everyplace else seems to be taken.

BETTY: Mm-hm.

BILL: Great place.

BETTY: Mm-hm.

BILL: What's the book?

BETTY: I just wanted to read in quiet, if you don't mind.

BILL: No. Sure thing.

[*Bell.*]

Everyplace else seems to be taken.

BETTY: Mm-hm.
BILL: Great place for reading.
BETTY: Yes, I like it.
BILL: What's the book?
BETTY: *The Sound and the Fury.*
BILL: Oh. Hemingway.

[*Bell.*]

What's the book?

BETTY: *The Sound and the Fury.*
BILL: Oh. Faulkner.
BETTY: Have you read it?
BILL: Not . . . actually. I've sure read *about* it, though. It's supposed to be great.
BETTY: It is great.
BILL: I hear it's great. [*Small pause.*] Waiter?

[*Bell.*]

What's the book?

BETTY: *The Sound and the Fury.*
BILL: Oh. Faulkner.
BETTY: Have you read it?
BILL: I'm a Mets fan, myself.

[*Bell.*]

BETTY: Have you read it?
BILL: Yeah, I read it in college.
BETTY: Where was college?
BILL: I went to Oral Roberts University.

[*Bell.*]

BETTY: Where was college?
BILL: I was lying. I never really went to college. I just like to party.

[*Bell.*]

BETTY: Where was college?
BILL: Harvard.
BETTY: Do you like Faulkner?
BILL: I love Faulkner. I spent a whole winter reading him once.
BETTY: I've just started.
BILL: I was so excited after ten pages that I went out and bought everything else
       he wrote. One of the greatest reading experiences of my life. I mean, all
       that incredible psychological understanding. Page after page of gorgeous
       prose. His profound grasp of the mystery of time and human existence.
       The smells of the earth . . . What do you think?
BETTY: I think it's pretty boring.

[*Bell.*]

BILL: What's the book?
BETTY: *The Sound and the Fury.*
BILL: Oh! Faulkner!

BETTY: Do you like Faulkner?

BILL: I love Faulkner.

BETTY: He's incredible.

BILL: I spent a whole winter reading him once.

BETTY: I was so excited after ten pages that I went out and bought everything else
he wrote.

BILL: All that incredible psychological understanding.

BETTY: And the prose is so gorgeous.

BILL: And the way he's grasped the mystery of time—

BETTY: —and human existence. I can't believe I've waited this long to read him.

BILL: You never know. You might not have liked him before.

BETTY: That's true.

BILL: You might not have been ready for him. You have to hit these things at the
right moment or it's no good.

BETTY: That's happened to me.

BILL: It's all in the timing. [*Small pause.*] My name's Bill, by the way.

BETTY: I'm Betty.

BILL: Hi.

BETTY: Hi. [*Small pause.*]

BILL: Yes I thought reading Faulkner was . . . a great experience.

BETTY: Yes. [*Small pause.*]

BILL: *The Sound and the Fury* . . . [*Another small pause.*]

BETTY: Well. Onwards and upwards. [*She goes back to her book.*]

BILL: Waiter—?

[*Bell.*]

You have to hit these things at the right moment or it's no good.

BETTY: That's happened to me.

BILL: It's all in the timing. My name's Bill, by the way.

BETTY: I'm Betty.

BILL: Hi.

BETTY: Hi.

BILL: Do you come in here a lot?

BETTY: Actually I'm just in town for two days from Pakistan.

BILL: Oh. Pakistan.

[*Bell.*]

My name's Bill, by the way.

BETTY: I'm Betty.

BILL: Hi.

BETTY: Hi.

BILL: Do you come in here a lot?

BETTY: Every once in a while. Do you?

BILL: Not so much anymore. Not as much as I used to. Before my nervous
breakdown.

[*Bell.*]

Do you come in here a lot?

BETTY: Why are you asking?

BILL: Just interested.

BETTY: Are you really interested, or do you just want to pick me up?

BILL: No, I'm really interested.

BETTY: Why would you be interested in whether I come in here a lot?

BILL: I'm just . . . getting acquainted.

BETTY: Maybe you're only interested for the sake of making small talk long enough
to ask me back to your place to listen to some music, or because you've
just rented this great tape for your VCR, or because you've got some
terrific unknown Django Reinhardt° record, only all you really want to do
is fuck—which you won't do very well—after which you'll go into the
bathroom and pee very loudly, then pad into the kitchen and get yourself
a beer from the refrigerator without asking me whether I'd like anything,
and then you'll proceed to lie back down beside me and confess that
you've got a girlfriend named Stephanie who's away at medical school in
Belgium for a year, and that you've been involved with her—off and on—
in what you'll call a very "intricate" relationship, for the past seven YEARS.
None of which interests me, mister!

BILL: Okay.

[*Bell.*]

Do you come in here a lot?

BETTY: Every other day, I think.

BILL: I come in here quite a lot and I don't remember seeing you.

BETTY: I guess we must be on different schedules.

BILL: Missed connections.

BETTY: Yes. Different time zones.

BILL: Amazing how you can live right next door to somebody in this town and
never even know it.

BETTY: I know.

BILL: City life.

BETTY: It's crazy.

BILL: We probably pass each other in the street every day. Right in front of this
place, probably.

BETTY: Yep.

BILL [*looks around*]: Well the waiters here sure seem to be in some different time
zone. I can't seem to locate one anywhere. . . . Waiter! [*He looks back.*]
So what do you—[*He sees that she's gone back to her book.*]

BETTY: I beg pardon?

BILL: Nothing. Sorry.

[*Bell.*]

BETTY: I guess we must be on different schedules.

BILL: Missed connections.

BETTY: Yes. Different time zones.

BILL: Amazing how you can live right next door to somebody in this town and
never even know it.

BETTY: I know.

BILL: City life.

BETTY: It's crazy.

BILL: You weren't waiting for somebody when I came in, were you?

Django Reinhardt: jazz guitarist (1910–1953), famous in Paris in the 1930s.

BETTY: Actually I was.
BILL: Oh. Boyfriend?
BETTY: Sort of.
BILL: What's a sort-of boyfriend?
BETTY: My husband.
BILL: Ah-ha.

[*Bell.*]

You weren't waiting for somebody when I came in, were you?

BETTY: Actually I was.
BILL: Oh. Boyfriend?
BETTY: Sort of.
BILL: What's a sort-of boyfriend?
BETTY: We were meeting here to break up.
BILL: Mm-hm . . .

[*Bell.*]

What's a sort-of boyfriend?

BETTY: My lover. Here she comes right now!

[*Bell.*]

BILL: You weren't waiting for somebody when I came in, were you?
BETTY: No, just reading.
BILL: Sort of a sad occupation for a Friday night, isn't it? Reading here, all by
        yourself?
BETTY: Do you think so?
BILL: Well sure. I mean, what's a good-looking woman like you doing out alone
        on a Friday night?
BETTY: Trying to keep away from lines like that.
BILL: No, listen—

[*Bell.*]

You weren't waiting for somebody when I came in, were you?

BETTY: No, just reading.
BILL: Sort of a sad occupation for a Friday night, isn't it? Reading here all by
        yourself?
BETTY: I guess it is, in a way.
BILL: What's a good-looking woman like you doing out alone on a Friday night
        anyway? No offense, but . . .
BETTY: I'm out alone on a Friday night for the first time in a very long time.
BILL: Oh.
BETTY: You see, I just recently ended a relationship.
BILL: Oh.
BETTY: Of rather long standing.
BILL: I'm sorry. [*Small pause.*] Well listen, since reading by yourself is such a sad
        occupation for a Friday night, would you like to go elsewhere?
BETTY: No . . .
BILL: Do something else?
BETTY: No thanks.

BILL: I was headed out to the movies in a while anyway.
BETTY: I don't think so.
BILL: Big chance to let Faulkner catch his breath. All those long sentences get him
     pretty tired.
BETTY: Thanks anyway.
BILL: Okay.
BETTY: I appreciate the invitation.
BILL: Sure thing.

[*Bell.*]

You weren't waiting for somebody when I came in, were you?

BETTY: No, just reading.
BILL: Sort of a sad occupation for a Friday night, isn't it? Reading here all by
     yourself?
BETTY: I guess I was trying to think of it as existentially romantic. You know—
     cappuccino, great literature, rainy night . . .
BILL: That only works in Paris. We *could* hop the late plane to Paris. Get on a
     Concorde. Find a café . . .
BETTY: I'm a little short on plane fare tonight.
BILL: Darn it, so am I.
BETTY: To tell you the truth, I was headed to the movies after I finished this
     section. Would you like to come along? Since you can't locate a waiter?
BILL: That's a very nice offer, but . . .
BETTY: Uh-huh. Girlfriend?
BILL: Two, actually. One of them's pregnant, and Stephanie—

[*Bell.*]

BETTY: Girlfriend?
BILL: No, I don't have a girlfriend. Not if you mean the castrating bitch I dumped
     last night.

[*Bell.*]

BETTY: Girlfriend?
BILL: Sort of. Sort of.
BETTY: What's a sort-of girlfriend?
BILL: My mother.

[*Bell.*]

I just ended a relationship, actually.

BETTY: Oh.
BILL: Of rather long standing.
BETTY: I'm sorry to hear it.
BILL: This is my first night out alone in a long time. I feel a little bit at sea, to tell
     you the truth.
BETTY: So you didn't stop to talk because you're a Moonie, or you have some
     weird political affiliation—?
BILL: Nope. Straight-down-the-ticket Republican.

[*Bell.*]

Straight-down-the-ticket Democrat.

[*Bell.*]

Can I tell you something about politics?

[*Bell.*]

I like to think of myself as a citizen of the universe.

[*Bell.*]

I'm unaffiliated.

BETTY: That's a relief. So am I.
BILL: I vote my beliefs.
BETTY: Labels are not important.
BILL: Labels are not important, exactly. Take me, for example. I mean, what does
    it matter if I had a two-point at—

[*Bell.*]

three-point at—

[*Bell.*]

four-point at college? Or if I did come from Pittsburgh—

[*Bell.*]

Cleveland—

[*Bell.*]

Westchester County?

BETTY: Sure.
BILL: I believe that a man is what he is.

[*Bell.*]

A person is what he is.

[*Bell.*]

A person is . . . what they are.

BETTY: I think so too.
BILL: So what if I admire Trotsky?

[*Bell.*]

So what if I once had a total-body liposuction?

[*Bell.*]

So what if I don't have a penis?

[*Bell.*]

So what if I spent a year in the Peace Corps? I was acting on my convictions.

BETTY: Sure.
BILL: You just can't hang a sign on a person.

BETTY: Absolutely. I'll bet you're a Scorpio.

[*Many bells ring.*]

Listen, I was headed to the movies after I finished this section. Would you like to come along?

BILL: That sounds like fun. What's playing?

BETTY: A couple of the really early Woody Allen movies.

BILL: Oh.

BETTY: You don't like Woody Allen?

BILL: Sure. I like Woody Allen.

BETTY: But you're not crazy about Woody Allen.

BILL: Those early ones kind of get on my nerves.

BETTY: Uh-huh.

[*Bell.*]

BILL: Y'know I was headed to the—

BETTY [*simultaneously*]: I was thinking about—

BILL: I'm sorry.

BETTY: No, go ahead.

BILL: I was going to say that I was headed to the movies in a little while, and . . .

BETTY: So was I.

BILL: The Woody Allen festival?

BETTY: Just up the street.

BILL: Do you like the early ones?

BETTY: I think anybody who doesn't ought to be run off the planet.

BILL: How many times have you seen *Bananas*?

BETTY: Eight times.

BILL: Twelve. So are you still interested? [*Long pause.*]

BETTY: Do you like Entenmann's crumb cake . . . ?

BILL: Last night I went out at two in the morning to get one. Did you have an Etch-a-Sketch as a child?

BETTY: Yes! And do you like Brussels sprouts? [*Pause.*]

BILL: No, I think they're disgusting.

BETTY: They *are* disgusting!

BILL: Do you still believe in marriage in spite of current sentiments against it?

BETTY: Yes.

BILL: And children?

BETTY: Three of them.

BILL: Two girls and a boy.

BETTY: Harvard, Vassar, and Brown.

BILL: And will you love me?

BETTY: Yes.

BILL: And cherish me forever?

BETTY: Yes.

BILL: Do you still want to go to the movies?

BETTY: Sure thing.

BILL AND BETTY [*together*]: Waiter!

BLACKOUT

[1988]

Joining the Conversation: Critical Thinking and Writing

1. Does *Sure Thing* have a plot? Does it follow the traditional formula of a beginning, a middle, and an end? (The conventional advice to playwrights is, "Get your guy up a tree, throw rocks at him, and get him down.") Is there an ending, a resolution, or do you think the play could go on and on? Please explain.
2. Ives's opening stage direction tells us that the play is set in a café, but no details are given. If you were staging the play, would you provide more than a table and two chairs? Some sort of atmosphere? Why, or why not?
3. Ives's text calls at the end for a blackout—a sudden darkening of the stage. Do you think this ending is preferable to a gradual fading of the lights, or a gradual closing of the curtain? Or, for that matter, why shouldn't the two characters leave some money on the table and walk out together? In short, staying with Ives's dialogue, evaluate other possible endings and present an argument for which one you believe is most effective. Ask yourself, "What kind of evidence do I need to make my argument as convincing as possible?"
4. If someone were to say to you that the play shows the need for people to keep revising their personalities, to (so to speak) keep reinventing themselves if they wish to function efficiently in the world, what might you reply? What does it mean to say that someone is "reinventing" himself or herself? Is that a desirable thing to do?

A Note on Greek Tragedy

Little or nothing is known for certain of the origin of Greek tragedy. The most common hypothesis holds that it developed from improvised speeches during choral dances honoring Dionysus, a Greek nature god associated with spring, fertility, and wine. Thespis (who perhaps never existed) is said to have introduced an actor into these choral performances in the sixth century BCE. Aeschylus (525–456 BCE), Greece's first great writer of tragedies, added the second actor, and Sophocles (496?–406 BCE) added the third actor and fixed the size of the chorus at fifteen. (Because the chorus leader often functioned as an additional actor, and because the actors sometimes doubled in their parts, a Greek tragedy could have more characters than might at first be thought.)

All the extant great Greek tragedy is of the fifth century BCE. It was performed at religious festivals in the winter and early spring, in large outdoor amphitheaters built on hillsides. Some of these theaters were enormous; the one at Epidaurus held about fifteen thousand people. The audience sat in tiers, looking down on the **orchestra** (a place for dancing), with the acting area behind it and the **skene** (the scene building) placed farther back. The scene building served as dressing room, background (suggesting a palace or temple), and place for occasional entrances and exits. Furthermore, this building helped to provide good acoustics, since speech travels well if there is a solid barrier behind the speakers and a hard, smooth surface in front of them, and if the audience sits in tiers. The wall of the scene building provided the barrier; the orchestra provided the surface in front of the actors; and the seats on the hillside fulfilled the third requirement. Moreover, the acoustics were somewhat improved by slightly elevating the actors above the orchestra, but it is not known exactly when this platform was first constructed in front of the scene building.

The theater at Epidaurus, located on the Peloponnesus, east of Nauplia, Greece.

A tragedy commonly begins with a ***prologos* (prologue)**, during which the exposition is given. Next comes the ***párodos***, the chorus's ode of entrance, sung while the chorus marches into the theater through the side aisles and onto the orchestra. The ***epeisodion* (episode)** is the ensuing scene; it is followed by a ***stasimon*** (choral song, ode). Usually, there are four or five *epeisodia,* alternating with *stasima*. Each of these choral odes has a **strophe** (lines presumably sung while the chorus dances in one direction) and an **antistrophe** (lines presumably sung while the chorus retraces its steps). Sometimes a third part, an **epode**, concludes an ode. (In addition to odes that are *stasima,* there can be odes within episodes; the fourth episode of *Antigonê* contains an ode complete with *epode*.) After the last part of the last ode comes the ***exodus***, the epilogue or final scene.

The actors (all male) wore masks, and they seem to have chanted much of the play. Perhaps the total result of combining speech with music and dancing was a sort of music–drama roughly akin to opera with some spoken dialogue, such as Mozart's *The Magic Flute* (1791).

A Greek Tragedy

Jane Lapotaire in *Antigone*. National Theatre, London, 1984. (Donald Cooper/Photostage)

SOPHOCLES

One of the three great writers of tragedies in ancient Greece, Sophocles (496?–406 BCE) was born in Colonus, near Athens, into a well-to-do family. Well educated, he first won public acclaim as a tragic poet at the age of twenty-seven, in 468 BCE, when he defeated Aeschylus in a competition for writing a tragic play. He is said to have written some 120 plays, but only seven tragedies are extant; among them are Oedipus the King Antigone, *and* Oedipus at Colonus. *He died, much honored, in his ninetieth year, in Athens, where he had lived his entire life.*

BACKGROUND TO THE STORY: Once King of Thebes, Oedipus was the Should be ISMENE of two sons, Polynices and Eteocles, and of two daughters, ANTIGONE and ISMENE. Oedipus unwittingly killed his father, Laius, and married his own mother, Jocasta. When he learned what he had done, he blinded himself and left Thebes. Eteocles and Polynices quarreled, Polynices was driven out but returned to assault Thebes. In the battle, each brother killed the other; CREON (uncle of Oedipus's four children) became king and ordered that Polynices (whom CREON regards as a traitor because he invaded his own land) be left to rot on the battlefield unburied.

Antigone

*Translated by Michael Townsend**

CHARACTERS

ANTIGONE	HAEMON	EURYDICE
ISMENE	TEIRESIAS	SERVANT
CREON	BOY	CHORUS
GUARD	MESSENGER	

*Stage directions and footnotes have been added by the editors.

[*Enter* ANTIGONE *and* ISMENE.]

ANTIGONE: My darling sister Ismene, we have had
    A fine inheritance from Oedipus.
    God has gone through the whole range of sufferings
    And piled them all on us,—grief upon grief,
    Humiliation upon humiliation.   5
    And now this latest thing that our dictator
    Has just decreed . . . you heard of it? Or perhaps
    You haven't noticed our enemies at work.
ISMENE: No news, either good or bad, has come
    To me, Antigone: nothing since the day   10
    We were bereaved of our two brothers. No,
    Since the withdrawal of the Argive army
    Last night, I've heard nothing about our loved ones
    To make me glad or sad.
ANTIGONE: I thought as much.
    That's why I brought you out, outside the gate,   15
    So we could have a talk here undisturbed.
ISMENE: You've something on your mind. What is it then?
ANTIGONE: Only that our friend Creon has decided
    To discriminate between our brothers' corpses.
    Eteocles he buried with full honors   20
    To light his way to hell in a blaze of glory.
    But poor dear Polynices,—his remains
    Are not allowed a decent burial.
    He must be left unmourned, without a grave,
    A happy hunting ground for birds   25
    To peck for tidbits. This ukase applies
    To you,—and me of course. What's more, friend Creon
    Is on his way here now to supervise
    Its circulation in person. And don't imagine
    He isn't serious,—the penalty   30
    For disobedience is to be stoned to death.
    So, there you have it. You're of noble blood.
    Soon you must show your mettle,—if you've any.
ISMENE: Oh my fire-eating sister, what am I
    Supposed to do about it, if this is the case?   35
ANTIGONE: Just think it over—if you'll give a hand . . .
ISMENE: In doing what? What do you have in mind?
ANTIGONE: Just helping me do something for the corpse.
ISMENE: You don't intend to bury him? It's forbidden.
ANTIGONE: He is my brother, and yours. My mind's made up.   40
    You please yourself.
ISMENE: But Creon has forbidden. . . .
ANTIGONE: What Creon says is quite irrelevant.
    He is my brother. I will bury him.
ISMENE: Oh God.
    Have you forgotten how our father died,   45
    Despised and hated? How he turned
    Detective to discover his own crimes,
    Then stabbed his own eyes out with his own hands?

And then Jocasta, who was both together
His mother and his wife,   50
Hanged herself with a rope? Next, our two brothers
Became each other's murderers. We are left,
We two. How terrible if we as well
Are executed for disobeying
The lawful orders of the head of state.   55
Oh please remember,—we are women, aren't we?
We shouldn't take on men. In times of crisis
It is the strongest men who take control.
We must obey their orders, however harsh.
So, while apologizing to the dead,   60
Regretting that I act under constraint,
I will comply with my superior's orders.
Sticking one's neck out would be merely foolish.

ANTIGONE: Don't think I'm forcing you. In fact, I wouldn't
Have your assistance if you offered it.   65
You've made your bed; lie on it. I intend
To give my brother burial. I'll be glad
To die in the attempt,—if it's a crime,
Then it's a crime that God commands. I then
Could face my brother as a friend and look   70
Him in the eyes. Why shouldn't I make sure
I get on with the dead rather than with
The living? There is all eternity
To while away below. And as for you,
By all means be an atheist if you wish.   75

ISMENE: I'm not. I'm simply powerless to act
Against this city's laws.

ANTIGONE: That's your excuse.
Good-bye. I'm going now to make a grave
For our brother, whom I love.

ISMENE: Oh, dear.
I'm terribly afraid for you.

ANTIGONE: Don't make a fuss   80
On my account,—look after your own skin.

ISMENE: At least then promise me that you will tell
No one of this; and I'll keep quiet too.

ANTIGONE: For God's sake don't do that,—you're sure to be
Far more unpopular if you keep quiet.   85
No; blurt it out, please do.

ISMENE: You're very cheerful.

ANTIGONE: That is because I'm helping those I know
That I should help.

ISMENE: I only hope you can,
But it's impossible.

ANTIGONE: Must I hang back
From trying, just because you say I can't?   90

ISMENE: If it's impossible, you shouldn't try
At all.

ANTIGONE: If that's your line, you've earned my hatred
　　　And that of our dead brother too, by rights.
　　　Oh, kindly let me go my foolish way,
　　　And take the consequences. I will suffer　　　　　　　　95
　　　Nothing worse than death in a good cause.
ISMENE: All right then, off you go. I'm bound to say
　　　You're being very loyal, but very silly.

　[*Exit* ANTIGONE *and* ISMENE, *separately. Enter* CHORUS.]

CHORUS: At last it has dawned, the day that sees
　　　The force that rode from Argos driven　　　　　　　　100
　　　Back upon its road again
　　　With headlong horses on a looser rein.

　　　Roused by Polynices to aid his claim,
　　　Like an eagle screaming,
　　　With snow-tipped wings and bloody claws　　　　　　105
　　　And mouth agape, it wheeled about our fortress doors.

　　　But Thebes, a hissing snake, fought back.
　　　The god of fire could get no grip
　　　Upon our crown of walls. That bird of prey,
　　　Its beak balked of our blood, has turned away.　　　　110

　　　God hates presumption. When he saw
　　　Those men in ostentatious force
　　　And clash of gold advancing,
　　　He singled out one man all set
　　　To shout the victory cry upon the parapet,　　　　　　115
　　　And flung at him a lightning bolt, to curtail his prancing.

　　　Covered in flame he dropped
　　　Down like an empty balance and drummed the earth;
　　　He who before had breathed
　　　The winds of hate against us. In many a foray and rout,　　120
　　　War, a runaway horse, was hitting out.

　　　Seven enemy kings at seven gates,
　　　Fighting at equal odds,
　　　Left their arms as trophies to Theban gods.

　　　Elsewhere, the hated pair,　　　　　　　　　　　125
　　　Sons of the same mother,
　　　Crossed their swords in combat and killed each other.

　　　But now that Victory has smiled on us,
　　　Let us forget the war, and dance
　　　At every temple all night long. And let　　　　　　　130
　　　Bacchus be king in Thebes, until the strong earth reels.

　　　Ah, here comes Creon, our ruler,—in haste.
　　　Something new has developed.
　　　He has something afoot . . .
　　　Else why has he summoned us to council?　　　　　135

[*Enter* CREON.]

CREON: Well, friends, our city has passed through stormy weather.
But now God has restored an even keel.
Why have I summoned you? Because I know
That you were at all times loyal to Laius.
And afterwards, when Oedipus put things right,   140
Then ruined them again, you showed
Your steadiness throughout his sons' dispute.
Well, now they're dead; and so, by due succession,
The power of the crown passes to me.
You cannot possibly judge a ruler's worth   145
Until he exercises the power he's got.
I've no time for the man who has full powers
Yet doesn't use them to enact good measures,
But adopts a timid policy of "do nothing."
Those aren't my principles. I'm not the man   150
To sit quietly by and watch my country
Sliding towards the precipice of ruin.
Nor can I be a friend to my country's foes.
This I believe—and God may witness it—
Our safety is bound up with that of our country. Therefore   155
All other loyalties are subject to
Our country's interests.
By such measures I'll make this city great;—
Measures like those that I have just enacted
Concerning Oedipus' sons. That Eteocles   165
Who died while fighting in his country's service,
Is to be buried with ceremonial honors.
But Polynices,—whose intention was
To fight his way back from exile, burn to the ground
His mother city and the temples of   165
His family's gods, to slaughter out of hand
And to enslave his fellow citizens—
He's not to have a grave or any mourning.
His corpse is to be left, a grim warning,
Pecked at by birds and worried by the dogs.   170
That is my policy. A malefactor mustn't
Have the same treatment as the loyal man.
I intend to see our country's friends rewarded
When they are dead, as well as while they live.
CHORUS: We understand the attitude you take   175
Towards these men. It's true your word is law,
And you can legislate for living and dead. . . .
CREON: What do you think then of this new enactment?
CHORUS: If I were younger, I might criticize. . . .
CREON: No turning back. The guard is set on the corpse.   180
CHORUS: What are the penalties for disobeying?
CREON: The penalty is death. As simple as that.
CHORUS: That ought to stop them. Who'd be such a fool?
CREON: You'd be surprised. Men led astray by hopes
Of gain will risk even their lives for money.   185

[*Enter* GUARD.]

GUARD: Sir, here I am. I can't pretend I'm puffed
    From running here with all possible speed.
    I kept changing my mind on the way.
    One moment I was thinking, "What's the hurry?
    You're bound to catch it when you get there." Then: 190
    "What are you dithering for? You'll get it hot
    And strong if Creon finds out from someone else."
    Torn by these doubts I seem to have taken my time.
    So what should be a short journey has become
    A long one. Anyway I have arrived.   195
    And now I'm going to tell you what I came
    To tell you, even if you've heard it. See,
    I've made up my mind to expect the worst.
    We can't avoid what's coming to us, can we?
CREON: Well then, what puts you in such deep despair?   200
GUARD: First I must make a statement—about myself.
    I didn't do it, and didn't see who did it.
    So I'm quite in the clear, you understand.
CREON: For God's sake tell me what it is, and then
    Get out.
GUARD: All right, all right. It amounts to this.   205
    Somebody's buried the body, thrown earth on it,
    And done the necessary purifications.
CREON: Someone has been a damn fool. Who was it?
GUARD: Dunno. There were no spade-marks in the earth.
    The ground was hard and dry, and so there was   210
    No sign of the intruder.
    See, when the man who had the first day watch
    Told us about it, we had the shock of our lives.
    The corpse had not been buried in a grave,
    But enough dust was thrown on to avoid   215
    The curse unburied bodies suffer from.
    There wasn't even a sign of any dog
    That might have come and scuffed the dust upon him.
    Then everyone started shouting. Each man blamed
    His mate. We very nearly came to blows.   220
    Everyone claimed that one of the others had done it,
    And tried to prove that he himself was blameless.
    To prove their innocence, some said they were
    Prepared to pick up red-hot coals or walk
    Through fire. While others swore on oath,   225
    By a catalog of gods, they didn't do it
    And weren't accomplices in any form.
    When our investigations made no progress,
    In the end one man came out with a sobering speech.
    We couldn't answer him, though what he said   230
    Was none too pleasant.
    He said we mustn't try to hush it up,
    But tell you everything. His view prevailed.
    Who was to bring the news? We tossed for it.

I was the lucky person. I can tell you,   235
I don't like being the bearer of bad news.
CHORUS: I think I see the hand of God in this,
Bringing about the body's burial.
CREON: Shut up, before I lose my temper.
You may be old, try not to be foolish as well.   240
How can you say God cares about this corpse?
Do you suppose God feels obliged to him
For coming to burn down his temples and
His statues, in defiance of his laws?
Ever noticed God being kind to evildoers?   245
No. Certain hostile elements in the city
Who don't like discipline and resent my rule,
Are in on this. They've worked upon the guards
By bribes. There is no human institution
As evil as money. Money ruins nations,   250
And makes men refugees. Money corrupts
The best of men into depravity.
The people who have done this thing for money
Will get what's coming to them. Listen here,
I swear to you by God who is my judge,   255
That if you and your friends do not divulge
The name of him who did the burying
One hell won't be enough for you. You'll all
Be hanged up and flogged until you tell.
That ought to teach you to be more selective   260
About what you get your money from.
GUARD: Am I dismissed?
Or may I speak?
CREON: I thought I made it plain
I couldn't stand your talk.
GUARD: Where does it hurt you,—
Your ears, or in your mind?
CREON: What do you mean?
What does it matter where you give me pain?   265
GUARD: The guilty party bothers you deep down.
But my offense is only at ear level.
CREON: My dear good man, you're much too talkative.
GUARD: I may be that, but I am not your culprit.
CREON: I think you are, and that you did it for money.   270
GUARD: Oh God! I tell you your suspicions are wrong.
CREON: Suspicion he calls it! Look here, if you
Don't tell me who the culprits are, you'll find
That ill-gotten gains are not without their drawbacks. [*Exit* CREON.]
GUARD: Good luck to you, I hope you find the man.   275
In any case I won't be in a hurry
To come back here again. I thank my stars
That I have saved my skin. I didn't expect to. [*Exit* GUARD.]
CHORUS: Many amazing things exist, and the most amazing is man.
He's the one, when the gale-force winds   280
Blow and the big waves
Tower and topple on every side,

Cruises over the deep on the gray tide.
He's the one that to and fro
Over the clods year after year   285
Wends with his horses and ploughing gear,
Works to his will the untiring Earth, the greatest of gods.

He traps the nitwit birds, and the wild
Beasts in their lairs. The ocean's myriad clan
In woven nets he catches,—ingenious man.   290

He has devised himself shelter against
The rigors of frost and the pelting weather.
Speech and science he's taught himself,
And the city's political arts for living together.

For incurable diseases he has found a cure;   295
By his inventiveness defying
Every eventuality there can be,—except dying.

But the most brilliant gifts
Can be misapplied.
On his moral road   300
Man swerves from side to side.

God and the government ordain
Just laws; the citizen
Who rules his life by them
Is worthy of acclaim.   305

But he that presumes
To set the law at naught
Is like a stateless person,
Outlawed, beyond the pale.

With such a man I'd have   310
No dealings whatsoever.
In public and in private
He'd get the cold shoulder.

What's this? What on earth?
My God. Can it be? Yes, Antigone.   315
Your father before, now you!
Is it so, you were caught disobeying the law?
How could you have been so stupid?

[*Enter* GUARD *with* ANTIGONE.]

GUARD: Here she is. She is the one,—the one that did it.
    We caught her in the act. Where's Creon gone?   320
CHORUS: There, by good luck he's coming out right now.

[*Enter* CREON.]

CREON: Soon as I leave the house, some trouble starts.
    What's happening?
GUARD: Well, well, I never thought
    That I'd be coming back here again so soon,

Considering how you swore at me just now.   325
But here I am, in spite of what I said.
I'm bringing in this girl. I caught her tending
The grave. I caught her, no one else. And so
I hand her over to you to stand her trial.
And now I reckon I'm entitled to beat it.   330
CREON: Give me full details, with the circumstances.
GUARD: This girl was burying him. As simple as that.
CREON: I trust you understand what you are saying.
GUARD: I saw her burying the corpse you said
    Was not permitted to be buried. Clear enough?   335
CREON: Tell me precisely how you saw and caught her.
GUARD: It was like this. When we got back,
    With your threats still smarting in our ears,
    We swept all the dust from off the corpse,
    And laid the moldering thing completely bare.   340
    Then we went and sat on the high ground to windward,
    To avoid the smell. And everyone gave hell
    To the man who was on duty, to keep him up
    To scratch. We watched till midday, when the sun
    Is hottest. Suddenly a squall came on,—   345
    A whirlwind with a thunderstorm; it ripped
    The leaves from every tree in all the plain.
    The air was full of it; we had to keep
    Our eyes tight shut against the wrath of heaven.
    At last, when all was over, there we see   350
    The girl,—crying like a bird that finds
    Its nest empty of chicks,—her having seen
    The corpse uncovered. Then she started cursing
    Whoever did it. Next she goes and fetches
    Dust in her hands; and from a jug she pours   355
    A set of three libations on the corpse.
    When we saw that of course we jumped straight up
    And grabbed the girl. She took it very calmly.
    We charged her with this crime and the previous one,
    And she admitted them. So I'm half glad,   360
    Half sorry. Glad that I am out of danger,
    But sorry someone that I like's in trouble.
    However, main thing is that I'm all right.
CREON: You, with your eyes fixed on the ground.
    Do you admit the charges or deny them?   365
ANTIGONE: I don't deny the charges. I admit them.
CREON: (*to* GUARD) All right, clear off. [*Exit* GUARD.] Consider yourself lucky
    To be absolved of guilt.
    (*to* ANTIGONE) Now tell me, briefly,—I don't want a speech.
    You knew about my edict which forbade this?   370
ANTIGONE: Of course I knew. You made it plain enough.
CREON: You took it on yourself to disobey?
ANTIGONE: Sorry, who made this edict? Was it God?
    Isn't a man's right to burial decreed
    By divine justice? I don't consider your   375
    Pronouncements so important that they can

Just . . . overrule the unwritten laws of heaven.
You are a man, remember.
These divine laws are not just temporary measures.
They stand forever. I would have to face   380
Them when I died. And I will die, without
Your troubling to arrange it. So, what matter
If I must die before my time? I'd welcome
An early death, living as I do now.
What I can't stand is passively submitting   385
To my own brother's body being unburied.
I dare say you think I'm being silly.
Perhaps you're not so very wise yourself.

CHORUS: She's difficult, just like her father was.
          She doesn't realize when to give in.   390

CREON: I know these rigid temperaments. They're the first
          To break. The hardest-tempered steel
          Will shatter at a blow. The highest-mettled
          Horses are broken in with a small bit.
          That's what is needed, discipline. This girl   395
          Knew damned well she was kicking over the traces,
          Breaking the law. And now when she has done it,
          She boasts about it, positively gloats.
          If she gets away with this behavior,
          Call me a woman and call her a man.   400
          I don't care if she is my sister's daughter.
          I don't care if she's closer to me than all
          My family. She and her sister won't get off.
          I'll execute them.
                              Oh yes, her as well.
          She's in it too. Go get her. She's inside.   405
          I saw her in there muttering, half-balmy.
          It is her conscience. She can't hide her guilt.
          At least she doesn't try to justify it.

ANTIGONE: Won't my death be enough? Do you want more?

CREON: No, that will do, as far as I'm concerned.   410

ANTIGONE: Then why not do it now? Our wills conflict
          Head-on. No chance of reconciliation.
          I can't think of a finer reason for dying,—
          Guilty of having buried my own brother.
          These men are on my side. But they daren't say so.   415

CREON: That's where you're wrong. You're quite alone in this.

ANTIGONE: They're on my side. They're forced to cringe to you.

CREON: These men obey. But you and you alone
          Decide to disobey. Aren't you ashamed?

ANTIGONE: Ashamed? Ashamed of what? Ashamed of being   420
          Loyal to my own family, my own brother?

CREON: Eteocles was also your own brother.

ANTIGONE: Indeed he was. Of course he was my brother.

CREON: Then why were you so disloyal to him?

ANTIGONE: If he were living now, he'd back me up.   425

CREON: For treating his brother no differently from him!

ANTIGONE: It was his brother that died, not just some servant.

CREON: Died while commanding an invading force!
  But Eteocles died fighting for his country.
ANTIGONE: That doesn't affect the laws of burial.   430
CREON: You can't treat friend and enemy the same.
ANTIGONE: Who knows what the rules are among the dead?
CREON: Your enemy doesn't become your friend by dying.
ANTIGONE: If we must have these groupings, let me say
  I'll join anyone in loving, but not in hating.   435
CREON: All right then, die, and love them both in hell.
  I'm not here to be shoved around by a woman.

  [*Enter* ISMENE, *guarded.*]

CHORUS: Oh, look, by the gate, here's Ismene.
  She's crying because of her sister.
  What a shame this heavy cloud of grief   440
  Should spoil her attractive appearance.
CREON: And now for you. You who've been skulking quiet,
  Injecting your slow poison like a viper.
  Imagine my not noticing,—I've been rearing
  Two furies in my house, ready to bite   445
  The hand that fed them. Just you tell me now—
  Will you confess you were party to this burial,
  Or will you swear you had no knowledge of it?
ISMENE: I did it, if she did it. I'm involved.
  I'm in with her and bear my share of blame.   450
ANTIGONE: That's quite unjustified. You didn't want
  To help me, and I didn't let you join me.
ISMENE: You are in trouble. May I then not make
  Myself your comrade in adversity?
ANTIGONE: The dead know who it was that did the deed.   455
  You took no action. Your speeches don't impress me.
ISMENE: How can you, being my sister, deny my wish
  To die with you for Polynices' sake?
ANTIGONE: Don't go and die as well as me, and don't
  Lay claim to what you haven't done. I'm going   460
  To die. One death's enough.
ISMENE: Will life be worth
  Living to me, left all alone without you?
ANTIGONE: May I suggest an object of affection?
  Creon. He is your uncle, after all.
ISMENE: Why do you try to hurt me? What's the point?   465
ANTIGONE: I may make fun of you, but I feel this deeply.
ISMENE: I only want to know how I can help you.
ANTIGONE: Well, save yourself then. I don't grudge you that.
ISMENE: I don't want that. I want to die with you.
ANTIGONE: You chose to live; I chose to die, remember?   470
ISMENE: I didn't express my innermost convictions.
ANTIGONE: You sounded pretty convinced at the time.
ISMENE: I still maintain that we two share the guilt.
ANTIGONE: Don't worry. You won't die. But I've already
  Sacrificed my life to help the dead.   475

CREON: These girls! One of them's been mad all her life.
    And now the other one's gone balmy too.
ISMENE: But, sir, however sensible one is,
    Adversity is bound to affect one's judgment.
CREON: Well, it has yours! You join this criminal,   480
    And identify yourself with her misdeeds . . .
ISMENE: There is no life left for me without her.
CREON: Forget about her. She's as good as dead.
ISMENE: So you would execute your own son's bride?
CREON: Plenty of other women in the world.   485
ISMENE: But they were so well suited to each other.
CREON: I won't have my son marrying a bitch.
ANTIGONE: Poor Haemon! See how much your father cares.
CREON: Oh, go to hell,—you and your marriage with you.
ISMENE: You really intend to take her from your son?   490
CREON: I won't stop the marriage. Death will stop it.
ISMENE: There's no way out? It is fixed that she dies?
CREON: Of course it's fixed. Stop wasting time.
    You servants, take her in. It's very important
    To keep women strictly disciplined.   495
    That's the deterrent. Even the bravest people
    Will step down quick when they see death loom up.

    [*Exit* ISMENE, ANTIGONE, *and* GUARDS.]

CHORUS: Happy the man whose life is uneventful.
    For once a family is cursed by God,
    Disasters come like earthquake tremors, worse   500
    With each succeeding generation.

    It's like when the sea is running rough
    Under stormy winds from Thrace.
    The black ooze is stirred up from the sea-bed,
    And louder and louder the waves crash on shore.   505

    Look now at the last sunlight that sustains
    The one surviving root of Oedipus' tree,—
    The sword of death is drawn to hack it down.

    And all through nothing more than intemperate
        language.
    All through nothing more than hasty temper.   510

    What power on earth can resist
    Your strength, O God? You stand supreme,
    Untouched by sleep that makes all else feel old,
    Untired by the passing years that wear all else away.

    I know one rule that has stood,   515
    And will stand, forever.
    That nothing in our life can be exempt
    From the universal forces that make for ruin.

    Hope, that tramps all roads, may help at times.
    More often, it deludes weak-minded men.   520

They never notice, till they feel the fire.

It is a wise saying, that
When God is set against you,
You welcome the path to ruin,—but not for long.

Here comes Haemon, your youngest son.   525
I expect he's grieved about his bride,
And this sudden bar to his marriage.

[*Enter* HAEMON.]

CREON: There's one way of finding out for certain.
My son, you've heard about this public decree.
Have you come here in a spirit of indignation   530
About your bride, or are you going to be
Loyal to me whatever I'm involved in?
HAEMON: I am your son. So while your policies
Are just, you have my full obedience.
I certainly wouldn't consider any marriage   535
As important as the right leadership by you.
CREON: Good, good. Your heart is in the right place. Nothing
Should come before your loyalty to your father.
Why else do fathers pray for well-behaved sons?
They do things together. Work together against   540
Their common enemy. Vie with each
Other in being good friends to their friends.
As for the man who brings up useless sons,
He's got himself a load of trouble,—all
His enemies laugh at them, a bad team.   545
Never get carried away by a woman, son.
Sex isn't everything. If she's a bitch,
You'll feel a coldness as she lies beside you.
Can there be anything worse than giving your love
To a bitch that doesn't deserve it? No, reject her,   550
And let her go and find a husband in hell.
Now that I've caught her flagrantly disobeying
When everybody else has toed the line,
The eyes of the nation are on me. I must stay
True to my principles. I must execute her.   555
I don't give a damn for all her talk
About family ties. If I allow
My own relations to get out of control,
That gives the cue to everybody else.
People who are loyal members of their families   560
Will be good citizens too. But if a person
Sets himself up above the law and tries
To tell his rulers what they ought to do,—
You can't expect me to approve of that.
Once a man has authority, he must be obeyed,—   565
In big things and in small, in every act,
Whether just or not so just. I tell you this,
The well-disciplined man is good

At giving orders and at taking them too.
In war, in a crisis, he's the sort of man   570
You like to have beside you. On the other hand,
There's nothing so disastrous as anarchy.
Anarchy means an ill-disciplined army,
A rabble that will break into a panic rout.
What follows? Plundered cities, homeless people.   575
A disciplined army loses few men;
Discipline pulls them through to victory.
We can't go about kowtowing to women.
If I must lose my throne, let it be a man
That takes it from me. I can't have people saying   580
My will has been defeated by a woman.

CHORUS: I think your observations very just,
     In general . . . though perhaps I'm old and silly.

HAEMON: Father, don't you agree,—
     Of all God's gifts, good sense is far the best.   585
I'm sure I'd be the last person to deny
That what you said is true. Yet there may be
A lot of justice in the opposite view.
I've one advantage over you,—I know
Before you what the people think about you,   590
Especially criticism. You're so held in awe
That people dare not say things to your face.
But I am able to hear their secret talk.
The people feel sorry for Antigone.
They say it isn't equitable she must die   595
A horrible death for such a noble action.
They say that she in fact deserves special
Honor for refusing to allow
The body of her brother to be left
Unburied for dogs and birds to pull to pieces.   600
That is their secret opinion, and it's gaining ground.
Of course I want your rule to be a success.
There's nothing more important to me than that.
Such feeling is mutual, between father and son,—
One's glad to see the other doing well.   605
Don't be too single-minded, then. Don't think
You have a complete monopoly of the truth.
Isn't it true that people who refuse
To see any other point of view but theirs
Often get shown up and discredited?   610
However acute one is, there's no disgrace
In being able to learn, being flexible.
In winter, when the streams turn into torrents,
You can see the trees that try to resist the water
Get rooted out and killed. But those that bend   615
A little, manage to survive the flood.
In a gale at sea if you cram on full sail,
You'll soon have the waves breaking aboard
And bowling over all the furniture.

Why not relax and change your mind for once?   620
Perhaps at my age I should not express
An opinion, but I would like to say this:—
Not everyone can be right on every issue,
But the next best thing is to take notice of
And learn from the judicious thoughts of others.   625
CHORUS: Yes, everyone can learn. You, sir, can learn
From him,—and he of course from you. There's much
Of substance in the arguments on both sides.
CREON: Am I to stand here and be lectured to
By a kid? A man of my experience!   630
HAEMON: I'm not suggesting anything illegal.
I may be young, but judge me by the facts.
CREON: The facts are, you're encouraging my detractors.
HAEMON: I'm not encouraging anything that's wrong.
CREON: You seem to have caught Antigone's disease.   635
HAEMON: The people of Thebes don't call it a disease.
CREON: Must I ask their permission for everything?
HAEMON: You're talking like an adolescent now.
CREON: Am I the king of Thebes, or am I not?
HAEMON: It takes more than one person to make a nation.   640
CREON: But a nation is personified in its ruler.
HAEMON: In that case Thebes has got no population.
CREON: I take it you are siding with this woman.
HAEMON: It is your interests I have at heart.
CREON: You show it by arguing against me?   645
HAEMON: Because I think you're making a mistake.
CREON: Must I let my authority be undermined?
HAEMON: Yes, rather your authority than God's.
CREON: What character! Subservient to a woman.
HAEMON: Subservient to what I think is right.   650
CREON: You've done nothing but back Antigone up.
HAEMON: Not only her, but God, and you as well.
CREON: Don't try to butter me up, you ladies' man.
HAEMON: You like to talk, but you're not prepared to listen.
CREON: This woman will not live to marry you.   655
HAEMON: Then she won't be the only one to die.
CREON: Oh, oh. Threats is it now? You've got a nerve.
HAEMON: I'm trying to show you that you're being perverse.
CREON: You will regret you tried to schoolmaster me.
HAEMON: If you weren't my father, I'd say you were deranged.   660
CREON: What's that? I've had enough of your abuse.
By heaven, I swear I'll make you suffer for it.
Take that hell-cat away. You'll watch her die.
Ha, she will die in front of her bridegroom's nose.
HAEMON: I won't give you that satisfaction.   665
I won't be around when she dies.
You must find other friends to condone your madness.
You will never set eyes on me again. [*Exit* HAEMON.]
CHORUS: He's rushed off in a really furious temper.   670
He's young,—I fear he may do something rash.

CREON: Let him.
>   Who does he think he is, God almighty?
>   In any case, he won't save these girls from death.

CHORUS: You don't mean to execute them both?

CREON: No, no. You're right. Not her that wasn't involved.   675

CHORUS: What sort of execution do you intend?

CREON: I'll take her to a deserted spot
>   And bury her alive in a trench.
>   She'll have enough food to avoid the curse,—
>   The people mustn't suffer because of her.   680
>   There she can pray to the god she likes so much,—
>   The god of death. Perhaps he'll save her life.
>   Either that, or she'll find out too late
>   That corpses are more trouble than they're worth.

CHORUS: What is it that nestles in   685
>   The soft cheeks of a girl,
>   And pervades the deep sea and the teeming earth,
>   And persecutes god and man, a force
>   Irresistible? We call it Love.
>   A man possessed by Love loses control.   690
>   Love drives the law-abiding into crime;
>   And sets a family against itself.
>
>   So here a lovely girl's appealing glance
>   Has prevailed, and destroyed the bonds of blood.
>   For Love makes mock of time-honored laws   695
>   Ordaining loyalty from son to father.
>
>   And grief also is irresistible.
>   The tears come to my eyes,—I cannot stop them;
>   Seeing Antigone go to such a bed,
>   The bed that puts all mortal things to sleep.   700

ANTIGONE: Take a good look. With life still strong in me,
>   I'm going on my last journey, seeing
>   For the last time the bright rays of the sun.
>   Unmarried, never having heard my wedding song,
>   Death takes me to the dark riverbanks to be his bride.   705

CHORUS: You have one glorious consolation.
>   By your own choice you go down to death
>   Alive, not wasted by disease,
>   Nor hacked by instruments of war.

ANTIGONE: I shall go to sleep like Niobe.°   710
>   I know her story well. On Mount Sipylus
>   The rock grew, like ivy, round her and weighed her down.
>   And now the rain and snow
>   Make tears that run across her stony face.

---

710 Niobe Niobe boasted of her numerous children, provoking Apollo's mother to destroy them. Niobe wept uncontrollably, and was turned into stone on Mount Sipylus, whose streams are her tears.

CHORUS: There's no comparison. For she was born   715
    Of divine parentage. You would be lucky
    To share the fate of mythical heroines.

ANTIGONE: Are you getting at me? Wait till I'm dead.
    I'm going to die,—do I merit no respect?
    O my city, O my friends, rich householders,   720
    O river Dirce, with the sacred grove
    Of Thebes the Charioteer, I call you all
    To witness that I die with nobody
    To shed a tear for me, the victim
    Of an unjust law. Who'd like to go with me   725
    To an eerie heap of stones, a tomb that is no tomb,
    A no-man's land between the living and the dead?

CHORUS: You tried to do the right thing by your brother.
    You stepped boldly towards the altar of Justice,
    But somehow stumbled. I fear you must suffer   730
    For your father's sins.

ANTIGONE: Don't speak of it again. It's only too well known,—
    My father's fate. To think how much
    Our family was admired, in generations past.
    Then came successive strokes of doom. My mother's   735
    Marriage to her son, the union
    From which I came, to end like this.
    My brother, dishonored, drags me down with him,
    And so I go to join my stricken family in hell.

CHORUS: We respect what you did for your brother.   740
    But there's no question that the orders
    Of those in authority must be obeyed.
    You were self-willed. That has been your undoing.

ANTIGONE: I see I have no friends to say good-bye.
    No friends, no tears for me, no marriage to look back on.   745
    Never again to see the face of the sun.

CREON: If I don't stop this blubbering, we'll be here
    All night. Stop wasting time. Take her away.
    As my instructions state, you are to place
    Her in the vaulted trench, and brick it in.   750
    It's up to her then,—either live or die.
    My hands are clean in this. I've merely
    Deprived her of all contact with the living.

ANTIGONE: This stone dugout, half tomb, half bridal-chamber,
    Will house me now for good. By this road   755
    I go below to Queen Persephone's kingdom,
    To see again so many of my family.
    As I am the latest recruit, so is my fate
    By far the cruelest. And I've not used
    My life's full span.   760
    At least I can look forward to a warm
    Welcome from my dear mother and father and
    My brother Eteocles. When they were dead,
    I washed them and prepared them for the grave   765
    With my own hands, and poured libations over them.

But now, for doing the same to Polynices,
This is my reward. Because Creon thinks
I have committed an act of brazen defiance.
For this I'm being dragged off by force,
Deprived of my chance to marry and raise children.   770
I'm to be buried alive, not very pleasant. . . .
I just want to ask, what moral law
Have I disobeyed? But what's the point
Of appealing to God? Or asking
Help from my fellow humans? It appears   775
That virtue is to be repaid by malice.
If that is God's idea of what is right,
Then I apologize; I made a mistake.
But if Creon is wrong, I only hope
He isn't treated any better than me.   780

CHORUS: A hurricane of passionate conviction
Still sweeps her mind.

CREON: Don't stand about, you lot; or else . . . .
Hurry, and off with her.

ANTIGONE: Oh, right before me now. Death.   785

CHORUS: If you had any hopes, I should forget them.
Your punishment is fixed. There's no appeal.

ANTIGONE: This is it. The time has come.
For doing what was right,
I'm dragged away to death.   790
And Thebes, city where I was born,
And you my friends, the rich people of Thebes,
Will you judge between us?
You might at least look and remember.

[*Exit* ANTIGONE *guarded.*]

CHORUS: My poor child, what must be   795
Must be. Console yourself,
Such things have happened before.

There's nothing that can win the fight
Against the force of destiny;
Not wealth, or military might,   800
Or city walls, or ships that breast the sea.

Lycurgus, king of Thrace, tried to stop
The bacchanal women and their torchlit orgies.
For his vindictive rage,
He lost his liberty with his temper, locked   805
By Bacchus in a mountain cave
To let his anger simmer down.

In Salmydessus on the Euxine Sea,
The two sons of Phineus lost their eyes.
In their stepmother's hand, a pointed shuttle   810
And their blood on her nails cried out for
    vengeance.

But their mother was jailed in a cavern
Under a steep mountain far away.
She was Cleopatra, the North Wind's daughter.
A god's daughter, but fate weighed her down. 815

[*Enter* TEIRESIAS, *led by a boy.*]

TEIRESIAS: Councillors of Thebes, I have come,—
 A man with four eyes, half of them blind . . .
CREON: It's old Teiresias. What's up, old fellow?
TEIRESIAS: Listen, and I will tell you. I'm no liar . . .
CREON: I've never suggested that. Quite the reverse. 820
TEIRESIAS: By doing so, you were able to save Thebes.
CREON: True, I have found what you have said most useful.
TEIRESIAS: Listen to me. You're on the razor's edge.
CREON: What's wrong? The way you talk gives me a turn.
TEIRESIAS: You may think nothing's wrong. But my skill 825
 Says differently.
 I went to my accustomed place
 Of augury, where there's a wide view of
 The sky, to observe the birds. There I heard
 An unprecedented din of birds, barbarous, 830
 Confused, as though some madness stung them into
 Screaming. I heard them fighting with their claws;
 The noise was unmistakable, their wings
 Whirring . . . and I felt fear. Immediately
 I tried the burnt sacrifices, but 835
 They gave no flame. Only a damp vapor
 Smoldered and spat. The gall burst in the fire,
 Exposing the thighbones bare of fat.
 The boy saw all this and told it me.
 Thus I interpret. These signs portend evil 840
 For Thebes; and the trouble stems from your policy.
 Why? Because our altars are polluted
 By flesh brought by dogs and birds, pickings
 From Polynices' corpse. Small wonder that
 The gods won't accept our sacrifices. 845
 My son, I ask you to consider well
 What you are doing. We all make mistakes.
 The wise man, having made an error of judgment,
 Will seek a remedy, not keep grinding on.
 Obstinacy isn't far removed from folly. 850
 The man is dead. No need to persecute him.
 You can give way, with good grace, to a corpse.
 He has died once, why try to kill him again?
 I'm saying this because I wish you well.
 A bit of sound advice is always welcome. 855
CREON: Money! Must everyone set their cap at me
 Because of money? Even you augurers
 Have formed a corporation to exploit me.
 For years now I have been traded about
 By your gang in the open market like 860

A piece of merchandise. All right, rake in
The cash, pile up the wealth of Lydia
And all the gold of India in bribes.
You'll never persuade me to bury that corpse.
Not even if the eagles of Zeus decide   865
To carry off its flesh in their claws
And place it right on their master's throne.
I refuse for the simple reason that
It's quite impossible for any man
To throw pollution on the gods. They are   870
Inviolate. But certain gifted men
That I could mention do not seem to mind
A little sharp practice, in the matter
Of telling a lie or two, strictly for cash.

TEIRESIAS: Well!   875
　　　　Can there exist a man who doesn't know . . .

CREON: Watch out, here comes another resounding cliché!

TEIRESIAS: . . . Good sense is a man's most precious attribute?

CREON: And bad judgment is a great encumbrance?

TEIRESIAS: It's an encumbrance you have plenty of.   880

CREON: . . . No.
　　　　You started it, but I won't insult a "seer."

TEIRESIAS: You've done that already,—accused me of lying.

CREON: The whole lot of you seers are on the make.

TEIRESIAS: Kings also have been known to make their pile.   885

CREON: Are you implying some reflection on me?

TEIRESIAS: You wouldn't be king now, but for me.

CREON: You're good at your job. But you've gone crooked.

TEIRESIAS: Much more of this, and you'll make me reveal . . .

CREON: Reveal away. But straight, and not for bribes.   890

TEIRESIAS: You'll wish you had bribed me not to speak . . .

CREON: Don't try to pull the wool over my eyes.

TEIRESIAS: The sun won't run its course for many days
　　　　Before you have to repay a corpse of your own,
　　　　One of your own children as recompense.   895
　　　　One body that belongs to this world
　　　　You have locked up in a tomb. Another body
　　　　That rightly should be in the underworld
　　　　You have forcibly retained here on earth.
　　　　Because of this, the Furies have been waiting   900
　　　　To pay you back in your own coin. And so
　　　　It won't be long before your house is full
　　　　Of grief; I can see men and women crying.
　　　　Make up your own mind whether I've been bribed
　　　　To say this. Yes, it hurts. But you provoked me.   905
　　　　My boy, take me home. I'm not so young,—
　　　　I dare not be around when he explodes.
　　　　I only hope he learns from this to show
　　　　A little sense and keep a civil tongue. [*Exit* TEIRESIAS.]

CHORUS: That was a horrible prophecy.   910
　　　　I'm bound to say I've never known him wrong
　　　　In any of his predictions.

CREON: Yes, I know,
        I know. I can't pretend that I'm not worried.
        The consequences of giving in are terrible.
        But if I hold out, I court disaster.   915
CHORUS: The right decision now is vitally important.
CREON: What should I do then? Tell me what to do.
CHORUS: You'll have to go and set Antigone free,
        And give the exposed corpse a burial.
CREON: Is that your real opinion? To give in?   920
CHORUS: And waste no time about it, for the wrath
        Of God will not be slow to catch you up.
CREON: Can't fight against what's destined. It is hard,
        But I'll change my mind. You servants,—
        Pick-axes, hurry, and come with me. I must   925
        Personally undo what I have done.
        I shouldn't have tried being unorthodox.
        I'll stick by the established laws in the future.
        [*Exit* CREON.]
CHORUS: We call on Bacchus, god of many names,
        And god of many places.   930
        You were once a little child
        In Thebes here, the darling of your mother's eye.
        Your father was Zeus, lord of the thundering sky;
        But your mother was Semele, a Theban girl.

        Are you among the rich cities   935
        Of Italy? Or presiding
        Over the cosmopolitan crowds
        That throng the Eleusinian Games?°

        Perhaps the firebrand lights your face
        Between the twin peaks of Mount Parnassus,   940
        Where the nymphs of Castaly°
        And Corycus° walk free.

        Perhaps you hear the songs of poets
        Where the ivy wreathes the crags
        On Nysa, looking over green   945
        Vineyards clustering on the plain.

        But this is your home,—the oil-like waters
        Of Ismene River, and the fields
        Where the dragon's teeth were sown.

        This is your mother city, Thebes.   950
        This is the city you honor most.
        If ever you heard us before, come to us now.
        Our nation is in the grip of a dread disease.
        Hasten to help us, speed to doctor our pain
        Over the slopes of Parnes Hill or over the roaring seas.   955

938 Eleusis in ancient Greece was the site of celebrations for cults celebrating Demeter and
Persephone. **941–42 Castly** and **Corycus** are the locations of springs and fountains.

[*Enter* MESSENGER.]

MESSENGER: Citizens of Thebes, who knows how long
>   Their luck will last? Whether you're up or down,
>   It's all pure chance. You can't predict what's coming.
>   Take Creon now. I thought he was doing well,—
>   The savior of his country, king of Thebes,   960
>   And the proud father of a lovely family.
>   He's lost the lot. Oh, yes, he's wealthy still;
>   But wealth can't buy you happiness. What's the use
>   Of money without the means of enjoying it?
>   His wealth's no more to him than a puff of smoke.   965
>   You can't say Creon lives; he's just a walking corpse.
CHORUS: About Creon's family, is there bad news then?
MESSENGER: They're dead. And those that live deserve to die.
CHORUS: How did they die? Who's dead? Why can't you tell me?
MESSENGER: Haemon is dead. Committed suicide.   970
CHORUS: He killed himself? His father didn't do it?
MESSENGER: Suicide, because Creon had murdered her.
CHORUS: Teiresias' prophecy was all too true.
MESSENGER: That's what has happened. Now it's up to you.

[*Enter* EURYDICE.]

CHORUS: Here is Eurydice, Creon's wife, poor woman.   975
>   Why is she coming out? Perhaps she's heard. . . .
EURYDICE: As I was going out, I heard you talking.
>   I was opening the door when I heard it,
>   Some more bad news about my children. I fainted,
>   But my maids held me up. Tell me about it.   980
>   I am quite used to suffering.
MESSENGER: I'll tell you everything, my dear mistress.
>   I was there, you know. No sense in glossing things over;
>   You've got to hear it sometime.
>   I went with my master, your husband, to the place   985
>   Where Polynices' corpse was exposed,
>   Cruelly torn by dogs. We said prayers
>   Placating Hecate and Pluto; then we washed
>   The body to purify it, gathered branches
>   Of olive, and cremated him or what   990
>   Was left of him. We piled him up a mound
>   Of his mother-earth; then went to get
>   Antigone. While we were on the way,
>   Somebody heard a sound of crying coming
>   From the stone chamber. He went up to Creon   995
>   And told him of it. Creon hurried on.
>   As we got near, the sound was all around us,—
>   Impossible to tell whose it was.
>   But Creon, in a voice breaking with grief,
>   Said, "Dare I prophesy? These yards of ground   1000
>   Will prove the bitterest journey of my life.
>   It's faint, but it's my son's voice. Hurry, men,
>   Get round the tomb, pull back the stones, and look

Inside. Is it Haemon's voice, or do the gods
Delude me?" At the far end of the tomb   1005
We saw Antigone hanging by the neck
In a noose of linen. He was hugging her
And talking bitterly of their marriage and
His father's action. Creon saw him and
Cried out and ran in, shouting, "Oh my son,   1010
What is this? What possessed you? Why are you trying
To kill yourself? Come out now, please, I beg you."
His son made no reply, just looked at him
Savagely with a look of deep contempt.
Then he suddenly drew his sword, evaded Creon,   1015
Held it out, and plunged the blade into his ribs.
He collapsed against Antigone's arms which were
Still warm, and hugged her. Then his blood came coughing,
And covered all her white cheeks with scarlet.
So now he lies, one corpse upon another;   1020
And thus their marriage is consummated,—in hell.
It only goes to show good sense is best,
When all this tragedy comes from one rash action.

[*Exit* EURYDICE *into palace.*]

CHORUS: What a strange thing. Eurydice has gone,
    Without saying a word.
MESSENGER: It is surprising.   1025
    I dare say she's too well-bred to go
    Showing her grief in public. I expect
    She's gone to have a good cry inside.
CHORUS: Perhaps. Noisy grief is a bad thing.
    But this extraordinary silence is ominous.   1030
MESSENGER: You're right. Let's go in then, and find out.
    She may have had her mind on something rash.
CHORUS: Who's coming? Creon with
    The body of his son.
    If truth be told, he is   1035
    Himself the murderer.

[*Enter* CREON *and* ATTENDANTS *carrying* HAEMON'S *body.*]

CREON: Wrong! How could I have been so wrong?
    And these deaths I caused—you have seen them—
    In my own family by my stubbornness.
    Oh my son, so young, to die so young,   1040
    And all because of me!
CHORUS: It's a bit late to find out you were wrong.
CREON: I know that. God has taken his revenge,
    Leapt on my head and beaten me
    And trampled on the only joy I had.
    And all the years that I have labored—wasted.   1045

[*Enter* SERVANT *from the palace.*]

SERVANT: My lord, what you see before your eyes,—
    It isn't all. You'd better come inside.
CREON: What fresh disaster could I suffer now?
SERVANT: Your wife, the mother of this corpse is dead.   1050
    Only a moment ago, she stabbed herself.
CREON: Oh death, can I never wash it away?
    Why are you destroying me? What
    Is your message now? Why stab me again?
    My wife dead too?   1055

[*The doors are opened, revealing* EURYDICE'S *body*.]

SERVANT: See for yourself. They've brought the body out.
CREON: Oh.
    Another blow. What else has fate in store?
    My wife, my son.
SERVANT: Stabbed herself by the altar, and so passed on.   1060
    But first she bewailed Megareus' death,
    Her first son, that was; then Haemon's death.
    And her last words were curses on your head.
CREON: Now I'm afraid. Why wasn't I killed?
    Why didn't somebody kill me, stab me to death?   1065
SERVANT: Before she died she made a point of planting
    The guilt of these two deaths squarely on you.
CREON: How did she die? How did she kill herself?
SERVANT: I told you. Stabbed herself. Under the heart.
    Soon as she heard about her son's death.   1070
CREON: Nobody else to share the blame. Just me . . .
    I killed you. I killed you, my dear.
    Servants, carry me in, away from all this.
    I wish I weren't alive.
CHORUS: Try to forget it. It is the only way.   1075
CREON: I invite Death. Do you only come uninvited?
    Come and take me. I cannot bear to live.
CHORUS: No time for such thoughts now. You're still in charge.
    You've got to see about these corpses, or
    We'll all be polluted
CREON: I meant what I said.   1080
CHORUS: No use in such prayers. You'll get what's destined.
CREON: Lead me away, a wreck, a useless wreck.
    I'll keep out of the way. I killed them both.
    Everything has crumbled. I feel
    A huge weight on my head. [*Exit* CREON.]   1085
CHORUS: Who wants happiness? The main
    Requirement is to be sensible.
    This means not rebelling against
    God's law, for that is arrogance.
    The greater your arrogance, the heavier God's revenge.   1090
    All old men have learned to be sensible;
    But their juniors will not take the lesson as proved. [*Exit* CHORUS.]

[441 BCE]

Joining the Conversation: Critical Thinking and Writing

1. Would you argue that masks should be used for some (or all) of the characters in *Antigone*? If so, would they be masks that fully cover the face, Greek style, or some sort of half-masks? (A full mask enlarges the face, and conceivably the mouthpiece can amplify the voice, but only an exceptionally large theater might require such help. Perhaps half-masks are enough if the aim is chiefly to distance the actors from the audience and from daily reality, and to force the actors to develop resources other than facial gestures. One director, arguing in favor of half-masks, has said that an actor who wears even a half-mask learns to act not with his eyes but with his neck.)
2. How would you costume the players? Would you dress them as the Greeks might have? Why? One argument sometimes used by those who hold that modern productions of Greek drama should use classical costumes is that Greek drama *ought* to be remote and ritualistic. Evaluate this view. What sort of modern dress might be effective?
3. If you were directing a college production of *Antigone,* how large a chorus would you use? (Sophocles is said to have used a chorus of fifteen.) Would you have the chorus recite (or chant) in unison, or would you assign lines to single speakers?
4. Although Sophocles called his play *Antigone,* many critics say that Creon is the real tragic hero, pointing out that Antigone is absent from the last third of the play. Argue for or against this view.
5. In some Greek tragedies, fate plays a great role in bringing about the downfall of the tragic hero. Though there are references to the curse on the House of Oedipus in *Antigone,* do we feel that Antigone goes to her death as a result of the workings of fate? Do we feel that fate is responsible for Creon's fall? Are both Antigone and Creon the creators of their own tragedy?
6. Are the words *hubris* (page 549) and *hamartia* (page 549) relevant to Antigone? To Creon? Argue your position.
7. Why does Creon, contrary to the Chorus's advice, bury the body of Polynices before he releases Antigone? Does his action show a zeal for piety as short-sighted as his earlier zeal for law? Is his action plausible in view of the facts that Teiresias has dwelt on the wrong done to Polynices and that Antigone has ritual food to sustain her? Or are we not to worry about Creon's motive?
8. A *foil* is a character who, by contrast, sets off or helps define another character. To what extent is Ismene a foil to Antigone? Is she entirely without courage?
9. What function does Eurydice serve? How deeply do we feel about her fate?

An Author in Depth: William Shakespeare

William Shakespeare

William Shakespeare (1564–1616) was born in Stratford-on-Avon, England, of middle-class parents. Nothing of interest is known about his early years, but by 1590 he was acting and writing plays in London. By the end of the following decade, he had worked in all three Elizabethan dramatic genres—tragedy, comedy, and history. Romeo and Juliet, for example, was written about 1595, the same year as

Richard II. Hamlet *was probably written in 1600–01. Among the plays that followed were* Othello *(1603–04),* King Lear *(1605–06),* Macbeth *(1605–06), and several "romances"—plays that have happy endings but that seem more meditative and closer to tragedy than such comedies as* A Midsummer Night's Dream *(c.1595),* As You Like It *(1598–1600), and* Twelfth Night *(1600–02).*

A Note on the Elizabethan Theater

Shakespeare's theater was wooden—round or polygonal (the Chorus in *Henry V* calls it a "wooden O"). About eight hundred spectators could stand in the yard in front of—and perhaps along the two sides of—the stage that jutted from the rear wall, and another fifteen hundred or so spectators could sit in the three roofed galleries that ringed the stage.

That portion of the galleries that was above the rear of the stage was sometimes used by actors. For instance, in *The Tempest*, 3.3, a stage direction following line 17 mentions "Prospero on the top, invisible"—that is, he is imagined to be invisible to the characters in the play.

Entry to the stage was normally gained by doors at the rear, but, apparently, on rare occasions, use was made of a curtained alcove—or perhaps a booth—between the doors, which allowed characters to be "discovered" (revealed) as in the modern proscenium theater, which normally employs a curtain. Such "discovery" scenes are rare.

Although the theater as a whole was unroofed, the stage was protected by a roof, supported by two pillars. They could serve (by an act of imagination) as trees behind which actors might pretend to conceal themselves.

A performance was probably uninterrupted by intermissions or by long pauses for the changing of scenery; a group of characters left the stage, another entered,

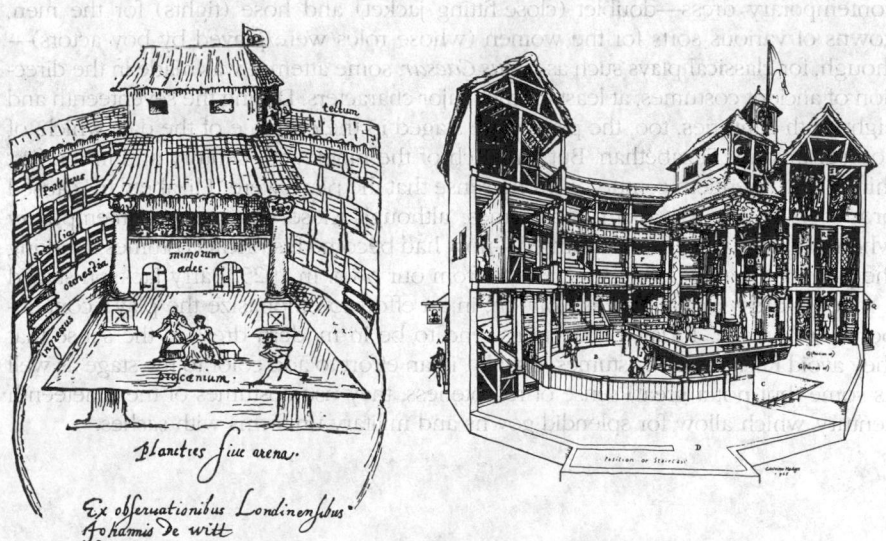

Left, Johannes de Witt, a Continental visitor to London, made a drawing of the Swan Theater in about the year 1596. The original drawing is lost; this is Arend van Buchel's copy of it. *Right,* C. Walter Hodges's drawing (1965) of an Elizabethan playhouse.

and, if the locale had changed, the new characters somehow told the audience. (Modern editors customarily add indications of locales to help a reader, but it should be remembered that the action on the Elizabethan stage was continuous.)

A Note on *Hamlet* on the Stage

We know that *Hamlet* was popular during Shakespeare's lifetime, but the earliest illustration (1709) showing a scene from the play was engraved more than a century after the play was written, so we know little about what *Hamlet* looked like on Shakespeare's stage. Still, we do have some idea. We know, for instance, that at least in the first scene, Hamlet wore black (he speaks of his "inky cloak"), and we know that, when the Ghost first appears, it is dressed in "the very armor he had on / When he the ambitious Norway combated" (1.1.64–65). We know, too, that when the Ghost appears later, in the Queen's chamber (3.4), he does not wear armor, a sign that his mood is different.

We also have a few tantalizing glimpses of Elizabethan acting. Thus, in the dumb show (pantomime) preceding *The Murder of Gonzago* that the touring players in 3.2 produce for the court, we get this stage direction: "Enter a King and a Queen [very lovingly]; the Queen embracing him, and he her." A little later, when the Queen in this dumb show finds that the King has been poisoned, she "makes passionate action," but then, when the poisoner woos her, "she seems harsh awhile, but in the end accepts love."

We know something, too, of the sound effects. Possibly the play begins with the bell tolling twelve (in 1.1, Bernardo says, "'Tis now struck twelve"), and, certainly in the first scene, we hear the crowing of a cock, which causes the Ghost to depart. Later, we hear the sound of drums, trumpets, and cannon when Claudius drinks toasts, and the play ends with the sound of cannon, when Fortinbras orders the soldiers to pay tribute to the dead Hamlet.

What about costumes? In their own day, Elizabethan plays were staged chiefly in contemporary dress—doublet (close-fitting jacket) and hose (tights) for the men, gowns of various sorts for the women (whose roles were played by boy actors)—though, for classical plays such as *Julius Caesar*, some attempt was made in the direction of ancient costumes, at least for the major characters. During the seventeenth and eighteenth centuries, too, the plays were staged in the costume of the day, which, of course, was not Elizabethan. But, in much of the nineteenth century and in the first third of the twentieth century, a strong sense that the plays were "Elizabethan" caused producers to use Elizabethan costumes, although these costumes—contemporary when the plays were first performed—now had become historical costumes, marking the plays as of an age that was remote from our own. In 1925, Barry Jackson staged a modern-dress production in London, in an effort to emphasize the play's contemporary relevance. Today, productions tend to be in modern dress in the sense that they avoid Elizabethan costumes. Usually, in an effort to add color to the stage as well as some (but not a great) sense of remoteness, they use costumes of the nineteenth century, which allow for splendid gowns and military uniforms with sashes.

Figure 1

Figure 1. The Murder of Gonzago, in 3.2. Because this episode is a play-within-the-play, Shakespeare uses a distinctive form of verse (pairs of rhyming lines, eight syllables to a line) that sets it off from the language of the rest of the play (chiefly prose, or unrhymed lines of ten syllables). The language, too, is different, for it is conspicuously old-fashioned (the sun is called "Phoebus' cart," the ocean is called "Neptune's salt wash"). In this modern-dress production done at Stratford, England, in 1975, Claudius wore a blue business suit and Fortinbras wore combat gear, but the characters in the play-within-the-play were masked, to emphasize their theatricality.

Figure 2

Figure 2. The "closet" scene, in 3.4. A line in the preceding scene specifically tells us that Hamlet is "going to his mother's closet." (In Elizabethan language, a "closet" is a private room rather than a public room—for instance, a room in which a monarch might pray, or relax, as opposed to an audience chamber in which he or she would engage in official actions.) In the twentieth century, at least as early as John Gielgud's production in New York in 1935, and probably in response to Freudian interpretations of the play, the Queen's closet was fitted with a bed on which Hamlet and Gertrude tussled, and indeed the scene is often wrongly called "the bedroom scene." In this 1989 Royal Shakespeare Company production, with Mark Rylance as Hamlet, a ranting Hamlet (at the left) confronts Gertrude. The Ghost, unknown to Gertrude, sits on the bed, presumably seeking to protect her from Hamlet's assault. The setting was not realistic but expressionistic; that is, the curtains stirred and the lighting changed, not because a physical wind was blowing or the sources of illumination were changing, but to express the characters' passions.

Figure 3

Figure 3 and (next page) 4. Hamlet meditates on death in the graveyard, in 5.1.
Both of these productions used costumes that suggested the late nineteenth
century. Kenneth Branagh portrayed Hamlet in 1993 for the Royal Shakespeare
Theatre.

In the photograph (next page) showing Kevin Kline as Hamlet in a New York
Shakespeare Festival production, Horatio is played by an African American. Other
than plays by black authors, and very few plays by whites about blacks (such as
Eugene O'Neill's *The Emperor Jones*), there are few roles in drama that are express-
ly written for blacks. Shakespeare offers only three: Othello, Aaron (a Moor in
Titus Andronicus), and the Prince of Morocco (in *The Merchant of Venice*). The
few black actors who played other Shakespearean roles, such as the great Ira
Aldridge who in the nineteenth century was known for his King Lear, performed
the roles in whiteface. Since the 1980s, however, directors have engaged in open
casting, using blacks (and Asians) in any and all roles without requiring white
makeup.

Figure 4. Reprinted by permission of the The New York Public Library.

A Note on the Text of *Hamlet*

Shakespeare's *Hamlet* comes to us in three versions. The first printed version, known as the First Quarto (Q1), was published in 1603. It is an illegitimate, garbled version, perhaps derived from the memory of the actor who played Marcellus (this part is conspicuously more accurate than the rest of the play) in a short version of the play.

The second printed version (Q2), which appeared in 1604–05, is almost twice as long as Q1; all in all, it is the best text we have, doubtless published (as Q1 was not) with the permission of Shakespeare's theatrical company.

The third printed version, in the First Folio (the collected edition of Shakespeare's plays, published in 1623), is also legitimate, but it seems to be an acting version, for it lacks some two hundred lines of Q2.

On the other hand, the First Folio text includes some ninety lines that are not found in Q2.

Because Q2 is the longest version, giving us more of the play as Shakespeare conceived it than either of the other texts two versions, it serves as the basic version for this text. Unfortunately, the printers of it often worked carelessly: Words and phrases are omitted, there are plain misreadings of what must have been in Shakespeare's manuscript, and speeches are sometimes wrongly assigned. It was therefore necessary to turn to the First Folio for many readings. It has been found useful, also, to divide the play into acts and scenes; these divisions, not found in Q2 (and only a few are found in the First Folio), are purely editorial additions, and they are therefore enclosed in square brackets.

We use the text edited by David Bevington.

The Tragedy of Hamlet

And so by continuance, and weakenesse of the braine
Iuto this frensie, which now possesseth him:
And if this be not true, take this from this.

    King Thinke you t'is so?

    Cor. How? so my Lord, I would very faine know
That thing that I haue saide t is so, positiuely,
And it hath fallen out otherwise.
Nay, if circumstances leade me on,
Ile finde it out, if it were hid
As deepe as the centre of the earth.

    King. how should wee trie this same?

    Cor. Mary my good lord thus,
The Princes walke is here in the galery,
There let *Ofelia*, walke vntill hee comes:
Your selfe and I will stand close in the study,
There shall you heare the effect of all his hart,
And if it proue any otherwise then loue,
Then let my censure faile an other time.

    King. see where hee comes poring vppon a booke.

Enter Hamlet.

    Cor. Madame, will it please your grace
To leaue vs here?

    Que. With all my hart.   *exit.*

    Cor. And here *Ofelia*, reade you on this booke,
And walke aloofe, the King shal be vnseene.

    Ham. To be, or not to be, I here's the point,
To Die, to sleepe, is that all? I all:
No, to sleepe, to dreame, I mary there it goes,
For in that dreame of death, when wee awake,
And borne before an euerlasting Iudge,
From whence no passenger euer returnd,
The vndiscouered country, at whose sight
The happy smile, and the accursed damn'd.
But for this, the ioyfull hope of this,
Whol'd beare the scornes and flattery of the world,
Scorned by the right rich, the rich cursfed of the poore?

                               The

On this page and on the next page, we give the text of "To be or not to be" from the First Quarto (Q1, 1603). On pages 649–50, we give the text from the Second Quarto (Q2, 1604–05), and on page 651, we give a third version, from the First Folio (F1, 1623), beginning at the bottom of the left-hand column.

Prince of Denmarke

The widow being oppressed the orphan wrong'd,
The taste of hunger, or a tirants raigne,
And thousand more calamities besides,
To grunt and sweate vnder this weary life,
When that he may his full *Quietus* make,
With a bare bodkin, who would this indure,
But for a hope of something after death?
Which pusles the braine, and doth confound the sence,
Which makes vs rather beare those euilles we haue,
Than flie to others that we know not of.
I that, O this conscience makes cowardes of vs all,
Lady in thy orizons, be all my sinnes remembred.

  Ofel. My Lord, I haue sought opportunitie, which now
I haue, to redeliuer to your worthy handes, a small remembrance, such tokens which I haue receiued of you.

  Ham. Are you faire?

  Ofel. My Lord.

  Ham. Are you honest?

  Ofel. What meanes my Lord?

  Ham. That if you be faire and honest,
Your beauty should admit no discourse to your honesty.

  Ofel. My Lord, can beauty haue better priuiledge than
with honesty?

  Ham. Yea mary may it; for Beauty may transforme
Honesty, from what she was into a bawd:
Then Honesty can transforme Beauty:
This was sometimes a Paradox,
But now the time giues it scope.
I neuer gaue you nothing.

  Ofel. My Lord, you know right well you did,
And with them such earnest vowes of loue,
As would haue moou'd the stoniest breast aliue,
But now too true I finde,
Rich giftes waxe poore, when giuers grow vnkinde.

  Ham. I neuer loued you.

  Ofel. You made me beleeue you did.

               E   *Ham.*

First Quarto continued.

That show of such an exercise may cullour
Your lowlines; we are oft too blame in this,
Tis too much proou'd, that with deuotions visage
And pious action, we doe sugar ore
The deuill himselfe.

   King. O tis too true,
How smart a lash that speech doth giue my conscience.
The harlots cheeke beautied with plastring art,
Is not more ougly to the thing that helps it,
Then is my deede to my most painted word :
O heauy burthen.

          Enter Hamlet.
   Pol. I heare him comming, with-draw my Lord.
   Ham. To be, or not to be, that is the question,
Whether tis nobler in the minde to suffer
The slings and arrowes of outragious fortune,
Or to take Armes against a sea of troubles,
And by opposing, end them; to die to sleepe
No more, and by a sleepe, to say we end
The hart-ake, and the thousand naturall shocks
That flesh is heire to; tis a consummation
Deuoutly to be wisht to die to sleepe,
To sleepe, perchance to dreame, I there's the rub,
For in that sleepe of death what dreames may come
When we haue shuffled off this mortall coyle
Must giue vs pause, there's the respect
That makes calamitie of so long life :
For who would beare the whips and scornes of time,
Th'oppressors wrong, the proude mans contumely,
The pangs of despiz'd loue, the lawes delay,
The insolence of office, and the spurnes
That patient merrit of th'vnworthy takes,
When he himselfe might his quietas make
With a bare bodkin; who would fardels beare,
To grunt and sweat vnder a wearie life,
But that the dread of something after death,
The vndiscouer'd country, from whose borne.

      G 2   **No**

On this page and the next page, we give "To be or not to be" as it appears in the Second Quarto (Q2, 1604–05).

The Tragedie of Hamlet

No trauiler returnes, puzzels the will,
And makes vs rather beare those ills we haue,
Then flie to others that we know not of.
Thus conscience dooes make cowards,
And thus the natiue hiew of resolution
Is sickled ore with the pale cast of thought,
And enterprises of great pitch and moment,
With this regard theyr currents turne awry,
And loose the name of action. Soft you now,
The faire *Ophelia*, Nimph in thy orizons
Be all my sinnes remembred.

   Oph. Good my Lord,
How dooes your honour for this many a day?
   Ham. I humbly thanke you well.
   Oph. My Lord, I haue remembrances of yours
That I haue longed long to redeliuer.
I pray you now receiue them.
   Ham. No, not I, I neuer gaue you ought.
   Oph. My honor'd Lord, you know right well you did,
And with them words of so sweet breath compos'd
As made these things more rich, their perfume lost,
Take these againe, for to the noble mind
Rich gifts wax poore when giuers prooue vnkind,
There my Lord.
   Ham. Ha, ha, are you honest.
   Oph. My Lord.
   Ham. Are you faire?
   Oph. What meanes your Lordship?
   Ham. That if you be honest & faire, you should admit
no discourse to your beautie.
   Oph. Could beauty my Lord haue better comerse
Then with honestie?
   Ham. I truly, for the power of beautie will sooner transforme ho-
nestie from what it is to a bawde, then the force of honestie can trans-
late beautie into his likenes, this was sometime a paradox, but now the
time giues it proofe, I did loue you once.
   Oph. Indeed my Lord you made me belieue so.
   Ham. You should not haue beleeu'd me, for vertue cannot so
euocutat our old stock, but we shall relish of it, I loued you not.

Second Quarto continued.

The Tragedie of Hamlet.   265

With turbulent and dangerous Lunacy.

Rosin. He does confesse he feeles himselfe distracted,
But from what cause he will by no meanes speake.

Gul. Nor do we finde him forward to be sounded,
But with a crafty Madnesse keepes aloofe:
When we would bring him on to some Confession
Of his true state.

Qu. Did he receiue you well?

Rosin. Most like a Gentleman.

Guild. But with much forcing of his disposition.

Rosin. Niggard of question, but of our demands
Most free in his reply.

Qu. Did you assay him to any pastime?

Rosin. Madam, it so fell out, that certaine Players
We ore-wrought on the way: of these we told him,
And there did seeme in him a kinde of ioy
To heare of it: They are about the Court,
And (as I thinke) they haue already order
This night to play before him.

Pol. 'Tis most true:
And he beseech'd me to intreate your Maiesties
To heare, and see the matter.

King. With all my heart, and it doth much content me
To heare him so inclin'd. Good Gentlemen,
Giue him a further edge, and driue his purpose on
To these delights.

Rosin. We shall my Lord.   *Exeunt.*

King. Sweet *Gertrude* leaue vs too,
For we haue closely sent for *Hamlet* hither,
That he, as 'twere by accident, may there
Affront *Ophelia.* Her Father, and my selfe (lawful espials)
Will so bestow our selues, that seeing vnseene
We may of their encounter frankely iudge,
And gather by him, as he is behaued,
Ift be th'affliction of his loue, or no.
That thus he suffers for.

Qu. I shall obey you,
And for your part *Ophelia*, I do wish
That your good Beauties be the happy cause
Of *Hamlets* wildenesse: so shall I hope your Vertues
Will bring him to his wonted way againe,
To both your Honors.

Ophe. Madam, I wish it may.

Pol. Ophelia, walke you heere. Gracious so please ye
We will bestow our selues: Reade on this booke,
That shew of such an exercise may colour
Your lonelinesse. We are oft too blame in this,
'Tis too much prou'd, that with Deuotions visage,
And pious Action, we do surge o're
The diuell himselfe.

King. Oh 'tis true:
How smart a lash that speech doth giue my Conscience?
The Harlots Cheeke beautied with plaist'ring Art
Is not more vgly to the thing that helpes it,
Then is my deede, to my most painted word.
Oh heauie burthen!

Pol. I heare him comming, let's withdraw my Lord.
                            Exeunt.

Enter Hamlet.

Ham. To be, or not to be, that is the Question:
Whether tis Nobler in the minde to suffer
The Slings and Arrowes of outragious Fortune,
Or to take Armes against a Sea of troubles,
And by opposing end them: to dye, to sleepe
No more; and by a sleepe, to say we end
The Heart-ake, and the thousand Naturall shockes

That Flesh is heyre too? 'Tis a consummation
Deuoutly to be wish'd. To dye to sleepe,
To sleepe, perchance to Dreame; I, there's the rub,
For in that sleepe of death, what dreames may come,
When we haue shuffel'd off this mortall coile,
Must giue vs pawse. There's the respect
That makes Calamity of so long life:
For who would beare the Whips and Scornes of time,
The Oppressors wrong, the poore mans Contumely,
The pangs of dispriz'd Loue, the Lawes delay,
The insolence of Office, and the Spurnes
That patient merit of the vnworthy takes,
When he himselfe might his *Quietus* make
With a bare Bodkin? Who would these Fardles beare
To grunt and sweat vnder a weary life,
But that the dread of something after death,
The vndiscouered Countrey, from whose Borne
No Traueller returnes, Puzels the will,
And makes vs rather beare those illes we haue,
Then flye to others that we know not of.
Thus Conscience does make Cowards of vs all,
And thus the Natiue hew of Resolution
Is sicklied o're, with the pale cast of Thought,
And enterprizes of great pith and moment,
With this regard their Currants turne away,
And loose the name of Action. Soft you now,
The faire *Ophelia?* Nimph, in thy Orizons
Be all my sinnes remembred.

Ophe. Good my Lord,
How does your Honor for this many a day?

Ham. I humbly thanke you: well, well, well.

Ophe. My Lord, I haue Remembrances of yours,
That I haue longed long to re-deliuer.
I pray you now, receiue them.

Ham. No, no, I neuer gaue you ought.

Ophe. My honor'd Lord, I know right well you did,
And with them words of so sweet breath compos'd,
As made the things more rich, then perfume left:
Take these againe, for to the Noble minde
Rich gifts wax poore, when giuers proue vnkinde.
There my Lord.

Ham. Ha, ha: Are you honest?

Ophe. My Lord.

Ham. Are you faire?

Ophe. What meanes your Lordship?

Ham. That if you be honest and faire, your Honesty
should admit no discourse to your Beautie.

Ophe. Could Beautie my Lord, haue better Comerce
then with Honestie?

Ham. I trulie: for the power of Beautie, will sooner
transforme Honestie from what it is, to a Bawd, then the
force of Honestie can translate Beautie into his likenesse.
This was sometime a Paradox, but now the time giues it
proofe. I did loue you once.

Ophe. Indeed my Lord, you made me beleeue so.

Ham. You should not haue beleeued me. For vertue
cannot so innoculate our old stocke, but we shall rellish
of it. I loued you not.

Ophe. I was the more deceiued.

Ham. Get thee to a Nunnerie. Why would'st thou
be a breeder of Sinners? I am my selfe indifferent honest,
but yet I could accuse me of such things, that it were better my Mother had not borne me. I am very prowd, re-
uengefull, Ambitious, with more offences at my becke,
then I haue thoughts to put them in imagination, to giue
them shape, or time to acte them in. What should such
Fel-

"To be or not to be," as given in the First Folio (F1, 1623).

The Tragedy of Hamlet, Prince of Denmark

DRAMATIS PERSONAE

GHOST *of Hamlet, the Former King of Denmark*
CLAUDIUS, *King of Denmark, the former King's brother*
GERTRUDE, *Queen of Denmark, widow of the former King and now wife of Claudius*
HAMLET, *Prince of Denmark, son of the late King and of Gertrude*
POLONIUS, *councillor to the King*
LAERTES, *his son*
OPHELIA, *his daughter*
REYNALDO, *his servant*

HORATIO, *Hamlet's friend and fellow student*

VOLTIMAND,
CORNELIUS,
ROSENCRANTZ,
GUILDENSTERN,　*members of the Danish court*
OSRIC,
A GENTLEMAN,
A LORD,

BERNARDO,
FRANCISCO,　*officers and soldiers on watch*
MARCELLUS,

FORTINBRAS, *Prince of Norway*
CAPTAIN *in his army*
Three or Four PLAYERS, *taking the roles of* PROLOGUE, PLAYER KING, PLAYER QUEEN, and LUCIANUS
Two MESSENGERS
FIRST SAILOR
Two CLOWNS, *a gravedigger and his companion*
PRIEST
FIRST AMBASSADOR *from England*
Lords, Soldiers, Attendants, Guards, other Players, Followers of Laertes, other Sailors, another Ambassador or Ambassadors from England
SCENE: *Denmark*

[1.1]

Enter BERNARDO *and* FRANCISCO, *two sentinels* [*meeting*].

BERNARDO: Who's there?
FRANCISCO: Nay, answer me.° Stand and unfold yourself.°
BERNARDO: Long live the King!
FRANCISCO: Bernardo?

Note: Stage directions that are enclosed within square brackets do not appear in the original text. They have been added by the editor.

[1.1] Location: Elsinore castle. A guard platform.   2 me (Francisco emphasizes that *he* is the sentry currently on watch.);   **unfold yourself** reveal your identity.

BERNARDO: He.   5
FRANCISCO: You come most carefully upon your hour.
BERNARDO: 'Tis now struck twelve. Get thee to bed, Francisco.
FRANCISCO: For this relief much thanks. 'Tis bitter cold,
     And I am sick at heart.
BERNARDO: Have you had quiet guard?   10
FRANCISCO: Not a mouse stirring.
BERNARDO: Well, good night.
     If you do meet Horatio and Marcellus,
     The rivals° of my watch, bid them make haste.

    Enter HORATIO *and* MARCELLUS.

FRANCISCO: I think I hear them.—Stand, ho! Who is there?   15
HORATIO: Friends to this ground.°
MARCELLUS: And liegemen to the Dane.°
FRANCISCO: Give° you good night.
MARCELLUS: O, farewell, honest soldier. Who hath relieved you?
FRANCISCO: Bernardo hath my place. Give you good night.   *Exit* FRANCISCO.   20
MARCELLUS: Holla! Bernardo!
BERNARDO: Say, what, is Horatio there?
HORATIO: A piece of him.
BERNARDO: Welcome, Horatio. Welcome, good Marcellus.
HORATIO: What, has this thing appeared again tonight?   25
BERNARDO: I have seen nothing.
MARCELLUS: Horatio says 'tis but our fantasy,°
     And will not let belief take hold of him
     Touching this dreaded sight twice seen of us.
     Therefore I have entreated him along°   30
     With us to watch° the minutes of this night,
     That if again this apparition come
     He may approve° our eyes and speak to it.
HORATIO: Tush, tush, 'twill not appear.
BERNARDO: Sit down awhile,
     And let us once again assail your ears,   35
     That are so fortified against our story,
     What° we have two nights seen.
HORATIO: Well, sit we down,
     And let us hear Bernardo speak of this.
BERNARDO: Last night of all,°
     When yond same star that's westward from the pole°
     Had made his° course t' illume° that part of heaven   40
     Where now it burns, Marcellus and myself,
     The bell then beating one—

---

14 rivals partners. **16 ground** ground, land. **17 liegemen to the Dane** men sworn to
serve the Danish king. **18 Give** i.e., may God give. **27 fantasy** imagination. **30 along** to
come along. **31 watch** keep watch during. **33 approve** corroborate. **37 What** with
what. **39 Last . . . all** i.e., this *very* last night (emphatic). **40 pole** Pole Star, North Star.
41 his its; **illume** illuminate.

Enter GHOST.

MARCELLUS: Peace, break thee off! Look where it comes again!

BERNARDO: In the same figure like the King that's dead.   45

MARCELLUS: Thou art a scholar.° Speak to it, Horatio.

BERNARDO: Looks 'a° not like the King? Mark it, Horatio.

HORATIO: Most like. It harrows me with fear and wonder.

BERNARDO: It would be spoke to.°

MARCELLUS: Speak to it, Horatio.

HORATIO: What art thou that usurp'st° this time of night,   50

       Together with that fair and warlike form

       In which the majesty of buried Denmark°

       Did sometime° march? By heaven, I charge thee, speak!

MARCELLUS: It is offended.

BERNARDO: See, it stalks away.

HORATIO: Stay! Speak, speak! I charge thee, speak!   *Exit* GHOST.   55

MARCELLUS: 'Tis gone and will not answer.

BERNARDO: How now, Horatio? You tremble and look pale.

       Is not this something more than fantasy?

       What think you on 't?°

HORATIO: Before my God, I might not this believe   60

       Without the sensible° and true avouch°

       Of mine own eyes.

MARCELLUS: Is it not like the King?

HORATIO: As thou art to thyself.

       Such was the very armor he had on

       When he the ambitious Norway° combated.   65

       So frowned he once when, in an angry parle,°

       He smote the sledded° Polacks° on the ice.

       'Tis strange.

MARCELLUS: Thus twice before, and jump° at this dead hour,

       With martial stalk° hath he gone by our watch.   70

HORATIO: In what particular thought to work° I know not,

       But in the gross and scope° of mine opinion

       This bodes some strange eruption to our state.

MARCELLUS: Good now,° sit down, and tell me, he that knows,

       Why this same strict and most observant watch   75

       So nightly toils° the subject° of the land,

       And why such daily cast° of brazen cannon

       And foreign mart° for implements of war,

       Why such impress° of shipwrights, whose sore task

---

46 scholar one learned enough to know how to question a ghost properly.   **47 'a** he.
49 It . . . to (It was commonly believed that a ghost could not speak until spoken to.)
50 usurp'st wrongfully takes over.   **52 buried Denmark** the buried King of Denmark.
53 sometime formerly.   **59 on 't** of it.   **61 sensible** confirmed by the sense;   **avouch**
warrant evidence.   **65 Norway** King of Norway.   **66 parle** parley.   **67 sledded** traveling
on sleds;   **Polacks** Poles.   **69 jump** exactly.   **70 stalk** stride.   **71 to work** i.e., to collect
my thoughts and try to understand this.   **72 gross and scope** general drift.   **74 Good now**
(An expression denoting entreaty or expostulation.)   **76 toils** causes to toil;   **subject** subjects.   **77 cast** casting.   **78 mart** buying and selling.   **79 impress** impressment, conscription.

Does not divide the Sunday from the week. 80
What might be toward,° that this sweaty haste
Doth make the night joint-laborer with the day?
Who is 't that can inform me?

HORATIO: That can I;
At least, the whisper goes so. Our last king,
Whose image even but now appeared to us, 85
Was, as you know, by Fortinbras of Norway,
Thereto pricked on° by a most emulate° pride,°
Dared to the combat; in which our valiant Hamlet—
For so this side of our known world° esteemed him—
Did slay this Fortinbras; who by a sealed° compact 90
Well ratified by law and heraldry
Did forfeit, with his life, all those his lands
Which he stood seized° of, to the conqueror;
Against the° which a moiety competent°
Was gagèd° by our king, which had returned° 95
To the inheritance° of Fortinbras
Had he been vanquisher, as, by the same cov'nant°
And carriage of the article designed,°
His fell to Hamlet. Now, sir, young Fortinbras,
Of unimprovèd mettle° hot and full, 100
Hath in the skirts° of Norway here and there
Sharked up° a list° of lawless resolutes°
For food and diet° to some enterprise
That hath a stomach° in 't, which is no other—
As it doth well appear unto our state— 105
But to recover of us, by strong hand
And terms compulsatory, those foresaid lands
So by his father lost. And this, I take it,
Is the main motive of our preparations,
The source of this our watch, and the chief head° 110
Of this posthaste and rummage° in the land.

BERNARDO: I think it be no other but e'en so.
Well may it sort° that this portentous figure
Comes armèd through our watch so like the King
That was and is the question° of these wars. 115

---

81 toward in preparation.   **87 pricked on** incited;   **emulate** emulous, ambitious;
Thereto . . . pride (refers to old Fortinbras, not the Danish King.)   **89 this . . . world** i.e.,
all Europe, the Western world.   **90 sealed** certified, confirmed.   **93 seized** possessed.
94 Against the in return for;   **moiety competent** corresponding portion.   **95 gagèd**
engaged, pledged;   **had returned** would have passed.   **96 inheritance** possession.
97 cov'nant i.e., the *sealed compact* on line 90.   **98 carriage . . . designed** carrying out
of the article or clause drawn up to cover the point.   **100 unimprovèd mettle** untried,
undisciplined spirits.   **101 skirts** outlying regions, outskirts.   **102 Sharked up** gathered
up, as a shark takes fish;   **list** i.e., troop;   **resolutes** Desperadoes.   **103 For food and diet**
i.e., they are to serve as *food,* or "means," *to some enterprises,* also they serve in return for
the rations they get.   **104 stomach** (1) a spirit of daring; (2) an appetite that is fed by the
lawless resolutes.   **110 head** source.   **111 rummage** bustle, commotion.   **113 sort** suit.
115 question focus of contention.

HORATIO: A mote° it is to trouble the mind's eye.
       In the most high and palmy° state of Rome,
       A little ere the mightiest Julius fell,
       The graves stood tenantless, and the sheeted° dead
       Did squeak and gibber in the Roman streets;   120
       As° stars with trains° of fire and dews of blood,
       Disasters° in the sun; and the moist star°
       Upon whose influence Neptune's° empire stands°
       Was sick almost to doomsday° with eclipse.
       And even the like precurse° of feared events,   125
       As harbingers° preceding still° the fates
       And prologue to the omen° coming on,
       Have heaven and earth together demonstrated
       Unto our climatures° and countrymen.

   Enter GHOST.

       But soft,° behold! Lo, where it comes again!   130
       I'll cross° it, though it blast° me. [*It spreads his° arms.*]
         Stay, *illusion!*
       If thou hast any sound or use of voice,
       Speak to me!
       If there be any good thing to be done
       That may to thee do ease and grace to me,   135
       Speak to me!
       If thou art privy to° thy country's fate,
       Which, happily,° foreknowing may avoid,
       O, speak!
       Or if thou hast uphoarded in thy life
       Extorted treasure in the womb of earth,   140
       For which, they say, you spirits oft walk in death,
       Speak of it! [*The cock crows.*] Stay and speak!—Stop it, Marcellus.
MARCELLUS: Shall I strike at it with my partisan?°
HORATIO: Do, if it will not stand.   [*They strike at it.*] 145
BERNARDO: 'Tis here!
HORATIO: 'Tis here!   [*Exit* GHOST.]
MARCELLUS: 'Tis gone.
       We do it wrong, being so majestical,
       To offer it the show of violence,   150
       For it is as the air invulnerable,
       And our vain blows malicious mockery.

---

116 mote speck of dust.   **117 palmy** flourishing.   **119 sheeted** shrouded.   **121 As**
(This abrupt transition suggests that matter is possibly omitted between lines 120 and
121.);   **trains** trails.   **122 Disasters** unfavorable signs or aspects;   **moist star** i.e., moon,
governing tides.   **123 Neptune** god of the sea;   **stands** depends.   **124 sick . . . doomsday**
(see Matthew 24:29 and Revelation 6:12.)   **125 precurse** heralding, foreshadowing.
126 harbingers forerunners;   **still** continually.   **127 omen** calamitous event.
129 climatures regions.   **130 soft** i.e., enough, break off.   **131 cross** stand in its path,
confront;   **blast** wither, strike with a curse;   **s.d. his** its.   **137 privy to** in on the secret
of.   **138 happily** haply, perchance.   **144 partisan** long-handled spear.

BERNARDO: It was about to speak when the cock crew.

HORATIO: And then it started like a guilty thing
    Upon a fearful summons. I have heard   155
    The cock, that is the trumpet° to the morn,
    Doth with his lofty and shrill-sounding throat
    Awake the god of day, and at his warning,
    Whether in sea or fire, in earth or air,
    Th' extravagant and erring° spirit hies°   160
    To his confine; and of the truth herein
    This present object made probation.°

MARCELLUS: It faded on the crowing of the cock.
    Some say that ever 'gainst° that season comes
    Wherein our Savior's birth is celebrated,   165
    This bird of dawning singeth all night long,
    And then, they say, no spirit dare stir abroad;
    The nights are wholesome, then no planets strike,°
    No fairy takes,° nor witch hath power to charm,
    So hallowed and so gracious° is that time.   170

HORATIO: So have I heard and do in part believe it.
    But, look, the morn in russet mantle clad
    Walks o'er the dew of yon high eastward hill.
    Break we our watch up, and by my advice
    Let us impart what we have seen tonight   175
    Unto young Hamlet; for upon my life,
    This spirit, dumb to us, will speak to him.
    Do you consent we shall acquaint him with it,
    As needful in our loves, fitting our duty?

MARCELLUS: Let's do 't, I pray, and I this morning know   180
    Where we shall find him most conveniently.   *Exeunt.*

[1.2]

Flourish. Enter CLAUDIUS, *King of Denmark,* GERTRUDE *the Queen,*
[the] *Council, as*° POLONIUS *and his son* LAERTES, HAMLET, *cum aliis*°
[*including* VOLTIMAND *and* CORNELIUS].

KING: Though yet of Hamlet our° dear brother's death
    The memory be green, and that it us befitted
    To bear our hearts in grief and our whole kingdom
    To be contracted in one brow of woe,
    Yet so far hath discretion fought with nature   5
    That we with wisest sorrow think on him
    Together with remembrance of ourselves.
    Therefore our sometime° sister, now our queen,
    Th' imperial jointress° to this warlike state,

---

156 trumpet trumpeter.   **160 extravagant and erring** wandering beyond bounds. (The
words have similar meaning.);   **hies** hastens.   **162 probation** proof.   **164 'gainst** just
before.   **168 strike** destroy by evil influence.   **169 takes** bewitches.   **170 gracious** full
of grace.   **[1.2] Location: The castle.   s.d. as** i.e., such as, including;   **cum aliis** with
others.   **1 our** my. (The royal "we"; also in the following lines.)   **8 sometime** former.
9 jointress woman possessing property with her husband.

Have we, as 'twere with a defeated joy— 　　　　　　　　　10
With an auspicious and a dropping eye,°
With mirth in funeral and with dirge in marriage,
In equal scale weighing delight and dole°—
Taken to wife: Nor have we herein barred
Your better wisdoms, which have freely gone 　　　　　15
With this affair along. For all, our thanks.
Now follows that you know° young Fortinbras,
Holding a weak supposal° of our worth,
Or thinking by our late dear brother's death
Our state to be disjoint and out of frame, 　　　　　　20
Co-leaguèd with° this dream of his advantage,°
He hath not failed to pester us with message
Importing° the surrender of those lands
Lost by his father, with all bonds° of law,
To our most valiant brother. So much for him. 　　　25
Now for ourself and for this time of meeting.
Thus much the business is: we have here writ
To Norway, uncle of young Fortinbras—
Who, impotent° and bed-rid, scarcely hears
Of this his nephew's purpose—to suppress 　　　　　30
His° further gait° herein, in that the levies,
The lists, and full proportions are all made
Out of his subject;° and we here dispatch
You, good Cornelius, and you, Voltimand,
For bearers of this greeting to old Norway, 　　　　35
Giving to you no further personal power
To business with the King more than the scope
Of these dilated° articles allow. 　　　　　　*[He gives a paper.]*
Farewell, and let your haste commend your duty.°
CORNELIUS, VOLTIMAND: In that, and all things, will we show our duty. 　40
KING: We doubt it nothing.° Heartily farewell.

　　　　　　　　　　　　　[Exeunt VOLTIMAND *and* CORNELIUS.]

And now, Laertes, what's the news with you?
You told us of some suit; what is 't, Laertes?
You cannot speak of reason to the Dane°
And lose your voice.° What wouldst thou beg, Laertes, 　　45
That shall not be my offer, not thy asking?
The head is not more native° to the heart,

---

11 With . . . eye with one eye smiling and the other weeping. 　**13 dole** grief. 　**17 that you know** what you know already, that; or, that you be informed as follows. 　**18 weak supposal** low estimate. 　**21 Co-leaguèd with** joined to, allied with; 　**dream . . . advantage** illusory hope of having the advantage. (His only ally is this hope.) 　**23 Importing** pertaining to. **24 bonds** contracts. 　**29 impotent** helpless. 　**31 His** i.e., Fortinbras'; 　**gait** proceeding. **31–33 in that . . . subject** since the levying of troops and supplies is drawn entirely from the King of Norway's own subjects. 　**38 dilated** set out at length. 　**39 let . . . duty** let your swift obeying of orders, rather than mere words, express your dutifulness. 　**41 nothing** not at all. 　**44 the Dane** the Danish king. 　**45 lose your voice** waste your speech. 　**47 native** closely connected, related.

The hand more instrumental° to the mouth,
Than is the throne of Denmark to thy father.
What wouldst thou have, Laertes?

LAERTES: My dread lord, 50
Your leave and favor° to return to France,
From whence though willingly I came to Denmark
To show my duty in your coronation,
Yet now I must confess, that duty done,
My thoughts and wishes bend again toward France 55
And bow them to your gracious leave and pardon.°

KING: Have you your father's leave? What says Polonius?

POLONIUS: H'ath,° my lord, wrung from me my slow leave
By laborsome petition, and at last
Upon his will I sealed° my hard° consent. 60
I do beseech you, give him leave to go.

KING: Take thy fair hour,° Laertes. Time be thine,
And thy best graces spend it at thy will!°
But now, my cousin° Hamlet, and my son—

HAMLET: A little more than kin, and less than kind.° 65

KING: How is it that the clouds still hang on you?

HAMLET: Not so, my lord. I am too much in the sun.°

QUEEN: Good Hamlet, cast thy nighted color° off,
And let thine eye look like a friend on Denmark.°
Do not forever with thy vailèd lids° 70
Seek for thy noble father in the dust.
Thou know'st 'tis common,° all that lives must die,
Passing through nature to eternity.

HAMLET: Ay, madam, it is common.

QUEEN: If it be,
Why seems it so particular° with thee? 75

HAMLET: Seems, madam? Nay, it is. I know not "seems."
'Tis not alone my inky cloak, good Mother,
Nor customary° suits of solemn black,
Nor windy suspiration° of forced breath,
No, nor the fruitful° river in the eye, 80

---

48 instrumental serviceable. **51 leave and favor** kind permission. **56 bow . . . pardon** entreatingly make a deep bow, asking your permission to depart. **58 H'ath** he has. **60 sealed** (as if sealing a legal document.); **hard** reluctant. **62 Take thy fair hour** enjoy your time of youth. **63 And . . . will** and may your finest qualities guide the way you choose to spend your time. **64 cousin** any kin not of the immediate family. **65 A little . . . kind** i.e., closer than an ordinary nephew (since I am stepson), and yet more separated in natural feeling (with pun on *kind* meaning "affectionate" and "natural," "lawful." This line is often read as an aside, but it need not be. The King chooses perhaps not to respond to Hamlet's cryptic and bitter remark.) **67 the sun** i.e., the sunshine of the King's royal favor (with pun on *son*). **68 nighted color** (1) mourning garments of black, (2) dark melancholy. **69 Denmark** the King of Denmark. **70 vailèd lids** lowered eyes. **72 common** of universal occurrence. (But Hamlet plays on the sense of "vulgar" in line 74.) **75 particular** personal. **78 customary** (1) socially conventional, (2) habitual with me. **79 suspiration** sighing. **80 fruitful** abundant.

Nor the dejected havior° of the visage,
Together with all forms, moods,° shapes of grief,
That can denote me truly. These indeed seem,
For they are actions that a man might play.
But I have that within which passes show;   85
These but the trappings and the suits of woe.

KING: 'Tis sweet and commendable in your nature, Hamlet,
To give these mourning duties to your father.
But you must know your father lost a father,
That father lost, lost his, and the survivor bound   90
In filial obligation for some term
To do obsequious° sorrow. But to persever°
In obstinate condolement° is a course
Of impious stubbornness. 'Tis unmanly grief.
It shows a will most incorrect to heaven,   95
A heart unfortified,° a mind impatient,
An understanding simple° and unschooled.
For what we know must be and is as common
As any the most vulgar thing to sense,°
Why should we in our peevish opposition   100
Take it to heart? Fie, 'tis a fault to heaven,
A fault against the dead, a fault to nature,
To reason most absurd, whose common theme
Is death of fathers, and who still° hath cried,
From the first corpse° till he that died today,   105
"This must be so." We pray you, throw to earth
This unprevailing° woe and think of us
As of a father; for let the world take note,
You are the most immediate° to our throne,
And with no less nobility of love   110
Than that which dearest father bears his son
Do I impart toward° you. For° your intent
In going back to school° in Wittenberg,°
It is most retrograde° to our desire,
And we beseech you bend you° to remain   115
Here in the cheer and comfort of our eye,
Our chiefest courtier, cousin, and our son.

QUEEN: Let not thy mother lose her prayers, Hamlet.
I pray thee, stay with us, go not to Wittenberg.

HAMLET: I shall in all my best° obey you, madam.   120

KING: Why, 'tis a loving and a fair reply.
Be as ourself in Denmark. Madam, come.

---

81 havior expression.   **82 moods** outward expression of feeling.   **92 obsequious** suited to
obsequies or funerals;   **persever** persevere.   **93 condolement** sorrowing.   **96 unfortified** i.e.,
against adversity.   **97 simple** ignorant.   **99 As . . . sense** as the most ordinary experience.
104 still always.   **105 the first corpse** (Abel's.)   **107 unprevailing** unavailing, useless.
109 most immediate next in succession.   **112 impart toward** i.e., bestow my affection on;
For as for.   **113 to school** i.e., to your studies;   **Wittenberg** famous German university founded
in 1502.   **114 retrograde** contrary.   **115 bend you** incline yourself.   **120 in all my best** to the
best of my ability.

This gentle and unforced accord of Hamlet
Sits smiling to° my heart, in grace° whereof
No jocund° health that Denmark drinks today   125
But the great cannon to the clouds shall tell,
And the King's rouse° the heaven shall bruit again,°
Respeaking earthly thunder.° Come away.

Flourish. Exeunt all but HAMLET.

HAMLET: O, that this too too sullied° flesh would melt,
Thaw, and resolve itself into a dew!   130
Or that the Everlasting had not fixed
His canon° 'gainst self-slaughter! O God, God,
How weary, stale, flat, and unprofitable
Seem to me all the uses° of this world!
Fie on 't, ah fie! 'Tis an unweeded garden   135
That grows to seed. Things rank and gross in nature
Possess it merely.° That it should come to this!
But two months dead—nay, not so much, not two.
So excellent a king, that was to° this
Hyperion° to a satyr,° so loving to my mother   140
That he might not beteem° the winds of heaven
Visit her face too roughly. Heaven and earth,
Must I remember? Why, she would hang on him
As if increase of appetite had grown
By what it fed on, and yet within a month—   145
Let me not think on 't; frailty, thy name is woman!—
A little month, or ere° those shoes were old
With which she followed my poor father's body,
Like Niobe;° all tears, why she, even she—
O God, a beast, that wants discourse of reason,°   150
Would have mourned longer—married with my uncle,
My father's brother, but no more like my father
Than I to Hercules. Within a month,
Ere yet the salt of most unrighteous tears
Had left the flushing in her gallèd° eyes,   155
She married. O, most wicked speed, to post°
With such dexterity to incestuous° sheets!
It is not, nor it cannot come to good.
But break, my heart, for I must hold my tongue.

---

124 to i.e., at; **grace** thanksgiving. **125 jocund** merry. **127 rouse** drinking of a draft of
liquor; **bruit again** loudly echo. **128 thunder** i.e., of trumpet and kettledrum, sounded
when the King drinks; see 1.4.8–12. **129 sullied** defiled. (The early quartos read *sallied;*
the Folio, *solid*.) **132 canon** law. **134 all the uses** the whole routine. **137 merely**
completely. **139 to** in comparison to. **140 Hyperion** Titan sun-god, father of Helios;
satyr a lecherous creature of classical mythology, half-human but with a goat's legs, tail, ears,
and horns. **141 beteem** allow. **147 or ere** even before. **149 Niobe** Tantalus' daughter,
Queen of Thebes, who boasted that she had more sons and daughters than Leto; for this,
Apollo and Artemis, children of Leto, slew her fourteen children. She was turned by Zeus into
a stone that continually dropped tears. **150 wants . . . reason** lacks the faculty of reason.
155 gallèd irritated, inflamed. **156 post** hasten. **157 incestuous** (In Shakespeare's day, the
marriage of a man like Claudius to his deceased brother's wife was considered incestuous.)

Enter HORATIO, MARCELLUS *and* BERNARDO.

HORATIO: Hail to your lordship!

HAMLET: I am glad to see you well.   160
    Horatio!—or I do forget myself.

HORATIO: The same, my lord, and your poor servant ever.

HAMLET: Sir, my good friend; I'll change that name° with you.
    And what make you from° Wittenberg, Horatio?
    Marcellus.   165

MARCELLUS: My good lord.

HAMLET: I am very glad to see you. [*To* BERNARDO.] Good even, sir.—
    But what in faith make you from Wittenberg?

HORATIO: A truant disposition, good my lord.

HAMLET: I would not hear your enemy say so,   170
    Nor shall you do my ear that violence
    To make it truster of your own report
    Against yourself. I know you are no truant.
    But what is your affair in Elsinore?
    We'll teach you to drink deep ere you depart.   175

HORATIO: My lord, I came to see your father's funeral.

HAMLET: I prithee, do not mock me, fellow student;
    I think it was to see my mother's wedding.

HORATIO: Indeed, my lord, it followed hard° upon.

HAMLET: Thrift, thrift, Horatio! The funeral baked meats°   180
    Did coldly° furnish forth the marriage tables.
    Would I had met my dearest° foe in heaven
    Or ever° I had seen that day, Horatio!
    My father!—Methinks I see my father.

HORATIO: Where, my lord?

HAMLET: In my mind's eye, Horatio.   185

HORATIO: I saw him once. 'A° was a goodly king.

HAMLET: 'A was a man. Take him for all in all,
    I shall not look upon his like again.

HORATIO: My lord, I think I saw him yesternight.

HAMLET: Saw? Who?   190

HORATIO: My lord, the King your father.

HAMLET: The King my father?

HORATIO: Season your admiration° for a while
    With an attent° ear till I may deliver,
    Upon the witness of these gentlemen,   195
    This marvel to you.

HAMLET: For God's love, let me hear!

HORATIO: Two nights together had these gentlemen,
    Marcellus and Bernardo, on their watch,
    In the dead waste° and middle of the night,
    Been thus encountered. A figure like your father,   200

163 change that name i.e., give and receive reciprocally the name of "friend" (rather than talk of "servant").   **164 make you from** are you doing away from.   **179 hard** close.
180 baked meats meat pies.   **181 coldly** i.e., as cold leftovers.   **182 dearest** closest (and therefore deadliest).   **183 Or ever** before.   **186 'A** he.   **193 Season your admiration** restrain your astonishment.   **194 attent** attentive.   **199 dead waste** desolate stillness.

Armèd at point° exactly, cap-à-pie,°
Appears before them, and with solemn march
Goes slow and stately by them. Thrice he walked
By their oppressed and fear-surprisèd eyes
Within his truncheon's° length, whilst they, distilled°   205
Almost to jelly with the act° of fear,
Stand dumb and speak not to him. This to me
In dreadful° secrecy impart they did,
And I with them the third night kept the watch,
Where, as they had delivered, both in time,   210
Form of the thing, each word made true and good,
The apparition comes. I knew your father;
These hands are not more like.

HAMLET: But where was this?
MARCELLUS: My lord, upon the platform where we watch.
HAMLET: Did you not speak to it?
HORATIO: My lord, I did,   215
But answer made it none. Yet once methought
It lifted up its head and did address
Itself to motion, like as it would speak;°
But even then° the morning cock crew loud,
And at the sound it shrunk in haste away   220
And vanished from our sight.
HAMLET: 'Tis very strange.
HORATIO: As I do live, my honored lord, 'tis true,
And we did think it writ down in our duty
To let you know of it.
HAMLET: Indeed, indeed, sirs. But this troubles me.   225
Hold you the watch tonight?
ALL: We do, my lord.
HAMLET: Armed, say you?
ALL: Armed, my lord.
HAMLET: From top to toe?
ALL: My lord, from head to foot.   230
HAMLET: Then saw you not his face?
HORATIO: O, yes, my lord, he wore his beaver° up.
HAMLET: What° looked he, frowningly?
HORATIO: A countenance more in sorrow than in anger.
HAMLET: Pale or red?   235
HORATIO: Nay, very pale.
HAMLET: And fixed his eyes upon you?
HORATIO: Most constantly.
HAMLET: I would I had been there.
HORATIO: It would have much amazed you.   240
HAMLET: Very like, very like. Stayed it long?

---

201 at point correctly in every detail;   **cap-à-pie** from head to foot.   **205 truncheon**
officer's staff;   **distilled** dissolved.   **206 act** action, operation.   **208 dreadful** full of
dread.   **217–18 did . . . speak** began to move as though it were about to speak.
219 even then at that very instant.   **232 beaver** visor on the helmet.   **233 What** how.

HORATIO: While one with moderate haste might tell° a hundred.

MARCELLUS, BERNARDO: Longer, longer.

HORATIO: Not when I saw 't.

HAMLET: His beard was grizzled°—no?   245

HORATIO: It was, as I have seen it in his life,
     A sable silvered.°

HAMLET: I will watch tonight.
     Perchance 'twill walk again.

HORATIO: I warrant° it will.

HAMLET: If it assume my noble father's person,
     I'll speak to it though hell itself should gape   250
     And bid me hold my peace. I pray you all,
     If you have hitherto concealed this sight,
     Let it be tenable° in your silence still,
     And whatsoever else shall hap tonight,
     Give it an understanding but no tongue.   255
     I will requite your loves. So, fare you well.
     Upon the platform twixt eleven and twelve
     I'll visit you.

ALL: Our duty to your honor.

HAMLET: Your loves, as mine to you. Farewell.   *Exeunt [all but* HAMLET].
     My father's spirit in arms! All is not well.   260
     I doubt° some foul play. Would the night were come!
     Till then sit still, my soul. Foul deeds will rise,
     Though all the earth o'erwhelm them, to men's eyes.   *Exit*.

[1.3]

Enter LAERTES *and* OPHELIA, *his sister.*

LAERTES: My necessaries are embarked. Farewell.
     And, sister, as the winds give benefit
     And convoy is assistant,° do not sleep
     But let me hear from you.

OPHELIA: Do you doubt that?

LAERTES: For Hamlet, and the trifling of his favor,   5
     Hold it a fashion and a toy in blood,°
     A violet in the youth of primy° nature,
     Forward,° not permanent, sweet, not lasting,
     The perfume and suppliance° of a minute—
     No more.

OPHELIA: No more but so?

LAERTES: Think it no more.   10
     For nature crescent° does not grow alone
     In thews° and bulk, but as this temple° waxes

---

242 tell count.   **245 grizzled** gray.   **247 sable silvered** black mixed with white.
248 warrant assure you.   **253 tenable** held.   **261 doubt** suspect.   **[1.3] Location:**
Polonius' chambers.   3 convoy is assistant means of conveyance are available.
6 toy in blood passing amorous fancy.   **7 primy** in its prime, springtime.   **8 Forward**
precocious.   **9 suppliance** supply, filler.   **11 crescent** growing, waxing.   **12 thews** bodily
strength;   **temple** i.e., body.

The inward service of the mind and soul
Grows wide withal.° Perhaps he loves you now,
And now no soil° nor cautel° doth besmirch 15
The virtue of his will,° but you must fear,
His greatness weighed,° his will is not his own.
For he himself is subject to his birth.
He may not, as unvalued persons do,
Carve° for himself, for on his choice depends 20
The safety and health of this whole state,
And therefore must his choice be circumscribed
Unto the voice and yielding° of that body
Whereof he is the head. Then if he says he loves you,
It fits your wisdom so far to believe it 25
As he in his particular act and place°
May give his saying deed, which is no further
Than the main voice° of Denmark goes withal.°
Then weigh what loss your honor may sustain
If with too credent° ear you list° his songs, 30
Or lose your heart, or your chaste treasure open
To his unmastered importunity.
Fear it, Ophelia, fear it, my dear sister,
And keep you in the rear of your affection,°
Out of the shot and danger of desire. 35
The chariest° maid is prodigal enough
If she unmask her beauty° to the moon.°
Virtue itself scapes not calumnious strokes.
The canker galls° the infants of the spring
Too oft before their buttons° be disclosed,° 40
And in the morn and liquid dew° of youth
Contagious blastments° are most imminent.
Be wary then; best safety lies in fear.
Youth to itself rebels,° though none else near.

OPHELIA: I shall the effect of this good lesson keep 45
As watchman to my heart. But, good my brother,
Do not, as some ungracious° pastors do,
Show me the steep and thorny way to heaven,
Whiles like a puffed° and reckless libertine
Himself the primrose path of dalliance treads, 50
And recks° not his own rede.°

Enter POLONIUS.

14 Grows wide withal grows along with it.   **15 soil** blemish;   **cautel** deceit.   **16 will**
desire.   **17 His greatness weighed** if you take into account his high position.   **20 Carve**
i.e., choose.   **23 voice and yielding** assent, approval.   **26 in . . . place** in his particular
restricted circumstances.   **28 main voice** general assent;   **withal** along with.   **30 credent**
credulous;   **list** listen to.   **34 keep . . . affection** don't advance as far as your affection
might lead you. (A military metaphor.)   **36 chariest** most scrupulously modest.
37 If she unmask her beauty if she does no more than show her beauty;   **moon** (symbol
of chastity.)   **39 canker galls** canker-worm destroys.   **40 buttons** buds;   **disclosed**
opened.   **41 liquid dew** i.e., time when dew is fresh and bright.   **42 blastments**
blights.   **44 Youth . . . rebels** youth is inherently rebellious.   **47 ungracious** ungodly.
49 puffed bloated, or swollen with pride.   **51 recks** heeds;   **rede** counsel.

LAERTES: O, fear me not.°
            I stay too long. But here my father comes.
            A double° blessing is a double grace;
            Occasion smiles upon a second leave.°
POLONIUS: Yet here, Laertes? Aboard, aboard, for shame!   55
            The wind sits in the shoulder of your sail,
            And you are stayed for. There—my blessing with thee!
            And these few precepts in thy memory
            Look° thou character.° Give thy thoughts no tongue,
            Nor any unproportioned° thought his° act.   60
            Be thou familiar,° but by no means vulgar.°
            Those friends thou hast, and their adoption tried,°
            Grapple them unto thy soul with hoops of steel,
            But do not dull thy palm° with entertainment
            Of each new-hatched, unfledged courage.° Beware   65
            Of entrance to a quarrel, but being in,
            Bear 't that° th' opposèd may beware of thee.
            Give every man thy ear, but few thy voice;
            Take each man's censure,° but reserve thy judgment.
            Costly thy habit° as thy purse can buy,   70
            But not expressed in fancy;° rich, not gaudy,
            For the apparel oft proclaims the man,
            And they in France of the best rank and station
            Are of a most select and generous chief in that.°
            Neither a borrower nor a lender be,   75
            For loan oft loses both itself and friend,
            And borrowing dulleth edge of husbandry.°
            This above all: to thine own self be true,
            And it must follow, as the night the day,
            Thou canst not then be false to any man.   80
            Farewell. My blessing season° this in thee!
LAERTES: Most humbly do I take my leave, my lord.
POLONIUS: The time invests° you. Go, your servants tend.°
LAERTES: Farewell, Ophelia, and remember well
            What I have said to you.   85
OPHELIA: 'Tis in my memory locked,
            And you yourself shall keep the key of it.
LAERTES: Farewell.   *Exit* LAERTES.
POLONIUS: What is 't, Ophelia, he hath said to you?
OPHELIA: So please you, something touching the Lord Hamlet.   90

51 fear me not don't worry on my account.   **53 double** (Laertes has already bid his father
good-bye.)   **54 Occasion . . . leave** happy is the circumstance that provides a second leave-
taking. (The goddess Occasion, or Opportunity, smiles.)   **59 Look** be sure that;   **character**
inscribe.   **60 unproportioned** badly calculated, intemperate;   **his** its.   **61 familiar** sociable;
vulgar common.   **62 and their adoption tried** and also their suitability for adoption as
friends having been tested.   **64 dull thy palm** i.e., shake hands so often as to make the
gesture meaningless.   **65 courage** young man of spirit.   **67 Bear 't that** manage it so that.
69 censure opinion, judgment.   **70 habit** clothing.   **71 fancy** excessive ornament, decadent
fashion.   **74 Are . . . that** are of a most refined and well-bred preeminence in choosing
what to wear.   **77 husbandry** thrift.   **81 season** mature.   **83 invests** besieges, presses
upon;   **tend** attend, wait.

POLONIUS: Marry,° well bethought.
     'Tis told me he hath very oft of late
     Given private time to you, and you yourself
     Have of your audience been most free and bounteous.
     If it be so—as so 'tis put on° me,   95
     And that in way of caution—I must tell you
     You do not understand yourself so clearly
     As it behooves° my daughter and your honor.
     What is between you? Give me up the truth.
OPHELIA: He hath, my lord, of late made many tenders°   100
     Of his affection to me.
POLONIUS: Affection? Pooh! You speak like a green girl,
     Unsifted° in such perilous circumstance.
     Do you believe his tenders, as you call them?
OPHELIA: I do not know, my lord, what I should think.   105
POLONIUS: Marry, I will teach you. Think yourself a baby
     That you have ta'en these tenders for true pay
     Which are not sterling.° Tender° yourself more dearly,
     Or—not to crack the wind° of the poor phrase,
     Running it thus—you'll tender me a fool.°   110
OPHELIA: My lord, he hath importuned me with love
     In honorable fashion.
POLONIUS: Ay, fashion° you may call it. Go to,° go to.
OPHELIA: And hath given countenance° to his speech, my lord,
     With almost all the holy vows of heaven.   115
POLONIUS: Ay, springes° to catch woodcocks.° I do know,
     When the blood burns, how prodigal° the soul
     Lends the tongue vows. These blazes, daughter,
     Giving more light than heat, extinct in both
     Even in their promise as it° is a making,   120
     You must not take for fire. From this time
     Be something° scanter of your maiden presence.
     Set your entreatments° at a higher rate
     Than a command to parle.° For Lord Hamlet,
     Believe so much in him° that he is young,   125
     And with a larger tether may he walk
     Than may be given you. In few,° Ophelia,
     Do not believe his vows, for they are brokers,°

---

91 Marry i.e., by the Virgin Mary. (A mild oath.)   **95 put on** impressed on, told to.
98 behooves befits.   **100 tenders** offers.   **103 Unsifted** i.e., untried.   **108 sterling** legal
currency; **Tender** hold, look after, offer.   **109 crack the wind** i.e., run it until it is broken-
winded.   **110 tender me a fool** (1) show yourself to me as a fool, (2) show me up as a fool,
(3) present me with a grandchild. (*Fool* was a term of endearment for a child.)   **113 fashion**
mere form, pretense; **Go to** (an expression of impatience.)   **114 countenance** credit,
confirmation.   **116 springes** snares; **woodcocks** birds easily caught; here used to connote
gullibility.   **117 prodigal** prodigally.   **120 it** i.e., the promise.   **122 something** somewhat.
123 entreatments negotiations for surrender. (A military term.)   **124 parle** discuss terms
with the enemy. (Polonius urges his daughter, in the metaphor of military language, not to
meet with Hamlet and consider giving in to him merely because he requests an interview.)
125 so . . . him this much concerning him.   **127 In few** briefly.   **128 brokers** go-betweens,
procurers.

Not of that dye° which their investments° show,
But mere implorators° of unholy suits,   130
Breathing° like sanctified and pious bawds,
The better to beguile. This is for all:°
I would not, in plain terms, from this time forth
Have you so slander° any moment° leisure
As to give words or talk with the Lord Hamlet.   135
Look to 't, I charge you. Come your ways.°

OPHELIA: I shall obey, my lord.   *Exeunt*.

[1.4]

Enter HAMLET, HORATIO, *and* MARCELLUS.

HAMLET: The air bites shrewdly,° it is very cold.
HORATIO: It is a nipping and an eager° air.
HAMLET: What hour now?
HORATIO: I think it lacks of° twelve.
MARCELLUS: No, it is struck.
HORATIO: Indeed? I heard it not.
It then draws near the season°   5
Wherein the spirit held his wont° to walk.
                    A flourish of trumpets, and two pieces° go off [within].
What does this mean, my lord?
HAMLET: The King doth wake° tonight and takes his rouse,°
Keeps wassail,° and the swaggering upspring° reels,°
And as he drains his drafts of Rhenish° down,   10
The kettledrum and trumpet thus bray out
The triumph of his pledge.°
HORATIO: It is a custom?
HAMLET: Ay, marry, is't,
But to my mind, though I am native here   15
And to the manner° born, it is a custom
More honored in the breach than the observance.°
This heavy-headed revel east and west°
Makes us traduced and taxed of° other nations.
They clepe° us drunkards, and with swinish phrase°   20
Soil our addition;° and indeed it takes
From our achievements, though performed at height,°
The pith and marrow of our attribute.°

129 dye color or sort;   **investments** clothes. (The vows are not what they seem.)   **130 mere
implorators** out-and-out solicitors.   **131 Breathing** speaking.   **132 for all** once for all, in sum.
134 slander abuse, misuse;   **moment** moment's.   **136 Come your ways** come along.
[1.4] Location: The guard platform.   1 shrewdly keenly, sharply.   **2 eager** biting.
3 lacks of is just short of.   **5 season** time.   **6 held his wont** was accustomed;   **s.d. pieces**
i.e., of ordnance, cannon.   **8 wake** stay awake and hold revel;   **takes his rouse** carouses.
9 wassail carousal;   **upspring** wild German dance;   **reels** dances.   **10 Rhenish** Rhine wine.
12 The triumph . . . pledge i.e., his feat in draining the wine in a single draft.   **16 manner**
custom (of drinking).   **17 More . . . observance** better neglected than followed.   **18 east and
west** i.e., everywhere.   **19 taxed of** censured by.   **20 clepe** call;   **with swinish phrase** i.e.,
by calling us swine.   **21 addition** reputation.   **22 at height** outstandingly.   **23 The pith . . .
attribute** the essence of the reputation that others attribute to us.

So, oft it chances in particular men,
That for° some vicious mole of nature° in them,   25
As in their birth—wherein they are not guilty,
Since nature cannot choose his° origin—
By their o'ergrowth of some complexion,°
Oft breaking down the pales° and forts of reason,
Or by some habit that too much o'erleavens°   30
The form of plausive° manners, that these men,
Carrying, I say, the stamp of one defect,
Being nature's livery° or fortune's star,°
His virtues else,° be they as pure as grace,
As infinite as man may undergo,°   35
Shall in the general censure° take corruption
From that particular fault. The dram of evil
Doth all the noble substance often dout
To his own scandal.°

    Enter GHOST.

HORATIO: Look, my lord, it comes!
HAMLET: Angels and ministers of grace° defend us!   40
        Be thou° a spirit of health° or goblin damned,
        Bring° with thee airs from heaven or blasts from hell,
        Be thy intents° wicked or charitable,
        Thou com'st in such a questionable° shape
        That I will speak to thee. I'll call thee Hamlet,   45
        King, father, royal Dane. O, answer me!
        Let me not burst in ignorance, but tell
        Why thy canonized° bones, hearsèd° in death,
        Have burst their cerements;° why the sepulcher
        Wherein we saw thee quietly inurned°   50
        Hath oped his ponderous and marble jaws
        To cast thee up again. What may this mean,
        That thou, dead corpse, again in complete steel,°
        Revisits thus the glimpses of the moon,°
        Making night hideous, and we fools of nature°   55
        So horridly to shake our disposition°

---

25 for on account of;   **mole of nature** natural blemish in one's constitution.   **27 his** its.
28 their o'ergrowth . . . complexion the excessive growth in individuals of some natural trait.
29 pales palings, fences (as of a fortification).   **30 o'erleavens** induces a change throughout
(as yeast works in dough).   **31 plausive** pleasing.   **33 nature's livery** sign of one's servitude
to nature;   **fortune's star** the destiny that chance brings.   **34 His virtues else** i.e., the other
qualities of *these men* (line 31).   **35 may undergo** can sustain.   **36 general censure** general
opinion that people have of him.   **37–39 The dram . . . scandal** i.e., the small drop of evil
blots out or works against the noble substance of the whole and brings it into disrepute. To
dout is to blot out. (A famous crux.)   **40 ministers of grace** messengers of God.   **41 Be thou**
whether you are;   **spirit of health** good angel.   **42 Bring** whether you bring.   **43 Be thy**
intents whether your intentions are.   **44 questionable** inviting question.   **48 canonized**
buried according to the canons of the church;   **hearsèd** coffined.   **49 cerements** grave
clothes.   **50 inurned** entombed.   **53 complete steel** full armor.   **54 glimpses of the moon**
pale and uncertain moonlight.   **55 fools of nature** mere men, limited to natural knowledge
and subject to nature.   **56 So . . . disposition** to distress our mental composure so violently.

With thoughts beyond the reaches of our souls?
Say, why is this? Wherefore? What should we do?

[*The* GHOST] *beckons* [HAMLET].

HORATIO: It beckons you to go away with it,
    As if it some impartment° did desire   60
    To you alone.
MARCELLUS: Look with what courteous action
    It wafts you to a more removèd ground.
    But do not go with it.
HORATIO: No, by no means.
HAMLET: It will not speak. Then I will follow it.
HORATIO: Do not, my lord!
HAMLET: Why, what should be the fear?   65
    I do not set my life at a pin's fee,°
    And for my soul, what can it do to that,
    Being a thing immortal as itself?
    It waves me forth again. I'll follow it.
HORATIO: What if it tempt you toward the flood,° my lord,   70
    Or to the dreadful summit of the cliff
    That beetles o'er° his° base into the sea,
    And there assume some other horrible form
    Which might deprive your sovereignty of reason°
    And draw you into madness? Think of it.   75
    The very place puts toys of desperation,°
    Without more motive, into every brain
    That looks so many fathoms to the sea
    And hears it roar beneath.
HAMLET: It wafts me still.—Go on, I'll follow thee.   80
MARCELLUS: You shall not go, my lord.   [*They try to stop him.*]
HAMLET: Hold off your hands!
HORATIO: Be ruled. You shall not go.
HAMLET: My fate cries out,°
    And makes each petty° artery° in this body
    As hardy as the Nemean lion's° nerve.°
    Still am I called. Unhand me, gentlemen.   85
    By heaven, I'll make a ghost of him that lets° me!
    I say, away!—Go on, I'll follow thee.   *Exeunt* GHOST *and* HAMLET.
HORATIO: He waxes desperate with imagination.
MARCELLUS: Let's follow. 'Tis not fit thus to obey him.
HORATIO: Have after.° To what issue° will this come?   90
MARCELLUS: Something is rotten in the state of Denmark.
HORATIO: Heaven will direct it.°
MARCELLUS: Nay, let's follow him.   *Exeunt.*

60 impartment communication. **66 fee** value. **70 flood** sea. **72 beetles o'er** overhangs
threateningly (like bushy eyebrows); **his** its. **74 deprive . . . reason** take away the rule of
reason over your mind. **76 toys of desperation** fancies of desperate acts, i.e., suicide.
82 My fate cries out my destiny summons me. **83 petty** weak; **artery** (through which the
vital spirits were thought to have been conveyed). **84 Nemean lion** one of the monsters
slain by Hercules in his twelve labors; **nerve** sinew. **86 lets** hinders. **90 Have after** let's
go after him; **issue** outcome. **92 it** i.e., the outcome.

[1.5]

Enter GHOST *and* HAMLET.

HAMLET: Whither wilt thou lead me? Speak. I'll go no further.
GHOST: Mark me.
HAMLET: I will.
GHOST: My hour is almost come,
    When I to sulfurous and tormenting flames
    Must render up myself.
HAMLET: Alas, poor ghost!
GHOST: Pity me not, but lend thy serious hearing   5
    To what I shall unfold.
HAMLET: Speak. I am bound° to hear.
GHOST: So art thou to revenge, when thou shalt hear.
HAMLET: What?
GHOST: I am thy father's spirit,   10
    Doomed for a certain term to walk the night,
    And for the day confined to fast° in fires,
    Till the foul crimes° done in my days of nature°
    Are burnt and purged away. But that° I am forbid
    To tell the secrets of my prison house,   15
    I could a tale unfold whose lightest word
    Would harrow up° thy soul, freeze thy young blood,
    Make thy two eyes like stars start from their spheres,°
    Thy knotted and combinèd locks° to part,
    And each particular hair to stand on end   20
    Like quills upon the fretful porcupine.
    But this eternal blazon° must not be
    To ears of flesh and blood. List, list, O, list!
    If thou didst ever thy dear father love—
HAMLET: O God!   25
GHOST: Revenge his foul and most unnatural murder.
HAMLET: Murder?
GHOST: Murder most foul, as in the best° it is,
    But this most foul, strange, and unnatural.
HAMLET: Haste me to know't, that I, with wings as swift   30
    As meditation or the thoughts of love,
    May sweep to my revenge.
GHOST: I find thee apt;
    And duller shouldst thou be° than the fat° weed
    That roots itself in ease on Lethe° wharf,

[1.5] Location: The battlements of the castle.   7 bound (1) ready, (2) obligated by duty
and fate. (The Ghost, in line 8, answers in the second sense.)   **12 fast** do penance by
fasting.   **13 crimes** sins;   **of nature** as a mortal.   **14 But that** were it not that.   **17 harrow
up** lacerate, tear.   **18 spheres** i.e., eye-sockets, here compared to the orbits or transparent
revolving spheres in which, according to Ptolemaic astronomy, the heavenly bodies were
fixed.   **19 knotted . . . locks** hair neatly arranged and confined.   **22 eternal blazon** revelation of the secrets of eternity.   **28 in the best** even at best.   **33 shouldst thou be** you would
have to be;   **fat** torpid, lethargic.   **34 Lethe** the river of forgetfulness in Hades.

  Wouldst thou not stir in this. Now, Hamlet, hear.   35
  'Tis given out that, sleeping in my orchard,°
  A serpent stung me. So the whole ear of Denmark
  Is by a forgèd process° of my death
  Rankly abused.° But know, thou noble youth,
  The serpent that did sting thy father's life   40
  Now wears his crown.
HAMLET: O, my prophetic soul! My uncle!
GHOST: Ay, that incestuous, that adulterate° beast,
  With witchcraft of his wit, with traitorous gifts°—
  O wicked wit and gifts, that have the power   45
  So to seduce!—won to his shameful lust
  The will of my most seeming-virtuous queen.
  O Hamlet, what a falling off was there!
  From me, whose love was of that dignity
  That it went hand in hand even with the vow°   50
  I made to her in marriage, and to decline
  Upon a wretch whose natural gifts were poor
  To° those of mine!
  But virtue, as it° never will be moved,
  Though lewdness court it in a shape of heaven,°   55
  So lust, though to a radiant angel linked,
  Will sate itself in a celestial bed°
  And prey on garbage.
  But soft, methinks I scent the morning air.
  Brief let me be. Sleeping within my orchard,   60
  My custom always of the afternoon,
  Upon my secure° hour thy uncle stole,
  With juice of cursèd hebona° in a vial,
  And in the porches of my ears° did pour
  The leprous distillment,° whose effect   65
  Holds such an enmity with blood of man
  That swift as quicksilver it courses through
  The natural gates and alleys of the body,
  And with a sudden vigor it doth posset°
  And curd, like eager° droppings into milk,   70
  The thin and wholesome blood. So did it mine,
  And a most instant tetter° barked° about,
  Most lazar-like,° with vile and loathsome crust,
  All my smooth body.

---

36 orchard garden. **38 forgèd process** falsified account. **39 abused** deceived.
43 adulterate adulterous. **44 gifts** (1) talents, (2) presents. **50 even with the vow** with
the very vow. **53 To** compared to. **54 virtue, as it** as virtue. **55 shape of heaven**
heavenly form. **57 sate . . . bed** cease to find sexual pleasure in a virtuously lawful
marriage. **62 secure** confident, unsuspicious. **63 hebona** a poison. (The word seems to
be a form of *ebony*, though it is thought perhaps to be related to *henbane*, a poison, or to
ebenus, "yew.") **64 porches of my ears** ears as a porch or entrance of the body.
65 leprous distillment distillation causing leprosylike disfigurement. **69 posset** coagulate,
curdle. **70 eager** sour, acid. **72 tetter** eruption of scabs; **barked** recovered with a rough
covering, like bark on a tree. **73 lazar-like** leperlike.

Thus was I, sleeping, by a brother's hand   75
Of life, of crown, of queen at once dispatched,°
Cut off even in the blossoms of my sin,
Unhouseled,° disappointed,° unaneled,°
No reckoning° made, but sent to my account
With all my imperfections on my head.   80
O, horrible! O, horrible, most horrible!
If thou hast nature° in thee, bear it not.
Let not the royal bed of Denmark be
A couch for luxury° and damnèd incest.
But, howsoever thou pursues this act,   85
Taint not thy mind nor let thy soul contrive
Against thy mother aught. Leave her to heaven
And to those thorns that in her bosom lodge,
To prick and sting her. Fare thee well at once.
The glowworm shows the matin° to be near,   90
And 'gins to pale his° uneffectual fire.
Adieu, adieu, adieu! Remember me.   [*Exit.*]

HAMLET: O all you host of heaven! O earth! What else?
And shall I couple° hell? O, fie! Hold,° hold, my heart,
And you, my sinews, grow not instant° old,   95
But bear me stiffly up. Remember thee?
Ay, thou poor ghost, whiles memory holds a seat
In this distracted globe.° Remember thee?
Yea, from the table° of my memory
I'll wipe away all trivial fond° records,   100
All saws° of books, all forms,° all pressures° past
That youth and observation copied there,
And thy commandment all alone shall live
Within the book and volume of my brain,
Unmixed with baser matter. Yes, by heaven!   105
O most pernicious woman!
O villain, villain, smiling, damnèd villain!
My tables°—meet it is° I set it down
That one may smile, and smile, and be a villain.
At least I am sure it may be so in Denmark.   [*Writing.*] 110
So uncle, there you are.° Now to my word:
It is "Adieu, adieu! Remember me."
I have sworn 't.

Enter HORATIO *and* MARCELLUS.

HORATIO: My lord, my lord!
MARCELLUS: Lord Hamlet!   115

---

76 dispatched suddenly deprived. **78 Unhouseled** without having received the Sacrament;
disappointed unready (spiritually) for the last journey; **unaneled** without having received
extreme unction. **79 reckoning** settling of accounts. **82 nature** i.e., the promptings of a son.
84 luxury lechery. **90 matin** morning. **91 his** its. **94 couple** add; **Hold** hold together.
95 instant instantly. **98 globe** (1) head, (2) world. **99 table** tablet, slate. **100 fond** foolish.
101 saws wise sayings; **forms** shapes or images copied onto the slate; general ideas;
pressures impressions stamped. **108 tables** writing tablets; **meet it is** it is fitting.
111 there you are i.e., there, I've written that down against you.

HORATIO: Heavens secure him!°
HAMLET: So be it.
MARCELLUS: Hilo, ho, ho, my lord!
HAMLET: Hillo, ho, ho, boy! Come, bird, come.°
MARCELLUS: How is 't, my noble lord?   120
HORATIO: What news, my lord?
HAMLET: O, wonderful!
HORATIO: Good my lord, tell it.
HAMLET: No, you will reveal it.
HORATIO: Not I, my lord, by heaven.   125
MARCELLUS: Nor I, my lord.
HAMLET: How say you, then, would heart of man once° think it?
    But you'll be secret?
HORATIO, MARCELLUS: Ay, by heaven, my lord.
HAMLET: There's never a villain dwelling in all Denmark
    But he's an arrant° knave.   130
HORATIO: There needs no ghost, my lord, come from the grave
    To tell us this.
HAMLET: Why, right, you are in the right.
    And so, without more circumstance° at all,
    I hold it fit that we shake hands and part,
    You as your business and desire shall point you—   135
    For every man hath business and desire,
    Such as it is—and for my own poor part,
    Look you, I'll go pray.
HORATIO: These are but wild and whirling words, my lord.
HAMLET: I am sorry they offend you, heartily;   140
    Yes, faith, heartily.
HORATIO: There's no offense, my lord.
HAMLET: Yes, by Saint Patrick,° but there is, Horatio,
    And much offense° too. Touching this vision here,
    It is an honest ghost,° that let me tell you.
    For your desire to know what is between us,   145
    O'ermaster 't as you may. And now, good friends,
    As you are friends, scholars, and soldiers,
    Give me one poor request.
HORATIO: What is 't, my lord? We will.
HAMLET: Never make known what you have seen tonight.   150
HORATIO, MARCELLUS: My lord, we will not.
HAMLET: Nay, but swear 't.
HORATIO: In faith, my lord, not I.°
MARCELLUS: Nor I, my lord, in faith.
HAMLET: Upon my sword.°   [*He holds out his sword.*]   155

---

116 secure him keep him safe.   **119 Hillo . . . come** (A falconer's call to a hawk in air. Hamlet mocks the halloing as though it were a part of hawking.)   **127 once** ever.   **130 arrant** thoroughgoing.   **133 circumstance** ceremony, elaboration.   **142 Saint Patrick** (the keeper of Purgatory and patron saint of all blunders and confusion.)   **143 offense** (Hamlet deliberately changes Horatio's "no offense against all decency.")   **144 an honest ghost** i.e., a real ghost and not an evil spirit.   **153 In faith . . . I** i.e., I swear not to tell what I have seen. (Horatio is not refusing to swear.)   **155 sword** i.e., the hilt in the form of a cross.

MARCELLUS: We have sworn, my lord, already.°
HAMLET: Indeed, upon my sword, indeed.
GHOST [*cries under the stage*]: Swear.
HAMLET: Ha, ha, boy, sayst thou so? Art thou there, truepenny?°
    Come on, you hear this fellow in the cellarage.   160
    Consent to swear.
HORATIO: Propose the oath, my lord.
HAMLET: Never to speak of this that you have seen,
    Swear by my sword.
GHOST [*beneath*]: Swear.   [*They swear.*°]
HAMLET: *Hic et ubique?* ° Then we'll shift our ground.   165
                             [*He moves to another spot.*]
    Come hither, gentlemen,
    And lay your hands again upon my sword.
    Swear by my sword
    Never to speak of this that you have heard.
GHOST [*beneath*]: Swear by his sword.   [*They swear.*]   170
HAMLET: Well said, old mole. Canst work i' th' earth so fast?
    A worthy pioneer!°—Once more removed, good friends.
                               [*He moves again.*]
HORATIO: O day and night, but this is wondrous strange!
HAMLET: And therefore as a stranger° give it welcome.
    There are more things in heaven and earth, Horatio,   175
    Than are dreamt of in your philosophy.°
    But come;
    Here, as before, never, so help you mercy,°
    How strange or odd soe'er I bear myself—
    As I perchance hereafter shall think meet   180
    To put an antic° disposition on—
    That you, at such times seeing me, never shall,
    With arms encumbered° thus, or this headshake,
    Or by pronouncing of some doubtful phrase
    As "Well, we know," or "We could, an if° we would,"   185
    Or "If we list° to speak," or "There be, an if they might,"°
    Or such ambiguous giving out,° to note°
    That you know aught° of me—this do swear,
    So grace and mercy at your most need help you.
GHOST [*beneath*]: Swear.   [*They swear.*]   190

---

156 We . . . already i.e., we swore in *faith*.   **159 truepenny** honest old fellow.   **164 s.d. They swear** (seemingly they swear here, and at lines 170 and 190, as they lay their hands on Hamlet's sword. Triple oaths would have particular force; these three oaths deal with what they have seen, what they have heard, and what they promise about Hamlet's *antic disposition*.)   **165 *Hic et ubique*** here and everywhere (Latin).   **172 pioneer** foot soldier assigned to dig tunnels and excavations.   **174 as a stranger** i.e., needing your hospitality.   **176 your philosophy** this subject called "natural philosophy" or "science" that people talk about.   **178 so help you mercy** as you hope for God's mercy when you are judged.   **181 antic** fantastic.   **183 encumbered** folded.   **185 an if** if.   **186 list** wished; **There . . . might** i.e., there are people here (we, in fact) who could tell news if we were at liberty to do so.   **187 giving out** intimation;   **note** draw attention to the fact.   **188 aught** i.e., something secret.

HAMLET: Rest, rest, perturbèd spirit! So, gentlemen,
With all my love I do commend me to you;°
And what so poor a man as Hamlet is
May do t' express his love and friending° to you,
God willing, shall not lack.° Let us go in together,   195
And still° your fingers on your lips, I pray.
The time° is out of joint. O cursèd spite°
That ever I was born to set it right!   [*They wait for him to leave first.*]
Nay, come, let's go together.°   *Exeunt.*

[2.1]

Enter old POLONIUS *with his man* [REYNALDO].

POLONIUS: Give him this money and these notes, Reynaldo.
[*He gives money and papers.*]
REYNALDO: I will, my lord.
POLONIUS: You shall do marvelous° wisely, good Reynaldo,
Before you visit him, to make inquire°
Of his behavior.
REYNALDO: My lord, I did intend it.   5
POLONIUS: Marry, well said, very well said. Look you, sir,
Inquire me first what Danskers° are in Paris,
And how, and who, what means,° and where they keep,°
What company, at what expense; and finding
By this encompassment° and drift° of question   10
That they do know my son, come you more nearer
Than your particular demands will touch it.°
Take you,° as 'twere, some distant knowledge of him,
As thus, "I know his father and his friends,
And in part him." Do you mark this, Reynaldo?   15
REYNALDO: Ay, very well, my lord.
POLONIUS: "And in part him, but," you may say, "not well.
But if 't be he I mean, he's very wild,
Addicted so and so," and there put on° him
What forgeries° you please—marry, none so rank°   20
As may dishonor him, take heed of that,
But, sir, such wanton,° wild, and usual slips
As are companions noted and most known
To youth and liberty.
REYNALDO: As gaming, my lord.   25
POLONIUS: Ay, or drinking, fencing, swearing,
Quarreling, drabbing°—you may go so far.

192 do . . . you entrust myself to you.   194 friending friendliness.   195 lack be
lacking.   196 still always.   197 The time the state of affairs;   spite i.e., the spite of
Fortune.   199 let's go together (probably they wait for him to leave first, but he refuses
this ceremoniousness.)   [2.1] Location: Polonius' chambers.   3 marvelous marvelously.
4 inquire inquiry.   7 Danskers Danes.   8 what means what wealth (they have);   keep
dwell.   10 encompassment roundabout talking;   drift gradual approach or course.
11–12 come . . . it you will find out more this way than by asking pointed questions
(*particular demands*).   13 Take you assume, pretend.   19 put on impute to.   20 forgeries
invented tales;   rank gross.   22 wanton sportive, unrestrained.   27 drabbing whoring.

REYNALDO: My lord, that would dishonor him.

POLONIUS: Faith, no, as you may season° it in the charge.
    You must not put another scandal on him 30
    That he is open to incontinency;°
    That's not my meaning. But breathe his faults so quaintly°
    That they may seem the taints of liberty,°
    The flash and outbreak of a fiery mind,
    A savageness in unreclaimèd blood, 35
    Of general assault.°

REYNALDO: But, my good lord—

POLONIUS: Wherefore should you do this?

REYNALDO: Ay, my lord, I would know that.

POLONIUS: Marry, sir, here's my drift, 40
    And I believe it is a fetch of warrant.°
    You laying these slight sullies on my son,
    As 'twere a thing a little soiled wi' the working,°
    Mark you,
    Your party in converse,° him you would sound,° 45
    Having ever° seen in the prenominate crimes°
    The youth you breathe° of guilty, be assured
    He closes with you in this consequence:°
    "Good sir," or so, or "friend," or "gentleman,"
    According to the phrase or the addition° 50
    Of man and country.

REYNALDO: Very good, my lord.

POLONIUS: And then, sir, does 'a this—'a does—what was I about to say? By the
    Mass, I was about to say something. Where did I leave?

REYNALDO: At "closes in the consequence."

POLONIUS: At "closes in the consequence," ay, marry. 55
    He closes thus: "I know the gentleman,
    I saw him yesterday," or "th' other day,"
    Or then, or then, with such or such, "and as you say,
    There was 'a gaming," "there o'ertook in 's rouse,"°
    "There falling out° at tennis," or perchance 60
    "I saw him enter such a house of sale,"
    Videlicet° a brothel, or so forth. See you now,
    Your bait of falsehood takes this carp° of truth;
    And thus do we of wisdom and of reach,°
    With windlasses° and with assays of bias,° 65

---

29 season temper, soften.   **31 incontinency** habitual sexual excess.   **32 quaintly** artfully, subtly.   **33 taints of liberty** faults resulting from free living.   **35–36 A savageness . . . assault** a wildness in untamed youth that assails all indiscriminately.   **41 fetch of warrant** legitimate trick.   **43 soiled wi' the working** soiled by handling while it is being made, i.e., by involvement in the ways of the world.   **45 converse** conversation;   **sound** i.e., sound out.   **46 Having ever** if he has ever;   **prenominate crimes** before-mentioned offenses.   **47 breathe** speak.   **48 closes . . . consequence** takes you into his confidence in some fashion, as follows.   **50 addition** title.   **59 o'ertook in 's rouse** overcome by drink.   **60 falling out** quarreling.   **62 Videlicet** namely.   **63 carp** a fish.   **64 reach** capacity, ability.   **65 windlasses** i.e., circuitous paths. (Literally, circuits made to head off the game in hunting);   **assays of bias** attempts through indirection (like the curving path of the bowling ball, which is biased or weighted to one side).

By indirections find directions° out.
So by my former lecture and advice
Shall you my son. You have° me, have you not?
REYNALDO: My lord, I have.
POLONIUS: God b'wi'° ye; fare ye well.
REYNALDO: Good my lord.   70
POLONIUS: Observe his inclination in yourself.°
REYNALDO: I shall, my lord.
POLONIUS: And let him ply his music.
REYNALDO: Well, my lord.
POLONIUS: Farewell.   *Exit* REYNALDO.

  Enter OPHELIA.

                          How now, Ophelia, what's the matter?   75
OPHELIA: O my lord, my lord, I have been so affrighted!
POLONIUS: With what, i' the name of God?
OPHELIA: My lord, as I was sewing in my closet,°
    Lord Hamlet, with his doublet° all unbraced,°
    No hat upon his head, his stockings fouled,   80
    Ungartered, and down-gyvèd° to his ankle,
    Pale as his shirt, his knees knocking each other,
    And with a look so piteous in purport°
    As if he had been loosèd out of hell
    To speak of horrors—he comes before me.   85
POLONIUS: Mad for thy love?
OPHELIA: My lord, I do not know,
    But truly I do fear it.
POLONIUS: What said he?
OPHELIA: He took me by the wrist and held me hard.
    Then goes he to the length of all his arm,
    And, with his other hand thus o'er his brow   90
    He falls to such perusal of my face
    As° 'a would draw it. Long stayed he so.
    At last, a little shaking of mine arm
    And thrice his head thus waving up and down,
    He raised a sigh so piteous and profound   95
    As it did seem to shatter all his bulk°
    And end his being. That done, he lets me go,
    And with his head over his shoulder turned
    He seemed to find his way without his eyes,
    For out o' doors he went without their helps,   100
    And to the last bended their light on me.
POLONIUS: Come, go with me. I will go seek the King.
    This is the very ecstasy° of love,
    Whose violent property° fordoes° itself
    And leads the will to desperate undertakings   105

66 directions i.e., the way things really are.   **68 have** understand.   **69 b' wi'** be with.
71 in yourself in your own person (as well as by asking questions).   **78 closet** private
chamber.   **79 doublet** close-fitting jacket;   **unbraced** unfastened.   **81 down-gyvèd** fallen to
the ankles (like gyves or fetters).   **83 in purport** in what it expressed.   **92 As** as if (also in
line 97).   **96 bulk** body.   **103 ecstasy** madness.   **104 property** nature;   **fordoes** destroys.

As oft as any passion under heaven
That does afflict our natures. I am sorry.
What, have you given him any hard words of late?

OPHELIA: No, my good lord, but as you did command
I did repel his letters and denied   110
His access to me.

POLONIUS: That hath made him mad.
I am sorry that with better heed and judgment
I had not quoted° him. I feared he did but trifle
And meant to wrack° thee. But beshrew my jealousy!°
By heaven, it is as proper to our age°   115
To cast beyond° ourselves in our opinions
As it is common for the younger sort
To lack discretion. Come, go we to the King.
This must be known,° which, being kept close,° might move
More grief to hide than hate to utter love.°   120
Come.   *Exeunt.*

[2.2]

Flourish. Enter KING *and* QUEEN, ROSENCRANTZ, *and* GUILDENSTERN [*with others*].

KING: Welcome, dear Rosencrantz and Guildenstern.
Moreover that° we much did long to see you,
The need we have to use you did provoke
Our hasty sending. Something have you heard
Of Hamlet's transformation—so call it,   5
Sith nor° th' exterior nor the inward man
Resembles that° it was. What it should be,
More than his father's death, that thus hath put him
So much from th' understanding of himself,
I cannot dream of. I entreat you both   10
That, being of so young days° brought up with him,
And sith so neighbored to° his youth and havior,°
That you vouchsafe your rest° here in our court
Some little time, so by your companies
To draw him on to pleasures, and to gather   15
So much as from occasion° you may glean,
Whether aught to us unknown afflicts him thus
That, opened,° lies within our remedy.

113 quoted observed.   **114 wrack** ruin, seduce;   **beshrew my jealousy** a plague upon my
suspicious nature.   **115 proper . . . age** characteristic of us (old) men.   **116 cast beyond**
over-shoot, miscalculate. (A metaphor from hunting.)   **119 known** made known (to the
King);   **close** secret.   **119–20 might . . . love** i.e., might cause more grief (because of what
Hamlet might do) by hiding the knowledge of Hamlet's strange behavior toward Ophelia
than unpleasantness by telling it.   **[2.2] Location: The castle.   2 Moreover that** besides
the fact that.   **6 Sith nor** since neither.   **7 that** what.   **11 of . . . days** From such early
youth.   **12 And sith so neighbored to** and since you are (or, and since that time you are)
intimately acquainted with;   **havior** demeanor.   **13 vouchsafe your rest** please to stay.
16 occasion opportunity.   **18 opened** being revealed.

QUEEN: Good gentlemen, he hath much talked of you,
     And sure I am two men there is not living   20
     To whom he more adheres. If it will please you
     To show us so much gentry° and good will
     As to expend your time with us awhile
     For the supply and profit of our hope,°
     Your visitation shall receive such thanks   25
     As fits a king's remembrance.°

ROSENCRANTZ: Both Your Majesties
     Might, by the sovereign power you have of° us,
     Put your dread° pleasures more into command
     Than to entreaty.

GUILDENSTERN: But we both obey,
     And here give up ourselves in the full bent°   30
     To lay our service freely at your feet,
     To be commanded.

KING: Thanks, Rosencrantz and gentle Guildenstern.

QUEEN: Thanks, Guildenstern and gentle Rosencrantz.
     And I beseech you instantly to visit   35
     My too much changèd son. Go, some of you,
     And bring these gentlemen where Hamlet is.

GUILDENSTERN: Heavens make our presence and our practices°
     Pleasant and helpful to him!

QUEEN: Ay, amen!
     Exeunt ROSENCRANTZ *and* GUILDENSTERN [*with some attendants*].

     Enter POLONIUS.

POLONIUS: Th' ambassadors from Norway, my good lord,   40
     Are joyfully returned.

KING: Thou still° hast been the father of good news.

POLONIUS: Have I, my lord? I assure my good liege
     I hold° my duty, as° I hold my soul,
     Both to my God and to my gracious king;   45
     And I do think, or else this brain of mine
     Hunts not the trail of policy° so sure
     As it hath used to do, that I have found
     The very cause of Hamlet's lunacy.

KING: O, speak of that! That do I long to hear.   50

POLONIUS: Give first admittance to th' ambassadors.
     My news shall be the fruit° to that great feast.

KING: Thyself do grace° to them and bring them in.   [*Exit* POLONIUS.]
     He tells me, my dear Gertrude, he hath found
     The head and source of all your son's distemper.   55

QUEEN: I doubt° it is no other but the main,°
     His father's death and our o'erhasty marriage.

---

22 gentry courtesy.　**24 supply . . . hope** aid and furtherance of what we hope for.　**26 As fits . . . remembrance** as would be a fitting gift of a king who rewards true service.　**27 of** over.　**28 dread** inspiring awe.　**30 in . . . bent** to the utmost degree of our capacity. (An archery metaphor.)　**38 practices** doings.　**42 still** always.　**44 hold** maintain;　**as** firmly as.　**47 policy** sagacity.　**52 fruit** dessert.　**53 grace** honor (punning on *grace* said before a *feast*, line 52.)　**56 doubt** fear, suspect;　**main** chief point, principal concern.

Enter Ambassadors VOLTIMAND *and* CORNELIUS, *with* POLONIUS.

KING: Well, we shall sift him.°—Welcome, my good friends!
　　　 Say, Voltimand, what from our brother° Norway?
VOLTIMAND: Most fair return of greetings and desires.°　　　　　　　　　 60
　　　 Upon our first,° he sent out to suppress
　　　 His nephew's levies, which to him appeared
　　　 To be a preparation 'gainst the Polack,
　　　 But, better looked into, he truly found
　　　 It was against Your Highness. Whereat grieved　　　　　　　　 65
　　　 That so his sickness, age, and impotence°
　　　 Was falsely borne in hand,° sends out arrests°
　　　 On Fortinbras, which he, in brief, obeys,
　　　 Receives rebuke from Norway, and in fine°
　　　 Makes vow before his uncle never more　　　　　　　　　　　 70
　　　 To give th' assay° of arms against Your Majesty.
　　　 Whereon old Norway, overcome with joy,
　　　 Gives him three thousand crowns in annual fee
　　　 And his commission to employ those soldiers,
　　　 So levied as before, against the Polack,　　　　　　　　　　　 75
　　　 With an entreaty, herein further shown,　　　　　 [*giving a paper*]
　　　 That it might please you to give quiet pass
　　　 Through your dominions for this enterprise
　　　 On such regards of safety and allowance°
　　　 As therein are set down.
KING:　　　　　　　　　　　 It likes° us well,　　　　　　　　　 80
　　　 And at our more considered° time we'll read,
　　　 Answer, and think upon this business.
　　　 Meantime we thank you for your well-took labor.
　　　 Go to your rest; at night we'll feast together.
　　　 Most welcome home!　　　　　　　　 *Exeunt Ambassadors.*
POLONIUS:　　　　　　　　　 This business is well ended.　　　　　 85
　　　 My liege, and madam, to expostulate°
　　　 What majesty should be, what duty is,
　　　 Why day is day, night night, and time is time,
　　　 Were nothing but to waste night, day, and time.
　　　 Therefore, since brevity is the soul of wit,°　　　　　　　　　 90
　　　 And tediousness the limbs and outward flourishes,
　　　 I will be brief. Your noble son is mad.
　　　 Mad call I it, for, to define true madness,
　　　 What is't but to be nothing else but mad?
　　　 But let that go.
QUEEN:　　　　　　　　　 More matter, with less art.　　　　　 95

---

58 sift him question Polonius closely.　**59 brother** fellow king.　**60 desires** good wishes.
61 Upon our first at our first words on the business.　**66 impotence** helplessness.　**67 borne in
hand** deluded, taken advantage of;　**arrests** orders to desist.　**69 in fine** in conclusion.　**71 give
th' assay** make trial of strength, challenge.　**78 On . . . allowance** i.e., with such considerations
for the safety of Denmark and permission for Fortinbras.　**80 likes** pleases.　**81 considered**
suitable for deliberation.　**86 expostulate** expound, inquire into.　**90 wit** sense or judgment.

POLONIUS: Madam, I swear I use no art at all.
That he's mad, 'tis true; 'tis true tis pity.
And pity 'tis 'tis true—a foolish figure,°
But farewell it, for I will use no art.
Mad let us grant him, then, and now remains   100
That we find out the cause of this effect,
Or rather say, the cause of this defect,
For this effect defective comes by cause.°
Thus it remains, and the remainder thus.
Perpend.°   105
I have a daughter—have while she is mine—
Who, in her duty and obedience, mark,
Hath given me this. Now gather and surmise.°
[*He reads the letter.*] "To the celestial and my soul's idol, the most
beautified Ophelia"—   110
That's an ill phrase, a vile phrase; "beautified" is a vile phrase. But you
shall hear. Thus: [*He reads.*]
"In her excellent white bosom,° these,° etc."
QUEEN: Came this from Hamlet to her?
POLONIUS: Good madam, stay° awhile, I will be faithful.°   [*He reads.*] 115
          "Doubt thou the stars are fire,
              Doubt that the sun doth move,
              Doubt° truth to be a liar,
              But never doubt I love.
O dear Ophelia, I am ill at these numbers.° I have not art to reckon° my   120
groans. But that I love thee best, O most best, believe it. Adieu.
          Thine evermore, most dear lady, whilst this machine° is to him,
                                                                Hamlet."
This in obedience hath my daughter shown me,
And, more above,° hath his solicitings,
As they fell out° by° time, by means, and place,   125
All given to mine ear.°
KING: But how hath she
Received his love?
POLONIUS: What do you think of me?
KING: As of a man faithful and honorable.
POLONIUS: I would fain° prove so. But what might you think,
When I had seen this hot love on the wing—   130
As I perceived it, I must tell you that,
Before my daughter told me—what might you,
Or my dear Majesty your queen here, think,
If I had played the desk or table book,°
Or given my heart a winking,° mute and dumb,   135

98 figure figure of speech.   **103 For . . . cause** i.e., for this defective behavior, his
madness, has a cause.   **105 Perpend** consider.   **108 gather and surmise** draw your own
conclusions.   **113 In . . . bosom** (The letter is poetically addressed to her heart.);   **these**
i.e., the letter.   **115 stay** wait;   **faithful** i.e., in reading the letter accurately.   **118 Doubt**
suspect.   **120 ill . . . numbers** unskilled at writing verses;   **reckon** (1) count, (2) number
metrically, scan.   **122 machine** i.e., body.   **124 more above** moreover.   **125 fell out**
occurred;   **by** according to.   **126 given . . . ear** i.e., told me about.   **129 fain** gladly.
134 played . . . table book i.e., remained shut up, concealing the information.
135 given . . . winking closed the eyes of my heart to this.

Or looked upon this love with idle sight?°
What might you think? No, I went round° to work,
And my young mistress thus I did bespeak:°
"Lord Hamlet is a prince out of thy star;°
This must not be." And then I prescripts° gave her,   140
That she should lock herself from his resort,°
Admit no messengers, receive no tokens.
Which done, she took the fruits of my advice;
And he, repellèd—a short tale to make—
Fell into a sadness, then into a fast,   145
Thence to a watch,° thence into a weakness,
Thence to a lightness,° and by this declension°
Into the madness wherein now he raves,
And all we° mourn for.

KING [*to the* QUEEN]:   Do you think 'tis this?
QUEEN: It may be, very like.   150
POLONIUS: Hath there been such a time—I would fain know that—
     That I have positively said "'Tis so,"
     When it proved otherwise?
KING: Not that I know.
POLONIUS: Take this from this,° if this be otherwise.
     If circumstances lead me, I will find   155
     Where truth is hid, though it were hid indeed
     Within the center.°
KING: How may we try° it further?
POLONIUS: You know sometimes he walks four hours together
     Here in the lobby.
QUEEN: So he does indeed.
POLONIUS: At such a time I'll loose° my daughter to him.   160
     Be you and I behind an arras° then.
     Mark the encounter. If he love her not
     And be not from his reason fall'n thereon,°
     Let me be no assistant for a state,
     But keep a farm and carters.°   165
KING: We will try it.

     Enter HAMLET [*reading on a book*].

QUEEN: But look where sadly° the poor wretch comes reading.
POLONIUS: Away, I do beseech you both, away.
     I'll board° him presently.° O, give me leave.°

---

136 with idle sight complacently or incomprehendingly.   **137 round** roundly, plainly.
138 bespeak address.   **139 out of thy star** above your sphere, position.   **140 prescripts**
orders.   **141 his resort** his visits.   **146 watch** state of sleeplessness.   **147 lightness** light-
headedness;   **declension** decline, deterioration (with a pun on the grammatical sense).
149 all we all of us, or, into everything that we.   **154 Take this from this** (The actor
probably gestures, indicating that he means his head from his shoulders, or his staff of office
or chain from his hands or neck, or something similar.)   **157 center** middle point of the
earth (which is also the center of the Ptolemaic universe);   **try** test, judge.   **160 loose** (as
one might release an animal that is being mated.)   **161 arras** hanging, tapestry.
163 thereon on that account.   **165 carters** wagon drivers.   **166 sadly** seriously.
168 board accost;   **presently** at once;   **give me leave** i.e., excuse me, leave me alone.
(Said to those he hurries offstage, including the King and Queen.)

Exeunt KING *and* QUEEN [*with attendants*].

How does my good Lord Hamlet?

HAMLET: Well, God-a-mercy.°   170

POLONIUS: Do you know me, my lord?

HAMLET: Excellent well. You are a fishmonger.°

POLONIUS: Not I, my lord.

HAMLET: Then I would you were so honest a man.

POLONIUS: Honest, my lord?   175

HAMLET: Ay, sir. To be honest, as this world goes, is to be one man picked out of
ten thousand.

POLONIUS: That's very true, my lord.

HAMLET: For if the sun breed maggots in a dead dog, being a good kissing carrion°—
Have you a daughter?   180

POLONIUS: I have, my lord.

HAMLET: Let her not walk i' the sun.° Conception° is a blessing, but as your daughter
may conceive, friend, look to 't.

POLONIUS [*aside*]: How say you by that? Still harping on my daughter. Yet he knew me
not at first; 'a° said I was a fishmonger. 'A is far gone. And truly in my   185
youth I suffered much extremity for love, very near this. I'll speak to him
again.—What do you read, my lord?

HAMLET: Words, words, words.

POLONIUS: What is the matter,° my lord?

HAMLET: Between who?   190

POLONIUS: I mean, the matter that you read, my lord.

HAMLET: Slanders, sir; for the satirical rogue says here that old men have gray
beards, that their faces are wrinkled, their eyes purging° thick amber° and
plum-tree gum, and that they have a plentiful lack of wit,° together with
most weak hams. All which, sir, though I most powerfully and potently   195
believe, yet I hold it not honesty° to have it thus set down, for yourself,
sir, shall grow old° as I am, if like a crab you could go backward.

POLONIUS [*aside*]: Though this be madness, yet there is method in 't.—Will you
walk out of the air,° my lord?

HAMLET: Into my grave.   200

POLONIUS: Indeed, that's out of the air. [*Aside.*] How pregnant° sometimes his
replies are! A happiness° that often madness hits on, which reason and
sanity could not so prosperously° be delivered of. I will leave him and
suddenly° contrive the means of meeting between him and my daughter.—
My honorable lord, I will most humbly take my leave of you.   205

HAMLET: You cannot, sir, take from me anything that I will more willingly part
withal°—except my life, except my life, except my life.

---

170 God-a-mercy God have mercy, i.e., thank you.   **172 fishmonger** fish merchant.
179 a good kissing carrion i.e., a good piece of flesh for kissing, or for the sun to kiss.
182 i' the sun in public (with additional implication of the sunshine of princely favors);
Conception (1) understanding, (2) pregnancy.   **185 'a** he.   **189 matter** substance. (But
Hamlet plays on the sense of "basis for a dispute.")   **193 purging** discharging;   **amber** i.e.,
resin, like the resinous **plum-tree gum**.   **194 wit** understanding.   **196 honesty** decency,
decorum.   **197 old** as old.   **199 out of the air** (The open air was considered dangerous
for sick people.)   **201 pregnant** quick-witted, full of meaning.   **202 happiness** felicity of
expression.   **203 prosperously** successfully.   **204 suddenly** immediately.   **207 withal** with.

Enter GUILDENSTERN *and* ROSENCRANTZ.

POLONIUS: Fare you well, my lord.

HAMLET: These tedious old fools!°

POLONIUS: You go to seek the Lord Hamlet. There he is. 210

ROSENCRANTZ [to POLONIUS]: God save you, sir! [*Exit* POLONIUS.]

GUILDENSTERN: My honored lord!

ROSENCRANTZ: My most dear lord!

HAMLET: My excellent good friends! How dost thou, Guildenstern? Ah, Rosencrantz!
    Good lads, how do you both? 215

ROSENCRANTZ: As the indifferent° children of the earth.

GUILDENSTERN: Happy in that we are not overhappy.
    On Fortune's cap we are not the very button.

HAMLET: Nor the soles of her shoe?

ROSENCRANTZ: Neither, my lord. 220

HAMLET: Then you live about her waist, or in the middle of her favors?°

GUILDENSTERN: Faith, her privates we.°

HAMLET: In the secret parts of Fortune? O, most true, she is a strumpet.°
    What news?

ROSENCRANTZ: None, my lord, but the world's grown honest. 225

HAMLET: Then is doomsday near. But your news is not true. Let me question more in par-
    ticular. What have you, my good friends, deserved at the hands of Fortune
    that she sends you to prison hither?

GUILDENSTERN: Prison, my lord?

HAMLET: Denmark's a prison. 230

ROSENCRANTZ: Then is the world one.

HAMLET: A goodly one, in which there are many confines,° wards,° and dungeons,
    Denmark being one o' the worst.

ROSENCRANTZ: We think not so, my lord.

HAMLET: Why then 'tis none to you, for there is nothing either good or bad but 235
    thinking makes it so. To me it is a prison.

ROSENCRANTZ: Why then, your ambition makes it one. 'Tis too narrow for your mind.

HAMLET: O God, I could be bounded in a nutshell and count myself a king of
    infinite space, were it not that I have bad dreams.

GUILDENSTERN: Which dreams indeed are ambition, for the very substance of the 240
    ambitious° is merely the shadow of a dream.

HAMLET: A dream itself is but a shadow.

ROSENCRANTZ: Truly, and I hold ambition of so airy and light a quality that it is
    but a shadow's shadow.

HAMLET: Then are our beggars bodies,° and our monarchs and outstretched° heroes 245
    the beggars' shadows. Shall we to the court? For, by my fay,° I cannot
    reason.

209 old fools i.e., old men like Polonius.   **216 indifferent** ordinary, at neither extreme of
fortune or misfortune.   **221 favors** i.e., sexual favors.   **222 her privates we** i.e., (1) we are
sexually intimate with Fortune, the fickle goddess who bestows her favors indiscriminately,
(2) we are her private citizens.   **223 strumpet** prostitute. (A common epithet for indiscrimi-
nate Fortune; see line 449.)   **232 confines** places of confinement; **wards** cells.   **240–41 the
very . . . ambitious** that seemingly very substantial thing that the ambitious pursue.
245 bodies i.e., solid substances rather than shadows (since beggars are not ambitious).
outstretched (1) far-reaching in their ambition, (2) elongated as shadows.   **246 fay** faith.

ROSENCRANTZ, GUILDENSTERN: We'll wait upon° you.

HAMLET: No such matter. I will not sort° you with the rest of my servants, for, to speak to you like an honest man, I am most dreadfully attended.° But, in the beaten way° of friendship, what make° you at Elsinore?   250

ROSENCRANTZ: To visit you, my lord, no other occasion.

HAMLET: Beggar that I am, I am even poor in thanks; but I thank you, and sure, dear friends, my thanks are too dear a halfpenny.° Were you not sent for? Is it your own inclining? Is it a free° visitation? Come, come, deal justly   255 with me. Come, come. Nay, speak.

GUILDENSTERN: What should we say, my lord?

HAMLET: Anything but to the purpose.° You were sent for, and there is a kind of confession in your looks which your modesties° have not craft enough to color.° I know the good King and Queen have sent for you.   260

ROSENCRANTZ: To what end, my lord?

HAMLET: That you must teach me. But let me conjure° you, by the rights of our fellowship, by the consonancy of our youth,° by the obligation of our ever-preserved love, and by what more dear a better° proposer could charge° you withal, be even° and direct with me whether you were sent for or no.   265

ROSENCRANTZ [*aside to* GUILDENSTERN]: What say you?

HAMLET [*aside*]: Nay, then, I have an eye of° you.—If you love me, hold not off.°

GUILDENSTERN: My lord, we were sent for.

HAMLET: I will tell you why; so shall my anticipation prevent your discovery,° and your secrecy to the King and Queen molt no feather.° I have of late—   270 but wherefore I know not—lost all my mirth, forgone all custom of exercises; and indeed it goes so heavily with my disposition that this goodly frame, the earth, seems to me a sterile promontory; this most excellent canopy, the air, look you, this brave° o'erhanging firmament, this majestical roof fretted° with golden fire, why, it appeareth nothing to me but a   275 foul and pestilent congregation° of vapors. What a piece of work° is a man! How noble in reason, how infinite in faculties, in form and moving how express° and admirable, in action how like an angel, in apprehension° how like a god! The beauty of the world, the paragon of animals! And yet, to me, what is this quintessence° of dust? Man delights not me—no, nor woman   280 neither, though by your smiling you seem to say so.

ROSENCRANTZ: My lord, there was no such stuff in my thoughts.

HAMLET: Why did you laugh, then, when I said man delights not me?

248 wait upon accompany, attend. (But Hamlet uses the phrase in the sense of providing menial service.)   **249 sort** class, categorize.   **250 dreadfully attended** waited upon in slovenly fashion.   **251 beaten way** familiar path, tried-and-true course;   **make** do.   **254 too dear a halfpenny** (1) too expensive at even a halfpenny, i.e., of little worth, (2) too expensive *by* a halfpenny in return for worthless kindness.   **255 free** voluntary.   **258 Anything but to the purpose** anything except a straightforward answer. (Said ironically.)   **259 modesties** sense of shame.   **260 color** disguise.   **262 conjure** adjure, entreat.   **263 the consonancy of our youth** our closeness in our younger days.   **264 better** more skillful;   **charge** urge.   **265 even** straight, honest.   **267 of** on;   **hold not off** don't hold back.   **269 so . . . discovery** in that way my saying it first will spare you from revealing the truth.   **270 molt no feather** i.e., not diminish in the least.   **274 brave** splendid.   **275 fretted** adorned (with fretwork, as in a vaulted ceiling). **276 congregation** mass;   **piece of work** masterpiece.   **278 express** well-framed, exact, expressive.   **278 apprehension** power of comprehending.   **280 quintessence** the fifth essence of ancient philosophy, beyond earth, water, air, and fire, supposed to be the substance of the heavenly bodies and to be latent in all things.

ROSENCRANTZ: To think, my lord, if you delight not in man, what Lenten entertainment° the players shall receive from you. We coted° them on the way, 285
and hither are they coming to offer you service.

HAMLET: He that plays the king shall be welcome; His Majesty shall have tribute° of° me. The adventurous knight shall use his foil and target,° the lover shall not sigh gratis,° the humorous man° shall end his part in peace,° the clown shall make those laugh whose lungs are tickle o' the sear,° and the 290
lady shall say her mind freely, or the blank verse shall halt° for 't. What players are they?

ROSENCRANTZ: Even those you were wont to take such delight in, the tragedians° of the city.

HAMLET: How chances it they travel? Their residence,° both in reputation and 295
profit, was better both ways.

ROSENCRANTZ: I think their inhibition° comes by the means of the late° innovation.°

HAMLET: Do they hold the same estimation they did when I was in the city? Are they so followed?

ROSENCRANTZ: No, indeed are they not. 300

HAMLET: How comes it? Do they grow rusty?

ROSENCRANTZ: Nay, their endeavor keeps° in the wonted° pace. But there is, sir, an aerie° of children, little eyases,° that cry out on the top of question° and are most tyrannically° clapped for 't. These are now the fashion, and so berattle° the common stages°—so they call them—that many wearing 305
rapiers° are afraid of goose quills° and dare scarce come thither.

HAMLET: What, are they children? Who maintains 'em? How are they escoted?° Will they pursue the quality° no longer than they can sing?° Will they not say afterwards, if they should grow themselves to common° players—as it is most like,° if their means are no better°—their writers do them 310
wrong to make them exclaim against their own succession?°

ROSENCRANTZ: Faith, there has been much to-do° on both sides, and the nation holds it no sin to tar° them to controversy. There was for a while no money bid for argument unless the poet and the player went to cuffs in the question.°

HAMLET: Is 't possible? 315

284–85 Lenten entertainment meager reception (appropriate to Lent);   **coted** overtook and passed by.   **287 tribute** (1) applause, (2) homage paid in money.   **288 of** from;   **foil and target** sword and shield.   **289 gratis** for nothing;   **humorous man** eccentric character, dominated by one trait or "humor";   **in peace** i.e., with full license.   **290 tickle o' the sear** easy on the trigger, ready to laugh easily. (A *sear* is part of a gunlock.)   **291 halt** limp.   **293 tragedians** actors.   **295 residence** remaining in their usual place, i.e., in the city.   **297 inhibition** formal prohibition (from acting plays in the city);   **late** recent;   **innovation** i.e., the new fashion in satirical plays performed by boy actors in the "private" theaters; or possibly a political uprising; or the strict limitations set on theaters in London in 1600.   **302 keeps** continues;   **wonted** usual.   **303 aerie** nest;   **eyases** young hawks;   **cry . . . question** speak shrilly, dominating the controversy (in decrying the public theaters).   **304 tyrannically** outrageously.   **305 berattle** berate, clamor against;   **common stages** public theaters.   **305–06 many wearing rapiers** i.e., many men of fashion, afraid to patronize the common players for fear of being satirized by the poets writing for the boy actors;   **goose quills** i.e., pens of satirists.   **307 escoted** maintained.   **308 quality** (acting) profession;   **no longer . . . sing** i.e., only until their voices change.   **309 common** regular, adult.   **310 like** likely;   **if . . . better** if they find no better way to support themselves.   **311 succession** i.e., future careers.   **312 to-do** ado.   **313 tar** set on (as dogs).   **313–14 There . . . question** i.e., for a while, no money was offered by the acting companies to playwrights for the plot to a play unless the satirical poets who wrote for the boys and the adult actors came to blows in the play itself.

GUILDENSTERN: O, there has been much throwing about of brains.

HAMLET: Do the boys carry it away?°

ROSENCRANTZ: Ay, that they do, my lord—Hercules and his load° too.°

HAMLET: It is not very strange; for my uncle is King of Denmark, and those that
would make mouths° at him while my father lived give twenty, forty,   320
fifty, a hundred ducats° apiece for his picture in little.° 'Sblood,° there is
something in this more than natural, if philosophy° could find it out.

A flourish [*of trumpets within*].

GUILDENSTERN: There are the players.

HAMLET: Gentlemen, you are welcome to Elsinore. Your hands, come then.
Th' appurtenance° of welcome is fashion and ceremony. Let me comply°   325
with you in this garb,° lest my extent° to the players, which, I tell you,
must show fairly outwards,° should more appear like entertainment° than
yours. You are welcome. But my uncle-father and aunt-mother are
deceived.

GUILDENSTERN: In what, my dear lord?   330

HAMLET: I am but mad north-north-west.° When the wind is southerly I know a
hawk from a handsaw.°

Enter POLONIUS.

POLONIUS: Well be with you, gentlemen!

HAMLET: Hark you, Guildenstern, and you too; at each ear a hearer. That great
baby you see there is not yet out of his swaddling clouts.°   335

ROSENCRANTZ: Haply° he is the second time come to them, for they say an old
man is twice a child.

HAMLET: I will prophesy he comes to tell me of the players. Mark it.—You say
right, sir, o' Monday morning, 'twas then indeed.

POLONIUS: My lord, I have news to tell you.   340

HAMLET: My lord, I have news to tell you. When Roscius° was an actor in Rome—

POLONIUS: The actors are come hither, my lord.

HAMLET: Buzz,° buzz!

POLONIUS: Upon my honor—

HAMLET: Then came each actor on his ass.   345

POLONIUS: The best actors in the world, either for tragedy, comedy, history,
pastoral, pastoral-comical, historical-pastoral, tragical-historical, tragical-
comical-historical-pastoral, scene individable,° or poem unlimited.°

317 carry it away i.e., win the day.   **318 Hercules . . . load** (thought to be an allusion
to the sign of the Globe Theatre, which was Hercules bearing the world on his shoulders.)   **301–18 How . . . load too** (The passage, omitted from the early quartos, alludes to
the so-called War of the Theaters, 1599–1602, the rivalry between the children's companies
and the adult actors.)   **320 mouths** faces.   **321 ducats** gold coins;   **in little** in miniature;   **'Sblood** by God's (Christ's) blood.   **322 philosophy** i.e., scientific inquiry.
325 appurtenance proper accompaniment;   **comply** observe the formalities of courtesy.
326 garb i.e., manner;   **my extent** that which I extend, i.e., my polite behavior.
327 show fairly outwards show every evidence of cordiality;   **entertainment** a (warm)
reception.   **331 north-north-west** just off true north, only partly.   **332 hawk, handsaw**
i.e., two very different things, though also perhaps meaning a mattock (or *back*) and
carpenter's cutting tools, respectively; also birds, with a play on *hernshaw,* or heron.
335 swaddling clouts cloths in which to wrap a newborn baby.   **336 Haply** perhaps.
341 Roscius a famous Roman actor who died in 62 BCE.   **343 Buzz** (an interjection used to
denote stale news.)   **348 scene individable** a play observing the unity of place; or perhaps
one that is unclassifiable, or performed without intermission;   **poem unlimited** a play disregarding the unities of time and place; one that is all-inclusive.

Seneca° cannot be too heavy, nor Plautus° too light. For the law of writ
and the liberty,° these° are the only men.   350

HAMLET: O Jephthah, judge of Israel,° what a treasure hadst thou!

POLONIUS: What a treasure had he, my lord?

HAMLET: Why,

> "One fair daughter, and no more,
> The which he lovèd passing° well."   355

POLONIUS [*aside*]: Still on my daughter.

HAMLET: Am I not i' the right, old Jephthah?

POLONIUS: If you call me Jephthah, my lord, I have a daughter that I love
passing well.

HAMLET: Nay, that follows not.   360

POLONIUS: What follows then, my lord?

HAMLET: Why,

> "As by lot,° God wot,"°

and then, you know,

> "It came to pass, as most like° it was"—   365

the first row° of the pious chanson° will show you more, for look where
my abridgement° comes.

Enter the PLAYERS.

You are welcome, masters; welcome, all. I am glad to see thee well.
Welcome, good friends. O, old friend! Why, thy face is valanced° since
I saw thee last. Com'st thou to beard° me in Denmark? What, my young   370
lady° and mistress! By 'r Lady,° your ladyship is nearer to heaven than
when I saw you last, by the altitude of a chopine.° Pray God your voice,
like a piece of uncurrent° gold, be not cracked within the ring.° Masters,
you are all welcome. We'll e'en to 't° like French falconers, fly at anything
we see. We'll have a speech straight.° Come, give us a taste of your   375
quality.° Come, a passionate speech.

FIRST PLAYER: What speech, my good lord?

HAMLET: I heard thee speak me a speech once, but it was never acted, or if it was,
not above once, for the play, I remember, pleased not the million; 'twas
caviar to the general.° But it was—as I received it, and others, whose   380
judgments in such matters cried in the top of° mine—an excellent play,
well digested° in the scenes, set down with as much modesty° as
cunning.° I remember one said there were no sallets° in the lines to make

---

349 Seneca writer of Latin tragedies;   **Plautus** writer of Latin comedies.   **349–50 law . . . liberty**
dramatic composition both according to the rules and disregarding the rules;   **these** i.e., the
actors.   **351 Jephthah . . . Israel** (Jephthah had to sacrifice his daughter; see Judges 11. Hamlet
goes on to quote from a ballad on the theme.)   **355 passing** surpassingly.   **363 lot** chance;
wot knows.   **365 like** likely, probable.   **366 row** stanza;   **chanson** ballad, song.   **367 my
abridgement** something that cuts short my conversation; also, a diversion.   **369 valanced** fringed
(with a beard).   **370 beard** confront, challenge (with obvious pun).   **370–71 young lady** i.e.,
boy playing women's parts;   **By 'r Lady** by Our Lady.   **372 chopine** thick-soled shoe of Italian
fashion.   **373 uncurrent** not passable as lawful coinage;   **cracked . . . ring** i.e., changed from
adolescent to male voice, no longer suitable for women's roles. (Coins featured rings enclosing the
sovereign's head; if the coin was cracked within this ring, it was unfit for currency.)   **374 e'en
to 't** go at it.   **375 straight** at once.   **376 quality** professional skill.   **380 caviar to the general**
caviar to the multitude, i.e., a choice dish too elegant for coarse tastes.   **381 cried in the top of**
i.e., spoke with greater authority than.   **382 digested** arranged, ordered;   **modesty** moderation,
restraint.   **383 cunning** skill;   **sallets** i.e., something savory, spicy improprieties.

the matter savory, nor no matter in the phrase that might indict° the
author of affectation, but called it an honest method, as wholesome as   385
sweet, and by very much more handsome° than fine.° One speech in 't I
chiefly loved: 'twas Aeneas' tale to Dido, and thereabout of it especially
when he speaks of Priam's slaughter.° If it live in your memory, begin at
this line: let me see, let me see—

"The rugged Pyrrhus,° like th' Hyrcanian beast°"—   390

'Tis not so. It begins with Pyrrhus:

"The rugged° Pyrrhus, he whose sable° arms,
Black as his purpose, did the night resemble
When he lay couchèd° in the ominous horse,°
Hath now this dread and black complexion smeared   395
With heraldry more dismal.° Head to foot
Now is he total gules,° horridly tricked°
With blood of fathers, mothers, daughters, sons,
Baked and impasted° with the parching streets,°
That lend a tyrannous° and a damnèd light   400
To their lord's° murder. Roasted in wrath and fire,
And thus o'ersizèd° with coagulate gore,
With eyes like carbuncles,° the hellish Pyrrhus
Old grandsire Priam seeks."

So proceed you.   405

POLONIUS: 'Fore God, my lord, well spoken, with good accent and good discretion.
FIRST PLAYER: "Anon he finds him
Striking too short at Greeks. His antique° sword,
Rebellious to his arm, lies where it falls,
Repugnant° to command. Unequal matched,   410
Pyrrhus at Priam drives, in rage strikes wide,
But with the whiff and wind of his fell° sword
Th' unnervèd° father falls. Then senseless Ilium,°
Seeming to feel this blow, with flaming top
Stoops to his° base, and with a hideous crash   415
Takes prisoner Pyrrhus' ear. For, lo! His sword,
Which was declining° on the milky° head

---

384 indict convict.   **386 handsome** well-proportioned;   **fine** elaborately ornamented,
showy.   **388 Priam's slaughter** the slaying of the ruler of Troy, when the Greeks finally
took the city.   **390 Pyrrhus** a Greek hero in the Trojan War, also known as Neoptolemus,
son of Achilles—another avenging son;   **Hyrcanian beast** i.e., tiger. (On the death of
Priam, see Virgil, *Aeneid,* 2.506 ff.; compare the whole speech with Marlowe's *Dido Queen
of Carthage,* 2.1.214. ff. On the *Hyrcanian* tiger, see *Aeneid,* 4.366–67. Hyrcania is on the
Caspian Sea.)   **392 rugged** shaggy, savage;   **sable** black (for reasons of camouflage during
the episode of the Trojan horse).   **394 couchèd** concealed;   **ominous horse** fateful Trojan
horse, by which the Greeks gained access to Troy.   **396 dismal** ill-omened.   **397 total
gules** entirely red. (A heraldic term);   **tricked** spotted and smeared. (Heraldic.)
399 impasted crusted, like a thick paste;   **with . . . streets** by the parching heat of the
streets (because of the fires everywhere).   **400 tyrannous** cruel.   **401 their lord's** i.e.,
Priam's.   **402 o'ersizèd** covered as with size or glue.   **403 carbuncles** large fiery-red precious
stones thought to emit their own light.   **408 antique** ancient, long-used.   **410 Repugnant** disobedient, resistant.   **412 fell** cruel.   **413 unnervèd** strengthless;   **senseless Ilium** inanimate
citadel of Troy.   **415 his** its.   **417 declining** descending;   **milky** white-haired.

Of reverend Priam, seemed i' th' air to stick.
So as a painted° tyrant Pyrrhus stood,
And, like a neutral to his will and matter,° 420
Did nothing.
But as we often see against° some storm
A silence in the heavens, the rack° stand still,
The bold winds speechless, and the orb° below
As hush as death, anon the dreadful thunder 425
Doth rend the region,° so, after Pyrrhus' pause,
A rousèd vengeance sets him new a-work
And never did the Cyclops'° hammers fall
On Mars's armor forged for proof eterne°
With less remorse° than Pyrrhus' bleeding sword 430
Now falls on Priam.
Out, out, thou strumpet Fortune! All you gods
In general synod° take away her power!
Break all the spokes and fellies° from her wheel,
And bowl the round nave° down the hill of heaven° 435
As low as to the fiends!"

POLONIUS: This is too long.

HAMLET: It shall to the barber's with your beard.—Prithee, say on. He's for a jig°
    or a tale of bawdry, or he sleeps. Say on; come to Hecuba.°

FIRST PLAYER: "But who, ah woe! had° seen the moblèd° queen"— 440

HAMLET: "The moblèd queen?"

POLONIUS: That's good. "Moblèd queen" is good.

FIRST PLAYER: "Run barefoot up and down, threat'ning the flames°
    With bisson rheum,° a clout° upon that head
    Where late° the diadem stood, and, for a robe, 445
    About her lank and all o'erteemd° loins
    A blanket, in the alarm of fear caught up—
    Who this had seen, with tongue in venom steeped,
    'Gainst Fortune's state° would treason have pronounced.°
    But if the gods themselves did see her then 450
    When she saw Pyrrhus make malicious sport
    In mincing with his sword her husband's limbs,
    The instant burst of clamor that she made,
    Unless things mortal move them not at all,
    Would have made milch° the burning eyes of heaven,° 455
    And passion° in the gods."

---

419 painted i.e., painted in a picture. **420 like . . . matter** i.e., as though suspended between his intention and its fulfillment. **422 against** just before. **423 rack** mass of clouds. **424 orb** globe, earth. **426 region** sky. **428 Cyclops** giant armor makers in the smithy of Vulcan. **429 proof eterne** eternal resistance to assault. **430 remorse** pity. **433 synod** assembly. **434 fellies** pieces of wood forming the rim of a wheel. **435 nave** hub; **hill of heaven** Mount Olympus. **438 jig** comic song and dance often given at the end of a play. **439 Hecuba** wife of Priam. **440 who . . . had** anyone who had; **mobled** muffled. **443 threat'ning the flames** i.e., weeping hard enough to dampen the flames. **444 bisson rheum** blinding tears; **clout** cloth. **445 late** lately. **446 all o'erteemèd** utterly worn out with bearing children. **449 state** rule, managing; **pronounced** proclaimed. **455 milch** milky, moist with tears; **burning eyes of heaven** i.e., heavenly bodies. **456 passion** overpowering emotion.

POLONIUS: Look whe'er° he has not turned his color and has tears in 's eyes.
　　　　　　 Prithee, no more.

HAMLET: 'Tis well; I'll have thee speak out the rest of this soon.—Good my lord, will
　　　　　 you see the players well bestowed?° Do you hear, let them be well used, for　　460
　　　　　 they are the abstract° and brief chronicles of the time. After your death you
　　　　　 were better have a bad epitaph than their ill report while you live.

POLONIUS: My lord, I will use them according to their desert.

HAMLET: God's bodikin,° man, much better. Use every man after his desert, and
　　　　　 who shall scape whipping? Use them after° your own honor and dignity.　　465
　　　　　 The less they deserve, the more merit is in your bounty. Take them in.

POLONIUS: Come, sirs.   [*Exit.*]

HAMLET: Follow him, friends. We'll hear a play tomorrow. [*As they start to leave,*
　　　　　 HAMLET *detains the* FIRST PLAYER.] Dost thou hear me, old friend? Can you
　　　　　 play *The Murder of Gonzago?*　　　　　　　　　　　　　　　　　　　　470

FIRST PLAYER: Ay, my lord.

HAMLET: We'll ha 't° tomorrow night. You could, for a need, study° a speech of
　　　　　 some dozen or sixteen lines which I would set down and insert in 't,
　　　　　 could you not?

FIRST PLAYER: Ay, my lord.　　　　　　　　　　　　　　　　　　　　　　　　　475

HAMLET: Very well. Follow that lord, and look you mock him not. [*Exeunt* PLAYERS.]
　　　　　 My good friends, I'll leave you till night. You are welcome to Elsinore.

ROSENCRANTZ: Good my lord!　　　*Exeunt* [ROSENCRANTZ *and* GUILDENSTERN].

HAMLET: Ay, so, goodbye to you.—Now I am alone.
　　　　　 O, what a rogue and peasant slave am I!　　　　　　　　　　　　　　480
　　　　　 Is it not monstrous that this player here,
　　　　　 But° in a fiction, in a dream of passion,
　　　　　 Could force his soul so to his own conceit°
　　　　　 That from her working° all his visage wanned,°
　　　　　 Tears in his eyes, distraction in his aspect,°　　　　　　　　　　　　485
　　　　　 A broken voice, and his whole function suiting
　　　　　 With forms to his conceit?° And all for nothing!
　　　　　 For Hecuba!
　　　　　 What's Hecuba to him, or he to Hecuba,
　　　　　 That he should weep for her? What would he do　　　　　　　　　490
　　　　　 Had he the motive and the cue for passion
　　　　　 That I have? He would drown the stage with tears
　　　　　 And cleave the general ear° with horrid° speech,
　　　　　 Make mad the guilty and appall° the free,°
　　　　　 Confound the ignorant,° and amaze° indeed　　　　　　　　　　　495
　　　　　 The very faculties of eyes and ears. Yet I,
　　　　　 A dull and muddy-mettled° rascal, peak°

---

457 whe'er whether.　**460 bestowed** lodged.　**461 abstract** summary account.　**464 God's**
bodikin by God's (Christ's) little body, *bodykin.* (Not to be confused with *bodkin,* "dagger.")
465 after according to.　**472 ha 't** have it;　**study** memorize.　**482 But** merely.　**483 force . . .**
conceit bring his innermost being so entirely into accord with his conception (of the role).
484 from her working as a result of, or in response to, his soul's activity;　**wanned** grew pale.
485 aspect look, glance.　**486–87 his whole . . . conceit** all his bodily powers responding
with actions to suit his thought.　**493 the general ear** everyone's ear;　**horrid** horrible.
494 appall (literally, make pale.);　**free** innocent.　**495 Confound the ignorant,** i.e., dumb-
found those who know nothing of the crime that has been committed;　**amaze** stun.
497 muddy-mettled dull-spirited;　**peak** mope, pine.

Like John-a-dreams,° unpregnant of° my cause,
And can say nothing—no, not for a king
Upon whose property° and most dear life   500
A damned defeat° was made. Am I a coward?
Who calls me villain? Breaks my pate° across?
Plucks off my beard and blows it in my face?
Tweaks me by the nose? Gives me the lie i' the throat°
As deep as to the lungs? Who does me this?   505
Ha, 'swounds,° I should take it; for it cannot be
But I am pigeon-livered° and lack gall
To make oppression bitter,° or ere this
I should ha' fatted all the region kites°
With this slave's offal.° Bloody, bawdy villain!   510
Remorseless,° treacherous, lecherous, kindless° villain!
O, vengeance!
Why, what an ass am I! This is most brave,°
That I, the son of a dear father murdered,
Prompted to my revenge by heaven and hell,   515
Must like a whore unpack my heart with words
And fall a-cursing, like a very drab,°
A scullion!° Fie upon 't, foh! About,° my brains!
Hum, I have heard
That guilty creatures sitting at a play   520
Have by the very cunning° of the scene°
Been struck so to the soul that presently°
They have proclaimed their malefactions;
For murder, though it have no tongue, will speak
With most miraculous organ. I'll have these players   525
Play something like the murder of my father
Before mine uncle. I'll observe his looks;
I'll tent° him to the quick.° If 'a do blench,°
I know my course. The spirit that I have seen
May be the devil, and the devil hath power   530
T' assume a pleasing shape; yea, and perhaps,
Out of my weakness and my melancholy,
As he is very potent with such spirits,°
Abuses° me to damn me. I'll have grounds
More relative° than this. The play's the thing   535
Wherein I'll catch the conscience of the King.   *Exit.*

---

498 John-a-dreams a sleepy, dreaming idler;   **unpregnant of** not quickened by.   **500 property**
i.e., the crown; also character, quality.   **501 damned defeat** damnable act of destruction.
502 pate head.   **504 Gives . . . throat** calls me an out-and-out liar.   **506 'swounds** by his
(Christ's) wounds.   **507 pigeon-livered** (The pigeon or dove was popularly supposed to be mild
because it secreted no gall.)   **508 bitter** i.e., bitter to me.   **509 region kites** kites (birds of prey)
of the air.   **510 offal** entrails.   **511 Remorseless** pitiless;   **kindless** unnatural.   **513 brave**
fine, admirable. (Said ironically.)   **517 drab** whore.   **518 scullion** menial kitchen servant
(apt to be foul-mouthed);   **About** about it, to work.   **521 cunning** art, skill;   **scene** dramatic
presentation.   **522 presently** at once.   **528 tent** probe;   **the quick** the tender part of a wound,
the core;   **blench** quail, flinch.   **533 spirits** humors (of melancholy).   **534 Abuses** deludes.
535 relative cogent, pertinent.

[3.1]

Enter KING, QUEEN, POLONIUS, OPHELIA, ROSENCRANTZ, GUILDENSTERN, *lords.*

KING: And can you by no drift of conference°
        Get from him why he puts on this confusion,
        Grating so harshly all his days of quiet
        With turbulent and dangerous lunacy?
ROSENCRANTZ: He does confess he feels himself distracted,   5
        But from what cause 'a will by no means speak.
GUILDENSTERN: Nor do we find him forward° to be sounded,°
        But with a crafty madness keeps aloof
        When we would bring him on to some confession
        Of his true state.
QUEEN: Did he receive you well?   10
ROSENCRANTZ: Most like a gentleman.
GUILDENSTERN: But with much forcing of his disposition.°
ROSENCRANTZ: Niggard° of question,° but of our demands
        Most free in his reply.
QUEEN: Did you assay° him
        To any pastime?   15
ROSENCRANTZ: Madam, it so fell out that certain players
        We o'erraught° on the way. Of these we told him,
        And there did seem in him a kind of joy
        To hear of it. They are here about the court,
        And, as I think, they have already order   20
        This night to play before him.
POLONIUS: 'Tis most true,
        And he beseeched me to entreat Your Majesties
        To hear and see the matter.
KING: With all my heart, and it doth much content me
        To hear him so inclined.   25
        Good gentlemen, give him a further edge°
        And drive his purpose into these delights.
ROSENCRANTZ: We shall, my lord.   *Exeunt* ROSENCRANTZ *and* GUILDENSTERN.
KING: Sweet Gertrude, leave us too
        For we have closely° sent for Hamlet hither,
        That he, as 'twere by accident, may here   30
        Affront° Ophelia.
        Her father and myself, lawful espials,°
        Will so bestow ourselves that seeing, unseen,
        We may of their encounter frankly judge,
        And gather by him, as he is behaved,   35
        If't be th' affliction of his love or no
        That thus he suffers for.
QUEEN: I shall obey you.
        And for your part, Ophelia, I do wish

[3.1] Location: The castle.   1 drift of conference directing of conversation.   **7 forward** willing;   **sounded** questioned.   **12 dispositon** inclination.   **13 Niggard** stingy;   **question** conversation.   **14 assay** try to win.   **17 o'erraught** overtook.   **26 edge** incitement. **29 closely** privately.   **31 Affront** confront, meet.   **32 espials** spies.

That your good beauties be the happy cause
Of Hamlet's wildness. So shall I hope your virtues   40
Will bring him to his wonted° way again,
To both your honors.
OPHELIA: Madam, I wish it may.   [*Exit* QUEEN.]
POLONIUS: Ophelia, walk you here.—Gracious,° so please you,
    We will bestow° ourselves. [*to* OPHELIA.] Read on this book,
                                             [*giving her a book*]
    That show of such an exercise° may color°   45
    Your loneliness.° We are oft to blame in this—
    'Tis too much proved°—that with devotion's visage
    And pious action we do sugar o'er
    The devil himself.
KING [*aside*]: O 'tis too true!   50
    How smart a lash that speech doth give my conscience!
    The harlot's cheek, beautied with plastering art,
    Is not more ugly to° the thing° that helps it
    Than is my deed to my most painted word.
    O heavy burden!   55
POLONIUS: I hear him coming. Let's withdraw, my lord.
                        [*The* KING *and* POLONIUS *withdraw.*°]
    Enter HAMLET. [OPHELIA *pretends to read a book.*]
HAMLET: To be, or not to be, that is the question:
    Whether 'tis nobler in the mind to suffer
    The slings° and arrows of outrageous fortune,
    Or to take arms against a sea of troubles   60
    And by opposing end them. To die, to sleep—
    No more—and by a sleep to say we end
    The heartache and the thousand natural shocks
    That flesh is heir to. 'Tis a consummation
    Devoutly to be wished. To die, to sleep;   65
    To sleep, perchance to dream. Ay, there's the rub,°
    For in that sleep of death what dreams may come,
    When we have shuffled° off this mortal coil,°
    Must give us pause. There's the respect°
    That makes calamity of so long life.°   70
    For who would bear the whips and scorns of time,
    Th' oppressor's wrong, the proud man's contumely,°
    The pangs of disprized° love, the law's delay,
    The insolence of office,° and the spurns°

---

41 wonted accustomed.   **43 Gracious** your Grace (i.e., the King).   **44 bestow** conceal.
45 exercise religious exercise. (The book she reads is one of devotion.);   **color** give
a plausible appearance to.   **46 loneliness** being alone.   **47 too much proved** too
often shown to be true, too often practiced.   **53 to** compared to;   **the thing** i.e., the
cosmetic.   **56 s.d. withdraw** (The King and Polonius may retire behind an arras. The stage
directions specify that they "enter" again near the end of the scene.)   **59 slings** missiles.
66 rub (literally, an obstacle in the game of bowls.)   **68 shuffled** sloughed, cast;   **coil**
turmoil.   **69 respect** consideration.   **70 of . . . life** so long-lived, something we willingly
endure for so long (also suggesting that long life is itself a calamity).   **72 contumely**
insolent abuse.   **73 disprized** unvalued.   **74 office** officialdom;   **spurns** insults.

That patient merit of th' unworthy takes,°   75
When he himself might his quietus° make
With a bare bodkin?° Who would fardels° bear,
To grunt and sweat under a weary life,
But that the dread of something after death,
The undiscovered country from whose bourn°   80
No traveler returns, puzzles the will,
And makes us rather bear those ills we have
Than fly to others that we know not of?
Thus conscience does make cowards of us all;
And thus the native hue° of resolution   85
Is sicklied o'er with the pale cast° of thought,
And enterprises of great pitch° and moment°
With this regard° their currents° turn awry
And lose the name of action.—Soft you° now,
The fair Ophelia. Nymph, in thy orisons°   90
Be all my sins remembered.

OPHELIA: Good my lord,
How does your honor for this many a day?

HAMLET: I humbly thank you; well, well, well.

OPHELIA: My lord, I have remembrances of yours,
That I have longèd long to redeliver.   95
I pray you, now receive them.   [*She offers tokens.*]

HAMLET: No, not I, I never gave you aught.

OPHELIA: My honored lord, you know right well you did,
And with them words of so sweet breath composed
As made the things more rich. Their perfume lost,   100
Take these again, for to the noble mind
Rich gifts wax poor when givers prove unkind.
There, my lord.   [*She gives tokens.*]

HAMLET: Ha, ha! Are you honest?°

OPHELIA: My lord?   105

HAMLET: Are you fair?°

OPHELIA: What means your lordship?

HAMLET: That if you be honest and fair, your honesty° should admit no discourse
to° your beauty.

OPHELIA: Could beauty, my lord, have better commerce° than with honesty?   110

HAMLET: Ay, truly, for the power of beauty will sooner transform honesty from
what it is to a bawd than the force of honesty can translate beauty into
his° likeness. This was sometime° a paradox,° but now the time° gives it
proof. I did love you once.

---

75 of . . . takes receives from unworthy persons.   **76 quietus** acquaintance; here, death.   **77 a
bare bodkin** a mere dagger, unsheathed;   **fardels** burdens.   **80 bourn** frontier, boundary.
85 native hue natural color, complexion.   **86 cast** tinge, shade of color.   **87 pitch** height
(as of a falcon's flight.);   **moment** importance.   **88 regard** respect, consideration;   **currents**
courses.   **89 Soft you** i.e., wait a minute, gently.   **90 orisons** prayers.   **104 honest** (1) truthful,
(2) chaste.   **106 fair** (1) beautiful, (2) just, honorable.   **108 your honesty** your chastity.
108–09 discourse to familiar dealings with.   **110 commerce** dealings, intercourse.
113 his its;   **sometime** formerly;   **a paradox** a view opposite to commonly held opinion;
the time the present age.

OPHELIA: Indeed, my lord, you made me believe so.   115

HAMLET: You should not have believed me, for virtue cannot so inoculate° our old stock but we shall relish of it.° I loved you not.

OPHELIA: I was the more deceived.

HAMLET: Get thee to a nunnery.° Why wouldst thou be a breeder of sinners? I am myself indifferent honest,° but yet I could accuse me of such things that it   120 were better my mother had not borne me: I am very proud, revengeful, ambitious, with more offenses at my beck° than I have thoughts to put them in, imagination to give them shape, or time to act them in. What should such fellows as I do crawling between earth and heaven? We are arrant knaves all; believe none of us. Go thy ways to a nunnery. Where's your father?   125

OPHELIA: At home, my lord.

HAMLET: Let the doors be shut upon him, that he may play the fool nowhere but in's own house. Farewell.

OPHELIA: O, help him, you sweet heavens!

HAMLET: If thou dost marry, I'll give thee this plague for thy dowry: be thou as   130 chaste as ice, as pure as snow, thou shalt not escape calumny. Get thee to a nunnery, farewell. Or, if thou wilt needs marry, marry a fool, for wise men know well enough what monsters° you° make of them. To a nunnery, go, and quickly too. Farewell.

OPHELIA: Heavenly powers, restore him!   135

HAMLET: I have heard of your paintings too, well enough. God hath given you one face, and you make yourselves another. You jig,° you amble,° and you lisp, you nickname God's creatures,° and make your wantonness your ignorance.° Go to, I'll no more on 't;° it hath made me mad. I say we will have no more marriage. Those that are married already—all but   140 one—shall live. The rest shall keep as they are. To a nunnery, go.

Exit.

OPHELIA: O, what a noble mind is here o'erthrown!
The courtier's, soldier's, scholar's, eye, tongue, sword,
Th' expectancy° and rose° of the fair state,
The glass of fashion and the mold of form,°   145
Th' observed of all observers,° quite, quite down!
And I, of ladies most deject and wretched,
That sucked the honey of his music° vows,
Now see that noble and most sovereign reason
Like sweet bells jangled out of tune and harsh,   150
That unmatched form and feature of blown° youth
Blasted° with ecstasy.° O, woe is me,
T' have seen what I have seen, see what I see!

---

116 inoculate graft, be engrafted to.   **117 but . . . it** that we do not still have about us a taste of the old stock, i.e., retain our sinfulness.   **119 nunnery** convent (with possibly an awareness that the word was also used derisively to denote a brothel).   **120 indifferent honest** reasonably virtuous.   **122 beck** command.   **133 monsters** (an illusion to the horns of a cuckold.);   **you** i.e., you women.   **137 jig** dance;   **amble** move coyly.   **138 you nickname . . . creatures** i.e., you give trendy names to things in place of their god-given names.   **139 make . . . ignorance** i.e., excuse your affectation on the grounds of pretended ignorance;   **on 't** of it.   **144 expectancy** hope;   **rose** ornament.   **145 The glass . . . form** the mirror of true fashioning and the pattern of courtly behavior.   **146 Th' observed . . . observers** i.e., the center of attention and honor in the court.   **148 music** musical, sweetly uttered.   **151 blown** blooming.   **152 Blasted** withered;   **ecstasy** madness.

Enter KING *and* POLONIUS.

KING: Love? His affections° do not that way tend;
    Nor what he spake, though it lacked form a little,   155
    Was not like madness. There's something in his soul
    O'er which his melancholy sits on brood,°
    And I do doubt° the hatch and the disclose°
    Will be some danger; which for to prevent,
    I have in quick determination   160
    Thus set it down:° he shall with speed to England
    For the demand of° our neglected tribute.
    Haply the seas and countries different
    With variable objects° shall expel
    This something-settled matter in his heart,°   165
    Whereon his brains still° beating puts him thus
    From fashion of himself.° What think you on 't?
POLONIUS: It shall do well. But yet do I believe
    The origin and commencement of his grief
    Sprung from neglected love.—How now, Ophelia?   170
    You need not tell us what Lord Hamlet said;
    We heard it all.—My lord, do as you please,
    But, if you hold it fit, after the play
    Let his queen-mother° all alone entreat him
    To show his grief. Let her be round° with him;   175
    And I'll be placed, so please you, in the ear
    Of all their conference. If she find him not,°
    To England send him, or confine him where
    Your wisdom best shall think.
KING: It shall be so.
    Madness in great ones must not unwatched go.   *Exeunt.*   180

[3.2]

Enter HAMLET *and three of the* PLAYERS.

HAMLET: Speak the speech, I pray you, as I pronounced it to you, trippingly on
   the tongue. But if you mouth it, as many of our players° do, I had as
   lief° the town crier spoke my lines. Nor do not saw the air too much
   with your hand, thus, but use all gently; for in the very torrent, tempest,
   and, as I may say, whirlwind of your passion, you must acquire and   5
   beget a temperance that may give it smoothness. O, it offends me to the
   soul to hear a robustious° periwig-pated° fellow tear a passion to tatters,
   to very rags, to split the ears of the groundlings,° who for the most part

---

154 **affections** emotions, feelings.   157 **sits on brood** sits like a bird on a nest, about to
hatch mischief (line 169).   158 **doubt** fear;   **disclose** disclosure, hatching.   161 **set it down**
resolved.   162 **For . . . of** to demand.   164 **variable objects** various sights and surroundings
to divert him.   165 **This something . . . heart** the strange matter settled in his heart.
166 **still** continually.   167 **From . . . himself** out of his natural manner.   174 **queen-mother**
queen and mother.   175 **round** blunt.   177 **find him not** fails to discover what is troubling
him.   **[3.2] Location:** The castle.   2 **our players** players nowadays.   2–3 **I had as lief**
I would just as soon.   7 **robustious** violent, boisterous;   **periwig-pated** wearing a wig.
8 **groundlings** spectators who paid least and stood in the yard of the theater.

are capable of° nothing but inexplicable dumb shows° and noise. I
would have such a fellow whipped for o'erdoing Termagant.° It out- 10
Herods Herod.° Pray you, avoid it.

FIRST PLAYER: I warrant your honor.

HAMLET: Be not too tame neither, but let your own discretion be your tutor. Suit the
action to the word, the word to the action, with this special observance,
that you o'erstep not the modesty° of nature. For anything so o'erdone 15
is from° the purpose of playing, whose end, both at the first and
now, was and is to hold as 't were the mirror up to nature, to show virtue
her feature, scorn° her own image, and the very age and body of the
time° his° form and pressure.° Now this overdone or come tardy off,°
though it makes the unskillful° laugh, cannot but make the judicious 20
grieve, the censure of the which one° must in your allowance° o'erweigh
a whole theater of others. O, there be players that I have seen play, and
heard others praise, and that highly, not to speak it profanely,° that, neither having th' accent of Christians° nor the gait of Christian, pagan, nor
man,° have so strutted and bellowed that I have thought some of nature's 25
journeymen° had made men and not made them well, they imitated humanity so abominably.°

FIRST PLAYER: I hope we have reformed that indifferently° with us, sir.

HAMLET: O, reform it altogether. And let those that play your clowns speak no
more than is set down for them; for there be of them° that will them- 30
selves laugh, to set on some quantity of barren° spectators to laugh too,
though in the meantime some necessary question of the play be then to
be considered. That's villainous, and shows a most pitiful ambition in
the fool that uses it. Go make you ready.   [*Exeunt* PLAYERS.]

Enter POLONIUS, GUILENSTERN *and* ROSENCRANTZ.

How now, my lord, will the King hear this piece of work? 35

POLONIUS: And the Queen too, and that presently.°

HAMLET: Bid the players make haste.   [*Exit* POLONIUS.]
Will you two help to hasten them?

ROSENCRANTZ: Ay, my lord.   *Exeunt they two*.

HAMLET: What ho, Horatio!

Enter HORATIO.

HORATIO: Here, sweet lord, at your service. 40

9 capable of able to understand; **dumb shows** mimed performances, often used before
Shakespeare's time to precede a play or each act. **10 Termagant** a supposed deity of the
Mohammedans, not found in any English medieval play but elsewhere portrayed as violent
and blustering. **11 Herod** Herod of Jewry. (A character in *The Slaughter of the Innocents*
and other cycle plays. The part was played with great noise and fury.) **15 modesty** restraint,
moderation. **16 from** contrary to. **18 scorn** i.e., something foolish and deserving of scorn.
18–19 the very . . . time i.e., the present state of affairs; **his** its; **pressure** stamp, impressed
character; **come tardy off** inadequately done. **20 the unskillful** those lacking in judgment. **21 the censure . . . one** the judgment of even one of whom; **your allowance** your
scale of values. **23 not . . . profanely** (Hamlet anticipates his idea in lines 25–27 that some
men were not made by God at all.) **24 Christians** i.e., ordinary decent folk. **24–25 nor
man** i.e., nor any human being at all. **26 journeymen** laborers who are not yet masters in
their trade. **27 abominably** (Shakespeare's usual spelling, *abhominably*, suggests a literal
though etymologically incorrect meaning, "removed from human nature.") **28 indifferently**
tolerably. **30 of them** some among them. **31 barren** i.e., of wit. **36 presently** at once.

HAMLET: Horatio, thou art e'en as just a man
　　　　As e'er my conversation coped withal.°
HORATIO: O, my dear lord—
HAMLET:　　　　　　　　Nay, do not think I flatter,
　　　　For what advancement may I hope from thee
　　　　That no revenue hast but thy good spirits　　　　　　　　45
　　　　To feed and clothe thee? Why should the poor be flattered?
　　　　No, let the candied° tongue lick absurd pomp,
　　　　And crook the pregnant° hinges of the knee
　　　　Where thrift° may follow fawning. Dost thou hear?
　　　　Since my dear soul was mistress of her choice　　　　　　50
　　　　And could of men distinguish her election,°
　　　　Sh' hath sealed thee° for herself, for thou hast been
　　　　As one, in suffering all, that suffers nothing,
　　　　A man that Fortune's buffets and rewards
　　　　Hast ta'en with equal thanks; and blest are those　　　　55
　　　　Whose blood° and judgment are so well commeddled°
　　　　That they are not a pipe for Fortune's finger
　　　　To sound what stop° she please. Give me that man
　　　　That is not passion's slave, and I will wear him
　　　　In my heart's core, ay, in my heart of heart,　　　　　　60
　　　　As I do thee.—Something too much of this.—
　　　　There is a play tonight before the King.
　　　　One scene of it comes near the circumstance
　　　　Which I have told thee of my father's death.
　　　　I prithee, when thou seest that act afoot,　　　　　　　　65
　　　　Even with the very comment of thy soul°
　　　　Observe my uncle. If his occulted° guilt
　　　　Do not itself unkennel° in one speech,
　　　　It is a damnéd° ghost that we have seen,
　　　　And my imaginations are as foul　　　　　　　　　　　　70
　　　　As Vulcan's stithy.° Give him heedful note,
　　　　For I mine eyes will rivet to his face,
　　　　And after we will both our judgments join
　　　　In censure of his seeming.°
HORATIO:　　　　　　　　　Well, my lord.
　　　　If 'a steal aught° the whilst this play is playing　　　　　75
　　　　And scape detecting, I will pay the theft.

　　[*Flourish.*] *Enter trumpets and kettledrums,* KING, QUEEN, POLONIUS, OPHELIA,
[ROSENCRANTZ, GUILDENSTERN, *and other lords, with guards carrying torches*].

HAMLET: They are coming to the play. I must be idle.°
　　　　Get you a place.　　　　　　　　　　　[*The* KING, QUEEN, *and courtiers sit.*]

42 my . . . withal my dealings encountered.　**47 candied** sugared, flattering.　**48 pregnant**
compliant.　**49 thrift** profit.　**51 could . . . election** could make distinguishing choices among
persons.　**52 sealed thee** (literally, as one would seal a legal document to mark possession.)
56 blood passion; **commeddled** commingled.　**58 stop** hole in a wind instrument for controlling the sound.　**66 very . . . soul** your most penetrating observation and consideration.
67 occulted hidden.　**68 unkennel** (as one would say of a fox driven from its lair.)
69 damnéd in league with Satan.　**71 stithy** smithy, place of stiths (anvils).　**74 censure of
his seeming** judgment of his appearance or behavior.　**75 If 'a steal aught** if he gets away
with anything.　**77 idle** (1) unoccupied, (2) mad.

KING: How fares our cousin° Hamlet?

HAMLET: Excellent, i' faith, of the chameleon's dish:° I eat the air, promise-   80
crammed. You cannot feed capons° so.

KING: I have nothing with° this answer, Hamlet. These words are not mine.°

HAMLET: No, nor mine now.° [*To* POLONIUS.] My lord, you played once i' th' university, you say?

POLONIUS: That did I, my lord, and was accounted a good actor.   85

HAMLET: What did you enact?

POLONIUS: I did enact Julius Caesar. I was killed i' the Capitol; Brutus killed me.

HAMLET: It was a brute° part° of him to kill so capital a calf° there.—Be the players ready?

ROSENCRANTZ: Ay, my lord. They stay upon° your patience.   90

QUEEN: Come hither, my dear Hamlet, sit by me.

HAMLET: No, good Mother, here's metal° more attractive.

POLONIUS [*to the* KING]: O, ho, do you mark that?

HAMLET: Lady, shall I lie in your lap?   [*Lying down at* OPHELIA's *feet.*]

OPHELIA: No, my lord.   95

HAMLET: I mean, my head upon your lap?

OPHELIA: Ay, my lord.

HAMLET: Do you think I meant country matters?°

OPHELIA: I think nothing, my lord.

HAMLET: That's a fair thought to lie between maids' legs.   100

OPHELIA: What is, my lord?

HAMLET: Nothing.°

OPHELIA: You are merry, my lord.

HAMLET: Who, I?

OPHELIA: Ay, my lord.   105

HAMLET: O God, your only jig maker.° What should a man do but be merry? For
look you how cheerfully my mother looks, and my father died within 's°
two hours.

OPHELIA: Nay, 'tis twice two months, my lord.

HAMLET: So long? Nay then, let the devil wear black, for I'll have a suit of sables.°   110
O heavens! Die two months ago, and not forgotten yet? Then there's

---

79 cousin i.e., close relative.   **80 chameleon's dish** (Chameleons were supposed to feed
on air. Hamlet deliberately misinterprets the King's *fares* as "feeds." By his phrase *eat the
air* he also plays on the idea of feeding himself with the promise of succession, of being the
heir.)   **81 capons** roosters castrated and crammed with feed to make them succulent.
82 have . . . with make nothing of, or gain nothing from;   **are not mine** do not respond
to what I asked.   **83 nor mine now** (once spoken, words are proverbially no longer the
speaker's own—and hence should be uttered warily.)   **88 brute** (the Latin meaning of *brutus*,
"stupid," was often used punningly with the name Brutus.);   **part** (1) deed, (2) role;   **calf**
fool.   **90 stay upon** await.   **92 metal** substance that is *attractive,* i.e., magnetic, but with suggestion also of *mettle*, "disposition."   **98 country matters** sexual intercourse (making a bawdy
pun on the first syllable of *country*).   **102 Nothing** the figure zero or naught, suggesting the
female sexual anatomy. (*Thing* not infrequently has a bawdy connotation of male or female
anatomy, and the reference here could be male.)   **106 only jig maker** very best composer of
jigs, i.e., pointless merriment. (Hamlet replies sardonically to Ophelia's observation that he is
merry by saying, "If you're looking for someone who is really merry, you've come to the right
person.")   **107 within 's** within this (i.e., these).   **110 suit of sables** garments trimmed with
the fur of the sable and hence suited for a wealthy person, not a mourner (but with a pun on
sable, "black," ironically suggesting mourning once again).

hope a great man's memory may outlive his life half a year. But, by 'r
Lady, 'a must build churches, then, or else shall 'a suffer not thinking on,°
with the hobbyhorse, whose epitaph is
"For O, for O, the hobbyhorse is forgot."°   115

The trumpets sound. Dumb show follows.

*Enter a King and a Queen [very lovingly]; the Queen embracing him, and
he her. [She kneels, and makes show of protestation unto him.] He takes her up,
and declines his head upon her neck. He lies him down upon a bank of flowers.
She, seeing him asleep, leaves him. Anon comes in another man, takes off his
crown, kisses it, pours poison in the sleeper's ears, and leaves him. The Queen
returns, finds the King dead, makes passionate action. The Poisoner with some
three or four come in again, seem to condole with her. The dead body is carried
away. The Poisoner woos the Queen with gifts; she seems harsh awhile, but in the
end accepts love.*

                                                          [*Exeunt* PLAYERS.]

OPHELIA: What means this, my lord?
HAMLET: Marry, this' miching mallico;° it means mischief.
OPHELIA: Belike° this show imports the argument° of the play.

    Enter PROLOGUE.

HAMLET: We shall know by this fellow. The players cannot keep counsel;° they'll
        tell all.   120
OPHELIA: Will 'a tell us what this show meant?
HAMLET: Ay, or any show that you will show him. Be not you° ashamed to show,
        he'll not shame to tell you what it means.
OPHELIA: You are naught,° you are naught. I'll mark the play.
PROLOGUE: For us, and for our tragedy,   125
        Here stooping° to your clemency,
        We beg your hearing patiently.   [*Exit.*]
HAMLET: Is this a prologue, or the posy of a ring?°
OPHELIA: 'Tis brief, my lord.
HAMLET: As woman's love.   130

    Enter [two PLAYERS *as]* King and Queen.

PLAYER KING: Full thirty times hath Phoebus' cart° gone round
        Neptune's salt wash° and Tellus'° orbèd ground,
        And thirty dozen moons with borrowed° sheen
        About the world have times twelve thirties been,
        Since love our hearts and Hymen° did our hands   135
        Unite commutual° in most sacred bands.°

113–14 suffer . . . on undergo oblivion.   **115 For . . . forgot** (verse of a song occurring also
in *Love's Labour's Lost*, 3.1.27–28. The hobbyhorse was a character made up to resemble a
horse and rider, appearing in the morris dance and such May-game sports. This song laments
the disappearance of such customs under pressure from the Puritans.)   **117 this' miching
mallico** this is sneaking mischief.   **118 Belike** probably;   **argument** plot.   **119 counsel**
secret.   **122 Be not you** provided you are not.   **124 naught** indecent. (Ophelia is reacting to
Hamlet's pointed remarks about not being ashamed to show all.)   **126 stooping** bowing.
128 posy . . . ring brief motto in verse inscribed in a ring.   **131 Phoebus' cart** the sun-god's
chariot, making its yearly cycle.   **132 salt wash** the sea;   **Tellus** goddess of the earth, of the
orbèd ground.   **133 borrowed** i.e., reflected.   **135 Hymen** god of matrimony.   **136 commutual**
mutually;   **bands** bonds.

PLAYER QUEEN: So many journeys may the sun and moon
    Make us again count o'er ere love be done!
    But, woe is me, you are so sick of late,
    So far from cheer and from your former state,   140
    That I distrust° you. Yet, though I distrust,
    Discomfort° you, my lord, it nothing° must.
    For women's fear and love hold quantity;°
    In neither aught, or in extremity.°
    Now, what my love is, proof° hath made you know,   145
    And as my love is sized,° my fear is so.
    Where love is great, the littlest doubts are fear;
    Where little fears grow great, great love grows there.
PLAYER KING: Faith, I must leave thee, love, and shortly too;
    My operant powers° their functions leave to do.°   150
    And thou shalt live in this fair world behind,°
    Honored, beloved; and haply one as kind
    For husband shalt thou—
PLAYER QUEEN: O, confound the rest!
    Such love must needs be treason in my breast.
    In second husband let me be accurst!   155
    None° wed the second but who° killed the first.
HAMLET: Wormwood,° wormwood.
PLAYER QUEEN: The instances° that second marriage move°
    Are base respects of thrift,° but none of love.
    A second time I kill my husband dead   160
    When second husband kisses me in bed.
PLAYER KING: I do believe you think what now you speak,
    But what we do determine oft we break.
    Purpose is but the slave to memory,°
    Of violent birth, but poor validity,°   165
    Which° now, like fruit unripe, sticks on the tree,
    But fall unshaken when they mellow be.
    Most necessary 'tis that we forget
    To pay ourselves what to ourselves is debt.°
    What to ourselves in passion we propose,   170
    The passion ending, doth the purpose lose.
    The violence of either grief or joy
    Their own enactures° with themselves destroy.
    Where joy most revels, grief doth most lament;
    Grief joys, joy grieves, on slender accident.°   175

---

141 distrust am anxious about. **142 Discomfort** distress; **nothing** not at all. **143 hold quantity** keep proportion with one another. **144 In . . . extremity** i.e., women fear and love either too little or too much, but the two, fear and love, are equal in either case. **145 proof** experience. **146 sized** in size. **150 operant powers** vital functions; **leave to do** cease to perform. **151 behind** after I have gone. **156 None** i.e., let no woman; **but who** except the one who. **157 Wormwood** i.e., how bitter. (Literally, a bitter-tasting plant.) **158 instances** motives; **move** motivate. **159 base . . . thrift** ignoble considerations of material prosperity. **164 Purpose . . . memory** our good intentions are subject to forgetfulness. **165 validity** strength, durability. **166 Which** i.e., purpose. **168–69 Most . . . debt** it's inevitable that in time we forget the obligations we have imposed on ourselves. **173 enactures** fulfillments. **174–75 Where . . . accident** the capacity for extreme joy and grief go together, and often one extreme is instantly changed into its opposite on the slightest provocation.

This world is not for aye,° nor 'tis not strange
That even our loves should with our fortunes change;
For 'tis a question left us yet to prove,
Whether love lead fortune, or else fortune love
The great man down,° you mark his favorite flies;   180
The poor advanced makes friends of enemies.°
And hitherto° doth love on fortune tend;°
For who not needs° shall never lack a friend,
And who in want° a hollow friend doth try°
Directly seasons him° his enemy.   185
But, orderly to end where I begun,
Our wills and fates do so contrary run°
That our devices still° are overthrown;
Our thoughts are ours, their ends° none of our own.
So think thou wilt no second husband wed,
But die thy thoughts when thy first lord is dead.   190

PLAYER QUEEN: Nor° earth to me give food, nor heaven light,
Sport and repose lock from me day and night,°
To desperation turn my trust and hope,
An anchor's cheer° in prison be my scope!°   195
Each opposite that blanks° the face of joy
Meet what I would have well and it destroy!°
Both here and hence° pursue me lasting strife
If, once a widow, ever I be wife!

HAMLET: If she should break it now!   200

PLAYER KING: 'Tis deeply sworn. Sweet, leave me here awhile;
My spirits° grow dull, and fain I would beguile
The tedious day with sleep.

PLAYER QUEEN: Sleep rock thy brain,
And never come mischance between us twain!

[He sleeps.] Exit [PLAYER QUEEN].

HAMLET: Madam, how like you this play?   205
QUEEN: The lady doth protest too much,° methinks.
HAMLET: O, but she'll keep her word.
KING: Have you heard the argument?° Is there no offense in 't?
HAMLET: No, no, they do but jest,° poison in jest. No offense° i' the world.
KING: What do you call the play?   210

---

176 aye ever.   **180 down** fallen in fortune.   **181 The poor . . . enemies** when one of
humble station is promoted, you see his enemies suddenly becoming his friends.   **182 hitherto** up to this point in the argument, or, to this extent;   **tend** attend.   **183 who not needs**
he who is not in need (of wealth).   **184 who in want** he who, being in need;   **try** test (his
generosity).   **185 seasons him** ripens him into.   **187 Our . . . run** what we want and what
we get go so contrarily.   **188 devices still** intentions continually.   **189 ends** results.
192 Nor let neither.   **193 Sport . . . night** may day deny me its pastimes and night its
repose.   **195 anchor's cheer** Anchorite's or hermit's fare;   **my scope** the extent of my
happiness.   **196 blanks** causes to blanch or grow pale.   **196–97 Each . . . destroy** may every
adverse thing that causes the face of joy to turn pale meet and destroy everything that I desire
to see prosper.   **198 hence** in the life hereafter.   **202 spirits** vital spirits.   **206 doth . . .
much** makes too many promises and protestations.   **208 argument** plot.   **209 jest** make
believe.   **208–09 offense . . . offense** cause for objection . . . actual injury, crime.

HAMLET: *The Mousetrap.* Marry, how? Tropically.° This play is the image of a
murder done in Vienna. Gonzago is the Duke's° name, his wife, Baptista.
You shall see anon. 'Tis a knavish piece of work, but what of that? Your
Majesty, and we that have free° souls, it touches us not. Let the galled
jade° wince, our withers° are unwrung.° 215

Enter LUCIANUS.

This is one Lucianus, nephew to the King.

OPHELIA: You are as good as a chorus,° my lord.

HAMLET: I could interpret° between you and your love, if I could see the puppets
dallying.°

OPHELIA: You are keen,° my lord, you are keen. 220

HAMLET: It would cost you a groaning to take off mine edge.

OPHELIA: Still better, and worse.°

HAMLET: So° you mis-take° your husbands. Begin, murder; leave thy damnable faces
and begin. Come, the croaking raven doth bellow for revenge.

LUCIANUS: Thoughts black, hands apt, drugs fit, and time agreeing, 225
Confederate season,° else° no creature seeing,°
Thou mixture rank, of midnight weeds collected,
With Hecate's ban° thrice blasted, thrice infected,
Thy natural magic and dire property°
On wholesome life usurp immediately. 230

[*He pours the poison into the sleeper's ear.*]

HAMLET: 'A poisons him i' the garden for his estate.° His° name's Gonzago. The
story is extant, and written in very choice Italian. You shall see anon how
the murderer gets the love of Gonzago's wife.

[CLAUDIUS *rises.*]

OPHELIA: The King rises.

HAMLET: What, frighted with false fire?° 235

QUEEN: How fares my lord?

POLONIUS: Give o'er the play.

KING: Give me some light. Away!

POLONIUS: Lights, lights, lights!

Exeunt all but HAMLET *and* HORATIO.

---

211 Tropically figuratively. (The First Quarto reading, *trapically*, suggests a pun on *trap* in
Mousetrap.)   **212 Duke's** i.e., king's (A slip that may be due to Shakespeare's possible source,
the alleged murder of the Duke of Urbino by Luigi Gonzaga in 1538.)   **214 free** guiltless.
214–15 galled jade horse whose hide is rubbed by saddle or harness.   **215 withers** the
part between the horse's shoulder blades; **unwrung** not rubbed sore.   **217 chorus** (In
many Elizabethan plays, the forthcoming action was explained by an actor known as the
"chorus"; at a puppet show, the actor who spoke the dialogue was known as an "interpreter," as indicated by the lines following.)   **218 interpret** (1) ventriloquize the dialogue, as
in a puppet show, (2) act as pander.   **218–19 puppets dallying** (with suggestion of sexual
play, continued in *keen*, "sexually aroused," *groaning*, "moaning in pregnancy," and *edge*,
"sexual desire" or "impetuosity.")   **220 keen** sharp, bitter.   **222 Still . . . worse** more keen,
always *bettering* what other people say with witty wordplay, but at the same time more offensive.   **223 So** even thus (in marriage);   **mis-take** take falseheartedly and cheat on. (The
marriage vows say "for better, for worse.")   **226 Confederate season** the time and occasion
conspiring (to assist the murderer);   **else** otherwise;   **seeing** seeing me.   **228 Hecate's
ban** the curse of Hecate, the goddess of witchcraft.   **229 dire property** baleful quality.
231 estate i.e., the kingship;   **His** i.e., the king's.   **235 false fire** the blank discharge of a
gun loaded with powder but no shot.

HAMLET:

> "Why,° let the strucken deer go weep,   240
>   The hart ungallèd° play.
> For some must watch,° while some must sleep;
>   Thus runs the world away."°

> Would not this,° sir, and a forest of feathers°—if the rest of my fortunes
> turn Turk with° me—with two Provincial roses° on my razed° shoes, get   245
> me a fellowship in a cry° of players?°

HORATIO: Half a share.

HAMLET: A whole one, I.

> "For thou dost know, O Damon° dear,
>   This realm dismantled° was   250
> Of Jove himself, and now reigns here
>   A very, very—pajock."°

HORATIO: You might have rhymed.

HAMLET: O good Horatio, I'll take the ghost's word for a thousand pound.
Didst perceive?   255

HORATIO: Very well, my lord.

HAMLET: Upon the talk of the poisoning?

HORATIO: I did very well note him.

Enter ROSENCRANTZ *and* GUILDENSTERN.

HAMLET: Aha! Come, some music! Come, the recorders.°

> "For if the King like not the comedy,   260
> Why then, belike, he likes it not, perdy."°

> Come, some music.

GUILDENSTERN: Good my lord, vouchsafe me a word with you.

HAMLET: Sir, a whole history.

GUILDENSTERN: The King, sir—   265

HAMLET: Ay, sir, what of him?

GUILDENSTERN: Is in his retirement° marvelous distempered.°

240–43 Why . . . away (probably from an old ballad, with allusion to the popular belief
that a wounded deer retires to weep and die; compare with *As You Like It*, 2.1.33–66.)
241 ungallèd unafflicted.   **242 watch** remain awake.   **243 Thus . . . away** thus the world
goes.   **244 this** i.e., the play;   **feathers** (allusion to the plumes that Elizabethan actors were
fond of wearing.)   **245 turn Turk with** turn renegade against, go back on;   **Provincial
roses** rosettes of ribbon, named for roses grown in a part of France;   **razed** with ornamental
slashing.   **246 cry** pack (of hounds);   **fellowship . . . players** partnership in a theatrical
company.   **249 Damon** the friend of Pythias, as Horatio is friend of Hamlet; or, a traditional
pastoral name.   **250 dismantled** stripped, divested.   **250–52 This realm . . . pajock** i.e.,
Jove, representing divine authority and justice, has abandoned this realm to its own devices,
leaving in his stead only a peacock or vain pretender to virtue (though the rhyme-word
expected in place of *pajock* or "peacock" suggests that the realm is now ruled over by an
"ass").   **259 recorders** wind instruments of the flute kind.   **261 perdy** (a corruption of the
French *par dieu*, "by god.")   **267 retirement** withdrawal to his chambers;   **distempered**
out of humor. (But Hamlet deliberately plays on the wider application to any illness of mind
or body, as in line 298, especially to drunkenness.)

HAMLET: With drink, sir?

GUILDENSTERN: No, my lord, with choler.°

HAMLET: Your wisdom should show itself more richer to signify this to the doctor, for for me to put him to his purgation° would perhaps plunge him into more choler. 270

GUILDENSTERN: Good my lord, put your discourse into some frame° and start° not so wildly from my affair.

HAMLET: I am tame, sir. Pronounce. 275

GUILDENSTERN: The Queen, your mother, in most great affliction of spirit, hath sent me to you.

HAMLET: You are welcome.

GUILDENSTERN: Nay, good my lord, this courtesy is not of the right breed.° If it shall please you to make me a wholesome answer, I will do your 280 mother's commandment; if not, your pardon° and my return shall be the end of my business.

HAMLET: Sir, I cannot.

ROSENCRANTZ: What, my lord?

HAMLET: Make you a wholesome answer; my wit's diseased. But, sir, such answer 285 as I can make, you shall command, or rather, as you say, my mother. Therefore no more, but to the matter. My mother, you say—

ROSENCRANTZ: Then thus she says: your behavior hath struck her into amazement and admiration.°

HAMLET: O wonderful son, that can so stonish a mother! But is there no sequel at 290 the heels of this mother's admiration? Impart.

ROSENCRANTZ: She desires to speak with you in her closet° ere you go to bed.

HAMLET: We shall obey, were she ten times our mother. Have you any further trade with us?

ROSENCRANTZ: My lord, you once did love me. 295

HAMLET: And do still, by these pickers and stealers.°

ROSENCRANTZ: Good my lord, what is your cause of distemper? You do surely bar the door upon your own liberty° if you deny° your griefs to your friend.

HAMLET: Sir, I lack advancement.

ROSENCRANTZ: How can that be, when you have the voice of the King himself for 300 your succession in Denmark?

HAMLET: Ay, sir, but "While the grass grows"°—the proverb is something° musty.

Enter the PLAYERS° *with recorders.*

O, the recorders. Let me see one. [*He takes a recorder.*]
To withdraw° with you: why do you go about to recover the wind° of me, as if you would drive me into a toil?° 305

---

269 choler anger. (But Hamlet takes the word in its more basic humoral sense of "bilious disorder.") **271 purgation** (Hamlet hints at something going beyond medical treatment to bloodletting and the extraction of confession.) **273 frame** order; **start** shy or jump away (like a horse; the opposite of *tame* in line 275). **279 breed** (1) kind, (2) breeding, manners. **281 pardon** permission to depart. **289 admiration** bewilderment. **292 closet** private chamber. **296 pickers and stealers** i.e., hands. (so called from the catechism, "to keep my hands from picking and stealing.") **298 liberty** i.e., being freed from *distemper*, line 297, but perhaps with a veiled threat as well; **deny** refuse to share. **302 While . . . grows** (the rest of the proverb is "the silly horse starves"; Hamlet may not live long enough to succeed to the kingdom.); **something** somewhat; **s.d. Players** actors. **304 withdraw** speak privately; **recover the wind** get to the windward side (thus driving the game into the *toil*, or "net"). **305 toil** snare.

GUILDENSTERN: O, my lord, if my duty be too bold, my love is too unmannerly.°
HAMLET: I do not well understand that.° Will you play upon this pipe?
GUILDENSTERN: My lord, I cannot.
HAMLET: I pray you.
GUILDENSTERN: Believe me, I cannot.   310
HAMLET: I do beseech you.
GUILDENSTERN: I know no touch of it, my lord.
HAMLET: It is as easy as lying. Govern these ventages° with your fingers and
    thumb, give it breath with your mouth, and it will discourse most
    eloquent music. Look you, these are the stops.   315
GUILDENSTERN: But these cannot I command to any utterance of harmony. I have
    not the skill.
HAMLET: Why, look you now, how unworthy a thing you make of me! You would
    play upon me, you would seem to know my stops, you would pluck out
    the heart of my mystery, you would sound° me from my lowest note to   320
    the top of my compass,° and there is much music, excellent voice, in this
    little organ,° yet cannot you make it speak. 'Sblood, do you think I am
    easier to be played on than a pipe? Call me what instrument you will,
    though you can fret° me, you cannot play upon me.

    Enter POLONIUS.

        God bless you, sir!   325
POLONIUS: My lord, the Queen would speak with you, and presently.°
HAMLET: Do you see yonder cloud that's almost in shape of a camel?
POLONIUS: By the Mass and 'tis, like a camel indeed.
HAMLET: Methinks it is like a weasel.
POLONIUS: It is backed like a weasel.   330
HAMLET: Or like a whale.
POLONIUS: Very like a whale.
HAMLET: Then I will come to my mother by and by.° [*Aside*.] They fool me° to
    the top of my bent.°—I will come by and by.
POLONIUS: I will say so.   [*Exit*.]   335
HAMLET: "By and by" is easily said. Leave me, friends.

                           [*Exeunt all but* HAMLET.]
    'Tis now the very witching time° of night,
    When churchyards yawn and hell itself breathes out
    Contagion to this world. Now could I drink hot blood
    And do such bitter business as the day   340
    Would quake to look on. Soft, now to my mother.
    O heart, lose not thy nature!° Let not ever
    The soul of Nero° enter this firm bosom.
    Let me be cruel, not unnatural;
    I will speak daggers to her, but use none.   345

306 if . . . unmannerly if I am using an unmannerly boldness, it is my love that occasions it.
307 I . . . that i.e., I don't understand how genuine love can be unmannerly.   **313 ventages**
finger-holes or *stops* (line 319) of the recorder.   **320 sound** (1) fathom, (2) produce sound in.
321 compass range (of voice).   **322 organ** musical instrument.   **324 fret** irritate (with a
quibble on *fret*, meaning the piece of wood, gut, or metal that regulates the fingering on
an instrument).   **326 presently** at once.   **333 by and by** quite soon.   **fool me** trifle with
me, humor my fooling.   **334 top of my bent** limit of my ability or endurance. (Literally, the
extent to which a bow may be bent.)   **337 witching time** time when spells are cast and evil
is abroad.   **342 nature** natural feeling.   **343 Nero** murderer of his mother, Agrippina.

My tongue and soul in this be hypocrites:
How in my words soever° she be shent,°
To give them seals° never my soul consent! *Exit.*

[3.3]

Enter KING, ROSENCRANTZ, *and* GUILDENSTERN.

KING: I like him° not, nor stands it safe with us
To let his madness range. Therefore prepare you.
I your commission will forthwith dispatch,°
And he to England shall along with you.
The terms of our estate° may not endure   5
Hazard so near 's as doth hourly grow
Out of his brows.°
GUILDENSTERN: We will ourselves provide.
Most holy and religious fear° it is
To keep those many many bodies safe
That live and feed upon Your Majesty.   10
ROSENCRANTZ: The single and peculiar° life is bound
With all the strength and armor of the mind
To keep itself from noyance,° but much more
That spirit upon whose weal depends and rests
The lives of many. The cess° of majesty   15
Dies not alone, but like a gulf° doth draw
What's near it with it; or it is a massy° wheel
Fixed on the summit of the highest mount,
To whose huge spokes ten thousand lesser things
Are mortised° and adjoined, which, when it falls,°   20
Each small annexment, petty consequence,°
Attends° the boisterous ruin. Never alone
Did the King sigh, but with a general groan.
KING: Arm° you, I pray you, to this speedy voyage,
For we will fetters put about this fear,   25
Which now goes too free-footed.
ROSENCRANTZ: We will haste us.

Exeunt gentlemen [ROSENCRANTZ *and* GUILDENSTERN].

Enter POLONIUS.

POLONIUS: My lord, he's going to his mother's closet.
Behind the arras° I'll convey myself

347 **How . . . soever** however much by my words;   **shent** rebuked.   348 **give them seals** i.e., confirm them with deeds.   [3.3] **Location: The castle.**   1 **him** i.e., his behavior.   3 **dispatch** prepare, cause to be drawn up.   5 **terms of our estate** circumstances of my royal position.   7 **Out of his brows** i.e., from his brain, in the form of plots and threats.   8 **religious fear** sacred concern.   11 **single and peculiar** individual and private.   13 **noyance** harm.   15 **cess** decease, cessation.   16 **gulf** whirlpool.   17 **massy** massive.   20 **mortised** fastened (as with a fitted joint);   **when it falls** i.e., when it descends, like the wheel of Fortune, bringing a king down with it.   21 **Each . . . consequence** i.e., every hanger-on and unimportant person or thing connected with the king.   22 **Attends** participates in.   24 **Arm** prepare.   28 **arras** screen of tapestry placed around the walls of household apartments. (On the Elizabethan stage, the arras was presumably over a door or discovery space in the tiring-house facade.)

To hear the process.° I'll warrant she'll tax him home,°
And, as you said—and wisely was it said—   30
'Tis meet° that some more audience than a mother,
Since nature makes them partial, should o'erhear
The speech, of vantage.° Fare you well, my liege.
I'll call upon you ere you go to bed
And tell you what I know.

KING: Thanks, dear my lord.   *Exit* [POLONIUS].   35
O, my offense is rank! It smells to heaven.
It hath the primal eldest curse° upon't,
A brother's murder. Pray can I not,
Though inclination be as sharp as will;°
My stronger guilt defeats my strong intent,   40
And like a man to double business bound°
I stand in pause where I shall first begin,
And both neglect. What if this cursèd hand
Were thicker than itself with brother's blood,
Is there not rain enough in the sweet heavens   45
To wash it white as snow? Whereto serves mercy
But to confront the visage of offense?°
And what's in prayer but this twofold force,
To be forestallèd° ere we come to fall,
Or pardoned being down? Then I'll look up.   50
My fault is past. But O, what form of prayer
Can serve my turn? "Forgive me my foul murder"?
That cannot be, since I am still possessed
Of those effects for which I did the murder:
My crown, mine own ambition, and my Queen.   55
May one be pardoned and retain th' offense?°
In the corrupted currents° of this world
Offense's gilded hand° may shove by° justice,
And oft 'tis seen the wicked prize° itself
Buys out the law. But 'tis not so above.   60
There° is no shuffling,° there the action lies°
In his° true nature, and we ourselves compelled,
Even to the teeth and forehead° of our faults,
To give in° evidence. What then? What rests?°
Try what repentance can. What can it not?   65
Yet what can it, when one cannot repent?
O wretched state, O bosom black as death,

---

29 process proceedings;   **tax him home** reprove him severely.   **31 meet** fitting.   **33 of
vantage** from an advantageous place, or, in addition.   **37 the primal eldest curse** the curse
of Cain, the first murderer; he killed his brother Abel.   **39 Though . . . will** though my desire
is as strong as my determination.   **41 bound** (1) destined, (2) obliged. (The King wants to
repent and still enjoy what he has gained.)   **46–47 Whereto . . . offense** What function
does mercy serve other than to meet sin face to face?   **49 forestallèd** prevented (from
sinning).   **56 th' offense** the thing for which one offended.   **57 currents** courses.
58 gilded hand hand offering gold as a bribe;   **shove by** thrust aside.   **59 wicked prize**
prize won by wickenness.   **61 There** i.e., in heaven;   **shuffling** escape by trickery;   **the
action lies** the accusation is made manifest. (A legal metaphor.)   **62 his** its.   **63 to the teeth
and forehead** face to face, concealing nothing.   **64 give in** provide;   **rests** remains.

limèd° soul that, struggling to be free,
Art more engaged!° Help, angels! Make assay.°
Bow, stubborn knees, and heart with strings of steel,   70
Be soft as sinews of the newborn babe!
All may be well.   [*He kneels.*]

Enter HAMLET.

HAMLET: Now might I do it pat,° now 'a is a-praying;
        And now I'll do 't. [*He draws his sword.*] And so 'a goes to heaven,
        And so am I revenged. That would be scanned:°   75
        A villain kills my father, and for that,
        I, his sole son, do this same villain send
        To heaven.
        Why, this is hire and salary, not revenge.
        'A took my father grossly, full of bread,°   80
        With all his crimes broad blown,° as flush° as May;
        And how his audit° stands who knows save° heaven?
        But in our circumstance and course of thought°
        'Tis heavy with him. And am I then revenged,
        To take him in the purging of his soul   85
        When he is fit and seasoned° for his passage?
        No!
        Up, sword, and know thou a more horrid hent.°

                                                            [*He puts up his sword.*]

        When he is drunk asleep, or in his rage,°
        Or in th' incestuous pleasure of his bed,   90
        At game,° a-swearing, or about some act
        That has no relish° of salvation in 't—
        Then trip him, that his heels may kick at heaven,
        And that his soul may be as damned and black
        As hell, whereto it goes. My mother stays.°   95
        This physic° but prolongs thy sickly days.   *Exit.*
KING: My words fly up, my thoughts remain below.
      Words without thoughts never to heaven go.   *Exit.*

                                    [3.4]

Enter [QUEEN] GERTRUDE *and* POLONIUS.

POLONIUS: 'A will come straight. Look you lay home° to him.
          Tell him his pranks have been too broad° to bear with,

---

68 limèd caught as with birdlime, a sticky substance used to ensnare birds.   **69 engaged**
entangled;   **assay** trial. (Said to himself.)   **73 pat** opportunely.   **75 would be scanned**
needs to be looked into, or, would be interpreted as follows.   **80 grossly, full of bread** i.e.,
enjoying his worldly pleasures rather than fasting. (See ezekiel 16:49.)   **81 crimes broad
blown** sins in full bloom;   **flush** vigorous.   **82 audit** account;   **save** except for.
83 in . . . thought As we see it from our mortal perspective.   **86 seasoned** matured,
readied.   **88 know . . . hent** await to be grasped by me on a more horrid occasion;   **hent**
act of seizing.   **89 drunk . . . rage** dead drunk, or in a fit of sexual passions.   **91 game**
gambling.   **92 relish** trace, savor.   **95 stays** awaits (me).   **96 physic** purging (by prayer),
or, Hamlet's postponement of the killing.   **[3.4] Location: The Queen's private chamber.**
1 lay home thrust to the heart, reprove him soundly.   **2 broad** unrestrained.

And that Your Grace hath screened and stood between
Much heat° and him. I'll shroud° me even here.
Pray you, be round° with him.   5

HAMLET [*within*]: Mother, Mother, Mother!
QUEEN: I'll warrant you, fear me not.
    Withdraw, I hear him coming.   [POLONIUS *hides behind the arras*.]

    Enter HAMLET.

HAMLET: Now, Mother, what's the matter?
QUEEN: Hamlet, thou hast thy father° much offended.   10
HAMLET: Mother, you have my father much offended.
QUEEN: Come, come, you answer with an idle° tongue.
HAMLET: Go, go, you question with a wicked tongue.
QUEEN: Why, how now, Hamlet?
HAMLET: What's the matter now?
QUEEN: Have you forgot me?°
HAMLET: No, by the rood,° not so: 15
    You are the Queen your husband's brother's wife,
    And—would it were not so!—you are my mother.
QUEEN: Nay, then, I'll set those to you that can speak.°
HAMLET: Come, come, and sit you down; you shall not budge.
    You go not till I set you up a glass   20
    Where you may see the inmost part of you.
QUEEN: What wilt thou do? Thou wilt not murder me?
    Help, ho!
POLONIUS [*behind the arras*]: What ho! Help!
HAMLET [*drawing*]: How now? A rat? Dead for a ducat,° dead!   25
                              [*He thrusts his rapier through the arras.*]
POLONIUS [*behind the arras*]: O, I am slain!   [*He falls and dies.*]
QUEEN: O me, what hast thou done?
HAMLET: Nay, I know not. Is it the King?
QUEEN: O, what a rash and bloody deed is this!
HAMLET: A bloody deed—almost as bad, good Mother,
    As kill a King, and marry with his brother.   30
QUEEN: As kill a King!
HAMLET: Ay, lady, it was my word.

                    [*He parts the arras and discovers* POLONIUS.]

    Thou wretched, rash, intruding fool, farewell!
    I took thee for thy better. Take thy fortune.
    Thou find'st to be too busy° is some danger.—
    Leave wringing of your hands. Peace, sit you down,   35
    And let me wring your heart, for so I shall,
    If it be made of penetrable stuff,
    If damnèd custom° have not brazed° it so
    That it be proof° and bulwark against sense.°

4 **Much heat** i.e., the King's anger;   **shroud** conceal. (With ironic fitness to Polonius'
imminent death. The word is only in the First Quarto: the second Quarto and the Folio
read "silence.")   5 **round** blunt.   10 **thy father** i.e., your stepfather, Claudius.   12 **idle**
foolish.   15 **forgot me** i.e., forgotten that I am your mother;   **rood** cross of Christ.
18 **speak** i.e., to someone so rude.   25 **Dead for a ducat** i.e., I bet a ducat he's dead; or,
a ducat is his life's fee.   34 **busy** nosy.   38 **damnèd custom** habitual wickedness;   **brazed**
brazened, hardened.   39 **proof** armor;   **sense** feeling.

QUEEN: What have I done, that thou dar'st wag thy tongue   40
    In noise so rude against me?

HAMLET: Such an act
    That blurs the grace and blush of modesty,
    Calls virtue hypocrite, takes off the rose
    From the fair forehead of an innocent love
    And sets a blister° there, makes marriage vows   45
    As false as dicers' oaths. O, such a deed
    As from the body of contraction° plucks
    The very soul, and sweet religion makes°
    A rhapsody° of words. Heaven's face does glow
    O'er this solidity and compound mass   50
    With tristful visage, as against the doom,
    Is thought-sick at the act.°

QUEEN: Ay me, what act,
    That roars so loud and thunders in the index?°

HAMLET [*showing her two likenesses*]: Look here upon this picture, and on this,
    The counterfeit presentment° of two brothers.   55
    See what a grace was seated on this brow:
    Hyperion's° curls, the front° of Jove himself,
    An eye like Mars° to threaten and command,
    A station° like the herald Mercury°
    New-lighted° on a heaven-kissing hill—   60
    A combination and a form indeed
    Where every god did seem to set his seal°
    To give the world assurance of a man.
    This was your husband. Look you now what follows:
    Here is your husband, like a mildewed ear,°   65
    Blasting° his wholesome brother. Have you eyes?
    Could you on this fair mountain leave° to feed
    And batten° on this moor?° Ha, have you eyes?
    You cannot call it love, for at your age
    The heyday° in the blood° is tame, it's humble,   70
    And waits upon the judgment, and what judgment
    Would step from this to this? Sense,° sure, you have,
    Else could you not have motion, but sure that sense
    Is apoplexed,° for madness would not err,°
    Nor sense to ecstasy was ne'er so thralled,   75

---

45 sets a blister i.e., brands as a harlot.   **47 contraction** the marriage contract.   **48 sweet religion makes** i.e., makes marriage vows.   **49 rhapsody** senseless string.   **49–52 Heaven's . . . act** Heaven's face blushes at this solid world compounded of the various elements, with sorrowful face as though the day of doom were near, and is sick with horror at the deed (i.e., Gertrude's marriage).   **54 index** table of contents, prelude or preface.   **55 counterfeit presentment** portrayed representation.   **57 Hyperion's** the sungod's;   **front** brow.   **58 Mars** god of war. **59 station** manner of standing;   **Mercury** winged messenger of the gods.   **60 New-lighted** newly alighted.   **62 set his seal** i.e., affix his approval.   **65 ear** i.e., of grain.   **66 Blasting** blighting.   **67 leave** cease.   **68 batten** gorge;   **moor** barren or marshy ground (suggesting also "darkskinned").   **70 heyday** state of excitement;   **blood** passion.   **72 Sense** perception through the five senses (the functions of the middle sensible soul).   **74 apoplexed** paralyzed (Hamlet goes on to explain that, without such a paralysis of will, mere madness would not so err, nor would the five senses so enthrall themselves to **ecstasy** or lunacy; even such deranged states of mind would be able to make the obvious choice between Hamlet Senior and Claudius.);   **err** so err.

But° it reserved some quantity of choice
To serve in such a difference.° What devil was 't
That thus hath cozened° you at hoodman-blind?°
Eyes without feeling, feeling without sight,
Ears without hands or eyes, smelling sans° all   80
Or but a sickly part of one true sense
Could not so mope.° O shame, where is thy blush?
Rebellious hell,
If thou canst mutine° in a matron's bones,
To flaming youth let virtue be as wax   85
And melt in her own fire.° Proclaim no shame
When the compulsive ardor gives the charge,
Since frost itself as actively doth burn,
And reason panders will.°

QUEEN: O Hamlet, speak no more!   90
Thou turn'st mine eyes into my very soul,
And there I see such black and grainèd° spots
As will not leave their tinct.°

HAMLET: Nay, but to live
In the rank sweat of an enseamèd° bed,
Stewed° in corruption, honeying and making love   95
Over the nasty sty!

QUEEN: O, speak to me no more!
These words like daggers enter in my ears.
No more, sweet Hamlet!

HAMLET: A murderer and a villain,
A slave that is not twentieth part the tithe°   100
Of your precedent lord,° a vice° of kings,
A cutpurse of the empire and the rule,
That from a shelf the precious diadem stole
And put it in his pocket!

QUEEN: No more!   105

Enter GHOST [*in his nightgown*].

HAMLET: A king of shreds and patches°—
Save me, and hover o'er me with your wings,
You heavenly guards! What would your gracious figure?

QUEEN: Alas, he's mad!

---

76 But but that.   **77 To . . . difference** to help in making a choice between two such men.
78 cozened cheated;   **hoodman-blind** blindman's buff. (In this game, says Hamlet, the devil
must have pushed Claudius toward Gertrude while she was blindfolded.)   **80 sans** without.   **82 mope** be dazed, act aimlessly.   **84 mutine** incite mutiny.   **85–86 be as wax . . .
fire** melt like a candle or stick of sealing wax held over the candle flame.   **86–89 Proclaim
. . . will** call it no shameful business when the compelling ardor of youth delivers the attack,
i.e., commits lechery, since the *frost* of advanced age burns with as active a fire of lust and
reason perverts itself by fomenting lust rather than restraining it.   **92 grainèd** dyed in grain,
indelible.   **93 leave their tinct** surrender their color.   **94 enseamèd** saturated in the grease
and filth of passionate lovemaking.   **95 Stewed** soaked, bathed (with a suggestion of "stew,"
brothel).   **100 tithe** tenth part.   **101 precedent lord** former husband;   **vice** buffoon.
(A reference to the Vice of the morality plays.)   **106 shreds and patches** i.e., motley, the
traditional costume of the clown or fool.

HAMLET: Do you not come your tardy son to chide,   110
  That, lapsed° in time and passion, lets go by
  Th' important° acting of your dread command?
  O, say!
GHOST: Do not forget. This visitation
  Is but to whet thy almost blunted purpose.   115
  But look, amazement° on thy mother sits.
  O, step between her and her fighting soul!
  Conceit° in weakest bodies strongest works.
  Speak to her, Hamlet.
HAMLET: How is it with you, lady?
QUEEN: Alas, how is 't with you,   120
  That you do bend your eye on vacancy,
  And with th' incorporal° air do hold discourse?
  Forth at your eyes your spirits wildly peep,
  And, as the sleeping soldiers in th' alarm,°
  Your bedded° hair, like life in excrements,°   125
  Start up and stand on end. O gentle son,
  Upon the heat and flame of thy distemper°
  Sprinkle cool patience. Whereon do you look?
HAMLET: On him, on him! Look you how pale he glares!
  His form and cause conjoined,° preaching to stones,   130
  Would make them capable.°—Do not look upon me,
  Lest with this piteous action you convert
  My stern effects.° Then what I have to do
  Will want true color—tears perchance for blood.°
QUEEN: To whom do you speak this?   135
HAMLET: Do you see nothing there?
QUEEN: Nothing at all, yet all that is I see.
HAMLET: Nor did you nothing hear?
QUEEN: No, nothing but ourselves.
HAMLET: Why, look you there, look how it steals away!   140
  My father, in his habit° as° he lived!
  Look where he goes even now out at the portal!   *Exit* GHOST.
QUEEN: This is the very° coinage of your brain.
  This bodiless creation ecstasy
  Is very cunning in.°   145
HAMLET: Ecstasy?
  My pulse as yours doth temperately keep time,
  And makes as healthful music. It is not madness

---

111 lapsed delaying. **112 important** importunate, urgent. **116 amazement** distraction.
118 Conceit imagination. **122 incorporal** immaterial. **124 as . . . alarm** like soldiers called
out of sleep by an alarum. **125 bedded** laid flat; **like life in excrements** i.e., as though
hair, an outgrowth of the body, had a life of its own. (Hair was thought to be lifeless because
it lacks sensation, and so its standing on end would be unnatural and ominous.) **127 distemper** disorder. **130 His . . . conjoined** his appearance joined to his cause for speaking.
131 capable receptive. **132–33 convert . . . effects** divert me from my stern duty.
134 want . . . blood lack plausibility so that (with a play on the normal sense of *color*) I
shall shed colorless tears instead of blood. **141 habit** clothes; **as** as when **143 very**
mere. **144–45 This . . . in** madness is skillful in creating this kind of hallucination.

That I have uttered. Bring me to the test,
And I the matter will reword,° which madness   150
Would gambol° from. Mother, for love of grace,
Lay not that flattering unction° to your soul
That not your trespass but my madness speaks.
It will but skin° and film the ulcerous place,
Whiles rank corruption, mining° all within,   155
Infects unseen. Confess yourself to heaven,
Repent what's past, avoid what is to come,
And do not spread the compost° on the weeds
To make them ranker. Forgive me this my virtue;°
For in the fatness° of these pursy° times   160
Virtue itself of vice must pardon beg,
Yea, curb° and woo for leave° to do him good.

QUEEN: O Hamlet, thou hast cleft my heart in twain.

HAMLET: O, throw away the worser part of it,
And live the purer with the other half.   165
Good night. But go not to my uncle's bed;
Assume a virtue, if you have it not.
That monster, custom, who all sense doth eat,°
Of habits devil,° is angel yet in this,
That to the use of actions fair and good   170
He likewise gives a frock or livery°
That aptly° is put on. Refrain tonight,
And that shall lend a kind of easiness
To the next abstinence; the next more easy;
For use° almost can change the stamp of nature,°   175
And either° . . . the devil, or throw him out
With wondrous potency. Once more, good night;
And when you are desirous to be blest,
I'll blessing beg of you.° For this same lord,   [*pointing to* POLONIUS.]
I do repent; but heaven hath pleased it so   180
To punish me with this, and this with me,
That I must be their scourge and minister.°
I will bestow° him, and will answer° well
The death I gave him. So, again, good night.
I must be cruel only to be kind.   185

---

150 reword repeat word for word.   **151 gambol** skip away.   **152 unction** ointment.
154 skin grow a skin for.   **155 mining** working under the surface.   **158 compost** manure.
159 this my virtue my virtuous talk in reproving you.   **160 fatness** grossness;   **pursy**
flabby, out of shape.   **162 curb** bow, bend the knee;   **leave** permission.   **168 who . . . eat**
which consumes all proper or natural feeling, all sensibility.   **169 Of habits devil** devil-like
in prompting evil habits.   **171 livery** an outer appearance, a customary garb (and hence a
predisposition easily assumed in time of stress).   **172 aptly** readily.   **175 use** habit;   **the
stamp of nature** our inborn traits.   **176 And either** (a defective line, usually emended by
inserting the word *master* after *either*, following the Fourth Quarto and early editors.)
178–79 when . . . you i.e., when you are ready to be penitent and seek God's blessing, I
will ask your blessing as a dutiful son should.   **182 their scourge and minister** i.e., agent
of heavenly retribution. (By *scourge*, Hamlet also suggests that he himself will eventually
suffer punishment in the process of fulfilling heaven's will.)   **183 bestow** stow, dispose of;
answer account or pay for.

This° bad begins, and worse remains behind.°
One word more, good lady.

QUEEN: What shall I do?

HAMLET: Not this by no means that I bid you do:
Let the bloat° King tempt you again to bed,
Pinch wanton° on your cheek, call you his mouse,   190
And let him, for a pair of reechy° kisses,
Or paddling° in your neck with his damned fingers,
Make you to ravel all this matter out°
That I essentially am not in madness,
But mad in craft.° 'Twere good° you let him know,   195
For who that's but a Queen, fair, sober, wise,
Would from a paddock,° from a bat, a gib,°
Such dear concernings° hide? Who would do so?
No, in despite of sense and secrecy,°
Unpeg the basket° on the house's top,   200
Let the birds fly, and like the famous ape,°
To try conclusions,° in the basket creep
And break your own neck down.°

QUEEN: Be thou assured, if words be made of breath,
And breath of life, I have no life to breathe   205
What thou hast said to me.

HAMLET: I must to England. You know that?

QUEEN: Alack,
I had forgot. 'Tis so concluded on.

HAMLET: There's letters sealed, and my two schoolfellows,
Whom I will trust as I will adders fanged,   210
They bear the mandate; they must sweep my way
And marshal me to knavery.° Let it work.°
For 'tis the sport to have the enginer°
Hoist with° his own petard,° and 't shall go hard
But I will° delve one yard below their mines°   215
And blow them at the moon. O, 'tis most sweet
When in one line° two crafts° directly meet.

---

186 This i.e., the killing of Polonius; **behind** to come.   **189 bloat** bloated.   **190 Pinch wanton** i.e., leave his love pinches on your cheeks, branding you as wanton.   **191 reechy** dirty, filthy.   **192 paddling** fingering amorously.   **193 ravel . . . out** unravel, disclose.   **195 in craft** by cunning;   **good** (said sarcastically; also the following eight lines.)   **197 paddock** toad;   **gib** tomcat.   **198 dear concernings** important affairs.   **199 sense and secrecy** secrecy that common sense requires.   **200 Unpeg the basket** open the cage, i.e., let out the secret.   **201 famous ape** (in a story now lost.)   **202 try conclusions** test the outcome (in which the ape apparently enters a cage from which birds have been released and then tries to fly out of the cage as they have done, falling to its death).   **203 down** in the fall; utterly.   **211–12 sweep . . . knavery** sweep a path before me and conduct me to some *knavery* or treachery prepared for me;   **work** proceed.   **213 enginer** maker of military contrivances.   **214 Hoist with** blown up by;   **petard** an explosive used to blow in a door or make a breach.   **214–15 't shall . . . will** unless luck is against me, I will;   **mines** tunnels used in warfare to undermine the enemy's emplacements; Hamlet will countermine by going under their mines.   **217 in one line** i.e., mines and countermines on a collision course, or the countermines directly below the mines;   **crafts** acts of guile, plots.

This man shall set me packing.°
I'll lug the guts into the neighbor room.
Mother, good night indeed. This counselor   220
Is now most still, most secret, and most grave,
Who was in life a foolish prating knave.—
Come, sir, to draw toward an end° with you.—
Good night, Mother.

> *Exeunt* [*separately,* HAMLET *dragging in* POLONIUS].

[4.1]

Enter KING *and* QUEEN,° *with* ROSENCRANTZ *and* GUILDENSTERN.

KING: There's matter° in these sighs, these profound heaves.°
      You must translate; 'tis fit we understand them.
      Where is your son?
QUEEN: Bestow this place on us a little while.

> [*Exeunt* ROSENCRANTZ *and* GUILDENSTERN.]

      Ah, mine own lord, what have I seen tonight!   5
KING: What, Gertrude? How does Hamlet?
QUEEN: Mad as the sea and wind when both contend
      Which is the mightier. In his lawless fit,
      Behind the arras hearing something stir,
      Whips out his rapier, cries, "A rat, a rat!"   10
      And in this brainish apprehension° kills
      The unseen good old man.
KING: O heavy° deed!
      It had been so with us,° had we been there.
      His liberty is full of threats to all—
      To you yourself, to us, to everyone.   15
      Alas, how shall this bloody deed be answered?°
      It will be laid to us, whose providence°
      Should have kept short,° restrained, and out of haunt°
      This mad young man. But so much was our love,
      We would not understand what was most fit,   20
      But, like the owner of a foul disease,
      To keep it from divulging,° let it feed
      Even on the pith of life. Where is he gone?
QUEEN: To draw apart the body he hath killed,
      O'er whom his very madness, like some ore°   25
      Among a mineral° of metals base,
      Shows itself pure: 'a weeps for what is done.

218 set me packing set me to making schemes, and set me to lugging (him), and, also,
send me off in a hurry.   **223 draw . . . end** finish up (with a pun on *draw*, "pull").
[4.1] Location: The castle.   s.d. Enter . . . Queen (Some editors argue that Gertrude
never exits in 3.4 and that the scene is continuous here, as suggested in the Folio, but the
second Quarto marks an entrance for her and at line 35 Claudius speaks of Gertrude's *closet*
as though it were elsewhere. A short time has elapsed, during which the King has become
aware of her highly wrought emotional state.)   **1 matter** significance;   **heaves** heavy
sighs.   **11 brainish apprehension** headstrong conception.   **12 heavy** grievous.   **13 us** i.e.,
me. (The royal "we"; also in line 15.)   **16 answered** explained.   **17 providence** foresight.
18 short i.e., on a short tether;   **out of haunt** secluded.   **22 divulging** becoming evident.
25 ore vein of gold.   **26 mineral** mine.

KING: O Gertrude, come away!
  The sun no sooner shall the mountains touch
  But we will ship him hence, and this vile deed   30
  We must with all our majesty and skill
  Both countenance° and excuse.—Ho, Guildenstern!

 Enter ROSENCRANTZ *and* GUILDENSTERN.

  Friends both, go join you with some further aid.
  Hamlet in madness hath Polonius slain,
  And from his mother's closet hath he dragged him.   35
  Go seek him out, speak fair, and bring the body
  Into the chapel. I pray you, haste in this.
      [*Exeunt* ROSENCRANTZ *and* GUILDENSTERN.]
  Come, Gertrude, we'll call up our wisest friends
  And let them know both what we mean to do
  And what's untimely done°.   40
  Whose whisper o'er the world's diameter,°
  As level° as the cannon to his blank,°
  Transports his poisoned shot, may miss our name
  And hit the woundless° air. O, come away!
  My soul is full of discord and dismay.   *Exeunt.* 45

       [4.2]

 Enter HAMLET.

HAMLET: Safely stowed.
ROSENCRANTZ, GUILDENSTERN [*within*]: Hamlet! Lord Hamlet!
HAMLET: But soft, what noise? Who calls on Hamlet? O, here they come.

 Enter ROSENCRANTZ *and* GUILDENSTERN.

ROSENCRANTZ: What have you done, my lord, with the dead body?
HAMLET: Compounded it with dust, whereto 'tis kin.   5
ROSENCRANTZ: Tell us where 'tis, that we may take it thence
  And bear it to the chapel.
HAMLET: Do not believe it.
ROSENCRANTZ: Believe what?
HAMLET: That I can keep your counsel and not mine own.° Besides, to be demanded 10
  of° a sponge, what replication° should be made by the son of a king?
ROSENCRANTZ: Take you me for a sponge, my lord?
HAMLET: Ay, sir, that soaks up the King's countenance,° his rewards, his authori-
  ties.° But such officers do the King best service in the end. He keeps
  them, like an ape, an apple, in the corner of his jaw, first mouthed to be 15
  last swallowed. When he needs what you have gleaned, it is but squeezing you, and, sponge, you shall be dry again.

32 countenance put the best face on. **40 And . . . done** (a defective line; conjectures as to
the missing words include *So, haply, slander* [Capell and other early editors]; *For, haply,
slander* [Theobald and others]; and *So envious slander* [Jenkins].) **41 diameter** extent
from side to side. **42 As level** with as direct aim; **his blank** its target at point-blank
range. **44 woundless** invulnerable. **[4.2] Location: The castle.** **10 That . . . own** i.e.,
that I can follow your advice (by telling where the body is) and still keep my own secret.
10–11 demanded of questioned by; **replication** reply. **13 countenance** favor.
13–14 authorities delegated power, influence.

ROSENCRANTZ: I understand you not, my lord.

HAMLET: I am glad of it. A knavish speech sleeps in° a foolish ear.

ROSENCRANTZ: My lord, you must tell us where the body is and go with us to the   20
King.

HAMLET: The body is with the King, but the King is not with the body.°
The King is a thing—

GUILDENSTERN: A thing, my lord?

HAMLET: Of nothing.° Bring me to him. Hide fox, and all after!°   25

Exeunt [*running*].

[4.3]

Enter KING, *and two or three.*

KING: I have sent to seek him, and to find the body.
How dangerous is it that this man goes loose!
Yet must not we put the strong law on him.
He's loved of° the distracted° multitude,
Who like not in their judgment, but their eyes,°   5
And where 'tis so, th' offender's scourge° is weighed,°
But never the offense. To bear all smooth and even,°
This sudden sending him away must seem
Deliberate pause.° Diseases desperate grown
By desperate appliance° are relieved,   10
Or not at all.

Enter ROSENCRANTZ, GUILDENSTERN, *and all the rest.*

How now, what hath befall'n?

ROSENCRANTZ: Where the dead body is bestowed, my lord,
We cannot get from him.

KING: But where is he?

ROSENCRANTZ: Without, my lord; guarded, to know your pleasure.

KING: Bring him before us.

ROSENCRANTZ: Ho! Bring in the lord.   15

They enter [*with* HAMLET].

KING: Now, Hamlet, where's Polonius?

HAMLET: At supper.

KING: At supper? Where?

19 sleeps in has no meaning to.   **22 The . . . body** (Perhaps alludes to the legal common-place of "the king's two bodies," which drew a distinction between the sacred office of king-ship and the particular mortal who possessed it at any given time. Hence, although Claudius' body is necessarily a part of him, true kingship is not contained in it. Similarly, Claudius will have Polonius' body when it is found, but there is no kingship in this business either.)
25 Of nothing (1) of no account, (2) lacking the essence of kingship, as in lines 24–25 and note;   **Hide . . . after** (an old signal cry in the game of hide-and-seek, suggesting that Hamlet now runs away from them.)   **[4.3] Location: The castle.   4 of** by;   **distracted** fickle, unstable.   **5 Who . . . eyes** who choose not by judgment but by appearance.   **6 scourge** punishment. (Literally, blow with a whip.);   **weighed** sympathetically considered.
7 To . . . even to manage the business in an unprovocative way.   **9 Deliberate pause** carefully considered action.   **10 appliance** remedies.

HAMLET: Not where he eats, but where 'a is eaten. A certain convocation of politic
    worms° are e'en° at him. Your worm° is your only emperor for diet.° We   20
    fat all creatures else to fat us, and we fat ourselves for maggots. Your fat
    king and your lean beggar is but variable service°—two dishes, but to
    one table. That's the end.

KING: Alas, alas!

HAMLET: A man may fish with the worm that hath eat° of a king, and eat of the   25
    fish that hath fed of that worm.

KING: What dost thou mean by this?

HAMLET: Nothing but to show you how a king may go a progress° through the guts
    of a beggar.

KING: Where is Polonius?   30

HAMLET: In heaven. Send thither to see. If your messenger find him not there,
    seek him i' th' other place yourself. But if indeed you find him not
    within this month, you shall nose him as you go up the stairs into the
    lobby.

KING [*to some attendants*]: Go seek him there.   35

HAMLET: 'A will stay till you come.   [*Exeunt attendants.*]

KING: Hamlet, this deed, for thine especial safety—
    Which we do tender,° as we dearly° grieve
    For that which thou hast done—must send thee hence
    With fiery quickness. Therefore prepare thyself.   40
    The bark° is ready, and the wind at help,
    Th' associates tend,° and everything is bent°
    For England.

HAMLET: For England!

KING: Ay, Hamlet.   45

HAMLET: Good.

KING: So is it, if thou knew'st our purposes.

HAMLET: I see a cherub° that sees them. But come, for England!
    Farewell, dear mother.

KING: Thy loving father, Hamlet.   50

HAMLET: My mother. Father and mother is man and wife, man and wife is one
    flesh, and so, my mother. Come, for England!   *Exit.*

KING: Follow him at foot;° tempt him with speed aboard.
    Delay it not. I'll have him hence tonight.
    Away! For everything is sealed and done   55
    That else leans on° th' affair. Pray you, make haste.
                     [*Exeunt all but the* KING.]
    And, England,° if my love thou hold'st at aught°—

19–20 politic worms crafty worms (suited to a master spy like Polonius); **e'en** even now;
Your worm your average worm. (Compare *your fat king and your lean beggar* in lines 21–22.);
diet food, eating (with a punning reference to the Diet of Worms, a famous *convocation* held
in 1521). **22 variable service** different courses of a single meal. **25 eat** eaten. (Pronounced *et.*)
28 progress royal journey of state. **38 tender** regard, hold dear; **dearly** intensely. **41 bark**
sailing vessel. **42 tend** wait; **bent** in readiness. **48 cherub** (Cherubim are angels of knowledge. Hamlet hints that both he and heaven are onto Claudius' tricks.) **53 at foot** close
behind, at heel. **56 leans on** bears upon, is related to. **57 England** i.e., King of England;
at aught at any value.

As my great power thereof may give thee sense,°
Since yet thy cicatrice° looks raw and red
After the Danish sword, and thy free awe°
Pays homage to us—thou mayst not coldly set°   60
Our sovereign process,° which imports at full,°
By letters congruing° to that effect,
The present° death of Hamlet. Do it, England,
For like the hectic° in my blood he rages,   65
And thou must cure me. Till I know 'tis done,
Howe'er my haps,° my joys were ne'er begun.   *Exit.*

[4.4]

Enter FORTINBRAS *with his army over the stage.*

FORTINBRAS: Go, Captain, from me greet the Danish king.
    Tell him that by his license° Fortinbras
    Craves the conveyance of° a promised march
    Over his kingdom. You know the rendezvous.
    If that His Majesty would aught with us,   5
    We shall express our duty° in his eye;°
    And let him know so.
CAPTAIN: I will do 't, my lord.
FORTINBRAS: Go softly° on.   *[Exeunt all but the* CAPTAIN*.]*

Enter HAMLET, ROSENCRANTZ, [GUILDENSTERN,] *etc.*

HAMLET: Good sir, whose powers° are these?   10
CAPTAIN: They are of Norway, sir.
HAMLET: How purposed, sir, I pray you?
CAPTAIN: Against some part of Poland.
HAMLET: Who commands them, sir?
CAPTAIN: The nephew to old Norway, Fortinbras.   15
HAMLET: Goes it against the main° of Poland, sir,
    Or for some frontier?
CAPTAIN: Truly to speak, and with no addition,°
    We go to gain a little patch of ground
    That hath in it no profit but the name.
    To pay° five ducats, five, I would not farm it;°   20
    Nor will it yield to Norway or the Pole
    A ranker° rate, should it be sold in fee.°
HAMLET: Why, then the Polack never will defend it.
CAPTAIN: Yes, it is already garrisoned.   25

---

58 As . . . sense for so my great power may give you a just appreciation of the importance of valuing my love.   **59 cicatrice** scar.   **60 free awe** voluntary show of respect.   **61 coldly set** regard with indifference.   **62 process** command;   **imports at full** conveys specific directions for.   **63 congruing** agreeing.   **64 present** immediate.   **65 hectic** persistent fever.   **67 haps** fortunes.   **[4.4] Location: The coast of Denmark**.   **2 license** permission.   **3 the conveyance** of escort during.   **6 duty** respect;   **eye** presence.   **9 softly** slowly, circumspectly.   **10 powers** forces.   **16 main** main part.   **18 addition** exaggeration.   **21 To pay** i.e., for a yearly rental of;   **farm it** take a lease on it.   **23 ranker** higher;   **in fee** fee simple, outright.

HAMLET: Two thousand souls and twenty thousand ducats
      Will not debate the question of this straw.°
      This is th' impostume° of much wealth and peace,
      That inward breaks, and shows no cause without
      Why the man dies. I humbly thank you, sir.   30
CAPTAIN: God b' wi' you, sir.   [*Exit.*]
ROSENCRANTZ: Will 't please you go, my lord?
HAMLET: I'll be with you straight. Go a little before.

                              [*Exeunt all except* HAMLET.]

      How all occasions do inform against° me
      And spur my dull revenge! What is a man,   35
      If his chief good and market of° his time
      Be but to sleep and feed? A beast, no more.
      Sure he that made us with such large discourse,°
      Looking before and after,° gave us not
      That capability and godlike reason   40
      To fust° in us unused. Now, whether it be
      Bestial oblivion,° or some craven° scruple
      Of thinking too precisely° on th' event°—
      A thought which, quartered, hath but one part wisdom
      And ever three parts coward—I do not know   45
      Why yet I live to say "This thing's to do,"
      Sith° I have cause, and will, and strength, and means
      To do 't. Examples gross° as earth exhort me:
      Witness this army of such mass and charge,°
      Led by a delicate and tender° prince,   50
      Whose spirit with divine ambition puffed
      Makes mouths° at the invisible event,°
      Exposing what is mortal and unsure
      To all that fortune, death, and danger dare,°
      Even for an eggshell. Rightly to be great   55
      Is not to stir without great argument,
      But greatly to find quarrel in a straw
      When honor's at the stake.° How stand I, then,
      That have a father killed, a mother stained,
      Excitements of° my reason and my blood,   60
      And let all sleep, while to my shame I see
      The imminent death of twenty thousand men
      That for a fantasy° and trick° of fame
      Go to their graves like beds, fight for a plot°

---

27 debate . . . straw settle this trifling matter.   **28 impostume** abscess.   **34 inform against**
denounce, betray; take shape against.   **36 market of** profit of, compensation for.   **38 discourse**
power of reasoning.   **39 Looking before and after** able to review past events and anticipate
the future.   **41 fust** grow moldy.   **42 oblivion** forgetfulness;   **craven** cowardly.   **43 precisely**
scrupulously;   **event** outcome.   **47 Sith** since.   **48 gross** obvious.   **49 charge** expense.
50 delicate and tender of fine and youthful qualities.   **52 Makes mouths** makes scornful faces;
invisible event unforeseeable outcome.   **54 dare** could do (to him).   **55–58 Rightly . . . stake**
true greatness does not normally consist of rushing into action over some trivial provocation; however, when one's honor is involved, even a trifling insult requires that one respond greatly (?);
at the stake (A metaphor from gambling or bear-baiting.)   **60 Excitements** of promptings by.
63 fantasy fanciful caprice, illusion;   **trick** trifle, deceit.   **64 plot** plot of ground.

Whereon the numbers cannot try the cause,°   65
Which is not tomb enough and continent°
To hide the slain? O, from this time forth
My thoughts be bloody or be nothing worth!   *Exit*.

[4.5]

Enter HORATIO, [QUEEN] GERTRUDE, *and a* GENTLEMAN.

QUEEN: I will not speak with her.
GENTLEMAN: She is importunate,
    Indeed distract.° Her mood will needs be pitied.
QUEEN: What would she have?
GENTLEMAN: She speaks much of her father, says she hears
    There's tricks° i' the world, and hems,° and beats her heart,°   5
    Spurns enviously at straws,° speaks things in doubt°
    That carry but half sense. Her speech is nothing,
    Yet the unshapèd use° of it doth move
    The hearers to collection;° they yawn° at it,
    And botch° the words up fit to their own thoughts,   10
    Which,° as her winks and nods and gestures yield° them,
    Indeed would make one think there might be thought,°
    Though nothing sure, yet much unhappily.°
HORATIO: 'Twere good she were spoken with, for she may strew
    Dangerous conjectures in ill-breeding° minds.   15
QUEEN: Let her come in.   [*Exit* GENTLEMAN.]
    [*Aside*.] To my sick soul, as sin's true nature is,
    Each toy° seems prologue to some great amiss.°
    So full of artless jealousy is guilt,
    It spills itself in fearing to be spilt.°   20

        Enter OPHELIA° [*distracted*].

OPHELIA: Where is the beauteous majesty of Denmark?
QUEEN: How now, Ophelia?
OPHELIA [*she sings*]:

    "How should I your true love know
        From another one?
    By his cockle hat° and staff,   25
        And his sandal shoon."°

QUEEN: Alas, sweet lady, what imports this song?

---

65 Whereon . . . cause on which there is insufficient room for the soldiers needed to engage in a military contest.   **66 continent** receptacle; container.   **[4.5] Location: The castle.**
2 distract distracted.   **5 tricks** deceptions;   **hems** makes "hmm" sounds;   **heart** i.e., breast.
6 Spurns . . . straws kicks spitefully, takes offense at trifles;   **in doubt** obscurely.   **8 unshapèd use** incoherent manner.   **9 collection** inference, a guess at some sort of meaning;   **yawn** gape, wonder; grasp. (The Folio reading, *aim*, is possible.)   **10 botch** patch.   **11 Which** which words;   **yield** deliver, represent.   **12 thought** intended.   **13 unhappily** unpleasantly near the truth, shrewdly.   **15 ill-breeding** prone to suspect the worst and to make mischief.   **18 toy** trifle;   **amiss** calamity.   **19–20 So . . . split** guilt is so full of suspicion that it unskilfully betrays itself in fearing betrayal.   **s.d. Enter Ophelia** (In the First Quarto, Ophelia enters, "playing on a lute, and her hair down, singing.")   **25 cockle hat** hat with cockle-shell stuck in it as a sign that the wearer had been a pilgrim to the shrine of saint James of Compostela in spain.   **26 shoon** shoes.

OPHELIA: Say you? Nay, pray you, mark.

   "He is dead and gone, lady,   [*Song.*]
      He is dead and gone;   30
   At his head a grass-green turf,
      At his heels a stone."
   O, ho!

QUEEN: Nay, but Ophelia—

OPHELIA: Pray you, mark.   [*Sings.*] 35

   "White his shroud as the mountain snow"—
   Enter KING.

QUEEN: Alas, look here, my lord.

OPHELIA:

   "Larded° with sweet flowers;   [*Song.*]
   Which bewept to the ground did not go
   With true-love showers."°   40

KING: How do you, pretty lady?

OPHELIA: Well, God 'ild° you! They say the owl° was a baker's daughter.
   Lord, we know what we are, but know not what we may be. God be at
   your table!

KING: Conceit° upon her father.   45

OPHELIA: Pray let's have no words of this; but when they ask you what
   it means, say you this:

   "Tomorrow is Saint Valentine's day,   [*Song.*]
     All in the morning betime,°
   And I a maid at your window,   50
     To be your Valentine.
   Then up he rose, and donned his clothes,
     And dupped° the chamber door,
   Let in the maid, that out a maid
     Never departed more."   55

KING: Pretty Ophelia—

OPHELIA: Indeed, la, without an oath, I'll make an end on 't: [*Sings.*]

   "By Gis° and by Saint Charity,
     Alack, and fie for shame!
   Young men will do 't, if they come to 't;   60
     By Cock,° they are to blame.
   Quoth she, 'Before you tumbled me,
     You promised me to wed.'"

   He answers:

   " 'So would I ha' done, by yonder sun,
     An° thou hadst not come to my bed.'"   65

38 Larded decorated.   **40 showers** i.e., tears.   **42 God 'ild** god yield or reward;   **owl** (refers
to a legend about a baker's daughter who was turned into an owl for being ungenerous when
Jesus begged a loaf of bread.)   **45 Conceit** brooding.   **49 betime** early.   **53 dupped** did up,
opened.   **58 Gis** Jesus.   **61 Cock** (a perversion of "god" in oaths; here also with a quibble
on the slang word for penis.)   **66 An** if.

KING: How long hath she been thus?

OPHELIA: I hope all will be well. We must be patient, but I cannot choose but
weep to think they would lay him i' the cold ground. My brother shall
know of it. And so I thank you for your good counsel. Come, my   70
coach! Good night, ladies, good night, sweet ladies, good night, good
night.   [*Exit.*]

KING [*to* HORATIO]: Follow her close. Give her good watch, I pray you.

[*Exit* HORATIO.]

O, this is the poison of deep grief; it springs
All from her father's death—and now behold!   75
O Gertrude, Gertrude,
When sorrows come, they come not single spies,°
But in battalions. First, her father slain;
Next, your son gone, and he most violent author
Of his own just remove;° the people muddied,°   80
Thick and unwholesome in their thoughts and whispers
For good Polonius' death—and we have done but greenly,°
In hugger-mugger° to inter him; poor Ophelia
Divided from herself and her fair judgment,
Without the which we are pictures or mere beasts;   85
Last, and as much containing° as all these,
Her brother is in secret come from France,
Feeds on this wonder, keeps himself in clouds,°
And wants° not buzzers° to infect his ear
With pestilent speeches of his father's death,   90
Wherein necessity,° of matter beggared,°
Will nothing stick our person to arraign
In ear and ear.° O my dear Gertrude, this,
Like to a murdering piece,° in many places
Gives me superfluous death.°   *A noise within.*   95

QUEEN: Alack, what noise is this?

KING: Attend!°
Where is my Switzers?° Let them guard the door.

Enter a MESSENGER.

What is the matter?

MESSENGER: Save yourself, my lord!
The ocean, overpeering of his list,°
Eats not the flats° with more impetuous° haste   100
Than young Laertes, in a riotous head,°
O'erbears your officers. The rabble call him lord,

---

77 spies scouts sent in advance of the main force.   **80 remove** removal;   **muddied** stirred up,
confused.   **82 greenly** in an inexperienced way, foolishly.   **83 hugger-mugger** secret haste.
86 as much containing as full of serious matter.   **88 Feeds . . . clouds** feeds his resentment
or shocked grievance, holds himself inscrutable and aloof amid all this rumor.   **89 wants** lacks;
buzzers gossipers, informers.   **91 necessity** i.e., the need to invent some plausible explanation;
of matter beggared unprovided with facts.   **92–93 Will . . . ear** will not hesitate to accuse my
(royal) person in everybody's ears.   **94 murdering piece** cannon loaded so as to scatter its shot.
95 Gives . . . death kills me over and over.   **97 Attend** i.e., guard me.   **98 Switzers** Swiss
guards, mercenaries.   **100 overpeering of his list** overflowing its shore, boundary.
101 flats i.e., flatlands near shore;   **impetuous** violent. (Perhaps also with the meaning of
impiteous [*impitious*, Q2], "pitiless.")   **102 head** insurrection.

And, as° the world were now but to begin,
Antiquity forgot, custom not known,   105
The ratifiers and props of every word,°
They cry, "Choose we! Laertes shall be king!"
Caps,° hands, and tongues applaud it to the clouds,
"Laertes shall be king, Laertes king!"

QUEEN: How cheerfully on the false trail they cry!   *A noise within.*   110
    O, this is counter,° you false Danish dogs!

    Enter LAERTES *with others.*

KING: The doors are broke.
LAERTES: Where is this King?—Sirs, stand you all without.
ALL: No, let's come in.
LAERTES: I pray you, give me leave.   115
ALL: We will, we will.
LAERTES: I thank you. Keep the door. [*Exeunt followers.*] O thou vile king,
    Give me my father!
QUEEN [*restraining him*]: Calmly, good Laertes.
LAERTES: That drop of blood that's calm proclaims me bastard,   120
    Cries cuckold to my father, brands the harlot
    Even here, between° the chaste unsmirchèd brow
    Of my true mother.
KING: What is the cause, Laertes,
    That thy rebellion looks so giantlike?
    Let him go, Gertrude. Do not fear our° person.   125
    There's such divinity doth hedge° a king
    That treason can but peep to what it would,°
    Acts little of his will.° Tell me, Laertes,
    Why thou art thus incensed. Let him go, Gertrude.
    Speak, man.
LAERTES: Where is my father?
KING: Dead.   130
QUEEN: But not by him.
KING: Let him demand his fill.
LAERTES: How came he dead? I'll not be juggled with.°
    To hell, allegiance! Vows, to the blackest devil!
    Conscience and grace, to the profoundest pit!
    I dare damnation. To this point I stand,°   135
    That both the worlds I give to negligence,°
    Let come what comes, only I'll be revenged
    Most throughly° for my father.
KING: Who shall stay you?

104 **as** as if.   106 **The ratifiers . . . word** i.e., *antiquity* (or tradition) and *custom* ought
to confirm (*ratify*) and underprop our every word or promise.   108 **Caps** (The caps are
thrown in the air.)   111 **counter** (a hunting term, meaning to follow the trail in a direction
opposite to that which the game has taken.)   122 **between** in the middle of.   125 **fear our**
fear for my.   126 **hedge** protect, as with a surrounding barrier.   127 **can . . . would** can
only peep furtively, as through a barrier, at what it would intend.   128 **Acts . . . will** (but)
performs little of what it intends.   132 **juggled with** cheated, deceived.   135 **To . . . stand**
I am resolved in this.   136 **both . . . negligence** i.e., both this world and the next are of no
consequence to me.   138 **throughly** thoroughly.

LAERTES: My will, not all the world's.°   140
      And for° my means, I'll husband them so well
      They shall go far with little.

KING: Good Laertes,
      If you desire to know the certainty
      Of your dear father, is 't writ in your revenge
      That, swoopstake,° you will draw both friend and foe,   145
      Winner and loser?

LAERTES: None but his enemies.

KING: Will you know them, then?

LAERTES: To his good friends thus wide I'll ope my arms,
      And like the kind life-rendering pelican°   150
      Repast° them with my blood.

KING: Why, now you speak
      Like a good child and a true gentleman.
      That I am guiltless of your father's death,
      And am most sensibly° in grief for it,
      It shall as level° to your judgment 'pear   155
      As day does to your eye.   *A noise within.*

LAERTES: How now, what noise is that?
    Enter OPHELIA.

KING: Let her come in.

LAERTES: O heat, dry up my brains! Tears seven times salt
      Burn out the sense and virtue° of mine eye!
      By heaven, thy madness shall be paid with weight°   160
      Till our scale turn the beam.° O rose of May!
      Dear maid, kind sister, sweet Ophelia!
      O heavens, is 't possible a young maid's wits
      Should be as mortal as an old man's life?
      Nature is fine in° love, and where 'tis fine   165
      It sends some precious instance° of itself
      After the thing it loves.°

OPHELIA: *[Song.]*

    "They bore him barefaced on the bier,
      Hey non nonny, nonny, hey nonny,
    And in his grave rained many a tear—"   170

    Fare you well, my dove!

LAERTES: Hadst thou thy wits and didst persuade° revenge,
      It could not move thus.

---

140 My will . . . world's I'll stop (*stay*) when my will is accomplished, not for anyone
else's.   **141 for** as for.   **145 swoopstake** i.e., indiscriminately. (Literally, taking all stakes
on the gambling table at once. *Draw* is also a gambling term, meaning "taken from.")
150 pelican (refers to the belief that the female pelican fed its young with its own blood.)
151 Repast feed.   **154 sensibly** feelingly.   **155 level** plain.   **159 virtue** faculty, power.
160 paid with weight repaid, avenged equally or more.   **161 beam** crossbar of a balance.
165 fine in refined by.   **166 instance** token.   **167 After . . . loves** i.e., into the grave, along
with Polonius.   **172 persuade** argue cogently for.

OPHELIA: You must sing "A-down a-down," and you "call him a-down-a."° O, how
the wheel° becomes it! It is the false steward° that stole his master's   175
daughter.

LAERTES: This nothing's more than matter.°

OPHELIA: There's rosemary,° that's for remembrance; pray you, love, remember.
And there is pansies;° that's for thoughts.

LAERTES: A document° in madness, thoughts and remembrance fitted.   180

OPHELIA: There's fennel° for you, and columbincs.° There's rue° for you, and
here's some for me; we may call it herb of grace o' Sundays. You must
wear your rue with a difference.° There's a daisy.° I would give you
some violets,° but they withered all when my father died. They say 'a
made a good end—   185

[*Sings.*] "For bonny sweet Robin is all my joy."

LAERTES: Thought° and affliction, passion,° hell itself,
She turns to favor° and to prettiness.

OPHELIA: [*Song.*]

"And will 'a not come again?
And will 'a not come again?   190
    No, no, he is dead.
    Go to thy deathbed,
He never will come again.

"His beard was as white as snow,
All flaxen was his poll.°   195
    He is gone, he is gone,
    And we cast away moan.
God ha' mercy on his soul!"

And of all Christian souls, I pray God. God b' wi' you.

[*Exit, followed by* GERTRUDE.]

LAERTES: Do you see this, O God?   200

KING: Laertes, I must commune with your grief,
Or you deny me right. Go but apart,
Make choice of whom° your wisest friends you will,
And they shall hear and judge twixt you and me.
If by direct or by collateral hand°   205
They find us touched,° we will our kingdom give,

---

174 You . . . a-down-a (Ophelia assigns the singing of refrains, like her own "Hey non nonny,"
to others present.)   **175 wheel** spinning wheel as accompaniment to the song, or refrain;
false steward (The story is unknown.)   **177 This . . . matter** This seeming nonsense is more
eloquent than sane utterance.   **178 rosemary** (used as a symbol of remembrance both at
weddings and at funerals.)   **179 pansies** (emblems of love and courtship; perhaps from
French *pensées*, "thoughts.")   **180 document** instruction, lesson.   **181 fennel** (emblem of
flattery.);   **columbines** (emblems of unchastity or ingratitude.);   **rue** (emblem of repentance—
a signification that is evident in its popular name, *herb of grace.*)   **183 with a difference**
(a device used in heraldry to distinguish one family from another on the coat of arms, here
suggesting that Ophelia and the others have different causes of sorrow and repentance;
perhaps with a play on *rue* in the sense of "ruth," "pity.");   **daisy** (emblem of dissembling,
faithlessness.)   **184 violets** (emblems of faithfulness.)   **187 Thought** melancholy;
passion suffering.   **188 favor** grace, beauty.   **195 poll** head.   **203 whom** whichever of.
205 collateral hand indirect agency.   **206 us touched** me implicated.

Our crown, our life, and all that we call ours
To you in satisfaction; but if not,
Be you content to lend your patience to us,
And we shall jointly labor with your soul   210
To give it due content.

LAERTES: Let this be so.
His means of death, his obscure funeral—
No trophy,° sword, nor hatchment° o'er his bones,
No noble rite, nor formal ostentation°—
Cry to be heard, as 'twere from heaven to earth,   215
That° I must call 't in question.°

KING: So you shall,
And where th' offense is, let the great ax fall.
I pray you, go with me.

Exeunt.

[4.6]

Enter HORATIO *and others.*

HORATIO: What are they that would speak with me?
GENTLEMAN: Seafaring men, sir. They say they have letters for you.
HORATIO: Let them come in.

[*Exit* GENTLEMAN.]

I do not know from what part of the world
I should be greeted, if not from Lord Hamlet.   5

Enter Sailors.

FIRST SAILOR: God bless you, sir.
HORATIO: Let him bless thee too.
FIRST SAILOR: 'A shall, sir, an 't° please him. There's a letter for you, sir—it came
from th' ambassador° that was bound for England—if your name be
Horatio, as I am let to know it is.   [*He gives a letter.*]   10
HORATIO [*reads*]: "Horatio, when thou shalt have overlooked° this, give these fel-
lows some means° to the King; they have letters for him. Ere we were
two days old at sea, a pirate of very warlike appointment° gave us chase.
Finding ourselves too slow of sail, we put on a compelled valor, and in
the grapple I boarded them. On the instant they got clear of our ship, so   15
I alone became their prisoner. They have dealt with me like thieves of
mercy,° but they knew what they did: I am to do a good turn for them.
Let the King have the letters I have sent, and repair° thou to me with as
much speed as thou wouldest fly death. I have words to speak in thine
ear will make thee dumb, yet are they much too light for the bore° of the   20
matter. These good fellows will bring thee where I am. Rosencrantz and
Guildenstern hold their course for England. Of them I have much to tell
thee. Farewell.

---

213 trophy memorial;   **hatchment** tablet displaying the armorial bearings of a deceased
person.   **214 ostentation** ceremony.   **216 That** so that;   **call 't in question** demand
an explanation.   **[4.6] Location: The castle.   8 an 't** if it.   **9 th' ambassador** (evidently
Hamlet. The sailor is being circumspect.)   **11 overlooked** looked over.   **12 means** means
of access.   **13 appointment** equipage.   **16–17 thieves of mercy** merciful thieves.
18 repair come.   **20 bore** caliber, i.e., importance.

He that thou knowest thine, Hamlet."
Come, I will give you way° for these your letters,   25
And do 't the speedier that you may direct me
To him from whom you brought them.   *Exeunt*.

[4.7]

Enter KING *and* LAERTES.

KING: Now must your conscience my acquittance seal,°
    And you must put me in your heart for friend,
    Sith° you have heard, and with a knowing ear,
    That he which hath your noble father slain
    Pursued my life.
LAERTES: It well appears. But tell me   5
    Why you proceeded not against these feats°
    So crimeful and so capital° in nature,
    As by your safety, greatness, wisdom, all things else,
    You mainly° were stirred up.
KING: O, for two special reasons,   10
    Which may to you perhaps seem much unsinewed,°
    But yet to me they're strong. The Queen his mother
    Lives almost by his looks, and for myself—
    My virtue or my plague, be it either which—
    She is so conjunctive° to my life and soul   15
    That, as the star moves not but in his° sphere,°
    I could not but by her. The other motive
    Why to a public count° I might not go
    Is the great love the general gender° bear him,
    Who, dipping all his faults in their affection,   20
    Work° like the spring° that turneth wood to stone,
    Convert his gyves° to graces, so that my arrows,
    Too slightly timbered° for so loud° a wind,
    Would have reverted° to my bow again
    But not where I had aimed them.   25
LAERTES: And so have I a noble father lost,
    A sister driven into desperate terms,°
    Whose worth, if praises may go back° again,
    Stood challenger on mount° of all the age
    For her perfections. But my revenge will come.   30
KING: Break not your sleeps for that. You must not think
    That we are made of stuff so flat and dull

---

25 way means of access.   **[4.7] Location: The castle.**   **1 my acquittance seal** confirm or
acknowledge my innocence.   **3 Sith** since.   **6 feats** acts.   **7 capital** punishable by death.
9 mainly greatly.   **11 unsinewed** weak.   **15 conjunctive** closely united. (An astronomical
metaphor.)   **16 his** its;   **sphere** one of the hollow spheres in which, according to Ptolematic
astronomy, the planets were supposed to move.   **18 count** account, reckoning, indictment.
19 general gender common people.   **21 Work** operate, act;   **spring** i.e., a spring with such
a concentration of lime that it coats a piece of wood with limestone, in effect gilding and
petrifying it.   **22 gyves** fetters (which, gilded by the people's praise, would look like badges
of honor).   **23 slightly timbered** light;   **loud** (suggesting public outcry on Hamlet's behalf).
24 reverted returned.   **27 terms** state, condition.   **28 go back** i.e., recall what she was.
29 on mount set up on high.

That we can let our beard be shook with danger
And think it pastime. You shortly shall hear more.
I loved your father, and we love ourself;　　　　　　　　　　35
And that, I hope, will teach you to imagine—

Enter a MESSENGER *with letters.*

How now? What news?
MESSENGER: Letters, my lord, from Hamlet:
This to Your Majesty, this to the queen.　　　　　　[*He gives letters.*]
KING: From Hamlet? Who brought them?　　　　　　　　　40
MESSENGER: Sailors, my lord, they say. I saw them not.
They were given me by Claudio. He received them
Of him that brought them.
KING:　　　　　　　　　　　Laertes, you shall hear them.—
Leave us.　　　　　　　　　　　　　　　[*Exit* MESSENGER.]
[*He reads.*] "High and mighty, you shall know I am set naked° on your　45
kingdom. Tomorrow shall I beg leave to see your kingly eyes, when I
shall, first asking your pardon,° thereunto recount the occasion of my
sudden and more strange return.　　　　　　　　　　　Hamlet."
What should this mean? Are all the rest come back?
Or is it some abuse,° and no such thing?°　　　　　　　　　50
LAERTES: Know you the hand?
KING:　　　　　　　　　'Tis Hamlet's character.° "Naked!"
And in a postscript here he says "alone."
Can you devise° me?
LAERTES: I am lost in it, my lord. But let him come.
It warms the very sickness in my heart　　　　　　　　　55
That I shall live and tell him to his teeth,
"Thus didst thou."°
KING:　　　　　　　　　　If it be so, Laertes—
As how should it be so? How otherwise?°—
Will you be ruled by me?
LAERTES:　　　　　　　　　　　Ay, my lord,
So° you will not o'errule me to a peace.　　　　　　　　　60
KING: To thine own peace. If he be now returned,
As checking at° his voyage, and that° he means
No more to undertake it, I will work him
To an exploit, now ripe in my device,°
Under the which he shall not choose but fall;　　　　　　　65
And for his death no wind of blame shall breathe,
But even his mother shall uncharge the practice°
And call it accident.

---

45 naked destitute, unarmed, without following.　**47 pardon** permission.　**50 abuse** deceit;
no such thing not what it appears.　**51 character** handwriting.　**53 devise** explain to.
57 Thus didst thou i.e., here's for what you did to my father.　**58 As . . . otherwise** How
can this (Hamlet's return) be true? Yet how otherwise than true (since we have the evidence
of his letter)?　**60 So** provided that.　**62 checking at** i.e., turning aside from (like a falcon
leaving the quarry to fly at a chance bird);　**that** if.　**64 device** devising, invention.
67 uncharge the practice acquit the stratagem of being a plot.

LAERTES: My lord, I will be ruled,
          The rather if you could devise it so
          That I might be the organ.°
KING: It falls right.   70
          You have been talked of since your travel much,
          And that in Hamlet's hearing, for a quality
          Wherein they say you shine. Your sum of parts°
          Did not together pluck such envy from him
          As did that one, and that, in my regard,   75
          Of the unworthiest siege.°
LAERTES: What part is that, my lord?
KING: A very ribbon in the cap of youth,
          Yet needful too, for youth no less becomes°
          The light and careless livery that it wears   80
          Than settled age his sables° and his weeds°
          Importing health and graveness.° Two months since
          Here was a gentleman of Normandy.
          I have seen myself, and served against, the French,
          And they can well° on horseback, but this gallant   85
          Had witchcraft in 't; he grew unto his seat,
          And to such wondrous doing brought his horse
          As had he been incorpsed and demi-natured°
          With the brave beast. So far he topped° my thought
          That I in forgery° of shapes and tricks   90
          Come short of what he did.
LAERTES: A Norman was 't?
KING: A Norman.
LAERTES: Upon my life, Lamord.
KING: The very same.
LAERTES: I know him well. He is the brooch° indeed
          And gem of all the nation.   95
KING: He made confession° of you,
          And gave you such a masterly report
          For art and exercise in your defense,°
          And for your rapier most especial,
          That he cried out 'twould be a sight indeed   100
          If one could match you. Th' escrimers° of their nation,
          He swore, had neither motion, guard, nor eye
          If you opposed them. Sir, this report of his
          Did Hamlet so envenom with his envy
          That he could nothing do but wish and beg   105
          Your sudden° coming o'er, to play° with you.
          Now, out of this—

---

70 organ agent, instrument.   **73 Your . . . parts** i.e., all your other virtues.   **76 unworthiest siege** least important rank.   **79 no less becomes** is no less suited by.   **81 his sables** its rich robes furred with sable;   **weeds** garments.   **82 Importing . . . graveness** signifying a concern for health and dignified prosperity; also, giving an impression of comfortable prosperity.   **85 can well** are skilled.   **88 As . . . demi-natured** as if he had been of one body and nearly of one nature (like the centaur).   **89 topped** surpassed.   **90 forgery** imagining.   **94 brooch** ornament.   **96 confession** testimonial, admission of superiority.   **98 For . . . defense** with respect to your skill and practice with your weapon.   **101 escrimers** fencers.   **106 sudden** immediate;   **play** fence.

LAERTES: What out of this, my lord?

KING: Laertes, was your father dear to you?
        Or are you like the painting of a sorrow,
        A face without a heart?

LAERTES: Why ask you this?   110

KING: Not that I think you did not love your father,
        But that I know love is begun by time,°
        And that I see, in passages of proof,°
        Time qualifies° the spark and fire of it.
        There lives within the very flame of love   115
        A kind of wick or snuff° that will abate it,
        And nothing is at a like goodness still,°
        For goodness, growing to a pleurisy,°
        Dies in his own too much.° That° we would do,
        We should do when we would; for this "would" changes   120
        And hath abatements° and delays as many
        As there are tongues, are hands, are accidents,°
        And then this "should" is like a spendthrift sigh,°
        That hurts by easing.° But, to the quick o' th' ulcer:°
        Hamlet comes back. What would you undertake   125
        To show yourself in deed your father's son
        More than in words?

LAERTES: To cut his throat i' the church.

KING: No place, indeed, should murder sanctuarize;°
        Revenge should have no bounds. But good Laertes,
        Will you do this,° keep close within your chamber.   130
        Hamlet returned shall know you are come home.
        We'll put on those shall° praise your excellence
        And set a double varnish on the fame
        The Frenchman gave you, bring you in fine° together,
        And wager on your heads. He, being remiss,°   135
        Most generous,° and free from all contriving,
        Will not peruse the foils, so that with ease,
        Or with a little shuffling, you may choose
        A sword unbated,° and in a pass of practice°
        Requite him for your father.

---

112 begun by time i.e., created by the right circumstance and hence subject to change.
113 passages of proof actual instances that prove it.   **114 qualifies** weakens, moderates.
116 snuff the charred part of a candlewick.   **117 nothing . . . still** nothing remains at a
constant level of perfection.   **118 pleurisy** excess, plethora. (Literally, a chest inflammation.)
119 in . . . much of its own excess;   **That** that which.   **121 abatements** diminutions.
122 As . . . accidents as there are tongues to dissuade, hands to prevent, and chance events
to intervene.   **123 spendthrift sigh** (an allusion to the belief that sighs draw blood from
the heart.)   **124 hurts by easing** i.e., costs the heart blood and wastes precious opportunity
even while it affords emotional relief;   **quick o' th' ulcer** i.e., heart of the matter.
128 sanctuarize protect from punishment. (Alludes to the right of sanctuary with which
certain religious places were invested.)   **130 Will you do this** if you wish to do this.
132 put on those shall arrange for some to.   **134 in fine** finally.   **135 remiss** negligently
unsuspicious.   **136 generous** noble-minded.   **139 unbated** not blunted, having no button;
pass of practice treacherous thrust.

LAERTES: I will do 't,   140
    And for that purpose I'll anoint my sword.
    I bought an unction° of a mountebank°
    So mortal that, but dip a knife in it,
    Where it draws blood no cataplasm° so rare,
    Collected from all simples° that have virtue°   145
    Under the moon,° can save the thing from death
    That is but scratched withal. I'll touch my point
    With this contagion, that if I gall° him slightly,
    It may be death.
KING: Let's further think of this,   150
    Weigh what convenience both of time and means
    May fit us to our shape.° If this should fail,
    And that our drift look through our bad performance,°
    'Twere better not assayed. Therefore this project
    Should have a back or second, that might hold   155
    If this did blast in proof.° Soft, let me see.
    We'll make a solemn wager on your cunnings°—
    I ha 't!
    When in your motion you are hot and dry—
    As° make your bouts more violent to that end—   160
    And that he calls for drink, I'll have prepared him
    A chalice for the nonce,° whereon but sipping,
    If he by chance escape your venomed stuck,°
    Our purpose may hold there. [*A cry within.*] But stay, what noise?

    Enter QUEEN.

QUEEN: One woe doth tread upon another's heel,   165
    So fast they follow. Your sister's drowned, Laertes.
LAERTES: Drowned! O, where?
QUEEN: There is a willow grows askant° the brook,
    That shows his hoar leaves° in the glassy stream;
    Therewith fantastic garlands did she make   170
    Of crowflowers, nettles, daisies, and long purples,°
    That liberal° shepherds give a grosser name,°
    But our cold° maids do dead men's fingers call them.
    There on the pendent° boughs her crownet° weeds
    Clamb'ring to hang, an envious sliver° broke,   175
    When down her weedy° trophies and herself

142 **unction** ointment; **mountebank** quack doctor.   144 **cataplasm** plaster or poultice.
145 **simples** herbs; **virtue** potency.   146 **Under the moon** i.e., anywhere (with reference
perhaps to the belief that herbs gathered at night had a special power).   148 **gall** graze,
wound.   152 **shape** part we propose to act.   153 **drift . . . performance** intention should
be made visible by our bungling.   156 **blast in proof** burst in the test (like a cannon).
157 **cunnings** respective skills.   160 **As** i.e., and you should.   162 **nonce** occasion.
163 **stuck** thrust. (From *stoccado,* a fencing term.)   168 **askant** aslant.   169 **hoar leaves**
white or gray undersides of the leaves.   171 **long purples** early purple orchids.   172 **liberal**
free-spoken;   **a grosser name** (the testicle-resembling tubers of the orchid, which also in
some cases resemble *dead men's fingers,* have earned various slang names like "dogstones"
and "cullions.")   173 **cold** chaste.   174 **pendent** over-hanging;   **crownet** made into a
chaplet or coronet.   175 **envious sliver** malicious branch.   176 **weedy** i.e., of plants.

Fell in the weeping brook. Her clothes spread wide,
And mermaidlike awhile they bore her up,
Which time she chanted snatches of old lauds,°
As one incapable of° her own distress,   180
Or like a creature native and endued°
Unto that element. But long it could not be
Till that her garments, heavy with their drink,
Pulled the poor wretch from her melodious lay
To muddy death.

LAERTES: Alas, then she is drowned?   185
QUEEN: Drowned, drowned.
LAERTES: Too much of water hast thou, poor Ophelia,
And therefore I forbid my tears. But yet
It is our trick;° nature her custom holds,
Let shame say what it will. [*He weeps.*] When these are gone,   190
The woman will be out.° Adieu, my lord.
I have a speech of fire that fain would blaze,
But that this folly douts° it.   *Exit.*
KING: Let's follow, Gertrude.
How much I had to do to calm his rage!
Now fear I this will give it start again;   195
Therefore let's follow.   *Exeunt.*

[5.1]

Enter two CLOWNS° [*with spades and mattocks*].

FIRST CLOWN: Is she to be buried in Christian burial, when she willfully seeks her own salvation?°
SECOND CLOWN: I tell thee she is; therefore make her grave straight.° The crowner° hath sat on her,° and finds it° Christian burial.
FIRST CLOWN: How can that be, unless she drowned herself in her own defense?   5
SECOND CLOWN: Why, 'tis found so.°
FIRST CLOWN: It must be *se offendendo*,° it cannot be else. For here lies the point: if I drown myself wittingly, it argues an act, and an act hath three branches—it is to act, to do, and to perform. Argal,° she drowned herself wittingly.   10
SECOND CLOWN: Nay, but hear you, goodman° delver—
FIRST CLOWN: Give me leave. Here lies the water; good. Here stands the man; good. If the man go to this water and drown himself, it is, will he, nill he,° he goes, mark you that. But if the water come to him and drown him, he drowns not himself. Argal, he that is not guilty of his own death shortens   15
not his own life.

179 lauds hymns.   **180 incapable of** lacking capacity to apprehend.   **181 endued** adapted by nature.   **189 It is our trick** i.e., weeping is our natural way (when sad).   **190–91 When . . . out** When my tears are all shed, the woman in me will be expended, satisfied.   **193 douts** extinguishes. (The Second Quarto reads "drowns.")   **[5.1] Location:** A churchyard.   **s.d. Clowns** rustics.
2 salvation (a blunder for "damnation," or perhaps a suggestion that Ophelia was taking her own shortcut to heaven.)   **3 straight** straightway, immediately. (But with a pun on *strait*, "narrow.")
4 crowner coroner;   **sat on her** conducted an inquest on her case;   **finds it** gives his official verdict that her means of death was consistent with.   **6 found so** determined so in the coroner's verdict.   **7 se offendendo** (a comic mistake for *se defendendo*, a term used in verdicts of justifiable homicide.)   **9 Argal** (corruption of *ergo*, "therefore.")   **11 goodman** (an honorific title often used with the name of a profession or craft.)   **13 will he, nill he** whether he will or no, willy-nilly.

SECOND CLOWN: But is this law?

FIRST CLOWN: Ay, marry, is 't—crowner's quest° law.

SECOND CLOWN: Will you ha' the truth on 't? If this had not been a gentlewoman, she should have been buried out o' Christian burial.   20

FIRST CLOWN: Why, there thou sayst.° And the more pity that great folk should have countenance° in this world to drown or hang themselves, more than their even-Christian.° Come, my spade. There is no ancient° gentlemen but gardeners, ditchers, and grave makers. They hold up° Adam's profession.

SECOND CLOWN: Was he a gentleman?   25

FIRST CLOWN: 'A was the first that ever bore arms.°

SECOND CLOWN: Why, he had none.

FIRST CLOWN: What, art a heathen? How dost thou understand the Scripture? The Scripture says Adam digged. Could he dig without arms?° I'll put another question to thee. If thou answerest me not to the purpose, confess   30
thyself°—

SECOND CLOWN: Go to.

FIRST CLOWN: What is he that builds stronger than either the mason, the shipwright, or the carpenter?

SECOND CLOWN: The gallows maker, for that frame° outlives a thousand tenants.   35

FIRST CLOWN: I like thy wit well, in good faith. The gallows does well.° But how does it well? It does well to those that do ill. Now thou dost ill to say the gallows is built stronger than the church. Argal, the gallows may do well to thee. To 't again, come.

SECOND CLOWN: "Who builds stronger than a mason, a shipwright, or a carpenter?"   40

FIRST CLOWN: Ay, tell me that, and unyoke.°

SECOND CLOWN: Marry, now I can tell.

FIRST CLOWN: To 't.

SECOND CLOWN: Mass,° I cannot tell.

Enter HAMLET *and* HORATIO [*at a distance*].

FIRST CLOWN: Cudgel thy brains no more about it, for your dull ass will not mend   45
his pace with beating; and when you are asked this question next, say "a grave maker." The houses he makes lasts till doomsday. Go get thee in and fetch me a stoup° of liquor.

[*Exit* SECOND CLOWN: FIRST CLOWN *digs*.]

Song.

"In youth, when I did love, did love,°
    Methought it was very sweet,   50
To contract—O—the time for—a—my behove,°
    O, methought there—a—was nothing—a—meet."°

18 quest inquest.   **21 there thou sayst** i.e., that's right.   **22 countenance** privilege.   **23 even-Christian** fellow christians;   **ancient** going back to ancient times.   **24 hold up** maintain.
26 bore arms (to be entitled to bear a coat of arms would make Adam a gentleman, but as one who bore a spade, our common ancestor was an ordinary delver in the earth.)
29 arms i.e., the arms of the body.   **31 confess thyself** (the saying continues, "and be hanged.")   **35 frame** (1) gallows, (2) structure.   **36 does well** (1) is an apt answer, (2) does a good turn.   **41 unyoke** i.e., after this great effort, you may unharness the team of your wits.
44 Mass by the Mass.   **48 stoup** two-quart measure.   **49 In . . . love** (This and the two following stanzas, with nonsensical variations, are from a poem attributed to lord Vaux and printed in *Tottel's Miscellany*, 1557. The O and a [for "ah"] seemingly are the grunts of the digger.)
51 To contract . . . behove i.e., to shorten the time for my own advantage. (Perhaps he means to *prolong* it.)   **52 meet** suitable, i.e., more suitable.

HAMLET: Has this fellow no feeling of his business, 'a° sings in gravemaking?
HORATIO: Custom hath made it in him a property of easiness.°
HAMLET: 'Tis e'en so. The hand of little employment hath the daintier sense.°   55
FIRST CLOWN: *Song.*

> "But age with his stealing steps
>   Hath clawed me in his clutch,
> And hath shipped me into the land,°
>   As if I had never been such."   [*He throws up a skull.*]

HAMLET: That skull had a tongue in it and could sing once. How the knave jowls°   60
    it to the ground, as if 'twere Cain's jawbone, that did the first murder! This
    might be the pate of a politician,° which this ass now o'erreaches,°
    one that would circumvent God, might it not?
HORATIO: It might, my lord.
HAMLET: Or of a courtier, which could say, "Good morrow, sweet lord! How dost   65
    thou, sweet lord?" This might be my Lord Such-a-one, that praised my
    Lord Such-a-one's horse when 'a meant to beg it, might it not?
HORATIO: Ay, my lord.
HAMLET: Why, e'en so, and now my Lady Worm's, chapless,° and knocked about
    the mazard° with a sexton's spade. Here's fine revolution,° an° we had   70
    the trick to see° 't. Did these bones cost no more the breeding but to°
    play at loggets° with them? Mine ache to think on 't.
FIRST CLOWN: *Song.*

> "A pickax and a spade, a spade,
>   For and° a shrouding sheet;
> O, a pit of clay for to be made   75
>   For such a guest is meet."   [*He throws up another skull.*]

HAMLET: There's another. Why may not that be the skull of a lawyer? Where be
    his quiddities° now, his quillities,° his cases, his tenures,° and his tricks?
    Why does he suffer this mad knave now to knock him about the sconce°
    with a dirty shovel, and will not tell him of his action of battery?° Hum,   80
    this fellow might be in 's time a great buyer of land, with his statutes, his
    recognizances,° his fines, his double° vouchers,° his recoveries.° Is this
    the fine of his fines and the recovery of his recoveries, to have his fine

---

53 'a that he.   **54 property of easiness** something he can do easily and indifferently.
55 daintier sense more delicate sense of feeling.   **58 into the land** i.e., toward my grave (?)
(But note the lack of rhyme in *steps, land*.)   **60 jowls** dashes (with a pun on *jowl*, "jawbone").
62 politician schemer, plotter;   **o'erreaches** circumvents, gets the better of (with a quibble
on the literal sense).   **69 chapless** having no lower jaw.   **70 mazard** i.e., head (Literally, a
drinking vessel.);   **revolution** turn of Fortune's wheel, change;   **an** if.   **71 trick to see** knack
of seeing;   **cost . . . to** involve so little expense and care in upbringing that we may.
72 loggets a game in which pieces of hard wood shaped like Indian clubs or bowling pins
are thrown to lie as near as possible to a stake.   **74 For and** and moreover.   **78 quiddities**
subtleties, quibbles. (From Latin *quid*, "a thing.");   **quillities** verbal niceties, subtle distinc-
tions. (Variation of *quiddities*.);   **tenures** the holding of a piece of property or office, or the
conditions or period of such holding.   **79 sconce** head.   **80 action of battery** lawsuit about
physical assault.   **81–82 statutes, recognizances** legal documents guaranteeing a debt by
attaching land and property.   **82 fines, recoveries** ways of converting entailed estates into
"fee simple" or freehold;   **double** signed by two signatories;   **vouchers** guarantees of the
legality of a title to real estate.

pate full of fine dirt?° Will his vouchers vouch him no more of his purchases, and double ones too, than the length and breadth of a pair of
indentures?° The very conveyances° of his lands will scarcely lie in this
box,° and must th' inheritor° himself have no more, ha?

HORATIO: Not a jot more, my lord.

HAMLET: Is not parchment made of sheepskins?

HORATIO: Ay, my lord, and of calves' skins too.

HAMLET: They are sheep and calves which seek out assurance in that.° I will
    speak to this fellow.—Whose grave's this, sirrah?°

FIRST CLOWN: Mine, sir.   [*Sings.*]
    "O, pit of clay for to be made
    For such a guest is meet."

HAMLET: I think it be thine, indeed, for thou liest in 't.

FIRST CLOWN: You lie out on 't, sir, and therefore 'tis not yours. For my part, I do
    not lie in 't, yet it is mine.

HAMLET: Thou dost lie in 't, to be in 't and say it is thine. 'Tis for the dead, not for
    the quick;° therefore thou liest.

FIRST CLOWN: 'Tis a quick lie, sir; 'twill away again from me to you.

HAMLET: What man dost thou dig it for?

FIRST CLOWN: For no man, sir.

HAMLET: What woman, then?

FIRST CLOWN: For none, neither.

HAMLET: Who is to be buried in 't?

FIRST CLOWN: One that was a woman, sir, but, rest her soul, she's dead.

HAMLET: How absolute° the knave is! We must speak by the card,° or equivoca-
    tion° will undo us. By the Lord, Horatio, this three years I have took°
    note of it: the age is grown so picked° that the toe of the peasant comes
    so near the heel of the courtier, he galls his kibe.°—How long hast thou
    been grave maker?

FIRST CLOWN: Of all the days i' the year, I came to 't that day that our last king
    Hamlet overcame Fortinbras.

HAMLET: How long is that since?

FIRST CLOWN: Cannot you tell that? Every fool can tell that. It was that very day
    that young Hamlet was born—he that is mad and sent into England.

HAMLET: Ay, marry, why was he sent into England?

FIRST CLOWN: Why, because 'a was mad. 'A shall recover his wits there, or if 'a do
    not, 'tis no great matter there.

HAMLET: Why?

FIRST CLOWN: 'Twill not be seen in him there. There the men are as mad as he.

HAMLET: How came he mad?

83–84 fine of his fines . . . fine pate . . . fine dirt end of his legal maneuvers . . . elegant
head . . . minutely sifted dirt.   **85–86 pair of indentures** legal document drawn up in
duplicate on a single sheet and then cut apart on a zigzag line so that each pair was uniquely
matched. (Hamlet may refer to two rows of teeth or dentures.)   **86 conveyances** deeds.
87 box (1) deed box, (2) coffin. ("Skull" has been suggested.);   **inheritor** possessor,
owner.   **91 assurance in that** safety in legal parchments.   **92 sirrah** (a term of address
to inferiors.)   **100 quick** living.   **108 absolute** strict, precise;   **by the card** i.e., with
precision. (Literally, by the mariner's compass-card, on which the points of the compass
were marked.)   **108–09 equivocation** ambiguity in the use of terms.   **109 took** taken.
110 picked refined, fastidious.   **111 galls his kibe** chafes the courtier's chilblain.

FIRST CLOWN: Very strangely, they say.

HAMLET: How strangely?   125

FIRST CLOWN: Faith, e'en with losing his wits.

HAMLET: Upon what ground?°

FIRST CLOWN: Why, here in Denmark. I have been sexton here, man and boy,
    thirty years.

HAMLET: How long will a man lie i' th' earth ere he rot?   130

FIRST CLOWN: Faith, if 'a be not rotten before 'a die—as we have many pocky°
    corpses nowadays, that will scarce hold the laying in°—'a will last you°
    some eight year or nine year. A tanner will last you nine year.

HAMLET: Why he more than another?

FIRST CLOWN: Why, sir, his hide is so tanned with his trade that 'a will keep out   135
    water a great while, and your water is a sore° decayer of your whoreson°
    dead body. [*He picks up a skull.*] Here's a skull now hath lien you° i' th'
    earth three-and-twenty years.

HAMLET: Whose was it?

FIRST CLOWN: A whoreson mad fellow's it was. Whose do you think it was?   140

HAMLET: Nay, I know not.

FIRST CLOWN: A pestilence on him for a mad rogue! 'A poured a flagon of
    Rhenish° on my head once. This same skull, sir, was, sir, Yorick's skull,
    the King's jester.

HAMLET: This?   145

FIRST CLOWN: E'en that.

HAMLET: Let me see. [*He takes the skull.*] Alas, poor Yorick! I knew him, Horatio, a
    fellow of infinite jest, of most excellent fancy. He hath bore° me on his
    back a thousand times, and now how abhorred in my imagination it is!
    My gorge rises° at it. Here hung those lips that I have kissed I know not   150
    how oft. Where be your gibes now? Your gambols, your songs, your
    flashes of merriment that were wont° to set the table on a roar? Not one
    now, to mock your own grinning?° Quite chopfallen?° Now get you to
    my lady's chamber and tell her, let her paint an inch thick, to this favor°
    she must come. Make her laugh at that. Prithee, Horatio, tell me one thing.   155

HORATIO: What's that, my lord?

HAMLET: Dost thou think Alexander looked o' this fashion i' th' earth?

HORATIO: E'en so.

HAMLET: And smelt so? Pah! [*He throws down the skull.*]

HORATIO: E'en so, my lord.   160

HAMLET: To what base uses we may return, Horatio! Why may not imagination
    trace the noble dust of Alexander till 'a find it stopping a bunghole?°

HORATIO: 'Twere to consider too curiously° to consider so.

---

127 ground cause. (But, in the next line, the gravedigger takes the word in the sense of
"land," "country.")   **131 pocky** rotten, diseased. (Literally, with the pox, or syphilis.)
132 hold the laying in hold together long enough to be interred;   **last you** last. (*You* is
used colloquially here and in the following lines.)   **136 sore** i.e., terrible, great;   **whoreson**
i.e., vile, scurvy.   **137 lien you** lain. (See the note at line 132.)   **143 Rhenish** Rhine wine.
148 bore borne.   **150 My gorge rises** i.e., I feel nauseated.   **152 were wont** used.
153 mock your own grinning mock at the way your skull seems to be grinning (just as
you used to mock at yourself and those who grinned at you);   **chopfallen** (1) lacking the
lower jaw, (2) dejected.   **154 favor** aspect, appearance.   **162 bunghole** hole for filling or
emptying a cask.   **163 curiously** minutely.

HAMLET: No, faith, not a jot, but to follow him thither with modesty° enough, and
 likelihood to lead it. As thus: Alexander died, Alexander was buried, 165
 Alexander returneth to dust, the dust is earth, of earth we make loam,° and
 why of that loam whereto he was converted might they not stop a beer
 barrel?

  Imperious° Caesar, dead and turned to clay,
 Might stop a hole to keep the wind away. 170
 O, that that earth which kept the world in awe
 Should patch a wall t' expel the winter's flaw!°

Enter KING, QUEEN, LAERTES, *and the corpse* [*of* OPHELIA, *in procession, with*
PRIEST, *lords, etc.*].

 But soft,° but soft awhile! Here comes the King,
 The Queen, the courtiers. Who is this they follow?
 And with such maimèd° rites? This doth betoken 175
 The corpse they follow did with desperate hand
 Fordo° its own life. 'Twas of some estate.°
 Couch we° awhile and mark.

[*He and* HORATIO *conceal themselves.* OPHELIA*'s body is taken to the grave.*]

LAERTES: What ceremony else?
HAMLET [*to* HORATIO]: That is Laertes, a very noble youth. Mark. 180
LAERTES: What ceremony else?
PRIEST: Her obsequies have been as far enlarged
 As we have warranty.° Her death was doubtful,
 And but that great command o'ersways the order°
 She should in ground unsanctified been lodged° 185
 Till the last trumpet. For° charitable prayers,
 Shards,° flints, and pebbles should be thrown on her.
 Yet here she is allowed her virgin crants,°
 Her maiden strewments,° and the bringing home
 Of bell and burial.° 190
LAERTES: Must there no more be done?
PRIEST: No more be done.
 We should profane the service of the dead
 To sing a requiem and such rest° to her
 As to peace-parted souls.°
LAERTES: Lay her i' th' earth,
 And from her fair and unpolluted flesh 195
 May violets° spring! I tell thee, churlish priest,

---

164 modesty plausible moderation. **166 loam** mortar consisting chiefly of moistened clay
and straw. **169 Imperious** imperial. **172 flaw** gust of wind. **173 soft** i.e., wait, be careful.
175 maimèd mutilated, incomplete. **177 Fordo** destroy; **estate** rank. **178 Couch we**
let's hide, lie low. **183 warranty** i.e., ecclesiastical authority. **184 great . . . order** orders
from on high overrule the prescribed procedures. **185 She should . . . lodged** she should
have been buried in unsanctified ground. **186 For** in place of. **187 Shards** broken bits of
pottery. **188 crants** garlands betokening maidenhood. **189 strewments** flowers strewn on
a coffin. **189–90 bringing . . . burial** laying the body to rest, to the sound of the bell.
193 such rest i.e., to pray for such rest. **194 peace-parted souls** those who have died at
peace with god. **196 violets** (see 4.5.184 and note.)

A ministering angel shall my sister be
When thou liest howling.°
HAMLET [*to* HORATIO]:   What, the fair Ophelia!
QUEEN [*scattering flowers*]: Sweets to the sweet! Farewell.
    I hoped thou shouldst have been my Hamlet's wife.   200
    I thought thy bride-bed to have decked, sweet maid,
    And not t' have strewed thy grave.
LAERTES: O, treble woe
    Fall ten times treble on that cursèd head
    Whose wicked deed thy most ingenious sense°
    Deprived thee of! Hold off the earth awhile,   205
    Till I have caught her once more in mine arms.

[*He leaps into the grave and embraces* OPHELIA.]

    Now pile your dust upon the quick and dead,
    Till of this flat a mountain you have made
    T' o'ertop old Pelion or the skyish head
    Of blue Olympus.°   210
HAMLET [*coming forward*]: What is he whose grief
    Bears such an emphasis,° whose phrase of sorrow
    Conjures the wandering stars° and makes them stand
    Like wonder-wounded° hearers? This is I,
    Hamlet the Dane.°   215
LAERTES [*grappling with him*°]: The devil take thy soul!
HAMLET: Thou pray'st not well.
    I prithee, take thy fingers from my throat,
    For though I am not splenitive° and rash,
    Yet have I in me something dangerous,   220
    Which let thy wisdom fear. Hold off thy hand.
KING: Pluck them asunder.
QUEEN: Hamlet, Hamlet!
ALL: Gentlemen!
HORATIO: Good my lord, be quiet.   225

[HAMLET *and* LAERTES *are parted.*]

HAMLET: Why, I will fight with him upon this theme
    Until my eyelids will no longer wag.°
QUEEN: O my son, what theme?
HAMLET: I loved Ophelia. Forty thousand brothers
    Could not with all their quantity of love   230
    Make up my sum. What wilt thou do for her?

198 howling i.e., in hell.   **204 ingenious sense** a mind that is quick, alert, of fine qualities.
209–10 Pelion, Olympus sacred mountains in the north of Thessaly; see also *Ossa*, below, at
line 243.   **212 emphasis** i.e., rhetorical and florid emphasis. (*Phrase* has a similar rhetorical
connotation.)   **213 wandering stars** planets.   **214 wonder-wounded** struck with amazement.
215 the Dane (This title normally signifies the king; see 1.1.17 and note.)   **s.d. grappling
with him** (The testimony of the First Quarto that "*Hamlet leaps in after Laertes*" and the "Elegy
on Burbage" ("Oft have I seen him leap into the grave") seem to indicate one way in which
this fight was staged; however, the difficulty of fitting two contenders and Ophelia's body
into a confined space (probably the trapdoor) suggests to many editors the alternative, that
Laertes jumps out of the grave to attack Hamlet.)   **219 splenitive** quick-tempered.   **227 wag**
move. (A fluttering eyelid is a conventional sign that life has not yet gone.)

KING: O, he is mad, Laertes.

QUEEN: For love of God, forbear him.°

HAMLET: 'Swounds,° show me what thou'lt do.

> Woo't° weep? Woo't fight? Woo't fast? Woo't tear thyself?   235
> Woo't drink up° eisel?° Eat a crocodile?°
> I'll do 't. Dost come here to whine?
> To outface me with leaping in her grave?
> Be buried quick° with her, and so will I.
> And if thou prate of mountains, let them throw   240
> Millions of acres on us, till our ground,
> Singeing his pate° against the burning zone,°
> Make Ossa° like a wart! Nay, an° thou'lt mouth,°
> I'll rant as well as thou.

QUEEN: This is mere° madness,

> And thus awhile the fit will work on him;   245
> Anon, as patient as the female dove
> When that her golden couplets° are disclosed,°
> His silence will sit drooping.

HAMLET: Hear you, sir,

> What is the reason that you use me thus?
> I loved you ever. But it is no matter.   250
> Let Hercules himself do what he may,
> The cat will mew, and dog will have his day.°   *Exit* HAMLET.

KING: I pray thee, good Horatio, wait upon him.   [*Exit*] HORATIO.

> [*To* LAERTES.] Strengthen your patience in° our last night's speech;
> We'll put the matter to the present push.°—   255
> Good Gertrude, set some watch over your son.—
> This grave shall have a living° monument.
> An hour of quiet° shortly shall we see;
> Till then, in patience our proceeding be.   *Exeunt.*

[5.2]

Enter HAMLET *and* HORATIO.

HAMLET: So much for this, sir; now shall you see the other.°

> You do remember all the circumstance?

HORATIO: Remember it, my lord!

---

233 forbear him leave him alone.   **234 'Swounds** by His (christ's) wounds.   **235 Woo't** wilt thou.   **236 drink up** drink deeply;   **eisel** vinegar;   **crocodile** (Crocodiles were tough and dangerous, and were supposed to shed hypocritical tears.)   **239 quick** alive.   **242 his pate** its head, i.e., top;   **burning zone** zone in the celestial sphere containing the sun's orbit, between the tropics of Cancer and Capricorn.   **243 Ossa** another mountain in Thessaly. (In their war against the Olympian gods, the giants attempted to heap Ossa on Pelion to scale Olympus.);   **an** if;   **mouth** i.e., rant.   **244 mere** utter.   **247 golden couplets** two baby pigeons, covered with yellow down;   **disclosed** hatched.   **251–52 Let . . . day** i.e., (1) even Hercules couldn't stop laertes' theatrical rant, (2) I, too, will have my turn; i.e., despite any blustering attempts at interference, every person will sooner or later do what he or she must do.   **254 in** i.e., by recalling.   **255 present push** immediate test.   **257 living** lasting. (For Laertes' private understanding, claudius also hints that Hamlet's death will serve as such a monument.)   **258 hour of quiet** time free of conflict.   **[5.2] Location:** The castle. **1 see the other** hear the other news.

HAMLET: Sir, in my heart there was a kind of fighting
        That would not let me sleep. Methought I lay   5
        Worse than the mutines° in the bilboes.° Rashly,°
        And praised be rashness for it—let us know°
        Our indiscretion° sometimes serves us well
        When our deep plots do pall,° and that should learn° us
        There's a divinity that shapes our ends,   10
        Rough-hew° them how we will—

HORATIO: That is most certain.

HAMLET: Up from my cabin,
        My sea-gown° scarfed° about me, in the dark
        Groped I to find out them,° had my desire,
        Fingered° their packet, and in fine° withdrew   15
        To mine own room again, making so bold,
        My fears forgetting manners, to unseal
        Their grand commission; where I found, Horatio—
        Ah, royal knavery!—an exact command,
        Larded° with many several° sorts of reasons   20
        Importing° Denmark's health and England's too,
        With, ho! such bugs° and goblins in my life,°
        That on the supervise,° no leisure bated,°
        No, not to stay° the grinding of the ax,
        My head should be struck off.

HORATIO: Is't possible?   25

HAMLET [*giving a document*]:
        Here's the commission. Read it at more leisure.
        But wilt thou hear now how I did proceed?

HORATIO: I beseech you.

HAMLET: Being thus benetted round with villainies—
        Ere I could make a prologue to my brains,   30
        They had begun the play°—I sat me down,
        Devised a new commission, wrote it fair.°
        I once did hold it, as our statists° do,
        A baseness° to write fair, and labored much
        How to forget that learning; but, sir, now   35
        It did me yeoman's° service. Wilt thou know
        Th' effect° of what I wrote?

HORATIO: Ay, good my lord.

HAMLET: An earnest conjuration° from the King,
        As England was his faithful tributary,

6 mutines mutineers; **bilboes** shackles; **Rashly** on impulse. (This adverb goes with line 13)
7 know acknowledge **8 indiscretion** lack of foresight and judgment (not an indiscreet act).
9 pall fail, falter, go stale; **learn** teach. **11 Rough-hew** shape roughly. **13 sea-gown** seaman's coat; **scarfed** loosely wrapped. **14 them** i.e., Rosencrantz and Guildenstern.
15 Fingered pilfered, pinched; **in fine** finally, in conclusion. **20 Larded** garnished;
several different. **21 Importing** relating to. **22 bugs** bugbears, hobgoblins; **in my life** i.e.,
to be feared if I were allowed to live. **23 supervise** reading; **leisure bated** delay allowed.
24 stay await. **30–31 Ere . . . play** before I could consciously turn my brain to the matter, it
had started working on a plan. **32 fair** in a clear hand. **33 statists** statesmen. **34 baseness**
i.e., lower-class trait. **36 yeoman's** i.e., substantial, faithful, loyal. **37 effect** purport.
38 conjuration entreaty.

As love between them like the palm° might flourish,   40
As peace should still° her wheaten garland° wear
And stand a comma° 'tween their amities,
And many suchlike "as"es° of great charge,°
That on the view and knowing of these contents,
Without debatement further more or less,   45
He should those bearers put to sudden death,
Not shriving time° allowed.

HORATIO: How was this sealed?

HAMLET: Why, even in that was heaven ordinant.°
I had my father's signet° in my purse,
Which was the model° of that Danish seal;   50
Folded the writ° up in the form of th' other,
Subscribed° it, gave 't th' impression,° placed it safely,
The changeling° never known. Now, the next day
Was our sea fight, and what to this was sequent°
Thou knowest already.   55

HORATIO: So Guildenstern and Rosencrantz go to 't.

HAMLET: Why, man, they did make love to this employment.
They are not near my conscience. Their defeat°
Does by their own insinuation° grow.
'Tis dangerous when the baser° nature comes   60
Between the pass° and fell° incensèd points
Of mighty opposites.°

HORATIO: Why, what a king is this!

HAMLET: Does it not, think thee, stand me now upon°—
He that hath killed my king and whored my mother,
Popped in between th' election° and my hopes,   65
Thrown out his angle° for my proper° life,
And with such cozenage°—is 't not perfect conscience
To quit° him with this arm? And is 't not to be damned
To let this canker° of our nature come
In° further evil?   70

HORATIO: It must be shortly known to him from England
What is the issue of the business there.

HAMLET: It will be short. The interim is mine,
And a man's life's no more than to say "one."°

---

40 palm (an image of health; see Psalm 92:12.)   **41 still** always;   **wheaten garland** (symbolic of fruitful agriculture, of peace and plenty.)   **42 comma** (indicating continuity, link.)   **43 "as"es** (1) the "whereases" of a formal document, (2) asses;   **charge** (1) import, (2) burden (appropriate to asses).   **47 shriving time** time for confession and absolution.   **48 ordinant** directing.   **49 signet** small seal.   **50 model** replica.   **51 writ** writing.   **52 Subscribed** signed (with forged signature);   **impression** i.e., with a wax seal.   **53 changeling** i.e., substituted letter. (Literally, a fairy child substituted for a human one.)   **54 was sequent** followed.   **58 defeat** destruction.   **59 insinuation** intrusive intervention, sticking their noses in my business.   **60 baser** of lower social station.   **61 pass** thrust;   **fell** fierce.   **62 opposites** antagonists.   **63 stand me now upon** become incumbent on me now.   **65 election** (The Danish monarch was "elected" by a small number of high-ranking electors.)   **66 angle** fishhook;   **proper** very.   **67 cozenage** trickery.   **68 quit** requite, pay back.   **69 canker** ulcer.   **69–70 come In** grow into.   **74 a man's . . .** "one" one's whole life occupies such a short time, only as long as it takes to count to 1.

	But I am very sorry, good Horatio,	75
	That to Laertes I forgot myself,	
	For by the image of my cause I see	
	The portraiture of his. I'll court his favors.	
	But, sure, the bravery° of his grief did put me	
	Into a tow'ring passion.	
HORATIO:	Peace, who comes here?	80

Enter a Courtier [OSRIC].

OSRIC: Your lordship is right welcome back to Denmark.

HAMLET: I humbly thank you, sir. [*To* HORATIO.] Dost know this water fly?

HORATIO: No, my good lord.

HAMLET: Thy state is the more gracious, for 'tis a vice to know him. He hath much land, and fertile. Let a beast be lord of beasts, and his crib° shall   85
stand at the King's mess.° 'Tis a chuff,° but, as I say, spacious in the possession of dirt.

OSRIC: Sweet lord, if your lordship were at leisure, I should impart a thing to you from His Majesty.

HAMLET: I will receive it, sir, with all diligence of spirit.   90
Put your bonnet° to his° right use; 'tis for the head.

OSRIC: I thank your lordship, it is very hot.

HAMLET: No, believe me, 'tis very cold. The wind is northerly.

OSRIC: It is indifferent° cold, my lord, indeed.

HAMLET: But yet methinks it is very sultry and hot for my complexion.°   95

OSRIC: Exceedingly, my lord. It is very sultry, as 'twere—I cannot tell how.
My lord, His Majesty bade me signify to you that 'a has laid a great wager on your head. Sir, this is the matter—

HAMLET: I beseech you, remember.

[HAMLET *moves him to put on his hat*.]

OSRIC: Nay, good my lord; for my ease,° in good faith. Sir, here is newly   100
come to court Laertes—believe me, an absolute° gentleman, full of most excellent differences,° of very soft society° and great showing.° Indeed, to speak feelingly° of him, he is the card° or calendar° of gentry,° for you shall find in him the continent of what part a gentleman would see.°   105

HAMLET: Sir, his definement° suffers no perdition° in you,° though I know to divide him inventorially° would dozy° th' arithmetic of memory, and yet but yaw° neither° in respect of° his quick sail. But, in the verity of

79 bravery bravado.   **85 crib** manger.   **85–86 Let . . . mess** i.e., if a man, no matter how beast-like, is as rich in livestock and possessions as Osric, he may eat at the King's table.   **86 chuff** boor, churl. (The second Quarto spelling, *chough,* is a variant spelling that also suggests the meaning here of "chattering jackdaw.")   **91 bonnet** any kind of cap or hat;   **his** its.   **94 indifferent** somewhat.   **95 complexion** temperament.   **100 for my ease** (a conventional reply declining the invitation to put his hat back on.)   **101 absolute** perfect.   **102 differences** special qualities;   **soft society** agreeable manners;   **great showing** distinguished appearance.   **103 feelingly** with just perception;   **card** chart, map;   **calendar** guide.   **104 gentry** good breeding.   **104–05 the continent . . . see** one who contains in him all the qualities a gentleman would like to see. (A *continent* is that which contains.)   **106 definement** definition (Hamlet proceeds to mock Osric by throwing his lofty diction back at him);   **perdition** loss, diminution;   **you** your description.   **107 divide him inventorially** enumerate his graces;   **dozy** dizzy.   **108 yaw** swing unsteadily off course. (Said of a ship.);   **neither** for all that;   **in respect of** in comparison with.

extolment,° I take him to be a soul of great article,° and his infusion° of
such dearth and rareness° as, to make true diction° of him, his semblable°   110
is his mirror and who else would trace° him his umbrage,° nothing more.

OSRIC: Your lordship speaks most infallibly of him.

HAMLET: The concernancy,° sir? Why do we wrap the gentleman in our more
rawer breath?°

OSRIC: Sir?   115

HORATIO: Is 't not possible to understand in another tongue?° You will do 't,° sir,
really.

HAMLET: What imports the nomination° of this gentleman?

OSRIC: Of Laertes?

HORATIO [*to* HAMLET]: His purse is empty already; all 's golden words are spent.   120

HAMLET: Of him, sir.

OSRIC: I know you are not ignorant—

HAMLET: I would you did, sir. Yet in faith if you did, it would not much approve°
me. Well, sir?

OSRIC: You are not ignorant of what excellence Laertes is—   125

HAMLET: I dare not confess that, lest I should compare with him in excellence.
But to know a man well were to know himself.°

OSRIC: I mean, sir, for° his weapon; but in the imputation laid on him by them,° in
his meed° he's unfellowed.°

HAMLET: What's his weapon?   130

OSRIC: Rapier and dagger.

HAMLET: That's two of his weapons—but well.°

OSRIC: The King, sir, hath wagered with him six Barbary horses, against the
which he° has impawned,° as I take it, six French rapiers and poniards,°
with their assigns,° as girdle, hangers,° and so.° Three of the carriages,°   135
in faith, are very dear to fancy,° very responsive° to the hilts, most deli-
cate° carriages, and of very liberal conceit.°

HAMLET: What call you the carriages?

HORATIO [*to* HAMLET]: I knew you must be edified by the margent° ere you had
done.   140

OSRIC: The carriages, sir, are the hangers.

108–09 in . . . extolment in true praise (of him).   **109 of great article** one with many articles
in his inventory;   **infusion** essence, character infused into him by nature.   **110 dearth and
rareness** rarity;   **make true diction** speak truly;   **semblable** only true likeness.   **111 who . . .
trace** any other person who would wish to follow;   **umbrage** shadow.   **113 concernancy**
import, relevance.   **114 rawer breath** unrefined speech that can only come short in praising
him.   **116 to understand . . . tongue** i.e., for you, Osric, to understand when someone else
speaks your language. (Horatio twits Osric for not being able to understand the kind of flowery
speech he himself uses, when Hamlet speaks in such a vein. Alternatively, all this could be
said to Hamlet.);   **You will do 't** i.e., you can if you try, or, you may well have to try (to speak
plainly).   **118 nomination** naming.   **123 approve** commend.   **126–27 I dare . . . himself**
I dare not boast of knowing Laertes' excellence lest I seem to imply a comparable excellence
in myself. Certainly, to know another person well, one must know oneself.   **128 for** i.e.,
with;   **imputation . . . them** reputation given him by others.   **129 meed** merit;   **unfellowed**
unmatched.   **132 but well** but never mind.   **134 he** i.e., Laertes;   **impawned** staked,
wagered;   **poniards** daggers.   **135 assigns** appurtenances;   **hangers** straps on the sword belt
(*girdle*), from which the sword hung;   **and so** and so on;   **carriages** (an affected way of saying
hangers, literally, gun carriages.)   **136 dear to fancy** delightful to the fancy;   **responsive** corresponding closely, matching or well adjusted.   **136–37 delicate** (i.e., in workmanship);   **liberal
conceit** elaborate design.   **139 margent** margin of a book, place for explanatory notes.

HAMLET: The phrase would be more germane to the matter if we could carry a
cannon by our sides; I would it might be hangers till then. But, on: six
Barbary horses against six French swords, their assigns, and three liberal-
conceited carriages; that's the French bet against the Danish. Why is this   145
impawned, as you call it?

OSRIC: The King, sir, hath laid,° sir, that in a dozen passes° between yourself and
him, he shall not exceed you three hits. He hath laid on twelve for nine,
and it would come to immediate trial, if your lordship would vouchsafe
the answer.°   150

HAMLET: How if I answer no?

OSRIC: I mean, my lord, the opposition of your person in trial.

HAMLET: Sir, I will walk here in the hall. If it please His Majesty, it is the breathing
time° of day with me. Let° the foils be brought, the gentleman willing,
and the King hold his purpose. I will win for him an I can; if not, I will   155
gain nothing but my shame and the odd hits.

OSRIC: Shall I deliver you° so?

HAMLET: To this effect, sir—after what flourish your nature will.

OSRIC: I commend° my duty to your lordship.

HAMLET: Yours, yours. [*Exit* OSRIC.] 'A does well to commend it himself; there are   160
no tongues else for 's turn.°

HORATIO: This lapwing° runs away with the shell on his head.

HAMLET: 'A did comply with his dug° before 'a sucked it. Thus has he—and many
more of the same breed that I know the drossy° age dotes on—only got
the tune° of the time and, out of an habit of encounter,° a kind of yeasty°   165
collection,° which carries them through and through the most fanned and
winnowed opinions;° and do° but blow them to their trial, the bubbles
are out.°

Enter a LORD.

LORD: My lord, His Majesty commended him to you by young Osric, who brings
back to him that you attend him in the hall. He sends to know if your   170
pleasure hold to play with Laertes, or that° you will take longer time.

---

147 laid wagered;   **passes** bouts. (The odds of the betting are hard to explain. Possibly the
King bets that Hamlet will win at least five out of twelve, at which point Laertes raises the
odds against himself by betting he will win nine.)   **149–50 vouchsafe the answer** be so
good as to accept the challenge. (Hamlet deliberately takes the phrase in its literal sense of
replying.)   **153–54 breathing time** exercise period;   **Let** i.e., if.   **157 deliver you** report
what you say.   **159 commend** commit to your favor. (A conventional salutation, but Hamlet
wryly uses a more literal meaning, "recommend," "praise," in line 160.)   **161 for 's turn** for
his purposes, i.e., to do it for him.   **162 lapwing** (a proverbial type of youthful forwardness.
Also, a bird that draws intruders away from its nest and was thought to run about with its head
in the shell when newly hatched; a seeming reference to Osric's hat.)   **163 comply . . . dug**
observe ceremonious formality toward his nurse's or mother's teat.   **164 drossy** laden with
scum and impurities, frivolous.   **165 tune** temper, mood, manner of speech;   **an habit of
encounter** a demeanor in conversing (with courtiers of his own kind);   **yeasty** frothy.
166 collection i.e., of current phrases.   **166–67 carries . . . opinions** sustains them right
through the scrutiny of persons whose opinions are select and refined. (Literally, like grain
separated from its chaff. Osric is both the chaff and the bubbly froth on the surface of the
liquor that is soon blown away.)   **167 and do** yet do.   **167–68 blow . . . out** test them by
merely blowing on them, and their bubbles burst.   **171 that** if.

HAMLET: I am constant to my purposes; they follow the King's pleasure. If his fitness speaks, mine is ready;° now or whensoever, provided I be so able
as now.

LORD: The King and Queen and all are coming down.   175

HAMLET: In happy time.°

LORD: The Queen desires you to use some gentle entertainment° to Laertes before
you fall to play.

HAMLET: She well instructs me.   [*Exit* LORD.]

HORATIO: You will lose, my lord.   180

HAMLET: I do not think so. Since he went into France, I have been in continual
practice; I shall win at the odds. But thou wouldst not think how ill all's
here about my heart; but it is no matter.

HORATIO: Nay, good my lord—

HAMLET: It is but foolery, but it is such a kind of gaingiving° as would perhaps   185
trouble a woman.

HORATIO: If your mind dislike anything, obey it. I will forestall their repair° hither
and say you are not fit.

HAMLET: Not a whit, we defy augury. There is special providence in the fall of a
sparrow. If it be now, 'tis not to come; if it be not to come, it will be now;   190
if it be not now, yet it will come. The readiness is all. Since no man of
aught he leaves knows, what is 't to leave betimes? Let be.°

   A table prepared. [*Enter*] *trumpets, drums, and officers with cushions;* KING,
QUEEN, [OSRIC,] *and all the state; foils, daggers,* [*and wine borne in;*] *and* LAERTES.

KING: Come, Hamlet, come and take this hand from me.

   [*The king puts* LAERTES' *hand into* HAMLET'*s.*]

HAMLET [*to* LAERTES]: Give me your pardon, sir. I have done you wrong,
But pardon 't as you are a gentleman.   195
This presence° knows,
And you must needs have heard, how I am punished°
With a sore distraction. What I have done
That might your nature, honor, and exception°
Roughly awake, I here proclaim was madness.   200
Was 't Hamlet wronged Laertes? Never Hamlet.
If Hamlet from himself be ta'en away,
And when he's not himself does wrong Laertes,
Then Hamlet does it not, Hamlet denies it.
Who does it, then? His madness. If 't be so,   205
Hamlet is of the faction° that is wronged;
His madness is poor Hamlet's enemy.
Sir, in this audience
Let my disclaiming from a purposed evil
Free me so far in your most generous thoughts   210

172–73 If . . . ready If he declares his readiness, my convenience waits on his. **176 In happy
time** (a phrase of courtesy indicating that the time is convenient). **177 entertainment** greeting.
185 gaingiving misgiving. **187 repair** coming. **191–92 Since . . . Let be** since no one has
knowledge of what he is leaving behind, what does an early death matter after all? enough; don't
struggle against it. **196 presence** royal assembly. **197 punished** afflicted. **199 exception**
disapproval. **206 faction** party.

That I have° shot my arrow o'er the house
And hurt my brother.

LAERTES: I am satisfied in nature,°
Whose motive° in this case should stir me most
To my revenge. But in my terms of honor
I stand aloof, and will no reconcilement   215
Till by some elder masters of known honor
I have a voice° and precedent of peace°
To keep my name ungored.° But till that time
I do receive your offered love like love,
And will not wrong it.

HAMLET: I embrace it freely,   220
And will this brothers' wager frankly° play.—
Give us the foils. Come on.

LAERTES: Come, one for me.

HAMLET: I'll be your foil,° Laertes. In mine ignorance
Your skill shall, like a star i' the darkest night,
Stick fiery off° indeed.

LAERTES: You mock me, sir.   225

HAMLET: No, by this hand.

KING: Give them the foils, young Osric. Cousin Hamlet,
You know the wager?

HAMLET: Very well, my lord.
Your Grace has laid the odds o'° the weaker side.

KING: I do not fear it; I have seen you both.   230
But since he is bettered,° we have therefore odds.

LAERTES: This is too heavy. Let me see another.

> [*He exchanges his foil for another.*]

HAMLET: This likes me° well. These foils have all a length?

> [*They prepare to play.*]

OSRIC: Ay, my good lord.

KING: Set me the stoups of wine upon that table.   235
If Hamlet give the first or second hit,
Or quit in answer of the third exchange,°
Let all the battlements their ordnance fire.
The King shall drink to Hamlet's better breath,°
And in the cup an union° shall he throw   240
Richer than that which four successive kings
In Denmark's crown have worn. Give me the cups,
And let the kettle° to the trumpet speak,
The trumpet to the cannoneer without,

211 That I have as if I had.   **212 in nature** i.e., as to my personal feelings.   **213 motive**
prompting.   **217 voice** authoritative pronouncement;   **of peace** for reconciliation.
218 name ungored reputation unwounded.   **221 frankly** without ill feeling or the burden
of rancor.   **223 foil** thin metal background which sets a jewel off (with pun on the blunted
rapier for fencing).   **225 Stick fiery off** stand out brilliantly.   **229 laid the odds o'** bet on,
backed.   **231 is bettered** has improved; is the odds-on favorite. (Laertes' handicap is the
"three hits" specified in line 148.)   **233 likes me** pleases me.   **237 Or . . . exchange** i.e., or
requites Laertes in the third bout for having won the first two.   **239 better breath** improved
vigor.   **240 union** pearl. (So called, according to Pliny's *Natural History*, 9, because pearls
are *unique*, never identical.)   **243 kettle** kettledrum.

The cannons to the heavens, the heaven to earth, 245
"Now the King drinks to Hamlet." Come, begin.   *Trumpets the while.*
And you, the judges, bear a wary eye.

HAMLET: Come on, sir.

LAERTES: Come, my lord.   [*They play.* HAMLET *scores a hit.*]

HAMLET: One.   250

LAERTES: No.

HAMLET: Judgment.

OSRIC: A hit, a very palpable hit.
                    Drum, trumpets, and shot. Flourish. A piece goes off.

LAERTES: Well, again.

KING: Stay, give me drink. Hamlet, this pearl is thine.
    [*He drinks, and throws a pearl in* HAMLET'*s cup.*]
    Here's to thy health. Give him the cup.   255

HAMLET: I'll play this bout first. Set it by awhile.
    Come. [*They play.*] Another hit; what say you?

LAERTES: A touch, a touch, I do confess 't.

KING: Our son shall win.

QUEEN: He's fat° and scant of breath.
    Here, Hamlet, take my napkin,° rub thy brows.   260
    The Queen carouses° to thy fortune, Hamlet.

HAMLET: Good madam!

KING: Gertrude, do not drink.

QUEEN: I will, my lord, I pray you pardon me.   [*She drinks.*]

KING [*aside*]: It is the poisoned cup. It is too late.   265

HAMLET: I dare not drink yet, madam; by and by.

QUEEN: Come, let me wipe thy face.

LAERTES [*to* KING]: My lord, I'll hit him now.

KING: I do not think 't.

LAERTES [*aside*]: And yet it is almost against my conscience.

HAMLET: Come, for the third, Laertes. You do but dally.   270
    I pray you, pass° with your best violence;
    I am afeard you make a wanton of me.°

LAERTES: Say you so? Come on.   [*They play.*]

OSRIC: Nothing neither way.

LAERTES: Have at you now!

    [LAERTES *wounds* HAMLET; *then, in scuffling, they change rapiers,*° *and* HAMLET
    wounds LAERTES.]

KING: Part them! They are incensed.   275

HAMLET: Nay, come, again.   [*The* QUEEN *falls.*]

OSRIC: Look to the Queen there, ho!

HORATIO: They bleed on both sides. How is it, my lord?

OSRIC: How is 't, Laertes?

LAERTES: Why, as a woodcock° to mine own springe,° Osric;
    I am justly killed with mine own treachery.   280

259 fat not physically fit, out of training.   **260 napkin** handkerchief.   **261 carouses** drinks
a toast.   **271 pass** thrust.   **272 make . . . me** i.e., treat me like a spoiled child, trifle with
me.   **275 s.d. in scuffling, they change rapiers** (This stage direction occurs in the Folio.
According to a widespread stage tradition, Hamlet receives a scratch, realizes that Laertes'
sword is unbated, and accordingly forces an exchange.)   **279 woodcock** a bird, a type of
stupidity or as a decoy;   **springe** trap, snare.

HAMLET: How does the Queen?

KING: She swoons to see them bleed.

QUEEN: No, no, the drink, the drink—O my dear Hamlet—
    The drink, the drink! I am poisoned.   [*She dies.*]

HAMLET: O villainy! Ho, let the door be locked!
    Treachery! Seek it out.   [LAERTES *falls. Exit* OSRIC.]   285

LAERTES: It is here, Hamlet. Hamlet, thou art slain.
    No med'cine in the world can do thee good;
    In thee there is not half an hour's life.
    The treacherous instrument is in thy hand,
    Unbated° and envenomed. The foul practice°   290
    Hath turned itself on me. Lo, here I lie,
    Never to rise again. Thy mother's poisoned.
    I can no more. The King, the King's to blame.

HAMLET: The point envenomed too? Then, venom, to thy work.

                                        [*He stabs the* KING.]

ALL: Treason! Treason!   295

KING: O, yet defend me, friends! I am but hurt.

HAMLET [*forcing the* KING *to drink*]:
    Here, thou incestuous, murderous, damnèd Dane,
    Drink off this potion. Is thy union° here?
    Follow my mother.   [*The* KING *dies.*]

LAERTES: He is justly served.
    It is a poison tempered° by himself.   300
    Exchange forgiveness with me, noble Hamlet.
    Mine and my father's death come not upon thee,
    Nor thine on me!   [*He dies.*]

HAMLET: Heaven make thee free of it! I follow thee.
    I am dead, Horatio. Wretched Queen, adieu!   305
    You that look pale and tremble at this chance,°
    That are but mutes° or audience to this act,
    Had I but time—as this fell° sergeant,° Death,
    Is strict° in his arrest°—O, I could tell you—
    But let it be. Horatio, I am dead;   310
    Thou livest. Report me and my cause aright
    To the unsatisfied.

HORATIO: Never believe it.
    I am more an antique Roman° than a Dane.
    Here's yet some liquor left.

    [*He attempts to drink from the poisoned cup.* HAMLET *prevents him.*]

HAMLET: As thou'rt a man,
    Give me the cup! Let go! By heaven, I'll ha 't.   315
    O God, Horatio, what a wounded name,

---

290 Unbated not blunted with a button;   **practice** plot.   **298 union** pearl. (See line 240;
with grim puns on the word's other meanings: marriage, shared death.)   **300 tempered**
mixed.   **306 chance** mischance.   **307 mutes** silent observers. (Literally, actors with
nonspeaking parts.)   **308 fell** cruel;   **sergeant** sheriff's officer.   **309 strict** (1) severely just,
(2) unavoidable;   **arrest** (1) taking into custody, (2) stopping my speech.   **313 Roman** (suicide
was an honorable choice for many Romans as an alternative to a dishonorable life.)

Things standing thus unknown, shall I leave behind me!
If thou didst ever hold me in thy heart,
Absent thee from felicity awhile,
And in this harsh world draw thy breath in pain   320
To tell my story.   *A march afar off* [*and a volley within*].
What warlike noise is this?

    Enter OSRIC.

OSRIC: Young Fortinbras, with conquest come from Poland,
    To th' ambassadors of England gives
    This warlike volley.
HAMLET: O, I die, Horatio!   325
    The potent poison quite o'ercrows° my spirit.
    I cannot live to hear the news from England,
    But I do prophesy th' election lights
    On Fortinbras. He has my dying voice.°
    So tell him, with th' occurents° more and less   330
    Which have solicited°—the rest is silence.   [*He dies.*]
HORATIO: Now cracks a noble heart. Good night, sweet prince,
    And flights of angels sing thee to thy rest!   [*March within.*]
    Why does the drum come hither?

    Enter FORTINBRAS, *with the* [*English*] *Ambassadors* [*with drum, colors, and attendants*].

FORTINBRAS: Where is this sight?
HORATIO: What is it you would see?   335
    If aught of woe or wonder, cease your search.
FORTINBRAS: This quarry° cries on havoc.° O proud Death,
    What feast° is toward° in thine eternal cell,
    That thou so many princes at a shot
    So bloodily hast struck?
FIRST AMBASSADOR: The sight is dismal,   340
    And our affairs from England come too late.
    The ears are senseless that should give us hearing,
    To tell him his commandment is fulfilled,
    That Rosencrantz and Guildenstern are dead.
    Where should we have our thanks?
HORATIO: Not from his° mouth,   345
    Had it th' ability of life to thank you.
    He never gave commandment for their death.
    But since, so jump° upon this bloody question,°
    You from the Polack wars, and you from England,
    And here arrived, give order that these bodies   350
    High on a stage° be placèd to the view,
    And let me speak to th' yet unknowing world

---

326 o'ercrows triumphs over (like the winner in a cockfight).   **329 voice** vote.   **330 occurrents** events, incidents.   **331 solicited** moved, urged. (Hamlet doesn't finish saying what the events have prompted—presumably, his acts of vengeance, or his reporting of those events to Fortinbras.)   **337 quarry** heap of dead;   **cries on havoc** proclaims a general slaughter.
338 feast i.e., Death feasting on those who have fallen;   **toward** in preparation.   **345 his** i.e., Claudius'.   **348 jump** precisely, immediately;   **question** dispute, affair.   **351 stage** platform.

How these things came about. So shall you hear
Of carnal, bloody, and unnatural acts,
Of accidental judgments,° casual° slaughters,   355
Of deaths put on° by cunning and forced cause,°
And, in this upshot, purposes mistook
Fall'n on th' inventors' heads. All this can I
Truly deliver.

FORTINBRAS: Let us haste to hear it,
And call the noblest to the audience.   360
For me, with sorrow I embrace my fortune.
I have some rights of memory° in this kingdom,
Which now to claim my vantage° doth invite me.

HORATIO: Of that I shall have also cause to speak,
And from his mouth whose voice will draw on more.°   365
But let this same be presently° performed,
Even while men's minds are wild, lest more mischance
On° plots and errors happen.

FORTINBRAS: Let four captains
Bear Hamlet, like a soldier, to the stage,
For he was likely, had he been put on,°   370
To have proved most royal; and for his passage,°
The soldiers' music and the rite of war
Speak° loudly for him.
Take up the bodies. Such a sight as this
Becomes the field,° but here shows much amiss.   375
Go bid the soldiers shoot.

Exeunt [marching, bearing off the dead bodies; a peal of ordnance is shot off].

[1603]

355 judgments retributions;   **casual** occurring by chance.   **356 put on** instigated;   **forced cause** contrivance.   **362 of memory** traditional, remembered, unforgotten.   **363 vantage** favorable opportunity   **365 voice . . . more** vote will influence still others.   **366 presently** immediately.   **368 On** on the basis of; on top of.   **370 put on** i.e., invested in royal office and so put to the test.   **371 passage** i.e., from life to death.   **373 Speak** let them speak. **375 Becomes the field** suits the field of battle.

Joining the Conversation: Critical Thinking and Writing

Act 1

1. The first scene (like many other scenes in this play) is full of expressions of uncertainty. What are some of these uncertainties? The Ghost first appears at 1.1.43. Does his appearance surprise us, or have we been prepared for it? Or is there both preparation and surprise? Do the last four speeches of 1.1 help to introduce a note of hope? If so, how?
2. Does the Claudius's opening speech in 1.2 reveal him to be an accomplished public speaker, or are lines 10–14 offensive? In his second speech (lines 41–49), what is the effect of naming Laertes four times? Claudius sometimes uses the

royal pronouns ("we," "our"), sometimes the more intimate "I" and "my." Study his use of these words in lines 1–4 and in 106–17. What do you think he is getting at?

3. Hamlet's first soliloquy (1.2.129–59) reveals that more than just his father's death distresses him. Be as specific as possible about the causes of Hamlet's anguish here.

4. What traits does Hamlet reveal in his conversation with Horatio (1.2.160–258)?

5. What do you make of Polonius's advice to Laertes (1.3.55–81)? Is it sound? Is it sound advice but here uttered by a fool? Is it ignoble advice? How would one follow the advice of line 78: "to thine own self be true"? In his words to Ophelia in 1.3.102–36, what does Polonius reveal about himself?

6. Can 1.4.17–38 reasonably be taken as a speech on the "tragic flaw"? (On this idea, see page 549.) Or is the passage a much more limited discussion, a comment simply on Danish drinking habits?

7. Hamlet is convinced in 1.5.93–105 that the Ghost has told the truth, indeed, the only important truth. But do we detect in 105–12 a hint of a tone suggesting that Hamlet delights in hating villainy? If so, can it be said that later this delight grows and that, in some scenes (e.g., 3.3), we feel that Hamlet has almost become a diabolic revenger? Explain your answer.

Act 2

1. Characterize Polonius on the basis of 2.1.1–75.

2. In light of what we have seen of Hamlet, is Ophelia's report of his strange behavior when he visits her understandable?

3. Why does 2.2.33–34 seem almost comic? How do these lines help us to form a view about Rosencrantz and Guildenstern?

4. Is "the hellish Pyrrhus" (2.2.405) Hamlet's version of Claudius? Or is he Hamlet, who soon will be responsible for the deaths of Polonius, Rosencrantz and Guildenstern, Claudius, Gertrude, Ophelia, and Laertes? Explain your answer.

5. Is the speech that Hamlet and the First Player recite, with some interruptions (2.2.392–453), an absurdly bombastic speech? If so, why? To distinguish it from the poetry of the play itself? To characterize the bloody deeds that Hamlet cannot descend to?

6. In 2.2.482–520, Hamlet rebukes himself for not acting. Why has he not acted? Is it because he is a coward (line 503)? Because he has a conscience? Because no action can restore his father and his mother's purity? Because he doubts the Ghost? What reason(s) can you offer?

Act 3

1. What do you make of Hamlet's assertion to Ophelia: "I loved you not" (3.1.117)? Of his characterization of himself as full of "offenses" (3.1.121–25)? Why is Hamlet so harsh to Ophelia?

2. In 3.3.36–72, Claudius's conscience afflicts him. Is he repentant? What makes you think so?

3. Is Hamlet other than abhorrent in 3.3.73–96? Do we want him to kill Claudius at this moment, when Claudius (presumably with his back to Hamlet) is praying? Why?

4. The Ghost speaks of Hamlet's "almost blunted purpose" (3.4.115). Is the accusation fair? Explain your answer.

5. How would you characterize Hamlet in 3.4.209–24?

Act 4

1. Is Gertrude protecting Hamlet when she says that he is mad (4.1.7), or does she believe that he is mad? If she believes that he is mad, does it follow that she no longer feels ashamed and guilty? Explain your answer.

2. Why should Hamlet hide Polonius's body (in 4.2)? Is he feigning madness? Is he on the edge of madness? Explain your answer.
3. How can we explain Hamlet's willingness to go to England (4.3.52)?
4. Judging from 4.5, what has driven Ophelia mad? Is Laertes heroic or somewhat foolish? Consider also the way Claudius treats Laertes in 4.7.

Act 5
1. Would anything be lost if the grave diggers in 5.1 were omitted?
2. To what extent do you judge Hamlet severely for sending Rosencrantz and Guildenstern to their deaths, as he reports in 5.2? On the whole, do you think of Hamlet as an intriguer? What other intrigues has he engendered? How successful were they?
3. Does 5.2.188–91 show a paralysis of the will or a wise recognition that more is needed than mere human scheming? Explain your answer.
4. Does 5.2.274 suggest that Laertes takes advantage of a momentary pause and unfairly stabs Hamlet? Is the exchange of weapons accidental, or does Hamlet (as in Olivier's film version), realizing that he has been betrayed, deliberately take possession of Laertes's deadly weapon?
5. Fortinbras is often cut from the play. How much is lost by the cut? Explain your answer.
6. Fortinbras gives Hamlet a soldier's funeral. Is this ridiculous? Can it fairly be said that, in a sense, Hamlet has been at war? Explain your answer.

General Questions

1. Hamlet in 5.2.10–11 speaks of "a divinity that shapes our ends." To what extent does "divinity" (or Fate or mysterious Chance) play a role in the happenings?
2. How do Laertes, Fortinbras, and Horatio help to define Hamlet for us?
3. T. S. Eliot says (in "Shakespeare and the Stoicism of Seneca") that Hamlet, having made a mess, "dies fairly well pleased with himself." Evaluate this statement.

ANNE BARTON

The Promulgation of Confusion[3]

The length of the play suggests that it was never, not even in Shakespeare's time, performed uncut. Other plays by Shakespeare are long; no other violates so strikingly the limits of audience attention, or asks for so much from its leading actor. Like *Titus*, like *The Spanish Tragedy* and that lost source play, the so-called *Ur-Hamlet*, which was probably the work of Kyd, Shakespeare's *Hamlet* is a tragedy of revenge. It concentrates, like them, upon a single, essentially sympathetic hero and it confronts precisely the same structural problem: how to linger out his vengeance for the necessary five acts. Kyd's Hieronymo (and probably his Hamlet), Shakespeare's Titus and Hamlet all require proof of the villain's identity before they can act. They are temporarily deflected from their purpose, not only by difficulties of strategy, but by a madness partly assumed and partly real. All make use of some kind of dramatic show to further their intention and all accomplish, in the end, a vengeance which, whatever the original provocation, has by this time become more than a little suspect.

[3]The title is the editors'.

As a tragic predicament, revenge has several inherent advantages. Intrigue and spectacle, madness and violence, are not the only elements native to the genre. The isolation naturally imposed upon the revenger not only encourages introspection, it destroys normal human relationships in a fundamentally tragic way. A detached, satirist's view of the society against which they war almost forces itself upon these characters. Their situation generates a corrosive doubt, reaching out to attack religious, moral and legal institutions. Kyd, Marlowe in *The Jew of Malta,* and the young Shakespeare of *Titus,* had all recognized and explored these inbuilt opportunities, at least to some extent. It was only with *Hamlet,* however, that a dramatist seized upon the form to trigger off an enquiry into the whole basis of human existence. Debate over man's right to encroach upon the prerogative of Heaven by undertaking himself what was properly God's act of retributive justice had been and, in the Jacobean period, would continue to be a feature of revenge tragedy.

• • •

Only *Hamlet* side-steps the ethic of revenge entirely. It is one of several great silences at the heart of this play. Deliberately, Shakespeare has shifted attention away from an expected centre, from the problem of whether the prince *ought* to kill Claudius—or even whether in practical terms he *can*—to the far more complicated and subjective issue of whether or not he ultimately *will*. It is not the peculiar status of acts of private vengeance that is under review here, but the validity of all and any human action.

Although other dramatists (Marston, Webster and Tourneur especially) later used *Hamlet* as a spring-board for their own exploration of the revenge form, none of them dared to attempt a focus so wide. The range of the play and, above all, of the role of Hamlet himself, is so great that any performance must necessarily be a matter of selection, of emphases more or less arbitrarily imposed. The impossibility of presenting *Hamlet* whole and uncut is not entirely a feature of its great length. It is also bound up with its inclusiveness, with the fact that Shakespeare seems to have been determined to subject a bewildering number of people, ideas, values, kinds of relationship, emotions and social forms to the distorted but strangely clear scrutiny of a revenger so complicated himself that no attempt to describe, or act, him can be more than partial. Even more than most plays of Shakespeare, *Hamlet* is a warning against the fallacy that any critical interpretation or stage production can be definitive, or even complete.

5 When Hamlet cautioned Rosencrantz and Guildenstern, after the play scene, against the attempt to "pluck out the heart of my mystery . . . sound me from my lowest note to the top of my compass" (3.2.319–21), he also provided a useful counsel for literary critics. The play as a whole is built upon contradiction, upon the promulgation of confusion. Shakespeare gives every indication of having constructed an imaginary Denmark intended to baffle, to resist explanation as stubbornly as those mysterious facts of human existence which it illuminates without rationalizing. A distrust of what might be described as a "play-shaped" view of the world of the falseness of clearly defined moral, theological or formal patterns imposed upon reality in the interests of art is, I think, characteristic of him throughout his dramatic career. It was to become particularly strong in his Jacobean plays. This antipathy may account, in part, for Shakespeare's apparent suspicion of *tragedy* as a term, and also for the variety and restlessness of his own formal development.

Certainly, the eschatology of *Hamlet* defies explication. The ghost of a murdered king appears from an almost embarrassingly specific Catholic Purgatory, a place of "sulph'rous and tormenting flames" (1.5.3) to which it has been confined "till the foul crimes done in my days of nature / Are burnt and purged away" (1.5.13–14). This spirit urges upon its beloved only son a revenge for which, by immutable Christian law, that son must be damned perpetually—sent not to Purgatory, but to the far greater torments of Hell. Neither Hamlet, the sensible Horatio nor the ghost itself ever remark upon this illogicality. Hamlet's worry is only about the truth of the ghost's accusation. If Claudius is guilty, and the Mouse-trap proves that he is, he must be killed. Not for an instant does Hamlet doubt the justice of such a course, let alone the propriety of a repentant soul spending its time in Purgatory meditating a murder. A similar inconsistency adds complications to what is already, on psychological grounds, a most ambiguous scene in Act 3. Hamlet declines to kill the king at prayers because he fears that Claudius' soul will ascend to Heaven. This, at least, is the reason he gives. He will wait to find his enemy

> drunk asleep, or in his rage,
> Or in th'incestuous pleasure of his bed,
> At game, a-swearing, or about some act
> That has no relish of salvation in't,
> Then trip him that his heels may kick at heaven,
> And that his soul may be as damned and black
> As hell whereto it goes.
>
> (3.3.89–95)

Here, the odd fact that Hamlet never considers that his own soul would be damned irrecoverably by the requirements of such a theology, is cunningly mingled with doubts as to whether he really means what he is saying in this speech, or whether it is a feeble excuse for postponing an explicably distasteful task.

In *Hamlet,* Shakespeare affirms a Christian supernatural in one moment to deny it in the next. The hereafter involves Purgatory, hell fire, and flights of angels. It is also silence, an eternal sleep that has nothing to do with punishment or reward. The prince talks about death as "the undiscovered country, from whose bourn / No traveller returns" (3.1.80–81) out of an anguish of mind created by the return of just such a traveller. A special Providence guides the fall of the sparrow, or at least Hamlet asserts that it does just before the fatal game with the foils in Act 5. He seems to die, however, in the agnostic spirit which, a moment later, prompts Horatio's account of the catastrophe as "accidental judgments, casual slaughters" (5.2.354). These conflicting views follow one another so closely in the action, and they are treated by the dramatist with such a non-committal equality, that it becomes impossible to characterize the supernatural in the play. Although we stumble from time to time over the partially submerged rocks of old beliefs, their presence only makes the obscurity of the total picture more poignant. In effect, Shakespeare has created his own, infinitely more complex version of the divided worlds of [Pickering's] *Horestes* and [Kyd's] *The Spanish Tragedy.* Hamlet's questions, instead of being halted artificially as Hieronymo's were by a tidy, Senecan supernatural visible to us in the audience although not to the hero, grope their way into a darkness without form or limit. Like Pickering, Shakespeare placed his spirit of Revenge inside the play itself, as a character who addresses the protagonist directly. Having done so, he proceeded disconcertingly to associate the ghost with a Christian hereafter, and refused to judge its ethic of blood vengeance. *Hamlet* never explains the nature of that silence towards which the hero moves gradually, away from us, and into which he finally vanishes. This is one reason why the tragedy has a terror, and also a relevance to the world as we know it, lacking in Pickering and Kyd.

More perhaps than any other Shakespearean tragedy, *Hamlet* is a play obsessed with words themselves. It displaces the accustomed centre of earlier revenge drama by subordinating plot for its own sake to a new concern with the mysterious gap between thought and action, between the verbal formulation of intent and its concrete realization. The prince himself is the most articulate of Shakespeare's tragic heroes, but he combines verbal fluency with a curious paralysis of the will. When Claudius asks Laertes in Act 4 what he would do "to show yourself in deed your father's son / More than in words" (4.7.126–27), Laertes replies instantly that, to be avenged, he would be happy to cut Hamlet's throat "i' the church." A demonstration that "in deed more than words" he is his father's son is conspicuously what the Hamlet of "O, what a rogue and peasant slave am I" and "How all occasions do inform against me" has not managed. We may respect him for this failing. Certainly, the sharply contrasted readiness of Laertes to act without thinking is unlovely. The fact remains that Hamlet is a man suffering from a peculiar malaise. In his mind, speech and event, language and its realization have become separate and disjunct. He can initiate action only when he has no time to subject it, first, to words: when he stabs impulsively through the arras and kills Polonius, when he sends Rosencrantz and Guildenstern to death *before* "I could make a prologue to my brains" (5.2.30), boards the pirate ship in the heat of the moment or finally, without premeditation, kills the king. The Norwegian captain tells Hamlet in the fourth scene of Act 4 that Fortinbras is hazarding twenty thousand ducats and an army of two thousand men to gain "a little patch of ground / That hath in it no profit but the name" (4.4.19–20). Fortinbras here, as in other respects, is Hamlet's diametric opposite. He has converted a mere word, a name, into a pretext for action. Hamlet, on the other hand, allows a tangible situation, the fact of a father's murder, to dissolve into words alone.

[1971]

STANLEY WELLS

On the First Soliloquy

More than most plays, *Hamlet* is a series of opportunities for virtuosity. This is true above all of the role of Hamlet himself. "Hamlet," wrote Max Beerbohm, is "a hoop through which every very eminent actor must, sooner or later, jump." There is no wonder that it has been such a favourite part with actors, and even with actresses. The performer has the opportunity to demonstrate a wide range of ability, to be melancholy and gay, charming and cynical, thoughtful and flippant, tender and cruel, calm and impassioned, noble and vindictive, downcast and witty, all within a few hours. He can wear a variety of costumes, he need not disguise good looks, he can demonstrate athletic ability, he has perhaps the longest role in drama—he could scarcely ask for more, except perhaps the opportunity to sing and dance.

And if the role of Hamlet is the greatest reason for the play's popularity with actors, the character of Hamlet is surely the greatest reason for its popularity with audiences. Hamlet is the most sympathetic of tragic heroes. We are drawn to him by his youth, his intelligence, and his vulnerability. As soon as he appears we are conscious of one of the sources of his appeal: his immense capacity for taking life seriously. It may sound like a slightly repellent quality, but I don't mean to imply that he is excessively gloomy or over-earnest. Often he is deeply dejected: but he has good cause. There is nothing exceptional about his emotional reactions except perhaps their intensity. He has a larger-than-life capacity for experience, a fullness of response, a depth of feeling, a vibrancy of living, which mark him out from the ordinary. He is a raw nerve in the court of Denmark, disconcertingly liable to make the instinctive rather than the conditioned response. This cuts him off from those around him, but it puts him into peculiar contact with the audience. And as Hamlet is to the other figures of the play, so his soliloquies are to the role, for in them Shakespeare shows us the raw nerves of Hamlet himself.

The use of soliloquy is one of the most brilliant features of the play, for in these speeches Shakespeare solves a major technical problem in the presentation of his central character. The young man who takes himself seriously, who persists in explaining himself and his problems, is someone we are apt—perhaps too apt— to regard as a bore. We have all had experience of him, and so probably have most of our friends. On the other hand, the desire to know someone to the depths is fundamental to human nature. Here was both a problem and a challenge: how to let Hamlet reveal himself without becoming an almighty bore? Shakespeare found a double solution. First, he caused Hamlet to conduct his deepest self-communings in solitude, so that there is none of the awkwardness associated with the presence of a confidant. And secondly, the soliloquies are written in a style which presents us not with conclusions but with the very processes of Hamlet's mind.

There had been nothing like this in drama before: nothing which, while retaining a verse form, at the same time so vividly revealed what Shakespeare elsewhere calls "the quick forge and working-house of thought". (*Henry the Fifth* [5.Pro.23]). Vocabulary, syntax, and rhythm all contribute to the effect. Consider the second half of Hamlet's first soliloquy, beginning with his contrast between his uncle and his dead father:

> That it should come to this!
> But two months dead—nay, not so much, not two.
> So excellent a king, that was to this
> Hyperion to a satyr, so loving to my mother
> That he might not beteem the winds of heaven
> Visit her face too roughly. Heaven and earth,
> Must I remember? Why, she would hang on him
> As if increase of appetite had grown
> By what it fed on, and yet within a month—
> Let me not think on 't; frailty, thy name is woman!—
> A little month, or ere those shoes were old
> With which she followed my poor father's body,
> Like Niobe, all tears, why she, even she—
> O God, a beast that wants discourse of reason,
> Would have mourned longer—married with my uncle,
> My father's brother, but no more like my father
> Than I to Hercules. Within a month,
> Ere yet the salt of most unrighteous tears
> Had left the flushing of her gallèd eyes,
> She married. O, most wicked speed, to post
> With such dexterity to incestuous sheets!
> It is not, nor it cannot come to good.
> But break, my heart, for I must hold my tongue.

(1.2.137–59)

5   The anguish that it causes Hamlet to think of his mother's over-hasty marriage is conveyed as much by the tortured syntax as by direct statement; we share his difficulty as he tries—and fails—to assimilate these unwelcome facts into his consciousness, seeking to bring under emotional control the discordant elements of his disrupted universe: his love of his dead father, his love of his mother combined

with disgust at her marriage to the uncle whom he loathes, and the disillusion with womankind that this has provoked in him. The short exclamations interrupting the sentence structure point his horror: the rhythms of ordinary speech within the verse give immediacy to the contrasts in phrases such as "Hyperion to a satyr" and "Than I to Hercules"; and the concreteness of the imagery betrays the effort it costs him to master the unwelcome nature of the facts which it expresses: his mother's haste to marry "or ere those shoes were old / With which she followed my poor father's body"—it is as if only by concentrating on the matter-of-fact, physical aspects of the scene can he bear to contemplate it, or bring it within his belief. He ends on a note of utter helplessness: he alone sees the truth; he knows that his mother's actions, which both he and she see as evil, must bring forth evil; but he, the only emotionally honest person there, cannot express his emotion—except to us.

[1995]

ELAINE SHOWALTER
Representing Ophelia

"Of all the characters in *Hamlet*," Bridget Lyons has pointed out, "Ophelia is most persistently presented in terms of symbolic meanings." Her behavior, her appearance, her gestures, her costume, her props, are freighted with emblematic significance, and for many generations of Shakespearean critics her part in the play has seemed to be primarily iconographic. Ophelia's symbolic meanings, moreover, are specifically feminine. Whereas for Hamlet madness is metaphysical, linked with culture, for Ophelia it is a product of the female body and female nature, perhaps that nature's purest form. On the Elizabethan stage, the conventions of female insanity were sharply defined. Ophelia dresses in white, decks herself with "fantastical garlands" of wild flowers, and enters, according to the stage directions of the "Bad" Quarto, "distracted" playing on a lute with her "hair down singing." Her speeches are marked by extravagant metaphors, lyrical free associations, and "explosive sexual imagery." She sings wistful and bawdy ballads, and ends her life by drowning.

All of these conventions carry specific messages about femininity and sexuality. Ophelia's virginal and vacant white is contrasted with Hamlet's scholar's garb, his "suits of solemn black." Her flowers suggest the discordant double images of female sexuality as both innocent blossoming and whorish contamination; she is the "green girl" of pastoral, the virginal "Rose of May" and the sexually explicit madwoman who, in giving away her wild flowers and herbs, is symbolically deflowering herself. The "weedy trophies" and phallic "long purples" which she wears to her death intimate an improper and discordant sexuality that Gertrude's lovely elegy cannot quite obscure. In Elizabethan and Jacobean drama, the stage direction that a woman enters with dishevelled hair indicates that she might either be mad or the victim of a rape; the disordered hair, her offense against decorum, suggests sensuality in each case. The mad Ophelia's bawdy songs and verbal license, while they give her access to "an entirely different range of experience" from what she is allowed as the dutiful daughter, seem to be her one sanctioned form of self-assertion as a woman, quickly followed, as if in retribution, by her death.

Drowning too was associated with the feminine, with female fluidity as opposed to masculine aridity. In his discussion of the "Ophelia complex," the phenomenologist Gaston Bachelard traces the symbolic connections between women, water, and death. Drowning, he suggests, becomes the truly feminine death in the dramas of literature and life, one which is a beautiful immersion and submersion in the female element. Water is the profound and organic symbol of the liquid woman whose eyes are so easily drowned in tears, as her body is the repository of blood, amniotic fluid, and milk. A man contemplating this feminine suicide understands it by reaching for what is feminine in himself, like Laertes, by a temporary surrender to his own fluidity—that is, his tears; and he becomes a man again in becoming once more dry—when his tears are stopped.

Clinically speaking, Ophelia's behavior and appearance are characteristic of the malady the Elizabethans would have diagnosed as female love-melancholy, or erotomania. From about 1580, melancholy had become a fashionable disease among young men, especially in London, and Hamlet himself is a prototype of the melancholy hero. Yet the epidemic of melancholy associated with intellectual and imaginative genius "curiously bypassed women." Women's melancholy was seen instead as biological, and emotional in origins.

[1985]

BERNICE W. KLIMAN

The BBC Hamlet: *A Television Production*

With *Hamlet*, the producers of the BBC Shakespeare Plays have finally met the demands of Shakespeare-on-television by choosing a relatively bare set, conceding only a few richly detailed movable panels and props to shape key locales. By avoiding both location and realistic settings, they point up the natural affinity between Shakespeare's stage and the undisguised sound set. This starkness of setting admits poetry, heightened intensity—and "what not that's sweet and happy."

The producers have thus made a valid choice from among television's three faces: one, broadcast films, whether made for television or not, which exploit location settings, long shots, and all the clichés we associate with movies, including sudden shifts of space and time and full use of distance, from the most extreme long shots to "eyes only" closeups; two, studio-shot television drama with naturalistic settings, such as the hospital corridors and middle-class living rooms of sitcoms and soap operas, mostly in mid- to close-shots, often interspersed, to be sure, with a bit of stock footage of highways and skylines to establish a realistic environment. This second style varies from a close representation of real action to frankly staged action, where canned laughter or even shadowy glimpses of the studio audience can heighten the staged effect. Three, there is bare space with little or no effort made to disguise that this is a televised activity with a television crew out of sight but nearby. News broadcasts, talk shows and some television drama fit into this third category. Because of its patently unrepresentational quality, this last type offers the most freedom in shooting style. To all three kinds of settings we bring particular expectations in response to their conventions.

Shakespeare's plays work best in the last kind of television space, I believe, because it avoids the clash between realism and poetry, between the unity often expected in realistic media and the disunity and ambiguity of many of the plays, especially *Hamlet*. Yet, while closest to the kind of stage Shakespeare wrote for, the bare television set can be stretched through creative camera work. For example, when Hamlet follows the ghost in the BBC play, the two repeatedly walk across the frame and out of it, first from one direction, then from another; framing fosters the illusion of extended space. Freeing this *Hamlet* from location (as in the BBC *As You Like It*) and from realistic sets (as in the BBC *Measure for Measure*—however well those sets worked for that play) allows the play to be as inconsistent as it is, with, as Bernard Beckerman has so brilliantly explained in *Shakespeare at the Globe, 1599–1609,* a rising and falling action in each individual scene rather than through the course of the drama as a whole. It also allows for acting, the bravura kind that Derek Jacobi is so capable of.

Although gradually coalescing like the pointillism of impressionistic paintings into a subtly textured portrait, at first his mannerisms suggesting madness seem excessive. It is to be expected, perhaps, that Hamlet is a bit unhinged after the ghost scene, but Jacobi's rapid, hard blows to his forehead with the flat of his hand as he says "My tables" recall the desperation of Lear's cry: "O, let me not be mad, not mad, sweet heaven." And soon after, following the last couplet of the scene, Hamlet, maniacally playful, widens his eyes and points, pretending to see the ghost again, then guffaws at Marcellus's fears. Even more unsettling is his laughter when he is alone, as while he is saying "The play's the thing / Wherein I'll catch the conscience of the King." More significantly, he breaks up his own "Mousetrap" by getting right into the play, destroying the distance between audience and stage (a very real raked proscenium-arch stage), spoiling it as a test, because Claudius has a right to be incensed at Hamlet's behavior. Of course, Hamlet does so because Claudius never gives himself away, an unusual and provocative but not impossible interpretation. Thus, Claudius can only have the court's sympathy as he calmly calls for light and uses it to examine Hamlet closely. Hamlet, in response, covers his face, then laughs.

5   Hamlet himself thinks he is mad. To Ophelia he says, as if the realization had suddenly struck him, "It *hath* made me mad [emphasis his]" (III.i.139). To his mother he stresses the word "essentially" in "I *essentially* am not in madness" (III.iv.194). That is, in all essential matters he can be considered sane, though mad around the edges. This indeed turns out to be the explanation.

However doubtful about Hamlet's sanity Jacobi's acting leaves us, in this production this question does not seem to make a difference because it does not have a bearing on the tragedy, and this is true at least partly because in each scene on this nonrealistic set we seem to start anew, ready to let Hamlet's behavior tell us if he is mad or not. Moreover, if Hamlet is mad, it is not so totally as to obscure reason or sensibility. Far from it. It is more as if exacerbated reason and sensibility sometimes tip him into madness. This madness is no excuse for action or delay; it is simply part of the suffering that Hamlet is heir to.

Hamlet, then, is left to struggle against himself—surely where Shakespeare intended the struggle to abide. One of the conflicts in this Hamlet results from his affinity, perhaps, more to the bureaucratic Claudius who handles war-scares with diplomacy and who sits at a desk while brooding over his sins than to the warlike King Hamlet who comes in full armor. Hamlet may admire Fortinbras but is himself more like the bookish Horatio. Through nuance of gesture, through body movement, through a face that is indeed a map of all emotions, Jacobi shapes a Hamlet who loves his father too much to disregard his command, yet who cannot hate his step-father enough to attend to it. Because Jacobi conveys so fully Hamlet's aloneness and vulnerability, one could be struck, for the first time, by the ghost's silence about his son. There is no declaration of love, no concern about Hamlet's ascension to the throne. Hamlet is doomed, it seems, to care about those who consistently care more for others than for him.

All of this production's richness and suggestiveness was realized not only because Jacobi is a marvelous actor—as indeed he is—but also because within the set's spareness that acting could unfold, an acting style that subsumes and transcends the "real." This production's space tells us what is possible for television presentations of Shakespeare. The more bare the set, it seems, the more glowing the words, the more immediate our apprehension of the enacted emotion.

[1988]

WILL SARETTA

What follows is an undergraduate's review, published in a college newspaper, of Kenneth Branagh's film version of Hamlet *(1996).*

Branagh's Film of Hamlet

Kenneth Branagh's *Hamlet* opened last night at the Harmon Auditorium, and will be shown again on Wednesday and Thursday at 7:30 p.m. According to the clock the evening will be long—the film runs for four hours, and in addition there is one ten-minute intermission—but you will enjoy every minute of it.

Well, almost every minute. Curiously, the film begins and ends relatively weakly, but most of what occurs in between is good and much of it is wonderful. The beginning is weak because it is too strong; Bernardo, the sentinel, offstage says "Who's there?" but before he gets a reply he crashes onto the screen and knocks Francisco down. The two soldiers grapple, swords flash in the darkness, and Francisco finally says, "Nay, answer me. Stand and unfold yourself." Presumably Branagh wanted to begin with a bang, but here, as often, more is less. A quieter, less physical opening in which Bernardo, coming on duty, hears a noise and demands that the maker of the noise identify himself and Francisco, the sentinel on duty, rightly demands that the newcomer identify *himself,* would catch the uneasiness and the mystery that pervades the play much better than does Branagh's showy beginning.

Similarly, at the end of the film, we get too much. For one thing, shots of Fortinbras's army invading Elsinore alternate with shots of the duel between Hamlet and King Claudius's pawn, Laertes, and they merely distract us from what really counts in this scene, the duel itself, which will result in Hamlet's death but also in Hamlet's successful completion of his mission to avenge his father. Second, at the very end we get shots of Fortinbras's men pulling down a massive statue of Hamlet Senior, probably influenced by television and newspaper shots of statues of Lenin being pulled down when the Soviet Union was dissolved a few years earlier. This is ridiculous; *Hamlet* is not a play about the fall of Communism, or about one form of tyranny replacing another. Shakespeare's *Hamlet* is not about the triumph of Fortinbras. It is about Hamlet's brave and ultimately successful efforts to do what is right, against overwhelming odds, and to offer us the consolation that in a world where death always triumphs there nevertheless is something that can be called nobility.

What, then, is good about the film? First of all, the film gives us the whole play, whereas almost all productions, whether on the stage or in the movie house, give us drastically abbreviated versions. Although less is often more, when it comes to the text of *Hamlet*, more is better, and we should be grateful to Branagh for letting us hear all of the lines. Second, it is very well performed, with only a few exceptions. Jack Lemmon as Marcellus is pretty bad, but fortunately the part is small. Other big-name actors in small parts—Charlton Heston as the Player King, Robin Williams as Osric, and Billy Crystal as the First Grave-digger—are admirable. But of course the success or failure of any production of *Hamlet* will depend chiefly on the actor who plays Hamlet, and to a considerable degree on the actors who play Claudius, Gertrude, Polonius, Ophelia, Laertes, and Horatio. There isn't space here to comment on all of these roles, but let it be said that Branagh's Prince Hamlet is indeed princely, a man who strikes us as having the ability to become a king, not a wimpy whining figure. When at the end Fortinbras says that if Hamlet had lived to become the king, he would "have proved most royal," we believe him. And his adversary, King Claudius, though morally despicable, is a man of great charm and great ability. The two men are indeed "mighty opposites," to use Hamlet's own words.

5 Branagh's decision to set the play in the late nineteenth century rather than in the Elizabethan period of Shakespeare's day and rather than in our own day contributes to this sense of powerful forces at work. If the play were set in Shakespeare's day, the men would wear tights, and if it were set in our day they would wear suits or trousers and sports jackets and sweaters, but in the film all of the men wear military costumes (black for Hamlet, scarlet for Claudius, white for Laertes) and the women wear ball gowns of the Victorian period. Branagh gives us a world that is closer to our own than would Elizabethan costumes, but yet it is, visually at least, also distant enough to convey a sense of grandeur, which modern dress cannot suggest. Of course *Hamlet* can be done in modern dress, just as *Romeo and Juliet* was done, successfully, in the recent film starring Claire Danes and Leonardo DiCaprio, set in a world that seemed to be Miami Beach, but *Romeo and Juliet* is less concerned with heroism and grandeur than *Hamlet* is, so Branagh probably did well to avoid contemporary costumes.

Although Branagh is faithful to the text, in that he gives us the entire text, he knows that a good film cannot be made merely by recording on film a stage production, and so he gives us handsome shots of landscape, and of rich interiors—for instance, a great mirrored hall—that would be beyond the resources of any theatrical production. I have already said that at the end, when Fortinbras's army swarms over the countryside and then invades the castle we get material that is distracting, indeed irrelevant, but there are also a few other distractions. It is all very well to let us *see* the content of long narrative speeches (for instance, when the Player King talks of the fall of Troy and the death of King Priam and the lament of Queen Hecuba, Branagh shows us these things, with John Gielgud as Priam and Judi Dench as Hecuba, performing in pantomime), but there surely is no need for us to see a naked Hamlet and a naked Ophelia in bed, when Polonius is warning Ophelia that Hamlet's talk of love cannot be trusted. Polonius's warning is not so long or so undramatic that we need to be entertained visually with an invention that finds not a word of support in the text. On the contrary, all of Ophelia's lines suggest that she would not be other than a dutiful young woman, obedient to the morals of the times and to her father's authority. Yet another of Branagh's unfortunate inventions is the prostitute who appears in Polonius's bedroom, during Polonius's interview with Reynaldo. A final example of unnecessary spectacle is Hamlet's killing of Claudius: He hurls his rapier the length of the hall, impaling Claudius, and then like some 1930's movie star he swings on the chandelier and drops down on Claudius to finish him off.

But it is wrong to end this review by pointing out faults in Branagh's film of *Hamlet*. There is so much in this film that is exciting, so much that is moving, so much that is . . . , well, so much that is *Hamlet* (which is to say that it is a great experience), that the film must be recommended without reservation. Go to see it. The four hours will fly.

A postscript. It is good to see that Branagh uses color-blind casting. Voltemand, Fortinbras's Captain, and the messenger who announces Laertes's return are all blacks—the messenger is a black woman—although of course medieval Denmark and Elizabethan England, and, for that matter, Victorian England, would not have routinely included blacks. These performers are effective, and it is appropriate that actors of color take their place in the world's greatest play.

[2000]

CHAPTER 15

Reading and Writing about Poems

Chapter Preview

After reading this chapter, you will be able to

- Identify and analyze the elements of poetry
- Explicate a poem
- Classify types of rhythm
- Write a successful paper about a poem, using a writing process that moves from first annotations to final draft

Elements of Poetry

The Speaker and the Poet

The **speaker**, **voice**, **mask**, or **persona** (Latin for *mask*) that speaks in a poem is not usually identical with the poet who writes it. The poet assumes a role or imitates the speech of a person in a particular situation. The nineteenth-century English poet Robert Browning, for instance, in "My Last Duchess," invented a Renaissance Italian duke who, in his palace, talks about his first wife and his art collection with an emissary from a count who is negotiating to offer his daughter in marriage to the duke.

In reading a poem, then, the first and most important question to ask yourself is this: Who is speaking? If an audience and a setting are suggested, keep them in mind, too, although they are not always indicated in a poem. Consider, for example, the following poem by Emily Dickinson.

EMILY DICKINSON

For biographical information on Emily Dickinson, see page 856.

I'm Nobody! Who are you?

I'm Nobody! Who are you?
Are you—Nobody—too?
Then there's a pair of us!
Don't tell! they'd banish us—you know!

How dreary—to be—Somebody!
How public—like a Frog—

5

To tell your name—the livelong June—
To an admiring Bog!

[1861?]

We cannot quite say that the speaker is Emily Dickinson, although, if we have read a fair number of her poems, we can say that the voice in this poem is familiar, and perhaps here we *can* talk of Dickinson rather than of "the speaker of the poem," since this speaker (unlike Browning's Renaissance duke) clearly is not a figure who is utterly remote from the poet.

Let's consider the sort of person we hear in "I'm Nobody! Who are you?" (Read it aloud to see if you agree with what we say. In fact, you should test each of our assertions by reading the poem aloud.)

- The voice in the first line is rather like that of a child playing a game with a friend.
- In the second and third lines, the speaker sees the reader as a fellow spirit ("Are you—Nobody—too?") and invites the reader to join the speaker ("Then there's a pair of us!"), to form a conspiracy of silence against outsiders ("Don't tell!").

In "they'd banish us," however, we hear a word that a child would not be likely to use, and we probably feel that the speaker is a shy but (with the right companion) playful adult, who here is speaking to an intimate friend, the reader. By means of "banish," a word that brings to mind images of a king's court, the speaker almost comically inflates and thereby makes fun of the "they" who are opposed to "us."

In the second stanza, or we might better say in the space between the two stanzas, the speaker puts aside the childlike manner. In "How dreary," the first words of the second stanza, we hear a sophisticated voice, one might even say a world-weary voice or a voice perhaps with more than a touch of condescension. But, since by now we are paired with the speaker in a conspiracy against outsiders, we enjoy the contrast that the speaker makes between the Nobodies and the Somebodies. Who are these Somebodies, these people who would imperiously "banish" the speaker and the friend? What are the Somebodies like?

How dreary—to be—Somebody!
How public—like a Frog—
To tell your name—the livelong June—
To an admiring Bog!

The last two lines do at least two things:

- They amusingly explain to the speaker's new friend (the reader) in what way a Somebody is public (it proclaims its presence all day), and
- they indicate the absurdity of the Somebody-Frog's behavior (the audience is "an admiring Bog").

By the end of the poem, we are convinced that it is better to be a Nobody (like Dickinson and the reader?) than a Somebody (a loudmouth).

Dickinson did not always speak in this persona, however. In another poem, "Wild Nights—Wild Nights," probably written in the same year as "I'm Nobody! Who are you?," Dickinson speaks as an impassioned lover, but we need not assume that the beloved is actually in the presence of the lover. Since the second line says,

"Were I with Thee," the reader must assume that the person addressed is *not* present. The poem represents a state of mind—a sort of talking to oneself—rather than an address to another person.

Wild Nights—Wild Nights

Wild Nights—Wild Nights,
Were I with Thee
Wild Nights should be
Our luxury

Futile—the Winds   5
To a Heart in port—
Done with the Compass—
Done with the Chart!

Rowing in Eden—
Ah, the Sea!   10
Might I but moor—Tonight—
In Thee.

[c. 1861]

This speaker is passionately in love. The following questions invite you to look more closely at how the speaker of "Wild Nights—Wild Nights" is characterized.

Joining the Conversation: Critical Thinking and Writing

1. How does this poem communicate the speaker's state of mind? For example, in the first stanza (lines 1–4), what—beyond the meaning of the words—is communicated by the repetition of "Wild Nights"? In the last stanza (lines 9–12), what is the tone of "Ah, the Sea!"? ("Tone" means something like emotional coloring, as for instance a "businesslike tone," a "bitter tone," or an "eager tone.")
2. Paraphrase (that is, put into your own words) the second stanza. What does this stanza communicate about the speaker's love for the beloved? Compare your paraphrase and the original. What does the form of the original sentences (the *omission,* for instance, of the verbs of lines 5 and 6 and of the subject in lines 7 and 8) communicate?
3. Paraphrase the last stanza. How does "Ah, the Sea!" fit into your paraphrase? If you had trouble fitting it in, do you think the poem would be better off without it? If not, why not?

The voice speaking in a poem may have the ring of the author's own voice, and to make a distinction between speaker and author may at times seem perverse. Some poetry (especially contemporary American poetry) is highly autobiographical. Still, even in autobiographical poems, it may be convenient to distinguish between author and speaker. The speaker of a given poem is, let's say, Sylvia Plath in her role as parent, or Sylvia Plath in her role as daughter, not simply Sylvia Plath the poet.

The Language of Poetry: Diction and Tone

How is a voice, mask, or persona created? From the whole of language, the author consciously or unconsciously selects certain words and grammatical constructions; this selection constitutes the persona's diction. It is, then, partly by the diction that we come to know the speaker of a poem. Just as in life there is a difference between people who speak of a "belly button," a "navel," or an "umbilicus," so in poetry there is a difference between speakers who use one word rather than another. It is also possible that all three of these terms may be part of a given speaker's vocabulary, and the speaker's choice among the three would depend on the situation. That is, in addressing a child, the speaker would probably use the phrase "belly button"; in addressing an adult other than a family member or a close friend, the speaker might be more likely to use "navel"; and, if the speaker is a physician addressing an audience of physicians, he or she most likely would use "umbilicus." But this is only to say, again, that the dramatic situation in which you find yourself helps to define you and helps to establish the particular role that you are playing.

Some words are used in virtually all poems: *I, see, and,* and the like. Still, the grammatical constructions in which they appear may help to define the speaker. In Dickinson's "Wild Nights—Wild Nights," for instance, expressions such as "Were I with Thee" and "Might I" indicate a speaker of an earlier century than ours, and probably an educated speaker.

Speakers have attitudes toward

- themselves,
- their subjects, and
- their audiences,

and, consciously or unconsciously, they choose their words, pitch, and modulation accordingly; all these add up to their tone. In written literature, tone must be detected without the aid of the ear, although it's a good idea to read poetry aloud, trying to find the appropriate tone of voice. The reader must understand by the selection and sequence of words the way the words are meant to sound—playful, angry, confidential, or ironic, for example. The reader must catch what Frost calls "the speaking tone of voice somehow entangled in the words and fastened to the page for the ear of the imagination."

WILLIAM SHAKESPEARE

For biographical information on William Shakespeare, see page 640. We print other sonnets on pages 188, 342, and 972.

Sonnet 146

Poor soul, the center of my sinful earth,
[My sinful earth] these rebel pow'rs that thee array,
Why dost thou pine within and suffer dearth,
Painting thy outward walls so costly gay?
Why so large cost,° having so short a lease,   5
Dost thou upon thy fading mansion spend?
Shall worms, inheritors of this excess,

5 cost expense.

Eat up thy charge? Is this thy body's end?
Then, soul, live thou upon thy servant's loss,
And let that pine to aggravate thy store;   10
Buy terms divine° in selling hours of dross;
Within be fed, without be rich no more.
So shalt thou feed on Death, that feeds on men,
    And death once dead, there's no more dying then.

[1609]

Joining the Conversation: Critical Thinking and Writing

1. "My sinful earth," in line 2, is doubtless an error made by the printer of the first edition (1609), who mistakenly repeated the end of the first line. Among suggested replacements are "Thrall to," "Fooled by," "Rebuke," "Leagued with," and "Feeding." If you wish, suggest your own correction. Which do you prefer?
2. In what tone of voice would you speak the first line? The last line? Trace the speaker's shifts in emotion throughout the poem.
3. Is the speaker presenting an argument? What is the argument (if you think there is one)? How does the speaker support it?

Figurative Language

Robert Frost once said, "Poetry provides the one permissible way of saying one thing and meaning another." This is an exaggeration, but it shrewdly suggests the importance of figurative language—saying one thing in terms of something else. Words have their literal meanings, but they can also be used so that something other than the literal meaning is implied. "My love is a rose" is, literally, nonsense, for a person is not a five-petaled, many-stamened plant with a spiny stem. But the suggestions of *rose* (at least for Robert Burns, who compared his beloved to a rose in the line "My love is like a red, red rose") include "delicate beauty," "soft," and "perfumed," and thus the word *rose* can be meaningfully applied—figuratively rather than literally—to "my love." The girl is fragrant; her skin is perhaps like a rose in texture and (in some measure) color; she will not keep her beauty long. The poet, that is, has communicated his perception very precisely.

People who write about poetry have found it convenient to name the various kinds of figurative language. Just as the student of geology employs such special terms as *kames* and *eskers*, the student of literature employs special terms to name things as accurately as possible. The following paragraphs discuss the most common terms.

In a **simile**, items from different classes are explicitly compared by a connective word such as *like, as,* or *than,* or by a verb such as *appears* or *seems.* (If the objects compared are from the same class, for example, "Tokyo is like Los Angeles," no simile is present.)

> It is a beauteous evening, calm and free.
> The holy time is quiet as a Nun,
> Breathless with adoration.

—William Wordsworth

11 buy terms divine buy ages of immortality.

A **metaphor** asserts the identity, without a connective word such as *like* or a verb such as *appears,* of terms that are literally incompatible.

> Umbrellas clothe the beach in every hue.

> —Elizabeth Bishop

Two common types of metaphor have Greek names. In **synecdoche**, the whole is replaced by the part, or the part is replaced by the whole. For example, *bread* in "Give us this day our daily bread" replaces all sorts of food. In **metonymy**, something is named that replaces something closely related to it. For example, James Shirley names certain objects, using them to replace social classes (royalty and the peasantry) to which they are related:

> Scepter and crown must tumble down
> And in the dust be equal made
> With the poor crooked scythe and spade.

The attribution of human feelings or characteristics or abstractions to inanimate objects is called **personification**.

> Memory,
> that exquisite blunderer.

> —Amy Clampitt

> There's Wrath who has learnt every trick of guerilla warfare,
> The shamming dead, the night-raid, the feinted retreat.

> —W. H. Auden

> Hope, thou bold taster of delight.

> —Richard Crashaw

Crashaw's personification, "Hope, thou bold taster of delight," is also an example of the figure called **apostrophe**, an address to a person or thing not literally listening. Wordsworth begins a sonnet by apostrophizing Milton:

> Milton, thou shouldst be living at this hour.

> —William Wordsworth

What conclusions can we draw about figurative language? First, figurative language, with its literally incompatible terms, forces the reader to attend to the **connotations** (suggestions, associations) rather than to the **denotations** (dictionary definitions) of one of the terms. Second, although figurative language is said to differ from ordinary speech, it is found in ordinary speech as well as in poetry and other literary forms. "It rained cats and dogs," "War is hell," "Don't be a pig," "Mr. Know-it-all," and other tired figures of speech are part of our daily utterances. But through repeated use, these, and most of the figures of speech that we use, have lost whatever impact they once had and are only a shade removed from expressions which, though once figurative, have become literal: the *eye* of a needle, a *branch* office, the *face* of a clock. Third, good figurative language is usually concrete, condensed, and interesting.

We should mention, too, that figurative language is not limited to literary writers; it is used by scientists and social scientists—by almost everyone who is concerned with effective expression.

Figures of speech are not a fancy way of speaking. Quite the opposite: Writers use figures of speech because they are forceful and exact. Literal language would be not only less interesting but also less precise.

We have already provided two sonnets by Shakespeare; here is a third, but before you read it, we might mention that, if you have read the other sonnets, you may recall that they abound with figurative language. For instance, in Sonnet 73 (page 188), the speaker says that he is aging, not by telling us how old he is, but by saying

> he is like a tree with "yellow leaves" [we might say, again using a figure of
>   speech, that he is in the autumn of his life],
>
> he is in his "twilight," and
>
> he is like a fire that now is merely embers lying on a bed of ashes.

In Sonnet 146 (page 769), the speaker compares his body to "earth" and to a "fading mansion," and he says that the body is the "servant" of the soul—expressions that are figurative, not literal. In the following poem, however, we see that Shakespeare can also laugh at figurative comparisons. His contemporaries wrote countless sonnets in which they compared their beloved's eyes to the sun, the redness of her lips to coral, her blonde hair to fine gold wire, her white complexion and red cheeks to damask roses (or perhaps to a silk called damask—mixed red and white), her breath to perfume, her speech to music, and her gait to that of a goddess (goddesses were said to walk on air, not on earth). Now see how Shakespeare describes his mistress. But, first, two cautions: In line 8, "reeks," in "the breath that from my mistress reeks," in Shakespeare's day did not have the strong negative suggestion of a bad smell that it has today; rather, it meant something like "emanates." Second, in the final line, "any she belied with false compare" means "any woman misrepresented by false comparisons."

Sonnet 130

My mistress' eyes are nothing like the sun;
Coral is far more red than her lips' red;
If snow be white, why then her breasts are dun;
If hairs be wires, black wires grow on her head.
I have seen roses damasked, red and white,   5
But no such roses see I in her cheeks;
And in some perfumes is there more delight
Than in the breath that from my mistress reeks.
I love to hear her speak, yet well I know
That music hath a far more pleasing sound;   10
I grant I never saw a goddess go;
My mistress, when she walks, treads on the ground.
And yet, by heaven, I think my love as rare
As any she belied with false compare.

[1609]

Joining the Conversation: Critical Thinking and Writing

1. Shakespeare here seems to ridicule figurative language, yet he uses figurative language in his sonnets and his plays. How can this be explained?

2. If Shakespeare is trying to convey his feelings of love, is this use of figurative language successful? Based on the imagery found in the poem, do you create a negative image of his beloved in your mind? Is his claim to love more true or less true because he denies that his mistress matches these images of beauty?

Imagery and Symbolism

When we read *rose*, we may more or less call to mind a picture of a rose, or perhaps we are reminded of the odor or texture of a rose. Whatever in a poem appeals to any of our senses (including sensations of heat as well as of sight, smell, taste, touch, and sound) is an image. In short, images are the sensory content of a work, whether literal or figurative. When a poet says "My rose" and is speaking about a rose, we have no figure of speech, although we still have an image. If, however, "My rose" is a shortened form of "My love is a rose," some would say that the poet is using a metaphor, but others would say that, because the first term is omitted ("My love is"), the rose is a symbol. A poem about the transience of a rose might compel the reader to feel that the transience of female beauty is the larger theme even though it is never explicitly stated.

Some symbols are **conventional symbols**; that is, people have agreed to accept them as standing for something other than their literal meanings. A poem about the cross would probably be about Christianity; similarly, the rose has long been a symbol for love. In Virginia Woolf's novel *Mrs. Dalloway,* the husband communicates his love by proffering this conventional symbol: "He was holding out flowers—roses, red and white roses. (But he could not bring himself to say he loved her; not in so many words.)." Here is a poem that uses the conventional symbol of the rose.

EDMUND WALLER

Edmund Waller (1606–87), born into a country family of wealth in Buckinghamshire in England, attended Eton College and the University of Cambridge before spending most of his life as a member of Parliament. When the Puritans came to power, he was imprisoned and eventually banished to France, although he was soon allowed to return to England. When the monarchy was restored, he returned to Parliament.

Song

   Go, lovely rose,
Tell her that wastes her time and me,
   That now she knows,
When I resemble her to thee,
   How sweet and fair she seems to be.   5

   Tell her that's young,
And shuns to have her graces spied,
   That hadst thou sprung
In deserts where no men abide,
   Thou must have uncommended died.   10
   Small is the worth

Of beauty from the light retired:
   Bid her come forth,
Suffer her self to be desired,
   And not blush so to be admired.   15

Then die, that she
The common fate of all things rare
    May read in thee,
How small a part of time they share,
    That are so wondrous sweet and fair.   20

[1645]

Joining the Conversation: Critical Thinking and Writing

1. In the first stanza, the poet says that the resemblance between the rose and the woman is that both are "sweet and fair," words that reappear at the end of the poem. In between these two passages, what additional resemblances does the poet find?
2. The poem contains a narrative of the brief life and the imminent death of a rose. In the third stanza, however, the rose is momentarily forgotten while the poet meditates and speaks directly about the woman. If you agree that this third stanza could conceivably stand as an independent poem, explain why it becomes a better poem when placed within the context of the address to the rose.

Let's now look at yet another poem that speaks of a rose, but in a much less traditional way.

WILLIAM BLAKE

For biographical information on William Blake, see page 1015.

The Sick Rose

O Rose, thou art sick.
The invisible worm,
That flies in the night
In the howling storm:

Has found out thy bed   5
Of crimson joy:
And his dark secret love
Does thy life destroy.

[1794]

A reader might perhaps argue that the worm is invisible (line 2) merely because it is hidden within the rose, but an "invisible worm / That flies in the night" is more than a long, slender, soft-bodied, creeping animal; and a rose that has, or is, a "bed / Of crimson joy" is more than a gardener's rose. Blake's worm and rose suggest things beyond themselves—a stranger, more vibrant world than the world we are usually aware of. They are, in short, symbolic, although readers will doubtless differ in their interpretations. Perhaps we find ourselves half thinking, for example, that the worm is male, the rose female, and that the poem is about the violation of virginity. Or, we may think that the poem is about the destruction of beauty: Woman's beauty, rooted in joy, is destroyed by a power that feeds on her.

These interpretations are not fully satisfying: The poem presents a worm and a rose, and yet it is not merely about a worm and a rose. These objects resonate, stimulating our thoughts toward something else, but the something else is elusive. This is not to say, however, that symbols mean whatever any reader says they mean. A reader could scarcely support, we imagine, an interpretation arguing that the poem is about the need to love all aspects of nature. All interpretations are not equally valid; it's the writer's job to offer a reasonably persuasive interpretation.

A symbol, then, is an image so loaded with significance that it is not simply literal and it does not simply stand for something else; it is both itself *and* something else that it richly suggests, a manifestation of something too complex or too elusive to be otherwise revealed. Blake's poem is about a blighted rose and at the same time about much more. In a symbol, as the nineteenth-century Scottish essayist and historian Thomas Carlyle wrote, "the Infinite is made to blend with the Finite, to stand visible, and as it were, attainable there."

Verbal Irony and Paradox

Among the most common devices in poems is **verbal irony**: The speaker's words mean more or less the opposite of what they seem to say. Sometimes verbal irony takes the form of **overstatement**, or **hyperbole**, as when Lady Macbeth says, while sleepwalking, "All the perfumes of Arabia will not sweeten this little hand." Sometimes it takes the form of **understatement**, as when Andrew Marvell's speaker in "To His Coy Mistress" remarks with cautious wryness, "The grave's a fine and private place, / But none, I think, do there embrace," or when Sylvia Plath sees an intended suicide as "the big strip tease." Speaking broadly, intensely emotional contemporary poems like those of Plath often use irony to undercut—and thus make acceptable—the emotion presented.

Another common device in poems is **paradox**: the assertion of an apparent contradiction, as in Marvell's "am'rous birds of prey" in "To His Coy Mistress." Normally, we think of amorous birds as gentle—doves, for example—and not as birds of prey, such as hawks. Another example of an apparent contradiction: In "Auld Lang Syne," there is the paradox that the remembrance of joy evokes sadness.

Structure

The arrangement of the parts, the organization of the entire poem, is its **structure**. Sometimes the poem is divided into blocks of, say, four lines each, but even if the poem is printed as a solid block, it probably has some principle of organization. It may move, for example, from sorrow in the first two lines to joy in the next two lines or from a question in the first three lines to an answer in the last line.

If a poem is broken down into blocks on the page, we can analyze the form of its stanzas. A **stanza** is an arranged grouping of lines, separated by space from the poem's other lines; the use of space forms a division in the poem that indicates a stanza. The stanza's grouping of lines might be marked by shared length, meter, or rhyme. One stanza's pattern of lines is often repeated in the poem's other stanzas. A movement from one stanza to another often marks a movement in theme, mood, time, or thought. We analyze different stanza forms in more detail below.

An individual line of a poem can also create structure. A line's length can be purposely short or long: A line can be so short that it is comprised of one word or letter, or it can be so long that it doesn't fit on a page's width. A line will often call attention to its length when that length captures the ideas it is expressing; for example, a short line might call attention to the speaker's thoughts being interrupted.

The blank or negative space created by the lines and surrounding a poem creates the poem's shape. Both the stanza and line are dependent on space: a stanza is created by the space of a skipped line. Similarly, a line's length, indentation, and placement are created by the space that comes before and after it. Space heightens the effect of the regular or irregular patterning of the poem. If a word is isolated on a line, we notice it. If a line is indented and appears "off-kilter" from the rest of the poem, we notice it. By seeing a poem's layout on a page, we can tell if the poem exhibits a consistent pattern or if it breaks a pattern, and we can then question why the poem is taking that shape.

Rhythm and Versification: A Glossary for Reference

Rhythm (most simply, in English poetry, stresses at regular intervals) has a power of its own. A highly pronounced rhythm is common in such forms of poetry as charms, college yells, and lullabies; all of them are aimed at inducing a special effect magically. It is not surprising that *carmen,* the Latin word for poem or song, is also the Latin word for *charm* and the word from which our word *charm* is derived.

In much poetry, rhythm is only half heard, but its presence is suggested by the way poetry is printed. Prose (from the Latin *prorsus,* meaning "forward," "straight on") keeps running across the paper until the right-hand margin is reached; then, merely because the paper has given out, the writer or printer starts again at the left, with a lowercase letter. But verse (from the Latin *versus,* meaning "a turning") often ends well short of the right-hand margin. The next line begins at the left—usually with a capital letter—not because paper has run out, but because the rhythmic pattern begins again. Lines of poetry are continually reminding us that they have a pattern.

Note that a mechanical, unvarying rhythm may be good to put a baby to sleep, but it can be deadly to readers who want to stay awake. Poets vary their rhythm according to their purposes; they ought not to be so regular that they are (in W. H. Auden's words) "accentual pests." In competent hands, rhythm contributes to meaning; it says something. Ezra Pound had a relevant comment: "Rhythm *must* have meaning. It cannot be merely a careless dash off, with no grip and no real hold to the words and sense, a tumty tum tumty tum tum ta."

Consider this description of Hell from John Milton's *Paradise Lost* (stressed syllables are marked by ´, and unstressed syllables, by ˘:

> Rócks, cáves, lákes, féns, bógs, déns, ănd shádes ŏf déath.

The normal line in *Paradise Lost* is written in iambic feet—alternate unstressed and stressed syllables—but, in this line, Milton immediately follows one heavy stress with another, helping to communicate the "meaning"—the oppressive monotony of Hell. As a second example, consider the function of the rhythm in two lines by Alexander Pope:

> When Ájăx stríves sŏme róck's vást wéight tŏ thrów,
> Thĕ líne tóo lábŏrs, ănd thĕ wórds móve slów.

The stressed syllables do not merely alternate with the unstressed ones; rather, the great weight of the rock is suggested by three consecutive stressed words, "rock's vast weight," and the great effort involved in moving it is suggested by another three consecutive stresses, "line too labors," and by yet another three, "words move slow." Note also the abundant pauses within the lines. In the first line, for example, unless one's speech is slovenly, one must pause at least slightly after "Ajax," "strives," "rock's," "vast," "weight," and "throw." The grating sounds in "Ajax" and "rock's" do their work, too, and so do the explosive *t*'s.

When Pope wishes to suggest lightness, he reverses his procedure, and he groups *un*stressed syllables:

> Not so, when swift Camilla scours the plain,
> Flíés o'ěr th' ŭnbéndǐng córn, ǎnd skíms ǎlóng thě máin.

This last line has twelve syllables and is thus longer than the line about Ajax, but the addition of "along" helps to communicate lightness and swiftness because, in this line (it can be argued), neither syllable of "along" is strongly stressed. If "along" is omitted, the line still makes grammatical sense and becomes more "regular," but it also becomes less imitative of lightness.

The very regularity of a line may be meaningful, too. Shakespeare begins a sonnet thus:

> Whěn Í dǒ cóunt thě clóck thǎt télls thě tíme.

This line about a mechanism runs with appropriate regularity. (It is worth noting, too, that "count the clock" and "tells the time" emphasize the regularity by the repetition of sounds and syntax.) Now, notice what Shakespeare does in the middle of the next line:

> Aňd sée thě bráve dáy súnk ǐn hídeǒus níght.

The technical vocabulary of **prosody** (the study of the principles of verse structure, including meter, rhyme and other sound effects, and stanzaic patterns) is large. An understanding of these terms will not turn you into a poet, but it will enable you to write about some aspects of poetry more efficiently. The chief terms of prosody presented in the sections that follow will provide a good base.

Meter

Most poetry written in English has a pattern of stressed (accented) sounds. This pattern is the **meter** (from the Greek word for "measure"). Strictly speaking, we should not talk of "unstressed" or "unaccented" syllables, since to utter a syllable—however lightly—is to give it some stress. It is a matter of *relative* stress, but the fact is that "unstressed" or "unaccented" are parts of the established terminology of versification.

In a line of poetry, the **foot** is the basic unit of measurement. It is, on rare occasions, a single stressed syllable; but generally a foot consists of two or three syllables, one of which is stressed. The repetition of feet, then, produces a pattern of stresses throughout the poem.

Two cautions:

- A poem will seldom contain only one kind of foot throughout; significant variations usually occur, but one kind of foot is dominant.
- When reading a poem, we chiefly pay attention to the sense, not to a presupposed metrical pattern. By paying attention to the sense, we often find (reading aloud is a great help) that the stress falls on a word that, according

to the metrical pattern, would be unstressed. Or a word that, according to the pattern, would be stressed may be seen to be unstressed. Furthermore, by reading for sense, we find that not all stresses are equally heavy; some are almost as light as unstressed syllables, and sometimes there is a **hovering stress**—that is, the stress is equally distributed over two adjacent syllables. To repeat: We read for sense, allowing the syntax to help indicate the stresses.

Metrical Feet. There are six common types of metrical feet in English poetry:

- **Iamb (adjective: iambic):** one unstressed syllable followed by one stressed syllable. The iamb, said to be the most common pattern in English speech, is surely the most common in English poetry. The following example has four iambic feet:

  Mў héart ĭs líke ă sínging bírd.

  —Christina Rossetti

- **Trochee (trochaic):** one stressed syllable followed by one unstressed syllable.

  Wé wĕre vérў tírĕd, wé wĕre vérў mérrў

  —Edna St. Vincent Millay

- **Anapest (anapestic):** two unstressed syllables followed by one stressed syllable.

  Thĕre ăre mánў whŏ sáy thăt ă dóg hăs hĭs dáy.

  —Dylan Thomas

- **Dactyl (dactylic):** one stressed syllable followed by two unstressed syllables. This trisyllabic foot, like the anapest, is common in light verse or verse suggesting joy, but its use is not limited to such material, as Longfellow's Evangeline shows. Thomas Hood's sentimental "The Bridge of Sighs" begins

  Táke hĕr ŭp téndĕrlў.

- **Spondee (spondaic):** two stressed syllables; it is most often used as a substitute for an iamb or trochee.

  Smárt lád, tŏ slíp bĕtímes áwáy.

  —A. E. Housman

- **Pyrrhic:** two unstressed syllables; it is often not considered a legitimate foot in English.

Metrical Lines. A metrical line consists of one or more feet and is named for the number of feet in it. The following names are used:

- **monometer:** one foot
- **dimeter:** two feet
- **trimeter:** three feet
- **tetrameter:** four feet
- **pentameter:** five feet
- **hexameter:** six feet
- **heptameter:** seven feet

A line is scanned for the kind and number of feet in it, and the **scansion** tells you if it is, say, anapestic trimeter (three anapests):

> Ăs Ĭ cáme tŏ thĕ édge ŏf thĕ wóods.

> —Robert Frost

Or, in another example, if it is iambic pentameter:

> Thĕ súmmĕr thúndĕr, líke ă wóodĕn béll

> —Louise Bogan

A line ending with a stress has a **masculine ending**; a line ending with an extra unstressed syllable has a **feminine ending**. The **caesura** (usually indicated by the symbol / /) is a slight pause within the line. It need not be indicated by punctuation (notice the fourth and fifth lines in the following passage), and it does not affect the metrical count:

> Awake, my St. John! / / leave all meaner things
> To low ambition, / / and the pride of kings.
> Let us / / (since Life can little more supply
> Than just to look about us / / and to die)
> Expatiate free / / o'er all this scene of Man;
> A mighty maze! / / but not without a plan;
> A wild, / / where weeds and flowers promiscuous shoot;
> Or garden, / / tempting with forbidden fruit.

> —Alexander Pope

The varying position of the caesura helps to give Pope's lines an informality that plays against the formality of the pairs of rhyming lines.

An **end-stopped line** concludes with a distinct syntactical pause, but a **run-on line** has its sense carried over into the next line without syntactical pause. (The running on of a line is called **enjambment**.) In the following passage, only the first is a run-on line:

> Yet if we look more closely we shall find
> Most have the seeds of judgment in their mind:
> Nature affords at least a glimmering light;
> The lines, though touched but faintly, are drawn right.

> —Alexander Pope

Meter produces **rhythm**, recurrences at equal intervals, but rhythm (from a Greek word meaning "flow") is usually applied to larger units than feet. Often, it depends most obviously on pauses. Thus, a poem with run-on lines will have a different rhythm from a poem with end-stopped lines, even though both are in the same meter. Further, prose, though it is unmetrical, can have rhythm, too.

In addition to being affected by syntactical pause, rhythm is affected by pauses that are attributable to consonant clusters and to the length of words. Polysyllabic words establish a different rhythm from monosyllabic words, even in metrically identical lines. We can say, then, that rhythm is altered by shifts in meter, syntax, and the length and ease of pronunciation. But even with no such shift, even if a line is repeated verbatim, a reader may sense a change in rhythm. The rhythm of the final line of a poem, for example, may well differ from that of the line before, even though in all other respects the lines are identical, as in Frost's "Stopping by Woods on a Snowy Evening" (page 269), which concludes by repeating "And miles to go before I sleep." The reader may simply sense that this final line ought to be spoken, say, more slowly and with more stress on "miles."

Patterns of Sound

Though rhythm is basic to poetry, **rhyme**—the repetition of identical or similar stressed sound or sounds—is not. Rhyme is, presumably, pleasant in itself; it suggests order; and it also may be related to meaning, for it brings two words sharply together, often implying a relationship, as in the now trite *dove* and *love*, or in the more imaginative *throne* and *alone*.

The commonest patterns are:

- **Perfect rhyme** (or **exact rhyme**): differing consonant sounds followed by identical stressed vowel sounds. The following sounds, if any, are identical (*foe—toe; meet—fleet; buffer—rougher*). Notice that perfect rhyme involves identity of sound, not of spelling. *Fix* and *sticks*, like *buffer* and *rougher*, are perfect rhymes.
- **Half-rhyme** (or **off-rhyme**): rhymes in which only the final consonant sounds of the words are identical; the stressed vowel sounds as well as the initial consonant sounds, if any, differ (*soul—oil; mirth—forth; trolley—bully*).
- **Eye rhyme**: sounds that do not, in fact, rhyme but look as though they would rhyme (*cough—bough*).
- **Masculine rhyme**: final syllables that are stressed and, after their differing initial consonant sounds, are identical in sound (*stark—mark; support—retort*).
- **Feminine rhyme** (or **double rhyme**): stressed rhyming syllables followed by identical unstressed syllables (*revival—arrival; flatter—batter*). **Triple rhyme**: a kind of feminine rhyme in which identical stressed vowel sounds are followed by two identical unstressed syllables (*machinery—scenery; tenderly—slenderly*).
- **End rhyme** (or **terminal rhyme**): rhyming words that occur at the ends of the lines.
- **Internal rhyme**: a type of rhyme in which at least one of the rhyming words occurs within the line (Oscar Wilde's "Each narrow *cell* in which we *dwell*").
- **Alliteration**: sometimes defined as the repetition of initial sounds ("*A*ll the *a*wful *a*uguries," or "*B*ring me my *b*ow of *b*urning gold") and sometimes defined as the prominent repetition of a consonant ("a*f*ter li*f*e's *f*it*f*ul *f*ever").
- **Assonance**: the repetition, in words of proximity, of identical vowel sounds preceded and followed by differing consonant sounds. Whereas *tide* and *hide* are rhymes, *tide* and *mine* are assonantal.
- **Consonance**: the repetition of identical consonant sounds and differing vowel sounds in words in proximity (*fail—feel; rough—roof; pitter—patter*). Sometimes consonance is more loosely defined merely as the repetition of a consonant (*fail—peel*).
- **Onomatopoeia**: the use of words that imitate sounds, such as *hiss* and *buzz*. There is a mistaken tendency to see onomatopoeia everywhere—for example, in *thunder* and *horror*. Many words that are sometimes

thought to be onomatopoeic are not clearly imitative of the thing they refer to; they merely contain some sounds that, when we know what the word means, seem to have some resemblance to the thing they denote. Tennyson's lines from "Come down, O maid" are usually cited as an example of onomatopoeia:

> The moan of doves in immemorial elms
> And murmuring of innumerable bees.

Stanzaic Patterns

Lines of poetry are commonly arranged in a rhythmical unit called a **stanza** (from an Italian word meaning "room" or "stopping-place"). Usually, all of the stanzas in a poem have the same rhyme pattern. A stanza is sometimes called a **verse**, although *verse* may also mean a single line of poetry. (In discussing stanzas, rhymes are indicated by identical letters. Thus, *abab* indicates that the first and third lines rhyme with each other, while the second and fourth lines are linked by a different rhyme. An unrhymed line is denoted by *x*.) Common stanzaic forms in English poetry are the following:

- **Couplet**: a stanza of two lines, usually, but not necessarily, with end-rhymes. *Couplet* is also used for a pair of rhyming lines. The **octosyllabic couplet** is iambic or trochaic tetrameter:

  > Had we but world enough, and time,
  > This coyness, lady, were no crime.

  > —Andrew Marvell

- **Heroic couplet**: a rhyming couplet of iambic pentameter, often "closed"— that is, containing a complete thought, with a fairly heavy pause at the end of the first line and a still heavier pause at the end of the second line. Commonly, there is a parallel or an *antithesis* (contrast) within a line or between the two lines. It is called heroic because in England, especially in the eighteenth century, it was much used for heroic (epic) poems.

  > Some foreign writers, some our own despise;
  > The ancients only, or the moderns, prize.

  > —Alexander Pope

- **Triplet** (or **tercet**): a three-line stanza, usually with one rhyme:

  > Whenas in silks my Julia goes
  > Then, then, methinks, how sweetly flows
  > That liquefaction of her clothes.

  > —Robert Herrick

- **Quatrain**: a four-line stanza, rhymed or unrhymed. The **heroic** (or **elegiac**) **quatrain** is iambic pentameter, rhyming *abab*. That is, the first and third lines rhyme (so they are designated *a*), and the second and fourth lines rhyme (so they are designated *b*).
- **Sonnet**: a fourteen-line poem, predominantly in iambic pentameter. The rhyme is usually according to one of two schemes. The **Italian** (or

Petrarchan[1]) **sonnet** has two divisions: The first eight lines (rhyming *abba abba*) are the **octave**, and the last six lines (rhyming *cd cd cd,* or a variant) are the **sestet**. The second kind of sonnet, the **English** (or **Shakespearean**) **sonnet**, is usually arranged into three quatrains and a couplet, rhyming *abab cdcd efef gg*. In many sonnets, there is a marked correspondence between the rhyme scheme and the development of the thought. Thus, an Italian sonnet may state a generalization in the octave and a specific example in the sestet. Or, an English sonnet may give three examples—one in each quatrain—and draw a conclusion in the couplet.

BILLY COLLINS

Born in New York City in 1941, Collins is a professor of English at Lehman College of the City University of New York. He is the author of many books of poetry and the recipient of numerous awards, including one from the National Endowment for the Arts. Collins's Sailing Alone around the Room: New and Selected Poems was published in 2001; in the same year, he was appointed poet laureate of the United States.

The following sonnet uses the Petrarchan form, which consists of an octave and a sestet. Petrarch is additionally present in the poem by the allusion in line 3 to "a little ship on love's storm-tossed seas," because Petrarch compared the hapless lover, denied the favor of his mistress, to a ship in a storm: The lover cannot guide his ship because the North Star is hidden (Petrarch's beloved Laura averts her eyes), and the sails of the ship are agitated by the lover's pitiful sighs. As you will see, Petrarch and Laura explicitly enter the poem in the last three lines.

In line 8, Collins refers to the stations of the cross. In some Christian denominations, one of the devotions consists of prayers and meditations before each of fourteen stations or images set up along a path that commemorates the fourteen places at which Jesus halted when, just before the Crucifixion, he was making his way in Jerusalem to Golgotha.

Sonnet

All we need is fourteen lines, well, thirteen now,
and after this next one just a dozen
to launch a little ship on love's storm-tossed seas,
then only ten more left like rows of beans.
How easily it goes unless you get Elizabethan   5
and insist the iambic bongos must be played
and rhymes positioned at the ends of lines,
one for every station of the cross.
But hang on here while we make the turn
into the final six where all will be resolved,   10
where longing and heartache will find an end,
where Laura will tell Petrarch to put down his pen,
take off those crazy medieval tights,
blow out the lights, and come at last to bed.

[1999]

[1] So called after Francesco Petrarch (1304–74), the Italian poet who perfected and popularized the form.

Joining the Conversation: Critical Thinking and Writing

1. The headnote explains the stations of the cross (line 8), but what is the point of introducing this image into a sonnet?
2. Normally, the "turn" (*volta*) in an Italian sonnet occurs at the beginning of the ninth line; the first eight lines (the octave) establish some sort of problem, and the final six lines (the sestet) respond, for instance, by answering a question or by introducing a contrasting emotion. In your view, how satisfactorily does Collins handle this form? Support your evaluation with reasons.
3. How is Collins both mocking and using the sonnet form? How does he call attention to the conventions of the sonnet—and how does he make those conventions funny? What ideas is he exploring about how the sonnet does or does not capture the emotions of love?

Blank Verse and Free Verse

A good deal of English poetry is unrhymed, much of it in **blank verse**, that is, unrhymed iambic pentameter. Introduced into English poetry by Henry Howard, Earl of Surrey, in the middle of the sixteenth century, late in the century it became the standard medium (especially in the hands of Christopher Marlowe and Shakespeare) of English drama. In the seventeenth century, Milton used blank verse for *Paradise Lost,* and it has continued to be used in both dramatic and nondramatic literature. For an example, see the first scene of *Hamlet* (page 652), until the Ghost appears.

The second kind of unrhymed poetry that is fairly common in English, especially in the twentieth century, is **free verse** (or ***vers libre***): rhythmical lines varying in length, adhering to no fixed metrical pattern and usually unrhymed. The pattern is often largely based on repetition and parallel grammatical structure. For examples, see Walt Whitman's "A Noiseless Patient Spider" (page 855) and T. S. Eliot's "The Love Song of J. Alfred Prufrock" (page 297).

If you are going to write about a short poem (say, under thirty lines), it's not a bad idea to copy out the poem, writing it out or typing it double-spaced. By writing it out, you will be forced to notice details, down to the punctuation. After you have copied the poem, proofread it carefully against the original. Catching an error—even the addition or omission of a comma—may help you to notice a detail in the original that you might otherwise have overlooked. Now that you have the poem with ample space between the lines, you have a worksheet with room for jottings.

✔ **CHECKLIST:** *Getting Ideas for Writing Arguments about Poems*

A good essay is based on a genuine response to a poem; a response may be stimulated in part by first reading the poem aloud and then considering the following questions.

First Response

☐ What was your response to the poem on first reading? Did some parts especially please or displease you, or puzzle you? After some study—perhaps checking the

(continued)

meanings of some words in a dictionary and reading the poem several times—did you modify your initial response to the parts and to the whole?

Speaker and Tone

☐ Who is the speaker? (Consider age, sex, personality, frame of mind, and tone of voice.) Is the speaker defined precisely (for instance, an older woman speaking to a child), or is the speaker simply a voice meditating? (Jot down your first impressions, and then reread the poem and make further jottings, if necessary.)

☐ Do you think the speaker is fully aware of what he or she is saying, or does the speaker unconsciously reveal his or her personality and values? What is your attitude toward this speaker?

☐ Is the speaker narrating or reflecting on an earlier experience or attitude? If so, does he or she convey a sense of new awareness, such as of regret for innocence lost?

Audience

☐ To whom is the speaker speaking? What is the situation (including time and place)? (In some poems, a listener is strongly implied, but in others, especially those in which the speaker is meditating, there may be no audience other than the reader, who "overhears" the speaker.)

Structure and Form

☐ Does the poem proceed in a straightforward way, or at some point or points does the speaker reverse course, altering his or her tone or perception? If there is a shift, what do you make of it?

☐ Is the poem organized into sections? If so, what are these sections—stanzas, for instance—and how does each section (characterized, perhaps, by a certain tone of voice, or a group of rhymes) grow out of what precedes it?

☐ What is the effect on you of the form—say, quatrains (stanzas of four lines) or blank verse (unrhymed lines of ten syllables)? If the sense overflows the form, running without pause from (for example) one quatrain into the next, what effect is created?

Center of Interest and Theme

☐ What is the poem about? Is the interest chiefly in a distinctive character, or in meditation? That is, is the poem chiefly psychological or chiefly philosophical?

☐ Is the theme stated explicitly (directly) or implicitly? How might you state the theme in a sentence?

Diction

☐ Do certain words have rich and relevant associations that relate to other words and help to define the speaker or the theme, or both?

☐ What is the role of figurative language, if any? Does it help to define the speaker or the theme?

☐ What do you think is to be taken figuratively or symbolically, and what is to be taken literally?

Sound Effects

☐ What is the role of sound effects, including repetitions of sound (for instance, alliteration) and of entire words, and shifts in versification?

☐ If there are off-rhymes (for instance "dizzy" and "easy," or "home" and "come"), what effect do they have on you? Do they, for instance, add a note of tentativeness or uncertainty?

☐ If there are unexpected stresses or pauses, what do they communicate about the speaker's experience? How do they affect you?

Student Writing Portfolio

EXPLICATION PAPER

Writing an Explication Paper

As we said in Chapter 6, a line-by-line commentary on a text is an explication (literally, an unfolding or spreading out). An explication assignment asks you to slow down and read a literary text carefully, explaining the text's lines as you read them. An explication is concerned with the relationship of the parts to the whole: How do the literary "parts" add up to the "whole" meaning of the poem? An explication assignment thus looks at literary details, exploring the connections among those details, the patterns created by those details, the literary forms that structure those details, and the possible meaning created by these rich relationships.

Although your explication will, for the most part, move steadily from the beginning to the end of the selection, try to avoid writing in a rigid, formal manner: "In the first line. . . . In the second line. . . . In the third line. . . ." That is, don't hesitate to vary your language:

The poem begins. . . . In the next line. . . . The speaker immediately adds. . . .

He then introduces. . . . The next stanza begins by complicating the tone. . . .

You can discuss the second line before the first when that seems the best way of handling the passage.

An explication is not a paraphrase (a rewording, a sort of translation),—although it may include paraphrase if a passage in the original seems unclear, perhaps because of an unusual word or an unfamiliar expression. On the whole, however, an explication goes beyond paraphrase, seeking to make explicit what the reader perceives as implicit in the work. It is chiefly concerned with

- connotations of words—for instance, "look" versus "behold";
- implications of syntax—for instance, whether it is notably complex (thereby implying one sort of speaker) or notably simple (implying a very different sort of speaker);

- implications of rhyme—for instance, the implied connection in meaning between "throne" and "alone";
- patterns of imagery—for instance, commercial imagery in a love poem.

As we said in Chapters 6 and 7, explication and analysis are not clearly distinct from each other; it is reasonable to think of explication as a kind of analysis operating on the level of verbal details.

The reader of an explication needs to see the text, and because the explicated text is usually short, it is advisable to quote it all. If the poem or passage of prose is longer than, say, six lines, you might number each line at the right for easy reference.

✔ CHECKLIST: *Explication*

On page 182, we provided a Checklist on explication. We repeat some of the key points here for your convenience.

Overall Considerations

- ☐ Does the poem imply a story of some sort If so, what is its beginning, middle, and end?
- ☐ If you detect a story in the speaker's mind, is this change communicated in part by the connotations of certain words? By syntax? By metrical shifts?

Detailed Considerations

- ☐ If the poem has a title other than the first line, what are the implications of the title?
- ☐ Are there clusters or patterns of imagery—for instance, religious images, economic images, or images drawn from nature? If so, how do they contribute to the meaning of the poem?
- ☐ Is irony (understatement or overstatement) used? To what effect?
- ☐ How do the connotations of certain words—for instance, "dad" rather than "father"—help to establish the meaning?
- ☐ What are the implications of the syntax—for instance, of notably simple or notably complex sentences? What do such sentences tell us about the speaker?
- ☐ Do metrical variations occur, and, if so, what is their significance?
- ☐ Do rhyming words have some meaningful connection, as in the clichés "moon" and "June," "dove" and "love"?
- ☐ What are the implications of the appearance of the poem on the page, for example, of an indented line, or of the stanzaic pattern? For instance, if the poem consists of two stanzas of four lines each, does the second stanza offer a reversal of the first?

As part of a course unit on poetry, students have been given an assignment to write a four-page explication paper. The assignment asks them to explicate Gwendolyn Brooks's "kitchenette building" and thus asks them to create a four-page paper out of a thirteen-line poem. Let's first look at the poem.

GWENDOLYN BROOKS

Gwendolyn Brooks (1917–2000) was born in Topeka, Kansas, but was raised in Chicago's South Side, where she spent most of her life. In 1950, when she won the Pulitzer Prize for Poetry, she became the first African American writer to win a Pulitzer Prize. In 1985 Brooks became Consultant in Poetry to the Library of Congress.

kitchenette building

We are things of dry hours and the involuntary plan,
Grayed in, and gray. "Dream" makes a giddy sound, not strong
Like "rent," "feeding a wife," "satisfying a man."

But could a dream send up through onion fumes
Its white and violet, fight with fried potatoes   5
And yesterday's garbage ripening in the hall,
Flutter, or sing an aria down these rooms

Even if we were willing to let it in,
Had time to warm it, keep it very clean,
Anticipate a message, let it begin?   10

We wonder. But not well! not for a minute!
Since Number Five is out of the bathroom now,
We think of lukewarm water, hope to get in it.

[1945]

When handed this assignment, Miguel Hernandez is at first intimidated: How will he get such a long paper out of such a short poem? However, Miguel comes to realize that the explication process outlined in Chapter 6 will allow him to develop this paper. The explication paper emphasizes the creation of an interpretation—and the prewriting, drafting, and revision process will allow that invention to take place. Miguel's reading and writing materials are reprinted here, allowing us to see how his understanding of the poem develops and deepens as he completes the assignment. Let's turn to the explication assignment, which emphasizes a careful close reading of Brooks's "kitchenette building."

Assignment

Four-page Explication Paper:

• This paper asks you to perform an explication of Gwendolyn Brooks's poem, "kitchenette building." An explication is a line-by-line close reading that analyzes the meaning of a literary text. An explication paper is a detail-driven assignment; you explore specific words and phrases, and explain how they create the text's meaning. As you perform this close reading, you must create an argument out of your understanding of the poem.

- Write a four-page explication paper that:
  1. creates an argument about the poem's meaning;
  2. performs a line-by-line analysis of the poem;
  3. analyzes literary form (the elements of poetry);
  4. explains how literary form, structure, and patterns create the poem's meaning; and
  5. quotes specific words and phrases.

Annotation: Highlighting First Reactions

As we've emphasized throughout this book, a strong understanding of a literary text often starts with annotation. The activity of marking up your text as you read, annotation provides a way of capturing your ideas as you create them. In an explication paper, you perform a careful close reading that slows you down so that you can consider the meaning of every word and then analyze how those words work together to create the larger meaning of the text as a whole. As seen in the annotations on stories in Chapter 12, literary annotation can explore both content, or the meaning of a text, and form, or the literary structures and devices used to convey that meaning. An explication paper emphasizes this analysis of both form and content.

With the explication assignment in mind, Miguel Hernandez decides to annotate the poem in a careful and comprehensive manner. Note how Miguel uses two different "levels" of annotation to capture his analysis process. First, Miguel uses his highlighter to record his reactions to the poem. Following the advice of his instructor, Miguel "notices what he notices" and uses his highlighter to emphasize words that he likes, that he questions, that he finds interesting, or that he thinks might lead to further analysis. Second, he makes some quick marginal notations that capture his initial thoughts about those highlighted words. These notes provide a foundation for his next step of more detailed brainstorming annotations.

Student Work: Annotation
Highlighting First Reactions to a Poem

kitchenette building

    We are things of dry hours and the involuntary plan,

    Grayed in, and gray. "Dream" makes a giddy sound, not strong   *why is dream giddy?*

    Like "rent," "feeding a wife," "satisfying a man."   *Strong words =*

    But could a dream send up through onion fumes   *responsibilities*

    Its white and violet, fight with fried potatoes   *strong imagery*

    And yesterday's garbage ripening in the hall,   *disgusting smell in hall!*

    Flutter, or sing an aria down these rooms

> Even if we were willing to let it in,
> Had time to warm it, keep it very clean,   *keep warm/clean—what*
> Anticipate a message, let it begin?   *is "it"?*
>
> We wonder. But not well! not for a minute!
> Since Number Five is out of the bathroom now,
> We think of lukewarm water, hope to get in it.   *wants bath—but lukewarm*

Explication as a Form of Critical Thinking

Any reading of literature usually will start with your personal reaction. What strikes you in these first two stanzas? If you had to highlight the most noticeable phrase in these lines, you might pick "yesterday's garbage ripening in the hall." This phrase is repulsive; with a few short words, Brooks has made us imagine a disgusting smell—we might even wrinkle our nose as we read it! This second stanza has additional phrases that seem designed to reach out and grab us. It is built on concrete images: The garbage is accompanied by the strong smell of "onion fumes" and "fried potatoes." In contrast, a dream is described as being able to "flutter" and "sing an aria"—language that seems weak or frivolous. Your first reaction to the poem might be to sense that it is powerful because it uses powerful language.

The critical thinking process required by explication encourages you to create a deeper understanding of the poem. Although Brooks uses simple language to describe the dream and its context, the meaning of these lines is far from simple. As we reread these lines, we start to understand that Brooks is describing the everyday lives of the people who comprise the poem's "we." Given the poem's title, we can make the assumption that the "we" lives in a kitchenette building.

If you don't know what a "kitchenette building" is, you might do a quick Internet search to check your understanding. For example, you can find a reputable source in the Chicago Historical Society's *Encyclopedia of Chicago* website; there, you will discover that a kitchenette building is a type of apartment building that was common in Chicago in the 1930s and 1940s.[2] A kitchenette is created when an apartment is divided into small, crowded rooms and each room is rented to a different family. The site explains that kitchenettes were most prevalent in African-American neighborhoods, where landlords could engage in unfair and predatory lending. Knowing that Brooks herself is African-American, it becomes clear that the poem is exploring the dreams of African-Americans and questioning what happens to those dreams when they are confined to a small kitchenette building—a space defined by race and racist social practices.

The explication paper expects that you will use close reading and rereading to generate your own insights into, and questions about, the poem. We have the basic scenario of the poem figured out: It describes a "we" living in a kitchenette building filled with disgusting smells. That "we" might be trying to create, or "send up," a dream, but that dream has to fight to come to life in a space defined by discomfort and racism.

Looking at the first stanza, it now becomes clear that Brooks is setting up a contrast between a "dream" and the everyday life of the "we" in the kitchenette

---

[2] Wendy Plotkin, "Kitchenettes." *Encyclopedia of Chicago*, Chicago Historical Society, 2005. Web 25 August 2015.

building. The dream seems frivolous and even silly—it "makes a giddy sound." In contrast, the concerns of everyday life seem solid and important—"rent," "feeding a wife," and "satisfying a man." As you reread these first two stanzas, you can continue to question exactly what they mean: Are the inhabitants of the kitchenette building weighed down by their situation? Is this what Brooks means by "grayed in"? How can the inhabitants fulfill their responsibilities, never mind follow their dreams? Further, this poem encourages us to ask even bigger questions. What causes a dream to die? What happens to people when their dreams die? Let's see how this type of critical thinking can be captured in more complete annotations.

Annotation: Rereading and Adding Inquiry Questions

At first, Miguel wonders if this thirteen-line poem will create enough material to fill a four-page paper. But, as he reads and rereads the short poem, he starts to see rich layers of imagery that he can use to develop his ideas. He knows that he will have to provide a very detailed explanation of how specific words can be connected to his specific interpretations. As a result, he decides to continue his annotation of the poem, using the annotation process to brainstorm possible interpretations. At the end of this process, notice how Miguel writes a short summary of his annotations and his most interesting insights, explaining to himself what types of words he highlighted and what ideas he has generated. In this way, Miguel uses his annotations to capture ideas that he can use in his paper draft.

Student Work: Annotation
Adding Inquiry Questions to a Poem

kitchenette building

We are things of dry hours and the involuntary plan,	*who is the we?*
Grayed in, and gray. "Dream" makes a giddy sound, not strong	*dream = giddy = weak*
Like "rent," "feeding a wife," "satisfying a man."	*strong words = responsibilities*
But could a dream send up through onion fumes	*what happens to dream?*
Its white and violet, fight with fried potatoes	*why is dream white and violet?*
And yesterday's garbage ripening in the hall,	*disgusting smell in hall!!*
Flutter, or sing an aria down these rooms	*who is fluttering? is the dream fluttering?*
Even if we were willing to let it in,	*let what in? let dream in*
Had time to warm it, keep it very clean,	*keep warm/clean: activities*
Anticipate a message, let it begin?	*to protect dream*

We wonder. But not well! not for a minute!

Since Number Five is out of the bathroom now,

We think of lukewarm water, hope to get in it.

apt. neighbor out of bathroom wants bath—lukewarm
This is what "we" wants: luke-warm water? That's it?!! Not a very big goal or dream!

Imagery: Imagery of dream vs. everyday life—strong contrast between the two. Dream is giddy, white, violet, fluttering, singing. Everyday life is real world—responsibilities, disgusting smells, waiting for bathroom

Note that images use senses (smell, taste)
***So, sensory images key part of poem*

Inquiry: Mapping, Clustering, and Creating Graphic Notes

The inquiry process uses note taking to trigger brainstorming. This brainstorming generates informal writing that will, in turn, develop into a more formal written analysis of the literary work. Miguel employs inquiry strategies in order to move toward a deeper understanding of the meaning of the poem: He needs to generate ideas, organize those ideas, and develop those ideas. Although he knows that the poem is about a dream trying to survive in a kitchenette building, he needs to create a more sophisticated understanding of that scenario. Miguel's note taking must investigate the exact words and phrases being used by Brooks.

As you look at Miguel's notes, you can imagine the types of inquiry questions that will lead to strong critical thinking and a successful paper: What precise words does Brooks use to describe the dream? How does she describe the kitchenette building and, by extension, the lives of the people who live in it? What sort of contrast is she creating between the dream and its setting? What larger point is she making about the dream? Will the dream survive?

When you are generating multilayered ideas, a more graphic approach that "maps out" your developing ideas can work well. You might want to experiment with this "mapping" approach or other forms of note taking that takes a more graphic or visual form. As Miguel works to develop his ideas, he uses a "clustering" form of mapping to capture the free-flowing, associative nature of his ideas. As seen here, Miguel creates notes that feel "right" for this poem and matches his thoughts. Miguel uses clustering to emphasize his central ideas and the connections between those ideas. Knowing that his prewriting is moving him toward an explication paper, Miguel includes many direct quotations from the poem in his clustering. He also employs the highlighting technique used in his marginal annotations, in which he highlights the key words that helped to form his ideas.

Student Work: Inquiry Notes
Cluster #1: Theme

Dream	vs.	Everyday Life
"giddy sound"		"rent"
"white and violet"		"feeding a wife"
"flutter, or sing an aria"		"satisfying a man"
let the dream in: keep warm, clean		"lukewarm water"
has message, "let it begin"		

note:

warm→"lukewarm water"

warm has become lukewarm

clean→shared water

bath water is not clean

why would they want this water?

"WE"

who is the "we"?

Group Persona?

"grey"

My Ideas:
Dream life vs. Everyday life
"We" caught between them

Student Work: Inquiry Notes
Cluster #2: Images

"WE"

who is the "we"?

Group Persona?

"grey"

"We" trapped in 2 key spaces:

Kitchenette Kitchen	Kitchenette Bathroom
"onion fumes"	"lukewarm water"
"fried potatoes"	"hope to get in" water
"yesterday's garbage"	

Sensory images

Visual

Touch

Sound

Verbal

My ideas:
Images overwhelm the "we"
Images trap the "we"
Images define the "we"?

Inquiry: Journal Writing

Journal writing offers a way of transforming your annotations and notes into sentences and paragraphs. Before Miguel even starts writing in sentence form, he decides to use the structure of the poem to structure his writing. He knows his explication paper will move through the poem line by line, so he maintains that structure in his journal writing. To trigger the writing process, Miguel records a few quick notes about each stanza before writing a short paragraph about each one. He then uses paragraphs to record his understanding of each stanza, explaining the key concepts that each stanza seems to be exploring. At the end of his journal writing, Miguel reminds himself to examine specific "compressed" phrases—phrases that need to be "opened up" and explained. He writes down the words he highlighted in his annotations, knowing that many of them will be cited in his paper. His journal writing contains many of the elements of a rough paper draft.

Student Work: Inquiry Notes
Listing and Journal Writing

Overview Notes: Quick Notes on Each Stanza
Stanza 1:

The "we" lives a life of "dry hours" and is "grayed in." In contrast, the dream is "giddy" (silly?). The lives of the people are responsible, solid, strong—worried about rent and food.

Stanza 2:

The dream wants to "send up" (to rise up?). Can it make it through the clouds of smells—the onions, potatoes, and garbage? The dream is still weak— fluttering—and seems less important than real life.

Stanza 3:

The "we" has to be willing to deal with the dream. They have to take care of it. Would it survive? Can a dream survive?

Stanza 4:

The "we" wonders if the dream would survive. Answer is: No! We can get into the bathroom (real life needs—body). The dream is no match for real life.
   Idea explanation: Explanation of ideas on each stanza:
   "kitchenette building" takes on a tough topic: a dream trying to live in a kitchenette building. The poem introduced this in stanza 1. The heart of the poem asks this tough question: Can a dream survive this life? The poem answers this question with a "No." This seems to be a rather depressing answer.

(continued)

However, Brooks gets across this idea that a dream can't survive by setting up a strong contrast in the second stanza. The strong contrast is between the dream and everyday life. The dream is weak and everyday life is strong. The strong contrast is between a dream defined as giddy and fluttering. In contrast, the everyday life is defined in really strong words—the image of onion fumes, fried potatoes, garbage ripening in the hall. In addition, real life is defined by living up to your responsibilities: "rent," feeding a wife," and "satisfying a man."

The dream needs help. It needs to be nurtured. It needs to be cared for. The third stanza explains that the dream needs to be kept warm and clean. It needs to be let in and "let it begin." It needs a lot of work. What type of work? Explore this idea.

I think the fourth stanza is the best. It shows that the people are thinking a little about the dream. But, then, the people have a chance to use the bathroom. The dream just disappears. The need to use the bathroom is more important. The needs of the body win out.

I also really like the poem's emphasis on the senses (sensory phrases/ images—see highlighted words on poem?). The poem seems to hit the eyes, ears, nose, even the sense of touch (warm):

"giddy sound"
"onion fumes"
"fried potatoes"
"garbage ripening in the hall"
"Flutter, or sing an aria"
"warm"—"clean"
"lukewarm water"
Sensory phrases/images

Drafting and Revision: Explaining a Close Reading

Let's turn to Miguel's draft of his explication paper. In this draft, Miguel explains his close reading and shapes an argument based on that close reading. The explication paper connects the structure of the poem to the structure of the paper. The assignment asks the writer to provide a line-by-line reading of the poem, explain the use of literary elements throughout the poem, and explore the ideas conveyed by the poem. Just like in his journal writing, Miguel provides a stanza-by-stanza reading of the poem. Miguel's first draft focuses on getting across his ideas rather than formulating those ideas into perfect sentences. Miguel shapes his ideas into a thesis and supporting paragraphs, but, notably, the draft contains ideas that are not fully developed. In addition, Miguel's earlier prewriting materials contain excellent ideas that do not appear in the paper's draft.

As you read Miguel's draft, critique it. Which ideas are Miguel's best ideas? Which ideas should Miguel develop further? Look back at Miguel's earlier note taking and journal writing. What ideas should Miguel add to his paper? Look back at

Miguel's annotations on the poem to see if he has any other missed ideas. What phrases are highlighted there that Miguel should add to this draft?

Student Explication Essay: "Life in a 'kitchenette building'" (Preliminary Draft)

In his first draft, Miguel pulls his best ideas from his prewriting and starts to order them through a line-by-line explication and paragraph-by-paragraph organization. Some of his ideas remain unclear or underdeveloped. However, it is important to feel that the first draft can be a rough draft; perfection is not possible on the first try! As we examine this draft, we note the strengths and weaknesses of the paper in a set of marginal annotations.

Hernandez 1

Miguel Hernandez

English 200

Professor Anderson

March 21, 2016

Life in a "kitchenette building"

Gwendolyn Brooks's poem "kitchenette building" wonders if a dream can survive everyday life in a kitchenette building. The poem highlights that a dream might die—especially if the dream faces a tough life. The poem gets this message across with a series of images. The poem makes the reader feel the tough life of the people in the kitchenette building. Because of these feelings, the reader can understand why the people might not have the time and space for dreams.

writer opens with a strong start—a clear thesis statement

A good place to start looking at the poem is its title: "kitchenette building." As explained in the Chicago Historical Society's *Encyclopedia of Chicago*, a kitchenette building is an apartment building in Chicago (Plotkin). During the 1930s–1940s, large apartments were chopped up into smaller apartments, cramming more and more people into the smaller apartments. As the *Encyclopedia of Chicago* explains, these apartments often housed African Americans who had moved to Chicago during the Great Depression and World War II (Plotkin). The African American families were

explication starts by exploring meaning of poem's title

writer makes sure to cite research sources

---

taken advantage of, pushed into overcrowded housing as they had nowhere

else to go, no place else to rent. Families could share one bathroom and

kitchen: "Entire families occupied single rooms, sharing with other

residents an inadequate number of bathrooms and kitchens, exceeding the

plumbing capacity, and leading to a serious deterioration in sanitary

writer could
more fully
explain how
research
connects to poem

conditions" (Plotkin). Brooks's poem describes the overcrowded space. The

title "kitchenette building" emphasizes this space. It also uses only small

letters.

an explication
paper moves
through the poem
in an orderly
way

   The first word of the poem is "we," which gets across the idea that

more than one person lives in this space. "We" also includes the reader. The

word "we" connects the reader to the people in the kitchenette building. The

first line of the poem emphasizes the "grayed in, and gray" lives of the

draft analyzes
poem on level of
specific words;
could be
developed further

people. The poem then contrasts these gray lives with the idea of a dream.

The poem explains that while a "dream" makes a "giddy sound," the people in

the kitchenette building are more concerned with words that make "strong"

sounds. Although the people might be "gray," they are taking life seriously.

They are living up to their responsibilities.

writer uses
poem's structure
(stanzas) to
organize analysis
(paragraphs)

   The second stanza provides a great image of a dream in a kitchenette

building. The stanza is filled with smells that make you feel how rough

everyday life is. The stanza describes the dream as trying to "send up" its

"white and violet," meaning that the dream is trying to rise up and help the

people rise up. The color violet is especially strong, showing that a dream is

passionate. But, around the dream, are smells of everyday life—the life that

is dragging it down. It is full of "onion fumes," "fried potatoes," and

"yesterday's garbage ripening in the hall." The poem shows how a dream can

be overwhelmed by the forces pushing it down. The smells seem to represent

body of paper
develops
conceptual ideas

these powerful forces—they are not just smells but something bigger. The

Hernandez 3

poem creates a strong contrast between the weak dream and the strong lives of the kitchenette inhabitants.

The third stanza shows the "we" questioning if the dream would succeed with a little help from its friends. This stanza focuses on the dream, questioning what the dream might need in order to survive. This stanza asks what would happen to the dream if the people "let it in" and then "had time to warm it, keep it very clean." The stanza ends by explaining that the dream would have to be allowed to begin. Its final words, "let it begin?" show that. The stanza demonstrates what a poem would need to survive—it would need some help.

interprets ideas presented by poem

The poem's fourth and last stanza shows the real world overwhelming these thoughts. The stanza starts with "we wonder," showing that the people are wondering what could be its future. But that wondering is short. The wondering is overwhelmed by reality. The next lines describe the thinking about the dream—the wondering is "not for a minute!" The importance is emphasized by the exclamation point. The thing about the dream is interrupted by the reality that the bathroom is empty—and that the "we" wants to get into the bathroom asap. The reality of everyday needs wipes away any thinking about the dream. The final line of the poem explains the need for a bath: "Since Number Five is out of the bathroom now, / We think of lukewarm water, hope to get in it." There are lots of things interesting about this line. It shows that the people in the Kitchenette building are numbers. And, it shows that the people are defined by their bodies and hoping to take a bath.

an explication paper analyzes literary form, such as the poem's punctuation

sentence is vague, can be strengthened

Thus, as the poem shows, the concerns of everyday life will overwhelm the dreams of the kitchenette building. Because the poem puts the characters as a "we," the reader feels for these people. We can feel the cramped life they lead. We can understand why the dream doesn't have a chance.

conclusion overviews paper's central argument

[New page]

Hernandez 4

Works Cited

Brooks, Gwendolyn. "kitchenette building." *Literature for Composition*. Ed. Sylvan

      Barnet, William Burto, Willian E. Cain, and Cheryl L. Nixon. 11th ed. Boston:

      Pearson, 2017. 787. Print.

Plotkin, Wendy. "Kitchenettes." *Encyclopedia of Chicago*. Chicago Historical Society,

      2005. Web. 25 August 2015.

Revision: Using a Revision Strategy

A paper is put through a revision process in order to improve its ideas, arguments, evidence, organization, and writing style. As seen in the Chapter 8, we can use this checklist to meet these revision goals. Let's see how Miguel applies selected aspects of this revision checklist to his paper.

✔ REVISION CHECKLIST

Strengthen Your Thesis

☐ Add focus and depth to your central argument.

Develop Your Ideas

☐ Revisit your best responses to literary form and content, adding more thinking to those responses.

Integrate and Explain Your Evidence

☐ Select and analyze rich, interesting quotations to provide evidence for your ideas.

Improve the Organization

☐ Structure your ideas to follow a clear sequence.

Clarify Your Style and Edit for Correctness

☐ Use a consistent, professional style to explain your ideas, correcting sentence structure, word usage, and grammar.

Revision: Revising to Strengthen the Thesis

A successful paper must have a strong thesis that states the paper's overarching argument. A thesis statement conveys the information that you could put in fill-in-the-blank sentences, such as "This paper's main idea is _____," "My paper's biggest argument is _____," or "When taken all together, the details in my paper add up to the idea that _____." Although these sentences are too overtly and simplistically stated, they indicate the type of argumentative clarity that your thesis should have. Obviously, a thesis should not be simplistic in its ideas but should be clear in its argument; your thesis should show off your sophisticated, original thinking—and show off that thinking in clear writing.

In an explication paper, the thesis must explain the reader's understanding of the poem's literary elements and central ideas. Although an explication is detail-driven, it must present a thesis about the meaning of the poem as a whole. Miguel's thesis argument can be seen in his paper's first two sentences: "Gwendolyn Brooks's poem 'kitchenette building,' wonders if a dream can survive everyday life in a kitchenette building. The poem highlights that a dream might die—especially if the dream faces a tough life." This thesis captures Miguel's overarching analysis of the poem and thus provides a good thesis for the paper. However, upon rereading, Miguel's realizes that his draft is missing one of the best ideas created by his prewriting: The poem explores a contrast between the weak dream and the strong lives of the kitchenette inhabitants. This contrast is an excellent one and should be added to the thesis. Let's see how Miguel located this contrast in his earlier writing and adds it to his thesis.

Student Work: Revision
Revising to Strengthen the Thesis

Rough Draft:

Gwendolyn Brooks's poem "kitchenette building," wonders if a dream can survive everyday life in a kitchenette building. The poem highlights that a dream might die—especially if the dream faces a tough life. The poem gets this message across with a series of images. The poem makes the reader feel the tough life of the people in the kitchenette building. Because of these feelings, the reader can understand why the people might not have the time and space for dreams.

First Revision:

Reexamine prewriting, including this passage from free writing:

However, Brooks gets across this idea that a dream can't survive by setting up a strong contrast. The strong contrast is between the dream and everyday life. The dream is weak and everyday life is strong. The strong contrast is between a dream defined as giddy and fluttering. In contrast, the everyday life is defined in really strong words—the image of "onion fumes," "fried potatoes," "yesterday's garbage

writer reexamines prewriting, searching for ideas not used in first draft

ripening in the hall." In addition, real life is defined by living up to your responsibilities: "rent," "feeding a wife," and "satisfying a man."

Reexamine rough draft, locating this passage:

The poem creates a strong contrast between the weak dream and the strong lives of the kitchenette inhabitants.

Add new sentences to first draft, capturing this idea:

In her poem "kitchenette building," Gwendolyn Brooks wonders if a dream can survive everyday life in a small kitchenette building. The poem sets up a strong contrast between the hopes of a dream and the demands of everyday life. The four stanzas of the poem emphasize this contrast by providing weak imagery connected to the dream and strong imagery connected to everyday life.

↓

Second Revision:

Revised thesis statement leads to revised transition into body of paper:

In her poem "kitchenette building," Gwendolyn Brooks wonders if a dream can survive everyday life in a small kitchenette building. The poem sets up a strong contrast between the hopes of a dream and the demands of everyday life. The four stanzas of the poem emphasize this contrast by providing weak imagery connected to the dream and strong imagery connected to everyday life.

The middle of the poem is a long question that asks if a dream can live in an overcrowded apartment. The beginning and end of the poem shows the everyday thoughts of the people that live in the kitchenette building. The poem ends with the message that these people have too many pressures to think about their dreams. The poem develops the differences between a dream and an everyday life through its use of sensory imagery.

Brooks's poem creates the contrast between dreams and life through a series of powerful images. The images are sensory, creating a strong feeling of life in the kitchenette building. These images help the reader understand the life of the people in the kitchenette building. As a result of these feelings, the reader can understand why the people might not have the time and space to think about their dreams.

— writer reexamines first draft, searching for its best ideas to further develop

— uses this revision to expand on the best ideas from earlier writing

— writer pushes his thesis, continues to develop new ideas

— writer improves phrasing of new ideas

— writer uses new ideas to transition from thesis into body

Revision: Revising to Integrate and Explain Evidence

Textual evidence is a crucial part of any paper—and especially so in an explication paper. An explication paper emphasizes close reading and must include meaningful quotations of words, phrases, and lines. These quotations must be followed by an "explication" of what they mean, showing how individual words are the foundation of conceptual analysis. An explication paper demonstrates that almost every paper can be strengthened by the close analysis of quotations from the text.

As Miguel revises his paper, he wants to show how his ideas are triggered by the language of the poem. This use of evidence demonstrates Miguel's ability to root his ideas in specific information. Miguel searches his earlier prewriting for ideas that he did not develop and that could lead to a more complete close reading of the poem. He discovers that his first draft leaves out one of the best ideas from his prewriting: the idea that Brooks's poem uses sensory imagery. Miguel's prewriting contains an excellent emphasis on sensory language and includes lists of Brooks's words that highlight the senses. Miguel decides that this key idea and this key evidence should be added to his final draft.

Student Work: Revision Revising to Integrate and Explain Evidence

Rough Draft:

The second stanza provides a great image of a dream in a kitchenette building. The stanza is filled with smells that make you feel how rough everyday life is. The stanza describes the dream as trying to "send up" its "white and violet," meaning that the dream is trying to rise up and help the people rise up. The color violet is especially strong, showing that a dream is passionate. But around the dream are smells of everyday life—the life that is dragging it down. It is full of "onion fumes," "fried potatoes," and "yesterday's garbage ripening in the hall." The poem shows how a dream can be overwhelmed by the forces pushing it down. The smells seem to represent these powerful forces—they are not just smells but something bigger.

↓

First Revision:

Reexamine prewriting, including this passage from journal writing:

I also really like the poem's emphasis on the senses (sensory phrases/ images—see list above?). The poem seems to hit the eyes, ears, nose, even the sense of touch (warm).

Add new sentence to draft, capturing this idea:

The images are very sensory, including auditory images that emphasize sound, gustatory images that emphasize taste, and olfactory images that emphasize smell.

writer reexamines prewriting for strong evidence not used in first draft

↓

Revised Draft:

The second stanza features a powerful image of a dream trying to live in a kitchenette building. Filled with strong images and smells, this stanza makes the reader feel how rough everyday life is for the kitchenette inhabitant. The stanza describes the dream as trying to "send up" its "white and violet," meaning that the dream is trying to rise up and thus help the people rise up. The color violet is especially strong, showing that a dream is passionate. Surrounding the dream, however, are the smells of the everyday life that are dragging it down. The images are very sensory, including auditory images that emphasize sound, gustatory images that emphasize taste, and olfactory images that emphasize smell. Describing food the reader can almost taste and smell, the poem puts the reader into the kitchen, with its "onion fumes" and "fried potatoes." Emphasizing these sensory images, the poem then describes "yesterday's garbage ripening in the hall." The poem shows how the dream can be overwhelmed by the powerful forces around it. The dream is described as wanting to "flutter" or "sing an aria." These images are visual, tactical, and auditory, making the fluttering, singing, dream something the reader can see, touch, and hear. These images show that the dream is not strong and could be easily knocked down. Up against the strong smells of the previous lines, the dream obviously will be overwhelmed by everyday life. The smells seem to represent powerful forces—they are not just smells but the bigger challenges of a tough life.

writer makes argument more precise, sets up next quotation more clearly.

adds new sentence, which connects to evidence

continues to revise, making evidence more powerful by connecting to reader's senses

emphasizes key concepts raised by evidence

final sentences connect ideas back to thesis

Student Analytical Essay: "The Contest between Dreams and Everyday Life in Brooks's 'kitchenette building'" (Final Draft)

Let's see how Miguel's rough draft evolves into a final draft. Compare this final draft to the first draft on page 759. The revision strategies explored here, which include strengthening the thesis and integrating evidence, have led to a much stronger paper. The ideas in this paper are much more fully developed, offering a more insightful and original analysis of the poem. In addition to improving his ideas, Miguel also has improved his writing style, creating clearer sentences and paragraphs.

Notice how Miguel has strengthened several aspects of his writing in his paper. He has

- clarified and deepened the thesis argument;
- developed the series of connected claims;
- created an organizational structure that captures his idea development;
- used evidence to support his ideas; and
- Improved his phrasing, style, and grammar.

Hernandez 1

Miguel Hernandez

English 122

Professor Anderson

20 April 2016

The Contest between Dreams and Everyday Life in Brooks's

"kitchenette building"

In her poem "kitchenette building," Gwendolyn Brooks wonders if a

dream can survive everyday life in a small kitchenette building. The poem

sets up a strong contrast between the hopes of a dream and the demands of

everyday life. The four stanzas of the poem emphasize this contrast by

providing weak imagery connected to the dream and strong imagery

connected to everyday life.

The middle of the poem is a long question that asks if a dream can live

in an overcrowded apartment. The beginning and end of the poem shows the

everyday thoughts of the people that live in the kitchenette building. The

poem ends with the message that these people have too many pressures to

think about their dreams. The poem develops the differences between a

dream and an everyday life through its use of sensory imagery.

Brooks's poem creates the contrast between dreams and life through a

series of powerful images. The images are sensory, creating a strong feeling

of life in the kitchenette building. These images help the reader understand

the life of the people in the kitchenette building. As a result of these

feelings, the reader can understand why the people might not have the time

and space to think about their dreams.

A good place to start an analysis of the poem is its title: "kitchenette

building." Brooks' title emphasizes the importance of place. As explained in

the Chicago Historical Society's *Encyclopedia of Chicago*, a kitchenette

building is an apartment building in Chicago (Plotkin). During the

strong thesis provides clear statement of central argument

previews paper structure, which follows structure of poem

thesis developed by exploring literary elements, such as imagery

creates strong argument by emphasizing larger meaning of poem

Hernandez 2

includes exploration of the poem's title (shows close reading, historical research)

1930s–1940s, large apartments were chopped up into smaller apartments, cramming more and more people into the small apartment space. As the *Encyclopedia of Chicago* explains, these apartments often housed African Americans who had moved to Chicago during the Great Depression and World War II (Plotkin). The African American families were taken advantage of, pushed into overcrowded housing because landlords would not rent to them

cites secondary sources

in other neighborhoods. In a kitchenette, several families would often share one bathroom and one kitchen: "Entire families occupied single rooms, sharing with other residents an inadequate number of bathrooms and kitchens, exceeding the plumbing capacity, and leading to a serious deterioration in sanitary conditions" (Plotkin). Brooks's title captures this

connects close readings of specific words to larger conceptual analysis

sense of overcrowded space. The title uses only small letters—it expresses the idea that these people's lives seem small. Just as small letters seem less important than capital letters, these people are made to feel unimportant.

uses clear organization, starting with poem's first stanza

The first word of the poem is "We," which captures the idea that more than one person lives in the kitchenette space. "We" reaches out and includes the reader. The word "we" connects the reader to a group persona— the people living in the kitchenette building. The opening line of the poem emphasizes the "Grayed in, and gray" lives of this group persona. The poem then contrasts their gray lives with the idea of a dream. The poem explains that while a "dream" makes "giddy sound," the people in the kitchenette building are more concerned with words that make "strong" sounds, like

uses concise quotations

"rent," "feeding a wife," and "satisfying a man." Although the people might be "gray" they are living up to their responsibilities. Interestingly, Brooks seems to be saying that although the people living in the kitchenette are worn down, they are responsible and take life seriously.

clear organization

The second stanza features a powerful image of a dream trying to live in a kitchenette building. Filled with strong images and smells, this stanza makes the reader feel how rough everyday life is for the kitchenette inhabitant. The stanza describes the dream as trying to "send up" its "white and violet," meaning that the dream is trying to rise up and thus help the people rise up. The color violet is especially strong, showing that a dream is passionate. Surrounding the dream, however, are the smells of the everyday life that is dragging it down. The images are very sensory, including auditory images that emphasize sound, gustatory images that emphasize taste, and olfactory images that emphasize smell. Describing food the reader can almost taste and smell, the poem puts the reader into the kitchen, with its "onion fumes" and "fried potatoes." Emphasizing these sensory images, the poem then describes "yesterday's garbage ripening in the hall." The poem shows how the dream can be overwhelmed by the powerful forces around it. The dream is described as wanting to "Flutter" or "sing an aria." These images are visual, tactical, and auditory, making the fluttering, singing, dream something the reader can see, touch, and hear. These images show that the dream is not strong and could be easily knocked down. Up against the strong smells of the previous lines, the dream obviously will be overwhelmed by everyday life. The smells seem to represent powerful forces—they are not just smells but the bigger challenges of a tough life.

clearly names, explains literary elements like sensory imagery

explains the meaning created by the literary elements

The poem then moves to showing the "we" persona questioning if the dream would succeed with help and assistance. The third stanza has a more thoughtful and less powerful tone. This stanza focuses on the dream, questioning what the dream might need in order to survive. This stanza asks what would happen to the dream if the kitchenette inhabitants "let it in" and then "Had time to warm it, keep it very clean." The stanza ends by explaining that the dream would have to be allowed to begin or get a start in life. The words "let it in" rhyme with "let it begin" in order to create the idea that a dream must be given a chance. A dream has to be accepted and then developed. The final words "let it begin?" show the need to let a dream grow, but use the question mark to show how uncertain that beginning is. The

moves to third stanza, continuing its clear organization

Hernandez 4

stanza demonstrates what a poem would need to survive—it would need help, care, and protection.

emphasizes key concepts central to paper's argument

    The poem's fourth and last stanza shows the real world overwhelming this questioning. The stanza starts with "We wonder," showing that the people are wondering about the future of a dream. But, that wondering lasts

moves to fourth stanza, maintaining organizational structure

for only those two words. Very quickly, the wondering is overwhelmed by reality. The next words describe how the "we" persona thinks about the dream—their wondering is "not well!" and lasts "not for a minute!" The importance of the shortness of the wondering is emphasized by the exclamation points. Thinking about the dream is interrupted by reality. This reality is that the bathroom is empty—and that the "we" wants to get into the bathroom. The reality of everyday needs intrudes and wipes away any thinking about the dream. The final lines of the poem explain the need for a bath: "Since Number Five is out of the bathroom now, / We think of lukewarm water, hope to get in it." These lines capture several interesting

uses quotations in every paragraph, connects to larger ideas.

ideas. First, the lines show that the people in the kitchenette building are treated like numbers. Second, they show that the people are defined by their bodies and their bodily needs (the people as simply hoping to take a bath). Third, they show the low level of the people's hopes—all they hope for is

breaks down ideas into sub-arguments

lukewarm water. This is the level of their dreams.

    The poem seems to predict that the concerns of everyday life will overwhelm the dreams of the people living in the kitchenette building. The imagery associated with everyday life is very strong and powerful, while the imagery associated with the dream is weak, dependent, and fluttery.

conclusion restates explication's thesis statement

The sensory imagery gets across the idea that the dream will not survive the contest with everyday life in the kitchenette building. Because the poem creates a group "we" persona in addition to creating sensory imagery, the reader feels for the people. The poem makes the reader sense the power of the

ends with strong, final argument.

forces that are lined up against the people living in a kitchenette building.

[New page]

Hernandez 5

Works Cited

Brooks, Gwendolyn. "kitchenette building." *Literature for Composition*. Ed. Sylvan

    Barnet, William Burto, William E. Cain, and Cheryl L. Nixon. 11th ed. Boston:

    Pearson, 2017. 787. Print.

Plotkin, Wendy. "Kitchenettes." *Encyclopedia of Chicago*. Chicago Historical Society,

    2005. Web. 25 August 2015.

Your Turn: Additional Poems for Analysis

ROBERT BROWNING

Born in a suburb of London into a middle-class family, Robert Browning (1812–89) was educated primarily at home, where he read widely. For a while, he wrote for the stage, and in 1846 he married Elizabeth Barrett—herself a poet—and lived with her in Italy until her death in 1861. He then returned to England and settled in London with their son. Regarded as one of the most distinguished poets of the Victorian period, he is buried in Westminster Abbey.

My Last Duchess

Ferrara°

That's my last Duchess painted on the wall,
Looking as if she were alive. I call
That piece a wonder, now; Frà Pandolf's° hands
Worked busily a day, and there she stands.
Will't please you sit and look at her? I said   5
"Frà Pandolf" by design, for never read
Strangers like you that pictured countenance,
The depth and passion of its earnest glance,
But to myself they turned (since none puts by
The curtain I have drawn for you, but I)   10
And seemed as they would ask me, if they durst,
How such a glance came there; so, not the first
Are you to turn and ask thus. Sir, 'twas not
Her husband's presence only, called that spot
Of joy into the Duchess' cheek; perhaps   15
Frà Pandolf chanced to say "Her mantle laps

° **Ferrara** a town in Italy. **3 Frà Pandolf** a fictitious painter.

Over my lady's wrist too much," or, "Paint
Must never hope to reproduce the faint
Half-flush that dies along her throat." Such stuff
Was courtesy, she thought, and cause enough   20
For calling up that spot of joy. She had
A heart—how shall I say?—too soon made glad,
Too easily impressed; she liked whate'er
She looked on, and her looks went everywhere.
Sir, 'twas all one! My favor at her breast,   25
The dropping of the daylight in the west,
The bough of cherries some officious fool
Broke in the orchard for her, the white mule
She rode with round the terrace—all and each
Would draw from her alike the approving speech,   30
Or blush, at least. She thanked men—good! but thanked
Somehow—I know not how—as if she ranked
My gift of a nine-hundred-years-old name
With anybody's gift. Who'd stoop to blame
This sort of trifling? Even had you skill   35
In speech—(which I have not)—to make your will
Quite clear to such an one, and say, "Just this
Or that in you disgusts me; here you miss,
Or there exceed the mark"—and if she let
Herself be lessoned so, nor plainly set   40
Her wits to yours, forsooth, and made excuse,
—E'en then would be some stooping; and I choose
Never to stoop. Oh, Sir, she smiled, no doubt,
Whene'er I passed her; but who passed without
Much the same smile? This grew; I gave commands;   45
Then all smiles stopped together. There she stands
As if alive. Will't please you rise? We'll meet
The company below, then. I repeat,
The Count your master's known munificence
Is ample warrant that no just pretense   50
Of mine for dowry will be disallowed;
Though his fair daughter's self, as I avowed
At starting, is my object. Nay, we'll go
Together down, Sir. Notice Neptune, though,
Taming a sea-horse, thought a rarity,   55
Which Claus of Innsbruck° cast in bronze for me!

[1842]

° **56 Claus of Innsbruck** a fictitious sculptor.

Joining the Conversation: Critical Thinking and Writing

1. Who is speaking to whom in "My Last Duchess"? On what occasion?
2. What words or lines especially convey the speaker's arrogance? What is our attitude toward the speaker? Loathing? Fascination? Respect? Explain your answer.
3. The time and place are Renaissance Italy; how do they affect our attitude toward the duke? What would be the effect if the poem were set in the twentieth century?

4. Years after writing this poem, Browning explained that the duke's "commands" (line 45) were "that she should be put to death, or he might have had her shut up in a convent." Should the poem have been more explicit? Does Browning's later uncertainty indicate that the poem is badly thought out? Suppose we did not have Browning's comment on line 45; could the line then mean only that he commanded her to stop smiling and that she obeyed? Explain your answer.

5. Elizabeth Barrett (not yet Mrs. Browning) wrote to Robert Browning that it was not "by the dramatic medium that poets teach most impressively. . . . It is too difficult for the common reader to analyze, and to discern between the vivid and the earnest." She went on, urging him to teach "in the directest and most impressive way, the mask thrown off." What teaching, if any, is in this poem? If there is any teaching in the poem, would it be more impressive if Browning had not used the mask of a Renaissance duke? Explain your answer.

6. You are the envoy, writing to the count, your master, a five-hundred-word report of your interview with the duke. What do you write?

7. You are the envoy, writing to the count, advising—as diplomatically as possible—for or against this marriage. Notice that this exercise, unlike the previous exercise, which calls for a *report,* calls for an *argument.*

E. E. CUMMINGS

E. E. Cummings was the pen name of Edwin Estlin Cummings (1894–1962), who grew up in Cambridge, Massachusetts, and was graduated from Harvard, where he became interested in modern literature and art, especially in the movements called Cubism and Futurism. His father, a conservative clergyman and a professor at Harvard, seems to have been baffled by the youth's interests, but Cummings's mother encouraged his artistic activities, including his use of unconventional punctuation and capitalization.

Politically liberal in his youth, Cummings became more conservative after a visit to Russia in 1931, but, in his early and late work, he emphasizes individuality and freedom of expression.

Anyone Lived in a Pretty How Town

anyone lived in a pretty how town
(with up so floating many bells down)
spring summer autumn winter
he sang his didn't he danced his did.

Women and men(both little and small)   5
cared for anyone not at all
they sowed their isn't they reaped their same
sun moon stars rain

children guessed(but only a few
and down they forgot as up they grew   10
autumn winter spring summer)
that noone loved him more by more

when by now and tree by leaf
she laughed his joy she cried his grief

bird by snow and stir by still   15
anyone's any was all to her

someones married their everyones
laughed their cryings and did their dance
(sleep wake hope and then)they
said their nevers they slept their dream   20

stars rain sun moon
(and only the snow can begin to explain
how children are apt to forget to remember
with up so floating many bells down)

one day anyone died i guess   25
(and noone stooped to kiss his face)
busy folk buried them side by side
little by little and was by was

all by all and deep by deep
and more by more they dream their sleep   30
noone and anyone earth by april
wish by spirit and if by yes.

Women and men(both dong and ding)
summer autumn winter spring
reaped their sowing and went their came   35
sun moon stars rain

                                                                            [1940]

Joining the Conversation: Critical Thinking and Writing

1. Put into normal order (as far as possible) the words of the first two stanzas and then compare your version with Cummings's. What does Cummings gain—or lose?
2. Characterize the "anyone" who "sang his didn't" and "danced his did." In your opinion, how does he differ from the people who "sowed their isn't they reaped their same"?
3. Some readers interpret "anyone died" (line 25) to mean that the child matured and became as dead as the other adults. How, in an argument, might you support or refute this interpretation?

Sylvia Plath

Sylvia Plath (1932–63) was born in Boston, Massachusetts, the daughter of German immigrants. While still an undergraduate at Smith College, she published in Seventeen *and* Mademoiselle, *but her years at college, like her later years, were marked by manic-depressive periods. After graduating from college, she went to England to study at Cambridge University, where she met the English poet Ted Hughes, whom she married in 1956. The marriage was unsuccessful, and they separated. She died of a suicide, just as her work was earning recognition.*

Daddy

You do not do, you do not do
Any more, black shoe
In which I have lived like a foot
For thirty years, poor and white,
Barely daring to breathe or Achoo.   5

Daddy, I have had to kill you.
You died before I had time—
Marble-heavy, a bag full of God,
Ghastly statue with one gray toe
Big as a Frisco seal   10

And a head in the freakish Atlantic
Where it pours bean green over blue
In the waters off beautiful Nauset.
I used to pray to recover you.
Ach, du.°   15

In the German tongue, in the Polish town
Scraped flat by the roller
Of wars, wars, wars.
But the name of the town is common.
My Polack friend   20

Says there are a dozen or two.
So I never could tell where you
Put your foot, your root,
I never could talk to you.
The tongue stuck in my jaw.   25

It stuck in a barb wire snare.
Ich, ich, ich, ich,°
I could hardly speak.
I thought every German was you.
And the language obscene   30

An engine, an engine
Chuffing me off like a Jew.
A Jew to Dachau, Auschwitz, Belsen.°
I began to talk like a Jew.
I think I may well be a Jew.   35

The snows of the Tyrol, the clear beer of Vienna
Are not very pure or true.
With my gypsy ancestress and my weird luck
And my Taroc pack and my Taroc pack
I may be a bit of a Jew.   40

I have always been scared of *you,*
With your Luftwaffe,° your gobbledygoo.

---

15 Ach, du O, you (German). **27 Ich, ich, ich, ich** I, I, I, I. **33 Dachau, Auschwitz, Belsen**
concentration camps. **42 Luftwaffe** German air force.

And your neat moustache
And your Aryan eye, bright blue,
Panzer-man,°panzer-man, O You—   45

Not God but a swastika
So black no sky could squeak through.
Every woman adores a Fascist,
The boot in the face, the brute
Brute heart of a brute like you.   50

You stand at the blackboard, daddy,
In the picture I have of you,
A cleft in your chin instead of your foot
But no less a devil for that, no not
Any less the black man who   55

Bit my pretty red heart in two.
I was ten when they buried you.
At twenty I tried to die
And get back, back, back to you.
I thought even the bones would do   60

But they pulled me out of the sack,
And they stuck me together with glue,
And then I knew what to do.
I made a model of you,
A man in black with a Meinkampf° look   65

And a love of the rack and the screw.
And I said I do, I do.
So daddy, I'm finally through.
The black telephone's off at the root,
The voices just can't worm through.   70

If I've killed one man, I've killed two—
The vampire who said he was you
And drank my blood for a year,
Seven years, if you want to know.
Daddy, you can lie back now.   75

There's a stake in your fat black heart
And the villagers never liked you.
They are dancing and stamping on you.
They always *knew* it was you.
Daddy, daddy, you bastard, I'm through.   80

[1965]

45 Panzer-man member of a tank crew.   **65 Mein Kampf** *My Struggle* (title of Hitler's autobiography).

Joining the Conversation: Critical Thinking and Writing

1. Many readers find in "Daddy" something that reminds them of nursery rhymes. If you are among these readers, specify the resemblance(s).
2. Some critics have called parts of the poem "surrealistic." Check a college dictionary, and then argue in a paragraph or two why the word is or is not appropriate.
3. Is this a poem whose experience a reader can share? Explain your answer.

GWENDOLYN BROOKS

For a biographical note on Gwendolyn Brooks, see page 787.

We Real Cool

The Pool Players.
Seven at the Golden Shovel.

We real cool. We
Left school. We

Lurk late. We
Strike straight. We

Sing sin. We   5
Thin gin. We

Jazz June. We
Die soon.

[1960]

Joining the Conversation: Critical Thinking and Writing

1. What does it mean for the pool players to say that they are "cool," and not just "cool," but "real cool"?
2. Why does Brooks give seven speakers? Why not simply one, as in "I real cool" and so on? Would that have been more focused and thus more effective?
3. The stanzas could have been written:

   We real cool.
   We left school.
   We lurk late.
   We strike straight.

   And so on. What does Brooks gain by organizing the lines as she does?
4. Brooks presents the poem in a first-person plural voice, "we." If someone claimed that Brooks would have made the poem more objective and, hence, better if she had presented it in third-personal plural, "they," what would be your argument in response?

5. One commentary we consulted says that this poem describes "pool-playing gang members at a bar called The Golden Shovel on the South Side of Chicago." Does this specific information add to or detract from your experience of the poem?
6. Is it accurate or is it misleading to say that this poem presents an argument?

ETHERIDGE KNIGHT

Etheridge Knight, born in Corinth, Mississippi, in 1931, dropped out of school in the eighth grade. He served in the U.S. Army from 1947 to 1951, but after his discharge became addicted to drugs and soon was involved in a life of crime. Arrested for robbery in 1960, Knight began to write poetry while in prison, encouraged by the African American poets Dudley Randall, Sonia Sanchez, and Gwendolyn Brooks. His first book, Poems from Prison, *was published in 1968 by Randall's Broadside Press. Knight was a leading figure in the Black Arts movement of the 1960s and 1970s, a form of radical cultural activity (related to the broader Black Power movement) that promoted "social engagement" as a crucial feature of literary practice. His* Belly Song and Other Poems *(1973) was one of the most influential books of the period for African American writers and critics. Knight died in 1985.*

The following poem was written a year after the assassination of the charismatic African American militant, writer, and orator Malcolm X (nicknamed "Red"). Born in Omaha, Nebraska, in 1925, Malcolm Little moved to Boston in the early 1940s, and there and in New York City he was a drug dealer and a thief. He was arrested in 1946 for armed robbery and spent the next six years in prisons in Massachusetts. While still in prison, he became acquainted with the teachings of Elijah Muhammed, the leader of the Nation of Islam, and he embarked upon an intensive program of self-education, especially in history. Upon his release from prison, Malcolm Little changed his name to Malcolm X, the "X" signifying the name, unknown to him, of his African ancestors who had been sold into slavery. He broke with Elijah Muhammed in 1963 and formed a rival organization, the Muslim Mosque, Inc. He then made a pilgrimage to Mecca, converted to orthodox Islam, and, while remaining a militant black nationalist, stated that he was no longer a racial separatist. In the Audubon Ballroom in Harlem, on February 21, 1965, Malcolm X was murdered by members of the Nation of Islam, though controversy still surrounds the conspiracy that led to his death. Malcolm X's writings and speeches are included in his Autobiography *(as told to Alex Haley, 1964) and* Malcolm X Speaks *(1965).*

For Malcolm, a Year After

Compose for Red a proper verse;
Adhere to foot and strict iamb;
Control the burst of angry words
Or they might boil and break the dam.
Or they might boil and overflow   5
And drench me, drown me, drive me mad.

So swear no oath, so shed no tear,
And sing no song blue Baptist sad.
Evoke no image, stir no flame,
And spin no yarn across the air.   10
Make empty anglo tea lace words—

Make them dead and white and dry bone bare.

Compose a verse for Malcolm man,
And make it rime and make it prim.
The verse will die—as all men do—   15
But not the memory of him!
Death might come singing sweet like C,
Or knocking like the old folk say,
The moon and stars may pass away,
But not the anger of that day.   20

[1966]

Joining the Conversation: Critical Thinking and Writing

1. Knight's poem is both about Malcolm X and about the writing of a poem about him. Why might Knight have wanted to connect the subject of this poem to the act of writing the poem in the first place? Do you think that Knight should have presented a more straightforward tribute?
2. Explain the meaning of line 8 and of line 11. Which line is more effective? Are these lines more or less effective than other lines in the poem?
3. Are the first two lines of the second stanza puzzling? Why the word "prim"?
4. What is the relationship of the fourth line of the second stanza to the final line of the poem?
5. Do you think that Knight's poem remains powerful today? How does a poem keyed to a specific historical event or person retain its power decades after the event or after the person's death? Or is it the case, in your view, that the passing of time always diminishes the impact of a poem like this one?

ANNE SEXTON

Anne Sexton (1928–74) was born in Newton, Massachusetts. She was a member of a well-educated New England family but did not attend college. After the birth of her second child, she suffered a mental breakdown, and, for much of the rest of her life, she was under psychiatric care. Indeed, a psychiatrist encouraged her to write poetry, and she was soon able to publish in national journals such as The New Yorker. *Despite her success, she continued to suffer mentally, and in 1974 she committed suicide.*

Her Kind

I have gone out, a possessed witch,
haunting the black air, braver at night;
dreaming evil, I have done my hitch
over the plain houses, light by light;
lonely thing, twelve-fingered, out of mind.   5
A woman like that is not a woman, quite.
I have been her kind.

I have found the warm caves in the woods,
filled them with skillets, carvings, shelves,

closets, silks, innumerable goods;   10
fixed the suppers for the worms and the elves:
whining, rearranging the disaligned.
A woman like that is misunderstood.
I have been her kind.

I have ridden in your cart, driver,   15
waved my nude arms at villages going by,
learning the last bright routes, survivor
where your flames still bite my thigh
and my ribs crack where your wheels wind.
A woman like that is not ashamed to die.   20
I have been her kind.

[1960]

Joining the Conversation: Critical Thinking and Writing

1. Whether you are male or female, can you categorically say that you are *not* "her kind"? Explain your answer.

JAMES WRIGHT

James Wright (1927–80) was born in Martins Ferry, Ohio, which provided him with the locale for many of his poems. He is often thought of as a poet of the Midwest, but (as in the example that we give here) his poems move beyond the scenery. Wright was educated at Kenyon College in Ohio and at the University of Washington. He wrote several books of poetry and published many translations of European and Latin American poetry.

Lying in a Hammock at William Duffy's Farm in Pine Island, Minnesota

Over my head, I see the bronze butterfly,
Asleep on the black trunk,
Blowing like a leaf in green shadow.
Down the ravine behind the empty house,
The cowbells follow one another   5
Into the distances of the afternoon.
To my right,
In a field of sunlight between two pines,
The droppings of last year's horses
Blaze up into golden stones.   10
I lean back, as the evening darkens and comes on.
A chicken hawk floats over, looking for home.
I have wasted my life.

[1963]

Joining the Conversation: Critical Thinking and Writing

1. How important is it that the poet is "lying in a hammock"? That he is at some place other than his own home?
2. Do you take the last line as a severe self-criticism, as a joking remark, or as something else?
3. Imagine yourself lying in a hammock—perhaps you can recall an actual moment when you were lying in a hammock, in bed, or on a blanket on the beach,, your eye taking in the surroundings. Write a description ending with some sort of judgment or concluding comment, as Wright does. You may want to parody Wright's poem, but you need not. (Keep in mind that the best parodies are written by people who regard the original with affection.)

An Author in Depth: Robert Frost

ROBERT FROST

Robert Frost (1874–1963) was born in California. After his father's death in 1885, Frost's mother took the family to New England, where she taught in high schools in Massachusetts and New Hampshire. Frost studied for part of one term at Dartmouth College in New Hampshire, then did odd jobs (including teaching), and from 1897 to 1899 was enrolled as a special student at Harvard. He then farmed in New Hampshire, published a few poems in local newspapers, left the farm and taught again, and in 1912 left for England, where he hoped to achieve more popular success as a writer. By 1915 he had won a considerable reputation, and he returned to the United States, settling on a farm in New Hampshire and cultivating the image of the country-wise farmer-poet. In fact he was well read in the classics, the Bible, and English and American literature.

Among Frost's many comments about literature, here are three: "Writing is unboring to the extent that it is dramatic"; "Every poem is . . . a figure of the will braving alien entanglements"; and, finally, a poem "begins in delight and ends in wisdom. . . . It runs a course of lucky events, and ends in a clarification of life—not necessarily a great clarification, such as sects and cults are founded on, but in a momentary stay against confusion."

Here is Frost, in a letter, writing about his own work:

> *You get more credit for thinking if you restate formulae or cite cases that fall in easily under formulae, but all the fun is outside[,] saying things that suggest formulae that won't formulate—that almost but don't quite formulate. I should like to be so subtle at this game as to seem to the casual person altogether obvious. The casual person would assume I meant nothing or else I came near enough meaning something he was familiar with to mean it for all practical purposes. Well, well, well.*

Robert Frost on Poetry

The Figure a Poem Makes

Abstraction is an old story with the philosophers, but it has been like a new toy in the hands of the artists of our day. Why can't we have any one quality of poetry we choose by itself? We can have in thought. Then it will go hard if we can't in practice. Our lives for it.

Granted no one but a humanist much cares how sound a poem is if it is only *a* sound. The sound is the gold in the ore. Then we will have the sound out alone and dispense with the inessential. We do till we make the discovery that the object in writing poetry is to make all poems sound as different as possible from each other, and the resources for that of vowels, consonants, punctuation, syntax, words, sentences, meter are not enough. We need the help of context—meaning—subject matter. That is the greatest help towards variety. All that can be done with words is soon told. So also with meters—particularly in our language where there are virtually but two, strict iambic and loose iambic. The ancients with many were still poor if they depended on meters for all tune. It is painful to watch our sprung-rhythmists straining at the point of omitting one short from a foot for relief from monotony. The possibilities for tune from the dramatic tones of meaning struck across the rigidity of a limited meter are endless. And we are back in poetry as merely one more art of having something to say, sound or unsound. Probably better if sound, because deeper and from wider experience.

Then there is this wildness whereof it is spoken. Granted again that it has an equal claim with sound to being a poem's better half. If it is a wild tune, it is a poem. Our problem then is, as modern abstractionists, to have the wildness pure: to be wild with nothing to be wild about. We bring up as aberrationists, giving way to undirected associations and kicking ourselves from one chance suggestion to another in all directions as of a hot afternoon in the life of a grasshopper. Theme alone can steady us down. Just as the first mystery was how a poem could have a tune in such a straightness as meter, so the second mystery is how a poem can have wildness and at the same time a subject that shall be fulfilled.

It should be of the pleasure of a poem itself to tell how it can. The figure a poem makes. It begins in delight and ends in wisdom. The figure is the same as for love. No one can really hold that the ecstasy should be static and stand still in one place. It begins in delight, it inclines to the impulse, it assumes direction with the first line laid down, it runs a course of lucky events, and ends in a clarification of life—not necessarily a great clarification, such as sects and cults are founded on, but in a momentary stay against confusion. It has denouement. It has an outcome that though unforeseen was predestined from the first image of the original mood—and indeed from the very mood. It is but a trick poem and no poem at all if the best of it was thought of first and saved for the last. It finds its own name as it goes and discovers the best waiting for it in some final phrase at once wise and sad—the happy-sad blend of the drinking song.

5   No tears in the writer, no tears in the reader. No surprise for the writer, no surprise for the reader. For me the initial delight is in the surprise of remembering something I didn't know I knew. I am in a place, in a situation, as if I had materialized from cloud or risen out of the ground. There is a glad recognition of the long lost and the rest follows. Step by step the wonder of unexpected supply keeps growing. The impressions most useful to my purpose seem always those I was unaware

of and so made no note of at the time when taken, and the conclusion is come to that like giants we are always hurling experience ahead of us to pave the future with against the day when we may want to strike a line of purpose across it for some- where. The line will have the more charm for not being mechanically straight. We enjoy the straight crookedness of a good walking stick. Modern instruments of preci- sion are being used to make things crooked as if by eye and hand in the old days.

I tell how there may be a better wildness of logic than of inconsequence. But the logic is backward, in retrospect, after the act. It must be more felt than seen ahead like prophecy. It must be a revelation, or a series of revelations, as much for the poet as for the reader. For it to be that there must have been the greatest free- dom of the material to move about in it and to establish relations in it regardless of time and space, previous relation, and everything but affinity. We prate of free- dom. We call our schools free because we are not free to stay away from them till we are sixteen years of age. I have given up my democratic prejudices and now willingly set the lower classes free to be completely taken care of by the upper classes. Political freedom is nothing to me. I bestow it right and left. All I would keep for myself is the freedom of my material—the condition of body and mind now and then to summons aptly from the vast chaos of all I have lived through.

Scholars and artists thrown together are often annoyed at the puzzle of where they differ. Both work from knowledge; but I suspect they differ most importantly in the way their knowledge is come by. Scholars get theirs with conscientious thor- oughness along projected lines of logic; poets theirs cavalierly and it happens in and out of books. They stick to nothing deliberately, but let what will stick to them like burrs where they walk in the fields. No acquirement is on assignment, or even self-assignment. Knowledge of the second kind is much more available in the wild free ways of wit and art. A school boy may be defined as one who can tell you what he knows in the order in which he learned it. The artist must value himself as he snatches a thing from some previous order in time and space into a new order with not so much as a ligature clinging to it of the old place where it was organic.

More than once I should have lost my soul to radicalism if it had been the original- ity it was mistaken for by young converts. Originality and initiative are what I ask for my country. For myself the originality need be no more than the freshness of a poem run in the way I have described: from delight to wisdom. The figure is the same as for love. Like a piece of ice on a hot stove the poem must ride on its own melting. A poem may be worked over once it is in being, but may not be worried into being. Its most precious quality will remain its having run itself and carried away the poet with it. Read it a hundred times: it will forever keep its freshness as a metal keeps its fragrance. It can never lose its sense of a meaning that once unfolded by surprise as it went.

[1939]

The Pasture

I'm going out to clean the pasture spring;
I'll only stop to rake the leaves away
(And wait to watch the water clear, I may):
I shan't be gone long.—You come too.

I'm going out to fetch the little calf   5
That's standing by the mother. It's so young,
It totters when she licks it with her tongue.
I shan't be gone long.—You come too.

[1914]

Joining the Conversation: Critical Thinking and Writing

1. Would the poem be just as good—maybe better?—if it consisted of only one stanza, either the first or the second? Explain your answer.
2. Although Frost had already published books of poems, after he wrote "The Pasture" he always placed this poem first in any collected edition of his poems. Why do you suppose he did this?

Mowing

There was never a sound beside the wood but one,
And that was my long scythe whispering to the ground.
What was it it whispered? I knew not well myself;
Perhaps it was something about the heat of the sun,
Something, perhaps, about the lack of sound—   5
And that was why it whispered and did not speak.
It was no dream of the gift of idle hours,
Or easy gold at the hand of fay or elf:
Anything more than the truth would have seemed too weak
To the earnest love that laid the swale in rows,   10
Not without feeble-pointed spikes of flowers
(Pale orchises), and scared a bright green snake.
The fact is the sweetest dream that labor knows.
My long scythe whispered and left the hay to make.

[1913]

Joining the Conversation: Critical Thinking and Writing

1. What associations come to mind from the title?
2. Please explain the distinction that Frost's speaker makes between whispering and speaking.
3. What is the speaker saying in lines 7–8?
4. Line 13 is well known to many readers. What does it mean? How is this line connected to the meaning of the poem as a whole?
5. Frost was keenly interested in tones of voice—in getting these tones into his poetry. How would you describe the tone or tones of voice in this poem?
6. Frost is a very popular poet, widely read and studied both inside and outside college classrooms. Is this a poem that you like? Explain your answer.
7. Could you imagine learning "Mowing" by heart? Why might someone want to memorize this poem?

The Wood-Pile

Out walking in the frozen swamp one grey day,
I paused and said, "I will turn back from here.
No, I will go on farther—and we shall see."
The hard snow held me, save where now and then   5
One foot went through. The view was all in lines

Straight up and down of tall slim trees
Too much alike to mark or name a place by
So as to say for certain I was here
Or somewhere else: I was just far from home.
A small bird flew before me. He was careful   10
To put a tree between us when he lighted,
And say no word to tell me who he was
Who was so foolish as to think what *he* thought.
He thought that I was after him for a feather—
The white one in his tail; like one who takes   15
Everything said as personal to himself.
One flight out sideways would have undeceived him.
And then there was a pile of wood for which
I forgot him and let his little fear
Carry him off the way I might have gone,   20
Without so much as wishing him good-night.
He went behind it to make his last stand.
It was a cord of maple, cut and split
And piled—and measured, four by four by eight.
And not another like it could I see.   25
No runner tracks in this year's snow looped near it.
And it was older sure than this year's cutting,
Or even last year's or the year's before.
The wood was grey and the bark warping off it
And the pile somewhat sunken. Clematis   30
Had wound strings round and round it like a bundle.
What held it though on one side was a tree
Still growing, and on one a stake and prop,
These latter about to fall. I thought that only
Someone who lived in turning to fresh tasks   35
Could so forget his handiwork on which
He spent himself, the labour of his axe,
And leave it there far from a useful fireplace
To warm the frozen swamps as best it could
With the slow smokeless burning of decay.   40

[1914]

Joining the Conversation: Critical Thinking and Writing

1. What is the contrast that Frost makes between human beings and nature?
2. What does he say about the relationship between human beings and nature?

The Oven Bird

There is a singer everyone has heard,
Loud, a mid-summer and a mid-wood bird,
Who makes the solid tree trunks sound again.
He says that leaves are old and that for flowers

Mid-summer is to spring as one to ten.   5
He says the early petal-fall is past
When pear and cherry bloom went down in showers
On sunny days a moment overcast;
And comes that other fall we name the fall.
He says the highway dust is over all.
The bird would cease and be as other birds   10
But that he knows in singing not to sing.
The question that he frames in all but words
Is what to make of a diminished thing.

                                                      [1916]

Joining the Conversation: Critical Thinking and Writing

1. Does the poem offer anything to a reader who has *not* heard an oven bird? If so, what?
2. Do you have an answer to "The question" raised in the last two lines? If so, what is the answer?

The Need of Being Versed in Country Things

The house had gone to bring again
To the midnight sky a sunset glow.
Now the chimney was all of the house that stood,
Like a pistil after the petals go.

The barn opposed across the way,   5
That would have joined the house in flame
Had it been the will of the wind, was left
To bear forsaken the place's name.

No more it opened with all one end
For teams that came by the stony road   10
To drum on the floor with scurrying hoofs
And brush the mow with the summer load.

The birds that came to it through the air
At broken windows flew out and in,
Their murmur more like the sigh we sigh   15
From too much dwelling on what has been.

Yet for them the lilac renewed its leaf,
And the aged elm, though touched with fire;
And the dry pump flung up an awkward arm;
And the fence post carried a strand of wire.   20

For them there was really nothing sad.
But though they rejoiced in the nest they kept,
One had to be versed in country things
Not to believe the phoebes wept.

                                                      [1923]

Joining the Conversation: Critical Thinking and Writing

1. By the end of the second stanza, the reader understands that the farmhouse has been destroyed by a fire. Why do you suppose (putting aside the matter of rhyme) in line 2 Frost wrote "a sunset glow" instead of (say) "a burst of flame"? And what is the effect of the simile in line 4? That is, what do these comparisons contribute to the poem? (If you are unsure of the meaning of "pistil," check a dictionary.)

2. In the fifth stanza, Frost uses personifications: "the lilac renewed its leaf," the "pump flung up an awkward arm," and "the fence post carried a strand of wire." What other personifications do you find in the poem? What effect do these personifications have on you? And why do you suppose there are no personifications in the last two lines of the poem?

3. In a sentence—or two or three—characterize the speaker. (You can probably characterize the speaker by means of one to three adjectives; use the rest of your answer to provide evidence, such as brief quotations.)

4. Much of the poem describes a scene, but the speaker also interprets the scene. How would you summarize the speaker's interpretation? How might you paraphrase the title? Does the speaker convince you of the "need" to be "versed in country things"?

5. Do you think the poem is sentimental? Or, on the other hand, is it cynical? Explain your answer.

6. Suppose you were to write a parody of "The Need of Being Versed in Country Things." What scene might you use, or what objects might you personify? (A parody is an amusing imitation of the style of another work, often with an inappropriate subject. Thus, one might parody a sports writer by imitating his or her style, but the subject would not be an athletic event but, say, students engaged in peer review.) Suggestion: Consider using your neighborhood or your workplace as a subject.

The Most of It

He thought he kept the universe alone;
For all the voice in answer he could wake
Was but the mocking echo of his own
From some tree-hidden cliff across the lake.
Some morning from the boulder-broken beach   5
He would cry out on life, that what it wants
Is not its own love back in copy speech,
But counter-love, original response.

And nothing ever came of what he cried
Unless it was the embodiment that crashed   10
In the cliff's talus on the other side,
And then in the far distant water splashed,
But after a time allowed for it to swim,
Instead of proving human when it neared
And someone else additional to him,   15
As a great buck it powerfully appeared,
Pushing the crumpled water up ahead,

And landed pouring like a waterfall,
And stumbled through the rocks with horny tread,
And forced the underbrush—and that was all.   20

[1942]

Joining the Conversation: Critical Thinking and Writing

1. How would you characterize the "He" of the first line?
2. Frost does *not* say "a great buck powerfully appeared." Rather, he says, "As a great buck it powerfully appeared." What is going on here?

Design

I found a dimpled spider, fat and white,
On a white heal-all, holding up a moth
Like a white piece of rigid satin cloth—
Assorted characters of death and blight
Mixed ready to begin the morning right,   5
Like the ingredients of a witches' broth—
A snow-drop spider, a flower like a froth,
And dead wings carried like a paper kite.

What had that flower to do with being white,
The wayside blue and innocent heal-all?   10
What brought the kindred spider to that height,
Then steered the white moth thither in the night?
What but design of darkness to appall?—
If design govern in a thing so small.

[1936]

Joining the Conversation: Critical Thinking and Writing

1. Do you find the spider, as described in line 1, cute or disgusting? Why?
2. What is the effect of "If" in the last line?
3. The word *design* can mean "pattern" (as in "a pretty design"), or it can mean "intention," especially an evil intention (as in "He had designs on her"). Does Frost use the word in one sense or in both? Explain your answer.
4. Is Frost offering an argument? If so, what is it?

CHAPTER 16

The World around Us

ESSAYS

HENRY DAVID THOREAU

Henry David Thoreau (1817–1862) was born in Concord, Massachusetts, where his most famous residence was a small self-built hut on Walden Pond where he lived for approximately two years (1845–1847). Thoreau's Walden *(1854) provides a personal account of the philosophical beliefs that led him to experiment with living a solitary, self-sufficient life on the pond. In addition to recording of the details of Thoreau's life, such as the building of his home and garden,* Walden *contains minutely observed descriptions of nature. Thoreau's description of the pond is deeply moving and is considered some of America's earliest and most important nature writing. The excerpts provided here include a short example of Thoreau's philosophical arguments and a lengthier example of Thoreau's poetic descriptions of the pond.*

Thoreau, a talented student at Harvard University, returned home to teach and work in his father's pencil factory. In Concord, he became close friends with Ralph Waldo Emerson, one of America's most famous writers and a leading proponent of Transcendentalism, which holds that the spiritual realm transcends the limits of the human realm and interconnects nature, man, and god. Emerson supported Thoreau and encouraged his writing. Thoreau died in 1862 due to complications from tuberculosis.

Walden

"Where I Lived, and What I Lived For"

I went to the woods because I wished to live deliberately, to front only the essential facts of life, and see if I could not learn what it had to teach, and not, when I came to die, discover that I had not lived. I did not wish to live what was not life, living is so dear; nor did I wish to practise resignation, unless it was quite necessary. I wanted to live deep and suck out all the marrow of life, to live so sturdily and Spartan-like as to put to rout all that was not life, to cut a broad swath and shave close, to drive life into a corner, and reduce it to its lowest terms, and, if it proved to be mean, why then to get the whole and genuine meanness of it, and publish its meanness to the world; or if it were sublime, to know it by experience, and be able to give a true account of it in my next excursion.

"The Ponds"

A lake is the landscape's most beautiful and expressive feature. It is earth's eye; looking into which the beholder measures the depth of his own nature. The fluviatile trees next the shore are the slender eyelashes which fringe it, and the wooded hills and cliffs around are its overhanging brows.

Standing on the smooth sandy beach at the east end of the pond, in a calm September afternoon, when a slight haze makes the opposite shore line indistinct, I have seen whence came the expression, "the glassy surface of a lake." When you invert your head, it looks like a thread of finest gossamer stretched across the valley, and gleaming against the distant pine woods, separating one stratum of the atmosphere from another. You would think that you could walk dry under it to the opposite hills, and that the swallows which skim over might perch on it. Indeed, they sometimes dive below the line, as it were by mistake, and are undeceived. As you look over the pond westward you are obliged to employ both your hands to defend your eyes against the reflected as well as true sun, for they are equally bright; and if, between the two, you survey its surface critically, it is literally as smooth as glass, except where the skater insects, at equal intervals scattered over its whole extent, by their motions in the sun produce the finest imaginable sparkle on it, or, perchance, a duck plumes itself, or, as I have said, a swallow skims so low as to touch it. It may be that in the distance a fish describes an arc of three or four feet in the air, and there is one bright flash where it emerges, and another where it strikes the water; sometimes the whole silvery arc is revealed; or here and there, perhaps, is a thistle-down floating on its surface, which the fishes dart at and so dimple it again. It is like molten glass cooled but not congealed, and the few motes in it are pure and beautiful like the imperfections in glass. You may often detect a yet smoother and darker water, separated from the rest as if by an invisible cobweb, boom of the water nymphs, resting on it. From a hill-top you can see a fish leap in almost any part; for not a pickerel or shiner picks an insect from this smooth surface but it manifestly disturbs the equilibrium of the whole lake. It is wonderful with what elaborateness this simple fact is advertised,—this piscine murder will out,—and from my distant perch I distinguish the circling undulations when they are half a dozen rods in diameter. You can even detect a water-bug, (*Gyrinus*) ceaselessly progressing over the smooth surface a quarter of a mile off; for they furrow the water slightly, making a conspicuous ripple bounded by two diverging lines, but the skaters glide over it without rippling it perceptibly. When the surface is considerably agitated there are no skaters nor water-bugs on it, but apparently, in calm days, they leave their havens and adventurously glide forth from the shore by short impulses till they completely cover it. It is a soothing employment, on one of those fine days in the fall when all the warmth of the sun is fully appreciated, to sit on a stump on such a height as this, overlooking the pond, and study the dimpling circles which are incessantly inscribed on its otherwise invisible surface amid the reflected skies and trees. Over this great expanse there is no disturbance but it is thus at once gently smoothed away and assuaged, as, when a vase of water is jarred, the trembling circles seek the shore and all is smooth again. Not a fish can leap or an insect fall on the pond but it is thus reported in circling dimples, in lines of beauty, as it were the constant welling up of its fountain, the gentle pulsing of its life, the heaving of its breast. The thrills of joy and thrills of pain are undistinguishable. How peaceful the phenomena of the lake! Again the works of man shine as in the spring. Ay, every leaf and twig and stone and cobweb sparkles now at mid-afternoon as when covered with dew in a spring morning. Every motion of an oar or an insect produces a flash of light; and if an oar falls, how sweet the echo!

In such a day, in September or October, Walden is a perfect forest mirror, set round with stones as precious to my eye as if fewer or rarer. Nothing so fair, so pure, and at the same time so large, as a lake, perchance, lies on the surface of the earth. Sky water. It needs no fence. Nations come and go defiling it. It is a mirror which no stone can crack, whose quicksilver will never wear off, whose gilding Nature continually repairs; no storms, no dust, can dim its surface ever fresh;—a mirror in which all impurity presented to it sinks, swept and dusted by the sun's hazy brush,—this the light dust-cloth,—which retains no breath that is breathed on it, but sends its own to float as clouds high above its surface, and be reflected in its bosom still.

A field of water betrays the spirit that is in the air. It is continually receiving new life and motion from above. It is intermediate in its nature between land and sky. On land only the grass and trees wave, but the water itself is rippled by the wind. I see where the breeze dashes across it by the streaks or flakes of light. It is remarkable that we can look down on its surface. We shall, perhaps, look down thus on the surface of air at length, and mark where a still subtler spirit sweeps over it.

The skaters and water-bugs finally disappear in the latter part of October, when the severe frosts have come; and then and in November, usually, in a calm day, there is absolutely nothing to ripple the surface. One November afternoon, in the calm at the end of a rain storm of several days' duration, when the sky was still completely overcast and the air was full of mist, I observed that the pond was remarkably smooth, so that it was difficult to distinguish its surface; though it no longer reflected the bright tints of October, but the sombre November colors of the surrounding hills. Though I passed over it as gently as possible, the slight undulations produced by my boat extended almost as far as I could see, and gave a ribbed appearance to the reflections. But, as I was looking over the surface, I saw here and there at a distance a faint glimmer, as if some skater insects which had escaped the frosts might be collected there, or, perchance, the surface, being so smooth, betrayed where a spring welled up from the bottom. Paddling gently to one of these places, I was surprised to find myself surrounded by myriads of small perch, about five inches long, of a rich bronze color in the green water, sporting there and constantly rising to the surface and dimpling it, sometimes leaving bubbles on it. In such transparent and seemingly bottomless water, reflecting the clouds, I seemed to be floating through the air as a balloon, and their swimming impressed me as a kind of flight or hovering, as if they were a compact flock of birds passing just beneath my level on the right or left, their fins, like sails, set all around them.

Joining the Conversation: Critical Thinking and Writing

1. Thoreau's descriptions of Walden Pond use highly evocative language. Find a series of sentences that you enjoy. Annotate the sentences, making sure to highlight Thoreau's poetic language. Then write a short response paper that explains how Thoreau uses language to convey his love of nature. In your opinion, which words, phrases, images, and symbols are the most successful?
2. At the end of the selection, "From 'The Ponds,'" Thoreau's describes paddling out to the middle of the pond. What is the optical illusion he describes? What does he compare the fish to?
3. What do you make of the short philosophical except from the chapter entitled "Where I Lived, and What I Lived For"? What are the central ideas Thoreau conveys? Write a short explication of this passage. Then, explain if you agree or disagree with Thoreau's argument.

BILL MCKIBBEN

Bill McKibben, born in California in 1960 and educated at Harvard, became a staff writer for the New Yorker, *then a freelance writer, publishing in numerous magazines, including the* New York Review of Books, Rolling Stone, *and the* New Republic. *Among his many books are* The End of Nature *(1989),* The Age of Missing Information *(1992), and* A Year of Living Strenuously *(2000).*

Now or Never

When global warming first emerged as a potential crisis in the late '80s, one academic analyst called it "the public policy problem from hell." The years since have only proven him more astute—15 years into our understanding of climate change, we have yet to figure out how we're going to tackle it. And environmentalists are just as clueless as anyone else: Do we need to work on lifestyles or on lobbying, on politics or on photovoltaics? And is there a difference? How well we handle global warming will determine what kind of century we inhabit—and indeed what kind of planet we leave behind to everyone and everything that follows us down into geologic time. It is *the* environmental question, the one that cuts closest to home and also floats off most easily into the abstract. So far it has been the ultimate "can't get there from here" problem, but the time has come to draw a roadmap— one that may help us deal with the handful of other issues on the list of real, world-shattering problems.

The first thing to know about global warming is this: The science is sound. In 1988, when scientists first testified before Congress about the potential for rapid and destabilizing climate change, they were still describing a hypothesis. It went like this: Every time human beings burn coal, gas, oil, wood or any other carbon-based fuel, they emit large quantities of carbon dioxide. (A car emits its own weight in carbon annually if you drive it the average American distance.) This carbon dioxide accumulates in the atmosphere. It's not a normal pollutant—it doesn't poison you, or change the color of the sunset. But it does have one interesting property: Its molecular structure traps heat near the surface of the planet that would otherwise radiate back out to space. It acts like the panes of glass on a greenhouse.

The hypothesis was that we were putting enough carbon dioxide into the atmosphere to make a difference. The doubters said no—that the earth would compensate for any extra carbon by forming extra clouds and cooling the planet, or through some other feedback mechanism. And so, as scientists will, they went at it. For five years—lavishly funded by governments that wanted to fund research instead of making politically unpopular changes—scientists produced paper after paper. They studied glacial cores and tree rings and old pollen sediments in lake beds to understand past climates; they took temperature measurements on the surface and from space; they refined their computer models and ran them backward in time to see if they worked. By 1995 they had reached a conclusion. That year the Intergovernmental Panel on Climate Change (IPCC), a group of all the world's climatologists assembled under the auspices of the United Nations, announced that human beings were indeed heating up the planet.

The scientists kept up the pace of their research for the next five years, and in the past five months have published a series of massive updates to their findings. These results are uniformly grimmer than even five years before. They include:

- The prediction that humans will likely heat the planet 4 to 6 degrees Fahrenheit in this century, twice as much as earlier forecasts, taking global temperatures to a level not seen in millions of years, and never before in human history.

- The worst-case possibility that we will raise the temperature by as much as 11 degrees Fahrenheit, a true science-fiction scenario that no one had seriously envisaged before.
- The near certainty that these temperature increases will lead to rises in sea level of at least a couple of feet.
- The well-documented fear that disease will spread quickly as vectors like mosquitoes expand their range to places that used to be too cool for their survival.

5   But it isn't just the scientists who are hard at work on this issue. For the past five years, it's almost as if the planet itself has been peer-reviewing their work. We've had the warmest years on record—including 1998, which was warmer than any year for which records exist. And those hot years have shown what even small changes in temperature—barely a degree Fahrenheit averaged globally—can do to the earth's systems.

Consider hydrology, for instance. Warm air holds more water vapor than cold air, so there is an increase in evaporation in dry areas, and hence more drought—something that has been documented on every continent. Once that water is in the atmosphere, it's going to come down somewhere—and indeed we have seen the most dramatic flooding ever recorded in recent years. In 1998, 300 million humans, one in 20 of us, had to leave their homes for a week, a month, a year, forever because of rising waters.

Or look at the planet's cryosphere, its frozen places. Every alpine glacier is in retreat; the snows of Kilimanjaro will have vanished by 2015; and the Arctic ice cap is thinning fast—data collected by U.S. and Soviet nuclear submarines show that it is almost half gone compared with just four decades ago.

In other words, human beings are changing the planet more fundamentally in the course of a couple of decades than in all the time since we climbed down from the trees and began making clever use of our opposable thumbs. There's never been anything like this.

Yet to judge from the political response, this issue ranks well below, say, the estate tax as a cause for alarm and worry. In 1988, there was enough public outcry that George Bush the Elder promised to combat "the greenhouse effect with the White House effect." In 1992, Bill Clinton promised that Americans would emit no more carbon dioxide by 2000 than they had in 1990—and that his administration would do the work of starting to turn around our ocean liner of an economy, laying the foundation for the transition to a world of renewable energy.

10   That didn't happen, of course. Fixated on the economy, Clinton and Gore presided over a decade when Americans, who already emitted a quarter of the world's carbon dioxide, actually managed to increase their total output by 12 percent. Now we have a president who seems unsure whether global warming is real, and far more concerned with increasing power production than with worrying about trifles like the collapse of the globe's terrestrial systems. In November, the hope of global controls on carbon dioxide production essentially collapsed at an international conference in the Hague, when the United States refused to make even modest concessions on its use of fossil fuels, and the rest of the world finally walked away from the table in disgust.

In the face of all this, what is an environmentalist to do? The normal answer, when you're mounting a campaign, is to look for self-interest, to scare people by saying what will happen to us if we don't do something: all the birds will die, the canyon will disappear beneath a reservoir, we will choke to death on smog.

But in the case of global warming, those kind of answers don't exactly do the trick, at least in the time frame we're discussing. At this latitude, climate change will creep up on us. Severe storms have already grown more frequent and more damaging. The seasons are less steady in their progression. Some agriculture is less reliable. But face it: Our economy is so enormous that it handles those kinds of changes in stride. Economists who work on this stuff talk about how it will shave a percentage or two off GNP over the next few decades—not enough to notice in the kind of generalized economic boom they describe. And most of us live lives so divorced from the natural world that we hardly notice the changes anyway. Hotter? Turn up the air conditioning. Stormier? Well, an enormous percentage of Americans commute from remote-controlled garage to office parking garage—they may have gone the last year without getting good and wet in a rainstorm. By the time the magnitude of the change is truly in our faces, it well be too late to do much about it: There's such a lag time with carbon dioxide in the atmosphere that we need to be making the switch to solar and wind and hydrogen right about now. Yesterday, in fact.

So maybe we should think of global warming in a different way—as the great moral crisis of our moment, the equivalent in our time of the civil rights movement of the '60s.

Why a moral question? In the first place, because we've never figured out a more effective way to screw the marginalized and poor of this planet. Having taken their dignity, their resources and their freedom under a variety of other schemes, we now are taking the very physical stability on which they depend for the most bottom-line of existences.

15   Our economy can absorb these changes for a while, but for a moment consider Bangladesh. A river delta that houses 130 million souls in an area the size of Wisconsin, Bangladesh actually manages food self-sufficiency most years. But in 1998, the sea level in the Bay of Bengal was higher than normal, just the sort of thing we can expect to become more frequent and severe. The waters sweeping down the Ganges and the Brahmaputra from the Himalayas could not drain easily into the ocean—they backed up across the country, forcing most of its inhabitants to spend three months in thigh-deep water. The fall rice crop didn't get planted. We've seen this same kind of disaster in the last few years in Mozambique or Honduras or Venezuela or any of a dozen other wretched spots.

And a moral crisis, too, if you place any value on the rest of creation. Coral reef researchers indicate that these spectacularly intricate ecosystems are also spectacularly vulnerable—rising water temperatures will likely bleach them to extinction by mid-century. In the Arctic, polar bears are 20 percent scrawnier than they were a decade ago: As pack ice melts, so does the opportunity for hunting seals. All in all, this century seems poised to see extinctions at a rate not observed since the last big asteroid slammed into the planet. But this time the asteroid is us.

A moral question, finally, if you think we owe any debt to the future. No one ever has figured out a more thorough-going way to stripmine the present and degrade what comes after. Forget the seventh generation—we're talking 70th generation, and 700th. All the people that will ever be related to you. Ever. No generation yet to come will ever forget us—we are the ones present at the moment when the temperature starts to spike, and so far we have not reacted. If it had been done to us, we would loathe the generation that did it, precisely as we will one day be loathed.

But trying to make a moral campaign is no easy task. In most moral crises, there is a villain—some person or class or institution that must be overcome. Once they're identified, the battle can commence. But you can't really get angry at carbon dioxide, and the people responsible for its production are, well, us. So perhaps we need some symbols to get us started, some places to sharpen the debate and rally ourselves to action. There are plenty to choose from: our taste for ever bigger houses and the heating and cooling bills that come with them; our penchant for jumping on airplanes at the drop of a hat; and so on. But if you wanted one glaring example of our lack of balance, you could do worse than point the finger at sport utility vehicles.

SUVs are more than mere symbol. They are a major part of the problem—one reason we emit so much more carbon dioxide now than we did a decade ago is because our fleet of cars and trucks actually has gotten steadily less fuel efficient for the past 10 years. If you switched today from the average American car to a big SUV, and drove it for just one year, the difference in carbon dioxide that you produced would be the equivalent of opening your refrigerator door and then forgetting to close it for six years. SUVs essentially are machines for burning fossil fuel that just happen to also move you and your stuff around.

20 But what makes them such a perfect symbol is the brute fact that they are simply unnecessary. Go to the parking lot of the nearest suburban supermarket and look around: the only conclusion you can draw is that to reach the grocery, people must drive through three or four raging rivers and up the side of a trackless canyon. These are semi-military machines (some, like the Hummer, are not semi at all), Brinks trucks on a slight diet. They don't keep their occupants safer, they do wreck whatever they plow into—they are the perfect metaphor for a heedless, supersized society. And a gullible one, which has been sold on these vast vehicles partly by the promise that they somehow allow us to commune with nature.

That's why we need a much broader politics than the White House-lobbying that's occupied the big enviros for the past decade, or the mass-market mailing that has been their stock in trade for the past quarter century. We need to take all the brilliant and energetic strategies of local grassroots groups fighting dumps and cleaning up rivers, and we need to make those tactics national and international. So that's why some pastors are starting to talk with their congregations about what car they're going to buy, and why some college seniors are passing around petitions pledging to stay away from the Ford Explorers and Excursions and Extraneouses, and why some few auto dealers have begun to notice informational picketers outside on Saturday mornings urging their customers to think about gas mileage when they go inside.

The point is not that by themselves such actions—any individual actions—will make any real dent in the production of carbon dioxide pouring into our atmosphere. Even if you got 10 percent of Americans really committed to changing energy use, their solar homes wouldn't make much of a dent in our national totals. But 10 percent would be enough to change the politics of the issue, to insure the passage of the laws that would cause us all to shift our habits. And so we need to begin to take an issue that is now the province of technicians and turn it into a political issue—just as bus boycotts began to take the issue of race and make it public, forcing the system to respond. That response is likely to be ugly—there are huge companies with a lot to lose, and many people so tied in to their current ways of life that advocating change smacks of subversion. But this has to become a political issue—and fast. The only way that may happen, short of a hideous drought or monster flood, is if it becomes a personal issue first.

[2001]

Joining the Conversation: Critical Thinking and Writing

1. McKibben argues that global warming constitutes "a moral crisis" (paragraph 13). What reasons does he offer?
2. In paragraphs 19–20, McKibben talks about SUVs, saying that "they are simply unnecessary." Do you agree? If you don't, explain why. If you do agree, explain why SUVs are popular.
3. What *persona* does McKibben convey in this essay? (On persona, see page 414.) Thoughtful? Belligerent? Hysterical? Concerned but eccentric? Support your answer with evidence.
4. McKibben often varies the length of his sentences, sometimes perhaps surprisingly. For instance, in the first paragraph, the first sentence contains twenty-four words, the second twenty-nine words, the third twenty-four, but the fourth—a question—contains only five words. What effect does he gain? Take another passage in his essay where there is a sharp contrast, and explain the effect.
5. Now that you have read McKibben's essay and thought further about it, do you plan to change your behavior in any way? Explain your answer.

STORIES

AESOP

In ancient Greece and Rome, many fables were attributed to Aesop, who was said to have been a Greek slave who lived in the sixth century BCE. In the first of the two that we print here, English versions speak of a grasshopper, but in Greek the insect is a cicada.

The Ant and the Grasshopper

One cold winter day an ant was dragging out a grain which he had buried during the winter. A hungry grasshopper asked for a bit of the grain.

"What did you do all summer?" asked the ant.

"I was busy all summer long, singing," replied the grasshopper.

"Well," said the ant, "since you sang all summer, now dance all winter."

The Moral: Negligence leads to hardship.

Joining the Conversation: Critical Thinking and Writing

1. Let's rewrite the ant's final remark, thus: "Well, since you spent the whole summer singing, I guess you'll dance now in the winter." We assume you agree that the original version is more effective. Exactly what makes the original better?
2. Do you think we can draw lessons from nature about how we should behave? Is a significant part of the argument (so to speak) of an Aesop fable that it is "natural," that it shows us "nature's way"? Think of other fables that draw on the nonhuman world, such as "The Fox and the Grapes." (The gist of "The Fox and the Grapes" is this: "A starving fox, seeing bunches of grapes hanging from a vine, but out of reach, went away saying, "Those grapes aren't ripe, they're sour.") What do such fables gain by being set in the nonhuman world? Why not

just say, "A starving man, seeing bunches of grapes that were out of reach. . . ."? Again, what, if anything, is gained by using talking animals? Is the moral enforced by nature?

The North Wind and the Sun

The North Wind and the Sun once got into an argument about which of the two was the most powerful. They agreed that whichever could make a certain traveler take off his overcoat would be declared the winner.

The North Wind was the first to try: He blew as hard as he could, but the harder he blew, the more the traveler buttoned up his coat and held it close to his body by folding his arms across his chest. The wind blew and blew, but finally he was out of breath.

Then it was the Sun's turn. The Sun smiled, sending beams of light that drove away the fog and the mist. He smiled a bit more, and the man unbuttoned his coat and after a little while, feeling pleasantly warm, took off the coat.

The North Wind agreed that the Sun was the winner.

The Moral: Gentleness is more persuasive than violence.

Joining the Conversation: Critical Thinking and Writing

1. Do you think the moral can reasonably be drawn from the story? Do you think the moral is true?
2. Do you think nature can teach us anything about moral behavior? If so, what sorts of things? Be as specific as possible. You may want to cite concrete instances. If you think it cannot teach us anything about morality, explain why you hold this view.

JACK LONDON

Jack London (1876–1916) was born in San Francisco and educated in Oakland High School and the University of California, Berkeley, but his formal education was intermittent. At thirteen or fourteen years old, he was a pirate raiding oyster beds in San Francisco Bay; a little later he worked in a cannery, and at seventeen years old, he joined a sealing expedition to Japan and Siberia. Back in the United States, he worked at odd jobs, became a socialist, finished high school in 1895, spent one semester at Berkeley, and then was off to the Klondike (age twenty-one) looking—unsuccessfully, it turned out—for gold. He published his first story in 1899, his first collection of stories (The Son of the Wolf) *in 1900, and his first novel* (The Call of the Wild) *in 1903. The novel was an immediate hit. London continued to write, both fiction and journalism, earning over a million dollars from his writing—at that time an astounding amount, especially for a writer.*

To Build a Fire

Day had broken cold and gray, exceedingly cold and gray, when the man turned aside from the main Yukon trail and climbed the high earth-bank, where a dim and little-travelled trail led eastward through the fat spruce timberland. It was a steep bank, and he paused for breath at the top, excusing the act to himself by looking at his watch. It was nine o'clock. There was no sun nor hint of sun, though there was not a cloud in the sky. It was a clear day, and yet there seemed an intangible pall over the face of things, a subtle gloom that made the day dark, and that was due to the absence of sun. This fact did not worry the man. He was used to the lack of sun. It had been days since he had seen the sun, and he knew that a few more days must pass before that cheerful orb, due south, should just peep above the sky line and dip immediately from view.

The man flung a look back along the way he had come. The Yukon[1] lay a mile wide and hidden under three feet of ice. On top of this ice were as many feet of snow. It was all pure white, rolling in gentle undulations where the ice jams of the freeze-up had formed. North and south, as far as his eye could see, it was unbroken white, save for a dark hairline that curved and twisted from around the spruce-covered island to the south, and that curved and twisted away into the north, where it disappeared behind another spruce-covered island. This dark hairline was the trail—the main trail—that led south five hundred miles to the Chilcoot Pass, Dyea, and salt water; and that led north seventy miles to Dawson, and still on to the north a thousand miles to Nulato, and finally to St. Michael, on Bering Sea, a thousand miles and a half a thousand more.

But all this—the mysterious, fair-reaching hairline trail, the absence of sun from the sky, the tremendous cold, and the strangeness and weirdness of it all— made no impression on the man. It was not because he was long used to it. He was a newcomer in the land, a *chechaquo,* and this was his first winter. The trouble with him was that he was without imagination. He was quick and alert in the things of life, but only in the things, and not in the significances. Fifty degrees below zero meant eighty-odd degrees of frost. Such fact impressed him as being cold and uncomfortable, and that was all. It did not lead him to meditate upon his frailty as a creature of temperature, and upon man's frailty in general, able only to live within certain narrow limits of heat and cold; and from there on it did not lead him to the conjectural field of immortality and man's place in the universe. Fifty degrees below zero stood for a bite of frost that hurt and that must be guarded against by the use of mittens, ear flaps, warm moccasins, and thick socks. Fifty degrees below zero was to him just precisely fifty degrees below zero. That there should be anything more to it than that was a thought that never entered his head.

As he turned to go on, he spat speculatively. There was a sharp, explosive crackle that startled him. He spat again. And again, in the air, before it could fall to the snow, the spittle crackled. He knew that at fifty below spittle crackled on the snow, but this spittle had crackled in the air. Undoubtedly it was colder than fifty below—how much colder he did not know. But the temperature did not matter. He was bound for the old claim on the left fork of Henderson Creek, where the boys were already. They had come over across the divide from the Indian Creek country, while he had come the roundabout way to take a look at the possibilities of getting out logs in the spring from the islands in the Yukon. He would be in to camp by six o'clock; a bit after dark, it was true, but the boys would be there, a fire would be going, and a hot supper would be ready. As for lunch, he pressed his hand against the protruding bundle under his jacket. It was also under his shirt, wrapped up in a handkerchief and lying against the naked skin. It was the only

[1]**Yukon** a major river in Alaska and western Canada.

way to keep the biscuits from freezing. He smiled agreeably to himself as he thought of those biscuits, each cut open and sopped in bacon grease, and each enclosing a generous slice of fried bacon.

5   He plunged in among the big spruce trees. The trail was faint. A foot of snow had fallen since the last sled had passed over, and he was glad he was without a sled, traveling light. In fact, he carried nothing but the lunch wrapped in the handkerchief. He was surprised, however, at the cold. It certainly was cold, he concluded, as he rubbed his numb nose and cheekbones with his mittened hand. He was a warm-whiskered man, but the hair on his face did not protect the high cheekbones and the eager nose that thrust itself aggressively into the frosty air.

At the man's heels trotted a dog, a big native husky, the proper wolf dog, gray-coated and without any visible or temperamental difference from its brother, the wild wolf. The animal was depressed by the tremendous cold. It knew that it was not time for traveling. Its instinct told it a truer tale than was told to the man by the man's judgment. In reality, it was not merely colder than fifty below zero; it was colder than sixty below, than seventy below. It was seventy-five below zero. Since the freezing point is thirty-two above zero, it meant that one hundred and seven degrees of frost obtained. The dog did not know anything about thermometers. Possibly in its brain there was no sharp consciousness of a condition of very cold such as was in the man's brain. But the brute had its instinct. It experienced a vague but menacing apprehension that subdued it and made it slink along at the man's heels, and that made it question eagerly every unwonted movement of the man as if expecting him to go into camp or to seek shelter somewhere and build a fire. The dog had learned fire, and it wanted fire, or else to burrow under the snow and cuddle its warmth away from the air.

The frozen moisture of its breathing had settled on its fur in a fine powder of frost, and especially were its jowls, muzzle, and eyelashes whitened by its crystalled breath. The man's red beard and mustache were likewise frosted, but more solidly, the deposit taking the form of ice and increasing with every warm, moist breath he exhaled. Also, the man was chewing tobacco, and the muzzle of ice held his lips so rigidly that he was unable to clear his chin when he expelled the juice. The result was that a crystal beard of the color and solidity of amber was increasing its length on his chin. If he fell down it would shatter itself, like glass, into brittle fragments. But he did not mind the appendage. It was the penalty all tobacco chewers paid in that country, and he had been out before in two cold snaps. They had not been so cold as this, he knew, but by the spirit thermometer at Sixty Mile he knew they had been registered at fifty below and at fifty-five.

He held on through the level stretch of woods for several miles, crossed a wide flat of nigger heads, and dropped down a bank to the frozen bed of a small stream. This was Henderson Creek, and he knew he was ten miles from the forks. He looked at his watch. It was ten o'clock. He was making four miles an hour, and he calculated that he would arrive at the forks at half-past twelve. He decided to celebrate that event by eating his lunch there.

The dog dropped in again at his heels, with a tail drooping discouragement, as the man swung along the creek bed. The furrow of the old sled trail was plainly visible, but a dozen inches of snow covered the marks of the last runners. In a month no man had come up or down that silent creek. The man held steadily on. He was not much given to thinking, and just then particularly he had nothing to think about save that he would eat lunch at the forks and that at six o'clock he would be in camp with the boys. There was nobody to talk to; and, had there been, speech would have been impossible because of the ice muzzle on his mouth. So he continued monotonously to chew tobacco and to increase the length of his amber beard.

10   Once in a while the thought reiterated itself that it was very cold and that he had never experienced such cold. As he walked along he rubbed his cheekbones and nose with the back of his mittened hand. He did this automatically, now and again changing hands. But, rub as he would, the instant he stopped his cheekbones went numb, and the following instant the end of his nose went numb. He was sure to frost his cheeks; he knew that, and experienced a pang of regret that he had not devised a nose strap of the sort Bud wore in cold snaps. Such a strap passed across the cheeks, as well, and saved them. But it didn't matter much, after all. What were frosted cheeks? A bit painful, that was all; they were never serious.

Empty as the man's mind was of thoughts, he was keenly observant, and he noticed the changes in the creek, the curves and bends and timber jams, and always he sharply noted where he placed his feet. Once, coming around a bend, he shied abruptly, like a startled horse, curved away from the place where he had been walking, and retreated several paces back along the trail. The creek he knew was frozen clear to the bottom—no creek could contain water in that arctic winter—but he knew also that there were springs that bubbled out from the hillsides and ran along under the snow and on top the ice of the creek. He knew that the coldest snaps never froze these springs, and he knew likewise their danger. They were traps. They hid pools of water under the snow that might be three inches deep, or three feet. Sometimes a skin of ice half an inch thick covered them, and in turn was covered by the snow. Sometimes there were alternate layers of water and ice skin, so that when one broke through he kept on breaking through for a while, sometimes wetting himself to the waist.

That was why he had shied in such panic. He had felt the give under his feet and heard the crackle of a snow-hidden ice skin. And to get his feet wet in such a temperature meant trouble and danger. At the very least it meant delay, for he would be forced to stop and build a fire, and under its protection to bare his feet while he dried his socks and moccasins. He stood and studied the creek bed and its banks, and decided that the flow of water came from the right. He reflected awhile, rubbing his nose and cheeks, then skirted to the left, stepping gingerly and testing the footing for each step. Once clear of the danger, he took a fresh chew of tobacco and swung along at his four-mile gait.

In the course of the next two hours he came upon several similar traps. Usually the snow above the hidden pools had a sunken, candied appearance that advertised the danger. Once again, however, he had a close call; and once, suspecting danger, he compelled the dog to go on in front. The dog did not want to go. It hung back until the man shoved it forward, and then it went quickly across the white, unbroken surface. Suddenly it broke through, floundered to one side, and got away to firmer footing. It had wet its forefeet and legs, and almost immediately the water that clung to it turned to ice. It made quick efforts to lick the ice off its legs, then dropped down in the snow and began to bite out the ice that had formed between the toes. This was a matter of instinct. To permit the ice to remain would mean sore feet. It did not know this. It merely obeyed the mysterious prompting that arose from the deep crypts of its being. But the man knew, having achieved a judgment on the subject, and he removed the mitten from his right hand and helped tear out the ice particles. He did not expose his fingers more than a minute, and was astonished at the swift numbness that smote them. It certainly was cold. He pulled on the mitten hastily, and beat the hand savagely across his chest.

At twelve o'clock the day was at its brightest. Yet the sun was too far south on its winter journey to clear the horizon. The bulge of the earth intervened between it and Henderson Creek, where the man walked under a clear sky at noon and cast no shadow. At half-past twelve, to the minute, he arrived at the forks of the creek. He was pleased at the speed he had made. If he kept it up, he would certainly be with the boys by six. He unbuttoned his jacket and shirt and drew forth his lunch. The action consumed no more than a quarter of a minute, yet in that brief moment the numbness laid hold of the exposed fingers. He did not put the mitten on, but, instead, struck the fingers a dozen sharp smashes against his leg. Then he sat down on a snow-covered log to eat. The sting that followed upon the striking of his fingers against his leg ceased so quickly that he was startled. He had had no chance to take a bite of biscuit. He struck the fingers repeatedly and returned them to the mitten, baring the other hand for the purpose of eating. He tried to take a mouthful, but the ice muzzle prevented. He had forgotten to build a fire and thaw out. He chuckled at his foolishness, and as he chuckled he noted the numbness creeping into the exposed fingers. Also, he noted that the stinging which had first come to his toes when he sat down was already passing away. He wondered whether the toes were warm or numb. He moved them inside the moccasins and decided that they were numb.

15   He pulled the mitten on hurriedly and stood up. He was a bit frightened. He stamped up and down until the stinging returned into the feet. It certainly was cold, was his thought. That man from Sulphur Creek had spoken the truth when telling how cold it sometimes got in the country. And he had laughed at him at the time! That showed one must not be too sure of things. There was no mistake about it, it *was* cold. He strode up and down, stamping his feet and threshing his arms, until reassured by the returning warmth. Then he got out matches and proceeded to make a fire. From the undergrowth, where high water of the previous spring had lodged a supply of seasoned twigs, he got his firewood. Working carefully from a small beginning, he soon had a roaring fire, over which he thawed the ice from his face and in the protection of which he ate his biscuits. For the moment the cold of space was outwitted. The dog took satisfaction in the fire, stretching out close enough for warmth and far enough away to escape being singed.

When the man had finished, he filled his pipe and took his comfortable time over a smoke. Then he pulled on his mittens, settled the ear flaps of his cap firmly about his ears, and took the creek trail up the left fork. The dog was disappointed and yearned back toward the fire. This man did not know cold. Possibly all the generations of his ancestry had been ignorant of cold, of real cold, of cold one hundred and seven degrees below freezing point. But the dog knew; all its ancestry knew, and it had inherited the knowledge. And it knew that it was not good to walk abroad in such fearful cold. It was the time to lie snug in a hole in the snow and wait for a curtain of cloud to be drawn across the face of outer space whence this cold came. On the other hand, there was no keen intimacy between the dog and the man. The one was the toil slave of the other, and the only caresses it had ever received were the caresses of the whip lash and of harsh and menacing throat sounds that threatened the whip lash. So the dog made no effort to communicate its apprehension to the man. It was not concerned in the welfare of the man; it was for its own sake that it yearned back toward the fire. But the man whistled, and spoke to it with the sound of whip lashes, and the dog swung in at the man's heels and followed after.

The man took a chew of tobacco and proceeded to start a new amber beard. Also, his moist breath quickly powdered with white his mustache, eyebrows, and lashes. There did not seem to be so many springs on the left fork of the Henderson, and for half an hour the man saw no signs of any. And then it happened. At a place where there were no signs, where the soft, unbroken snow seemed to advertise solidity beneath, the man broke through. It was not deep. He wet himself halfway to the knees before he floundered out to the firm crust.

He was angry, and cursed his luck aloud. He had hoped to get into camp with the boys at six o'clock, and this would delay him an hour, for he would have to build a fire and dry out his footgear. This was imperative at that low temperature— he knew that much; and he turned aside to the bank, which he climbed. On top, tangled in the underbrush about the trunks of several small spruce trees, was a highwater deposit of dry firewood—sticks and twigs, principally, but also larger portions of seasoned branches and fine dry last year's grasses. He threw down several large pieces on top of the snow. This served for a foundation and pre- vented the young flame from drowning itself in the snow it otherwise would melt. The flame he got by touching a match to a small shred of birch bark that he took from his pocket. This burned even more readily than paper. Placing it on the foundation, he fed the young flame with wisps of dry grass and with the tiniest dry twigs.

He worked slowly and carefully, keenly aware of his danger. Gradually, as the flame grew stronger, he increased the size of the twigs with which he fed it. He squatted in the snow, pulling the twigs out from their entanglement in the brush and feeding directly to the flame. He knew there must be no failure. When it is seventy-five below zero, a man must not fail in his first attempt to build a fire—that is, if his feet are wet. If his feet are dry, and he fails, he can run along the trail for half a mile and restore his circulation. But the circulation of wet and freezing feet cannot be restored by running when it is seventy-five below. No matter how fast he runs, the wet feet will freeze the harder.

20   All this the man knew. The old-timer on Sulphur Creek had told him about it the previous fall, and now he was appreciating the advice. Already all sensation had gone out of his feet. To build the fire he had been forced to remove his mittens, and the fingers had quickly gone numb. His pace of four miles an hour had kept his heart pumping blood to the surface of his body and to all the extrem- ities. But the instant he stopped, the action of the pump eased down. The cold of space smote the unprotected tip of the planet, and he, being on that unprotected tip, received the full force of the blow. The blood of his body recoiled before it. The blood was alive, like the dog, and like the dog it wanted to hide away and cover itself up from the fearful cold. So long as he walked four miles an hour, he pumped that blood, willy-nilly, to the surface; but now it ebbed away and sank down into the recesses of his body. The extremities were the first to feel its absence. His wet feet froze the faster, and his exposed fingers numbed the faster, though they had not yet begun to freeze. Nose and cheeks were already freezing, while the skin of all his body chilled as it lost its blood.

But he was safe. Toes and nose and cheeks would be only touched by the frost, for the fire was beginning to burn with strength. He was feeding it with twigs the size of his finger. In another minute he would be able to feed it with branches the size of his wrist, and then he could remove his wet footgear, and, while it dried, he could keep his naked feet warm by the fire, rubbing them at first, of course, with snow. The fire was a success. He was safe. He remembered the advice of the old-timer on Sulphur Creek, and smiled. The old-timer had been very serious in laying down the law that no man must travel alone in the Klondike after fifty below. Well, here he was; he had had the accident; he was alone; and he had saved himself. Those old-timers were rather womanish, some of them, he thought. All a man had to do was to keep his head, and he was all right. Any man who was a man could travel alone. But it was surprising, the rapidity with which his cheeks and nose were freezing. And he had not thought his fingers could go lifeless in so short a time. Lifeless they were, for he could scarcely make them move together to grip a twig, and they seemed remote from his body and from him. When he touched a twig, he had to look and see whether or not he had hold of it. The wires were pretty well down between him and his finger ends.

All of which counted for little. There was the fire, snapping and crackling and promising life with every dancing flame. He started to untie his moccasins. They were coated with ice; the thick German socks were like sheaths of iron halfway to the knees; and the moccasin strings were like rods of steel all twisted and knotted as by some conflagration. For a moment he tugged with his numb fingers, then, realizing the folly of it, he drew his sheath knife.

But before he could cut the strings, it happened. It was his own fault or, rather, his mistake. He should not have built the fire under the spruce tree. He should have built it in the open. But it had been easier to pull the twigs from the brush and drop them directly on the fire. Now the tree under which he had done this carried a weight of snow on its boughs. No wind had blown for weeks, and each bough was fully freighted. Each time he had pulled a twig he had communicated a slight agitation to the tree—an imperceptible agitation, so far as he was concerned, but an agitation sufficient to bring about the disaster. High up in the tree one bough capsized its load of snow. This fell on the boughs beneath, capsizing them. This process continued, spreading out and involving the whole tree. It grew like an avalanche, and it descended without warning upon the man and the fire, and the fire was blotted out! Where it had burned was a mantle of fresh and disordered snow.

The man was shocked. It was as though he had just heard his own sentence of death. For a moment he sat and stared at the spot where the fire had been. Then he grew very calm. Perhaps the old-timer on Sulphur Creek was right. If he had only had a trail mate he would have been in no danger now. The trail mate could have built the fire. Well, it was up to him to build the fire over again, and this second time there must be no failure. Even if he succeeded, he would most likely lose some toes. His feet must be badly frozen by now, and there would be some time before the second fire was ready.

25   Such were his thoughts, but he did not sit and think them. He was busy all the time they were passing through his mind. He made a new foundation for a fire, this time in the open, where no treacherous tree could blot it out. Next he gathered dry grasses and tiny twigs from the high-water flotsam. He could not bring his fingers together to pull them out, but he was able to gather them by the handful. In this way he got many rotten twigs and bits of green moss that were undesirable, but it was the best he could do. He worked methodically, even collecting an armful of the larger branches to be used later when the fire gathered strength. And all the while the dog sat and watched him, a certain yearning wistfulness in its eyes, for it looked upon him as the fire provider, and the fire was slow in coming.

When all was ready, the man reached in his pocket for a second piece of birch bark. He knew the bark was there, and, though he could not feel it with his fingers, he could hear its crisp rustling as he fumbled for it. Try as he would, he could not clutch hold of it. And all the time, in his consciousness, was the knowledge that each instant his feet were freezing. This thought tended to put him in a panic, but he fought against it and kept calm. He pulled on his mittens with his teeth, and threshed his arms back and forth, beating his hands with all his might against his sides. He did this sitting down, and he stood up to do it; and all the while the dog sat in the snow, its wolf brush of a tail curled around warmly over its forefeet, its sharp wolf ears pricked forward intently as it watched the man. And the man, as he beat and threshed with his arms and hands, felt a great surge of envy as he regarded the creature that was warm and secure in its natural covering.

After a time he was aware of the first faraway signals of sensation in his beaten fingers. The faint tingling grew stronger till it evolved into a stinging ache that was excruciating, but which the man hailed with satisfaction. He stripped the mitten from his right hand and fetched forth the birch bark. The exposed fingers were quickly going numb again. Next he brought out his bunch of sulphur matches. But the tremendous cold had already driven the life out of his fingers. In his effort to separate one match from the others, the whole bunch fell in the snow. He tried to pick it out of the snow, but failed. The dead fingers could neither touch nor clutch. He was very careful. He drove the thought of his freezing feet, and nose, and cheeks, out of his mind, devoting his whole soul to the matches. He watched, using the sense of vision in place of that of touch, and when he saw his fingers on each side the bunch, he closed them—that is he willed to close them, for the wires were down, and the fingers did not obey. He pulled the mitten on the right hand, and beat it fiercely against his knee. Then, with both mittened hands, he scooped the bunch of matches, along with much snow, into his lap. Yet he was no better off.

After some manipulation he managed to get the bunch between the heels of his mittened hands. In this fashion he carried it to his mouth. The ice crackled and snapped when by a violent effort he opened his mouth. He drew the lower jaw in, curled the upper lip out of the way, scraped the bunch with his upper teeth in order to separate a match. He succeeded in getting one, which he dropped on his lap. He was no better off. He could not pick it up. Then he devised a way. He picked it up in his teeth and scratched it on his leg. Twenty times he scratched before he succeeded in lighting it. As it flamed he held it with his teeth to the birch bark. But the burning brimstone went up his nostrils and into his lungs, causing him to cough spasmodically. The match fell into the snow and went out.

The old-timer on Sulphur Creek was right, he thought in the moment of controlled despair that ensued: after fifty below, a man should travel with a partner. He beat his hands, but failed in exciting any sensation. Suddenly he bared both hands, removing the mittens with his teeth. He caught the whole bunch between the heels of his hands. His arm muscles not being frozen enabled him to press the hand heels tightly against the matches. Then he scratched the bunch along his leg. It flared into flame, seventy sulphur matches at once! There was no wind to blow them out. He kept his head to one side to escape the strangling fumes, and held the blazing bunch to the birch bark. As he so held it, he became aware of sensation in his hand. His flesh was burning. He could smell it. Deep down below the surface he could feel it. The sensation developed into pain that grew acute. And still he endured it, holding the flame of the matches clumsily to the bark that would not light readily because his own burning hands were in the way, absorbing most of the flame.

30   At last, when he could endure no more, he jerked his hands apart. The blazing matches fell sizzling into the snow, but the birch bark was alight. He began laying dry grasses and the tiniest twigs on the flame. He could not pick and choose, for he had to lift the fuel between the heels of his hands. Small pieces of rotten wood and green moss clung to the twigs, and he bit them off as well as he could with

his teeth. He cherished the flame carefully and awkwardly. It meant life, and it must not perish. The withdrawal of blood from the surface of his body now made him begin to shiver, and he grew more awkward. A large piece of green moss fell squarely on the little fire. He tried to poke it out with his fingers, but his shivering frame made him poke too far, and he disrupted the nucleus of the little fire, the burning grasses and tiny twigs separating and scattering. He tried to poke them together again, but in spite of the tenseness of the effort, his shivering got away with him, and the twigs were hopelessly scattered. Each twig gushed a puff of smoke and went out. The fire provider had failed. As he looked apathetically about him, his eyes chanced on the dog, sitting across the ruins of the fire from him, in the snow, making restless, hunching, movements, slightly lifting one fore-foot and then the other, shifting its weight back and forth on them with wistful eagerness.

The sight of the dog put a wild idea into his head. He remembered the tale of the man, caught in a blizzard, who killed a steer and crawled inside the carcass, and so was saved. He would kill the dog and bury his hands in the warm body until the numbness went out of them. Then he could build another fire. He spoke to the dog, calling it to him; but in his voice was a strange note of fear that fright-ened the animal, who had never known the man to speak in such way before. Something was the matter, and its suspicious nature sensed danger—it knew not what danger, but somewhere, somehow, in its brain arose an apprehension of the man. It flattened its ears down at the sound of the man's voice, and its restless, hunching movements and the liftings and shiftings of its forefeet became more pronounced; but it would not come to the man. He got on his hands and knees and crawled toward the dog. This unusual posture again excited suspicion, and the animal sidled mincingly away.

The man sat up in the snow for a moment and struggled for calmness. Then he pulled on his mittens, by means of his teeth, and got upon his feet. He glanced down at first in order to assure himself that he was really standing up, for the absence of sensation in his feet left him unrelated to the earth. His erect position in itself started to drive the webs of suspicion from the dog's mind; and when he spoke peremptorily, with the sound of whip lashes in his voice, the dog rendered its customary allegiance and came to him. As it came within reaching distance the man lost his control. His arms flashed out to the dog, and he experienced genuine surprise when he discovered that his hands could not clutch, that there was neither bend nor feeling in the fingers. He had forgotten for the moment that they were frozen and that they were freezing more and more. All this happened quickly, and before the animal could get away, he encircled its body with his arms. He sat down in the snow, and in this fashion held the dog, while it snarled and whined and struggled.

But it was all he could do, hold its body encircled in his arms and sit there. He realized that he could not kill the dog. There was no way to do it. With his helpless hands he could neither draw nor hold his sheath knife nor throttle the animal. He released it, and it plunged wildly away, with tail between its legs, and still snarling. It halted forty feet away and surveyed him curiously, with ears sharply pricked forward.

The man looked down at his hands in order to locate them, and found them hanging on the ends of his arms. It struck him as curious that one should have to use his eyes in order to find out where his hands were. He began threshing his arms back and forth, beating the mittened hands against his sides. He did this for five minutes, violently, and his heart pumped enough blood up to the surface to put a stop to his shivering. But no sensation was aroused in the hands. He had an impression that they hung like weights on the ends of his arms, but when he tried to run the impression down, he could not find it.

35   A certain fear of death, dull and oppressive, came to him. This fear quickly became poignant as he realized that it was no longer a mere matter of freezing his fingers and toes, or of losing his hands and feet, but that it was a matter of life and death with the chances against him. This threw him into a panic, and he turned and ran up the creek bed along the old, dim trail. The dog joined in behind and kept up with him. He ran blindly, without intention, in fear such as he had never known in his life. Slowly, as he plowed and floundered through the snow, he began to see things again—the banks of the creek, the old timber jams, the leafless aspens, and the sky. The running made him feel better. He did not shiver. Maybe, if he ran on, his feet would thaw out; and, anyway, if he ran far enough, he would reach camp and the boys. Without doubt he would lose some fingers and toes and some of his face; but the boys would take care of him, and save the rest of him when he got there. And at the same time there was another thought in his mind that said he would never get to the camp and the boys; that it was too many miles away, that the freezing had too great a start on him, and that he would soon be stiff and dead. This thought he kept in the background and refused to consider. Sometimes it pushed itself forward and demanded to be heard, but he thrust it back and strove to think of other things.

It struck him as curious that he could run at all on feet so frozen that he could not feel them when they struck the earth and took the weight of his body. He seemed to himself to skim along above the surface, and to have no connection with the earth. Somewhere he had once seen a winged Mercury,[2] and he wondered if Mercury felt as he felt when skimming over the earth.

His theory of running until he reached camp and the boys had one flaw in it: he lacked the endurance. Several times he stumbled, and finally he tottered, crumpled up, and fell. When he tried to rise, he failed. He must sit and rest, he decided, and next time he would merely walk and keep on going. As he sat and regained his breath, he noted that he was feeling quite warm and comfortable. He was not shivering, and it even seemed that a warm glow had come to this chest and trunk. And yet, when he touched his nose or cheeks, there was no sensation. Running would not thaw them out. Nor would it thaw out his hands and feet. Then the thought came to him that the frozen portions of his body must be extending. He tried to keep this thought down, to forget it, to think of something else; he was aware of the panicky feeling that it caused, and he was afraid of the panic. But the thought asserted itself, and persisted, until it produced a vision of his body totally frozen. This was too much, and he made another wild run along the trail. Once he slowed down to a walk, but the thought of the freezing extending itself made him run again.

And all the time the dog ran with him, at his heels. When he fell down a second time, it curled its tail over its forefeet and sat in front of him, facing him, curiously eager and intent. The warmth and security of the animal angered him, and he cursed it till it flattened down its ears appeasingly. This time the shivering came more quickly upon the man. He was losing his battle with the frost. It was creeping into his body from all sides. The thought of it drove him on, but he ran no more than a hundred feet, when he staggered and pitched headlong. It was his

---

[2]**winged Mercury** the winged messenger of Roman mythology.

last panic. When he had recovered his breath and control, he sat up and entertained in his mind the conception of meeting death with dignity. However, the conception did not come to him in such terms. His idea of it was that he had been making a fool of himself, running around like a chicken with its head cut off—such was the simile that occurred to him. Well, he was bound to freeze anyway, and he might as well take it decently. With this new-found peace of mind came the first glimmerings of drowsiness. A good idea, he thought, to sleep off to death. It was like taking an anesthetic. Freezing was not so bad as people thought. There were lots worse ways to die.

He pictured the boys finding his body next day. Suddenly he found himself with them, coming along the trail and looking for himself. And, still with them, he came around a turn in the trail and found himself lying in the snow. He did not belong with himself any more, for even then he was out of himself, standing with the boys and looking at himself in the snow. It certainly was cold, was his thought. When he got back to the States he could tell the folks what real cold was. He drifted on from this to a vision of the old-timer on Sulphur Creek. He could see him quite clearly, warm and comfortable, and smoking a pipe.

40   "You were right, old hoss; you were right," the man mumbled to the old-timer of Sulphur Creek.

Then the man drowsed off into what seemed to him the most comfortable and satisfying sleep he had ever known. The dog sat facing him and waiting. The brief day drew to a close in a long, slow twilight. There were no signs of a fire to be made, and, besides, never in the dog's experience had it known a man to sit like that in the snow and make no fire. As the twilight drew on, its eager yearning for the fire mastered it, and with a great lifting and shifting of forefeet, it whined softly, then flattened its ears down in anticipation of being chidden by the man. But the man remained silent. Later the dog whined loudly. And still later it crept close to the man and caught the scent of death. This made the animal bristle and back away. A little longer it delayed, howling under the stars that leaped and danced and shone brightly in the cold sky. Then it turned and trotted up the trail in the direction of the camp it knew, where were the other food providers and fire providers.

[1908]

Joining the Conversation: Critical Thinking and Writing

1. In a paragraph, explain the significance of the sentence, "The trouble with him was that he was without imagination" (paragraph 3).
2. In a letter to a young writer, London said: "Don't you tell the reader. . . . BUT HAVE YOUR CHARACTERS TELL IT BY THEIR DEEDS, ACTIONS, TALK, ETC. . . . The reader . . . doesn't want your dissertations on the subject, . . . your ideas—BUT PUT ALL THOSE THINGS WHICH ARE YOURS INTO THE STORIES." Good advice for a storyteller. Judging from this story, what do you suppose London's "ideas" were? Write a short dissertation—about 250 words—setting forth what you assume was London's view of man and nature.

SARAH ORNE JEWETT

Sarah Orne Jewett (1849–1909) was born and raised in South Berwick, Maine. A sickly girl, Jewett received little formal education, but her father, a doctor, introduced her to British and American fiction. Inspired by the writings of Harriet Beecher Stowe, Jewett determined in her teens to become a writer and began writing sketches and stories about the rural people of her native region. (Although South Berwick in Jewett's day was beginning to become industrialized, it had once been a busy port in a rural setting; Jewett's grandfather had been a sea captain and a leading owner of ships.) When she was twenty years old, she published her first story in the Atlantic Monthly, *and she continued to publish in national magazines stories about the vanishing era of her childhood.*

A White Heron

I

The woods were already filled with shadows one June evening, just before eight o'clock, though a bright sunset still glimmered faintly among the trunks of the trees. A little girl was driving home her cow, a plodding, dilatory, provoking creature in her behavior, but a valued companion for all that. They were going away from whatever light there was, and striking deep into the woods, but their feet were familiar with the path, and it was no matter whether their eyes could see it or not.

There was hardly a night the summer through when the old cow could be found waiting at the pasture bars; on the contrary, it was her greatest pleasure to hide herself away among the huckleberry bushes, and though she wore a loud bell she had made the discovery that if one stood perfectly still it would not ring. So Sylvia had to hunt for her until she found her, and call Co'! Co'! with never an answering Moo, until her childish patience was quite spent. If the creature had not given good milk and plenty of it, the case would have seemed very different to her owners. Besides, Sylvia had all the time there was, and very little use to make of it. Sometimes in pleasant weather it was a consolation to look upon the cow's pranks as an intelligent attempt to play hide and seek, and as the child had no playmates she lent herself to this amusement with a good deal of zest. Though this chase had been so long that the wary animal herself had given an unusual signal of her whereabouts, Sylvia had only laughed when she came upon Mistress Moolly at the swamp-side, and urged her affectionately homeward with a twig of birch leaves. The old cow was not inclined to wander farther, she even turned in the right direction for once as they left the pasture, and stepped along the road at a good pace. She was quite ready to be milked now, and seldom stopped to browse. Sylvia wondered what her grandmother would say because they were so late. It was a great while since she had left home at half-past five o'clock, but everybody knew the difficulty of making this errand a short one. Mrs. Tilley had chased the hornéd torment too many summer evenings herself to blame any one else for lingering, and was only thankful as she waited that she had Sylvia, nowadays, to give such valuable assistance. The good woman suspected that Sylvia loitered occasionally on her own account; there never was such a child for straying about out-of-doors since the world was made! Everybody said that it was a good change for a little maid who had tried to grow for eight years in a crowded manufacturing town, but as for Sylvia herself, it seemed as if she never had been alive at all before she came to live at the farm. She thought often with wistful compassion of a wretched geranium that belonged to a town neighbor.

"'Afraid of folks,'" old Mrs. Tilley said to herself, with a smile, after she had made the unlikely choice of Sylvia from her daughter's houseful of children, and was returning to the farm. "'Afraid of folks,' they said! I guess she won't be troubled no great with 'em up to the old place!" When they reached the door of the lonely house and stopped to unlock it, and the cat came to purr loudly, and rub against them, a deserted pussy, indeed, but fat with young robins, Sylvia whispered that this was a beautiful place to live in, and she never should wish to go home.

The companions followed the shady wood-road, the cow taking slow steps and the child very fast ones. The cow stopped long at the brook to drink, as if the pasture were not half a swamp, and Sylvia stood still and waited, letting her bare feet cool themselves in the shoal water, while the great twilight moths struck softly against her. She waded on through the brook as the cow moved away, and listened to the thrushes with a heart that beat fast with pleasure. There was a stirring in the great boughs overhead. They were full of little birds and beasts that seemed to be wide awake, and going about their world, or else saying goodnight to each other in sleepy twitters. Sylvia herself felt sleepy as she walked along. However, it was not much farther to the house, and the air was soft and sweet. She was not often in the woods so late as this, and it made her feel as if she were a part of the gray shadows and the moving leaves. She was just thinking how long it seemed since she first came to the farm a year ago, and wondering if everything went on in the noisy town just the same as when she was there; the thought of the great red-faced boy who used to chase and frighten her made her hurry along the path to escape from the shadow of the trees.

5   Suddenly this little woods-girl is horror-stricken to hear a clear whistle not very far away. Not a bird's-whistle, which would have a sort of friendliness, but a boy's whistle, determined, and somewhat aggressive. Sylvia left the cow to whatever sad fate might await her, and stepped discreetly aside into the brushes, but she was just too late. The enemy had discovered her, and called out in a very cheerful and persuasive tone, "Halloa, little girl, how far is it to the road?" and trembling Sylvia answered almost inaudibly, "A good ways."

She did not dare to look boldly at the tall young man, who carried a gun over his shoulder, but she came out of her bush and again followed the cow, while he walked alongside.

"I have been hunting for some birds," the stranger said kindly, "and I have lost my way, and need a friend very much. Don't be afraid," he added gallantly. "Speak up and tell me what your name is, and whether you think I can spend the night at your house, and go out gunning early in the morning."

Sylvia was more alarmed than before. Would not her grandmother consider her much to blame? But who could have foreseen such an accident as this? It did not seem to be her fault, and she hung her head as if the stem of it were broken, but managed to answer "Sylvy," with much effort when her companion again asked her name.

Mrs. Tilley was standing in the doorway when the trio came into view. The cow gave a loud moo by way of explanation.

10   "Yes, you'd better speak up for yourself, you old trial! Where'd she tucked herself away this time, Sylvy?" But Sylvia kept an awed silence; she knew by instinct that her grandmother did not comprehend the gravity of the situation. She must be mistaking the stranger for one of the farmer-lads of the region.

The young man stood his gun beside the door, and dropped a lumpy gamebag beside it; then he bade Mrs. Tilley good-evening, and repeated his wayfarer's story, and asked if he could have a night's lodging.

"Put me anywhere you like," he said. "I must be off early in the morning, before day; but I am very hungry indeed. You can give me some milk at any rate, that's plain."

"Dear sakes, yes," responded the hostess, whose long slumbering hospitality seemed to be easily awakened. "You might fare better if you went out to the main road a mile or so, but you're welcome to what we've got. I'll milk right off, and you make yourself at home. You can sleep on husks or feathers," she proffered graciously. "I raised them all myself. There's good pasturing for geese just below here towards the ma'sh. Now step round and set a plate for the gentleman, Sylvy!" And Sylvia promptly stepped. She was glad to have something to do, and she was hungry herself.

It was a surprise to find so clean and comfortable a little dwelling in this New England wilderness. The young man had known the horrors of its most primitive housekeeping, and the dreary squalor of that level of society which does not rebel at the companionship of hens. This was the best thrift of an old-fashioned farmstead, though on such a small scale that it seemed like a hermitage. He listened eagerly to the old woman's quaint talk, he watched Sylvia's pale face and shining gray eyes with ever growing enthusiasm, and insisted that this was the best supper he had eaten for a month, and afterward the new-made friends sat down in the doorway together while the moon came up.

15   Soon it would be berry-time, and Sylvia was a great help at picking. The cow was a good milker, though a plaguy thing to keep track of, the hostess gossiped frankly, adding presently that she had buried four children, so Sylvia's mother, and a son (who might be dead) in California were all the children she had left. "Dan, my boy, was a great hand to go gunning," she explained sadly. "I never wanted for pa'tridges or gray squer'ls while he was to home. He's been a great wand'rer, I expect, and he's no hand to write letters. There, I don't blame him, I'd ha' seen the world myself if it had been so I could."

"Sylvy takes after him," the grandmother continued affectionately, after a minute's pause. "There ain't a foot o' ground she don't know her way over, and the wild creaturs counts her one o' themselves. Squer'ls she'll tame to come an' feed right out o' her hands, and all sorts o' birds. Last winter she got the jaybirds to bangeing here, and I believe she'd 'a' scanted herself of her own meals to have plenty to throw out amongst 'em, if I hadn't kep' watch. Anything but crows, I tell her, I'm willin' to help support— though Dan he had a tamed one o' them that did seem to have reason same as folks. It was round here a good spell after he went away. Dan an' his father they didn't hitch,—but he never held up his head ag'in after Dan had dared him an' gone off."

The guest did not notice this hint of family sorrows in his eager interest in something else.

"So Sylvy knows all about birds, does she?" he exclaimed, as he looked round at the little girl who sat, very demure but increasingly sleepy, in the moonlight. "I am making a collection of birds myself. I have been at it ever since I was a boy." (Mrs. Tilley smiled.) "There are two or three very rare ones I have been hunting for these five years. I mean to get them on my own ground if they can be found."

"Do you cage 'em up?" asked Mrs. Tilley doubtfully, in response to this enthusiastic announcement.

20   "Oh no, they're stuffed and preserved, dozens and dozens of them," said the ornithologist, "and I have shot or snared every one myself. I caught a glimpse of a white heron a few miles from here on Saturday, and I have followed it in this direction. They have never been found in this district at all. The little white heron, it is," and he turned again to look at Sylvia with the hope of discovering that the rare bird was one of her acquaintances.

But Sylvia was watching a hop-toad in the narrow footpath.

"You would know the heron if you saw it," the stranger continued eagerly. "A queer tall white bird with soft feathers and long thin legs. And it would have a nest perhaps in the top of a high tree, made of sticks, something like a hawk's nest."

Sylvia's heart gave a wild beat; she knew that strange white bird, and had once stolen softly near where it stood in some bright green swamp grass, away over at the other side of the woods. There was an open place where the sunshine always seemed strangely yellow and hot, where tall, nodding rushes grew, and her grandmother had warned her that she might sink in the soft black mud underneath and never be heard of more. Not far beyond were the salt marshes just this side the sea itself, which Sylvia wondered and dreamed much about, but never had seen, whose great voice could sometimes be heard above the noise of the woods on stormy nights.

"I can't think of anything I should like so much as to find that heron's nest," the handsome stranger was saying. "I would give ten dollars to anybody who could show it to me," he added desperately, "and I mean to spend my whole vacation hunting for it if need be. Perhaps it was only migrating, or had been chased out of its own region by some bird of prey."

25   Mrs. Tilley gave amazed attention to all this, but Sylvia still watched the toad, not divining, as she might have done at some calmer time, that the creature wished to get to its hole under the door-step, and was much hindered by the unusual spectators at that hour of the evening. No amount of thought, that night, could decide how many wished-for treasures the ten dollars, so lightly spoken of, would buy.

The next day the young sportsman hovered about the woods, and Sylvia kept him company, having lost her first fear of the friendly lad, who proved to be most kind and sympathetic. He told her many things about the birds and what they knew and where they lived and what they did with themselves. And he gave her a jack-knife, which she thought as great a treasure as if she were a desert-islander. All day long he did not once make her troubled or afraid except when he brought down some unsuspecting singing creature from its bough. Sylvia would have liked him vastly better without his gun: she could not understand why he killed the very birds he seemed to like so much. But as the day waned, Sylvia still watched the young man with loving admiration. She had never seen anybody so charming and delightful; the woman's heart, asleep in the child, was vaguely thrilled by a dream of love. Some premonition of that great power stirred and swayed these young creatures who traversed the solemn woodlands with soft-footed silent care. They stopped to listen to a bird's song; they pressed forward again eagerly, parting the branches— speaking to each other rarely and in whispers; the young man going first and Sylvia following, fascinated, a few steps behind, with her gray eyes dark with excitement.

She grieved because the longed-for white heron was elusive, but she did not lead the guest, she only followed, and there was no such thing as speaking first. The sound of her own unquestioned voice would have terrified her—it was hard enough to answer yes or no when there was need of that. At last evening began to fall, and they drove the cow home together, and Sylvia smiled with pleasure when they came to the place where she heard the whistle and was afraid only the night before.

II

Half a mile from home, at the farther edge of the woods, where the land was highest, a great pine-tree stood, the last of its generation. Whether it was left for a boundary mark, or for what reason, no one could say; the woodchoppers who had felled its mates were dead and gone long ago, and a whole forest of sturdy trees, pines and oaks and maples, had grown again. But the stately head of this old pine towered above them all and made a landmark for sea and shore miles and miles away. Sylvia knew it well. She had always believed that whoever climbed to the top of it could see the ocean; and the little girl had often laid her hand on the great rough trunk and looked up wistfully at those dark boughs that the wind always stirred, no matter how hot and still the air might be below. Now she thought of the tree with a new excitement, for why, if one climbed it at break of day could not one see all the world, and easily discover from whence the white heron flew, and mark the place, and find the hidden nest?

What a spirit of adventure, what wild ambition! What fancied triumph and delight and glory for the later morning when she could make known the secret! It was almost too real and too great for the childish heart to bear.

30   All night the door of the little house stood open and the whippoorwills came and sang upon the very step. The young sportsman and his old hostess were sound asleep, but Sylvia's great design kept her broad awake and watching. She forgot to think of sleep. The short summer night seemed as long as the winter darkness, and at last when the whippoorwills ceased, and she was afraid the morning would after all come too soon, she stole out of the house and followed the pasture path through the woods, hastening toward the open ground beyond, listening with a sense of comfort and companionship to the drowsy twitter of a half-awakened bird, whose perch she had jarred in passing. Alas, if the great wave of human interest which flooded for the first time this dull little life should sweep away the satisfactions of an existence heart to heart with nature and the dumb life of the forest!

There was the huge tree asleep yet in the paling moonlight, and small and silly Sylvia began with utmost bravery to mount to the top of it, with tingling, eager blood coursing the channels of her whole frame, with her bare feet and fingers, that pinched and held like bird's claws to the monstrous ladder reaching up, up, almost to the sky itself. First she must mount the white oak tree that grew alongside, where she was almost lost among the dark branches and the green leaves heavy and wet with dew; a bird fluttered off its nest, and a red squirrel ran to and fro and scolded pettishly at the harmless housebreaker. Sylvia felt her way easily. She had often climbed there, and knew that higher still one of the oak's upper branches chafed against the pine trunk, just where its lower boughs were set close together. There, when she made the dangerous pass from one tree to the other, the great enterprise would really begin.

She crept out along the swaying oak limb at last, and took the daring step across into the old pine-tree. The way was harder than she thought; she must reach far and hold fast, the sharp dry twigs caught and held her and scratched her like angry talons, the pitch made her thin little fingers clumsy and stiff as she went round and round the tree's great stem, higher and higher upward. The sparrows and robins in the woods below were beginning to wake and twitter to the dawn, yet it seemed much lighter there aloft in the pine-tree, and the child knew she must hurry if her project were to be of any use.

The tree seemed to lengthen itself out as she went up, and to reach farther and farther upward. It was like a great main-mast to the voyaging earth; it must truly have been amazed that morning through all its ponderous frame as it felt this determined spark of human spirit wending its way from higher branch to branch. Who knows how steadily the least twigs held themselves to advantage this light, weak creature on her way! The old pine must have loved his new dependent. More than all the hawks, and bats, and moths, and even the sweet voiced thrushes, was the brave, beating heart of the solitary gray-eyed child. And the tree stood still and frowned away the winds that June morning while the dawn grew bright in the east.

Sylvia's face was like a pale star, if one had seen it from the ground, when the last thorny bough was past, and she stood trembling and tired but wholly triumphant, high in the treetop. Yes, there was the sea with the dawning sun making a golden dazzle over it, and toward that glorious east flew two hawks with slow-moving pinions. How low they looked in the air from that height when one had only seen them before far up, and dark against the blue sky. Their gray feathers were as soft as moths; they seemed only a little way from the tree, and Sylvia felt as if she too could go flying away among the clouds. Westward, the woodlands and farms reached miles and miles into the distance; here and there were church steeples, and white villages, truly it was a vast and awesome world!

35   The birds sang louder and louder. At last, the sun came up bewilderingly bright. Sylvia could see the white sails of ships out at sea, and the clouds that were purple and rose-colored and yellow at first began to fade away. Where was the white heron's nest in the sea of green branches, and was this wonderful sight and pageant of the world the only reward for having climbed to such a giddy height? Now look down again, Sylvia, where the green marsh is set among the shining birches and dark hemlocks; there where you saw the white heron once you will see him again; look, look! a white spot of him like a single floating feather comes up from the dead hemlock and grows larger, and rises, and comes close at last, and goes by the landmark pine with steady sweep of wing and outstretched slender neck and crested head. And wait! wait! do not move a foot or a finger, little girl, do not send an arrow of light and consciousness from your two eager eyes, for the heron has perched on a pine bough not far beyond yours, and cries back to his mate on the nest and plumes his feathers for the new day!

The child gives a long sigh a minute later when a company of shouting catbirds comes also to the tree, and vexed by their fluttering and lawlessness the solemn heron goes away. She knows his secret now, the wild, light, slender bird that floats and wavers, and goes back like an arrow presently to his home in the green world beneath. Then Sylvia, well satisfied, makes her perilous way down again, not daring to look far below the branch she stands on, ready to cry sometimes because her fingers ache and her lamed feet slip. Wondering over and over again what the stranger would say to her, and what he would think when she told him how to find his way straight to the heron's nest.

"Sylvy, Sylvy!" called the busy old grandmother again and again, but nobody answered, and the small husk bed was empty and Sylvia had disappeared.

The guest waked from a dream, and remembering his day's pleasure hurried to dress himself that might it sooner begin. He was sure from the way the shy little girl looked once or twice yesterday that she had at least seen the white heron, and now she must really be made to tell. Here she comes now, paler than ever, and her worn old frock is torn and tattered, and smeared with pine pitch. The grandmother and the sportsman stand in the door together and question her, and the splendid moment has come to speak of the dead hemlock-tree by the green marsh.

But Sylvia does not speak after all, though the old grandmother fretfully rebukes her, and the young man's kind, appealing eyes are looking straight in her own. He can make them rich with money; he has promised it, and they are poor now. He is so well worth making happy, and he waits to hear the story she can tell.

40   No, she must keep silence! What is it that suddenly forbids her and makes her dumb? Has she been nine years growing and now, when the great world for the first

time puts out a hand to her, must she thrust it aside for a bird's sake? The murmur of the pine's green branches is in her ears, she remembers how the white heron came flying through the golden air and how they watched the sea and the morning together, and Sylvia cannot speak; she cannot tell the heron's secret and give its life away.

Dear loyalty, that suffered a sharp pang as the guest went away disappointed later in the day, that could have served and followed him and loved him as a dog loves! Many a night Sylvia heard the echo of his whistle haunting the pasture path as she came home with the loitering cow. She forgot even her sorrow at the sharp report of his gun and the sight of thrushes and sparrows dropping silent to the ground, their songs hushed and their pretty feathers stained and wet with blood. Were the birds better friends than their hunter might have been,—who can tell? Whatever treasures were lost to her, woodlands and summer-time, remember! Bring your gifts and graces and tell your secrets to this lonely country child!

[1886]

Joining the Conversation: Critical Thinking and Writing

1. What does the name "Sylvia" mean? Why is this name appropriate to the central figure and to the theme of the story?
2. Why does Jewett include the passage about the grandmother's son, Dan? To what extent does Sylvia take after Dan?
3. In 250 words or so, discuss whether or not the final paragraph of "A White Heron" is appropriate and effective.
4. Many fairy tales tell of a hero or heroine who strays (usually into a wood), encounters a villain who seems friendly, passes a test, enters a new world, escapes from the villain, and returns safely home. If you can think of such a fairy tale, perhaps "Little Red Riding Hood" or "Jack and the Beanstalk," write an essay of 750 to 1,000 words, set down its framework, and then see to what extent it corresponds to the framework of "A White Heron."

PATRICIA GRACE

Patricia Grace was born in Wellington, New Zealand, in 1937, of Ngati Raukawa, Ngati Toa, and Te Ati Awa descent. In 1974, she received the first grant awarded to a Maori writer, and in 1975 she became the first Maori woman to publish a book of stories. She is the author of five novels, a play, a book of poems, and several volumes of short stories.

Butterflies

The grandmother plaited her granddaughter's hair and then she said, "Get your lunch. Put it in your bag. Get your apple. You come straight back after school, straight home here. Listen to the teacher," she said. "Do what she say."

Her grandfather was out on the step. He walked down the path with her and out onto the footpath. He said to a neighbor, "Our granddaughter goes to school. She lives with us now."

"She's fine," the neighbor said. "She's terrific with her two plaits in her hair."

"And clever," the grandfather said. "Writes every day in her book."

5   "She's fine," the neighbor said.
     The grandfather waited with his granddaughter by the crossing and then he
said, "Go to school. Listen to the teacher. Do what she say."
     When the granddaughter came home from school her grandfather was hoeing
around the cabbages. Her grandmother was picking beans. They stopped their work.
     "You bring your book home?" the grandmother asked.
     "Yes."
10   "You write your story?"
     "Yes."
     "What's your story?"
     "About the butterflies."
     "Get your book then. Read your story."
15   The granddaughter took her book from her schoolbag and opened it.
     "I killed all the butterflies," she read. "This is me and this is all the butterflies."
     "And your teacher like your story, did she?"
     "I don't know."
     "What your teacher say?"
20   "She said butterflies are beautiful creatures. They hatch out and fly in the sun.
The butterflies visit all the pretty flowers, she said. They lay their eggs and then
they die. You don't kill butterflies, that's what she said."
     The grandmother and the grandfather were quiet for a long time, and their
granddaughter, holding the book, stood quite still in the warm garden.
     "Because you see," the grandfather said, "your teacher, she buy all her cabbages
from the supermarket and that's why."

                                                                          [1988]

Joining the Conversation: Critical Thinking and Writing

1. On the basis of the first six paragraphs, how would you characterize the grandparents? How would you characterize the grandfather at the end of the story?
2. Why do you suppose Grace makes the relationship between a girl and her grandparents rather than between the girl and her parents? Or, for that matter, why not
   a boy and his parents? Would the story have a different feel? Explain your answer.
3. The story is told from an objective point of view. Suppose Grace had told it from
   the grandfather's point of view. Rewrite the final paragraph, using his point of
   view, and compare your version with Grace's. Which do you prefer? Why?
4. You are a teacher. You have just read this story, and you recognize yourself in
   it. Record your response in your journal (that is, record the teacher's response).
5. You are a teacher. A student tells you that this story advocates the use of
   pesticides. How do you respond?

POEMS

MATTHEW ARNOLD

*Matthew Arnold (1822–88) is a central figure in nineteenth-century English
literature. After his graduation from Oxford University in 1844, he became an
inspector of schools, a post he held nearly his entire life. He is admired both for his
poetry and for his influential essays on culture and literature.*

In the title of the following sonnet, "Nature" apparently means the world of things other than human beings, a world without human morality.

In Harmony with Nature

To a Preacher

"In Harmony with Nature?" Restless fool,
Who with such heat dost preach what were to thee,
When true, the last impossibility—
To be like Nature strong, like Nature cool!
Know, man hath all which Nature hath, but more,   5
And in that *more* lie all his hopes of good.
Nature is cruel, man is sick of blood;
Nature is stubborn, man would fain adore;

Nature is fickle, man hath need of rest;
Nature forgives no debt, and fears no grave;   10
Man would be mild, and with safe conscience blest.

Man must begin, know this, where Nature ends;
Nature and man can never be fast friends.
Fool, if thou canst not pass her, rest her slave!

[1849]

Joining the Conversation: Critical Thinking and Writing

1. In the first stanza, the speaker is replying to someone, perhaps a preacher, who has espoused the goal of being "in harmony with Nature." Nature is said (line 4) to be "strong" and "cool." Do these adjectives make sense?
2. Having said that nature is "strong" and "cool," Arnold goes on to stay, in lines 5–8, that Nature is "cruel" and "stubborn." Is the speaker contradicting himself? Please explain how the first two stanzas do, or do not, fit together.
3. In the remainder of the poem, the speaker objects to the idea of living "in Harmony with Nature." Exactly what are the grounds of his objection?
4. Please make your way through the poem, line by line, stating in your own words what the speaker is saying about Nature and about man. What is the speaker's overall argument?
5. In line 10, Arnold says "Nature forgives no debt." What do you think this means? Do you think that Arnold is establishing a contrast between an amoral Nature and the morality that Jesus preached when he said, in the Lord's Prayer, "Forgive us our debts, as we forgive our debtors" (Matthew 6:12)?
6. What does "Harmony" mean? Do you believe we can live "in Harmony with Nature"? How would you define "Nature"?
7. Read Whitman's "A Noiseless Patient Spider" (page 855), and then respond to the fourth question that follows Whitman's poem.

THOMAS HARDY

Thomas Hardy (1840–1928) was born near Dorchester, in southwest England, where at fifteen years old he was apprenticed to an architect. At the age of twenty-one, he went to London to practice as an architect, but he soon turned to writing fiction and poetry. Between 1872 and 1896, he achieved fame as a novelist; among his novels are The Return of the Native *(1878) and* Tess of the D'Urbervilles *(1891). After the hostile reception of* Jude the Obscure *(1896), he abandoned writing fiction and concentrated on writing poetry.*

Transformations

Portion of this yew
Is a man my grandsire knew,
Bosomed here at its foot:
This branch may be his wife,
A ruddy human life   5
Now turned to a green shoot.

These grasses must be made
Of her who often prayed,
Last century, for repose;
And the fair girl long ago   10
Whom I often tried to know
May be entering this rose.

So, they are not underground,
But as nerves and veins abound
In the growths of upper air,   15
And they feel the sun and rain,
And the energy again
That made them what they were!

[1917]

Joining the Conversation: Critical Thinking and Writing

1. What is your sense of the speaker's tone in the first stanza? In the last stanza? In lines 7–8, the speaker conjectures that "These grasses must be made / Of her who often prayed." What sort of visual connection is suggested between the grasses and the woman?
2. How might the speaker know that someone "often prayed, / Last century, for repose"?
3. At what stage of life is the speaker? How do you know?
4. What do you think Hardy means by "the energy . . . / That made them what they were!"?
5. Do you find the poem far-fetched, or do you feel that the poet has made his assertions plausible? Explain your answer.

GERARD MANLEY HOPKINS

Gerard Manley Hopkins (1844—89) was born near London and was educated at Oxford, where he studied the classics. A convert from Anglicanism to Roman Catholicism, he was ordained a Jesuit priest in 1877. After serving as a parish priest and teacher, he was appointed professor of Greek at the Catholic University of Ireland in Dublin.

Hopkins published only a few poems during his lifetime, partly because he believed that the pursuit of literary fame was incompatible with his vocation as a priest and partly because he was aware that his highly individual style might puzzle readers.

God's Grandeur

The world is charged with the grandeur of God.
    It will flame out, like shining from shook foil;
    It gathers to a greatness, like the ooze of oil
Crushed. Why do men then now not reck his rod?
Generations have trod, have trod, have trod;   5
    And all is seared with trade; bleared, smeared with toil;
    And wears man's smudge and shares man's smell: the soil
Is bare now, nor can foot feel, being shod.

And for all this, nature is never spent;
    There lives the dearest freshness deep down things;   10
And though the last lights off the black West went
    Oh, morning, at the brown brink eastward, springs—
Because the Holy Ghost over the bent
    World broods with warm breast and with ah! bright wings.

[1877]

Joining the Conversation: Critical Thinking and Writing

1. How would you define "charged" in the first line? How does the meaning connect with "flame out" in the next line? The Judeo-Christian tradition, unlike some ancient religions, insists that there are no thunder gods, lightning gods, river gods, and so forth; God is independent of nature, and therefore nature is not to be worshipped. Taking the poem as a whole, do you think Hopkins has slipped into nature-worship? Explain your answer.

2. Hopkins in a letter explained "foil" in the second line thus: "I mean foil in its sense of leaf or tinsel. . . . Shaken goldfoil gives off broad glares like sheet lightning and also, and this is true of nothing else, owing to its zigzag dints and creasings and network of small many cornered facets, a sort of fork lightning too." Suppose Hopkins had not explained it, and a reader thought that "foil" referred to a fencing sword. Might the meaning of the passage—the concept of nature that the line conveys—be equally interesting? How would you characterize Hopkins's view of nature, based on the first four lines of the poem ("the ooze of oil / Crushed" probably evokes an image of oil crushed from olives or from seed.)

3. Hopkins was a Roman Catholic priest. Does it therefore make sense to say that, in line 7, "man's smudge" probably refers not only to a polluted environment (for instance, from factory smoke) but also to the doctrine of original sin? (If you are unfamiliar with this doctrine, begin by looking up "original sin" in a dictionary.)

4. The poem is a sonnet (14 lines), and, like many (but not all) sonnets, it is constructed with a unit of eight lines (the octave) followed by a unit of six lines (the sestet). What change in voice, in tone, do you hear at the beginning of the sestet? Do the following writing assignment: Is the second part of the sonnet

(lines 9–14) more unified or less unified than first part? Probably, after writing a first draft, you will be able to form a thesis that describes an overall pattern. As you revise your drafts, make sure (a) that the thesis is clear to the reader and (b) that it is adequately supported by quotations that provide evidence.

5. The "Holy Ghost" (line 13) is described in Luke 3:22 as descending in the form of a dove. Given this information, explicate the final two lines of the poem.

6. Do you think that a reader has to be a Roman Catholic (as Hopkins was) or at least some sort of believer in the Judeo-Christian God in order to find the poem meaningful? Explain your answer.

WALT WHITMAN

Walt Whitman (1819–92) was born on Long Island, New York, the son of a farmer. The young Whitman taught school and worked as a carpenter, a printer, a newspaper editor, and, during the Civil War, as a volunteer nurse on the Union side. After the war, he supported himself by doing secretarial jobs. In Whitman's own day, his poetry was highly controversial because of its unusual form (formlessness, many people said) and (though not in the following poem) its abundant erotic implications.

A Noiseless Patient Spider

A noiseless patient spider,
I mark'd where on a little promontory it stood isolated,
Mark'd how to explore the vacant vast surrounding,
It launch'd forth filament, filament, filament, out of itself,
Ever unreeling them, ever tirelessly speeding them.   5

And you O my soul where you stand,
Surrounded, detached, in measureless oceans of space,
Ceaselessly musing, venturing, throwing, seeking the spheres to
    connect them,
Till the bridge you will need be form'd, till the ductile anchor hold,
Till the gossamer thread you fling catch somewhere, O my soul.   10

[1862–63]

Joining the Conversation: Critical Thinking and Writing

1. How are the suggestions in "launch'd" (line 4) and "unreeling" (line 5) continued in the second stanza?

2. How are the varying lengths of lines 1, 4, and 8 relevant to their ideas?

3. The second stanza is not a complete sentence. Why? The poem is unrhymed. What effect does the near-rhyme *(hold—soul)* in the last two lines have on you?

4. Whitman apparently thinks we can learn something about ourselves by observing nature. Read Matthew Arnold's "In Harmony with Nature" (page 852), and then write a dialogue of about five hundred words in which Arnold and Whitman talk about nature.

EMILY DICKINSON

Emily Dickinson (1830–86) was one of the most influential American poets. Her amazing gift for vivid, piercing language and her extraordinary ability to suggest and represent complex movements of thought and feeling is evidenced in nearly everything she composed. Born in Amherst, Massachusetts, where she spent most of her life, she rigorously maintained her privacy in the family home. Dickinson composed over 1,800 poems in her lifetime, but only a handful were published—anonymously—while she was alive.

A Narrow Fellow in the Grass

A narrow Fellow in the Grass
Occasionally rides—
You may have met Him—did you not
His notice sudden is—

The Grass divides as with a Comb—   5
A spotted shaft is seen—
And then it closes at your feet
And opens further on—

He likes a Boggy Acre
A Floor too cool for Corn—   10
Yet when a Boy, and Barefoot—
I more than once at Noon
Have passed, I thought, a Whip lash
Unbraiding in the Sun
When stooping to secure it   15
It wrinkled, and was gone—

Several of Nature's People
I know, and they know me—
I feel for them a transport
Of cordiality—   20

But never met this Fellow
Attended, or alone
Without a tighter breathing
And Zero at the Bone—

[c. 1865]

Joining the Conversation: Critical Thinking and Writing

1. What sorts of things is Dickinson implying by referring to the snake as "a narrow Fellow"?
2. Why does she address the reader in line 3, and then again in line 7? Do you like this effect?
3. How would you reply to someone who says, "I find it confusing that Dickinson presents herself here as a boy."

4. Is this a serious poem or a humorous one? Please point to evidence in the text to support your view.
5. Please rewrite this poem in prose, and punctuate it as you see fit. What is your response to this prose version?

There's a certain Slant of light

There's a certain Slant of light
Winter Afternoons—
That oppresses, like the Heft°
Of Cathedral Tunes—

Heavenly Hurt, it gives us—   5
We can find no scar,
But internal difference,
Where the Meanings, are—

None may teach it—Any—
'Tis the Seal Despair—   10
An imperial affliction
Sent us of the Air—

When it comes, the Landscape listens—
Shadows—hold their breath—
When it goes, 'tis like the Distance   15
On the look of Death—

[c. 1861]

³**Heft** weight.

Joining the Conversation: Critical Thinking and Writing

1. Dickinson's poem describes the way a winter afternoon oppresses the spirit. What language does the poem use to convey this negative impression of winter? Circle specific words in the poem that you find the most evocative.
2. What do you think the phrase "where the Meanings, are" (line 8) means?
3. Do you feel that your outlook on life changes with the seasons? What is your own sense of how winter affects your mood? Write a short personal reflection that explains your response to winter.

The name—of it—is 'Autumn'

The name—of it—is 'Autumn'—
The hue—of it—is Blood—
An Artery—upon the Hill—
A Vein—along the Road—

Great Globules—in the Alleys—   5
And Oh, the Shower of Stain—
When Winds—upset the Basin—
And spill the Scarlet Rain—

It sprinkles Bonnets—far below—
It gathers ruddy Pools—   10
Then—eddies like a Rose—away—
Upon Vermilion Wheels—

[c. 1862]

Joining the Conversation: Critical Thinking and Writing

1. Re read the poem, making sure that you understand its imagery. What is the "Blood" (line 2)? How can there be blood on a hill and road? What does "eddies like a Rose" (line 11) describe?
2. After reading the poem closely, write an explication of its imagery and meaning. What is the meaning constructed by this imagery? What images in the poem are most important to that meaning?
3. What do you make of all of the dashes in this poem? Do the dashes help you to understand the poem? Or do you find the dashes distracting? Why do you think Dickinson relied on dashes?

JOY HARJO

Joy Harjo, a Creek Indian, was born in Tulsa, Oklahoma, in 1951. She was educated at the Institute of American Indian Arts in Santa Fe, New Mexico, and at the University of Iowa Writers' Workshop. She now teaches at the University of Colorado in Boulder. Her chief books are poetry collections, including The Last Song *(1975),* What Moon Drove Me to This *(1979),* She Had Some Horses *(1983), and* Secrets from the Center of the World *(1989).*

Vision

The rainbow touched down
"somewhere in the Rio Grande,"
we said. And saw the light of it
from your mother's house in Isleta.°
How it curved down between earth   5
and the deepest sky to give us horses
of color

            horses that were within us all of this time
but we didn't see them because
we wait for the easiest vision   10
                    to save us.

In Isleta the rainbow was a crack
in the universe. We saw the barest
of all life that is possible.
Bright horses rolled over   15

---

⁴**Isleta** a pueblo in New Mexico.

and over the dusking sky.
I heard the thunder of their beating
hearts. Their lungs hit air
and sang. All the colors of horses
formed the rainbow,   20
                    and formed us
watching them.

[1983]

Joining the Conversation: Critical Thinking and Writing

1. Who are the "we," the "us," referred to in this poem?
2. What main point is the speaker making?
3. Is there anything in this poem that you do not understand or that you find confusing?
4. Do you like this poem? Yes, no? A lot, a little, not at all?
5. What is the significance of the horses? Would the poem be equally effective, or less so, if Harjo had used a different animal?

MARY OLIVER

*Mary Oliver, born in Cleveland, Ohio, in 1935, attended Ohio State University and Vassar College. She is the author of six books of poetry—*American Primitive *received the Pulitzer Prize for Poetry in 1984, and* New and Selected Poems *received a National Book Award in 1992—and she has served as a visiting professor or a poet in residence at several colleges.*

Two of her prose comments may be of special interest. Of today's readers she has said, "The question asked today is: What does it mean? Nobody says, how does it feel?" And of her work she has said, "I am trying in my poems to vanish and have the reader be the experiencer. I do not want to be there. It is not even a walk we take together."

The Black Walnut Tree

My mother and I debate:
we could sell
the black walnut tree
to the lumberman,
and pay off the mortgage.   5
Likely some storm anyway
will churn down its dark boughs,
smashing the house. We talk
slowly, two women trying
in a difficult time to be wise.   10
Roots in the cellar drains,
I say, and she replies
that the leaves are getting heavier
every year, and the fruit   15
harder to gather away.

But something brighter than money
moves in our blood—an edge
sharp and quick as a trowel
that wants us to dig and sow.
So we talk, but we don't do   20
anything. That night I dream
of my fathers out of Bohemia
filling the blue fields
of fresh and generous Ohio
with leaves and vines and orchards.   25
What my mother and I both know
is that we'd crawl with shame
in the emptiness we'd made
in our own and our fathers' backyard.
So the black walnut tree   30
swings through another year
of sun and leaping winds,
of leaves and bounding fruit,
and, month after month, the whip
crack of the mortgage.   35

[1992]

Joining the Conversation: Critical Thinking and Writing

1. Why are the mother and daughter unable to sell the black walnut tree? Do you believe that they should?
2. What is the "something brighter than money" to which the speaker refers in line 16?
3. Do you know what a black walnut tree looks like? Does it matter that Oliver has keyed her poem to this kind of tree, as opposed to some other kind?
4. Please write a response (one page) to someone who says: "These poets are too sentimental about Nature; after all, it's just a tree."

KAY RYAN

Kay Ryan, born in San Jose, California, in 1945, holds a bachelor's and a master's degree in English from the University of California, Los Angeles. She has published a number of books of poetry, and in 2009 she was appointed the sixteenth Poet Laureate Consultant in Poetry to the Library of Congress.

Turtle

Who would be a turtle who could help it?
A barely mobile hard roll, a four-oared helmet,
she can ill afford the chances she must take
in rowing toward the grasses that she eats.
Her track is graceless, like dragging   5
a packing-case places, and almost any slope
defeats her modest hopes. Even being practical,

she's often stuck up to the axle on her way
to something edible, With everything optimal,
she skirts the ditch which would convert 10
her shell into a serving dish. She lives
below luck-level, never imagining some lottery
will change her load of pottery to wings.
Her only levity is patience,
the sport of truly chastened things. 15

[1994]

Joining the Conversation: Critical Thinking and Writing

1. Elsewhere in this book, we say that a poem is (to quote Robert Frost) "a performance in words." In what ways is this poem a "performance"?
2. Does this poem have a point? If so, what is it?
3. Is Ryan saying anything about turtles that is relevant to human beings? If so,
   what? If not, is there any point to the poem?

Chapter Overview: Looking Backward/Looking Forward

1. Does it make sense for hunters and fishers to say that their activity shows they
   are lovers of nature? Whatever your personal view, write two essays, each of
   500 words, one essay taking one side and the other essay taking the other side.
2. Do you "love nature"? What does it mean to say such a thing?
3. When someone says, "you should take more interest in the world around you,"
   what does this person mean?
4. Could a person live a good life without paying any attention to nature?
5. A well-known contemporary writer who lives in New York City has said, "I hate
   nature." Please compose a letter of 500–750 words, in which you explain to this
   writer why she is wrong to feel this way.
6. Would you enjoy living on a farm and making your living from the crops you
   grew and the animals you raised and cared for?
7. Please describe your most rewarding experience of living or traveling in an
   unusual natural setting, here or abroad—a setting that you found very different
   from where you live most of the time.

CHAPTER 17

Technology and Human Identity

ESSAY

NICHOLAS CARR

Nicholas Carr is a nonfiction writer whose work focuses on technology and culture. In addition to writing numerous articles for such publications as The Atlantic, Wired, The New York Times, *and* The Wall Street Journal, *Carr has written several books, including* The Glass Cage: Automation and Us *(2014) and* The Big Switch: Rewriting the World, from Edison to Google *(2008). He is best known for his book* The Shallows: What the Internet Is Doing to Our Brains *(2010), which encouraged widespread cultural debate about our use of the Internet and how that use is restructuring the brain. The book was a* New York Times *best seller and a Pulitzer Prize finalist. Born in 1959, he earned a BA from Dartmouth College and an MA in English from Harvard University.*

Is Google Making Us Stupid?

"Dave, stop. Stop, will you? Stop, Dave. Will you stop, Dave?" So the supercomputer HAL pleads with the implacable astronaut Dave Bowman in a famous and weirdly poignant scene toward the end of Stanley Kubrick's *2001: A Space Odyssey*. Bowman, having nearly been sent to a deep-space death by the malfunctioning machine, is calmly, coldly disconnecting the memory circuits that control its artificial brain. "Dave, my mind is going," HAL says, forlornly. "I can feel it. I can feel it."

I can feel it, too. Over the past few years I've had an uncomfortable sense that someone, or something, has been tinkering with my brain, remapping the neural circuitry, reprogramming the memory. My mind isn't going—so far as I can tell—but it's changing. I'm not thinking the way I used to think. I can feel it most strongly when I'm reading. Immersing myself in a book or a lengthy article used to be easy. My mind would get caught up in the narrative or the turns of the argument, and I'd spend hours strolling through long stretches of prose. That's rarely the case anymore. Now my concentration often starts to drift after two or three pages. I get fidgety, lose the thread, begin looking for something else to do. I feel as if I'm always dragging my wayward brain back to the text. The deep reading that used to come naturally has become a struggle.

I think I know what's going on. For more than a decade now, I've been spending a lot of time online, searching and surfing and sometimes adding to the great databases of the Internet. The Web has been a godsend to me as a writer. Research that once required days in the stacks or periodical rooms of libraries can now be done in minutes. A few Google searches, some quick clicks on hyperlinks, and I've got the telltale fact or pithy quote I was after. Even when I'm not working, I'm as likely as not to be foraging in the Web's info-thickets' reading and writing e-mails, scanning headlines and blog posts, watching videos and listening to podcasts, or just tripping from link to link to link. (Unlike footnotes, to which they're sometimes likened, hyperlinks don't merely point to related works; they propel you toward them.)

For me, as for others, the Net is becoming a universal medium, the conduit for most of the information that flows through my eyes and ears and into my mind. The advantages of having immediate access to such an incredibly rich store of information are many, and they've been widely described and duly applauded. "The perfect recall of silicon memory," *Wired*'s Clive Thompson has written, "can be an enormous boon to thinking." But that boon comes at a price. As the media theorist Marshall McLuhan pointed out in the 1960s, media are not just passive channels of information. They supply the stuff of thought, but they also shape the process of thought. And what the Net seems to be doing is chipping away my capacity for concentration and contemplation. My mind now expects to take in information the way the Net distributes it: in a swiftly moving stream of particles. Once I was a scuba diver in the sea of words. Now I zip along the surface like a guy on a Jet Ski.

5   I'm not the only one. When I mention my troubles with reading to friends and acquaintances—literary types, most of them—many say they're having similar experiences. The more they use the Web, the more they have to fight to stay focused on long pieces of writing. Some of the bloggers I follow have also begun mentioning the phenomenon. Scott Karp, who writes a blog about online media, recently confessed that he has stopped reading books altogether. "I was a lit major in college, and used to be [a] voracious book reader," he wrote. "What happened?" He speculates on the answer: "What if I do all my reading on the web not so much because the way I read has changed, i.e. I'm just seeking convenience, but because the way I THINK has changed?"

Bruce Friedman, who blogs regularly about the use of computers in medicine, also has described how the Internet has altered his mental habits. "I now have almost totally lost the ability to read and absorb a longish article on the web or in print," he wrote earlier this year. A pathologist who has long been on the faculty of the University of Michigan Medical School, Friedman elaborated on his comment in a telephone conversation with me. His thinking, he said, has taken on a "staccato" quality, reflecting the way he quickly scans short passages of text from many sources online. "I can't read *War and Peace* anymore," he admitted. "I've lost the ability to do that. Even a blog post of more than three or four paragraphs is too much to absorb. I skim it."

Anecdotes alone don't prove much. And we still await the long-term neurological and psychological experiments that will provide a definitive picture of how Internet use affects cognition. But a recently published study of online research habits, conducted by scholars from University College London, suggests that we may well be in the midst of a sea change in the way we read and think. As part of the five-year research program, the scholars examined computer logs documenting the behavior of visitors to two popular research sites, one operated by the British Library and one by a U.K. educational consortium, that provide access to journal articles, e-books, and other sources of written information. They found that people using the sites exhibited "a form of skimming activity," hopping from one source to another and rarely returning to any source they'd already visited. They typically read no more than one or two pages of an article or book before they would "bounce" out to another site. Sometimes they'd save a long article, but there's no evidence that they ever went back and actually read it. The authors of the study report:

> It is clear that users are not reading online in the traditional sense; indeed there are signs that new forms of "reading" are emerging as users "power browse" horizontally through titles, contents pages and abstracts going for quick wins. It almost seems that they go online to avoid reading in the traditional sense.

Thanks to the ubiquity of text on the Internet, not to mention the popularity of text-messaging on cell phones, we may well be reading more today than we did in the 1970s or 1980s, when television was our medium of choice. But it's a different kind of reading, and behind it lies a different kind of thinking—perhaps even a new sense of the self. "We are not only *what* we read," says Maryanne Wolf, a developmental psychologist at Tufts University and the author of *Proust and the Squid: The Story and Science of the Reading Brain*. "We are *how* we read." Wolf worries that the style of reading promoted by the Net, a style that puts "efficiency" and "immediacy" above all else, may be weakening our capacity for the kind of deep reading that emerged when an earlier technology, the printing press, made long and complex works of prose commonplace. When we read online, she says, we tend to become "mere decoders of information." Our ability to interpret text, to make the rich mental connections that form when we read deeply and without distraction, remains largely disengaged.

Reading, explains Wolf, is not an instinctive skill for human beings. It's not etched into our genes the way speech is. We have to teach our minds how to translate the symbolic characters we see into the language we understand. And the media or other technologies we use in learning and practicing the craft of reading play an important part in shaping the neural circuits inside our brains. Experiments demonstrate that readers of ideograms, such as the Chinese, develop a mental circuitry for reading that is very different from the circuitry found in those of us whose written language employs an alphabet. The variations extend across many regions of the brain, including those that govern such essential cognitive functions as memory and the interpretation of visual and auditory stimuli. We can expect as well that the circuits woven by our use of the Net will be different from those woven by our reading of books and other printed works.

10   Sometime in 1882, Friedrich Nietzsche bought a typewriter—a Malling-Hansen Writing Ball, to be precise. His vision was failing, and keeping his eyes focused on a page had become exhausting and painful, often bringing on crushing headaches. He had been forced to curtail his writing, and he feared that he would soon have to give it up. The typewriter rescued him, at least for a time. Once he had mastered touch-typing, he was able to write with his eyes closed, using only the tips of his fingers. Words could once again flow from his mind to the page.

But the machine had a subtler effect on his work. One of Nietzsche's friends, a composer, noticed a change in the style of his writing. His already terse prose had become even tighter, more telegraphic. "Perhaps you will through this instrument even take to a new idiom," the friend wrote in a letter, noting that, in his own work, his "'thoughts' in music and language often depend on the quality of pen and paper."

Also see:
James Fallows, "Living with a Computer," *The Atlantic*, July 1982.
"The process works this way. When I sit down to write a letter or start the first draft of an article, I simply type on the keyboard and the words appear on the screen."

"You are right," Nietzsche replied, "our writing equipment takes part in the forming of our thoughts." Under the sway of the machine, writes the German media scholar Friedrich A. Kittler, Nietzsche's prose "changed from arguments to aphorisms, from thoughts to puns, from rhetoric to telegram style."

The human brain is almost infinitely malleable. People used to think that our mental meshwork, the dense connections formed among the 100 billion or so neurons inside our skulls, was largely fixed by the time we reached adulthood. But brain researchers have discovered that that's not the case. James Olds, a professor of neuroscience who directs the Krasnow Institute for Advanced Study at George Mason University, says that even the adult mind "is very plastic." Nerve cells routinely break old connections and form new ones. "The brain," according to Olds, "has the ability to reprogram itself on the fly, altering the way it functions."

As we use what the sociologist Daniel Bell has called our "intellectual technologies"—the tools that extend our mental rather than our physical capacities—we inevitably begin to take on the qualities of those technologies. The mechanical clock, which came into common use in the 14th century, provides a compelling example. In *Technics and Civilization*, the historian and cultural critic Lewis Mumford described how the clock "disassociated time from human events and helped create the belief in an independent world of mathematically measurable sequences." The "abstract framework of divided time" became "the point of reference for both action and thought."

15   The clock's methodical ticking helped bring into being the scientific mind and the scientific man. But it also took something away. As the late MIT computer scientist Joseph Weizenbaum observed in his 1976 book, *Computer Power and Human Reason: From Judgment to Calculation,* the conception of the world that emerged from the widespread use of timekeeping instruments "remains an impoverished version of the older one, for it rests on a rejection of those direct experiences that formed the basis for, and indeed constituted, the old reality." In deciding when to eat, to work, to sleep, to rise, we stopped listening to our senses and started obeying the clock.

The process of adapting to new intellectual technologies is reflected in the changing metaphors we use to explain ourselves to ourselves. When the mechanical clock arrived, people began thinking of their brains as operating "like clockwork." Today, in the age of software, we have come to think of them as operating "like computers." But the changes, neuroscience tells us, go much deeper than metaphor. Thanks to our brain's plasticity, the adaptation occurs also at a biological level.

The Internet promises to have particularly far-reaching effects on cognition. In a paper published in 1936, the British mathematician Alan Turing proved that a digital computer, which at the time existed only as a theoretical machine, could be programmed to perform the function of any other information-processing device. And that's what we're seeing today. The Internet, an immeasurably powerful computing system, is subsuming most of our other intellectual technologies. It's becoming our map and our clock, our printing press and our typewriter, our calculator and our telephone, and our radio and TV.

When the Net absorbs a medium, that medium is re-created in the Net's image. It injects the medium's content with hyperlinks, blinking ads, and other digital gewgaws, and it surrounds the content with the content of all the other media it has absorbed. A new e-mail message, for instance, may announce its arrival as we're glancing over the latest headlines at a newspaper's site. The result is to scatter our attention and diffuse our concentration.

The Net's influence doesn't end at the edges of a computer screen, either. As people's minds become attuned to the crazy quilt of Internet media, traditional media have to adapt to the audience's new expectations. Television programs add text crawls and pop-up ads, and magazines and newspapers shorten their articles, introduce capsule summaries, and crowd their pages with easy-to-browse info-snippets. When, in March of this year, *The New York Times* decided to devote the second and third pages of every edition to article abstracts, its design director, Tom Bodkin, explained that the "shortcuts" would give harried readers a quick "taste" of the day's news, sparing them the "less efficient" method of actually turning the pages and reading the articles. Old media have little choice but to play by the new-media rules.

20   Never has a communications system played so many roles in our lives—or exerted such broad influence over our thoughts—as the Internet does today. Yet, for all that's been written about the Net, there's been little consideration of how, exactly, it's reprogramming us. The Net's intellectual ethic remains obscure.

About the same time that Nietzsche started using his typewriter, an earnest young man named Frederick Winslow Taylor carried a stopwatch into the Midvale Steel plant in Philadelphia and began a historic series of experiments aimed at improving the efficiency of the plant's machinists. With the approval of Midvale's owners, he recruited a group of factory hands, set them to work on various metal-working machines, and recorded and timed their every movement as well as the operations of the machines. By breaking down every job into a sequence of small, discrete steps and then testing different ways of performing each one, Taylor created a set of precise instructions—an "algorithm," we might say today—for how each worker should work. Midvale's employees grumbled about the strict new regime, claiming that it turned them into little more than automatons, but the factory's productivity soared.

More than a hundred years after the invention of the steam engine, the Industrial Revolution had at last found its philosophy and its philosopher. Taylor's tight industrial choreography—his "system," as he liked to call it—was embraced by manufacturers throughout the country and, in time, around the world. Seeking maximum speed, maximum efficiency, and maximum output, factory owners used time-and-motion studies to organize their work and configure the jobs of their workers. The goal, as Taylor defined it in his celebrated 1911 treatise, *The Principles of Scientific Management*, was to identify and adopt, for every job, the "one best method" of work and thereby to effect "the gradual substitution of science for rule of thumb throughout the mechanic arts." Once his system was applied to all acts of manual labor, Taylor assured his followers, it would bring about a restructuring not only of industry but of society, creating a utopia of perfect efficiency. "In the past the man has been first," he declared; "in the future the system must be first."

Taylor's system is still very much with us; it remains the ethic of industrial manufacturing. And now, thanks to the growing power that computer engineers and software coders wield over our intellectual lives, Taylor's ethic is beginning to govern the realm of the mind as well. The Internet is a machine designed for the efficient and automated collection, transmission, and manipulation of information, and its legions of programmers are intent on finding the "one best method"—the perfect algorithm—to carry out every mental movement of what we've come to describe as "knowledge work."

Google's headquarters, in Mountain View, California—the Googleplex—is the Internet's high church, and the religion practiced inside its walls is Taylorism. Google, says its chief executive, Eric Schmidt, is "a company that's founded around the science of measurement," and it is striving to "systematize everything" it does. Drawing on the terabytes of behavioral data it collects through its search engine and other sites, it carries out thousands of experiments a day, according to the *Harvard Business Review*, and it uses the results to refine the algorithms that increasingly control how people find information and extract meaning from it. What Taylor did for the work of the hand, Google is doing for the work of the mind.

25   The company has declared that its mission is "to organize the world's information and make it universally accessible and useful." It seeks to develop "the perfect search engine," which it defines as something that "understands exactly what you mean and gives you back exactly what you want." In Google's view, information is a kind of commodity, a utilitarian resource that can be mined and processed with industrial efficiency. The more pieces of information we can "access" and the faster we can extract their gist, the more productive we become as thinkers.

Where does it end? Sergey Brin and Larry Page, the gifted young men who founded Google while pursuing doctoral degrees in computer science at Stanford, speak frequently of their desire to turn their search engine into an artificial intelligence, a HAL-like machine that might be connected directly to our brains. "The ultimate search engine is something as smart as people—or smarter," Page said in a speech a few years back. "For us, working on search is a way to work on artificial intelligence." In a 2004 interview with *Newsweek*, Brin said, "Certainly if you had all the world's information directly attached to your brain, or an artificial brain that was smarter than your brain, you'd be better off." Last year, Page told a convention of scientists that Google is "really trying to build artificial intelligence and to do it on a large scale."

Such an ambition is a natural one, even an admirable one, for a pair of math whizzes with vast quantities of cash at their disposal and a small army of computer scientists in their employ. A fundamentally scientific enterprise, Google is motivated by a desire to use technology, in Eric Schmidt's words, "to solve problems that have never been solved before," and artificial intelligence is the hardest problem out there. Why wouldn't Brin and Page want to be the ones to crack it?

Still, their easy assumption that we'd all "be better off" if our brains were supplemented, or even replaced, by an artificial intelligence is unsettling. It suggests a belief that intelligence is the output of a mechanical process, a series of discrete steps that can be isolated, measured, and optimized. In Google's world, the world we enter when we go online, there's little place for the fuzziness of contemplation. Ambiguity is not an opening for insight but a bug to be fixed. The human brain is just an outdated computer that needs a faster processor and a bigger hard drive.

The idea that our minds should operate as high-speed data-processing machines is not only built into the workings of the Internet, it is the network's reigning business model as well. The faster we surf across the Web—the more links we click and pages we view—the more opportunities Google and other companies gain to collect information about us and to feed us advertisements. Most of the proprietors of the commercial Internet have a financial stake in collecting the crumbs of data we leave behind as we flit from link to link—the more crumbs, the better. The last thing these companies want is to encourage leisurely reading or slow, concentrated thought. It's in their economic interest to drive us to distraction.

30   Maybe I'm just a worrywart. Just as there's a tendency to glorify technological progress, there's a countertendency to expect the worst of every new tool or machine. In Plato's *Phaedrus*, Socrates bemoaned the development of writing. He feared that, as people came to rely on the written word as a substitute for the

knowledge they used to carry inside their heads, they would, in the words of one of the dialogue's characters, "cease to exercise their memory and become forgetful." And because they would be able to "receive a quantity of information without proper instruction," they would "be thought very knowledgeable when they are for the most part quite ignorant." They would be "filled with the conceit of wisdom instead of real wisdom." Socrates wasn't wrong—the new technology did often have the effects he feared—but he was shortsighted. He couldn't foresee the many ways that writing and reading would serve to spread information, spur fresh ideas, and expand human knowledge (if not wisdom).

The arrival of Gutenberg's printing press, in the 15th century, set off another round of teeth gnashing. The Italian humanist Hieronimo Squarciafico worried that the easy availability of books would lead to intellectual laziness, making men "less studious" and weakening their minds. Others argued that cheaply printed books and broadsheets would undermine religious authority, demean the work of scholars and scribes, and spread sedition and debauchery. As New York University professor Clay Shirky notes, "Most of the arguments made against the printing press were correct, even prescient." But, again, the doomsayers were unable to imagine the myriad blessings that the printed word would deliver.

So, yes, you should be skeptical of my skepticism. Perhaps those who dismiss critics of the Internet as Luddites or nostalgists will be proved correct, and from our hyperactive, data-stoked minds will spring a golden age of intellectual discovery and universal wisdom. Then again, the Net isn't the alphabet, and although it may replace the printing press, it produces something altogether different. The kind of deep reading that a sequence of printed pages promotes is valuable not just for the knowledge we acquire from the author's words but for the intellectual vibrations those words set off within our own minds. In the quiet spaces opened up by the sustained, undistracted reading of a book, or by any other act of contemplation, for that matter, we make our own associations, draw our own inferences and analogies, foster our own ideas. Deep reading, as Maryanne Wolf argues, is indistinguishable from deep thinking.

If we lose those quiet spaces, or fill them up with "content," we will sacrifice something important not only in our selves but in our culture. In a recent essay, the playwright Richard Foreman eloquently described what's at stake:

> I come from a tradition of Western culture, in which the ideal (my ideal) was the complex, dense and "cathedral-like" structure of the highly educated and articulate personality—a man or woman who carried inside themselves a personally constructed and unique version of the entire heritage of the West. [But now] I see within us all (myself included) the replacement of complex inner density with a new kind of self—evolving under the pressure of information overload and the technology of the "instantly available."

As we are drained of our "inner repertory of dense cultural inheritance," Foreman concluded, we risk turning into "'pancake people'—spread wide and thin as we connect with that vast network of information accessed by the mere touch of a button."

35   I'm haunted by that scene in *2001*. What makes it so poignant, and so weird, is the computer's emotional response to the disassembly of its mind: its despair as one circuit after another goes dark, its childlike pleading with the astronaut—"I can feel it. I can feel it. I'm afraid"—and its final reversion to what can only be called a state of innocence. HAL's outpouring of feeling contrasts with the emotionlessness that characterizes the human figures in the film, who go about their business

with an almost robotic efficiency. Their thoughts and actions feel scripted, as if they're following the steps of an algorithm. In the world of *2001*, people have become so machinelike that the most human character turns out to be a machine. That's the essence of Kubrick's dark prophecy: as we come to rely on computers to mediate our understanding of the world, it is our own intelligence that flattens into artificial intelligence.

[2008]

Joining the Conversation: Critical Thinking and Writing

1. Annotate "Is Google Making Us Stupid?" highlighting its central arguments. Work to create a "reverse outline" of the essay, in which you generate an outline out of a fully written text. Locate the essay's thesis and subpoints, creating a conceptual outline of its argument. For example, you can imagine yourself adding headers and subheaders to the essay, calling attention to its argument. Then, locate its central evidence, noting how it supports its main arguments with details. As you create this "reverse outline," note how the argument is organized and developed. When you write an analytical paper of your own, remember the "reverse outline" exercise, and see if you can create a clear argumentative structure that can be neatly reverse outlined.

2. Carr's essay contrasts "deep reading" and "deep thinking" with "minds [that] operate as high-speed data-processing machines." Using Carr's essay, define these two types of thinking. Create a chart that develops your understanding of each type of thinking. For example, list the details that Carr provides to explore each type of thinking. Ultimately, how does he assess and value each type of thinking? Are there ideas about each type of thinking that Carr seems to overlook? If Carr were to continue to develop his article, what ideas would you encourage him to explore about each type of thinking?

3. Notice that Carr opens his essay by discussing his use of the Internet and how it seems to shape his own thought patterns. Think of your own experience using the Internet. Do you agree or disagree with Carr's central arguments? Using your own experiences as evidence, write an analytical paper that agrees or disagrees with Carr. Create a strong argument, and support it with details from your use of technology.

STORIES

KURT VONNEGUT, JR.

Kurt Vonnegut, Jr. (1922–2007) was born in Indianapolis and studied biochemistry at Cornell University. He was drafted into the army and was captured by the Germans in the Battle of the Bulge in late 1944. A survivor of the Allied fire-bombing of Dresden in February 1945, he was required along with other prisoners to search for corpses hidden in the rubble. Two months later, he was freed. After the war, he studied anthropology at the University of Chicago and then worked as a publicist for General Electric from 1947 until 1950, when he became a full-time writer.

Vonnegut wrote stories, novels, and plays. His two most famous works are probably Cat's Cradle *(1963), which ends with the freezing of the world, and* Slaughterhouse-Five *(1969), which draws on his wartime experience in Dresden.*

Harrison Bergeron

The year was 2081, and everybody was finally equal. They weren't only equal before God and the law. They were equal every which way. Nobody was smarter than anybody else. Nobody was better looking than anybody else. Nobody was stronger or quicker than anybody else. All this equality was due to the 211th, 212th, and 213th Amendments to the Constitution, and to the unceasing vigilance of agents of the United States Handicapper General.

Some things about living still weren't quite right, though. April, for instance, still drove people crazy by not being springtime. And it was in that clammy month that the H-G men took George and Hazel Bergeron's fourteen-year-old son, Harrison, away.

It was tragic, all right, but George and Hazel couldn't think about it very hard. Hazel had a perfectly average intelligence, which meant she couldn't think about anything except in short bursts. And George, while his intelligence was way above normal, had a little mental handicap radio in his ear. He was required by law to wear it at all times. It was tuned to a government transmitter. Every twenty seconds or so, the transmitter would send out some sharp noise to keep people like George from taking unfair advantage of their brains.

George and Hazel were watching television. There were tears on Hazel's cheeks, but she'd forgotten for the moment what they were about.

5   On the television screen, were ballerinas.

A buzzer sounded in George's head. His thoughts fled in panic, like bandits from a burglar alarm.

"That was a real pretty dance, that dance they just did," said Hazel.

"Huh?" said George.

"That dance—it was nice," said Hazel.

10   "Yup," said George. He tried to think a little about the ballerinas. They weren't really very good—no better than anybody else would have been, anyway. They were burdened with sashweights and bags of birdshot, and their faces were masked, so that no one, seeing a free and graceful gesture or a pretty face, would feel like something the cat drug in. George was toying with the vague notion that maybe dancers shouldn't be handicapped. But he didn't get very far with it before another noise in his ear radio scattered his thoughts.

George winced. So did two out of the eight ballerinas.

Hazel saw him wince. Having no mental handicap herself, she had to ask George what the latest sound had been.

"Sounded like somebody hitting a milk bottle with a ball peen hammer," said George.

"I'd think it would be real interesting, hearing all the different sounds," said Hazel, a little envious. "All the things they think up."

15   "Um," said George.

"Only, if I was Handicapper General, you know what I would do?" said Hazel. Hazel, as a matter of fact, bore a strong resemblance to the Handicapper General, a woman named Diana Moon Glampers. "If I was Diana Moon Glampers," said Hazel, "I'd have chimes on Sunday—just chimes. Kind of in honor of religion."

"I could think, if it was just chimes," said George.

"Well—maybe make 'em real loud," said Hazel. "I think I'd make a good Handicapper General."

"Good as anybody else," said George.

20 "Who knows better'n I do what normal is?" said Hazel.

"Right," said George. He began to think glimmeringly about his abnormal son who was now in jail, about Harrison, but a twenty-one-gun salute in his head stopped that.

"Boy!" said Hazel, "that was a doozy, wasn't it?"

It was such a doozy that George was white and trembling, and tears stood on the rims of his red eyes. Two of the eight ballerinas had collapsed to the studio floor, and were holding their temples.

"All of a sudden you look so tired," said Hazel. "Why don't you stretch out on the sofa, so's you can rest your handicap bag on the pillows, honeybunch." She was referring to the forty-seven pounds of birdshot in a canvas bag, which was padlocked around George's neck. "Go on and rest the bag for a little while," she said. "I don't care if you're not equal to me for a while."

25 George weighed the bag with his hands. "I don't mind it," he said. "I don't notice it any more. It's just a part of me."

"You been so tired lately—kind of wore out," said Hazel. "If there was just some way we could make a little hole in the bottom of the bag, and just take out a few of them lead balls. Just a few."

"Two years in prison and two thousand dollars fine for every ball I took out," said George. "I don't call that a bargain."

"If you could just take a few out when you came home from work," said Hazel. "I mean—you don't compete with anybody around here. You just set around."

"If I tried to get away with it," said George, "then other people'd get away with it—and pretty soon we'd be right back to the dark ages again, with everybody competing against everybody else. You wouldn't like that, would you?"

30 "I'd hate it," said Hazel.

"There you are," said George. "The minute people start cheating on laws, what do you think happens to society?"

If Hazel hadn't been able to come up with an answer to this question, George couldn't have supplied one. A siren was going off in his head.

"Reckon it'd fall apart," said Hazel.

"What would?" said George blankly.

35 "Society," said Hazel uncertainly. "Wasn't that what you just said?"

"Who knows?" said George.

The television program was suddenly interrupted for a news bulletin. It wasn't clear at first as to what the bulletin was about, since the announcer, like all announcers, had a serious speech impediment. For about half a minute, and in a state of high excitement, the announcer tried to say, "Ladies and gentlemen—"

He finally gave up, handed the bulletin to a ballerina to read.

"That's all right—" Hazel said of the announcer, "he tried. That's the big thing. He tried to do the best he could with what God gave him. He should get a nice raise for trying so hard."

40 "Ladies and gentlemen—" said the ballerina, reading the bulletin. She must have been extraordinarily beautiful, because the mask she wore was hideous. And it was easy to see that she was the strongest and most graceful of all the dancers, for her handicap bags were as big as those worn by two-hundred-pound men.

And she had to apologize at once for her voice, which was a very unfair voice for a woman to use. Her voice was a warm, luminous, timeless melody. "Excuse me—" she said, and she began again, making her voice absolutely uncompetitive.

"Harrison Bergeron, age fourteen," she said in a grackle squawk, "has just escaped from jail, where he was held on suspicion of plotting to overthrow the government. He is a genius and an athlete, is under-handicapped, and should be regarded as extremely dangerous."

A police photograph of Harrison Bergeron was flashed on the screen upside down, then sideways, upside down again, then right side up. The picture showed the full length of Harrison against a background calibrated in feet and inches. He was exactly seven feet tall.

The rest of Harrison's appearance was Halloween and hardware. Nobody had ever borne heavier handicaps. He had outgrown hindrances faster than the H-G men could think them up. Instead of a little ear radio for a mental handicap, he wore a tremendous pair of earphones, and spectacles with thick wavy lenses. The spectacles were intended to make him not only half blind, but to give him whanging headaches besides.

45   Scrap metal was hung all over him. Ordinarily, there was a certain symmetry, a military neatness to the handicaps issued to strong people, but Harrison looked like a walking junkyard. In the race of life, Harrison carried three hundred pounds.

And to offset his good looks, the H-G men required that he wear at all times a red rubber ball for a nose, keep his eyebrows shaved off, and cover his even white teeth with black caps at snaggle-tooth random.

"If you see this boy," said the ballerina, "do not—I repeat, do not—try to reason with him."

There was the shriek of a door being torn from its hinges.

Screams and barking cries of consternation came from the television set. The photograph of Harrison Bergeron on the screen jumped again and again, as though dancing to the tune of an earthquake.

50   George Bergeron correctly identified the earthquake, and well he might have—for many was the time his own home had danced to the same crashing tune. "My God—" said George, "that must be Harrison!"

The realization was blasted from his mind instantly by the sound of an automobile collision in his head.

When George could open his eyes again, the photograph of Harrison was gone. A living, breathing Harrison filled the screen.

Clanking, clownish, and huge, Harrison stood in the center of the studio. The knob of the uprooted studio door was still in his hand. Ballerinas, technicians, musicians, and announcers cowered on their knees before him, expecting to die.

"I am the Emperor!" cried Harrison. "Do you hear? I am the Emperor! Everybody must do what I say at once!" He stamped his foot and the studio shook.

55   "Even as I stand here—" he bellowed, "crippled, hobbled, sickened—I am a greater ruler than any man who ever lived! Now watch me become what I *can* become!"

Harrison tore the straps of his handicap harness like wet tissue paper, tore straps guaranteed to support five thousand pounds.

Harrison's scrap-iron handicaps crashed to the floor.

Harrison thrust his thumbs under the bar of the padlock that secured his head harness. The bar snapped like celery. Harrison smashed his headphones and spectacles against the wall.

He flung away his rubber-ball nose, revealed a man that would have awed Thor, the god of thunder.

60   "I shall now select my Empress!" he said, looking down on the cowering people. "Let the first woman who dares rise to her feet claim her mate and her throne!"

A moment passed, and then a ballerina arose, swaying like a willow.

Harrison plucked the mental handicap from her ear, snapped off her physical handicaps with marvelous delicacy. Last of all, he removed her mask.

She was blindingly beautiful.

"Now—" said Harrison, taking her hand, "shall we show the people the meaning of the word dance? Music!" he commanded.

65 The musicians scrambled back into their chairs, and Harrison stripped them of their handicaps, too. "Play your best," he told them, "and I'll make you barons and dukes and earls."

The music began. It was normal at first—cheap, silly, false. But Harrison snatched two musicians from their chairs, waved them like batons as he sang the music as he wanted it played. He slammed them back into their chairs.

The music began again and was much improved.

Harrison and his Empress merely listened to the music for a while—listened gravely, as though synchronizing their heartbeats with it.

They shifted their weights to their toes.

70 Harrison placed his big hands on the girl's tiny waist, letting her sense the weightlessness that would soon be hers.

And then, in an explosion of joy and grace, into the air they sprang!

Not only were the laws of the land abandoned, but the law of gravity and the laws of motion as well.

They reeled, whirled, swiveled, flounced, capered, gamboled, and spun.

They leaped like deer on the moon.

75 The studio ceiling was thirty feet high, but each leap brought the dancers nearer to it.

It became their obvious intention to kiss the ceiling.

They kissed it.

And then, neutralizing gravity with love and pure will, they remained suspended in air inches below the ceiling, and they kissed each other for a long, long time.

It was then that Diana Moon Glampers, the Handicapper General, came into the studio with a double-barreled ten-gauge shotgun. She fired twice, and the Emperor and the Empress were dead before they hit the floor.

80 Diana Moon Glampers loaded the gun again. She aimed it at the musicians and told them they had ten seconds to get their handicaps back on.

It was then that the Bergerons' television tube burned out.

Hazel turned to comment about the blackout to George. But George had gone out into the kitchen for a can of beer.

George came back in with the beer, paused while a handicap signal shook him up. And then he sat down again. "You been crying?" he said to Hazel.

"Yup," she said.

85 "What about?" he said.

"I forget," she said. "Something real sad on television."

"What was it?" he said.

"It's all kind of mixed up in my mind," said Hazel.

"Forget sad things," said George.

90 "I always do," said Hazel.

"That's my girl," said George. He winced. There was the sound of a riveting gun in his head.

"Gee—I could tell that one was a doozy," said Hazel.

"You can say that again," said George.

"Gee—" said Hazel, "I could tell that one was a doozy."

[1961]

Joining the Conversation: Critical Thinking and Writing

1. The Declaration of Independence, drafted by Thomas Jefferson, tells us that "all men are created equal." What does this statement mean? Does the society of Harrison Bergeron—a society in which, according to the first sentence of the story, "everybody was finally equal"—show us a society in which Jefferson's words are at last fulfilled? Exactly what are the values of the world in 2081?
2. One sometimes hears that it is the duty of government to equalize society. Hence, for instance, inheritance taxes are sometimes said to be a device employed in an effort to equalize wealth. What forces, if any, can you point to, for example in educational or political systems, that seek to equalize people? If there are such forces at work, do you think they represent unwise and perhaps unlawful government meddling, and are essentially at odds with a basic American idea of rugged individualism and wholesome competition?
3. Speaking of competition, George says (paragraph 31) to Hazel, "The minute people start cheating on laws, what do you think happens to society?" Hazel replies, "Reckon it'd fall all apart" (paragraph 33). What do you think that we, as readers, are supposed to make of this statement? In your response—an essay of five hundred words—consider the actions of Harrison Bergeron, who declares himself Emperor and who says (paragraph 54), "Everybody must do what I say at once!" Is Vonnegut suggesting, in George's behavior, that only laws can keep talented individuals from tyrannizing others?

AMY STERLING CASIL

Amy Sterling Casil, born in Los Angeles, California, in 1962 and educated at Scripps College and Chapman University, teaches English at Saddleback College in Southern California. Her mother, Sterling Sturtevant, was an Academy Award and Cannes Golden Palm–winning art director who redesigned Mr. Magoo and Charlie Brown, among other well-known characters. Casil has published more than one hundred short stories, three novels, two collections of short fiction and poetry, and a number of nonfiction books. She has twice been nominated for science fiction's Nebula Award.

The following story first appeared in the Magazine of Fantasy & Science Fiction *in 2006. It was inspired by and is dedicated to her son Anthony, who was born with Down syndrome. Casil has said that "every therapy mentioned in the story is currently being developed. The story is fiction; the feelings are real."*

Perfect Stranger

The rain falls in sheets across the yard, another pane of glass beyond our windows.

Would you like it warmer, Mr. Gill?

The house pings once. Twice.

"No," I say. "It's fine the way it is."

5   *Thank you very much*, the house says.

Just like anybody else, the house likes to talk to somebody. I imagined this as a great feature. I'm an ergonomic architect; I designed it.

Denny is asleep in his room. You'd think at fifteen, he'd be too old to take a nap. But he's wiped out after soccer.

Carolyn threw Denny's football out today. The foam rubber football I gave him when he was four years old.

It was old, she said. Falling apart. He didn't want it any more. I thought, if he really doesn't want the football, maybe he could say. I tried asking.

10 But right then, Denny was off to soccer practice, then a study session, then the game. Now, he's sleeping. This is what happens when they're in high school.

Carolyn says I should be proud. Proud he's such an athlete. And a scholar.

And I guess I'm a gentleman.

The rain comes down like liquid leaded glass.

The gardeners have taken the trash all the way to the curb once again.

15 It's a very long way to the end of the driveway.

I return with half of Denny's football.

She must have taken shears to it. A lightning strike of rage flashes. If she were home right now . . .

Your body temperature is lower than normal, Mr. Gill, the house chimes in its chimey voice.

"I've been out in the rain," I mutter.

20 *Would you like some soft, fluffy towels?* the house asks. I want the other half of the football. I'll glue it back together. But I smile and grunt an assent, to which the house responds.

Outside, the rain sleets down, a thousand tiny sticks pattering on a thousand tin drums. Nah, not drums. It's just our solar panels.

Denny was born with HLHS. That's an acronym for hypoplastic left heart syndrome. Hypoplastic left heart syndrome is universally fatal, if left untreated. Even now, there are babies that do not survive, even with full-length clone DNA therapy administered in-utero.

When at five months of pregnancy, Carolyn went for a high-level ultrasound that determined Denny had HLHS, it seemed like the most natural thing in the world to try gene therapy. The doctors explained how the heart healed itself as the baby grew.

It was raining that day.

25 Pouring outside while we listened to the neonatal geneticist explain how the procedure worked. We were so lucky, she said. Before gene therapy, babies like Denny could only survive with full heart transplants. She told us about a doctor that had tried baboon hearts to replace broken baby ones.

Apparently, some parents aborted babies diagnosed with HLHS.

"I'd never accept that," I said.

"What?" Carolyn snapped, her hand over her swollen belly. "You'd rather let my baby suffer?"

I guess I hadn't thought of it that way.

30 The geneticist explained in the past, babies born with this heart defect were simply left to die. Their hearts that barely pumped blood. And they would just fade away.

Maybe that could be less humane than an abortion.

At least that was what we discussed on the way home.

It was a miracle that we had the gene therapy, and that Denny was born whole. And totally healthy.

It was the best moment of my life.

35 The rain rattles the solar panels as I sort pictures on the computer. Denny in his baby swing. Denny playing with blocks.

I should be working. But I can't focus on the Recreation Center today.

There was one of him holding the fuzzy book he got from his grandmother. She was so frightened—my mother—when I told her about Denny's heart problem. She didn't understand gene therapy.

Carolyn got on the phone and explained it to her. When Denny was born perfectly healthy, I don't think any of us gave it much more thought. My mother and Denny sat for hours, reading that little book. *Pat the Bunny*. Her favorite—she insisted on buying it. I have it in my study, in the right drawer of my desk.

At one past garage sale, it had been another item bound for the dumpster.

40   I put the half-football with *Pat the Bunny*.

Denny was about three when he learned to read.

I sorted those pictures, too.

They say a man's not supposed to be interested in pictures. Mementos.

The man lives his life, and the woman saves it.

45   Well, what they say is true and what happens are sometimes two different things.

There was another book Denny liked. *Stan the Hotdog Man*. We read it over and over.

And one day, Denny started talking about Stan. It dawned on me that he was reading.

"Carolyn, come here!" I called.

She came running in from the kitchen, alarmed.

50   "Honey, I think he's reading."

Her face changed. "Horse manure," she said.

"No, really," I said.

Denny then read a whole page of *Stan the Hotdog Man* in his small voice. He beamed proudly up at me.

"See?" I said.

55   "You've read it to him so many times, he's memorized it," she said.

"Oh," I said.

It was some time later when I learned that by memorizing the book, Denny was, indeed, reading. By that time, he was in kindergarten.

I sorted some more of the pictures from later years, and looked pensively out at the rain. Denny was still sleeping.

I think I always hoped that my son would play football.

60   Back before I met Carolyn, I played ball. Played all the way through sophomore year in college. Sidelined by a knee injury. I guess I was a pretty good running back, if a little bit underweight. The guys were all into steroids back in those days. There was no such thing as gene augmentation. All we had were good, old-fashioned workouts and protein shakes.

And maybe a shot in the butt for guys that were really dedicated. Or crazy.

You could blow your heart out on steroids. They made you break out all over. Gave you erectile dysfunction. Made you crazy.

Happened to a lot of my friends. It's a good thing I figured out that trap before I fell into it.

I guess I did try it a few times.

65   Drops of rain dappled the window.

Your heart rate has increased, Mr. Gill, the house chimed. *Your core body temperature has dropped.*

"So turn up the heat," I told the house.

I had to say something. Otherwise, it wouldn't leave me alone.

I folded the blue ribbon neatly into my desk drawer. For math excellence. Why they'd give a math prize to a kid in second grade was beyond me.

70   When Denny hit second grade, his teacher pointed out that he was reading like a pro, but having trouble with his figures.

"I was never too good with math," I told her. Wasn't that great in reading, either, but I didn't feel compelled to share.

"You might want to look into some tutoring," she said.

"He's in second grade!" I said.

Carolyn hushed me. "How far is he behind?" she asked.

75 "Behind?" the teacher asked. "Oh, no—he's not behind."

"Well, there's no reason to worry," I said. "He'll pick it up."

"His times tables," Carolyn said. "Next year he's got to learn the times tables."

"We don't do it that way any more, Mrs. Gill. Each child is tested individually against his or her own standards."

I didn't precisely follow how there could be enough time to set individual standards seeing as the kid had just started second grade.

80 "How far is he behind?" Carolyn asked again.

"He's not behind," the teacher said, a stubborn tone creeping into her voice. "Denny is so bright. I'm sure you'd agree with me that he could do better if he applied himself. That's all I'm trying to say."

"Maybe he just wants to play outside," I said.

"Hush!" Carolyn said. "Gary and I both agree that Denny is bright. And he's got plenty of motivation."

"Well," the teacher said smiling. "Why don't you try that tutoring service, or a math buddy."

85 A math buddy was like an English buddy, or a foreign language buddy. It was a small, silver, pain-in-the-ass robot that could also vacuum the floor. They were notorious for tripping guys foolish enough to buy them for their kids. A guy in Cleveland broke his neck that way.

I was going to be damned if I'd get one. I would have rather gotten Denny another football.

On the way out to the car, Carolyn looked up at me, concern wrinkling her forehead. "He's falling behind in math," she whispered.

"You don't have to whisper," I told her. "Nobody can hear. Besides, the teacher said he's not behind. We can encourage him."

"Encourage him!" Carolyn snapped. "He can do better, and he will."

90 "Well, do you think we should try a tutor?" I asked. The thought of locking Denny inside with some greasy-haired high school math geek made me cringe. But even that was a more appealing choice than bringing a gibbering, tortoise-like "math buddy" into the house, so it could trip me on the stairs and turn me into a paraplegic.

"No," Carolyn said. "Not a tutor."

I felt relieved.

"Have you heard about the new gene therapy?" she asked. "It's just like what they did for Denny's heart defect. Only it can strengthen a child's brain power. I was reading all about it yesterday."

"Oh," I said. I had pretty favorable memories of how they'd fixed Denny's heart. "How does that work?"

95 "Maybe it's like what they did before. Only they inject the new genetic material into someone's brain. Then it makes a few changes and the person gets smarter."

"Oh," I said. I didn't like the thought of anybody injecting anything into Denny's brain. But I'd learned it was best not to interrupt Carolyn when she was thinking like this. Frankly, it was almost always better just to wait things out. Half the time she forgot about this stuff and never mentioned it again.

"If you're concerned about your son's logical and mathematical abilities, I don't think you've got much to worry about with Denny," Dr. Mandel said. "He's a bright, normal boy."

"But his teacher says he's falling behind in math," Carolyn said. "Can't we do something?"

"I'd recommend a math buddy," the doctor said. "My own daughter has one. She's about Denny's age. She used to hate math, and now she loves it."

100   "Doesn't that thing get in your way?" I asked—about the math buddy.

"Thing?" the doctor said, looking puzzled. "Oh!" he said, chuckling. "Yeah, it did trip me up once. I fell right off the deck into the pool."

"There's something I don't like about those little robots," I said. "The teacher also suggested a tutor."

"A wise choice," the doctor said. He started to check his personal assistant, a sure sign our time was up. I started to rise, but Carolyn put her hand on my arm.

"Wait," she said. "Can you explain how the procedure works, doctor?"

105   He paused. I suddenly understood that he was one of those guys who never missed a chance to wow others with his special, technical knowledge.

"Well," he said, smiling. "Years ago, we discovered that viruses could be effective transports to load different types of DNA into human—or any other type—of brains. Now we've identified a specific enzyme or cocktail of enzymes that enhances almost every type of brain function. We load the enzymes into a virus, which then transcribes the DNA, and delivers the desired changes to what we once thought were 'unchangeable' brain cells. I'm sure you've heard of people building up their 'extra-sensory perception.'"

Carolyn and I nodded. We'd seen a show about wild-eyed lunatics bending iron and starting fires at a distance the night before.

"It's like an infection," Dr. Mandel said. "But it's one that most people wouldn't mind catching."

"Like a cold?" Carolyn asked.

110   "Exactly!" Dr. Mandel said. "You do understand. Only in this case, the subject catches the cold in their cerebral cortex, and as healing occurs, so do changes for the better."

"Wow," Carolyn said.

"I'm not sure about this," I said.

"Shhh!" she hushed.

"How old is your son?" the doctor asked.

115   "Seven," Carolyn said.

"Ah, the perfect age. Look—" he said, leaning across his shiny titanium desk—everybody who was anybody had one of those a few years back—"It's not cheap. But you could make your son into a math genius if you wanted. He wouldn't feel a thing, and a few days later, his abilities would manifest. They'd grow day by day."

"I don't know," I said. It sounded like mad scientist stuff to me. Weren't they trying these techniques on psychotic murderers? If this was so safe and healthy, I figured we would have heard about it in other areas besides criminal rehabilitation and iron-bending firestarters.

"People are doing it all the time," Dr. Mandel said. "You just don't hear about it on the newslinks because improving kids' test scores isn't nearly as big a story as turning a mass-murderer into Mother Teresa."

Carolyn squeezed my hand under the table. "Doctor, we'd like to try," she said.

120   "I suppose we could—" Dr. Mandel said, voice slightly uncertain.

"Is this necess—"

Carolyn cut me short. "I know he can benefit," she said. "I don't think we mentioned it earlier, but Denny received gene therapy before he was born, to cure a congenital heart defect."

"Oh!" the doctor said. "In that case, he's pre-qualified. Be sure to fill out all the forms, you two. We're conducting multi-treatment longitudinal studies and your son is an ideal candidate."

So, Denny got the blue ribbon in math.

125   He got so into math that he stayed inside almost all the time. He hardly wanted to play with his friends any more. We were supposed to start Pony League football.

But Denny didn't want to play. He didn't want to try for T-Ball, either.

The only thing he'd talk about was math.

One day, Carolyn pointed out that Denny was getting a little chunky.

"He was size eight last month," she said. "Now I've got to buy the next size up."

130   "So? My mom told me I grew three sizes and four inches one summer."

"Your mom said all kinds of things," Carolyn said.

Mom had passed last spring. We used to joke about her seeing Denny through high school. It wasn't meant to be.

"Could you give it a rest, Carolyn?" My wife thought that seven months was long enough. For mourning.

She forged ahead. "Denny's getting fat, Gary. We can't let him get overweight."

135   "So, we'll put him on a diet," I said. I'd been a little chunky when I was his age. When my mom found out how much time I could waste playing video games, she ripped the whole console out of the wall. It was the cold-turkey video game withdrawal method. I lost the weight.

We tried a diet, but Denny was too young to understand why he couldn't eat everything he liked. I wasn't surprised when a couple of frustrating weeks later, Carolyn told me that she'd called Dr. Mandel.

There was of course a gene therapy—the most popular one of all—to deal with unwanted weight gain. This time, the virus carrying altered DNA helped to increase some of the hormones in the brain that controlled appetite and metabolism.

Voila! A thin kid.

That was Denny's third treatment.

140   The rain is imploding on the roof. It's almost in my head.

"Turn up the heat!" I scream.

The house complies. If I didn't know better, I'd almost think that the house was sulking.

After the obesity treatment, Denny started getting into soccer. And discovered his talent for art.

By thirteen, Denny was Dr. Mandel's best patient. He had even been featured on the cover of *Parenting* with two other kids that had been helped by Dr. Mandel's gene practice. It wasn't exactly as if gene therapy was cutting-edge any more. Dr. Mandel was known for his "boutique" practice. That meant that he helped parents with money and fine-edged concerns about their children's growth and well-being.

145   No one really took the dire warnings of the early part of the millennium seriously. Creating a "master race" and so-on. Well, heck. If a person could get a little bit better in some way, and it wasn't hurting them or anybody else, how did that qualify as a "master race"? People without genetic improvements were never looked down upon.

Sure, it was a generational thing. I mean, there were some skin therapies for people my age and Carolyn's age. And they had learned how to rejuvenate most of the vital organs. When I was young, it was a big deal for anybody to make it to age 100. These days, you had to hit 120 and look really good to get your picture on the newslinks.

It was the kids that benefited. If somebody would have told me back in the day that a Pugsley kid could turn into a hunk in a matter of weeks, or a kid with no chin could suddenly acquire a nice, square one without surgery, I would have laughed out loud. You were what you were born to be.

Up until he was nine or ten, Denny's eyes were kind of a hazel color. Now they were piercing, bright blue. The girls went crazy over his eyes. I mean, the kid was a good-looking fifteen, but—

150   The house chimed. Somebody was calling.

"Gary here," I answered.

"Is Denny home?" came a petite, snippy little voice.

"Yes, but he's sleeping. Tired out after his game." I didn't share that he'd had yet another treatment—this one to deal with a few pimples, of all things. Kids slept a lot after a treatment. Body change and metabolic readjustment, supposedly. Dr. Mandel likened it to "growing pains."

"Oh, well, like we were supposed to be . . . studying . . . for chemistry tonight," the little voice said. After a moment's pause, she added, "This is Candy."

155   "I thought you were Apple," I said. She sounded like the girl Denny had introduced me to named "Apple." Apple was a cheerleader, and—

"No, I'm Candy," she said vehemently. "I don't see how you could confuse us. Apple is completely shallow and self-centered and she can't pass math. I'm the captain of the Debate Team."

"Oh," I said. *Of course* she was Debate Team Captain. "My mistake. Apple calls a lot."

"Oh," Candy said. "I see."

"Denny hardly ever takes her calls," I said. This was utterly untrue, but for some reason, I enjoyed the thought of the little white lie that was involved.

160   "Oh," she said, voice brightening. "Well, just tell Denny that I called."

"Thank you, Mr. Gill." And she broke the connection.

So I went upstairs.

"Hey," I said, waking Denny. "A girl called."

Denny rose, shaking sleep out of his eyes. "Yeah? Who was it, Dad?"

165   "Apple," I said. "Wait—no, Candy."

"Candy," Denny said, smiling slyly. "She likes me, I think."

"She's the jealous type too," I said. "What are you doing to attract all these girls, Denny?"

Denny scooted up in bed and swung his legs to the floor. He started rubbing his shoulder. "Hurt it a little bit in the game," he said.

"How'd it go?"

170   "Not bad," he said. "We won by two goals. I got the last goal."

Of course you did, I thought. I hadn't gone to the game. Somehow, I just hadn't wanted to. It was raining. I said it was crazy to play soccer in the rain. Watching soccer in the rain was even crazier.

I couldn't put my finger on the real reason I hadn't gone to the game.

Carolyn was at work, of course. She had a fulfilling, demanding job at the local art museum. She put together their brochures and maintained their web presence. Everybody says what artistic talent she has. It's really amazing how

Denny has the same abilities—maybe even more so. Paintings, drawings, vector art—Denny does it all. He would be taking sculpture, if it didn't conflict with soccer practice.

Denny got up and started to strip off his clothes. He was only fifteen, but his chest and biceps were more muscular than mine. Not just at that age—now.

175   He sprinted into his bathroom and called for the house to turn on the shower.

"Did you order more after-shave, Dad?" he called.

"Yeah," I said. "Yesterday."

"Oh, right," Denny said. "It's all full now—I can see it."

Of course I ordered after-shave. When you work from home, all those little chores seem to fall on you. Tell the house what to cook for dinner, tell it to keep the different meals ready at different times for everyone's schedule, see to it the laundry schedule isn't too full and somebody—namely Denny—isn't going to have to run to a soccer game and play in a dirty jersey. Make sure all the plants are watered and trimmed and the rug is vacuumed and the floor polished and there are no lights out and there—

180   "Hey Dad, what should I do about Candy?" Denny asked from the shower.

"Do about what?"

"She *likes* me, Dad. I like her fine as a friend, but I don't want to get serious. She's just not—"

"What's wrong with her?"

"Nothing," Denny said.

185   "Well, if there's nothing wrong with her, why don't you like her?" I knew perfectly well what he meant, but I was just playing with his mind.

"I mean *like*, Dad. As in . . . you know. . . ."

"You're supposed to be the genius," I said. "I don't know, so explain it to me."

I don't know what I expected to hear. "She's homely, Dad." Or, "She comes on too strong." Or, maybe, "She's pretty nerdy."

"She's a mundane, Dad," Denny said. "I just can't get interested in a girl who's never had any type of modifications."

190   I said, "Oh."

I sat on the bed. I think it was the way he said it.

Denny came out of the shower, a towel wrapped around his Adonis-like frame. "Dad, you know how it is," he said.

"Yeah," I said.

"I mean, look at Apple. She might not be that smart, but she's got a great body. She does a five-minute mile, and her nails are perfect. I know her hair's not real, but what does that matter? It looks great."

195   "Apple's a nice girl," I said.

A long time ago when Denny was a baby, my mother came over and we spent the whole day playing. Building towers of blocks. Reading books. Setting up paper and finger paints on the kitchen table. She baked cookies.

I watched my son and my mother playing together. His hair was light brown and wispy over his hazel eyes. Maybe he looked like an old, balding fat guy, but he was just a baby. There was a funny little cleft in his chin. He was clumsy. We worked with him to use his right hand, then his left. Just letting him experiment. She grabbed his outstretched hands in hers and lifted him up. He giggled and stood and toddled, then soon sat back down.

He was only nine months.

Even a genetically modified baby can't walk at nine months.

200   And it comes to me.

Why I didn't go to the game.

I looked in Denny's eyes a long while. Bright blue, they were. There's been nobody with blue eyes in my family for a long time. Maybe there never were. I can't say those were Carolyn's eyes, either. She has muddy brown eyes, and hates them.

Denny started to laugh, feeling uncomfortable. "Hey, Dad, what are you looking at me like that for?"

I can't reply.

205   "I'm just—you know—" I say, finally. I look over at Denny's artwork.

At the trophies for soccer. Math ribbons. His poster, running for class president last year.

Yeah, he won.

"Your mom threw your little kid football out this morning," I said. "What football?" Denny asked.

It was no big deal, I guess. I really didn't know how to explain.

210   I heard him on the phone after dinner.

Talking up that Apple.

"Yeah, baby. I know it's hard. But everyone's parents are pretty much mundanes. You should see my Dad."

It wasn't like I hadn't had my own rough spots with my Dad. I wanted to run in and grab the vox away from Denny. Yell. Tell her to respect her parents. Tell him.

Denny never knew my father. Carolyn's Dad was an old fart who painted bowls of fruit and sad-eyed clowns.

215   He wasn't a bad guy. He was just kind of . . . distant.

There was no way to make Denny comprehend that my Dad had been a great guy. I mean, I hated Dad when he grounded me. I hated him when he took my car away. I hated him when he flushed my sad little pot stash down the can.

He taught me responsibility. He taught me what it meant to be a man. A mundane.

Hush my feet, I told the house much later that night. The house could do that, you know. Make it quiet to walk, or very noisy. Only the administrator could tell it to do that. I know a lot of parents that use this feature.

I was sleeping in my study again. No. I was lying on the couch in the study, pretending to sleep.

220   It was easier. Carolyn always has some book she's reading or some work she's going over and that light in my eyes drives me crazy.

I was turning the whole thing over in my mind.

All the little treatments. Yeah, it was right to fix Denny's heart.

We had to fix Denny's heart.

Denny was the only son Carolyn and I were ever going to have. I used, back in the day, you know. Stacking. I was juiced up all the time. I thought it made me more of a man.

225   They said it was a minor miracle that Carolyn had gotten pregnant, since I had a sperm count of about 3. Three million particles per ml. And after that, it went down even more. They call that sterile.

She could have left me. Maybe if I had been in her shoes, I would have.

She could have had a lot more kids with a healthy man.

But this was our son. This was Denny.

One time, my Dad was watching me at football practice. I caught a right screen pass we'd been practicing a long time and raced away. My legs were wings. The scrimmagers hurled themselves at me in slow motion. I was flying, the wind whipping through the bars of my helmet. Nobody could touch me.

230   My Dad had this look on his face when he ran out on the field after that scrimmage.

We didn't need to say too much. In fact, we didn't say anything. I was his son, and he was my Dad.

Then it started to rain, and we headed for our car.

I wandered into the kitchen, still remembering.

"Hey house, I'm going to make a sandwich," I whispered. "I want to use the last of that good bread."

235   "Do you want me to slice it?" the house asked.

"No," I said. "You know I cut it myself."

"That's right," the house said. It put the bread and knife out on the counter.

"Mustard?"

"Yes."

240   "Lettuce?"

"No, just bologna."

"Very good," the house said. "Low-fat, high protein."

"Right, house," I said. "Thanks."

I cut the bread for the sandwich. Put mustard on the bread. Slapped down the meat, slapped the whole thing together and stuffed it in my mouth.

245   Then I started upstairs on quiet feet.

"Don't forget to put your knife in the dishwasher," the house said. To some questions, house did not require an immediate answer.

In terms of his eyes, they were blue.

A tear rolls down my mundane cheek.

His chest moves slowly, up and down. His breathing soft, like a cat. Denny stirs. Moans slightly.

250   So they dream.

But what dreams come, I can never know.

There was no such face, ever. Not in my house. Not in my line. None of my father's strength. None of my mother's cleft chin. None of us were ever so broad-shouldered.

None of us were any good at math.

We were good with people. We were fast runners, me and Dad. Denny's a fast runner, too, but different.

255   One time I visited Dad in the care home. Premature Alzheimers, they said. It was the last time he'd know my face. Be able to say my name.

"Carolyn and I are having a baby," I told him. "It's going to be a little boy."

He took my hand.

"I'm so glad, Son," he said, his brown eyes warm and lucid. Knowing me and what I said.

I wonder what it will feel like when I'm an old man. Denny won't come.

260   I can't imagine him ever telling me he's going to have a son.

I dream what it will feel like to look into those ice-blue, strange eyes.

Just one stroke. Quick. Hard.

Down into his changed heart. The heart of a perfect stranger.

Denny turns and sighs.

265   Like a vision, I see my Dad's face. He speaks.

Why did you lose us, Gary? Your Mom—me? For this?

He taught me what it was to be a man.

Outside, the rain falls. It's tapping on the roof like a hundred little cats running up and down.

270   I listen.

Then I turn and go on my quiet feet back down the stairs.

Outside, the rain is a cold curtain of ice knifing my face. I look up, into the clear, black sky. No stars, nothing. Pines shadowed against the midnight fog.

I know if I just look hard enough, I'll find the other half of the football.

Let the sky darken like soot. Let the wind gather.

Let it rain.

For Anthony Sterling Rodgers

[2006]

Joining the Conversation: Critical Thinking and Writing

1. Why is the narrator of "Perfect Stranger" so concerned with retrieving the foam rubber football (paragraphs 8 and 272)?
2. How would you characterize the narrator? How would you characterize the relationship between the narrator and Carolyn, his wife? Suppose Carolyn were the narrator. Write the last paragraph or two or three paragraphs of the story that Carolyn might narrate.
3. Are the treatments given in the story believable? Do you think that they are advisable? Are they moral?
4. Do you think that we are on the road toward the society that the story depicts? Why, or why not?

MARK TWAIN

One of America's most original and influential writers, Mark Twain is best known for his novels The Adventures of Tom Sawyer *(1876) and the* Adventures of Huckleberry Finn *(1885). Born Samuel Langhorne Clements in Missouri in 1835, Twain started his writing career as a newspaper journalist and experienced his first success with the tall tale story, "The Celebrated Jumping Frog of Calaveras County." Famous for his satirical wit, Twain's work includes humor writing, travel writing, autobiographical essays, and literary criticism. He also became famous for his public speaking tours. Addressing American themes (such as slavery) in an American style (such as using local dialect), Twain's writing is essential to the development of American literature.*

A Telephonic Conversation

I consider that a conversation by telephone—when you are simply sitting by and not taking any part in that conversation—is one of the solemnest curiosities of this modern life. Yesterday I was writing a deep article on a sublime philosophical subject while such a conversation was going on in the room. I notice that one can always write best when somebody is talking through a telephone close by. Well, the thing began in this way. A member of our household came in and asked me to have our house put into communication with Mr. Bagley's, down town. I have observed, in many cities, that the gentle sex always shrink from calling up the central office themselves. I don't know why, but they do. So I touched the bell, and this talk ensued:—

  Central Office. [Gruffly.] Hello!

  I. Is it the Central Office?

  C. O. Of course it is. What do you want?

5 *I.* Will you switch me on to the Bagleys, please?

  C. O. All right. Just keep your ear to the telephone.

  Then I heard, *k-look, k-look, k'look—klook-klook-klook-look-look!* then a horrible "gritting" of teeth, and finally a piping female voice: Y-e-s? [Rising inflection.] Did you wish to speak to me?"

  Without answering, I handed the telephone to the applicant, and sat down. Then followed that queerest of all the queer things in this world,—a conversation with only one end to it. You hear questions asked; you don't hear the answer. You hear invitations given; you hear no thanks in return. You have listening pauses of dead silence, followed by apparently irrelevant and unjustifiable exclamations of glad surprise, or sorrow, or dismay. You can't make head or tail of the talk, because you never hear anything that the person at the other end of the wire says. Well, I heard the following remarkable series of observations, all from the one tongue, and all shouted,—for you can't ever persuade the gentle sex to speak gently into a telephone:—

  Yes? Why, how did *that* happen?

10 Pause.

  What did you say?

  Pause.

  Oh, no, I don't think it was.

  Pause.

15 *No!* Oh, no, I didn't mean *that.* I meant, put it in while it is still boiling,—or just before it *comes* to a boil.

  Pause.

  WHAT?

  Pause.

  I turned it over with a back stitch on the selvage edge.

20 Pause.

  Yes, I like that way, too; but I think it's better to baste it on with Valenciennes or bombazine, or something of that sort. It gives it such an air,—and attracts so much notice.

  Pause.

  It's forty-ninth Deuteronomy, sixty-fourth to ninety-seventh inclusive. I think we ought all to read it often.

  Pause.

25 Perhaps so; I generally use a hair-pin.

  Pause.

  What did you say? [*Aside*] Children, do be quiet!

  Pause.

  Oh! B *flat!* Dear me, I thought you said it was the cat!

30 Pause.

  Since *when?*

  Pause.

  Why, *I* never heard of it.

Pause.

35   You astound me! It seems utterly impossible!

Pause.

Who did?

Pause.

Good-ness gracious!

40   Pause.

Well, what *is* this world coming to? Was it right in *church*?

Pause.

And was her *mother* there?

Pause.

45   Why, Mrs. Bagley, I should have died of humiliation! What did they *do*?

Long Pause.

I can't be perfectly sure, because I haven't the notes by me; but I think it goes
something like this: te-rolly-loll-loll, loll lolly-loll-loll, O tolly-loll-loll-*lee-ly-li-i*-do!
And then *repeat*, you know.

Pause.

Yes, I think it *is* very sweet,—and very solemn and impressive, if you get the
andantino and the pianissimo right.

50   Pause.

Oh, gum-drops, gum-drops! But I never allow them to eat striped candy. And
of course they *can't*, till they get their teeth, any way.

Pause.

What?

Pause.

55   Oh, not in the least,—go right on. He's here writing,—it doesn't bother *him*.

Pause.

Very well, I'll come if I can. [*Aside.*] Dear me, how it does tire a person's arm
to hold this thing up so long! I wish she'd—

Pause.

Oh, no, not at all; I *like* to talk,—but I'm afraid I'm keeping you from your
affairs.

60   Pause.

Visitors?

Pause.

No, we never use butter on them.

Pause.

65   Yes, that is a very good way; but all the cook-books say they are very unhealthy
when they are out of season. And *he* doesn't like them, any way,—especially
canned.

Pause.

Oh, I think that is too high for them; we have never paid over fifty cents a
bunch.

Pause.

Must you go? Well, *good*-by.

70   Pause.

Yes, I think so. *Good*-by.

Pause.

Four, o'clock then—I'll be ready. *Good*-by.

Pause.

75   Thank you ever so much. *Good*-by.

Pause.

Oh, not at all!—just as fresh—*Which?* Oh, I'm glad to hear you say that. *Good*-by. [Hangs up the telephone and says, "Oh, it *does* tire a person's arm so!"]

A man delivers a single brutal "Good-by," and that is the end of it. Not so with the gentle sex,—I say it in their praise; they cannot abide abruptness.

[1880]

Joining the Conversation: Critical Thinking and Writing

1. The first telephone transmission took place in 1876, and Twain's "A Telephonic Conversation" was published in 1880. How is Twain responding to this new form of technology? Does Twain praise the telephone or critique it?
2. Twain's comic sketch presents only one side of a telephone conversation. Why is this form of conversation funny? Locate specific lines that convey a comic meaning.
3. We tend to think of the phone as enabling communication. What type of communication is depicted in "A Telephonic Conversation"? What are the topics covered in the telephone conversation? Make a list of the different topics discussed. Also, note that the story contains the repeated word "pause." How many times does this word appear? Why is only half the conversation recorded, and why is that conversation constantly interrupted by "pause"? Does this short story show that communication is improved by the telephone?

MARIA SEMPLE

Born in Santa Monica, California, in 1964, Maria Semple received a BA in English from Barnard College in 1984. She works as a television writer and producer, and her screenwriting credits include such well-known television shows as Beverly Hills, 90210; Mad about You; *and* Arrested Development. *Semple has also written the best-selling novels* This One is Mine *(2008) and* Where'd You Go, Bernadette *(2012). She currently lives in Seattle, Washington, and actively supports the literary scene there.*

Dear Mountain Room Parents

Hi, everyone!

The Mountain Room is gearing up for its Day of the Dead celebration on Friday. Please send in photos of loved ones for our altar. All parents are welcome to come by on Wednesday afternoon to help us make candles and decorate skulls.

Thanks!

Emily

Hi again.

Because I've gotten sonic questions about my last e-mail, there is nothing "wrong" with Halloween. The Day of the Dead is the Mexican version, a time of remembrance. Many of you chose Little Learners because of our emphasis on global awareness. Our celebration on Friday is an example of that. The skulls we're decorating are sugar skulls. I should have made that more clear.

Emily

Parents:

Some of you have expressed concern about your children celebrating a holiday with the word "dead" in it. I asked Eleanor's mom, who's a pediatrician, and here's what she said: "Preschoolers tend to see death as temporary and reversible. Therefore, I see nothing traumatic about the Day of the Dead." I hope this helps.

Emily

Dear Parents:

In response to the e-mail we all received from Maddie's parents, in which they shared their decision to raise their daughter dogma-free, yes, there will be an altar, but please be assured that the Day of the Dead is a pagan celebration of life and has nothing to do with God. Keep those photos coming!

Emily

Hello.

Perhaps "pagan" was a poor word choice. I feel like were veering a bit off track, so here's what I'll do. I'll start setting up our altar now, so that today at pickup you can see for yourselves how colorful and harmless the Day of the Dead truly is.

Emily

Parents:

The photos should be of loved ones who have passed. Max's grandma was understandably shaken when she came in and saw a photo of herself on our altar. But the candles and skulls were cute, right?

Emily

Mountain Room Parents:

It's late and I can't possibly respond to each and every e-mail. (Not that it comes up a lot in conversation, but I have children, too.) As the skulls have clearly become a distraction, I decided to throw them away. They're in the compost. I'm looking at them now. You can, too, tomorrow at drop-off. I just placed a "NO BASURA" card on the bin to make sure it doesn't get emptied. Finally, to those parents who are offended by our Day of the Dead celebration, I'd like to point out that there are parents who are offended that you are offended.

Emily

Dear Parents:

Thanks to their group e-mail, we now know that the families of Millie and Jaden M. recognize Jesus Christ as their Saviour. There still seems to be some confusion about why, if we want to celebrate life, we're actually celebrating death. To better explain this "bewildering detour," I've asked Adela, who works in the office and makes waffles for us on Wednesdays, and who was born in Mexico, to write you directly.

Emily

Hola a los Padres:

El Día de los Muertos begins with a parade through the zócalo, where we toss oranges into decorated coffins. The skeletons drive us in the bus to the cemetery and we molest the spirits from under the ground with candy and traditional Mexican music. We write poems called calaveras, which laugh at the living. In Mexico, it is a rejoicing time of ofrendas, picnics, and dancing on graves.

Adela

Parents:

I sincerely apologize for Adela's e-mail. I would have looked it over, but I was at my daughter's piano recital. (Three kids, in case you're wondering, one who's allergic to everything, even wind.) For now, let's agree that e-mail has reached its limits. How about we process our feelings face to face? 9 A.M. tomorrow?

Emily

Dear Parents:

Some of you chose to engage in our dialogue. Some chose to form a human chain. Others had jobs (!) to go to. So we're all up to speed, let me recap this morning's discussion:

- Satan isn't driving our bus. Little Learners does not have a bus. If we did, I wouldn't still need parent drivers for the field trip to the cider mill. Anyone? I didn't think so.
- Ofrenda means "offering." It's just a thing we put on the altar. Any random thing. A bottle of Fanta. Unopened, not poisoned. Just a bottle of Fanta.
- We're moving past the word "altar" and calling it what it really is: a Seahawks blanket draped over some cinder blocks.
- Adela will not be preparing food anymore and Waffle Wednesdays will be suspended. (That didn't make us any new friends in the Rainbow and Sunshine Rooms!)
- On Friday morning, I will divide the Mountain Room into three groups: those who wish to celebrate the Day of the Dead; those who wish to celebrate Halloween; and Maddie, who will make nondenominational potato prints in the corner.

Dear Mountain Room Parents:

Today I learned not to have open flames in the same room as a costume parade. I learned that a five-dollar belly-dancer outfit purchased at a pop-up costume store can easily catch fire, but, really, I knew that just by looking at it. I learned that Fanta is effective in putting out fires. I learned that a child's emerging completely unscathed from a burning costume isn't a good enough outcome for some parents. I learned that I will be unemployed on Monday. For me, the Day of the Dead will always be a time of remembrance.

Happy Halloween!
Emily ♦

[2011]

Joining the Conversation: Critical Thinking and Writing

1. Annotate the short story as you read it. When you have finished, write a summary of the story's main events. What events happen, and in what order? "Plot" is often defined as a series of "cause-effect" relationships. In "Dear Mountain

Room Parents," how does one event cause or lead to the next event? What sorts of misunderstandings lead to unexpected events?

2. The short story is written as if it were the record of an e-mail chain written by the schoolteacher, Emily, to her students' parents. How is this form of communication humorous? How does e-mail encourage misinformation and misunderstanding? Examine one of the story's most interesting or most comic examples of misunderstanding, and analyze how the misunderstanding occurred.

3. How does the story end? Does this ending provide a critique of e-mail communication?

4. Compare "Dear Mountain School Parents" to Twain's "A Telephonic Conversation." How does each story use recent technology to create a one-sided conversation?

ROBIN HEMLEY

Robin Hemley was born in 1958, earned a BA from Indiana University and a MFA from the University of Iowa, and taught at the University of Iowa and Vermont College. Author of eleven books, Hemley's stories and essays have appeared in The Believer, *the* New York Times, New York Magazine, *and numerous literary magazines. His writing includes fiction, nonfiction, memoir, and a guide to writing. As in "Reply All," his short stories often use humor to provide insights into contemporary culture. He has won numerous awards, including a Guggenheim Fellowship, three Pushcart Prizes, and the Nelson Algren Award for Fiction from the* Chicago Tribune.

Reply All

To: Poetry Association of the Western Suburbs Listserve <7/17>
From: Lisa Drago-Harse
Subject: Next Meeting

Hi all,

I wanted to confirm that our next meeting will be held in the Sir Francis Drake Room at the Bensonville Hampton Inn on August 3rd. Minutes from our last meeting and an agenda for the next meeting will follow shortly.

Peace and Poetry,
Lisa Drago-Harse
Secretary/PAWS

To: Poetry Association of the Western Suburbs Listserve <7/17>
From: Michael Stroud
Re: Re: Next Meeting

Dearest Lisa,

First of all, I LOVE your mole and don't find it unsightly in the least! There is absolutely no reason for you to be ashamed of it (though it might be a good idea to have it checked out). But please don't remove it! Heaven forbid, my darling! As I recall, I gave you considerable pleasure when I sucked and licked it like a nipple. A nipple it is, in size and shape, if not placement. That no one else knows your mole's position on your body (other than your benighted husband, poor limp

Richard, that Son(net) of a Bitch as you call him) is more the pity (if Marvell had known such a mole, he undoubtedly would have added an extra stanza to his poem). But my coy mistress is not SO terribly coy as all that. When you started massaging my crotch with your foot underneath the table in the Sir Francis Drake Room, I was at first shocked. I thought perhaps the unseen massager was none other than our esteemed president, the redoubtable Darcy McFee (makeup and wardrobe courtesy of Yoda). Is that terrible of me? I have nothing personal against her, really, except for her execrable taste in poetry, and the fact that you should be president, not she. And her breath. And that habit of pulling her nose when she speaks and that absolutely horrific expression of hers, Twee. As in, "I find his poetry just so twee." What does twee mean and why does she keep inflicting it upon us! So imagine my horror when I felt this foot in my crotch and I stared across the table at the two of you—she twitching like a slug that's had salt poured on it and you immobile except for your Mont Blanc pen taking down the minutes. Ah, to think that the taking down of minutes could be such an erotic activity, but in your capable hands, it is. To think that mere hours later, it would be my Mont Blanc you'd grasp so firmly, guiding me into the lyrical book of your body. But initially, I thought the worst, that it was Darcy, not you. My only consolation was the idea that at least I had her on a sexual harassment suit, her being my boss after all at Roosevelt. Another reason I thought it was her and not you was because I know you're married and she isn't and I knew that Richard is a member of our esteemed organization, too (and he was in the room, seated beside you no less!). It was only that sly smile in your eyes that tipped me off. I, too, love the danger that illicit public sex brings, as long as it's kept under the table, so to speak. And yes, maybe someday we can make love on that very same table in the Sir Francis Drake Room, my darling. Thinking of you now makes me so hot. I want to nibble you. I want to live in your panties. I want to make metaphors of your muscles, of your thighs, of the fecund wetness bursting with your being and effulgence.

With undying love and erotic daydreams,
Mikey

To: PAWS Listserve <//17>
From: Darcy McFee
Re: Re: Re: Next Meeting

I am traveling now and will not be answering e-mails until I return on July 21st.

Thanks!
Darcy

To: PAWS Listserve <7/17>
From: Sam Fulgram, Jr.
Re: Re: Re: Re: Next Meeting

Whoa boy! Do you realize you just sent out your love note to the entire Poetry Association of the Western Suburbs listserve?

Cheers,
Sam

P.S.—That mole? You've got my imagination running wild. As long as the entire organization knows about it now, would you mind divulging its location? I'd sleep better at night knowing it.

To: PAWS Listserve <7/17>
From: Betsy Midchester
Re: Re: Re: Re: Re: Next Meeting

Hi all.

Well! That last message from "Mikey" Stroud certainly made my day. I thought at first the message was addressed to me. As I had no memory of placing my foot in Mike's crotch, I naturally assumed that I needed an adjustment of my medication so that I wouldn't forget such episodes in the future. Now I see its simply Michael ("Down Boy") Stroud and our esteemed Secretary of the Galloping Mont Blaaaaanc who need the medication adjustments. Thanks, in any case, for a much needed lift in an otherwise humdrum day.

Betsy Midchester
Treasurer/PAWS

To: PAWS Listserve <7/17>
From: Lisa Drago-Harse
Re: Re: Re: Re: Re: Re: Next Meeting

This is a nightmare. I'm not quite sure what to say except that life is unpredictable and often irreversible. While I do not wish to go into details or make excuses for the above e-mail from Michael Stroud, I would like to clarify one thing: that was not my foot in your crotch, Michael. But your belief that it was my foot in your crotch explains a few things concerning your subsequent behavior towards me that were up until this moment a mystery.

LDH

To: PAWS Listserve <7/17>
From: Michael Stroud
Re: Re: Re: Re: Re: Re: Re: Next Meeting

I'm

To: PAWS Listserve <7/17>
From: Michael Stroud
Re: Re: Re: Re: Re: Re: Re: Re: Next Meeting

I hit the send button by mistake before I was ready. This isn't my day, to say the least! I'm sorry!!!! I'd like to apologize to the entire PAWS community, and also to Lisa's husband Richard and to Darcy. And to you, Lisa. I don't mean to make excuses for myself, but I would like to say that I've been under a tremendous amount of pressure of late, at school, at home, and I am nothing if not vulnerable and flawed. All I can say is that in poetry I find some solace for the petty actions of others and the sometimes monstrous actions of which I'm all too capable. I ask you all to blame me, not Lisa, for what has happened.

But if not your foot, Lisa, then whose?

Michael Stroud

To: PAWS Listserve <7/17>
From: Greg Rudolfsky
Re: Re: Re: Re: Re: Re: Re: Re: Re: RESPECT
Just a little bit, Just a little bit.
Sock it to me, sock it to me, sock it to me, sock it to me,

sock it to me, sock it to me, sock it to me, sock it to me,
RESPECT, Just a little bit, just a little bit ....

To: PAWS Listserve <7/17>
From: Samantha M. Poulsen, RN
Subject: Fecund Poets

I do not care whose foot is in whose crotch, but I think it's insulting and idiotic that
so-called educated people would use such phrases as, "the fecund wetness bursting with your being and effulgence." And officers of the PAWS at that!

To: PAWS Listserve <7/17>
From: Richard Harse
Re: Fecund Poets

I would like to tender my resignation in the Poets of the Western Suburbs, as I will
be tendering my resignation in several other areas of my life. I only belonged to
PAWS in any case because of my wife's interest in poetry. I wanted to share her
interests, but clearly not all of them.

To: PAWS Listserve <7/22>
From: Darcy McFee
Re: Fecund Poets

Well, it seems that our little organization has been busy in my absence. I have over
300 new messages in my e-mail account, all, it seems, from my fellow poetry lovers! I haven't yet had a chance to read your exchanges, but I will soon. In the
meantime, I wanted to convey some exciting news. This weekend, while attending
a workshop at Wright State in Dayton, I ran into the former Poet Laureate, Billy
Collins, who has agreed to be our special guest at our annual Poetry Bash in Oak
Park. He said he's heard quite a lot about our organization in recent days and that
our board had achieved near legendary status in the poetry community. I knew this
would make you as proud as it makes me.

To: PAWS Listserve <7/24>
From: Darcy McFee
Subject: Twee

So this is how it is. Upon reading the 300 e-mails that collected in my inbox over the
weekend, my mind is a riot of emotions. I have not slept for nearly 48 hours. Never
before have I been so insulted. Yet, I also know that I am, at least in part, to blame.
Had I not stuck my foot in Michael Stroud's crotch, none of this would have happened. Twitching like a slug that's had salt poured on it? That hurts, Michael. It
really does. I didn't realize you were so shallow. But in reading your collective
e-mails, I see that at least half our membership has a decidedly sadistic bent. In any
case, it was not your crotch I aimed for, Michael, but the crotch of our Vice-President,
Amir Bathshiri, with whom I have long been intimately acquainted, both of us having
lost our spouses several years ago. If the seating arrangements in the Sir Francis
Drake Room were any less cramped, none of these misunderstandings would have
occurred. Of course, I never would have tried to fondle you, Michael. In the first
place, you are the most boring, tedious person I have met in my life, and believe me,
as Chair of the English Dept. at Roosevelt, I have met my share of boring, tedious
people. You recite poetry with all the grace of a highway sign that cautions one to
beware of falling rocks. But enough! I know that it is my errant foot to blame. Amir
and I have talked this over and have decided to withdraw from PAWS as well as from

academia. Early retirement calls, Michael and Lisa, and I will give neither of you a thought as I walk along the beach hand in hand with Amir in the months and years to come, listening to the mermaids singing each to each.

Yes, Michael, I find you and your crotch and your paramour the very essence of Twee.

To: PAWS Listserve <7/30>
From: Betsy Midchester/Treasurer
Subject: New Elections

Please note that the agenda for our next meeting has changed. We will spend most of the meeting on new elections to be held for the positions of President, Vice-President and Secretary of our organization. Note, too, that we will no longer be meeting in the Sir Francis Drake Room of the Bensonville Hampton Inn. Instead, we will be meeting in the cafeteria of Enchanted Gardens Residence for Seniors in Glen Ellyn. The change in venue was planned well in advance of recent events, so members should not read anything into this (though if any organization's members are skilled at reading between the lines, it should be ours). Please think about whom you would like to nominate for these important positions in our organization. And in the meantime, please remember to always be conscious and considerate of your audience.

Peace and poetry,
Betsy Midchester
Treasurer and Acting President/PAWS

[2012]

Joining the Conversation: Critical Thinking and Writing

1. "Reply All" relies on a common e-mail mistake as the source of the story: A private email has been sent "reply all" to a large list of readers. Why is this mistake humorous? What information is contained in the private e-mail that should not have been made public?
2. Analyze the recipients of the e-mails. Why are the recipients poets? What are the relationships among the recipients? What are the different organizational posts held by the recipients? How do the e-mail recipients add to the humor of the story?
3. Locate a particularly funny e-mail that you have received, and provide a close reading of it. Write a short two-page explication of what occurs in the e-mail. Examine the details of the selected e-mail text, such as the name of recipient list ("To: PAWS Listserve"). Analyze how the e-mail builds on a humorous situation and how it uses humorous language.

JOHN CHEEVER

John Cheever (1912–82) was an American novelist and short-story writer known for his careful examination of mid-twentieth-century suburban life. Born and raised in Quincy, Massachusetts, Cheever's fiction is set in small New England towns, in addition to the urban centers of Manhattan and Rome. His work often reveals the moral turmoil underlying the seeming order and propriety of the well-manicured suburbs. He won a Pulitzer Prize, National Book Critics Circle Award, and National Book Award for his collected short stories, The Stories of John Cheever *(1978); "The Enormous Radio" is included in this collection. He is considered one of the most important masters of the short-story form.*

The Enormous Radio

Jim and Irene Westcott were the kind of people who seem to strike that satisfactory average of income, endeavor, and respectability that is reached by the statistical reports in college alumni bulletins. They were the parents of two young children, they had been married nine years, they lived on the twelfth floor of an apartment house near Sutton Place, they went to the theatre on an average of 10.3 times a year, and they hoped someday to live in Westchester. Irene Westcott was a pleasant, rather plain girl with soft brown hair and a wide, fine forehead upon which nothing at all had been written, and in the cold weather she wore a coat of fitch skins dyed to resemble mink. You could not say that Jim Westcott looked younger than he was, but you could at least say of him that he seemed to feel younger. He wore his graying hair cut very short, he dressed in the kind of clothes his class had worn at Andover, and his manner was earnest, vehement, and intentionally naive. The Westcotts differed from their friends, their classmates, and their neighbors only in an interest they shared in serious music. They went to a great many concerts—although they seldom mentioned this to anyone—and they spent a good deal of time listening to music on the radio.

Their radio was an old instrument, sensitive, unpredictable, and beyond repair. Neither of them understood the mechanics of radio—or of any of the other appliances that surrounded them—and when the instrument faltered, Jim would strike the side of the cabinet with his hand. This sometimes helped. One Sunday afternoon, in the middle of a Schubert quartet, the music faded away altogether. Jim struck the cabinet repeatedly, but there was no response; the Schubert was lost to them forever. He promised to buy Irene a new radio, and on Monday when he came home from work he told her that he had got one. He refused to describe it, and said it would be a surprise for her when it came.

The radio was delivered at the kitchen door the following afternoon, and with the assistance of her maid and the handyman Irene uncrated it and brought it into the living room. She was struck at once with the physical ugliness of the large gumwood cabinet. Irene was proud of her living room, she had chosen its furnishings and colors as carefully as she chose her clothes, and now it seemed to her that the new radio stood among her intimate possessions like an aggressive intruder. She was confounded by the number of dials and switches on the instrument panel, and she studied them thoroughly before she put the plug into a wall socket and turned the radio on. The dials flooded with a malevolent green light, and in the distance she heard the music of a piano quintet. The quintet was in the distance for only an instant; it bore down upon her with a speed greater than light and filled the apartment with the noise of music amplified so mightily that it knocked a china ornament from a table to the floor. She rushed to the instrument and reduced the volume. The violent forces that were snared in the ugly gumwood cabinet made her uneasy. Her children came home from school then, and she took them to the Park. It was not until later in the afternoon that she was able to return to the radio.

The maid had given the children their suppers and was supervising their baths when Irene turned on the radio, reduced the volume, and sat down to listen to a

Mozart quintet that she knew and enjoyed. The music came through clearly. The new instrument had a much purer tone, she thought, than the old one. She decided that tone was most important and that she could conceal the cabinet behind a sofa. But as soon as she had made her peace with the radio, the interference began. A crackling sound like the noise of a burning powder fuse began to accompany the singing of the strings. Beyond the music, there was a rustling that reminded Irene unpleasantly of the sea, and as the quintet progressed, these noises were joined by many others. She tried all the dials and switches but nothing dimmed the interference, and she sat down, disappointed and bewildered, and tried to trace the flight of the melody. The elevator shaft in her building ran beside the living-room wall, and it was the noise of the elevator that gave her a clue to the character of the static. The rattling of the elevator cables and the opening and closing of the elevator doors were reproduced in her loudspeaker, and, realizing that the radio was sensitive to electrical currents of all sorts, she began to discern through the Mozart the ringing of telephone bells, the dialing of phones, and the lamentation of a vacuum cleaner. By listening more carefully, she was able to distinguish doorbells, elevator bells, electric razors, and Waring mixers, whose sounds had been picked up from the apartments that surrounded hers and transmitted through her loudspeaker. The powerful and ugly instrument, with its mistaken sensitivity to discord, was more than she could hope to master, so she turned the thing off and went into the nursery to see her children.

5   When Jim Westcott came home that night, he went to the radio confidently and worked the controls. He had the same sort of experience Irene had had. A man was speaking on the station Jim had chosen, and his voice swung instantly from the distance into a force so powerful that it shook the apartment. Jim turned the volume control and reduced the voice. Then, a minute or two later, the interference began. The ringing of telephones and doorbells set in, joined by the rasp of the elevator doors and the whir of cooking appliances. The character of the noise had changed since Irene had tried the radio earlier; the last of the electric razors was being unplugged, the vacuum cleaners had all been returned to their closets, and the static reflected that change in pace that overtakes the city after the sun goes down. He fiddled with the knobs but couldn't get rid of the noises, so he turned the radio off and told Irene that in the morning he'd call the people who had sold it to him and give them hell.

The following afternoon, when Irene returned to the apartment from a luncheon date, the maid told her that a man had come and fixed the radio. Irene went into the living room before she took off her hat or her furs and tried the instrument. From the loudspeaker came a recording of the "Missouri Waltz." It reminded her of the thin, scratchy music from an old-fashioned phonograph that she sometimes heard across the lake where she spent her summers. She waited until the waltz had finished, expecting an explanation of the recording, but there was none. The music was followed by silence, and then the plaintive and scratchy record was repeated. She turned the dial and got a satisfactory burst of Caucasian music—the thump of bare feet in the dust and the rattle of coin jewelry—but in the background she could hear the ringing of bells and a confusion of voices. Her children came home from school then, and she turned off the radio and went to the nursery.

When Jim came home that night, he was tired, and he took a bath and changed his clothes. Then he joined Irene in the living room. He had just turned on the radio when the maid announced dinner, so he left it on, and he and Irene went to the table.

Jim was too tired to make even a pretense of sociability, and there was nothing about the dinner to hold Irene's interest, so her attention wandered from the food to the deposits of silver polish on the candlesticks and from there to the music in the other room. She listened for a few minutes to a Chopin prelude and then was surprised to hear a man's voice break in. "For Christ's sake, Kathy," he said, "do you always have to play the piano when I get home?" The music stopped abruptly. "It's the only chance I have," a woman said. "I'm at the office all day." "So am I," the man said. He added something obscene about an upright piano, and slammed a door. The passionate and melancholy music began again.

"Did you hear that?" Irene asked.

10   "What?" Jim was eating his dessert.

"The radio. A man said something while the music was still going on—something dirty."

"It's probably a play."

"I don't think it *is* a play," Irene said.

They left the table and took their coffee into the living room. Irene asked Jim to try another station. He turned the knob. "Have you seen my garters?" a man asked. "Button me up," a woman said. "Have you seen my garters?" the man said again. "Just button me up and I'll find your garters," the woman said. Jim shifted to another station. "I wish you wouldn't leave apple cores in the ashtrays," a man said. "I hate the smell."

15   "This is strange," Jim said.

"Isn't it?" Irene said.

Jim turned the knob again. "'On the coast of Coromandel where the early pumpkins blow,'" a woman with a pronounced English accent said, "'in the middle of the woods lived the Yonghy-Bonghy-Bò. Two old chairs, and half a candle, one old jug without a handle . . .'"

"My God!" Irene cried. "That's the Sweeneys' nurse."

"'These were all his worldly goods,'" the British voice continued.

20   "Turn that thing off," Irene said. "Maybe they can hear *us*." Jim switched the radio off. "That was Miss Armstrong, the Sweeneys' nurse," Irene said. "She must be reading to the little girl. They live in 17-B. I've talked with Miss Armstrong in the Park. I know her voice very well. We must be getting other people's apartments."

"That's impossible," Jim said.

"Well, that was the Sweeneys' nurse," Irene said hotly. "I know her voice. I know it very well. I'm wondering if they can hear us."

Jim turned the switch. First from a distance and then nearer, nearer, as if borne on the wind came the pure accents of the Sweeneys' nurse again: "*Lady Jingly! Lady Jingly!*" she said, "*sitting where the pumpkins blow, will you come and be my wife?* said the Yonghy-Bonghy-Bò . . .'"

Jim went over to the radio and said "Hello" loudly into the speaker.

25   "*I am tired of living singly,*'" the nurse went on, "*on this coast so wild and shingly, I'm a-weary of my life; if you'll come and be my wife, quite serene would be my life . . .*'"

"I guess she can't hear us," Irene said. "Try something else."

Jim turned to another station, and the living room was filled with the uproar of a cocktail party that had overshot its mark. Someone was playing the piano and singing the "Whiffenpoof Song," and the voices that surrounded the piano were vehement and happy. "Eat some more sandwiches," a woman shrieked. There were screams of laughter and a dish of some sort crashed to the floor.

"Those must be the Fullers, in 11-E," Irene said. "I knew they were giving a party this afternoon. I saw her in the liquor store. Isn't this too divine? Try something else. See if you can get those people in 18-C."

The Westcotts overheard that evening a monologue on salmon fishing in Canada, a bridge game, running comments on home movies of what had apparently been a fortnight at Sea Island, and a bitter family quarrel about an overdraft at the bank. They turned off their radio at midnight and went to bed, weak with laughter. Sometime in the night, their son began to call for a glass of water and Irene got one and took it to his room. It was very early. All the lights in the neighborhood were extinguished, and from the boy's window she could see the empty street. She went into the living room and tried the radio. There was some faint coughing, a moan, and then a man spoke. "Are you all right, darling?" he asked. "Yes," a woman said wearily. "Yes, I'm all right, I guess," and then she added with great feeling, "But, you know, Charlie, I don't feel like myself any more. Sometimes there are about fifteen or twenty minutes in the week when I feel like myself. I don't like to go to another doctor, because the doctor's bills are so awful already, but I just don't feel like myself, Charlie. I just never feel like myself." They were not young, Irene thought. She guessed from the timbre of their voices that they were middle-aged. The restrained melancholy of the dialogue and the draft from the bedroom window made her shiver, and she went back to bed.

30   The following morning, Irene cooked breakfast for the family—the maid didn't come up from her room in the basement until ten—braided her daughter's hair, and waited at the door until her children and her husband had been carried away in the elevator. Then she went into the living room and tried the radio. "I don't want to go to school," a child screamed. "I hate school. I won't go to school. I hate school." "You will go to school," an enraged woman said. "We paid eight hundred dollars to get you into that school and you'll go if it kills you." The next number on the dial produced the worn record of the "Missouri Waltz." Irene shifted the control and invaded the privacy of several breakfast tables. She overheard demonstrations of indigestion, carnal love, abysmal vanity, faith, and despair. Irene's life was nearly as simple and sheltered as it appeared to be, and the forthright and sometimes brutal language that came from the loudspeaker that morning astonished and troubled her. She continued to listen until her maid came in. Then she turned off the radio quickly, since this insight, she realized, was a furtive one.

Irene had a luncheon date with a friend that day, and she left her apartment at a little after twelve. There were a number of women in the elevator when it stopped at her floor. She stared at their handsome and impassive faces, their furs, and the cloth flowers in their hats. Which one of them had been to Sea Island? she wondered. Which one had overdrawn her bank account? The elevator stopped at the tenth floor and a woman with a pair of Skye terriers joined them. Her hair was rigged high on her head and she wore a mink cape. She was humming the "Missouri Waltz."

Irene had two Martinis at lunch, and she looked searchingly at her friend and wondered what her secrets were. They had intended to go shopping after lunch, but Irene excused herself and went home. She told the maid that she was not to be disturbed; then she went into the living room, closed the doors, and switched on the radio. She heard, in the course of the afternoon, the halting conversation of a woman entertaining her aunt, the hysterical conclusion of a luncheon party, and a hostess briefing her maid about some cocktail guests. "Don't give the best Scotch to anyone who hasn't white hair," the hostess said. "See if you can get rid of that liver paste before you pass those hot things, and could you lend me five dollars? I want to tip the elevator man."

As the afternoon waned, the conversations increased in intensity. From where Irene sat, she could see the open sky above the East River. There were hundreds of clouds in the sky, as though the south wind had broken the winter into pieces and were blowing it north, and on her radio she could hear the arrival of cocktail guests and the return of children and businessmen from their schools and offices. "I found a good-sized diamond on the bathroom floor this morning," a woman said. "It must have fallen out of that bracelet Mrs. Dunston was wearing last night." "We'll sell it," a man said. "Take it down to the jeweler on Madison Avenue and sell it. Mrs. Dunston won't know the difference, and we could use a couple of hundred bucks . . ." "'Oranges and lemons, say the bells of St. Clement's,'" the Sweeneys' nurse sang. "'Halfpence and farthings, say the bells of St. Martin's. When will you pay me? say the bells at old Bailey . . .'" "It's not a hat," a woman cried, and at her back roared a cocktail party. "It's not a hat, it's a love affair. That's what Walter Florell said. He said it's not a hat, it's a love affair," and then, in a lower voice, the same woman added, "Talk to somebody, for Christ's sake, honey, talk to somebody. If she catches you standing here not talking to anybody, she'll take us off her invitation list, and I love these parties."

The Westcotts were going out for dinner that night, and when Jim came home, Irene was dressing. She seemed sad and vague, and he brought her a drink. They were dining with friends in the neighborhood, and they walked to where they were going. The sky was broad and filled with light. It was one of those splendid spring evenings that excite memory and desire, and the air that touched their hands and faces felt very soft. A Salvation Army band was on the corner playing "Jesus Is Sweeter." Irene drew on her husband's arm and held him there for a minute, to hear the music. "They're really such nice people, aren't they?" she said. "They have such nice faces. Actually, they're so much nicer than a lot of the people we know". She took a bill from her purse and walked over and dropped it into the tambourine. There was in her face, when she returned to her husband, a look of radiant melancholy that he was not familiar with. And her conduct at the dinner party that night seemed strange to him, too. She interrupted her hostess rudely and stared at the people across the table from her with an intensity for which she would have punished her children.

35   It was still mild when they walked home from the party, and Irene looked up at the spring stars. "'How far that little candle throws its beams,'" she exclaimed. "'So shines a good deed in a naughty world.'" She waited that night until Jim had fallen asleep, and then went into the living room and turned on the radio.

Jim came home at about six the next night. Emma, the maid, let him in, and he had taken off his hat and was taking off his coat when Irene ran into the hall. Her face was shining with tears and her hair was disordered. "Go up to 16-C, Jim!" she screamed. "Don't take off your coat. Go up to 16-C. Mr. Osborn's beating his wife. They've been quarreling since four o'clock, and now he's hitting her. Go up there and stop him."

From the radio in the living room, Jim heard screams, obscenities, and thuds. "You know you don't have to listen to this sort of thing," he said. He strode into the living room and turned the switch. "It's indecent," he said. "It's like looking in windows. You know you don't have to listen to this sort of thing. You can turn it off."

"Oh, it's so horrible, it's so dreadful," Irene was sobbing. "I've been listening all day, and it's so depressing."

"Well, if it's so depressing, why do you listen to it? I bought this damned radio to give you some pleasure," he said. "I paid a great deal of money for it. I thought it might make you happy. I wanted to make you happy."

40   "Don't, don't, don't, don't quarrel with me," she moaned, and laid her head on his shoulder. "All the others have been quarreling all day. Everybody's been quarreling. They're all worried about money. Mrs. Hutchinson's mother is dying of cancer in Florida and they don't have enough money to send her to the Mayo Clinic. At least, Mr. Hutchinson says they don't have enough money. And some woman in this building is having an affair with the handyman—with that hideous handyman. It's too disgusting. And Mrs. Melville has heart trouble and Mr. Hendricks is going to lose his job in April and Mrs. Hendricks is horrid about the whole thing and that girl who plays the 'Missouri Waltz' is a whore, a common whore, and the elevator man has tuberculosis and Mr. Osborn has been beating Mrs. Osborn." She wailed, she trembled with grief and checked the stream of tears down her face with the heel of her palm.

"Well, why do you have to listen?" Jim asked again. "Why do you have to listen to this stuff if it makes you so miserable?"

"Oh, don't, don't, don't," she cried. ("Life is too terrible, too sordid and awful.) But we've never been like that, have we, darling? Have we? I mean, we've always been good and decent and loving to one another, haven't we? And we have two children, two beautiful children. Our lives aren't sordid, are they, darling? Are they?" She flung her arms around his neck and drew his face down to hers. "We're happy, aren't we, darling? We are happy, aren't we?"

"Of course we're happy," he said tiredly. He began to surrender his resentment. "Of course we're happy. I'll have that damned radio fixed or taken away tomorrow." He stroked her soft hair. "My poor girl," he said.

"You love me, don't you?" she asked. "And we're not hypercritical or worried about money or dishonest, are we?"

45   "No, darling," he said.

A man came in the morning and fixed the radio. Irene turned it on cautiously and was happy to hear a California-wine commercial and a recording of Beethoven's Ninth Symphony, including Schiller's "Ode to Joy." She kept the radio on all day and nothing untoward came from the speaker.

A Spanish suite was being played when Jim came home. "Is everything all right?" he asked. His face was pale, she thought. They had some cocktails and went in to dinner to the "Anvil Chorus" from *Il Trovatore*. This was followed by Debussy's "La Mer."

"I paid the bill for the radio today," Jim said. "It cost four hundred dollars. I hope you'll get some enjoyment out of it."

"Oh, I'm sure I will," Irene said.

50   "Four hundred dollars is a good deal more than I can afford," he went on. "I wanted to get something that you'd enjoy. It's the last extravagance we'll be able to indulge in this year. I see that you haven't paid your clothing bills yet. I saw them on your dressing table." He looked directly at her. "Why did you tell me you'd paid them? Why did you lie to me?"

"I just didn't want you to worry, Jim," she said. She drank some water. "I'll be able to pay my bills out of this month's allowance. There were the slipcovers last month, and that partly)'."

"You've got to learn to handle the money I give you a little more intelligently, Irene," he said. "You've got to understand that we won't have as much money this year as we had last. I had a very sobering talk with Mitchell today. No one is buying anything. We're spending all our time promoting new issues, and you know how long that takes. I'm not getting any younger, you know. I'm thirty-seven. My hair will be gray next year. I haven't done as well as I'd hoped to do. And I don't suppose things will get any better."

"Yes, dear," she said.

"We've got to start cutting down," Jim said. "We've got to think of the children. To be perfectly frank with you, I worry about money a great deal. I'm not at all sure of the future. No one is. If anything should happen to me, there's the insurance, but that wouldn't go very far today. I've worked awfully hard to give you and the children a comfortable life," he said bitterly. "I don't like to see all of my energies, all of my youth, wasted in fur coats and radios and slipcovers and—"

55   "Please, Jim," she said. "Please. They'll hear us."

"*Who'll hear us?* Emma can't hear us."

"The radio."

"Oh, I'm sick!" he shouted. "I'm sick to death of your apprehensiveness. The radio can't hear us. Nobody can hear us. And what if they can hear us? Who cares?"

Irene got up from the table and went into the living room. Jim went to the door and shouted at her from there. "Why are you so Christly all of a sudden? What's turned you overnight into a convent girl? You stole your mother's jewelry before they probated her will. You never gave your sister a cent of that money that was intended for her—not even when she needed it. You made Grace Howland's life miserable, and where was all your piety and your virtue when you went to that abortionist? I'll never forget how cool you were. You packed your bag and went off to have that child murdered as if you were going to Nassau. If you'd had any reasons, if you'd had any good reasons—"

60   Irene stood for a minute before the hideous cabinet, disgraced and sickened, but she held her hand on the switch before she extinguished the music and the voices, hoping that the instrument might speak to her kindly, that she might hear the Sweeneys' nurse. Jim continued to shout at her from the door. The voice on the radio was suave and non-committal. "An early-morning railroad disaster in Tokyo," the loudspeaker said, "killed twenty-nine people. A fire in a Catholic hospital near Buffalo for the care of blind children was extinguished early this morning by nuns. The temperature is forty-seven. The humidity is eighty-nine."

[1947]

Joining the Conversation: Critical Thinking and Writing

1. Describe and explain the enormous radio. What does the radio look like? What is the strange power of the radio?
2. What does the radio reveal about the Westcott's neighbors? What sorts of activities and concerns comprise the lives of their neighbors? What does the radio reveal about the everyday lives of the respectable middle class?
3. Why does Irene become distraught by what she hears on the radio? After listening to the radio, she feels the need to quiz her husband. What does she question

her husband about? Consider the terms she uses, such as "sordid." What key
ideas does she feel she must ask her husband about?

4. Take inquiry notes that help to determine the meaning of the ending of the
story. Question elements of the ending, and then see if your answers to those
questions create an interpretation of the story. Why does Jim criticize Irene?
What past histories and current stresses are revealed? Why does the story end
with the broadcast of a set of disasters?

RAY BRADBURY

*Ray Bradbury (1920–2012) was born in Waukegan, Illinois, and he was educated
there and in Los Angeles, California. While he was a high school student, he
published his first work of science fiction in the school's magazine, and by 1941 he
was publishing professionally. The story printed here is from* The Illustrated Man
(1951), a collection of short stories. Among his other works are Fahrenheit 451
(1953), Something Wicked This Way Comes *(1962), and* Death Is a Lonely
Business *(1985).*

The Veldt

"George, I wish you'd look at the nursery."

"What's wrong with it?"

"I don't know."

"Well, then."

5   "I just want you to look at it, is all, or call a psychologist in to look at it."

"What would a psychologist want with a nursery?"

"You know very well what he'd want." His wife paused in the middle of the
kitchen and watched the stove busy humming to itself, making supper for four.

"It's just that the nursery is different now than it was."

"All right, let's have a look."

10   They walked down the hall of their soundproofed Happylife Home, which
had cost them thirty thousand dollars installed, this house which clothed and fed
and rocked them to sleep and played and sang and was good to them. Their
approach sensitized a switch somewhere and the nursery light flicked on when
they came within ten feet of it. Similarly, behind them, in the halls, lights went on
and off as they left them behind, with a soft automaticity.

"Well," said George Hadley.

They stood on the thatched floor of the nursery. It was forty feet across by
forty feet long and thirty feet high; it had cost half again as much as the rest of the
house. "But nothing's too good for our children," George had said.

The nursery was silent. It was empty as a jungle glade at hot high noon. The
walls were blank and two dimensional. Now, as George and Lydia Hadley stood in
the center of the room, the walls began to purr and recede into crystalline distance,
it seemed, and presently an African veldt appeared, in three dimensions, on all
sides, in color, reproduced to the final pebble and bit of straw. The ceiling above
them became a deep sky with a hot yellow sun.

George Hadley felt the perspiration start on his brow.

15   "Let's get out of this sun," he said. "This is a little too real. But I don't see anything wrong."

"Wait a moment, you'll see," said his wife.

Now the hidden odorophonics were beginning to blow a wind of odor at the two people in the middle of the baked veldtland. The hot straw smell of lion grass, the cool green smell of the hidden water hole, the great rusty smell of animals, the smell of dust like a red paprika in the hot air. And now the sounds: the thump of distant antelope feet on grassy sod, the papery rustling of vultures. A shadow passed through the sky. The shadow flickered on George Hadley's upturned, sweating face.

"Filthy creatures," he heard his wife say.

"The vultures."

20   "You see, there are the lions, far over, that way. Now they're on their way to the water hole. They've just been eating," said Lydia. "I don't know what."

"Some animal." George Hadley put his hand up to shield off the burning light from his squinted eyes. "A zebra or a baby giraffe, maybe."

"Are you sure?" His wife sounded peculiarly tense.

"No, it's a little late to be sure," he said, amused. "Nothing over there I can see but cleaned bone, and the vultures dropping for what's left."

"Did you hear that scream?" she asked.

25   "No."

"About a minute ago?"

"Sorry, no."

The lions were coming. And again George Hadley was filled with admiration for the mechanical genius who had conceived this room. A miracle of efficiency selling for an absurdly low price. Every home should have one. Oh, occasionally they frightened you with their clinical accuracy, they startled you, gave you a twinge, but most of the time what fun for everyone, not only your own son and daughter, but for yourself when you felt like a quick jaunt to a foreign land, a quick change of scenery. Well, here it was!

And here were the lions now, fifteen feet away, so real, so feverishly and startlingly real that you could feel the prickling fur on your hand, and your mouth was stuffed with the dusty upholstery smell of their heated pelts, and the yellow of them was in your eyes like the yellow of an exquisite French tapestry, the yellows of lions and summer grass, and the sound of the matted lion lungs exhaling on the silent noontide, and the smell of meat from the panting, dripping mouths.

30   The lions stood looking at George and Lydia Hadley with terrible green-yellow eyes.

"Watch out!" screamed Lydia.

The lions came running at them.

Lydia bolted and ran. Instinctively, George sprang after her. Outside, in the hall, with the door slammed, he was laughing and she was crying, and they both stood appalled at the other's reaction.

"George!"

35   "Lydia! Oh, my dear poor sweet Lydia!"

"They almost got us!"

"Walls, Lydia, remember; crystal walls, that's all they are. Oh, they look real, I must admit—Africa in your parlor—but it's all dimensional, superreactionary, supersensitive color film and mental tape film behind glass screens. It's all odorophonics and sonics, Lydia. Here's my handkerchief."

"I'm afraid." She came to him and put her body against him and cried steadily. "Did you see? Did you *feel*? It's too real."

"Now, Lydia . . ."

40   "You've got to tell Wendy and Peter not to read any more on Africa."

"Of course—of course." He patted her.

"Promise?"

"Sure."

"And lock the nursery for a few days until I get my nerves settled."

45   "You know how difficult Peter is about that. When I punished him a month ago by locking the nursery for even a few hours—the tantrum he threw! And Wendy too. They *live* for the nursery."

"It's got to be locked, that's all there is to it."

"All right." Reluctantly he locked the huge door. "You've been working too hard. You need a rest."

"I don't know—I don't know," she said, blowing her nose, sitting down in a chair that immediately began to rock and comfort her. "Maybe I don't have enough to do. Maybe I have time to think too much. Why don't we shut the whole house off for a few days and take a vacation?"

"You mean you want to fry my eggs for me?"

50   "Yes." She nodded.

"And darn my socks?"

"Yes." A frantic, watery-eyed nodding.

"And sweep the house?"

"Yes, yes—oh, yes!"

55   "But I thought that's why we bought this house, so we wouldn't have to do anything?"

"That's just it. I feel like I don't belong here. The house is wife and mother now, and nursemaid. Can I compete with an African veldt? Can I give a bath and scrub the children as efficiently or quickly as the automatic scrub bath can? I cannot. And it isn't just me. It's you. You've been awfully nervous lately."

"I suppose I have been smoking too much."

"You look as if you didn't know what to do with yourself in this house, either. You smoke a little more every morning and drink a little more every afternoon and need a little more sedative every night. You're beginning to feel unnecessary too."

"Am I?" He paused and tried to feel into himself to see what was really there.

60   "Oh, George!" She looked beyond him, at the nursery door. "Those lions can't get out of there, can they?"

He looked at the door and saw it tremble as if something had jumped against it from the other side.

"Of course not," he said.

At dinner they ate alone, for Wendy and Peter were at a special plastic carnival across town and had televised home to say they'd be late, to go ahead eating. So George Hadley, bemused, sat watching the dining-room table produce warm dishes of food from its mechanical interior.

"We forgot the ketchup," he said.

65   "Sorry," said a small voice within the table, and ketchup appeared.

As for the nursery, thought George Hadley, it won't hurt for the children to be locked out of it awhile. Too much of anything isn't good for anyone. And it was clearly indicated that the children had been spending a little too much time on Africa. That *sun*. He could feel it on his neck, still, like a hot paw. And the *lions*. And the smell of blood. Remarkable how the nursery caught the telepathic emanations of the children's minds and created life to fill their every' desire.

The children thought lions, and there were lions. The children thought zebras, and there were zebras. Sun—sun. Giraffes—giraffes. Death and death.

That *last*. He chewed tastelessly on the meat that the table had cut for him. Death thoughts. They were awfully young, Wendy and Peter, for death thoughts. Or, no, you were never too young, really. Long before you knew what death was you were wishing it on someone else. When you were two years old you were shooting people with cap pistols.

But this—the long, hot African veldt—the awful death in the jaws of a lion. And repeated again and again.

"Where are you going?"

He didn't answer Lydia. Preoccupied, he let the lights glow softly on ahead of him, extinguish behind him as he padded to the nursery door. He listened against it. Far away, a lion roared.

He unlocked the door and opened it. Just before he stepped inside, he heard a faraway scream. And then another roar from the lions, which subsided quickly.

He stepped into Africa. How many times in the last year had he opened this door and found Wonderland, Alice, the Mock Turtle, or Aladdin and his Magical Lamp, or Jack Pumpkinhead of Oz, or Dr. Doolittle, or the cow jumping over a very real-appearing moon—all the delightful contraptions of a make-believe world. How often had he seen Pegasus flying in the sky ceiling, or seen fountains of red fireworks, or heard angel voices singing. But now, this yellow hot Africa, this bake oven with murder in the heat. Perhaps Lydia was right. Perhaps they needed a little vacation from the fantasy which was growing a bit too real for ten-year-old children. It was all right to exercise one's mind with gymnastic fantasies, but when the lively child mind settled on *one* pattern . . . ? It seemed that, at a distance, for the past month, he had heard lions roaring, and smelled their strong odor seeping as far away as his study door. But, being busy, he had paid it no attention.

George Hadley stood on the African grassland alone. The lions looked up from their feeding, watching him. The only flaw to the illusion was the open door through which he could see his wife, far down the dark hall, like a framed picture, eating her dinner abstractedly.

"Go away," he said to the lions.

They did not go.

He knew the principle of the room exactly. You sent out your thoughts. Whatever you thought would appear.

"Let's have Aladdin and his lamp," he snapped.

The veldtland remained; the lions remained.

"Come on, room! I demand Aladdin!" he said.

Nothing happened. The lions mumbled in their baked pelts.

"Aladdin!"

He went back to dinner. "The fool room's out of order," he said. "It won't respond."

"Or—"

"Or what?"

"Or it *can't* respond," said Lydia, "because the children have thought about Africa and lions and killing so many days that the room's in a rut."

"Could be."

"Or Peter's set it to remain that way."

"Set it?"

"He may have got into the machinery and fixed something."

"Peter doesn't know machinery."

"He's a wise one for ten. That I.Q. of his—"

"Nevertheless—"

"Hello, Mom. Hello, Dad."

The Hadleys turned. Wendy and Peter were coming in the front door, cheeks like peppermint candy, eyes like bright blue agate marbles, a smell of ozone on their jumpers from their trip in the helicopter.

95   "You're just in time for supper," said both parents.

"We're full of strawberry ice cream and hot dogs," said the children, holding hands. "But we'll sit and watch."

"Yes, come tell us about the nursery," said George Hadley.

The brother and sister blinked at him and then at each other. "Nursery?"

"All about Africa and everything," said the father with false joviality.

100   "I don't understand," said Peter.

"Your mother and I were just traveling through Africa with rod and reel; Tom Swift and his Electric Lion," said George Hadley.

"There's no Africa in the nursery," said Peter simply.

"Oh, come now, Peter. We know better."

"I don't remember any Africa," said Peter to Wendy. "Do you?"

105   "No."

"Run see and come tell."

She obeyed.

"Wendy, come back here!" said George Hadley, but she was gone. The house lights followed her like a flock of fireflies. Too late, he realized he had forgotten to lock the nursery door after his last inspection.

"Wendy'll look and come tell us," said Peter.

110   "She doesn't have to tell *me*. I've seen it."

"I'm sure you're mistaken, Father."

"I'm not, Peter. Come along now."

But Wendy was back. "It's not Africa," she said breathlessly.

"We'll see about this," said George Hadley, and they all walked down the hall together and opened the nursery door.

115   There was a green, lovely forest, a lovely river, a purple mountain, high voices singing, and Rima, lovely and mysterious, lurking in the trees with colorful flights of butterflies, like animated bouquets, lingering in her long hair. The African veldt-land was gone. The lions were gone. Only Rima was here now, singing a song so beautiful that it brought tears to your eyes.

George Hadley looked in at the changed scene. "Go to bed," he said to the children.

They opened their mouths.

"You heard me," he said.

They went off to the air closet, where a wind sucked them like brown leaves up the flue to their slumber rooms.

120   George Hadley walked through the singing glade and picked up something that lay in the corner where the lions had been. He walked slowly back to his wife.

"What is that?" she asked.

"An old wallet of mine," he said.

He showed it to her. The smell of hot grass was on it and the smell of a lion. There were drops of saliva on it, it had been chewed, and there were blood smears on both sides.

He closed the nursery' door and locked it, tight.

125 In the middle the night he was still awake and he knew his wife was awake. "Do you think Wendy changed it?" she said at last, in the dark room.

"Of course."

"Made it from a veldt into a forest and put Rima there instead of lions?"

"Yes."

"Why?"

130 "I don't know. But it's staying locked until I find out."

"How did your wallet get there?"

"I don't know anything," he said, "except that I'm beginning to be sorry we bought that room for the children. If children are neurotic at all, a room like that—"

"It's supposed to help them work off their neuroses in a healthful way."

"I'm starting to wonder." He stared at the ceiling.

135 "We've given the children everything they ever wanted. Is this our reward—secrecy, disobedience?"

"Who was it said, 'Children are carpets, they should be stepped on occasionally'? We've never lifted a hand. They're insufferable—let's admit it. They come and go when they like; they treat us as if we were offspring. They're spoiled and we're spoiled."

"They've been acting funny ever since you forbade them to take the rocket to New York a few months ago."

"They're not old enough to do that alone, I explained."

"Nevertheless, I've noticed they've been decidedly cool toward us since."

140 "I think I'll have David McClean come tomorrow morning to have a look at Africa."

"But it's not Africa now, it's *Green Mansions* country and Rima."

"I have a feeling it'll be Africa again before then."

A moment later they heard the screams.

Two screams. Two people screaming from downstairs. And then a roar of lions.

145 "Wendy and Peter aren't in their rooms," said his wife.

He lay in his bed with his beating heart. "No," he said. "They've broken into the nursery."

"Those, screams—they sound familiar."

"Do they?"

"Yes, awfully."

150 And although their beds tried very hard, the two adults couldn't be rocked to sleep for another hour. A smell of cats was in the night air.

"Father?" said Peter.

"Yes."

Peter looked at his shoes. He never looked at his father anymore, nor at his mother. "You aren't going to lock up the nursery for good, are you?"

"That all depends."

155 "On what?" snapped Peter.

"On you and your sister. If you intersperse this Africa with a little variety—oh, Sweden perhaps, or Denmark or China—"

"I thought we were free to play as we wished."

"You are, within reasonable bounds."

"What's wrong with Africa, Father?"

160 "Oh, so now you admit you have been conjuring up Africa, do you?"

"I wouldn't want the nursery locked up," said Peter coldly. "Ever."

"Matter of fact, we're thinking of turning the whole house off for about a month. Live sort of a carefree one-for-all existence."

"That sounds dreadful! Would I have to tie my own shoes instead of letting the shoe tier do it? And brush my own teeth and comb my hair and give myself a bath?"

"It would be fun for a change, don't you think?"

165   "No, it would be horrid. I didn't like it when you took out the picture painter last month."

"That's because I wanted you to learn to paint all by yourself, son."

"I don't want to do anything but look and listen and smell; what else *is* there to do?"

"All right, go play in Africa."

"Will you shut off the house sometime soon?"

170   "We're considering it."

"I don't think you'd better consider it any more, Father."

"I won't have any threats from my son!"

"Very well." And Peter strolled off to the nursery.

"Am I on time?" said David McClean.

175   "Breakfast?" asked George Hadley.

"Thanks, had some. What's the trouble?"

"David, you're a psychologist."

"I should hope so."

"Well, then, have a look at our nursery. You saw it a year ago when you dropped by; did you notice anything peculiar about it then?"

180   "Can't say I did; the usual violence, a tendency toward a slight paranoia here or there, usual in children because they feel persecuted by parents constantly, but, oh, really nothing."

They walked down the hall. "I locked the nursery up," explained the father, "and the children broke back into it during the night. I let them stay so they could form the patterns for you to see."

"There was a terrible screaming from the nursery."

"There it is," said George Hadley. "See what you make of it."

They walked in on the children without rapping.

185   The screams had faded. The lions were feeding.

"Run outside a moment, children," said George Hadley. "No, don't change the mental combination. Leave the walls as they are. Get!"

With the children gone, the two men stood studying the lions clustered at a distance, eating with great relish whatever it was they had caught.

"I wish I knew what it was," said George Hadley. "Sometimes I can almost see. Do you think if I brought high-powered binoculars here and—"

David McClean laughed dryly. "Hardly." He turned to study all four walls. "How long has this been going on?"

190   "A little over a month."

"It certainly doesn't *feel* good."

"I want facts, not feelings."

"My dear George, a psychologist never saw a fact in his life. He only hears about feelings; vague things. This doesn't feel good, I tell you. Trust my hunches and my instincts. I have a nose for something bad. This is very bad. My advice to you is to have the whole damn room torn down and your children brought to me every day during the next year for treatment."

"Is it that bad?"

195 "I'm afraid so. One of the original uses of these nurseries was so that we could study the patterns left on the walls by the child's mind, study at our leisure, and help the child. In this case, however, the room has become a channel toward—destructive thoughts, instead of a release away from them."

"Didn't you sense this before?"

"I sensed only that you had spoiled your children more than most. And now you're letting them down in some way. What way?"

"I wouldn't let them go to New York."

"What else?"

200 "I've taken a few machines from the house and threatened them, a month ago, with closing up the nursery unless they did their homework. I did close it for a few days to show I meant business."

"Ah, ha!"

"Does that mean anything?"

"Everything. Where before they had a Santa Claus now they have a Scrooge. Children prefer Santas. You've let this room and this house replace you and your wife in your children's affections. This room is their mother and father, far more important in their lives than their real parents. And now you come along and want to shut it off. No wonder there's hatred here. You can feel it coming out of the sky. Feel that sun. George, you'll have to change your life. Like too many others, you've built it around creature comforts. Why, you'd starve tomorrow if something went wrong in your kitchen. You wouldn't know how to tap an egg. Nevertheless, turn everything off. Start new. It'll take time. But we'll make good children out of bad in a year, wait and see."

"But won't the shock be too much for the children, shutting the room up abruptly, for good?"

205 "I don't want them going any deeper into this, that's all."

The lions were finished with their red feast.

The lions were standing on the edge of the clearing watching the two men.

"Now *I'm* feeling persecuted," said McClean. "Let's get out of here. I never have cared for these damned rooms. Make me nervous."

"The lions look real, don't they?" said George Hadley. "I don't suppose there's any way—"

210 "What?"

"—that they could *become* real?"

"Not that I know."

"Some flaw in the machinery, a tampering or something?"

"No."

215 They went to the door.

"I don't imagine the room will like being turned off," said the father.

"Nothing ever likes to die—even a room."

"I wonder if it hates me for wanting to switch it off?"

"Paranoia is thick around here today," said David McClean. "You can follow it like a spoor. Hello." He bent and picked up a bloody scarf. "This yours?"

220 "No." George Hadley's face was rigid. "It belongs to Lydia."

They went to the fuse box together and threw the switch that killed the nursery.

The two children were in hysterics. They screamed and pranced and threw things. They yelled and sobbed and swore and jumped at the furniture.

"You can't do that to the nursery, you can't!"

"Now, children."

225   The children flung themselves onto a couch, weeping.

"George," said Lydia Hadley, "turn on the nursery', just for a few moments. You can't be so abrupt."

"No."

"You can't be so cruel."

"Lydia, it's off, and it stays off. And the whole damn house dies as of here and now. The more I see of the mess we've put ourselves in, the more it sickens me. We've been contemplating our mechanical, electronic navels for too long. My God, how we need a breath of honest air!"

230   And he marched about the house turning off the voice clocks, the stoves, the heaters, the shoe shiners, the shoe lacers, the body scrubbers and swabbers and massagers, and every' other machine he could put his hand to.

The house was full of dead bodies, it seemed. It felt like a mechanical cemetery. So silent. None of the humming hidden energy of machines waiting to function at the tap of a button.

"Don't let them do it!" wailed Peter at the ceiling, as if he was talking to the house, the nursery. "Don't let Father kill everything." He turned to his father. "Oh, I hate you!"

"Insults won't get you anywhere."

"I wish you were dead!"

235   "We were, for a long while. Now we're going to really start living. Instead of being handled and massaged, we're going to *live*."

Wendy was still crying and Peter joined her again. "Just a moment, just one moment, just another moment of nursery," they wailed.

"Oh, George," said the wife, "it can't hurt."

"All right—all right, if they'll just shut up. One minute, mind you, and then off forever."

"Daddy, Daddy, Daddy!" sang the children, smiling with wet faces.

240   "And then we're going on a vacation. David McClean is coming back in half an hour to help us move out and get to the airport. I'm going to dress. You turn the nursery on for a minute, Lydia, just a minute, mind you."

And the three of them went babbling off while he let himself be vacuumed upstairs through the air flue and set about dressing himself. A minute later Lydia appeared.

"I'll be glad when we get away," she sighed.

"Did you leave them in the nursery?"

"I wanted to dress too. Oh, that horrid Africa. What can they see in it?"

245   "Well, in five minutes we'll be on our way to Iowa. Lord, how did we ever get in this house? What prompted us to buy a nightmare?"

"Pride, money, foolishness."

"I think we'd better get downstairs before those kids get engrossed with those damned beasts again."

Just then they heard the children calling, "Daddy, Mommy, come quick—quick!"

They went downstairs in the air flue and ran down the hall. The children were nowhere in sight. "Wendy? Peter!"

250   They ran into the nursery. The veldtland was empty save for the lions waiting, looking at them. "Peter, Wendy?"

The door slammed.

"Wendy, Peter!"

George Hadley and his wife whirled and ran back to the door.

"Open the door!" cried George Hadley, trying the knob. "Why, they've locked it from the outside! Peter!" He beat at the door. "Open up!"

255 He heard Peter's voice outside, against the door.

"Don't let them switch off the nursery' and the house," he was saying.

Mr. and Mrs. George Hadley beat at the door. "Now, don't be ridiculous, children. It's time to go. Mr. McClean'll be here in a minute and . . ."

And then they heard the sounds.

The lions on three sides of them, in the yellow veldt grass, padding through the dry straw, rumbling and roaring in their throats.

260 The lions.

Mr. Hadley looked at his wife and they turned and looked back at the beasts edging slowly forward, crouching, tails stiff.

Mr. and Mrs. Hadley screamed.

And suddenly they realized why those other screams had sounded familiar.

"Well, here I am," said David McClean in the nursery doorway. "Oh, hello." He stared at the two children seated in the center of the open glade eating a little picnic lunch. Beyond them was the water hole and the yellow veldtland; above was the hot sun. He began to perspire. "Where are your father and mother?"

265 The children looked up and smiled. "Oh, they'll be here directly."

"Good, we must get going." At a distance, Mr. McClean saw the lions fighting and clawing and then quieting down to feed in silence under the shady trees.

He squinted at the lions with his hand up to his eyes.

Now the lions were done feeding. They moved to the water hole to drink.

A shadow flickered over Mr. McClean's hot face. Many shadows flickered. The vultures were dropping down the blazing sky.

270 "A cup of tea?" asked Wendy in the silence.

[1950]

Joining the Conversation: Critical Thinking and Writing

1. The Veldt features a "Happylife" home. Explain the technology that has been installed in the nursery. What does this technology do?
2. What happens at the end of the story? Why is the ending horrific? The final events are not explained, but they are left for the reader to deduce. How does Bradbury make the ending more horrific by relying on the reader's understanding of the situation?
3. Write an analytical paper that focuses on the relationship between the children, Wendy and Peter, and their parents, George and Lydia. How do the children manipulate their parents? What is the character David McClean's analysis of the relationship and the nursery?
4. Explore how the story builds suspense. Trace the imagery of the eating lions. How does the image become more ominous over the course of the story?

STEPHEN KING

Stephen King, with more than three hundred and fifty million copies of his books in print, is one of America's most popular authors. King was born in Portland, Maine, in 1947. After graduating from the University of Maine, he taught high school English until he was able to devote himself full-time to writing. The author of numerous stories and novels, King is lauded as one of the most important and innovative practitioners of contemporary horror fiction. Many of King's novels have been made into popular films, reaching a huge audience and attesting to his cultural influence. His most well-known novels include Carrie *(1974),* The Shining *(1977), and* Misery *(1987).*

Word Processor of the Gods

At first glance it looked like a Wang word processor—it had a Wang keyboard and a Wang casing. It was only on second glance that Richard Hagstrom saw that the casing had been split open (and not gently, either; it looked to him as if the job had been done with a hacksaw blade) to admit a slightly larger IBM cathode tube. The archive discs, which had come with this odd mongrel, were not floppy at all; they were as hard as the 45's Richard had listened to as a kid.

"What in the name of God is that?" Lina asked as he and Mr. Nordhoff lugged it over to his study piece by piece. Mr. Nordhoff had lived next door to Richard Hagstrom's brother's family . . . Roger, Belinda, and their boy, Jonathan.

"Something Jon built," Richard said. "Meant for me to have it, Mr. Nordhoff says. It looks like a word processor."

"Oh yeah," Nordhoff said. He would not see his sixties again and he was badly out of breath. "That's what he said it was, the poor kid . . . think we could set it down for a minute, Mr. Hagstrom? I'm pooped."

5   "You bet," Richard said, and then called to his son, Seth, who was tooling odd, atonal chords out of his Fender guitar downstairs—the room Richard had envisioned as a "family room" when he had first paneled it had become his son's "rehearsal hall" instead.

"Seth!" he yelled. "Come give us a hand!"

Downstairs, Seth just went on warping chords out of the Fender. Richard looked at Mr. Nordhoff and shrugged, ashamed and unable to hide it. Nordhoff shrugged back as if to say Kids! Who expects anything better from them these days? Except they both knew that Jon—poor doomed Jon Hagstrom, his crazy brother's son—had been better.

"You were good to help me with this," Richard said.

Nordhoff shrugged. "What else has an old man got to do with his time? And I guess it was the least I could do for Johnny. He used to cut my lawn gratis, do you know that? I wanted to pay him, but the kid wouldn't take it. He was quite a boy." Nordhoff was still out of breath. "Do you think I could have a glass of water, Mr. Hagstrom?"

10   "You bet." He got it himself when his wife didn't move from the kitchen table, where she was reading a bodice-ripper paperback and eating a Twinkie. "Seth!" he yelled again. "Come on up here and help us, okay?"

But Seth just went on playing muffled and rather sour bar chords on the Fender for which Richard was still paying.

He invited Nordhoff to stay for supper, but Nordhoff refused politely. Richard nodded, embarrassed again but perhaps hiding it a little better this time. What's a nice guy like you doing with a family like that? his friend Bernie Epstein had asked him once, and Richard had only been able to shake his head, feeling the same dull embarrassment he was feeling now. He was a nice guy. And yet somehow this was what he had come out with—an overweight, sullen wife who felt cheated out of the good things in life, who felt that she had backed the losing horse (but who would never come right out and say so), and an uncommunicative fifteen-year-old son who was doing marginal work in the same school where Richard taught . . . a son who played weird chords on the guitar morning, noon and night (mostly night) and who seemed to think that would somehow be enough to get him through.

"Well, what about a beer?" Richard asked. He was reluctant to let Nordhoff go—he wanted to hear more about Jon.

"A beer would taste awful good," Nordhoff said, and Richard nodded gratefully. "Fine," he said, and went back to get them a couple of Buds.

15   His study was in a small shed-like building that stood apart from the house—like the family room, he had fixed it up himself. But unlike the family room, this was a place he thought of as his own—a place where he could shut out the stranger he had married and the stranger she had given birth to.

Lina did not, of course, approve of him having his own place, but she had not been able to stop it—it was one of the few little victories he had managed over her.

He supposed that in a way she had backed a losing horse—when they had gotten married sixteen years before, they had both believed he would write wonderful, lucrative novels and they would both soon be driving around in Mercedes-Benzes. But the one novel he had published had not been lucrative, and the critics had been quick to point out that it wasn't very wonderful, either. Una had seen things the critics' way, and that had been the beginning of their drifting apart.

So the high school teaching job which both of them had seen as only a stepping-stone on their way to fame, glory, and riches, had now been their major source of income for the last fifteen years—one helluva long stepping-stone, he sometimes thought. But he had never quite let go of his dream. He wrote short stories and the occasional article. He was a member in good standing of the Authors Guild. He brought in about $5,000 in additional income with his typewriter each year, and no matter how much Una might grouse about it, that rated him his own study . . . especially since she refused to work.

"You've got a nice place here," Nordhoff said, looking around the small room with the mixture of old-fashioned prints on the walls. The mongrel word processor sat on the desk with the CPU tucked underneath. Richard's old Olivetti electric had been put aside for the time being on top of one of the filing cabinets.

20   "It serves the purpose," Richard said. He nodded at the word processor. "You don't suppose that thing really works, do you? Jon was only fourteen."

"Looks funny, doesn't it?"

"It sure does," Richard agreed.

Nordhoff laughed. "You don't know the half of it," he said. "I peeked down into the back of the video unit. Some of the wires are stamped IBM, and some are stamped Radio Shack. There's most of a Western Electric telephone in there. And believe it or not, there's a small motor from an Erector Set." He sipped his beer and said in a kind of afterthought: "Fifteen. He just turned fifteen. A couple of days before the accident." He paused and said it again, looking down at his bottle of beer. "Fifteen." He didn't say it loudly.

"Erector Set?" Richard blinked at the old man.

25   "That's right. Erector Set puts out an electric model kit. Jon had one of them, since he was . . . oh, maybe six. I gave it to him for Christmas one year. He was crazy for gadgets even then. Any kind of gadget would do him, and did that little box of Erector Set motors tickle him? I guess it did. He kept it for almost ten years. Not many kids do that, Mr. Hagstrom."

"No," Richard said, thinking of the boxes of Seth's toys he had lugged out over the years—discarded, forgotten, or wantonly broken. He glanced at the word processor. "It doesn't work, then."

"I wouldn't bet on that until you try it," Nordhoff said. "The kid was damn near an electrical genius."

"That's sort of pushing it, I think. I know he was good with gadgets, and he won the State Science Fair when he was in the sixth grade—"

"Competing against kids who were much older—high school seniors some of them," Nordhoff said. "Or that's what his mother said."

30   "It's true. We were all very proud of him." Which wasn't exactly true. Richard had been proud, and Jon's mother had been proud; the boy's father didn't give a shit at all. "But Science Fair projects and building your very own hybrid word-cruncher—" He shrugged.

Nordhoff set his beer down. "There was a kid back in the fifties," he said, "who made an atom smasher out of two soup cans and about five dollars' worth of electrical equipment. Jon told me about that. And he said there was a kid out in some hick town in New Mexico who discovered tachyons—negative particles that are supposed to travel backwards through time—in 1954. A kid in Waterbury, Connecticut—eleven years old—who made a pipe-bomb out of the celluloid he scraped off the backs of a deck of playing cards. He blew up an empty dog-house with it. Kids're funny sometimes. The super smart ones in particular. You might be surprised."

"Maybe. Maybe I will be."

"He was a fine boy, regardless."

"You loved him a little, didn't you?"

35   "Mr. Hagstrom," Nordhoff said, "I loved him a lot. He was a genuinely all-right kid."

And Richard thought how strange it was—his brother, who had been an utter shit since the age of six, had gotten a fine woman and a fine bright son. He himself, who had always tried to be gentle and good (whatever "good" meant in this crazy world), had married Lina, who had developed into a silent, piggy woman, and had gotten Seth by her. Looking at Nordhoff's honest, tired face, he found himself wondering exactly how that had happened and how much of it had been his own fault, a natural result of his own quiet weakness.

"Yes," Richard said. "He was, wasn't he?"

"Wouldn't surprise me if it worked," Nordhoff said. "Wouldn't surprise me at all." After Nordhoff had gone, Richard Hagstrom plugged the word processor in and turned it on. There was a hum, and he waited to see if the letters IBM would come up on the face of the screen. They did not. Instead, eerily, like a voice from the grave, these words swam up, green ghosts, from the darkness:

HAPPY BIRTHDAY, UNCLE RICHARD! JON.

40   "Christ," Richard whispered, sitting down hard. The accident that had killed his brother, his wife, and their son had happened two weeks before—they had been coming back from some sort of day trip and Roger had been drunk. Being drunk was a perfectly ordinary occurrence in the life of Roger Hagstrom. But this time his luck had simply run out and he had driven his dusty old van off the edge of a ninety-foot drop. It had crashed and burned. Jon was fourteen—no, fifteen. Just turned fifteen a couple of days before the accident, the old man said. Another three years and he would have gotten free of that hulking, stupid bear. His birthday . . . and mine coming up soon.

A week from today. The word processor had been Jon's birthday present for him.

That made it worse, somehow. Richard could not have said precisely how, or why, but it did. He reached out to turn off the screen and then withdrew his hand.

Some kid made an atom smasher out of two soup cans and five dollars' worth of auto electrical parts.

Yeah, and the New York City sewer system is full of alligators and the U.S. Air Force has the body of an alien on ice somewhere in Nebraska. Tell me a few more.

It's bullshit. But maybe that's something I don't want to know for sure.

He got up, went around to the back of the VDT, and looked through the slots. Yes, it was as Nordhoff had said. Wires stamped RADIO SHACK MADE IN TAIWAN. Wires stamped WESTERN ELECTRIC and WESTREX and ERECTOR SET, with the little circled trademark r. And he saw something else, something Nordhoff had either missed or hadn't wanted to mention. There was a Lionel Train transformer in there, wired up like the Bride of Frankenstein.

"Christ," he said, laughing but suddenly near tears. "Christ, Jonny, what did you think you were doing?"

But he knew that, too. He had dreamed and talked about owning a word processor for years, and when Lina's laughter became too sarcastic to bear, he had talked about it to Jon. "I could write faster, rewrite faster, and submit more," he remembered telling Jon last summer—the boy had looked at him seriously, his light blue eyes, intelligent but always so carefully wary, magnified behind his glasses. "It would be great . . . really great."

"Then why don't you get one, Uncle Rich?"

"They don't exactly give them away," Richard had said, smiling. "The Radio Shack model starts at around three grand. From there you can work yourself up into the eighteen-thousand-dollar range."

"Well, maybe I'll build you one sometime," Jon had said.

"Maybe you just will," Richard had said, clapping him on the back. And until Nordhoff had called, he had thought no more about it.

Wires from hobby-shop electrical models.

A Lionel Train transformer.

Christ.

He went around to the front again, meaning to turn it off, as if to actually try to write something on it and fail would somehow defile what his earnest, fragile (doomed) nephew had intended.

Instead, he pushed the EXECUTE button on the board. A funny little chill scraped across his spine as he did it—EXECUTE was a funny word to use, when you thought of it. It wasn't a word he associated with writing; it was a word he associated with gas chambers and electric chairs . . . and, perhaps, with dusty old vans plunging off the sides of roads.

EXECUTE.

The CPU was humming louder than any he had ever heard on the occasions when he had window-shopped word processors; it was, in fact, almost roaring. What's in the memory-box, Jon? he wondered. Bed springs? Train transformers all in a row? Soup cans? He thought again of Jon's eyes, of his still and delicate face. Was it strange, maybe even sick, to be jealous of another man's son?

But he should have been mine. I knew it . . . and I think he knew it, too. And then there was Belinda, Roger's wife. Belinda who wore sunglasses too often on cloudy days. The big ones, because those bruises around the eyes have a nasty way of spreading. But he looked at her sometimes, sitting there still and watchful in the loud umbrella of Roger's laughter, and he thought almost the exact same thing: She should have been mine.

It was a terrifying thought, because they had both known Belinda in high school and had both dated her. He and Roger had been two years apart in age and

Belinda had been perfectly between them, a year older than Richard and a year younger than Roger. Richard had actually been the first to date the girl who would grow up to become Jon's mother. Then Roger had stepped in, Roger who was older and bigger, Roger who always got what he wanted, Roger who would hurt you if you tried to stand in his way.

I got scared. 1 got scared and I let her get away. Was it as simple as that? Dear God help me, I think it was. I'd like to have it a different way, but perhaps it's best not to lie to yourself about such things as cowardice. And shame.

And if those things were true—if Lina and Seth had somehow belonged with his no-good of a brother and if Belinda and Jon had somehow belonged with him, what did that prove? And exactly how was a thinking person supposed to deal with such an absurdly balanced screw-up? Did you laugh? Did you scream? Did you shoot yourself for a yellow dog?

Wouldn't surprise me if it worked. Wouldn't surprise me at all.

65   EXECUTE.

His fingers moved swiftly over the keys. He looked at the screen and saw these letters floating green on the surface of the screen:

MY BROTHER WAS A WORTHLESS DRUNK.

They floated there and Richard suddenly thought of a toy he had had when he was a kid. It was called a Magic Eight-Ball. You asked it a question that could be answered yes or no and then you turned the Magic Eight-Ball over to see what it had to say on the subject—its phony yet somehow entrancingly mysterious responses included such things as IT IS ALMOST CERTAIN, I WOULD NOT PLAN ON IT, and ASK AGAIN LATER

Roger had been jealous of that toy, and finally, after bullying Richard into giving it to him one day, Roger had thrown it onto the sidewalk as hard as he could, breaking it. Then he had laughed. Sitting here now, listening to the strangely choppy roar from the CPU cabinet Jon had jury-rigged, Richard remembered how he had collapsed to the sidewalk, weeping, unable to believe his brother had done such a thing.

70   "Bawl-baby, bawl-baby, look at the baby bawl," Roger had taunted him. "It wasn't nothing but a cheap, shitty toy anyway, Richie. Lookit there, nothing in it but a bunch of little signs and a lot of water."

"I'M TELLING!" Richard had shrieked at the top of his lungs. His head felt hot. His sinuses were stuffed shut with tears of outrage. "I'M TELLING ON YOU, ROGER! I'M TELLING MOM!"

"You tell and I'll break your arm," Roger said, and in his chilling grin Richard had seen he meant it. He had not told.

MY BROTHER WAS A WORTHLESS DRUNK.

Well, weirdly put together or not, it screen-printed. Whether it would store information in the CPU still remained to be seen, but Jon's mating of a Wang board to an IBM screen had actually worked. Just coincidentally it called up some pretty crappy memories, but he didn't suppose that was Jon's fault.

75   He looked around his office, and his eyes happened to fix on the one picture in here that he hadn't picked and didn't like. It was a studio portrait of Lina, her Christmas present to him two years ago. I want you to hang it in your study, she'd said, and so of course he had done just that. It was, he supposed, her way of keeping an eye on him even when she wasn't here. Don't forget me, Richard. I'm here. Maybe I backed the wrong horse, but I'm still here. And you better remember it.

The studio portrait with its unnatural tints went oddly with the amiable mixture of prints by Whistler, Homer, and N. C. Wyeth. Lina's eyes were half-lidded, the heavy Cupid's bow of her mouth composed in something that was not quite a smile. Still here, Richard, her mouth said to him. And don t you forget it.

He typed:

MY WIFE'S PHOTOGRAPH HANGS ON THE WEST WALL OF MY STUDY

He looked at the words and liked them no more than he liked the picture itself. He punched the DELETE button. The words vanished. Now there was nothing at all on the screen but the steadily pulsing cursor.

80   He looked up at the wall and saw that his wife's picture had also vanished.

He sat there for a very long time—it felt that way, at least—looking at the wall where the picture had been. What finally brought him out of his daze of utter unbelieving shock was the smell from the CPU—a smell he remembered from his childhood as clearly as he remembered the Magic Eight-Ball Roger had broken because it wasn't his. The smell was essence of electric train transformer. When you smelled that you were supposed to turn the thing off so it could cool down.

And so he would.

In a minute.

He got up and walked over to the wall on legs which felt numb. He ran his fingers over the Armstrong paneling. The picture had been here, yes, right here. But it was gone now, and the hook it had hung on was gone, and there was no hole where he had screwed the hook into the paneling.

85   Gone.

The world abruptly went gray and he staggered backwards, thinking dimly that he was going to faint. He held on grimly until the world swam back into focus.

He looked from the blank place on the wall where Lina's picture had been to the word processor his dead nephew had cobbled together.

You might be surprised, he heard Nordhoff saying in his mind. You might be surprised, you might be surprised, oh yes, if some kid in the fifties could discover particles that travel backwards through time, you might be surprised what your genius of a nephew could do with a bunch of discarded word processor elements and some wires and electrical components. You might be so surprised that you'll feel as if you're going insane.

The transformer smell was richer, stronger now, and he could see wisps of smoke rising from the vents in the screen housing. The noise from the CPU was louder, too. It was time to turn it off—smart as Jon had been, he apparently hadn't had time to work out all the bugs in the crazy thing.

90   But had he known it would do this?

Feeling like a figment of his own imagination, Richard sat down in front of the screen again and typed:

MY WIFE'S PICTURE IS ON THE WALL

He looked at this for a moment, looked back at the keyboard, and then hit the EXECUTE key.

He looked at the wall.

95   Lina's picture was back, right where it had always been.

"Jesus," he whispered. "Jesus Christ."

He rubbed a hand up his cheek, looked at the keyboard (blank again now except for the cursor), and then typed:

MY FLOOR IS BARE

He then touched the INSERT button and typed:

100   EXCEPT FOR TWELVE TWENTY-DOLLAR GOLD PIECES IN A SMALL COTTON SACK He pressed EXECUTE.

He looked at the floor, where there was now a small white cotton sack with a drawstring top. WELLS FARGO was stenciled on the bag in faded black ink.

"Dear Jesus," he heard himself saying in a voice that wasn't his. "Dear Jesus, dear good Jesus—"

He might have gone on invoking the Savior's name for minutes or hours if the word processor had not started beeping at him steadily. Flashing across the top of the screen was the word OVERLOAD.

Richard turned off everything in a hurry and left his study as if all the devils of hell were after him.

105   But before he went he scooped up the small drawstring sack and put it in his pants pocket.

When he called Nordhoff that evening, a cold November wind was playing tuneless bagpipes in the trees outside. Seth s group was downstairs, murdering a Bob Seger tune. Lina was out at Our Lady of Perpetual Sorrows, playing bingo.

"Does the machine work?" Nordhoff asked.

"It works, all right," Richard said. He reached into his pocket and brought out a coin. It was heavy—heavier than a Rolex watch. An eagle's stern profile was embossed on one side, along with the date 1871. "It works in ways you wouldn't believe."

"I might," Nordhoff said evenly. "He was a very bright boy, and he loved you very much, Mr. Hagstrom. But be careful. A boy is only a boy, bright or otherwise, and love can be misdirected. Do you take my meaning?"

110   Richard didn't take his meaning at all. He felt hot and feverish. That day's paper had listed the current market price of gold at $514 an ounce. The coins had weighed out at an average of 4.5 ounces each on his postal scale. At the current market rate that added up to $27,756. And he guessed that was perhaps only a quarter of what he could realize for those coins if he sold them as coins.

"Mr. Nordhoff, could you come over here? Now? Tonight?"

"No," Nordhoff said. "No, I don't think I want to do that, Mr. Hagstrom. I think this ought to stay between you and Jon."

"But—"

"Just remember what I said. For Christ's sake, be careful." There was a small click and Nordhoff was gone.

115   He found himself out in his study again half an hour later, looking at the word processor. He touched the ON/OFF key but didn't turn it on just yet. The second time Nordhoff said it, Richard had heard it. For Christ's sake, be careful. Yes. He would have to be careful. A machine that could do such a thing—How could a machine do such a thing?

He had no idea . . . but in a way, that made the whole crazy thing easier to accept. He was an English teacher and sometime writer, not a technician, and he had a long history of not understanding how things worked: phonographs, gasoline engines, telephones, televisions, the flushing mechanism in his toilet. His life had been a history of understanding operations rather than principles. Was there any difference here, except in degree?

He turned the machine on. As before it said: HAPPY BIRTHDAY, UNCLE RICHARD! JON. He pushed EXECUTE and the message from his nephew disappeared.

This machine is not going to work for long, he thought suddenly. He felt sure that Jon must have still been working on it when he died, confident that there was time, Uncle Richard's birthday wasn't for three weeks, after all—But time had run out for Jon, and so this totally amazing word processor, which could apparently insert new things or delete old things from the real world, smelled like a frying train transformer and started to smoke after a few minutes. Jon hadn't had a chance to perfect it. He had been—Confident that there was time?

But that was wrong. That was all wrong. Richard knew it Jon's still, watchful face, the sober eyes behind the thick spectacles . . . there was no confidence there, no belief in the comforts of time. What was the word that had occurred to him earlier that day? Doomed. It wasn't just a good word for Jon; it was the right word. That sense of doom had hung about the boy so palpably that there had been times when Richard had wanted to hug him, to tell him to lighten up a little bit, that sometimes there were happy endings and the good didn't always die young.

120   Then he thought of Roger throwing his Magic Eight-Ball at the sidewalk, throwing it just as hard as he could; he heard the plastic splinter and saw the Eight-Ball's magic fluid—just water after all—running down the sidewalk. And this picture merged with a picture of Roger's mongrel van, HAGSTROM'S WHOLESALE DELIVERIES written on the side, plunging over the edge of some dusty, crumbling cliff out in the country, hitting dead squat on its nose with a noise that was, like Roger himself, no big deal. He saw—although he didn't want to—the face of his brother's wife disintegrate into blood and bone. He saw Jon burning in the wreck, screaming, turning black.

No confidence, no real hope. He had always exuded a sense of time running out. And in the end he had turned out to be right.

"What does that mean?" Richard muttered, looking at the blank screen.

How would the Magic Eight-Ball have answered that? ASK AGAIN LATER "OUTCOME IS MURKY" Or perhaps IT IS CERTAINLY SO?

The noise coming from the CPU was getting louder again, and more quickly than this afternoon. Already he could smell the train transformer Jon had lodged in the machinery behind the screen getting hot.

125   Magic dream machine.

Word processor of the gods.

Was that what it was? Was that what Jon had intended to give his uncle for his birthday? The space-age equivalent of a magic lamp or a wishing well?

He heard the back door of the house bang open and then the voices of Seth and the other members of Seth's band. The voices were too loud, too raucous. They had either been drinking or smoking dope.

"Where's your old man, Seth?" he heard one of them ask.

130   "Goofing off in his study, like usual, I guess," Seth said. "I think he—" The wind rose again then, blurring the rest, but not blurring their vicious tribal laughter.

Richard sat listening to them, his head cocked a little to one side, and suddenly he typed:

MY SON IS SETH ROBERT HAGSTROM

His finger hovered over the DELETE button.

What are you doing? his mind screamed at him. Can you be serious? Do you intend to murder your own son?

135   "He must do somethin in there," one of the others said.

"He's a goddam dimwit," Seth answered. "You ask my mother sometime. She'll tell you. He—"

I'm not going to murder him. I'm going to . . . to DELETE him.

His finger stabbed down on the button.

"—ain't never done nothing but—"

140   The words MY SON is SETH ROBERT HAGSTROM vanished from the screen.

Outside, Seth's words vanished with them.

There was no sound out there now but the cold November wind, blowing grim advertisements for winter.

Richard turned off the word processor and went outside. The driveway was empty. The group's lead guitarist, Norm somebody, drove a monstrous and somehow sinister old LTD station wagon in which the group carried their equipment to their infrequent gigs. It was not parked in the driveway now. Perhaps it was somewhere in the world, tooling down some highway or parked in the parking lot of some greasy hamburger hangout, and Norm was also somewhere in the world, as was Davey, the bassist, whose eyes were frighteningly blank and who wore a safety pin dangling from one earlobe, as was the drummer, who had no front teeth. They were somewhere in the world, somewhere, but not here, because Seth wasn't here, Seth had never been here.

Seth had been DELETED.

145   "I have no son," Richard muttered. How many times had he read that melodramatic phrase in bad novels? A hundred? Two hundred? It had never rung true to him. But here it was true. Now it was true. Oh yes.

The wind gusted, and Richard was suddenly seized by a vicious stomach cramp that doubled him over, gasping. He passed explosive wind.

When the cramps passed, he walked into the house.

The first thing he noticed was that Seth's ratty tennis shoes—he had four pairs of them and refused to throw any of them out—were gone from the front hall. He went to the stairway banister and ran his thumb over a section of it. At age ten (old enough to know better, but Lina had refused to allow Richard to lay a hand on the boy in spite of that), Seth had carved his initials deeply into the wood of that banister, wood which Richard had labored over for almost one whole summer. He had sanded and filled and revarnished, but the ghost of those initials had remained. They were gone now.

Upstairs Seth's room. It was neat and clean and unlived-in, dry and devoid of personality. It might as well have had a sign on the doorknob reading GUEST ROOM Downstairs. And it was here that Richard lingered the longest. The snarls of wire were gone; the amplifiers and microphones were gone; the litter of tape recorder parts that Seth was always going to "fix up" were gone (he did not have Jon's hands or concentration). Instead the room bore the deep (if not particularly pleasant) stamp of Lina's personality—heavy, florid furniture and saccharin velvet tapestries (one depicting a Last Supper at which Christ looked like Wayne Newton, another showing deer against a sunset Alaskan sky-line), a glaring rug as bright as arterial blood. There was no longer the faintest sense that a boy named Seth Hagstrom had once inhabited this room. This room, or any of the other rooms in the house.

150   Richard was still standing at the foot of the stairs and looking around when he heard a car pull into the driveway.

Lina, he thought, and felt a surge of almost frantic guilt. It's Lina, back from bingo, and what's she going to say when she sees that Seth is gone? What . . . what . . . Murderer! he heard her screaming. You murdered my boy!

But he hadn't murdered Seth.

"I DELETED him," he muttered, and went upstairs to meet her in the kitchen.

Lina was fatter.

155   He had sent a woman off to bingo who weighed a hundred and eighty pounds or so. The woman who came back in weighed at least three hundred, perhaps more; she had to twist slightly sideways to get in through the back door. Elephantine hips and thighs rippled in tidal motions beneath polyester slacks the color of overripe green olives. Her skin, merely sallow three hours ago, was now sickly and

pale. Although he was no doctor, Richard thought he could read serious liver dam-age or incipient heart disease in that skin. Her heavy-lidded eyes regarded Richard with a steady, even contempt.

She was carrying the frozen corpse of a huge turkey in one of her flabby hands. It twisted and turned within its cellophane wrapper like the body of a bizarre suicide. "What are you staring at, Richard?" she asked.

You, Lina. I'm staring at you. Because this is how you turned out in a world where we had no children. This is how you turned out in a world where there was no object for your love—poisoned as your love might be. This is how Lina looks in a world where everything comes in and nothing at all goes out. You, Lina. That's what I'm staring at. You.

"That bird, Lina," he managed finally. "That's one of the biggest damn turkeys I've ever seen."

"Well don't just stand there looking at it, idiot! Help me with it!"

160   He took the turkey and put it on the counter, feeling its waves of cheerless cold.

It sounded like a block of wood.

"Not there!" she cried impatiently, and gestured toward the pantry. "It's not going to fit in there! Put it in the freezer!"

"Sorry," he murmured. They had never had a freezer before. Never in the world where there had been a Seth.

He took the turkey into the pantry, where a long Amana freezer sat under cold white fluorescent tubes like a cold white coffin. He put it inside along with the cryogenically preserved corpses of other birds and beasts and then went back into the kitchen. Lina had taken the jar of Reese's peanut butter cups from the cupboard and was eating them methodically, one after the other.

165   "It was the Thanksgiving bingo," she said. "We had it this week instead of next because next week Father Phillips has to go in hospital and have his gall-bladder out. I won the coverall." She smiled. A brown mixture of chocolate and peanut butter dripped and ran from her teeth.

"Lina," he said, "are you ever sorry we never had children?"

She looked at him as if he had gone utterly crazy. "What in the name of God would I want a rug-monkey for?" she asked. She shoved the jar of peanut butter cups, now reduced by half, back into the cupboard. "I'm going to bed. Are you com-ing, or are you going back out there and moon over your typewriter some more?"

"I'll go out for a little while more, I think," he said. His voice was surprisingly steady. "I won't be long."

"Does that gadget work?"

170   "What—" Then he understood and he felt another flash of guilt. She knew about the word processor, of course she did. Seth's DELETION had not affected Roger and the track that Roger's family had been on. "Oh. Oh, no. It doesn't do anything."

She nodded, satisfied. "That nephew of yours. Head always in the clouds. Just like you, Richard. If you weren't such a mouse, I'd wonder if maybe you'd been putting it where you hadn't ought to have been putting it about fifteen years ago." She laughed a coarse, surprisingly powerful laugh—the laugh of an aging, cynical bawd—and for a moment he almost leaped at her. Then he felt a smile surface on his own lips—a smile as thin and white and cold as the Amana freezer that had replaced Seth on this new track.

"I won't be long," he said. "I just want to note down a few things."

"Why don't you write a Nobel Prize-winning short story, or something?" she asked indifferently. The hall floorboards creaked and muttered as she swayed her huge way toward the stairs. "We still owe the optometrist for my reading glasses and we're a payment behind on the Betamax. Why don't you make us some damn money?"

"Well," Richard said, "I don't know, Lina. But I've got some good ideas tonight. I really do."

175   She turned to look at him, seemed about to say something sarcastic—something about how none of his good ideas had put them on easy street but she had stuck with him anyway—and then didn't. Perhaps something about his smile deterred her. She went upstairs. Richard stood below, listening to her thundering tread. He could feel sweat on his forehead. He felt simultaneously sick and exhilarated.

He turned and went back out to his study.

This time when he turned the unit on, the CPU did not hum or roar; it began to make an uneven howling noise. That hot train transformer smell came almost immediately from the housing behind the screen, and as soon as he pushed the EXECUTE button, erasing the HAPPY BIRTHDAY, UNCLE RICHARD! message, the unit began to smoke.

Not much time, he thought. No . . . that's not right. No time at all. Jon knew it, and now I know it, too.

The choices came down to two: Bring Seth back with the INSERT button (he was sure he could do it; it would be as easy as creating the Spanish doubloons had been) or finish the job.

180   The smell was getting thicker, more urgent. In a few moments, surely no more, the screen would start blinking its OVERLOAD message.

He typed: MY WIFE IS ADELINA MABEL WARREN HAGSTROM

He punched the DELETE button. He typed: I AM A MAN WHO LIVES ALONE.

Now the word began to blink steadily in the upper right-hand corner of the screen: OVERLOAD OVERLOAD OVERLOAD. Please. Please let me finish. Please, please, please . . . The smoke coming from the vents in the video cabinet was thicker and grayer now. He looked down at the screaming CPU and saw that smoke was also coming from its vents . . . and down in that smoke he could see a sullen red spark of fire.

Magic Eight-Ball, will I be healthy, wealthy, or wise? Or will I live alone and perhaps kill myself in sorrow? Is there time enough?

185   CANNOT SEE NOW TRY AGAIN LATER Except there was no later.

He struck the INSERT button and the screen went dark, except for the constant OVERLOAD message, which was now blinking at a frantic, stuttery rate.

He typed: EXCEPT FOR MY WIFE, BELINDA, AND MY SON, JONATHAN Please. Please.

He hit the EXECUTE button.

The screen went blank. For what seemed like ages it remained blank, except for OVERLOAD, which was now blinking so fast that, except for a faint shadow, it seemed to remain constant, like a computer executing a closed loop of command. Something inside the CPU popped and sizzled, and Richard groaned.

190   Then green letters appeared on the screen, floating mystically on the black: I AM AN WHO LIVES ALONE EXCEPT FOR MY WIFE, BELINDA, AND MY SON, JONATHAN He hit the EXECUTE button twice.

Now, he thought. Now I will type: ALL THE BUGS IN THIS WORD PROCESSOR WERE FULLY WORKED OUT BEFORE MR. NORDHOFF BROUGHT IT OVER HERE. Or I'll type: I HAVE IDEAS FOR AT LEAST TWENTY BEST-SELLING NOVELS. Or I'll type: MY FAMILY AND I ARE GOING TO LIVE HAPPILY EVER AFTER. Or I'll type—But he typed nothing. His fingers hovered stupidly over the keys as he felt—literally felt—all the circuits in his brain jam up like cars grid-locked into the worst manhattan traffic jam in the history of internal combustion. The screen suddenly filled up with the word: LOADOVERLOADOVERLOADOVERLOADOVER-LOADOVERLOADOVERLOAD

There was another pop, and then an explosion from the CPU. Flames belched out of the cabinet and then died away.

Richard leaned back in his chair, shielding his face in case the screen should implode. It didn't. It only went dark. He sat there, looking at the darkness of the screen.

CANNOT TELL FOR SURE ASK AGAIN LATER.

195 "Dad?"

He swiveled around in his chair, heart pounding so hard he felt that it might actually tear itself out of his chest.

Jon stood there, Jon Hagstrom, and his face was the same but somehow different—the difference was subtle but noticeable. Perhaps, Richard thought, the difference was the difference in paternity between two brothers. Or perhaps it was simply that that wary, watching expression was gone from the eyes, slightly over-magnified by thick spectacles (wire-rims now, he noticed, not the ugly industrial horn-rims that Roger had always gotten the boy because they were fifteen bucks cheaper).

Maybe it was something even simpler: that look of doom was gone from the boy's eyes. "Jon?" he said hoarsely, wondering if he had actually wanted something more than this. Had he? It seemed ridiculous, but he supposed he had. He supposed people always did. "Jon, it's you, isn't it?"

"Who else would it be?" He nodded toward the word processor. "You didn't hurt yourself when that baby went to data heaven, did you?"

200 Richard smiled. "No. I'm fine."

Jon nodded. "I'm sorry it didn't work. I don't know what ever possessed me to use all those cruddy parts." He shook his head. "Honest to God I don't. It's like I had to. Kid's stuff."

"Well," Richard said, joining his son and putting an arm around his shoulders, "you'll do better next time, maybe."

"Maybe. Or I might try something else."

"That might be just as well."

205 "Mom said she had cocoa for you, if you wanted it."

"I do," Richard said, and the two of them walked together from the study to a house into which no frozen turkey won in a bingo coverall game had ever come. "A cup of cocoa would go down just fine right now."

"I'll cannibalize anything worth cannibalizing out of that thing tomorrow and then take it to the dump," Jon said.

Richard nodded. "Delete it from our lives," he said, and they went into the house and the smell of hot cocoa, laughing together.

[1983]

Joining the Conversation: Critical Thinking and Writing

1. Richard Hagstrom is trapped in an unhappy family situation. Define his relationship with his wife Lina and his son Seth. Annotate the story, locating and marking up the quotations that capture how both Lina and Seth treat Richard. How would you describe this family?

2. The story focuses on a marvelous piece of technology: a word processer with magical powers. Who made the word processor? What is the word processor made out of? Explain the word processor's powers. How does Richard learn of and then use the word processor's powers? What words does he type on the word processor's screen, and what actions result?

3. Richard's unhappy family is doubled in that of his brother Roger, Roger's wife Belinda, and their son Jon. Explain the tragic story that defines Roger's family.

4. The story ends with an unexpected choice. Write a short paper that explains and analyzes this choice. What does Richard do at the end of the story? What happens to Lina and Seth? What happens to Belinda and Jon? Is this a moral choice? Is this a justifiable choice? Would you make this same choice?

KIT REED

Currently a resident writer at Wesleyan University, Kit Reed (1932–) writes speculative fiction and psychological thrillers (often under a pen name) in addition to literary fiction. The author of numerous short stories and novels, many of her works feature dystopian settings. Her work often has a satirical or feminist edge, exploring what happens to communities of people when they are placed under stress or siege. Her stories are published in numerous collections dedicated to her work, most recently The Story Until Now: A Great Big Book of Stories *(2013).*

The New You

"Now—The New You," the ad said. It was a two-page spread in one of the glossier fashion magazines, and it was accompanied by a shadowed, grainy art shot that hinted at the possibility of a miraculous transformation which hovered at every woman's fingertips.

Raptly, Martha Merriam hunched over the magazine, tugging at her violet-sprigged housedress so that it almost covered her plump knees. She contemplated the photograph, the list of promises framed in elegant italics, unaware as she did so that her mouth was working, gnawing a strand of dirty, dun-colored hair.

In her more wistful, rebellious moments, Martha Merriam forgot her dumpy body and imagined herself the svelte, impeccable Marnie, taller by six inches and lighter by forty pounds. When a suaver, better-dressed woman cut her at a luncheon or her husband left her alone at parties she would retreat into dialogs with Marnie. Marnie knew just the right, devastating thing to say to chic, overconfident women, and Marnie was expert in all the wiles that keep a man at home. In the person of Marnie, Martha could pretend.

"Watch the Old You Melt Away," Martha read, and as she mouthed the words for the second time Marnie strained inside her, waiting for release. Martha straightened imperceptibly, patting her doughy throat with a stubby hand, and as her eyes found the hooker—the price tag for the New You in small print in the lower right-hand corner—longing consumed her, and Marnie took over.

5   "We could use a New You," Marnie said.

"But three thousand dollars." Martha nibbled at the strand of hair.

"You have those stocks."

"But those were Howard's wedding present to me—part of his *business*."

    "He won't mind . . ." Marnie twisted and became one with the photograph.

10   "But a hundred shares . . ." The hank off hair was sodden now, and Martha was chewing faster.

    "He won't mind when he sees us," Marnie said.

    And Martha, eyes aglow, got up and went to the telephone almost without realizing what she was doing, and got her broker on the line.

    The New You arrived two weeks later, as advertised, and when it came Martha was too excited to touch it, alone in the house as she was, with this impossibly beautiful future.

    In mid-afternoon, when she had looked at the coffin-shaped crate from every possible angle and smoothed the rough, splintered edges of the wood, she nerved herself to pull the ripcord the company had provided—and let her future begin. She jumped back with a squeak as the hard crate sides fell away to reveal a black and richly molded box. Trembling, she twiddled the gold-plated clasp with the rosebud emblem and opened the lid.

15   For a moment, all she saw was an instruction booklet, centered on top of fold upon fold of purple tissue paper, but as she looked closer she saw that the paper was massed to protect a mysterious, promising form which lay beneath.

    IMPORTANT: READ THIS BEFORE PROCEEDING, the booklet warned. Distracted, she threw it aside, reflecting as she did so that the last time she had seen paper folded in this way was around long-stemmed American Beauties, a dozen roses Howard had sent her a dozen years before.

    The last piece of paper came way in her fingers, revealing the figure beneath, and Martha gasped. It was a long-stemmed American Beauty—everything she had hoped for. She recognized her own expression in its face, but it was a superb, glamorous version of her face, and at the same time it was Marnie, Helen, Cleopatra—more than she had dared anticipate. It was the new her. Quivering with impatience to get into it, she bent over it without another thought for the instruction book and plunged her arms to the elbows in the rustling, rising swirl of purple tissue paper. The sudden aura of perfume, the movement of the paper, a sense of mounting excitement overcame her and the last thing she remembered was clasping the figure's silken hands into her own stubby fingers and holding them to her bosom as the two figures, new and old, tossed on a rushing purple sea. Then the moiling sheets of purple kaleidoscoped and engulfed her and she lost consciousness.

    She was awakened by a squashy thud. She lay in the midst of the purple tissue, stretching luxuriously, thinking that she ought to get up to see what the thud had been. She raised one knee, in the beginning of a move to get to her feet, and then stopped, delighted by the golden sleekness of the knee. She stretched the leg she knew must be just beyond that perfect knee and then hugged shoulders as lithe and smooth as those of a jungle cat, expanding in a gradual awareness of what had happened. Then, remembering that the new her was quite naked and that Howard would be home any minute, she pulled herself together in one fluid glide of muscles and got to her feet. With the air of a queen, she lifted one foot delicately and stepped out of the box.

    She remembered the line from the advertisement, "Watch the Old You Melt Away," and she smiled languidly as she flowed away from the box. Yawning, she reached in the closet, picked up her old quilted wrapper and discarded it for the silk kimono Howard had brought her from Japan. It had fitted her ten years before and then it had gotten too small. She looped the sash twice around her middle and then—still not too good to be an orderly housewife—she began folding the tissue paper that seemed to have exploded all over the room. As she came to the side where the old her had first touched the gold-plated rosebud, she swooped up a whole armful of tissue in a gesture of exuberance—and dropped it with a little scream. Her toe had hit something. Not wanting to look, she poked at the remaining pieces of paper with a gilded toenail. Her foot connected with something soft. She made herself look down. And stifled a moan.

20   The old her had not melted away. It was still there, dowdy as ever in its violet-sprigged housedress. Its drab hair trailed like seaweed and its hips seemed to spread where it lay, settling on the rug.

"But you promised!" the new, sleek Martha yelped. With a sudden sinking feeling, she rooted around in the rest of the purple tissue until she found the castoff instruction book.

"Care must be exercised in effecting the transfer," the book warned in urgent italics. Then it went on with a number of complicated technical directions about transfer and grounding, which Martha didn't understand. When she had grasped the new her's hands she had plunged right into the transfer without a thought for the body she was leaving behind. And it had to be dematerialized at the time of transfer, no later. It was pointless to send botched jobs back to the company, the booklet warned. The company would send them back. Apparently, the new Martha was stuck with the old her.

"Oh . . ." There was a little moan from the figure on the floor. And the old Martha sat up and looked dully around the room.

"You—" the new Martha looked at it in growing hatred. "You leave me alone," she said. She was about to lunge at it in a fit of irritation when there was a sound in the driveway. "Oh-oh. Howard." Without another thought, she pushed the lumpy, unresisting old her into the hall closet, locked it in and pocketed the key.

25   Then, pulling the robe around her, she went to the door. "Howard, darling," she began.

He recognized her and he didn't recognize her. He stood just inside the doorway with the look of a child who has just been given his own soda fountain, listening as she explained (leaving out certain details: the sale of his stock, the matter of the old her) in vibrant, intimate tones.

"Martha, darling," he said at last, pulling her toward him.

"Call me Marnie, dear. Hm?" She purred, and nestled against his chest.

Of course the change involved a new wardrobe and new things for Howard too, as Marnie had read in a dozen glamour magazines how important an accessory a well-dressed man could be. The Merriams were swept up in a round of parties and were admitted, for the first time, to the city's most glittering homes. Howard's business flourished and Marnie, surrounded by admirers, Marnie, far more attractive than the most fashionable of her rivals, thrived. There were parties, meetings, theater dates, luncheon engagements and a number of attractive men. And what with one thing and another, Marnie didn't have much time for piddling around the house. The black box from the New You Company lay where she had left it, and the old her was still stacked (like an old vacuum cleaner, as Marnie saw it, outmoded and unused) in the closet in the hall.

30   In the second week of her new life, Marnie began to notice things. The tissue paper around he New You box was disarrayed, and the instruction book was gone. Once, when she had stepped out of the bedroom for a moment, she thought she saw a shadow moving in the hall. "Oh, it's you," Howard said with an ambiguous look when she returned to their room. "For a minute I thought . . ." He sounded almost wistful.

And there were crumbs—little trails of them—and empty food containers left in odd corners of the house.

Disturbed by the dirt which had begun to collect, Marnie refused two luncheon dates and a cocktail invitation and spent one of her rare afternoons at home. In slippers and the quilted house coat she had discarded the fist day of her transformation, she began to clean the house. She was outraged to find a damp trail leading from the kitchen to the hall closet. With a rug-cleaning preparation she began scrubbing at the hall carpet, and she straightened her back, indignant, when she reached a particularly sordid little mixture of liquid and crumbs right at the closet door. Fumbling in her pocket, she brought out the key and applied herself to the lock.

"You," she said disgustedly. She had almost forgotten.

"Yes—yes ma'am," the old her said humbly, almost completely cowed. The dumpy, violet-sprigged Martha was sitting in one corner of the closet, a milk carton in one hand and a box of marshmallow cookies open in her lap.

35   "Why can't you just . . . Why can't you . . ." Marnie snorted in disgust. There was chocolate at the corners of the creature's mouth, and it had gained another five pounds.

"A body has to live," the old her said humbly, trying to wipe away the chocolate. "You forgot—I had a key to the closet too."

"If you're going to be wandering around," Marnie said, tapping one fingernail on a flawless tooth, "you might as well be of some use. Come on," she said, pulling at the old her. "We're going to clear out the old maid's room. Move!"

The old Martha came to its feet and shambled behind Marnie, making little sounds of obedience.

The experiment was a flop. The creature ate constantly and had a number of (to Marnie) disgusting habits, and when Marnie invited some of Howard's more attractive business contacts in for dinner, it refused to wear a maid's cap and apron, and made a terrible mess of serving the soup. When she called it down at table, Howard protested mildly, but Marnie was too engrossed in conversation with a Latin type who dealt in platinum to notice. Nor did she notice, in the days that followed, that Howard was putting on weight. She was slimmer than she had been in the first day of her new life and she stalked the house impatiently, nervous and well groomed as a high-bred horse. Howard seemed unusually quiet and withdrawn and Marnie laid it to the effect of having the Old Her around, flat-footed and quiet in its violet-sprigged dress. When she caught it feeding Howard fudge cake at the kitchen table the very day she found he could no longer button his tuxedo, she knew the Old Her had to go.

40   She had a Disposal installed in her kitchen sink and began a quiet investigation into the properties of various poisons, in hopes of finding a permanent way of getting rid of it. But when she brought a supply of sharp-edged instruments into the house the violet-sprigged Martha seemed to sense what she was planning. It stood in front of her, wringing its hands humbly until she noticed it.

"Well?" Marnie said, perhaps more sharply than she had intended.

"I—just wanted to say you can't get rid of me that way," it offered, almost apologetically. "What way?" Marnie asked, trying to cover, and then, with a little gesture of indifference, she raised one eyebrow. "OK, smarty, why not?"

"Killing's against the law," the creature said patiently.

"This would hardly be killing," Marnie said in her most biting tones. "It's like giving your old clothes to the rag man or the Goodwill or burning them. Getting rid of old clothes has never been murder."

45   "Not murder," the old her said, and it produced the instruction book. Patiently, it guided Marnie's eyes over the well-thumbed pages to a paragraph marked in chocolate. "Suicide."

Desperate, she gave it a thousand dollars and a ticket to California.

And for a few days, the gay life went on as it had before. The Merriams were entertained or entertaining day and night now, and Howard hardly had time to notice that the quiet old Martha was missing. Marnie's new autochef made her dinner parties the talk of the city's smarter social set, and she found herself the center of an inexhaustible crowd of attentive, handsome young men in tuxedos. While Howard had abandoned the old her at parties, she saw little more of him now because the good-looking young men adored her too much to leave her alone. She was welcome in the very best places and there wasn't a woman in town who dared exclude her from her invitation list. Marnie went everywhere.

If she was dissatisfied, it was only because Howard seemed lumpier and less attractive than usual, and the bumps and wrinkles in his evening clothes made him something less than the perfect accessory. She slipped away from him early in the evening each time they went out together and she looked for him again only in the small hours, when it was time to go home.

But for all that she still loved him, and it came as something of a blow when she discovered that it was no longer she who avoided him at parties—he was avoiding her. She first noticed it after an evening of dinner and dancing. She had been having a fascinating conversation with someone in consolidated metals and it seemed to her the right touch, the final fillip, for the evening would be for the gentleman in question to see her standing next to Howard in the soft light, serene, beautiful, the doting wife.

50   "You must meet my husband," she murmured, stroking the metal magnate's lapel.

"Have you seen Howard?" she asked a friend nearby, and something in the way the friend shook his head and turned away from her made her uneasy.

Several minutes later the metal magnate had taken his leave and Marnie was still looking for Howard. She found him at last, on a balcony, and she could have sworn that she saw him wave to a dark figure which touched its hands to its lips and disappeared into the bushes just as she closed the balcony door.

"It's not very flattering, you know," she said, coiling around his arm.

"Mmmmm?" He hardly looked at her.

"Having to track you down like this," she said, fitting against him.

55   "Mmmmmm?"

She started to go on, but instead led him through the apartment and down to the front door. Even in the cab, she couldn't shake his reverie. She tucked his coat tails into a cab with a solicitous little frown. And she brooded. There had been something disturbingly familiar about that figure on the balcony.

The next morning Marnie was up at an unaccustomed hour, dressing with exquisite care. She had been summoned to a morning coffee with Edna Hotchkiss-Baines. For the first time, she had been invited to help with the Widows' and Orphans' Bazaar. ("I've found somebody wonderful to help with the planning," the chichi Edna had confided. "You'll never guess who.")

Superb in an outfit that could withstand even Edna's scrutiny, Marnie presented herself at the Hotchkiss-Baines door and followed the butler into the Hotchkiss-Baines breakfast room.

60   Edna Hotchkiss-Baines barely greeted her. She was engrossed in conversation with a squat, unassuming figure that slumped across the table from her, shoes slit

to accommodate feet that were spreading now, violet-sprigged dress growing a little tight.

Face afire, Marnie fell back. She took a chair without speaking and leveled a look of hatred at the woman who held the town's most fashionable social leader enthralled—the dowdy, frumpy, lumpy, old her.

It was only the beginning. Apparently the creature had cashed in the California ticket and used the fare and the thousand dollars to rent a small flat and buy a modest wardrobe. Now, to Marnie's helpless fury, it seemed to be going everywhere. It appeared at cocktail parties in a series of matronly crepe dresses ranging in color from taupe to dove gray. It sat on the most important committees and appeared at the most elegant dinners. No matter how exclusive the guest list or now festive the company, no matter how high Marnie's hopes that it had not been included, somebody had always invited it. It appeared behind her in clothing-store mirrors when she was trying on new frocks and looked over her shoulder in restaurants when she dined with one of her devastating young men. It haunted her steps, looking just enough like her to make everyone uncomfortable, enough like everything Marnie hated to embarrass her.

Then one night she found Howard kissing it at a party.

At home a few hours later, he confronted her. "Marnie, I want a divorce."

65   "Howard." She made clutching motions. "Is there . . ."

He sounded grave. "My dear, there's someone else. Well, it isn't exactly someone else."

"You don't mean . . . Howard, you can't be serious."

"I'm in love with the girl I married," he said. "A quiet girl, a grey-and-brown girl."

"That—" Her fashionable body was trembling. Her gemlike eyes were aflame. That frumpy . . ."

70   "A home girl . . ." He was getting rhapsodic now. "Like the girl I married so many years ago."

"After all that money—the transformation—the new body—" Marnie's voice rose with every word. "—the CHANGE?"

"I never asked you to change, Marnie." He smiled mistily. "You were so . . ."

"You'd drop me for that piece of suet?" She was getting shrill. "How could I face my *friends*?"

"You deserve somebody better looking," he said with a little sigh. "Somebody tall and slim. I'll just pack and go . . ."

75   "All right, Howard." She managed a noble tone. "But not just yet." She was thinking fast. "There has to be a Decent Waiting Period . . ."

A period that would give her time to handle this.

"If you wish, my dear." He had changed into his favorite flannel bathrobe. In times past, the old Martha had sat next to him on the couch in front of the television, she in her quilted house coat, he in his faithful robe. He stroked its lapels. "I just want you to realize that my mind is made up—we'll all be happier . . ."

"Of course," she said, and a hundred plans went through her mind. "Of course."

She sat alone for the rest of the night, drumming opalescent nails on here dressing-table, tapping one slender foot.

80   And by morning, she had it. Something Howard had said had sent her mind churning. "You deserve somebody better looking."

"He's right," she said aloud. "I do."

And by the time it had begun to get light she had conceived of a way to get rid of the persistent embarrassment of the old her and the—*homier* elements of

Howard at one stroke. As soon as Howard left for the office she began a series of long-distance inquiries, and once she had satisfied her curiosity she called a number of friends and floated several discreet loans in the course of drinks over lunch.

There was a crate in the living room just two weeks later. "Howard," Marnie said, beckoning. "I have a surprise for you . . ."

He was just coming in, with the old Martha, from a date. They liked to sit in the kitchen over cocoa and talk. At a look from Marnie, the old Martha settled in a chair. It couldn't take its eyes off the coffin-shaped box. Howard stepped forward, brows wrinkling furrily. "What's this?" he asked, and then without waiting for her to answer, he murmured, "Didn't we have one of these around a few months ago?" and pulled the cord attached to the corner of the crate. It fell open—perhaps a little too easily—and the lid of the smooth ebony box sprang up under his fingers almost before he had touched the rosebud catch. The tissue paper was green this time, and if there had been an instruction book nestled on top, it was gone now.

85   Both the new Marnie and the old her watched raptly as Howard, oblivious of them both, broke through the layers of tissue paper and with a spontaneous sound of pleasure grasped the figure in the box.

Both the new and the old woman watched as the papers began to swirl and rise, and they sat transfixed until there was a thud and the papers settled again.

When it was over, Marnie turned to the old her with a malicious grin. "Satisfied?" she asked. And then, eyes gleaming, she waited for the new Howard to rise from the box.

He came forth like a new Adam, ignoring both of them, and went to his own room for clothes.

While he was gone the old Howard, a little frayed at the corners, almost buried under a fall of tissue, stirred and tried to rise.

90   "That's yours," Marnie said, giving the old her a dig in the ribs. "Better help it up." And then she presented herself, facing the doorway, waiting with arms spread for the new Howard to reappear. After a few moments he came, godlike in one of Howard's pinstriped business suits.

"Darling," Marnie murmured, mentally canceling the dinner at the Hotchkiss-Bainses' and a Westport party with a new man.

"Darling," the new Howard said. And he swept past her to the old Martha, still scrabbling around in the tissue paper on the floor. Gently, with the air of a prince who has discovered his Cinderella, he helped her to her feet.

"Shall we go?"

Marnie watched, openmouthed.

95   They did.

On the floor, the old Howard had gotten turned on its stomach somehow, and was floundering like a displaced fish. Marnie watched, taut with rage, too stricken to speak. The old Howard flapped a few times, made it to its knees and then slipped on the tissue paper again. Hardly looking at it, Marnie smoothed the coif she had prepared for the Hotchkiss-Baines dinner that night. There was always the dinner—and there was the party in Westport. Dispassionately, she moved forward and kicked a piece of tissue out of the way. She drew herself up, supple, beautiful, and she seemed to find new strength. The old Howard flapped again.

"Oh, get *up*," she said, and poked it with her toe. She was completely composed now. "Get up—*darling*," she spat.

[1962]

Joining the Conversation: Critical Thinking and Writing

1. "The New You" dramatizes a fantasy of creating a new self. Explain how Martha is able to trade in herself for the "new you" of Marnie. What mistake does she make as part of the transfer?
2. Write an analytical paper that compares Marnie and Martha. What are the key characteristics of each woman? Use quotations from the story to define each woman's physical, social, and intellectual qualities.
3. The story contains several unexpected plot twists. Explain the unexpected complications involving Howard and his attraction to Martha. Marnie seems to create a solution to this issue, but at the very end of the story, another twist occurs in the plot. Explain the complications involving the "new Howard." What seems to be the larger message conveyed by these complications?

POEMS

WALT WHITMAN

For a biographical note on Walt Whitman, see page 855.

To a Locomotive in Winter

Thee for my recitative!
Thee in the driving storm, even as now—the snow—the
    winter-day declining;
Thee in thy panoply, thy measured dual throbbing, and thy
    beat convulsive;
Thy black cylindric body, golden brass, and silvery steel;
Thy ponderous side-bars, parallel and connecting rods,   5
    gyrating, shuttling at thy sides;
Thy metrical, now swelling pant and roar—now tapering in
    the distance;
Thy great protruding head-light, fix'd in front;
Thy long, pale, floating vapor-pennants, tinged with delicate
    purple;
The dense and murky clouds out-belching from thy
    smoke-stack;
Thy knitted frame—thy springs and valves—the tremulous   10
    twinkle of thy wheels;
Thy train of cars behind, obedient, merrily-following,
Through gale or calm, now swift, now slack, yet steadily
    careering:
Type of the modem! emblem of motion and power! pulse of
    the continent!
For once, come serve the Muse, and merge in verse, even as
    here I see thee,
With storm, and buffeting gusts of wind, and falling snow;   15
By day, thy warning, ringing bell to sound its notes,
By night, thy silent signal lamps to swing.

Fierce-throated beauty!
Roll through my chant, with all thy lawless music! thy
swinging lamps at night;
Thy piercing, madly-whistled laughter! thy echoes, rumbling   20
like an earthquake, rousing all!
Law of thyself complete, thine own track firmly holding;
(No sweetness debonair of tearful harp or glib piano thine,)
Thy trills of shrieks by rocks and hills return'd,
Launch'd o'er the prairies wide—across the lakes,
To the free skies, unpent, and glad, and strong.   25

[1876]

Joining the Conversation: Critical Thinking and Writing

1. How does Whitman's language capture the force of a locomotive? What are some of the most powerful descriptive words that Whitman uses?
2. In line 13, Whitman calls the locomotive a "Type of the modern!" How does Whitman connect the train to the idea of modern technology? How does Whitman view the modern world? For example, is "the modern" positive or negative?
3. Why does Whitman address the train at the start of each line? How does this use of repetition help to convey the themes of the poem? Does this repetition create a compelling pattern of sound?

EMILY DICKINSON

For a biographical note on Emily Dickinson, see page 856.

I like to see it lap the Miles

I like to see it lap the Miles—
And lick the Valleys up—
And stop to feed itself at Tanks—
And then—prodigious step

Around a Pile of Mountains—   5
And supercilious peer
In Shanties—by the sides of Roads—
And then a Quarry pare

To fit it's sides
And crawl between   10
Complaining all the while
In horrid—hooting stanza—
Then chase itself down Hill—

And neigh like Boanerges—
Then—prompter than a Star   15
Stop—docile and omnipotent
At it's own stable door—

[1890]

Joining the Conversation: Critical Thinking and Writing

1. What is the subject of "I like to see it lap the Miles"? The manuscript version of the poem does not include the word "locomotive" or "train," but the first published edition of the poem titles it "The Railway Train." What images in the poem reveal that the poem describes a train?
2. The railroad was a new technology during Dickinson's time. What lines in the poem express a fascination with this technology?
3. How does the poem express the different relationships that a train might have with the surrounding world? What attitudes does the train seem to have toward its surrounding world? Write a short journal entry that catalogs the many different ways in which the train interacts with the surrounding world.

DANIEL NYIKOS

A native of Germany, Daniel Nyikos earned a BA and MA from Utah State University and is a doctoral student in fiction at the University of Nebraska. He was awarded a 2013–14 Fulbright Scholarship to study in Hungary, which allowed him to work on his current novel-in-progress, which is set in that country. He has served as an editorial assistant for the creative writing journal Prairie Schooner.

Potato Soup

I set up my computer and webcam in the kitchen
so I can ask my mother's and aunt's advice
as I cook soup for the first time alone.
My mother is in Utah. My aunt is in Hungary.
I show the onions to my mother with the webcam.   5
"Cut them smaller," she advises.
"You only need a taste."
I chop potatoes as the onions fry in my pan.
When I say I have no paprika to add to the broth,
they argue whether it can be called potato soup.   10
My mother says it will be white potato soup,
my aunt says potato soup must be red.
When I add sliced peppers, I ask many times
if I should put the water in now,
but they both say to wait until I add the potatoes.   15
I add Polish sausage because I can't find Hungarian,
and I cook it so long the potatoes fall apart.
"You've made stew," my mother says
when I hold up the whole pot to the camera.
They laugh and say I must get married soon.   20
I turn off the computer and eat alone.

[2010]

Joining the Conversation: Critical Thinking and Writing

1. How does technology allow the poem's narrator to connect with his family? Have you ever used technology in a similar fashion? Write an informal journal

entry that summarizes the poem. Then, describe a scene in which you used technology to create connections with family or friends. Reflect on the poem and your own experiences: What are the similarities and differences? Does the poem capture how and why you use technology?

2. Examine the poem's last line. How do you interpret this line? Is it a sad ending? Why does the poem end on this note? Does this final line provide a commentary on technology?

3. How does the poem capture the voices of the mother and aunt? How does technology allow this conversation to take place?

A. E. STALLINGS

Born in 1968 in Decatur, Georgia, A. E. (Alicia Elsbeth) Stallings is a poet and translator who is interested in using the themes of ancient mythology and traditional forms of rhyme and meter to explore contemporary life. For her innovative fusing of ancient and contemporary poetic forms and ideas, she received a MacArthur ("Genius") Fellowship in 2011. She has published collections of poetry, including Archaic Style *(1999) and* Olives *(2012), and a translation of Lucretius. She earned a BA from the University of Georgia in 1990 and an MSt from the University of Oxford, and currently lives in Athens, Greece.*

Sestina: Like

With a nod to Jonah Winter

Now we're all "friends," there is no love but Like,
A semi-demi goddess, something like
A reality-TV star look-alike,
Named Simile or Me Two. So we like
In order to be liked. It isn't like   5
There's Love or Hate now. Even plain "dislike"

Is frowned on: there's no button for it. Like
Is something you can quantify: each "like"
You gather's almost something money-like,
Token of virtual support. "Please like   10
This page to stamp out hunger." And you'd *like*
To end hunger and climate change alike,

But it's unlikely Like does diddly. Like
Just twiddles its unopposing thumbs-ups, like
Wise props up scarecrow silences. *"I'm like,*   15
So OVER him," I overhear. "But, like,
He doesn't get it. Like, you know? He's like
It's all OK. Like I don't even LIKE

Him anymore. Whatever. I'm all like . . . "
Take "like" out of our chat, we'd all alike   20
Flounder, agape, gesticulating like
A foreign film sans subtitles, fall like
Dumb phones to mooted desuetude. Unlike
With other crutches, um, when we use "like,"

We're not just buying time on credit: Like   25
Displaces other words; crowds, cuckoo-like,
Endangered hatchlings from the nest. (Click "like"
If you're against extinction!) Like is like
Invasive zebra mussels, or it's like
Those nutria-things, or kudzu, or belike   30

Redundant fast food franchises, each like
(More like) the next. Those poets who dislike
Inversions, archaisms, who just like
Plain English as she's spoke —why isn't "like"
Their (literally) every other word? I'd like   35
Us just to admit that's what real speech is like.

But as you like, my friend. Yes, we're alike,
How we pronounce, say, lichen, and dislike
Cancer and war. So like this page. Click *Like*.

[2013]

Joining the Conversation: Critical Thinking and Writing

1. How is "Sestina: Like" using the vocabulary of current technology, specifically social networking sites? How does the poem call attention to our new definitions and uses of such words as "like" and "friends"?
2. Look at the last word of each line of the poem. What is the pattern of repetition that Stallings has created here? Did you notice this pattern when you first read the poem? Why has Stallings created this repetition?
3. Annotate the poem's use of the word "like," circling each time it is used. Note how Stallings uses multiple forms of "like," such as "alike" and "dislike." As you mark up the poem, keep track of how the word "like" morphs into different forms. Also note how he word "like" increases in use throughout the poem. After you have annotated the poem, write a short response paper that explains your understanding of how the poem wants us to respond to the word "like." For example, is the poem encouraging us to be critical of, or to accept, our use of the word "like"?
4. What is a "sestina"? How does this poem use the sestina form?

MARCUS WICKER

Born in Ann Arbor, Michigan, in 1984, Marcus Wicker is currently an assistant professor of English at the University of Southern Indiana. His first book of poetry, Maybe the Saddest Thing *(2012), was selected by D. A. Powell to be published as part of the National Poetry Series; Powell praised the collection's hip-hop sensibility and energetic lyrics. Wicker has published poetry in journals such as* Poetry *and* American Poetry Review, *and has received numerous poetry awards, including the 2011 Ruth Lilly Fellowship.*

Ode to Browsing the Web

Two spiky-haired Russian cats hit kick flips
on a vert ramp. The camera pans to another

pocket of the room where six kids rocking holey
T-shirts etch aerosol lines on warehouse walls

in words I cannot comprehend. All of this   5
happening in a time no older than your last

heartbeat. I've been told the internet is
an unholy place — an endless intangible

stumbling ground of false deities
dogma and loneliness, sad as a pile of shit   10

in a world without flies. My loneliness exists
in every afterthought. Yesterday, I watched

a neighbor braid intricate waves of cornrows
into her son's tiny head and could have lived

in her focus-wrinkled brow for a living. Today   15
I think I practice the religion of blinking too much.

Today, I know no neighbor's name and won't
know if I like it or not. O holy streaming screen

of counterculture punks, linger my lit mind
on landing strips —through fog, rain, hail —   20

without care for time or density. O world
wide web, o viral video, o god of excrement

thought. Befriend me. Be fucking infectious.
Move my eyes from one sight to the next.

[2013]

Joining the Conversation: Critical Thinking and Writing

1. "Ode to Browsing the Web" opens with images of the content of the Internet. Take notes on those images and how they impact the poem's narrator. The poem then moves on to descriptions of how the narrator feels when he is browsing the Internet (such as feeling "loneliness" in lines 10 and 11); take notes on these descriptions. Consider the notes that you have generated. How does the poem depict the Internet and how the Internet shapes its user?

2. The poem describes a mother braiding her son's hair (lines 13–14). The narrator states, "I . . . . could have lived in her focus-wrinkled brow." What does this mean? How does this "focus" compare to "blinking too much" described in the next line?

3. Look up the definition of the word *ode*. How is this poem an "ode"?

4. How would you characterize the poem's attitude toward the Internet? Is the poem praising the Internet or criticizing it? Does the poem's narrator enjoy the Internet or dislike it? Write a short analytical paper that creates an argument about the poem's stance toward the Internet. Support your argument with specific quotations from the poem.

PLAY

Luis Valdez

Luis Valdez was born into a family of migrant farm workers in Delano, California, in 1940. After completing high school, he entered San José State College on a scholarship. He wrote his first plays while still an undergraduate, and after receiving his degree (in English and drama) from San José in 1964, he joined the San Francisco Mime Troupe, a left-wing group that performed in parks and streets. Revolutionary in technique as well as in political content, the Mime Troupe rejected the traditional forms of drama and, instead, drew on the traditions of the circus and the carnival.

In 1965, Valdez returned to Delano, where César Chávez had organized a strike of farm workers and a boycott against grape growers. It was here, under the wing of the United Farm Workers, that he established El Teatro Campesino (the Farm Workers' Theater), which at first specialized in doing short, improvised, satirical skits called actos. *When the El Teatro Campesino moved to Del Rey, California, it expanded its repertoire beyond farm issues, and it became part of a cultural center that gave workshops (in English and Spanish) in such subjects as history, drama, and politics.*

The actos, *performed by amateurs on college campuses, on flatbed trucks, and at the edges of vineyards, were highly political. Making use of stereotypes (the boss, the scab), the* actos *sought not to present the individual thoughts of a gifted playwright but to present the social vision of ordinary people—the pueblo—though it was acknowledged that, in an oppressive society, the playwright might have to help guide the people to see their own best interests.*

Valdez moved from actos *to* mitos (*myths*)—*plays that drew on Aztec mythology, Mexican folklore, and Christianity—and then to* Zoot Suit, *a play that ran for many months in California and that became the first Mexican American play to be produced on Broadway. More recently, he wrote and directed a hit movie,* La Bamba, *and in 1991, he received an award from the AT&T Foundation for his musical,* Bandido, *presented by El Teatro Campesino. Valdez teaches at California State University, Monterey Bay.*

Los Vendidos was written in 1967, when Ronald Reagan, a conservative Republican, was governor of California.

Los Vendidos[1]

LIST OF CHARACTERS

HONEST SANCHO
SECRETARY
FARM WORKER
JOHNNY
REVOLUCIONARIO
MEXICAN-AMERICAN

SCENE: *Honest Sancho's Used Mexican Lot and Mexican Curio Shop. Three models are on display in Honest* SANCHO's *shop: to the right, there is a* REVOLUCIONARIO, *complete with sombrero, carrilleras,*[2] *and carabina 30-30. At center, on the floor,*

---

[1]**Los Vendidos** the sellouts.   [2]**carrilleras** cartridge belts.

there is the FARM WORKER *under a broad straw sombrero. At stage left is the* PACHUCO[3]
filero[4] in hand.

[*Honest* SANCHO *is moving among his models, dusting them off and preparing for another day of business*]

SANCHO: Bueno, bueno, mis monos, vamos a ver a quien vendemos ahora, ¿no?[5] [*To audience.*] ¡Quihubo! I'm Honest Sancho and this is my shop. Antes fui contratista pero ahora logré tener mi negocito.[6] All I need now is a customer. [A bell rings offstage.] Ay, a customer!

SECRETARY: [*Entering*] Good morning, I'm Miss Jiménez from—

SANCHO: ¡Ah, una chicana! Welcome, welcome Señorita Jiménez.

SECRETARY: [*Anglopronunciation*] JIM-enez.

SANCHO: ¿Qué?

SECRETARY: My name is Miss JIM-enez. Don't you speak English? What's wrong with you?

SANCHO: Oh, nothing, Señorita JIM-enez. I'm here to help you.

SECRETARY: That's better. As I was starting to say, I'm a secretary from Governor Reagan's office, and we're looking for a Mexican type for the administration.

SANCHO: Well, you come to the right place, lady. This is Honest Sancho's Used Mexican lot, and we got all types here. Any particular type you want?

SECRETARY: Yes, we were looking for somebody suave—

SANCHO: Suave.

SECRETARY: Debonair.

SANCHO: De buen aire.

SECRETARY: Dark.

SANCHO: Prieto.

SECRETARY: But of course not too dark.

SANCHO: No muy prieto.

SECRETARY: Perhaps, beige.

SANCHO: Beige, just the tone. Así como cafecito con leche,[7] ¿no?

SECRETARY: One more thing. He must be hard-working.

SANCHO: That could only be one model. Step right over here to the center of the shop, lady. [*They cross to the* FARM WORKER.] This is our standard FARM WORKER model. As you can see, in the words of our beloved Senator George Murphy, he is "built close to the ground." Also take special notice of his four-ply Goodyear huaraches, made from the rain tire. This wide-brimmed sombrero is an extra added feature—keeps off the sun, rain, and dust.

SECRETARY: Yes, it does look durable.

SANCHO: And our farm worker model is friendly. Muy amable.[8] Watch. [*Snaps his fingers.*]

FARM WORKER [*Lifts up head*]: Buenos días, señorita. [*His head drops.*]

SECRETARY: My, he's friendly.

SANCHO: Didn't I tell you? Loves his patrones! But his most attractive feature is that he's hard working. Let me show you. [*Snaps fingers,* FARM WORKER *stands.*]

FARM WORKER: ¡El jale![9] [*He begins to work.*]

---

[3]**Pachuco** an urban tough guy.   [4]**filero** blade.   [5]**Bueno . . . ¿no?** Well, well darlings, let's see who we can sell now, O.K.?   [6]**Antes . . . negocito** I used to be a contractor, but now I've succeeded in having my little business.   [7]**Así . . . leche** like coffee with milk.   [8]**Muy amable** very friendly.   [9]**¡El jale!** the job!

SANCHO: As you can see, he is cutting grapes.

SECRETARY: Oh, I wouldn't know.

SANCHO: He also picks cotton. [*Snap.* FARM WORKER *begins to pick cotton.*]

SECRETARY: Versatile isn't he?

SANCHO: He also picks melons. [*Snap.* FARM WORKER *picks melons.*] That's his slow speed for late in the season. Here's his fast speed. [*Snap.* FARM WORKER *picks faster.*]

SECRETARY: ¡Chihuahua! . . . I mean, goodness, he sure is a hard worker.

SANCHO [*Pulls the* FARM WORKER *to his feet*]: And that isn't the half of it. Do you see these little holes on his arms that appear to be pores? During those hot sluggish days in the field, when the vines or the branches get so entangled, it's almost impossible to move; these holes emit a certain grease that allow our model to slip and slide right through the crop with no trouble at all.

SECRETARY: Wonderful. But is he economical?

SANCHO: Economical? Señorita, you are looking at the Volkswagen of Mexicans. Pennies a day is all it takes. One plate of beans and tortillas will keep him going all day. That, and chile. Plenty of chile. Chile jalapeños, chile verde, chile colorado. But, of course, if you do give him chile [*Snap.* FARM WORKER *turns left face. Snap.* FARM WORKER *bends over.*] then you have to change his oil filter once a week.

SECRETARY: What about storage?

SANCHO: No problem. You know these new farm labor camps our Honorable Governor Reagan has built out by Parlier or Raisin City? They were designed with our model in mind. Five, six, seven, even ten in one of those shacks will give you no trouble at all. You can also put him in old barns, old cars, river banks. You can even leave him out in the field overnight with no worry!

SECRETARY: Remarkable.

SANCHO: And here's an added feature: Every year at the end of the season, this model goes back to Mexico and doesn't return, automatically, until next Spring.

SECRETARY: How about that. But tell me: does he speak English?

SANCHO: Another outstanding feature is that last year this model was programmed to go out on STRIKE! [*Snap.*]

FARM WORKER: ¡ HUELGA! ¡HUELGA! Hermanos, sálganse de esos files.[10] [*Snap. He stops.*]

SECRETARY: No! Oh no, we can't strike in the State Capitol.

SANCHO: Well, he also scabs. [*Snap.*]

FARM WORKER: Me vendo barato, ¿y qué?[11] [*Snap.*]

SECRETARY: That's much better, but you didn't answer my question. Does he speak English?

SANCHO: Bueno . . . no, pero[12] he has other—

SECRETARY: No.

SANCHO: Other features.

SECRETARY: NO! He just won't do!

SANCHO: Okay, okay pues. We have other models.

SECRETARY: I hope so. What we need is something a little more sophisticated.

SANCHO: Sophisti—¿qué?

---

[10]**¡HUELGA! . . . files** Strike! Strike! Brothers, leave those rows.   [11]**Me . . . qué?** I come cheap. So what?   [12]**Bueno . . . no, pero** well, no, but.

SECRETARY: An urban model.

SANCHO: Ah, from the city! Step right back. Over here in this corner of the shop is exactly what you're looking for. Introducing our new 1969 JOHNNY PACHUCO model! This is our fast-back model. Streamlined. Built for speed, low-riding, city life. Take a look at some of these features. Mag shoes, dual exhausts, green chartreuse paint-job, dark-tint windshield, a little poof on top. Let me just turn him on. [*Snap.* JOHNNY *walks to stage center with a pachuco bounce.*]

SECRETARY: What was that?

SANCHO: That, señorita, was the Chicano shuffle.

SECRETARY: Okay, what does he do?

SANCHO: Anything and everything necessary for city life. For instance, survival: He knife fights. [*Snap.* JOHNNY *pulls out switchblade and swings at* SECRETARY.]

   [SECRETARY *screams.*]

SANCHO: He dances. [*Snap.*]

JOHNNY [*Singing*]: "Angel Baby, my Angel Baby . . ." [*Snap.*]

SANCHO: And here's a feature no city model can be without. He gets arrested, but not without resisting, of course. [*Snap.*]

JOHNNY: ¡En la madre, la placa![13] I didn't do it! I didn't do it! [JOHNNY *turns and stands up against an imaginary wall, legs spread out, arms behind his back.*]

SECRETARY: Oh no, we can't have arrests! We must maintain law and order.

SANCHO: But he's bilingual!

SECRETARY: Bilingual?

SANCHO: Simón que yes.[14] He speaks English! Johnny, give us some English. [*Snap*]

JOHNNY [*Comes downstage*]: Fuck-you!

SECRETARY [*Gasps*]: Oh! I've never been so insulted in my whole life!

SANCHO: Well, he learned it in your school.

SECRETARY: I don't care where he learned it.

SANCHO: But he's economical!

SECRETARY: Economical?

SANCHO: Nickels and dimes. You can keep Johnny running on hamburgers, Taco Bell tacos, Lucky Lager beer, Thunderbird wine, yesca—

SECRETARY: Yesca?

SANCHO: Mota.

SECRETARY: Mota?

SANCHO: Leños[15] . . . Marijuana. [*Snap;* JOHNNY *inhales on an imaginary joint*]

SECRETARY: That's against the law!

JOHNNY [*Big smile, holding his breath*]: Yeah.

SANCHO: He also sniffs glue. [*Snap.* JOHNNY *inhales glue, big smile.*]

JOHNNY: That's too much man, ése.[16]

SECRETARY: No, Mr. Sancho, I don't think this—

SANCHO: Wait a minute, he has other qualities I know you'll love. For example, an inferiority complex. [*Snap.*]

JOHNNY [*To* SANCHO]: You think you're better than me, huh ése? [*Swings switchblade.*]

SANCHO: He can also be beaten and he bruises, cut him and he bleeds; kick him and he—[*He beats, bruises and kicks* PACHUCO.] would you like to try it?

---

[13]**¡En . . . la placa!** Wow, the cops!   [14]**Simón que yes** Yea, sure.   [15]**Leños** joints (marijuana).   [16]**ése** fellow.

SECRETARY: Oh, I couldn't.

SANCHO: Be my guest. He's a great scapegoat.

SECRETARY: No, really.

SANCHO: Please.

SECRETARY: Well, all right. Just once. [She *kicks* PACHUCO.] Oh, he's so soft.

SANCHO: Wasn't that good? Try again.

SECRETARY [*Kicks* PACHUCO]: Oh, he's so wonderful! [She *kicks him again*.]

SANCHO: Okay, that's enough, lady. You ruin the merchandise. Yes, our Johnny Pachuco model can give you many hours of pleasure. Why, the L.A.P.D. just bought twenty of these to train their rookie cops on. And talk about maintenance. Señorita, you are looking at an entirely self-supporting machine. You're never going to find our Johnny Pachuco model on the relief rolls. No, sir, this model knows how to liberate.

SECRETARY: Liberate?

SANCHO: He steals. [*Snap.* JOHNNY *rushes the* SECRETARY *and steals her purse*]

JOHNNY: ¡Dame esa bolsa, vieja!¹⁷ [*He grabs the purse and runs. Snap by* SANCHO. *He stops.*]

[SECRETARY *runs after* JOHNNY *and grabs purse away from him, kicking him as she goes.*]

SECRETARY: No, no, no! We can't have any *more* thieves in the State Administration. Put him back.

SANCHO: Okay, we still got other models. Come on, Johnny, we'll sell you to some old lady. [SANCHO *takes* JOHNNY *back to his place.*]

SECRETARY: Mr. Sancho, I don't think you quite understand what we need. What we need is something that will attract the women voters. Something more traditional, more romantic.

SANCHO: Ah, a lover. [He *smiles meaningfully*.] Step right over here, señorita. Introducing our standard Revolucionario and/or Early California Bandit type. As you can see he is well-built, sturdy, durable. This is the International Harvester of Mexicans.

SECRETARY: What does he do?

SANCHO: You name it, he does it. He rides horses, stays in the mountains, crosses deserts, plains, rivers, leads revolutions, follows revolutions, kills, can be killed, serves as a martyr, hero, movie star—did I say movie star? Did you ever see *Viva Zapata? Viva Villa? Villa Rides? Pancho Villa Returns? Pancho Villa Goes Back? Pancho Villa Meets Abbott and Costello*—

SECRETARY: I've never seen any of those.

SANCHO: Well, he was in all of them. Listen to this. [*Snap.*]

REVOLUCIONARIO [Scream]: ¡VIVA VILLAAAAA!

SECRETARY: That's awfully loud.

SANCHO: He has a volume control. [He *adjusts volume. Snap.*]

REVOLUCIONARIO [*Mousey voice*]: ¡Viva Villa!

SECRETARY: That's better.

SANCHO: And even if you didn't see him in the movies, perhaps you saw him on TV He makes commercials. [*Snap.*]

REVOLUCIONARIO: Is there a Frito Bandito in your house?

SECRETARY: Oh yes, I've seen that one!

---

¹⁷¡**Dame . . . vieja!** Give me that bag, old lady!

SANCHO: Another feature about this one is that he is economical. He runs on raw horsemeat and tequila.

SECRETARY: Isn't that rather savage?

SANCHO: Al contrario,[18] it makes him a lover. [*Snap.*]

REVOLUCIONARIO [*To* SECRETARY]: ¡Ay, mamasota, cochota, ven pa'ca![19] [*He grabs* SECRETARY *and folds her back—Latin-Lover style.*]

SANCHO [*Snap.* REVOLUCIONARIO *goes back upright.*]: Now wasn't that nice?

SECRETARY: Well, it was rather nice.

SANCHO: And finally, there is one outstanding feature about this model I KNOW the ladies are going to love: He's a GENUINE antique! He was made in Mexico in 1910!

SECRETARY: Made in Mexico?

SANCHO: That's right. Once in Tijuana, twice in Guadalajara, three times in Cuernavaca.

SECRETARY: Mr. Sancho, I thought he was an American product.

SANCHO: No, but—

SECRETARY: No, I'm sorry. We can't buy anything but American-made products. He just won't do.

SANCHO: But he's an antique!

SECRETARY: I don't care. You still don't understand what we need. It's true we need Mexican models such as these, but it's more important that he be *American.*

SANCHO: American?

SECRETARY: That's right, and judging from what you've shown me, I don't think you have what we want. Well, my lunch hour's almost over: I better—

SANCHO: Wait a minute! Mexican but American?

SECRETARY: That's correct.

SANCHO: Mexican but . . . [*A sudden flash*] AMERICAN! Yeah, I think we've got exactly what you want. He just came in today! Give me a minute. [*He exits. Talks from backstage.*] Here he is in the shop. Let me just get some papers off. There. Introducing our new 1970 Mexican-American! Ta-ra-ra-ra-ra-ra-RA-RAAA!

[SANCHO *brings out the* MEXICAN-AMERICAN *model, a clean-shaven middle-class type in a business suit, with glasses.*]

SECRETARY [*Impressed*]: Where have you been hiding this one?

SANCHO: He just came in this morning. Ain't he a beauty? Feast your eyes on him! Sturdy US STEEL frame, streamlined, modern. As a matter of fact, he is built exactly like our Anglo models except that he comes in a variety of darker shades: naugahyde, leather, or leatherette.

SECRETARY: Naugahyde.

SANCHO: Well, we'll just write that down. Yes, señorita, this model represents the apex of American engineering! He is bilingual, college educated, ambitious! Say the word "acculturate" and he accelerates. He is intelligent, well-mannered, clean—did I say clean? [*Snap.* MEXICAN-AMERICAN *raises his arm.*] Smell.

SECRETARY [*Smells*]: Old Sobaco, my favorite.

SANCHO [*Snap.* MEXICAN-AMERICAN *turns toward* SANCHO]: Eric! [To SECRETARY.] We call him Eric García. [*To* ERIC.] I want you to meet Miss JIM-enez, Eric.

---

[18]**Al contrario** On the contrary.   [19]**¡Ay . . . pa'ca!** Get over here!

MEXICAN-AMERICAN: Miss JIM-enez, I am delighted to make your acquaintance. [*He kisses her hand.*]

SECRETARY: Oh, my, how charming!

SANCHO: Did you feel the suction? He has seven especially engineered suction cups right behind his lips. He's a charmer all right!

SECRETARY: How about boards? Does he function on boards?

SANCHO: You name them, he is on them. Parole boards, draft boards, school boards, taco quality control boards, surf boards, two-by-fours.

SECRETARY: Does he function in politics?

SANCHO: Señorita, you are looking at a political MACHINE. Have you ever heard of the OEO, EOC, COD, WAR ON POVERTY? That's our model! Not only that, he makes political speeches.

SECRETARY: May I hear one?

SANCHO: With pleasure. [*Snap.*] Eric, give us a speech.

MEXICAN-AMERICAN: Mr. Congressman, Mr. Chairman, members of the board, honored guests, ladies and gentlemen. [SANCHO *and* SECRETARY *applaud.*] Please, please. I come before you as a Mexican-American to tell you about the problems of the Mexican. The problems of the Mexican stem from one thing and one thing alone: He's stupid. He's uneducated. He needs to stay in school. He needs to be ambitious, forward-looking, harder-working. He needs to think American, American, American, AMERICAN, AMERICAN, AMERICAN. GOD BLESS AMERICA! GOD BLESS AMERICA! GOD BLESS AMERICA!! [*He goes out of control.*]

[SANCHO *snaps frantically and the* MEXICAN-AMERICAN *finally slumps forward, bending at the waist.*]

SECRETARY: Oh my, he's patriotic too!

SANCHO: Sí, señorita, he loves his country. Let me just make a little adjustment here. [*Stands* MEXICAN-AMERICAN *up.*]

SECRETARY: What about upkeep? Is he economical?

SANCHO: Well, no, I won't lie to you. The Mexican-American costs a little bit more, but you get what you pay for. He's worth every extra cent. You can keep him running on dry Martinis, Langendorf bread.

SECRETARY: Apple pie?

SANCHO: Only Mom's. Of course, he's also programmed to eat Mexican food on ceremonial functions, but I must warn you: an overdose of beans will plug up his exhaust.

SECRETARY: Fine! There's just one more question: HOW MUCH DO YOU WANT FOR HIM?

SANCHO: Well, I tell you what I'm gonna do. Today and today only, because you've been so sweet, I'm gonna let you steal this model from me! I'm gonna let you drive him off the lot for the simple price of—let's see taxes and license included—$15,000.

SECRETARY: Fifteen thousand DOLLARS? For a MEXICAN!

SANCHO: Mexican? What are you talking, lady? This is a Mexican-AMERICAN! We had to melt down two pachucos, a farm worker and three gabachos[20] to make this model! You want quality, but you gotta pay for it! This is no cheap runabout. He's got class!

[20]**gabachos** whites.

SECRETARY: Okay, I'll take him.

SANCHO: You will?

SECRETARY: Here's your money.

SANCHO: You mind if I count it?

SECRETARY: Go right ahead.

SANCHO: Well, you'll get your pink slip in the mail. Oh, do you want me to wrap him up for you? We have a box in the back.

SECRETARY: No, thank you. The Governor is having a luncheon this afternoon, and we need a brown face in the crowd. How do I drive him?

SANCHO: Just snap your fingers. He'll do anything you want.

[SECRETARY *snaps.* MEXICAN-AMERICAN *steps forward.*]

MEXICAN-AMERICAN: RAZA QUERIDA, ¡VAMOS LEVANTANDO ARMAS PARA LIBER-ARNOS DE ESTOS DESGRACIADOS GABACHOS QUE NOS EXPLOTAN! VAMOS.[21]

SECRETARY: What did he say?

SANCHO: Something about lifting arms, killing white people, etc.

SECRETARY: But he's not supposed to say that!

SANCHO: Look, lady, don't blame me for bugs from the factory. He's your Mexican-American; you bought him, now drive him off the lot!

SECRETARY: But he's broken!

SANCHO: Try snapping another finger.

[SECRETARY *snaps.* MEXICAN-AMERICAN *comes to life again.*]

MEXICAN-AMERICAN: ¡ESTA GRAN HUMANIDAD HA DICHO BASTA! Y SE HA PUES-TO EN MARCHA! ¡BASTA! ¡BASTA! ¡VIVA LA RAZA! ¡VIVA LA CAUSA! ¡VIVA LA HUELGA! ¡VIVAN LOS BROWN BERETS! ¡VIVAN LOS ESTUDI-ANTES![22] ¡CHICANO POWER!

[*The* MEXICAN-AMERICAN *turns toward the* SECRETARY, *who gasps and backs up.*

He keeps turning toward the PACHUCO, FARM WORKER, *and* REVOLUCIONARIO, *snapping his fingers and turning each of them on, one by one.*]

PACHUCO [*Snap. To* SECRETARY]: I'm going to get you, baby! ¡Viva La Raza!

FARM WORKER [*Snap. To* SECRETARY]: ¡Viva la huelga! ¡Viva la Huelga! ¡VIVA LA HUELGA!

REVOLUCIONARIO [*Snap. To* SECRETARY]: ¡Viva la revolución! ¡VIVA LA REVOLUCIÓN!

[*The three models join together and advance toward the* SECRETARY, *who backs up and runs out of the shop screaming.* SANCHO *is at the other end of the shop hold-ing his money in his hand. All freeze. After a few seconds of silence, the* PACHUCO *moves and stretches, shaking his arms and loosening up. The* FARM WORKER *and* REVOLUCIONARIO *do the same.* SANCHO *stays where he is, frozen to his spot.*]

JOHNNY: Man, that was a long one, ése.[23] [*Others agree with him.*]

FARM WORKER: How did we do?

---

[21]**RAZA . . . VAMOS** Beloved Raza [persons of Mexican descent], let's take up arms to liberate ourselves from those damned whites who exploit us. Let's get going.   [22]**¡ESTA . . . ESTUDIANTES!** This great mass of humanity has said enough! And it has begun to march. Enough! Enough! Long live La Raza! Long live the Cause! Long live the strike! Long live the Brown Berets! Long live the students!   [23]**ése** fellow.

JOHNNY: Perty good, look at all that lana,[24] man! [*He goes over to* SANCHO *and removes the money from his hand.* SANCHO *stays where he is.*] REVOLUCIONARIO: En la madre, look at all the money.

JOHNNY: We keep this up, we're going to be rich.

FARM WORKER: They think we're machines.

REVOLUCIONARIO: Burros.

JOHNNY: Puppets.

MEXICAN-AMERICAN: The only thing I don't like is—how come I always got to play the godamn Mexican-American?

JOHNNY: That's what you get for finishing high school.

FARM WORKER: How about our wages, ése?

JOHNNY: Here it comes right now. $3,000 for you, $3,000 for you, $3,000 for you, and $3,000 for me. The rest we put back into the business.

MEXICAN-AMERICAN: Too much, man. Heh, where you vatos[25] going tonight?

FARM WORKER: I'm going over to Concha's. There's a party.

JOHNNY: Wait a minute, vatos. What about our salesman? I think he needs an oil job.

REVOLUCIONARIO: Leave him to me.

[*The* PACHUCO, FARM WORKER, *and* MEXICAN-AMERICAN *exit, talking loudly about their plans for the night. The* REVOLUCIONARIO *goes over to* SANCHO, *removes his derby hat and cigar, lifts him up and throws him over his shoulder.* SANCHO *hangs loose, lifeless.*]

REVOLUCIONARIO [To *audience*]: He's the best model we got! ¡Ajua![26]

[*Exit.*]

THE END

[1967]

Joining the Conversation: Critical Thinking and Writing

1. If you are an Anglo (shorthand for a Caucasian with traditional northern European values), do you find *Los Vendidos* deeply offensive? Why, or why not? If you are a Mexican American, do you find the play entertaining—or do you find parts of it offensive? What might Anglos enjoy in the play, and what might Mexican Americans find offensive? Set forth your views in a detailed argument.

2. What stereotypes of Mexican Americans are presented here? At the end of the play, what image of the Mexican American is presented? How does it compare with the stereotypes?

3. If you are a member of some other minority group, in a few sentences indicate how *Los Vendidos* might be adapted into a play about that group.

4. Putting aside the politics of the play (and your own politics), what do you think are the strengths of *Los Vendidos?* What do you think are its weaknesses?

5. The play was written in 1967. Do you find it dated? If not, why not? Please point to specific passages to support your analysis and argument.

---

[24]**lana** money.   [25]**vatos** guys.   [26]**¡Ajua!** Wow!

6. In 1971 when *Los Vendidos* was produced by El Teatro de la Esperanza, the group altered the ending by having the men decide to use the money to build a community center. Evaluate this ending.

7. When the play was videotaped by KNBC in Los Angeles for broadcast in 1973, Valdez changed the ending. In the revised version we discover that a scientist (played by Valdez) masterminds the operation, placing Mexican American models wherever there are persons of Mexican descent. These models soon will become Chicanos (as opposed to persons with Anglo values) and will aid rather than work against their fellows. Evaluate this ending.

8. In his short essay "The Actos," Valdez says, "Actos: Inspire the audience to social action. Illuminate specific points about social problems. Satirize the opposition. Show or hint at a solution. Express what people are feeling." How many of these things do you think *Los Vendidos* does?

9. Many people assume that politics gets in the way of serious art. That is, they assume that artists ought to be concerned with issues that transcend politics. Does this point make any sense to you? Why, or why not?

Chapter Overview: Looking Backward/Looking Forward

1. How would you define technology's role in your life? For one day, keep a "technology log," in which you keep track of how often you use a computer, cell phone, television, or any other form of technology. Note the type and function of the technology that you use and how long you use it. Analyze this log, and reflect on your use of technology. What does the log reveal about your reliance on technology? Does the log reveal anything surprising or reassuring to you?

2. Our popular culture generates many images of technology—some positive, some negative. For example, one science fiction movie might present a utopian world filled with high-tech spaceships, while another might present a dystopian world in which robots control humans. How do you imagine the technologies of the future? Do you imagine a utopian or a dystopian world of technology?

3. Do you ever feel that you control technology or that technology controls you?

4. Some of the literary selections in this chapter feature writers depicting outdated forms of technology, such a locomotives and telephones. Informally interview your parents, grandparents, or older friends or relatives about the forms of technology that were new when they were children. What was their reaction to that form of technology? How has that technology evolved? Do you use that form of technology today?

5. Is it possible to escape technology? Have you ever made a purposeful decision, such as going on a hike or studying without your cell phone, to leave technology behind? Would you like to escape technology? Why or why not?

6. A common modern fear expresses the belief that "computers will take over the world." Do you share this fear?

7. Technology is now interwoven into our social relationships, such as when we "friend" or "like" someone. How has technology shaped your social relationships? Has technology strengthened or weakened, helped or hindered those relationships?

8. What might be some future uses of technology? Think of a problem—large or small—that could be aided or solved by technology. For example, can technology help with global issues of world hunger, local issues such as traffic-filled highways, or everyday issues such as making the use of tap water more efficient? Or, think of an artificial intelligence type of activity that might show off the potential of technology. For example, would you like to see a computer play a game of monopoly or assess the risks of different types of surgery? After you locate a topic, search the Internet, using terms for the topic and phrases such as "technology," to see what sort of research is being done in that area. Can you define an issue and imagine progress being made in that area due to technology?

CHAPTER 18

Love and Hate, Men and Women

ESSAY

JUDITH ORTIZ COFER

Born in Puerto Rico in 1952 of a Puerto Rican mother and a U.S. mainland father who served in the navy, Judith Ortiz Cofer was educated both in Puerto Rico and on the mainland. After earning a BA and an MA in English, she did further graduate work at Oxford and then taught English in Florida. Her publications include books of poetry, a novel, and collections of stories and essays. She is now a professor of English and creative writing at the University of Georgia.

The following selection comes from Cofer's autobiography, Silent Dancing *(1990).*

I Fell in Love, or My Hormones Awakened

I fell in love, or my hormones awakened from their long slumber in my body, and suddenly the goal of my days was focused on one thing: to catch a glimpse of my secret love. And it had to remain secret, because I had, of course, in the great tradition of tragic romance, chosen to love a boy who was totally out of my reach. He was not Puerto Rican; he was Italian and rich. He was also an older man. He was a senior at the high school when I came in as a freshman. I first saw him in the hall, leaning casually on a wall that was the border line between girlside and boyside for underclassmen. He looked extraordinarily like a young Marlon Brando[1]—down to the ironic little smile. The total of what I knew about the boy who starred in every one of my awkward fantasies was this: that he was the nephew of the man who owned the supermarket on my block; that he often had parties at his parents' beautiful home in the suburbs which I would hear about; that his family had money (which came to our school in many ways)—and this fact made my knees weak: and that he worked at the store near my apartment building on weekends and in the summer.

My mother could not understand why I became so eager to be the one sent out on her endless errands. I pounced on every opportunity from Friday to late Saturday afternoon to go after eggs, cigarettes, milk (I tried to drink as much of it as possible, although I hated the stuff)—the staple items that she would order from the "American" store.

[1] **Marlon Brando** charismatic American stage and screen actor (1924–2004)

Week after week I wandered up and down the aisles, taking furtive glances at the stock room in the back, breathlessly hoping to see my prince. Not that I had a plan. I felt like a pilgrim waiting for a glimpse of Mecca. I did not expect him to notice me. It was sweet agony.

One day I did see him. Dressed in a white outfit like a surgeon: white pants and shirt, white cap, and (gross sight, but not to my love-glazed eyes) blood-smeared butcher's apron. He was helping to drag a side of beef into the freezer storage area of the store. I must have stood there like an idiot, because I remember that he did see me, he even spoke to me! I could have died. I think he said, "Excuse me," and smiled vaguely in my direction.

5   After that, I *willed* occasions to go to the supermarket. I watched my mother's pack of cigarettes empty ever so slowly. I wanted her to smoke them fast. I drank milk and forced it on my brother (although a second glass for him had to be bought with my share of Fig Newton cookies which we both liked, but we were restricted to one row each). I gave my cookies up for love, and watched my mother smoke her L&M's with so little enthusiasm that I thought (God, no!) that she might be cutting down on her smoking or maybe even giving up the habit. At this crucial time!

I thought I had kept my lonely romance a secret. Often I cried hot tears on my pillow for the things that kept us apart. In my mind there was no doubt that he would never notice me (and that is why I felt free to stare at him—I was invisible). He could not see me because I was a skinny Puerto Rican girl, a freshman who did not belong to any group he associated with.

At the end of the year I found out that I had not been invisible. I learned one little lesson about human nature—adulation leaves a scent, one that we are all equipped to recognize, and no matter how insignificant the source, we seek it.

In June the nuns at our school would always arrange for some cultural extravaganza. In my freshman year it was a Roman banquet. We had been studying Greek drama (as a prelude to church history—it was at a fast clip that we galloped through Sophocles and Euripides toward the early Christian martyrs), and our young, energetic Sister Agnes was in the mood for spectacle. She ordered the entire student body (it was a small group of under 300 students) to have our mothers make us togas out of sheets. She handed out a pattern on mimeo pages fresh out of the machine. I remember the intense smell of the alcohol on the sheets of paper, and how almost everyone in the auditorium brought theirs to their noses and inhaled deeply—mimeographed handouts were the school-day buzz that the new Xerox generation of kids is missing out on. Then, as the last couple of weeks of school dragged on, the city of Paterson becoming a concrete oven, and us wilting in our uncomfortable uniforms, we labored like frantic Roman slaves to build a splendid banquet hall in our small auditorium. Sister Agnes wanted a raised dais where the host and hostess would be regally enthroned.

She had already chosen our Senator and Lady from among our ranks. The Lady was to be a beautiful new student named Sophia, a recent Polish immigrant, whose English was still practically unintelligible, but whose features, classically perfect without a trace of makeup, enthralled us. Everyone talked about her gold hair cascading past her waist, and her voice which could carry a note right up to heaven in choir. The nuns wanted her for God. They kept saying that she had vocation. We just looked at her in awe, and the boys seemed afraid of her. She just smiled and did as she was told. I don't know what she thought of it all. The main privilege of beauty is that others will do almost everything for you, including thinking.

10   Her partner was to be our best basketball player, a tall, red-haired senior whose family sent its many offspring to our school. Together, Sophia and her senator looked like the best combination of immigrant genes our community could produce. It did not occur to me to ask then whether anything but their physical beauty qualified them for the starring roles in our production. I had the highest average in the church history class, but I was given the part of one of many "Roman Citizens." I was to sit in front of the plastic fruit and recite a greeting in Latin along with the rest of the school when our hosts came into the hall and took their places on their throne.

On the night of our banquet, my father escorted me in my toga to the door of our school. I felt foolish in my awkwardly draped sheet (blouse and skirt required underneath). My mother had no great skill as a seamstress. The best she could do was hem a skirt or a pair of pants. That night I would have traded her for a peasant woman with a golden needle. I saw other Roman ladies emerging from their parents' cars looking authentic in sheets of material that folded over their bodies like the garments on a statue by Michelangelo. How did they do it? How was it that I always got it just slightly wrong, and worse, I believed that other people were just too polite to mention it. "The poor little Puerto Rican girl," I could hear them thinking. But in reality, I must have been my worst critic, self-conscious as I was.

Soon, we were all sitting at our circle of tables joined together around the dais. Sophia glittered like a golden statue. Her smile was beatific: a perfect, silent Roman lady. Her "senator" looked uncomfortable, glancing around at his buddies, perhaps waiting for the ridicule that he would surely get in the locker room later. The nuns in their black habits stood in the background watching us. What were they supposed to be, the Fates? Nubian slaves? The dancing girls did their modest little dance to tinny music from their finger cymbals, then the speeches were made. Then the grape juice "wine" was raised in a toast to the Roman Empire we all knew would fall within the week—before finals anyway.

All during the program I had been in a state of controlled hysteria. My secret love sat across the room from me looking supremely bored. I watched his every move, taking him in gluttonously. I relished the shadow of his eyelashes on his ruddy cheeks, his pouty lips smirking sarcastically at the ridiculous sight of our little play. Once he slumped down on his chair, and our sergeant-at-arms nun came over and tapped him sharply on his shoulder. He drew himself up slowly, with disdain. I loved his rebellious spirit. I believed myself still invisible to him in my "nothing" status as I looked upon my beloved. But toward the end of the evening, as we stood chanting our farewells in Latin, he looked straight across the room and into my eyes! How did I survive the killing power of those dark pupils? I trembled in a new way. I was not cold—I was burning! Yet I shook from the inside out, feeling light-headed, dizzy.

The room began to empty and I headed for the girls' lavatory. I wanted to relish the miracle in silence. I did not think for a minute that anything more would follow. I was satisfied with the enormous favor of a look from my beloved. I took my time, knowing that my father would be waiting outside for me, impatient, perhaps glowing in the dark in his phosphorescent white Navy uniform. The others would ride home. I would walk home with my father, both of us in costume. I wanted as few witnesses as possible. When I could no longer hear the crowds in the hallway, I emerged from the bathroom, still under the spell of those mesmerizing eyes.

15   The lights had been turned off in the hallway and all I could see was the lighted stairwell, at the bottom of which a nun would be stationed. My father would be waiting just outside. I nearly screamed when I felt someone grab me by

the waist. But my mouth was quickly covered by someone else's mouth. I was being kissed. My first kiss and I could not even tell who it was. I pulled away to see that face not two inches away from mine. It was he. He smiled down at me. Did I have a silly expression on my face? My glasses felt crooked on my nose. I was unable to move or to speak. More gently, he lifted my chin and touched his lips to mine. This time I did not forget to enjoy it. Then, like the phantom lover that he was, he walked away into the darkened corridor and disappeared.

I don't know how long I stood there. My body was changing right there in the hallway of a Catholic school. My cells were tuning up like musicians in an orchestra, and my heart was a chorus. It was an opera I was composing, and I wanted to stand very still and just listen. But, of course, I heard my father's voice talking to the nun. I was in trouble if he had had to ask about me. I hurried down the stairs making up a story on the way about feeling sick. That would explain my flushed face and it would buy me a little privacy when I got home.

The next day Father announced at the breakfast table that he was leaving on a six month tour of Europe with the Navy in a few weeks and that at the end of the school year my mother, my brother, and I would be sent to Puerto Rico to stay for half a year at Mamá's (my mother's mother) house. I was devastated. This was the usual routine for us. We had always gone to Mamá's to stay when Father was away for long periods. But this year it was different for me. I was in love, and . . . my heart knocked against my bony chest at this thought . . . he loved me too? I broke into sobs and left the table.

In the next week I discovered the inexorable truth about parents. They can actually carry on with their plans right through tears, threats, and the awful spectacle of a teenager's broken heart. My father left me to my mother who impassively packed while I explained over and over that I was at a crucial time in my studies and that if I left my entire life would be ruined. All she would say was, "You are an intelligent girl, you'll catch up." Her head was filled with visions of *casa*[2] and family reunions, long gossip sessions with her mamá and sisters. What did she care that I was losing my one chance at true love?

In the meantime I tried desperately to see him. I thought he would look for me too. But the few times I saw him in the hallway, he was always rushing away. It would be long weeks of confusion and pain before I realized that the kiss was nothing but a little trophy for his ego. He had no interest in me other than as his adorer. He was flattered by my silent worship of him, and he had *bestowed* a kiss on me to please himself, and to fan the flames. I learned a lesson about the battle of the sexes then that I have never forgotten: the object is not always to win, but most times simply to keep your opponent (synonymous at times with "the loved one") guessing.

20　　But this is too cynical a view to sustain in the face of that overwhelming rush of emotion that is first love. And in thinking back about my own experience with it, I can be objective only to the point where I recall how sweet the anguish was, how caught up in the moment I felt, and how every nerve in my body was involved in this salute to life. Later, much later, after what seemed like an eternity of dragging the weight of unrequited love around with me, I learned to make myself visible and to relish the little battles required to win the greatest prize of all. And much later, I read and understood Camus'[3] statement about the subject that concerns both adolescent and philosopher alike: if love were easy, life would be too simple.

[1990]

---

[2]*casa* home.　[3]**Albert Camus** (1913–60), French novelist and philosopher.

Joining the Conversation: Critical Thinking and Writing

1. If you agree with us that Cofer's essay is amusing, try to analyze the sources of its humor. Why are some passages funny?
2. In paragraph 9 Cofer says, "The main privilege of beauty is that others will do almost everything for you, including thinking." Do you agree that the beautiful are privileged? If so, draw on your experience (as one of the privileged or the unprivileged) to recount an example or two. By the way, Cofer seems to imply (paragraph 10) that the academically gifted should be privileged, or at least should be recognized as candidates for leading roles (for example, that of "a perfect, silent Roman lady") in school productions. Is it any fairer to privilege brains than to privilege beauty? Explain your answer.
3. In her final paragraph, Cofer speaks of the experience as a "salute to life." What do you think she means by that?
4. Cofer is describing a state that is (or used to be) called "puppy love." If you have experienced anything like what Cofer experienced, write your own autobiographical essay. (You can, of course, amplify or censor as you wish.) If you have experienced a love that you think is more serious, more lasting, write about *that.*

STORIES

ZORA NEALE HURSTON

Zora Neale Hurston (1891–1960) was brought up in Eaton-ville, Florida, a town said to be the first all-black, self-governing town in the United States. Her mother died in 1904, and when Hurston's father remarried, Hurston felt out of place. In 1914, she joined a traveling theatrical group as a maid, hoping to save money for school. Later, by working at such jobs as manicurist and waitress, she put herself through college, entering Howard University in 1923. After receiving a scholarship, she transferred in 1926 to Barnard College in New York, where she was the first African American student in the college. After graduating from Barnard in 1928, she taught drama, worked as an editor, and studied anthropology. But, when grant money ran out in 1932, she returned to Eatonville to edit the folk material that she had collected during four years of fieldwork and to do further writing. She published steadily from 1932 to 1938—stories, folklore, and two novels—but she made very little money. Furthermore, although she played a large role in the Harlem Renaissance in the 1930s, she was criticized by Richard Wright and other influential black authors for portraying blacks as stereotypes and for being politically conservative. To many in the 1950s, her writing seemed reactionary and almost embarrassing in an age of black protest, and she herself—working as a domestic, a librarian, and a substitute teacher—was almost forgotten. Hurston died in a county wel-fare home in Florida and is buried in an unmarked grave. But literary scholars now judge her to be one of the major authors of her era, and her work is widely read and taught.

Sweat

It was eleven o'clock of a Spring night in Florida. It was Sunday. Any other night, Delia Jones would have been in bed for two hours by this time. But she was a washwoman, and Monday morning meant a great deal to her. So she collected the soiled clothes on Saturday when she returned the clean things. Sunday night after church, she sorted them and put the white things to soak. It saved her almost a half day's start. A great hamper in the bedroom held the clothes that she brought home. It was so much neater than a number of bundles lying around.

She squatted in the kitchen floor beside the great pile of clothes, sorting them into small heaps according to color, and humming a song in a mournful key, but wondering through it all where Sykes, her husband, had gone with her horse and buckboard.[1]

Just then something long, round, limp and black fell upon her shoulders and slithered to the floor beside her. A great terror took hold of her. It softened her knees and dried her mouth so that it was a full minute before she could cry out or move. Then she saw that it was the big bull whip her husband liked to carry when he drove.

She lifted her eyes to the door and saw him standing there bent over with laughter at her fright. She screamed at him.

5　"Sykes, what you throw dat whip on me like dat? You know it would skeer me—looks just like a snake, an' you knows how skeered Ah is of snakes."

"Course Ah knowed it! That's how come Ah done it." He slapped his leg with his hand and almost rolled on the ground in his mirth. "If you such a big fool dat you got to have a fit over a earth worm or a string, Ah don't keer how bad Ah skeer you."

"You aint got no business doing it. Gawd knows it's a sin. Some day Ah'm gointuh drop dead from some of yo' foolishness. 'Nother thing, where you been wid mah rig? Ah feeds dat pony. He aint fuh you to be drivin' wid no bull whip."

"Yo sho is one aggravatin' nigger woman!" he declared and stepped into the room. She resumed her work and did not answer him at once. "Ah done tole you time and again to keep them white folks' clothes outa dis house."

He picked up the whip and glared down at her. Delia went on with her work. She went out into the yard and returned with a galvanized tub and set it on the washbench. She saw that Sykes had kicked all of the clothes together again, and now stood in her way truculently, his whole manner hoping, *praying,* for an argument. But she walked calmly around him and commenced to re-sort the things.

10　"Next time, Ah'm gointer to kick 'em outdoors," he threatened as he struck a match along the leg of his corduroy breeches.

Delia never looked up from her work, and her thin, stooped shoulders sagged further.

"Ah aint for no fuss t'night Sykes. Ah just come from taking sacrament at the church house."

He snorted scornfully. "Yeah, you just come from de church house on a Sunday night, but heah you is gone to work on them clothes. You aint nothing but a hypocrite. One of them amen-corner Christians—sing, whoop, shout, then come home and wash white folks clothes on the Sabbath."

He stepped roughly upon the whitest pile of things, kicking them helter-skelter as he crossed the room. His wife gave a little scream of dismay, and quickly gathered them together again.

---

[1]**buckboard** an open wagon.

15   "Sykes, you quit grindin' dirt into these clothes! How can Ah git through by Sat'day if Ah don't start on Sunday?"

"Ah don't keer if you never git through. Anyhow, Ah done promised Gawd and a couple of other men, Ah aint gointer have it in mah house. Don't gimme no lip neither, else Ah'll throw 'em out and put mah fist up side yo' head to boot."

Delia's habitual meekness seemed to slip from her shoulders like a blown scarf. She was on her feet; her poor little body, her bare knuckly hands bravely defying the strapping hulk before her.

"Looka heah, Sykes, you done gone too fur. Ah been married to you fur fifteen years, and Ah been takin' in washin' for fifteen years. Sweat, sweat, sweat! Work and sweat, cry and sweat, pray and sweat!"

"What's that got to do with me?" he asked brutally.

20   "What's it got to do with you, Sykes? Mah tub of suds is filled yo' belly with vittles more times than yo' hands is filled it. Mah sweat is done paid for this house and Ah reckon Ah kin keep on sweatin in it."

She seized the iron skillet from the stove and struck a defensive pose, which act surprised him greatly, coming from her. It cowed him and he did not strike her as he usually did.

"Naw you won't," she panted, "that ole snaggle-toothed black woman you runnin' with aint comin' heah to pile up on *mah* sweat and blood. You aint paid for nothin' on this place, and Ah'm gointer stay right heah till Ah'm toted out foot foremost."

"Well, you better quit gittin' me riled up, else they'll be totin' you out sooner than you expect. Ah'm so tired of you Ah don't know whut to do. Gawd! how Ah hates skinny wimmen!"

A little awed by this new Delia, he sidled out of the door and slammed the back gate after him. He did not say where he had gone, but she knew too well. She knew very well that he would not return until nearly daybreak also. Her work over, she went on to bed but not to sleep at once. Things had come to a pretty pass!

25   She lay awake, gazing upon the debris that cluttered their matrimonial trail. Not an image left standing along the way. Anything like flowers had long ago been drowned in the salty stream that had been pressed from her heart. Her tears, her sweat, her blood. She had brought love to the union and he had brought a longing for the flesh. Two months after the wedding, he had given her the first brutal beating. She had the memory of numerous trips to Orlando with all of his wages when he had returned to her penniless, even before the first year had passed. She was young and soft then, but now she thought of her knotty, muscled limbs, her harsh knuckly hands, and drew herself up into an unhappy little ball in the middle of the big feather bed. Too late now to hope for love, even if it were not Bertha it would be someone else. This case differed from the others only in that she was bolder than the others. Too late for everything except her little home. She had built it for her old days, and planted one by one the trees and flowers there. It was lovely to her, lovely.

Somehow before sleep came, she found herself saying aloud: "Oh well, whatever goes over the Devil's back, is got to come under his belly. Sometime or ruther, Sykes, like everybody else, is gointer reap his sowing." After that she was able to build a spiritual earthworks against her husband. His shells could no longer reach her. *Amen.* She went to sleep and slept until he announced his presence in bed by kicking her feet and rudely snatching the cover away.

"Gimme some kivah heah, an' git yo' damn foots over on yo' own side! Ah oughter mash you in yo' mouf fuh drawing dat skillet on me."

Delia went clear to the rail without answering him. A triumphant indifference to all that he was or did.

The week was as full of work for Delia as all other weeks, and Saturday found her behind her little pony, collecting and delivering clothes.

30 It was a hot, hot day near the end of July. The village men on Joe Clarke's porch even chewed cane listlessly. They did not hurl the cane-knots as usual. They let them dribble over the edge of the porch. Even conversation had collapsed under the heat.

"Heah comes Delia Jones," Jim Merchant said, as the shaggy pony came round the bend of the road toward them. The rusty buckboard was heaped with baskets of crisp, clean laundry.

"Yep," Joe Lindsay agreed, "Hot or col', rain or shine, jes ez reg'lar ez de weeks roll roun' Delia carries 'em an' fetches 'em on Sat'day."

"She better if she wanter eat," said Moss. "Syke Jones aint wuth de shot an' powder hit would tek tuh kill 'em. Not to *bub* he aint."

"He sho' aint," Walter Thomas chimed in. "It's too bad, too, cause she wuz a right pritty lil trick when he got huh. Ah'd uh mah'ied huh mahseft' it' he hadnter beat me to it."

35 Delia nodded briefly at the men as she drove past.

"Too much knockin will ruin *any* 'oman. He done beat huh nough tuh kill three women, let 'lone change they looks," said Elijah Mosely. "How Syke kin stom-muck dat big black greasy Mogu[2] he's layin' roun' wid, gits me. Ah swear dat cight-rock couldn't kiss a sardine can Ah done thowed out de back do' 'way las' yeah."

"Aw, she's fat, thass how come. He's allus been crazy 'bout fat women," put in Merchant. "He'd a' been tied up wid one long time ago if he could a' found one tuh have him. Did Ah tell yuh 'bout him come sidlin' roun' *mah* 'wife—bringin' her a basket uh pee-cans outa his yard fuh a present? Yes-sir, mah wife! She tol' him tuh take 'em right straight back home, cause Delia works so hard ovah dat washtub she reckon everything en de place taste lak sweat an' soap-suds. Ah jus' wisht Ah'd a' caught 'im 'roun' dere! Ah'd a' made his hips ketch on fiah down dat shell road."

"Ah know he done it, too. Ah sees 'im grinnin' at every 'oman dat passes," Walter Thomas said. "But even so, he useter eat some mighty big hunks uh humble pie tuh git dat lil' 'oman he got. She wuz ez pritty ez a speckled pup! Dat wuz fif-teen yeahs ago. He useter be so skeered uh losin' huh, she could make him do some parts of a husband's duty. Dey never wuz de same in de mind."

"There oughter be a law about him," said Lindsay. "He aint fit tuh carry guts tuh a bear."

40 Clarke spoke for the first time. "Taint no law on earth dat kin make a man be decent if it aint in 'im. There's plenty men dat takes a wife lak dey do a joint uh sugar-cane. It's round, juicy an' sweet when dey gits it. But dey squeeze an' grind, squeeze an' grind an' wring tell dey wring every drop uh pleasure dat's in 'em out. When dey's satisfied dat dey is wring dry, dey treats 'em jes lak dey do a cane-chew. Dey thows 'em away. Dey knows whut dey is doin' while dey is at it, an' hates theirselves fuh it but they keeps on hangin' after huh tell she's empty. Den dey hates huh fuh bein' a cane-chew an' in de way."

"We oughter take Syke an' dat stray 'oman uh his'n down in Lake Howell swamp an' lay on de rawhide till they cain't say 'Lawd a' mussy.' He allus wuz uh ovahbearin' niggah, but since dat white 'oman from up north done teached 'im

[2]**Mogu** big person.

how to run a automobile, he done got too biggety to live—an' we oughter kill 'im," Old Man Anderson advised.

A grunt of approval went around the porch. But the heat was melting their civic virtue and Elijah Moseley began to bait Joe Clarke.

"Come on, Joe, git a melon outa dere an' slice it up for yo' customers. We'se all sufferin' wid de heat. De bear's done got *me!*"

"Thass right. Joe, a watermelon is jes' whut Ah needs tuh cure de eppizu-dicks."[3] Walter Thomas joined forces with Moseley. "Come on dere, Joe. We all is steady customers an' you aint set us up in a long time. Ah chooses dat long, bow-legged Floridy favorite."

45   "A god, an' be dough. You all gimme twenty cents and slice away," Clarke retorted. "Ah needs a col' slice m'self. Heah, everybody chip in. Ah'll lend y'll mah meat knife."

The money was quickly subscribed and the huge melon brought forth. At that moment, Sykes and Bertha arrived. A determined silence fell on the porch and the melon was put away again.

Merchant snapped down the blade of his jackknife and moved toward the store door.

"Come on in, Joe, an' gimme a slab uh sow belly an' uh pound uh coffee—almost fuhgot 'twas Sat'day. Got to git on home." Most of the men left also.

Just then Delia drove past on her way home, as Sykes was ordering magnifi-cently for Bertha. It pleased him for Delia to see.

50   "Git whutsoever yo' heart desires, Honey. Wait a minute, Joe. Give huh two bottles uh strawberry soda-water, uh quart uh parched groundpeas, an' a block uh chewin' gum."

With all this they left the store, with Sykes reminding Bertha that this was his town and she could have it if she wanted it.

The men returned soon after they left, and held their watermelon feast. "Where did Syke Jones git dat 'oman from nohow?" Lindsay asked.

"Ovah Apopka. Guess dey musta been cleanin' out de town when she lef. She don't look lak a thing but a hunk uh liver wid hair on it."

"Well, she sho' kin squall," Dave Carter contributed. "When she gits ready tuh laff, she jes' opens huh mouf an' latches it back tuh de las' notch. No ole grandpa alligator down in Lake Bell aint got nothin' on huh."

55   Bertha had been in town three months now. Sykes was still paying her room rent at Della Lewis'—the only house in town that would have taken her in. Sykes took her frequently to Winter Park to "stomps."[4] He still assured her that he was the swellest man in the state.

"Sho' you kin have dat lil' ole house soon's Ah kin git dat 'oman outa dere. Everything b'longs tuh me an' you sho' kin have it. Ah sho' 'bominates uh skinny 'oman. Lawdy, you sho' is got one portly shape on you! You kin git *anything* you wants. Dis is *mah* town an' you sho' kin have it."

Delia's work-worn knees crawled over the earth in Gethsemane and on the rocks of Calvary[5] many, many times during these months. She avoided the villagers and meeting places in her effort to be blind and deaf. But Bertha nullified this to a degree, by coming to Delia's house to call Sykes out to her at the gate.

---

[3]**eppizudicks** i.e., epizootic, an epidemic among animals.   [4]**stomps** dances.
[5]**Gethsemane** the garden where Jesus prayed just before he was betrayed (Matthew 26.36–47); **Calvary** the hill where he was crucified.

Delia and Sykes fought all the time now with no peaceful interludes. They slept and ate in silence. Two or three times Delia had attempted a timid friendliness, but she was repulsed each time. It was plain that the breaches must remain agape.

The sun had burned July to August. The heat streamed down like a million hot arrows, smiting all things living upon the earth. Grass withered, leaves browned, snakes went blind in shedding and men and dogs went mad. Dog days!

60   Delia came home one day and found Sykes there before her. She wondered, but started to go on into the house without speaking, even though he was standing in the kitchen door and she must either stoop under his arm or ask him to move. He made no room for her. She noticed a soap box beside the steps, but paid no particular attention to it, knowing that he must have brought it there. As she was stooping to pass under his outstretched arm, he suddenly pushed her backward, laughingly.

"Look in de box dere Delia. Ah done brung yuh somethin'!"

She nearly fell upon the box in her stumbling, and when she saw what it held, she all but fainted outright.

"Syke! Syke, mah Gawd! You take dat rattlesnake 'way from heah! You *gottuh*. Oh, Jesus, have mussy!"

"Ah aint gut tuh do nuthin' uh de kin'—fact is Ah aint got tuh do nothin' but die. Taint no use uh you puttin' on airs makin' out lak you sceered uh dat snake— he's gointer stay right heah tell he die. He wouldn't bite me cause Ah knows how tuh handle 'im. Nohow he wouldn't risk breakin' out his fangs 'gin *yo'* skinny laigs."

65   "Naw, now Syke, don't keep dat thing 'roun' heah tuh skeer me tuh death. You knows Ah'm even feared uh earth worms. Thass de biggest snake Ah evah did see. Kill 'im Syke, please."

"Doan ast me tuh do nothin 'fuh yuh. Goin' 'roun' tryin' to be so damn aster-perious. Naw, Ah aint gonna kill it. Ah think uh damn sight mo' uh him dan you! Dat's a nice snake an' anybody doan lak 'im kin jes' hit de grit."

The village soon heard that Sykes had the snake, and came to see and ask questions.

"How de hen-fire did you ketch dat six-foot rattler, Syke?" Thomas asked.

"He's full uh frogs so he caint hardly move, thass how Ah eased up on 'm. But Ah'm a snake charmer an' knows how tuh handle 'em. Shux, dat aint nothin'. Ah could ketch one eve'y day if Ah so wanted tuh."

70   "Whut he needs is a heavy hick'ry club leaned real heavy on his head. Dat's de bes 'way tuh charm a rattlesnake."

"Naw, Walt, y'll jes' don't understand dese diamon' backs lak Ah do," said Sykes in a superior tone of voice.

The village agreed with Walter, but the snake stayed on. His box remained by the kitchen door with its screen wire covering. Two or three days later it had digested its meal of frogs and literally came to life. It rattled at every movement in the kitchen or the yard. One day as Delia came down the kitchen steps she saw his chalky-white fangs curved like scimitars hung in the wire meshes. This time she did not run away with averted eyes as usual. She stood for a long time in the door-way in a red fury that grew bloodier for every second that she regarded the crea-ture that was her torment.

That night she broached the subject as soon as Sykes sat down to the table.

"Syke, Ah wants you tuh take dat snake 'way fum heah. You done starved me an' Ah put up widcher, you done beat me an Ah took dat, but you done kilt all mah insides bringin' dat varmint heah."

75   Sykes poured out a saucer full of coffee and drank it deliberately before he answered her.

"A whole lot Ah keer 'bout how you feels inside uh out. Dat snake aint goin' no damn wheah till Ah gits ready fuh 'im tuh go. So fur as beatin' is concerned, yuh aint took near all dat you gointer take ef yuh stay 'roun' *me*."

Delia pushed back her plate and got up from the table. "Ah hates you. Sykes," she said calmly. "Ah hates you tuh de same degree dat Ah useter love yuh. Ah done took an' took till mah belly is full up tuh mah neck. Dat's de reason Ah got mah letter fum de church an' moved mah membership tuh Woodbridge—so Ah don't haftuh take no sacrament wid yuh. Ah don't wantuh see yuh, 'roun' me atall. Lay 'roun' wid dat 'oman all yuh wants tuh, but gwan 'way fum me an' mah house. Ah hates yuh lak uh suck-egg dog."

Sykes almost let the huge wad of corn bread and collard greens he was chewing fall out of his mouth in amazement. He had a hard time whipping himself to the proper fury to try to answer Delia.

"Well, Ah'm glad you does hate me. Ah'm sho' tiahed uh you hangin' ontuh me. Ah don't want yuh. Look at yuh stringey ole neck! Yo' raw-bony laigs an' arms is enough tuh cut uh man tuh death. You looks jes' lak de devvul's doll-baby tuh *me*. You cain't hate me no worse dan Ah hates you. Ah been hatin' *you* fuh years."

80   "Yo' ole black hide don't look lak nothin' tuh me, but uh passle uh wrinkled up rubber, wid yo' big ole yeahs flappin' on each side lak uh paih uh buzzard wings. Don't think Ah'm gointuh be run 'way fum mah house neither. Ah'm goin' tuh de white folks about *you,* mah young man, de very nex' time you lay yo' han's on me. Mah cup is done run ovah." Delia said this with no signs of fear and Sykes departed from the house, threatening her, but made not the slightest move to carry out any of them.

That night he did not return at all, and the next day being Sunday, Delia was glad that she did not have to quarrel before she hitched up her pony and drove the four miles to Woodbridge.

She stayed to the night service—"love feast"—which was very warm and full of spirit. In the emotional winds her domestic trials were borne far and wide so that she sang as she drove homeward.

"Jurden water,[6] black an' col'
Chills de body, not de soul
An' Ah wantah cross Jurden in uh calm time."

She came from the barn to the kitchen door and stopped.

"Whut's de mattah, ol' satan, you aint kickin' up yo' racket?" She addressed the snake's box. Complete silence. She went on into the house with a new hope in its birth struggles. Perhaps her threat to go to the white folks had frightened Sykes! Perhaps he was sorry! Fifteen years of misery and suppression had brought Delia to the place where she would hope *anything* that looked towards a way over or through her wall of inhibitions.

85   She felt in the match safe behind the stove at once for a match. There was only one there.

"Dat niggah wouldn't fetch nothin heah tuh save his rotten neck, but he kin run thew whut Ah brings quick enough. Now he done toted off nigh on tuh haff uh box uh matches. He done had dat 'oman heah in mah house, too."

Nobody but a woman could tell how she knew this even before she struck the match. But she did and it put her into a new fury.

[6]**Jurden** the river Jordan, which the Israelites had to cross in order to reach the Promised Land.

Presently she brought in the tubs to put the white things to soak. This time she decided she need not bring the hamper out of the bedroom; she would go in there and do the sorting. She picked up the pot-bellied lamp and went in. The room was small and the hamper stood hard by the foot of the white iron bed. She could sit and reach through the bedposts—resting as she worked.

"Ah wantah cross Jurden in uh calm time." She was singing again. The mood of the "love feast" had returned. She threw back the lid of the basket almost gaily. Then, moved by both horror and terror, she sprang back toward the door. *There lay the snake in the basket!* He moved sluggishly at first, but even as she turned round and round, jumped up and down in an insanity of fear, he began to stir vigorously. She saw him pouring his awful beauty from the basket upon the bed, then she seized the lamp and ran as fast as she could to the kitchen. The wind from the open door blew out the light and the darkness added to her terror. She sped to the darkness of the yard, slamming the door after her before she thought to set down the lamp. She did not feel safe even on the ground, so she climbed up in the hay barn.

90   There for an hour or more she lay sprawled upon the hay a gibbering wreck. Finally she grew quiet, and after that, coherent thought. With this, stalked through her a cold, bloody rage. Hours of this. A period of introspection, a space of retrospection, then a mixture of both. Out of this an awful calm.

"Well, Ah done de bes' Ah could. If things aint right, Gawd knows taint mah fault."

She went to sleep—a twitchy sleep—and woke up to a faint gray sky. There was a loud hollow sound below. She peered out. Sykes was at the wood-pile, demolishing a wire-covered box.

He hurried to the kitchen door, but hung outside there some minutes before he entered, and stood some minutes more inside before he closed it after him.

95   The gray in the sky was spreading. Delia descended without fear now, and crouched beneath the low bedroom window. The drawn shade shut out the dawn, shut in the night. But the thin walls held back no sound.

"Dat ol' scratch is woke up now!" She mused at the tremendous whirr inside, which every woodsman knows, is one of the sound illusions. The rattler is a ventriloquist. His whirr sounds to the right, to the left, straight ahead, behind, close under foot—everywhere but where it is. Woe to him who guesses wrong unless he is prepared to hold up his end of the argument! Sometimes he strikes without rattling at all.

Inside, Sykes heard nothing until he knocked a pot lid off the stove while trying to reach the match safe in the dark. He had emptied his pockets at Bertha's.

The snake seemed to wake up under the stove and Sykes made a quick leap into the bedroom. In spite of the gin he had had, his head was clearing now.

"Mah Gawd!" he chattered. "Ef Ah could only strack uh light!"

100   The rattling ceased for a moment as he stood paralyzed. He waited. It seemed that the snake waited also.

"Oh, fuh de light! Ah thought he'd be too sick"—Sykes was muttering to himself when the whirr began again, closer, right underfoot this time. Long before this, Sykes' ability to think had been flattened down to primitive instinct and he leaped—onto the bed.

Outside Delia heard a cry that might have come from a maddened chimpanzee, a stricken gorilla. All the terror, all the horror, all the rage that man possibly could express, without a recognizable human sound.

A tremendous stir inside there, another series of animal screams, the intermittent whirr of the reptile. The shade torn violently down from the window, letting in the red dawn, a huge brown hand seizing the window stick, great dull blows upon the wooden floor punctuating the gibberish of sound long after the rattle of the snake had abruptly subsided. All this Delia could see and hear from her place beneath the window, and it made her ill. She crept over to the four-o'clocks[7] and stretched herself on the cool earth to recover.

She lay there. "Delia, Delia!" She could hear Sykes calling in a most despairing tone as one who expected no answer. The sun crept on up, and he called. Delia could not move—her legs were gone flabby. She never moved, he called, and the sun kept rising.

"Mah Gawd!" She heard him moan. "Mah Gawd fum Heben!" She heard him stumbling about and got up from her flower-bed. The sun was growing warm. As she approached the door she heard him call out hopefully. "Delia, is dat you Ah heah?"

She saw him on his hands and knees as soon as she reached the door. He crept an inch or two toward her—all that he was able, and she saw his horribly swollen neck and his one open eye shining with hope. A surge of pity too strong to support bore her away from that eye that must, could not, fail to see the tubs. He would see the lamp. Orlando with its doctors was too far. She could scarcely reach the Chinaberry tree, where she waited in the growing heat while inside she knew the cold river was creeping up and up to extinguish that eye which must know by now that she knew.

[1926]

[7]**four-o'clocks** flowers that open in the late afternoon.

Joining the Conversation: Critical Thinking and Writing

1. Summarize the relationship of Delia and Sykes before the time of the story.
2. How do the men on Joe Clark's porch further your understanding of Delia and Sykes and of the relationship between the two?
3. To what extent is Delia responsible for Sykes's death? To what extent is Sykes responsible? Do you think that Delia's action (or inaction) at the end of the story is immoral? Why, or why not?
4. To what extent does the relationship between African Americans and whites play a role in the lives of the characters in "Sweat" and in the outcome of the story?
5. Are the African Americans in "Sweat" portrayed stereotypically, as some of Hurston's critics charged? (See the biographical note, page 705.) How, on the evidence available in this story, might Hurston's fiction be defended from that charge?

JHUMPA LAHIRI

Indian American author Jhumpa Lahiri was born in London in 1967 to Indian immigrants who moved to the United States when she was two years old. Her fiction is praised for its sensitive depiction of the Indian American experience, including the difficulties of managing marital and parent/child relationships when families are placed in new cultural contexts. Her 1999 short story collection, Interpreter of Maladies, *which includes "This Blessed House," won the Pulitzer Prize and PEN/Hemingway Award. Her 2003 novel,* The Namesake, *received widespread acclaim and was made into a movie of the same name. Raised in Rhode Island, she earned a BA degree from Barnard College and an MA in English, MFA in Creative Writing, and a PhD in English from Boston University.*

This Blessed House

They discovered the first one in a cupboard above the stove, beside an unopened bottle of malt vinegar.

"Guess what I found." Twinkle walked into the living room, lined from end to end with taped-up packing boxes, waving the vinegar in one hand and a white porcelain effigy of Christ, roughly the same size as the vinegar bottle, in the other.

Sanjeev looked up. He was kneeling on the floor, marking, with ripped bits of a Post-it, patches on the baseboard that needed to be retouched with paint. "Throw it away."

"Which?"

5   "Both."

"But I can cook something with the vinegar. It's brand-new."

"You've never cooked anything with vinegar."

"I'll look something up. In one of those books we got for our wedding."

Sanjeev turned back to the baseboard, to replace a Post-it scrap that had fallen to the floor. "Check the expiration. And at the very least get rid of that idiotic statue."

10   "But it could be worth something. Who knows?" She turned it upside down, then stroked, with her index finger, the minuscule frozen folds of its robes. "It's pretty."

"We're not Christian," Sanjeev said. Lately he had begun noticing the need to state the obvious to Twinkle. The day before he had to tell her that if she dragged her end of the bureau instead of lifting it, the parquet floor would scratch.

She shrugged. "No, we're not Christian. We're good little Hindus." She planted a kiss on top of Christ's head, then placed the statue on top of the fireplace mantel, which needed, Sanjeev observed, to be dusted.

By the end of the week the mantel had still not been dusted; it had, however, come to serve as the display shelf for a sizable collection of Christian paraphernalia. There was a 3-D post-card of Saint Francis done in four colors, which Twinkle had found taped to the back of the medicine cabinet, and a wooden cross key chain, which Sanjeev had stepped on with bare feet as he was installing extra shelving in Twinkle's study. There was a framed paint-by-number of the three wise men, against a black velvet background, tucked in the linen closet. There was also a tile trivet depicting a blond, unbearded Jesus, delivering a sermon on a mountaintop, left in one of the drawers of the built-in china cabinet in the dining room.

"Do you think the previous owners were born-agains?" asked Twinkle, making room the next day for a small plastic snow-filled dome containing a miniature Nativity scene, found behind the pipes of the kitchen sink.

15   Sanjeev was organizing his engineering texts from MIT in alphabetical order on a bookshelf, though it had been several years since he had needed to consult any of them. After graduating, he moved from Boston to Connecticut, to work for a firm near Hartford, and he had recently learned that he was being considered for the position of vice president. At thirty-three he had a secretary of his own and a dozen people working under his supervision who gladly supplied him with any information he needed. Still, the presence of his college books in the room reminded him of a time in his life he recalled with fondness, when he would walk each evening across the Mass. Avenue bridge to order Mughlai chicken with spinach from his favorite Indian restaurant on the other side of the Charles, and return to his dorm to write out clean copies of his problem sets.

"Or perhaps it's an attempt to convert people," Twinkle mused.

"Clearly the scheme has succeeded in your case."

She disregarded him, shaking the little plastic dome so that the snow swirled over the manger.

He studied the items on the mantel. It puzzled him that each was in its own way so silly. Clearly they lacked a sense of sacredness. He was further puzzled that Twinkle, who normally displayed good taste, was so charmed. These objects meant something to Twinkle, but they meant nothing to him. They irritated him. "We should call the Realtor. Tell him there's all this nonsense left behind. Tell him to take it away."

20   "Oh, Sanj." Twinkle groaned. "Please. I would feel terrible throwing them away. Obviously they were important to the people who used to live here. It would feel, I don't know, sacrilegious or something."

"If they're so precious, then why are they hidden all over the house? Why didn't they take them with them?"

"There must be others," Twinkle said. Her eyes roamed the bare off-white walls of the room, as if there were other things concealed behind the plaster. "What else do you think we'll find?"

But as they unpacked their boxes and hung up their winter clothes and the silk paintings of elephant processions bought on their honeymoon in Jaipur, Twinkle, much to her dismay, could not find a thing. Nearly a week had passed before they discovered, one Saturday afternoon, a larger-than-life-sized watercolor poster of Christ, weeping translucent tears the size of peanut shells and sporting a crown of thorns, rolled up behind a radiator in the guest bedroom. Sanjeev had mistaken it for a window shade.

"Oh, we must, we simply must put it up. It's too spectacular." Twinkle lit a cigarette and began to smoke it with relish, waving it around Sanjeev's head as if it were a conductor's baton as Mahler's Fifth Symphony roared from the stereo downstairs.

25   "Now, look. I will tolerate, for now, your little biblical menagerie in the living room. But I refuse to have this," he said, flicking at one of the painted peanut-tears, "displayed in our home."

Twinkle stared at him, placidly exhaling, the smoke emerging in two thin blue streams from her nostrils. She rolled up the poster slowly, securing it with one of the elastic bands she always wore around her wrist for tying back her thick, unruly hair, streaked here and there with henna. "I'm going to put it in my study," she informed him. "That way you don't have to look at it."

"What about the housewarming? They'll want to see all the rooms. I've invited people from the office."

She rolled her eyes. Sanjeev noted that the symphony, now in its third movement, had reached a crescendo, for it pulsed with the telltale clashing of cymbals.

"I'll put it behind the door," she offered. "That way, when they peek in, they won't see. Happy?"

30   He stood watching her as she left the room, with her poster and her cigarette; a few ashes had fallen to the floor where she'd been standing. He bent down, pinched them between his fingers, and deposited them in his cupped palm. The tender fourth movement, the *adagietto,* began. During breakfast, Sanjeev had read in the liner notes that Mahler had proposed to his wife by sending her the manuscript of this portion of the score. Although there were elements of tragedy and struggle in the Fifth Symphony, he had read, it was principally music of love and happiness.

He heard the toilet flush. "By the way," Twinkle hollered, "if you want to impress people, I wouldn't play this music. It's putting me to sleep."

Sanjeev went to the bathroom to throw away the ashes. The cigarette butt still bobbed in the toilet bowl, but the tank was refilling, so he had to wait a moment before he could flush it again. In the mirror of the medicine cabinet he inspected his long eyelashes—like a girl's, Twinkle liked to tease. Though he was of average build, his cheeks had a plumpness to them; this, along with the eyelashes, detracted, he feared, from what he hoped was a distinguished profile. He was of average height as well, and had wished ever since he had stopped growing that he were just one inch taller. For this reason it irritated him when Twinkle insisted on wearing high heels, as she had done the other night when they ate dinner in Manhattan. This was the first weekend after they'd moved into the house; by then the mantel had already filled up considerably, and they had bickered about it in the car on the way down. But then Twinkle had drunk four glasses of whiskey in a nameless bar in Alphabet City, and forgot all about it. She dragged him to a tiny bookshop on St. Mark's Place, where she browsed for nearly an hour, and when they left she insisted that they dance a tango on the sidewalk in front of strangers.

Afterward, she tottered on his arm, rising faintly over his line of vision, in a pair of suede three-inch leopard-print pumps. In this manner they walked the endless blocks back to a parking garage on Washington Square, for Sanjeev had heard far too many stories about the terrible things that happened to cars in Manhattan. "But I do nothing all day except sit at my desk" she fretted when they were driving home, after he had mentioned that her shoes looked uncomfortable and suggested that perhaps she should not wear them. "I can't exactly wear heels when I'm typing." Though he abandoned the argument, he knew for a fact that she didn't spend all day at her desk; just that afternoon, when he got back from a run, he found her inexplicably in bed, reading. When he asked why she was in bed in the middle of the day she told him she was bored. He had wanted to say to her then, You could unpack some boxes. You could sweep the attic. You could retouch the paint on the bathroom windowsill, and after you do it you could warn me so that I don't put my watch on it. They didn't bother her, these scattered, unsettled matters. She seemed content with whatever clothes she found at the front of the closet, with whatever magazine was lying around, with whatever song was on the radio—content yet curious. And now all of her curiosity centered around discovering the next treasure.

A few days later when Sanjeev returned from the office, he found Twinkle on the telephone, smoking and talking to one of her girlfriends in California even though it was before five o'clock and the long-distance rates were at their peak "Highly devout people," she was saying, pausing every now and then to exhale. "Each day is like a treasure hunt. I'm serious. This you won't believe. The switch plates in the bedrooms were decorated with scenes from the Bible. You know, Noah's Ark and all that. Three bedrooms, but one is my study. Sanjeev went to the hardware store right away and replaced them, can you imagine, he replaced every single one."

35   Now it was the friend's turn to talk. Twinkle nodded, slouched on the floor in front of the fridge, wearing black stirrup pants and a yellow chenille sweater, groping for her lighter. Sanjeev could smell something aromatic on the stove, and he picked his way carefully across the extra-long phone cord tangled on the Mexican terra cotta tiles. He opened the lid of a pot with some sort of reddish brown sauce dripping over the sides, boiling furiously.

"It's a stew made with fish. I put the vinegar in it," she said to him, interrupting her friend, crossing her fingers. "Sorry, you were saying?" She was like that, excited and delighted by little things, crossing her fingers before any remotely unpredictable event, like tasting a new flavor of ice cream, or dropping a letter in a mailbox. It was a quality he did not under stand. It made him feel stupid, as if the world contained hidden wonders he could not anticipate, or see. He looked at her face, which, it occurred to him, had not grown out of its girlhood, the eyes untroubled, the pleasing features unfirm, as if they still had to settle into some sort of permanent expression. Nicknamed after a nursery rhyme, she had yet to shed a childhood endearment. Now, in the second month of their marriage, certain things nettled him—the way she sometimes spat a little when she spoke, or left her undergarments after removing them at night at the foot of their bed rather than depositing them in the laundry hamper.

They had met only four months before. Her patents who lived in California, and his, who still lived in Calcutta, were old friends, and across continents they had arranged the occasion at which Twinkle and Sanjeev were introduces—a sixteenth birthday party for a daughter in their circle—when Sanjeev was in Palo Alto on business. At the restaurant they were seated side by side at a round table with a revolving platter of spareribs and egg rolls and chicken wings, which, they concurred, all tasted the same. They had concurred too on their adolescent but still persistent fondness for Wodehouse novels, and their dislike for the sitar, and later Twinkle confessed that she was charmed by the way Sanjeev had dutifully refilled her teacup during their conversation.

And so the phone calls began, and grew longer, and then the visits, first he to Stanford, then she to Connecticut, after which Sanjeev would save in an ashtray left on the balcony the crushed cigarettes she had smoked during the weekend—saved them, that is, until the next time she came to visit him, and then he vacuumed the apartment, washed the sheets, even dusted the plant leaves in her honor. She was twenty-seven and recently abandoned, he had gathered, by an American who had tried and failed to be an actor; Sanjeev was lonely, with an excessively generous income for a single man, and had never been in love. At the urging of their matchmakers, they married in India, amid hundreds of well-wishers whom he barely remembered from his childhood, in incessant August rains, under a red and orange tent strung with Christmas tree lights on Mandeville Road.

"Did you sweep the attic?" he asked Twinkle later as she was folding paper napkins and wedging them by their plates. The attic was the only part of the house they had not yet given an initial cleaning.

40 "Not yet. I will, I promise. I hope this tastes good," she said, planting the steaming pot on top of the Jesus trivet. There was a loaf of Italian bread in a little basket, and iceberg lettuce and grated carrots tossed with bottled dressing and croutons, and glasses of red wine. She was not terribly ambitious in the kitchen. She bought preroasted chickens from the super-market and served them with potato salad prepared who knew when, sold in little plastic containers. Indian food, she complained, was a bother; she detested chopping garlic, and peeling ginger, and could not operate a blender, and so it was Sanjeev who, on weekends, seasoned mustard oil with cinnamon sticks and cloves in order to produce a proper curry.

He had to admit, though, that whatever it was that she had cooked today, it was unusually tasty, attractive even, with bright white cubes of fish, and flecks of parsley, and fresh tomatoes gleaming in the dark brown-red broth.

"How did you make it?"

"I made it up."

"What did you do?"

45   "I just put some things into the pot and added the malt vinegar at the end."

"How much vinegar?"

She shrugged, ripping off some bread and plunging it into her bowl.

What do you mean you don't know? You should write it down. What if you need to make it again, for a party or something?"

"I'll remember," she said. She covered the bread basket with a dishtowel that had, he suddenly noticed, the Ten Commandments printed on it. She flashed him a smile, giving his knee a little squeeze under the table. "Face it. This house is blessed."

50   The housewarming party was scheduled for the last Saturday in October, and they had invited about thirty people. All were Sanjeev's acquaintances, people from the office, and a number of Indian couples in the Connecticut area, many of whom he barely knew, but who had regularly invited him, in his bachelor days, to supper on Saturdays. He often wondered why they included him in their circle. He had little in common with any of them, but he always attended their gatherings, to eat spiced chickpeas and shrimp cutlets, and gossip and discuss politics, for he seldom had other plans. So far, no one had met Twinkle; back when they were still dating, Sanjeev didn't want to waste their brief weekends together with people he associated with being alone. Other than Sanjeev and an ex-boyfriend who she believed worked in a pottery studio in Brookfield, she knew no one in the state of Connecticut. She was completing her master's thesis at Stanford, a study of an Irish poet whom Sanjeev had never heard of.

Sanjeev had found the house on his own before leaving for the wedding, for a good price, in a neighborhood with a fine school system. He was impressed by the elegant curved staircase with its wrought-iron banister, and the dark wooden wainscoting, and the solarium overlooking rhododendron bushes, and the solid brass 22, which also happened to be the date of his birth, nailed impressively to the vaguely Tudor facade. There were two working fireplaces, a two-car garage, and an attic suitable for converting into extra bedrooms if, the Realtor mentioned, the need should arise. By then Sanjeev had already made up his mind, was determined that he and Twinkle should live there together, forever, and so he had not bothered to notice the switch plates covered with biblical stickers, or the transparent decal of the Virgin on the half shell, as Twinkle liked to call it, adhered to the window in the master bedroom. When, after moving in, he tried to scrape it off, he scratched the glass.

The weekend before the party they were raking the lawn when he heard Twinkle shriek. He ran to her, clutching his rake, worried that she had discovered a dead animal, or a snake. A brisk October breeze stung the tops of his ears as his sneakers crunched over brown and yellow leaves. When he reached her, she had collapsed on the grass, dissolved in nearly silent laughter. Behind an overgrown forsythia bush was a plaster Virgin Mary as tall as their waists, with a blue painted hood draped over her head in the manner of an Indian bride. Twinkle grabbed the hem of her T-shirt and began wiping away the dirt staining the statue's brow.

I suppose you want to put her by the foot of our bed," Sanjeev said.

She looked at him, astonished. Her belly was exposed, and he saw that there were goose bumps around her navel. "What do you think? Of course we can't put this in our bedroom."

55   "We can't?"

"No, silly Sanj. This is meant for outside. For the lawn."

"Oh God, no. Twinkle, no."

"But we must. It would be bad luck not to."

"All the neighbors will see. They'll think we're insane."

60   "Why, for having a statue of the Virgin Mary on our lawn? Every other person in this neighborhood has a statue of Mary on the lawn. We'll fit right in."

"We're not Christian."

"So you keep reminding me." She spat onto the tip of her finger and started to rub intently at a particularly stubborn stain on Mary's chin. "Do you think this is dirt, or some kind of fungus?"

He was getting nowhere with her, with this woman whom he had known for only four months and whom he had married, this woman with whom he now shared his life. He thought with a flicker of regret of the snapshots his mother used to send him from Calcutta, of prospective brides who could sing and sew and season lentils without consulting a cookbook. Sanjeev had considered these women, had even ranked them in order of preference, but then he had met Twinkle. "Twinkle, I can't have the people I work with see this statue on my lawn."

"They can't fire you for being a believer. It would be discrimination."

65   "That's not the point."

"Why does it matter to you so much what other people think?"

"Twinkle, please." He was tired. He let his weight rest against his rake as she began dragging the statue toward an oval bed of myrtle, beside the lamppost that flanked the brick pathway. "Look, Sanj. She's so lovely."

He returned to his pile of leaves and began to deposit them by handfuls into a plastic garbage bag. Over his head the blue sky was cloudless. One tree on the lawn was still full of leaves, red and orange, like the tent in which he had married Twinkle.

He did not know if he loved her. He said he did when she had first asked him, one afternoon in Palo Alto as they sat side by side in a darkened, nearly empty movie theater. Before the film, one of her favorites, something in German that he found extremely depressing, she had pressed the tip of her nose to his so that he could feel the flutter of her mascara-coated eyelashes. That afternoon he had replied, yes, he loved her, and she was delighted, and fed him a piece of popcorn, letting her finger linger an instant between his lips, as if it were his reward for coming up with the right answer.

70   Though she did not say it herself, he assumed then that she loved him too, but now he was no longer sure. In truth, Sanjeev did not know what love was, only what he thought it was not. It was not, he had decided, returning to an empty carpeted condominium each night, and using only the top fork in his cutlery drawer, and turning away politely at those weekend dinner parties when the other men eventually put their arms around the waists of their wives and girlfriends, leaning over every now and again to kiss their shoulders or necks. It was not sending away for classical music CDs by mail, working his way methodically through the major composers that the catalogue recommended, and always sending his payments in on time. In the months before meeting Twinkle, Sanjeev had begun to realize this. "You have enough money in the bank to raise three families," his mother reminded him when they spoke at the start of each month on the phone. "You need a wife to look after and love." Now he had one, a pretty one, from a suitably high caste, who would soon have a master's degree. What was there not to love?

That evening Sanjeev poured himself a gin and tonic, drank it and most of another during one segment of the news, and then approached Twinkle, who was taking a bubble bath, for she announced that her limbs ached from raking the lawn, something she had never done before. He didn't knock. She had applied a bright blue mask to her face, was smoking and sipping some bourbon with ice and leafing through a fat paperback book whose pages had buckled and turned gray from the water. He glanced at the cover; the only thing written on it was the word "Sonnets" in dark red letters. He took a breath, and then he informed her very calmly that after finishing his drink he was going to put on his shoes and go outside and remove he Virgin from the front lawn.

"Where are you going to put it?" she asked him dreamily, her eyes closed. One of her legs emerged, unfolding gracefully, from the layer of suds. She flexed and pointed her toes.

"For now I am going to put it in the garage. Then tomorrow morning on my way to work I am going to take it to the dump."

"Don't you dare." She stood up, letting the book fall into the water, bubbles dripping down her thighs. "I hate you," she informed him, her eyes narrowing at the word "hate." She reached for her bathrobe, tied it tightly about her waist, and padded down the winding staircase, leaving sloppy wet footprints along the parquet floor. When she reached the foyer, Sanjeev said, "Are you planning on leaving the house that way?" He felt a throbbing in his temples, and his voice revealed an unfamiliar snarl when he spoke.

75 "Who cares? Who cares what way I leave this house?"

"Where are you planning on going at this hour?"

"You can't throw away that statue. I won't let you." Her mask, now dry, had assumed an ashen quality, and water from her hair dripped onto the caked contours of her face.

"Yes I can. I will."

"No," Twinkle said, her voice suddenly small. "This is our house. We own it together. The statue is a part of our property." She had begun to shiver. A small pool of bathwater had collected around her ankles. He went to shut a window, fearing that she would catch cold. Then he noticed that some of the water dripping down her hard blue face was tears.

80 "Oh God, Twinkle, please, I didn't mean it." He had never seen her cry before, had never seen such sadness in her eyes. She didn't turn away or try to stop the tears; instead she looked strangely at peace. For a moment she closed her lids, pale and unprotected compared to the blue that caked the rest of her face. Sanjeev felt ill, as if he had eaten either too much or too little.

She went to him, placing her damp toweled arms about his neck, sobbing into his chest, soaking his shirt. The mask flaked onto his shoulders.

In the end they settled on a compromise: the statue would be placed in a recess at the side of the house, so that it wasn't obvious to passersby, but was still clearly visible to all who came.

The menu for the party was fairly simple: there would be a case of champagne, and samosas from an Indian restaurant in Hartford, and big trays of rice with chicken and almonds and orange peels, which Sanjeev had spent the greater part of the morning and afternoon preparing. He had never entertained on such a large scale before and, worried that there would not be enough to drink, ran out at one point to buy another case of champagne just in case. For this reason he burned one of the rice trays and had to start it over again. Twinkle swept the floors and volunteered to pick up the samosas; she had an appointment for a manicure and a pedicure in that direction, anyway. Sanjeev had planned to ask if she would consider clearing the menagerie off the mantel, if only for the party, but she left while he was in the shower. She was gone for a good three hours, and so it was Sanjeev who did the rest of the cleaning. By five-thirty the entire house sparkled, with scented candles that Twinkle had picked up in Hartford illuminating the items on the mantel, and slender stalks of burning incense planted into the soil of potted plants. Each time he passed the mantel he winced, dreading the raised eyebrows of his guests as they viewed the flickering ceramic saints, the salt and pepper shakers designed to resemble Mary and Joseph. Still, they would be impressed, he hoped, by the lovely bay windows, the shining parquet floors, the impressive winding staircase, the wooden wainscoting, as they sipped champagne and dipped samosas in chutney.

Douglas, one of the new consultants at the firm, and his girlfriend Nora were the first to arrive. Both were tall and blond, wearing matching wire-rimmed glasses and long black overcoats. Nora wore a black hat full of sharp thin feathers that corresponded to the sharp thin angles of her face. Her left hand was joined with Douglas's. In her right hand was a bottle of cognac with a red ribbon wrapped around its neck, which she gave to Twinkle.

85   "Great lawn, Sanjeev," Douglas remarked. "We've got to get that rake out ourselves, sweetie. And this must be . . ."

"My wife. Tanima."

"Call me Twinkle."

"What an unusual name," Nora remarked.

Twinkle shrugged. "Not really. There's an actress in Bombay named Dimple Kapadia. She even has a sister named Simple."

90   Douglas and Nora raised their eyebrows simultaneously, nodding slowly, as if to let the absurdity of the names settle in. "Pleased to meet you, Twinkle."

"Help yourself to champagne. There's gallons."

"I hope you don't mind my asking," Douglas said, "but I noticed the statue outside, and are you guys Christian? I thought you were Indian."

"There are Christians in India," Sanjeev replied, "but we're not."

"I love your outfit," Nora told Twinkle.

95   "And I adore your hat. Would you like the grand tour?"

The bell rang again, and again and again. Within minutes, it seemed, the house had filled with bodies and conversations and unfamiliar fragrances. The women wore heels and sheer stockings, and short black dresses made of crepe and chiffon. They handed their wraps and coats to Sanjeev, who draped them carefully on hangers in the spacious coat closet, though Twinkle told people to throw their things on the ottomans in the solarium. Some of the Indian women wore their finest saris, made with gold filigree that draped in elegant pleats over their shoulders. The men wore jackets and ties and citrus-scented aftershaves. As people filtered from one room to the next, presents piled onto the long cherry-wood table that ran from one end of the downstairs hall to the other.

It bewildered Sanjeev that it was for him, and his house, and his wife, that they had all gone to so much care. The only other time in his life that something similar had happened was his wedding day, but somehow this was different, for these were not his family, but people who knew him only casually, and in a sense owed him nothing. Everyone congratulated him. Lester, another coworker, predicted that Sanjeev would be promoted to vice president in two months maximum. People devoured the samosas, and dutifully admired the freshly painted ceilings and walls, the hanging plants, the bay windows, the silk paintings from Jaipur. But most of all they admired Twinkle, and her brocaded *salwar-kameez,* which was the shade of a persimmon with a low scoop in the back, and the little string of white rose petals she had coiled cleverly around her head, and the pearl choker with a sapphire at its center that adorned her throat. Over hectic jazz records, played under Twinkle's supervision, they laughed at her anecdotes and observations, forming a widening circle around her, while Sanjeev replenished the samosas that he kept warming evenly in the oven, and getting ice for people's drinks, and opening more bottles of champagne with some difficulty, and explaining for the fortieth time that he wasn't Christian. It was Twinkle who led them in separate groups up and down the winding stairs, to gaze at the back lawn, to peer down the cellar steps. "Your friends adore the poster in my study," she mentioned to him triumphantly, placing her hand on the small of his back as they, at one point, brushed past each other.

Sanjeev went to the kitchen, which was empty, and ate a piece of chicken out of the tray on the counter with his fingers because he thought no one was looking. He ate a second piece, then washed it down with a gulp of gin straight from the bottle.

"Great house. Great rice." Sunil, an anesthesiologist, walked in, spooning food from his paper plate into his mouth. "Do you have more champagne?"

"Your wife's wow," added Prabal, following behind. He was an unmarried professor of physics at Yale. For a moment Sanjeev stared at him blankly, then blushed; once at a dinner party Prabal had pronounced that Sophia Loren was wow, as was Audrey Hepburn. "Does she have a sister?"

Sunil picked a raisin out of the rice tray. "Is her last name Little Star?"

The two men laughed and started eating more rice from the tray, plowing through it with their plastic spoons. Sanjeev went down to the cellar for more liquor. For a few minutes he paused on the steps, in the damp, cool silence, hugging the second crate of champagne to his chest as the party drifted above the rafters. Then he set the reinforcements on the dining table.

"Yes, everything, we found them all in the house, in the most unusual places," he heard Twinkle saying in the living room. "In fact we keep finding them."

"No!"

"Yes! Every day is like a treasure hunt. It's too good. God only knows what else we'll find, no pun intended."

That was what started it. As if by some unspoken pact, the whole party joined forces and began combing through each of the rooms, opening closets on their own, peering under chairs and cushions, feeling behind curtains, removing books from bookcases. Groups scampered, giggling and swaying, up and down the winding staircase.

"We've never explored the attic," Twinkle announced suddenly, and so everybody followed.

"How do we get up there?"

"There's a ladder in the hallway, somewhere in the ceiling."

Wearily Sanjeev followed at the back of the crowd, to point out the location of the ladder, but Twinkle had already found it on her own. "Eureka!" she hollered.

Douglas pulled the chain that released the steps. His face was flushed and he was wearing Nora's feather hat on his head. One by one the guests disappeared, men helping women as they placed their strappy high heels on the narrow slats of the ladder, the Indian women wrapping the free ends of their expensive saris into their waistbands. The men followed behind, all quickly disappearing, until Sanjeev alone remained at the top of the winding staircase. Footsteps thundered over his head. He had no desire to join them. He wondered if the ceiling would collapse, imagined, for a split second, the sight of all the tumbling drunk perfumed bodies crashing, tangled, around him. He heard a shriek, and then rising, spreading waves of laughter in discordant tones. Something fell, something else shattered. He could hear them babbling about a trunk. They seemed to be struggling to get it open, banging feverishly on its surface.

He thought perhaps Twinkle would call for his assistance, but he was not summoned. He looked about the hallway and to the landing below, at the champagne glasses and half-eaten samosas and napkins smeared with lipstick abandoned in every corner, on every available surface. Then he noticed that Twinkle, in her haste, had discarded her shoes altogether, for they lay by the foot of the ladder, black patent-leather mules with heels like golf tees, open toes, and slightly soiled silk labels on the instep where her soles had rested. He placed them in the doorway of the master bedroom so that no one would trip when they descended.

He heard something creaking open slowly. The strident voices had subsided to an even murmur. It occurred to Sanjeev that he had the house all to himself. The music had ended and he could hear, if he concentrated, the hum of the refrigerator, and the rustle of the last leaves on the trees outside, and the tapping of their branches against the windowpanes. With one flick of his hand he could snap the ladder back on its spring into the ceiling, and they would have no way of getting down unless he were to pull the chain and let them. He thought of all the things he could do, undisturbed. He could sweep Twinkle's menagerie into a garbage bag and get in the car and drive it all to the dump, and tear down the poster of weeping Jesus, and take a hammer to the Virgin Mary while he was at it. Then he would return to the empty house; he could easily clear up the cups and plates in an hour's time, and pour himself a gin and tonic, and eat a plate of warmed rice and listen to his new Bach CD while reading the liner notes so as to understand it properly. He nudged the ladder slightly, but it was sturdily planted against the floor. Budging it would require some effort.

"My God, I need a cigarette," Twinkle exclaimed from above.

115   Sanjeev felt knots forming at the back of his neck. He felt dizzy. He needed to lie down. He walked toward the bedroom, but stopped short when he saw Twinkle's shoes facing him in the doorway. He thought of her slipping them on her feet. But instead of feeling irritated, as he had ever since they'd moved into the house together, he felt a pang of anticipation at the thought of her rushing unsteadily down the winding staircase in them, scratching the floor a bit in her path. The pang intensified as he thought of her rushing to the bathroom to brighten her lipstick, and eventually rushing to get people their coats, and finally rushing to the cherrywood table when the last guest had left, to begin opening their housewarming presents. It was the same pang he used to feel before they were married, when he would hang up the phone after one of their conversations, or when he would drive back from the airport, wondering which ascending plane in the sky was hers.

"Sanj, you won't believe this."

She emerged with her back to him, her hands over her head, the tops of her bare shoulder blades perspiring, supporting something still hidden from view.

"You got it, Twinkle?" someone asked.

"Yes, you can let go."

120   Now he saw that her hands were wrapped around it: a solid silver bust of Christ, the head easily three times the size of his own. It had a patrician bump on its nose, magnificent curly hair that rested atop a pronounced collarbone, and a broad forehead that reflected in miniature the walls and doors and lampshades around them. Its expression was confident, as if assured of its devotees, the unyielding lips sensuous and full. It was also sporting Nora's feather hat. As Twinkle

descended, Sanjeev put his hands around her waist to balance her, and he relieved her of the bust when she had reached the ground. It weighed a good thirty pounds. The others began lowering themselves slowly, exhausted from the hunt. Some trickled downstairs in search of a fresh drink.

She took a breath, raised her eyebrows, crossed her fingers. "Would you mind terribly if we displayed it on the mantel? Just for tonight? I know you hate it."

He did hate it. He hated its immensity, and its flawless, polished surface, and its undeniable value. He hated that it was in his house, and that he owned it. Unlike the other things they'd found, this contained dignity, solemnity, beauty even. But to his surprise these qualities made him hate it all the more. Most of all he hated it because he knew that Twinkle loved it.

"I'll keep it in my study from tomorrow," Twinkle added. "I promise."

She would never put it in her study, he knew. For the rest of their days together she would keep it on the center of the mantel, flanked on either side by the rest of the menagerie. Each time they had guests Twinkle would explain how she had found it, and they would admire her as they listened. He gazed at the crushed rose petals in her hair, at the pearl and sapphire choker at her throat, at the sparkly crimson polish on her toes. He decided these were among the things that made Prabal think she was wow. His head ached from gin and his arms ached from the weight of the statue. He said, "I put your shoes in the bedroom."

125 "Thanks. But my feet are killing me." Twinkle gave his elbow a little squeeze and headed for the living room.

Sanjeev pressed the massive silver face to his ribs, careful not to let the feather hat slip, and followed her.

[1999]

Joining the Conversation: Critical Thinking and Writing

1. This story focuses on the two distinctly different characters, Twinkle and Sanjeev, and their unique personalities. Take inquiry notes on each character, and write a journal entry that describes each character. What are the notable qualities of each character? What actions define each character? What objects are associated with each character? In your notes, select and analyze quotations that capture each character's personality.

2. The conflict between Twinkle and Sanjeev focuses on the Christian religious objects that they find in their new home. How does Twinkle react to these objects? How does Sanjeev react? These objects are obviously symbols of the Christian faith. How do they take on more symbolic meaning within the context of the story; how does Lahiri add to their symbolic meaning? How do the objects become symbols of the two main characters and the tensions in their marriage? For example, why does the statue of the Virgin Mary become a source of conflict?

3. Why is the housewarming party important for these two characters? Reread and annotate the section that provides details of the housewarming party. What does the party reveal about Twinkle and Sanjeev and their social world?

4. How is the Indian American experience depicted in "This Blessed House"? Locate moments in the story that refer to India. What cultural pressures, conflicts, freedoms, and opportunities arise from being from India and living in America? Do Twinkle and Sanjeev offer different depictions of the Indian American experience?

5. Analyze the ending of the story. Write an essay that uses the events described at the end of the story to predict the future success or failure of Twinkle and Sanjeev's marriage. Why does Twinkle invite the party guests up into the attic? What do they find there? How does Sanjeev react to the guests' visit to the attic and to finding the new treasure?

POEMS

ANONYMOUS

Western Wind

Westron° wind, when will thou blow?
The small rain down can rain.
Christ, that my love were in my arms,
And I in my bed again.

[c. 1500]

1 **Westron** western.

Joining the Conversation: Critical Thinking and Writing

1. In "Western Wind," what do you think is the tone of the speaker's voice in the first two lines? Angry? Impatient? Supplicating? Be as precise as possible. What is the tone in the last two lines?
2. In England, the west wind, warmed by the Gulf Stream, rises in the spring. What associations link the wind and rain of lines 1 and 2 with lines 3 and 4?
3. Should we have been told why the lovers are separated? Explain your answer.

WILLIAM SHAKESPEARE

For biographical information on William Shakespeare, see pages 187–88.

Sonnet 116

Let me not to the marriage of true minds
Admit impediments; love is not love
Which alters when it alteration finds,
Or bends with the remover to remove.
O, no, it is an ever-fixèd mark°   5
That looks on tempests and is never shaken;
It is the star° to every wand'ring bark,
Whose worth's unknown, although his height be taken.
Love's not Time's fool,° though rosy lips and cheeks

5 **ever-fixèd** mark seamark, guide to mariners.   7 **the star** the North Star.   9 **fool** plaything.

Within his bending sickle's compass° come;   10
Love alters not with his° brief hours and weeks
But bears° it out even to the edge of doom.°
If this be error and upon° me proved,
I never writ, nor no man ever loved.

[c. 1600]

10 **compass** range, circle.   11 **his** time's.   12 **bears** survives;   **doom** Judgment Day.
13 **upon** against.

Joining the Conversation: Critical Thinking and Writing

1. Paraphrase (that is, put into your own words) "Let me not to the marriage of true minds / Admit impediments." Is there more than one appropriate meaning of "Admit"?
2. Notice that the poem celebrates "the marriage of true minds," not bodies. In a sentence or two, using only your own words, summarize Shakespeare's idea of the nature of such love, both what it is and what it is not.
3. Paraphrase lines 13–14. What is the speaker's tone here? Would you say that the tone is different from the tone in the rest of the poem?
4. Write a paragraph or a poem defining either love or hate.
5. Find a definition of love or hate in a popular song. Bring the lyrics to class. Why is this definition a good one?

JOHN DONNE

For biographical information on John Donne, see page 188.

A Valediction: Forbidding Mourning

As virtuous men pass mildly away,
    And whisper to their souls, to go,
Whilst some of their sad friends do say,
    "The breath goes now," and some say, "No":

So let us melt, and make no noise,   5
    No tear-floods, nor sigh-tempests move;
'Twere profanation of our joys
    To tell the laity our love.

Moving of th' earth° brings harms and fears;
    Men reckon what it did and meant;   10
But trepidation of the spheres,
    Though greater far, is innocent.°

9 **Moving of th' earth** an earthquake.   11–12 **But trepidation . . . innocent** But the movement of the heavenly spheres (in Ptolemaic astronomy), though far greater, is harmless.

Dull sublunary° lovers' love
　　(Whose soul is sense) cannot admit
Absence, because it doth remove　　　　　　　　　　　　　　15
　　Those things which elemented it.

But we, by a love so much refined
　　That our selves know not what it is,
Inter-assurèd of the mind,
　　Care less, eyes, lips, and hands to miss.　　　　　　　　20

Our two souls therefore, which are one,
　　Though I must go, endure not yet
A breach, but an expansion,
　　Like gold to airy thinness beat.

If they be two, they are two so　　　　　　　　　　　　　25
　　As stiff twin compasses° are two:
Thy soul, the fixed foot, makes no show
　　To move, but doth, if the other do.

And though it in the center sit,
　　Yet when the other far doth roam,　　　　　　　　　　30
It leans, and hearkens after it,
　　And grows erect as that comes home.

Such wilt thou be to me, who must,
　　Like the other foot, obliquely run;
Thy firmness makes my circle just,　　　　　　　　　　35
　　And makes me end where I begun.

　　　　　　　　　　　　　　　　　　　　　　　[1611]

13 **sublunary** under the moon, i.e., earthly.　26 **compasses** i.e., a carpenter's compass.

Joining the Conversation: Critical Thinking and Writing

1. The first stanza describes the death of "virtuous men." To what is their death compared in the second stanza?
2. Who is the speaker of this poem? To whom does he speak, and what is the occasion? Explain the title.
3. What is the meaning of "laity" in line 8? What does it imply about the speaker and his beloved?
4. In the fourth stanza, the speaker contrasts the love of "dull sublunary lovers" (that is, ordinary mortals) with the love that he and his beloved share. What is the difference?
5. In the figure of the carpenter's or draftsperson's compass (lines 25–36), the speaker offers reasons—some stated clearly, some not so clearly—why he will end where he began. In 250 words, explain these reasons.
6. In line 35, Donne speaks of his voyage as a "circle." Explain in a paragraph why the circle is traditionally a symbol of perfection.
7. Write a farewell note or poem to someone you love (or hate).

EDNA ST. VINCENT MILLAY

Edna St. Vincent Millay (1892–1950) was born in Rockland, Maine. Even as a child she wrote poetry, and, by the time she graduated from Vassar College in 1917, she had achieved some notice as a poet. Millay settled for a while in Greenwich Village, a center of bohemian activity in New York City, where she wrote, performed in plays, and engaged in feminist causes. In 1923, the year she married, she became the first woman to win the Pulitzer Prize for Poetry. Numerous other awards followed. Though she is best known as a lyric poet— especially as a writer of sonnets—she also wrote political poetry and nature poetry, as well as short stories, plays, and a libretto for an opera.

Love Is Not All: It Is Not Meat nor Drink

Love is not all: it is not meat nor drink
Nor slumber nor a roof against the rain;
Nor yet a floating spar to men that sink
And rise and sink and rise and sink again;
Love can not fill the thickened lung with breath, 5
Nor clean the blood, nor set the fractured bone;
Yet many a man is making friends with death
Even as I speak, for lack of love alone.
It well may be that in a difficult hour,
Pinned down by pain and moaning for release, 10
Or nagged by want past resolution's power,
I might be driven to sell your love for peace,
Or trade the memory of this night for food.
It well may be. I do not think I would.

[1931]

Joining the Conversation: Critical Thinking and Writing

1. "Love Is Not All" is a sonnet. Using your own words, briefly summarize the argument of the octet (the first eight lines). Next, paraphrase the sestet (the last six lines), line by line. On the whole, does the sestet repeat the idea of the octet, or does it add a new idea?

2. Whom did you imagine to be speaking in the octet? What does the sestet add to your knowledge of the speaker and the occasion? (And how did you paraphrase line 11?)

3. The first and last lines of the poem consist of words of one syllable, and both lines have a distinct pause in the middle. Do you imagine the lines to be spoken in the same tone of voice? If not, can you describe the difference and account for it?

4. Lines 7 and 8 appear to mean that the absence of love can be a cause of death. To what degree do you believe that to be true?

5. Would you call "Love Is Not All" a love poem? Why or why not? Describe the kind of person who might include the poem in a love letter or valentine, or who would be happy to receive it.

6. One of our friends recited this poem at her wedding. What do you think of that idea?

ROBERT BROWNING

Born in a suburb of London into a middle-class family, Robert Browning (1812–89) was educated primarily at home, where he read widely. For a while, he wrote for the stage, and in 1846 he married Elizabeth Barrett—herself a poet—and lived with her in Italy until her death in 1861. He then returned to England and settled in London with their son. Regarded as one of the most distinguished poets of the Victorian period, he is buried in Westminster Abbey.

Porphyria's Lover

The rain set early in to-night,
    The sullen wind was soon awake,
It tore the elm-tops down for spite,
    And did its worst to vex the lake:
    I listened with heart fit to break.   5
When glided in Porphyria; straight
    She shut the cold out and the storm,
And kneeled and made the cheerless grate
    Blaze up, and all the cottage warm;
    Which done, she rose, and from her form   10
Withdrew the dripping cloak and shawl,
    And laid her soiled gloves by, untied
Her hat and let the damp hair fall,
    And, last, she sat down by my side
    And called me. When no voice replied,   15
She put my arm about her waist,
    And made her smooth white shoulder bare,
And all her yellow hair displaced,
    And, stooping, made my cheek lie there,
    And spread, o'er all, her yellow hair,   20
Murmuring how she loved me—she
    Too weak, for all her heart's endeavour,
To set its struggling passion free
    From pride, and vainer ties dissever,
    And give herself to me for ever.   25
But passion sometimes would prevail,
    Nor could to-night's gay feast restrain
A sudden thought of one so pale
    For love of her, and all in vain:
    So, she was come through wind and rain.   30
Be sure I looked up at her eyes
    Happy and proud; at last I knew
Porphyria worshipped me; surprise

Made my heart swell, and still it grew
    While I debated what to do.   35
That moment she was mine, mine, fair,
    Perfectly pure and good: I found
A thing to do, and all her hair
    In one long yellow string I wound
    Three times her little throat around,   40
And strangled her. No pain felt she;
    I am quite sure she felt no pain.
As a shut bud that holds a bee,
    I warily oped her lids: again
    Laughed the blue eyes without a stain.   45
And I untightened next the tress
    About her neck; her cheek once more
Blushed bright beneath my burning kiss:
    I propped her head up as before,
    Only, this time my shoulder bore   50
Her head, which droops upon it still:
    The smiling rosy little head,
So glad it has its utmost will,
    That all it scorned at once is fled,
    And I, its love, am gained instead!   55
Porphyria's love: she guessed not how
    Her darling one wish would be heard.
And thus we sit together now,
    And all night long we have not stirred,
    And yet God has not said a word!   60

[1836]

Joining the Conversation: Critical Thinking and Writing

1. What are the events that "Porphyria's Lover" dramatizes? What is the shocking act that provides the poem's central event? Examine carefully the words that describe this act. What do you find interesting about the language that conveys the act?

2. Annotate the poem, noting the complex emotions that accompany or trigger the poem's central events. Who is narrating these events and emotions? What are the emotions that the narrator feels? For example, why does the narrator feel "surprise" that makes his "heart swell"?

3. What did the narrator hope to accomplish through his violent act? What is he trying to express through his actions? Write a short essay that explores the narrator's motivations.

4. What do you make of the final line of the poem? Why is God evoked? Does the narrator seem satisfied with his situation at the end of the poem?

5. Describe Porphyria. What do we know about her physical appearance at the beginning of the poem? What do we know about her physical appearance at the end of the poem? Write a short analysis that compares Porphyria's physical state at the beginning of the poem to her physical state at the end of the poem.

NIKKI GIOVANNI

Nikki Giovanni was born in Knoxville, Tennessee, in 1943 and was educated at Fisk University, the University of Pennsylvania School of Social Work, and Columbia University. She has taught at Queens College, Rutgers University, and Ohio State University, and she now teaches at Virginia Tech in Blacksburg, Virginia. Giovanni has published many books of poems, an autobiography (Gemini: An Extended Autobiographical Statement on My First Twenty-Five Years of Being a Black Poet), *a book of essays, and a book consisting of a conversation with James Baldwin (1972).*

Love in Place

I really don't remember falling in love all that much
I remember wanting to bake corn bread and boil a ham and I
certainly remember making lemon pie and when I used to smoke I
stopped in the middle of my day to contemplate

I know I must have fallen in love once because I quit biting   5
my cuticles and my hair is gray and that must indicate
something and I all of a sudden had a deeper appreciation
for Billie Holiday° and Billy Strayhorn° so if it wasn't love I don't
know what it was

I see the old photographs and I am smiling and I'm sure quite   10
happy but what I mostly see is me
through your eyes
and I am still young and slim and very much committed to the
love we still have

[1997]

8 **Billie Holiday** jazz singer (1915–59);   **Billy Strayhorn** jazz composer and musician (1915–67).

Joining the Conversation: Critical Thinking and Writing

1. What reasons does the speaker offer for supposing that she once fell in love? How seriously does she expect us to take those reasons?
2. Read the poem again, but begin with the third stanza and then read the first and second stanzas. Does it make a difference? If so, what is the difference?
3. In line 14 we learn of the "love we still have." Does "still" refer to the present or to the time of "the old photographs" (line 10), as the "still" in line 13 does?
4. Why are two of the lines in the final stanza much shorter than the other three lines?
5. What do you make of the title?
6. In the first line, Giovanni speaks of "falling in love," and she returns to the idea in the fifth line. Judging from your own experience (which includes your knowledge of the people around you), is the term "falling in love" apt, or do people

come to love one another in a more gradual fashion than "falling in love" implies? In an essay of five hundred words, explain your understanding or "falling in love." When, why, and how do people "fall in love?"

ANONYMOUS

The following lines have been attributed to various writers, including the American philosopher William James (1842–1910), but, to the best of our knowledge, the author is unknown.

> Higamus, Hogamus,
> Woman's monogamous;
> Hogamus, Higamus,
> Man is polygamous.

Joining the Conversation: Critical Thinking and Writing

1. If you find these lines engaging, how do you account for their appeal? Does it make any difference—even a tiny difference—if the pairs are reversed; that is, if the first two lines are about men and the second two are about women?
2. The underlying idea largely coincides with the saying, "Men are from Mars, women are from Venus." But consider the four lines of verse: Do you agree that in the form we have just given them, they are more effective than "Men are from Mars, women are from Venus"? And how about "Women are from Venus, men are from Mars"? Admittedly, the differences are small, but would you argue that one form is decidedly more effective than the others? How do you explain the greater effectiveness?

DOROTHY PARKER

Dorothy Parker (1893–1967) was born in West End, New Jersey, but brought up in New York City. From 1917 to 1920, she served as drama critic for the magazine Vanity Fair, *where her witty, satiric reviews gained her the reputation of being hard to please. She distinguished between wit and wisecracking: "Wit has truth in it; wisecracking is simply calisthenics with words."*

In addition to essays and stories, Parker wrote light verse, especially about love.

General Review of the Sex Situation

> Woman wants monogamy;
> Man delights in novelty.
> Love is woman's moon and sun;
> Man has other forms of fun.

> Woman lives but in her lord;   5
> Count to ten, and man is bored.
> With this the gist and sum of it,
> What earthly good can come of it?

[1926]

Joining the Conversation: Critical Thinking and Writing

1. How would you characterize Parker's message? (For instance, is it sad, happy, pitiful?) How would you characterize her tone—her attitude, as you perceive it?
2. How much truth do you think there is in Parker's lines? (Remember: No poem, or, for that matter, no novel—however long—can tell the whole truth about life.) As for truth, how would you compare the validity of the poem's assertion with the following passage, from Barbara Dafoe Whitehead's review (*Times Literary Supplement*, June 9, 1995) of two sociological studies, *The Social Organization of Sexuality: Sexual Practice in the U.S.* and *Sex in America*:

> Men and women have different sexual interests, stakes and appetites, with men more oriented to the sex act and women more interested in sex as an expression of affiliative and romantic love.

FRANK O'HARA

Frank O'Hara (1926–66) was born in Baltimore, Maryland, and died in a tragic accident—he was run over by a beach vehicle—on Fire Island, New York. O'Hara was not only a prolific writer of verse but also an astute critic of sculpture and painting who worked as an assistant curator at the Museum of Modern Art in New York (on West 53rd Street; see line 16) and as an editor of Art News. *O'Hara's first volume of poetry was* A City Winter, and Other Poems *(1952).* Collected Poems *was issued in 1971, but it was not complete; it has been supplemented by two additional volumes,* Early Poems *(1977) and* Poems Retrieved *(1977).*

Homosexuality

So we are taking off our masks, are we, and keeping
our mouths shut? as if we'd been pierced by a glance!

The song of an old cow is not more full of judgment
than the vapors which escape one's soul when one is sick;

so I pull the shadows around me like a puff   5
and crinkle my eyes as if at the most exquisite moment

of a very long opera, and then we are off!
without reproach and without hope that our delicate feet

will touch the earth again, let alone "very soon."
It is the law of my own voice I shall investigate.   10

I start like ice, my finger to my ear, my ear
to my heart, that proud cur at the garbage can

in the rain. It's wonderful to admire oneself
with complete candor, tallying up the merits of each

of the latrines. 14th Street is drunken and credulous,   15
53rd tries to tremble but is too at rest. The good

love a park and the inept a railway station,
and there are the divine ones who drag themselves up

and down the lengthening shadow of an Abyssinian head
in the dust, trailing their long elegant heels of hot air   20

crying to confuse the brave "It's a summer day,
and I want to be wanted more than anything else in the world."

[1971]

Joining the Conversation: Critical Thinking and Writing

1. Describe your response to the word that is O'Hara's title. In what ways does the poem define and explore the word's meanings and our responses to it?
2. Characterize the point of view and tone of the speaker. Who is or are the "we" named in line 1?
3. In line 1, the speaker declares that "we are taking off our masks" but then immediately seems to confuse or contradict his point when he says "we" are "keeping / our mouths shut." Explain as clearly as you can what the speaker is suggesting in this first stanza.
4. Some of the language in this poem is ugly or unpleasant—for example, the "cur at the garbage can," "the latrines." What is the purpose of such language? What is its place in the structure of the poem as a whole? Can one argue that such language has no place in a decent poem?
5. Could O'Hara's poem be reasonably described as an argument on behalf of gays and lesbians? Please explain.

MARGE PIERCY

Marge Piercy, born in Detroit, Michigan, in 1936, was the first member of her family to attend college. After earning a BA from the University of Michigan in 1957 and an MA from Northwestern University in 1958, she moved to Chicago. There she worked at odd jobs while writing novels (unpublished) and engaging in action on behalf of women and African Americans and against the war in Vietnam. In 1969—the year she moved to Wellfleet, Massachusetts, where she still lives—she published her first book, a novel, Going Down Fast. *Since then she has published other novels, short stories, poems, and essays.*

Barbie Doll

This girlchild was born as usual
and presented dolls that did pee-pee
and miniature GE stoves and irons
and wee lipsticks the color of cherry candy.
Then in the magic of puberty, a classmate said: 5
You have a great big nose and fat legs.

She was healthy, tested intelligent,
possessed strong arms and back,
abundant sexual drive and manual dexterity.
She went to and fro apologizing.   10
Everyone saw a fat nose on thick legs.

She was advised to play coy,
exhorted to come on hearty,

exercise, diet, smile and wheedle.
Her good nature wore out   15
like a fan belt.
So she cut off her nose and her legs
and offered them up.

In the casket displayed on satin she lay
with the undertaker's cosmetics painted on,   20
a turned-up putty nose,
dressed in a pink and white nightie.
Doesn't she look pretty? everyone said.
Consummation at last.
To every woman a happy ending.   25

[1969]

Joining the Conversation: Critical Thinking and Writing

1. Why is the poem called "Barbie Doll"?
2. What voice do you hear in lines 1–4? Line 6 is, we are told, the voice of "a classmate." How do these voices differ? What voice do you hear in the first three
   lines of the second stanza?
3. Explain in your own words what Piercy is saying about women in this poem.
   Does her view seem to you fair, slightly exaggerated, or greatly exaggerated?
   Support your thesis with reasons.

PLAY

TERRENCE MCNALLY

*Terrence McNally, born in 1939 in St. Petersburg, Florida, grew up in Corpus
Christi, Texas, and did his undergraduate work at Columbia University. "I'm a gay
man who writes plays," he has said, and most of his work concerns gay people—or
the responses of straight people to gay people.*

We give the original script of Andre's Mother *(1988); McNally later amplified it for
a 1990 television broadcast (running time is 58 minutes) that was awarded an Emmy.*

Andre's Mother

CHARACTERS

CAL, a young man
ARTHUR, his father
PENNY, his sister
ANDRE'S MOTHER
Time: *Now*
Place: *New York City, Central Park*

*Four people—*CAL, ARTHUR, PENNY, *and* ANDRE'S MOTHER—*enter: They are nicely
dressed and each carries a white helium-filled balloon on a string.*

CAL: You know what's really terrible? I can't think of anything terrific to say. Good-bye. I love you. I'll miss you. And I'm supposed to be so great with words!

PENNY: What's that over there?

ARTHUR: Ask your brother.

CAL: It's a theatre. An outdoor theatre. They do plays there in the summer. Shakespeare's plays. [*To* ANDRE'S MOTHER.] God, how much he wanted to play Hamlet again. He would have gone to Timbuktu to have another go at that part. The summer he did it in Boston, he was so happy!

PENNY: Cal, I don't think she . . . ! It's not the time. Later.

ARTHUR: Your son was a . . . the Jews have a word for it . . .

PENNY [QUIETLY APPALLED]: Oh my God!

ARTHUR: Mensch, I believe it is, and I think I'm using it right. It means warm, solid, the real thing. Correct me if I'm wrong.

PENNY: Fine, Dad, fine. Just quit while you're ahead.

ARTHUR: I won't say he was like a son to me. Even my son isn't always like a son to me. I mean . . . ! In my clumsy way, I'm trying to say how much I liked Andre. And how much he helped me to know my own boy. Cal was always two handsful but Andre and I could talk about anything under the sun. My wife was very fond of him, too.

PENNY: Cal, I don't understand about the balloons.

CAL: They represent the soul. When you let go, it means you're letting his soul ascend to Heaven. That you're willing to let go. Breaking the last earthly ties.

PENNY: Does the Pope know about this?

ARTHUR: Penny!

PENNY: Andre loved my sense of humor. Listen, you can hear him laughing. [*She lets go of her white balloon.*] So long, you glorious, wonderful, I-know-what-Cal-means-about-words . . . *man!* God forgive me for wishing you were straight every time I laid eyes on you. But if any man was going to have you, I'm glad it was my brother! Look how fast it went up. I bet that means something. Something terrific.

ARTHUR [LETS HIS BALLOON GO]: Good-bye. God speed.

PENNY: Cal?

CAL: I'm not ready yet.

PENNY: Okay. We'll be over there. Come on, Pop, you can buy your little girl a Good Humor.

ARTHUR: They still make Good Humor?

PENNY: Only now they're called Dove Bars and they cost twelve dollars.

[PENNY TAKES ARTHUR OFF. CAL AND ANDRE'S MOTHER *stand with their balloons.*]

CAL: I wish I knew what you were thinking. I think it would help me. You know almost nothing about me and I only know what Andre told me about you. I'd always had it in my mind that one day we would be friends, you and me. But if you didn't know about Andre and me . . . If this hadn't happened, I wonder if he would have ever told you. When he was sick, if I asked him once I asked him a thousand times, tell her. She's your mother. She won't mind. But he was so afraid of hurting you and of your disapproval. I don't know which was worse. [*No response. He sighs.*] God, how many of us live in this city because we don't want to hurt our mothers and live in mortal terror of their disapproval. We lose ourselves here. Our lives aren't furtive, just our feelings toward people like you are! A city of fugitives from our parents' scorn or heartbreak. Sometimes he'd seem a little down and I'd say, "What's the matter, babe?" and this funny sweet, sad smile would cross his face and he'd say, "Just a little homesick, Cal, just a little bit." I always accused him of being a country boy just playing at being a hotshot, sophisticated New Yorker. [*He sighs.*]

It's bullshit. It's all bullshit. [*Still no response.*]

Do you remember the comic strip *Little Lulu?* Her mother had no name, she was so remote, so formidable to all the children. She was just Lulu's mother. "Hello, Lulu's Mother," Lulu's friends would say. She was almost anonymous in her remoteness. You remind me of her. Andre's Mother. Let me answer the questions you can't ask and then I'll leave you alone and you won't ever have to see me again. Andre died of AIDS. I don't know how he got it. I tested negative. He died bravely. You would have been proud of him. The only thing that frightened him was you. I'll have everything that was his sent to you. I'll pay for it. There isn't much. You should have come up the summer he played Hamlet. He was magnificent. Yes, I'm bitter. I'm bitter I've lost him. I'm bitter what's happening. I'm bitter even now, after all this, I can't reach you. I'm beginning to feel your disapproval and it's making me ill. [*He looks at his balloon.*] Sorry, old friend. I blew it. [*He lets go of the balloon.*]

Good night, sweet prince, and flights of angels sing thee to they rest![1] [*Beat.*]

Goodbye, Andre's Mother.

[*He goes.* ANDRE'S MOTHER *stands alone holding her white balloon. Her lips tremble. She looks on the verge of breaking down. She is about to let go of the balloon when she pulls it down to her. She looks at it awhile before she gently kisses it. She lets go of the balloon. She follows it with her eyes as it rises and rises. The lights are beginning to fade.* ANDRE'S MOTHER *'s eyes are still on the balloon. The lights fade.*]

[1988]

---

[1]**Good night . . . rest!** Cal is quoting lines that Hamlet's friend Horatio speaks (5.2.336–37) at the moment of Hamlet's death.

Joining the Conversation: Critical Thinking and Writing

1. Andre's Mother doesn't speak in the play, but we learn something about her through Cal's words and something more through the description in the final stage direction. In a paragraph, characterize Andre's Mother.
2. Let's assume that you drafted this play, and now, on rereading it, you decide that you want to give Andre's Mother one speech, and one speech only. Write the speech—it can go anywhere in the play that you think best—and then in a brief essay explain why you think the speech is effective.
3. Cal tells Penny that the balloons "represent the soul. When you let go, it means you're letting his soul ascend to Heaven." Is that exactly the way you see the balloons or would see them if you attended a funeral where white balloons were distributed? Explain your answer.

Chapter Overview: Looking Backward/Looking Forward

1. Do you think it is possible to love many people? Or is love so special that it can only be felt for a few people? Would you go further and say that love—real love, love in the deepest sense—can in truth only be felt for one person in your life?

2. How do we know when we have moved from "liking" someone to "loving" him or her? What are the signs? What is the evidence?

3. What does it mean to say that we have "fallen out of love" with someone? Is this change in us the result of something specific? Or does it somehow simply happen? Once you fall out of love, can you ever fall back in, or is that feeling lost forever?

4. Have you ever hated someone? How did this come about? Do you still hate the person, or have your feelings changed?

5. "Love" is a term that is often used in literature courses—love poetry, for instance, or love in the modern novel. What do you imagine a course in literature could teach you about love? Have you read a literary work that made you think and feel differently about love?

6. Do you find it hard to say, "I love you"? Why is that?

7. Do you think that it is a good experience to write about personal feelings, such as love and hate? Would you prefer not to? Would you like to do more of this kind of personal writing in your courses, or less?

8. Are you a religious person? Do you love God? How is this love felt and expressed in your life from day to day?

CHAPTER 19

Innocence and Experience

ESSAY

GEORGE ORWELL

George Orwell (1903–50), an Englishman, adopted this name; he was born Eric Blair, in India. He was educated at Eton, in England, but in 1921 he went to Burma (now Myanmar), where he served for five years as a police officer. He then returned to Europe, doing odd jobs while writing novels and stories. In 1936, he fought in the Spanish Civil War on the side of the Republicans, an experience that he reported in Homage to Catalonia *(1938). Orwell is best known for his novels* Animal Farm *(1945) and* Nineteen Eighty-Four *(1949).*

Shooting an Elephant

In Moulmein, in Lower Burma, I was hated by large numbers of people—the only time in my life that I have been important enough for this to happen to me. I was sub-divisional police officer of the town, and in an aimless, petty kind of way anti-European feeling was very bitter. No one had the guts to raise a riot, but if a European woman went through the bazaars alone somebody would probably spit betel juice over her dress. As a police officer I was an obvious target and was baited whenever it seemed safe to do so. When a nimble Burman tripped me up on the football field and the referee (another Burman) looked the other way, the crowd yelled with hideous laughter. This happened more than once. In the end the sneering yellow faces of young men that met me everywhere, the insults hooted after me when I was at a safe distance, got badly on my nerves. The young Buddhist priests were the worst of all. There were several thousands of them in the town and none of them seemed to have anything to do except stand on street corners and jeer at Europeans.

All this was perplexing and upsetting. For at that time I had already made up my mind that imperialism was an evil thing and the sooner I chucked up my job and got out of it the better. Theoretically—and secretly, of course—I was all for the Burmese and all against their oppressors, the British. As for the job I was doing, I hated it more bitterly than I can perhaps make clear. In a job like that you see the dirty work of the Empire at close quarters. The wretched prisoners huddling in the stinking cages of the lockups, the grey, cowed faces of the long-term convicts, the scarred buttocks of the men who had been flogged with bamboos—all these oppressed me with an intolerable sense of guilt. But I could get nothing into perspective. I was young and ill-educated and I had had to think out my problems in the utter silence that is imposed on every Englishman in the East. I did not even know that the British Empire is dying, still less did I know that it is a great deal better than the younger empires that are going to supplant it. All I knew was that I was stuck between my hatred of the empire I served and my rage against the evil-spirited little beasts who tried to make my job impossible. With one part of my mind I thought of the British Raj as an unbreakable tyranny, as something clamped down, in *saecula saeculorum*,[1] upon the will of prostrate peoples; with another part I thought that the greatest joy in the world would be to drive a bayonet into a Buddhist priest's guts. Feelings like these are the normal by-products of imperialism; ask any Anglo-Indian official, if you can catch him off duty.

One day something happened which in a roundabout way was enlightening. It was a tiny incident in itself, but it gave me a better glimpse than I had had before of the real nature of imperialism—the real motives for which despotic governments act. Early one morning the sub-inspector at a police station at the other end of the town rang me up on the 'phone and said that an elephant was ravaging the bazaar. Would I please come and do something about it? I did not know what I could do, but I wanted to see what was happening and I got onto a pony and started out. I took my rifle, an old .44 Winchester and much too small to kill an elephant, but I thought the noise might be useful *in terrorem*.[2] Various Burmans stopped me on the way and told me about the elephant's doings. It was not, of course, a wild elephant, but a tame one which had gone "must." It had been chained up, as tame elephants always are when their attack of "must" is due, but on the previous night it had broken its chain and escaped. Its mahout, the only person who could manage it when it was in that state, had set out in pursuit, but had taken the wrong direction and was now twelve hours' journey away, and in the morning the elephant had suddenly reappeared in the town. The Burmese population had no weapons and were quite helpless against it. It had already destroyed somebody's bamboo hut, killed a cow and raided some fruit-stalls and devoured the stock; also it had met the municipal rubbish van and, when the driver jumped out and took to his heels, had turned the van over and inflicted violences upon it.

The Burmese sub-inspector and some Indian constables were waiting for me in the quarter where the elephant had been seen. It was a very poor quarter, a labyrinth of squalid bamboo huts, thatched with palmleaf, winding all over a steep hillside. I remember that it was a cloudy, stuffy morning at the beginning of the rains. We began questioning the people as to where the elephant had gone and, as usual, failed to get any definite information. That is invariably the case in the East; a story always sounds clear enough at a distance, but the nearer you get to the scene of events the vaguer it becomes. Some of the people said that the elephant had gone in one direction, some said that he had gone in another, some professed not even to have heard of any elephant. I had almost made up my mind that the whole story was a pack of lies, when we heard yells a little distance away. There was a loud, scandalized cry of "Go away, child! Go away this instant!" and an old woman with a switch in her hand came round the corner of a hut, violently shooing away a crowd of naked children. Some more women followed, clicking their tongues and exclaiming; evidently there was something that the children ought not to have seen. I rounded the hut and saw a man's dead body sprawling in the mud. He was an Indian, a black Dravidian coolie, almost naked, and he could not have been dead many minutes. The people said that the elephant had come suddenly upon him round the corner of the hut, caught him with

---

[1] *saecula saeculorum* Latin, "world without end"; literally, "a century of centuries."
[2] *in terrorem* as a warning.

its trunk, put its foot on his back and ground him into the earth. This was the rainy season and the ground was soft, and his face had scored a trench a foot deep and a couple of yards long. He was lying on his belly with arms crucified and head sharply twisted to one side. His face was coated with mud, the eyes wide open, the teeth bared and grinning with an expression of unendurable agony. (Never tell me, by the way, that the dead look peaceful. Most of the corpses I have seen look devilish.) The friction of the great beast's foot had stripped the skin from his back as neatly as one skins a rabbit. As soon as I saw the dead man I sent an orderly to a friend's house nearby to borrow an elephant rifle. I had already sent back the pony, not wanting it to go mad with fright and throw me if it smelt the elephant.

5   The orderly came back in a few minutes with a rifle and five cartridges, and meanwhile some Burmans had arrived and told us that the elephant was in the paddy fields below, only a few hundred yards away. As I started forward practically the whole population of the quarter flocked out of the houses and followed me. They had seen the rifle and were all shouting excitedly that I was going to shoot the elephant. They had not shown much interest in the elephant when he was merely ravaging their homes, but it was different now that he was going to be shot. It was a bit of fun to them, as it would be to an English crowd; besides they wanted the meat. It made me vaguely uneasy. I had no intention of shooting the elephant—I had merely sent for the rifle to defend myself if necessary—and it is always unnerving to have a crowd following you. I marched down the hill, looking and feeling a fool, with the rifle over my shoulder and an ever-growing army of people jostling at my heels. At the bottom, when you got away from the huts, there was a metalled road and beyond that a miry waste of paddy fields a thousand yards across, not yet ploughed but soggy from the first rains and dotted with coarse grass. The elephant was standing eight yards from the road, his left side towards us. He took not the slightest notice of the crowd's approach. He was tearing up bunches of grass, beating them against his knees to clean them and stuffing them into his mouth.

I had halted on the road. As soon as I saw the elephant I knew with perfect certainty that I ought not to shoot him. It is a serious matter to shoot a working elephant—it is comparable to destroying a huge and costly piece of machinery— and obviously one ought not to do it if it can possibly be avoided. And at that distance, peacefully eating, the elephant looked no more dangerous than a cow. I thought then and I think now that his attack of "must" was already passing off; in which case he would merely wander harmlessly about until the mahout came back and caught him. Moreover, I did not in the least want to shoot him. I decided that I would watch him for a little while to make sure that he did not turn savage again, and then go home.

But at that moment I glanced round at the crowd that had followed me. It was an immense crowd, two thousand at the least and growing every minute. It blocked the road for a long distance on either side. I looked at the sea of yellow faces above the garish clothes—faces all happy and excited over this bit of fun, all certain that the elephant was going to be shot. They were watching me as they would watch a conjurer about to perform a trick. They did not like me, but with the magical rifle in my hands I was momentarily worth watching. And suddenly I realized that I should have to shoot the elephant after all. The people expected it of me and I had got to do it; I could feel their two thousand wills pressing me forward, irresistibly. And it was at this moment, as I stood there with the rifle in my hands, that I first grasped the hollowness, the futility of the white man's dominion in the East. Here was I, the white man with his gun, standing in front of the unarmed native crowd—seemingly the leading actor of the piece; but in reality I was only an absurd puppet pushed to and fro by the will of those yellow faces behind. I perceived in this moment that when the white man turns tyrant it is his own freedom that he destroys. He becomes a sort of hollow, posing dummy, the conventionalized figure of a sahib. For it is the condition of his rule that he shall spend his life in trying to impress the "natives," and so in every crisis he has got to do what the "natives" expect of him. He wears a mask, and his face grows to fit it. I had got to shoot the elephant. I had committed myself to doing it when I sent for the rifle. A sahib has got to act like a sahib; he has got to appear resolute, to know his own mind and do definite things. To come all that way, rifle in hand, with two thousand people marching at my heels, and then to trail feebly away, having done nothing—no, that was impossible. The crowd would laugh at me. And my whole life, every white man's life in the East, was one long struggle not to be laughed at.

But I did not want to shoot the elephant. I watched him beating his bunch of grass against his knees, with that preoccupied grandmotherly air that elephants have. It seemed to me that it would be murder to shoot him. At that age I was not squeamish about killing animals, but I had never shot an elephant and never wanted to. (Somehow it always seems worse to kill a *large* animal.) Besides, there was the beast's owner to be considered. Alive, the elephant was worth at least a hundred pounds; dead, he would only be worth the value of his tusks, five pounds, possibly. But I had got to act quickly. I turned to some experienced-looking Burmans who had been there when we arrived, and asked them how the elephant had been behaving. They all said the same thing; he took no notice of you if you left him alone, but he might charge if you went too close to him.

It was perfectly clear to me what I ought to do. I ought to walk up to within, say, twenty-five yards of the elephant and test his behavior. If he charged, I could shoot; if he took no notice of me, it would be safe to leave him until the mahout came back. But also I knew that I was going to do no such thing. I was a poor shot with a rifle and the ground was soft mud into which one would sink at every step. If the elephant charged and I missed him, I should have about as much chance as a toad under a steam-roller. But even then I was not thinking particularly of my own skin, only of the watchful yellow faces behind. For at that moment, with the crowd watching me, I was not afraid in the ordinary sense, as I would have been if I had been alone. A white man mustn't be frightened in front of "natives"; and so, in general, he isn't frightened. The sole thought in my mind was that if anything went wrong those two thousand Burmans would see me pursued, caught, trampled on and reduced to a grinning corpse like that Indian up the hill. And if that happened it was quite probable that some of them would laugh. That would never do. There was only one alternative. I shoved the cartridges into the magazine and lay down on the road to get a better aim.

10   The crowd grew very still, and a deep, low, happy sigh, as of people who see the theatre curtain go up at last breathed from innumerable throats. They were going to have their bit of fun after all. The rifle was a beautiful German thing with cross-hair sights. I did not then know that in shooting an elephant one would shoot to cut an imaginary bar running from ear-hole to ear-hole. I ought, therefore, as the elephant was sideways on, to have aimed straight at his ear-hole; actually I aimed several inches in front of this, thinking the brain would be further forward.

When I pulled the trigger I did not hear the bang or feel the kick—one never does when a shot goes home—but I heard the devilish roar of glee that went up from the crowd. In that instant, in too short a time, one would have thought, even for the bullet to get there, a mysterious, terrible change had come over the elephant. He neither stirred nor fell, but every line of his body had altered. He looked suddenly stricken, shrunken, immensely old, as though the frightful impact of the bullet had paralysed him without knocking him down. At last, after what seemed a long time—it might have been five seconds, I dare say—he sagged flab-bily to his knees. His mouth slobbered. An enormous senility seemed to have settled upon him. One could have imagined him thousands of years old. I fired again into the same spot. At the second shot he did not collapse but climbed with desperate slowness to his feet and stood weakly upright, with legs sagging and head dropping. I fired a third time. That was the shot that did for him. You could see the agony of it jolt his whole body and knock the last remnant of strength from his legs. But in falling he seemed for a moment to rise, for as his hind legs col-lapsed beneath him he seemed to tower upward like a huge rock toppling, his trunk reaching skywards like a tree. He trumpeted, for the first and only time. And then down he came, his belly towards me, with a crash that seemed to shake the ground even where I lay.

I got up. The Burmans were already racing past me across the mud. It was obvious that the elephant would never rise again, but he was not dead. He was breathing very rhythmically with long rattling gasps, his great mound of a side painfully rising and falling. His mouth was wide open. I could see far down into caverns of pale pink throat. I waited a long time for him to die, but his breathing did not weaken. Finally I fired my two remaining shots into the spot where I thought his heart must be. The thick blood welled out of him like red velvet, but still he did not die. His body did not even jerk when the shots hit him, the tortured breathing continued without a pause. He was dying, very slowly and in great agony, but in some world remote from me where not even a bullet could damage him further. I felt I had got to put an end to that dreadful noise. It seemed dreadful to see the great beast lying there, powerless to move and yet powerless to die, and not even to be able to finish him. I sent back for my small rifle and poured shot after shot into his heart and down his throat. They seemed to make no impression. The tortured gasps continued as steadily as the ticking of a clock.

In the end I could not stand it any longer and went away. I heard later that it took him half an hour to die. Burmans were bringing dahs[3] and baskets even before I left, and I was told they had stripped his body almost to the bones by the afternoon.

Afterwards, of course, there were endless discussions about the shooting of the elephant. The owner was furious, but he was only an Indian and could do nothing. Besides, legally I had done the right thing, for a mad elephant has to be killed, like a mad dog, if its owner fails to control it. Among the Europeans opinion was divided. The older men said I was right, the younger men said it was a damn shame to shoot an elephant for killing a coolie, because an elephant was worth more than any damn Coringhee coolie. And afterwards I was very glad that the coolie had been killed; it put me legally in the right and it gave me a sufficient pretext for shooting the elephant. I often wondered whether any of the others grasped that I had done it solely to avoid looking a fool.

[1936]

---

[3]**dahs** knives.

Joining the Conversation: Critical Thinking and Writing

1. How does Orwell characterize himself at the time of the events that he describes? What evidence in the essay suggests that he wrote it some years later?
2. Orwell says that the incident was "enlightening." What does he mean? Picking up this clue, state in a sentence or two the thesis or main point of the essay.
3. Compare Orwell's description of the dead coolie (in the fourth paragraph) with his description of the elephant's death (in the eleventh and twelfth paragraphs). Why does Orwell devote more space to the death of the elephant?
4. How would you describe the tone of the last paragraph, particularly of the last two sentences? Do you find the paragraph an effective conclusion to the essay? Explain your answer.

STORIES

CHARLOTTE PERKINS GILMAN

Charlotte Perkins Gilman (1860–1935) was born in Hartford, Connecticut. Her father deserted the family soon after Charlotte's birth; she was brought up by her mother, who found it difficult to support her family. For a while, Charlotte worked as an artist and teacher of art, and in 1884, when she was twenty-four years old, she married an artist. In 1885, she had a daughter, but soon after the birth of the girl, Charlotte had a nervous breakdown. At her husband's urging, she spent a month in the sanitarium of Dr. S. Weir Mitchell, a physician who specialized in treating women with nervous disorders. (Mitchell is specifically named in "The Yellow Wallpaper.")
Because the treatment—isolation and total rest—nearly drove her to insanity, she fled Mitchell and her husband. In California, she began a career as a lecturer and writer on feminist topics. (She also supported herself by teaching school and by keeping a boardinghouse.) Among her books are Women and Economics *(1899) and* The Man-Made World *(1911), which have been revived by the feminist movement. In 1900, she married a cousin, George Gilman. From all available evidence, the marriage was successful. Certainly, it did not restrict her activities as a feminist. In 1935, suffering from inoperable cancer, she took her own life.*

"The Yellow Wallpaper," written in 1892—that is, written after she had been treated by S. Weir Mitchell for her nervous breakdown—was at first interpreted either as a ghost story or as a Poe-like study of insanity. Only in recent years has it been seen as a feminist story. (One might ask oneself if these interpretations are mutually exclusive.)

The Yellow Wallpaper

It is very seldom that mere ordinary people like John and myself secure ancestral halls for the summer.

A colonial mansion, a hereditary estate. I would say a haunted house, and reach the height of romantic felicity—but that would be asking too much of fate!

Still I will proudly declare that there is something queer about it.

Else, why should it be let so cheaply? And why have stood so long untenanted?

John laughs at me, of course, but one expects that in marriage.

John is practical in the extreme. He has no patience with faith, an intense horror of superstition, and he scoffs openly at any talk of things not to be felt and seen and put down in figures.

John is a physician, and *perhaps*—(I would not say it to a living soul, of course, but this is dead paper and a great relief to my mind)—*perhaps* that is one reason I do not get well faster.

You see he does not believe I am sick! And what can one do?

If a physician of high standing, and one's own husband, assures friends and relatives that there is really nothing the matter with one but temporary nervous depression—a slight hysterical tendency—what is one to do?

10 My brother is also a physician, and also of high standing, and he says the same thing.

So I take phosphates or phosphites—whichever it is, and tonics, and journeys, and air, and exercise, and am absolutely forbidden to "work" until I am well again.

Personally, I disagree with their ideas.

Personally, I believe that congenial work, with excitement and change, would do me good.

But what is one to do?

15 I did write for a while in spite of them: but it *does* exhaust me a good deal—having to be so sly about it, or else meet with heavy opposition.

I sometimes fancy that in my condition if I had less opposition and more society and stimulus—but John says the very worst thing I can do is to think about my condition, and I confess it always makes me feel bad.

So I will let it alone and talk about the house.

The most beautiful place! It is quite alone, standing well back from the road, quite three miles from the village. It makes me think of English places that you read about, for there are hedges and walls and gates that lock, and lots of separate little houses for the gardeners and people.

There is a *delicious* garden! I never saw such a garden—large and shady, full of box-bordered paths, and lined with long grape-covered arbors with seats under them. There were greenhouses, too, but they are all broken now.

20 There was some legal trouble, I believe, something about the heirs and coheirs: anyhow, the place has been empty for years.

That spoils my ghostliness, I am afraid, but I don't care—there is something strange about the house—I can feel it.

I even said so to John one moonlight evening, but he said what I felt was a *draught,* and shut the window.

I get unreasonably angry with John sometimes. I'm sure I never used to be so sensitive. I think it is due to this nervous condition.

But John says if I feel so, I shall neglect proper self-control: so I take pains to control myself—before him, at least, and that makes me very tired.

25 I don't like our room a bit. I wanted one downstairs that opened on the piazza and had roses all over the window, and such pretty old-fashioned chintz hangings! But John would not hear of it.

He said there was only one window and not room for two beds, and no near room for him if he took another.

He is very careful and loving, and hardly lets me stir without special direction.

I have a schedule prescription for each hour in the day: he takes all care from me, and so I feel basely ungrateful not to value it more.

He said we came here solely on my account, that I was to have perfect rest and all the air I could get. "Your exercise depends on your strength, my dear," said he, "and your food somewhat on your appetite; but air you can absorb all the time." So we took the nursery at the top of the house.

30 It is a big, airy room, the whole floor nearly, with windows that look all ways, and air and sunshine galore. It was nursery first and then playroom and gymnasium, I should judge; for the windows are barred for little children, and there are rings and things in the walls.

The paint and paper look as if a boys' school had used it. It is stripped off—the paper—in great patches all around the head of my bed, about as far as I can reach, and in a great place on the other side of the room low down. I never saw a worse paper in my life.

One of those sprawling flamboyant patterns committing every artistic sin.

It is dull enough to confuse the eye in following, pronounced enough to constantly irritate and provoke study, and when you follow the lame uncertain curves for a little distance they suddenly commit suicide—plunge off at outrageous angles, destroy themselves in unheard of contradictions.

The color is repellent, almost revolting: a smouldering unclean yellow, strangely faded by the slow-turning sunlight. It is a dull yet lurid orange in some places, a sickly sulphur tint in others.

35 No wonder the children hated it! I should hate it myself if I had to live in this room long.

There comes John, and I must put this away,—he hates to have me write a word.

We have been here two weeks, and I haven't felt like writing before, since that first day.

I am sitting by the window now, up in this atrocious nursery, and there is nothing to hinder my writing as much as I please, save lack of strength.

John is away all day, and even some nights when his cases are serious.

40 I am glad my case is not serious!

But these nervous troubles are dreadfully depressing.

John does not know how much I really suffer. He knows there is no *reason* to suffer, and that satisfies him.

Of course it is only nervousness. It does weigh on me so not to do my duty in any way!

I meant to be such a help to John, such a real rest and comfort, and here I am a comparative burden already!

45 Nobody would believe what an effort it is to do what little I am able,—to dress and entertain, and order things.

It is fortunate Mary is so good with the baby. Such a dear baby!

And yet I *cannot* be with him, it makes me so nervous.

I suppose John never was nervous in his life. He laughs at me so about this wallpaper!

At first he meant to repaper the room, but afterwards he said that I was letting it get the better of me, and that nothing was worse for a nervous patient than to give way to such fancies.

50 He said that after the wallpaper was changed it would be the heavy bedstead, and then the barred windows, and then that gate at the head of the stairs, and so on.

"You know the place is doing you good," he said, "and really, dear, I don't care to renovate the house just for a three months' rental."

"Then do let us go downstairs," I said, "there are such pretty rooms there."

[margin notes: "is she thinking of suicide?"; "it's like a diary"; "she belittles herself a lot"]

Then he took me in his arms and called me a blessed little goose, and said he would go down to the cellar, if I wished, and have it whitewashed into the bargain. But he is right enough about the beds and windows and things.

55 It is an airy and comfortable room as any one need wish, and, of course, I would not be so silly as to make him uncomfortable just for a whim.

I'm really getting quite fond of the big room, all but that horrid paper.

Out of one window I can see the garden, those mysterious deep-shaded arbors, the riotous old-fashioned flowers, and bushes and gnarly trees.

Out of another I get a lovely view of the bay and a little private wharf belonging to the estate. There is a beautiful shaded lane that runs down there from the house. I always fancy I see people walking in these numerous paths and arbors, but John has cautioned me not to give way to fancy in the least. He says that with my imaginative power and habit of story-making, a nervous weakness like mine is sure to lead to all manner of excited fancies, and that I ought to use my will and good sense to check the tendency. So I try.

I think sometimes that if I were only well enough to write a little it would relieve the press of ideas and rest me.

60 But I find I get pretty tired when I try.

It is so discouraging not to have any advice and companionship about my work. When I get really well, John says we will ask Cousin Henry and Julia down for a long visit; but he says he would as soon put fireworks in my pillow-case as to let me have those stimulating people about now.

I wish I could get well faster.

But I must not think about that. This paper looks to me as if it *knew* what a vicious influence it had!

There is a recurrent spot where the pattern lolls like a broken neck and two bulbous eyes stare at you upside down.

65 I get positively angry with the impertinence of it and the everlastingness. Up and down and sideways they crawl, and those absurd, unblinking eyes are everywhere. There is one place where two breadths didn't match, and the eyes go all up and down the line, one a little higher than the other.

I never saw so much expression in an inanimate thing before, and we all know how much expression they have! I used to lie awake as a child and get more entertainment and terror out of blank walls and plain furniture than most children could find in a toystore.

I remember what a kindly wink the knobs of our big, old bureau used to have, and there was one chair that always seemed like a strong friend.

I used to feel that if any of the other things looked too fierce I could always hop into that chair and be safe.

The furniture in this room is no worse than inharmonious, however, for we had to bring it all from downstairs. I suppose when this was used as a playroom they had to take the nursery things out, and no wonder! I never saw such ravages as the children have made here.

70 The wallpaper, as I said before, is torn off in spots, and it sticketh closer than a brother—they must have had perseverance as well as hatred.

Then the floor is scratched and gouged and splintered, the plaster itself is dug out here and there, and this great heavy bed which is all we found in the room, looks as if it had been through the wars.

But I don't mind it a bit—only the paper.

There comes John's sister. Such a dear girl as she is, and so careful of me! I must not let her find me writing.

She is a perfect and enthusiastic housekeeper, and hopes for no better profession. I verily believe she thinks it is the writing which made me sick!

But I can write when she is out, and see her a long way off from these windows.

There is one that commands the road, a lovely shaded winding road, and one that just looks off over the country. A lovely country, too, full of great elms and velvet meadows.

This wallpaper has a kind of sub-pattern in a different shade, a particularly irritating one, for you can only see it in certain lights, and not clearly then.

But in the places where it isn't faded and where the sun is just so—I can see a strange, provoking, formless sort of figure, that seems to skulk about behind that silly and conspicuous front design.

There's sister on the stairs!

Well, the Fourth of July is over! The people are all gone and I am tired out. John thought it might do me good to see a little company, so we just had mother and Nellie and the children down for a week.

Of course I didn't do a thing. Jennie sees to everything now.

But it tired me all the same.

John says if I don't pick up faster he shall send me to Weir Mitchell in the fall.

But I don't want to go there at all. I had a friend who was in his hands once, and she says he is just like John and my brother, only more so!

Besides, it is such an undertaking to go so far.

I don't feel as if it was worthwhile to turn my hand over for anything, and I'm getting dreadfully fretful and querulous.

I cry at nothing, and cry most of the time.

Of course I don't when John is here, or anybody else, but when I am alone.

And I am alone a good deal just now. John is kept in town very often by serious cases, and Jennie is good and lets me alone when I want her to.

So I walk a little in the garden or down that lovely lane, sit on the porch under the roses, and lie down up here a good deal.

I'm getting really fond of the room in spite of the wallpaper. Perhaps *because* of the wallpaper.

It dwells in my mind so!

I lie here on this great immovable bed—it is nailed down, I believe—and follow that pattern about by the hour. It is as good as gymnastics, I assure you. I start, we'll say, at the bottom, down in the corner over there where it has not been touched, and I determine for the thousandth time that I *will* follow that pointless pattern to some sort of a conclusion.

I know a little of the principle of design, and I know this thing was not arranged on any laws of radiation, or alternation, or repetition, or symmetry, or anything else that I ever heard of.

It is repeated, of course, by the breadths, but not otherwise.

Looked at in one way each breadth stands alone, the bloated curves and flourishes—a kind of "debased Romanesque" with *delirium tremens*—go waddling up and down in isolated columns of fatuity.

But, on the other hand, they connect diagonally, and the sprawling outlines run off in great slanting waves of optic horror, like a lot of wallowing seaweeds in full chase.

The whole thing goes horizontally, too, at least it seems so, and I exhaust myself in trying to distinguish the order of its going in that direction.

They have used a horizontal breadth for a frieze, and that adds wonderfully to the confusion.

100   There is one end of the room where it is almost intact, and there, when the crosslights fade and the low sun shines directly upon it, I can almost fancy radiation after all,—the interminable grotesques seem to form around a common center and rush off in headlong plunges of equal distraction.

It makes me tired to follow it. I will take a nap I guess.

I don't know why I should write this.

I don't want to.

I don't feel able.

105   And I know John would think it absurd. But I *must* say what I feel and think in some way—it is such a relief.

But the effort is getting to be greater than the relief!

Half the time now I am awfully lazy, and lie down ever so much. John says I mustn't lose my strength, and has me take cod liver oil and lots of tonics and things, to say nothing of ale and wine and rare meat.

Dear John! He loves me very dearly, and hates to have me sick. I tried to have a real earnest reasonable talk with him the other day, and tell him how I wish he would let me go and make a visit to Cousin Henry and Julia.

But he said I wasn't able to go, nor able to stand it after I got there: and I did not make out a very good case for myself, for I was crying before I had finished.

110   It is getting to be a great effort for me to think straight. Just this nervous weakness I suppose.

And dear John gathered me up in his arms, and just carried me upstairs and laid me on the bed, and sat by me and read to me till it tired my head.

He said I was his darling and his comfort and all he had, and that I must take care of myself for his sake, and keep well.

He says no one but myself can help me out of it, that I must use my will and self-control and not let any silly fancies run away with me.

There's one comfort, the baby is well and happy, and does not have to occupy this nursery with the horrid wallpaper.

115   If we had not used it, that blessed child would have! What a fortunate escape! Why, I wouldn't have a child of mine, an impressionable little thing, live in such a room for worlds.

I never thought of it before, but it is lucky that John kept me here after all. I can stand it so much easier than a baby, you see.

Of course I never mention it to them any more—I am too wise,—but I keep watch of it all the same.

There are things in that paper that nobody knows but me, or ever will.

Behind that outside pattern the dim shapes get clearer every day.

120   It is always the same shape, only very numerous.

And it is like a woman stooping down and creeping about behind that pattern. I don't like it a bit. I wonder—I begin to think—I wish John would take me away from here!

It is so hard to talk with John about my case, because he is so wise, and because he loves me so.

But I tried last night.

It was moonlight. The moon shines in all around just as the sun does.

125   I hate to see it sometimes, it creeps so slowly, and always comes in by one window or another.

John was asleep and I hated to waken him, so I kept still and watched the moonlight on that undulating wallpaper till I felt creepy.

The faint figure behind seemed to shake the pattern, just as if she wanted to get out.

I got up softly and went to feel and see if the paper *did* move, and when I came back John was awake.

"What is it, little girl?" he said. "Don't go walking about like that—you'll get cold."

130 I thought it was a good time to talk, so I told him that I really was not gaining here, and that I wished he would take me away.

"Why darling!" said he, "our lease will be up in three weeks, and I can't see how to leave before."

"The repairs are not done at home, and I cannot possibly leave town just now. Of course if you were in any danger, I could and would, but you really are better, dear, whether you can see it or not. I am a doctor, dear, and I know. You are gaining flesh and color, your appetite is better, I feel really much easier about you."

"I don't weigh a bit more," said I, "nor as much: and my appetite may be better in the evening when you are here, but it is worse in the morning when you are away!"

"Bless her little heart!" said he with a big hug, "she shall be as sick as she pleases! But now let's improve the shining hours by going to sleep, and talk about it in the morning!"

135 "And you won't go away?" I asked gloomily.

"Why, how can I, dear? It is only three weeks more and then we will take a nice little trip of a few days while Jennie is getting the house ready. Really, dear, you are better!"

"Better in body perhaps——" I began, and stopped short, for he sat up straight and looked at me with such a stern, reproachful look that I could not say another word.

"My darling," said he, "I beg of you, for my sake and for our child's sake, as well as for your own, that you will never for one instant let that idea enter your mind! There is nothing so dangerous, so fascinating, to a temperament like yours. It is a false and foolish fancy. Can you not trust me as a physician when I tell you so?"

So of course I said no more on that score, and we went to sleep before long. He thought I was asleep first, but I wasn't and lay there for hours trying to decide whether that front pattern and the back pattern really did move together or separately.

140 On a pattern like this, by daylight, there is a lack of sequence, a defiance of law, that is a constant irritant to a normal mind.

The color is hideous enough, and unreliable enough, and infuriating enough, but the pattern is torturing.

You think you have mastered it, but just as you get well underway in following, it turns a back-somersault and there you are. It slaps you in the face, knocks you down, and tramples upon you. It is like a bad dream.

The outside pattern is a florid arabesque, reminding one of a fungus. If you can imagine a toadstool in joints, an interminable string of toadstools, budding and sprouting in endless convolutions—why, that is something like it.

That is, sometimes!

145 There is one marked peculiarity about this paper, a thing nobody seems to notice but myself, and that is that it changes as the light changes.

When the sun shoots in through the east window—I always watch for that first long, straight ray—it changes so quickly that I never can quite believe it.

That is why I watch it always.

By moonlight—the moon shines in all night when there is a moon—I wouldn't know it was the same paper.

At night in any kind of light, in twilight, candlelight, lamplight, and worst of all by moonlight, it becomes bars! The outside pattern I mean, and the woman behind it is as plain as can be.

150   I didn't realize for a long time what the thing was that showed behind, that dim sub-pattern, but now I am quite sure it is a woman.

By daylight she is subdued, quiet. I fancy it is the pattern that keeps her so still. It is so puzzling. It keeps me quiet by the hour.

I lie down ever so much now. John says it is good for me, and to sleep all I can.

Indeed he started the habit by making me lie down for an hour after each meal.

It is a very bad habit I am convinced, for you see I don't sleep.

155   And that cultivates deceit, for I don't tell them I'm awake—O no!

The fact is I am getting a little afraid of John.

He seems very queer sometimes, and even Jennie has an inexplicable look.

It strikes me occasionally, just as a scientific hypothesis—that perhaps it is the paper!

I have watched John when he did not know I was looking, and come into the room suddenly on the most innocent excuses, and I've caught him several times *looking at the paper!* And Jennie too. I caught Jennie with her hand on it once.

160   She didn't know I was in the room, and when I asked her in a quiet, a very quiet voice, with the most restrained manner possible, what she was doing with the paper—she turned around as if she had been caught stealing, and looked quite angry—asked me why I should frighten her so!

Then she said that the paper stained everything it touched, that she had found yellow smooches on all my clothes and John's, and she wished we would be more careful!

Did not that sound innocent? But I know she was studying that pattern, and I am determined that nobody shall find it out but myself!

Life is very much more exciting now than it used to be. You see I have something more to expect, to look forward to, to watch. I really do eat better, and am more quiet than I was.

John is so pleased to see me improve! He laughed a little the other day, and said I seemed to be flourishing in spite of my wallpaper.

165   I turned it off with a laugh. I had no intention of telling him it was *because* of the wallpaper—he would make fun of me. He might even want to take me away.

I don't want to leave now until I have found it out. There is a week more, and I think that will be enough.

I'm feeling ever so much better! I don't sleep much at night, for it is so interesting to watch developments, but I sleep a good deal in the daytime.

In the daytime it is tiresome and perplexing.

There are always new shoots on the fungus, and new shades of yellow all over it. I cannot keep count of them, though I have tried conscientiously.

170   It is the strangest yellow, that wallpaper! It makes me think of all the yellow things I ever saw—not beautiful ones like buttercups, but old, foul, bad yellow things.

But there is something else about that paper—the smell! I noticed it the moment we came into the room, but with so much air and sun it was not bad. Now we have had a week of fog and rain, and whether the windows are open or not, the smell is here.

It creeps all over the house.

I find it hovering in the dining-room, skulking in the parlor, hiding in the hall, lying in wait for me on the stairs.

It gets into my hair.

175   Even when I go to ride, if I turn my head suddenly and surprise it—there is that smell!

Such a peculiar odor, too! I have spent hours in trying to analyze it, to find what it smelled like.

It is not bad—at first, and very gentle, but quite the subtlest, most enduring odor I ever met.

In this damp weather it is awful, I wake up in the night and find it hanging over me.

It used to disturb me at first. I thought seriously of burning the house—to reach the smell.

180   But now I am used to it. The only thing I can think of that it is like is the *color* of the paper! A yellow smell.

There is a very-funny mark on this wall, low down, near the mopboard. A streak that runs round the room. It goes behind every piece of furniture, except the bed, a long, straight, even *smooch,* as if it had been rubbed over and over.

I wonder how it was done and who did it, and what they did it for. Round and round and round—round and round and round—it makes me dizzy!

I really have discovered something at last.

Through watching so much at night, when it changes so, I have finally found out.

185   The front pattern *does* move—and no wonder! The woman behind shakes it! Sometimes I think there are a great many women behind, and sometimes only one, and she crawls around fast, and her crawling shakes it all over.

Then in the very bright spots she keeps still, and in the very shady spots she just takes hold of the bars and shakes them hard.

And she is all the time trying to climb through. But nobody could climb through that pattern—it strangles so: I think that is why it has so many heads.

They get through, and then the pattern strangles them off and turns them upside down, and makes their eyes white!

190   If those heads were covered or taken off it would not be half so bad.

I think that woman gets out in the daytime!

And I'll tell you why—privately—I've seen her!

I can see her out of every one of my windows!

It is the same woman, I know, for she is always creeping, and most women do not creep by daylight.

195   I see her in that long shaded lane, creeping up and down. I see her in those dark grape arbors, creeping all round the garden.

I see her on that long road under the trees, creeping along, and when a carriage comes she hides under the blackberry vines.

I don't blame her a bit. It must be very humiliating to be caught creeping by daylight!

I always lock the door when I creep by daylight. I can't do it at night, for I know John would suspect something at once.

And John is so queer now, that I don't want to irritate him. I wish he would take another room! Besides, I don't want anybody to get that woman out at night but myself.

I often wonder if I could see her out of all the windows at once.

But, turn as fast as I can, I can only see out of one at one time. And though I always see her, she *may* be able to creep faster than I can turn!

I have watched her sometimes away off in the open country, creeping as fast as a cloud shadow in a high wind.

If only that top pattern could be gotten off from the under one! I mean to try it, little by little.

I have found out another funny thing, but I shan't tell at this time! It does not do to trust people too much.

There are only two more days to get this paper off, and I believe John is beginning to notice. I don't like the look in his eyes.

And I heard him ask Jennie a lot of professional questions about me. She had a very good report to give.

She said I slept a good deal in the daytime.

John knows I don't sleep very well at night, for all I'm so quiet!

He asked me all sorts of questions, too, and pretended to be very loving and kind.

As if I couldn't see through him!

Still, I don't wonder he acts so, sleeping under this paper for three months. It only interests me, but I feel sure John and Jennie are secretly affected by it.

Hurrah! This is the last day, but it is enough. John is to stay in town over night, and won't be out until this evening.

Jennie wanted to sleep with me—the sly thing! But I told her I should undoubtedly rest better for a night all alone.

That was clever, for really I wasn't alone a bit! As soon as it was moonlight and that poor thing began to crawl and shake the pattern, I got up and ran to help her.

I pulled and she shook, I shook and she pulled, and before morning we had peeled off yards of that paper.

A strip about as high as my head and half round the room.

And then when the sun came and that awful pattern began to laugh at me, I declared I would finish it today!

We go away tomorrow, and they are moving all the furniture down again to leave things as they were before.

Jennie looked at the wall in amazement, but I told her merrily that I did it out of pure spite at the vicious thing.

She laughed and said she wouldn't mind doing it herself, but I must not get tired.

How she betrayed herself that time!

But I am here, and no person touches this paper but me—not *alive!*

She tried to get me out of the room—it was too patent! But I said it was so quiet and empty and clean now that I believed I would lie down again and sleep all I could; and not to wake me even for dinner—I would call when I woke.

So now she is gone, and the servants are gone, and the things are gone, and there is nothing left but that great bedstead nailed down, with the canvas mattress we found on it.

We shall sleep downstairs tonight, and take the boat home tomorrow.

I quite enjoy the room, now it is bare again.

How those children did tear about here!

This bedstead is fairly gnawed!

230 But I must get to work.

I have locked the door and thrown the key down into the front path.

I don't want to go out, and I don't want to have anybody come in, till John comes.

I want to astonish him.

I've got a rope up here that even Jennie did not find. If that woman does get out, and tries to get away, I can tie her!

235 But I forgot I could not reach far without anything to stand on! This bed will *not* move!

I tried to lift and push it until I was lame, and then I got so angry I bit off a little piece at one corner—but it hurt my teeth.

Then I peeled off all the paper I could reach standing on the floor. It sticks horribly and the pattern just enjoys it! All those strangled heads and bulbous eyes and waddling fungus growths just shriek with derision!

I am getting angry enough to do something desperate. To jump out of the window would be admirable exercise, but the bars are too strong even to try.

Besides I wouldn't do it. Of course not, I know well enough that a step like that is improper and might be misconstrued.

240 I don't like to *look* out of the windows even—there are so many of those creeping women, and they creep so fast.

I wonder if they all come out of that wallpaper as I did?

But I am securely fastened now by my well-hidden rope—you don't get *me* out in the road there!

I suppose I shall have to get back behind the pattern when it comes night, and that is hard!

It is so pleasant to be out in this great room and creep around as I please!

245 I don't want to go outside. I won't, even if Jennie asks me to.

For outside you have to creep on the ground, and everything is green instead of yellow.

But here I can creep smoothly on the floor, and my shoulder just fits in that long smooch around the wall, so I cannot lose my way.

Why there's John at the door!

It is no use, young man, you can't open it!

250 How he does call and pound!

Now he's crying for an axe.

It would be a shame to break down that beautiful door!

"John, dear!" said I in the gentlest voice, "the key is down by the front steps, under a plantain leaf!"

That silenced him for a few moments.

255 Then he said—very quietly indeed, "Open the door, my darling!"

"I can't," said I. "The key is down by the front door under a plantain leaf!"

And then I said it again, several times, very gently and slowly, and said it so often that he had to go and see, and he got it of course, and came in. He stopped short by the door.

"What is the matter?" he cried. "For God's sake, what are you doing!"

I kept on creeping just the same, but I looked at him over my shoulder.

260 "I've got out at last," said I, "in spite of you and Jane. And I've pulled off most of the paper, so you can't put me back!"

Now why should that man have fainted? But he did, and right across my path by the wall, so that I had to creep over him every time!

[1892]

Joining the Conversation: Critical Thinking and Writing

1. Is the narrator insane at the start of "The Yellow Wallpaper," or does she become insane at some point during the narrative? Or can't we be sure? Support your view with evidence from the story.
2. How reliable do you think the narrator's characterization of her husband is? Support your answer with reasons.
3. The narrator says that she cannot get better because her husband is a physician. What do you take this to mean? Do you think the story is about a husband who deliberately drives his wife insane?
4. Is Gilman attacking men in this story? If so, is that a bad thing? If she is not, then what is she doing?

JOHN STEINBECK

John Steinbeck (1902–68) was born in Salinas, California, and much of his fiction concerns this landscape and its people. As a young man, he worked on ranches, farms, and road gangs, and sometimes attended Stanford University—he never graduated—but he wrote whenever he could find the time. His early efforts at writing, however, were uniformly rejected by publishers. Even when he did break into print, he did not achieve much notice for several years: a novel in 1929, a book of stories in 1932, and another novel in 1933 attracted little attention. But the publication of Tortilla Flat *(1935), a novel about Mexican Americans, changed all that. It was followed by other successful novels—*In Dubious Battle *(1936) and* Of Mice and Men *(1937)—and by* The Long Valley *(1938), a collection of stories that included "The Chrysanthemums." His next book,* The Grapes of Wrath *(1939), about dispossessed sharecropper migrants from the Oklahoma dust bowl, was immensely popular and won a Pulitzer Prize. During World War II, Steinbeck sent reports from battlefields in Italy and Africa. In 1962, he was awarded the Nobel Prize in Literature.*

The Chrysanthemums

The high grey-flannel fog of winter closed off the Salinas Valley[1] from the sky and from all the rest of the world. On every side it sat like a lid on the mountains and made of the great valley a closed pot. On the broad, level land floor the gang plows bit deep and left the black earth shining like metal where the shares had cut. On the foothill ranches across the Salinas River, the yellow stubble fields seemed to be bathed in pale cold sunshine, but there was no sunshine in the valley now in December. The thick willow scrub along the river flamed with sharp and positive yellow leaves.

It was a time of quiet and of waiting. The air was cold and tender. A light wind blew up from the southwest so that the farmers were mildly hopeful of a good rain before long; but fog and rain do not go together.

Across the river, on Henry Allen's foothill ranch there was little work to be done, for the hay was cut and stored and the orchards were plowed up to receive the rain deeply when it should come. The cattle on the higher slopes were becoming shaggy and rough-coated.

[1]the **Salinas Valley** a fertile area in central California.

Elisa Allen, working in her flower garden, looked down across the yard and saw Henry, her husband, talking to two men in business suits. The three of them stood by the tractor shed, each man with one foot on the side of the little Fordson.[2] They smoked cigarettes and studied the machine as they talked.

5   Elisa watched them for a moment and then went back to her work. She was thirty-five. Her face was lean and strong and her eyes were as clear as water. Her figure looked blocked and heavy in her gardening costume, a man's black hat pulled low down over her eyes, clod-hopper shoes, a figured print dress almost completely covered by a big corduroy apron with four big pockets to hold the snips, the trowel and scratcher, the seeds and the knife she worked with. She wore heavy leather gloves to protect her hands while she worked.

She was cutting down the old year's chrysanthemum stalks with a pair of short and powerful scissors. She looked down toward the men by the tractor shed now and then. Her face was eager and mature and handsome; even her work with the scissors was over-eager, over-powerful. The chrysanthemum stems seemed too small and easy for her energy.

She brushed a cloud of hair out of her eyes with the back of her glove, and left a smudge of earth on her cheek in doing it. Behind her stood the neat white farm house with red geraniums close-banked around it as high as the windows. It was a hard-swept looking little house with hard-polished windows, and a clean mud-mat on the front steps.

Elisa cast another glance toward the tractor shed. The strangers were getting into their Ford coupe. She took off a glove and put her strong fingers down into the forest of new green chrysanthemum sprouts that were growing around the old roots. She spread the leaves and looked down among the close-growing stems. No aphids were there, no sowbugs or snails or cutworms. Her terrier fingers destroyed such pests before they could get started.

Elisa started at the sound of her husband's voice. He had come near quietly, and he leaned over the wire fence that protected her flower garden from cattle and dogs and chickens.

10   "At it again," he said. "You've got a strong new crop coming."

Elisa straightened her back and pulled on the gardening glove again. "Yes. They'll be strong this coming year." In her tone and on her face there was a little smugness.

"You've got a gift with things," Henry observed. "Some of those yellow chrysanthemums you had this year were ten inches across. I wish you'd work out in the orchard and raise some apples that big."

Her eyes sharpened. "Maybe I could do it, too. I've a gift with things, all right. My mother had it. She could stick anything in the ground and make it grow. She said it was having planters' hands that knew how to do it."

"Well, it sure works with flowers," he said.

15   "Henry, who were those men you were talking to?"

"Why, sure, that's what I came to tell you. They were from the Western Meat Company. I sold those thirty head of three-year-old steers. Got nearly my own price, too."

"Good," she said. "Good for you."

"And I thought," he continued, "I thought how it's Saturday afternoon, and we might go into Salinas for dinner at a restaurant, and then to a picture show—to celebrate, you see."

---

[2]**Fordson** a two-door Ford car.

"Good," she repeated. "Oh, yes. That will be good."

20　　Henry put on his joking tone. "There's fights tonight. How'd you like to go to the fights?"

"Oh, no," she said breathlessly. "No, I wouldn't like fights."

"Just fooling, Elisa. We'll go to a movie. Let's see. It's two now. I'm going to take Scotty and bring down those steers from the hill. It'll take us maybe two hours. We'll go in town about five and have dinner at the Cominos Hotel. Like that?"

"Of course I'll like it. It's good to eat away from home."

"All right, then. I'll go get up a couple of horses."

25　　She said, "I'll have plenty of time to transplant some of these sets, I guess."

She heard her husband calling Scotty down by the barn. And a little later she saw the two men ride up the pale yellow hillside in search of the steers.

There was a little square sandy bed kept for rooting the chrysanthemums. With her trowel she turned the soil over and over, and smoothed it and patted it firm. Then she dug ten parallel trenches to receive the sets. Back at the chrysanthemum bed she pulled out the little crisp shoots, trimmed off the leaves of each one with her scissors and laid it on a small orderly pile.

A squeak of wheels and plod of hoofs came from the road. Elisa looked up. The country road ran along the dense bank of willows and cottonwoods that bordered the river, and up this road came a curious vehicle, curiously drawn. It was an old springwagon, with a round canvas top on it like the cover of a prairie schooner. It was drawn by an old bay horse and a little grey-and-white burro. A big stubble-bearded man sat between the cover flaps and drove the crawling team. Underneath the wagon, between the hind wheels, a lean and rangy mongrel dog walked sedately. Words were painted on the canvas, in clumsy, crooked letters. "Pots, pans, knives, sisors, lawn mores, Fixed." Two rows of articles, and the triumphantly definitive "Fixed" below. The black paint had run down in little sharp points beneath each letter.

Elisa, squatting on the ground, watched to see the crazy, loose-jointed wagon pass by. But it didn't pass. It turned into the farm road in front of her house, crooked old wheels skirling and squeaking. The rangy dog darted from between the wheels and ran ahead. Instantly the two ranch shepherds flew out at him. Then all three stopped, and with stiff and quivering tails, with taut straight legs, with ambassadorial dignity, they slowly circled, sniffing daintily. The caravan pulled up to Elisa's wire fence and stopped. Now the newcomer dog, feeling out-numbered, lowered his tail and retired under the wagon with raised hackles and bared teeth.

30　　The man on the wagon seat called out, "That's a bad dog in a fight when he gets started."

Elisa laughed. "I see he is. How soon does he generally get started?"

The man caught up her laughter and echoed it heartily. "Sometimes not for weeks and weeks," he said. He climbed stiffly down, over the wheel. The horse and the donkey drooped like unwatered flowers.

Elisa saw that he was a very big man. Although his hair and beard were greying, he did not look old. His worn black suit was wrinkled and spotted with grease. The laughter had disappeared from his face and eyes the moment his laughing voice ceased. His eyes were dark, and they were full of the brooding that gets in the eyes of teamsters and of sailors. The calloused hands he rested on the wire fence were cracked, and every crack was a black line. He took off his battered hat.

"I'm off my general road, ma'am," he said. "Does this dirt road cut over across the river to the Los Angeles highway?"

35   Elisa stood up and shoved the thick scissors in her apron pocket. "Well, yes, it does, but it winds around and then fords the river. I don't think your team could pull through the sand."

He replied with some asperity. "It might surprise you what them beasts can pull through."

"When they get started?" she asked.

He smiled for a second. "Yes. When they get started."

"Well," said Elisa, "I think you'll save time if you go back to the Salinas road and pick up the highway there."

40   He drew a big finger down the chicken wire and made it sing. "I ain't in any hurry, ma'am. I go from Seattle to San Diego and back every year. Takes all my time. About six months each way. I aim to follow nice weather."

Elisa took off her gloves and stuffed them in the apron pocket with the scissors. She touched the under edge of her man's hat, searching for fugitive hairs. "That sounds like a nice kind of way to live," she said.

He leaned confidentially over the fence. "Maybe you noticed the writing on my wagon. I mend pots and sharpen knives and scissors. You got any of them things to do?"

"Oh, no," she said quickly. "Nothing like that." Her eyes hardened with resistance.

"Scissors is the worst thing," he explained. "Most people just ruin scissors trying to sharpen 'em, but I know how. I got a special tool. It's a little bobbit kind of thing, and patented. But it sure does the trick."

45   "No. My scissors are all sharp."

"All right, then. Take a pot," he continued earnestly, "a bent pot, or a pot with a hole. I can make it like new so you don't have to buy no new ones. That's a saving for you."

"No," she said shortly. "I tell you I have nothing like that for you to do."

His face fell to an exaggerated sadness. His voice took on a whining undertone. "I ain't had a thing to do today. Maybe I won't have no supper tonight. You see I'm off my regular road. I know folks on the highway clear from Seattle to San Diego. They save their things for me to sharpen up because they know I do it so good and save them money."

"I'm sorry," Elisa said irritably. "I haven't anything for you to do."

50   His eyes left her face and fell to searching the ground. They roamed about until they came to the chrysanthemum bed where she had been working. "What's them plants, ma'am?"

The irritation and resistance melted from Elisa's face. "Oh, those are chrysanthemums, giant whites and yellows. I raise them every year, bigger than anybody around here."

"Kind of a long-stemmed flower? Looks like a quick puff of colored smoke?" he asked.

"That's it. What a nice way to describe them."

"They smell kind of nasty till you get used to them," he said.

55   "It's a good bitter smell," she retorted, "not nasty at all."

He changed his tone quickly. "I like the smell myself."

"I had ten-inch blooms this year," she said.

The man leaned farther over the fence. "Look. I know a lady down the road a piece, has got the nicest garden you ever seen. Got nearly every kind of flower but no chrysanthemums. Last time I was mending a copper-bottom wash-tub for her (that's a hard job but I do it good), she said to me, 'If you ever run acrost some nice chrysanthemums I wish you'd try to get me a few seeds.' That's what she told me."

Elisa's eyes grew alert and eager. "She couldn't have known much about chrysanthemums. You *can* raise them from seed, but it's much easier to root the little sprouts you see there."

60   "Oh," he said. "I s'pose I can't take none to her, then."

"Why yes you can," Elisa cried. "I can put some in damp sand, and you can carry them right along with you. They'll take root in the pot if you keep them damp. And then she can transplant them."

"She'd sure like to have some, ma'am. You say they're nice ones?"

"Beautiful," she said. "Oh, beautiful." Her eyes shone. She tore off the battered hat and shook out her dark pretty hair. "I'll put them in a flower pot, and you can take them right with you. Come into the yard."

While the man came through the picket gate Elisa ran excitedly along the geranium-bordered path to the back of the house. And she returned carrying a big red flower pot. The gloves were forgotten now. She kneeled on the ground by the starting bed and dug up the sandy soil with her fingers and scooped it into the bright new flower pot. Then she picked up the little pile of shoots she had prepared. With her strong fingers she pressed them into the sand and tamped around them with her knuckles. The man stood over her. "I'll tell you what to do," she said. "You remember so you can tell the lady."

65   "Yes, I'll try to remember."

"Well, look. These will take root in about a month. Then she must set them out, about a foot apart in good rich earth like this, see?" She lifted a handful of dark soil for him to look at. "They'll grow fast and tall. Now remember this: In July tell her to cut them down, about eight inches from the ground."

"Before they bloom?" he asked.

"Yes, before they bloom." Her face was tight with eagerness. "They'll grow right up again. About the last of September the buds will start."

She stopped and seemed perplexed. "It's the budding that takes the most care," she said hesitantly. "I don't know how to tell you." She looked deep into his eyes, searchingly. Her mouth opened a little, and she seemed to be listening. "I'll try to tell you," she said. "Did you ever hear of planting hands?"

70   "Can't say I have, ma'am."

"Well, I can only tell you what it feels like. It's when you're picking off the buds you don't want. Everything goes right down into your fingertips. You watch your fingers work. They do it themselves. You can feel how it is. They pick and pick the buds. They never make a mistake. They're with the plant. Do you see? Your fingers and the plant. You can feel that, right up your arm. They know. They never make a mistake. You can feel it. When you're like that you can't do anything wrong. Do you see that? Can you understand that?"

She was kneeling on the ground looking up at him. Her breast swelled passionately.

The man's eyes narrowed. He looked away self-consciously. "Maybe I know," he said. "Sometimes in the night in the wagon there—"

Elisa's voice grew husky. She broke in on him, "I've never lived as you do, but I know what you mean. When the night is dark—why, the stars are sharp-pointed, and there's quiet. Why, you rise up and up! Every pointed star gets driven into your body. It's like that. Hot and sharp and—lovely."

75   Kneeling there, her hand went out toward his legs in the greasy black trousers. Her hesitant fingers almost touched the cloth. Then her hand dropped to the ground. She crouched low like a fawning dog.

He said, "It's nice, just like you say. Only when you don't have no dinner, it ain't."

She stood up then, very straight, and her face was ashamed. She held the flower pot out to him and placed it gently in his arms. "Here. Put it in your wagon, on the seat, where you can watch it. Maybe I can find something for you to do."

At the back of the house she dug in the can pile and found two old and battered aluminum saucepans. She carried them back and gave them to him. "Here, maybe you can fix these."

His manner changed. He became professional. "Good as new I can fix them." At the back of his wagon he set a little anvil, and out of an oily tool box dug a small machine hammer. Elisa came through the gate to watch him while he pounded out the dents in the kettles. His mouth grew sure and knowing. At a difficult part of the work he sucked his under-lip.

80 "You sleep right in the wagon?" Elisa asked.

"Right in the wagon, ma'am. Rain or shine I'm dry as a cow in there."

"It must be nice," she said. "It must be very nice. I wish women could do such things."

"It ain't the right kind of a life for a woman."

Her upper lip raised a little, showing her teeth. "How do you know? How can you tell?" she said.

85 "I don't know, ma'am," he protested. "Of course I don't know. Now here's your kettles, done. You don't have to buy no new ones."

"How much?"

"Oh, fifty cents'll do. I keep my prices down and my work good. That's why I have all them satisfied customers up and down the highway."

Elisa brought him a fifty-cent piece from the house and dropped it in his hand. "You might be surprised to have a rival some time. I can sharpen scissors, too. And I can beat the dents out of little pots. I could show you what a woman might do."

He put his hammer back in the oily box and shoved the little anvil out of sight. "It would be a lonely life for a woman, ma'am, and a scarey life, too, with animals creeping under the wagon all night." He climbed over the singletree, steadying himself with a hand on the burro's white rump. He settled himself in the seat, picked up the lines. "Thank you kindly, ma'am," he said. "I'll do like you told me; I'll go back and catch the Salinas road."

90 "Mind," she called, "if you're long in getting there, keep the sand damp."

"Sand, ma'am? . . . Sand? Oh, sure. You mean around the chrysanthemums. Sure I will." He clucked his tongue. The beasts leaned luxuriously into their collars. The mongrel dog took his place between the back wheels. The wagon turned and crawled out the entrance road and back the way it had come, along the river.

Elisa stood in front of her wire fence watching the slow progress of the caravan. Her shoulders were straight, her head thrown back, her eyes half-closed, so that the scene came vaguely into them. Her lips moved silently, forming the words "Goodbye—good-bye." Then she whispered, "That's a bright direction. There's a glowing there." The sound of her whisper startled her. She shook herself free and looked about to see whether anyone had been listening. Only the dogs had heard. They lifted their heads toward her from their sleeping in the dust, and then stretched out their chins and settled asleep again. Elisa turned and ran hurriedly into the house.

In the kitchen she reached behind the stove and felt the water tank. It was full of hot water from the noonday cooking. In the bathroom she tore off her soiled clothes and flung them into the corner. And then she scrubbed herself with a little block of pumice, legs and thighs, loins and chest and arms, until her skin was scratched and red. When she had dried herself she stood in front of a mirror in her bedroom and looked at her body. She tightened her stomach and threw out her chest. She turned and looked over her shoulder at her back.

After a while she began to dress, slowly. She put on her newest underclothing and her nicest stockings and the dress which was the symbol of her prettiness. She worked carefully on her hair, penciled her eyebrows and rouged her lips.

95   Before she was finished she heard the little thunder of hoofs and the shouts of Henry and his helper as they drove the red steers into the corral. She heard the gate bang shut and set herself for Henry's arrival.

His step sounded on the porch. He entered the house calling, "Elisa, where are you?"

"In my room, dressing. I'm not ready. There's hot water for your bath. Hurry up. It's getting late."

When she heard him splashing in the tub, Elisa laid his dark suit on the bed, and shirt and socks and tie beside it. She stood his polished shoes on the floor beside the bed. Then she went to the porch and sat primly and stiffly down. She looked toward the river road where the willow-line was still yellow with frosted leaves so that under the high grey fog they seemed a thin band of sunshine. This was the only color in the grey afternoon. She sat unmoving for a long time. Her eyes blinked rarely.

Henry came banging out of the door shoving his tie inside his vest as he came. Elisa stiffened and her face grew tight. Henry stopped short and looked at her. "Why—why, Elisa. You look so nice!"

100   "Nice? You think I look nice? What do you mean by 'nice'?"

Henry blundered on. "I don't know. I mean you look different, strong and happy."

"I am strong? Yes, strong. What do you mean 'strong'?"

He looked bewildered. "You're playing some kind of a game," he said helplessly. "It's a kind of a play. You look strong enough to break a calf over your knee, happy enough to eat it like a watermelon."

For a second she lost her rigidity. "Henry! Don't talk like that. You didn't know what you said." She grew complete again. "I'm strong," she boasted. "I never knew before how strong."

105   Henry looked down toward the tractor shed, and when he brought his eyes back to her, they were his own again. "I'll get out the car. You can put on your coat while I'm starting."

Elisa went into the house. She heard him drive to the gate and idle down his motor, and then she took a long time to put on her hat. She pulled it here and pressed it there. When Henry turned the motor off she slipped into her coat and went out.

The little roadster bounced along on the dirt road by the river, raising the birds and driving the rabbits into the brush. Two cranes flapped heavily over the willowline and dropped into the river-bed.

Far ahead on the road Elisa saw a dark speck. She knew.

She tried not to look as they passed it, but her eyes would not obey. She whispered to herself sadly, "He might have thrown them off the road. That wouldn't have been much trouble, not very much. But he kept the pot," she explained. "He had to keep the pot. That's why he couldn't get them off the road."

110   The roadster turned a bend and she saw the caravan ahead. She swung full around toward her husband so she could not see the little covered wagon and the mismatched team as the car passed them.

In a moment it was over. The thing was done. She did not look back.

She said loudly, to be heard above the motor, "It will be good, tonight, a good dinner."

"Now you're changed again," Henry complained. He took one hand from the wheel and patted her knee. "I ought to take you in to dinner oftener. It would be good for both of us. We get so heavy out on the ranch."

"Henry," she asked, "could we have wine at dinner?"

115 "Sure we could. Say! That will be fine."

She was silent for a while; then she said, "Henry, at those prize fights, do the men hurt each other very much?"

"Sometimes a little, not often. Why?"

"Well, I've read how they break noses, and blood runs down their chests. I've read how the fighting gloves get heavy and soggy with blood."

He looked around at her. "What's the matter, Elisa? I didn't know you read things like that." He brought the car to a stop, then turned to the right over the Salinas River bridge.

120 "Do any women ever go to the fights?" she asked.

"Oh, sure, some. What's the matter, Elisa? Do you want to go? I don't think you'd like it, but I'll take you if you really want to go."

She relaxed limply in the seat. "Oh, no. No. I don't want to go. I'm sure I don't." Her face was turned away from him. "It will be enough if we can have wine. It will be plenty." She turned up her coat collar so he could not see that she was crying weakly—like an old woman.

[1937]

Joining the Conversation: Critical Thinking and Writing

1. In the first paragraph of "The Chrysanthemums," the valley, shut off by fog, is said to be "a closed pot." Is this setting significant? Would any other setting do equally well? Why, or why not?
2. What physical descriptions in the story—literal or figurative—suggest that Elisa is frustrated?
3. Describe Elisa and Henry's marriage.
4. In an argument, evaluate the view that Elisa is responsible for her troubles.

ALICE WALKER

Alice Walker was born in 1944 in Eatonton, Georgia, where her parents eked out a living as sharecroppers and dairy farmers; her mother also worked as a domestic. Walker attended Spelman College in Atlanta, and in 1965, she finished her undergraduate work at Sarah Lawrence College near New York City. She then became active in the welfare rights movement in New York and in the voter registration movement in Georgia. Later she taught writing and literature in Mississippi, at Jackson State College and Tougaloo College, and at Wellesley College, the University of Massachusetts, and Yale University.

Walker has written essays, poetry, and fiction. Her best-known novel, The Color Purple *(1982), won a Pulitzer Prize and the National Book*

Award. She has said that her chief concern is "exploring the oppressions, the insanities, the loyalties, and the triumphs of black women."

Everyday Use

For your grandmama

I will wait for her in the yard that Maggie and I made so clean and wavy yesterday afternoon. A yard like this is more comfortable than most people know. It is not just a yard. It is like an extended living room. When the hard clay is swept clean as a floor and the fine sand around the edges lined with tiny, irregular grooves, anyone can come and sit and look up into the elm tree and wait for the breezes that never come inside the house.

Maggie will be nervous until after her sister goes: she will stand hopelessly in corners homely and ashamed of the burn scars down her arms and legs, eyeing her sister with a mixture of envy and awe. She thinks her sister had held life always in the palm of one hand, that "no" is a word the world never learned to say to her.

You've no doubt seen those TV shows where the child who has "made it" is confronted, as a surprise, by her own mother and father, tottering in weakly from backstage. (A pleasant surprise, of course: What would they do if parent and child came on the show only to curse out and insult each other?) On TV mother and child embrace and smile into each other's faces. Sometimes the mother and father weep, the child wraps them in her arms and leans across the table to tell how she would not have made it without their help. I have seen these programs.

Sometimes I dream a dream in which Dee and I are suddenly brought together on a TV program of this sort. Out of a dark and soft-seated limousine I am ushered into a bright room filled with many people. There I meet a smiling, gray, sporty man like Johnny Carson[1] who shakes my hand and tells me what a fine girl I have. Then we are on the stage and Dee is embracing me with tears in her eyes. She pins on my dress a large orchid, even though she has told me once that she thinks orchids are tacky flowers.

5   In real life I am a large, big-boned woman with rough, man-working hands. In the winter I wear flannel nightgowns to bed and overalls during the day. I can kill and clean a hog as mercilessly as a man. My fat keeps me hot in zero weather. I can work outside all day, breaking ice to get water for washing. I can eat pork liver cooked over the open fire minutes after it comes steaming from the hog. One winter I knocked a bull calf straight in the brain between the eyes with a sledge hammer and had the meat hung up to chill before nightfall. But of course all this does not show on television. I am the way my daughter would want me to be: a hundred pounds lighter, my skin like an uncooked barley pancake. My hair glistens in the hot bright lights. Johnny Carson has much to do to keep up with my quick and witty tongue.

But that is a mistake. I know even before I wake up. Who ever knew a Johnson with a quick tongue? Who can even imagine me looking a strange white man in the eye? It seems to me I have talked to them always with one foot raised in flight, with my head turned in whichever way is farthest from them. Dee, though. She would always look anyone in the eye. Hesitation was no part of her nature.

"How do I look, Mama?" Maggie says, showing just enough of her thin body enveloped in pink skirt and red blouse for me to know she's there, almost hidden by the door.

---

[1]**Johnny Carson** (1925–2005), U.S. television personality and comedian.

"Come out into the yard," I say.

Have you ever seen a lame animal, perhaps a dog run over by some careless person rich enough to own a car, sidle up to someone who is ignorant enough to be kind to him? That is the way my Maggie walks. She has been like this, chin on chest, eyes on ground, feet in shuffle, ever since the fire that burned the other house to the ground.

10   Dee is lighter than Maggie, with nicer hair and a fuller figure. She's a woman now, though sometimes I forget. How long ago was it that the other house burned? Ten, twelve years? Sometimes I can still hear the flames and feel Maggie's arms sticking to me, her hair smoking and her dress falling off her in little black papery flakes. Her eyes seemed stretched open, blazed open by the flames reflected in them. And Dee. I see her standing off under the sweet gum tree she used to dig gum out of; a look of concentration on her face as she watched the last dingy gray board of the house fall in toward the red-hot brick chimney. Why don't you do a dance around the ashes? I'd wanted to ask her. She had hated the house that much.

I used to think she hated Maggie, too. But that was before we raised the money, the church and me, to send her to Augusta to school. She used to read to us without pity; forcing words, lies, other folks' habits, whole lives upon us two, sitting trapped and ignorant underneath her voice. She washed us in a river of make-believe, burned us with a lot of knowledge we didn't necessarily need to know. Pressed us to her with the serious way she read, to shove us away at just the moment, like dimwits, we seemed about to understand.

Dee wanted nice things. A yellow organdy dress to wear to her graduation from high school; black pumps to match a green suit she'd made from an old suit somebody gave me. She was determined to stare down any disaster in her efforts. Her eyelids would not flicker for minutes at a time. Often I fought off the temptation to shake her. At sixteen she had a style of her own: and knew what style was.

I never had an education myself. After second grade the school was closed down. Don't ask me why: in 1927 colored asked fewer questions than they do now. Sometimes Maggie reads to me. She stumbles along goodnaturedly but can't see well. She knows she is not bright. Like good looks and money, quickness passed her by. She will marry John Thomas (who has mossy teeth in an earnest face) and then I'll be free to sit here and I guess just sing church songs to myself. Although I never was a good singer. Never could carry a tune. I was always better at a man's job. I used to love to milk till I was hoofed in the side in '49. Cows are soothing and slow and don't bother you, unless you try to milk them the wrong way.

I have deliberately turned my back on the house. It is three rooms, just like the one that burned, except the roof is tin; they don't make shingle roofs any more. There are no real windows, just some holes cut in the sides, like the portholes in a ship, but not round and not square, with rawhide holding the shutters up on the outside. This house is in a pasture, too, like the other one. No doubt when Dee sees it she will want to tear it down. She wrote me once that no matter where we "choose" to live, she will manage to come see us. But she will never bring her friends. Maggie and I thought about this and Maggie asked me, "Mama, when did Dee ever *have* any friends?"

15   She had a few. Furtive boys in pink shirts hanging about on washday after school. Nervous girls who never laughed. Impressed with her they worshiped the well-turned phrase, the cute shape, the scalding humor that erupted like bubbles in lye. She read to them.

When she was courting Jimmy T she didn't have much time to pay to us, but turned all her faultfinding power on him. He *flew* to marry a cheap gal from a family of ignorant flashy people. She hardly had time to recompose herself.

When she comes I will meet—but there they are!

Maggie attempts to make a dash for the house, in her shuffling way, but I stay her with my hand. "Come back here," I say. And she stops and tries to dig a well in the sand with her toe.

It is hard to see them clearly through the strong sun. But even the first glimpse of leg out of the car tells me it is Dee. Her feet were always neat-looking, as if God himself had shaped them with a certain style. From the other side of the car comes a short, stocky man. Hair is all over his head a foot long and hanging from his chin like a kinky mule tail. I hear Maggie suck in her breath. "Uhnnnh," is what it sounds like. Like when you see the wriggling end of a snake just in front of your foot on the road. "Uhnnnh."

20   Dee next. A dress down to the ground, in this hot weather. A dress so loud it hurts my eyes. There are yellows and oranges enough to throw back the light of the sun. I feel my whole face warming from the heat waves it throws out. Earrings, too, gold and hanging down to her shoulders. Bracelets dangling and making noises when she moves her arm up to shake the folds of the dress out of her armpits. The dress is loose and flows, and as she walks closer, I like it. I hear Maggie go "Uhnnnh" again. It is her sister's hair. It stands straight up like the wool on a sheep. It is black as night and around the edges are two long pigtails that rope about like small lizards disappearing behind her ears.

"Wa-su-zo-Tean-o!" she says, coming on in that gliding way the dress makes her move. The short stocky fellow with the hair to his navel is all grinning and he follows up with "Asalamalakim, my mother and sister!" He moves to hug Maggie but she falls back, right up against the back of my chair. I feel her trembling there and when I look up I see the perspiration falling off her chin.

"Don't get up," says Dee. Since I am stout it takes something of a push. You can see me trying to move a second or two before I make it. She turns, showing white heels through her sandals, and goes back to the car. Out she peeks next with a Polaroid. She stoops down quickly and lines up picture after picture of me sitting there in front of the house with Maggie cowering behind me. She never takes a shot without making sure the house is included. When a cow comes nibbling around the edge of the yard she snaps it and me and Maggie *and* the house. Then she puts the Polaroid in the back seat of the car, and comes up and kisses me on the forehead.

Meanwhile Asalamalakim is going through the motions with Maggie's hand. Maggie's hand is as limp as a fish, and probably as cold, despite the sweat, and she keeps trying to pull it back. It looks like Asalamalakim wants to shake hands but wants to do it fancy. Or maybe he don't know how people shake hands. Anyhow, he soon gives up on Maggie.

"Well," I say. "Dee."

25   "No, Mama," she says. "Not 'Dee,' Wangero Leewanika Kemanjo!"

"What happened to 'Dee'?" I wanted to know.

"She's dead," Wangero said. "I couldn't bear it any longer being named after the people who oppress me."

"You know as well as me you was named after your aunt Dicie," I said. Dicie is my sister. She named Dee. We called her "Big Dee" after Dee was born.

"But who was *she* named after?" asked Wangero.

30   "I guess after Grandma Dee," I said.

"And who was she named after?" asked Wangero.

"Her mother," I said, and saw Wangero was getting tired. "That's about as far back as I can trace it," I said. Though, in fact, I probably could have carried it back beyond the Civil War through the branches.

"Well," said Asalamalakim, "there you are."

"Uhnnnh," I heard Maggie say.

35   "There I was not," I said, "before 'Dicie' cropped up in our family, so why should I try to trace it that far back?"

He just stood there grinning, looking down on me like somebody inspecting a Model A car. Every once in a while he and Wangero sent eye signals over my head.

"How do you pronounce this name?" I asked.

"You don't have to call me by it if you don't want to," said Wangero.

"Why shouldn't I?" I asked. "If that's what you want us to call you, we'll call you."

40   "I know it might sound awkward at first," said Wangero.

"I'll get used to it," I said. "Ream it out again."

Well, soon we got the name out of the way. Asalamalakim had a name twice as long and three times as hard. After I tripped over it two or three times he told me to just call him Hakim-a-barber. I wanted to ask him was he a barber, but I didn't really think he was, so I didn't ask.

"You must belong to those beef-cattle peoples down the road," I said. They said "Asalamalakim" when they met you, too, but they didn't shake hands. Always too busy: feeding the cattle, fixing the fences, putting up saltlick shelters, throwing down hay. When the white folks poisoned some of the herd the men stayed up all night with rifles in their hands. I walked a mile and a half just to see the sight.

Hakim-a-barber said, "I accept some of their doctrines, but farming and raising cattle is not my style." (They didn't tell me, and I didn't ask, whether Wangero [Dee] had really gone and married him.)

45   We sat down to eat and right away he said he didn't eat collards and pork was unclean. Wangero, though, went on through the chitlins and corn bread, the greens and everything else. She talked a blue streak over the sweet potatoes. Everything delighted her. Even the fact that we still used the benches her daddy made for the table when we couldn't afford to buy chairs.

"Oh, Mama!" she cried. Then turned to Hakim-a-barber. "I never knew how lovely these benches are. You can feel the rump prints," she said, running her hands underneath her and along the bench. Then she gave a sigh and her hand closed over Grandma Dee's butter dish. "That's it!" she said. "I knew there was something I wanted to ask you if I could have." She jumped up from the table and went over in the corner where the churn stood, the milk in it clabber by now. She looked at the churn and looked at it.

"This churn top is what I need," she said. "Didn't Uncle Buddy whittle it out of a tree you all used to have?"

"Yes," I said.

"Uh huh," she said happily. "And I want the dasher, too."

50   "Uncle Buddy whittle that, too?" asked the barber.

Dee (Wangero) looked up at me.

"Aunt Dee's first husband whittled the dash," said Maggie so low you almost couldn't hear her. "His name was Henry, but they called him Stash."

"Maggie's brain is like an elephant's," Wangero said, laughing. "I can use the churn top as a centerpiece for the alcove table," she said, sliding a plate over the churn, "and I'll think of something artistic to do with the dasher."

When she finished wrapping the dasher the handle stuck out. I took it for a moment in my hands. You didn't even have to look close to see where hands pushing the dasher up and down to make butter had left a kind of sink in the wood. In fact, there were a lot of small sinks; you could see where thumbs and fingers had sunk into the wood. It was beautiful light yellow wood, from a tree that grew in the yard where Big Dee and Stash had lived.

55   After dinner Dee (Wangero) went to the trunk at the foot of my bed and started rifling through it. Maggie hung back in the kitchen over the dishpan. Out came Wangero with two quilts. They had been pieced by Grandma Dee and then Big Dee and me had hung them on the quilt frames on the front porch and quilted them. One was in the Lone Star pattern. The other was Walk Around the Mountain. In both of them were scraps of dresses Grandma Dee had worn fifty and more years ago. Bits and pieces of Grandpa Jarrell's paisley shirts. And one teeny faded blue piece, about the size of a penny matchbox, that was from Great Grandpa Ezra's uniform that he wore in the Civil War.

"Mama," Wangero said sweet as a bird. "Can I have these old quilts?"

I heard something fall in the kitchen, and a minute later the kitchen door slammed.

"Why don't you take one or two of the others?" I asked. "These old things was just done by me and Big Dee from some tops your grandma pieced before she died."

"No," said Wangero. "I don't want those. They are stitched around the borders by machine."

60   "That'll make them last better," I said.

"That's not the point," said Wangero. "These are all pieces of dresses Grandma used to wear. She did all this stitching by hand. Imagine!" She held the quilts securely in her arms, stroking them.

"Some of the pieces, like those lavender ones, come from old clothes her mother handed down to her," I said, moving up to touch the quilts. Dee (Wangero) moved back just enough so that I couldn't reach the quilts. They already belonged to her.

"Imagine!" she breathed again, clutching them closely to her bosom.

"The truth is," I said, "I promised to give them quilts to Maggie, for when she marries John Thomas."

65   She gasped like a bee had stung her.

"Maggie can't appreciate these quilts!" she said. "She'd probably be backward enough to put them to everyday use."

"I reckon she would," I said. "God knows I been saving 'em for long enough with nobody using 'em. I hope she will!" I didn't want to bring up how I had offered Dee (Wangero) a quilt when she went away to college. Then she had told me they were old-fashioned, out of style.

"But they're *priceless!*" she was saying now, furiously; for she has a temper. "Maggie would put them on the bed and in five years they'd be in rags. Less than that!"

"She can always make some more," I said. "Maggie knows how to quilt."

70   Dee (Wangero) looked at me with hatred. "You just will not understand. The point is these quilts, *these* quilts!"

"Well," I said, stumped. "What would *you* do with them?"

"Hang them," she said. As if that was the only thing you *could* do with quilts.

Maggie by now was standing in the door. I could almost hear the sound her feet made as they scraped over each other.

"She can have them, Mama," she said, like somebody used to never winning anything, or having anything reserved for her. "I can 'member Grandma Dee without the quilts."

75   I looked at her hard. She had filled her bottom lip with checkerberry snuff and it gave her face a kind of dopey, hangdog look. It was Grandma Dee and Big Dee who

taught her how to quilt herself. She stood there with her scarred hands hidden in the folds of her skirt. She looked at her sister with something like fear but she wasn't mad at her. This was Maggie's portion. This was the way she knew God to work.

When I looked at her like that something hit me in the top of my head and ran down to the soles of my feet. Just like when I'm in church and the spirit of God touches me and I get happy and shout. I did something I never had done before: hugged Maggie to me, then dragged her on into the room, snatched the quilts out of Miss Wangero's hands and dumped them into Maggie's lap. Maggie just sat there on my bed with her mouth open.

"Take one or two of the others," I said to Dee.

But she turned without a word and went out to Hakim-a-barber.

"You just don't understand," she said, as Maggie and I came out to the car.

"What don't I understand?" I wanted to know.

"Your heritage," she said. And then she turned to Maggie, kissed her, and said, "You ought to try to make something of yourself, too, Maggie. It's really a new day for us. But from the way you and Mama still live you'd never know it."

She put on some sunglasses that hid everything above the tip of her nose and her chin.

Maggie smiled; maybe at the sunglasses. But a real smile, not scared. After we watched the car dust settle I asked Maggie to bring me a dip of snuff. And then the two of us sat there just enjoying, until it was time to go in the house and go to bed.

[1973]

Joining the Conversation: Critical Thinking and Writing

1. Alice Walker wrote "Everyday Use," but the story is narrated by one of the characters, Mama. How would you characterize Mama?
2. At the end of the story, Dee tells Maggie, "It's really a new day for us. But from the way you and Mama still live you'd never know it." What does Dee mean? And how do Maggie and Mama respond?
3. In paragraph 76, the narrator says, speaking of Maggie, "When I looked at her like that something hit me in the top of my head and ran down to the soles of my feet." What "hit" Mama? That is, what does she understand at this moment that she had not understood before?
4. In "Everyday Use," why does the family quarrel about who will possess the quilts? Why are the quilts important? What do they symbolize?

POEMS

WILLIAM BLAKE

William Blake (1757–1827) was born in London and at fourteen years old was apprenticed for seven years to an engraver. A Christian visionary poet, he made his living by giving drawing lessons and by illustrating books, including his own Songs of Innocence *(1789) and* Songs of Experience *(1794). These two books represent, he said, "two contrary states of the human soul." ("Infant Joy" and "The Echoing Green" come from* Songs of Innocence, *"Infant Sorrow" comes from* Songs of

Experience.) In 1809, Blake exhibited his art, but the show was a failure. Not until he was in his sixties, when he stopped writing poetry, did he achieve any public recognition—and then it was as a painter.

"Infant Joy" by William Blake, from *Songs of Innocence*.

Infant Joy

"I have no name,
I am but two days old."
What shall I call thee?
"I happy am,
Joy is my name."   5

Sweet joy befall thee!
Pretty joy!
Sweet joy but two days old,
Sweet joy I call thee;
Thou dost smile,   10
I sing the while—
Sweet joy befall thee.

[1789]

"Infant Sorrow" by William Blake, from *Songs of Experience*.

Infant Sorrow

My mother groand! my father wept.
Into the dangerous world I leapt,
Helpless, naked, piping loud;
Like a fiend hid in a cloud.

Struggling in my father's hands,   5
Striving against my swadling bands;
Bound and weary I thought best
To sulk upon my mother's breast.

[1794]

Joining the Conversation: Critical Thinking and Writing

1. "Infant Joy" begins "I have no name," but by line 5, the infant says "Joy is my name." What does the mother reply? Does she know the infant's name?

2. In line 9, the mother says, "Sweet joy I call thee." Does the line suggest how the mother has learned the name? What is the child's response?
3. In "Infant Sorrow," why is the infant sorrowful? What does the baby struggle against? Does "Like a fiend" suggest that it is inherently wicked and therefore should be repressed? Or does the adult world wickedly repress energy?
4. Why does the mother groan? Why does the father weep? Is the world "dangerous" to the infant in other than an obviously physical sense? To what degree are its parents its enemies? To what degree does the infant yield to them? In the last line, one might expect a newborn baby to nurse. What does this infant do?
5. Compare "Infant Joy" with "Infant Sorrow." What differences in sound do you hear? In "Infant Sorrow," for instance, look at lines 3, 5, 6, and 7. What repeated sounds do you hear?
6. One scholar has said that each of these poems is a "refutation" of the other one. Do you agree? Explain your answer.
7. What is your response to Blake's illustrations?

The Lamb

Little Lamb, who made thee?
  Dost thou know who made thee?
Gave thee life, and bid thee feed
By the stream and o'er the mead;
Gave thee clothing of delight,   5
Softest clothing, wooly, bright;
Gave thee such a tender voice,
Making all the vales rejoice?
  Little Lamb, who made thee?
  Dost thou know who made thee?   10

Little Lamb, I'll tell thee,
  Little Lamb, I'll tell thee:
He is calléd by thy name,
For he calls himself a Lamb.
He is meek, and he is mild;   15
He became a little child.
I a child, and thou a lamb,
We are calléd by his name.
  Little Lamb, God bless thee!
  Little Lamb, God bless thee!   20

[1789]

The Tyger

Tyger! Tyger! burning bright
In the forests of the night,
What immortal hand or eye
Could frame thy fearful symmetry?

In what distant deeps or skies   5
Burnt the fire of thine eyes?
On what wings dare he aspire?
What the hand dare seize the fire?

And what shoulder, and what art,
Could twist the sinews of thy heart?   10
And, when thy heart began to beat,
What dread hand? and what dread feet?

What the hammer? what the chain?
In what furnace was thy brain?
What the anvil? what dread grasp   15
Dare its deadly terrors clasp?

When the stars threw down their spears,
And watered heaven with their tears,
Did he smile his work to see?
Did he who made the lamb make thee?   20

Tyger! Tyger! burning bright
In the forests of the night,
What immortal hand or eye,
Dare frame thy fearful symmetry?

[1794]

Joining the Conversation: Critical Thinking and Writing

Why does Blake answer his question in "The Lamb" but not in "The Tyger"?

THOMAS HARDY

Thomas Hardy (1840–1928) was born in Dorset, England, the son of a stonemason. Despite great obstacles, he studied the classics and architecture, and in 1862 he moved to London to study and practice as an architect. Ill health forced him to return to Dorset, where he continued to work as an architect and to write. Best known for his novels, Hardy ceased writing fiction after the hostile reception of Jude the Obscure *in 1896 and turned to writing lyric poetry.*

The Ruined Maid

"O 'Melia, my dear, this does everything crown!
Who could have supposed I should meet you in Town?
And whence such fair garments, such prosperi-ty?"—
"O didn't you know I'd been ruined?" said she.

—"You left us in tatters, without shoes or socks,   5
Tired of digging potatoes, and spudding up docks;
And now you've gay bracelets and bright feathers three!"—
"Yes: that's how we dress when we're ruined," said she.

—"At home in the barton you said thee' and thou,'
And thik oon,' and theäs oon,' and t'other'; but now   10
Your talking quite fits 'ee for high compa-ny!"—
"Some polish is gained with one's ruin," said she.

—"Your hands were like paws then, your face blue and bleak
But now I'm bewitched by your delicate cheek,
And your little gloves fit as on any la-dy!"—   15
"We never do work when we're ruined," said she.

—"You used to call home-life a hag-ridden dream,
And you'd sigh, and you'd sock; but at present you seem
To know not of megrims or melancho-ly!"—
"True. One's pretty lively when ruined," said she.   20

—"I wish I had feathers, a fine sweeping gown,
And a delicate face, and could strut about Town!"—
"My dear—a raw country girl, such as you be,
Cannot quite expect that. You ain't ruined," said she.

                                                                        [1901]

Joining the Conversation: Critical Thinking and Writing

1. What is the work that 'Melia is engaged in?
2. Explore the structural elements of the poem. How does it function as a dialogue? What is its stanza structure and rhyme scheme? What is its meter? How does the poem's structure contribute to its meaning?
3. Why is the word "ruined" repeated? What are the attractions of the "ruined" life to the speaker?
4. How does the poem compare country life and city life? What are the key images that are associated with the country and the city?

E. E. CUMMINGS

For biographical information on e.e. cummings, see page 809.

in Just-

in Just-
spring   when the world is mud-
luscious the little
lame baloonman

whistles   far   and wee   5

and eddyandbill come
running from marbles and
piracies and it's
spring

when the world is puddle-wonderful   10

the queer
old baloonman whistles
far   and   wee
and bettyandisbel come dancing

from hop-scotch and jump-rope and   15

it's
spring
and

        the

                goat-footed   20

baloonMan   whistles
far
and
wee

                                                    [1920]

Joining the Conversation: Critical Thinking and Writing

1. Why "eddyandbill" and "bettyandisbel" rather than "eddy and bill" and "betty and isabel"? And why not "eddy and betty," and "bill and isabel"?
2. What are some effects that Cummings may be getting at by his unusual arrangement of words on the page? Compare, for instance, the physical appearance of "whistles far and wee" in line 5 with the appearance of the same words in lines 12–13 and 21–24.
3. Because the "baloonman" is "lame" (line 4) or "goat-footed" (line 20), many readers find an allusion to the Greek god Pan, the goat-footed god of woods, fields, and flocks, and the inventor of a primitive wind instrument consisting of a series of reeds, "Pan's pipes." (If you are unfamiliar with Pan, consult an encyclopedia or a guide to mythology.) Do you agree that Cummings is alluding to Pan? If so, what is the point of the allusion?
4. A critic has said: "Cummings cares more about words than about their meanings." What is this critic saying? Please argue why you agree or disagree.

LOUISE GLÜCK

Louise Glück was born in 1943 in New York City and attended Sarah Lawrence College and Columbia University. She has taught at Goddard College in Vermont and at Warren Wilson College in North Carolina. Her volume of poems The Triumph of Achilles *(1985) won the National Book Critics Circle Award for poetry. She now teaches creative writing at Yale and Boston University.*

The School Children

The children go forward with their little satchels.
And all morning the mothers have labored
to gather the late apples, red and gold,
like words of another language.

And on the other shore   5
are those who wait behind great desks
to receive these offerings.

How orderly they are—the nails
on which the children hang
their overcoats of blue or yellow wool.   10

And the teachers shall instruct them in silence
and the mothers shall scour the orchards for a way out,
drawing to themselves the gray limbs of the fruit trees
bearing so little ammunition.

[1975]

Joining the Conversation: Critical Thinking and Writing

1. Which words in the poem present a cute picture-postcard view of small children going to school?
2. Which words undercut this happy scene?
3. In the last stanza, we read that "the teachers shall instruct" and "the mothers shall scour." What, if anything, is changed if we substitute "will" for "shall"?
4. In this poem about schoolchildren, is the poet herself seeking to teach us something? Explain your answer.

LINDA PASTAN

Linda Pastan was born in New York City in 1932 and educated at Radcliffe College, Simmons College, and Brandeis University. The author of ten books of poems, she has won numerous prizes, including a Pushcart Prize and the 2003 Ruth Lilly Poetry Prize, and she has received a grant from the National Endowment for the Arts.

Ethics

In ethics class so many years ago
our teacher asked this question every fall:
if there were a fire in a museum
which would you save, a Rembrandt painting
or an old woman who hadn't many   5
years left anyhow? Restless on hard chairs
caring little for pictures or old age
we'd opt one year for life, the next for art
and always half-heartedly. Sometimes
the woman borrowed my grandmother's face   10
leaving her usual kitchen to wander
some drafty, half-imagined museum.
One year, feeling clever, I replied
why not let the woman decide herself?
Linda, the teacher would report, eschews   15
the burdens of responsibility.

This fall in a real museum I stand
before a real Rembrandt, old woman,
or nearly so, myself. The colors
within this frame are darker than autumn,   20
darker even than winter—the browns of earth,
though earth's most radiant elements burn
through the canvas. I know now that woman
and painting and season are almost one
and all beyond saving by children.   25

[1980]

Joining the Conversation: Critical Thinking and Writing

1. What do we know about the teacher in the poem? Do you think you would like to take a course with this teacher? Why?
2. Lines 3–6 report a question that a teacher asked. Does the rest of the poem answer the question? If so, what is the answer? If not, what does the rest of the poem do?
3. Do you assume that, for this poem, the responses of younger readers (say, ages seventeen to twenty-two) as a group would differ from those of older readers? If so, set forth your response in a short argumentative essay.
4. Do you think high schools should offer courses in ethics? If so, do you think the question posed by the teacher in the poem is an appropriate question for such a course? And do you think that Pastan's poem suggests that high schools should or should not teach such courses?

THEODORE ROETHKE

Theodore Roethke (1908–63) was born in Saginaw, Michigan, and was educated at the University of Michigan and Harvard. From 1947 until his death, he taught at the University of Washington in Seattle, where he exerted considerable influence on the next generation of poets. Many of Roethke's best poems are lyrical memories of his childhood.

My Papa's Waltz

The whiskey on your breath
Could make a small boy dizzy;
but I hung on like death:
Such waltzing was not easy.

We romped until the pans   5
Slid from the kitchen shelf;
My mother's countenance
Could not unfrown itself.

The hand that held my wrist
Was battered on one knuckle;   10
At every step you missed
My right ear scraped a buckle.

You beat time on my head
With a palm caked hard by dirt,
Then waltzed me off to bed   15
Still clinging to your shirt.

[1948]

Joining the Conversation: Critical Thinking and Writing

1. Do the syntactical pauses vary much from stanza to stanza? Be specific. Would you say that the rhythm suggests lightness? Why?
2. Does the rhythm parallel or ironically contrast with the episode described? Was the dance a graceful waltz? Explain.
3. What would you say is the function of the stresses in lines 13–14?
4. How different would the poem be if the speaker were female and "girl" instead of "boy" appeared in line 2?

SHARON OLDS

Sharon Olds, born in San Francisco in 1942 and educated at Stanford University and Columbia University, has published many volumes of poetry and received major awards. Olds held the position of New York State Poet from 1998 to 2000, and she currently teaches poetry workshops in the Graduate Creative Writing Program at New York University.

Rites of Passage

As the guests arrive at my son's party
They gather in the living room—
short men, men in first grade
with smooth jaws and chins.
Hands in pockets, they stand around   5
jostling, jockeying for place, small fights
breaking out and calming. One says to another
How old are you? Six. I'm seven. So?
They eye each other, seeing themselves
tiny in the other's pupils. They clear their   10
throats a lot, a room of small bankers,
they fold their arms and frown. *I could beat you
up,* a seven says to a six,
the dark cake, round and heavy as a
turret, behind them on the table. My son,   15

freckles like specks of nutmeg on his cheeks,
chest narrow as the balsa keel of a
model boat, long hands
cool and thin as the day they guided him
out of me, speaks up as a host   20
for the sake of the group.
We could easily kill a two-year-old,
he says in his clear voice. The other
men agree, they clear their throats
like Generals, they relax and get down to   25
playing war, celebrating my son's life.

                                                        [1983]

Joining the Conversation: Critical Thinking and Writing

1. Focus on the details that the speaker provides about the boys—how they look, how they speak. What do the details reveal about them?
2. Is the speaker's son the same as, or different from, the other boys?
3. Some readers find the ironies in this poem (for instance, "short men") to be somewhat comical, while others, noting such phrases as *kill a two-year-old* and "playing war," conclude that the poem as a whole is meant to be upsetting, even frightening. How would you describe the kinds of irony that Olds uses here?
4. Here is an experiment in irony and point of view: Try writing a poem like this one, from the point of view of a father about the birthday party of his son, and then try writing another one, by either a father or a mother, about a daughter's party.

NATASHA TRETHEWEY

Born in Mississippi in 1966, Natasha Trethewey was named the Poet Laureate of the United States in 2012 and won the Pulitzer Prize for her third book of poems, Native Guard, *in 2007. One of contemporary America's most celebrated poets, she raises important questions about race and class by presenting memorable characters and drawing on her own mixed-race heritage. For example, her first poetry collection,* Domestic Work *(2000), depicts working-class black men and women of the South, and her second poetry collection,* Bellocq's Ophelia *(2002), presents a fictional prostitute in early twentieth-century New Orleans. Tretheway earned a BA in English at the University of Georgia, an MA in English at Hollins University, and an MFA in poetry from the University of Massachusetts Amherst, and she has held appointments at Duke University, the University of North Carolina-Chapel Hill, and Yale University.*

White Lies

The lies I could tell,
when I was growing up
light-bright, near-white,
high-yellow, red-boned
in a black place,   5
were just white lies.

I could easily tell the white folks
that we lived uptown,
not in that pink and green
shanty-fled shotgun section   10
along the tracks. I could act
like my homemade dresses
came straight out the window
of Maison Blanche. I could even
keep quiet, quiet as kept,   15
like the time a white girl said
(squeezing my hand), *Now
we have three of us in this class.*

But I paid for it every time
Mama found out.   20
She laid her hands on me,
then washed out my mouth
with Ivory soap. *This
is to purify,* she said,
and cleanse your lying tongue.   25
Believing her, I swallowed suds
thinking they'd work
from the inside out.

                                          [2000]

Joining the Conversation: Critical Thinking and Writing

1. What are the "white lies" that the narrator of this poem tells? Annotate the poem, using your notes to determine what lies the narrator is telling. What mistruth do these lies add up to? What lines lead you to determine the content of the lie?
2. We typically think of a "white lie" as a minor, unimportant, or trivial lie, often told with good intentions or to avoid hurting someone's feelings. Do the lies the narrator tells fit into this definition of a white lie?
3. Explore the image of "Ivory soap" in line 23. Write a response paragraph explaining how the soap functions as a complex symbol and is central to a set of interesting actions. What is the soap supposed to "*purify*"? Why is the soap "Ivory"? How does the soap connect to earlier use of the word "white"? Why is the mother so angry at the narrator? Why does the narrator swallow the soap suds?
4. Have you ever told a serious lie or been punished for telling a lie? Write a personal reflection on what that lie meant at the time you told it and how your thinking about that lie has or has not changed as you reflect back on it.

Chapter Overview: Looking Backward/Looking Forward

1. Sometimes we say a person is "so innocent." Is this a compliment or a criticism?
2. Was there a moment in your own life when you moved in a significant way from "innocence" to "experience"? How did you feel when this event occurred? How do you feel about it now?

3. Do you think it is possible to know something well even without having direct experience of it? Can someone know what being a parent means, for example, if he or she does not have a child? Can someone comment expertly on baseball without having played on a major-league team?

4. Name and describe some things that you have experienced once but never want to experience again.

5. Name and describe some things that you have not experienced but that you hope to experience some day. If you do not experience them, will your life be affected a lot or a little?

6. Name and describe some things that you feel you must experience at some point in your life. Why are these things so important to you?

7. If you could have been present at any historical event, however long ago, what would it be? Why would you want to be there? What would this experience give you that you do not now possess?

CHAPTER 20

All in a Day's Work

ESSAY

BARBARA EHRENREICH

Barbara Ehrenreich was born in Butte, Montana, in 1941, of parents whom she characterized as strongly pro-union. The two family rules, she told an interviewer, were "Never cross a picket line and never vote Republican." She did her undergraduate work (in chemistry) at Reed College, and she earned a PhD (in cellular biology) at Rockefeller University, but her career has been as a writer, not a scientist. Ehrenreich has written more than twenty books, chiefly on social issues.

We give an extract from Nickel and Dimed: On (Not) Getting By in America *(2001). In this book, she recounts her experiences while working during 1998–2000 in minimum-wage jobs as a waitress, hotel maid, nursing-home aide, house cleaner, and Wal-Mart associate. These jobs tended to pay about seven or eight dollars an hour, close to the minimum wage established by the federal government, which at the time was $7.25. In 2012, the minimum hourly wage for nontip jobs was $7.40, and for jobs that get tips, $3.70. Almost 30 percent of the workers in the United States earn about eight dollars an hour.*

In the following pages, Ehrenreich discusses the orientation procedure at Wal-Mart. The title of this extract from Ehrenreich's book is our own.

Wal-Mart Orientation Program

For sheer grandeur, scale, and intimidation value, I doubt if any corporate orientation exceeds that of Wal-Mart. I have been told that the process will take eight hours, which will include two fifteen-minute breaks and one half-hour break for a meal, and will be paid for like a regular shift. When I arrive, dressed neatly in khakis and clean T-shirt, as befits a potential Wal-Mart "associate," I find there are ten new hires besides myself, mostly young and Caucasian, and a team of three, headed by Roberta, to do the "orientating." We sit around a long table in the same windowless room where I was interviewed, each with a thick folder of paperwork in front of us, and hear Roberta tell once again about raising six children, being a "people person," discovering that the three principles of Wal-Mart philosophy were the same as her own, and so on. We begin with a video, about fifteen minutes long, on the history and philosophy of Wal-Mart, or, as an anthropological observer might call it, the Cult of Sam. First young Sam Walton, in uniform, comes back from the war. He starts a store, a sort of five-and-dime; he marries and fathers four attractive children; he receives a Medal of Freedom from President Bush, after which he promptly dies, making way for the eulogies.

But the company goes on, yes indeed. Here the arc of the story soars upward unstoppably, pausing only to mark some fresh milestone of corporate expansion. 1992: Wal-Mart becomes the largest retailer in the world. 1997: Sales top $100 billion. 1998: The number of Wal-Mart associates hits 825,000, making Wal-Mart the largest private employer in the nation. Each landmark date is accompanied by a clip showing throngs of shoppers, swarms of associates, or scenes of handsome new stores and their adjoining parking lots. Over and over we hear in voiceover or see in graphic display the "three principles," which are maddeningly, even defiantly, nonparallel: "respect for the individual, exceeding customers' expectations; strive for excellence."

"Respect for the individual" is where we, the associates, come in, because vast as Wal-Mart is, and tiny as we may be as individuals, everything depends on us. Sam always said, and is shown saying, that "the best ideas come from the associates"—for example, the idea of having a "people greeter," an elderly employee (excuse me, associate) who welcomes each customer as he or she enters the store. Three times during the orientation, which began at three and stretches to nearly eleven, we are reminded that this brainstorm originated in a mere associate, and who knows what revolutions in retailing each one of us may propose? Because our ideas are welcome, more than welcome, and we are to think of our managers not as bosses but as "servant leaders," serving us as well as the customers. Of course, all is not total harmony, in every instance, between associates and their servant leaders. A video on "associate honesty" shows a cashier being caught on videotape as he pockets some bills from the cash register. Drums beat ominously as he is led away in handcuffs and sentenced to four years.

The theme of covert tensions, overcome by right thinking and positive attitude, continues in the twelve-minute video entitled *You've Picked a Great Place to Work*. Here various associates testify to the "essential feeling of family for which Wal-Mart is so well-known," leading up to the conclusion that we don't need a union. Once, long ago, unions had a place in American society, but they "no longer have much to offer workers," which is why people are leaving them "by the droves." Wal-Mart is booming; unions are declining: judge for yourself. But we are warned that "unions have been targeting Wal-Mart for years." Why? For the dues money of course. Think of what you would lose with a union: first, your dues money, which could be $20 a month "and sometimes much more." Second, you would lose "your voice" because the union would insist on doing your talking for you. Finally, you might lose even your wages and benefits because they would all be "at risk on the bargaining table." You have to wonder— and I imagine some of my teenage fellow orientees may be doing so—why such fiends as these union organizers, such outright extortionists, are allowed to roam free in the land.

There is more, much more than I could ever absorb, even if it were spread out over a semester-long course. On the reasonable assumption that none of us is planning to go home and curl up with the "Wal-Mart Associate Handbook," our trainers start reading it out loud to us, pausing every few paragraphs to ask, "Any questions?" There never are. Barry, the seventeen-year-old to my left, mutters that his "butt hurts." Sonya, the tiny African American woman across from me, seems frozen in terror. I have given up on looking perky and am fighting to keep my eyes open. No nose or other facial jewelry, we learn; earrings must be small and discreet, not dangling; no blue jeans except on Friday, and then you have to pay $1 for the privilege of wearing them. No "grazing," that is, eating from food packages that somehow become open; no "time theft." This last sends me drifting off in a sci-fi direction: *And as the time thieves headed back to the year 3420, loaded with week-ends and days off looted from the twenty-first century* . . . Finally, a question. The old guy who is being hired as a people greeter wants to know, "What is time theft?" Answer: Doing anything other than working during company time, anything at all. Theft of *our* time is not, however, an issue. There are stretches amounting to many minutes when all three of our trainers wander off, leaving us to sit there in silence or take the opportunity to squirm. Or our junior trainers go through a section of the handbook, and then Roberta, returning from some other business, goes over the same section again. My eyelids droop and I consider walking out. I have seen time move more swiftly during seven-hour airline delays. In fact, I am getting nostalgic about seven-hour airline delays. At least you can read a book or get up and walk around, take a leak.

5   On breaks, I drink coffee purchased at the Radio Grill, as the in-house fast food place is called, the real stuff with caffeine, more because I'm concerned about being alert for the late-night drive home than out of any need to absorb all the Wal-Mart trivia coming my way. Now, here's a drug the drug warriors ought to take a little more interest in. Since I don't normally drink it at all—iced tea can usually be counted on for enough of a kick—the coffee has an effect like reagent-grade Dexedrine: my pulse races, my brain overheats, and the result in this instance is a kind of delirium. I find myself overly challenged by the little kindergarten-level tasks we are now given to do, such as affixing my personal bar code to my ID card, then sticking on the punch-out letters to spell my name. The letters keep curling up and sticking to my fingers, so I stop at "Barb," or more precisely, "BARB," drift-ing off to think of all the people I know who have gentrified their names in recent years—Patsy to Patricia, Dick to Richard, and so forth—while I am going in the other direction. Now we start taking turns going to the computers to begin our CBL, or Computer-Based Learning, and I become transfixed by the HIV-inspired module entitled "Bloodborne Pathogens," on what to do in the event that pools of human blood should show up on the sales floor. All right, you put warning cones around the puddles, don protective gloves, etc., but I can't stop trying to envision the circumstances in which these pools might arise: an associate uprising? a guest riot? I have gone through six modules, three more than we are supposed to do tonight—the rest are to be done in our spare moments over the next few weeks—when one of the trainers gently pries me away from the computer. We are allowed now to leave.

[2001]

Joining the Conversation: Critical Thinking and Writing

1. What is the effect of putting quotation marks around "associate" and "orientation"?
2. Imagine that you are working for a publisher, as the editor of Ehrenreich's manuscript. Have you any suggestions? (Remember that we are reprinting only an extract, so it is *not* appropriate, for instance, to suggest that she should iden-tify Roberta, who in fact is fully identified earlier in the chapter.)
3. Write a 500–750 word essay on an orientation program—perhaps the one in your college for incoming students. Do not be merely descriptive: Let your reader sense your attitude toward the program, but communicate this attitude throughout the essay rather than merely in an opening or concluding paragraph.

4. If you were a manager at Wal-Mart and you had read Ehrenreich's essay, would you be likely to hire her? In a paragraph, explain why or why not. In another paragraph, explain why you would or would not be eager to take a course with Ehrenreich if she were teaching at your college.

STORIES

JACOB GRIMM AND WILHELM GRIMM

The brothers Jacob Grimm (1785–1863) and Wilhelm Grimm (1786–1859) were German scholars who collected folktales, chiefly from peasant women who told the stories to children, though the stories also circulated among adults. The first Grimm collection, Children's and Household Tales *(1812), contained more than two hundred stories, including such now-classic tales as "The Frog Prince," "Sleeping Beauty," and "Snow White."*

Short narratives of this sort are commonly called fairy tales. *In fact, relatively few of them include fairies, although almost all of them do include such supernatural elements as talking animals, gnomes, giants, and witches. They also include archetypal human beings, such as the beautiful princess, the handsome prince, and the wicked stepmother.*

Mother Holle

Translated by Margaret Taylor

There was once a widow who had two daughters—one of whom was pretty and industrious, whilst the other was ugly and idle. But she was much fonder of the ugly and idle one, because she was her own daughter, and the other, who was a step-daughter, was obliged to do all the work, and be the Cinderella of the house. Every day the poor girl had to sit by a well, in the highway, and spin and spin till her fingers bled.

Now it happened that one day the shuttle was marked with her blood, so she dipped it in the well, to wash the mark off; but it dropped out of her hand and fell to the bottom. She began to weep, and ran to her step-mother and told her of the mishap. But she scolded her sharply, and was so merciless as to say, "Since you have let the shuttle fall in, you must fetch it out again." So the girl went back to the well, and did not know what to do; and in the sorrow of her heart she jumped into the well to get the shuttle. She lost her senses; and when she awoke and came to herself again, she was in a lovely meadow where the sun was shining and many thousands of flowers were growing. Along this meadow she went, and at last came to a baker's oven full of bread, and the bread cried out, "Oh, take me out! take me out! or I shall burn; I have been baked a long time!" So she went up to it, and took out all the loaves one after another with the bread-shovel. After that she went on till she came to a tree covered with apples, which called out to her, "Oh, shake me! shake me! we apples are all ripe!" So she shook the tree till the apples fell like rain, and went on shaking till they were all down, and when she had gathered them into a heap, she went on her way.

At last she came to a little house, out of which an old woman peeped; but she had such large teeth that the girl was frightened, and was about to run away. But the old woman called out to her, "What are you afraid of, dear child? Stay with me; if you will do all the work in the house properly, you shall be the better for it. Only you must take care to make my bed well, and shake it thoroughly till the feathers fly—for then there is snow on the earth. I am Mother Holle.

As the old woman spoke so kindly to her, the girl took courage and agreed to enter her service. She attended to everything to the satisfaction of her mistress, and always shook her bed so vigorously that the feathers flew about like snow-flakes. So she had a pleasant life with her; never an angry word; and boiled or roast meat every day.

5   She stayed some time with Mother Holle, and then she became sad. At first she did not know what was the matter with her, but found at length that it was home-sickness: although she was many thousand times better off here than at home, still she had a longing to be there. At last she said to the old woman, "I have a longing for home; and however well off I am down here, I cannot stay any longer; I must go up again to my own people." Mother Holle said, "I am pleased that you long for your home again, and as you have served me so truly, I myself will take you up again." Thereupon she took her by the hand, and led her to a large door. The door was opened, and just as the maiden was standing beneath the doorway, a heavy shower of golden rain fell, and all the gold remained sticking to her, so that she was completely covered over with it.

"You shall have that because you have been so industrious," said Mother Holle, and at the same time she gave her back the shuttle which she had let fall into the well. Thereupon the door closed, and the maiden found herself up above upon the earth, not far from her mother's house. And as she went into the yard the cock was standing by the well-side, and cried—

> "Cock-a-doodle-doo!
> Your golden girl's come back to you!"

So she went in to her mother, and as she arrived thus covered with gold, she was well received, both by her and her sister.

The girl told all that had happened to her; and as soon as the mother heard how she had come by so much wealth, she was very anxious to obtain the same good luck for the ugly and lazy daughter. She had to seat herself by the well and spin; and in order that her shuttle might be stained with blood, she stuck her hand into a thorn bush and pricked her finger. Then she threw her shuttle into the well, and jumped in after it.

She came, like the other, to the beautiful meadow and walked along the very same path. When she got to the oven the bread again cried, "Oh, take me out! take me out! or I shall burn; I have been baked a long time!" But the lazy thing answered, "As if I had any wish to make myself dirty?" and on she went. Soon she came to the apple-tree, which cried, "Oh, shake me! shake me! we apples are all ripe!" But she answered, "I like that! one of you might fall on my head," and so went on.

10   When she came to Mother Holle's house she was not afraid, for she had already heard of her big teeth, and she hired herself to her immediately.

The first day she forced herself to work diligently, and obeyed Mother Holle when she told her to do anything, for she was thinking of all the gold that she would give her. But on the second day she began to be lazy, and on the third day still more so, and then she would not get up in the morning at all. Neither did she make Mother Holle's bed as she ought, and did not shake it so as to make the feathers fly up. Mother Holle was soon tired of this, and gave her notice to leave.

The lazy girl was willing enough to go, and thought that now the golden rain would come. Mother Holle led her also to the great door; but while she was standing beneath it, instead of the gold a big kettleful of pitch was emptied over her. "That is the reward for your service," said Mother Holle, and shut the door.

So the lazy girl went home; but she was quite covered with pitch, and the cock by the well-side, as soon as he saw her, cried out—

> "Cock-a-doodle-doo!
> Your pitchy girl's come back to you!"

But the pitch stuck fast to her, and could not be got off as long as she lived.

[1884]

Joining the Conversation: Critical Thinking and Writing

1. In this story, work is associated with goodness and laziness is associated with evil. In short, the story illustrates "the work ethic" (sometimes called "the Protestant work ethic"), which holds that work enhances character and that laziness is morally bad. On the other hand, some people argue that the work ethic is essentially a trick, a con game, by which those in power delude the lower classes into working mindlessly while the rich exploit their loyal service. What are your thoughts?

2. We often hear today that youngsters may be damaged by the kinds of stories implicit in computer games that seem to celebrate violence. And we hear that children do not read enough or, if the children are very young, that parents do not read enough to their children. But consider "Mother Holle," a traditional story found in many older books of fairy tales. Can a good argument be made that the tale is based on a vicious idea that physically attractive people are virtuous (the beautiful daughter is industrious) and that unattractive or deformed people are morally deficient (the ugly daughter is indolent). After all, our physical appearances often are beyond our control, and, although good looks have been said to be the EZ Pass of life, surely our degree of attractiveness is not correlated with our morality. Further, the lifetime punishment of the ugly girl ("the pitch stuck fast to her . . . as long as she lived") implies that human beings cannot repent, cannot reform—or, if they can, they nevertheless should be horribly punished for life. Do you think, then, that this fairy tale (and there are many others like it in its implicit morality) may have a destructive effect on children? Or, on balance, do you think that this fairy tale may have a beneficial effect on young readers? Explain your answer.

WILLIAM CARLOS WILLIAMS

William Carlos Williams (1883–1963) was the son of an English traveling salesman and a Basque Jewish woman. The couple met in Puerto Rico and settled in Rutherford, New Jersey, where Williams was born. He spent his life there, practicing as a pediatrician and writing poems in the moments between seeing patients who were visiting his office.

The Use of Force

They were new patients to me, all I had was the name, Olson. Please come down as soon as you can, my daughter is very sick. When I arrived I was met by the mother, a big startled looking woman, very clean and apologetic who merely said, Is this the doctor? and let me in. In the back, she added. You must excuse us, doctor, we have her in the kitchen where it is warm. It is very damp here sometimes.

The child was fully dressed and sitting on her father's lap near the kitchen table. He tried to get up, but I motioned for him not to bother, took off my overcoat and started to look things over. I could see that they were all very nervous, eyeing me up and down distrustfully. As often, in such cases, they weren't telling me more than they had to, it was up to me to tell them; that's why they were spending three dollars on me.

The child was fairly eating me up with her cold, steady eyes, and no expression to her face whatever. She did not move and seemed, inwardly, quiet; an unusually attractive little thing, and as strong as a heifer in appearance. But her face was flushed, she was breathing rapidly, and I realized that she had a high fever. She had magnificent blond hair, in profusion. One of those picture children often reproduced in advertising leaflets and the photogravure sections of the Sunday papers.

She's had a fever for three days, began the father and we don't know what it comes from. My wife has given her things, you know, like people do, but it don't do no good. And there's been a lot of sickness around. So we tho't you'd better look her over and tell us what is the matter.

5   As doctors often do I took a trial shot at it as a point of departure. Has she had a sore throat?

Both parents answered me together, No . . . No, she says her throat don't hurt her.

Does your throat hurt you? added the mother to the child. But the little girl's expression didn't change nor did she move her eyes from my face.

Have you looked?

I tried to, said the mother, but I couldn't see.

10   As it happens we had been having a number of cases of diphtheria in the school to which the child went during that month and we were all, quite apparently, thinking of that, though no one had as yet spoken of the thing.

Well, I said, suppose we take a look at the throat first. I smiled in my best professional manner and asking for the child's first name I said, come on, Mathilda, open your mouth and let's take a look at your throat.

Nothing doing.

Aw, come on, I coaxed, just open your mouth wide and let me take a look. Look, I said opening both hands wide, I haven't anything in my hands. Just open up and let me see.

Such a nice man, put in the mother. Look how kind he is to you. Come on, do what he tells you to, he won't hurt you.

15   At that I ground my teeth in disgust. If only they wouldn't use the word "hurt" I might be able to get somewhere. But I did not allow myself to be hurried or disturbed but speaking quietly and slowly I approached the child again.

As I moved my chair a little nearer suddenly with one catlike movement both her hands clawed instinctively for my eyes and she almost reached them too. In fact she knocked my glasses flying and they fell, though unbroken, several feet away from me on the kitchen floor.

Both the mother and father almost turned themselves inside out in embarrassment and apology. You bad girl, said the mother, taking her and shaking her by one arm. Look what you've done. The nice man . . .

For heaven's sake, I broke in. Don't call me a nice man to her. I'm here to look at her throat on the chance that she might have diphtheria and possibly die of it. But that's nothing to her. Look here, I said to the child, we're going to look at your throat. You're old enough to understand what I'm saying. Will you open it now by yourself or shall we have to open it for you?

Not a move. Even her expression hadn't changed. Her breaths however were coming faster and faster. Then the battle began. I had to do it. I had to have a throat culture for her own protection. But first I told the parents that it was entirely up to them. I explained the danger but said that I would not insist on a throat examination so long as they would take the responsibility.

20   If you don't do what the doctor says you'll have to go to the hospital, the mother admonished her severely.

Oh yeah? I had to smile to myself. After all, I had already fallen in love with the savage brat, the parents were contemptible to me. In the ensuing struggle they grew more and more abject, crushed, exhausted while she surely rose to magnificent heights of insane fury of effort bred of her terror of me.

The father tried his best, and he was a big man but the fact that she was his daughter, his shame at her behavior and his dread of hurting her made him release her just at the critical times when I had almost achieved success, till I wanted to kill him. But his dread also that she might have diphtheria made him tell me to go on, go on though he himself was almost fainting, while the mother moved back and forth behind us raising and lowering her hands in an agony of apprehension.

Put her in front of you on your lap, I ordered, and hold both her wrists.

But as soon as he did the child let out a scream. Don't, you're hurting me. Let go of my hands. Let them go I tell you. Then she shrieked terrifyingly, hysterically. Stop it! Stop it! You're killing me!

25   Do you think she can stand it, doctor! said the mother.

You get out, said the husband to his wife. Do you want her to die of diphtheria?

Come on now, hold her, I said.

Then I grasped the child's head with my left hand and tried to get the wooden tongue depressor between her teeth. She fought, with clenched teeth, desperately! But now I also had grown furious—at a child. I tried to hold myself down but I couldn't. I know how to expose a throat for inspection. And I did my best. When finally I got the wooden spatula behind the last teeth and just the point of it into the mouth cavity, she opened up for an instant but before I could see anything she came down again and gripped the wooden blade between her molars. She reduced it to splinters before I could get it out again.

Aren't you ashamed, the mother yelled at her. Aren't you ashamed to act like that in front of the doctor?

30   Get me a smooth-handled spoon of some sort, I told the mother. We're going through with this. The child's mouth was already bleeding. Her tongue was cut and she was screaming in wild hysterical shrieks. Perhaps I should have desisted and come back in an hour or more. No doubt it would have been better. But I have seen at least two children lying dead in bed of neglect in such cases, and feeling that I must get a diagnosis now or never I went at it again. But the worst of it was that I too had got beyond reason. I could have torn the child apart in

my own fury and enjoyed it. It was a pleasure to attack her. My face was burning with it.

The damned little brat must be protected against her own idiocy, one says to one's self at such times. Others must be protected against her. It is a social necessity. And all these things are true. But a blind fury, a feeling of adult shame, bred of a longing for muscular release are the operatives. One goes on to the end.

In the final unreasoning assault I overpowered the child's neck and jaws. I forced the heavy silver spoon back of her teeth and down her throat till she gagged. And there it was—both tonsils covered with membrane. She had fought valiantly to keep me from knowing her secret. She had been hiding that sore throat for three days at least and lying to her parents in order to escape just such an outcome as this.

Now truly she was furious. She had been on the defensive before but now she attacked. Tried to get off her father's lap and fly at me while tears of defeat blinded her eyes.

[1938]

Joining the Conversation: Critical Thinking and Writing

1. The characters in "The Use of Force" are the doctor, the girl, and her parents. What can you say about each of them—their characters, their classes—on the basis of the first paragraph? What can you say about the doctor as we perceive him by the end of the fifteenth paragraph?

2. According to popular stereotypes, children are supposed to be nice, sweet, innocent things, and doctors are supposed to be kind, wise, relatively unemotional persons. Do Williams's figures seem to you to be utterly improbable? Explain your answer.

3. The narrator is the doctor, but he occasionally lets us hear other voices. For instance, we hear the voice of one of the parents in the second sentence ("Please come down as soon as you can, my daughter is very sick"), the voice of the father in the fourth paragraph ("She's had a fever for three days, began the father and we don't know what it comes from. My wife has given her things, you know, like people do, but it don't do no good"), and the voice of the mother in the fourteenth paragraph ("Such a nice man, put in the mother"). Still, the doctor is the narrator, and we chiefly hear his voice. Now, consider the fact that he says such things as "I wanted to kill [the father]" (paragraph 22), "But now I also had grown furious—at a child" (paragraph 28), and "the worst of it was that I too had got beyond reason" (paragraph 30). Can we reasonably say that there are *two* conflicts in the story—the doctor versus the child, and the doctor versus himself, that is, the doctor as a dispassionate professional, and the doctor as a human being? The first conflict is resolved—the child is defeated—but would you add that the second conflict is never resolved? If you believe it is not resolved, do you think this is a weakness in the story?

4. One of our students, in an analysis of the story, argued that it is really a story about rape, perhaps in the form of a rapist's memoir, written for himself. Her evidence included such passages as "I had already fallen in love with the savage brat" (paragraph 21) and "Will you open it now by yourself or shall we have to open it for you?" (paragraph 18). Do you think the episode describes a rape? What is your evidence?

WILL EISNER

For biographical information on Will Eisner, see page 527.

THE DAY I BECAME A PROFESSIONAL

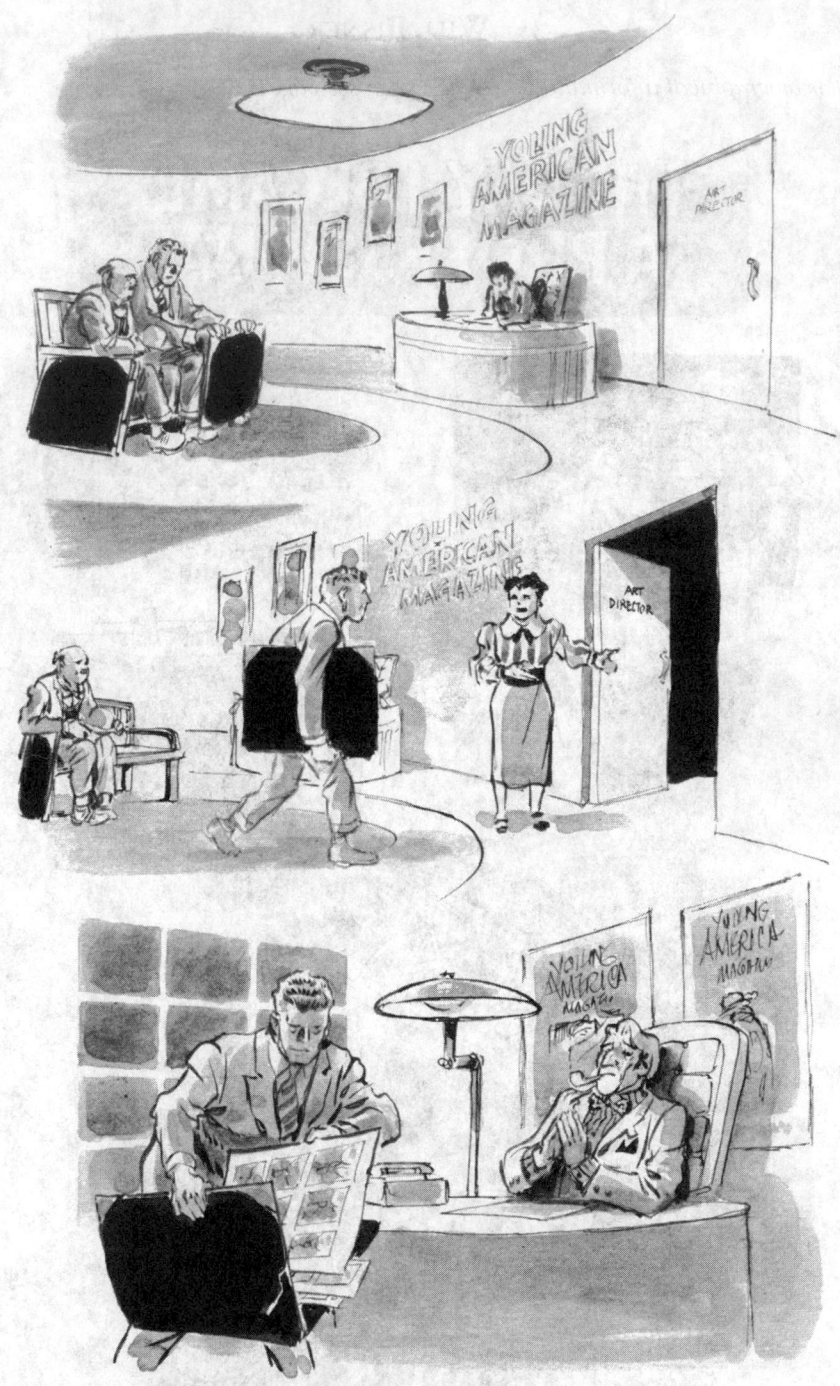

Will Eisner Studios. Inc.

Joining the Conversation: Critical Thinking and Writing

1. The last line of this story is something like the punch line of a joke: It conveys the point of all that precedes it, but, alas, most of today's readers are not familiar with the charming illustrations of Ludwig Bemelmans. (Fifty or sixty years ago, Bemelmans was widely known, especially for a series of children's books about a girl called Madeline.) If you have no sense of Bemelmans's work, substitute the name of any illustrator whose work you greatly admire—perhaps Walt Disney or Garry Trudeau. Presumably, Bemelmans was, in fact, tubby and balding, as depicted. Would the story be more effective or less effective if he were more like the central character, a tall, good-looking guy? Explain your answer.
2. In the first drawing, we see an older man standing behind the artist. Who do you suppose this person is, and what is his attitude? How do you know? Why does the author/cartoonist include this figure? And why does the author/cartoonist include the second drawing, showing the artist tightening his necktie? How relevant is this image to the rest of the story? In the next image, if you were creating the strip, would you show the artist standing, as Eisner does? Why didn't the author/cartoonist show the artist seated, with the other passengers?
3. Explain the title of the story.
4. If you were writing this text book, would you have included this piece? Why, or why not?

DANIEL OROZCO

Daniel Orozco, born in San Francisco in 1957, is known chiefly for his short stories. A professor of creative writing at the University of Idaho, Orozco has received several important awards, including a grant from the National Endowment for the Arts.

Orientation

Those are the offices and these are the cubicles. That's my cubicle there, and this is your cubicle. This is your phone. Never answer your phone. Let the Voicemail System answer it. This is your Voicemail System Manual. There are no personal phone calls allowed. We do, however, allow for emergencies. If you must make an emergency phone call, ask your supervisor first. If you can't find your supervisor, ask Phillip Spiers, who sits over there. He'll check with Clarissa Nicks, who sits over there. If you make an emergency phone call without asking, you may be let go.

These are your in- and out-boxes. All the forms in your in-box must be logged in by the date shown in the upper left-hand corner, initialed by you in the upper right-hand corner, and distributed to the Processing Analyst whose name is numerically coded in the lower left-hand corner. The lower right-hand corner is left blank. Here's your Processing Analyst Numerical Code Index. And here's your Forms Processing Procedures Manual.

You must pace your work. What do I mean? I'm glad you asked that. We pace our work according to the eight-hour workday. If you have twelve hours of work in your in-box, for example, you must compress that work into the eight-hour day. If you have one hour of work in your in-box, you must expand that work to fill the eight-hour day. That was a good question. Feel free to ask questions. Ask too many questions, however, and you may be let go.

That is our receptionist. She is a temp. We go through receptionists here. They quit with alarming frequency. Be polite and civil to the temps. Learn their names, and invite them to lunch occasionally. But don't get close to them, as it only makes it more difficult when they leave. And they always leave. You can be sure of that.

5   The men's room is over there. The women's room is over there. John LaFountaine, who sits over there, uses the women's room occasionally. He says it is accidental. We know better, but we let it pass. John LaFountaine is harmless, his forays into the forbidden territory of the women's room simply a benign thrill, a faint blip on the dull flat line of his life.

Russell Nash, who sits in the cubicle to your left, is in love with Amanda Pierce, who sits in the cubicle to your right. They ride the same bus together after work. For Amanda Pierce, it is just a tedious bus ride made less tedious by the idle nattering of Russell Nash. But for Russell Nash, it is the highlight of his day. It is the highlight of his life. Russell Nash has put on forty pounds, and grows fatter with each passing month, nibbling on chips and cookies while peeking glumly over the partitions at Amanda Pierce and gorging himself at home on cold pizza and ice cream while watching adult videos on TV.

Amanda Pierce, in the cubicle to your right, has a six-year-old son named Jamie, who is autistic. Her cubicle is plastered from top to bottom with the boy's crayon artwork—sheet after sheet of precisely drawn concentric circles and ellipses, in black and yellow. She rotates them every other Friday. Be sure to comment on them. Amanda Pierce also has a husband, who is a lawyer. He subjects her to an escalating array of painful and humiliating sex games, to which Amanda Pierce reluctantly submits. She comes to work exhausted and freshly wounded each morning, wincing from the abrasions on her breasts, or the bruises on her abdomen, or the second-degree burns on the backs of her thighs.

But we're not supposed to know any of this. Do not let on. If you let on, you may be let go.

Amanda Pierce, who tolerates Russell Nash, is in love with Albert Bosch, whose office is over there. Albert Bosch, who only dimly registers Amanda Pierce's existence, has eyes only for Ellie Tapper, who sits over there. Ellie Tapper, who hates Albert Bosch, would walk through fire for Curtis Lance. But Curtis Lance hates Ellie Tapper. Isn't the world a funny place? Not in the ha-ha sense, of course.

10   Anika Bloom sits in that cubicle. Last year, while reviewing quarterly reports in a meeting with Barry Hacker, Anika Bloom's left palm began to bleed. She fell into a trance, stared into her hand, and told Barry Hacker when and how his wife would die. We laughed it off. She was, after all, a new employee. But Barry Hacker's wife is dead. So unless you want to know exactly when and how you'll die, never talk to Anika Bloom.

Colin Heavey sits in that cubicle over there. He was new once, just like you. We warned him about Anika Bloom. But at last year's Christmas Potluck he felt sorry for her when he saw that no one was talking to her. Colin Heavey brought her a drink. He hasn't been himself since. Colin Heavey is doomed. There's nothing he can do about it, and we are powerless to help him. Stay away from Colin Heavey. Never give any of your work to him. If he asks you to do something, tell him you have to check with me. If he asks again, tell him I haven't gotten back to you.

This is the fire exit. There are several on this floor, and they are marked accordingly. We have a Floor Evacuation Review every three months, and an Escape Route Quiz once a month. We have our Biannual Fire Drill twice a year, and our Annual Earthquake Drill once a year. These are precautions only. These things never happen.

For your information, we have a comprehensive health plan. Any catastrophic illness, any unforeseen tragedy is completely covered. All dependents are completely covered. Larry Bagdikian, who sits over there, has six daughters. If anything were to happen to any of his girls, or to all of them, if all six were to simultaneously fall victim to illness or injury—stricken with a hideous degenerative muscle disease or some rare toxic blood disorder, sprayed with semiautomatic gunfire while on a class field trip, or attacked in their bunk beds by some prowling nocturnal lunatic—if any of this were to pass, Larry's girls would all be taken care of. Larry Bagdikian would not have to pay one dime. He would have nothing to worry about.

We also have a generous vacation and sick leave policy. We have an excellent disability insurance plan. We have a stable and profitable pension fund. We get group discounts for the symphony, and block seating at the ballpark. We get commuter ticket books for the bridge. We have direct deposit. We are all members of Costco.

15   This is our kitchenette. And this, this is our Mr. Coffee. We have a coffee pool, into which we each pay two dollars a week for coffee, filters, sugar, and Coffee-Mate. If you prefer Cremora or half-and-half to Coffee-Mate, there is a special pool for three dollars a week. If you prefer Sweet 'N Low to sugar, there is a special pool for two-fifty a week. We do not do decaf. You are allowed to join the coffee pool of your choice, but you are not allowed to touch the Mr. Coffee.

This is the microwave oven. You are allowed to *heat* food in the microwave oven. You are not, however, allowed to *cook* food in the microwave oven.

We get one hour for lunch. We also get one fifteen-minute break in the morning, and one fifteen-minute break in the afternoon. Always take your breaks. If you skip a break, it is gone forever. For your information, your break is a privilege, not a right. If you abuse the break policy, we are authorized to rescind your breaks. Lunch, however, is a right, not a privilege. If you abuse the lunch policy, our hands will be tied, and we will be forced to look the other way. We will not enjoy that.

This is the refrigerator. You may put your lunch in it. Barry Hacker, who sits over there, steals food from this refrigerator. His petty theft is an outlet for his grief. Last New Year's Eve, while kissing his wife, a blood vessel burst in her brain. Barry Hacker's wife was two months pregnant at the time, and lingered in a coma for half a year before she died. It was a tragic loss for Barry Hacker. He hasn't been himself since. Barry Hacker's wife was a beautiful woman. She was also completely covered. Barry Hacker did not have to pay one dime. But his dead wife haunts him. She haunts all of us. We have seen her, reflected in the monitors of our computers, moving past our cubicles. We have seen the dim shadow of her face in our photocopies. She pencils herself in the receptionist's appointment book, with the notation To see Barry Hacker. She has left messages in the receptionist's Voicemail box, messages garbled by the electronic chirrups and buzzes in the phone line, her voice echoing from an immense distance within the ambient hum. But the voice is hers. And beneath her voice, beneath the tidal whoosh of static and hiss, the gurgling and crying of a baby can be heard.

In any case, if you bring a lunch, put a little something extra in the bag for Barry Hacker. We have four Barrys in this office. Isn't that a coincidence?

20   This is Matthew Payne's office. He is our Unit Manager, and his door is always closed. We have never seen him, and you will never see him. But he is here. You can be sure of that. He is all around us.

This is the Custodian's Closet. You have no business in the Custodian's Closet.

And this, this is our Supplies Cabinet. If you need supplies, see Curtis Lance. He will log you in on the Supplies Cabinet Authorization Log, then give you a Supplies Authorization Slip. Present your pink copy of the Supplies Authorization Slip to Ellie Tapper. She will log you in on the Supplies Cabinet Key Log, then give you the key. Because the Supplies Cabinet is located outside the Unit Manager's office, you must be very quiet. Gather your supplies quietly. The Supplies Cabinet is divided into four sections. Section One contains letterhead stationery, blank paper and envelopes, memo pads and notepads, and so on. Section Two contains pens and pencils and typewriter and printer ribbons, and the like. In Section Three we have erasers, correction fluids, transparent tapes, glue sticks, et cetera. And in Section Four we have paper clips and push pins and scissors and razor blades. And here are the spare blades for the shredder. Do not touch the shredder, which is located over there. The shredder is of no concern to you.

Gwendolyn Stich sits in that office there. She is crazy about penguins and collects penguin knickknacks: penguin posters and coffee mugs and stationery, penguin stuffed animals, penguin jewelry, penguin sweaters and T-shirts and socks. She has a pair of penguin fuzzy slippers she wears when working late at the office. She has a tape cassette of penguin sounds, which she listens to for relaxation. Her favorite colors are black and white. She has personalized license plates that read PEN GWEN. Every morning, she passes through all the cubicles to wish each of us a *good* morning. She brings Danish on Wednesdays for Hump Day morning break, and doughnuts on Fridays for TGIF afternoon break. She organizes the Annual Christmas Potluck and is in charge of the Birthday List. Gwendolyn Stich's door is always open to all of us. She will always lend an ear, and put in a good word for you; she will always give you a hand, or the shirt off her back, or a shoulder to cry on. Because her door is always open, she hides and cries in a stall in the women's room. And John LaFountaine—who, enthralled when a woman enters, sits quietly in his stall with his knees to his chest—John LaFountaine has heard her vomiting in there. We have come upon Gwendolyn Stich huddled in the stairwell, shivering in the updraft, sipping a Diet Mr. Pibb and hugging her knees. She does not let any of this interfere with her work. If it interfered with her work, she might have to be let go.

Kevin Howard sits in that cubicle over there. He is a serial killer, the one they call the Carpet Cutter, responsible for the mutilations across town. We're not supposed to know that, so do not let on. Don't worry. His compulsion inflicts itself on strangers only, and the routine established is elaborate and unwavering. The victim must be a white male, a young adult no older than thirty, heavyset, with dark hair and eyes, and the like. The victim must be chosen at random, before sunset, from a public place; the victim is followed home and must put up a struggle, et cetera. The carnage inflicted is precise: the angle and direction of the incisions, the layering of skin and muscle tissue, the rearrangement of the visceral organs, and so on. Kevin Howard does not let any of this interfere with his work. He is, in fact, our fastest typist. He types as if he were on fire. He has a secret crush on Gwendolyn Stich and leaves a red-foil-wrapped Hershey's Kiss on her desk every afternoon. But he hates Anika Bloom and keeps well away from her. In his presence, she has uncontrollable fits of shaking and trembling. Her left palm does not stop bleeding.

25   In any case, when Kevin Howard gets caught, act surprised. Say that he seemed like a nice person, a bit of a loner, perhaps, but always quiet and polite.

This is the photocopier room. And this, this is our view. It faces southwest. West is down there, toward the water. North is back there. Because we are on the seventeenth floor, we are afforded a magnificent view. Isn't it beautiful? It overlooks the park, where the tops of those trees are. You can see a segment of the bay between those two buildings there. You can see the sun set in the gap between those two buildings over there. You can see this building reflected in the glass panels of that building across the way. There. See? That's you, waving. And look there. There's Anika Bloom in the kitchenette, waving back.

Enjoy this view while photocopying. If you have problems with the photocopier, see Russell Nash. If you have any questions, ask your supervisor. If you can't find your supervisor, ask Phillip Spiers. He sits over there. He'll check with Clarissa Nicks. She sits over there. If you can't find them, feel free to ask me. That's my cubicle. I sit in there.

[1994]

Joining the Conversation: Critical Thinking and Writing

1. How would you characterize the narrator? Is the narrator thoroughly experienced? Innocent in some ways?
2. Write your own "Orientation" instructions (250–500 words) for someone who is about to take a job that you have had.

POEMS

WILLIAM WORDSWORTH

William Wordsworth (1770–1850), the son of an attorney, grew up in the Lake District of England. After graduating from Cambridge University in 1791, he spent a year in France, falling in love with a French girl, by whom he had a daughter. His enthusiasm for the French Revolution waned, and he returned alone to England where, with the help of a legacy, he devoted his life to poetry. With his friend Samuel Taylor Coleridge, in 1798, he published anonymously a volume of poetry, Lyrical Ballads, *which changed the course of English poetry. In 1799, he and his sister Dorothy settled in Grasmere in the Lake District, where he married and was given the office of distributor of stamps. In 1843, he was appointed poet laureate.*

The Solitary Reaper

Behold her, single in the field,
Yon solitary Highland Lass!
Reaping and singing by herself;
Stop here, or gently pass!
Alone she cuts and binds the grain,   5
And sings a melancholy strain;
O listen! for the vale profound
Is overflowing with the sound.

No Nightingale did ever chant   10
More welcome notes to weary bands
Of travellers in some shady haunt,
Among Arabian sands:
A voice so thrilling ne'er was heard
In spring-time from the Cuckoo-bird,
Breaking the silence of the seas   15
Among the farthest Hebrides.

Will no one tell me what she sings?°—
Perhaps the plaintive numbers flow
For old, unhappy, far-off things,
And battles long ago: 20
Or is it some more humble lay,
Familiar matter of today?
Some natural sorrow, loss, of pain,
That has been, and may be again?

Whate'er the theme, the maiden sang   25
As if her song could have no ending;
I saw her singing at her work,
And o'er the sickle bending;—
I listened, motionless and still;
And, as I mounted up the hill,   30
The music in my heart I bore
Long after it was heard no more.

[1805]

¹⁷**Will . . . sings?** Wordsworth had read an account of a woman reaping. The author
had specified that the reaper sang in Erse, hence Wordsworth—imagining himself in the
scene—cannot understand the song.

Joining the Conversation: Critical Thinking and Writing

Why do people sometimes sing while they work? And why do people sometimes
sing *sad* songs?

CARL SANDBURG

*Born in Galesburg, Illinois, Carl Sandburg (1878–1967) was the son of Swedish
immigrants. His first book, a pamphlet of poems,* Reckless Ecstasy, *was published in
1904. His other books include* Chicago Poems *(1916),* Cornhuskers *(1918),* Smoke
and Steel *(1920), and* Slabs of the Sunburnt West *(1922). "Chicago," written in
1913, first published in 1914, and later included in* Chicago Poems, *shows his rugged realism and his tone of uplift.*

Chicago

Hog Butcher for the World,
Tool Maker, Stacker of Wheat,
Player with Railroads and the Nation's Freight Handler;
Stormy, husky, brawling,
City of the Big Shoulders: 5

They tell me you are wicked and I believe them, for I have seen your painted
    women under the gas lamps luring the farm boys.
And they tell me you are crooked and I answer: Yes, it is true I have seen
    the gunman kill and go free to kill again.

And they tell me you are brutal and my reply is: On the faces of women and
   children I have seen the marks of wanton hunger.
And having answered so I turn once more to those who sneer at this my city,
   and I give them back the sneer and say to them:
Come and show me another city with lifted head singing so proud to be
   alive and coarse and strong and cunning.   10
Flinging magnetic curses amid the toil of piling job on job, here is a tall bold
   slugger set vivid against the little soft cities;
Fierce as a dog with tongue lapping for action, cunning as a savage
   pitted against the wilderness,
   Bareheaded,
   Shoveling,
   Wrecking,   15
   Planning,
   Building, breaking, rebuilding,
Under the smoke, dust all over his mouth, laughing with white teeth,
Under the terrible burden of destiny laughing as a young man laughs,
Laughing even as an ignorant fighter laughs who has never lost a battle,   20
Bragging and laughing that under his wrist is the pulse, and under his ribs
   the heart of the people,
                         Laughing!
Laughing the stormy, husky, brawling laughter of Youth, half-naked,
   sweating, proud to be Hog Butcher, Tool Maker, Stacker of Wheat,
   Player with Railroads and Freight Handler to the Nation.

                                                                      [1914]

Joining the Conversation: Critical Thinking and Writing

1. Describe how, from the beginning to the end, you would read "Chicago" out
   loud.
2. In your view, which line or lines in the poem are the most expressive—that is,
   they express most effectively what Sandburg says that Chicago is?
3. Does Sandburg make Chicago a city where you would like to live?
4. After you have given careful study to Sandburg's poem, write a poem of your
   own in this style to a city that you know well. If you do not know a city well,
   write a poem about your hometown instead.

GARY SNYDER

*Gary Snyder, born in 1930, grew up on a farm north of Seattle, Washington, and
then in Portland, Oregon. By the age of fifteen, he was deeply concerned with indigenous cultures of the American Northwest. He then went to Reed College, working
during the summers in logging camps. When he moved to San Francisco, he became part of the Beat movement, which included Allen Ginsberg and Jack Kerouac.
(He is the hero of Kerouac's novel* The Dharma Bums.*) In 1956, in order to deepen
his understanding of Buddhism, he went to Japan, where he remained for ten years.
When he returned to the United States, he settled with his family in the foothills of the
northwestern Sierra Nevada. He is the author of several books of poetry, one of
which,* Turtle Island *(1974), won the Pulitzer Prize.*

Hay for the Horses

He had driven half the night
From far down San Joaquin
Through Mariposa, up the
Dangerous mountain roads,
And pulled in at eight a.m.   5
With his big truckload of hay
       behind the barn.
With winch and ropes and hooks
We stacked the bales up clean
To splintery redwood rafters   10
High in the dark, flecks of alfalfa
Whirling through shingle-cracks of light,
Itch of haydust in the
       sweaty shirt and shoes.
At lunchtime under Black oak   15
Out in the hot corral,
—The old mare nosing lunchpails,
Grasshoppers crackling in the weeds—
"I'm sixty-eight" he said,
"I first bucked hay when I was seventeen.   20
I thought, that day I started,
I sure would hate to do this all my life.
And dammit, that's just what
I've gone and done."

[1964]

Joining the Conversation: Critical Thinking and Writing

1. The speaker does not explicitly offer his opinion of the man who "had driven half the night," but do the first two sentences (lines 1–14) communicate at least a hint of an attitude?
2. The old man who speaks lines 19–24 sums up his life. He seems to regard it as wasted, but, as we hear his words, do we hear bitterness? Self-pity? What is our attitude toward him; how does it compare with that of the speaker of the poem?

Robert Hayden

Robert Hayden (1913–80) was born in Detroit, Michigan. His parents divorced when he was a child, and he was brought up by a neighboring family, whose name he adopted. In 1942, at the age of twenty-nine, he graduated from Detroit City College (now Wayne State University); he received an MA from the University of Michigan. He taught at Fisk University from 1946 to 1969 and after that, for the remainder of his life, at the University of Michigan. In 1979, he was appointed Consultant in Poetry to the Library of Congress, the first African American to hold the post.

Those Winter Sundays

Sundays too my father got up early
and put his clothes on in the blueblack cold,
then with cracked hands that ached
from labor in the weekday weather made
banked fires blaze. No one ever thanked him.   5

I'd wake and hear the cold splintering, breaking.
When the rooms were warm, he'd call,
and slowly I would rise and dress,
fearing the chronic angers of that house.

Speaking indifferently to him,   10
who had driven out the cold
and polished my good shoes as well.
What did I know, what did I know
of love's austere and lonely offices?

[1962]

Joining the Conversation: Critical Thinking and Writing

1. In line 1, what does the word "too" tell us about the father? What does it suggest about the speaker and the implied hearer of the poem?
2. How old do you believe the speaker was at the time he recalls in the second and third stanzas? What details suggest this age?
3. What is the meaning of "offices" in the last line? What does this word suggest that other words Hayden might have chosen do not?
4. What do you take to be the speaker's present attitude toward his father? What circumstances do you think prompted his memory of "Those Winter Sundays"?
5. In a page or two, try to get down the exact circumstances when you spoke "indifferently," or not at all, to someone who had deserved your gratitude.

SEAMUS HEANEY

For biographical information on Seamus Heaney, see page 356.

Digging

Between my finger and my thumb
The squat pen rests; snug as a gun.

Under my window, a clean rasping sound
When the spade sinks into gravelly ground:
My father, digging, I look down   5
Till his straining rump among the flowerbeds
Bends low, comes up twenty years away
Stooping in rhythm through potato drills
Where he was digging.
The coarse boot nestled on the lug, the shaft   10

Against the inside knee was levered firmly.
He rooted out tall tops, buried the bright edge deep
To scatter new potatoes that we picked
Loving their cool hardness in our hands.

By God, the old man could handle a spade.   15
Just like his old man.

My grandfather cut more turf in a day
Than any other man on Toner's bog.
Once I carried him milk in a bottle
Corked sloppily with paper. He straightened up   20
To drink it, then fell to right away
Nicking and slicing neatly, heaving sods
Over his shoulder, going down and down
For the good turf. Digging.

The cold smell of potato mould, the squelch and slap   25
Of soggy peat, the curt cuts of an edge
Through living roots awaken in my head.
But I've no spade to follow men like them.

Between my finger and my thumb
The squat pen rests.   30
I'll dig with it.

[1966]

Joining the Conversation: Critical Thinking and Writing

1. The poem ends with the speaker saying that he will "dig" with his pen. Given all the preceding lines, what will he dig?
2. The first lines compare the pen with a gun. What implications are suggested by this comparison?

JULIA ALVAREZ

The Latina author Julia Alvarez, born in 1950 in New York of Dominican descent, has written fiction, poetry, and nonfictional prose. Her books include the novel How the Garcia Girls Lost Their Accents *(1991), which tells the story of four sisters and their parents who emigrate from the Dominican Republic to the United States;* Something to Declare: Essays *(1998); and* Homecoming: New and Collected Poems *(1996), which include her first book of poetry,* Homecoming *(1984), as well as more recent work. The following poem is taken from that collection.*

Woman's Work

Who says a woman's work isn't high art?
She'd challenge as she scrubbed the bathroom tiles.
Keep house as if the address were your heart.

We'd clean the whole upstairs before we'd start
downstairs. I'd sigh, hearing my friends outside.   5
Doing her woman's work was a hard art

to practice when the summer sun would bar
the floor I swept till she was satisfied.
She kept me prisoner in her housebound heart.

She'd shine the tines of forks, the wheels of carts,   10
cut lacy lattices for all her pies.
Her woman's work was nothing less than art.

And, I, her masterpiece since I was smart,
was primed, praised, polished, scolded and advised
to keep a house much better than my heart.   15

I did not want to be her counterpart!
I struck out . . . but became my mother's child:
a woman working at home on her art,
housekeeping paper as if it were her heart.

                                                                  [1996]

Joining the Conversation: Critical Thinking and Writing

1. The poet explores the relationship between mother and daughter through the
   work that each performs. Describe this work, and, in particular, the lessons that
   the mother teaches through what she does and how she does it.
2. What is the meaning of line 3?
3. How do you interpret the phrase "I struck out"?
4. Do you feel inclined to argue for or against Alvarez's conception of "woman's
   work"? Please explain, and cite evidence from the poem.

MARGE PIERCY

For biographical information on Marge Piercy, see page 981.

To be of use

The people I love the best
jump into work head first
without dallying in the shallows
and swim off with sure strokes almost out of sight.
They seem to become natives of that element,   5
the black sleek heads of seals
bouncing like half-submerged balls.

I love people who harness themselves, an ox to a heavy cart,
who pull like water buffalo, with massive patience,
who strain in the mud and the muck to move things forward,   10
who do what has to be done, again and again.

I want to be with people who submerge
in the task, who go into the fields to harvest
and work in a row and pass the bags along,
who are not parlor generals and field deserters   15
but move in a common rhythm
when the food must come in or the fire be put out.

The work of the world is common as mud.
Botched, it smears the hands, crumbles to dust.
But the thing worth doing well done   20
has a shape that satisfies, clean and evident.
Greek amphoras for wine or oil,
Hopi vases that held corn, are put in museums
but you know they were made to be used.
The pitcher cries for water to carry   25
and a person for work that is real.

[1974]

Joining the Conversation: Critical Thinking and Writing

1. Write a short poem—perhaps seven lines, the length of Piercy's first stanza—
   beginning with Piercy's first line, "The people I love the best."
2. Suppose someone argued that Piercy's first stanza is the best and, moreover, that
   this stanza can stand by itself. How might you argue that the next three stanzas
   contribute to the poem, making a better poem than the first stanza by itself?

JIMMY SANTIAGO BACA

*Jimmy Santiago Baca, of Chicano and Apache descent, was
born in 1952. When he was two years old, his parents divorced, and a grandparent brought him up until he was five
years old, at which time he was placed in an orphanage in
New Mexico. He ran away when he was eleven years old, lived
on the streets, took drugs, and at the age of twenty was convicted of drug possession. In prison, he taught himself to read
and write, and he began to compose poetry. A fellow inmate
urged him to send some poems to* Mother Jones *magazine,
and the work was accepted. In 1979, Louisiana State University Press published a book of his poems,* Immigrants in Our
Own Land. *Since then, he has published several other books.*

So Mexicans Are Taking Jobs from Americans

O Yes? Do they come on horses
with rifles, and say,
          Ese gringo,° gimmee your job?
And do you, gringo, take off your ring,
drop your wallet into a blanket   5

---
³ **Ese gringo** Hey, whitey.

spread over the ground, and walk away?
I hear Mexicans are taking your jobs away.
Do they sneak into town at night,
and as you're walking home with a whore,
do they mug you, a knife at your throat,   10
saying, I want your job?

Even on TV, an asthmatic leader
crawls turtle heavy, leaning on an assistant,
and from a nest of wrinkles on his face,
a tongue paddles through flashing waves   15
of lightbulbs, of cameramen, rasping
"They're taking our jobs away."

Well, I've gone about trying to find them,
asking just where the hell are these fighters.

The rifles I hear sound in the night   20
are white farmers shooting blacks and browns
whose ribs I see jutting out
and starving children,
I see the poor marching for a little work,
I see small white farmers selling out   25
to clean-suited farmers living in New York,
who've never been on a farm,
don't know the look of a hoof or the smell
of a woman's body bending all day long in fields.

I see this, and I hear only a few people   30
got all the money in this world, the rest
count their pennies to buy bread and butter.

Below that cool green sea of money,
millions and millions of people fight to live,
search for pearls in the darkest depths   35
of their dreams, hold their breath for years
trying to cross poverty to just having something.

The children are dead already. We are killing them,
that is what America should be saying;
on TV, in the streets, in offices, should be saying,   40
"We aren't giving the children a chance to live."

Mexicans are taking our jobs, they say instead.
What they really say is, let them die,
and the children too.

[1979]

Joining the Conversation: Critical Thinking and Writing

1. When you read the title, what was your response to it? What happened to this
   first response as you read and then reread the poem?
2. To whom is the poem addressed?

3. Is the speaker angry? If so, is the speaker too angry?
4. Identify and comment on the section of the poem that you think is the most effective. Is the poem effective throughout, or is there a section or sections where, in your view, it is not?
5. One critic, in praise of the poem, said that in it Baca "uses words as a weapon." Explain what you think this phrase means. Does it strike you as a good insight about the poem? Point to evidence in the text to support your argument.
6. Prepare an essay of one to two pages in which you argue that Baca's poem should be included on the required reading list for first-year high school students. Then prepare an essay of the same length in which you argue that it should not.

PLAYS

JANE MARTIN

Jane Martin has never given an interview and has never been photographed. The name presumably is the pseudonym of a writer who works with the Actors Theatre of Louisville, Kentucky. Rodeo *is one of a collection of monologues,* Talking With . . . , *first presented at the Actors Theatre during the 1981 Humana Festival of New American Plays. Jane Martin has also written full-length plays.*

Rodeo

A young woman in her late twenties sits working on a piece of tack.[1] Beside her is a Lone Star beer in the can. As the lights come up we hear the last verse of a Tanya Tucker song or some other female country-western vocalist. She is wearing old worn jeans and boots plus a long-sleeved workshirt with the sleeves rolled up. She works until the song is over and then speaks.

BIG EIGHT: Shoot—Rodeo's just goin' to hell in a handbasket. Rodeo used to be somethin'. I loved it. I did. Once Daddy an' a bunch of 'em was foolin' around with some old bronc over to our place and this ol' red nose named Cinch got bucked off and my Daddy hooted and said he had him a nine-year-old girl, namely me, wouldn't have no damn trouble cowboyin' that horse. Well, he put me on up there, stuck that ridin' rein in my hand, gimme a kiss, and said, "Now there's only one thing t' remember Honey Love, if ya fall off you jest don't come home." Well I stayed up. You gotta stay on a bronc eight seconds. Otherwise the ride don't count. So from that day on my daddy called me Big Eight. Heck! That's all the name I got anymore . . . Big Eight.

Used to be fer cowboys, the rodeo did. Do it in some open field, folks would pull their cars and pick-ups round it, sit on the hoods, some ranch hand'd bulldog him some rank steer and everybody'd wave their hats and call him by name. Ride us some buckin' stock, rope a few calves, git throwed off a bull, and then we'd jest git us to a bar and tell each other lies about how good we were.

Used to be a family thing. Wooly Billy Tilson and Tammy Lee had them five kids on the circuit. Three boys, two girls and Wooly and Tammy. Wasn't no

---

[1] **tack** harness for a horse, including the bridle and saddle.

two-beer rodeo in Oklahoma didn't have a Tilson entered. Used to call the oldest girl Tits. Tits Tilson. Never seen a girl that top-heavy could ride so well. Said she only fell off when the gravity got her. Cowboys used to say if she landed face down you could plant two young trees in the holes she'd leave. Ha! Tits Tilson.

Used to be people came to a rodeo had a horse of their own back home. Farm people, ranch people—lord, they knew what they were lookin' at. Knew a good ride from a bad ride, *knew* hard from easy. You broke some bones er spent the day eatin' dirt, at least ya got appreciated.

Now they bought the rodeo. Them. Coca-Cola, Pepsi Cola, Marlboro damn cigarettes. You know the ones I mean. Them. Hire some New York faggot t' sit on some ol' stuffed horse in front of a sagebrush photo n' smoke that junk. Hell, tobacco wasn't made to smoke, honey, it was made to chew. Lord wanted ya filled up with smoke he would've set ya on fire. Damn it gets me!

There's some guy in a banker's suit runs the rodeo now. Got him a pinky ring and a digital watch, honey. Told us we oughta have a watchamacallit, choriographus or somethin', ol' ballbuster used to be with the Ice damn Capades. Wants us to ride around dressed up like Mickey Mouse, Pluto, crap like that. Told me I had to haul my butt through the barrel race done up like Minnie damn Mouse in a tu-tu. Huh uh, honey! Them people is so screwed-up they probably eat what they run over in the road.

Listen, they got the clowns wearin' Astronaut suits! I ain't lyin'. You know what a rodeo clown does! You go down, fall off whatever—the clown runs in front of the bull so's ya don't git stomped. Pinstripes, he got 'em in space suits tellin' jokes on a microphone. First horse see 'em, done up like the Star Wars went crazy. Best buckin' horse on the circuit, name of Piss 'N' Vinegar, took one look at them clowns, had him a heart attack and died. Cowboy was ridin' him got hisself squashed. Twelve hundred pounds of coronary arrest jes fell right through 'em. Blam! Vio con dios. Crowd thought that was funnier than the astronauts. I swear it won't be long before they're strappin' ice-skates on the ponies. Big crowds now. Ain't hardly no ranch people, no farm people, nobody I know. Buncha disco babies and deevorce lawyers—designer jeans and day-glo Stetsons. Hell, the whole bunch of 'em wears French perfume. Oh it smells like money now! Got it on the cable T and V—hey, you know what, when ya rodeo yer just bound to kick yerself up some dust—well now, seems like that fogs up the ol' TV camera, so they told us a while back that from now on we was gonna ride on some new stuff called Astro-dirt. Dust free. Artificial damn dirt, honey. Lord have mercy.

Banker Suit called me in the other day said "Lurlene . . ." "Hold it," I said. "Who's this Lurlene? Round here they call me Big Eight." "Well, Big Eight," he said, "my name's Wallace." "Well that's a real surprise t' me," I said, "cause aroun' here everybody jes calls you Dumbass." My, he laughed real big, slapped his big ol' desk, an' then he said I wasn't suitable for the rodeo no more. Said they was lookin' fer another type, somethin' a little more in the showgirl line, like the Dallas Cowgirls maybe. Said the ridin' and ropin' wasn't the thing no more. Talked on about floats, costumes, dancin' choreogaphy. If I was a man I woulda pissed on his shoe. Said he'd give me a lifetime pass though. Said I could come to his rodeo any time I wanted.

Rodeo used to be people ridin' horses for the pleasure of people who rode horses—made you feel good about what you could do. Rodeo wasn't worth no money to nobody. Money didn't have nothing to do with it! Used to be seven Tilsons riding in the rodeo. Wouldn't none of 'em dress up like Donald damn Duck so they quit. That there's the law of gravity!

There's a bunch of assholes in this country sneak around until they see ya havin' fun and then they buy the fun and start in sellin' it. See, they figure if ya love it, they can sell it. Well you look out, honey! They want to make them a dollar out of what you love. Dress *you* up like Minnie Mouse. Sell your rodeo. Turn *yer* pleasure into Ice damn Capades. You hear what I'm sayin'? You're jus' merchandise to them, sweetie. You're jus' merchandise to them.
    Blackout.

[1981]

Joining the Conversation: Critical Thinking and Writing

1. Try to recall your response to the title and the first paragraph or two of *Rodeo*. Did Big Eight fit your view (perhaps a stereotypical view) of what a cowgirl might sound like?
2. Reread *Rodeo*, this time paying attention not only to what Big Eight says but also to your responses to her. By the end of the play, has she become a some-what more complicated figure than she seems to be after the first paragraph, or does she seem the same? Do you find that you become increasingly sympa-thetic? Increasingly unsympathetic? Or does your opinion not change?
3. If you have ever seen a rodeo, do you think Big Eight's characterization is on the mark? Or is she simply bitter because she has been fired?
4. If a local theater group were staging *Rodeo,* presumably with some other short plays, would you go to see it? Why, or why not?
5. If you were directing a production of *Rodeo,* would you keep the actor seated, or would you have her get up, move around the stage, perhaps hang up one piece of tack and take down another? Why?
6. If you were directing *Rodeo,* would you tell Big Eight that her speech is essentially an interior monologue—a soliloquy—or would you tell her that she is speaking directly to the audience—that the audience is, collectively, a character in the play?
7. The play ends with a stage direction, "Blackout"; that is, the stage suddenly darkens. One director of a recent production, however, chose to end with a "fade out": The illumination decreased slowly by means of dimmers (mechan-ical devices that regulate the intensity of a lighting unit). If you were directing a production of *Rodeo,* what sort of lighting would you use at the end? Why?

ARTHUR MILLER

Arthur Miller (1915–2005) was born in New York. In 1938, he graduated from the University of Michigan, where he won prizes for drama. Six years later, he had his first Broadway production, The Man Who Had All the Luck, *but the play was unlucky and closed after four days. By the time of his first com-mercial success,* All My Sons *(1947), he had already written several plays. In 1949, he won a Pulitzer Prize for* Death of a Salesman *and achieved an international reputation. Among his other works are an adaptation (1950) of Ibsen's* Enemy of the People *and a play about the Salem witch trials,* The Crucible *(1953), both containing political implications, and* The Misfits *(1961, a screenplay), After the Fall *(1964), and* Incident at Vichy *(1965).*

Death of a Salesman

Certain Private Conversations in Two Acts and a Requiem

CHARACTERS

WILLY LOMAN
LINDA
BIFF
HAPPY
BERNARD
THE WOMAN
CHARLEY
UNCLE BEN
HOWARD WAGNER
JENNY
STANLEY
MISS FORSYTHE
LETTA

SCENE: The action takes place in WILLY LOMAN's house and yard and in various places he visits in the New York and Boston of today.

ACT 1

A melody is heard, played upon a flute. It is small and fine, telling of grass and trees and the horizon. The curtain rises.

Before us is the Salesman's house. We are aware of towering, angular shapes behind it, surrounding it on all sides. Only the blue light of the sky falls upon the house and forestage; the surrounding area shows an angry glow of orange. As more light appears, we see a solid vault of apartment houses around the small, fragile-seeming home. An air of the dream clings to the place, a dream rising out of reality. The kitchen at center seems actual enough, for there is a kitchen table with three chairs, and a refrigerator. But no other fixtures are seen. At the back of the kitchen there is a draped entrance, which leads to the living room. To the right of the kitchen, on a level raised two feet, is a bedroom furnished only with a brass bedstead and a straight chair. On a shelf over the bed a silver athletic trophy stands. A window opens onto the apartment house at the side.

Behind the kitchen, on a level raised six and a half feet, is the boys' bedroom, at present barely visible. Two beds are dimly seen, and at the back of the room a dormer window. (This bedroom is above the unseen living room.) At the left a stairway curves up to it from the kitchen.

The entire setting is wholly or, in some places, partially transparent. The roof-line of the house is one-dimensional; under and over it we see the apartment buildings. Before the house lies an apron, curving beyond the forestage into the orchestra. This forward area serves as the back yard as well as the locale of all WILLY's imaginings and of his city scenes. Whenever the action is in the present the actors observe the imaginary wall-lines, entering the house only through its door at the left. But in the scenes of the past these boundaries are broken, and characters enter or leave a room by stepping "through" a wall onto the forestage.

From the right, WILLY LOMAN, *the Salesman, enters, carrying two large sample cases. The flute plays on. He hears but is not aware of it. He is past sixty years of age, dressed quietly. Even as he crosses the stage to the doorway of the house, his exhaustion is apparent. He unlocks the door, comes into the kitchen, and thankfully lets his burden down, feeling the soreness of his palms. A word-sigh escapes his lips—it might be "Oh, boy, oh, boy." He closes the door, then carries his cases out into the living room, through the draped kitchen doorway.*

LINDA, *his wife, has stirred in her bed at the right. She gets out and puts on a robe, listening. Most often jovial, she has developed an iron repression of her exceptions to* WILLY'S *behavior—she more than loves him, she admires him, as though his mercurial nature, his temper, his massive dreams and little cruelties, served her only as sharp reminders of the turbulent longings within him, longings which she shares but lacks the temperament to utter and follow to their end.*

LINDA (*hearing* WILLY *outside the bedroom, calls with some trepidation*): Willy!

WILLY: It's all right. I came back.

LINDA: Why? What happened? (*Slight pause.*) Did something happen, Willy?

WILLY: No, nothing happened.

LINDA: You didn't smash the car, did you?

WILLY (*with casual irritation*): I said nothing happened. Didn't you hear me?

LINDA: Don't you feel well?

WILLY: I'm tired to the death. (*The flute has faded away. He sits on the bed beside her, a little numb.*) I couldn't make it. I just couldn't make it, Linda.

LINDA (*very carefully, delicately*): Where were you all day? You look terrible.

WILLY: I got as far as a little above Yonkers. I stopped for a cup of coffee. Maybe it was the coffee.

LINDA: What?

WILLY (*after a pause*): I suddenly couldn't drive any more. The car kept going off onto the shoulder, y'know?

LINDA (*helpfully*): Oh. Maybe it was the steering again. I don't think Angelo knows the Studebaker.

Dustin Hoffman as Willy Loman, and John Malkovich as Biff, in the 1984 production.

WILLY: No, it's me, it's me. Suddenly I realize I'm goin' sixty miles an hour and I don't remember the last five minutes. I'm—I can't seem to—keep my mind to it.

LINDA: Maybe it's your glasses. You never went for your new glasses.

WILLY: No, I see everything. I came back ten miles an hour. It took me nearly four hours from Yonkers.

LINDA (*resigned*): Well, you'll just have to take a rest, Willy, you can't continue this way.

WILLY: I just got back from Florida.

LINDA: But you didn't rest your mind. Your mind is overactive, and the mind is what counts, dear.

WILLY: I'll start out in the morning. Maybe I'll feel better in the morning. (*She is taking off his shoes.*) These goddam arch supports are killing me.

LINDA: Take an aspirin. Should I get you an aspirin? It'll soothe you.

WILLY (*with wonder*): I was driving along, you understand? And I was fine. I was even observing the scenery. You can imagine, me looking at scenery, on the road every week of my life. But it's so beautiful up there, Linda, the trees are so thick, and the sun is warm. I opened the windshield and just let the warm air bathe over me. And then all of a sudden I'm goin' off the road! I'm tellin' ya, I absolutely forgot I was driving. If I'd've gone the other way over the white line I might've killed somebody. So I went on again—and five minutes later I'm dreamin' again, and I nearly . . . (*He presses two fingers against his eyes.*) I have such thoughts, I have such strange thoughts.

LINDA: Willy, dear. Talk to them again. There's no reason why you can't work in New York.

WILLY: They don't need me in New York. I'm the New England man. I'm vital in New England.

LINDA: But you're sixty years old. They can't expect you to keep traveling every week.

WILLY: I'll have to send a wire to Portland. I'm supposed to see Brown and Morrison tomorrow morning at ten o'clock to show the line. Goddammit, I could sell them! (*He starts putting on his jacket.*)

LINDA (*taking the jacket from him*): Why don't you go down to the place tomorrow and tell Howard you've simply got to work in New York? You're too accommodating, dear.

WILLY: If old man Wagner was alive I'd a been in charge of New York now! That man was a prince, he was a masterful man. But that boy of his, that Howard, he don't appreciate. When I went north the first time, the Wagner Company didn't know where New England was!

LINDA: Why don't you tell those things to Howard, dear?

WILLY (*encouraged*): I will, I definitely will. Is there any cheese?

LINDA: I'll make you a sandwich.

WILLY: No, go to sleep. I'll take some milk. I'll be up right away. The boys in?

LINDA: They're sleeping. Happy took Biff on a date tonight.

WILLY (*interested*): That so?

LINDA: It was so nice to see them shaving together, one behind the other, in the bathroom. And going out together. You notice? The whole house smells of shaving lotion.

WILLY: Figure it out. Work a lifetime to pay off a house. You finally own it, and there's nobody to live in it.

LINDA: Well, dear, life is a casting off. It's always that way.

WILLY: No, no, some people—some people accomplish something. Did Biff say anything after I went this morning?

LINDA: You shouldn't have criticized him, Willy, especially after he just got off the train. You mustn't lose your temper with him.

WILLY: When the hell did I lose my temper? I simply asked him if he was making any money. Is that a criticism?

LINDA: But, dear, how could he make any money?

WILLY (*worried and angered*): There's such an undercurrent in him. He became a moody man. Did he apologize when I left this morning?

LINDA: He was crestfallen, Willy. You know how he admires you. I think if he finds himself, then you'll both be happier and not fight any more.

WILLY: How can he find himself on a farm? Is that a life? A farm hand? In the beginning, when he was young, I thought, well, a young man, it's good for him to tramp around, take a lot of different jobs. But it's more than ten years now and he has yet to make thirty-five dollars a week!

LINDA: He's finding himself, Willy.

WILLY: Not finding yourself at the age of thirty-four is a disgrace!

LINDA: Shh!

WILLY: The trouble is he's lazy, goddammit!

LINDA: Willy, please!

WILLY: Biff is a lazy bum!

LINDA: They're sleeping. Get something to eat. Go on down.

WILLY: Why did he come home? I would like to know what brought him home.

LINDA: I don't know. I think he's still lost, Willy. I think he's very lost.

WILLY: Biff Loman is lost. In the greatest country in the world a young man with such—personal attractiveness, gets lost. And such a hard worker. There's one thing about Biff—he's not lazy.

LINDA: Never.

WILLY (*with pity and resolve*): I'll see him in the morning; I'll have a nice talk with him. I'll get him a job selling. He could be big in no time. My God! Remember how they used to follow him around in high school? When he smiled at one of them their faces lit up. When he walked down the street . . . (*He loses himself in reminiscences.*)

LINDA (*trying to bring him out of it*): Willy, dear, I got a new kind of American-type cheese today. It's whipped.

WILLY: Why do you get American when I like Swiss?

LINDA: I just thought you'd like a change . . . .

WILLY: I don't want a change! I want Swiss cheese. Why am I always being contradicted?

LINDA (*with a covering laugh*): I thought it would be a surprise.

WILLY: Why don't you open a window in here, for God's sake?

LINDA (*with infinite patience*): They're all open, dear.

WILLY: The way they boxed us in here. Bricks and windows, windows and bricks.

LINDA: We should've bought the land next door.

WILLY: The street is lined with cars. There's not a breath of fresh air in the neighborhood. The grass don't grow any more, you can't raise a carrot in the back yard. They should've had a law against apartment houses. Remember those two beautiful elm trees out there? When I and Biff hung the swing between them?

LINDA: Yeah, like being a million miles from the city.

WILLY: They should've arrested the builder for cutting those down. They massacred the neighborhood. (*Lost.*) More and more I think of those days, Linda. This time of year it was lilac and wisteria. And then the peonies would come out, and the daffodils. What fragrance in this room!

LINDA: Well, after all, people had to move somewhere.

WILLY: No, there's more people now.

LINDA: I don't think there's more people. I think . . .

WILLY: There's more people! That's what's ruining this country! Population is getting out of control. The competition is maddening! Smell the stink from that apartment house! And another one on the other side . . . How can they whip cheese?

On WILLY'S *last line,* BIFF *and* HAPPY *raise themselves up in their beds, listening.*

LINDA: Go down, try it. And be quiet.

WILLY (*turning to* LINDA, *guiltily*): You're not worried about me, are you, sweetheart?

BIFF: What's the matter?

HAPPY: Listen!

LINDA: You've got too much on the ball to worry about.

WILLY: You're my foundation and my support, Linda.

LINDA: Just try to relax, dear. You make mountains out of molehills.

WILLY: I won't fight with him any more. If he wants to go back to Texas, let him go.

LINDA: He'll find his way.

WILLY: Sure. Certain men just don't get started till later in life. Like Thomas Edison, I think. Or B. F. Goodrich. One of them was deaf. (*He starts for the bedroom doorway.*) I'll put my money on Biff.

LINDA: And Willy—if it's warm Sunday we'll drive in the country. And we'll open the windshield, and take lunch.

WILLY: No, the windshields don't open on the new cars.

LINDA: But you opened it today.

WILLY: Me? I didn't. (*He stops.*) Now isn't that peculiar! Isn't that a remarkable . . . (*He breaks off in amazement and fright as the flute is heard distantly.*)

LINDA: What, darling?

WILLY: That is the most remarkable thing.

LINDA: What, dear?

WILLY: I was thinking of the Chevvy. (*Slight pause.*) Nineteen twenty-eight . . . when I had that red Chevvy . . . (*Breaks off.*) That funny? I coulda sworn I was driving that Chevvy today.

LINDA: Well, that's nothing. Something must've reminded you.

WILLY: Remarkable. Ts. Remember those days? The way Biff used to simonize that car? The dealer refused to believe there was eighty thousand miles on it. (*He shakes his head.*) Heh! (*To Linda.*) Close your eyes, I'll be right up. (*He walks out of the bedroom.*)

HAPPY (*to* BIFF): Jesus, maybe he smashed up the car again!

LINDA (*calling after* WILLY): Be careful on the stairs, dear! The cheese is on the middle shelf. (*She turns, goes over to the bed, takes his jacket, and goes out of the bedroom.*)

Light has risen on the boys' room. Unseen, WILLY *is heard talking to himself; "Eighty thousand miles," and a little laugh.* BIFF *gets out of bed, comes downstage a bit, and stands attentively.* BIFF *is two years older than his brother* HAPPY, *well built, but in these days bears a worn air and seems less self-assured. He has succeeded less, and his dreams are stronger and less acceptable than* HAPPY*'s.* HAPPY *is tall, powerfully made. Sexuality is like a visible color on him, or a scent that many women have discovered. He, like his brother, is lost, but in a different way, for he has never allowed himself to turn his face toward defeat and is thus more confused and hard-skinned, although seemingly more content.*

HAPPY (*getting out of bed*): He's going to get his license taken away if he keeps that up. I'm getting nervous about him, y'know, Biff?

BIFF: His eyes are going.

HAPPY: No, I've driven with him. He sees all right. He just doesn't keep his mind on it. I drove into the city with him last week. He stops at a green light and then it turns red and he goes. (*He laughs.*)

BIFF: Maybe he's color-blind.

HAPPY: Pop? Why he's got the finest eye for color in the business. You know that.

BIFF (*sitting down on his bed*): I'm going to sleep.

HAPPY: You're not still sour on Dad, are you, Biff?

BIFF: He's all right, I guess.

WILLY (*underneath them, in the living room*): Yes, sir, eighty thousand miles—eighty-two thousand!

BIFF: You smoking?

HAPPY (*holding out a pack of cigarettes*): Want one?

BIFF (*taking a cigarette*): I can never sleep when I smell it.

WILLY: What a simonizing job, heh!

HAPPY (*with deep sentiment*): Funny, Biff, y'know? Us sleeping in here again? The old beds. (*He pats his bed affectionately.*) All the talk that went across those beds, huh? Our whole lives.

BIFF: Yeah. Lotta dreams and plans.

HAPPY (*with a deep and masculine laugh*): About five hundred women would like to know what was said in this room. (*They share a soft laugh.*)

BIFF: Remember that big Betsy something—what the hell was her name—over on Bushwick Avenue?

HAPPY (*combing his hair*): With the collie dog!

BIFF: That's the one. I got you in there, remember?

HAPPY: Yeah, that was my first time—I think. Boy, there was a pig. (*They laugh, almost crudely.*) You taught me everything I know about women. Don't forget that.

BIFF: I bet you forgot how bashful you used to be. Especially with girls.

HAPPY: Oh, I still am, Biff.

BIFF: Oh, go on.

HAPPY: I just control it, that's all. I think I got less bashful and you got more so. What happened, Biff? Where's the old humor, the old confidence? (*He shakes* BIFF*'s knee.* BIFF *gets up and moves restlessly about the room.*) What's the matter?

BIFF: Why does Dad mock me all the time?

HAPPY: He's not mocking you, he . . .

BIFF: Everything I say there's a twist of mockery on his face. I can't get near him.

HAPPY: He just wants you to make good, that's all. I wanted to talk to you about Dad for a long time, Biff. Something's—happening to him. He—talks to himself.

BIFF: I noticed that this morning. But he always mumbled.

HAPPY: But not so noticeable. It got so embarrassing I sent him to Florida. And you know something? Most of the time he's talking to you.

BIFF: What's he say about me?

HAPPY: I can't make it out.

BIFF: What's he say about me?

HAPPY: I think the fact that you're not settled, that you're still kind of up in the air . . .

BIFF: There's one or two other things depressing him, Happy.

HAPPY: What do you mean?

BIFF: Never mind. Just don't lay it all to me.

HAPPY: But I think if you just got started—I mean—is there any future for you out there?

BIFF: I tell ya, Hap, I don't know what the future is. I don't know—what I'm supposed to want.

HAPPY: What do you mean?

BIFF: Well, I spent six or seven years after high school trying to work myself up. Shipping clerk, salesman, business of one kind or another. And it's a measly manner of existence. To get on that subway on the hot mornings in summer. To devote your whole life to keeping stock, or making phone calls, or selling or buying. To suffer fifty weeks of the year for the sake of a two-week vacation, when all you really desire is to be outdoors, with your shirt off. And always to have to get ahead of the next fella. And still—that's how you build a future.

HAPPY: Well, you really enjoy it on a farm? Are you content out there?

BIFF (*with rising agitation*): Hap, I've had twenty or thirty different kinds of jobs since I left home before the war, and it always turns out the same. I just realized it lately. In Nebraska when I herded cattle, and the Dakotas, and Arizona, and now in Texas. It's why I came home now, I guess, because I realized it. This farm I work on, it's spring there now, see? And they've got about fifteen new colts. There's nothing more inspiring or—beautiful than the sight of a mare and a new colt. And it's cool there now, see? Texas is cool now, and it's spring. And whenever spring comes to where I am, I suddenly get the feeling, my God, I'm not gettin' anywhere! What the hell am I doing, playing around with horses, twenty-eight dollars a week! I'm thirty-four years old, I oughta be makin' my future. That's when I come running home. And now, I get here, and I don't know what to do with myself. (*After a pause.*) I've always made a point of not wasting my life, and everytime I come back here I know that all I've done is to waste my life.

HAPPY: You're a poet, you know that, Biff? You're a—you're an idealist!

BIFF: No, I'm mixed up very bad. Maybe I oughta get married. Maybe I oughta get stuck into something. Maybe that's my trouble. I'm like a boy. I'm not married, I'm not in business, I just—I'm like a boy. Are you content, Hap? You're a success, aren't you? Are you content?

HAPPY: Hell, no!

BIFF: Why? You're making money, aren't you?

HAPPY (*moving about with energy, expressiveness*): All I can do now is wait for the merchandise manager to die. And suppose I get to be merchandise manager? He's a good friend of mine, and he just built a terrific estate on Long Island. And he lived there about two months and sold it, and now he's building another one. He can't enjoy it once it's finished. And I know that's just what I would do. I don't know what the hell I'm workin' for. Sometimes I sit in my apartment—all alone. And I think of the rent I'm paying. And it's crazy. But then, it's what I always wanted. My own apartment, a car, and plenty of women. And still, goddammit, I'm lonely.

BIFF (*with enthusiasm*): Listen, why don't you come out West with me?

HAPPY: You and I, heh?

BIFF: Sure, maybe we could buy a ranch. Raise cattle, use our muscles. Men built like we are should be working out in the open.

HAPPY (*avidly*): The Loman Brothers, heh?

BIFF (*with vast affection*): Sure, we'd be known all over the counties!

HAPPY (*enthralled*): That's what I dream about, Biff. Sometimes I want to just rip my clothes off in the middle of the store and outbox that goddam merchandise manager. I mean I can outbox, outrun, and outlift anybody in that store, and I have to take orders from those common, petty sons-of-bitches till I can't stand it any more.

BIFF: I'm tellin' you, kid, if you were with me I'd be happy out there.

HAPPY (*enthused*): See, Biff, everybody around me is so false that I'm constantly lowering my ideals . . .

BIFF: Baby, together we'd stand up for one another, we'd have someone to trust.

HAPPY: If I were around you . . .

BIFF: Hap, the trouble is we weren't brought up to grub for money. I don't know how to do it.

HAPPY: Neither can I!

BIFF: Then let's go!

HAPPY: The only thing is—what can you make out there?

BIFF: But look at your friend. Builds an estate and then hasn't the peace of mind to live in it.

HAPPY: Yeah, but when he walks into the store the waves part in front of him. That's fifty-two thousand dollars a year coming through the revolving door, and I got more in my pinky finger than he's got in his head.

BIFF: Yeah, but you just said . . .

HAPPY: I gotta show some of those pompous, self-important executives over there that Hap Loman can make the grade. I want to walk into the store the way he walks in. Then I'll go with you, Biff. We'll be together yet, I swear. But take those two we had tonight. Now weren't they gorgeous creatures?

BIFF: Yeah, yeah, most gorgeous I've had in years.

HAPPY: I get that any time I want, Biff. Whenever I feel disgusted. The only trouble is, it gets like bowling or something. I just keep knockin' them over and it doesn't mean anything. You still run around a lot?

BIFF: Naa. I'd like to find a girl—steady, somebody with substance.

HAPPY: That's what I long for.

BIFF: Go on! You'd never come home.

HAPPY: I would! Somebody with character, with resistance! Like Mom, y'know? You're gonna call me a bastard when I tell you this. That girl Charlotte I was with tonight is engaged to be married in five weeks. (*He tries on his new hat.*)

BIFF: No kiddin'!

HAPPY: Sure, the guy's in line for the vice-presidency of the store. I don't know what gets into me, maybe I just have an over-developed sense of competition or something, but I went and ruined her, and furthermore I can't get rid of her. And he's the third executive I've done that to. Isn't that a crummy characteristic? And to top it all, I go to their weddings! (*Indignantly, but laughing.*) Like I'm not supposed to take bribes. Manufacturers offer me a hundred-dollar bill now and then to throw an order their way. You know how honest I am, but it's like this girl, see. I hate myself for it. Because I don't want the girl, and, still, I take it and—I love it!

BIFF: Let's go to sleep.

HAPPY: I guess we didn't settle anything, heh?

BIFF: I just got one idea that I think I'm going to try.

HAPPY: What's that?

BIFF: Remember Bill Oliver?

HAPPY: Sure, Oliver is very big now. You want to work for him again?

BIFF: No, but when I quit he said something to me. He put his arm on my shoulder, and he said, "Biff, if you ever need anything, come to me."

HAPPY: I remember that. That sounds good.

BIFF: I think I'll go to see him. If I could get ten thousand or even seven or eight thousand dollars I could buy a beautiful ranch.

HAPPY: I bet he'd back you. 'Cause he thought highly of you, Biff. I mean, they all do. You're well liked, Biff. That's why I say to come back here, and we both have the apartment. And I'm tellin' you, Biff, any babe you want . . .

BIFF: No, with a ranch I could do the work I like and still be something. I just wonder though. I wonder if Oliver still thinks I stole that carton of basketballs.

HAPPY: Oh, he probably forgot that long ago. It's almost ten years. You're too sensitive. Anyway, he didn't really fire you.

BIFF: Well, I think he was going to. I think that's why I quit. I was never sure whether he knew or not. I know he thought the world of me, though. I was the only one he'd let lock up the place.

WILLY (*below*): You gonna wash the engine, Biff?

HAPPY: Shh!

  BIFF *looks at* HAPPY, *who is gazing down, listening.* WILLY *is mumbling in the parlor.*

HAPPY: You hear that?

  They listen. WILLY *laughs warmly.*

BIFF (*growing angry*): Doesn't he know Mom can hear that?

WILLY: Don't get your sweater dirty, Biff!

  A look of pain crosses BIFF'S *face.*

HAPPY: Isn't that terrible? Don't leave again, will you? You'll find a job here. You gotta stick around. I don't know what to do about him, it's getting embarrassing.

WILLY: What a simonizing job!

BIFF: Mom's hearing that!

WILLY: No kiddin', Biff, you got a date? Wonderful!

HAPPY: Go on to sleep. But talk to him in the morning, will you?

BIFF (*reluctantly getting into bed*): With her in the house. Brother!

HAPPY (*getting into bed*): I wish you'd have a good talk with him.

  The light on their room begins to fade.

BIFF (*to himself in bed*): That selfish, stupid . . .

HAPPY: Sh . . . Sleep, Biff.

Their light is out. Well before they have finished speaking, WILLY'S *form is dimly seen below in the darkened kitchen. He opens the refrigerator, searches in there, and takes out a bottle of milk. The apartment houses are fading out, and the entire house and surroundings become covered with leaves. Music insinuates itself as the leaves appear.*

WILLY: Just wanna be careful with those girls, Biff, that's all. Don't make any promises. No promises of any kind. Because a girl, y'know, they always believe what you tell 'em, and you're very young, Biff, you're too young to be talking seriously to girls.

Light rises on the kitchen. WILLY, *talking, shuts the refrigerator door and comes downstage to the kitchen table. He pours milk into a glass. He is totally immersed in himself, smiling faintly.*

WILLY: Too young entirely, Biff. You want to watch your schooling first. Then when you're all set, there'll be plenty of girls for a boy like you. *(He smiles broadly at a kitchen chair.)* That so? The girls pay for you? *(He laughs.)* Boy, you must really be makin' a hit.

WILLY *is gradually addressing—physically—a point offstage, speaking through the wall of the kitchen, and his voice has been rising in volume to that of a normal conversation.*

WILLY: I been wondering why you polish the car so careful. Ha! Don't leave the hubcaps, boys. Get the chamois to the hubcaps. Happy, use newspaper on the windows, it's the easiest thing. Show him how to do it, Biff! You see, Happy? Pad it up, use it like a pad. That's it, that's it, good work. You're doin' all right, Hap. *(He pauses, then nods in approbation for a few seconds, then looks upward.)* Biff, first thing we gotta do when we get time is clip that big branch over the house. Afraid it's gonna fall in a storm and hit the roof. Tell you what. We get a rope and sling her around, and then we climb up there with a couple of saws and take her down. Soon as you finish the car, boys, I wanna see ya. I got a surprise for you, boys.
BIFF *(offstage)*: Whatta ya got, Dad?
WILLY: No, you finish first. Never leave a job till you're finished—remember that. *(Looking toward the "big trees.")* Biff, up in Albany I saw a beautiful hammock. I think I'll buy it next trip, and we'll hang it right between those two elms. Wouldn't that be something? Just swingin' there under those branches. Boy, that would be . . .

Young BIFF *and Young* HAPPY *appear from the direction* WILLY *was addressing.* HAPPY *carries rags and a pail of water.* BIFF, *wearing a sweater with a block "S," carries a football.*

BIFF *(pointing in the direction of the car offstage)*: How's that, Pop, professional?
WILLY: Terrific. Terrific job, boys. Good work, Biff.
HAPPY: Where's the surprise, Pop?
WILLY: In the back seat of the car.
HAPPY: Boy! *(He runs off.)*
BIFF: What is it, Dad? Tell me, what'd you buy?
WILLY *(laughing, cuffs him)*: Never mind, something I want you to have.

BIFF (*turns and starts off*): What is it, Hap?

HAPPY (*offstage*): It's a punching bag!

BIFF: Oh, Pop!

WILLY: It's got Gene Tunney's signature on it!

 HAPPY *runs onstage with a punching bag.*

BIFF: Gee, how'd you know we wanted a punching bag?

WILLY: Well, it's the finest thing for the timing.

HAPPY (*lies down on his back and pedals with his feet*): I'm losing weight, you notice, Pop?

WILLY (*to* HAPPY): Jumping rope is good too.

BIFF: Did you see the new football I got?

WILLY (*examining the ball*): Where'd you get a new ball?

BIFF: The coach told me to practice my passing.

WILLY: That so? And he gave you the ball, heh?

BIFF: Well, I borrowed it from the locker room. (*He laughs confidentially.*)

WILLY (*laughing with him at the theft*): I want you to return that.

HAPPY: I told you he wouldn't like it!

BIFF (*angrily*): Well, I'm bringing it back!

WILLY (*stopping the incipient argument, to* HAPPY): Sure, he's gotta practice with a regulation ball, doesn't he? (*To* BIFF.) *Coach'll probably congratulate you on your initiative!*

BIFF: Oh, he keeps congratulating my initiative all the time, Pop.

WILLY: That's because he likes you. If somebody else took that ball there'd be an uproar. So what's the report, boys, what's the report?

BIFF: Where'd you go this time, Dad? Gee we were lonesome for you.

WILLY (*pleased, puts an arm around each boy and they come down to the apron*): Lonesome, heh?

BIFF: Missed you every minute.

WILLY: Don't say? Tell you a secret, boys. Don't breathe it to a soul. Someday I'll have my own business, and I'll never have to leave home any more.

HAPPY: Like Uncle Charley, heh?

WILLY: Bigger than Uncle Charley! Because Charley is not—liked. He's liked, but he's not—well liked.

BIFF: Where'd you go this time, Dad?

WILLY: Well, I got on the road, and I went north to Providence. Met the Mayor.

BIFF: The Mayor of Providence!

WILLY: He was sitting in the hotel lobby.

BIFF: What'd he say?

WILLY: He said, "Morning!" And I said, "Morning!" And I said, "You got a fine city here, Mayor." And then he had coffee with me. And then I went to Waterbury. Waterbury is a fine city. Big clock city, the famous Waterbury clock. Sold a nice bill there. And then Boston—Boston is the cradle of the Revolution. A fine city. And a couple of other towns in Mass., and on to Portland and Bangor and straight home!

BIFF: Gee, I'd love to go with you sometime, Dad.

WILLY: Soon as summer comes.

HAPPY: Promise?

WILLY: You and Hap and I, and I'll show you all the towns. America is full of beautiful towns and fine, upstanding people. And they know me, boys, they know me up and down New England. The finest people. And when

I bring you fellas up, there'll be open sesame for all of us, 'cause one thing, boys: I have friends. I can park my car in any street in New England, and the cops protect it like their own. This summer, heh?

BIFF AND HAPPY (*together*): Yeah! You bet!

WILLY: We'll take our bathing suits.

HAPPY: We'll carry your bags, Pop!

WILLY: Oh, won't that be something! Me comin' into the Boston stores with you boys carryin' my bags. What a sensation!

BIFF *is prancing around, practicing passing the ball.*

WILLY: You nervous, Biff, about the game?

BIFF: Not if you're gonna be there.

WILLY: What do they say about you in school, now that they made you captain?

HAPPY: There's a crowd of girls behind him everytime the classes change.

BIFF (*taking* WILLY'*s hand*): This Saturday, Pop, this Saturday—just for you, I'm going to break through for a touchdown.

HAPPY: You're supposed to pass.

BIFF: I'm takin' one play for Pop. You watch me, Pop, and when I take off my helmet, that means I'm breakin' out. Then you watch me crash through that line!

WILLY (*kisses* BIFF): Oh, wait'll I tell this in Boston!

BERNARD *enters in knickers. He is younger than* BIFF, *earnest and loyal, a worried boy.*

BERNARD : Biff, where are you? You're supposed to study with me today.

WILLY: Hey, looka Bernard. What're you lookin' so anemic about, Bernard?

BERNARD: He's gotta study, Uncle Willy. He's got Regents next week.

HAPPY (*tauntingly, spinning* BERNARD *around*): Let's box, Bernard!

BERNARD: Biff! (*He gets away from* HAPPY.) Listen, Biff, I heard Mr. Birnbaum say that if you don't start studyin' math he's gonna flunk you, and you won't graduate. I heard him!

WILLY: You better study with him, Biff. Go ahead now.

BERNARD: I heard him!

BIFF: Oh, Pop, you didn't see my sneakers! (*He holds up a foot for* WILLY *to look at.*)

WILLY: Hey, that's a beautiful job of printing!

BERNARD (*wiping his glasses*): Just because he printed University of Virginia on his sneakers doesn't mean they've got to graduate him, Uncle Willy!

WILLY (*angrily*): What're you talking about? With scholarships to three universities they're gonna flunk him?

BERNARD: But I heard Mr. Birnbaum say . . .

WILLY: Don't be a pest, Bernard! (*To his boys.*) What an anemic!

BERNARD: Okay, I'm waiting for you in my house, Biff.

BERNARD *goes off. The* LOMANS *laugh.*

WILLY: Bernard is not well liked, is he?

BIFF: He's liked, but he's not well liked.

HAPPY: That's right, Pop.

WILLY: That's just what I mean. Bernard can get the best marks in school, y'understand, but when he gets out in the business world, y'understand, you are going to be five times ahead of him. That's why I thank Almighty

God you're both built like Adonises. Because the man who makes an appearance in the business world, the man who creates personal interest, is the man who gets ahead. Be liked and you will never want. You take me, for instance. I never have to wait in line to see a buyer. "Willy Loman is here!" That's all they have to know, and I go right through.

BIFF: Did you knock them dead, Pop?

WILLY: Knocked 'em cold in Providence, slaughtered 'em in Boston.

HAPPY (*on his back, pedaling again*): I'm losing weight, you notice, Pop?

LINDA *enters as of old, a ribbon in her hair, carrying a basket of washing.*

LINDA (*with youthful energy*): Hello, dear!

WILLY: Sweetheart!

LINDA: How'd the Chevvy run?

WILLY: Chevrolet, Linda, is the greatest car ever built. (*To the boys.*) Since when do you let your mother carry wash up the stairs?

BIFF: Grab hold there, boy!

HAPPY: Where to, Mom?

LINDA: Hang them up on the line. And you better go down to your friends, Biff. The cellar is full of boys. They don't know what to do with themselves.

BIFF: Ah, when Pop comes home they can wait!

WILLY (*laughs appreciatively*): You better go down and tell them what to do, Biff.

BIFF: I think I'll have them sweep out the furnace room.

WILLY: Good work, Biff.

BIFF (*goes through wall-line of kitchen to doorway at back and calls down*): Fellas! Everybody sweep out the furnace room! I'll be right down!

VOICES: All right! Okay, Biff.

BIFF: George and Sam and Frank, come out back! We're hangin' up the wash! Come on, Hap, on the double! (*He and* HAPPY *carry out the basket.*)

LINDA: The way they obey him!

WILLY: Well, that's training, the training. I'm tellin' you, I was sellin' thousands and thousands, but I had to come home.

LINDA: Oh, the whole block'll be at that game. Did you sell anything?

WILLY: I did five hundred gross in Providence and seven hundred gross in Boston.

LINDA: No! Wait a minute. I've got a pencil. (*She pulls pencil and paper out of her apron pocket.*) That makes your commission . . . Two hundred—my God! Two hundred and twelve dollars!

WILLY: Well, I didn't figure it yet, but . . .

LINDA: How much did you do?

WILLY: Well, I—I did—about a hundred and eighty gross in Providence. Well, no— it came to—roughly two hundred gross on the whole trip.

LINDA (*without hesitation*): Two hundred gross. That's . . . (*She figures.*)

WILLY: The trouble was that three of the stores were half-closed for inventory in Boston. Otherwise I woulda broke records.

LINDA: Well, it makes seventy dollars and some pennies. That's very good.

WILLY: What do we owe?

LINDA: Well, on the first there's sixteen dollars on the refrigerator . . . .

WILLY: Why sixteen?

LINDA: Well, the fan belt broke, so it was a dollar eighty.

WILLY: But it's brand new.

LINDA: Well, the man said that's the way it is. Till they work themselves in, y'know. *They move through the wall-line into the kitchen.*

WILLY: I hope we didn't get stuck on that machine.

LINDA: They got the biggest ads of any of them!

WILLY: I know, it's a fine machine. What else?

LINDA: Well, there's nine-sixty for the washing machine. And for the vacuum cleaner there's three and a half due on the fifteenth. Then the roof, you got twenty one dollars remaining.

WILLY: It don't leak, does it?

LINDA: No, they did a wonderful job. Then you owe Frank for the carburetor.

WILLY: I'm not going to pay that man! That goddam Chevrolet, they ought to prohibit the manufacture of that car!

LINDA: Well, you owe him three and a half. And odds and ends, comes to around a hundred and twenty dollars by the fifteenth.

WILLY: A hundred and twenty dollars! My God, if business don't pick up I don't know what I'm gonna do!

LINDA: Well, next week you'll do better.

WILLY: Oh, I'll knock 'em dead next week. I'll go to Hartford. I'm very well liked in Hartford. You know, the trouble is, Linda, people don't seem to take to me.

They move onto the forestage.

LINDA: Oh, don't be foolish.

WILLY: I know it when I walk in. They seem to laugh at me.

LINDA: Why? Why would they laugh at you? Don't talk that way, Willy.

WILLY *moves to the edge of the stage.* LINDA *goes into the kitchen and starts to darn stockings.*

WILLY: I don't know the reason for it, but they just pass me by. I'm not noticed.

LINDA: But you're doing wonderful, dear. You're making seventy to a hundred dollars a week.

WILLY: But I gotta be at it ten, twelve hours a day. Other men—I don't know—they do it easier. I don't know why—I can't stop myself—I talk too much. A man oughta come in with a few words. One thing about Charley. He's a man of few words, and they respect him.

LINDA: You don't talk too much, you're just lively.

WILLY *(smiling)*: Well, I figure, what the hell, life is short, a couple of jokes. *(To himself:)* I joke too much! *(The smile goes.)*

LINDA: Why? You're . . .

WILLY: I'm fat. I'm very—foolish to look at, Linda. I didn't tell you, but Christmas time I happened to be calling on F. H. Stewarts, and a salesman I know, as I was going in to see the buyer I heard him say something about—walrus. And I—I cracked him right across the face. I won't take that. I simply will not take that. But they do laugh at me. I know that.

LINDA: Darling . . .

WILLY: I gotta overcome it. I know I gotta overcome it. I'm not dressing to advantage, maybe.

LINDA: Willy, darling, you're the handsomest man in the world . . .

WILLY: Oh, no, Linda.

LINDA: To me you are. *(Slight pause.)* The handsomest.

From the darkness is heard the laughter of a woman. WILLY *doesn't turn to it, but it continues through* LINDA's *lines.*

LINDA: And the boys, Willy. Few men are idolized by their children the way you are.

Music is heard as behind a scrim, to the left of the house; THE WOMAN, *dimly seen, is dressing.*

WILLY (*with great feeling*): You're the best there is. Linda, you're a pal, you know that? On the road—on the road I want to grab you sometimes and just kiss the life outa you.

The laughter is loud now, and he moves into a brightening area at the left, where THE WOMAN *has come from behind the scrim and is standing, putting on her hat, looking into a "mirror" and laughing.*

WILLY: 'Cause I get so lonely—especially when business is bad and there's nobody to talk to. I get the feeling that I'll never sell anything again, that I won't make a living for you, or a business, a business for the boys. (*He talks through* THE WOMAN'*s subsiding laughter;* THE WOMAN *primps at the "mirror."*) There's so much I want to make for . . .

THE WOMAN: Me? You didn't make me, Willy. I picked you.

WILLY (*pleased*): You picked me?

THE WOMAN (*who is quite proper-looking,* WILLY'*s age*): I did. I've been sitting at that desk watching all the salesmen go by, day in, day out. But you've got such a sense of humor, and we do have such a good time together, don't we?

WILLY: Sure, sure. (*He takes her in his arms.*) Why do you have to go now?

THE WOMAN: It's two o'clock . . .

WILLY: No, come on in! (*He pulls her.*)

THE WOMAN: . . . my sisters'll be scandalized. When'll you be back?

WILLY: Oh, two weeks about. Will you come up again?

THE WOMAN: Sure thing. You do make me laugh. It's good for me. (*She squeezes his arm, kisses him.*) And I think you're a wonderful man.

WILLY: You picked me, heh?

THE WOMAN: Sure. Because you're so sweet. And such a kidder.

WILLY: Well, I'll see you next time I'm in Boston.

THE WOMAN: I'll put you right through to the buyers.

WILLY (*slapping her bottom*): Right. Well, bottoms up!

THE WOMAN (*slaps him gently and laughs*): You just kill me, Willy. (*He suddenly grabs her and kisses her roughly.*) You kill me. And thanks for the stockings. I love a lot of stockings. Well, good night.

WILLY: Good night. And keep your pores open!

THE WOMAN: Oh, Willy!

THE WOMAN *bursts out laughing, and* LINDA'*s laughter blends in.* THE WOMAN *disappears into the dark. Now the area at the kitchen table brightens.* LINDA *is sitting where she was at the kitchen table, but now is mending a pair of her silk stockings.*

LINDA: You are, Willy. The handsomest man. You've got no reason to feel that . . .

WILLY (*coming out of* THE WOMAN'*s dimming area and going over to* LINDA): I'll make it all up to you, Linda, I'll . . .

LINDA: There's nothing to make up, dear. You're doing fine, better than . . .

WILLY (*noticing her mending*): What's that?

LINDA: Just mending my stockings. They're so expensive . . .

WILLY (*angrily, taking them from her*): I won't have you mending stockings in this house! Now throw them out!

LINDA *puts the stockings in her pocket.*

BERNARD (*entering on the run*): Where is he? If he doesn't study!

WILLY (*moving to the forestage, with great agitation*): You'll give him the answers!

BERNARD: I do, but I can't on a Regents! That's a state exam! They're liable to arrest me!

WILLY: Where is he? I'll whip him, I'll whip him!

LINDA: And he'd better give back that football, Willy, it's not nice.

WILLY: Biff! Where is he? Why is he taking everything?

LINDA: He's too rough with the girls, Willy. All the mothers are afraid of him!

WILLY: I'll whip him!

BERNARD: He's driving the car without a license!

THE WOMAN's *laugh is heard.*

WILLY: Shut up!

LINDA: All the mothers . . .

WILLY: Shut up!

BERNARD (*backing quietly away and out*): Mr. Birnbaum says he's stuck up.

WILLY: Get outa here!

BERNARD: If he doesn't buckle down he'll flunk math! (*He goes off.*)

LINDA: He's right, Willy, you've gotta . . .

WILLY (*exploding at her*): There's nothing the matter with him! You want him to be a worm like Bernard? He's got spirit, personality . . . .

As he speaks, LINDA, *almost in tears, exits into the living room.* WILLY *is alone in the kitchen, wilting and staring. The leaves are gone. It is night again, and the apartment houses look down from behind.*

WILLY: Loaded with it. Loaded! What is he stealing? He's giving it back, isn't he? Why is he stealing? What did I tell him? I never in my life told him anything but decent things.

HAPPY *in pajamas has come down the stairs;* WILLY *suddenly becomes aware of* HAPPY's *presence.*

HAPPY: Let's go now, come on.

WILLY (*sitting down at the kitchen table*): Huh! Why did she have to wax the floors herself? Everytime she waxes the floors she keels over. She knows that!

HAPPY: Shh! Take it easy. What brought you back tonight?

WILLY: I got an awful scare. Nearly hit a kid in Yonkers. God! Why didn't I go to Alaska with my brother Ben that time! Ben! That man was a genius, that man was success incarnate! What a mistake! He begged me to go.

HAPPY: Well, there's no use in . . .

WILLY: You guys! There was a man started with the clothes on his back and ended up with diamond mines!

HAPPY: Boy, someday I'd like to know how he did it.

WILLY: What's the mystery? The man knew what he wanted and went out and got it! Walked into a jungle, and comes out, the age of twenty-one, and he's rich! The world is an oyster, but you don't crack it open on a mattress!

HAPPY: Pop, I told you I'm gonna retire you for life.

WILLY: You'll retire me for life on seventy goddam dollars a week? And your women and your car and your apartment, and you'll retire me for life! Christ's sake, I couldn't get past Yonkers today! Where are you guys, where are you? The woods are burning! I can't drive a car!

CHARLEY *has appeared in the doorway. He is a large man, slow of speech, laconic, immovable. In all he says, despite what he says, there is pity, and, now, trepidation. He has a robe over pajamas, slippers on his feet. He enters the kitchen.*

CHARLEY: Everything all right?
HAPPY: Yeah, Charley, everything's . . .
WILLY: What's the matter?
CHARLEY: I heard some noise. I thought something happened. Can't we do something about the walls? You sneeze in here, and in my house hats blow off.
HAPPY: Let's go to bed, Dad. Come on.

CHARLEY *signals to* HAPPY *to go.*

WILLY: You go ahead, I'm not tired at the moment.
HAPPY (*to* WILLY): Take it easy, huh? (*He exits.*)
WILLY: What're you doin' up?
CHARLEY (*sitting down at the kitchen table opposite* WILLY): Couldn't sleep good. I had a heartburn.
WILLY: Well, you don't know how to eat.
CHARLEY: I eat with my mouth.
WILLY: No, you're ignorant. You gotta know about vitamins and things like that.
CHARLEY: Come on, let's shoot. Tire you out a little.
WILLY (*hesitantly*): All right. You got cards?
CHARLEY (*taking a deck from his pocket*): Yeah, I got them. Someplace. What is it with those vitamins?
WILLY (*dealing*): They build up your bones. Chemistry.
CHARLEY: Yeah, but there's no bones in a heartburn.
WILLY: What are you talkin' about? Do you know the first thing about it?
CHARLEY: Don't get insulted.
WILLY: Don't talk about something you don't know anything about.

They are playing. pause.

CHARLEY: What're you doin' home?
WILLY: A little trouble with the car.
CHARLEY: Oh. (*Pause.*) I'd like to take a trip to California.
WILLY: Don't say.
CHARLEY: You want a job?
WILLY: I got a job, I told you that. (*After a slight pause.*) What the hell are you offering me a job for?
CHARLEY: Don't get insulted.
WILLY: Don't insult me.
CHARLEY: I don't see no sense in it. You don't have to go on this way.
WILLY: I got a good job. (*Slight pause.*) What do you keep comin' in here for?
CHARLEY: You want me to go?

WILLY (*after a pause, withering*): I can't understand it. He's going back to Texas again. What the hell is that?

CHARLEY: Let him go.

WILLY: I got nothin' to give him, Charley, I'm clean, I'm clean.

CHARLEY: He won't starve. None a them starve. Forget about him.

WILLY: Then what have I got to remember?

CHARLEY: You take it too hard. To hell with it. When a deposit bottle is broken you don't get your nickel back.

WILLY: That's easy enough for you to say.

CHARLEY: That ain't easy for me to say.

WILLY: Did you see the ceiling I put up in the living room?

CHARLEY: Yeah, that's a piece of work. To put up a ceiling is a mystery to me. How do you do it?

WILLY: What's the difference?

CHARLEY: Well, talk about it.

WILLY: You gonna put up a ceiling?

CHARLEY: How could I put up a ceiling?

WILLY: Then what the hell are you bothering me for?

CHARLEY: You're insulted again.

WILLY: A man who can't handle tools is not a man. You're disgusting.

CHARLEY: Don't call me disgusting, Willy.

> UNCLE BEN, *carrying a valise and an umbrella, enters the forestage from around the right corner of the house. He is a stolid man, in his sixties, with a mustache and an authoritative air. He is utterly certain of his destiny, and there is an aura of far places about him. He enters exactly as* WILLY *speaks.*

WILLY: I'm getting awfully tired, Ben.

> BEN's *music is heard.* BEN *looks around at everything.*

CHARLEY: Good, keep playing; you'll sleep better. Did you call me Ben?

> BEN *looks at his watch.*

WILLY: That's funny. For a second there you reminded me of my brother Ben.

BEN: I only have a few minutes. (*He strolls, inspecting the place.* WILLY *and* CHARLEY *continue playing.*)

CHARLEY: You never heard from him again, heh? Since that time?

WILLY: Didn't Linda tell you? Couple of weeks ago we got a letter from his wife in Africa. He died.

CHARLEY: That so.

BEN (*chuckling*): So this is Brooklyn, eh?

CHARLEY: Maybe you're in for some of his money.

WILLY: Naa, he had seven sons. There's just one opportunity I had with that man . . .

BEN: I must make a train, William. There are several properties I'm looking at in Alaska.

WILLY: Sure, sure! If I'd gone with him to Alaska that time, everything would've been totally different.

CHARLEY: Go on, you'd froze to death up there.

WILLY: What're you talking about?

BEN: Opportunity is tremendous in Alaska, William. Surprised you're not up there.

WILLY: Sure, tremendous.

CHARLEY: Heh?

WILLY: There was the only man I ever met who knew the answers.

CHARLEY: Who?

BEN: How are you all?

WILLY (*taking a pot, smiling*): Fine, fine.

CHARLEY: Pretty sharp tonight.

BEN: Is Mother living with you?

WILLY: No, she died a long time ago.

CHARLEY: Who?

BEN: That's too bad. Fine specimen of a lady, Mother.

WILLY (*to* CHARLEY): Heh?

BEN: I'd hoped to see the old girl.

CHARLEY: Who died?

BEN: Heard anything from Father, have you?

WILLY (*unnerved*): What do you mean, who died?

CHARLEY (*taking a pot*): What're you talkin' about?

BEN (*looking at his watch*): William, it's half-past eight!

WILLY (*as though to dispel his confusion he angrily stops* CHARLEY's *hand*): That's my build!

CHARLEY: I put the ace . . . .

WILLY: If you don't know how to play the game I'm not gonna throw my money away on you!

CHARLEY (*rising*): It was my ace, for God's sake!

WILLY: I'm through, I'm through!

BEN: When did Mother die?

WILLY: Long ago. Since the beginning you never knew how to play cards.

CHARLEY (*picks up the cards and goes to the door*): All right! Next time I'll bring a deck with five aces.

WILLY: I don't play that kind of game!

CHARLEY (*turning to him*): You ought to be ashamed of yourself!

WILLY: Yeah?

CHARLEY: Yeah! (*He goes out.*)

WILLY (*slamming the door after him*): Ignoramus!

BEN (*as* WILLY *comes toward him through the wall-line of the kitchen*): So you're William.

WILLY (*shaking* BEN's *hand*): Ben! I've been waiting for you so long! What's the answer? How did you do it?

BEN: Oh, there's a story in that.

LINDA *enters the forestage, as of old, carrying the wash basket.*

LINDA: Is this Ben?

BEN (*gallantly*): How do you do, my dear.

LINDA: Where've you been all these years? Willy's always wondered why you . . .

WILLY (*pulling* BEN *away from her impatiently*): Where is Dad? Didn't you follow him? How did you get started?

BEN: Well, I don't know how much you remember.

WILLY: Well, I was just a baby, of course, only three or four years old . . . .

BEN: Three years and eleven months.

WILLY: What a memory, Ben!

BEN: I have many enterprises, William, and I have never kept books.

WILLY: I remember I was sitting under the wagon in—was it Nebraska?

BEN: It was South Dakota, and I gave you a bunch of wild flowers.

WILLY: I remember you walking away down some open road.

BEN (*laughing*): I was going to find Father in Alaska.

WILLY: Where is he?

BEN: At that age I had a very faulty view of geography, William. I discovered after a few days that I was heading due south, so instead of Alaska, I ended up in Africa.

LINDA: Africa!

WILLY: The Gold Coast!

BEN: Principally diamond mines.

LINDA: Diamond mines!

BEN: Yes, my dear. But I've only a few minutes . . .

WILLY: No! Boys! Boys! (*Young* BIFF *and* HAPPY *appear.*) Listen to this. This is your Uncle Ben, a great man! Tell my boys, Ben!

BEN: Why, boys, when I was seventeen I walked into the jungle, and when I was twenty-one I walked out. (*He laughs.*) And by God I was rich.

WILLY (*to the boys*): You see what I been talking about? The greatest things can happen!

BEN (*glancing at his watch*): I have an appointment in Ketchikan Tuesday week.

WILLY: No, Ben! Please tell about Dad. I want my boys to hear. I want them to know the kind of stock they spring from. All I remember is a man with a big beard, and I was in Mamma's lap, sitting around a fire, and some kind of high music.

BEN: His flute. He played the flute.

WILLY: Sure, the flute, that's right!

New music is heard, a high, rollicking tune.

BEN: Father was a very great and a very wild-hearted man. We would start in Boston, and he'd toss the whole family into the wagon, and then he'd drive the team right across the country; through Ohio, and Indiana, Michigan, Illinois, and all the Western states. And we'd stop in the towns and sell the flutes that he'd made on the way. Great inventor, Father. With one gadget he made more in a week than a man like you could make in a lifetime.

WILLY: That's just the way I'm bringing them up, Ben—rugged, well liked, all-around.

BEN: Yeah? (*To* BIFF.) Hit that, boy—hard as you can. (*He pounds his stomach.*)

BIFF: Oh, no, sir!

BEN (*taking boxing stance*): Come on, get to me! (*He laughs.*)

WILLY: Go to it. Biff! Go ahead, show him!

BIFF: Okay! (*He cocks his fists and starts in.*)

LINDA (*to* WILLY): Why must he fight, dear?

BEN (*sparring with* BIFF): Good boy! Good boy!

WILLY: How's that, Ben, heh?

HAPPY: Give him the left, Biff!

LINDA: Why are you fighting?

BEN: Good boy! (*Suddenly comes in, trips* BIFF, *and stands over him, the point of his umbrella poised over* BIFF's *eye.*)

LINDA: Look out, Biff!

BIFF: Gee!

BEN (*patting* BIFF's *knee*): Never fight fair with a stranger, boy. You'll never get out of the jungle that way. (*Taking* LINDA's *hand and bowing.*) It was an honor and a pleasure to meet you, Linda.

LINDA (*withdrawing her hand coldly, frightened*): Have a nice—trip.

BEN (*to* WILLY): And good luck with your—what do you do?

WILLY: Selling.

BEN: Yes. Well . . . (*He raises his hand in farewell to all.*)

WILLY: No, Ben, I don't want you to think . . . (*He takes* BEN's *arm to show him.*) It's Brooklyn, I know, but we hunt too.

BEN: Really, now.

WILLY: Oh, sure, there's snakes and rabbits and—that's why I moved out here. Why, Biff can fell any one of these trees in no time! Boys! Go right over to where they're building the apartment house and get some sand. We're gonna rebuild the entire front stoop right now! Watch this, Ben!

BIFF: Yes, sir! On the double, Hap!

HAPPY (*as he and* BIFF *run off*): I lost weight, Pop, you notice?

CHARLEY *enters in knickers, even before the boys are gone.*

CHARLEY: Listen, if they steal any more from that building the watchman'll put the cops on them!

LINDA (*to* WILLY): Don't let Biff . . .

BEN *laughs lustily.*

WILLY: You shoulda seen the lumber they brought home last week. At least a dozen six-by-tens worth all kinds a money.

CHARLEY: Listen, if that watchman . . .

WILLY: I gave them hell, understand. But I got a couple of fearless characters there.

CHARLEY: Willy, the jails are full of fearless characters.

BEN (*clapping* WILLY *on the back, with a laugh at* CHARLEY): And the stock exchange, friend!

WILLY (*joining in* BEN's *laughter*): Where are the rest of your pants?

CHARLEY: My wife bought them.

WILLY: Now all you need is a golf club and you can go upstairs and go to sleep. (*To* BEN.) Great athlete! Between him and his son Bernard they can't hammer a nail!

BERNARD (*rushing in*): The watchman's chasing Biff!

WILLY (*angrily*): Shut up! He's not stealing anything!

LINDA (*alarmed, hurrying off left*): Where is he? Biff, dear! (*She exits.*)

WILLY (*moving toward the left, away from* BEN): There's nothing wrong. What's the matter with you?

BEN: Nervy boy. Good!

WILLY (*laughing*): Oh, nerves of iron, that Biff!

CHARLEY: Don't know what it is. My New England man comes back and he's bleedin', they murdered him up there.

WILLY: It's contacts, Charley, I got important contacts!

CHARLEY (*sarcastically*): Glad to hear it, Willy. Come in later, we'll shoot a little casino. I'll take some of your Portland money. (*He laughs at* WILLY *and exits.*)

WILLY (*turning to* BEN): Business is bad, it's murderous. But not for me, of course.

BEN: I'll stop by on my way back to Africa.

WILLY (*longingly*): Can't you stay a few days? You're just what I need, Ben, because I—I have a fine position here, but I—well, Dad left when I was such a baby and I never had a chance to talk to him and I still feel—kind of temporary about myself.

BEN: I'll be late for my train.

They are at opposite ends of the stage.

WILLY: Ben, my boys—can't we talk? They'd go into the jaws of hell for me, see, but I . . .

BEN: William, you're being first-rate with your boys. Outstanding, manly chaps!

WILLY (*hanging on to his words*): Oh, Ben, that's good to hear! Because sometimes I'm afraid that I'm not teaching them the right kind of—Ben, how should I teach them?

BEN (*giving great weight to each word, and with a certain vicious audacity*): William, when I walked into the jungle, I was seventeen. When I walked out I was twenty-one. And, by God, I was rich! (*He goes off into darkness around the right corner of the house.*)

WILLY: . . . was rich! That's just the spirit I want to imbue them with! To walk into a jungle! I was right! I was right! I was right!

BEN *is gone, but* WILLY *is still speaking to him as* LINDA, *in nightgown and robe, enters the kitchen, glances around for* WILLY, *then goes to the door of the house, looks out and sees him. Comes down to his left. He looks at her.*

LINDA: Willy, dear? Willy?

WILLY: I was right!

LINDA: Did you have some cheese? (*He can't answer.*) It's very late, darling. Come to bed, heh?

WILLY (*looking straight up*): Gotta break your neck to see a star in this yard.

LINDA: You coming in?

WILLY: Whatever happened to that diamond watch fob? Remember? When Ben came from Africa that time? Didn't he give me a watch fob with a diamond in it?

LINDA: You pawned it, dear. Twelve, thirteen years ago. For Biff's radio correspondence course.

WILLY: Gee, that was a beautiful thing. I'll take a walk.

LINDA: But you're in your slippers.

WILLY (*starting to go around the house at the left*): I was right! I was! (*Half to* LINDA, *as he goes, shaking his head.*) What a man! There was a man worth talking to. I was right!

LINDA (*calling after* WILLY): But in your slippers, Willy!

WILLY *is almost gone when* BIFF, *in his pajamas, comes down the stairs and enters the kitchen.*

BIFF: What is he doing out there?

LINDA: Sh!

BIFF: God Almighty, Mom, how long has he been doing this?

LINDA: Don't, he'll hear you.

BIFF: What the hell is the matter with him?

LINDA: It'll pass by morning.

BIFF: Shouldn't we do anything?

LINDA: Oh, my dear, you should do a lot of things, but there's nothing to do, so go to sleep.

HAPPY *comes down the stairs and sits on the steps.*

HAPPY: I never heard him so loud, Mom.

LINDA: Well, come around more often; you'll hear him. (*She sits down at the table and mends the lining of* WILLY's *jacket.*)

BIFF: Why didn't you ever write me about this, Mom?

LINDA: How would I write to you? For over three months you had no address.

BIFF: I was on the move. But you know I thought of you all the time. You know that, don't you, pal?

LINDA: I know, dear, I know. But he likes to have a letter. Just to know that there's still a possibility for better things.

BIFF: He's not like this all the time, is he?

LINDA: It's when you come home he's always the worst.

BIFF: When I come home?

LINDA: When you write you're coming, he's all smiles, and talks about the future, and—he's just wonderful. And then the closer you seem to come, the more shaky he gets, and then, by the time you get here, he's arguing, and he seems angry at you. I think it's just that maybe he can't bring himself to—to open up to you. Why are you so hateful to each other? Why is that?

BIFF (*evasively*): I'm not hateful, Mom.

LINDA: But you no sooner come in the door than you're fighting!

BIFF: I don't know why. I mean to change. I'm tryin', Mom, you understand?

LINDA: Are you home to stay now?

BIFF: I don't know. I want to look around, see what's doin'.

LINDA: Biff, you can't look around all your life, can you?

BIFF: I just can't take hold, Mom. I can't take hold of some kind of a life.

LINDA: Biff, a man is not a bird, to come and go with the spring time.

BIFF: Your hair . . . (*He touches her hair.*) Your hair got so gray.

LINDA: Oh, it's been gray since you were in high school. I just stopped dyeing it, that's all.

BIFF: Dye it again, will ya? I don't want my pal looking old. (*He smiles.*)

LINDA: You're such a boy! You think you can go away for a year and . . . You've got to get it into your head now that one day you'll knock on this door and there'll be strange people here . . .

BIFF: What are you talking about? You're not even sixty, Mom.

LINDA: But what about your father?

BIFF (*lamely*): Well, I meant him too.

HAPPY: He admires Pop.

LINDA: Biff, dear, if you don't have any feeling for him, then you can't have any feeling for me.

BIFF: Sure I can, Mom.

LINDA: No. You can't just come to see me, because I love him. (*With a threat, but only a threat, of tears.*) He's the dearest man in the world to me, and I won't have anyone making him feel unwanted and low and blue. You've got to make up your mind now, darling, there's no leeway any more. Either he's your father and you pay him that respect, or else you're not to come here. I know he's not easy to get along with—nobody knows that better than me—but . . .

WILLY (*from the left, with a laugh*): Hey, hey, Biffo!

BIFF (*starting to go out after* WILLY): What the hell is the matter with him? (HAPPY *stops him.*)

LINDA: Don't—don't go near him!

BIFF: Stop making excuses for him! He always, always wiped the floor with you. Never had an ounce of respect for you.

HAPPY: He's always had respect for . . .

BIFF: What the hell do you know about it?

HAPPY (*surlily*): Just don't call him crazy!

BIFF: He's got no character—Charley wouldn't do this. Not in his own house— spewing out that vomit from his mind.

HAPPY: Charley never had to cope with what he's got to.

BIFF: People are worse off than Willy Loman. Believe me, I've seen them!

LINDA: Then make Charley your father, Biff. You can't do that, can you? I don't say he's a great man. Willy Loman never made a lot of money. His name was never in the paper. He's not the finest character that ever lived. But he's a human being, and a terrible thing is happening to him. So attention must be paid. He's not to be allowed to fall into his grave like an old dog. Attention, attention must be finally paid to such a person. You called him crazy . . .

BIFF: I didn't mean . . .

LINDA: No, a lot of people think he's lost his—balance. But you don't have to be very smart to know what his trouble is. The man is exhausted.

HAPPY: Sure!

LINDA: A small man can be just as exhausted as a great man. He works for a company thirty-six years this March, opens up unheard-of territories to their trademark, and now in his old age they take his salary away.

HAPPY (*indignantly*): I didn't know that, Mom.

LINDA: You never asked, my dear! Now that you get your spending money someplace else you don't trouble your mind with him.

HAPPY: But I gave you money last . . .

LINDA: Christmas time, fifty dollars! To fix the hot water it cost ninety-seven fifty! For five weeks he's been on straight commission, like a beginner, an unknown!

BIFF: Those ungrateful bastards!

LINDA: Are they any worse than his sons? When he brought them business, when he was young, they were glad to see him. But now his old friends, the old buyers that loved him so and always found some order to hand him in a pinch— they're all dead, retired. He used to be able to make six, seven calls a day in Boston. Now he takes his valises out of the car and puts them back and takes them out again and he's exhausted. Instead of walking he talks now. He drives seven hundred miles, and when he gets there no one knows him any more, no one welcomes him. And what goes through a man's mind, driving seven hundred miles home without having earned a cent? Why shouldn't he talk to himself? Why? When he has to go to Charley and borrow fifty dollars a week and pretend to me that it's his pay? How long can that go on? How long? You see what I'm sitting here and waiting for? And you tell me he has no character? The man who never worked a day but for your benefit? When does he get the medal for that? Is this his reward—to turn around at the age of sixty-three and find his sons, who he loved better than his life, one a philandering bum . . .

HAPPY: Mom!

LINDA: That's all you are, my baby! (*To* BIFF.) And you! What happened to the love you had for him? You were such pals! How you used to talk to him on the phone every night! How lonely he was till he could come home to you!

BIFF: All right, Mom. I'll live here in my room, and I'll get a job. I'll keep away from him, that's all.

LINDA: No, Biff. You can't stay here and fight all the time.

BIFF: He threw me out of this house, remember that.

LINDA: Why did he do that? I never knew why.

BIFF: Because I know he's a fake and he doesn't like anybody around who knows!

LINDA: Why a fake? In what way? What do you mean?

BIFF: Just don't lay it all at my feet. It's between me and him—that's all I have to say. I'll chip in from now on. He'll settle for half my paycheck. He'll be all right. I'm going to bed. (*He starts for the stairs.*)

LINDA: He won't be all right.

BIFF (*turning on the stairs, furiously*): I hate this city and I'll stay here. Now what do you want?

LINDA: He's dying, Biff.

HAPPY *turns quickly to her, shocked.*

BIFF (*after a pause*): Why is he dying?

LINDA: He's been trying to kill himself.

BIFF (*with great horror*): How?

LINDA: I live from day to day.

BIFF: What're you talking about?

LINDA: Remember I wrote you that he smashed up the car again? In February?

BIFF: Well?

LINDA: The insurance inspector came. He said that they have evidence. That all these accidents in the last year—weren't—weren't—accidents.

HAPPY: How can they tell that? That's a lie.

LINDA: It seems there's a woman . . . (*She takes a breath as:*)

BIFF (*sharply but contained*): What woman?

LINDA (*simultaneously*): . . . and this woman . . .

LINDA: What?

BIFF: Nothing. Go ahead.

LINDA: What did you say?

BIFF: Nothing. I just said what woman?

HAPPY: What about her?

LINDA: Well, it seems she was walking down the road and saw his car. She says that he wasn't driving fast at all, and that he didn't skid. She says he came to that little bridge, and then deliberately smashed into the railing, and it was only the shallowness of the water that saved him.

BIFF: Oh, no, he probably just fell asleep again.

LINDA: I don't think he fell asleep.

BIFF: Why not?

LINDA: Last month . . . (*With great difficulty.*) Oh, boys, it's so hard to say a thing like this! He's just a big stupid man to you, but I tell you there's more good in him than in many other people. (*She chokes, wipes her eyes.*) I was looking for a fuse. The lights blew out, and I went down the cellar. And behind the fuse box—it happened to fall out—was a length of rubber pipe—just short.

HAPPY: No kidding!

LINDA: There's a little attachment on the end of it. I knew right away. And sure enough, on the bottom of the water heater there's a new little nipple on the gas pipe.

HAPPY (*angrily*): That—jerk.

BIFF: Did you have it taken off?

LINDA: I'm—I'm ashamed to. How can I mention it to him? Every day I go down and take away that little rubber pipe. But, when he comes home, I put it back where it was. How can I insult him that way? I don't know what to do. I live from day to day, boys. I tell you, I know every thought in his mind. It sounds so old-fashioned and silly, but I tell you he put his whole life into you and you've turned your backs on him. (*She is bent over in the chair, weeping, her face in her hands.*) Biff, I swear to God! Biff, his life is in your hands!

HAPPY (*to* BIFF): How do you like that damned fool!

BIFF (*kissing her*): All right, pal, all right. It's all settled now. I've been remiss. I know that, Mom. But now I'll stay, and I swear to you, I'll apply myself. (*Kneeling in front of her, in a fever of self-reproach.*) It's just—you see, Mom, I don't fit in business. Not that I won't try. I'll try, and I'll make good.

HAPPY: Sure you will. The trouble with you in business was you never tried to please people.

BIFF: I know, I . . .

HAPPY: Like when you worked for Harrison's. Bob Harrison said you were tops, and then you go and do some damn fool thing like whistling whole songs in the elevator like a comedian.

BIFF (*against* HAPPY): So what? I like to whistle sometimes.

HAPPY: You don't raise a guy to a responsible job who whistles in the elevator!

LINDA: Well, don't argue about it now.

HAPPY: Like when you'd go off and swim in the middle of the day instead of taking the line around.

BIFF (*his resentment rising*): Well, don't you run off? You take off sometimes, don't you? On a nice summer day?

HAPPY: Yeah, but I cover myself!

LINDA: Boys!

HAPPY: If I'm going to take a fade the boss can call any number where I'm supposed to be and they'll swear to him that I just left. I'll tell you something that I hate to say, Biff, but in the business world some of them think you're crazy.

BIFF (*angered*): Screw the business world!

HAPPY: All right, screw it! Great, but cover yourself!

LINDA: Hap, Hap!

BIFF: I don't care what they think! They've laughed at Dad for years, and you know why? Because we don't belong in this nuthouse of a city! We should be mixing cement on some open plain or—or carpenters. A carpenter is allowed to whistle!

WILLY *walks in from the entrance of the house, at left.*

WILLY: Even your grandfather was better than a carpenter. (*Pause. They watch him.*) You never grew up. Bernard does not whistle in the elevator, I assure you.

BIFF (*as though to laugh* WILLY *out of it*): Yeah, but you do, Pop.

WILLY: I never in my life whistled in an elevator! And who in the business world thinks I'm crazy?

BIFF: I didn't mean it like that, Pop. Now don't make a whole thing out of it, will ya?

WILLY: Go back to the West! Be a carpenter, a cowboy, enjoy yourself!

LINDA: Willy, he was just saying . . .

WILLY: I heard what he said!

HAPPY (*trying to quiet* WILLY): Hey, Pop, come on now . . .

WILLY (*continuing over* HAPPY'*s line*): They laugh at me, heh? Go to Filene's, go to the Hub, go to Slattery's, Boston. Call out the name Willy Loman and see what happens! Big shot!

BIFF: All right, Pop.

WILLY: Big!

BIFF: All right!

WILLY: Why do you always insult me?

BIFF: I didn't say a word. (*To* LINDA.) Did I say a word?

LINDA: He didn't say anything, Willy.

WILLY (*going to the doorway of the living room*): All right, good night, good night.

LINDA: Willy, dear, he just decided . . .

WILLY (*to* BIFF): If you get tired hanging around tomorrow, paint the ceiling I put up in the living room.

BIFF: I'm leaving early tomorrow.

HAPPY: He's going to see Bill Oliver, Pop.

WILLY (*interestedly*): Oliver? For what?

BIFF (*with reserve, but trying, trying*): He always said he'd stake me. I'd like to go into business, so maybe I can take him up on it.

LINDA: Isn't that wonderful?

WILLY: Don't interrupt. What's wonderful about it? There's fifty men in the City of New York who'd stake him. (*To* BIFF.) Sporting goods?

BIFF: I guess so. I know something about it and . . .

WILLY: He knows something about it! You know sporting goods better than Spalding, for God's sake! How much is he giving you?

BIFF: I don't know, I didn't even see him yet, but . . .

WILLY: Then what're you talkin' about?

BIFF (*getting angry*): Well, all I said was I'm gonna see him, that's all!

WILLY (*turning away*): Ah, you're counting your chickens again.

BIFF (*starting left for the stairs*): Oh, Jesus, I'm going to sleep!

WILLY (*calling after him*): Don't curse in this house!

BIFF (*turning*): Since when did you get so clean?

HAPPY (*trying to stop them*): Wait a . . .

WILLY: Don't use that language to me! I won't have it!

HAPPY (*grabbing* BIFF, *shouts*): Wait a minute! I got an idea. I got a feasible idea. Come here, Biff, let's talk this over now, let's talk some sense here. When I was down in Florida last time, I thought of a great idea to sell sporting goods. It just came back to me. You and I, Biff—we have a line, the Loman Line. We train a couple of weeks, and put on a couple of exhibitions, see?

WILLY: That's an idea!

HAPPY: Wait! We form two basketball teams, see? Two water-polo teams. We play each other. It's a million dollars' worth of publicity. Two brothers, see? The Loman Brothers. Displays in the Royal Palms—all the hotels. And banners over the ring and the basketball court: "Loman Brothers." Baby, we could sell sporting goods!

WILLY: That is a one-million-dollar idea!

LINDA: Marvelous!

BIFF: I'm in great shape as far as that's concerned.

HAPPY: And the beauty of it is, Biff, it wouldn't be like a business. We'd be out playin' ball again.

BIFF (*enthused*): Yeah, that's . . .

WILLY: Million-dollar . . .

HAPPY: And you wouldn't get fed up with it, Biff. It'd be the family again. There'd be the old honor, and comradeship, and if you wanted to go off for a swim or somethin'—well, you'd do it! Without some smart cooky gettin' up ahead of you!

WILLY: Lick the world! You guys together could absolutely lick the civilized world.

BIFF: I'll see Oliver tomorrow. Hap, if we could work that out . . .

LINDA: Maybe things are beginning to . . .

WILLY (*wildly enthused, to* LINDA): Stop interrupting! (*To* BIFF.) But don't wear sport jacket and slacks when you see Oliver.

BIFF: No, I'll . . .

WILLY: A business suit, and talk as little as possible, and don't crack any jokes.

BIFF: He did like me. Always liked me.

LINDA: He loved you!

WILLY (*to* LINDA): Will you stop! (*To* BIFF.) Walk in very serious. You are not applying for a boy's job. Money is to pass. Be quiet, fine, and serious. Everybody likes a kidder, but nobody lends him money.

HAPPY: I'll try to get some myself, Biff. I'm sure I can.

WILLY: I see great things for you kids, I think your troubles are over. But remember, start big and you'll end big. Ask for fifteen. How much you gonna ask for?

BIFF: Gee, I don't know . . .

WILLY: And don't say "Gee." "Gee" is a boy's word. A man walking in for fifteen thousand dollars does not say "Gee!"

BIFF: Ten, I think, would be top though.

WILLY: Don't be so modest. You always started too low. Walk in with a big laugh. Don't look worried. Start off with a couple of your good stories to lighten things up. It's not what you say, it's how you say it—because personality always wins the day.

LINDA: Oliver always thought the highest of him . . .

WILLY: Will you let me talk?

BIFF: Don't yell at her, Pop, will ya?

WILLY (*angrily*): I was talking, wasn't I?

BIFF: I don't like you yelling at her all the time, and I'm tellin' you, that's all.

WILLY: What're you, takin' over this house?

LINDA: Willy . . .

WILLY (*turning to her*): Don't take his side all the time, goddammit!

BIFF (*furiously*): Stop yelling at her!

WILLY (*suddenly pulling on his cheek, beaten down, guilt ridden*): Give my best to Bill Oliver—he may remember me. (*He exits through the living room doorway.*)

LINDA (*her voice subdued*): What'd you have to start that for? (BIFF *turns away.*) You see how sweet he was as soon as you talked hopefully? (*She goes over to* BIFF.) Come up and say good night to him. Don't let him go to bed that way.

HAPPY: Come on, Biff, let's buck him up.

LINDA: Please, dear. Just say good night. It takes so little to make him happy. Come. (*She goes through the living room doorway, calling upstairs from within the living room.*) Your pajamas are hanging in the bathroom, Willy!

HAPPY (*looking toward where* LINDA *went out*): What a woman! They broke the mold when they made her. You know that, Biff.

BIFF: He's off salary. My God, working on commission!

HAPPY: Well, let's face it: he's no hot-shot selling man. Except that sometimes, you have to admit, he's a sweet personality.

BIFF (*deciding*): Lend me ten bucks, will ya? I want to buy some new ties.

HAPPY: I'll take you to a place I know. Beautiful stuff. Wear one of my striped shirts tomorrow.

BIFF: She got gray. Mom got awful old. Gee, I'm gonna go in to Oliver tomorrow and knock him for a . . .

HAPPY: Come on up. Tell that to Dad. Let's give him a whirl. Come on.

BIFF (*steamed up*): You know, with ten thousand bucks, boy!

HAPPY (*as they go into the living room*): That's the talk, Biff, that's the first time I've heard the old confidence out of you! (*From within the living room, fading off*) You're gonna live with me, kid, and any babe you want just say the word . . . (*The last lines are hardly heard. They are mounting the stairs to their parents' bedroom.*)

LINDA (*entering her bedroom and addressing* WILLY, *who is in the bathroom. She is straightening the bed for him*): Can you do anything about the shower? It drips.

WILLY (*from the bathroom*): All of a sudden everything falls to pieces. Goddam plumbing, oughta be sued, those people. I hardly finished putting it in and the thing . . . (*His words rumble off.*)

LINDA: I'm just wondering if Oliver will remember him. You think he might?

WILLY (*coming out of the bathroom in his pajamas*): Remember him? What's the matter with you, you crazy? If he'd've stayed with Oliver he'd be on top by now! Wait'll Oliver gets a look at him. You don't know the average caliber any more. The average young man today—(*he is getting into bed*)—is got a caliber of zero. Greatest thing in the world for him was to bum around.

BIFF *and* HAPPY *enter the bedroom. Slight pause.*

WILLY (*stops short, looking at* BIFF): Glad to hear it, boy.

HAPPY: He wanted to say good night to you, sport.

WILLY (*to* BIFF): Yeah. Knock him dead, boy. What'd you want to tell me?

BIFF: Just take it easy, Pop. Good night. (*He turns to go.*)

WILLY (*unable to resist*): And if anything falls off the desk while you're talking to him—like a package or something—don't you pick it up. They have office boys for that.

LINDA: I'll make a big breakfast . . .

WILLY: Will you let me finish? (*To* BIFF.) Tell him you were in the business in the West. Not farm work.

BIFF: All right, Dad.

LINDA: I think everything . . .

WILLY (*going right through her speech*): And don't undersell yourself. No less than fifteen thousand dollars.

BIFF (*unable to bear him*): Okay. Good night, Mom. (*He starts moving.*)

WILLY: Because you got a greatness in you, Biff, remember that. You got all kinds of greatness . . . (*He lies back, exhausted.* BIFF *walks out.*)

LINDA (*calling after* BIFF): Sleep well, darling!

HAPPY: I'm gonna get married, Mom. I wanted to tell you.

LINDA: Go to sleep, dear.

HAPPY (*going*): I just wanted to tell you.

WILLY: Keep up the good work. (HAPPY *exits.*) God . . . remember that Ebbets Field game? The championship of the city?

LINDA: Just rest. Should I sing to you?

WILLY: Yeah. Sing to me. (LINDA *hums a soft lullaby.*) When that team came out—he was the tallest, remember?

LINDA: Oh, yes. And in gold.

BIFF *enters the darkened kitchen, takes a cigarette, and leaves the house. He comes downstage into a golden pool of light. He smokes, staring at the night.*

WILLY: Like a young god. Hercules—something like that. And the sun, the sun all around him. Remember how he waved to me? Right up from the field, with the representatives of three colleges standing by? And the buyers I brought, and the cheers when he came out—Loman, Loman, Loman! God Almighty, he'll be great yet. A star like that, magnificent, can never really fade away!

The light on WILLY *is fading. The gas heater begins to glow through the kitchen wall, near the stairs, a blue flame beneath red coils.*

LINDA (*timidly*): Willy dear, what has he got against you?

WILLY: I'm so tired. Don't talk any more.

BIFF *slowly returns to the kitchen. He stops, stares toward the heater.*

LINDA: Will you ask Howard to let you work in New York?

WILLY: First thing in the morning. Everything'll be all right.

BIFF *reaches behind the heater and draws out a length of rubber tubing. He is horrified and turns his head toward* WILLY*'s room, still dimly lit, from which the strains of* LINDA*'s desperate but monotonous humming rise.*

WILLY (*staring through the window into the moonlight*): Gee, look at the moon moving between the buildings!

BIFF *wraps the tubing around his hand and quickly goes up the stairs.*

ACT 2

Music is heard, gay and bright. The curtain rises as the music fades away. WILLY, *in shirt sleeves, is sitting at the kitchen table, sipping coffee, his hat in his lap.* LINDA *is filling his cup when she can.*

WILLY: Wonderful coffee. Meal in itself.

LINDA: Can I make you some eggs?

WILLY: No. Take a breath.

LINDA: You look so rested, dear.

WILLY: I slept like a dead one. First time in months. Imagine, sleeping till ten on a Tuesday morning. Boys left nice and early, heh?

LINDA: They were out of here by eight o'clock.

WILLY: Good work!

LINDA: It was so thrilling to see them leaving together. I can't get over the shaving lotion in this house!

WILLY (*smiling*): Mmm . . .

LINDA: Biff was very changed this morning. His whole attitude seemed to be hopeful. He couldn't wait to get downtown to see Oliver.

WILLY: He's heading for a change. There's no question, there simply are certain men that take longer to get—solidified. How did he dress?

LINDA: His blue suit. He's so handsome in that suit. He could be a—anything in that suit!

WILLY *gets up from the table.* LINDA *holds his jacket for him.*

WILLY: There's no question, no question at all. Gee, on the way home tonight I'd like to buy some seeds.

LINDA (*laughing*): That'd be wonderful. But not enough sun gets back there. Nothing'll grow any more.

WILLY: You wait, kid, before it's all over we're gonna get a little place out in the country, and I'll raise some vegetables, a couple of chickens . . .

LINDA: You'll do it yet, dear.

WILLY *walks out of his jacket.* LINDA *follows him.*

WILLY: And they'll get married, and come for a weekend. I'd build a little guest house. 'Cause I got so many fine tools, all I'd need would be a little lumber and some peace of mind.

LINDA (*joyfully*): I sewed the lining . . .

WILLY: I could build two guest houses, so they'd both come. Did he decide how much he's going to ask Oliver for?

LINDA (*getting him into the jacket*): He didn't mention it, but I imagine ten or fifteen thousand. You going to talk to Howard today?

WILLY: Yeah. I'll put it to him straight and simple. He'll just have to take me off the road.

LINDA: And Willy, don't forget to ask for a little advance, because we've got the insurance premium. It's the grace period now.

WILLY: That's a hundred . . . ?

LINDA: A hundred and eight, sixty-eight. Because we're a little short again.

WILLY: Why are we short?

LINDA: Well, you had the motor job on the car . . .

WILLY: That goddam Studebaker!

LINDA: And you got one more payment on the refrigerator . . .

WILLY: But it just broke again!

LINDA: Well, it's old, dear.

WILLY: I told you we should've bought a well-advertised machine. Charley bought a General Electric and it's twenty years old and it's still good, that son-of-a-bitch.

LINDA: But, Willy . . .

WILLY: Whoever heard of a Hastings refrigerator? Once in my life I would like to own something outright before it's broken! I'm always in a race with the junkyard! I just finished paying for the car and it's on its last legs. The refrigerator consumes belts like a goddam maniac. They time those things. They time them so when you finally paid for them, they're used up.

LINDA (*buttoning up his jacket as he unbuttons it*): All told, about two hundred dollars would carry us, dear. But that includes the last payment on the mortgage. After this payment, Willy, the house belongs to us.

WILLY: It's twenty-five years!

LINDA: Biff was nine years old when we bought it.

WILLY: Well, that's a great thing. To weather a twenty-five year mortgage is . . .

LINDA: It's an accomplishment.

WILLY: All the cement, the lumber, the reconstruction I put in this house! There ain't a crack to be found in it any more.

LINDA: Well, it served its purpose.

WILLY: What purpose? Some stranger'll come along, move in, and that's that. If only Biff would take this house, and raise a family . . . (*He starts to go.*) Goodby, I'm late.

LINDA (*suddenly remembering*): Oh, I forgot! You're supposed to meet them for dinner.

WILLY: Me?

LINDA: At Frank's Chop House on Forty-eighth near Sixth Avenue.

WILLY: Is that so! How about you?

LINDA: No, just the three of you. They're gonna blow you to a big meal!

WILLY: Don't say! Who thought of that?

LINDA: Biff came to me this morning, Willy, and he said, "Tell Dad, we want to blow him to a big meal." Be there six o'clock. You and your two boys are going to have dinner.

WILLY: Gee whiz! That's really somethin'. I'm gonna knock Howard for a loop, kid. I'll get an advance, and I'll come home with a New York job. Goddammit, now I'm gonna do it!

LINDA: Oh, that's the spirit, Willy!

WILLY: I will never get behind a wheel the rest of my life!

LINDA: It's changing, Willy, I can feel it changing!

WILLY: Beyond a question. G'by, I'm late. (*He starts to go again.*)

LINDA (*calling after him as she runs to the kitchen table for a handkerchief*): You got your glasses?

WILLY (*feels for them, then comes back in*): Yeah, yeah, got my glasses.

LINDA (*giving him the handkerchief*): And a handkerchief.

WILLY: Yeah, handkerchief.

LINDA: And your saccharine?

WILLY: Yeah, my saccharine.

LINDA: Be careful on the subway stairs.

She kisses him, and a silk stocking is seen hanging from her hand. WILLY *notices it.*

WILLY: Will you stop mending stockings? At least while I'm in the house. It gets me nervous. I can't tell you. Please.

LINDA *hides the stocking in her hand as she follows* WILLY *across the forestage in front of the house.*

LINDA: Remember, Frank's Chop House.

WILLY (*passing the apron*): Maybe beets would grow out there.

LINDA (*laughing*): But you tried so many times.

WILLY: Yeah. Well, don't work hard today. (*He disappears around the right corner of the house.*)

LINDA: Be careful!

As WILLY *vanishes,* LINDA *waves to him. Suddenly the phone rings. She runs across the stage and into the kitchen and lifts it.*

LINDA: Hello? Oh, Biff! I'm so glad you called, I just . . . Yes, sure, I just told him. Yes, he'll be there for dinner at six o'clock, I didn't forget. Listen, I was just dying to tell you. You know that little rubber pipe I told you about? That he connected to the gas heater? I finally decided to go down the cellar this morning and take it away and destroy it. But it's gone! Imagine? He took it away himself, it isn't there! (*She listens.*) When? Oh, then you took it. Oh— nothing, it's just that I'd hoped he'd taken it away himself. Oh, I'm not worried, darling, because this morning he left in such high spirits, it was like the old days! I'm not afraid any more. Did Mr. Oliver see you? . . . Well, you wait there then. And make a nice impression on him, darling. Just don't perspire too much before you see him. And have a nice time with Dad. He may have big news too! . . . That's right, a New York job. And be sweet to him tonight, dear. Be loving to him. Because he's only a little boat looking for a harbor. (*She is trembling with sorrow and joy.*) Oh, that's wonderful, Biff, you'll save his life. Thanks, darling. Just put your arm around him when he comes into the restaurant. Give him a smile. That's the boy . . . Good-by, dear. . . . You got your comb? . . . That's fine. Good- by, Biff dear.

In the middle of her speech, HOWARD WAGNER, *thirty-six, wheels in a small type- writer table on which is a wire-recording machine and proceeds to plug it in. This is on the left forestage. Light slowly fades on* LINDA *as it rises on* HOWARD. HOWARD *is intent on threading the machine and only glances over his shoulder as* WILLY *appears.*

WILLY: Pst! Pst!

HOWARD: Hello, Willy, come in.

WILLY: Like to have a little talk with you, Howard.

HOWARD: Sorry to keep you waiting. I'll be with you in a minute.

WILLY: What's that, Howard?

HOWARD: Didn't you ever see one of these? Wire recorder.

WILLY: Oh. Can we talk a minute?

HOWARD: Records things. Just got delivery yesterday. Been driving me crazy, the most terrific machine I ever saw in my life. I was up all night with it.

WILLY: What do you do with it?

HOWARD: I bought it for dictation, but you can do anything with it. Listen to this. I had it home last night. Listen to what I picked up. The first one is my daughter. Get this. (*He flicks the switch and "Roll out the Barrel" is heard being whistled.*) Listen to that kid whistle.

WILLY: That is lifelike, isn't it?

HOWARD: Seven years old. Get that tone.

WILLY: Ts, ts. Like to ask a little favor if you . . .

The whistling breaks off, and the voice of HOWARD'*s daughter is heard.*

HIS DAUGHTER: "Now you, Daddy."

HOWARD: She's crazy for me! (*Again the same song is whistled.*) That's me! Ha! (*He winks.*)

WILLY: You're very good!

The whistling breaks off again. The machine runs silent for a moment.

HOWARD: Sh! Get this now, this is my son.

HIS SON: "The capital of Alabama is Montgomery; the capital of Arizona is Phoenix; the capital of Arkansas is Little Rock; the capital of California is Sacramento . . . " (*and on, and on.*)

HOWARD (*holding up five fingers*): Five years old, Willy!

WILLY: He'll make an announcer some day!

HIS SON (*continuing*): "the capital . . ."

HOWARD: Get that—alphabetical order! (*The machine breaks off suddenly.*) Wait a
minute. The maid kicked the plug out.

WILLY: It certainly is a . . .

HOWARD: Sh, for God's sake!

HIS SON: "It's nine o'clock, Bulova watch time. So I have to go to sleep."

WILLY: That really is . . .

HOWARD: Wait a minute! The next is my wife.

They wait.

HOWARD'S VOICE: "Go on, say something." (*Pause.*) "Well, you gonna talk?"

HIS WIFE: "I can't think of anything."

HOWARD'S VOICE: "Well, talk—it's turning."

HIS WIFE (*shyly, beaten*): "Hello." (*Silence.*) "Oh, Howard, I can't talk into this . . ."

HOWARD (*snapping the machine off*): That was my wife.

WILLY: That is a wonderful machine. Can we . . .

HOWARD: I tell you, Willy, I'm gonna take my camera, and my bandsaw, and all my
hobbies, and out they go. This is the most fascinating relaxation I ever
found.

WILLY: I think I'll get one myself.

HOWARD: Sure, they're only a hundred and a half. You can't do without it. Supposing
you wanna hear Jack Benny, see? But you can't be at home at that hour.
So you tell the maid to turn the radio on when Jack Benny comes on, and
this automatically goes on with the radio . . .

WILLY: And when you come home you . . .

HOWARD: You can come home twelve o'clock, one o'clock, any time you like, and
you get yourself a Coke and sit yourself down, throw the switch, and
there's Jack Benny's program in the middle of the night!

WILLY: I'm definitely going to get one. Because lots of times I'm on the road, and
I think to myself, what I must be missing on the radio!

HOWARD: Don't you have a radio in the car?

WILLY: Well, yeah, but who ever thinks of turning it on?

HOWARD: Say, aren't you supposed to be in Boston?

WILLY: That's what I want to talk to you about, Howard. You got a minute? (*He
draws a chair in from the wing.*)

HOWARD: What happened? What're you doing here?

WILLY: Well . . .

HOWARD: You didn't crack up again, did you?

WILLY: Oh, no. No . . .

HOWARD: Geez, you had me worried there for a minute. What's the trouble?

WILLY: Well, tell you the truth, Howard. I've come to the decision that I'd rather not
travel any more.

HOWARD: Not travel! Well, what'll you do?

WILLY: Remember, Christmas time, when you had the party here? You said you'd try
to think of some spot for me here in town.

HOWARD: With us?

WILLY: Well, sure.

HOWARD: Oh, yeah, yeah. I remember. Well, I couldn't think of anything for you,
Willy.

WILLY: I tell ya, Howard. The kids are all grown up, y'know. I don't need much any more. If I could take home—well, sixty-five dollars a week, I could swing it.

HOWARD: Yeah, but Willy, see I . . .

WILLY: I tell ya why, Howard. Speaking frankly and between the two of us, y'know— I'm just a little tired.

HOWARD: Oh, I could understand that, Willy. But you're a road man, Willy, and we do a road business. We've only got a half-dozen salesmen on the floor here.

WILLY: God knows, Howard. I never asked a favor of any man. But I was with the firm when your father used to carry you in here in his arms.

HOWARD: I know that, Willy, but . . .

WILLY: Your father came to me the day you were born and asked me what I thought of the name Howard, may he rest in peace.

HOWARD: I appreciate that, Willy, but there just is no spot here for you. If I had a spot I'd slam you right in, but I just don't have a single solitary spot.

He looks for his lighter. WILLY *has picked it up and gives it to him. Pause.*

WILLY (*with increasing anger*): Howard, all I need to set my table is fifty dollars a week.

HOWARD: But where am I going to put you, kid?

WILLY: Look, it isn't a question of whether I can sell merchandise, is it?

HOWARD: No, but it's business, kid, and everybody's gotta pull his own weight.

WILLY (*desperately*): Just let me tell you a story, Howard . . .

HOWARD: 'Cause you gotta admit, business is business.

WILLY (*angrily*): Business is definitely business, but just listen for a minute. You don't understand this. When I was a boy—eighteen, nineteen—I was already on the road. And there was a question in my mind as to whether selling had a future for me. Because in those days I had a yearning to go to Alaska. See, there were three gold strikes in one month in Alaska, and I felt like going out. Just for the ride, you might say.

HOWARD (*barely interested*): Don't say.

WILLY: Oh, yeah, my father lived many years in Alaska. He was an adventurous man. We've got quite a little streak of self-reliance in our family. I thought I'd go out with my older brother and try to locate him, and maybe settle in the North with the old man. And I was almost decided to go, when I met a salesman in the Parker House. His name was Dave Singleman. And he was eightyfour years old, and he'd drummed merchandise in thirty-one states. And old Dave, he'd go up to his room, y'understand, put on his green velvet slippers— I'll never forget—and pick up his phone and call the buyers, and without ever leaving his room, at the age of eighty-four, he made his living. And when I saw that, I realized that selling was the greatest career a man could want. 'Cause what could be more satisfying than to be able to go, at the age of eighty-four, into twenty or thirty different cities, and pick up a phone, and be remembered and loved and helped by so many different people? Do you know? when he died—and by the way he died the death of a salesman, in his green velvet slippers in the smoker of the New York, New Haven and Hartford, going into Boston—when he died, hundreds of salesmen and buyers were at his funeral. Things were sad on a lotta trains for months after that. (*He stands up,* HOWARD *has not looked at him.*) In those days there was personality in it, Howard. There was respect, and comradeship, and gratitude in it. Today, it's all cut and dried, and there's no chance for bringing friendship to bear—or personality. You see what I mean? They don't know me any more.

HOWARD (*moving away, to the right*): That's just the thing, Willy.

WILLY: If I had forty dollars a week—that's all I'd need. Forty dollars, Howard.

HOWARD: Kid, I can't take blood from a stone, I . . .

WILLY (*desperation is on him now*): Howard, the year Al Smith was nominated, your father came to me and . . .

HOWARD (*starting to go off*): I've got to see some people, kid.

WILLY (*stopping him*): I'm talking about your father! There were promises made across this desk! You mustn't tell me you've got people to see—I put thirtyfour years into this firm, Howard, and now I can't pay my insurance! You can't eat the orange and throw the peel away—a man is not a piece of fruit! (*After a pause.*) Now pay attention. Your father—in 1928 I had a big year. I averaged a hundred and seventy dollars a week in commissions.

HOWARD (*impatiently*): Now, Willy, you never averaged . . .

WILLY (*banging his hand on the desk*): I averaged a hundred and seventy dollars a week in the year of 1928! And your father came to me—or rather, I was in the office here—it was right over this desk—and he put his hand on my shoulder . . .

HOWARD (*getting up*): You'll have to excuse me, Willy, I gotta see some people. Pull yourself together. (*Going out.*) I'll be back in a little while.

On HOWARD's *exit, the light on his chair grows very bright and strange.*

WILLY: Pull myself together! What the hell did I say to him? My God, I was yelling at him! How could I? (WILLY *breaks off, staring at the light, which occupies the chair, animating it. He approaches this chair, standing across the desk from it.*) Frank, Frank, don't you remember what you told me that time? How you put your hand on my shoulder, and Frank . . . (*He leans on the desk and as he speaks the dead man's name he accidentally switches on the recorder, and instantly*)

HOWARD's son: ". . . New York is Albany. The capital of Ohio is Cincinnati, the capital of Rhode Island is . . . " (*The recitation continues.*)

WILLY (*leaping away with fright, shouting*): Ha! Howard! Howard! Howard!

HOWARD (*rushing in*): What happened?

WILLY (*pointing at the machine, which continues nasally, childishly, with the capital cities*): Shut it off! Shut it off!

HOWARD (*pulling the plug out*): Look, Willy . . .

WILLY (*pressing his hands to his eyes*): I gotta get myself some coffee. I'll get some coffee . . .

WILLY *starts to walk out.* HOWARD *stops him.*

HOWARD (*rolling up the cord*): Willy, look . . .

WILLY: I'll go to Boston.

HOWARD: Willy, you can't go to Boston for us.

WILLY: Why can't I go?

HOWARD: I don't want you to represent us. I've been meaning to tell you for a long time now.

WILLY: Howard, are you firing me?

HOWARD: I think you need a good long rest, Willy.

WILLY: Howard . . .

HOWARD: And when you feel better, come back, and we'll see if we can work something out.

WILLY: But I gotta earn money, Howard. I'm in no position to . . .

HOWARD: Where are your sons? Why don't your sons give you a hand?

WILLY: They're working on a very big deal.

HOWARD: This is no time for false pride, Willy. You go to your sons and you tell them that you're tired. You've got two great boys, haven't you?

WILLY: Oh, no question, no question, but in the meantime . . .

HOWARD: Then that's that, heh?

WILLY: All right, I'll go to Boston tomorrow.

HOWARD: No, no.

WILLY: I can't throw myself on my sons. I'm not a cripple!

HOWARD: Look, kid, I'm busy this morning.

WILLY (*grasping* HOWARD's *arm*): Howard, you've got to let me go to Boston!

HOWARD (*hard, keeping himself under control*): I've got a line of people to see this morning. Sit down, take five minutes, and pull yourself together, and then go home, will ya? I need the office, Willy. (*He starts to go, turns, remembering the recorder, starts to push off the table holding the recorder.*) Oh, yeah. Whenever you can this week, stop by and drop off the samples. You'll feel better, Willy, and then come back and we'll talk. Pull yourself together, kid, there's people outside.

HOWARD *exits, pushing the table off left.* WILLY *stares into space, exhausted. Now the music is heard—*BEN's *music—first distantly, then closer, closer. As* WILLY *speaks,* BEN *enters from the right. He carries valise and umbrella.*

WILLY: Oh, Ben, how did you do it? What is the answer? Did you wind up the Alaska deal already?

BEN: Doesn't take much time if you know what you're doing. Just a short business trip. Boarding ship in an hour. Wanted to say good-by.

WILLY: Ben, I've got to talk to you.

BEN (*glancing at his watch*): Haven't the time, William.

WILLY (*crossing the apron to* BEN): Ben, nothing's working out. I don't know what to do.

BEN: Now, look here, William. I've bought timberland in Alaska and I need a man to look after things for me.

WILLY: God, timberland! Me and my boys in those grand outdoors!

BEN: You've a new continent at your doorstep, William. Get out of these cities, they're full of talk and time payments and courts of law. Screw on your fists and you can fight for a fortune up there.

WILLY: Yes, yes! Linda, Linda!

LINDA *enters as of old, with the wash.*

LINDA: Oh, you're back?

BEN: I haven't much time.

WILLY: No, wait! Linda, he's got a proposition for me in Alaska.

LINDA: But you've got . . . (*To* BEN.) He's got a beautiful job here.

WILLY: But in Alaska, kid, I could . . .

LINDA: You're doing well enough, Willy!

BEN (*To* LINDA): Enough for what, my dear?

LINDA (*frightened of* BEN *and angry at him*): Don't say those things to him! Enough to be happy right here, right now. (*To* WILLY, *while* BEN *laughs.*) Why must everybody conquer the world? You're well liked, and the boys love you, and someday—(*To* BEN)—why, old man Wagner told him just the other day that if he keeps it up he'll be a member of the firm, didn't he, Willy?

WILLY: Sure, sure. I am building something with this firm, Ben, and if a man is building something he must be on the right track, mustn't he?

BEN: What are you building? Lay your hand on it. Where is it?

WILLY (*hesitantly*): That's true, Linda, there's nothing.

LINDA: Why? (*To* BEN.) There's a man eighty-four years old . . .

WILLY: That's right, Ben, that's right. When I look at that man I say, what is there to worry about?

BEN: Bah!

WILLY: It's true, Ben. All he has to do is go into any city, pick up the phone, and he's making his living and you know why?

BEN (*picking up his valise*): I've got to go.

WILLY (*holding* BEN *back*): Look at this boy!

BIFF, *in his high school sweater, enters carrying suitcase.* HAPPY *carries* BIFF's *shoulder guards, gold helmet, and football pants.*

WILLY: Without a penny to his name, three great universities are begging for him, and from there the sky's the limit, because it's not what you do, Ben. It's who you know and the smile on your face! It's contacts, Ben, contacts! The whole wealth of Alaska passes over the lunch table at the Commodore Hotel, and that's the wonder, the wonder of this country, that a man can end with diamonds here on the basis of being liked! (*He turns to* BIFF.) And that's why when you get out on that field today it's important. Because thousands of people will be rooting for you and loving you. (*To* BEN, *who has again begun to leave.*) And Ben! when he walks into a business office his name will sound out like a bell and all the doors will open to him! I've seen it, Ben, I've seen it a thousand times! You can't feel it with your hand like timber, but it's there!

BEN: Good-by, William.

WILLY: Ben, am I right? Don't you think I'm right? I value your advice.

BEN: There's a new continent at your doorstep, William. You could walk out rich. Rich! (*He is gone.*)

WILLY: We'll do it here, Ben! You hear me? We're gonna do it here!

Young BERNARD *rushes in. The gay music of the Boys is heard.*

BERNARD: Oh, gee, I was afraid you left already!

WILLY: Why? What time is it?

BERNARD: It's half-past one!

WILLY: Well, come on, everybody! Ebbets Field next stop! Where's the pennants? (*He rushes through the wall-line of the kitchen and out into the living room.*)

LINDA (*to* BIFF): Did you pack fresh underwear?

BIFF (*who has been limbering up*): I want to go!

BERNARD: Biff, I'm carrying your helmet, ain't I?

HAPPY: No, I'm carrying the helmet.

BERNARD: Oh, Biff, you promised me.

HAPPY: I'm carrying the helmet.

BERNARD: How am I going to get in the locker room?

LINDA: Let him carry the shoulder guards. (*She puts her coat and hat on in the kitchen.*)

BERNARD: Can I, Biff? 'Cause I told everybody I'm going to be in the locker room.

HAPPY: In Ebbets Field it's the clubhouse.

BERNARD: I meant the clubhouse. Biff!

HAPPY: Biff!

BIFF (*grandly, after a slight pause*): Let him carry the shoulder guards.

HAPPY (*as he gives* BERNARD *the shoulder guards*): Stay close to us now.

> WILLY *rushes in with the pennants.*

WILLY (*handing them out*): Everybody wave when Biff comes out on the field. (HAPPY *and* BERNARD *run off.*) You set now, boy?

> *The music has died away.*

BIFF: Ready to go, Pop. Every muscle is ready.

WILLY (*at the edge of the apron*): You realize what this means?

BIFF: That's right, Pop.

WILLY (*feeling* BIFF's *muscles*): You're comin' home this afternoon captain of the All-Scholastic Championship Team of the City of New York.

BIFF: I got it, Pop. And remember, pal, when I take off my helmet, that touchdown is for you.

WILLY: Let's go! (*He is starting out, with his arm around* BIFF, *when* CHARLEY *enters, as of old, in knickers.*) I got no room for you, Charley.

CHARLEY: Room? For what?

WILLY: In the car.

CHARLEY: You goin' for a ride? I wanted to shoot some casino.

WILLY (*furiously*): Casino! (*Incredulously.*) Don't you realize what today is?

LINDA: Oh, he knows, Willy. He's just kidding you.

WILLY: That's nothing to kid about!

CHARLEY: No, Linda, what's goin' on?

LINDA: He's playing in Ebbets Field.

CHARLEY: Baseball in this weather?

WILLY: Don't talk to him. Come on, come on! (*He is pushing them out.*)

CHARLEY: Wait a minute, didn't you hear the news?

WILLY: What?

CHARLEY: Don't you listen to the radio? Ebbets Field just blew up.

WILLY: You go to hell! (CHARLEY *laughs. Pushing them out.*) Come on, come on! We're late.

CHARLEY (*as they go*): Knock a homer, Biff, knock a homer!

WILLY (*the last to leave, turning to* CHARLEY): I don't think that was funny, Charley. This is the greatest day of his life.

CHARLEY: Willy, when are you going to grow up?

WILLY: Yeah, heh? When this game is over, Charley, you'll be laughing out of the other side of your face. They'll be calling him another Red Grange. Twenty five thousand a year.

CHARLEY (*kidding*): Is that so?

WILLY: Yeah, that's so.

CHARLEY: Well, then, I'm sorry, Willy. But tell me something.

WILLY: What?

CHARLEY: Who is Red Grange?

WILLY: Put up your hands. Goddam you, put up your hands!

> CHARLEY, *chuckling, shakes his head and walks away, around the left corner of the stage.* WILLY *follows him. The music rises to a mocking frenzy.*

WILLY: Who the hell do you think you are, better than everybody else? You don't know everything, you big, ignorant, stupid . . . Put up your hands!

> *Light rises, on the right side of the forestage, on a small table in the reception room of* CHARLEY's *office. Traffic sounds heard.* BERNARD, *now mature, sits whistling to himself. A pair of tennis rackets and an old overnight bag are on the floor beside him.*

WILLY (*offstage*): What are you walking away for? Don't walk away! If you're going to say something say it to my face! I know you laugh at me behind my back. You'll laugh out of the other side of your goddam face after this game. Touchdown! Touchdown! Eighty thousand people! Touchdown! Right between the goal posts.

> (BERNARD *is a quiet, earnest, but self-assured young man.* WILLY's *voice is coming from right upstage now.* BERNARD *lowers his feet off the table and listens.* JENNY, *his father's secretary, enters.*)

JENNY (*distressed*): Say, Bernard, will you go out in the hall?

BERNARD: What is that noise? Who is it?

JENNY: Mr. Loman. He just got off the elevator.

BERNARD (*getting up*): Who's he arguing with?

JENNY: Nobody. There's nobody with him. I can't deal with him any more, and your father gets all upset every time he comes. I've got a lot of typing to do, and your father's waiting to sign it. Will you see him?

WILLY (*entering*): Touchdown! Touch— (*He sees* JENNY.) Jenny, Jenny, good to see you. How're ya? Workin'? Or still honest?

JENNY: Fine. How've you been feeling?

WILLY: Not much any more, Jenny. Ha, ha! (*He is surprised to see the rackets.*)

BERNARD: Hello, Uncle Willy.

WILLY (*almost shocked*): Bernard! Well, look who's here! (*He comes quickly, guiltily, to* BERNARD *and warmly shakes his hand.*)

BERNARD: How are you? Good to see you.

WILLY: What are you doing here?

BERNARD: Oh, just stopped by to see Pop. Get off my feet till my train leaves. I'm going to Washington in a few minutes.

WILLY: Is he in?

BERNARD: Yes, he's in his office with the accountant. Sit down.

WILLY (*sitting down*): What're you going to do in Washington?

BERNARD: Oh, just a case I've got there, Willy.

WILLY: That so? (*Indicating the rackets.*) You going to play tennis there?

BERNARD: I'm staying with a friend who's got a court.

WILLY: Don't say. His own tennis court. Must be fine people, I bet.

BERNARD: They are, very nice. Dad tells me Biff's in town.

WILLY (*with a big smile*): Yeah, Biff's in. Working on a very big deal, Bernard.

BERNARD: What's Biff doing?

WILLY: Well, he's been doing very big things in the West. But he decided to establish himself here. Very big. We're having dinner. Did I hear your wife had a boy?

BERNARD: That's right. Our second.

WILLY: Two boys! What do you know!

BERNARD: What kind of a deal has Biff got?

WILLY: Well, Bill Oliver—very big sporting-goods man—he wants Biff very badly. Called him in from the West. Long distance, carte blanche, special deliveries. Your friends have their own private tennis court?

BERNARD: You still with the old firm, Willy?

WILLY (*after a pause*): I'm—I'm overjoyed to see how you made the grade, Bernard, overjoyed. It's an encouraging thing to see a young man really— really . . . Looks very good for Biff—very . . . (*He breaks off, then.*) Bernard . . . . (*He is so full of emotion, he breaks off again.*)

BERNARD: What is it, Willy?

WILLY (*small and alone*): What—what's the secret?

BERNARD: What secret?

WILLY: How—how did you? Why didn't he ever catch on?

BERNARD: I wouldn't know that, Willy.

WILLY (*confidentially, desperately*): You were his friend, his boyhood friend. There's something I don't understand about it. His life ended after that Ebbets Field game. From the age of seventeen nothing good ever happened to him.

BERNARD: He never trained himself for anything.

WILLY: But he did, he did. After high school he took so many correspondence courses. Radio mechanics; television; God knows what, and never made the slightest mark.

BERNARD (*taking off his glasses*): Willy, do you want to talk candidly?

WILLY (*rising, faces* BERNARD): I regard you as a very brilliant man, Bernard. I value your advice.

BERNARD: Oh, the hell with the advice, Willy. I couldn't advise you. There's just one thing I've always wanted to ask you. When he was supposed to graduate, and the math teacher flunked him . . .

WILLY: Oh, that son-of-a-bitch ruined his life.

BERNARD: Yeah, but, Willy, all he had to do was go to summer school and make up that subject.

WILLY: That's right, that's right.

BERNARD: Did you tell him not to go to summer school?

WILLY: Me? I begged him to go. I ordered him to go!

BERNARD: Then why wouldn't he go?

WILLY: Why? Why! Bernard, that question has been trailing me like a ghost for the last fifteen years. He flunked the subject, and laid down and died like a hammer hit him!

BERNARD: Take it easy, kid.

WILLY: Let me talk to you—I got nobody to talk to. Bernard, Bernard, was it my fault? Y'see? It keeps going around in my mind, maybe I did something to him. I got nothing to give him.

BERNARD: Don't take it so hard.

WILLY: Why did he lay down? What is the story there? You were his friend!

BERNARD: Willy, I remember, it was June, and our grades came out. And he'd flunked math.

WILLY: That son-of-a-bitch!

BERNARD: No, it wasn't right then. Biff just got very angry, I remember, and he was ready to enroll in summer school.

WILLY (*surprised*): He was?

BERNARD: He wasn't beaten by it at all. But then, Willy, he disappeared from the block for almost a month. And I got the idea that he'd gone up to New England to see you. Did he have a talk with you then?

WILLY *stares in silence*.

BERNARD: Willy?

WILLY (*with a strong edge of resentment in his voice*): Yeah, he came to Boston. What about it?

BERNARD: Well, just that when he came back—I'll never forget this, it always mystifies me. Because I'd thought so well of Biff, even though he'd always taken advantage of me. I loved him, Willy, y'know? And he came back after that month and took his sneakers—remember those sneakers with "University of Virginia" printed on them? He was so proud of those, wore them every day. And he took them down in the cellar, and burned them up in the furnace. We had a fist fight. It lasted at least half an hour. Just the two of us, punching each other down the cellar, and crying right through it. I've often thought of how strange it was that I knew he'd given up his life. What happened in Boston, Willy?

WILLY *looks at him as at an intruder*.

BERNARD : I just bring it up because you asked me.

WILLY (*angrily*): Nothing. What do you mean, "What happened?" What's that got to do with anything?

BERNARD: Well, don't get sore.

WILLY: What are you trying to do, blame it on me? If a boy lays down is that my fault?

BERNARD: Now, Willy, don't get . . .

WILLY: Well, don't—don't talk to me that way! What does that mean, "What happened?"

CHARLEY *enters. He is in his vest, and he carries a bottle of bourbon*.

CHARLEY: Hey, you're going to miss that train. (*He waves the bottle*.)

BERNARD: Yeah, I'm going. (*He takes the bottle*.) Thanks, Pop. (*He picks up his rackets and bag*.) Good-by, Willy, and don't worry about it. You know, "If at first you don't succeed . . ."

WILLY: Yes, I believe in that.

BERNARD: But sometimes, Willy, it's better for a man just to walk away.

WILLY: Walk away?

BERNARD: That's right.

WILLY: But if you can't walk away?

BERNARD (*after a slight pause*): I guess that's when it's tough. (*Extending his hand*.) Good-by, Willy.

WILLY (*shaking* BERNARD's *hand*): Good-by, boy.

CHARLEY (*an arm on* BERNARD's *shoulder*): How do you like this kid? Gonna argue a case in front of the Supreme Court.

BERNARD (*protesting*): Pop!

WILLY (*genuinely shocked, pained, and happy*): No! The Supreme Court!

BERNARD: I gotta run. 'By, Dad!

CHARLEY: Knock 'em dead, Bernard!

BERNARD *goes off.*

WILLY (*as* CHARLEY *takes out his wallet*): The Supreme Court! And he didn't even mention it!

CHARLEY (*counting out money on the desk*): He don't have to—he's gonna do it.

WILLY: And you never told him what to do, did you? You never took any interest in him.

CHARLEY: My salvation is that I never took any interest in anything. There's some money—fifty dollars. I got an accountant inside.

WILLY: Charley, look . . . (*with difficulty*). I got my insurance to pay. If you can manage it—I need a hundred and ten dollars.

CHARLEY *doesn't reply for a moment; merely stops moving.*

WILLY: I'd draw it from my bank but Linda would know, and I . . .

CHARLEY: Sit down, Willy.

WILLY (*moving toward the chair*): I'm keeping an account of everything, remember. I'll pay every penny back. (*He sits.*)

CHARLEY: Now listen to me, Willy.

WILLY: I want you to know I appreciate . . .

CHARLEY (*sitting down on the table*): Willy, what're you doin'? What the hell is going on in your head?

WILLY: Why? I'm simply . . .

CHARLEY: I offered you a job. You make fifty dollars a week. And I won't send you on the road.

WILLY: I've got a job.

CHARLEY: Without pay? What kind of a job is a job without pay? (*He rises.*) Now, look, kid, enough is enough. I'm no genius but I know when I'm being insulted.

WILLY: Insulted!

CHARLEY: Why don't you want to work for me?

WILLY: What's the matter with you? I've got a job.

CHARLEY: Then what're you walkin' in here every week for?

WILLY (*getting up*): Well, if you don't want me to walk in here . . .

CHARLEY: I'm offering you a job.

WILLY: I don't want your goddam job!

CHARLEY: When the hell are you going to grow up?

WILLY (*furiously*): You big ignoramus, if you say that to me again I'll rap you one! I don't care how big you are! (*He's ready to fight.*)

Pause.

CHARLEY (*kindly, going to him*): How much do you need, Willy?

WILLY: Charley, I'm strapped. I'm strapped. I don't know what to do. I was just fired.

CHARLEY: Howard fired you?

WILLY: That snotnose. Imagine that? I named him. I named him Howard.

CHARLEY: Willy, when're you gonna realize that them things don't mean anything? You named him Howard, but you can't sell that. The only thing you got in this world is what you can sell. And the funny thing is that you're a salesman, and you don't know that.

WILLY: I've always tried to think otherwise, I guess. I always felt that if a man was impressive, and well liked, that nothing . . .

CHARLEY: Why must everybody like you? Who liked J. P. Morgan? Was he impressive? In a Turkish bath he'd look like a butcher. But with his pockets on he was very well liked. Now listen, Willy, I know you don't like me, and nobody can say I'm in love with you, but I'll give you a job because—just for the hell of it, put it that way. Now what do you say?

WILLY: I—I just can't work for you, Charley.

CHARLEY: What're you, jealous of me?

WILLY: I can't work for you, that's all, don't ask me why.

CHARLEY (*angered, takes out more bills*): You been jealous of me all your life, you damned fool! Here, pay your insurance. (*He puts the money in* WILLY'S *hand*.)

WILLY: I'm keeping strict accounts.

CHARLEY: I've got some work to do. Take care of yourself. And pay your insurance.

WILLY (*moving to the right*): Funny, y'know? After all the highways, and the trains, and the appointments, and the years, you end up worth more dead than alive.

CHARLEY: Willy, nobody's worth nothin' dead. (*After a slight pause.*) Did you hear what I said?

WILLY *stands still, dreaming*.

CHARLEY: Willy!

WILLY: Apologize to Bernard for me when you see him. I didn't mean to argue with him. He's a fine boy. They're all fine boys, and they'll end up big—all of them. Someday they'll all play tennis together. Wish me luck, Charley. He saw Bill Oliver today.

CHARLEY: Good luck.

WILLY (*on the verge of tears*): Charley, you're the only friend I got. Isn't that a remarkable thing? (*He goes out.*)

CHARLEY: Jesus!

CHARLEY *stares after him a moment and follows. All light blacks out. Suddenly raucous music is heard, and a red glow rises behind the screen at right.* STANLEY, *a young waiter, appears, carrying a table, followed by* HAPPY, *who is carrying two chairs.*

STANLEY (*putting the table down*): That's all right, Mr. Loman, I can handle it myself. (*He turns and takes the chairs from* HAPPY *and places them at the table.*)

HAPPY (*glancing around*): Oh, this is better.

STANLEY: Sure, in the front there you're in the middle of all kinds of noise. Whenever you got a party, Mr. Loman, you just tell me and I'll put you back here. Y'know, there's a lotta people they don't like it private, because when they go out they like to see a lotta action around them because they're sick and tired to stay in the house by theirself. But I know you, you ain't from Hackensack. You know what I mean?

HAPPY (*sitting down*): So how's it coming, Stanley?

STANLEY: Ah, it's a dog life. I only wish during the war they'd a took me in the Army. I coulda been dead by now.

HAPPY: My brother's back, Stanley.

STANLEY: Oh, he come back, heh? From the Far West.

HAPPY: Yeah, big cattle man, my brother, so treat him right. And my father's coming too.

STANLEY: Oh, your father too!

HAPPY: You got a couple of nice lobsters?

STANLEY: Hundred percent, big.

HAPPY: I want them with the claws.

STANLEY: Don't worry, I don't give you no mice. (HAPPY *laughs.*) How about some wine? It'll put a head on the meal.

HAPPY: No. You remember, Stanley, that recipe I brought you from overseas? With the champagne in it?

STANLEY: Oh, yeah, sure. I still got it tacked up yet in the kitchen. But that'll have to cost a buck apiece anyways.

HAPPY: That's all right.

STANLEY: What'd you, hit a number or somethin'?

HAPPY: No, it's a little celebration. My brother is—I think he pulled off a big deal today. I think we're going into business together.

STANLEY: Great! That's the best for you. Because a family business, you know what I mean?—that's the best.

HAPPY: That's what I think.

STANLEY: 'Cause what's the difference? Somebody steals? It's in the family. Know what I mean? (*Sotto voce.*) Like this bartender here. The boss is goin' crazy what kinda leak he's got in the cash register. You put it in but it don't come out.

HAPPY (*raising his head*): Sh!

STANLEY: What?

HAPPY: You notice I wasn't lookin' right or left, was I?

STANLEY: No.

HAPPY: And my eyes are closed.

STANLEY: So what's the . . . ?

HAPPY: Strudel's comin'.

STANLEY (*catching on, looks around*): Ah, no, there's no . . .

He breaks off as a furred, lavishly dressed GIRL *enters and sits at the next table. Both follow her with their eyes.*

STANLEY: Geez, how'd ya know?

HAPPY: I got radar or something. (*Staring directly at her profile.*) Oooooooo . . . Stanley.

STANLEY: I think that's for you, Mr. Loman.

HAPPY: Look at that mouth. Oh, God. And the binoculars.

STANLEY: Geez, you got a life, Mr. Loman.

HAPPY: Wait on her.

STANLEY (*going to the* GIRL'S *table*): Would you like a menu, ma'am?

GIRL: I'm expecting someone, but I'd like a . . .

HAPPY: Why don't you bring her—excuse me, miss, do you mind? I sell champagne, and I'd like you to try my brand. Bring her a champagne, Stanley.

GIRL: That's awfully nice of you.

HAPPY: Don't mention it. It's all company money. (*He laughs.*)

GIRL: That's a charming product to be selling, isn't it?

HAPPY: Oh, gets to be like everything else. Selling is selling, y'know.

GIRL: I suppose.

HAPPY: You don't happen to sell, do you?

GIRL: No, I don't sell.

HAPPY: Would you object to a compliment from a stranger? You ought to be on a magazine cover.

GIRL (*looking at him a little archly*): I have been.

STANLEY *comes in with a glass of champagne.*

HAPPY: What'd I say before, Stanley? You see? She's a cover girl.

STANLEY: Oh, I could see, I could see.

HAPPY (*to the* GIRL): What magazine?

GIRL: Oh, a lot of them. (*She takes the drink.*) Thank you.

HAPPY: You know what they say in France, don't you? "Champagne is the drink of the complexion"—Hya, Biff!

BIFF *has entered and sits with* HAPPY.

BIFF: Hello, kid. Sorry I'm late.

HAPPY: I just got here. Uh, Miss . . . ?

GIRL: Forsythe.

HAPPY: Miss Forsythe, this is my brother.

BIFF: Is Dad here?

HAPPY: His name is Biff. You might've heard of him. Great football player.

GIRL: Really? What team?

HAPPY: Are you familiar with football?

GIRL: No, I'm afraid I'm not.

HAPPY: Biff is quarterback with the New York Giants.

GIRL: Well, that is nice, isn't it? (*She drinks.*)

HAPPY: Good health.

GIRL: I'm happy to meet you.

HAPPY: That's my name. Hap. It's really Harold, but at West Point they called me Happy.

GIRL (*now really impressed*): Oh, I see. How do you do? (*She turns her profile.*)

BIFF: Isn't Dad coming?

HAPPY: You want her?

BIFF: Oh, I could never make that.

HAPPY: I remember the time that idea would never come into your head. Where's the old confidence, Biff?

BIFF: I just saw Oliver . . .

HAPPY: Wait a minute. I've got to see that old confidence again. Do you want her? She's on call.

BIFF: Oh, no. (*He turns to look at the* GIRL.)

HAPPY: I'm telling you. Watch this. (*Turning to the* GIRL.) Honey? (*She turns to him.*) Are you busy?

GIRL: Well, I am . . . but I could make a phone call.

HAPPY: Do that, will you, honey? And see if you can get a friend. We'll be here for a while. Biff is one of the greatest football players in the country.

GIRL (*standing up*): Well, I'm certainly happy to meet you.

HAPPY: Come back soon.

GIRL: I'll try.

HAPPY: Don't try, honey, try hard.

The GIRL *exits.* STANLEY *follows, shaking his head in bewildered admiration.*

HAPPY: Isn't that a shame now? A beautiful girl like that? That's why I can't get married. There's not a good woman in a thousand. New York is loaded with them, kid!

BIFF: Hap, look . . .

HAPPY: I told you she was on call!

BIFF (*strangely unnerved*): Cut it out, will ya? I want to say something to you.

HAPPY: Did you see Oliver?

BIFF: I saw him all right. Now look, I want to tell Dad a couple of things and I want you to help me.

HAPPY: What? Is he going to back you?

BIFF: Are you crazy? You're out of your goddam head, you know that?

HAPPY: Why? What happened?

BIFF (*breathlessly*): I did a terrible thing today, Hap. It's been the strangest day I ever went through. I'm all numb, I swear.

HAPPY: You mean he wouldn't see you?

BIFF: Well, I waited six hours for him, see? All day. Kept sending my name in. Even tried to date his secretary so she'd get me to him, but no soap.

HAPPY: Because you're not showin' the old confidence, Biff. He remembered you, didn't he?

BIFF (*stopping* HAPPY *with a gesture*): Finally, about five o'clock, he comes out. Didn't remember who I was or anything. I felt like such an idiot, Hap.

HAPPY: Did you tell him my Florida idea?

BIFF: He walked away. I saw him for one minute. I got so mad I could've torn the walls down! How the hell did I ever get the idea I was a salesman there? I even believed myself that I'd been a salesman for him! And then he gave me one look and—I realized what a ridiculous lie my whole life has been! We've been talking in a dream for fifteen years. I was a shipping clerk.

HAPPY: What'd you do?

BIFF (*with great tension and wonder*): Well, he left, see. And the secretary went out. I was all alone in the waiting room. I don't know what came over me, Hap. The next thing I know I'm in his office—paneled walls, everything. I can't explain it. I—Hap. I took his fountain pen.

HAPPY: Geez, did he catch you?

BIFF: I ran out. I ran down all eleven flights. I ran and ran and ran.

HAPPY: That was an awful dumb—what'd you do that for?

BIFF (*agonized*): I don't know, I just—wanted to take something, I don't know. You gotta help me, Hap. I'm gonna tell Pop.

HAPPY: You crazy? What for?

BIFF: Hap, he's got to understand that I'm not the man somebody lends that kind of money to. He thinks I've been spiting him all these years and it's eating him up.

HAPPY: That's just it. You tell him something nice.

BIFF: I can't.

HAPPY: Say you got a lunch date with Oliver tomorrow.

BIFF: So what do I do tomorrow?

HAPPY: You leave the house tomorrow and come back at night and say Oliver is thinking it over. And he thinks it over for a couple of weeks, and gradually it fades away and nobody's the worse.

BIFF: But it'll go on forever!

HAPPY: Dad is never so happy as when he's looking forward to something!

WILLY *enters.*

HAPPY: Hello, scout!

WILLY: Gee, I haven't been here in years!

STANLEY *has followed* WILLY *in and sets a chair for him.* STANLEY *starts off but* HAPPY *stops him.*

HAPPY: Stanley!

STANLEY *stands by, waiting for an order.*

BIFF (*going to* WILLY *with guilt, as to an invalid*): Sit down, Pop. You want a drink?

WILLY: Sure, I don't mind.

BIFF: Let's get a load on.

WILLY: You look worried.

BIFF: N-no. (*To* STANLEY.) Scotch all around. Make it doubles.

STANLEY: Doubles, right. (*He goes.*)

WILLY: You had a couple already, didn't you?

BIFF: Just a couple, yeah.

WILLY: Well, what happened, boy? (*Nodding affirmatively, with a smile.*) Everything go all right?

BIFF (*takes a breath, then reaches out and grasps* WILLY's *hand*): Pal . . . (*He is smiling bravely, and* WILLY *is smiling too.*) I had an experience today.

HAPPY: Terrific, Pop.

WILLY: That so? What happened?

BIFF (*high, slightly alcoholic, above the earth*): I'm going to tell you everything from first to last. It's been a strange day. (*Silence. He looks around, composes himself as best he can, but his breath keeps breaking the rhythm of his voice.*) I had to wait quite a while for him, and . . .

WILLY: Oliver?

BIFF: Yeah, Oliver. All day, as a matter of cold fact. And a lot of—instances—facts, Pop, facts about my life came back to me. Who was it, Pop? Who ever said I was a salesman with Oliver?

WILLY: Well, you were.

BIFF: No, Dad, I was a shipping clerk.

WILLY: But you were practically . . .

BIFF (*with determination*): Dad, I don't know who said it first, but I was never a salesman for Bill Oliver.

WILLY: What're you talking about?

BIFF: Let's hold on to the facts tonight, Pop. We're not going to get anywhere bullin' around. I was a shipping clerk.

WILLY (*angrily*): All right, now listen to me . . .

BIFF: Why don't you let me finish?

WILLY: I'm not interested in stories about the past or any crap of that kind because the woods are burning, boys, you understand? There's a big blaze going on all around. I was fired today.

BIFF (*shocked*): How could you be?

WILLY: I was fired, and I'm looking for a little good news to tell your mother, because the woman has waited and the woman has suffered. The gist of it is that I haven't got a story left in my head, Biff. So don't give me a lecture about facts and aspects. I am not interested. Now what've you got to say to me?

STANLEY *enters with three drinks. They wait until he leaves.*

WILLY: Did you see Oliver?

BIFF: Jesus, Dad!

WILLY: You mean you didn't go up there?

HAPPY: Sure he went up there.

BIFF: I did. I—saw him. How could they fire you?

WILLY (*on the edge of his chair*): What kind of a welcome did he give you?

BIFF: He won't even let you work on commission?

WILLY: I'm out! (*Driving.*) So tell me, he gave you a warm welcome?

HAPPY: Sure, Pop, sure!

BIFF (*driven*): Well, it was kind of . . .

WILLY: I was wondering if he'd remember you. (*To* HAPPY.) Imagine, man doesn't see him for ten, twelve years and gives him that kind of a welcome!

HAPPY: Damn right!

BIFF (*trying to return to the offensive*): Pop, look . . .

WILLY: You know why he remembered you, don't you? Because you impressed him in those days.

BIFF: Let's talk quietly and get this down to the facts, huh?

WILLY (*as though* BIFF *had been interrupting*): Well, what happened? It's great news, Biff. Did he take you into his office or'd you talk in the waiting room?

BIFF: Well, he came in, see, and . . .

WILLY (*with a big smile*): What'd he say? Betcha he threw his arm around you.

BIFF: Well, he kinda . . .

WILLY: He's a fine man. (*To* HAPPY.) Very hard man to see, y'know.

HAPPY (*agreeing*): Oh, I know.

WILLY (*to* BIFF): Is that where you had the drinks?

BIFF: Yeah, he gave me a couple of—no, no!

HAPPY (*cutting in*): He told him my Florida idea.

WILLY: Don't interrupt. (*To* BIFF.) How'd he react to the Florida idea?

BIFF: Dad, will you give me a minute to explain?

WILLY: I've been waiting for you to explain since I sat down here! What happened? He took you into his office and what?

BIFF: Well—I talked. And—and he listened, see.

WILLY: Famous for the way he listens, y'know. What was his answer?

BIFF: His answer was— (*He breaks off, suddenly angry.*) Dad, you're not letting me tell you what I want to tell you!

WILLY (*accusing, angered*): You didn't see him, did you?

BIFF: I did see him!

WILLY: What'd you insult him or something? You insulted him, didn't you?

BIFF: Listen, will you let me out of it, will you just let me out of it!

HAPPY: What the hell!

WILLY: Tell me what happened!

BIFF (*to* HAPPY): I can't talk to him!

> *A single trumpet note jars the ear. The light of green leaves stains the house, which holds the air of night and a dream.* YOUNG BERNARD *enters and knocks on the door of the house.*

YOUNG BERNARD (*frantically*): Mrs. Loman, Mrs. Loman!

HAPPY: Tell him what happened!

BIFF (*to* HAPPY): Shut up and leave me alone!

WILLY: No, no! You had to go and flunk math!

BIFF: What math? What're you talking about?

YOUNG BERNARD: Mrs. Loman, Mrs. Loman!

LINDA *appears in the house, as of old.*

WILLY (*wildly*): Math, math, math!

BIFF: Take it easy, Pop!

YOUNG BERNARD: Mrs. Loman!

WILLY (*furiously*): If you hadn't flunked you'd've been set by now!

BIFF: Now, look, I'm gonna tell you what happened, and you're going to listen to me.

YOUNG BERNARD: Mrs. Loman!

BIFF: I waited six hours . . .

HAPPY: What the hell are you saying?

BIFF: I kept sending in my name but he wouldn't see me. So finally he . . . (*He continues unheard as light fades low on the restaurant.*)

YOUNG BERNARD: Biff flunked math!

LINDA: No!

YOUNG BERNARD: Birnbaum flunked him! They won't graduate him!

LINDA: But they have to. He's gotta go to the university. Where is he? Biff! Biff!

YOUNG BERNARD: No, he left. He went to Grand Central.

LINDA: Grand—You mean he went to Boston!

YOUNG BERNARD: Is Uncle Willy in Boston?

LINDA: Oh, maybe Willy can talk to the teacher. Oh, the poor, poor boy!

Light on house area snaps out.

BIFF (*at the table, now audible, holding up a gold fountain pen*): . . . so I'm washed up with Oliver, you understand? Are you listening to me?

WILLY (*at a loss*): Yeah, sure. If you hadn't flunked . . .

BIFF: Flunked what? What're you talking about?

WILLY: Don't blame everything on me! I didn't flunk math—you did! What pen?

HAPPY: That was awful dumb, Biff, a pen like that is worth—

WILLY (*seeing the pen for the first time*): You took Oliver's pen?

BIFF (*weakening*): Dad, I just explained it to you.

WILLY: You stole Bill Oliver's fountain pen!

BIFF: I didn't exactly steal it! That's just what I've been explaining to you!

HAPPY: He had it in his hand and just then Oliver walked in, so he got nervous and stuck it in his pocket!

WILLY: My God, Biff!

BIFF: I never intended to do it, Dad!

OPERATOR'S VOICE: Standish Arms, good evening!

WILLY (*shouting*): I'm not in my room!

BIFF (*frightened*): Dad, what's the matter? (*He and* HAPPY *stand up.*)

OPERATOR: Ringing Mr. Loman for you!

WILLY: I'm not there, stop it!

BIFF (*horrified, gets down on one knee before* WILLY): Dad, I'll make good, I'll make good. (WILLY *tries to get to his feet.* BIFF *holds him down.*) Sit down now.

WILLY: No, you're no good, you're no good for anything.

BIFF: I am, Dad, I'll find something else, you understand? Now don't worry about anything. (*He holds up* WILLY's *face.*) Talk to me, Dad.

OPERATOR: Mr. Loman does not answer. Shall I page him?

WILLY (*attempting to stand, as though to rush and silence the* OPERATOR): No, no, no!

HAPPY: He'll strike something, Pop.

WILLY: No, no . . .

BIFF (*desperately, standing over* WILLY): Pop, listen! Listen to me! I'm telling you something good. Oliver talked to his partner about the Florida idea. You listening? He—he talked to his partner, and he came to me . . . I'm going to be all right, you hear? Dad, listen to me, he said it was just a question of the amount!

WILLY: Then you . . . got it?

HAPPY: He's gonna be terrific, Pop!

WILLY (*trying to stand*): Then you got it, haven't you? You got it! You got it!

BIFF (*agonized, holds* WILLY *down*): No, no. Look, Pop. I'm supposed to have lunch with them tomorrow. I'm just telling you this so you'll know that I can still make an impression, Pop. And I'll make good somewhere, but I can't go tomorrow, see.

WILLY: Why not? You simply . . .

BIFF: But the pen, Pop!

WILLY: You give it to him and tell him it was an oversight!

HAPPY: Sure, have lunch tomorrow!

BIFF: I can't say that . . .

WILLY: You were doing a crossword puzzle and accidentally used his pen!

BIFF: Listen, kid, I took those balls years ago, now I walk in with his fountain pen? That clinches it, don't you see? I can't face him like that! I'll try elscwhere.

PAGE'S VOICE: Paging Mr. Loman!

WILLY: Don't you want to be anything?

BIFF: Pop, how can I go back?

WILLY: You don't want to be anything, is that what's behind it?

BIFF (*now angry at* WILLY *for not crediting his sympathy*): Don't take it that way! You think it was easy walking into that office after what I'd done to him? A team of horses couldn't have dragged me back to Bill Oliver!

WILLY: Then why'd you go?

BIFF: Why did I go? Why did I go! Look at you! Look at what's become of you!

Off left, THE WOMAN *laughs.*

WILLY: Biff, you're going to go to that lunch tomorrow, or . . .

BIFF: I can't go. I've got no appointment!

HAPPY: Biff, for . . . !

WILLY: Are you spiting me?

BIFF: Don't take it that way! Goddammit!

WILLY (*strikes* BIFF *and falters away from the table*): You rotten little louse! Are you spiting me?

THE WOMAN: Someone's at the door, Willy!

BIFF: I'm no good, can't you see what I am?

HAPPY (*separating them*): Hey, you're in a restaurant! Now cut it out, both of you! (*The girls enter.*) Hello, girls, sit down.

THE WOMAN *laughs, off left.*

MISS FORSYTHE: I guess we might as well. This is Letta.

THE WOMAN: Willy, are you going to wake up?

BIFF (*ignoring* WILLY): How're ya, miss, sit down. What do you drink?

MISS FORSYTHE: Letta might not be able to stay long.

LETTA: I gotta get up very early tomorrow. I got jury duty. I'm so excited! Were you fellows ever on a jury?

BIFF: No, but I been in front of them! (*The girls laugh.*) This is my father.

LETTA: Isn't he cute? Sit down with us, Pop.

HAPPY: Sit him down, Biff!

BIFF (*going to him*): Come on, slugger, drink us under the table. To hell with it! Come on, sit down, pal.

On BIFF's *last insistence,* WILLY *is about to sit.*

THE WOMAN (now urgently): Willy, are you going to answer the door!

THE WOMAN's *call pulls* WILLY *back. He starts right, befuddled.*

BIFF: Hey, where are you going?

WILLY: Open the door.

BIFF: The door?

WILLY: The washroom . . . the door . . . where's the door?

BIFF (*leading* WILLY *to the left*): Just go straight down.

WILLY *moves left.*

THE WOMAN: Willy, Willy, are you going to get up, get up, get up, get up?

WILLY *exits left.*

LETTA: I think it's sweet you bring your daddy along.

MISS FORSYTHE: Oh, he isn't really your father!

BIFF (*at left, turning to her resentfully*): Miss Forsythe, you've just seen a prince walk by. A fine, troubled prince. A hardworking, unappreciated prince. A pal, you understand? A good companion. Always for his boys.

LETTA: That's so sweet.

HAPPY: Well, girls, what's the program? We're wasting time. Come on, Biff. Gather round. Where would you like to go?

BIFF: Why don't you do something for him?

HAPPY: Me!

BIFF: Don't you give a damn for him, Hap?

HAPPY: What're you talking about? I'm the one who . . .

BIFF: I sense it, you don't give a good goddam about him. (*He takes the rolled-up hose from his pocket and puts it on the table in front of* HAPPY.) Look what I found in the cellar, for Christ's sake. How can you bear to let it go on?

HAPPY: Me? Who goes away? Who runs off and . . .

BIFF: Yeah, but he doesn't mean anything to you. You could help him—I can't! Don't you understand what I'm talking about? He's going to kill himself, don't you know that?

HAPPY: Don't I know it! Me!

BIFF: Hap, help him! Jesus . . . help him . . . Help me, help me, I can't bear to look at his face! (*Ready to weep, he hurries out, up right.*)

HAPPY (*starting after him*): Where are you going?

MISS FORSYTHE: What's he so mad about?

HAPPY: Come on, girls, we'll catch up with him.

MISS FORSYTHE (*as* HAPPY *pushes her out*): Say, I don't like that temper of his!

HAPPY: He's just a little overstrung, he'll be all right!

WILLY (*off left, as* THE WOMAN *laughs*): Don't answer! Don't answer!

LETTA: Don't you want to tell your father . . .

HAPPY: No, that's not my father. He's just a guy. Come on, we'll catch Biff, and, honey, we're going to paint this town! Stanley, where's the check! Hey, Stanley!

They exit. STANLEY *looks toward left.*

STANLEY (calling to HAPPY indignantly): Mr. Loman! Mr. Loman!

STANLEY *picks up a chair and follows them off. Knocking is heard off left.* THE WOMAN *enters, laughing.* WILLY *follows her. She is in a black slip; he is buttoning his shirt. Raw, sensuous music accompanies their speech.*

WILLY: Will you stop laughing? Will you stop?

THE WOMAN: Aren't you going to answer the door? He'll wake the whole hotel.

WILLY: I'm not expecting anybody.

THE WOMAN: Whyn't you have another drink, honey, and stop being so damn self-centered?

WILLY: I'm so lonely.

THE WOMAN: You know you ruined me, Willy? From now on, whenever you come to the office, I'll see that you go right through to the buyers. No waiting at my desk anymore, Willy. You ruined me.

WILLY: That's nice of you to say that.

THE WOMAN: Gee, you are self-centered! Why so sad? You are the saddest, selfcen-teredest soul I ever did see-saw. (*She laughs. He kisses her.*) Come on inside, drummer boy. It's silly to be dressing in the middle of the night. (*As knocking is heard.*) Aren't you going to answer the door?

WILLY: They're knocking on the wrong door.

THE WOMAN: But I felt the knocking. And he heard us talking in here. Maybe the hotel's on fire!

WILLY (*his terror rising*): It's a mistake.

THE WOMAN: Then tell him to go away!

WILLY: There's nobody there.

THE WOMAN: It's getting on my nerves, Willy. There's somebody standing out there and it's getting on my nerves!

WILLY (*pushing her away from him*): All right, stay in the bathroom here, and don't come out. I think there's a law in Massachusetts about it, so don't come out. It may be that new room clerk. He looked very mean. So don't come out. It's a mistake, there's no fire.

The knocking is heard again. he takes a few steps away from her, and she vanishes into the wing. The light follows him, and now he is facing YOUNG BIFF, *who carries a suitcase.* BIFF *steps toward him. The music is gone.*

BIFF: Why didn't you answer?

WILLY: Biff! What are you doing in Boston?

BIFF: Why didn't you answer? I've been knocking for five minutes, I called you on the phone . . .

WILLY: I just heard you. I was in the bathroom and had the door shut. Did anything happen home?

BIFF: Dad—I let you down.

WILLY: What do you mean?

BIFF: Dad . . .

WILLY: Biffo, what's this about? (*Putting his arm around* BIFF.) Come on, let's go downstairs and get you a malted.

BIFF: Dad, I flunked math.

WILLY: Not for the term?

BIFF: The term. I haven't got enough credits to graduate.

WILLY: You mean to say Bernard wouldn't give you the answers?

BIFF: He did, he tried, but I only got a sixty-one.

WILLY: And they wouldn't give you four points?

BIFF: Birnbaum refused absolutely. I begged him, Pop, but he won't give me those points. You gotta talk to him before they close the school. Because if he saw the kind of man you are, and you just talked to him in your way, I'm sure he'd come through for me. The class came right before practice, see, and I didn't go enough. Would you talk to him? He'd like you, Pop. You know the way you could talk.

WILLY: You're on. We'll drive right back.

BIFF: Oh, Dad, good work! I'm sure he'll change it for you!

WILLY: Go downstairs and tell the clerk I'm checkin' out. Go right down.

BIFF: Yes, sir! See, the reason he hates me, Pop—one day he was late for class so I got up at the blackboard and imitated him. I crossed my eyes and talked with a lithp.

WILLY (*laughing*): You did? The kids like it?

BIFF: They nearly died laughing!

WILLY: Yeah? What'd you do?

BIFF: The thquare root of thixty twee is . . . (WILLY *bursts out laughing;* BIFF *joins.*) And in the middle of it he walked in!

WILLY *laughs and* THE WOMAN *joins in offstage.*

WILLY (*without hesitation*): Hurry downstairs and . . .

BIFF: Somebody in there?

WILLY: No, that was next door.

THE WOMAN *laughs offstage.*

BIFF: Somebody got in your bathroom!

WILLY: No, it's the next room, there's a party . . .

THE WOMAN (*enters, laughing; she lisps this*): Can I come in? There's something in the bathtub, Willy, and it's moving!

WILLY *looks at* BIFF, *who is staring open-mouthed and horrified at* THE WOMAN.

WILLY: Ah—you better go back to your room. They must be finished painting by now. They're painting her room so I let her take a shower here. Go back, go back . . . (*He pushes her.*)

THE WOMAN (*resisting*): But I've got to get dressed, Willy, I can't . . .

WILLY: Get out of here! Go back, go back . . . (*Suddenly striving for the ordinary.*) This is Miss Francis, Biff, she's a buyer. They're painting her room. Go back, Miss Francis, go back . . .

THE WOMAN: But my clothes, I can't go out naked in the hall!

WILLY (*pushing her offstage*): Get outa here! Go back, go back!

BIFF *slowly sits down on his suitcase as the argument continues offstage.*

THE WOMAN: Where's my stockings? You promised me stockings, Willy!

WILLY: I have no stockings here!

THE WOMAN: You had two boxes of size nine sheers for me, and I want them!

WILLY: Here, for God's sake, will you get outa here!

THE WOMAN (*enters holding a box of stockings*): I just hope there's nobody in the hall. That's all I hope. (*To* BIFF.) Are you football or baseball?

BIFF: Football.

THE WOMAN (*angry, humiliated*): That's me too. G'night. (*She snatches her clothes from* WILLY, *and walks out.*)

WILLY (*after a pause*): Well, better get going. I want to get to the school first thing in the morning. Get my suits out of the closet. I'll get my valise. (BIFF *doesn't move.*) What's the matter! (BIFF *remains motionless, tears falling.*) She's a buyer. Buys for J. H. Simmons. She lives down the hall—they're painting. You don't imagine—(*He breaks off. After a pause.*) Now listen, pal, she's just a buyer. She sees merchandise in her room and they have to keep it looking just so . . . (*Pause. Assuming command.*) All right, get my suits. (BIFF *doesn't move.*) Now stop crying and do as I say. I gave you an order. Biff, I gave you an order! Is that what you do when I give you an order? How dare you cry! (*Putting his arm around* BIFF.) Now look, Biff, when you grow up you'll understand about these things. You mustn't—you mustn't overemphasize a thing like this. I'll see Birnbaum first thing in the morning.

BIFF: Never mind.

WILLY (*getting down beside* BIFF): Never mind! He's going to give you those points. I'll see to it.

BIFF: He wouldn't listen to you.

WILLY: He certainly will listen to me. You need those points for the U. of Virginia.

BIFF: I'm not going there.

WILLY: Heh? If I can't get him to change that mark you'll make it up in summer school. You've got all summer to . . .

BIFF (*his weeping breaking from him*): Dad . . .

WILLY (*infected by it*): Oh, my boy . . .

BIFF: Dad . . .

WILLY: She's nothing to me, Biff. I was lonely, I was terribly lonely.

BIFF: You—you gave her Mama's stockings! (*His tears break through and he rises to go.*)

WILLY (*grabbing for* BIFF): I gave you an order!

BIFF: Don't touch me, you—liar!

WILLY: Apologize for that!

BIFF: You fake! You phony little fake! You fake! (*Overcome, he turns quickly and weeping fully goes out with his suitcase.* WILLY *is left on the floor on his knees.*)

WILLY: I gave you an order! Biff, come back here or I'll beat you! Come back here! I'll whip you!

STANLEY *comes quickly in from the right and stands in front of* WILLY.

WILLY (*shouts at* STANLEY): I gave you an order . . .

STANLEY: Hey, let's pick it up, pick it up, Mr. Loman. (*He helps* WILLY *to his feet.*) Your boys left with the chippies. They said they'll see you home.

A second waiter watches some distance away.

WILLY: But we were supposed to have dinner together.

    Music is heard, WILLY*'s theme.*

STANLEY: Can you make it?

WILLY: I'll—sure, I can make it. (*Suddenly concerned about his clothes.*) Do I—I
      look all right?

STANLEY: Sure, you look all right. (*He flicks a speck off* WILLY*'s lapel.*)

WILLY: Here—here's a dollar.

STANLEY: Oh, your son paid me. It's all right.

WILLY (*putting it in* STANLEY*'s hand*): No, take it. You're a good boy.

STANLEY: Oh, no, you don't have to . . .

WILLY: Here—here's some more, I don't need it any more. (*After a slight pause.*) Tell
      me—is there a seed store in the neighborhood?

STANLEY: Seeds? You mean like to plant?

    As WILLY *turns,* STANLEY *slips the money back into his jacket pocket.*

WILLY: Yes. Carrots, peas . . .

STANLEY: Well, there's hardware stores on Sixth Avenue, but it may be too late now.

WILLY (*anxiously*): Oh, I'd better hurry. I've got to get some seeds. (*He starts off to
      the right.*) I've got to get some seeds, right away. Nothing's planted. I don't
      have a thing in the ground.

    WILLY *hurries out as the light goes down.* STANLEY *moves over to the right after
him, watches him off. The other waiter has been staring at* WILLY.

STANLEY (*to the waiter*): Well, whatta you looking at?

    The waiter picks up the chairs and moves off right. STANLEY *takes the table and
follows him. The light fades on this area. There is a long pause, the sound of the
flute coming over. The light gradually rises on the kitchen, which is empty.*
HAPPY *appears at the door of the house, followed by* BIFF. HAPPY *is carrying a
large bunch of long-stemmed roses. He enters the kitchen, looks around for*
LINDA. *Not seeing her, he turns to* BIFF, *who is just outside the house door, and
makes a gesture with his hands, indicating "Not here, I guess." He looks into the
living room and freezes. Inside,* LINDA, *unseen, is seated,* WILLY*'s coat on her lap.
She rises ominously and quietly and moves toward* HAPPY, *who backs up into
the kitchen, afraid.*

HAPPY: Hey, what're you doing up? (LINDA *says nothing but moves toward him
      implacably.*) Where's Pop? (*He keeps backing to the right, and now* LINDA
      is in full view in the doorway to the living room.) Is he sleeping?

LINDA: Where were you?

HAPPY (*trying to laugh it off*): We met two girls, Mom, very fine types. Here, we
      brought you some flowers. (*Offering them to her.*) Put them in your room,
      Ma.

    She knocks them to the floor at BIFF*'s feet. He has now come inside and closed
the door behind him. She stares at* BIFF, *silent.*

HAPPY: Now what'd you do that for? Mom, I want you to have some flowers . . .

LINDA (*cutting* HAPPY *off, violently to* BIFF): Don't you care whether he lives or dies?

HAPPY (*going to the stairs*): Come upstairs, Biff.

BIFF (*with a flare of disgust, to* HAPPY): Go away from me! (*To* LINDA.) What do you
  mean, lives or dies? Nobody's dying around here, pal.

LINDA: Get out of my sight! Get out of here!

BIFF: I wanna see the boss.

LINDA: You're not going near him!

BIFF: Where is he? (*He moves into the living room and* LINDA *follows.*)

LINDA (*shouting after* BIFF): You invite him for dinner. He looks forward to it all
  day— (BIFF *appears in his parents' bedroom, looks around, and exits*)—
  and then you desert him there. There's no stranger you'd do that to!

HAPPY: Why? He had a swell time with us. Listen, when I— (LINDA *comes back into
  the kitchen*)—desert him I hope I don't outlive the day!

LINDA: Get out of here!

HAPPY: Now look, Mom . . .

LINDA: Did you have to go to women tonight? You and your lousy rotten whores!

  BIFF *re-enters the kitchen.*

HAPPY: Mom, all we did was follow Biff around trying to cheer him up! (*To* BIFF.)
  Boy, what a night you gave me!

LINDA: Get out of here, both of you, and don't come back! I don't want you tormenting him any more. Go on now, get your things together! (*To* BIFF.)
  You can sleep in his apartment. (*She starts to pick up the flowers and stops
  herself.*) Pick up this stuff, I'm not your maid any more. Pick it up, you
  bum, you!

  HAPPY *turns his back to her in refusal.* BIFF *slowly moves over and gets down on
  his knees, picking up the flowers.*

LINDA: You're a pair of animals! Not one, not another living soul would have had
  the cruelty to walk out on that man in a restaurant!

BIFF (*not looking at her*): Is that what he said?

LINDA: He didn't have to say anything. He was so humiliated he nearly limped when
  he came in.

HAPPY: But, Mom, he had a great time with us . . .

BIFF (*cutting him off violently*): Shut up!

  Without another word, HAPPY *goes upstairs.*

LINDA: You! You didn't even go in to see if he was all right!

BIFF (*still on the floor in front of* LINDA, *the flowers in his hand; with self-loathing*):
  No. Didn't. Didn't do a damned thing. How do you like that, heh? Left him
  babbling in a toilet.

LINDA: You louse. You . . .

BIFF: Now you hit it on the nose! (*He gets up, throws the flowers in the wastebasket.*)
  The scum of the earth, and you're looking at him!

LINDA: Get out of here!

BIFF: I gotta talk to the boss, Mom. Where is he?

LINDA: You're not going near him. Get out of this house!

BIFF (*with absolute assurance, determination*): No. We're gonna have an abrupt
  conversation, him and me.

LINDA: You're not talking to him.

  Hammering is heard from outside the house, off right. BIFF *turns toward the noise.*

LINDA (*suddenly pleading*): Will you please leave him alone?
BIFF: What's he doing out there?
LINDA: He's planting the garden!
BIFF (*quietly*): Now? Oh, my God!

> BIFF *moves outside,* LINDA *following. The light dies down on them and comes up on the center of the apron as* WILLY *walks into it. He is carrying a flashlight, a hoe, and a handful of seed packets. He raps the top of the hoe sharply to fix it firmly, and then moves to the left, measuring off the distance with his foot. He holds the flashlight to look at the seed packets, reading off the instructions. He is in the blue of night.*

WILLY: Carrots . . . quarter-inch apart. Rows . . . one-foot rows. (*He measures it off.*) One foot. (*He puts down a package and measures off.*) Beets. (*He puts down another package and measures again.*) Lettuce. (*He reads the package, puts it down.*) One foot— (*He breaks off as* BEN *appears at the right and moves slowly down to him.*) What a proposition, ts, ts. Terrific, terrific. 'Cause she's suffered, Ben, the woman has suffered. You understand me? A man can't go out the way he came in, Ben, a man has got to add up to something. You can't, you can't— (BEN *moves toward him as though to interrupt.*) You gotta consider now. Don't answer so quick. Remember, it's a guaranteed twenty-thousand-dollar proposition. Now look, Ben, I want you to go through the ins and outs of this thing with me. I've got nobody to talk to, Ben, and the woman has suffered, you hear me?
BEN (*standing still, considering*): What's the proposition?
WILLY: It's twenty thousand dollars on the barrelhead. Guaranteed, gilt-edged, you understand?
BEN: You don't want to make a fool of yourself. They might not honor the policy.
WILLY: How can they dare refuse? Didn't I work like a coolie to meet every premium on the nose? And now they don't pay off? Impossible!
BEN: It's called a cowardly thing, William.
WILLY: Why? Does it take more guts to stand here the rest of my life ringing up a zero?
BEN (*yielding*): That's a point, William. (*He moves, thinking, turns.*) And twenty thousand—that is something one can feel with the hand, it is there.
WILLY (*now assured, with rising power*): Oh, Ben, that's the whole beauty of it! I see it like a diamond, shining in the dark, hard and rough, that I can pick up and touch in my hand. Not like—like an appointment! This would not be another damned-fool appointment, Ben, and it changes all the aspects. Because he thinks I'm nothing, see, and so he spites me. But the funeral—. (*Straightening up.*) Ben, that funeral will be massive! They'll come from Maine, Massachusetts, Vermont, New Hampshire! All the old-timers with the strange license plates—that boy will be thunderstruck, Ben, because he never realized—I am known! Rhode Island, New York, New Jersey—I am known, Ben, and he'll see it with his eyes once and for all. He'll see what I am, Ben! He's in for a shock, that boy!
BEN (*coming down to the edge of the garden*): He'll call you a coward.
WILLY (*suddenly fearful*): No, that would be terrible.
BEN: Yes. And a damned fool.
WILLY: No, no, he mustn't, I won't have that! (*He is broken and desperate.*)
BEN: He'll hate you, William.

> *The gay music of the Boys is heard.*

WILLY: Oh, Ben, how do we get back to all the great times? Used to be so full of light, and comradeship, the sleigh-riding in winter, and the ruddiness on his cheeks. And always some kind of good news coming up, always something nice coming up ahead. And never even let me carry the valises in the house, and simonizing, simonizing that little red car! Why, why can't I give him something and not have him hate me?

BEN: Let me think about it. (*He glances at his watch.*) I still have a little time. Remarkable proposition, but you've got to be sure you're not making a fool of yourself.

BEN *drifts off upstage and goes out of sight.* BIFF *comes down from the left.*

WILLY (*suddenly conscious of* BIFF, *turns and looks up at him, then begins picking up the packages of seeds in confusion*): Where the hell is that seed? (*Indignantly.*) You can't see nothing out here! They boxed in the whole goddam neighborhood!

BIFF: There are people all around here. Don't you realize that?

WILLY: I'm busy. Don't bother me.

BIFF (*taking the hoe from* WILLY): I'm saying good-by to you, Pop. (WILLY *looks at him, silent, unable to move.*) I'm not coming back any more.

WILLY: You're not going to see Oliver tomorrow?

BIFF: I've got no appointment, Dad.

WILLY: He put his arm around you, and you've got no appointment?

BIFF: Pop, get this now, will you? Everytime I've left it's been a—fight that sent me out of here. Today I realized something about myself and I tried to explain it to you and I—I think I'm just not smart enough to make any sense out of it for you. To hell with whose fault it is or anything like that. (*He takes* WILLY's *arm.*) Let's just wrap it up, heh? Come on in, we'll tell Mom. (*He gently tries to pull* WILLY *to left.*)

WILLY (*frozen, immobile, with guilt in his voice*): No, I don't want to see her.

BIFF: Come on! (*He pulls again, and* WILLY *tries to pull away.*)

WILLY (*highly nervous*): No, no, I don't want to see her.

BIFF (*tries to look into* WILLY's *face, as if to find the answer there*): Why don't you want to see her?

WILLY (*more harshly now*): Don't bother me, will you?

BIFF: What do you mean, you don't want to see her? You don't want them calling you yellow, do you? This isn't your fault; it's me, I'm a bum. Now come inside! (WILLY *strains to get away.*) Did you hear what I said to you?

WILLY *pulls away and quickly goes by himself into the house.* BIFF *follows.*

LINDA (*to* WILLY): Did you plant, dear?

BIFF (*at the door, to* LINDA): All right, we had it out. I'm going and I'm not writing any more.

LINDA (*going to* WILLY *in the kitchen*): I think that's the best way, dear. 'Cause there's no use drawing it out, you'll just never get along.

WILLY *doesn't respond.*

BIFF: People ask where I am and what I'm doing, you don't know, and you don't care. That way it'll be off your mind and you can start brightening up again. All right? That clears it, doesn't it? (WILLY *is silent, and* BIFF *goes to him.*) You gonna wish me luck, scout? (*He extends his hand.*) What do you say?

LINDA: Shake his hand, Willy.

WILLY (*turning to her, seething with hurt*): There's no necessity—to mention the pen at all, y'know.

BIFF (*gently*): I've got no appointment, Dad.

WILLY (*erupting fiercely*): He put his arm around . . . ?

BIFF: Dad, you're never going to see what I am, so what's the use of arguing? If I strike oil I'll send you a check. Meantime forget I'm alive.

WILLY (*to* LINDA): Spite, see?

BIFF: Shake hands, Dad.

WILLY: Not my hand.

BIFF: I was hoping not to go this way.

WILLY: Well, this is the way you're going. Good-by.

> BIFF *looks at him a moment, then turns sharply and goes to the stairs.*

WILLY (*stops him with*): May you rot in hell if you leave this house!

BIFF (*turning*): Exactly what is it that you want from me?

WILLY: I want you to know, on the train, in the mountains, in the valleys, wherever you go, that you cut down your life for spite!

BIFF: No, no.

WILLY: Spite, spite, is the word of your undoing! And when you're down and out, remember what did it. When you're rotting somewhere beside the railroad tracks, remember, and don't you dare blame it on me!

BIFF: I'm not blaming it on you!

WILLY: I won't take the rap for this, you hear?

> HAPPY *comes down the stairs and stands on the bottom step, watching.*

BIFF: That's just what I'm telling you!

WILLY (*sinking into a chair at a table, with full accusation*): You're trying to put a knife in me—don't think I don't know what you're doing!

BIFF: All right, phony! Then let's lay it on the line. (*He whips the rubber tube out of his pocket and puts it on the table.*)

HAPPY: You crazy . . .

LINDA: Biff! (*She moves to grab the hose, but* BIFF *holds it down with his hand.*)

BIFF: Leave it there! Don't move it!

WILLY (*not looking at it*): What is that?

BIFF: You know goddam well what that is.

WILLY (*caged, wanting to escape*): I never saw that.

BIFF: You saw it. The mice didn't bring it into the cellar! What is this supposed to do, make a hero out of you? This supposed to make me sorry for you?

WILLY: Never heard of it.

BIFF: There'll be no pity for you, you hear it? No pity!

WILLY (*to* LINDA): You hear the spite!

BIFF: No, you're going to hear the truth—what you are and what I am!

LINDA: Stop it!

WILLY: Spite!

HAPPY (*coming down toward* BIFF): You cut it now!

BIFF (*to* HAPPY): The man don't know who we are! The man is gonna know! (*To* WILLY.) We never told the truth for ten minutes in this house!

HAPPY: We always told the truth!

BIFF (*turning on him*): You big blow, are you the assistant buyer? You're one of the two assistants to the assistant, aren't you?

HAPPY: Well, I'm practically . . .

BIFF: You're practically full of it! We all are! and I'm through with it. (*To* WILLY.) Now hear this, Willy, this is me.

WILLY: I know you!

BIFF: You know why I had no address for three months? I stole a suit in Kansas City and I was in jail. (*To* LINDA, *who is sobbing*.) Stop crying. I'm through with it.

LINDA *turns away from them, her hands covering her face.*

WILLY: I suppose that's my fault!

BIFF: I stole myself out of every good job since high school!

WILLY: And whose fault is that?

BIFF: And I never got anywhere because you blew me so full of hot air I could never stand taking orders from anybody! That's whose fault it is!

WILLY: I hear that!

LINDA: Don't, Biff!

BIFF: It's goddam time you heard that! I had to be boss big shot in two weeks, and I'm through with it!

WILLY: Then hang yourself! For spite, hang yourself!

BIFF: No! Nobody's hanging himself, Willy! I ran down eleven flights with a pen in my hand today. And suddenly I stopped, you hear me? And in the middle of that office building, do you hear this? I stopped in the middle of that building and I saw—the sky. I saw the things that I love in this world. The work and the food and time to sit and smoke. And I looked at the pen and said to myself, what the hell am I grabbing this for? Why am I trying to become what I don't want to be? What am I doing in an office, making a contemptuous, begging fool of myself, when all I want is out there, waiting for me the minute I say I know who I am! Why can't I say that, Willy? (*He tries to make* WILLY *face him, but* WILLY *pulls away and moves to the left.*)

WILLY (*with hatred, threateningly*): The door of your life is wide open!

BIFF: Pop! I'm a dime a dozen, and so are you!

WILLY (*turning on him now in an uncontrolled outburst*): I am not a dime a dozen! I am Willy Loman, and you are Biff Loman!

BIFF *starts for* WILLY, *but is blocked by* HAPPY. *In his fury,* BIFF *seems on the verge of attacking his father.*

BIFF: I am not a leader of men, Willy, and neither are you. You were never anything but a hard-working drummer who landed in the ash can like all the rest of them! I'm one dollar an hour, Willy! I tried seven states and couldn't raise it. A buck an hour! Do you gather my meaning? I'm not bringing home any prizes any more, and you're going to stop waiting for me to bring them home!

WILLY (*directly to* BIFF): You vengeful, spiteful mutt!

BIFF *breaks from* HAPPY. WILLY, *in fright, starts up the stairs.* BIFF *grabs him.*

BIFF (*at the peak of his fury*): Pop! I'm nothing! I'm nothing, Pop. Can't you understand that? There's no spite in it any more. I'm just what I am, that's all.

BIFF'*s fury has spent itself and he breaks down, sobbing, holding on to* WILLY, *who dumbly fumbles for* BIFF'*s face.*

WILLY (*astonished*): What're you doing? What're you doing? (*To* LINDA.) Why is he crying?

BIFF (*crying, broken*): Will you let me go, for Christ's sake? Will you take that phony dream and burn it before something happens? (*Struggling to contain himself he pulls away and moves to the stairs.*) I'll go in the morning. Put him—put him to bed. (*Exhausted,* BIFF *moves up the stairs to his room.*)

WILLY (*after a long pause, astonished, elevated*): Isn't that—isn't that remarkable? Biff—he likes me!

LINDA: He loves you, Willy!

HAPPY (*deeply moved*): Always did, Pop.

WILLY: Oh, Biff! (*Staring wildly.*) He cried! Cried to me. (*He is choking with his love, and now cries out his promise.*) That boy—that boy is going to be magnificent!

BEN *appears in the light just outside the kitchen.*

BEN: Yes, outstanding, with twenty thousand behind him.

LINDA (*sensing the racing of his mind, fearfully, carefully*). Now come to bed, Willy. It's all settled now.

WILLY (*finding it difficult not to rush out of the house*): Yes, we'll sleep. Come on. Go to sleep, Hap.

BEN: And it does take a great kind of a man to crack the jungle.

In accents of dread, BEN's *idyllic music starts up.*

HAPPY (*his arm around* LINDA): I'm getting married, Pop, don't forget it. I'm changing everything. I'm gonna run that department before the year is up. You'll see, Mom. (*He kisses her.*)

BEN: The jungle is dark but full of diamonds, Willy.

WILLY *turns, moves, listening to* BEN.

LINDA: Be good. You're both good boys, just act that way, that's all.

HAPPY: 'Night, Pop. (*He goes upstairs.*)

LINDA (*to* WILLY): Come, dear.

BEN (*with greater force*): One must go in to fetch a diamond out.

WILLY (*to* LINDA, *as he moves slowly along the edge of the kitchen, toward the door*): I just want to get settled down, Linda. Let me sit alone for a little.

LINDA (*almost uttering her fear*): I want you upstairs.

WILLY (*taking her in his arms*): In a few minutes, Linda. I couldn't sleep right now. Go on, you look awful tired. (*He kisses her.*)

BEN: Not like an appointment at all. A diamond is rough and hard to the touch.

WILLY: Go on now. I'll be right up.

LINDA: I think this is the only way, Willy.

WILLY: Sure, it's the best thing.

BEN: Best thing!

WILLY: The only way. Everything is gonna be—go on, kid, get to bed. You look so tired.

LINDA: Come right up.

WILLY: Two minutes.

LINDA *goes into the living room, then reappears in her bedroom.* WILLY *moves just outside the kitchen door.*

WILLY: Loves me. (*Wonderingly.*) Always loved me. Isn't that a remarkable thing? Ben, he'll worship me for it!

BEN (*with promise*): It's dark there, but full of diamonds.

WILLY: Can you imagine that magnificence with twenty thousand dollars in his pocket?

LINDA (*calling from her room*): Willy! Come up!

WILLY (*calling into the kitchen*): Yes! Yes. Coming! It's very smart, you realize that, don't you, sweetheart? Even Ben sees it. I gotta go, baby. 'By! 'By! (*Going over to* BEN, *almost dancing.*) Imagine? When the mail comes he'll be ahead of Bernard again!

BEN: A perfect proposition all around.

WILLY: Did you see how he cried to me? Oh, if I could kiss him, Ben!

BEN: Time, William, time!

WILLY: Oh, Ben, I always knew one way or another we were gonna make it, Biff and I.

BEN (*looking at his watch*): The boat. We'll be late. (*He moves slowly off into the darkness.*)

WILLY (*elegiacally, turning to the house*): Now when you kick off, boy, I want a seventy-yard boot, and get right down the field under the ball, and when you hit, hit low and hit hard, because it's important, boy. (*He swings around and faces the audience.*) There's all kinds of important people in the stands, and the first thing you know . . . (*Suddenly realizing he is alone.*) Ben! Ben, where do I . . . ? (*He makes a sudden movement of search.*) Ben, how do I . . . ?

LINDA (*calling*): Willy, you coming up?

WILLY (*uttering a gasp of fear, whirling about as if to quiet her*): Sh! (*He turns around as if to find his way; sounds, faces, voices, seem to be swarming in upon him and he flicks at them, crying.*) Sh! Sh! (*Suddenly music, faint and high, stops him. It rises in intensity, almost to an unbearable scream. He goes up and down on his toes, and rushes off around the house.*) Shhh!

LINDA: Willy?

There is no answer. LINDA *waits.* BIFF *gets up off his bed. He is still in his clothes.* HAPPY *sits up.* BIFF *stands listening.*

LINDA (*with real fear*): Willy, answer me! Willy!

There is the sound of a car starting and moving away at full speed.

LINDA: No!

BIFF (*rushing down the stairs*): Pop!

As the car speeds off the music crashes down in a frenzy of sound, which becomes the soft pulsation of a single cello string. BIFF *slowly returns to his bedroom. He and* HAPPY *gravely don their jackets.* LINDA *slowly walks out of her room. The music has developed into a dead march. The leaves of day are appearing over everything.* CHARLEY *and* BERNARD, *somberly dressed, appear and knock on the kitchen door.* BIFF *and* HAPPY *slowly descend the stairs to the kitchen as* CHARLEY *and* BERNARD *enter. All stop a moment when* LINDA, *in clothes of mourning, bearing a little bunch of roses, comes through the draped doorway into the kitchen. She goes to* CHARLEY *and takes his arm. Now all move toward the audience, through the wall-line of the kitchen. At the limit of the apron,* LINDA *lays down the flowers, kneels, and sits back on her heels. All stare down at the grave.*

Requiem

CHARLEY: It's getting dark, Linda.

    LINDA *doesn't react. She stares at the grave.*

BIFF: How about it, Mom? Better get some rest, heh? They'll be closing the gate soon.

    LINDA *makes no move. Pause.*

HAPPY (*deeply angered*): He had no right to do that. There was no necessity for it. We would've helped him.

CHARLEY (*grunting*): Hmmm.

BIFF: Come along, Mom.

LINDA: Why didn't anybody come?

CHARLEY: It was a very nice funeral.

LINDA: But where are all the people he knew? Maybe they blame him.

CHARLEY: Naa. It's a rough world, Linda. They wouldn't blame him.

LINDA: I can't understand it. At this time especially. First time in thirty-five years we were just about free and clear. He only needed a little salary. He was even finished with the dentist.

CHARLEY: No man only needs a little salary.

LINDA: I can't understand it.

BIFF: There were a lot of nice days. When he'd come home from a trip; or on Sundays, making the stoop; finishing the cellar; putting on the new porch; when he built the extra bathroom; and put up the garage. You know something, Charley, there's more of him in that front stoop than in all the sales he ever made.

CHARLEY: Yeah. He was a happy man with a batch of cement.

LINDA: He was so wonderful with his hands.

BIFF: He had the wrong dreams. All, all, wrong.

HAPPY (*almost ready to fight* BIFF): Don't say that!

BIFF: He never knew who he was.

CHARLEY (*stopping* HAPPY's *movement and reply; to* BIFF): Nobody dast blame this man. You don't understand: Willy was a salesman. And for a salesman, there is no rock bottom to the life. He don't put a bolt to a nut, he don't tell you the law or give you medicine. He's a man way out there in the blue, riding on a smile and a shoeshine. And when they start not smiling back—that's an earthquake. And then you get yourself a couple of spots on your hat, and you're finished. Nobody dast blame this man. A salesman is got to dream, boy. It comes with the territory.

BIFF: Charley, the man didn't know who he was.

HAPPY (*infuriated*): Don't say that!

BIFF: Why don't you come with me, Happy?

HAPPY: I'm not licked that easily. I'm staying right in this city, and I'm gonna beat this racket! (*He looks at* BIFF, *his chin set.*) The Loman Brothers!

BIFF: I know who I am, kid.

HAPPY: All right, boy. I'm gonna show you and everybody else that Willy Loman did not die in vain. He had a good dream. It's the only dream you can have— to come out number-one man. He fought it out here, and this is where I'm gonna win it for him.

BIFF (*with a hopeless glance at* HAPPY, *bends toward his mother*): Let's go, Mom.

LINDA: I'll be with you in a minute. Go on, Charley. (*He hesitates.*) I want to, just for a minute. I never had a chance to say good-by.

CHARLEY *moves away, followed by* HAPPY. BIFF *remains a slight distance up and left of* LINDA. *She sits there, summoning herself. The flute begins, not far away, playing behind her speech.*

LINDA: Forgive me, dear. I can't cry. I don't know what it is, but I can't cry. I don't understand it. Why did you ever do that? Help me, Willy, I can't cry. It seems to me that you're just on another trip. I keep expecting you. Willy, dear, I can't cry. Why did you do it? I search and search and I search, and I can't understand it, Willy. I made the last payment on the house today. Today, dear. And there'll be nobody home. (*A sob rises in her throat.*) We're free and clear. (*Sobbing mournfully, released.*) We're free. (BIFF *comes slowly toward her.*) We're free . . . We're free . . .

BIFF *lifts her to her feet and moves out up right with her in his arms.* LINDA *sobs quietly.* BERNARD *and* CHARLEY *come together and follow them, followed by* HAPPY. *Only the music of the flute is left on the darkening stage as over the house the hard towers of the apartment buildings rise into sharp focus and the curtain falls.*

[1949]

Joining the Conversation: Critical Thinking and Writing

The Play on the Page

1. Arthur Miller said in the *New York Times* (February 27, 1949) that tragedy shows man's struggle to secure "his sense of personal dignity" and that "his destruction in the attempt posits a wrong or an evil in his environment." Does this make sense when applied to some earlier tragedy (for example, *Oedipus the King* or *Hamlet*), and does it apply convincingly to *Death of a Salesman*? Is this the tragedy of an individual's own making? Or is society at fault for corrupting and exploiting Willy? Or both?
2. Is Willy pathetic rather than tragic? If pathetic, does this imply that the play is less worthy than if he is tragic?
3. Do you feel that Miller is straining too hard to turn a play about a little man into a big, impressive play? For example, do the musical themes, the unrealistic setting, the appearances of Ben, and the speech at the grave seem out of keeping in a play about the death of a salesman?
4. We don't know what Willy sells, and we don't know whether or not the insurance will be paid after his death. Do you consider these uncertainties to be faults in the play?
5. Is Howard a villain?
6. Characterize Linda.

The Play on the Stage

7. It is sometimes said that, in this realistic play that includes symbolic and expressionistic elements, Biff and Happy can be seen as two aspects of Willy. In this view, Biff more or less represents Willy's spiritual needs, and Happy represents his materialism and his sexuality. If you were directing the play, would you adopt this point of view? Whatever your interpretation is, how would you costume the brothers?
8. Although Miller envisioned Willy as a small man (literally, small), the role was first performed by Lee J. Cobb, a large man. If you were casting the play, what actor would you select? Why? Whom would you choose for Linda, Biff, Happy, Bernard, and Charley?
9. Select roughly thirty lines of dialogue, and discuss the movements (gestures and blocking) that as a director you would suggest to the performers.

Chapter Overview: Looking Backward/Looking Forward

1. What work, if any, have you done that was rewarding beyond a financial sense? Please explain.
2. What work, if any, have you done that was rewarding *only* financially? Please explain.
3. How important do you think your work will be, to your life as a whole, in the years after your graduation? Would you say that it will matter 25 percent, 40 percent, or some other figure? What other categories would you include as significant parts of your life, and what percentage would you assign to them?
4. If you think you know what line of work you want to go into after graduation, explain why this line interests you. Because, for instance, you have already done it? Or because a member of your family does it and you esteem this person?

CHAPTER 21

American Dreams and Nightmares

ESSAYS

CHIEF SEATTLE

Seattle (1786–1866), for whom the city in Washington is named, was a chief of the Suquamish and Duwamish tribes on the coast of the Pacific Northwest region of what is now the United States. There is some uncertainty about exactly when he delivered this speech—perhaps late in 1853, when the white governor of the Washington Territory first visited the territory, or perhaps early in 1855, when Seattle signed the Port Elliott Treaty, which confined the tribes to a reservation.

Seattle spoke little or no English. The speech was given through an interpreter and was transcribed by Henry Smith, who published it in 1887, with a concluding note saying, "The above is but a fragment of his speech." Because Smith's notes are not extant, it is now impossible to know exactly what Seattle said, but one point can be made: The text we print here is based entirely on Smith's version, the only text with any claim to authenticity. Since 1931, Smith's version has occasionally been reprinted with embellishments, the most popular of which is the addition of three sentences at the end: "Dead—did I say? There is no death. Only a change of worlds." Fine words, but they belong to an editor of 1931, not to Seattle.

My People

Yonder sky has wept tears of compassion on our fathers for centuries untold, and which, to us, looks eternal, may change. To-day it is fair, to-morrow it may be overcast with clouds. My words are like the stars that never set. What Seattle says the great chief, Washington, (the Indians in early times thought that Washington was still alive. They knew the name to be that of a president, and when they heard of the president at Washington they mistook the name of the city for the name of the reigning chief. They thought, also, that King George was still England's monarch, because the Hudson Bay traders called themselves "King George men." This innocent deception the company was shrewd enough not to explain away for the Indians had more respect for them than they would have had, had they known England was ruled by a woman. Some of us have learned better.) can rely upon, with as much certainty as our pale-face brothers can rely upon the return of the seasons. The son of the white chief says his father sends us greetings of friendship and good-will. This is kind, for we know he has little need of our friendship in return, because his people are many. They are like the grass that covers the vast prairies, while my people are few, and resemble the scattering trees of a wind-swept plain.

The great, and I presume also good, white chief sends us word that he wants to buy our lands but is willing to allow us to reserve enough to live on comfortably. This indeed appears generous, for the red man no longer has rights that he need respect, and the offer may be wise, also, for we are no longer in need of a great country. There was a time when our people covered the whole land as the waves of a wind-ruffled sea cover its shell-paved floor. But that time has long since passed away with the greatness of tribes almost forgotten. I will not mourn over our untimely decay, nor reproach my pale-face brothers with hastening it, for we, too, may have been somewhat to blame.

When our young men grow angry at some real or imaginary wrong and disfigure their faces with black paint, their hearts, also, are disfigured and turn black, and then their cruelty is relentless and knows no bounds, and our old men are not able to restrain them.

But let us hope that hostilities between the red man and his pale face brothers may never return. We would have everything to lose and nothing to gain.

5   True it is that revenge, with our young braves, is considered gain, even at the cost of their own lives, but old men who stay at home in times of war, and old women who have sons to lose, know better.

Our great father Washington, for I presume he is now our father as well as yours, since George has moved his boundaries to the north; our great and good father, I say, sends us word by his son, who, no doubt, is a great chief among his people, that if we do as he desires, he will protect us. His brave armies will be to us a bristling wall of strength, and his great ships of war will fill our harbors so that our ancient enemies far to the northward, the Simsiams and Hydas, will no longer frighten our women and old men. Then he will be our father and we will be his children. But can this ever be? Your God loves your people and hates mine; he folds his strong arms lovingly around the white man and leads him as a father leads his infant son, but he has forsaken his red children; he makes your people wax strong every day, and soon they will fill the land; while our people are ebbing away like a fast-receding tide, that will never flow again. The white man's God cannot love his red children or he would protect them. They seem to be orphans and can look nowhere for help. How then can we become brothers? How can your father become our father and bring us prosperity and awaken in us dreams of returning greatness?

Your God seems to be partial. He came to the white man. We never saw Him; never even heard His voice; He gave the white man laws but He had no word for His red children whose teeming millions filled this vast continent as the stars fill the firmament. No, we are two distinct races and must ever remain so. There is little in common between us. The ashes of our ancestors are sacred and their final resting place is hallowed ground, while you wander away from the tombs of your fathers seemingly without regret.

Your religion was written on tables of stone by the iron finger of an angry God, lest you might forget it. The red man could never remember nor comprehend it.

Our religion is the traditions of our ancestors, the dreams of our old men, given them by the great Spirit, and the visions of our sachems, and is written in the hearts of our people.

10   Your dead cease to love you and the homes of their nativity as soon as they pass the portals of the tomb. They wander off beyond the stars, are soon forgotten and never return. Our dead never forget the beautiful world that gave them being. They still love its winding rivers, its great mountains and its sequestered vales, and they ever yearn in tenderest affection over the lonely hearted living and often return to visit and comfort them.

Day and night cannot dwell together. The red man has ever fled the approach of the white man, as the changing mists on the mountain side flee before the blazing morning sun.

However, your proposition seems a just one, and I think my folks will accept it and will retire to the reservation you offer them, and we will dwell apart and in peace, for the words of the great white chief seem to be the voice of nature speaking to my people out of the thick darkness that is fast gathering around them like a dense fog floating inward from a midnight sea.

It matters but little where we pass the remainder of our days. They are not many. The Indian's night promises to be dark. No bright star hovers about the horizon. Sad-voiced winds moan in the distance. Some grim Nemesis of our race is on the red man's trail, and wherever he goes he will still hear the sure approaching footsteps of the fell destroyer and prepare to meet his doom, as does the wounded doe that hears the approaching footsteps of the hunter. A few more moons, a few more winters and not one of all the mighty hosts that once filled this broad land or that now roam in fragmentary bands through these vast solitudes will remain to weep over the tombs of a people once as powerful and as hopeful as your own.

But why should we repine? Why should I murmur at the fate of my people? Tribes are made up of individuals and are no better than they. Men come and go like the waves of the sea. A tear, a tamanamus,[1] a dirge, and they are gone from our longing eyes forever. Even the white man, whose God walked and talked with him, as friend to friend, is not exempt from the common destiny. *We may* be brothers after all. We shall see.

15   We will ponder your proposition, and when we have decided we will tell you. But should we accept it, I here and now make this the first condition: That we will not be denied the privilege, without molestation, of visiting at will the graves of our ancestors and friends. Every part of this country is sacred to my people. Every hillside, every valley, every plain and grove has been hallowed by some fond memory or some sad experience of my tribe. Even the rocks that seem to lie dumb as they swelter in the sun along the silent seashore in solemn grandeur thrill with memories of past events connected with the fate of my people, and the very dust under your feet responds more lovingly to our footsteps than to yours, because it is the ashes of our ancestors, and our bare feet are conscious of the sympathetic touch, for the soil is rich with the life of our kindred.

The sable braves, and fond mothers, and glad-hearted maidens, and the little children who lived and rejoiced here, and whose very names are now forgotten, still love these solitudes, and their deep fastnesses at eventide grow shadowy with the presence of dusky spirits. And when the last red man shall have perished from the earth and his memory among white men shall have become a myth, these shores shall swarm with the invisible dead of my tribe, and when your children's children shall think themselves alone in the field, the shop, upon the highway or in the silence of the woods they will not be alone. In all the earth there is no place dedicated to solitude. At night when the streets of your cities and villages shall be silent, and you think them deserted, they will throng with the returning hosts that once filled and still love this beautiful land. The white man will never be alone. Let him be just and deal kindly with my people, for the dead are not altogether powerless.

[c. 1853]

---

[1]**tamanamus** guardian spirit.

Joining the Conversation: Critical Thinking and Writing

1. In a paragraph, explain why Chief Seattle believes white people have a different God from that of American Indians.
2. Chief Seattle says that he thinks the offer of the whites is "fair" and that he thinks his people will accept the offer and retire to the reservation. Judging from his speech, do you think his main reason for approving the proposal is that it is fair?
3. In 250 words, explain why Chief Seattle believes that whites and American Indians can never be reconciled, and evaluate his view.
4. Chief Seattle's speech is rich in metaphors and other figures of speech. List three examples. From what areas are most of his figures of speech drawn?

ELIZABETH CADY STANTON

Elizabeth Cady Stanton (1815–1902), a lawyer's daughter and journalist's wife, proposed in 1848 a convention to address the "social, civil, and religious condition and rights of women." Responding to Stanton's call, women from all over the Northeast convened in the village of Seneca Falls, New York. Her Declaration of Sentiments and Resolutions *that was adopted by the Seneca Falls Convention—but only after vigorous debate and some amendments by others—became the platform for the women's movement in this country.*

Declaration of Sentiments and Resolutions

When, in the course of human events, it becomes necessary for one portion of the family of man to assume among the people of the earth a position different from that which they have hitherto occupied, but one to which the laws of nature and of nature's God entitle them, a decent respect to the opinions of mankind requires that they should declare the causes that impel them to such a course.

We hold these truths to be self-evident: that all men and women are created equal; that they are endowed by their Creator with certain inalienable rights; that among these are life, liberty and the pursuit of happiness; that to secure these rights governments are instituted, deriving their just powers from the consent of the governed. Whenever any form of government becomes destructive of these ends, it is the right of those who suffer from it to refuse allegiance to it, and to insist upon the institution of a new government, laying its foundation on such principles, and organizing its powers in such form, as to them shall seem most likely to effect their safety and happiness. Prudence, indeed, will dictate that governments long established should not be changed for light and transient causes; and accordingly all experience hath shown that mankind are more disposed to suffer, while evils are sufferable, than to right themselves by abolishing the forms to which they were accustomed. But when a long train of abuses and usurpations, pursuing invariably the same object, evinces a design to reduce them under absolute despotism, it is their duty to throw off such government, and to provide new guards for their future security. Such has been the patient sufferance of the women under this government, and such is now the necessity which constrains them to demand the equal station to which they are entitled.

The history of mankind is a history of repeated injuries and usurpations on the part of man toward woman, having in direct object the establishment of an absolute tyranny over her. To prove this, let facts be submitted to a candid world.

He has never permitted her to exercise her inalienable right to the elective franchise.

5   He has compelled her to submit to laws, in the formation of which she had no voice.

He has withheld from her rights which are given to the most ignorant and degraded men—both natives and foreigners.

Having deprived her of this first right of a citizen, the elective franchise, thereby leaving her without representation in the halls of legislation, he has oppressed her on all sides.

He has made her, if married, in the eye of the law, civilly dead.

He has taken from her all right in property, even to the wages she earns.

10   He has made her, morally, an irresponsible being, as she can commit many crimes with impunity, provided they be done in the presence of her husband. In the covenant of marriage, she is compelled to promise obedience to her husband, he becoming to all intents and purposes, her master—the law giving him power to deprive her of her liberty, and to administer chastisement.

He has so framed the laws of divorce, as to what shall be the proper causes, and in case of separation, to whom the guardianship of the children shall be given, as to be wholly regardless of the happiness of women—the law, in all cases, going upon a false supposition of the supremacy of man, and giving all power into his hands.

After depriving her of all rights as a married woman, if single, and the owner of property, he has taxed her to support a government which recognizes her only when her property can be made profitable to it.

He has monopolized nearly all the profitable employments, and from those she is permitted to follow, she receives but a scanty remuneration. He closes against her all the avenues to wealth and distinction which he considers most honorable to himself. As a teacher of theology, medicine, or law, she is not known.

He has denied her the facilities for obtaining a thorough education, all colleges being closed against her.

15   He allows her in Church, as well as State, but a subordinate position, claiming Apostolic authority for her exclusion from the ministry, and, with some exceptions, from any public participation in the affairs of the Church.

He has created a false public sentiment by giving to the world a different code of morals for men and women, by which moral delinquencies which exclude women from society, are not only tolerated, but deemed of little account in man.

He has usurped the prerogative of Jehovah himself, claiming it as his right to assign for her a sphere of action, when that belongs to her conscience and to her God.

He has endeavored, in every way that he could, to destroy her confidence in her own powers, to lessen her self-respect, and to make her willing to lead a dependent and abject life.

Now, in view of this entire disfranchisement of one-half the people of this country, their social and religious degradation—in view of the unjust laws above mentioned, and because women do feel themselves aggrieved, oppressed, and fraudulently deprived of their most sacred rights, we insist that they have immediate admission to all the rights and privileges which belong to them as citizens of the United States.

20   In entering upon the great work before us, we anticipate no small amount of misconception, misrepresentation, and ridicule; but we shall use every

instrumentality within our power to effect our object. We shall employ agents, circulate tracts, petition the State and National legislatures, and endeavor to enlist the pulpit and the press in our behalf. We hope this Convention will be followed by a series of Conventions embracing every part of the country.

[The following resolutions were discussed by Lucretia Mott, Thomas and Mary Ann McClintock, Amy Post, Catharine A. F. Stebbins, and others, and were adopted:]

Whereas, The great precept of nature is conceded to be, that "man shall pursue his own true and substantial happiness." Blackstone in his Commentaries remarks, that this law of Nature being coeval with mankind, and dictated by God himself, is of course superior in obligation to any other. It is binding over all the globe, in all countries, and at all times; no human laws are of any validity if contrary to this, and such of them as are valid, derive all their force, and all their validity, and all their authority, mediately and immediately, from this original; therefore.

Resolved, That such laws as conflict, in any way, with the true and substantial happiness of woman, are contrary to the great precept of nature and of no validity, for this is "superior in obligation to any other."

Resolved, That all laws which prevent woman from occupying such a station in society as her conscience shall dictate, or which place her in a position inferior to that of man, are contrary to the great precept of nature, and therefore of no force or authority.

Resolved, That woman is man's equal—was intended to be so by the Creator, and the highest good of the race demands that she should be recognized as such.

25 *Resolved*, That the women of this country ought to be enlightened in regard to the laws under which they live, that they may no longer publish their degradation by declaring themselves satisfied with their present position, nor their ignorance, by asserting that they have all the rights they want.

Resolved, That inasmuch as man, while claiming for himself intellectual superiority, does accord to woman moral superiority, it is preeminently his duty to encourage her to speak and teach, as she has an opportunity, in all religious assemblies.

Resolved, That the same amount of virtue, delicacy, and refinement of behavior that is required of woman in the social state, should also be required of man, and the same transgressions should be visited with equal severity on both man and woman.

Resolved, That the objection of indelicacy and impropriety, which is so often brought against woman when she addresses a public audience, comes with a very ill-grace from those who encourage, by their attendance, her appearance on the stage, in the concert, or in feats of the circus.

Resolved, That woman has too long rested satisfied in the circumscribed limits which corrupt customs and a perverted application of the Scriptures have marked out for her, and that it is time she should move in the enlarged sphere which her great Creator has assigned her.

30 *Resolved*, That it is the duty of the women of this country to secure to themselves their sacred right to the elective franchise.

Resolved, That the equality of human rights results necessarily from the fact of the identity of the race in capabilities and responsibilities.

Resolved, therefore, That, being invested by the Creator with the same capabilities, and the same consciousness of responsibility for their exercise, it is demonstrably the right and duty of woman, equally with man, to promote every righteous cause by every righteous means; and especially in regard to the great subjects of morals and religion, it is self-evidently her right to participate with her brother in teaching them, both in private and in public, by writing and by speaking, by any instrumentalities proper to be used, and in any assemblies proper to be held; and this being a self-evident truth growing out of the divinely implanted principles of human nature, any custom or authority adverse to it, whether modern or wearing the hoary sanction of antiquity, is to be regarded as a self-evident falsehood, and at war with mankind.

[At the last session Lucretia Mott offered and spoke to the following resolution:]

Resolved, That the speedy success of our cause depends upon the zealous and untiring efforts of both men and women, for the overthrow of the monopoly of the pulpit, and for the securing to woman an equal participation with men in the various trades, professions, and commerce.

[1848]

Joining the Conversation: Critical Thinking and Writing

1. Stanton echoes the Declaration of Independence because she wishes to associate her ideas and the movement that she supports with a document and a movement that her readers esteem. And, of course, she must have believed that, if readers esteem the Declaration of Independence, they must grant the justice of her goals. Does her strategy work, or does it backfire by making her essay seem strained?
2. When Stanton insists that women have an "inalienable right to the elective franchise" (paragraph 4), what does she mean by "inalienable"?
3. Stanton complains that men have made women, "in the eye of the law, civilly dead" (paragraph 8). What does she mean by "civilly dead"? How is it possible for a person to be biologically alive yet "civilly dead"?
4. Stanton objects that women are "not known" as teachers of "theology, medicine, or law" (paragraph 13). Is this still true today? Do some research in the library or online, and then write three 100-word biographical sketches, one each on a well-known woman professor of theology, medicine, and law.
5. How might you go about proving (rather than merely asserting) that, as paragraph 24 says, "woman is man's equal—was intended to be so by the Creator"?
6. Stanton's *Declaration* claims that women have "the same capabilities" as men (paragraph 32). Yet, in 1848, Stanton and the others at Seneca Falls knew, or should have known, that history recorded no example of an outstanding woman philosopher to compare with Plato or Kant, a great composer to compare with Beethoven or Chopin, a scientist to compare with Galileo or Newton, or a creative mathematician to compare with Euclid or Descartes. Do these facts contradict the *Declaration*'s claim? If not, why not? How else but by different intellectual capabilities do you think such facts are to be explained?
7. Stanton's *Declaration* is about 165 years old. Have all of the issues that she raised been satisfactorily resolved? If not, which ones remain?
8. In our society, children have very few rights. For instance, a child cannot decide to drop out of elementary school or high school, and a child cannot decide to leave his or her parents to reside with some other family that he or she finds more compatible. Whatever your view of children's rights, compose the best declaration of the rights of children that you can.

ABRAHAM LINCOLN

Abraham Lincoln (1809–65), sixteenth president of the United States, is not usually thought of as a writer, but his published speeches and writings comprise about 1,078,000 words, the equivalent of about four thousand pages of double-spaced typing. They were all composed without the assistance of a speechwriter.

The Gettysburg campaign—a series of battles fought near Gettysburg in southeastern Pennsylvania—took place in June and July of 1863. Each side lost over twenty-three thousand men. The battle is regarded as a turning point in the war, but the Confederate army escaped and the war continued until April 1865.

On November 19, 1863, Lincoln delivered this short speech at the dedication of a national cemetery on the battlefield at Gettysburg.

Address at the Dedication of the Gettysburg National Cemetery

Four score and seven years ago our fathers brought forth on this continent, a new nation, conceived in Liberty, and dedicated to the proposition that all men are created equal.

Now we are engaged in a great civil war; testing whether that nation, or any nation so conceived and so dedicated, can long endure. We are met on a great battlefield of that war. We have come to dedicate a portion of that field as a final resting-place for those who here gave their lives that that nation might live. It is altogether fitting and proper that we should do this.

But, in a larger sense, we cannot dedicate—we cannot consecrate—we cannot hallow—this ground. The brave men, living and dead, who struggled here have consecrated it, far above our poor power to add or detract. The world will little note, nor long remember, what we say here, but it can never forget what they did here. It is for us the living, rather, to be dedicated here to the unfinished work which they who fought here have thus far so nobly advanced. It is rather for us to be here dedicated to the great task remaining before us—that from these honored dead we take increased devotion to that cause for which they gave the last full measure of devotion; that we here highly resolve that these dead shall not have died in vain; that this nation, under God, shall have a new birth of freedom; and that government of the people, by the people, for the people, shall not perish from the earth.

[1863]

Joining the Conversation: Critical Thinking and Writing

1. Why do you suppose Lincoln began by saying, "Four score and seven years ago" rather than "Eighty-seven years ago"? By the way, Martin Luther King Jr. began his speech, *I Have a Dream* (delivered in 1963 in front of the Lincoln Memorial), with the words "Five score years ago."
2. Some people have objected that (in the final sentence) "government of the people" is the same as "[government] by the people," and the passage is pointlessly redundant. Do you agree? If you were speaking this passage ("of the people, by the people, for the people"), would you emphasize "of," "by," and "for," or would you emphasize "people"? Explain your answer.

3. Do you think that Lincoln says enough in his address about the dead soldiers? Should he have said more about them? How might the family of one of the dead responded to Lincoln's words?
4. What is the "unfinished work" that Lincoln enjoins us to perform? How are we to perform it, and how will we know whether we have done this work successfully or not?

STUDS TERKEL

Studs Terkel (1912–2008) was born Louis Terkel in New York City. After earning a PhD and a law degree from the University of Chicago, he worked as a civil servant and an actor before becoming a radio and television broadcaster. Much of his broadcasting work consisted of interviewing people for "Studs' Place," and he later published numerous books of interviews. His American Dreams *presents transcriptions that Terkel recorded. This interview took place in the 1970s, decades before Schwarzenegger served as governor of California.*

Arnold Schwarzenegger's Dream

Call me Arnold.

I was born in a little Austrian town, outside Graz. It was a 300-year-old house.

When I was ten years old, I had the dream of being the best in the world in something. When I was fifteen, I had a dream that I wanted to be the best body builder in the world and the most muscular man. It was not only a dream I dreamed at night. It was also a daydream. It was so much in my mind that I felt it had to become a reality. It took me five years of hard work. Five years later, I turned this dream into reality and became Mr. Universe, the best-built man in the world.

"Winning" is a very important word. There is one that achieves what he wanted to achieve and there are hundreds of thousands that failed. It singles you out: the winner.

5   I came out second three times, but that is not what I call losing. The bottom line for me was: Arnold has to be the winner. I have to win more often the Mr. Universe title than anybody else. I won it five times consecutively. I hold the record as Mr. Olympia, the top professional body-building championship. I won it six times. That's why I retired. There was nobody even close to me. Everybody gave up competing against me. That's what I call a winner.

When I was a small boy, my dream was not to be big physically, but big in a way that everybody listens to me when I talk, that I'm a very important person, that people recognize me and see me as something special. I had a big need for being singled out.

Also my dream was to end up in America. When I was ten years old, I dreamed of being an American. At the time I didn't know much about America, just that it was a wonderful country. I felt it was where I belonged. I didn't like being in a little country like Austria. I did everything possible to get out. I did so in 1968, when I was twenty-one years old.

If I would believe in life after death, I would say my before-life I was living in America. That's why I feel so good here. It is the country where you can turn your dream into reality. Other countries don't have those things. When I came over here to America, I felt I was in heaven. In America, we don't have an obstacle. Nobody's holding you back.

Number One in America pretty much takes care of the rest of the world. You kind of run through the rest of the world like nothing. I'm trying to make people in America aware that they should appreciate what they have here. You have the best tax advantages here and the best prices here and the best products here.

10   One of the things I always had was a business mind. When I was in high school, a majority of my classes were business classes. Economics and accounting and mathematics. When I came over here to this country, I really didn't speak English almost at all. I learned English and then started taking business courses, because that's what America is best known for: business. Turning one dollar into a million dollars in a short period of time. Also when you make money, how do you keep it?

That's one of the most important things when you have money in your hand, how can you keep it? Or make more out of it? Real estate is one of the best ways of doing that. I own apartment buildings, office buildings, and raw land. That's my love, real estate.

I have emotions. But what you do, you keep them cold or you store them away for a time. You must control your emotions, you must have command over yourself. Three, four months before a competition, I could not be interfered by other people's problems. This is sometimes called selfish. It's the only way you can be if you want to achieve something. Any emotional things inside me, I try to keep cold so it doesn't interfere with my training.

Many times things really touched me. I felt them and I felt sensitive about them. But I had to talk myself out of it. I had to suppress those feelings in order to go on. Sport is one of those activities where you really have to concentrate. You must pay attention a hundred percent to the particular thing you're doing. There must be nothing else on your mind. Emotions must not interfere. Otherwise, you're thinking about your girlfriend. You're in love, your positive energies get channeled into another direction rather than going into your weight room or making money.

You have to choose at a very early date what you want: a normal life or to achieve things you want to achieve. I never wanted to win a popularity contest in doing things the way people want me to do it. I went the road I thought was best for me. A few people thought I was cold, selfish. Later they found out that's not the case. After I achieve my goal, I can be Mr. Nice Guy. You know what I mean?

15   California is to me a dreamland. It is the absolute combination of everything I was always looking for. It has all the money in the world there, show business there, wonderful weather there, beautiful country, ocean is there. Snow skiing in the winter, you can go in the desert the same day. You have beautiful-looking people there. They all have a tan.

I believe very strongly in the philosophy of staying hungry. If you have a dream and it becomes a reality, don't stay satisfied with it too long. Make up a new dream and hunt after that one and turn it into reality. When you have that dream achieved, make up a new dream.

I am a strong believer in Western philosophy, the philosophy of success, of progress, of getting rich. The Eastern philosophy is passive, which I believe in maybe three percent of the times, and the ninety-seven percent is Western, conquering and going on. It's a beautiful philosophy, and America should keep it up.

[1980]

Joining the Conversation: Critical Thinking and Writing

1. After saying that America "is the country where you can turn your dream into reality. Other countries don't have those things," Schwarzenegger goes on to say, "In America . . . nobody's holding you back." What do you suppose he means by "those things," and by saying that here "nobody's holding you back"?
2. If you have some firsthand knowledge of another country, indicate, in an essay of 250–500 words, in what ways that country might differ from America in the matter of allowing individuals to fulfill their dreams. By the way, is it your guess that Schwarzenegger's particular dream ("to be the best body builder in the world") is more easily fulfilled in the United States than elsewhere—say in Canada, or Cuba, or Russia, or Austria? Why?
3. In one paragraph, set forth what you think Schwarzenegger's view of America is.
4. In one paragraph, sketch Schwarzenegger as objectively as possible, as you perceive him in this interview. In a second paragraph, again drawing only on this interview, evaluate him, calling attention to what you think are his strengths and weaknesses.

ANDREW LAM

Born in South Vietnam in 1964, Andrew Lam, essayist and short-story writer, is the web editor of the Pacific News Service. *We reprint a* PNS *essay that originally appeared on May 7, 2003.*

Who Will Light Incense When Mother's Gone?

My mother turned 70 recently, and though she remains a vivacious woman—her hair is still mostly black and there is a girlish twang in her laughter—mortality nevertheless weighs heavily on her soul. After the gifts were opened and the cake eaten, mother whispered this confidence to her younger sister: "Who will light incense to the dead when we're gone?"

"Honestly, I don't know," my aunt replied. "None of my children will do it, and we can forget the grandchildren. They don't even understand what we are doing. I guess when we're gone, the ritual ends."

Such is the price of living in America. I can't remember the last time I lit incense sticks and talked to my dead ancestors. Having fled so far from Vietnam, I no longer know to whom I should address my prayers or what promises I could possibly make to the long departed.

My mother, on the other hand, lives in America the way she would in Vietnam. Every morning in my parents' suburban home north of San Jose, she climbs a chair and piously lights a few joss sticks for the ancestral altar that sits on top of the living room bookcase. Every morning she talks to ghosts. She mumbles solemn prayers to the spirits of our dead ancestors, asks them for protection.

5   By contrast, on the shelves below stand my older siblings' engineering and business degrees, my own degree in biochemistry, our combined sports trophies and, last but not least, the latest installments of my own unending quest for self-reinvention—plaques and obelisk-shaped crystals—my journalism awards.

What mother's altar and the shelves beneath it seek to tell is the narrative of many an Asian immigrant family's journey to America. The collective, agrarian-based ethos in which ancestor worship is central slowly gives way to the glories of individual ambitions.

At that far end of the Asian immigrant trajectory, however, I cannot help but feel a certain twinge of guilt and regret upon hearing my mother's remark. Once when I was still a rebellious teenager and living at home, Mother asked me to speak more Vietnamese inside the house. "No," I answered in English, "what good is it to speak it? It's not as if I'm going to use it after I move out."

Mother, I remember, had a pained look in her eyes and called me the worst thing she could muster. "You've become a little American now, haven't you? A cowboy."

Vietnamese appropriated the word "cowboy" from the movies to imply selfishness. A cowboy in Vietnamese estimation is a rebel who, as in the spaghetti westerns, leaves town—the communal life—to ride alone into the sunset.

10   America, it had seemed, had stolen my mother's children, especially her youngest and once obedient son. America seduced him with its optimism, twisted his thinking, bent his tongue and dulled his tropic memories. America gave him freeways and fast food and silly cartoons and sitcoms, imbuing him with sappy, happy-ending incitements.

If we have reconciled since then, it does not mean I have become a traditional, incense-lighting Vietnamese son. I visit. I take her to lunch. I come home for important dates—New Year, Thanksgiving, Tet.[1]

But these days in front of the family altar, with all those faded photos of the dead staring down at me, I often feel oddly removed, as if staring at a relic of my distant past. And when, upon my mother's insistence, I light incense, I do not feel as if I am participating in a living tradition so much as pleasing a traditional mother.

We live in two different worlds, Mother and I. Mine is a world of travel and writing and public speaking, of immersing myself in contemporary history. Hers is a world of consulting the Vietnamese horoscope, of attending Buddhist temple on the day of her parents' death anniversaries and of telling and retelling stories of the past.

But on her 70th birthday, having listened to her worries, I have to wonder: What will survive my mother?

15   I wish I could assure my mother that, after she is gone, each morning I would light incense for her and all the ancestor spirits before her, but I can't.

In that odd, contradictory space in which immigrants' children find themselves, I feel strangely comforted when watching my mother's pious gesture each morning in front of the ancestors' altar. She is what connects me and my generation to a traditional past. And essentially, I share her fear that her generation and its memories of the Old World, what preserves us as a community, will fade away like incense smoke. I fear she'll leave me stranded in America, becoming more American than I expected, a lonely cowboy cursed with amnesia.

[2003]

Joining the Conversation: Critical Thinking and Writing

1. What does Andrew Lam mean when he refers to his mother as "a vivacious woman"? What does he mean when he refers to his own "unending quest for self-reinvention"? And what does the phrase "collective, agrarian-based ethos" mean?

2. How does Lam's mother feel about America? What about Lam himself: What are his feelings about America?

[1]**Tet** the Vietnamese New Year.

3. Does this essay give you a new perspective on the immigrant experience, or a familiar one? Do you think Lam intends to show the reader something new? Or does he have a different purpose in mind?

4. Imagine that you know this author and that, before publishing this essay, he asked for your "response and any suggestions" you might have. Compose a letter of one to two pages, beginning "Dear Andrew," in which you reply to him.

STORIES

SHERMAN ALEXIE

Sherman Alexie, born in 1966 in Spokane, Washington, holds a BA from Washington State University. The author of novels, stories, and poems, he adapted a volume of his short stories, The Lone Ranger and Tonto Fistfight in Heaven *(1994), into the film* Smoke Signals *(1998). Of his life and work Alexie has said, "I am a Spokane Coeur d'Alene Indian. . . . everything I do now, writing and otherwise, has its origin in that."*

The Lone Ranger, an immensely popular radio program that began in 1933, successfully made the transition to television (1949–57) and to comic books and films. The chief figure, the Lone Ranger, fought the bad guys of the Old West. He was assisted by the loyal Tonto, an American Indian who played a helpful but decidedly minor role. Tonto's name (it means "stupid" in Spanish, though in fact the character is not stupid) and his primitive English (he said things like "Me help Lone Ranger") make him an unacceptable figure today. Alexie's story never (after its title) mentions either the Lone Ranger or Tonto, nor does a fistfight occur, but a reader of the story presumably keeps in mind the problems that an American Indian faced—and faces—in a white world, in which whites and Indians do not easily co-exist, or at least do not coexist in a Lone Ranger-and-Tonto way.

The Lone Ranger and Tonto Fistfight in Heaven

Too hot to sleep so I walked down to the Third Avenue 7-11 for a Creamsicle and the company of a graveyard-shift cashier. I know that game. I worked graveyard for a Seattle 7-11 and got robbed once too often. The last time the bastard locked me in the cooler. He even took my money and basketball shoes.

The graveyard-shift worker in the Third Avenue 7-11 looked like they all do. Acne scars and a bad haircut, work pants that showed off his white socks, and those cheap black shoes that have no support. My arches still ache from my year at the Seattle 7-11.

"Hello," he asked when I walked into his store. "How you doing?"

I gave him a half-wave as I headed back to the freezer. He looked me over so he could describe me to the police later. I knew the look. One of my old girlfriends said I started to look at her that way, too. She left me not long after that. No, I left her and don't blame her for anything. That's how it happened. When one person starts to look at another like a criminal, then the love is over. It's logical.

5   "I don't trust you," she said to me. "You get too angry."

She was white and I lived with her in Seattle. Some nights we fought so bad that I would just get in my car and drive all night, only stop to fill up on gas. In fact,

I worked the graveyard shift to spend as much time away from her as possible. But I learned all about Seattle that way, driving its back ways and dirty alleys.

Sometimes, though, I would forget where I was and get lost. I'd drive for hours, searching for something familiar. Seems like I'd spent my whole life that way, looking for anything I recognized. Once, I ended up in a nice residential neighborhood and somebody must have been worried because the police showed up and pulled me over.

"What are you doing out here?" the police officer asked me as he looked over my license and registration.

"I'm lost."

10   "Well, where are you supposed to be?" he asked me, and I knew there were plenty of places I wanted to be, but none where I was supposed to be.

"I got in a fight with my girlfriend," I said. "I was just driving around, blowing off steam, you know?"

"Well, you should be more careful where you drive," the officer said. "You're making people nervous. You don't fit the profile of the neighborhood."

I wanted to tell him that I didn't really fit the profile of the country but I knew it would just get me into trouble.

"Can I help you?" the 7-11 clerk asked me loudly, searching for some response that would reassure him that I wasn't an armed robber. He knew this dark skin and long, black hair of mine was dangerous. I had potential.

15   "Just getting a Creamsicle," I said after a long interval. It was a sick twist to pull on the guy, but it was late and I was bored. I grabbed my Creamsicle and walked back to the counter slowly, scanned the aisles for effect. I wanted to whistle low and menacingly but I never learned to whistle.

"Pretty hot out tonight?" he asked, that old rhetorical weather bullshit question designed to put us both at ease.

"Hot enough to make you go crazy," I said and smiled. He swallowed hard like a white man does in those situations. I looked him over. Same old green, red, and white 7-11 jacket and thick glasses. But he wasn't ugly, just misplaced and marked by loneliness. If he wasn't working there that night, he'd be at home alone, flipping through channels and wishing he could afford HBO or Showtime.

"Will this be all?" he asked me, in that company effort to make me do some impulse shopping. Like adding a clause onto a treaty. *We'll take Washington and Oregon, and you get six pine trees and a brand-new Chrysler Cordoba.* I knew how to make and break promises.

"No," I said and paused. "Give me a Cherry Slushie, too."

20   "What size?" he asked, relieved.

"Large," I said, and he turned his back to me to make the drink. He realized his mistake but it was too late. He stiffened, ready for the gunshot or the blow behind the ear. When it didn't come, he turned back to me.

"I'm sorry," he said. "What size did you say?"

"Small," I said and changed the story.

"But I thought you said large."

25   "If you knew I wanted a large, then why did you ask me again?" I asked him and laughed. He looked at me, couldn't decide if I was giving him serious shit or just goofing. There was something about him I liked, even if it was three in the morning and he was white.

"Hey," I said. "Forget the Slushie. What I want to know is if you know all the words to the theme from 'The Brady Bunch'?"

He looked at me, confused at first, then laughed.

"Shit," he said. "I was hoping you weren't crazy. You were scaring me."

"Well, I'm going to get crazy if you don't know the words."

30   He laughed loudly then, told me to take the Creamsicle for free. He was the graveyard-shift manager and those little demonstrations of power tickled him. All seventy-five cents of it. I knew how much everything cost.

"Thanks," I said to him and walked out the door. I took my time walking home, let the heat of the night melt the Creamsicle all over my hand. At three in the morning I could act just as young as I wanted to act. There was no one around to ask me to grow up.

In Seattle, I broke lamps. She and I would argue and I'd break a lamp, just pick it up and throw it down. At first she'd buy replacement lamps, expensive and beautiful. But after a while she'd buy lamps from Goodwill or garage sales. Then she just gave up the idea entirely and we'd argue in the dark.

"You're just like your brother," she'd yell. "Drunk all the time and stupid."

"My brother don't drink that much."

35   She and I never tried to hurt each other physically. I did love her, after all, and she loved me. But those arguments were just as damaging as a fist. Words can be like that, you know? Whenever I get into arguments now, I remember her and I also remember Muhammad Ali. He knew the power of his fists but, more importantly, he knew the power of his words, too. Even though he only had an IQ of 80 or so, Ali was a genius. And she was a genius, too. She knew exactly what to say to cause me the most pain.

But don't get me wrong. I walked through that relationship with an executioner's hood. Or more appropriately, with war paint and sharp arrows. She was a kindergarten teacher and I continually insulted her for that.

"Hey, schoolmarm," I asked. "Did your kids teach you anything new today?"

And I always had crazy dreams. I always have had them, but it seemed they became nightmares more often in Seattle.

In one dream, she was a missionary's wife and I was a minor war chief. We fell in love and tried to keep it secret. But the missionary caught us fucking in the barn and shot me. As I lay dying, my tribe learned of the shooting and attacked the whites all across the reservation. I died and my soul drifted above the reservation.

40   Disembodied, I could see everything that was happening. Whites killing Indians and Indians killing whites. At first it was small, just my tribe and the few whites who lived there. But my dream grew, intensified. Other tribes arrived on horseback to continue the slaughter of whites, and the United States Cavalry rode into battle.

The most vivid image of that dream stays with me. Three mounted soldiers played polo with a dead Indian woman's head. When I first dreamed it, I thought it was just a product of my anger and imagination. But since then, I've read similar accounts of that kind of evil in the old West. Even more terrifying, though, is the fact that those kinds of brutal things are happening today in places like El Salvador.

All I know for sure, though, is that I woke from that dream in terror, packed up all my possessions, and left Seattle in the middle of the night.

"I love you," she said as I left her. "And don't ever come back."

I drove through the night, over the Cascades, down into the plains of central Washington, and back home to the Spokane Indian Reservation.

45   When I finished the Creamsicle that the 7-11 clerk gave me, I held the wooden stick up into the air and shouted out very loudly. A couple lights flashed on in windows and a police car cruised by me a few minutes later. I waved to the men

in blue and they waved back accidentally. When I got home it was still too hot to sleep so I picked up a week-old newspaper from the floor and read.

There was another civil war, another terrorist bomb exploded, and one more plane crashed and all aboard were presumed dead. The crime rate was rising in every city with populations larger than 100,000, and a farmer in Iowa shot his banker after foreclosure on his 1,000 acres.

A kid from Spokane won the local spelling bee by spelling the word *rhinoceros*.

When I got back to the reservation, my family wasn't surprised to see me. They'd been expecting me back since the day I left for Seattle. There's an old Indian poet who said that Indians can reside in the city, but they can never live there. That's as close to truth as any of us can get.

Mostly I watched television. For weeks I flipped through channels, searched for answers in the game shows and soap operas. My mother would circle the want ads in red and hand the paper to me.

50   "What are you going to do with the rest of your life?" she asked.

"Don't know," I said, and normally, for almost any other Indian in the country, that would have been a perfectly fine answer. But I was special, a former college student, a smart kid. I was one of those Indians who was supposed to make it, to rise above the rest of the reservation like a fucking eagle or something. I was the new kind of warrior.

For a few months I didn't even look at the want ads my mother circled, just left the newspaper where she had set it down. After a while, though, I got tired of television and started to play basketball again. I'd been a good player in high school, nearly great, and almost played at the college I attended for a couple years. But I'd been too out of shape from drinking and sadness to ever be good again. Still, I liked the way the ball felt in my hands and the way my feet felt inside my shoes.

At first I just shot baskets by myself. It was selfish, and I also wanted to learn the game again before I played against anybody else. Since I had been good before and embarrassed fellow tribal members, I knew they would want to take revenge on me. Forget about the cowboys versus Indians business. The most intense competition on any reservation is Indians versus Indians.

But on the night I was ready to play for real, there was this white guy at the gym, playing with all the Indians.

55   "Who is that?" I asked Jimmy Seyler.

"He's the new BIA[1] chief's kid."

"Can he play?"

"Oh, yeah."

And he could play. He played Indian ball, fast and loose, better than all the Indians there.

60   "How long's he been playing here?" I asked.

"Long enough."

I stretched my muscles, and everybody watched me. All these Indians watched one of their old and dusty heroes. Even though I had played most of my ball at the white high school I went to, I was still all Indian, you know? I was Indian when it counted, and this BIA kid needed to be beaten by an Indian, any Indian.

[1]**BIA** Bureau of Indian Affairs.

I jumped into the game and played well for a little while. It felt good. I hit a few shots, grabbed a rebound or two, played enough defense to keep the other team honest. Then that white kid took over the game. He was too good. Later, he'd play college ball back East and would nearly make the Knicks team a couple years on. But we didn't know any of that would happen. We just knew he was better that day and every other day.

The next morning I woke up tired and hungry, so I grabbed the want ads, found a job I wanted, and drove to Spokane to get it. I've been working at the high school exchange program ever since, typing and answering phones. Sometimes I wonder if the people on the other end of the line know that I'm Indian and if their voices would change if they did know.

65   One day I picked up the phone and it was her, calling from Seattle.

"I got your number from your mom," she said. "I'm glad you're working."

"Yeah, nothing like a regular paycheck."

"Are you drinking?"

"No, I've been on the wagon for almost a year."

70   "Good."

The connection was good. I could hear her breathing in the spaces between our words. How do you talk to the real person whose ghost has haunted you? How do you tell the difference between the two?

"Listen," I said. "I'm sorry for everything."

"Me, too."

"What's going to happen to us?" I asked her and wished I had the answer for myself.

75   "I don't know," she said. "I want to change the world."

These days, living alone in Spokane, I wish I lived closer to the river, to the falls where ghosts of salmon jump. I wish I could sleep. I put down my paper or book and turn off all the lights, lie quietly in the dark. It may take hours, even years, for me to sleep again. There's nothing surprising or disappointing in that. I know how all my dreams end anyway.

[1993]

Joining the Conversation: Critical Thinking and Writing

1. Given the fact that neither the Lone Ranger nor Tonto appears in the story, what do you make of the title?
2. Paragraphs 54–63 introduce a white man from the Bureau of Indian Affairs. Why do you suppose Alexie includes this episode in his story?
3. How would you characterize the narrator? How do you think he would characterize himself? In thinking about these matters, you might ask yourself, "What are his chief problems?" and "How well does he understand himself and the social world around him?"
4. What do you make of the narrator's statement, in the next-to-last paragraph, that he wishes he "lived closer to the river, to the falls where ghosts of salmon jump"?
5. Alexie has said that there is "a political purpose" to everything he writes. In your view, does his statement apply to this story? If so, does it increase your enjoyment

and your understanding of the story? Or do you think that storytellers—once they have told their story—should let readers draw their own conclusions? In an essay of 250–500 words, offer a comment on Alexie's comment.

RALPH ELLISON

Ralph Ellison (1914–94) was born in Oklahoma City. His father died when Ellison was three years old, and his mother supported herself and her child by working as a domestic. A trumpeter since boyhood, Ellison studied music at Tuskegee Institute, an historically black college in Alabama founded by Booker T. Washington. In 1936, he dropped out of Tuskegee and went to Harlem to study music composition and the visual arts; there he met Langston Hughes and Richard Wright, who encouraged him to turn to fiction. Ellison published stories and essays, and in 1942, he became the managing editor of Negro Quarterly. *During World War II, he served in the U. S. Merchant Marine. After the war, he returned to writing and later taught in universities.*

"Battle Royal" was first published in 1947 and was slightly revised (a transitional paragraph was added at the end of the story) for the opening chapter of Ellison's novel, Invisible Man *(1952), a book cited by* Book-Week *as "the most significant work of fiction written by an American" in the years between 1945 and 1965. In addition to stories and his one novel, Ellison published critical essays, which are brought together in* The Collected Essays of Ralph Ellison *(1995).*

Battle Royal

It goes a long way back, some twenty years. All my life I had been looking for something, and everywhere I turned someone tried to tell me what it was. I accepted their answers too, though they were often in contradiction and even self-contradictory. I was naïve. I was looking for myself and asking everyone except myself questions which I, and only I, could answer. It took me a long time and much painful boomeranging of my expectations to achieve a realization everyone else appears to have been born with: That I am nobody but myself. But first I had to discover that I am an invisible man!

And yet I am no freak of nature, nor of history. I was in the cards, other things having been equal (or unequal) eighty-five years ago. I am not ashamed of my grandparents for having been slaves. I am only ashamed of myself for having at one time been ashamed. About eighty-five years ago they were told that they were free, united with others of our country in everything pertaining to the common good, and, in everything social, separate like the fingers of the hand. And they believed it. They exulted in it. They stayed in their place, worked hard, and brought up my father to do the same. But my grandfather is the one. He was an odd old guy, my grandfather, and I am told I take after him. It was he who caused the trouble. On his deathbed he called my father to him and said, "Son, after I'm gone I want you to keep up the good fight. I never told you, but our life is a war and I have been a traitor all my born days, a spy in the enemy's country ever since I give up my gun back in the Reconstruction. Live with your head in the lion's mouth. I want you to overcome 'em with yeses, undermine 'em with grins, agree 'em to death and destruction, let 'em swoller you till they vomit or bust wide open." They thought the old man had gone out of his mind. He had been the meekest of men. The younger children were rushed from the room, the shades drawn and the flame of the lamp turned so low that it sputtered on the wick like the old man's breathing. "Learn it to the younguns," he whispered fiercely; then he died.

But my folks were more alarmed over his last words than over his dying. It was as though he had not died at all, his words caused so much anxiety. I was warned emphatically to forget what he had said and, indeed, this is the first time it has been mentioned outside the family circle. It had a tremendous effect upon me, however. I could never be sure of what he meant. Grandfather had been a quiet old man who never made any trouble, yet on his deathbed he had called himself a traitor and a spy, and he had spoken of his meekness as a dangerous activity. It became a constant puzzle which lay unanswered in the back of my mind. And whenever things went well for me I remembered my grandfather and felt guilty and uncomfortable. It was as though I was carrying out his advice in spite of myself. And to make it worse, everyone loved me for it. I was praised by the most lily-white men of the town. I was considered an example of desirable conduct— just as my grandfather had been. And what puzzled me was that the old man had defined it as *treachery*. When I was praised for my conduct I felt a guilt that in some way I was doing something that was really against the wishes of the white folks, that if they had understood they would have desired me to act just the opposite, that I should have been sulky and mean, and that that really would have been what they wanted, even though they were fooled and thought they wanted me to act as I did. It made me afraid that some day they would look upon me as a traitor and I would be lost. Still I was more afraid to act any other way because they didn't like that at all. The old man's words were like a curse. On my graduation day I delivered an oration in which I showed that humility was the secret, indeed, the very essence of progress. (Not that I believed this—how could I, remembering my grandfather?—I only believed that it worked.) It was a great success. Everyone

Gordon Parks, *Ralph Ellison*. Parks, an African American photographer with an international reputation, published many books of photographs, including *Camera Portraits*, where this picture appears.

praised me and I was invited to give the speech at a gathering of the town's leading white citizens. It was a triumph for our whole community.

It was in the main ballroom of the leading hotel. When I got there I discovered that it was on the occasion of a smoker, and I was told that since I was to be there anyway I might as well take part in the battle royal to be fought by some of my schoolmates as part of the entertainment. The battle royal came first.

5   All of the town's big shots were there in their tuxedoes, wolfing down the buffet foods, drinking beer and whiskey and smoking black cigars. It was a large room with a high ceiling. Chairs were arranged in neat rows around three sides of a portable boxing ring. The fourth side was clear, revealing a gleaming space of polished floor. I had some misgivings over the battle royal, by the way. Not from a distaste for fighting, but because I didn't care too much for the other fellows who were to take part. They were tough guys who seemed to have no grandfather's curse worrying their minds. No one could mistake their toughness. And besides, I suspected that fighting a battle royal might detract from the dignity of my speech. In those pre-invisible days I visualized myself as a potential Booker T. Washington.[1] But the other fellows didn't care too much for me either, and there were nine of them. I felt superior to them in my way, and I didn't like the manner in which we were all crowded together into the servants' elevator. Nor did they like my being there. In fact, as the warmly lighted floors flashed past the elevator we had words over the fact that I, by taking part in the fight, had knocked one of their friends out of a night's work.

We were led out of the elevator through a rococo hall into an anteroom and told to get into our fighting togs. Each of us was issued a pair of boxing gloves and ushered out into the big mirrored hall, which we entered looking cautiously about us and whispering, lest we might accidentally be heard above the noise of the room. It was foggy with cigar smoke. And already the whiskey was taking effect. I was shocked to see some of the most important men of the town quite tipsy. They were all there—bankers, lawyers, judges, doctors, fire chiefs, teachers, merchants. Even one of the more fashionable pastors. Something we could not see was going on up front. A clarinet was vibrating sensuously and the men were standing up and moving eagerly forward. We were a small tight group, clustered together, our bare upper bodies touching and shining with anticipatory sweat; while up front the big shots were becoming increasingly excited over something we still could not see. Suddenly I heard the school superintendent, who had told me to come, yell. "Bring up the shines, gentlemen! Bring up the little shines!"

We were rushed up to the front of the ballroom, where it smelled even more strongly of tobacco and whiskey. Then we were pushed into place. I almost wet my pants. A sea of faces, some hostile, some amused, ringed around us, and in the center, facing us, stood a magnificent blonde—stark naked. There was dead silence. I felt a blast of cold air chill me. I tried to back away, but they were behind me and around me. Some of the boys stood with lowered heads, trembling. I felt a wave of irrational guilt and fear. My teeth chattered, my skin turned to goose flesh, my knees knocked. Yet I was strongly attracted and looked in spite of myself. Had the price of looking been blindness, I would have looked. The hair was yellow like that of a circus kewpie doll, the face heavily powdered and rouged, as though to form an abstract mask, the eyes hollow and smeared a cool blue, the color of a baboon's butt. I felt a desire to spit upon her as my eyes brushed slowly over her

[1]**Booker T. Washington** (1856–1915), African American educator and leader.

body. Her breasts were firm and round as the domes of East Indian temples, and I stood so close as to see the fine skin texture and beads of pearly perspiration glistening like dew around the pink and erected buds of her nipples. I wanted at one and the same time to run from the room, to sink through the floor, or go to her and cover her from my eyes and the eyes of the others with my body; to feel the soft thighs, to caress her and destroy her, to love her and murder her, to hide from her, and yet to stroke where below the small American flag tattooed upon her belly her thighs formed a capital V. I had a notion that of all in the room she saw only me with her impersonal eyes.

And then she began to dance, a slow sensuous movement; the smoke of a hundred cigars clinging to her like the thinnest of veils. She seemed like a fair bird-girl girdled in veils calling to me from the angry surface of some gray and threatening sea. I was transported. Then I became aware of the clarinet playing and the big shots yelling at us. Some threatened us if we looked and others if we did not. On my right I saw one boy faint. And now a man grabbed a silver pitcher from a table and stepped close as he dashed ice water upon him and stood him up and forced two of us to support him as his head hung and moans issued from his thick bluish lips. Another boy began to plead to go home. He was the largest of the group, wearing dark red fighting trunks much too small to conceal the erection which projected from him as though in answer to the insinuating low-registered moans of the clarinet. He tried to hide himself with his boxing gloves.

And all the while the blonde continued dancing, smiling faintly at the big shots who watched her with fascination, and faintly smiling at our fear. I noticed a certain merchant who followed her hungrily, his lips loose and drooling. He was a large man who wore diamond studs in a shirtfront which swelled with the ample paunch underneath, and each time the blonde swayed her undulating hips he ran his hand through the thin hair of his bald head and, with his arms upheld, his posture clumsy like that of an intoxicated panda, wound his belly in a slow and obscene grind. This creature was completely hypnotized. The music had quickened. As the dancer flung herself about with a detached expression on her face, the men began reaching out to touch her. I could see their beefy fingers sink into her soft flesh. Some of the others tried to stop them and she began to move around the floor in graceful circles, as they gave chase, slipping and sliding over the polished floor. It was mad. Chairs went crashing, drinks were spilt, as they ran laughing and howling after her. They caught her just as she reached a door, raised her from the floor, and tossed her as college boys are tossed at a hazing, and above her red, fixed-smiling lips I saw the terror and disgust in her eyes, almost like my own terror and that which I saw in some of the other boys. As I watched, they tossed her twice and her soft breasts seemed to flatten against the air and her legs flung wildly as she spun. Some of the more sober ones helped her to escape. And I started off the floor, heading for the anteroom with the rest of the boys.

10   Some were still crying and in hysteria. But as we tried to leave we were stopped and ordered to get into the ring. There was nothing to do but what we were told. All ten of us climbed under the ropes and allowed ourselves to be blindfolded with broad bands of white cloth. One of the men seemed to feel a bit sympathetic and tried to cheer us up as we stood with our backs against the ropes. Some of us tried to grin. "See that boy over there?" one of the men said. "I want you to run across at the bell and give it to him right in the belly. If you don't get him, I'm going to get you. I don't like his looks." Each of us was told the same. The blindfolds were put on. Yet even then I had been going over my speech. In my

mind each word was as bright as flame. I felt the cloth pressed into place, and frowned so that it would be loosened when I relaxed.

But now I felt a sudden fit of blind terror. I was unused to darkness. It was as though I had suddenly found myself in a dark room filled with poisonous cotton-mouths. I could hear the bleary voices yelling insistently for the battle royal to begin.

"Get going in there!"

"Let me at that big nigger!"

I strained to pick up the school superintendent's voice, as though to squeeze some security out of that slightly more familiar sound.

15   "Let me at those black sonsabitches!" someone yelled.

"No, Jackson, no!" another voice yelled. "Here, somebody, help me hold Jack."

"I want to get at that ginger-colored nigger. Tear him limb from limb," the first voice yelled.

I stood against the ropes trembling. For in those days I was what they called ginger-colored, and he sounded as though he might crunch me between his teeth like a crisp ginger cookie.

Quite a struggle was going on. Chairs were being kicked about and I could hear voices grunting as with a terrific effort. I wanted to see, to see more desperately than ever before. But the blindfold was as tight as a thick skin-puckering scab and when I raised my gloved hands to push the layers of white aside a voice yelled, "Oh, no you don't, black bastard! Leave that alone!"

20   "Ring the bell before Jackson kills him a coon!" someone boomed in the sudden silence. And I heard the bell clang and the sound of the feet scuffling forward.

A glove smacked against my head. I pivoted, striking out stiffly as someone went past, and felt the jar ripple along the length of my arm to my shoulder. Then it seemed as though all nine of the boys had turned upon me at once. Blows pounded me from all sides while I struck out as best I could. So many blows landed upon me that I wondered if I were not the only blindfolded fighter in the ring, or if the man called Jackson hadn't succeeded in getting me after all.

Blindfolded, I could no longer control my motions. I had no dignity. I stumbled about like a baby or a drunken man. The smoke had become thicker and with each new blow it seemed to sear and further restrict my lungs. My saliva became like hot bitter glue. A glove connected with my head, filling my mouth with warm blood. It was everywhere. I could not tell if the moisture I felt upon my body was sweat or blood. A blow landed hard against the nape of my neck. I felt myself going over, my head hitting the floor. Streaks of blue light filled the black world behind the blindfold. I lay prone, pretending that I was knocked out, but felt myself seized by hands and yanked to my feet. "Get going, black boy! Mix it up!" My arms were like lead, my head smarting from blows. I managed to feel my way to the ropes and held on, trying to catch my breath. A glove landed in my midsection and I went over again, feeling as though the smoke had become a knife jabbed into my guts. Pushed this way and that by the legs milling around me, I finally pulled erect and discovered that I could see the black, sweat-washed forms weaving in the smoky-blue atmosphere like drunken dancers weaving to the rapid drum-like thuds of blows.

Everyone fought hysterically. It was complete anarchy. Everybody fought everybody else. No group fought together for long. Two, three, four, fought one, ⁓n turned to fight each other, were themselves attacked. Blows landed below ⁓elt and in the kidney, with the gloves open as well as closed, and with my ⁓rtly opened now there was not so much terror. I moved carefully, avoiding blows, although not too many to attract attention, fighting from group to group. The boys groped about like blind, cautious crabs crouching to protect their mid-sections, their heads pulled in short against their shoulders, their arms stretched nervously before them, with their fists testing the smoke-filled air like the knobbed feelers of hypersensitive snails. In one corner I glimpsed a boy violently punching the air and heard him scream in pain as he smashed his hand against a ring post. For a second I saw him bent over holding his hand, then going down as a blow caught his unprotected head. I played one group against the other, slipping and throwing a punch then stepping out of range while pushing the others into the melee to take the blows blindly aimed at me. The smoke was agonizing and there were no rounds, no bells at three minute intervals to relieve our exhaustion. The room spun round me, a swirl of lights, smoke, sweating bodies surrounded by tense white faces. I bled from both nose and mouth, the blood spattering upon my chest.

The men kept yelling, "Slug him, black boy! Knock his guts out!"

25   "Uppercut him! Kill him! Kill that big boy!"

Taking a fake fall, I saw a boy going down heavily beside me as though we were felled by a single blow, saw a sneaker-clad foot shoot into his groin as the two who had knocked him down stumbled upon him. I rolled out of range, feeling a twinge of nausea.

The harder we fought the more threatening the men became. And yet, I had begun to worry about my speech again. How would it go? Would they recognize my ability? What would they give me?

I was fighting automatically and suddenly I noticed that one after another of the boys was leaving the ring. I was surprised, filled with panic, as though I had been left alone with an unknown danger. Then I understood. The boys had arranged it among themselves. It was the custom for the two men left in the ring to slug it out for the winner's prize. I discovered this too late. When the bell sounded two men in tuxedoes leaped into the ring and removed the blindfold. I found myself facing Tatlock, the biggest of the gang. I felt sick at my stomach. Hardly had the bell stopped ringing in my ears than it clanged again and I saw him moving swiftly toward me. Thinking of nothing else to do I hit him smash on the nose. He kept coming, bringing the rank sharp violence of stale sweat. His face was a black blank of a face, only his eyes alive—with hate of me and aglow with a feverish terror from what had happened to us all. I became anxious. I wanted to deliver my speech and he came at me as though he meant to beat it out of me. I smashed him again and again, taking his blows as they came. Then on a sudden impulse I struck him lightly as we clinched, I whispered, "Fake like I knocked you out, you can have the prize."

"I'll break your behind," he whispered hoarsely.

30   "For *them*?"

"For *me*, sonofabitch!"

They were yelling for us to break it up and Tatlock spun me half around with a blow, and as a joggled camera sweeps in a reeling scene, I saw the howling red faces crouching tense beneath the cloud of blue-gray smoke. For a moment the world wavered, unraveled, flowed, then my head cleared and Tatlock bounced before me. That fluttering shadow before my eyes was his jabbing left hand. Then falling forward, my head against his damp shoulder, I whispered,

"I'll make it five dollars more."

"Go to hell!"

35   But his muscles relaxed a trifle beneath my pressure and I breathed, "Seven!"

"Give it to your ma," he said, ripping me beneath the heart.

And while I still held him I butted him and moved away. I felt myself bombarded with punches. I fought back with hopeless desperation. I wanted to deliver my speech more than anything else in the world, because I felt that only these men could judge truly my ability, and now this stupid clown was ruining my chances. I began fighting carefully now, moving in to punch him and out again with my greater speed. A lucky blow to his chin and I had him going too—until I heard a loud voice yell, "I got my money on the big boy."

Hearing this, I almost dropped my guard. I was confused: Should I try to win against the voice out there? Would not this go against my speech, and was not this a moment for humility, for nonresistance? A blow to my head as I danced about sent my right eye popping like a jack-in-the-box and settled my dilemma. The room went red as I fell. It was a dream fall, my body languid and fastidious as to where to land, until the floor became impatient and smashed up to meet me. A moment later I came to. An hypnotic voice said FIVE emphatically. And I lay there, hazily watching a dark red spot of my own blood shaping itself into a butterfly, glistening and soaking into the soiled gray world of the canvas.

When the voice drawled TEN I was lifted up and dragged to a chair. I sat dazed. My eye pained and swelled with each throb of my pounding heart and I wondered if now I would be allowed to speak. I was wringing wet, my mouth still bleeding. We were grouped along the wall now. The other boys ignored me as they congratulated Tatlock and speculated as to how much they would be paid. One boy whimpered over his smashed hand. Looking up front, I saw attendants in white jackets rolling the portable ring away and placing a small square rug in the vacant space surrounded by chairs. Perhaps, I thought, I will stand on the rug to deliver my speech.

40   Then the M.C. called to us, "Come on up here boys and get your money."

We ran forward to where the men laughed and talked in their chairs, waiting. Everyone seemed friendly now.

"There it is on the rug," the man said. I saw the rug covered with coins of all dimensions and a few crumpled bills. But what excited me, scattered here and there, were the gold pieces.

"Boys, it's all yours," the man said. "You get all you grab."

"That's right, Sambo," a blond man said, winking at me confidentially.

45   I trembled with excitement, forgetting my pain. I would get the gold and the bills, I thought. I would use both hands. I would throw my body against the boys nearest me to block them from the gold.

"Get down around the rug now," the man commanded, "and don't anyone touch it until I give the signal."

"This ought to be good," I heard.

As told, we got around the square rug on our knees. Slowly the man raised his freckled hand as we followed it upward with our eyes.

I heard, "These niggers look like they're about to pray!"

50   Then, "Ready," the man said. "Go!"

I lunged for a yellow coin lying on the blue design of the carpet, touching it and sending a surprised shriek to join those rising around me. I tried frantically to remove my hand but could not let go. A hot, violent force tore through my body, shaking me like a wet rat. The rug was electrified. The hair bristled up on my head as I shook myself free. My muscles jumped, my nerves jangled, writhed. But I saw this was not stopping the other boys. Laughing in fear and embarrassment, some were holding back and scooping up the coins knocked off by the painful contortions of the others. The men roared above us as we struggled.

"Pick it up, goddamnit, pick it up!" someone called like a bass-voiced parrot. "Go on, get it!"

I crawled rapidly around the floor, picking up the coins, trying to avoid the coppers and to get greenbacks and the gold. Ignoring the shock by laughing, as I brushed the coins off quickly, I discovered that I could contain the electricity— a contradiction, but it works. Then the men began to push us onto the rug. Laughing embarrassedly, we struggled out of their hands and kept after the coins. We were all wet and slippery and hard to hold. Suddenly I saw a boy lifted into the air, glistening with sweat like a circus seal, and dropped, his wet back landing flush upon the charged rug, heard him yell and saw him literally dance upon his back, his elbows beating a frenzied tattoo upon the floor, his muscles twitching like the flesh of a horse stung by many flies. When he finally rolled off, his face was gray and no one stopped him when he ran from the floor amid booming laughter.

"Get the money," the M.C. called. "That's good hard American cash!"

55   And we snatched and grabbed, snatched and grabbed. I was careful not to come too close to the rug now, and when I felt the hot whiskey breath descend upon me like a cloud of foul air I reached out and grabbed the leg of a chair. It was occupied and I held on desperately.

"Leggo, nigger! Leggo!"

The huge face wavered down to mine as he tried to push me free. But my body was slippery and he was too drunk. It was Mr. Colcord, who owned a chain of movie houses and "entertainment palaces." Each time he grabbed me I slipped out of his hands. It became a real struggle. I feared the rug more than I did the drunk, so I held on, surprising myself for a moment by trying to topple *him* upon the rug. It was such an enormous idea that I found myself actually carrying it out. I tried not to be obvious, yet when I grabbed his leg, trying to tumble him out of the chair, he raised up roaring with laughter, and, looking at me with soberness dead in the eye, kicked me viciously in the chest. The chair leg flew out of my hand. I felt myself going and rolled. It was as though I had rolled through a bed of hot coals. It seemed a whole century would pass before I would roll free, a century in which I was seared through the deepest levels of my body to the fearful breath within me and the breath seared and heated to the point of explosion. It'll all be over in a flash, I thought as I rolled clear. It'll all be over in a flash.

But not yet, the men on the other side were waiting, red faces swollen as though from apoplexy as they bent forward in their chairs. Seeing their fingers coming toward me I rolled away as a fumbled football rolls off the receiver's fingertips, back into the coals. That time I luckily sent the rug sliding out of place and heard the coins ringing against the floor and the boys scuffling to pick them up and the M.C. calling, "All right, boys, that's all. Go get dressed and get your money."

I was limp as a dish rag. My back felt as though it had been beaten with wires.

60   When we had dressed the M.C. came in and gave us each five dollars, except Tatlock, who got ten for being the last in the ring. Then he told us to leave. I was not to get a chance to deliver my speech, I thought. I was going out into the dim alley in despair when I was stopped and told to go back. I returned to the ballroom, where the men were pushing back their chairs and gathering in groups to talk.

The M.C. knocked on a table for quiet. "Gentlemen," he said, "we almost forgot an important part of the program. A most serious part, gentlemen. This boy was brought here to deliver a speech which he made at his graduation yesterday. . . ."

"Bravo!"

"I'm told that he is the smartest boy we've got out there in Greenwood. I'm told that he knows more big words than a pocket-sized dictionary."

Much applause and laughter.

65   "So now, gentlemen, I want you to give him your attention."

There was still laughter as I faced them, my mouth dry, my eye throbbing. I began slowly, but evidently my throat was tense, because they began shouting, "Louder! Louder!"

"We of the younger generation extol the wisdom of that great leader and educator," I shouted, "who first spoke these flaming words of wisdom: 'A ship lost at sea for many days suddenly sighted a friendly vessel. From the mast of the unfortunate vessel was seen a signal: "Water, water; we die of thirst!" The answer from the friendly vessel came back: "Cast down your bucket where you are." The captain of the distressed vessel, at last heeding the injunction, cast down his bucket, and it came up full of fresh sparkling water from the mouth of the Amazon River.' And like him I say, and in his words, 'To those of my race who depend upon bettering their condition in a foreign land, or who underestimate the importance of cultivating friendly relations with the Southern white man, who is his next-door neighbor, I would say: "Cast down your bucket where you are"—cast it down in making friends in every manly way of the people of all races by whom we are surrounded. . . .'"

I spoke automatically and with such fervor that I did not realize that the men were still talking and laughing until my dry mouth, filling up with blood from the cut, almost strangled me. I coughed, wanting to stop and go to one of the tall brass, sand-filled spittoons to relieve myself, but a few of the men, especially the superintendent, were listening and I was afraid. So I gulped it down, blood, saliva and all, and continued. (What powers of endurance I had during those days! What enthusiasm! What a belief in the rightness of things!) I spoke even louder in spite of the pain. But still they talked and still they laughed, as though deaf with cotton in dirty ears. So I spoke with greater emotional emphasis. I closed my ears and swallowed blood until I was nauseated. The speech seemed a hundred times as long as before, but I could not leave out a single word. All had to be said, each memorized nuance considered, rendered. Nor was that all. Whenever I uttered a word of three or more syllables a group of voices would yell for me to repeat it. I used the phrase "social responsibility" and they yelled:

"What's the word you say, boy?"

70   "Social responsibility," I said.

"What?"

"Social . . ."

"Louder."

". . . responsibility."

75   "More!"

"Respon—"

"Repeat!"

"—sibility."

The room filled with the uproar of laughter until, no doubt, distracted by having to gulp down my blood, I made a mistake and yelled a phrase I had often seen denounced in newspaper editorials, heard debated in private.

80   "Social . . ."

"What?" they yelled.

". . . equality—"

The laughter hung smokelike in the sudden stillness. I opened my eyes, puzzled. Sounds of displeasure filled the room. The M.C. rushed forward. They shouted hostile phrases at me. But I did not understand.

A small dry mustached man in the front row blared out, "Say that slowly, son!"

85   "What sir?"

"What you just said!"

"Social responsibility, sir," I said.

"You weren't being smart, were you, boy?" he said, not unkindly.

"No, sir!"

90   "You sure that about 'equality' was a mistake?"

"Oh, yes, sir," I said. "I was swallowing blood."

"Well, you had better speak more slowly so we can understand. We mean to do right by you, but you've got to know your place at all times. All right, now, go on with your speech."

I was afraid. I wanted to leave but I wanted also to speak and I was afraid they'd snatch me down.

"Thank you, sir," I said, beginning where I had left off, and having them ignore me as before.

95   Yet when I finished there was a thunderous applause. I was surprised to see the superintendent come forth with a package wrapped in white tissue paper, and gesturing for quiet, address the men.

"Gentlemen, you see that I did not overpraise this boy. He makes a good speech and some day he'll lead his people in the proper paths. And I don't have to tell you that that is important in these days and times. This is a good, smart boy, and so to encourage him in the right direction, in the name of the Board of Education I wish to present him a prize in the form of this . . ."

He paused, removing the tissue paper and revealing a gleaming calfskin brief case.

". . . in the form of this first-class article from Shad Whitmore's shop."

"Boy," he said, addressing me, "take this prize and keep it well. Consider it a badge of office. Prize it. Keep developing as you are and some day it will be filled with important papers that will help shape the destiny of your people."

100   I was so moved that I could hardly express my thanks. A rope of bloody saliva forming a shape like an undiscovered continent drooled upon the leather and I wiped it quickly away. I felt an importance that I had never dreamed.

"Open it and see what's inside," I was told.

My fingers a-tremble, I complied, smelling the fresh leather and finding an official-looking document inside. It was a scholarship to the state college for Negroes. My eyes filled with tears and I ran awkwardly off the floor.

I was overjoyed; I did not even mind when I discovered that the gold pieces I had scrambled for were brass pocket tokens advertising a certain make of automobile.

When I reached home everyone was excited. Next day the neighbors came to congratulate me. I even felt safe from grandfather, whose deathbed curse usually spoiled my triumphs. I stood beneath his photograph with my brief case in hand and smiled triumphantly into his stolid black peasant's face. It was a face that fascinated me. The eyes seemed to follow everywhere I went.

105   That night I dreamed I was at a circus with him and that he refused to laugh
at the clowns no matter what they did. Then later he told me to open my brief case
and read what was inside and I did, finding an official envelope stamped with the
state seal; and inside the envelope I found another and another, endlessly, and I
thought I would fall of weariness. "Them's years," he said. "Now open that one."
And I did and in it I found an engraved document containing a short message in
letters of gold. "Read it," my grandfather said. "Out loud."
        "To Whom It May Concern," I intoned, "Keep This Nigger-Boy Running."
        I awoke with the old man's laughter ringing in my ears.
        (It was a dream I was to remember and dream again for many years after. But
at the time I had no insight into its meaning. First I had to attend college.)

[1947]

Joining the Conversation: Critical Thinking and Writing

1. Now that you have read the entire story, the opening paragraph of "Battle
   Royal" may be clearer than it was when you first read it. What does the narrator
   mean when he declares at the end of this paragraph, "I am an invisible man"?
   Explain how the events described in the story taught him this painful truth.
2. The narrator says of his grandfather's dying speech, "I could never be sure of
   what he meant." What do you think the grandfather meant by calling himself a
   traitor and a spy in the enemy's territory?
3. What is the significance of the scene involving the naked blonde woman? How
   is this scene related to the narrator's discovery that he is invisible?
4. This story is a powerful, indeed shocking, study of racism, but in essays and
   interviews, Ellison often noted that he intended his stories and his novel *Invisible
   Man* to illuminate "universal truths" about human experience as well. In your
   view, does "Battle Royal" achieve this goal? What insights does it offer about the
   nature of self-knowledge and human identity?

TONI CADE BAMBARA

*Toni Cade Bambara (1939–95) was born in New York City
and grew up in various African American neighborhoods of
the city. After studying at the University of Florence in Italy and
at City College in New York, where she received an MA degree,
she worked for a while as a case investigator for the New York
State Welfare Department. Later, she directed a recreation program for hospital patients. After her literary reputation became
established, she spent most of her time writing, though she also
served as writer in residence at Spelman College in Atlanta.*

The Lesson

Back in the days when everyone was old and stupid or young and foolish and me
and Sugar were the only ones just right, this lady moved on our block with nappy
hair and proper speech and no makeup. And quite naturally we laughed at her,
laughed the way we did at the junk man who went about his business like he was

some big-time president and his sorry-ass horse his secretary. And we kinda hated her too, hated the way we did the winos who cluttered up our parks and pissed on our handball walls and stank up our hallways and stairs so you couldn't halfway play hide-and-seek without a goddamn gas mask. Miss Moore was her name. The only woman on the block with no first name. And she was black as hell, cept for her feet, which were fish-white and spooky. And she was always planning these boring-ass things for us to do, us being my cousin, mostly, who lived on the block cause we all moved North the same time and to the same apartment then spread out gradual to breathe. And our parents would yank our heads into some kinda shape and crisp up our clothes so we'd be presentable for travel with Miss Moore, who always looked like she was going to church, though she never did. Which is just one of the things the grownups talked about when they talked behind her back like a dog. But when she came calling with some sachet she'd sewed up or some gingerbread she'd made or some book, why then they'd all be too embarrassed to turn her down and we'd get handed over all spruced up. She'd been to college and said it was only right that she should take responsibility for the young ones' education, and she not even related by marriage or blood. So they'd go for it. Specially Aunt Gretchen. She was the main gofer in the family. You got some ole dumb shit foolishness you want somebody to go for, you send for Aunt Gretchen. She been screwed into the go-along for so long, it's a blood-deep natural thing with her. Which is how she got saddled with me and Sugar and Junior in the first place while our mothers were in a la-de-da apartment up the block having a good ole time.

So this one day Miss Moore rounds us all up at the mailbox and it's puredee hot and she's knockin herself out about arithmetic. And school suppose to let up in summer I heard, but she don't never let up. And the starch in my pinafore scratching the shit outta me and I'm really hating this nappy-head bitch and her goddamn college degree. I'd much rather go to the pool or to the show where it's cool. So me and Sugar leaning on the mailbox being surly, which is a Miss Moore word. And Flyboy checking out what everybody brought for lunch. And Fat Butt already wasting his peanut-butter-and-jelly sandwich like the pig he is. And Junebug punchin on Q.T.'s arm for potato chips. And Rosie Giraffe shifting from one hip to the other waiting for somebody to step on her foot or ask her if she from Georgia so she can kick ass, preferably Mercedes'. And Miss Moore asking us do we know what money is, like we a bunch of retards. I mean real money, she say, like it's only poker chips or monopoly papers we lay on the grocer. So right away I'm tired of this and say so. And would much rather snatch Sugar and go to the Sunset and terrorize the West Indian kids and take their hair ribbons and their money too. And Miss Moore files that remark away for next week's lesson on brotherhood, I can tell. And finally I say we oughta get to the subway cause it's cooler and besides we might meet some cute boys. Sugar done swiped her mama's lipstick, so we ready.

So we heading down the street and she's boring us silly about what things cost and what our parents make and how much goes for rent and how money ain't divided up right in this country. And then she gets to the part about we all poor and live in the slums, which I don't feature. And I'm ready to speak on that, but she steps out in the street and hails two cabs just like that. Then she hustles half the crew in with her and hands me a five-dollar bill and tells me to calculate 10 percent tip for the driver. And we're off. Me and Sugar and Junebug and Flyboy hangin out the window and hollering to everybody, putting lipstick on each other cause Flyboy a faggot anyway, and making farts with our sweaty armpits.

But I'm mostly trying to figure how to spend this money. But they all fascinated with the meter ticking and Junebug starts laying bets to how much it'll read when Flyboy can't hold his breath no more. Then Sugar lays bets as to how much it'll be when we get there. So I'm stuck. Don't nobody want to go for my plan, which is to jump out at the next light and run off to the first bar-b-que we can find. Then the driver tells us to get the hell out cause we there already. And the meter reads eighty-five cents. And I'm stalling to figure out the tip and Sugar say give him a dime. And I decide he don't need it as bad as I do, so later for him. But then he tries to take off with Junebug foot still in the door so we talk about his mama something ferocious. Then we check out that we on Fifth Avenue and everybody dressed up in stockings. One lady in a fur coat, hot as it is. White folks crazy.

"This is the place," Miss Moore say, presenting it to us in the voice she uses at the museum. "Let's look in the windows before we go in."

5   "Can we steal?" Sugar asks very serious like she's getting the ground rules squared away before she plays. "I beg your pardon," say Miss Moore, and we fall out. So she leads us around the windows of the toy store and me and Sugar screamin, "This is mine, that's mine, I gotta have that, that was made for me, I was born for that," till Big Butt drowns us out.

"Hey, I'm goin to buy that there."

"That there? You don't even know what it is, stupid."

"I do so," he say punchin on Rosie Giraffe. "It's a microscope."

"Whatcha gonna do with a microscope, fool?"

10   "Look at things."

"Like what, Ronald?" ask Miss Moore. And Big Butt ain't got the first notion. So here go Miss Moore gabbing about the thousands of bacteria in a drop of water and the somethinorother in a speck of blood and the million and one living things in the air around us is invisible to the naked eye. And what she say that for? Junebug go to town on that "naked" and we rolling. Then Miss Moore ask what it cost. So we all jam into the window smudgin it up and the price tag say $300. So then she ask how long'd take for Big Butt and Junebug to save up their allowances. "Too long," I say. "Yeh," adds Sugar, "outgrown it by that time." And Miss Moore say no, you never outgrow learning instruments. "Why, even medical students and interns and," blah, blah, blah. And we ready to choke Big Butt for bringing it up in the first damn place.

"This here costs four hundred eighty dollars," say Rosie Giraffe. So we pile up all over her to see what she pointin out. My eyes tell me it's a chunk of glass cracked with something heavy, and different-color inks dripped into the splits, then the whole thing put into a oven or something. But for $480 it don't make sense.

"That's a paperweight made of semi-precious stones fused together under tremendous pressure," she explains slowly, and her hands doing the mining and all the factory work.

"So what's a paperweight?" asks Rosie Giraffe.

15   "To weigh paper with, dumbbell," say Flyboy, the wise man from the East.

"Not exactly," say Miss Moore, which is what she say when you warm or way off too. "It's to weigh paper down so it won't scatter and make your desk untidy." So right away me and Sugar curtsy to each other and then to Mercedes who is more the tidy type.

"We don't keep paper on top of the desk in my class," say Junebug, figuring Miss Moore crazy or lyin one.

"At home, then," she say. "Don't you have a calendar and a pencil case and a blotter and a letter-opener on your desk at home where you do your homework?" And she know damn well what our homes look like cause she nosys around in them every chance she gets.

"I don't even have a desk," say Junebug. "Do we?"

20   "No. And I don't get no homework neither," says Big Butt.

"And I don't even have a home," say Flyboy like he do at school to keep the white folks off his back and sorry for him. Send this poor kid to camp posters, is his specialty.

"I do," says Mercedes. "I have a box of stationery on my desk and a picture of my cat. My godmother bought the stationery and the desk. There's a big rose on each sheet and the envelopes smell like roses."

"Who wants to know about your smelly-ass stationery," say Rosie Giraffe fore I can get my two cents in.

"It's important to have a work area all your own so that . . ."

25   "Will you look at this sailboat, please," say Flyboy, cuttin her off and pointin to the thing like it was his. So once again we tumble all over each other to gaze at this magnificent thing in the toy store which is just big enough to maybe sail two kittens across the pond if you strap them to the posts tight. We all start reciting the price tag like we in assembly. "Handcrafted sailboat of fiberglass at one thousand one hundred ninety-five dollars."

"Unbelievable," I hear myself say and am really stunned. I read it again for myself just in case the group recitation put me in a trance. Same thing. For some reason this pisses me off. We look at Miss Moore and she lookin at us, waiting for I dunno what.

"Who'd pay all that when you can buy a sailboat set for a quarter at Pop's, a tube of glue for a dime, and a ball of string for eight cents? It must have a motor and a whole lot else besides," I say. "My sailboat cost me about fifty cents."

"But will it take water?" say Mercedes with her smart ass.

"Took mine to Alley Pond Park once," say Flyboy. "String broke. Lost it. Pity."

30   "Sailed mine in Central Park and it keeled over and sank. Had to ask my father for another dollar."

"And you got the strap," laugh Big Butt. "The jerk didn't even have a string on it. My old man wailed on his behind."

Little Q.T. was staring hard at the sailboat and you could see he wanted it bad. But he too little and somebody'd just take it from him. So what the hell. "This boat for kids, Miss Moore?"

"Parents silly to buy something like that just to get all broke up," say Rosie Giraffe.

"That much money it should last forever," I figure.

35   "My father'd buy it for me if I wanted it."

"Your father, my ass," say Rosie Giraffe getting a chance to finally push Mercedes.

"Must be rich people shop here," say Q.T.

"You are a very bright boy," say Flyboy. "What was your first clue?" And he rap him on the head with the back of his knuckles, since Q.T. the only one he could get away with. Though Q.T. liable to come up behind you years later and get his licks in when you half expect it.

"What I want to know is," I says to Miss Moore though I never talk to her, I wouldn't give the bitch that satisfaction, "is how much a real boat costs? I figure a thousand'd get you a yacht any day."

40   "Why don't you check that out," she says, "and report back to the group?" Which really pains my ass. If you gonna mess up a perfectly good swim day least you could do is have some answers. "Let's go in," she say like she got something up her sleeve. Only she don't lead the way. So me and Sugar turn the corner to where the entrance is, but when we get there I kinda hang back. Not that I'm scared, what's there to be afraid of, just a toy store. But I feel funny, shame. But what I got to be shamed about? Got as much right to go in as anybody. But somehow I can't seem to get hold of the door, so I step away for Sugar to lead. But she hangs back too. And I look at her and she looks at me and this is ridiculous. I mean, damn, I have never ever been shy about doing nothing or going nowhere. But then Mercedes steps up and then Rosie Giraffe and Big Butt crowd in behind and shove, and next thing we all stuffed into the doorway with only Mercedes squeezing past us, smoothing out her jumper and walking right down the aisle. Then the rest of us tumble in like a glued-together jigsaw done all wrong. And people lookin at us. And it's like the time me and Sugar crashed into the Catholic church on a dare. But once we got in there and everything so hushed and holy and the candles and the bowin and the handkerchiefs on all the drooping heads, I just couldn't go through with the plan. Which was for me to run up to the altar and do a tap dance while Sugar played the nose flute and messed around in the holy water. And Sugar kept givin me the elbow. Then later teased me so bad I tied her up in the shower and turned it on and locked her in. And she'd be there till this day if Aunt Gretchen hadn't finally figured I was lyin about the boarder takin a shower.

Same thing in the store. We all walkin on tiptoe and hardly touchin the games and puzzles and things. And I watched Miss Moore who is steady watchin us like she waitin for a sign. Like Mama Drewery watches the sky and sniffs the air and takes note of just how much slant is in the bird formation. Then me and Sugar bump smack into each other, so busy gazing at the toys, 'specially the sailboat. But we don't laugh and go into our fat-lady bumpstomach routine. We just stare at that price tag. Then Sugar run a finger over the whole boat. And I'm jealous and want to hit her. Maybe not her, but I sure want to punch somebody in the mouth.

"Whatcha bring us here for, Miss Moore?"

"You sound angry, Sylvia. Are you mad about something?" Givin me one of them grins like she tellin a grown-up joke that never turns out to be funny. And she's lookin very closely at me like maybe she plannin to do my portrait from memory. I'm mad, but I won't give her that satisfaction. So I slouch around the store bein very bored and say, "Let's go."

Me and Sugar at the back of the train watchin the tracks whizzin by large then small then gettin gobbled up in the dark. I'm thinkin about this tricky toy I saw in the store. A clown that somersaults on a bar then does chin-ups just cause you yank lightly at his leg. Cost $35. I could see me askin my mother for a $35 birthday clown. "You wanna who that costs what?" she'd say, cocking her head to the side to get a better view of the hole in my head. Thirty-five dollars could buy new bunk beds for Junior and Gretchen's boy. Thirty-five dollars and the whole household could go visit Granddaddy Nelson in the country. Thirty-five dollars would pay for the rent and the piano bill too. Who are these people that spend that much for performing clowns and $1000 for toy sailboats? What kinda work they do and how they live and how come we ain't in on it? Where we are is who we are, Miss Moore always pointin out. But it don't necessarily have to be that way, she always adds then waits for somebody to say that poor people have to wake up and demand their share of the pie and don't none of us know what kind of pie she talkin about in the first damn place. But she ain't so smart cause I still got her four dollars from the taxi and she sure ain't gettin it. Messin up my day with this shit. Sugar nudges me in my pocket and winks.

45   Miss Moore lines us up in front of the mailbox where we started from, seem like years ago, and I got a headache for thinkin so hard. And we lean all over each other so we can hold up under the draggy-ass lecture she always finishes us off with at the end before we thank her for borin us to tears. But she just looks at us like she readin tea leaves. Finally she say, "Well, what do you think of F. A. O. Schwarz?"

Rosie Giraffe mumbles, "White folks crazy."

"I'd like to go there again when I get my birthday money," says Mercedes, and we shove her out the pack so she has to lean on the mailbox by herself.

"I'd like a shower. Tiring day," say Flyboy.

Then Sugar surprises me by sayin, "You know, Miss Moore, I don't think all of us here put together eat in a year what that sailboat costs." And Miss Moore lights up like somebody goosed her. "And?" she say, urging Sugar on. Only I'm standin on her foot so she don't continue.

50   "Imagine for a minute what kind of society it is in which some people can spend on a toy what would cost to feed a family of six or seven. What do you think?"

"I think," say Sugar pushing me off her feet like she never done before, cause I whip her ass in a minute, "that this is not much of a democracy if you ask me. Equal chance to pursue happiness means an equal crack at the dough, don't it?" Miss Moore is besides herself and I am disgusted with Sugar's treachery. So I stand on her foot one more time to see if she'll shove me. She shuts up, and Miss Moore looks at me, sorrowfully I'm thinkin. And somethin weird is goin on, I can feel it in my chest.

"Anybody else learn anything today?" lookin dead at me. I walk away and Sugar has to run to catch up and don't even seem to notice when I shrug her arm off my shoulder.

"Well, we got four dollars anyway," she says.

"Uh hunh."

55   "We could go to Hascombs and get half a chocolate layer and then go to the Sunset and still have plenty money for potato chips and ice cream sodas."

"Uh hunh."

"Race you to Hascombs," she say.

We start down the block and she gets ahead which is O.K. by me cause I'm going to the West End and then over to the Drive to think this day through. She can run if she want to and even run faster. But ain't nobody gonna beat me at nuthin.

[1972]

Joining the Conversation: Critical Thinking and Writing

1. What is the point of Miss Moore's lesson? Why does Sylvia resist it?
2. Describe the relationship between Sugar and Sylvia. What is Sugar's function in the story?

3. What does the last line of the story suggest?
4. In a paragraph or two, characterize the narrator. Do not summarize the story—
   assume that your reader is familiar with it—but support your characterization
   by references to episodes in the story and perhaps by a few brief quotations.

AMY TAN

Amy Tan was born in Oakland, California, in 1952, of Chinese immigrant parents. When she was eight years old, she won first prize among elementary students with an essay titled "What the Library Means to Me." She attended Linfield College in Oregon and then transferred to San Jose State University in California, where, while working two part-time jobs, she became an honors student and a President's Scholar. In 1973, she earned an MA in linguistics, also at San Jose, and she later enrolled as a doctoral student at the University of California, Berkeley, though she left this program after the murder of a close friend. For the next five years, she worked as a language development consultant and a project director, and then she became a freelance business writer. In 1986, she published her first short story; reprinted in Seventeen, *it was noticed by an agent who encouraged her to continue writing fiction. In 1989,* The Joy Luck Club *(a collection of linked short stories, including "Two Kinds") was published. Other books include* The Kitchen God's Wife *(1991),* The Hundred Secret Senses *(1995), and* The Bonesetter's Daughter *(2001). She has also written two books for children,* The Moon Lady *(1992) and* SAGWA The Chinese Siamese Cat *(1994).*

Two Kinds

My mother believed you could be anything you wanted to be in America. You could open a restaurant. You could work for the government and get good retirement. You could buy a house with almost no money down. You could become rich. You could become instantly famous.

"Of course, you can be prodigy, too," my mother told me when I was nine. "You can be best anything. What does Auntie Lindo know? Her daughter, she is only best tricky."

America was where all my mother's hopes lay. She had come here in 1949 after losing everything in China: her mother and father, her family home, her first husband, and two daughters, twin baby girls. But she never looked back with regret. There were so many ways for things to get better.

We didn't immediately pick the right kind of prodigy. At first my mother thought I could be a Chinese Shirley Temple.[1] We'd watch Shirley's old movies on TV as though they were training films. My mother would poke my arm and say, "*Ni kan.*"—You watch. And I would see Shirley tapping her feet, or singing a sailor song, or pursing her lips into a very round O while saying "Oh, my goodness."

---

[1]**Shirley Temple** (1928–), U.S. child movie star.

5   "*Ni kan,*" said my mother as Shirley's eyes flooded with tears. "You already know how. Don't need talent for crying!"

Soon after my mother got this idea about Shirley Temple, she took me to a beauty training school in the Mission district and put me in the hands of a student who could barely hold the scissors without shaking. Instead of getting big fat curls, I emerged with an uneven mass of crinkly black fuzz. My mother dragged me off to the bathroom and tried to wet down my hair.

"You look like Negro Chinese," she lamented, as if I had done this on purpose.

The instructor of the beauty training school had to lop off these soggy clumps to make my hair even again. "Peter Pan is very popular these days," the instructor assured my mother. I now had hair the length of a boy's, with straight-across bangs that hung at a slant two inches above my eyebrows. I liked the haircut and it made me actually look forward to my future fame.

In fact, in the beginning, I was just as excited as my mother, maybe even more so. I pictured this prodigy part of me as many different images, trying each one on for size. I was a dainty ballerina girl standing by the curtains, waiting to hear the music that would send me floating on my tiptoes. I was like the Christ child lifted out of the straw manger, crying with holy indignity. I was Cinderella stepping from her pumpkin carriage with sparkly cartoon music filling the air.

10   In all of my imaginings, I was filled with a sense that I would soon become *perfect*. My mother and father would adore me. I would be beyond reproach. I would never feel the need to sulk for anything.

But sometimes the prodigy in me became impatient. "If you don't hurry up and get me out of here, I'm disappearing for good," it warned. "And then you'll always be nothing."

Every night after dinner, my mother and I would sit at the Formica kitchen table. She would present new tests, taking her examples from stories of amazing children she had read in *Ripley's Believe It or Not,* or *Good Housekeeping, Reader's Digest,* and a dozen other magazines she kept in a pile in our bathroom. My mother got these magazines from people whose houses she cleaned. And since she cleaned many houses each week, we had a great assortment. She would look through them all, searching for stories about remarkable children.

The first night she brought out a story about a three-year-old boy who knew the capitals of all the states and even most of the European countries. A teacher was quoted as saying the little boy could also pronounce the names of the foreign cities correctly.

"What's the capital of Finland?" my mother asked me, looking at the magazine story.

15   All I knew was the capital of California, because Sacramento was the name of the street we lived on in Chinatown. "Nairobi!" I guessed, saying the most foreign word I could think of. She checked to see if that was possibly one way to pronounce "Helsinki" before showing me the answer.

The tests got harder—multiplying numbers in my head, finding the queen of hearts in a deck of cards, trying to stand on my head without using my hands, predicting the daily temperatures in Los Angeles, New York, and London.

One night I had to look at a page from the Bible for three minutes and then report everything I could remember. "Now Jehoshaphat had riches and honor in abundance and . . . . that's all I remember, Ma," I said.

And after seeing my mother's disappointed face once again, something inside of me began to die. I hated the tests, the raised hopes and failed expectations.

Before going to bed that night, I looked in the mirror above the bathroom sink and when I saw only my face staring back—and that it would always be this ordinary face—I began to cry. Such a sad, ugly girl! I made high-pitched noises like a crazed animal, trying to scratch out the face in the mirror.

And then I saw what seemed to be the prodigy side of me—because I had never seen that face before. I looked at my reflection, blinking so I could see more clearly. The girl staring back at me was angry, powerful. This girl and I were the same. I had new thoughts, willful thoughts, or rather thoughts filled with lots of won'ts. I won't let her change me, I promised myself. I won't be what I'm not.

20   So now on nights when my mother presented her tests, I performed listlessly, my head propped on one arm. I pretended to be bored. And I was. I got so bored I started counting the bellows of the foghorns out on the bay while my mother drilled me in other areas. The sound was comforting and reminded me of the cow jumping over the moon. And the next day, I played a game with myself, seeing if my mother would give up on me before eight bellows. After a while I usually counted only one, maybe two bellows at most. At last she was beginning to give up hope.

Two or three months had gone by without any mention of my being a prodigy again. And then one day my mother was watching *The Ed Sullivan Show*[2] on TV. The TV was old and the sound kept shorting out. Every time my mother got half-way up from the sofa to adjust the set, the sound would go back on and Ed would be talking. As soon as she sat down, Ed would go silent again. She got up, the TV broke into loud piano music. She sat down. Silence. Up and down, back and forth, quiet and loud. It was like a stiff embraceless dance between her and the TV set. Finally she stood by the set with her hand on the sound dial.

She seemed entranced by the music, a little frenzied piano piece with this mesmerizing quality, sort of quick passages and then teasing lilting ones before it returned to the quick playful parts.

"*Ni kan*," my mother said, calling me over with hurried hand gestures, "Look here."

I could see why my mother was fascinated by the music. It was being pounded out by a little Chinese girl, about nine years old, with a Peter Pan haircut. The girl had the sauciness of a Shirley Temple. She was proudly modest like a proper Chinese child. And she also did this fancy sweep of a curtsy, so that the fluffy skirt of her white dress cascaded slowly to the floor like the petals of a large carnation.

25   In spite of these warning signs, I wasn't worried. Our family had no piano and we couldn't afford to buy one, let alone reams of sheet music and piano lessons. So I could be generous in my comments when my mother bad-mouthed the little girl on TV.

"Play note right, but doesn't sound good! No singing sound," my mother complained.

"What are you picking on her for?" I said carelessly. "She's pretty good. Maybe she's not the best, but she's trying hard." I knew almost immediately I would be sorry I said that.

"Just like you," she said. "Not the best. Because you not trying." She gave a little huff as she let go of the sound dial and sat down on the sofa.

The little Chinese girl sat down also to play an encore of "Anitra's Dance,"[3] by Grieg. I remember the song, because later on I had to learn how to play it.

---

[2]*The Ed Sullivan Show* popular television variety show (1948–71).   [3]**Anitra's Dance** a section from the incidental music that Edvard Grieg (1843–1907) wrote for *Peer Gynt*, a play by Henrik Ibsen.

30   Three days after watching *The Ed Sullivan Show*, my mother told me what my schedule would be for piano lessons and piano practice. She had talked to Mr. Chong, who lived on the first floor of our apartment building. Mr. Chong was a retired piano teacher and my mother had traded housecleaning services for weekly lessons and a piano for me to practice on every day, two hours a day, from four until six.

When my mother told me this, I felt as though I had been sent to hell. I whined and then kicked my foot a little when I couldn't stand it anymore.

"Why don't you like me the way I am? I'm not a genius! I can't play the piano. And even if I could, I wouldn't go on TV if you paid me a million dollars!" I cried.

My mother slapped me. "Who ask you be genius?" she shouted. "Only ask you be your best. For you sake. You think I want you be genius? Hnnh! What for! Who ask you!"

"So ungrateful," I heard her mutter in Chinese. "If she had as much talent as she has temper, she would be famous now."

35   Mr. Chong, whom I secretly nicknamed Old Chong, was very strange, always tapping his fingers to the silent music of an invisible orchestra. He looked ancient in my eyes. He had lost most of the hair on top of his head and he wore thick glasses and had eyes that always looked tired and sleepy. But he must have been younger than I thought, since he lived with his mother and was not yet married.

I met Old Lady Chong once and that was enough. She had this peculiar smell like a baby that had done something in its pants. And her fingers felt like a dead person's, like an old peach I once found in the back of the refrigerator; the skin just slid off the meat when I picked it up.

I soon found out why Old Chong had retired from teaching piano. He was deaf. "Like Beethoven!" he shouted to me. "We're both listening only in our head!" And he would start to conduct his frantic silent sonatas.

Our lessons went like this. He would open the book and point to different things, explaining their purpose: "Key! Treble! Bass! No sharps or flats! So this is C major! Listen now and play after me!"

And then he would play the C scale a few times, a simple chord, and then, as if inspired by an old, unreachable itch, he gradually added more notes and running trills and a pounding bass until the music was really something quite grand.

40   I would play after him, the simple scale, the simple chord, and then I just played some nonsense that sounded like a cat running up and down on top of garbage cans. Old Chong smiled and applauded and then said, "Very good! But now you must learn to keep time!"

So that's how I discovered that Old Chong's eyes were too slow to keep up with the wrong notes I was playing. He went through the motions in half-time. To help me keep rhythm, he stood behind me, pushing down on my right shoulder for every beat. He balanced pennies on top of my wrists so I would keep them still as I slowly played scales and arpeggios. He had me curve my hand around an apple and keep that shape when playing chords. He marched stiffly to show me how to make each finger dance up and down, staccato like an obedient little soldier.

He taught me all these things, and that was how I also learned I could be lazy and get away with mistakes, lots of mistakes. If I hit the wrong notes because I hadn't practiced enough, I never corrected myself. I just kept playing in rhythm. And Old Chong kept conducting his own private reverie.

So maybe I never really gave myself a fair chance. I did pick up the basics pretty quickly, and I might have become a good pianist at that young age. But I was so determined not to try, not to be anybody different that I learned to play only the most ear-splitting preludes, the most discordant hymns.

Over the next year I practiced like this, dutifully in my own way. And then one day I heard my mother and her friend Lindo Jong both talking in a loud bragging tone of voice so others could hear. It was after church, and I was leaning against the brick wall wearing a dress with stiff white petticoats. Auntie Lindo's daughter, Waverly, who was about my age, was standing farther down the wall about five feet away. We had grown up together and shared all the closeness of two sisters squabbling over crayons and dolls. In other words, for the most part, we hated each other. I thought she was snotty. Waverly Jong had gained a certain amount of fame as "Chinatown's Littlest Chinese Chess Champion."

45   "She bring home too many trophy," lamented Auntie Lindo that Sunday. "All day she play chess. All day I have no time do nothing but dust off her winnings." She threw a scolding look at Waverly, who pretended not to see her.

"You lucky you don't have this problem," said Auntie Lindo with a sigh to my mother.

And my mother squared her shoulders and bragged: "Our problem worser than yours. If we ask Jing-mei wash dish, she hear nothing but music. It's like you can't stop this natural talent."

And right then, I was determined to put a stop to her foolish pride.

A few weeks later, Old Chong and my mother conspired to have me play in a talent show which would be held in the church hall. By then, my parents had saved up enough to buy me a secondhand piano, a black Wurlitzer spinet with a scarred bench. It was the showpiece of our living room.

50   For the talent show, I was to play a piece called "Pleading Child" from Schumann's *Scenes from Childhood*.[4] It was a simple, moody piece that sounded more difficult than it was. I was supposed to memorize the whole thing, playing the repeat parts twice to make the piece sound longer. But I dawdled over it, playing a few bars and then cheating, looking up to see what notes followed. I never really listened to what I was playing. I daydreamed about being somewhere else, about being someone else.

The part I liked to practice best was the fancy curtsy: right foot out, touch the rose on the carpet with a pointed foot, sweep to the side, left leg bends, look up and smile.

My parents invited all the couples from the Joy Luck Club to witness my debut. Auntie Lindo and Uncle Tin were there. Waverly and her two older brothers had also come. The first two rows were filled with children both younger and older than I was. The littlest ones got to go first. They recited simple nursery rhymes, squawked out tunes on miniature violins, twirled Hula Hoops, pranced in pink ballet tutus, and when they bowed or curtsied, the audience would sigh in unison, "Awww," and then clap enthusiastically.

When my turn came, I was very confident. I remember my childish excitement. It was as if I knew, without a doubt, that the prodigy side of me really did exist. I had no fear whatsoever, no nervousness. I remember thinking to myself, This is it! This is it! I looked out over the audience, at my mother's blank face, my father's yawn, Auntie Lindo's stiff-lipped smile, Waverly's sulky expression. I had on a white dress layered with sheets of lace, and a pink bow in my Peter Pan haircut. As I sat down I envisioned people jumping to their feet and Ed Sullivan rushing up to introduce me to everyone on TV.

[4]***Scenes from Childhood*** a piano work by Robert Schumann (1810–56) with twelve titled sections and an epilogue.

And I started to play. It was so beautiful. I was so caught up in how lovely I looked that at first I didn't worry how I would sound. So it was a surprise to me when I hit the first wrong note and I realized something didn't sound quite right. And then I hit another and another followed that. A chill started at the top of my head and began to trickle down. Yet I couldn't stop playing, as though my hands were bewitched. I kept thinking my fingers would adjust themselves back, like a train switching to the right track. I played this strange jumble through two repeats, the sour notes staying with me all the way to the end.

55   When I stood up, I discovered my legs were shaking. Maybe I had just been nervous and the audience, like Old Chong, had seen me go through the right motions and had not heard anything wrong at all. I swept my right foot out, went down on my knee, looked up and smiled. The room was quiet, except for Old Chong, who was beaming and shouting, "Bravo! Bravo! Well done!" But then I saw my mother's face, her stricken face. The audience clapped weakly, and as I walked back to my chair, with my whole face quivering as I tried not to cry, I heard a little boy whisper loudly to his mother, "That was awful," and the mother whispered back, "Well, she certainly tried."

And now I realized how many people were in the audience, the whole world it seemed. I was aware of eyes burning into my back. I felt the shame of my mother and father as they sat stiffly throughout the rest of the show.

We could have escaped during intermission. Pride and some strange sense of honor must have anchored my parents to their chairs. And so we watched it all: the eighteen-year-old boy with a fake moustache who did a magic show and juggled flaming hoops while riding a unicycle. The breasted girl with white make-up who sang from *Madame Butterfly* and got honorable mention. And the eleven-year-old boy who won first prize playing a tricky violin song that sounded like a busy bee.

After the show, the Hsus, the Jongs, and the St. Clairs from the Joy Luck Club, came up to my mother and father.

"Lots of talented kids," Auntie Lindo said vaguely, smiling broadly.

60   "That was somethin' else," said my father, and I wondered if he was referring to me in a humorous way, or whether he even remembered what I had done.

Waverly looked at me and shrugged her shoulders. "You aren't a genius like me," she said matter-of-factly. And if I hadn't felt so bad, I would have pulled her braids and punched her stomach.

But my mother's expression was what devastated me: a quiet, blank look that said she had lost everything. I felt the same way, and it seemed as if everybody were now coming up, like gawkers at the scene of an accident, to see what parts were actually missing. When we got on the bus to go home, my father was humming the busy-bee tune and my mother was silent. I kept thinking she wanted to wait until we got home before shouting at me. But when my father unlocked the door to our apartment, my mother walked in and then went to the back, into the bedroom. No accusations. No blame. And in a way, I felt disappointed. I had been waiting for her to start shouting, so I could shout back and cry and blame her for all my misery.

I assumed my talent-show fiasco meant I never had to play the piano again. But two days later, after school, my mother came out of the kitchen and saw me watching TV.

"Four clock," she reminded me as if it were any other day. I was stunned, as though she were asking me to go through the talent-show torture again. I wedged myself more tightly in front of the TV.

65   "Turn off TV," she called from the kitchen five minutes later.

I didn't budge. And then I decided. I didn't have to do what my mother said anymore. I wasn't her slave. This wasn't China. I had listened to her before and look what happened. She was the stupid one.

She came out from the kitchen and stood in the arched entryway of the living room. "Four clock," she said once again, louder.

"I'm not going to play anymore," I said nonchalantly. "Why should I? I'm not a genius."

She walked over and stood in front of the TV. I saw her chest was heaving up and down in an angry way.

70   "No!" I said, and I now felt stronger, as if my true self had finally emerged. So this was what had been inside me all along.

"No! I won't!" I screamed.

She yanked me by the arm, pulled me off the floor, snapped off the TV. She was frighteningly strong, half pulling, half carrying me toward the piano as I kicked the throw rugs under my feet. She lifted me up and onto the hard bench. I was sobbing by now, looking at her bitterly. Her chest was heaving even more and her mouth was open, smiling crazily as if she were pleased I was crying.

"You want me to be someone that I'm not!" I sobbed. "I'll never be the kind of daughter you want me to be!"

"Only two kinds of daughters," she shouted in Chinese. "Those who are obedient and those who follow their own mind! Only one kind of daughter can live in this house. Obedient daughter!"

75   "Then I wish I wasn't your daughter. I wish you weren't my mother," I shouted. As I said these things I got scared. It felt like worms and toads and slimy things crawling out of my chest, but it also felt good, as if this awful side of me had surfaced, at last.

"Too late change this," said my mother shrilly.

And I could sense her anger rising to its breaking point. I wanted to see it spill over. And that's when I remembered the babies she had lost in China, the ones we never talked about. "Then I wish I'd never been born!" I shouted. "I wish I were dead! Like them."

It was as if I had said the magic words. Alakazam!—and her face went blank, her mouth closed, her arms went slack, and she backed out of the room, stunned, as if she were blowing away like a small brown leaf, thin, brittle, lifeless.

It was not the only disappointment my mother felt in me. In the years that followed, I failed her so many times, each time asserting my own will, my right to fall short of expectations. I didn't get straight As. I didn't become class president. I didn't get into Stanford. I dropped out of college.

80   For unlike my mother, I did not believe I could be anything I wanted to be. I could only be me.

And for all those years, we never talked about the disaster at the recital or my terrible accusations afterward at the piano bench. All of that remained unchecked, like a betrayal that was now unspeakable. So I never found a way to ask her why she had hoped for something so large that failure was inevitable.

And even worse, I never asked her what frightened me the most: Why had she given up hope?

For after our struggle at the piano, she never mentioned my playing again. The lessons stopped. The lid to the piano was closed, shutting out the dust, my misery, and her dreams.

So she surprised me. A few years ago, she offered to give me the piano, for my thirtieth birthday. I had not played in all those years. I saw the offer as a sign of forgiveness, a tremendous burden removed.

85   "Are you sure?" I asked shyly. "I mean, won't you and Dad miss it?"

"No, this your piano," she said firmly. "Always your piano. You only one can play."

"Well, I probably can't play anymore," I said. "It's been years."

"You pick up fast," said my mother, as if she knew this was certain. "You have natural talent. You could been genius if you want to."

"No I couldn't."

90   "You just not trying," said my mother. And she was neither angry nor sad. She said it as if to announce a fact that could never be disproved. "Take it," she said.

But I didn't at first. It was enough that she had offered it to me. And after that, every time I saw it in my parents' living room, standing in front of the bay windows, it made me feel proud, as if it were a shiny trophy I had won back.

Last week I sent a tuner over to my parents' apartment and had the piano reconditioned, for purely sentimental reasons. My mother had died a few months before and I had been getting things in order for my father, a little bit at a time. I put the jewelry in special silk pouches. The sweaters she had knitted in yellow, pink, bright orange—all the colors I hated—I put those in moth-proof boxes. I found some old Chinese silk dresses, the kind with little slits up the sides. I rubbed the old silk against my skin, then wrapped them in tissue and decided to take them home with me.

After I had the piano tuned, I opened the lid and touched the keys. It sounded even richer than I remembered. Really, it was a very good piano. Inside the bench were the same exercise notes with handwritten scales, the same secondhand music books with their covers held together with yellow tape.

I opened up the Schumann book to the dark little piece I had played at the recital. It was on the left-hand side of the page, "Pleading Child." It looked more difficult than I remembered. I played a few bars, surprised at how easily the notes came back to me.

95   And for the first time, or so it seemed, I noticed the piece on the right-hand side. It was called "Perfectly Contented." I tried to play this one as well. It had a lighter melody but the same flowing rhythm and turned out to be quite easy. "Pleading Child" was shorter but slower; "Perfectly Contented" was longer, but faster. And after I played them both a few times, I realized they were two halves of the same song.

[1989]

Joining the Conversation: Critical Thinking and Writing

1. Try to recall your responses when you had read just the first three paragraphs. At that point, how did the mother strike you? Now that you have read the entire story, is your view of her different? If so, in what way(s)?

2. When the narrator looks in the mirror, she discovers "the prodigy side," a face she had never seen before. What do you think she is discovering?

3. If you enjoyed "Two Kinds," point out two or three passages that you found particularly engaging, and briefly explain why they appeal to you. Create an argument that would convince someone to share your view.

4. Do you think this story is interesting only because it may give a glimpse of life in a Chinese American family? Or do you find it interesting for additional reasons? Explain your answer.

5. Conceivably, the story could have ended with paragraph 91. What do the last four paragraphs contribute? Argue your case.

POEMS

ROBERT HAYDEN

Robert Hayden (1913–80) was born in Detroit, Michigan. His parents divorced when he was a child, and he was brought up by a neighboring family, whose name he adopted. In 1942, at the age of twenty-nine, he graduated from Detroit City College (now Wayne State University), and he received an MA from the University of Michigan. He taught at Fisk University from 1946 to 1969 and after that, for the remainder of his life, at the University of Michigan. In 1979, he was appointed Consultant in Poetry to the Library of Congress, the first African American to hold the post.

Frederick Douglass*

When it is finally ours, this freedom, this liberty, this beautiful
and terrible thing, needful to man as air,
usable as earth; when it belongs at last to all,
when it is truly instinct, brain matter, diastole, systole,
reflex action; when it is finally won; when it is more   5
than the gaudy mumbo jumbo of politicians:
this man, this Douglass, this former slave, this Negro
beaten to his knees, exiled, visioning a world
where none is lonely, none hunted, alien,
this man, superb in love and logic, this man   10
shall be remembered. Oh, not with statues' rhetoric,
not with legends and poems and wreaths of bronze alone,
but with the lives grown out of his life, the lives
fleshing his dream of the beautiful, needful thing.

[1947]

*Frederick Douglass (1818–95) Born a slave, Douglass escaped and became an important spokesman for the abolitionist movement and later for civil rights for African Americans.

Joining the Conversation: Critical Thinking and Writing

1. When, according to Hayden, will Douglass "be remembered"? And *how* will he be remembered?

2. "Frederick Douglass" consists of two sentences (or one sentence and a fragment). In what line do you find the subject of the first sentence? What is the main verb (the predicate), and where do you find it? How would you describe the effect of the long delaying of the subject? And of the predicate?

3. Does Hayden assume or seem to predict that there *will* come a time when freedom "is finally ours" (line 1) and "belongs at last to all" (line 3)?
4. Hayden wrote "Frederick Douglass" in 1947. In your opinion, are we closer now to Hayden's vision, or are we farther away? (You may find that we are closer in some ways and farther in others.) In your answer—perhaps an essay of five hundred words—try to be as specific as possible.
5. "Frederick Douglass" consists of fourteen lines. Is it a sonnet?

LORNA DEE CERVANTES

Lorna Dee Cervantes, born in San Francisco, California, in 1954, founded a press and a poetry magazine, Mango, *which was chiefly devoted to Chicano literature. In 1978, she received a fellowship from the National Endowment for the Arts, and in 1981, she published her first book of poems. She lives in Boulder, Colorado. "Refugee Ship," originally written in 1974, was revised for the book,* Emplumada *(1981). We print the revised version.*

Refugee Ship

Like wet cornstarch, I slide
past my grandmother's eyes. Bible
at her side, she removes her glasses.
The pudding thickens.

Mama raised me without language.   5
I'm orphaned from my Spanish name.
The words are foreign, stumbling
on my tongue. I see in the mirror
my reflection: bronzed skin, black hair.

I feel I am a captive   10
aboard the refugee ship.
The ship that will never dock.
El barco que nunca atraca.°

[1981]

13 *El barco que nunca atraca* The ship that never docks.

Joining the Conversation: Critical Thinking and Writing

1. What do you think the speaker in "Refugee Ship" means by the comparison with "wet cornstarch" in line 1? What do you take her to mean in line 7 when she says, "I'm orphaned from my Spanish name"?
2. Judging from the poem as a whole, why does the speaker feel she is "a captive / aboard the refugee ship"? How would you characterize such feelings?
3. In an earlier version of the poem, instead of "my grandmother's eyes" Cervantes wrote "*mi abuelita's* eyes"; that is, she used the Spanish words for "my grandmother." In line 5, instead of "Mama," she wrote "*mamá*" (again, the Spanish equivalent), and in line 9, she wrote "brown skin" instead of "bronzed skin." The final line of the original version was not in Spanish but in English, a repetition

of the preceding line, which ran thus: "A ship that will never dock." How does each of these changes strike you?

EDWIN ARLINGTON ROBINSON

Edwin Arlington Robinson (1869–1935) grew up in Gardiner, Maine, spent two years at Harvard, and then returned to Maine, where he published his first book of poetry, The Torrent and The Night Before, *in 1896. Though he received encouragement from neighbors, his finances were precarious, even after President Theodore Roosevelt, having been made aware of the book, secured for him an appointment as customs inspector in New York from 1905 to 1909. Additional books won fame for Robinson, and in 1922, he was awarded the first of three Pulitzer Prizes for poetry.*

Richard Cory

Whenever Richard Cory went down town,
We people on the pavement looked at him:
He was a gentleman from sole to crown,
Clean favored, and imperially slim.

And he was always quietly arrayed,   5
And he was always human when he talked;
But still he fluttered pulses when he said,
"Good-morning," and he glittered when he walked.

And he was rich—yes, richer than a king—
And admirably schooled in every grace: 10
In fine,° we thought that he was everything
To make us wish that we were in his place.

So on we worked, and waited for the light,
And went without the meat, and cursed the bread;
And Richard Cory, one calm summer night,   15
Went home and put a bullet through his head.

[1896]

11 **In fine** in short.

Joining the Conversation: Critical Thinking and Writing

1. What do you think were Richard Cory's thoughts shortly before he "put a bullet through his head"? In five hundred words, set forth his thoughts and actions (what he sees and does). If you wish, you can write in the first person, from Cory's point of view. Further, if you wish, your essay can be in the form of a suicide note.
2. Write a sketch (250–350 words) setting forth your early impression or understanding of someone whose later actions revealed that you had not understood that person.

W. H. AUDEN

Wystan Hugh Auden (1907–73) was born in York, England, and was educated at Oxford. In the 1930s, his left-wing poetry earned him wide acclaim as the leading poet of his generation. He went to Spain during the Spanish Civil War, intending to serve as an ambulance driver for the Republicans in their struggle against fascism, but he was so distressed by the violence of the Republicans that he almost immediately returned to England. In 1939, he came to America, and in 1946, he became a citizen of the United States, though he returned to England for his last years. Much of his poetry is characterized by a combination of colloquial diction and technical dexterity.

The Unknown Citizen

(To JS/07/M/378
This Marble Monument
Is Erected by the State)

He was found by the Bureau of Statistics to be
One against whom there was no official complaint,
And all the reports on his conduct agree
That, in the modern sense of an old-fashioned word, he was a saint,
For in everything he did he served the Greater Community.   5
Except for the War till the day he retired
He worked in a factory and never got fired,
But satisfied his employers, Fudge Motors Inc.
Yet he wasn't a scab or odd in his views,
For his Union reports that he paid his dues,   10
(Our report on his Union shows it was sound)
And our Social Psychology workers found
That he was popular with his mates and liked a drink.
The Press are convinced that he bought a paper every day
And that his reactions to advertisements were normal in every way. 15
Policies taken out in His name prove that he was fully insured,
And his Health-card shows he was once in hospital but left it
     cured.
Both Producers Research and High-Grade Living declare
He was fully sensible to the advantages of the Installment Plan
And had everything necessary to the Modern Man,   20
A phonograph, radio, a car and a frigidaire.
Our researchers into Public Opinion are content
That he held the proper opinions for the time of year;
When there was peace, he was for peace; when there was war,
     he went.
He was married and added five children to the population,   25
Which our Eugenist says was the right number for a parent of
     his generation,
And our teachers report that he never interfered with their
     education.
Was he free? Was he happy? The question is absurd:
Had anything been wrong, we should certainly have heard.

[1940]

Joining the Conversation: Critical Thinking and Writing

1. What is Auden satirizing in "The Unknown Citizen"? You will want to spend some time thinking about whether Auden is satirizing the speaker, the citizen, conformism, totalitarianism, technology, or something else.
2. Write a prose eulogy of 250 words satirizing contemporary conformity or, if you prefer, contemporary individualism.
3. Was the citizen free? Was he happy? Explain your answer.
4. In a paragraph or two, sketch the values of the speaker of the poem and then sum them up in a sentence or two. Finally, in as much space as you feel you need, judge these values.

EMMA LAZARUS

Emma Lazarus (1849–87) was of German Jewish descent on her mother's side and of Sephardic descent on her father's side. (Sephardic Jews trace their ancestry back to Spain under Moslem rule, before the Jews were expelled by the Christians in 1492.)

In 1883, a committee was formed to raise funds for a pedestal for the largest statue in the world, Liberty Enlightening the People, to be installed on a small island in New York Harbor. Authors were asked to donate manuscripts that were then auctioned to raise money. Emma Lazarus, keenly aware of ancient persecutions and of contemporary Jewish refugees fleeing Russian persecutions, contributed the following poem. It was read when the statue was unveiled in 1886, and the words of Liberty, spoken in the last five lines, were embossed on a plaque inside the pedestal.

For the ancients, a colossus was a statue that was larger than life. The "brazen giant of Greek fame," mentioned in Lazarus's first line, was a statue of the sun god, erected in the harbor of the Greek island of Rhodes, celebrating the island's success in resisting the Macedonians in 305–304 BCE. More than one hundred feet tall, it stood in the harbor until it toppled during an earthquake in 225 BCE. In later years, its size became mythical; it was said to have straddled the harbor (Lazarus speaks of "limbs astride from land to land") so that ships supposedly entered the harbor by sailing between its legs.

In Lazarus's poem, the "imprisoned lightning" (line 5) in the torch is electricity. The harbor is said to be "air-bridged" because in 1883, the year of the poem, the Brooklyn Bridge was completed, connecting Brooklyn with New York. (These are the "twin cities" of the poem.)

The New Colossus

Not like the brazen giant of Greek fame,
With conquering limbs astride from land to land;
Here at our sea-washed, sunset gates shall stand
A mighty woman with a torch, whose flame
Is the imprisoned lightning, and her name   5
Mother of Exiles. From her beacon-hand
Glows world-wide welcome; her mild eyes command
The air-bridged harbor that twin cities frame.

"Keep, ancient lands, your storied pomp!" cries she
With silent lips. "Give me your tired, your poor,   10
Your huddled masses yearning to breathe free,
The wretched refuse of your teeming shore.
Send these, the homeless, tempest-tost to me,
I lift my lamp beside the golden door!"

[1883]

Joining the Conversation: Critical Thinking and Writing

1. Does this poem have a message? In a paragraph, please state what this message is.
2. Do you find this poem to be clear, confusing, or both? Please point to details that are either clear in their meaning or confusing to you.
3. Emma Lazarus uses the word *new* in her title. What is the relationship between the old Colossus and this new one?
4. Have you ever visited the Statue of Liberty? If you have, describe this experience. If you have not, please explain why you have not, and explain, too, why you do or do not intend to visit this site sometime soon.
5. A prominent historian has said that the Statue of Liberty is the nation's "greatest monument to the true meaning of America." Do you agree with this statement? Please argue for or against it.

THOMAS BAILEY ALDRICH

Thomas Bailey Aldrich (1836–1907) was born in Portsmouth, New Hampshire. He wrote poetry from his youth to his old age, and he also wrote short stories and essays, but his literary career was chiefly that of a journalist and an editor. (One magazine that he edited from 1881 to 1890, Atlantic Monthly, *continues to be important.) As the following poem indicates, Aldrich was deeply conservative. The view that he here expresses is known as Nativism, or the Nativist view, favoring the interests of established inhabitants rather than those of immigrants and newcomers.*

The Unguarded Gates

Wide open and unguarded stand our gates,
And through them press a wild, a motley throng—
Men from the Volga and the Tartar steppes,
Featureless figures of the Hoang-Ho,
Malayan, Scythian, Teuton, Kelt, and Slav,   5
Flying the Old World's poverty and scorn;
These bringing with them unknown gods and rites,
Those tiger passions, here to stretch their claws.
In street and alley what strange tongues are these,
Accents of menace alien to our air,   10
Voices that once the tower of Babel knew!

O, Liberty, white goddess, is it well
To leave the gate unguarded? On thy breast

Fold sorrow's children, soothe the hurts of fate,
Lift the downtrodden, but with the hand of steel   15
Stay those who to thy sacred portals come
To waste the fight of freedom. Have a care
Lest from thy brow the clustered stars be torn
And trampled in the dust. For so of old
The thronging Goth and Vandal trampled Rome,   20
And where the temples of the Caesars stood
The lean wolf unmolested made her lair.

[1885]

Joining the Conversation: Critical Thinking and Writing

1. Using a good dictionary and other reference books or Internet resources, identify the terms in lines 3, 4, 5, 11, 20, and 21.
2. Do you think that this poet is a racist? Explain your answer.
3. Could someone say, "Aldrich is a racist, but he is making a defensible point"? What is Aldrich's point? In the poem, does he argue effectively for it?
4. How would Aldrich respond to Lazarus's poem? How would she respond to his poem?

JOSEPH BRUCHAC III

Joseph Bruchac III (the name is pronounced "Brewshack") was born in Saratoga Springs, New York, in 1942, and was educated at Cornell University, Syracuse University, and Union Graduate School. Like many other Americans, he has a multicultural ethnic heritage, and he includes Native Americans as well as Slovaks among his ancestors. Bruchac, who has taught in Ghana and also in the United States, has chiefly worked as an editor and educator. He lives in Saratoga County, New York.

"Much of my writing and my life," Bruchac says, "relates to the problem of being an American. . . . While in college I was active in Civil Rights work and in the antiwar movement. . . . I went to Africa to teach—but more than that to be taught. It showed me many things. How much we have as Americans and take for granted. How much our eyes refuse to see because they are blinded to everything in a man's face except his color."

Ellis Island

Beyond the red brick of Ellis Island
where the two Slovak children
who became my grandparents
waited the long days of quarantine,
after leaving the sickness,   5
the old Empires of Europe,
a Circle Line ship slips easily
on its way to the island
of the tall woman, green

Slavic women arrive at Ellis Island in the winter of 1910.

as dreams of forests and meadows   10
waiting for those who'd worked
a thousand years
yet never owned their own.
Like millions of others,
I too come to this island,   15
nine decades the answerer
of dreams.
Yet only one part of my blood loves that memory.
Another voice speaks
of native lands   20
within this nation.
Lands invaded
when the earth became owned.
Lands of those who followed
the changing Moon,   25
knowledge of the seasons
in their veins.

[1978]

Joining the Conversation: Critical Thinking and Writing

1. The poet tells of a visit he made to Ellis Island. What did he learn there?
2. Do you think that the poem would be effective if it ended at line 17? If so, in what way would it be effective?
3. How is the effect of the poem changed by lines 18–27?
4. Should every American be required to visit Ellis Island? What would be the benefit of such a requirement?
5. Consider this question in relation to the poem: Should America be celebrated or criticized? Is Bruchac doing one or the other, or both?

AURORA LEVINS MORALES

Aurora Levins Morales, born in Puerto Rico in 1954, moved to the mainland United States with her family in 1967. She has lived in Chicago and New Hampshire, and she now lives in the San Francisco Bay Area. A member of the Latina Feminist Group, Levins Morales has published stories, essays, prose poems, and poems.

Child of the Americas

I am a child of the Americas,
a light-skinned mestiza of the Caribbean,
a child of many diaspora,° born into this continent at a crossroads.
I am a U.S. Puerto Rican Jew,
a product of the ghettos of New York I have never known.   5
An immigrant and the daughter and granddaughter of
    immigrants.
I speak English with passion: it's the tongue of my
    consciousness,
a flashing knife blade of crystal, my tool, my craft.

I am Caribeña,° island grown. Spanish is in my flesh,
ripples from my tongue, lodges in my hips: 10
the language of garlic and mangoes,
the singing in my poetry, the flying gestures of my hands.

I am of Latinoamerica, rooted in the history of my continent:
I speak from that body.

I am not african. African is in me, but I cannot return.   15
I am not taína.° Taíno is in me, but there is no way back.
I am not european. Europe lives in me, but I have no home
    there.

---

3 diaspora literally, "scattering"; the term is used especially to refer to the dispersion of the Jews outside Israel from the sixth century BCE, when they were exiled to Babylonia, to the present time.   **9 Caribeña** Caribbean woman.   **16 taína** The Taínos were the Indian tribe native to Puerto Rico.

I am new. History made me. My first language was spanglish.°
I was born at the crossroads
and I am whole.   20

                                                              [1986]

18 spanglish a mixture of Spanish and English.

Joining the Conversation: Critical Thinking and Writing

1. In the first stanza, Levins Morales speaks of herself as "a child of many diaspora." *Diaspora* often means "a scattering" or "a dispersion of a homogeneous people." What does it refer to here?
2. In the second stanza, Levins Morales says that she is "a product of the ghettos of New York I have never known." What does she apparently refer to?
3. What attitude does "Child of the Americas" have toward the writer's ethnicity? What words or lines particularly communicate it?

GLORIA ANZALDÚA

Gloria Anzaldúa, a seventh-generation American, was born in 1942 on a ranch settlement in Texas. When she was eleven years old her family moved to Hargill, Texas, and in the next few years, the family traveled as migrant workers between Texas and Arkansas. In 1969, she earned a BA from Pan American University, and later she earned an MA from the University of Texas at Austin and did further graduate work at the University of California, Santa Cruz. Anzaldúa taught at the University of Texas at Austin; San Francisco State University; Oakes College at the University of California, Santa Cruz; and Vermont College. She died in 2004.

   We provide a poem from Anzaldúa's Borderlands: La Frontera—The New Mestiza *(1987), a work that combines seven prose essays with poems. For Anzaldúa— a woman, a Latina, and a lesbian—the "borderlands" are spiritual as well as geographic.*

To Live in the Borderlands Means You

To live in the Borderlands means you
    are neither *hispana india negra española*
    ni gabacha,° eres mestiza, mulata,° half-breed
    caught in the crossfire between camps
    while carrying all five races on your back
    not knowing which side to turn to, run from;   5

2–3 neither . . . *mulata* neither Hispanic Indian black Spanish woman nor white you are mixed, a mixed breed. **3 *gabacha*** a Chicano term for a white woman.

To live in the Borderlands means knowing
    that the *india* in you, betrayed for 500 years,
    is no longer speaking to you,
    that *mexicanas* call you *rajetas*,°   10
    that denying the Anglo inside you
    is as bad as having denied the Indian or Black;

Cuando vives en la frontera°
    people walk through you, the wind steals your voice,
    you're a *burra, buey,*° scapegoat,   15
    forerunner of a new race,
    half and half—both woman and man, neither—
    a new gender;

To live in the Borderlands means to
    put *chile* in the borscht,   20
    eat whole wheat *tortillas*,
    speak Tex-Mex with a Brooklyn accent;
    be stopped by *la migra*° at the border checkpoints;

Living in the Borderlands means you fight hard to
    resist the gold elixer beckoning from the bottle,   25
    the pull of the gun barrel,
    the rope crushing the hollow of your throat;

In the Borderlands
    you are the battleground
    where enemies are kin to each other;   30
    you are at home, a stranger,
    the border disputes have been settled
    the volley of shots have shattered the truce
    you are wounded, lost in action
    dead, fighting back;   35

To live in the Borderlands means
    the mill with the razor white teeth wants to shred off
    your olive-red skin, crush out the kernel, your heart
    pound you pinch you roll you out
    smelling like white bread but dead;   40

To survive the Borderlands
    you must live *sin fronteras*°
    be a crossroads.

                                                      [1987]

---

10 *rajetas* literally, "split," that is, having betrayed your word (author's note).
13 *Cuando . . . frontera* when you live in the borderlands. **15 *burra, buey*** donkey, oxen
(author's note). **23 *la migra*** immigration officials. **42 *sin fronteras*** without borders.

Joining the Conversation: Critical Thinking and Writing

1. When you first read the title, what was your response to it? After studying the poem, has your understanding of the title changed?
2. What is your response to Anzaldúa's use of Spanish terms? Why might she have wanted this mix of English and Spanish languages?
3. In no more than a paragraph, summarize what it means "to live in the Borderlands."
4. Is the tone of the poem celebratory, despairing, or something else? Does the tone change as the poem unfolds?
5. From your own personal background and experience, do you feel a special connection to Anzaldúa's poem? If you do not have such a background and experience, how does this fact affect your response to the poem?
6. Do some people live more in the Borderlands than do others? Why is that?

MITSUYE YAMADA

Mitsuye Yamada, the daughter of Japanese immigrants to the United States, was born in Japan in 1923, during her mother's return visit to her native land. Yamada was raised in Seattle, Washington, but in 1942, she and her family were incarcerated and then relocated to a camp in Idaho, when Executive Order 9066 gave military authorities the right to remove any and all persons from "military areas." In 1955, she became an American citizen. Later, she became a member of the Asian American Studies Program at the University of California at Irvine. She is the author of poems and stories.

To the Lady

The one in San Francisco who asked:
Why did the Japanese Americans let
the government put them in
those camps without protest?

Come to think of it I   5
   should've run off to Canada
   should've hijacked a plane to Algeria
   should've pulled myself up from my
   bra straps
   and kicked'm in the groin   10
   should've bombed a bank
   should've tried self-immolation
   should've holed myself up in a
   woodframe house
   and let you watch me   15
   burn up on the six o'clock news
   should've run howling down the street
   naked and assaulted you at breakfast
   by AP wirephoto

Dorothea Lange, "Grandfather and Grandchildren Awaiting
Evacuation Bus."

should've screamed bloody murder   20
like Kitty Genovese°

Then
YOU would've
come to my aid in shining armor
laid yourself across the railroad track   25
marched on Washington
tatooed a Star of David on your arm
written six million enraged
letters to Congress

But we didn't draw the line   30
anywhere
law and order Executive Order 9066°
social order moral order internal order

21 Kitty Genovese In 1964 Kitty Genovese of Kew Gardens, New York, was stabbed to
death when she left her car and walked toward her home. Thirty-eight persons heard her
screams, but no one came to her assistance.   **32 Executive Order 9066** an authorization,
signed in 1941 by President Franklin D. Roosevelt, allowing military authorities to relocate
Japanese and Japanese Americans who resided on the Pacific Coast of the United States.

You let'm
I let'm
All are punished.   35

[1976]

Joining the Conversation: Critical Thinking and Writing

1. Has the lady's question (lines 2–4) ever crossed your mind? If so, what answers did you think of?
2. What, in effect, is the speaker really saying in lines 5–21 and in lines 24–29?
3. Explain the last line.

nILA nORTHSUN

nila northSun was born in 1951 in Schurz, Nevada, of Shoshone-Chippewa stock. She studied at the California State University campuses at Hayward and Humboldt and the University of Montana at Missoula, beginning as a psychology major but switching to art history, specializing in American Indian art. She is a photographer, a teacher, and the author of three books of poetry.

Moving Camp Too Far

i can't speak of
    many moons
    moving camp on travois°
i can't tell of
    the last great battle   5
    counting coup° or
    taking scalp
i don't know what it
    was to hunt buffalo
    or do the ghost dance
    but   10
i can see an eagle
    almost extinct
    on slurpee plastic cups
i can travel to powwows   15
    in campers & winnebagos
i can eat buffalo meat
    at the tourist burger stand
i can dance to indian music
    rock-n-roll hey-a-hey-o   20
i can
    & unfortunately
    i do

[1977]

3 travois a frame slung between trailing poles that are pulled by a horse. Plains Indians used the device to transport their goods.   **6 counting coup** recounting one's exploits in battle.

Joining the Conversation: Critical Thinking and Writing

1. What is the speaker's attitude toward the world that she has lost? What is her attitude toward herself?
2. The first ten lines are presented in a negative form, and the final ten lines are presented in a positive form. How would you respond to someone who argued, "This poem is too formulaic"?

YUSEF KOMUNYAKAA

Yusef Komunyakaa was born in 1947 in Bogalusa, Louisiana. After graduating from high school, he entered the army and served in Vietnam, where he was awarded the Bronze Star. On his return to the United States, he earned a BA at the University of Colorado and then an MA at Colorado State University and an MFA in creative writing at the University of California, Irvine. The author of several books of poetry, Komunyakaa teaches at New York University. "Facing It" is the last poem in a book of poems about Vietnam, Dien Cai Dau *(1988). The title of the book is a slang term for "crazy."*

Facing It

My black face fades,
hiding inside the black granite.
I said I wouldn't,
dammit: No tears.
I'm stone. I'm flesh.   5
My clouded reflection eyes me
like a bird of prey, the profile of night
slanted against morning. I turn
this way—the stone lets me go.
I turn that way—I'm inside   10
the Vietnam Veterans Memorial
again, depending on the light
to make a difference.
I go down the 58,022 names,
half-expecting to find   15
my own in letters like smoke.
I touch the name Andrew Johnson;
I see the booby trap's white flash.
Names shimmer on a woman's blouse
but when she walks away   20
the names stay on the wall.
Brushstrokes flash, a red bird's
wings cutting across my stare.
The sky. A plane in the sky.
A white vet's image floats   25
closer to me, then his pale eyes
look through mine. I'm a window.
He's lost his right arm

Vietnam Veterans Memorial, Washington, DC.

inside the stone. In the black mirror
a woman's trying to erase names: 30
No, she's brushing a boy's hair.

[1988]

Joining the Conversation: Critical Thinking and Writing

1. The poem's title is "Facing It." What is the speaker facing? How would you describe his attitude?
2. Three people, whose names we don't know, briefly appear on the wall. How might we describe their actions? Try to paraphrase these lines: "I'm a window. / He's lost his right arm / inside the stone."
3. At the poem's end, has the speaker "faced it"? What is your evidence?
4. If you have seen the Vietnam Veterans Memorial, describe it and your reaction to it in a paragraph or two. If you haven't seen it, try to describe it from "Facing It" and any written or photographic accounts that you have seen.

BILLY COLLINS

"Billy Collins writes lovely poems," the late novelist, critic, and poet John Updike said. "Limpid, gently and consistently startling, more serious than they seem, they describe all the worlds that are and were and some others besides." The recipient of many honors and awards, and a former poet laureate of the United States, Collins

was born in New York City in 1941. He has taught at both the City University of New York and Sarah Lawrence College. His Sailing Alone around the Room: New and Selected Poems *was published in 2002.*

Collins wrote the following poem on the first anniversary of the terrorist attack on the World Trade Center in New York City, on September 11, 2001, which killed about 3,000 people and destroyed the Twin Towers.

The Names

Yesterday, I lay awake in the palm of the night.
A soft rain stole in, unhelped by any breeze,
And when I saw the silver glaze on the windows,
I started with A, with Ackerman, as it happened,
Then Baxter and Calabro,   5
Davis and Eberling, names falling into place
As droplets fell through the dark.

Names printed on the ceiling of the night.
Names slipping around a watery bend.
Twenty-six willows on the banks of a stream.   10

In the morning, I walked out barefoot
Among thousands of flowers
Heavy with dew like the eyes of tears,
And each had a name—
Fiori inscribed on a yellow petal   15
Then Gonzalez and Han, Ishikawa and Jenkins.

Names written in the air
And stitched into the cloth of the day.
A name under a photograph taped to a mailbox.
Monogram on a torn shirt,   20
I see you spelled out on storefront windows
And on the bright unfurled awnings of this city.
I say the syllables as I turn a corner—
Kelly and Lee,
Medina, Nardella, and O'Connor.   25

When I peer in to the woods,
I see a thick tangle where letters are hidden
As in a puzzle concocted for children.
Parker and Quigley in the twigs of an ash,
Rizzo, Schubert, Torres, and Upton,   30
Secrets in the boughs of an ancient maple.

Names written in the pale sky.
Names rising in the updraft amid buildings.
Names silent in stone
Or cried out behind a door.   35
Names blown over the earth and out to sea.

In the evening—weakening light, the last swallows.
A boy on a lake lifts his oars.

A woman by a window puts a match to a candle,
And the names are outlined on the rose clouds—
Vanacore and Wallace,   40
(let X stand, if it can, for the ones unfound)
Then Young and Ziminsky, the final jolt of Z.

Names etched on the head of a pin.
One name spanning a bridge, another undergoing a tunnel.   45
A blue name needled into the skin.
Names of citizens, workers, mothers and fathers,
The bright-eyed daughter, the quick son.
Alphabet of names in a green field.
Names in the small tracks of birds.   50
Names lifted from a hat
Or balanced on the tip of the tongue.
Names wheeled into the dim warehouse of memory.
So many names, there is barely room on the walls of the heart.

[2002]

Joining the Conversation: Critical Thinking and Writing

1. In an interview that appeared several years before "The Names" was published, Collins said of his intention as a poet: "By the end of the poem, the reader should be in a different place from where he started." When you finished reading "The Names," did you find yourself in a "different place"? How would you describe this place?

2. Collins also observed, again in an interview before he wrote "The Names": "Poetry is clearly very serious for me, but without heaviness or a glib sense of spirituality." Do you perceive a "spiritual" dimension to this poem—one that is not "glib"? What does it mean to say that a poem is "spiritual," that is, creates a spiritual effect? Is this the same thing as saying that a poem is "religious," or is it something different?

3. Many readers have expressed their high regard for "The Names," referring to it as a "great poem." Do you agree? What defines a great poem? Do you think a poet does or does not face a special challenge in trying to write a poem, great or simply good, about the tragedy of September 11, 2001? Explain your answer.

4. One critic, who otherwise admires Collins's work, has objected to "The Names" for being "too sentimental." How would you define "sentimentality"? (Clarify your definition with an example.) Can you locate evidence in the text that might support the judgment that Collins's poem is sentimental? Are there other passages that you could cite and analyze in order to argue against it? And what's the matter with sentimentality? Is sentimentality something that poets should always avoid?

5. How do you feel about your own name? Is it something that you give much thought to? Any thought? Why is that? Now that you have read Collins's poem, has your relationship to your own name changed in any way?

PLAY

LORRAINE HANSBERRY

Lorraine Hansberry (1930–65) was born in Chicago, Illinois, to middle-class black parents who lived on the city's South Side. When she was still a child, her father was barred from purchasing a house in a white neighborhood. He sued and pursued the case all the way to the Supreme Court, which ruled in his favor. Hansberry attended the University of Wisconsin as an undergraduate. Following college, she began a career as a painter, studying at the Art Institute of Chicago and in Mexico before she decided to move to New York to take up her interest in writing. There she wrote for Freedom, *a magazine founded by the great singer–actor turned political activist, Paul Robeson. When her first play,* A Raisin in the Sun, *premiered at the Ethel Barrymore Theater in 1959, it was the first play written by an African American*

The 1959 opening night cast for the Broadway production of *A Raisin in the Sun* included Sidney Poitier, Claudia MacNeil, Ruby Dee, Diana Sands, Louis Gossett Jr., Ivan Dixon, Glynn Turman, John Fielder, Lonne Elder III, Ed Hall, and Douglas Turner Ward.

woman to be performed on Broadway. She wrote only one other play, The Sign in Sidney Brustein's Window *(1965), before she died of cancer at the age of thirty-four. The title of* A Raisin in the Sun *is taken from the poem "A Dream Deferred" by Langston Hughes.*

A Raisin in the Sun

CHARACTERS IN ORDER OF APPEARANCE

RUTH YOUNGER, *Walter's wife, about thirty*

TRAVIS YOUNGER, *her son and Walter's*

WALTER LEE YOUNGER, *(Brother) Ruth's husband, mid-thirties*

BENEATHA YOUNGER, *Walter's sister, about twenty*

LENA YOUNGER, *(Mama) mother of Walter and Beneatha*

JOSEPH ASAGAI, *Nigerian, Beneatha's suitor*

GEORGE MURCHISON, *Beneatha's date, wealthy*

KARL LINDNER, *white, chairman of the Clybourne Park New Neighbors Orientation Committee*

BOBO, *one of Walter's business partners*

MOVING MEN

The action of the play is set in Chicago's South Side, sometime between World War II and the present.

ACT I
SCENE 1. *Friday morning*
SCENE 2. *The following morning*

ACT II
SCENE 1. *Later, the same day*
SCENE 2. *Friday night, a few weeks later*
SCENE 3. *Moving day, one week later*

ACT III
An hour later

ACT I

Scene 1

The Younger living room would be a comfortable and well-ordered room if it were not for a number of indestructible contradictions to this state of being. Its furnishings are typical and undistinguished and their primary feature now is that they have clearly had to accommodate the living of too many people for too many years—and they are tired. Still, we can see that at some time, a time probably no longer remembered by the family (except perhaps for MAMA) *the furnishings of this room were actually selected with care and love and even hope—and brought to this apartment and arranged with taste and pride.*

That was a long time ago. Now the once loved pattern of the couch upholstery has to fight to show itself from under acres of crocheted doilies and couch covers which have themselves finally come to be more important than the upholstery. And here a table or a chair has been moved to disguise the worn places in the carpet; but the carpet has fought back by showing its weariness, with depressing uniformity, elsewhere on its surface.

Weariness has, in fact, won in this room. Everything has been polished, washed, sat on, used, scrubbed too often. All pretenses but living itself have long since vanished from the very atmosphere of this room.

Moreover, a section of this room, for it is not really a room unto itself, though the landlord's lease would make it seem so, slopes backward to provide a small kitchen area, where the family prepares the meals that are eaten in the living room proper, which must also serve as dining room. The single window that has been provided for these "two" rooms is located in this kitchen area. The sole natural light the family may enjoy in the course of a day is only that which fights its way through this little window.

At left, a door leads to a bedroom which is shared by MAMA *and her daughter,* BENEATHA. *At right, opposite, is a second room (which in the beginning of the life of this apartment was probably a breakfast room) which serves as a bedroom for* WALTER *and his wife,* RUTH.

TIME: *Sometime between World War II and the present.*
PLACE: *Chicago's South Side.*

AT RISE: *It is morning dark in the living room.* TRAVIS *is asleep on the makedown bed at center. An alarm clock sounds from within the bedroom at right, and presently* RUTH *enters from that room and closes the door behind her. She crosses sleepily toward the window. As she passes her sleeping son she reaches down and shakes him a little. At the window she raises the shade and a dusky South Side morning light comes in feebly. She fills a pot with water and puts it on to boil. She calls to the boy, between yawns, in a slightly muffled voice.*

RUTH *is about thirty. We can see that she was a pretty girl, even exceptionally so, but now it is apparent that life has been little that she expected, and disappointment has already begun to hang in her face. In a few years, before thirty-five even, she will be known among her people as a "settled woman."*

She crosses to her son and gives him a good, final, rousing shake.

RUTH: Come on now, boy, it's seven thirty! [*Her son sits up at last, in a stupor of sleepiness.*] I say hurry up, Travis! You ain't the only person in the world got to use a bathroom! [*The child, a sturdy, handsome little boy of ten or eleven, drags himself out of the bed and almost blindly takes his towels and "today's clothes" from drawers and a closet and goes out to the bathroom, which is in an outside hall and which is shared by another family or families on the same floor.* RUTH *crosses to the bedroom door at right and opens it and calls in to her husband.*] Walter Lee! . . . It's after seven thirty! Lemme see you do some waking up in there now! [*She waits.*] You better get up from there, man! It's after seven thirty I tell you. [*She waits again.*] All right, you just go ahead and lay there and next thing you know Travis be finished and Mr. Johnson'll be in there and you'll be fussing and cussing round here like a mad man! And be late too! [*She waits, at the end of patience.*] Walter Lee—it's time for you to get up! [*She waits another second and then starts to go into the bedroom, but is apparently satisfied that her husband has begun to get up. She stops, pulls the door to, and returns to the kitchen area. She wipes her face with a moist cloth and runs her fingers through her sleep-disheveled hair in a vain effort and ties an apron around her housecoat. The bedroom door at right opens and her husband stands in the doorway in his pajamas, which are rumpled and mismated. He is a lean, intense young man in his middle thirties, inclined to quick*

> *nervous movements and erratic speech habits—and always in his voice there is a quality of indictment.*]

WALTER: Is he out yet?

RUTH: What you mean *out?* He ain't hardly got in there good yet.

WALTER [*wandering in, still more oriented to sleep than to a new day*]: Well, what was you doing all that yelling for if I can't even get in there yet? [*stopping and thinking*] Check coming today?

RUTH: They *said* Saturday and this is just Friday and I hopes to God you ain't going to get up here first thing this morning and start talking to me 'bout no money—'cause I 'bout don't want to hear it.

WALTER: Something the matter with you this morning?

RUTH: No—I'm just sleepy as the devil. What kind of eggs you want?

WALTER: Not scrambled. [RUTH *starts to scramble eggs.*] Paper come? [RUTH *points impatiently to the rolled up* Tribune *on the table, and he gets it and spreads it out and vaguely reads the front page.*] Set off another bomb yesterday.

RUTH [*maximum indifference*]: Did they?

WALTER [*looking up*]: What's the matter with you?

RUTH: Ain't nothing the matter with me. And don't keep asking me that this morning.

WALTER: Ain't nobody bothering you. [*reading the news of the day absently again*] Say Colonel McCormick is sick.

RUTH [*affecting tea-party interest*]: Is he now? Poor thing.

WALTER [*sighing and looking at his watch*]: Oh, me. [*He waits.*] Now what is that boy doing in that bathroom all this time? He just going to have to start getting up earlier. I can't be being late to work on account of him fooling around in there.

RUTH [*turning on him*]: Oh, no he ain't going to be getting up earlier no such thing! It ain't his fault that he can't get to bed no earlier nights 'cause he got a bunch of crazy good-for-nothing clowns sitting up running their mouths in what is supposed to be his bedroom after ten o'clock at night . . .

WALTER: That's what you mad about, ain't it? The things I want to talk about with my friends just couldn't be important in your mind, could they? [*He rises and finds a cigarette in her handbag on the table and crosses to the little window and looks out, smoking and deeply enjoying this first one.*]

RUTH [*almost matter of factly, a complaint too automatic to deserve emphasis*]: Why you always got to smoke before you eat in the morning?

WALTER [*at the window*]: Just look at 'em down there. . . . Running and racing to work . . . [*He turns and faces his wife and watches her a moment at the stove, and then, suddenly*] You look young this morning, baby.

RUTH [*indifferently*]: Yeah?

WALTER: Just for a second—stirring them eggs. It's gone now—just for a second it was—you looked real young again. [*then, drily*] It's gone now—you look like yourself again.

RUTH: Man, if you don't shut up and leave me alone.

WALTER [*looking out to the street again*]: First thing a man ought to learn in life is not to make love to no colored woman first thing in the morning. You all some evil people at eight o'clock in the morning. [TRAVIS *appears in the hall doorway, almost fully dressed and quite wide awake now, his towels and pajamas across his shoulders. He opens the door and signals for his father to make the bathroom in a hurry.*]

TRAVIS [*watching the bathroom*]: Daddy, come on! [WALTER *gets his bathroom utensils and flies out to the bathroom.*]

RUTH: Sit down and have your breakfast, Travis.

TRAVIS: Mama, this is Friday. [*gleefully*] Check coming tomorrow, huh?

RUTH: You get your mind off money and eat your breakfast.

TRAVIS [*eating*]: This is the morning we supposed to bring the fifty cents to school.

RUTH: Well, I ain't got no fifty cents this morning.

TRAVIS: Teacher say we have to.

RUTH: I don't care what teacher say. I ain't got it. Eat your breakfast, Travis.

TRAVIS: I *am* eating.

RUTH: Hush up now and just eat! [*The boy gives her an exasperated look for her lack of understanding, and eats grudgingly.*]

TRAVIS: You think Grandmama would have it?

RUTH: No! And I want you to stop asking your grandmother for money, you hear me?

TRAVIS [*outraged*]: Gaaaleee! I don't ask her, she just gimme it sometimes!

RUTH: Travis Willard Younger—I got too much on me this morning to be—

TRAVIS: Maybe Daddy—

RUTH: *Travis.* [*The boy hushes abruptly. They are both quiet and tense for several seconds.*]

TRAVIS [*presently*]: Could I maybe go carry some groceries in front of the supermarket for a little while after school then?

RUTH: Just hush, I said. [TRAVIS *jabs his spoon into his cereal bowl viciously, and rests his head in anger upon his fists.*] If you through eating, you can get over there and make up your bed. [*The boy obeys stiffly and crosses the room, almost mechanically, to the bed and more or less carefully folds the covering. He carries the bedding into his mother's room and returns with his books and cap.*]

TRAVIS [*sulking and standing apart from her unnaturally*]: I'm gone.

RUTH [*looking up from the stove to inspect him automatically*]: Come here. [*He crosses to her and she studies his head.*] If you don't take this comb and fix this here head, you better! [TRAVIS *puts down his books with a great sigh of oppression, and crosses to the mirror. His mother mutters under her breath about his "stubbornness."*] 'Bout to march out of here with that head looking just like chickens slept in it! I just don't know where you get your stubborn ways . . . And get your jacket, too. Looks chilly out this morning.

TRAVIS [*with conspicuously brushed hair and jacket*]: I'm gone.

RUTH: Get carfare and milk money—[*waving one finger*]—and not a single penny for no caps, you hear me?

TRAVIS [*with sullen politeness*]: Yes'm. [*He turns in outrage to leave. His mother watches after him as in his frustration he approaches the door almost comically. When she speaks to him, her voice has become a very gentle tease.*]

RUTH [*mocking, as she thinks he would say it*]: Oh, Mama makes me so mad sometimes, I don't know what to do! [*She waits and continues to his back as he stands stock-still in front of the door.*] I wouldn't kiss that woman good-bye for nothing in this world this morning! [*The boy finally turns around and rolls his eyes at her, knowing the mood has changed and he is vindicated; he does not, however, move toward her yet.*] Not for nothing in this world! [*She finally laughs aloud at him and holds out her arms to him and we see that it is a way between them, very old and practiced. He crosses to her and allows her to embrace him warmly but keeps his face fixed with masculine rigidity. She holds him back from her presently and looks at him and runs*

her fingers over the features of his face. With utter gentleness—] Now—
whose little old angry man are you?

TRAVIS [*The masculinity and gruffness start to fade at last.*]: Aw gaalee—Mama . . .

RUTH [*mimicking*]: Aw—gaaaaalleeeee, Mama! [*She pushes him, with rough playfulness and finality, toward the door.*] Get on out of here or you going to be late.

TRAVIS [*in the face of love, new aggressiveness*]: Mama, could I *please* go carry groceries?

RUTH: Honey, it's starting to get so cold evenings.

WALTER [*coming in from the bathroom and drawing a make-believe gun from a make-believe holster and shooting at his son*]: What is it he wants to do?

RUTH: Go carry groceries after school at the supermarket.

WALTER: Well, let him go . . .

TRAVIS [*quickly, to the ally*]: I *have* to—she won't gimme the fifty cents . . .

WALTER [*to his wife only*]: Why not?

RUTH [*simply, and with flavor*]: 'Cause we don't have it.

WALTER [*to RUTH only*]: What you tell the boy things like that for? [*reaching down into his pants with a rather important gesture*] Here, son—[*He hands the boy the coin, but his eyes are directed to his wife's.* TRAVIS *takes the money happily.*]

TRAVIS: Thanks, Daddy. [*He starts out.* RUTH *watches both of them with murder in her eyes.* WALTER *stands and stares back at her with defiance, and suddenly reaches into his pocket again on an afterthought.*]

WALTER [*without even looking at his son, still staring hard at his wife*]: In fact, here's another fifty cents . . . Buy yourself some fruit today—or take a taxicab to school or something!

TRAVIS: Whoopee—[*He leaps up and clasps his father around the middle with his legs, and they face each other in mutual appreciation; slowly* WALTER LEE *peeks around the boy to catch the violent rays from his wife's eyes and draws his head back as if shot.*]

WALTER: You better get down now—and get to school, man.

TRAVIS [*at the door*]: O.K. Good-bye. [*He exits.*]

WALTER [*after him, pointing with pride*]: That's *my* boy. [*She looks at him in disgust and turns back to her work.*] You know what I was thinking 'bout in the bathroom this morning?

RUTH: No.

WALTER: How come you always try to be so pleasant!

RUTH: What is there to be pleasant 'bout!

WALTER: You want to know what I was thinking 'bout in the bathroom or not!

RUTH: I know what you thinking 'bout.

WALTER [*ignoring her*]: 'Bout what me and Willy Harris was talking about last night.

RUTH [*immediately—a refrain*]: Willy Harris is a good-for-nothing loudmouth.

WALTER: Anybody who talks to me has got to be a good-for-nothing loudmouth, ain't he? And what you know about who is just a good-for-nothing loudmouth? Charlie Atkins was just a "good-for-nothing loudmouth" too, wasn't he! When he wanted me to go in the dry-cleaning business with him. And now—he's grossing a hundred thousand a year. A hundred thousand dollars a year! You still call *him* a loudmouth!

RUTH [*bitterly*]: Oh, Walter Lee . . . [*She folds her head on her arms over the table.*]

WALTER [*rising and coming to her and standing over her*]: You tired, ain't you? Tired of everything. Me, the boy, the way we live—this beat-up hole—everything. Ain't you? [*She doesn't look up, doesn't answer.*] So tired—moaning and groaning all the time, but you wouldn't do nothing to help, would you? You couldn't be on my side that long for nothing, could you?

RUTH: Walter, please leave me alone.

WALTER: A man needs for a woman to back him up . . .

RUTH: Walter—

WALTER: Mama would listen to you. You know she listen to you more than she do me and Bennie. She think more of you. All you have to do is just sit down with her when you drinking your coffee one morning and talking 'bout things like you do and—[*He sits down beside her and demonstrates graphically what he thinks her methods and tone should be.*]—you just sip your coffee, see, and say easy like that you been thinking 'bout that deal Walter Lee is so interested in, 'bout the store and all, and sip some more coffee, like what you saying ain't really that important to you—And the next thing you know, she be listening good and asking you questions and when I come home—I can tell her the details. This ain't no fly-by-night proposition, baby. I mean we figured it out, me and Willy and Bobo.

RUTH [*with a frown*]: Bobo?

WALTER: Yeah. You see, this little liquor store we got in mind cost seventy-five thousand and we figured the initial investment on the place be 'bout thirty thousand, see. That be ten thousand each. Course, there's a couple of hundred you got to pay so's you don't spend your life just waiting for them clowns to let your license get approved—

RUTH: You mean graft?

WALTER [*frowning impatiently*]: Don't call it that. See there, that just goes to show you what women understand about the world. Baby, don't *nothing* happen for you in this world 'less you pay *somebody* off!

RUTH: Walter, leave me alone! [*She raises her head and stares at him vigorously—then says, more quietly.*] Eat your eggs, they gonna be cold.

WALTER [*straightening up from her and looking off*]: That's it. There you are. Man say to his woman: I got me a dream. His woman say: Eat your eggs. [*sadly, but gaining in power*] Man say: I got to take hold of this here world, baby! And a woman will say: Eat your eggs and go to work. [*passionately now*] Man say: I got to change my life, I'm choking to death, baby! And his woman say—[*in utter anguish as he brings his fists down on his thighs*]—Your eggs is getting cold!

RUTH [*softly*]: Walter, that ain't none of our money.

WALTER [*not listening at all or even looking at her*]: This morning, I was lookin' in the mirror and thinking about it . . . I'm thirty-five years old; I been married eleven years and I got a boy who sleeps in the living room—[*very, very quietly*]—and all I got to give him is stories about how rich white people live . . .

RUTH: Eat your eggs, Walter.

WALTER: *Damn my eggs . . . damn all the eggs that ever was!*

RUTH: Then go to work.

WALTER [*looking up at her*]: See—I'm trying to talk to you 'bout myself—[*shaking his head with the repetition*]—and all you can say is eat them eggs and go to work.

RUTH [*wearily*]: Honey, you never say nothing new. I listen to you every day, every night and every morning, and you never say nothing new. [*shrugging*] So you would rather *be* Mr. Arnold than be his chauffeur. So—I would *rather* be living in Buckingham Palace.

WALTER: That is just what is wrong with the colored woman in this world . . . Don't understand about building their men up and making 'em feel like they somebody. Like they can do something.

RUTH [*drily, but to hurt*]: There *are* colored men who do things.

WALTER: No thanks to the colored woman.

RUTH: Well, being a colored woman, I guess I can't help myself none. [*She rises and gets the ironing board and sets it up and attacks a huge pile of roughdried clothes, sprinkling them in preparation for the ironing and then rolling them into tight fat balls.*]

WALTER [*mumbling*]: We one group of men tied to a race of women with small minds.

[*His sister* BENEATHA *enters. She is about twenty, as slim and intense as her brother. She is not as pretty as her sister-in-law, but her lean, almost intellectual face has a handsomeness of its own. She wears a bright-red flannel nightie, and her thick hair stands wildly about her head. Her speech is a mixture of many things; it is different from the rest of the family's insofar as education has permeated her sense of English—and perhaps the Midwest rather than the South has finally—at last— won out in her inflection; but not altogether, because over all of it is a soft slurring and transformed use of vowels which is the decided influence of the South Side. She passes through the room without looking at either* RUTH *or* WALTER *and goes to the outside door and looks, a little blindly, out to the bathroom. She sees that it has been lost to the Johnsons. She closes the door with a sleepy vengeance and crosses to the table and sits down a little defeated.*]

BENEATHA: I am going to start timing those people.

WALTER: You should get up earlier.

BENEATHA [*her face in her hands; she is still fighting the urge to go back to bed*]: Really—would you suggest dawn? Where's the paper?

WALTER [*pushing the paper across the table to her as he studies her almost clinically, as though he has never seen her before*]: You a horrible-looking chick at this hour.

BENEATHA [*drily*]: Good morning, everybody.

WALTER [*senselessly*]: How is school coming?

BENEATHA [*in the same spirit*]: Lovely, Lovely. And you know, biology is the great- est. [*looking up at him*] I dissected something that looked just like you yesterday.

WALTER: I just wondered if you've made up your mind and everything.

BENEATHA [*gaining in sharpness and impatience*]: And what did I answer yesterday morning—and the day before that?

RUTH [*from the ironing board, like someone disinterested and old*]: Don't be so nasty, Bennie.

BENEATHA [*still to her brother*]: And the day before that and the day before that!

WALTER [*defensively*]: I'm interested in you. Something wrong with that? Ain't many girls who decide—

WALTER AND BENEATHA [*in unison*]: —"to be a doctor." [*silence*]

WALTER: Have we figured out yet just exactly how much medical school is going to cost?

RUTH: Walter Lee, why don't you leave that girl alone and get out of here to work?

BENEATHA [*exits to the bathroom and bangs on the door*]: Come on out of there, please! [*She comes back into the room.*]

WALTER [*looking at his sister intently*]: You know the check is coming tomorrow.

BENEATHA [*turning on him with a sharpness all her own*]: That money belongs to
 Mama, Walter and it's for her to decide how she wants to use it. I don't
 care if she wants to buy a house or a rocket ship or just nail it up somewhere and look at it. It's hers. Not ours—hers.

WALTER [*bitterly*]: Now ain't that fine! You just got your mother's interest at heart,
 ain't you, girl? You such a nice girl—but if Mama got that money she can
 always take a few thousand and help you through school too—can't
 she?

BENEATHA: I have never asked anyone around here to do anything for me!

WALTER: No! And the line between asking and just accepting when the time comes
 is big and wide—ain't it!

BENEATHA [*with fury*]: What do you want from me, Brother—that I quit school or just
 drop dead, which!

WALTER: I don't want nothing but for you to stop acting holy 'round here. Me and
 Ruth done made some sacrifices for you—why can't you do something for
 the family?

RUTH: Walter, don't be dragging me in it.

WALTER: You are in it—Don't you get up and go work in somebody's kitchen for the
 last three years to help put clothes on her back?

RUTH: Oh, Walter—that's not fair . . .

WALTER: It ain't that nobody expects you to get on your knees and say thank you,
 Brother; thank you, Ruth; thank you, Mama—and thank you, Travis, for
 wearing the same pair of shoes for two semesters—

BENEATHA [*dropping to her knees*]: Well—I do—all right?—thank everybody . . . and
 forgive me for ever wanting to be anything at all . . . forgive me, forgive
 me!

RUTH: Please stop it! Your mama'll hear you.

WALTER: Who the hell told you you had to be a doctor? If you so crazy 'bout messing
 'round with sick people—then go be a nurse like other women—or just
 get married and be quiet . . .

BENEATHA: Well—you finally got it said . . . It took you three years but you finally
 got it said. Walter, give up; leave me alone—it's Mama's money.

WALTER: *He was my father, too!*

BENEATHA: So what? He was mine, too—and Travis' grandfather—but the insurance
 money belongs to Mama. Picking on me is not going to make her give it
 to you to invest in any liquor stores—[*under breath, dropping into a
 chair*]—and I for one say, God bless Mama for that!

WALTER [*to* RUTH]: See—did you hear? Did you hear!

RUTH: Honey, please go to work.

WALTER: Nobody in this house is ever going to understand me.

BENEATHA: Because you're a nut.

WALTER: Who's a nut?

BENEATHA: You—you are a nut. Thee is mad, boy.

WALTER [*looking at his wife and his sister from the door, very sadly*]: The world's most
 backward race of people, and that's a fact.

BENEATHA [*turning slowly in her chair*]: And then there are all those prophets who
 would lead us out of the wilderness—[WALTER *slams out of the house.*]—
 into the swamps!

RUTH: Bennie, why you always gotta be pickin' on your brother? Can't you be a
 little sweeter sometimes? [*Door opens.* WALTER *walks in.*]

WALTER [*to* RUTH]: I need some money for carfare.

RUTH [*looks at him, then warms; teasing, but tenderly*]: Fifty cents? [*She goes to her bag and gets money.*] Here, take a taxi. [WALTER *exits.* MAMA *enters. She is a woman in her early sixties, full-bodied and strong. She is one of those women of a certain grace and beauty who wear it so unobtrusively that it takes a while to notice. Her dark-brown face is surrounded by the total whiteness of her hair, and, being a woman who has adjusted to many things in life and overcome many more, her face is full of strength. She has, we can see, wit and faith of a kind that keep her eyes lit and full of interest and expectancy. She is, in a word, a beautiful woman. Her bearing is perhaps most like the noble bearing of the women of the Hereros of Southwest Africa—rather as if she imagines that as she walks she still bears a basket or a vessel upon her head. Her speech, on the other hand, is as careless as her carriage is precise—she is inclined to slur everything—but her voice is perhaps not so much quiet as simply soft.*]

MAMA: Who that 'round here slamming doors at this hour? [*She crosses through the room, goes to the window, opens it, and brings in a feeble little plant growing doggedly in a small pot on the window sill. She feels the dirt and puts it back out.*]

RUTH: That was Walter Lee. He and Bennie was at it again.

MAMA: My children and they tempers. Lord, if this little old plant don't get more sun that it's been getting it ain't never going to see spring again. [*She turns from the window.*] What's the matter with you this morning, Ruth? You looks right peaked. You aiming to iron all them things? Leave some for me. I'll get to 'em this afternoon. Bennie honey, it's too drafty for you to be sitting 'round half dressed. Where's your robe?

BENEATHA: In the cleaners.

MAMA: Well, go get mine and put it on.

BENEATHA: I'm not cold, Mama, honest.

MAMA: I know—but you so thin . . .

BENEATHA [*irritably*]: Mama, I'm not cold.

MAMA [*seeing the make-down bed as* TRAVIS *has left it*]: Lord have mercy, look at that poor bed. Bless his heart—he tries, don't he? [*She moves to the bed* TRAVIS *has sloppily made up.*]

RUTH: No—he don't half try at all 'cause he knows you going to come along behind him and fix everything. That's just how come he don't know how to do nothing right now—you done spoiled that boy so.

MAMA: Well—he's a little boy. Ain't supposed to know 'bout housekeeping. My baby, that's what he is. What you fix for his breakfast this morning?

RUTH [*angrily*]: I feed my son, Lena!

MAMA: I ain't meddling—[*under breath, busy-bodyish*]: I just noticed all last week he had cold cereal, and when it starts getting this chilly in the fall a child ought to have some hot grits or something when he goes out in the cold—

RUTH [*furious*]: I gave him hot oats—is that all right!

MAMA: I ain't meddling. [*pause*] Put a lot of nice butter on it? [RUTH *shoots her an angry look and does not reply.*] He likes lots of butter.

RUTH [*exasperated*]: Lena—

MAMA [*to* BENEATHA; MAMA *is inclined to wander conversationally sometimes*]: What was you and your brother fussing 'bout this morning?

BENEATHA: It's not important, Mama. [*She gets up and goes to look out at the bathroom, which is apparently free, and she picks up her towels and rushes out.*]

MAMA: What was they fighting about?

RUTH: Now you know as well as I do.

MAMA [*shaking her head*]: Brother still worrying hisself sick about that money?

RUTH: You know he is.

MAMA: You had breakfast?

RUTH: Some coffee.

MAMA: Girl, you better start eating and looking after yourself better. You almost thin
     as Travis.

RUTH: Lena—

MAMA: Uh-hunh?

RUTH: What are you going to do with it?

MAMA: Now don't you start, child. It's too early in the morning to be talking about
     money. It ain't Christian.

RUTH: It's just that he got his heart set on that store—

MAMA: You mean that liquor store that Willy Harris want him to invest in?

RUTH: Yes—

MAMA: We ain't no business people, Ruth. We just plain working folks.

RUTH: Ain't nobody business people till they go into business. Walter Lee say col-
     ored people ain't never going to start getting ahead till they start gam-
     bling on some different kinds of things in the world—investments and
     things.

MAMA: What done got into you, girl? Walter Lee done finally sold you on investing.

RUTH: No. Mama, something is happening between Walter and me. I don't know
     what it is—but he needs something—something I can't give him any
     more. He needs this chance, Lena.

MAMA [*frowning deeply*]: But liquor, honey—

RUTH: Well—like Walter say—I spec people going to always be drinking themselves
     some liquor.

MAMA: Well—whether they drinks it or not ain't none of my business. But whether
     I go into business selling it to 'em is, and I don't want that on my ledger
     this late in life. [*stopping suddenly and studying her daughter-in-law*] Ruth
     Younger, what's the matter with you today? You look like you could fall
     over right there.

RUTH: I'm tired.

MAMA: Then you better stay home from work today.

RUTH: I can't stay home. She'd be calling up the agency and screaming at them, "My
     girl didn't come in today—send me somebody! My girl didn't come in!"
     Oh, she just have a fit . . .

MAMA: Well, let her have it. I'll just call her up and say you got the flu—

RUTH [*laughing*]: Why the flu?

MAMA: 'Cause it sounds respectable to 'em. Something white people get, too. They
     know 'bout the flu. Otherwise they think you been cut up or something
     when you tell 'em you sick.

RUTH: I got to go in. We need the money.

MAMA: Somebody would of thought my children done all but starved to death the
     way they talk about money here late. Child, we got a great big old check
     coming tomorrow.

RUTH [*sincerely, but also self-righteously*]: Now that's your money. It ain't got noth-
     ing to do with me. We all feel like that—Walter and Bennie and me—even
     Travis.

MAMA [*thoughtfully, and suddenly very far away*]: Ten thousand dollars—

RUTH: Sure is wonderful.

MAMA: Ten thousand dollars.

RUTH: You know what you should do, Miss Lena? You should take yourself a trip somewhere. To Europe or South America or someplace—

MAMA [*throwing up her hands at the thought*]: Oh, child!

RUTH: I'm serious. Just pack up and leave! Go on away and enjoy yourself some. Forget about the family and have yourself a ball for once in your life—

MAMA [*drily*]: You sound like I'm just about ready to die. Who'd go with me? What I look like wandering 'round Europe by myself?

RUTH: Shoot—these here rich white women do it all the time. They don't think nothing of packing up they suitcases and piling on one of them big steamships and—swoosh!—they gone, child.

MAMA: Something always told me I wasn't no rich white woman.

RUTH: Well—what are you going to do with it then?

MAMA: I ain't rightly decided. [*Thinking. She speaks now with emphasis.*] Some of it got to be put away for Beneatha and her schoolin'—and ain't nothing going to touch that part of it. Nothing. [*She waits several seconds, trying to make up her mind about something, and looks at* RUTH *little tentatively before going* on.] Been thinking that we maybe could meet the notes on a little old two-story somewhere, with a yard where Travis could play in the summertime, if we use part of the insurance for a down payment and everybody kind of pitch in. I could maybe take on a little day work again, few days a week—

RUTH [*studying her mother-in-law furtively and concentrating on her ironing, anxious to encourage without seeming to*]: Well, Lord knows, we've put enough rent into this here rat trap to pay for four houses by now . . .

MAMA [*looking up at the words "rat trap" and then looking around and leaning back and sighing—in a suddenly reflective mood*]: "Rat trap"—yes, that's all it is. [*smiling*] I remember just as well the day me and Big Walter moved in here. Hadn't been married but two weeks and wasn't planning on living here no more than a year. [*She shakes her head at the dissolved dream.*] We was going to set away, little by little, don't you know, and buy a little place out in Morgan Park. We had even picked out the house. [*chuckling a little*] Looks right dumpy today. But Lord, child, you should know all the dreams I had 'bout buying that house and fixing it up and making me a little garden in the back—[*She waits and stops smiling.*] And didn't none of it happen [*dropping her hands in a futile gesture*].

RUTH [*keeps her head down, ironing*]: Yes, life can be a barrel of disappointments, sometimes.

MAMA: Honey, Big Walter would come in here some nights back then and slump down on that couch there and just look at the rug, and look at me and look at the rug and then back at me—and I'd know he was down then . . . really down. [*After a second very long and thoughtful pause; she is seeing back to times that only she can see.*] And then, Lord, when I lost that baby—little Claude—I almost thought I was going to lose Big Walter too. Oh, that man grieved hisself! He was one man to love his children.

RUTH: Ain't nothin' can tear at you like losin' your baby.

MAMA: I guess that's how come that man finally worked hisself to death like he done. Likely he was fighting his own war with this here world that took his baby from him.

RUTH: He sure was a fine man, all right. I always liked Mr. Younger.

MAMA: Crazy 'bout his children! God knows there was plenty wrong with Walter Younger—hard-headed, mean, kind of wild with women—plenty wrong with him. But he sure loved his children. Always wanted them to have something—be something. That's where Brother gets all these notions, I reckon. Big Walter used to say, he'd get right wet in the eyes sometimes, lean his head back with the water standing in his eyes and say, "Seem like God didn't see fit to give the black man nothing but dreams—but He did give us children to make them dreams seem worth while." [*She smiles.*] He could talk like that, don't you know.

RUTH: Yes, he sure could. He was a good man, Mr. Younger.

MAMA: Yes, a fine man—just couldn't never catch up with his dreams, that's all. [BENEATHA *comes in, brushing her hair and looking up to the ceiling, where the sound of a vacuum cleaner has started up.*]

BENEATHA: What could be so dirty on that woman's rugs that she has to vacuum them every single day?

RUTH: I wish certain young women 'round here who I could name would take inspiration about certain rugs in a certain apartment I could also mention.

BENEATHA [*shrugging*]: How much cleaning can a house need, for Christ's sakes?

MAMA [*not liking the Lord's name used thus*]: Bennie!

RUTH: Just listen to her—just listen!

BENEATHA: Oh, God!

MAMA: If you use the Lord's name just one more time—

BENEATHA [*a bit of a whine*]: Oh, Mama—

RUTH: Fresh—just fresh as salt, this girl!

BENEATHA [*drily*]: Well—if the salt loses its savor—

MAMA: Now that will do. I just ain't going to have you 'round here reciting the scriptures in vain—you hear me?

BENEATHA: How did I manage to get on everybody's wrong side by just walking into a room?

RUTH: If you weren't so fresh—

BENEATHA: Ruth, I'm twenty years old.

MAMA: What time you be home from school today?

BENEATHA: Kind of late. [*with enthusiasm*] Madeline is going to start my guitar lessons today. [MAMA *and* RUTH *look up with the same expression.*]

MAMA: Your *what* kind of lessons?

BENEATHA: Guitar.

RUTH: Oh, Father!

MAMA: How come you done taken it in your mind to learn to play the guitar?

BENEATHA: I just want to, that's all.

MAMA [*smiling*]: Lord, child, don't you know what to do with yourself? How long it going to be before you get tired of this now—like you got tired of that little play-acting group you joined last year? [*looking at* RUTH] And what was it the year before that?

RUTH: The horseback-riding club for which she bought that fifty-five-dollar riding habit that's been hanging in the closet ever since!

MAMA [*to* BENEATHA]: Why you got to flit so from one thing to another, baby?

BENEATHA [*sharply*]: I just want to learn to play the guitar. Is there anything wrong with that?

MAMA: Ain't nobody trying to stop you. I just wonders sometimes why you has to flit so from one thing to another all the time. You ain't never done nothing with all that camera equipment you brought home—

BENEATHA: I don't flit! I—I experiment with different forms of expression—

RUTH: Like riding a horse?

BENEATHA: —People have to express themselves one way or another.

MAMA: What is it you want to express?

BENEATHA [*angrily*]: Me! [MAMA *and* RUTH *look at each other and burst into raucous laughter*] Don't worry—I don't expect you to understand.

MAMA [*to change the subject*]: Who you going out with tomorrow night?

BENEATHA [*with displeasure*]: George Murchison again.

MAMA [*pleased*]: Oh—you getting a little sweet on him?

RUTH: You ask me, this child ain't sweet on nobody but herself—[*under breath*] Express herself! [*They laugh.*]

BENEATHA: Oh—I like George all right, Mama. I mean I like him enough to go out with him and stuff, but—

RUTH [*for devilment*]: What does and stuff mean?

BENEATHA: Mind your own business.

MAMA: Stop picking at her now, Ruth. [*a thoughtful pause, and then a suspicious sudden look at her daughter as she turns in her chair for emphasis*] What does it mean?

BENEATHA [*wearily*]: Oh, I just mean I couldn't ever really be serious about George. He's—he's so shallow.

RUTH: Shallow—what do you mean he's shallow? He's *Rich!*

MAMA: Hush, Ruth.

BENEATHA: I know he's rich. He knows he's rich, too.

RUTH: Well—what other qualities a man got to have to satisfy you, little girl?

BENEATHA: You wouldn't even begin to understand. Anybody who married Walter could not possibly understand.

MAMA [*outraged*]: What kind of way is that to talk about your brother?

BENEATHA: Brother is a flip—let's face it.

MAMA [*to* RUTH, *helplessly*]: What's a flip?

RUTH [*glad to add kindling*]: She's saying he's crazy.

BENEATHA: Not crazy. Brother isn't really crazy yet—he—he's an elaborate neurotic.

MAMA: Hush your mouth!

BENEATHA: As for George. Well. George looks good—he's got a beautiful car and he takes me to nice places and, as my sister-in-law says, he is probably the richest boy I will ever get to know and I even like him sometimes—but if the Youngers are sitting around waiting to see if their little Bennie is going to tie up the family with the Murchisons, they are wasting their time.

RUTH: You mean you wouldn't marry George Murchison if he asked you someday? That pretty, rich thing? Honey, I knew you was odd—

BENEATHA: No I would not marry him if all I felt for him was what I feel now. Besides, George's family wouldn't really like it.

MAMA: Why not?

BENEATHA: Oh, Mama—The Murchisons are honest-to-God-real-*live*-rich colored people, and the only people in the world who are more snobbish than rich white people are rich colored people. I thought everybody knew that. I've met Mrs. Murchison. She's a scene!

MAMA: You must not dislike people 'cause they well off, honey.

BENEATHA: Why not? It makes just as much sense as disliking people 'cause they are poor, and lots of people do that.

RUTH [*a wisdom-of-the-ages manner; to* MAMA]: Well, she'll get over some of this—

BENEATHA: Get over it? What are you talking about, Ruth? Listen, I'm going to be a doctor. I'm not worried about who I'm going to marry yet—if I ever get married.

MAMA AND RUTH: *If!*

MAMA: Now, Bennie—

BENEATHA: Oh, I probably will . . . but first I'm going to be a doctor, and George, for one, still thinks that's pretty funny. I couldn't be bothered with that. I am going to be a doctor and everybody around here better understand that!

MAMA [*kindly*]: 'Course you going to be a doctor, honey, God willing.

BENEATHA [*drily*]: God hasn't got a thing to do with it.

MAMA: Beneatha—that just wasn't necessary.

BENEATHA: Well—neither is God. I get sick of hearing about God.

MAMA: Beneatha!

BENEATHA: I mean it! I'm just tired of hearing about God all the time. What has He got to do with anything? Does he pay tuition?

MAMA: You 'bout to get your fresh little jaw slapped!

RUTH: That's just what she needs, all right!

BENEATHA: Why? Why can't I say what I want to around here, like everybody else?

MAMA: It don't sound nice for a young girl to say things like that—you wasn't brought up that way. Me and your father went to trouble to get you and Brother to church every Sunday.

BENEATHA: Mama, you don't understand. It's all a matter of ideas, and God is just one idea I don't accept. It's not important. I am not going out and be immoral or commit crimes because I don't believe in God. I don't even think about it. It's just that I get tired of Him getting credit for all the things the human race achieves through its own stubborn effort. There simply is no blasted God—there is only man and it is he who makes miracles! [MAMA *absorbs this speech, studies her daughter and rises slowly and crosses to* BENEATHA *and slaps her powerfully across the face. After, there is only silence and the daughter drops her eyes from her mother's face, and* MAMA *is very tall before her.*]

MAMA: Now—you say after me, in my mother's house there is still God. [*There is a long pause and* BENEATHA *stares at the floor wordlessly.* MAMA *repeats the phrase with precision and cool emotion.*] In my mother's house there is still God.

BENEATHA: In my mother's house there is still God [*a long pause*].

MAMA [*walking away from* BENEATHA, *too disturbed for triumphant posture; stopping and turning back to her daughter*]: There are some ideas we ain't going to have in this house. Not long as I am at the head of this family.

BENEATHA: Yes, ma'am. [MAMA *walks out of the room.*]

RUTH [*almost gently, with profound understanding*]: You think you a woman, Bennie—but you still a little girl. What you did was childish—so you got treated like a child.

BENEATHA: I see. [*quietly*] I also see that everybody thinks it's all right for Mama to be a tyrant. But all the tyranny in the world will never put a God in the heavens! [*She picks up her books and goes out.*]

RUTH [*goes to* MAMA's *door*]: She said she was sorry.

MAMA [*coming out, going to her plant*]: They frightens me, Ruth. My children.

RUTH: You got good children, Lena. They just a little off sometimes—but they're good.

MAMA: No—There's something come down between me and them that don't let us understand each other and I don't know what it is. One done almost lost his mind thinking 'bout money all the time and the other done commence to talk about things I can't seem to understand in no form or fashion. What is it that's changing, Ruth?

RUTH [*soothingly, older than her years*]: Now . . . you taking it all too seriously. You just got strong-willed children and it takes a strong woman like you to keep 'em in hand.

MAMA [*looking at her plant and sprinkling a little water on it*]: They spirited all right, my children. Got to admit they got spirit—Bennie and Walter. Like this little old plant that ain't never had enough sunshine or nothing—and look at it . . . [*She has her back to* RUTH, *who has had to stop ironing and lean against something and put the back of her hand to her forehead.*]

RUTH [*trying to keep* MAMA *from noticing*]: You . . . sure . . . loves that little old thing, don't you? . . .

MAMA: Well, I always wanted me a garden like I used to see sometimes at the back of the houses down home. This plant is close as I ever got to having one. [*She looks out of the window as she replaces the plant.*] Lord, ain't nothing as dreary as the view from this window on a dreary day, is there? Why ain't you singing this morning, Ruth? Sing that "No Ways Tired." That song always lifts me up so—[*She turns at last to see that* RUTH *has slipped quietly into a chair, in a state of semiconsciousness.*] Ruth! Ruth honey—what's the matter with you . . . Ruth!

CURTAIN

Scene 2

It is the following morning; a Saturday morning, and house cleaning is in progress at the Youngers. Furniture has been shoved hither and yon and MAMA *is giving the kitchen-area walls a washing down.* BENEATHA, *in dungarees, with a handkerchief tied around her face, is spraying insecticide into the cracks in the walls. As they work, the radio is on and a South Side disk jockey program is inappropriately filling the house with a rather exotic saxophone blues.* TRAVIS, *the sole idle one, is leaning on his arms, looking out of the window.*

TRAVIS: Grandmama, that stuff Bennie is using smells awful. Can I go downstairs, please?

MAMA: Did you get all them chores done already? I ain't seen you doing much.

TRAVIS: Yes'm—finished early. Where did Mama go this morning?

MAMA [*looking at* BENEATHA]: She had to go on a little errand.

TRAVIS: Where?

MAMA: To tend to her business.

TRAVIS: Can I go outside then?

MAMA: Oh, I guess so. You better stay right in front of the house, though . . . and keep a good lookout for the postman.

TRAVIS: Yes'm. [*He starts out and decides to give his* AUNT BENEATHA *a good swat on the legs as he passes her.*] Leave them poor little old cockroaches alone, they ain't bothering you none. [*He runs as she swings the spray gun at him both viciously and playfully.* WALTER *enters from the bedroom and goes to the phone.*]

MAMA: Look out there, girl, before you be spilling some of that stuff on that child!

TRAVIS [*teasing*]: That's right—look out now! [*He exits.*]

BENEATHA [*drily*]: I can't imagine that it would hurt him—it has never hurt the roaches.

MAMA: Well, little boys' hides ain't as tough as South Side roaches.

WALTER [*into phone*]: Hello—Let me talk to Willy Harris.

MAMA: You better get over there behind the bureau. I seen one marching out of there like Napoleon yesterday.

WALTER: Hello, Willy? It ain't come yet. It'll be here in a few minutes. Did the lawyer give you the papers?

BENEATHA: There's really only one way to get rid of them, Mama—

MAMA: How?

BENEATHA: Set fire to this building.

WALTER: Good. Good. I'll be right over.

BENEATHA: Where did Ruth go, Walter?

WALTER: I don't know. [*He exits abruptly.*]

BENEATHA: Mama, where did Ruth go?

MAMA [*looking at her with meaning*]: To the doctor, I think.

BENEATHA: The doctor? What's the matter? [*They exchange glances.*] You don't think—

MAMA [*with her sense of drama*]: Now I ain't saying what I think. But I ain't never been wrong 'bout a woman neither. [*The phone rings.*]

BENEATHA [*at the phone*]: Hay-lo . . . [*pause, and a moment of recognition*] Well— when did you get back! . . . And how was it? . . . Of course I've missed you—in my way . . . This morning? No . . . house cleaning and all that and Mama hates it if I let people come over when the house is like this . . . You *have?* Well, that's different . . . What is it—Oh, what the hell, come on over . . . Right, see you then. [*She hangs up.*]

MAMA [*who has listened vigorously, as is her habit*]: Who is that you inviting over here with this house looking like this? You ain't got the pride you was born with!

BENEATHA: Asagai doesn't care how houses look, Mama—he's an intellectual.

MAMA: *Who?*

BENEATHA: Asagai—Joseph Asagai. He's an African boy I met on campus. He's been studying in Canada all summer.

MAMA: What's his name?

BENEATHA: Asagai, Joseph. Ah-sah-guy . . . He's from Nigeria.

MAMA: Oh, that's the little country that was founded by slaves way back . . .

BENEATHA: No, Mama—that's Liberia.

MAMA: I don't think I never met no African before.

BENEATHA: Well, do me a favor and don't ask him a whole lot of ignorant questions about Africans. I mean, do they wear clothes and all that—

MAMA: Well, now, I guess if you think we so ignorant 'round here maybe you shouldn't bring your friends here—

BENEATHA: It's just that people ask such crazy things. All anyone seems to know about when it comes to Africa is Tarzan—

MAMA [*indignantly*]: Why should I know anything about Africa?

BENEATHA: Why do you give money at church for the missionary work?

MAMA: Well, that's to help save people.

BENEATHA: You mean save them from *heathenism*—

MAMA [*innocently*]: Yes.

BENEATHA: I'm afraid they need more salvation from the British and the French. [RUTH *comes in forlornly and pulls off her coat with dejection. They both turn to look at her.*]

RUTH [*dispiritedly*]: Well, I guess from all the happy faces—everybody knows.

BENEATHA: You pregnant?

MAMA: Lord have mercy, I sure hope it's a little old girl. Travis ought to have a sister [BENEATHA *and* RUTH *give her a hopeless look for this grandmotherly enthusiasm*].

BENEATHA: How far along are you?

RUTH: Two months.

BENEATHA: Did you mean to? I mean did you plan it or was it an accident?

MAMA: What do you know about planning or not planning?

BENEATHA: Oh, Mama.

RUTH [*wearily*]: She's twenty years old, Lena.

BENEATHA: Did you plan it, Ruth?

RUTH: Mind your own business.

BENEATHA: It is my business—where is he going to live, on the roof? [*There is silence following the remark as the three women react to the sense of it.*] Gee—I didn't mean that, Ruth, honest. Gee, I don't feel like that at all. I—I think it is wonderful.

RUTH [*dully*]: Wonderful.

BENEATHA: Yes—really.

MAMA [*looking at* RUTH, *worried*]: Doctor say everything going to be all right?

RUTH [*far away*]: Yes—she says everything is going to be fine . . .

MAMA [*immediately suspicious*]: "She"—What doctor you went to? [RUTH *folds over, near hysteria.*]

MAMA [*worriedly hovering over* RUTH]: Ruth, honey—what's the matter with you— you sick? [RUTH *has her fists clenched on her thighs and is fighting hard to suppress a scream that seems to be rising in her.*]

BENEATHA: What's the matter with her, Mama?

MAMA [*working her fingers in* RUTH's *shoulder to relax her*]: She be all right. Women gets right depressed sometimes when they get her way. [*speaking softly, expertly, rapidly*] Now you just relax. That's right . . . just lean back, don't think 'bout nothing at all . . . nothing at all—

RUTH: I'm all right . . . [*The glassy-eyed look melts and then she collapses into a fit of heavy sobbing. The bell rings.*]

BENEATHA: Oh, my God—that must be Asagai.

MAMA [*to* RUTH]: Come on now, honey. You need to lie down and rest awhile . . . then have some nice hot food. [*They exit,* RUTH's *weight on her mother-in-law.* BENEATHA, *herself profoundly disturbed, opens the door to admit a rather dramatic-looking young man with a large package.*]

ASAGAI: Hello, Alaiyo—

BENEATHA [*holding the door open and regarding him with pleasure*]: Hello . . . [*long pause*] Well—come in. And please excuse everything. My mother was very upset about my letting anyone come here with the place like this.

ASAGAI [*coming into the room*]: You look disturbed too . . . Is something wrong?

BENEATHA [*still at the door, absently*]: Yes . . . we've all got acute ghetto-itis. [*She smiles and comes toward him, finding a cigarette and sitting.*] So—sit down! How was Canada?

ASAGAI [*a sophisticate*]: Canadian.

BENEATHA [*looking at him*]: I'm very glad you are back.

ASAGAI [*looking back at her in turn*]: Are you really?

BENEATHA: Yes—very.

ASAGAI: Why—you were quite glad when I went away. What happened?

BENEATHA: You went away.

ASAGAI: Ahhhhhhhh.

BENEATHA: Before—you wanted to be so serious before there was time.

ASAGAI: How much time must there be before one knows what one feels?

BENEATHA [*stalling this particular conversation; her hands pressed together, in a deliberately childish gesture*]: What did you bring me?

ASAGAI [*handing her the package*]: Open it and see.

BENEATHA [*eagerly opening the package and drawing out some records and the colorful robes of a Nigerian woman*]: Oh, Asagai! . . . You got them for me! . . . How beautiful . . . and the records too! [*She lifts out the robes and runs to the mirror with them and holds the drapery up in front of herself.*]

ASAGAI [*coming to her at the mirror*]: I shall have to teach you how to drape it properly. [*He flings the material about her for the moment and stands back to look at her.*] Ah—Oh-pay-gay-day, oh-gbah-mu-shay. [*a Yoruba exclamation for admiration*] You wear it well . . . very well . . . mutilated hair and all.

BENEATHA [*turning suddenly*]: My hair—what's wrong with my hair?

ASAGAI [*shrugging*]: Were you born with it like that?

BENEATHA [*reaching up to touch it*]: No . . . of course not. [*She looks back to the mirror, disturbed.*]

ASAGAI [*smiling*]: How then?

BENEATHA: You know perfectly well how . . . as crinkly as yours . . . that's how.

ASAGAI: And it is ugly to you that way?

BENEATHA [*quickly*]: Oh, no—not ugly . . . [*more slowly, apologetically*] But it's so hard to manage when it's, well—raw.

ASAGAI: And so to accommodate that—you mutilate it every week?

BENEATHA: It's not mutilation!

ASAGAI [*laughing aloud at her seriousness*]: Oh . . . please! I am only teasing you because you are so very serious about these things. [*He stands back from her and folds his arms across his chest as he watches her pulling at her hair and frowning in the mirror.*] Do you remember the first time you met me at school? . . . [*He laughs.*] You came up to me and said—and I thought you were the most serious little thing I had ever seen—you said: [*He imitates her.*] "Mr. Asagai—I want very much to talk with you. About Africa. You see, Mr. Asagai, I am looking for my *identity!*" [*He laughs.*]

BENEATHA [*turning to him, not laughing*]: Yes—[*Her face is quizzical, profoundly disturbed.*]

ASAGAI [*still teasing and reaching out and taking her face in his hands and turning her profile to him*]: Well . . . it is true that this is not so much a profile of a Hollywood queen as perhaps a queen of the Nile—[*a mock dismissal of the importance of the question*] But what does it matter? Assimilationism is so popular in your country.

BENEATHA [*wheeling, passionately, sharply*]: I am not an assimilationist!

ASAGAI [*the protest hangs in the room for a moment and* ASAGAI *studies her, his laughter fading*]: Such a serious one. [*There is a pause.*] So—you like the robes? You must take excellent care of them—they are from my sister's personal wardrobe.

BENEATHA [*with incredulity*]: You—you sent all the way home—for me?

ASAGAI [*with charm*]: For you—I would do much more . . . Well, that is what I came for. I must go.

BENEATHA: Will you call me Monday?

ASAGAI: Yes . . . We have a great deal to talk about. I mean about identity and time and all that.

BENEATHA: Time?

ASAGAI: Yes. About how much time one needs to know what one feels.

BENEATHA: You never understood that there is more than one kind of feeling which can exist between a man and a woman—or, at least, there should be.

ASAGAI [*shaking his head negatively but gently*]: No. Between a man and a woman there need be only one kind of feeling. I have that for you . . . Now even . . . right this moment . . .

BENEATHA: I know—and by itself—it won't do. I can find that anywhere.

ASAGAI: For a woman it should be enough.

BENEATHA: I know—because that's what it says in all the novels that men write. But it isn't. Go ahead and laugh—but I'm not interested in being someone's little episode in America or—[*with feminine vengeance*]—one of them! [ASAGAI *has burst into laughter again.*] That's funny as hell, huh!

ASAGAI: It's just that every American girl I have known has said that to me. White— black—in this you are all the same. And the same speech, too!

BENEATHA [*angrily*]: Yuk, yuk, yuk!

ASAGAI: It's how you can be sure that the world's most liberated women are not liberated at all. You all talk about it too much! [MAMA *enters and is immediately all social charm because of the presence of a guest.*]

BENEATHA: Oh—Mama—this is Mr. Asagai.

MAMA: How do you do?

ASAGAI [*total politeness to an elder*]: How do you do, Mrs. Younger. Please forgive me for coming at such an outrageous hour on a Saturday.

MAMA: Well, you are quite welcome. I just hope you understand that our house don't always look like this. [*chatterish*] You must come again. I would love to hear all about—[*not sure of the name*]—your country. I think it's so sad the way our American Negroes don't know nothing about Africa 'cept Tarzan and all that. And all that money they pour into these churches when they ought to be helping you people over there drive out them French and Englishmen done taken away your land. [*The mother flashes a slightly superior look at her daughter upon completion of the recitation.*]

ASAGAI [*taken aback by this sudden and acutely unrelated expression of sympathy*]: Yes . . . yes . . .

MAMA [*smiling at him suddenly and relaxing and looking him over*]: How many miles is it from here to where you come from?

ASAGAI: Many thousands.

MAMA [*looking at him as she would* WALTER]: I bet you don't half look after yourself, being away from your mama either. I spec you better come 'round here from time to time and get yourself some decent home-cooked meals . . .

ASAGAI [*moved*]: Thank you. Thank you very much. [*They are all quiet, then—*] Well . . . I must go. I will call you Monday, Alaiyo.

MAMA: What's that he call you?

ASAGAI: Oh—"Alaiyo." I hope you don't mind. It is what you would call a nickname, I think. It is a Yoruba word. I am a Yoruba.

MAMA [*looking at* BENEATHA]: I—I thought he was from—

ASAGAI [*understanding*]: Nigeria is my country. Yoruba is my tribal origin—

BENEATHA: You didn't tell us what Alaiyo means . . . for all I know, you might be calling me Little Idiot or something . . .

ASAGAI: Well . . . let me see . . . I do not know how just to explain it . . . The sense of a thing can be so different when it changes languages.

BENEATHA: You're evading.

ASAGAI: No—really it is difficult . . . [*thinking*] It means . . . it means One for Whom Bread—Food—Is Not Enough. [*He looks at her.*] Is that all right?

BENEATHA [*understanding, softly*]: Thank you.

MAMA [*looking from one to the other and not understanding any of it*]: Well . . . that's nice . . . You must come see us again—Mr.—

ASAGAI: Ah-sah-guy . . .

MAMA: Yes . . . Do come again.

ASAGAI: Good-bye. [*He exits.*]

MAMA [*after him*]: Lord, that's a pretty thing just went out here! [*insinuatingly, to her daughter*] Yes, I guess I see why we done commence to get so interested in Africa 'round here. Missionaries my aunt Jenny! [*She exits.*]

BENEATHA: Oh, Mama! . . . [*She picks up the Nigerian dress and holds it up to her in front of the mirror again. She sets the headdress on haphazardly and then notices her hair again and clutches at it and then replaces the headdress and frowns at herself. Then she starts to wriggle in front of the mirror as she thinks a Nigerian woman might.* TRAVIS *enters and regards her.*]

TRAVIS: You cracking up?

BENEATHA: Shut up. [*She pulls the headdress off and looks at herself in the mirror and clutches at her hair again and squinches her eyes as if trying to imagine something. Then, suddenly, she gets her raincoat and kerchief and hurriedly prepares for going out.*]

MAMA [*coming back into the room*]: She's resting now. Travis, baby, run next door and ask Miss Johnson to please let me have a little kitchen cleanser. This here can is empty as Jacob's kettle.

TRAVIS: I just came in.

MAMA: Do as you told. [*He exits and she looks at her daughter.*] Where you going?

BENEATHA [*halting at the door*]: To become a queen of the Nile! [*She exits in a breathless blaze of glory.* RUTH *appears in the bedroom doorway.*]

MAMA: Who told you to get up?

RUTH: Ain't nothing wrong with me to be lying in no bed for. Where did Bennie go?

MAMA [*drumming her fingers*]: Far as I could make out—to Egypt. [RUTH *just looks at her.*] What time is it getting to?

RUTH: Ten twenty. And the mailman going to ring that bell this morning just like he done every morning for the last umpteen years. [TRAVIS *comes in with the cleanser can.*]

TRAVIS: She say to tell you that she don't have much.

MAMA [*angrily*]: Lord, some people I could name sure is tight-fisted! [*directing her grandson*] Mark two cans of cleanser down on the list there. If she that hard up for kitchen cleanser, I sure don't want to forget to get her none!

RUTH: Lena—maybe the woman is just short on cleanser—

MAMA [*not listening*]: —Much baking powder as she done borrowed from me all these years, she could of done gone into the baking business! [*The bell sounds suddenly and sharply and all three are stunned—serious and silent—mid-speech. In spite of all the other conversation and distractions of the morning, this is what they have been waiting for, even* TRAVIS, *who looks helplessly from his mother to his grandmother.* RUTH *is the first to come to life again.*]

RUTH [*to* TRAVIS]: Get down them steps, boy! [TRAVIS *snaps to life and flies out to get the mail.*]

MAMA [*her eyes wide, her hand to her breast*]: You mean it done really come?

RUTH [*excited*]: Oh, Miss Lena!

MAMA [*collecting herself*]: Well . . . I don't know what we all so excited about 'round here for. We known it was coming for months.

RUTH: That's a whole lot different from having it come and being able to hold it in your hands . . . a piece of paper worth ten thousand dollars . . . [TRAVIS *bursts back into the room. He holds the envelope high above his head, like a little dancer, his face is radiant and he is breathless. He moves to his grandmother with sudden slow ceremony and puts the envelope into her hands. She accepts it, and then merely holds it and looks at it.*] Come on! Open it . . . Lord have mercy, I wish Walter Lee was here!

TRAVIS: Open it, Grandmama!

MAMA [*staring at it*]: Now you all be quiet. It's just a check.

RUTH: Open it . . .

MAMA [*still staring at it*]: Now don't act silly . . . We ain't never been no people to act silly 'bout no money—

RUTH [*swiftly*]: We ain't never had none before—*open it!* [MAMA *finally makes a good strong tear and pulls out the thin blue slice of paper and inspects it closely. The boy and his mother study it raptly over* MAMA*'s shoulders.*]

MAMA: Travis! [*She is counting off with doubt.*] Is that the right number of zeros?

TRAVIS: Yes'm . . . ten thousand dollars. Gaalee, Grandmama, you rich.

MAMA [*She holds the check away from her, still looking at it. Slowly her face sobers into a mask of unhappiness.*]: Ten thousand dollars. [*She hands it to* RUTH.] Put it away somewhere, Ruth. [*She does not look at* RUTH; *her eyes seem to be seeing something somewhere very far off.*] Ten thousand dollars they give you. Ten thousand dollars.

TRAVIS [*to his mother, sincerely*]: What's the matter with Grandmama—don't she want to be rich?

RUTH [*distractedly*]: You go on out and play now, baby. [TRAVIS *exits.* MAMA *starts wiping dishes absently, humming intently to herself.* RUTH *turns to her, with kind exasperation.*] You've gone and got yourself upset.

MAMA [*not looking at her*]: I spec if it wasn't for you all . . . I would just put that money away or give it to the church or something.

RUTH: Now what kind of talk is that. Mr. Younger would just be plain mad if he could hear you talking foolish like that.

MAMA [*stopping and staring off*]: Yes . . . he sure would. [*sighing*] We got enough to do with that money, all right. [*She halts then, and turns and looks at her daughter-in-law hard;* RUTH *avoids her eyes and* MAMA *wipes her hands with finality and starts to speak firmly to* RUTH.] Where did you go today, girl?

RUTH: To the doctor.

MAMA [*impatiently*]: Now, Ruth . . . you know better than that. Old Doctor Jones is strange enough in his way but there ain't nothing 'bout him make somebody slip and call him "she"—like you done this morning.

RUTH: Well, that's what happened—my tongue slipped.

MAMA: You went to see that woman, didn't you?

RUTH [*defensively, giving herself away*]: What woman you talking about?

MAMA [*angrily*]: That woman who—[WALTER *enters in great excitement.*]

WALTER: Did it come?

MAMA [*quietly*]: Can't you give people a Christian greeting before you start asking about money?

WALTER [*to* RUTH]: Did it come? [RUTH *unfolds the check and lays it quietly before him, watching him intently with thoughts of her own.* WALTER *sits down and grasps it close and counts off the zeros.*] Ten thousand dollars—[*He turns suddenly, frantically to his mother and draws some papers out of his breast pocket.*] Mama—look. Old Willy Harris put everything on paper—

MAMA: Son—I think you ought to talk to your wife . . . I'll go on out and leave you alone if you want—

WALTER: I can talk to her later—Mama, look—

MAMA: Son—

WALTER: WILL SOMEBODY PLEASE LISTEN TO ME TODAY!

MAMA [*quietly*]: I don't 'low no yellin' in this house, Walter Lee, and you know it—[WALTER *stares at them in frustration and starts to speak several times.*] And there ain't going to be no investing in no liquor stores. I don't aim to have to speak on that again [*a long pause*].

WALTER: Oh—so you don't aim to have to speak on that again? So you have decided . . . [*crumpling his papers*] Well, *you* tell that to my boy tonight when you put him to sleep on the living-room couch . . . [*turning to* MAMA *and speaking directly to her*]: Yeah—and tell it to my wife, Mama, tomorrow when she has to go out of here to look after somebody else's kids. And tell it to *me,* Mama, every time we need a new pair of curtains and I have to watch *you* go out and work in somebody's kitchen. Yeah, you tell me then! [WALTER *starts out.*]

RUTH: Where you going?

WALTER: I'm going out!

RUTH: Where?

WALTER: Just out of this house somewhere—

RUTH [*getting her coat*]: I'll come too.

WALTER: I don't want you to come!

RUTH: I got something to talk to you about, Walter.

WALTER: That's too bad.

MAMA [*still quietly*]: Walter Lee—[*She waits and he finally turns and looks at her.*] Sit down.

WALTER: I'm a grown man, Mama.

MAMA: Ain't nobody said you wasn't grown. But you still in my house and my presence. And as long as you are—you'll talk to your wife civil. Now sit down.

RUTH [*suddenly*]: Oh, let him go on out and drink himself to death! He makes me sick to my stomach! [*She flings her coat against him.*]

WALTER [*violently*]: And you turn mine, too, baby! [RUTH *goes into their bedroom and slams the door behind her.*] That was my greatest mistake—

MAMA [*still quietly*]: Walter, what is the matter with you?

WALTER: Matter with me? Ain't nothing the matter with *me!*

MAMA: Yes there is. Something eating you up like a crazy man. Something more than me not giving you this money. The past few years I been watching it happen to you. You get all nervous acting and kind of wild in the eyes—[WALTER *jumps up impatiently at her words.*] I said sit there now, I'm talking to you!

WALTER: Mama—I don't need no nagging at me today.

MAMA: Seem like you getting to a place where you always tied up in some kind of knot about something. But if anybody ask you 'bout it you just yell at 'em and bust out the house and go out and drink somewheres. Walter Lee, people can't live with that. Ruth's a good, patient girl in her way—but you getting to be too much. Boy, don't make the mistake of driving that girl away from you.

WALTER: Why—what she do for me?

MAMA: She loves you.

WALTER: Mama—I'm going out. I want to go off somewhere and be by myself for a while.

MAMA: I'm sorry 'bout your liquor store, son. It just wasn't the thing for us to do. That's what I want to tell you about—

WALTER: I got to go out, Mama—[*He rises.*]

MAMA: It's dangerous, son.

WALTER: What's dangerous?

MAMA: When a man goes outside his home to look for peace.

WALTER [*beseechingly*]: Then why can't there never be no peace in this house then?

MAMA: You done found it in some other house?

WALTER: No—there ain't no woman! Why do women always think there's a woman somewhere when a man gets restless. [*coming to her*] Mama—Mama—I want so many things . . .

MAMA: Yes, son—

WALTER: I want so many things that they are driving me kind of crazy . . . Mama—look at me.

MAMA: I'm looking at you. You a good-looking boy. You got a job, a nice wife, a fine boy and—

WALTER: A job. [*looks at her*] Mama, a job? I open and close car doors all day long. I drive a man around in his limousine and I say, "Yes, sir; no, sir; very good, sir; shall I take the Drive, sir?" Mama, that ain't no kind of job . . . that ain't nothing at all. [*very quietly*] Mama, I don't know if I can make you understand.

MAMA: Understand what, baby?

WALTER [*quietly*]: Sometimes it's like I can see the future stretched out in front of me—just plain as day. The future, Mama. Hanging over there at the edge of my days. Just waiting for me—a big, looming blank space—full of *nothing*. Just waiting for *me*. [*pause*] Mama—sometimes when I'm downtown and I pass them cool, quiet-looking restaurants where them white boys are sitting back and talking 'bout things . . . sitting there turning deals worth millions of dollars . . . sometimes I see guys don't look much older than me—

MAMA: Son—how come you talk so much 'bout money?

WALTER [*with immense passion*]: Because it is life, Mama!

MAMA [*quietly*]: Oh—[*very quietly*] So now it's life. Money is life. Once upon a time freedom used to be life—now it's money. I guess the world really do change . . .

WALTER: No—it was always money, Mama. We just didn't know about it.

MAMA: No . . . something has changed. [*She looks at him.*] You something new, boy. In my time we was worried about not being lynched and getting to the North if we could and how to stay alive and still have a pinch of dignity too . . . Now here come you and Beneatha—talking 'bout things we ain't never even thought about hardly, me and your daddy. You ain't satisfied or proud of nothing we done. I mean that you had a home; that we kept you out of trouble till you was grown; that you don't have to ride to work on the back of nobody's streetcar—You my children—but how different we done become.

WALTER: You just don't understand, Mama, you just don't understand.

MAMA: Son—do you know your wife is expecting another baby? [WALTER *stands, stunned, and absorbs what his mother has said.*] That's what she wanted to talk to you about. [walter *sinks down into a chair.*] This ain't for me to be telling—but you ought to know. [*She waits*] I think Ruth is thinking 'bout getting rid of that child.

WALTER [*slowly understanding*]: No—no—Ruth wouldn't do that.

MAMA: When the world gets ugly enough—a woman will do anything for her family. *The part that's already living.*

WALTER: You don't know Ruth, Mama, if you think she would do that. [RUTH *opens the bedroom door and stands there a little limp.*]

RUTH [*beaten*]: Yes I would too, Walter, [*pause*] I gave her a five-dollar down payment. [*There is total silence as the man stares at his wife and the mother stares at her son.*]

MAMA [*presently*]: Well—[*tightly*] Well—son, I'm waiting to hear you say something . . . I'm waiting to hear how you be your father's son. Be the man he was . . . [*pause*] Your wife say she going to destroy your child. And I'm waiting to hear you talk like him and say we a people who give children life, not who destroys them—[*She rises.*] I'm waiting to see you stand up and look like your daddy and say we done give up one baby to poverty and that we ain't going to give up nary another one . . . I'm waiting.

WALTER: Ruth—

MAMA: If you a son of mine, tell her! [WALTER *turns, looks at her and can say nothing. She continues, bitterly.*] You . . . you are a disgrace to your father's memory. Somebody get me my hat.

CURTAIN

ACT II

Scene 1

TIME: *Later the same day.*

AT RISE: RUTH *is ironing again. She has the radio going. Presently* BENEATHA*'s bedroom door opens and* RUTH*'s mouth falls and she puts down the iron in fascination.*

RUTH: What have we got on tonight!

BENEATHA [*emerging grandly from the doorway so that we can see her thoroughly robed in the costume* ASAGAI *brought*]: You are looking at what a well-dressed Nigerian woman wears—[*She parades for* RUTH, *her hair completely hidden by the headdress; she is coquettishly fanning herself with an ornate oriental fan, mistakenly more like Butterfly than any Nigerian that ever was.*] Isn't it beautiful? [*She promenades to the radio and, with an arrogant flourish, turns off the good loud blues that is playing.*] Enough of this assimilationist junk! [RUTH *follows her with her eyes as she goes to the phonograph and puts on a record and turns and waits ceremoniously for the music to come up. Then with a shout—*] OCOMOGOSIAY! [RUTH *jumps. The music comes up, a lovely Nigerian melody.* BENEATHA *listens, enraptured, her eyes far away—"back to the past." She begins to dance.* RUTH *is dumbfounded.*]

RUTH: What kind of dance is that?

BENEATHA: A folk dance.

RUTH [*Pearl Bailey*]: What kind of folks do that, honey?

BENEATHA: It's from Nigeria. It's a dance of welcome.

RUTH: Who you welcoming?

BENEATHA: The men back to the village.

RUTH: Where they been?

BENEATHA: How should I know—out hunting or something. Anyway, they are coming back now . . .

RUTH: Well, that's good.

BENEATHA [*with the record*]: *Alundi, alundi*
    Alundi alunya
    Jop pu a jeepua
    Ang gu soooooooooo
    Ai yai yae . . .
    Ayehaye—alundi . . .

[WALTER *comes in during this performance; he has obviously been drinking. He leans
against the door heavily and watches his sister, at first with distaste. Then his eyes
look off—"back to the past"—as he lifts both his fists to the roof, screaming.*]

WALTER: YEAH . . . AND ETHIOPIA STRETCH FORTH HER HANDS AGAIN! . . .

RUTH [*drily, looking at him*]: Yes—and Africa sure is claiming her own tonight. [*She
gives them both up and starts ironing again.*]

WALTER [*all in a drunken, dramatic shout*]: Shut up! . . . I'm digging them drums . . .
them drums move me! . . . [*He makes his weaving way to his wife's face
and leans in close to her.*] In my heart of hearts—[*He thumps his chest.*]—
I am much warrior!

RUTH [*without even looking up*]: In your heart of hearts you are much drunkard.

WALTER [*coming away from her and starting to wander around the room, shouting*]:
Me and Jomo . . . [*Intently, in his sister's face. She has stopped dancing to
watch him in this unknown mood.*] That's my man, Kenyatta. [*Shouting
and thumping his chest.*] FLAMING SPEAR! HOT DAMN! [*He is suddenly in
possession of an imaginary spear and actively spearing enemies all over
the room.*] OCOMOGOSIAY . . . THE LION IS WAKING . . . OWIMOWEH! [*He pulls his
shirt open and leaps up on a table and gestures with his spear. The bell
rings.* RUTH *goes to answer.*]

BENEATHA [*to encourage* WALTER, *thoroughly caught up with this side of him*]:
OCOMOGOSIAY, FLAMING SPEAR!

WALTER [*On the table, very far gone, his eyes pure glass sheets. He sees what we cannot, that he is a leader of his people, a great chief, a descendant of Chaka,
and that the hour to march has come.*]: Listen, my black brothers—

BENEATHA: OCOMOGOSIAY!

WALTER: —Do you hear the waters rushing against the shores of the coast-lands—

BENEATHA: OCOMOGOSIAY!

WALTER: —Do you hear the screeching of the cocks in yonder hills beyond where
the chiefs meet in council for the coming of the mighty war—

BENEATHA: OCOMOGOSIAY!

WALTER: —Do you hear the beating of the wings of the birds flying low over the
mountains and the low places of our land—[RUTH *opens the door,* GEORGE
MURCHISON *enters.*]

BENEATHA: OCOMOGOSIAY!

WALTER: —Do you hear the singing of the women, singing the war songs of our fathers to the babies in the great houses . . . singing the sweet war songs? OH, DO YOU HEAR, MY BLACK BROTHERS?

BENEATHA [*completely gone*]: We hear you, Flaming Spear—

WALTER: Telling us to prepare for the greatness of the time—[*to* GEORGE] Black Brother! [*He extends his hand for the fraternal clasp.*]

GEORGE: Black Brother, hell!

RUTH [*having had enough, and embarrassed for the family*]: Beneatha, you got company—what's the matter with you? Walter Lee Younger, get down off that table and stop acting like a fool . . . [WALTER *comes down off the table suddenly and makes a quick exit to the bathroom.*]

RUTH: He's had a little to drink . . . I don't know what her excuse is.

GEORGE [*to* BENEATHA]: Look honey, we're going *to* the theatre—we're not going to be *in* it . . . so go change, huh?

RUTH: You expect this boy to go out with you looking like that?

BENEATHA [*looking at* GEORGE]: That's up to George. If he's ashamed of his heritage—

GEORGE: Oh, don't be so proud of yourself, Bennie—just because you look eccentric.

BENEATHA: How can something that's natural be eccentric?

GEORGE: That's what being eccentric means—being natural. Get dressed.

BENEATHA: I don't like that, George.

RUTH: Why must you and your brother make an argument out of everything people say?

BENEATHA: Because I hate assimilationist Negroes!

RUTH: Will somebody please tell me what assimila-who-ever means!

GEORGE: Oh, it's just a college girl's way of calling people Uncle Toms—but that isn't what it means at all.

RUTH: Well, what does it mean?

BENEATHA [*cutting* GEORGE *off and staring at him as she replies to* RUTH]: It means someone who is willing to give up his own culture and submerge himself completely in the dominant, and in this case, *oppressive* culture!

GEORGE: Oh, dear, dear, dear! Here we go! A lecture on the African past! On our Great West African Heritage! In one second we will hear all about the great Ashanti empires; the great Songhay civilizations; and the great sculpture of Benin—and then some poetry in the Bantu—and the whole monologue will end with the word *heritage!* [*nastily*] Let's face it, baby, your heritage is nothing but a bunch of raggedy-assed spirituals and some grass huts!

BENEATHA: *Grass huts!* [RUTH *crosses to her and forcibly pushes her toward the bedroom.*] See there . . . you are standing there in your splendid ignorance talking about people who were the first to smelt iron on the face of the earth! [RUTH *is pushing her through the door.*] The Ashanti were performing surgical operations when the English—[RUTH *pulls the door to, with* BENEATHA *on the other side, and smiles graciously at* GEORGE. BENEATHA *opens the door and shouts the end of the sentence defiantly at* GEORGE.]— were still tattooing themselves with blue dragons . . . [*She goes back inside.*]

RUTH: Have a seat, George. [*They both sit.* RUTH *folds her hands rather primly on her lap, determined to demonstrate the civilization of the family.*] Warm, ain't it? I mean for September. [*pause*] Just like they always say about Chicago weather: If it's too hot or cold for you, just wait a minute and it'll change. [*She smiles happily at this cliché of clichés.*] Everybody say it's got to do with them bombs and things they keep setting off. [*pause*] Would you like a nice cold beer?

GEORGE: No, thank you. I don't care for beer. [*He looks at his watch.*] I hope she hurries up.

RUTH: What time is the show?

GEORGE: It's an eight-thirty curtain. That's just Chicago, though. In New York standard curtain time is eight forty. [*He is rather proud of this knowledge.*]

RUTH [*properly appreciating it*]: You get to New York a lot?

GEORGE [*offhand*]: Few times a year.

RUTH: Oh—that's nice. I've never been to New York. [WALTER *enters. We feel he has relieved himself, but the edge of unreality is still with him.*]

WALTER: New York ain't got nothing Chicago ain't. Just a bunch of hustling people all squeezed up together—being "Eastern." [*He turns his face into a screw of displeasure.*]

GEORGE: Oh—you've been?

WALTER: Plenty of times.

RUTH [*shocked at the lie*]: Walter Lee Younger!

WALTER [*staring her down*]: Plenty! [*pause*] What we got to drink in this house? Why don't you offer this man some refreshment. [*to* GEORGE] They don't know how to entertain people in this house, man.

GEORGE: Thank you—I don't really care for anything.

WALTER [*feeling his head; sobriety coming*]: Where's Mama?

RUTH: She ain't come back yet.

WALTER [*looking* MURCHISON *over from head to toe, scrutinizing his carefully casual tweed sports jacket over cashmere V-neck sweater over soft eyelet shirt and tie, and soft slacks, finished off with white buckskin shoes*]: Why all you college boys wear them fairyish-looking white shoes?

RUTH: Walter Lee! [GEORGE MURCHISON *ignores the remark.*]

WALTER [*to* RUTH]: Well, they look crazy as hell—white shoes, cold as it is.

RUTH [*crushed*]: You have to excuse him—

WALTER: No he don't! Excuse me for what? What you always excusing me for! I'll excuse myself when I needs to be excused! [*a pause*] They look as funny as them black knee socks Beneatha wears out of here all the time.

RUTH: It's the college *style,* Walter.

WALTER: Style, hell. She looks like she got burnt legs or something!

RUTH: Oh, Walter—

WALTER [*an irritable mimic*]: Oh, Walter! Oh, Walter! [*to* MURCHISON] How's your old man making out? I understand you all going to buy that big hotel on the Drive?[1] [*He finds a beer in the refrigerator, wanders over to* MURCHISON, *sipping and wiping his lips with the back of his hand, and straddling a chair backwards to talk to the other man.*] Shrewd move. Your old man is all right, man. [*tapping his head and half winking for emphasis*] I mean he knows how to operate. I mean he thinks big, you know what I mean, I mean for a home,[2] you know? But I think he's kind of running out of ideas now. I'd like to talk to him. Listen, man, I got some plans that could turn this city upside down. I mean I think like he does. *Big.* Invest big, gamble big, hell, lose *big* if you have to, you know what I mean. It's hard to find a man on this whole Southside who understands my kind of thinking—

[1]**Drive** Chicago's Outer Drive running along Lake Michigan.   [2]**Home** home-boy; one of us.

you dig? [*He scrutinizes* MURCHISON *again, drinks his beer, squints his eyes and leans in close, confidential, man to man.*] Me and you ought to sit down and talk sometimes, man. Man, I got me some ideas . . .

MURCHISON [*with boredom*]: Yeah—sometimes we'll have to do that, Walter.

WALTER [*understanding the indifference, and offended*]: Yeah—well, when you get the time, man. I know you a busy little boy.

RUTH: Walter, please—

WALTER [*bitterly, hurt*]: I know ain't nothing in this world as busy as you colored college boys with your fraternity pins and white shoes . . .

RUTH [*covering her face with humiliation*]: Oh, Walter Lee—

WALTER: I see you all all the time—with the books tucked under your arms—going to your [*British A—a mimic*] "clahsses." And for what! What the hell you learning over there? Filling up your heads—[*counting off on his fingers*]— with the sociology and the psychology—but they teaching you how to be a man? How to take over and run the world? They teaching you how to run a rubber plantation or a steel mill? Naw—just to talk proper and read books and wear white shoes . . .

GEORGE [*looking at him with distaste, a little above it all*]: You're all wacked up with bitterness, man.

WALTER [*intently, almost quietly, between the teeth, glaring at the boy*]: And you— ain't you bitter, man? Ain't you just about had it yet? Don't you see no stars gleaming that you can't reach out and grab? You happy?—You contented son-of-a-bitch—you happy? You got it made? Bitter? Man, I'm a volcano. Bitter? Here I am a giant—surrounded by ants! Ants who can't even under- stand what it is the giant is talking about.

RUTH [*passionately and suddenly*]: Oh, Walter—ain't you with nobody!

WALTER [*violently*]: No! 'Cause ain't nobody with me! Not even my own mother!

RUTH: Walter, that's a terrible thing to say! [BENEATHA *enters, dressed for the evening in a cocktail dress and earrings.*]

GEORGE: Well—hey, you look great.

BENEATHA: Let's go, George. See you all later.

RUTH: Have a nice time.

GEORGE: Thanks. Good night. [*to* WALTER, *sarcastically*] Good night, *Prometheus*. [BENEATHA *and* GEORGE *exit.*]

WALTER [*to* RUTH]: Who is Prometheus?

RUTH: I don't know. Don't worry about it.

WALTER [*in fury, pointing after* GEORGE]: See there—they get to a point where they can't insult you man to man—they got to go talk about something ain't nobody never heard of!

RUTH: How do you know it was an insult? [*to humor him*] Maybe Prometheus is a nice fellow.

WALTER: Prometheus! I bet there ain't even no such thing! I bet that simple-minded clown—

RUTH: Walter—[*She stops what she is doing and looks at him.*]

WALTER [*yelling*]: Don't start!

RUTH: Start what?

WALTER: Your nagging! Where was I? Who was I with? How much money did I spend?

RUTH [*plaintively*]: Walter Lee—why don't we just try to talk about it . . .

WALTER [*not listening*]: I been out talking with people who understand me. People who care about the things I got on my mind.

RUTH [*wearily*]: I guess that means people like Willy Harris.

WALTER: Yes, people like Willy Harris.

RUTH [*with a sudden flash of impatience*]: Why don't you all just hurry up and go into the banking business and stop talking about it!

WALTER: Why? You want to know why? 'Cause we all tied up in a race of people that don't know how to do nothing but moan, pray and have babies! [*The line is too bitter even for him and he looks at her and sits down.*]

RUTH: Oh, Walter . . . [*softly*] Honey, why can't you stop fighting me?

WALTER [*without thinking*]: Who's fighting you? Who even cares about you? [*This line begins the retardation of his mood.*]

RUTH: Well—[*She waits a long time, and then with resignation starts to put away her things.*] I guess I might as well go on to bed . . . [*more or less to herself*] I don't know where we lost it . . . but we have . . . [*Then, to him.*] I—I'm sorry about this new baby, Walter. I guess maybe I better go on and do what I started . . . I guess I just didn't realize how bad things was with us . . . I guess I just didn't really realize—[*She starts out to the bedroom and stops.*] You want some hot milk?

WALTER: Hot milk?

RUTH: Yes—hot milk.

WALTER: Why hot milk?

RUTH: 'Cause after all that liquor you come home with you ought to have something hot in your stomach.

WALTER: I don't want no milk.

RUTH: You want some coffee then?

WALTER: No, I don't want no coffee. I don't want nothing hot to drink. [*almost plaintively*] Why you always trying to give me something to eat?

RUTH [*standing and looking at him helplessly*]: What else can I give you, Walter Lee Younger? [*She stands and looks at him and presently turns to go out again. He lifts his head and watches her going away from him in a new mood which began to emerge when he asked her, "Who cares about you?"*]

WALTER: It's been rough, ain't it, baby? [*She hears and stops but does not turn around and he continues to her back.*] I guess between two people there ain't never as much understood as folks generally thinks there is. I mean like between me and you—[*She turns to face him.*] How we gets to the place where we scared to talk softness to each other. [*He waits, thinking hard himself.*] Why you think it got to be like that? [*He is thoughtful, almost as a child would be.*] Ruth, what is it gets into people ought to be close?

RUTH: I don't know, honey. I think about it a lot.

WALTER: On account of you and me, you mean? The way things are with us. The way something done come down between us.

RUTH: There ain't so much between us, Walter . . . Not when you come to me and try to talk to me. Try to be with me . . . a little even.

WALTER [*total honesty*]: Sometimes . . . sometimes . . . I don't even know how to try.

RUTH: Walter—

WALTER: Yes?

RUTH [*coming to him, gently and with misgiving, but coming to him*]: Honey . . . life don't have to be like this. I mean sometimes people can do things so that things are better . . . You remember how we used to talk when Travis was born . . . about the way we were going to live . . . the kind of house . . . [*She is stroking his head.*] Well, it's all starting to slip away from us . . . [MAMA *enters, and* WALTER *jumps up and shouts at her.*]

WALTER: Mama, where have you been?

MAMA: My—them steps is longer than they used to be. Whew! [*She sits down and ignores him.*] How you feeling this evening, Ruth! [RUTH *shrugs, disturbed some at having been prematurely interrupted and watching her husband knowingly.*]

WALTER: Mama, where have you been all day?

MAMA [*still ignoring him and leaning on the table and changing to more comfortable shoes*]: Where's Travis?

RUTH: I let him go out earlier and he ain't come back yet. Boy, is he going to get it!

WALTER: Mama!

MAMA [*as if she has heard him for the first time*]: Yes, son?

WALTER: Where did you go this afternoon?

MAMA: I went downtown to tend to some business that I had to tend to.

WALTER: What kind of business?

MAMA: You know better than to question me like a child, Brother.

WALTER [*rising and bending over the table*]: Where were you, Mama? [*bringing his fists down and shouting*] Mama, you didn't go do something with that insurance money, something crazy? [*The front door opens slowly, interrupting him, and* TRAVIS *peeks his head in, less than hopefully.*]

TRAVIS [*to his mother*]: Mama, I—

RUTH: "Mama I" nothing! You're going to get it, boy! Get on in that bedroom and get yourself ready!

TRAVIS: But I—

MAMA: Why don't you all never let the child explain hisself.

RUTH: Keep out of it now, Lena. [MAMA *clamps her lips together, and* RUTH *advances toward her son menacingly.*]

RUTH: A thousand times I have told you not to go off like that—

MAMA [*holding out her arms to her grandson*]: Well—at least let me tell him something. I want him to be the first one to hear . . . Come here, Travis. [*the boy obeys, gladly*] Travis—[*She takes him by the shoulder and looks into his face.*]—you know that money we got in the mail this morning?

TRAVIS: Yes'm—

MAMA: Well—what you think your grandmama gone and done with that money?

TRAVIS: I don't know, Grandmama.

MAMA [*putting her finger on his nose for emphasis*]: She went out and she bought you a house! [*The explosion comes from* WALTER *at the end of the revelation and he jumps up and turns away from all of them in a fury.* MAMA *continues, to* TRAVIS.] You glad about the house? It's going to be yours when you get to be a man.

TRAVIS: Yeah—I always wanted to live in a house.

MAMA: All right, gimme some sugar then—[TRAVIS *puts his arms around her neck as she watches her son over the boy's shoulder. Then, to* TRAVIS, *after the embrace.*] Now when you say your prayers tonight, you thank God and your grandfather—'cause it was him who give you the house—in his way.

RUTH [*taking the boy from* MAMA *and pushing him toward the bedroom*]: Now you get out of here and get ready for your beating.

TRAVIS: Aw, Mama—

RUTH: Get on in there—[*closing the door behind him and turning radiantly to her mother-in-law*] So you went and did it!

MAMA [*quietly, looking at her son with pain*]: Yes, I did.

RUTH [*raising both arms classically*]: *Praise God!* [*Looks at* WALTER *a moment, who says nothing. She crosses rapidly to her husband.*] Please, honey—let me be glad . . . you be glad too. [*She has laid her hands on his shoulders, but he shakes himself free of her roughly, without turning to face her.*] Oh, Walter . . . a home . . . *a home.* [*She comes back to* MAMA.] Well—where is it? How big is it? How much it going to cost?

MAMA: Well—

RUTH: When we moving?

MAMA [*smiling at her*]: First of the month.

RUTH [*throwing back her head with jubilance*]: *Praise God!*

MAMA [*tentatively, still looking at her son's back turned against her and* RUTH]: It's—it's a nice house too . . . [*She cannot help speaking directly to him. An imploring quality in her voice, her manner, makes her almost like a girl now.*] Three bedrooms—nice big one for you and Ruth . . Me and Beneatha still have to share our room, but Travis have one of his own—and [*with difficulty*] I figure if the—new baby—is a boy, we could get one of them double-decker outfits . . . And there's a yard with a little patch of dirt where I could maybe get to grow me a few flowers . . . And a nice big basement . . .

RUTH: Walter honey, be glad—

MAMA [*still to his back, fingering things on the table*]: 'Course I don't want to make it sound fancier than it is . . . It's just a plain little old house—but it's made good and solid—and it will be *ours*. Walter Lee—it makes a difference in a man when he can walk on floors that belong to *him* . . .

RUTH: Where is it?

MAMA [*frightened at this telling*]: Well—well—it's out there in Clybourne Park— [RUTH's *radiance fades abruptly, and* WALTER *finally turns slowly to face his mother with incredulity and hostility.*]

RUTH: Where?

MAMA [*matter-of-factly*]: Four o six Clybourne Street, Clybourne Park.

RUTH: Clybourne Park? Mama, there ain't no colored people living in Clybourne Park.

MAMA [*almost idiotically*]: Well, I guess there's going to be some now.

WALTER [*bitterly*]: So that's the peace and comfort you went out and bought for us today!

MAMA [*raising her eyes to meet his finally*]: Son—I just tried to find the nicest place for the least amount of money for my family.

RUTH [*trying to recover from the shock*]: Well—well—'course I ain't one never been 'fraid of no crackers, mind you—but—well, wasn't there no other houses nowhere?

MAMA: Them houses they put up for colored in them areas way out all seem to cost twice as much as other houses. I did the best I could.

RUTH [*struck senseless with the news, in its various degrees of goodness and trouble, she sits a moment, her fists propping her chin in thought, and then she starts to rise, bringing her fists down with vigor, the radiance spreading from cheek to cheek again*]: Well—well!—All I can say is—if this is my time in life—my time—to say good-bye—[*And she builds with momentum as she starts to circle the room with an exuberant, almost tearfully happy release*]—to these Goddamned cracking walls!—[*she pounds the walls*]—and these marching roaches—[*she wipes at an imaginary army of marching roaches*]—and this cramped little closet which ain't now or never was no kitchen! . . . then I say it loud and good, *Hallelujah! and good-bye misery . . . I don't never want to see your ugly face again!* [*She laughs joyously, having practically destroyed the apartment, and flings her arms up and lets them come down happily, slowly, reflectively, over her abdomen, aware for the first time perhaps that the life therein pulses with happiness and not despair.*] Lena?

MAMA [*moved, watching her happiness*]: Yes, honey?

RUTH [*looking off*]: Is there—is there a whole lot of sunlight?

MAMA [*understanding*]: Yes, child, there's a whole lot of sunlight [*long pause*].

RUTH [*collecting herself and going to the door of the room* TRAVIS *is in*]: Well—I guess I better see 'bout Travis. [*to* MAMA] Lord, I sure don't feel like whipping nobody today! [*She exits.*]

MAMA [*the mother and son are left alone now and the mother waits a long time, considering deeply, before she speaks*]: Son—you—you understand what I done, don't you? [WALTER *is silent and sullen.*] I—I just seen my family falling apart today . . . just falling to pieces in front of my eyes . . . We couldn't of gone on like we was today. We was going backwards 'stead of forwards—talking 'bout killing babies and wishing each other was dead . . . When it gets like that in life—you just got to do something different, push on out and do something bigger . . . [*She waits.*] I wish you say something, son . . . I wish you'd say how deep inside you you think I done the right thing—

WALTER [*crossing slowly to his bedroom door and finally turning there and speaking measuredly*]: What you need me to say you done right for? You the head of this family. You run our lives like you want to. It was your money and you did what you wanted with it. So what you need for me to say it was all right for? [*bitterly, to hurt her as deeply as he knows is possible*] So you butchered up a dream of mine—you—who always talking 'bout your children's dreams . . .

MAMA: Walter Lee—[*He just closes the door behind him.* MAMA *sits alone, thinking heavily.*]

CURTAIN

Scene 2

TIME: *Friday night. A few weeks later.*

AT RISE: *Packing crates mark the intention of the family to move.* BENEATHA *and* GEORGE *come in, presumably from an evening out again.*

GEORGE: O.K. . . . O.K., whatever you say . . . [*They both sit on the couch. He tries to kiss her. She moves away.*] Look, we've had a nice evening; let's not spoil it, huh? . . . [*He again turns her head and tries to nuzzle in and she turns away from him, not with distaste but with momentary lack of interest; in a mood to pursue what they were talking about.*]

BENEATHA: I'm trying to talk to you.

GEORGE: We always talk.

BENEATHA: Yes—and I love to talk.

GEORGE [*exasperated; rising*]: I know it and I don't mind it sometimes . . . I want you to cut it out, see—The moody stuff, I mean. I don't like it. You're a nice-looking girl . . . all over. That's all you need, honey, forget the atmosphere. Guys aren't going to go for the atmosphere—they're going to go for what they see. Be glad for that. Drop the Garbo routine. It doesn't go with you. As for myself, I want a nice—[*groping*]—simple [*thoughtfully*]—sophisticated girl . . . not a poet—O.K.? [*She rebuffs him again and he starts to leave.*]

BENEATHA: Why are you angry?

GEORGE: Because this is stupid! I don't go out with you to discuss the nature of "quiet desperation" or to hear all about your thoughts—because the world will go on thinking what it thinks regardless—

BENEATHA: Then why read books? Why go to school?

GEORGE [*with artificial patience, counting on his fingers*]: It's simple. You read books—to learn facts—to get grades—to pass the course—to get a degree. That's all—it has nothing to do with thoughts [*a long pause*].

BENEATHA: I see. [*a longer pause as she looks at him*] Good night, George. [GEORGE *looks at her a little oddly, and starts to exit. He meets* MAMA *coming in.*]

GEORGE: Oh—hello, Mrs. Younger.

MAMA: Hello, George, how you feeling?

GEORGE: Fine—fine, how are you?

MAMA: Oh, a little tired. You know them steps can get you after a day's work. You all have a nice time tonight?

GEORGE: Yes—a fine time. Well, good night.

MAMA: Good night. [*He exits.* MAMA *closes the door behind her.*] Hello, honey. What you sitting like that for?

BENEATHA: I'm just sitting.

MAMA: Didn't you have a nice time?

BENEATHA: No.

MAMA: No? What's the matter?

BENEATHA: Mama, George is a fool—honest. [*She rises.*]

MAMA [*hustling around unloading the packages she has entered with; she stops*]: Is he, baby?

BENEATHA: Yes. [BENEATHA *makes up* TRAVIS' *bed as she talks.*]

MAMA: You sure?

BENEATHA: Yes.

MAMA: Well—I guess you better not waste your time with no fools. [BENEATHA *looks up at her mother, watching her put groceries in the refrigerator. Finally she gathers up her things and starts into the bedroom. At the door she stops and looks back at her mother.*]

BENEATHA: Mama—

MAMA: Yes, baby—

BENEATHA: Thank you.

MAMA: For what?

BENEATHA: For understanding me this time. [*She exits quickly and the mother stands, smiling a little, looking at the place where* BENEATHA *had stood.* RUTH *enters.*]

RUTH: Now don't you fool with any of this stuff, Lena—

MAMA: Oh, I just thought I'd sort a few things out. [*The phone rings.* RUTH *answers.*]

RUTH [*at the phone*]: Hello—Just a minute. [*goes to door*] Walter, it's Mrs. Arnold. [*Waits. Goes back to the phone. Tense.*] Hello. Yes, this is his wife speaking . . . He's lying down now. Yes . . . well, he'll be in tomorrow. He's been very sick. Yes—I know we should have called, but we were so sure he'd be able to come in today. Yes—yes, I'm very sorry. Yes . . . Thank you very much. [*She hangs up.* WALTER *is standing in the doorway of the bedroom behind her.*] That was Mrs. Arnold.

WALTER [indifferently]: Was it?

RUTH: She said if you don't come in tomorrow that they are getting a new man . . .

WALTER: Ain't that sad—ain't that crying sad.

RUTH: She said Mr. Arnold has had to take a cab for three days . . . Walter, you ain't
been to work for three days! [This is a revelation to her.] Where you been,
Walter Lee Younger? [WALTER looks at her and starts to laugh.] You're going
to lose your job.

WALTER: That's right . . .

RUTH: Oh, Walter, and with your mother working like a dog every day—

WALTER: That's sad too—Everything is sad.

MAMA: What you been doing for these three days, son?

WALTER: Mama—you don't know all the things a man what got leisure can find to
do in this city . . . What's this—Friday night? Well—Wednesday I borrowed
Willy Harris' car and I went for a drive . . . just me and myself and I drove
and drove . . . Way out . . . way past South Chicago, and I parked the car
and I sat and looked at the steel mills all day long. I just sat in the car and
looked at them big black chimneys for hours. Then I drove back and I went
to the Green Hat. [pause] And Thursday—Thursday I borrowed the car
again and I got in it and I pointed it the other way and I drove the other
way—for hours—way, way up to Wisconsin, and I looked at the farms.
I just drove and looked at the farms. Then I drove back and I went to the
Green Hat. [pause] And today—today I didn't get the car. Today I just
walked. All over the Southside. And I looked at the Negroes and they
looked at me and finally I just sat down on the curb at Thirty-ninth and
South Parkway and I just sat there and watched the Negroes go by. And
then I went to the Green Hat. You all sad? You all depressed? And you
know where I am going right now—[RUTH goes out quietly.].

MAMA: Oh, Big Walter, is this the harvest of our days?

WALTER: You know what I like about the Green Hat? [He turns the radio on and a
steamy, deep blues pours into the room.] I like this little cat they got there
who blows a sax . . . He blows. He talks to me. He ain't but 'bout five feet
tall and he's got a conked head and his eyes is always closed and he's all
music—

MAMA [rising and getting some papers out of her handbag]: Walter—

WALTER: And there's this other guy who plays the piano . . . and they got a sound.
I mean they can work on some music . . . They got the best little combo
in the world in the Green Hat . . . You can just sit there and drink and
listen to them three men play and you realize that don't nothing matter
worth a damn, but just being there—

MAMA: I've helped do it to you, haven't I, son? Walter, I been wrong.

WALTER: Naw—you ain't never been wrong about nothing, Mama.

MAMA: Listen to me, now. I say I been wrong, son. That I been doing to you what
the rest of the world been doing to you. [She stops and he looks up slowly
at her and she meets his eyes pleadingly.] Walter—what you ain't understood is that I ain't got nothing, don't own nothing, ain't never really
wanted nothing that wasn't for you. There ain't nothing as precious to me
. . . There ain't nothing worth holding on to, money, dreams, nothing
else—if it means—if it means it's going to destroy my boy. [She puts her
papers in front of him and he watches her without speaking or moving.] I
paid the man thirty-five hundred dollars down on the house. That leaves
sixty-five hundred dollars. Monday morning I want you to take this money

and take three thousand dollars and put it in a savings account for Beneatha's medical schooling. The rest you put in a checking account—with your name on it. And from now on any penny that come out of it or that go in it is for you to look after. For you to decide. [*She drops her hands a little helplessly.*] It ain't much, but it's all I got in the world and I'm putting it in your hands. I'm telling you to be the head of this family from now on like you supposed to be.

WALTER [*stares at the money*]: You trust me like that, Mama?

MAMA: I ain't never stop trusting you. Like I ain't never stop loving you. [*She goes out, and* WALTER *sits looking at the money on the table as the music continues in its idiom, pulsing in the room. Finally, in a decisive gesture, he gets up, and, in mingled joy and desperation, picks up the money. At the same moment,* TRAVIS *enters for bed.*]

TRAVIS: What's the matter, Daddy? You drunk?

WALTER [*sweetly, more sweetly than we have ever known him*]: No, Daddy ain't drunk. Daddy ain't going to never be drunk again. . . .

TRAVIS: Well, good night, Daddy. [*The father has come from behind the couch and leans over, embracing his son.*]

WALTER: Son, I feel like talking to you tonight.

TRAVIS: About what?

WALTER: Oh, about a lot of things. About you and what kind of man you going to be when you grow up. . . . Son—son, what do you want to be when you grow up?

TRAVIS: A bus driver.

WALTER [*laughing a little*]: A what? Man, that ain't nothing to want to be!

TRAVIS: Why not?

WALTER: 'Cause, man—it ain't big enough—you know what I mean.

TRAVIS: I don't know then. I can't make up my mind. Sometimes Mama asks me that too. And sometimes when I tell her I just want to be like you—she says she don't want me to be like that and sometimes she says she does . . .

WALTER [*gathering him up in his arms*]: You know what, Travis? In seven years you going to be seventeen years old. And things is going to be very different with us in seven years, Travis. . . . One day when you are seventeen I'll come home—home from my office downtown somewhere—

TRAVIS: You don't work in no office, Daddy.

WALTER: No—but after tonight. After what your daddy gonna do tonight, there's going to be offices—a whole lot of offices. . . .

TRAVIS: What you gonna do tonight, Daddy?

WALTER: You wouldn't understand yet, son, but your daddy's gonna make a transaction . . . a business transaction that's going to change our lives . . . That's how come one day when you 'bout seventeen years old I'll come home and I'll be pretty tired, you know what I mean, after a day of conferences and secretaries getting things wrong the way they do . . . 'cause an executive's life is hell, man—[*The more he talks the farther away he gets.*] And I'll pull the car up on the driveway . . . just a plain black Chrysler, I think, with white walls—no—black tires. More elegant. Rich people don't have to be flashy . . . though I'll have to get something a little sportier for Ruth—maybe a Cadillac convertible to do her shopping in. . . . And I'll come up the steps to the house and the gardener will be clipping away at the hedges and he'll say, "Good evening, Mr. Younger." And I'll say, "Hello, Jefferson, how are you this evening?" And I'll go

inside and Ruth will come downstairs and meet me at the door and we'll
kiss each other and she'll take my arm and we'll go up to your room to
see you sitting on the floor with the catalogues of all the great schools in
America around you. . . . All the great schools in the world! And—and I'll
say, all right son—it's your seventeenth birthday, what is it you've
decided? . . . Just tell me where you want to go to school and you'll *go*.
Just tell me, what it is you want to be—and you'll be it. . . . Whatever you
want to be—Yessir! [*He holds his arms open for* TRAVIS.] You just name it,
son . . . [TRAVIS *leaps into them*] and I hand you the world! [WALTER*'s voice
has risen in pitch and hysterical promise and on the last line he lifts* TRAVIS
high.]

BLACKOUT

Scene 3

TIME: *Saturday, moving day, one week later.*

Before the curtain rises, RUTH*'s voice, a strident, dramatic church alto, cuts
through the silence.*

It is, in the darkness, a triumphant surge, a penetrating statement of expectation: "Oh, Lord, I don't feel no ways tired! Children, oh, glory hallelujah!"*

As the curtain rises we see that* RUTH *is alone in the living room, finishing up
the family's packing. It is moving day. She is nailing crates and tying cartons.*
BENEATHA *enters, carrying a guitar case, and watches her exuberant sister-in-law.*

RUTH: Hey!
BENEATHA [*putting away the case*]: Hi.
RUTH [*pointing at a package*]: Honey—look in that package there and see what I
found on sale this morning at the South Center. [RUTH *gets up and moves
to the package and draws out some curtains.*] Lookahere—hand-turned
hems!
BENEATHA: How do you know the window size out there?
RUTH [*who hadn't thought of that*]: Oh—Well, they bound to fit something in the
whole house. Anyhow, they was too good a bargain to pass up. [RUTH
slaps her head, suddenly remembering something.] Oh, Bennie—I meant
to put a special note on that carton over there. That's your mama's good
china and she wants 'em to be very careful with it.
BENEATHA: I'll do it. [BENEATHA *finds a piece of paper and starts to draw large letters
on it.*]
RUTH: You know what I'm going to do soon as I get in that new house?
BENEATHA: What?
RUTH: Honey—I'm going to run me a tub of water up to here . . . [*with her fingers
practically up to her nostrils*] And I'm going to get in it—and I am going
to sit . . . and sit . . . and sit in that hot water and the first person who
knocks to tell *me* to hurry up and come out—
BENEATHA: Gets shot at sunrise.
RUTH [*laughing happily*]: You said it, sister! [*noticing how large* BENEATHA *is absent-
mindedly making the note*] Honey, they ain't going to read that from no
airplane.
BENEATHA [*laughing herself*]: I guess I always think things have more emphasis if
they are big, somehow.

RUTH [*looking up at her and smiling*]: You and your brother seem to have that as a philosophy of life. Lord, that man—done changed so 'round here. You know—you know what we did last night? Me and Walter Lee?

BENEATHA: What?

RUTH [*smiling to herself*]: We went to the movies. [*looking at* BENEATHA *to see if she understands*] We went to the movies. You know the last time me and Walter went to the movies together?

BENEATHA: No.

RUTH: Me neither. That's how long it been. [*smiling again*] But we went last night. The picture wasn't much good, but that didn't seem to matter. We went— and we held hands.

BENEATHA: Oh, Lord!

RUTH: We held hands—and you know what?

BENEATHA: What?

RUTH: When we come out of the show it was late and dark and all the stores and things was closed up . . . and it was kind of chilly and there wasn't many people on the streets . . . and we was still holding hands, me and Walter.

BENEATHA: You're killing me. [WALTER *enters with a large package. His happiness is deep in him; he cannot keep still with his new-found exuberance. He is singing and wiggling and snapping his fingers. He puts his package in a corner and puts a phonograph record, which he has brought in with him, on the record player. As the music comes up he dances over to* RUTH *and tries to get her to dance with him. She gives in at last to his raunchiness and in a fit of giggling allows herself to be drawn into his mood and together they deliberately burlesque an old social dance of their youth.*]

BENEATHA [*regarding them a long time as they dance, then drawing in her breath for a deeply exaggerated comment which she does not particularly mean*]: Talk about—oldddddddddd—fashionedddddddd—Negroes!

WALTER [*stopping momentarily*]: What kind of Negroes? [*He says this in fun. He is not angry with her today, nor with anyone. He starts to dance with his wife again.*]

BENEATHA: Old-fashioned.

WALTER [*as he dances with* RUTH]: You know, when these *New Negroes* have their convention—[*pointing at his sister*]—that is going to be the chairman of the Committee on Unending Agitation. [*He goes on dancing, then stops.*] Race, race, race! . . . Girl, I do believe you are the first person in the history of the entire human race to successfully brainwash yourself. [BENEATHA *breaks up and he goes on dancing. He stops again, enjoying his tease.*] Damn, even the N double A C P takes a holiday sometimes! [BENEATHA *and* RUTH *laugh. He dances with* RUTH *some more and starts to laugh and stops and pantomimes someone over an operating table.*] I can just see that chick someday looking down at some poor cat on an operating table before she starts to slice him, saying . . . [*pulling his sleeves back maliciously*] "By the way, what are your views on civil rights down there? . . ." [*He laughs at her again and starts to dance happily. The bell sounds.*]

BENEATHA: Sticks and stones may break my bones but . . . words will never hurt me! [BENEATHA *goes to the door and opens it as* WALTER *and* RUTH *go on with the clowning.* BENEATHA *is somewhat surprised to see a quiet-looking middle-aged white man in a business suit holding his hat and a briefcase in his hand and consulting a small piece of paper.*]

MAN: Uh—how do you do, miss. I am looking for a Mrs.—[*He looks at the slip of paper.*] Mrs. Lena Younger?

BENEATHA [*smoothing her hair with slight embarrassment*]: Oh—yes, that's my mother. Excuse me. [*She closes the door and turns to quiet the other two.*] Ruth! Brother! Somebody's here. [*Then she opens the door. The man casts a curious quick glance at all of them.*] Uh—come in please.

MAN [*coming in*]: Thank you.

BENEATHA: My mother isn't here just now. Is it business?

MAN: Yes . . . well, of a sort.

WALTER [*freely, the Man of the House*]: Have a seat. I'm Mrs. Younger's son. I look after most of her business matters. [RUTH *and* BENEATHA *exchange amused glances.*]

MAN [*regarding* WALTER, *and sitting*]: Well—My name is Karl Lindner . . .

WALTER [*stretching out his hand*]: Walter Younger. This is my wife—[RUTH *nods politely.*]—and my sister.

LINDNER: How do you do.

WALTER [*amiably, as he sits himself easily on a chair, leaning with interest forward on his knees and looking expectantly into the newcomer's face*]: What can we do for you, Mr. Lindner!

LINDNER [*some minor shuffling of the hat and briefcase on his knees*]: Well—I am a representative of the Clybourne Park Improvement Association—

WALTER [*pointing*]: Why don't you sit your things on the floor?

LINDNER: Oh—yes. Thank you. [*He slides the briefcase and hat under the chair.*] And as I was saying—I am from the Clybourne Park Improvement Association and we have had it brought to our attention at the last meeting that you people—or at least your mother—has bought a piece of residential property at—[*He digs for the slip of paper again.*]—four o six at Clybourne Street . . .

WALTER: That's right. Care for something to drink? Ruth, get Mr. Lindner a beer.

LINDNER [*upset for some reason*]: Oh—no, really, I mean thank you very much, but no thank you.

RUTH [*innocently*]: Some coffee?

LINDNER: Thank you, nothing at all. [BENEATHA *is watching the man carefully.*]

LINDNER: Well, I don't know how much you folks know about our organization. [*He is a gentle man; thoughtful and somewhat labored in his manner.*] It is one of these community organizations set up to look after—oh, you know, things like block upkeep and special projects and we also have what we call our New Neighbors Orientation Committee . . .

BENEATHA [*drily*]: Yes—and what do they do?

LINDNER [*turning a little to her and then returning the main force to* WALTER]: Well—it's what you might call a sort of welcoming committee, I guess. I mean they, we, I'm the chairman of the committee—go around and see the new people who move into the neighborhood and sort of give them the lowdown on the way we do things out in Clybourne Park.

BENEATHA [*with appreciation of the two meanings, which escape* RUTH *and* WALTER]: Uh-huh.

LINDNER: And we also have the category of what the association calls—[*He looks elsewhere.*]—uh—special community problems . . .

BENEATHA: Yes—and what are some of those?

WALTER: Girl, let the man talk.

LINDNER [*with understated relief*]: Thank you. I would sort of like to explain this thing in my own way. I mean I want to explain to you in a certain way.

WALTER: Go ahead.

LINDNER: Yes. Well. I'm going to try to get right to the point. I'm sure we'll all appreciate that in the long run.

BENEATHA: Yes.

WALTER: Be still now!

LINDNER: Well—

RUTH [*still innocently*]: Would you like another chair—you don't look comfortable.

LINDNER [*more frustrated than annoyed*]: No, thank you very much. Please. Well—to get right to the point I—[*a great breath, and he is off at last*] I am sure you people must be aware of some of the incidents which have happened in various parts of the city when colored people have moved into certain areas—[BENEATHA *exhales heavily and starts tossing a piece of fruit up and down in the air.*] Well—because we have what I think is going to be a unique type of organization in American community life—not only do we deplore that kind of thing—but we are trying to do something about it. [BENEATHA *stops tossing and turns with a new and quizzical interest to the man.*] We feel—[*gaining confidence in his mission because of the interest in the faces of the people he is talking to*]—we feel that most of the trouble in this world, when you come right down to it—[*He hits his knee for emphasis.*]—most of the trouble exists because people just don't sit down and talk to each other.

RUTH [*nodding as she might in church, pleased with the remark*]: You can say that again, mister.

LINDNER [*more encouraged by such affirmation*]: That we don't try hard enough in this world to understand the other fellow's problem. The other guy's point of view.

RUTH: Now that's right. [BENEATHA *and* WALTER *merely watch and listen with genuine interest.*]

LINDNER: Yes—that's the way we feel out in Clybourne Park. And that's why I was elected to come here this afternoon and talk to you people. Friendly like, you know, the way people should talk to each other and see if we couldn't find some way to work this thing out. As I say, the whole business is a matter of caring about the other fellow. Anybody can see that you are a nice family of folks, hard working and honest I'm sure. [BENEATHA *frowns slightly, quizzically, her head tilted regarding him.*] Today everybody knows what it means to be on the outside of *something*. And of course, there is always somebody who is out to take the advantage of people who don't always understand.

WALTER: What do you mean?

LINDNER: Well—you see our community is made of people who've worked hard as the dickens for years to build up that little community. They're not rich and fancy people; just hardworking, honest people who don't really have much but those little homes and a dream of the kind of community they want to raise their children in. Now, I don't say we are perfect and there is a lot wrong in some of the things they want. But you've got to admit that a man, right or wrong, has the right to want to have the neighborhood he lives in a certain kind of way. And at the moment the overwhelming majority of our people out there feel that people get along better, take more of a common interest in the life of the community, when they share a common background. I want you to believe me when I tell you that race prejudice simply doesn't enter into it. It is a matter of the people of Clybourne Park believing, rightly or wrongly, as I say, that for the happiness of all concerned that our Negro families are happier when they live in their *own* communities.

BENEATHA [*with a grand and bitter gesture*]: This, friends, is the Welcoming Committee!

WALTER [*dumbfounded, looking at* LINDNER]: Is this what you came marching all the way over here to tell us?

LINDNER: Well, now we've been having a fine conversation. I hope you'll hear me all the way through.

WALTER [*tightly*]: Go ahead, man.

LINDNER: You see—in the face of all things I have said, we are prepared to make your family a very generous offer . . .

BENEATHA: Thirty pieces and not a coin less!

WALTER: Yeah?

LINDNER [*putting on his glasses and drawing a form out of the briefcase*]: Our association is prepared, through the collective effort of our people, to buy the house from you at a financial gain to your family.

RUTH: Lord have mercy, ain't this the living gall!

WALTER: All right, you through?

LINDNER: Well, I want to give you the exact terms of the financial arrangement—

WALTER: We don't want to hear no exact terms of no arrangements. I want to know if you got any more to tell us 'bout getting together?

LINDNER [*taking off his glasses*]: Well—I don't suppose that you feel . . .

WALTER: Never mind how I feel—you got any more to say 'bout how people ought to sit down and talk to each other? . . . Get out of my house, man. [*He turns his back and walks to the door.*]

LINDNER [*looking around at the hostile faces and reaching and assembling his hat and briefcase*]: Well—I don't understand why you people are reacting this way. What do you think you are going to gain by moving into a neighborhood where you just aren't wanted and where some elements—well—people can get awful worked up when they feel that their whole way of life and everything they've ever worked for is threatened.

WALTER: Get out.

LINDNER [*at the door, holding a small card*]: Well—I'm sorry it went like this.

WALTER: Get out.

LINDNER [*almost sadly regarding* WALTER]: You just can't force people to change their hearts, son. [*He turns and put his card on a table and exits.* WALTER *pushes the door to with stinging hatred, and stands looking at it.* RUTH *just sits and* BENEATHA *just stands. They say nothing.* MAMA *and* TRAVIS *enter.*]

MAMA: Well—this all the packing got done since I left out of here this morning. I testify before God that my children got all the energy of the dead. What time the moving men due?

BENEATHA: Four o'clock. You had a caller, Mama. [*She is smiling, teasingly.*]

MAMA: Sure enough—who?

BENEATHA [*her arms folded saucily*]: The Welcoming Committee. [WALTER *and* RUTH *giggle.*]

MAMA [*innocently*]: Who?

BENEATHA: The Welcoming Committee. They said they're sure going to be glad to see you when you get there.

WALTER [*devilishly*]: Yeah, they said they can't hardly wait to see your face. [*laughter*]

MAMA [*sensing their facetiousness*]: What's the matter with you all?

WALTER: Ain't nothing the matter with us. We just telling you 'bout the gentleman who came to see you this afternoon. From the Clybourne Park Improvement Association.

MAMA: What he want?

RUTH [*in the same mood as* BENEATHA *and* WALTER]: To welcome you, honey.

WALTER: He said they can't hardly wait. He said the one thing they don't have, that they just dying to have out there is a fine family of colored people! [*to* RUTH *and* BENEATHA] Ain't that right!

RUTH AND BENEATHA [*mockingly*]: Yeah! He left his card in case—[*They indicate the card, and* MAMA *picks it up and throws it on the floor—understanding and looking off as she draws her chair up to the table on which she has put her plant and some sticks and some cord.*]

MAMA: Father, give us strength. [*knowingly—and without fun*] Did he threaten us?

BENEATHA: Oh—Mama—they don't do it like that any more. He talked Brotherhood. He said everybody ought to learn how to sit down and hate each other with good Christian fellowship. [*She and* WALTER *shake hands to ridicule the remark.*]

MAMA [*sadly*]: Lord, protect us . . . .

RUTH: You should hear the money those folks raised to buy the house from us. All we paid and then some.

BENEATHA: What they think we going to do—eat 'em?

RUTH: No, honey, marry 'em.

MAMA [*shaking her head*]: Lord, Lord, Lord . . .

RUTH: Well—that's the way the crackers crumble. Joke.

BENEATHA [*laughingly noticing what her mother is doing*]: Mama, what are you doing?

MAMA: Fixing my plant so it won't get hurt none on the way . . .

BENEATHA: Mama, you going to take that to the new house?

MAMA: Uh-huh—

BENEATHA: That raggedy-looking old thing?

MAMA [*stopping and looking at her*]: It expresses *me*.

RUTH [*with delight, to* BENEATHA]: So there, Miss Thing! [WALTER *comes to* MAMA *suddenly and bends down behind her and squeezes her in his arms with all his strength. She is overwhelmed by the suddenness of it and, though delighted, her manner is like that of* RUTH *with* TRAVIS.]

MAMA: Look out now, boy! You make me mess up my thing here!

WALTER [*his face lit, he slips down on his knees beside her, his arms still about her*]: Mama . . . you know what it means to climb up in the chariot?

MAMA [*gruffly, very happy*]: Get on away from me now . . .

RUTH [*near the gift-wrapped package, trying to catch* WALTER's *eye*]: Psst—

WALTER: What the old song say, Mama . . .

RUTH: Walter—Now? [*She is pointing at the package.*]

WALTER [*speaking the lines, sweetly, playfully, in his mother's face*]:
 I got wings . . . you got wings . . .
 All God's children got wings . . . .

MAMA: Boy—get out of my face and do some work . . .

WALTER: *When I get to heaven gonna put on my wings,*
 Gonna fly all over God's heaven . . . .

BENEATHA [*teasingly, from across the room*]: Everybody talking 'bout heaven ain't going there!

WALTER [*to* RUTH, *who is carrying the box across to them*]: I don't know, you think we ought to give her that . . . Seems to me she ain't been very appreciative around here.

MAMA [*eying the box, which is obviously a gift*]: What is that?

WALTER [*taking it from* RUTH *and putting it on the table in front of* MAMA]: Well—what you all think? Should we give it to her?

RUTH: Oh—she was pretty good today.

MAMA: I'll good you—[*She turns her eyes to the box again.*]

BENEATHA: Open it, Mama. [*She stands up, looks at it, turns and looks at all of them, and then presses her hands together and does not open the package.*]

WALTER [*sweetly*]: Open it, Mama. It's for you. [MAMA *looks in his eyes. It is the first present in her life without its being Christmas. Slowly she opens her package and lifts out, one by one, a brand-new sparkling set of gardening tools.* WALTER *continues, prodding.*] Ruth made up the note—read it . . .

MAMA [*picking up the card and adjusting her glasses*]: "To our own Mrs. Miniver— Love from Brother, Ruth and Beneatha." Ain't that lovely . . .

TRAVIS [*tugging at his father's sleeve*]: Daddy, can I give her mine now?

WALTER: All right, son. [TRAVIS *flies to get his gift.*] Travis didn't want to go in with the rest of us, Mama. He got his own. [*somewhat amused*] We don't know what it is . . .

TRAVIS [*racing back in the room with a large hatbox and putting it in front of his grandmother*]: Here!

MAMA: Lord have mercy, baby. You done gone and bought your grandmother a hat?

TRAVIS [*very proud*]: Open it! [*She does and lifts out an elaborate, but very elaborate, wide gardening hat, and all the adults break up at the sight of it.*]

RUTH: Travis, honey, what is that?

TRAVIS [*who thinks it is beautiful and appropriate*]: It's a gardening hat! Like the ladies always have on in the magazines when they work in their gardens.

BENEATHA [*giggling fiercely*]: Travis—we were trying to make Mama Mrs. Miniver— not Scarlett O'Hara!

MAMA [*indignantly*]: What's the matter with you all! This here is a beautiful hat! [*absurdly*] I always wanted me one just like it! [*She pops it on her head to prove it to her grandson, and the hat is ludicrous and considerably oversized.*]

RUTH: Hot dog! Go, Mama!

WALTER [*doubled over with laughter*]: I'm sorry, Mama—but you look like you ready to go out and chop you some cotton sure enough! [*They all laugh except* MAMA, *out of deference to* TRAVIS*'s feelings.*]

MAMA [*gathering the boy up to her*]: Bless your heart—this is the prettiest hat I ever owned—[WALTER, RUTH *and* BENEATHA *chime in—noisily, festively and insincerely congratulating* TRAVIS *on his gift.*] What are we all standing around here for? We ain't finished packin' yet. Bennie, you ain't packed one book. [*The bell rings.*]

BENEATHA: That couldn't be the movers . . . it's not hardly two o'clock yet— [BENEATHA *goes into her room.* MAMA *starts for door.*]

WALTER [*turning, stiffening*]: Wait—wait—I'll get it. [*He stands and looks at the door.*]

MAMA: You expecting company, son?

WALTER [*just looking at the door*]: Yeah—yeah . . . [MAMA *looks at* RUTH, *and they exchange innocent and unfrightened glances.*]

MAMA [*not understanding*]: Well, let them in, son.

BENEATHA [*from her room*]: We need some more string.

MAMA: Travis—you run to the hardware and get me some string cord. [MAMA *goes out and* WALTER *turns and looks at* RUTH. TRAVIS *goes to a dish for money.*]

RUTH: Why don't you answer the door, man?

WALTER [*suddenly bounding across the floor to her*]: 'Cause sometimes it hard to let the future begin! [*stooping down in her face*].

> *I got wings! You got wings!*
> *All God's children got wings!*

[*He crosses to the door and throws it open. Standing there is a very slight little man in a not too prosperous business suit and with haunted frightened eyes and a hat pulled down tightly, brim up, around his forehead.* TRAVIS *passes between the men and exits.* WALTER *leans deep in the man's face, still in his jubilance.*]

> *When I get to heaven gonna put on my wings,*
> *Gonna fly all over God's heaven . . .*

[*The little man just stares at him*]

> Heaven—

[*Suddenly he stops and looks past the little man into the empty hallway.*]

> Where's Willy, man?

BOBO: He ain't with me.

WALTER [*not disturbed*]: Oh—come on in. You know my wife.

BOBO [*dumbly, taking off his hat*]: Yes—h'you, Miss Ruth.

RUTH [*quietly, a mood apart from her husband already, seeing* BOBO]: Hello, Bobo.

WALTER: You right on time today . . . Right on time. That's the way! [*He slaps* BOBO *on his back.*] Sit down . . . lemme hear. [RUTH *stands stiffly and quietly in back of them, as though somehow she senses death, her eyes fixed on her husband.*]

BOBO [*his frightened eyes on the floor, his hat in his hands*]: Could I please get a drink of water, before I tell you about it, Walter Lee? [WALTER *does not take his eyes off the man.* RUTH *goes blindly to the tap and gets a glass of water and brings it to* BOBO.]

WALTER: There ain't nothing wrong, is there?

BOBO: Lemme tell you—

WALTER: Man—didn't nothing go wrong?

BOBO: Lemme tell you—Walter Lee. [*Looking at* RUTH *and talking to her more than to* WALTER.] You know how it was. I got to tell you how it was. I mean first I got to tell you how it was all the way . . . I mean about the money I put in, Walter Lee . . .

WALTER [*with taut agitation now*]: What about the money you put in?

BOBO: Well—it wasn't much as we told you—me and Willy—[*He stops.*] I'm sorry, Walter. I got a bad feeling about it. I got a real bad feeling about it . . .

WALTER: Man, what you telling me about all this for? . . . Tell me what happened in Springfield . . .

BOBO: Springfield.

RUTH [*like a dead woman*]: What was supposed to happen in Springfield?

BOBO [*to her*]: This deal that me and Walter went into with Willy—Me and Willy was going to go down to Springfield and spread some money 'round so's we wouldn't have to wait so long for the liquor license . . . That's what we were going to do. Everybody said that was the way you had to do, you understand, Miss Ruth?

WALTER: Man—what happened down there?

BOBO [*a pitiful man, near tears*]: I'm trying to tell you, Walter.

WALTER [*screaming at him suddenly*]: THEN TELL ME, GODDAMMIT . . . WHAT'S THE MATTER WITH YOU?

BOBO: Man . . . I didn't go to no Springfield, yesterday.

WALTER [*halted, life hanging in the moment*]: Why not?

BOBO [*the long way, the hard way to tell*]: 'Cause I didn't have no reasons to . . .

WALTER: Man, what are you talking about!

BOBO: I'm talking about the fact that when I got to the train station yesterday morning—eight o'clock like we planned . . . Man—*Willy didn't never show up.*

WALTER: Why . . . where was he . . . where is he?

BOBO: That's what I'm trying to tell you . . . I don't know . . . I waited six hours . . . I called his house . . . and I waited . . . six hours . . . I waited in that train station six hours . . . [*breaking into tears*] That was all the extra money I had in the world . . . [*looking up at* WALTER *with the tears running down his face*] Man, *Willy is gone.*

WALTER: Gone, what you mean Willy is gone? Gone where? You mean he went by himself. You mean he went off to Springfield by himself—to take care of getting the license—[*turns and looks anxiously at* RUTH] You mean maybe he didn't want too many people in on the business down there? [*looks to* RUTH *again, as before*] You know Willy got his own ways. [*looks back to* BOBO] Maybe you was late yesterday and he just went on down there without you. Maybe—maybe—he's been callin' you at home tryin' to tell you what happened or something. Maybe—maybe—he just got sick. He's somewhere—he's got to be somewhere. We just got to find him—me and you got to find him. [*grabs* BOBO *senselessly by the collar and starts to shake him*] We got to!

BOBO [*in sudden angry, frightened agony*]: What's the matter with you, Walter! When a cat take off with your money he don't leave you no maps!

WALTER [*turning madly, as though he is looking for* WILLY *in the very room*]: Willy! . . . Willy . . . don't do it . . . Please don't do it . . . Man, not with that money . . . Man, please, not with that money . . . Oh, God . . . Don't let it be true . . . [*He is wandering around, crying out for* WILLY *and looking for him or perhaps for help from God.*] Man . . . I trusted you . . . Man, I put my life in your hands . . . [*He starts to crumple down on the floor as* RUTH *just covers her face in horror,* MAMA *opens the door and comes into the room, with* BENEATHA *behind her.*] Man . . . [*He starts to pound the floor with his fists, sobbing wildly.*] *That money is made out of my father's flesh* . . .

BOBO [*standing over him helplessly*]: I'm sorry, Walter . . . [*Only* WALTER'S *sobs reply.* BOBO *puts on his hat.*] I had my life staked on this deal, too . . . [*He exits.*]

MAMA [*to* WALTER]: Son—[*She goes to him, bends down to him, talks to his bent head.*] Son . . . Is it gone? Son, I gave you sixty-five hundred dollars. Is it gone? All of it? Beneatha's money too?

WALTER [*lifting his head slowly*]: Mama . . . I never . . . went to the bank at all . . .

MAMA [*not wanting to believe him*]: You mean . . . your sister's school money . . . you used that too . . . Walter? . . .

WALTER: Yessss! . . . All of it . . . It's all gone . . . [*There is total silence.* RUTH *stands with her face covered with her hands;* BENEATHA *leans forlornly against a wall, fingering a piece of red ribbon from the mother's gift.* MAMA *stops and looks at her son without recognition and then, quite without thinking about it, starts to beat him senselessly in the face.* BENEATHA *goes to them and stops it.*]

BENEATHA: Mama! [MAMA *stops and looks at both of her children and rises slowly and wanders vaguely, aimlessly away from them.*]

MAMA: I seen . . . him . . . night after night . . . come in . . . and look at that rug . . . and then look at me . . . the red showing in his eyes . . . the veins moving in his head . . . I seen him grow thin and old before he was forty . . . working and working and working like somebody's old horse . . . killing himself . . . and you—you give it all away in a day . . .

BENEATHA: Mama—

MAMA: Oh, God . . . [*She looks up to Him.*] Look down here—and show me the strength.

BENEATHA: Mama—

MAMA [*folding over*]: Strength . . .

BENEATHA [*plaintively*]: Mama . . .

MAMA: Strength!

CURTAIN

ACT III

An hour later.

At curtain, there is a sullen light of gloom in the living room, gray light not unlike that which began the first scene of Act I. At left we can see WALTER within his room, alone with himself. He is stretched out on the bed, his shirt out and open, his arms under his head. He does not smoke, he does not cry out, he merely lies there, looking up at the ceiling, much as if he were alone in the world.

In the living room BENEATHA sits at the table, still surrounded by the now almost ominous packing crates. She sits looking off. We feel that this is a mood struck perhaps an hour before, and it lingers now, full of the empty sound of profound disappointment. We see on a line from her brother's bedroom the sameness of their attitudes. Presently the bell rings and BENEATHA rises without ambition or interest in answering. It is ASAGAI, smiling broadly, striding into the room with energy and happy expectation and conversation.

ASAGAI: I came over . . . I had some free time. I thought I might help with the packing. Ah, I like the look of packing crates! A household in preparation for a journey! It depresses some people . . . but for me . . . it is another feeling. Something full of the flow of life, do you understand? Movement, progress . . . It makes me think of Africa.

BENEATHA: Africa!

ASAGAI: What kind of a mood is this? Have I told you how deeply you move me?

BENEATHA: He gave away the money, Asagai . . .

ASAGAI: Who gave away what money?

BENEATHA: The insurance money. My brother gave it away.

ASAGAI: Gave it away?

BENEATHA: He made an investment! With a man even Travis wouldn't have trusted.

ASAGAI: And it's gone?

BENEATHA: Gone!

ASAGAI: I'm very sorry . . . And you, now?

BENEATHA: Me? . . . Me? . . . Me, I'm nothing . . . Me. When I was very small . . . we used to take our sleds out in the wintertime and the only hills we had were the ice-covered stone steps of some houses down the street. And we used to fill them in with snow and make them smooth and slide down them all day . . . and it was very dangerous you know . . . far too steep . . . and sure enough one day a kid named Rufus came down too fast and hit the sidewalk . . . and we saw his face just split open right there in front of us . . . And I remember standing there looking at his bloody open face thinking that was the end of Rufus. But the ambulance came and they took him to the hospital and they fixed the broken bones and they sewed it all up . . . and the next time I saw Rufus he just had a little line down the middle of his face . . . I never got over that . . . [WALTER *sits up, listening on the bed. Throughout this scene it is important that we feel his reaction at all times, that he visibly respond to the words of his sister and* ASAGAI.]

ASAGAI: What?

BENEATHA: That that was what one person could do for another, fix him up—sew up the problem, make him all right again. That was the most marvelous thing in the world . . . I wanted to do that. I always thought it was the one concrete thing in the world that a human being could do. Fix up the sick, you know—and make them whole again. This was truly being God . . .

ASAGAI: You wanted to be God?

BENEATHA: No—I wanted to cure. It used to be so important to me. I wanted to cure. It used to matter. I used to care. I mean about people and how their bodies hurt . . .

ASAGAI: And you've stopped caring?

BENEATHA: Yes—I think so.

ASAGAI: Why? [WALTER *rises, goes to the door of his room and is about to open it, then stops and stands listening, leaning on the door jamb.*]

BENEATHA: Because it doesn't seem deep enough, close enough to what ails mankind—I mean this thing of sewing up bodies or administering drugs. Don't you understand? It was a child's reaction to the world. I thought that doctors had the secret to all the hurts . . . That's the way a child sees things—or an idealist.

ASAGAI: Children see things very well sometimes—and idealists even better.

BENEATHA: I know that's what you think. Because you are still where I left off—you still care. This is what you see for the world, for Africa. You with the dreams of the future will patch up all Africa—you are going to cure the Great Sore of colonialism with Independence—

ASAGAI: Yes!

BENEATHA: Yes—and you think that one word is the penicillin of the human spirit: "Independence!" But then what?

ASAGAI: That will be the problem for another time. First we must get there.

BENEATHA: And where does it end?

ASAGAI: End? Who even spoke of an end? To life? To living?

BENEATHA: An end to misery!

ASAGAI [*smiling*]: You sound like a French intellectual.

BENEATHA: No! I sound like a human being who just had her future taken right out of her hands! While I was sleeping in my bed in there, things were happening in this world that directly concerned me—and nobody asked me, consulted me—they just went out and did things—and changed my life. Don't you see there isn't any real progress, Asagai, there is only one large circle that we march in, around and around, each of us with our own little picture—in front of us—our own little mirage that we think is the future.

ASAGAI: That is the mistake.

BENEATHA: What?

ASAGAI: What you just said—about the circle. It isn't a circle—it is simply a long line—as in geometry, you know, one that reaches into infinity. And because we cannot see the end—we also cannot see how it changes. And it is very odd but those who see the changes are called "idealists"— and those who cannot, or refuse to think, they are the "realists." It is very strange, and amusing too, I think.

BENEATHA: You—you are almost religious.

ASAGAI: Yes . . . I think I have the religion of doing what is necessary in the world— and of worshipping man—because he is so marvelous, you see.

BENEATHA: Man is foul! And the human race deserves its misery!

ASAGAI: You see: *you* have become the religious one in the old sense. Already, and after such a small defeat, you are worshipping despair.

BENEATHA: From now on, I worship the truth—and the truth is that people are puny, small and selfish . . .

ASAGAI: Truth? Why is it that you despairing ones always think that only you have the truth? I never thought to see *you* like that. You! Your brother made a stupid, childish mistake—and you are grateful to him. So that now you can give up the ailing human race on account of it. You talk about what good is struggle; what good is anything? Where are we all going? And why are we bothering?

BENEATHA: *And you cannot answer it!* All your talk and dreams about Africa and Independence. Independence and then what? What about all the crooks and petty thieves and just plain idiots who will come into power to steal and plunder the same as before—only now they will be black and do it in the name of the new Independence—You cannot answer that.

ASAGAI [*shouting over her*]: *I live the answer!* [*pause*] In my village at home it is the exceptional man who can even read a newspaper . . . or who ever *sees* a book at all. I will go home and much of what I will have to say will seem strange to the people of my village. . . . But I will teach and work and things will happen, slowly and swiftly. At times it will seem that nothing changes at all . . . and then again . . . the sudden dramatic events which make history leap into the future. And then quiet again. Retrogression even. Guns, murder, revolution. And I even will have moments when I wonder if the quiet was not better than all that death and hatred. But I will look about my village at the illiteracy and disease and ignorance and I will not wonder long. And perhaps . . . perhaps I will be a great man . . . I mean perhaps I will hold on to the substance of truth and find my way always with the right course . . . and perhaps for it I will be butchered in my bed some night by the servants of empire . . .

BENEATHA: *The martyr!*

ASAGAI: . . . or perhaps I shall live to be a very old man, respected and es- teemed in my new nation . . . And perhaps I shall hold office and this is what I'm trying to tell you, Alaiyo; perhaps the things I believe now for my country will be wrong and outmoded, and I will not understand and do terrible things to have things my way or merely to keep my power. Don't you see that there will be young men and women, not British soldiers then, but my own black countrymen . . . to step out of the shadows some evening

and slit my then useless throat? Don't you see they have always been there
. . . that they always will be. And that such a thing as my own death will
be an advance? They who might kill me even . . . actually replenish me!

BENEATHA: Oh, Asagai, I know all that.

ASAGAI: Good! Then stop moaning and groaning and tell me what you plan to do.

BENEATHA: Do?

ASAGAI: I have a bit of a suggestion.

BENEATHA: What?

ASAGAI [*rather quietly for him*]: That when it is all over—that you come home with
me—

BENEATHA [*slapping herself on the forehead with exasperation born of misunderstanding*]: Oh—Asagai—at this moment you decide to be romantic!

ASAGAI [*quickly understanding the misunderstanding*]: My dear, young creature of
the New World—I do not mean across the city—I mean across the ocean;
home—to Africa.

BENEATHA [*slowly understanding and turning to him with murmured amazement*]:
To—to Nigeria?

ASAGAI: Yes! . . . [*smiling and lifting his arms playfully*]. Three hundred years later
the African Prince rose up out of the seas and swept the maiden back
across the middle passage over which her ancestors had come—

BENEATHA [*unable to play*]: Nigeria?

ASAGAI: Nigeria. Home. [*coming to her with genuine romantic flippancy*] I will show
you our mountains and our stars; and give you cool drinks from gourds
and teach you the old songs and the ways of our people—and, in time,
we will pretend that—[*very softly*]—you have only been away for a day—
[*She turns her back to him, thinking. He swings her around and takes her
full in his arms in a long embrace which proceeds to passion.*]

BENEATHA [*pulling away*]: You're getting me all mixed up—

ASAGAI: Why?

BENEATHA: Too many things—too many things have happened today. I must sit
down and think. I don't know what I feel about anything right this minute.
[*She promptly sits down and props her chin on her fist.*]

ASAGAI [*charmed*]: All right, I shall leave you. No—don't get up. [*touching her, gently, sweetly*] Just sit awhile and think . . . Never be afraid to sit awhile and
think. [*He goes to door and looks at her.*] How often I have looked at you
and said, "Ah—so this is what the New World hath finally wrought . . ."
[*He exits.* BENEATHA *sits on alone. Presently* WALTER *enters from his room and
starts to rummage through things, feverishly looking for something. She
looks up and turns in her seat.*]

BENEATHA [*hissingly*]: Yes—just look at what the New World hath wrought! . . . Just
look! [*She gestures with bitter disgust.*] There he is! *Monsieur le petit bou-
geois noir*—himself! There he is—Symbol of a Rising Class! Entrepreneur!
Titan of the system! [WALTER *ignores her completely and continues frantically and destructively looking for something and hurling things to the
floor and tearing things out of their place in his search.* BENEATHA *ignores
the eccentricity of his actions and goes on with the monologue of insult.*]
Did you dream of yachts on Lake Michigan, Brother? Did you see yourself
on that Great Day sitting down at the Conference Table, surrounded by all
the mighty bald-headed men in America? All halted, waiting, breathless,
waiting for your pronouncements on industry? Waiting for you—Chairman of the Board? [WALTER *finds what he is looking for—a small piece of*

white paper—and pushes it in his pocket and puts on his coat and rushes out without ever having looked at her. She shouts after him.] I look at you and I see the final triumph of stupidity in the world! [*The door slams and she returns to just sitting again.* RUTH *comes quickly out of* MAMA's *room.*]

RUTH: Who was that?

BENEATHA: Your husband.

RUTH: Where did he go?

BENEATHA: Who knows—maybe he has an appointment at U.S. Steel.

RUTH [*anxiously, with frightened eyes*]: You didn't say nothing bad to him, did you?

BENEATHA: Bad? Say anything bad to him? No—I told him he was a sweet boy and full of dreams and everything is strictly peachy keen, as the ofay[3] kids say!

[MAMA *enters from her bedroom. She is lost, vague, trying to catch hold, to make some sense of her former command of the world, but it still eludes her. A sense of waste overwhelms her gait; a measure of apology rides on her shoulders. She goes to her plant, which has remained on the table, looks at it, picks it up and takes it to the window sill and sets it outside, and she stands and looks at it a long moment. Then she closes the window, straightens her body with effort and turns around to her children.*]

MAMA: Well—ain't it a mess in here, though? [*a false cheerfulness, a beginning of something*] I guess we all better stop moping around and get some work done. All this unpacking and everything we got to do. [RUTH *raises her head slowly in response to the sense of the line; and* BENEATHA *in similar manner turns very slowly to look at her mother.*] One of you all better call the moving people and tell 'em not to come.

RUTH: Tell 'em not to come?

MAMA: Of course, baby. Ain't no need in 'em coming all the way here and having to go back. They charges for that too. [*She sits down, fingers to her brow, thinking.*] Lord, ever since I was a little girl, I always remembers people saying, "Lena—Lena Eggleston, you aims too high all the time. You needs to slow down and see life a little more like it is. Just slow down some." That's what they always used to say down home—"Lord, that Lena Eggleston is a highminded thing. She'll get her due one day!"

RUTH: No, Lena . . .

MAMA: Me and Big Walter just didn't never learn right.

RUTH: Lena, no! We gotta go. Bennie—tell her . . . [*She rises and crosses to* BENEATHA *with her arms outstretched.* BENEATHA *doesn't respond.*] Tell her we can still move . . . the notes ain't but a hundred and twenty-five a month. We got four grown people in this house—we can work . . .

MAMA [*to herself*]: Just aimed too high all the time—

RUTH [*turning and going to* MAMA *fast—the words pouring out with urgency and desperation*]: Lena—I'll work . . . I'll work twenty hours a day in all the kitchens in Chicago . . . I'll strap my baby on my back if I have to and scrub all the floors in America and wash all the sheets in America if I have to—but we got to move . . . We got to get out of here . . . [MAMA *reaches out absently and pats* RUTH's *hand.*]

MAMA: No—I sees things differently now. Been thinking 'bout some of the things we could do to fix this place up some. I seen a second-hand bureau over on Maxwell Street just the other day that could fit right there. [*She points*

---

[3]**ofay** White (pig Latin meaning "foe").

to where the new furniture might go. RUTH *wanders away from her.*]
Would need some new handles on it and then a little varnish and then it
look like something brand-new. And—we can put up them new curtains
in the kitchen . . . Why this place be looking fine. Cheer us all up so that
we forget trouble ever came . . . [*to* RUTH] And you could get some nice
screens to put up in your room round the baby's bassinet . . . [*She looks
at both of them, pleadingly.*] Sometimes you just got to know when to
give up some things . . . and hold on to what you got. [WALTER *enters from
the outside, looking spent and leaning against the door, his coat hanging
from him.*]

MAMA: Where you been, son?

WALTER [*breathing hard*]: Made a call.

MAMA: To who, son?

WALTER: To the Man.

MAMA: What man, baby?

WALTER: The Man, Mama. Don't you know who The Man is?

RUTH: Walter Lee?

WALTER: *The Man.* Like the guys in the street say—*the Man.* Captain Boss—Mistuh
　　　Charley . . . Old Captain Please Mr. Bossman . . .

BENEATHA [*suddenly*]: Lindner!

WALTER: That's right! That's good. I told him to come right over.

BENEATHA [*fiercely, understanding*]: For what? What do you want to see him for?

WALTER [*looking at his sister*]: We are going to do business with him.

MAMA: What you talking 'bout, son?

WALTER: Talking 'bout life, Mama. You all always telling me to see life like it is.
　　　Well—I laid in there on my back today . . . and I figured it out. Life just
　　　like it is. Who gets and who don't get. [*He sits down with his coat on and
　　　laughs.*] Mama, you know it's all divided up. Life is. Sure enough. Between
　　　the takers and the "tooken." [*He laughs.*] I've figured it out finally. [*He looks
　　　around at them.*] Yeah. Some of us always getting "tooken." [*He laughs.*]
　　　People like Willy Harris, they don't never get "tooken." And you know
　　　why the rest of us do? 'Cause we all mixed up. Mixed up bad. We get to
　　　looking 'round for the right and the wrong; and we worry about it and cry
　　　about it and stay up nights trying to figure out 'bout the wrong and the
　　　right of things all the time . . . And all the time, man, them takers is out
　　　there operating, just taking and taking. Willy Harris? Shoot—Willy Harris
　　　don't even count. He don't even count in the big scheme of things. But I'll
　　　say one thing for old Willy Harris . . . he's taught me something. He's
　　　taught me to keep my eye on what counts in this world. Yeah—[*shouting
　　　out a little*] Thanks, Willy!

RUTH: What did you call that man for, Walter Lee!

WALTER: Called him to tell him to come on over to the show. Gonna put on a show
　　　for the man. Just what he wants to see. You see, Mama, the man came here
　　　today and he told us that them people out there where you want us to
　　　move—well they so upset they willing to pay us not to move out there. [*He
　　　laughs again.*] And—and oh, Mama—you would of been proud of the way
　　　me and Ruth and Bennie acted. We told him to get out . . . Lord have mercy!
　　　We told the man to get out. Oh, we was some proud folks this afternoon,
　　　yeah. [*He lights a cigarette.*] We were still full of that old-time stuff . . .

RUTH [*coming toward him slowly*]: You talking 'bout taking them people's money to
　　　keep us from moving in that house?

WALTER: I ain't just talking 'bout it, baby—I'm telling you that's what's going to happen.

BENEATHA: Oh, God! Where is the bottom! Where is the real honest-to-God bottom so he can't go any farther!

WALTER: See—that's the old stuff. You and that boy that was here today. You all want everybody to carry a flag and a spear and sing some marching songs, huh? You wanna spend your life looking into things and trying to find the right and the wrong part, huh? Yeah. You know what's going to happen to that boy someday—he'll find himself sitting in a dungeon, locked in forever— and the takers will have the key! Forget it, baby! There ain't no causes— there ain't nothing but taking in this world, and he who takes most is smartest—and it don't make a damn bit of difference *how*.

MAMA: You making something inside me cry, son. Some awful pain inside me.

WALTER: Don't cry, Mama. Understand. That white man is going to walk in that door able to write checks for more money than we ever had. It's important to him and I'm going to help him . . . I'm going to put on the show, Mama.

MAMA: Son—I come from five generations of people who was slaves and sharecrop- pers—but ain't nobody in my family never let nobody pay 'em no money that was a way of telling us we wasn't fit to walk the earth. We ain't never been that poor. [*raising her eyes and looking at him*] We ain't never been that dead inside.

BENEATHA: Well—we are dead now. All the talk about dreams and sunlight that goes on in this house. All dead.

WALTER: What's the matter with you all! I didn't make this world! It was give to me this way! Hell, yes, I want me some yachts someday! Yes, I want to hang some real pearls 'round my wife's neck. Ain't she supposed to wear no pearls? Somebody tell me—tell me, who decides which women is sup- pose to wear pearls in this world. I tell you I am a *man*—and I think my wife should wear some pearls in this world! [*This last line hangs a good while and* WALTER *begins to move about the room. The word "Man" has penetrated his consciousness; he mumbles it to himself repeatedly between strange agitated pauses as he moves about.*]

MAMA: Baby, how you going to feel on the inside?

WALTER: Fine! . . . Going to feel fine . . . a man . . .

MAMA: You won't have nothing left then, Walter Lee.

WALTER [*coming to her*]: I'm going to feel fine, Mama. I'm going to look that son-of-a- bitch in the eyes and say—[*He falters.*]—and say, "All right, Mr. Lindner— [*He falters even more.*]—that's your neighborhood out there. You got the right to keep it like you want. You got the right to have it like you want. Just write the check and—the house is yours." And, and I am going to say—[*His voice almost breaks.*] And you—you people just put the money in my hand and you won't have to live next to this bunch of stinking nig- gers! . . . [*He straightens up and moves away from his mother, walking around the room.*] Maybe—maybe I'll just get down on my black knees . . . [*He does so;* RUTH *and* BENNIE *and* MAMA *watch him in frozen horror.*] Cap- tain, Mistuh, Bossman. [*He starts crying.*] Ahee-hee-hee! [*wringing his hands in profoundly anguished imitation*] Yassssssuh! Great White Father, just gi' ussen de money, fo' God's sake, and we's ain't gwine come out deh and dirty up yo' white folks neighborhood . . . [*He breaks down com- pletely, then gets up and goes into the bedroom.*]

BENEATHA: That is not a man. That is nothing but a toothless rat.

MAMA: Yes—death done come in this here house. [*She is nodding, slowly, reflec-tively.*] Done come walking in my house. On the lips of my children. You what supposed to be my beginning again. You—what supposed to be my harvest. [*to* BENEATHA] You—you mourning your brother?

BENEATHA: He's no brother of mine.

MAMA: What you say?

BENEATHA: I said that that individual in that room is no brother of mine.

MAMA: That's what I thought you said. You feeling like you better than he is today? [BENEATHA *does not answer.*] Yes? What you tell him a minute ago? That he wasn't a man? Yes? You give him up for me? You done wrote his epitaph too—like the rest of the world? Well, who give you the privilege?

BENEATHA: Be on my side for once! You saw what he just did, Mama! You saw him—down on his knees. Wasn't it you who taught me—to despise any man who would do that? Do what he's going to do.

MAMA: Yes—I taught you that. Me and your daddy. But I thought I taught you some-thing else too . . . I thought I taught you to love him.

BENEATHA: Love him? There is nothing left to love.

MAMA: There is always something left to love. And if you ain't learned that, you ain't learned nothing. [*looking at her*] Have you cried for that boy today? I don't mean for yourself and for the family 'cause we lost the money. I mean for him; what he been through and what it done to him. Child, when do you think is the time to love somebody the most; when they done good and made things easy for everybody? Well then, you ain't through learning—because that ain't the time at all. It's when he's at his lowest and can't believe in hisself 'cause the world done whipped him so. When you starts measuring somebody, measure him right, child, measure him right. Make sure you done taken into account what hills and valleys he come through before he got to wherever he is. [TRAVIS *bursts into the room at the end of the speech, leaving the door open.*]

TRAVIS: Grandmama—the moving men are downstairs! The truck just pulled up.

MAMA [*turning and looking at him*]: Are they, baby? They downstairs? [*She sighs and sits.* LINDNER *appears in the doorway. He peers in and knocks lightly, to gain attention, and comes in. All turn to look at him.*]

LINDNER [*hat and briefcase in hand*]: Uh—hello . . . [RUTH *crosses mechanically to the bedroom door and opens it and lets it swing open freely and slowly as the lights come up on* WALTER *within, still in his coat, sitting at the far corner of the room. He looks up and out through the room to* LINDNER.]

RUTH: He's here. [*A long minute passes and* WALTER *slowly gets up.*]

LINDNER [*coming to the table with efficiency, putting his briefcase on the table and starting to unfold papers and unscrew fountain pens*]: Well, I certainly was glad to hear from you people. [WALTER *has begun the trek out of the room, slowly and awkwardly, rather like a small boy, passing the back of his sleeve across his mouth from time to time.*] Life can really be so much simpler than people let it be most of the time. Well—with whom do I negotiate? You, Mrs. Younger, or your son here? [MAMA *sits with her hands folded on her lap and her eyes closed as* WALTER *advances.* TRAVIS *goes close to* LINDNER *and looks at the papers curiously.*] Just some official papers, sonny.

RUTH: Travis, you go downstairs.

MAMA [*opening her eyes and looking into* WALTER'S]: No. Travis, you stay right here. And you make him understand what you doing, Walter Lee. You teach

him good. Like Willy Harris taught you. You show where our five generations done come to. Go ahead, son—

WALTER [*Looks down into his boy's eyes.* TRAVIS *grins at him merrily and* WALTER *draws
him beside him with his arm lightly around his shoulders.*]: Well,
Mr. Lindner. [BENEATHA *turns away.*] We called you—[*There is a profound,
simple groping quality in his speech.*]—because, well, me and my family
[*He looks around and shifts from one foot to the other.*] Well—we are very
plain people . . .

LINDNER: Yes—

WALTER: I mean—I have worked as a chauffeur most of my life—and my wife here,
she does domestic work in people's kitchens. So does my mother. I
mean—we are plain people . . .

LINDNER: Yes, Mr. Younger—

WALTER [*really like a small boy, looking down at his shoes and then up at the man*]:
And—uh—well, my father, well, he was a laborer most of his life.

LINDNER [*absolutely confused*]: Uh, yes—

WALTER [*looking down at his toes once again*]: My father almost beat a man to death
once because this man called him a bad name or something, you know
what I mean?

LINDNER: No, I'm afraid I don't.

WALTER [*finally straightening up*]: Well, what I mean is that we come from people
who had a lot of pride. I mean—we are very proud people. And that's my
sister over there and she's going to be a doctor—and we are very proud—

LINDNER: Well—I am sure that is very nice, but—

WALTER [*starting to cry and facing the man eye to eye*]: What I am telling you is that
we called you over here to tell you that we are very proud and that this
is—this is my son, who makes the sixth generation of our family in this
country, and that we have all thought about your offer and we have
decided to move into our house because my father—my father—he
earned it. [MAMA *has her eyes closed and is rocking back and forth as
though she were in church, with her head nodding the amen yes.*] We don't
want to make no trouble for nobody or fight no causes—but we will try
to be good neighbors. That's all we got to say. [*He looks the man absolutely in the eyes.*] We don't want your money. [*He turns and walks away
from the man.*]

LINDNER [*looking around at all of them*]: I take it then that you have decided to
occupy.

BENEATHA: That's what the man said.

LINDNER [*to* MAMA *in her reverie*]: Then I would like to appeal to you, Mrs. Younger.
You are older and wiser and understand things better I am sure . . .

MAMA [*rising*]: I am afraid you don't understand. My son said we was going to move
and there ain't nothing left for me to say. [*Shaking her head with double
meaning.*] You know how these young folks is nowadays, mister. Can't do
a thing with 'em. Good-bye.

LINDNER [*folding up his materials*]: Well—if you are that final about it . . . There is
nothing left for me to say. [*He finishes. He is almost ignored by the family,
who are concentrating on* WALTER LEE. *At the door* LINDNER *halts and looks
around.*] I sure hope you people know what you're doing. [*He shakes his
head and exits.*]

RUTH [*looking around and coming to life*]: Well, for God's sake—if the moving men
are here—LET'S GET THE HELL OUT OF HERE!

MAMA [*into action*]: Ain't it the truth! Look at all this here mess. Ruth, put Travis' good jacket on him . . . Walter Lee, fix your tie and tuck your shirt in, you look just like somebody's hoodlum. Lord have mercy, where is my plant? [*She flies to get it amid the general bustling of the family, who are deliberately trying to ignore the nobility of the past moment.*] You all start on down . . . Travis child, don't go empty-handed . . . Ruth, where did I put that box with my skillets in it? I want to be in charge of it myself . . . I'm going to make us the biggest dinner we ever ate tonight . . . Beneatha, what's the matter with them stockings? Pull them things up, girl . . . [*The family starts to file out as two moving men appear and begin to carry out the heavier pieces of furniture, bumping into the family as they move about.*]

BENEATHA: Mama, Asagai—asked me to marry him today and go to Africa—

MAMA [*in the middle of her getting-ready activity*]: He did? You ain't old enough to marry nobody—[*Seeing the moving men lifting one of her chairs precariously.*] Darling, that ain't no bale of cotton, please handle it so we can sit in it again. I had that chair twenty-five years . . . [*The movers sigh with exasperation and go on with their work.*]

BENEATHA [*girlishly and unreasonably trying to pursue the conversation*]: To go to Africa, Mama—be a doctor in Africa . . .

MAMA [*distracted*]: Yes, baby—

WALTER: Africa! What he want to go to Africa for?

BENEATHA: To practice there . . .

WALTER: Girl, if you don't get all them silly ideas out your head! You better marry yourself a man with some loot . . .

BENEATHA [*angrily, precisely as in the first scene of the play*]: What have you got to do with who I marry!

WALTER: Plenty. Now I think George Murchison—[*He and* BENEATHA *go out yelling at each other vigorously;* BENEATHA *is heard saying that she would not marry* GEORGE MURCHISON *if he were Adam and she were Eve, etc. The anger is loud and real till their voices diminish.* RUTH *stands at the door and turns to* MAMA *and smiles knowingly.*]

MAMA [*fixing her hat at last*]: Yeah—they something all right, my children . . .

RUTH: Yeah—they're something. Let's go, Lena.

MAMA [*stalling, starting to look around at the house*]: Yes—I'm coming. Ruth—

RUTH: Yes?

MAMA [*quietly, woman to woman*]: He finally come into his manhood today, didn't he? Kind of like a rainbow after the rain . . .

RUTH [*biting her lip lest her own pride explode in front of* MAMA]: Yes, Lena. [BENEATHA'*s voice calls for them raucously.*]

MAMA [*waving* RUTH *out vaguely*]: All right, honey—go on down. I be down directly. [RUTH *hesitates, then exits.* MAMA *stands, at last alone in the living room, her plant on the table before her as the lights start to come down. She looks around at all the walls and ceilings and suddenly, despite herself, while the children call below, a great heaving thing rises in her and she puts her fist to her mouth, takes a final desperate look, pulls her coat about her, pats her hat and goes out. The lights dim down. The door opens and she comes back in, grabs her plant, and goes out for the last time.*]

CURTAIN

[1958]

Joining the Conversation: Critical Thinking and Writing

1. On pages 170–81, we discuss Langston Hughes's "Harlem," the poem from which Hansberry chose her title. Please describe why this choice of title is a good one.

2. Imagine that Hansberry has asked your help in selecting a title for her play and that the title she actually selected, *A Raisin in the Sun,* is not an option. Write a letter to her, of about one to two pages, in which you recommend a title of your own choosing based on your reading of the text.

3. A scholar has observed, "the main point of the play is that the characters find they must defer their dreams." Present an argument in which you discuss and provide evidence for this claim.

4. Please list, in two or three sentences each, three key insights that Hansberry offers about race. Describe how you would organize and connect these insights into an effective argument.

5. If you were assigned to give an analysis in class of a crucial passage or scene in the play, which one would you choose? What would be the key questions about it that you would ask the students? What would you be trying to help them discover and understand about Hansberry's work?

6. Walter says money "is life." What does he mean? Is his view supported by the play as a whole? How does Mama respond to this idea?

7. Consider the phrase "money is life" in a more general sense. In an essay of one to two pages, please argue that it is indeed the case that "money is life," and then in a second essay of the same length, argue that it is not.

8. Mama also says, "There is always something left to love." What does she mean by this statement? Does the play as a whole support her view?

9. Commenting on the historical context of *A Raisin the Sun,* a scholar has stated, "The play is best understood in relation to the American civil rights movement of the 1950s and 1960s." Making use of at least three sources, write a two to three page essay that summarizes the play in this context. Remember to include a bibliography of the Internet and print sources that you consult.

10. Another scholar has noted that Hansberry's play "has been translated into over thirty languages on every continent, and has been produced in such diverse countries as the former Czechoslovakia, England, the former Soviet Union, and France." In your view, what explains this worldwide appeal? Please point to specific passages to support your argument.

11. Do you agree that *A Raisin in the Sun* is not only about race but also about gender and class? Locate passages in the text that support your response.

12. Are you familiar with the phrase "the American dream"? What does it mean? How does it apply to the characters in this play?

13. Is "the American dream" for these characters the same as, or different from, what it is for you? Do you expect that you will be able to achieve your dream when you want to or that you will be obliged to defer it? Please explain as clearly as you can.

14. Why is having a home of one's own so important in this play? Is it important for you as well?

15. Often it is said that each of us—whatever our race, religion, ethnicity, or gender—"wants the same things in life." Do you agree or disagree? How would you go about developing an argument to explain and support your view? What kinds of evidence would you present?

16. Imagine that you are preparing a new edition of Hansberry's play. Making use of library or Internet sources, locate a photograph or an image of some other kind for the cover of this edition. Please explain your choice. (Be sure to include the image with your essay.)

Chapter Overview: Looking Backward/Looking Forward

1. Do you think it is important for Americans to love their country? In what ways would this love be shown?
2. Is it possible to love one's country and, at the same time, to be critical of it? Should love of country be complete and unconditional?
3. If you are not an American, but you are, for example, attending school here, what is the relationship between your feelings about the United States and your feelings about your homeland?
4. Do you think Americans are the same as, or different from, people everywhere else? How would you argue that they are the same? How would you argue that they are different? Which argument, in your view, is more convincing?
5. In five hundred words, set forth your idea of the American Dream.

CHAPTER 22

Law and Disorder

ESSAY

MARTIN LUTHER KING JR.

Martin Luther King Jr. (1929–68) was born in Atlanta, Georgia, and was educated at Morehouse College, Crozer Theological Seminary, and Boston University. In 1954, he was called to serve as a Baptist minister in Montgomery, Alabama. During the next two years, he achieved national fame when, using a policy of nonviolent resistance, he successfully led a boycott of the segregated bus lines in Montgomery. He then organized the Southern Christian Leadership Conference, which furthered the pursuit of civil rights, first in the South and then nationwide. In 1964, he was awarded the Nobel Peace Prize. Four years later, he was assassinated in Memphis, Tennessee.

Before we turn to Dr. Martin Luther King's "Letter from Birmingham Jail," it is helpful to have a sense of the historical context of the letter, which is widely considered one of the most important essays in American history. Written during the civil rights movement, the letter decries the injustice that defines segregation. Explaining the need for civil disobedience, it provides a clear argument for the need to counter injustice with nonviolent protest. King highlights the unequal application of the law to different racial groups, and maintains that an unjust law can and must be broken in order for it to be remedied. Calling attention to the oppression of black Americans, King argues that the cause of racial equality has suffered due to white moderates' calls for order and patience. King supports his arguments with references to the Bible, American history, and the recent events of the civil rights movement. Although the letter provides a series of clear and logical arguments, it builds towards an emotional appeal to the reader's sense of moral justice. It thus stands as one of America's most inspirational texts.

The letter was written in reaction to a specific series of events. On April 12, 1963, King was arrested in Birmingham, Alabama, for participating in a Good Friday protest march. A permit for the march had not been been issued by the city officials, and the protesters ignored the recently-passed local law requiring that public gatherings have an official permit. As King's letter explains, the protest sought to call attention to the racist practices of white-owned businesses. The protest was part of a larger anti-segregation campaign designed to attack the racism and prejudice that defined Birmingham, one of the most segregated cities in America. The campaign included lunch counter sit-ins, kneel-ins at churches, marches on city hall, and a boycott of local businesses. On April 10, the city obtained a court injunction against the protests, but the campaign leaders decided to disobey the order. As a result, King and almost 50 other protesters were arrested. King was later released from jail on April 20. King strategically employed this tactic of peaceful protest and subsequent arrest to call attention to segregation; his arrest in Birmingham was his thirteenth arrest.

Events in Birmingham continued to worsen. On May 7, four thousand protesters were dispersed with high-pressure fire hoses and police dogs; images of this treatment of peaceful protesters lead to widespread outrage. On May 10, a "Birmingham Truce Agreement" was signed, detailing plans to reverse segregationist structures by removing "white only" and "blacks only" signs on restrooms and water fountains and by integrating lunch counters. That night, an explosion went off at a hotel where King had stayed and, the next day, the home of King's brother was bombed. On August 28, King delivered his "I Have a Dream" speech as part of a march on Washington. On September 15, the Birmingham Sixteenth Street Baptist Church was bombed by Ku Klux Klan members and four young girls died as a result.

While in the Birmingham jail, King wrote a response to a letter, titled "A Call for Unity," that eight local clergymen had published in the Birmingham News. The clergymen's letter opens by asking that the decisions of the courts be "peacefully obeyed." It explains that there is hope for new solutions to racial problems, but maintains that those solutions are being undermined by the protests, especially because the protests are being lead by "outsiders," or organizers from out of town. The letter continues to argue that the problems of segregation would best be addressed by the people from Birmingham, and calls for local "white and Negro" people to meet and engage in "open negotiation." However, the letter also calls for the local black community to "withdraw support" for the ongoing protests. The letter praises the protesters' peaceful demonstrations and urges the police to show restraint, but ultimately aims to end the protests by removing local participation in them. The letter ends by calling for the black and white citizens of Birmingham to "observe the principles of law and order and common sense."

King penned his reactions to the clergymen's letter in the margins of the paper, and his writing was circulated as a mimeographed copy before being published as a pamphlet and in several magazines.

Letter from Birmingham Jail

April 16, 1963

My Dear Fellow Clergymen:

While confined here in the Birmingham city jail, I came across your recent statement calling my present activities "unwise and untimely."[1] Seldom do I pause to answer criticism of my work and ideas. If I sought to answer all the criticisms that cross my desk, my secretaries would have little time for anything other than such correspondence in the course of the day, and I would have no time for constructive work. But since I feel that you are men of genuine good will and that your criticisms are sincerely set forth, I want to try to answer your statement in what I hope will be patient and reasonable terms.

---

[1] This response to a published statement by eight fellow clergymen from Alabama (Bishop C.C.J. Carpenter, Bishop Joseph A. Durick, Rabbi Milton L. Grafman, Bishop Paul Hardin, Bishop Nolan B. Harmon, the Reverend George M. Murray, the Reverend Edward V. Ramage, and the Reverend Earl Stallings) was composed under somewhat constricting circumstances. Begun on the margins of the newspaper in which the statement appeared while I was in jail, the letter was continued on scraps of writing paper supplied by a friendly Negro trusty, and concluded on a pad my attorneys were eventually permitted to leave me. Although the text remains in substance unaltered, I have indulged in the author's prerogative of polishing it for publication. [King's note.]

I think I should indicate why I am here in Birmingham, since you have been influenced by the view which argues against "outsiders coming in." I have the honor of serving as president of the Southern Christian Leadership Conference, an organization operating in every southern state, with headquarters in Atlanta, Georgia. We have some eighty-five affiliated organizations across the South, and one of them is the Alabama Christian Movement for Human Rights. Frequently we share staff, educational, and financial resources with our affiliates. Several months ago the affiliate here in Birmingham asked us to be on call to engage in a nonviolent direct-action program if such were deemed necessary. We readily consented, and when the hour came we lived up to our promise. So I, along with several members of my staff, am here because I was invited here. I am here because I have organizational ties here.

But more basically, I am in Birmingham because injustice is here. Just as the prophets of the eighth century B.C. left their villages and carried their "thus saith the Lord" far beyond the boundaries of their home towns, and just as the Apostle Paul left his village of Tarsus and carried the gospel of Jesus Christ to the far corners of the Greco-Roman world, so am I compelled to carry the gospel of freedom beyond my own home town. Like Paul, I must constantly respond to the Macedonian call for aid.

Moreover, I am cognizant of the interrelatedness of all communities and states. I cannot sit idly by in Atlanta and not be concerned about what happens in Birmingham. Injustice anywhere is a threat to justice everywhere. We are caught in an inescapable network of mutuality; tied in a single garment of destiny. Whatever affects one directly, affects all indirectly. Never again can we afford to live with the narrow, provincial "outside agitator" idea. Anyone who lives inside the United States can never be considered an outsider anywhere within its bounds.

5   You deplore the demonstrations taking place in Birmingham. But your statement, I am sorry to say, fails to express a similar concern for the conditions that brought about the demonstrations. I am sure that none of you would want to rest content with the superficial kind of social analysis that deals merely with effects and does not grapple with underlying causes. It is unfortunate that demonstrations are taking place in Birmingham, but it is even more unfortunate that the city's white power structure left the Negro community with no alternative.

In any nonviolent campaign there are four basic steps: collection of the facts to determine whether injustices exist; negotiation; self-purification; and direct action. We have gone through all these steps in Birmingham. There can be no gainsaying the fact that racial injustice engulfs this community. Birmingham is probably the most thoroughly segregated city in the United States. Its ugly record of brutality is widely known. Negroes have experienced grossly unjust treatment in the courts. There have been more unsolved bombings of Negro homes and churches in Birmingham than in any other city in the nation. These are the hard, brutal facts of the case. On the basis of these conditions, Negro leaders sought to negotiate with the city fathers. But the latter consistently refused to engage in good-faith negotiation.

Then, last September, came the opportunity to talk with leaders of Birmingham's economic community. In the course of the negotiations, certain promises were made by the merchants—for example, to remove the stores' humiliating racial signs. On the basis of these promises, the Reverend Fred Shuttleworth and the leaders of the Alabama Christian Movement for Human Rights agreed to a moratorium on all demonstrations. As the weeks and months went by, we realized that we were the victims of a broken promise. A few signs, briefly removed, returned; the others remained.

Martin Luther King Jr.,
in Birmingham Jail

As in so many past experiences, our hopes had been blasted, and the shadow of deep disappointment settled upon us. We had no alternative except to prepare for direct action, whereby we would present our very bodies as a means of laying our case before the conscience of the local and the national community. Mindful of the difficulties involved, we decided to undertake a process of self-purification. We began a series of workshops on nonviolence, and we repeatedly asked ourselves: "Are you able to accept blows without retaliating?" "Are you able to endure the ordeal of jail?" We decided to schedule our direct-action program for the Easter season, realizing that except for Christmas, this is the main shopping period of the year. Knowing that a strong economic-withdrawal program would be the by-product of direct action, we felt that this would be the best time to bring pressure to bear on the merchants for the needed change.

Then it occurred to us that Birmingham's mayoralty election was coming up in March, and we speedily decided to postpone action until after election day. When we discovered that the Commissioner of Public Safety, Eugene "Bull" Connor, had piled up enough votes to be in the run-off, we decided again to postpone action until the day after the run-off so that the demonstrations could not be used to cloud the issues. Like many others, we waited to see Mr. Connor defeated, and to this end we endured postponement after postponement. Having aided in this community need, we felt that our direct-action program could be delayed no longer.

10   You may well ask: "Why direct action? Why sit-ins, marches, and so forth? Isn't negotiation a better path?" You are quite right in calling for negotiation. Indeed, this is the very purpose of direct action. Nonviolent direct action seeks to create such a crisis and foster such a tension that a community which has constantly refused to negotiate is forced to confront the issue. It seeks so to dramatize the issue that it can no longer be ignored. My citing the creation of tension as part of the work of the nonviolent-resister may sound rather shocking. But I must confess that I am not afraid of the word "tension." I have earnestly opposed violent tension, but there is a type of constructive, nonviolent tension which is necessary for growth. Just as Socrates felt that it was necessary to create a tension in the mind so that individuals could rise from the bondage of myths and half-truths to the unfettered realm of creative analysis and objective appraisal, so must we see the need for nonviolent gadflies to create the kind of tension in society that will help men rise from the dark depths of prejudice and racism to the majestic heights of understanding and brotherhood.

The purpose of our direct-action program is to create a situation so crisis-packed that it will inevitably open the door to negotiation. I therefore concur with you in your call for negotiation. Too long has our beloved Southland been bogged down in a tragic effort to live in monologue rather than dialogue.

One of the basic points in your statement is that the action that I and my associates have taken in Birmingham is untimely. Some have asked: "Why didn't you give the new city administration time to act?" The only answer that I can give to this query is that the new Birmingham administration must be prodded about as much as the outgoing one, before it will act. We are sadly mistaken if we feel that the election of Albert Boutwell as mayor will bring the millennium to Birmingham. While Mr. Boutwell is a much more gentle person than Mr. Connor, they are both segregationists, dedicated to maintenance of the status quo. I have hope that Mr. Boutwell will be reasonable enough to see the futility of massive resistance to desegregation. But he will not see this without pressure from devotees of civil rights. My friends, I must say to you that we have not made a single gain in civil rights without determined legal and nonviolent pressure. Lamentably, it is an historical fact that privileged groups seldom give up their privileges voluntarily. Individuals may see the moral light and voluntarily give up their unjust posture; but as Reinhold Niebuhr[2] has reminded us, groups tend to be more immoral than individuals.

We know through painful experience that freedom is never voluntarily given by the oppressor; it must be demanded by the oppressed. Frankly, I have yet to engage in a direct-action campaign that was "well timed" in the view of those who have not suffered unduly from the disease of segregation. For years now I have heard the word "Wait!" It rings in the ear of every Negro with piercing familiarity. This "Wait" has almost always meant "Never." We must come to see, with one of our distinguished jurists, that "justice too long delayed is justice denied."[3]

We have waited for more than 340 years for our constitutional and God-given rights. The nations of Asia and Africa are moving with jetlike speed toward gaining political independence, but we still creep at horse-and-buggy pace toward gaining a cup of coffee at a lunch counter. Perhaps it is easy for those who have never felt the stinging darts of segregation to say, "Wait." But when you have seen vicious

[2]**Reinhold Niebuhr** Niebuhr (1892–1971) was a minister, political activist, author, and professor at Union Theological Seminary in New York City. [All notes are the editors' unless otherwise specified.]   [3]**Justice . . . denied** a quotation attributed to William E. Gladstone (1809–98), British statesman and prime minister.

mobs lynch your mothers and fathers at will and drown your sisters and brothers at whim; when you have seen hate-filled policemen curse, kick, and even kill your black brothers and sisters; when you see the vast majority of your twenty million Negro brothers smothering in an airtight cage of poverty in the midst of an affluent society; when you suddenly find your tongue twisted and your speech stammering as you seek to explain to your six-year-old daughter why she can't go to the public amusement park that has just been advertised on television, and see tears welling up in her eyes when she is told that Funtown is closed to colored children, and see ominous clouds of inferiority beginning to form in her little mental sky, and see her beginning to distort her personality by developing an unconscious bitterness toward white people; when you have to concoct an answer for a five-year-old son who is asking: "Daddy, why do white people treat colored people so mean?"; when you take a cross-country drive and find it necessary to sleep night after night in the uncomfortable corners of your automobile because no motel will accept you; when you are humiliated day in and day out by nagging signs reading "white" and "colored"; when your first name becomes "nigger," your middle name becomes "boy" (however old you are) and your last name becomes "John," and your wife and mother are never given the respected title "Mrs."; when you are harried by day and haunted by night by the fact that you are a Negro, living constantly at tiptoe stance, never quite knowing what to expect next, and are plagued with inner fears and outer resentments; when you are forever fighting a degenerating sense of "nobodiness"— then you will understand why we find it difficult to wait. There comes a time when the cup of endurance runs over, and men are no longer willing to be plunged into the abyss of despair. I hope, sirs, you can understand our legitimate and unavoidable impatience.

15   You express a great deal of anxiety over our willingness to break laws. This is certainly a legitimate concern. Since we so diligently urge people to obey the Supreme Court's decision of 1954 outlawing segregation in the public schools, at first glance it may seem rather paradoxical for us consciously to break laws. One may well ask: "How can you advocate breaking some laws and obeying others?" The answer lies in the fact that there are two types of laws: just and unjust. I would be the first to advocate obeying just laws. One has not only a legal but a moral responsibility to obey just laws. Conversely, one has a moral responsibility to disobey unjust laws. I would agree with St. Augustine that "an unjust law is no law at all."

Now, what is the difference between the two? How does one determine whether a law is just or unjust? A just law is a man-made code that squares with the moral law or the law of God. An unjust law is a code that is out of harmony with the moral law. To put it in the terms of St. Thomas Aquinas: An unjust law is a human law that is not rooted in eternal law and natural law. Any law that uplifts human personality is just. Any law that degrades human personality is unjust. All segregation statutes are unjust because segregation distorts the soul and damages the personality. It gives the segregator a false sense of superiority and the segregated a false sense of inferiority. Segregation, to use the terminology of the Jewish philosopher Martin Buber,[4] substitutes an "I-it" relationship for an "I-thou" relationship and ends up relegating persons to the status of things. Hence segregation is

[4]**Martin Buber** Israeli religious philosopher (1878–1965), author of *Land Thou* (1923).
[5]**Paul Tillich** Tillich (1886–1965), born in Germany, taught theology at several German universities until in 1933 he was dismissed from his post at the University of Frankfurt because of his opposition to the Nazi regime. At the invitation of Reinhold Niebuhr, he came to the United States and taught at Union Theological Seminary.

not only politically, economically, and sociologically unsound, it is morally wrong and sinful. Paul Tillich[5] has said that sin is separation. Is not segregation an existential expression of man's tragic separation, his awful estrangement, his terrible sinfulness? Thus it is that I can urge men to obey the 1954 decision of the Supreme Court, for it is morally right; and I can urge them to disobey segregation ordinances, for they are morally wrong.

Let us consider a more concrete example of just and unjust laws. An unjust law is a code that a numerical or power majority group compels a minority group to obey but does not make binding on itself. This is *difference* made legal. By the same token, a just law is a code that a majority compels a minority to follow and that it is willing to follow itself. This is *sameness* made legal.

Let me give another explanation. A law is unjust if it is inflicted on a minority that, as a result of being denied the right to vote, had no part in enacting or devising the law. Who can say that the legislature of Alabama which set up that state's segregation laws was democratically elected? Throughout Alabama all sorts of devious methods are used to prevent Negroes from becoming registered voters, and there are some counties in which, even though Negroes constitute a majority of the population, not a single Negro is registered. Can any law enacted under such circumstances be considered democratically structured?

Sometimes a law is just on its face and unjust in its application. For instance, I have been arrested on a charge of parading without a permit. Now, there is nothing wrong in having an ordinance which requires a permit for a parade. But such an ordinance becomes unjust when it is used to maintain segregation and to deny citizens the First Amendment privilege of peaceful assembly and protest.

20   I hope you are able to see the distinction I am trying to point out. In no sense do I advocate evading or defying the law, as would the rabid segregationist. That would lead to anarchy. One who breaks an unjust law must do so openly, lovingly, and with a willingness to accept the penalty. I submit that an individual who breaks a law that conscience tells him is unjust, and who willingly accepts the penalty of imprisonment in order to arouse the conscience of the community over its injustice, is in reality expressing the highest respect for law.

Of course, there is nothing new about this kind of civil disobedience. It was evidenced sublimely in the refusal of Shadrach, Meshach, and Abednego to obey the laws of Nebuchadnezzar, on the ground that a higher moral law was at stake. It was practiced superbly by the early Christians, who were willing to face hungry lions and the excruciating pain of chopping blocks rather than submit to certain unjust laws of the Roman Empire. To a degree, academic freedom is a reality today because Socrates practiced civil disobedience. In our own nation, the Boston Tea Party represented a massive act of civil disobedience.

We should never forget that everything Adolf Hitler did in Germany was "legal" and everything the Hungarian freedom fighters did in Hungary was "illegal." It was "illegal" to aid and comfort a Jew in Hitler's Germany. Even so, I am sure that, had I lived in Germany at the time, I would have aided and comforted my Jewish brothers. If today I lived in a Communist country where certain principles dear to the Christian faith are suppressed, I would openly advocate disobeying that country's anti-religious laws.

I must make two honest confessions to you, my Christian and Jewish brothers. First, I must confess that over the past few years I have been gravely disappointed with the white moderate. I have almost reached the regrettable conclusion that the Negro's great stumbling block in his stride toward freedom is not the White Citizen's Counciler or the Ku Klux Klanner, but the white moderate, who is more devoted to "order" than to justice; who prefers a negative peace which is the absence of tension to a positive peace which is the presence of justice; who constantly says: "I agree with you in the goal you seek, but I cannot agree with your methods or direct action"; who paternalistically believes he can set the timetable for another man's freedom; who lives by a mythical concept of time and who constantly advises the Negro to wait for a "more convenient season." Shallow understanding from people of good will is more frustrating than absolute misunderstanding from people of ill will. Lukewarm acceptance is much more bewildering than outright rejection.

I had hoped that the white moderate would understand that law and order exist for the purpose of establishing justice and that when they fail in this purpose they become the dangerously structured dams that block the flow of social progress. I had hoped that the white moderate would understand that the present tension in the South is a necessary phase of the transition from an obnoxious negative peace, in which the Negro passively accepted his unjust plight, to a substantive and positive peace, in which all men will respect the dignity and worth of human personality. Actually, we who engage in nonviolent direct action are not the creators of tension. We merely bring to the surface the hidden tension that is already alive. We bring it out in the open, where it can be seen and dealt with. Like a boil that can never be cured so long as it is covered up but must be opened with all its ugliness to the natural medicines of air and light, injustice must be exposed, with all the tension its exposure creates, to the light of human conscience and the air of national opinion before it can be cured.

25   In your statement you assert that our actions, even though peaceful, must be condemned because they precipitate violence. But is this a logical assertion? Isn't this like condemning a robbed man because his possession of money precipitated the evil act of robbery? Isn't this like condemning Socrates because his unswerving commitment to truth and his philosophical inquiries precipitated the act by the misguided populace in which they made him drink hemlock? Isn't this like condemning Jesus because his unique God-consciousness and never-ceasing devotion to God's will precipitated the evil act of crucifixion? We must come to see that, as the federal courts have consistently affirmed, it is wrong to urge an individual to cease his efforts to gain his basic constitutional rights because the quest may precipitate violence. Society must protect the robbed and punish the robber.

I had also hoped that the white moderate would reject the myth concerning time in relation to the struggle for freedom. I have just received a letter from a white brother in Texas. He writes: "All Christians know that the colored people will receive equal rights eventually, but it is possible that you are in too great a religious hurry. It has taken Christianity almost two thousand years to accomplish what it has. The teachings of Christ take time to come to earth." Such an attitude stems from a tragic misconception of time, from the strangely irrational notion that there is something in the very flow of time that will inevitably cure all ills. Actually, time itself is neutral; it can be used either destructively or constructively. More and more I feel that the people of ill will have used time much more effectively than have the people of good will. We will have to repent in this generation not merely for the hateful words and actions of the bad people but for the appalling silence of the good people. Human progress never rolls in on wheels of inevitability; it comes through the tireless efforts of men willing to be co-workers with God, and without this hard work, time itself becomes an ally of the forces of social stagnation. We must use time creatively, in the knowledge that the time is always ripe to do right. Now is the time to make real the promise of democracy and transform our pending national elegy into a creative psalm of brotherhood. Now is the time to lift our national policy from the quicksand of racial injustice to the solid rock of human dignity.

You speak of our activity in Birmingham as extreme. At first I was rather disappointed that fellow clergymen would see my nonviolent efforts as those of an extremist. I began thinking about the fact that I stand in the middle of two opposing forces in the Negro community. One is a force of complacency, made up in part of Negroes who, as a result of long years of oppression, are so drained of self-respect and a sense of "somebodiness" that they have adjusted to segregation; and in part of a few middle-class Negroes who, because of a degree of academic and economic security and because in some ways they profit by segregation, have become insensitive to the problems of the masses. The other force is one of bitterness and hatred, and it comes perilously close to advocating violence. It is expressed in the various black nationalist groups that are springing up across the nation, the largest and best-known being Elijah Muhammad's Muslim movement. Nourished by the Negro's frustration over the continued existence of racial discrimination, this movement is made up of people who have lost faith in America, who have absolutely repudiated Christianity, and who have concluded that the white man is an incorrigible "devil."

I have tried to stand between these two forces, saying that we need emulate neither the "do-nothingism" of the complacent nor the hatred and despair of the black nationalist. For there is the more excellent way of love and nonviolent protest. I am grateful to God that, through the influence of the Negro church, the way of nonviolence became an integral part of our struggle.

If this philosophy had not emerged, by now many streets of the South should, I am convinced, be flowing with blood. And I am further convinced that if our white brothers dismiss as "rabble-rousers" and "outside agitators" those of us who employ nonviolent direct action, and if they refuse to support our nonviolent efforts, millions of Negroes will, out of frustration and despair, seek solace and security in black-nationalist ideologies—a development that would inevitably lead to a frightening racial nightmare.

30   Oppressed people cannot remain oppressed forever. The yearning for freedom eventually manifests itself, and that is what has happened to the American Negro. Something within has reminded him of his birthright of freedom, and something without has reminded him that it can be gained. Consciously or unconsciously, he has been caught up by the *Zeitgeist*,[6] and with his black brothers of Africa and his brown and yellow brothers of Asia, South America, and the Caribbean, the United States Negro is moving with a sense of great urgency toward the promised land of racial justice. If one recognizes this vital urge that has engulfed the Negro community, one should readily understand why public demonstrations are taking place. The Negro has many pent-up resentments and latent frustrations, and he must release them. So let him march; let him make prayer pilgrimages to the city hall; let him go on freedom rides—and try to understand why he must do so. If his repressed emotions are not released in nonviolent ways, they will seek expression through violence; this is not a threat but a fact of history. So I have not said to my people: "Get rid of your discontent." Rather, I have tried to say that this normal and healthy discontent can be channeled into the creative outlet of nonviolent direct action. And now this approach is being termed extremist.

But though I was initially disappointed at being categorized as an extremist, as I continued to think about the matter I gradually gained a measure of satisfaction from the label. Was not Jesus an extremist for love: "Love your enemies, bless them that curse you, do good to them that hate you, and pray for them which despitefully use you, and persecute you." Was not Amos an extremist for justice: "Let justice roll down like waters and righteousness like an ever-flowing stream." Was not Paul an extremist for the Christian gospel: "I bear in my body the marks of the Lord Jesus." Was not Martin Luther an extremist: "Here I stand; I cannot do otherwise, so help me God." And John Bunyan:[7] "I will stay in jail to the end of my days before I make a butchery of my conscience." And Abraham Lincoln: "This nation cannot survive half slave and half free." And Thomas Jefferson: "We hold these truths to be self-evident, that all men are created equal. . . ." So the question is not whether we will be extremists, but what kind of extremists we will be. Will we be extremists for hate or for love? Will we be extremists for the preservation of injustice or for the extension of justice? In that dramatic scene on Calvary's hill three men were crucified. We must never forget that all three were crucified for the same crime— the crime of extremism. Two were extremists for immorality, and thus fell below their environment. The other, Jesus Christ, was an extremist for love, truth, and goodness, and thereby rose above his environment. Perhaps the South, the nation, and the world are in dire need of creative extremists.

I had hoped that the white moderate would see this need. Perhaps I was too optimistic; perhaps I expected too much. I suppose I should have realized that few members of the oppressor race can understand the deep groans and passionate yearnings of the oppressed race, and still fewer have the vision to see that injustice must be rooted out by strong, persistent, and determined action. I am thankful, however, that some of our white brothers in the South have grasped the meaning of this social revolution and committed themselves to it. They are still all too few in quantity, but they are big in quality. Some—such as Ralph McGill, Lillian Smith, Harry Golden, James McBride Dabbs, Ann Braden, and Sarah Patton Boyle—have written about our struggle in eloquent and prophetic terms. Others have marched with us down nameless streets of the South. They have languished in filthy, roach-infested jails, suffering the abuse and brutality of policemen who view them as "dirty nigger-lovers." Unlike so many of their moderate brothers and sisters, they have recognized the urgency of the moment and sensed the need for powerful "action" antidotes to combat the disease of segregation.

Let me take note of my other major disappointment. I have been so greatly disappointed with the white church and its leadership. Of course, there are some notable exceptions. I am not unmindful of the fact that each of you has taken some significant stands on this issue. I commend you, Reverend Stallings, for your Christian stand on this past Sunday, in welcoming Negroes to your worship service on a nonsegregated basis. I commend the Catholic leaders of this state for integrating Spring Hill College several years ago.

But despite these notable exceptions, I must honestly reiterate that I have been disappointed with the church. I do not say this as one of those negative critics who can always find something wrong with the church. I say this as a minister of the gospel, who loves the church; who was nurtured in its bosom; who has been sustained by its spiritual blessings and who will remain true to it as long as the cord of life shall lengthen.

35   When I was suddenly catapulted into the leadership of the bus protest in Montgomery, Alabama, a few years ago, I felt we would be supported by the white church. I felt that the white ministers, priests, and rabbis of the South would be among our strongest allies. Instead, some have been outright opponents, refusing to understand the freedom movement and misrepresenting its leaders; all too many

[7]**John Bunyan** English writer (1628–88) best known for his *Pilgrim's Progress* (two parts, 1678 and 1684); from 1660 to 1672 he was imprisoned for his political and religious views.

others have been more cautious than courageous and have remained silent behind the anesthetizing security of stained-glass windows.

In spite of my shattered dreams, I came to Birmingham with the hope that the white religious leadership of this community would see the justice of our cause and, with deep moral concern, would serve as the channel through which our just grievances could reach the power structure. I had hoped that each of you would understand. But again I have been disappointed.

I have heard numerous southern religious leaders admonish their worshipers to comply with a desegregation decision because it is the law, but I have longed to hear white ministers declare: "Follow this decree because integration is morally right and because the Negro is your brother." In the midst of blatant injustices inflicted upon the Negro, I have watched white churchmen stand on the sideline and mouth pious irrelevancies and sanctimonious trivialities. In the midst of a mighty struggle to rid our nation of racial and economic injustice, I have heard many ministers say: "Those are social issues, with which the gospel has no real concern." And I have watched many churches commit themselves to a completely otherworldly religion which makes a strange, unbiblical distinction between body and soul, between the sacred and the secular.

I have traveled the length and breadth of Alabama, Mississippi, and all the other southern states. On sweltering summer days and crisp autumn mornings I have looked at the South's beautiful churches with their lofty spires pointing heavenward. I have beheld the impressive outlines of her massive religious-education buildings. Over and over I have found myself saying. "What kind of people worship here? Who is their God? Where were their voices when the lips of Governor Barnett dripped with words of interposition and nullification? Where were they when Governor Wallace gave a clarion call for defiance and hatred? Where were their voices of support when bruised and weary Negro men and women decided to rise from the dark dungeons of complacency to the bright hills of creative protest?"

Yes, these questions are still in my mind. In deep disappointment I have wept over the laxity of the church. But be assured that my tears have been tears of love. There can be no deep disappointment where there is not deep love. Yes, I love the church. How could I do otherwise? I am in the rather unique position of being the son, the grandson, and the great-grandson of preachers. Yes, I see the church as the body of Christ. But, Oh! How we have blemished and scarred that body through social neglect and through fear of being nonconformists.

40   There was a time when the church was very powerful—in the time when the early Christians rejoiced at being deemed worthy to suffer for what they believed. In those days the church was not merely a thermometer that recorded the ideas and principles of popular opinion; it was a thermostat that transformed the mores of society. Whenever the early Christians entered a town, the people in power became disturbed and immediately sought to convict the Christians for being "disturbers of the peace" and "outside agitators." But the Christians pressed on, in the conviction that they were "a colony of heaven," called to obey God rather than man. Small in number, they were big in commitment. They were too God-intoxicated to be "astronomically intimidated." By their effort and example they brought an end to such ancient evils as infanticide and gladiatorial contests.

Things are different now. So often the contemporary church is a weak, ineffectual voice with an uncertain sound. So often it is an archdefender of the status quo. Far from being disturbed by the presence of the church, the power structure of the average community is consoled by the church's silent—and often even vocal—sanction of things as they are.

But the judgment of God is upon the church as never before. If today's church does not recapture the sacrificial spirit of the early church, it will lose its authenticity, forfeit the loyalty of millions, and be dismissed as an irrelevant social club with no meaning for the twentieth century. Every day I meet young people whose disappointment with the church has turned into outright disgust.

Perhaps I have once again been too optimistic. Is organized religion too inextricably bound to the status quo to save our nation and the world? Perhaps I must turn my faith to the inner spiritual church, the church within the church, as the true *ekklesia*[8] and the hope of the world. But again I am thankful to God that some noble souls from the ranks of organized religion have broken loose from the paralyzing chains of conformity and joined us as active partners in the struggle for freedom. They have left their secure congregations and walked the streets of Albany, Georgia, with us. They have gone down the highways of the South on tortuous rides for freedom. Yes, they have gone to jail with us. Some have been dismissed from their churches, have lost the support of their bishops and fellow ministers. But they have acted in the faith that right defeated is stronger than evil triumphant. Their witness has been the spiritual salt that has preserved the true meaning of the gospel in these troubled times. They have carved a tunnel of hope through the dark mountain of disappointment.

I hope the church as a whole will meet the challenge of this decisive hour. But even if the church does not come to the aid of justice, I have no despair about the future. I have no fear about the outcome of our struggle in Birmingham, even if our motives are at present misunderstood. We will reach the goal of freedom in Birmingham and all over the nation, because the goal of America is freedom. Abused and scorned though we may be, our destiny is tied up with America's destiny. Before the pilgrims landed at Plymouth, we were here. Before the pen of Jefferson etched the majestic words of the Declaration of Independence across the pages of history, we were here. For more than two centuries our forebears labored in this country without wages; they made cotton king; they built the homes of their masters while suffering gross injustice and shameful humiliation—and yet out of a bottomless vitality they continue to thrive and develop. If the inexpressible cruelties of slavery could not stop us, the opposition we now face will surely fail. We will win our freedom because the sacred heritage of our nation and the eternal will of God are embodied in our echoing demands.

45   Before closing I feel impelled to mention one other point in your statement that has troubled me profoundly. You warmly commended the Birmingham police force for keeping "order" and "preventing violence." I doubt that you would have so warmly commended the police force if you had seen its dogs sinking their teeth into unarmed, nonviolent Negroes. I doubt that you would so quickly commend the policemen if you were to observe their ugly and inhumane treatment of Negroes here in the city jail; if you were to watch them push and curse old Negro women and young Negro girls; if you were to see them slap and kick old Negro men and young boys; if you were to observe them, as they did on two occasions, refuse to give us food because we wanted to sing our grace together. I cannot join you in your praise of the Birmingham police department.

It is true that the police have exercised a degree of discipline in handling the demonstrators. In this sense they have conducted themselves rather "nonviolently" in public. But for what purpose? To preserve the evil system of segregation. Over

[8]*ekklesia* the word "church" in the New Testament is translated from the Greek word "ekklesia," from "el" meaning "out" and "kaleo" meaning to "call."

the past few years I have consistently preached that nonviolence demands that the means we use must be as pure as the ends we seek. I have tried to make clear that it is wrong to use immoral means to attain moral ends. But now I must affirm that it is just as wrong, or perhaps even more so, to use moral means to preserve immoral ends. Perhaps Mr. Connor and his policemen have been rather nonviolent in public, as was Chief Pritchett in Albany, Georgia, but they used the moral means of nonviolence to maintain the immoral end of racial injustice. As T. S. Eliot has said: "The last temptation is the greatest treason: To do the right deed for the wrong reason."

I wish you had commended the Negro sit-inners and demonstrators of Birmingham for their sublime courage, their willingness to suffer, and their amazing discipline in the midst of great provocation. One day the South will recognize its real heroes. They will be the James Merediths,[9] with the noble sense of purpose that enables them to face jeering and hostile mobs, and with the agonizing loneliness that characterizes the life of the pioneer. They will be old, oppressed, battered Negro women, symbolized in a seventy-two-year-old woman in Montgomery, Alabama, who rose up with a sense of dignity and with her people decided not to ride segregated buses, and who responded with ungrammatical profundity to one who inquired about her weariness: "My feets is tired, but my soul is at rest." They will be the young high school and college students, the young ministers of the gospel and a host of their elders, courageously and non-violently sitting in at lunch counters and willingly going to jail for conscience' sake. One day the South will know that when these disinherited children of God sat down at lunch counters, they were in reality standing up for what is best in the American dream and for the most sacred values in our Judaeo-Christian heritage, thereby bringing our nation back to those great wells of democracy which were dug deep by the founding fathers in their formulation of the Constitution and the Declaration of Independence.

Never before have I written so long a letter. I'm afraid it is much too long to take your precious time. I can assure you that it would have been much shorter if I had been writing from a comfortable desk, but what else can one do when he is alone in a narrow jail cell, other than write long letters, think long thoughts, and pray long prayers?

If I have said anything in this letter that overstates the truth and indicates an unreasonable impatience, I beg you to forgive me. If I have said anything that understates the truth and indicates my having a patience that allows me to settle for anything less than brotherhood, I beg God to forgive me.

50   I hope this letter finds you strong in the faith. I also hope that circumstances will soon make it possible for me to meet each of you, not as an integrationist or a civil-rights leader but as a fellow clergyman and a Christian brother. Let us all hope that the dark clouds of racial prejudice will soon pass away and the deep fog of misunderstanding will be lifted from our fear-drenched communities, and in some not too distant tomorrow the radiant stars of love and brotherhood will shine over our great nation with all their scintillating beauty.

Yours for the cause of Peace and Brotherhood,

Martin Luther King Jr.

[1963]

[9]**James Meredith** On 1 October 1962, in the face of widespread opposition, James Meredith became the first African American to attend the University of Mississippi.

Joining the Conversation: Critical Thinking and Writing

1. In his first five paragraphs, how does King assure his audience that he is not a meddlesome intruder but a man of goodwill?
2. In paragraph 3, King refers to Hebrew prophets and to the Apostle Paul, and later (paragraph 10) to Socrates. What is the point of these references?
3. In paragraph 11, what does King mean when he says that "our beloved South-land" has long tried to "live in monologue rather than dialogue"?
4. King begins paragraph 23 with "I must make two honest confessions to you, my Christian and Jewish brothers." What would have been gained or lost if he had used this paragraph as his opening?
5. King's last three paragraphs do not advance his argument. What do they do?
6. Why does King advocate breaking unjust laws "openly, lovingly" (paragraph 20)? What does he mean by these words? What other motives or attitudes do these words rule out?
7. Construct two definitions of "civil disobedience," and explain whether and to what extent it is easier (or harder) to justify civil disobedience, depending on how you have defined the term.
8. If you feel that you wish to respond to King's letter on some point, write a letter nominally addressed to King. You may, if you wish, adopt the persona of one of the eight clergymen whom King initially addressed.
9. King writes (paragraph 46) that "nonviolence demands that the means we use must be as pure as the ends we seek." How do you think King would evaluate the following acts of civil disobedience: (a) occupying a college administration building in order to protest the administration's unsatisfactory response to a racial incident on campus or in order to protest the failure of the administration to hire minority persons as staff and faculty; (b) sailing on a collision course with a whaling ship to protest against whaling; (c) trespassing on an abortion clinic to protest abortion? Set down your answer in an essay of five hundred words.

STORIES

ELIZABETH BISHOP

Elizabeth Bishop (1911–79) is known chiefly as a poet. Here, however, we give a prose piece. In a letter (February 3, 1937), Bishop mentions the act that served as the immediate trigger for the piece, but of course far more experience of life is in the work than the trivial act she specifies: "I once hung [my cat's] artificial mouse on a string to a chairback, without thinking what I had done—it looked very sad."

The Hanging of the Mouse

Early, early in the morning, even before five o'clock, the mouse was brought out, but already there were large crowds. Some of the animals had not gone to bed the night before, but had stayed up later and later; at first because of a vague feeling of celebration, and then, after deciding several times that they might as well wander about the town for an hour more, to conclude the night by arriving at the square in time for the hanging became only sensible. These animals hiccuped a little and had an air of cynical lassitude. Those who had got up out of bed to come also appeared weary and silent, but not so bored.

The mouse was led in by two enormous brown beetles in the traditional picturesque armor of an earlier day. They came on to the square through the small black door and marched between the lines of soldiers standing at attention: straight ahead, to the right, around two sides of the hollow square, to the left, and out into the middle where the gallows stood. Before each turn the beetle on the right glanced quickly at the beetle on the left; their traditional long, long antennae swerved sharply in the direction they were to turn and they did it to perfection. The mouse, of course, who had had no military training and who, at the moment, was crying so hard he could scarcely see where he was going, rather spoiled the precision and snap of the beetles. At each corner he fell slightly forward, and when he was jerked in the right direction his feet became tangled together. The beetles, however, without even looking at him, each time lifted him quickly into the air for a second until his feet were untangled.

At that hour in the morning the mouse's gray clothes were almost indistinguishable from the light. But his whimpering could be heard, and the end of his nose was rose-red from crying so much. The crowd of small animals tipped back their heads and sniffed with pleasure.

A raccoon, wearing the traditional black mask, was the executioner. He was very fastidious and did everything just so. One of his young sons, also wearing a black mask, waited on him with a small basin and a pitcher of water. First he washed his hands and rinsed them carefully; then he washed the rope and rinsed it. At the last minute he again washed his hands and drew on a pair of elegant black kid gloves.

5   A large praying mantis was in charge of the religious end of the ceremonies. He hurried up on the stage after the mouse and his escorts, but once there a fit of nerves seemed to seize him. He glided to the left a few steps, to the right a few steps, lifted his arms gracefully, but could not seem to begin; and it was quite apparent that he would have liked nothing better than to have jumped quickly down and left the whole affair. When his arms were stretched to Heaven his large eyes flashed toward the crowd, and when he looked up, his body was twitching and he moved about in a really pathetic way. He seemed to feel ill at ease with the low characters around him: the beetles, the hangmen, and the criminal mouse. At last he made a great effort to pull himself together and, approaching the mouse, said a few words in a high, incomprehensible voice. The mouse jumped from nervousness, and cried harder than ever.

At this point the spectators would all undoubtedly have burst out laughing, but just then the King's messenger appeared on the balcony above the small black door the mouse and his guards had lately come through. He was a very large, overweight bullfrog, also dressed in the traditional costume and carrying the traditional long scroll that dragged for several feet on the ground and had the real speech, on a little slip of paper, pasted inside it. The scroll and the white plume on his hat made him look comically like something in a nursery tale, but his voice was impressive enough to awe the crowd into polite attention. It was a deep bass: "Glug! Glug! Berrr-up!" No one could understand a word of the mouse's death sentence.

With the help of some pushes and pinches from the beetles, the executioner got the mouse into position. The rope was tied exquisitely behind one of his little round ears. The mouse raised a hand and wiped his nose with it, and most of the crowd interpreted this gesture as a farewell wave and spoke of it for weeks afterwards. The hangman's young son, at a signal from his father, sprang the trap.

"Squee-eek! Squee-eek!" went the mouse.

His whiskers rowed hopelessly round and round in the air a few times and his feet flew up and curled into little balls like young fern-plants.

10   The praying mantis, with an hysterical fling of his long limbs, had disappeared in the crowd. It was all so touching that a cat, who had brought her child in her mouth, shed several large tears. They rolled down on to the child's back and he began to squirm and shriek, so that the mother thought that the sight of the hanging had perhaps been too much for him, but an excellent moral lesson, nevertheless.

[1937]

Joining the Conversation: Critical Thinking and Writing

1. We have several times quoted Robert Frost's observation that a poem (he could have said any work of literature) is "a performance in words." Reread Bishop's first paragraph, and discuss it in terms of "performance." Why, for instance, do you think she repeats the word "early" in the first sentence? In this paragraph, notice that Bishop says the animals decided "several times that they might as well wander about the town for an hour more." What do you make of deciding "several times"? And then Bishop says that the idea of concluding the night by "arriving at the square in time for the hanging became only sensible." What do you make of "sensible," especially in the context that immediately follows it: "These animals hiccupped a little and had an air of cynical lassitude." What does "cynical lassitude" mean? How has Bishop juggled her words to convey what you assume is her attitude toward the animals?
2. Would you agree that there are humorous touches in the piece? If so, point them out. If you don't think there is anything humorous in it, point to something that someone might conceivably find amusing, and explain why you do not find it so.
3. Describe your response to the sentence, "The rope was tied exquisitely behind one of his little round ears."
4. In the final paragraph, Bishop tells us that the cat believed "the sight of the hanging [provided] . . . an excellent moral lesson. . . ." Do you assume that Bishop agrees? By the way, executions used to be public, partly because it was felt that they served to educate the general public. As the proverb puts it, "Who hangs one corrects a thousand." Do you think Bishop would agree or disagree? Why?

URSULA K. LE GUIN

Ursula K. Le Guin was born in 1929 in Berkeley, California, the daughter of a distinguished mother (Theodora Kroeber, a folklorist) and father (Alfred L. Kroeber, an anthropologist). After graduating from Radcliffe College, she earned an MA at Columbia University; in 1952, she held a Fulbright Fellowship for study in Paris, where she met and married Charles Le Guin, a historian. Although her work is most widely known to fans of science fiction, because it usually has larger moral or political dimensions it interests many readers who normally do not care for science fiction.

Le Guin has said that she was prompted to write the following story because of a remark that she encountered in William James's "The Moral Philosopher and the Moral Life." James suggests there that, if millions of people could be "kept permanently happy on the one simple condition that a certain lost soul on the far-off edge of things should lead a life of lonely torment," our moral sense "would make us immediately feel" it would be "hideous" to accept such a bargain. This story first appeared in New Dimensions 3 *(1973).*

The Ones Who Walk Away from Omelas

With a clamor of bells that set the swallows soaring, the Festival of Summer came to the city Omelas, bright-towered by the sea. The rigging of the boats in harbor sparkled with flags. In the streets between houses with red roofs and painted walls, between old moss-grown gardens and under avenues of trees, past great parks and public buildings, processions moved. Some were decorous: old people in long stiff robes of mauve and gray, grave master workmen, quiet, merry women carrying their babies and chatting as they walked. In other streets the music beat faster, a shimmering of gong and tambourine, and the people went dancing, the procession was a dance. Children dodged in and out, their high calls rising like the swallows' crossing flights over the music and the singing. All the processions wound towards the north side of the city, where on the great water-meadow called the Green Fields boys and girls, naked in the bright air, with mudstained feet and ankles and long, lithe arms, exercised their restive horses before the race. The horses wore no gear at all but a halter without bit. Their manes were braided with streamers of silver, gold, and green. They flared their nostrils and pranced and boasted to one another; they were vastly excited, the horse being the only animal who has adopted our ceremonies as his own. Far off to the north and west the mountains stood up half encircling Omelas on her bay. The air of morning was so clear that the snow still crowning the Eighteen Peaks burned with white-gold fire across the miles of sunlit air, under the dark blue of the sky. There was just enough wind to make the banners that marked the racecourse snap and flutter now and then. In the silence of the broad green meadows one could hear the music winding through the city streets, farther and nearer and ever approaching, a cheerful faint sweetness of the air that from time to time trembled and gathered together and broke out into the great joyous clanging of the bells.

Joyous! How is one to tell about joy? How describe the citizens of Omelas?

They were not simple folk, you see, though they were happy. But we do not say the words of cheer much any more. All smiles have become archaic. Given a description such as this one tends to make certain assumptions. Given a description such as this one tends to look next for the King, mounted on a splendid stallion and surrounded by his noble knights, or perhaps in a golden litter borne by great-muscled slaves. But there was no king. They did not use swords, or keep slaves. They were not barbarians. I do not know the rules and laws of their society, but I suspect that they were singularly few. As they did without monarchy and slavery, so they also got on without the stock exchange, the advertisement, the secret police, and the bomb. Yet I repeat that these were not simple folk, not dulcet shepherds, noble savages, bland utopians. They were not less complex than us. The trouble is that we have a bad habit, encouraged by pedants and sophisticates, of considering happiness as something rather stupid. Only pain is intellectual, only evil interesting. This is the treason of the artist: a refusal to admit the banality of evil and the terrible boredom of pain. If you can't lick 'em, join 'em. If it hurts, repeat it. But to praise despair is to condemn delight, to embrace violence is to lose hold of everything else. We have almost lost hold, we can no longer describe a happy man, nor make any celebration of joy. How can I tell you about the people of Omelas? They were not naïve and happy children—though their children were, in fact, happy. They were mature, intelligent, passionate adults whose lives were not wretched. O miracle! But I wish I could describe it better. I wish I could convince you. Omelas sounds in my words like a city in a fairy tale, long ago and far away, once upon a time. Perhaps it would be best if you imagined it as your own fancy bids, assuming it will rise to the occasion, for certainly I cannot suit you all. For instance, how about technology? I think that there would be no cars or helicopters in and above the streets; this follows from the fact that the people of Omelas are happy people. Happiness is based on a just discrimination of what is necessary, what is neither necessary nor destructive, and what is destructive. In the middle category, however— that of the unnecessary but undestructive, that of comfort, luxury, exuberance, etc.—they could perfectly well have central heating, subway trains, washing machines, and all kinds of marvelous devices not yet invented here, floating light-sources, fuelless power, a cure for the common cold. Or they could have none of that: it doesn't matter. As you like it. I incline to think that people from towns up and down the coast have been coming in to Omelas during the last days before the Festival on very fast little trains and double-decked trams, and that the train station of Omelas is actually the handsomest building in town, though plainer than the magnificent Farmers' Market. But even granted trains, I fear that Omelas so far strikes some of you as goody-goody. Smiles, bells, parades, horses, bleh. If so, please add an orgy. If an orgy would help, don't hesitate. Let us not, however, have temples from which issue beautiful nude priests and priestesses already half in ecstasy and ready to copulate with any man or woman, lover or stranger, who desires union with the deep godhead of the blood, although that was my first idea. But really it would be better not to have any temples in Omelas—at least, not manned temples. Religion yes, clergy no. Surely the beautiful nudes can just wander about, offering themselves like divine soufflés to the hunger of the needy and the rapture of the flesh. Let them join the processions. Let tambourines be struck above the copulations, and the glory of desire be proclaimed upon the gongs, and (a not unimportant point) let the offspring of these delightful rituals be beloved and looked after by all. One thing I know there is none of in Omelas is guilt. But what else should there be? I thought that first there were no drugs, but that is puritanical. For those who like it, the faint insistent sweetness of *drooz* may perfume the ways of the city, *drooz* which first brings a great lightness and brilliance to the mind and limbs, and then after some hours a dreamy languor, and wonderful visions at last of the very arcana and inmost secrets of the Universe, as well as exciting the pleasure of sex beyond all belief; and it is not habit-forming. For more modest tastes I think there ought to be beer. What else, what else belongs in the joyous city? The sense of victory, surely, the celebration of courage. But as we did without clergy, let us do without soldiers. The joy built upon successful slaughter is not the right kind of joy; it will not do; it is fearful and it is trivial. A boundless and generous contentment, a magnanimous triumph felt not against some outer enemy but in communion with the finest and fairest in the souls of all men everywhere and the splendor of the world's summer: this is what swells the hearts of the people of Omelas, and the victory they celebrate is that of life. I really don't think many of them need to take *drooz*.

Most of the processions have reached the Green Fields by now. A marvelous smell of cooking goes forth from the red and blue tents of the provisioners. The faces of small children are amiably sticky; in the benign grey beard of a man a couple of crumbs of rich pastry are entangled. The youths and girls have mounted their horses and are beginning to group around the starting line of the course. An old woman, small, fat, and laughing, is passing out flowers from a basket, and tall young men wear her flowers in their shining hair. A child of nine or ten sits at the edge of the crowd, alone, playing on a wooden flute. People pause to listen, and they smile, but they do not speak to him, for he never ceases playing and never sees them, his dark eyes wholly rapt in the sweet, thin magic of the tune.

5   He finishes, and slowly lowers his hands holding the wooden flute.

As if that little private silence were the signal, all at once a trumpet sounds from the pavilion near the starting line: imperious, melancholy, piercing. The horses rear on their slender legs, and some of them neigh in answer. Sober-faced, the young riders stroke the horses' necks and soothe them, whispering, "Quiet, quiet, there my beauty, my hope. . . ." They begin to form in rank along the starting line. The crowds along the racecourse are like a field of grass and flowers in the wind. The Festival of Summer has begun.

Do you believe? Do you accept the festival, the city, the joy? No? Then let me describe one more thing.

In a basement under one of the beautiful public buildings of Omelas, or perhaps in the cellar of one of its spacious private homes, there is a room. It has one locked door, and no window. A little light seeps in dustily between cracks in the boards, secondhand from a cobwebbed window somewhere across the cellar. In one corner of the little room a couple of mops, with stiff, clotted, foul-smelling heads, stand near a rusty bucket. The floor is dirt, a little damp to the touch, as cellar dirt usually is. The room is about three paces long and two wide: a mere broom closet or disused tool room. In the room a child is sitting. It could be a boy or a girl. It looks about six, but actually is nearly ten. It is feebleminded. Perhaps it was born defective, or perhaps it has become imbecile through fear, malnutrition, and neglect. It picks its nose and occasionally fumbles vaguely with its toes or genitals, as it sits hunched in the corner farthest from the bucket and the two mops. It is afraid of the mops. It finds them horrible. It shuts its eyes, but it knows the mops are still standing there; and the door is locked; and nobody will come. The door is always locked; and nobody ever comes, except that sometimes—the child has no understanding of time or interval—sometimes the door rattles terribly and opens, and a person, or several people, are there. One of them may come in and kick the child to make it stand up. The others never come close, but peer in at it with frightened, disgusted eyes. The food bowl and the water jug are hastily filled, the door is locked, the eyes disappear. The people at the door never say anything, but the child, who has not always lived in the tool room, and can remember sunlight and its mother's voice, sometimes speaks. "I will be good," it says. "Please let me out. I will be good!" They never answer. The child used to scream for help at night, and cry a good deal, but now it only makes a kind of whining "eh-haa, eh-haa," and it speaks less and less often. It is so thin there are no calves to its legs; its belly protrudes; it lives on a half-bowl of corn meal and grease a day. It is naked. Its buttocks and thighs are a mass of festered sores, as it sits in its own excrement continually.

They all know it is there, all the people of Omelas. Some of them have come to see it, others are content merely to know it is there. They all know that it has to be there. Some of them understand why, and some do not, but they all understand that their happiness, the beauty of their city, the tenderness of their friendships, the health of their children, the wisdom of their scholars, the skill of their makers, even the abundance of their harvest and the kindly weathers of their skies, depend wholly on this child's abominable misery.

This is usually explained to children when they are between eight and twelve, whenever they seem capable of understanding; and most of those who come to see the child are young people, though often enough an adult comes, or comes back, to see the child. No matter how well the matter has been explained to them, these young spectators are always shocked and sickened at the sight. They feel disgust, which they had thought themselves superior to. They feel anger, outrage, impotence, despite all the explanations. They would like to do something for the child. But there is nothing they can do. If the child were brought up into the sunlight out of that vile place, if it were cleaned and fed and comforted, that would be a good thing, indeed; but if it were done, in that day and hour all the prosperity and beauty and delight of Omelas would wither and be destroyed. Those are the terms. To exchange all the goodness and grace of every life in Omelas for that single, small improvement: to throw away the happiness of thousands for the chance of the happiness of one: that would be to let guilt within the walls indeed.

The terms are strict and absolute; there may not even be a kind word spoken to the child.

Often the young people go home in tears, or in a tearless rage, when they have seen the child and faced this terrible paradox. They may brood over it for weeks or years. But as time goes on they begin to realize that even if the child could be released, it would not get much good of its freedom: a little vague pleasure of warmth and food, no doubt, but little more. It is too degraded and imbecile to know any real joy. It has been afraid too long ever to be free of fear. Its habits are too uncouth for it to respond to humane treatment. Indeed, after so long it would probably be wretched without walls about it to protect it, and darkness for its eyes, and its own excrement to sit in. Their tears at the bitter injustice dry when they begin to perceive the terrible justice of reality, and to accept it. Yet it is their tears and anger, the trying of their generosity and the acceptance of their helplessness, which are perhaps the true source of the splendor of their lives. Theirs is no vapid, irresponsible happiness. They know that they, like the child, are not free. They know compassion. It is the existence of the child, and their knowledge of its existence, that makes possible the nobility of their architecture, the poignancy of their music, the profundity of their science. It is because of the child that they are so gentle with children. They know that if the wretched one were not there snivelling in the dark, the other one, the flute-player, could make no joyful music as the young riders line up in their beauty for the race in the sunlight of the first morning of summer.

Now do you believe in them? Are they not more credible? But there is one more thing to tell, and this is quite incredible.

At times one of the adolescent girls or boys who go to see the child does not go home to weep or rage, does not, in fact, go home at all. Sometimes also a man or woman much older falls silent for a day or two, and then leaves home. These people go out into the street, and walk down the street alone. They keep walking, and walk straight out of the city of Omelas, through the beautiful gates. They keep walking across the farmlands of Omelas. Each one goes alone, youth or girl, man or woman. Night falls; the traveler must pass down village streets, between the houses with yellow-lit windows, and on out into the darkness of the fields. Each alone, they go west or north, towards the mountains. They go on. They leave Omelas, they walk ahead into the darkness, and they do not come back. The place they go towards is a place even less imaginable to most of us than the city of happiness. I cannot describe it at all. It is possible that it does not exist. But they seem to know where they are going, the ones who walk away from Omelas.

[1973]

Joining the Conversation: Critical Thinking and Writing

1. Summarize the point of "The Ones Who Walk Away from Omelas"—not the plot, but what the story adds up to, what the author is getting at. Next, set forth what you would probably do (and why) if you were born in Omelas.
2. Consider the narrator's assertion (paragraph 3) that happiness "is based on a just discrimination of what is necessary." Please argue for or against this statement.
3. Do you think the story implies a criticism of contemporary American society? Explain your answer.

SHIRLEY JACKSON

Shirley Jackson (1919–65) was born in San Francisco, California, and went to college in New York State, first at the University of Rochester and then at Syracuse University. Although one of her stories was published in The Best American Short Stories 1944, *she did not receive national attention until 1948, when the* New Yorker *published "The Lottery." The magazine later reported that none of its earlier publications had produced so strong a response.*

In 1962, she experienced a breakdown and was unable to write, but she recovered and worked on a new novel. Before completing the book, however, she died of cardiac arrest at the age of forty-six. The book was published posthumously under the title Come Along with Me.

Two of her books, Life among the Savages *(1953) and* Raising Demons *(1957), are engaging self-portraits of a harried mother in a house full of children. But what seems amusing also has its dark underside. After her breakdown, Jackson said, "I think all my books laid end to end would be one long documentary of anxiety."*

Her husband, Stanley Edgar Hyman (her college classmate and later a professor of English), said of Jackson, "If she used the resources of supernatural terror, it was to provide metaphors for the all-too-real terrors of the natural."

The Lottery

The morning of June 27th was clear and sunny, with the fresh warmth of a full-summer day; the flowers were blossoming profusely and the grass was richly green. The people of the village began to gather in the square, between the post office and the bank, around ten o'clock; in some towns there were so many people that the lottery took two days and had to be started on June 26th, but in this village, where there were only about three hundred people, the whole lottery took less than two hours, so it could begin at ten o'clock in the morning and still be through in time to allow the villagers to get home for noon dinner.

The children assembled first, of course. School was recently over for the summer, and the feeling of liberty sat uneasily on most of them; they tended to gather together quietly for a while before they broke into boisterous play, and their talk was still of the classroom and the teacher, of books and reprimands. Bobby Martin had already stuffed his pockets full of stones, and the other boys soon followed his example, selecting the smoothest and roundest stones; Bobby and Harry Jones and Dickie Delacroix—the villagers pronounced this name "Dellacroy"—eventually made a great pile of stones in one corner of the square and guarded it against the raids of the other boys. The girls stood aside, talking among themselves, looking over their shoulders at the boys, and the very small children rolled in the dust or clung to the hands of their older brothers or sisters.

Soon the men began to gather, surveying their own children, speaking of planting and rain, tractors and taxes. They stood together, away from the pile of stones in the corner, and their jokes were quiet and they smiled rather than laughed. The women, wearing faded house dresses and sweaters, came shortly after their menfolk. They greeted one another and exchanged bits of gossip as they went to join their husbands. Soon the women, standing by their husbands, began to call to their children, and the children came reluctantly, having to be called four or five times. Bobby Martin ducked under his mother's grasping hand and ran, laughing, back to the pile of stones. His father spoke up sharply, and Bobby came quickly, and took his place between his father and his oldest brother.

The lottery was conducted—as were the square dances, the teenage club, the Halloween program—by Mr. Summers, who had time and energy to devote to civic activities. He was a roundfaced, jovial man and he ran the coal business, and people were sorry for him, because he had no children and his wife was a scold. When he arrived in the square, carrying the black wooden box, there was a murmur of conversation among the villagers and he waved and called, "Little late today, folks." The postmaster, Mr. Graves, followed him, carrying a three-legged stool, and the stool was put in the center of the square and Mr. Summers set the black box down on it. The villagers kept their distance, leaving a space between themselves and the stool, and when Mr. Summers said, "Some of you fellows want to give me a hand?" there was a hesitation before two men, Mr. Martin and his oldest son, Baxter, came forward to hold the box steady on the stool while Mr. Summers stirred up the papers inside it.

5   The original paraphernalia for the lottery had been lost long ago, and the black box now resting on the stool had been put into use even before Old Man Warner, the oldest man in town, was born. Mr. Summers spoke frequently to the villagers about making a new box, but no one liked to upset even as much tradition as was represented by the black box. There was a story that the present box had been made with some pieces of the box that had preceded it, the one that had been constructed when the first people settled down to make a village here. Every year, after the lottery, Mr. Summers began talking again about a new box, but every year the subject was allowed to fade off without anything's being done. The black box grew shabbier each year; by now it was no longer completely black but splintered badly along one side to show the original wood color, and in some places faded or stained.

Mr. Martin and his oldest son, Baxter, held the black box securely on the stool until Mr. Summers had stirred the papers thoroughly with his hand. Because so much of the ritual had been forgotten or discarded, Mr. Summers had been successful in having slips of paper substituted for the chips of wood that had been used for generations. Chips of wood, Mr. Summers had argued, had been all very well when the village was tiny, but now that the population was more than three hundred and likely to keep on growing, it was necessary to use something that would fit more easily into the black box. The night before the lottery, Mr. Summers and Mr. Graves made up the slips of paper and put them in the box, and it was then taken to the safe of Mr. Summers's coal company and locked up until Mr. Summers was ready to take it to the square next morning. The rest of the year, the box was put away, sometimes one place, sometimes another; it had spent one year in Mr. Graves's barn and another year underfoot in the post office, and sometimes it was set on a shelf in the Martin grocery and left there.

There was a great deal of fussing to be done before Mr. Summers declared the lottery open. There were lists to make up—of heads of families, heads of households in each family, members of each household in each family. There was the proper swearing in of Mr. Summers by the postmaster, as the official of the lottery; at one time, some people remembered, there had been a recital of some sort, performed by the official of the lottery, a perfunctory, tuneless chant that had been rattled off duly each year; some people believed that the official of the lottery used to stand just so when he said or sang it, others believed that he was supposed to walk among the people, but years and years ago this part of the ritual had been allowed to lapse. There had been, also, a ritual salute, which the official of the lottery had had to use in addressing each person who came up to draw from the box, but this also had changed with time, until now it was felt necessary only for the official to speak to each person approaching. Mr. Summers was very good at all this; in his clean white shirt and blue jeans, with one hand resting carelessly on the black box, he seemed very proper and important as he talked interminably to Mr. Graves and the Martins.

Just as Mr. Summers left off talking and turned to the assembled villagers, Mrs. Hutchinson came hurriedly along the path to the square, her sweater thrown over her shoulders, and slid into place in the back of the crowd. "Clean forgot what day it was," she said to Mrs. Delacroix, who stood next to her, and they both laughed softly. "Thought my old man was out back stacking wood," Mrs. Hutchinson went on, "and then I looked out the window and the kids were gone, and then I remembered it was the twenty-seventh and came a-running." She dried her hands on her apron, and Mrs. Delacroix said, "You're in time, though. They're still talking away up there."

Mrs. Hutchinson craned her neck to see through the crowd and found her husband and children standing near the front. She tapped Mrs. Delacroix on the arm as a farewell and began to make her way through the crowd. The people separated good humoredly to let her through, two or three people said, in voices just loud enough to be heard across the crowd, "Here comes your Missus, Hutchinson," and "Bill, she made it after all." Mrs. Hutchinson reached her husband, and Mr. Summers, who had been waiting, said cheerfully, "Thought we were going to have to get on without you, Tessie." Mrs. Hutchinson said, grinning, "Wouldn't have me leave m'dishes in the sink, now would you, Joe?," and soft laughter ran through the crowd as the people stirred back into position after Mrs. Hutchinson's arrival.

10   "Well, now," Mr. Summers said soberly, "guess we better get started, get this over with, so's we can go back to work. Anybody ain't here?"

"Dunbar," several people said. "Dunbar, Dunbar."

Mr. Summers consulted his list. "Clyde Dunbar," he said. "That's right. He's broke his leg, hasn't he? Who's drawing for him?"

"Me, I guess," a woman said, and Mr. Summers turned to look at her. "Wife draws for her husband," Mr. Summers said. "Don't you have a grown boy to do it for you, Janey?" Although Mr. Summers and everyone else in the village knew the answer perfectly well, it was the business of the official of the lottery to ask such questions formally. Mr. Summers waited with an expression of polite interest while Mrs. Dunbar answered.

"Horace's not but sixteen yet," Mrs. Dunbar said regretfully. "Guess I gotta fill in for the old man this year."

15   "Right," Mr. Summers said. He made a note on the list he was holding. Then he asked, "Watson boy drawing this year?"

A tall boy in the crowd raised his hand. "Here," he said. "I'm drawing for m'- mother and me." He blinked his eyes nervously and ducked his head as several voices in the crowd said things like "Good fellow, Jack," and "Glad to see your mother's got a man to do it."

"Well," Mr. Summers said, "guess that's everyone. Old Man Warner make it?"

"Here," a voice said, and Mr. Summers nodded.

A sudden hush fell on the crowd as Mr. Summers cleared his throat and looked at the list. "All ready?" he called. "Now, I'll read the names—heads of families first—and the men come up and take a paper out of the box. Keep the paper folded in your hand without looking at it until everyone has had a turn. Everything clear?"

20   The people had done it so many times that they only half listened to the directions; most of them were quiet, wetting their lips, not looking around. Then Mr. Summers raised one hand high and said, "Adams." A man disengaged himself from the crowd and came forward. "Hi, Steve," Mr. Summers said, and Mr. Adams said, "Hi, Joe." They grinned at one another humorlessly and nervously. Then Mr. Adams reached into the black box and took out a folded paper. He held it firmly by one corner as he turned and went hastily back to his place in the crowd, where he stood a little apart from his family, not looking down at his hand.

"Allen," Mr. Summers said. "Anderson. . . . Bentham."

"Seems like there's no time at all between lotteries any more," Mrs. Delacroix said to Mrs. Graves in the back row. "Seems like we got through with the last one only last week."

"Time sure goes fast," Mrs. Graves said.

"Clark. . . . Delacroix."

25   "There goes my old man," Mrs. Delacroix said. She held her breath while her husband went forward.

"Dunbar," Mr. Summers said, and Mrs. Dunbar went steadily to the box while one of the women said, "Go on, Janey," and another said, "There she goes."

"We're next," Mrs. Graves said. She watched while Mr. Graves came around from the side of the box, greeted Mr. Summers gravely, and selected a slip of paper from the box. By now, all through the crowd there were men holding the small folded papers in their large hands, turning them over and over nervously. Mrs. Dunbar and her two sons stood together. Mrs. Dunbar holding the slip of paper.

"Harburt. . . . Hutchinson."

"Get up there, Bill," Mrs. Hutchinson said, and the people near her laughed.

30   "Jones."

"They do say," Mr. Adams said to Old Man Warner, who stood next to him, "that over in the north village they're talking of giving up the lottery."

Old Man Warner snorted. "Pack of crazy fools," he said. "Listening to the young folks, nothing's good enough for *them*. Next thing you know, they'll be wanting to go back to living in caves, nobody work any more, live *that* way for a while. Used to be a saying about 'Lottery in June, corn be heavy soon.' First thing you know, we'd all be eating stewed chickweed and acorns. There's *always* been a lottery," he added petulantly. "Bad enough to see young Joe Summers up there joking with everybody."

"Some places have already quit lotteries," Mrs. Adams said.

"Nothing but trouble in *that*," Old Man Warner said stoutly. "Pack of young fools."

35   "Martin." And Bobby Martin watched his father go forward. "Overdyke. . . . Percy."

"I wish they'd hurry," Mrs. Dunbar said to her older son. "I wish they'd hurry."

"They're almost through," her son said.

"You get ready to run tell Dad," Mrs. Dunbar said.

Mr. Summers called his own name and then stepped forward precisely and selected a slip from the box. Then he called, "Warner."

40   "Seventy-seventh year I been in the lottery," Old Man Warner said as he went through the crowd. "Seventy-seventh time."

"Watson." The tall boy came awkwardly through the crowd. Someone said, "Don't be nervous, Jack," and Mr. Summers said, "Take your time, son."

"Zanani."

After that, there was a long pause, a breathless pause, until Mr. Summers, holding his slip of paper in the air, said, "All right, fellows." For a minute, no one moved, and then all of the slips of paper were opened. Suddenly, all women began to speak at once, saying, "Who is it?" "Who's got it?" "Is it the Dunbars?" "Is it the Watsons?" Then the voices began to say, "It's Hutchinson. It's Bill." "Bill Hutchinson's got it."

"Go tell your father," Mrs. Dunbar said to her older son.

45   People began to look around to see the Hutchinsons. Bill Hutchinson was standing quiet, staring down at the paper in his hand. Suddenly, Tessie Hutchinson shouted to Mr. Summers, "You didn't give him time enough to take any paper he wanted. I saw you. It wasn't fair!"

"Be a good sport, Tessie," Mrs. Delacroix called, and Mrs. Graves said, "All of us took the same chance."

"Shut up, Tessie," Bill Hutchinson said.

"Well, everyone," Mr. Summers said, "That was done pretty fast, and now we've got to be hurrying a little more to get done in time." He consulted his next list. "Bill," he said, "you draw for the Hutchinson family. You got any other households in the Hutchinsons?"

"There's Don and Eva," Mrs. Hutchinson yelled. "Make *them* take their chance!"

50   "Daughters draw with their husbands' families, Tessie," Mr. Summers said gently. "You know that as well as anyone else."

"It wasn't fair," Tessie said.

"I guess no, Joe," Bill Hutchinson said regretfully. "My daughter draws with her husband's family, that's only fair. And I've got no other family except the kids."

"Then, as far as drawing for families is concerned, it's you," Mr. Summers said in explanation, "and as far as drawing for households is concerned, that's you, too. Right?"

"Right," Bill Hutchinson said.

55   "How many kids, Bill?" Mr. Summers asked formally.

"Three," Bill Hutchinson said. "There's Bill, Jr., and Nancy, and little Dave. And Tessie and me."

"All right, then," Mr. Summers said. "Harry, you got their tickets back?"

Mr. Graves nodded and held up the slips of paper. "Put them in the box, then," Mr. Summers directed. "Take Bill's and put it in."

"I think we ought to start over," Mrs. Hutchinson said, as quietly as she could. "I tell you it wasn't *fair*. You didn't give him time enough to choose. *Everybody* saw that."

60   Mr. Graves had selected the five slips and put them in the box, and he dropped all the papers but those onto the ground, where the breeze caught them and lifted them off.

"Listen, everybody," Mrs. Hutchinson was saying to the people around her.

"Ready, Bill?" Mr. Summers asked, and Bill Hutchinson, with one quick glance around at his wife and children, nodded.

"Remember," Mr. Summers said, "Take the slips and keep them folded until each person has taken one. Harry, you help little Dave." Mr. Graves took the hand of the little boy, who came willingly with him up to the box. "Take a paper out of the box, Davy," Mr. Summers said. Davy put his hand into the box and laughed. "Take just *one* paper," Mr. Summers said. "Harry, you hold it for him." Mr. Graves took the child's hand and removed the folded paper from the tight fist and held it while little Dave stood next to him and looked up at him wonderingly.

"Nancy next," Mr. Summers said. Nancy was twelve, and her school friends breathed heavily as she went forward, switching her skirt, and took a slip daintily from the box. "Bill, Jr.," Mr. Summers said, and Billy, his face red and his feet overlarge, nearly knocked the box over as he got a paper out. "Tessie," Mr. Summers said. She hesitated for a minute, looking around defiantly, and then set her lips and went up to the box. She snatched a paper out and held it behind her.

65   "Bill," Mr. Summers said, and Bill Hutchinson reached into the box and felt around, bringing his hand out at last with the slip of paper in it.

The crowd was quiet. A girl whispered, "I hope it's not Nancy," and the sound of the whisper reached the edges of the crowd.

"It's not the way it used to be," Old Man Warner said clearly. "People ain't the way they used to be."

"All right," Mr. Summers said. "Open the papers. Harry, you open little Dave's."

Mr. Graves opened the slip of paper and there was a general sigh through the crowd as he held it up and everyone could see that it was blank. Nancy and Bill, Jr., opened theirs at the same time, and both beamed and laughed, turning around to the crowd and holding their slips of paper above their heads.

70   "Tessie," Mr. Summers said. There was a pause, and then Mr. Summers looked at Bill Hutchinson, and Bill unfolded his paper and showed it. It was blank.

"It's Tessie," Mr. Summers said, and his voice was hushed. "Show us her paper, Bill."

Bill Hutchinson went over to his wife and forced the slip of paper out of her hand. It had a black spot on it, the black spot Mr. Summers had made the night before with the heavy pencil in the coal-company office. Bill Hutchinson held it up, and there was a stir in the crowd.

"All right, folks," Mr. Summers said, "let's finish quickly."

Although the villagers had forgotten the ritual and lost the original black box, they still remembered to use stones. The pile of stones the boys had made earlier was ready; there were stones on the ground with the blowing scraps of paper that had come out of the box. Mrs. Delacroix selected a stone so large she had to pick it up with both hands and turned to Mrs. Dunbar. "Come on," she said. "Hurry up."

75   Mrs. Dunbar had small stones in both hands, and she said, gasping for breath, "I can't run at all. You'll have to go ahead and I'll catch up with you."

The children had stones already, and someone gave little Davy Hutchinson a few pebbles.

Tessie Hutchinson was in the center of a cleared space by now, and she held her hands out desperately as the villagers moved in on her. "It isn't fair," she said. A stone hit her on the side of the head.

Old Man Warner was saying, "Come on, come on, everyone." Steve Adams was front of the crowd of villagers, with Mrs. Graves beside him.

n't fair, it isn't right," Mrs. Hutchinson screamed, and then they were upon

[1948]

Joining the Conversation: Critical Thinking and Writing

1. Is "The Lottery" more than a shocker?
2. What is the community's attitude toward tradition?
3. Doubtless a good writer could tell this story effectively from the point of view of a participant, but Jackson chose a nonparticipant point of view. What does she gain?
4. Let's say you were writing this story, and you had decided to write it from Tessie's point of view. What would your first paragraph, or your first 250 words, be?
5. Suppose someone claimed that the story is an attack on religious orthodoxy. What might be your response? (Whether you agree or disagree, set forth your reasons in a thoughtful argument.)

WILLIAM FAULKNER

For a biographical note on William Faulkner, see page 449.

Barn Burning

The store in which the Justice of the Peace's court was sitting smelled of cheese. The boy, crouched on his nail keg at the back of the crowded room, knew he smelled cheese, and more: from where he sat he could see the ranked shelves close-packed with the solid, squat, dynamic shapes of tin cans whose labels his stomach read, not from the lettering which mean nothing to his mind but from the scarlet devils and the silver curve of fish—this, the cheese which he knew he smelled and the hermetic meat which his intestines believed he smelled coming in intermittent gusts momentary and brief between the other constant one, the smell and sense just a little of fear because mostly of despair and grief, the old fierce pull of blood. He could not see the table where the Justice sat and before which his father and his father's enemy (*our enemy* he thought in that despair; *ourn! mine and hisn both! He's my father!*) stood, but he could hear them, the two of them that is, because his father had said no word yet:

"But what proof have you, Mr. Harris?"

"I told you. The hog got into my corn. I caught it up and sent it back to him. He had no fence that would hold it. I told him so, warned him. The next time I put the hog in my pen. When he came to get it I gave him enough wire to patch up his pen. The next time I put the hog up and kept it. I rode down to his house and saw the wire I gave him still rolled on to the spool in his yard. I told him he could have the hog when he paid me a dollar pound fee. That evening a nigger came with the dollar and got the hog. He was a strange nigger. He said, 'He say to tell you wood and hay kin burn.' I said, 'What?' 'That whut he say to tell you,' the nigger said. 'Wood and hay kin burn.' That night my barn burned. I got the stock out but I lost the barn."

"Where is the nigger? Have you got him?"

5   "He was a strange nigger, I tell you. I don't know what became of him."

"But that's not proof. Don't you see that's not proof?"

"Get that boy up here. He knows." For a moment the boy thought too that the man meant his older brother until Harris said, "Not him. The little one. The boy," and, crouching, small for his age, small and wiry like his father, in patched and faded jeans even too small for him, with straight, uncombed, brown hair and eyes gray and wild as storm scud, he saw the men between himself and the table part and become a lane of grim faces, at the end of which he saw the Justice, a shabby, collarless, graying man in spectacles, beckoning him. He felt no floor under his bare feet; he seemed to walk beneath the palpable weight of the grim turning faces. His father, stiff in his black Sunday coat donned not for the trial but for the moving, did not even look at him. *He aims for me to lie*, he thought, again with that frantic grief and despair. *And I will have to do hit.*

"What's your name, boy?" the Justice said.

"Colonel Sartoris Snopes," the boy whispered.

10   "Hey?" the Justice said. "Talk louder. Colonel Sartoris? I reckon anybody named for Colonel Sartoris in this country can't help but tell the truth, can they?" The boy said nothing. *Enemy! Enemy!* he thought; for a moment he could not even see, could not see that the Justice's face was kindly nor discern that his voice was troubled when he spoke to the man named Harris: "Do you want me to question this boy?" But he could hear, and during those subsequent long seconds while there was absolutely no sound in the crowded little room save that of quiet and intent breathing it was as if he had swung outward at the end of a grape vine, over a ravine, and at the top of the swing had been caught in a prolonged instant of mesmerized gravity, weightless in time.

"No!" Harris said violently, explosively. "Damnation! Send him out of here!" Now time, the fluid world, rushed beneath him again, the voices coming to him again through the smell of cheese and sealed meat, the fear and despair and the old grief of blood:

"This case is closed. I can't find against you, Snopes, but I can give you advice. Leave this country and don't come back to it."

His father spoke for the first time, his voice cold and harsh, level, without emphasis: "I aim to. I don't figure to stay in a country among people who . . ." he said something unprintable and vile, addressed to no one.

"That'll do," the Justice said. "Take your wagon and get out of this country before dark. Case dismissed."

15   His father turned, and he followed the stiff black coat, the wiry figure walking a little stiffly from where a Confederate provost's man's musket ball had taken him in the heel on a stolen horse thirty years ago, followed the two backs now, since his older brother had appeared from somewhere in the crowd, no taller than the father but thicker, chewing tobacco steadily, between the two lines of grim-faced men and out of the store and across the worn gallery and down the sagging steps and among the dogs and half-grown boys in the mild May dust, where as he passed a voice hissed:

"Barn burner!"

Again he could not see, whirling; there was a face in a red haze, moonlike, bigger than the full moon, the owner of it half again his size, he leaping in the red haze toward the face, feeling no blow, feeling no shock when his head struck the earth, scrabbling up and leaping again, feeling no blow this time either and tasting no blood, scrabbling up to see the other boy in full flight and himself already leaping into pursuit as his father's hand jerked him back, the harsh, cold voice speaking above him: "Go get in the wagon."

It stood in a grove of locusts and mulberries across the road. His two hulking n in their Sunday dresses and his mother and her sister in calico and sunbon- e already in it, sitting on and among the sorry residue of the dozen and ings which even the boy could remember—the battered stove, the and chairs, the clock inlaid with mother-of-pearl, which would not run, stopped at some fourteen minutes past two o'clock of a dead and forgotten day and time, which had been his mother's dowry. She was crying, though when she saw him she drew her sleeve across her face and began to descend from the wagon. "Get back," the father said.

"He's hurt. I got to get some water and wash his . . ."

20   "Get back in the wagon," his father said. He got in too, over the tail-gate. His father mounted to the seat where the older brother already sat and struck the gaunt mules two savage blows with the peeled willow, but without heat. It was not even sadistic; it was exactly that same quality which in later years would cause his descendants to over-run the engine before putting a motor car into motion, striking and reining back in the same movement. The wagon went on, the store with its quiet crowd of grimly watching men dropped behind; a curve in the road hid it. *Forever* he thought. *Maybe he's done satisfied now, now that he has . . .* stopping himself, not to say it aloud even to himself. His mother's hand touched his shoulder.

"Does hit hurt?" she said.

"Naw," he said. "Hit don't hurt. Lemme be."

"Can't you wipe some of the blood off before hit dries?" *blood from what?*

"I'll wash to-night," he said. "Lemme be, I tell you."

25   The wagon went on. He did not know where they were going. None of them ever did or ever asked, because it was always somewhere, always a house of sorts waiting for them a day or two days or even three days away. Likely his father had already arranged to make a crop on another farm before he . . . Again he had to stop himself. He (the father) always did. There was something about his wolflike independence and even courage when the advantage was at least neutral which impressed strangers, as if they got from his latent ravening ferocity not so much a sense of dependability as a feeling that his ferocious conviction in the rightness of his own actions would be of advantage to all whose interest lay with his.

That night they camped, in a grove of oaks and beeches where a spring ran. The nights were still cool and they had a fire against it, of a rail lifted from a near-by fence and cut into lengths—a small fire, neat, niggard almost, a shrewd fire; such fires were his father's habit and custom always, even in freezing weather. Older, the boy might have remarked this and wondered why not a big one; why should not a man who had not only seen the waste and extravagance of war, but who had in his blood an inherent voracious prodigality with material not his own, have burned everything in sight? Then he might have gone a step farther and thought that that was the reason: that niggard blaze was the living fruit of nights passed during those four years in the woods hiding from all men, blue or gray, with his strings of horses (captured horses, he called them). And older still, he might have divined the true reason: that the element of fire spoke to some deep mainspring of his father's being, as the element of steel or of powder spoke to other men, as the one weapon for the preservation of integrity, else breath were not worth the breathing, and hence to be regarded with respect and used with discretion. *what*

But he did not think this now and he had seen those same niggard blazes all *are*
his life. He merely ate his supper beside it and was already half asleep over his iron *they?*
plate when his father called him, and once more he followed the stiff back, the stiff and ruthless limp, up the slope and on to the starlit road where, turning, he could see his father against the stars but without face or depth—a shape black, flat, and bloodless as though cut from tin in the iron folds of the frockcoat which had not been made for him, the voice harsh like tin and without heat like tin:

"You were fixing to tell them. You would have told him." He didn't answer. His father struck him with the flat of his hand on the side of the head, hard but without heat, exactly as he had struck the two mules at the store, exactly as he would strike either of them with any stick in order to kill a horse fly, his voice still without heat or anger: "You're getting to be a man. You got to learn. You got to learn to stick to your own blood or you ain't going to have any blood to stick to you. Do you think either of them, any man there this morning, would? Don't you know all they wanted was a chance to get at me because they knew I had them beat? Eh?" Later, twenty years later, he was to tell himself, "If I had said they wanted only truth, justice, he would have hit me again." But now he said nothing. He was not crying. He just stood there. "Answer me," his father said.

"Yes," he whispered. His father turned.

30   "Get on to bed. We'll be there to-morrow."

To-morrow they were there. In the early afternoon the wagon stopped before a paintless two-room house identical almost with the dozen others it had stopped before even in the boy's ten years, and again, as on the other dozen occasions, his mother and aunt got down and began to unload the wagon, although his two sisters and his father and brother had not moved.

"Likely hit ain't fitten for hawgs," one of the sisters said.

"Nevertheless, fit it will and you'll hog it and like it," his father said. "Get out of them chairs and help your Ma unload."

The two sisters got down, big, bovine, in a flutter of cheap ribbons; one of them drew from the jumbled wagon bed a battered lantern, the other a worn broom. His father handed the reins to the older son and began to climb stiffly over the wheel. "When they get unloaded, take the team to the barn and feed them." Then he said, and at first the boy thought he was still speaking to his brother: "Come with me."

35   "Me?" he said.

"Yes," his father said. "You."

"Abner," his mother said. His father paused and looked back—the harsh level stare beneath the shaggy, graying, irascible brows.

"I reckon I'll have a word with the man that aims to begin to-morrow owning me body and soul for the next eight months."

They went back up the road. A week ago—or before last night, that is—he would have asked where they were going, but not now. His father had struck him before last night but never before had he paused afterward to explain why; it was as if the blow and the following calm, outrageous voice still rang, repercussed, divulging nothing to him save the terrible handicap of being young, the light weight of his few years, just heavy enough to prevent his soaring free of the world as it seemed to be ordered but not heavy enough to keep him footed solid in it, to resist it and try to change the course of its events.

40   Presently he could see the grove of oaks and cedars and the other flowering trees and shrubs where the house would be, though not the house yet. They walked beside a fence massed with honeysuckle and Cherokee roses and came to a gate swinging open between two brick pillars, and now, beyond a sweep of drive, he saw the house for the first time and at that instant he forgot his father and the terror and despair both, and even when he remembered his father again (who had not stopped) the terror and despair did not return. Because, for all the twelve movings, they had sojourned until now in a poor country, a land of small farms and fields and houses, and he had never seen a house like this before. *Hit's big as a courthouse* he thought quietly, with a surge of peace and joy whose reason he could not have thought into words, being too young for that: *They are safe from him. People whose lives are a part of this peace and dignity are beyond his touch,*

*be no more to them than a buzzing wasp: capable of stinging for a little moment but
that's all; the spell of this peace and dignity rendering even the barns and stable and
cribs which belong to it impervious to the puny flames he might contrive . . .* this, the
peace and joy, ebbing for an instant as he looked again at the stiff black back,
the stiff and implacable limp of the figure which was not dwarfed by the house,
for the reason that it had never looked big anywhere and which now, against the
serene columned backdrop, had more than ever that impervious quality of something cut ruthlessly from tin, depthless, as though, sidewise to the sun, it would
cast no shadow. Watching him, the boy remarked the absolutely undeviating course
which his father held and saw the stiff foot come squarely down in a pile of fresh
droppings where a horse had stood in the drive and which his father could have
avoided by a simple change of stride. But it ebbed only for a moment, though he
could not have thought this into words either, walking on in the spell of the house,
which he could even want but without envy, without sorrow, certainly never with
that ravening and jealous rage which unknown to him walked in the ironlike black
coat before him: *Maybe he will feel it too. Maybe it will even change him now from
what maybe he couldn't help but be.*

They crossed the portico. Now he could hear his father's stiff foot as it came
down on the boards with clocklike finality, a sound out of all proportion to the
displacement of the body it bore and which was not dwarfed either by the white
door before it, as though it had attained to a sort of vicious and ravening minimum
not to be dwarfed by anything—the flat, wide, black hat, the formal coat of broad-
cloth which had once been black but which had now that friction-glazed greenish
cast of the bodies of old house flies, the lifted sleeve which was too large, the
lifted hand like a curled claw. The door opened so promptly that the boy knew the
Negro must have been watching them all the time, an old man with neat grizzled
hair, in a linen jacket, who stood barring the door with his body, saying, "Wipe yo
foots, white man, fo you come in here. Major ain't home nohow."

"Get out of my way, nigger," his father said, without heat too, flinging the door
back and the Negro also and entering, his hat still on his head. And now the boy
saw the prints of the stiff foot on the doorjamb and saw them appear on the pale
rug behind the machinelike deliberation of the foot which seemed to bear (or
transmit) twice the weight which the body compassed. The Negro was shouting
"Miss Lula! Miss Lula!" somewhere behind them, then the boy, deluged as though
by a warm wave by a suave turn of carpeted stair and a pendant glitter of chande-
liers and a mute gleam of gold frames, heard the swift feet and saw her too, a
lady—perhaps he had never seen her like before either—in a gray, smooth gown
with lace at the throat and an apron tied at the waist and the sleeves turned back,
wiping cake or biscuit dough from her hands with a towel as she came up the hall,
looking not at his father at all but at the tracks on the blond rug with an expression
of incredulous amazement.

"I tried," the Negro cried. "I tole him to . . ."

"Will you please go away?" she said in a shaking voice. "Major de Spain is not
at home. Will you please go away?"

45   His father had not spoken again. He did not speak again. He did not even look
at her. He just stood stiff in the center of the rug, in his hat, the shaggy iron-gray
brows twitching slightly above the pebble-colored eyes as he appeared to examine
the house with brief deliberation. Then with the same deliberation he turned; the
boy watched him pivot on the good leg and saw the stiff foot drag round the arc
of the turning, leaving a final long and fading smear. His father never looked at it,
he never once looked down at the rug. The Negro held the door. It closed behind

them, upon the hysteric and indistinguishable woman-wail. His father stopped at the top of the steps and scraped his boot clean on the edge of it. At the gate he stopped again. He stood for a moment, planted stiffly on the stiff foot, looking back at the house. "Pretty and white, ain't it?" he said. "That's sweat. Nigger sweat. Maybe it ain't white enough yet to suit him. Maybe he wants to mix some white sweat with it."

Two hours later the boy was chopping wood behind the house within which his mother and aunt and the two sisters (the mother and aunt, not the two girls, he knew that; even at this distance and muffled by walls the flat loud voices of the two girls emanated an incorrigible idle inertia) were setting up the stove to prepare a meal, when he heard the hooves and saw the linen-clad man on a fine sorrel mare, whom he recognized even before he saw the rolled rug in front of the Negro youth following on a fat bay carriage horse—a suffused, angry face vanishing, still at full gallop, behind the corner of the house where his father and brother were sitting in the two tilted chairs; and a moment later, almost before he could have put the axe down, he heard the hooves again and watched the sorrel mare go back out of the yard, already galloping again. Then his father began to shout one of the sisters' names, who presently emerged backward from the kitchen door dragging the rolled rug along the ground by one end while the other sister walked behind it.

"If you ain't going to tote, go on and set up the wash pot," the first said.

"You, Sarty!" the second shouted. "Set up the wash pot!" His father appeared at the door, framed against that shabbiness, as he had been against that other bland perfection, impervious to either, the mother's anxious face at his shoulder.

"Go on," the father said. "Pick it up." The two sisters stooped, broad, lethargic; stooping, they presented an incredible expanse of pale cloth and a flutter of tawdry ribbons.

50   "If I thought enough of a rug to have to git hit all the way from France I wouldn't keep hit where folks coming in would have to tromp on hit," the first said. They raised the rug.

"Abner," the mother said. "Let me do it."

"You go back and git dinner," his father said. "I'll tend to this."

From the woodpile through the rest of the afternoon the boy watched them, the rug spread flat in the dust beside the bubbling wash-pot, the two sisters stooping over it with that profound and lethargic reluctance, while the father stood over them in turn, implacable and grim, driving them though never raising his voice again. He could smell the harsh homemade lye they were using; he saw his mother come to the door once and look toward them with an expression not anxious now but very like despair; he saw his father turn, and he fell to with the axe and saw from the corner of his eye his father raise from the ground a flattish fragment of field stone and examine it and return to the pot, and this time his mother actually spoke: "Abner. Abner. Please don't. Please, Abner."

Then he was done too. It was dusk; the whippoorwills had already begun. He could smell coffee from the room where they would presently eat the cold food remaining from the midafternoon meal, though when he entered the house he realized they were having coffee again probably because there was a fire on the hearth, before which the rug now lay spread over the backs of the two chairs. The tracks of his father's foot were gone. Where they had been were now long, water-cloudy scoriations resembling the sporadic course of a liliputian[1] mowing machine.

---

[1]**liliputian** trivial or very small, from the imaginary country Liliput, in Jonathan Swift's *Gulliver's Travels* (1726), inhabited by people 6 inches tall.

55   It still hung there while they ate the cold food and then went to bed, scattered without order or claim up and down the two rooms, his mother in one bed, where his father would later lie, the older brother in the other, himself, the aunt, and the two sisters on pallets on the floor. But his father was not in bed yet. The last thing the boy remembered was the depthless, harsh silhouette of the hat and coat bending over the rug and it seemed to him that he had not even closed his eyes when the silhouette was standing over him, the fire almost dead behind it, the stiff foot prodding him awake. "Catch up the mule," his father said.

When he returned with the mule his father was standing in the back door, the rolled rug over his shoulder. "Ain't you going to ride?" he said.

"No. Give me your foot."

He bent his knee into his father's hand, the wiry, surprising power flowed smoothly, rising, he rising with it, on to the mule's bare back (they had owned a saddle once; the boy could remember it though not when or where) and with the same effortlessness his father swung the rug up in front of him. Now in the starlight they retraced the afternoon's path, up the dusty road rife with honeysuckle, through the gate and up the black tunnel of the drive to the lightless house, where he sat on the mule and felt the rough warp of the rug drag across his thighs and vanish.

"Don't you want me to help?" he whispered. His father did not answer and now he heard again that stiff foot striking the hollow portico with that wooden and clocklike deliberation, that outrageous overstatement of the weight it carried. The rug, hunched, not flung (the boy could tell that even in the darkness) from his father's shoulder struck the angle of wall and floor with a sound unbelievably loud, thunderous, then the foot again, unhurried and enormous; a light came on in the house and the boy sat, tense, breathing steadily and quietly and just a little fast, though the foot itself did not increase its beat at all, descending the steps now; now the boy could see him.

60   "Don't you want to ride now?" he whispered. "We kin both ride now," the light within the house altering now, flaring up and sinking. *He's coming down the stairs now*, he thought. He had already ridden the mule up beside the horse block; presently his father was up behind him and he doubled the reins over and slashed the mule across the neck, but before the animal could begin to trot the hard, thin arm came round him, the hard, knotted hand jerking the mule back to a walk.

In the first red rays of the sun they were in the lot, putting plow gear on the mules. This time the sorrel mare was in the lot before he heard it at all, the rider collarless and even bareheaded, trembling, speaking in a shaking voice as the woman in the house had done. His father merely looking up once before stooping again to the hame he was buckling, so that the man on the mare spoke to his stooping back:

"You must realize you have ruined that rug. Wasn't there anybody here, any of your women . . ." he ceased, shaking, the boy watching him, the older brother leaning now in the stable door, chewing, blinking slowly and steadily at nothing apparently. "It cost a hundred dollars. But you never had a hundred dollars. You never will. So I'm going to charge you twenty bushels of corn against your crop. I'll add it in your contract and when you come to the commissary you can sign it. That won't keep Mrs. de Spain quiet but maybe it will teach you to wipe your feet off before you enter her house again."

Then he was gone. The boy looked at his father, who still had not spoken or even looked up again, who was now adjusting the loggerhead in the hame.

"Pap," he said. His father looked at him—the inscrutable face, the shaggy brows beneath which the gray eyes glinted coldly. Suddenly the boy went toward him, fast, stopping as suddenly. "You done the best you could!" he cried. "If he wanted hit done different why didn't he wait and tell you how? He won't git no twenty bushels! He won't git none! We'll gether hit and hide hit! I kin watch . . ."

65   "Did you put the cutter back in that straight stock like I told you?"

"No, sir," he said.

"Then go do it."

That was Wednesday. During the rest of that week he worked steadily, at what was within his scope and some which was beyond it, with an industry that did not need to be driven nor even commanded twice; he had this from his mother, with the difference that some at least of what he did he liked to do, such as splitting wood with the half-size axe which his mother and aunt had earned, or saved money somehow, to present him with at Christmas. In company with the two older women (and on one afternoon, even one of the sisters), he built pens for the shoat and the cow which were a part of his father's contract with the landlord, and one afternoon, his father being absent, gone somewhere on one of the mules, he went to the field.

They were running a middle buster now, his brother holding the plow straight while he handled the reins, and walking beside the straining mule, the rich black soil shearing cool and damp against his bare ankles, he thought *Maybe this is the end of it. Maybe even that twenty bushels that seems hard to have to pay for just a rug will be a cheap price for him to stop forever and always from being what he used to be;* thinking, dreaming now, so that his brother had to speak sharply to him to mind the mule: *Maybe he even won't collect the twenty bushels. Maybe it will all add up and balance and vanish—corn, rug, fire; the terror and grief, the being pulled two ways like between two teams of horses—gone, done with for ever and ever.*

70   Then it was Saturday; he looked up from beneath the mule he was harnessing and saw his father in the black coat and hat. "Not that," his father said. "The wagon gear." And then, two hours later, sitting in the wagon bed behind his father and brother on the seat, the wagon accomplished a final curve, and he saw the weathered paintless store with its tattered tobacco- and patent-medicine posters and the tethered wagons and saddle animals below the gallery. He mounted the gnawed steps behind his father and brother, and there again was the lane of quiet, watching faces for the three of them to walk through. He saw the man in spectacles sitting at the plank table and he did not need to be told this was a Justice of the Peace; he sent one glare of fierce, exultant, partisan defiance at the man in collar and cravat now, whom he had seen but twice before in his life, and that on a galloping horse, who now wore on his face an expression not of rage but of amazed unbelief which the boy could not have known was at the incredible circumstance of being sued by one of his own tenants, and came and stood against his father and cried at the Justice: "He ain't done it! He ain't burnt . . ."

"Go back to the wagon," his father said.

"Burnt?" the Justice said. "Do I understand this rug was burned too?"

"Does anybody here claim it was?" his father said. "Go back to the wagon." But he did not, he merely retreated to the rear of the room, crowded as that other had been, but not to sit down this time, instead, to stand pressing among the motionless bodies, listening to the voices:

"And you claim twenty bushels of corn is too high for the damage you did to the rug?"

75   "He brought the rug to me and said he wanted the tracks washed out of it. I washed the tracks out and took the rug back to him."

"But you didn't carry the rug back to him in the same condition it was in before you made the tracks on it."

His father did not answer, and now for perhaps half a minute there was no sound at all save that of breathing, the faint, steady suspiration of complete and intent listening.

"You decline to answer that, Mr. Snopes?" Again his father did not answer. "I'm going to find against you, Mr. Snopes. I'm going to find that you were responsible for the injury to Major de Spain's rug and hold you liable for it. But twenty bushels of corn seems a little high for a man in your circumstances to have to pay. Major de Spain claims it costs a hundred dollars. October corn will be worth about fifty cents. I figure that if Major de Spain can stand a ninety-five-dollar loss on something he paid cash for, you can stand a five-dollar loss you haven't earned yet. I hold you in damages to Major de Spain to the amount of ten bushels of corn over and above your contract with him, to be paid to him out of your crop at gathering time. Court adjourned."

It had taken no time hardly, the morning was but half begun. He thought they would return home and perhaps back to the field, since they were late, far behind all other farmers. But instead his father passed on behind the wagon, merely indicating with his hand for the older brother to follow with it, and crossed the road toward the blacksmith shop opposite, pressing on after his father, overtaking him, speaking, whispering up at the harsh, calm face beneath the weathered hat: "He won't git no ten bushels neither. He won't git one. We'll . . ." until his father glanced for an instant down at him, the face absolutely calm, the grizzled eyebrows tangled above the cold eyes, the voice almost pleasant, almost gentle:

80   "You think so? Well, we'll wait till October anyway."

The matter of the wagon—the setting of a spoke or two and the tightening of the tires—did not take long either, the business of the tires accomplished by driving the wagon into the spring branch behind the shop and letting it stand there, the mules nuzzling into the water from time to time, and the boy on the seat with the idle reins, looking up the slope and through the sooty tunnel of the shed where the slow hammer rang and where his father sat on an upended cypress bolt, easily, either talking or listening, still sitting there when the boy brought the dripping wagon up out of the branch and halted it before the door.

"Take them on to the shade and hitch," his father said. He did so and returned. His father and the smith and a third man squatting on his heels inside the door were talking, about crops and animals; the boy, squatting too in the ammoniac dust and hoof-parings and scales of rust, heard his father tell a long and unhurried story out of the time before the birth of the older brother even when he had been a professional horsetrader. And then his father came up beside him where he stood before a tattered last year's circus poster on the other side of the store, gazing rapt and quiet at the scarlet horses, the incredible poisings and convolutions of tulle and tights and the painted leers of comedians, and said, "It's time to eat."

But not at home. Squatting beside his brother against the front wall, he watched his father emerge from the store and produce from a paper sack a segment of cheese and divide it carefully and deliberately into three with his pocket knife and produce crackers from the same sack. They all three squatted on the gallery and ate, slowly, without talking; then in the store again, they drank from a tin dipper tepid water smelling of the cedar bucket and of living beech trees. And still they did not go home. It was a horse lot this time, a tall rail fence upon and along which men stood and sat and out of which one by one horses were led, to be talked and trotted and then cantered back and forth along the road while the slow swapping and buying went on and the sun began to slant westward, they—the three of them—watching and listening, the older brother with his muddy eyes and his steady, inevitable tobacco, the father commenting now and then on certain of the animals, to no one in particular.

It was after sundown when they reached home. They ate supper by lamplight, then, sitting on the doorstep, the boy watched the night fully accomplish, listening to the whippoorwills and the frogs, when he heard his mother's voice: "Abner! No! No! Oh, God. Oh, God. Abner!" and he rose, whirled, and saw the altered light through the door where a candle stub now burned in a bottle neck on the table and his father, still in the hat and coat, at once formal and burlesque as though dressed carefully for some shabby and ceremonial violence, emptying the reservoir of the lamp back into the five-gallon kerosene can from which it had been filled, while the mother tugged at his arm until he shifted the lamp to the other hand and flung her back, not savagely or viciously, just hard, into the wall, her hands flung out against the wall for balance, her mouth open and in her face the same quality of hopeless despair as had been in her voice. Then his father saw him standing in the door.

85   "Go to the barn and get that can of oil we were oiling the wagon with," he said. The boy did not move. Then he could speak.

"What . . ." he cried. "What are you . . ."

"Go get that oil," his father said. "Go."

Then he was moving, running, outside the house, toward the stable: this the old habit, the old blood which he had not been permitted to choose for himself, which had been bequeathed him willy nilly and which had run for so long (and who knew where, battening on what of outrage and savagery and lust) before it came to him. *I could keep on, he thought. I could run on and on and never look back, never need to see his face again. Only I can't. I can't,* the rusted can in his hand now, the liquid sploshing in it as he ran back to the house and into it, into the sound of his mother's weeping in the next room, and handed the can to his father.

"Ain't you going to even send a nigger?" he cried. "At least you sent a nigger before!"

90   This time his father didn't strike him. The hand came even faster than the blow had, the same hand which had set the can on the table with almost excruciating care flashing from the can toward him too quick for him to follow it, gripping him by the back of his shirt and on to tiptoe before he had seen it quit the can, the face stooping at him in breathless and frozen ferocity, the cold, dead voice speaking over him to the older brother who leaned against the table, chewing with that steady, curious, sidewise motion of cows:

"Empty the can into the big one and go on. I'll catch up with you."

"Better tie him up to the bedpost," the brother said.

"Do like I told you," the father said. Then the boy was moving, his bunched shirt and the hard, bony hand between his shoulderblades, his toes just touching the floor, across the room and into the other one, past the sisters sitting with spread heavy thighs in the two chairs over the cold hearth, and to where his mother and aunt sat side by side on the bed, the aunt's arms about his mother's shoulders.

"Hold him," the father said. The aunt made a startled movement. "Not you," the father said. "Lennie. Take hold of him. I want to see you do it." His mother took him by the wrist. "You'll hold him better than that. If he gets loose don't you know what he is going to do? He will go up yonder." He jerked his head toward the road. "Maybe I'd better tie him."

95   "I'll hold him," his mother whispered.

"See you do then." Then his father was gone, the stiff foot heavy and measured upon the boards, ceasing at last.

Then he began to struggle. His mother caught him in both arms, he jerking and wrenching at them. He would be stronger in the end, he knew that. But he had no time to wait for it. "Lemme go!" he cried. "I don't want to have to hit you!"

"Let him go!" the aunt said. "If he don't go, before God, I am going up there myself!"

"Don't you see I can't?" his mother cried. "Sarty! Sarty! No! No! Help me, Lizzie!"

100   Then he was free. His aunt grasped at him but it was too late. He whirled, running, his mother stumbled forward on to her knees behind him, crying to the nearer sister: "Catch him, Net! Catch him!" But that was too late too, the sister (the sisters were twins, born at the same time, yet either of them now gave the impression of being, encompassing as much living meat and volume and weight as any other two of the family) not yet having begun to rise from the chair, her head, face, alone merely turned, presenting to him in the flying instant an astonishing expanse of young female features untroubled by any surprise even, wearing only an expression of bovine interest. Then he was out of the room, out of the house, in the mild dust of the starlit road and the heavy rifeness of honeysuckle, the pale ribbon unspooling with terrific slowness under his running feet, reaching the gate at last and turning in, running, his heart and lungs drumming, on up the drive toward the lighted house, the lighted door. He did not knock, he burst in, sobbing for breath, incapable for the moment of speech; he saw the astonished face of the Negro in the linen jacket without knowing when the Negro had appeared.

"De Spain!" he cried, panted. "Where's . . ." then he saw the white man too emerging from a white door down the hall. "Barn!" he cried. "Barn!"

"What?" the white man said. "Barn?"

"Yes!" the boy cried. "Barn!"

105   "Catch him!" the white man shouted.

But it was too late this time too. The Negro grasped his shirt, but the entire sleeve, rotten with washing, carried away, and he was out that door too and in the drive again, and had actually never ceased to run even while he was screaming into the white man's face.

Behind him the white man was shouting, "My horse! Fetch my horse!" and he thought for an instant of cutting across the park and climbing the fence into the road, but he did not know the park nor how high the vine-massed fence might be and he dared not risk it. So he ran on down the drive, blood and breath roaring; presently he was in the road again though he could not see it. He could not hear either: the galloping mare was almost upon him before he heard her, and even then he held his course, as if the very urgency of his wild grief and need must in a moment more find him wings, waiting until the ultimate instant to hurl himself aside and into the weed-choked roadside ditch as the horse thundered past and on, for an instant in furious silhouette against the stars, the tranquil early summer night sky which, even before the shape of the horse and rider vanished, stained abruptly and violently upward: a long, swirling roar incredible and soundless, blotting the stars, and he springing up and into the road again, running again, knowing it was too late yet still running even after he heard the shot and, an instant later, two shots, pausing now without knowing he had ceased to run, crying "Pap! Pap!",

what does the honeysuckle me[an]

running again before he knew he had begun to run, stumbling, tripping over something and scrabbling up again without ceasing to run, looking backward over his shoulder at the glares as he got up, running on among the invisible trees, panting, sobbing, "Father! Father!"

At midnight he was sitting on the crest of a hill. He did not know it was midnight and he did not know how far he had come. But there was no glare behind him now and he sat now, his back toward what he had called home for four days anyhow, his face toward the dark woods which he would enter when breath was strong again, small, shaking steadily in the chill darkness, hugging himself into the remainder of his thin, rotten shirt, the grief and despair now no longer terror and fear but just grief and despair. *Father. My father*, he thought. "He was brave!" He cried suddenly, aloud but not loud, no more than a whisper: "He was! He was in the war! He was in Colonel Sartoris' cav'ry!" not knowing that his father had gone to that war a private in the fine old European sense, wearing no uniform, admitting the authority of and giving fidelity to no man or army or flag, going to war as Malbrouck himself did: for booty—it meant nothing and less than nothing to him if it were enemy booty or his own.

The slow constellations wheeled on. It would be dawn and then sun-up after a while and he would be hungry. But that would be to-morrow and now he was only cold, and walking would cure that. His breathing was easier now and he decided to get up and go on, and then he found that he had been asleep because he knew it was almost dawn, the night almost over. He could tell that from the whippoorwills. They were everywhere now among the dark trees below him, constant and inflectioned and ceaseless, so that, as the instant for giving over to the day birds drew nearer and nearer, there was no interval at all between them. He got up. He was a little stiff, but walking would cure that too as it would the cold, and soon there would be the sun. He went on down the hill, toward the dark woods within which the liquid silver voices of the birds called unceasing—the rapid and urgent beating of the urgent and quiring heart of the late spring night. He did not look back.

[1939]

Joining the Conversation: Critical Thinking and Writing

1. Discuss "point of view" in this story. Identify passages in the text where we are made aware of the narrator's or a character's point of view.
2. Is Faulkner on Major de Spain's side, or Abner Snopes's, or both, or neither?
3. By the end of the story, how has Sarty changed? Does Faulkner show us this process of change in a convincing way? Do we believe it? In your argument, make sure to cite evidence from the text.
4. While you were reading "Barn Burning," did you feel at any point that you needed "background information" in order to understand and appreciate it? Or do you think that the story itself contains everything that you need to know?
5. Many people claim that Faulkner is one of the greatest American writers. Do you think that this story supports such a view? Is this a great story or a good story?

TOBIAS WOLFF

Tobias Wolff was born in Alabama in 1945, but he was raised in the state of Washington. He served for four years in the army (1964–68), including a tour of duty in Vietnam. He graduated from Oxford University in 1972 and then studied creative writing at Stanford University. Wolff's first two books were collections of short stories, In the Garden of North American Martyrs *(1981) and* Back in the World *(1985), and both received good reviews, but he achieved greater success and acclaim with the publication of* This Boy's Life *(1989), his memoir of his teenage years. He has also written a memoir of his military service,* In Pharaoh's Army *(1994). The author of many short stories and two novels, his recent publications include* Our Story Begins: New and Selected Stories *(2008). From 1980 to 1997, Wolff taught courses in English and creative writing at Syracuse University, and since then he has taught at Stanford, where he is the Ward W. and Priscilla B. Woods Professor in the School of Humanities and Sciences.*

Powder

Just before Christmas my father took me skiing at Mount Baker. He'd had to fight for the privilege of my company, because my mother was still angry with him for sneaking me into a nightclub during his last visit, to see Thelonius Monk.

He wouldn't give up. He promised, hand on heart, to take good care of me and have me home for dinner on Christmas Eve, and she relented. But as we were checking out of the lodge that morning it began to snow, and in this snow he observed some quality that made it necessary for us to get in one last run. We got in several last runs. He was indifferent to my fretting. Snow whirled around us in bitter, blinding squalls, hissing like sand, and still we skied. As the lift bore us to the peak yet again, my father looked at his watch and said: "Criminey. This'll have to be a fast one."

By now I couldn't see the trail. There was no point in trying. I stuck to him like white on rice and did what he did and somehow made it to the bottom without sailing off a cliff. We returned our skis and my father put chains on the Austin-Healy while I swayed from foot to foot, clapping my mittens and wishing I were home. I could see everything. The green tablecloth, the plates with the holly pattern, the red candles waiting to be lit.

We passed a diner on our way out. "You want some soup?" my father asked. I shook my head. "Buck up," he said. "I'll get you there. Right, doctor?"

5   I was supposed to say, "Right, doctor," but I didn't say anything.

A state trooper waved us down outside the resort. A pair of sawhorses were blocking the road. The trooper came up to our car and bent down to my father's window. His face was bleached by the cold. Snowflakes clung to his eyebrows and to the fur trim of his jacket and cap.

"Don't tell me," my father said.

The trooper told him. The road was closed. It might get cleared, it might not. Storm took everyone by surprise. So much, so fast. Hard to get people moving. Christmas Eve. What can you do?

My father said: "Look. We're talking about four, five inches. I've taken this car through worse than that."

10   The trooper straightened up, boots creaking. His face was out of sight but I could hear him. "The road is closed."

My father sat with both hands on the wheel, rubbing the wood with his thumbs. He looked at the barricade for a long time. He seemed to be trying to master the

idea of it. Then he thanked the trooper, and with a weird, old-maidy show of caution turned the car around. "Your mother will never forgive me for this," he said.

"We should have left before," I said. "Doctor."

He didn't speak to me again until we were both in a booth at the diner, waiting
for our burgers. "She won't forgive me," he said. "Do you understand? Never."

"I guess," I said, but no guesswork was required; she wouldn't forgive him.

15   "I can't let that happen." He bent toward me. "I'll tell you what I want. I want
us to be all together again. Is that what you want?"

"Yes, sir."

He bumped my chin with his knuckles. "That's all I needed to hear."

When we finished eating he went to the pay phone in the back of the dinner,
then joined me in the booth again. I figured he'd called my mother, but he didn't
give a report. He sipped at his coffee and stared out the window at the empty road.
"Come on, come on," he said. A little while later he said, "Come on!" When the
trooper's car went past, lights flashing, he got up and dropped some money on the
check. "O.K. Vámanos."

The wind had died. The snow was falling straight down, less of it now; lighter.
We drove away from the resort, right up to the barricade. "Move it," my father told
me. When I looked at him he said, "What are you waiting for?" I got out and
dragged one of the sawhorses aside, then put it back after he drove through. He
pushed the door open for me. "Now you're an accomplice," he said. "We go down
together." He put the car into gear and gave me a look. "Joke, doctor."

20   "Funny, doctor."

Down the first long stretch I watched the road behind us, to see if the trooper
was on our tail. The barricade vanished. Then there was nothing but snow: snow
on the road, snow kicking up from the chains, snow on the trees, snow in the sky;
and our trail in the snow. I faced around and had a shock. The lie of the road
behind us had been marked by our own tracks, but there were no tracks ahead of
us. My father was breaking virgin snow between a line of tall trees. He was humming "Stars Fell on Alabama." I felt snow brush along the floorboards under my
feet. To keep my hands from shaking, I clamped them between my knees.

My father grunted in a thoughtful way and said, "Don't ever try this yourself."

"I won't."

"That's what you say now, but someday you'll get your license and then you'll
think you can do anything. Only you won't be able to do this. You need, I don't
know—a certain instinct."

25   "Maybe I have it."

"You don't. You have your strong points, but not . . . this. I only mention it,
because I don't want you to get the idea this is something just anybody can do. I'm
a great driver. That's not a virtue, O.K.? It's just a fact, and one you should be aware
of. Of course you have to give the old heap some credit, too—there aren't many
cars I'd try this with. Listen!"

I listened. I heard the slap of the chains, the stiff, jerky rasps of the wipers, the
purr of the engine. It really did purr. The car was almost new. My father couldn't
afford it, and kept promising to sell it, but here it was.

I said, "Where do you think that policeman went to?"

"Are you warm enough?" He reached over and cranked up the blower. Then
he turned off the wipers. We didn't need them. The clouds had brightened. A few
sparse, feathery flakes drifted into our slipstream and were swept away. We left the
trees and entered a broad field of snow that ran level for a while and then tilted
sharply downward. Orange stakes had been planted at intervals in two parallel
lines and my father steered a course between them, though they were far enough

apart to leave considerable doubt in my mind as to where exactly the road lay. He was humming again, doing little scat riffs around the melody.

30   "O.K. then. What are my strong points?"

"Don't get me started," he said. "It'd take all day."

"Oh, right. Name one."

"Easy. You always think ahead."

True. I always thought ahead. I was a boy who kept his clothes on numbered hangers to insure proper rotation. I bothered my teachers for homework assignments far ahead of their due dates so I could make up schedules. I thought ahead, and that was why I knew that there would be other troopers waiting for us at the end of our ride, if we got there. What I did not know was that my father would wheedle and plead his way past them—he didn't sing "O Tannenbaum"[1] but just about—and get me home for dinner, buying a little more time before my mother decided to make the split final. I knew we'd get caught; I was resigned to it. And maybe for this reason I stopped moping and began to enjoy myself.

35   Why not? This was one for the books. Like being in a speedboat, but better. You can't go downhill in a boat. And it was all ours. And it kept coming, the laden trees, the unbroken surface of snow, the sudden white vistas. Here and there I saw hints of the road, ditches, fences, stakes, but not so many that I could have found my way. But then I didn't have to. My father was driving. My father in his 48th year, rumpled, kind, bankrupt of honor, flushed with certainty. He was a great driver. All persuasion, no coercion. Such subtlety at the wheel, such tactful pedalwork. I actually trusted him. And the best was yet to come—the switchbacks and hairpins. Impossible to describe. Except maybe to say this: If you haven't driven fresh powder, you haven't driven.

[1992]

[1]**"O Tannenbaum"** a German song known in English as "O Christmas Tree."

Joining the Conversation: Critical Thinking and Writing

1. How would you characterize the father in "Powder"?
2. How does the boy feel about his father?
3. What argument might you offer to someone who said that this story glorified an irresponsible father?
4. What is the main point of the story? What is your evidence? Or does this story have more than one "main point"? Again, please support your view with evidence.

POEMS

ANONYMOUS

Birmingham Jail was famous, not only in the South but throughout the United States, for many decades before Martin Luther King Jr. was arrested and imprisoned there in 1963. A song called "Birmingham Jail" is at least as old as the early twentieth century (a version was published in 1909), and, like many popular ballads, it draws on older songs, notably "Down in the Valley," which has been sung at least since the late nineteenth century. Like all folk songs, "Birmingham Jail" exists in many versions: Singers make small changes within a line, or sometimes drop or add whole verses. For instance, in what may be the most common version, some lines run thus:

Send me a letter, send it by mail,
Send it in care of the Birmingham jail.

But we have also heard

Send me a letter, send it by mail,
Back it in care of Birmingham jail.

and another version sung by Huddie Ledbetter, known as Leadbelly (1888–1949):

Send me a letter, send it by mail,
'Dress it all over, that Birmingham jail.

We print one version as it was actually sung, and then we offer additional stanzas from other versions, that is, from performances by other singers. You can pick and choose and thus create the version that strikes you as the one that is most effective. (Inventing new lines and stanzas, or adding lines or stanzas from other ballads, is entirely acceptable.)

Birmingham Jail

Down in the valley, the valley so low,
Put your head out the window, and hear the wind blow.
Hear the wind blow, hear the wind blow,
Put your head out the window, and hear the wind blow.

Write me a letter, send it by mail   5
'Dress it all over, that Birmingham jail.
Birmingham jail, boys, Birmingham jail,
'Dress it all over, that Birmingham jail.

Ty Shek [?] will 'rrest you, bound you over in jail,
Can't get nobody, to go your bail.   10
To go your bail, boys, to go your bail,
Can't get nobody, to go your bail.

Send for your lawyer, come down to your cell,
He swear he can clear you, in spite of all hell.
Spite of all hell, boys, spite of all hell,   15
He swear he can clear you, in spite of all hell.

Get the biggest your money, come back for the rest,
Tell you plead guilty, for he know that is best.
He know that is best, boys, he know that is best,
Tell you plead guilty, he know that is best.   20

Down in the valley, the valley so low,
Put your head out the window, and hear the wind blow.
Hear the wind blow, hear the wind blow,
Put your head out the window, and hear the wind blow.

Joining the Conversation: Critical Thinking and Writing

1. Here are some additional verses, taken from other singers. If you were singing "Birmingham Jail," which verses might you include, and which exclude? Why?

Writing this letter, containing three lines,
Answer my question, will you be mine?
Will you be mine, dear, will you be mine,
Answer my question, will you be mine?

The roses are red, and the vi'lets are blue,
Angels in Heaven sing "I love you."
Angels in Heaven, Angels in Heaven,
Angels in Heaven, sing "I love you."

Roses love sunshine, violets love dew,
Angels in Heaven know I love you,
Know I love you, dear, know I love you,
Angels in Heaven know I love you.

Go build me a castle, forty feet high,
So I can see her, as she goes by.
As she goes by, love, as she goes by,
So I can see her, as she goes by.

Bird in a cage, love, bird in a cage,
Dying for freedom, ever a slave.
Ever a slave love, ever a slave,
Dying for freedom, ever a slave.

2. We have never heard a version of "Birmingham Jail" in which the singer tells *why* he is in jail. Other songs talk about gambling debts, drunkenness, or disorderly or criminal behavior, but in "Birmingham Jail," no explanation is offered, not even that the singer is unjustly imprisoned. Would the song be better if we were given such information? Why, or why not?
3. How is it that we as readers can feel pleasure in response to a poem that is sorrowful in tone and situation? What kind of pleasure is it? Do we share the speaker's sorrow, or do we remain somewhat at a distance from it?

A. E. HOUSMAN

Alfred Edward Housman (1859–1936) was born near rural Shropshire, England, and was educated in classics and philosophy at Oxford University. Although he was a brilliant student, he failed his final examination and did not receive the academic appointment that he had anticipated. He began working as a civil servant at the British Patent Office, but in his spare time, he wrote scholarly articles on Latin literature. These writings in 1892 won him an appointment as Professor of Latin at the University of London. In 1911, he was appointed to Cambridge University. During his lifetime, he published (in addition to his scholarly writings) only two thin books of poetry, A Shropshire Lad *(1896) and* Last Poems *(1922), and a highly readable lecture called* The Name and Nature of Poetry *(1933). After his death, a third book of poems,* More Poems *(1936), was published. The best edition of Housman's poems (containing not only the three books of poems already mentioned but also additional poems, fragments, translations, light verse, and Latin verse) is* The Poems of A. E. Housman *(1997), edited by Archie Burnett.*

The usual explanation for Housman's failure at his examination is that he was in a state of shock resulting from his repressed homosexual love for a fellow student. In any case, Housman, like almost all homosexuals of the period, kept his homosexuality a secret. This is not surprising; in England, "unnatural acts" between men were punishable by death until 1885, when the penalty was modified to a maximum of two years at hard labor. (Not until 1967 was homosexual behavior between consenting adults legalized in England.) In the poetry published in Housman's lifetime, there is nothing explicitly homosexual, but today readers who are aware of his sexual orientation can easily and reasonably perceive the sexual implications in the voice of the man who believes he is doomed to be an outsider.

The first of the two poems that we print here, "The Carpenter's Son," was written in 1895 and was published the next year in A Shropshire Lad. *In this poem, Housman sets forth, in nineteenth-century rural imagery, the story of a carpenter's son—Jesus was the son of a carpenter—who is carried in a cart to a gallows, where he will be hanged between two thieves. The youth who speaks the poem differs from his two fellow victims, he says, in that he "dies for love."*

The second poem, "Oh who is that young sinner," was written in August 1895, shortly after Oscar Wilde (1854–1900), the most popular British playwright of the period, was convicted of sodomy and given the maximum prison sentence. Although the poem does not mention homosexuality, Wilde's conviction unquestionably inspired it. Housman never published it, but after Housman died, his brother, Laurence Housman, published it in A.E.H.: Some Poems, Some Letters and a Personal Memoir by His Brother *(1936).*

The Carpenter's Son*

"Here the hangman stops his cart:
Now the best of friends must part.
Fare you well, for ill fare I:
Live, lads, and I will die.

"Oh, at home had I but stayed   5
'Prenticed to my father's trade,
Had I stuck to plane and adze,
I had not been lost, my lads.

"Then I might have built perhaps
Gallows-trees for other chaps,   10
Never dangled on my own,
Had I but left ill alone.

"Now, you see, they hang me high,
And the people passing by
Stop to shake their fists and curse;   15
So 'tis come from ill to worse.

"Here hang I, and right and left
Two poor fellows hang for theft:
All the same's the luck we prove,
Though the midmost hangs for love.   20

---

*The Carpenter's Son The Gospels according to Matthew (13:55) and Mark (6:3) identify Jesus as a carpenter's son. Lines 18–19 in the poem allude to the two thieves between whom Jesus was crucified (Matthew 27:38; Mark 15:27; Luke 23:39–40).

"Comrades all, that stand and gaze,
Walk henceforth in other ways;
See my neck and save your own:
Comrades all, leave ill alone.

"Make some day a decent end,   25
Shrewder fellows than your friend.
Fare you well, for ill fare I:
Live, lads, and I will die."

[1895]

Joining the Conversation: Critical Thinking and Writing

1. We think you will agree that even separated from the context of the other
poems in *A Shropshire Lad*—a world in which Housman speaks of lads, barns,
ploughing, country fairs, and so forth—"The Carpenter's Son" evokes a folksy,
rural nineteenth-century world. What words make it seem to be set in relatively
modern times rather than the time of the crucifixion of Jesus? Or put it this way:
Why does the speaker sound like a youth of the modern world (nineteenth
century) rather than Jesus?
2. The speaker says that he "hangs for love," but he never amplifies what he
means. Should he have?
3. Is the poem blasphemous? (If you are not a Christian, try to put yourself into
the shoes of a Christian while thinking about this question.)

Oh who is that young sinner

Oh who is that young sinner with the handcuffs on his wrists?
And what has he been after that they groan and shake their fists?
And wherefore is he wearing such a conscience-stricken air?
Oh they're taking him to prison for the colour of his hair.

'Tis a shame to human nature, such a head of hair as his;   5
In the good old time 'twas hanging for the colour that it is;
Though hanging isn't bad enough and flaying would be fair
For the nameless and abominable colour of his hair.

Oh a deal of pains he's taken and a pretty price he's paid
To hide his poll° or dye it of a mentionable shade;   10
But they've pulled the beggar's hat off for the world to see and stare,
And they're haling him to justice for the colour of his hair.

Now 'tis oakum for his fingers° and the treadmill for his feet
And the quarry-gang on Portland in the cold and in the heat,
And between his spells of labour in the time he has to spare   15
He can curse the God that made him for the colour of his hair.

[1895]

10 poll the hair-covered back and top of the human head.   **13 oakum for his fingers**
Prisoners sentenced to hard labor had to shred jute, a coarse fiber mixed with tar to make
oakum, used for caulking wooden ships. The task bloodied their fingers.

Joining the Conversation: Critical Thinking and Writing

1. Characterize the tone of the speaker in the first two stanzas. He begins by asking a simple question, but what causes him to change to the tone that we hear in the second stanza? What is the tone of the last line of the poem?
2. In a draft of the first line, Housman wrote "fellow", but he then replaced it with "sinner." Why do you suppose he made the change?
3. No one in England, or probably anywhere else, is or was put into prison "for the colour of his hair." What is Housman getting at?

Dorothy Parker

For a biographical note on Dorothy Parker, see page 979.

Résumé

> Razors pain you;
> Rivers are damp;
> Acids stain you;
> And drugs cause cramp.
> Guns aren't lawful;   5
> Nooses give;
> Gas smells awful;
> You might as well live.

[1926]

Joining the Conversation: Critical Thinking and Writing

1. "Exactly what is a *résumé?* How does Parker's *résumé* differ from the usual one?
2. Is the poem amusing? Is it more than amusing; that is, does it offer insight into an interesting state of feeling, or perhaps does it offer a view worth thinking about?

Claude McKay

Born in Jamaica, Claude McKay (1890–1948) wrote his first poems there, in dialect that drew upon the island's folk culture. In 1912, he left Jamaica to pursue a literary career in the United States. McKay attended school and worked at a number of jobs in the 1910s, but above all he continued to write poems, which were well received. During the 1920s, he became part of the Harlem literary and cultural renaissance. A political radical, McKay was also active in left-wing groups and causes; in 1922–23, he traveled to the Soviet Union, where he lectured on politics and literature. McKay's books of poems include Songs of Jamaica *(1912) and* Harlem Shadows *(1922). His most notable novel,* Home to Harlem *(1928), tells the story of an African American soldier who deserts from the army in France and then returns to the United States; it was the first novel by an African American to become a best seller. McKay's autobiography is* A Long Way from Home *(1937). "If We Must Die," printed here, is McKay's best-known poem. A response to a horrific outbreak of racial violence in the summer of 1919 in Chicago and other major cities, the poem was first published in July of that year in the radical journal* Liberator.

If We Must Die

If we must die, let it not be like hogs
Hunted and penned in an inglorious spot,
While round us bark the mad and hungry dogs,
Making their mock at our accursed lot.
If we must die, O let us nobly die,   5
So that our precious blood may not be shed
In vain: then even the monsters we defy
Shall be constrained to honor us though dead!
O kinsmen! we must meet the common foe!
Though far outnumbered let us show us brave,   10
And for their thousand blows deal one deathblow!
What though before us lies the open grave?
Like men we'll face the murderous, cowardly pack,
Pressed to the wall, dying, but fighting back!

[1919]

Joining the Conversation: Critical Thinking and Writing

1. In line 9, the speaker refers to "the common foe." In what other ways in the poem is this "foe" characterized?
2. We know that "If We Must Die" is a poem about racial violence. How would you interpret the poem if you did not know this?
3. Some would argue that violence should never be the response to injustice, no matter how cruel the injustice might be. Do you believe this yourself? Or can you think of instances when violence might be justified?

JIMMY SANTIAGO BACA

For a biographical note on Jimmy Santiago Baca, see page 1052. Immigrants in Our Own Land, *published in 1979, was Baca's first book, and it includes the poem printed here. Among his other books are* Black Mesa Poems *(1989) and* Healing Earthquakes: Poems *(2001).*

Cloudy Day

It is windy today. A wall of wind crashes against,
windows clunk against, iron frames
as wind swings past broken glass
and seethes, like a frightened cat
in empty spaces of the cellblock.   5

In the exercise yard
we sat huddled in our prison jackets,
on our haunches against the fence,
and the wind carried our words
over the fence,
while the vigilant guard on the tower   10
held his cap at the sudden gust.

I could see the main tower from where I sat,
and the wind in my face
gave me the feeling I could grasp   15
the tower like a cornstalk,
and snap it from its roots of rock.
The wind plays it like a flute,
this hollow shoot of rock.
The brim girded with barbwire   20
with a guard sitting there also,
listening intently to the sounds
as clouds cover the sun.

I thought of the day I was coming to prison,
in the back seat of a police car,   25
hands and ankles chained, the policeman pointed,
"See that big water tank? The big
silver one out there, sticking up?
That's the prison."

And here I am, I cannot believe it.   30
Sometimes it is such a dream, a dream,
where I stand up in the face of the wind,
like now, it blows at my jacket,
and my eyelids flick a little bit,
while I stare disbelieving. . . .   35

The third day of spring,
and four years later, I can tell you,
how a man can endure, how a man
can become so cruel, how he can die
or become so cold. I can tell you this,   40
I have seen it every day, every day,
and still I am strong enough to love you,
love myself and feel good;
even as the earth shakes and trembles,
and I have not a thing to my name,   45
I feel as if I have everything, everything.

[1979]

Joining the Conversation: Critical Thinking and Writing

1. In an interview in 1997, Baca noted that he wrote "Cloudy Day" in prison. How do the details of the poem's language bear witness to Baca's own experience of imprisonment? Do you think that a person who had never been imprisoned could write such a poem?
2. In the same interview, Baca was asked about this poem: "Was that written for a person?" He replied: "It was written for me." Baca did not say any more than that. What do you think he means? And how, specifically, is this meaning reflected in the poem?
3. In the final stanza, Baca recalls that he has now been in prison for four years. What has he learned about himself, and about the realities of prison, during this period of time?

4. Who is the "you" referred to in the final stanza? How do you interpret the last line? And why does Baca repeat the word "everything"?

CAROLYN FORCHÉ

Carolyn Forché was born in Detroit in 1950. After earning a BA from Michigan State University and an MA from Bowling Green State University, she traveled widely in the Southwest, living among Pueblo Indians. Between 1978 and 1986, she made several visits to El Salvador, documenting human rights violations for Amnesty International. Her first book of poems, Gathering the Tribes, *won the Yale Younger Poets award in 1975. Forché is Director of the Lannan Center for Poetry and Poetics and holds the Lannan Chair in Poetry at Georgetown University in Washington, DC. Her second book of poems,* The Country between Us *(1981), includes "The Colonel," which has been called a prose poem, that is, a short work that looks like prose but that is highly rhythmical or rich in images, or both.*

The Colonel

What you have heard is true. I was in his house. His wife carried a tray of coffee and sugar. His daughter filed her nails, his son went out for the night. There were daily papers, pet dogs, a pistol on the cushion beside him. The moon swung bare on its black cord over the house. On the television was a cop show. It was in English. Broken bottles were embedded in the walls around the house to scoop the knee-caps from a man's legs or cut his hands to lace. On the windows there were gratings like those in liquor stores. We had dinner, rack of lamb, good wine, a gold bell was on the table for calling the maid. The maid brought green mangoes, salt, a type of bread. I was asked how I enjoyed the country. There was a brief commercial in Spanish. His wife took everything away. There was some talk then of how difficult it had become to govern. The parrot said hello on the terrace. The colonel told it to shutup, and pushed himself from the table. My friend said to me with his eyes: say nothing. The colonel returned with a sack used to bring groceries home. He spilled many human ears on the table. They were like dried peach halves. There is no other way to say this. He took one of them in his hands, shook it in our faces, dropped it into a water glass. It came alive there. I am tired of fooling around he said. As for the rights of anyone, tell your people they can go fuck themselves. He swept the ears to the floor with his arm and held the last of his wine in the air. Something for your poetry, no? he said. Some of the ears on the floor caught this scrap of his voice. Some of the ears on the floor were pressed to the ground. *May 1978*

[1981]

Joining the Conversation: Critical Thinking and Writing

1. How would you characterize the colonel in a few sentences?
2. We are told that the colonel spoke of "how difficult it had become to govern." What do you suppose the colonel assumes is the purpose of government? What do you assume its purpose is?
3. How much do we know about the narrator? Can we guess the narrator's purpose in visiting the colonel? How would you characterize the narrator's tone? Do you believe the narrator?
4. What is your response to the last sentence?

HAKI MADHUBUTI

Haki Madhubuti is an African American poet who is known for his inventive use of language that captures the rhythms and sounds of black speech. Born as Don L. Lee in Little Rock, Arkansas, in 1942, Madhubuti has initiated or engaged in many social causes that are dedicated to improving educational, economic, and social opportunities for African Americans. He has published over twenty books of poetry and nonfiction, and his work is frequently anthologized. He is one of the founders of Third World Press, which has published works by important African American writers and has played an influential role in the development of American literature.

The B Network

brothers bop & pop and be-bop in cities locked up
and chained insane by crack and other acts
of desperation computerized in pentagon cellars producing
boppin brothers boastin of being better, best & beautiful.
if the boppin brothers are beautiful where are the sisters   5
who seek brotherman with a drugless head unbossed or beaten
by the bodacious West?

in a time of big wind being blown by boastful brothers,
will other brothers beat back backwardness to better & best
without braggart bosses beatin butts,   10
takin names and diggin graves?

beatin badness into bad may be urban but is it beautiful & serious?
or is it betrayal in an era of prepared easy death hangin on corners
trappin young brothers before they know the difference between
big death and big life?   15

brothers bop & pop and be-bop in cities locked up
and chained insane by crack and other acts
of desperation computerized in pentagon cellars producing
boppin brothers boastin of being better, best, beautiful
and definitely not *Black*.   20

the critical best is that
brothers better be the best if they are to avoid backwardness
brothers better be the best if they are to conquer beautiful bigness
Comprehend that bad is only *bad* if it s big, Black and better than
boastful braggarts belittling our best and brightest   25
with bosses seeking inches when miles are better.
brothers need to bop to being Black & bright & above board
the black train of beautiful wisdom that is bending this bind
towards a new & knowledgeable beginning that is
bountiful & bountiful & beautiful   30
While be-boppin to be
better than the test,
brotherman.

better yet write the exam.

[1990]

Joining the Conversation: Critical Thinking and Writing

1. "The B Network" is a poem that is defined by rhythm and sound. Examine how Madhubuti uses poetic techniques to make his poem "bop & pop and be-bop," as he says in its first line. How does the repetition of the sound "b" make this an effective poem?
2. What is the larger theme of "The B Network"? Does Madhubuti have a message or a lesson that he is conveying to the reader? For example, what is his message about how "brothers better be the best"? According to the poem, how can a "brother" be the best?
3. How does Madhubuti characterize the urban lives of black men? What are some of the details that he uses to create an image of the city?
4. What ideas about power is Madhubuti exploring? Why does he evoke the pentagon? Why does he mention "bosses"?
5. Look at the form of this poem on the page. How would you describe the look and feel of the poem? For example, how does the poem use different line lengths to express its energy?

JILL MCDONOUGH

Born in Hartford, Connecticut in 1972, Jill McDonough has received numerous awards for her poetry, including a Lannan Fellowship, three Pushcart Prizes, a National Endowment for the Arts fellowship, and fellowships from the New York Public Library and the Library of Congress. Her poetry is notable for its direct and intimate portrayal of the complexities of contemporary life. Her collections of poetry include Where You Live *and* Habeas Corpus. *In addition to teaching as a professor at the University of Massachusetts, Boston, she has taught incarcerated college students through Boston University's Prison Education Program.*

Three a.m.

Our cabdriver tells us how Somalia is better
than here because in Islam we execute murderers.
So, fewer murders. *But isn't there civil war
there now? Aren't there a lot of murders?*
Yes, but in general it's better. Not   5
now, but most of the time. He tells us about how
smart the system is, how it's hard to bear
false witness. We nod. We're learning a lot.
I say—once we are close to the house—I say, *What
about us?* Two women, married to each other.   10
Don't be offended, he says, gravely. *But a man
with a man, a woman with a woman: it would be
a public execution.* We nod. A little silence along
the Southeast Corridor. Then I say, *Yeah,
I love my country.* This makes him laugh; we all laugh.   15
We aren't offended, says Josey. *We love you.* Sometimes
I feel like we're proselytizing, spreading the Word of Gay.
The cab is shaking with laughter, the poor man
relieved we're not mad he sort of wants us dead.

The two of us soothing him, wanting him comfortable,   20
wanting him to laugh. *We love our country,*
we tell him. And Josey tips him. She tips him well.

[2012]

Joining the Conversation: Critical Thinking and Writing

1. Write a short summary of the poem. Explain the conversation that takes place in the cab. Who is engaged in the dialogue? What topic is being discussed? What are the opinions being expressed on that topic?
2. What is the uneasy realization that the narrator comes to during the course of the poem? How would you describe the insight that the narrator and her partner, Josey, have? What lines capture that insight? Why are the narrator and her partner troubled by that insight?
3. Notice that the line, "I love my country," is repeated as "We love our country." Why is the sentiment of "love" repeated throughout the poem? What does "love of country" express?
4. How does the poem address the issue of gay marriage? What are the different opinions on gay marriage expressed in the poem? What is the "Word of Gay"?
5. Analyze the last lines of the poem. Why does Josey give the cabdriver a good tip? What does that tip represent? Imagine a different ending to the poem. Why would Josey be justified in giving a small tip? Thinking through the discussion during the cab ride, would you expect a larger or a smaller tip to be given? Why is the size of the tip meaningful?

PLAY

BILLY GODA

Billy Goda, playwright and screenwriter, holds an MFA from Columbia University. No Crime was first published in Best American Short Plays *1998–99. His most recent publication is* Dust *(2009), a thriller that ran in New York in 2008–09.*

No Crime

CHARACTERS

CAL ROBERTS, a good looking thirty-year-old man
JIM ABNER, a big, egotistical fifty-year-old man
CAL *is in* JIM ABNER'S *office. It is a large office with a great deal of room, light, and a nice view.* JIM *has his cowboy boots up on his desk.*

JIM: A time comes in a man's life when fifteen minutes can change his future, change his life; these could be your fifteen minutes, Cal.

Pause as JIM *takes a tin of Skoal chewing tobacco out of his desk, packs it down, and takes a dip. He will spit throughout the scene.*

You're one of three finalists for this position. Now it all depends upon your interview. Whichever one of you has the best interview, that's the one I'll hire. (JIM *spits*). Nasty habit. I've already met with the other two, so it's up to you now, Cal. It's up to you. (JIM *spits*.) What do you have to say about that?

CAL: I look forward to the challenge . . .

JIM: Yeah, yeah, yeah, one of the others said that also. Every time we interview I get that answer: "looking forward to something." You must get it out of a book. Were you reading one of those "what to say in an interview" books?

CAL: I wasn't . . .

5   JIM: I hope not. We need original thinking here. This law firm's been around for fifty-two years, and we've become so damn successful by original thinking; not by memorizing some damn answers in a how to be interviewed book. Are you aware of the success this firm has accomplished?

CAL: I am very aware of that . . . .

JIM: We've been involved in some of the most important criminal cases in this country, and you know what nearly every one of them have in common? (*Pause.*) I'm asking what do these cases have in common? You said you know about our firm . . .

CAL: That you've improved the situation of the defendant. You've either plea bargained for a much lesser charge or you've had your client acquitted.

JIM: That's good, very good. Dave told you to say that, didn't he? (*Laughing.*) That s.o.b.'s ruining all my fun. That question usually scares the pants off the applicant . . .

10 CAL: However, in 1988, the state versus Max Mainer, he received a life sentence. In 1994, Tony Giovano received three consecutive life sentences for multiple murders, and I wonder if you shouldn't have gone with the insanity plea . . .

JIM: All right, Cal, you've done your homework; I don't need a history lesson. (*Pause.*) There is only one thing that matters when a client walks through that door. Do you know what that is?

CAL: That he can pay the bill for our legal services.

JIM: (*Laughing.*) Well, yes that too. Make that two things that matter. If he can pay our bill and if there is at least a slight chance of our improving his situation. If there is not that possibility we will reject the case no matter how much money they offer. If you lose cases you lose your reputation. We do not take kindly to losing cases here.

CAL: I understand.

15 JIM: When we went down with the Giovano fiasco, two very prestigious clients walked out the door with his guilty verdict. (JIM *spits*.) How is Dave?

CAL: He's fine.

JIM: Dave speaks very highly of you.

CAL: Thank you.

JIM: I said Dave does, not me. I don't know you yet. That's one of the main reasons you're sitting in that chair right now—that crazy bastard's a very good friend of mine. At Harvard Law, he saved my butt more than once forcing me to study something other than women and beer. I never understood why he decided to become a professor, without a doubt he could have been one of the top litigaters in the country. We could have been partners. (*Pause.*) I have numerous applications with excellent resumes, but you have an ace in your pocket by the name of Dave Horowitz. That recommendation gives you the rail position. What do you have to say about that?

20   CAL: I think Dave's an excellent judge of character.

JIM: (*Laughing.*) I'm sure you do. He says you'll do whatever it takes to improve your situation—that's the feeling he gets from you. That's an important feeling, very important. What did Dave teach you, Cal? You better not give me a course title.

CAL: How to shoot a gun. How to aim and hit a target.

JIM: Well that's good, but I'm not interviewing you for our rifle team.

CAL: Everyone has a price, that becomes, that is, a weakness, and it's up to me, as a lawyer, as a thinking man, to find out what that is, and then, if need be, to use it. Ready, aim, fire, so to speak.

Long pause.

JIM *spits.*

25   JIM: A client walks into your office, sits down in your leather arm chair, Cal, lights a cigar, and then tells you the truth of his case, let's say he cracked some lady on the head with a baseball bat splattering her brains all over the sidewalk . . . (JIM *spits.*) . . . and he played Mickey Mantle on her head because he was ordered to by his, let's call it a supervisor, and he did not question his supervisor's authority. What would you do? How would you feel, Cal? This client has confessed his guilt to you. He has confessed to this horrible, this heinous crime of an innocent lady's head being smashed open. What would you do in defending a client that was guilty, and your only hope of winning the case was by twisting the truth?

Long pause.

CAL: I cannot accurately answer that question.

JIM: Why not?

CAL: He is my client?

JIM: That's what I said . . .

30   CAL: He has already agreed to use our firm as his representation?

JIM: Correct . . .

CAL: He is not guilty.

JIM: Cal, he has confessed to you . . .

35   CAL: He is innocent . . .

JIM: He has told you about the murder . . .

CAL: He did not commit . . .

JIM: He bashed a lady's head in with a bat! Splattering her blood . . .

CAL: Blood on the sidewalk from someone else's bat . . .

JIM: Are you stupid, son?! What is wrong with you? I have told you, he has told you . . .

40   CAL: You say that my client is guilty, well I say that is impossible, Jim. It is impossible to say he is guilty. He is innocent until someone from the DA's office can persuade a jury of twelve to say he is not innocent. He is innocent until a verdict of guilty is returned. This is why I can not accurately answer your question; this is why your question becomes irrelevant. If he is my client then he is innocent, and it was someone else's bat. Who are the witnesses, Jim? Do you have eyewitnesses? Did he confess to the police? I don't think he confessed or he wouldn't be in my office. Only if he confessed to the police would I start with the idea of his guilt as a possibility. A possibility that I would evaluate and attempt to repudiate. Has our hypothetical client confessed to the police?

JIM: We'll say he has not.

CAL: Then he is not guilty. Then the only thing which can be proved is that some lady's head has been struck with a blunt object causing her death. What other evidence exists, Jim? Is there any other evidence?

JIM *spits*.

JIM: Your conscience.
CAL: My conscience is not on trial.

Pause.

45 JIM: Would you like a dip of tobacco? Green, Skoal, longcut. Dave's the idiot that started me dipping; he thinks he's a Jewish cowboy from New York. I always chew tobacco when I think—that's as long as no women are around.
CAL: Yes, thank you.

JIM *passes the tin to* CAL. CAL *packs it down and places a dip in his mouth.*

JIM: I spit in this bronze cup. It was a present from my daughter. See that: "World's Greatest Dad."
CAL: That's a nice spit cup, sir.
JIM: I never hired a lawyer that dips tobacco.
50 CAL: It helps me think.
JIM: So your hypothetical client is not guilty?
CAL: No, he isn't.
JIM: I like that answer. I like the logic. The logic of truth not existing until it's been proven again.
CAL: And it can be a very difficult thing to prove.

Pause.
JIM *spits and then gives* CAL *an empty cup to spit in.*

55 JIM: My instincts seem to be the same as Dave's, and I go with my instincts, Cal. I'm betting you'll be a fine addition to this team.
CAL: Thank you. I'll do my best . . .
JIM: Is that another answer out of that damn book?
CAL: No, it's not.
JIM: When you start at this firm, you start on probation, so I can see if you have what it takes to succeed.
60 CAL: That's fine.
JIM: You'll do some leg work for me, gathering some background information. Let's see what questions you come up with, what possibilities you create. (JIM *spits.*) I ask everyone if they'd like a dip of tobacco. No one ever says yes. Most people think it's disgusting.
CAL: Maybe that's why we like it.
JIM: Yes, yes, maybe that is why. I want you to meet someone, Cal. (JIM *buzzes the secretary.*) Send him in.

A man enters the office.

Cal, this will be your first client. His name is John Stutts. He bashed an elderly lady's head in with a baseball bat.

Lights down.

[1998]

Joining the Conversation: Critical Thinking and Writing

1. At the very beginning of *No Crime*, Cal is described as "good looking" and Jim is described as "big." What difference(s) might it make in seeing, reading, or viewing the play if Cal were "big" and Jim were "good looking"?
2. If you were asked to perform in this play, which role would you select? Please explain why.
3. Many people find it disgusting to watch someone chew—and spit—tobacco. *Why* are these people revolted by this practice? Why, in your view, did Goda give this habit to Jim, and why did Goda have Cal join Jim in chewing tobacco?
4. In an interview, Goda said that he admired the film director Martin Scorcese because "There is always an edge to his work, always a feeling of danger and violence." Would you say that in *No Crime* there is "always an edge"? Please explain.
5. Cal's basic argument is that the job of a lawyer is to make the district attorney *prove* the guilt of a client who the defending lawyer *knows* is guilty. Thus, a guilty person should be vigorously defended and should go free if the guilt is not *proved*. As many lawyers say, "Cases are tried in a court of *law*, not a court of justice." Do you believe that it is immoral for a lawyer who thinks the evidence is inconclusive to argue on behalf of a person who he knows is guilty? Set forth your response in an essay of 250–500 words.

Chapter Overview: Looking Backward/Looking Forward

1. Should a defense attorney defend a client whose guilt is obvious to everybody? If you were defending a client you believed to be innocent but then discovered evidence of the client's guilt, would you tell the judge or keep this information to yourself?
2. During the civil rights campaigns of the 1950s and 1960s, Martin Luther King Jr. and many other activists frequently broke the law. What was their aim in doing so? Isn't it always wrong to break the law?
3. Often we say to ourselves or to someone else, "There should be a law against that." Is there an activity or specific form of behavior that you believe should be outlawed? Do you think that most people agree with you about this, or are you clearly in the minority? If your position on this issue became "the law," what would be the consequences?
4. Should a judge strictly abide by the letter of the law all the time? Can you imagine a situation in which a judge knew a defendant to be guilty but nonetheless found him or her not guilty? Would such a decision make you respect the law more, or less?
5. Does the study of literature affect a person's attitude toward the law? Do you think that it makes a person more respectful of the law, or less? Which literary works have affected your own views about law and order?
6. Has the study of literature made you a better person? How would you prove this to someone?

CHAPTER 23

Journeys

ESSAY

JOAN DIDION

Joan Didion, born in Sacramento, California, in 1934 and educated at the University of California, Berkeley, worked for a while as a features editor at Vogue *but then turned to freelance writing. Among her novels are* Play It as It Lays *(1970),* A Book of Common Prayer *(1977), and* The Last Thing He Wanted *(1996). Collections of her magazine essays include* Slouching towards Bethlehem *(1968), which is the source of the piece we reprint;* The White Album *(1979); and* The Year of Magical Thinking, *which won the National Book Award in 2005.*

On Going Home

I am home for my daughter's first birthday. By "home" I do not mean the house in Los Angeles where my husband and I and the baby live, but the place where my family is, in the Central Valley of California. It is a vital although troublesome distinction. My husband likes my family but is uneasy in their house, because once there I fall into their ways, which are difficult, oblique, deliberately inarticulate, not my husband's ways. We live in dusty houses ("D-U-S-T," he once wrote with his finger on surfaces all over the house, but no one noticed it) filled with mementos quite without value to him (what could the Canton dessert plates mean to him? How could he have known about the assay scales, why should he care if he did know?), and we appear to talk exclusively about people we know who have been committed to mental hospitals, about people we know who have been booked on drunk-driving charges, and about property, particularly about property, land, price per acre and C-2 zoning and assessments, and freeway access. My brother does not understand my husband's inability to perceive the advantage in the rather common real-estate transaction known as "sale-leaseback," and my husband in turn does not understand why so many of the people he hears about in my father's house have recently been committed to mental hospitals or booked on drunk-driving charges. Nor does he understand that when we talk about sale-leasebacks and right-of-way condemnations we are talking in code about the things we like best, the yellow fields and the cottonwoods and the rivers rising and falling and the mountain roads closing when the heavy snow comes in. We miss each other's points, have another drink and regard the fire. My brother refers to my husband, in his presence, as "Joan's husband." Marriage is the classic betrayal.

Or perhaps it is not any more. Sometimes I think that those of us who are now in our thirties were born into the last generation to carry the burden of "home," to find in family life the source of all tension and drama. I had by all objective accounts a "normal" and a "happy" family situation, and yet I was almost thirty years old before I could talk to my family on the telephone without crying after

I had hung up. We did not fight. Nothing was wrong. And yet some nameless anxiety colored the emotional charges between me and the place that I came from. The question of whether or not you could go home again was a very real part of the sentimental and largely literary baggage with which we left home in the fifties; I suspect that it is irrelevant to the children born of the fragmentation after World War II. A few weeks ago in a San Francisco bar I saw a pretty young girl on crystal take off her clothes and dance for the cash prize in an "amateur-topless" contest. There was no particular sense of moment about this, none of the effect of romantic degradation, of "dark journey," for which my generation strived so assiduously. What sense could that girl possibly make of, say, *Long Day's Journey into Night*[1] Who is beside the point?

That I am trapped in this particular irrelevancy is never more apparent to me than when I am home. Paralyzed by the neurotic lassitude engendered by meeting one's past at every turn, around every corner, inside every cupboard, I go aimlessly from room to room. I decide to meet it head-on and clean out a drawer, and I spread the contents on the bed. A bathing suit I wore the summer I was seventeen. A letter of rejection from *The Nation*, an aerial photograph of the site for a shopping center my father did not build in 1954. Three teacups hand-painted with cabbage roses and signed "E.M.," my grandmother's initials. There is no final solution for letters of rejection from *The Nation* and teacups hand-painted in 1900. Nor is there any answer to snapshots of one's grandfather as a young man on skis, surveying around Donner Pass in the year 1910. I smooth out the snapshot and look into his face, and do and do not see my own. I close the drawer, and have another cup of coffee with my mother. We get along very well, veterans of a guerilla war we never understood.

Days pass. I see no one. I come to dread my husband's evening call, not only because he is full of news of what by now seems to me our remote life in Los Angeles, people he has seen, letters which require attention, but because he asks what I have been doing, suggests uneasily that I get out, drive to San Francisco or Berkeley. Instead I drive across the river to a family graveyard. It has been vandalized since my last visit and the monuments are broken, overturned in the dry grass. Because I once saw a rattlesnake in the grass I stay in the car and listen to a country-and-Western station. Later I drive with my father to a ranch he has in the foothills. The man who runs his cattle on it asks us to the roundup, a week from Sunday, and although I know I will be in Los Angeles I say, in the oblique way my family talks, that I will come. Once home I mention the broken monuments in the graveyard. My mother shrugs.

5   I go to visit my great-aunts. A few of them think now that I am my cousin, or their daughter who died young. We recall an anecdote about a relative last seen in 1948, and they ask if I still like living in New York City. I have lived in Los Angeles for three years, but I say that I do. The baby is offered a horehound drop, and I am slipped a dollar bill "to buy a treat." Questions trail off, answers are abandoned, the baby plays with the dust motes in a shaft of afternoon sun.

It is time for the baby's birthday party: a white cake, strawberry-marshmellow ice cream, a bottle of champagne saved from another party. In the evening, after she has gone to sleep, I kneel beside the crib and touch her face, where it is pressed against the slats, with mine. She is an open and trusting child, unprepared for and unaccustomed to the ambushes of family life, and perhaps it is just as well

---

[1]**Long Days Journey into Night** family drama (written 1941–42, published 1956) by Eugene O'Neill (1888–1953).

that I can offer her a little of that life. I would like to give her more. I would like to promise her that she will grow up with a sense of her cousins and of rivers and of her great-grandmother's teacups, would like to pledge her a picnic on a river with fried chicken and her hair uncombed, would like to give her *home* for her birthday, but we live differently now and I can promise her nothing like that. I give her a xylophone and a sundress from Madeira, and promise to tell her a funny story.

[1968]

Joining the Conversation: Critical Thinking and Writing

1. Didion reveals that members of her family are difficult, inarticulate, poor housekeepers, and so forth. Do you find these revelations about her family distasteful? Would you mind seeing in print similarly unflattering things that you had written about your own family? How might such revelations be justified? Are they justified in this essay?
2. Summarize the point of the second paragraph. Do you find Didion's speculations about the difference between her generation and succeeding generations meaningful? Are they accurate for your generation?
3. Do you think that growing up necessarily involves estrangement from one's family? Support your thesis with reasons.

STORIES

NATHANIEL HAWTHORNE

Nathaniel Hawthorne (1804–64) was born in Salem, Massachusetts, the son of a sea captain. Two of his ancestors were judges; one had persecuted Quakers, and another had served at the Salem witch trials. After graduating from Bowdoin College in Maine, Hawthorne went back to Salem in order to write in relative seclusion. In 1835, he published one of his best stories, "Young Goodman Brown."

From 1839 to 1841, Hawthorne worked in the Boston Customs House and then spent a few months as a member of a communal society, Brook Farm. In 1842, he married and settled with his wife in Concord, Massachusetts, where they became friendly with Emerson and Thoreau. From 1846 to 1849, he was a surveyor at the Custom-House in Salem; from 1849 to 1850, he wrote The Scarlet Letter, *the book that made him famous. From 1853 to 1857, he served as American consul in Liverpool, England, a plum awarded him in exchange for writing a campaign biography of a former college classmate, President Franklin Pierce. In 1860, after living in England and Italy, he returned to the United States, settling in Concord, Massachusetts.*

In his stories and novels, Hawthorne keeps returning to the Puritan past, studying guilt, sin, and isolation.

Young Goodman Brown

Young Goodman Brown came forth at sunset into the street at Salem village; but put his head back, after crossing the threshold, to exchange a parting kiss with his young wife. And Faith, as the wife was aptly named, thrust her own pretty head into the street, letting the wind play with the pink ribbons of her cap while she called to Goodman Brown.

"Dearest heart," whispered she, softly and rather sadly, when her lips were close to his ear, "prithee put off your journey until sunrise and sleep in your own bed to-night. A lone woman is troubled with such dreams and such thoughts that she's afeared of herself sometimes. Pray tarry with me this night, dear husband, of all nights in the year."

"My love and my Faith," replied young Goodman Brown, "of all nights in the year, this one night must I tarry away from thee. My journey, as thou callest it, forth and back again, must needs be done 'twixt now and sunrise. What, my sweet, pretty wife, dost thou doubt me already, and we but three months married?"

"Then God bless you!" said Faith, with the pink ribbons; "and may you find all well when you come back."

5   "Amen!" cried Goodman Brown. "Say thy prayers, dear Faith, and go to bed at dusk, and no harm will come to thee."

So they parted; and the young man pursued his way until, being about to turn the corner by the meeting-house, he looked back and saw the head of Faith still peeping after him with a melancholy air, in spite of her pink ribbons.

"Poor little Faith!" thought he, for his heart smote him. "What a wretch am I to leave her on such an errand! She talks of dreams, too. Methought as she spoke there was trouble in her face, as if a dream had warned her what work is to be done to-night. But no, no; 'twould kill her to think it. Well, she's a blessed angel on earth; and after this one night I'll cling to her skirts and follow her to heaven."

With this excellent resolve for the future, Goodman Brown felt himself justified in making more haste on his present evil purpose. He had taken a dreary road, darkened by all the gloomiest trees of the forest, which barely stood aside to let the narrow path creep through, and closed immediately behind. It was all as lonely as could be; and there is this peculiarity in such a solitude, that the traveller knows not who may be concealed by the innumerable trunks and the thick boughs overhead; so that with lonely footsteps he may yet be passing through an unseen multitude.

"There may be a devilish Indian behind every tree," said Goodman Brown to himself; and he glanced fearfully behind him as he added, "What if the devil himself should be at my very elbow!"

10   His head being turned back, he passed a crook of the road, and, looking forward again, beheld the figure of a man, in grave and decent attire, seated at the foot of an old tree. He arose at Goodman Brown's approach and walked onward side by side with him.

"You are late, Goodman Brown," said he. "The clock of the Old South was striking as I came through Boston, and that is full fifteen minutes agone."

"Faith kept me back a while," replied the young man, with a tremor in his voice, caused by the sudden appearance of his companion, though not wholly unexpected.

It was now deep dusk in the forest, and deepest in that part of it where these two were journeying. As nearly as could be discerned, the second traveller was about fifty years old, apparently in the same rank of life as Goodman Brown, and bearing a considerable resemblance to him, though perhaps more in expression than features. Still they might have been taken for father and son. And yet, though the elder person was as simply clad as the younger, and as simple in manner too, he had an indescribable air of one who knew the world, and who would not have felt abashed at the governor's dinner table or in King William's court,[1] were it

---

[1]**King William's court** refers to the English king who ruled from 1688 to 1694.

possible that his affairs should call him thither. But the only thing about him that could be fixed upon as remarkable was his staff, which bore the likeness of a great black snake, so curiously wrought that it might almost be seen to twist and wriggle itself like a living serpent. This, of course, must have been an ocular deception, assisted by the uncertain light.

"Come, Goodman Brown," cried his fellow-traveller, "this is a dull pace for the beginning of a journey. Take my staff, if you are so soon weary."

15 "Friend," said the other, exchanging his slow pace for a full stop, "having kept covenant by meeting thee here, it is my purpose now to return whence I came. I have scruples touching the matter thou wot'st of."

"Sayest thou so?" replied he of the serpent, smiling apart. "Let us walk on, nevertheless, reasoning as we go; and if I convince thee not thou shalt turn back. We are but a little way in the forest yet."

"Too far! too far!" exclaimed the goodman, unconsciously resuming his walk. "My father never went into the woods on such an errand, nor his father before him. We have been a race of honest men and good Christians since the days of the martyrs; and shall I be the first of the name of Brown that ever took this path and kept—"

"Such company, thou wouldst say," observed the elder person, interpreting his pause. "Well said, Goodman Brown! I have been as well acquainted with your family as with ever a one among the Puritans; and that's no trifle to say. I helped your grandfather, the constable, when he lashed the Quaker woman so smartly through the streets of Salem; and it was I that brought your father a pitch-pine knot, kindled at my own hearth, to set fire to an Indian village, in King Philip's war. They were my good friends, both; and many a pleasant walk have we had along this path, and returned merrily after midnight. I would fain be friends with you for their sake."

"If it be as thou sayest," replied Goodman Brown, "I marvel they never spoke of these matters; or, verily, I marvel not, seeing that the least rumor of the sort would have driven them from New England. We are a people of prayer, and good works to boot, and abide no such wickedness."

20 "Wickedness or not," said the traveller with the twisted staff, "I have a very general acquaintance here in New England. The deacons of many a church have drunk the communion wine with me; the selectmen of divers towns make me their chairman; and a majority of the Great and General Court are firm supporters of my interest. The governor and I, too—But these are state secrets."

"Can this be so?" cried Goodman Brown, with a stare of amazement at his undisturbed companion. "Howbeit, I have nothing to do with the governor and council; they have their own ways, and are no rule for a simple husbandman like me. But, were I to go on with thee, how should I meet the eye of that good old man, our minister, at Salem village? Oh, his voice would make me tremble both Sabbath day and lecture day."

Thus far the elder traveller had listened with due gravity; but now burst into a fit of irrepressible mirth, shaking himself so violently that his snake-like staff actually seemed to wriggle in sympathy.

"Ha! ha! ha!" shouted he again and again; then composing himself, "Well, go on, Goodman Brown, go on; but, prithee, don't kill me with laughing."

"Well, then, to end the matter at once," said Goodman Brown, considerably nettled, "there is my wife, Faith. It would break her dear little heart; and I'd rather break my own."

25 "Nay, if that be the case," answered the other, "e'en go thy ways, Goodman Brown. I would not for twenty old women like the one hobbling before us that Faith should come to any harm."

As he spoke he pointed his staff at a female figure on the path, in whom Goodman Brown recognized a very pious and exemplary dame, who had taught him his catechism in youth, and was still his moral and spiritual adviser, jointly with the minister and Deacon Gookin.

"A marvel, truly, that Goody Cloyse should be so far in the wilderness at night-fall," said he. "But with your leave, friend, I shall take a cut through the woods until we have left this Christian woman behind. Being a stranger to you, she might ask whom I was consorting with and whither I was going."

"Be it so," said his fellow-traveller. "Betake you to the woods, and let me keep the path."

Accordingly the young man turned aside, but took care to watch his companion, who advanced softly along the road until he had come within a staff's length of the old dame. She, meanwhile, was making the best of her way, with singular speed for so aged a woman, and mumbling some indistinct words—a prayer, doubtless—as she went. The traveller put forth his staff and touched her withered neck with what seemed the serpent's tail.

30   "The devil!" screamed the pious old lady.

"Then Goody Cloyse knows her old friend?" observed the traveller, confronting her and leaning on his writhing stick.

"Ah, forsooth, and is it your worship indeed?" cried the good dame. "Yea, truly is it, and in the very image of my old gossip, Goodman Brown, the grandfather of the silly fellow that now is. But—would your worship believe it?—my broomstick hath strangely disappeared, stolen, as I suspect, by that unhanged witch, Goody Cory, and that, too, when I was all anointed with the juice of smallage, and cinque-foil, and wolf's bane—"

"Mingled with fine wheat and the fat of a new-born babe," said the shape of old Goodman Brown.

"Ah, your worship knows the recipe," cried the old lady, cackling aloud. "So, as I was saying, being all ready for the meeting, and no horse to ride on, I made up my mind to foot it; for they tell me there is a nice young man to be taken into communion to-night. But now your good worship will lend me your arm, and we shall be there in a twinkling."

35   "That can hardly be," answered her friend. "I may not spare you my arm, Goody Cloyse; but here is my staff, if you will."

So saying, he threw it down at her feet, where, perhaps, it assumed life, being one of the rods which its owner had formerly lent to the Egyptian magi. Of this fact, however, Goodman Brown could not take cognizance. He had cast up his eyes in astonishment, and, looking down again, beheld neither Goody Cloyse nor the serpentine staff, but his fellow-traveller alone, who waited for him as calmly as if nothing had happened.

"That old woman taught me my catechism," said the young man; and there was a world of meaning in this simple comment.

They continued to walk onward, while the elder traveller exhorted his companion to make good speed and persevere in the path, discoursing so aptly that his arguments seemed rather to spring up in the bosom of his auditor than to be suggested by himself. As they went, he plucked a branch of maple to serve for a walking stick, and began to strip it of the twigs and the little boughs, which were wet with evening dew. The moment his fingers touched them they became strangely withered and dried up as with a week's sunshine. Thus the pair proceeded, at a good free pace, until suddenly, in a gloomy hollow of the road, Goodman Brown sat himself down on the stump of a tree and refused to go any farther.

"Friend," said he, stubbornly, "my mind is made up. Not another step will I budge on this errand. What if a wretched old woman do choose to go to the devil when I thought she was going to heaven: is that any reason why I should quit my dear Faith and go after her?"

40   "You will think better of this by and by," said his acquaintance, composedly. "Sit here and rest yourself a while; and when you feel like moving again, there is my staff to help you along."

Without more words, he threw his companion the maple stick, and was as speedily out of sight as if he had vanished into the deepening gloom. The young man sat a few moments by the roadside, applauding himself greatly, and thinking with how clear a conscience he should meet the minister in his morning walk, nor shrink from the eye of good old Deacon Gookin. And what calm sleep would be his that very night, which was to have been spent so wickedly, but so purely and sweetly now, in the arms of Faith! Amidst these pleasant and praiseworthy meditations, Goodman Brown heard the tramp of horses along the road, and deemed it advisable to conceal himself within the verge of the forest, conscious of the guilty purpose that had brought him thither, though now so happily turned from it.

On came the hoof tramps and the voices of the riders, two grave old voices, conversing soberly as they drew near. These mingled sounds appeared to pass along the road, within a few yards of the young man's hiding-place; but, owing doubtless to the depth of the gloom at that particular spot, neither the travellers nor their steeds were visible. Though their figures brushed the small boughs by the wayside, it could not be seen that they intercepted, even for a moment, the faint gleam from the strip of bright sky athwart which they must have passed. Goodman Brown alternately crouched and stood on tiptoe, pulling aside the branches and thrusting forth his head as far as he durst without discerning so much as a shadow. It vexed him the more, because he could have sworn, were such a thing possible, that he recognized the voices of the minister and Deacon Gookin, jogging along quietly, as they were wont to do, when bound to some ordination or ecclesiastical council. While yet within hearing, one of the riders stopped to pluck a switch.

"Of the two, reverend sir," said the voice like the deacon's, "I had rather miss an ordination dinner than to-night's meeting. They tell me that some of our community are to be here from Falmouth and beyond, and others from Connecticut and Rhode Island, besides several of the Indian powwows, who, after their fashion, know almost as much deviltry as the best of us. Moreover, there is a goodly young woman to be taken into communion."

"Mighty well, Deacon Gookin!" replied the solemn old tones of the minister. "Spur up, or we shall be late. Nothing can be done, you know, until I get on the ground."

45   The hoofs clattered again; and the voices, talking so strangely in the empty air, passed on through the forest, where no church had ever been gathered or solitary Christian prayed. Whither, then, could these holy men be journeying so deep into the heathen wilderness? Young Goodman Brown caught hold of a tree for support, being ready to sink down on the ground, faint and overburdened with the heavy sickness of his heart. He looked up to the sky, doubting whether there really was a heaven above him. Yet there was the blue arch, and the stars brightening in it.

"With heaven above and Faith below, I will yet stand firm against the devil!" cried Goodman Brown.

While he still gazed upward into the deep arch of the firmament and had lifted his hands to pray, a cloud, though no wind was stirring, hurried across the zenith and hid the brightening stars. The blue sky was still visible, except directly overhead, where this black mass of cloud was sweeping swiftly northward. Aloft in the air, as if from the depths of the cloud, came a confused and doubtful sound of voices. Once the listener fancied that he could distinguish the accents of towns-people of his own, men and women, both pious and ungodly, many of whom he had met at the communion table, and had seen others rioting at the tavern. The next moment, so indistinct were the sounds, he doubted whether he had heard aught but the murmur of the old forest, whispering without a wind. Then came a stronger swell of those familiar tones, heard daily in the sunshine at Salem village, but never until now from a cloud of night. There was one voice, of a young wom-an, uttering lamentations, yet with an uncertain sorrow, and entreating for some favor, which, perhaps, it would grieve her to obtain; and all the unseen multitude, both saints and sinners, seemed to encourage her onward.

"Faith!" shouted Goodman Brown, in a voice of agony and desperation; and the echoes of the forest mocked him, crying, "Faith! Faith!" as if bewildered wretches were seeking her all through the wilderness.

The cry of grief, rage, and terror was yet piercing the night, when the unhappy husband held his breath for a response. There was a scream, drowned immediately in a louder murmur of voices, fading into far-off laughter, as the dark cloud swept away, leaving the clear and silent sky above Goodman Brown. But something flut-tered lightly down through the air and caught on the branch of a tree. The young man seized it, and beheld a pink ribbon.

"My Faith is gone!" cried he, after one stupefied moment. "There is no good on earth; and sin is but a name. Come, devil; for to thee is this world given."

And, maddened with despair, so that he laughed loud and long, did Goodman Brown grasp his staff and set forth again, at such a rate that he seemed to fly along the forest path rather than to walk or run. The road grew wilder and drearier and more faintly traced, and vanished at length, leaving him in the heart of the dark wilderness, still rushing onward with the instinct that guides mortal man to evil. The whole forest was peopled with frightful sounds—the creaking of the trees, the howling of wild beasts, and the yell of Indians; while sometimes the wind tolled like a distant church bell, and sometimes gave a broad roar around the traveller, as if all Nature were laughing him to scorn. But he was himself the chief horror of the scene, and shrank not from its other horrors.

"Ha! ha! ha!" roared Goodman Brown when the wind laughed at him. "Let us hear which will laugh loudest. Think not to frighten me with your deviltry. Come witch, come wizard, come Indian powwow, come devil himself, and here comes Goodman Brown. You may as well fear him as he fear you."

In truth, all through the haunted forest there could be nothing more frightful than the figure of Goodman Brown. On he flew among the black pines, brandish-ing his staff with frenzied gestures, now giving vent to an inspiration of horrid blasphemy, and now shouting forth such laughter as set all the echoes of the for-est laughing like demons around him. The fiend in his own shape is less hideous than when he rages in the breast of man. Thus sped the demoniac on his course, until, quivering among the trees, he saw a red light before him, as when the felled trunks and branches of a clearing have been set on fire, and throw up their lurid blaze against the sky, at the hour of midnight. He paused, in a lull of the tempest that had driven him onward, and heard the swell of what seemed a hymn, rolling solemnly from a distance with the weight of many voices. He knew the tune; it was a familiar one in the choir of the village meeting-house. The verse died heav-ily away, and was lengthened by a chorus, not of human voices, but of all the sounds of the benighted wilderness pealing in awful harmony together. Goodman

Brown cried out, and his cry was lost to his own ear by its unison with the cry of the desert.

In the interval of silence he stole forward until the light glared full upon his eyes. At one extremity of an open space, hemmed in by the dark wall of the forest, arose a rock, bearing some rude, natural resemblance either to an altar or a pulpit, and surrounded by four blazing pines, their tops aflame, their stems untouched, like candles at an evening meeting. The mass of foliage that had overgrown the summit of the rock was all on fire, blazing high into the night and fitfully illuminating the whole field. Each pendent twig and leafy festoon was in a blaze. As the red light arose and fell, a numerous congregation alternately shone forth, then disappeared in shadow, and again grew, as it were, out of the darkness, peopling the heart of the solitary woods at once.

55   "A grave and dark-clad company," quoth Goodman Brown.

In truth they were such. Among them, quivering to and fro between gloom and splendor, appeared faces that would be seen next day at the council board of the province, and others which, Sabbath after Sabbath, looked devoutly heavenward, and benignantly over the crowded pews, from the holiest pulpits in the land. Some affirm that the lady of the governor was there. At least three were high dames well known to her, and wives of honored husbands, and widows, a great multitude, and ancient maidens, all of excellent repute, and fair young girls, who trembled lest their mothers should espy them. Either the sudden gleams of light flashing over the obscure field bedazzled Goodman Brown, or he recognized a score of the church members of Salem village famous for their especial sanctity. Good old Deacon Gookin had arrived, and waited at the skirts of that venerable saint, his revered pastor. But, irreverently consorting with these grave, reputable, and pious people, these elders of the church, these chaste dames and dewy virgins, there were men of dissolute lives and women of spotted fame, wretches given over to all mean and filthy vice, and suspected even of horrid crimes. It was strange to see that the good shrank not from the wicked, nor were the sinners abashed by the saints. Scattered also among their pale-faced enemies were the Indian priests, or powwows, who had often scared their native forest with more hideous incantations than any known to English witchcraft.

"But where is Faith?" thought Goodman Brown; and, as hope came into his heart, he trembled.

Another verse of the hymn arose, a slow and mournful strain, such as the pious love, but joined to words which expressed all that our nature can conceive of sin, and darkly hinted at far more. Unfathomable to mere mortals is the lore of fiends. Verse after verse was sung; and still the chorus of the desert swelled between like the deepest tone of a mighty organ; and with the final peal of that dreadful anthem there came a sound, as if the roaring wind, the rushing streams, the howling beasts, and every other voice of the unconcerted wilderness were mingling and according with the voice of guilty man in homage to the prince of all. The four blazing pines threw up a loftier flame, and obscurely discovered shapes and visages of horror on the smoke wreaths above the impious assembly. At the same moment the fire on the rock shot redly forth and formed a glowing arch above its base, where now appeared a figure. With reverence be it spoken, the figure bore no slight similitude, both in garb and manner, to some grave divine of the New England churches.

"Bring forth the converts!" cried a voice that echoed through the field and rolled into the forest.

60   At the word, Goodman Brown stepped forth from the shadow of the trees and approached the congregation, with whom he felt a loathful brotherhood by the sympathy of all that was wicked in his heart. He could have well-nigh sworn that

the shape of his own dead father beckoned him to advance, looking downward from a smoke wreath, while a woman, with dim features of despair, threw out her hand to warn him back. Was it his mother? But he had no power to retreat one step, nor to resist, even in thought, when the minister and good old Deacon Gookin seized his arms and led him to the blazing rock. Thither came also the slender form of a veiled female, led between Goody Cloyse, that pious teacher of the catechism, and Martha Carrier, who had received the devil's promise to be queen of hell. A rampant hag was she. And there stood the proselytes beneath the canopy of fire.

"Welcome, my children," said the dark figure, "to the communion of your race. Ye have found thus young your nature and your destiny. My children, look behind you!"

They turned; and flashing forth, as it were, in a sheet of flame, the fiend worshippers were seen; the smile of welcome gleamed darkly on every visage.

"There," resumed the sable form, "are all whom ye have reverenced from youth. Ye deemed them holier than yourselves, and shrank from your own sin, contrasting it with their lives of righteousness and prayerful aspirations heavenward. Yet here are they all in my worshipping assembly. This night it shall be granted you to know their secret deeds: how hoary-bearded elders of the church have whispered wanton words to the young maids of their households; how many a woman, eager for widows' weeds, has given her husband a drink at bedtime and let him sleep his last sleep in her bosom; how beardless youths have made haste to inherit their fathers' wealth; and how fair damsels—blush not, sweet ones—have dug little graves in the garden, and bidden me, the sole guest, to an infant's funeral. By the sympathy of your human hearts for sin ye shall scent out all the places—whether in church, bedchamber, street, field, or forest—where crime has been committed, and shall exult to behold the whole earth one stain of guilt, one mighty blood spot. Far more than this. It shall be yours to penetrate, in every bosom, the deep mystery of sin, the fountain of all wicked arts, and which inexhaustibly supplies more evil impulses than human power—than my power at its utmost— can make manifest in deeds. And now, my children, look upon each other."

They did so; and, by the blaze of the hell-kindled torches, the wretched man beheld his Faith, and the wife her husband, trembling before that unhallowed altar.

65   "Lo, there ye stand, my children," said the figure, in a deep and solemn tone, almost sad with its despairing awfulness, as if his once angelic nature could yet mourn for our miserable race. "Depending upon one another's hearts, ye had still hoped that virtue were not all a dream. Now are ye undeceived. Evil is the nature of mankind. Evil must be your only happiness. Welcome again, my children, to the communion of your race."

"Welcome," repeated the fiend worshippers, in one cry of despair and triumph.

And there they stood, the only pair, as it seemed, who were yet hesitating on the verge of wickedness in this dark world. A basin was hollowed, naturally, in the rock. Did it contain water, reddened by the lurid light? or was it blood? or, perchance, a liquid flame? Herein did the shape of evil dip his hand and prepare to lay the mark of baptism upon their foreheads, that they might be partakers of the mystery of sin, more conscious of the secret guilt of others, both in deed and thought, than they could now be of their own. The husband cast one look at his pale wife, and Faith at him. What polluted wretches would the next glance show them to each other, shuddering alike at what they disclosed and what they saw!

"Faith! Faith!" cried the husband, "look up to heaven, and resist the wicked one."

Whether Faith obeyed he knew not. Hardly had he spoken when he found himself amid calm night and solitude, listening to a roar of the wind which died heavily away through the forest. He staggered against the rock, and felt it chill and damp; while a hanging twig, that had been all on fire, besprinkled his cheek with the coldest dew.

70   The next morning young Goodman Brown came slowly into the street of Salem village, staring around him like a bewildered man. The good old minister was taking a walk along the graveyard to get an appetite for breakfast and meditate his sermon, and bestowed a blessing, as he passed, on Goodman Brown. He shrank from the venerable saint as if to avoid an anathema. Old Deacon Gookin was at domestic worship, and the holy words of his prayer were heard through the open window. "What God doth the wizard pray to?" quoth Goodman Brown. Goody Cloyse, that excellent old Christian, stood in the early sunshine at her own lattice, catechizing a little girl who had brought her a pint of morning's milk. Goodman Brown snatched away the child as from the grasp of the fiend himself. Turning the corner by the meeting-house, he spied the head of Faith, with the pink ribbons, gazing anxiously forth, and bursting into such joy at sight of him that she skipped along the street and almost kissed her husband before the whole village. But Goodman Brown looked sternly and sadly into her face, and passed on without a greeting.

Had Goodman Brown fallen asleep in the forest and only dreamed a wild dream of a witch-meeting?

Be it so if you will; but alas! it was a dream of evil omen for young Goodman Brown. A stern, a sad, a darkly meditative, a distrustful, if not a desperate man did he become from the night of that fearful dream. On the Sabbath day, when the congregation were singing a holy psalm, he could not listen because an anthem of sin rushed loudly upon his ear and drowned all the blessed strain. When the minister spoke from the pulpit with power and fervid eloquence, and, with his hand on the open Bible, of the sacred truths of our religion, and of saint-like lives and triumphant deaths, and of future bliss or misery unutterable, then did Goodman Brown turn pale, dreading lest the roof should thunder down upon the gray blasphemer and his hearers. Often, awaking suddenly at midnight, he shrank from the bosom of Faith; and at morning or eventide, when the family knelt down at prayer, he scowled and muttered to himself, and gazed sternly at his wife, and turned away. And when he had lived long, and was borne to his grave a hoary corpse, followed by Faith, an aged woman, and children and grandchildren, a goodly procession, besides neighbors not a few, they carved no hopeful verse upon his tombstone, for his dying hour was gloom.

[1835]

Joining the Conversation: Critical Thinking and Writing

1. What do you think Hawthorne gains (or loses) by the last sentence?
2. Evaluate the view that, when young Goodman Brown enters the dark forest, he is really entering his own evil mind. Why, by the way, does he go into the forest at night? (Hawthorne gives no explicit reason, but you may want to offer a conjecture.)
3. In a sentence or two, summarize the plot, and then, in another sentence or two, state the theme of the story.
4. If you have undergone a religious experience, write an essay discussing your experience before, during, and after the experience.

EUDORA WELTY

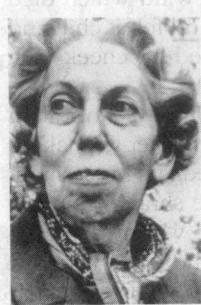

Eudora Welty (1909–2001) was born in Jackson, Mississippi. Although she earned a BA from the University of Wisconsin and spent a year studying advertising in New York City at the Columbia University Graduate School of Business, she lived almost all of her life in Jackson.

In the preface to her Collected Stories, *she says:*

> *I have been told, both in approval and in accusation, that I seem to love all my characters. What I do in writing of any character is to try to enter into the mind, heart and skin of a human being who is not myself. Whether this happens to be a man or a woman, old or young, with skin black or white, the primary challenge lies in making the jump itself. It is the act of a writer's imagination that I set most high.*

In addition to writing stories and novels, Welty wrote a book about fiction, The Eye of the Story *(1977), and a memoir,* One Writer's Beginnings *(1984).*

A Worn Path

It was December—a bright frozen day in the early morning. Far out in the country there was an old Negro woman with her head tied in a red rag, coming along a path through the pinewoods. Her name was Phoenix Jackson. She was very old and small and she walked slowly in the dark pine shadows, moving a little from side to side in her steps, with the balanced heaviness and lightness of a pendulum in a grandfather clock. She carried a thin, small cane made from an umbrella, and with this she kept tapping the frozen earth in front of her. This made a grave and persistent noise in the still air, that seemed meditative like the chirping of a solitary little bird.

She wore a dark striped dress reaching down to her shoe tops, and an equally long apron of bleached sugar sacks, with a full pocket: all neat and tidy, but every time she took a step she might have fallen over her shoelaces, which dragged from her unlaced shoes. She looked straight ahead. Her eyes were blue with age. Her skin had a pattern all its own of numberless branching wrinkles and as though a whole little tree stood in the middle of her forehead, but a golden color ran underneath, and the two knobs of her cheeks were illuminated by a yellow burning under the dark. Under the red rag her hair came down on her neck in the frailest of ringlets, still black, and with an odor like copper.

Now and then there was a quivering in the thicket. Old Phoenix said, "Out of my way, all you foxes, owls, beetles, jack rabbits, coons, and wild animals! . . . Keep out from under these feet, little bob-whites. . . . Keep the big wild hogs out of my path. Don't let none of those come running my direction. I got a long way." Under her small black-freckled hand her cane, limber as a buggy whip, would switch at the brush as if to rouse up any hiding things.

On she went. The woods were deep and still. The sun made the pine needles almost too bright to look at, up where the wind rocked. The cones dropped as light as feathers. Down in the hollow was the mourning dove—it was not too late for him.

5   The path ran up a hill. "Seem like there is chains about my feet, time I get this far," she said, in the voice of argument old people keep to use with themselves. "Something always take a hold of me on this hill—pleads I should stay."

After she got to the top she turned and gave a full, severe look behind her where she had come. "Up through pines," she said at length. "Now down through oaks."

Her eyes opened their widest, and she started down gently. But before she got to the bottom of the hill a bush caught her dress.

Her fingers were busy and intent, but her skirts were full and long, so that before she could pull them free in one place they were caught in another. It was not possible to allow the dress to tear. "I in the thorny bush," she said. "Thorns, you doing your appointed work. Never want to let folks pass—no sir. Old eyes thought you was a pretty little *green* bush."

Finally, trembling all over, she stood free, and after a moment dared to stoop for her cane.

10   "Sun so high!" she cried, leaning back and looking, while the thick tears went over her eyes. "The time getting all gone here."

At the foot of this hill was a place where a log was laid across the creek.

"Now comes the trial," said Phoenix.

Putting her right foot out, she mounted the log and shut her eyes. Lifting her skirt, levelling her cane fiercely before her, like a festival figure in some parade, she began to march across. Then she opened her eyes and she was safe on the other side.

"I wasn't as old as I thought," she said.

15   But she sat down to rest. She spread her skirts on the bank around her and folded her hands over her knees. Up above her was a tree in a pearly cloud of mistletoe. She did not dare to close her eyes, and when a little boy brought her a little plate with a slice of marble-cake on it she spoke to him. "That would be acceptable," she said. But when she went to take it there was just her own hand in the air.

So she left that tree, and had to go through a barbed-wire fence. There she had to creep and crawl, spreading her knees and stretching her fingers like a baby trying to climb the steps. But she talked loudly to herself: she could not let her dress be torn now, so late in the day, and she could not pay for having her arm or leg sawed off if she got caught fast where she was.

At last she was safe through the fence and risen up out in the clearing. Big dead trees, like black men with one arm, were standing in the purple stalks of the withered cotton field. There sat a buzzard.

"Who you watching?"

In the furrow she made her way along.

20   "Glad this not the season for bulls," she said, looking sideways, "and the good Lord made his snakes to curl up and sleep in the winter. A pleasure I don't see no two-headed snake coming around that tree, where it come once. It took a while to get by him, back in the summer."

She passed through the old cotton and went into a field of dead corn. It whispered and shook and was taller than her head. "Through the maze now," she said, for there was no path.

Then there was something tall, black, and skinny there, moving before her.

At first she took it for a man. It could have been a man dancing in the field. But she stood still and listened, and it did not make a sound. It was as silent as a ghost.

"Ghost," she said sharply, "who be you the ghost of? For I have heard of nary death close by."

25   But there was no answer—only the ragged dancing in the wind.

She shut her eyes, reached out her hand, and touched a sleeve. She found a coat and inside that an emptiness, cold as ice.

"You scarecrow," she said. Her face lighted. "I ought to be shut up for good," she said with laughter. "My senses is gone, I too old. I the oldest people I ever know. Dance, old scarecrow," she said, "while I dancing with you."

She kicked her foot over the furrow, and with mouth drawn down, shook her head once or twice in a little strutting way. Some husks blew down and whirled in streamers about her skirts.

Then she went on, parting her way from side to side with the cane, through the whispering field. At last she came to the end, to a wagon track where the silver grass blew between the red ruts. The quail were walking around like pullets, seeming all dainty and unseen.

30   "Walk pretty," she said. "This the easy place. This the easy going."

She followed the track, swaying through the quiet bare fields, through the little strings of trees silver in their dead leaves, past cabins silver from weather, with the doors and windows boarded shut, all like old women under a spell sitting there. "I walking in their sleep," she said, nodding her head vigorously.

In a ravine she went where a spring was silently flowing through a hollow log. Old Phoenix bent and drank. "Sweet-gum makes the water sweet," she said, and drank more. "Nobody know who made this well, for it was here when I was born."

The track crossed a swampy part where the moss hung as white as lace from every limb. "Sleep on, alligators, and blow your bubbles." Then the track went into the road.

Deep, deep the road went down between the high green-colored banks. Overhead the live-oaks met, and it was as dark as a cave.

35   A black dog with a lolling tongue came up out of the weeds by the ditch. She was meditating, and not ready, and when he came at her she only hit him a little with her cane. Over she went in the ditch, like a little puff of milk-weed.

Down there, her senses drifted away. A dream visited her, and she reached her hand up, but nothing reached down and gave her a pull. So she lay there and presently went to talking. "Old woman," she said to herself, "that black dog come up out of the weeds to stall you off, and now there he sitting on his fine tail, smiling at you."

A white man finally came along and found her—a hunter, a young man, with his dog on a chain.

"Well, Granny!" he laughed. "What are you doing there?"

"Lying on my back like a June-bug waiting to be turned over, mister," she said, reaching up her hand.

40   He lifted her up, gave her a swing in the air, and set her down. "Anything broken, Granny?"

"No sir, them old dead weeds is springy enough," said Phoenix, when she had got her breath. "I thank you for your trouble."

"Where do you live, Granny?" he asked, while the two dogs were growling at each other.

"Away back yonder, sir, behind the ridge. You can't even see it from here."

"On your way home?"

45   "No, sir, I going to town."

"Why, that's too far! That's as far as I walk when I come out myself, and I get something for my trouble." He patted the stuffed bag he carried, and there hung down a little closed claw. It was one of the bob-whites, with its beak hooked bitterly to show it was dead. "Now you go on home, Granny!"

"I bound to go to town, mister," said Phoenix. "The time come around."

He gave another laugh, filling the whole landscape. "I know you old colored people! Wouldn't miss going to town to see Santa Claus!"

But something held Old Phoenix very still. The deep lines in her face went into a fierce and different radiation. Without warning, she had seen with her own eyes a flashing nickel fall out of the man's pocket onto the ground.

50 "How old are you, Granny?" he was saying.

"There is no telling, mister," she said, "no telling."

Then she gave a little cry and clapped her hands and said, "Git on away from here, dog! Look! Look at that dog!" She laughed as if in admiration. "He ain't scared of nobody. He a big black dog." She whispered, "Sic him!"

"Watch me get rid of that cur," said the man. "Sic him, Pete! Sic him!"

Phoenix heard the dogs fighting, and heard the man running and throwing sticks. She even heard a gunshot. But she was slowly bending forward by that time, further and further forward, the lids stretched down over her eyes, as if she were doing this in her sleep. Her chin was lowered almost to her knees. The yellow palm of her hand came out from the fold of her apron. Her fingers slid down and along the ground under the piece of money with the grace and care they would have in lifting an egg from under a sitting hen. Then she slowly straightened up, she stood erect, and the nickel was in her apron pocket. A bird flew by. Her lips moved. "God watching me the whole time. I come to stealing."

55 The man came back, and his own dog panted about them. "Well, I scared him off that time," he said, and then he laughed and lifted his gun and pointed it at Phoenix.

She stood straight and faced him.

"Doesn't the gun scare you?" he said, still pointing it.

"No, sir, I seen plenty go off closer by, in my day, and for less than what I done," she said, holding utterly still.

He smiled, and shouldered the gun. "Well, Granny," he said, "you must be a hundred years old, and scared of nothing. I'd give you a dime if I had any money with me. But you take my advice and stay home, and nothing will happen to you."

60 "I bound to go on my way, mister," said Phoenix. She inclined her head in the red rag. Then they went in different directions, but she could hear the gun shooting again and again over the hill.

She walked on. The shadows hung from the oak trees to the road like curtains. Then she smelled wood-smoke, and smelled the river, and she saw a steeple and the cabins on their steep steps. Dozens of little black children whirled around her. There ahead was Natchez shining. Bells were ringing. She walked on.

In the paved city it was Christmas time. There were red and green electric lights strung and crisscrossed everywhere, and all turned on in the daytime. Old Phoenix would have been lost if she had not distrusted her eyesight and depended on her feet to know where to take her.

She paused quietly on the sidewalk where people were passing by. A lady came along in the crowd, carrying an armful of red-, green-, and silver-wrapped presents; she gave off perfume like the red roses in hot summer, and Phoenix stopped her.

"Please, missy, will you lace up my shoe?" She held up her foot.

65 "What do you want, Grandma?"

"See my shoe," said Phoenix. "Do all right for out in the country, but wouldn't look right to go in a big building."

"Stand still then, Grandma," said the lady. She put her packages down on the sidewalk beside her and laced and tied both shoes tightly.

"Can't lace 'em with a cane," said Phoenix. "Thank you, missy. I doesn't mind asking a nice lady to tie up my shoe, when I gets out on the street."

Moving slowly and from side to side, she went into the big building and into a tower of steps, where she walked up and around and around until her feet knew to stop.

70　　She entered a door, and there she saw nailed up on the wall the document that had been stamped with the gold seal and framed in the gold frame, which matched the dream that was hung up in her head.

"Here I be," she said. There was a fixed and ceremonial stiffness over her body.

"A charity case, I suppose," said an attendant who sat at the desk before her.

But Phoenix only looked above her head. There was sweat on her face, the wrinkles in her skin shone like a bright net.

"Speak up, Grandma," the woman said. "What's your name? We must have your history, you know. Have you been here before? What seems to be the trouble with you?"

75　　Old Phoenix only gave a twitch to her face as if a fly were bothering her.

"Are you deaf?" cried the attendant.

But then the nurse came in.

"Oh, that's just old Aunt Phoenix," she said. "She doesn't come for herself—she has a little grandson. She makes these trips just as regular as clockwork. She lives away back off the old Natchez Trace." She bent down. "Well, Aunt Phoenix, why don't you just take a seat? We won't keep you standing after your long trip." She pointed.

The old woman sat down, bolt upright in the chair.

80　　"Now, how is the boy?" asked the nurse.

Old Phoenix did not speak.

"I said, how is the boy?"

But Phoenix only waited and stared straight ahead, her face very solemn and withdrawn into rigidity.

"Is his throat any better?" asked the nurse. "Aunt Phoenix, don't you hear me? Is your grandson's throat any better since the last time you came for the medicine?"

85　　With her hands on her knees, the old woman waited, silent, erect and motionless, just as if she were in armor.

"You mustn't take up our time this way, Aunt Phoenix," the nurse said. "Tell us quickly about your grandson, and get it over. He isn't dead, is he?"

At last there came a flicker and then a flame of comprehension across her face, and she spoke.

"My grandson. It was my memory had left me. There I sat and forgot why I made my long trip."

"Forgot?" The nurse frowned. "After you came so far?"

90　　Then Phoenix was like an old woman begging a dignified forgiveness for waking up frightened in the night. "I never did go to school, I was too old at the Surrender," she said in a soft voice. "I'm an old woman without an education. It was my memory fail me. My little grandson, he is just the same, and I forgot it in the coming."

"Throat never heals, does it?" said the nurse, speaking in a loud, sure voice to Old Phoenix. By now she had a card with something written on it, a little list. "Yes. Swallowed lye. When was it—January—two-three years ago—"

Phoenix spoke unasked now. "No, missy, he not dead, he just the same. Every little while his throat begin to close up again, and he not able to swallow. He not get his breath. He not able to help himself. So the time come around, and I go on another trip for the soothing medicine."

"All right. The doctor said as long as you came to get it, you could have it," said the nurse. "But it's an obstinate case."

"My little grandson, he sit up there in the house all wrapped up, waiting by himself," Phoenix went on. "We is the only two left in the world. He suffer and it

don't seem to put him back at all. He got a sweet look. He going to last. He wear
a little patch quilt and peep out holding his mouth open like a little bird. I remembers so plain now. I not going to forget him again, no, the whole enduring time. I
could tell him from all the others in creation."

95   "All right." The nurse was trying to hush her now. She brought her a bottle of
medicine. "Charity," she said, making a check mark in a book.

         Old Phoenix held the bottle close to her eyes and then carefully put it into her
pocket.

         "I thank you," she said.

         "It's Christmas time, Grandma," said the attendant. "Could I give you a few
pennies out of my purse?"

         "Five pennies is a nickel," said Phoenix stiffly.

100   "Here's a nickel," said the attendant.

         Phoenix rose carefully and held out her hand. She received the nickel and
then fished the other nickel out of her pocket and laid it beside the new one. She
stared at her palm closely, with her head on one side.

         Then she gave a tap with her cane on the floor.

         "This is what come to me to do," she said. "I going to the store and buy my
child a little windmill they sells, made out of paper. He going to find it hard to
believe there such a thing in the world. I'll march myself back where he waiting,
holding it straight up in his hand."

         She lifted her free hand, gave a little nod, turned round, and walked out of the
doctor's office. Then her slow step began on the stairs, going down.

                                                                        [1941]

Joining the Conversation: Critical Thinking and Writing

1. If you do not know the legend of the phoenix, look it up in a dictionary or,
   better, in an online encyclopedia. Then carefully reread the story, to learn
   whether the story in any way connects with the legend.
2. What do you think of the hunter?
3. What would be lost if the episode (with all of its dialogue) of Phoenix falling
   into the ditch and being helped out of it by the hunter were omitted?
4. Is Christmas a particularly appropriate time in which to set the story? Why or
   why not?
5. In an argument of no more than one page, explain the significance of the story's
   title.

JAMES JOYCE

For a biographical note on James Joyce, see page 220.

Eveline

She sat at the window watching the evening invade the avenue. Her head was leaned against the window curtains and
in her nostrils was the odor of dusty cretonne. She was tired.

Few people passed. The man out of the last house
passed on his way home; she heard his footsteps clacking
along the concrete pavement and afterwards crunching on
the cinder path before the new red houses. One time there

used to be a field there in which they used to play every evening with other people's children. Then a man from Belfast[1] bought the field and built houses in it—not like their little brown houses but bright brick houses with shining roofs. The children of the avenue used to play together in that field—the Devines, the Waters, the Dunns, little Keogh the cripple, she and her brothers and sisters. Ernest, however, never played: he was too grown up. Her father used often to hunt them in out of the field with his blackthorn stick; but usually little Keogh used to keep *nix*[2] and call out when he saw her father coming. Still they seemed to have been rather happy then. Her father was not so bad then; and besides, her mother was alive. That was a long time ago; she and her brothers and sisters were all grown up; her mother was dead. Tizzie Dunn was dead, too, and the Waters had gone back to England. Everything changes. Now she was going to go away like the others, to leave her home.

Home! She looked around the room, reviewing all its familiar objects which she had dusted once a week for so many years, wondering where on earth all the dust came from. Perhaps she would never see again those familiar objects from which she had never dreamed of being divided. And yet during all those years she had never found out the name of the priest whose yellowing photograph hung on the wall above the broken harmonium beside the colored print of the promises made to Blessed Margaret Mary Alacoque. He had been a school friend of her father. Whenever he showed the photograph to a visitor her father used to pass it with a casual word:

"He is in Melbourne now."

5   She had consented to go away, to leave her home. Was that wise? She tried to weigh each side of the question. In her home anyway she had shelter and food; she had those whom she had known all her life about her. Of course she had to work hard both in the house and at business. What would they say of her in the Stores when they found out that she had run away with a fellow? Say she was a fool, perhaps; and her place would be filled up by advertisement. Miss Gavan would be glad. She had always had an edge on her, especially whenever there were people listening.

"Miss Hill, don't you see these ladies are waiting?"

"Look lively, Miss Hill, please."

She would not cry many tears at leaving the Stores.

But in her new home, in a distant unknown country, it would not be like that. Then she would be married—she, Eveline. People would treat her with respect then. She would not be treated as her mother had been. Even now, though she was over nineteen, she sometimes felt herself in danger of her father's violence. She knew it was that that had given her the palpitations. When they were growing up he had never gone for her, like he used to go for Harry and Ernest, because she was a girl; but latterly he had begun to threaten her and say what he would do to her only for her dead mother's sake. And now she had nobody to protect her. Ernest was dead and Harry, who was in the church decorating business, was nearly always down somewhere in the country. Besides, the invariable squabble for money on Saturday nights had begun to weary her unspeakably. She always gave her entire wages—seven shillings—and Harry always sent up what he could but the trouble was to get any money from her father. He said she used to squander the money, that she had no head, that he wasn't going to give her his hard-earned

---

[1]**a man from Belfast** i.e., man of the Protestant faith.   [2]**to keep *nix*** to stand guard.

money to throw about the streets, and much more, for he was usually fairly bad of a Saturday night. In the end he would give her the money and ask her had she any intention of buying Sunday dinner. Then she had to rush out as quickly as she could and do her marketing, holding her black leather purse tightly in her hand as she elbowed her way through the crowds and returning home late under her load of provisions. She had hard work to keep the house together and to see that the two young children, who had been left to her charge went to school regularly and got their meals regularly. It was hard work—a hard life—but now that she was about to leave it she did not find it a wholly undesirable life.

10 　　She was about to explore another life with Frank. Frank was very kind, manly, open-hearted. She was to go away with him by the night-boat to be his wife and to live with him in Buenos Aires where he had a home waiting for her. How well she remembered the first time she had seen him; he was lodging in a house on the main road where she used to visit. It seemed a few weeks ago. He was standing at the gate, his peaked cap pushed back on his head and his hair tumbled forward over a face of bronze. Then they had come to know each other. He used to meet her outside the Stores every evening and see her home. He took her to see *The Bohemian Girl*[3] and she felt elated as she sat in an unaccustomed part of the theater with him. He was awfully fond of music and sang a little. People knew that they were courting and, when he sang about the lass that loves a sailor, she always felt pleasantly confused. He used to call her Poppens out of fun. First of all it had been an excitement for her to have a fellow and then she had begun to like him. He had tales of distant countries. He had started as a deck boy at a pound a month on a ship of the Allan Line going out to Canada. He told her the names of the ships he had been on and the names of the different services. He had sailed through the Straits of Magellan and he told her stories of the terrible Patagonians. He had fallen on his feet in Buenos Aires, he said, and had come over to the old country just for a holiday. Of course, her father had found out the affair and had forbidden her to have anything to say to him.

"I know these sailor chaps," he said.

One day he had quarreled with Frank and after that she had to meet her lover secretly.

The evening deepened in the avenue. The white of two letters in her lap grew indistinct. One was to Harry; the other was to her father. Ernest had been her favorite but she liked Harry too. Her father was becoming old lately, she noticed; he would miss her. Sometimes he could be very nice. Not long before, when she had been laid up for a day, he had read her out a ghost story and made toast for her at the fire. Another day, when their mother was alive, they had all gone for a picnic to the Hill of Howth. She remembered her father putting on her mother's bonnet to make the children laugh.

Her time was running out but she continued to sit by the window, leaning her head against the window curtain, inhaling the odor of dusty cretonne. Down far in the avenue she could hear a street organ playing. She knew the air. Strange that it should come that very night to remind her of the promise to her mother, her promise to keep the home together as long as she could. She remembered the last night of her mother's illness; she was again in the close dark room at the other side of the hall and outside she heard a melancholy air of Italy. The organ player had been

---

[3]**The Bohemian Girl** an opera composed by Michael William Balfe with a libretto by Alfred Bunn, first performed in Dublin in 1844.

ordered to go away and given sixpence. She remembered her father strutting back into the sickroom saying:

15   "Damned Italians! coming over here!"

As she mused the pitiful vision of her mother's life laid its spell on the very quick of her being—that life of commonplace sacrifices closing in final craziness. She trembled as she heard again her mother's voice saying constantly with foolish insistence:

"Derevaun Seraun! Derevaun Seraun!"[4]?

She stood up in a sudden impulse of terror. Escape! She must escape! Frank would save her. He would give her life, perhaps love, too. But she wanted to live. Why should she be unhappy? She had a right to happiness. Frank would take her in his arms, fold her in his arms. He would save her.

She stood among the swaying crowd in the station at the North Wall. He held her hand and she knew that he was speaking to her, saying something about the passage over and over again. The station was full of soldiers with brown baggages. Through the wide doors of the sheds she caught a glimpse of the black mass of the boat, lying in beside the quay wall, with illumined portholes. She answered nothing. She felt her cheek pale and cold and, out of a maze of distress, she prayed to God to direct her, to show her what was her duty. The boat blew a long mournful whistle into the mist. If she went, tomorrow she would be on the sea with Frank, steaming towards Buenos Aires. Their passage had been booked. Could she still draw back after all he had done for her? Her distress awoke a nausea in her body and she kept moving her lips in silent, fervent prayer.

20   A bell clanged upon her heart. She felt him seize her hand:

"Come!"

All the seas of the world tumbled about her heart. He was drawing her into them: he would drown her. She gripped with both hands at the iron railing.

"Come!"

No! No! No! It was impossible. Her hands clutched the iron in frenzy. Amid the seas she sent a cry of anguish!

25   "Eveline! Evvy!"

He rushed beyond the barrier and called to her to follow. He was shouted at to go on but he still called to her. She set her white face to him, passive, like a helpless animal. Her eyes gave him no sign of love or farewell or recognition.

[1914]

Joining the Conversation: Critical Thinking and Writing

1. Why, in your opinion, does Eveline not join Frank?
2. What do you think are Eveline's virtues, and what are her weaknesses? How sympathetic are you to Eveline?
3. In paragraph 18, Eveline tells herself that "She had a right to happiness." Do we have a right to happiness? If so, where does this right come from? Does it make sense for us to speak of such a right?

---

[4]**Derevaun Seraun** possibly a garbled version of Gaelic for "The end of pleasure is pain," but perhaps meaningless syllables uttered by the dying woman.

RAYMOND CARVER

For a biographical note on Raymond Carver, see page 329.

Cathedral

This blind man, an old friend of my wife's, he was on his way to spend the night. His wife had died. So he was visiting the dead wife's relatives in Connecticut. He called my wife from his in-laws'. Arrangements were made. He would come by train, a five-hour trip, and my wife would meet him at the station. She hadn't seen him since she worked for him one summer in Seattle ten years ago. But she and the blind man had kept in touch. They made tapes and mailed them back and forth. I wasn't enthusiastic about his visit. He was no one I knew. And his being blind bothered me. My idea of blindness came from the movies. In the movies, the blind moved slowly and never laughed. Sometimes they were led by seeing-eye dogs. A blind man in my house was not something I looked forward to.

That summer in Seattle she had needed a job. She didn't have any money. The man she was going to marry at the end of the summer was in officers' training school. He didn't have any money, either. But she was in love with the guy, and he was in love with her, etc. She'd seen something in the paper: HELP WANTED—*Reading to Blind Man,* and a telephone number. She phoned and went over, was hired on the spot. She'd worked with this blind man all summer. She read stuff to him, case studies, reports, that sort of thing. She helped him organize his little office in the county social-service department. They'd become good friends, my wife and the blind man. How do I know these things? She told me. And she told me something else. On her last day in the office, the blind man asked if he could touch her face. She agreed to this. She told me he touched his fingers to every part of her face, her nose—even her neck! She never forgot it. She even tried to write a poem about it. She was always trying to write a poem. She wrote a poem or two every year, usually after something really important had happened to her.

When we first started going out together, she showed me the poem. In the poem, she recalled his fingers and the way they had moved around over her face. In the poem, she talked about what she had felt at the time, about what went through her mind when the blind man touched her nose and lips. I can remember I didn't think much of the poem. Of course, I didn't tell her that. Maybe I just don't understand poetry. I admit it's not the first thing I reach for when I pick up something to read.

Anyway, this man who'd first enjoyed her favors, the officer-to-be, he'd been her childhood sweetheart. So okay. I'm saying that at the end of the summer she let the blind man run his hands over her face, said goodbye to him, married her childhood etc., who was now a commissioned officer, and she moved away from Seattle. But they'd kept in touch, she and the blind man. She made the first contact after a year or so. She called him up one night from an Air Force base in Alabama. She wanted to talk. They talked. He asked her to send a tape and tell him about her life. She did this. She sent the tape. On the tape, she told the blind man about her husband and about their life together in the military. She told the blind man she loved her husband but she didn't like it where they lived and she didn't like it that he was part of the military-industrial thing. She told the blind man she'd written a poem and he was in it. She told him that she was writing a poem about what it was like to be an Air Force officer's wife. The poem wasn't finished yet. She was still writing it. The blind man made a tape. He sent her the tape. She made a tape. This went on for years. My wife's officer was posted to one base and then another. She sent tapes from Moody AFB, McGuire, McConnell, and finally Travis, near Sacramento, where one night she got to feeling lonely and cut off from people she kept losing in that moving-around life. She got to feeling she couldn't go it another step. She went in and swallowed all the pills and capsules in the medicine chest and washed them down with a bottle of gin. Then she got into a hot bath and passed out.

5   But instead of dying, she got sick. She threw up. Her officer—why should he have a name? he was the childhood sweetheart, and what more does he want?— came home from somewhere, found her, and called the ambulance. In time, she put it all on a tape and sent the tape to the blind man. Over the years, she put all kinds of stuff on tapes and sent the tapes off lickety-split. Next to writing a poem every year, I think it was her chief means of recreation. On one tape, she told the blind man she'd decided to live away from her officer for a time. On another tape, she told him about her divorce. She and I began going out, and of course she told her blind man about it. She told him everything, or so it seemed to me. Once she asked me if I'd like to hear the latest tape from the blind man. This was a year ago. I was on the tape, she said. So I said okay, I'd listen to it. I got us drinks and we settled down in the living room. We made ready to listen. First she inserted the tape into the player and adjusted a couple of dials. Then she pushed a lever. The tape squeaked and someone began to talk in this loud voice. She lowered the volume. After a few minutes of harmless chitchat, I heard my own name in the mouth of this stranger, this blind man I didn't even know! And then this: "From all you've said about him, I can only con- clude—" But we were interrupted, a knock at the door, something, and we didn't ever get back to the tape. Maybe it was just as well. I'd heard all I wanted to.

Now this same blind man was coming to sleep in my house.

"Maybe I could take him bowling," I said to my wife. She was at the draining board doing scalloped potatoes. She put down the knife she was using and turned around.

"If you love me," she said, "you can do this for me. If you don't love me, okay. But if you had a friend, any friend, and the friend came to visit, I'd make him feel comfortable." She wiped her hands with the dish towel.

"I don't have any blind friends," I said.

10   "You don't have *any* friends," she said. "Period. Besides," she said, "goddamn it, his wife's just died! Don't you understand that? The man's lost his wife!"

I didn't answer. She'd told me a little about the blind man's wife. Her name was Beulah. Beulah! That's a name for a colored woman.

"Was his wife a Negro?" I asked.

"Are you crazy?" my wife said. "Have you just flipped or something?" She picked up a potato. I saw it hit the floor, then roll under the stove. "What's wrong with you?" she said. "Are you drunk?"

"I'm just asking," I said.

15   Right then my wife filled me in with more detail than I cared to know. I made a drink and sat at the kitchen table to listen. Pieces of the story began to fall into place.

Beulah had gone to work for the blind man the summer after my wife had stopped working for him. Pretty soon Beulah and the blind man had themselves a church wedding. It was a little wedding—who'd want to go to such a wedding in the first place?—just the two of them, plus the minister and the minister's wife. But it was a church wedding just the same. It was what Beulah had wanted, he'd said. But even then Beulah must have been carrying the cancer in her glands. After they had been inseparable for eight years—my wife's word, *inseparable*—Beulah's health went into a rapid decline. She died in a Seattle hospital room, the blind man sitting beside the bed and holding on to her hand. They'd married, lived and worked together, slept together—had sex, sure—and then the blind man had to bury her. All this without his having ever seen what the goddamned woman looked like. It was beyond my understanding. Hearing this, I felt sorry for the blind man for a little bit. And then I found myself thinking what a pitiful life this woman must have led. Imagine a woman who could never see herself as she was seen in the eyes of her loved one. A woman who could go on day after day and never receive the smallest compliment from her beloved. A woman whose husband could never read the expression on her face, be it misery or something better. Someone who could wear makeup or not—what difference to him? She could, if she wanted, wear green eye-shadow around one eye, a straight pin in her nostril, yellow slacks, and purple shoes, no matter. And then to slip off into death, the blind man's hand on her hand, his blind eyes streaming tears—I'm imagining now—her last thought maybe this: that he never even knew what she looked like, and she on an express to the grave. Robert was left with a small insurance policy and a half of a twenty-peso Mexican coin. The other half of the coin went into the box with her. Pathetic.

So when the time rolled around, my wife went to the depot to pick him up. With nothing to do but wait—sure, I blamed him for that—I was having a drink and watching the TV when I heard the car pull into the drive. I got up from the sofa with my drink and went to the window to have a look.

I saw my wife laughing as she parked the car. I saw her get out of the car and shut the door. She was still wearing a smile. Just amazing. She went around to the other side of the car to where the blind man was already starting to get out. This blind man, feature this, he was wearing a full beard! A beard on a blind man! Too much, I say. The blind man reached into the back seat and dragged out a suitcase. My wife took his arm, shut the car door, and, talking all the way, moved him down the drive and then up the steps to the front porch. I turned off the TV. I finished my drink, rinsed the glass, dried my hands. Then I went to the door.

My wife said, "I want you to meet Robert. Robert, this is my husband. I've told you all about him." She was beaming. She had this blind man by his coat sleeve.

20   The blind man let go of his suitcase and up came his hand. I took it. He squeezed hard, held my hand, and then he let it go.

"I feel like we've already met," he boomed.

"Likewise," I said. I didn't know what else to say. Then I said, "Welcome. I've heard a lot about you." We began to move then, a little group, from the porch into the living room, my wife guiding him by the arm. The blind man was carrying his suitcase in his other hand. My wife said things like, "To your left here, Robert. That's right. Now watch it, there's a chair. That's it. Sit down right here. This is the sofa. We just bought this sofa two weeks ago."

I started to say something about the old sofa. I'd liked that old sofa. But I didn't say anything. Then I wanted to say something else, small-talk, about the scenic ride along the Hudson. How going *to* New York, you should sit on the right-hand side of the train, and coming *from* New York, the left-hand side.

"Did you have a good train ride?" I said. "Which side of the train did you sit on, by the way?"

25   "What a question, which side!" my wife said. "What's it matter which side?" she said.

"I just asked," I said.

"Right side," the blind man said. "I hadn't been on a train in nearly forty years. Not since I was a kid. With my folks. That's been a long time. I'd nearly forgotten the sensation. I have winter in my beard now," he said. "So I've been told, anyway. Do I look distinguished, my dear?" the blind man said to my wife.

"You look distinguished, Robert," she said. "Robert," she said. "Robert, it's just so good to see you."

My wife finally took her eyes off the blind man and looked at me. I had the feeling she didn't like what she saw. I shrugged.

30   I've never met, or personally known, anyone who was blind. This blind man was late forties, a heavy-set, balding man with stooped shoulders, as if he carried a great weight there. He wore brown slacks, brown shoes, a light-brown shirt, a tie, a sports coat. Spiffy. He also had this full beard. But he didn't use a cane and he didn't wear dark glasses. I'd always thought dark glasses were a must for the blind. Fact was, I wished he had a pair. At first glance, his eyes looked like anyone else's eyes. But if you looked close, there was something different about them. Too much white in the iris, for one thing, and the pupils seemed to move around in the sockets without his knowing it or being able to stop it. Creepy. As I stared at his face, I saw the left pupil turn in toward his nose while the other made an effort to keep in one place. But it was only an effort, for that eye was on the roam without his knowing it or wanting it to be.

I said, "Let me get you a drink. What's your pleasure? We have a little of everything. It's one of our pastimes."

"Bub, I'm a Scotch man myself," he said fast enough in this big voice.

"Right," I said. Bub! "Sure you are. I knew it."

He let his fingers touch his suitcase, which was sitting alongside the sofa. He was taking his bearings. I didn't blame him for that.

35   "I'll move that up to your room," my wife said.

"No, that's fine," the blind man said loudly. "It can go up when I go up."

"A little water with the Scotch?" I said.

"Very little," he said.

"I knew it," I said.

40   He said, "Just a tad. The Irish actor, Barry Fitzgerald? I'm like that fellow. When I drink water, Fitzgerald said, I drink water. When I drink whiskey, I drink whiskey." My wife laughed. The blind man brought his hand up under his beard. He lifted his beard slowly and let it drop.

I did the drinks, three big glasses of Scotch with a splash of water in each. Then we made ourselves comfortable and talked about Robert's travels. First the long flight from the West Coast to Connecticut, we covered that. Then from Connecticut up here by train. We had another drink concerning that leg of the trip.

I remembered having read somewhere that the blind didn't smoke because, as speculation had it, they couldn't see the smoke they exhaled. I thought I knew that much and that much only about blind people. But this blind man smoked his cigarette down to the nubbin and then lit another one. This blind man filled his ashtray and my wife emptied it.

When we sat down at the table for dinner, we had another drink. My wife heaped Robert's plate with cube steak, scalloped potatoes, green beans. I buttered him up two slices of bread. I said, "Here's bread and butter for you." I swallowed some of my drink. "Now let us pray," I said, and the blind man lowered his head. My wife looked at me, her mouth agape. "Pray the phone won't ring and the food doesn't get cold," I said.

We dug in. We ate everything there was to eat on the table. We ate like there was no tomorrow. We didn't talk. We ate. We scarfed. We grazed that table. We were into serious eating. The blind man had right away located his foods, he knew just where everything was on his plate. I watched with admiration as he used his knife and fork on the meat. He'd cut two pieces of meat, fork the meat into his mouth, and then go all out for the scalloped potatoes, the beans next, and then he'd tear off a hunk of buttered bread and eat that. He'd follow this up with a big drink of milk. It didn't seem to bother him to use his fingers once in a while, either.

45   We finished everything, including half a strawberry pie. For a few moments, we sat as if stunned. Sweat beaded on our faces. Finally, we got up from the table and left the dirty plates. We didn't look back. We took ourselves into the living room and sank into our places again. Robert and my wife sat on the sofa. I took the big chair. We had us two or three more drinks while they talked about the major things that had come to pass for them in the past ten years. For the most part, I just listened. Now and then I joined in. I didn't want him to think I'd left the room, and I didn't want her to think I was feeling left out. They talked of things that had happened to them—to them!—these past ten years. I waited in vain to hear my name on my wife's sweet lips: "And then my dear husband came into my life"—something like that. But I heard nothing of the sort. More talk of Robert. Robert had done a little of everything, it seemed, a regular blind jack-of-all-trades. But most recently he and his wife had had an Amway distributorship, from which, I gathered, they'd earned their living, such as it was. The blind man was also a ham radio operator. He talked in his loud voice about conversations he'd had with fellow operators in Guam, in the Philippines, in Alaska, and even in Tahiti. He said he'd have a lot of friends there if he ever wanted to go visit those places. From time to time, he'd turn his blind face toward me, put his hand under his beard, ask me something. How long had I been in my present position? (Three years.) Did I like my work? (I didn't.) Was I going to stay with it? (What were the options?) Finally, when I thought he was beginning to run down, I got up and turned on the TV.

    My wife looked at me with irritation. She was heading toward a boil. Then she looked at the blind man and said, "Robert, do you have a TV?"

    The blind man said, "My dear, I have two TVs. I have a color set and a black-and-white thing, an old relic. It's funny, but if I turn the TV on, and I'm always turning it on, I turn on the color set. It's funny, don't you think?"

    I didn't know what to say to that. I had absolutely nothing to say to that. No opinion. So I watched the news program and tried to listen to what the announcer was saying.

    "This is a color TV," the blind man said. "Don't ask me how, but I can tell."

50   "We traded up a while ago," I said.

    The blind man had another taste of his drink. He lifted his beard, sniffed it, and let it fall. He leaned forward on the sofa. He positioned his ashtray on the coffee table, then put the lighter to his cigarette. He leaned back on the sofa and crossed his legs at the ankles.

    My wife covered her mouth, and then she yawned. She stretched. She said, "I think I'll go upstairs and put on my robe. I think I'll change into something else. Robert, you make yourself comfortable," she said.

    "I'm comfortable," the blind man said.

    "I want you to feel comfortable in this house," she said.

55   "I am comfortable," the blind man said.

    After she'd left the room, he and I listened to the weather report and then to the sports roundup. By that time, she'd been gone so long I didn't know if she was going to come back. I thought she might have gone to bed. I wished she'd come back downstairs. I didn't want to be left alone with a blind man. I asked him if he wanted another drink, and he said sure. Then I asked if he wanted to smoke some dope with me. I said I'd just rolled a number. I hadn't, but I planned to do so in about two shakes.

"I'll try some with you," he said.

"Damn right," I said. "That's the stuff."

I got our drinks and sat down on the sofa with him. Then I rolled us two fat numbers. I lit one and passed it. I brought it to his fingers. He took it and inhaled.

60 "Hold it as long as you can," I said. I could tell he didn't know the first thing.

My wife came back downstairs wearing her pink robe and her pink slippers.

"What do I smell?" she said.

"We thought we'd have us some cannabis," I said.

My wife gave me a savage look. Then she looked at the blind man and said, "Robert, I didn't know you smoked."

65 He said, "I do now, my dear. There's a first time for everything. But I don't feel anything yet."

"This stuff is pretty mellow," I said. "This stuff is mild. It's dope you can reason with," I said. "It doesn't mess you up."

"Not much it doesn't, bub," he said, and laughed.

My wife sat on the sofa between the blind man and me. I passed her the number. She took it and toked and then passed it back to me. "Which way is this going?" she said. Then she said, "I shouldn't be smoking this. I can hardly keep my eyes open as it is. That dinner did me in. I shouldn't have eaten so much."

"It was the strawberry pie," the blind man said. "That's what did it," he said, and he laughed his big laugh. Then he shook his head.

70 "There's more strawberry pie," I said.

"Do you want some more, Robert?" my wife said.

"Maybe in a little while," he said.

We gave our attention to the TV. My wife yawned again. She said, "Your bed is made up when you feel like going to bed, Robert. I know you must have had a long day. When you're ready to go to bed, say so." She pulled his arm. "Robert?"

He came to and said, "I've had a real nice time. This beats tapes, doesn't it?"

75 I said, "Coming at you," and I put the number between his fingers. He inhaled, held the smoke, and then let it go. It was like he'd been doing it since he was nine years old.

"Thanks, bub," he said. "But I think this is all for me. I think I'm beginning to feel it," he said. He held the burning roach out for my wife.

"Same here," she said. "Ditto. Me, too." She took the roach and passed it to me. "I may just sit here for a while between you two guys with my eyes closed. But don't let me bother you, okay? Either one of you. If it bothers you, say so. Otherwise, I may just sit here with my eyes closed until you're ready to go to bed," she said. "Your bed's made up, Robert, when you're ready. It's right next to our room at the top of the stairs. We'll show you up when you're ready. You wake me up now, you guys, if I fall asleep." She said that and then she closed her eyes and went to sleep.

The news program ended. I got up and changed the channel. I sat back down on the sofa. I wished my wife hadn't pooped out. Her head lay across the back of the sofa, her mouth open. She'd turned so that her robe slipped away from her legs, exposing a juicy thigh. I reached to draw her robe back over her, and it was then that I glanced at the blind man. What the hell! I flipped the robe open again. "You say when you want some strawberry pie," I said.

80   "I will," he said.

I said, "Are you tired? Do you want me to take you up to your bed? Are you ready to hit the hay?"

"Not yet," he said. "No, I'll stay up with you, bub. If that's all right. I'll stay up until you're ready to turn in. We haven't had a chance to talk. Know what I mean? I feel like me and her monopolized the evening." He lifted his beard and he let it fall. He picked up his cigarettes and his lighter.

"That's all right," I said. Then I said, "I'm glad for the company."

And I guess I was. Every night I smoked dope and stayed up as long as I could before I fell asleep. My wife and I hardly ever went to bed at the same time. When I did go to sleep, I had these dreams. Sometimes I'd wake up from one of them, my heart going crazy.

85   Something about the church and the Middle Ages was on the TV. Not your run-of-the-mill TV fare. I wanted to watch something else. I turned to the other channels. But there was nothing on them, either. So I turned back to the first channel and apologized.

"Bub, it's all right," the blind man said. "It's fine with me. Whatever you want to watch is okay. I'm always learning something. Learning never ends. It won't hurt me to learn something tonight. I got ears," he said.

We didn't say anything for a time. He was leaning forward with his head turned at me, his right ear aimed in the direction of the set. Very disconcerting. Now and then his eyelids drooped and then they snapped open again. Now and then he put his fingers into his beard and tugged, like he was thinking about something he was hearing on the television.

On the screen, a group of men wearing cowls was being set upon and tormented by men dressed in skeleton costumes and men dressed as devils. The men dressed as devils wore devil masks, horns, and long tails. This pageant was part of a procession. The Englishman who was narrating the thing said it took place in Spain once a year. I tried to explain to the blind man what was happening.

"Skeletons," he said. "I know about skeletons," he said, and he nodded.

90   The TV showed this one cathedral. Then there was a long, slow look at another one. Finally, the picture switched to the famous one in Paris, with its flying buttresses and its spires reaching up to the clouds. The camera pulled away to show the whole of the cathedral rising above the skyline.

There were times when the Englishman who was telling the thing would shut up, would simply let the camera move around the cathedrals. Or else the camera would tour the countryside, men in fields walking behind oxen. I waited as long as I could. Then I felt I had to say something. I said, "They're showing the outside of this cathedral now. Gargoyles. Little statues carved to look like monsters. Now I guess they're in Italy. Yeah, they're in Italy. There's paintings on the walls of this one church."

"Are those fresco paintings, bub?" he asked, and he sipped from his drink.

I reached for my glass. But it was empty. I tried to remember what I could remember. "You're asking me are those frescoes?" I said. "That's a good question. I don't know."

The camera moved to a cathedral outside Lisbon. The differences in the Portuguese cathedral compared with the French and Italian were not that great. But they were there. Mostly the interior stuff. Then something occurred to me, and I said, "Something has occurred to me. Do you have any idea what a cathedral is? What they look like, that is? Do you follow me? If somebody says cathedral to you, do you have any notion what they're talking about? Do you know the difference between that and a Baptist church, say?"

95   He let the smoke dribble from his mouth. "I know they took hundreds of workers fifty or a hundred years to build," he said. "I just heard the man say that, of course. I know generations of the same families worked on a cathedral. I heard him say that, too. The men who began their life's work on them, they never lived to see the completion of their work. In that wise, bub, they're no different from the rest of us, right?" He laughed. Then his eyelids drooped again. His head nodded. He seemed to be snoozing. Maybe he was imagining himself in Portugal. The TV was showing another cathedral now. This one was in Germany. The Englishman's voice droned on. "Cathedrals," the blind man said. He sat up and rolled his head back and forth. "If you want the truth, bub, that's about all I know. What I just said. What I heard him say. But maybe you could describe one to me? I wish you'd do it. I'd like that. If you want to know, I really don't have a good idea."

I stared hard at the shot of the cathedral on the TV. How could I even begin to describe it? But say my life depended on it. Say my life was being threatened by an insane guy who said I had to do it or else.

I stared some more at the cathedral before the picture flipped off into the countryside. There was no use. I turned to the blind man and said, "To begin with, they're very tall." I was looking around the room for clues. "They reach way up. Up and up. Toward the sky. They're so big, some of them, they have to have these supports. To help hold them up, so to speak. These supports are called buttresses. They remind me of viaducts, for some reason. But maybe you don't know viaducts, either? Sometimes the cathedrals have devils and such carved into the front. Sometimes lords and ladies. Don't ask why this is," I said.

He was nodding. The whole upper part of his body seemed to be moving back and forth.

"I'm not doing so good, am I?" I said.

100   He stopped nodding and leaned forward on the edge of the sofa. As he listened to me, he was running his fingers through his beard. I wasn't getting through to him, I could see that. But he waited for me to go on just the same. He nodded, like he was trying to encourage me. I tried to think what else to say. "They're really big," I said. "They're massive. They're built of stone. Marble, too, sometimes. In those olden days, when they built cathedrals, men wanted to be close to God. In those olden days, God was an important part of everyone's life. You could tell this from their cathedral-building. I'm sorry," I said, "but it looks like that's the best I can do for you. I'm just no good at it."

"That's all right, bub," the blind man said. "Hey, listen. I hope you don't mind my asking you. Can I ask you something? Let me ask you a simple question, yes or no. I'm just curious and there's no offense. You're my host. But let me ask if you are in any way religious? You don't mind my asking?"

I shook my head. He couldn't see that, though. A wink is the same as a nod to a blind man. "I guess I don't believe in it. In anything. Sometimes it's hard. You know what I'm saying?"

"Sure, I do," he said.

"Right," I said.

105   The Englishman was still holding forth. My wife sighed in her sleep. She drew a long breath and went on with her sleeping.

"You'll have to forgive me," I said. "But I can't tell you what a cathedral looks like. It just isn't in me to do it. I can't do any more than I've done."

The blind man sat very still, his head down, as he listened to me.

I said, "The truth is, cathedrals don't mean anything special to me. Nothing. Cathedrals. They're something to look at on late-night TV. That's all they are."

It was then that the blind man cleared his throat. He brought something up. He took a handkerchief from his back pocket. Then he said, "I get it, bub. It's okay. It happens. Don't worry about it," he said. "Hey, listen to me. Will you do me a favor? I got an idea. Why don't you find us some heavy paper? And a pen. We'll do something. We'll draw one together. Get us a pen and some heavy paper. Go on, bub, get the stuff," he said.

110   So I went upstairs. My legs felt like they didn't have any strength in them. They felt like they did after I'd done some running. In my wife's room, I looked around. I found some ballpoints in a little basket on her table. And then I tried to think where to look for the kind of paper he was talking about.

Downstairs, in the kitchen, I found a shopping bag with onion skins in the bottom of the bag. I emptied the bag and shook it. I brought it into the living room and sat down with it near his legs. I moved some things, smoothed the wrinkles from the bag, spread it out on the coffee table.

The blind man got down from the sofa and sat next to me on the carpet.

He ran his fingers over the paper. He went up and down the sides of the paper. The edges, even the edges. He fingered the corners.

"All right," he said. "All right, let's do her."

115   He found my hand, the hand with the pen. He closed his hand over my hand. "Go ahead, bub, draw," he said. "Draw. You'll see. I'll follow along with you. It'll be okay. Just begin now like I'm telling you. You'll see. Draw," the blind man said.

So I began. First I drew a box that looked like a house. It could have been the house I lived in. Then I put a roof on it. At either end of the roof, I drew spires. Crazy.

"Swell," he said. "Terrific. You're doing fine," he said. "Never thought anything like this could happen in your lifetime, did you, bub? Well, it's a strange life, we all know that. Go on now. Keep it up."

I put in windows with arches. I drew flying buttresses. I hung great doors. I couldn't stop. The TV station went off the air. I put down the pen and closed and opened my fingers. The blind man felt around over the paper. He moved the tips of his fingers over the paper, all over what I had drawn, and he nodded.

"Doing fine," the blind man said.

120   I took up the pen again, and he found my hand. I kept at it. I'm no artist. But I kept drawing just the same.

My wife opened up her eyes and gazed at us. She sat up on the sofa, her robe hanging open. She said, "What are you doing? Tell me, I want to know."

I didn't answer her.

The blind man said, "We're drawing a cathedral. Me and him are working on it. Press hard," he said to me. "That's right. That's good," he said. "Sure. You got it, bub, I can tell. You didn't think you could. But you can, can't you? You're cooking with gas now. You know what I'm saying? We're going to really have us something here in a minute. How's the old arm?" he said. "Put some people in there now. What's a cathedral without people?"

My wife said, "What's going on? Robert, what are you doing? What's going on?"

125   "It's all right," he said to her. "Close your eyes now," the blind man said to me.

I did it. I closed them just like he said.

"Are they closed?" he said. "Don't fudge."

"They're closed," I said.

"Keep them that way," he said. He said, "Don't stop now. Draw."

130   So we kept on with it. His fingers rode my fingers as my hand went over the paper. It was like nothing else in my life up to now.

Then he said, "I think that's it. I think you got it," he said. "Take a look. What do you think?"

But I had my eyes closed. I thought I'd keep them that way for a little longer. I thought it was something I ought to do.

"Well?" he said. "Are you looking?"

My eyes were still closed. I was in my house. I knew that. But I didn't feel like I was inside anything.

"It's really something," I said.

[1983]

Joining the Conversation: Critical Thinking and Writing

1. How does "Cathedral" dramatize the idea of an internal journey? How would you define an internal journey as opposed to an external or physical journey? Can you provide evidence that any of the characters in the story undergo an internal change or transformation?
2. Why does the narrator feel threatened by the blind man? Has he any reason to feel threatened?
3. What attitude does the narrator reveal in the following passage:

> She'd turned so that her robe slipped away from her legs, exposing a juicy thigh. I reached to draw her robe back over her and it was then that I glanced at the blind man. What the hell! I flipped the robe open again.

POEMS

JOHN KEATS

John Keats (1795–1821), son of a London stable keeper, was taken out of school when he was fifteen years old and apprenticed to a surgeon and apothecary. In 1816, he was licensed to practice as an apothecary–surgeon, but he almost immediately abandoned medicine and decided to make a career as a poet. His progress was amazing; he quickly moved from routine verse to major accomplishments, publishing books of poems in 1817, 1818, and 1820, before dying of tuberculosis at the age of twenty-five.

On First Looking into Chapman's Homer*

Much have I traveled in the realms of gold,
And many goodly states and kingdoms seen;
Round many western islands have I been

*__*Chapman's Homer__ George Chapman (1559–1634?), Shakespeare's contemporary, is chiefly known for his translations (from the Greek) of Homer's *Odyssey* and *Iliad*. In lines 11–14 Keats mistakenly says that Cortés was the first European to see the Pacific Ocean, from the heights of Darien, in Panama. In fact, Balboa was the first.*

Which bards in fealty to Apollo° hold.
Oft of one wide expanse have I been told   5
That deep-browed Homer ruled as his demesne;°
Yet did I never breathe its pure serene°
Till I heard Chapman speak out loud and bold;
Then felt I like some watcher of the skies
When a new planet swims into his ken;   10
Or like stout Cortez when with eagle eyes
He stared at the Pacific—and all his men
Looked at each other with a wild surmise—
Silent, upon a peak in Darien.

[1816]

4 **Apollo** god of poetry.   6 **demesne** domain.   7 **serene** open space.

Joining the Conversation: Critical Thinking and Writing

1. In line 1, what do you think "realms of gold" stands for? Chapman was an Elizabethan; how does this fact add relevance to the metaphor in the first line?
2. Does line 9 introduce a totally new idea, or can you somehow connect it to the opening metaphor?
3. Do you like this poem? As specifically as you can, please explain why or why not.

PERCY BYSSHE SHELLEY

Percy Bysshe Shelley (1792–1822) was born in Sussex in England, the son of a prosperous country squire. Educated at Eton, he went on to Oxford but was expelled for having written a pamphlet supporting a belief in atheism. Like John Keats, he was a member of the second generation of English romantic poets. (The first generation included Wordsworth and Coleridge.) And, like Keats, Shelley died young; he drowned during a violent storm off the western coast of Italy while sailing with a friend.

Ozymandias

I met a traveler from an antique land
Who said: Two vast and trunkless legs of stone
Stand in the desert . . . Near them, on the sand,
Half sunk, a shattered visage lies, whose frown,
And wrinkled lip, and sneer of cold command,   5
Tell that its sculptor well those passions read
Which yet survive, stamped on these lifeless things,
The hand that mocked them, and the heart that fed:
And on the pedestal these words appear:
"My name is Ozymandias, king of kings: 10
Look on my works, ye Mighty, and despair!"
Nothing beside remains. Round the decay
Of that colossal wreck, boundless and bare
The lone and level sands stretch far away.

[1817]

Joining the Conversation: Critical Thinking and Writing

1. What elements of the poem do you find confusing? Re-read the poem and take inquiry notes on it, investigating the lines that you find unclear. For example, lines 4–8 are somewhat obscure, but the point is that the passions, which are still evident in the "shattered visage," survive the sculptor's hand that "mocked"— that is, (1) imitated or copied, (2) derided—them, and the passions also survive the king's heart that had nourished them.
2. There is an irony of plot here: Ozymandias believed that he created enduring works, but his intentions came to nothing. However, another irony is also present: How are his words, in a way that he did not intend, true?

ALFRED, LORD TENNYSON

Alfred, Lord Tennyson (1809–92), the son of an English clergyman, was born in Lincolnshire, where he began writing verse at age five. Educated at Cambridge, Alfred had to leave without a degree when his father died, and Alfred had to accept responsibility for bringing up his brothers and sisters. In fact, the family had inherited ample funds, but for some years, the money was tied up by litigation. Following Wordsworth's death in 1850, Tennyson was made poet laureate. With his government pension, he moved with his family to the Isle of Wight, where he lived in comfort until his death.

*Ulysses**

It little profits that an idle king,
By this still hearth, among these barren crags,
Matched with an aged wife, I mete and dole
Unequal laws unto a savage race,
That hoard, and sleep, and feed, and know not me.   5
I cannot rest from travel; I will drink
Life to the lees. All times I have enjoyed
Greatly, have suffered greatly, both with those
That loved me, and alone; on shore, and when
Thro' scudding drifts the rainy Hyades   10
Vext the dim sea. I am become a name;
For always roaming with a hungry heart
Much have I seen and known,—cities of men
And manners, climates, councils, governments,
Myself not least, but honored of them all,—   15
And drunk delight of battle with my peers,
Far on the ringing plains of windy Troy.
I am a part of all that I have met;
Yet all experience is an arch wherethro'
Gleams that untravelled world whose margin fades   20
For ever and for ever when I move.

* **Ulysses** Odysseus, King of Ithaca, a leader of the Greeks in the Trojan War, famous for his ten years of journeying to remote places.

How dull it is to pause, to make an end,
To rust unburnished, not to shine in use!
As tho' to breathe were life! Life piled on life
Were all too little, and of one to me   25
Little remains; but every hour is saved
From that eternal silence, something more,
A bringer of new things; and vile it were
For some three suns to store and hoard myself,
And this gray spirit yearning in desire   30
To follow knowledge like a sinking star
Beyond the utmost bound of human thought.

   This is my son, mine own Telemachus,
To whom I leave the scepter and the isle,—
Well-loved of me, discerning to fulfill   35
This labor, by slow prudence to make mild
A rugged people, and thro' soft degrees
Subdue them to the useful and the good.
Most blameless is he, centered in the sphere
Of common duties, decent not to fail   40
In offices of tenderness, and pay
Meet adoration to my household gods,
When I am gone. He works his work, I mine.

   There lies the port; the vessel puffs her sail;
There gloom the dark, broad seas. My mariners,   45
Souls that have toiled, and wrought, and thought with me,—
That ever with a frolic welcome took
The thunder and the sunshine, and opposed
Free hearts, free foreheads,—you and I are old;
Old age hath yet his honor and his toil.   50
Death closes all; but something ere the end,
Some work of noble note, may yet be done,
Not unbecoming men that strove with Gods.
The lights begin to twinkle from the rocks;
The long day wanes; the slow moon climbs; the deep   55
Moans round with many voices. Come, my friends.
'Tis not too late to seek a newer world.
Push off, and sitting well in order smite
The sounding furrows; for my purpose holds
To sail beyond the sunset, and the baths   60
Of all the western stars, until I die.
It may be that the gulfs will wash us down;
It may be we shall touch the Happy Isles,
And see the great Achilles, whom we knew.
Tho' much is taken, much abides; and tho'   65
We are not now that strength which in old days
Moved earth and heaven, that which we are, we are.
One equal temper of heroic hearts,
Made weak by time and fate, but strong in will
To strive, to seek, to find, and not to yield.   70

[1833]

Joining the Conversation: Critical Thinking and Writing

1. Given the fact that Ulysses is a king and therefore a person with great responsibilities, does such a line as "I cannot rest from travel" (line 6) strike you as irresponsible? Explain your answer.
2. It has been said that, although at first glance the poem seems optimistic and highly positive—the final line is "To strive, to seek, to find, and not to yield"— the poem, in fact, is melancholy and filled with suggestions of death. What is Your view?
3. Is Tennyson presenting an argument here for how we should live? If so, what is your response?

COUNTEE CULLEN

Countee Cullen (1903–46) was born Countee Porter in New York City, raised by his grandmother, and then adopted by the Reverend Frederick A. Cullen, a Methodist minister in Harlem. Countee Cullen received a BA from New York University (Phi Beta Kappa) and an MA from Harvard. He earned his living as a high school teacher of French, but his literary gifts were recognized in his own day.

Incident

(For Eric Walrond)

Once riding in old Baltimore,
   Heart-filled, head-filled with glee,
I saw a Baltimorean
   Keep looking straight at me.

Now I was eight and very small,   5
   And he was no whit bigger,
And so I smiled, but he poked out
   His tongue, and called me, "Nigger."

I saw the whole of Baltimore
   From May until December;   10
Of all the things that happened there
   That's all that I remember.

[1925]

Joining the Conversation: Critical Thinking and Writing

1. How would you define an "incident"? A serious occurrence? A minor occurrence? Or what? Think about the word, and then think about Cullen's use of it as a title for the event recorded in this poem. Test out one or two other possible titles as a way of helping yourself to see the strengths or weaknesses of Cullen's title.
2. The dedicatee, Eric Walrond (1898–1966), was an African American essayist and writer of fiction who in an essay, "On Being Black," had described his experiences of racial prejudice. How does the presence of the dedication bear on our response to Cullen's account of the "incident"?

3. What is the tone of the poem: indifferent, angry, sad, or another emotion? What do you think is the speaker's attitude toward the "incident"? What is your attitude?
4. Ezra Pound, poet and critic, once defined literature as "news that *stays* news." What do you think he meant by this? Do you think that the definition fits Cullen's poem?

WILLIAM STAFFORD

William Stafford (1914–93) was born in Hutchinson, Kansas, and was educated at the University of Kansas and the State University of Iowa. A conscientious objector during World War II, he worked for the Brethren Service and the Church World Service. After the war, he taught at several universities and then settled at Lewis and Clark College in Portland, Oregon. In addition to several books of poems, Stafford wrote Down in My Heart *(1947), an account of his experiences as a conscientious objector.*

Traveling through the Dark

Traveling through the dark I found a deer
dead on the edge of the Wilson River road.
It is usually best to roll them into the canyon:
the road is narrow; to swerve might make more dead.

By glow of the tail-light I stumbled back of the car   5
and stood by the heap, a doe, a recent killing;
she had stiffened already, almost cold.
I dragged her off; she was large in the belly.

My fingers touching her side brought me the reason—
her side was warm; her fawn lay there waiting,   10
alive, still, never to be born.
Beside that mountain road I hesitated.

The car aimed ahead its lowered parking lights;
under the hood purred the steady engine.
I stood in the glare of the warm exhaust turning red;   15
around our group I could hear the wilderness listen.

I thought hard for us all—my only swerving—
Then pushed her over the edge into the river.

[1960]

Joining the Conversation: Critical Thinking and Writing

1. Look at the first sentence (the first two lines), and try to recall what your impression of the speaker was, based only on these two lines, or pretend that you have not read the entire poem, and characterize him based merely on these two lines. Then take the entire poem into consideration, and characterize him.
2. What do you make of the title? Do you think it is a good title for this poem? Explain your answer.

ADRIENNE RICH

Adrienne Rich (1929–2012) was born in Baltimore, Maryland. She published over sixteen volumes of poetry and five volumes of critical prose. Her most recent books include Tonight No Poetry Will Serve: Poems 2007–2010 *and* Telephone Ringing in the Labyrinth: Poems 2004–2006. A Human Eye: Essays on Art in Society, *appeared in 2009. She edited Muriel Rukeyser's* Selected Poems *for the Library of America. Among numerous other recognitions, she was the 2006 recipient of the National Book Foundation's Medal for Distinguished Contribution to American Letters. Her poetry and essays have been widely translated and published internationally.*

Diving into the Wreck

First having read the book of myths,
and loaded the camera,
and checked the edge of the knife-blade,
I put on
the body-armor of black rubber   5
the absurd flippers
the grave and awkward mask.
I am having to do this
not like Cousteau° with his
assiduous team   10
aboard the sun-flooded schooner
but here alone.

There is a ladder.
The ladder is always there
hanging innocently   15
close to the side of the schooner.
We know what it is for,
we who have used it.
Otherwise
it's a piece of maritime floss   20
some sundry equipment.

I go down.
Rung after rung and still
the oxygen immerses me
the blue light   25
the clear atoms
of our human air.
I go down.
My flippers cripple me,
I crawl like an insect down the ladder   30

9 **Cousteau** Jacques Cousteau (1910–97), French underwater explorer.

and there is no one
to tell me when the ocean
will begin.

First the air is blue and then
it is bluer and then green and then   35
black I am blacking out and yet
my mask is powerful
it pumps my blood with power
the sea is another story
the sea is not a question of power   40
I have to learn alone
to turn my body without force
in the deep element.

And now: it is easy to forget
what I came for   45
among so many who have always
lived here
swaying their crenellated fans
between the reefs
and besides   50
you breathe differently down here.

I came to explore the wreck.
The words are purposes.
The words are maps.
I came to see the damage that was done   55
and the treasures that prevail.
I stroke the beam of my lamp
slowly along the flank
of something more permanent
than fish or weed   60

the thing I came for:
the wreck and not the story of the wreck
the thing itself and not the myth
the drowned face always staring
toward the sun   65
the evidence of damage
worn by salt and sway into this threadbare beauty
the ribs of the disaster
curving their assertion
among the tentative haunters.   70

This is the place.
And I am here, the mermaid whose dark hair
streams black, the merman in his armored body
We circle silently
about the wreck   75

we dive into the hold.
I am she: I am he

whose drowned face sleeps with open eyes
whose breasts still bear the stress
whose silver, copper, vermeil cargo lies   80
obscurely inside barrels
half-wedged and left to rot
we are the half-destroyed instruments
that once held to a course
the water-eaten log   85
the fouled compass

We are, I am, you are
by cowardice or courage
the one who find our way
back to this scene   90
carrying a knife, a camera
a book of myths
in which
our names do not appear.

[1972]

Joining the Conversation: Critical Thinking and Writing

1. Rich emphasizes the physical sensation of scuba diving. Reread the poem and highlight your favorite descriptions of the feelings that accompany diving. Note any particularly interesting words or phrases that make this experience come alive.
2. In lines 61-62, the poem's speaker explains that she "came for:/the wreck and not the story of the wreck." What does this mean? Why did she come for "the thing itself" (63)? Why is she emphasizing her need to understand the reality of the wreck rather than the story of the wreck?
3. In the poem's last stanzas, the poem's speaker explains that she and her co-diver are swimming like a mermaid and merman. In the last lines of the poem, she explains that the two divers are carrying a book of myths. Obviously, this book of myths has influenced how the narrator is experiencing the ocean. Why does the poem emphasize that the narrator's name does not appear in the book of myths?

DEREK WALCOTT

Derek Walcott, born in 1930 on the Caribbean island of St. Lucia, was awarded the Nobel Prize in Literature in 1992. Although in the United States he is known chiefly as a poet, Walcott is also an important playwright and director of plays. Much of his work is concerned with his mixed heritage—a black writer from the Caribbean, whose language is English. Walcott taught for many years in the Creative Writing Program at Boston University. Walcott's books include Collected Poems *(1986) and* Omeros *(1989), a Caribbean epic that echoes Homer's* Iliad *and* Odyssey *as it explores the Caribbean's past and present.*

A Far Cry from Africa

A wind is ruffling the tawny pelt
Of Africa. Kikuyu,° quick as flies,
Batten upon the bloodstreams of the veldt.°
Corpses are scattered through a paradise.
Only the worm, colonel of carrion, cries: 5
"Waste no compassion on these separate dead!"
Statistics justify and scholars seize
The salients of colonial policy.
What is that to the white child hacked in bed?
To savages, expendable as Jews?   10

Threshed out by beaters, the long rushes break
In a white dust of ibises whose cries
Have wheeled since civilization's dawn
From the parched river or beast-teeming plain.
The violence of beast on beast is read   15
As natural law, but upright man
Seeks his divinity by inflicting pain.
Delirious as these worried beasts, his wars
Dance to the tightened carcass of a drum,
While he calls courage still that native dread   20
Of the white peace contracted by the dead.

Again brutish necessity wipes its hands
Upon the napkins of a dirty cause, again
A waste of our compassion, as with Spain,°
The gorilla wrestles with the superman.   25

I who am poisoned with the blood of both,
Where shall I turn, divided to the vein?
I who have cursed
The drunken officer of British rule, how choose
Between this Africa and the English tongue I love?   30
Betray them both, or give back what they give?
How can I face such slaughter and be cool?
How can I turn from Africa and live?

[1962]

24 **Spain** a reference to the triumph of fascism in Spain after the civil war of 1936–39.

Joining the Conversation: Critical Thinking and Writing

1. Now that you have read the poem, explain the meaning of the title.
2. Do you find the first stanza hard to understand? Why, or why not?
3. Focus on lines 15–17: What is Walcott saying here? Do you think that the poem might be even more effective if these lines were placed at the beginning? Or do they belong exactly where they are?

4. Imagine that Walcott sent this poem to you with a letter that asked for your response. In a letter ("Dear Mr. Walcott . . .") of one page in length, give your response to the poem.
5. What is the meaning of line 25?
6. Walcott uses the first-person "I" in the final stanza. How would you answer each of the questions that he asks in it? Or do you think the point is that these questions cannot be answered?
7. What is your own experience of Africa? Have you lived or traveled there? Would you like to? Has Walcott given you a new perspective on Africa and its history and culture?

SHERMAN ALEXIE

Sherman Alexie, born in 1966 in Spokane, Washington, holds a BA from Washington State University. Author of novels, stories, and poems, and author and director of the highly praised film Smoke Signals *(1998), Alexie was awarded a grant from the National Endowment for the Arts. Of his life and his work he says, "I am a Spokane Coeur d'Alene Indian. . . . I live on the Spokane Indian Reservation. Everything I do now, writing and otherwise, has its origin in that."*

On the Amtrak from Boston to New York City

The white woman across the aisle from me says, "Look,
look at all the history, that house
on the hill there is over two hundred years old,"
as she points out the window past me

into what she has been taught. I have learned   5
little more about American history during my few days
back East than what I expected and far less
of what we should all know of the tribal stories

whose architecture is 15,000 years older
than the corners of the house that sits   10
museumed on the hill. "Walden Pond,"°
the woman on the train asks, "Did you see Walden Pond?"

and I don't have a cruel enough heart to break
her own by telling her there are five Walden Ponds°
on my little reservation out West   15
and at least a hundred more surrounding Spokane,

the city I pretend to call my home. "Listen,"
I could have told her. "I don't give a shit
about Walden. I know the Indians were living stories
around that pond before Walden's grandparents were born   20

11 **Walden Pond** site in Massachusetts where Henry David Thoreau (1817–62) lived from July 4, 1845 to September 6, 1847, and about which he wrote in his most famous book, *Walden* (1854). An excerpt from *Walden* is provided on pages 825–27.

and before his grandparents' grandparents were born.
I'm tired of hearing about Don-fucking-Henley° saving it, too,
because that's redundant. If Don Henley's brothers and sisters
and mothers and fathers hadn't come here in the first place

then nothing would need to be saved."   25
But I didn't say a word to the woman about Walden
Pond because she smiled so much and seemed delighted
that I thought to bring her an orange juice

back from the food car. I respect elders
of every color. All I really did was eat   30
my tasteless sandwich, drink my Diet Pepsi
and nod my head whenever the woman pointed out

another little piece of her country's history
while I, as all Indians have done
since this war began, made plans   35
for what I would do and say the next time

somebody from the enemy thought I was one of their own.

[1993]

22 **Don Henley** rock singer who was active in preserving Walden from building developers.

Joining the Conversation: Critical Thinking and Writing

1. Characterize the speaker.
2. Take the common idea that "Columbus discovered America." What attitude toward the history of this land and toward Indians is implicit in these words?

WILLIAM BUTLER YEATS

William Butler Yeats (1865–1939) was born in Dublin, Ireland. The early Yeats was very interested in highly lyrical, romantic poetry, often drawing on Irish mythology. The later poems, from about 1910 (and especially after Yeats met Ezra Pound in 1911), are often more colloquial. Although the later poems often employ mythological references too, many believe that these poems are more down-to-earth. Yeats was awarded the Nobel Prize in Literature in 1923.

In the seventh century BCE, the ancient Greeks founded the city of Byzantium in Thrace, where Istanbul, Turkey, now stands. (Constantine, the first Christian ruler of the Roman Empire, built a new city there in 330 ce. Named Constantinople, the city served as the capital of the Roman Empire until 1453, when the Turks captured it. In 1930, the name was officially changed to Istanbul.) The capital of the Roman Empire and the "holy city" of the Greek Orthodox Church, Byzantium had two golden ages. The first, in its early centuries, continued the traditions of the antique Greco-Roman world. The second, which is what Yeats had in mind, extended from the mid-ninth to the mid-thirteenth century and was a distinctive blend of classical, Christian, Slavic, and even Islamic culture. This period is noted for mysticism, for the preservation of ancient learning, and for exquisitely refined symbolic art. In short, Byzantium (as Yeats saw it) was wise and passionless. In A Vision, *his prose treatment of his complex mystical system, Yeats says:*

> I think that in early Byzantium, maybe never before or since in recorded history, religious, aesthetic and practical life were one, that architect and artificers—though not, it may be, poets, for language has been the instrument of controversy and must have grown abstract—spoke to the multitude and the few alike. The painter, the mosaic worker, the worker in gold and silver, the illuminator of sacred books, were almost impersonal, almost perhaps without the consciousness of individual design, absorbed in their subject matter and that the vision of the whole people. They could copy out of old Gospel books those pictures that seemed as sacred as the text, and yet weave all into a vast design, the work of many that seemed the work of one, that made building, picture, pattern, metal-work of rail and lamp, seem but a single image.

Sailing to Byzantium

I

That is no country for old men. The young
In one another's arms, birds in the trees
—Those dying generations—at their song,
The salmon-falls, the mackerel-crowded seas,
Fish, flesh, or fowl, commend all summer long   5
Whatever is begotten, born, and dies.
Caught in that sensual music all neglect
Monuments of unaging intellect.

II

An aged man is but a paltry thing,
A tattered coat upon a stick, unless   10
Soul clap its hands and sing, and louder sing
For every tatter in its mortal dress.
Nor is there singing school but studying
Monuments of its own magnificence;
And therefore I have sailed the seas and come   15
To the holy city of Byzantium.

III

O sages standing in God's holy fire
As in the gold mosaic of a wall,
Come from the holy fire, perne° in a gyre,
And be the singing-masters of my soul.   20
Consume my heart away; sick with desire
And fastened to a dying animal
It knows not what it is; and gather me
Into the artifice of eternity.

19 **perne** whirl down.

IV

Once out of nature I shall never take   25
My bodily form from any natural thing,
But such a form as Grecian goldsmiths make
Of hammered gold and gold enameling
To keep a drowsy Emperor awake;
Or set upon a golden bough to sing   30
To lords and ladies of Byzantium
Of what is past, or passing, or to come.

[1926]

Joining the Conversation: Critical Thinking and Writing

1. What is "that . . . country," mentioned in the first line?
2. By the end of the first stanza, the speaker seems to be dismissing the natural world. Do you agree that even in this stanza, however, he sounds attracted to it?
3. The poem is filled with oppositions—for instance, "old men" versus "The young" (both in line 1), and "birds in the trees" (line 2) versus the mechanical bird in the final stanza. List as many opposites as you see in the poem, and then explain what Yeats is getting at.
4. The first stanza speaks of "monuments of unaging intellect." What might be some examples of these?
5. After reading and rereading this poem, do you think you will—even if only briefly—*act* differently, redirect any of your choices? Support your response with reasons.
6. Have you ever visited any place—perhaps the place where you or your parents or grandparents were born, or perhaps a house of worship, or perhaps a college campus—that you have come to see symbolically, standing for a way of life or for some aspect of life? If so, describe the place and the significance that you give it.

CHRISTINA ROSSETTI

Christina Rossetti (1830–94) was the daughter of an exiled Italian patriot who lived in London and the sister of the poet and painter Dante Gabriel Rossetti. After her father became an invalid, she led an extremely ascetic life, devoting most of her life to doing charitable work. Her first and best-known volume of poetry, Goblin Market and Other Poems, *was published in 1862.*

Uphill

Does the road wind uphill all the way?
　　Yes, to the very end.
Will the day's journey take the whole long day?
　　From morn to night, my friend.

But is there for the night a resting-place?   5
　　A roof for when the slow dark hours begin.
May not the darkness hide it from my face?
　　You cannot miss that inn.

Shall I meet other wayfarers at night?
   Those who have gone before.   10
Then must I knock, or call when just in sight?
   They will not keep you standing at that door.

Shall I find comfort, travel-sore and weak?
   Of labor you shall find the sum.
Will there be beds for me and all who seek?   15
   Yea, beds for all who come.

[1858]

Joining the Conversation: Critical Thinking and Writing

1. Who is the questioner? A woman? A man? All human beings collectively? "Uphill" does not use quotation marks to distinguish between the two speakers. Can one say that in "Uphill" the questioner and the answerer are the same person?
2. Are the answers unambiguously comforting? Or can it, for instance, be argued that the "roof" is (perhaps among other things) the lid of a coffin—hence, the questioner will certainly not be kept "standing at that door"? If the poem can be read along these lines, is it chilling rather than comforting?

PLAY

HENRIK IBSEN

Henrik Ibsen (1828–1906) was born in Skien, Norway, of wealthy parents who soon after his birth lost their money. Ibsen worked as a pharmacist's apprentice, but at the age of twenty-two, he had written his first play, a promising melodrama titled Cataline *(or* Catalina*). He engaged in theater work first in Norway and then in Denmark and Germany. By 1865, his plays had won him a state pension that enabled him to settle in Rome. After writing romantic, historic, and poetic plays, he turned to realistic drama with* The League of Youth *(1869). Among his major realistic "problem plays" are* A Doll's House *(1879),* Ghosts *(1881), and* An Enemy of the People *(1882). In* The Wild Duck *(1884), he moved toward a more symbolic tragicomedy, and his last plays, written in the nineties, are highly symbolic.* Hedda Gabler *(1890) looks backward to the plays of the eighties rather than forward to the plays of the nineties.*

A Doll's House

Translated by R. Farquharson Sharp

CHARACTERS

TORVALD HELMER, *a lawyer and bank manager*
NORA, *his wife*
DOCTOR RANK
MRS. CHRISTINE LINDE
NILS KROGSTAD, *a lawyer and bank clerk*
IVAR, BOB, AND EMMY, *the Helmers' three young children*
ANNE, *their nurse*

A Doll's House. Photofest, Inc.

HELEN, *a housemaid*
A porter

The action takes place in HELMER's *apartment.*

ACT 1

SCENE: *A room furnished comfortably and tastefully, but not extravagantly. At the back, a door to the right leads to the entrance hall, another to the left leads to* HELMER'S *study. Between the doors stands a piano. In the middle of the left-hand wall is a door, and beyond it a window. Near the window are a round table, armchairs and a small sofa. In the right-hand wall, at the farther end, another door; and on the same side, nearer the footlights, a stove, two easy chairs and a rocking-chair; between the stove and the door, a small table. Engravings on the walls; a cabinet with china and other small objects; a small book case with well-bound books. The floors are carpeted, and a fire burns in the stove. It is winter.*

A bell rings in the hall; shortly afterwards the door is heard to open. Enter NORA, *humming a tune and in high spirits. She is in outdoor dress and carries a number of parcels; these she lays on the table to the right. She leaves the outer door open after her, and through it is seen a* PORTER *who is carrying a Christmas Tree and a basket, which he gives to the* MAID *who has opened the door.*

NORA: Hide the Christmas Tree carefully, Helen. Be sure the children do not see it till this evening, when it is dressed. [*to the* PORTER, *taking out her purse.*] How much?

PORTER: Sixpence.

NORA: There is a shilling. No, keep the change. [*The* PORTER *thanks her, and goes out.* NORA *shuts the door. She is laughing to herself, as she takes off*

> *her hat and coat. She takes a packet of macaroons from her pocket and eats one or two; then goes cautiously to her husband's door and listens.*] Yes, he is in.

[*Still humming, she goes to the table on the right.*]

HELMER [*calls out from his room*]: Is that my little lark twittering out there?

NORA [*busy opening some of the parcels*]: Yes, it is!

HELMER: Is my little squirrel bustling about?

NORA: Yes!

HELMER: When did my squirrel come home?

NORA: Just now. [*puts the bag of macaroons into her pocket and wipes her mouth.*] Come in here, Torvald, and see what I have bought.

HELMER: Don't disturb me. [*A little later, he opens the door and looks into the room, pen in hand.*] Bought, did you say? All these things? Has my little spendthrift been wasting money again?

NORA: Yes, but, Torvald, this year we really can let ourselves go a little. This is the first Christmas that we have not needed to economise.

HELMER: Still, you know, we can't spend money recklessly.

NORA: Yes, Torvald, we may be a wee bit more reckless now, mayn't we? Just a tiny wee bit! You are going to have a big salary and earn lots and lots of money.

HELMER: Yes, after the New Year; but then it will be a whole quarter before the salary is due.

NORA: Pooh! we can borrow till then.

HELMER: Nora! [*goes up to her and takes her playfully by the ear.*] The same little featherhead! Suppose, now, that I borrowed fifty pounds to-day, and you spent it all in the Christmas week, and then on New Year's Eve a slate fell on my head and killed me, and—

NORA [*putting her hands over his mouth*]: Oh! don't say such horrid things.

HELMER: Still, suppose that happened—what then?

NORA: If that were to happen, I don't suppose I should care whether I owed money or not.

HELMER: Yes, but what about the people who had lent it?

NORA: They? Who would bother about them? I should not know who they were.

HELMER: That is like a woman! But seriously, Nora, you know what I think about that. No debt, no borrowing. There can be no freedom or beauty about a home life that depends on borrowing and debt. We two have kept bravely on the straight road so far, and we will go on the same way for the short time longer that there need be any struggle.

NORA [*moving towards the stove*]: As you please, Torvald.

HELMER [*following her*]: Come, come, my little skylark must not droop her wings. What is this! Is my little squirrel out of temper? [*taking out his purse.*] Nora, what do you think I have got here?

NORA [*turning around quickly*]: Money!

HELMER: There you are. [*gives her some money*] Do you think I don't know what a lot is wanted for housekeeping at Christmas-time?

NORA [*counting*]: Ten shillings—a pound—two pounds! Thank you, thank you, Torvald; that will keep me going for a long time.

HELMER: Indeed it must.

NORA: Yes, yes, it will. But come here and let me show you what I have bought. And all so cheap! Look, here is a new suit for Ivar, and a sword; and a horse and a trumpet for Bob; and a doll and dolly's bedstead for Emmy— they are very plain, but anyway she will soon break them in pieces. And here are dress-lengths and handkerchiefs for the maids; old Anne ought really to have something better.

HELMER: And what is in this parcel?

NORA [*crying out*]: No, no! you mustn't see that till this evening.

HELMER: Very well. But now tell me, you extravagant little person, what would you like for yourself?

NORA: For myself? Oh, I am sure I don't want anything.

HELMER: Yes, but you must. Tell me something reasonable that you would particularly like to have.

NORA: No, I really can't think of anything—unless, Torvald—

HELMER: Well?

NORA [*playing with his coat buttons, and without raising her eyes to his*]: If you really want to give me something, you might—you might—

HELMER: Well, out with it!

NORA [*speaking quickly*]: You might give me money, Torvald. Only just as much as you can afford; and then one of these days I will buy something with it.

HELMER: But, Nora—

NORA: Oh, do! dear Torvald; please, please do! Then I will wrap it up in beautiful gilt paper and hang it on the Christmas Tree. Wouldn't that be fun?

HELMER: What are little people called that are always wasting money?

NORA: Spendthrifts—I know. Let us do as you suggest, Torvald, and then I shall have time to think what I am most in want of. That is a very sensible plan, isn't it?

HELMER [*smiling*]: Indeed it is—that is to say, if you were really to save out of the money I give you, and then really buy something for yourself. But if you spend it all on the housekeeping and any number of unnecessary things, then I merely have to pay up again.

NORA: Oh but, Torvald—

HELMER: You can't deny it, my dear little Nora. [*puts his arm round her waist*] It's a sweet little spendthrift, but she uses up a deal of money. One would hardly believe how expensive such little persons are!

NORA: It's a shame to say that. I do really save all I can.

HELMER [*laughing*]: That's very true—all you can. But you can't save anything!

NORA [*smiling quietly and happily*]: You haven't any idea how many expenses we skylarks and squirrels have, Torvald.

HELMER: You are an odd little soul. Very like your father. You always find some new way of wheedling money out of me, and, as soon as you have got it, it seems to melt in your hands. You never know where it has gone. Still, one must take you as you are. It is in the blood; for indeed it is true that you can inherit these things, Nora.

NORA: Ah, I wish I had inherited many of papa's qualities.

HELMER: And I would not wish you to be anything but just what you are, my sweet little skylark. But, do you know, it strikes me that you are looking rather— what shall I say—rather uneasy to-day?

NORA: Do I?

HELMER: You do, really. Look straight at me.

NORA [*looks at him*]: Well?

HELMER [*wagging his finger at her*]: Hasn't Miss Sweet-Tooth been breaking rules in town to-day?

NORA: No; what makes you think that?

HELMER: Hasn't she paid a visit to the confectioner's?

NORA: No, I assure you, Torvald—

HELMER: Not been nibbling sweets?

NORA: No, certainly not.

HELMER: Not even taken a bite at a macaroon or two?

NORA: No, Torvald, I assure you really—

HELMER: There, there, of course I was only joking.

NORA [*going to the table on the right*]: I should not think of going against your wishes.

HELMER: No, I am sure of that! besides, you gave me your word—[*going up to her*] Keep your little Christmas secrets to yourself, my darling. They will all be revealed to-night when the Christmas Tree is lit, no doubt.

NORA: Did you remember to invite Doctor Rank?

HELMER: No. But there is no need; as a matter of course he will come to dinner with us. However, I will ask him when he comes in this morning. I have ordered some good wine. Nora, you can't think how I am looking forward to this evening.

NORA: So am I! And how the children will enjoy themselves, Torvald!

HELMER: It is splendid to feel that one has a perfectly safe appointment, and a big enough income. It's delightful to think of, isn't it?

NORA: It's wonderful!

HELMER: Do you remember last Christmas? For a full three weeks beforehand you shut yourself up every evening till long after midnight, making ornaments for the Christmas Tree and all the other fine things that were to be a surprise to us. It was the dullest three weeks I ever spent!

NORA: I didn't find it dull.

HELMER [*smiling*]: But there was precious little result, Nora.

NORA: Oh, you shouldn't tease me about that again. How could I help the cat's going in and tearing everything to pieces?

HELMER: Of course you couldn't, poor little girl. You had the best of intentions to please us all, and that's the main thing. But it is a good thing that our hard times are over.

NORA: Yes, it is really wonderful.

HELMER: This time I needn't sit here and be dull all alone, and you needn't ruin your dear eyes and your pretty little hands—

NORA [*clapping her hands*]: No, Torvald, I needn't any longer, need I! It's wonderfully lovely to hear you say so! [*taking his arm*] Now I will tell you how I have been thinking we ought to arrange things, Torvald. As soon as Christmas is over—[*A bell rings in the hall.*] There's the bell. [*She tidies the room a little.*] There's someone at the door. What a nuisance!

HELMER: If it is a caller, remember I am not at home.

MAID [*in the doorway*]: A lady to see you, ma'am—a stranger.

NORA: Ask her to come in.

MAID: [*to* HELMER] The doctor came at the same time, sir.

HELMER: Did he go straight into my room?

MAID: Yes sir.

[HELMER *goes into his room. The* MAID *ushers in* MRS. LINDE, *who is in travelling dress, and shuts the door.*]

MRS. LINDE [*in a dejected and timid voice*]: How do you do, Nora?

NORA [*doubtfully*]: How do you do—

MRS. LINDE: You don't recognise me, I suppose.

NORA: No, I don't know—yes, to be sure, I seem to—[*suddenly*] Yes! Christine! Is it really you?

MRS. LINDE: Yes, it is I.

NORA: Christine! To think of my not recognising you! And yet how could I—[*in a gentle voice*] How you have altered, Christine!

MRS. LINDE: Yes, I have indeed. In nine, ten long years—

NORA: Is it so long since we met? I suppose it is. The last eight years have been a happy time for me, I can tell you. And so now you have come into the town, and have taken this long journey in winter—that was plucky of you.

MRS. LINDE: I arrived by steamer this morning.

NORA: To have some fun at Christmas-time, of course. How delightful! We will have such fun together! But take off your things. You are not cold, I hope. [*helps her*] Now we will sit down by the stove, and be cosy. No, take this arm-chair; I will sit here in the rocking-chair. [*takes her hands*] Now you look like your old self again; it was only the first moment—You are a little paler, Christine, and perhaps a little thinner.

MRS. LINDE: And much, much older, Nora.

NORA: Perhaps a little older; very, very little; certainly not much. [*stops suddenly and speaks seriously*] What a thoughtless creature I am, chattering away like this. My poor, dear Christine, do forgive me.

MRS. LINDE: What do you mean, Nora?

NORA [*gently*]: Poor Christine, you are a widow.

MRS. LINDE: Yes; it is three years ago now.

NORA: Yes, I knew; I saw it in the papers. I assure you, Christine, I meant ever so often to write to you at the time, but I always put it off and something always prevented me.

MRS. LINDE: I quite understand, dear.

NORA: It was very bad of me, Christine. Poor thing, how you must have suffered. And he left you nothing?

MRS. LINDE: No.

NORA: And no children?

MRS. LINDE: No.

NORA: Nothing at all, then?

MRS. LINDE: Not even any sorrow or grief to live upon.

NORA [*looking incredulously at her*]: But, Christine, is that possible?

MRS. LINDE [*smiles sadly and strokes her hair*]: It sometimes happens, Nora.

NORA: So you are quite alone. How dreadfully sad that must be. I have three lovely children. You can't see them just now, for they are out with their nurse. But now you must tell me all about it.

MRS. LINDE: No, no; I want to hear you.

NORA: No, you must begin. I mustn't be selfish to-day; to-day I must only think of your affairs. But there is one thing I must tell you. Do you know we have just had a great piece of good luck?

MRS. LINDE: No, what is it?

NORA: Just fancy, my husband has been made manager of the Bank!

MRS. LINDE: Your husband? What good luck!

NORA: Yes, tremendous! A barrister's profession is such an uncertain thing, especially if he won't undertake unsavoury cases; and naturally Torvald has never been willing to do that, and I quite agree with him. You may imagine how pleased we are! He is to take up his work in the Bank at the New Year, and then he will have a big salary and lots of commissions. For the future we can live quite differently—we can do just as we like. I feel so relieved and so happy, Christine! It will be splendid to have heaps of money and not need to have any anxiety, won't it?

MRS. LINDE: Yes, anyhow I think it would be delightful to have what one needs.

NORA: No, not only what one needs, but heaps and heaps of money.

MRS. LINDE [*smiling*]: Nora, Nora haven't you learnt sense yet? In our schooldays you were a great spendthrift.

NORA [*laughing*]: Yes, that is what Torvald says now. [*wags her finger at her*] But "Nora, Nora" is not so silly as you think. We have not been in a position for me to waste money. We have both had to work.

MRS. LINDE: You too?

NORA: Yes; odds and ends, needlework, crochet-work, embroidery, and that kind of thing. [*dropping her voice*] And other things as well. You know Torvald left his office when we were married? There was no prospect of promotion there, and he had to try and earn more than before. But during the first year he overworked himself dreadfully. You see, he had to make money every way he could, and he worked early and late; but he couldn't stand it, and fell dreadfully ill, and the doctors said it was necessary for him to go south.

MRS. LINDE: You spent a whole year in Italy didn't you?

NORA: Yes. It was no easy matter to get away, I can tell you. It was just as Ivar was born; but naturally we had to go. It was a wonderfully beautiful journey, and it saved Torvald's life. But it cost a tremendous lot of money, Christine.

MRS. LINDE: So I should think.

NORA: It cost about two hundred and fifty pounds. That's a lot, isn't it?

MRS. LINDE: Yes, and in emergencies like that it is lucky to have the money.

NORA: I ought to tell you that we had it from papa.

MRS. LINDE: Oh, I see. It was just about that time that he died, wasn't it?

NORA: Yes; and, just think of it, I couldn't go and nurse him. I was expecting little Ivar's birth every day and I had my poor sick Torvald to look after. My dear, kind father—I never saw him again, Christine. That was the saddest time I have known since our marriage.

MRS. LINDE: I know how fond you were of him. And then you went off to Italy?

NORA: Yes; you see we had money then, and the doctors insisted on our going, so we started a month later.

MRS. LINDE: And your husband came back quite well?

NORA: As sound as a bell!

MRS. LINDE: But—the doctor?

NORA: What doctor?

MRS. LINDE: I thought your maid said the gentleman who arrived here just as I did was the doctor?

NORA: Yes, that was Doctor Rank, but he doesn't come here professionally. He is our greatest friend, and comes in at least once every day. No, Torvald has not had an hour's illness since then, and our children are strong and healthy and so am I. [*jumps up and claps her hands*] Christine! Christine! it's good to be alive and happy!—But how horrid of me; I am talking of nothing but my own affairs. [*sits on a stool near her, and rests her arms on her knees*] You mustn't be angry with me. Tell me, is it really true that you did not love your husband? Why did you marry him?

MRS. LINDE: My mother was alive then, and was bedridden and helpless, and I had to provide for my two younger brothers; so I did not think I was justified in refusing his offer.

NORA: No, perhaps you were quite right. He was rich at that time, then?

MRS. LINDE: I believe he was quite well off. But his business was a precarious one; and, when he died, it all went to pieces and there was nothing left.

NORA: And then?—

MRS. LINDE: Well, I had to turn my hand to anything I could find—first a small shop, then a small school, and so on. The last three years have seemed like one long working-day, with no rest. Now it is at an end, Nora. My poor mother needs me no more, for she is gone; and the boys do not need me either; they have got situations and can shift for themselves.

NORA: What a relief you must feel it—

MRS. LINDE: No, indeed; I only feel my life unspeakably empty. No one to live for any more. [*gets up restlessly*] That was why I could not stand the life in my little backwater any longer. I hope it may be easier here to find something which will busy me and occupy my thoughts. If only I could have the good luck to get some regular work—office work of some kind—

NORA: But, Christine, that is so frightfully tiring, and you look tired out now. You had far better go away to some watering-place.

MRS. LINDE [*walking to the window*]: I have no father to give me money for a journey, Nora.

NORA [*rising*]: Oh, don't be angry with me.

MRS. LINDE [*going up to her*]: It is you that must not be angry with me, dear. The worst of a position like mine is that it makes one so bitter. No one to work for, and yet obliged to be always on the look-out for chances. One must live, and so one becomes selfish. When you told me of the happy turn your fortunes have taken—you will hardly believe it—I was delighted not so much on your account as on my own.

NORA: How do you mean?—Oh, I understand. You mean that perhaps Torvald could get you something to do.

MRS. LINDE: Yes, that was what I was thinking of.

NORA: He must, Christine. Just leave it to me; I will broach the subject very cleverly—I will think of something that will please him very much. It will make me so happy to be of some use to you.

MRS. LINDE: How kind you are, Nora, to be so anxious to help me! It is doubly kind in you, for you know so little of the burdens and troubles of life.

NORA: I—? I know so little of them?

MRS. LINDE [*smiling*]: My dear! Small household cares and that sort of thing!—You are a child, Nora.

NORA [*tosses her head and crosses the stage*]: You ought not to be so superior.

MRS. LINDE: No?

NORA: You are just like the others. They all think that I am incapable of anything really serious—

MRS. LINDE: Come, come—

NORA: —that I have gone through nothing in this world of cares.

MRS. LINDE: But, my dear Nora, you have just told me all your troubles.

NORA: Pooh!—those were trifles. [*lowering her voice*] I have not told you the important thing.

MRS. LINDE: The important thing? What do you mean?

NORA: You look down upon me altogether, Christine—but you ought not to. You are proud, aren't you, of having worked so hard and so long for your mother?

MRS. LINDE: Indeed, I don't look down on any one. But it is true that I am both proud and glad to think that I was privileged to make the end of my mother's life almost free from care.

NORA: And you are proud to think of what you have done for your brothers.

MRS. LINDE: I think I have the right to be.

NORA: I think so, too. But now, listen to this; I too have something to be proud of
          and glad of.

MRS. LINDE: I have no doubt you have. But what do you refer to?

NORA: Speak low. Suppose Torvald were to hear! He mustn't on any account—no
          one in the world must know, Christine, except you.

MRS. LINDE: But what is it?

NORA: Come here [*pulls her down on the sofa beside her*] Now I will show you that
          I too have something to be proud and glad of. It was I who saved Tor-
          vald's life.

MRS. LINDE: "Saved"? How?

NORA: I told you about our trip to Italy. Torvald would never have recovered if he
          had not gone there—

MRS. LINDE: Yes, but your father gave you the necessary funds.

NORA [*smiling*]: Yes, that is what Torvald and all the others think, but—

MRS. LINDE: But—

NORA: Papa didn't give us a shilling. It was I who procured the money.

MRS. LINDE: You? All that large sum?

NORA: Two hundred and fifty pounds. What do you think of that?

MRS. LINDE: But, Nora, how could you possibly do it? Did you win a prize in the
          Lottery?

NORA [*contemptuously*]: In the Lottery? There would have been no credit in that.

MRS. LINDE: But where did you get it from, then?

NORA [*humming and smiling with an air of mystery*]: Hm, hm! Aha!

MRS. LINDE: Because you couldn't have borrowed it.

NORA: Couldn't I? Why not?

MRS. LINDE: No, a wife cannot borrow without her husband's consent.

NORA [*tossing her head*]: Oh, if it is a wife who has any head for business—a wife
          who has the wit to be a little bit clever—

MRS. LINDE: I don't understand it at all, Nora.

NORA: There is no need you should. I never said I had borrowed the money. I may
          have got it some other way. [*lies back on the sofa*] Perhaps I got it from
          some other admirer. When anyone is as attractive as I am—

MRS. LINDE: You are a mad creature.

NORA: Now, you know you're full of curiosity, Christine.

MRS. LINDE: Listen to me, Nora dear. Haven't you been a little bit imprudent?

NORA [*sits up straight*]: Is it imprudent to save your husband's life?

MRS. LINDE: It seems to me imprudent, without his knowledge, to—

NORA: But it was absolutely necessary that he should not know! My goodness,
          can't you understand that? It was necessary he should have no idea what
          a dangerous condition he was in. It was to me that the doctors came and
          said that his life was in danger, and that the only thing to save him was
          to live in the south. Do you suppose I didn't try, first of all, to get what I
          wanted as if it were for myself? I told him how much I should love to
          travel abroad like other young wives; I tried tears and entreaties with
          him; I told him that he ought to remember the condition I was in, and
          that he ought to be kind and indulgent to me; I even hinted that he might
          raise a loan. That nearly made him angry, Christine. He said I was
          thoughtless, and that it was his duty as my husband not to indulge me in
          my whims and caprices—as I believe he called them. Very well I thought,
          you must be saved—and that was how I came to devise a way out of the
          difficulty—

MRS. LINDE: And did your husband never get to know from your father that the money had not come from him?

NORA: No, never. Papa died just at that time. I had meant to let him into the secret and beg him never to reveal it. But he was so ill then—alas, there never was any need to tell him.

MRS. LINDE: And since then have you never told your secret to your husband?

NORA: Good Heavens, no! How could you think so? A man who has such strong opinions about these things! And besides, how painful and humiliating it would be for Torvald, with his manly independence, to know that he owed me anything! It would upset our mutual relations altogether; our beautiful happy home would no longer be what it is now.

MRS. LINDE: Do you mean never to tell him about it?

NORA [*meditatively, and with a half smile*]: Yes—some day, perhaps, after many years, when I am no longer as nice-looking as I am now. Don't laugh at me! I mean of course, when Torvald is no longer as devoted to me as he is now; when my dancing and dressing-up and reciting have palled on him; then it may be a good thing to have something in reserve— [*breaking off*] What nonsense! That time will never come. Now, what do you think of my great secret, Christine? Do you still think I am of no use? I can tell you, too, that this affair has caused me a lot of worry. It has been by no means easy for me to meet my engagements punctually. I may tell you that there is something that is called, in business, quarterly interest, and another thing called payment in installments, and it is always so dreadfully difficult to manage them. I have had to save a little here and there, where I could, you understand. I have not been able to put aside much from my housekeeping money, for Torvald must have a good table. I couldn't let my children be shabbily dressed; I have felt obliged to use up all he gave me for them, the sweet little darlings!

MRS. LINDE: So it has all had to come out of your own necessaries of life, poor Nora?

NORA: Of course. Besides, I was the one responsible for it. Whenever Torvald has given me the money for new dresses and such things, I have never spent more than half of it; I have always bought the simplest and cheapest things. Thank Heaven, any clothes look well on me, and so Torvald has never noticed it. But it was often very hard on me, Christine—because it is delightful to be really well dressed, isn't it?

MRS. LINDE: Quite so.

NORA: Well, then I have found other ways of earning money. Last winter I was lucky enough to get a lot of copying to do; so I locked myself up and sat writing every evening until quite late at night. Many a time I was desperately tired; but all the same it was a tremendous pleasure to sit there working and earning money. It was like being a man.

MRS. LINDE: How much have you been able to pay off in that way?

NORA: I can't tell you exactly. You see, it is very difficult to keep an account of a business matter of that kind. I only know that I have paid every penny that I could scrape together. Many a time I was at my wit's end. [*smiles*] Then I used to sit here and imagine that a rich old gentleman had fallen in love with me—

MRS. LINDE: What! Who was it?

NORA: Be quiet!—that he had died; and that when his will was opened it contained, written in big letters, the instruction: "The lovely Mrs. Nora Helmer is to have all I possess paid over to her at once in cash."

MRS. LINDE: But, my dear Nora—who could the man be?

NORA: Good gracious, can't you understand? There was no old gentleman at all; it was only something that I used to sit here and imagine, when I couldn't think of any way of procuring money. But it's all the same now; the tiresome old person can stay where he is, as far as I am concerned; I don't care about him or his will either, for I am free from care now. [*jumps up*] My goodness, it's delightful to think of, Christine! Free from care! To be able to be free from care, quite free from care; to be able to play and romp with the children; to be able to keep the house beautifully and have everything just as Torvald likes it! And, think of it, soon the spring will come and the big blue sky! Perhaps we shall be able to take a little trip—perhaps I shall see the sea again! Oh, it's a wonderful thing to be alive and be happy. [*A bell is heard in the hall.*]

MRS. LINDE [*rising*]: There is the bell; perhaps I had better go.

NORA: No, don't go; no one will come in here; it is sure to be for Torvald.

SERVANT [*at the hall door*]: Excuse me, ma'am—there is a gentleman to see the master, and as the doctor is with him—

NORA: Who is it?

KROGSTAD [*at the door*]: It is I, Mrs. Helmer. [*Mrs. Linde starts, trembles, and turns to the window.*]

NORA [*takes a step towards him, and speaks in a strained, low voice*]: You? What is it? What do you want to see my husband about?

KROGSTAD: Bank business—in a way. I have a small post in the Bank, and I hear your husband is to be our chief now—

NORA: Then it is—

KROGSTAD: Nothing but dry business matters, Mrs. Helmer; absolutely nothing else.

NORA: Be so good as to go into the study, then. [*She bows indifferently to him and shuts the door into the hall; then comes back and makes up the fire in the stove.*]

MRS. LINDE: Nora—who was that man?

NORA: A lawyer, of the name of Krogstad.

MRS. LINDE: Then it really was he.

NORA: Do you know the man?

MRS. LINDE: I used to—many years ago. At one time he was a solicitor's clerk in our town.

NORA: Yes, he was.

MRS. LINDE: He is greatly altered.

NORA: He made a very unhappy marriage.

MRS. LINDE: He is a widower now, isn't he?

NORA: With several children. There now, it is burning up.

[*Shuts the door of the stove and moves the rocking-chair aside.*]

MRS. LINDE: They say he carries on various kinds of business.

NORA: Really! Perhaps he does; I don't know anything about it. But don't let us think of business; it is so tiresome.

DOCTOR RANK [*comes out of* HELMER'S *study. before he shuts the door he calls to him*]: No, my dear fellow, I won't disturb you; I would rather go in to your wife for a little while. [*shuts the door and sees* MRS. LINDE] I beg your pardon; I am afraid I am disturbing you too.

NORA: No, not at all. [*introducing him*] Doctor Rank, Mrs. Linde.

RANK: I have often heard Mrs. Linde's name mentioned here. I think I passed you on the stairs when I arrived, Mrs. Linde?

MRS. LINDE: Yes, I go up very slowly; I can't manage stairs well.

RANK: Ah! some slight internal weakness?

MRS. LINDE: No, the fact is I have been overworking myself.

RANK: Nothing more than that? Then I suppose you have come to town to amuse yourself with our entertainments?

MRS. LINDE: I have come to look for work.

RANK: Is that a good cure for overwork?

MRS. LINDE: One must live, Doctor Rank.

RANK: Yes, the general opinion seems to be that it is necessary.

NORA: Look here, Doctor Rank—you know you want to live.

RANK: Certainly. However wretched I may feel, I want to prolong the agony as long as possible. All my patients are like that. And so are those who are morally diseased; one of them, and a bad case too, is at this very moment with Helmer—

MRS. LINDE [*sadly*]: Ah!

NORA: Whom do you mean?

RANK: A lawyer of the name of Krogstad, a fellow you don't know at all. He suffers from a diseased moral character, Mrs. Helmer; but even he began talking of its being highly important that he should live.

NORA: Did he? What did he want to speak to Torvald about?

RANK: I have no idea; I only heard that it was something about the Bank.

NORA: I didn't know this—what's his name—Krogstad had anything to do with the Bank.

RANK: Yes, he has some sort of appointment there. [*to* MRS. LINDE] I don't know whether you find also in your part of the world that there are certain people who go zealously snuffing about to smell out moral corruption, and, as soon as they have found some, put the person concerned into some lucrative position where they can keep their eye on him. Healthy natures are left out in the cold.

MRS. LINDE: Still I think the sick are those who most need taking care of.

RANK [*shrugging his shoulders*]: Yes, there you are. That is the sentiment that is turning Society into a sickhouse.

[NORA, *who has been absorbed in her thoughts, breaks out into smothered laughter and claps her hands.*]

RANK: Why do you laugh at that? Have you any notion what Society really is?

NORA: What do I care about tiresome Society? I am laughing at something quite different, something extremely amusing. Tell me, Doctor Rank, are all the people who are employed in the Bank dependent on Torvald now?

RANK: Is that what you find so extremely amusing?

NORA [*smiling and humming*]: That's my affair! [*walking about the room*] It's perfectly glorious to think that we have—that Torvald has so much power over so many people. [*takes the packet from her pocket*] Doctor Rank, what do you say to a macaroon?

RANK: What, macaroons? I thought they were forbidden here.

NORA: Yes, but these are some Christine gave me.

MRS. LINDE: What! I?—

NORA: Oh, well, don't be alarmed! You couldn't know that Torvald had forbidden them. I must tell you that he is afraid they will spoil my teeth. But, bah!— once in a way—That's so, isn't it, Doctor Rank? By your leave? [*puts a macaroon into his mouth*] You must have one too, Christine. And I shall have one, just a little one—or at most two. [*walking about*] I am tremendously happy. There is just one thing in the world now that I should dearly love to do.

RANK: Well, what is that?

NORA: It's something I should dearly love to say, if Torvald could hear me.

RANK: Well, why can't you say it?

NORA: No, I daren't; it's so shocking.

MRS. LINDE: Shocking?

RANK: Well, I should not advise you to say it. Still, with us you might. What is it you would so much like to say if Torvald could hear you?

NORA: I should just love to say—Well, I'm damned!

RANK: Are you mad?

MRS. LINDE: Nora, dear—!

RANK: Say it, here he is!

NORA [*hiding the packet*]: Hush! Hush! Hush!

[HELMER *comes out of his room, with his coat over his arm and his hat in his hands.*]

NORA: Well, Torvald dear, have you got rid of him?

HELMER: Yes, he has just gone.

NORA: Let me introduce you—this is Christine, who has come to town.

HELMER: Christine—? Excuse me, but I don't know—

NORA: Mrs. Linde, dear; Christine Linde.

HELMER: Of course. A school friend of my wife's, I presume?

MRS. LINDE: Yes, we have known each other since then.

NORA: And just think, she has taken a long journey in order to see you.

HELMER: What do you mean?

MRS. LINDE: No, really, I—

NORA: Christine is tremendously clever at book-keeping, and she is frightfully anxious to work under some clever man, so as to perfect herself—

HELMER: Very sensible, Mrs. Linde.

NORA: And when she heard you had been appointed manager of the Bank—the news was telegraphed, you know—she travelled here as quick as she could. Torvald, I am sure you will be able to do something for Christine, for my sake, won't you?

HELMER: Well, it is not altogether impossible. I presume you are a widow, Mrs. Linde?

MRS. LINDE: Yes.

HELMER: And have had some experience of book-keeping?

MRS. LINDE: Yes, a fair amount.

HELMER: Ah! well, it's very likely I may be able to find something for you—

NORA [*clapping her hands*]: What did I tell you? What did I tell you?

HELMER: You have just come at a fortunate moment, Mrs. Linde.

MRS. LINDE: How am I to thank you?

HELMER: There is no need. [*puts on his coat*] But to-day you must excuse me—

RANK: Wait a minute; I will come with you.

[*Brings his fur coat from the hall and warms it at the fire.*]

NORA: Don't be long away, Torvald dear.

HELMER: About an hour, not more.

NORA: Are you going too, Christine?

MRS. LINDE [*putting on her cloak*]: Yes, I must go and look for a room.

HELMER: Oh, well then, we can walk down the street together.

NORA [*helping her*]: What a pity it is we are so short of space here: I am afraid it is impossible for us—

MRS. LINDE: Please don't think of it! Good-bye, Nora dear, and many thanks.

NORA: Good-bye for the present. Of course you will come back this evening. And you too, Dr. Rank. What do you say? If you are well enough? Oh, you must be! Wrap yourself up well.

[*They go to the door all talking together. Children's voices are heard on the staircase.*]

NORA: There they are. There they are! [*She runs to open the door. The* NURSE *comes in with the children.*] Come in! Come in! [*stoops and kisses them*] Oh, you sweet blessings! Look at them, Christine! Aren't they darlings?

RANK: Don't let us stand here in the draught.

HELMER: Come along, Mrs. Linde; the place will only be bearable for a mother now!

[RANK, HELMER *and* MRS. LINDE *go downstairs. The* NURSE *comes forward with the children;* NORA *shuts the hall door.*]

NORA: How fresh and well you look! Such red cheeks!—like apples and roses. [*The children all talk at once while she speaks to them.*] Have you had great fun? That's splendid! What, you pulled both Emmy and Bob along on the sledge?— both at once?—that was good. You are a clever boy, Ivar. Let me take her for a little, Anne. My sweet little baby doll! [*takes the baby from the* MAID *and dances it up and down*] Yes, yes, mother will dance with Bob too. What! Have you been snowballing? I wish I had been there too! No, no, I will take their things off, Anne; please let me do it, it is such fun. Go in now, you look half frozen. There is some coffee for you on the stove.

[*The* NURSE *goes into the room on the left.* NORA *takes off the children's things and throws them about, while they all talk to her at once.*]

NORA: Really! Did a big dog run after you? But it didn't bite you? No, dogs don't bite nice little dolly children. You mustn't look at the parcels, Ivar. What are they? Ah, I daresay you would like to know. No, no—it's something nasty! Come, let us have a game! What shall we play at? Hide and Seek? Yes, we'll play Hide and Seek. Bob shall hide first. Must I hide? Very well, I'll hide first.

[*She and the children laugh and shout, and romp in and out of the room; at last* NORA *hides under the table, the children rush in and look for her, but do not see her; they hear her smothered laughter, run to the table, lift up the cloth and find her. Shouts of laughter. She crawls forward and pretends to frighten them. Fresh laughter. Meanwhile there has been a knock at the hall door, but none of them has noticed it. The door is half opened, and* KROGSTAD *appears. He waits a little; the game goes on.*]

KROGSTAD: Excuse me, Mrs. Helmer.

NORA [*with a stifled cry, turns round and gets up on to her knees*]: Ah! what do you want?

KROGSTAD: Excuse me, the outer door was ajar; I suppose someone forgot to shut it.

NORA [*rising*]: My husband is out, Mr. Krogstad.

KROGSTAD: I know that.

NORA: What do you want here, then?

KROGSTAD: A word with you.

NORA: With me?—[*to the children, gently*] Go in to nurse. What? No, the strange man won't do mother any harm. When he has gone we will have another game. [*She takes the children into the room on the left, and shuts the door after them.*] You want to speak to me?

KROGSTAD: Yes, I do.

NORA: To-day? It is not the first of the month yet.

KROGSTAD: No, it is Christmas Eve, and it will depend on yourself what sort of a Christmas you will spend.

NORA: What do you want? To-day it is absolutely impossible for me—

KROGSTAD: We won't talk about that till later on. This is something different. I presume you can give me a moment?

NORA: Yes—yes, I can—although—

KROGSTAD: Good. I was in Olsen's Restaurant and saw your husband going down the street—

NORA: Yes?

KROGSTAD: With a lady.

NORA: What then?

KROGSTAD: May I make so bold as to ask if it was a Mrs. Linde?

NORA: It was.

KROGSTAD: Just arrived in town?

NORA: Yes, to-day.

KROGSTAD: She is a great friend of yours, isn't she?

NORA: She is. But I don't see—

KROGSTAD: I knew her too, once upon a time.

NORA: I am aware of that.

KROGSTAD: Are you? So you know all about it; I thought as much. Then I can ask you, without beating about the bush—is Mrs. Linde to have an appointment in the Bank?

NORA: What right have you to question me, Mr. Krogstad?—You, one of my husband's subordinates! But since you ask, you shall know. Yes, Mrs. Linde *is* to have an appointment. And it was I who pleaded her cause, Mr. Krogstad, let me tell you that.

KROGSTAD: I was right in what I thought, then.

NORA [*walking up and down the stage*]: Sometimes one has a tiny little bit of influence, I should hope. Because one is a woman, it does not necessarily follow that—. When anyone is in a subordinate position, Mr. Krogstad, they should really be careful to avoid offending anyone who—who—

KROGSTAD: Who has influence?

NORA: Exactly.

KROGSTAD [*changing his tone*]: Mrs. Helmer, you will be so good as to use your influence on my behalf.

NORA: What? What do you mean?

KROGSTAD: You will be so kind as to see that I am allowed to keep my subordinate position in the Bank.

NORA: What do you mean by that? Who proposes to take your post away from you?

KROGSTAD: Oh, there is no necessity to keep up the pretence of ignorance. I can quite understand that your friend is not very anxious to expose herself to the chance of rubbing shoulders with me; and I quite understand, too, whom I have to thank for being turned out.

NORA: But I assure you—

KROGSTAD: Very likely; but, to come to the point, the time has come when I should advise you to use your influence to prevent that.

NORA: But, Mr. Krogstad, I *have* no influence.

KROGSTAD: Haven't you? I thought you said yourself just now—

NORA: Naturally I did not mean you to put that construction on it. I! What should make you think I have any influence of that kind with my husband?

KROGSTAD: Oh, I have known your husband from our student days. I don't suppose he is any more unassailable than other husbands.

NORA: If you speak slightingly of my husband, I shall turn you out of the house.

KROGSTAD: You are bold, Mrs. Helmer.

NORA: I am not afraid of you any longer. As soon as the New Year comes, I shall in a very short time be free of the whole thing.

KROGSTAD [*controlling himself*]: Listen to me, Mrs. Helmer. If necessary, I am prepared to fight for my small post in the Bank as if I were fighting for my life.

NORA: So it seems.

KROGSTAD: It is not only for the sake of the money; indeed, that weighs least with me in the matter. There is another reason—well, I may as well tell you. My position is this. I daresay you know, like everybody else, that once, many years ago, I was guilty of an indiscretion.

NORA: I think I have heard something of the kind.

KROGSTAD: The matter never came into court; but every way seemed to be closed to me after that. So I took to the business that you know of. I had to do something; and, honestly, I don't think I've been one of the worst. But now I must cut myself free from all that. My sons are growing up; for their sake I must try and win back as much respect as I can in the town. This post in the Bank was like the first step up for me—and now your husband is going to kick me downstairs again into the mud.

NORA: But you must believe me, Mr. Krogstad; it is not in my power to help you at all.

KROGSTAD: Then it is because you haven't the will; but I have means to compel you.

NORA: You don't mean that you will tell my husband that I owe you money?

KROGSTAD: Hm!—suppose I were to tell him?

NORA: It would be perfectly infamous of you. [*sobbing*] To think of his learning my secret, which has been my joy and pride, in such an ugly, clumsy way— that he should learn it from you! And it would put me in a horribly disagreeable position—

KROGSTAD: Only disagreeable?

NORA [*impetuously*]: Well, do it, then!—and it will be the worse for you. My husband will see for himself what a blackguard you are, and you certainly won't keep your post then.

KROGSTAD: I asked you if it was only a disagreeable scene at home that you were afraid of?

NORA: If my husband does get to know of it, of course he will at once pay you what is still owing, and we shall have nothing more to do with you.

KROGSTAD [*coming a step nearer*]: Listen to me, Mrs. Helmer. Either you have a very bad memory or you know very little of business. I shall be obliged to remind you of a few details.

NORA: What do you mean?

KROGSTAD: When your husband was ill, you came to me to borrow two hundred and fifty pounds.

NORA: I didn't know any one else to go to.

KROGSTAD: I promised to get you that amount—

NORA: Yes, and you did so.

KROGSTAD: I promised to get you that amount, on certain conditions. Your mind
       was so taken up with your husband's illness, and you were so anxious to
       get the money for your journey, that you seem to have paid no attention
       to the conditions of our bargain. Therefore it will not be amiss if I remind
       you of them. Now, I promised to get the money on the security of a bond
       which I drew up.

NORA: Yes, and which I signed.

KROGSTAD: Good. But below your signature there were a few lines constituting your
       father a surety for the money; those lines your father should have signed.

NORA: Should? He did sign them.

KROGSTAD: I had left the date blank; that is to say your father should himself have
       inserted the date on which he signed the paper. Do you remember that?

NORA: Yes, I think I remember—

KROGSTAD: Then I gave you the bond to send by post to your father. Is that not so?

NORA: Yes.

KROGSTAD: And you naturally did so at once, because five or six days afterwards you
       brought me the bond with your father's signature. And then I gave you the
       money.

NORA: Well, haven't I been paying it off regularly?

KROGSTAD: Fairly so, yes. But—to come back to the matter in hand—that must have
       been a very trying time for you, Mrs. Helmer?

NORA: It was, indeed.

KROGSTAD: Your father was very ill, wasn't he?

NORA: He was very near his end.

KROGSTAD: And died soon afterwards?

NORA: Yes.

KROGSTAD: Tell me, Mrs. Helmer, can you by any chance remember what day your
       father died?—on what day of the month, I mean.

NORA: Papa died on the 29th of September.

KROGSTAD: That is correct; I have ascertained it for myself. And, as that is so, there is
       a discrepancy [*taking a paper from his pocket*] which I cannot account for.

NORA: What discrepancy? I don't know—

KROGSTAD: The discrepancy consists, Mrs. Helmer, in the fact that your father signed
       this bond three days after his death.

NORA: What do you mean? I don't understand—

KROGSTAD: Your father died on the 29th of September. But, look here; your father
       has dated his signature the 2nd of October. It is a discrepancy, isn't it?
       [NORA *is silent.*] Can you explain it to me? [NORA *is still silent.*] It is a remark-
       able thing, too, that the words "2nd of October," as well as the year, are
       not written in your father's handwriting but in one that I think I know.
       Well, of course it can be explained; your father may have forgotten to date
       his signature, and someone else may have dated it haphazard before they
       knew of his death. There is no harm in that. It all depends on the signa-
       ture of the name; and *that* is genuine, I suppose, Mrs. Helmer? It was your
       father himself who signed his name here?

NORA [*after a short pause, throws her head up and looks defiantly at him*]: No, it was
       not. It was I that wrote papa's name.

KROGSTAD: Are you aware that is a dangerous confession?

NORA: In what way? You shall have your money soon.

KROGSTAD: Let me ask you a question; why did you not send the paper to your father?

NORA: It was impossible; papa was so ill. If I had asked him for his signature, I should have had to tell him what the money was to be used for; and when he was so ill himself I couldn't tell him that my husband's life was in danger—it was impossible.

KROGSTAD: It would have been better for you if you had given up your trip abroad.

NORA: No, that was impossible. That trip was to save my husband's life; I couldn't give that up.

KROGSTAD: But did it never occur to you that you were committing a fraud on me?

NORA: I couldn't take that into account; I didn't trouble myself about you at all. I couldn't bear you, because you put so many heartless difficulties in my way, although you knew what a dangerous condition my husband was in.

KROGSTAD: Mrs. Helmer, you evidently do not realise clearly what it is that you have been guilty of. But I can assure you that my one false step, which lost me all my reputation, was nothing more or nothing worse than what you have done.

NORA: You? Do you ask me to believe that you were brave enough to run a risk to save your wife's life?

KROGSTAD: The law cares nothing about motives.

NORA: Then it must be a very foolish law.

KROGSTAD: Foolish or not, it is the law by which you will be judged, if I produce this paper in court.

NORA: I don't believe it. Is a daughter not to be allowed to spare her dying father anxiety and care? Is a wife not to be allowed to save her husband's life? I don't know much about law; but I am certain that there must be laws permitting such things as that. Have you no knowledge of such laws—you who are a lawyer? You must be a very poor lawyer, Mr. Krogstad.

KROGSTAD: Maybe. But matters of business—such business as you and I have had together—do you think I don't understand that? Very well. Do as you please. But let me tell you this—if I lose my position a second time, you shall lose yours with me.

[*He bows, and goes out through the hall.*]

NORA [*appears buried in thought for a short time, then tosses her head*]: Nonsense! Trying to frighten me like that!—I am not so silly as he thinks. [*begins to busy herself putting the children's things in order*] And yet—? No, it's impossible! I did it for love's sake.

THE CHILDREN [*in the doorway on the left*]: Mother, the stranger man has gone out through the gate.

NORA: Yes, dears, I know. But, don't tell anyone about the stranger man. Do you hear? Not even papa.

CHILDREN: No, mother; but will you come and play again?

NORA: No, no—not now.

CHILDREN: But, mother, you promised us.

NORA: Yes, but I can't now. Run away in; I have such a lot to do. Run away in, my sweet little darlings. [*She gets them into the room by degrees and shuts the door on them; then sits down on the sofa, takes up a piece of needlework and sews a few stitches, but soon stops.*] No! [*throws down the work, gets up, goes to the hall door and calls out*] Helen! bring the Tree in. [*goes to the table on the left, opens a drawer, and stops again*] No, no! it is quite impossible!

MAID [*coming in with the Tree*]: Where shall I put it, ma'am?

NORA: Here, in the middle of the floor.

MAID: Shall I get you anything else?

NORA: No, thank you. I have all I want.

[*Exit* MAID.]

NORA [*begins dressing the tree*]: A candle here—and flowers here—. The horrible man! It's all nonsense—there's nothing wrong. The Tree shall be splendid! I will do everything I can think of to please you, Torvald!—I will sing for you, dance for you— [HELMER *comes in with some papers under his arm*] Oh! are you back already?

HELMER: Yes. Has anyone been here?

NORA: Here? No.

HELMER: That is strange. I saw Krogstad going out of the gate.

NORA: Did you? Oh yes, I forgot, Krogstad was here for a moment.

HELMER: Nora, I can see from your manner that he has been here begging you to say a good word for him.

NORA: Yes.

HELMER: And you were to appear to do it of your own accord; you were to conceal from me the fact of his having been here; didn't he beg that of you too?

NORA: Yes, Torvald, but—

HELMER: Nora, Nora, and you would be a party to that sort of thing? To have any talk with a man like that, and give him any sort of promise? And to tell me a lie into the bargain?

NORA: A lie—?

HELMER: Didn't you tell me no one had been here? [*shakes his finger at her*] My little song-bird must never do that again. A song-bird must have a clean beak to chirp with—no false notes! [*puts his arm round her waist*] That is so, isn't it? Yes, I am sure it is. [*lets her go*] We will say no more about it. [*sits down by the stove*] How warm and snug it is here!

[*Turns over his papers.*]

NORA [*after a short pause, during which she busies herself with the Christmas Tree*]: Torvald!

HELMER: Yes.

NORA: I am looking forward tremendously to the fancy dress ball at the Stenborgs' the day after to-morrow.

HELMER: And I am tremendously curious to see what you are going to surprise me with.

NORA: It was very silly of me to want to do that.

HELMER: What do you mean?

NORA: I can't hit upon anything that will do; everything I think of seems so silly and insignificant.

HELMER: Does my little Nora acknowledge that at last?

NORA [*standing behind his chair with her arms on the back of it*]: Are you very busy, Torvald?

HELMER: Well—

NORA: What are all those papers?

HELMER: Bank business.

NORA: Already?

HELMER: I have got authority from the retiring manager to undertake the necessary changes in the staff and in the rearrangement of the work; and I must make use of the Christmas week for that, so as to have everything in order for the new year.

NORA: Then that was why this poor Krogstad—

HELMER: Hm!

NORA [*leans against the back of his chair and strokes his hair*]: If you hadn't been so busy I should have asked you a tremendously big favour, Torvald.

HELMER: What is that? Tell me.

NORA: There is no one has such good taste as you. And I do so want to look nice at the fancy-dress ball. Torvald, couldn't you take me in hand and decide what I shall go as, and what sort of a dress I shall wear?

HELMER: Aha! so my obstinate little woman is obliged to get someone to come to her rescue?

NORA: Yes, Torvald, I can't get along a bit without your help.

HELMER: Very well, I will think it over, we shall manage to hit upon something.

NORA: That is nice of you. [*Goes to the Christmas Tree. A short pause.*] How pretty the red flowers look—. But, tell me, was it really something very bad that this Krogstad was guilty of?

HELMER: He forged someone's name. Have you any idea what that means?

NORA: Isn't it possible that he was driven to do it by necessity?

HELMER: Yes; or, as in so many cases, by imprudence. I am not so heartless as to condemn a man altogether because of a single false step of that kind.

NORA: No you wouldn't, would you, Torvald?

HELMER: Many a man has been able to retrieve his character, if he has openly confessed his fault and taken his punishment.

NORA: Punishment—?

HELMER: But Krogstad did nothing of that sort; he got himself out of it by a cunning trick, and that is why he has gone under altogether.

NORA: But do you think it would—?

HELMER: Just think how a guilty man like that has to lie and play the hypocrite with everyone, how he has to wear a mask in the presence of those near and dear to him, even before his own wife and children. And about the children—that is the most terrible part of it all, Nora.

NORA: How?

HELMER: Because such an atmosphere of lies infects and poisons the whole life of a home. Each breath the children take in such a house is full of the germs of evil.

NORA [*coming nearer him*]: Are you sure of that?

HELMER: My dear, I have often seen it in the course of my life as a lawyer. Almost everyone who has gone to the bad early in life has had a deceitful mother.

NORA: Why do you only say—mother?

HELMER: It seems most commonly to be the mother's influence, though naturally a bad father's would have the same result. Every lawyer is familiar with the fact. This Krogstad, now, has been persistently poisoning his own children with lies and dissimulation; that is why I say he has lost all moral character. [*holds out his hands to her*] That is why my sweet little Nora must promise me not to plead his cause. Give me your hand on it. Come, come, what is this? Give me your hand. There now, that's settled. I assure you it would be quite impossible for me to work with him; I literally feel physically ill when I am in the company of such people.

NORA [*takes her hand out of his and goes to the opposite side of the Christmas Tree*]: How hot it is in here; and I have such a lot to do.

HELMER [*getting up and putting his papers in order*]: Yes, and I must try and read through some of these before dinner; and I must think about your costume, too. And it is just possible I may have something ready in gold paper to hang up on the Tree. [*Puts his hand on her head.*] My precious little singing-bird!

[*He goes into his room and shuts the door after him.*]

NORA [*after a pause, whispers*]: No, no—it isn't true. It's impossible; it must be impossible.

[*The* NURSE *opens the door on the left.*]

NURSE: The little ones are begging so hard to be allowed to come in to mamma.

NORA: No, no, no! Don't let them come in to me! You stay with them, Anne.

NURSE: Very well, ma'am.

[*Shuts the door.*]

NORA [*pale with terror*]: Deprave my little children? Poison my home? [*a short pause. Then she tosses her head.*] It's not true. It can't possibly be true.

ACT 2

THE SAME SCENE. *The Christmas Tree is in the corner by the piano, stripped of its ornaments and with burnt-down candle-ends on its dishevelled branches.* NORA's *cloak and hat are lying on the sofa. She is alone in the room, walking about uneasily. She stops by the sofa and takes up her cloak.*

NORA [*drops the cloak*]: Someone is coming now! [*goes to the door and listens*] No—
it is no one. Of course, no one will come to-day, Christmas Day—nor tomorrow either. But, perhaps—[*opens the door and looks out*] No, nothing in the letter-box; it is quite empty. [*comes forward*] What rubbish! of course he can't be in earnest about it. Such a thing couldn't happen; it is impossible—I have three little children.

[*Enter the* NURSE *from the room on the left, carrying a big cardboard box.*]

NURSE: At last I have found the box with the fancy dress.

NORA: Thanks; put it on the table.

NURSE [*doing so*]: But it is very much in want of mending.

NORA: I should like to tear it into a hundred thousand pieces.

NURSE: What an idea! It can easily be put in order—just a little patience.

NORA: Yes, I will go and get Mrs. Linde to come and help me with it.

NURSE: What, out again? In this horrible weather? You will catch cold, ma'am, and make yourself ill.

NORA: Well, worse than that might happen. How are the children?

NURSE: The poor little souls are playing with their Christmas presents, but—

NORA: Do they ask much for me?

NURSE: You see, they are so accustomed to have their mamma with them.

NORA: Yes, but, nurse, I shall not be able to be so much with them now as I was before.

NURSE: Oh well, young children easily get accustomed to anything.

NORA: Do you think so? Do you think they would forget their mother if she went away altogether?

NURSE: Good heavens!—went away altogether?

NORA: Nurse, I want you to tell me something I have often wondered about—how could you have the heart to put your own child out among strangers?

NURSE: I was obliged to, if I wanted to be little Nora's nurse.

NORA: Yes, but how could you be willing to do it?

NURSE: What, when I was going to get such a good place by it? A poor girl who has got into trouble should be glad to. Besides, that wicked man didn't do a single thing for me.

NORA: But I suppose your daughter has quite forgotten you.

NURSE: No, indeed she hasn't. She wrote to me when she was confirmed, and when she was married.

NORA [*putting her arms round her neck*]: Dear old Anne, you were a good mother to me when I was little.

NURSE: Little Nora, poor dear, had no other mother but me.

NORA: And if my little ones had no other mother, I am sure you would——What nonsense I am talking! [*opens the box*] Go in to them. Now I must——. You will see tomorrow how charming I shall look.

NURSE: I am sure there will be no one at the ball so charming as you, ma'am.

[*Goes into the room on the left.*]

NORA [*begins to unpack the box, but soon pushes it away from her*]: If only I dared go out. If only no one would come. If only I could be sure nothing would happen here in the meantime. Stuff and nonsense! No one will come. Only I mustn't think about it. I will brush my muff. What, lovely gloves! Out of my thoughts, out of my thoughts! One, two, three, four, five, six— [*Screams.*] Ah! there is someone coming—

[*Makes a movement towards the door, but stands irresolute.*]

[*Enter* MRS. LINDE *from the hall, where she has taken off her cloak and hat.*]

NORA: Oh, it's you, Christine. There is no one else out there, is there? How good of you to come!

MRS. LINDE: I heard you were up asking for me.

NORA: Yes, I was passing by. As a matter of fact, it is something you could help me with. Let us sit down here on the sofa. Look here. To-morrow evening there is to be a fancy-dress ball at the Stenborgs', who live above us; and Torvald wants me to go as a Neapolitan fisher-girl, and dance the Tarantella that I learnt at Capri.

MRS. LINDE: I see; you are going to keep up the character.

NORA: Yes, Torvald wants me to. Look, here is the dress; Torvald had it made for me there, but now it is all so torn, and I haven't any idea—

MRS. LINDE: We will easily put that right. It is only some of the trimming come unsewn here and there. Needle and thread? Now then, that's all we want.

NORA: It *is* nice of you.

MRS. LINDE [*sewing*]: So you are going to be dressed up to-morrow, Nora. I will tell you what—I shall come in for a moment and see you in your fine feathers. But I have completely forgotten to thank you for a delightful evening yesterday.

NORA [*gets up, and crosses the stage*]: Well I don't think yesterday was as pleasant as usual. You ought to have come to town a little earlier, Christine. Certainly Torvald does understand how to make a house dainty and attractive.

MRS. LINDE: And so do you, it seems to me; you are not your father's daughter for nothing. But tell me, is Doctor Rank always as depressed as he was yesterday?

NORA: No; yesterday it was very noticeable. I must tell you that he suffers from a very dangerous disease. He has consumption of the spine, poor creature. His father was a horrible man who committed all sorts of excesses; and that is why his son was sickly from childhood, do you understand?

MRS. LINDE [*dropping her sewing*]: But, my dearest Nora, how do you know anything about such things?

NORA [*walking about*]: Pooh! When you have three children, you get visits now and then from—from married women, who know something of medical matters, and they talk about one thing and another.

MRS. LINDE [*goes on sewing. A short silence*]: Does Doctor Rank come here every day?

NORA: Every day regularly. He is Torvald's most intimate friend, and a great friend of mine too. He is just like one of the family.

MRS. LINDE: But tell me this—is he perfectly sincere? I mean, isn't he the kind of man that is very anxious to make himself agreeable?

NORA: Not in the least. What makes you think that?

MRS. LINDE: When you introduced him to me yesterday, he declared he had often heard my name mentioned in this house; but afterwards I noticed that your husband hadn't the slightest idea who I was. So how could Doctor Rank—?

NORA: That is quite right, Christine. Torvald is so absurdly fond of me that he wants me absolutely to himself, as he says. At first he used to seem almost jealous if I mentioned any of the dear folk at home, so naturally I gave up doing so. But I often talk about such things with Doctor Rank, because he likes hearing about them.

MRS. LINDE: Listen to me, Nora. You are still very like a child in many things, and I am older than you in many ways and have a little more experience. Let me tell you this—you ought to make an end of it with Doctor Rank.

NORA: What ought I to make an end of?

MRS. LINDE: Of two things, I think. Yesterday you talked some nonsense about a rich admirer who was to leave you money—

NORA: An admirer who doesn't exist, unfortunately! But what then?

MRS. LINDE: Is Doctor Rank a man of means?

NORA: Yes, he is.

MRS. LINDE: And has no one to provide for?

NORA: No, no one; but—

MRS. LINDE: And comes here every day?

NORA: Yes, I told you so.

MRS. LINDE: But how can this well-bred man be so tactless?

NORA: I don't understand you at all.

MRS. LINDE: Don't prevaricate, Nora. Do you suppose I don't guess who lent you the two hundred and fifty pounds?

NORA: Are you out of your senses? How can you think of such a thing! A friend of ours, who comes here every day! Do you realise what a horribly painful position that would be?

MRS. LINDE: Then it really isn't he?

NORA: No, certainly not. It would never have entered into my head for a moment. Besides, he had no money to lend then; he came into his money afterwards.

MRS. LINDE: Well, I think that was lucky for you, my dear Nora.

NORA: No, it would never have come into my head to ask Doctor Rank. Although I am quite sure that if I had asked him—

MRS. LINDE: But of course you won't.

NORA: Of course not. I have no reason to think it could possibly be necessary. But I am quite sure that if I told Doctor Rank—

MRS. LINDE: Behind your husband's back?

NORA: I *must* make an end of it with the other one, and that will be behind his back too. I *must* make an end of it with him.

MRS. LINDE: Yes, that is what I told you yesterday, but—

NORA [*walking up and down*]: A man can put a thing like that straight much easier than a woman—

MRS. LINDE: One's husband, yes.

NORA: Nonsense! [*standing still*] When you pay off a debt you get your bond back, don't you?

MRS. LINDE: Yes, as a matter of course.

NORA: And can tear it into a hundred thousand pieces, and burn it up—the nasty dirty paper!

MRS. LINDE [*looks hard at her, lays down her sewing and gets up slowly*]: Nora, you are concealing something from me.

NORA: Do I look as if I were?

MRS. LINDE: Something has happened to you since yesterday morning. Nora, what is it?

NORA [*going nearer to her*]: Christine! [*listens*] Hush! there's Torvald come home. Do you mind going in to the children for the present? Torvald can't bear to see dressmaking going on. Let Anne help you.

MRS. LINDE [*gathering some of the things together*]: Certainly—but I am not going away from here till we have had it out with one another.

[*She goes into the room on the left, as* helmer *comes in from the hall.*]

NORA [*going up to* HELMER]: I have wanted you so much, Torvald dear.

HELMER: Was that the dressmaker?

NORA: No, it was Christine; she is helping me to put my dress in order. You will see I shall look quite smart.

HELMER: Wasn't that a happy thought of mine, now?

NORA: Splendid! But don't you think it is nice of me, too, to do as you wish?

HELMER: Nice?—because you do as your husband wishes? Well, well, you little rogue, I am sure you did not mean it in that way. But I am not going to disturb you; you will want to be trying on your dress, I expect.

NORA: I suppose you are going to work.

HELMER: Yes. [*shows her a bundle of papers*] Look at that. I have just been into the bank. [*Turns to go into his room.*]

NORA: Torvald.

HELMER: Yes.

NORA: If your little squirrel were to ask you for something very, very prettily—?

HELMER: What then?

NORA: Would you do it?

HELMER: I should like to hear what it is, first.

NORA: Your squirrel would run about and do all her tricks if you would be nice, and do what she wants.

HELMER: Speak plainly.

NORA: Your skylark would chirp about in every room, with her song rising and falling—

HELMER: Well, my skylark does that anyhow.

NORA: I would play the fairy and dance for you in the moonlight, Torvald.

HELMER: Nora—you surely don't mean that request you made of me this morning?

NORA [*going near him*]: Yes, Torvald, I beg you so earnestly—

HELMER: Have you really the courage to open up that question again?

NORA: Yes, dear, you *must* do as I ask; you *must* let Krogstad keep his post in the Bank.

HELMER: My dear Nora, it is his post that I have arranged Mrs. Linde shall have.

NORA: Yes, you have been awfully kind about that; but you could just as well dismiss some other clerk instead of Krogstad.

HELMER: This is simply incredible obstinacy! Because you chose to give him a thoughtless promise that you would speak for him, I am expected to—

NORA: That isn't the reason, Torvald. It is for your own sake. This fellow writes in the most scurrilous newspapers; you have told me so yourself. He can do you an unspeakable amount of harm. I am frightened to death of him—

HELMER: Ah, I understand; it is recollections of the past that scare you.

NORA: What do you mean?

HELMER: Naturally you are thinking of your father.

NORA: Yes—yes, of course. Just recall to your mind what these malicious creatures wrote in the papers about papa, and how horribly they slandered him. I believe they would have procured his dismissal if the Department had not sent you over to inquire into it, and if you had not been so kindly disposed and helpful to him.

HELMER: My little Nora, there is an important difference between your father and me. Your father's reputation as a public official was not above suspicion. Mine is, and I hope it will continue to be so, as long as I hold my office.

NORA: You never can tell what mischief these men may contrive. We ought to be so well off, so snug and happy here in our peaceful home, and have no cares—you and I and the children, Torvald! That is why I beg you so earnestly—

HELMER: And it is just by interceding for him that you make it impossible for me to keep him. It is already known at the Bank that I mean to dismiss Krogstad. Is it to get about now that the new manager has changed his mind at his wife's bidding—

NORA: And what if it did?

HELMER: Of course!—if only this obstinate little person can get her way! Do you suppose I am going to make myself ridiculous before my whole staff, to let people think that I am a man to be swayed by all sorts of outside influence? I should very soon feel the consequences of it, I can tell you! And besides, there is one thing that makes it quite impossible for me to have Krogstad in the Bank as long as I am manager.

NORA: Whatever is that?

HELMER: His moral failings I might perhaps have overlooked, if necessary—

NORA: Yes, you could—couldn't you?

HELMER: And I hear he is a good worker, too. But I knew him when we were boys. It was one of those rash friendships that so often prove an incubus in afterlife. I may as well tell you plainly, we were once on very intimate terms with one another. But this tactless fellow lays no restraint on himself when other people are present. On the contrary, he thinks it gives him the right to adopt a familiar tone with me, and every minute it is "I say, Helmer, old fellow!" and that sort of thing. I assure you it is extremely painful for me. He would make my position in the Bank intolerable.

NORA: Torvald, I don't believe you mean that.

HELMER: Don't you? Why not?

NORA: Because it is such a narrow-minded way of looking at things.

HELMER: What are you saying? Narrow-minded? Do you think I am narrow-minded?

NORA: No, just the opposite, dear—and it is exactly for that reason.

HELMER: It's the same thing. You say my point of view is narrow-minded, so I must be so too. Narrow-minded! Very well—I must put an end to this. [*Goes to the hall-door and calls.*] Helen!

NORA: What are you going to do?

HELMER [*looking among his papers*]: Settle it. [*Enter* MAID.] Look here; take this letter and go downstairs with it at once. Find a messenger and tell him to deliver it, and be quick. The address is on it, and here is the money.

MAID: Very well, sir.

[*Exits with the letter.*]

HELMER [*putting his papers together*]: Now then, little Miss Obstinate.

NORA [*breathlessly*]: Torvald—what was that letter?

HELMER: Krogstad's dismissal.

NORA: Call her back, Torvald! There is still time. Oh Torvald, call her back! Do it for my sake—for your own sake—for the children's sake! Do you hear me, Torvald? Call her back!! You don't know what that letter can bring upon us.

HELMER: It's too late.

NORA: Yes, it's too late.

HELMER: My dear Nora, I can forgive the anxiety you are in, although really it is an insult to me. It is, indeed. Isn't it an insult to think that I should be afraid of a starving quill-driver's vengeance? But I forgive you nevertheless, because it is such eloquent witness to your great love for me. [*takes her in his arms*] And that is as it should be, my own darling Nora. Come what will, you may be sure I shall have both courage and strength if they be needed. You will see I am man enough to take everything upon myself.

NORA [*in a horror-stricken voice*]: What do you mean by that?

HELMER: Everything, I say—

NORA [*recovering herself*]: You will never have to do that.

HELMER: That's right. Well, we will share it, Nora, as man and wife should. That is how it shall be. [*caressing her*] Are you content now? There! there!—not these frightened dove's eyes! The whole thing is only the wildest fancy!—Now, you must go and play through the Tarantella and practise with your tambourine. I shall go into the inner office and shut the door, and I shall hear nothing; you can make as much noise as you please. [*turns back at the door*] And when Rank comes, tell him where he will find me.

[*Nods to her, takes his papers and goes into his room, and shuts the door after him*]

NORA [*bewildered with anxiety, stands as if rooted to the spot, and whispers*]: He is capable of doing it. He will do it. He will do it in spite of everything.—No, not that! Never, never! Anything rather than that! Oh, for some help, some way out of it! [*The door-bell rings.*] Doctor Rank! Anything rather than that—anything, whatever it is!

[*She puts her hands over her face, pulls herself together, goes to the door and opens it.* RANK *is standing without, hanging up his coat. During the following dialogue it begins to grow dark.*]

NORA: Good-day, Doctor Rank. I knew your ring. But you mustn't go in to Torvald now; I think he is busy with something.

RANK: And you?

NORA [*brings him in and shuts the door after him*]: Oh, you know very well I always have time for you.

RANK: Thank you. I shall make use of as much of it as I can.

NORA: What do you mean by that? As much of it as you can?

RANK: Well, does that alarm you?

NORA: It was such a strange way of putting it. Is anything likely to happen?

RANK: Nothing but what I have long been prepared for. But I certainly didn't expect it to happen so soon.

NORA [*gripping him by the arm*]: What have you found out? Doctor Rank, you must tell me.

RANK [*sitting down by the stove*]: It is all up with me. And it can't be helped.

NORA [*with a sigh of relief*]: Is it about yourself?

RANK: Who else? It is no use lying to one's self. I am the most wretched of all my patients, Mrs. Helmer. Lately I have been taking stock of my internal economy. Bankrupt! Probably within a month I shall lie rotting in the churchyard.

NORA: What an ugly thing to say!

RANK: The thing itself is cursedly ugly, and the worst of it is that I shall have to face so much more that is ugly before that. I shall only make one more examination of myself; when I have done that, I shall know pretty certainly when it will be that the horrors of dissolution will begin. There is something I want to tell you. Helmer's refined nature gives him an unconquerable disgust at everything that is ugly; I won't have him in my sick-room.

NORA: Oh, but, Doctor Rank—

RANK: I won't have him there. Not on any account. I bar my door to him. As soon as I am quite certain that the worst has come, I shall send you my card with a black cross on it, and then you will know that the loathsome end has begun.

NORA: You are quite absurd to-day. And I wanted you so much to be in a really good humour.

RANK: With death stalking beside me?—To have to pay this penalty for another man's sin! Is there any justice in that? And in every single family, in one way or another, some such inexorable retribution is being exacted—

NORA [*putting her hands over her ears*]: Rubbish! Do talk of something cheerful.

RANK: Oh, it's a mere laughing matter, the whole thing. My poor innocent spine has to suffer for my father's youthful amusements.

NORA [*sitting at the table on the left*]: I suppose you mean that he was too partial to asparagus and pâté de foie gras, don't you?

RANK: Yes, and to truffles.

NORA: Truffles, yes. And oysters too, I suppose?

RANK: Oysters, of course, that goes without saying.

NORA: And heaps of port and champagne. It is sad that all these nice things should take their revenge on our bones.

RANK: Especially that they should revenge themselves on the unlucky bones of those who have not had the satisfaction of enjoying them.

NORA: Yes, that's the saddest part of it all.

RANK [*with a searching look at her*]: Hm!—

NORA [*after a short pause*]: Why did you smile?

RANK: No, it was you that laughed.

NORA: No, it was you that smiled, Doctor Rank!

RANK [*rising*]: You are a greater rascal than I thought.

NORA: I am in a silly mood to-day.

RANK: So it seems.

NORA [*putting her hands on his shoulders*]: Dear, dear Doctor Rank, death mustn't take you away from Torvald and me.

RANK: It is a loss you would easily recover from. Those who are gone are soon forgotten.

NORA [*looking at him anxiously*]: Do you believe that?

RANK: People form new ties, and then—

NORA: Who will form new ties?

RANK: Both you and Helmer, when I am gone. You yourself are already on the high road to it, I think. What did that Mrs. Linde want here last night?

NORA: Oho!—you don't mean to say you are jealous of poor Christine?

RANK: Yes, I am. She will be my successor in this house. When I am done for, this woman will—

NORA: Hush! don't speak so loud. She is in that room.

RANK: To-day again. There, you see.

NORA: She has only come to sew my dress for me. Bless my soul, how unreasonable you are! [*sits down on the sofa*] Be nice now, Doctor Rank, and tomorrow you will see how beautifully I shall dance, and you can imagine I am doing it all for you—and for Torvald too, of course. [*takes various things out of the box*] Doctor Rank, come and sit down here, and I will show you something.

RANK [*sitting down*]: What is it?

NORA: Just look at those!

RANK: Silk stockings.

NORA: Flesh-coloured. Aren't they lovely? It is so dark here now, but to-morrow—. No, no, no! you must only look at the feet. Oh well, you may have leave to look at the legs too.

RANK: Hm!—

NORA: Why are you looking so critical? Don't you think they will fit me?

RANK: I have no means of forming an opinion about that.

NORA [*looks at him for a moment*]: For shame! [*hits him lightly on the ear with the stockings*] That's to punish you. [*folds them up again*]

RANK: And what other nice things am I to be allowed to see?

NORA: Not a single thing more, for being so naughty. [*She looks among the things, humming to herself.*]

RANK [*after a short silence*]: When I am sitting here, talking to you as intimately as this, I cannot imagine for a moment what would have become of me if I had never come into this house.

NORA [*smiling*]: I believe you do feel thoroughly at home with us.

RANK [*in a lower voice, looking straight in front of him*]: And to be obliged to leave it all—

NORA: Nonsense, you are not going to leave it.

RANK [*as before*]: And not be able to leave behind one the slightest token of one's gratitude, scarcely even a fleeting regret—nothing but an empty place which the first comer can fill as well as any other.

NORA: And if I asked you now for a—? No!

RANK: For what?

NORA: For a big proof of your friendship—

RANK: Yes, yes!

NORA: I mean a tremendously big favour—

RANK: Would you really make me so happy for once?

NORA: Ah, but you don't know what it is yet.

RANK: No—but tell me.

NORA: I really can't, Doctor Rank. It is something out of all reason; it means advice, and help, and a favour—

RANK: The bigger a thing it is the better. I can't conceive what it is you mean. Do tell me. Haven't I your confidence?

NORA: More than anyone else. I know you are my truest and best friend, and so I will tell you what it is. Well, Doctor Rank, it is something you must help me to prevent. You know how devotedly, how inexpressibly deeply Torvald loves me; he would never for a moment hesitate to give his life for me.

RANK [*leaning towards her*]: Nora—do you think he is the only one—?

NORA [*with a slight start*]: The only one—?

RANK: The only one who would gladly give his life for your sake.

NORA [*sadly*]: Is that it?

RANK: I was determined you should know it before I went away, and there will never be a better opportunity than this. Now you know it, Nora. And now you know, too, that you can trust me as you would trust no one else.

NORA [*rises, deliberately and quietly*]: Let me pass.

RANK [*makes room for her to pass him, but sits still*]: Nora!

NORA [*at the hall door*]: Helen, bring in the lamp. [*goes over to the stove*] Dear Doctor Rank, that was really horrid of you.

RANK: To have loved you as much as anyone else does? Was that horrid?

NORA: No, but to go and tell me so. There was really no need—

RANK: What do you mean? Did you know—? [MAID *enters with lamp, puts it down on the table, and goes out.*] Nora—Mrs. Helmer—tell me, had you any idea of this?

NORA: Oh, how do I know whether I had or whether I hadn't? I really can't tell you—To think you could be so clumsy, Doctor Rank! We were getting on so nicely.

RANK: Well, at all events you know now that you can command me, body and soul. So won't you speak out?

NORA [*looking at him*]: After what happened?

RANK: I beg you to let me know what it is.

NORA: I can't tell you anything now.

RANK: Yes, yes. You mustn't punish me in that way. Let me have permission to do for you whatever a man may do.

NORA: You can do nothing for me now. Besides, I really don't need any help at all. You will find that the whole thing is merely fancy on my part. It really is so—of course it is! [*Sits down in the rocking-chair, and looks at him with a smile*] You are a nice sort of man, Doctor Rank!—don't you feel ashamed of yourself, now the lamp has come?

RANK: Not a bit. But perhaps I had better go—for ever?

NORA: No, indeed, you shall not. Of course you must come here just as before. You know very well Torvald can't do without you.

RANK: Yes, but you?

NORA: Oh, I am always tremendously pleased when you come.

RANK: It is just that, that put me on the wrong track. You are a riddle to me. I have often thought that you would almost as soon be in my company as in Helmer's.

NORA: Yes—you see there are some people one loves best, and others whom one would almost always rather have as companions.

RANK: Yes, there is something in that.

NORA: When I was at home, of course I loved papa best. But I always thought it tremendous fun if I could steal down into the maid's room, because they never moralised at all, and talked to each other about such entertaining things.

RANK: I see—it is *their* place I have taken.

NORA [*jumping up and going to him*]: Oh, dear, nice Doctor Rank, I never meant that at all. But surely you can understand that being with Torvald is a little like being with papa—

[*Enter* MAID *from the hall*]

MAID: If you please, ma'am. [*whispers and hands her a card*]

NORA [*glancing at the card*]: Oh! [*puts it in her pocket*]

RANK: Is there anything wrong?

NORA: No, no, not in the least. It is only something—it is my new dress—

RANK: What? Your dress is lying there.

NORA: Oh, yes, that one; but this is another. I ordered it. Torvald mustn't know about it—

RANK: Oho! Then that was the great secret.

NORA: Of course. Just go in to him; he is sitting in the inner room. Keep him as long as—

RANK: Make your mind easy; I won't let him escape. [*goes into* HELMER'*s room*]

NORA [*to the* MAID]: And he is standing waiting in the kitchen?

MAID: Yes; he came up the back stairs.

NORA: But didn't you tell him no one was in?

MAID: Yes, but it was no good.

NORA: He won't go away?

MAID: No; he says he won't until he has seen you, ma'am.

NORA: Well, let him come in—but quietly. Helen, you mustn't say anything about it to anyone. It is a surprise for my husband.

MAID: Yes, ma'am, I quite understand.

[*Exit.*]

NORA: This dreadful thing is going to happen! It will happen in spite of me! No, no, no, it can't happen—it shan't happen!

[*She bolts the door of* HELMER'*s room. The* MAID *opens the hall door for* KROGSTAD *and shuts it after him. He is wearing a fur coat, high boots and a fur cap.*]

NORA [*advancing towards him*]: Speak low—my husband is at home.

KROGSTAD: No matter about that.

NORA: What do you want of me?

KROGSTAD: An explanation of something.

NORA: Make haste then. What is it?

KROGSTAD: You know, I suppose, that I have got my dismissal.

NORA: I couldn't prevent it, Mr. Krogstad. I fought as hard as I could on your side, but it was no good.

KROGSTAD: Does your husband love you so little, then? He knows that what I can expose you to, and yet he ventures—

NORA: How can you suppose that he has any knowledge of the sort?

KROGSTAD: I didn't suppose so at all. It would not be the least like our dear Torvald Helmer to show so much courage—

NORA: Mr. Krogstad, a little respect for my husband, please.

KROGSTAD: Certainly—all the respect he deserves. But since you have kept the matter so carefully to yourself, I make bold to suppose that you have a little clearer idea, than you had yesterday, of what it actually is that you have done?

NORA: More than you could ever teach me.

KROGSTAD: Yes, such a bad lawyer as I am.

NORA: What is it you want of me?

KROGSTAD: Only to see how you were, Mrs. Helmer. I have been thinking about you all day long. A mere cashier, a quill-driver, a—well, a man like me—even he has a little of what is called feeling, you know.

NORA: Show it, then; think of my little children.

KROGSTAD: Have you and your husband thought of mine? But never mind about that. I only wanted to tell you that you need not take this matter too seriously. In the first place there will be no accusation made on my part.

NORA: No, of course not; I was sure of that.

KROGSTAD: The whole thing can be arranged amicably; there is no reason why anyone should know anything about it. It will remain a secret between us three.

NORA: My husband must never get to know anything about it.

KROGSTAD: How will you be able to prevent it? Am I to understand that you can pay the balance that is owing?

NORA: No, not just at present.

KROGSTAD: Or perhaps that you have some expedient for raising the money soon?

NORA: No expedient that I mean to make use of.

KROGSTAD: Well, in any case, it would have been of no use to you now. If you stood there with ever so much money in your hand, I would never part with your bond.

NORA: Tell me what purpose you mean to put it to.

KROGSTAD: I shall only preserve it—keep it in my possession. No one who is not concerned in the matter shall have the slightest hint of it. So that if the thought of it has driven you to any desperate resolution—

NORA: It has.

KROGSTAD: If you had it in your mind to run away from your home—

NORA: I had.

KROGSTAD: Or even something worse—

NORA: How could you know that?

KROGSTAD: Give up the idea.

NORA: How did you know I had thought of *that?*

KROGSTAD: Most of us think of that at first. I did, too—but I hadn't the courage.

NORA [*faintly*]: No more had I.

KROGSTAD [*in a tone of relief*]: No, that's it, isn't it—you hadn't the courage either?

NORA: No, I haven't—I haven't.

KROGSTAD: Besides, it would have been a great piece of folly. Once the first storm at home is over—. I have a letter for your husband in my pocket.

NORA: Telling him everything?

KROGSTAD: In as lenient a manner as I possibly could.

NORA [*quickly*]: He mustn't get the letter. Tear it up. I will find some means of getting money.

KROGSTAD: Excuse me, Mrs. Helmer, but I think I told you just now—

NORA: I am not speaking of what I owe you. Tell me what sum you are asking my husband for, and I will get the money.

KROGSTAD: I am not asking your husband for a penny.

NORA: What do you want, then?

KROGSTAD: I will tell you. I want to rehabilitate myself, Mrs. Helmer; I want to get on; and in that your husband must help me. For the last year and a half I have not had a hand in anything dishonourable, and all that time I have been struggling in most restricted circumstances. I was content to work my way up step by step. Now I am turned out, and I am not going to be satisfied with merely being taken into favour again. I want to get on, I tell you. I want to get into the Bank again, in a higher position. Your husband must make a place for me—

NORA: That he will never do!

KROGSTAD: He will; I know him; he dare not protest. And as soon as I am in there again with him, then you will see! Within a year I shall be the manager's right hand. It will be Nils Krogstad and not Torvald Helmer who manages the Bank.

NORA: That's a thing you will never see!

KROGSTAD: Do you mean that you will—?

NORA: I have courage enough for it now.

KROGSTAD: Oh, you can't frighten me. A fine, spoilt lady like you—

NORA: You will see, you will see.

KROGSTAD: Under the ice, perhaps? Down into the cold, coal-black water? And then, in the spring, to float up to the surface, all horrible and unrecognisable, with your hair fallen out—

NORA: You can't frighten me.

KROGSTAD: Nor you me. People don't do such things, Mrs. Helmer. Besides, what use would it be? I should have him completely in my power all the same.

NORA: Afterwards? When I am no longer—

KROGSTAD: Have you forgotten that it is I who have the keeping of your reputation? [NORA *stands speechlessly looking at him.*] Well, now, I have warned you. Do not do anything foolish. When Helmer has had my letter, I shall expect a message from him. And be sure you remember that it is your husband himself who has forced me into such ways as this again. I will never forgive him for that. Good-bye, Mrs. Helmer.

[*Exit through the hall*]

NORA [*goes to the hall door, opens it slightly and listens*]: He is going. He is not putting the letter in the box. Oh no, no! that's impossible! [*opens the door by degrees*] What is that? He is standing outside. He is not going downstairs. Is he hesitating? Can he—

[*A letter drops into the box; then* KROGSTAD's *footsteps are heard, till they die away as he goes downstairs.* NORA *utters a stifled cry and runs across the room to the table by the sofa. A short pause.*]

NORA: In the letter-box. [*steals across to the hall door*] There it lies—Torvald, Torvald, there is no hope for us now!

[MRS. LINDE *comes in from the room on the left, carrying the dress.*]

MRS. LINDE: There, I can't see anything more to mend now. Would you like to try it on—?

NORA [*in a hoarse whisper*]: Christine, come here.

MRS. LINDE [*throwing the dress down on the sofa*]: What is the matter with you? You look so agitated!

NORA: Come here. Do you see that letter? There, look—you can see it through the glass in the letter-box.

MRS. LINDE: Yes, I see it.

NORA: That letter is from Krogstad.

MRS. LINDE: Nora—it was Krogstad who lent you the money!

NORA: Yes, and now Torvald will know all about it.

MRS. LINDE: Believe me, Nora, that's the best thing for both of you.

NORA: You don't know all. I forged a name.

MRS. LINDE: Good heavens—!

NORA: I only want to say this to you, Christine—you must be my witness.

MRS. LINDE: Your witness? What do you mean? What am I to—?

NORA: If I should go out of my mind—and it might easily happen—

MRS. LINDE: Nora!

NORA: Or if anything else should happen to me—anything, for instance, that might prevent my being here—

MRS. LINDE: Nora! Nora! you are quite out of your mind.

NORA: And if it should happen that there were someone who wanted to take all the responsibility, all the blame, you understand—

MRS. LINDE: Yes, yes—but how can you suppose—?

NORA: Then you must be my witness, that it is not true, Christine. I am not out of my mind at all; I am in my right senses now, and I tell you no one else has known anything about it; I, and I alone, did the whole thing. Remember that.

MRS. LINDE: I will, indeed. But I don't understand all this.

NORA: How should you understand it? A wonderful thing is going to happen.

MRS. LINDE: A wonderful thing?

NORA: Yes, a wonderful thing!—But it is so terrible, Christine; it *mustn't* happen, not for all the world.

MRS. LINDE: I will go at once and see Krogstad.

NORA: Don't go to him; he will do you some harm.

MRS. LINDE: There was a time when he would gladly do anything for my sake.

NORA: He?

MRS. LINDE: Where does he live?

NORA: How should I know—? Yes [*feeling in her pocket*] here is his card. But the letter, the letter—!

HELMER [*calls from his room, knocking at the door*]: Nora!

NORA [*cries out anxiously*]: Oh, what's that? What do you want?

HELMER: Don't be so frightened. We are not coming in; you have locked the door. Are you trying on your dress?

NORA: Yes, that's it. I look so nice, Torvald.

MRS. LINDE [*who has read the card*]: I see he lives at the corner here.

NORA: Yes, but it's no use. It is hopeless. The letter is lying there in the box.

MRS. LINDE: And your husband keeps the key?

NORA: Yes, always.

MRS. LINDE: Krogstad must ask for his letter back unread, he must find some pretence—

NORA: But it is just at this time that Torvald generally—

MRS. LINDE: You must delay him. Go in to him in the meantime. I will come back as soon as I can.

[*She goes out hurriedly through the hall door.*]

NORA [*goes to* HELMER'S *door, opens it and peeps in*]: Torvald!

HELMER [*from the inner room*]: Well? May I venture at last to come into my own room again? Come along, Rank, now you will see—[*halting in the doorway*] But what is this?

NORA: What is what, dear?

HELMER: Rank led me to expect a splendid transformation.

RANK [*in the doorway*]: I understood so, but evidently I was mistaken.

NORA: Yes, nobody is to have the chance of admiring me in my dress until tomorrow.

HELMER: But, my dear Nora, you look so worn out. Have you been practising too much?

NORA: No, I have not practised at all.

HELMER: But you will need to—

NORA: Yes, indeed I shall, Torvald. But I can't get on a bit without you to help me; I have absolutely forgotten the whole thing.

HELMER: Oh, we will soon work it up again.

NORA: Yes, help me, Torvald. Promise that you will! I am so nervous about it—all the people—. You must give yourself up to me entirely this evening. Not the tiniest bit of business—you mustn't even take a pen in your hand. Will you promise, Torvald dear?

HELMER: I promise. This evening I will be wholly and absolutely at your service, you helpless little mortal. Ah, by the way, first of all I will just—

[*Goes towards the hall door.*]

NORA: What are you going to do there?

HELMER: Only see if any letters have come.

NORA: No, no! don't do that, Torvald!

HELMER: Why not?

NORA: Torvald, please don't. There is nothing there.

HELMER: Well, let me look. [*Turns to go to the letter-box.* NORA, *at the piano, plays the first bars of the Tarantella.* HELMER *stops in the doorway.*] Aha!

NORA: I can't dance to-morrow if I don't practise with you.

HELMER [*going up to her*]: Are you really so afraid of it, dear.

NORA: Yes, so dreadfully afraid of it. Let me practise at once; there is time now, before we go to dinner. Sit down and play for me, Torvald dear; criticise me, and correct me as you play.

HELMER: With great pleasure, if you wish me to.

[*Sits down at the piano.*]

NORA [*takes out of the box a tambourine and a long variegated shawl. She hastily drapes the shawl round her. Then she springs to the front of the stage and calls out*]: Now play for me! I am going to dance!

[HELMER *plays and* NORA *dances.* RANK *stands by the piano behind* HELMER *and looks on.*]

HELMER [*as he plays*]: Slower, slower!

NORA: I can't do it any other way.

HELMER: Not so violently, Nora!

NORA: This is the way.

HELMER [*stops playing*]: No, no—that is not a bit right.

NORA [*laughing and swinging the tambourine*]: Didn't I tell you so?

RANK: Let me play for her.

HELMER [*getting up*]: Yes, do. I can correct her better then.

[RANK *sits down at the piano and plays.* NORA *dances more and more wildly.* HELMER *has taken up a position beside the stove, and during her dance gives her frequent instructions. She does not seem to hear him; her hair comes down and falls over her shoulders; she pays no attention to it, but goes on dancing. Enter* MRS. LINDE.]

MRS. LINDE [*standing as if spell-bound in the doorway*]: Oh!—

NORA [*as she dances*]: Such fun, Christine!

HELMER: My dear darling Nora, you are dancing as if your life depended on it.

NORA: So it does.

HELMER: Stop, Rank; this is sheer madness. Stop, I tell you! [RANK *stops playing, and* NORA *suddenly stands still.* HELMER *goes up to her.*] I could never have believed it. You have forgotten everything I taught you.

NORA [*throwing away the tambourine*]: There, you see.

HELMER: You will want a lot of coaching.

NORA: Yes, you see how much I need it. You must coach me up to the last minute. Promise me that, Torvald!

HELMER: You can depend on me.

NORA: You must not think of anything but me, either to-day or to-morrow; you mustn't open a single letter—not even open the letter-box—

HELMER: Ah, you are still afraid of that fellow—

NORA: Yes, indeed I am.

HELMER: Nora, I can tell from your looks that there is a letter from him lying there.

NORA: I don't know; I think there is; but you must not read anything of that kind now. Nothing horrid must come between us till this is all over.

RANK [*whispers to* HELMER]: You mustn't contradict her.

HELMER [*taking her in his arms*]: The child shall have her way. But to-morrow night, after you have danced—

NORA: Then you will be free.

[MAID *appears in the doorway to the right.*]

MAID: Dinner is served, ma'am.

NORA: We will have champagne, Helen.

MAID: Very good, ma'am.

[*Exit.*]

HELMER: Hullo!—are we going to have a banquet?

NORA: Yes, a champagne banquet till the small hours. [*calls out*] And a few macaroons, Helen—lots, just for once!

HELMER: Come, come, don't be so wild and nervous. Be my own little skylark, as you used.

NORA: Yes, dear, I will. But go in now, and you too, Doctor Rank. Christine, you must help me to do up my hair.

RANK [*whispers to* HELMER *as they go out*]: I suppose there is nothing—she is not expecting anything?

HELMER: Far from it, my dear fellow; it is simply nothing more than this childish nervousness I was telling you of.

[*They go into the right-hand room.*]

NORA: Well!

MRS. LINDE: Gone out of town.

NORA: I could tell from your face.

MRS. LINDE: He is coming home to-morrow evening. I wrote a note for him.

NORA: You should have let it alone; you must prevent nothing. After all, it is splendid to be waiting for a wonderful thing to happen.

MRS. LINDE: What is it that you are waiting for?

NORA: Oh, you wouldn't understand. Go in to them, I will come in a moment.
[MRS. LINDE *goes into the dining-room.* NORA *stands still for a little while,
as if to compose herself. Then she looks at her watch.*] Five o'clock. Seven
hours till midnight; and then four-and-twenty hours till the next midnight. Then the Tarantella will be over. Twenty-four and seven? Thirty-
one hours to live.

HELMER [*from the doorway on the right*]: Where's my little skylark?

NORA [*going to him with her arms outstretched*]: Here she is!

ACT 3

THE SAME SCENE *The table has been placed in the middle of the stage, with chairs
round it. A lamp is burning on the table. The door into the hall stands open. Dance
music is heard in the room above.* MRS. LINDE *is sitting at the table idly turning over
the leaves of a book; she tries to read, but does not seem able to collect her thoughts.
Every now and then she listens intently for a sound at the outer door.*

MRS. LINDE [*looking at her watch*]: Not yet—and the time is nearly up. If only he does
not—. [*listens again*] Ah, there he is. [*Goes into the hall and opens the
outer door carefully. Light footsteps are heard on the stairs. She whispers.*]
Come in. There is no one here.

KROGSTAD [*in the doorway*]: I found a note from you at home. What does this mean?

MRS. LINDE: It is absolutely necessary that I should have a talk with you.

KROGSTAD: Really? And is it absolutely necessary that it should be here?

MRS. LINDE: It is impossible where I live; there is no private entrance to my rooms.
Come in; we are quite alone. The maid is asleep, and the Helmers are at
the dance upstairs.

KROGSTAD [*coming into the room*]: Are the Helmers really at a dance to-night?

MRS. LINDE: Yes, why not?

KROGSTAD: Certainly—why not?

MRS. LINDE: Now, Nils, let us have a talk.

KROGSTAD: Can we two have anything to talk about?

MRS. LINDE: We have a great deal to talk about.

KROGSTAD: I shouldn't have thought so.

MRS. LINDE: No, you have never properly understood me.

KROGSTAD: Was there anything else to understand except what was obvious to all the
world—a heartless woman jilts a man when a more lucrative chance turns up?

MRS. LINDE: Do you believe I am as absolutely heartless as all that? And do you
believe that I did it with a light heart?

KROGSTAD: Didn't you?

MRS. LINDE: Nils, did you really think that?

KROGSTAD: If it were as you say, why did you write to me as you did at the time?

MRS. LINDE: I could do nothing else. As I had to break with you, it was my duty also
to put an end to all that you felt for me.

KROGSTAD [*wringing his hands*]: So that was it, and all this—only for the sake of
money!

MRS. LINDE: You must not forget that I had a helpless mother and two little brothers. We couldn't wait for you, Nils; your prospects seemed hopeless then.

KROGSTAD: That may be so, but you had no right to throw me over for anyone else's sake.

MRS. LINDE: Indeed I don't know. Many a time did I ask myself if I had the right to do it.

KROGSTAD [*more gently*]: When I lost you, it was as if all the solid ground went from under my feet. Look at me now—I am a shipwrecked man clinging to a bit of wreckage.

MRS. LINDE: But help may be near.

KROGSTAD: It *was* near; but then you came and stood in my way.

MRS. LINDE: Unintentionally, Nils. It was only to-day that I learnt it was your place I was going to take in the Bank.

KROGSTAD: I believe you, if you say so. But now that you know it, are you not going to give it up to me?

MRS. LINDE: No, because that would not benefit you in the least.

KROGSTAD: Oh, benefit, benefit—I would have done it whether or no.

MRS. LINDE: I have learnt to act prudently. Life, and hard, bitter necessity have taught me that.

KROGSTAD: And life has taught me not to believe in fine speeches.

MRS. LINDE: Then life has taught you something very reasonable. But deeds you must believe in?

KROGSTAD: What do you mean by that?

MRS. LINDE: You said you were like a shipwrecked man clinging to some wreckage.

KROGSTAD: I had good reason to say so.

MRS. LINDE: Well, I am like a shipwrecked woman clinging to some wreckage—no one to mourn for, no one to care for.

KROGSTAD: It was your own choice.

MRS. LINDE: There was no other choice—then.

KROGSTAD: Well, what now?

MRS. LINDE: Nils, how would it be if we two shipwrecked people could join forces?

KROGSTAD: What are you saying?

MRS. LINDE: Two on the same piece of wreckage would stand a better chance than each on their own.

KROGSTAD: Christine!

MRS. LINDE: What do you suppose brought me to town?

KROGSTAD: Do you mean that you gave me a thought?

MRS. LINDE: I could not endure life without work. All my life, as long as I can remember, I have worked, and it has been my greatest and only pleasure. But now I am quite alone in the world—my life is so dreadfully empty and I feel so forsaken. There is not the least pleasure in working for one's self. Nils, give me someone and something to work for.

KROGSTAD: I don't trust that. It is nothing but a woman's overstrained sense of generosity that prompts you to make such an offer of yourself.

MRS. LINDE: Have you ever noticed anything of the sort in me?

KROGSTAD: Could you really do it? Tell me—do you know all about my past life?

MRS. LINDE: Yes.

KROGSTAD: And do you know what they think of me here?

MRS. LINDE: You seemed to me to imply that with me you might have been quite another man.

KROGSTAD: I am certain of it.

MRS. LINDE: Is it too late now?

KROGSTAD: Christine, are you saying this deliberately? Yes, I am sure you are. I see it in your face. Have you really the courage, then—?

MRS. LINDE: I want to be a mother to someone, and your children need a mother. We two need each other. Nils, I have faith in your real character—I can dare anything together with you.

KROGSTAD [*grasps her hands*]: Thanks, thanks, Christine! Now I shall find a way to clear myself in the eyes of the world. Ah, but I forgot—

MRS. LINDE [*listening*]: Hush! The Tarantella! Go, go!

KROGSTAD: Why? What is it?

MRS. LINDE: Do you hear them up there? When that is over, we may expect them back.

KROGSTAD: Yes, yes—I will go. But it is all no use. Of course you are not aware what steps I have taken in the matter of the Helmers.

MRS. LINDE: Yes, I know all about that.

KROGSTAD: And in spite of that have you the courage to—?

MRS. LINDE: I understand very well to what lengths a man like you might be driven by despair.

KROGSTAD: If I could only undo what I have done!

MRS. LINDE: You can. Your letter is lying in the letter-box now.

KROGSTAD: Are you sure of that?

MRS. LINDE: Quite sure, but—

KROGSTAD [*with a searching look at her*]: Is that what it all means?—that you want to save your friend at any cost? Tell me frankly. Is that it?

MRS. LINDE: Nils, a woman who has once sold herself for another's sake, doesn't do it a second time.

KROGSTAD: I will ask for my letter back.

MRS. LINDE: No, no.

KROGSTAD: Yes, of course I will. I will wait here till Helmer comes; I will tell him he must give me my letter back—that it only concerns my dismissal—that he is not to read it—

MRS. LINDE: No, Nils, you must not recall your letter.

KROGSTAD: But, tell me, wasn't it for that very purpose that you asked me to meet you here?

MRS. LINDE: In my first moment of fright, it was. But twenty-four hours have elapsed since then, and in that time I have witnessed incredible things in this house. Helmer must know all about it. This unhappy secret must be disclosed; they must have a complete understanding between them, which is impossible with all this concealment and falsehood going on.

KROGSTAD: Very well, if you will take the responsibility. But there is one thing I can do in any case, and I shall do it at once.

MRS. LINDE [*listening*]: You must be quick and go! The dance is over; we are not safe a moment longer.

KROGSTAD: I will wait for you below.

MRS. LINDE: Yes, do. You must see me back to my door.

KROGSTAD: I have never had such an amazing piece of good fortune in my life.

[*Goes out through the outer door. The door between the room and the hall remains open.*]

MRS. LINDE [*tidying up the room and laying her hat and cloak ready*]: What a difference! what a difference! Someone to work for and live for—a home to bring comfort into. That I will do, indeed. I wish they would be quick and come— [*listens*] Ah, there they are now. I must put on my things.

[*Takes up her hat and cloak.* HELMER's *and* NORA's *voices are heard outside; a key is turned, and* HELMER *brings* NORA *almost by force into the hall. She is in an Italian costume with a large black shawl round her; he is in evening dress and a black domino which is flying open.*]

NORA [*hanging back in the doorway, and struggling with him*]: No, no, no!—don't take me in. I want to go upstairs again; I don't want to leave so early.

HELMER: But, my dearest Nora—

NORA: Please, Torvald dear—please, *please*—only an hour more.

HELMER: Not a single minute, my sweet Nora. You know that was our agreement. Come along into the room; you are catching cold standing there.

[*He brings her gently into the room, in spite of her resistance.*]

MRS. LINDE: Good evening.

NORA: Christine!

HELMER: You here, so late, Mrs. Linde?

MRS. LINDE: Yes, you must excuse me; I was so anxious to see Nora in her dress.

NORA: Have you been sitting here waiting for me?

MRS. LINDE: Yes, unfortunately I came too late, you had already gone upstairs; and I thought I couldn't go away without having seen you.

HELMER [*taking off* NORA's *shawl*]: Yes, take a good look at her. I think she is worth looking at. Isn't she charming, Mrs. Linde?

MRS. LINDE: Yes, indeed she is.

HELMER: Doesn't she look remarkably pretty? Everyone thought so at the dance. But she is terribly self-willed, this sweet little person. What are we to do with her? You will hardly believe that I had almost to bring her away by force.

NORA: Torvald, you will repent not having let me stay, even if it were only for half an hour.

HELMER: Listen to her, Mrs. Linde! She had danced her Tarantella, and it had been a tremendous success, as it deserved—although possibly the performance was a trifle too realistic—a little more so, I mean, than was strictly compatible with the limitations of art. But never mind about that! The chief thing is, she had made a success—she had made a tremendous success. Do you think I was going to let her remain there after that, and spoil the effect? No indeed! I took my charming little Capri maiden—my capricious little Capri maiden, I should say—on my arm; took one quick turn round the room; a curtsey on either side, and, as they say in novels, the beautiful apparition disappeared. An exit ought always to be effective, Mrs. Linde; but that is what I cannot make Nora understand. Pooh! this room is hot. [*throws his domino on a chair and opens the door of his room*] Hullo! it's all dark in here. Oh, of course—excuse me—.

[*He goes in and lights some candles.*]

NORA [*in a hurried and breathless whisper*]: Well?

MRS. LINDE [*in a low voice*]: I have had a talk with him.

NORA: Yes, and—

MRS. LINDE: Nora, you must tell your husband all about it.

NORA [*in an expressionless voice*]: I knew it.

MRS. LINDE: You have nothing to be afraid of as far as Krogstad is concerned; but you must tell him.

NORA: I won't tell him.

MRS. LINDE: Then the letter will.

NORA: Thank you, Christine. Now I know what I must do. Hush—!

HELMER [*coming in again*]: Well, Mrs. Linde, have you admired her?

MRS. LINDE: Yes, and now I will say good-night.

HELMER: What, already? Is this yours, this knitting?

MRS. LINDE [*taking it*]: Yes, thank you, I had very nearly forgotten it.

HELMER: So you knit?

MRS. LINDE: Of course.

HELMER: Do you know, you ought to embroider.

MRS. LINDE: Really? Why?

HELMER: Yes, it's far more becoming. Let me show you. You hold the embroidery thus in your left hand, and use the needle with the right—like this—with a long, easy sweep. Do you see?

MRS. LINDE: Yes, perhaps—

HELMER: But in the case of knitting—that can never be anything but ungraceful; look here—the arms close together, the knitting-needles going up and down— it has a sort of Chinese effect—. That was really excellent champagne they gave us.

MRS. LINDE: Well,—good-night, Nora, and don't be self-willed any more.

HELMER: That's right, Mrs. Linde.

MRS. LINDE: Good-night, Mr. Helmer.

HELMER [*accompanying her to the door*]: Good-night, good-night. I hope you will get home all right. I should be very happy to—but you haven't any great distance to go. Good-night, good-night. [*She goes out; he shuts the door after her, and comes in again.*] Ah!—at last we have got rid of her. She is a frightful bore, that woman.

NORA: Aren't you very tired, Torvald?

HELMER: No, not in the least.

NORA: Nor sleepy?

HELMER: Not a bit. On the contrary, I feel extraordinarily lively. And you?—you really look both tired and sleepy.

NORA: Yes, I am very tired. I want to go to sleep at once.

HELMER: There, you see it was quite right of me not to let you stay there any longer.

NORA: Everything you do is quite right, Torvald.

HELMER [*kissing her on the forehead*]: Now my little skylark is speaking reasonably. Did you notice what good spirits Rank was in this evening?

NORA: Really? Was he? I didn't speak to him at all.

HELMER: And I very little, but I have not for a long time seen him in such good form. [*looks for a while at her and then goes nearer to her*] It is delightful to be at home by ourselves again, to be all alone with you—you fascinating, charming little darling!

NORA: Don't look at me like that, Torvald.

HELMER: Why shouldn't I look at my dearest treasure?—at all the beauty that is mine, all my very own?

NORA [*going to the other side of the table*]: You mustn't say things like that to me to-night.

HELMER [*following her*]: You have still got the Tarantella in your blood, I see. And it makes you more captivating than ever. Listen—the guests are beginning to go now. [*in a lower voice*] Nora—soon the whole house will be quiet.

NORA: Yes, I hope so.

HELMER: Yes, my own darling Nora. Do you know, when I am out at a party with you like this, why I speak so little to you, keep away from you, and only send a stolen glance in your direction now and then?—do you know why

I do that? It is because I make believe to myself that we are secretly in love, and you are my secretly promised bride, and that no one suspects there is anything between us.

NORA: Yes, yes—I know very well your thoughts are with me all the time.

HELMER: And when we are leaving, and I am putting the shawl over your beautiful young shoulders—on your lovely neck—then I imagine that you are my young bride and that we have just come from the wedding, and I am bringing you for the first time into our home—to be alone with you for the first time—quite alone with my shy little darling! All this evening I have longed for nothing but you. When I watched the seductive figures of the Tarantella, my blood was on fire; I could endure it no longer, and that was why I brought you down so early—

NORA: Go away, Torvald! You must let me go. I won't—

HELMER: What's that? You're joking, my little Nora! You won't—you won't? Am I not your husband—?

[*A knock is heard at the outer door.*]

NORA [*starting*]: Did you hear—?

HELMER [*going into the hall*]: Who is it?

RANK [*outside*]: It is I. May I come in for a moment?

HELMER [*in a fretful whisper*]: Oh, what does he want now? [*aloud*] Wait a minute! [*unlocks the door*] Come, that's kind of you not to pass by our door.

RANK: I thought I heard your voice, and felt as if I should like to look in. [*with a swift glance round*] Ah, yes!—these dear familiar rooms. You are very happy and cosy in here, you two.

HELMER: It seems to me that you looked after yourself pretty well upstairs too.

RANK: Excellently. Why shouldn't I? Why shouldn't one enjoy everything in this world?—at any rate as much as one can, and as long as one can. The wine was capital—

HELMER: Especially the champagne.

RANK: So you noticed that too? It is almost incredible how much I managed to put away!

NORA: Torvald drank a great deal of champagne tonight, too.

RANK: Did he?

NORA: Yes, and he is always in such good spirits afterwards.

RANK: Well, why should one not enjoy a merry evening after a well-spent day?

HELMER: Well spent? I am afraid I can't take credit for that.

RANK [*clapping him on the back*]: But I can, you know!

NORA: Doctor Rank, you must have been occupied with some scientific investigation to-day.

RANK: Exactly.

HELMER: Just listen!—little Nora talking about scientific investigations!

NORA: And may I congratulate you on the result?

RANK: Indeed you may.

NORA: Was it favourable, then?

RANK: The best possible, for both doctor and patient—certainty.

NORA [*quickly and searchingly*]: Certainty?

RANK: Absolute certainty. So wasn't I entitled to make a merry evening of it after that?

NORA: Yes, you certainly were, Doctor Rank.

HELMER: I think so too, so long as you don't have to pay for it in the morning.

RANK: Oh well, one can't have anything in this life without paying for it.

NORA: Doctor Rank—are you fond of fancy-dress balls?

RANK: Yes, if there is a fine lot of pretty costumes.

NORA: Tell me—what shall we two wear at the next?

HELMER: Little featherbrain!—are you thinking of the next already?

RANK: We two? Yes, I can tell you. You shall go as a good fairy—

HELMER: Yes, but what do you suggest as an appropriate costume for that?

RANK: Let your wife go dressed just as she is in everyday life.

HELMER: That was really very prettily turned. But can't you tell us what you will be?

RANK: Yes, my dear friend, I have quite made up my mind about that.

HELMER: Well?

RANK: At the next fancy dress ball I shall be invisible.

HELMER: That's a good joke!

RANK: There is a big black hat—have you never heard of hats that make you invisible? If you put one on, no one can see you.

HELMER [*suppressing a smile*]: Yes, you are quite right.

RANK: But I am clean forgetting what I came for. Helmer, give me a cigar—one of the dark Havanas.

HELMER: With the greatest pleasure [*offers him his case*].

RANK [*takes a cigar and cuts off the end*]: Thanks.

NORA [*striking a match*]: Let me give you a light.

RANK: Thank you. [*She holds the match for him to light his cigar.*] And now good-bye!

HELMER: Good-bye, good-bye, dear old man!

NORA: Sleep well, Doctor Rank.

RANK: Thank you for that wish.

NORA: Wish me the same.

RANK: You? Well, if you want me to: sleep well! And thanks for the light.

[*He nods to them both and goes out.*]

HELMER [*in a subdued voice*]: He has drunk more than he ought.

NORA [*absently*]: Maybe. [HELMER *takes a bunch of keys out of his pocket and goes into the hall.*] Torvald! what are you going to do there?

HELMER: Empty the letter-box; it is quite full; there will be no room to put the newspaper in to-morrow morning.

NORA: Are you going to work to-night?

HELMER: You know quite well I'm not. What is this? Some one has been at the lock.

NORA: At the lock—?

HELMER: Yes, someone has. What can it mean? I should never have thought the maid—. Here is a broken hairpin. Nora, it is one of yours.

NORA [*quickly*]: Then it must have been the children—

HELMER: Then you must get them out of those ways. There, at last I have got it open. [*Takes out the contents of the letter-box, and calls to the kitchen.*] Helen!— Helen, put out the light over the front door. [*Goes back into the room and shuts the door into the hall. He holds out his hand full of letters.*] Look at that—look what a heap of them there are. [*turning them over*] What on earth is that?

NORA [*at the window*]: The letter—No! Torvald, no!

HELMER: Two cards—of Rank's.

NORA: Of Doctor Rank's?

HELMER [*looking at them*]: Doctor Rank. They were on the top. He must have put them in when he went out.

NORA: Is there anything written on them?

HELMER: There is a black cross over the name. Look there—what an uncomfortable idea! It looks as if he were announcing his own death.

NORA: It is just what he is doing.

HELMER: What? Do you know anything about it? Has he said anything to you?

NORA: Yes. He told me that when the cards came it would be his leave-taking from us. He means to shut himself up and die.

HELMER: My poor old friend. Certainly I knew we should not have him very long with us. But so soon! And so he hides himself away like a wounded animal.

NORA: If it has to happen, it is best it should be without a word—don't you think so, Torvald?

HELMER [*walking up and down*]: He had so grown into our lives. I can't think of him as having gone out of them. He, with his sufferings and his loneliness, was like a cloudy background to our sunlit happiness. Well, perhaps it is best so. For him, anyway. [*standing still*] And perhaps for us too, Nora. We two are thrown quite upon each other now. [*puts his arms round her*] My darling wife, I don't feel as if I could hold you tight enough. Do you know, Nora, I have often wished that you might be threatened by some great danger, so that I might risk my life's blood, and everything, for your sake.

NORA [*disengages herself, and says firmly and decidedly*]: Now you must read your letters, Torvald.

HELMER: No, no; not to-night. I want to be with you, my darling wife.

NORA: With the thought of your friend's death—

HELMER: You are right, it has affected us both. Something ugly has come between us—the thought of the horrors of death. We must try and rid our minds of that. Until then—we will each go to our own room.

NORA [*hanging on his neck*]: Good-night, Torvald—Good-night!

HELMER [*kissing her on the forehead*]: Good-night, my little singing-bird. Sleep sound, Nora. Now I will read my letters through.

> [*He takes his letters and goes into his room, shutting the door after him.*]

NORA [*gropes distractedly about, seizes* HELMER's *domino, throws it round her, while she says in quick, hoarse, spasmodic whispers*]: Never to see him again. Never! Never! [*puts her shawl over her head*] Never to see my children again either— never again. Never! Never!—Ah! the icy, black water—the unfathomable depths—If only it were over! He has got it now—now he is reading it. Goodby, Torvald and my children!

> [*She is about to rush out through the hall, when* HELMER *opens his door hurriedly and stands with an open letter in his hand.*]

HELMER: Nora!

NORA: Ah!—

HELMER: What is this? Do you know what is in this letter?

NORA: Yes, I know. Let me go! Let me get out!

HELMER [*holding her back*]: Where are you going?

NORA [*trying to get free*]: You shan't save me, Torvald!

HELMER [*reeling*]: True? Is this true, that I read here? Horrible! No, no—it is impossible that it can be true.

NORA: It is true. I have loved you above everything else in the world.

HELMER: Oh, don't let us have any silly excuses.

NORA [*taking a step towards him*]: Torvald—!

HELMER: Miserable creature—what have you done?

NORA: Let me go. You shall not suffer for my sake. You shall not take it upon yourself.

HELMER: No tragedy airs, please. [*locks the hall door*] Here you shall stay and give me an explanation. Do you understand what you have done? Answer me? Do you understand what you have done?

NORA [*looks steadily at him and says with a growing look of coldness in her face*]: Yes, now I am beginning to understand thoroughly.

HELMER [*walking about the room*]: What a horrible awakening! All these eight years—she who was my joy and pride—a hypocrite, a liar—worse, worse—a criminal! The unutterable ugliness of it all! For shame! For shame! [NORA *is silent and looks steadily at him. He stops in front of her.*] I ought to have suspected that something of the sort would happen. I ought to have foreseen it. All your father's want of principle—be silent!—all your father's want of principle has come out in you. No religion, no morality, no sense of duty—. How I am punished for having winked at what he did! I did it for your sake, and this is how you repay me.

NORA: Yes, that's just it.

HELMER: Now you have destroyed all my happiness. You have ruined all my future. It is horrible to think of! I am in the power of an unscrupulous man; he can do what he likes with me, ask anything he likes of me, give me any orders he pleases— I dare not refuse. And I must sink to such miserable depths because of a thoughtless woman!

NORA: When I am out of the way, you will be free.

HELMER: No fine speeches, please. Your father had always plenty of those ready, too. What good would it be to me if you were out of the way, as you say? Not the slightest. He can make the affair known everywhere; and if he does, I may be falsely suspected of having been a party to your criminal action. Very likely people will think I was behind it all—that it was I who prompted you! And I have to thank you for all this—you whom I have cherished during the whole of our married life. Do you understand now what it is you have done for me?

NORA [*coldly and quietly*]: Yes.

HELMER: It is so incredible that I can't take it in. But we must come to some understanding. Take off that shawl. Take it off, I tell you. I must try and appease him some way or another. The matter must be hushed up at any cost. And as for you and me, it must appear as if everything between us were just as before— but naturally only in the eyes of the world. You will still remain in my house, that is a matter of course. But I shall not allow you to bring up the children; I dare not trust them to you. To think that I should be obliged to say so to one whom I have loved so dearly, and whom I still—. No, that is all over. From this moment happiness is not the question; all that concerns us is to save the remains, the fragments, the appearance—

[*A ring is heard at the front-door bell.*]

HELMER [*with a start*]: What is that? So late! Can the worst—? Can he—? Hide yourself, Nora. Say you are ill.

[NORA *stands motionless.* HELMER *goes and unlocks the hall door.*]

MAID [*half-dressed, comes to the door*]: A letter for the mistress.

HELMER: Give it to me. [*takes the letter, and shuts the door*] Yes, it is from him. You shall not have it; I will read it myself.

NORA: Yes, read it.

HELMER [*standing by the lamp*]: I scarcely have the courage to do it. It may mean ruin for both of us. No, I must know. [*tears open the letter, runs his eye over a few lines, looks at a paper enclosed and gives a shout of joy*] Nora! [*She looks at him questioningly.*] Nora!—No, I must read it once again—. Yes, it is true! I am saved! Nora, I am saved!

NORA: And I?

HELMER: You too, of course; we are both saved, both you and I. Look, he sends you your bond back. He says he regrets and repents—that a happy change in his life—never mind what he says! We are saved, Nora! No one can do anything to you. Oh, Nora, Nora!—no, first I must destroy these hateful things. Let me see—. [*takes a look at the bond*] No, no, I won't look at it. The whole thing shall be nothing but a bad dream to me. [*tears up the bond and both letters, throws them all into the stove, and watches them burn*] There—now it doesn't exist any longer. He says that since Christmas Eve you—. These must have been three dreadful days for you, Nora.

NORA: I have fought a hard fight these three days.

HELMER: And suffered agonies, and seen no way out but—. No, we won't call any of the horrors to mind. We will only shout with joy, and keep saying "It's all over! It's all over!" Listen to me, Nora. You don't seem to realise that it is all over. What is this?—such a cold, set face! My poor little Nora, I quite understand; you don't feel as if you could believe that I have forgiven you. But it is true, Nora, I swear it; I have forgiven you everything. I know that what you did, you did out of love for me.

NORA: That is true.

HELMER: You have loved me as a wife ought to love her husband. Only you had not sufficient knowledge to judge of the means you used. But do you suppose you are any the less dear to me, because you don't understand how to act on your own responsibility? No, no; only lean on me; I will advise you and direct you. I should not be a man if this womanly helplessness did not just give you a double attractiveness in my eyes. You must not think any more about the hard things I said in my first moment of consternation, when I thought everything was going to overwhelm me. I have forgiven you, Nora; I swear to you I have forgiven you.

NORA: Thank you for your forgiveness.

[*She goes out through the door to the right.*]

HELMER: No, don't go—. [*looks in*] What are you doing in there?

NORA [*from within*]: Taking off my fancy dress.

HELMER [*standing at the open door*]: Yes, do. Try and calm yourself, and make your mind easy again, my frightened little singing-bird. Be at rest, and feel secure; I have broad wings to shelter you under. [*walks up and down by the door*] How warm and cosy our home is, Nora. Here is shelter for you; here I will protect you like a hunted dove that I have saved from a hawk's claws. I will bring peace to your poor beating heart. It will come, little by little, Nora, believe me. Tomorrow morning you will look upon it all quite differently; soon everything will be just as it was before. Very soon you won't need me to assure you that I have forgiven you; you will yourself feel the certainty that I have done so. Can you suppose I should ever think of such a thing as repudiating you, or even reproaching you? You have no idea what a true man's heart is like, Nora. There is something so indescribably sweet and satisfying, to a man, in the knowledge that he has forgiven his wife—forgiven her freely, and with all his heart. It seems as if that had made her, as it were, doubly his own; he has given her a new life, so to speak; and she has in a way become both wife and child to him. So you shall be for me after this, my little scared, helpless darling. Have no anxiety about anything, Nora; only be frank and open with me, and I will serve as will and conscience both to you—. What is this? Not gone to bed? Have you changed your things?

NORA [*in everyday dress*]: Yes, Torvald, I have changed my things now.

HELMER: But what for?—so late as this.

NORA: I shall not sleep to-night.

HELMER: But, my dear Nora—

NORA [*looking at her watch*]: It is not so very late. Sit down here, Torvald. You and I have much to say to one another.

[*She sits down at one side of the table.*]

HELMER: Nora—what is this?—this cold, set face?

NORA: Sit down. It will take some time; I have a lot to talk over with you.

HELMER [*sits down at the opposite side of the table*]: You alarm me, Nora!—and I don't understand you.

NORA: No, that is just it. You don't understand me, and I have never understood you either—before to-night. No, you mustn't interrupt me. You must simply listen to what I say. Torvald, this is a settling of accounts.

HELMER: What do you mean by that?

NORA [*after a short silence*]: Isn't there one thing that strikes you as strange in our sitting here like this?

HELMER: What is that?

NORA: We have been married now eight years. Does it not occur to you that this is the first time we two, you and I, husband and wife, have had a serious conversation?

HELMER: What do you mean by serious?

NORA: In all these eight years—longer than that—from the very beginning of our acquaintance, we have never exchanged a word on any serious subject.

HELMER: Was it likely that I would be continually and for ever telling you about worries that you could not help me to bear?

NORA: I am not speaking about business matters. I say that we have never sat down in earnest together to try and get at the bottom of anything.

HELMER: But, dearest Nora, would it have been any good to you?

NORA: That is just it; you have never understood me. I have been greatly wronged, Torvald—first by papa and then by you.

HELMER: What! By us two—by us two, who have loved you better than anyone else in the world?

NORA [*shaking her head*]: You have never loved me. You have only thought it pleasant to be in love with me.

HELMER: Nora, what do I hear you saying?

NORA: It is perfectly true, Torvald. When I was at home with papa, he told me his opinion about everything, and so I had the same opinions; and if I differed from him I concealed the fact, because he would not have liked it. He called me his doll-child, and he played with me just as I used to play with my dolls. And when I came to live with you—

HELMER: What sort of an expression is that to use about our marriage?

NORA [*undisturbed*]: I mean that I was simply transferred from papa's hands into yours. You arranged everything according to your own taste, and so I got the same tastes as you—or else I pretended to, I am really not quite sure which— I think sometimes the one and sometimes the other. When I look back on it, it seems to me as if I had been living here like a poor woman—just from hand to mouth. I have existed merely to perform tricks for you, Torvald. But you would have it so. You and papa have committed a great sin against me. It is your fault that I have made nothing of my life.

HELMER: How unreasonable and how ungrateful you are, Nora! Have you not been happy here?

NORA: No, I have never been happy. I thought I was, but it has never really been so.

HELMER: Not—not happy!

NORA: No, only merry. And you have always been so kind to me. But our home has been nothing but a playroom. I have been your doll-wife, just as at home I was papa's doll-child; and here the children have been my dolls. I thought it great fun when you played with me, just as they thought it great fun when I played with them. That is what our marriage has been, Torvald.

HELMER: There is some truth in what you say—exaggerated and strained as your view of it is. But for the future it shall be different. Playtime shall be over, and lesson-time shall begin.

NORA: Whose lessons? Mine, or the children's?

HELMER: Both yours and the children's, my darling Nora.

NORA: Alas, Torvald, you are not the man to educate me into being a proper wife for you.

HELMER: And you can say that!

NORA: And I—how am I fitted to bring up the children?

HELMER: Nora!

NORA: Didn't you say so yourself a little while ago—that you dare not trust me to bring them up?

HELMER: In a moment of anger! Why do you pay any heed to that?

NORA: Indeed, you were perfectly right. I am not fit for the task. There is another task I must undertake first. I must try and educate myself—you are not the man to help me in that. I must do that for myself. And that is why I am going to leave you now.

HELMER [*springing up*]: What do you say?

NORA: I must stand quite alone, if I am to understand myself and everything about me. It is for that reason that I cannot remain with you any longer.

HELMER: Nora! Nora!

NORA: I am going away from here now, at once. I am sure Christine will take me in for the night—

HELMER: You are out of your mind! I won't allow it! I forbid you!

NORA: It is no use forbidding me anything any longer. I will take with me what belongs to myself. I will take nothing from you, either now or later.

HELMER: What sort of madness is this!

NORA: To-morrow I shall go home—I mean, to my old home. It will be easiest for me to find something to do there.

HELMER: You blind, foolish woman!

NORA: I must try and get some sense, Torvald.

HELMER: To desert your home, your husband and your children! And you don't consider what people will say!

NORA: I cannot consider that at all. I only know that it is necessary for me.

HELMER: It's shocking. This is how you would neglect your most sacred duties.

NORA: What do you consider my most sacred duties?

HELMER: Do I need to tell you that? Are they not your duties to your husband and your children?

NORA: I have other duties just as sacred.

HELMER: That you have not. What duties could those be?

NORA: Duties to myself.

HELMER: Before all else, you are a wife and a mother.

NORA: I don't believe that any longer. I believe that before all else I am a reasonable human being, just as you are—or, at all events, that I must try and become one. I know quite well, Torvald, that most people would think you right, and that views of that kind are to be found in books; but I can no longer content myself with what most people say, or with what is found in books. I must think over things for myself and get to understand them.

HELMER: Can you not understand your place in your own home? Have you not a reliable guide in such matters as that?—have you no religion?

NORA: I am afraid, Torvald, I do not exactly know what religion is.

HELMER: What are you saying?

NORA: I know nothing but what the clergyman said when I went to be confirmed. He told us that religion was this, and that, and the other. When I am away from all this, and am alone, I will look into that matter too. I will see if what the clergyman said is true, or at all events if it is true for me.

HELMER: This is unheard of in a girl of your age! But if religion cannot lead you aright, let me try and awaken your conscience. I suppose you have some moral sense? Or—answer me—am I to think you have none?

NORA: I assure you, Torvald, that is not an easy question to answer. I really don't know. The thing perplexes me altogether. I only know that you and I look at it in quite a different light. I am learning, too, that the law is quite another thing from what I supposed; but I find it impossible to convince myself that the law is right. According to it a woman has no right to spare her old dying father, or to save her husband's life. I can't believe that.

HELMER: You talk like a child. You don't understand the conditions of the world in which you live.

NORA: No, I don't. But now I am going to try. I am going to see if I can make out who is right, the world or I.

HELMER: You are ill, Nora; you are delirious; I almost think you are out of your mind.

NORA: I have never felt my mind so clear and certain as to-night.

HELMER: And is it with a clear and certain mind that you forsake your husband and your children?

NORA: Yes, it is.

HELMER: Then there is only one possible explanation.

NORA: What is that?

HELMER: You do not love me any more.

NORA: No, that is just it.

HELMER: Nora!—and you can say that?

NORA: It gives me great pain, Torvald, for you have always been so kind to me, but I cannot help it. I do not love you any more.

HELMER [*regaining his composure*]: Is that a clear and certain conviction too?

NORA: Yes, absolutely clear and certain. That is the reason why I will not stay here any longer.

HELMER: And can you tell me what I have done to forfeit your love?

NORA: Yes, indeed I can. It was to-night, when the wonderful thing did not happen; then I saw you were not the man I had thought you.

HELMER: Explain yourself better—I don't understand you.

NORA: I have waited so patiently for eight years; for, goodness knows, I knew very well that wonderful things don't happen every day. Then this horrible misfortune came upon me; and then I felt quite certain that the wonderful thing was going to happen at last. When Krogstad's letter was lying out there, never for a moment did I imagine that you would consent to accept this man's conditions. I was so absolutely certain that you would say to him: Publish the thing to the whole world. And when that was done—

HELMER: Yes, what then?—when I had exposed my wife to shame and disgrace?

NORA: When that was done, I was so absolutely certain, you would come forward and take everything upon yourself, and say: I am the guilty one.

HELMER: Nora—!

NORA: You mean that I would never have accepted such a sacrifice on your part? No, of course not. But what would my assurances have been worth against yours? That was the wonderful thing which I hoped for and feared; and it was to prevent that, that I wanted to kill myself.

HELMER: I would gladly work night and day for you, Nora—bear sorrow and want for your sake. But no man would sacrifice his honour for the one he loves.

NORA: It is a thing hundreds of thousands of women have done.

HELMER: Oh, you think and talk like a heedless child.

NORA: Maybe. But you neither think nor talk like the man I could bind myself to. As soon as your fear was over—and it was not fear for what threatened me, but for what might happen to you—when the whole thing was past, as far as you were concerned it was exactly as if nothing at all had happened. Exactly as before, I was your little skylark, your doll, which you would in future treat with doubly gentle care, because it was so brittle and fragile. [*getting up*] Torvald— it was then it dawned upon me that for eight years I had been living here with a strange man, and had borne him three children—. Oh, I can't bear to think of it! I could tear myself into little bits!

HELMER [*sadly*]: I see, I see. An abyss has opened between us—there is no denying it. But, Nora, would it not be possible to fill it up?

NORA: As I am now, I am no wife for you.

HELMER: I have it in me to become a different man.

NORA: Perhaps—if your doll is taken away from you.

HELMER: But to part!—to part from you! No, no, Nora, I can't understand that idea.

NORA [*going out to the right*]: That makes it all the more certain that it must be done.

[*She comes back with her cloak and hat and a small bag which she puts on a chair by the table.*]

HELMER: Nora, Nora, not now! Wait till to-morrow.

NORA [*putting on her cloak*]: I cannot spend the night in a strange man's room.

HELMER: But can't we live here like brother and sister—?

NORA [*putting on her hat*]: You know very well that would not last long. [*puts the shawl round her*] Good-bye, Torvald. I won't see the little ones. I know they are in better hands than mine. As I am now, I can be of no use to them.

HELMER: But some day, Nora—some day?

NORA: How can I tell? I have no idea what is going to become of me.

HELMER: But you are my wife, whatever becomes of you.

NORA: Listen, Torvald. I have heard that when a wife deserts her husband's house, as I am doing now, he is legally freed from all obligations towards her. In

any case I set you free from all your obligations. You are not to feel yourself bound in the slightest way, any more than I shall. There must be
perfect freedom on both sides. See here is your ring back. Give me mine.

HELMER: That too?

NORA: That too.

HELMER: Here it is.

NORA: That's right. Now it is all over. I have put the keys here. The maids know all
about everything in the house—better than I do. To-morrow, after I have
left her, Christine will come here and pack up my own things that I
brought with me from home. I will have them sent after me.

HELMER: All over! All over!—Nora, shall you never think of me again?

NORA: I know I shall often think of you and the children and this house.

HELMER: May I write to you, Nora?

NORA: No—never. You must not do that.

HELMER: But at least let me send you—

NORA: Nothing—nothing—

HELMER: Let me help you if you are in want.

NORA: No. I can receive nothing from a stranger.

HELMER: Nora—can I never be anything more than a stranger to you?

NORA [*taking her bag*]: Ah, Torvald, the most wonderful thing of all would have to
happen.

HELMER: Tell me what that would be!

NORA: Both you and I would have to be so changed that—. Oh, Torvald, I don't
believe any longer in wonderful things happening.

HELMER: But I will believe in it. Tell me? So changed that—?

NORA: That our life together would be a real wedlock. Good-bye.

[*She goes out through the hall.*]

HELMER [*sinks down on a chair at the door and buries his face in his hands*]: Nora!
Nora! [*looks round, and rises*] Empty. She is gone. [*A hope flashes across
his mind.*] The most wonderful thing of all—?

[*The sound of a door slamming is heard from below.*]

[1879]

Joining the Conversation: Critical Thinking and Writing

1. Near the beginning of the play, how does Mrs. Linde's presence help to define
Nora's character? How does Nora's response to Krogstad's entrance tell us
something about Nora?

2. What does Dr. Rank contribute to the play? If he were eliminated, what would
be lost?

3. Can it be argued that, although at the end Nora goes out to achieve self-
realization, her abandonment of her children—especially to Torvald's loathsome conventional morality—is a crime?

4. Why does Nora leave the children? She seems to imply in some passages that,
because she forged a signature, she is unfit to bring them up. Do you agree with
her?

5. Michael Meyer, in his splendid biography *Henrik Ibsen*, says that the play is not
so much about women's rights as about "the need of every individual to find

out the kind of person he or she really is, and to strive to become that person." What evidence can you offer to support or refute this interpretation?

6. In *The Quintessence of Ibsenism*, Bernard Shaw says that Ibsen, reacting against a common theatrical preference for strange situations,

> saw that . . . the more familiar the situation, the more interesting the play. Shakespeare had put ourselves on the stage but not our situations. Our uncles seldom murder our fathers and . . . marry our mothers. . . . Ibsen . . . gives us not only ourselves, but ourselves in our own situations. The things that happen to his stage figures are things that happen to us. One consequence is that his plays are much more important to us than Shakespeare's. Another is that they are capable both of hurting us cruelly and of filling us with excited hopes of escape from idealistic tyrannies, and with visions of intenser life in the future.

How much of this do you believe? Support your response with reasons.

Chapter Overview: Looking Backward/Looking Forward

1. Write a short essay that defends travel, explaining the benefits that result from a journey. Rewrite your essay as a single paragraph, summarizing your best arguments. Next, try to do the same in just a single sentence.

2. Review the essay that you wrote for the first question, in defense of travel. What are the strengths and weaknesses of your argument? Do you see any weaknesses? How might you revise this essay to make it more effective? Do you think you should introduce counterarguments into your essay—arguments "on the other side" that you could address and try to answer? Or would this prove confusing to your reader?

3. When someone says to you that he or she "hates to travel," what is your response? Do you think that such a position can be defended? If you had to argue that traveling is a bad idea, what main points would you make? Would you cite any of the quotations given at the beginning of this chapter? Which ones? What would you gain from such a citation? What, if anything, might you lose?

4. If someone surprised you with a gift of a free trip, what destination would excite you the most? Which one would excite you the least?

5. Do you spend much time exploring your own thoughts and feelings? Do you set aside a specific time for this? Is there a specific place where it occurs? Is this an activity that you undertake by yourself, or with someone else, or with some group? Describe an occasion when you explored your thoughts and feelings, and explain what happened next.

APPENDIX A

Writing about Literature: An Overview of Critical Strategies

The Nature of Critical Writing

We have said that in everyday talk the commonest meaning of **criticism** is something like "finding fault" but that a critic can see excellences as well as faults. Because we turn to criticism with the hope that the critic has seen something that we have missed, the most valuable criticism is not that which shakes its finger at faults but that which calls our attention to interesting things going on in the work of art.

How would a critic introduce an author and his or her writing to a reader? It's not enough just to name the author; almost surely the critic would give *reasons* why we should read a particular book: "It will really grip you"; "It's the funniest thing I've read in months"; "I was moved to tears." Criticism is largely a matter of showing and thereby convincing. We cannot just announce that we like or dislike something and expect people to agree; we have to point to evidence (that's the showing part) if we are going to convince.

The writer D. H. Lawrence asserted that criticism is *a reasoned account*—writing about literature is a rational activity, not a mere pouring out of emotion—that is rooted in *feeling*. As suggested, when we read, we respond (perhaps with an intense interest or perhaps with a yawn). Our responses are worth examining. *Why* do we find this character memorable or that character unbelievable?

As we examine our responses and check the text to make sure that we have properly remembered it, we may find our responses changing, but finally we think we know what we think of the literary work, and we know *why* we think it. We are, in Lawrence's words, able to give "a reasoned account of the feeling produced . . . by the book."

Criticism as Argument: Assumptions and Evidence

Even when we are talking about a so-so movie or television show, what we say depends in large measure on certain conscious or unconscious assumptions that we make:

- "I liked it because the characters were very believable" (here the assumption is that characters ought to be believable);

- "I didn't like it; there was too much violence" (here the assumption is that violence ought not to be shown or, if it is shown, it should be condemned);
- "I didn't like it; it was awfully slow" (here the assumption is probably that there ought to be a fair amount of physical action, perhaps even changes of scene, rather than characters just talking in the kitchen);
- "I didn't like it; I don't think topics of this sort should be discussed publicly" (here the assumption is a moral one, that it is indecent to present certain topics);
- "I liked it partly because it was refreshing to hear such frankness" (here, again, the assumption is moral and more or less the reverse of the previous one).

In short, whether we realize it or not, our responses are rooted in assumptions. These assumptions, we may believe, are so self-evident that they do not need to be stated. Our readers, however, may disagree.

If we are to hold our readers' interest and perhaps convince them to see things the way we do, we must recognize our assumptions and offer evidence—point to things in the literary work—that will convince our readers that our assumptions are reasonable. If we want to say that a short story ought to be realistic, we will call our readers' attention to unrealistic aspects in a particular story and, with this evidence in front of our readers, argue that the story is not worth much. Or, conversely, we might say that, in a satiric story, realism is not a valid criterion; what readers want is (as in a political caricature in a newspaper) exaggeration and humor, and in our critical study we will call attention to the delight that this or that bit of exaggeration offers.

In brief, as we suggested earlier in this text, argument consists of offering statements that are *reasons* for other statements ("The work means X *because* . . ."), and the words that follow "because" normally point to the evidence that we believe supports the earlier assertion.

Some Critical Strategies

Professional critics, like the ordinary moviegoer who recommends a movie to a friend, work from assumptions, but their assumptions are usually highly conscious, and the critics may define their assumptions at length. They regard themselves as, for instance, Freudians or Marxists or gay critics. They read all texts through the lens of a particular theory, and their focus enables them to see things that otherwise might go unnoticed. Most critics realize, however, that, if a lens, a critical perspective, or an interpretive strategy helps us to see certain things, it also limits our vision. They therefore regard their method not as an exclusive way of thinking but only as a useful tool.

What follows is a brief survey of the chief current approaches to literature. You may find as you read these pages that one or another approach sounds congenial, and you may want to make use of it in your reading and writing. On the other hand, it's important to remember that works of literature are highly varied, and we read them for various purposes: to kill time, to enjoy fanciful visions, to be amused, to learn about alien ways of feeling, and to learn about ourselves.

It may be best, therefore, to try to respond to each literary work in the way that the work seems to require rather than to read all literary works according to a single formula. You'll find, of course, that some works will lead you to want to think about them from several angles. A play by Shakespeare may stimulate you to read a book about the Elizabethan playhouse, another book that offers a Marxist interpretation of the English Renaissance, and still another that offers a feminist analysis of Shakespeare's plays. All of these approaches, and others, may help to deepen your understanding of the literary works that you read.

Formalist Criticism (New Criticism)

Formalist criticism emphasizes the work as an independent creation, a self-contained unity, that is, something to be studied in itself and not as part of some larger context, such as the author's life or a historical period. This kind of study is called formalist criticism because the emphasis is on the *form* of the work, the relationships between the parts: the construction of the plot, the contrasts between characters, the functions of rhymes, the point of view, and so on. Formalist critics explain how and why literary works—*these* words, in *this* order—constitute unique, complex structures that embody or set forth meanings.

Formalist criticism is, in essence, *intrinsic* rather than extrinsic criticism, for it concentrates on the work itself, independent of its writer and the writer's background—that is, independent of biography, psychology, sociology, and history. The discussion of "The Span of Life," a short poem by Frost on page 167 is a brief example.

In practice, of course, we usually bring outside knowledge to the work. For instance, a reader who is familiar with, say, *Hamlet* can hardly study some other tragedy by Shakespeare, such as *Romeo and Juliet*, without bringing to the second play some conception of what Shakespearean tragedy is or can be. A reader of Alice Walker's *The Color Purple* inevitably brings unforgettable outside material (perhaps the experience of being an African American or some knowledge of the history of African Americans) to the literary work. It is difficult to talk only about *Hamlet* or *The Color Purple* and not at the same time talk about, or at least have in mind, aspects of human experience.

Formalist criticism begins with a personal response to the literary work, but it goes on to try to account for that response by closely examining the work. It assumes that the author shaped the poem, play, or story so fully that the work guides the reader's responses.

The assumption that "meaning" is fully and completely presented within the text is not much in favor today, when many literary critics argue that the active or subjective reader (or even what Judith Fetterley, a feminist critic, has called "the resisting reader"), not the author of the text, makes the "meaning." Still, even if we grant that the reader is active, not passive or coolly objective, we can hold with the formalists that the author is active too, constructing a text that in some measure controls the reader's responses.

Formalist criticism usually takes one of two forms: **explication** (the unfolding of meaning, line by line or even word by word) and **analysis** (the examination of the relations of parts). The essay on Langston Hughes's "Harlem" (page 178) is an explication, a setting forth of the implicit meanings of the words. The essay on Kate Chopin's "The Story of an Hour" (page 73) is an analysis. The two essays on Frost's "Stopping by Woods on a Snowy Evening" (pages 271 and 275) are chiefly analyses but with some passages of explication.

Formalist criticism, also called the **New Criticism** (to distinguish it from the historical and biographical writing that in earlier decades had dominated literary study), began to achieve prominence in the late 1920s and was dominant from the late 1930s until about 1970, and even today it is widely considered the best way for a student to begin to study a work of literature. Formalist criticism empowers the student; that is, the student confronts the work immediately and is not told first to spend days, weeks, or months in preparation—for instance, reading Freud and his followers in order to write a psychoanalytic essay, reading Marx and Marxists in order to write a Marxist essay, or doing research on "necessary historical background" in order to write a historical essay.

Deconstruction

Deconstruction, or deconstructive or poststructuralist criticism, can almost be characterized as the opposite of everything that formalist criticism stands for. Deconstruction begins with the assumptions that language is unstable, elusive, and unreliable (Language is all of these things because meaning is largely generated by opposition: *hot* means something in opposition to *cold*, but a hot day may be 90 degrees whereas a hot oven is at least 400 degrees, and a "hot item" may be of any temperature.) Deconstructionists seek to show that a literary work (usually called "a text" or "a discourse") is inevitably self-contradictory. Unlike formalist critics, who hold that an author constructs a coherent work with a stable meaning and that competent readers can perceive this meaning, deconstructionists hold that a work has no coherent meaning at its center.

Despite the emphasis on indeterminacy, it is sometimes possible to detect in deconstructionist interpretations a view that is associated with Marxism. This is the idea that authors are "socially constructed" from the "discourses of power" or "signifying practices" that surround them. Thus, although authors may think that they are individuals with independent minds, their works usually reveal—unknown to the authors—powerful social, cultural, or philosophical assumptions. Deconstructionists "interrogate" a text, and they reveal what the authors were unaware of or had thought they had kept safely out of sight. That is, deconstructionists often find a rather specific meaning, although this meaning is one that might surprise the author.

Deconstruction is valuable insofar as—like the New Criticism—it encourages close, rigorous attention to the text. The problem with deconstruction, however, is that too often it is reductive, telling the same story about every text—that here, yet again, and again, we see how a text is incoherent and heterogeneous.

Reader-Response Criticism

Probably all reading includes some sort of response—"This is terrific," "This is a bore," "I don't know what's going on here"—and almost all writing about literature begins with some such response, but specialists in literature disagree greatly about the role that response plays, or should play, in experiencing literature and in writing about it.

At one extreme are those who say that our response to a work of literature should be a purely aesthetic response—a response to a work of art—and not the response that we would have to something comparable in real life. To take an obvious point, if in real life we heard someone plotting a murder, we would intervene, perhaps by calling the police or by attempting to warn the victim. However, when we hear Macbeth and Lady Macbeth plot to kill King Duncan, we watch with deep *interest*; we hear their words with *pleasure*, and maybe with horror and fascination we even look forward to seeing the murder and to what the characters then will say and what will happen to the murderers.

When you think about it, the vast majority of works of literature do not have a close, obvious resemblance to the reader's life. Most readers of *Macbeth* are not Scots, and no readers are Scottish kings or queens. The connections that readers make between themselves and the lives in most of the books that they read are not, on the whole, connections based on ethnic or professional identities. Rather, they are connections with states of consciousness—for instance, a young person's sense of isolation from the family or a young person's sense of guilt for initial sexual experiences.

Before we reject a work because it seems either too close to us ("I'm a man, and I don't like the depiction of this man") or too far from our experience ("I'm not a woman, so how can I enjoy reading about these women?"), we should probably try to follow the advice of Virginia Woolf, who said, "Do not dictate to your author; try to become him." Nevertheless, some literary works of the past may today seem intolerable, at least in part. There are passages in Mark Twain's *Adventures of Huckleberry Finn* in which African Americans are stereotyped or called derogatory names that deeply upset us today. We should, however, try to reconstruct the cultural assumptions of the age in which the work was written. If we do so, we may find that, if in some ways it reflected its historical era, in other ways it challenged it.

Reader-response criticism, then, says that the "meaning" of a work is not merely something put into the work by the writer; rather, the "meaning" is an interpretation that is created, constructed, or produced by the reader as well as the writer.

Does every reader see his or her individual image in each literary work? Even *Hamlet*, a play that has generated an enormous range of interpretation, is universally seen as a tragedy that deals with painful realities. If someone were to tell us that *Hamlet* is a comedy and that the end, with a pile of corpses, is especially funny, we would not say, "Oh, well, we all see things in our own way." We would conclude that we have just heard a misinterpretation.

Many people who subscribe to one version or another of a reader-response theory would agree that they are concerned not with all readers but with what they call *informed readers* or *competent readers*. Informed or competent readers are familiar with the conventions of literature and understand that, in a play such as *Hamlet*, the characters usually speak in verse. Such readers, then, do not express amazement that Hamlet often speaks metrically and sometimes uses rhyme. These readers understand that verse is the normal language for most of the characters in the play, and therefore such readers do not characterize Hamlet as a poet. Informed readers, in short, know the rules of the game.

There will still be plenty of room for differences of interpretation. Some people will find Hamlet not at all blameworthy, others will find him somewhat blameworthy, and still others may find him highly blameworthy. In short, we can say that a writer works against a background that is *shared* by readers. As readers, we are familiar with various kinds of literature, and we read or see *Hamlet* as a particular kind of literary work, a tragedy, a play that evokes (in Shakespeare's words) "woe or wonder," sadness, and astonishment. Knowing (in a large degree) how we ought to respond, our responses are not merely private.

Archetypal Criticism (Myth Criticism)

Carl G. Jung, the Swiss psychiatrist, in *Contributions to Analytical Psychology* (1928), postulates the existence of a "collective unconscious," an inheritance in our brains consisting of "countless typical experiences [such as birth, escape from danger, selection of a mate] of our ancestors." Few people today believe in an inherited "collective unconscious," but many people agree that certain repeated experiences, such as going to sleep and hours later awakening, the perception of the setting and rising sun, or of the annual death and rebirth of vegetation, manifest themselves in dreams, myths, and literature—in these instances, as stories of apparent death and rebirth. This archetypal plot of death and rebirth is said to be evident in Coleridge's *The Rime of the Ancient Mariner* (1798), for example. The ship suffers a death-like calm and then is miraculously restored to motion, and, in a sort of parallel rebirth, the mariner moves from spiritual death to renewed perception of the holiness of life. Another archetypal plot is the quest, which usually involves the testing and initiation of a hero, and thus essentially represents the movement from innocence to experience.

In addition to archetypal plots, there are archetypal characters, since an **archetype** is any recurring unit. Among archetypal characters are the scapegoat (as in Shirley Jackson's "The Lottery"), the hero (savior, deliverer), the terrible mother (witch, stepmother, or even the wolf "grandmother" in the tale of Little Red Riding Hood), and the wise old man (father figure, magician).

Because, the theory holds, both writer and reader share unconscious memories, the tale that an author tells (derived from the collective unconscious) may strangely move the reader, speaking to his or her collective unconscious. The critic looks for certain characters or patterns of action and values of the work if the motifs are there, meanwhile overlooking what is unique, subtle, distinctive, and truly interesting about the work. That is, a work is regarded as good if it closely resembles other works, with the usual motifs and characters. A second weakness in some archetypal criticism is that, in his or her search for the deepest meaning of a work, the critic may crudely impose a pattern, seeing the quest in every walk down a street.

If archetypal criticism sometimes seems far-fetched, it is nevertheless true that one of its strengths is that it invites us to use comparisons, and comparing is often an excellent way to see not only what a work shares with other works but also what is distinctive in the work. The most successful practitioner of archetypal criticism was Northrop Frye (1912–91), whose numerous books help readers to see fascinating connections between works. For Frye's explicit comments about archetypal criticism, as well as examples of such criticism in action, see especially his *Anatomy of Criticism* (1957) and *The Educated Imagination* (1964). On archetypes, see also Chapter 16, "Archetypal Patterns," in Norman Friedman, *Form and Meaning in Fiction* (1975).

Historical Criticism

Historical criticism studies a work within its historical context. Thus, a student of *Julius Caesar, Hamlet,* or *Macbeth*—plays in which ghosts appear—may try to learn about Elizabethan attitudes toward ghosts. We may find that the Elizabethans took ghosts more seriously than we do, or, on the other hand, we may find that ghosts were explained in various ways—for instance, sometimes as figments of the imagination and sometimes as shapes taken by the devil in order to mislead the virtuous. Similarly, a historical essay concerned with *Othello* may be devoted to Elizabethan attitudes toward Moors, to Elizabethan ideas of love, or, for that matter, to Elizabethan ideas of a daughter's obligations toward her father's wishes concerning her suitor.

The historical critic assumes (and the assumption can hardly be disputed) that writers, however individualistic, are shaped by the social contexts in which they live. Put another way, the goal of historical criticism is to understand how people in the past thought and felt. It assumes that such knowledge can enrich our understanding of a particular work. The assumption is, however, disputable because it may be argued that the artist may *not* have shared the age's view on this or that. All of the half-dozen or so Moors in Elizabethan plays other than *Othello* are villainous or foolish, but this evidence does not prove that *therefore* Othello is villainous or foolish.

Biographical Criticism

One kind of historical research is the study of *biography*, which for our purposes includes not only biographies but also autobiographies, diaries, journals, letters, and so on. What experiences did Mark Twain undergo? Are some of the apparently sensational aspects of *Huckleberry Finn* in fact close to events that Twain experienced? If so, is he a "realist"? If not, is he writing in the tradition of the "tall tale"?

The really good biographies not only tell us about the life of the author but also enable us to return to the literary texts with a deeper understanding of how they came to be what they are. If, for example, you read Richard B. Sewall's biography of Emily Dickinson, you will find a wealth of material concerning her family and the world in which she lived—for instance, the religious ideas that were part of her upbringing.

Biographical criticism may illuminate even the work of a contemporary author. If you are writing about the poetry of Adrienne Rich, for example, you may want to consider what she has told us in many essays about her life, in *On Lies, Secrets, and Silence* (1979) and *Blood, Bread, and Poetry* (1986), especially about her relations with her father and her husband.

Marxist Criticism

One form of historical criticism is **Marxist criticism**, named for Karl Marx (1818–83). Actually, to say "one form" is misleading because Marxist criticism today is varied, but essentially it sees history primarily as a struggle between socioeconomic classes, and it sees literature (and everything else, too) as the product of the economic forces of the period.

For Marxists, economics is the "base" or "infrastructure"; on this base rests a "superstructure" of ideology (law, politics, philosophy, religion, and the arts, including literature), reflecting the interests of the dominant class. Literature is a material product, produced—like bread or battleships—in order to be consumed in a given society. Marxist critics are concerned with Shakespeare's plays as part of a market economy: show *business*, the economics of the theater, including payments to authors and actors and revenue from audiences.

Few critics would disagree that works of art in some measure reflect the age in which they were produced, but most contemporary Marxist critics go further. First, they assert—in a repudiation of what has been called "vulgar Marxist theory"—that the deepest historical meaning of a literary work is to be found in what it does *not* say, what its ideology does not permit it to express. Second, Marxists take seriously Marx's famous comment that "the philosophers have only *interpreted* the world in various ways: the point is to *change* it." The critic's job is to change the world by revealing the economic basis of the arts. Not surprisingly, most Marxists are skeptical of such concepts as "genius" and "masterpiece." These concepts, they say, are part of the bourgeois myth that idealizes the individual and detaches art from its economic context. For an introduction to Marxist criticism, see Terry Eagleton, *Marxism and Literary Criticism* (1976).

New Historicist Criticism

A recent school of scholarship, called **New Historicism**, insists that there is no "history" in the sense of a narrative of indisputable past events. Rather, New Historicism holds that there is only our version—our narrative, our representation—of the past. In this view, each age projects its own preconceptions on the past: Historians may think that they are revealing the past, but they are revealing only their own historical situation and their personal preferences.

For example, in the nineteenth century, and in the twentieth century almost up to 1992, Columbus was represented as the heroic benefactor of humankind who discovered the New World. But, even while plans were being made to celebrate the five-hundredth anniversary of his first voyage across the Atlantic, voices were raised in protest: Columbus did not "discover" a New World; after all, the indigenous people knew where they were, and it was Columbus who was lost because he thought he was in India. In short, people who wrote history in, say, 1900 projected onto the past their current views (colonialism was a good thing), and people who wrote history in 1992 projected onto that same period a very different set of views (colonialism was a bad thing).

Similarly, ancient Greece, once celebrated by historians as the source of democracy and rational thinking, is now more often regarded as a society that was built on slavery and on the oppression of women. Further, the Renaissance, once glorified as an age of enlightened thought, is now often seen as an age that tyrannized women, enslaved colonial people, and enslaved itself with its belief in witchcraft and astrology. Thinking about these changing views, we feel the truth of the witticism that the only thing more uncertain than the future is the past.

On the New Historicism, see *The New Historicism* (1989), edited by H. Aram Veeser, and *The New Historicism Reader* (1994), also edited by H. Aram Veeser.

Psychological or Psychoanalytic Criticism

One form that biographical study may take is **psychological criticism**, or *psychoanalytic criticism*, which usually examines the author and the author's writings within the framework of Freudian psychology. A central doctrine of Sigmund Freud (1856–1939) is the Oedipus complex, the view that all males (Freud seems not to have made his mind up about females) unconsciously wish to displace their fathers and to sleep with their mothers. According to Freud, hatred for the father and love of the mother, normally repressed, may appear disguised in dreams. Works of art, like dreams, are disguised versions of repressed wishes.

In *Hamlet and Oedipus* (1949), Ernest Jones, amplifying some comments by Freud, argued that Hamlet delays killing Claudius because Claudius (who has killed Hamlet's father and married Hamlet's mother) has done exactly what Hamlet himself wanted to do. For Hamlet to kill Claudius, then, would be to kill himself.

If this approach interests you, take a look at Norman N. Holland's *Psychoanalysis and Shakespeare* (1966) or Frederick Crews's study of Hawthorne, *The Sins of the Fathers* (1966). Crews finds in Hawthorne's work evidence of unresolved Oedipal conflicts, and he accounts for the appeal of the fictions thus: The stories "rest on fantasy, but on the shared fantasy of mankind, and this makes for a more penetrating fiction than would any illusionistic slice of life.". For applications to other authors, consider Simon O. Lesser's *Fiction and the Unconscious* (1957), or an anthology of criticism, *Literature and Psychoanalysis*, edited by Edith Kurzweil and William Phillips (1983).

Psychological criticism can also turn from the author and the work to the reader, seeking to explain why we, as readers, respond in certain ways. Why is *Hamlet* so widely popular? A Freudian answer is that it is universal because it deals with a universal (Oedipal) impulse. We can, however, ask whether it appeals as strongly to women as to men (again, Freud was unsure about the Oedipus complex in women) and, if so, why it appeals to them. Or, more generally, we can ask if males and females read in the same way.

Gender Criticism (Feminist, and Lesbian and Gay Criticism)

This last question brings us to **gender criticism**. As we have seen, a person writing about literature usually seeks to answer questions. Historical scholarship, for instance, tries to answer such questions as "What did Shakespeare and his contemporaries believe about ghosts?" or "How did Victorian novelists and poets respond to Darwin's theory of evolution?" Gender criticism, too, asks questions. It is especially concerned with two issues, one about reading and one about writing: "Do men and women read in different ways?" and "Do they write in different ways?"

Feminist criticism can be traced back to the work of Virginia Woolf (1882–1941), but chiefly it grew out of the women's movement of the 1960s. The women's movement at first tended to hold that women are pretty much the same as men and therefore should be treated equally, but much recent feminist criticism has emphasized and explored the differences between women and men. Because the experiences of the sexes are different, the argument goes, their values and sensibilities are different, and their responses to literature are different. Further, literature written by women is different from literature written by men. Works written by women are seen by some feminist critics as embodying the experiences of a minority culture—a group marginalized by the dominant male culture. If you have read Susan Glaspell's *Trifles* (page 558), you'll recall that this literary work itself is largely concerned with the differing ways in which males and females perceive the world. Not all women are feminist critics, and not all feminist critics are women; further, there are varieties of feminist criticism. For a good introduction, see *The New Feminist Criticism: Essays on Women, Literature, and Theory* (1985), edited by Elaine Showalter, and *Feminism: An Anthology of Literary Theory and Criticism*, edited by Robyn R. Warhol and Diane Price Herndl (1997). For the role of men in feminist criticism, see *Engendering Men*, edited by Joseph A. Boone and Michael Cadden (1990).

Feminist critics rightly point out that men have established the conventions of literature and that men have established the canon—that is, the body of literature that is said to be worth reading. Speaking a bit broadly, in this patriarchal or male-dominated body of literature, men are valued for being strong and active, whereas women are expected to be weak and passive. Thus, in the world of fairy tales, the admirable male is the energetic hero (Jack, the Giant-Killer) but the admirable female is the passive Sleeping Beauty. Active women, such as the wicked stepmother—or a disguised form of the same thing, the witch—are generally villainous. (There are exceptions, such as Gretel in "Hansel and Gretel.") A woman hearing or reading the story of Sleeping Beauty or of Little Red Riding Hood (rescued by the powerful woodcutter), or any other work in which women seem to be trivialized, will respond differently than a man. For instance, a woman may be socially conditioned to admire Sleeping Beauty but only at great cost to her mental well-being. A more resistant female reader may recognize in herself no kinship with the beautiful, passive Sleeping Beauty and may respond to the story indignantly. Another way to put it is this: The male reader perceives a romantic story, but the resistant female reader perceives a story of oppression.

For discussions of the ways in which, it is argued, women *ought* to read, you may want to look at *Gender and Reading*, edited by Elizabeth A. Flynn and Patrocino Schweikart, and Judith Fetterley's *The Resisting Reader* (1978).

Feminist criticism has been concerned not only with the depiction of women and men in a male-determined literary canon and with women's responses to these images but also with yet another topic: women's writing. Women have had fewer opportunities than men to become writers of fiction, poetry, and drama. For one thing, they have been less well educated in the things that the male patriarchy has valued. However, even when they *have* managed to write, men have sometimes neglected their work simply because it was written by a woman. Feminists have further argued that certain forms of writing have been especially the province of women—for instance, journals, diaries, and letters—and, predictably, that these forms have not been given adequate space in the traditional, male-oriented canon. Poet and essayist Adrienne Rich effectively sums up the matter in her 1972 essay, "When We Dead Awaken: Writing as Re-Vision."

Much feminist criticism concerned with women writers has emphasized connections between the writer's biography and her work, such as Suzanne Juhasz, in her introduction to *Feminist Critics Read Emily Dickinson* (1983). Feminist criticism has made many readers—men as well as women—increasingly aware of gender relationships within literary works.

Lesbian criticism and **gay criticism** have their roots in feminist criticism; that is, feminist criticism introduced many of the questions that these other, newer developments are now exploring.

Before turning to some of the questions that lesbian and gay critics address, it is necessary to say that lesbian criticism and gay criticism are not symmetrical, because lesbian and gay relationships themselves are not symmetrical. Straight society has traditionally been more tolerant of—or blinder to—lesbianism than male homosexuality. Further, lesbian literary theory has tended to see its affinities more with feminist theory than with gay theory; that is, the emphasis has been on gender (male/female) rather than on sexuality (homosexuality/bisexuality/ heterosexuality). On the other hand, some gays and lesbians have been writing what is now being called "queer theory."

These are some of the questions that this criticism addresses: (1) Do lesbians and gays read in ways that differ from the ways in which straight people read? (2) Do they write in ways that differ from those of straight people? (3) How have straight writers portrayed lesbians and gays, and how have lesbian and gay writers portrayed straight women and men? (4) What strategies did lesbian and gay writers use to make their work acceptable to a general public in an age when lesbian and gay behavior was unmentionable?

The examination of gender by gay and lesbian critics can help to illuminate literary works, but it should be added, too, that some—perhaps most—gay and lesbian critics write also as activists, reporting their findings not only to enable us to understand and to enjoy the works of (say) Whitman but also to change society's view of sexuality. Thus, in *Disseminating Whitman* (1991), Michael Moon is impatient with earlier critical rhapsodies about Whitman's universalism. It used to be said that Whitman's celebration of the male body was a sexless celebration of brotherly love in a democracy, but Moon's view is that we must neither whitewash Whitman's poems with such high-minded talk nor reject them as indecent; rather, we must see exactly what Whitman is saying about a kind of experience to which society had shut its eyes, and we must take Whitman's view seriously.

One assumption in much lesbian and gay critical writing is that, although gender greatly influences the ways in which we read, reading is a skill that can be learned, and therefore straight people (aided by lesbian and gay critics) can learn to read, with pleasure and profit, lesbian and gay writers. This assumption also underlies much feminist criticism, which often assumes that men must stop ignoring books by women and must learn (with the help of feminist critics) how to read them, and, in fact, how to read—with newly opened eyes—the sexist writings of men of the past and present.

In addition to the titles mentioned earlier concerning gay and lesbian criticism, consult Eve Kosofsky Sedgwick, *Between Men: English Literature and Male Homosocial Desire* (1985), and an essay by Sedgwick, "Gender Criticism," in *Redrawing the Boundaries*, edited by Stephen Greenblatt and Giles Gunn (1992).

Works that concern gay or lesbian experience include those by A. E. Housman, Gloria Naylor, Adrienne Rich, and Walt Whitman.

This appendix began by making the point that all readers, whether or not they consciously adopt a particular approach to literature, necessarily read through particular lenses. More precisely, a reader begins with a frame of interpretation and from within that frame of interpretation selects one of the several competing methodologies.

When we talk about a critical approach, sometimes our point is made by saying that readers decode a text by applying a grid to it: The grid enables readers to see certain things clearly. What is sometimes forgotten, however, is that a lens or a grid—an angle of vision or interpretive frame and a methodology—also prevents a reader from seeing certain other things. This is to be expected. What is important, then, is to remember this fact and thus not to deceive ourselves by thinking that our keen tools enable us to see the whole. A psychoanalytic reading of *Hamlet* may be helpful, but it does not reveal all that is in *Hamlet*, and it does not refute the perceptions of another approach, let's say a historical study. Each approach may illuminate aspects neglected by others.

It is too much to expect a reader to apply all useful methods (or even several) at once; that would be rather like looking through a telescope with one eye and through a microscope with the other. However, it is not too much to expect readers to be aware of the limitations of their methods. If you read much criticism, you will find two kinds of critics. There are, on the one hand, critics who methodically and mechanically peer through a lens or a grid, and they find what can be easily predicted that they will find. On the other hand, there are critics who (despite what may be inevitable class and gender biases) are relatively open-minded in their approach and who, one might say, do not at the outset of their reading believe that their method assures them that they have got the text's number and that by means of this method they will expose the text for what it is.

Your Turn: Putting Critical Strategies to Work

1. Which of the critical strategies described in this appendix do you find the most interesting? Which interests you the least?
2. In Chapter 4, we present three stories by Kate Chopin, "The Story of an Hour," "Desiree's Baby," and "The Storm." Which critical strategy do you think is the

most rewarding for the study of this author ? Explain why, using your favorite story of the three as a "case study" for your arguments.

3. Select a poem in this book that you especially enjoy, and explain why you value it so highly. Next, reread and think about this poem in relation to each of the critical strategies outlined in this appendix. In what ways do these strategies, one by one, enable you to respond to and understand the poem more deeply? Does one of them seem to you especially helpful? Are any of them unhelpful?

4. Imagine that you have been assigned to prepare a mini-anthology of three or four poems and two or three stories that are particularly suited to one of these critical strategies. List your selections, and then explain how your critical strategy gives a special insight into each one, and into the group of works as a whole.

5. Do you think that any of these critical strategies could be usefully combined with one or more of the others? Could, for example, reader-response criticism go hand-in-hand with gender criticism? Select a poem or a story to show how your combination of two or more strategies can be brought together effectively.

6. Do you find that some of these critical strategies are in conflict with one another? Can you, for instance, be a formalist critic and, say, a reader-response critic or a gender critic at the same time? Is it a problem if our interpretation of a literary work changes, depending on the critical strategy that we use?

7. As you review and think further about the critical strategies that we have described, do you find anything missing? How would you respond to someone who says, "What really matters is our own interpretation of a literary work, not the interpretation that this or that critical strategy produces"?

APPENDIX B

The Basics of Manuscript Form

Basic Manuscript Form

Much of what follows is nothing more than common sense.

- Use good quality **8½″ × 11″** paper. Print out a second copy, in case the instructor's copy goes astray. Make sure also to back up the file on an external hard drive or in your e-mail account.
- **Double-space**, and print on one side of the page only.
- Use **1-inch margins** on all sides.
- Put your last name and then the **page number** (in arabic numerals) so that the number is flush with the right-hand margin and one-half inch from the top margin.
- On the first page, below the top margin and flush with the left-hand margin, put your **full name**, your **instructor's name**, the **course number** (including the section), and the **date**, one item per line, double-spaced.
- **Center the title** of your essay. Remember that the title is important because it gives the readers their first glimpse of your essay. **Create your own title**—one that reflects your topic or thesis. For example, an essay on Charlotte Perkins Gilman's "The Yellow Wallpaper" should not be called "The Yellow Wallpaper" but might be called

Disguised Tyranny in Gilman's "The Yellow Wallpaper"

or

How to Drive a Woman Mad

These titles at least do a little in the way of rousing a reader's interest.

- **Capitalize the title thus**: Begin the first word of the title with a capital letter, and capitalize each subsequent word except articles (*a, an, the*), conjunctions (*and, but, if, when,* etc.), and prepositions (*in, on, with,* and so forth):

A Word on Behalf of Love

Notice that you do *not* enclose your title within quotation marks, and you do *not* italicize or underline it. However, if it includes the title of a poem or a story, *that* title is enclosed within quotation marks, or if it includes the title of a novel or a play, *that* title is set in italics. Thus,

Gilman's "The Yellow Wallpaper" and Medical Practice

and

Gender Stereotypes in *Hamlet*

- **After writing your title, double-spaced**, indent one-half inch and begin your first sentence.
- Unless your instructor tells you otherwise, **use a staple** to hold the pages together. (Do not use a stiff binder; it will only add to the bulk of the instructor's stack of papers.)
- Extensive revisions should have been made in your drafts, but minor **last-minute revisions** may be made—neatly—on the finished copy if your instructor permits. If you proofread your essay, you may catch some typographical errors, and you may also notice some minor weaknesses.

Quotations and Quotation Marks

First, a word about the *point* of using quotations. Don't use quotations to pad the length of an essay. Rather, give quotations from the work that you are discussing so that your readers will see the material being considered and (especially in a research paper) so that your readers will know what some of the chief interpretations are and your responses to them.

Note: The next few paragraphs do *not* discuss how to include citations of sources, a topic that will be taken up a little later in this appendix, under the heading "Documentation."

The Golden Rule: If you quote, *comment on* the quotation. Let the reader know what you make of it and why you quote it.

Additional principles:

1. **Identify the speaker or writer of the quotation** so that the reader is not left with a sense of uncertainty. Usually, in accordance with the principle of letting readers know where they are going, this identification precedes the quoted material, but occasionally it may follow the quoted material, especially if it will provide something of a pleasant surprise. For instance, in a discussion of Flannery O'Connor's stories, you might quote a disparaging comment on one of the stories and then reveal that O'Connor herself was the speaker.

2. If the quotation is part of your own sentence, **be sure to fit the quotation grammatically and logically into your sentence**.

> *Incorrect:* Holden Caulfield tells us very little about "what my lousy childhood was like."
>
> *Correct:* Holden Caulfield tells us very little about what his "lousy childhood was like."

3. **Indicate any omissions or additions.** The quotation must be exact. Any material that you add—even one or two words—must be enclosed within square brackets, as in the following example:

> Hawthorne tells us that "owing doubtless to the depth of the gloom at that particular spot [in the forest], neither the travellers nor their steeds were visible."

If you wish to omit material from within a quotation, indicate the ellipsis by three spaced periods. That is, at the point where you are omitting material, type a space, a period, a space, a period, a space, and a third period. If you are omitting material from the end of a quoted sentence, type a period (no space) immediately following the last quoted word and then a space, a period, a space, a third period, a space, and a final period to indicate the end of your sentence. The following example is based on a quotation from the sentences immediately preceding this one:

> The instructions say, "If you . . . omit material from within a quotation, [you
>
> must] indicate the ellipsis. . . . If you are omitting material from the end of a
>
> quoted sentence, type . . . a final period to indicate the end. . . .

Notice that, although material preceded "If you," an ellipsis mark is not needed to indicate the omission because "If you" began a sentence in the original. Customarily, initial and terminal omissions are indicated only when they are part of the sentence that you are quoting. Even such omissions need not be indicated when the quoted material is obviously incomplete—when, for instance, it is a word or a phrase.

4. **Distinguish between short and long quotations**, and treat each appropriately. **Short quotations** (usually defined as four or fewer lines of typed prose or up to three lines of poetry) are enclosed within quotation marks and run into the text (rather than being set off, without quotation marks), as in the following example:

> Hawthorne begins the story by telling us that "Young Goodman Brown came forth
>
> at sunset into the street at Salem village" (640), thus at the outset connecting the
>
> village with daylight. A few paragraphs later, when Hawthorne tells us that the
>
> road Brown takes was "darkened by all of the gloomiest trees of the forest" (640),
>
> he begins to associate the forest with darkness—and a very little later with evil.

If your short quotation is from a poem, be sure to follow the capitalization of the original, and use a slash mark (with a space before and after it) to indicate separate lines. Give the line numbers, if your source gives them, in parentheses, immediately after the closing quotation marks and before the closing punctuation, as in the following example:

> In "Diving into the Wreck," Adrienne Rich's speaker says that she puts on
>
> "body-armor" (5). Obviously the journey is dangerous.

To set off a **long quotation** (more than four typed lines of prose or more than two lines of poetry), indent the entire quotation ten spaces, or 1 inch from the left margin. Usually, a long quotation is introduced by a clause ending with a colon—for instance,

> The following passage will make this point clear:

Or:

> The closest we come to hearing an editorial voice is a long passage in the middle
>
> of the story:

or some such lead-in. After typing your lead-in, double-spaced, then type the quotation, indented and double-spaced.

5. **Commas and periods go inside the quotation marks.** If you are quoting material within a sentence of your own and you need to use a comma or a period, these marks of punctuation go *before* the closing quotation mark, as in the following example, in which the author uses a comma after "trouble" and a period after "disease."

> Chopin tells us in the first sentence that "Mrs. Mallard was afflicted with
>
> heart trouble," and in the last sentence the doctors say that Mrs. Mallard
>
> "died of heart disease."

Exception: When the quotation is immediately followed by material in parentheses or in square brackets, close the quotation, then give the parenthetic or bracketed material, and then, after the closing parenthesis or bracket, insert the comma or period.

> Chopin tells us in the first sentence that "Mrs. Mallard was afflicted with
>
> heart trouble" (57), and in the last sentence the doctors say that Mrs. Mallard
>
> "died of heart disease" (58).

Semicolons, colons, and dashes go outside (after) the closing quotation mark.
Question marks and exclamation points go inside if they are part of the quotation or outside if they are your own.

In the following passage from a student's essay, notice the difference in the position of the question marks. The first question mark is part of the quotation, so it is enclosed within the quotation marks. The second question mark, however, is the student's, so it comes after the closing quotation mark.

> The older man says to Goodman Brown, "Sayest thou so?" Doesn't a reader
>
> become uneasy when the man immediately adds, "We are but a little way in
>
> the forest yet"?

Quotation Marks or Italics?

Use quotation marks around titles of short stories and other short works—that is, titles of chapters in books, essays, and poems that might not be published by themselves. Use italics for titles of books, periodicals, collections of essays, plays, and long poems such as *The Rime of the Ancient Mariner.*

A Note on the Possessive

It is awkward to use the possessive case for titles of literary works and secondary sources. Rather than "*The Great Gatsby*'s final chapter," write instead "the final chapter of *The Great Gatsby.*" Do not say "*The Oxford Companion to American Literature*'s entry on Emerson" but, instead, "the entry on Emerson in *The Oxford Companion to American Literature.*"

Documentation: Internal Parenthetical Citations and a List of Works Cited (MLA Format)

Documentation tells your reader exactly what your sources are. Here we describe how to create internal parenthetical citations and the Works Cited list.

Internal Parenthetical Citations

On page 1403, we distinguish between embedded quotations (which are short, are made part of your own sentence, and are enclosed in quotation marks) and quotations that are set off on the page and are not enclosed in quotation marks (for example, three or more lines of poetry, or five or more lines of typed prose).

For an embedded quotation, put the page reference in parentheses immediately after the closing quotation marks *without* any intervening punctuation. Then, after the parenthesis that follows the number, insert the necessary punctuation (for instance, a comma or a period):

> Brent Staples says that he "learned to smother the rage" he felt at "often being
>
> taken for a criminal" (337).

The period comes *after* the parenthetical citation. In the next example, *no* punctuation comes after the first citation—because none is needed—and a comma comes *after* (not before or within) the second citation, because a comma is needed in the sentence:

> This is ironic because almost at the start of the story, in the second paragraph,
>
> Richards with the best of motives "hastened" (57) to bring his sad message; if he
>
> had at the start been "too late" (58), Mallard would have arrived at home first.

For a quotation that is not embedded within the text but is set off (by being indented ten spaces), put the parenthetical citation on the last line of the quotation, one space *after* the punctuation that ends the quoted sentence.

We note four additional points:

- "The abbreviations *p., pg.,* and *pp.* are *not* used in citing pages.
- "If a story is very short, perhaps running for only a page or two, your instructor may tell you that there is no need to keep citing the page reference for each quotation. Simply include on your Works Cited list the story's page numbers, say, 205–06.
- "If you are referring to a poem, your instructor may tell you to use parenthetical citations of line numbers rather than of page numbers. But, again, your Works Cited list will tell the reader where the poem can be found.
- "If you are referring to a play with numbered lines, your instructor may prefer that in your parenthetical citations you give act, scene, and line rather than page numbers. Use arabic (not roman) numerals, separating the act from the scene, and the scene from the line, by periods. Here, then, is how a reference to Act 3, Scene 2, line 105 would be given:

> When Hamlet says to Ophelia, "That's a fair thought to lie between maids'
>
> legs" (3.2.105), she does not understand that he is making a lewd comment.

Parenthetical Citations and List of Works Cited

Parenthetical citations are clarified by means of a list, headed "Works Cited," that appears at the end of the essay. In this list, you give alphabetically (last name first) the authors and titles that you have quoted or referred to in the essay, and full publication information.

Briefly, the idea is that the reader of your essay will encounter an author's name and a parenthetical citation of pages. By checking the author's name in Works Cited, the reader can find the passage in the book. Suppose you are writing about Kate Chopin's "The Story of an Hour." Let's assume that you have already mentioned the author and the title of the story—that is, you have let the reader know the subject of the essay—and now you introduce a quotation from the story in a sentence such as the one following. (Notice the parenthetical citation of page numbers immediately after the quotation.)

> True, Mrs. Mallard at first expresses grief when she hears the news, but soon
>
> (unknown to her friends) she finds joy in it. So, Richards's "sad message" (57),
>
> though sad in Richards's eyes, is in fact a happy message.

Turning to Works Cited, the reader, knowing the quoted words are by Chopin, looks for Chopin and finds the following:

> Chopin, Kate. "The Story of an Hour." *Literature for Composition.*
>
> Ed. Sylvan Barnet, William Burto, William E. Cain, and Cheryl L. Nixon. 11th ed.
>
> Boston: Pearson, 2017. 65–66. Print.

Thus, in your essay, you inform the reader that the quoted words ("sad message") are to be found on page 65 of this anthology.

If you have not mentioned Chopin's name in some sort of lead-in, you will have to give her name within the parentheses so that the reader will know the author of the quoted words:

> What are we to make out of a story that ends by telling us that the leading
>
> character has died "of joy that kills" (Chopin 66)?

If you are referring to several works reprinted within one volume, instead of listing each item fully, it is acceptable in Works Cited to list each item simply by giving the author's name, the title of the work, then a period, a space, and the name of the anthologist, followed by the page numbers that the selection spans. Thus, a reference to Chopin's "The Story of an Hour" would be followed only by this: Barnet 00–000. This form requires that the anthology itself be cited under the name of the first-listed editor, as shown in the following example:

> Barnet, Sylvan, William Burto, William E. Cain, and Cheryl L. Nixon, eds. *Literature*
>
> *for Composition.* 11th ed. Boston: Pearson, 2017. Print.
>
> Chopin, Kate. "The Story of an Hour." Barnet 65–66.

If you are writing a research essay you will use many sources. In the essay itself, you will mention an author's name, quote or summarize from this author, and follow the quotation or summary with a parenthetical citation of the pages. In Works Cited, you will give the full title, place of publication, and other bibliographic material.

Here are a few examples, all referring to an article by Joan Templeton, "The *Doll House* Backlash: Criticism, Feminism, and Ibsen." The article appeared in *PMLA* 104 (1989): 28–40, but this information is given only in Works Cited, not within the text of the student's essay.

If in the text of your essay you mention the author's name, the citation following a quotation (or a summary of a passage) will be merely a page number in parentheses, followed by a period, as shown in the following example:

> In 1989 Joan Templeton argued that many critics, unhappy with recognizing
>
> Ibsen as a feminist, sought "to render Nora inconsequential" (29).

Or:

> In 1989 Joan Templeton noted that many critics, unhappy with recognizing
>
> Ibsen as a feminist, have sought to make Nora trivial (29).

If you don't mention the name of the author in a lead-in, you will have to give the name within the parenthetical citation:

> Many critics, attempting to argue that Ibsen was not a feminist, have tried to
>
> make Nora trivial (Templeton 29).

Notice in all of these examples that the final period comes after the parenthetical citation. *Exception:* When the quotation is longer than four lines and is therefore set off by being indented ten spaces from the left margin, end the quotation with the appropriate punctuation (period, question mark, or exclamation mark), hit the space bar, then type (in parentheses) the page number. In this case, do not put a period after the citation.

Another point: If your list of Works Cited includes more than one work by an author, in your essay when you quote or refer to one or the other, you'll have to identify *which* work you are drawing on. You can provide the title in a lead-in, as shown in the following example:

> In "The *Doll House* Backlash: Criticism, Feminism, and Ibsen," Templeton says,
>
> "Nora's detractors have often been, from the first, her husband's defenders" (30).

Alternatively, you can provide the information in the parenthetical citation, giving a shortened version of the title. This usually consists of the first word, unless it is *A, An,* or *The,* in which case including the second word is usually enough. Certain titles may require still another word or two, as in this example:

> According to Templeton, "Nora's detractors have often been, from the first, her
>
> husband's defenders" ("*Doll House* Backlash" 30).

Forms of Citation in Works Cited

In looking over the following sample entries in a Works Cited list, remember:

- The list of Works Cited appears at the end of the essay. It begins on a new page, and that page continues the numbering of the text pages.
- The list of Works Cited is arranged alphabetically by author (last name first).
- If a work is anonymous, list it under the first word of the title, unless the first word is *A, An,* or *The,* in which case list it under the second word.
- If a work is by two authors, although the book is listed alphabetically under the first author's last name, the second author's name is given in the normal order, first name first.
- If you list two or more works by the same author, the author's name is not repeated after the first entry but is represented by three hyphens, followed by a period and a space.

- Each item begins flush left; if an entry is longer than one line, subsequent lines in the entry are indented five spaces.

For details about preparing almost every imaginable kind of citation, consult the *MLA Handbook for Writers of Research Papers,* 7th ed. (New York: Modern Language Association, 2009). Here we give samples of the kinds of citations that you are most likely to include in your list of Works Cited. (For citations of electronic sources, see pages 1414–16.)

A book by one author:

> Douglas, Ann. *The Feminization of American Culture*. New York: Knopf, 1977. Print.

Take the title from the title page and italicize both the title and the subtitle. The place of publication is indicated by the name of the city. If several cities have the same name (for instance, Cambridge, Massachusetts, and Cambridge, England) the name of the state or country may be added. If the title page lists several cities, give only the first one. You may also shorten the publisher's name—for example, from *Oxford University Press* to *Oxford UP.* For a print source, add the word "Print" at the end of the entry.

A book by two or three authors:

> Gilbert, Sandra M., and Susan Gubar. *The Madwoman in the Attic: The Woman Writer and*
>
> *the Nineteenth-Century Literary Imagination*. New Haven: Yale UP, 1979. Print.

Notice that the book is listed under the last name of the first author (Gilbert) and that the second author's name is then given with first name (Susan) first. *If the book has more than three authors,* give the name of the first author only (last name first) and follow it with *et al.* (Latin for "and others").

A book by more than three authors:

> Beidler, Peter G., et al. *A Reader's Companion to J. D. Salinger's* The Catcher in the Rye.
>
> Seattle: Coffeetown Press, 2009. Print.

A book in several volumes:

> McQuade, Donald, et al., eds. *The Harper American Literature*. 2nd ed. 2 vols.
>
> New York: Harper, 1994. Print.

> Pope, Alexander. *The Correspondence of Alexander Pope*. Ed. George Sherburn.
>
> 5 vols. Oxford: Clarendon, 1955. Print.

The total number of volumes is given, regardless of the number of volumes that you have used.

If you have used more than one volume, within your essay you will parenthetically indicate a reference to, for instance, page 30 of volume 3, thus: (3: 30). If you have used only one volume of a multivolume work—let's say you used only volume 2 of McQuade's anthology—in your entry in Works Cited, you will write, after the period following the date, Vol. 2. In your parenthetical citation within the essay, you will therefore cite only the page reference (without the volume number) because the reader will (on consulting Works Cited) understand that in this example the reference is in volume 2.

If, instead of using the volumes as a whole, you used only an independent work within one volume—say, an essay in volume 2—in Works Cited you will omit the abbreviation *Vol.* Instead, give an arabic 2 (indicating volume 2), followed by a colon, a space, and the page numbers that encompass the selection that you used, as shown in the following example:

> McPherson, James Alan. "Why I Like Country Music." *The Harper American Literature*. Ed.
>
> Donald McQuade et al. 2nd ed. 2 vols. New York: Longman, 1994. 2: 2304-15. Print.

Notice that this entry for McPherson specifies not only that the book consists of two volumes but also that only one selection ("Why I Like Country Music," occupying pages 2304–2315 in volume 2) was used. If you use this sort of citation in Works Cited, in the body of your essay a documentary reference to this work will be only to the page; the volume number will *not* be added.

A book with a separate title in a set of volumes:

> Churchill, Winston. *The Age of Revolution*. Vol. 3 of *A History of the English-Speaking*
>
> *Peoples*. New York: Dodd, 1957. Print.
>
> Jonson, Ben. *The Complete Masques*. Ed. Stephen Orgel. Vol. 4 of *The Yale Ben Jonson*.
>
> New Haven: Yale UP, 1969. Print.

A revised edition of a book:

> Chaucer, Geoffrey. *The Riverside Chaucer*. Ed. Larry Benson. 3rd ed. Boston: Houghton,
>
> 1987. Print.
>
> Ellmann, Richard. *James Joyce*. Rev. ed. New York: Oxford UP, 1982. Print.

A reprint, such as a paperback version of an older hardcover book:

> Rourke, Constance. *American Humor*. 1931. Garden City: Doubleday, 1953. Print.

Notice that the entry cites the original date (1931) but indicates that the writer is using the Doubleday reprint of 1953.

An edited book other than an anthology:

> Keats, John. *The Letters of John Keats*. Ed. Hyder Edward Rollins. 2 vols. Cambridge:
>
> Harvard UP, 1958. Print.

An anthology: You can list an anthology either under the editor's name or under the title.

A work in a volume of works by one author:

> Sontag, Susan. "The Aesthetics of Silence." *Styles of Radical Will*. New York: Farrar,
>
> 1969. 3-34. Print.

This entry indicates that Sontag's essay "The Aesthetics of Silence" appears in a book of hers titled *Styles of Radical Will*. Notice that the page numbers of the short work are cited (not the page numbers that you may happen to refer to, but the page numbers of the entire essay).

A work in an anthology, that is, in a collection of works by several authors: Begin with the author and the title of the work that you are citing, not with the name of the anthologist or the title of the anthology. The entry ends with the pages occupied by the selection that you are citing, as shown in the following example:

> Ng, Fae Myenne. "A Red Sweater." *Charlie Chan Is Dead: An Anthology of Contemporary Asian*
>
> *American Fiction*. Ed. Jessica Hagedorn. New York: Penguin, 1993. 358-68. Print.

Normally, you will give the title of the work that you are citing (probably an essay, a short story, or a poem) in quotation marks. If you are referring to a book-length work (for instance, a novel or a full-length play), italicize it. If the work is translated, after the period that follows the title, write *Trans.* and give the name of the translator, followed by a period and the name of the anthology.

If the collection is a multivolume work and you are using only one volume, in Works Cited you will specify the volume, as in the example on page 1415 of McPherson's essay. Because the list of Works Cited specifies the volume, your parenthetical documentary reference within your essay will specify (as mentioned earlier) only the page numbers, not the volume. Thus, although McPherson's essay appears on pages 2304–15 in the second volume of a two-volume work, a parenthetical citation will refer only to the page numbers, because the citation in Works Cited specifies the volume.

Remember that the pages specified in the entry in your list of Works Cited are those of the *entire selection,* not simply the pages that you refer to within your essay.

If you are referring to a *reprint of a scholarly article,* give details of the original publication:

> Mack, Maynard. "The World of Hamlet." *Yale Review* 41 (1952): 502-23. Rpt. in *Hamlet*.
>
> By William Shakespeare. Ed. Sylvan Barnet. New York: Penguin Putnam, 1998.
>
> 265-87. Print.

Two or more works in an anthology: If you are referring to more than one work in an anthology, in order to avoid repeating all the information about the anthology in each entry in Works Cited, under each author's name (in the appropriate alphabetical place), give the author and title of the work, then a period, a space, and the name of the anthologist, followed by the page numbers that the selection spans. A reference to Shakespeare's *Hamlet* would appear as follows:

> Shakespeare, William. *Hamlet*. Barnet 878-980.

rather than by a full citation of Barnet's anthology. This form requires that the anthology itself also be listed, under Barnet.

Two or more works by the same author: Notice that the works are given in alphabetical order (*Fables* precedes *Fools*) and that the author's name is not repeated but is represented by three hyphens, followed by a period and a space. If the author is the translator or the editor of a volume, the three hyphens are followed not by a period but by a comma, then a space, then the appropriate abbreviation (*Trans.* or *Ed.*), and then the title:

> Frye, Northrop. *Fables of Identity: Studies in Poetic Mythology*. New York: Harcourt,
>
> 1963. Print.
>
> ---. *Fools of Time: Studies in Shakespearean Tragedy*. Toronto: U of Toronto P, 1967. Print.

A translated book:

> Gogol, Nikolai. *Dead Souls*. Trans. Andrew McAndrew. New York: New American Library,
>
> 1961. Print.

If you are discussing the translation itself, as opposed to the book, list the work under the translator's name. Then put a comma, a space, and "trans." After the period following "trans," skip a space, then give the title of the book, a period, a space, and then "By" and the author's name, first name first. Continue with information about the place of publication, publisher, and date, as in any entry for a book.

An introduction, foreword, afterword, or other editorial apparatus:

> Fromm, Erich. Afterword. *1984*. By George Orwell. New York: New American Library, 1961.
>
> Print.

Usually a book with an introduction or comparable section is listed under the name of the author of the book rather than the name of the author of the editorial material (see the citation of Pope on page 1409). However, if you are referring to the editor's apparatus rather than to the work itself, use the form just given.

Words such as *preface, introduction, afterword,* and *conclusion* are capitalized in the entry but are neither enclosed within quotation marks nor underlined.

A book review: First, here is an example of a review that does not have a title.

> Vendler, Helen. Rev. of *Essays on Style*, ed. Roger Fowler. *Essays in Criticism* 16 (1966):
>
> 457-63. Print.

If the review has a title, give the title after the period following the reviewer's name, before "Rev." If the review is unsigned, list it under the first word of the title, or the second word if the first word is *A, An,* or *The*. If an unsigned review has no title, begin the entry with "Rev. of" and alphabetize it under the title of the work being reviewed.

An article in a scholarly journal: Some journals are paginated consecutively; that is, the pagination of the second issue picks up where the first issue left off. Other journals begin each issue with a new page one. The forms of the citations in Works Cited differ slightly.

First, the citation of a *journal that uses continuous pagination:*

> Burbick, Joan. "Emily Dickinson and the Economics of Desire." *American Literature* 58
>
> (1986): 361-78. Print.

This article appeared in volume 58, which was published in 1986. (Notice that the volume number is followed by a space, then by the year in parentheses, and then by a colon, a space, and the page numbers of the entire article.) Although each volume consists of four issues, you do *not* specify the issue number when the journal is paginated continuously.

For a *journal that paginates each issue separately* (a quarterly journal will have four page ones each year), give the issue number directly after the volume number and a period, with no space before or after the period:

> Spillers, Hortense J. "Martin Luther King and the Style of the Black Sermon." *The Black*
>
> *Scholar* 3.1 (1971): 14-27. Print.

An article in a weekly, biweekly, or monthly publication:

> McCabe, Bernard. "Taking Dickens Seriously." *Commonweal* 14 May 1965: 24. Print.

Notice that the volume number and the issue number are omitted for popular weeklies or monthlies such as *Time* and *Atlantic*.

An article in a newspaper: Because newspapers usually consist of several sections, a section number may precede the page number. The following example indicates that an article begins on page 3 of section 2 and continues on a later page:

> Wu, Jim. "Authors Praise New Forms." *New York Times* 8 Mar. 1996, late ed., sec. 2: 3+. Print.

You may have occasion to cite other than a printed source, for instance, a lecture. Here are the forms for the chief nonprint sources.

An interview:

> Saretta, Howard. Personal interview. 3 Nov. 2015.

A lecture:

> Heaney, Seamus. Tufts University, Medford, MA. 15 Oct. 1998. Lecture.

A television or radio program:

> *60 Minutes*. CBS. WCBS, New York. 30 Jan. 1994. Television.

A film or video recording:

> *Modern Times*. Dir. Charles Chaplin. United Artists, 1936. DVD.

A sound recording:

> Frost, Robert. "The Road Not Taken." *Robert Frost Reads His Poetry*. Caedmon,
>
> TC 1060, 1956. MP3.

A performance:

> *The Cherry Orchard*. By Anton Chekhov. Dir. Ron Daniels. American Repertory Theatre,
>
> Cambridge, MA. 3 Feb. 1994. Performance.

Citing Internet Sources

Many websites and web pages are not prepared according to the style and form in which you want to cite them. Sometimes the name of the author is unknown, and other information may be missing or difficult to find. Perhaps the main point to remember is that a source on the Internet is as much a source as is a book or an article that you can track down and read in the library. If you have made use of it, you must acknowledge that you have done so and include the bibliographical information, as fully as you can, in your list of Works Cited.

✔ **CHECKLIST:** *Citing Sources on the Web*

Provide the following information:

☐ Author's name.
☐ Title of work in quotation marks, or in italics if it's a longer work or book title.
☐ Title of website in italics, followed by a period.
☐ Publisher or sponsor of website, followed by a comma. (Use *N.p.* if that information is not available.)
☐ Date of publication, followed by a period. (Use *n.d.* if that information is not available.)
☐ Publication medium—*Web*—followed by a period.
☐ Date of access—the date when you accessed the site.
☐ Include the URL only when your reader cannot locate the source without it.

A short work within a scholarly project:

Whitman, Walt. "Crossing Brooklyn Ferry." *The Walt Whitman Archive*. Ed. Kenneth M.

Price and Ed Folson. The Walt Whitman Archive, 16 Mar. 1998. Web. 3 Apr. 2016.

A personal or professional site:

Winter, Mick. *How to Talk New Age*. The Well, 6 Jan. 2004. Web. 6 Apr. 2016.

An online book published independently:

Smith, Adam. *The Wealth of Nations*. New York: Methuen. 1904. *Bibliomania*, n.d.

Web. 3 Mar. 2016.

An online book within a scholarly project:

Whitman, Walt. *Leaves of Grass*. Philadelphia: McKay, 1891-92. *The Walt Whitman*

Archive. Ed. Kenneth M. Price and Ed Folson. The Walt Whitman Archive, 16

Mar. 1998. Web. 3 Apr. 2016.

An article in an online scholarly journal:

Jackson, Francis L. "Mexican Freedom: The Ideal of the Indigenous State." *Animus*

2.3 (1997): n. pag. Web. 4 Apr. 2016.

An article from a database:

Farley-Hills, David. "Hamlet's Account of the Pirates." *Review of English Studies*
50.199 (1999): 320-31. *JSTOR*. Web. 1 Apr. 2015.

An unsigned article in a newspaper or on a newswire:

"Drug Czar Wants to Sharpen Drug War." *TopNews* 6 Apr. 1998. Web. 6 Apr. 2015.

An unsigned article in a newspaper or on a website:

"Hiking: Richard W. DeKorte Park, Lyndhurst." *North Jersey.com*. North Jersey Media
Group, 2 July 2009. Web. 10 July 2015.

An article in a magazine:

Pitta, Julie. "Un-Wired?" Forbes.com. Forbes, 20 Apr. 1998. Web. 6 Apr. 2015.

A review:

Beer, Francis A. Rev. of *Evolutionary Paradigms in the Social Sciences, Special Issue,*
International Studies Quarterly 40.3 (Sept. 1996). *Journal of Memetics* 1
(1997). Web. 4 Jan. 2016.

An editorial or letter to the editor:

"The Net Escape Censorship? Ha!" Editorial. *Wired* Sept. 1995. Web. 1 Apr. 2015.

E-mail:

Mendez, Michael R. "Re: Solar power." Message to Edgar V. Atamian. 11 Sept. 2015. E-mail.

Armstrong, David J. Message to the author. 30 Aug. 2015. E-mail.

An Online Posting: For online postings or synchronous communications, try to cite
a version stored as a web file, if one exists, as a courtesy to the reader. Label sources
as needed (for example, "Online posting," "Online defense of dissertation," and so forth,
with neither underlining nor quotation marks). Follow these models as appropriate:

Listserv (electronic mailing list):

Kosten, A. "Major update of the WWWVL Migration and Ethnic Relations." 7 Apr. 1998.

Online posting. ERCOMER News. 7 May 2015.

A video accessed online:

The Poet's View: C. K. Williams. YouTube. The Academy of American Poets,
17 Mar. 2009. Web. 1 Apr. 2015.

Photograph or painting accessed online:

Manet, Edouard. *Le Déjeuner sur l'herbe.* 1863. *Wikimedia Commons.* Wikimedia
Foundation, 26 Nov. 2008. Web. 1 Apr. 2015.

Literary Credits

p. 337: Cisneros, Sandra. "Barbie-Q" from *Woman Hollering Creek*. Copyright © 1991 by Sandra Cisneros. Published by Vintage Books, a division of Penguin Random House, New York and originally in hardcover by Random House. By permission of Susan Bergholtz Literary Services, New York, NY and Lamy NM. All rights reserved. **p. 338:** O'Hara, Maryanne. "Diverging Paths and All That" © Maryanne O'Hara. Reprinted by permission of The Gernert Company as agents for the author. **p. 339:** Phillips, Jayne, Anne. "Sweethearts" by Jayne Anne Phillips. Copyright © 1979 by Jayne Anne Phillips. Originally published in *Black Tickets*. Reprinted by permission of the author. **p. 342:** Shakespeare, William. "Sonnet 18: Shall I Compare Thee to a Summer's Day?" *The Sonnets of William Shakespeare*, 1609, published by Thomas Thorpe. **p. 342:** Moss, Howard. "Sonnet 18: Shall I Compare Thee to a Summer Day?" in *A Swimmer in the Air* (New York: Scribner, 1957) © 1957. Reprinted by permission. **p. 348:** Herrick, Robert. "To the Virgins, to Make Much of Time" Hesperides: or, the works both humane and divine of Robert Herrick, Esq. 1648. **p. 349:** Marlowe, Christopher. "The Passionate Shepherd to His Love "*England's Helicon* edited by John Flasket 1600, (London: Printed by I.R. for John Flasket 1600). **p. 350:** Raleigh, Walter, "The Nymph's Reply to the Shepherd" from *The Poems of Sir Walter Raleigh Collected and Authenticated with those of Sir Henry Wotton and other Courtly Poets From 1540 to 1650*, edited by J. Hannah D.C.L. (London: George Bell and Sons, 1892) p. 11. **p. 351:** Marvell, Andrew. "To His Coy Mistress" from *Miscellaneous Poems* (London: Printed for Robert Boulter at the Turks-Head in Cornhill, 1681). **p. 353:** Donne, John. "The Bait" from *Poems on Several Occasions*. By the Reverend John Donne, D.D. (London Printed for Jacob Tonson and sold by William Taylor, 1719) p. 33. **p. 354:** Kinnell, Galway. "Blackberrying Eating" from *Mortal Acts, Mortal Words* by Galway Kinnell. copyright © 1980, renewed 2008 by Galway Kinnell. Reprinted by permission of Houghton Mifflin Harcourt Publishing Company. All rights reserved. **p. 355:** Plath, Sylvia. All lines from "Blackberrying" from *Crossing the Water* by Sylvia Plath. Copyright © 1962 by Ted Hughes. This poem originally appeared in *Uncollected Poems*, Turret Books, London, and in the Hudson Review. Reprinted with permission of HarperCollins Publishers and Faber and Faber Publishers. **p. 356:** Heaney, Seamus "Blackberry-Picking" from *Opened Ground: Selected Poems 1966–1996*. Copyright © 199 by Seamus Heaney Used by permission of Farrar, Straus & Giroux, LLC and Faber and Faber Publishers. **p. 356:** Heaney, Seamus "Blackberry-Picking" from *Opened Ground: Selected Poems 1966–1996*. Copyright © 1998 by Seamus Heaney Used by permission of Farrar, Straus & Giroux, LLC and Faber and Faber Publishers. **p. 357:** Komunyakaa, Yusef. "Facing It" from *Dien Cai Dau* © 1988 by Yusef Komunyakaa. Reprinted with permission of Wesleyan University Press. **p. 359:** Hughes, Langston. "I, Too [Sing America]" from *Collected Poems of Langston Hughes* by Langston Hughes. By permission of Harold Ober Associates Incorporated. Copyright © 1994 by The Estate of Langston Hughes. **p. 359:** Whitman, Walt. "I Hear America Singing." *Leaves of Grass*. Brooklyn: Fulton Street Printing, 1855. **p. 361:** Cortázar, Julio. "Continuidad de los parques" *Final Del Juego* © Sucesion Julio Cortázar, 1956. Reprinted with permission. **p. 361:** Cortázar, Julio. "Continuity of Parks" from *End of the Game and Other Stories* by Julio Cortázar, copyright © 1963, 1967 by Random House LLC. Used by permission of Pantheon Books, an imprint of the Knopf Doubleday Publishing Group, a division of Penguin Random House LLC. All rights reserved. **p. 362:** Homes, A.M. "Things You Should Know" by A.M. Homes collected in *Things You Should Know*. Copyright © 2002 by A.M. Homes, used by permission of The Wylie Agency LLC. **p. 362:** Homes, A.M. "Things You Should Know" [pp. 132–4] from *Things You Should Know* by A.M. Homes. Copyright © 1998 by A.M. Homes. Reprinted by permission of HarperCollins Publishers. **p. 364:** Chang, Samantha, Lan. "Water Names" from *Hunger* by Lan Samantha Chang. Copyright © 1998 by Lan Samantha Chang. Used by permission of W.W. Norton & Company, Inc. **p. 368:** Porter, Katherine, Anne. "The Jilting of Granny Weatherall from *Flowering Judas an Other Stories* by Katherine Anne Porter. Copyright © Renewed 1958 by Katherine Anne Porter. Reprinted by permission of Houghton Mifflin Harcourt Publishing Company, and by The Katherine Ann Porter Literary Trust c/o The Permissions Company, Inc. www.permissionscompany.com. All rights reserved. **p. 389:** Rutgers University Press. **p. 389:** The Poetry Foundation. **p. 390:** Houghton Library website. Harvard University. Copyright © 2015 President and Fellows of Harvard College. **p. 391:** Cody, David. "Blood in the Basin: The Civil War in Emily Dickinson's 'The name—of it—is "Autumn"— ". *The Emily Dickinson Journal 12:1* (2003), 25, © 2003 The John Hopkins University Press. Reprinted with permission of Johns Hopkins University Press. **p. 391:** © 2015 Microsoft. **p. 419:** Staples, Brent. "Black Men and Public Space" Originally appeared in *Harper's* 12/86. Copyright © 1986 Brent Staples. Reprinted by permission of the author. **p. 432:** Hughes, Langston. "Salvation" from *The Big Sea* by Langston Hughes. Copyright © 1940 by Langston Hughes. Copyright renewed 1968 by Arna Bontemps and George Houston Bass. Reprinted by permission of Hill and Wang, a division of Farrar, Straus and Giroux, LLC. **p. 433:** Vanderkam, Laura. "Hookups Starve the Soul" *USA Today* (Editorial/Opinion) 7/25/01. Copyright 2001. Reprinted by permission of the author. Laura Vanderkam is the author of several books, including *168 Hours*. Visit her website at www.lauravanderkam.com. **p. 434:** Doloff, Steven. "The Opposite Sex." Originally appeared in *The Washington Post*, January 1983. Copyright © 1983. Reprinted by permission of the author. **p. 437:** Ehrlich, Greta. "About Men," from *The Solace of Open Spaces* by Gretel Ehrlich, copyright © 1985 by Greta Ehrlich. Used by permission of Viking Books, an imprint of Penguin Publishing Group, a division of Penguin Random House LLC. **p. 437:** Ehrlich, Gretel. "About Men," Gretel Ehrlich in *The Solace of Open Spaces* (Viking, 1985). Copyright © 1985 by Gretel Ehrlich. All rights reserved. Used with permission. **p. 441:** Paley, Grace. "Samuel" from *The Collected Stories by Grace Paley*. Copyright © 1994 by Grace Paley. Reprinted by permission of Farrar, Straus and Giroux, LLC. **p. 451:** Faulkner, William. "A Rose for Emily" copyright © 1930 and renewed 1958 by William Faulkner from *Collected Stories of William Faulkner* by William Faulkner. Used by permission of Random House, an imprint and division of Penguin

Children" from *The First Four Books of Poems* by Louise Gluck, Copyright © 1968, 1971, 1972, 1973, 1974, 1975, 1976, 1977, 1978, 1979, 1980, 19854, 1995 by Louise Gluck. Reprinted by permission of HarperCollins Publishers. **p. 1022:** Pastan, Linda. "Ethics" from *Waiting for My Life* by Linda Pastan. Copyright © 1981 by Linda Pastan. Used by permission of Linda Pastan in care of the Jean V. Naggar Literary Agency, Inc. (permissions@jvnla.com). **p. 1023:** Roethke, Theodore. "My Papa's Waltz," copyright © 1942 by Hearst Magazines, Inc.; from *Collected Poems* by Theodore Roethke. Used by permission of Doubleday, an imprint of the Knopf Doubleday Publishing Group, a division of Penguin Random House, LLC, All rights reserved. **p. 1024:** Olds, Sharon. "The Rites of Passage from *The Dead and the Living*. Copyright ©1987 by Sharon Olds. Used by permission of Alfred A. Knopf Inc., an imprint of the Knopf Doubleday Publishing Group, a division of Penguin Random House, LLC. **p. 1025:** Trethewey, Natasha. "White Lies from *Domestic Work*. Copyright © 1988, 2000 by Natasha Trethewey. Reprinted with the permission of The Permissions Company, Inc., on behalf of Graywolf Press, www.graywolfpress.org. **p. 1028:** Ehrenreich, Barbara. Wal-Mart Orientation Program from "Selling in Minnesota" from the book *Nickled and Dimed: On (Not) Getting by in America* by Barbara Ehrenreich. Copyright © 2001 by Barbara Ehrenreich. Used by permission of Henry Holt and Company, LLC. All rights reserved. **p. 1031:** Grimm, Jacob and Wilhelm Grimm, *Children's and Household Tales*, 1812. **p. 1034:** William, William, Carlos, "The Use of Force" by William Carlos Williams from *The Collected Stories of William Carlos Williams*, copyright © 1938 by William Carlos Williams. Reprinted by permission of New Directions Publishing Corp. **p. 1037:** Eisner, Will. "The Day I Became a Professional" from *Life in Pictures: Autobiographical Stories* by Will Eisner. Copyright © 2007 by Will Eisner Studios, Inc. Used by permission of W.W. Norton & Company. **p. 1041:** Orozco, Daniel. "Orientation" from *Orientation and Other Stories* by Daniel Orozco. Copyright © 2011 by Daniel Orozco. Reprinted by permission of Farrar, Straus, and Giroux, LLC. **p. 1045:** Wordsworth, William. "The Solitary Reaper" in *Poems, in Two Volumes, Vol. 1* (London: Longman, Hurst, Rees and Ormn, Paternoster-Row, 1807). **p. 1046:** Sandburg, Carol. "Chicago" in "Chicago Poems" *Poetry*, March 1914. **p. 1048:** Snyder, Gary. "Hay for Horses" Copyright © 1965 by Gary Snyder, from *Riprap and Could Mountain Poems*. Reprinted by permission of Counterpoint. **p. 1049:** Hayden, Robert. "Those Winter Sundays" Copyright © 1966 by Robert Hayden, from *Collected Poems of Robert Hayden* by Robert Hayden, edited by Frederick Glaysher. Used by permission of Liveright Publishing Corporation. **p. 1049:** Heaney, Seamus. "Digging" from *Opened Ground: Selected Poems 1966–1996* by Seamus Heaney. Copyright © 1998 by Seamus Heaney. Reprinted by permission of Farrar, Straus & Giroux, LLC. **p. 1049:** Heaney, Seamus. "Digging" from *Opened Ground* by Seamus Heaney. Copyright © Reprinted by permission of Faber and Faber Ltd. **p. 1050:** Alvarez, Julia. "Woman's Work" from *Homecoming*. Copyright © 1984, 1996 by Julia Alvarez. Published by Plume, an imprint of Penguin Random House; originally published by Grove Press. By permission of Susan Bergholz Literary Services, New York, NY and Lamy, NM. All rights reserved. **p. 1051:** Piercy, Marge. "To be of use" from *Circles on the Water* by Marge Piercy, Copyright © 1982 by Middlemarsh, Inc. Used by permission of Alfred A. Knopf, an imprint of the Knopf Doubleday Publishing Group, a division of Penguin Random House LLC. All rights reserved. **p. 1052:** Barca, Jimmy, Santiago. "So Mexicans are Taking Jobs From Americans" by Jimmy Santiago Barca, from *Immigrants in Our Own Land*, copyright © 1979 by Jimmy Santiago Barca. Reprinted by permission of New Directions Publishing Corp. **p. 1054:** Martin, Jane. "Rodeo" from In *Talking With* by Jane Martin. © Reprinted by permission. **p. 1057:** Miller, Arthur. "Death of a Salesman "from *Death of a Salesman* by Arthur Miller, copyright 1949, renewed © 1977 by Arthur Miller. Used by permission of Viking Books, an imprint of Penguin Publishing Group, a division of Penguin Random House, LLC. **p. 1125:** Chief Seattle's 1854 Treaty Oration, *Seattle Star*, October 29, 1887 in a column by Dr. Henry A. Smith. **p. 1128:** Stanton, Elizabeth, Cady, Susan B. Anthony, and Matilda Joslyn Gage, eds., "Declaration of Sentiments and Resolutions" in *History of Woman Suffrage, 2 vols.* (New York, 1881), vol. 1, pp. 70–73. **p. 1132:** Lincoln, Abraham. "The Gettysburg Address." 19 November 1863. **p. 1133:** Terkel, Studs. Excerpt from *American Dreams: Lost and Found*. Copyright © 1980 by Studs Terkel. Reprinted by permission of The New Press. www.thenewpress.com **p. 1135:** Lam, Andrew. "Who Will Light Incense When Mother's Gone?" by Andrew Lam. Originally published in The *Huffington Post*, 5/11/13. Copyright © 2013. Reprinted by permission of the author. **p. 1137:** Alexie, Sherman. Excerpt from *The Lone Ranger and Tonto Fistfight in Heaven*, copyright © 1993, 2005 by Sherman Alexie. Used by permission of Grove/Atlantic, Inc. Any third party use of this material outside of this publication is prohibited. **p. 1142:** Ellison, Ralph. "Chapter 1 [Battle Royale]" copyright © 1948 and renewed 1976 by Ralph Ellison; from *Invisible Man* by Ralph Ellison. Used by permission of Random House, an imprint and division of Penguin Random House LLC. All rights reserved. **p. 1152:** Bambara, Toni, Cade. "The Lesson," copyright © 1972 by Toni Cade Bambara; from *Gorilla, My Love* by Toni Cade Bambara. Used by permission of Random House, an imprint and division of Penguin Random House LLC. All rights reserved. **p. 1158:** Tan, Amy. "Two Kinds," from *The Joy Luck Club* by Amy Tan. Copyright © 1987 by Amy Tan. First appeared in Seventeen Magazine. Reprinted by permission of the author and the Sandra Dijkstra Literary Agency. **p. 1158:** Tan, Amy. "Two Kinds," from *The Joy Luck Club* by Amy Tan, copyright © 1989 by Amy Tan. Used by permission of G.P. Putnam's Sons, an imprint of Penguin Publishing Group, a division of Penguin Random House LLC. **p. 1166:** Hayden, Robert. "Frederick Douglass" copyright © 1966 by Robert Hayden from *Collected Poems* of Robert Hayden by Robert Hayden, edited by Frederick Glaysher. Reprinted by permission of Liveright Publishing Corporation. **p. 1167:** Cervantes, Lorna, Dee. "Refugee Ship" from *Emplumada* by Lorna Dee Cervantes (University of Pittsburgh Press, 1981); first appeared in Revista Chicanco—Riquena. Copyright © 1981 Reprinted by permission of the author. . **p. 1168:** Robinson, Edward, Arlington. "Richard Cory" in *The Children*

Photo Credits

Index of Authors, Titles, and First Lines of Poetry